8 Pop Change. Indicates the percentage by which the county's population has increased or decreased between the 2000 census and the 2005 population estimate, as well as between the 1990 and 2000 censuses.

9 Pop 2000. The total population reported in the decennial census conducted by the US Bureau of the Census, followed (parenthetically) by the racial/ethnic breakdown of the population figures into five categories: White; Black or African American; Hispanic or Latino; Asian; and Other. The "Other" designation includes respondents categorized in the 2000 Census as American Indian/Alaska Native, Native Hawaiian/Other Pacific Islander, or persons who are members of more than one race. If the population of a county includes more than 1% American Indian/Alaska Native or Native Hawaiian/Other Pacific Islander, then this percentage is noted at the end of the racial/ethnic breakdown.

10 Foreign born. Percentage of the county population born in a country other than the United States.

11 Median age. The median age for that county's residents.

12 Income 2000. Income figures are presented in terms of both per capita income and median household income. Per capita means per person. *Per capita income* for a county represents the total income of county residents divided by the number of county residents. *Household income* refers to the sum of money received in the previous calendar year by all household members aged 15 and older, including those not related to the householder, as well as persons living alone and others in nonfamily households.

13 Pop below poverty level. The percentage of the population that falls below the amount of income designated as "poverty level." Poverty thresholds incorporate a number of varying factors such as family size, age of householder, number of children under 18, etc., and are updated annually to reflect changes in the Consumer Price Index.

14 Personal per capita income 2000-2003. This figure is calculated by the U.S. Bureau of Economic Analysis and represents the personal income of residents of a given area divided by the resident population of the area (based on the Census Bureau's annual midyear population estimates). The *per capita income* data produced by the Census Bureau includes only income that is received by individuals in cash and its equivalents, whereas the *personal per capita income data* produced by the Bureau of Economic Analysis includes other types of income as well (e.g., employer contributions to private health and pension funds, Medicaid or Medicare payments, food stamps, etc.).

15 Unemployment. The percentage of the county's residents who are unemployed. (Persons are classified as *unemployed* if they do not have a job, have actively looked for work in the prior four weeks, and are currently available for work. Persons are considered *employed* if they did any work at all for pay or profit during the previous survey week, including part-time or temporary work as well as regular full-time, year-round employment. Persons are also considered employed if they have a job but did not work during the survey week due to illness, vacation, etc.)

16 Change from 2000. The percentage of change in unemployment from 2000 to 2004.

17 Median travel time to work. The median amount of time that it takes county residents who are 16 years of age or older, and who do not work at home, to get from their homes to their places of work.

18 Working outside county of residence: The percentage of residents who work in a county other than the one in which they reside.

19 Cities with pop over 10,000. If a county has five or fewer cities with populations above 10,000, those cities are included here in descending order of population. If a county has six or more cities in this category, the cities are listed on page 33 under the heading Cities with Populations Over 10,000.

Counties USA

A Directory of United States Counties

3rd Edition

Containing Addresses, Telephone Numbers, Fax Numbers, and Web Site Addresses for All U.S. Counties and County-Equivalent Entities, as well as Descriptive Information, Population-Related Statistics, and Other Statistical Data Related to Income and Employment. Arranged Alphabetically by State, with Maps Provided for Each State. Also includes Counties Index and Other Features.

Omnigraphics

615 Griswold Street • Detroit, Michigan 48226

ISBN 0-7808-0821-5

Printed in the United States of America

Omnigraphics, Inc.
615 Griswold Street • Detroit, MI 48226
Phone Orders: 800-234-1340 • Fax Orders: 800-875-1340
Mail Orders: P.O. Box 625 • Holmes, PA 19043
www.omnigraphics.com

Contents

Counties USA

See page 11, U.S. Counties in State Order, for an expanded table of contents that includes page references for county listings in each state.

Foreword

It is my distinct pleasure to introduce this directory of the counties of the United States. County governments are a unique form of government in the federal structure. Counties were one of the first forms of local government established when colonists settled our country in the 1600s. County governments are thriving today and meeting the needs of Americans with a wide range of services.

Counties are diverse. They are called parishes in Louisiana and boroughs in Alaska. The officials that lead county governments are called commissioners, supervisors, police jurors, council members, county executives and freeholders.

Their populations range in size from nearly 10 million in Los Angeles County, California, to fewer than 100 people in Loving County, Texas. Two thirds of the counties in the U.S. have populations less than 50,000. There are many smaller counties, but most of the people live in the 200 largest counties.

Counties are created by and carry out responsibilities for state governments. For that reason, the roles and responsibilities of counties vary from state to state. In the northeastern part of the United States, the role of county governments is limited. In fact, Connecticut and Rhode Island do not have county governments. There are geographical boundaries for counties in those states, but no working county governments.

But in the south and the west, counties have considerably more authority and responsibility because of the large areas of unincorporated land. Counties in those areas also provide more services to their residents.

The services provided by counties include courts and corrections, record keeping, solid waste management, road maintenance, elections, health care, planning and zoning, libraries, emergency management and public safety. As counties have grown in population, the responsibilities have grown as well. Many counties are now providing recreation and parks programs, transportation systems, recycling programs and homeland security.

County names are interesting to study. Counties are named for U.S. Presidents, early leaders of our country, those who fought for independence in the Revolutionary War, Native American names, and families and locations in the old country, wherever that may be.

The leading name for counties is Washington. Thirty counties are named for the first President of the U.S. Not too far behind is Jefferson with 24 counties named for the author of the Declaration of Independence and the third President. Tied at 23 are Franklin County, Jackson County and Lincoln County. Nineteen counties are named Madison and 18 are named Montgomery.

The list of county names runs from A to Z. Abbeville County, South Carolina is the first. Ziebach County, South Dakota is the last. In between are Yazoo County, Mississippi; Wirt County, West Virginia; Transylvania County, North Carolina; Otter Tail County, Minnesota; Love County, Oklahoma; Eureka County, Nevada; and Bee County, Texas.

This directory lists all counties and is an excellent source of basic information about counties. You can learn more about each county by going to the county's Web site, a link to which is included in each listing.

You can also learn more about counties through the National Association of Counties (NACo). NACo is the only national organization representing counties in the United States. It is a full-service association that provides legislative, research, technical and public affairs assistance to county governments. Created in 1935, NACo continues to ensure that the message from the nation's counties is heard and understood in the White House and Congress. To find NACo's Web site, go to *www.naco.org*.

Learning about counties is great fun. I hope that you find the directory interesting and informative.

Larry E. Naake
Executive Director
National Association of Counties

An Overview of County Government

Forty-eight of the fifty U.S. states have operational county governments. Connecticut and Rhode Island are divided into geographic regions that are called counties but don't have functioning governments. Alaska and Louisiana have county governments but they call their counties boroughs and parishes, respectively. Counties vary greatly in size, ranging in area from 26 square miles in Arlington County, Virginia, to 87,860 square miles in North Slope Borough, Alaska. Counties also vary greatly in population – Loving County, Texas has just 62 residents, while Los Angeles County, California has 9,935,475. On the whole, county populations are not exceptionally large. Counties with populations under 50,000 accounted for nearly three-fourths of all county governments in 2000.

Counties trace their roots to the English shire of a thousand years ago, which acted as both the administrative arm of the national government and as the citizens' local government. The colonists along the eastern seaboard of North America adopted the structural form of the shire and adapted it to suit the diverse economic and geographic needs of each of the colonies. When our national government was formed, the framers of the Constitution did not provide for local governments. That was left to the states, and early state constitutions generally conceptualized county government as an arm of the state.

After World War I, with the growth in population and development of the suburbs, the government reform movement strengthened the role of local governments. Post-World War II urbanization brought changes in structure, greater autonomy from the states, rising revenues, and stronger political accountability, and counties began providing an ever-widening range of services.

Traditionally, counties performed state-mandated duties, which included assessment of property, record keeping (e.g., property and vital statistics), maintenance of rural roads, administration of election and judicial functions, and providing relief for the poor. Today, counties are moving into other areas as well, with programs relating to child welfare, consumer protection, economic development, employment and training, planning and zoning, and water quality, among others.

Service delivery responsibilities vary widely among counties. For example, construction and maintenance of local roads is one of the primary duties of most counties, but North Carolina counties have no responsibilities in this area. In addition, the mix of services often involves shared responsibilities with cities. In Indiana, cities and towns provide police protection only within their boundaries, and the county police (i.e., the Sheriff's Department) handle calls in the unincorporated areas (although all police units are expected to provide mutual aid when needed). Similarly, cities and towns handle their own planning, zoning, and building permits, while the county provides these services in the unincorporated areas.

Per capita spending is another area that points up the differences in county roles and responsibilities. In 2001, Menominee County, Wisconsin had the highest per capita spending in the state for public safety expenditures: $1,508. Walworth County, on the other hand, reported per capita spending of $179.37.

The three basic forms of county government are commission, commission/administrator, and council-executive. Under all three, many administrative responsibilities are vested by state constitution or statute to independently elected row officers (e.g., clerk, coroner, sheriff, and treasurer).

With the **Commission** type of structure, both legislative authority and executive powers are exercised jointly by an elected commission or board of supervisors. (Although governing body members are most frequently called commissioners or supervisors, these are not universal titles — in Louisiana, for example, governing body members are called parish police jurors, and the county governing body in most New Jersey counties is the board of chosen freeholders.)

Under the **Commission/Administrator** form of government, the county board of commissioners appoints an administrator who serves at its pleasure. That individual may be vested with a wide range of powers, including the authority to hire and fire department heads and to formulate a budget.

The separation-of-powers principle forms the basis of the **Council-Executive** system of governance, in which a county executive is the chief administrative officer of the jurisdiction. Typically, he or she has the authority to veto ordinances enacted by the county board (subject to their possible override) and hire or fire department heads.

Although most counties still operate under the commission form of government, more than 40 percent have shifted to either the county administrator or the elected executive type. State policymakers have contributed to this trend, as Arkansas, Kentucky, and Tennessee now mandate that an elected executive head counties in those states.

The states also dictate, through state constitutions and statutes, the revenue sources counties may use. Barely half the states allow counties to impose a sales tax, and a tax on income is a significant county revenue source only in Indiana and Maryland. Nevertheless, taxes are the number one revenue-generating source for counties, with property taxes accounting for the single most important revenue source. (However, for the 25 largest counties, state aid provides a larger percentage of revenue than property taxes.)

County expenditures fall generally into the areas of education services, social services and income maintenance, transportation, public safety, environment and housing, and general governmental administration. In addition, to fulfill their service responsibilities, county governments employ millions of professional, technical, and clerical personnel.

Continuing to provide these services when states are experiencing budget problems has not been easy for county governments. According to a survey conducted in 2003 on the budgetary crisis facing counties, 81% of the responding counties have experienced revenue shortfalls, and 56% of those stated that their state either proposed cutbacks or has cut back on funding for state-mandated programs. One in four counties reported the level of state cutbacks could be as much as 10%.

This overview is based on information provided to the editors by the National Association of Counties (NACo).

Introduction

Counties USA provides statistical, descriptive, and contact information for the 3,140 counties and county-equivalent entities in the United States. Similar information is also provided for the 50 U.S. states and for the United States as a whole. Statistics presented in *Counties USA* include data from the U.S. Bureau of the Census, U.S. Bureau of Labor Statistics, and U.S. Bureau of Economic Analysis.

What's New in This Edition

This third edition of *Counties USA* contains more categories of information for each county listing than previous editions, as well as additional statistical tables and other new features.

New information provided for each county includes:

1. Population per square mile
2. Estimated population in 2005
3. Percentage of population increase or decrease from 2000-2005 (as well as from 1990-2000)
4. Personal per capita income
5. Change in unemployment from 2000 through 2004
6. Percentage of the county's residents who work outside the county
7. Cities within each county that have a population of 10,000 or higher

Statistical tables are included in this edition for 23 categories of data—more than four times the number included in last edition.

Other new features in this third edition of *Counties USA* include:

1. A table that lists the cities in each county that have populations greater than 10,000
2. A listing for the United States that contains the same types of data found in the county listings, which can be used to compare county or state statistics against statistics for the country as a whole

3. A feature that lists all Counties Associations in the U.S., with addresses, phone and fax numbers, and websites given for each association
4. Enhanced state maps that pinpoint the location of every county seat

Counties and County-Equivalent Entities

Forty-eight of the 50 states have governmental entities that operate at a county level. Alaska and Louisiana call their county-type governments boroughs and parishes, respectively; Connecticut and Rhode Island are divided into geographic regions *called* counties, but these regions don't have functioning governments as defined by the U.S. Census Bureau.

The 3,140 county listings in this directory comprise the following entities:

- 3007 counties
- 64 parishes (Louisiana)
- 16 boroughs (Alaska)
- 11 census areas (Alaska)
- 42 independent cities

The parishes of Louisiana were originally formed as ecclesiastical districts of the Roman Catholic Church under Spanish rule. Today they function the same as counties, as do the boroughs of Alaska. Cities that have consolidated government functions with their surrounding counties include Jacksonville, FL (Duval County), Kansas City, KS (Wyandotte County), and the Alaskan cities of Juneau, Sitka, and Yakutat (with counties by the same name). Of the 42 independent cities listed, 39 are in Virginia; the others are Baltimore, MD, St. Louis, MO, and Carson City, NV. Independent cities function with an autonomy similar to counties, but legally they are separate entities from the counties in which they are located.

Arrangement of Information

Information in *Counties USA* is organized by states, with the following types of information included for each state grouping:

1. A state map outlining the names and boundaries of the counties and statistically equivalent areas for each state. Each state map also identifies the county seat for each county.

2. A brief listing for that state, with a number to call for general information about the state; the state's website; and statistical data in the same categories as the data provided for county listings.

3. Detailed listings for each of the counties/county equivalents in that state, including contact and statistical data as well as some descriptive information.

Content of Counties Listings

Information provided for each county includes:

Contact data. The name of the county seat and its address and telephone number; fax numbers and county websites also are given as available.

Description. A brief description of the general location of the county, as well as other background information such as dates of incorporation or organization, if available.

Name origin. Historical notes on the origin of the county name.

Area. Total county area in square miles, along with separate figures for land and water areas. This edition also gives the population per square mile in each county.

Statistical data. Includes population and related data as well as statistics on income and employment. The specific categories in which statistics are provided in this edition are described in detail in the **sample entry** inside the front cover of this book.

Definition of Terms

Statistical data provided in several of the listing categories are identified as ***median*** figures (e.g., median age, median income). The term 'median' refers to a value such that half the data in the population set is above that number and half is below it. This should not be confused with *mean*, or *average*, which is the sum of the data elements, or values, divided by the number of data elements in the set.

Income statistics given in *Counties USA* include both ***per capita income*** and ***personal per capita income***. Per capita income data are produced by the U.S. Bureau of the Census and include only income that is received by individuals in cash and its equivalents. Personal per capita income is calculated by the U.S. Bureau of Economic Analysis and represents the personal income of residents of a given area divided by the resident population of the area (based on the Census Bureau's annual midyear population estimates). Personal per capita income includes not only cash income or its equivalent, but also Medicaid or Medicare payments, food stamps, employer contributions to private health and pension funds, and similar forms of compensation.

Statistical Tables and Other Special Features

As noted at the beginning of this Introduction, this edition of *Counties USA* includes 23 separate Statistical Tables, which are presented as a group following the main body of listings. These tables provide rankings for various types of population, income, and employment statistics, as well as lists of counties ranked by total area and a list of the most common names for counties in the United States.

Features introduced for the first time in this edition of *Counties USA* include: a table that lists for each applicable county the cities in it with populations greater than 10,000; a United States listing containing the same types of data found in the county listings, which can be used to compare county or state statistics against statistics for the country as a whole; and a list of all of the associations of counties in the U.S., with addresses, phone and fax numbers, and websites given for each association.

Index to Counties

All of the counties and comparable legal entities listed in *Counties USA* are interfiled alphabetically in the **County Index** located at the back of the book. Index citations include the telephone number for each county, together with a reference to the page on which that county's listing appears in the main body of the book. (A detailed state-by-state list of all counties in *Counties USA* is provided as part of the book's table of contents.

Acknowledgments

The editors are grateful for the cooperation and assistance provided to us by representatives of the U.S. Bureau of the Census, the U.S. Bureau of Labor Statistics, and the U.S. Bureau of Economic Analysis. Special thanks are due the National Association of Counties (NACo) for providing information for *An Overview of County Government*, and to Larry E. Naake, Executive Director of NACo, for writing the foreword to *Counties USA*.

Comments Welcome

Comments from readers concerning this publication, including corrections and/or suggestions for additions or improvement, are welcome. Please send to:

Editor – Counties USA
Omnigraphics, Inc.
615 Griswold St., Suite 1400
Detroit, MI 48226
editorial@omnigraphics.com

U.S. Counties in State Order

Mississippi

Missouri

U.S. Counties in State Order

Cities with Populations over 10,000

Counties that have more than five cities with populations above 10,000 are listed here, together with the names of those cities and their populations. Information is organized alphabetically by county names in state-by-state order. The cities are listed in ranked order under each county's name, beginning with the city having the largest population.

If a county has five or fewer cities with populations in excess of 10,000, that information is provided within the individual county listings in the main body of the book.

Jefferson County, AL

City	Pop.	City	Pop.
Birmingham 🏛	233,149	Hueytown	15,313
Hoover	66,346	Center Point	15,130
Vestavia Hills	31,012	Gardendale	12,532
Bessemer	28,727	Fairfield	11,866
Homewood	24,259	Leeds	11,020
Mountain Brook	20,747	Pleasant Grove	10,377
Trussville	15,744		

Maricopa County, AZ

City	Pop.	City	Pop.
Mesa	437,454	Surprise	60,686
Glendale	235,591	Avondale	59,180
Chandler	223,991	Goodyear	37,496
Scottsdale	221,792	Fountain Hills	22,557
Tempe	160,676	El Mirage	20,914
Gilbert	156,917	Paradise Valley	14,330
Phoenix 🏛	141,804	Queen Creek	13,866
Peoria	132,487		

Alameda County, CA

City	Pop.	City	Pop.
Oakland 🏛	397,976	Union City	68,938
Fremont	202,373	Pleasanton	65,951
Hayward	140,795	Newark	42,511
Berkeley	101,517	Dublin	36,995
San Leandro	79,183	Albany	16,216
Livermore	77,983	Piedmont	10,713
Alameda	71,136		

Contra Costa County, CA

City	Pop.	City	Pop.
Concord	124,328	San Pablo	31,041
Richmond	102,318	Oakley	26,818
Antioch	100,923	Lafayette	24,665
Walnut Creek	64,822	Hercules	23,425
Pittsburg	62,600	El Cerrito	23,138
San Ramon	45,616	Pinole	19,272
Danville	42,199	Orinda	18,176
Martinez 🏛	36,305	Moraga	16,797
Pleasant Hill	33,529	Clayton	11,126

Fresno County, CA

City	Pop.	City	Pop.
Fresno 🏛	457,719	Coalinga	17,102
Clovis	82,374	Parlier	12,981
Reedley	22,264	Kingsburg	11,049
Selma	21,919	Kerman	10,238
Sanger	21,040		

Kern County, CA

City	Pop.	City	Pop.
Bakersfield 🏛	283,936	Shafter	14,155
Delano	43,988	Tehachapi	11,653
Ridgecrest	25,854	California City	11,422
Wasco	23,240	McFarland	10,074
Arvin	14,404		

Los Angeles County, CA

City	Pop.	City	Pop.
Long Beach	476,564	Redondo Beach	66,683
Los Angeles 🏛	384,554	Pico Rivera	65,198
Glendale	201,326	Montebello	63,700
Santa Clarita	164,800	Huntington Park	62,979
Pomona	155,448	Monterey Park	62,398
Pasadena	144,068	Gardena	59,727
Torrance	142,841	Diamond Bar	58,326
Palmdale	131,153	Paramount	56,899
Lancaster	128,928	Arcadia	55,992
El Monte	122,123	Rosemead	55,296
Inglewood	115,313	Cerritos	52,898
Downey	110,318	Glendora	50,889
West Covina	108,668	La Mirada	49,636
Norwalk	106,683	Covina	48,091
Burbank	104,114	Azusa	47,388
South Gate	99,627	Bell Gardens	45,372
Compton	96,235	Rancho Palos Verdes	42,310
Carson	93,733	La Puente	42,058
Alhambra	87,995	San Gabriel	41,260
Santa Monica	87,823	Culver City	39,896
Hawthorne	86,279	Brentwood	39,827
Whittier	85,509	Monrovia	38,174
Lakewood	81,088	Bell	37,779
Baldwin Park	78,887	West Hollywood	36,933
Bellflower	74,964	Temple City	36,911
Lynwood	71,632	Manhattan Beach	36,321

🏛 County Seat

31

City	Pop.	City	Pop.
San Dimas	36,067	La Canada Flintridge	21,063
Claremont	35,097	Lomita	20,549
Beverly Hills	35,088	Hermosa Beach	19,537
La Verne	33,146	Santa Fe Springs	17,060
Lawndale	32,436	Artesia	16,782
Walnut	31,607	El Segundo	16,492
Maywood	28,816	Hawaiian Gardens	15,406
Cudahy	25,191	Palos Verdes Estates	13,868
South Pasadena	25,048	Commerce	13,405
San Fernando	24,355	Malibu	13,305
Agoura Hills	22,863	San Marino	13,272
Duarte	22,273	Sierra Madre	11,023
South El Monte	21,801	Signal Hill	10,698
Calabasas	21,629		

Monterey County, CA

City	Pop.	City	Pop.
Salinas 🏛	148,183	Marina	19,324
Seaside	34,130	Pacific Grove	15,280
Monterey	29,669	Greenfield	12,845
Soledad	26,325	King City	11,162

Orange County, CA

City	Pop.	City	Pop.
Santa Ana 🏛	342,715	San Clemente	59,550
Anaheim	333,776	Fountain Valley	56,352
Huntington Beach	195,305	Rancho Santa	
Irvine	178,317	Margarita	50,004
Garden Grove	167,347	Placentia	49,949
Orange	133,819	Cypress	47,614
Fullerton	133,439	Aliso Viejo	41,468
Costa Mesa	110,411	Brea	38,522
Mission Viejo	96,253	Stanton	37,923
Westminster	89,855	Dana Point	36,019
Newport Beach	79,957	San Juan Capistrano	34,882
Buena Park	79,357	Laguna Hills	32,380
Lake Forest	77,012	Seal Beach	24,459
Tustin	68,612	Laguna Beach	24,250
Laguna Niguel	64,946	Laguna Woods	18,306
Yorba Linda	63,660	La Palma	15,935
La Habra	59,803	Los Alamitos	11,780

Riverside County, CA

City	Pop.	City	Pop.
Riverside 🏛	288,384	Lake Elsinore	37,009
Moreno Valley	166,290	La Quinta	35,363
Corona	145,398	Coachella	30,194
Temecula	82,083	Banning	28,686
Murrieta	74,513	San Jacinto	28,043
Hemet	66,563	Norco	26,668
Indio	63,326	Blythe	22,428
Cathedral City	50,756	Desert Hot Springs	19,273
Palm Desert	46,615	Beaumont	18,115
Palm Springs	46,436	Rancho Mirage	16,230
Perris	45,793	Canyon Lake	11,161

Sacramento County, CA

City	Pop.	City	Pop.
Sacramento 🏛	454,330	Folsom	63,960
Elk Grove	100,760	Rancho Cordova	56,508
Citrus Heights	87,383	Galt	22,965

San Bernardino County, CA

City	Pop.	City	Pop.
San Bernardino 🏛	198,406	Apple Valley	62,639
Ontario	170,057	Colton	51,382
Rancho Cucamonga	159,346	Highland	50,236
Fontana	158,715	Yucaipa	47,864
Rialto	99,659	Montclair	35,245
Victorville	82,790	Twentynine Palms	30,081
Chino	76,042	Barstow	23,528
Chino Hills	75,622	Adelanto	21,642
Upland	73,526	Loma Linda	20,332
Hesperia	73,376	Yucca Valley	19,031
Redlands	69,682	Grand Terrace	12,349

San Diego County, CA

City	Pop.	City	Pop.
Chula Vista	204,879	National City	54,572
Oceanside	167,438	La Mesa	53,855
Escondido	135,462	Santee	52,577
San Diego 🏛	126,375	Poway	48,977
El Cajon	93,987	Imperial Beach	26,710
Vista	91,585	Lemon Grove	24,537
Carlsbad	89,042	Coronado	23,774
San Marcos	68,347	Solana Beach	12,860
Encinitas	60,057		

San Joaquin County, CA

City	Pop.	City	Pop.
Stockton 🏛	279,888	Manteca	61,407
Tracy	76,900	Ripon	12,980
Lodi	61,961	Lathrop	12,642

San Luis Obispo County, CA

City	Pop.	City	Pop.
San Luis Obispo 🏛	44,032	Arroyo Grande	16,183
Atascadero	27,158	Grover Beach	13,036
El Paso de Robles (Paso Robles)	26,887	Morro Bay	10,309

San Mateo County, CA

City	Pop.	City	Pop.
Daly City	100,620	Foster City	28,847
San Mateo	91,275	Burlingame	27,420
Redwood City 🏛	73,346	San Carlos	26,915
South San Francisco	59,897	Belmont	24,449
San Bruno	39,661	Millbrae	20,419
Pacifica	37,182	Half Moon Bay	12,208
Menlo Park	29,759	Hillsborough	10,600

🏛 County Seat

Santa Clara County, CA

City	Pop.	City	Pop.
San Jose 🏛	904,522	Gilroy	44,356
Sunnyvale	128,012	Campbell	37,013
Santa Clara	104,001	Morgan Hill	34,885
Mountain View	69,011	East Palo Alto	32,042
Milpitas	62,698	Saratoga	29,633
Palo Alto	56,862	Los Gatos	27,930
Cupertino	51,405	Los Altos	26,992

Stanislaus County, CA

City	Pop.	City	Pop.
Modesto 🏛	206,769	Riverbank	20,207
Turlock	65,484	Oakdale	17,679
Ceres	38,546	Patterson	14,793

Ventura County, CA

City	Pop.	City	Pop.
Oxnard	183,587	Camarillo	60,890
Thousand Oaks	125,054	Moorpark	35,894
Simi Valley	118,893	Santa Paula	28,732
San Buenaventura		Port Hueneme	22,041
(Ventura)	104,068	Fillmore	14,967

Boulder County, CO

City	Pop.	City	Pop.
Boulder 🏛	92,196	Louisville	18,493
Longmont	80,627	Superior	10,404
Lafayette	23,762	Erie	10,064

Jefferson County, CO

City	Pop.	City	Pop.
Denver 🏛	556,835	Arvada	102,562
Aurora	291,843	Wheat Ridge	31,411
Lakewood	141,301	Golden 🏛	17,436
Westminster	104,759		

New Haven County, CT

City	Pop.	City	Pop.
New Haven 🏛	124,829	Milford	52,726
Waterbury	108,429	Naugatuck	31,805
Meriden	59,136	Ansonia	18,844
West Haven	53,087	Derby	12,608

Brevard County, FL

City	Pop.	City	Pop.
Palm Bay	88,758	Cocoa	16,693
Melbourne	75,366	West Melbourne	13,797
Titusville 🏛	42,614	Cocoa Beach	12,588
Rockledge	23,295		

Broward County, FL

City	Pop.	City	Pop.
Fort Lauderdale 🏛	164,578	Coral Springs	128,355
Pembroke Pines	150,104	Miramar	101,486
Hollywood	144,535	Sunrise	90,227
Pompano Beach	88,874	Hallandale Beach	36,349
Plantation	85,497	North Lauderdale	34,403
Davie	82,579	Lauderdale Lakes	31,639
Deerfield Beach	66,189	Oakland Park	31,512
Weston	63,534	Cooper City	29,446
Lauderhill	59,542	Dania Beach	28,479
Tamarac	59,278	Parkland	20,556
Margate	55,152	Wilton Manors	12,844
Coconut Creek	48,889	Lighthouse Point	11,212

Lake County, FL

City	Pop.	City	Pop.
Leesburg	18,079	Tavares 🏛	11,368
Eustis	17,235	Clermont	11,125
Lady Lake	13,042	Mount Dora	10,658

Miami-Dade County, FL

City	Pop.	City	Pop.
Miami 🏛	379,724	Hialeah Gardens	19,969
Hialeah	224,522	Pinecrest	19,432
Miami Gardens	100,887	Sunny Isles Beach	15,399
Miami Beach	89,104	Opa Locka	15,327
North Miami	58,750	Sweetwater	13,992
Coral Gables	42,459	Miami Springs	13,422
North Miami Beach	39,921	South Miami	11,274
Homestead	37,957	Key Biscayne	10,324
Aventura	27,236	Miami Shores	10,195
Miami Lakes	22,688		

Orange County, FL

City	Pop.	City	Pop.
Orlando 🏛	205,648	Winter Park	26,608
Apopka	32,062	Winter Garden	22,070
Ocoee	28,248	Maitland	14,099

Palm Beach County, FL

City	Pop.	City	Pop.
West Palm Beach 🏛	95,344	Riviera Beach	32,522
Boca Raton	78,069	Greenacres	32,019
Boynton Beach	64,775	Royal Palm Beach	30,371
Delray Beach	64,150	Belle Glade	15,318
Wellington	49,976	Palm Springs	14,690
Jupiter	46,752	North Palm Beach	12,645
Palm Beach Gardens	44,315	Lantana	10,389
Lake Worth	35,485		

Pinellas County, FL

City	Pop.	City	Pop.
Saint Petersburg	249,090	Seminole	18,226
Clearwater 🏛	108,606	Safety Harbor	17,550
Largo	71,704	Oldsmar	13,706
Pinellas Park	47,166	Gulfport	12,740
Dunedin	36,632	Saint Pete Beach	10,027
Tarpon Springs	22,554		

🏛 County Seat

Polk County, FL

City	Pop.	City	Pop.
Lakeland	88,357	Haines City	14,530
Winter Haven	27,855	Auburndale	12,154
Bartow 🏛	15,824	Lake Wales	11,802

Seminole County, FL

City	Pop.	City	Pop.
Sanford 🏛	45,460	Casselberry	24,142
Altamonte Springs	40,786	Lake Mary	13,918
Winter Springs	31,972	Longwood	13,571
Oviedo	28,802		

Volusia County, FL

City	Pop.	City	Pop.
Deltona	79,749	New Smyrna Beach	21,464
Daytona Beach	64,422	Edgewater	20,721
Port Orange	52,793	De Bary	16,211
Ormond Beach	37,929	South Daytona	13,758
De Land	22,857	Holly Hill	12,586

Fulton County, GA

City	Pop.	City	Pop.
Atlanta 🏛	419,122	Alpharetta	34,245
Roswell	85,044	College Park	18,353
East Point	35,457	Union City	13,355

Gwinnett County, GA

City	Pop.	City	Pop.
Lawrenceville 🏛	26,925	Lilburn	11,419
Duluth	24,255	Buford	10,966
Snellville	18,782	Suwanee	10,956
Sugar Hill	14,982		

Cook County, IL

City	Pop.	City	Pop.
Chicago 🏛	286,224	Park Ridge	37,185
Cicero	83,102	Streamwood	37,125
Arlington Heights	75,181	Wheeling	36,766
Evanston	74,811	Northbrook	34,209
Schaumburg	73,346	Elk Grove Village	34,136
Palatine	66,401	Chicago Heights	31,688
Bolingbrook	66,206	Niles	29,617
Skokie	63,965	Harvey	29,030
Tinley Park	56,274	Oak Forest	28,078
Des Plaines	56,229	Burbank	27,741
Mount Prospect	55,028	Lansing	27,574
Orland Park	54,781	Wilmette	27,104
Oak Lawn	54,257	Maywood	26,081
Berwyn	52,000	Dolton	24,765
Oak Park	50,993	Elmwood Park	24,653
Hoffman Estates	49,823	Rolling Meadows	23,990
Glenview	44,655	Park Forest	23,189
Calumet City	38,172	Blue Island	23,010

City	Pop.	City	Pop.
Melrose Park	22,734	Chicago Ridge	13,728
Morton Grove	22,383	Hickory Hills	13,652
South Holland	21,731	Richton Park	12,879
Evergreen Park	20,086	La Grange Park	12,857
Bellwood	19,754	Justice	12,649
Alsip	19,239	Western Springs	12,562
Homewood	19,112	Winnetka	12,473
Franklin Park	18,701	Palos Heights	12,440
Brookfield	18,678	Markham	12,348
Palos Hills	17,399	Lincolnwood	12,101
Prospect Heights	16,544	Schiller Park	11,726
Westchester	16,367	Northlake	11,473
Country Club Hills	16,283	River Forest	11,371
La Grange	15,557	Crestwood	11,255
Forest Park	15,251	Burr Ridge	10,822
Bridgeview	15,061	Worth	10,718
Riverdale	14,759	Sauk Village	10,490
Matteson	14,668	Lyons	10,480
Lemont	14,643	Summit	10,391
Hazel Crest	14,555	River Grove	10,293
Norridge	14,159	Steger	10,201
Midlothian	14,072		

DuPage County, IL

City	Pop.	City	Pop.
Aurora	166,614	Glen Ellyn	27,214
Naperville	140,106	West Chicago	26,063
Wheaton 🏛	54,979	Westmont	24,820
Downers Grove	49,302	Roselle	23,367
Elmhurst	44,352	Darien	22,923
Lombard	42,975	Villa Park	22,795
Carol Stream	40,267	Lisle	22,321
Bartlett	37,773	Bloomingdale	21,903
Hanover Park	37,391	Bensenville	20,594
Addison	37,040	Hinsdale	17,632
Woodridge	33,943	Wood Dale	13,388
Glendale Heights	32,729	Warrenville	13,293

Kane County, IL

City	Pop.	City	Pop.
Elgin	97,761	Geneva 🏛	22,913
Carpentersville	35,980	South Elgin	20,746
Saint Charles	32,134	North Aurora	13,677
Batavia	26,901		

Lake County, IL

City	Pop.	City	Pop.
Waukegan 🏛	91,602	Round Lake Beach	28,208
Buffalo Grove	43,152	Zion	24,086
North Chicago	33,271	Vernon Hills	23,446
Mundelein	32,651	Libertyville	21,665
Highland Park	31,221	Lake Forest	20,922
Gurnee	30,709	Grayslake	20,459
Deerfield	19,426	Antioch	11,223
Lake Zurich	19,325	Fox Lake	10,367
Lindenhurst	14,353	Barrington	10,170
Round Lake	12,166	Wauconda	10,104
Beach Park	12,104		

🏛 County Seat

Madison County, IL

City	Pop.	City	Pop.
Granite City	31,223	Godfrey	16,974
Alton	29,774	Glen Carbon	11,714
Collinsville	25,384	Wood River	11,085
Edwardsville 🏛	23,953		

McHenry County, IL

City	Pop.	City	Pop.
Crystal Lake	40,496	Woodstock 🏛	21,556
Algonquin	28,223	Cary	18,717
Lake in the Hills	28,220	Huntley	15,065
McHenry	23,997		

Saint Clair County, IL

City	Pop.	City	Pop.
East Saint Louis	30,266	Fairview Heights	15,805
O'Fallon	24,547	Cahokia	15,794
Belleville 🏛	41,429	Swansea	11,842

Will County, IL

City	Pop.	City	Pop.
Joliet 🏛	129,519	Crest Hill	18,025
Romeoville	35,020	Mokena	16,529
Plainfield	24,647	Frankfort	14,667
Homer Glen	24,138	Channahon	11,038
New Lenox	22,528	Shorewood	10,987
Lockport	20,587		

Lake County, IN

City	Pop.	City	Pop.
Gary	99,516	Highland	23,290
Hammond	79,985	Munster	22,240
Merrillville	31,258	Crown Point 🏛	21,822
East Chicago	31,237	Griffith	16,806
Hobart	27,510	Dyer	14,793
Schererville	27,451	Lake Station	13,657

Polk County, IA

City	Pop.	City	Pop.
Des Moines 🏛	194,311	Clive	13,598
West Des Moines	51,363	Altoona	12,107
Ankeny	34,439	Johnston	11,770
Urbandale	33,379		

Johnson County, KS

City	Pop.	City	Pop.
Overland Park	162,728	Leawood	29,504
Olathe 🏛	108,390	Prairie Village	21,511
Shawnee	56,178	Gardner	12,937
Lenexa	42,615	Merriam	10,774

Prince George's County, MD

City	Pop.	City	Pop.
Bowie	53,840	Laurel	21,048
College Park	25,350	Hyattsville	15,186
Greenbelt	22,176	New Carrollton	13,029

Essex County, MA

City	Pop.	City	Pop.
Lynn	89,485	Salem 🏛	41,912
Lawrence	71,858	Beverly	40,166
Haverhill	60,482	Gloucester	30,817
Peabody	50,370	Newburyport	17,552
Methuen	44,845		

Hampden County, MA

City	Pop.	City	Pop.
Springfield 🏛	152,091	Holyoke	40,058
Chicopee	54,838	Agawam	28,616
Westfield	40,559	West Springfield	28,048

Middlesex County, MA

City	Pop.	City	Pop.
Lowell	103,655	Medford	54,197
Cambridge 🏛	100,771	Marlborough	37,699
Newton	83,802	Woburn	37,448
Somerville	75,621	Everett	37,195
Waltham	59,232	Watertown	32,603
Malden	55,340	Melrose	26,533

Kent County, MI

City	Pop.	City	Pop.
Grand Rapids 🏛	195,115	Walker	23,315
Wyoming	70,300	Grandville	16,680
Kentwood	46,538	East Grand Rapids	10,482

Macomb County, MI

City	Pop.	City	Pop.
Warren	136,118	Eastpointe	33,384
Sterling Heights	127,476	Mount Clemens 🏛	17,108
Saint Clair Shores	61,864	Fraser	15,130
Roseville	47,960	New Baltimore	10,857

Oakland County, MI

City	Pop.	City	Pop.
Troy	81,432	Royal Oak	58,573
Farmington Hills	80,787	Novi	51,934
Southfield	77,491	Madison Heights	30,510
Rochester Hills	69,480	Oak Park	29,074
Pontiac 🏛	67,582	Ferndale	21,666
Auburn Hills	20,737	Clawson	12,443
Birmingham	19,217	Rochester	11,217
Hazel Park	18,553	South Lyon	11,017
Berkley	15,236	Beverly Hills	10,186
Wixom	13,514	Farmington	10,146

🏛 County Seat

Wayne County, MI

City	Pop.	City	Pop.
Detroit ⛁	900,198	Romulus	23,609
Livonia	98,936	Hamtramck	22,241
Dearborn	95,470	Trenton	19,468
Westland	86,316	Wayne	18,780
Taylor	65,383	Grosse Pointe Woods	16,546
Dearborn Heights	56,828	Highland Park	15,675
Lincoln Park	38,744	Harper Woods	13,815
Southgate	29,919	Riverview	12,909
Garden City	29,310	Woodhaven	12,853
Inkster	29,239	Grosse Pointe Park	12,064
Allen Park	28,481	Ecorse	10,896
Wyandotte	27,247	Melvindale	10,719

Anoka County, MN

City	Pop.	City	Pop.
Coon Rapids	62,721	Lino Lakes	19,123
Blaine	52,137	Columbia Heights	18,258
Andover	29,450	Anoka ⛁	17,797
Fridley	26,942	Ham Lake	14,559
Ramsey	20,735	East Bethel	11,856

Dakota County, MN

City	Pop.	City	Pop.
Eagan	64,105	South Saint Paul	19,478
Burnsville	59,384	West Saint Paul	19,183
Apple Valley	49,606	Rosemount	17,997
Lakeville	49,440	Farmington	17,344
Inver Grove Heights	32,338	Mendota Heights	11,378
Hastings ⛁	20,353		

Hennepin County, MN

City	Pop.	City	Pop.
Minneapolis ⛁	373,943	Richfield	33,911
Bloomington	81,875	Brooklyn Center	27,851
Plymouth	69,797	Champlin	23,293
Brooklyn Park	67,927	Crystal	21,883
Eden Prairie	60,430	Golden Valley	20,200
Maple Grove	58,628	New Hope	19,983
Minnetonka	50,077	Hopkins	16,957
Edina	46,081	Robbinsdale	13,490
Saint Louis Park	43,607		

Ramsey County, MN

City	Pop.	City	Pop.
Saint Paul ⛁	276,963	New Brighton	21,145
Maplewood	35,528	Vadnais Heights	12,869
Roseville	32,695	Mounds View	12,360
Shoreview	26,991	North Saint Paul	11,600
White Bear Lake	24,051		

Jackson County, MO

City	Pop.	City	Pop.
Kansas City ⛁	444,387	Raytown	29,348
Independence ⛁	111,023	Grandview	24,848
Blue Springs	49,467	Lee's Summit	78,659

Saint Charles County, MO

City	Pop.	City	Pop.
O'Fallon	67,009	Lake Saint Louis	12,893
Saint Charles ⛁	61,411	Saint Ann	13,235
Saint Peters	53,907	Wentzville	14,601

Saint Louis County, MO

City	Pop.	City	Pop.
Florissant	51,583	Manchester	19,059
Chesterfield	47,110	Creve Coeur	16,642
University City	37,493	Overland	16,272
Wildwood	34,588	Clayton ⛁	15,944
Ballwin	30,778	Bridgeton	15,382
Kirkwood	27,156	Jennings	15,056
Hazelwood	25,651	Crestwood	11,757
Maryland Heights	25,407	Town and Country	10,851
Webster Groves	23,076	Bellefontaine Neighbors	
Ferguson	21,677		10,732

Atlantic County, NJ

City	Pop.	City	Pop.
Atlantic City	40,580	Ventnor City	12,831
Pleasantville	19,113	Brigantine	12,769
Hammonton	13,280	Somers Point	11,731

Bergen County, NJ

City	Pop.	City	Pop.
Hackensack ⛁	43,681	North Arlington	15,254
Fort Lee	37,310	Ramsey	14,601
Fair Lawn	31,613	Tenafly	14,214
Garfield	29,833	Oakland	13,707
Paramus	26,624	Fairview	13,561
Englewood	26,353	Ridgefield Park	12,822
Bergenfield	26,210	Hasbrouck Heights	11,679
Ridgewood	24,916	Wallington	11,558
Lodi	24,336	Glen Rock	11,525
Cliffside Park	23,012	Franklin Lakes	11,260
Elmwood Park	19,005	Westwood	11,051
Palisades Park	18,301	Ridgefield	11,005
Rutherford	18,084	River Edge	10,966
Dumont	17,571	Little Ferry	10,840
New Milford	16,397	Hillsdale	10,138

Camden County, NJ

City	Pop.	City	Pop.
Camden ⛁	79,948	Haddonfield	11,596
Lindenwold	17,297	Pine Hill	11,221
Collingswood	14,138	Bellmawr	11,184
Gloucester City	11,608		

Hudson County, NJ

City	Pop.	City	Pop.
Jersey City ⛁	239,079	Kearny	39,496
Union City	66,167	Secaucus	15,663
Bayonne	60,748	Harrison	14,164
West New York	46,231	Guttenberg	11,011
Hoboken	40,175		

⛁ County Seat

Middlesex County, NJ

City	Pop.	City	Pop.
New Brunswick 🏛	50,010	South River	16,025
Perth Amboy	48,823	Highland Park	14,172
Sayreville	42,663	Middlesex	13,967
South Plainfield	23,034	Metuchen	13,335
Carteret	21,523		

Monmouth County, NJ

City	Pop.	City	Pop.
Long Branch	31,526	Red Bank	11,940
Asbury Park	16,819	Freehold 🏛	11,527
Tinton Falls	16,206	Keansburg	10,739
Eatontown	14,139		

Morris County, NJ

City	Pop.	City	Pop.
Morristown 🏛	18,842	Lincoln Park	10,894
Dover	18,463	Point Pleasant	19,821
Madison	16,005	Beachwood	10,740
Florham Park	12,556		

Passaic County, NJ

City	Pop.	City	Pop.
Paterson 🏛	150,869	Pompton Lakes	11,389
Clifton	79,944	West Paterson	11,298
Passaic	68,662	Wanaque	10,440
Hawthorne	18,378	Totowa	10,360
Ringwood	12,769		

Union County, NJ

City	Pop.	City	Pop.
Elizabeth 🏛	124,724	Roselle	21,415
Plainfield	47,987	Summit	21,267
Linden	40,004	Roselle Park	13,296
Westfield	30,062	New Providence	11,981
Rahway	27,578		

Erie County, NY

City	Pop.	City	Pop.
Buffalo 🏛	282,864	Kenmore	15,749
Lackawanna	18,394	Tonawanda	15,515
Depew	16,003	Lancaster	11,594

Nassau County, NY

City	Pop.	City	Pop.
Hempstead	53,145	Lynbrook	19,795
Freeport	43,726	Mineola 🏛	19,129
Valley Stream	36,131	Massapequa Park	17,400
Long Beach	35,553	Floral Park	15,850
Glen Cove	26,787	Westbury	14,259
Rockville Centre	24,392	East Rockaway	10,327
Garden City	21,848		

Westchester County, NY

City	Pop.	City	Pop.
Yonkers	197,126	Ossining	23,656
New Rochelle	72,985	Mamaroneck	18,463
Mount Vernon	68,321	Scarsdale	17,888
White Plains 🏛	56,509	Rye	15,067
Port Chester	27,902	Tarrytown	11,402
Harrison	25,553	Dobbs Ferry	11,136
Peekskill	23,782	Mount Kisco	10,057

Wake County, NC

City	Pop.	City	Pop.
Raleigh 🏛	326,653	Wake Forest	17,390
Cary	101,265	Holly Springs	13,740
Apex	27,509	Morrisville	11,595
Garner	21,772	Fuquay-Varina	11,110

Cuyahoga County, OH

City	Pop.	City	Pop.
Cleveland 🏛	458,684	Rocky River	19,910
Parma	82,672	Mayfield Heights	18,538
Lakewood	53,971	Berea	18,276
Euclid	50,398	Broadview Heights	17,223
Cleveland Heights	48,643	Fairview Park	16,754
Strongsville	44,315	Middleburg Heights	15,527
North Olmsted	33,105	Bay Village	15,439
Westlake	31,535	Lyndhurst	14,600
North Royalton	29,497	Warrensville Heights	14,444
Garfield Heights	29,445	Bedford	13,583
Shaker Heights	28,084	University Heights	13,553
East Cleveland	25,924	Brecksville	13,377
Maple Heights	25,068	Seven Hills	12,002
South Euclid	22,504	Beachwood	11,680
Solon	22,309	Brooklyn	11,051
Parma Heights	20,954	Bedford Heights	11,015
Brook Park	20,296	Richmond Heights	10,623

Franklin County, OH

City	Pop.	City	Pop.
Columbus 🏛	730,008	Grove City	30,502
Westerville	34,846	Hilliard	26,449
Dublin	34,301	Whitehall	18,258
Reynoldsburg	32,943	Worthington	13,335
Gahanna	32,791	Bexley	12,411
Upper Arlington	31,860		

Hamilton County, OH

City	Pop.	City	Pop.
Cincinnati 🏛	314,154	Blue Ash	11,917
Norwood	20,405	Loveland	11,285
Forest Park	18,381	Reading	10,521
Sharonville	13,299	Montgomery	10,147

Lake County, OH

City	Pop.	City	Pop.
Mentor	51,332	Painesville 🏛	17,599
Willoughby	22,493	Willowick	14,175
Eastlake	19,901	Wickliffe	13,355

🏛 County Seat

37

Lorain County, OH

City	Pop.	City	Pop.
Lorain	67,915	Avon Lake	20,233
Elyria 🏛	56,175	Avon	14,880
North Ridgeville	25,204	Amherst	11,805

Montgomery County, OH

City	Pop.	City	Pop.
Dayton 🏛	160,293	Miamisburg	19,809
Kettering	55,903	Vandalia	14,304
Beavercreek	39,421	West Carrollton City	13,299
Huber Heights	38,229	Clayton	13,215
Trotwood	26,800	Englewood	12,598
Centerville	23,122		

Summit County, OH

City	Pop.	City	Pop.
Akron 🏛	212,179	Hudson	23,054
Cuyahoga Falls	50,515	Twinsburg	17,286
Stow	34,394	Tallmadge	17,180
Barberton	27,362	Norton	11,596
Green	23,433	Macedonia	10,147

Oklahoma County, OK

City	Pop.	City	Pop.
Oklahoma City 🏛	528,042	Del City	22,029
Edmond	73,080	Bethany	19,871
Midwest City	54,822	Choctaw	10,276
Moore	46,208		

Tulsa County, OK

City	Pop.	City	Pop.
Tulsa 🏛	383,764	Bixby	17,729
Broken Arrow	84,399	Sand Springs	17,642
Owasso	22,582	Jenks	12,079

Clackamas County, OR

City	Pop.	City	Pop.
Lake Oswego	36,368	Wilsonville	15,514
Oregon City 🏛	29,767	Canby	14,715
West Linn	25,051	Gladstone	12,131
Milwaukie	20,755		

Washington County, OR

City	Pop.	City	Pop.
Beaverton	82,907	Forest Grove	19,261
Hillsboro 🏛	81,854	Sherwood	14,540
Tigard	46,860	Cornelius	10,346
Tualatin	25,268		

Allegheny County, PA

City	Pop.	City	Pop.
Pittsburgh 🏛	322,450	West Mifflin	21,563
Bethel Park	32,670	Baldwin	19,138
Municipality of Monroeville	28,486	Wilkinsburg	18,302
Plum	26,684	Whitehall	13,923
McKeesport	23,053	Franklin Park	11,708
		Munhall	11,697

Providence County, RI

City	Pop.	City	Pop.
Providence 🏛	178,126	East Providence	49,765
Cranston	81,986	Woonsocket	44,534
Pawtucket	74,254	Central Falls	19,292

Brazoria County, TX

City	Pop.	City	Pop.
Pearland	52,402	Angleton 🏛	18,704
Lake Jackson	27,022	Freeport	12,759
Alvin	22,142	Clute	10,763

Collin County, TX

City	Pop.	City	Pop.
Plano	245,411	Frisco	62,372
McKinney 🏛	88,409	The Colony	36,316
Allen	66,341	Wylie	25,743

Dallas County, TX

City	Pop.	City	Pop.
Garland	217,176	Coppell	38,939
Irving	194,547	Duncanville	35,346
Grand Prairie	140,320	Lancaster	30,304
Mesquite	129,710	Farmers Branch	26,706
Dallas 🏛	121,039	University Park	23,686
Carrollton	117,823	Balch Springs	19,343
Richardson	99,263	Sachse	16,077
Rowlett	52,779	Addison	13,778
DeSoto	43,050	Seagoville	11,071
Cedar Hill	40,219		

Denton County, TX

City	Pop.	City	Pop.
Denton 🏛	98,288	Corinth	17,212
Lewisville	89,142	Little Elm	14,884
Flower Mound	62,209	Highland Village	14,589

Galveston County, TX

City	Pop.	City	Pop.
League City	57,981	Dickinson	17,749
Galveston 🏛	57,355	La Marque	13,733
Texas City	43,535	Santa Fe	10,371
Friendswood	32,717		

🏛 County Seat

Harris County, TX

City	Pop.	City	Pop.
Houston 🏛	201,262	West University Place	14,820
Pasadena	144,174	Humble	14,757
Baytown	67,321	Katy	13,012
La Porte	33,265	Seabrook	10,856
Deer Park	28,647	Galena Park	10,341
Bellaire	16,940	Jacinto City	10,048
South Houston	16,350		

Hidalgo County, TX

City	Pop.	City	Pop.
McAllen	120,743	San Juan	29,741
Edinburg 🏛	58,448	Alamo	15,928
Mission	57,812	Donna	15,611
Pharr	56,839	Mercedes	14,164
Weslaco	31,081	Hidalgo	10,073

Tarrant County, TX

City	Pop.	City	Pop.
Fort Worth 🏛	603,337	Mansfield	34,735
Arlington	359,467	Southlake	24,490
North Richland Hills	60,483	Watauga	23,649
Euless	50,575	Colleyville	21,720
Bedford	48,417	Benbrook	21,646
Grapevine	47,265	Saginaw	16,874
Haltom City	40,132	White Settlement	15,652
Hurst	37,893	Forest Hill	13,275
Keller	34,915	Azle	10,301

Davis County, UT

City	Pop.	City	Pop.
Layton	61,205	Clinton	16,447
Bountiful	41,173	Syracuse	16,158
Clearfield	27,227	Centerville	14,670
Kaysville	21,749	Farmington 🏛	13,882

Salt Lake County, UT

City	Pop.	City	Pop.
Salt Lake City 🏛	178,605	South Jordan	36,791
West Valley City	112,678	Draper	33,042
Sandy	89,979	Riverton	30,119
West Jordan	89,011	Midvale	27,019
Taylorsville	58,179	South Salt Lake	21,510
Murray	43,328	Holladay	19,311

Utah County, UT

City	Pop.	City	Pop.
Provo 🏛	99,624	American Fork	22,387
Orem	88,619	Springville	21,507
Pleasant Grove	27,116	Payson	14,542
Lehi	25,665	Highland	12,332
Spanish Fork	22,839		

King County, WA

City	Pop.	City	Pop.
Seattle 🏛	571,480	Bothell	30,671
Bellevue	116,914	Des Moines	28,847
Kent	81,631	SeaTac	25,155
Federal Way	81,356	Mercer Island	22,182
Renton	54,807	Kenmore	19,353
Shoreline	51,950	Tukwila	16,992
Redmond	46,965	Covington	16,205
Kirkland	45,557	Issaquah	15,570
Auburn	44,980	Maple Valley	14,286
Sammamish	34,269	Lake Forest Park	12,474
Burien	30,887	Enumclaw	10,940

Snohomish County, WA

City	Pop.	City	Pop.
Everett 🏛	96,101	Mukilteo	19,434
Edmonds	39,601	Monroe	15,178
Lynnwood	33,418	Arlington	14,491
Marysville	28,804	Mill Creek	13,506
Mountlake Terrace	20,310		

Brown County, WI

City	Pop.	City	Pop.
Green Bay 🏛	101,100	Howard	15,774
De Pere	22,875	Allouez	15,043
Ashwaubenon	17,050	Bellevue	14,386

Milwaukee County, WI

City	Pop.	City	Pop.
Milwaukee 🏛	583,624	Cudahy	18,112
West Allis	59,508	Greendale	13,995
Wauwatosa	45,602	Whitefish Bay	13,672
Greenfield	35,865	Shorewood	13,351
Franklin	32,405	Glendale	13,008
Oak Creek	32,155	Brown Deer	11,895
South Milwaukee	21,051		

Waukesha County, WI

City	Pop.	City	Pop.
Waukesha 🏛	67,258	Muskego	22,600
Brookfield	39,890	Oconomowoc	13,528
New Berlin	38,719	Pewaukee	12,709
Menomonee Falls	33,877		

🏛 County Seat

Counties Associations

National Association of Counties (NACo)
440 1st St NW
Washington, DC 20001
www.naco.org
Ph: 202-393-6226
Fax: 202-393-2630

Alaska Municipal League
217 2nd St Suite 200
Juneau, AK 99801
www.akml.org
Ph: 907-586-1325
Fax: 907-463-5480

Arizona Association of Counties (AACo)
1910 W Jefferson
Phoenix, AZ 85009
www.azcounties.org
Ph: 602-252-6563
Fax: 602-254-0969

Association of Arkansas Counties
1415 W 3rd St
Little Rock, AR 72201
www.arcounties.org
Ph: 501-372-7550
Fax: 501-372-0611

Association of County Commissioners of Oklahoma (ACCO)
429 NE 50th St
Oklahoma City, OK 73105
www.okacco.com
Ph: 405-524-3200
Fax: 405-524-3700

Association of County Commissions of Alabama (ACCA)
100 N Jackson St
Montgomery, AL 36104
www.acca-online.org
Ph: 334-263-7594
Fax: 334-263-7678

Association County Commissioners of Georgia (ACCG)
50 Hurt Plaza Suite 1000
Atlanta, GA 30303
www.accg.org
Ph: 404-522-5022
Fax: 404-525-2477
TF: 800-858-2224

Association of Indiana Counties
10 W Market St Suite 1060
Indianapolis, IN 46204
www.indianacounties.org
Ph: 317-684-3710
Fax: 317-684-3713

Association of Minnesota Counties
125 Charles Ave
Saint Paul, MN 55103
www.mncounties.org
Ph: 651-224-3344
Fax: 651-224-6540

Association of Oregon Counties
PO Box 12729
Salem, OR 97309
www.aocweb.org
Ph: 503-585-8351
Fax: 503-373-7876

California State Association of Counties
1100 K St Suite 101
Sacramento, CA 95814
www.csac.counties.org
Ph: 916-327-7500
Fax: 916-441-5507

Colorado Counties Inc
800 Grant St Suite 500
Denver, CO 80203
www.ccionline.org
Ph: 303-861-4076
Fax: 303-861-2818

County Commissioners Association of Ohio
37 W Broad St Suite 650
Columbus, OH 43215
www.ccao.org
Ph: 614-221-5627
Fax: 614-221-6986

County Commissioners Association of Pennsylvania
PO Box 60769
Harrisburg, PA 17106
www.pacounties.org
Ph: 717-232-7554
Fax: 717-232-2162

County Commissioners' Association of West Virginia
2309 Washington St E
Charleston, WV 25311
www.polsci.wvu.edu/wv/
Ph: 304-345-4639
Fax: 304-346-3512

Delaware Association of Counties
12 N Washington Ave
Lewes, DE 19958
Ph: 302-645-0432
Fax: 302-645-2232

Florida Association of Counties
PO Box 549
Tallahassee, FL 32302
www.fl-counties.com
Ph: 850-922-4300
Fax: 850-488-7501

Hawaii State Association of Counties
200 S High St
Wailuku, HI 96793
Ph: 808-270-7760
Fax: 808-270-7639

Idaho Association of Counties (IAC)
PO Box 1623
Boise, ID 83701
www.idcounties.org
Ph: 208-345-9126
Fax: 208-345-0379

**Illinois Association of County Board
Members & Commissioners**
413 W Monroe St 2nd Fl   **Ph:** 217-528-5331
Springfield, IL 62704   **Fax:** 217-528-5562

Iowa State Association of Counties (ISAC)
501 SW 7th St Suite Q   **Ph:** 515-244-7181
Des Moines, IA 50309   **Fax:** 515-244-6397
www.iowacounties.org

Kentucky Association of Counties (KAC)
380 King's Daughters Dr   **Ph:** 502-223-7667
Frankfort, KY 40601   **Fax:** 502-223-1502
www.kaco.org   **TF:** 800-264-5226

Maine County Commissioners Association
11 Columbia St   **Ph:** 207-623-4697
Augusta, ME 04330   **Fax:** 207-622-4437
www.mainecounties.org

**Massachusetts Association of
County Commissioners**
614 High St   **Ph:** 781-461-6105
Dedham, MA 02027   **Fax:** 781-326-6480

Metro Counties of Illinois
1303 Brandywine Rd   **Ph:** 847-816-0889
Libertyville, IL 60048
www.co.cook.il.us/secretary/HomePage_Links/
collar_counties.htm

Michigan Association of Counties (MAC)
935 N Washington Ave   **Ph:** 517-372-5374
Lansing, MI 48906   **Fax:** 517-482-4599
www.micounties.org   **TF:** 800-258-1152

Mississippi Association of Supervisors
793 N President St   **Ph:** 601-353-2741
Jackson, MS 39202   **Fax:** 601-353-2749
www.masnetwork.org

Missouri Association of Counties (MAC)
516 E Capitol Ave PO Box 234   **Ph:** 573-634-2120
Jefferson City, MO 65102   **Fax:** 573-634-3549
www.mocounties.com

Montana Association of Counties
2715 Skyway Dr   **Ph:** 406-444-4380
Helena, MT 59602   **Fax:** 406-442-5238
maco.cog.mt.us

**Nebraska Association of County
Officials (NACO)**
625 S 14th St Suite A   **Ph:** 402-434-5660
Lincoln, NE 68508   **Fax:** 402-434-5673
www.nacone.org

Nevada Association of Counties (NACO)
201 S Roop St Suite 101   **Ph:** 775-883-7863
Carson City, NV 89701   **Fax:** 775-883-7398
www.nvnaco.org

**New Hampshire Association of
Counties (NHAC)**
46 Donovan St Suite 2   **Ph:** 603-224-9222
Concord, NH 03301   **Fax:** 603-224-8312
www.nhcounties.org

New Jersey Association of Counties
150 W State St   **Ph:** 609-394-3467
Trenton, NJ 08608   **Fax:** 609-989-8567
www.njac.org

New Mexico Association of Counties (NMAC)
613 Old Santa Fe Trail   **Ph:** 505-983-2101
Santa Fe, NM 87505   **Fax:** 505-983-4396
www.nmcounties.org   **TF:** 800-333-6438

New York State Association of Counties (NYSAC)
111 Pine St   **Ph:** 518-465-1473
Albany, NY 12207   **Fax:** 518-465-0506
www.nysac.org

**North Carolina Association of County
Commissioners (NCACC)**
PO Box 1488   **Ph:** 919-715-2893
Raleigh, NC 27602   **Fax:** 919-733-1065
www.ncacc.org

**North Dakota Association of
Counties (NDACO)**
1661 Capitol Way   **Ph:** 701-328-7300
Bismarck, ND 58502   **Fax:** 701-328-7308
www.ndaco.org

Police Jury Association of Louisiana
707 N 7th St   **Ph:** 225-343-2835
Baton Rouge, LA 70802   **Fax:** 225-336-1344
www.lpgov.org

South Carolina Association of Counties
1919 Thurmond Mall   **Ph:** 803-252-7255
Columbia, SC 29202   **Fax:** 803-252-0379
www.sccounties.org

**South Dakota Association of
County Commissioners**
222 E Capitol Ave Suite 1   **Ph:** 605-224-4554
Pierre, SD 57501   **Fax:** 605-224-9128
www.sdcounties.org   **TF:** 800-439-5672

**South Dakota Association of
County Officials**
207 E Capitol Ave Suite 8   **Ph:** 605-224-1968
Pierre, SD 57501   **Fax:** 605-224-9128
www.sdcounties.org

Tennessee County Services Association
226 Capitor Blvd Bldg Suite 700   **Ph:** 615-532-3767
Nashville, TN 37219   **Fax:** 615-532-3769
www.tncounties.org

Texas Association of Counties
PO Box 2131   **Ph:** 512-478-8753
Austin, TX 78768   **Fax:** 512-478-0519
www.county.org

Utah Association of Counties
5397 S Vine St   **Ph:** 801-265-1331
Salt Lake City, UT 84107   **Fax:** 801-265-9485
uacnet.org

Virginia Association of Counties
1001 E Broad St Suite LL20   **Ph:** 804-788-6652
Richmond, VA 23219   **Fax:** 804-788-0083
www.vaco.org

Washington Association of County Officials
206 10th Ave SE   **Ph:** 360-753-7319
Olympia, WA 98501   **Fax:** 360-664-2812
www.wacounties.org

Washington State Association of Counties
206 10th Ave SE   **Ph:** 360-753-1886
Olympia, WA 98501   **Fax:** 360-753-2842
www.wacounties.org

Wisconsin Counties Association
22 E Mifflin St Suite 900   **Ph:** 608 663-7188
Madison, WI 53703   **Fax:** 608-663-7189
www.wicounties.org   **TF:** 866-404-2700

Wyoming County Commissioners Association
PO Box 86   **Ph:** 307-632-5409
Cheyenne, WY 82003   **Fax:** 307-632-6533
www.wyo-wcca.org

Counties USA

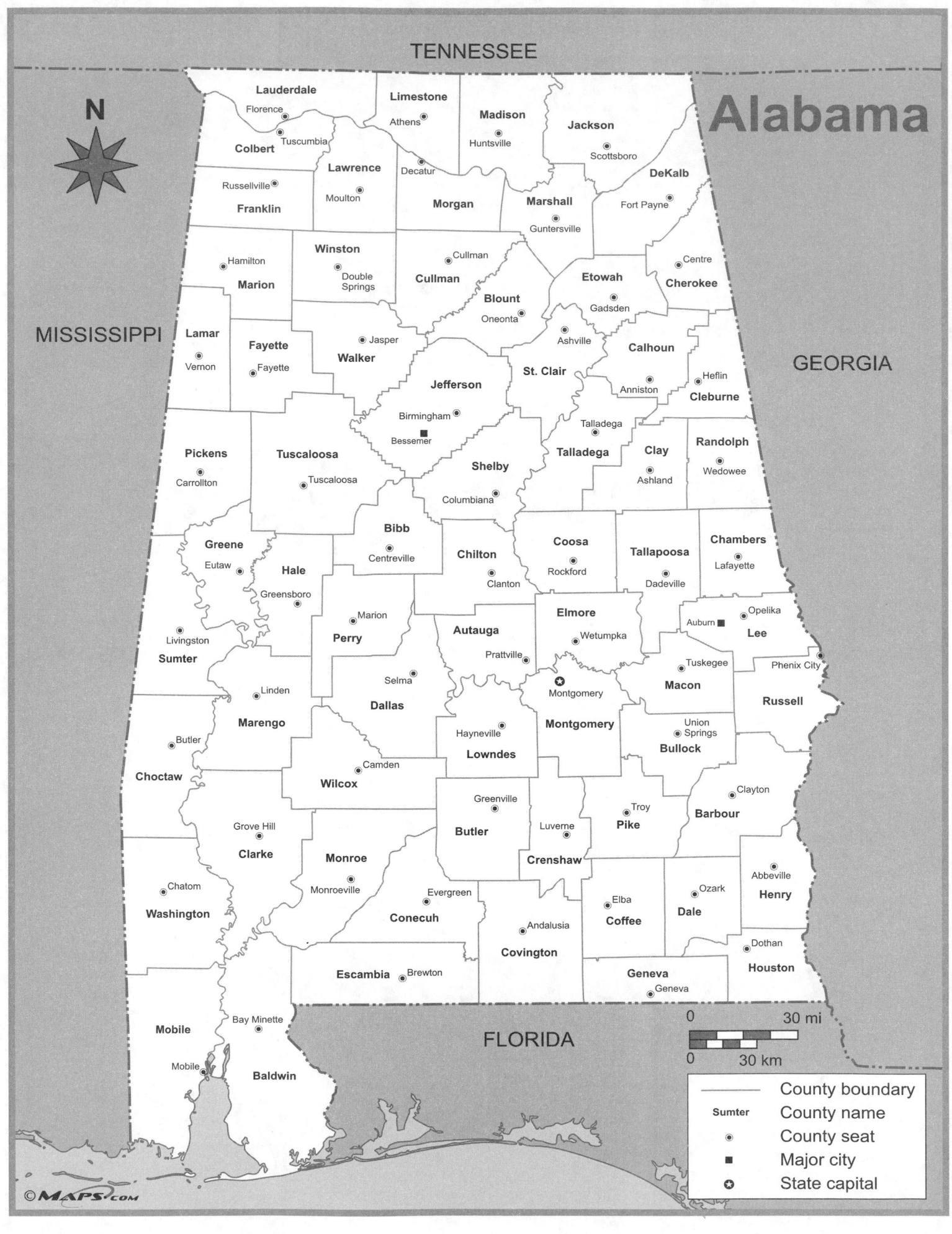

Alabama

ALABAMA STATE INFORMATION

www.alabama.gov   **Ph:** 334-242-8000

Area (sq mi): 52,419.02 (land 50,744; water 1675.01). **Pop per sq mi:** 89.8.

Pop 2005: 4,557,808. **Pop change:** 2000-20005 +2.5%; 1990-2000 +10.1%. **Pop 2000:** 4,447,100 (White 70.3%; Black or African American 26%; Hispanic or Latino 1.7%; Asian 0.7%; Other 2.2%). **Foreign born:** 2%. **Median age:** 35.8.

Income 2000: per capita $18,189; median household $34,135; **Pop below poverty level:** 16.1%. *Personal per capita income 2000-2003: $23,764-$26,505.

Unemployment 2004: 5.2%. **Change from 2000:** +1%. **Median travel time to work:** 24.8 minutes. **Working outside county of residence:** 25.2%.

AUTAUGA COUNTY

134 N Court St Rm 106   **Ph:** 334-361-3701
Prattville, AL 36067   **Fax:** 334-361-3724

In central AL, northwest of Montgomery; organized Nov 30, 1818 (prior to statehood) from Montgomery County. **Name Origin:** For Autauga Creek, probably from Creek Indian *atigi* 'border.'

Area (sq mi): 604.45 (land 595.97; water 8.48). **Pop per sq mi:** 81.6.

Pop 2005: 48,612. **State rank:** 27. **Pop change:** 2000-20005 +11.3%; 1990-2000 +27.6%. **Pop 2000:** 43,671 (White 79.7%; Black or African American 17.1%; Hispanic or Latino 1.4%; Asian 0.5%; Other 1.7%). **Foreign born:** 1.2%. **Median age:** 35.1.

Income 2000: per capita $18,518; median household $42,013; **Pop below poverty level:** 10.9%. *Personal per capita income 2000-2003: $23,018-$25,664.

Unemployment 2004: 4.6%. **Change from 2000:** +0.9%. **Median travel time to work:** 26.5 minutes. **Working outside county of residence:** 60.3%.

Cities with pop over 10,000: Prattville 🏛 (27,500).

BALDWIN COUNTY

312 Court House Sq Suite 12   **Ph:** 251-937-9561
Bay Minette, AL 36507   **Fax:** 251-580-2500
www.co.baldwin.al.us

In southwestern AL, east of Mobile, forms part of border with Florida; organized Dec 21, 1809 from Washington County (prior to statehood). **Name Origin:** For Abraham Baldwin (1754-1807), American clergyman and U.S. senator from GA (1799-1807); founded Franklin College (now University of Georgia).

Area (sq mi): 2026.93 (land 1596.35; water 430.58). **Pop per sq mi:** 101.8.

Pop 2005: 162,586. **State rank:** 7. **Pop change:** 2000-20005 +15.8%; 1990-2000 +42.9%. **Pop 2000:** 140,415 (White 86.1%; Black or African American 10.3%; Hispanic or Latino 1.8%; Asian 0.4%; Other 2.1%). **Foreign born:** 2.1%. **Median age:** 39.

Income 2000: per capita $20,826; median household $40,250; **Pop below poverty level:** 10.1%. *Personal per capita income 2000-2003: $26,120-$27,945.

Unemployment 2004: 4.8%. **Change from 2000:** +0.7%. **Median travel time to work:** 25.9 minutes. **Working outside county of residence:** 27.3%.

Cities with pop over 10,000: Daphne (18,115); Fairhope (14,602); Foley (10,421).

BARBOUR COUNTY

PO Box 398   **Ph:** 334-775-3203
Clayton, AL 36016   **Fax:** 334-775-1102

On southeastern border of AL, southwest of Columbus; organized Dec 18, 1832 from Pike County and territorial land. **Name Origin:** For James Barbour (1775-1842), governor of VA (1812-14), minister to England (1828-29).

Area (sq mi): 904.52 (land 884.9; water 19.61). **Pop per sq mi:** 32.1.

Pop 2005: 28,414. **State rank:** 39. **Pop change:** 2000-20005 -2.1%; 1990-2000 +14.2%. **Pop 2000:** 29,038 (White 50.9%; Black or African American 46.3%; Hispanic or Latino 1.6%; Asian 0.3%; Other 2.1%). **Foreign born:** 1.5%. **Median age:** 35.8.

Income 2000: per capita $13,316; median household $25,101; **Pop below poverty level:** 26.8%. *Personal per capita income 2000-2003: $18,820-$20,889.

Unemployment 2004: 7.2%. **Change from 2000:** -0.5%. **Median travel time to work:** 23.1 minutes. **Working outside county of residence:** 16.5%.

Cities with pop over 10,000: Eufaula (13,521).

BIBB COUNTY

PO Box 185   **Ph:** 205-926-3103
Centreville, AL 35042
www.dbtech.net/bibbco

In central AL, southeast of Tuscaloosa; organized Feb 9, 1818 (prior to statehood) from Monroe and Montgomery counties. **Name Origin:** For William Wyatt Bibb (1781-1820), U.S. senator from GA (1813-16) and first governor of AL (1817-20).

Area (sq mi): 626.16 (land 623.03; water 3.14). **Pop per sq mi:** 34.5.

🏛 *County Seat*

Bibb County (cont'd)

Pop 2005: 21,516. **State rank:** 48. **Pop change:** 2000-20005 +3.3%; 1990-2000 +25.6%. **Pop 2000:** 20,826 (White 76.2%; Black or African American 22.2%; Hispanic or Latino 1%; Asian 0.1%; Other 1%). **Foreign born:** 0.4%. **Median age:** 34.7.

Income 2000: per capita $14,105; median household $31,420; **Pop below poverty level:** 20.6%. ***Personal per capita income 2000-2003:** $17,724-$19,130.

Unemployment 2004: 5.4%. **Change from 2000:** -4.6%. **Median travel time to work:** 31.6 minutes. **Working outside county of residence:** 59.4%.

Cities with pop over 10,000: None.

BLOUNT COUNTY
220 2nd Ave E Rm 106   **Ph:** 205-625-4160
Oneonta, AL 35121   **Fax:** 205-625-5961
www.coveredbridge.org

In north-central AL, east of Gadsden; organized Feb 6, 1818 (prior to statehood) from Montgomery County. **Name Origin:** For William Blount (1749-1800), NC delegate to Continental Congress and U.S. senator from Tennessee (1796-97).

Area (sq mi): 650.6 (land 645.59; water 5.02). **Pop per sq mi:** 86.3.

Pop 2005: 55,725. **State rank:** 22. **Pop change:** 2000-20005 +9.2%; 1990-2000 +30%. **Pop 2000:** 51,024 (White 92.1%; Black or African American 1.2%; Hispanic or Latino 5.3%; Asian 0.1%; Other 3.6%). **Foreign born:** 3.1%. **Median age:** 36.4.

Income 2000: per capita $16,325; median household $35,241; **Pop below poverty level:** 11.7%. ***Personal per capita income 2000-2003:** $19,973-$21,623.

Unemployment 2004: 4%. **Change from 2000:** +1.2%. **Median travel time to work:** 34.7 minutes. **Working outside county of residence:** 59.7%.

Cities with pop over 10,000: None.

BULLOCK COUNTY
PO Box 472   **Ph:** 334-738-3883
Union Springs, AL 36089   **Fax:** 334-738-3839
www.unionspringsalabama.com/

In southeastern AL, southeast of Montgomery; organized Dec 5, 1866 from Barbour, Pike, Macon, and Montgomery counties. **Name Origin:** For E.C. Bullock, a local citizen.

Area (sq mi): 626.06 (land 625.01; water 1.04). **Pop per sq mi:** 17.7.

Pop 2005: 11,055. **State rank:** 66. **Pop change:** 2000-20005 -5.6%; 1990-2000 +6.1%. **Pop 2000:** 11,714 (White 23.6%; Black or African American 73.1%; Hispanic or Latino 2.7%; Asian 0.2%; Other 1.5%). **Foreign born:** 3.1%. **Median age:** 35.

Income 2000: per capita $10,163; median household $20,605; **Pop below poverty level:** 33.5%. ***Personal per capita income 2000-2003:** $15,395-$17,993.

Unemployment 2004: 11.6%. **Change from 2000:** +0%. **Median travel time to work:** 26 minutes. **Working outside county of residence:** 33.9%.

Cities with pop over 10,000: None.

BUTLER COUNTY
PO Box 756   **Ph:** 334-382-3612
Greenville, AL 36037   **Fax:** 334-382-3506

In south-central AL; organized Dec 13, 1819 from Conecuh and Montgomery counties. **Name Origin:** For William Butler (?-1818), GA legislator and soldier, killed by Indians.

Area (sq mi): 777.92 (land 776.87; water 1.05). **Pop per sq mi:** 26.7.

Pop 2005: 20,766. **State rank:** 49. **Pop change:** 2000-20005 -3%; 1990-2000 -2.3%. **Pop 2000:** 21,399 (White 58.1%; Black or African American 40.8%; Hispanic or Latino 0.7%; Asian 0.2%; Other 0.7%). **Foreign born:** 0.4%. **Median age:** 37.7.

Income 2000: per capita $15,715; median household $24,791; **Pop below poverty level:** 24.6%. ***Personal per capita income 2000-2003:** $18,924-$22,993.

Unemployment 2004: 9.4%. **Change from 2000:** -0.5%. **Median travel time to work:** 26.3 minutes. **Working outside county of residence:** 27.6%.

Cities with pop over 10,000: None.

CALHOUN COUNTY
1702 Noble St Suite 103   **Ph:** 256-241-2800
Anniston, AL 36201   **Fax:** 256-231-1744
www.calhounchamber.com

In northeastern AL, southeast of Gadsden; organized as Benton County Dec 18, 1832 from Creek cession; name changed Jan 29, 1858. **Name Origin:** For John Caldwell Calhoun (1782-1850), U.S. statesman and champion of Southern causes. Originally for Thomas Hart Benton (1782-1858), U.S. senator from MO, but his views on the Missouri Compromise angered the residents.

Area (sq mi): 612.32 (land 608.46; water 3.86). **Pop per sq mi:** 184.3.

Pop 2005: 112,141. **State rank:** 10. **Pop change:** 2000-20005 -0.1%; 1990-2000 -3.3%. **Pop 2000:** 112,249 (White 78%; Black or African American 18.5%; Hispanic or Latino 1.6%; Asian 0.6%; Other 2.1%). **Foreign born:** 1.7%. **Median age:** 37.2.

Income 2000: per capita $17,367; median household $31,768; **Pop below poverty level:** 16.1%. ***Personal per capita income 2000-2003:** $21,388-$24,492.

Unemployment 2004: 5.4%. **Change from 2000:** -0.2%. **Median travel time to work:** 23.4 minutes. **Working outside county of residence:** 15.5%.

Cities with pop over 10,000: Anniston ▥ (23,822); Oxford (15,648).

CHAMBERS COUNTY
2 Lafayette St Courthouse   **Ph:** 334-864-4348
Lafayette, AL 36862
www.chamberscounty.com

On eastern border of AL, north of Auburn; organized Dec 18, 1832 from Creek cession. **Name Origin:** For Henry H. Chambers (1790-1826), physician and U.S. senator (1825-26).

Area (sq mi): 603.11 (land 597.17; water 5.94). **Pop per sq mi:** 59.4.

Pop 2005: 35,460. **State rank:** 34. **Pop change:** 2000-20005 -3.1%; 1990-2000 -0.8%. **Pop 2000:** 36,583 (White 60.4%; Black or African

*Source: Personal per capita income data are from the Bureau of Economic Analysis; per capita income data are from the Bureau of the Census. See Introduction for explanation of differences.

48

Chambers County (cont'd)

American 38.1%; Hispanic or Latino 0.8%; Asian 0.2%; Other 0.8%). **Foreign born:** 0.8%. **Median age:** 37.7.

Income 2000: per capita $15,147; median household $29,667; **Pop below poverty level:** 17%. ***Personal per capita income 2000-2003:** $19,958-$22,278.

Unemployment 2004: 6.9%. **Change from 2000:** +0.4%. **Median travel time to work:** 22 minutes. **Working outside county of residence:** 40%.

Cities with pop over 10,000: None.

CHEROKEE COUNTY
260 Cedar Bluff Rd Suite 103   **Ph:** 256-927-3668
Centre, AL 35960   **Fax:** 256-927-3669
www.cherokee-chamber.org

On northeastern border of AL, east of Gadsden; organized Jun 9, 1836 from Cherokee cession. **Name Origin:** For the Indian tribe of Iroquoian linguistic stock. Name may derive from Creek *tciloki* 'people of a different speech.'

Area (sq mi): 599.95 (land 553.12; water 46.83). **Pop per sq mi:** 44.3.

Pop 2005: 24,522. **State rank:** 42. **Pop change:** 2000-20005 +2.2%; 1990-2000 +22.7%. **Pop 2000:** 23,988 (White 92.4%; Black or African American 5.5%; Hispanic or Latino 0.9%; Asian 0.1%; Other 1.4%). **Foreign born:** 1.1%. **Median age:** 40.

Income 2000: per capita $15,543; median household $30,874; **Pop below poverty level:** 15.6%. ***Personal per capita income 2000-2003:** $18,472-$20,798.

Unemployment 2004: 4.6%. **Change from 2000:** +0.2%. **Median travel time to work:** 30 minutes. **Working outside county of residence:** 53.6%.

Cities with pop over 10,000: None.

CHILTON COUNTY
PO Box 1948   **Ph:** 205-755-1551
Clanton, AL 35046   **Fax:** 205-280-7204

In central AL, south of Birmingham; organized as Baker County Dec 30, 1868 from Bibb, Perry, Autauga, and Shelby counties; name changed Dec 17, 1874. **Name Origin:** For William Parish Chilton (1810-71), legislator, jurist, and member of the Confederate Congress.

Area (sq mi): 700.76 (land 693.98; water 6.78). **Pop per sq mi:** 60.2.

Pop 2005: 41,744. **State rank:** 30. **Pop change:** 2000-20005 +5.4%; 1990-2000 +22%. **Pop 2000:** 39,593 (White 85.6%; Black or African American 10.6%; Hispanic or Latino 2.9%; Asian 0.2%; Other 2.5%). **Foreign born:** 1.9%. **Median age:** 35.9.

Income 2000: per capita $15,303; median household $32,588; **Pop below poverty level:** 15.7%. ***Personal per capita income 2000-2003:** $19,655-$21,416.

Unemployment 2004: 4.6%. **Change from 2000:** -0.5%. **Median travel time to work:** 33.2 minutes. **Working outside county of residence:** 52.7%.

Cities with pop over 10,000: None.

CHOCTAW COUNTY
117 S Mulberry St Suite 9   **Ph:** 205-459-2417
Butler, AL 36904   **Fax:** 205-459-4248

On western border of AL; organized Dec 29, 1847 from Sumter and Washington counties. **Name Origin:** For the Indian tribe of Muskohegean linguistic stock; meaning of the name unknown.

Area (sq mi): 920.85 (land 913.51; water 7.34). **Pop per sq mi:** 16.2.

Pop 2005: 14,807. **State rank:** 56. **Pop change:** 2000-20005 -7%, 1990-2000 -0.6%. **Pop 2000:** 15,922 (White 54.8%; Black or African American 44.1%; Hispanic or Latino 0.7%; Asian 0%; Other 0.7%). **Foreign born:** 0.6%. **Median age:** 37.9.

Income 2000: per capita $14,635; median household $24,749; **Pop below poverty level:** 24.5%. ***Personal per capita income 2000-2003:** $19,524-$21,269.

Unemployment 2004: 8.6%. **Change from 2000:** -0.5%. **Median travel time to work:** 37.8 minutes. **Working outside county of residence:** 35.5%.

Cities with pop over 10,000: None.

CLARKE COUNTY
PO Box 548   **Ph:** 251-275-3507
Grove Hill, AL 36451   **Fax:** 251-275-8517

In southwestern AL, northeast of Mobile; organized Dec 10, 1812 (prior to statehood) from Washington County. **Name Origin:** For John Clarke, a local Indian fighter.

Area (sq mi): 1252.51 (land 1238.38; water 14.13). **Pop per sq mi:** 22.

Pop 2005: 27,269. **State rank:** 40. **Pop change:** 2000-20005 -2.1%; 1990-2000 +2.3%. **Pop 2000:** 27,867 (White 55.7%; Black or African American 43%; Hispanic or Latino 0.6%; Asian 0.2%; Other 0.9%). **Foreign born:** 0.5%. **Median age:** 35.5.

Income 2000: per capita $14,581; median household $27,388; **Pop below poverty level:** 22.6%. ***Personal per capita income 2000-2003:** $20,209-$21,867.

Unemployment 2004: 8.8%. **Change from 2000:** -2.8%. **Median travel time to work:** 26.2 minutes. **Working outside county of residence:** 24.7%.

Cities with pop over 10,000: None.

CLAY COUNTY
PO Box 187   **Ph:** 256-354-7888
Ashland, AL 36251   **Fax:** 256-354-3208

In east-central AL, south of Anniston; organized Dec 7, 1866 from Talladega and Randolph counties. **Name Origin:** For Henry Clay (1777-1852), U.S. senator from KY, known as the 'Great Pacificator' for his advocacy of compromise to avert national crises.

Area (sq mi): 606 (land 605.07; water 0.93). **Pop per sq mi:** 23.1.

Pop 2005: 13,964. **State rank:** 58. **Pop change:** 2000-20005 -2%; 1990-2000 +7.6%. **Pop 2000:** 14,254 (White 81.5%; Black or African American 15.7%; Hispanic or Latino 1.8%; Asian 0.1%; Other 1.6%). **Foreign born:** 0.9%. **Median age:** 38.7.

Income 2000: per capita $13,785; median household $27,885; **Pop below poverty level:** 17.1%. ***Personal per capita income 2000-2003:** $18,391-$20,585.

Clay County (cont'd)

Unemployment 2004: 6.3%. **Change from 2000:** +0.4%. **Median travel time to work:** 26.6 minutes. **Working outside county of residence:** 34.1%.

Cities with pop over 10,000: None.

CLEBURNE COUNTY

120 Vickery St Rm 202   **Ph:** 256-463-2651
Heflin, AL 36264   **Fax:** 256-463-2257

On eastern border of AL, east of Anniston; organized Dec 6, 1866 from Calhoun and Randolph counties. **Name Origin:** For Confederate Gen. Patrick R. Cleburne (1828-64).

Area (sq mi): 561.02 (land 560.21; water 0.81). **Pop per sq mi:** 25.8.

Pop 2005: 14,460. **State rank:** 57. **Pop change:** 2000-20005 +2.4%; 1990-2000 +10.9%. **Pop 2000:** 14,123 (White 93.7%; Black or African American 3.7%; Hispanic or Latino 1.4%; Asian 0.1%; Other 1.4%). **Foreign born:** 0.9%. **Median age:** 37.5.

Income 2000: per capita $14,762; median household $30,820; **Pop below poverty level:** 13.9%. ***Personal per capita income 2000-2003:** $18,331-$20,470.

Unemployment 2004: 5.2%. **Change from 2000:** -0.3%. **Median travel time to work:** 30.3 minutes. **Working outside county of residence:** 60.1%.

Cities with pop over 10,000: None.

COFFEE COUNTY

230-M Court Ave   **Ph:** 334-897-2954
Elba, AL 36323

In southeastern AL, northwest of Dothan; organized Dec 29, 1841 from Dale County. **Name Origin:** For Gen. John Coffee (1772-1833), TN surveyor and officer who oversaw the removal of the Choctaws and Chickasaws to the OK Territory.

Area (sq mi): 680.48 (land 678.99; water 1.49). **Pop per sq mi:** 67.1.

Pop 2005: 45,567. **State rank:** 28. **Pop change:** 2000-20005 +4.5%; 1990-2000 +8.4%. **Pop 2000:** 43,615 (White 75.6%; Black or African American 18.4%; Hispanic or Latino 2.7%; Asian 0.9%; Other 3.6%). **Foreign born:** 2.7%. **Median age:** 37.2.

Income 2000: per capita $18,321; median household $33,664; **Pop below poverty level:** 14.7%. ***Personal per capita income 2000-2003:** $23,452-$26,837.

Unemployment 2004: 5.3%. **Change from 2000:** -1.4%. **Median travel time to work:** 21.4 minutes. **Working outside county of residence:** 35.3%.

Cities with pop over 10,000: Enterprise (22,231).

COLBERT COUNTY

201 N Main St   **Ph:** 256-386-8500
Tuscumbia, AL 35674   **Fax:** 256-386-8510
www.colbertcounty.org

On northwestern border of AL, south of Florence; organized Feb 6, 1867 from Franklin County. **Name Origin:** For George and Levi Colbert, two Cherokee Indian brothers.

Area (sq mi): 623.61 (land 594.53; water 29.08). **Pop per sq mi:** 91.9.

Pop 2005: 54,660. **State rank:** 23. **Pop change:** 2000-20005 -0.6%; 1990-2000 +6.4%. **Pop 2000:** 54,984 (White 80.9%; Black or African American 16.6%; Hispanic or Latino 1.1%; Asian 0.2%; Other 1.6%). **Foreign born:** 0.9%. **Median age:** 38.7.

Income 2000: per capita $17,533; median household $31,954; **Pop below poverty level:** 14%. ***Personal per capita income 2000-2003:** $21,216-$23,219.

Unemployment 2004: 6.9%. **Change from 2000:** -1.5%. **Median travel time to work:** 23.8 minutes. **Working outside county of residence:** 34.9%.

Cities with pop over 10,000: Muscle Shoals (12,395).

CONECUH COUNTY

409 Bellville St   **Ph:** 251-578-2066
Evergreen, AL 36401   **Fax:** 251-578-7013

In south-central AL; organized Feb 13, 1818 (prior to statehood) from Monroe County. **Name Origin:** Probably from Creek Indian *kono ika* 'polecat's head.'

Area (sq mi): 852.51 (land 850.79; water 1.71). **Pop per sq mi:** 15.6.

Pop 2005: 13,257. **State rank:** 61. **Pop change:** 2000-20005 -5.9%; 1990-2000 +0.2%. **Pop 2000:** 14,089 (White 55.1%; Black or African American 43.6%; Hispanic or Latino 0.7%; Asian 0.1%; Other 0.9%). **Foreign born:** 0.4%. **Median age:** 38.

Income 2000: per capita $12,964; median household $22,111; **Pop below poverty level:** 26.6%. ***Personal per capita income 2000-2003:** $19,086-$20,544.

Unemployment 2004: 8.5%. **Change from 2000:** +0.6%. **Median travel time to work:** 26.2 minutes. **Working outside county of residence:** 46.9%.

Cities with pop over 10,000: None.

COOSA COUNTY

PO Box 10   **Ph:** 256-377-2420
Rockford, AL 35136   **Fax:** 256-377-2524

In east-central AL, north of Montgomery; organized Dec 18, 1832 from Creek cession. **Name Origin:** For the Coosa River, which flows through the county.

Area (sq mi): 666.36 (land 652.44; water 13.91). **Pop per sq mi:** 17.1.

Pop 2005: 11,162. **State rank:** 65. **Pop change:** 2000-20005 -8.5%; 1990-2000 +10.3%. **Pop 2000:** 12,202 (White 63.4%; Black or African American 34.2%; Hispanic or Latino 1.3%; Asian 0%; Other 1.8%). **Foreign born:** 0.3%. **Median age:** 37.7.

Income 2000: per capita $14,875; median household $29,873; **Pop below poverty level:** 14.9%. ***Personal per capita income 2000-2003:** $18,255-$20,214.

Unemployment 2004: 7.1%. **Change from 2000:** -0.9%. **Median travel time to work:** 27.7 minutes. **Working outside county of residence:** 75%.

Cities with pop over 10,000: None.

COVINGTON COUNTY

1 Court Sq County Courthouse **Ph:** 334-428-2540
Andalusia, AL 36420 **Fax:** 334-428-2575

On south-central border of AL; organized Dec 7, 1821 from Henry County. **Name Origin:** For Leonard Wales Covington (1768-1813), MD-born legislator and army officer.

Area (sq mi): 1043.86 (land 1033.82; water 10.05). **Pop per sq mi.** 35.0.

Pop 2005: 37,003. **State rank:** 33. **Pop change:** 2000-20005 -1.7%; 1990-2000 +3.2%. **Pop 2000:** 37,631 (White 85.7%; Black or African American 12.4%; Hispanic or Latino 0.8%; Asian 0.2%; Other 1.3%). **Foreign born:** 0.6%. **Median age:** 39.8.

Income 2000: per capita $15,365; median household $26,336; **Pop below poverty level:** 18.4%. ***Personal per capita income 2000-2003:** $19,496-$23,656.

Unemployment 2004: 6.6%. **Change from 2000:** -0.8%. **Median travel time to work:** 23.6 minutes. **Working outside county of residence:** 17.8%.

Cities with pop over 10,000: None.

CRENSHAW COUNTY

PO Box 227 **Ph:** 334-335-6568
Luverne, AL 36049 **Fax:** 334-335-3616

In south-central AL, south of Montgomery; organized Nov 24, 1866 from Covington, Butler, Coffee, Lowndes, and Pike counties. **Name Origin:** For Anderson Crenshaw (1783-1847), lawyer, statesman, and jurist.

Area (sq mi): 610.88 (land 609.58; water 1.3). **Pop per sq mi:** 22.5.

Pop 2005: 13,727. **State rank:** 60. **Pop change:** 2000-20005 +0.5%; 1990-2000 +0.2%. **Pop 2000:** 13,665 (White 73.5%; Black or African American 24.8%; Hispanic or Latino 0.6%; Asian 0.1%; Other 1.3%). **Foreign born:** 0.3%. **Median age:** 38.8.

Income 2000: per capita $14,565; median household $26,054; **Pop below poverty level:** 22.1%. ***Personal per capita income 2000-2003:** $21,900-$23,897.

Unemployment 2004: 6.7%. **Change from 2000:** -0.9%. **Median travel time to work:** 31.8 minutes. **Working outside county of residence:** 51.4%.

Cities with pop over 10,000: None.

CULLMAN COUNTY

500 2nd Ave SW Rm 202 **Ph:** 256-739-3530
Cullman, AL 35055 **Fax:** 256-739-3525
www.co.cullman.al.us

In north-central AL, north of Birmingham; organized Jan 24, 1877 from Blount, Morgan, and Winston counties. **Name Origin:** For the city of Cullman.

Area (sq mi): 754.82 (land 738.43; water 16.39). **Pop per sq mi:** 108.2.

Pop 2005: 79,886. **State rank:** 16. **Pop change:** 2000-20005 +3.1%; 1990-2000 +14.6%. **Pop 2000:** 77,483 (White 95.4%; Black or African American 1%; Hispanic or Latino 2.2%; Asian 0.2%; Other 2%). **Foreign born:** 1.7%. **Median age:** 37.5.

Income 2000: per capita $16,922; median household $32,256; **Pop below poverty level:** 13%. ***Personal per capita income 2000-2003:** $21,239-$24,253.

Unemployment 2004: 5.1%. **Change from 2000:** +0.9%. **Median travel time to work:** 28.2 minutes. **Working outside county of residence:** 28.5%.

Cities with pop over 10,000: Cullman ⚖ (14,544).

DALE COUNTY

202 Hwy 123 S Suite C **Ph:** 334-774-6025
Ozark, AL 36360 **Fax:** 334-774-1841

In southeastern AL, northwest of Dothan; organized Dec 22, 1824 from Covington and Henry counties. **Name Origin:** For Samuel Dale (1772-1841), officer and scout in the Indian wars, and legislator in AL and MS.

Area (sq mi): 562.67 (land 561.07; water 1.6). **Pop per sq mi:** 86.9.

Pop 2005: 48,748. **State rank:** 26. **Pop change:** 2000-20005 -0.8%; 1990-2000 -1%. **Pop 2000:** 49,129 (White 72.8%; Black or African American 20.4%; Hispanic or Latino 3.3%; Asian 1.1%; Other 4.1%). **Foreign born:** 3.1%. **Median age:** 34.3.

Income 2000: per capita $16,010; median household $31,998; **Pop below poverty level:** 15.1%. ***Personal per capita income 2000-2003:** $20,266-$22,124.

Unemployment 2004: 5.4%. **Change from 2000:** +0.1%. **Median travel time to work:** 20.7 minutes. **Working outside county of residence:** 35.6%.

Cities with pop over 10,000: Ozark ⚖ (14,953).

DALLAS COUNTY

PO Box 987 **Ph:** 334-874-2560
Selma, AL 36702 **Fax:** 334-874-2587

In southwest-cental AL, west of Montgomery; organized Feb 9, 1818 (prior to statehood) from Montgomery County. **Name Origin:** For Alexander James Dallas (1759-1817), PA statesman, secretary of the treasury (1814-16) and acting secretary of war (1815); father of George Mifflin Dallas (1792-1864).

Area (sq mi): 993.37 (land 980.71; water 12.66). **Pop per sq mi:** 45.2.

Pop 2005: 44,366. **State rank:** 29. **Pop change:** 2000-20005 -4.3%; 1990-2000 -3.7%. **Pop 2000:** 46,365 (White 35.4%; Black or African American 63.3%; Hispanic or Latino 0.6%; Asian 0.3%; Other 0.7%). **Foreign born:** 0.7%. **Median age:** 35.3.

Income 2000: per capita $13,638; median household $23,370; **Pop below poverty level:** 31.1%. ***Personal per capita income 2000-2003:** $19,247-$21,469.

Unemployment 2004: 10.1%. **Change from 2000:** -1.6%. **Median travel time to work:** 23.6 minutes. **Working outside county of residence:** 13.8%.

Cities with pop over 10,000: Selma ⚖ (19,618).

DEKALB COUNTY

111 Grand Ave SW Suite 200 **Ph:** 256-845-8500
Fort Payne, AL 35967 **Fax:** 256-845-8502
www.dekalbcountyal.us

On northeastern border AL, north of Gadsden; organized Jan 9,

Dekalb County (cont'd)

1836 form Cherokee cession. **Name Origin:** For Johann, Baron de Kalb (1721-80), German-born French soldier who fought with the Americans during the Revolutionary War.

Area (sq mi): 778.65 (land 777.91; water 0.74). **Pop per sq mi:** 86.5.

Pop 2005: 67,271. **State rank:** 21. **Pop change:** 2000-20005 +4.4%; 1990-2000 +17.9%. **Pop 2000:** 64,452 (White 90.7%; Black or African American 1.7%; Hispanic or Latino 5.6%; Asian 0.2%; Other 5.6%). **Foreign born:** 4.1%. **Median age:** 36.3.

Income 2000: per capita $15,818; median household $30,137; **Pop below poverty level:** 15.4%. ***Personal per capita income 2000-2003:** $20,942-$22,950.

Unemployment 2004: 5.6%. **Change from 2000:** +1%. **Median travel time to work:** 23.9 minutes. **Working outside county of residence:** 25.1%.

Cities with pop over 10,000: Fort Payne ⚖ (13,435).

ELMORE COUNTY

PO Box 310   **Ph:** 334-567-1124
Wetumpka, AL 36092   **Fax:** 334-567-5957
elmoreco.org

In east-central AL, north of Montgomery; organized Feb 15, 1866 from Montgomery, Coosa, and Autauga counties, and from Tallapoosa County in 1867. **Name Origin:** For Revolutionary War veteran John Archer Elmore, an early settler (1821) and state legislator.

Area (sq mi): 657.21 (land 621.26; water 35.96). **Pop per sq mi:** 119.

Pop 2005: 73,937. **State rank:** 17. **Pop change:** 2000-20005 +12.2%; 1990-2000 +33.9%. **Pop 2000:** 65,874 (White 76.5%; Black or African American 20.6%; Hispanic or Latino 1.2%; Asian 0.4%; Other 1.9%). **Foreign born:** 1.1%. **Median age:** 35.3.

Income 2000: per capita $17,650; median household $41,243; **Pop below poverty level:** 10.2%. ***Personal per capita income 2000-2003:** $23,089-$25,015.

Unemployment 2004: 4.7%. **Change from 2000:** +0.8%. **Median travel time to work:** 28.7 minutes. **Working outside county of residence:** 66.5%.

Cities with pop over 10,000: Millbrook (13,248).

ESCAMBIA COUNTY

PO Box 856   **Ph:** 251-867-0305
Brewton, AL 36427   **Fax:** 251-867-0365
www.co.escambia.al.us

On southern border of AL; organized Dec 10, 1868 from Baldwin and Conecuh counties. **Name Origin:** For Escambia River, probably a Spanish rendering of a Choctaw or Chickasaw Indian word but origin is in dispute. There may be a connection to Spanish *cambiar* 'to exchange, trade, barter.' River formerly called the *Pensacola*.

Area (sq mi): 952.95 (land 947.38; water 5.57). **Pop per sq mi:** 40.2.

Pop 2005: 38,082. **State rank:** 32. **Pop change:** 2000-20005 -0.9%; 1990-2000 +8.2%. **Pop 2000:** 38,440 (White 63.9%; Black or African American 30.8%; Hispanic or Latino 1%; Asian 0.2%; Other 4.5%, including 3% American Indian/Alaska Native). **Foreign born:** 0.6%. **Median age:** 36.9.

Income 2000: per capita $14,396; median household $28,319; **Pop below poverty level:** 20.9%. ***Personal per capita income 2000-2003:** $18,687-$19,758.

Unemployment 2004: 7.5%. **Change from 2000:** +1.7%. **Median travel time to work:** 25.5 minutes. **Working outside county of residence:** 22%.

Cities with pop over 10,000: None.

ETOWAH COUNTY

800 Forrest Ave   **Ph:** 256-549-5300
Gadsden, AL 35901   **Fax:** 256-549-5400
www.etowahcounty.org

In northeastern AL, northwest of Anniston; organized as Baine County Dec 7, 1866; name changed Dec 1, 1868. **Name Origin:** Originally for David W. Baine, Confederate officer killed in the war. County abolished Dec 3, 1867 because he was a secessionist. Recreated and renamed for the Etowah Indian mound in GA. Meaning of Cherokee *itawa* is unknown but may be related to Creek *italwa* 'town, tribe.'

Area (sq mi): 548.75 (land 534.82; water 13.93). **Pop per sq mi:** 192.9.

Pop 2005: 103,189. **State rank:** 11. **Pop change:** 2000-20005 -0.3%; 1990-2000 +3.6%. **Pop 2000:** 103,459 (White 82.1%; Black or African American 14.7%; Hispanic or Latino 1.7%; Asian 0.4%; Other 1.9%). **Foreign born:** 1.6%. **Median age:** 38.3.

Income 2000: per capita $16,783; median household $31,170; **Pop below poverty level:** 15.7%. ***Personal per capita income 2000-2003:** $21,410-$23,744.

Unemployment 2004: 6.3%. **Change from 2000:** -1.1%. **Median travel time to work:** 24.5 minutes. **Working outside county of residence:** 24.8%.

Cities with pop over 10,000: Gadsden ⚖ (37,640).

FAYETTE COUNTY

103 1st Ave NW Courthouse Annex Suite 2   **Ph:** 205-932-4510
Fayette, AL 35555   **Fax:** 205-932-2902

In west-central AL, north of Tuscaloosa; organized Dec 20, 1824 from Marion and Pickens counties. **Name Origin:** For the Marquis de Layfayette (1757-1834), French statesman and soldier who fought with Americans during the Revolutionary War.

Area (sq mi): 629.34 (land 627.66; water 1.68). **Pop per sq mi:** 29.

Pop 2005: 18,228. **State rank:** 52. **Pop change:** 2000-20005 -1.4%; 1990-2000 +3%. **Pop 2000:** 18,495 (White 86.5%; Black or African American 11.9%; Hispanic or Latino 0.8%; Asian 0.2%; Other 1%). **Foreign born:** 0.7%. **Median age:** 39.

Income 2000: per capita $14,439; median household $28,539; **Pop below poverty level:** 17.3%. ***Personal per capita income 2000-2003:** $18,928-$21,204.

Unemployment 2004: 6.7%. **Change from 2000:** -0.8%. **Median travel time to work:** 28.5 minutes. **Working outside county of residence:** 40.4%.

Cities with pop over 10,000: None.

Source: Personal per capita income data are from the Bureau of Economic Analysis; per capita income data are from the Bureau of the Census.
See Introduction for explanation of differences.

FRANKLIN COUNTY

PO Box 1028   **Ph:** 256-332-8851
Russellville, AL 35653   **Fax:** 256-332-8855
www.franklincountychamber.org

On northwestern border of AL, south of Florence; organized Feb 4, 1818 (prior to statehood) from Cherokee cession. **Name Origin:** For Benjamin Franklin (1706-90), U.S. patriot, diplomat, and statesman.

Area (sq mi): 646.51 (land 635.64; water 10.86). **Pop per sq mi:** 48.4.

Pop 2005: 30,737. **State rank:** 36. **Pop change:** 2000-20005 -1.6%; 1990-2000 +12.3%. **Pop 2000:** 31,223 (White 87.3%; Black or African American 4.2%; Hispanic or Latino 7.4%; Asian 0.1%; Other 6%). **Foreign born:** 5.6%. **Median age:** 36.7.

Income 2000: per capita $14,814; median household $27,177; **Pop below poverty level:** 18.9%. ***Personal per capita income 2000-2003:** $20,127-$22,364.

Unemployment 2004: 7%. **Change from 2000:** -1.4%. **Median travel time to work:** 24.4 minutes. **Working outside county of residence:** 34.9%.

Cities with pop over 10,000: None.

GENEVA COUNTY

PO Box 86   **Ph:** 334-684-5620
Geneva, AL 36340   **Fax:** 334-684-5605

On southern border of AL, south of Dothan; organized Dec 26, 1868 from Coffee, Dale, and Henry counties. **Name Origin:** For Geneva, Switzerland, former home of the early settlers.

Area (sq mi): 578.9 (land 576.28; water 2.62). **Pop per sq mi:** 44.7.

Pop 2005: 25,735. **State rank:** 41. **Pop change:** 2000-20005 -0.1%; 1990-2000 +9%. **Pop 2000:** 25,764 (White 86.1%; Black or African American 10.6%; Hispanic or Latino 1.8%; Asian 0.1%; Other 2.1%). **Foreign born:** 0.8%. **Median age:** 39.3.

Income 2000: per capita $14,620; median household $26,448; **Pop below poverty level:** 19.6%. ***Personal per capita income 2000-2003:** $20,151-$23,596.

Unemployment 2004: 4.8%. **Change from 2000:** -4.4%. **Median travel time to work:** 27.2 minutes. **Working outside county of residence:** 49.4%.

Cities with pop over 10,000: None.

GREENE COUNTY

PO Box 307   **Ph:** 205-372-3598
Eutaw, AL 35462   **Fax:** 205-372-1510
greenecountyalabama.com

In western AL, southwest of Tuscaloosa; organized Dec 13, 1819 from Marengo and Tuscaloosa counties. **Name Origin:** For Gen. Nathanael Greene (1742-86), hero of the Revolutionary War and quartermaster general (1778-80).

Area (sq mi): 659.93 (land 645.87; water 14.07). **Pop per sq mi:** 15.

Pop 2005: 9,661. **State rank:** 67. **Pop change:** 2000-20005 -3.1%; 1990-2000 -1.8%. **Pop 2000:** 9,974 (White 19%; Black or African American 80.3%; Hispanic or Latino 0.6%; Asian 0.1%; Other 0.5%). **Foreign born:** 0.7%. **Median age:** 35.9.

Income 2000: per capita $13,686; median household $19,819; **Pop below poverty level:** 34.3%. ***Personal per capita income 2000-2003:** $17,548-$20,029.

Unemployment 2004: 8.4%. **Change from 2000:** -2.3%. **Median travel time to work:** 28.8 minutes. **Working outside county of residence:** 51.7%.

Cities with pop over 10,000: None.

HALE COUNTY

PO Box 396   **Ph:** 334-624-4257
Greensboro, AL 36744   **Fax:** 334-624-1715
www.halecoal.org

In west-central AL, south of Tuscaloosa; organized Jan 30, 1867 from Greene, Marengo, and Perry counties. **Name Origin:** For Stephen F. Hale (1816-78), early settler, lawyer, and Confederate army officer.

Area (sq mi): 656.47 (land 643.74; water 12.74). **Pop per sq mi:** 28.5.

Pop 2005: 18,316. **State rank:** 51. **Pop change:** 2000-20005 +6.6%; 1990-2000 +10.9%. **Pop 2000:** 17,185 (White 39.6%; Black or African American 59%; Hispanic or Latino 0.9%; Asian 0.2%; Other 1.1%). **Foreign born:** 0.3%. **Median age:** 34.4.

Income 2000: per capita $12,661; median household $25,807; **Pop below poverty level:** 26.9%. ***Personal per capita income 2000-2003:** $16,292-$18,368.

Unemployment 2004: 7%. **Change from 2000:** -2.7%. **Median travel time to work:** 29 minutes. **Working outside county of residence:** 51.8%.

Cities with pop over 10,000: None.

HENRY COUNTY

101 Court Sq Suite J   **Ph:** 334-585-2753
Abbeville, AL 36310   **Fax:** 334-585-5006

On southeastern border of AL, north of Dothan; organized Dec 13, 1819 from Conecuh County. **Name Origin:** For Patrick Henry (1736-99), patriot, governor of VA (1776-79; 1784-86), and statesman, famous for declaring 'Give me liberty or give me death.'

Area (sq mi): 568.33 (land 561.8; water 6.53). **Pop per sq mi:** 29.6.

Pop 2005: 16,610. **State rank:** 54. **Pop change:** 2000-20005 +1.8%; 1990-2000 +6.1%. **Pop 2000:** 16,310 (White 65.3%; Black or African American 32.3%; Hispanic or Latino 1.5%; Asian 0.1%; Other 1.9%). **Foreign born:** 1.1%. **Median age:** 39.3.

Income 2000: per capita $15,681; median household $30,353; **Pop below poverty level:** 19.1%. ***Personal per capita income 2000-2003:** $19,792-$22,750.

Unemployment 2004: 5.5%. **Change from 2000:** -1%. **Median travel time to work:** 25.5 minutes. **Working outside county of residence:** 53.7%.

Cities with pop over 10,000: None.

HOUSTON COUNTY

PO Drawer 6406   **Ph:** 334-677-4741
Dothan, AL 36302   **Fax:** 334-794-6633
www.houstoncounty.org

In southeastern corner of AL; organized Feb 9, 1903 from Dale,

Houston County (cont'd)

Geneva, and Henry counties. **Name Origin:** For George Smith Houston (1808-79), U.S. senator and governor of AL (1874-78).

Area (sq mi): 581.65 (land 580.36; water 1.29). **Pop per sq mi:** 162.4.

Pop 2005: 94,249. **State rank:** 12. **Pop change:** 2000-20005 +6.2%; 1990-2000 +9.2%. **Pop 2000:** 88,787 (White 72.4%; Black or African American 24.6%; Hispanic or Latino 1.3%; Asian 0.6%; Other 1.7%). **Foreign born:** 1.6%. **Median age:** 36.7.

Income 2000: per capita $18,759; median household $34,431; **Pop below poverty level:** 15%. *Personal per capita income 2000-2003: $24,455-$27,702.

Unemployment 2004: 4.6%. **Change from 2000:** +0.4%. **Median travel time to work:** 20 minutes. **Working outside county of residence:** 12.3%.

Cities with pop over 10,000: Dothan 🏛 (61,287).

JACKSON COUNTY

102 E Laurel St Suite 47 Courthouse   **Ph:** 256-574-9280
Scottsboro, AL 35768   **Fax:** 256-574-9321

On northeastern corner of AL; organized Dec 13, 1819 from Cherokee cession. **Name Origin:** For Andrew Jackson (1767-1845), seventh U.S. president.

Area (sq mi): 1126.77 (land 1078.74; water 48.02). **Pop per sq mi:** 49.7.

Pop 2005: 53,650. **State rank:** 24. **Pop change:** 2000-20005 -0.5%; 1990-2000 +12.8%. **Pop 2000:** 53,926 (White 91.2%; Black or African American 3.7%; Hispanic or Latino 1.1%; Asian 0.2%; Other 4.2%, including 1.8% American Indian/Alaska Native). **Foreign born:** 0.7%. **Median age:** 37.6.

Income 2000: per capita $16,000; median household $32,020; **Pop below poverty level:** 13.7%. *Personal per capita income 2000-2003: $21,373-$22,416.

Unemployment 2004: 6.7%. **Change from 2000:** -1.7%. **Median travel time to work:** 27 minutes. **Working outside county of residence:** 31.8%.

Cities with pop over 10,000: Scottsboro 🏛 (14,806).

JEFFERSON COUNTY

716 Richard Arrington Jr Blvd N Suite 210   **Ph:** 205-325-5555
Birmingham, AL 35203   **Fax:** 205-325-4860
www.jeffcointouch.com

In central AL; organized Dec 13, 1819 from Blount County. **Name Origin:** For Thomas Jefferson (1743-1826), U.S. patriot and statesman; third U.S. president.

Area (sq mi): 1123.8 (land 1112.61; water 11.2). **Pop per sq mi:** 590.7.

Pop 2005: 657,229. **State rank:** 1. **Pop change:** 2000-20005 -0.7%; 1990-2000 +1.6%. **Pop 2000:** 662,047 (White 57.4%; Black or African American 39.4%; Hispanic or Latino 1.6%; Asian 0.9%; Other 1.6%). **Foreign born:** 2.3%. **Median age:** 36.

Income 2000: per capita $20,892; median household $36,868; **Pop below poverty level:** 14.8%. *Personal per capita income 2000-2003: $30,406-$34,323.

Unemployment 2004: 5.3%. **Change from 2000:** +1.5%. **Median travel time to work:** 24.3 minutes. **Working outside county of residence:** 9.3%.

Cities with pop over 10,000: 13 (see page 31 for cities).

LAMAR COUNTY

PO Box 338   **Ph:** 205-695-7333
Vernon, AL 35592   **Fax:** 205-695-8522

On western border of AL, west of Birmingham; organized as Jones County Feb 14, 1867 from Marion, Pickens, and Fayette counties; abolished the same year; recreated as Sanford County Oct 8, 1868; renamed Feb 8, 1877. **Name Origin:** For Lucius Quintus Cincinnatus Lamar (1825-93), U.S. representative from MS (1857-60; 1873-77), U.S. senator (1877-85), secretary of the interior (1885-88), and a justice of the U.S. Supreme Court (1888-93).

Area (sq mi): 605.47 (land 604.85; water 0.62). **Pop per sq mi:** 24.7.

Pop 2005: 14,962. **State rank:** 55. **Pop change:** 2000-20005 -5.9%; 1990-2000 +1.2%. **Pop 2000:** 15,904 (White 86.1%; Black or African American 12%; Hispanic or Latino 1.3%; Asian 0.1%; Other 1.1%). **Foreign born:** 0.8%. **Median age:** 38.2.

Income 2000: per capita $14,435; median household $28,059; **Pop below poverty level:** 16.1%. *Personal per capita income 2000-2003: $18,625-$20,645.

Unemployment 2004: 8.2%. **Change from 2000:** -2.3%. **Median travel time to work:** 23.9 minutes. **Working outside county of residence:** 36%.

Cities with pop over 10,000: None.

LAUDERDALE COUNTY

PO Box 1059   **Ph:** 256-760-5750
Florence, AL 35631   **Fax:** 256-760-5703
lauderdalecountyonline.com

On northwestern border of AL; organized Feb 13, 1818 (prior to statehood) from Cherokee cession. **Name Origin:** At suggestion of Gen. John Coffee (1772-1833), for Col. James Lauderdale (?-1814), who died fighting under Coffee at the Battle of Talladega.

Area (sq mi): 718.78 (land 669.46; water 49.32). **Pop per sq mi:** 131.

Pop 2005: 87,691. **State rank:** 13. **Pop change:** 2000-20005 -0.3%; 1990-2000 +10.4%. **Pop 2000:** 87,966 (White 87.8%; Black or African American 9.8%; Hispanic or Latino 1%; Asian 0.4%; Other 1.5%). **Foreign born:** 1%. **Median age:** 37.6.

Income 2000: per capita $18,626; median household $33,354; **Pop below poverty level:** 14.4%. *Personal per capita income 2000-2003: $22,117-$24,435.

Unemployment 2004: 6.3%. **Change from 2000:** -1.8%. **Median travel time to work:** 23.7 minutes. **Working outside county of residence:** 29.5%.

Cities with pop over 10,000: Florence 🏛 (36,258).

LAWRENCE COUNTY

PO Box 307   **Ph:** 256-974-0663
Moulton, AL 35650   **Fax:** 256-974-2403
www.naiap.com

In northwest AL, west of Decatur; organized Feb 14, 1818 (prior to statehood) from Cherokee cession. **Name Origin:** For Capt.

*Source: Personal per capita income data are from the Bureau of Economic Analysis; per capita income data are from the Bureau of the Census.
See Introduction for explanation of differences.

54

Lawrence County (cont'd)

James Lawrence (1781-1813), U.S. Navy commander in War of 1812 who said, 'Don't give up the ship!'

Area (sq mi): 718.07 (land 693.38; water 24.68). **Pop per sq mi:** 49.9.

Pop 2005: 34,605. **State rank:** 35. **Pop change:** 2000-20005 -0.6%; 1990-2000 +10.4%. **Pop 2000:** 34,803 (White 77.3%, Black or African American 13.4%; Hispanic or Latino 1.1%; Asian 0.1%, Other 8.8%, including 5.4% American Indian/Alaska Native). **Foreign born:** 0.5%. **Median age:** 35.9.

Income 2000: per capita $16,515; median household $31,549; **Pop below poverty level:** 15.3%. ***Personal per capita income 2000-2003:** $19,949-$22,599.

Unemployment 2004: 6.4%. **Change from 2000:** -0.4%. **Median travel time to work:** 27 minutes. **Working outside county of residence:** 62.5%.

Cities with pop over 10,000: None.

LEE COUNTY

PO Box 666   **Ph:** 334-745-9767
Opelika, AL 36803   **Fax:** 334-742-9478

On eastern border of AL, north of Columbus; organized Dec 15, 1866 from Chambers and Macon counties. **Name Origin:** For Robert E. Lee (1807-70), American general and commander in chief of the Confederate forces during the Civil War.

Area (sq mi): 615.55 (land 608.71; water 6.84). **Pop per sq mi:** 202.5.

Pop 2005: 123,254. **State rank:** 8. **Pop change:** 2000-20005 +7.1%; 1990-2000 +32.1%. **Pop 2000:** 115,092 (White 73.2%; Black or African American 22.7%; Hispanic or Latino 1.4%; Asian 1.6%; Other 1.6%). **Foreign born:** 2.7%. **Median age:** 27.5.

Income 2000: per capita $17,158; median household $30,952; **Pop below poverty level:** 21.8%. ***Personal per capita income 2000-2003:** $20,254-$22,227.

Unemployment 2004: 4.2%. **Change from 2000:** +0.4%. **Median travel time to work:** 20.6 minutes. **Working outside county of residence:** 31.8%.

Cities with pop over 10,000: Auburn (48,348); Opelika ⛪ (23,483).

LIMESTONE COUNTY

310 W Washington St   **Ph:** 256-233-6400
Athens, AL 35611   **Fax:** 256-233-6403
www.co.limestone.al.us

On central northern border of AL, north of Decatur; organized Feb 6, 1818 (prior to statehood) from Cherokee and Chickasaw cessions. **Name Origin:** For Limestone Creek, which flows through it.

Area (sq mi): 607.08 (land 568.05; water 39.03). **Pop per sq mi:** 124.1.

Pop 2005: 70,469. **State rank:** 19. **Pop change:** 2000-20005 +7.3%; 1990-2000 +21.3%. **Pop 2000:** 65,676 (White 82.4%; Black or African American 13.3%; Hispanic or Latino 2.6%; Asian 0.4%; Other 2.5%). **Foreign born:** 1.7%. **Median age:** 35.8.

Income 2000: per capita $17,782; median household $37,405; **Pop below poverty level:** 12.3%. ***Personal per capita income 2000-2003:** $22,258-$25,475.

Unemployment 2004: 5%. **Change from 2000:** +0.6%. **Median travel time to work:** 26.4 minutes. **Working outside county of residence:** 46.1%.

Cities with pop over 10,000: Madison (35,012); Athens ⛪ (20,316).

LOWNDES COUNTY

PO Box 65   **Ph:** 334-548-2331
Hayneville, AL 36040   **Fax:** 334-548-5101

In south-central AL, southwest of Montgomery; organized Jan 20, 1830 from Butler and Dallas counties. **Name Origin:** For William Jones Lowndes (1782-1822), SC legislator and U.S. representative (1811-22).

Area (sq mi): 725.03 (land 717.94; water 7.1). **Pop per sq mi:** 18.2.

Pop 2005: 13,076. **State rank:** 62. **Pop change:** 2000-20005 -2.9%; 1990-2000 +6.4%. **Pop 2000:** 13,473 (White 25.7%; Black or African American 73.4%; Hispanic or Latino 0.6%; Asian 0.1%; Other 0.6%). **Foreign born:** 0.3%. **Median age:** 33.9.

Income 2000: per capita $12,457; median household $23,050; **Pop below poverty level:** 31.4%. ***Personal per capita income 2000-2003:** $17,478-$18,870.

Unemployment 2004: 9%. **Change from 2000:** -0.4%. **Median travel time to work:** 36.3 minutes. **Working outside county of residence:** 69%.

Cities with pop over 10,000: None.

MACON COUNTY

101 E Northside St Courthouse   **Ph:** 334-727-5120
Tuskegee, AL 36083   **Fax:** 334-724-2621

In southwestern AL, west of Columbus; organized Dec 18, 1832 from Creek cession. **Name Origin:** For Nathaniel Macon (1757-1837), NC legislator, U.S. representative (1791-1815), U.S. senator (1815-28), and president of the NC constitutional convention (1835).

Area (sq mi): 613.24 (land 610.52; water 2.72). **Pop per sq mi:** 37.4.

Pop 2005: 22,810. **State rank:** 45. **Pop change:** 2000-20005 -5.4%; 1990-2000 -3.3%. **Pop 2000:** 24,105 (White 13.8%; Black or African American 84.6%; Hispanic or Latino 0.7%; Asian 0.4%; Other 1%). **Foreign born:** 1.5%. **Median age:** 32.

Income 2000: per capita $13,714; median household $21,180; **Pop below poverty level:** 32.8%. ***Personal per capita income 2000-2003:** $15,621-$17,319.

Unemployment 2004: 6.6%. **Change from 2000:** +0.3%. **Median travel time to work:** 25.4 minutes. **Working outside county of residence:** 47.3%.

Cities with pop over 10,000: Tuskegee ⛪ (11,741).

MADISON COUNTY

100 Northside Sq   **Ph:** 256-532-3492
Huntsville, AL 35801   **Fax:** 256-532-6994
www.co.madison.al.us

On central northern border of AL; organized Dec 13, 1808 from

Madison County (cont'd)

Cherokee cession (prior to statehood). **Name Origin:** For James Madison (1751-1836), fourth U.S. president.

Area (sq mi): 812.85 (land 804.92; water 7.93). **Pop per sq mi:** 370.5.

Pop 2005: 298,192. **State rank:** 3. **Pop change:** 2000-20005 +7.8%; 1990-2000 +15.8%. **Pop 2000:** 276,700 (White 71%; Black or African American 22.8%; Hispanic or Latino 1.9%; Asian 1.9%; Other 3.4%). **Foreign born:** 4%. **Median age:** 35.7.

Income 2000: per capita $23,091; median household $44,704; **Pop below poverty level:** 10.5%. ***Personal per capita income 2000-2003:** $28,825-$31,797.

Unemployment 2004: 4.5%. **Change from 2000:** +1.1%. **Median travel time to work:** 20.9 minutes. **Working outside county of residence:** 5.8%.

Cities with pop over 10,000: Huntsville 🏛 (164,146).

MARENGO COUNTY
PO Box 480715   **Ph:** 334-295-2200
Linden, AL 36748   **Fax:** 334-295-2254

In west-central AL, south of Tuscaloosa; organized Feb 7, 1818 (prior to statehood) from Choctaw cession. **Name Origin:** Commemorates Napoleon's (1769-1821) victory over the Austrian army at Marengo, Italy (Jun 14, 1800).

Area (sq mi): 982.85 (land 977.04; water 5.8). **Pop per sq mi:** 22.4.

Pop 2005: 21,879. **State rank:** 47. **Pop change:** 2000-20005 -2.9%; 1990-2000 -2.4%. **Pop 2000:** 22,539 (White 46.9%; Black or African American 51.7%; Hispanic or Latino 1%; Asian 0.2%; Other 0.9%). **Foreign born:** 0.7%. **Median age:** 36.4.

Income 2000: per capita $15,308; median household $27,025; **Pop below poverty level:** 25.9%. ***Personal per capita income 2000-2003:** $21,304-$24,188.

Unemployment 2004: 6.2%. **Change from 2000:** +0.9%. **Median travel time to work:** 25.5 minutes. **Working outside county of residence:** 29.2%.

Cities with pop over 10,000: None.

MARION COUNTY
PO Box 1595   **Ph:** 205-921-7451
Hamilton, AL 35570   **Fax:** 205-952-9851
www.sonet.net/marioncounty/

On northwestern border of AL, south of Florence; organized Dec 13, 1818 (prior to statehood) from Indian lands. **Name Origin:** For Gen. Francis Marion (c. 1732-95), SC soldier and legislator, known as 'The Swamp Fox' for his tactics during the Revolutionary War.

Area (sq mi): 743.57 (land 741.41; water 2.16). **Pop per sq mi:** 40.7.

Pop 2005: 30,154. **State rank:** 37. **Pop change:** 2000-20005 -3.4%; 1990-2000 +4.6%. **Pop 2000:** 31,214 (White 94.1%; Black or African American 3.6%; Hispanic or Latino 1.2%; Asian 0.2%; Other 1.4%). **Foreign born:** 0.5%. **Median age:** 38.9.

Income 2000: per capita $15,321; median household $27,475; **Pop below poverty level:** 15.6%. ***Personal per capita income 2000-2003:** $18,514-$19,937.

Unemployment 2004: 6.3%. **Change from 2000:** -4.2%. **Median travel time to work:** 23.6 minutes. **Working outside county of residence:** 30%.

Cities with pop over 10,000: None.

MARSHALL COUNTY
424 Blount Ave   **Ph:** 256-571-7701
Guntersville, AL 35976   **Fax:** 256-571-7703
www.marshallco.org

In northeastern AL, south of Huntsville; organized Jan 9, 1836 from Blount County and Cherokee cession. **Name Origin:** For John Marshall (1755-1835), American jurist; fourth Chief Justice of the U.S. Supreme Court (1801-35).

Area (sq mi): 623.16 (land 567.06; water 56.1). **Pop per sq mi:** 151.

Pop 2005: 85,634. **State rank:** 14. **Pop change:** 2000-20005 +4.1%; 1990-2000 +16.1%. **Pop 2000:** 82,231 (White 91.3%; Black or African American 1.5%; Hispanic or Latino 5.7%; Asian 0.2%; Other 4.8%). **Foreign born:** 4%. **Median age:** 36.9.

Income 2000: per capita $17,089; median household $32,167; **Pop below poverty level:** 14.7%. ***Personal per capita income 2000-2003:** $21,546-$24,654.

Unemployment 2004: 4.8%. **Change from 2000:** -1.4%. **Median travel time to work:** 24.2 minutes. **Working outside county of residence:** 26.1%.

Cities with pop over 10,000: Albertville (18,251).

MOBILE COUNTY
205 Government St Rm C-936   **Ph:** 251-574-8786
Mobile, AL 36644
www.mobilecounty.org

In southwestern corner of AL on Mobile Bay; organized Aug 1, 1812 (prior to statehood) from Louisiana Purchase. **Name Origin:** For the city and the bay.

Area (sq mi): 1644.02 (land 1233.09; water 410.93). **Pop per sq mi:** 325.5.

Pop 2005: 401,427. **State rank:** 2. **Pop change:** 2000-20005 +0.4%; 1990-2000 +5.6%. **Pop 2000:** 399,843 (White 62.5%; Black or African American 33.4%; Hispanic or Latino 1.2%; Asian 1.4%; Other 2.1%). **Foreign born:** 2.3%. **Median age:** 34.4.

Income 2000: per capita $17,178; median household $33,710; **Pop below poverty level:** 18.5%. ***Personal per capita income 2000-2003:** $21,590-$23,164.

Unemployment 2004: 6.5%. **Change from 2000:** +0.5%. **Median travel time to work:** 25.2 minutes. **Working outside county of residence:** 8.1%.

Cities with pop over 10,000: Mobile 🏛 (192,759); Prichard (27,622); Saraland (12,603).

MONROE COUNTY
PO Box 8   **Ph:** 251-743-4107
Monroeville, AL 36461   **Fax:** 251-575-7934
www.monroecountyal.com

In southwest-central AL; organized Jan 29, 1815 (prior to statehood) from Creek cession. **Name Origin:** For James Monroe (1758-1831), fifth U.S. president.

---

*Source: Personal per capita income data are from the Bureau of Economic Analysis; per capita income data are from the Bureau of the Census. See Introduction for explanation of differences.

Monroe County (cont'd)

Area (sq mi): 1034.53 (land 1025.85; water 8.67). **Pop per sq mi:** 23.1.

Pop 2005: 23,733. **State rank:** 44. **Pop change:** 2000-20005 -2.4%; 1990-2000 +1.5%. **Pop 2000:** 24,324 (White 57.4%; Black or African American 40.1%; Hispanic or Latino 0.8%; Asian 0.3%; Other 1.9%, including 1% American Indian/Alaska Native). **Foreign born:** 0.3%. **Median age:** 35.4.

Income 2000: per capita $14,862; median household $29,093; **Pop below poverty level:** 21.3%. ***Personal per capita income 2000-2003:** $19,457-$21,110.

Unemployment 2004: 7.5%. **Change from 2000:** -2.2%. **Median travel time to work:** 23.3 minutes. **Working outside county of residence:** 15.4%.

Cities with pop over 10,000: None.

MONTGOMERY COUNTY

PO Box 1667   **Ph:** 334-832-1210
Montgomery, AL 36102   **Fax:** 334-832-2533
www.mc-ala.org

In south-central AL; organized Dec 6, 1816 (prior to statehood) from Monroe County. **Name Origin:** For Gen. Richard Montgomery (1738-75), American Revolutionary War officer who captured Montreal, Canada.

Area (sq mi): 799.76 (land 789.76; water 9.99). **Pop per sq mi:** 280.6.

Pop 2005: 221,619. **State rank:** 4. **Pop change:** 2000-20005 -0.8%; 1990-2000 +6.9%. **Pop 2000:** 223,510 (White 48.3%; Black or African American 48.6%; Hispanic or Latino 1.2%; Asian 1%; Other 1.6%). **Foreign born:** 2%. **Median age:** 33.5.

Income 2000: per capita $19,358; median household $35,962; **Pop below poverty level:** 17.3%. ***Personal per capita income 2000-2003:** $27,256-$31,381.

Unemployment 2004: 5.7%. **Change from 2000:** +1.6%. **Median travel time to work:** 20.2 minutes. **Working outside county of residence:** 6.7%.

Cities with pop over 10,000: Montgomery ⛪ (200,983).

MORGAN COUNTY

PO Box 668   **Ph:** 256-351-4730
Decatur, AL 35602   **Fax:** 256-351-4738
www.co.morgan.al.us

In north-central AL; organized as Cotaco County Jun 8, 1818 (prior to statehood) from Indian lands; name changed Jun 14, 1821. **Name Origin:** For Gen. Daniel Morgan (1736-1802), an officer in the Revolutionary War and U.S. representative from VA (1797-99). Originally for Cotaco Creek, which runs through it.

Area (sq mi): 599.06 (land 582.21; water 16.84). **Pop per sq mi:** 195.4.

Pop 2005: 113,740. **State rank:** 9. **Pop change:** 2000-20005 +2.4%; 1990-2000 +11%. **Pop 2000:** 111,064 (White 83.4%; Black or African American 11.2%; Hispanic or Latino 3.3%; Asian 0.4%; Other 3.3%). **Foreign born:** 2.7%. **Median age:** 36.6.

Income 2000: per capita $19,223; median household $37,803; **Pop below poverty level:** 12.3%. ***Personal per capita income 2000-2003:** $24,875-$27,475.

Unemployment 2004: 6%. **Change from 2000:** +0.5%. **Median travel time to work:** 23.3 minutes. **Working outside county of residence:** 27.7%.

Cities with pop over 10,000: Decatur ⛪ (54,528); Hartselle (12,866)

PERRY COUNTY

PO Box 505   **Ph:** 334-683-6106
Marion, AL 36756

In west-central AL, southeast of Tuscaloosa; organized Dec 13, 1819 from Tuscaloosa County. **Name Origin:** For Oliver Hazard Perry (1785-1819), U.S. naval officer during the War of 1812, famous for the message, 'We have met the enemy and they are ours.'

Area (sq mi): 724.08 (land 719.48; water 4.59). **Pop per sq mi:** 15.8.

Pop 2005: 11,371. **State rank:** 64. **Pop change:** 2000-20005 -4.1%; 1990-2000 -7%. **Pop 2000:** 11,861 (White 30.7%; Black or African American 68.4%; Hispanic or Latino 0.9%; Asian 0%; Other 0.7%). **Foreign born:** 0.5%. **Median age:** 33.3.

Income 2000: per capita $10,948; median household $20,200; **Pop below poverty level:** 35.4%. ***Personal per capita income 2000-2003:** $16,894-$18,389.

Unemployment 2004: 9.9%. **Change from 2000:** -3.7%. **Median travel time to work:** 33.7 minutes. **Working outside county of residence:** 49.2%.

Cities with pop over 10,000: None.

PICKENS COUNTY

PO Box 460   **Ph:** 205-367-2020
Carrollton, AL 35447   **Fax:** 205-367-2025

On central-western border of AL, west of Tuscaloosa; organized Dec 19, 1820 from Tuscaloosa County. **Name Origin:** Probably for Gen. Andrew Pickens (1739-1817), Revolutionary War hero, and U.S. representative from SC (1793-95). Others claim Israel Pickens, GA governor (1821-25).

Area (sq mi): 890.05 (land 881.42; water 8.63). **Pop per sq mi:** 22.9.

Pop 2005: 20,178. **State rank:** 50. **Pop change:** 2000-20005 -3.7%; 1990-2000 +1.2%. **Pop 2000:** 20,949 (White 55.7%; Black or African American 43%; Hispanic or Latino 0.7%; Asian 0.1%; Other 0.9%). **Foreign born:** 0.4%. **Median age:** 36.9.

Income 2000: per capita $13,746; median household $26,254; **Pop below poverty level:** 24.9%. ***Personal per capita income 2000-2003:** $18,309-$20,679.

Unemployment 2004: 7.5%. **Change from 2000:** -3.9%. **Median travel time to work:** 30 minutes. **Working outside county of residence:** 46.9%.

Cities with pop over 10,000: None.

PIKE COUNTY

PO Box 1147   **Ph:** 334-566-6374
Troy, AL 36081   **Fax:** 334-566-0142

In southeastern AL, southeast of Montgomery; organized Dec 17,

Pike County (cont'd)

1821 from Henry and Montgomery counties. **Name Origin:** For Zebulon Montgomery Pike (1779-1813), U.S. army officer and discoverer of Pikes Peak in CO.

Area (sq mi): 672.1 (land 671.03; water 1.06). **Pop per sq mi:** 44.2.

Pop 2005: 29,639. **State rank:** 38. **Pop change:** 2000-20005 +0.1%; 1990-2000 +7.3%. **Pop 2000:** 29,605 (White 60.1%; Black or African American 36.6%; Hispanic or Latino 1.2%; Asian 0.4%; Other 2.4%). **Foreign born:** 1.9%. **Median age:** 32.5.

Income 2000: per capita $14,904; median household $25,551; **Pop below poverty level:** 23.1%. ***Personal per capita income 2000-2003:** $21,011-$24,856.

Unemployment 2004: 5.3%. **Change from 2000:** -0.4%. **Median travel time to work:** 22 minutes. **Working outside county of residence:** 20.2%.

Cities with pop over 10,000: Troy 🏛 (13,737).

RANDOLPH COUNTY

PO Box 328   **Ph:** 256-357-4551
Wedowee, AL 36278   **Fax:** 256-357-9012

On central-eastern border of AL; organized Dec 18, 1832 from Creek cession. **Name Origin:** For John Randolph (1773-1833), U.S. congressman from VA during the years of 1799-1827, and U.S. minister to Russia (1830-31).

Area (sq mi): 584.11 (land 581.05; water 3.06). **Pop per sq mi:** 39.1.

Pop 2005: 22,717. **State rank:** 46. **Pop change:** 2000-20005 +1.5%; 1990-2000 +12.6%. **Pop 2000:** 22,380 (White 75.7%; Black or African American 22.2%; Hispanic or Latino 1.2%; Asian 0.2%; Other 1.1%). **Foreign born:** 1.2%. **Median age:** 37.7.

Income 2000: per capita $14,147; median household $28,675; **Pop below poverty level:** 17%. ***Personal per capita income 2000-2003:** $17,976-$19,645.

Unemployment 2004: 6.5%. **Change from 2000:** -1.3%. **Median travel time to work:** 31.2 minutes. **Working outside county of residence:** 41.7%.

Cities with pop over 10,000: None.

RUSSELL COUNTY

501 14th St   **Ph:** 334-298-0516
Phenix City, AL 36867   **Fax:** 334-297-6250

On southeastern border of AL; organized Dec 18, 1832 from Creek cession. **Name Origin:** For Col. Gilbert Christian Russell, U.S. Army officer.

Area (sq mi): 647.38 (land 641.32; water 6.06). **Pop per sq mi:** 76.9.

Pop 2005: 49,326. **State rank:** 25. **Pop change:** 2000-20005 -0.9%; 1990-2000 +6.2%. **Pop 2000:** 49,756 (White 56.1%; Black or African American 40.8%; Hispanic or Latino 1.5%; Asian 0.4%; Other 2.2%). **Foreign born:** 2%. **Median age:** 35.4.

Income 2000: per capita $14,015; median household $27,492; **Pop below poverty level:** 19.9%. ***Personal per capita income 2000-2003:** $19,412-$21,586.

Unemployment 2004: 6.1%. **Change from 2000:** +0.4%. **Median travel time to work:** 24.6 minutes. **Working outside county of residence:** 64.5%.

Cities with pop over 10,000: Phenix City 🏛 (28,936).

SAINT CLAIR COUNTY

PO Box 397   **Ph:** 205-594-2103
Ashville, AL 35953   **Fax:** 205-594-2110
www.stclairco.com

In east-central AL, east of Birmingham; organized Nov 20, 1818 (prior to statehood) from Shelby County. **Name Origin:** For Gen. Arthur Saint Clair (1736-1818), soldier, president of the Continental Congress (1787), and governor of the Northwest Territory (1787-1805).

Area (sq mi): 653.61 (land 633.75; water 19.86). **Pop per sq mi:** 114.1.

Pop 2005: 72,330. **State rank:** 18. **Pop change:** 2000-20005 +11.7%; 1990-2000 +29.5%. **Pop 2000:** 64,742 (White 89.5%; Black or African American 8.1%; Hispanic or Latino 1.1%; Asian 0.2%; Other 1.7%). **Foreign born:** 0.6%. **Median age:** 36.4.

Income 2000: per capita $17,960; median household $37,285; **Pop below poverty level:** 12.1%. ***Personal per capita income 2000-2003:** $21,305-$23,453.

Unemployment 2004: 4.8%. **Change from 2000:** +1.1%. **Median travel time to work:** 32.3 minutes. **Working outside county of residence:** 61.7%.

Cities with pop over 10,000: Pell City (10,602).

SHELBY COUNTY

PO Box 1810   **Ph:** 205-669-3760
Columbiana, AL 35051   **Fax:** 205-669-3786
www.shelbycountyalabama.com

In central AL, south of Birmingham; organized Feb 7, 1817 (prior to statehood) from Montgomery County. **Name Origin:** For Gen. Isaac Shelby (1750-1826), officer in the Revolutionary War, NC legislator, and governor of KY (1792-96; 1812-16).

Area (sq mi): 809.53 (land 794.69; water 14.83). **Pop per sq mi:** 215.8.

Pop 2005: 171,465. **State rank:** 5. **Pop change:** 2000-20005 +19.7%; 1990-2000 +44.2%. **Pop 2000:** 143,293 (White 88.6%; Black or African American 7.4%; Hispanic or Latino 2%; Asian 1%; Other 1.7%). **Foreign born:** 2.4%. **Median age:** 34.9.

Income 2000: per capita $27,176; median household $55,440; **Pop below poverty level:** 6.3%. ***Personal per capita income 2000-2003:** $32,913-$34,697.

Unemployment 2004: 3.2%. **Change from 2000:** +1.2%. **Median travel time to work:** 28.6 minutes. **Working outside county of residence:** 55.8%.

Cities with pop over 10,000: Alabaster (26,830); Pelham (18,113); Helena (12,433).

SUMTER COUNTY

PO Box 936   **Ph:** 205-652-2291
Livingston, AL 35470

On central-western border of AL, southwest of Tuscaloosa; organized Dec 18, 1832 from Choctaw cession. **Name Origin:** For Gen.

**Source: Personal per capita income data are from the Bureau of Economic Analysis; per capita income data are from the Bureau of the Census.
See Introduction for explanation of differences.*

Sumter County (cont'd)

Thomas Sumter (1734-1832), American Revolutionary officer nicknamed the 'Gamecock of the Revolution,' U.S. representative from GA (1789-93;1797-1801), and U.S. senator (1801-10).

Area (sq mi): 913.3 (land 904.94; water 8.37). **Pop per sq mi:** 15.3.

Pop 2005: 13,819. **State rank:** 59. **Pop change:** 2000-20005 -6.6%; 1990-2000 -8.5%. **Pop 2000:** 14,798 (White 25.0%, Black or African American 73.2%; Hispanic or Latino 1.1%; Asian 0.1%, Other 0.8%). **Foreign born:** 0.5%. **Median age:** 32.1.

Income 2000: per capita $11,491; median household $18,911; **Pop below poverty level:** 38.7%. ***Personal per capita income 2000-2003:** $16,508-$18,319.

Unemployment 2004: 9.5%. **Change from 2000:** -1.1%. **Median travel time to work:** 28 minutes. **Working outside county of residence:** 31.3%.

Cities with pop over 10,000: None.

TALLADEGA COUNTY

PO Box 6170   **Ph:** 256-362-1357
Talladega, AL 35161   **Fax:** 256-761-2147
www.talladegacounty.com

In east-central AL, southeast of Birmingham; organized Dec 18, 1832 from Creek cession. **Name Origin:** For the town, from Cree *talwa* 'town' and *atigi* 'border,' being the boundary between the Creeks and the Natchez.

Area (sq mi): 760.25 (land 739.53; water 20.72). **Pop per sq mi:** 108.8.

Pop 2005: 80,457. **State rank:** 15. **Pop change:** 2000-20005 +0.2%; 1990-2000 +8.4%. **Pop 2000:** 80,321 (White 66.5%; Black or African American 31.5%; Hispanic or Latino 1%; Asian 0.2%; Other 1.2%). **Foreign born:** 0.7%. **Median age:** 36.6.

Income 2000: per capita $15,704; median household $31,628; **Pop below poverty level:** 17.6%. ***Personal per capita income 2000-2003:** $19,014-$24,182.

Unemployment 2004: 6.7%. **Change from 2000:** -1.3%. **Median travel time to work:** 25.1 minutes. **Working outside county of residence:** 34.6%.

Cities with pop over 10,000: Talladega ⚏ (17,090); Sylacauga (12,883).

TALLAPOOSA COUNTY

125 N Broadnax St Rm 131   **Ph:** 256-825-4268
Dadeville, AL 36853   **Fax:** 256-825-1009

In east-central AL, west of Auburn; organized Dec 18, 1832 from Chickasaw cession. **Name Origin:** For the Tallapoosa River, which runs through it.

Area (sq mi): 766.23 (land 717.93; water 48.3). **Pop per sq mi:** 56.7.

Pop 2005: 40,717. **State rank:** 31. **Pop change:** 2000-20005 -1.8%; 1990-2000 +6.8%. **Pop 2000:** 41,475 (White 73.2%; Black or African American 25.4%; Hispanic or Latino 0.6%; Asian 0.2%; Other 1%). **Foreign born:** 0.4%. **Median age:** 39.3.

Income 2000: per capita $16,909; median household $30,745; **Pop below poverty level:** 16.6%. ***Personal per capita income 2000-2003:** $21,238-$23,452.

Unemployment 2004: 6.1%. **Change from 2000:** -0.6%. **Median travel time to work:** 25.1 minutes. **Working outside county of residence:** 28.7%.

Cities with pop over 10,000: Alexander City (14,971).

TUSCALOOSA COUNTY

PO Box 20113   **Ph:** 205-349-3870
Tuscaloosa, AL 35402   **Fax:** 205-469-6313
www.co.tuscaloosa.al.us

In west-central AL, west of Birmingham; organized Feb 7, 1818 (prior to statehood) from Indian lands. **Name Origin:** Indian name for the Black Warrior River, which runs through it.

Area (sq mi): 1351.23 (land 1324.37; water 26.85). **Pop per sq mi:** 127.5.

Pop 2005: 168,908. **State rank:** 6. **Pop change:** 2000-20005 +2.4%; 1990-2000 +9.5%. **Pop 2000:** 164,875 (White 67.5%; Black or African American 29.3%; Hispanic or Latino 1.3%; Asian 0.9%; Other 1.6%). **Foreign born:** 2.1%. **Median age:** 31.9.

Income 2000: per capita $18,998; median household $34,436; **Pop below poverty level:** 17%. ***Personal per capita income 2000-2003:** $24,496-$27,845.

Unemployment 2004: 4.6%. **Change from 2000:** +1.3%. **Median travel time to work:** 21.2 minutes. **Working outside county of residence:** 10.9%.

Cities with pop over 10,000: Tuscaloosa ⚏ (80,181); Northport (20,451).

WALKER COUNTY

PO Box 1447   **Ph:** 205-384-7230
Jasper, AL 35502   **Fax:** 205-384-7003
www.walkercounty.com

In west-central AL, northwest of Birmingham; organized Dec 20, 1823 from Marion and Tuscaloosa counties. **Name Origin:** For John Williams Walker (1783-1823), U.S. senator from AL (1819-22).

Area (sq mi): 805.3 (land 794.39; water 10.91). **Pop per sq mi:** 88.3.

Pop 2005: 70,117. **State rank:** 20. **Pop change:** 2000-20005 -0.8%; 1990-2000 +4.5%. **Pop 2000:** 70,713 (White 91.7%; Black or African American 6.2%; Hispanic or Latino 0.9%; Asian 0.2%; Other 1.5%). **Foreign born:** 0.7%. **Median age:** 38.3.

Income 2000: per capita $15,546; median household $29,076; **Pop below poverty level:** 16.5%. ***Personal per capita income 2000-2003:** $20,711-$23,449.

Unemployment 2004: 6.1%. **Change from 2000:** -1.3%. **Median travel time to work:** 33.2 minutes. **Working outside county of residence:** 37%.

Cities with pop over 10,000: Jasper ⚏ (13,907).

WASHINGTON COUNTY

PO Box 146   **Ph:** 251-847-2208
Chatom, AL 36518   **Fax:** 251-847-3677
www.washingtoncountyalgov.com

On southwestern border of AL, north of Mobile; original county; organized Jun 4, 1800 (prior to statehood). **Name Origin:** For George Washington (1732-1799), American patriot and first U.S. president.

⚏ *County Seat*

Washington County (cont'd)

Area (sq mi): 1088.54 (land 1080.66; water 7.89). **Pop per sq mi:** 16.4.

Pop 2005: 17,773. **State rank:** 53. **Pop change:** 2000-20005 -1.8%; 1990-2000 +8.4%. **Pop 2000:** 18,097 (White 64.5%; Black or African American 26.9%; Hispanic or Latino 0.9%; Asian 0.1%; Other 8%, including 7.1% American Indian/Alaska Native). **Foreign born:** 0.5%. **Median age:** 34.9.

Income 2000: per capita $14,081; median household $30,815; **Pop below poverty level:** 18.5%. ***Personal per capita income 2000-2003:** $18,197-$19,157.

Unemployment 2004: 9.6%. **Change from 2000:** -6.2%. **Median travel time to work:** 34.6 minutes. **Working outside county of residence:** 48.1%.

Cities with pop over 10,000: None.

WILCOX COUNTY

PO Box 608   **Ph:** 334-682-4126
Camden, AL 36726   **Fax:** 334-682-4025

In southwest-central AL, southwest of Montgomery; organized Dec 13, 1819 from Dallas and Monroe counties. **Name Origin:** For Lt. Joseph M. Wilcox, killed in 1814 by Creek Indians.

Area (sq mi): 907.46 (land 888.68; water 18.78). **Pop per sq mi:** 14.6.

Pop 2005: 12,937. **State rank:** 63. **Pop change:** 2000-20005 -1.9%; 1990-2000 -2.8%. **Pop 2000:** 13,183 (White 27.4%; Black or African American 71.9%; Hispanic or Latino 0.7%; Asian 0.1%; Other 0.4%). **Foreign born:** 0.3%. **Median age:** 33.8.

Income 2000: per capita $10,903; median household $16,646; **Pop below poverty level:** 39.9%. ***Personal per capita income 2000-2003:** $15,835-$17,441.

Unemployment 2004: 12%. **Change from 2000:** -1.2%. **Median travel time to work:** 31.3 minutes. **Working outside county of residence:** 36.9%.

Cities with pop over 10,000: None.

WINSTON COUNTY

PO Box 309   **Ph:** 205-489-5533
Double Springs, AL 35553   **Fax:** 205-489-1225

In northwest-central AL, northwest of Birmingham; organized as Hancock County Feb 12, 1858 from Walker County; renamed Jan 22, 1858. **Name Origin:** Originally for John Hancock (1737-93), noted signer of the Declaration of Independence; then for John Anthony Winston (1812-71), Confederate army officer and governor of AL (1854-1857).

Area (sq mi): 631.86 (land 614.44; water 17.42). **Pop per sq mi:** 39.9.

Pop 2005: 24,498. **State rank:** 43. **Pop change:** 2000-20005 -1.4%; 1990-2000 +12.7%. **Pop 2000:** 24,843 (White 96.8%; Black or African American 0.4%; Hispanic or Latino 1.5%; Asian 0.1%; Other 2.2%). **Foreign born:** 1%. **Median age:** 38.

Income 2000: per capita $15,738; median household $28,435; **Pop below poverty level:** 17.1%. ***Personal per capita income 2000-2003:** $19,058-$20,407.

Unemployment 2004: 7.3%. **Change from 2000:** -5.2%. **Median travel time to work:** 26.4 minutes. **Working outside county of residence:** 28.7%.

Cities with pop over 10,000: None.

---

*Source: Personal per capita income data are from the Bureau of Economic Analysis; per capita income data are from the Bureau of the Census. See Introduction for explanation of differences.

Alaska

RUSSIA

CANADA

Arctic Ocean

Bering Sea

Gulf of Alaska

Pacific Ocean

North Slope

Northwest Arctic

Nome

Wade-Hampton

Bethel

Yukon-Koyukuk

Fairbanks North Star

Denali

Southeast Fairbanks

Matanuska-Susitna

Valdez-Cordova

Anchorage

Kenai Peninsula

Dillingham

Bristol Bay

Lake and Peninsula

Aleutians East

Aleutians West

Skagway-Yakutat-Angoon

Haines

Wrangell-Petersburg

Ketchikan Gateway

Prince of Wales-Outer Ketchikan

Barrow

Kotzebue

Fairbanks

Healy

Palmer

Soldotna

Anchorage

Naknek

King Salmon

Sand Point

Kodiak

Sitka

Juneau

Haines

Yakutat

Ketchikan

County boundary

Haines — County name

⊙ County seat

■ Major city

✪ State capital

0   400 km
0   400 mi

N

© MAPS.com

Alaska

ALASKA STATE INFORMATION

www.state.ak.us   **Ph:** 907-465-2111

Area (sq mi): 663,267.26 (land 571,951.26; water 91,316). **Pop per sq mi:** 1.2.

Pop 2005: 663,661. **Pop change:** 2000-20005 +5.9%; 1990-2000 +14%. **Pop 2000:** 626,932 (White 67.6%; Black or African American 3.5%; Hispanic or Latino 4.1%; Asian 4%; Other 23.1%, including 15.6% American Indian/Alaska Native). **Foreign born:** 5.9%. **Median age:** 32.4.

Income 2000: per capita $22,660; median household $51,571; **Pop below poverty level:** 9.4%. ***Personal per capita income 2000-2003:** $29,867-$33,213.

Unemployment 2004: 7.4%. **Change from 2000:** +1.2%. **Median travel time to work:** 19.6 minutes. **Working outside county of residence:** 6%.

ALEUTIANS EAST BOROUGH

PO Box 349   **Ph:** 907-383-2699

Sand Point, AK 99661   **Fax:** 907-383-3496

www.aleutianseast.org

In southwestern AK, extending south and west from the Alaska Peninsula as far west as Akutan Island; bounded on south and east by Pacific Ocean, on north by Bering Sea. Established Oct 23, 1987 from the eastern portion of the former Aleutian Islands Census Area and the southwestern portion of the Dillingham Census Area **Name Origin:** Adjective form of *Aleut*, the natives of the Aleutian Islands.

Area (sq mi): 15011.6 (land 6988.14; water 8023.46). **Pop per sq mi:** 0.4.

Pop 2005: 2,713. **State rank:** 22. **Pop change:** 2000-20005 +0.6%; 1990-2000 +9.5%. **Pop 2000:** 2,697 (White 19.3%; Black or African American 1.7%; Hispanic or Latino 12.6%; Asian 26.5%; Other 47.9%, including 37.3% American Indian/Alaska Native). **Foreign born:** 18.3%. **Median age:** 37.

Income 2000: per capita $18,421; median household $47,875; **Pop below poverty level:** 21.8%. ***Personal per capita income 2000-2003:** $22,694-$24,522.

Unemployment 2004: 8.8%. **Change from 2000:** +4.5%. **Median travel time to work:** 6.3 minutes. **Working outside county of residence:** 0.5%.

Cities with pop over 10,000: None.

ALEUTIANS WEST CENSUS AREA

Southwest of Alaska Peninsula, from the Andreanof Islands in east to the Near Islands in west; bounded on north by Bering Sea and on south and east by Pacific Ocean. **Name Origin:** Adjective form of *Aleut*, the natives of the Aleutian Islands. Originally called the Aleutian Islands Census Area; name officially changed Jan 1, 1990.

Area (sq mi): 14,116.51 (land 4396.77; water 9719.74). **Pop per sq mi:** 1.2.

Pop 2005: 5,382. **State rank:** 19. **Pop change:** 2000-20005 -1.5%; 1990 2000 -12.3%. **Pop 2000:** 5,465 (White 37.7%; Black or African American 3%; Hispanic or Latino 10.5%; Asian 24.6%; Other 32.4%, including 21% American Indian/Alaska Native). **Foreign born:** 21.5%. **Median age:** 36.1.

Income 2000: per capita $24,037; median household $61,406; **Pop below poverty level:** 11.9%. ***Personal per capita income 2000-2003:** $21,057-$25,885.

Unemployment 2004: 6.6%. **Change from 2000:** -2.6%. **Median travel time to work:** 11.3 minutes. **Working outside county of residence:** 7.6%.

Cities with pop over 10,000: None.

ANCHORAGE BOROUGH

PO Box 196650   **Ph:** 907-343-4311

Anchorage, AK 99519   **Fax:** 907-343-4313

www.ci.anchorage.ak.us

On the south-central coast of AK, at the head of Cook Inlet, 470 mi. south of Fairbanks. Founded 1914. Borough and city were consolidated as the municipality of Anchorage; includes Glen Alps and Girdwood. **Name Origin:** For Knik Anchorage, a settlement just offshore. This was named for a Tanaina village spelled *Kinik* and *Kinnick* 'fire'. Previously called *Ship Creek* and *Woodrow*.

Area (sq mi): 1961.09 (land 1697.21; water 263.88). **Pop per sq mi:** 162.1.

Pop 2005: 275,043. **State rank:** 1. **Pop change:** 2000-20005 +5.7%; 1990-2000 +15%. **Pop 2000:** 260,283 (White 69.9%; Black or African American 5.8%; Hispanic or Latino 5.7%; Asian 5.5%; Other 16.4%, including 7.3% American Indian/Alaska Native). **Foreign born:** 8.2%. **Median age:** 32.4.

Income 2000: per capita $25,287; median household $55,546; **Pop below poverty level:** 7.3%. ***Personal per capita income 2000-2003:** $33,697-$37,750.

Unemployment 2004: 5.9%. **Change from 2000:** +1.6%. **Median travel time to work:** 19.5 minutes. **Working outside county of residence:** 3.3%.

Cities with pop over 10,000: Anchorage 🏛 (272,687).

BETHEL CENSUS AREA

In southwestern AK with coastal area on Bering Sea. Established from the former *Kuskokwim Division*. **Name Origin:** For the city.

Area (sq mi): 45,508.46 (land 40,633.31; water 4875.15). **Pop per sq mi:** 0.4.

Pop 2005: 17,127. **State rank:** 6. **Pop change:** 2000-20005 +7%; 1990-2000 +17.2%. **Pop 2000:** 16,006 (White 12.2%; Black or African American 0.4%; Hispanic or Latino 0.9%; Asian 1%; Other 86.1%, including 81.9% American Indian/Alaska Native). **Foreign born:** 1.4%. **Median age:** 25.3.

Income 2000: per capita $12,603; median household $35,701; **Pop below poverty level:** 20.6%. ***Personal per capita income 2000-2003:** $19,392-$22,883.

Unemployment 2004: 12.9%. **Change from 2000:** +2.3%. **Median travel time to work:** 8.6 minutes. **Working outside county of residence:** 1.5%.

Cities with pop over 10,000: None.

BRISTOL BAY BOROUGH

PO Box 189 **Ph:** 907-246-4224
Naknek, AK 99633 **Fax:** 907-246-6633
www.theborough.com

In southwestern AK at head of Kvichak Bay, an inlet of the Bering Sea, west of Katmai National Park. **Name Origin:** For the bay, named in 1778 by Capt. James Cook (1728-79) for the Earl of Bristol (England). Formerly the *Bristol Bay Borough Division*.

Area (sq mi): 887.68 (land 504.92; water 382.77). **Pop per sq mi:** 2.2.

Pop 2005: 1,112. **State rank:** 26. **Pop change:** 2000-20005 -11.6%; 1990-2000 -10.8%. **Pop 2000:** 1,258 (White 52.1%; Black or African American 0.6%; Hispanic or Latino 0.6%; Asian 0.2%; Other 46.7%, including 43.7% American Indian/Alaska Native). **Foreign born:** 0.6%. **Median age:** 36.

Income 2000: per capita $22,210; median household $52,167; **Pop below poverty level:** 9.5%. ***Personal per capita income 2000-2003:** $34,596-$40,769.

Unemployment 2004: 6.6%. **Change from 2000:** -3.4%. **Median travel time to work:** 10 minutes. **Working outside county of residence:** 1.4%.

Cities with pop over 10,000: None.

DENALI BOROUGH

PO Box 480 **Ph:** 907-683-1330
Healy, AK 99743 **Fax:** 907-683-1340
www.denaliborough.govoffice.com

In south-central AK, southwest of Fairbanks. Includes Denali National Park, where Mount McKinley, the highest point in North America, is located. Established Dec 28, 1990, primarily from the Yukon-Koyukuk Census Area and a small part of the Southeast Fairbanks Census Area. **Name Origin:** The Tanana Indian name for Mount McKinley, meaning 'the great one' or 'the high one.'

Area (sq mi): 12,774.53 (land 12,749.65; water 24.88). **Pop per sq mi:** 0.1.

Pop 2005: 1,881. **State rank:** 24. **Pop change:** 2000-20005 -0.6%; 1990-2000 +7.3%. **Pop 2000:** 1,893 (White 84.5%; Black or African

American 1.4%; Hispanic or Latino 2.5%; Asian 1.5%; Other 11.4%, including 4.8% American Indian/Alaska Native). **Foreign born:** 2.9%. **Median age:** 37.6.

Income 2000: per capita $26,251; median household $53,654; **Pop below poverty level:** 7.9%. ***Personal per capita income 2000-2003:** $37,129-$39,487.

Unemployment 2004: 7.9%. **Change from 2000:** -0.9%. **Median travel time to work:** 16.2 minutes. **Working outside county of residence:** 12.3%.

Cities with pop over 10,000: None.

DILLINGHAM CENSUS AREA

In southwestern AK, along Bristol Bay, northwest of Katmai National Park. Has been reduced in area as portions have been separated off to create new boroughs and census areas. **Name Origin:** For the city.

Area (sq mi): 20,928.41 (land 18,674.78; water 2253.63). **Pop per sq mi:** 0.3.

Pop 2005: 4,926. **State rank:** 20. **Pop change:** 2000-20005 +0.1%; 1990-2000 +22.7%. **Pop 2000:** 4,922 (White 20.9%; Black or African American 0.4%; Hispanic or Latino 2.3%; Asian 0.6%; Other 77.3%, including 70.1% American Indian/Alaska Native). **Foreign born:** 1%. **Median age:** 28.9.

Income 2000: per capita $16,021; median household $43,079; **Pop below poverty level:** 21.4%. ***Personal per capita income 2000-2003:** $26,368-$28,485.

Unemployment 2004: 11.2%. **Change from 2000:** +2%. **Median travel time to work:** 10 minutes. **Working outside county of residence:** 2.4%.

Cities with pop over 10,000: None.

FAIRBANKS NORTH STAR BOROUGH

809 Pioneer Rd **Ph:** 907-459-1000
Fairbanks, AK 99701 **Fax:** 907-459-1224
www.co.fairbanks.ak.us

In east-central AK. **Name Origin:** Formerly called the *Fairbanks Division*, for the city.

Area (sq mi): 7444.02 (land 7366.24; water 77.78). **Pop per sq mi:** 11.9.

Pop 2005: 87,560. **State rank:** 2. **Pop change:** 2000-20005 +5.7%; 1990-2000 +6.6%. **Pop 2000:** 82,840 (White 76%; Black or African American 5.8%; Hispanic or Latino 4.2%; Asian 2.1%; Other 14.3%, including 6.9% American Indian/Alaska Native). **Foreign born:** 4%. **Median age:** 29.5.

Income 2000: per capita $21,553; median household $49,076; **Pop below poverty level:** 7.8%. ***Personal per capita income 2000-2003:** $27,842-$30,583.

Unemployment 2004: 6.6%. **Change from 2000:** +0.9%. **Median travel time to work:** 17.3 minutes. **Working outside county of residence:** 2.3%.

Cities with pop over 10,000: Fairbanks 🏛 (30,435).

Source: Personal per capita income data are from the Bureau of Economic Analysis; per capita income data are from the Bureau of the Census. See Introduction for explanation of differences.

HAINES BOROUGH

PO Box 1209
Haines, AK 99827
www.haines.ak.us

Ph: 907-766-2711
Fax: 907-766-2716

In AK, panhandle, northeastern (inner) portion of Alexander Archipelago, north of Juneau, bordering the province of British Colombia, Canada, to the east. **Name Origin:** For the city.

Area (sq mi): 2725.82 (land 2343.73; water 382.09). **Pop per sq mi:** 1.

Pop 2005: 2,272. **State rank:** 23. **Pop change:** 2000-20005 -5%; 1990-2000 +13%. **Pop 2000:** 2,392 (White 81.9%; Black or African American 0.1%; Hispanic or Latino 1.4%; Asian 0.7%; Other 16.6%, including 11.5% American Indian/Alaska Native). **Foreign born:** 4.1%. **Median age:** 40.7.

Income 2000: per capita $22,090; median household $40,772; **Pop below poverty level:** 10.7%. ***Personal per capita income 2000-2003:** $31,750-$35,542.

Unemployment 2004: 10.1%. **Change from 2000:** -0.4%. **Median travel time to work:** 12.7 minutes. **Working outside county of residence:** 6%.

Cities with pop over 10,000. None.

JUNEAU CITY & BOROUGH

155 S Seward St
Juneau, AK 99801
www.juneau.org

Ph: 907-586-5278
Fax: 907-586-5385

In panhandle, southeastern AK on the Gastineau Channel, 90 mi. northeast of Sitka. State capital and largest city in the U.S. (by area). Founded 1880; designated to replace Sitka as capital in 1900, but the move to Juneau did not take place until 1906. Major industries: fishing, lumbering, tourism. Borough and city were consolidated in 1970; includes Douglas. **Name Origin:** For miner Joseph Juneau (1826-99), who discovered gold here in 1880. Formerly Harrisburg.

Area (sq mi): 3255.01 (land 2716.67; water 538.34). **Pop per sq mi:** 11.4.

Pop 2005: 30,987. **State rank:** 5. **Pop change:** 2000-20005 +0.9%; 1990-2000 +14.8%. **Pop 2000:** 30,711 (White 73.3%; Black or African American 0.8%; Hispanic or Latino 3.4%; Asian 4.7%; Other 19.8%, including 11.4% American Indian/Alaska Native). **Foreign born:** 5.7%. **Median age:** 35.3.

Income 2000: per capita $26,719; median household $62,034; **Pop below poverty level:** 6%. ***Personal per capita income 2000-2003:** $34,762-$36,668.

Unemployment 2004: 6%. **Change from 2000:** +1.2%. **Median travel time to work:** 16.4 minutes. **Working outside county of residence:** 1.3%.

Cities with pop over 10,000: Juneau 🏛 (31,118).

KENAI PENINSULA BOROUGH

144 N Binkley St
Soldotna, AK 99669
www.borough.kenai.ak.us

Ph: 907-262-4441
Fax: 907-262-8615

In south-central AK, bounded on west by Cook Inlet, on east by the Gulf of Alaska, inlets of the Pacific. Established by combining the former divisions of *Kenai-Cook Inlet* and *Seward*. **Name Origin:** For a local Indian tribe; meaning of name unknown.

Area (sq mi): 24754.6 (land 16,013.26; water 8741.34). **Pop per sq mi:** 3.2.

Pop 2005: 51,960. **State rank:** 4. **Pop change:** 2000-20005 +4.6%; 1990-2000 +21.8%. **Pop 2000:** 49,691 (White 85.1%; Black or African American 0.5%; Hispanic or Latino 2.2%; Asian 1%; Other 12.4%, including 7.5% American Indian/Alaska Native). **Foreign born:** 2.7%. **Median age:** 36.3.

Income 2000: per capita $20,949; median household $46,397; **Pop below poverty level:** 10%. ***Personal per capita income 2000-2003:** $28,156-$29,362.

Unemployment 2004: 9.6%. **Change from 2000:** +0%. **Median travel time to work:** 25.6 minutes. **Working outside county of residence:** 7.3%.

Cities with pop over 10,000: None.

KETCHIKAN GATEWAY BOROUGH

344 Front St
Ketchikan, AK 99901
www.borough.ketchikan.ak.us

Ph: 907-228-6605
Fax: 907-247-8439

In AK panhandle, southern Alexander Archipelago, east of Prince of Wales Island. **Name Origin:** For the city, which is in the southernmost portion of AK. Formerly called *Ketchican Division*.

Area (sq mi): 1753.98 (land 1233.22; water 520.75). **Pop per sq mi:** 10.8.

Pop 2005: 13,262. **State rank:** 7. **Pop change:** 2000-20005 -5.7%; 1990-2000 +1.8%. **Pop 2000:** 14,070 (White 72.9%; Black or African American 0.5%; Hispanic or Latino 2.6%; Asian 4.3%; Other 20.9%, including 15% American Indian/Alaska Native). **Foreign born:** 5.7%. **Median age:** 36.

Income 2000: per capita $23,994; median household $51,344; **Pop below poverty level:** 6.5%. ***Personal per capita income 2000-2003:** $34,389-$38,343.

Unemployment 2004: 7.7%. **Change from 2000:** +0%. **Median travel time to work:** 14.8 minutes. **Working outside county of residence:** 3.1%.

Cities with pop over 10,000: None.

KODIAK ISLAND BOROUGH

710 Mill Bay Rd
Kodiak, AK 99615
www.kib.co.kodiak.ak.us

Ph: 907-486-9311
Fax: 907-486-9391

Off southern coast of AK, east of the Alaska Peninsula in the Gulf of Alaska. **Name Origin:** For the island. Formerly called *Kodiak Division*.

Area (sq mi): 12,023.67 (land 6559.85; water 5463.83). **Pop per sq mi:** 2.

Pop 2005: 13,051. **State rank:** 8. **Pop change:** 2000-20005 -6.2%; 1990-2000 +4.5%. **Pop 2000:** 13,913 (White 57.5%; Black or African American 1%; Hispanic or Latino 6.1%; Asian 16%; Other 23.4%, including 14.6% American Indian/Alaska Native). **Foreign born:** 16.7%. **Median age:** 31.6.

Kodiak Island Borough (cont'd)

Income 2000: per capita $22,195; median household $54,636; **Pop below poverty level:** 6.6%. ***Personal per capita income 2000-2003:** $26,695-$29,479.

Unemployment 2004: 9.2%. **Change from 2000:** +0.2%. **Median travel time to work:** 10.8 minutes. **Working outside county of residence:** 1.8%.

Cities with pop over 10,000: None.

LAKE & PENINSULA BOROUGH

PO Box 495   **Ph:** 907-246-3421
King Salmon, AK 99613   **Fax:** 907-246-6602

In southwestern AK, including most of the upper Alaska Peninsula. Established April 24, 1989 from eastern portions of the Dillingham Census Area plus the Alaska Peninsula. **Name Origin:** For Iliamna Lake and the Alaska Peninsula.

Area (sq mi): 30,906.96 (land 23,781.96; water 7125). **Pop per sq mi:** 0.1.

Pop 2005: 1,570. **State rank:** 25. **Pop change:** 2000-20005 -13.9%; 1990-2000 +9.3%. **Pop 2000:** 1,823 (White 18.8%; Black or African American 0.1%; Hispanic or Latino 1.2%; Asian 0.2%; Other 81%, including 73.5% American Indian/Alaska Native). **Foreign born:** 0.7%. **Median age:** 29.2.

Income 2000: per capita $15,361; median household $36,442; **Pop below poverty level:** 18.9%. ***Personal per capita income 2000-2003:** $21,076-$22,697.

Unemployment 2004: 10.2%. **Change from 2000:** -0.6%. **Median travel time to work:** 7.9 minutes. **Working outside county of residence:** 3.2%.

Cities with pop over 10,000: None.

MATANUSKA-SUSITNA BOROUGH

350 E Dahlia Ave   **Ph:** 907-745-4801
Palmer, AK 99645   **Fax:** 907-745-9845
www.co.mat-su.ak.us

In south-central AK, north of Anchorage. **Name Origin:** For the Metanuska River, derived from Russian for 'copper river people,' variously spelled *Matanooski, Mednofski, Miduuski*; and the Susitna River, from Tanaina Indian meaning 'sandy river'; also spelled *Sushitna, Sushit, Sutschitna, Sustchino*.

Area (sq mi): 25,259.79 (land 24,681.54; water 578.25). **Pop per sq mi:** 3.1.

Pop 2005: 76,006. **State rank:** 3. **Pop change:** 2000-20005 +28.1%; 1990-2000 +49.5%. **Pop 2000:** 59,322 (White 86.3%; Black or African American 0.7%; Hispanic or Latino 2.5%; Asian 0.7%; Other 11.1%, including 5.5% American Indian/Alaska Native). **Foreign born:** 2.6%. **Median age:** 34.1.

Income 2000: per capita $21,105; median household $51,221; **Pop below poverty level:** 11%. ***Personal per capita income 2000-2003:** $25,902-$29,483.

Unemployment 2004: 8.3%. **Change from 2000:** +0.6%. **Median travel time to work:** 40.7 minutes. **Working outside county of residence:** 35.3%.

Cities with pop over 10,000: None.

NOME CENSUS AREA

In west-central AK, including much of Seward Peninsula. **Name Origin:** For the city.

Area (sq mi): 28,283.33 (land 23,000.91; water 5282.42). **Pop per sq mi:** 0.4.

Pop 2005: 9,328. **State rank:** 10. **Pop change:** 2000-20005 +1.4%; 1990-2000 +11%. **Pop 2000:** 9,196 (White 19.1%; Black or African American 0.4%; Hispanic or Latino 1%; Asian 0.7%; Other 79.6%, including 75.2% American Indian/Alaska Native). **Foreign born:** 1.5%. **Median age:** 27.6.

Income 2000: per capita $15,476; median household $41,250; **Pop below poverty level:** 17.4%. ***Personal per capita income 2000-2003:** $21,436-$24,774.

Unemployment 2004: 11.9%. **Change from 2000:** +0.5%. **Median travel time to work:** 6.3 minutes. **Working outside county of residence:** 2%.

Cities with pop over 10,000: None.

NORTH SLOPE BOROUGH

PO Box 69   **Ph:** 907-852-2611
Barrow, AK 99723   **Fax:** 907-852-0229
www.co.north-slope.ak.us

Across northernmost AK from Pt. Hope in west to border of Yukon province, Canada in east; bounded on the north by the Arctic Ocean and Beaufort Sea. **Name Origin:** Formerly called *Barrow-North Slope Division*.

Area (sq mi): 94,762.64 (land 88,817.12; water 5945.53). **Pop per sq mi:** 0.1.

Pop 2005: 6,924. **State rank:** 14. **Pop change:** 2000-20005 -6.2%; 1990-2000 +23.5%. **Pop 2000:** 7,385 (White 16.6%; Black or African American 0.7%; Hispanic or Latino 2.4%; Asian 5.9%; Other 76.3%, including 68.4% American Indian/Alaska Native). **Foreign born:** 5.8%. **Median age:** 27.

Income 2000: per capita $20,540; median household $63,173; **Pop below poverty level:** 9.1%. ***Personal per capita income 2000-2003:** $29,960-$36,613.

Unemployment 2004: 10.7%. **Change from 2000:** +2.4%. **Median travel time to work:** 7.9 minutes. **Working outside county of residence:** 1.1%.

Cities with pop over 10,000: None.

NORTHWEST ARCTIC BOROUGH

PO Box 1110   **Ph:** 907-442-2500
Kotzebue, AK 99752   **Fax:** 907-442-2930
www.nwabor.org

On northwestern coast of AK on Kotzebue Sound, north of Nome. Known as the Kobak Census Area until change to borough status on Jun 2, 1986. **Name Origin:** For its location.

Area (sq mi): 40,762 (land 35,898.34; water 4863.66). **Pop per sq mi:** 0.2.

Pop 2005: 7,621. **State rank:** 12. **Pop change:** 2000-20005 +5.7%; 1990-2000 +17.9%. **Pop 2000:** 7,208 (White 12.2%; Black or African American 0.2%; Hispanic or Latino 0.8%; Asian 0.9%; Other 86.7%, including 82.5% American Indian/Alaska Native). **Foreign born:** 1.1%. **Median age:** 23.9.

---

*Source: Personal per capita income data are from the Bureau of Economic Analysis; per capita income data are from the Bureau of the Census. See Introduction for explanation of differences.

Northwest Arctic Borough (cont'd)

Income 2000: per capita $15,286; median household $45,976; **Pop below poverty level:** 17.4%. ***Personal per capita income 2000-2003:** $22,174-$24,425.

Unemployment 2004: 13.6%. **Change from 2000:** -1.1%. **Median travel time to work:** 8.9 minutes. **Working outside county of residence:** 0.6%.

Cities with pop over 10,000: None.

PRINCE OF WALES-OUTER KETCHIKAN CENSUS AREA

In AK panhandle, southern outer portion of Alexander Archipelago, including Prince of Wales Island. Established by combining the former divisions of *Prince of Wales* and *Outer Ketchikan*. **Name Origin:** For the Prince of Wales Archipelago and nearby Ketchikan.

Area (sq mi): 12706.3 (land 7410.62; water 5295.67). **Pop per sq mi:** 0.8.

Pop 2005: 5,660. **State rank:** 18. **Pop change:** 2000-20005 -7.9%; 1990-2000 -2.1%. **Pop 2000:** 6,146 (White 52.5%; Black or African American 0.1%; Hispanic or Latino 1.7%; Asian 0.4%; Other 46.3%, including 38.7% American Indian/Alaska Native). **Foreign born:** 1.8%. **Median age:** 34.7.

Income 2000: per capita $18,395; median household $40,636; **Pop below poverty level:** 12.1%. ***Personal per capita income 2000-2003:** $20,945-$21,492.

Unemployment 2004: 14.1%. **Change from 2000:** +1.8%. **Median travel time to work:** 20.9 minutes. **Working outside county of residence:** 4.3%.

Cities with pop over 10,000: None.

SITKA CITY & BOROUGH

100 Lincoln St
Sitka, AK 99835
www.cityofsitka.com

Ph: 907-747-3294
Fax: 907-747-7403

In AK panhandle, western (outer) portion of the central Alexander Archipelago, southwest of Juneau. City center on the west coast of Baranof Island, 930 mi. north of Seattle, WA. **Name Origin:** From Tlingit term for 'by the sea' or 'on Shi,' the Tlingit name for Baranof Island.

Area (sq mi): 4811.53 (land 2873.98; water 1937.55). **Pop per sq mi:** 3.1.

Pop 2005: 8,986. **State rank:** 11. **Pop change:** 2000-20005 +1.7%; 1990-2000 +2.9%. **Pop 2000:** 8,835 (White 67.1%; Black or African American 0.3%; Hispanic or Latino 3.3%; Asian 3.8%; Other 27.4%, including 18.6% American Indian/Alaska Native). **Foreign born:** 5.1%. **Median age:** 35.2.

Income 2000: per capita $23,622; median household $51,901; **Pop below poverty level:** 7.8%. ***Personal per capita income 2000-2003:** $29,078-$31,467.

Unemployment 2004: 6.4%. **Change from 2000:** +1.6%. **Median travel time to work:** 13.5 minutes. **Working outside county of residence:** 2.8%.

Cities with pop over 10,000: None.

SKAGWAY-HOONAH-ANGOON CENSUS AREA

In AK panhandle, north of the Alexander Archipelago. Created from the remainder of the former Skagway-Yakutat-Angoon Census Area when the new Yakutat City and Borough was created effective September 22, 1992. **Name Origin:** For the towns that define its northern, western and eastern extent.

Area (sq mi): 11,376.73 (land 7896.48; water 3480.25). **Pop per sq mi:** 0.4.

Pop 2005: 3,126. **State rank:** 21. **Pop change:** 2000-20005 -9%; 1990-2000 -6.6%. **Pop 2000:** 3,436 (White 57.5%; Black or African American 0.1%; Hispanic or Latino 2.8%; Asian 0.4%; Other 41.3%, including 35% American Indian/Alaska Native). **Foreign born:** 2%. **Median age:** 37.8.

Income 2000: per capita $19,974; median household $40,879; **Pop below poverty level:** 12.8%. ***Personal per capita income 2000-2003:** $29,104-$34,508.

Unemployment 2004: 13.5%. **Change from 2000:** +2.8%. **Median travel time to work:** 12 minutes. **Working outside county of residence:** 10.6%.

Cities with pop over 10,000: None.

SOUTHEAST FAIRBANKS CENSUS AREA

In east-central AK, southeast of Fairbanks, bordering the Yukon Territory of Canada to the east. Includes portion of former *Upper Yukon Division*. A small portion of the census area was removed to establish Denali Borough on Dec. 28, 1990. **Name Origin:** For its location.

Area (sq mi): 25,061.19 (land 24,814.86; water 246.33). **Pop per sq mi:** 0.3.

Pop 2005: 6,614. **State rank:** 15. **Pop change:** 2000-20005 +7.1%; 1990-2000 +4.4%. **Pop 2000:** 6,174 (White 77.4%; Black or African American 2%; Hispanic or Latino 2.7%; Asian 0.7%; Other 18.3%, including 12.7% American Indian/Alaska Native). **Foreign born:** 9.9%. **Median age:** 33.7.

Income 2000: per capita $16,679; median household $38,776; **Pop below poverty level:** 18.9%. ***Personal per capita income 2000-2003:** $22,756-$28,404.

Unemployment 2004: 12.4%. **Change from 2000:** +1.7%. **Median travel time to work:** 15.7 minutes. **Working outside county of residence:** 6.5%.

Cities with pop over 10,000: None.

VALDEZ-CORDOVA CENSUS AREA

In southeastern AK, bounded on east by Yukon Territory of Canada and on south by the Gulf of Alaska. Established by combining the former divisions of Cordova-McCarthy and Valdez-Chitina-Whittier with part of Southeast Fairbanks Division. **Name Origin:** For the city of Valdez.

Area (sq mi): 40,199.15 (land 34319.1; water 5880.05). **Pop per sq mi:** 0.3.

Pop 2005: 9,899. **State rank:** 9. **Pop change:** 2000-20005 -2.9%; 1990-2000 +2.4%. **Pop 2000:** 10,195 (White 74.7%; Black or African American 0.3%; Hispanic or Latino 2.8%; Asian 3.6%; Other 20.3%, including 13.3% American Indian/Alaska Native). **Foreign born:** 5.1%. **Median age:** 36.1.

Income 2000: per capita $23,046; median household $48,734; **Pop below poverty level:** 9.8%. ***Personal per capita income 2000-2003:** $30,011-$33,321.

Valdez-Cordova Census Area (cont'd)

Unemployment 2004: 10.2%. **Change from 2000:** +0.8%. **Median travel time to work:** 12.7 minutes. **Working outside county of residence:** 3.7%.

Cities with pop over 10,000: None.

WADE HAMPTON CENSUS AREA

On central-western coast of AK, north of Bethel. **Name Origin:** Named for Wade Hampton, a lieutenant general in the Civil War, governor of South Carolina and U.S. Senator from South Carolina.

Area (sq mi): 19,669.24 (land 17193.5; water 2475.74). **Pop per sq mi:** 0.4.

Pop 2005: 7,541. **State rank:** 13. **Pop change:** 2000-20005 +7.3%; 1990-2000 +21.4%. **Pop 2000:** 7,028 (White 4.7%; Black or African American 0.1%; Hispanic or Latino 0.3%; Asian 0.1%; Other 95%, including 92.5% American Indian/Alaska Native). **Foreign born:** 0.3%. **Median age:** 20.

Income 2000: per capita $8,717; median household $30,184; **Pop below poverty level:** 26.2%. ***Personal per capita income 2000-2003:** $14,070-$15,748.

Unemployment 2004: 20.5%. **Change from 2000:** +2.4%. **Median travel time to work:** 6.3 minutes. **Working outside county of residence:** 2.3%.

Cities with pop over 10,000: None.

WRANGELL-PETERSBURG CENSUS AREA

In AK panhandle in central-eastern Alexander Archipelago, south of Juneau. **Name Origin:** For the two chief cities.

Area (sq mi): 9021.21 (land 5834.94; water 3186.27). **Pop per sq mi:** 1.1.

Pop 2005: 6,245. **State rank:** 16. **Pop change:** 2000-20005 -6.6%; 1990-2000 -5.1%. **Pop 2000:** 6,684 (White 72.5%; Black or African American 0.2%; Hispanic or Latino 2%; Asian 1.6%; Other 25.1%, including 16.1% American Indian/Alaska Native). **Foreign born:** 2.8%. **Median age:** 37.2.

Income 2000: per capita $23,494; median household $46,434; **Pop below poverty level:** 7.9%. ***Personal per capita income 2000-2003:** $27,852-$31,861.

Unemployment 2004: 12.6%. **Change from 2000:** +3.8%. **Median travel time to work:** 12.7 minutes. **Working outside county of residence:** 3.2%.

Cities with pop over 10,000: None.

YAKUTAT CITY & BOROUGH
PO Box 160   **Ph:** 907-784-3323
Yakutat, AK 99689   **Fax:** 907-784-3281
www.yakutat.net

In AK panhandle, north of the Alexander Archipelago. Established Sep 22, 1992 from the former Skagway-Yakutat-Angoon Census Area (now Skagway-Hoonah-Angoon Census Area). **Name Origin:** Probably for Yakutat Bay, from the name of a Tlingit Indian village; meaning of name unknown.

Area (sq mi): 9459.28 (land 7650.46; water 1808.82). **Pop per sq mi:** 0.1.

Pop 2005: 722. **State rank:** 27. **Pop change:** 2000-20005 -10.6%; 1990-2000 +14.6%. **Pop 2000:** 808 (White 50.2%; Black or African American 0.1%; Hispanic or Latino 0.7%; Asian 1.2%; Other 48.2%, including 39.6% American Indian/Alaska Native). **Foreign born:** 0.6%. **Median age:** 37.2.

Income 2000: per capita $22,579; median household $46,786; **Pop below poverty level:** 13.5%. ***Personal per capita income 2000-2003:** $29,237-$31,352.

Unemployment 2004: 10.9%. **Change from 2000:** -1.9%. **Median travel time to work:** 9.2 minutes. **Working outside county of residence:** 5.7%.

Cities with pop over 10,000: None.

YUKON-KOYUKUK CENSUS AREA

In Alaska's Interior, stretching across more than 148,250 square miles from Canada's Yukon Territories to the lower Yukon River. **Name Origin:** For the Yukon River and one of its principal tributaries, the Koyukuk River.

Area (sq mi): 147,842.51 (land 145,899.69; water 1942.83). **Pop per sq mi:** 0.04.

Pop 2005: 6,143. **State rank:** 17. **Pop change:** 2000-20005 -6.2%; 1990-2000 -2.4%. **Pop 2000:** 6,551 (White 24%; Black or African American 0.1%; Hispanic or Latino 1.2%; Asian 0.4%; Other 75.2%, including 70.9% American Indian/Alaska Native). **Foreign born:** 1%. **Median age:** 31.1.

Income 2000: per capita $13,720; median household $28,666; **Pop below poverty level:** 23.8%. ***Personal per capita income 2000-2003:** $19,363-$22,907.

Unemployment 2004: 12.2%. **Change from 2000:** -2.2%. **Median travel time to work:** 8.9 minutes. **Working outside county of residence:** 7.3%.

Cities with pop over 10,000: None.

*Source: Personal per capita income data are from the Bureau of Economic Analysis; per capita income data are from the Bureau of the Census. See Introduction for explanation of differences.

Arizona

CO.

N

UTAH

NEVADA

Mohave

Kingman

Bullhead City

Coconino

Flagstaff

Apache

Navajo

Winslow

Holbrook

Yavapai

Cottonwood

Prescott

Saint Johns

Lake Havasu City

CALIF.

Parker

La Paz

Payson

Gila

Greenlee

Globe

Phoenix

Maricopa

Clifton

Yuma

Florence

Graham

Safford

Pinal

Yuma

Tucson

Cochise

Pima

Green Valley

Santa Cruz

Sierra Vista

Bisbee

Douglas

Nogales

MEXICO

Gulf of California

©MAPS.COM

NEW MEXICO

———	County boundary
Yuma	County name
◉	County seat
■	Major city
✪	State capital

0   50 mi

0   50 km

Arizona

ARIZONA STATE INFORMATION

www.az.gov   **Ph:** 602-542-4900

Area (sq mi): 11,3998.3 (land 113,634.57; water 363.73). **Pop per sq mi:** 52.3.

Pop 2005: 5,939,292. **Pop change:** 2000-20005 +15.8%; 1990-2000 +40%. **Pop 2000:** 5,130,632 (White 63.8%; Black or African American 3.1%; Hispanic or Latino 25.3%; Asian 1.8%; Other 19.6%, including 5% American Indian/Alaska Native). **Foreign born:** 12.8%. **Median age:** 34.2.

Income 2000: per capita $20,275; median household $40,558; **Pop below poverty level:** 13.9%. ***Personal per capita income 2000-2003:** $25,660-$27,232.

Unemployment 2004: 5%. **Change from 2000:** +1%. **Median travel time to work:** 24.9 minutes. **Working outside county of residence:** 4.8%.

APACHE COUNTY

PO Box 365   **Ph:** 928-337-4364
Saint Johns, AZ 85936   **Fax:** 928-337-2771
www.co.apache.az.us

On eastern border of AZ; organized Feb 14, 1879 (prior to statehood) from Mohave County. **Name Origin:** For the Apache Indian tribe, of Athapascan linguistic stock, who inhabited the land for centuries. The name is variously said to mean 'man,' 'battles,' or 'enemy.'

Area (sq mi): 11,218.42 (land 11,204.88; water 13.54). **Pop per sq mi:** 6.2.

Pop 2005: 69,343. **State rank:** 10. **Pop change:** 2000-20005 -0.1%; 1990-2000 +12.7%. **Pop 2000:** 69,423 (White 17.7%; Black or African American 0.2%; Hispanic or Latino 4.5%; Asian 0.1%; Other 80.2%, including 76.9% American Indian/Alaska Native). **Foreign born:** 0.9%. **Median age:** 27.

Income 2000: per capita $8,986; median household $23,344; **Pop below poverty level:** 37.8%. ***Personal per capita income 2000-2003:** $13,632-$16,476.

Unemployment 2004: 12.1%. **Change from 2000:** +0.1%. **Median travel time to work:** 28 minutes. **Working outside county of residence:** 22%.

Cities with pop over 10,000: None.

COCHISE COUNTY

1415 W Melody Ln   **Ph:** 520-432-9200
Bisbee, AZ 85603   **Fax:** 520-432-5016
www.co.cochise.az.us

In southeastern corner of AZ; organized Feb 1, 1881 (prior to statehood) from Pima County. **Name Origin:** For the famous Chiricahua Apache chief (c. 1812-74), who conducted raids against the U.S. after brutal treatment by U.S. Army officers and surrendered in 1871.

Area (sq mi): 6218.77 (land 6169.45; water 49.32). **Pop per sq mi:** 20.4.

Pop 2005: 126,106. **State rank:** 7. **Pop change:** 2000-20005 +7.1%; 1990-2000 +20.6%. **Pop 2000:** 117,755 (White 60.1%; Black or African American 4.5%; Hispanic or Latino 30.7%; Asian 1.6%; Other 17.2%, including 1.1% American Indian/Alaska Native). **Foreign born:** 12.3%. **Median age:** 36.9.

Income 2000: per capita $15,988; median household $32,105; **Pop below poverty level:** 17.7%. ***Personal per capita income 2000-2003:** $19,734-$23,217.

Unemployment 2004: 5%. **Change from 2000:** +0.4%. **Median travel time to work:** 19.8 minutes. **Working outside county of residence:** 6.6%.

Cities with pop over 10,000: Sierra Vista (40,820); Douglas (16,706).

COCONINO COUNTY

219 E Cherry Ave   **Ph:** 928-774-5011
Flagstaff, AZ 86001   **Fax:** 928-779-6785
co.coconino.az.us

In north-central AZ; organized Feb 19, 1891 (prior to statehood) from Yavapai County. **Name Origin:** Possibly from the Hopi Indian name, *Kohnina*, for the Havasupai tribe that inhabits the Grand Canyon region, which is within the county. Or derived from a Havasupai word meaning 'little water.'

Area (sq mi): 18,661.21 (land 18,617.42; water 43.79). **Pop per sq mi:** 6.7.

Pop 2005: 123,866. **State rank:** 8. **Pop change:** 2000-20005 +6.5%; 1990-2000 +20.4%. **Pop 2000:** 116,320 (White 57.6%; Black or African American 1%; Hispanic or Latino 10.9%; Asian 0.8%; Other 35.1%, including 28.5% American Indian/Alaska Native). **Foreign born:** 4.3%. **Median age:** 29.6.

Income 2000: per capita $17,139; median household $38,256; **Pop below poverty level:** 18.2%. ***Personal per capita income 2000-2003:** $22,814-$25,345.

Coconino County (cont'd)

Unemployment 2004: 5.5%. **Change from 2000:** +0.1%. **Median travel time to work:** 19 minutes. **Working outside county of residence:** 8.1%.

Cities with pop over 10,000: Flagstaff 🏛 (57,038).

GILA COUNTY

1400 E Ash St
Globe, AZ 85501
www.co.gila.az.us

Ph: 928-425-3231
Fax: 928-425-0319

In east-central AZ, east of Phoenix; organized Feb 8, 1881 (prior to statehood) from Maricopa and Pinal counties. **Name Origin:** For the Gila River, which forms part of the county's southern boundary. Some sources suggest the name may refer to the Gila monster.

Area (sq mi): 4795.74 (land 4767.7; water 28.03). **Pop per sq mi:** 10.8.

Pop 2005: 51,663. **State rank:** 11. **Pop change:** 2000-20005 +0.6%; 1990-2000 +27.6%. **Pop 2000:** 51,335 (White 68.9%; Black or African American 0.4%; Hispanic or Latino 16.6%; Asian 0.4%; Other 21.4%, including 12.9% American Indian/Alaska Native). **Foreign born:** 3.6%. **Median age:** 42.3.

Income 2000: per capita $16,315; median household $30,917; **Pop below poverty level:** 17.4%. ***Personal per capita income 2000-2003:** $18,945-$21,454.

Unemployment 2004: 6.6%. **Change from 2000:** +0.7%. **Median travel time to work:** 20.3 minutes. **Working outside county of residence:** 12.3%.

Cities with pop over 10,000: Payson (14,473).

GRAHAM COUNTY

800 W Main
Safford, AZ 85546
www.graham.az.gov

Ph: 928-428-3250
Fax: 928-428-5951

In southeastern AZ, northeast of Tucson; organized Mar 10, 1881 (prior to statehood) from Apache and Pima counties. **Name Origin:** For its most prominent feature, Mount Graham, in the Pinaleno Mountains; elevation 10,720 ft.

Area (sq mi): 4641.14 (land 4629.32; water 11.83). **Pop per sq mi:** 7.1.

Pop 2005: 33,073. **State rank:** 13. **Pop change:** 2000-20005 -1.2%; 1990-2000 +26.1%. **Pop 2000:** 33,489 (White 55.2%; Black or African American 1.9%; Hispanic or Latino 27%; Asian 0.6%; Other 30.3%, including 14.9% American Indian/Alaska Native). **Foreign born:** 2.6%. **Median age:** 30.9.

Income 2000: per capita $12,139; median household $29,668; **Pop below poverty level:** 23%. ***Personal per capita income 2000-2003:** $14,158-$16,994.

Unemployment 2004: 6.8%. **Change from 2000:** -0.5%. **Median travel time to work:** 22.6 minutes. **Working outside county of residence:** 21.9%.

Cities with pop over 10,000: None.

GREENLEE COUNTY

PO Box 908
Clifton, AZ 85533
www.co.greenlee.az.us

Ph: 928-865-2072
Fax: 928-865-4417

On southeastern border of AZ; organized Mar 10, 1909 (prior to statehood) from Graham County. **Name Origin:** For Mason Greenlee (1835-1903), a Virginian who settled in the area in the 1870s.

Area (sq mi): 1848.42 (land 1847; water 1.42). **Pop per sq mi:** 4.1.

Pop 2005: 7,521. **State rank:** 15. **Pop change:** 2000-20005 -12%; 1990-2000 +6.7%. **Pop 2000:** 8,547 (White 53.9%; Black or African American 0.5%; Hispanic or Latino 43.1%; Asian 0.2%; Other 25.2%, including 1.7% American Indian/Alaska Native). **Foreign born:** 3.4%. **Median age:** 33.6.

Income 2000: per capita $15,814; median household $39,384; **Pop below poverty level:** 9.9%. ***Personal per capita income 2000-2003:** $20,195-$21,575.

Unemployment 2004: 5.6%. **Change from 2000:** -3.4%. **Median travel time to work:** 20.3 minutes. **Working outside county of residence:** 6.3%.

Cities with pop over 10,000: None.

LA PAZ COUNTY

1108 Joshua Ave
Parker, AZ 85344
www.co.la-paz.az.us

Ph: 928-669-6115
Fax: 928-669-9709

On western border of AZ, west of Phoenix; organized Jan 1, 1983 from Yuma County. **Name Origin:** For the once-prominent AZ city of La Paz, an important gold-mining center in the 1860s that eventually was abandoned. Gold had been discovered near the site on Jan 12, 1862, the date on which many Mexican and Mexican-American Catholics in early Arizona celebrated the Feast of our Lady of Peace (in Spanish, Nuestra Senora de la Paz).

Area (sq mi): 4513.36 (land 4499.95; water 13.4). **Pop per sq mi:** 4.5.

Pop 2005: 20,238. **State rank:** 14. **Pop change:** 2000-20005 +2.7%; 1990-2000 +42.4%. **Pop 2000:** 19,715 (White 63.8%; Black or African American 0.8%; Hispanic or Latino 22.4%; Asian 0.4%; Other 24.7%, including 12.5% American Indian/Alaska Native). **Foreign born:** 9.7%. **Median age:** 46.8.

Income 2000: per capita $14,916; median household $25,839; **Pop below poverty level:** 19.6%. ***Personal per capita income 2000-2003:** $15,672-$18,653.

Unemployment 2004: 6.7%. **Change from 2000:** +0.4%. **Median travel time to work:** 17.2 minutes. **Working outside county of residence:** 13.8%.

Cities with pop over 10,000: None.

MARICOPA COUNTY

301 W Jefferson St 10th Fl
Phoenix, AZ 85003
www.maricopa.gov

Ph: 602-506-3415
Fax: 602-506-6402

In south-central AZ; organized Feb 14, 1871 (prior to statehood) from Yavapai and Yuma counties. **Name Origin:** From the name of an Indian tribe of Yuman linguistic stock. The name may be a variant of the spanish *mariposa*, or 'butterfly,' as the Spanish found

Source: Personal per capita income data are from the Bureau of Economic Analysis; per capita income data are from the Bureau of the Census. See Introduction for explanation of differences.

72

Maricopa County (cont'd)

the tribe wearing bright paints. The tribe called itself *Pipatsje*, 'people.'

Area (sq mi): 9224.27 (land 9203.14; water 21.13). **Pop per sq mi:** 395.

Pop 2005: 3,635,528. **State rank:** 1. **Pop change:** 2000-20005 +18.3%; 1990-2000 +44.8%. **Pop 2000:** 3,072,149 (White 66.2%; Black or African American 3.7%; Hispanic or Latino 24.8%; Asian 2.2%; Other 16.7%, including 1.8% American Indian/Alaska Native). **Foreign born:** 14.4%. **Median age:** 33.

Income 2000: per capita $22,251; median household $45,358; **Pop below poverty level:** 11.7%. ***Personal per capita income 2000-2003:** $28,992-$30,160.

Unemployment 2004: 4.4%. **Change from 2000:** +0.5%. **Median travel time to work:** 26.1 minutes. **Working outside county of residence:** 1.8%.

Cities with pop over 10,000: 15 (see page 31 for cities).

MOHAVE COUNTY

PO Box 7000　　　　　　　**Ph:** 928-753-0729
Kingman, AZ 86402　　　　**Fax:** 928-753-5103
www.co.mohave.az.us

On western border of AZ; original county; organized Dec 21, 1864 (prior to statehood); in 1871 annexed Pah-Ute County, which had been organized in 1865. **Name Origin:** For a tribe of Yuman linguistic stock, who inhabited both the CA and AZ sides of the Colorado River. Name means 'three mountains' and refers to the Needles, the three pointed mountain peaks at the center of tribal activities. Also spelled *Mojave*.

Area (sq mi): 13,469.71 (land 13,311.64; water 158.07). **Pop per sq mi:** 14.1.

Pop 2005: 187,200. **State rank:** 5. **Pop change:** 2000-20005 +20.7%; 1990-2000 +65.8%. **Pop 2000:** 155,032 (White 84%; Black or African American 0.5%; Hispanic or Latino 11.1%; Asian 0.8%; Other 8.6%, including 2.4% American Indian/Alaska Native). **Foreign born:** 5.9%. **Median age:** 42.9.

Income 2000: per capita $16,788; median household $31,521; **Pop below poverty level:** 13.9%. ***Personal per capita income 2000-2003:** $18,610-$20,327.

Unemployment 2004: 4.1%. **Change from 2000:** -0.4%. **Median travel time to work:** 20.6 minutes. **Working outside county of residence:** 25.3%.

Cities with pop over 10,000: Lake Havasu City (53,204); Bullhead City (37,568); Kingman 🏛 (24,174).

NAVAJO COUNTY

PO Box 668　　　　　　　**Ph:** 928-524-4188
Holbrook, AZ 86025　　　**Fax:** 928-524-4261
www.co.navajo.az.us

In northeastern AZ, east of Flagstaff; organized Mar 21, 1895 (prior to statehood). **Name Origin:** For the Navajo Indian tribe. Site of the Navajo National Monument.

Area (sq mi): 9959.49 (land 9953.18; water 6.31). **Pop per sq mi:** 10.9.

Pop 2005: 108,432. **State rank:** 9. **Pop change:** 2000-20005 +11.2%; 1990-2000 +25.5%. **Pop 2000:** 97,470 (White 42.3%; Black or African American 0.9%; Hispanic or Latino 8.2%; Asian 0.3%; Other 52.7%, including 47.7% American Indian/Alaska Native). **Foreign born:** 1.7%. **Median age:** 30.2.

Income 2000: per capita $11,609; median household $28,569; **Pop below poverty level:** 29.5%. ***Personal per capita income 2000-2003:** $14,506-$16,421.

Unemployment 2004: 8.7%. **Change from 2000:** -1.8%. **Median travel time to work:** 22.9 minutes. **Working outside county of residence:** 9.9%.

Cities with pop over 10,000: None.

PIMA COUNTY

130 W Congress St 10th Fl　　　**Ph:** 520-740-8661
Tucson, AZ 85701　　　　　　　**Fax:** 520-740-8171
www.co.pima.az.us

On south-central border of AZ; original county; organized Dec 15, 1864 (prior to statehood). **Name Origin:** For the Pima Indian tribe, who inhabited the Gila and Salt River valleys of AZ. *Pima* was the name given the tribe by the Spanish; it means 'no' or 'I don't know,' the response the Spanish received to their questions and mistook for the tribe's name.

Area (sq mi): 9188.83 (land 9186.27; water 2.57). **Pop per sq mi:** 100.7.

Pop 2005: 924,786. **State rank:** 2. **Pop change:** 2000-20005 +9.6%; 1990-2000 +26.5%. **Pop 2000:** 843,746 (White 61.5%; Black or African American 3%; Hispanic or Latino 29.3%; Asian 2%; Other 19.8%, including 3.2% American Indian/Alaska Native). **Foreign born:** 11.9%. **Median age:** 35.7.

Income 2000: per capita $19,785; median household $36,758; **Pop below poverty level:** 14.7%. ***Personal per capita income 2000-2003:** $24,175-$25,906.

Unemployment 2004: 4.6%. **Change from 2000:** +1.1%. **Median travel time to work:** 23.9 minutes. **Working outside county of residence:** 2.7%.

Cities with pop over 10,000: Tucson 🏛 (512,023); Oro Valley (37,653); Marana (23,099).

PINAL COUNTY

31 N Pinal St　　　　　　**Ph:** 520-866-6000
Florence, AZ 85232　　　**Fax:** 520-866-6512
www.co.pinal.az.us

In south-central AZ, southeast of Phoenix; organized Feb 1, 1875 (prior to statehood) from Pima County. **Name Origin:** Probably for the Pinal tribe of the Apaches, or for an Apache chief. Name means 'deer' in Apache; in Spanish it means 'pine' or possibly 'the Apaches who live in the pines.' Pine groves and deer can be found on nearby mountains.

Area (sq mi): 5374.09 (land 5369.59; water 4.5). **Pop per sq mi:** 42.7.

Pop 2005: 229,549. **State rank:** 3. **Pop change:** 2000-20005 +27.7%; 1990-2000 +54.4%. **Pop 2000:** 179,727 (White 58.8%; Black or African American 2.8%; Hispanic or Latino 29.9%; Asian 0.6%; Other 26.3%, including 7.8% American Indian/Alaska Native). **Foreign born:** 9%. **Median age:** 37.1.

🏛 *County Seat*

Pinal County (cont'd)

Income 2000: per capita $16,025; median household $35,856; **Pop below poverty level:** 16.9%. ***Personal per capita income 2000-2003:** $17,651-$20,153.

Unemployment 2004: 5.8%. **Change from 2000:** +0.7%. **Median travel time to work:** 27.4 minutes. **Working outside county of residence:** 40.1%.

Cities with pop over 10,000: Apache Junction (33,457); Casa Grande (31,192); Florence ⚖ (17,198); Eloy (10,695).

SANTA CRUZ COUNTY
2150 N Congress Dr   **Ph:** 520-761-7800
Nogales, AZ 85621   **Fax:** 520-761-7700
www.co.santa-cruz.az.us

On south-central border of AZ; organized Mar 15, 1899 (prior to statehood) from Pima County. **Name Origin:** For the Santa Cruz River, which flows through the county. From the Spanish meaning 'holy cross.'

Area (sq mi): 1238.11 (land 1237.63; water 0.47). **Pop per sq mi:** 33.9.

Pop 2005: 42,009. **State rank:** 12. **Pop change:** 2000-20005 +9.5%; 1990-2000 +29.3%. **Pop 2000:** 38,381 (White 17.8%; Black or African American 0.4%; Hispanic or Latino 80.8%; Asian 0.5%; Other 23.1%). **Foreign born:** 37.7%. **Median age:** 31.8.

Income 2000: per capita $13,278; median household $29,710; **Pop below poverty level:** 24.5%. ***Personal per capita income 2000-2003:** $16,873-$18,621.

Unemployment 2004: 9.7%. **Change from 2000:** -3.1%. **Median travel time to work:** 19.7 minutes. **Working outside county of residence:** 13.7%.

Cities with pop over 10,000: Nogales ⚖ (20,619).

YAVAPAI COUNTY
1015 Fair St Rm 310   **Ph:** 928-771-3200
Prescott, AZ 86305   **Fax:** 928-771-3257
www.co.yavapai.az.us

In central AZ, north of Phoenix; original county; organized Dec 21, 1860 (prior to statehood). **Name Origin:** For a tribe of Yuman linguistic stock who lived in western AZ. Name has been variously explained. Most probable is 'sun people,' from *enyaeva* 'sun'; *pai* 'people'. Other theories include 'hill country' from *yava* 'hill'; Spanish *pais* 'country'; and 'crooked-mouth (surly) people.'

Area (sq mi): 8127.78 (land 8123.3; water 4.48). **Pop per sq mi:** 24.5.

Pop 2005: 198,701. **State rank:** 4. **Pop change:** 2000-20005 +18.6%; 1990-2000 +55.5%. **Pop 2000:** 167,517 (White 86.6%; Black or African American 0.4%; Hispanic or Latino 9.8%; Asian 0.5%; Other 7.2%, including 1.6% American Indian/Alaska Native). **Foreign born:** 5.9%. **Median age:** 44.5.

Income 2000: per capita $19,727; median household $34,901; **Pop below poverty level:** 11.9%. ***Personal per capita income 2000-2003:** $21,150-$22,075.

Unemployment 2004: 4.3%. **Change from 2000:** +1.4%. **Median travel time to work:** 22.5 minutes. **Working outside county of residence:** 11.9%.

Cities with pop over 10,000: Prescott ⚖ (38,930); Prescott Valley (30,231); Sedona (11,067); Cottonwood (10,424); Camp Verde (10,033).

YUMA COUNTY
198 S Main St   **Ph:** 928-329-2104
Yuma, AZ 85364   **Fax:** 928-329-2001
www.co.yuma.az.us

In southwestern corner of AZ; original county; organized Dec 21, 1864 (prior to statehood). **Name Origin:** For the Yuma Indian tribe, who lived principally along the Colorado River. The name, given to the tribe by the Spanish, may mean 'son of the captain' or may come from the Spanish *umo* 'smoke.'

Area (sq mi): 5518.96 (land 5514.09; water 4.87). **Pop per sq mi:** 32.9.

Pop 2005: 181,277. **State rank:** 6. **Pop change:** 2000-20005 +13.3%; 1990-2000 +49.7%. **Pop 2000:** 160,026 (White 44.3%; Black or African American 2.2%; Hispanic or Latino 50.5%; Asian 0.9%; Other 28.5%, including 1.6% American Indian/Alaska Native). **Foreign born:** 24%. **Median age:** 33.9.

Income 2000: per capita $14,802; median household $32,182; **Pop below poverty level:** 19.2%. ***Personal per capita income 2000-2003:** $16,509-$19,158.

Unemployment 2004: 15.4%. **Change from 2000:** -9%. **Median travel time to work:** 18.6 minutes. **Working outside county of residence:** 4.5%.

Cities with pop over 10,000: Yuma ⚖ (83,322); San Luis (20,539).

Source: Personal per capita income data are from the Bureau of Economic Analysis; per capita income data are from the Bureau of the Census. See Introduction for explanation of differences.

Arkansas

N

MISSOURI

Bentonville
Eureka
Springs
Berryville
Boone
Marion
Mountain
Home
Salem
Randolph
Corning
Piggott

Benton
Carroll
Harrison
Yellville
Baxter
Fulton
Pocahontas
Clay

Fayetteville
Huntsville
Jasper
Ash
Flat
Greene

Washington
Madison
Newton
Searcy
Melbourne
Izard
Sharp
Lawrence
Walnut Ridge
Paragould

Marshall
Stone
Mountain View
Independence
Jonesboro
Blytheville
Mississippi

Clinton
Heber
Springs
Batesville
Craighead
Lake City
Osceola

Crawford
Franklin
Johnson
Pope
Van Buren
Cleburne
Jackson
Newport
Poinsett
Harrisburg

Van Buren
Ozark
Clarksville
Conway
Faulkner
Searcy
Augusta
Cross
Wynne
Crittenden

Fort Smith
Charleston
Russellville
White
Woodruff
Marion

Sebastian
Greenwood
Logan
Paris
Dardanelle
Morrilton
Conway
St. Francis
Forrest City
TENN.

Booneville
Danville
Perryville
Des Arc
Prairie
Marianna
Lee

Waldron
Yell
Perry
Pulaski
Lonoke
De Valls
Bluff
Helena

Scott
Little
Rock
Lonoke
Clarendon
Monroe
Phillips

Mena
Mount Ida
Garland
Saline
Benton
Lonoke
Stuttgart

Polk
Montgomery
Hot Springs
Arkansas
De Witt

Howard
Pike
Malvern
Hot Spring
Sheridan
Grant
Jefferson
Pine Bluff

Sevier
De Queen
Arkadelphia
Rison
Star City
Desha

Nashville
Murfreesboro
Clark
Dallas
Fordyce
Cleveland
Lincoln
Arkansas
City

Hempstead
Prescott
Ouachita
Warren
Monticello
Lake
Village

Little River
Ashdown
Hope
Nevada
Camden
Calhoun
Hampton
Bradley
Drew
Chicot

Texarkana
Lewisville
Magnolia
El Dorado
Hamburg

Miller
Columbia
Union
Ashley

Lafayette

TEXAS

MISSISSIPPI

OKLAHOMA

LOUISIANA

	County boundary
Miller	County name
⊙	County seat
■	Major city
✪	State capital

0   50 mi
0   50 km

©MAPS.com

Arkansas

ARKANSAS STATE INFORMATION

www.arkansas.gov   **Ph:** 501-682-3000

Area (sq mi): 53,178.62 (land 52,068.17; water 1110.45). **Pop per sq mi:** 53.4.

Pop 2005: 2,779,154. **Pop change:** 2000-20005 +4%; 1990-2000 +13.7%. **Pop 2000:** 2,673,400 (White 78.6%; Black or African American 15.7%; Hispanic or Latino 3.2%; Asian 0.8%; Other 3.6%). **Foreign born:** 2.8%. **Median age:** 36.

Income 2000: per capita $16,904; median household $32,182; **Pop below poverty level:** 15.8%. ***Personal per capita income 2000-2003:** $21,925-$24,384.

Unemployment 2004: 5.6%. **Change from 2000:** +0.7%. **Median travel time to work:** 21.9 minutes. **Working outside county of residence:** 23.4%.

ARKANSAS COUNTY

PO Box 719   **Ph:** 870-673-7311
Stuttgart, AR 72160

In east-central AR, east of Pine Bluff; original county; organized Dec 31, 1813 (prior to statehood). **Name Origin:** For the Arkansas Indians.

Area (sq mi): 1033.79 (land 988.49; water 45.3). **Pop per sq mi:** 20.3.

Pop 2005: 20,073. **State rank:** 38. **Pop change:** 2000-20005 -3.3%; 1990-2000 -4.2%. **Pop 2000:** 20,749 (White 74.8%; Black or African American 23.4%; Hispanic or Latino 0.8%; Asian 0.4%; Other 1.1%). **Foreign born:** 0.4%. **Median age:** 38.7.

Income 2000: per capita $16,401; median household $30,316; **Pop below poverty level:** 17.8%. ***Personal per capita income 2000-2003:** $21,572-$26,489.

Unemployment 2004: 6%. **Change from 2000:** +1.1%. **Median travel time to work:** 16.5 minutes. **Working outside county of residence:** 7.8%.

Cities with pop over 10,000: None.

ASHLEY COUNTY

205 E Jefferson St Box 5   **Ph:** 870-853-2020
Hamburg, AR 71646   **Fax:** 870-853-2082

On southern border of AR; organized Nov 30, 1848 from Union and Drew counties. **Name Origin:** For Chester Ashley (1790-1848), U.S. senator from AR (1844-48).

Area (sq mi): 939.08 (land 921.15; water 17.93). **Pop per sq mi:** 25.2.

Pop 2005: 23,178. **State rank:** 32. **Pop change:** 2000-20005 -4.3%; 1990-2000 -0.5%. **Pop 2000:** 24,209 (White 69%; Black or African American 27.1%; Hispanic or Latino 3.2%; Asian 0.2%; Other 2.9%). **Foreign born:** 2.2%. **Median age:** 36.2.

Income 2000: per capita $15,702; median household $31,758; **Pop below poverty level:** 17.5%. ***Personal per capita income 2000-2003:** $21,058-$22,884.

Unemployment 2004: 9.5%. **Change from 2000:** +0.4%. **Median travel time to work:** 18.5 minutes. **Working outside county of residence:** 12.8%.

Cities with pop over 10,000: None.

BAXTER COUNTY

1 E 7th St Room 103   **Ph:** 870-425-3475
Mountain Home, AR 72653   **Fax:** 870-424-5105
www.baxtercounty.org

On central-northern border of AR; organized Mar 24, 1873 from Fulton County. **Name Origin:** For Elisha Baxter (1827-99), AR legislator, chief justice (1864), circuit judge (1868-72), and governor (1872-74).

Area (sq mi): 586.74 (land 554.36; water 32.38). **Pop per sq mi:** 72.8.

Pop 2005: 40,330. **State rank:** 18. **Pop change:** 2000-20005 +5.1%; 1990-2000 +23.1%. **Pop 2000:** 38,386 (White 97.1%; Black or African American 0.1%; Hispanic or Latino 1%; Asian 0.3%; Other 1.7%). **Foreign born:** 1.6%. **Median age:** 48.1.

Income 2000: per capita $16,859; median household $29,106; **Pop below poverty level:** 11.1%. ***Personal per capita income 2000-2003:** $22,026-$24,535.

Unemployment 2004: 5.8%. **Change from 2000:** +0.1%. **Median travel time to work:** 18.4 minutes. **Working outside county of residence:** 10.6%.

Cities with pop over 10,000: Mountain Home ⚖ (11,709).

BENTON COUNTY

215 E Central St Suite 217   **Ph:** 479-271-1013
Bentonville, AR 72712   **Fax:** 479-271-1019
www.co.benton.ar.us

In northwest corner of AR; organized 1836 from Washington County. **Name Origin:** For Thomas Hart Benton (1782-1858), U.S. journalist and statesman; nicknamed 'Old Bullion' for championing use of gold and silver currency rather than paper money.

Area (sq mi): 880.24 (land 845.99; water 34.25). **Pop per sq mi:** 221.

Benton County (cont'd)

Pop 2005: 186,938. **State rank:** 2. **Pop change:** 2000-20005 +21.9%; 1990-2000 +57.3%. **Pop 2000:** 153,406 (White 86.8%; Black or African American 0.4%; Hispanic or Latino 8.8%; Asian 1.1%; Other 7.6%, including 1.6% American Indian/Alaska Native). **Foreign born:** 6.4%. **Median age:** 35.3.

Income 2000: per capita $19,377; median household $40,281; **Pop below poverty level:** 10.1%. *****Personal per capita income 2000-2003:** $25,013-$27,604.

Unemployment 2004: 3.4%. **Change from 2000:** +1.2%. **Median travel time to work:** 19.5 minutes. **Working outside county of residence:** 17.6%.

Cities with pop over 10,000: Rogers (44,885); Bentonville 🏛 (27,765); Siloam Springs (13,246).

BOONE COUNTY

100 N Main St Suite 201   **Ph:** 870-741-8428
Harrison, AR 72601   **Fax:** 870-741-9724

On northern border of AR; organized Apr 9, 1869 from Carroll and Marion counties. **Name Origin:** For Daniel Boone (1734?-1820), U.S. frontiersman and KY pioneer.

Area (sq mi): 601.82 (land 591.18; water 10.64). **Pop per sq mi:** 60.5.

Pop 2005: 35,793. **State rank:** 20. **Pop change:** 2000-20005 +5.4%; 1990-2000 +20%. **Pop 2000:** 33,948 (White 96.9%; Black or African American 0.1%; Hispanic or Latino 1.1%; Asian 0.3%; Other 1.9%). **Foreign born:** 1%. **Median age:** 38.9.

Income 2000: per capita $16,175; median household $29,988; **Pop below poverty level:** 14.8%. *****Personal per capita income 2000-2003:** $20,650-$21,941.

Unemployment 2004: 5.8%. **Change from 2000:** -0.2%. **Median travel time to work:** 20 minutes. **Working outside county of residence:** 12.1%.

Cities with pop over 10,000: Harrison 🏛 (12,563).

BRADLEY COUNTY

101 E Cedar St   **Ph:** 870-226-3853
Warren, AR 71671   **Fax:** 870-226-8401

In south-central AR; organized Dec 18, 1840 from Union County. **Name Origin:** For William L. Bradley, a local settler.

Area (sq mi): 654.38 (land 650.63; water 3.75). **Pop per sq mi:** 18.7.

Pop 2005: 12,192. **State rank:** 58. **Pop change:** 2000-20005 -3.2%; 1990-2000 +6.8%. **Pop 2000:** 12,600 (White 62.3%; Black or African American 28.6%; Hispanic or Latino 8.3%; Asian 0.1%; Other 8%). **Foreign born:** 4.3%. **Median age:** 38.

Income 2000: per capita $13,895; median household $24,821; **Pop below poverty level:** 26.3%. *****Personal per capita income 2000-2003:** $18,235-$20,503.

Unemployment 2004: 7.7%. **Change from 2000:** -1.4%. **Median travel time to work:** 23.2 minutes. **Working outside county of residence:** 26.8%.

Cities with pop over 10,000: None.

CALHOUN COUNTY

PO Box 1175   **Ph:** 870-798-2517
Hampton, AR 71744   **Fax:** 870-798-2428

In south-central AR; organized Dec 6, 1850 from Dallas, Ouachita, and Union counties. **Name Origin:** For John Caldwell Calhoun (1782-1850), U.S. statesman and champion of Southern causes.

Area (sq mi): 632.54 (land 628.27; water 4.27). **Pop per sq mi:** 8.9.

Pop 2005: 5,589. **State rank:** 75. **Pop change:** 2000-20005 -2.7%; 1990-2000 -1.4%. **Pop 2000:** 5,744 (White 74%; Black or African American 23.4%; Hispanic or Latino 1.5%; Asian 0%; Other 2%). **Foreign born:** 0.9%. **Median age:** 39.2.

Income 2000: per capita $15,555; median household $28,438; **Pop below poverty level:** 16.5%. *****Personal per capita income 2000-2003:** $18,366-$20,574.

Unemployment 2004: 6.9%. **Change from 2000:** -0.3%. **Median travel time to work:** 24.8 minutes. **Working outside county of residence:** 52.3%.

Cities with pop over 10,000: None.

CARROLL COUNTY

210 W Church St   **Ph:** 870-423-2022
Berryville, AR 72616   **Fax:** 870-423-7400

On northern border of AR; organized Nov 1, 1833 (prior to statehood) from Izard County. **Name Origin:** For Charles Carroll (1737-1832), signer of the Declaration of Independence, U.S. senator from MD (1789-92), and founder of the Baltimore and Ohio railroad.

Area (sq mi): 638.81 (land 630.27; water 8.54). **Pop per sq mi:** 42.8.

Pop 2005: 26,999. **State rank:** 25. **Pop change:** 2000-20005 +6.5%; 1990-2000 +35.9%. **Pop 2000:** 25,357 (White 87.7%; Black or African American 0.1%; Hispanic or Latino 9.7%; Asian 0.4%; Other 5.9%). **Foreign born:** 7.5%. **Median age:** 39.4.

Income 2000: per capita $16,003; median household $27,924; **Pop below poverty level:** 15.5%. *****Personal per capita income 2000-2003:** $18,301-$18,819.

Unemployment 2004: 4.8%. **Change from 2000:** +0.6%. **Median travel time to work:** 19.7 minutes. **Working outside county of residence:** 12.5%.

Cities with pop over 10,000: None.

CHICOT COUNTY

108 Main St County Courthouse   **Ph:** 870-265-8000
Lake Village, AR 71653   **Fax:** 870-265-8018

In southeastern corner of AR; organized Oct 25, 1823 (prior to statehood) from Arkansas County. **Name Origin:** For Point Chicot on the Mississippi River; *chicot* in French means 'stump,' referring to navigational difficulties there.

Area (sq mi): 690.88 (land 644.03; water 46.86). **Pop per sq mi:** 20.2.

Pop 2005: 13,027. **State rank:** 57. **Pop change:** 2000-20005 -7.7%; 1990-2000 -10.2%. **Pop 2000:** 14,117 (White 42.4%; Black or African American 54%; Hispanic or Latino 2.9%; Asian 0.4%; Other 2.4%). **Foreign born:** 2.3%. **Median age:** 36.2.

*****Source: Personal per capita income data are from the Bureau of Economic Analysis; per capita income data are from the Bureau of the Census.*
See Introduction for explanation of differences.

Chicot County (cont'd)

Income 2000: per capita $12,825; median household $22,024; **Pop below poverty level:** 28.6%. ***Personal per capita income 2000-2003:** $17,164-$19,526.

Unemployment 2004: 11%. **Change from 2000:** +0.7%. **Median travel time to work:** 19.4 minutes. **Working outside county of residence:** 24.1%.

Cities with pop over 10,000: None.

CLARK COUNTY

401 Clay St   **Ph:** 870-246-4491
Arkadelphia, AR 71923   **Fax:** 870-246-6505
www.clarkcountyarkansas.com

In west-central AR, south of Hot Springs; organized Dec 15, 1818 (prior to statehood) from Arkansas County. **Name Origin:** For William Clark (1770-1838), explorer, and co-leader of the Lewis and Clark Expedition.

Area (sq mi): 882.6 (land 865.43; water 17.17). **Pop per sq mi:** 26.5.

Pop 2005: 22,916. **State rank:** 34. **Pop change:** 2000-20005 -2.7%; 1990-2000 +9.8%. **Pop 2000:** 23,546 (White 73.5%; Black or African American 22%; Hispanic or Latino 2.4%; Asian 0.6%; Other 3.1%). **Foreign born:** 2%. **Median age:** 31.8.

Income 2000: per capita $14,533; median household $28,845; **Pop below poverty level:** 19.1%. ***Personal per capita income 2000-2003:** $18,814-$21,387.

Unemployment 2004: 6.1%. **Change from 2000:** +2.4%. **Median travel time to work:** 19.4 minutes. **Working outside county of residence:** 17%.

Cities with pop over 10,000: Arkadelphia ⛫ (10,665).

CLAY COUNTY

PO Box 306   **Ph:** 870-598-2813
Piggott, AR 72454   **Fax:** 870-598-2813

In northeastern corner of AR; organized Mar 24, 1873 from Randolph County. **Name Origin:** For Henry Clay (1777-1852), U.S. senator from KY, known as the 'Great Pacificator' for his advocacy of compromise to avert national crises.

Area (sq mi): 641.42 (land 639.3; water 2.12). **Pop per sq mi:** 25.9.

Pop 2005: 16,578. **State rank:** 48. **Pop change:** 2000-20005 -5.9%; 1990-2000 -2.8%. **Pop 2000:** 17,609 (White 97.5%; Black or African American 0.2%; Hispanic or Latino 0.8%; Asian 0.1%; Other 1.7%). **Foreign born:** 0.3%. **Median age:** 40.5.

Income 2000: per capita $14,512; median household $25,345; **Pop below poverty level:** 17.5%. ***Personal per capita income 2000-2003:** $18,164-$20,953.

Unemployment 2004: 8%. **Change from 2000:** -0.2%. **Median travel time to work:** 21.4 minutes. **Working outside county of residence:** 29.7%.

Cities with pop over 10,000: None.

CLEBURNE COUNTY

301 W Main St   **Ph:** 501-362-4620
Heber Springs, AR 72543   **Fax:** 501-362-4622

In north-central AR, north of Little Rock; organized Feb 20, 1883 from White and Van Buren counties. **Name Origin:** For Gen. Patrick R. Cleburne (1828-64), Confederate officer.

Area (sq mi): 591.91 (land 553.05; water 38.86). **Pop per sq mi:** 45.9.

Pop 2005: 25,391. **State rank:** 26. **Pop change:** 2000-20005 +5.6%; 1990-2000 +23.9%. **Pop 2000:** 24,046 (White 97.3%; Black or African American 0.1%; Hispanic or Latino 1.2%; Asian 0.1%; Other 1.5%). **Foreign born:** 1.1%. **Median age:** 43.7.

Income 2000: per capita $17,250; median household $31,531; **Pop below poverty level:** 13.1%. ***Personal per capita income 2000-2003:** $21,745-$23,149.

Unemployment 2004: 5.1%. **Change from 2000:** +0.4%. **Median travel time to work:** 27.1 minutes. **Working outside county of residence:** 32%.

Cities with pop over 10,000: None.

CLEVELAND COUNTY

PO Box 368   **Ph:** 870-325-6521
Rison, AR 71665   **Fax:** 870-325-6144

In south-central AR, south of Pine Bluff; organized Apr 17, 1873 from Dallas County. **Name Origin:** For Grover Cleveland (1837-1908), twenty-second and twenty-fourth U.S. president.

Area (sq mi): 598.8 (land 597.74; water 1.06). **Pop per sq mi:** 14.9.

Pop 2005: 8,903. **State rank:** 69. **Pop change:** 2000-20005 +3.9%; 1990-2000 +10.2%. **Pop 2000:** 8,571 (White 84%; Black or African American 13.2%; Hispanic or Latino 1.6%; Asian 0.1%; Other 1.8%). **Foreign born:** 1.4%. **Median age:** 36.9.

Income 2000: per capita $15,362; median household $32,405; **Pop below poverty level:** 15.2%. ***Personal per capita income 2000-2003:** $20,773-$22,725.

Unemployment 2004: 6.7%. **Change from 2000:** +0.3%. **Median travel time to work:** 31.7 minutes. **Working outside county of residence:** 70.4%.

Cities with pop over 10,000: None.

COLUMBIA COUNTY

1 Court Sq Suite 1   **Ph:** 870-235-3774
Magnolia, AR 71753   **Fax:** 870-235-3773

On southern border of AR; organized Dec 17, 1852 from Lafayette County. **Name Origin:** Feminine form of Columbus, a poetic and honorific reference to Christopher Columbus (1451-1506) and America.

Area (sq mi): 766.86 (land 766.11; water 0.75). **Pop per sq mi:** 32.2.

Pop 2005: 24,695. **State rank:** 28. **Pop change:** 2000-20005 -3.5%; 1990-2000 -0.3%. **Pop 2000:** 25,603 (White 61.6%; Black or African American 36.1%; Hispanic or Latino 1.1%; Asian 0.3%; Other 1.6%). **Foreign born:** 0.9%. **Median age:** 35.7.

Income 2000: per capita $15,322; median household $27,640; **Pop below poverty level:** 21.1%. ***Personal per capita income 2000-2003:** $21,776-$23,647.

Unemployment 2004: 6.5%. **Change from 2000:** +1.2%. **Median travel time to work:** 18.4 minutes. **Working outside county of residence:** 15.3%.

Cities with pop over 10,000: Magnolia ⛫ (10,458).

⛫ County Seat

CONWAY COUNTY

117 S Moose St   **Ph:** 501-354-9621
Morrilton, AR 72110   **Fax:** 501-354-9610

In central AR, northwest of Little Rock; organized Oct 20, 1825 (prior to statehood) from Pulaski County. **Name Origin:** For Henry W. Conway (1793-1827), soldier, early settler, and delegate to Congress at the time of establishment.

Area (sq mi): 566.66 (land 556.15; water 10.51). **Pop per sq mi:** 37.3.

Pop 2005: 20,739. **State rank:** 36. **Pop change:** 2000-20005 +2%; 1990-2000 +6.2%. **Pop 2000:** 20,336 (White 83.5%; Black or African American 13.1%; Hispanic or Latino 1.8%; Asian 0.2%; Other 2.4%). **Foreign born:** 1.2%. **Median age:** 37.9.

Income 2000: per capita $16,056; median household $31,209; **Pop below poverty level:** 16.1%. ***Personal per capita income 2000-2003:** $21,610-$22,749.

Unemployment 2004: 5.7%. **Change from 2000:** +0.4%. **Median travel time to work:** 24.9 minutes. **Working outside county of residence:** 41%.

Cities with pop over 10,000: None.

CRAIGHEAD COUNTY

PO Box 1167   **Ph:** 870-933-4520
Jonesboro, AR 72403   **Fax:** 870-933-4514
www.craigheadcounty.org

In northeastern AR; organized Feb 19, 1859 from Mississippi County. **Name Origin:** For Thomas C. Craighead, state senator at the time of establishment.

Area (sq mi): 712.98 (land 710.84; water 2.14). **Pop per sq mi:** 122.

Pop 2005: 86,735. **State rank:** 8. **Pop change:** 2000-20005 +5.6%; 1990-2000 +19.1%. **Pop 2000:** 82,148 (White 88.2%; Black or African American 7.8%; Hispanic or Latino 2.1%; Asian 0.6%; Other 2.3%). **Foreign born:** 2%. **Median age:** 33.

Income 2000: per capita $17,091; median household $32,425; **Pop below poverty level:** 15.4%. ***Personal per capita income 2000-2003:** $21,731-$24,434.

Unemployment 2004: 5.4%. **Change from 2000:** +1%. **Median travel time to work:** 18.2 minutes. **Working outside county of residence:** 11.5%.

Cities with pop over 10,000: Jonesboro ⛪ (58,799).

CRAWFORD COUNTY

300 Main St County Courthouse Rm 7   **Ph:** 479-474-1312
Van Buren, AR 72956   **Fax:** 479-471-3236

On western border of AR, north of Fort Smith; organized Oct 18, 1820 (prior to statehood) from Pulaski County. **Name Origin:** For William Harris Crawford (1772-1834), VA statesman.

Area (sq mi): 604.2 (land 595.39; water 8.81). **Pop per sq mi:** 96.8.

Pop 2005: 57,630. **State rank:** 12. **Pop change:** 2000-20005 +8.2%; 1990-2000 +25.3%. **Pop 2000:** 53,247 (White 90.7%; Black or African American 0.9%; Hispanic or Latino 3.3%; Asian 1.2%; Other 5.7%, including 2% American Indian/Alaska Native). **Foreign born:** 2.4%. **Median age:** 35.1.

Income 2000: per capita $15,015; median household $32,871; **Pop below poverty level:** 14.2%. ***Personal per capita income 2000-2003:** $18,791-$20,361.

Unemployment 2004: 5.1%. **Change from 2000:** +1%. **Median travel time to work:** 23.7 minutes. **Working outside county of residence:** 53.2%.

Cities with pop over 10,000: Van Buren ⛪ (20,637).

CRITTENDEN COUNTY

100 Court St County Courthouse   **Ph:** 870-739-4434
Marion, AR 72364   **Fax:** 870-739-3072

On eastern border of AR, east of TN; organized Oct 22, 1825 (prior to statehood) from Phillips County. **Name Origin:** For Robert Crittenden, veteran of the War of 1812 and Arkansas Territory official.

Area (sq mi): 636.69 (land 610.17; water 26.52). **Pop per sq mi:** 85.

Pop 2005: 51,882. **State rank:** 14. **Pop change:** 2000-20005 +2%; 1990-2000 +1.9%. **Pop 2000:** 50,866 (White 50.4%; Black or African American 47.1%; Hispanic or Latino 1.4%; Asian 0.5%; Other 1.5%). **Foreign born:** 1.2%. **Median age:** 32.

Income 2000: per capita $14,424; median household $30,109; **Pop below poverty level:** 25.3%. ***Personal per capita income 2000-2003:** $19,761-$22,266.

Unemployment 2004: 7%. **Change from 2000:** +1.1%. **Median travel time to work:** 22.8 minutes. **Working outside county of residence:** 40.6%.

Cities with pop over 10,000: West Memphis (28,117).

CROSS COUNTY

705 E Union St Rm 8   **Ph:** 870-238-5735
Wynne, AR 72396   **Fax:** 870-238-5739

In northeastern AR, west of Memphis, TN; organized Nov 15, 1862 from Crittenden, Poinsett, and Saint Francis counties. **Name Origin:** For Edward Cross (1798-1887), jurist and U.S. representative from AR (1839-45).

Area (sq mi): 622.33 (land 615.85; water 6.49). **Pop per sq mi:** 31.2.

Pop 2005: 19,237. **State rank:** 39. **Pop change:** 2000-20005 -1.5%; 1990-2000 +1.6%. **Pop 2000:** 19,526 (White 74.4%; Black or African American 23.7%; Hispanic or Latino 0.9%; Asian 0.3%; Other 1.1%). **Foreign born:** 1%. **Median age:** 35.9.

Income 2000: per capita $15,726; median household $29,362; **Pop below poverty level:** 19.9%. ***Personal per capita income 2000-2003:** $17,515-$20,624.

Unemployment 2004: 8.2%. **Change from 2000:** +0.7%. **Median travel time to work:** 23.4 minutes. **Working outside county of residence:** 32.3%.

Cities with pop over 10,000: None.

DALLAS COUNTY

206 W 3rd St   **Ph:** 870-352-2307
Fordyce, AR 71742   **Fax:** 870-352-7179

In south-central AR, southeast of Hot Springs; organized Jan 1, 1845 from Clark and Hot Springs counties. **Name Origin:** For George Mifflin Dallas (1792-1864), U.S. statesman and U.S. vice president (1845-49).

*Source: Personal per capita income data are from the Bureau of Economic Analysis; per capita income data are from the Bureau of the Census. See Introduction for explanation of differences.

80

Dallas County (cont'd)

Area (sq mi): 668.16 (land 667.42; water 0.74). **Pop per sq mi:** 12.8.

Pop 2005: 8,524. **State rank:** 70. **Pop change:** 2000-20005 -7.4%; 1990-2000 -4.2%. **Pop 2000:** 9,210 (White 56.4%; Black or African American 41%; Hispanic or Latino 1.9%; Asian 0.2%; Other 1.8%). **Foreign born:** 0.9%. **Median age:** 38.4.

Income 2000: per capita $14,610; median household $26,608; **Pop below poverty level:** 18.9%. ***Personal per capita income 2000-2003:** $19,919-$21,547.

Unemployment 2004: 7.6%. **Change from 2000:** -1.6%. **Median travel time to work:** 23.5 minutes. **Working outside county of residence:** 38.2%.

Cities with pop over 10,000: None.

DESHA COUNTY
PO Box 188   **Ph:** 870-877-2426
Arkansas City, AR 71630   **Fax:** 870-877-2531

On southeastern border of AR, southeast of Pine Bluff; organized Dec 12, 1838 from Arkansas County. **Name Origin:** For Capt. Benjamin Desha (?-1835), officer in the War of 1812.

Area (sq mi): 819.52 (land 764.99; water 54.53). **Pop per sq mi:** 18.8.

Pop 2005: 14,358. **State rank:** 53. **Pop change:** 2000-20005 -6.4%; 1990-2000 -8.7%. **Pop 2000:** 15,341 (White 49.6%; Black or African American 46.3%; Hispanic or Latino 3.2%; Asian 0.3%; Other 2.9%). **Foreign born:** 2.1%. **Median age:** 35.5.

Income 2000: per capita $13,446; median household $24,121; **Pop below poverty level:** 28.9%. ***Personal per capita income 2000-2003:** $17,542-$21,078.

Unemployment 2004: 9.4%. **Change from 2000:** -1.7%. **Median travel time to work:** 18.9 minutes. **Working outside county of residence:** 19.6%.

Cities with pop over 10,000: None.

DREW COUNTY
210 S Main St   **Ph:** 870-460-6250
Monticello, AR 71655   **Fax:** 870-460-6246

In southeastern AR, southeast of Pine Bluff; organized Nov 26, 1846 from Arkansas County. **Name Origin:** For Thomas Stevenson Drew (1802-79), governor of AR (1844-49).

Area (sq mi): 835.65 (land 828.18; water 7.47). **Pop per sq mi:** 22.6.

Pop 2005: 18,693. **State rank:** 40. **Pop change:** 2000-20005 -0.2%; 1990-2000 +7.8%. **Pop 2000:** 18,723 (White 69.7%; Black or African American 27.2%; Hispanic or Latino 1.8%; Asian 0.4%; Other 2.2%). **Foreign born:** 1.5%. **Median age:** 34.

Income 2000: per capita $16,264; median household $28,627; **Pop below poverty level:** 18.2%. ***Personal per capita income 2000-2003:** $19,238-$21,737.

Unemployment 2004: 8%. **Change from 2000:** -2.1%. **Median travel time to work:** 20.2 minutes. **Working outside county of residence:** 24.5%.

Cities with pop over 10,000: None.

FAULKNER COUNTY
801 Locust St   **Ph:** 501-450-4909
Conway, AR 72034   **Fax:** 501-450-4938

In central AR, north of Little Rock; organized Apr 12, 1873 from Pulaski County. **Name Origin:** Said to be for Sanford C. Faulkner, who wrote 'The Arkansas Traveler,' the state song. Other Faulkner family names occur in the area.

Area (sq mi): 664.01 (land 647.38; water 16.63). **Pop per sq mi:** 150.1.

Pop 2005: 97,147. **State rank:** 5. **Pop change:** 2000-20005 +12.9%; 1990-2000 +43.3%. **Pop 2000:** 86,014 (White 87.4%; Black or African American 8.5%; Hispanic or Latino 1.8%; Asian 0.7%; Other 2.4%). **Foreign born:** 1.7%. **Median age:** 31.

Income 2000: per capita $17,988; median household $38,204; **Pop below poverty level:** 12.5%. ***Personal per capita income 2000-2003:** $22,470-$24,370.

Unemployment 2004: 4.9%. **Change from 2000:** -0.1%. **Median travel time to work:** 24.8 minutes. **Working outside county of residence:** 32.9%.

Cities with pop over 10,000: Conway 🏛 (50,358).

FRANKLIN COUNTY
211 W Commercial St   **Ph:** 479 667 3607
Ozark, AR 72949   **Fax:** 479-667-4247

In northwestern AR, east of Fort Smith; organized Dec 19, 1837 from Crawford County. **Name Origin:** For Benjamin Franklin (1706-90), U.S. patriot, diplomat, and statesman.

Area (sq mi): 619.69 (land 609.55; water 10.13). **Pop per sq mi:** 29.9.

Pop 2005: 18,218. **State rank:** 42. **Pop change:** 2000-20005 +2.5%; 1990-2000 +19.3%. **Pop 2000:** 17,771 (White 95.3%; Black or African American 0.6%; Hispanic or Latino 1.7%; Asian 0.3%; Other 3%). **Foreign born:** 1.3%. **Median age:** 37.6.

Income 2000: per capita $14,616; median household $30,848; **Pop below poverty level:** 15.2%. ***Personal per capita income 2000-2003:** $19,452-$20,830.

Unemployment 2004: 4.8%. **Change from 2000:** +1.4%. **Median travel time to work:** 26.6 minutes. **Working outside county of residence:** 45.4%.

Cities with pop over 10,000: None.

FULTON COUNTY
PO Box 219   **Ph:** 870-895-3310
Salem, AR 72576   **Fax:** 870-895-3383

On north-central border of AR; organized Dec 21, 1842 from Izard County. **Name Origin:** For William Savin Fulton (1795-1844), governor of the Arkansas Territory and U.S. senator (1836-44).

Area (sq mi): 620.31 (land 618.16; water 2.16). **Pop per sq mi:** 19.3.

Pop 2005: 11,934. **State rank:** 59. **Pop change:** 2000-20005 +2.5%; 1990-2000 +16%. **Pop 2000:** 11,642 (White 97.3%; Black or African American 0.2%; Hispanic or Latino 0.5%; Asian 0.2%; Other 2%). **Foreign born:** 0.4%. **Median age:** 43.

🏛 *County Seat*

Fulton County (cont'd)

Income 2000: per capita $15,712; median household $25,529; **Pop below poverty level:** 16.3%. ***Personal per capita income 2000-2003:** $16,204-$18,485.

Unemployment 2004: 5.9%. **Change from 2000:** +0.4%. **Median travel time to work:** 26.7 minutes. **Working outside county of residence:** 50.1%.

Cities with pop over 10,000: None.

GARLAND COUNTY
501 Ouachita Ave   **Ph:** 501-622-3610
Hot Springs, AR 71901   **Fax:** 501-624-0665
www.garlandcounty.org

In west-central AR; organized Apr 5, 1873 from Montgomery County. **Name Origin:** For Augustus Hill Garland (1832-99), AR governor (1874-76) and U.S. senator (1877-85).

Area (sq mi): 734.57 (land 677.22; water 57.35). **Pop per sq mi:** 138.1.

Pop 2005: 93,551. **State rank:** 6. **Pop change:** 2000-20005 +6.2%; 1990-2000 +20%. **Pop 2000:** 88,068 (White 87.3%; Black or African American 7.8%; Hispanic or Latino 2.6%; Asian 0.5%; Other 2.8%). **Foreign born:** 2.6%. **Median age:** 42.5.

Income 2000: per capita $18,631; median household $31,724; **Pop below poverty level:** 14.6%. ***Personal per capita income 2000-2003:** $23,963-$25,497.

Unemployment 2004: 5.9%. **Change from 2000:** +1.6%. **Median travel time to work:** 21.1 minutes. **Working outside county of residence:** 11.5%.

Cities with pop over 10,000: Hot Springs ⛪ (37,245).

GRANT COUNTY
101 W Center St County Courthouse Rm 106 **Ph:** 870-942-2631
Sheridan, AR 72150   **Fax:** 870-942-3564

In south-central AR, south of Little Rock; organized Feb 4, 1869 from Jefferson County. **Name Origin:** For Ulysses S. Grant (1822-85), Civil War general and eighteenth U.S. president.

Area (sq mi): 633.01 (land 631.78; water 1.23). **Pop per sq mi:** 27.5.

Pop 2005: 17,348. **State rank:** 45. **Pop change:** 2000-20005 +5.4%; 1990-2000 +18%. **Pop 2000:** 16,464 (White 95.1%; Black or African American 2.5%; Hispanic or Latino 1.1%; Asian 0.1%; Other 1.7%). **Foreign born:** 0.6%. **Median age:** 36.6.

Income 2000: per capita $17,547; median household $37,182; **Pop below poverty level:** 10.2%. ***Personal per capita income 2000-2003:** $22,132-$24,637.

Unemployment 2004: 5.5%. **Change from 2000:** -0.6%. **Median travel time to work:** 31.5 minutes. **Working outside county of residence:** 59%.

Cities with pop over 10,000: None.

GREENE COUNTY
PO Box 62   **Ph:** 870-239-6311
Paragould, AR 72451   **Fax:** 870-239-3550
www.greenecounty.org

On northeastern border of AR; organized Nov 5, 1833 (prior to statehood) from Lawrence County. **Name Origin:** For Gen. Nathanael Greene (1742-86), hero of the Revolutionary War, quartermaster general (1778-80), and commander of the Army of the South (1780).

Area (sq mi): 579.65 (land 577.51; water 2.14). **Pop per sq mi:** 68.2.

Pop 2005: 39,401. **State rank:** 19. **Pop change:** 2000-20005 +5.5%; 1990-2000 +17.4%. **Pop 2000:** 37,331 (White 96.8%; Black or African American 0.1%; Hispanic or Latino 1.2%; Asian 0.2%; Other 2.2%). **Foreign born:** 0.5%. **Median age:** 36.2.

Income 2000: per capita $16,403; median household $30,828; **Pop below poverty level:** 13.3%. ***Personal per capita income 2000-2003:** $19,166-$21,106.

Unemployment 2004: 6.1%. **Change from 2000:** -1.7%. **Median travel time to work:** 19.2 minutes. **Working outside county of residence:** 18.3%.

Cities with pop over 10,000: Paragould ⛪ (23,397).

HEMPSTEAD COUNTY
PQ Box 1420   **Ph:** 870-777-2241
Hope, AR 71802   **Fax:** 870-777-7829

In southwestern AR, northeast of Texarkana; organized Dec 15, 1818 (prior to statehood) from Arkansas County. **Name Origin:** For Edward Hempstead (1780-1817), delegate to Congress from MO.

Area (sq mi): 741.36 (land 728.77; water 12.59). **Pop per sq mi:** 32.1.

Pop 2005: 23,383. **State rank:** 31. **Pop change:** 2000-20005 -0.9%; 1990-2000 +9.1%. **Pop 2000:** 23,587 (White 59.8%; Black or African American 30.4%; Hispanic or Latino 8.3%; Asian 0.2%; Other 6.2%). **Foreign born:** 6.4%. **Median age:** 35.2.

Income 2000: per capita $14,103; median household $28,622; **Pop below poverty level:** 20.3%. ***Personal per capita income 2000-2003:** $18,681-$20,320.

Unemployment 2004: 6%. **Change from 2000:** +1.1%. **Median travel time to work:** 19.2 minutes. **Working outside county of residence:** 26.9%.

Cities with pop over 10,000: Hope ⛪ (10,462).

HOT SPRING COUNTY
210 Locust St   **Ph:** 501-332-2291
Malvern, AR 72104   **Fax:** 501-332-2221

In central AR, south of Hot Springs; organized Apr 17, 1829 (prior to statehood) from Clark County. **Name Origin:** At the time of organization the famous Hot Springs were within the county boundaries.

Area (sq mi): 622.16 (land 614.93; water 7.22). **Pop per sq mi:** 50.8.

Pop 2005: 31,264. **State rank:** 22. **Pop change:** 2000-20005 +3%; 1990-2000 +16.2%. **Pop 2000:** 30,353 (White 86.6%; Black or African American 10.3%; Hispanic or Latino 1.3%; Asian 0.2%; Other 2.1%). **Foreign born:** 1.2%. **Median age:** 38.4.

Income 2000: per capita $15,216; median household $31,543; **Pop below poverty level:** 14%. ***Personal per capita income 2000-2003:** $18,349-$20,017.

*Source: Personal per capita income data are from the Bureau of Economic Analysis; per capita income data are from the Bureau of the Census. See Introduction for explanation of differences.

Hot Spring County (cont'd)

Unemployment 2004: 6.1%. **Change from 2000:** +0.1%. **Median travel time to work:** 27.9 minutes. **Working outside county of residence:** 48%.

Cities with pop over 10,000: None.

HOWARD COUNTY

421 N Main St Rm 10   **Ph:** 870-845-7502
Nashville, AR 71852   **Fax:** 870-845-7505

In southwestern AR, north of Texarkana; organized Apr 17, 1873 from Pike County. **Name Origin:** Said to be named for James Howard, a state senator.

Area (sq mi): 595.2 (land 587.42; water 7.78). **Pop per sq mi:** 24.8.

Pop 2005: 14,552. **State rank:** 52. **Pop change:** 2000-20005 +1.8%; 1990-2000 +5.4%. **Pop 2000:** 14,300 (White 71.5%; Black or African American 21.9%; Hispanic or Latino 5.1%; Asian 0.5%; Other 4.1%). **Foreign born:** 3.5%. **Median age:** 36.1.

Income 2000: per capita $15,586; median household $28,699; **Pop below poverty level:** 15.5%. ***Personal per capita income 2000-2003:** $21,064-$20,940.

Unemployment 2004: 6.1%. **Change from 2000:** +0.6%. **Median travel time to work:** 19.2 minutes. **Working outside county of residence:** 13.6%.

Cities with pop over 10,000: None.

INDEPENDENCE COUNTY

192 E Main St   **Ph:** 870-793-8828
Batesville, AR 72501   **Fax:** 870-793-8831

In north-central AR; organized Oct 23, 1820 (prior to statehood) from Arkansas County. **Name Origin:** To honor the Declaration of Independence.

Area (sq mi): 771.57 (land 763.78; water 7.79). **Pop per sq mi:** 45.5.

Pop 2005: 34,737. **State rank:** 21. **Pop change:** 2000-20005 +1.5%; 1990-2000 +9.7%. **Pop 2000:** 34,233 (White 94.2%; Black or African American 2%; Hispanic or Latino 1.5%; Asian 0.6%; Other 2.4%). **Foreign born:** 1.2%. **Median age:** 37.7.

Income 2000: per capita $16,163; median household $31,920; **Pop below poverty level:** 13%. ***Personal per capita income 2000-2003:** $20,409-$22,212.

Unemployment 2004: 6.4%. **Change from 2000:** +0.3%. **Median travel time to work:** 21.5 minutes. **Working outside county of residence:** 11.5%.

Cities with pop over 10,000: None.

IZARD COUNTY

PO Box 95   **Ph:** 870-368-4316
Melbourne, AR 72556   **Fax:** 870-368-4748

In north-central AR; organized Oct 27, 1825 (prior to statehood) from Independence County. **Name Origin:** For George Izard (1777-1828), general in the War of 1812 and governor of Arkansas Territory (1825-28).

Area (sq mi): 584.02 (land 580.68; water 3.34). **Pop per sq mi:** 23.1.

Pop 2005: 13,430. **State rank:** 55. **Pop change:** 2000-20005 +1.4%; 1990-2000 +16.6%. **Pop 2000:** 13,249 (White 95.9%; Black or African American 1.4%; Hispanic or Latino 1%; Asian 0.1%; Other 2%). **Foreign born:** 0.8%. **Median age:** 42.6.

Income 2000: per capita $14,397; median household $25,670; **Pop below poverty level:** 17.2%. ***Personal per capita income 2000-2003:** $17,083-$18,926.

Unemployment 2004: 6.8%. **Change from 2000:** +0.2%. **Median travel time to work:** 26.8 minutes. **Working outside county of residence:** 35.6%.

Cities with pop over 10,000: None.

JACKSON COUNTY

208 Main St County Courthouse   **Ph:** 870-523-7420
Newport, AR 72112   **Fax:** 870-523-7404

In northeast-central AR; organized Nov 5, 1829 (prior to statehood) from Independence County. **Name Origin:** For Andrew Jackson (1767-1845), seventh U.S. president.

Area (sq mi): 641.45 (land 633.52; water 7.92). **Pop per sq mi:** 27.8.

Pop 2005: 17,601. **State rank:** 43. **Pop change:** 2000-20005 -4.4%; 1990-2000 -2.8%. **Pop 2000:** 18,418 (White 79.9%; Black or African American 17.6%; Hispanic or Latino 1.3%; Asian 0.2%; Other 1.7%). **Foreign born:** 0.5%. **Median age:** 38.2.

Income 2000: per capita $14,564; median household $25,081; **Pop below poverty level:** 17.4%. ***Personal per capita income 2000-2003:** $18,956-$22,150.

Unemployment 2004: 8.7%. **Change from 2000:** +0%. **Median travel time to work:** 20.2 minutes. **Working outside county of residence:** 24%.

Cities with pop over 10,000: None.

JEFFERSON COUNTY

PO Box 6317   **Ph:** 870-541-5322
Pine Bluff, AR 71611   **Fax:** 870-541-5324
www.jeffersoncountyark.com

In southeast-central AR; organized Nov 2, 1829 (prior to statehood) from Arkansas and Pulaski counties. **Name Origin:** For Thomas Jefferson (1743-1826), U.S. patriot and statesman; third U.S. president.

Area (sq mi): 913.7 (land 884.82; water 28.88). **Pop per sq mi:** 92.3.

Pop 2005: 81,700. **State rank:** 9. **Pop change:** 2000-20005 -3.1%; 1990-2000 -1.4%. **Pop 2000:** 84,278 (White 48%; Black or African American 49.6%; Hispanic or Latino 1%; Asian 0.7%; Other 1.3%). **Foreign born:** 1.1%. **Median age:** 35.1.

Income 2000: per capita $15,417; median household $31,327; **Pop below poverty level:** 20.5%. ***Personal per capita income 2000-2003:** $19,634-$22,451.

Unemployment 2004: 7.9%. **Change from 2000:** -0.3%. **Median travel time to work:** 21.6 minutes. **Working outside county of residence:** 15.4%.

Cities with pop over 10,000: Pine Bluff ⛪ (53,419).

⛪ County Seat

JOHNSON COUNTY

215 Main St   **Ph:** 479-754-3967
Clarksville, AR 72830   **Fax:** 479-754-2286

In northwestern AR, northeast of Fort Smith; organized Nov 16, 1833 (prior to statehood) from Pope County. **Name Origin:** For Benjamin Johnson, a territorial judge.

Area (sq mi): 682.74 (land 662.17; water 20.57). **Pop per sq mi:** 36.3.

Pop 2005: 24,042. **State rank:** 30. **Pop change:** 2000-20005 +5.5%; 1990-2000 +25%. **Pop 2000:** 22,781 (White 90%; Black or African American 1.4%; Hispanic or Latino 6.7%; Asian 0.3%; Other 4.6%). **Foreign born:** 4.5%. **Median age:** 36.4.

Income 2000: per capita $15,097; median household $27,910; **Pop below poverty level:** 16.4%. ***Personal per capita income 2000-2003:** $17,842-$19,057.

Unemployment 2004: 5.3%. **Change from 2000:** +1%. **Median travel time to work:** 20.5 minutes. **Working outside county of residence:** 20.9%.

Cities with pop over 10,000: None.

LAFAYETTE COUNTY

1 Courthouse Sq   **Ph:** 870-921-4858
Lewisville, AR 71845   **Fax:** 870-921-4505

On southwestern border of AR; organized Oct 15, 1827 (prior to statehood) from Hempstead County. **Name Origin:** For the Marquis de Lafayette (1757-1834), French statesman and soldier who fought with the Americans during the Revolutionary War.

Area (sq mi): 545.07 (land 526.5; water 18.57). **Pop per sq mi:** 15.2.

Pop 2005: 8,027. **State rank:** 73. **Pop change:** 2000-20005 -6.2%; 1990-2000 -11.2%. **Pop 2000:** 8,559 (White 61.5%; Black or African American 36.5%; Hispanic or Latino 1%; Asian 0.2%; Other 1.2%). **Foreign born:** 1%. **Median age:** 39.3.

Income 2000: per capita $14,128; median household $24,831; **Pop below poverty level:** 23.2%. ***Personal per capita income 2000-2003:** $17,633-$19,107.

Unemployment 2004: 7.3%. **Change from 2000:** +2.1%. **Median travel time to work:** 26.8 minutes. **Working outside county of residence:** 43.2%.

Cities with pop over 10,000: None.

LAWRENCE COUNTY

PO Box 526   **Ph:** 870-886-1111
Walnut Ridge, AR 72476   **Fax:** 870-886-1122

In northeastern AR; organized Jan 15, 1815 (prior to statehood) from New Madrid County, MO. **Name Origin:** For Capt. James Lawrence (1781-1813), U.S. Navy commander in War of 1812 who said 'Don't give up the ship!'

Area (sq mi): 592.34 (land 586.57; water 5.78). **Pop per sq mi:** 29.2.

Pop 2005: 17,153. **State rank:** 46. **Pop change:** 2000-20005 -3.5%; 1990-2000 +1.8%. **Pop 2000:** 17,774 (White 97.4%; Black or African American 0.4%; Hispanic or Latino 0.7%; Asian 0.1%; Other 1.7%). **Foreign born:** 0.6%. **Median age:** 38.2.

Income 2000: per capita $13,785; median household $27,139; **Pop below poverty level:** 18.4%. ***Personal per capita income 2000-2003:** $17,175-$19,608.

Unemployment 2004: 8.1%. **Change from 2000:** +0.1%. **Median travel time to work:** 23.6 minutes. **Working outside county of residence:** 35.1%.

Cities with pop over 10,000: None.

LEE COUNTY

15 E Chestnut St   **Ph:** 870-295-7715
Marianna, AR 72360   **Fax:** 870-295-7766

On central-eastern border of AR; organized Apr 17, 1873 from Phillips and Monroe counties. **Name Origin:** For Robert E. Lee (1807-70), American general and commander in chief of the Confederate forces during the Civil War.

Area (sq mi): 619.47 (land 601.66; water 17.8). **Pop per sq mi:** 19.2.

Pop 2005: 11,545. **State rank:** 61. **Pop change:** 2000-20005 -8.2%; 1990-2000 -3.6%. **Pop 2000:** 12,580 (White 40.3%; Black or African American 57.2%; Hispanic or Latino 2.2%; Asian 0.3%; Other 1.1%). **Foreign born:** 0.3%. **Median age:** 34.6.

Income 2000: per capita $10,983; median household $20,510; **Pop below poverty level:** 29.9%. ***Personal per capita income 2000-2003:** $14,795-$19,594.

Unemployment 2004: 11.6%. **Change from 2000:** +2.2%. **Median travel time to work:** 22.5 minutes. **Working outside county of residence:** 33.8%.

Cities with pop over 10,000: None.

LINCOLN COUNTY

300 S Drew St   **Ph:** 870-628-5114
Star City, AR 71667   **Fax:** 870-628-5794

In southeastern AR; organized Mar 28, 1871 from Arkansas, Bradley, Desha, Drew, and Jefferson counties. **Name Origin:** For Abraham Lincoln (1809-65), sixteenth U.S. president.

Area (sq mi): 572.17 (land 561.2; water 10.97). **Pop per sq mi:** 25.4.

Pop 2005: 14,262. **State rank:** 54. **Pop change:** 2000-20005 -1.6%; 1990-2000 +5.9%. **Pop 2000:** 14,492 (White 64.3%; Black or African American 32.9%; Hispanic or Latino 1.8%; Asian 0.1%; Other 2.1%). **Foreign born:** 0.7%. **Median age:** 34.7.

Income 2000: per capita $12,479; median household $29,607; **Pop below poverty level:** 19.5%. ***Personal per capita income 2000-2003:** $14,796-$16,977.

Unemployment 2004: 7.9%. **Change from 2000:** +1.8%. **Median travel time to work:** 25.9 minutes. **Working outside county of residence:** 46.2%.

Cities with pop over 10,000: None.

LITTLE RIVER COUNTY

351 N 2nd St   **Ph:** 870-898-7208
Ashdown, AR 71822   **Fax:** 870-898-7207

On southwestern border; organized Mar 5, 1867 from Hempstead County. **Name Origin:** For the Little River, which forms its northern boundary.

Source: Personal per capita income data are from the Bureau of Economic Analysis; per capita income data are from the Bureau of the Census. See Introduction for explanation of differences.

Little River County (cont'd)

Area (sq mi): 564.87 (land 531.73; water 33.14). **Pop per sq mi:** 24.9.

Pop 2005: 13,227. **State rank:** 56. **Pop change:** 2000-20005 -2.9%; 1990-2000 -2.4%. **Pop 2000:** 13,628 (White 73.8%; Black or African American 21.3%; Hispanic or Latino 1.7%; Asian 0.2%; Other 4.1%, including 1.5% American Indian/Alaska Native). **Foreign born:** 1.7%. **Median age:** 38.2.

Income 2000: per capita $15,899; median household $29,417; **Pop below poverty level:** 15.4%. *Personal per capita income 2000-2003: $20,567-$21,924.

Unemployment 2004: 5.1%. **Change from 2000:** +0.7%. **Median travel time to work:** 24.5 minutes. **Working outside county of residence:** 38.9%.

Cities with pop over 10,000: None.

LOGAN COUNTY

366 N Broadway Ave   **Ph:** 479-675-2951
Booneville, AR 72927   **Fax:** 479-675-2952

In west-central AR, southeast of Fort Smith; organized as Sarber County Mar 22, 1871 from Franklin County; name changed Dec 14, 1875. **Name Origin:** For James Logan, an early settler.

Area (sq mi): 731.5 (land 709.87; water 21.63). **Pop per sq mi:** 32.3.

Pop 2005: 22,944. **State rank:** 33. **Pop change:** 2000-20005 +2%; 1990-2000 +9.4%. **Pop 2000:** 22,486 (White 95.7%; Black or African American 1%; Hispanic or Latino 1.2%; Asian 0.1%; Other 2.4%). **Foreign born:** 0.9%. **Median age:** 38.

Income 2000: per capita $14,527; median household $28,344; **Pop below poverty level:** 15.4%. *Personal per capita income 2000-2003: $18,176-$19,767.

Unemployment 2004: 5.4%. **Change from 2000:** +0%. **Median travel time to work:** 24.5 minutes. **Working outside county of residence:** 33.1%.

Cities with pop over 10,000: None.

LONOKE COUNTY

301 N Center St   **Ph:** 501-676-2368
Lonoke, AR 72086   **Fax:** 501-676-3038

In central AR, east of Little Rock; organized Apr 16, 1873 from Pulaski and Jefferson counties. **Name Origin:** Variant spelling of *lone oak*, a former landmark at the county seat.

Area (sq mi): 802.43 (land 765.96; water 36.47). **Pop per sq mi:** 79.2.

Pop 2005: 60,658. **State rank:** 11. **Pop change:** 2000-20005 +14.8%; 1990-2000 +34.5%. **Pop 2000:** 52,828 (White 90%; Black or African American 6.4%; Hispanic or Latino 1.7%; Asian 0.4%; Other 2.1%). **Foreign born:** 1.4%. **Median age:** 34.7.

Income 2000: per capita $17,397; median household $40,314; **Pop below poverty level:** 10.5%. *Personal per capita income 2000-2003: $22,026-$24,358.

Unemployment 2004: 4.6%. **Change from 2000:** +1.1%. **Median travel time to work:** 27.5 minutes. **Working outside county of residence:** 61.9%.

Cities with pop over 10,000: Cabot (19,607).

MADISON COUNTY

201 Main St   **Ph:** 479-738-2747
Huntsville, AR 72740   **Fax:** 479-738-2735

In northwestern AR, east of Fayetteville; organized Sep 30, 1836 from Washington County. **Name Origin:** For James Madison (1751-1836), fourth U.S. president.

Area (sq mi): 837.06 (land 836.81; water 0.25). **Pop per sq mi:** 17.9.

Pop 2005: 14,962. **State rank:** 51. **Pop change:** 2000-20005 +5%; 1990-2000 +22.6%. **Pop 2000:** 14,243 (White 94.5%; Black or African American 0.1%; Hispanic or Latino 3.1%; Asian 0.1%; Other 3.9%, including 1.2% American Indian/Alaska Native). **Foreign born:** 1.8%. **Median age:** 37.7.

Income 2000: per capita $14,736; median household $27,895; **Pop below poverty level:** 18.6%. *Personal per capita income 2000-2003: $18,651-$18,742.

Unemployment 2004: 4%. **Change from 2000:** +1%. **Median travel time to work:** 32.9 minutes. **Working outside county of residence:** 46.5%.

Cities with pop over 10,000: None.

MARION COUNTY

PO Box 545   **Ph:** 870-449-6231
Yellville, AR 72687   **Fax:** 870-449-4979

On north-central border of AR; organized Nov 3, 1835 (prior to statehood) from Izard County. **Name Origin:** For Gen. Francis Marion (c. 1732-95), SC soldier and legislator, known as 'The Swamp Fox' for his tactics during the Revolutionary War.

Area (sq mi): 640.35 (land 597.7; water 42.65). **Pop per sq mi:** 28.

Pop 2005: 16,735. **State rank:** 47. **Pop change:** 2000-20005 +3.7%; 1990-2000 +34.5%. **Pop 2000:** 16,140 (White 96.9%; Black or African American 0.1%; Hispanic or Latino 0.8%; Asian 0.2%; Other 2.1%). **Foreign born:** 1.1%. **Median age:** 44.1.

Income 2000: per capita $14,588; median household $26,737; **Pop below poverty level:** 15.2%. *Personal per capita income 2000-2003: $17,071-$18,579.

Unemployment 2004: 5.8%. **Change from 2000:** +0.2%. **Median travel time to work:** 26 minutes. **Working outside county of residence:** 39.4%.

Cities with pop over 10,000: None.

MILLER COUNTY

400 Laurel St Rm 105   **Ph:** 870-774-1501
Texarkana, AR 71854   **Fax:** 870-773-4090

On southwestern corner of AR; organized Apr 1, 1820 (prior to statehood). **Name Origin:** For Gen. James Miller (1776-1851), first territorial governor of AR (1819-25).

Area (sq mi): 637.48 (land 623.98; water 13.5). **Pop per sq mi:** 69.2.

Pop 2005: 43,162. **State rank:** 17. **Pop change:** 2000-20005 +6.7%; 1990-2000 +5.1%. **Pop 2000:** 40,443 (White 73.2%; Black or African American 23%; Hispanic or Latino 1.6%; Asian 0.4%; Other 2.5%). **Foreign born:** 1.1%. **Median age:** 34.9.

Miller County (cont'd)

Income 2000: per capita $16,444; median household $30,951; **Pop below poverty level:** 19.3%. ***Personal per capita income 2000-2003:** $20,992-$23,619.

Unemployment 2004: 4.8%. **Change from 2000:** +0.5%. **Median travel time to work:** 21.1 minutes. **Working outside county of residence:** 55.1%.

Cities with pop over 10,000: Texarkana 🏛 (29,494).

MISSISSIPPI COUNTY
200 W Walnut St Rm 103   **Ph:** 870-762-2411
Blytheville, AR 72315   **Fax:** 870-838-7784
mcagov.missconet.com

On the northeastern border of AR, north of Memphis, TN; organized Nov 1, 1883 from Crittenden County. **Name Origin:** For the Mississippi River, which forms its eastern border.

Area (sq mi): 919.73 (land 898.25; water 21.48). **Pop per sq mi:** 53.3.

Pop 2005: 47,911. **State rank:** 15. **Pop change:** 2000-20005 -7.8%; 1990-2000 -9.6%. **Pop 2000:** 51,979 (White 63.6%; Black or African American 32.7%; Hispanic or Latino 2.2%; Asian 0.4%; Other 2.5%). **Foreign born:** 1.2%. **Median age:** 33.1.

Income 2000: per capita $13,978; median household $27,479; **Pop below poverty level:** 23%. ***Personal per capita income 2000-2003:** $18,376-$21,738.

Unemployment 2004: 10.5%. **Change from 2000:** -3.4%. **Median travel time to work:** 19 minutes. **Working outside county of residence:** 9%.

Cities with pop over 10,000: Blytheville 🏛 (16,868).

MONROE COUNTY
123 Madison St   **Ph:** 870-747-3632
Clarendon, AR 72029   **Fax:** 870-747-5961

In east-central AR, east of Little Rock; organized Nov 2, 1839 from Phillips and Arkansas counties. **Name Origin:** For James Monroe (1758-1831), fifth U.S. president.

Area (sq mi): 621.41 (land 606.65; water 14.76). **Pop per sq mi:** 15.3.

Pop 2005: 9,302. **State rank:** 66. **Pop change:** 2000-20005 -9.3%; 1990-2000 -9.5%. **Pop 2000:** 10,254 (White 58.5%; Black or African American 38.8%; Hispanic or Latino 1.3%; Asian 0.1%; Other 1.7%). **Foreign born:** 0.5%. **Median age:** 38.3.

Income 2000: per capita $13,096; median household $22,632; **Pop below poverty level:** 27.5%. ***Personal per capita income 2000-2003:** $17,062-$20,713.

Unemployment 2004: 7.4%. **Change from 2000:** +0%. **Median travel time to work:** 21.5 minutes. **Working outside county of residence:** 32.8%.

Cities with pop over 10,000: None.

MONTGOMERY COUNTY
PO Box 717   **Ph:** 870-867-3114
Mount Ida, AR 71957   **Fax:** 870-867-4354

In west-central AR, west of Hot Springs; organized Dec 9, 1842

from Clark County. **Name Origin:** For Gen. Richard Montgomery (1736-75), American Revolutionary War officer who captured Montreal, Canada.

Area (sq mi): 800.29 (land 780.93; water 19.36). **Pop per sq mi:** 11.9.

Pop 2005: 9,274. **State rank:** 67. **Pop change:** 2000-20005 +0.3%; 1990-2000 +17.9%. **Pop 2000:** 9,245 (White 94.5%; Black or African American 0.3%; Hispanic or Latino 2.5%; Asian 0.4%; Other 3.9%, including 1.1% American Indian/Alaska Native). **Foreign born:** 2%. **Median age:** 41.5.

Income 2000: per capita $14,668; median household $28,421; **Pop below poverty level:** 17%. ***Personal per capita income 2000-2003:** $18,010-$19,113.

Unemployment 2004: 5.4%. **Change from 2000:** +1.2%. **Median travel time to work:** 28.5 minutes. **Working outside county of residence:** 42.1%.

Cities with pop over 10,000: None.

NEVADA COUNTY
PO Box 621   **Ph:** 870-887-2710
Prescott, AR 71857   **Fax:** 870-887-5795

In southwestern AR, northeast of Texarkana; organized Mar 20, 1871 from Hempstead County. **Name Origin:** In reference to the state of Nevada. Possibly because the outline of the county, viewed upside down, roughly resembles that of Nevada.

Area (sq mi): 620.78 (land 619.95; water 0.83). **Pop per sq mi:** 15.4.

Pop 2005: 9,550. **State rank:** 65. **Pop change:** 2000-20005 -4.1%; 1990-2000 -1.4%. **Pop 2000:** 9,955 (White 66.5%; Black or African American 31.2%; Hispanic or Latino 1.5%; Asian 0.1%; Other 1.9%). **Foreign born:** 1.1%. **Median age:** 37.7.

Income 2000: per capita $14,184; median household $26,962; **Pop below poverty level:** 22.8%. ***Personal per capita income 2000-2003:** $18,872-$21,118.

Unemployment 2004: 6.2%. **Change from 2000:** +1.3%. **Median travel time to work:** 23.4 minutes. **Working outside county of residence:** 47.2%.

Cities with pop over 10,000: None.

NEWTON COUNTY
PO Box 410   **Ph:** 870-446-5125
Jasper, AR 72641   **Fax:** 870-446-5775

In northwest-central AR, east of Fayetteville; organized Dec 14, 1842 from Carroll County. **Name Origin:** For Thomas Willoughby Newton (1804-53), AR legislator and U.S. representative.

Area (sq mi): 823.18 (land 822.97; water 0.21). **Pop per sq mi:** 10.3.

Pop 2005: 8,452. **State rank:** 71. **Pop change:** 2000-20005 -1.8%; 1990-2000 +12.3%. **Pop 2000:** 8,608 (White 96.8%; Black or African American 0.1%; Hispanic or Latino 1.1%; Asian 0.2%; Other 2.3%). **Foreign born:** 0.5%. **Median age:** 40.1.

Income 2000: per capita $13,788; median household $24,756; **Pop below poverty level:** 20.4%. ***Personal per capita income 2000-2003:** $14,766-$16,765.

---

*Source: Personal per capita income data are from the Bureau of Economic Analysis; per capita income data are from the Bureau of the Census. See Introduction for explanation of differences.

Newton County (cont'd)

Unemployment 2004: 6.1%. Change from 2000: -0.6%. Median travel time to work: 35.9 minutes. Working outside county of residence: 56.7%.

Cities with pop over 10,000: None.

OUACHITA COUNTY

PO Box 644　　　　　　　　　　Ph: 870-837-2210
Camden, AR 71711　　　　　　　Fax: 870-837-2218

In south-central AR; organized Nov 29, 1842 from Clark County. Name Origin: For the Ouachita River, which runs through the county.

Area (sq mi): 739.63 (land 732.45; water 7.18). Pop per sq mi: 37.

Pop 2005: 27,102. State rank: 24. Pop change: 2000-20005 -5.9%; 1990-2000 -5.8%. Pop 2000: 28,790 (White 59.4%; Black or African American 38.6%; Hispanic or Latino 0.7%; Asian 0.2%; Other 1.4%). Foreign born: 0.7%. Median age: 38.7.

Income 2000: per capita $15,118; median household $29,341; Pop below poverty level: 19.5%. *Personal per capita income 2000-2003: $19,264-$21,059.

Unemployment 2004: 7.1%. Change from 2000: -2.6%. Median travel time to work: 21.9 minutes. Working outside county of residence: 27.7%.

Cities with pop over 10,000: Camden 🏛 (12,342).

PERRY COUNTY

310 W Main St Suite 105　　　　Ph: 501-889-5126
Perryville, AR 72126　　　　　　Fax: 501-889-5759

In central AR, northwest of Little Rock; organized Dec 18, 1840 from Pulaski County. Name Origin: For Oliver Hazard Perry (1785-1819), U.S. naval officer during the War of 1812, famous for the message, 'We have met the enemy and they are ours.'

Area (sq mi): 560.47 (land 550.94; water 9.53). Pop per sq mi: 19.

Pop 2005: 10,468. State rank: 64. Pop change: 2000-20005 +2.5%; 1990-2000 +28.1%. Pop 2000: 10,209 (White 95.1%; Black or African American 1.7%; Hispanic or Latino 1.2%; Asian 0.1%; Other 2.5%, including 1% American Indian/Alaska Native). Foreign born: 0.8%. Median age: 38.

Income 2000: per capita $16,216; median household $31,083; Pop below poverty level: 14%. *Personal per capita income 2000-2003: $20,214-$21,948.

Unemployment 2004: 5.7%. Change from 2000: -1.5%. Median travel time to work: 36.1 minutes. Working outside county of residence: 70.7%.

Cities with pop over 10,000: None.

PHILLIPS COUNTY

620 Cherry St Suite 202 County Courthouse　Ph: 870-338-5505
Helena, AR 72342　　　　　　　　　　　　Fax: 870-338-5509

On central-eastern border of AR; organized May 1, 1820 (prior to statehood) from Arkansas County. Name Origin: For Sylvanus Phillips (1766-1830), who explored the area along the Arkansas River in the 1790s.

Area (sq mi): 727.29 (land 692.67; water 34.62). Pop per sq mi: 34.8.

Pop 2005: 24,107. State rank: 29. Pop change: 2000-20005 -8.8%; 1990-2000 -8.3%. Pop 2000: 26,445 (White 38.7%; Black or African American 59%; Hispanic or Latino 1.4%; Asian 0.3%; Other 1.4%). Foreign born: 1.1%. Median age: 33.

Income 2000: per capita $12,288; median household $22,231; Pop below poverty level: 32.7%. *Personal per capita income 2000-2003: $16,753-$19,845.

Unemployment 2004: 9.5%. Change from 2000: -0.7%. Median travel time to work: 20.5 minutes. Working outside county of residence: 18.9%.

Cities with pop over 10,000: None.

PIKE COUNTY

PO Box 219　　　　　　　　　　Ph: 870-285-2231
Murfreesboro, AR 71958　　　　　Fax: 870-285-3281

In southwestern AR, southwest of Hot Springs; organized Nov 1, 1833 (prior to statehood) from Carroll and Clark counties. Name Origin: For Zebulon Montgomery Pike (1779-1813), U.S. army officer and discoverer of Pikes Peak in CO.

Area (sq mi): 613.88 (land 603.01; water 10.87). Pop per sq mi: 18.3.

Pop 2005: 11,038. State rank: 63. Pop change: 2000-20005 -2.3%; 1990-2000 +12.1%. Pop 2000: 11,303 (White 91.2%; Black or African American 3.5%; Hispanic or Latino 3.6%; Asian 0.2%; Other 4.3%). Foreign born: 2.2%. Median age: 38.9.

Income 2000: per capita $15,385; median household $27,695; Pop below poverty level: 16.8%. *Personal per capita income 2000-2003: $18,919-$20,746.

Unemployment 2004: 5.6%. Change from 2000: +0.1%. Median travel time to work: 26.7 minutes. Working outside county of residence: 42.5%.

Cities with pop over 10,000: None.

POINSETT COUNTY

County Courthouse 401 Market St　　Ph: 870-578-5333
Harrisburg, AR 72432

In northeastern AR, northwest of Memphis, TN; organized Feb 28, 1838 from Greene County. Name Origin: For Joel Roberts Poinsett (1779-1851), SC statesman and secretary of war (1837-41). He introduced the cultivation of the poinsettia flower to the U.S., having imported it from Mexico after he was a U.S. minister there (1825-29).

Area (sq mi): 763.39 (land 757.74; water 5.65). Pop per sq mi: 33.5.

Pop 2005: 25,349. State rank: 27. Pop change: 2000-20005 -1%; 1990-2000 +3.9%. Pop 2000: 25,614 (White 90.5%; Black or African American 7.1%; Hispanic or Latino 1.4%; Asian 0.2%; Other 1.6%). Foreign born: 0.9%. Median age: 36.6.

Income 2000: per capita $13,087; median household $26,558; Pop below poverty level: 21.2%. *Personal per capita income 2000-2003: $17,764-$20,682.

Unemployment 2004: 6.4%. Change from 2000: -3.1%. Median travel time to work: 23.5 minutes. Working outside county of residence: 41.2%.

🏛 County Seat

Poinsett County (cont'd)

Cities with pop over 10,000: None.

POLK COUNTY

507 Church Ave   **Ph:** 479-394-8123
Mena, AR 71953   **Fax:** 479-394-8115

On western border of AR; organized Nov 30, 1844 from Montgomery County. **Name Origin:** For James Knox Polk (1795-1849), eleventh U.S. president.

Area (sq mi): 862.42 (land 859.38; water 3.04). **Pop per sq mi:** 23.5.

Pop 2005: 20,176. **State rank:** 37. **Pop change:** 2000-20005 -0.3%; 1990-2000 +16.6%. **Pop 2000:** 20,229 (White 93.1%; Black or African American 0.2%; Hispanic or Latino 3.5%; Asian 0.2%; Other 5%, including 1.5% American Indian/Alaska Native). **Foreign born:** 2.7%. **Median age:** 38.6.

Income 2000: per capita $14,063; median household $25,180; **Pop below poverty level:** 18.2%. ***Personal per capita income 2000-2003:** $17,529-$18,689.

Unemployment 2004: 6.1%. **Change from 2000:** +1.7%. **Median travel time to work:** 20.4 minutes. **Working outside county of residence:** 9.9%.

Cities with pop over 10,000: None.

POPE COUNTY

102 W Main St County Courthouse Suite 6   **Ph:** 479-968-6064
Russellville, AR 72801   **Fax:** 479-967-2291

In northwest-central AR, east of Fort Smith; organized Nov 2, 1829 (prior to statehood) from Pulaski County. **Name Origin:** For John Pope (1770-1845), KY legislator and governor of Arkansas Territory (1829-35).

Area (sq mi): 830.79 (land 811.9; water 18.89). **Pop per sq mi:** 69.7.

Pop 2005: 56,580. **State rank:** 13. **Pop change:** 2000-20005 +3.9%; 1990-2000 +18.7%. **Pop 2000:** 54,469 (White 92.8%; Black or African American 2.6%; Hispanic or Latino 2.1%; Asian 0.6%; Other 3%). **Foreign born:** 1.7%. **Median age:** 34.8.

Income 2000: per capita $15,918; median household $32,069; **Pop below poverty level:** 15.2%. ***Personal per capita income 2000-2003:** $20,898-$22,353.

Unemployment 2004: 5.3%. **Change from 2000:** +1.2%. **Median travel time to work:** 19.8 minutes. **Working outside county of residence:** 16.5%.

Cities with pop over 10,000: Russellville ⛪ (25,179).

PRAIRIE COUNTY

PO Box 1011   **Ph:** 870-256-4434
Des Arc, AR 72040

In east-central AR, east of Little Rock; organized Nov 25, 1846 from Monroe County. **Name Origin:** For its open countryside.

Area (sq mi): 675.76 (land 645.93; water 29.83). **Pop per sq mi:** 14.1.

Pop 2005: 9,113. **State rank:** 68. **Pop change:** 2000-20005 -4.5%; 1990-2000 +0.2%. **Pop 2000:** 9,539 (White 84.5%; Black or African

American 13.7%; Hispanic or Latino 0.8%; Asian 0.2%; Other 1.3%). **Foreign born:** 0.4%. **Median age:** 40.1.

Income 2000: per capita $15,907; median household $29,990; **Pop below poverty level:** 15.5%. ***Personal per capita income 2000-2003:** $17,791-$21,205.

Unemployment 2004: 5.3%. **Change from 2000:** +0.5%. **Median travel time to work:** 26.8 minutes. **Working outside county of residence:** 47.2%.

Cities with pop over 10,000: None.

PULASKI COUNTY

401 W Markham St Suite 102   **Ph:** 501-340-8431
Little Rock, AR 72201   **Fax:** 501-340-8420
www.co.pulaski.ar.us

In central AR; organized Dec 15, 1818 (prior to statehood) from Arkansas County. **Name Origin:** For Count Casimir Pulaski (1747-79), a Polish soldier who fought for America during the Revolutionary War.

Area (sq mi): 807.84 (land 770.82; water 37.02). **Pop per sq mi:** 475.4.

Pop 2005: 366,463. **State rank:** 1. **Pop change:** 2000-20005 +1.4%; 1990-2000 +3.4%. **Pop 2000:** 361,474 (White 62.9%; Black or African American 31.9%; Hispanic or Latino 2.4%; Asian 1.2%; Other 2.9%). **Foreign born:** 3%. **Median age:** 35.

Income 2000: per capita $21,466; median household $38,120; **Pop below poverty level:** 13.3%. ***Personal per capita income 2000-2003:** $30,021-$33,620.

Unemployment 2004: 5.3%. **Change from 2000:** +1.2%. **Median travel time to work:** 20.8 minutes. **Working outside county of residence:** 5.5%.

Cities with pop over 10,000: Little Rock ⛪ (184,081); North Little Rock (59,474); Jacksonville (30,600); Sherwood (22,564); Maumelle (13,273).

RANDOLPH COUNTY

107 W Broadway   **Ph:** 870-892-5264
Pocahontas, AR 72455   **Fax:** 870-892-2269

On northern border; organized Oct 29, 1835 (prior to statehood) from Lawrence County. **Name Origin:** For John Randolph (1773-1833), U.S. congressman from VA during the years 1799-1827, and U.S. minister to Russia (1830).

Area (sq mi): 656.04 (land 651.82; water 4.21). **Pop per sq mi:** 28.3.

Pop 2005: 18,465. **State rank:** 41. **Pop change:** 2000-20005 +1.5%; 1990-2000 +9.9%. **Pop 2000:** 18,195 (White 96.5%; Black or African American 1%; Hispanic or Latino 0.8%; Asian 0.1%; Other 1.9%). **Foreign born:** 0.9%. **Median age:** 38.8.

Income 2000: per capita $14,502; median household $27,583; **Pop below poverty level:** 15.3%. ***Personal per capita income 2000-2003:** $16,778-$18,599.

Unemployment 2004: 8.2%. **Change from 2000:** -0.4%. **Median travel time to work:** 23.3 minutes. **Working outside county of residence:** 26.1%.

Cities with pop over 10,000: None.

*Source: Personal per capita income data are from the Bureau of Economic Analysis; per capita income data are from the Bureau of the Census. See Introduction for explanation of differences.

SAINT FRANCIS COUNTY

PO Box 1653
Forrest City, AR 72336

Ph: 870-261-1725
Fax: 870-630-1210

In eastern AR, west of Memphis, TN; organized Oct 13, 1827 (prior to statehood) from Phillips County. **Name Origin:** For the Saint Francis River, which bisects the county.

Area (sq mi): 642.4 (land 633.84; water 8.56). **Pop per sq mi:** 44.

Pop 2005: 27,902. **State rank:** 23. **Pop change:** 2000-20005 -4.9%; 1990-2000 +2.9%. **Pop 2000:** 29,329 (White 45.1%; Black or African American 49%; Hispanic or Latino 4.9%; Asian 0.6%; Other 2%). **Foreign born:** 0.3%. **Median age:** 33.8.

Income 2000: per capita $12,483; median household $26,146; **Pop below poverty level:** 27.5%. *Personal per capita income 2000-2003: $16,100-$18,546.

Unemployment 2004: 9.4%. **Change from 2000:** +0.5%. **Median travel time to work:** 22.2 minutes. **Working outside county of residence:** 26.4%.

Cities with pop over 10,000: Forrest City ⛪ (14,242).

SALINE COUNTY

215 N Main St Suite 9
Benton, AR 72015
www.salinecounty.org

Ph: 501-303-5630
Fax: 501-776-2412

In central AR, west of Little Rock; organized Nov 2, 1835 (prior to statehood) from Pulaski County. **Name Origin:** For the Saline River, which has its source within the county.

Area (sq mi): 730.46 (land 723.46; water 7). **Pop per sq mi:** 126.

Pop 2005: 91,188. **State rank:** 7. **Pop change:** 2000-20005 +9.2%; 1990-2000 +30.1%. **Pop 2000:** 83,529 (White 94.5%; Black or African American 2.2%; Hispanic or Latino 1.3%; Asian 0.6%; Other 1.9%). **Foreign born:** 1.3%. **Median age:** 36.8.

Income 2000: per capita $19,214; median household $42,569; **Pop below poverty level:** 7.2%. *Personal per capita income 2000-2003: $23,285-$26,004.

Unemployment 2004: 4.6%. **Change from 2000:** +1.3%. **Median travel time to work:** 27 minutes. **Working outside county of residence:** 62.8%.

Cities with pop over 10,000: Benton ⛪ (24,695); Bryant (12,543).

SCOTT COUNTY

190 W 1st St Box 10
Waldron, AR 72958

Ph: 479-637-2642
Fax: 479-637-0124

On central-western border of AR; organized Nov 5, 1833 (prior to statehood) from Crawford and Pope counties. **Name Origin:** For Andrew Scott, superior court justice for the Arkansas Territory (1819-21).

Area (sq mi): 898.09 (land 893.88; water 4.21). **Pop per sq mi:** 12.5.

Pop 2005: 11,150. **State rank:** 62. **Pop change:** 2000-20005 +1.4%; 1990-2000 +7.8%. **Pop 2000:** 10,996 (White 90.5%; Black or African American 0.2%; Hispanic or Latino 5.7%; Asian 1%; Other 5.3%, including 1.4% American Indian/Alaska Native). **Foreign born:** 3.5%. **Median age:** 37.3.

Income 2000: per capita $13,609; median household $26,412; **Pop below poverty level:** 18.2%. *Personal per capita income 2000-2003: $18,364-$18,834.

Unemployment 2004: 5.2%. **Change from 2000:** +1.7%. **Median travel time to work:** 23.6 minutes. **Working outside county of residence:** 27.8%.

Cities with pop over 10,000: None.

SEARCY COUNTY

PO Box 998
Marshall, AR 72650

Ph: 870-448-3807
Fax: 870-448-5005

In north-central AR; first established Nov 3, 1835; name changed to Marion in 1836, then in 1838 a new Searcy County was formed from Marion County. **Name Origin:** For Richard Searcy (1796-1832), lawyer, jurist, and legislator.

Area (sq mi): 668.51 (land 667.15; water 1.36). **Pop per sq mi:** 11.9.

Pop 2005: 7,969. **State rank:** 74. **Pop change:** 2000-20005 -3.5%; 1990-2000 +5.4%. **Pop 2000:** 8,261 (White 96.8%; Black or African American 0%; Hispanic or Latino 1%; Asian 0.1%; Other 2.5%). **Foreign born:** 0.6%. **Median age:** 42.3.

Income 2000: per capita $12,536; median household $21,397; **Pop below poverty level:** 23.8%. *Personal per capita income 2000-2003: $15,032-$16,793.

Unemployment 2004: 5.7%. **Change from 2000:** +0.7%. **Median travel time to work:** 32 minutes. **Working outside county of residence:** 33.8%.

Cities with pop over 10,000: None.

SEBASTIAN COUNTY

35 S 6th St
Fort Smith, AR 72901
www.sebastiancountyonline.com

Ph: 479-782-5065
Fax: 479-784-1567

On western border of AR; organized Jan 6, 1851 from Crawford County. **Name Origin:** For William King Sebastian (1812-65), jurist and U.S. senator from AR (1846-61).

Area (sq mi): 546.04 (land 536.24; water 9.79). **Pop per sq mi:** 221.4.

Pop 2005: 118,750. **State rank:** 4. **Pop change:** 2000-20005 +3.2%; 1990-2000 +15.5%. **Pop 2000:** 115,071 (White 80%; Black or African American 6.2%; Hispanic or Latino 6.7%; Asian 3.5%; Other 8%, including 1.6% American Indian/Alaska Native). **Foreign born:** 6.9%. **Median age:** 35.5.

Income 2000: per capita $18,424; median household $33,889; **Pop below poverty level:** 13.6%. *Personal per capita income 2000-2003: $25,303-$28,149.

Unemployment 2004: 4.8%. **Change from 2000:** +0.8%. **Median travel time to work:** 19.3 minutes. **Working outside county of residence:** 12.2%.

Cities with pop over 10,000: Fort Smith ⛪ (81,849).

SEVIER COUNTY

County Courthouse 115 N 3rd St Rm 102
De Queen, AR 71832

Ph: 870-642-2852
Fax: 870-642-3896

On southwestern border of AR; organized Oct 17, 1828 (prior to

⛪ County Seat

89

Sevier County (cont'd)

statehood) from Hempstead County. **Name Origin:** For Ambrose Hundley Sevier (1801-48), territorial legislator (1823-27) and delegate to U.S. Congress (1828-36), later U.S. senator from AR (1836-48), and minister to Mexico (1848).

Area (sq mi): 581.35 (land 563.94; water 17.41). **Pop per sq mi:** 29.2.

Pop 2005: 16,456. **State rank:** 50. **Pop change:** 2000-20005 +4.4%; 1990-2000 +15.5%. **Pop 2000:** 15,757 (White 72.5%; Black or African American 4.9%; Hispanic or Latino 19.7%; Asian 0.1%; Other 15.3%, including 1.8% American Indian/Alaska Native). **Foreign born:** 12.7%. **Median age:** 33.6.

Income 2000: per capita $14,122; median household $30,144; **Pop below poverty level:** 19.2%. ***Personal per capita income 2000-2003:** $18,469-$19,926.

Unemployment 2004: 4.7%. **Change from 2000:** +0.6%. **Median travel time to work:** 22.2 minutes. **Working outside county of residence:** 26%.

Cities with pop over 10,000: None.

SHARP COUNTY
PO Box 307
Ash Flat, AR 72513
www.sharpcounty.org

Ph: 870-994-7361
Fax: 870-994-7712

In northeast-central AR; organized Jul 18, 1868 from Izard County. **Name Origin:** For Ephraim Sharp, AR state legislator for the district when the county was formed.

Area (sq mi): 606.35 (land 604.35; water 1.99). **Pop per sq mi:** 28.8.

Pop 2005: 17,397. **State rank:** 44. **Pop change:** 2000-20005 +1.6%; 1990-2000 +21.3%. **Pop 2000:** 17,119 (White 96.4%; Black or African American 0.5%; Hispanic or Latino 1%; Asian 0.1%; Other 2.3%). **Foreign born:** 0.8%. **Median age:** 44.3.

Income 2000: per capita $14,143; median household $25,152; **Pop below poverty level:** 18.2%. ***Personal per capita income 2000-2003:** $16,285-$17,247.

Unemployment 2004: 7.6%. **Change from 2000:** +0.8%. **Median travel time to work:** 26.4 minutes. **Working outside county of residence:** 37.4%.

Cities with pop over 10,000: None.

STONE COUNTY
107 W Main St Suite C
Mountain View, AR 72560

Ph: 870-269-3351
Fax: 870-269-3176

In north-central AR; organized Apr 21, 1873 from Izard and Independence counties. **Name Origin:** For natural stone formations in the area.

Area (sq mi): 609.43 (land 606.59; water 2.84). **Pop per sq mi:** 19.3.

Pop 2005: 11,716. **State rank:** 60. **Pop change:** 2000-20005 +1.9%; 1990-2000 +17.6%. **Pop 2000:** 11,499 (White 96.5%; Black or African American 0.1%; Hispanic or Latino 1.1%; Asian 0.1%; Other 2.5%). **Foreign born:** 0.8%. **Median age:** 43.1.

Income 2000: per capita $14,134; median household $22,209; **Pop below poverty level:** 18.9%. ***Personal per capita income 2000-2003:** $17,139-$18,597.

Unemployment 2004: 7.4%. **Change from 2000:** +2.5%. **Median travel time to work:** 26.5 minutes. **Working outside county of residence:** 24.6%.

Cities with pop over 10,000: None.

UNION COUNTY
101 N Washington Rm 102
County Courthouse
El Dorado, AR 71730

Ph: 870-864-1910
Fax: 870-864-1927

On central-southern border of AR; organized Nov 2, 1829 (prior to statehood) from Hempstead and Clark counties. **Name Origin:** For a group of citizens who had presented petitions to the legislature in a spirit of 'Union and Unity.'

Area (sq mi): 1055.27 (land 1038.9; water 16.37). **Pop per sq mi:** 42.5.

Pop 2005: 44,186. **State rank:** 16. **Pop change:** 2000-20005 -3.2%; 1990-2000 -2.3%. **Pop 2000:** 45,629 (White 65.6%; Black or African American 32%; Hispanic or Latino 1.1%; Asian 0.4%; Other 1.5%). **Foreign born:** 1.2%. **Median age:** 37.7.

Income 2000: per capita $16,063; median household $29,809; **Pop below poverty level:** 18.7%. ***Personal per capita income 2000-2003:** $25,395-$28,354.

Unemployment 2004: 7.4%. **Change from 2000:** +2%. **Median travel time to work:** 18 minutes. **Working outside county of residence:** 6.2%.

Cities with pop over 10,000: El Dorado 🏛 (20,682).

VAN BUREN COUNTY
451 Main St Suite 2
Clinton, AR 72031

Ph: 501-745-4140
Fax: 501-745-7400

In north-central AR; organized Nov 11, 1833 (prior to statehood) from Independence County. **Name Origin:** For Martin Van Buren (1782-1862), eighth U.S. president.

Area (sq mi): 724.32 (land 711.51; water 12.81). **Pop per sq mi:** 23.2.

Pop 2005: 16,529. **State rank:** 49. **Pop change:** 2000-20005 +2.1%; 1990-2000 +15.6%. **Pop 2000:** 16,192 (White 96%; Black or African American 0.3%; Hispanic or Latino 1.3%; Asian 0.2%; Other 2.7%). **Foreign born:** 1.4%. **Median age:** 44.2.

Income 2000: per capita $16,603; median household $27,004; **Pop below poverty level:** 15.4%. ***Personal per capita income 2000-2003:** $17,767-$18,714.

Unemployment 2004: 6.8%. **Change from 2000:** -0.1%. **Median travel time to work:** 32.9 minutes. **Working outside county of residence:** 36.2%.

Cities with pop over 10,000: None.

WASHINGTON COUNTY
280 N College Ave Suite 300
Fayetteville, AR 72701
www.co.washington.ar.us

Ph: 479-444-1711
Fax: 479-444-1894

On northwestern border of AR; organized Oct 17, 1828 (prior to statehood) from the eastern portion of former Lovely County. **Name Origin:** For George Washington (1732-99), American patriot and first U.S. president.

Source: Personal per capita income data are from the Bureau of Economic Analysis; per capita income data are from the Bureau of the Census. See Introduction for explanation of differences.

Washington County (cont'd)

Area (sq mi): 956.01 (land 949.72; water 6.29). **Pop per sq mi:** 189.9.

Pop 2005: 180,357. **State rank:** 3. **Pop change:** 2000-20005 +14.4%; 1990-2000 +39.1%. **Pop 2000:** 157,715 (White 84.6%; Black or African American 2.2%; Hispanic or Latino 8.2%; Asian 1.5%; Other 8.3%, including 1.3% American Indian/Alaska Native). **Foreign born:** 7.4%. **Median age:** 30.8.

Income 2000: per capita $17,347; median household $34,691; **Pop below poverty level:** 14.6%. ***Personal per capita income 2000-2003:** $21,828-$24,286.

Unemployment 2004: 3.7%. **Change from 2000:** +1.4%. **Median travel time to work:** 19.7 minutes. **Working outside county of residence:** 13.5%.

Cities with pop over 10,000: Fayetteville ⛪ (64,190); Springdale (55,971).

WHITE COUNTY

300 N Spruce St   **Ph:** 501-279-6200
Searcy, AR 72143   **Fax:** 501-279-6233
www.whitecountyar.org

In central AR, northeast of Little Rock; organized Oct 23, 1835 (prior to statehood) from Pulaski, Jackson, and Independence counties. **Name Origin:** For Hugh Lawson White (1773-1840), TN legislator and U.S. senator (1825-40); candidate for U.S. president in 1836.

Area (sq mi): 1042.36 (land 1034.03; water 8.33). **Pop per sq mi:** 69.

Pop 2005: 71,332. **State rank:** 10. **Pop change:** 2000-20005 +6.2%; 1990-2000 +22.8%. **Pop 2000:** 67,165 (White 92.6%; Black or African American 3.6%; Hispanic or Latino 1.9%; Asian 0.3%; Other 2.5%). **Foreign born:** 1.5%. **Median age:** 35.1.

Income 2000: per capita $15,890; median household $32,203; **Pop below poverty level:** 14%. ***Personal per capita income 2000-2003:** $18,809-$21,128.

Unemployment 2004: 6.3%. **Change from 2000:** +1.1%. **Median travel time to work:** 23.8 minutes. **Working outside county of residence:** 25%.

Cities with pop over 10,000: Searcy ⛪ (20,429).

WOODRUFF COUNTY

Woodruff County Courthouse 500 N 3rd St   **Ph:** 870-347-2871
Augusta, AR 72006   **Fax:** 870-347-2608

In east-central AR, west of Memphis, TN; organized Nov 26, 1862 from White County. **Name Origin:** For William Edward Woodruff (1795-1885), publisher who established the *Arkansas Gazette*, the state's first newspaper.

Area (sq mi): 594.05 (land 586.56; water 7.49). **Pop per sq mi:** 13.8.

Pop 2005: 8,098. **State rank:** 72. **Pop change:** 2000-20005 -7.4%; 1990-2000 -8.2%. **Pop 2000:** 8,741 (White 67.5%; Black or African American 30.8%; Hispanic or Latino 0.8%; Asian 0.1%; Other 1.3%). **Foreign born:** 0.6%. **Median age:** 38.4.

Income 2000: per capita $13,269; median household $22,099; **Pop below poverty level:** 27%. ***Personal per capita income 2000-2003:** $17,122-$21,064.

Unemployment 2004: 10.2%. **Change from 2000:** +2.3%. **Median travel time to work:** 18.4 minutes. **Working outside county of residence:** 25.5%.

Cities with pop over 10,000: None.

YELL COUNTY

PO Box 219   **Ph:** 479-495-4850
Danville, AR 72833

In west-central AR, northwest of Hot Springs; organized Dec 5, 1840 from Pope County. **Name Origin:** For Archibald Yell (1797-1847), U.S. representative from AR (1836-39) and governor (1840-44).

Area (sq mi): 948.84 (land 927.89; water 20.95). **Pop per sq mi:** 23.1.

Pop 2005: 21,391. **State rank:** 35. **Pop change:** 2000-20005 +1.2%; 1990-2000 +19%. **Pop 2000:** 21,139 (White 83.5%; Black or African American 1.5%; Hispanic or Latino 12.7%; Asian 0.7%; Other 11.2%). **Foreign born:** 10.2%. **Median age:** 36.1.

Income 2000: per capita $15,383; median household $28,916; **Pop below poverty level:** 15.4%. ***Personal per capita income 2000-2003:** $18,784-$20,261.

Unemployment 2004: 5%. **Change from 2000:** +1.7%. **Median travel time to work:** 22.8 minutes. **Working outside county of residence:** 37.5%.

Cities with pop over 10,000: None.

⛪ *County Seat*

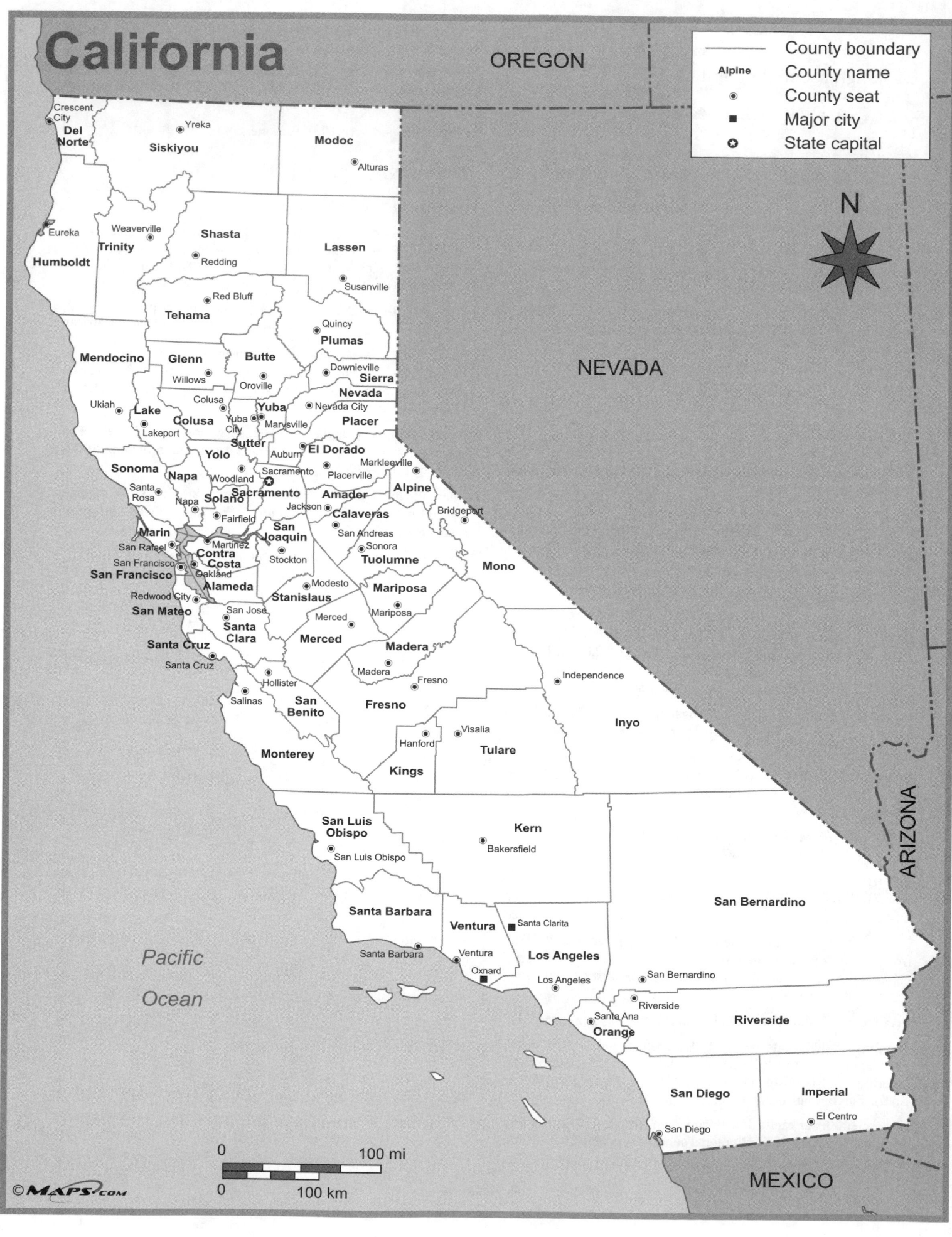

California

CALIFORNIA STATE INFORMATION
www.ca.gov   **Ph:** 916-657-9900

Area (sq mi): 163,695.57 (land 155,959.34; water 7736.23). **Pop per sq mi:** 231.7.

Pop 2005: 36,132,147. **Pop change:** 2000-20005 +6.7%; 1990-2000 +13.8%. **Pop 2000:** 33,871,648 (White 46.7%; Black or African American 6.7%; Hispanic or Latino 32.4%; Asian 10.9%; Other 22.8%, including 1% American Indian/Alaska Native). **Foreign born:** 26.2%. **Median age:** 33.3.

Income 2000: per capita $22,711; median household $47,493; **Pop below poverty level:** 14.2%. ***Personal per capita income 2000-2003:** $32,464-$33,415.

Unemployment 2004: 6.2%. **Change from 2000:** +1.3%. **Median travel time to work:** 27.7 minutes. **Working outside county of residence:** 17.1%.

ALAMEDA COUNTY
1221 Oak St Suite 555   **Ph:** 510-272-6984
Oakland, CA 94612   **Fax:** 510-272-3784
www.acgov.org

Along San Francisco Bay E of San Francisco; organized in Mar 25, 1853 from Contra Costa and Santa Clara counties. **Name Origin:** From Spanish 'grove of poplar trees.'

Area (sq mi): 821.15 (land 737.57; water 83.57). **Pop per sq mi:** 1964.4.

Pop 2005: 1,448,905. **State rank:** 7. **Pop change:** 2000-20005 +0.4%; 1990-2000 +12.9%. **Pop 2000:** 1,443,741 (White 40.9%; Black or African American 14.9%; Hispanic or Latino 19%; Asian 20.4%; Other 15.7%). **Foreign born:** 27.2%. **Median age:** 34.5.

Income 2000: per capita $26,680; median household $55,946; **Pop below poverty level:** 11%. ***Personal per capita income 2000-2003:** $38,466-$38,521.

Unemployment 2004: 6%. **Change from 2000:** +1.5%. **Median travel time to work:** 30.8 minutes. **Working outside county of residence:** 33.1%.

Cities with pop over 10,000: 13 (see page 31 for cities).

ALPINE COUNTY
99 Waters St   **Ph:** 530-694-2281
Markleeville, CA 96120   **Fax:** 530-694-2491
www.alpinecountyca.com

In NE CA on Nevada border, E of Sacramento; organized Mar 16, 1864 from Calaveras, Amador, El Dorado, and Mono counties. **Name Origin:** For the mountainous terrain of the Sierra Nevada.

Area (sq mi): 743.19 (land 738.62; water 4.57). **Pop per sq mi:** 1.6.

Pop 2005: 1,159. **State rank:** 58. **Pop change:** 2000-20005 -4.1%; 1990-2000 +8.5%. **Pop 2000:** 1,208 (White 71.8%; Black or African American 0.6%; Hispanic or Latino 7.8%; Asian 0.3%; Other 25.4%, including 18.9% American Indian/Alaska Native). **Foreign born:** 3.2%. **Median age:** 39.3.

Income 2000: per capita $24,431; median household $41,875; **Pop below poverty level:** 19.5%. ***Personal per capita income 2000-2003:** $26,401-$28,222.

Unemployment 2004: 8.1%. **Change from 2000:** -0.9%. **Median travel time to work:** 17.3 minutes. **Working outside county of residence:** 35.6%.

Cities with pop over 10,000: None.

AMADOR COUNTY
500 Argonaut Ln   **Ph:** 209-223-6470
Jackson, CA 95642   **Fax:** 209-257-0619
www.co.amador.ca.us

In NE CA, due E of Sacramento; organized May 11, 1854 from Calaveras County. **Name Origin:** For Jose Maria Amador, a construction foreman at the San Jose Mission, miner, and early land-owner.

Area (sq mi): 604.69 (land 592.97; water 11.73). **Pop per sq mi:** 64.9.

Pop 2005: 38,471. **State rank:** 46. **Pop change:** 2000-20005 +9.6%; 1990-2000 +16.8%. **Pop 2000:** 35,100 (White 82.4%; Black or African American 3.9%; Hispanic or Latino 8.9%; Asian 1%; Other 9.3%, including 1.8% American Indian/Alaska Native). **Foreign born:** 3.4%. **Median age:** 42.7.

Income 2000: per capita $22,412; median household $42,280; **Pop below poverty level:** 9.2%. ***Personal per capita income 2000-2003:** $23,783-$25,781.

Unemployment 2004: 5.4%. **Change from 2000:** +1.5%. **Median travel time to work:** 29.1 minutes. **Working outside county of residence:** 26.4%.

Cities with pop over 10,000: None.

BUTTE COUNTY
25 County Center Dr   **Ph:** 530-538-7691
Oroville, CA 95965   **Fax:** 530-538-7975
www.buttecounty.net

In N central CA; original county; organized Feb 18, 1850 (prior to statehood). **Name Origin:** For the Sutter Buttes of the Sacramento Valley, or the Butte River, which flows through the county.

Butte County (cont'd)

Area (sq mi): 1677.11 (land 1639.49; water 37.62). **Pop per sq mi:** 130.6.

Pop 2005: 214,185. **State rank:** 27. **Pop change:** 2000-20005 +5.4%; 1990-2000 +11.6%. **Pop 2000:** 203,171 (White 80%; Black or African American 1.4%; Hispanic or Latino 10.5%; Asian 3.3%; Other 10.7%, including 1.9% American Indian/Alaska Native). **Foreign born:** 7.7%. **Median age:** 35.8.

Income 2000: per capita $17,517; median household $31,924; **Pop below poverty level:** 19.8%. ***Personal per capita income 2000-2003:** $22,428-$23,799.

Unemployment 2004: 7.2%. **Change from 2000:** +0.2%. **Median travel time to work:** 20.9 minutes. **Working outside county of residence:** 9.3%.

Cities with pop over 10,000: Chico (70,204); Paradise (26,671).

CALAVERAS COUNTY
891 Mountain Ranch Rd   **Ph:** 209-754-6370
San Andreas, CA 95249   **Fax:** 209-754-6733
www.co.calaveras.ca.us

In NE CA, SE of Sacramento; original county; organized Feb 18, 1850 (prior to statehood). **Name Origin:** For the Calaveras River, which flows through the county, from the Spanish 'skulls,' so named because skulls were found on the river's banks in the 1830s.

Area (sq mi): 1036.84 (land 1020.04; water 16.81). **Pop per sq mi:** 46.

Pop 2005: 46,871. **State rank:** 44. **Pop change:** 2000-20005 +15.6%; 1990-2000 +26.7%. **Pop 2000:** 40,554 (White 87.5%; Black or African American 0.7%; Hispanic or Latino 6.8%; Asian 0.9%; Other 7.2%, including 1.7% American Indian/Alaska Native). **Foreign born:** 3%. **Median age:** 44.6.

Income 2000: per capita $21,420; median household $41,022; **Pop below poverty level:** 11.8%. ***Personal per capita income 2000-2003:** $24,745-$25,395.

Unemployment 2004: 6.5%. **Change from 2000:** +0.6%. **Median travel time to work:** 34.5 minutes. **Working outside county of residence:** 41.2%.

Cities with pop over 10,000: None.

COLUSA COUNTY
546 Jay St   **Ph:** 530-458-0500
Colusa, CA 95932   **Fax:** 530-458-0512
www.colusacountyclerk.com

In N CA, NW of Sacramento; original county; organized Feb 18, 1850 (prior to statehood). **Name Origin:** From the name of a former village of the Patwin Indians; earlier spelled *Colusi*.

Area (sq mi): 1156.22 (land 1150.68; water 5.54). **Pop per sq mi:** 18.3.

Pop 2005: 21,095. **State rank:** 51. **Pop change:** 2000-20005 +12.2%; 1990-2000 +15.5%. **Pop 2000:** 18,804 (White 48%; Black or African American 0.5%; Hispanic or Latino 46.5%; Asian 1.2%; Other 33.9%, including 2.3% American Indian/Alaska Native). **Foreign born:** 27.6%. **Median age:** 31.5.

Income 2000: per capita $14,730; median household $35,062; **Pop below poverty level:** 16.1%. ***Personal per capita income 2000-2003:** $23,402-$26,711.

Unemployment 2004: 13.4%. **Change from 2000:** -4.2%. **Median travel time to work:** 22 minutes. **Working outside county of residence:** 19.7%.

Cities with pop over 10,000: None.

CONTRA COSTA COUNTY
651 Pine St 3rd Fl   **Ph:** 925-335-1080
Martinez, CA 94553   **Fax:** 925-335-1098
www.co.contra-costa.ca.us

On San Pablo Bay, E of San Francisco; original county; organized Feb 18, 1850 (prior to statehood). **Name Origin:** From Spanish 'opposite coast' designating the coast opposite Marin County, north of San Francisco.

Area (sq mi): 802.15 (land 719.95; water 82.2). **Pop per sq mi:** 1413.7.

Pop 2005: 1,017,787. **State rank:** 9. **Pop change:** 2000-20005 +7.3%; 1990-2000 +18.1%. **Pop 2000:** 948,816 (White 57.9%; Black or African American 9.4%; Hispanic or Latino 17.7%; Asian 11%; Other 14.2%). **Foreign born:** 19%. **Median age:** 36.4.

Income 2000: per capita $30,615; median household $63,675; **Pop below poverty level:** 7.6%. ***Personal per capita income 2000-2003:** $44,479-$43,957.

Unemployment 2004: 5.4%. **Change from 2000:** +2.1%. **Median travel time to work:** 34.4 minutes. **Working outside county of residence:** 42.4%.

Cities with pop over 10,000: 18 (see page 31 for cities).

DEL NORTE COUNTY
981 H St Suite 200   **Ph:** 707-464-7204
Crescent City, CA 95531   **Fax:** 707-464-1165
www.co.del-norte.ca.us

In NW corner of CA; organized Mar 2, 1857 from Klamath County. **Name Origin:** Spanish 'of the North,' for the county's position in the state.

Area (sq mi): 1229.75 (land 1007.81; water 221.94). **Pop per sq mi:** 28.5.

Pop 2005: 28,705. **State rank:** 48. **Pop change:** 2000-20005 +4.4%; 1990-2000 +17.3%. **Pop 2000:** 27,507 (White 70.1%; Black or African American 4.3%; Hispanic or Latino 13.9%; Asian 2.3%; Other 14.5%, including 6.4% American Indian/Alaska Native). **Foreign born:** 5.7%. **Median age:** 36.4.

Income 2000: per capita $14,573; median household $29,642; **Pop below poverty level:** 20.2%. ***Personal per capita income 2000-2003:** $18,024-$18,893.

Unemployment 2004: 8.1%. **Change from 2000:** -0.6%. **Median travel time to work:** 14.8 minutes. **Working outside county of residence:** 5.9%.

Cities with pop over 10,000: None.

---

*Source: Personal per capita income data are from the Bureau of Economic Analysis; per capita income data are from the Bureau of the Census. See Introduction for explanation of differences.

EL DORADO COUNTY

360 Fair Ln Bldg B   **Ph:** 530-621-5490
Placerville, CA 95667   **Fax:** 530-621-2147
co.el-dorado.ca.us

In NE CA, E of Sacramento; original county; organized Feb 18, 1850 (prior to statehood). **Name Origin:** From Spanish 'the gilded' or 'the golden,' originally applied to a legendary chief and city sought by the early Spanish explorers; here the name refers to gold discovered in the area in 1848.

Area (sq mi): 1788.1 (land 1710.85; water 77.25). **Pop per sq mi:** 103.4.

Pop 2005: 176,841. **State rank:** 30. **Pop change:** 2000-20005 +13.1%; 1990-2000 +24.1%. **Pop 2000:** 156,299 (White 84.9%; Black or African American 0.5%; Hispanic or Latino 9.3%; Asian 2.1%; Other 7.6%, including 1% American Indian/Alaska Native). **Foreign born:** 7.2%. **Median age:** 39.4.

Income 2000: per capita $25,560; median household $51,484; **Pop below poverty level:** 7.1%. ***Personal per capita income 2000-2003:** $35,597-$36,373.

Unemployment 2004: 5.1%. **Change from 2000:** +1.3%. **Median travel time to work:** 29.7 minutes. **Working outside county of residence:** 44.9%.

Cities with pop over 10,000: South Lake Tahoe (23,926); Placerville 🏛 (10,151).

FRESNO COUNTY

2281 Tulare St Rm 304 Hall of Records   **Ph:** 559-488-1710
Fresno, CA 93721   **Fax:** 559-488-1830
www.co.fresno.ca.us

In central CA; organized Apr 19, 1856 from Mariposa and Merced counties. **Name Origin:** From the Spanish 'ash (tree)'; name originally applied to the river, for the ash trees that grew near it.

Area (sq mi): 6017.42 (land 5962.73; water 54.7). **Pop per sq mi:** 147.2.

Pop 2005: 877,584. **State rank:** 10. **Pop change:** 2000-20005 +9.8%; 1990-2000 +19.8%. **Pop 2000:** 799,407 (White 39.7%; Black or African American 5.3%; Hispanic or Latino 44%; Asian 8.1%; Other 32.3%, including 1.6% American Indian/Alaska Native). **Foreign born:** 21.1%. **Median age:** 29.9.

Income 2000: per capita $15,495; median household $34,725; **Pop below poverty level:** 22.9%. ***Personal per capita income 2000-2003:** $21,975-$24,277.

Unemployment 2004: 10.4%. **Change from 2000:** -3.3%. **Median travel time to work:** 22.2 minutes. **Working outside county of residence:** 7.4%.

Cities with pop over 10,000: 9 (see page 31 for cities).

GLENN COUNTY

526 W Sycamore St   **Ph:** 530-934-6400
Willows, CA 95988   **Fax:** 530-934-6419
www.countyofglenn.net

In NW CA; organized Mar 11, 1891 from Colusa County. **Name Origin:** For Dr. Hugh James Glenn (1824-83), the most important wheatgrower in California during the latter half of the 1800s.

Area (sq mi): 1327.16 (land 1314.79; water 12.36). **Pop per sq mi:** 21.1.

Pop 2005: 27,759. **State rank:** 49. **Pop change:** 2000-20005 +4.9%; 1990-2000 +6.7%. **Pop 2000:** 26,453 (White 62.6%; Black or African American 0.6%; Hispanic or Latino 29.6%; Asian 3.4%; Other 24.3%, including 2.1% American Indian/Alaska Native). **Foreign born:** 17.8%. **Median age:** 33.7.

Income 2000: per capita $14,069; median household $32,107; **Pop below poverty level:** 18.1%. ***Personal per capita income 2000-2003:** $19,334-$20,641.

Unemployment 2004: 9.3%. **Change from 2000:** -1.9%. **Median travel time to work:** 21.1 minutes. **Working outside county of residence:** 29.2%.

Cities with pop over 10,000: None.

HUMBOLDT COUNTY

825 5th St   **Ph:** 707-445-7256
Eureka, CA 95501
www.co.humboldt.ca.us

On NW coast of CA; organized Mar 12, 1853 from Trinity County, and in 1874 annexed part of Klamath County. **Name Origin:** For Humboldt Bay, which was named for German naturalist and traveler, [Friedrich Heinrich] Alexander von Humboldt (1769-1859).

Area (sq mi): 4052.22 (land 3572.49; water 479.74). **Pop per sq mi:** 35.9.

Pop 2005: 128,376. **State rank:** 35. **Pop change:** 2000-20005 +1.5%; 1990-2000 +6.2%. **Pop 2000:** 126,518 (White 81.6%; Black or African American 0.9%; Hispanic or Latino 6.5%; Asian 1.7%; Other 12.7%, including 5.7% American Indian/Alaska Native). **Foreign born:** 4.5%. **Median age:** 36.3.

Income 2000: per capita $17,203; median household $31,226; **Pop below poverty level:** 19.5%. ***Personal per capita income 2000-2003:** $23,236-$24,895.

Unemployment 2004: 6.5%. **Change from 2000:** +0.4%. **Median travel time to work:** 17.8 minutes. **Working outside county of residence:** 2%.

Cities with pop over 10,000: Eureka 🏛 (25,803); Arcata (16,929); Fortuna (10,995).

IMPERIAL COUNTY

940 W Main St Rm 202   **Ph:** 760-482-4427
El Centro, CA 92243   **Fax:** 760-482-4271
www.co.imperial.ca.us

In SE CA on border with Baja California; organized Aug 15, 1907 from San Diego County. **Name Origin:** For the Imperial Valley, itself named for the Imperial Land Company that was organized to colonize the southern Colorado Desert.

Area (sq mi): 4481.73 (land 4174.73; water 307). **Pop per sq mi:** 37.3.

Pop 2005: 155,823. **State rank:** 31. **Pop change:** 2000-20005 +9.5%; 1990-2000 +30.2%. **Pop 2000:** 142,361 (White 20.2%; Black or African American 4%; Hispanic or Latino 72.2%; Asian 2%; Other 44.7%, including 1.9% American Indian/Alaska Native). **Foreign born:** 32.2%. **Median age:** 31.

Income 2000: per capita $13,239; median household $31,870; **Pop below poverty level:** 22.6%. ***Personal per capita income 2000-2003:** $17,752-$20,674.

🏛 *County Seat*

Imperial County (cont'd)

Unemployment 2004: 17.1%. **Change from 2000:** -4.2%. **Median travel time to work:** 20.3 minutes. **Working outside county of residence:** 7%.

Cities with pop over 10,000: El Centro ⛪ (38,350); Calexico (34,326); Brawley (22,255).

INYO COUNTY
PO Drawer N   **Ph:** 760-878-0292
Independence, CA 93526   **Fax:** 760-878-2241
www.countyofinyo.org

On E border of CA, E of Fresno; organized Mar 22, 1866 from Tulare County. **Name Origin:** For the Inyo Mountains, from an Indian name said to mean 'where the great spirit dwells.'

Area (sq mi): 10,226.98 (land 10203.1; water 23.88). **Pop per sq mi:** 1.8.

Pop 2005: 18,156. **State rank:** 52. **Pop change:** 2000-20005 +1.2%; 1990-2000 -1.8%. **Pop 2000:** 17,945 (White 74.4%; Black or African American 0.2%; Hispanic or Latino 12.6%; Asian 0.9%; Other 18.8%, including 10% American Indian/Alaska Native). **Foreign born:** 7.6%. **Median age:** 42.8.

Income 2000: per capita $19,639; median household $35,006; **Pop below poverty level:** 12.6%. ***Personal per capita income 2000-2003:** $24,270-$25,619.

Unemployment 2004: 5.3%. **Change from 2000:** +0.4%. **Median travel time to work:** 15.2 minutes. **Working outside county of residence:** 7.3%.

Cities with pop over 10,000: None.

KERN COUNTY
1115 Truxtun Ave 5th Fl   **Ph:** 661-868-3198
Bakersfield, CA 93301   **Fax:** 661-868-3190
www.co.kern.ca.us

In SW CA, N of Los Angeles; organized Apr 2, 1866 from Los Angeles and Tulare counties. **Name Origin:** For the Kern River, which was named in 1845 by explorer John C. Fremont (1813-90) for Edward M. Kern, the topographer and artist for the expedition.

Area (sq mi): 8161.42 (land 8140.96; water 20.46). **Pop per sq mi:** 93.

Pop 2005: 756,825. **State rank:** 12. **Pop change:** 2000-20005 +14.4%; 1990-2000 +21.7%. **Pop 2000:** 661,645 (White 49.5%; Black or African American 6%; Hispanic or Latino 38.4%; Asian 3.4%; Other 28.9%, including 1.5% American Indian/Alaska Native). **Foreign born:** 16.9%. **Median age:** 30.6.

Income 2000: per capita $15,760; median household $35,446; **Pop below poverty level:** 20.8%. ***Personal per capita income 2000-2003:** $20,928-$22,947.

Unemployment 2004: 9.8%. **Change from 2000:** -0.7%. **Median travel time to work:** 23.2 minutes. **Working outside county of residence:** 6.4%.

Cities with pop over 10,000: 9 (see page 31 for cities).

KINGS COUNTY
1400 W Lacey Blvd   **Ph:** 559-582-3211
Hanford, CA 93230   **Fax:** 559-582-6639
www.co.kings.ca.us

In central CA, S of Fresno; organized Mar 22, 1893 from Tulare County. **Name Origin:** For the Kings River, which flows through the county, itself from Spanish *Rio de los Santos Reyes* 'River of the Holy Kings,' for the Biblical figures known in English as the Three Wise Men or Magi; river discovered on Jan 6, 1806, their feast day.

Area (sq mi): 1391.49 (land 1390.99; water 0.5). **Pop per sq mi:** 103.1.

Pop 2005: 143,420. **State rank:** 32. **Pop change:** 2000-20005 +10.8%; 1990-2000 +27.6%. **Pop 2000:** 129,461 (White 41.6%; Black or African American 8.3%; Hispanic or Latino 43.6%; Asian 3.1%; Other 35%, including 1.7% American Indian/Alaska Native). **Foreign born:** 16%. **Median age:** 30.2.

Income 2000: per capita $15,848; median household $35,749; **Pop below poverty level:** 19.5%. ***Personal per capita income 2000-2003:** $16,312-$19,390.

Unemployment 2004: 10.8%. **Change from 2000:** -3%. **Median travel time to work:** 20.8 minutes. **Working outside county of residence:** 20.7%.

Cities with pop over 10,000: Hanford ⛪ (46,820); Corcoran (22,434); Lemoore (22,231); Avenal (16,681).

LAKE COUNTY
255 N Forbes St   **Ph:** 707-263-2371
Lakeport, CA 95453   **Fax:** 707-263-2207
www.co.lake.ca.us

In NW CA, N of San Francisco; organized May 20, 1861 from Napa County. **Name Origin:** For Clear Lake, the principal feature of the county.

Area (sq mi): 1329.48 (land 1257.96; water 71.52). **Pop per sq mi:** 51.8.

Pop 2005: 65,147. **State rank:** 40. **Pop change:** 2000-20005 +11.7%; 1990-2000 +15.2%. **Pop 2000:** 58,309 (White 80.5%; Black or African American 2.1%; Hispanic or Latino 11.4%; Asian 0.8%; Other 10.8%, including 3% American Indian/Alaska Native). **Foreign born:** 6.6%. **Median age:** 42.7.

Income 2000: per capita $16,825; median household $29,627; **Pop below poverty level:** 17.6%. ***Personal per capita income 2000-2003:** $23,687-$25,099.

Unemployment 2004: 8.8%. **Change from 2000:** +1.5%. **Median travel time to work:** 29.1 minutes. **Working outside county of residence:** 21.7%.

Cities with pop over 10,000: Clearlake (14,513).

LASSEN COUNTY
220 S Lassen St Suite 5   **Ph:** 530-251-8217
Susanville, CA 96130   **Fax:** 530-257-3480
www.co.lassen.ca.us

In NE CA; organized Apr 1, 1864 from Plumas and Shasta counties. **Name Origin:** For Peter Lassen (1793-1895), a Danish-born pioneer.

Source: Personal per capita income data are from the Bureau of Economic Analysis; per capita income data are from the Bureau of the Census. See Introduction for explanation of differences.

Lassen County (cont'd)

Area (sq mi): 4720.37 (land 4557.27; water 163.1). **Pop per sq mi:** 7.6.

Pop 2005: 34,751. **State rank:** 47. **Pop change:** 2000-20005 +2.7%; 1990-2000 +22.6%. **Pop 2000:** 33,828 (White 70.6%; Black or African American 8.8%; Hispanic or Latino 13.8%; Asian 0.7%; Other 9.6%, including 3.3% American Indian/Alaska Native). **Foreign born:** 2.3%. **Median age:** 34.6.

Income 2000: per capita $14,749; median household $36,310; **Pop below poverty level:** 14%. *Personal per capita income 2000-2003: $17,454-$19,205.

Unemployment 2004: 7.7%. **Change from 2000:** +0.9%. **Median travel time to work:** 19.4 minutes. **Working outside county of residence:** 10.2%.

Cities with pop over 10,000: Susanville ⛪ (18,043).

LOS ANGELES COUNTY

500 W Temple St   **Ph:** 213-974-1311
Los Angeles, CA 90012   **Fax:** 213-680-1122
lacounty.info

On SW coast of CA; original county; organized Feb 18, 1850 (prior to statehood). **Name Origin:** For the city.

Area (sq mi): 4752.32 (land 4060.87; water 691.45). **Pop per sq mi:** 2446.6.

Pop 2005: 9,935,475. **State rank:** 1. **Pop change:** 2000-20005 +4.4%; 1990-2000 +7.4%. **Pop 2000:** 9,519,338 (White 31.1%; Black or African American 9.8%; Hispanic or Latino 44.6%; Asian 11.9%; Other 29.5%). **Foreign born:** 36.2%. **Median age:** 32.

Income 2000: per capita $20,683; median household $42,189; **Pop below poverty level:** 17.9%. *Personal per capita income 2000-2003: $29,233-$31,569.

Unemployment 2004: 6.6%. **Change from 2000:** +1%. **Median travel time to work:** 29.4 minutes. **Working outside county of residence:** 7.3%.

Cities with pop over 10,000: 79 (see page 31 for cities).

MADERA COUNTY

209 W Yosemite Ave   **Ph:** 559-675-7721
Madera, CA 93637   **Fax:** 559-675-7870
www.madera-county.com

In central CA, N of Fresno; organized Mar 11, 1893 from Fresno County. **Name Origin:** Spanish for 'lumber' because the town around which the county developed was a lumbering center.

Area (sq mi): 2153.32 (land 2135.86; water 17.46). **Pop per sq mi:** 66.9.

Pop 2005: 142,788. **State rank:** 33. **Pop change:** 2000-20005 +16%; 1990-2000 +39.8%. **Pop 2000:** 123,109 (White 46.6%; Black or African American 4.1%; Hispanic or Latino 44.3%; Asian 1.3%; Other 32.4%, including 2.6% American Indian/Alaska Native). **Foreign born:** 20.1%. **Median age:** 32.7.

Income 2000: per capita $14,682; median household $36,286; **Pop below poverty level:** 21.4%. *Personal per capita income 2000-2003: $18,317-$20,382.

Unemployment 2004: 8.8%. **Change from 2000:** -3.3%. **Median travel time to work:** 26.3 minutes. **Working outside county of residence:** 31.2%.

Cities with pop over 10,000: Madera ⛪ (50,043); Chowchilla (15,693).

MARIN COUNTY

3501 Civic Center Dr   **Ph:** 415-499-6407
San Rafael, CA 94903
www.marin.org

Located on N coast of California, N of San Francisco; organized in 1850. **Name Origin:** Two main theories: 1) From the old Spanish name of San Rafael Bay, *Bahia de Nuestra Senora del Rosario la Marinera*, 'Bay of Our Lady of the Rosary, Mariner's Patron'; this name was given in 1775 by the surveyor Ayala. 2) For the name of a mythical Indian leader, transliterated to Marin; also applied to the islands in San Rafael Bay.

Area (sq mi): 828.2 (land 519.8; water 308.39). **Pop per sq mi:** 475.1.

Pop 2005: 246,960. **State rank:** 25. **Pop change:** 2000-20005 -0.1%; 1990-2000 +7.5%. **Pop 2000:** 247,289 (White 78.6%; Black or African American 2.9%; Hispanic or Latino 11.1%; Asian 4.5%; Other 8.6%). **Foreign born:** 16.6%. **Median age:** 41.3.

Income 2000: per capita $44,962; median household $71,306; **Pop below poverty level:** 6.6%. *Personal per capita income 2000-2003: $67,694-$65,642.

Unemployment 2004: 4.4%. **Change from 2000:** +1.9%. **Median travel time to work:** 32.3 minutes. **Working outside county of residence:** 37.9%.

Cities with pop over 10,000: San Rafael ⛪ (55,560); Novato (49,238); Mill Valley (13,359); San Anselmo (12,110); Larkspur (11,797).

MARIPOSA COUNTY

PO Box 28   **Ph:** 209-966-2005
Mariposa, CA 95338   **Fax:** 209-742-6860
www.mariposacounty.org

In central CA, E of San Francisco; original county; organized Feb 18, 1850 (prior to statehood). **Name Origin:** Spanish 'butterfly,' a name originally applied to an area in the county in which butterflies were numerous.

Area (sq mi): 1462.79 (land 1451.12; water 11.67). **Pop per sq mi:** 12.5.

Pop 2005: 18,069. **State rank:** 53. **Pop change:** 2000-20005 +5.5%; 1990-2000 +19.8%. **Pop 2000:** 17,130 (White 84.9%; Black or African American 0.7%; Hispanic or Latino 7.8%; Asian 0.7%; Other 9.7%, including 3.5% American Indian/Alaska Native). **Foreign born:** 2.8%. **Median age:** 42.9.

Income 2000: per capita $18,190; median household $34,626; **Pop below poverty level:** 14.8%. *Personal per capita income 2000-2003: $22,112-$22,716.

Unemployment 2004: 6.6%. **Change from 2000:** +0.3%. **Median travel time to work:** 32.1 minutes. **Working outside county of residence:** 27.6%.

Cities with pop over 10,000: None.

⛪ *County Seat*

MENDOCINO COUNTY

501 Low Gap Rd Rm 1020   **Ph:** 707-463-4376
Ukiah, CA 95482   **Fax:** 707-463-4257
www.co.mendocino.ca.us

On N coast of California; original county; organized Feb 18, 1850 (prior to statehood). **Name Origin:** For Cabo (Cape) Mendocino, which early records indicate was named for Antonio de Mendoza (c. 1485-1552), viceroy of New Spain in 1542, or Lorenzo Suarez de Mendoza, viceroy of New Spain (1580-83). Name merely means someone from Mendoza.

Area (sq mi): 3878.14 (land 3508.97; water 369.17). **Pop per sq mi:** 25.1.

Pop 2005: 88,161. **State rank:** 38. **Pop change:** 2000-20005 +2.2%; 1990-2000 +7.4%. **Pop 2000:** 86,265 (White 74.9%; Black or African American 0.6%; Hispanic or Latino 16.5%; Asian 1.2%; Other 17.4%, including 4.8% American Indian/Alaska Native). **Foreign born:** 10.2%. **Median age:** 38.9.

Income 2000: per capita $19,443; median household $35,996; **Pop below poverty level:** 15.9%. ***Personal per capita income 2000-2003:** $24,891-$25,886.

Unemployment 2004: 6.5%. **Change from 2000:** -0.1%. **Median travel time to work:** 20.3 minutes. **Working outside county of residence:** 5.9%.

Cities with pop over 10,000: Ukiah 🏛 (15,580).

MERCED COUNTY

2222 M St   **Ph:** 209-385-7637
Merced, CA 95340   **Fax:** 209-385-7375
www.co.merced.ca.us

In central CA, SE of San Francisco; organized Apr 19, 1855 from Mariposa County. **Name Origin:** Spanish 'mercy', from the original Spanish name of Lake Merced, *Nuestra Senora de la Merced* 'Our Lady of Mercy.'

Area (sq mi): 1971.87 (land 1928.69; water 43.18). **Pop per sq mi:** 125.3.

Pop 2005: 241,706. **State rank:** 26. **Pop change:** 2000-20005 +14.8%; 1990-2000 +18%. **Pop 2000:** 210,554 (White 40.6%; Black or African American 3.8%; Hispanic or Latino 45.3%; Asian 6.8%; Other 33.2%, including 1.2% American Indian/Alaska Native). **Foreign born:** 24.8%. **Median age:** 29.

Income 2000: per capita $14,257; median household $35,532; **Pop below poverty level:** 21.7%. ***Personal per capita income 2000-2003:** $19,530-$21,365.

Unemployment 2004: 10.8%. **Change from 2000:** -3.2%. **Median travel time to work:** 26 minutes. **Working outside county of residence:** 25%.

Cities with pop over 10,000: Merced 🏛 (72,487); Los Banos (31,830); Atwater (26,370); Livingston (12,093).

MODOC COUNTY

204 S Court St Rm 204   **Ph:** 530-233-6200
Alturas, CA 96101   **Fax:** 530-233-2434
www.modoccounty.us

In NE CA; organized Feb 17, 1874 from Siskiyou County. **Name Origin:** For the Modoc Indian tribe, who had been subdued in the Modoc War of 1872-73. The name, derived from *moatokni*, means 'southerners.'

Area (sq mi): 4203.37 (land 3944.1; water 259.28). **Pop per sq mi:** 2.4.

Pop 2005: 9,524. **State rank:** 56. **Pop change:** 2000-20005 +0.8%; 1990-2000 -2.4%. **Pop 2000:** 9,449 (White 81.1%; Black or African American 0.7%; Hispanic or Latino 11.5%; Asian 0.6%; Other 12.8%, including 4.2% American Indian/Alaska Native). **Foreign born:** 5.9%. **Median age:** 41.8.

Income 2000: per capita $17,285; median household $27,522; **Pop below poverty level:** 21.5%. ***Personal per capita income 2000-2003:** $20,796-$24,091.

Unemployment 2004: 8.6%. **Change from 2000:** +1.6%. **Median travel time to work:** 13.4 minutes. **Working outside county of residence:** 16.1%.

Cities with pop over 10,000: None.

MONO COUNTY

PO Box 237   **Ph:** 760-932-5530
Bridgeport, CA 93517   **Fax:** 760-932-5531
www.monocounty.ca.gov

On W central border of CA and NV; organized Apr 24, 1861 from Calaveras and Fresno counties. **Name Origin:** For Mono Lake; the lake's name is probably a Spanish-influenced shortened form of a Shoshonean tribal name, *monache* or *monachi* 'fly people'; their staple food was the pupae of a fly.

Area (sq mi): 3131.8 (land 3044.4; water 87.4). **Pop per sq mi:** 4.1.

Pop 2005: 12,509. **State rank:** 55. **Pop change:** 2000-20005 -2.7%; 1990-2000 +29.1%. **Pop 2000:** 12,853 (White 76.5%; Black or African American 0.5%; Hispanic or Latino 17.7%; Asian 1.1%; Other 14.2%, including 2.4% American Indian/Alaska Native). **Foreign born:** 12.4%. **Median age:** 36.

Income 2000: per capita $23,422; median household $44,992; **Pop below poverty level:** 11.5%. ***Personal per capita income 2000-2003:** $25,632-$30,771.

Unemployment 2004: 5.2%. **Change from 2000:** +0%. **Median travel time to work:** 16.4 minutes. **Working outside county of residence:** 15%.

Cities with pop over 10,000: None.

MONTEREY COUNTY

PO Box 180   **Ph:** 831-755-5115
Salinas, CA 93902   **Fax:** 831-757-5792
www.co.monterey.ca.us

On central coast of CA; original county; organized Feb 18, 1850 (prior to statehood). **Name Origin:** For Monterey Bay.

Area (sq mi): 3771.07 (land 3321.95; water 449.12). **Pop per sq mi:** 124.1.

Pop 2005: 412,104. **State rank:** 18. **Pop change:** 2000-20005 +2.6%; 1990-2000 +13%. **Pop 2000:** 401,762 (White 40.3%; Black or African American 3.7%; Hispanic or Latino 46.8%; Asian 6%; Other 34.2%, including 1% American Indian/Alaska Native). **Foreign born:** 29%. **Median age:** 31.7.

Source: Personal per capita income data are from the Bureau of Economic Analysis; per capita income data are from the Bureau of the Census. See Introduction for explanation of differences.

Monterey County (cont'd)

Income 2000: per capita $20,165; median household $48,305; **Pop below poverty level:** 13.5%. *****Personal per capita income 2000-2003:** $30,005-$31,801.

Unemployment 2004: 8.2%. **Change from 2000:** -1.1%. **Median travel time to work:** 23.2 minutes. **Working outside county of residence:** 11%.

Cities with pop over 10,000: 8 (see page 32 for cities).

NAPA COUNTY
1195 3rd St Rm 310
Napa, CA 94559
www.co.napa.ca.us

Ph: 707-253-4421
Fax: 707-253-4176

In NW CA, N of San Francisco; original county; organized Feb 18, 1850 (prior to statehood). World-famous wine-making area. **Name Origin:** For the valley, whose name is possibly that of an Indian tribe that formerly inhabited the area.

Area (sq mi): 788.27 (land 753.73; water 34.53). **Pop per sq mi:** 176.1.

Pop 2005: 132,764. **State rank:** 34. **Pop change:** 2000-20005 +6.8%; 1990-2000 +12.2%. **Pop 2000:** 124,279 (White 69.1%; Black or African American 1.3%; Hispanic or Latino 23.7%; Asian 3%; Other 15.6%). **Foreign born:** 18.1%. **Median age:** 38.3.

Income 2000: per capita $26,395; median household $51,738; **Pop below poverty level:** 8.3%. *****Personal per capita income 2000-2003:** $37,828-$38,364.

Unemployment 2004: 4.6%. **Change from 2000:** +1.3%. **Median travel time to work:** 24.3 minutes. **Working outside county of residence:** 22.7%.

Cities with pop over 10,000: Vallejo (118,349); Napa ⛪ (75,465); American Canyon (13,887).

NEVADA COUNTY
201 Church St Suite 5
Nevada City, CA 95959
www.co.nevada.ca.us

Ph: 530-265-1293

On NE border of CA and NV; organized Apr 25, 1851 from Yuba County. **Name Origin:** For Nevada City, named for the Sierra Nevada range, from the Spanish words meaning 'snow-covered mountain range.'

Area (sq mi): 974.49 (land 957.61; water 16.88). **Pop per sq mi:** 102.7.

Pop 2005: 98,394. **State rank:** 36. **Pop change:** 2000-20005 +6.9%; 1990-2000 +17.2%. **Pop 2000:** 92,033 (White 90.3%; Black or African American 0.3%; Hispanic or Latino 5.7%; Asian 0.8%; Other 5.5%). **Foreign born:** 4.4%. **Median age:** 43.1.

Income 2000: per capita $24,007; median household $45,864; **Pop below poverty level:** 8.1%. *****Personal per capita income 2000-2003:** $30,544-$31,737.

Unemployment 2004: 5.2%. **Change from 2000:** +1.5%. **Median travel time to work:** 26 minutes. **Working outside county of residence:** 27.6%.

Cities with pop over 10,000: Truckee (15,451); Grass Valley (11,986).

ORANGE COUNTY
12 Civic Center Plaza
Santa Ana, CA 92702
www.oc.ca.gov

Ph: 714-834-2500
Fax: 714-834-2675

On SW coast of CA, S of Los Angeles; organized Mar 11, 1889 from Los Angeles County. **Name Origin:** For local orange groves.

Area (sq mi): 947.98 (land 789.4; water 158.57). **Pop per sq mi:** 3785.2.

Pop 2005: 2,988,072. **State rank:** 2. **Pop change:** 2000-20005 +5%; 1990-2000 +18.1%. **Pop 2000:** 2,846,289 (White 51.3%; Black or African American 1.7%; Hispanic or Latino 30.8%; Asian 13.6%; Other 19.9%). **Foreign born:** 29.9%. **Median age:** 33.3.

Income 2000: per capita $25,826; median household $58,820; **Pop below poverty level:** 10.3%. *****Personal per capita income 2000-2003:** $37,103-$39,268.

Unemployment 2004: 4.3%. **Change from 2000:** +1.3%. **Median travel time to work:** 27.2 minutes. **Working outside county of residence:** 17%.

Cities with pop over 10,000: 33 (see page 32 for cities).

PLACER COUNTY
2954 Richardson Dr
Auburn, CA 95603
www.placer.ca.gov

Ph: 530-886-5600
Fax: 530-886-5687

On NE border of CA and NV; county organized 1851 from Yuba and Sutter counties. **Name Origin:** For the many placer deposits in the county's territory.

Area (sq mi): 1502.78 (land 1404.37; water 98.41). **Pop per sq mi:** 225.7.

Pop 2005: 317,028. **State rank:** 22. **Pop change:** 2000-20005 +27.6%; 1990-2000 +43.8%. **Pop 2000:** 248,399 (White 83.4%; Black or African American 0.8%; Hispanic or Latino 9.7%; Asian 2.9%; Other 7.7%). **Foreign born:** 7.1%. **Median age:** 38.

Income 2000: per capita $27,963; median household $57,535; **Pop below poverty level:** 5.8%. *****Personal per capita income 2000-2003:** $36,419-$36,613.

Unemployment 2004: 4.6%. **Change from 2000:** +1%. **Median travel time to work:** 27 minutes. **Working outside county of residence:** 40.3%.

Cities with pop over 10,000: Roseville (103,609); Rocklin (48,637); Lincoln (28,134); Auburn ⛪ (12,775).

PLUMAS COUNTY
520 Main St Rm 104
Quincy, CA 95971
www.countyofplumas.com

Ph: 530-283-6305
Fax: 530-283-6415

On NE border of CA and NV; organized Mar 18, 1854, from Butte County. **Name Origin:** Spanish 'feathers,' for the Feather River, once known as *Rio de las Plumas*. Named by John A. Sutter, first settler in the Sacramento Valley, for the quantities of feathers found all around it with which the Indians decorated themselves and made blankets.

Area (sq mi): 2613.48 (land 2553.69; water 59.78). **Pop per sq mi:** 8.4.

⛪ *County Seat*

Plumas County (cont'd)

Pop 2005: 21,477. **State rank:** 50. **Pop change:** 2000-20005 +3.1%; 1990-2000 +5.5%. **Pop 2000:** 20,824 (White 88.7%; Black or African American 0.6%; Hispanic or Latino 5.7%; Asian 0.5%; Other 7%, including 2.5% American Indian/Alaska Native). **Foreign born:** 2.5%. **Median age:** 44.2.

Income 2000: per capita $19,391; median household $36,351; **Pop below poverty level:** 13.1%. ***Personal per capita income 2000-2003:** $25,939-$28,013.

Unemployment 2004: 9.4%. **Change from 2000:** +1%. **Median travel time to work:** 19.5 minutes. **Working outside county of residence:** 13.2%.

Cities with pop over 10,000: Oroville ⚏ (13,209).

RIVERSIDE COUNTY
4080 Lemon St 4th Fl   **Ph:** 951-955-1100
Riverside, CA 92501   **Fax:** 951-955-1105
www.co.riverside.ca.us

In S CA; organized Mar 11, 1893, from San Bernardino and San Diego counties. **Name Origin:** For the city.

Area (sq mi): 7303.13 (land 7207.37; water 95.76). **Pop per sq mi:** 270.1.

Pop 2005: 1,946,419. **State rank:** 5. **Pop change:** 2000-20005 +26%; 1990-2000 +32%. **Pop 2000:** 1,545,387 (White 51%; Black or African American 6.2%; Hispanic or Latino 36.2%; Asian 3.7%; Other 24.6%, including 1.2% American Indian/Alaska Native). **Foreign born:** 19%. **Median age:** 33.1.

Income 2000: per capita $18,689; median household $42,887; **Pop below poverty level:** 14.2%. ***Personal per capita income 2000-2003:** $23,728-$25,032.

Unemployment 2004: 5.8%. **Change from 2000:** +0.6%. **Median travel time to work:** 31.2 minutes. **Working outside county of residence:** 29.4%.

Cities with pop over 10,000: 22 (see page 32 for cities).

SACRAMENTO COUNTY
700 H St Rm 7650   **Ph:** 916-874-5833
Sacramento, CA 95814   **Fax:** 916-874-5885
www.saccounty.net

In N central CA; original county; organized Feb 18, 1850 (prior to statehood). **Name Origin:** For the Sacramento River.

Area (sq mi): 995.48 (land 965.65; water 29.83). **Pop per sq mi:** 1412.

Pop 2005: 1,363,482. **State rank:** 8. **Pop change:** 2000-20005 +11.4%; 1990-2000 +17.5%. **Pop 2000:** 1,223,499 (White 57.8%; Black or African American 10%; Hispanic or Latino 16%; Asian 11%; Other 15%, including 1.1% American Indian/Alaska Native). **Foreign born:** 16.1%. **Median age:** 33.8.

Income 2000: per capita $21,142; median household $43,816; **Pop below poverty level:** 14.1%. ***Personal per capita income 2000-2003:** $28,463-$30,129.

Unemployment 2004: 5.5%. **Change from 2000:** +1.3%. **Median travel time to work:** 25.4 minutes. **Working outside county of residence:** 15.5%.

Cities with pop over 10,000: 6 (see page 32 for cities).

SAN BENITO COUNTY
440 5th St Rm 206   **Ph:** 831-636-4029
Hollister, CA 95023   **Fax:** 831-636-2939
www.san-benito.ca.us

In W central CA, east of Monterey; organized Feb 12, 1874 from Monterey County. **Name Origin:** For San Benito, 'Saint Benedict,' the original name of San Juan Creek.

Area (sq mi): 1390.73 (land 1389.06; water 1.68). **Pop per sq mi:** 40.3.

Pop 2005: 55,936. **State rank:** 43. **Pop change:** 2000-20005 +5.1%; 1990-2000 +45.1%. **Pop 2000:** 53,234 (White 46%; Black or African American 1.1%; Hispanic or Latino 47.9%; Asian 2.4%; Other 31.4%, including 1.2% American Indian/Alaska Native). **Foreign born:** 18.8%. **Median age:** 31.4.

Income 2000: per capita $20,932; median household $57,469; **Pop below poverty level:** 10%. ***Personal per capita income 2000-2003:** $28,984-$29,109.

Unemployment 2004: 9.5%. **Change from 2000:** +1.2%. **Median travel time to work:** 33.7 minutes. **Working outside county of residence:** 48.5%.

Cities with pop over 10,000: Hollister ⚏ (36,330).

SAN BERNARDINO COUNTY
222 W Hospitality Ln   **Ph:** 909-387-8306
San Bernardino, CA 92415   **Fax:** 909-376-8940
www.co.san-bernardino.ca.us

In SE CA, east of Los Angeles; organized in 1853 from Los Angeles County. Largest county in the U.S. in land area, 20,105 sq. mi. **Name Origin:** Named for the city, Spanish 'Saint Bernard [of Siena].'

Area (sq mi): 20,105.32 (land 20052.5; water 52.82). **Pop per sq mi:** 97.9.

Pop 2005: 1,963,535. **State rank:** 4. **Pop change:** 2000-20005 +14.9%; 1990-2000 +20.5%. **Pop 2000:** 1,709,434 (White 44%; Black or African American 9.1%; Hispanic or Latino 39.2%; Asian 4.7%; Other 27.3%, including 1.2% American Indian/Alaska Native). **Foreign born:** 18.6%. **Median age:** 30.3.

Income 2000: per capita $16,856; median household $42,066; **Pop below poverty level:** 15.8%. ***Personal per capita income 2000-2003:** $21,972-$24,042.

Unemployment 2004: 5.6%. **Change from 2000:** +0.8%. **Median travel time to work:** 31 minutes. **Working outside county of residence:** 30.7%.

Cities with pop over 10,000: 22 (see page 32 for cities).

SAN DIEGO COUNTY
1600 Pacific Hwy 2nd Fl Rm 260   **Ph:** 619-237-0502
San Diego, CA 92101   **Fax:** 619-557-4155
www.co.san-diego.ca.us

In SW CA on border with Baja California; original county; organized Feb 18, 1850 (prior to statehood). **Name Origin:** For the bay, named for San Diego de Alcala de Henares (Saint Didacus), Spanish Franciscan saint of the 15th century.

*Source: Personal per capita income data are from the Bureau of Economic Analysis; per capita income data are from the Bureau of the Census. See Introduction for explanation of differences.

San Diego County (cont'd)

Area (sq mi): 4525.52 (land 4199.89; water 325.62). **Pop per sq mi:** 698.5.

Pop 2005: 2,933,462. **State rank:** 3. **Pop change:** 2000-20005 +4.3%; 1990-2000 +12.6%. **Pop 2000:** 2,813,833 (White 55%; Black or African American 5.7%; Hispanic or Latino 26.7%; Asian 8.9%; Other 18.9%). **Foreign born:** 21.5%. **Median age:** 33.2.

Income 2000: per capita $22,926; median household $47,067; **Pop below poverty level:** 12.4%. *Personal per capita income 2000-2003: $32,803-$35,841.

Unemployment 2004: 4.7%. **Change from 2000:** +1.5%. **Median travel time to work:** 25.3 minutes. **Working outside county of residence:** 3.5%.

Cities with pop over 10,000: 17 (see page 32 for cities).

SAN FRANCISCO CITY & COUNTY

1 Dr Carlton B Goodlett Pl City Hall Rm 168   **Ph:** 415-554-4950
San Francisco, CA 94102   **Fax:** 415-554-4951
www.sfgov.org

On N coast of CA; original county; organized Feb 18, 1850 (prior to statehood). **Name Origin:** For the bay, named for Saint Francis of Assisi (c. 1181-1226).

Area (sq mi): 231.92 (land 46.69; water 185.22). **Pop per sq mi:** 15836.9.

Pop 2005: 739,426. **State rank:** 13. **Pop change:** 2000-20005 -4.8%; 1990-2000 +7.3%. **Pop 2000:** 776,733 (White 43.6%; Black or African American 7.8%; Hispanic or Latino 14.1%; Asian 30.8%; Other 11.7%). **Foreign born:** 36.8%. **Median age:** 36.5.

Income 2000: per capita $34,556; median household $55,221; **Pop below poverty level:** 11.3%. *Personal per capita income 2000-2003: $55,730-$55,720.

Unemployment 2004: 5.9%. **Change from 2000:** +0.7%. **Median travel time to work:** 30.7 minutes. **Working outside county of residence:** 23.1%.

Cities with pop over 10,000: San Francisco 🏛 (744,230).

SAN JOAQUIN COUNTY

222 E Weber Ave Rm 707   **Ph:** 209-468-3211
Stockton, CA 95202   **Fax:** 209-468-2875
www.sjgov.org

In N central CA, E of San Francisco; original county; organized Feb 18, 1850 (prior to statehood). **Name Origin:** For the river, named for Saint Joachim, father of the Virgin Mary.

Area (sq mi): 1426.25 (land 1399.28; water 26.97). **Pop per sq mi:** 474.6.

Pop 2005: 664,116. **State rank:** 15. **Pop change:** 2000-20005 +17.8%; 1990-2000 +17.3%. **Pop 2000:** 563,598 (White 47.4%; Black or African American 6.7%; Hispanic or Latino 30.5%; Asian 11.4%; Other 23.7%, including 1.1% American Indian/Alaska Native). **Foreign born:** 19.5%. **Median age:** 31.9.

Income 2000: per capita $17,365; median household $41,282; **Pop below poverty level:** 17.7%. *Personal per capita income 2000-2003: $24,210-$24,397.

Unemployment 2004: 8.5%. **Change from 2000:** -0.2%. **Median travel time to work:** 29.2 minutes. **Working outside county of residence:** 23.5%.

Cities with pop over 10,000: 6 (see page 32 for cities).

SAN LUIS OBISPO COUNTY

1155 Monterey St Rm D-120   **Ph:** 805-781-5245
San Luis Obispo, CA 93408   **Fax:** 805-781-1111
www.slocounty.org

On central coast of CA; original county; organized Feb 18, 1850 (prior to statehood). **Name Origin:** For the mission, named for Saint Louis, Bishop of Toulouse, son of King Charles II of Naples and Sicily.

Area (sq mi): 3615.54 (land 3304.32; water 311.22). **Pop per sq mi:** 77.3.

Pop 2005: 255,478. **State rank:** 23. **Pop change:** 2000-20005 +3.6%; 1990-2000 +13.6%. **Pop 2000:** 246,681 (White 76.1%; Black or African American 2%; Hispanic or Latino 16.3%; Asian 2.7%; Other 10.6%). **Foreign born:** 8.9%. **Median age:** 37.3.

Income 2000: per capita $21,864; median household $42,428; **Pop below poverty level:** 12.8%. *Personal per capita income 2000-2003: $27,455-$30,228.

Unemployment 2004: 4.4%. **Change from 2000:** +1.6%. **Median travel time to work:** 21.1 minutes. **Working outside county of residence:** 10.3%.

Cities with pop over 10,000: 6 (see page 32 for cities).

SAN MATEO COUNTY

555 County Ctr   **Ph:** 650-363-4712
Redwood City, CA 94063   **Fax:** 650-363-4843
www.co.sanmateo.ca.us

On N central coast of CA, S of San Francisco; organized Apr 19, 1856 from San Francisco County. **Name Origin:** For the creek, named for Saint Matthew the Apostle.

Area (sq mi): 741.01 (land 449.07; water 291.95). **Pop per sq mi:** 1557.9.

Pop 2005: 699,610. **State rank:** 14. **Pop change:** 2000-20005 -1.1%; 1990-2000 +8.9%. **Pop 2000:** 707,161 (White 49.8%; Black or African American 3.5%; Hispanic or Latino 21.9%; Asian 20%; Other 16.9%, including 1.3% Native Hawaiian/Other Pacific Islander). **Foreign born:** 32.3%. **Median age:** 36.8.

Income 2000: per capita $36,045; median household $70,819; **Pop below poverty level:** 5.8%. *Personal per capita income 2000-2003: $58,905-$52,841.

Unemployment 2004: 5%. **Change from 2000:** +2.2%. **Median travel time to work:** 27 minutes. **Working outside county of residence:** 41.8%.

Cities with pop over 10,000: 14 (see page 32 for cities).

SANTA BARBARA COUNTY

PO Box 159   **Ph:** 805-568-2550
Santa Barbara, CA 93102   **Fax:** 805-568-3247
www.countyofsb.org

On S coast of CA, northwest of Los Angeles; original county; organized Feb 18, 1850 (prior to statehood). **Name Origin:** For the channel named for Saint Barbara.

🏛 *County Seat*

Santa Barbara County (cont'd)

Area (sq mi): 3789.08 (land 2737.01; water 1052.07). **Pop per sq mi:** 146.4.

Pop 2005: 400,762. **State rank:** 21. **Pop change:** 2000-20005 +0.4%; 1990-2000 +8%. **Pop 2000:** 399,347 (White 56.9%; Black or African American 2.3%; Hispanic or Latino 34.2%; Asian 4.1%; Other 20.9%, including 1.2% American Indian/Alaska Native). **Foreign born:** 21.2%. **Median age:** 33.4.

Income 2000: per capita $23,059; median household $46,677; **Pop below poverty level:** 14.3%. ***Personal per capita income 2000-2003:** $32,302-$33,624.

Unemployment 2004: 4.7%. **Change from 2000:** +1.2%. **Median travel time to work:** 19.3 minutes. **Working outside county of residence:** 5.9%.

Cities with pop over 10,000: Santa Barbara 🏛 (87,370); Santa Maria (83,756); Lompoc (40,908); Goleta (28,181); Carpinteria (13,829).

SANTA CLARA COUNTY

70 W Hedding St 11th Fl East Wing   **Ph:** 408-299-5105
San Jose, CA 95110   **Fax:** 408-293-5649
claraweb.co.santa-clara.ca.us

In W central CA, north of Monterey; original county; organized Feb 18, 1850 (prior to statehood). **Name Origin:** For the river named for Saint Clare of Assisi.

Area (sq mi): 1304.01 (land 1290.69; water 13.32). **Pop per sq mi:** 1316.4.

Pop 2005: 1,699,052. **State rank:** 6. **Pop change:** 2000-20005 +1%; 1990-2000 +12.4%. **Pop 2000:** 1,682,585 (White 44.2%; Black or African American 2.8%; Hispanic or Latino 24%; Asian 25.6%; Other 17.8%). **Foreign born:** 34.1%. **Median age:** 34.

Income 2000: per capita $32,795; median household $74,335; **Pop below poverty level:** 7.5%. ***Personal per capita income 2000-2003:** $54,195-$46,640.

Unemployment 2004: 6.6%. **Change from 2000:** +2.1%. **Median travel time to work:** 26.1 minutes. **Working outside county of residence:** 12.2%.

Cities with pop over 10,000: 14 (see page 33 for cities).

SANTA CRUZ COUNTY

701 Ocean St Rm 230   **Ph:** 831-454-2800
Santa Cruz, CA 95060
www.co.santa-cruz.ca.us

On S central coast of CA; original county; organized Feb 18, 1850 (prior to statehood). **Name Origin:** Spanish 'holy cross,' a common Spanish placename. Originally named *Branciforte* for the viceroy, but changed Apr 6, 1850.

Area (sq mi): 607.16 (land 445.24; water 161.92). **Pop per sq mi:** 560.7.

Pop 2005: 249,666. **State rank:** 24. **Pop change:** 2000-20005 -2.3%; 1990-2000 +11.3%. **Pop 2000:** 255,602 (White 65.5%; Black or African American 1%; Hispanic or Latino 26.8%; Asian 3.4%; Other 20.5%, including 1% American Indian/Alaska Native). **Foreign born:** 18.2%. **Median age:** 35.

Income 2000: per capita $26,396; median household $53,998; **Pop below poverty level:** 11.9%. ***Personal per capita income 2000-2003:** $39,149-$38,126.

Unemployment 2004: 7%. **Change from 2000:** +0.9%. **Median travel time to work:** 27.8 minutes. **Working outside county of residence:** 26.2%.

Cities with pop over 10,000: Santa Cruz 🏛 (54,213); Watsonville (47,152); Scotts Valley (11,205).

SHASTA COUNTY

1643 Market St   **Ph:** 530-225-5378
Redding, CA 96099   **Fax:** 530-225-5454
www.co.shasta.ca.us

In N central CA, north of Chico; original county; organized Feb 18, 1850 (prior to statehood). **Name Origin:** For the Indian tribe of Hokan linguistic stock; the original meaning is uncertain. Also spelled *Sasty, Sastise, Chasty, Chasta*.

Area (sq mi): 3847.44 (land 3785.19; water 62.24). **Pop per sq mi:** 47.5.

Pop 2005: 179,904. **State rank:** 29. **Pop change:** 2000-20005 +10.2%; 1990-2000 +11%. **Pop 2000:** 163,256 (White 86.4%; Black or African American 0.8%; Hispanic or Latino 5.5%; Asian 1.9%; Other 8.1%, including 2.8% American Indian/Alaska Native). **Foreign born:** 4%. **Median age:** 38.9.

Income 2000: per capita $17,738; median household $34,335; **Pop below poverty level:** 15.4%. ***Personal per capita income 2000-2003:** $24,443-$26,161.

Unemployment 2004: 7.4%. **Change from 2000:** +0.7%. **Median travel time to work:** 20.9 minutes. **Working outside county of residence:** 7.4%.

Cities with pop over 10,000: Redding 🏛 (88,573); Anderson (10,375); Shasta Lake (10,117).

SIERRA COUNTY

110 Courthouse Sq Rm 11   **Ph:** 530-289-3295
Downieville, CA 95936   **Fax:** 530-289-2830
www.sierracounty.ws/

On NE border of CA with NV; organized Apr 16, 1852 from Yuba County. **Name Origin:** Spanish 'mountain range,' for its location in the northern part of the Sierra Nevada.

Area (sq mi): 961.97 (land 953.38; water 8.59). **Pop per sq mi:** 3.6.

Pop 2005: 3,434. **State rank:** 57. **Pop change:** 2000-20005 -3.4%; 1990-2000 +7.1%. **Pop 2000:** 3,555 (White 90.3%; Black or African American 0.2%; Hispanic or Latino 6%; Asian 0.2%; Other 5.4%, including 1.9% American Indian/Alaska Native). **Foreign born:** 3%. **Median age:** 43.7.

Income 2000: per capita $18,815; median household $35,827; **Pop below poverty level:** 11.3%. ***Personal per capita income 2000-2003:** $22,646-$22,533.

Unemployment 2004: 9.9%. **Change from 2000:** +0.2%. **Median travel time to work:** 29 minutes. **Working outside county of residence:** 39.3%.

Cities with pop over 10,000: None.

---

*Source: Personal per capita income data are from the Bureau of Economic Analysis; per capita income data are from the Bureau of the Census. See Introduction for explanation of differences.

SISKIYOU COUNTY

201 4th St   **Ph:** 530-842-8005
Yreka, CA 96097   **Fax:** 530-842-8013
www.co.siskiyou.ca.us

In N central CA on OR border; organized Mar 22, 1852 from Klamath and Shasta counties, and in 1874 annexed part of Klamath County. Site of Mt. Shasta, 14,162 ft. **Name Origin:** Possibly Chinook from Cree for 'bob-tailed horse,' or French *six cailloux* 'six boulders.'

Area (sq mi): 6347.46 (land 6286.78; water 60.68). **Pop per sq mi:** 7.2.

Pop 2005: 45,259. **State rank:** 45. **Pop change:** 2000-20005 +2.2%; 1990-2000 +1.8%. **Pop 2000:** 44,301 (White 83.3%; Black or African American 1.3%; Hispanic or Latino 7.6%; Asian 1.2%; Other 10.4%, including 3.9% American Indian/Alaska Native). **Foreign born:** 5.4%. **Median age:** 43.

Income 2000: per capita $17,570; median household $29,530; **Pop below poverty level:** 18.6%. *Personal per capita income 2000-2003: $22,315-$23,807.

Unemployment 2004: 9.3%. **Change from 2000:** -0.1%. **Median travel time to work:** 18.2 minutes. **Working outside county of residence:** 6.2%.

Cities with pop over 10,000: None.

SOLANO COUNTY

675 Texas St Suite 1900 **Ph:** 707-784-7485
Fairfield, CA 94533   **Fax:** 707-784-6311
www.co.solano.ca.us

In N central CA, NE of San Francisco; original county; organized Feb 18, 1850 (prior to statehood). **Name Origin:** For Saint Francis Solano and for Sem-yeto, a chief of the Soscol and Suisun Indians, who had accepted the Christian name of the saint at his baptism.

Area (sq mi): 906.67 (land 829.19; water 77.48). **Pop per sq mi:** 496.4.

Pop 2005: 411,593. **State rank:** 19. **Pop change:** 2000-20005 +4.3%; 1990-2000 +15.9%. **Pop 2000:** 394,542 (White 49.2%; Black or African American 14.9%; Hispanic or Latino 17.6%; Asian 12.7%; Other 16%). **Foreign born:** 16.9%. **Median age:** 33.9.

Income 2000: per capita $21,731; median household $54,099; **Pop below poverty level:** 8.3%. *Personal per capita income 2000-2003: $27,576-$30,259.

Unemployment 2004: 5.9%. **Change from 2000:** +1.8%. **Median travel time to work:** 31.8 minutes. **Working outside county of residence:** 43.2%.

Cities with pop over 10,000: Fairfield ⛫ (103,949); Vacaville (94,303); Suisun City (26,945); Benicia (26,828); Dixon (16,710).

SONOMA COUNTY

575 Administration Dr Suite 104A **Ph:** 707-565-2431
Santa Rosa, CA 95403   **Fax:** 707-565-3778
www.sonoma-county.org

On NW coast of CA, north of San Francisco; original county; organized Feb 18, 1850 (prior to statehood). **Name Origin:** For the city, named for a Wintun Indian group that lived in the Sacramento Valley. The name means 'nose' but the reason in unknown; possibly referring to the shape of a peak. A fanciful interpretation is 'valley of the moon.'

Area (sq mi): 1768.23 (land 1575.88; water 192.35). **Pop per sq mi:** 296.

Pop 2005: 466,477. **State rank:** 17. **Pop change:** 2000-20005 +1.7%; 1990-2000 +18.1%. **Pop 2000:** 458,614 (White 74.5%; Black or African American 1.4%; Hispanic or Latino 17.3%; Asian 3.1%; Other 13.9%, including 1.2% American Indian/Alaska Native). **Foreign born:** 14.3%. **Median age:** 37.5.

Income 2000: per capita $25,724; median household $53,076; **Pop below poverty level:** 8.1%. *Personal per capita income 2000-2003: $36,439-$36,466.

Unemployment 2004: 4.9%. **Change from 2000:** +2%. **Median travel time to work:** 26.8 minutes. **Working outside county of residence:** 18%.

Cities with pop over 10,000: Santa Rosa ⛫ (153,636); Petaluma (55,359); Rohnert Park (41,966); Windsor (24,751); Healdsburg (11,130).

STANISLAUS COUNTY

1021 'I' St   **Ph:** 209-525-5251
Modesto, CA 95354   **Fax:** 209-525-5239
www.co.stanislaus.ca.us

In central CA, E of San Francisco; organized Apr 1, 1854, from Tuolumne County. **Name Origin:** For the Stanislaus River, the baptismal name of an Indian leader who fought bravely there. John C. Fremont (1813-90) used the anglicization of Spanish *Estanislao*.

Area (sq mi): 1514.67 (land 1493.79; water 20.88). **Pop per sq mi:** 338.4.

Pop 2005: 505,505. **State rank:** 16. **Pop change:** 2000-20005 +13.1%; 1990-2000 +20.6%. **Pop 2000:** 446,997 (White 57.3%; Black or African American 2.6%; Hispanic or Latino 31.7%; Asian 4.2%; Other 23.8%, including 1.3% American Indian/Alaska Native). **Foreign born:** 18.3%. **Median age:** 31.7.

Income 2000: per capita $16,913; median household $40,101; **Pop below poverty level:** 16%. *Personal per capita income 2000-2003: $23,502-$24,276.

Unemployment 2004: 9.1%. **Change from 2000:** -1.1%. **Median travel time to work:** 26.8 minutes. **Working outside county of residence:** 20.9%.

Cities with pop over 10,000: 6 (see page 33 for cities).

SUTTER COUNTY

433 2nd St   **Ph:** 530-822-7120
Yuba City, CA 95991   **Fax:** 530-822-7214
www.co.sutter.ca.us

In N central CA, NW of Sacramento; original county; organized Feb 18, 1850 (prior to statehood). **Name Origin:** For Sutter's Creek, named for John Augustus Sutter (Johann August Suter 1803-80), on whose property gold was discovered in 1848, the beginning of the California Gold Rush.

Area (sq mi): 608.58 (land 602.54; water 6.04). **Pop per sq mi:** 147.5.

Pop 2005: 88,876. **State rank:** 37. **Pop change:** 2000-20005 +12.6%; 1990-2000 +22.5%. **Pop 2000:** 78,930 (White 60.2%;

Sutter County (cont'd)

Black or African American 1.9%; Hispanic or Latino 22.2%; Asian 11.3%; Other 19.4%, including 1.6% American Indian/Alaska Native). **Foreign born:** 19.3%. **Median age:** 34.1.

Income 2000: per capita $17,428; median household $38,375; **Pop below poverty level:** 15.5%. ***Personal per capita income 2000-2003:** $24,487-$25,606.

Unemployment 2004: 10.5%. **Change from 2000:** -1.8%. **Median travel time to work:** 25.4 minutes. **Working outside county of residence:** 43.9%.

Cities with pop over 10,000: Yuba City 🏛 (52,124).

TEHAMA COUNTY
633 Washington St Rm 11   **Ph:** 530-527-3350
Red Bluff, CA 96080   **Fax:** 530-527-1745
www.co.tehama.ca.us

In N central CA, north of Chico; organized Apr 9, 1856 from Butte, Colusa, and Shasta counties. **Name Origin:** For the city, origin and meaning uncertain. It is almost certainly Indian, though an Arabian generic *tihama* 'hot lowlands' is frequently found in Arabic placenames. The Indian parallel term may also mean 'lowlands' or shallow,' as in a ford of a river.

Area (sq mi): 2962.27 (land 2950.99; water 11.28). **Pop per sq mi:** 20.7.

Pop 2005: 61,197. **State rank:** 41. **Pop change:** 2000-20005 +9.2%; 1990-2000 +12.9%. **Pop 2000:** 56,039 (White 78.5%; Black or African American 0.6%; Hispanic or Latino 15.8%; Asian 0.8%; Other 13.9%, including 2.1% American Indian/Alaska Native). **Foreign born:** 7.9%. **Median age:** 37.8.

Income 2000: per capita $15,793; median household $31,206; **Pop below poverty level:** 17.3%. ***Personal per capita income 2000-2003:** $19,029-$20,711.

Unemployment 2004: 7.3%. **Change from 2000:** +0.9%. **Median travel time to work:** 22.4 minutes. **Working outside county of residence:** 23.8%.

Cities with pop over 10,000: Red Bluff 🏛 (13,911).

TRINITY COUNTY
101 Court St   **Ph:** 530-623-1222
Weaverville, CA 96093   **Fax:** 530-623-8398
www.trinitycounty.org

In NW CA, west of Redding; original county; organized Feb 18, 1850 (prior to statehood). **Name Origin:** For the Trinity River, named by Pierson B. Reading in 1845, who believed it entered Trinidad Bay. (Trinity is the English version of the Spanish Trinidad.)

Area (sq mi): 3207.54 (land 3178.61; water 28.93). **Pop per sq mi:** 4.3.

Pop 2005: 13,622. **State rank:** 54. **Pop change:** 2000-20005 +4.6%; 1990-2000 -0.3%. **Pop 2000:** 13,022 (White 86.6%; Black or African American 0.4%; Hispanic or Latino 4%; Asian 0.5%; Other 10.2%, including 4.8% American Indian/Alaska Native). **Foreign born:** 1.6%. **Median age:** 44.6.

Income 2000: per capita $16,868; median household $27,711; **Pop below poverty level:** 18.7%. ***Personal per capita income 2000-2003:** $19,918-$21,756.

Unemployment 2004: 10.8%. **Change from 2000:** -0.1%. **Median travel time to work:** 24 minutes. **Working outside county of residence:** 16.7%.

Cities with pop over 10,000: None.

TULARE COUNTY
2800 W Burrel Ave   **Ph:** 559-733-6271
Visalia, CA 93291   **Fax:** 559-733-6898
www.co.tulare.ca.us

In central CA, southeast of Fresno; organized Apr 20, 1852, from Mariposa County. **Name Origin:** For Tulare Lake, Mexican-Spanish 'rush' or 'reed,' perhaps originally from Aztec *tullin* or *tollin*, 'cattail' or 'bulrush.'

Area (sq mi): 4839.09 (land 4823.97; water 15.12). **Pop per sq mi:** 85.2.

Pop 2005: 410,874. **State rank:** 20. **Pop change:** 2000-20005 +11.6%; 1990-2000 +18%. **Pop 2000:** 368,021 (White 41.8%; Black or African American 1.6%; Hispanic or Latino 50.8%; Asian 3.3%; Other 37.1%, including 1.6% American Indian/Alaska Native). **Foreign born:** 22.6%. **Median age:** 29.2.

Income 2000: per capita $14,006; median household $33,983; **Pop below poverty level:** 23.9%. ***Personal per capita income 2000-2003:** $19,567-$21,388.

Unemployment 2004: 11.5%. **Change from 2000:** -3.9%. **Median travel time to work:** 21.9 minutes. **Working outside county of residence:** 11.8%.

Cities with pop over 10,000: Visalia 🏛 (104,655); Tulare (48,697); Porterville (44,011); Dinuba (18,479); Lindsay (10,734).

TUOLUMNE COUNTY
2 S Green St   **Ph:** 209-533-5511
Sonora, CA 95370   **Fax:** 209-533-5510
portal.co.tuolumne.ca.us

In E central CA, east of Stockton; original county; organized Feb 18, 1850 (prior to statehood). **Name Origin:** For the Tuolumne River, named for either the Central Miwok or Yokut Indians, of Penutian linguistic stock. Name is believed to be a corruption of Indian *talmalamne* 'cluster of stone wigwams': they lived in caves or recesses in the rocks. Variously spelled *Taulamne, Tahualamne,* and *Tavalames*.

Area (sq mi): 2274.34 (land 2235.41; water 38.93). **Pop per sq mi:** 26.6.

Pop 2005: 59,380. **State rank:** 42. **Pop change:** 2000-20005 +9%; 1990-2000 +12.5%. **Pop 2000:** 54,501 (White 85.1%; Black or African American 2.1%; Hispanic or Latino 8.2%; Asian 0.7%; Other 7.7%, including 1.8% American Indian/Alaska Native). **Foreign born:** 3.2%. **Median age:** 42.9.

Income 2000: per capita $21,015; median household $38,725; **Pop below poverty level:** 11.4%. ***Personal per capita income 2000-2003:** $23,204-$24,860.

Unemployment 2004: 6.8%. **Change from 2000:** +1.3%. **Median travel time to work:** 26.8 minutes. **Working outside county of residence:** 17%.

*Source: Personal per capita income data are from the Bureau of Economic Analysis; per capita income data are from the Bureau of the Census. See Introduction for explanation of differences.

104

Tuolumne County (cont'd)

Cities with pop over 10,000: None.

VENTURA COUNTY

800 S Victoria Ave	**Ph:** 805-654-2267
Ventura, CA 93009	**Fax:** 805-662-6543
www.countyofventura.org	

On S coast of CA, N of Los Angeles; organized Mar 22, 1873 from Santa Barbara County. **Name Origin:** For the city, abbreviation of Spanish *San Buenaventura* 'St Bonaventure.'

Area (sq mi): 2208.2 (land 1845.3; water 362.9). **Pop per sq mi:** 431.4.

Pop 2005: 796,106. **State rank:** 11. **Pop change:** 2000-20005 +5.7%; 1990-2000 +12.6%. **Pop 2000:** 753,197 (White 56.8%; Black or African American 1.9%; Hispanic or Latino 33.4%; Asian 5.3%; Other 22.7%). **Foreign born:** 20.7%. **Median age:** 34.2.

Income 2000: per capita $24,600; median household $59,666; **Pop below poverty level:** 9.2%. ***Personal per capita income 2000-2003:** $33,521-$35,241.

Unemployment 2004: 5.3%. **Change from 2000:** +0.8%. **Median travel time to work:** 25.4 minutes. **Working outside county of residence:** 23.8%.

Cities with pop over 10,000: 9 (see page 33 for cities).

YOLO COUNTY

625 Court St Suite 202	**Ph:** 530-666-8150
Woodland, CA 95695	**Fax:** 530-668-4029
www.yolocounty.org	

In N central CA, NE of San Francisco; original county; organized Feb 18, 1850 (prior to statehood). **Name Origin:** For a subtribe of Patwin Indians, of Wintun linguistic stock; meaning of name unclear. Possibly a corruption of *Yoloy* 'place abounding with rushes,' or *Yodoi* a Patwin village, or for a chief named *Yodo*. There was also a captain of a ranch who was named Yolo.

Area (sq mi): 1022.89 (land 1013.27; water 9.62). **Pop per sq mi:** 182.5.

Pop 2005: 184,932. **State rank:** 28. **Pop change:** 2000-20005 +9.6%; 1990-2000 +19.5%. **Pop 2000:** 168,660 (White 58.1%; Black or African American 2%; Hispanic or Latino 25.9%; Asian 9.9%; Other 20.5%, including 1.2% American Indian/Alaska Native). **Foreign born:** 20.3%. **Median age:** 29.5.

Income 2000: per capita $19,365; median household $40,769; **Pop below poverty level:** 18.4%. ***Personal per capita income 2000-2003:** $26,331-$27,932.

Unemployment 2004: 5.9%. **Change from 2000:** +1.7%. **Median travel time to work:** 21.2 minutes. **Working outside county of residence:** 32.8%.

Cities with pop over 10,000: Davis (63,722); Woodland ⛪ (51,693), West Sacramento (39,351).

YUBA COUNTY

915 8th St Suite 115	**Ph:** 530-749-7575
Marysville, CA 95901	**Fax:** 530-749-7312
www.co.yuba.ca.us	

In N central CA, N of Sacramento; original county; organized Feb 18, 1850 (prior to statehood). **Name Origin:** For the Yuba River, the name of which came from a Maidu Indian village and tribal name. Also spelled *Yubu, Yupu, Jubu.*

Area (sq mi): 643.73 (land 630.69; water 13.04). **Pop per sq mi:** 106.5.

Pop 2005: 67,153. **State rank:** 39. **Pop change:** 2000-20005 +11.5%; 1990-2000 +3.4%. **Pop 2000:** 60,219 (White 65.3%; Black or African American 3.2%; Hispanic or Latino 17.4%; Asian 7.5%; Other 18.6%, including 2.6% American Indian/Alaska Native). **Foreign born:** 13.2%. **Median age:** 31.4.

Income 2000: per capita $14,124; median household $30,460; **Pop below poverty level:** 20.8%. ***Personal per capita income 2000-2003:** $19,140-$21,903.

Unemployment 2004: 9.7%. **Change from 2000:** -2%. **Median travel time to work:** 26.2 minutes. **Working outside county of residence:** 43.9%.

Cities with pop over 10,000: Marysville ⛪ (12,518).

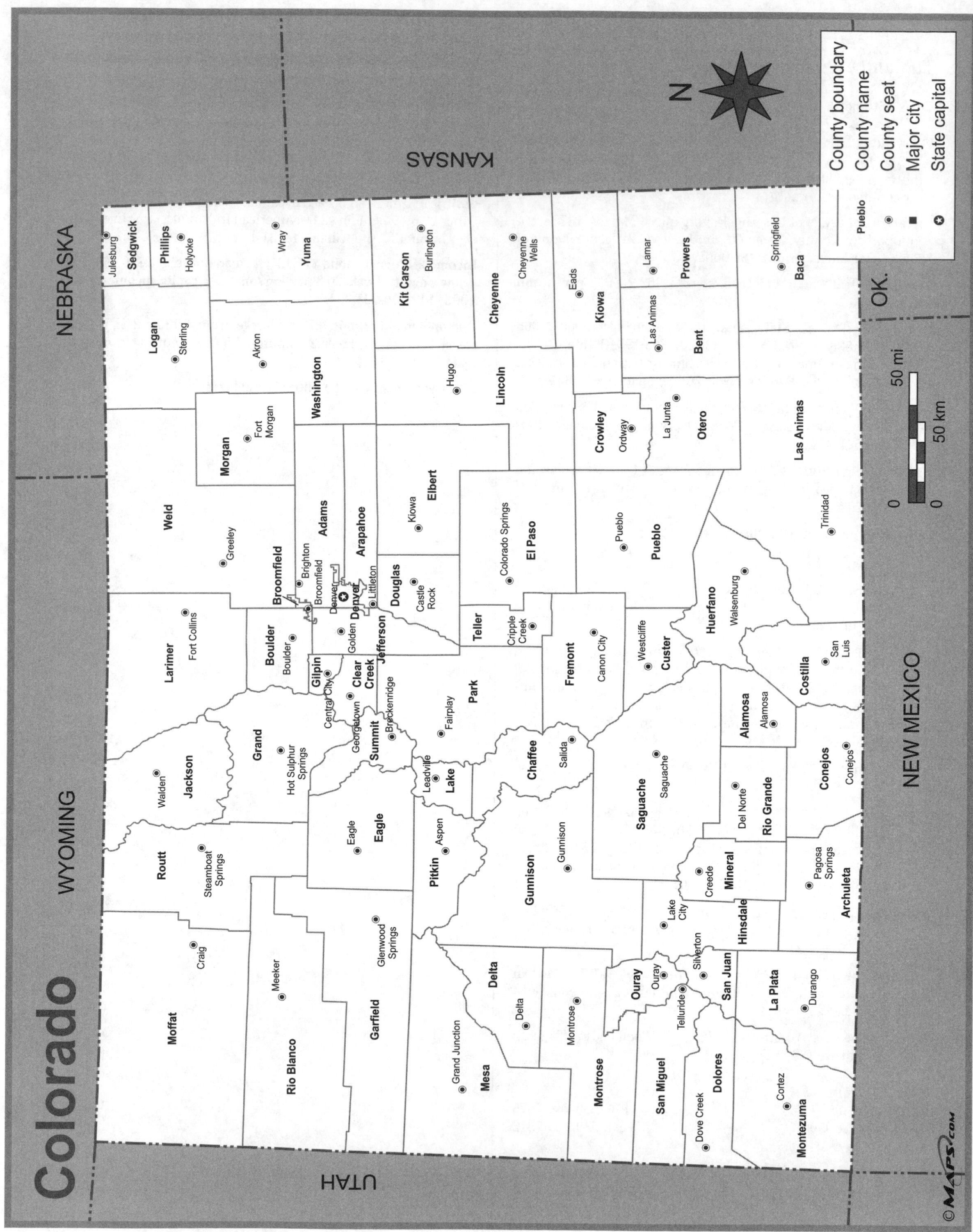

Colorado

Colorado

COLORADO STATE INFORMATION

www.colorado.gov   **Ph:** 303-866-5000

Area (sq mi): 104,093.57 (land 103,717.53; water 376.04). **Pop per sq mi:** 45.

Pop 2005: 4,665,177. **Pop change:** 2000-20005 +8.5%; 1990-2000 +30.6%. **Pop 2000:** 4,301,261 (White 74.5%; Black or African American 3.8%; Hispanic or Latino 17.1%; Asian 2.2%; Other 11.1%, including 1% American Indian/Alaska Native). **Foreign born:** 8.6%. **Median age:** 34.3.

Income 2000: per capita $24,049; median household $47,203; **Pop below poverty level:** 9.3%. ***Personal per capita income 2000-2003:** $33,370-$34,561.

Unemployment 2004: 5.6%. **Change from 2000:** +2.9%. **Median travel time to work:** 24.3 minutes. **Working outside county of residence:** 33%.

ADAMS COUNTY

450 S 4th Ave   **Ph:** 303-659-2120
Brighton, CO 80601   **Fax:** 303-654-6011
www.co.adams.co.us

In east-central CO, east of Denver; organized Apr 15, 1901 from Arapahoe County; annexed part of Denver County in 1909. A portion of the county was used to create Broomfield County on November 15, 2001. **Name Origin:** For Alva Adams (1850-1922), statesman and governor (1887-89; 1897-99; 1905).

Area (sq mi): 1197.71 (land 1191.93; water 5.78). **Pop per sq mi:** 335.1.

Pop 2005: 399,426. **State rank:** 5. **Pop change:** 2000-20005 +9.8%; 1990-2000 +37.3%. **Pop 2000:** 363,857 (White 63.3%; Black or African American 3%; Hispanic or Latino 28.2%; Asian 3.2%; Other 16.5%, including 1.2% American Indian/Alaska Native). **Foreign born:** 12.5%. **Median age:** 31.4.

Income 2000: per capita $19,944; median household $47,323; **Pop below poverty level:** 8.9%. ***Personal per capita income 2000-2003:** $26,722-$27,620.

Unemployment 2004: 6.4%. **Change from 2000:** +2.6%. **Median travel time to work:** 27.6 minutes. **Working outside county of residence:** 60.7%.

Cities with pop over 10,000: Northglenn (33,234); Commerce City (29,734); Brighton 🏛 (26,927); Federal Heights (11,809).

ALAMOSA COUNTY

PO Box 178   **Ph:** 719-589-4848
Alamosa, CO 81101   **Fax:** 719-589-1900
www.ccionline.org/counties/alamosa.html

In south-central CO, southwest of Pueblo; organized Mar 8, 1913 from Costilla County. **Name Origin:** Spanish 'cottonwood trees.'

Area (sq mi): 723.53 (land 722.74; water 0.78). **Pop per sq mi:** 21.1.

Pop 2005: 15,282. **State rank:** 30. **Pop change:** 2000-20005 +2.1%; 1990-2000 +9.9%. **Pop 2000:** 14,966 (White 54%; Black or African American 1%; Hispanic or Latino 41.4%; Asian 0.8%; Other 27%, including 2.3% American Indian/Alaska Native). **Foreign born:** 4.7%. **Median age:** 30.6.

Income 2000: per capita $15,037; median household $29,447; **Pop below poverty level:** 21.3%. ***Personal per capita income 2000-2003:** $20,568-$23,216.

Unemployment 2004: 6.2%. **Change from 2000:** +0.6%. **Median travel time to work:** 13.5 minutes. **Working outside county of residence:** 13.1%.

Cities with pop over 10,000: None.

ARAPAHOE COUNTY

5334 S Prince St   **Ph:** 303-795-4200
Littleton, CO 80166   **Fax:** 303-794-4625
www.co.arapahoe.co.us

In east-central CO, south of Denver; original county, organized Nov 1, 1861 (prior to statehood). **Name Origin:** For a tribe of Algonquian linguistic stock. Name is probably Pawnee *tirapihu* 'trader.' Also suggested, but not documented, 'blue-sky men' and 'cloud men.'

Area (sq mi): 805.43 (land 803.14; water 2.29). **Pop per sq mi:** 658.8.

Pop 2005: 529,090. **State rank:** 3. **Pop change:** 2000-20005 +8.4%; 1990-2000 +24.6%. **Pop 2000:** 487,967 (White 73.9%; Black or African American 7.7%; Hispanic or Latino 11.8%; Asian 3.9%; Other 8.5%). **Foreign born:** 11%. **Median age:** 34.5.

Income 2000: per capita $28,147; median household $53,570; **Pop below poverty level:** 5.8%. ***Personal per capita income 2000-2003:** $42,829-$45,013.

Unemployment 2004: 5.5%. **Change from 2000:** +2.3%. **Median travel time to work:** 26.1 minutes. **Working outside county of residence:** 49.9%.

Cities with pop over 10,000: Centennial (98,245); Littleton 🏛 (40,456); Englewood (32,432); Greenwood Village (12,678).

ARCHULETA COUNTY

PO Box 2589
Pagosa Springs, CO 81147
www.archuletacounty.org

Ph: 970-264-5633
Fax: 970-264-6423

On southern border, east of Durango; organized Apr 14, 1885 from Conejos County. **Name Origin:** For Antonio D. Archuleta, a CO legislator.

Area (sq mi): 1355.48 (land 1350.22; water 5.26). **Pop per sq mi:** 8.8.

Pop 2005: 11,886. **State rank:** 37. **Pop change:** 2000-20005 +20.1%; 1990-2000 +85.2%. **Pop 2000:** 9,898 (White 80.1%; Black or African American 0.4%; Hispanic or Latino 16.8%; Asian 0.3%; Other 11%, including 1.4% American Indian/Alaska Native). **Foreign born:** 2.9%. **Median age:** 40.8.

Income 2000: per capita $21,683; median household $37,901; **Pop below poverty level:** 11.7%. ***Personal per capita income 2000-2003:** $19,156-$20,122.

Unemployment 2004: 5.2%. **Change from 2000:** +0.9%. **Median travel time to work:** 19.2 minutes. **Working outside county of residence:** 10.4%.

Cities with pop over 10,000: None.

BACA COUNTY

741 Main St
Springfield, CO 81073
www.springfieldcolorado.com/countygov.html

Ph: 719-523-4372
Fax: 719-523-4881

On southeastern border of CO; organized Apr 16 1889 from Las Animas County. **Name Origin:** For an early pioneer family from Trinidad, CO.

Area (sq mi): 2557.09 (land 2555.72; water 1.37). **Pop per sq mi:** 1.6.

Pop 2005: 4,069. **State rank:** 54. **Pop change:** 2000-20005 -9.9%; 1990-2000 -0.9%. **Pop 2000:** 4,517 (White 90.4%; Black or African American 0%; Hispanic or Latino 7%; Asian 0.2%; Other 6.1%, including 1.2% American Indian/Alaska Native). **Foreign born:** 2.5%. **Median age:** 42.9.

Income 2000: per capita $15,068; median household $28,099; **Pop below poverty level:** 16.9%. ***Personal per capita income 2000-2003:** $23,527-$26,502.

Unemployment 2004: 3.9%. **Change from 2000:** +1%. **Median travel time to work:** 15.2 minutes. **Working outside county of residence:** 5.7%.

Cities with pop over 10,000: None.

BENT COUNTY

PO Box 350
Las Animas, CO 81054
www.bentcounty.org

Ph: 719-456-1600
Fax: 719-456-0375

In southeastern CO, southwest of Pueblo; organized Feb 11, 1870, from Greenwood County (prior to statehood), which was organized in 1874 and abolished in 1878 by being divided between Bent and Elbert counties. **Name Origin:** For Bent's Fort on the north bank of the Arkansas River and for the Bent brothers who built it, or for one of the brothers, William Bent (1809-69), early settler, fur trader, and Indian agent.

Area (sq mi): 1541.12 (land 1513.9; water 27.22). **Pop per sq mi:** 3.7.

Pop 2005: 5,558. **State rank:** 48. **Pop change:** 2000-20005 -7.3%; 1990-2000 +18.8%. **Pop 2000:** 5,998 (White 63.3%; Black or African American 3.7%; Hispanic or Latino 30.2%; Asian 0.6%; Other 16.3%, including 2.2% American Indian/Alaska Native). **Foreign born:** 4.4%. **Median age:** 37.3.

Income 2000: per capita $13,567; median household $28,125; **Pop below poverty level:** 19.5%. ***Personal per capita income 2000-2003:** $17,788-$18,428.

Unemployment 2004: 7.6%. **Change from 2000:** +3.1%. **Median travel time to work:** 18.6 minutes. **Working outside county of residence:** 29.7%.

Cities with pop over 10,000: None.

BOULDER COUNTY

1750 33rd St Suite 201
Boulder, CO 80301
www.co.boulder.co.us

Ph: 303-413-7770
Fax: 303-413-7775

In north-central CO, northwest of Denver; original county, organized Nov 1, 1861 (prior to statehood). A portion of the county was used to create Broomfield County on November 15, 2001. **Name Origin:** For Boulder City and Boulder Creek, themselves named for the huge rock formations in the area.

Area (sq mi): 751.37 (land 742.46; water 8.91). **Pop per sq mi:** 377.7.

Pop 2005: 280,440. **State rank:** 6. **Pop change:** 2000-20005 -3.7%; 1990-2000 +29.3%. **Pop 2000:** 291,288 (White 83.6%; Black or African American 0.9%; Hispanic or Latino 10.5%; Asian 3.1%; Other 7.6%). **Foreign born:** 9.4%. **Median age:** 33.4.

Income 2000: per capita $28,976; median household $55,861; **Pop below poverty level:** 9.5%. ***Personal per capita income 2000-2003:** $40,360-$41,110.

Unemployment 2004: 4.9%. **Change from 2000:** +1.4%. **Median travel time to work:** 22.4 minutes. **Working outside county of residence:** 20.1%.

Cities with pop over 10,000: 6 (see page 33 for cities).

BROOMFIELD CITY & COUNTY

1 DesCombes Dr
Broomfield, CO 80020
www.ci.broomfield.co.us

Ph: 303-469-3301
Fax: 303-438-6296

Broomfield was the only city in CO to lie in portions of four counties (Jefferson, Adams, Weld, and Boulder), which caused problems for local residents in accessing services. Consequently, on Nov 3, 1998, the City and County of Broomfield was created by constitutional amendment. After a three-year period in which to organize, it became CO's 64th county on Nov 15, 2001. The US Bureau of the Census recognized the new county in Feb of 2002, and its census status will become official after the 2010 Census.

Area (sq mi): 33.6 (land 32.6; water 1). **Pop per sq mi:** 1333.7.

Pop 2005: 43,478. **State rank:** 16. **Pop 2000:** 0 (White 0%; Black or African American 0%; Hispanic or Latino 0%; Asian 0%; Other 0%). **Foreign born:** 0%. **Median age:** 0.

*Source: Personal per capita income data are from the Bureau of Economic Analysis; per capita income data are from the Bureau of the Census. See Introduction for explanation of differences.

Broomfield City & County (cont'd)

Income 2000: per capita $0; median household $0; **Pop below poverty level:** 0%. ***Personal per capita income 2000-2003:** $0-$33,376.

Unemployment 2004: 5.5%. **Change from 2000:** +0%. **Median travel time to work:** 0 minutes.

Cities with pop over 10,000: Thornton (102,072); Broomfield 🏛 (42,901).

CHAFFEE COUNTY

PO Box 699   **Ph:** 719-539-4004
Salida, CO 81201   **Fax:** 719-539-8588
www.chaffeecounty.org

In central CO; organized as Lake County Nov 1, 1861 (prior to statehood); name changed Feb 10, 1879. **Name Origin:** For Jerome Bounty Chaffee (1825-86), CO territorial legislator and U.S. senator (1876-79); one of the founders of Denver.

Area (sq mi): 1015.01 (land 1013.45; water 1.55). **Pop per sq mi:** 16.7.

Pop 2005: 16,968. **State rank:** 27. **Pop change:** 2000-20005 +4.5%; 1990-2000 +28.1%. **Pop 2000:** 16,242 (White 87.3%; Black or African American 1.6%; Hispanic or Latino 8.6%; Asian 0.4%; Other 7%, including 1.1% American Indian/Alaska Native). **Foreign born:** 2%. **Median age:** 41.8.

Income 2000: per capita $19,430; median household $34,368; **Pop below poverty level:** 11.7%. ***Personal per capita income 2000-2003:** $21,649-$22,536.

Unemployment 2004: 5.5%. **Change from 2000:** +2.7%. **Median travel time to work:** 14.8 minutes. **Working outside county of residence:** 7.7%.

Cities with pop over 10,000: None.

CHEYENNE COUNTY

PO Box 567   **Ph:** 719-767-5685
Cheyenne Wells, CO 80810   **Fax:** 719-767-5540

On central-eastern border of CO, east of Colorado Springs; organized Mar 25, 1889 from Bent and Elbert counties. **Name Origin:** For the Dakota Indian tribe of Algonquian linguistic stock; name means 'red talkers.'

Area (sq mi): 1781.37 (land 1781.35; water 0.02). **Pop per sq mi:** 1.1.

Pop 2005: 1,953. **State rank:** 58. **Pop change:** 2000-20005 -12.5%; 1990-2000 -6.9%. **Pop 2000:** 2,231 (White 90.5%; Black or African American 0.5%; Hispanic or Latino 8.1%; Asian 0.1%; Other 6.5%). **Foreign born:** 4.1%. **Median age:** 37.9.

Income 2000: per capita $17,850; median household $37,054; **Pop below poverty level:** 11.1%. ***Personal per capita income 2000-2003:** $23,581-$29,933.

Unemployment 2004: 3.6%. **Change from 2000:** +1.3%. **Median travel time to work:** 13.5 minutes. **Working outside county of residence:** 11.8%.

Cities with pop over 10,000: None.

CLEAR CREEK COUNTY

PO Box 2000   **Ph:** 303-679-2312
Georgetown, CO 80444   **Fax:** 303-679-2440
www.co.clear-creek.co.us

In north-central CO, west of Denver; original county, organized Nov 1, 1861 (prior to statehood). **Name Origin:** For the name of a stream in the county, which was originally called Vasquez Fork, but present name adopted by 1860.

Area (sq mi): 396.46 (land 395.45; water 1.01). **Pop per sq mi:** 23.3.

Pop 2005: 9,197. **State rank:** 39. **Pop change:** 2000-20005 -1.3%; 1990-2000 +22.4%. **Pop 2000:** 9,322 (White 94%; Black or African American 0.3%; Hispanic or Latino 3.9%; Asian 0.4%; Other 2.9%). **Foreign born:** 1.9%. **Median age:** 40.2.

Income 2000: per capita $28,160; median household $50,997; **Pop below poverty level:** 5.4%. ***Personal per capita income 2000-2003:** $34,449-$42,225.

Unemployment 2004: 5.5%. **Change from 2000:** +1.7%. **Median travel time to work:** 32.6 minutes. **Working outside county of residence:** 56.4%.

Cities with pop over 10,000: None.

CONEJOS COUNTY

PO Box 157   **Ph:** 719-376-5565
Conejos, CO 81129   **Fax:** 719-376-5661

On central southern border, east of Durango; original county, organized as Guadalupe County Nov 1, 1861 (prior to statehood); name changed Nov 7, 1861. **Name Origin:** For the river (which runs through the county) and town called Conejos, from the Spanish meaning 'rabbits,' for the local abundance of the animals.

Area (sq mi): 1290.87 (land 1287.22; water 3.65). **Pop per sq mi:** 6.6.

Pop 2005: 8,512. **State rank:** 40. **Pop change:** 2000-20005 +1.3%; 1990-2000 +12.7%. **Pop 2000:** 8,400 (White 39.3%; Black or African American 0.2%; Hispanic or Latino 58.9%; Asian 0.2%; Other 26.9%, including 1.7% American Indian/Alaska Native). **Foreign born:** 3%. **Median age:** 34.2.

Income 2000: per capita $12,050; median household $24,744; **Pop below poverty level:** 23%. ***Personal per capita income 2000-2003:** $15,649-$17,724.

Unemployment 2004: 8.2%. **Change from 2000:** +0.3%. **Median travel time to work:** 22.4 minutes. **Working outside county of residence:** 36.7%.

Cities with pop over 10,000: None.

COSTILLA COUNTY

PO Box 301   **Ph:** 719-672-3681
San Luis, CO 81152   **Fax:** 719-672-4493
www.costilla-county.com

On central southern border of CO, southwest of Pueblo; original county, organized Nov 1, 1861 (prior to statehood). **Name Origin:** Probably for Costilla Creek, which runs through the county; Spanish 'rib' or 'furring timber'; or possibly for a local family of this name.

Area (sq mi): 1230.44 (land 1227.1; water 3.34). **Pop per sq mi:** 2.8.

Costilla County (cont'd)

Pop 2005: 3,424. **State rank:** 56. **Pop change:** 2000-20005 -6.5%; 1990-2000 +14.8%. **Pop 2000:** 3,663 (White 28.2%; Black or African American 0.8%; Hispanic or Latino 67.6%; Asian 1%; Other 37.3%, including 2.5% American Indian/Alaska Native). **Foreign born:** 6.9%. **Median age:** 42.1.

Income 2000: per capita $10,748; median household $19,531; **Pop below poverty level:** 26.8%. *Personal per capita income 2000-2003: $17,755-$20,158.

Unemployment 2004: 10.1%. **Change from 2000:** +0.7%. **Median travel time to work:** 23.3 minutes. **Working outside county of residence:** 28.2%.

Cities with pop over 10,000: None.

CROWLEY COUNTY
631 Main St Suite 102   **Ph:** 719-267-4643
Ordway, CO 81063   **Fax:** 719-267-4608
crowleycounty.net

In southeastern CO, east of Pueblo; organized May 29, 1911 from Otero County. **Name Origin:** For John H. Crowley (1849-?), state senator from Otero County when Crowley County was formed.

Area (sq mi): 800.33 (land 788.99; water 11.34). **Pop per sq mi:** 6.8.

Pop 2005: 5,401. **State rank:** 49. **Pop change:** 2000-20005 -2.1%; 1990-2000 +39.8%. **Pop 2000:** 5,518 (White 66.5%; Black or African American 7%; Hispanic or Latino 22.5%; Asian 0.8%; Other 9.2%, including 2.6% American Indian/Alaska Native). **Foreign born:** 1.1%. **Median age:** 36.6.

Income 2000: per capita $12,836; median household $26,803; **Pop below poverty level:** 18.5%. *Personal per capita income 2000-2003: $15,344-$15,646.

Unemployment 2004: 8.5%. **Change from 2000:** +4%. **Median travel time to work:** 22.2 minutes. **Working outside county of residence:** 38.7%.

Cities with pop over 10,000: None.

CUSTER COUNTY
205 S 6th St   **Ph:** 719-783-2441
Westcliffe, CO 81252   **Fax:** 719-783-2885
www.custercountygov.com

In south-central CO, southwest of Pueblo; organized Mar 9, 1877 from Fremont County. **Name Origin:** For Gen. George Armstrong Custer (1839-76), U.S. soldier and Indian fighter.

Area (sq mi): 739.9 (land 738.89; water 1.02). **Pop per sq mi:** 5.2.

Pop 2005: 3,860. **State rank:** 55. **Pop change:** 2000-20005 +10.2%; 1990-2000 +81.9%. **Pop 2000:** 3,503 (White 94.2%; Black or African American 0.4%; Hispanic or Latino 2.5%; Asian 0.3%; Other 3.4%, including 1.1% American Indian/Alaska Native). **Foreign born:** 1.7%. **Median age:** 44.9.

Income 2000: per capita $19,817; median household $34,731; **Pop below poverty level:** 13.3%. *Personal per capita income 2000-2003: $20,892-$24,381.

Unemployment 2004: 5%. **Change from 2000:** +1.5%. **Median travel time to work:** 26.4 minutes. **Working outside county of residence:** 27.2%.

Cities with pop over 10,000: None.

DELTA COUNTY
501 Palmer St Suite 211   **Ph:** 970-874-2150
Delta, CO 81416   **Fax:** 970-874-2161
www.deltacounty.com

In west-central CO, southeast of Grand Junction; organized Feb 11, 1883 from Gunnison County. **Name Origin:** For the city, named for its location on the delta of the Uncompahgre River.

Area (sq mi): 1148.52 (land 1142.11; water 6.42). **Pop per sq mi:** 26.2.

Pop 2005: 29,947. **State rank:** 18. **Pop change:** 2000-20005 +7.6%; 1990-2000 +32.7%. **Pop 2000:** 27,834 (White 86%; Black or African American 0.5%; Hispanic or Latino 11.4%; Asian 0.3%; Other 6.9%). **Foreign born:** 4.2%. **Median age:** 42.3.

Income 2000: per capita $17,152; median household $32,785; **Pop below poverty level:** 12.1%. *Personal per capita income 2000-2003: $20,881-$21,518.

Unemployment 2004: 5.2%. **Change from 2000:** +1.1%. **Median travel time to work:** 23.5 minutes. **Working outside county of residence:** 21.4%.

Cities with pop over 10,000: None.

DENVER CITY & COUNTY
201 W Colfax Ave 1st Fl   **Ph:** 720-865-8400
Denver, CO 80202
www.denvergov.org

In north-central CO; organized Mar 18, 1901 from Adams County. The city and county are coterminous. **Name Origin:** For Gen. James William Denver (1817-92), CA legislator, commissioner of Indian affairs, and governor of KS Territory (1857-58).

Area (sq mi): 154.94 (land 153.35; water 1.59). **Pop per sq mi:** 3638.2.

Pop 2005: 557,917. **State rank:** 2. **Pop change:** 2000-20005 +0.6%; 1990-2000 +18.6%. **Pop 2000:** 554,636 (White 51.9%; Black or African American 11.1%; Hispanic or Latino 31.7%; Asian 2.8%; Other 20.7%, including 1.3% American Indian/Alaska Native). **Foreign born:** 17.4%. **Median age:** 33.1.

Income 2000: per capita $24,101; median household $39,500; **Pop below poverty level:** 14.3%. *Personal per capita income 2000-2003: $39,152-$43,117.

Unemployment 2004: 6.7%. **Change from 2000:** +2.2%. **Median travel time to work:** 24.5 minutes. **Working outside county of residence:** 36.6%.

Cities with pop over 10,000: None.

DOLORES COUNTY
PO Box 608   **Ph:** 970-677-2383
Dove Creek, CO 81324   **Fax:** 970-677-2815
www.dolorescounty.org

On southwestern border of CO, south of Grand Junction; organized Feb 19, 1881 from Ouray County. **Name Origin:** For the Dolores River, which runs through it; from Spanish *Rio de Nuestra Senora de los Dolores*, ' River of Our Lay of Sorrows.'

Source: Personal per capita income data are from the Bureau of Economic Analysis; per capita income data are from the Bureau of the Census. See Introduction for explanation of differences.

Dolores County (cont'd)

Area (sq mi): 1068.09 (land 1066.97; water 1.13). **Pop per sq mi:** 1.7.

Pop 2005: 1,827. **State rank:** 59. **Pop change:** 2000-20005 -0.9%; 1990-2000 +22.6%. **Pop 2000:** 1,844 (White 92.8%; Black or African American 0.1%; Hispanic or Latino 3.9%; Asian 0.4%; Other 4.4%, including 2% American Indian/Alaska Native). **Foreign born:** 0.9%. **Median age:** 42.4.

Income 2000: per capita $17,106; median household $32,196; **Pop below poverty level:** 13.1%. *Personal per capita income 2000-2003:** $20,180-$24,384.

Unemployment 2004: 6.9%. **Change from 2000:** -0.2%. **Median travel time to work:** 25.6 minutes. **Working outside county of residence:** 43.3%.

Cities with pop over 10,000: None.

DOUGLAS COUNTY
100 3rd St　　　　　　　　**Ph:** 303-660-7401
Castle Rock, CO 80104　　　**Fax:** 303-688-1293
www.douglas.co.us

In central CO, between Denver and Colorado Springs; original county, organized Nov 1, 1861 (prior to statehood). **Name Origin:** For Stephen Arnold Douglas (1813-61), U.S. orator and statesman.

Area (sq mi): 842.75 (land 840.11; water 2.64). **Pop per sq mi:** 296.9.

Pop 2005: 249,416. **State rank:** 8. **Pop change:** 2000-20005 +41.9%; 1990-2000 +191%. **Pop 2000:** 175,766 (White 89.7%; Black or African American 1%; Hispanic or Latino 5.1%; Asian 2.5%; Other 3.8%). **Foreign born:** 5.2%. **Median age:** 33.7.

Income 2000: per capita $34,848; median household $82,929; **Pop below poverty level:** 2.1%. *Personal per capita income 2000-2003:** $43,471 $38,900.

Unemployment 2004: 4.2%. **Change from 2000:** +1.4%. **Median travel time to work:** 29.3 minutes. **Working outside county of residence:** 68.6%.

Cities with pop over 10,000: Parker (36,962); Castle Rock ⚏ (32,709).

EAGLE COUNTY
PO Box 850　　　　　　　　**Ph:** 970-328-8612
Eagle, CO 81631　　　　　　**Fax:** 970-328-8716
www.eaglecounty.us

In west-central CO, west of Denver; organized Feb 11, 1883, from Summit County. **Name Origin:** For the Eagle River, which flows through the county; the river was named for the bird.

Area (sq mi): 1691.8 (land 1687.88; water 3.93). **Pop per sq mi:** 28.2.

Pop 2005: 47,530. **State rank:** 14. **Pop change:** 2000-20005 +14.1%; 1990-2000 +90%. **Pop 2000:** 41,659 (White 74.2%; Black or African American 0.3%; Hispanic or Latino 23.2%; Asian 0.8%; Other 13.5%). **Foreign born:** 18.2%. **Median age:** 31.2.

Income 2000: per capita $32,011; median household $62,682; **Pop below poverty level:** 7.8%. *Personal per capita income 2000-2003:** $37,769-$38,252.

Unemployment 2004: 4.6%. **Change from 2000:** +1.8%. **Median travel time to work:** 21.3 minutes. **Working outside county of residence:** 15.2%.

Cities with pop over 10,000: None.

EL PASO COUNTY
200 S Cascade Ave　　　　　**Ph:** 719-520-6200
Colorado Springs, CO 80903　**Fax:** 719-520-6212
www.elpasoco.com

In central CO, south of Denver; original county, organized Nov 1, 1861 (prior to statehood). **Name Origin:** Spanish 'the pass' [through the mountains], referring to Ute Pass, west of Colorado Springs.

Area (sq mi): 2129.56 (land 2126.45; water 3.11). **Pop per sq mi:** 266.

Pop 2005: 565,582. **State rank:** 1. **Pop change:** 2000-20005 +9.4%; 1990-2000 +30.2%. **Pop 2000:** 516,929 (White 76.2%; Black or African American 6.5%; Hispanic or Latino 11.3%; Asian 2.5%; Other 9.7%). **Foreign born:** 6.4%. **Median age:** 33.

Income 2000: per capita $22,005; median household $46,844; **Pop below poverty level:** 8%. *Personal per capita income 2000-2003:** $29,603-$30,811.

Unemployment 2004: 5.7%. **Change from 2000:** +1.3%. **Median travel time to work:** 22.3 minutes. **Working outside county of residence:** 4.8%.

Cities with pop over 10,000: Colorado Springs ⚏ (369,363); Fountain (15,663).

ELBERT COUNTY
PO Box 597　　　　　　　　**Ph:** 303-621-3132
Kiowa, CO 80117　　　　　　**Fax:** 303-621-3166
www.elbertcolorado.com

In east-central CO, southeast of Denver; organized Feb 2, 1874, from Douglas and Greenwood counties (prior to statehood), the latter of which was organized in 1874 and abolished in 1878 by being divided between Bent and Elbert counties. **Name Origin:** For Samuel H. Elbert (1833-1907), CO territorial governor (1873-74) and chief justice of CO Supreme Court (1880-83).

Area (sq mi): 1850.89 (land 1850.78; water 0.11). **Pop per sq mi:** 12.3.

Pop 2005: 22,788. **State rank:** 22. **Pop change:** 2000-20005 +14.7%; 1990-2000 +106%. **Pop 2000:** 19,872 (White 93.2%; Black or African American 0.6%; Hispanic or Latino 3.9%; Asian 0.4%; Other 3.8%). **Foreign born:** 1.9%. **Median age:** 37.2.

Income 2000: per capita $24,960; median household $62,480; **Pop below poverty level:** 4%. *Personal per capita income 2000-2003:** $31,124-$30,522.

Unemployment 2004: 4.6%. **Change from 2000:** +1.8%. **Median travel time to work:** 41.1 minutes. **Working outside county of residence:** 71.6%.

Cities with pop over 10,000: None.

FREMONT COUNTY
136 Justice Ctr Rd Rm 103　**Ph:** 719-269-0100
Canon City, CO 81212　　　**Fax:** 719-269-0134
www.fremontco.com

In central CO, southwest of Colorado Springs; original county,

Fremont County (cont'd)

organized Nov 1, 1861 (prior to statehood). **Name Origin:** For John Charles Fremont (1813-90), soldier and explorer who led five expeditions to the West, U.S. senator from CA (1850-51), and governor of the AZ Territory (1878-81).

Area (sq mi): 1533.95 (land 1532.93; water 1.02). **Pop per sq mi:** 31.2.

Pop 2005: 47,766. **State rank:** 13. **Pop change:** 2000-20005 +3.5%; 1990-2000 +43%. **Pop 2000:** 46,145 (White 81.1%; Black or African American 5.3%; Hispanic or Latino 10.3%; Asian 0.5%; Other 4.6%, including 1.5% American Indian/Alaska Native). **Foreign born:** 1.5%. **Median age:** 38.8.

Income 2000: per capita $17,420; median household $34,150; **Pop below poverty level:** 11.7%. ***Personal per capita income 2000-2003:** $18,727-$19,084.

Unemployment 2004: 6.8%. **Change from 2000:** +2.9%. **Median travel time to work:** 23.9 minutes. **Working outside county of residence:** 20.6%.

Cities with pop over 10,000: Canon City ⛪ (15,813).

GARFIELD COUNTY

109 8th St Suite 200   **Ph:** 970-945-2377
Glenwood Springs, CO 81601   **Fax:** 970-947-1078
www.garfield-county.com

On central-western border of CO, north of Grand Junction; organized Feb 10, 1883 from Summit County. **Name Origin:** For James Abram Garfield (1831-81), twentieth U.S. president.

Area (sq mi): 2955.76 (land 2947.06; water 8.7). **Pop per sq mi:** 16.9.

Pop 2005: 49,810. **State rank:** 12. **Pop change:** 2000-20005 +13.7%; 1990-2000 +46.1%. **Pop 2000:** 43,791 (White 81%; Black or African American 0.4%; Hispanic or Latino 16.7%; Asian 0.4%; Other 9.1%). **Foreign born:** 10.4%. **Median age:** 34.2.

Income 2000: per capita $21,341; median household $47,016; **Pop below poverty level:** 7.5%. ***Personal per capita income 2000-2003:** $28,056-$27,127.

Unemployment 2004: 4.4%. **Change from 2000:** +1.9%. **Median travel time to work:** 30.6 minutes. **Working outside county of residence:** 26.4%.

Cities with pop over 10,000: None.

GILPIN COUNTY

203 Eureka St   **Ph:** 303-582-5321
Central City, CO 80427   **Fax:** 303-582-3086
www.co.gilpin.co.us

In central CO, west of Denver; original county; organized Nov 1, 1861 (prior to statehood). **Name Origin:** For Col. William Gilpin (1822-94), first territorial governor of CO (1861-62).

Area (sq mi): 150.25 (land 149.87; water 0.39). **Pop per sq mi:** 32.9.

Pop 2005: 4,932. **State rank:** 50. **Pop change:** 2000-20005 +3.7%; 1990-2000 +55%. **Pop 2000:** 4,757 (White 92%; Black or African American 0.5%; Hispanic or Latino 4.2%; Asian 0.7%; Other 4.4%). **Foreign born:** 3.4%. **Median age:** 38.3.

Income 2000: per capita $26,148; median household $51,942; **Pop below poverty level:** 4%. ***Personal per capita income 2000-2003:** $34,222-$36,180.

Unemployment 2004: 5.4%. **Change from 2000:** +2.3%. **Median travel time to work:** 34.7 minutes. **Working outside county of residence:** 59.3%.

Cities with pop over 10,000: None.

GRAND COUNTY

308 Byers Ave PO Box 120   **Ph:** 970-725-3347
Hot Sulphur Springs, CO 80451   **Fax:** 970-725-0100
co.grand.co.us

In north-central CO, west of Boulder; organized Feb 2, 1874 (prior to statehood) from Summit County. **Name Origin:** For Grand Lake and the Grand River; the latter was renamed the Colorado.

Area (sq mi): 1869.6 (land 1846.67; water 22.93). **Pop per sq mi:** 7.2.

Pop 2005: 13,211. **State rank:** 35. **Pop change:** 2000-20005 +6.2%; 1990-2000 +56.2%. **Pop 2000:** 12,442 (White 93%; Black or African American 0.5%; Hispanic or Latino 4.4%; Asian 0.7%; Other 3.6%). **Foreign born:** 3.4%. **Median age:** 36.9.

Income 2000: per capita $25,198; median household $47,759; **Pop below poverty level:** 7.3%. ***Personal per capita income 2000-2003:** $27,639-$30,639.

Unemployment 2004: 4.3%. **Change from 2000:** +1.2%. **Median travel time to work:** 22.7 minutes. **Working outside county of residence:** 12.2%.

Cities with pop over 10,000: None.

GUNNISON COUNTY

221 N Wisconsin St Suite C   **Ph:** 970-641-1516
Gunnison, CO 81230   **Fax:** 970-641-7956
www.co.gunnison.co.us

In west-central CO, west of Colorado Springs; organized Mar 9, 1877, from Lake County. **Name Origin:** For John William Gunnison (1812-53), killed by Indians while surveying for a proposed railroad.

Area (sq mi): 3259.75 (land 3238.81; water 20.93). **Pop per sq mi:** 4.4.

Pop 2005: 14,226. **State rank:** 32. **Pop change:** 2000-20005 +1.9%; 1990-2000 +35.9%. **Pop 2000:** 13,956 (White 92.3%; Black or African American 0.5%; Hispanic or Latino 5%; Asian 0.5%; Other 3.8%). **Foreign born:** 2.9%. **Median age:** 30.4.

Income 2000: per capita $21,407; median household $36,916; **Pop below poverty level:** 15%. ***Personal per capita income 2000-2003:** $22,468-$26,581.

Unemployment 2004: 4.2%. **Change from 2000:** -0.6%. **Median travel time to work:** 15.9 minutes. **Working outside county of residence:** 4.4%.

Cities with pop over 10,000: None.

HINSDALE COUNTY

PO Box 277   **Ph:** 970-944-2225
Lake City, CO 81235   **Fax:** 970-944-2630
www.hinsdalecountycolorado.us

In southwest CO, northeast of Durango; organized Feb 10, 1874,

---

Source: Personal per capita income data are from the Bureau of Economic Analysis; per capita income data are from the Bureau of the Census. See Introduction for explanation of differences.

Hinsdale County (cont'd)

from Conejos and Summit counties (prior to statehood). **Name Origin:** For George A. Hinsdale, a former lieutenant governor of the state.

Area (sq mi): 1123.14 (land 1117.68; water 5.46). **Pop per sq mi:** 0.7.

Pop 2005: 765. **State rank:** 63. **Pop change:** 2000-20005 -3.2%; 1990-2000 +69.2%. **Pop 2000:** 790 (White 96.6%; Black or African American 0%; Hispanic or Latino 1.5%; Asian 0.3%; Other 2.4%, including 1.5% American Indian/Alaska Native). **Foreign born:** 2%. **Median age:** 43.9.

Income 2000: per capita $22,360; median household $37,279; **Pop below poverty level:** 7.2%. ***Personal per capita income 2000-2003:** $23,811-$25,210.

Unemployment 2004: 2.8%. **Change from 2000:** +0.1%. **Median travel time to work:** 16 minutes. **Working outside county of residence:** 14.5%.

Cities with pop over 10,000: None.

HUERFANO COUNTY

401 Main St Suite 201   **Ph:** 719-738-2370
Walsenburg, CO 81089   **Fax:** 719-738-3996
www.huerfanococc.com

In south-central CO, south of Pueblo; original county, organized Nov 1, 1861 (prior to statehood). **Name Origin:** For the Huerfano River, Spanish 'orphan,' referring to an isolated butte in the river.

Area (sq mi): 1593.24 (land 1590.87; water 2.38). **Pop per sq mi:** 4.9.

Pop 2005: 7,771. **State rank:** 41. **Pop change:** 2000-20005 -1.2%; 1990-2000 +30.8%. **Pop 2000:** 7,862 (White 58.4%; Black or African American 2.7%; Hispanic or Latino 35.1%; Asian 0.4%; Other 15.9%, including 2.7% American Indian/Alaska Native). **Foreign born:** 1.6%. **Median age:** 41.7.

Income 2000: per capita $15,242; median household $25,775; **Pop below poverty level:** 18%. ***Personal per capita income 2000-2003:** $16,733-$18,067.

Unemployment 2004: 8.2%. **Change from 2000:** +2.5%. **Median travel time to work:** 24.7 minutes. **Working outside county of residence:** 15.9%.

Cities with pop over 10,000: None.

JACKSON COUNTY

404 4th St   **Ph:** 970-723-4660
Walden, CO 80480   **Fax:** 970-723-4706

On central northern border of CO, west of Ft. Collins; organized May 5, 1909 from Larimer County. **Name Origin:** For Andrew Jackson (1767-1845), seventh U.S. president.

Area (sq mi): 1620.95 (land 1613.21; water 7.74). **Pop per sq mi:** 0.9.

Pop 2005: 1,448. **State rank:** 60. **Pop change:** 2000-20005 -8.2%; 1990-2000 -1.7%. **Pop 2000:** 1,577 (White 92.1%; Black or African American 0.3%; Hispanic or Latino 6.5%; Asian 0.1%; Other 3.6%). **Foreign born:** 1.9%. **Median age:** 40.5.

Income 2000: per capita $17,826; median household $31,821; **Pop below poverty level:** 14%. ***Personal per capita income 2000-2003:** $19,941-$21,292.

Unemployment 2004: 4.1%. **Change from 2000:** -0.5%. **Median travel time to work:** 14.4 minutes. **Working outside county of residence:** 7%.

Cities with pop over 10,000: None.

JEFFERSON COUNTY

100 Jefferson County Pkwy   **Ph:** 303-271-8106
Golden, CO 80419   **Fax:** 303-271-8197
www.jeffco.us

In central CO, west of Denver; original county, organized Nov 1, 1861 (prior to statehood). A portion of the county was used to create Broomfield County on November 15, 2001. **Name Origin:** From Jefferson Territory, the extra-legal government that preceded CO Territory. Named in honor of Thomas Jefferson (1743-1826), U.S. patriot and statesman; third U.S. president.

Area (sq mi): 778.06 (land 772.09; water 5.97). **Pop per sq mi:** 682.3.

Pop 2005: 526,801. **State rank:** 4. **Pop change:** 2000-20005 +0%; 1990-2000 +20.2%. **Pop 2000:** 527,056 (White 84.9%; Black or African American 0.9%; Hispanic or Latino 10%; Asian 2.3%; Other 6.3%). **Foreign born:** 5.4%. **Median age:** 36.8.

Income 2000: per capita $28,066; median household $57,339; **Pop below poverty level:** 5.2%. ***Personal per capita income 2000-2003:** $38,234-$39,069.

Unemployment 2004: 5.4%. **Change from 2000:** +2.4%. **Median travel time to work:** 27.4 minutes. **Working outside county of residence:** 52.1%.

Cities with pop over 10,000: 7 (see page 33 for cities).

KIOWA COUNTY

PO Box 37   **Ph:** 719-438-5421
Eads, CO 81036   **Fax:** 719-438-5327
www.kiowacountycolo.com

On southeastern border of CO, east of Pueblo; organized Apr 11, 1889, from Bent County. **Name Origin:** For the Indian tribe of Tanoan linguistic stock; name means 'principal people.'

Area (sq mi): 1785.76 (land 1770.99; water 14.76). **Pop per sq mi:** 0.8.

Pop 2005: 1,422. **State rank:** 61. **Pop change:** 2000-20005 -12.3%; 1990-2000 -3.9%. **Pop 2000:** 1,622 (White 94.3%; Black or African American 0.5%; Hispanic or Latino 3.1%; Asian 0%; Other 3.4%, including 1.1% American Indian/Alaska Native). **Foreign born:** 1.4%. **Median age:** 39.7.

Income 2000: per capita $16,382; median household $30,494; **Pop below poverty level:** 12.2%. ***Personal per capita income 2000-2003:** $34,665-$33,431.

Unemployment 2004: 5.8%. **Change from 2000:** +3.3%. **Median travel time to work:** 18.3 minutes. **Working outside county of residence:** 14.8%.

Cities with pop over 10,000: None.

KIT CARSON COUNTY

PO Box 249   **Ph:** 719-346-8638
Burlington, CO 80807   **Fax:** 719-346-7242
www.kitcarsoncounty.org

On central eastern border of CO; organized Apr 11, 1889 from Elbert County. **Name Origin:** For Christopher (Kit) Carson (1809-68), frontiersman, guide, and Indian agent.

Area (sq mi): 2161.56 (land 2160.87; water 0.69). **Pop per sq mi:** 3.5.

Pop 2005: 7,642. **State rank:** 43. **Pop change:** 2000-20005 -4.6%; 1990-2000 +12.2%. **Pop 2000:** 8,011 (White 83.4%; Black or African American 1.7%; Hispanic or Latino 13.7%; Asian 0.3%; Other 10.6%). **Foreign born:** 5.8%. **Median age:** 37.4.

Income 2000: per capita $16,964; median household $33,152; **Pop below poverty level:** 12.1%. ***Personal per capita income 2000-2003:** $23,846-$26,637.

Unemployment 2004: 4%. **Change from 2000:** +2%. **Median travel time to work:** 14.6 minutes. **Working outside county of residence:** 6.6%.

Cities with pop over 10,000: None.

LA PLATA COUNTY

1060 E 2nd Ave Suite 134   **Ph:** 970-382-6280
Durango, CO 81301   **Fax:** 970-382-6285
www.co.laplata.co.us

On southwestern border of CO; organized Feb 10, 1874, from Conejos and Lake counties (prior to statehood). **Name Origin:** For La Plata River, which runs through the county; from Spanish 'silver,' for the mines in the area.

Area (sq mi): 1699.93 (land 1692.15; water 7.78). **Pop per sq mi:** 28.

Pop 2005: 47,452. **State rank:** 15. **Pop change:** 2000-20005 +8%; 1990-2000 +36.1%. **Pop 2000:** 43,941 (White 82.3%; Black or African American 0.3%; Hispanic or Latino 10.4%; Asian 0.4%; Other 12.1%, including 5.8% American Indian/Alaska Native). **Foreign born:** 2.7%. **Median age:** 35.6.

Income 2000: per capita $21,534; median household $40,159; **Pop below poverty level:** 11.7%. ***Personal per capita income 2000-2003:** $27,408-$29,807.

Unemployment 2004: 4%. **Change from 2000:** +0.3%. **Median travel time to work:** 20.7 minutes. **Working outside county of residence:** 5.6%.

Cities with pop over 10,000: Durango ⛪ (15,020).

LAKE COUNTY

PO Box 917   **Ph:** 719-486-1410
Leadville, CO 80461   **Fax:** 719-486-3972

In central CO, southwest of Denver; original county, organized Nov 1, 1861 (prior to statehood); name changed from Carbonate Feb 10, 1879. **Name Origin:** For the Twin Lakes, a major feature of the county.

Area (sq mi): 383.9 (land 376.89; water 7.01). **Pop per sq mi:** 20.5.

Pop 2005: 7,738. **State rank:** 42. **Pop change:** 2000-20005 -0.9%; 1990-2000 +30%. **Pop 2000:** 7,812 (White 61.6%; Black or African American 0.2%; Hispanic or Latino 36.1%; Asian 0.3%; Other 22%,

including 1.3% American Indian/Alaska Native). **Foreign born:** 15.6%. **Median age:** 30.5.

Income 2000: per capita $18,524; median household $37,691; **Pop below poverty level:** 12.9%. ***Personal per capita income 2000-2003:** $20,599-$20,699.

Unemployment 2004: 6.2%. **Change from 2000:** +1.5%. **Median travel time to work:** 35.8 minutes. **Working outside county of residence:** 52.1%.

Cities with pop over 10,000: None.

LARIMER COUNTY

PO Box 1280   **Ph:** 970-498-7860
Fort Collins, CO 80522   **Fax:** 970-498-7830
www.larimer.org

On central northern border of CO; original county, organized Nov 1, 1861 (prior to statehood). **Name Origin:** For Gen. William Larimer, a founder of Denver and prominent early settler.

Area (sq mi): 2633.86 (land 2601.3; water 32.56). **Pop per sq mi:** 104.5.

Pop 2005: 271,927. **State rank:** 7. **Pop change:** 2000-20005 +8.1%; 1990-2000 +35.1%. **Pop 2000:** 251,494 (White 87.5%; Black or African American 0.7%; Hispanic or Latino 8.3%; Asian 1.6%; Other 6.4%). **Foreign born:** 4.3%. **Median age:** 33.2.

Income 2000: per capita $23,689; median household $48,655; **Pop below poverty level:** 9.2%. ***Personal per capita income 2000-2003:** $30,274-$32,037.

Unemployment 2004: 4.6%. **Change from 2000:** +1.1%. **Median travel time to work:** 21.4 minutes. **Working outside county of residence:** 15.8%.

Cities with pop over 10,000: Fort Collins ⛪ (126,967); Loveland (57,784); Windsor (13,832).

LAS ANIMAS COUNTY

PO Box 115   **Ph:** 719-846-3314
Trinidad, CO 81082   **Fax:** 719-845-2573
www.trinidadco.com/Main/CityCounty.asp

On southeastern border of CO, south of Pueblo; organized Feb 9, 1866 from Huerfano County (prior to statehood). **Name Origin:** From part of the original name of the Purgatoire River, which runs through the county, *El Rio de las Animas Perdidas en Purgatorio*, Spanish 'river of souls lost in Purgatory,' in memory of people killed at the river by Indians c. 1595 who died without absolution. Shortened to El Purgatorio; then to its present form by French trappers; also known by Americanized *Picketwire*.

Area (sq mi): 4775.42 (land 4772.63; water 2.79). **Pop per sq mi:** 3.2.

Pop 2005: 15,446. **State rank:** 29. **Pop change:** 2000-20005 +1.6%; 1990-2000 +10.5%. **Pop 2000:** 15,207 (White 55.2%; Black or African American 0.4%; Hispanic or Latino 41.5%; Asian 0.4%; Other 16.5%, including 2.5% American Indian/Alaska Native). **Foreign born:** 2.3%. **Median age:** 40.9.

Income 2000: per capita $16,829; median household $28,273; **Pop below poverty level:** 17.3%. ***Personal per capita income 2000-2003:** $19,880-$21,865.

*Source: Personal per capita income data are from the Bureau of Economic Analysis; per capita income data are from the Bureau of the Census. See Introduction for explanation of differences.

114

Las Animas County (cont'd)

Unemployment 2004: 5.4%. Change from 2000: +1%. Median travel time to work: 20.6 minutes. Working outside county of residence: 9.8%.

Cities with pop over 10,000: None.

LINCOLN COUNTY

PO Box 67
Hugo, CO 80821
www.lincolncountyco.us.

Ph: 719-743-2444
Fax: 719-743-2524

In east-central CO, east of Colorado Springs; organized Apr 11, 1889 , from Bent and Elbert counties. **Name Origin:** For Abraham Lincoln (1809-65), sixteenth U.S. president.

Area (sq mi): 2586.39 (land 2586.09; water 0.3). Pop per sq mi: 2.2.

Pop 2005: 5,618. State rank: 47. Pop change: 2000-20005 -7.7%; 1990-2000 +34.4%. Pop 2000: 6,087 (White 84.2%; Black or African American 5%; Hispanic or Latino 8.5%; Asian 0.6%; Other 8.2%). Foreign born: 1.8%. Median age: 37.8.

Income 2000: per capita $15,510; median household $31,914; Pop below poverty level: 11.7%. *Personal per capita income 2000-2003: $17,378-$18,864.

Unemployment 2004: 4.5%. Change from 2000: +2.9%. Median travel time to work: 19.2 minutes. Working outside county of residence: 10.2%.

Cities with pop over 10,000: None.

LOGAN COUNTY

315 Main St
Sterling, CO 80751
www.loganco.gov

Ph: 970-522-0888
Fax: 970-522-4018

On northeastern border of CO, northeast of Greeley; organized Feb 25, 1887 from Weld County. **Name Origin:** For Gen. John Alexander Logan (1826-86), officer in the Mexican-American War and Civil War; U.S. senator from IL (1871-77; 1879-86).

Area (sq mi): 1844.86 (land 1838.52; water 6.33). Pop per sq mi: 11.3.

Pop 2005: 20,719. State rank: 25. Pop change: 2000-20005 +1%; 1990-2000 +16.7%. Pop 2000: 20,504 (White 84.4%; Black or African American 2%; Hispanic or Latino 11.9%; Asian 0.4%; Other 5.9%). Foreign born: 3.1%. Median age: 36.5.

Income 2000: per capita $16,721; median household $32,724; Pop below poverty level: 12.2%. *Personal per capita income 2000-2003: $24,290-$25,038.

Unemployment 2004: 4.4%. Change from 2000: +1.1%. Median travel time to work: 15.2 minutes. Working outside county of residence: 9.2%.

Cities with pop over 10,000: Sterling 🏛 (12,730).

MESA COUNTY

PO Box 20000-5007
Grand Junction, CO 81502
www.co.mesa.co.us

Ph: 970-244-1800
Fax: 970-256-1588

On central western border of CO; organized Feb 14, 1883 from

Gunnison County. **Name Origin:** Spanish 'table,' for the high, flat tablelands with sharply eroded sides common to the area.

Area (sq mi): 3341.11 (land 3327.75; water 13.36). Pop per sq mi: 39.

Pop 2005: 129,872. State rank: 11. Pop change: 2000-20005 +11.7%; 1990-2000 +24.8%. Pop 2000: 116,255 (White 87%; Black or African American 0.5%; Hispanic or Latino 10%; Asian 0.5%; Other 6.7%). Foreign born: 3%. Median age: 38.1.

Income 2000: per capita $18,715; median household $35,864; Pop below poverty level: 10.2%. *Personal per capita income 2000-2003: $24,921-$26,035.

Unemployment 2004: 5.1%. Change from 2000: +1.1%. Median travel time to work: 18.4 minutes. Working outside county of residence: 4.3%.

Cities with pop over 10,000: Grand Junction 🏛 (44,693).

MINERAL COUNTY

PO Box 70
Creede, CO 81130
www.creede.com

Ph: 719-658-2440
Fax: 719-658-2931

In south-central CO, northeast of Durango; organized Mar 27, 1893, from Saguache and Rio Grande counties. **Name Origin:** For the rich mineral resources of the area.

Area (sq mi): 877.7 (land 875.72; water 1.99). Pop per sq mi: 1.1.

Pop 2005: 932. State rank: 62. Pop change: 2000-20005 +12.2%; 1990-2000 +48.9%. Pop 2000: 831 (White 95.4%; Black or African American 0%; Hispanic or Latino 2%; Asian 0%; Other 3.1%). Foreign born: 0.7%. Median age: 45.

Income 2000: per capita $24,475; median household $34,844; Pop below poverty level: 10.2%. *Personal per capita income 2000-2003: $22,100-$24,863.

Unemployment 2004: 3.9%. Change from 2000: +1.5%. Median travel time to work: 15.9 minutes. Working outside county of residence: 17.2%.

Cities with pop over 10,000: None.

MOFFAT COUNTY

221 W Victory Way
Craig, CO 81625
www.co.moffat.co.us

Ph: 970-824-9104
Fax: 970-824-4975

On northwestern border of CO; organized Feb 27, 1911, from Routt County. **Name Origin:** For David Halliday Moffat (1839-1911), president of the Rio Grande Railroad (1884-91).

Area (sq mi): 4750.94 (land 4742.25; water 8.69). Pop per sq mi: 2.8.

Pop 2005: 13,417. State rank: 34. Pop change: 2000-20005 +1.8%; 1990-2000 +16.1%. Pop 2000: 13,184 (White 88.2%; Black or African American 0.2%; Hispanic or Latino 9.5%; Asian 0.3%; Other 5.9%). Foreign born: 4.1%. Median age: 35.4.

Income 2000: per capita $18,540; median household $41,528; Pop below poverty level: 8.3%. *Personal per capita income 2000-2003: $22,358-$24,850.

Moffat County (cont'd)

Unemployment 2004: 5.4%. **Change from 2000:** +0.5%. **Median travel time to work:** 23.4 minutes. **Working outside county of residence:** 27.6%.

Cities with pop over 10,000: None.

MONTEZUMA COUNTY

109 W Main St Rm 302   **Ph:** 970-565-8317
Cortez, CO 81321   **Fax:** 970-565-3420
www.co.montezuma.co.us

On southwesternmost border of CO; organized Apr 16, 1889, from La Plata County. The corners of four states, CO, AZ, NM, and UT, meet at this point, the only place in the U.S. where this occurs. **Name Origin:** For Montezuma (1479?-1520), Aztec Indian emperor of Mexico who was conquered by Hernan Cortez (1485-1547).

Area (sq mi): 2039.97 (land 2036.63; water 3.34). **Pop per sq mi:** 12.2.

Pop 2005: 24,778. **State rank:** 21. **Pop change:** 2000-20005 +4%; 1990-2000 +27.6%. **Pop 2000:** 23,830 (White 77.5%; Black or African American 0.1%; Hispanic or Latino 9.5%; Asian 0.2%; Other 18%, including 11.2% American Indian/Alaska Native). **Foreign born:** 2.2%. **Median age:** 38.

Income 2000: per capita $17,003; median household $32,083; **Pop below poverty level:** 16.4%. ***Personal per capita income 2000-2003:** $22,490-$23,752.

Unemployment 2004: 5.7%. **Change from 2000:** +0.7%. **Median travel time to work:** 21.8 minutes. **Working outside county of residence:** 14.5%.

Cities with pop over 10,000: None.

MONTROSE COUNTY

161 S Townsend   **Ph:** 970-249-3362
Montrose, CO 81401   **Fax:** 970-249-7761
www.co.montrose.co.us

On central western border of CO, south of Grand Junction; organized Feb 11, 1883 from Gunnison County. **Name Origin:** For the city, named for *The Legend of Montrose*, by Sir Walter Scott (1771-1832), for the similarity of the surrounding country; also possibly an allusion to Montrose, Scotland.

Area (sq mi): 2242.57 (land 2240.61; water 1.96). **Pop per sq mi:** 16.7.

Pop 2005: 37,482. **State rank:** 17. **Pop change:** 2000-20005 +12.1%; 1990-2000 +36.9%. **Pop 2000:** 33,432 (White 82.4%; Black or African American 0.3%; Hispanic or Latino 14.9%; Asian 0.4%; Other 9.3%, including 1% American Indian/Alaska Native). **Foreign born:** 5.6%. **Median age:** 38.8.

Income 2000: per capita $17,158; median household $35,234; **Pop below poverty level:** 12.6%. ***Personal per capita income 2000-2003:** $22,145-$24,658.

Unemployment 2004: 5.1%. **Change from 2000:** +0.2%. **Median travel time to work:** 21.5 minutes. **Working outside county of residence:** 14.7%.

Cities with pop over 10,000: Montrose 🏛 (14,771).

MORGAN COUNTY

PO Box 1399   **Ph:** 970-542-3521
Fort Morgan, CO 80701   **Fax:** 970-542-3520
www.co.morgan.co.us

In northeastern CO, east of Boulder; organized Feb 19, 1889, from Weld County. **Name Origin:** For Fort Morgan, named for Col. Christopher Anthony Morgan (1825?-66), an army officer and inspector general of the Department of Missouri.

Area (sq mi): 1293.87 (land 1285.36; water 8.51). **Pop per sq mi:** 21.8.

Pop 2005: 27,995. **State rank:** 19. **Pop change:** 2000-20005 +3%; 1990-2000 +23.8%. **Pop 2000:** 27,171 (White 67%; Black or African American 0.3%; Hispanic or Latino 31.2%; Asian 0.2%; Other 19.9%). **Foreign born:** 14.6%. **Median age:** 33.5.

Income 2000: per capita $15,492; median household $34,568; **Pop below poverty level:** 12.4%. ***Personal per capita income 2000-2003:** $21,789-$23,319.

Unemployment 2004: 4.9%. **Change from 2000:** +2.2%. **Median travel time to work:** 18.5 minutes. **Working outside county of residence:** 10.7%.

Cities with pop over 10,000: Fort Morgan 🏛 (10,992).

OTERO COUNTY

PO Box 511   **Ph:** 719-383-3020
La Junta, CO 81050   **Fax:** 719-383-3026

In southeastern CO, southeast of Pueblo; organized Mar 25, 1889, from Bent County. **Name Origin:** For Miguel Antonio Otero (1859-1944), NM territorial governor (1896-1906).

Area (sq mi): 1269.74 (land 1262.86; water 6.89). **Pop per sq mi:** 15.4.

Pop 2005: 19,495. **State rank:** 26. **Pop change:** 2000-20005 -4%; 1990-2000 +0.6%. **Pop 2000:** 20,311 (White 59.2%; Black or African American 0.8%; Hispanic or Latino 37.6%; Asian 0.7%; Other 19.6%, including 1.4% American Indian/Alaska Native). **Foreign born:** 4.9%. **Median age:** 37.7.

Income 2000: per capita $15,113; median household $29,738; **Pop below poverty level:** 18.8%. ***Personal per capita income 2000-2003:** $22,097-$23,348.

Unemployment 2004: 6.5%. **Change from 2000:** +1.5%. **Median travel time to work:** 18 minutes. **Working outside county of residence:** 16%.

Cities with pop over 10,000: None.

OURAY COUNTY

PO Box C   **Ph:** 970-325-4961
Ouray, CO 81427   **Fax:** 970-325-0452
www.co.ouray.co.us

In southwestern CO, north of Durango; organized as Uncompahgre County Jan 18, 1877, from San Juan County; name changed Mar 2, 1883. **Name Origin:** For the Ute Indian chief Ouray (1820-80), possibly 'the arrow.' He was chief of Uncompahgre Utes and signed a treaty with U.S. in 1863 as 'U-ray' or 'Arrow'; signed one in 1868 'U-re,' and later that year 'Ouray.'

Area (sq mi): 542.21 (land 540.47; water 1.74). **Pop per sq mi:** 7.9.

Source: Personal per capita income data are from the Bureau of Economic Analysis; per capita income data are from the Bureau of the Census. See Introduction for explanation of differences.

Ouray County (cont'd)

Pop 2005: 4,260. **State rank:** 53. **Pop change:** 2000-20005 +13.8%; 1990-2000 +63.1%. **Pop 2000:** 3,742 (White 93.2%; Black or African American 0.1%; Hispanic or Latino 4.1%; Asian 0.3%; Other 3.2%). **Foreign born:** 3.2%. **Median age:** 43.4.

Income 2000: per capita $24,335; median household $42,019; **Pop below poverty level:** 7.2%. *Personal per capita income 2000-2003: $26,424-$31,364.

Unemployment 2004: 4.4%. **Change from 2000:** +1.2%. **Median travel time to work:** 23.6 minutes. **Working outside county of residence:** 27.8%.

Cities with pop over 10,000: None.

PARK COUNTY

PO Box 220
Fairplay, CO 80440
www.co.park.co.us

Ph: 719-836-4227
Fax: 719-836-4348

In central CO, west of Colorado Springs; original county, organized Nov 1, 1861 (prior to statehood). **Name Origin:** For the large mountain valley known as the 'South Park.'

Area (sq mi): 2210.69 (land 2200.69; water 10). **Pop per sq mi:** 7.7.

Pop 2005: 16,949. **State rank:** 28. **Pop change:** 2000-20005 +16.7%; 1990-2000 +102.4%. **Pop 2000:** 14,523 (White 92.5%; Black or African American 0.5%; Hispanic or Latino 4.3%; Asian 0.4%; Other 3.9%). **Foreign born:** 2.2%. **Median age:** 40.

Income 2000: per capita $25,019; median household $51,899; **Pop below poverty level:** 5.6%. *Personal per capita income 2000-2003: $29,418-$27,424.

Unemployment 2004: 5.2%. **Change from 2000:** 2.1%. **Median travel time to work:** 44.8 minutes. **Working outside county of residence:** 64%.

Cities with pop over 10,000: None.

PHILLIPS COUNTY

221 S Interocean Ave
Holyoke, CO 80734
www.phillipscountyco.org

Ph: 970-854-3131
Fax: 970-854-4745

On northeastern border of CO; organized Mar 27, 1889, from Logan County. **Name Origin:** For R. O. Phillips, an offical in the Lincoln Land Company, which organized many of the towns in eastern CO.

Area (sq mi): 687.74 (land 687.62; water 0.12). **Pop per sq mi:** 6.7.

Pop 2005: 4,586. **State rank:** 52. **Pop change:** 2000-20005 +2.4%; 1990-2000 +6.9%. **Pop 2000:** 4,480 (White 86.3%; Black or African American 0.2%; Hispanic or Latino 11.8%; Asian 0.4%; Other 6.3%). **Foreign born:** 8.1%. **Median age:** 39.8.

Income 2000: per capita $16,394; median household $32,177; **Pop below poverty level:** 11.6%. *Personal per capita income 2000-2003: $24,675-$24,910.

Unemployment 2004: 3.7%. **Change from 2000:** +1.4%. **Median travel time to work:** 15.3 minutes. **Working outside county of residence:** 11.3%.

Cities with pop over 10,000: None.

PITKIN COUNTY

530 E Main St Suite 101
Aspen, CO 81611
county.aspenpitkin.com

Ph: 970-920-5180
Fax: 970-920-5196

In west-central CO, west of Leadville; organized Feb 23, 1881, from Gunnison County. **Name Origin:** For Frederick Walker Pitkin (1837-86), governor of CO (1879-83).

Area (sq mi): 973.23 (land 970.42; water 2.81). **Pop per sq mi:** 15.4.

Pop 2005: 14,914. **State rank:** 31. **Pop change:** 2000-20005 +0.3%; 1990-2000 +17.5%. **Pop 2000:** 14,872 (White 90.6%; Black or African American 0.5%; Hispanic or Latino 6.5%; Asian 1.1%; Other 4%). **Foreign born:** 10.9%. **Median age:** 38.4.

Income 2000: per capita $40,811; median household $59,375; **Pop below poverty level:** 6.2%. *Personal per capita income 2000-2003: $66,605-$68,504.

Unemployment 2004: 5.2%. **Change from 2000:** +1.9%. **Median travel time to work:** 17.3 minutes. **Working outside county of residence:** 8.9%.

Cities with pop over 10,000: None.

PROWERS COUNTY

301 S Main St Suite 210
Lamar, CO 81052
www.prowerscounty.net

Ph: 719-336-8011
Fax: 719-336-5306

On southeastern border of CO; organized Apr 11, 1889, from Bent County. **Name Origin:** For John Wesley Prowers (1839-84), a member of CO General Assembly who married Amanche, daughter of a Cheyenne chief, and worked with Indian agent Col. William Bent.

Area (sq mi): 1644.35 (land 1640.38; water 3.97). **Pop per sq mi:** 8.5.

Pop 2005: 13,892. **State rank:** 33. **Pop change:** 2000-20005 -4.1%; 1990-2000 +8.5%. **Pop 2000:** 14,483 (White 65.1%; Black or African American 0.3%; Hispanic or Latino 32.9%; Asian 0.4%; Other 20.7%, including 1.2% American Indian/Alaska Native). **Foreign born:** 10.6%. **Median age:** 32.4.

Income 2000: per capita $14,150; median household $29,935; **Pop below poverty level:** 19.5%. *Personal per capita income 2000-2003: $22,109-$24,406.

Unemployment 2004: 4.8%. **Change from 2000:** +1.7%. **Median travel time to work:** 15.9 minutes. **Working outside county of residence:** 6.6%.

Cities with pop over 10,000: None.

PUEBLO COUNTY

215 W 10th St
Pueblo, CO 81003
www.co.pueblo.co.us

Ph: 719-583-6000
Fax: 719-583-4894

In south-central CO; original county, organized Nov 1, 1861, (prior to statehood). **Name Origin:** For the city, from Spanish 'town'.

Area (sq mi): 2397.73 (land 2388.69; water 9.04). **Pop per sq mi:** 63.3.

Pop 2005: 151,322. **State rank:** 10. **Pop change:** 2000-20005 +7%; 1990-2000 +15%. **Pop 2000:** 141,472 (White 57.7%; Black or African American 1.9%; Hispanic or Latino 38%; Asian 0.7%; Other

Pueblo County (cont'd)

18%, including 1.6% American Indian/Alaska Native). **Foreign born:** 3%. **Median age:** 36.7.

Income 2000: per capita $17,163; median household $32,775; **Pop below poverty level:** 14.9%. ***Personal per capita income 2000-2003:** $22,992-$24,830.

Unemployment 2004: 7.2%. **Change from 2000:** +2.1%. **Median travel time to work:** 20.7 minutes. **Working outside county of residence:** 10.3%.

Cities with pop over 10,000: Pueblo 🏛 (103,621).

RIO BLANCO COUNTY

PO box 1067   **Ph:** 970-878-5068
Meeker, CO 81641   **Fax:** 970-878-3587
www.co.rio-blanco.co.us

On northwestern border of CO, north of Grand Junction; organized Mar 25, 1889, from Garfield County. **Name Origin:** Spanish name for the White River, which flows through the county; possibly referring to the white caps of the rapids; probably translated from the Ute name.

Area (sq mi): 3222.91 (land 3220.97; water 1.94). **Pop per sq mi:** 1.9.

Pop 2005: 5,973. **State rank:** 46. **Pop change:** 2000-20005 -0.2%; 1990-2000 +0.2%. **Pop 2000:** 5,986 (White 92.6%; Black or African American 0.2%; Hispanic or Latino 4.9%; Asian 0.3%; Other 4.5%). **Foreign born:** 3.2%. **Median age:** 37.5.

Income 2000: per capita $17,344; median household $37,711; **Pop below poverty level:** 9.6%. ***Personal per capita income 2000-2003:** $26,605-$27,048.

Unemployment 2004: 4.2%. **Change from 2000:** +1.8%. **Median travel time to work:** 17.4 minutes. **Working outside county of residence:** 10.9%.

Cities with pop over 10,000: None.

RIO GRANDE COUNTY

965 6th St PO Box 160   **Ph:** 719-657-3334
Del Norte, CO 81132   **Fax:** 719-657-2621
www.riograndecounty.org

In south-central CO; organized Feb 10, 1874, from Conejos County. **Name Origin:** For the Rio Grande, which flows through the county; shortened from Spanish *Rio Grande del Norte* 'Great River of the North.'

Area (sq mi): 912.14 (land 911.6; water 0.53). **Pop per sq mi:** 13.4.

Pop 2005: 12,227. **State rank:** 36. **Pop change:** 2000-20005 -1.5%; 1990-2000 +15.3%. **Pop 2000:** 12,413 (White 56.6%; Black or African American 0.3%; Hispanic or Latino 41.7%; Asian 0.2%; Other 25.5%, including 1.3% American Indian/Alaska Native). **Foreign born:** 6%. **Median age:** 37.3.

Income 2000: per capita $15,650; median household $31,836; **Pop below poverty level:** 14.5%. ***Personal per capita income 2000-2003:** $22,272-$25,580.

Unemployment 2004: 5.8%. **Change from 2000:** -2.1%. **Median travel time to work:** 19.3 minutes. **Working outside county of residence:** 21.7%.

Cities with pop over 10,000: None.

ROUTT COUNTY

136 6th St   **Ph:** 970-879-0108
Steamboat Springs, CO 80477   **Fax:** 970-879-3992
www.co.routt.co.us

On central northern border of CO; organized Jan 29, 1877, from Grand County. **Name Origin:** For John Long Routt (1826-1907), last territorial governor (1876-79) and first CO state governor (1891-93).

Area (sq mi): 2368.02 (land 2361.59; water 6.43). **Pop per sq mi:** 9.

Pop 2005: 21,313. **State rank:** 24. **Pop change:** 2000-20005 +8.2%; 1990-2000 +39.8%. **Pop 2000:** 19,690 (White 94.8%; Black or African American 0.1%; Hispanic or Latino 3.2%; Asian 0.4%; Other 2.6%). **Foreign born:** 4.1%. **Median age:** 35.

Income 2000: per capita $28,792; median household $53,612; **Pop below poverty level:** 6.1%. ***Personal per capita income 2000-2003:** $32,746-$36,900.

Unemployment 2004: 4.2%. **Change from 2000:** +2%. **Median travel time to work:** 18.5 minutes. **Working outside county of residence:** 4.7%.

Cities with pop over 10,000: None.

SAGUACHE COUNTY

501 4th St PO Box 176   **Ph:** 719-655-2512
Saguache, CO 81149   **Fax:** 719-655-2730
saguache.org

In south-central CO, west of Pueblo; organized Dec 29, 1866, from Costilla County (prior to statehood). **Name Origin:** For Saguache Creek, which flows through the county; from a Ute Indian word meaning 'blue earth,' or 'water at the blue earth.'

Area (sq mi): 3170.25 (land 3168.44; water 1.82). **Pop per sq mi:** 2.2.

Pop 2005: 7,031. **State rank:** 45. **Pop change:** 2000-20005 +18.8%; 1990-2000 +28.1%. **Pop 2000:** 5,917 (White 51.6%; Black or African American 0.1%; Hispanic or Latino 45.3%; Asian 0.5%; Other 28.2%, including 2.1% American Indian/Alaska Native). **Foreign born:** 14.5%. **Median age:** 36.9.

Income 2000: per capita $13,121; median household $25,495; **Pop below poverty level:** 22.6%. ***Personal per capita income 2000-2003:** $15,260-$18,063.

Unemployment 2004: 7%. **Change from 2000:** -1.3%. **Median travel time to work:** 19.8 minutes. **Working outside county of residence:** 32.2%.

Cities with pop over 10,000: None.

SAN JUAN COUNTY

PO Box 466   **Ph:** 970-387-5671
Silverton, CO 81433   **Fax:** 970-387-5671

In southwestern CO, north of Durango; organized 1876, from La Plata County. **Name Origin:** Spanish Saint John (the Baptist). Name was given by early Spanish explorers to the river, the mountain range, and then the whole region.

Area (sq mi): 388.29 (land 387.42; water 0.86). **Pop per sq mi:** 1.5.

---

*Source: Personal per capita income data are from the Bureau of Economic Analysis; per capita income data are from the Bureau of the Census. See Introduction for explanation of differences.

San Juan County (cont'd)

Pop 2005: 577. **State rank:** 64. **Pop change:** 2000-20005 +3.4%; 1990-2000 -25.1%. **Pop 2000:** 558 (White 91.2%; Black or African American 0%; Hispanic or Latino 7.3%; Asian 0.2%; Other 2.7%). **Foreign born:** 2.5%. **Median age:** 43.7.

Income 2000: per capita $17,584; median household $30,764; **Pop below poverty level:** 20.9%. ***Personal per capita income 2000-2003:** $24,475-$28,461.

Unemployment 2004: 5.9%. **Change from 2000:** -10.3%. **Median travel time to work:** 16.1 minutes. **Working outside county of residence:** 25%.

Cities with pop over 10,000: None.

SAN MIGUEL COUNTY

PO Box 548   **Ph:** 970-728-3954
Telluride, CO 81435   **Fax:** 970-728-4808
www.sanmiguelcounty.org

On southwestern border of CO; organized Nov 1, 1861, from Ouray County (prior to statehood). **Name Origin:** For the river, which flows through the county; Spanish for Saint Michael (the Archangel).

Area (sq mi): 1288.49 (land 1286.5; water 1.98). **Pop per sq mi:** 5.6.

Pop 2005: 7,213. **State rank:** 44. **Pop change:** 2000-20005 +9.4%; 1990-2000 +80.5%. **Pop 2000:** 6,594 (White 90.4%; Black or African American 0.3%; Hispanic or Latino 6.7%; Asian 0.7%; Other 5.4%). **Foreign born:** 7.3%. **Median age:** 34.2.

Income 2000: per capita $35,329; median household $48,514; **Pop below poverty level:** 10.4%. ***Personal per capita income 2000-2003:** $34,193-$33,234.

Unemployment 2004: 5.2%. **Change from 2000:** +1.4%. **Median travel time to work:** 18.8 minutes. **Working outside county of residence:** 4.7%.

Cities with pop over 10,000: None.

SEDGWICK COUNTY

PO Box 50   **Ph:** 970-474-3346
Julesburg, CO 80737   **Fax:** 970-474-0954

On northeasternmost border of CO; organized Apr 9, 1889, from Logan County. **Name Origin:** For Fort Sedgwick, named for Maj. Gen. John Sedgwick (1813-64), Indian fighter and Union officer in the Civil War.

Area (sq mi): 549.6 (land 548.24; water 1.36). **Pop per sq mi:** 4.6.

Pop 2005: 2,529. **State rank:** 57. **Pop change:** 2000-20005 -7.9%; 1990-2000 +2.1%. **Pop 2000:** 2,747 (White 86.5%; Black or African American 0.5%; Hispanic or Latino 11.4%; Asian 0.8%; Other 8.2%). **Foreign born:** 2.7%. **Median age:** 43.2.

Income 2000: per capita $16,125; median household $28,278; **Pop below poverty level:** 10%. ***Personal per capita income 2000-2003:** $23,625-$24,323.

Unemployment 2004: 3.5%. **Change from 2000:** +0.5%. **Median travel time to work:** 15.7 minutes. **Working outside county of residence:** 19.2%.

Cities with pop over 10,000: None.

SUMMIT COUNTY

PO Box 1538   **Ph:** 970-453-2561
Breckenridge, CO 80424   **Fax:** 970-453-3540
www.co.summit.co.us

In central CO west of Denver; original county, organized 1861, (prior to statehood). **Name Origin:** For the mountainous terrain of the county; part of its southeastern border follows the Continental Divide.

Area (sq mi): 619.25 (land 608.16; water 11.09). **Pop per sq mi:** 40.9.

Pop 2005: 24,892. **State rank:** 20. **Pop change:** 2000-20005 +5.7%; 1990-2000 +82.8%. **Pop 2000:** 23,548 (White 86.7%; Black or African American 0.7%; Hispanic or Latino 9.8%; Asian 0.9%; Other 6.7%). **Foreign born:** 11.6%. **Median age:** 30.8.

Income 2000: per capita $28,676; median household $56,587; **Pop below poverty level:** 9%. ***Personal per capita income 2000-2003:** $34,627-$32,382.

Unemployment 2004: 4.7%. **Change from 2000:** +2%. **Median travel time to work:** 16.9 minutes. **Working outside county of residence:** 5.7%.

Cities with pop over 10,000: None.

TELLER COUNTY

PO Box 959   **Ph:** 719-689-2988
Cripple Creek, CO 80813   **Fax:** 719-686-7900
www.co.teller.co.us

In central CO, west of Colorado Springs; organized Mar 23, 1899, from El Paso and Fremont Counties. **Name Origin:** For Henry Moore Teller (1830-1914), U.S. senator from CO (1876-82; 1885-1909), and U.S. secretary of the interior (1882-85).

Area (sq mi): 558.96 (land 557.06; water 1.89). **Pop per sq mi:** 39.3.

Pop 2005: 21,918. **State rank:** 23. **Pop change:** 2000-20005 +6.6%; 1990-2000 +64.9%. **Pop 2000:** 20,555 (White 92.9%; Black or African American 0.5%; Hispanic or Latino 3.5%; Asian 0.6%; Other 4%, including 1% American Indian/Alaska Native). **Foreign born:** 1.8%. **Median age:** 39.4.

Income 2000: per capita $23,412; median household $50,165; **Pop below poverty level:** 5.4%. ***Personal per capita income 2000-2003:** $29,832-$28,858.

Unemployment 2004: 5.4%. **Change from 2000:** +2.5%. **Median travel time to work:** 30.1 minutes. **Working outside county of residence:** 43.9%.

Cities with pop over 10,000: None.

WASHINGTON COUNTY

150 Ash Ave   **Ph:** 970-345-2701
Akron, CO 80720   **Fax:** 970-345-2702

In northeastern CO, east of Denver; organized Feb 9, 1887, from Weld County. **Name Origin:** For George Washington (1732-1799), American patriot and first U.S. president.

Area (sq mi): 2524.12 (land 2520.98; water 3.13). **Pop per sq mi:** 1.8.

Pop 2005: 4,633. **State rank:** 51. **Pop change:** 2000-20005 -5.9%; 1990-2000 +2.4%. **Pop 2000:** 4,926 (White 92.7%; Black or African

Washington County (cont'd)

American 0%; Hispanic or Latino 6.3%; Asian 0.1%; Other 3.5%). **Foreign born:** 2.5%. **Median age:** 40.2.

Income 2000: per capita $17,788; median household $32,431; **Pop below poverty level:** 11.4%. ***Personal per capita income 2000-2003:** $22,100-$24,832.

Unemployment 2004: 4%. **Change from 2000:** +1.6%. **Median travel time to work:** 21 minutes. **Working outside county of residence:** 26.6%.

Cities with pop over 10,000: None.

WELD COUNTY

PO Box 758
Greeley, CO 80632
www.co.weld.co.us

Ph: 970-336-7204
Fax: 970-352-0242

On central northern border of CO, east of Fort Collins; original county, organized Nov 1, 1861, (prior to statehood). A portion of the county was used to create Broomfield County on November 15, 2001. **Name Origin:** For Lewis Ledyard Weld, first Secretary of the CO Territory.

Area (sq mi): 4021.56 (land 3992.45; water 29.11). **Pop per sq mi:** 57.3.

Pop 2005: 228,943. **State rank:** 9. **Pop change:** 2000-20005 +26.5%; 1990-2000 +37.3%. **Pop 2000:** 180,936 (White 70%; Black or African American 0.6%; Hispanic or Latino 27%; Asian 0.8%; Other 17%). **Foreign born:** 9.3%. **Median age:** 30.9.

Income 2000: per capita $18,957; median household $42,321; **Pop below poverty level:** 12.5%. ***Personal per capita income 2000-2003:** $25,038-$24,279.

Unemployment 2004: 5.4%. **Change from 2000:** +1.3%. **Median travel time to work:** 23.7 minutes. **Working outside county of residence:** 33%.

Cities with pop over 10,000: Greeley ⛫ (84,815); Evans (16,314).

YUMA COUNTY

310 Ash St Suite F
Wray, CO 80758
www.yumacounty.net

Ph: 970-332-5809
Fax: 970-332-5919

On eastern border of CO, east of Denver; organized Mar 15, 1889, from Washington County. **Name Origin:** For the Yuma Indian tribe. The name, given to the tribe by the Spanish, may mean 'children of the sun' or may come from the Spanish *umo* 'smoke.'

Area (sq mi): 2369.1 (land 2365.79; water 3.3). **Pop per sq mi:** 4.1.

Pop 2005: 9,789. **State rank:** 38. **Pop change:** 2000-20005 -0.5%; 1990-2000 +9.9%. **Pop 2000:** 9,841 (White 86.1%; Black or African American 0.1%; Hispanic or Latino 12.9%; Asian 0.1%; Other 5.6%). **Foreign born:** 7.9%. **Median age:** 37.3.

Income 2000: per capita $16,005; median household $33,169; **Pop below poverty level:** 12.9%. ***Personal per capita income 2000-2003:** $23,742-$26,707.

Unemployment 2004: 3.5%. **Change from 2000:** +1.4%. **Median travel time to work:** 15.4 minutes. **Working outside county of residence:** 6.3%.

Cities with pop over 10,000: None.

---

*Source: Personal per capita income data are from the Bureau of Economic Analysis; per capita income data are from the Bureau of the Census. See Introduction for explanation of differences.

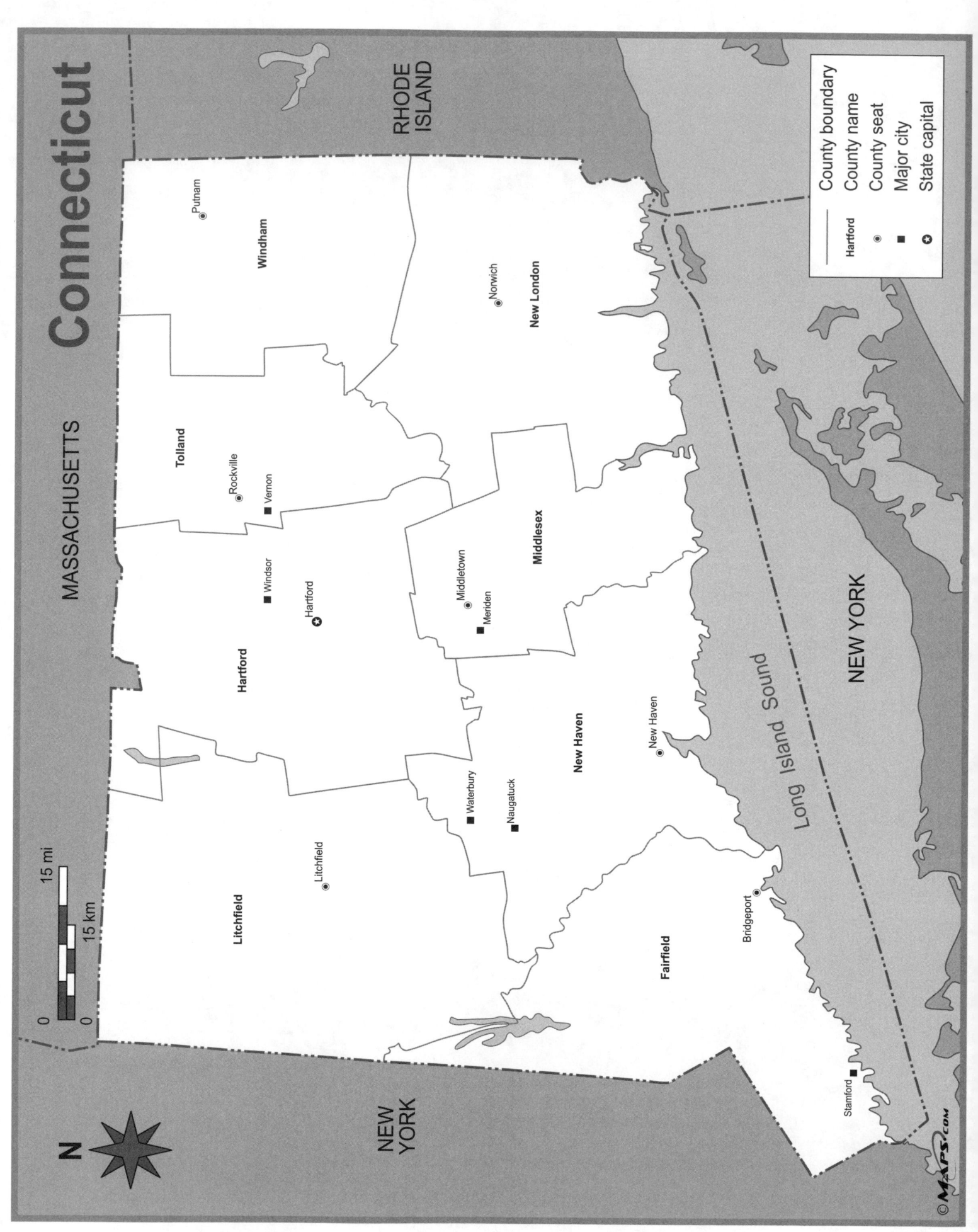

Connecticut

CONNECTICUT STATE INFORMATION
www.ct.gov   **Ph:** 860-622-2200

Area (sq mi): 5543.33 (land 4844.8; water 698.53). **Pop per sq mi:** 724.5.

Pop 2005: 3,510,297. **Pop change:** 2000-20005 +3.1%; 1990-2000 +3.6%. **Pop 2000:** 3,405,565 (White 77.5%; Black or African American 9.1%; Hispanic or Latino 9.4%; Asian 2.4%; Other 6.8%). **Foreign born:** 10.9%. **Median age:** 37.4.

Income 2000: per capita $28,766; median household $53,935; **Pop below poverty level:** 7.9%. ***Personal per capita income 2000-2003:** $41,489-$42,972.

Unemployment 2004: 4.9%. **Change from 2000:** +2.6%. **Median travel time to work:** 24.4 minutes. **Working outside county of residence:** 24.8%.

FAIRFIELD COUNTY
1061 Main St   **Ph:** 203-579-6527
Bridgeport, CT 06604   **Fax:** 203-382-8406

In southwestern CT, bordered on the west by NY and on the south by Long Island Sound. Original county, organized May 10, 1666. **Name Origin:** Descriptive of the area.

Area (sq mi): 836.96 (land 625.8; water 211.15). **Pop per sq mi:** 1442.6.

Pop 2005: 902,775. **State rank:** 1. **Pop change:** 2000-20005 +2.3%; 1990-2000 +6.6%. **Pop 2000:** 882,567 (White 73.1%; Black or African American 10%; Hispanic or Latino 11.9%; Asian 3.3%; Other 7.4%). **Foreign born:** 16.9%. **Median age:** 37.3.

Income 2000: per capita $38,350; median household $65,249; **Pop below poverty level:** 6.9%. ***Personal per capita income 2000-2003:** $58,986-$60,803.

Unemployment 2004: 4.4%. **Change from 2000:** +1.3%. **Median travel time to work:** 28 minutes. **Working outside county of residence:** 20%.

Cities with pop over 10,000: Bridgeport 🏛 (139,910); Stamford (120,226); Norwalk (84,401); Danbury (78,263); Shelton (39,321).

HARTFORD COUNTY
550 Main St   **Ph:** 860-543-8580
Hartford, CT 06103   **Fax:** 860-722-8041
www.hartford.gov

In north-central CT. Original county, organized May 10, 1666. **Name Origin:** For Hertford or Hertfordshire, England. Spelling reflects English pronunciation.

Area (sq mi): 750.57 (land 735.44; water 15.13). **Pop per sq mi:** 1193.

Pop 2005: 877,393. **State rank:** 2. **Pop change:** 2000-20005 +2.4%; 1990-2000 +0.6%. **Pop 2000:** 857,183 (White 73%; Black or African American 11.7%; Hispanic or Latino 11.5%; Asian 2.4%; Other 8.9%). **Foreign born:** 11.7%. **Median age:** 37.7.

Income 2000: per capita $26,047; median household $50,756; **Pop below poverty level:** 9.3%. ***Personal per capita income 2000-2003:** $37,451-$38,805.

Unemployment 2004: 5.5%. **Change from 2000:** +2%. **Median travel time to work:** 21.9 minutes. **Working outside county of residence:** 13.1%.

Cities with pop over 10,000: Hartford 🏛 (124,848); New Britain (71,699); Bristol (61,005).

LITCHFIELD COUNTY
15 West St   **Ph:** 860-567-0885
Litchfield, CT 06759   **Fax:** 860-567-4779
www.litchfieldcty.com

In northwestern CT, bordered on the west by NY and on the north by MA; organized Oct 14, 1751 from Hartford and Fairfield counties. **Name Origin:** For the town in England, in Hampshire County.

Area (sq mi): 944.57 (land 919.92; water 24.65). **Pop per sq mi:** 206.6.

Pop 2005: 190,071. **State rank:** 5. **Pop change:** 2000-20005 +4.3%; 1990-2000 +4.7%. **Pop 2000:** 182,193 (White 94.5%; Black or African American 1.1%; Hispanic or Latino 2.1%; Asian 1.2%; Other 2%). **Foreign born:** 5.4%. **Median age:** 39.6.

Income 2000: per capita $28,408; median household $56,273; **Pop below poverty level:** 4.5%. ***Personal per capita income 2000-2003:** $38,042-$38,225.

Unemployment 2004: 4.6%. **Change from 2000:** +1.6%. **Median travel time to work:** 26.2 minutes. **Working outside county of residence:** 45.2%.

Cities with pop over 10,000: Torrington (35,930).

MIDDLESEX COUNTY
1 Court St   **Ph:** 860-343-6400
Middletown, CT 06457   **Fax:** 860-343-6423

In south-central CT, east of New Haven, with Long Island Sound to the south and the Connecticut River to the east; organized May 2, 1785 (prior to statehood) from Hartford, New London, and New Haven counties. **Name Origin:** For a former county in southeast England.

🏛 *County Seat*

123

Middlesex County (cont'd)

Area (sq mi): 439.07 (land 369.26; water 69.81). **Pop per sq mi:** 442.

Pop 2005: 163,214. **State rank:** 6. **Pop change:** 2000-20005 +5.3%; 1990-2000 +8.3%. **Pop 2000:** 155,071 (White 89.6%; Black or African American 4.4%; Hispanic or Latino 3%; Asian 1.6%; Other 2.8%). **Foreign born:** 6%. **Median age:** 38.6.

Income 2000: per capita $28,251; median household $59,175; **Pop below poverty level:** 4.6%. ***Personal per capita income 2000-2003:** $37,893-$38,712.

Unemployment 2004: 4.1%. **Change from 2000:** +1.4%. **Median travel time to work:** 24.5 minutes. **Working outside county of residence:** 48.4%.

Cities with pop over 10,000: Middletown 🏛 (47,157).

NEW HAVEN COUNTY
165 Church St   **Ph:** 203-946-8200
New Haven, CT 06510   **Fax:** 203-946-7683
www.cityofnewhaven.com

In south-central CT on Long Island Sound, south of Hartford. Original county, organized May 10, 1666. **Name Origin:** For the colonial settlement at New Haven.

Area (sq mi): 862.02 (land 605.64; water 256.38). **Pop per sq mi:** 1398.1.

Pop 2005: 846,766. **State rank:** 3. **Pop change:** 2000-20005 +2.8%; 1990-2000 +2.5%. **Pop 2000:** 824,008 (White 74.8%; Black or African American 11.3%; Hispanic or Latino 10.1%; Asian 2.3%; Other 6.9%). **Foreign born:** 9%. **Median age:** 37.

Income 2000: per capita $24,439; median household $48,834; **Pop below poverty level:** 9.5%. ***Personal per capita income 2000-2003:** $34,396-$36,127.

Unemployment 2004: 5.2%. **Change from 2000:** +1.5%. **Median travel time to work:** 23.2 minutes. **Working outside county of residence:** 25.2%.

Cities with pop over 10,000: 8 (see page 33 for cities).

NEW LONDON COUNTY
70 Huntington St   **Ph:** 860-443-5363
New London, CT 06320   **Fax:** 860-442-7703

In southeastern CT on Long Island Sound and east of the Connecticut River. Original county, organized May 10, 1666. **Name Origin:** For the city in England.

Area (sq mi): 771.66 (land 665.91; water 105.75). **Pop per sq mi:** 400.4.

Pop 2005: 266,618. **State rank:** 4. **Pop change:** 2000-20005 +2.9%; 1990-2000 +1.6%. **Pop 2000:** 259,088 (White 84.7%; Black or African American 5.3%; Hispanic or Latino 5.1%; Asian 2%; Other 5.9%, including 1% American Indian/Alaska Native). **Foreign born:** 5.4%. **Median age:** 37.

Income 2000: per capita $24,678; median household $50,646; **Pop below poverty level:** 6.4%. ***Personal per capita income 2000-2003:** $32,810-$35,147.

Unemployment 2004: 4.4%. **Change from 2000:** +1.6%. **Median travel time to work:** 22.2 minutes. **Working outside county of residence:** 17.2%.

Cities with pop over 10,000: Norwich 🏛 (36,645); New London 🏛 (26,319).

TOLLAND COUNTY
69 Brooklyn St   **Ph:** 860-896-4920
Rockville, CT 06066

In north-central CT, east of Hartford; organized Oct 17, 1785 (prior to statehood) from Windham County. **Name Origin:** For the town in western England, in Somerset County.

Area (sq mi): 417.01 (land 410.07; water 6.94). **Pop per sq mi:** 360.

Pop 2005: 147,634. **State rank:** 7. **Pop change:** 2000-20005 +8.3%; 1990-2000 +6%. **Pop 2000:** 136,364 (White 90.9%; Black or African American 2.7%; Hispanic or Latino 2.8%; Asian 2.3%; Other 2.7%). **Foreign born:** 5.9%. **Median age:** 35.7.

Income 2000: per capita $25,474; median household $59,044; **Pop below poverty level:** 5.6%. ***Personal per capita income 2000-2003:** $32,997-$33,441.

Unemployment 2004: 4%. **Change from 2000:** +1.7%. **Median travel time to work:** 25.4 minutes. **Working outside county of residence:** 62.5%.

Cities with pop over 10,000: None.

WINDHAM COUNTY
PO Box 191   **Ph:** 860-928-7749
Putnam, CT 06260   **Fax:** 860-928-7076

In northeastern CT, bordered on the east by RI and on the north by MA; organized May 12, 1726 from Hartford and New London counties. **Name Origin:** For Wymondham, Norfolk, England; spelling reflects pronunciation.

Area (sq mi): 521.47 (land 512.75; water 8.71). **Pop per sq mi:** 225.9.

Pop 2005: 115,826. **State rank:** 8. **Pop change:** 2000-20005 +6.2%; 1990-2000 +6.4%. **Pop 2000:** 109,091 (White 88.6%; Black or African American 1.9%; Hispanic or Latino 7.1%; Asian 0.8%; Other 6%). **Foreign born:** 4.3%. **Median age:** 36.3.

Income 2000: per capita $20,443; median household $45,115; **Pop below poverty level:** 8.5%. ***Personal per capita income 2000-2003:** $27,209-$28,759.

Unemployment 2004: 5.4%. **Change from 2000:** +1.7%. **Median travel time to work:** 25.7 minutes. **Working outside county of residence:** 43%.

Cities with pop over 10,000: None.

Source: Personal per capita income data are from the Bureau of Economic Analysis; per capita income data are from the Bureau of the Census. See Introduction for explanation of differences.

0 ____ 15 mi
0 ____ 15 km

N

PENNSYLVANIA

Wilmington ⊙

■ Newark

New Castle

NEW JERSEY

MARYLAND

⊛ Dover

Kent

Delaware Bay

Chesapeake Bay

Sussex

⊙ Georgetown

Atlantic Ocean

	County boundary
Kent	County name
⊙	County seat
■	Major city
✪	State capital

©MAPS.COM

Delaware

Delaware

DELAWARE STATE INFORMATION

www.delaware.gov   **Ph:** 302-739-4000

Area (sq mi): 2489.27 (land 1953.56; water 535.71). **Pop per sq mi:** 431.8.

Pop 2005: 843,524. **Pop change:** 2000-20005 +7.6%; 1990-2000 +17.6%. **Pop 2000:** 783,600 (White 72.5%; Black or African American 19.2%; Hispanic or Latino 4.8%; Asian 2.1%; Other 4%). **Foreign born:** 5.7%. **Median age:** 36.

Income 2000: per capita $23,305; median household $47,381; **Pop below poverty level:** 9.2%. *Personal per capita income 2000-2003: $30,869-$34,199.

Unemployment 2004: 4%. **Change from 2000:** +0.7%. **Median travel time to work:** 24 minutes. **Working outside county of residence:** 17.1%.

KENT COUNTY

555 Bay Rd   **Ph:** 302-744-2305
Dover, DE 19901   **Fax:** 302-736-2279
www.co.kent.de.us

In central DE; organized as Saint Jones County in 1680 from Horre Kill District, which was organized in 1664; name changed in 1682. **Name Origin:** For the county in England.

Area (sq mi): 800.12 (land 589.72; water 210.4). **Pop per sq mi:** 244.1.

Pop 2005: 143,968. **State rank:** 3. **Pop change:** 2000-20005 +13.6%; 1990-2000 +14.1%. **Pop 2000:** 126,697 (White 72.1%; Black or African American 20.7%; Hispanic or Latino 3.2%; Asian 1.7%; Other 4.1%). **Foreign born:** 4%. **Median age:** 34.4.

Income 2000: per capita $18,662; median household $40,950; **Pop below poverty level:** 10.7%. *Personal per capita income 2000-2003: $23,768-$26,438.

Unemployment 2004: 3.6%. **Change from 2000:** -0.1%. **Median travel time to work:** 22.7 minutes. **Working outside county of residence:** 20.7%.

Cities with pop over 10,000: Dover 🏛 (33,618).

NEW CASTLE COUNTY

87 Reads Way New Castle
Corporate Commons   **Ph:** 302-395-5555
New Castle, DE 19720   **Fax:** 302-395-5268
www.co.new-castle.de.us

In northern DE; original county, organized 1673. **Name Origin:**

Col. Richard Nicolls, in Oct. 1664, renamed the former Swedish-Dutch settlement of New Amstel to honor William Cavendish (1592-1676), Duke of Newcastle.

Area (sq mi): 493.51 (land 426.27; water 67.24). **Pop per sq mi:** 1226.9.

Pop 2005: 523,008. **State rank:** 1. **Pop change:** 2000-20005 +4.5%; 1990-2000 +13.2%. **Pop 2000:** 500,265 (White 70.7%; Black or African American 20.2%; Hispanic or Latino 5.3%; Asian 2.6%; Other 4%). **Foreign born:** 6.6%. **Median age:** 35.

Income 2000: per capita $25,413; median household $52,419; **Pop below poverty level:** 8.4%. *Personal per capita income 2000-2003: $34,750-$38,636.

Unemployment 2004: 4.4%. **Change from 2000:** +1%. **Median travel time to work:** 24.3 minutes. **Working outside county of residence:** 14.4%.

Cities with pop over 10,000: Wilmington 🏛 (72,784); Newark (29,821).

SUSSEX COUNTY

PO Box 589   **Ph:** 302-855-7743
Georgetown, DE 19947   **Fax:** 302-855 7749
www.sussexcounty.net

In southern DE; organized as Deale County in 1680 from Horre Kill District, which was organized in 1664; name changed in 1682. **Name Origin:** For the county in England.

Area (sq mi): 1195.65 (land 937.58; water 258.07). **Pop per sq mi:** 188.3.

Pop 2005: 176,548. **State rank:** 2. **Pop change:** 2000-20005 +12.7%; 1990-2000 +38.3%. **Pop 2000:** 156,638 (White 78.5%; Black or African American 14.9%; Hispanic or Latino 4.4%; Asian 0.7%; Other 4%). **Foreign born:** 4.5%. **Median age:** 41.1.

Income 2000: per capita $20,328; median household $39,208; **Pop below poverty level:** 10.5%. *Personal per capita income 2000-2003: $24,233-$26,832.

Unemployment 2004: 3.6%. **Change from 2000:** -0.3%. **Median travel time to work:** 24 minutes. **Working outside county of residence:** 23.6%.

Cities with pop over 10,000: None.

🏛 *County Seat*

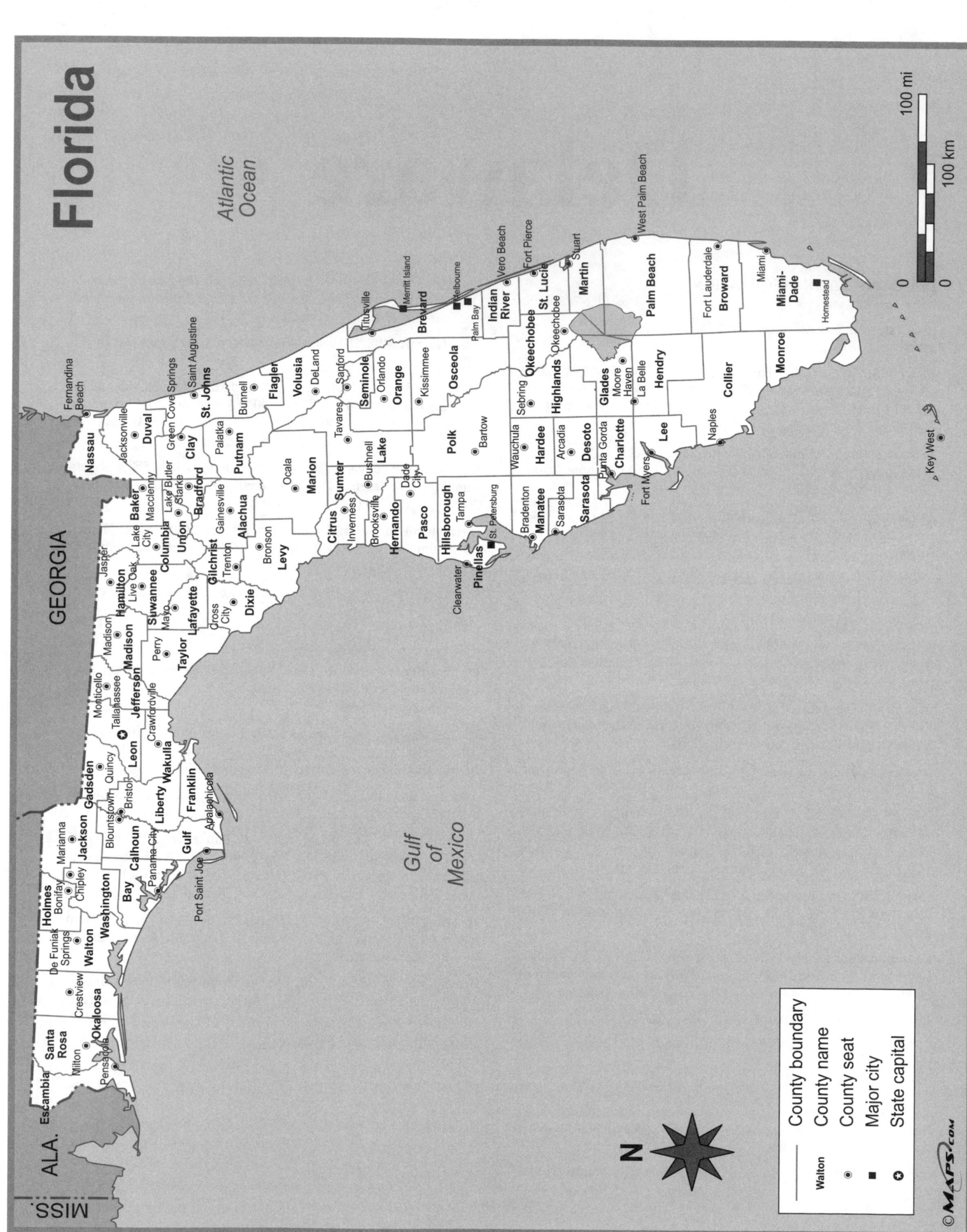

Florida

Florida

FLORIDA STATE INFORMATION

www.myflorida.com   **Ph:** 850-488-1234

Area (sq mi): 65,754.59 (land 53,926.82; water 11,827.77). **Pop per sq mi:** 329.9.

Pop 2005: 17,789,864. **Pop change:** 2000-20005 +11.3%; 1990-2000 +23.5%. **Pop 2000:** 15,982,378 (White 65.4%; Black or African American 14.6%; Hispanic or Latino 16.8%; Asian 1.7%; Other 5.8%). **Foreign born:** 16.7%. **Median age:** 38.7.

Income 2000: per capita $21,557; median household $38,819; **Pop below poverty level:** 12.5%. ***Personal per capita income 2000-2003:** $28,509-$30,098.

Unemployment 2004: 4.7%. **Change from 2000:** +0.9%. **Median travel time to work:** 26.2 minutes. **Working outside county of residence:** 18.1%.

ALACHUA COUNTY

12 SE 1st St   **Ph:** 352-374-5210
Gainesville, FL 32601   **Fax:** 352-338-7303
www.co.alachua.fl.us

In north-central FL, north of Ocala; organized Dec 29, 1824 (prior to statehood) from Duval and Saint Johns counties. **Name Origin:** For a Seminole Indian town settled by Creek Indians from Oconee, GA. Name derives from *luchuwa* 'jug,' descriptive of a chasm, probably the Devil's Millhopper, near Gainesville, FL.

Area (sq mi): 969.12 (land 874.25; water 94.88). **Pop per sq mi:** 256.1.

Pop 2005: 223,852. **State rank:** 23. **Pop change:** 2000-20005 +2.7%; 1990-2000 +20%. **Pop 2000:** 217,955 (White 69.7%; Black or African American 19.3%; Hispanic or Latino 5.7%; Asian 3.5%; Other 3.6%). **Foreign born:** 7.3%. **Median age:** 29.

Income 2000: per capita $18,465; median household $31,426; **Pop below poverty level:** 22.8%. ***Personal per capita income 2000-2003:** $24,010-$26,041.

Unemployment 2004: 3.4%. **Change from 2000:** +0.8%. **Median travel time to work:** 21.1 minutes. **Working outside county of residence:** 6.9%.

Cities with pop over 10,000: Gainesville ⛪ (108,856).

BAKER COUNTY

339 E Macclenny Ave   **Ph:** 904-259-8113
Macclenny, FL 32063   **Fax:** 904-259-4176
bakercountyfl.org

On northern border of FL, west of Jacksonville; organized Feb 8, 1861 from New River County. **Name Origin:** For James McNair Baker (1821-92), FL legislator and jurist, associate justice of the FL supreme court (1866).

Area (sq mi): 588.89 (land 585.21; water 3.67). **Pop per sq mi:** 42.

Pop 2005: 24,569. **State rank:** 52. **Pop change:** 2000-20005 +10.4%; 1990-2000 +20.4%. **Pop 2000:** 22,259 (White 82.6%; Black or African American 13.9%; Hispanic or Latino 1.9%; Asian 0.4%; Other 1.6%). **Foreign born:** 1.1%. **Median age:** 34.

Income 2000: per capita $15,164; median household $40,035; **Pop below poverty level:** 14.7%. ***Personal per capita income 2000-2003:** $19,256-$20,686.

Unemployment 2004: 4.4%. **Change from 2000:** -0.1%. **Median travel time to work:** 32.7 minutes. **Working outside county of residence:** 51.7%.

Cities with pop over 10,000: None.

BAY COUNTY

300 E 4th St   **Ph:** 850-763-9061
Panama City, FL 32401   **Fax:** 850-747-5188
www.co.bay.fl.us

On northern coast of the Gulf of Mexico; organized Apr 24, 1913 from Calhoun and Washington counties; name changed from New River County in 1861. **Name Origin:** For Saint Andrews Bay, in the southeastern part of the county.

Area (sq mi): 1033.27 (land 763.68; water 269.6). **Pop per sq mi:** 211.6.

Pop 2005: 161,558. **State rank:** 26. **Pop change:** 2000-20005 +9%; 1990-2000 +16.7%. **Pop 2000:** 148,217 (White 82.8%; Black or African American 10.6%; Hispanic or Latino 2.4%; Asian 1.7%; Other 3.5%). **Foreign born:** 3.6%. **Median age:** 37.4.

Income 2000: per capita $18,700; median household $36,092; **Pop below poverty level:** 13%. ***Personal per capita income 2000-2003:** $23,756-$26,120.

Unemployment 2004: 4.6%. **Change from 2000:** -1.4%. **Median travel time to work:** 21.6 minutes. **Working outside county of residence:** 5%.

Cities with pop over 10,000: Panama City ⛪ (37,079); Lynn Haven (14,663); Callaway (14,510); Panama City Beach (10,199).

BRADFORD COUNTY

PO Drawer B   **Ph:** 904-964-6280
Starke, FL 32091   **Fax:** 904-964-4454
www.bradford-co-fla.org

In north-central FL between Gainesville and Jacksonville; organized as New River County Dec 21, 1858; name changed Dec 6,

Bradford County (cont'd)

1861. **Name Origin:** For Capt. Richard Bradford (1839?-61), the first Florida officer killed in the Civil War.

Area (sq mi): 300.04 (land 293.13; water 6.91). **Pop per sq mi:** 95.9.

Pop 2005: 28,118. **State rank:** 51. **Pop change:** 2000-20005 +7.8%; 1990-2000 +15.9%. **Pop 2000:** 26,088 (White 75%; Black or African American 20.8%; Hispanic or Latino 2.4%; Asian 0.6%; Other 2.3%). **Foreign born:** 1.8%. **Median age:** 37.2.

Income 2000: per capita $14,226; median household $33,140; **Pop below poverty level:** 14.6%. *****Personal per capita income 2000-2003:** $18,550-$20,018.

Unemployment 2004: 4.3%. **Change from 2000:** +1.1%. **Median travel time to work:** 27.9 minutes. **Working outside county of residence:** 51.7%.

Cities with pop over 10,000: None.

BREVARD COUNTY

400 South St County Courthouse   **Ph:** 321-264-6942
Titusville, FL 32780   **Fax:** 321-633-2115
www.brevardcounty.us

On central east coast of FL, east of Orlando; organized as Saint Lucie County Mar 14, 1844 from Mosquito County; name changed Jan 6, 1855. **Name Origin:** For Theodore Washington Brevard (1804-77), FL state comptroller (1853-61).

Area (sq mi): 1556.95 (land 1018.19; water 538.76). **Pop per sq mi:** 521.8.

Pop 2005: 531,250. **State rank:** 10. **Pop change:** 2000-20005 +11.6%; 1990-2000 +19.4%. **Pop 2000:** 476,230 (White 83.7%; Black or African American 8.4%; Hispanic or Latino 4.6%; Asian 1.5%; Other 3.4%). **Foreign born:** 6.5%. **Median age:** 41.4.

Income 2000: per capita $21,484; median household $40,099; **Pop below poverty level:** 9.5%. *****Personal per capita income 2000-2003:** $26,925-$28,669.

Unemployment 2004: 4.4%. **Change from 2000:** +0.1%. **Median travel time to work:** 24.5 minutes. **Working outside county of residence:** 7.8%.

Cities with pop over 10,000: 7 (see page 33 for cities).

BROWARD COUNTY

115 S Andrews Ave Rm 421   **Ph:** 954-357-7000
Fort Lauderdale, FL 33301   **Fax:** 954-357-7295
www.co.broward.fl.us

On southeastern coast of FL, north of Miami; organized Apr 30, 1915 from Dade and Palm Beach counties. **Name Origin:** For Napoleon Bonaparte Broward (1857-1910), FL governor (1905-09).

Area (sq mi): 1319.63 (land 1205.4; water 114.24). **Pop per sq mi:** 1474.7.

Pop 2005: 1,777,638. **State rank:** 2. **Pop change:** 2000-20005 +9.5%; 1990-2000 +29.3%. **Pop 2000:** 1,623,018 (White 58%; Black or African American 20.5%; Hispanic or Latino 16.7%; Asian 2.3%; Other 6.7%). **Foreign born:** 25.3%. **Median age:** 37.8.

Income 2000: per capita $23,170; median household $41,691; **Pop below poverty level:** 11.5%. *****Personal per capita income 2000-2003:** $30,709-$32,844.

Unemployment 2004: 4.7%. **Change from 2000:** -0.2%. **Median travel time to work:** 27.4 minutes. **Working outside county of residence:** 23.9%.

Cities with pop over 10,000: 24 (see page 33 for cities).

CALHOUN COUNTY

20859 Central Ave E Rm 130   **Ph:** 850-674-4545
Blountstown, FL 32424   **Fax:** 850-674-5553
www.calhounco.org/index.htm

In the central panhandle of FL, west of Tallahassee; organized Jan 26, 1838 (prior to statehood) from Jackson County. **Name Origin:** For John Caldwell Calhoun (1782-1850), U.S. statesman and champion of Southern causes.

Area (sq mi): 574.34 (land 567.31; water 7.03). **Pop per sq mi:** 23.4.

Pop 2005: 13,290. **State rank:** 63. **Pop change:** 2000-20005 +2.1%; 1990-2000 +18.2%. **Pop 2000:** 13,017 (White 77.6%; Black or African American 15.8%; Hispanic or Latino 3.8%; Asian 0.5%; Other 3.9%, including 1.3% American Indian/Alaska Native). **Foreign born:** 2.2%. **Median age:** 36.2.

Income 2000: per capita $12,379; median household $26,575; **Pop below poverty level:** 20%. *****Personal per capita income 2000-2003:** $15,904-$17,566.

Unemployment 2004: 5.2%. **Change from 2000:** +0.1%. **Median travel time to work:** 28 minutes. **Working outside county of residence:** 43.8%.

Cities with pop over 10,000: None.

CHARLOTTE COUNTY

18500 Murdoch Cir   **Ph:** 941-743-1200
Port Charlotte, FL 33948   **Fax:** 941-743-1530
www.co.charlotte.fl.us

On the Gulf coast of FL, north of Fort Myers; organized Apr 23, 1921 from DeSoto County. **Name Origin:** For Charlotte Harbor, possibly originally named for the Calusa tribe of southwestern FL, which the Spanish corrupted to Carlos or Calos. The name was later changed by English surveyors to honor Charlotte Sophia (1744-1818), wife of King George III of England.

Area (sq mi): 859.12 (land 693.6; water 165.51). **Pop per sq mi:** 227.1.

Pop 2005: 157,536. **State rank:** 29. **Pop change:** 2000-20005 +11.2%; 1990-2000 +27.6%. **Pop 2000:** 141,627 (White 90.4%; Black or African American 4.4%; Hispanic or Latino 3.3%; Asian 0.9%; Other 2.1%). **Foreign born:** 8%. **Median age:** 54.3.

Income 2000: per capita $21,806; median household $36,379; **Pop below poverty level:** 8.2%. *****Personal per capita income 2000-2003:** $25,649-$26,479.

Unemployment 2004: 5%. **Change from 2000:** +1.6%. **Median travel time to work:** 23.6 minutes. **Working outside county of residence:** 26%.

Cities with pop over 10,000: Punta Gorda 🏛 (17,215).

CITRUS COUNTY

110 N Apopka Ave   **Ph:** 352-341-6400
Inverness, FL 34450   **Fax:** 352-341-6491
www.clerk.citrus.fl.us

On the Gulf coast of FL, southwest of Ocala; organized Jun 2, 1887

Source: Personal per capita income data are from the Bureau of Economic Analysis; per capita income data are from the Bureau of the Census. See Introduction for explanation of differences.

Citrus County (cont'd)

from Hernando County. **Name Origin:** For the major agricultural crop of the region.

Area (sq mi): 773.15 (land 583.81; water 189.34). **Pop per sq mi:** 230.2.

Pop 2005: 134,370. **State rank:** 32. **Pop change:** 2000-20005 +13.8%; 1990-2000 +26.3%. **Pop 2000:** 118,085 (White 93%; Black or African American 2.4%; Hispanic or Latino 2.7%; Asian 0.8%; Other 1.9%). **Foreign born:** 4.9%. **Median age:** 52.6.

Income 2000: per capita $18,585; median household $31,001; **Pop below poverty level:** 11.7%. *Personal per capita income 2000-2003: $22,211-$23,513.

Unemployment 2004: 5.1%. **Change from 2000:** -0.9%. **Median travel time to work:** 26.6 minutes. **Working outside county of residence:** 22.3%.

Cities with pop over 10,000: None.

CLAY COUNTY

825 N Orange Ave
Green Cove Springs, FL 32043
www.claycountygov.com

Ph: 904-269-6302

In northeastern FL, southwest of Jacksonville; organized Dec 31, 1858 from Duval County. **Name Origin:** For Henry Clay (1777-1852), U.S. senator from KY, known as the 'Great Pacificator' for his advocacy of compromise to avert national crises.

Area (sq mi): 643.69 (land 601.11; water 42.59). **Pop per sq mi:** 284.6.

Pop 2005: 171,095. **State rank:** 25. **Pop change:** 2000-20005 +21.5%; 1990-2000 +32.9%. **Pop 2000:** 140,814 (White 84.9%; Black or African American 6.7%; Hispanic or Latino 4.3%; Asian 2%; Other 3.9%). **Foreign born:** 4.5%. **Median age:** 35.9.

Income 2000: per capita $20,868; median household $48,854; **Pop below poverty level:** 6.8%. *Personal per capita income 2000-2003: $26,329-$27,084.

Unemployment 2004: 4.3%. **Change from 2000:** +0.7%. **Median travel time to work:** 33.5 minutes. **Working outside county of residence:** 60.4%.

Cities with pop over 10,000: None.

COLLIER COUNTY

3301 Tamiami Trail E
Naples, FL 34112
www.co.collier.fl.us

Ph: 239-774-8383
Fax: 239-774-4010

On the southwestern Gulf coast of FL, west of Fort Lauderdale; organized May 8, 1923 from Lee and Monroe counties. **Name Origin:** For Barron Gift Collier (1873-1939), a promoter active in the development of southern FL.

Area (sq mi): 2304.93 (land 2025.34; water 279.59). **Pop per sq mi:** 151.7.

Pop 2005: 307,242. **State rank:** 15. **Pop change:** 2000-20005 +22.2%; 1990-2000 +65.3%. **Pop 2000:** 251,377 (White 73.8%; Black or African American 4.5%; Hispanic or Latino 19.6%; Asian 0.6%; Other 8.8%). **Foreign born:** 18.3%. **Median age:** 44.1.

Income 2000: per capita $31,195; median household $48,289; **Pop below poverty level:** 10.3%. *Personal per capita income 2000-2003: $39,403-$41,513.

Unemployment 2004: 4%. **Change from 2000:** +0.1%. **Median travel time to work:** 24 minutes. **Working outside county of residence:** 7.8%.

Cities with pop over 10,000: Naples 🏛 (21,480); Marco Island (15,828).

COLUMBIA COUNTY

PO Box 2069
Lake City, FL 32056
www.columbiacountyfla.com

Ph: 386-755-4100
Fax: 386-758-1337

On northern border of FL, west of Jacksonville; organized Feb 4, 1832 (prior to statehood) from Alachua County. **Name Origin:** Feminine form of Columbus, a poetic and honorific reference to Christopher Columbus (1451-1506) and America.

Area (sq mi): 801.04 (land 797.05; water 3.99). **Pop per sq mi:** 80.3.

Pop 2005: 61,040. **State rank:** 40. **Pop change:** 2000-20005 +13.3%; 1990-2000 +32.6%. **Pop 2000:** 56,513 (White 78%; Black or African American 17%; Hispanic or Latino 2.7%; Asian 0.7%; Other 2.5%). **Foreign born:** 2.3%. **Median age:** 37.3.

Income 2000: per capita $14,598; median household $30,881; **Pop below poverty level:** 15%. *Personal per capita income 2000-2003: $18,734-$19,517.

Unemployment 2004: 4.5%. **Change from 2000:** -1.9%. **Median travel time to work:** 24.1 minutes. **Working outside county of residence:** 25.4%.

Cities with pop over 10,000: Lake City 🏛 (10,699).

DESOTO COUNTY

201 E Oak St
Arcadia, FL 34266
www.co.desoto.fl.us

Ph: 863-993-4800
Fax: 863-993-4809

In southwest-central FL, east of Sarasota; organized May 19, 1887 from Manatee County. **Name Origin:** For Hernando De Soto (c. 1500-42), Spanish explorer of southern U.S.

Area (sq mi): 639.5 (land 637.27; water 2.23). **Pop per sq mi:** 55.6.

Pop 2005: 35,406. **State rank:** 48. **Pop change:** 2000-20005 +9.9%; 1990-2000 +35%. **Pop 2000:** 32,209 (White 61.2%; Black or African American 12.7%; Hispanic or Latino 24.9%; Asian 0.4%; Other 13.5%, including 1.6% American Indian/Alaska Native). **Foreign born:** 18.7%. **Median age:** 36.5.

Income 2000: per capita $14,000; median household $30,714; **Pop below poverty level:** 23.6%. *Personal per capita income 2000-2003: $16,454-$16,458.

Unemployment 2004: 5.5%. **Change from 2000:** -0.5%. **Median travel time to work:** 27.9 minutes. **Working outside county of residence:** 26.9%.

Cities with pop over 10,000: None.

DIXIE COUNTY

PO Box 1206
Cross City, FL 32628   **Ph:** 352-498-1200
www.dixiecounty.org   **Fax:** 352-498-1201

On the Gulf coast of FL, west of Gainesville; organized Apr 25, 1921 from Lafayette County. **Name Origin:** For the name applied to the Confederate States, from the song composed in 1859 by Daniel Decatur Emmett (1815-1904), said to be derived from a Creole pronunciation of the second name in the Mason and Dixon Line.

Area (sq mi): 863.66 (land 704.01; water 159.65). **Pop per sq mi:** 20.8.

Pop 2005: 14,647. **State rank:** 59. **Pop change:** 2000-20005 +5.9%; 1990-2000 +30.6%. **Pop 2000:** 13,827 (White 87.7%; Black or African American 9%; Hispanic or Latino 1.8%; Asian 0.2%; Other 1.9%). **Foreign born:** 2%. **Median age:** 40.7.

Income 2000: per capita $13,559; median household $26,082; **Pop below poverty level:** 19.1%. ***Personal per capita income 2000-2003:** $15,295-$16,239.

Unemployment 2004: 5.6%. **Change from 2000:** -1.1%. **Median travel time to work:** 30.2 minutes. **Working outside county of residence:** 37.4%.

Cities with pop over 10,000: None.

DUVAL COUNTY/CITY OF JACKSONVILLE

117 W Duval St
Jacksonville, FL 32202   **Ph:** 904-630-1178
www.coj.net   **Fax:** 904-630-2906

On the northeastern coast of FL; organized Aug 12, 1822 from Saint Johns County (prior to statehood). **Name Origin:** For William Pope DuVal (1784-1854), governor of the Florida Territory (1822-34).

Area (sq mi): 918.24 (land 773.67; water 144.57). **Pop per sq mi:** 1068.2.

Pop 2005: 826,436. **State rank:** 7. **Pop change:** 2000-20005 +6.1%; 1990-2000 +15.7%. **Pop 2000:** 778,879 (White 63.5%; Black or African American 27.8%; Hispanic or Latino 4.1%; Asian 2.7%; Other 3.7%). **Foreign born:** 5.9%. **Median age:** 34.1.

Income 2000: per capita $20,753; median household $40,703; **Pop below poverty level:** 11.9%. ***Personal per capita income 2000-2003:** $28,920-$30,212.

Unemployment 2004: 5.2%. **Change from 2000:** +0.7%. **Median travel time to work:** 25.2 minutes. **Working outside county of residence:** 6.6%.

Cities with pop over 10,000: Jacksonville 🏛 (777,704); Jacksonville Beach (21,353); Atlantic Beach (13,553).

ESCAMBIA COUNTY

PO Box 1591
Pensacola, FL 32591   **Ph:** 850-595-4900
www.co.escambia.fl.us   **Fax:** 850-595-4908

On northwestern border of FL, bordered on the south by the Gulf of Mexico; original county; organized Jul 21, 1822 (prior to statehood). It is one of the two first counties; the other is Saint Johns. **Name Origin:** For the river, which forms its eastern border; probably a Spanish rendering of a Choctaw or Chickasaw Indian word but origin is in dispute. River formerly called the *Pensacola*. There may be a connection to Spanish *cambiar* 'to trade.'

Area (sq mi): 875.57 (land 662.35; water 213.21). **Pop per sq mi:** 448.1.

Pop 2005: 296,772. **State rank:** 18. **Pop change:** 2000-20005 +0.8%; 1990-2000 +12%. **Pop 2000:** 294,410 (White 70.9%; Black or African American 21.4%; Hispanic or Latino 2.7%; Asian 2.2%; Other 4.1%). **Foreign born:** 3.7%. **Median age:** 35.4.

Income 2000: per capita $18,641; median household $35,234; **Pop below poverty level:** 15.4%. ***Personal per capita income 2000-2003:** $23,279-$25,168.

Unemployment 2004: 4.9%. **Change from 2000:** -0.1%. **Median travel time to work:** 23 minutes. **Working outside county of residence:** 10.4%.

Cities with pop over 10,000: Pensacola 🏛 (54,734).

FLAGLER COUNTY

1200 E Moody Blvd Suite 1
Bunnell, FL 32110   **Ph:** 386-437-7480
www.flaglercounty.org   **Fax:** 386-437-7399

On northeastern Atlantic coast of FL, north of Daytona Beach; organized Apr 28, 1917 from Saint Johns and Volusia counties. **Name Origin:** For Henry Morrison Flagler (1830-1913), founder of the Florida East Coast Railroad (1886) and a leader in developing Florida's east coast as a resort area.

Area (sq mi): 570.76 (land 485; water 85.77). **Pop per sq mi:** 157.5.

Pop 2005: 76,410. **State rank:** 35. **Pop change:** 2000-20005 +53.3%; 1990-2000 +73.6%. **Pop 2000:** 49,832 (White 83.6%; Black or African American 8.8%; Hispanic or Latino 5.1%; Asian 1.2%; Other 2.8%). **Foreign born:** 9.9%. **Median age:** 50.4.

Income 2000: per capita $21,879; median household $40,214; **Pop below poverty level:** 8.7%. ***Personal per capita income 2000-2003:** $23,610-$23,929.

Unemployment 2004: 4.6%. **Change from 2000:** +0%. **Median travel time to work:** 25.9 minutes. **Working outside county of residence:** 37.9%.

Cities with pop over 10,000: Palm Coast (44,427).

FRANKLIN COUNTY

33 Market St Suite 203
Apalachicola, FL 32320   **Ph:** 850-653-8861
www.franklincountyflorida.com   **Fax:** 850-653-2261

In eastern FL panhandle, southwest of Tallahassee and bordered on south by the Gulf of Mexico; organized Feb 8, 1832 from Jackson County (prior to statehood). **Name Origin:** For Benjamin Franklin (1706-1790), U.S. patriot, diplomat, and statesman.

Area (sq mi): 1037.48 (land 544.34; water 493.14). **Pop per sq mi:** 18.7.

Pop 2005: 10,177. **State rank:** 65. **Pop change:** 2000-20005 -8%; 1990-2000 +23.3%. **Pop 2000:** 11,057 (White 79.8%; Black or African American 16.3%; Hispanic or Latino 2.4%; Asian 0.2%; Other 2.2%). **Foreign born:** 1.9%. **Median age:** 40.8.

Income 2000: per capita $16,140; median household $26,756; **Pop below poverty level:** 17.7%. ***Personal per capita income 2000-2003:** $20,859-$22,585.

*Source: Personal per capita income data are from the Bureau of Economic Analysis; per capita income data are from the Bureau of the Census.
See Introduction for explanation of differences.*

Franklin County (cont'd)

Unemployment 2004: 4%. **Change from 2000:** +1.3%. **Median travel time to work:** 19.9 minutes. **Working outside county of residence:** 11.8%.

Cities with pop over 10,000: None.

GADSDEN COUNTY
PO Box 1649   **Ph:** 850-875-8601
Quincy, FL 32353   **Fax:** 850-875-8612
www.gadsdengov.net

On northern border of FL panhandle, west of Tallahassee; organized Jun 24, 1823 (prior to statehood) from Jackson County. **Name Origin:** For James Gadsden (1788-1858), SC soldier and politician, negotiator of the Gadsden Purchase (1853).

Area (sq mi): 528.49 (land 516.13; water 12.35). **Pop per sq mi:** 90.

Pop 2005: 46,428. **State rank:** 43. **Pop change:** 2000-20005 +3%; 1990-2000 +9.7%. **Pop 2000:** 45,087 (White 35.9%; Black or African American 57.1%; Hispanic or Latino 6.2%; Asian 0.3%; Other 3.9%). **Foreign born:** 4.1%. **Median age:** 35.5.

Income 2000: per capita $14,499; median household $31,240. **Pop below poverty level:** 19.9%. ***Personal per capita income 2000-2003:** $19,588-$20,535.

Unemployment 2004: 5.1%. **Change from 2000:** +0.5%. **Median travel time to work:** 29.3 minutes. **Working outside county of residence:** 51%.

Cities with pop over 10,000: None.

GILCHRIST COUNTY
PO Box 37   **Ph:** 352-463-3170
Trenton, FL 32693   **Fax:** 352-463-3166
www.co.gilchrist.fl.us

In north-central FL, west of Gainesville; organized Dec 4, 1925 from Alachua County. **Name Origin:** For Capt. Albert Waller Gilchrist (1858-1926), officer, FL legislator, and governor (1909-13).

Area (sq mi): 355.47 (land 348.89; water 6.58). **Pop per sq mi:** 47.

Pop 2005: 16,402. **State rank:** 57. **Pop change:** 2000-20005 +13.6%; 1990-2000 +49.3%. **Pop 2000:** 14,437 (White 88.7%; Black or African American 7%; Hispanic or Latino 2.8%; Asian 0.2%; Other 2.4%). **Foreign born:** 1.7%. **Median age:** 35.4.

Income 2000: per capita $13,985; median household $30,328; **Pop below poverty level:** 14.1%. ***Personal per capita income 2000-2003:** $19,448-$20,946.

Unemployment 2004: 3.9%. **Change from 2000:** -1.1%. **Median travel time to work:** 33.5 minutes. **Working outside county of residence:** 59.8%.

Cities with pop over 10,000: None.

GLADES COUNTY
500 Ave J Suite 102   **Ph:** 863-946-6010
Moore Haven, FL 33471   **Fax:** 863-946-0560
www.gladescofl.us

In south-central FL, includes part of Lake Okeechobee; organized Apr 23, 1921 from DeSoto County. **Name Origin:** A shortened form of *Everglades*: the county is at their northern extent.

Area (sq mi): 986.43 (land 773.64; water 212.79). **Pop per sq mi:** 14.5.

Pop 2005: 11,252. **State rank:** 64. **Pop change:** 2000-20005 +6.4%; 1990-2000 +39.3%. **Pop 2000:** 10,576 (White 68.6%; Black or African American 10.5%; Hispanic or Latino 15.1%; Asian 0.3%; Other 12.1%, including 4.9% American Indian/Alaska Native). **Foreign born:** 7.9%. **Median age:** 40.2.

Income 2000: per capita $15,338; median household $30,774; **Pop below poverty level:** 15.2%. ***Personal per capita income 2000-2003:** $15,391-$17,159.

Unemployment 2004: 5.3%. **Change from 2000:** -4.3%. **Median travel time to work:** 29.1 minutes. **Working outside county of residence:** 54.2%.

Cities with pop over 10,000: None.

GULF COUNTY
1000 Cecil Costin Sr Blvd   **Ph:** 850-229-6113
Port Saint Joe, FL 32456   **Fax:** 850-229-6174
www.gulfcountygovernment.com

In FL panhandle, southwest of Tallahassee; organized Jun 6, 1925 from Calhoun County. **Name Origin:** For the Gulf of Mexico, which forms its southern border.

Area (sq mi): 744.59 (land 554.6; water 190). **Pop per sq mi:** 25.2.

Pop 2005: 13,975. **State rank:** 62. **Pop change:** 2000-20005 +4.8%; 1990-2000 +15.9%. **Pop 2000:** 13,332 (White 78.7%; Black or African American 16.9%; Hispanic or Latino 2%; Asian 0.4%; Other 2.7%). **Foreign born:** 2.1%. **Median age:** 40.3.

Income 2000: per capita $14,449; median household $30,276; **Pop below poverty level:** 16.7%. ***Personal per capita income 2000-2003:** $16,604-$20,571.

Unemployment 2004: 4.5%. **Change from 2000:** -1.2%. **Median travel time to work:** 25.8 minutes. **Working outside county of residence:** 31.9%.

Cities with pop over 10,000: None.

HAMILTON COUNTY
207 NE 1st St Rm 106   **Ph:** 386-792-1288
Jasper, FL 32052   **Fax:** 386-792-3524
www.hamiltoncountyflorida.com

On northern border of FL, between Jacksonville and Tallahassee; organized Dec 26, 1827 from Duval County (prior to statehood). **Name Origin:** For Alexander Hamilton (1757-1804), first U.S. secretary of the treasury (1789-95).

Area (sq mi): 519.31 (land 514.86; water 4.45). **Pop per sq mi:** 27.2.

Pop 2005: 13,983. **State rank:** 61. **Pop change:** 2000-20005 +4.9%; 1990-2000 +21.9%. **Pop 2000:** 13,327 (White 55%; Black or African American 37.7%; Hispanic or Latino 6.4%; Asian 0.2%; Other 3.3%). **Foreign born:** 2.3%. **Median age:** 35.1.

Income 2000: per capita $10,562; median household $25,638; **Pop below poverty level:** 26%. ***Personal per capita income 2000-2003:** $14,569-$13,932.

Unemployment 2004: 5.7%. **Change from 2000:** -4.7%. **Median travel time to work:** 24.1 minutes. **Working outside county of residence:** 41.9%.

Hamilton County (cont'd)

Cities with pop over 10,000: None.

HARDEE COUNTY
412 W Orange St Rm A-203   **Ph:** 863-773-6952
Wauchula, FL 33873   **Fax:** 863-773-0958
www.hardeecounty.net

In south-central FL, south of Winter Haven; organized Apr 23, 1921 from DeSoto County. **Name Origin:** For Cary Augustus Hardee (1876-1957), governor of FL (1921-25).

Area (sq mi): 638.33 (land 637.3; water 1.03). **Pop per sq mi:** 44.4.

Pop 2005: 28,286. **State rank:** 49. **Pop change:** 2000-20005 +5%; 1990-2000 +38.2%. **Pop 2000:** 26,938 (White 54.6%; Black or African American 8.3%; Hispanic or Latino 35.7%; Asian 0.3%; Other 20.8%). **Foreign born:** 17.5%. **Median age:** 32.7.

Income 2000: per capita $12,445; median household $30,183; **Pop below poverty level:** 24.6%. *****Personal per capita income 2000-2003:** $16,616-$17,257.

Unemployment 2004: 6.6%. **Change from 2000:** -3%. **Median travel time to work:** 26.7 minutes. **Working outside county of residence:** 30.6%.

Cities with pop over 10,000: None.

HENDRY COUNTY
PO Box 1760   **Ph:** 863-675-5217
La Belle, FL 33975   **Fax:** 863-675-5238
www.hendryfla.net

In south-central FL, east of Fort Myers; organized May 11, 1923 from Calhoun County. **Name Origin:** For Capt. Francis Asbury Hendry (?-1917), Confederate officer, dubbed the 'Cattle King of South Florida.'

Area (sq mi): 1189.79 (land 1152.53; water 37.26). **Pop per sq mi:** 34.3.

Pop 2005: 39,561. **State rank:** 45. **Pop change:** 2000-20005 +9.3%; 1990-2000 +40.5%. **Pop 2000:** 36,210 (White 43.9%; Black or African American 14.7%; Hispanic or Latino 39.6%; Asian 0.4%; Other 18.7%). **Foreign born:** 24%. **Median age:** 29.5.

Income 2000: per capita $13,663; median household $33,592; **Pop below poverty level:** 24.1%. *****Personal per capita income 2000-2003:** $18,088-$19,461.

Unemployment 2004: 8.2%. **Change from 2000:** -4.1%. **Median travel time to work:** 26.5 minutes. **Working outside county of residence:** 30.8%.

Cities with pop over 10,000: None.

HERNANDO COUNTY
20 N Main St Rm 460   **Ph:** 352-754-4000
Brooksville, FL 34601   **Fax:** 352-754-4477
www.co.hernando.fl.us

On central Gulf coast of FL, north of Tampa; organized Feb 24, 1843 (prior to statehood). Name changed to Benton County Mar 6, 1844, and back again Dec 24, 1850. **Name Origin:** For Hernando De Soto (c. 1500-42), Spanish explorer of southern U.S. Changed to honor Thomas Hart Benton (1782-53) who sponsored legislation

to open central FL to settlement; name changed back because of his moderate position on the Missouri Compromise.

Area (sq mi): 589.08 (land 478.31; water 110.77). **Pop per sq mi:** 331.2.

Pop 2005: 158,409. **State rank:** 28. **Pop change:** 2000-20005 +21.1%; 1990-2000 +29.4%. **Pop 2000:** 130,802 (White 89.2%; Black or African American 4.1%; Hispanic or Latino 5%; Asian 0.6%; Other 2.4%). **Foreign born:** 5.3%. **Median age:** 49.5.

Income 2000: per capita $18,321; median household $32,572; **Pop below poverty level:** 10.3%. *****Personal per capita income 2000-2003:** $23,475-$24,555.

Unemployment 2004: 5.6%. **Change from 2000:** +1.4%. **Median travel time to work:** 29.3 minutes. **Working outside county of residence:** 33.3%.

Cities with pop over 10,000: None.

HIGHLANDS COUNTY
430 S Commerce Ave   **Ph:** 863-402-6500
Sebring, FL 33870   **Fax:** 863-402-6507
www.hcbcc.net

In central FL, west of Ft. Pierce; organized Apr 23, 1921 from DeSoto County. **Name Origin:** For the hilliness of the area, in a state almost completely flat.

Area (sq mi): 1106.28 (land 1028.27; water 78.01). **Pop per sq mi:** 92.9.

Pop 2005: 95,496. **State rank:** 34. **Pop change:** 2000-20005 +9.3%; 1990-2000 +27.7%. **Pop 2000:** 87,366 (White 76.5%; Black or African American 9.3%; Hispanic or Latino 12.1%; Asian 1%; Other 6%). **Foreign born:** 9.1%. **Median age:** 50.

Income 2000: per capita $17,222; median household $30,160; **Pop below poverty level:** 15.2%. *****Personal per capita income 2000-2003:** $20,246-$22,111.

Unemployment 2004: 5.1%. **Change from 2000:** -0.8%. **Median travel time to work:** 23 minutes. **Working outside county of residence:** 10.6%.

Cities with pop over 10,000: Sebring 🏛 (10,076).

HILLSBOROUGH COUNTY
800 E Twigg St   **Ph:** 813-276-8100
Tampa, FL 33602   **Fax:** 813-276-2437
www.hillsboroughcounty.org

On Tampa Bay on the central Gulf coast of FL; organized Jan 25, 1834 (prior to statehood) from Alachua and Monroe counties. **Name Origin:** For Wills Hills, Earl of Hillsborough (1718-93), Irish peer and secretary of state for the colonies (1768-72) who had received a large grant of land in FL. Named by Bernard Romans, his surveyor.

Area (sq mi): 1266.22 (land 1050.91; water 215.31). **Pop per sq mi:** 1077.3.

Pop 2005: 1,132,152. **State rank:** 4. **Pop change:** 2000-20005 +13.3%; 1990-2000 +19.8%. **Pop 2000:** 998,948 (White 63.3%; Black or African American 15%; Hispanic or Latino 18%; Asian 2.2%; Other 7.8%). **Foreign born:** 11.5%. **Median age:** 35.1.

Income 2000: per capita $21,812; median household $40,663; **Pop below poverty level:** 12.5%. *****Personal per capita income 2000-2003:** $28,556-$29,748.

Source: Personal per capita income data are from the Bureau of Economic Analysis; per capita income data are from the Bureau of the Census. See Introduction for explanation of differences.

Hillsborough County (cont'd)

Unemployment 2004: 4.4%. **Change from 2000:** +0.8%. **Median travel time to work:** 25.8 minutes. **Working outside county of residence:** 10.8%.

Cities with pop over 10,000: Tampa ⛫ (321,772); Plant City (30,906); Temple Terrace (21,694).

HOLMES COUNTY

PO Box 397   **Ph:** 850-547-1100
Bonifay, FL 32425   **Fax:** 850-547-6630
www.holmescountyonline.com

On northern border of FL panhandle, north of Panama City; organized Jan 8, 1848 from Walton and Calhoun counties. **Name Origin:** For Holmes Creek, which forms the eastern boundary of the county. The creek was named for the valley, which was probably named for a Creek Indian chief, killed (1818) by troops under the command of Andrew Jackson (1767-1845); or possibly for Thomas J. Holmes, a settler from NC about 1830.

Area (sq mi): 488.71 (land 482.45; water 6.26). **Pop per sq mi:** 39.9.

Pop 2005: 19,264. **State rank:** 55. **Pop change:** 2000-20005 +3.8%; 1990-2000 +17.7%. **Pop 2000:** 18,564 (White 88.9%; Black or African American 6.5%; Hispanic or Latino 1.9%; Asian 0.4%; Other 3.3%, including 1% American Indian/Alaska Native). **Foreign born:** 1.7%. **Median age:** 37.5.

Income 2000: per capita $14,135; median household $27,923; **Pop below poverty level:** 19.1%. ***Personal per capita income 2000-2003:** $17,611-$18,742.

Unemployment 2004: 4.9%. **Change from 2000:** -2.1%. **Median travel time to work:** 34 minutes. **Working outside county of residence:** 53.8%.

Cities with pop over 10,000: None.

INDIAN RIVER COUNTY

1840 25th St   **Ph:** 772-567-8000
Vero Beach, FL 32960   **Fax:** 772-978-1822
indian-river.fl.us

On south-central Atlantic coast of FL, north of Fort Pierce; organized May 30, 1925 from Saint Lucie County. **Name Origin:** For the Indian River, which forms its eastern border.

Area (sq mi): 616.92 (land 503.23; water 113.69). **Pop per sq mi:** 255.5.

Pop 2005: 128,594. **State rank:** 33. **Pop change:** 2000-20005 +13.9%; 1990-2000 +25.2%. **Pop 2000:** 112,947 (White 83.4%; Black or African American 8.2%; Hispanic or Latino 6.5%; Asian 0.7%; Other 3.5%). **Foreign born:** 8.1%. **Median age:** 47.

Income 2000: per capita $27,227; median household $39,635; **Pop below poverty level:** 9.3%. ***Personal per capita income 2000-2003:** $37,110-$39,953.

Unemployment 2004: 6.6%. **Change from 2000:** -0.7%. **Median travel time to work:** 20.3 minutes. **Working outside county of residence:** 12.9%.

Cities with pop over 10,000: Sebastian (18,671); Vero Beach ⛫ (17,209).

JACKSON COUNTY

PO Box 510   **Ph:** 850-482-9552
Marianna, FL 32447   **Fax:** 850-482-7849
www.jacksoncounty-fl.com

On northern border of FL panhandle, northwest of Tallahassee; organized Aug 12, 1822 (prior to statehood) from Escambia County; in 1834 annexed Fayette County, which was organized in 1832. **Name Origin:** For Andrew Jackson (1767-1845), seventh U.S. president.

Area (sq mi): 954.58 (land 915.64; water 38.94). **Pop per sq mi:** 53.5.

Pop 2005: 48,985. **State rank:** 42. **Pop change:** 2000-20005 +4.8%; 1990-2000 +13%. **Pop 2000:** 46,755 (White 68.6%; Black or African American 26.6%; Hispanic or Latino 2.9%; Asian 0.4%; Other 2.9%). **Foreign born:** 1.5%. **Median age:** 37.6.

Income 2000: per capita $13,905; median household $29,744; **Pop below poverty level:** 17.2%. ***Personal per capita income 2000-2003:** $18,013-$20,548.

Unemployment 2004: 4.5%. **Change from 2000:** +0.2%. **Median travel time to work:** 23.5 minutes. **Working outside county of residence:** 25.6%.

Cities with pop over 10,000: None.

JEFFERSON COUNTY

County Courthouse Rm 10   **Ph:** 850-342-0218
Monticello, FL 32344   **Fax:** 850-342-0222
www.co.jefferson.fl.us

On northern Gulf coast of FL, east of Tallahassee; organized Jan 20, 1827 (prior to statehood) from Leon County. **Name Origin:** For Thomas Jefferson (1743-1826), U.S. patriot and statesman; third U.S. president.

Area (sq mi): 636.65 (land 597.74; water 38.91). **Pop per sq mi:** 24.2.

Pop 2005: 14,490. **State rank:** 60. **Pop change:** 2000-20005 +12.3%; 1990-2000 +14.2%. **Pop 2000:** 12,902 (White 58.3%; Black or African American 38.3%; Hispanic or Latino 2.2%; Asian 0.3%; Other 2.1%). **Foreign born:** 1.2%. **Median age:** 39.4.

Income 2000: per capita $17,006; median household $32,998; **Pop below poverty level:** 17.1%. ***Personal per capita income 2000-2003:** $23,815-$22,906.

Unemployment 2004: 3.9%. **Change from 2000:** -2%. **Median travel time to work:** 29.2 minutes. **Working outside county of residence:** 56.8%.

Cities with pop over 10,000: None.

LAFAYETTE COUNTY

PO Box 88   **Ph:** 386-294-1600
Mayo, FL 32066   **Fax:** 386-294-4231

In northern FL, northwest of Gainesville; organized Dec 23, 1856 from Madison County. **Name Origin:** For the Marquis de Lafayette (1757-1834), French statesman and soldier who fought with Americans during the Revolutionary War.

Area (sq mi): 547.92 (land 542.84; water 5.08). **Pop per sq mi:** 14.7.

Lafayette County (cont'd)

Pop 2005: 7,953. **State rank:** 66. **Pop change:** 2000-20005 +13.3%; 1990-2000 +25.9%. **Pop 2000:** 7,022 (White 75.3%; Black or African American 14.4%; Hispanic or Latino 9.1%; Asian 0.1%; Other 6.2%). **Foreign born:** 6.6%. **Median age:** 34.8.

Income 2000: per capita $13,087; median household $30,651; **Pop below poverty level:** 17.5%. ***Personal per capita income 2000-2003:** $14,979-$14,880.

Unemployment 2004: 4.1%. **Change from 2000:** +0.4%. **Median travel time to work:** 22.8 minutes. **Working outside county of residence:** 36.7%.

Cities with pop over 10,000: None.

LAKE COUNTY

PO Box 7800   **Ph:** 352-742-4102
Tavares, FL 32778   **Fax:** 352-742-4110
www.lakegovernment.com

In central FL, west of Orlando; organized May 27, 1887 from Orange and Sumter counties. **Name Origin:** For the more than 500 lakes of 10 acres or more in the county.

Area (sq mi): 1156.4 (land 953.15; water 203.25). **Pop per sq mi:** 290.7.

Pop 2005: 277,035. **State rank:** 19. **Pop change:** 2000-20005 +31.6%; 1990-2000 +38.4%. **Pop 2000:** 210,528 (White 84.2%; Black or African American 8.3%; Hispanic or Latino 5.6%; Asian 0.8%; Other 3.4%). **Foreign born:** 5.1%. **Median age:** 45.1.

Income 2000: per capita $20,199; median household $36,903; **Pop below poverty level:** 9.6%. ***Personal per capita income 2000-2003:** $25,651-$26,189.

Unemployment 2004: 4.5%. **Change from 2000:** +0.8%. **Median travel time to work:** 27.6 minutes. **Working outside county of residence:** 36.4%.

Cities with pop over 10,000: 6 (see page 33 for cities).

LEE COUNTY

PO Box 398   **Ph:** 239-335-2227
Fort Myers, FL 33902   **Fax:** 239-335-2599
www.lee-county.com

On southwestern Gulf coast of FL, north of Naples; organized May 13, 1887 from Monroe County. **Name Origin:** For Robert E. Lee (1807-70), American general and commander in chief of the Confederate forces during the Civil War.

Area (sq mi): 1211.89 (land 803.63; water 408.26). **Pop per sq mi:** 677.9.

Pop 2005: 544,758. **State rank:** 8. **Pop change:** 2000-20005 +23.6%; 1990-2000 +31.6%. **Pop 2000:** 440,888 (White 82%; Black or African American 6.6%; Hispanic or Latino 9.5%; Asian 0.8%; Other 5%). **Foreign born:** 9.2%. **Median age:** 45.2.

Income 2000: per capita $24,542; median household $40,319; **Pop below poverty level:** 9.7%. ***Personal per capita income 2000-2003:** $29,006-$31,487.

Unemployment 2004: 3.9%. **Change from 2000:** +0.7%. **Median travel time to work:** 25 minutes. **Working outside county of residence:** 11.3%.

Cities with pop over 10,000: Cape Coral (127,985); Fort Myers 🏛 (52,901); Bonita Springs (35,850).

LEON COUNTY

301 S Monroe St Suite 108   **Ph:** 850-487-2220
Tallahassee, FL 32301   **Fax:** 850-488-6293
www.co.leon.fl.us

In eastern end of FL panhandle; organized Dec 9, 1824 (prior to statehood) from Gadsden County. **Name Origin:** For Juan Ponce de Leon (1460-1521), Spanish colonial governor and discoverer of Florida while in search of the 'fountain of youth.'

Area (sq mi): 701.78 (land 666.74; water 35.04). **Pop per sq mi:** 368.6.

Pop 2005: 245,756. **State rank:** 20. **Pop change:** 2000-20005 +2.6%; 1990-2000 +24.4%. **Pop 2000:** 239,452 (White 64.1%; Black or African American 29.1%; Hispanic or Latino 3.5%; Asian 1.9%; Other 2.6%). **Foreign born:** 4.7%. **Median age:** 29.5.

Income 2000: per capita $21,024; median household $37,517; **Pop below poverty level:** 18.2%. ***Personal per capita income 2000-2003:** $26,068-$28,109.

Unemployment 2004: 3.8%. **Change from 2000:** +0.9%. **Median travel time to work:** 21.7 minutes. **Working outside county of residence:** 5%.

Cities with pop over 10,000: Tallahassee 🏛 (156,612).

LEVY COUNTY

PO Box 610   **Ph:** 352-486-5100
Bronson, FL 32621   **Fax:** 352-486-5166
www.naturecoast.org

On Gulf coast of FL, west of Ocala; organized Mar 10, 1845 from Alachua and Marion counties. **Name Origin:** For David Levy [Yulee] (1810-86), West Indian-born FL legislator, first U.S. senator from FL (1845-51; 1855-61), and member of the Confederate Congress (1861-65).

Area (sq mi): 1412.32 (land 1118.38; water 293.94). **Pop per sq mi:** 34.

Pop 2005: 37,998. **State rank:** 47. **Pop change:** 2000-20005 +10.3%; 1990-2000 +32.9%. **Pop 2000:** 34,450 (White 83.2%; Black or African American 11%; Hispanic or Latino 3.9%; Asian 0.4%; Other 2.8%). **Foreign born:** 2.6%. **Median age:** 41.1.

Income 2000: per capita $14,746; median household $26,959; **Pop below poverty level:** 18.6%. ***Personal per capita income 2000-2003:** $18,143-$19,146.

Unemployment 2004: 4.8%. **Change from 2000:** -0.2%. **Median travel time to work:** 31.4 minutes. **Working outside county of residence:** 46.4%.

Cities with pop over 10,000: None.

LIBERTY COUNTY

PO Box 399   **Ph:** 850-643-5404
Bristol, FL 32321   **Fax:** 850-643-2866
www.libertycountyflorida.com

In eastern end of FL panhandle, southwest of Tallahassee; organized Dec 15, 1855 from Franklin and Gadsden counties. **Name Origin:** For the objective of the people who founded the U.S.

Source: Personal per capita income data are from the Bureau of Economic Analysis; per capita income data are from the Bureau of the Census. See Introduction for explanation of differences.

Liberty County (cont'd)

Area (sq mi): 843.16 (land 835.87; water 7.29). **Pop per sq mi:** 9.3.

Pop 2005: 7,773. **State rank:** 67. **Pop change:** 2000-20005 +10.7%; 1990-2000 +26.1%. **Pop 2000:** 7,021 (White 74.5%; Black or African American 18.4%; Hispanic or Latino 4.5%; Asian 0.1%; Other 5%, including 1.8% American Indian/Alaska Native). **Foreign born:** 2.1%. **Median age:** 35.

Income 2000: per capita $17,225; median household $28,840; **Pop below poverty level:** 19.9%. ***Personal per capita income 2000-2003:** $16,975-$18,590.

Unemployment 2004: 4%. **Change from 2000:** 0.6%. **Median travel time to work:** 33.2 minutes. **Working outside county of residence:** 51.8%.

Cities with pop over 10,000: None.

MADISON COUNTY

PO Box 237   **Ph:** 850-973-1500
Madison, FL 32341   **Fax:** 850-973-2059
www.madisonfl.org

On northern border of FL, east of Tallahassee; organized Dec 26, 1827 (prior to statehood) from Jefferson County. **Name Origin:** For James Madison (1751-1836), fourth U.S. president.

Area (sq mi): 715.8 (land 691.79; water 24). **Pop per sq mi:** 27.6.

Pop 2005: 19,092. **State rank:** 56. **Pop change:** 2000-20005 +1.9%; 1990-2000 +13.1%. **Pop 2000:** 18,733 (White 55.4%; Black or African American 40.3%; Hispanic or Latino 3.2%; Asian 0.3%; Other 1.8%). **Foreign born:** 2%. **Median age:** 36.3.

Income 2000: per capita $12,511; median household $26,533; **Pop below poverty level:** 23.1%. ***Personal per capita income 2000-2003:** $16,652-$17,793.

Unemployment 2004: 5.8%. **Change from 2000:** +1.6%. **Median travel time to work:** 23.1 minutes. **Working outside county of residence:** 29.9%.

Cities with pop over 10,000: None.

MANATEE COUNTY

PO Box 25400   **Ph:** 941-749-1800
Bradenton, FL 34206   **Fax:** 941-741-4083
www.co.manatee.fl.us

On central Gulf coast, south of Tampa; organized Jan 9, 1855 from Hillsborough County. **Name Origin:** For the manatee, or sea cow, an endangered aquatic mammal found in the local waterways.

Area (sq mi): 892.75 (land 741.03; water 151.72). **Pop per sq mi:** 414.

Pop 2005: 306,779. **State rank:** 16. **Pop change:** 2000-20005 +16.2%; 1990-2000 +24.7%. **Pop 2000:** 264,002 (White 80.6%; Black or African American 8.2%; Hispanic or Latino 9.3%; Asian 0.9%; Other 4.6%). **Foreign born:** 8.4%. **Median age:** 43.6.

Income 2000: per capita $22,388; median household $38,673; **Pop below poverty level:** 10.1%. ***Personal per capita income 2000-2003:** $30,439-$31,669.

Unemployment 2004: 4.1%. **Change from 2000:** +0.8%. **Median travel time to work:** 23.3 minutes. **Working outside county of residence:** 26%.

Cities with pop over 10,000: Bradenton ▥ (53,136); Palmetto (13,132).

MARION COUNTY

601 SE 25th Ave   **Ph:** 352-620-3307
Ocala, FL 34471   **Fax:** 352-620-3392
www.marioncountyfl.org

In north-central FL, south of Gainesville; organized Mar 14, 1844 (prior to statehood) from Alachua County. **Name Origin:** For Gen. Francis Marion (c. 1732-1795), SC soldier and legislator, known as 'The Swamp Fox' for his tactics during the Revolutionary War.

Area (sq mi): 1663.01 (land 1578.86; water 84.15). **Pop per sq mi:** 192.2.

Pop 2005: 303,442. **State rank:** 17. **Pop change:** 2000-20005 +17.2%; 1990-2000 +32.9%. **Pop 2000:** 258,916 (White 80.4%; Black or African American 11.5%; Hispanic or Latino 6%; Asian 0.7%; Other 3.5%). **Foreign born:** 5.2%. **Median age:** 43.8.

Income 2000: per capita $17,848; median household $31,944; **Pop below poverty level:** 13.1%. ***Personal per capita income 2000-2003:** $22,640-$23,512.

Unemployment 2004: 4.6%. **Change from 2000:** -0.3%. **Median travel time to work:** 25.8 minutes. **Working outside county of residence:** 13.8%.

Cities with pop over 10,000: Ocala ▥ (48,901).

MARTIN COUNTY

PO Box 9016   **Ph:** 772-288-5576
Stuart, FL 34995   **Fax:** 772-288-5548
www.martin.fl.us

On central Atlantic coast of FL, north of Palm Beach; organized May 30, 1925 from Palm Beach County. **Name Origin:** For John W. Martin (1884-1958), governor of FL (1925-29).

Area (sq mi): 752.79 (land 555.62; water 197.18). **Pop per sq mi:** 251.5.

Pop 2005: 139,728. **State rank:** 31. **Pop change:** 2000-20005 +10.3%; 1990-2000 +25.6%. **Pop 2000:** 126,731 (White 85.8%; Black or African American 5.3%; Hispanic or Latino 7.5%; Asian 0.6%; Other 4.2%). **Foreign born:** 8.1%. **Median age:** 47.3.

Income 2000: per capita $29,584; median household $43,083; **Pop below poverty level:** 8.8%. ***Personal per capita income 2000-2003:** $42,065-$42,248.

Unemployment 2004: 4.8%. **Change from 2000:** -0.8%. **Median travel time to work:** 25.5 minutes. **Working outside county of residence:** 32%.

Cities with pop over 10,000: Stuart ▥ (15,728).

MIAMI-DADE COUNTY

111 NW 1st St Suite 320   **Ph:** 305-375-5124
Miami, FL 33128   **Fax:** 305-375-5569
miamidade.gov

In southeastern FL, south of Fort Lauderdale; organized Feb 4, 1836 (prior to statehood) from Monroe County. Renamed as Miami-Dade County effective July 22, 1997. **Name Origin:** For Maj. Francis Langhorne Dade (1793-1835), officer killed in the Seminole War (1835-42).

Miami-Dade County (cont'd)

Area (sq mi): 2431.26 (land 1946.06; water 485.19). **Pop per sq mi:** 1220.9.

Pop 2005: 2,376,014. **State rank:** 1. **Pop change:** 2000-20005 +5.4%; 1990-2000 +16.3%. **Pop 2000:** 2,253,362 (White 20.7%; Black or African American 20.3%; Hispanic or Latino 57.3%; Asian 1.4%; Other 8.6%). **Foreign born:** 50.9%. **Median age:** 35.6.

Income 2000: per capita $18,497; median household $35,966; **Pop below poverty level:** 18%. ***Personal per capita income 2000-2003:** $25,626-$27,593.

Unemployment 2004: 5.6%. **Change from 2000:** -1.3%. **Median travel time to work:** 30.1 minutes. **Working outside county of residence:** 8.4%.

Cities with pop over 10,000: 19 (see page 33 for cities).

MONROE COUNTY
500 Whitehead St   **Ph:** 305-292-3540
Key West, FL 33040   **Fax:** 305-295-3970
www.co.monroe.fl.us

In southwestern FL, includes the Florida Keys; organized Jul 3, 1823 (prior to statehood) from Saint Johns County. **Name Origin:** For James Monroe (1758-1831), fifth U.S. president.

Area (sq mi): 3737.15 (land 996.91; water 2740.24). **Pop per sq mi:** 76.6.

Pop 2005: 76,329. **State rank:** 36. **Pop change:** 2000-20005 -4.1%; 1990-2000 +2%. **Pop 2000:** 79,589 (White 77.2%; Black or African American 4.8%; Hispanic or Latino 15.8%; Asian 0.8%; Other 3.7%). **Foreign born:** 14.7%. **Median age:** 42.6.

Income 2000: per capita $26,102; median household $42,283; **Pop below poverty level:** 10.2%. ***Personal per capita income 2000-2003:** $37,009-$37,901.

Unemployment 2004: 3.3%. **Change from 2000:** +0.7%. **Median travel time to work:** 18.4 minutes. **Working outside county of residence:** 4.6%.

Cities with pop over 10,000: Key West 🏛 (24,768); Marathon (10,002).

NASSAU COUNTY
PO Box 456   **Ph:** 904-548-4600
Fernandina Beach, FL 32035   **Fax:** 904-321-5723
www.nassauclerk.org

In northeastern corner of FL, north of Jacksonville; organized Dec 29, 1824 (prior to statehood) from Duval County. **Name Origin:** For the Nassau River, which forms part of the northern border of the county, and Nassau Sound; named for the duchy in Germany associated with the House of Orange.

Area (sq mi): 725.86 (land 651.55; water 74.3). **Pop per sq mi:** 99.4.

Pop 2005: 64,746. **State rank:** 38. **Pop change:** 2000-20005 +12.3%; 1990-2000 +31.2%. **Pop 2000:** 57,663 (White 89%; Black or African American 7.7%; Hispanic or Latino 1.5%; Asian 0.5%; Other 1.7%). **Foreign born:** 2.7%. **Median age:** 38.3.

Income 2000: per capita $22,836; median household $46,022; **Pop below poverty level:** 9.1%. ***Personal per capita income 2000-2003:** $30,143-$32,042.

Unemployment 2004: 4.2%. **Change from 2000:** +0.2%. **Median travel time to work:** 28.2 minutes. **Working outside county of residence:** 46%.

Cities with pop over 10,000: Fernandina Beach 🏛 (11,241).

OKALOOSA COUNTY
101 E James Lee Blvd   **Ph:** 850-689-5000
Crestview, FL 32536   **Fax:** 850-689-5818
www.co.okaloosa.fl.us

In northwestern FL panhandle, east of Pensacola; organized Jun 13, 1915 from Santa Rosa and Walton counties. **Name Origin:** From Choctaw Indian name for the Blackwater River, which runs through the county; from *oka* 'water' and *lusa* 'black.'

Area (sq mi): 1082 (land 935.63; water 146.37). **Pop per sq mi:** 194.7.

Pop 2005: 182,172. **State rank:** 24. **Pop change:** 2000-20005 +6.8%; 1990-2000 +18.6%. **Pop 2000:** 170,498 (White 81%; Black or African American 9.1%; Hispanic or Latino 4.3%; Asian 2.5%; Other 5%). **Foreign born:** 5.3%. **Median age:** 36.1.

Income 2000: per capita $20,918; median household $41,474; **Pop below poverty level:** 8.8%. ***Personal per capita income 2000-2003:** $26,977-$30,440.

Unemployment 2004: 3.5%. **Change from 2000:** +0.2%. **Median travel time to work:** 21.9 minutes. **Working outside county of residence:** 8.8%.

Cities with pop over 10,000: Fort Walton Beach (19,992); Crestview 🏛 (16,826); Niceville (12,515); Destin (12,162).

OKEECHOBEE COUNTY
304 NW 2nd St   **Ph:** 863-763-6441
Okeechobee, FL 34972   **Fax:** 863-763-9529
www.co.okeechobee.fl.us

In east-central FL, west of Fort Pierce; organized May 8, 1917 from Osceola and Palm Beach counties. **Name Origin:** For Lake Okeechobee, which forms the county's southern boundary; from Hitchiti (Muskhogan) Indian *oki* 'water' and *chobi* 'big.'

Area (sq mi): 891.57 (land 773.94; water 117.63). **Pop per sq mi:** 51.5.

Pop 2005: 39,836. **State rank:** 44. **Pop change:** 2000-20005 +10.9%; 1990-2000 +21.2%. **Pop 2000:** 35,910 (White 71.6%; Black or African American 7.9%; Hispanic or Latino 18.6%; Asian 0.7%; Other 12.1%). **Foreign born:** 11.5%. **Median age:** 36.7.

Income 2000: per capita $14,553; median household $30,456; **Pop below poverty level:** 16%. ***Personal per capita income 2000-2003:** $17,003-$18,726.

Unemployment 2004: 6.3%. **Change from 2000:** -0.7%. **Median travel time to work:** 27.7 minutes. **Working outside county of residence:** 24.5%.

Cities with pop over 10,000: None.

ORANGE COUNTY
201 S Rosalind Ave   **Ph:** 407-836-7350
Orlando, FL 32801   **Fax:** 407-836-5879
www.orangecountyfl.net

In central FL, southwest of Daytona Beach; organized as Mosquito

*Source: Personal per capita income data are from the Bureau of Economic Analysis; per capita income data are from the Bureau of the Census. See Introduction for explanation of differences.

Orange County (cont'd)

County Dec 29, 1824 (prior to statehood) from Indian lands; name changed Jan 30, 1845. **Name Origin:** For the major crop in the region.

Area (sq mi): 1004.19 (land 907.45; water 96.74). **Pop per sq mi:** 1127.4.

Pop 2005: 1,023,023. **State rank:** 5. **Pop change:** 2000-20005 +14.1%; 1990-2000 +32.3%. **Pop 2000:** 896,344 (White 57.5%, Black or African American 18.2%; Hispanic or Latino 18.8%; Asian 3.4%; Other 9.8%). **Foreign born:** 14.4%. **Median age:** 33.3.

Income 2000: per capita $20,916; median household $41,311; **Pop below poverty level:** 12.1%. *Personal per capita income 2000-2003:* $27,084-$28,031.

Unemployment 2004: 4.6%. **Change from 2000:** +0.5%. **Median travel time to work:** 26.6 minutes. **Working outside county of residence:** 14.3%.

Cities with pop over 10,000: 6 (see page 33 for cities).

OSCEOLA COUNTY

2 Courthouse Sq   **Ph:** 407-343-3500
Kissimmee, FL 34741   **Fax:** 407-343-3699
www.osceola.org

In east-central FL, west of Melbourne; organized May 12, 1887 from Brevard and Orange counties. **Name Origin:** For Osceola (c. 1804-38), Seminole leader during the early years of the Second Seminole War (1835-42). Name is from Creek *asi-yahola* 'black drink cry,' and refers to a ceremonial drink made from leaves of the yaupon bush (Ilex vomitoria).

Area (sq mi): 1506.35 (land 1321.9; water 184.45). **Pop per sq mi:** 175.2.

Pop 2005: 231,578. **State rank:** 22. **Pop change:** 2000-20005 +34.3%; 1990-2000 +60.1%. **Pop 2000:** 172,493 (White 59.6%; Black or African American 7.4%; Hispanic or Latino 29.4%; Asian 2.2%; Other 13.3%). **Foreign born:** 14%. **Median age:** 34.6.

Income 2000: per capita $17,022; median household $38,214; **Pop below poverty level:** 11.5%. *Personal per capita income 2000-2003:* $20,112-$20,400.

Unemployment 2004: 4.8%. **Change from 2000:** +0.3%. **Median travel time to work:** 28.1 minutes. **Working outside county of residence:** 50.7%.

Cities with pop over 10,000: Kissimmee 🏛 (56,153); Saint Cloud (22,385).

PALM BEACH COUNTY

301 N Olive Ave   **Ph:** 561-355-2001
West Palm Beach, FL 33401   **Fax:** 561-355-3990
www.co.palm-beach.fl.us

On south-central Atlantic coast, north of Fort Lauderdale; organized Apr 30, 1909 from Dade County. **Name Origin:** For the coconut palms that are common in the area.

Area (sq mi): 2386.33 (land 1974.11; water 412.22). **Pop per sq mi:** 642.6.

Pop 2005: 1,268,548. **State rank:** 3. **Pop change:** 2000-20005 +12.1%; 1990-2000 +31%. **Pop 2000:** 1,131,184 (White 70.6%;

Black or African American 13.8%; Hispanic or Latino 12.4%; Asian 1.5%; Other 5.7%). **Foreign born:** 17.4%. **Median age:** 41.8.

Income 2000: per capita $28,801; median household $45,062; **Pop below poverty level:** 9.9%. *Personal per capita income 2000-2003:* $43,102-$44,050.

Unemployment 2004: 5.1%. **Change from 2000:** -0.4%. **Median travel time to work:** 25.7 minutes. **Working outside county of residence:** 11.3%.

Cities with pop over 10,000: 15 (see page 33 for cities).

PASCO COUNTY

7530 Little Rd   **Ph:** 727-847-8190
New Port Richey, FL 34654
www.pascocountyfl.net

On central Gulf coast of FL, north of Tampa; organized Jun 2, 1887 from Hernando County. **Name Origin:** For Samuel Pasco (1834-1917), English-born FL legislator, and U.S. senator (1887-99).

Area (sq mi): 867.95 (land 744.85; water 123.1). **Pop per sq mi:** 576.

Pop 2005: 429,065. **State rank:** 13. **Pop change:** 2000-20005 +24.5%; 1990-2000 +22.6%. **Pop 2000:** 344,765 (White 89.9%; Black or African American 2.1%; Hispanic or Latino 5.7%; Asian 0.9%; Other 3.3%). **Foreign born:** 7%. **Median age:** 44.9.

Income 2000: per capita $18,439; median household $32,969; **Pop below poverty level:** 10.7%. *Personal per capita income 2000-2003:* $22,582-$24,025.

Unemployment 2004: 5%. **Change from 2000:** +0.8%. **Median travel time to work:** 30 minutes. **Working outside county of residence:** 45.7%.

Cities with pop over 10,000: New Port Richey 🏛 (16,675); Zephyrhills (11,854).

PINELLAS COUNTY

315 Court St   **Ph:** 727-464-3485
Clearwater, FL 33756   **Fax:** 727-464-4384
www.pinellascounty.org

On central Gulf coast of FL, west of Tampa, largely a peninsula, bounded on the east by Old Tampa Bay; organized May 23, 1911 from Hillsborough County. **Name Origin:** Derived from Spanish *punta pinal* 'point of pines.'

Area (sq mi): 607.67 (land 279.92; water 327.75). **Pop per sq mi:** 3315.3.

Pop 2005: 928,032. **State rank:** 6. **Pop change:** 2000-20005 +0.7%; 1990-2000 +8.2%. **Pop 2000:** 921,482 (White 82.8%; Black or African American 9%; Hispanic or Latino 4.6%; Asian 2.1%; Other 3.1%). **Foreign born:** 9.5%. **Median age:** 43.

Income 2000: per capita $23,497; median household $37,111; **Pop below poverty level:** 10%. *Personal per capita income 2000-2003:* $31,784-$33,316.

Unemployment 2004: 4.5%. **Change from 2000:** +0.8%. **Median travel time to work:** 23.6 minutes. **Working outside county of residence:** 13.9%.

Cities with pop over 10,000: 11 (see page 33 for cities).

POLK COUNTY

PO Box 9005 Drawer BC01   **Ph:** 863-534-6000
Bartow, FL 33831   **Fax:** 863-534-7655
www.polk-county.net

In central FL, east of Tampa; organized Feb 8, 1861 from Brevard and Hillsborough counties. **Name Origin:** For James Knox Polk (1795-1849), eleventh U.S. president.

Area (sq mi): 2009.99 (land 1874.38; water 135.6). **Pop per sq mi:** 289.6.

Pop 2005: 542,912. **State rank:** 9. **Pop change:** 2000-20005 +12.2%; 1990-2000 +19.4%. **Pop 2000:** 483,924 (White 74.7%; Black or African American 13.5%; Hispanic or Latino 9.5%; Asian 0.9%; Other 5.9%). **Foreign born:** 6.9%. **Median age:** 38.6.

Income 2000: per capita $18,302; median household $36,036; **Pop below poverty level:** 12.9%. ***Personal per capita income 2000-2003:** $23,723-$25,323.

Unemployment 2004: 5%. **Change from 2000:** -1.2%. **Median travel time to work:** 25.4 minutes. **Working outside county of residence:** 15.7%.

Cities with pop over 10,000: 6 (see page 34 for cities).

PUTNAM COUNTY

PO Box 758   **Ph:** 386-329-0361
Palatka, FL 32178   **Fax:** 386-329-0888
www.co.putnam.fl.us

In northeastern FL, east of Gainesville; organized Jan 13, 1849 from Alachua, Duval, Marion, Mosquito (now Orange), and Saint Johns counties. **Name Origin:** For Gen. Benjamin Alexander Putnam (1801-69), officer in the Seminole Indian War (1835-42), FL legislator, and surveyor-general of FL (1848-54).

Area (sq mi): 827.16 (land 721.89; water 105.27). **Pop per sq mi:** 101.9.

Pop 2005: 73,568. **State rank:** 37. **Pop change:** 2000-20005 +4.5%; 1990-2000 +8.2%. **Pop 2000:** 70,423 (White 75.4%; Black or African American 17%; Hispanic or Latino 5.9%; Asian 0.4%; Other 4.5%). **Foreign born:** 3.4%. **Median age:** 40.5.

Income 2000: per capita $15,603; median household $28,180; **Pop below poverty level:** 20.9%. ***Personal per capita income 2000-2003:** $18,195-$20,371.

Unemployment 2004: 5.5%. **Change from 2000:** -0.4%. **Median travel time to work:** 29.3 minutes. **Working outside county of residence:** 32.8%.

Cities with pop over 10,000: Palatka 🏛 (10,796).

SAINT JOHNS COUNTY

PO Box 300   **Ph:** 904-823-2500
Saint Augustine, FL 32085   **Fax:** 904-819-3666
www.co.st-johns.fl.us

In northeastern FL, south of Jacksonville; original county; organized Aug 12, 1822 (prior to statehood). **Name Origin:** For the Saint Johns River, which forms its western border.

Area (sq mi): 821.43 (land 609.01; water 212.42). **Pop per sq mi:** 265.2.

Pop 2005: 161,525. **State rank:** 27. **Pop change:** 2000-20005 +31.2%; 1990-2000 +46.9%. **Pop 2000:** 123,135 (White 89%; Black

or African American 6.3%; Hispanic or Latino 2.6%; Asian 1%; Other 1.9%). **Foreign born:** 4.9%. **Median age:** 40.6.

Income 2000: per capita $28,674; median household $50,099; **Pop below poverty level:** 8%. ***Personal per capita income 2000-2003:** $37,709-$37,040.

Unemployment 2004: 3.7%. **Change from 2000:** +0.2%. **Median travel time to work:** 26.3 minutes. **Working outside county of residence:** 39.8%.

Cities with pop over 10,000: Saint Augustine 🏛 (12,157).

SAINT LUCIE COUNTY

PO Box 700   **Ph:** 772-462-6900
Fort Pierce, FL 34954
www.stlucieco.gov

On central Atlantic coast of FL, north of Palm Beach; organized Mar 14, 1844 (prior to statehood) from Mosquito County; name changed to Brevard County on Jan 6, 1855. The present-day Saint Lucie County was organized from Brevard County May 24, 1905. **Name Origin:** For Saint Lucy (c.283-303), early Christian martyr.

Area (sq mi): 688.08 (land 572.45; water 115.63). **Pop per sq mi:** 421.5.

Pop 2005: 241,305. **State rank:** 21. **Pop change:** 2000-20005 +25.2%; 1990-2000 +28.3%. **Pop 2000:** 192,695 (White 74.1%; Black or African American 15.4%; Hispanic or Latino 8.2%; Asian 0.9%; Other 4.5%). **Foreign born:** 10.5%. **Median age:** 42.

Income 2000: per capita $18,790; median household $36,363; **Pop below poverty level:** 13.4%. ***Personal per capita income 2000-2003:** $22,237-$23,051.

Unemployment 2004: 6.2%. **Change from 2000:** -2.1%. **Median travel time to work:** 25.9 minutes. **Working outside county of residence:** 34.5%.

Cities with pop over 10,000: Port Saint Lucie (118,396); Fort Pierce 🏛 (37,959).

SANTA ROSA COUNTY

68655 Caroline St   **Ph:** 850-983-1974
Milton, FL 32570   **Fax:** 850-983-1986
www.co.santa-rosa.fl.us

In western end of FL panhandle, east of Pensacola; organized Feb 18, 1842 (prior to statehood) from Escambia County. **Name Origin:** For Santa Rosa Island, which lies off its southern coast; named for Santa Rosa de Viterbo (1235-52), Christian saint.

Area (sq mi): 1173.57 (land 1016.93; water 156.65). **Pop per sq mi:** 140.7.

Pop 2005: 143,105. **State rank:** 30. **Pop change:** 2000-20005 +21.5%; 1990-2000 +44.3%. **Pop 2000:** 117,743 (White 89.1%; Black or African American 4.2%; Hispanic or Latino 2.5%; Asian 1.3%; Other 3.8%, including 1% American Indian/Alaska Native). **Foreign born:** 3%. **Median age:** 36.8.

Income 2000: per capita $20,089; median household $41,881; **Pop below poverty level:** 9.8%. ***Personal per capita income 2000-2003:** $24,066-$25,027.

Unemployment 2004: 4.3%. **Change from 2000:** -0.1%. **Median travel time to work:** 29.2 minutes. **Working outside county of residence:** 55.4%.

---

*Source: Personal per capita income data are from the Bureau of Economic Analysis; per capita income data are from the Bureau of the Census. See Introduction for explanation of differences.

Santa Rosa County (cont'd)

Cities with pop over 10,000: None.

SARASOTA COUNTY

PO Box 3079   **Ph:** 941-861-7400
Sarasota, FL 34230
www.co.sarasota.fl.us

On central Gulf coast of FL, south of Tampa; organized May 14, 1921 from Manatee County. **Name Origin:** Variously attributed to Spanish and Indian sources. One version states that the Spanish gave this name to the area, with the meaning 'place of dancing'; another explanation is that this was the site of a Seminole village named Sarasota, meaning 'point of rocks.'

Area (sq mi): 725.18 (land 571.55; water 153.63). **Pop per sq mi:** 640.8.

Pop 2005: 366,256. **State rank:** 14. **Pop change:** 2000-20005 +12.4%; 1990-2000 +17.3%. **Pop 2000:** 325,957 (White 89.8%; Black or African American 4.2%; Hispanic or Latino 4.3%; Asian 0.8%; Other 2.3%). **Foreign born:** 9.3%. **Median age:** 50.5.

Income 2000: per capita $28,326; median household $41,957; **Pop below poverty level:** 7.8%. ***Personal per capita income 2000-2003:** $39,564-$41,627.

Unemployment 2004: 4%. **Change from 2000:** +1.2%. **Median travel time to work:** 21.8 minutes. **Working outside county of residence:** 14.4%.

Cities with pop over 10,000: Sarasota 🏛 (53,349); North Port (35,272); Venice (19,990).

SEMINOLE COUNTY

1101 E 1st St   **Ph:** 407-665-7945
Sanford, FL 32771   **Fax:** 407-665-7939
www.seminolecountyfl.gov

In east-central FL, north of Orlando; organized Apr 25, 1913 from Orange County. **Name Origin:** For the Muskhogean tribe who lived in FL until the end of the Seminole War (1835-42). Remnants of the tribe moved into the Everglades and their descendants are still there. The name may be from Creek *ishti semoli* 'wild men' or 'separate ones.'

Area (sq mi): 344.87 (land 308.2; water 36.67). **Pop per sq mi:** 1303.1.

Pop 2005: 401,619. **State rank:** 13. **Pop change:** 2000-20005 +10%; 1990-2000 +27%. **Pop 2000:** 365,196 (White 75.2%; Black or African American 9.5%; Hispanic or Latino 11.2%; Asian 2.5%; Other 5.6%). **Foreign born:** 9.1%. **Median age:** 36.2.

Income 2000: per capita $24,591; median household $49,326; **Pop below poverty level:** 7.4%. ***Personal per capita income 2000-2003:** $30,925-$33,676.

Unemployment 2004: 4.3%. **Change from 2000:** +0.6%. **Median travel time to work:** 27 minutes. **Working outside county of residence:** 48.7%.

Cities with pop over 10,000: 7 (see page 34 for cities).

SUMTER COUNTY

209 N Florida St   **Ph:** 352-793-0200
Bushnell, FL 33513   **Fax:** 352-793-0207
www.bocc.co.sumter.fl.us

In west-central FL, west of Orlando; organized 1853 from Marion and Orange counties. **Name Origin:** For Gen. Thomas Sumter (1734-1832), American Revolutionary officer nicknamed the 'Gamecock of the Revolution,' U.S. representative from GA (1789-93; 1797-1801), and U.S. senator (1801-10).

Area (sq mi): 580.31 (land 545.73; water 34.58). **Pop per sq mi:** 117.6.

Pop 2005: 64,182. **State rank:** 39. **Pop change:** 2000-20005 +20.3%; 1990-2000 +68.9%. **Pop 2000:** 53,345 (White 78.4%; Black or African American 13.8%; Hispanic or Latino 6.3%; Asian 0.4%; Other 3.3%). **Foreign born:** 5.5%. **Median age:** 49.2.

Income 2000: per capita $16,830; median household $32,073; **Pop below poverty level:** 13.7%. ***Personal per capita income 2000-2003:** $15,421-$17,793.

Unemployment 2004: 4.7%. **Change from 2000:** +0.4%. **Median travel time to work:** 28.6 minutes. **Working outside county of residence:** 45.8%.

Cities with pop over 10,000: None.

SUWANNEE COUNTY

200 S Ohio Ave   **Ph:** 386-364-3498
Live Oak, FL 32064   **Fax:** 386-362-0548
www.suwanneechamber.com

In northern FL, west of Jacksonville; organized Dec 21, 1858 from Columbia County. **Name Origin:** For the Suwanee River, which forms the northern and western borders of the county.

Area (sq mi): 691.9 (land 687.64; water 4.26). **Pop per sq mi:** 56.2.

Pop 2005: 38,624. **State rank:** 46. **Pop change:** 2000-20005 +10.8%; 1990-2000 +30.1%. **Pop 2000:** 34,844 (White 81.1%; Black or African American 12.1%; Hispanic or Latino 4.9%; Asian 0.5%; Other 2.8%). **Foreign born:** 4.7%. **Median age:** 39.7.

Income 2000: per capita $14,678; median household $29,963; **Pop below poverty level:** 18.5%. ***Personal per capita income 2000-2003:** $18,995-$20,439.

Unemployment 2004: 4.3%. **Change from 2000:** -1.3%. **Median travel time to work:** 27.9 minutes. **Working outside county of residence:** 34.7%.

Cities with pop over 10,000: None.

TAYLOR COUNTY

PO Box 620   **Ph:** 850-838-3506
Perry, FL 32348   **Fax:** 850-838-3549
taco.perryfl.com

On northern Gulf coast of FL, southeast of Tallahassee; organized Dec 23, 1856 from Madison County. **Name Origin:** For Zachary Taylor (1784-1850), twelfth U.S. president.

Area (sq mi): 1232.01 (land 1041.91; water 190.1). **Pop per sq mi:** 18.8.

Pop 2005: 19,622. **State rank:** 54. **Pop change:** 2000-20005 +1.9%; 1990-2000 +12.5%. **Pop 2000:** 19,256 (White 76.9%; Black or African American 19%; Hispanic or Latino 1.5%; Asian 0.4%; Other

Taylor County (cont'd)

2.7%, including 1% American Indian/Alaska Native). **Foreign born:** 1.7%. **Median age:** 37.8.

Income 2000: per capita $15,281; median household $30,032; **Pop below poverty level:** 18%. ***Personal per capita income 2000-2003:** $19,239-$19,965.

Unemployment 2004: 5.8%. **Change from 2000:** -3.8%. **Median travel time to work:** 20.9 minutes. **Working outside county of residence:** 12.6%.

Cities with pop over 10,000: None.

UNION COUNTY
55 W Main St Rm 103   **Ph:** 386-496-3711
Lake Butler, FL 32054   **Fax:** 386-496-1718
www.unioncofl.com

In north-central FL, southwest of Jacksonville; organized May 20, 1921 from Bradford County. **Name Origin:** An expression of unity between political parties in the division of Bradford County, from which this was formed, and in the location of the county seat.

Area (sq mi): 249.71 (land 240.29; water 9.42). **Pop per sq mi:** 62.1.

Pop 2005: 14,916. **State rank:** 58. **Pop change:** 2000-20005 +11%; 1990-2000 +31.1%. **Pop 2000:** 13,442 (White 71.9%; Black or African American 22.8%; Hispanic or Latino 3.5%; Asian 0.3%; Other 3.2%). **Foreign born:** 2.1%. **Median age:** 35.7.

Income 2000: per capita $12,333; median household $34,563; **Pop below poverty level:** 14%. ***Personal per capita income 2000-2003:** $13,249-$14,021.

Unemployment 2004: 4.8%. **Change from 2000:** +0.8%. **Median travel time to work:** 28.6 minutes. **Working outside county of residence:** 53.6%.

Cities with pop over 10,000: None.

VOLUSIA COUNTY
123 W Indiana Ave   **Ph:** 386-736-5920
DeLand, FL 32720   **Fax:** 386-822-5707
volusia.org

On central Atlantic coast of FL, northeast of Orlando; organized Dec 29, 1854 from Saint Lucie County. **Name Origin:** For Volusia Landing on the Saint Johns River, the latter forms the western border of the county. Origin uncertain.

Area (sq mi): 1432.44 (land 1103.25; water 329.19). **Pop per sq mi:** 444.2.

Pop 2005: 490,055. **State rank:** 11. **Pop change:** 2000-20005 +10.5%; 1990-2000 +19.6%. **Pop 2000:** 443,343 (White 81.9%; Black or African American 9.3%; Hispanic or Latino 6.6%; Asian 1%; Other 3.5%). **Foreign born:** 6.4%. **Median age:** 42.4.

Income 2000: per capita $19,664; median household $35,219; **Pop below poverty level:** 11.6%. ***Personal per capita income 2000-2003:** $23,327-$25,403.

Unemployment 2004: 4.6%. **Change from 2000:** +0.3%. **Median travel time to work:** 25.4 minutes. **Working outside county of residence:** 19.4%.

Cities with pop over 10,000: 10 (see page 34 for cities).

WAKULLA COUNTY
3056 Crawfordville Hwy   **Ph:** 850-926-0905
Crawfordville, FL 32327   **Fax:** 850-926-0938
www.clerk.wakulla.fl.us

On north Gulf coast of FL, south of Tallahassee; organized Mar 11, 1843 (prior to statehood) from Leon County. **Name Origin:** Possibly from Creek *wahkola* 'loon,'

Area (sq mi): 735.74 (land 606.66; water 129.08). **Pop per sq mi:** 46.5.

Pop 2005: 28,212. **State rank:** 50. **Pop change:** 2000-20005 +23.4%; 1990-2000 +61%. **Pop 2000:** 22,863 (White 84.8%; Black or African American 11.5%; Hispanic or Latino 1.9%; Asian 0.2%; Other 2.1%). **Foreign born:** 1.5%. **Median age:** 36.8.

Income 2000: per capita $17,678; median household $37,149; **Pop below poverty level:** 11.3%. ***Personal per capita income 2000-2003:** $22,266-$21,753.

Unemployment 2004: 3.5%. **Change from 2000:** +0.1%. **Median travel time to work:** 35.5 minutes. **Working outside county of residence:** 61.4%.

Cities with pop over 10,000: None.

WALTON COUNTY
PO Box 1260   **Ph:** 850-892-8115
De Funiak Springs, FL 32435   **Fax:** 850-892-7551
www.co.walton.fl.us

In central part of FL panhandle, east of Pensacola; organized Dec 29, 1824 (prior to statehood) from Jackson County. **Name Origin:** For Col. George William Walton (1740-1804), secretary of the Territory of West Florida under Andrew Jackson (1821-22).

Area (sq mi): 1238.03 (land 1057.56; water 180.47). **Pop per sq mi:** 47.6.

Pop 2005: 50,324. **State rank:** 41. **Pop change:** 2000-20005 +23.9%; 1990-2000 +46.3%. **Pop 2000:** 40,601 (White 87.3%; Black or African American 7%; Hispanic or Latino 2.2%; Asian 0.5%; Other 4.2%, including 1.3% American Indian/Alaska Native). **Foreign born:** 3.2%. **Median age:** 40.5.

Income 2000: per capita $18,198; median household $32,407; **Pop below poverty level:** 14.4%. ***Personal per capita income 2000-2003:** $18,504-$20,750.

Unemployment 2004: 3.4%. **Change from 2000:** +0.1%. **Median travel time to work:** 31.3 minutes. **Working outside county of residence:** 34.7%.

Cities with pop over 10,000: None.

WASHINGTON COUNTY
PO Box 647   **Ph:** 850-638-6285
Chipley, FL 32428   **Fax:** 850-638-6297
www.washingtonfl.com

In central part of FL panhandle, north of Panama City; organized Dec 9, 1825 (prior to statehood) from Jackson and Walton counties. **Name Origin:** For George Washington (1732-99), American patriot and first U.S. president.

Area (sq mi): 615.79 (land 579.93; water 35.86). **Pop per sq mi:** 38.5.

Source: Personal per capita income data are from the Bureau of Economic Analysis; per capita income data are from the Bureau of the Census. See Introduction for explanation of differences.

Washington County (cont'd)

Pop 2005: 22,299. **State rank:** 53. **Pop change:** 2000-20005 +6.3%; 1990-2000 +24%. **Pop 2000:** 20,973 (White 80.5%; Black or African American 13.7%; Hispanic or Latino 2.3%; Asian 0.4%; Other 4.2%, including 1.5% American Indian/Alaska Native). **Foreign born:** 2.5%. **Median age:** 38.8.

Income 2000: per capita $14,980; median household $27,922; **Pop below poverty level:** 19.2%. ***Personal per capita Income 2000-2003:** $17,628-$18,545.

Unemployment 2004: 4.8%. **Change from 2000:** -0.2%. **Median travel time to work:** 28.9 minutes. **Working outside county of residence:** 46.8%.

Cities with pop over 10,000: None.

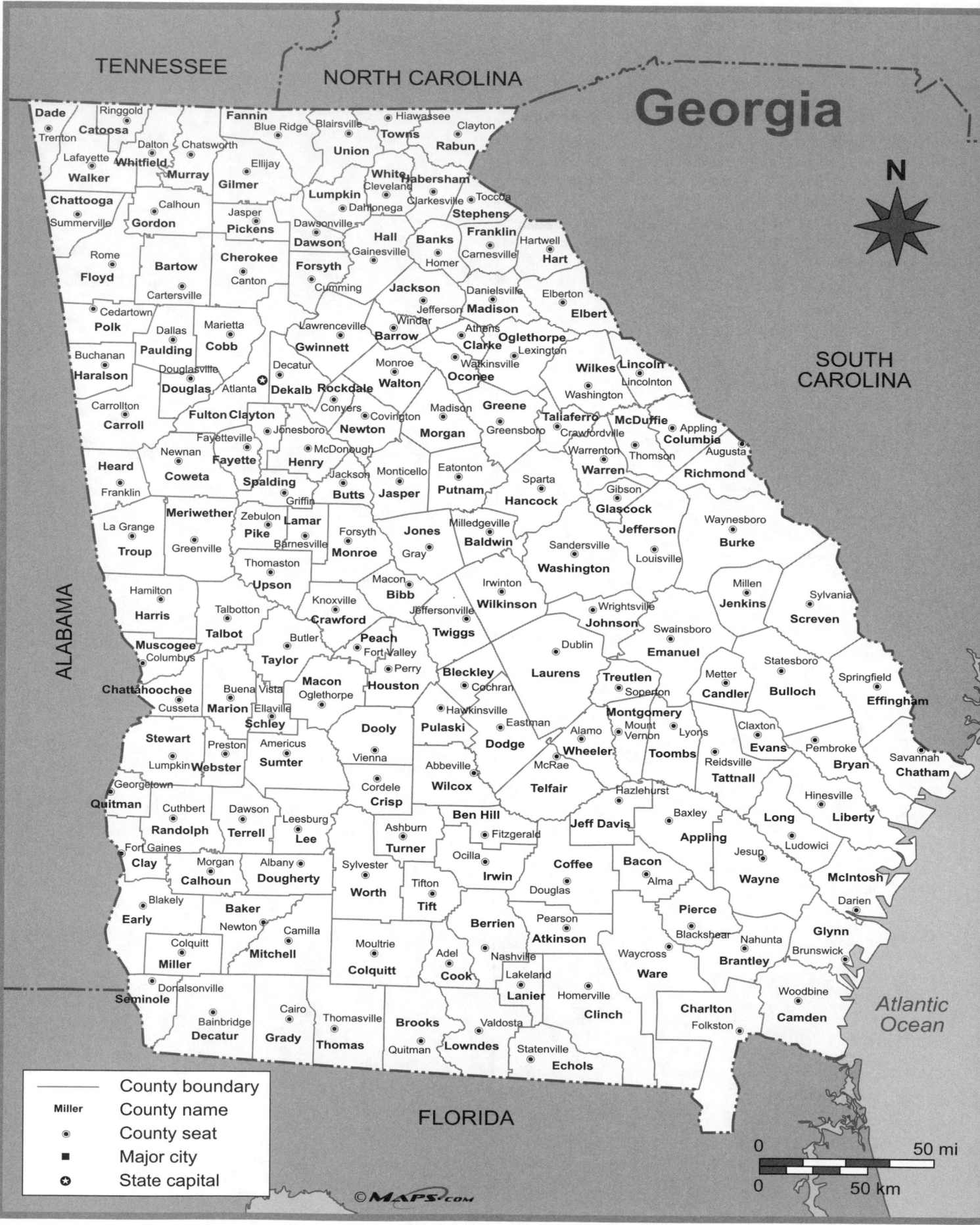

Georgia

TENNESSEE

NORTH CAROLINA

ALABAMA

SOUTH CAROLINA

FLORIDA

Atlantic Ocean

N

	County boundary
Miller	County name
⊙	County seat
■	Major city
✪	State capital

0   50 mi

0   50 km

©MAPS.com

Georgia

GEORGIA STATE INFORMATION
www.georgia.gov   **Ph:** 404-656-2000

Area (sq mi): 59,424.77 (land 57,906.14; water 1518.63). **Pop per sq mi:** 156.7.

Pop 2005: 9,072,576. **Pop change:** 2000-20005 +10.8%; 1990-2000 +26.4%. **Pop 2000:** 8,186,453 (White 62.6%; Black or African American 28.7%; Hispanic or Latino 5.3%; Asian 2.1%; Other 4.2%). **Foreign born:** 7.1%. **Median age:** 33.4.

Income 2000: per capita $21,154; median household $42,433; **Pop below poverty level:** 13%. ***Personal per capita income 2000-2003:** $27,989-$29,000.

Unemployment 2004: 4.8%. **Change from 2000:** +1.3%. **Median travel time to work:** 27.7 minutes. **Working outside county of residence:** 41.5%.

APPLING COUNTY
60 Tippins St Suite 201   **Ph:** 912-367-8100
Baxley, GA 31513   **Fax:** 912-367-8161
www.baxley.org/site/

In southeast-central GA; organized 1818 (prior to statehood) from Creek cession. **Name Origin:** For Daniel Appling (1787-1818), an officer in the War of 1812.

Area (sq mi): 512.11 (land 508.51; water 3.61). **Pop per sq mi:** 35.3.

Pop 2005: 17,954. **State rank:** 91. **Pop change:** 2000-20005 +3.1%; 1990-2000 +10.6%. **Pop 2000:** 17,419 (White 74.9%; Black or African American 19.6%; Hispanic or Latino 4.5%; Asian 0.3%; Other 3.3%). **Foreign born:** 3.4%. **Median age:** 35.4.

Income 2000: per capita $15,044; median household $30,266; **Pop below poverty level:** 18.6%. ***Personal per capita income 2000-2003:** $19,214-$19,747.

Unemployment 2004: 6.1%. **Change from 2000:** -2.8%. **Median travel time to work:** 24.1 minutes. **Working outside county of residence:** 28.3%.

Cities with pop over 10,000: None.

ATHENS-CLARKE COUNTY
PO Box 1868   **Ph:** 706-613-3031
Athens, GA 30603   **Fax:** 706-613-3033
www.athensclarkecounty.com

In north-central GA, northeast of Atlanta; organized Dec 5, 1801 from Jackson and Greene counties. **Name Origin:** For Gen. Elijah Clarke (1733-99), an officer in the American Revolution.

Area (sq mi): 121.28 (land 120.79; water 0.49). **Pop per sq mi:** 864.6.

Pop 2005: 104,439. **State rank:** 19. **Pop change:** 2000-20005 +2.9%; 1990-2000 +15.9%. **Pop 2000:** 101,489 (White 62%; Black or African American 27.3%; Hispanic or Latino 6.3%; Asian 3.1%; Other 4.7%). **Foreign born:** 8.4%. **Median age:** 25.4.

Income 2000: per capita $17,123; median household $28,403; **Pop below poverty level:** 28.3%. ***Personal per capita income 2000-2003:** $21,253-$23,125.

Unemployment 2004: 3.6%. **Change from 2000:** +0.2%. **Median travel time to work:** 18.6 minutes. **Working outside county of residence:** 19.1%.

Cities with pop over 10,000: Athens 🏛 (102,744).

ATKINSON COUNTY
PO Box 518   **Ph:** 912-422-3391
Pearson, GA 31642   **Fax:** 912-422-3429

In south-central GA, northeast of Valdosta; organized Aug 15, 1917 from Coffee and Clinch counties. **Name Origin:** For William Yates Atkinson (1854-99), GA governor (1894-99).

Area (sq mi): 344.1 (land 338.04; water 6.05). **Pop per sq mi:** 23.8.

Pop 2005: 8,030. **State rank:** 140. **Pop change:** 2000-20005 +5.5%; 1990-2000 +22.5%. **Pop 2000:** 7,609 (White 62.6%; Black or African American 19.6%; Hispanic or Latino 17%; Asian 0.1%; Other 13.5%). **Foreign born:** 12.1%. **Median age:** 30.7.

Income 2000: per capita $12,178; median household $26,470; **Pop below poverty level:** 23%. ***Personal per capita income 2000-2003:** $17,856-$19,595.

Unemployment 2004: 7.5%. **Change from 2000:** -1.6%. **Median travel time to work:** 23.9 minutes. **Working outside county of residence:** 42.9%.

Cities with pop over 10,000: None.

AUGUSTA-RICHMOND COUNTY
530 Greene St   **Ph:** 706-821-2400
Augusta, GA 30911   **Fax:** 706-821-2819
www.augustaga.gov

On central east coast of GA; original county; organized Feb 5, 1777 (prior to statehood) from Saint Paul Parish. **Name Origin:** For Charles Lennox, 1st Duke of Richmond (1672-1723).

Area (sq mi): 328.45 (land 324.04; water 4.41). **Pop per sq mi:** 604.2.

Pop 2005: 195,769. **State rank:** 7. **Pop change:** 2000-20005 -2%; 1990-2000 +5.3%. **Pop 2000:** 199,775 (White 44.4%; Black or

Augusta-Richmond County (cont'd)

African American 49.8%; Hispanic or Latino 2.8%; Asian 1.5%; Other 3.2%). **Foreign born:** 3.4%. **Median age:** 32.3.

Income 2000: per capita $17,088; median household $33,086; **Pop below poverty level:** 19.6%. *****Personal per capita income 2000-2003:** $22,105-$24,320.

Unemployment 2004: 5.9%. **Change from 2000:** +0.4%. **Median travel time to work:** 22.2 minutes. **Working outside county of residence:** 20.3%.

Cities with pop over 10,000: Augusta ⚏ (191,326).

BACON COUNTY

PO Box 356   **Ph:** 912-632-5214
Alma, GA 31510   **Fax:** 912-632-2757

In southeast-central GA, northwest of Brunswick; organized Jul 27, 1914 from Appling, Pierce, and Ware counties. **Name Origin:** For Capt. Augustus Octavius Bacon (1839-1914), Confederate army officer and U.S. senator (1895-1914) from GA.

Area (sq mi): 285.92 (land 284.95; water 0.97). **Pop per sq mi:** 36.4.

Pop 2005: 10,379. **State rank:** 124. **Pop change:** 2000-20005 +2.7%; 1990-2000 +5.6%. **Pop 2000:** 10,103 (White 79.9%; Black or African American 15.7%; Hispanic or Latino 3.4%; Asian 0.3%; Other 2.5%). **Foreign born:** 1.6%. **Median age:** 34.8.

Income 2000: per capita $14,289; median household $26,910; **Pop below poverty level:** 23.7%. *****Personal per capita income 2000-2003:** $18,926-$19,554.

Unemployment 2004: 5.2%. **Change from 2000:** -1.3%. **Median travel time to work:** 24.4 minutes. **Working outside county of residence:** 32%.

Cities with pop over 10,000: None.

BAKER COUNTY

PO Box 10   **Ph:** 229-734-3004
Newton, GA 39870   **Fax:** 229-734-7770

In southwestern GA, southwest of Albany; organized Dec 12, 1825 from Early County. **Name Origin:** For Col. John Baker (?-1792), Army officer and GA legislator.

Area (sq mi): 349.17 (land 343.22; water 5.95). **Pop per sq mi:** 12.1.

Pop 2005: 4,154. **State rank:** 153. **Pop change:** 2000-20005 +2%; 1990-2000 +12.7%. **Pop 2000:** 4,074 (White 46.4%; Black or African American 50.4%; Hispanic or Latino 2.7%; Asian 0%; Other 2.1%). **Foreign born:** 1.9%. **Median age:** 35.

Income 2000: per capita $16,969; median household $30,338; **Pop below poverty level:** 23.4%. *****Personal per capita income 2000-2003:** $20,150-$19,708.

Unemployment 2004: 4.2%. **Change from 2000:** -0.9%. **Median travel time to work:** 28.3 minutes. **Working outside county of residence:** 65.5%.

Cities with pop over 10,000: None.

BALDWIN COUNTY

121 N Wilkinson St Suite 314   **Ph:** 478-445-4791
Milledgeville, GA 31061   **Fax:** 478-445-6320
www.baldwincountyga.com

In central GA, northeast of Macon; original county; organized May 11, 1803 from Creek Indian lands and Hancock, Washington, and Wilkinson counties. **Name Origin:** For Abraham Baldwin (1754-1807), member of the Continental Congress, and U.S. senator from GA (1799-1807).

Area (sq mi): 267.5 (land 258.45; water 9.05). **Pop per sq mi:** 175.

Pop 2005: 45,230. **State rank:** 43. **Pop change:** 2000-20005 +1.2%; 1990-2000 +13.1%. **Pop 2000:** 44,700 (White 53.5%; Black or African American 43.4%; Hispanic or Latino 1.4%; Asian 1%; Other 1.4%). **Foreign born:** 1.9%. **Median age:** 34.2.

Income 2000: per capita $16,271; median household $35,159; **Pop below poverty level:** 16.8%. *****Personal per capita income 2000-2003:** $21,285-$22,835.

Unemployment 2004: 4.5%. **Change from 2000:** +0.8%. **Median travel time to work:** 19.9 minutes. **Working outside county of residence:** 20.4%.

Cities with pop over 10,000: Milledgeville ⚏ (19,268).

BANKS COUNTY

144 Yonah Homer Rd PO Box 337   **Ph:** 706-677-6240
Homer, GA 30547   **Fax:** 706-677-6294
www.bankscountyga.org

In northeastern GA, north of Athens; organized Dec 11, 1858 from Franklin and Habersham counties. **Name Origin:** For Richard Banks (1784-1850), a noted local surgeon.

Area (sq mi): 233.87 (land 233.67; water 0.2). **Pop per sq mi:** 68.7.

Pop 2005: 16,055. **State rank:** 102. **Pop change:** 2000-20005 +11.3%; 1990-2000 +39.9%. **Pop 2000:** 14,422 (White 91.9%; Black or African American 3.2%; Hispanic or Latino 3.4%; Asian 0.6%; Other 3.1%). **Foreign born:** 2.1%. **Median age:** 35.2.

Income 2000: per capita $17,424; median household $38,523; **Pop below poverty level:** 12.5%. *****Personal per capita income 2000-2003:** $21,669-$24,059.

Unemployment 2004: 3.4%. **Change from 2000:** -0.4%. **Median travel time to work:** 30.1 minutes. **Working outside county of residence:** 75.2%.

Cities with pop over 10,000: None.

BARROW COUNTY

233 E Broad St   **Ph:** 770-307-3005
Winder, GA 30680   **Fax:** 770-307-3141
www.barrowga.org

In north-central GA, west of Athens; organized Jul 7, 1914 from Jackson, Walton, and Gwinnett counties. **Name Origin:** For David Crenshaw Barrow (1852-1929), professor and chancellor of the University of Georgia.

Area (sq mi): 162.84 (land 162.17; water 0.67). **Pop per sq mi:** 369.7.

Pop 2005: 59,954. **State rank:** 36. **Pop change:** 2000-20005 +29.9%; 1990-2000 +55.3%. **Pop 2000:** 46,144 (White 83.5%;

*Source: Personal per capita income data are from the Bureau of Economic Analysis; per capita income data are from the Bureau of the Census. See Introduction for explanation of differences.

146

Barrow County (cont'd)

Black or African American 9.7%; Hispanic or Latino 3.2%; Asian 2.2%; Other 3.2%). **Foreign born:** 3.6%. **Median age:** 32.5.

Income 2000: per capita $18,350; median household $45,019; **Pop below poverty level:** 8.3%. ***Personal per capita income 2000-2003:** $23,246-$23,360.

Unemployment 2004: 4.3%. **Change from 2000:** -0.2%. **Median travel time to work:** 33.7 minutes. **Working outside county of residence:** 65.7%.

Cities with pop over 10,000: Winder ⛫ (12,083).

BARTOW COUNTY

135 W Cherokee Ave Suite 251   **Ph:** 770-387-5030
Cartersville, GA 30120   **Fax:** 770-387-5023
www.bartowga.org

In northwestern GA, east of Rome; organized as Cass County Dec 3, 1832 from Indian lands; name changed Dec 6, 1861. **Name Origin:** For Confederate Gen. Francis S. Bartow (? 1861), first officer of such rank to be killed in action during the Civil War.

Area (sq mi): 470.11 (land 459.43; water 10.69). **Pop per sq mi:** 194.2.

Pop 2005: 89,229. **State rank:** 26. **Pop change:** 2000-20005 +17.4%; 1990-2000 +36%. **Pop 2000:** 76,019 (White 86.4%; Black or African American 8.7%; Hispanic or Latino 3.3%; Asian 0.5%; Other 3%). **Foreign born:** 2.5%. **Median age:** 33.7.

Income 2000: per capita $18,989; median household $43,660; **Pop below poverty level:** 8.6%. ***Personal per capita income 2000-2003:** $25,820-$26,265.

Unemployment 2004: 5%. **Change from 2000:** +0.5%. **Median travel time to work:** 29.6 minutes. **Working outside county of residence:** 42.4%.

Cities with pop over 10,000: Cartersville ⛫ (17,403).

BEN HILL COUNTY

402A E Pine St   **Ph:** 229-426-5112
Fitzgerald, GA 31750   **Fax:** 229-426-5106
www.benhillcounty.com

In south-central GA, northeast of Albany; organized Jul 31, 1906 from Irwin and Wilcox counties. **Name Origin:** For Benjamin Harvey Hill (1823-82), GA legislator and U.S. senator.

Area (sq mi): 254.03 (land 251.79; water 2.23). **Pop per sq mi:** 68.8.

Pop 2005: 17,316. **State rank:** 93. **Pop change:** 2000-20005 -1%; 1990-2000 +7.6%. **Pop 2000:** 17,484 (White 61.9%; Black or African American 32.6%; Hispanic or Latino 4.6%; Asian 0.3%; Other 3.9%). **Foreign born:** 3.4%. **Median age:** 34.8.

Income 2000: per capita $14,093; median household $27,100; **Pop below poverty level:** 22.3%. ***Personal per capita income 2000-2003:** $20,603-$22,475.

Unemployment 2004: 4.9%. **Change from 2000:** -0.5%. **Median travel time to work:** 18.3 minutes. **Working outside county of residence:** 21.4%.

Cities with pop over 10,000: None.

BERRIEN COUNTY

PO Box 446   **Ph:** 229-686-5421
Nashville, GA 31639   **Fax:** 229-686-2785

In south-central GA, north of Valdosta; organized Feb 25, 1856 from Lowndes, Coffee, and Irwin counties. **Name Origin:** For John Macpherson Berrien (1781-1856), U.S. senator from GA (1825-29; 1841-52) and U.S. Attorney General (1829-31).

Area (sq mi): 457.78 (land 452.41; water 5.37). **Pop per sq mi:** 36.9.

Pop 2005: 16,708. **State rank:** 96. **Pop change:** 2000-20005 +2.9%; 1990-2000 +14.7%. **Pop 2000:** 16,235 (White 84.8%; Black or African American 11.4%; Hispanic or Latino 2.4%; Asian 0.3%; Other 2.8%). **Foreign born:** 1.4%. **Median age:** 35.2.

Income 2000: per capita $16,375; median household $30,044; **Pop below poverty level:** 17.7%. ***Personal per capita income 2000-2003:** $20,928-$23,288.

Unemployment 2004: 3.6%. **Change from 2000:** -1.6%. **Median travel time to work:** 21.9 minutes. **Working outside county of residence:** 44.7%.

Cities with pop over 10,000: None.

BIBB COUNTY

601 Mulberry St   **Ph:** 478-621-6400
Macon, GA 31201   **Fax:** 478-621-6329
www.co.bibb.ga.us

In central GA; organized Dec 9, 1822 from Jones, Monroe, Twiggs, and Houston counties. **Name Origin:** For William Wyatt Bibb (1781-1820), U.S. senator from GA (1813-16) and first governor of AL (1817-20).

Area (sq mi): 255.13 (land 249.96; water 5.17). **Pop per sq mi:** 619.8.

Pop 2005: 154,918. **State rank:** 12. **Pop change:** 2000-20005 +0.7%; 1990-2000 +2.6%. **Pop 2000:** 153,887 (White 49.6%; Black or African American 47.3%; Hispanic or Latino 1.3%; Asian 1.1%; Other 1.5%). **Foreign born:** 1.9%. **Median age:** 34.7.

Income 2000: per capita $19,058; median household $34,532; **Pop below poverty level:** 19.1%. ***Personal per capita income 2000-2003:** $27,053-$29,405.

Unemployment 2004: 5.1%. **Change from 2000:** +0.8%. **Median travel time to work:** 22.2 minutes. **Working outside county of residence:** 14.4%.

Cities with pop over 10,000: Macon ⛫ (94,990).

BLECKLEY COUNTY

306 SE 2nd St   **Ph:** 478-934-3200
Cochran, GA 31014   **Fax:** 478-934-0822
www.bleckley.org

In central GA, southeast of Macon; organized Jul 30, 1912 from Pulaski County. **Name Origin:** For Logan Edwin Bleckley (1827-1907), Confederate soldier and chief justice of GA supreme court.

Area (sq mi): 219.14 (land 217.39; water 1.74). **Pop per sq mi:** 55.8.

Pop 2005: 12,141. **State rank:** 114. **Pop change:** 2000-20005 +4.1%; 1990-2000 +11.9%. **Pop 2000:** 11,666 (White 72.9%; Black or African American 24.6%; Hispanic or Latino 0.9%; Asian 0.9%; Other 1.2%). **Foreign born:** 1.4%. **Median age:** 35.1.

Bleckley County (cont'd)

Income 2000: per capita $15,934; median household $33,448; **Pop below poverty level:** 15.9%. ***Personal per capita income 2000-2003:** $21,677-$23,904.

Unemployment 2004: 5.4%. **Change from 2000:** +0.9%. **Median travel time to work:** 26.1 minutes. **Working outside county of residence:** 45%.

Cities with pop over 10,000: None.

BRANTLEY COUNTY

PO Box 398   **Ph:** 912-462-6285
Nahunta, GA 31553   **Fax:** 912-462-5538
www.brantleycounty.org

In southeastern GA, west of Brunswick; organized Aug 4, 1920 from Charlton, Pierce, and Wayne counties. **Name Origin:** For William Gordon Brantley (1860-1934), state senator. Some claim Benjamin D. Brantley (1832-91).

Area (sq mi): 447.42 (land 444.4; water 3.02). **Pop per sq mi:** 34.9.

Pop 2005: 15,491. **State rank:** 105. **Pop change:** 2000-20005 +5.9%; 1990-2000 +32.1%. **Pop 2000:** 14,629 (White 93.7%; Black or African American 4%; Hispanic or Latino 1%; Asian 0.1%; Other 1.5%). **Foreign born:** 0.9%. **Median age:** 34.6.

Income 2000: per capita $13,713; median household $30,361; **Pop below poverty level:** 15.6%. ***Personal per capita income 2000-2003:** $17,685-$19,589.

Unemployment 2004: 4.7%. **Change from 2000:** -0.9%. **Median travel time to work:** 34 minutes. **Working outside county of residence:** 71.1%.

Cities with pop over 10,000: None.

BROOKS COUNTY

PO Box 272   **Ph:** 229-263-5561
Quitman, GA 31643   **Fax:** 229-263-9345
www.brooks-county.org

On central southern border of GA, west of Valdosta; organized Dec 11, 1858 from Lowndes and Thomas counties. **Name Origin:** For a local citizen.

Area (sq mi): 497.77 (land 493.62; water 4.15). **Pop per sq mi:** 33.1.

Pop 2005: 16,327. **State rank:** 99. **Pop change:** 2000-20005 -0.7%; 1990-2000 +6.8%. **Pop 2000:** 16,450 (White 56.6%; Black or African American 39.3%; Hispanic or Latino 3.1%; Asian 0.3%; Other 3%). **Foreign born:** 1.7%. **Median age:** 36.3.

Income 2000: per capita $13,977; median household $26,911; **Pop below poverty level:** 23.4%. ***Personal per capita income 2000-2003:** $20,236-$21,345.

Unemployment 2004: 3.6%. **Change from 2000:** -1.3%. **Median travel time to work:** 24.6 minutes. **Working outside county of residence:** 51.5%.

Cities with pop over 10,000: None.

BRYAN COUNTY

116 Lanier St PO Box 430   **Ph:** 912-653-3819
Pembroke, GA 31321   **Fax:** 912-653-4691
www.bryancountyga.org

In southeastern GA, west of Savannah; organized Dec 19, 1793 from Chatham County. **Name Origin:** For Jonathan Bryan (1708-88), a founder of the Georgia Colony at Savannah, jurist, and GA legislator.

Area (sq mi): 454.49 (land 441.71; water 12.78). **Pop per sq mi:** 64.6.

Pop 2005: 28,549. **State rank:** 56. **Pop change:** 2000-20005 +21.9%; 1990-2000 +51.7%. **Pop 2000:** 23,417 (White 81.7%; Black or African American 14.1%; Hispanic or Latino 2%; Asian 0.8%; Other 2.3%). **Foreign born:** 2.5%. **Median age:** 33.3.

Income 2000: per capita $19,794; median household $48,345; **Pop below poverty level:** 11.7%. ***Personal per capita income 2000-2003:** $24,088-$26,871.

Unemployment 2004: 3.3%. **Change from 2000:** +0.8%. **Median travel time to work:** 31.3 minutes. **Working outside county of residence:** 74.8%.

Cities with pop over 10,000: None.

BULLOCH COUNTY

PO Box 347   **Ph:** 912-764-6245
Statesboro, GA 30459   **Fax:** 912-764-8634
www.bullochcounty.net

In central eastern GA, northwest of Savannah; organized Feb 8, 1796 from Bryan and Screven counties. **Name Origin:** For Archibald Bulloch (1730-77), soldier, legislator, and first governor of GA (1776-77).

Area (sq mi): 688.84 (land 682.07; water 6.77). **Pop per sq mi:** 90.1.

Pop 2005: 61,454. **State rank:** 33. **Pop change:** 2000-20005 +9.8%; 1990-2000 +29.8%. **Pop 2000:** 55,983 (White 67.9%; Black or African American 28.8%; Hispanic or Latino 1.9%; Asian 0.8%; Other 1.7%). **Foreign born:** 3.1%. **Median age:** 26.1.

Income 2000: per capita $16,080; median household $29,499; **Pop below poverty level:** 24.5%. ***Personal per capita income 2000-2003:** $19,595-$19,872.

Unemployment 2004: 4.3%. **Change from 2000:** +0.6%. **Median travel time to work:** 22.7 minutes. **Working outside county of residence:** 22.6%.

Cities with pop over 10,000: Statesboro ⛪ (24,604).

BURKE COUNTY

PO Box 89   **Ph:** 706-554-2324
Waynesboro, GA 30830   **Fax:** 706-554-0350
www.burkecounty-ga.gov

On central east coast of GA, south of Augusta; original county; organized Feb 5, 1777 (prior to statehood) from Saint George Parish. **Name Origin:** For Edmund Burke (1729-97), British statesman, orator, and defender of the American colonies.

Area (sq mi): 834.99 (land 830.47; water 4.52). **Pop per sq mi:** 28.1.

*Source: Personal per capita income data are from the Bureau of Economic Analysis; per capita income data are from the Bureau of the Census. See Introduction for explanation of differences.

Burke County (cont'd)

Pop 2005: 23,299. **State rank:** 75. **Pop change:** 2000-20005 +4.7%; 1990-2000 +8.1%. **Pop 2000:** 22,243 (White 46.5%; Black or African American 51%; Hispanic or Latino 1.4%; Asian 0.3%; Other 1.8%). **Foreign born:** 0.8%. **Median age:** 33.

Income 2000: per capita $13,136; median household $27,877; **Pop below poverty level:** 28.7%. ***Personal per capita income 2000-2003:** $17,407-$19,215.

Unemployment 2004: 6.8%. **Change from 2000:** -1.1%. **Median travel time to work:** 29 minutes. **Working outside county of residence:** 42.3%.

Cities with pop over 10,000: None.

BUTTS COUNTY

25 3rd St Suite 4   **Ph:** 770-775-8200
Jackson, GA 30233   **Fax:** 770-775-8211
www.buttscounty.org

In west-central GA, northwest of Macon; organized Dec 24, 1825 from Henry and Monroe counties. **Name Origin:** For Capt. Sam Butts (1777-1814), army officer killed in the War of 1812.

Area (sq mi): 190.01 (land 186.61; water 3.4). **Pop per sq mi:** 112.8.

Pop 2005: 21,045. **State rank:** 84. **Pop change:** 2000-20005 +7.8%; 1990-2000 +27.4%. **Pop 2000:** 19,522 (White 68.5%; Black or African American 28.8%; Hispanic or Latino 1.4%; Asian 0.3%; Other 1.6%). **Foreign born:** 0.9%. **Median age:** 35.9.

Income 2000: per capita $17,016; median household $39,879; **Pop below poverty level:** 11.5%. ***Personal per capita income 2000-2003:** $21,813-$21,898.

Unemployment 2004: 5%. **Change from 2000:** +0%. **Median travel time to work:** 31 minutes. **Working outside county of residence:** 55.4%.

Cities with pop over 10,000: None.

CALHOUN COUNTY

PO Box 226   **Ph:** 229-849-4835
Morgan, GA 39866   **Fax:** 229-849-2100

In southwestern GA, west of Albany; organized Feb 20, 1854 from Early and Baker counties. **Name Origin:** For John Caldwell Calhoun (1782-1850), U.S. statesman and champion of Southern causes.

Area (sq mi): 283.57 (land 280.18; water 3.39). **Pop per sq mi:** 21.3.

Pop 2005: 5,972. **State rank:** 150. **Pop change:** 2000-20005 -5.5%; 1990-2000 +26.1%. **Pop 2000:** 6,320 (White 37.5%; Black or African American 60.6%; Hispanic or Latino 3%; Asian 0.1%; Other 1%). **Foreign born:** 1.9%. **Median age:** 35.6.

Income 2000: per capita $11,839; median household $24,588; **Pop below poverty level:** 26.5%. ***Personal per capita income 2000-2003:** $15,735 $19,271.

Unemployment 2004: 5.9%. **Change from 2000:** -1%. **Median travel time to work:** 26.4 minutes. **Working outside county of residence:** 49.8%.

Cities with pop over 10,000: None.

CAMDEN COUNTY

PO Box 99   **Ph:** 912-576-5649
Woodbine, GA 31569   **Fax:** 912-576-5647
www.co.camden.ga.us

On southeastern Atlantic coast; original county; organized Feb 5, 1777 (prior to statehood) from Saint Mary and Saint Thomas parishes. **Name Origin:** For Charles Pratt, 1st Earl of Camden (1714-94), English statesman who supported the American colonies before the Revolutionary War.

Area (sq mi): 782.52 (land 629.91; water 152.61). **Pop per sq mi:** 72.6.

Pop 2005: 45,759. **State rank:** 42. **Pop change:** 2000-20005 +4.8%; 1990-2000 +44.7%. **Pop 2000:** 43,664 (White 73.2%; Black or African American 20.1%; Hispanic or Latino 3.6%; Asian 1%; Other 3.9%). **Foreign born:** 2.3%. **Median age:** 28.2.

Income 2000: per capita $16,445; median household $41,056; **Pop below poverty level:** 10.1%. ***Personal per capita income 2000-2003:** $20,939-$22,730.

Unemployment 2004: 4.5%. **Change from 2000:** +1%. **Median travel time to work:** 21.6 minutes. **Working outside county of residence:** 22.4%.

Cities with pop over 10,000: Saint Marys (16,187); Kingsland (11,588).

CANDLER COUNTY

705 N Lewis St   **Ph:** 912-685-2835
Metter, GA 30439   **Fax:** 912-685-4823

In east-central GA, northwest of Savannah; organized Jul 1914 from Bulloch, Emanuel, and Tattnall counties. **Name Origin:** For Col. Allen Daniel Candler (1834-1910), GA legislator and governor (1898-1902).

Area (sq mi): 248.81 (land 246.88; water 1.94). **Pop per sq mi:** 41.8.

Pop 2005: 10,321. **State rank:** 125. **Pop change:** 2000-20005 +7.8%; 1990-2000 +23.7%. **Pop 2000:** 9,577 (White 62.9%; Black or African American 27.1%; Hispanic or Latino 9.2%; Asian 0.3%; Other 7.2%). **Foreign born:** 6.1%. **Median age:** 35.6.

Income 2000: per capita $12,958; median household $25,022; **Pop below poverty level:** 26.1%. ***Personal per capita income 2000-2003:** $18,960-$19,691.

Unemployment 2004: 4.4%. **Change from 2000:** +0%. **Median travel time to work:** 24.4 minutes. **Working outside county of residence:** 40.5%.

Cities with pop over 10,000: None.

CARROLL COUNTY

PO Box 338   **Ph:** 770-830-5800
Carrollton, GA 30112   **Fax:** 770-830-5992
www.carrollcountyga.com

On central western border of GA, southwest of Atlanta; original county; established Jun 9, 1825 from Indian lands. **Name Origin:** For Charles Carroll (1737-1832), a signer of the Declaration of Independence, U.S. senator from MD (1789-92), and founder of the Baltimore and Ohio Railroad.

Area (sq mi): 503.83 (land 498.93; water 4.89). **Pop per sq mi:** 211.4.

Carroll County (cont'd)

Pop 2005: 105,453. **State rank:** 18. **Pop change:** 2000-20005 +20.8%; 1990-2000 +22.2%. **Pop 2000:** 87,268 (White 79.4%; Black or African American 16.3%; Hispanic or Latino 2.6%; Asian 0.6%; Other 2.5%). **Foreign born:** 2.9%. **Median age:** 32.5.

Income 2000: per capita $17,656; median household $38,799; **Pop below poverty level:** 13.7%. ***Personal per capita income 2000-2003:** $21,606-$22,476.

Unemployment 2004: 4.7%. **Change from 2000:** -0.3%. **Median travel time to work:** 28 minutes. **Working outside county of residence:** 38.1%.

Cities with pop over 10,000: Carrollton ⛪ (21,010).

CATOOSA COUNTY
875 Lafayette St   **Ph:** 706-935-4231
Ringgold, GA 30736
www.catoosa.com

On the northern border of GA, southeast of Chattanooga, TN; organized Dec 5, 1853 from Walker and Whitfield counties. **Name Origin:** For the Cherokee Indian chief.

Area (sq mi): 162.66 (land 162.23; water 0.44). **Pop per sq mi:** 374.9.

Pop 2005: 60,813. **State rank:** 35. **Pop change:** 2000-20005 +14.1%; 1990-2000 +25.5%. **Pop 2000:** 53,282 (White 95.7%; Black or African American 1.3%; Hispanic or Latino 1.2%; Asian 0.7%; Other 1.6%). **Foreign born:** 1.7%. **Median age:** 35.8.

Income 2000: per capita $18,009; median household $39,998; **Pop below poverty level:** 9.4%. ***Personal per capita income 2000-2003:** $22,372-$23,543.

Unemployment 2004: 3.3%. **Change from 2000:** +0.7%. **Median travel time to work:** 23.7 minutes. **Working outside county of residence:** 73.2%.

Cities with pop over 10,000: None.

CHARLTON COUNTY
100 S 3rd St   **Ph:** 912-496-2549
Folkston, GA 31537   **Fax:** 912-496-1156

In southeastern GA, southwest of Brunswick; organized Feb 11, 1854 from Camden County. **Name Origin:** For Robert Milledge Charlton (1807-54), GA legislator, jurist, and U.S. senator (1852-52).

Area (sq mi): 782.97 (land 780.77; water 2.2). **Pop per sq mi:** 13.8.

Pop 2005: 10,790. **State rank:** 121. **Pop change:** 2000-20005 +4.9%; 1990-2000 +21%. **Pop 2000:** 10,282 (White 68.2%; Black or African American 29.3%; Hispanic or Latino 0.8%; Asian 0.3%; Other 1.8%). **Foreign born:** 0.9%. **Median age:** 33.4.

Income 2000: per capita $12,920; median household $27,869; **Pop below poverty level:** 20.9%. ***Personal per capita income 2000-2003:** $15,585-$16,108.

Unemployment 2004: 4.8%. **Change from 2000:** +0.9%. **Median travel time to work:** 33.8 minutes. **Working outside county of residence:** 50.9%.

Cities with pop over 10,000: None.

CHATHAM COUNTY
124 Bull St   **Ph:** 912-652-7869
Savannah, GA 31401   **Fax:** 912-652-7874
www.chathamcounty.org

On the southeastern Atlantic coast of GA; original county; organized Feb 5, 1777 (prior to statehood) from Saint Phillips and Christ Church parishes. **Name Origin:** For William Pitt (the Elder; 1708-78), 1st Earl of Chatham, known as 'the Great Commoner,' for his support of the American colonies before the Revolutionary War.

Area (sq mi): 632.28 (land 438.11; water 194.17). **Pop per sq mi:** 544.2.

Pop 2005: 238,410. **State rank:** 6. **Pop change:** 2000-20005 +2.7%; 1990-2000 +7%. **Pop 2000:** 232,048 (White 54.2%; Black or African American 40.5%; Hispanic or Latino 2.3%; Asian 1.7%; Other 2.5%). **Foreign born:** 4%. **Median age:** 34.4.

Income 2000: per capita $21,152; median household $37,752; **Pop below poverty level:** 15.6%. ***Personal per capita income 2000-2003:** $27,804-$30,022.

Unemployment 2004: 4.2%. **Change from 2000:** +0.8%. **Median travel time to work:** 22.3 minutes. **Working outside county of residence:** 6.1%.

Cities with pop over 10,000: Savannah ⛪ (129,808).

CHATTOOGA COUNTY
PO Box 211   **Ph:** 706-857-0701
Summerville, GA 30747   **Fax:** 706-857-0742

On the northwestern border of GA, north of Rome; organized Dec 28, 1838 from Floyd and Walker counties. **Name Origin:** For the Chattooga River, which runs diagonally through the county; a Cherokee word whose meaning is unclear.

Area (sq mi): 313.55 (land 313.33; water 0.23). **Pop per sq mi:** 84.8.

Pop 2005: 26,570. **State rank:** 66. **Pop change:** 2000-20005 +4.3%; 1990-2000 +14.5%. **Pop 2000:** 25,470 (White 85.5%; Black or African American 11.2%; Hispanic or Latino 2.1%; Asian 0.1%; Other 1.9%). **Foreign born:** 1.9%. **Median age:** 36.5.

Income 2000: per capita $14,508; median household $30,664; **Pop below poverty level:** 14.3%. ***Personal per capita income 2000-2003:** $17,998-$18,951.

Unemployment 2004: 4.7%. **Change from 2000:** +0.3%. **Median travel time to work:** 23.9 minutes. **Working outside county of residence:** 36.1%.

Cities with pop over 10,000: None.

CHEROKEE COUNTY
90 North St Suite 310   **Ph:** 678-493-6000
Canton, GA 30114   **Fax:** 678-493-6013
www.cherokeega.com/ie.cfm

In northwest-central GA, north of Atlanta; original county; established Dec 21, 1830 from Cherokee lands. **Name Origin:** For the Indian tribe of Iroquoian linguistic stock who occupied the land at the time. Name may derive from Creek *tciloki* 'people of a different speech.'

Area (sq mi): 433.99 (land 423.68; water 10.31). **Pop per sq mi:** 434.8.

*Source: Personal per capita income data are from the Bureau of Economic Analysis; per capita income data are from the Bureau of the Census. See Introduction for explanation of differences.

150

Cherokee County (cont'd)

Pop 2005: 184,211. **State rank:** 9. **Pop change:** 2000-20005 +29.8%; 1990-2000 +57.3%. **Pop 2000:** 141,903 (White 89.9%; Black or African American 2.5%; Hispanic or Latino 5.4%; Asian 0.8%; Other 4.3%). **Foreign born:** 5.8%. **Median age:** 34.

Income 2000: per capita $24,871; median household $60,896; **Pop below poverty level:** 5.3%. ***Personal per capita income 2000-2003:** $31,150-$30,059.

Unemployment 2004: 3.6%. **Change from 2000:** +1.3%. **Median travel time to work:** 34.4 minutes. **Working outside county of residence:** 64.6%.

Cities with pop over 10,000: Woodstock (17,214); Canton 🏛 (15,094).

CLAY COUNTY

PO Box 519   **Ph:** 229-768-3238
Fort Gaines, GA 39851   **Fax:** 229-768-3672
www.fortgaines.com

On the southwestern border of GA, west of Albany; organized Feb 16, 1854 from Early and Randolph counties. **Name Origin:** For Henry Clay (1777-1852), U.S. senator from KY, known as the 'Great Pacificator' for his advocacy of compromise to avert national crises.

Area (sq mi): 216.99 (land 195.21; water 21.79). **Pop per sq mi:** 16.6.

Pop 2005: 3,242. **State rank:** 155. **Pop change:** 2000-20005 -3.4%; 1990-2000 -0.2%. **Pop 2000:** 3,357 (White 38.2%; Black or African American 60.5%; Hispanic or Latino 1%; Asian 0.3%; Other 0.9%). **Foreign born:** 0.7%. **Median age:** 41.9.

Income 2000: per capita $16,819; median household $21,448; **Pop below poverty level:** 31.3%. ***Personal per capita income 2000-2003:** $19,973-$23,718.

Unemployment 2004: 5%. **Change from 2000:** -0.8%. **Median travel time to work:** 25.9 minutes. **Working outside county of residence:** 52%.

Cities with pop over 10,000: None.

CLAYTON COUNTY

112 Smith St   **Ph:** 770-477-3211
Jonesboro, GA 30236   **Fax:** 770-477-3217
www.co.clayton.ga.us

In west-central GA, south of Atlanta; organized Nov 30, 1858 from Fayette and Henry counties. **Name Origin:** For Augustin Smith Clayton (1783-1839), GA jurist and U.S. representative (1832-35).

Area (sq mi): 144.28 (land 142.62; water 1.66). **Pop per sq mi:** 1878.9.

Pop 2005: 267,966. **State rank:** 5. **Pop change:** 2000-20005 +13.3%; 1990-2000 +29.9%. **Pop 2000:** 236,517 (White 34.9%; Black or African American 51.6%; Hispanic or Latino 7.5%; Asian 4.5%; Other 6%). **Foreign born:** 10.9%. **Median age:** 30.2.

Income 2000: per capita $18,079; median household $42,697; **Pop below poverty level:** 10.1%. ***Personal per capita income 2000-2003:** $21,609-$21,569.

Unemployment 2004: 5.6%. **Change from 2000:** +1.6%. **Median travel time to work:** 29.8 minutes. **Working outside county of residence:** 61.9%.

Cities with pop over 10,000: Forest Park (21,184); Riverdale (15,611).

CLINCH COUNTY

PO Box 433   **Ph:** 912-487-5854
Homerville, GA 31634   **Fax:** 912-487-2083

On southern border, east of Valdosta; organized Feb 14, 1850 from Ware and Lowndes counties. **Name Origin:** For Brig. Gen. Duncan Lamont Clinch (1787-1849), Army officer and U.S. representative from GA (1844-45).

Area (sq mi): 824.17 (land 809.29; water 14.88). **Pop per sq mi:** 8.6.

Pop 2005: 6,996. **State rank:** 144. **Pop change:** 2000-20005 +1.7%; 1990-2000 +11.7%. **Pop 2000:** 6,878 (White 68.5%; Black or African American 29.5%; Hispanic or Latino 0.8%; Asian 0.1%; Other 1.4%). **Foreign born:** 1.4%. **Median age:** 34.9.

Income 2000: per capita $13,023; median household $26,755; **Pop below poverty level:** 23.4%. ***Personal per capita income 2000-2003:** $16,985-$17,772.

Unemployment 2004: 5.7%. **Change from 2000:** -1.3%. **Median travel time to work:** 19.6 minutes. **Working outside county of residence:** 19.6%.

Cities with pop over 10,000: None.

COBB COUNTY

100 Cherokee St Suite 300   **Ph:** 770-528-3300
Marietta, GA 30090   **Fax:** 770-528-2606
www.cobbcounty.org

In northwest-central GA, northwest of Atlanta; organized Dec 3, 1832 from Cherokee County. **Name Origin:** For Thomas Willis Cobb (1784-1830), U.S. senator from GA (1824-28) and judge of the GA superior court (1828).

Area (sq mi): 344.51 (land 340.15; water 4.36). **Pop per sq mi:** 1951.5.

Pop 2005: 663,818. **State rank:** 4. **Pop change:** 2000-20005 +9.2%; 1990-2000 +35.7%. **Pop 2000:** 607,751 (White 68.8%; Black or African American 18.8%; Hispanic or Latino 7.7%; Asian 3.1%; Other 5.8%). **Foreign born:** 11.6%. **Median age:** 33.2.

Income 2000: per capita $27,863; median household $58,289; **Pop below poverty level:** 6.5%. ***Personal per capita income 2000-2003:** $36,447-$36,175.

Unemployment 2004: 4.2%. **Change from 2000:** +1.2%. **Median travel time to work:** 31.3 minutes. **Working outside county of residence:** 44.8%.

Cities with pop over 10,000: Marietta 🏛 (60,547); Smyrna (45,755); Kennesaw (27,433); Acworth (18,093); Powder Springs (14,300).

COFFEE COUNTY

101 S Peterson Ave   **Ph:** 912-384-4799
Douglas, GA 31533   **Fax:** 912-384-0291

In south-central GA, northeast of Valdosta; organized Feb 9, 1854 from Clinch, Irwin, Telfair, and Ware counties. **Name Origin:** For

Coffee County (cont'd)

Gen. John Coffee (1782-1836), an officer in the Indian wars, U.S. representative from GA (1833-36), and cousin to John Coffee of TN.

Area (sq mi): 602.61 (land 598.9; water 3.72). **Pop per sq mi:** 66.2.

Pop 2005: 39,674. **State rank:** 49. **Pop change:** 2000-20005 +6%; 1990-2000 +26.4%. **Pop 2000:** 37,413 (White 66%; Black or African American 25.9%; Hispanic or Latino 6.8%; Asian 0.6%; Other 5.2%). **Foreign born:** 5.4%. **Median age:** 32.1.

Income 2000: per capita $15,530; median household $30,710; **Pop below poverty level:** 19.1%. ***Personal per capita income 2000-2003:** $20,510-$21,549.

Unemployment 2004: 5.8%. **Change from 2000:** +0.5%. **Median travel time to work:** 20.7 minutes. **Working outside county of residence:** 12.4%.

Cities with pop over 10,000: Douglas ⚒ (10,916).

COLQUITT COUNTY

PO Box 517   **Ph:** 229-890-1805
Moultrie, GA 31776

In south-central GA, northwest of Valdosta; organized Feb 25, 1856 from Thomas and Lowndes counties. **Name Origin:** For Walter Terry Colquitt (1799-1855), jurist, Methodist minister, and U.S. senator (1843-48).

Area (sq mi): 556.55 (land 552.27; water 4.28). **Pop per sq mi:** 79.5.

Pop 2005: 43,915. **State rank:** 45. **Pop change:** 2000-20005 +4.4%; 1990-2000 +14.8%. **Pop 2000:** 42,053 (White 64.8%; Black or African American 23.5%; Hispanic or Latino 10.8%; Asian 0.2%; Other 8.5%). **Foreign born:** 6.5%. **Median age:** 33.7.

Income 2000: per capita $14,457; median household $28,539; **Pop below poverty level:** 19.8%. ***Personal per capita income 2000-2003:** $19,219-$20,384.

Unemployment 2004: 4.7%. **Change from 2000:** -2%. **Median travel time to work:** 22.5 minutes. **Working outside county of residence:** 23%.

Cities with pop over 10,000: Moultrie ⚒ (14,792).

COLUMBIA COUNTY

PO Box 498   **Ph:** 706-868-3379
Evans, GA 30809   **Fax:** 706-868-3348
www.columbiacountyga.gov

On central eastern coast of GA, north of Augusta; organized Dec 10, 1790 from Richmond County. **Name Origin:** Feminine form of Columbus, a poetic and honorific reference to Christopher Columbus (1451-1506) and America.

Area (sq mi): 307.78 (land 290.01; water 17.76). **Pop per sq mi:** 358.

Pop 2005: 103,812. **State rank:** 21. **Pop change:** 2000-20005 +16.3%; 1990-2000 +35.2%. **Pop 2000:** 89,288 (White 81.1%; Black or African American 11.2%; Hispanic or Latino 2.6%; Asian 3.4%; Other 2.8%). **Foreign born:** 4.8%. **Median age:** 35.4.

Income 2000: per capita $23,496; median household $55,682; **Pop below poverty level:** 5.1%. ***Personal per capita income 2000-2003:** $29,751-$31,562.

Unemployment 2004: 3.7%. **Change from 2000:** +1.2%. **Median travel time to work:** 25.3 minutes. **Working outside county of residence:** 67.3%.

Cities with pop over 10,000: None.

COLUMBUS-MUSCOGEE COUNTY

PO Box 1340   **Ph:** 706-653-4013
Columbus, GA 31902   **Fax:** 706-653-4016
www.columbusga.com

On central western border of GA, southwest of Macon; organized Dec 11, 1826 from Creek lands. **Name Origin:** For the Muskogee Indians, a Shawnee tribe of Muskhogean linguistic stock.

Area (sq mi): 221 (land 216.26; water 4.74). **Pop per sq mi:** 856.7.

Pop 2005: 185,271. **State rank:** 8. **Pop change:** 2000-20005 -0.5%; 1990-2000 +3.9%. **Pop 2000:** 186,291 (White 48.7%; Black or African American 43.7%; Hispanic or Latino 4.5%; Asian 1.5%; Other 4.3%). **Foreign born:** 4.7%. **Median age:** 32.6.

Income 2000: per capita $18,262; median household $34,798; **Pop below poverty level:** 15.7%. ***Personal per capita income 2000-2003:** $25,070-$28,724.

Unemployment 2004: 5.1%. **Change from 2000:** +0.3%. **Median travel time to work:** 19.9 minutes. **Working outside county of residence:** 13.4%.

Cities with pop over 10,000: Columbus ⚒ (182,850).

COOK COUNTY

209 N Parrish Ave   **Ph:** 229-896-2266
Adel, GA 31620   **Fax:** 229-896-7629

In south-central GA, northwest of Valdosta; organized Jul 30, 1918 from Berrien County. **Name Origin:** For Gen. Philip Cook (1817-94), Confederate officer and U.S. representative from GA (1873-83).

Area (sq mi): 233.22 (land 229.02; water 4.2). **Pop per sq mi:** 71.5.

Pop 2005: 16,366. **State rank:** 98. **Pop change:** 2000-20005 +3.8%; 1990-2000 +17.2%. **Pop 2000:** 15,771 (White 66.7%; Black or African American 29.1%; Hispanic or Latino 3.1%; Asian 0.4%; Other 2.5%). **Foreign born:** 2.3%. **Median age:** 34.3.

Income 2000: per capita $13,465; median household $27,582; **Pop below poverty level:** 20.7%. ***Personal per capita income 2000-2003:** $17,964-$18,849.

Unemployment 2004: 5.1%. **Change from 2000:** +0.2%. **Median travel time to work:** 21.3 minutes. **Working outside county of residence:** 40.2%.

Cities with pop over 10,000: None.

COWETA COUNTY

22 E Broad St   **Ph:** 770-254-2601
Newnan, GA 30263   **Fax:** 770-254-2606
www.coweta.ga.us

In west-central GA, southwest of Atlanta; organized Jun 9, 1825 from Indian lands. **Name Origin:** For Gen. William McIntosh (1775-1825), a half-blooded Creek Indian and the head chief of the Coweta Indians of the Creek nation. The name may mean 'falls,' with reference to those on the Chattahoochee River.

Area (sq mi): 445.98 (land 442.62; water 3.36). **Pop per sq mi:** 248.3.

---

*Source: Personal per capita income data are from the Bureau of Economic Analysis; per capita income data are from the Bureau of the Census. See Introduction for explanation of differences.

Coweta County (cont'd)

Pop 2005: 109,903. **State rank:** 17. **Pop change:** 2000-20005 +23.2%; 1990-2000 +65.7%. **Pop 2000:** 89,215 (White 77.2%; Black or African American 18%; Hispanic or Latino 3.1%; Asian 0.7%; Other 2.4%). **Foreign born:** 3.7%. **Median age:** 33.6.

Income 2000: per capita $21,949; median household $52,706; **Pop below poverty level:** 7.8%. ***Personal per capita income 2000-2003:** $27,067-$26,869.

Unemployment 2004: 3.8%. **Change from 2000:** +0.5%. **Median travel time to work:** 29.7 minutes. **Working outside county of residence:** 52.3%.

Cities with pop over 10,000: Newnan 🏛 (22,520).

CRAWFORD COUNTY

1011 Hwy 341 N   **Ph:** 478-836-3782
Roberta, GA 31078   **Fax:** 478-836-5818

In west-central GA, southwest of Macon; organized Dec 9, 1822 from Houston County. **Name Origin:** For William Harris Crawford (1772-1834), VA statesman.

Area (sq mi): 326.45 (land 325.01; water 1.45). **Pop per sq mi:** 39.6.

Pop 2005: 12,874. **State rank:** 113. **Pop change:** 2000-20005 +3%; 1990-2000 +39%. **Pop 2000:** 12,495 (White 72.3%; Black or African American 23.8%; Hispanic or Latino 2.4%; Asian 0.2%; Other 3.2%). **Foreign born:** 0.5%. **Median age:** 35.2.

Income 2000: per capita $15,768; median household $37,848; **Pop below poverty level:** 15.4%. ***Personal per capita income 2000-2003:** $19,630-$22,999.

Unemployment 2004: 4.8%. **Change from 2000:** +1%. **Median travel time to work:** 32.3 minutes. **Working outside county of residence:** 82.7%.

Cities with pop over 10,000: None.

CRISP COUNTY

210 S 7th St   **Ph:** 229-276-2672
Cordele, GA 31015   **Fax:** 229-276-2675
www.crispcounty.com

In south-central GA, northeast of Albany; organized Aug 17, 1905 from Dooly County. **Name Origin:** For Charles Frederick Crisp (1845-96), Confederate army officer and U.S. representative from GA (1883-96).

Area (sq mi): 281.2 (land 273.82; water 7.38). **Pop per sq mi:** 80.4.

Pop 2005: 22,017. **State rank:** 79. **Pop change:** 2000-20005 +0.1%; 1990-2000 +9.9%. **Pop 2000:** 21,996 (White 53.5%; Black or African American 43.4%; Hispanic or Latino 1.7%; Asian 0.7%; Other 1.9%). **Foreign born:** 2.1%. **Median age:** 34.4.

Income 2000: per capita $14,695; median household $26,547; **Pop below poverty level:** 29.3%. ***Personal per capita income 2000-2003:** $19,653-$20,908.

Unemployment 2004: 5.5%. **Change from 2000:** -0.6%. **Median travel time to work:** 19 minutes. **Working outside county of residence:** 20.6%.

Cities with pop over 10,000: Cordele 🏛 (11,557).

CUSSETA-CHATTAHOOCHEE COUNTY

PO Box 299   **Ph:** 706-989-3602
Cusseta, GA 31805   **Fax:** 706-989-2005
chattahoocheecounty.georgia.gov

On the central western border of GA, south of Columbus; organized Feb 13, 1854 from Muscogee and Marion counties. **Name Origin:** For the Chattahoochee River, which forms its western border. From an Indian word probably meaning 'marked rocks,' for painted stones found in the river.

Area (sq mi): 251.17 (land 248.77; water 2.4). **Pop per sq mi:** 59.

Pop 2005: 14,679. **State rank:** 107. **Pop change:** 2000-20005 -1.4%; 1990-2000 -12.1%. **Pop 2000:** 14,882 (White 55%; Black or African American 29.9%; Hispanic or Latino 10.4%; Asian 1.8%; Other 10.3%). **Foreign born:** 6%. **Median age:** 23.2.

Income 2000: per capita $14,049; median household $37,106; **Pop below poverty level:** 10.6%. ***Personal per capita income 2000-2003:** $15,743-$20,163.

Unemployment 2004: 6.8%. **Change from 2000:** +0.8%. **Median travel time to work:** 14.3 minutes. **Working outside county of residence:** 35.8%.

Cities with pop over 10,000: None.

DADE COUNTY

PO Box 417   **Ph:** 706-657-4778
Trenton, GA 30752   **Fax:** 706-657-8284
www.dadega.com

In northwestern corner of GA, south of Chattanooga, TN; organized Dec 25, 1837 from Walker County. **Name Origin:** For Maj. Francis Langhorne Dade (1793-1835), officer killed in the Seminole War (1835-42).

Area (sq mi): 174.16 (land 173.98; water 0.18). **Pop per sq mi:** 92.2.

Pop 2005: 16,040. **State rank:** 103. **Pop change:** 2000-20005 +5.8%; 1990-2000 +15.3%. **Pop 2000:** 15,154 (White 96.9%; Black or African American 0.6%; Hispanic or Latino 0.9%; Asian 0.4%; Other 1.5%). **Foreign born:** 1.4%. **Median age:** 36.1.

Income 2000: per capita $16,127; median household $35,259; **Pop below poverty level:** 9.7%. ***Personal per capita income 2000-2003:** $20,803-$21,648.

Unemployment 2004: 3.9%. **Change from 2000:** +1%. **Median travel time to work:** 26.7 minutes. **Working outside county of residence:** 66.2%.

Cities with pop over 10,000: None.

DAWSON COUNTY

76 Howard Ave E Suite 120   **Ph:** 706-344-3501
Dawsonville, GA 30534   **Fax:** 706-344-3504
www.dawsoncounty.org

In north-central GA, northeast of Atlanta; organized Dec 3, 1857 from Gilmer and Lumpkin counties. **Name Origin:** For William Crosby Dawson (1798-1856), soldier, jurist, and U.S. senator from GA (1849-55).

Area (sq mi): 213.93 (land 211.04; water 2.9). **Pop per sq mi:** 93.5.

Pop 2005: 19,731. **State rank:** 89. **Pop change:** 2000-20005 +23.3%; 1990-2000 +69.7%. **Pop 2000:** 15,999 (White 96.4%;

Dawson County (cont'd)

Black or African American 0.4%; Hispanic or Latino 1.6%; Asian 0.3%; Other 2.1%). **Foreign born:** 1.4%. **Median age:** 36.2.

Income 2000: per capita $22,520; median household $47,486; **Pop below poverty level:** 7.6%. ***Personal per capita income 2000-2003:** $26,571-$28,010.

Unemployment 2004: 3.6%. **Change from 2000:** +1%. **Median travel time to work:** 34 minutes. **Working outside county of residence:** 65.5%.

Cities with pop over 10,000: None.

DECATUR COUNTY

PO Box 726   **Ph:** 229-248-3030
Bainbridge, GA 39818   **Fax:** 229-246-2062

On the southwestern border of GA, southwest of Albany; organized Dec 8, 1823 from Early county. **Name Origin:** For Stephen F. Decatur (1779-1820), U.S. naval officer during the War of 1812 and in actions against the Barbary pirates near Tripoli, who said '. . . may she always be in the right; but our country, right or wrong!'

Area (sq mi): 623.16 (land 596.8; water 26.36). **Pop per sq mi:** 48.

Pop 2005: 28,618. **State rank:** 55. **Pop change:** 2000-20005 +1.3%; 1990-2000 +10.7%. **Pop 2000:** 28,240 (White 55.9%; Black or African American 39.9%; Hispanic or Latino 3.2%; Asian 0.3%; Other 2.5%). **Foreign born:** 2.3%. **Median age:** 34.4.

Income 2000: per capita $15,063; median household $28,820; **Pop below poverty level:** 22.7%. ***Personal per capita income 2000-2003:** $19,931-$21,038.

Unemployment 2004: 6.4%. **Change from 2000:** -0.1%. **Median travel time to work:** 22.5 minutes. **Working outside county of residence:** 22.1%.

Cities with pop over 10,000: Bainbridge ⚖ (12,106).

DEKALB COUNTY

556 N McDonough St   **Ph:** 404-371-2000
Decatur, GA 30030   **Fax:** 404-371-2002
www.co.dekalb.ga.us

In northwest-central GA, east of Atlanta; organized Dec 9, 1822 from Fayette, Henry, Gwinnett, and Newton counties. **Name Origin:** For Johann, Baron de Kalb (1721-80), German-born French soldier who fought with the Americans during the Revolutionary War.

Area (sq mi): 270.91 (land 268.21; water 2.7). **Pop per sq mi:** 2527.7.

Pop 2005: 677,959. **State rank:** 3. **Pop change:** 2000-20005 +1.8%; 1990-2000 +22%. **Pop 2000:** 665,865 (White 32.2%; Black or African American 54.2%; Hispanic or Latino 7.9%; Asian 4%; Other 5.8%). **Foreign born:** 15.2%. **Median age:** 32.3.

Income 2000: per capita $23,968; median household $49,117; **Pop below poverty level:** 10.8%. ***Personal per capita income 2000-2003:** $32,068-$34,745.

Unemployment 2004: 5.3%. **Change from 2000:** +1.1%. **Median travel time to work:** 31.7 minutes. **Working outside county of residence:** 56%.

Cities with pop over 10,000: Decatur ⚖ (18,251); Doraville (10,032).

DODGE COUNTY

5016 Courthouse Cir Suite 102   **Ph:** 478-374-4361
Eastman, GA 31023   **Fax:** 478-374-8121

In central GA, southwest of Macon; organized Oct 26, 1870 from Montgomery, Pulaski, and Telfair counties. **Name Origin:** For William Earle Dodge (1805-83), U.S. representative from NY (1866-67) and owner of a vast estate in GA, who was active in the attempt to avoid the Civil War.

Area (sq mi): 503.17 (land 500.29; water 2.88). **Pop per sq mi:** 39.1.

Pop 2005: 19,574. **State rank:** 90. **Pop change:** 2000-20005 +2.1%; 1990-2000 +8.9%. **Pop 2000:** 19,171 (White 68.6%; Black or African American 29.4%; Hispanic or Latino 1.3%; Asian 0.2%; Other 1.5%). **Foreign born:** 1.4%. **Median age:** 35.8.

Income 2000: per capita $14,468; median household $27,607; **Pop below poverty level:** 17.4%. ***Personal per capita income 2000-2003:** $18,049-$19,134.

Unemployment 2004: 4.9%. **Change from 2000:** +0.4%. **Median travel time to work:** 26.1 minutes. **Working outside county of residence:** 34.3%.

Cities with pop over 10,000: None.

DOOLY COUNTY

PO Box 322   **Ph:** 229-268-4228
Vienna, GA 31092   **Fax:** 229-268-4230
www.doolychamber.com

In west-central GA, south of Macon; original county; organized May 15, 1821 from Indian lands. **Name Origin:** For Capt. John Dooly (1740-80), American Revolutionary officer in GA, killed by British sympathizers.

Area (sq mi): 397.07 (land 392.88; water 4.19). **Pop per sq mi:** 29.9.

Pop 2005: 11,749. **State rank:** 116. **Pop change:** 2000-20005 +1.9%; 1990-2000 +16.4%. **Pop 2000:** 11,525 (White 44.8%; Black or African American 49.5%; Hispanic or Latino 4.7%; Asian 0.4%; Other 4.1%). **Foreign born:** 1.5%. **Median age:** 35.1.

Income 2000: per capita $13,628; median household $27,980; **Pop below poverty level:** 22.1%. ***Personal per capita income 2000-2003:** $19,071-$20,535.

Unemployment 2004: 5.8%. **Change from 2000:** -0.5%. **Median travel time to work:** 22.5 minutes. **Working outside county of residence:** 42.3%.

Cities with pop over 10,000: None.

DOUGHERTY COUNTY

PO Box 1827   **Ph:** 229-431-2121
Albany, GA 31702   **Fax:** 229-438-3967
www.dougherty.ga.us

In southwestern GA, southeast of Columbus; organized Dec 15, 1853 from Baker County. **Name Origin:** For Charles Dougherty (1801-53), lawyer and western circuit judge.

Area (sq mi): 334.64 (land 329.6; water 5.04). **Pop per sq mi:** 287.9.

*Source: Personal per capita income data are from the Bureau of Economic Analysis; per capita income data are from the Bureau of the Census.
See Introduction for explanation of differences.

Dougherty County (cont'd)

Pop 2005: 94,882. **State rank:** 23. **Pop change:** 2000-20005 -1.2%; 1990-2000 -0.3%. **Pop 2000:** 96,065 (White 37.3%; Black or African American 60.1%; Hispanic or Latino 1.3%; Asian 0.6%; Other 1.4%). **Foreign born:** 1.7%. **Median age:** 32.2.

Income 2000: per capita $16,645; median household $30,934; **Pop below poverty level:** 24.8%. *Personal per capita income 2000-2003:** $21,608-$24,399.

Unemployment 2004: 5.9%. **Change from 2000:** -0.2%. **Median travel time to work:** 18.7 minutes. **Working outside county of residence:** 9.6%.

Cities with pop over 10,000: Albany ⛪ (76,253).

DOUGLAS COUNTY

8700 Hospital Dr   **Ph:** 770-920-7266
Douglasville, GA 30134   **Fax:** 770-920-7357
www.co.douglas.ga.us

In west-central GA, west of Atlanta; organized Oct 17, 1870 from Carroll and Campbell counties. **Name Origin:** For Stephen Arnold Douglas (1813-61), U.S. orator and statesman.

Area (sq mi): 200.26 (land 199.3; water 0.96). **Pop per sq mi:** 565.8.

Pop 2005: 112,760. **State rank:** 15. **Pop change:** 2000-20005 +22.3%; 1990-2000 +29.6%. **Pop 2000:** 92,174 (White 75.9%; Black or African American 18.5%; Hispanic or Latino 2.9%; Asian 1.2%; Other 3%). **Foreign born:** 3.9%. **Median age:** 33.8.

Income 2000: per capita $21,172; median household $50,108; **Pop below poverty level:** 7.8%. *Personal per capita income 2000-2003:** $26,290-$26,273.

Unemployment 2004: 4.6%. **Change from 2000:** +1.8%. **Median travel time to work:** 32.3 minutes. **Working outside county of residence:** 63.3%.

Cities with pop over 10,000: Douglasville ⛪ (26,461).

EARLY COUNTY

PO Box 849   **Ph:** 229-723-3033
Blakely, GA 31723   **Fax:** 229-723-4411

On southwestern border, southwest of Albany; original county; organized Dec 15, 1818 from Creek Indian lands. **Name Origin:** For Peter Early (1773-1817), U.S. representative from GA, jurist, and governor (1813-15).

Area (sq mi): 516.27 (land 511.23; water 5.04). **Pop per sq mi:** 23.6.

Pop 2005: 12,056. **State rank:** 115. **Pop change:** 2000-20005 -2.4%; 1990-2000 +4.2%. **Pop 2000:** 12,354 (White 49.9%; Black or African American 48.1%; Hispanic or Latino 1.2%; Asian 0.2%; Other 1.5%). **Foreign born:** 0.7%. **Median age:** 36.4.

Income 2000: per capita $14,936; median household $25,629; **Pop below poverty level:** 25.7%. *Personal per capita income 2000-2003:** $20,874-$25,410.

Unemployment 2004: 4.9%. **Change from 2000:** -1%. **Median travel time to work:** 22.8 minutes. **Working outside county of residence:** 29.9%.

Cities with pop over 10,000: None.

ECHOLS COUNTY

PO Box 190   **Ph:** 229-559-6538
Statenville, GA 31648   **Fax:** 229-559-6158

On southern border of GA, east of Valdosta; organized Dec 13, 1858 from Clinch and Lowndes counties. **Name Origin:** For Gen. Robert M. Echols (1800?-47), a GA officer killed during the Mexican War.

Area (sq mi): 420.8 (land 404.13; water 16.67). **Pop per sq mi:** 10.5.

Pop 2005: 4,253. **State rank:** 152. **Pop change:** 2000-20005 +13.3%; 1990-2000 +60.8%. **Pop 2000:** 3,754 (White 71.6%; Black or African American 6.9%; Hispanic or Latino 19.7%; Asian 0.1%; Other 15.8%, including 1.1% American Indian/Alaska Native). **Foreign born:** 12.6%. **Median age:** 29.7.

Income 2000: per capita $15,727; median household $25,851; **Pop below poverty level:** 28.7%. *Personal per capita income 2000-2003:** $15,023-$16,030.

Unemployment 2004: 3%. **Change from 2000:** -2%. **Median travel time to work:** 25.3 minutes. **Working outside county of residence:** 85%.

Cities with pop over 10,000: None.

EFFINGHAM COUNTY

601 N Laurel St   **Ph:** 912-754-2153
Springfield, GA 31329   **Fax:** 912-754-4157
www.effinghamcounty.org

On the central eastern border of GA, north of Savannah; original county; organized Feb 5, 1777 (prior to statehood) from Saint Mathew and Saint Phillips parishes. **Name Origin:** For Thomas Howard (1746-91), Earl of Effingham, a pro-colonist English army officer.

Area (sq mi): 482.82 (land 479.41; water 3.4). **Pop per sq mi:** 97.9.

Pop 2005: 46,924. **State rank:** 40. **Pop change:** 2000-20005 +25%; 1990-2000 +46.1%. **Pop 2000:** 37,535 (White 83.9%; Black or African American 13%; Hispanic or Latino 1.4%; Asian 0.5%; Other 1.8%). **Foreign born:** 1.3%. **Median age:** 33.6.

Income 2000: per capita $18,873; median household $46,505; **Pop below poverty level:** 9.3%. *Personal per capita income 2000-2003:** $22,589-$23,553.

Unemployment 2004: 3.5%. **Change from 2000:** +0.8%. **Median travel time to work:** 31.3 minutes. **Working outside county of residence:** 66.7%.

Cities with pop over 10,000: None.

ELBERT COUNTY

PO Box 619   **Ph:** 706-283-2005
Elberton, GA 30635   **Fax:** 706-213-7286
www.elbertga.com

On northeastern border of GA, northeast of Athens; organized Dec 10, 1790 from Wilkes County. **Name Origin:** For Gen. Samuel Elbert (1743-88), Revolutionary War hero and GA governor (1785-86).

Area (sq mi): 374.54 (land 368.76; water 5.78). **Pop per sq mi:** 56.4.

⛪ *County Seat*

Elbert County (cont'd)

Pop 2005: 20,799. **State rank:** 85. **Pop change:** 2000-20005 +1.4%; 1990-2000 +8.2%. **Pop 2000:** 20,511 (White 65.8%; Black or African American 30.9%; Hispanic or Latino 2.4%; Asian 0.2%; Other 2%). **Foreign born:** 1.9%. **Median age:** 37.2.

Income 2000: per capita $14,535; median household $28,724; **Pop below poverty level:** 17.3%. ***Personal per capita income 2000-2003:** $20,898-$22,274.

Unemployment 2004: 5.2%. **Change from 2000:** -2%. **Median travel time to work:** 21.2 minutes. **Working outside county of residence:** 27.3%.

Cities with pop over 10,000: None.

EMANUEL COUNTY

101 N Main St   **Ph:** 478-237-3881
Swainsboro, GA 30401   **Fax:** 478-237-2593

In east-central GA, northwest of Savannah; organized Dec 10, 1812 from Montgomery and Bulloch counties. **Name Origin:** For David Emanuel (1742-1808), GA legislator and governor (1801).

Area (sq mi): 690.33 (land 685.79; water 4.54). **Pop per sq mi:** 32.2.

Pop 2005: 22,108. **State rank:** 78. **Pop change:** 2000-20005 +1.2%; 1990-2000 +6.3%. **Pop 2000:** 21,837 (White 62.6%; Black or African American 33.3%; Hispanic or Latino 3.4%; Asian 0.2%; Other 2.7%). **Foreign born:** 4.1%. **Median age:** 34.9.

Income 2000: per capita $13,627; median household $24,383; **Pop below poverty level:** 27.4%. ***Personal per capita income 2000-2003:** $18,754-$20,719.

Unemployment 2004: 5%. **Change from 2000:** -3.3%. **Median travel time to work:** 23.1 minutes. **Working outside county of residence:** 26.6%.

Cities with pop over 10,000: None.

EVANS COUNTY

3 Freeman St   **Ph:** 912-739-1141
Claxton, GA 30417   **Fax:** 912-739-0111
www.claxtonevanschamber.com

In east-central GA, west of Savannah; organized Aug 11, 1914 from Bulloch and Tattnall counties. **Name Origin:** For Gen. Clement Anselm Evans (1833-1911), GA officer during the Civil War, jurist, and Methodist minister.

Area (sq mi): 186.88 (land 184.92; water 1.96). **Pop per sq mi:** 61.9.

Pop 2005: 11,443. **State rank:** 117. **Pop change:** 2000-20005 +9%; 1990-2000 +20.3%. **Pop 2000:** 10,495 (White 60.3%; Black or African American 33%; Hispanic or Latino 6%; Asian 0.3%; Other 5%). **Foreign born:** 4.3%. **Median age:** 34.

Income 2000: per capita $12,758; median household $25,447; **Pop below poverty level:** 27%. ***Personal per capita income 2000-2003:** $19,166-$20,075.

Unemployment 2004: 3.8%. **Change from 2000:** +0.1%. **Median travel time to work:** 21.7 minutes. **Working outside county of residence:** 33.5%.

Cities with pop over 10,000: None.

FANNIN COUNTY

400 W Main St Suite 100   **Ph:** 706-632-2203
Blue Ridge, GA 30513   **Fax:** 706-632-2507
www.fannincountyga.org

On the central northern border of GA northeast of Rome; organized Jan 12, 1854 from Gilmer and Union counties. **Name Origin:** For James Walker Fannin (1809-36), GA soldier killed in action in the Texas War of Independence.

Area (sq mi): 391.43 (land 385.74; water 5.69). **Pop per sq mi:** 56.7.

Pop 2005: 21,887. **State rank:** 81. **Pop change:** 2000-20005 +10.6%; 1990-2000 +23.8%. **Pop 2000:** 19,798 (White 97.5%; Black or African American 0.1%; Hispanic or Latino 0.7%; Asian 0.2%; Other 1.7%). **Foreign born:** 1.1%. **Median age:** 43.1.

Income 2000: per capita $16,269; median household $30,612; **Pop below poverty level:** 12.4%. ***Personal per capita income 2000-2003:** $21,469-$22,002.

Unemployment 2004: 4.5%. **Change from 2000:** +0.8%. **Median travel time to work:** 31.8 minutes. **Working outside county of residence:** 40.3%.

Cities with pop over 10,000: None.

FAYETTE COUNTY

140 Stonewall Ave W   **Ph:** 770-460-5730
Fayetteville, GA 30214   **Fax:** 770-460-9412
www.fayettecountyga.gov

In west-central GA, south of Atlanta; original county; organized May 15, 1821 from Indian lands. **Name Origin:** For the Marquis de Lafayette (1757-1834), French statesman and soldier who fought with the Americans during the Revolutionary War.

Area (sq mi): 199.25 (land 197.05; water 2.2). **Pop per sq mi:** 529.

Pop 2005: 104,248. **State rank:** 20. **Pop change:** 2000-20005 +14.2%; 1990-2000 +46.2%. **Pop 2000:** 91,263 (White 82%; Black or African American 11.5%; Hispanic or Latino 2.8%; Asian 2.4%; Other 2.2%). **Foreign born:** 5%. **Median age:** 38.2.

Income 2000: per capita $29,464; median household $71,227; **Pop below poverty level:** 2.6%. ***Personal per capita income 2000-2003:** $36,727-$37,185.

Unemployment 2004: 3.4%. **Change from 2000:** +1.5%. **Median travel time to work:** 30.6 minutes. **Working outside county of residence:** 62.5%.

Cities with pop over 10,000: Peachtree City (33,810); Fayetteville ⛪ (13,858).

FLOYD COUNTY

12 E 4th Ave Suite 209   **Ph:** 706-291-5110
Rome, GA 30162   **Fax:** 706-291-5248
www.floydcountyga.org

On northwestern border of GA; organized Dec 3, 1832 from Cherokee County. **Name Origin:** For Gen. John Floyd (1769-1839), officer in the GA militia and U.S. representative (1827-29).

Area (sq mi): 518.46 (land 513.13; water 5.33). **Pop per sq mi:** 183.6.

Pop 2005: 94,198. **State rank:** 24. **Pop change:** 2000-20005 +4%; 1990-2000 +11.5%. **Pop 2000:** 90,565 (White 79.1%; Black or

*Source: Personal per capita income data are from the Bureau of Economic Analysis; per capita income data are from the Bureau of the Census. See Introduction for explanation of differences.

156

Floyd County (cont'd)

African American 13.3%; Hispanic or Latino 5.5%; Asian 0.9%; Other 4.4%). **Foreign born:** 5.2%. **Median age:** 35.7.

Income 2000: per capita $17,808; median household $35,615; **Pop below poverty level:** 14.4%. ***Personal per capita income 2000-2003:** $23,236-$25,337.

Unemployment 2004: 4.6%. **Change from 2000:** +0.3%. **Median travel time to work:** 23.7 minutes. **Working outside county of residence:** 18.1%.

Cities with pop over 10,000: Rome ⛪ (35,551).

FORSYTH COUNTY

100 Courthouse Sq Suite 010   **Ph:** 770-781-2120
Cumming, GA 30040   **Fax:** 770-886-2858
www.co.forsyth.ga.us

In north-central GA, northeast of Atlanta; organized Dec 3, 1832 from Cherokee County. **Name Origin:** For John Forsyth (1780-1841), governor of GA (1827-29) and U.S. secretary of state (1834-41).

Area (sq mi): 247.37 (land 225.8; water 21.57). **Pop per sq mi:** 621.8.

Pop 2005: 140,393. **State rank:** 13. **Pop change:** 2000-20005 +42.7%; 1990-2000 +123.2%. **Pop 2000:** 98,407 (White 92.3%; Black or African American 0.7%; Hispanic or Latino 5.6%; Asian 0.8%; Other 3.5%). **Foreign born:** 6%. **Median age:** 34.6.

Income 2000: per capita $29,114; median household $68,890; **Pop below poverty level:** 5.5%. ***Personal per capita income 2000-2003:** $36,174-$30,555.

Unemployment 2004: 3.1%. **Change from 2000:** +0.8%. **Median travel time to work:** 33.2 minutes. **Working outside county of residence:** 58.9%.

Cities with pop over 10,000: None.

FRANKLIN COUNTY

9492 Lavonia Rd PO Box 70   **Ph:** 706-384-2514
Carnesville, GA 30521
www.franklin-county.com

On northeast border of GA, northeast of Athens; original county; organized Feb 25, 1784 (prior to statehood) from Cherokee lands. **Name Origin:** For Benjamin Franklin (1706-90), U.S. patriot, diplomat, and statesman.

Area (sq mi): 266.37 (land 263.29; water 3.07). **Pop per sq mi:** 82.

Pop 2005: 21,590. **State rank:** 83. **Pop change:** 2000-20005 +6.4%; 1990-2000 +21.8%. **Pop 2000:** 20,285 (White 89.1%; Black or African American 8.8%; Hispanic or Latino 0.9%; Asian 0.3%; Other 1.4%). **Foreign born:** 1.2%. **Median age:** 37.6.

Income 2000: per capita $15,767; median household $32,134; **Pop below poverty level:** 13.9%. ***Personal per capita income 2000-2003:** $22,323-$23,594.

Unemployment 2004: 4.7%. **Change from 2000:** -0.4%. **Median travel time to work:** 25.7 minutes. **Working outside county of residence:** 46.1%.

Cities with pop over 10,000: None.

FULTON COUNTY

141 Pryor St SW Suite 10061   **Ph:** 404-730-8320
Atlanta, GA 30303   **Fax:** 404-730-8341
www.co.fulton.ga.us

In west-central GA; organized Dec 20, 1853 from De Kalb County; on Jan 1, 1932 annexed Campbell County (organized 1828 from Carroll, Coweta, De Kalb, Fayette, and Cherokee counties) and Milton County (organized 1857 from Cobb, Cherokee, and Forsyth counties). **Name Origin:** For Robert Fulton (1765-1815), builder of the Clermont, the first commercially successful steamboat. Some believe for Hamilton Fulton, the English engineer who surveyed a railroad through the present county.

Area (sq mi): 534.61 (land 528.66; water 5.95). **Pop per sq mi:** 1732.

Pop 2005: 915,623. **State rank:** 1. **Pop change:** 2000-20005 +12.2%; 1990-2000 +25.7%. **Pop 2000:** 816,006 (White 45.3%; Black or African American 44.6%; Hispanic or Latino 5.9%; Asian 3%; Other 4.3%). **Foreign born:** 9.6%. **Median age:** 32.7.

Income 2000: per capita $30,003; median household $47,321; **Pop below poverty level:** 15.7%. ***Personal per capita income 2000-2003:** $45,916-$48,647.

Unemployment 2004: 5.3%. **Change from 2000:** +1%. **Median travel time to work:** 29.1 minutes. **Working outside county of residence:** 31%.

Cities with pop over 10,000: 6 (see page 34 for cities).

GILMER COUNTY

1 West Side Sq   **Ph:** 706-635-4361
Ellijay, GA 30540   **Fax:** 706-635-4359
www.gilmerchamber.com

In north-central GA, north of Atlanta; organized Dec 3, 1832 from Cherokee County. **Name Origin:** For George Rockingham Gilmer (1790-1859), U.S. representative from GA (1821-23; 1827-29; 1833-35) and twice governor (1829-31; 1837-39).

Area (sq mi): 431.83 (land 426.69; water 5.14). **Pop per sq mi:** 64.1.

Pop 2005: 27,335. **State rank:** 62. **Pop change:** 2000-20005 +16.5%; 1990-2000 +75.5%. **Pop 2000:** 23,456 (White 90.8%; Black or African American 0.3%; Hispanic or Latino 7.7%; Asian 0.2%; Other 6%). **Foreign born:** 5.8%. **Median age:** 37.3.

Income 2000: per capita $17,147; median household $35,140; **Pop below poverty level:** 12.5%. ***Personal per capita income 2000-2003:** $19,631-$21,517.

Unemployment 2004: 3.8%. **Change from 2000:** +0.3%. **Median travel time to work:** 31.1 minutes. **Working outside county of residence:** 38.1%.

Cities with pop over 10,000: None.

GLASCOCK COUNTY

PO Box 231   **Ph:** 706-598-2084
Gibson, GA 30810   **Fax:** 706-598-2577

In east-central GA, southwest of Augusta; organized Dec 19, 1857 from Warren County. **Name Origin:** For Gen. Thomas Glascock (1790-1841), GA army officer during the War of 1812 and the Seminole War (1817), state legislator, and U.S. representative from GA (1835-39).

Area (sq mi): 144.45 (land 144.14; water 0.31). **Pop per sq mi:** 18.8.

⛪ *County Seat*

157

Glascock County (cont'd)

Pop 2005: 2,705. **State rank:** 156. **Pop change:** 2000-20005 +5.8%; 1990-2000 +8.4%. **Pop 2000:** 2,556 (White 90.3%; Black or African American 8.3%; Hispanic or Latino 0.5%; Asian 0%; Other 1%). **Foreign born:** 0%. **Median age:** 39.6.

Income 2000: per capita $14,185; median household $29,743; **Pop below poverty level:** 17.2%. ***Personal per capita income 2000-2003:** $19,714-$21,054.

Unemployment 2004: 4.3%. **Change from 2000:** -0.4%. **Median travel time to work:** 35.3 minutes. **Working outside county of residence:** 74.4%.

Cities with pop over 10,000: None.

GLYNN COUNTY
1803 Gloucester St Rm 114　　　　**Ph:** 912-554-7400
Brunswick, GA 31520　　　　　　**Fax:** 912-267-5691
www.glynncounty.com

On southeastern Atlantic coast of GA; original county; organized Feb 5, 1777 (prior to statehood) from Saint David and Saint Patrick parishes. **Name Origin:** For John Glynn (1722-79), a pro-colonist member of the British Parliament.

Area (sq mi): 585.17 (land 422.37; water 162.8). **Pop per sq mi:** 170.2.

Pop 2005: 71,874. **State rank:** 30. **Pop change:** 2000-20005 +6.4%; 1990-2000 +8.1%. **Pop 2000:** 67,568 (White 68.9%; Black or African American 26.5%; Hispanic or Latino 3%; Asian 0.6%; Other 2.3%). **Foreign born:** 3.3%. **Median age:** 37.9.

Income 2000: per capita $21,707; median household $38,765; **Pop below poverty level:** 15.1%. ***Personal per capita income 2000-2003:** $28,945-$30,032.

Unemployment 2004: 3.8%. **Change from 2000:** +0.5%. **Median travel time to work:** 19.6 minutes. **Working outside county of residence:** 6.4%.

Cities with pop over 10,000: Brunswick ⛪ (15,978).

GORDON COUNTY
201 N Wall St　　　　　　　　**Ph:** 706-629-3795
Calhoun, GA 30701　　　　　　**Fax:** 706-629-9516
www.gordoncounty.org

In northwestern GA, northeast of Rome; organized Feb 13, 1850 from Bartow (then called Cass) and Floyd counties. **Name Origin:** For William Washington Gordon (1796-1842), prominent GA railroad official.

Area (sq mi): 358.01 (land 355.54; water 2.48). **Pop per sq mi:** 141.4.

Pop 2005: 50,279. **State rank:** 39. **Pop change:** 2000-20005 +14%; 1990-2000 +25.8%. **Pop 2000:** 44,104 (White 87.6%; Black or African American 3.5%; Hispanic or Latino 7.4%; Asian 0.5%; Other 6.4%). **Foreign born:** 6.4%. **Median age:** 34.1.

Income 2000: per capita $17,586; median household $38,831; **Pop below poverty level:** 9.9%. ***Personal per capita income 2000-2003:** $21,974-$23,442.

Unemployment 2004: 4.3%. **Change from 2000:** -2.3%. **Median travel time to work:** 23.2 minutes. **Working outside county of residence:** 31.1%.

Cities with pop over 10,000: Calhoun ⛪ (13,103).

GRADY COUNTY
250 N Broad St　　　　　　　**Ph:** 229-377-1512
Cairo, GA 39828　　　　　　　**Fax:** 229-377-1039

On southern border of GA, west of Valdosta; organized Aug 17, 1905 from Decatur and Thomas counties. **Name Origin:** For Henry Woodfin Grady (1850-89), GA orator and journalist, editor, and part-owner of the *Atlanta Constitution*.

Area (sq mi): 460.34 (land 458.12; water 2.22). **Pop per sq mi:** 53.4.

Pop 2005: 24,466. **State rank:** 69. **Pop change:** 2000-20005 +3.4%; 1990-2000 +16.7%. **Pop 2000:** 23,659 (White 63.2%; Black or African American 30.1%; Hispanic or Latino 5.2%; Asian 0.3%; Other 4.9%). **Foreign born:** 3.9%. **Median age:** 35.5.

Income 2000: per capita $14,278; median household $28,656; **Pop below poverty level:** 21.3%. ***Personal per capita income 2000-2003:** $18,840-$21,122.

Unemployment 2004: 4.3%. **Change from 2000:** -0.8%. **Median travel time to work:** 24.4 minutes. **Working outside county of residence:** 43.7%.

Cities with pop over 10,000: None.

GREENE COUNTY
113 N Main St 3rd Fl Suite 306　　**Ph:** 706-453-7716
Greensboro, GA 30642　　　　　**Fax:** 706-453-9555
www.greenecountyga.gov

In east-central GA, southeast of Athens; organized Feb 3, 1786 (prior to statehood) from Washington, Oglethorpe, and Wilkes counties. **Name Origin:** For Gen. Nathanael Greene (1742-86), hero of the Revolutionary War, quartermaster general (1778-80), and commander of the Army of the South.

Area (sq mi): 406.24 (land 388.28; water 17.96). **Pop per sq mi:** 40.4.

Pop 2005: 15,693. **State rank:** 104. **Pop change:** 2000-20005 +8.9%; 1990-2000 +22.2%. **Pop 2000:** 14,406 (White 51.9%; Black or African American 44.4%; Hispanic or Latino 2.9%; Asian 0.2%; Other 2.4%). **Foreign born:** 2.6%. **Median age:** 39.1.

Income 2000: per capita $23,389; median household $33,479; **Pop below poverty level:** 22.3%. ***Personal per capita income 2000-2003:** $23,392-$24,549.

Unemployment 2004: 5.9%. **Change from 2000:** -2.7%. **Median travel time to work:** 26 minutes. **Working outside county of residence:** 31.3%.

Cities with pop over 10,000: None.

GWINNETT COUNTY
75 Langley Dr
Gwinnett Justice & Administration Ctr　**Ph:** 770-822-7000
Lawrenceville, GA 30045　　　　　**Fax:** 770-822-7097
www.co.gwinnett.ga.us

In north-central GA, northeast of Atlanta; original county; organized Dec 15, 1818 from Cherokee lands. **Name Origin:** For Button

*Source: Personal per capita income data are from the Bureau of Economic Analysis; per capita income data are from the Bureau of the Census. See Introduction for explanation of differences.

Gwinnett County (cont'd)

Gwinnett (c. 1735-77), a signer of the Declaration of Independence and acting president of GA (1777).

Area (sq mi): 436.72 (land 432.73; water 3.99). **Pop per sq mi:** 1678.4.

Pop 2005: 726,273. **State rank:** 2. **Pop change:** 2000-20005 +23.4%; 1990-2000 +66.7%. **Pop 2000:** 588,448 (White 67%; Black or African American 13.3%; Hispanic or Latino 10.9%; Asian 7.2%; Other 6.8%). **Foreign born:** 16.9%. **Median age:** 32.5.

Income 2000: per capita $25,006; median household $60,537; **Pop below poverty level:** 5.7%. ***Personal per capita income 2000-2003:** $31,863-$30,277.

Unemployment 2004: 4%. **Change from 2000:** +1%. **Median travel time to work:** 32.2 minutes. **Working outside county of residence:** 45.4%.

Cities with pop over 10,000: 7 (see page 34 for cities).

HABERSHAM COUNTY
555 Monroe St Unit 20   **Ph:** 706-754-6270
Clarkesville, GA 30523   **Fax:** 706-754-1014
www.co.habersham.ga.us

In northeastern GA; original county; organized Dec 15, 1818 from Cherokee lands. **Name Origin:** For Col. Joseph Habersham (1751-1815), member of the Continental Congress and U.S. postmaster general (1795-1801).

Area (sq mi): 279.2 (land 278.17; water 1.03). **Pop per sq mi:** 142.4.

Pop 2005: 39,603. **State rank:** 50. **Pop change:** 2000-20005 +10.3%; 1990-2000 +30%. **Pop 2000:** 35,902 (White 84.9%; Black or African American 4.5%; Hispanic or Latino 7.7%; Asian 1.9%; Other 4.8%). **Foreign born:** 7.8%. **Median age:** 36.4.

Income 2000: per capita $17,706; median household $36,321; **Pop below poverty level:** 12.2%. ***Personal per capita income 2000-2003:** $21,916-$23,202.

Unemployment 2004: 3.5%. **Change from 2000:** -1%. **Median travel time to work:** 23.8 minutes. **Working outside county of residence:** 31.4%.

Cities with pop over 10,000: None.

HALL COUNTY
PO Box 1275   **Ph:** 770-531-7025
Gainesville, GA 30503   **Fax:** 770-531-7070
www.hallcounty.org

In north-central GA, northwest of Athens; original county; organized Dec 15, 1818 from Cherokee lands. **Name Origin:** For Lyman Hall (1731-90), a signer of the Declaration of Independence, and GA governor (1783-84).

Area (sq mi): 429.19 (land 393.66; water 35.53). **Pop per sq mi:** 421.1.

Pop 2005: 165,771. **State rank:** 11. **Pop change:** 2000-20005 +19%; 1990-2000 +45.9%. **Pop 2000:** 139,277 (White 71%; Black or African American 7.3%; Hispanic or Latino 19.6%; Asian 1.3%; Other 10.7%). **Foreign born:** 16.2%. **Median age:** 32.2.

Income 2000: per capita $19,690; median household $44,908; **Pop below poverty level:** 12.4%. ***Personal per capita income 2000-2003:** $24,734-$25,132.

Unemployment 2004: 3.8%. **Change from 2000:** +0.9%. **Median travel time to work:** 26.1 minutes. **Working outside county of residence:** 28.6%.

Cities with pop over 10,000: Gainesville 🏛 (31,107).

HANCOCK COUNTY
601 Broad St Courthouse Sq   **Ph:** 706-444-5746
Sparta, GA 31087   **Fax:** 706-444-6221

In east-central GA, southwest of Augusta; organized Dec 17, 1793 from Greene and Washington counties. **Name Origin:** For John Hancock (1737-93), noted signer of the Declaration of Independence, governor of MA (1780-85; 1787-93), and statesman.

Area (sq mi): 478.76 (land 473.28; water 5.48). **Pop per sq mi:** 20.4.

Pop 2005: 9,643. **State rank:** 131. **Pop change:** 2000-20005 -4.3%; 1990-2000 +13.1%. **Pop 2000:** 10,076 (White 21.2%; Black or African American 77.8%; Hispanic or Latino 0.5%; Asian 0.1%; Other 0.7%). **Foreign born:** 0.3%. **Median age:** 35.8.

Income 2000: per capita $10,916; median household $22,003; **Pop below poverty level:** 29.4%. ***Personal per capita income 2000-2003:** $13,747-$15,673.

Unemployment 2004: 6.4%. **Change from 2000:** -4.3%. **Median travel time to work:** 36.2 minutes. **Working outside county of residence:** 63.8%.

Cities with pop over 10,000: None.

HARALSON COUNTY
PO Box 489   **Ph:** 770-646-2002
Buchanan, GA 30113   **Fax:** 770-646-2035
www.haralsoncountyga.org

On the western border of GA, west of Atlanta; organized Jan 26, 1856 from Carroll and Polk counties. **Name Origin:** For Gen. Hugh Anderson Haralson (1805-54), U.S. representative from GA (1843-51).

Area (sq mi): 283.16 (land 282.11; water 1.05). **Pop per sq mi:** 100.5.

Pop 2005: 28,338. **State rank:** 59. **Pop change:** 2000-20005 +10.3%; 1990-2000 +17%. **Pop 2000:** 25,690 (White 92.6%; Black or African American 5.4%; Hispanic or Latino 0.6%; Asian 0.3%; Other 1.3%). **Foreign born:** 0.9%. **Median age:** 36.1.

Income 2000: per capita $15,823; median household $31,656; **Pop below poverty level:** 15.5%. ***Personal per capita income 2000-2003:** $21,080-$21,742.

Unemployment 2004: 4.9%. **Change from 2000:** -0.7%. **Median travel time to work:** 30.3 minutes. **Working outside county of residence:** 54.4%.

Cities with pop over 10,000: None.

HARRIS COUNTY
PO Box 528   **Ph:** 706-628-4944
Hamilton, GA 31811   **Fax:** 706-628-7039
www.harriscountychamber.org

On central western border of GA, north of Columbus; organized

Harris County (cont'd)

Dec 14, 1827 from Muscogee and Troup counties. **Name Origin:** For Charles Harris (1772-1827), a Savannah lawyer and city official.

Area (sq mi): 472.93 (land 463.69; water 9.24). **Pop per sq mi:** 59.9.

Pop 2005: 27,779. **State rank:** 60. **Pop change:** 2000-20005 +17.2%; 1990-2000 +33.2%. **Pop 2000:** 23,695 (White 77.8%; Black or African American 19.5%; Hispanic or Latino 1.1%; Asian 0.5%; Other 1.6%). **Foreign born:** 1.9%. **Median age:** 38.5.

Income 2000: per capita $21,680; median household $47,763; **Pop below poverty level:** 8.2%. ***Personal per capita income 2000-2003:** $30,537-$32,173.

Unemployment 2004: 3.7%. **Change from 2000:** +0.6%. **Median travel time to work:** 29.9 minutes. **Working outside county of residence:** 75.7%.

Cities with pop over 10,000: None.

HART COUNTY
800 Chandler St   **Ph:** 706-376-2024
Hartwell, GA 30643   **Fax:** 706-376-9477
www.hartcountyga.org

On the northeastern border of GA, northeast of Athens; organized Dec 7, 1853 from Elbert and Franklin counties. **Name Origin:** For Nancy (Morgan) Hart (1735?-1830?), spy, sharpshooter, and heroine of the American Revolution. Called 'War Woman' by the Indians.

Area (sq mi): 256.42 (land 232.21; water 24.21). **Pop per sq mi:** 103.5.

Pop 2005: 24,036. **State rank:** 72. **Pop change:** 2000-20005 +4.5%; 1990-2000 +16.7%. **Pop 2000:** 22,997 (White 78.6%; Black or African American 19.4%; Hispanic or Latino 0.9%; Asian 0.5%; Other 1%). **Foreign born:** 1.3%. **Median age:** 39.2.

Income 2000: per capita $16,714; median household $32,833; **Pop below poverty level:** 14.8%. ***Personal per capita income 2000-2003:** $21,115-$21,663.

Unemployment 2004: 4.7%. **Change from 2000:** -2.3%. **Median travel time to work:** 20.7 minutes. **Working outside county of residence:** 34.1%.

Cities with pop over 10,000: None.

HEARD COUNTY
PO Box 40   **Ph:** 706-675-3821
Franklin, GA 30217   **Fax:** 706-675-2493

On central western border of GA, southwest of Atlanta; organized Dec 22, 1830 from Carroll, Coweta, and Troup counties. **Name Origin:** For Stephen Heard (1740-1815), chief justice of the GA inferior court and governor of GA (1780-81).

Area (sq mi): 301.08 (land 296.03; water 5.06). **Pop per sq mi:** 38.3.

Pop 2005: 11,346. **State rank:** 118. **Pop change:** 2000-20005 +3%; 1990-2000 +27.6%. **Pop 2000:** 11,012 (White 87%; Black or African American 10.8%; Hispanic or Latino 1.1%; Asian 0.1%; Other 1.6%). **Foreign born:** 0.7%. **Median age:** 34.1.

Income 2000: per capita $15,132; median household $33,038; **Pop below poverty level:** 13.6%. ***Personal per capita income 2000-2003:** $18,766-$19,172.

Unemployment 2004: 5.2%. **Change from 2000:** -0.3%. **Median travel time to work:** 37.5 minutes. **Working outside county of residence:** 68.5%.

Cities with pop over 10,000: None.

HENRY COUNTY
140 Henry Pkwy   **Ph:** 770-954-2400
McDonough, GA 30253   **Fax:** 770-954-2418
www.co.henry.ga.us

In west-central GA, southeast of Atlanta; county organized May 15, 1821 from Indian lands. **Name Origin:** For Patrick Henry (1736-99), patriot, governor of VA (1776-79; 1784-86), and statesman, famous for declaring, 'Give me liberty or give me death.'

Area (sq mi): 324.48 (land 322.71; water 1.77). **Pop per sq mi:** 520.1.

Pop 2005: 167,848. **State rank:** 10. **Pop change:** 2000-20005 +40.6%; 1990-2000 +103.2%. **Pop 2000:** 119,341 (White 80.1%; Black or African American 14.7%; Hispanic or Latino 2.3%; Asian 1.8%; Other 2.1%). **Foreign born:** 3.4%. **Median age:** 33.4.

Income 2000: per capita $22,945; median household $57,309; **Pop below poverty level:** 4.9%. ***Personal per capita income 2000-2003:** $26,993-$26,468.

Unemployment 2004: 4%. **Change from 2000:** +1.5%. **Median travel time to work:** 32.7 minutes. **Working outside county of residence:** 68.9%.

Cities with pop over 10,000: McDonough (13,622); Stockbridge (12,541).

HOUSTON COUNTY
201 Perry Pkwy County Courthouse   **Ph:** 478-542-2115
Perry, GA 31069   **Fax:** 478-923-5697
www.houstoncountyga.com

In central GA, south of Macon; original county; organized May 15, 1821 from Indian lands. **Name Origin:** For John Houstoun (1744-96), American Revolutionary patriot and GA governor (1778; 1784). Spelling changed by clerical error.

Area (sq mi): 379.83 (land 376.75; water 3.08). **Pop per sq mi:** 334.9.

Pop 2005: 126,163. **State rank:** 14. **Pop change:** 2000-20005 +13.9%; 1990-2000 +24.2%. **Pop 2000:** 110,765 (White 69%; Black or African American 24.8%; Hispanic or Latino 3%; Asian 1.6%; Other 3.1%). **Foreign born:** 3.4%. **Median age:** 34.

Income 2000: per capita $19,515; median household $43,638; **Pop below poverty level:** 10.2%. ***Personal per capita income 2000-2003:** $24,390-$26,379.

Unemployment 2004: 3.8%. **Change from 2000:** +0.8%. **Median travel time to work:** 20.2 minutes. **Working outside county of residence:** 37.2%.

Cities with pop over 10,000: Warner Robins (56,305); Perry (10,660).

IRWIN COUNTY
207 S Irwin Ave Suite 2   **Ph:** 229-468-9441
Ocilla, GA 31774   **Fax:** 229-468-9672

In south-central GA, north of Valdosta; original county; organized

---

*Source: Personal per capita income data are from the Bureau of Economic Analysis; per capita income data are from the Bureau of the Census. See Introduction for explanation of differences.

Irwin County (cont'd)

Dec 15, 1818 from Indian lands. **Name Origin:** For Gen. Jared Irwin (1750-1818), twice GA governor (1796-98; 1806-09).

Area (sq mi): 362.73 (land 356.81; water 5.92). **Pop per sq mi:** 28.3.

Pop 2005: 10,093. **State rank:** 129. **Pop change:** 2000-20005 +1.6%; 1990-2000 +14.8%. **Pop 2000:** 9,931 (White 71.5%; Black or African American 25.9%; Hispanic or Latino 2%; Asian 0.3%; Other 1.8%). **Foreign born:** 1.3%. **Median age:** 34.6.

Income 2000: per capita $14,867; median household $30,257; **Pop below poverty level:** 17.8%. *Personal per capita income 2000-2003:** $19,206-$20,590.

Unemployment 2004: 4.7%. **Change from 2000:** 1.3%. **Median travel time to work:** 22.5 minutes. **Working outside county of residence:** 56.6%.

Cities with pop over 10,000: None.

JACKSON COUNTY
67 Athens St   **Ph:** 706-367-6312
Jefferson, GA 30549   **Fax:** 706-367-9083
www.jacksoncountygov.com

In northeastern GA, northwest of Athens; organized Feb 11, 1796 from Franklin County. **Name Origin:** For Gen. James Jackson (1757-1806), an officer in the American Revolution, GA governor (1798-1801), and U.S. senator (1793-95; 1801-06).

Area (sq mi): 343 (land 342.36; water 0.64). **Pop per sq mi:** 152.7.

Pop 2005: 52,292. **State rank:** 38. **Pop change:** 2000-20005 +25.7%; 1990-2000 +38.6%. **Pop 2000:** 41,589 (White 87.3%; Black or African American 7.8%; Hispanic or Latino 3%; Asian 1%; Other 2.3%). **Foreign born:** 2.5%. **Median age:** 34.6.

Income 2000: per capita $17,808; median household $40,349; **Pop below poverty level:** 12%. *Personal per capita income 2000-2003: $23,421 $24,445.

Unemployment 2004: 4%. **Change from 2000:** +0.1%. **Median travel time to work:** 29.9 minutes. **Working outside county of residence:** 58.4%.

Cities with pop over 10,000: None.

JASPER COUNTY
126 W Greene St Suite 18   **Ph:** 706-468-4900
Monticello, GA 31064   **Fax:** 706-468-4942

In central GA, north of Macon; organized as Randolph County Dec 10, 1807 from Baldwin County; name changed Dec 10, 1812. **Name Origin:** For Sgt. William Jasper (1750-79), Revolutionary War soldier from SC. Originally for John Randolph (1773-1833), U.S. congressman from VA, home of many early settlers; his opposition to the War of 1812 angered the populace.

Area (sq mi): 373.58 (land 370.42; water 3.16). **Pop per sq mi:** 35.5.

Pop 2005: 13,147. **State rank:** 111. **Pop change:** 2000-20005 +15.1%; 1990-2000 +35.2%. **Pop 2000:** 11,426 (White 69.7%; Black or African American 27.3%; Hispanic or Latino 2.1%; Asian 0.2%; Other 1.6%). **Foreign born:** 2.1%. **Median age:** 36.3.

Income 2000: per capita $19,249; median household $39,890; **Pop below poverty level:** 14.2%. *Personal per capita income 2000-2003: $22,178-$22,211.

Unemployment 2004: 4.7%. **Change from 2000:** +0.7%. **Median travel time to work:** 34.2 minutes. **Working outside county of residence:** 62.7%.

Cities with pop over 10,000: None.

JEFF DAVIS COUNTY
PO Box 609   **Ph:** 912-375-6611
Hazlehurst, GA 31539   **Fax:** 912-375-0378

In southeast-central GA; organized Aug 18, 1905 from Appling and Coffee counties. **Name Origin:** For Jefferson Davis (1808-89), president of the Confederate States of America (1862-65).

Area (sq mi): 335.42 (land 333.38; water 2.04). **Pop per sq mi:** 39.2.

Pop 2005: 13,083. **State rank:** 112. **Pop change:** 2000-20005 +3.1%; 1990-2000 +5.4%. **Pop 2000:** 12,684 (White 78.8%; Black or African American 15.1%; Hispanic or Latino 5.1%; Asian 0.4%; Other 3.2%). **Foreign born:** 3.8%. **Median age:** 35.

Income 2000: per capita $13,780; median household $27,310; **Pop below poverty level:** 19.4%. *Personal per capita income 2000-2003: $20,114-$21,088.

Unemployment 2004: 6.8%. **Change from 2000:** -3.3%. **Median travel time to work:** 21.7 minutes. **Working outside county of residence:** 28.4%.

Cities with pop over 10,000: None.

JEFFERSON COUNTY
217 E Broad St   **Ph:** 478-625-3332
Louisville, GA 30434   **Fax:** 478-625-4007
www.jeffersoncounty.org

In east-central GA, southwest of Augusta; organized Feb 20, 1796 from Burke and Warren counties. **Name Origin:** For Thomas Jefferson (1743-1826), U.S. patriot and statesman; third U.S. president.

Area (sq mi): 529.56 (land 527.65; water 1.91). **Pop per sq mi:** 32.1.

Pop 2005: 16,926. **State rank:** 95. **Pop change:** 2000-20005 -2%; 1990-2000 -0.8%. **Pop 2000:** 17,266 (White 41.8%; Black or African American 56.3%; Hispanic or Latino 1.5%; Asian 0.2%; Other 1.4%). **Foreign born:** 0.5%. **Median age:** 34.9.

Income 2000: per capita $13,491; median household $26,120; **Pop below poverty level:** 23%. *Personal per capita income 2000-2003: $18,036-$19,905.

Unemployment 2004: 7.7%. **Change from 2000:** -2.1%. **Median travel time to work:** 29 minutes. **Working outside county of residence:** 34.2%.

Cities with pop over 10,000: None.

JENKINS COUNTY
611 Winthrop Ave   **Ph:** 478-982-2563
Millen, GA 30442   **Fax:** 478-982-4750

In east-central GA, south of Augusta; organized Aug 17, 1905 from Bulloch, Burke, Screven, and Emanuel counties. **Name Origin:** For Charles Jones Jenkins (1805-83), GA legislator, jurist, and governor (1865-67).

Area (sq mi): 352.45 (land 349.81; water 2.64). **Pop per sq mi:** 25.

Pop 2005: 8,729. **State rank:** 137. **Pop change:** 2000-20005 +1.8%; 1990-2000 +4%. **Pop 2000:** 8,575 (White 55.6%; Black or African

Jenkins County (cont'd)

American 40.5%; Hispanic or Latino 3.3%; Asian 0.2%; Other 3.1%). **Foreign born:** 0.9%. **Median age:** 35.4.

Income 2000: per capita $13,400; median household $24,025; **Pop below poverty level:** 28.4%. ***Personal per capita income 2000-2003:** $17,776-$18,753.

Unemployment 2004: 5.9%. **Change from 2000:** -0.1%. **Median travel time to work:** 22.6 minutes. **Working outside county of residence:** 35%.

Cities with pop over 10,000: None.

JOHNSON COUNTY

PO Box 321   **Ph:** 478-864-3484
Wrightsville, GA 31096   **Fax:** 478-864-1343

In east-central GA, east of Macon; organized Dec 11, 1858 from Emanuel, Laurens, and Washington counties. **Name Origin:** For Herschel Vespasian Johnson (1812-80), middle circuit court judge, U.S. senator (1848-49), and GA governor (1853-57).

Area (sq mi): 306.52 (land 304.26; water 2.26). **Pop per sq mi:** 31.3.

Pop 2005: 9,538. **State rank:** 132. **Pop change:** 2000-20005 +11.4%; 1990-2000 +2.8%. **Pop 2000:** 8,560 (White 62%; Black or African American 37%; Hispanic or Latino 0.9%; Asian 0.1%; Other 0.5%). **Foreign born:** 0.2%. **Median age:** 34.9.

Income 2000: per capita $12,384; median household $23,848; **Pop below poverty level:** 22.6%. ***Personal per capita income 2000-2003:** $18,171-$17,582.

Unemployment 2004: 5.2%. **Change from 2000:** -2%. **Median travel time to work:** 29.7 minutes. **Working outside county of residence:** 55.4%.

Cities with pop over 10,000: None.

JONES COUNTY

PO Box 1359   **Ph:** 478-986-6405
Gray, GA 31032   **Fax:** 478-986-9682
www.jonescounty.org

In central GA, north of the Macon city center; organized Dec 10, 1807 from Baldwin County. **Name Origin:** For James Jones (?-1801), GA legislator and U.S. representative (1799-1801).

Area (sq mi): 395.39 (land 393.75; water 1.64). **Pop per sq mi:** 68.2.

Pop 2005: 26,836. **State rank:** 65. **Pop change:** 2000-20005 +13.5%; 1990-2000 +14%. **Pop 2000:** 23,639 (White 74.7%; Black or African American 23.3%; Hispanic or Latino 0.7%; Asian 0.5%; Other 1.1%). **Foreign born:** 1%. **Median age:** 36.1.

Income 2000: per capita $19,126; median household $43,301; **Pop below poverty level:** 10.2%. ***Personal per capita income 2000-2003:** $23,312-$23,761.

Unemployment 2004: 4.2%. **Change from 2000:** +1.1%. **Median travel time to work:** 27.8 minutes. **Working outside county of residence:** 76.6%.

Cities with pop over 10,000: None.

LAMAR COUNTY

326 Thomaston St   **Ph:** 770-358-5146
Barnesville, GA 30204   **Fax:** 770-358-5149
www.barnesville.org

In west-central GA, northwest of Macon; organized Aug 17, 1920 from Monroe and Pike counties. **Name Origin:** For Lucius Quintus Cincinnatus Lamar (1825-93), U.S. statesman and a justice of the U.S. Supreme Court (1888-93).

Area (sq mi): 185.79 (land 184.82; water 0.97). **Pop per sq mi:** 88.6.

Pop 2005: 16,378. **State rank:** 97. **Pop change:** 2000-20005 +2.9%; 1990-2000 +22%. **Pop 2000:** 15,912 (White 67.1%; Black or African American 30.4%; Hispanic or Latino 1.1%; Asian 0.4%; Other 1.5%). **Foreign born:** 1%. **Median age:** 35.7.

Income 2000: per capita $16,666; median household $37,087; **Pop below poverty level:** 11.2%. ***Personal per capita income 2000-2003:** $21,096-$23,004.

Unemployment 2004: 5.5%. **Change from 2000:** -0.5%. **Median travel time to work:** 28.1 minutes. **Working outside county of residence:** 64.5%.

Cities with pop over 10,000: None.

LANIER COUNTY

100 W Main St   **Ph:** 229-482-2088
Lakeland, GA 31635   **Fax:** 229-482-8187

In south-central GA, northeast of Valdosta; organized Aug 7, 1920 from Berrien, Lowndes, and Clinch counties. **Name Origin:** For Sidney Lanier (1842-81), soldier, lawyer, musician, and important post-Civil War southern poet.

Area (sq mi): 199.83 (land 186.82; water 13.01). **Pop per sq mi:** 40.4.

Pop 2005: 7,553. **State rank:** 141. **Pop change:** 2000-20005 +4.3%; 1990-2000 +30.9%. **Pop 2000:** 7,241 (White 70.7%; Black or African American 25.6%; Hispanic or Latino 1.7%; Asian 0.4%; Other 2.4%). **Foreign born:** 1.1%. **Median age:** 33.3.

Income 2000: per capita $13,690; median household $29,171; **Pop below poverty level:** 18.5%. ***Personal per capita income 2000-2003:** $18,461-$20,818.

Unemployment 2004: 3.6%. **Change from 2000:** -0.2%. **Median travel time to work:** 26.8 minutes. **Working outside county of residence:** 65.3%.

Cities with pop over 10,000: None.

LAURENS COUNTY

117 E Jackson St   **Ph:** 478-272-4755
Dublin, GA 31040   **Fax:** 478-272-3895
www.co.laurens.ga.us

In central GA, southeast of Macon; organized Dec 10, 1807 from Wilkinson County. **Name Origin:** For Lt. John Laurens (1753-82), officer in the American Revolution, who received the sword of Gen. Charles Cornwallis when the latter surrendered at Yorktown, VA.

Area (sq mi): 818.51 (land 812.27; water 6.24). **Pop per sq mi:** 57.7.

Pop 2005: 46,896. **State rank:** 41. **Pop change:** 2000-20005 +4.5%; 1990-2000 +12.2%. **Pop 2000:** 44,874 (White 62.8%; Black or African American 34.5%; Hispanic or Latino 1.2%; Asian 0.8%; Other 1.2%). **Foreign born:** 1.1%. **Median age:** 35.8.

Source: Personal per capita income data are from the Bureau of Economic Analysis; per capita income data are from the Bureau of the Census. See Introduction for explanation of differences.

Laurens County (cont'd)

Income 2000: per capita $16,763; median household $32,010; **Pop below poverty level:** 18.4%. ***Personal per capita income 2000-2003:** $21,569-$22,655.

Unemployment 2004: 5.4%. **Change from 2000:** +1%. **Median travel time to work:** 23.6 minutes. **Working outside county of residence:** 15.5%.

Cities with pop over 10,000: Dublin 🏛 (16,689).

LEE COUNTY

PO Box 889   **Ph:** 229-759-6000
Leesburg, GA 31763   **Fax:** 229-759-6050
www.lee.ga.us

In southwestern GA, north of Albany; original county; established Jun 9, 1826 from Indian lands. **Name Origin:** For Richard Henry Lee (1732-94), signer of the Declaration of Independence, VA legislator, and U.S. senator (1789-92).

Area (sq mi): 362.01 (land 355.77; water 6.24). **Pop per sq mi:** 87.4.

Pop 2005: 31,099. **State rank:** 53. **Pop change:** 2000-20005 +25.6%; 1990-2000 +52.4%. **Pop 2000:** 24,757 (White 81.6%; Black or African American 15.5%; Hispanic or Latino 1.2%; Asian 0.8%; Other 1.4%). **Foreign born:** 1.7%. **Median age:** 32.6.

Income 2000: per capita $19,897; median household $48,600; **Pop below poverty level:** 8.2%. ***Personal per capita income 2000-2003:** $22,724-$21,811.

Unemployment 2004: 3.2%. **Change from 2000:** -0.4%. **Median travel time to work:** 21.4 minutes. **Working outside county of residence:** 82%.

Cities with pop over 10,000: None.

LIBERTY COUNTY

PO Box 829   **Ph:** 912-876-2164
Hinesville, GA 31310   **Fax:** 912-369-0204
www.libertycounty.org

In southeastern GA, southwest of Savannah; original county; organized Feb 5, 1777 (prior to statehood) from Saint Andrew, Saint James, Saint Johns, and Tatnall parishes. **Name Origin:** For the fervent patriotism of the Midway community during the Revolutionary War, and to honor American independence.

Area (sq mi): 602.52 (land 519.05; water 83.47). **Pop per sq mi:** 110.9.

Pop 2005: 57,544. **State rank:** 37. **Pop change:** 2000-20005 -6.6%; 1990-2000 +16.8%. **Pop 2000:** 61,610 (White 44.2%; Black or African American 42.8%; Hispanic or Latino 8.2%; Asian 1.8%; Other 8.7%). **Foreign born:** 5.7%. **Median age:** 25.

Income 2000: per capita $13,855; median household $33,477; **Pop below poverty level:** 15%. ***Personal per capita income 2000-2003:** $16,913-$19,064.

Unemployment 2004: 5.8%. **Change from 2000:** +0.9%. **Median travel time to work:** 21.4 minutes. **Working outside county of residence:** 19.5%.

Cities with pop over 10,000: Hinesville 🏛 (30,566).

LINCOLN COUNTY

PO Box 340   **Ph:** 706-359-4444
Lincolnton, GA 30817   **Fax:** 706-359-4729
www.lincolncountyga.com

On central-eastern border of GA, north of Augusta; organized Feb 20, 1796 from Wilkes County. **Name Origin:** For Gen. Benjamin Lincoln (1733-1810), Revolutionary War officer, U.S. secretary of war (1781-83), and lt. gov. of MA (1788).

Area (sq mi): 257.28 (land 211.09, water 46.19). **Pop per sq mi:** 38.9.

Pop 2005: 8,207. **State rank:** 139. **Pop change:** 2000-20005 -1.7%; 1990-2000 +12.2%. **Pop 2000:** 8,348 (White 63.7%; Black or African American 34.4%; Hispanic or Latino 1%; Asian 0.2%; Other 1.2%). **Foreign born:** 0.7%. **Median age:** 39.3.

Income 2000: per capita $15,351; median household $31,952; **Pop below poverty level:** 15.3%. ***Personal per capita income 2000-2003:** $19,390-$21,156.

Unemployment 2004: 6%. **Change from 2000:** 6%. **Median travel time to work:** 33.1 minutes. **Working outside county of residence:** 58.5%.

Cities with pop over 10,000: None.

LONG COUNTY

49 E McDonald St   **Ph:** 912-545-2143
Ludowici, GA 31316   **Fax:** 912-545-2150

In southeastern GA, northwest of Brunswick; organized Aug 14, 1920 from Liberty County. **Name Origin:** For Crawford Williamson Long (1815-78), prominent GA surgeon, first in history to use sulphuric ether as an anesthetic, Mar 30, 1842.

Area (sq mi): 403.49 (land 400.92; water 2.57). **Pop per sq mi:** 27.6.

Pop 2005: 11,083. **State rank:** 119. **Pop change:** 2000-20005 +7.6%; 1990-2000 +66.1%. **Pop 2000:** 10,304 (White 64.8%; Black or African American 24.3%; Hispanic or Latino 8.4%; Asian 0.6%; Other 6.8%). **Foreign born:** 5.4%. **Median age:** 26.5.

Income 2000: per capita $12,586; median household $30,640; **Pop below poverty level:** 19.5%. ***Personal per capita income 2000-2003:** $15,015-$16,831.

Unemployment 2004: 4.1%. **Change from 2000:** +1.4%. **Median travel time to work:** 29.5 minutes. **Working outside county of residence:** 86.2%.

Cities with pop over 10,000: None.

LOWNDES COUNTY

325 W Savannah Ave   **Ph:** 229-671-2400
Valdosta, GA 31601   **Fax:** 229-245-5222
www.lowndescounty.com

On central southern border of GA; organized Dec 23, 1825 from Irwin County. **Name Origin:** For William Jones Lowndes (1782-1822), SC legislator and U.S. representative (1811-22).

Area (sq mi): 510.63 (land 504.22; water 6.41). **Pop per sq mi:** 191.8.

Pop 2005: 96,705. **State rank:** 22. **Pop change:** 2000-20005 +5%; 1990-2000 +21.2%. **Pop 2000:** 92,115 (White 60.8%; Black or African American 34%; Hispanic or Latino 2.7%; Asian 1.2%; Other 2.8%). **Foreign born:** 2.7%. **Median age:** 30.2.

🏛 *County Seat*

Lowndes County (cont'd)

Income 2000: per capita $16,683; median household $32,132; **Pop below poverty level:** 18.3%. ***Personal per capita income 2000-2003:** $21,280-$24,236.

Unemployment 2004: 3.5%. **Change from 2000:** -0.2%. **Median travel time to work:** 18.7 minutes. **Working outside county of residence:** 8.6%.

Cities with pop over 10,000: Valdosta 🏛 (45,373).

LUMPKIN COUNTY

99 Courthouse Hill Suite A   **Ph:** 706-864-3742
Dahlonega, GA 30533   **Fax:** 706-864-4760
www.lumpkincounty.gov

In north-central GA, northeast of Atlanta; organized Dec 3, 1832 from Cherokee, Hall, and Habersham counties. **Name Origin:** For Wilson Lumpkin (1783-1870), GA governor (1831-35) and U.S. senator (1837-41).

Area (sq mi): 284.87 (land 284.47; water 0.4). **Pop per sq mi:** 85.5.

Pop 2005: 24,324. **State rank:** 70. **Pop change:** 2000-20005 +15.7%; 1990-2000 +44.2%. **Pop 2000:** 21,016 (White 92.2%; Black or African American 1.5%; Hispanic or Latino 3.5%; Asian 0.4%; Other 4.2%, including 1% American Indian/Alaska Native). **Foreign born:** 2.9%. **Median age:** 32.5.

Income 2000: per capita $18,062; median household $39,167; **Pop below poverty level:** 13.2%. ***Personal per capita income 2000-2003:** $21,937-$22,282.

Unemployment 2004: 3.8%. **Change from 2000:** +1.5%. **Median travel time to work:** 29.6 minutes. **Working outside county of residence:** 48.7%.

Cities with pop over 10,000: None.

MACON COUNTY

121 S Sumter St   **Ph:** 478-472-7021
Oglethorpe, GA 31068   **Fax:** 478-472-5643
www.maconcountyga.org

In central GA, southeast of Atlanta; organized Dec 14, 1837 from Houston and Marion counties. **Name Origin:** For Nathaniel Macon (1757-1837), NC legislator, U.S. representative (1791-1815), U.S. senator (1815-28), and president of the NC constitutional convention (1835).

Area (sq mi): 405.95 (land 403.28; water 2.67). **Pop per sq mi:** 34.1.

Pop 2005: 13,745. **State rank:** 108. **Pop change:** 2000-20005 -2.3%; 1990-2000 +7.3%. **Pop 2000:** 14,074 (White 36.8%; Black or African American 59.5%; Hispanic or Latino 2.6%; Asian 0.6%; Other 2.5%). **Foreign born:** 1.8%. **Median age:** 35.1.

Income 2000: per capita $11,820; median household $24,224; **Pop below poverty level:** 25.8%. ***Personal per capita income 2000-2003:** $18,152-$19,832.

Unemployment 2004: 7.8%. **Change from 2000:** +0.1%. **Median travel time to work:** 24.5 minutes. **Working outside county of residence:** 41.4%.

Cities with pop over 10,000: None.

MADISON COUNTY

PO Box 147   **Ph:** 706-795-5664
Danielsville, GA 30633   **Fax:** 706-795-2997
www.madisonco.us

In northeastern GA, northeast of Athens; organized Dec 5, 1811 from Clarke, Elbert, Franklin, Jackson, and Oglethorpe counties. **Name Origin:** For James Madison (1751-1836), fourth U.S. president.

Area (sq mi): 285.57 (land 283.88; water 1.69). **Pop per sq mi:** 96.1.

Pop 2005: 27,289. **State rank:** 63. **Pop change:** 2000-20005 +6.1%; 1990-2000 +22.2%. **Pop 2000:** 25,730 (White 88.3%; Black or African American 8.5%; Hispanic or Latino 2%; Asian 0.3%; Other 2.2%). **Foreign born:** 2%. **Median age:** 35.8.

Income 2000: per capita $16,998; median household $36,347; **Pop below poverty level:** 11.6%. ***Personal per capita income 2000-2003:** $22,548-$24,349.

Unemployment 2004: 3.6%. **Change from 2000:** +0%. **Median travel time to work:** 26.7 minutes. **Working outside county of residence:** 72%.

Cities with pop over 10,000: None.

MARION COUNTY

PO Box 481   **Ph:** 229-649-2603
Buena Vista, GA 31803   **Fax:** 229-649-3702

In west-central GA, east of Columbus; organized Dec 14, 1827 from Lee and Muscogee counties. **Name Origin:** For Gen. Francis Marion (c. 1732-1795), SC soldier and legislator, known as 'The Swamp Fox' for his tactics during the Revolutionary War.

Area (sq mi): 367.49 (land 367; water 0.49). **Pop per sq mi:** 19.7.

Pop 2005: 7,244. **State rank:** 143. **Pop change:** 2000-20005 +1.4%; 1990-2000 +27.8%. **Pop 2000:** 7,144 (White 58.5%; Black or African American 34.1%; Hispanic or Latino 5.8%; Asian 0.2%; Other 5%). **Foreign born:** 5%. **Median age:** 35.2.

Income 2000: per capita $14,044; median household $29,145; **Pop below poverty level:** 22.4%. ***Personal per capita income 2000-2003:** $19,228-$22,008.

Unemployment 2004: 5%. **Change from 2000:** -0.6%. **Median travel time to work:** 34.4 minutes. **Working outside county of residence:** 53.6%.

Cities with pop over 10,000: None.

MCDUFFIE COUNTY

PO Box 158   **Ph:** 706-595-2134
Thomson, GA 30824   **Fax:** 706-595-9150
www.dca.state.ga.us/snapshots

In eastern GA, west of Augusta; organized Oct 18, 1870 from Columbia and Warren counties. **Name Origin:** For George McDuffie (1790-1851), SC governor (1834-36) and U.S. senator (1842-46).

Area (sq mi): 266.3 (land 259.77; water 6.52). **Pop per sq mi:** 83.7.

Pop 2005: 21,743. **State rank:** 82. **Pop change:** 2000-20005 +2.4%; 1990-2000 +5.5%. **Pop 2000:** 21,231 (White 60.3%; Black or African American 37.5%; Hispanic or Latino 1.3%; Asian 0.3%; Other 1.3%). **Foreign born:** 0.6%. **Median age:** 35.2.

*Source: Personal per capita income data are from the Bureau of Economic Analysis; per capita income data are from the Bureau of the Census. See Introduction for explanation of differences.

McDuffie County (cont'd)

Income 2000: per capita $18,005; median household $31,920; **Pop below poverty level:** 18.4%. ***Personal per capita income 2000-2003:** $22,591-$24,777.

Unemployment 2004: 5.7%. **Change from 2000:** -1.2%. **Median travel time to work:** 24 minutes. **Working outside county of residence:** 38.9%.

Cities with pop over 10,000: None.

MCINTOSH COUNTY

PO Box 584
Darien, GA 31305
www.mcintoshcounty.com

Ph: 912-437-6671
Fax: 912-437-6416

On southeastern coast of GA, north of Brunswick; organized Dec 19, 1793 from Liberty County. **Name Origin:** Either for the McIntosh family of early settlers; or for William McIntosh (1775-1825), Creek Indian leader who fought in the Seminole War (1817-18), then became a brigadier general in the U.S. Army. He was killed as a traitor by the Creek Indians.

Area (sq mi): 574.53 (land 433.45; water 141.08). **Pop per sq mi:** 25.5.

Pop 2005: 11,068. **State rank:** 120. **Pop change:** 2000-20005 +2%; 1990-2000 +25.6%. **Pop 2000:** 10,847 (White 60.9%; Black or African American 36.8%; Hispanic or Latino 0.9%; Asian 0.3%; Other 1.6%). **Foreign born:** 1%. **Median age:** 37.

Income 2000: per capita $14,253; median household $30,102; **Pop below poverty level:** 18.7%. ***Personal per capita income 2000-2003:** $17,635-$19,783.

Unemployment 2004: 4.5%. **Change from 2000:** +0.1%. **Median travel time to work:** 29.6 minutes. **Working outside county of residence:** 52.7%.

Cities with pop over 10,000: None.

MERIWETHER COUNTY

PO Box 428
Greenville, GA 30222

Ph: 706-672-1314
Fax: 706-672-1886

In west-central GA, northeast of Columbus; organized Dec 24, 1827 from Troup County. **Name Origin:** For Gen. David Meriwether (1755-1823), officer in the Revolutionary War, U.S. representative from GA (1802-07), and commissioner to the Creek Indians (1804).

Area (sq mi): 505.34 (land 503.28; water 2.06). **Pop per sq mi:** 45.5.

Pop 2005: 22,919. **State rank:** 77. **Pop change:** 2000-20005 +1.7%; 1990-2000 +0.5%. **Pop 2000:** 22,534 (White 55.8%; Black or African American 42.2%; Hispanic or Latino 0.8%; Asian 0.2%; Other 1.4%). **Foreign born:** 0.7%. **Median age:** 36.4.

Income 2000: per capita $15,708; median household $31,870; **Pop below poverty level:** 17.8%. ***Personal per capita income 2000-2003:** $20,385-$20,730.

Unemployment 2004: 6.4%. **Change from 2000:** -0.5%. **Median travel time to work:** 31.2 minutes. **Working outside county of residence:** 53.7%.

Cities with pop over 10,000: None.

MILLER COUNTY

179 S Cuthbert St
Colquitt, GA 39837

Ph: 229-758-4104
Fax: 229-758-2229

In southwestern GA, southwest of Albany; organized Feb 26, 1856 from Baker and Early counties. **Name Origin:** For Andrew Jackson Miller (1806-56), GA legislator and superior court judge.

Area (sq mi): 283.72 (land 283.05; water 0.68). **Pop per sq mi:** 22.

Pop 2005: 6,228. **State rank:** 148. **Pop change:** 2000-20005 -2.4%; 1990-2000 +1.6%. **Pop 2000:** 6,383 (White 69.8%; Black or African American 28.9%; Hispanic or Latino 0.7%; Asian 0%; Other 0.8%). **Foreign born:** 0.4%. **Median age:** 38.2.

Income 2000: per capita $15,435; median household $27,335; **Pop below poverty level:** 21.2%. ***Personal per capita income 2000-2003:** $21,371-$23,619.

Unemployment 2004: 4.1%. **Change from 2000:** -0.4%. **Median travel time to work:** 21.9 minutes. **Working outside county of residence:** 46.6%.

Cities with pop over 10,000: None.

MITCHELL COUNTY

PO Box 187
Camilla, GA 31730
www.mitchellcountyga.net

Ph: 229-336-2000
Fax: 229-336-2003

In southwestern GA, south of Albany; organized Dec 21, 1857 from Baker County. **Name Origin:** For Gen. Henry Mitchell (1760-1839), Revolutionary War hero and president of the GA Senate. Some claim David Brydie Mitchell (1766-1837), GA governor.

Area (sq mi): 513.81 (land 511.96; water 1.85). **Pop per sq mi:** 46.5.

Pop 2005: 23,791. **State rank:** 73. **Pop change:** 2000-20005 -0.6%; 1990-2000 +18%. **Pop 2000:** 23,932 (White 49.1%; Black or African American 47.9%; Hispanic or Latino 2.1%; Asian 0.3%; Other 2.3%). **Foreign born:** 1.6%. **Median age:** 34.

Income 2000: per capita $13,042; median household $26,581; **Pop below poverty level:** 26.4%. ***Personal per capita income 2000-2003:** $17,344-$18,466.

Unemployment 2004: 5.8%. **Change from 2000:** +0.6%. **Median travel time to work:** 26.5 minutes. **Working outside county of residence:** 36.4%.

Cities with pop over 10,000: None.

MONROE COUNTY

38 W Main St
Forsyth, GA 31029
www.monroecountygeorgia.com

Ph: 478-994-7000
Fax: 478-994-7294

In central GA, northwest of Macon; original county; organized May 15, 1821 from Indian lands. **Name Origin:** For James Monroe (1758-1831), fifth U.S. president.

Area (sq mi): 397.8 (land 395.63; water 2.17). **Pop per sq mi:** 60.1.

Pop 2005: 23,785. **State rank:** 74. **Pop change:** 2000-20005 +9.3%; 1990-2000 +27.1%. **Pop 2000:** 21,757 (White 69.6%; Black or African American 27.9%; Hispanic or Latino 1.3%; Asian 0.3%; Other 1.2%). **Foreign born:** 1%. **Median age:** 36.4.

Monroe County (cont'd)

Income 2000: per capita $19,580; median household $44,195; **Pop below poverty level:** 9.8%. ***Personal per capita income 2000-2003:** $23,792-$25,207.

Unemployment 2004: 4.1%. **Change from 2000:** -0.6%. **Median travel time to work:** 27.6 minutes. **Working outside county of residence:** 60.1%.

Cities with pop over 10,000: None.

MONTGOMERY COUNTY
PO Box 295   **Ph:** 912-583-2363
Mount Vernon, GA 30445   **Fax:** 912-583-2026

In east-central GA, west of Savannah; organized Dec 19, 1793 from Washington County. **Name Origin:** For Gen. Richard Montgomery (1736-75), American Revolutionary War officer who captured Montreal, Canada.

Area (sq mi): 247.32 (land 245.33; water 1.99). **Pop per sq mi:** 36.3.

Pop 2005: 8,909. **State rank:** 135. **Pop change:** 2000-20005 +7.7%; 1990-2000 +15.5%. **Pop 2000:** 8,270 (White 68.7%; Black or African American 27.2%; Hispanic or Latino 3.3%; Asian 0.2%; Other 2.8%). **Foreign born:** 3.9%. **Median age:** 33.6.

Income 2000: per capita $14,182; median household $30,240; **Pop below poverty level:** 19.9%. ***Personal per capita income 2000-2003:** $17,669-$19,457.

Unemployment 2004: 5.5%. **Change from 2000:** -3%. **Median travel time to work:** 27 minutes. **Working outside county of residence:** 68.2%.

Cities with pop over 10,000: None.

MORGAN COUNTY
355 Hancock St   **Ph:** 706-342-0725
Madison, GA 30650   **Fax:** 706-343-6450
www.morganga.org

In central GA, southeast of Atlanta; organized as Cotaco County Dec 10, 1807 from Baldwin County; name changed Jun 14, 1821. **Name Origin:** For Gen. Daniel Morgan (1736-1802), an officer in the Revolutionary War and U.S. representative from VA (1797-99).

Area (sq mi): 354.6 (land 349.64; water 4.96). **Pop per sq mi:** 50.

Pop 2005: 17,492. **State rank:** 92. **Pop change:** 2000-20005 +13.2%; 1990-2000 +20%. **Pop 2000:** 15,457 (White 68.7%; Black or African American 28.5%; Hispanic or Latino 1.6%; Asian 0.3%; Other 1.4%). **Foreign born:** 1.1%. **Median age:** 36.8.

Income 2000: per capita $18,823; median household $40,249; **Pop below poverty level:** 10.9%. ***Personal per capita income 2000-2003:** $26,105-$27,922.

Unemployment 2004: 4%. **Change from 2000:** +0.8%. **Median travel time to work:** 25 minutes. **Working outside county of residence:** 37.2%.

Cities with pop over 10,000: None.

MURRAY COUNTY
PO Box 1129   **Ph:** 706-695-2413
Chatsworth, GA 30705   **Fax:** 706-695-8721

On northern border of GA, southeast of Chattanooga, TN; organized

Dec 3, 1832 from Cherokee County. **Name Origin:** For Thomas W. Murray (1790-1832), GA legislator.

Area (sq mi): 346.88 (land 344.41; water 2.47). **Pop per sq mi:** 118.5.

Pop 2005: 40,812. **State rank:** 46. **Pop change:** 2000-20005 +11.8%; 1990-2000 +39.6%. **Pop 2000:** 36,506 (White 92.8%; Black or African American 0.6%; Hispanic or Latino 5.5%; Asian 0.3%; Other 3.8%). **Foreign born:** 3.6%. **Median age:** 32.6.

Income 2000: per capita $16,230; median household $36,996; **Pop below poverty level:** 12.7%. ***Personal per capita income 2000-2003:** $19,930-$20,579.

Unemployment 2004: 3.9%. **Change from 2000:** -0.6%. **Median travel time to work:** 24.6 minutes. **Working outside county of residence:** 54.5%.

Cities with pop over 10,000: None.

NEWTON COUNTY
1124 Clark St   **Ph:** 770-784-2000
Covington, GA 30014   **Fax:** 770-784-2007
www.co.newton.ga.us

In central GA, southeast of Atlanta; organized Dec 24, 1821 from Henry, Walton, and Jasper counties. **Name Origin:** For Sgt. John Newton (1752-80), soldier under Gen. Francis Marion (1732?-95) in the Revolutionary War, who saved several colonial patriots from execution by surprising and capturing the British soldiers guarding them.

Area (sq mi): 279.19 (land 276.43; water 2.76). **Pop per sq mi:** 313.7.

Pop 2005: 86,713. **State rank:** 27. **Pop change:** 2000-20005 +39.9%; 1990-2000 +48.3%. **Pop 2000:** 62,001 (White 74.2%; Black or African American 22.2%; Hispanic or Latino 1.9%; Asian 0.7%; Other 1.8%). **Foreign born:** 2.5%. **Median age:** 33.3.

Income 2000: per capita $19,317; median household $44,875; **Pop below poverty level:** 10%. ***Personal per capita income 2000-2003:** $23,594-$22,458.

Unemployment 2004: 4.9%. **Change from 2000:** +1.4%. **Median travel time to work:** 30.5 minutes. **Working outside county of residence:** 59.6%.

Cities with pop over 10,000: Covington 🏭 (13,464).

OCONEE COUNTY
PO Box 145   **Ph:** 706-769-5120
Watkinsville, GA 30677   **Fax:** 706-769-0705
www.oconeecounty.net

In northeast-central GA, south of Athens; organized Feb 25, 1875 from Clarke County. **Name Origin:** For an Indian tribe of Muskhogean linguistic stock; meaning of name uncertain.

Area (sq mi): 186.14 (land 185.7; water 0.44). **Pop per sq mi:** 160.2.

Pop 2005: 29,748. **State rank:** 54. **Pop change:** 2000-20005 +13.4%; 1990-2000 +48.9%. **Pop 2000:** 26,225 (White 88.1%; Black or African American 6.4%; Hispanic or Latino 3.2%; Asian 1.4%; Other 2.6%). **Foreign born:** 4.4%. **Median age:** 35.2.

Income 2000: per capita $24,153; median household $55,211; **Pop below poverty level:** 6.5%. ***Personal per capita income 2000-2003:** $29,015-$29,922.

Source: Personal per capita income data are from the Bureau of Economic Analysis; per capita income data are from the Bureau of the Census. See Introduction for explanation of differences.

Oconee County (cont'd)

Unemployment 2004: 2.6%. **Change from 2000:** +0.9%. **Median travel time to work:** 25 minutes. **Working outside county of residence:** 71.9%.

Cities with pop over 10,000: None.

OGLETHORPE COUNTY
PO Box 261   **Ph:** 706-743-5270
Lexington, GA 30648   **Fax:** 706-743-8371

In northeastern GA, southeast of Athens; organized Dec 19, 1793 from Wilkes County. **Name Origin:** For Gen. James Edward Oglethorpe (1696-1785), founder of GA and English humanitarian who proposed that GA be settled by former prisoners; first governor of GA under the charter granted to him.

Area (sq mi): 442.17 (land 441.11; water 1.06). **Pop per sq mi:** 30.9.

Pop 2005: 13,609. **State rank:** 109. **Pop change:** 2000-20005 +7.7%; 1990-2000 +29.4%. **Pop 2000:** 12,635 (White 77.7%; Black or African American 19.8%; Hispanic or Latino 1.4%; Asian 0.2%; Other 1.6%). **Foreign born:** 0.8%. **Median age:** 36.8.

Income 2000: per capita $17,089; median household $35,578; **Pop below poverty level:** 13.2%. ***Personal per capita income 2000-2003:** $21,533-$22,979.

Unemployment 2004: 3.5%. **Change from 2000:** -0.2%. **Median travel time to work:** 31.6 minutes. **Working outside county of residence:** 78.2%.

Cities with pop over 10,000: None.

PAULDING COUNTY
166 Confederate Ave   **Ph:** 770-505-1352
Dallas, GA 30132   **Fax:** 770-505-1353
www.paulding.gov

In northwestern GA, northwest of Atlanta; organized Dec 3, 1832 from Cherokee County. **Name Origin:** For John Paulding (1758-1818), one of the captors (1780) of John Andre (1750-80), British spy, during the American Revolution.

Area (sq mi): 315.06 (land 313.43; water 1.63). **Pop per sq mi:** 358.6.

Pop 2005: 112,411. **State rank:** 16. **Pop change:** 2000-20005 +37.6%; 1990-2000 +96.3%. **Pop 2000:** 81,678 (White 89.6%; Black or African American 7%; Hispanic or Latino 1.7%; Asian 0.4%; Other 2.1%). **Foreign born:** 2.1%. **Median age:** 31.2.

Income 2000: per capita $19,974; median household $52,161; **Pop below poverty level:** 5.5%. ***Personal per capita income 2000-2003:** $23,578-$23,191.

Unemployment 2004: 4%. **Change from 2000:** +1.6%. **Median travel time to work:** 39.1 minutes. **Working outside county of residence:** 75.3%.

Cities with pop over 10,000: None.

PEACH COUNTY
205 W Church St   **Ph:** 478-825-2535
Fort Valley, GA 31030   **Fax:** 478-825-2678
www.peachcounty.net

In central GA, southeast of Macon; organized Jul 18, 1924 from Houston and Macon counties; the last county formed. **Name Origin:** For its location in one of the most fertile peach-growing areas of the state.

Area (sq mi): 151.46 (land 151.06; water 0.4). **Pop per sq mi:** 164.1.

Pop 2005: 24,794. **State rank:** 68. **Pop change:** 2000-20005 +4.8%; 1990-2000 +11.7%. **Pop 2000:** 23,668 (White 49.2%; Black or African American 45.4%; Hispanic or Latino 4.2%; Asian 0.3%; Other 2.9%). **Foreign born:** 3.8%. **Median age:** 31.8.

Income 2000: per capita $16,031; median household $34,453; **Pop below poverty level:** 20.2%. ***Personal per capita income 2000-2003:** $21,591-$22,732.

Unemployment 2004: 6.3%. **Change from 2000:** +1.9%. **Median travel time to work:** 25.1 minutes. **Working outside county of residence:** 57.5%.

Cities with pop over 10,000: None.

PICKENS COUNTY
PO Box 130   **Ph:** 706-253-8766
Jasper, GA 30143
www.georgiamarble-mountain.org

In north-central GA, north of Atlanta, organized Dec 5, 1853 from Cherokee and Gilmer counties. **Name Origin:** For Andrew Pickens (1739-1817), soldier and U.S. representative from SC (1793-95).

Area (sq mi): 232.78 (land 232.13; water 0.65). **Pop per sq mi:** 122.5.

Pop 2005: 28,442. **State rank:** 57. **Pop change:** 2000-20005 +23.8%; 1990-2000 +59.3%. **Pop 2000:** 22,983 (White 95.3%; Black or African American 1.3%; Hispanic or Latino 2%; Asian 0.2%; Other 2.2%). **Foreign born:** 2%. **Median age:** 37.9.

Income 2000: per capita $19,774; median household $41,387; **Pop below poverty level:** 9.2%. ***Personal per capita income 2000-2003:** $26,504-$27,730.

Unemployment 2004: 3.6%. **Change from 2000:** +0.6%. **Median travel time to work:** 32.5 minutes. **Working outside county of residence:** 52.2%.

Cities with pop over 10,000: None.

PIERCE COUNTY
PO Box 679   **Ph:** 912-449-2022
Blackshear, GA 31516   **Fax:** 912-449-2024

In southeastern GA, west of Brunswick; organized Dec 18, 1857 from Appling and Ware counties. **Name Origin:** For Franklin Pierce (1804-69), fourteenth U.S. president.

Area (sq mi): 343.9 (land 343.25; water 0.65). **Pop per sq mi:** 49.9.

Pop 2005: 17,119. **State rank:** 94. **Pop change:** 2000-20005 +9.5%; 1990-2000 +17.3%. **Pop 2000:** 15,636 (White 85.9%; Black or African American 10.9%; Hispanic or Latino 2.3%; Asian 0.2%; Other 2.1%). **Foreign born:** 2.1%. **Median age:** 36.2.

Income 2000: per capita $14,230; median household $29,895; **Pop below poverty level:** 18.4%. ***Personal per capita income 2000-2003:** $19,904-$21,945.

Unemployment 2004: 4.3%. **Change from 2000:** +0.3%. **Median travel time to work:** 26.2 minutes. **Working outside county of residence:** 56.4%.

Pierce County (cont'd)

Cities with pop over 10,000: None.

PIKE COUNTY

PO Box 377   **Ph:** 770-567-3406
Zebulon, GA 30295   **Fax:** 770-567-2006
www.co.pike.ga.us

In west-central GA, northwest of Macon; organized Dec 9, 1822 from Monroe County. **Name Origin:** For Gen. Zebulon Montgomery Pike (1779-1813), U.S. army officer and discoverer of Pikes Peak in CO.

Area (sq mi): 219.43 (land 218.37; water 1.06). **Pop per sq mi:** 73.9.

Pop 2005: 16,128. **State rank:** 100. **Pop change:** 2000-20005 +17.8%; 1990-2000 +33.9%. **Pop 2000:** 13,688 (White 82.9%; Black or African American 14.8%; Hispanic or Latino 1.2%; Asian 0.4%; Other 1.2%). **Foreign born:** 1%. **Median age:** 35.7.

Income 2000: per capita $17,661; median household $44,370; **Pop below poverty level:** 9.6%. *Personal per capita income 2000-2003: $22,452-$23,561.

Unemployment 2004: 4.6%. **Change from 2000:** +0.6%. **Median travel time to work:** 30.6 minutes. **Working outside county of residence:** 75.6%.

Cities with pop over 10,000: None.

POLK COUNTY

PO Box 948   **Ph:** 770-749-2114
Cedartown, GA 30125   **Fax:** 770-749-2148
www.polkcountygeorgia.us

On northwestern border of GA, south of Rome; organized Dec 20, 1851 from Paulding and Floyd counties. **Name Origin:** For James Knox Polk (1795-1849), eleventh U.S. president.

Area (sq mi): 312.13 (land 311.14; water 0.99). **Pop per sq mi:** 130.1.

Pop 2005: 40,479. **State rank:** 48. **Pop change:** 2000-20005 +6.2%; 1990-2000 +12.8%. **Pop 2000:** 38,127 (White 77.9%; Black or African American 13.3%; Hispanic or Latino 7.7%; Asian 0.3%; Other 5.7%). **Foreign born:** 6%. **Median age:** 35.1.

Income 2000: per capita $15,617; median household $32,328; **Pop below poverty level:** 15.5%. *Personal per capita income 2000-2003: $18,725-$20,102.

Unemployment 2004: 4.7%. **Change from 2000:** -0.4%. **Median travel time to work:** 30 minutes. **Working outside county of residence:** 44.8%.

Cities with pop over 10,000: None.

PULASKI COUNTY

105 Lumpkin St   **Ph:** 478-783-4154
Hawkinsville, GA 31036   **Fax:** 478-783-9209

In central GA, southeast of Macon; organized Dec 13, 1808 from Laurens County. **Name Origin:** For Count Casimir Pulaski (1747-79), Polish soldier who fought for America during the Revolutionary War.

Area (sq mi): 249.89 (land 247.42; water 2.47). **Pop per sq mi:** 39.4.

Pop 2005: 9,737. **State rank:** 130. **Pop change:** 2000-20005 +1.6%; 1990-2000 +18.3%. **Pop 2000:** 9,588 (White 61.9%; Black or African American 34.3%; Hispanic or Latino 2.8%; Asian 0.3%; Other 2.4%). **Foreign born:** 2.6%. **Median age:** 36.7.

Income 2000: per capita $16,435; median household $31,895; **Pop below poverty level:** 16.4%. *Personal per capita income 2000-2003: $23,001-$25,001.

Unemployment 2004: 4.1%. **Change from 2000:** -2.8%. **Median travel time to work:** 20.8 minutes. **Working outside county of residence:** 42.4%.

Cities with pop over 10,000: None.

PUTNAM COUNTY

108 S Madison Ave Suite 300   **Ph:** 706-485-5826
Eatonton, GA 31024   **Fax:** 706-485-5578
www.putnamcountyga.us

In central GA, northeast of Macon; organized Dec 10, 1807 from Baldwin County. **Name Origin:** For Gen. Israel Putnam (1718-90), Revolutionary War officer and American commander at the Battle of Bunker Hill.

Area (sq mi): 360.63 (land 344.53; water 16.1). **Pop per sq mi:** 57.6.

Pop 2005: 19,829. **State rank:** 87. **Pop change:** 2000-20005 +5.4%; 1990-2000 +33.1%. **Pop 2000:** 18,812 (White 66.3%; Black or African American 29.9%; Hispanic or Latino 2.2%; Asian 0.7%; Other 1.9%). **Foreign born:** 2.5%. **Median age:** 39.6.

Income 2000: per capita $20,161; median household $36,956; **Pop below poverty level:** 14.6%. *Personal per capita income 2000-2003: $23,057-$24,427.

Unemployment 2004: 4.1%. **Change from 2000:** +0.8%. **Median travel time to work:** 26.5 minutes. **Working outside county of residence:** 44.4%.

Cities with pop over 10,000: None.

QUITMAN COUNTY

PO Box 307   **Ph:** 229-334-2578
Georgetown, GA 39854   **Fax:** 229-334-3991

On southwestern border of GA, south of Columbus; organized Dec 10, 1858 from Randolph (organized 1828) and Stewart counties. **Name Origin:** For John Anthony Quitman (1799-1858), tenth and sixteenth governor of MS (1835-36; 1850-51), and U.S. representative (1855-58).

Area (sq mi): 160.92 (land 151.54; water 9.38). **Pop per sq mi:** 16.3.

Pop 2005: 2,467. **State rank:** 157. **Pop change:** 2000-20005 -5%; 1990-2000 +17.6%. **Pop 2000:** 2,598 (White 52%; Black or African American 46.9%; Hispanic or Latino 0.5%; Asian 0%; Other 0.9%). **Foreign born:** 0.7%. **Median age:** 42.

Income 2000: per capita $14,301; median household $25,875; **Pop below poverty level:** 21.9%. *Personal per capita income 2000-2003: $18,644-$22,000.

Unemployment 2004: 6.4%. **Change from 2000:** -0.2%. **Median travel time to work:** 27.6 minutes. **Working outside county of residence:** 76.4%.

Cities with pop over 10,000: None.

Source: Personal per capita income data are from the Bureau of Economic Analysis; per capita income data are from the Bureau of the Census. See Introduction for explanation of differences.

RABUN COUNTY

25 Courthouse Sq Suite 201   **Ph:** 706-782-5271
Clayton, GA 30525   **Fax:** 706-782-7588
www.gamountains.com

In northeastern corner of GA; organized Dec 21, 1819 from Cherokee land. **Name Origin:** For William Rabun (1771-1819), GA legislator and governor (1817-19).

Area (sq mi): 376.99 (land 371.05; water 5.94). **Pop per sq mi:** 43.4.

Pop 2005: 16,087. **State rank:** 101. **Pop change:** 2000-20005 +6.9%; 1990-2000 +29.2%. **Pop 2000:** 15,050 (White 93.2%; Black or African American 0.8%; Hispanic or Latino 4.5%; Asian 0.4%; Other 3.9%). **Foreign born:** 4.1%. **Median age:** 42.

Income 2000: per capita $20,608; median household $33,899; **Pop below poverty level:** 11.1%. ***Personal per capita income 2000-2003:** $22,874-$23,281.

Unemployment 2004: 3.5%. **Change from 2000:** +0.7%. **Median travel time to work:** 24.1 minutes. **Working outside county of residence:** 18.1%.

Cities with pop over 10,000: None.

RANDOLPH COUNTY

PO Box 221   **Ph:** 229-732-6440
Cuthbert, GA 39840   **Fax:** 229-732-5364

In southwestern GA, northwest of Albany; organized Dec 20, 1828 from Lee County (an earlier Randolph County was renamed Jasper County in 1812). **Name Origin:** For John Randolph (1773-1833), VA statesman and U.S. minister to Russia (1830).

Area (sq mi): 430.89 (land 429.25; water 1.64). **Pop per sq mi:** 17.

Pop 2005: 7,310. **State rank:** 142. **Pop change:** 2000-20005 -6.2%; 1990-2000 -2.9%. **Pop 2000:** 7,791 (White 38.7%; Black or African American 59.5%; Hispanic or Latino 1.2%; Asian 0.2%; Other 1.3%). **Foreign born:** 0.7%. **Median age:** 36.1.

Income 2000: per capita $11,809; median household $22,004; **Pop below poverty level:** 27.7%. ***Personal per capita income 2000-2003:** $17,314-$20,569.

Unemployment 2004: 6.6%. **Change from 2000:** -2.7%. **Median travel time to work:** 23.6 minutes. **Working outside county of residence:** 31.3%.

Cities with pop over 10,000: None.

ROCKDALE COUNTY

922 Court St   **Ph:** 770-929-4021
Conyers, GA 30012
www.rockdalecounty.org

In central GA, southeast of Atlanta; organized Oct 18, 1870 from Henry and Newton counties. **Name Origin:** For the Rockdale Church, which was named for the underlying bed of granite in this part of the state.

Area (sq mi): 132.13 (land 130.63; water 1.5). **Pop per sq mi:** 601.3.

Pop 2005: 78,545. **State rank:** 28. **Pop change:** 2000-20005 +12%; 1990-2000 +29.6%. **Pop 2000:** 70,111 (White 72.7%; Black or African American 18.2%; Hispanic or Latino 6%; Asian 1.9%; Other 4.2%). **Foreign born:** 7.6%. **Median age:** 35.4.

Income 2000: per capita $22,300; median household $53,599; **Pop below poverty level:** 8.2%. ***Personal per capita income 2000-2003:** $27,825-$28,343.

Unemployment 2004: 4.8%. **Change from 2000:** +2.1%. **Median travel time to work:** 29.5 minutes. **Working outside county of residence:** 56.3%.

Cities with pop over 10,000: Conyers 🏛 (12,147).

SCHLEY COUNTY

PO Box 352   **Ph:** 229-937-2609
Ellaville, GA 31806   **Fax:** 229-937-5880

In west-central GA, southeast of Columbus; organized Dec 22, 1857 from Marion and Sumter counties. **Name Origin:** For William Schley (1786-1858), U.S. representative from GA and governor (1835-37).

Area (sq mi): 167.82 (land 167.61; water 0.21). **Pop per sq mi:** 24.6.

Pop 2005: 4,122. **State rank:** 154. **Pop change:** 2000-20005 +9.5%; 1990-2000 +5%. **Pop 2000:** 3,766 (White 65.4%; Black or African American 31.3%; Hispanic or Latino 2.4%; Asian 0.1%; Other 2.9%). **Foreign born:** 1.8%. **Median age:** 34.5.

Income 2000: per capita $14,981; median household $32,035; **Pop below poverty level:** 19.9%. ***Personal per capita income 2000-2003:** $19,799-$20,284.

Unemployment 2004: 5.6%. **Change from 2000:** +0.7%. **Median travel time to work:** 25.8 minutes. **Working outside county of residence:** 59.4%.

Cities with pop over 10,000: None.

SCREVEN COUNTY

PO Box 159   **Ph:** 912-564-7535
Sylvania, GA 30467   **Fax:** 912-564-2562

On central east coast of GA, north of Savannah; organized Dec 14, 1793 from Burke and Effingham counties. **Name Origin:** For Gen. James Screven (1744-78), an officer in the Revolutionary War. Originally spelled *Scriven*.

Area (sq mi): 655.59 (land 648.44; water 7.14). **Pop per sq mi:** 23.8.

Pop 2005: 15,430. **State rank:** 106. **Pop change:** 2000-20005 +0.4%; 1990-2000 +11.1%. **Pop 2000:** 15,374 (White 53.2%; Black or African American 45.3%; Hispanic or Latino 1%; Asian 0.3%; Other 0.9%). **Foreign born:** 1.7%. **Median age:** 36.2.

Income 2000: per capita $13,894; median household $29,312; **Pop below poverty level:** 20.1%. ***Personal per capita income 2000-2003:** $17,995-$19,034.

Unemployment 2004: 5.1%. **Change from 2000:** -4.4%. **Median travel time to work:** 29.1 minutes. **Working outside county of residence:** 38.9%.

Cities with pop over 10,000: None.

SEMINOLE COUNTY

200 S Knox Ave   **Ph:** 229-524-2878
Donalsonville, GA 39845   **Fax:** 229-524-8984
www.donalsonvillega.com

In southwestern corner of GA; organized Jul 8, 1920 from Decatur and Early counties. **Name Origin:** For the Muskhogean tribe. Name is from Creek 'the separate ones.'

🏛 *County Seat*

Seminole County (cont'd)

Area (sq mi): 256.56 (land 238.04; water 18.52). **Pop per sq mi:** 38.8.

Pop 2005: 9,226. **State rank:** 134. **Pop change:** 2000-20005 -1.5%; 1990-2000 +4%. **Pop 2000:** 9,369 (White 61.2%; Black or African American 34.7%; Hispanic or Latino 3.7%; Asian 0.2%; Other 3.4%). **Foreign born:** 1.1%. **Median age:** 37.5.

Income 2000: per capita $14,635; median household $27,094; **Pop below poverty level:** 23.2%. ***Personal per capita income 2000-2003:** $21,468-$24,351.

Unemployment 2004: 5.3%. **Change from 2000:** +0.9%. **Median travel time to work:** 24.6 minutes. **Working outside county of residence:** 44.9%.

Cities with pop over 10,000: None.

SPALDING COUNTY

PO Box 1046   **Ph:** 770-467-4309
Griffin, GA 30224
www.spaldingcounty.com

In west-central GA, south of Atlanta; organized Dec 20, 1851 from Henry, Pike, and Fayette counties. **Name Origin:** For Thomas Spalding (1774-1851), GA legislator, U.S. representative (1805-06), and member of the GA Constitutional Convention of 1798.

Area (sq mi): 199.6 (land 197.95; water 1.65). **Pop per sq mi:** 309.6.

Pop 2005: 61,289. **State rank:** 34. **Pop change:** 2000-20005 +4.9%; 1990-2000 +7.3%. **Pop 2000:** 58,417 (White 65.8%; Black or African American 31.1%; Hispanic or Latino 1.6%; Asian 0.7%; Other 1.8%). **Foreign born:** 2.2%. **Median age:** 34.6.

Income 2000: per capita $16,791; median household $36,221; **Pop below poverty level:** 15.5%. ***Personal per capita income 2000-2003:** $22,637-$24,058.

Unemployment 2004: 5.9%. **Change from 2000:** +1.1%. **Median travel time to work:** 27.5 minutes. **Working outside county of residence:** 45%.

Cities with pop over 10,000: Griffin 🏛 (23,397).

STEPHENS COUNTY

PO Box 386   **Ph:** 706-886-9491
Toccoa, GA 30577   **Fax:** 706-886-2185
www.stephenscounty-ga.gov

On northeastern border of GA, northeast of Athens; organized Aug 18, 1905 from Franklin and Habersham counties. **Name Origin:** For Alexander Hamilton Stephens (1812-83), GA statesman and a vice president of the Confederacy (1861).

Area (sq mi): 184.23 (land 179.26; water 4.97). **Pop per sq mi:** 139.8.

Pop 2005: 25,060. **State rank:** 67. **Pop change:** 2000-20005 -1.5%; 1990-2000 +9.4%. **Pop 2000:** 25,435 (White 85.2%; Black or African American 12%; Hispanic or Latino 1%; Asian 0.6%; Other 1.7%). **Foreign born:** 1.4%. **Median age:** 37.5.

Income 2000: per capita $15,529; median household $29,466; **Pop below poverty level:** 15.1%. ***Personal per capita income 2000-2003:** $22,102-$23,779.

Unemployment 2004: 6%. **Change from 2000:** +0%. **Median travel time to work:** 20.7 minutes. **Working outside county of residence:** 23.3%.

Cities with pop over 10,000: None.

STEWART COUNTY

PO Box 157   **Ph:** 229-838-6769
Lumpkin, GA 31815   **Fax:** 229-838-9856

On central-western border of GA, south of Columbus; organized Dec 23, 1830 from Randolph County. **Name Origin:** For Gen. Daniel Stewart (1759-1829), an officer in the American Revolution and the War of 1812.

Area (sq mi): 463.23 (land 458.7; water 4.53). **Pop per sq mi:** 10.6.

Pop 2005: 4,882. **State rank:** 151. **Pop change:** 2000-20005 -7%; 1990-2000 -7.1%. **Pop 2000:** 5,252 (White 36.7%; Black or African American 61.5%; Hispanic or Latino 1.5%; Asian 0.2%; Other 1.1%). **Foreign born:** 1.6%. **Median age:** 38.8.

Income 2000: per capita $16,071; median household $24,789; **Pop below poverty level:** 22.2%. ***Personal per capita income 2000-2003:** $19,415-$20,976.

Unemployment 2004: 10.1%. **Change from 2000:** +2.8%. **Median travel time to work:** 28.6 minutes. **Working outside county of residence:** 49%.

Cities with pop over 10,000: None.

SUMTER COUNTY

PO Box 295   **Ph:** 229-928-4500
Americus, GA 31709   **Fax:** 229-928-4503
www.sumter-ga.com

In west-central GA, north of Albany; organized Dec 26, 1831 from Lee County. **Name Origin:** For Gen. Thomas Sumter (1734-1832), American Revolutionary officer nicknamed the 'Gamecock of the Revolution,' U.S. representative from GA (1789-93; 1797-1801), and U.S. senator (1801-10).

Area (sq mi): 492.54 (land 485.28; water 7.26). **Pop per sq mi:** 67.8.

Pop 2005: 32,912. **State rank:** 52. **Pop change:** 2000-20005 -0.9%; 1990-2000 +9.8%. **Pop 2000:** 33,200 (White 47.2%; Black or African American 49%; Hispanic or Latino 2.7%; Asian 0.6%; Other 2.2%). **Foreign born:** 2%. **Median age:** 32.6.

Income 2000: per capita $15,083; median household $30,904; **Pop below poverty level:** 21.4%. ***Personal per capita income 2000-2003:** $21,039-$22,881.

Unemployment 2004: 5.6%. **Change from 2000:** -1%. **Median travel time to work:** 19.2 minutes. **Working outside county of residence:** 16.6%.

Cities with pop over 10,000: Americus 🏛 (16,737).

TALBOT COUNTY

PO Box 325   **Ph:** 706-665-3239
Talbotton, GA 31827   **Fax:** 706-665-8637
www.talbotgeorgia.com

In west-central GA, northeast of Columbus; organized Dec 14, 1827 from Muscogee County. **Name Origin:** For Matthew Talbot (1762-1827), GA legislator and ex-officio governor (1819).

Source: Personal per capita income data are from the Bureau of Economic Analysis; per capita income data are from the Bureau of the Census. See Introduction for explanation of differences.

Talbot County (cont'd)

Area (sq mi): 394.74 (land 393.21; water 1.52). **Pop per sq mi:** 17.1.

Pop 2005: 6,709. **State rank:** 146. **Pop change:** 2000-20005 +3.2%; 1990-2000 -0.4%. **Pop 2000:** 6,498 (White 36.2%; Black or African American 61.6%; Hispanic or Latino 1.3%; Asian 0.3%; Other 1.3%). **Foreign born:** 0.7%. **Median age:** 39.5.

Income 2000: per capita $14,539; median household $26,611; **Pop below poverty level:** 24.2%. ***Personal per capita income 2000-2003:** $17,626-$19,693.

Unemployment 2004: 5.7%. **Change from 2000:** -1%. **Median travel time to work:** 32.8 minutes. **Working outside county of residence:** 76%.

Cities with pop over 10,000: None.

TALIAFERRO COUNTY

PO Box 182
Crawfordville, GA 30631

Ph: 706-456-2123
Fax: 706-456-2749

In east-central GA, northwest of Augusta; organized Dec 24, 1825 from Greene, Hancock, Oglethorpe, Warren, and Wilkes counties. **Name Origin:** For Capt. Benjamin Taliaferro (1750-1821), GA superior court judge, legislator, and U.S. representative (1799-1802).

Area (sq mi): 195.47 (land 195.39; water 0.08). **Pop per sq mi:** 9.3.

Pop 2005: 1,826. **State rank:** 159. **Pop change:** 2000-20005 -12.1%; 1990-2000 +8.5%. **Pop 2000:** 2,077 (White 37.9%; Black or African American 60.3%; Hispanic or Latino 0.9%; Asian 0%; Other 1.4%). **Foreign born:** 0.5%. **Median age:** 40.2.

Income 2000: per capita $15,498; median household $23,750; **Pop below poverty level:** 23.4%. ***Personal per capita income 2000-2003:** $16,158-$19,163.

Unemployment 2004: 6.2%. **Change from 2000:** -5.7%. **Median travel time to work:** 31.2 minutes. **Working outside county of residence:** 70.7%.

Cities with pop over 10,000: None.

TATTNALL COUNTY

PO Box 25
Reidsville, GA 30453
www.tattnall.com

Ph: 912-557-4335
Fax: 912-557-6088

In east-central GA, west of Savannah; organized Dec 5, 1801 from Montgomery County. **Name Origin:** For Gen. Josiah Tattnall (1764-1803), an officer in the American Revolution, U.S. senator from GA (1796-99), and governor (1801-02).

Area (sq mi): 488.22 (land 483.69; water 4.53). **Pop per sq mi:** 48.

Pop 2005: 23,211. **State rank:** 76. **Pop change:** 2000-20005 +4.1%; 1990-2000 +25.9%. **Pop 2000:** 22,305 (White 59.3%; Black or African American 31.4%; Hispanic or Latino 8.4%; Asian 0.3%; Other 7.7%). **Foreign born:** 5.8%. **Median age:** 33.9.

Income 2000: per capita $13,439; median household $28,664; **Pop below poverty level:** 23.9%. ***Personal per capita income 2000-2003:** $18,911-$20,099.

Unemployment 2004: 5.3%. **Change from 2000:** +0.1%. **Median travel time to work:** 27.5 minutes. **Working outside county of residence:** 40.4%.

Cities with pop over 10,000: None.

TAYLOR COUNTY

109 Ivy St
Butler, GA 31006

Ph: 478-862-3336
Fax: 478-862-2871

In west-central GA, east of Columbus; organized Jan 15, 1852 from Macon, Marion, and Talbot counties. **Name Origin:** For Zachary Taylor (1784-1850), twelfth U.S. president.

Area (sq mi): 379.61 (land 377.44; water 2.17). **Pop per sq mi:** 23.5.

Pop 2005: 8,887. **State rank:** 136. **Pop change:** 2000-20005 +0.8%; 1990-2000 +15.3%. **Pop 2000:** 8,815 (White 55%; Black or African American 42.6%; Hispanic or Latino 1.8%; Asian 0.2%; Other 1.8%). **Foreign born:** 1%. **Median age:** 35.7.

Income 2000: per capita $13,432; median household $25,148; **Pop below poverty level:** 26%. ***Personal per capita income 2000-2003:** $18,320-$19,351.

Unemployment 2004: 6.4%. **Change from 2000:** +1.1%. **Median travel time to work:** 28.6 minutes. **Working outside county of residence:** 47.4%.

Cities with pop over 10,000: None.

TELFAIR COUNTY

713 Telfair Ave
McRae, GA 31055

Ph: 229-868-5688
Fax: 229-868-7950

In central GA, southeast of Macon; organized Dec 10, 1807 from Wilkinson County. **Name Origin:** For Edward Telfair (1735-1807), member of the Continental Congress (1777-79; 1780-83), and GA governor (1786-87; 1790-93).

Area (sq mi): 444.08 (land 441.09; water 2.99). **Pop per sq mi:** 29.9.

Pop 2005: 13,205. **State rank:** 110. **Pop change:** 2000-20005 +12%; 1990-2000 +7.2%. **Pop 2000:** 11,794 (White 59.3%; Black or African American 38.4%; Hispanic or Latino 1.8%; Asian 0.2%; Other 1.7%). **Foreign born:** 1.1%. **Median age:** 36.8.

Income 2000: per capita $14,197; median household $26,097; **Pop below poverty level:** 21.2%. ***Personal per capita income 2000-2003:** $17,062-$16,611.

Unemployment 2004: 7.1%. **Change from 2000:** -6.3%. **Median travel time to work:** 24.2 minutes. **Working outside county of residence:** 33.8%.

Cities with pop over 10,000: None.

TERRELL COUNTY

PO Box 525
Dawson, GA 39842

Ph: 229-995-4476
Fax: 229-995-4320

In southwestern GA, northwest of Albany; organized Feb 16, 1856 from Lee and Randolph counties. **Name Origin:** For Dr. William Terrell (1778-1855), GA legislator and U.S. representative (1817-21).

Area (sq mi): 337.63 (land 335.37; water 2.26). **Pop per sq mi:** 31.9.

Pop 2005: 10,711. **State rank:** 122. **Pop change:** 2000-20005 -2.4%; 1990-2000 +3%. **Pop 2000:** 10,970 (White 37.4%; Black or African American 60.7%; Hispanic or Latino 1.2%; Asian 0.3%; Other 1%). **Foreign born:** 1.7%. **Median age:** 35.4.

Terrell County (cont'd)

Income 2000: per capita $13,894; median household $26,969; **Pop below poverty level:** 28.6%. ***Personal per capita income 2000-2003:** $18,670-$20,519.

Unemployment 2004: 5.8%. **Change from 2000:** -2.3%. **Median travel time to work:** 23 minutes. **Working outside county of residence:** 46%.

Cities with pop over 10,000: None.

THOMAS COUNTY

PO Box 920   **Ph:** 229-225-4100
Thomasville, GA 31799   **Fax:** 229-226-3430
www.thomascountyboc.org

On southern border of GA, west of Valdosta; organized Dec 23, 1825 from Decatur and Irwin counties. **Name Origin:** For Gen. Jett Thomas (1776-1817), officer of the GA militia; supervisor of the construction of the state capitol at Milledgeville and the first university building at Athens.

Area (sq mi): 552.08 (land 548.3; water 3.78). **Pop per sq mi:** 81.5.

Pop 2005: 44,692. **State rank:** 44. **Pop change:** 2000-20005 +4.6%; 1990-2000 +9.6%. **Pop 2000:** 42,737 (White 58.2%; Black or African American 38.9%; Hispanic or Latino 1.7%; Asian 0.4%; Other 1.8%). **Foreign born:** 1.4%. **Median age:** 36.3.

Income 2000: per capita $16,211; median household $31,115; **Pop below poverty level:** 17.4%. ***Personal per capita income 2000-2003:** $23,166-$25,192.

Unemployment 2004: 4.3%. **Change from 2000:** +0.2%. **Median travel time to work:** 19.1 minutes. **Working outside county of residence:** 13.9%.

Cities with pop over 10,000: Thomasville 🏛 (18,526).

TIFT COUNTY

PO Box 354   **Ph:** 229-386-7810
Tifton, GA 31793   **Fax:** 229-386-7813
www.tiftcounty.org

In south-central GA, east of Albany; organized Aug 17, 1905 from Berrien, Irwin, and Worth counties. **Name Origin:** For Capt. Nelson Tift (1810-91), GA legislator, officer in the Confederate Navy, and U.S. representative (1868-69). Founder of the city of Albany, GA (1836).

Area (sq mi): 268.86 (land 265.05; water 3.81). **Pop per sq mi:** 153.9.

Pop 2005: 40,793. **State rank:** 47. **Pop change:** 2000-20005 +6.2%; 1990-2000 +9.7%. **Pop 2000:** 38,407 (White 62.7%; Black or African American 28%; Hispanic or Latino 7.7%; Asian 1%; Other 5.7%). **Foreign born:** 5.5%. **Median age:** 33.

Income 2000: per capita $16,833; median household $32,616; **Pop below poverty level:** 19.9%. ***Personal per capita income 2000-2003:** $21,878-$22,596.

Unemployment 2004: 4.3%. **Change from 2000:** -0.2%. **Median travel time to work:** 17.9 minutes. **Working outside county of residence:** 15.5%.

Cities with pop over 10,000: Tifton 🏛 (16,197).

TOOMBS COUNTY

100 Courthouse Sq   **Ph:** 912-526-3311
Lyons, GA 30436   **Fax:** 912-526-1004

In east-central GA, west of Savannah; organized Aug 18, 1905 from Emanuel, Montgomery, and Tattnall counties. **Name Origin:** For Gen. Robert Toombs (1810-85), U.S. senator (1853-61), secretary of state of the Confederacy, and officer in the Confederate Army.

Area (sq mi): 368.64 (land 366.65; water 1.99). **Pop per sq mi:** 74.4.

Pop 2005: 27,274. **State rank:** 64. **Pop change:** 2000-20005 +4.6%; 1990-2000 +8.3%. **Pop 2000:** 26,067 (White 66.1%; Black or African American 24.2%; Hispanic or Latino 8.9%; Asian 0.5%; Other 6.2%). **Foreign born:** 5.9%. **Median age:** 34.2.

Income 2000: per capita $14,252; median household $26,811; **Pop below poverty level:** 23.9%. ***Personal per capita income 2000-2003:** $20,138-$21,984.

Unemployment 2004: 6%. **Change from 2000:** -1.7%. **Median travel time to work:** 21.9 minutes. **Working outside county of residence:** 25.3%.

Cities with pop over 10,000: Vidalia (10,868).

TOWNS COUNTY

48 River St Suite B   **Ph:** 706-896-2276
Hiawassee, GA 30546   **Fax:** 706-896-4628
www.mountaintopga.com

On northern border of GA, northwest of Athens; organized Mar 6, 1856 from Rabun and Union counties. **Name Origin:** For George Washington Bonaparte Towns (1801-54), U.S. representative from GA (1835-36; 1837-39; 1846-47) and governor (1847-51).

Area (sq mi): 172.01 (land 166.66; water 5.35). **Pop per sq mi:** 61.9.

Pop 2005: 10,315. **State rank:** 126. **Pop change:** 2000-20005 +10.7%; 1990-2000 +38%. **Pop 2000:** 9,319 (White 98.3%; Black or African American 0.1%; Hispanic or Latino 0.7%; Asian 0.3%; Other 0.8%). **Foreign born:** 2.7%. **Median age:** 48.6.

Income 2000: per capita $18,221; median household $31,950; **Pop below poverty level:** 11.8%. ***Personal per capita income 2000-2003:** $22,678-$24,036.

Unemployment 2004: 3%. **Change from 2000:** +0.3%. **Median travel time to work:** 28.5 minutes. **Working outside county of residence:** 41.8%.

Cities with pop over 10,000: None.

TREUTLEN COUNTY

PO Box 79   **Ph:** 912-529-3664
Soperton, GA 30457   **Fax:** 912-529-6062

In east-central GA; organized Aug 21, 1917 from Emanuel and Montgomery counties. **Name Origin:** For John Adam Treutlen (1726-83), first governor of GA (1777-78).

Area (sq mi): 202.19 (land 200.66; water 1.53). **Pop per sq mi:** 33.7.

Pop 2005: 6,753. **State rank:** 145. **Pop change:** 2000-20005 -1.5%; 1990-2000 +14.3%. **Pop 2000:** 6,854 (White 65.1%; Black or African American 33.1%; Hispanic or Latino 1.2%; Asian 0.3%; Other 1%). **Foreign born:** 1.9%. **Median age:** 33.9.

---

*Source: Personal per capita income data are from the Bureau of Economic Analysis; per capita income data are from the Bureau of the Census.
See Introduction for explanation of differences.

Treutlen County (cont'd)

Income 2000: per capita $13,122; median household $24,644; **Pop below poverty level:** 26.3%. ***Personal per capita income 2000-2003:** $15,346-$16,788.

Unemployment 2004: 6%. **Change from 2000:** -0.9%. **Median travel time to work:** 27.8 minutes. **Working outside county of residence:** 54.1%.

Cities with pop over 10,000: None.

TROUP COUNTY

PO Box 866
LaGrange, GA 30241
www.troupcountyga.org

Ph: 706-883-1740
Fax: 706-883-1724

On central western border of GA, north of Columbus; original county; organized Dec 11, 1826 from Indian lands. **Name Origin:** For George Michael Troup (1780-1856), U.S. senator from GA (1816-18; 1829-33) and governor (1823-27).

Area (sq mi): 445.96 (land 413.9; water 32.06). **Pop per sq mi:** 149.8.

Pop 2005: 62,015. **State rank:** 32. **Pop change:** 2000-20005 +5.5%; 1990-2000 +5.8%. **Pop 2000:** 58,779 (White 65.1%; Black or African American 31.9%; Hispanic or Latino 1.7%; Asian 0.6%; Other 1.8%). **Foreign born:** 2%. **Median age:** 34.6.

Income 2000: per capita $17,626; median household $35,469; **Pop below poverty level:** 14.8%. ***Personal per capita income 2000-2003:** $24,070-$25,318.

Unemployment 2004: 5.4%. **Change from 2000:** +0.7%. **Median travel time to work:** 21.1 minutes. **Working outside county of residence:** 16.2%.

Cities with pop over 10,000: LaGrange ⛪ (26,955).

TURNER COUNTY

PO Box 106
Ashburn, GA 31714
www.turnerchamber.com

Ph: 229-567-2011
Fax: 229-567-0450

In south-central GA, northeast of Albany; organized 1905 from Dooly, Irwin, Wilcox, and Worth counties. **Name Origin:** For Capt. Henry Gray Turner (1839-1904), officer in the Confederate Army, U.S. representative from GA (1881-97), and associate justice of the GA supreme court (1903).

Area (sq mi): 289.85 (land 286.03; water 3.83). **Pop per sq mi:** 33.1.

Pop 2005: 9,474. **State rank:** 133. **Pop change:** 2000-20005 -0.3%; 1990-2000 +9.2%. **Pop 2000:** 9,504 (White 55.9%; Black or African American 41%; Hispanic or Latino 2.6%; Asian 0.3%; Other 2.3%). **Foreign born:** 2.4%. **Median age:** 33.3.

Income 2000: per capita $13,454; median household $25,676; **Pop below poverty level:** 26.7%. ***Personal per capita income 2000-2003:** $17,637-$20,162.

Unemployment 2004: 5.4%. **Change from 2000:** -3.6%. **Median travel time to work:** 22.4 minutes. **Working outside county of residence:** 38.3%.

Cities with pop over 10,000: None.

TWIGGS COUNTY

425 N Railroad St
Jeffersonville, GA 31044
www.twiggscounty.us

Ph: 478-945-3629
Fax: 478-945-3988

In central GA, east of Macon; organized Dec 14, 1809 from Wilkinson County. The geographic center of GA is within the county. **Name Origin:** For Maj. Gen. John Twiggs, an officer in the American Revolution.

Area (sq mi): 302.95 (land 300.29, water 2.66). **Pop per sq mi:** 20.6.

Pop 2005: 10,299. **State rank:** 127. **Pop change:** 2000-20005 -2.7%; 1990-2000 +8%. **Pop 2000:** 10,590 (White 54.6%; Black or African American 43.7%; Hispanic or Latino 1.1%; Asian 0.1%; Other 1.3%). **Foreign born:** 0.8%. **Median age:** 35.4.

Income 2000: per capita $14,259; median household $31,608; **Pop below poverty level:** 19.7%. ***Personal per capita income 2000-2003:** $17,342-$20,252.

Unemployment 2004: 5.4%. **Change from 2000:** -0.9%. **Median travel time to work:** 29.3 minutes. **Working outside county of residence:** 75.1%.

Cities with pop over 10,000: None.

UNION COUNTY

114 Courthouse St Box 1
Blairsville, GA 30512
www.unioncounty.gov

Ph: 706-439-6000
Fax: 706-439-6004

On northern border of GA, northwest of Athens; organized Dec 3, 1832 from Cherokee County. **Name Origin:** By John Thomas, state legislator at the time of naming: 'Union, for none but Union men reside in it.'

Area (sq mi): 329.02 (land 322.55; water 6.47). **Pop per sq mi:** 61.3.

Pop 2005: 19,782. **State rank:** 88. **Pop change:** 2000-20005 +14.4%; 1990-2000 +44.2%. **Pop 2000:** 17,289 (White 97.4%; Black or African American 0.6%; Hispanic or Latino 0.9%; Asian 0.2%; Other 1.2%). **Foreign born:** 1.3%. **Median age:** 44.8.

Income 2000: per capita $18,845; median household $31,893; **Pop below poverty level:** 12.5%. ***Personal per capita income 2000-2003:** $21,328-$22,354.

Unemployment 2004: 3.6%. **Change from 2000:** +1%. **Median travel time to work:** 27.3 minutes. **Working outside county of residence:** 31%.

Cities with pop over 10,000: None.

UPSON COUNTY

106 E Lee St Suite 110
Thomaston, GA 30286

Ph: 706-647-7012
Fax: 706-647-7030

In west-central GA, west of Macon; organized Dec 15, 1824 from Crawford and Pike counties. **Name Origin:** For Stephen Upson (1786-1824), attorney, jurist, and GA legislator.

Area (sq mi): 327.64 (land 325.48; water 2.15). **Pop per sq mi:** 85.

Pop 2005: 27,679. **State rank:** 61. **Pop change:** 2000-20005 +0.3%; 1990-2000 +4.9%. **Pop 2000:** 27,597 (White 69.8%; Black or African American 27.9%; Hispanic or Latino 1.2%; Asian 0.4%; Other 1.1%). **Foreign born:** 2%. **Median age:** 37.4.

Upson County (cont'd)

Income 2000: per capita $17,053; median household $31,201; **Pop below poverty level:** 14.7%. ***Personal per capita income 2000-2003:** $20,114-$19,920.

Unemployment 2004: 5.7%. **Change from 2000:** -4.8%. **Median travel time to work:** 25.1 minutes. **Working outside county of residence:** 26.9%.

Cities with pop over 10,000: None.

WALKER COUNTY

PO Box 445
La Fayette, GA 30728
www.co.walker.ga.us

Ph: 706-638-1437
Fax: 706-638-1453

On the northern border of GA, south of Chattanooga, TN; organized Dec 18, 1833 from Murray County. **Name Origin:** For Maj. Freeman Walker (1780-1827), GA legislator, U.S. senator (1819-21), and mayor of Augusta (1818-19; 1823).

Area (sq mi): 447.03 (land 446.58; water 0.45). **Pop per sq mi:** 143.1.

Pop 2005: 63,890. **State rank:** 31. **Pop change:** 2000-20005 +4.6%; 1990-2000 +4.7%. **Pop 2000:** 61,053 (White 93.9%; Black or African American 3.8%; Hispanic or Latino 0.9%; Asian 0.3%; Other 1.5%). **Foreign born:** 1%. **Median age:** 37.1.

Income 2000: per capita $15,867; median household $32,406; **Pop below poverty level:** 12.5%. ***Personal per capita income 2000-2003:** $21,833-$22,286.

Unemployment 2004: 4.2%. **Change from 2000:** +0.3%. **Median travel time to work:** 26.5 minutes. **Working outside county of residence:** 58.7%.

Cities with pop over 10,000: None.

WALTON COUNTY

303 S Hammond Dr Suite 330
Monroe, GA 30655
www.waltoncountyga.org

Ph: 770-267-1301
Fax: 770-267-1400

In central GA, east of Atlanta; original county; organized Dec 15, 1818 from Cherokee lands. **Name Origin:** For George Walton (1741-1804), a signer of the Declaration of Independence, GA governor (1779-80; 1789), and U.S. senator (1795-96).

Area (sq mi): 330.05 (land 329.18; water 0.87). **Pop per sq mi:** 229.8.

Pop 2005: 75,647. **State rank:** 29. **Pop change:** 2000-20005 +24.7%; 1990-2000 +57.3%. **Pop 2000:** 60,687 (White 81.9%; Black or African American 14.4%; Hispanic or Latino 1.9%; Asian 0.7%; Other 1.8%). **Foreign born:** 2%. **Median age:** 33.9.

Income 2000: per capita $19,470; median household $46,479; **Pop below poverty level:** 9.7%. ***Personal per capita income 2000-2003:** $23,525-$23,925.

Unemployment 2004: 4.2%. **Change from 2000:** +0.7%. **Median travel time to work:** 33.5 minutes. **Working outside county of residence:** 61.4%.

Cities with pop over 10,000: Monroe 🏛 (11,903).

WARE COUNTY

800 Church St
Waycross, GA 31501
www.warecounty.com

Ph: 912-287-4300
Fax: 912-287-4301

In southeastern GA, west of Brunswick; organized Dec 15, 1824 from Appling County. **Name Origin:** For Nicholas Ware (1769-1824), GA legislator, mayor of Augusta (1819-21), and U.S. senator (1821-24).

Area (sq mi): 906.31 (land 902.29; water 4.02). **Pop per sq mi:** 38.2.

Pop 2005: 34,492. **State rank:** 51. **Pop change:** 2000-20005 -2.8%; 1990-2000 +0%. **Pop 2000:** 35,483 (White 68.9%; Black or African American 28%; Hispanic or Latino 1.9%; Asian 0.5%; Other 1.9%). **Foreign born:** 1.8%. **Median age:** 36.8.

Income 2000: per capita $14,384; median household $28,360; **Pop below poverty level:** 20.5%. ***Personal per capita income 2000-2003:** $19,514-$21,101.

Unemployment 2004: 5.3%. **Change from 2000:** +0%. **Median travel time to work:** 20.2 minutes. **Working outside county of residence:** 18.7%.

Cities with pop over 10,000: Waycross 🏛 (15,187).

WARREN COUNTY

521 Main St PO Box 46
Warrenton, GA 30828
www.warrencountyga.com

Ph: 706-465-2171
Fax: 706-465-1300

In east-central GA, west of Augusta; organized Dec 19, 1793 from Hancock, Wilkes, Richmond, and Columbus counties. **Name Origin:** For Gen. Joseph Warren (1741-75), Revolutionary War patriot and member of the Committee of Safety who dispatched Paul Revere (1735-1818) on his famous ride.

Area (sq mi): 286.74 (land 285.52; water 1.22). **Pop per sq mi:** 21.4.

Pop 2005: 6,101. **State rank:** 149. **Pop change:** 2000-20005 -3.7%; 1990-2000 +4.2%. **Pop 2000:** 6,336 (White 39.2%; Black or African American 59.5%; Hispanic or Latino 0.8%; Asian 0.1%; Other 1%). **Foreign born:** 0.5%. **Median age:** 37.8.

Income 2000: per capita $14,022; median household $27,366; **Pop below poverty level:** 27%. ***Personal per capita income 2000-2003:** $17,870-$19,830.

Unemployment 2004: 6.9%. **Change from 2000:** -3.3%. **Median travel time to work:** 27.9 minutes. **Working outside county of residence:** 56.9%.

Cities with pop over 10,000: None.

WASHINGTON COUNTY

119 Jones St
Sandersville, GA 31082
www.washingtoncounty-ga.com

Ph: 478-552-2325
Fax: 478-552-7424

In east-central GA, east of Macon; organized Feb 25, 1784 (prior to statehood) from Indian lands. **Name Origin:** For George Washington (1732-99), American patriot and first U.S. president.

Area (sq mi): 684.37 (land 680.34; water 4.03). **Pop per sq mi:** 29.6.

Pop 2005: 20,118. **State rank:** 86. **Pop change:** 2000-20005 -5%; 1990-2000 +10.8%. **Pop 2000:** 21,176 (White 45.4%; Black or African American 53.2%; Hispanic or Latino 0.6%; Asian 0.3%; Other 0.8%). **Foreign born:** 0.5%. **Median age:** 35.6.

---

*Source: Personal per capita income data are from the Bureau of Economic Analysis; per capita income data are from the Bureau of the Census.
See Introduction for explanation of differences.

Washington County (cont'd)

Income 2000: per capita $15,565; median household $29,910; **Pop below poverty level:** 22.9%. ***Personal per capita income 2000-2003:** $20,143-$22,771.

Unemployment 2004: 5.3%. **Change from 2000:** +0.4%. **Median travel time to work:** 23.9 minutes. **Working outside county of residence:** 21.1%.

Cities with pop over 10,000: None.

WAYNE COUNTY

PO Box 270   **Ph:** 912-427-5900
Jesup, GA 31598   **Fax:** 912-427-5906
www.co.wayne.ga.us

In southeastern GA, northwest of Brunswick; original county; organized May 11, 1803 from Indian lands. **Name Origin:** For Gen. Anthony Wayne (1745-96), PA soldier and statesman; nicknamed 'Mad Anthony' for his daring during the Revolutionary War.

Area (sq mi): 648.8 (land 644.66; water 4.13). **Pop per sq mi:** 44.

Pop 2005: 28,390. **State rank:** 58. **Pop change:** 2000-20005 +6.9%; 1990-2000 +18.8%. **Pop 2000:** 26,565 (White 74.7%; Black or African American 20.3%; Hispanic or Latino 3.8%; Asian 0.4%; Other 2.5%). **Foreign born:** 1.5%. **Median age:** 35.5.

Income 2000: per capita $15,628; median household $32,766; **Pop below poverty level:** 16.7%. ***Personal per capita income 2000-2003:** $20,152-$21,013.

Unemployment 2004: 5.4%. **Change from 2000:** +0.2%. **Median travel time to work:** 26.2 minutes. **Working outside county of residence:** 25.1%.

Cities with pop over 10,000: None.

WEBSTER COUNTY

PO Box 29   **Ph:** 229-828-5775
Preston, GA 31824   **Fax:** 229-828-2105

In west-central GA, southeast of Columbus; organized as Kinchafoonee County Dec 16, 1853 from Stewart County; name changed Feb 21, 1856. Originally named for the creek that runs through the county; from Creek 'nutcracker.' **Name Origin:** For Daniel Webster (1782-1852), U.S. statesman and orator from MA.

Area (sq mi): 210.26 (land 209.54; water 0.72). **Pop per sq mi:** 10.9.

Pop 2005: 2,289. **State rank:** 158. **Pop change:** 2000-20005 -4.2%; 1990-2000 +5.6%. **Pop 2000:** 2,390 (White 49.6%; Black or African American 47%; Hispanic or Latino 2.8%; Asian 0%; Other 2.5%). **Foreign born:** 2%. **Median age:** 37.5.

Income 2000: per capita $14,772; median household $27,992; **Pop below poverty level:** 19.3%. ***Personal per capita income 2000-2003:** $19,658-$24,022.

Unemployment 2004: 6.8%. **Change from 2000:** +2%. **Median travel time to work:** 24.7 minutes. **Working outside county of residence:** 64.7%.

Cities with pop over 10,000: None.

WHEELER COUNTY

PO Box 181   **Ph:** 912-568-7135
Alamo, GA 30411   **Fax:** 912-568-1909

In central GA, west of Savannah; organized Aug 14, 1912 from Montgomery County. **Name Origin:** For Joseph Wheeler (1836-1906), Confederate general, author, and U.S. representative from AL (1881-82; 1883; 1885-1900).

Area (sq mi): 300.14 (land 297.72; water 2.42). **Pop per sq mi:** 22.5.

Pop 2005: 6,706. **State rank:** 147. **Pop change:** 2000-20005 +8.5%; 1990-2000 +26%. **Pop 2000:** 6,179 (White 62.6%; Black or African American 33.2%; Hispanic or Latino 3.5%; Asian 0.1%; Other 2.1%). **Foreign born:** 1.9%. **Median age:** 36.1.

Income 2000: per capita $13,005; median household $24,053; **Pop below poverty level:** 25.3%. ***Personal per capita income 2000-2003:** $14,720-$15,327.

Unemployment 2004: 6.5%. **Change from 2000:** -3.9%. **Median travel time to work:** 29.9 minutes. **Working outside county of residence:** 59.6%.

Cities with pop over 10,000: None.

WHITE COUNTY

59 S Main St Suite A   **Ph:** 706-865-2235
Cleveland, GA 30528   **Fax:** 706-865-1324
www.whitecounty.net

In northeastern GA, northwest of Athens; organized Dec 22, 1857 from Habersham County. **Name Origin:** Believed to be for David Thomas White (1812-71), supporter of a bill to create the county. Some claim Col. John White, a hero of the American Revolution.

Area (sq mi): 242.16 (land 241.58; water 0.58). **Pop per sq mi:** 99.6.

Pop 2005: 24,055. **State rank:** 71. **Pop change:** 2000-20005 +20.6%; 1990-2000 +53.3%. **Pop 2000:** 19,944 (White 94.3%; Black or African American 2.2%; Hispanic or Latino 1.6%; Asian 0.5%; Other 2.2%). **Foreign born:** 2%. **Median age:** 38.3.

Income 2000: per capita $17,193; median household $36,084; **Pop below poverty level:** 10.5%. ***Personal per capita income 2000-2003:** $22,807-$21,890.

Unemployment 2004: 3.6%. **Change from 2000:** +0.3%. **Median travel time to work:** 29.6 minutes. **Working outside county of residence:** 47.7%.

Cities with pop over 10,000: None.

WHITFIELD COUNTY

PO Box 868   **Ph:** 706-275-7450
Dalton, GA 30722   **Fax:** 706-275-7456
www.whitfieldcountyga.com

On northern border of GA, northeast of Rome; organized Dec 20, 1851 from Murray County. **Name Origin:** For the Rev. George Whitefield (1714-70), prominent Church of England clergyman who established Bethesda, one of the first orphanages in the U.S. Spelling changed by clerical error.

Area (sq mi): 290.65 (land 289.99; water 0.66). **Pop per sq mi:** 313.4.

Pop 2005: 90,889. **State rank:** 25. **Pop change:** 2000-20005 +8.8%; 1990-2000 +15.3%. **Pop 2000:** 83,525 (White 72.2%; Black or

Whitfield County (cont'd)

African American 3.8%; Hispanic or Latino 22.1%; Asian 0.9%; Other 14.3%). **Foreign born:** 16.6%. **Median age:** 33.

Income 2000: per capita $18,515; median household $39,377; **Pop below poverty level:** 11.5%. ***Personal per capita income 2000-2003:** $25,391-$27,072.

Unemployment 2004: 4.2%. **Change from 2000:** +0%. **Median travel time to work:** 20.8 minutes. **Working outside county of residence:** 13.1%.

Cities with pop over 10,000: Dalton 🏛 (31,478).

WILCOX COUNTY

103 N Broad St   **Ph:** 229-467-2737
Abbeville, GA 31001   **Fax:** 229-467-2000

In central GA, northeast of Albany; organized Dec 22, 1857 from Dooly, Irwin, and Pulaski counties. **Name Origin:** Either for the Abbeville District of SC, or for the wife of David Fitzgerald, who donated the land for the county seat.

Area (sq mi): 383.3 (land 380.3; water 3). **Pop per sq mi:** 22.9.

Pop 2005: 8,721. **State rank:** 138. **Pop change:** 2000-20005 +1.7%; 1990-2000 +22.4%. **Pop 2000:** 8,577 (White 61.8%; Black or African American 36.2%; Hispanic or Latino 1.6%; Asian 0.2%; Other 1%). **Foreign born:** 0.8%. **Median age:** 36.7.

Income 2000: per capita $14,014; median household $27,483; **Pop below poverty level:** 21%. ***Personal per capita income 2000-2003:** $18,184-$20,759.

Unemployment 2004: 5.4%. **Change from 2000:** -0.2%. **Median travel time to work:** 26 minutes. **Working outside county of residence:** 51.8%.

Cities with pop over 10,000: None.

WILKES COUNTY

23 E Court St Rm 222   **Ph:** 706-678-2511
Washington, GA 30673   **Fax:** 706-678-3033
www.washingtonwilkes.org

In eastern GA, southeast of Athens; organized Feb 5, 1777 (prior to statehood) from original territory. **Name Origin:** For John Wilkes (1725-97), member of the British House of Commons who supported the American colonies before the Revolutionary War.

Area (sq mi): 474 (land 471.37; water 2.62). **Pop per sq mi:** 22.2.

Pop 2005: 10,457. **State rank:** 123. **Pop change:** 2000-20005 -2.2%; 1990-2000 +0.8%. **Pop 2000:** 10,687 (White 53.9%; Black or African American 43.1%; Hispanic or Latino 2%; Asian 0.2%; Other 1.6%). **Foreign born:** 1.3%. **Median age:** 39.

Income 2000: per capita $15,020; median household $27,644; **Pop below poverty level:** 17.5%. ***Personal per capita income 2000-2003:** $20,333-$20,598.

Unemployment 2004: 7%. **Change from 2000:** -3.2%. **Median travel time to work:** 21.6 minutes. **Working outside county of residence:** 22.3%.

Cities with pop over 10,000: None.

WILKINSON COUNTY

100 Bacon St   **Ph:** 478-946-2236
Irwinton, GA 31042   **Fax:** 478-946-3767

In central GA, east of Macon; original county; organized May 11, 1803 from Creek cession. **Name Origin:** For James Wilkinson (1757-1825), officer under Washington, negotiated for the Louisiana Purchase, and first governor of the Louisiana Territory.

Area (sq mi): 452.01 (land 446.56; water 5.45). **Pop per sq mi:** 22.7.

Pop 2005: 10,143. **State rank:** 128. **Pop change:** 2000-20005 -0.8%; 1990-2000 -0.1%. **Pop 2000:** 10,220 (White 57.7%; Black or African American 40.7%; Hispanic or Latino 1%; Asian 0.1%; Other 1.3%). **Foreign born:** 1.4%. **Median age:** 35.8.

Income 2000: per capita $14,658; median household $32,723; **Pop below poverty level:** 17.9%. ***Personal per capita income 2000-2003:** $19,759-$21,101.

Unemployment 2004: 5%. **Change from 2000:** +0.3%. **Median travel time to work:** 28.6 minutes. **Working outside county of residence:** 52.4%.

Cities with pop over 10,000: None.

WORTH COUNTY

201 N Main St Rm 30   **Ph:** 229-776-8200
Sylvester, GA 31791   **Fax:** 229-776-8232
www.worthcounty.com

In southwest-central GA, east of Albany; organized Dec 20, 1853 from Dooly and Irwin counties. **Name Origin:** For William Jenkins Worth (1794-1849), general during the Mexican War, cited by Congress for bravery.

Area (sq mi): 574.58 (land 569.73; water 4.86). **Pop per sq mi:** 38.6.

Pop 2005: 21,996. **State rank:** 80. **Pop change:** 2000-20005 +0.1%; 1990-2000 +11.3%. **Pop 2000:** 21,967 (White 68.3%; Black or African American 29.6%; Hispanic or Latino 1.1%; Asian 0.2%; Other 1.6%). **Foreign born:** 1%. **Median age:** 35.7.

Income 2000: per capita $15,856; median household $32,384; **Pop below poverty level:** 18.5%. ***Personal per capita income 2000-2003:** $20,349-$22,249.

Unemployment 2004: 5%. **Change from 2000:** -1%. **Median travel time to work:** 24.8 minutes. **Working outside county of residence:** 61.6%.

Cities with pop over 10,000: None.

Hawaii

Pacific Ocean

NIIHAU

KAUAI

Kauai
Lihue ⊙

Kauai Channel

OAHU

Honolulu ✪
Honolulu

MOLOKAI

KALAWAO

LANAI

MAUI

Maui

Wailuku ⊙

KAHOOLAWE

Alenuihaha

Pacific Ocean

HAWAII

Hawaii

Hilo ⊙

Pacific Ocean

N

	County boundary
Hawaii	County name
⊙	County seat
■	Major city
✪	State capital

50 mi

50 km

0

0

© MAPS.com

Hawaii

HAWAII STATE INFORMATION

www.hawaii.gov   **Ph:** 808-586-2211

Area (sq mi): 10,930.98 (land 6422.62; water 4508.36). **Pop per sq mi:** 198.5.

Pop 2005: 1,275,194. **Pop change:** 2000-20005 +5.3%; 1990-2000 +9.3%. **Pop 2000:** 1,211,537 (White 22.9%; Black or African American 1.8%; Hispanic or Latino 7.2%; Asian 41.6%; Other 32.4%, including 9.4% Native Hawaiian/Other Pacific Islander). **Foreign born:** 17.5%. **Median age:** 36.2.

Income 2000: per capita $21,525; median household $49,820; **Pop below poverty level:** 10.7%. ***Personal per capita income 2000-2003:** $28,422-$30,441.

Unemployment 2004: 3.3%. **Change from 2000:** -0.7%. **Median travel time to work:** 26.1 minutes. **Working outside county of residence:** 1.3%.

HAWAII COUNTY

25 Aupuni St Rm 209   **Ph:** 808-961-8255

Hilo, HI 96720   **Fax:** 808-961-8912

www.hawaii-county.com

Southernmost of the Islands, bordered on the north by Alenuihaha Channel; county is coextensive with the island. Established 1905 (prior to statehood). **Name Origin:** In Hawaii the name has no meaning, but in the rest of Polynesia it is the name of the underworld or of the ancestral home. Sometimes translated as 'beyond the doors of death.' Called the 'Big Island.'

Area (sq mi): 5086.7 (land 4028.02; water 1058.69). **Pop per sq mi:** 41.5.

Pop 2005: 167,293. **State rank:** 2. **Pop change:** 2000-20005 +12.5%; 1990-2000 +23.6%. **Pop 2000:** 148,677 (White 29.7%; Black or African American 0.5%; Hispanic or Latino 9.5%; Asian 26.7%; Other 41.1%, including 11.2% Native Hawaiian/Other Pacific Islander). **Foreign born:** 10.2%. **Median age:** 38.6.

Income 2000: per capita $18,791; median household $39,805; **Pop below poverty level:** 15.7%. ***Personal per capita income 2000-2003:** $21,403-$23,500.

Unemployment 2004: 3.8%. **Change from 2000:** -3%. **Median travel time to work:** 24.5 minutes. **Working outside county of residence:** 2%.

Cities with pop over 10,000: None.

HONOLULU CITY & COUNTY

530 S King St Rm 100   **Ph:** 808-523-4352

Honolulu, HI 96813   **Fax:** 808-527-6888

www.co.honolulu.hi.us

Between the islands of Kauai and Molokai; bordered on west by Kauai Channel and on southeast by Kaiwi Channel. Established 1905 (prior to statehood); legally the City and County of Honolulu with one municipal government; includes the islands of Oahu and small ones northwest of Kauai. About 80% of the state's population lives in Honolulu County. **Name Origin:** From two Polynesian words, *hono* 'fair haven' and *lulu* 'calm' or 'quiet,' referring to Mamala Bay, into which Pearl Harbor opens.

Area (sq mi): 2126.85 (land 599.77; water 1527.08). **Pop per sq mi:** 1509.4.

Pop 2005: 905,266. **State rank:** 1. **Pop change:** 2000-20005 +3.3%; 1990-2000 +4.8%. **Pop 2000:** 876,156 (White 20%; Black or African American 2.4%; Hispanic or Latino 6.7%; Asian 46%; Other 30.3%, including 8.9% Native Hawaiian/Other Pacific Islander). **Foreign born:** 19.2%. **Median age:** 35.7.

Income 2000: per capita $21,998; median household $51,914; **Pop below poverty level:** 9.9%. ***Personal per capita income 2000-2003:** $30,393-$32,463.

Unemployment 2004: 3.2%. **Change from 2000:** -0.9%. **Median travel time to work:** 27.3 minutes. **Working outside county of residence:** 1.1%.

Cities with pop over 10,000: Honolulu 🏛 (377,260).

KALAWAO COUNTY

On the island of Molokai, southeast of the island of Oahu. Established 1905 (prior to statehood); has no county government. For statistical purposes is considered as one of the judicial districts of Maui County. Site of a colony for victims of leprosy or Hansen's disease; administered by the state department of health.

Area (sq mi): 52.33 (land 13.21; water 39.12). **Pop per sq mi:** 8.4.

Pop 2005: 111. **State rank:** 5. **Pop change:** 2000-20005 -24.5%; 1990-2000 +13.1%. **Pop 2000:** 147 (White 22.4%; Black or African American 0%; Hispanic or Latino 4.1%; Asian 17%; Other 57.1%, including 48.3% Native Hawaiian/Other Pacific Islander). **Foreign born:** 20.4%. **Median age:** 58.6.

Income 2000: per capita $13,756; median household $9,333; **Pop below poverty level:** 40.1%. ***Personal per capita income 2000-2003:** $25,135-$27,310 (includes Maui County & Kalawao).

Unemployment 2004: 0%. **Median travel time to work:** 12.9 minutes. **Working outside county of residence:** 0%.

Cities with pop over 10,000: None.

🏛 *County Seat*

KAUAI COUNTY

4396 Rice St Rm 206   **Ph:** 808-241-6371
Lihue, HI 96766   **Fax:** 808-241-6349
www.kauai.gov

Westernmost of the Islands; county includes Kauai and Niihau islands; bordered on east by Kauai Channel. Established 1905 (prior to statehood). **Name Origin:** From the Polynesian meaning 'drying place.'

Area (sq mi): 1266.37 (land 622.44; water 643.93). **Pop per sq mi:** 100.6.

Pop 2005: 62,640. **State rank:** 4. **Pop change:** 2000-20005 +7.1%; 1990-2000 +14.2%. **Pop 2000:** 58,463 (White 27.9%; Black or African American 0.3%; Hispanic or Latino 8.2%; Asian 36%; Other 34.2%, including 9.1% Native Hawaiian/Other Pacific Islander). **Foreign born:** 13%. **Median age:** 38.4.

Income 2000: per capita $20,301; median household $45,020; **Pop below poverty level:** 10.5%. ***Personal per capita income 2000-2003:** $24,090-$25,838.

Unemployment 2004: 3.3%. **Change from 2000:** -3.7%. **Median travel time to work:** 21.5 minutes. **Working outside county of residence:** 1.7%.

Cities with pop over 10,000: None.

MAUI COUNTY

200 S High St   **Ph:** 808-270-7748
Wailuku, HI 96793   **Fax:** 808-270-7171
www.co.maui.hi.us

Separated from Hawaii County to the southeast by Alenuihaha Channel and from Honolulu to the northwest by Kaiwi Channel. Established 1905 (prior to statehood). Includes Molokai, Lanai, Kahoolawe, and Maui islands. **Name Origin:** A Polynesian demigod.

Area (sq mi): 2398.74 (land 1159.2; water 1239.54). **Pop per sq mi:** 120.7.

Pop 2005: 139,884. **State rank:** 3. **Pop change:** 2000-20005 +9.2%; 1990-2000 +27.6%. **Pop 2000:** 128,094 (White 31.9%; Black or African American 0.4%; Hispanic or Latino 7.8%; Asian 31%; Other 34.7%, including 10.7% Native Hawaiian/Other Pacific Islander). **Foreign born:** 16.5%. **Median age:** 36.8.

Income 2000: per capita $22,033; median household $49,489; **Pop below poverty level:** 10.5%. ***Personal per capita income 2000-2003:** $25,135-$27,310 (includes Maui County & Kalawao).

Unemployment 2004: 3.1%. **Change from 2000:** -1.7%. **Median travel time to work:** 21.7 minutes. **Working outside county of residence:** 1.5%.

Cities with pop over 10,000: None.

*Source: Personal per capita income data are from the Bureau of Economic Analysis; per capita income data are from the Bureau of the Census. See Introduction for explanation of differences.

180

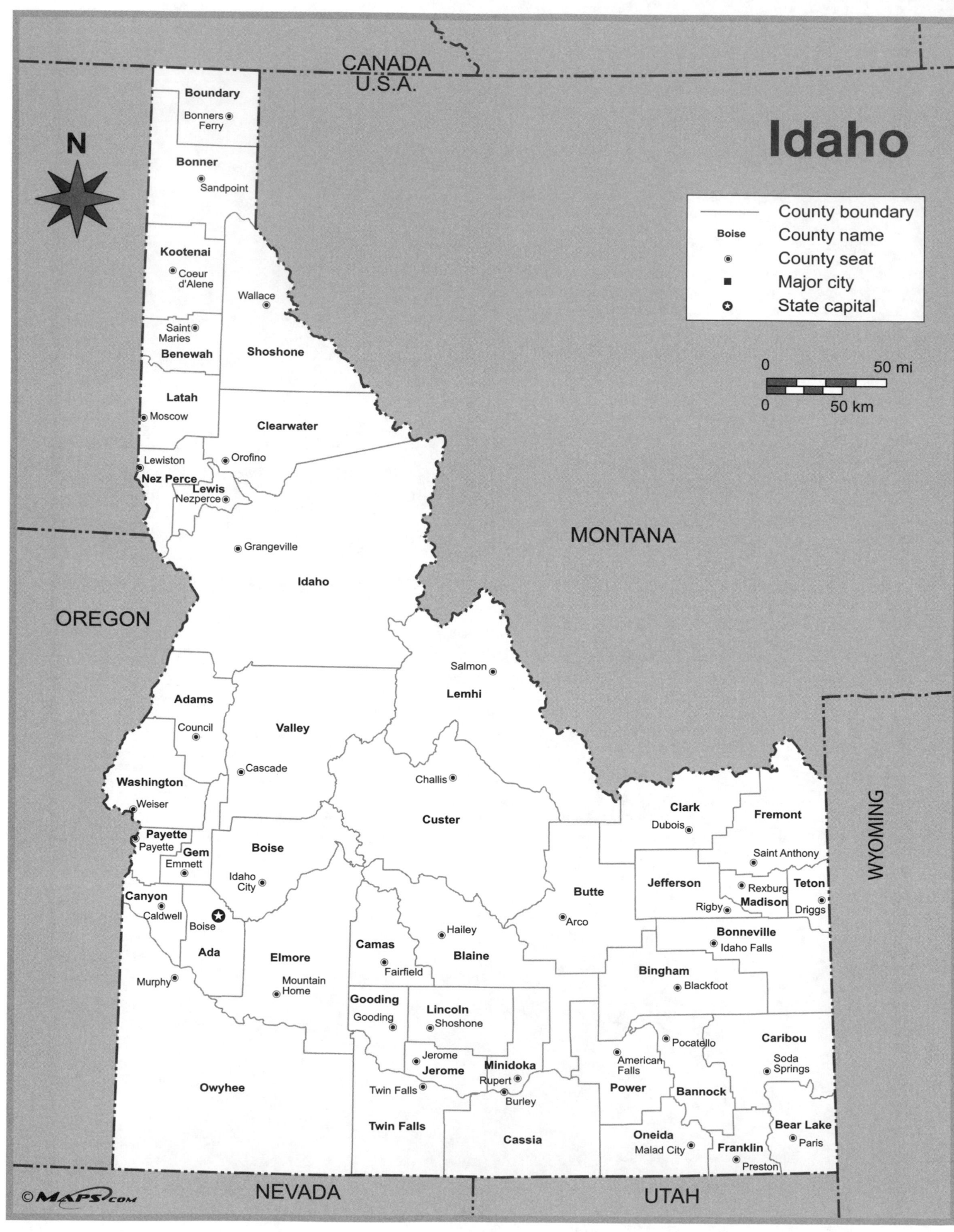

Idaho

Idaho

IDAHO STATE INFORMATION

www.idaho.gov   **Ph:** 208-334-2411

Area (sq mi): 83,570.08 (land 82,747.21; water 822.87). **Pop per sq mi:** 17.3.

Pop 2005: 1,429,096. **Pop change:** 2000-20005 +10.4%; 1990-2000 +28.5%. **Pop 2000:** 1,293,953 (White 88%; Black or African American 0.4%; Hispanic or Latino 7.9%; Asian 0.9%; Other 7.7%, including 1.4% American Indian/Alaska Native). **Foreign born:** 5%. **Median age:** 33.2.

Income 2000: per capita $17,841; median household $37,572; **Pop below poverty level:** 11.8%. ***Personal per capita income 2000-2003:** $24,075-$25,902.

Unemployment 2004: 4.7%. **Change from 2000:** +0.1%. **Median travel time to work:** 20 minutes. **Working outside county of residence:** 19.1%.

ADA COUNTY

200 W Front St Suite 3255   **Ph:** 208-287-7000
Boise, ID 83702   **Fax:** 208-287-7009
www.adaweb.net

In southwestern ID; organized Dec 22, 1864 (prior to statehood) from Boise County. **Name Origin:** For Ada Riggs (1863-?), the first white child born in Boise, daughter of H. C. Riggs.

Area (sq mi): 1060.33 (land 1054.99; water 5.34). **Pop per sq mi:** 326.8.

Pop 2005: 344,727. **State rank:** 1. **Pop change:** 2000-20005 +14.6%; 1990-2000 +46.2%. **Pop 2000:** 300,904 (White 90.6%; Black or African American 0.6%; Hispanic or Latino 4.5%; Asian 1.7%; Other 4.7%). **Foreign born:** 4.3%. **Median age:** 32.8.

Income 2000: per capita $22,519; median household $46,140; **Pop below poverty level:** 7.7%. ***Personal per capita income 2000-2003:** $33,511-$35,324.

Unemployment 2004: 3.9%. **Change from 2000:** +0.4%. **Median travel time to work:** 19.3 minutes. **Working outside county of residence:** 6.9%.

Cities with pop over 10,000: Boise 🏛 (190,122); Meridian (44,962); Eagle (16,176); Garden City (11,173).

ADAMS COUNTY

PO Box 48   **Ph:** 208-253-4561
Council, ID 83612   **Fax:** 208-253-4880
www.co.adams.id.us

On the central western border of ID, north of Boise; organized Mar 3, 1911 from Washington County. **Name Origin:** For John Adams (1735-1826), second U.S. president.

Area (sq mi): 1370 (land 1364.58; water 5.43). **Pop per sq mi:** 2.6.

Pop 2005: 3,591. **State rank:** 41. **Pop change:** 2000-20005 +3.3%; 1990-2000 +6.8%. **Pop 2000:** 3,476 (White 95.5%; Black or African American 0.1%; Hispanic or Latino 1.6%; Asian 0.1%; Other 3.5%, including 1.4% American Indian/Alaska Native). **Foreign born:** 1.7%. **Median age:** 44.4.

Income 2000: per capita $14,908; median household $28,423; **Pop below poverty level:** 15.1%. ***Personal per capita income 2000-2003:** $21,750-$23,061.

Unemployment 2004: 11.6%. **Change from 2000:** -1.9%. **Median travel time to work:** 22.2 minutes. **Working outside county of residence:** 25.3%.

Cities with pop over 10,000: None.

BANNOCK COUNTY

PO Box 4016   **Ph:** 208-236-7210
Pocatello, ID 83205   **Fax:** 208-236-7363
www.co.bannock.id.us

In southeastern ID; organized Mar 6, 1893 from Bingham County. **Name Origin:** For the Bannack Indians whose name in Shoshonean means 'hair in backward motion,' for their habit of wearing a lock of hair tossed back over their heads. Early settlers spelled the name 'Bannock,' with an 'o' instead of an 'a'.

Area (sq mi): 1147.46 (land 1113.3; water 34.16). **Pop per sq mi:** 70.2.

Pop 2005: 78,155. **State rank:** 5. **Pop change:** 2000-20005 +3.4%; 1990-2000 +14.4%. **Pop 2000:** 75,565 (White 89.5%; Black or African American 0.6%; Hispanic or Latino 4.7%; Asian 1%; Other 7.2%, including 2.9% American Indian/Alaska Native). **Foreign born:** 2.2%. **Median age:** 29.8.

Income 2000: per capita $17,148; median household $36,683; **Pop below poverty level:** 13.9%. ***Personal per capita income 2000-2003:** $20,856-$23,724.

Unemployment 2004: 4.7%. **Change from 2000:** +0%. **Median travel time to work:** 17.2 minutes. **Working outside county of residence:** 13%.

Cities with pop over 10,000: Pocatello 🏛 (50,723); Chubbuck (10,492).

🏛 *County Seat*

183

BEAR LAKE COUNTY

7 E Center St PO Box 190   **Ph:** 208-945-2212
Paris, ID 83261   **Fax:** 208-945-2780
www.bearlakecounty.info

On the southeastern border of ID, southeast of Pocatello; organized Jan 5, 1875 from Oneida County. **Name Origin:** For Bear Lake, which lies half in ID and half in UT.

Area (sq mi): 1049.44 (land 971.38; water 78.05). **Pop per sq mi:** 6.4.

Pop 2005: 6,176. **State rank:** 36. **Pop change:** 2000-20005 -3.7%; 1990-2000 +5.4%. **Pop 2000:** 6,411 (White 96.6%; Black or African American 0.1%; Hispanic or Latino 2.4%; Asian 0.1%; Other 2.1%). **Foreign born:** 1.1%. **Median age:** 35.8.

Income 2000: per capita $13,592; median household $32,162; **Pop below poverty level:** 9.6%. ***Personal per capita income 2000-2003:** $16,689-$19,680.

Unemployment 2004: 4.7%. **Change from 2000:** -0.3%. **Median travel time to work:** 21.3 minutes. **Working outside county of residence:** 25.4%.

Cities with pop over 10,000: None.

BENEWAH COUNTY

701 College Ave   **Ph:** 208-245-2234
Saint Maries, ID 83861   **Fax:** 208-245-9152

On the western border of ID, southeast of Spokane, WA; organized Jan 23, 1915 from Kootenai County. **Name Origin:** For Benewah, a chief of the Coeur d'Alene Indian tribe.

Area (sq mi): 783.98 (land 776.07; water 7.91). **Pop per sq mi:** 11.9.

Pop 2005: 9,218. **State rank:** 28. **Pop change:** 2000-20005 +0.5%; 1990-2000 +15.5%. **Pop 2000:** 9,171 (White 87.8%; Black or African American 0.1%; Hispanic or Latino 1.5%; Asian 0.2%; Other 11.1%, including 8.9% American Indian/Alaska Native). **Foreign born:** 0.6%. **Median age:** 39.2.

Income 2000: per capita $15,285; median household $31,517; **Pop below poverty level:** 14.1%. ***Personal per capita income 2000-2003:** $20,213-$21,987.

Unemployment 2004: 8.8%. **Change from 2000:** -1.4%. **Median travel time to work:** 19.2 minutes. **Working outside county of residence:** 16.1%.

Cities with pop over 10,000: None.

BINGHAM COUNTY

501 N Maple St Suite 205   **Ph:** 208-782-3163
Blackfoot, ID 83221   **Fax:** 208-785-4131
www.co.bingham.id.us

In southeastern ID, south of Idaho Falls; organized Jan 13, 1885 (prior to statehood) from Oneida County. **Name Origin:** By ID Territorial Governor William M. Bunn for his friend Henry Harrison Bingham (1841-1912), U.S. representative from PA (1879-1912) and a former Union officer who was awarded the Congressional Medal of Honor in 1864.

Area (sq mi): 2120.24 (land 2094.73; water 25.51). **Pop per sq mi:** 20.9.

Pop 2005: 43,739. **State rank:** 7. **Pop change:** 2000-20005 +4.8%; 1990-2000 +11%. **Pop 2000:** 41,735 (White 78.6%; Black or African American 0.2%; Hispanic or Latino 13.3%; Asian 0.6%; Other 16.8%, including 6.7% American Indian/Alaska Native). **Foreign born:** 6.1%. **Median age:** 29.7.

Income 2000: per capita $14,365; median household $36,423; **Pop below poverty level:** 12.4%. ***Personal per capita income 2000-2003:** $19,267-$20,589.

Unemployment 2004: 4.4%. **Change from 2000:** -0.2%. **Median travel time to work:** 21.2 minutes. **Working outside county of residence:** 32.5%.

Cities with pop over 10,000: Blackfoot ⛴ (10,707).

BLAINE COUNTY

206 1st Ave S Suite 200   **Ph:** 208-788-5505
Hailey, ID 83333   **Fax:** 208-788-5501
www.co.blaine.id.us

In south-central ID, west of Pocatello; organized Mar 5, 1895 from Alturas County, which was organized in 1864 and abolished in 1895, and from Logan County, which was organized in 1889 and abolished in 1895. **Name Origin:** For James Gillespie Blaine (1830-93), U.S. representative from ME (1863-76), U.S. senator (1876-81), and U.S. secretary of state (1881; 1889-92).

Area (sq mi): 2661.02 (land 2644.78; water 16.24). **Pop per sq mi:** 8.

Pop 2005: 21,166. **State rank:** 16. **Pop change:** 2000-20005 +11.5%; 1990-2000 +40.1%. **Pop 2000:** 18,991 (White 87%; Black or African American 0.1%; Hispanic or Latino 10.7%; Asian 0.7%; Other 8.4%). **Foreign born:** 10.6%. **Median age:** 37.4.

Income 2000: per capita $31,346; median household $50,496; **Pop below poverty level:** 7.8%. ***Personal per capita income 2000-2003:** $42,945-$43,060.

Unemployment 2004: 3.5%. **Change from 2000:** +0.6%. **Median travel time to work:** 18.7 minutes. **Working outside county of residence:** 3.7%.

Cities with pop over 10,000: None.

BOISE COUNTY

420 Main St PO Box 1300   **Ph:** 208-392-4431
Idaho City, ID 83631   **Fax:** 208-392-4473
www.co.boise.id.us

In west-central ID, northeast of Boise; original county, established Feb 4, 1864. **Name Origin:** For the Boise River, which forms part of its eastern border from French *boise* 'woods.'

Area (sq mi): 1906.76 (land 1902.46; water 4.3). **Pop per sq mi:** 4.

Pop 2005: 7,535. **State rank:** 33. **Pop change:** 2000-20005 +13%; 1990-2000 +90.1%. **Pop 2000:** 6,670 (White 93.3%; Black or African American 0.1%; Hispanic or Latino 3.4%; Asian 0.3%; Other 4.3%). **Foreign born:** 2.4%. **Median age:** 40.4.

Income 2000: per capita $18,787; median household $38,651; **Pop below poverty level:** 12.9%. ***Personal per capita income 2000-2003:** $21,542-$21,871.

Unemployment 2004: 4.8%. **Change from 2000:** -0.2%. **Median travel time to work:** 37.5 minutes. **Working outside county of residence:** 58.2%.

Cities with pop over 10,000: None.

---

*Source: Personal per capita income data are from the Bureau of Economic Analysis; per capita income data are from the Bureau of the Census. See Introduction for explanation of differences.

BONNER COUNTY

215 S 1st Ave   **Ph:** 208-265-1432
Sandpoint, ID 83864   **Fax:** 208-265-1447
www.co.bonner.id.us

In the north of the ID panhandle, northeast of Spokane, WA; organized Feb 21, 1907 from Kootenai County. **Name Origin:** For Edwin L. Bonner, an early settler of northern ID who operated a ferry on the Kootenai River.

Area (sq mi): 1919.59 (land 1737.67; water 181.92). **Pop per sq mi:** 23.5.

Pop 2005: 40,908. **State rank:** 8. **Pop change:** 2000-20005 +11.1%; 1990-2000 +38.4%. **Pop 2000:** 36,835 (White 95.6%; Black or African American 0.1%; Hispanic or Latino 1.6%; Asian 0.3%; Other 3%). **Foreign born:** 2%. **Median age:** 40.8.

Income 2000: per capita $17,263; median household $32,803; **Pop below poverty level:** 15.5%. ***Personal per capita income 2000-2003:** $20,362-$21,764.

Unemployment 2004: 5.9%. **Change from 2000:** -2.2%. **Median travel time to work:** 25.5 minutes. **Working outside county of residence:** 16.7%.

Cities with pop over 10,000: None.

BONNEVILLE COUNTY

605 N Capital Ave   **Ph:** 208-529-1354
Idaho Falls, ID 83402   **Fax:** 208-529-1379
www.co.bonneville.id.us

On the southeastern border of ID, northeast of Pocatello; organized Feb 7, 1911 from Bingham County. **Name Origin:** For Benjamin Louis Eulalie de Bonneville (1796-1878), French-born officer in the Mexican-American War and explorer of California and the Rocky Mountains region (1831-31); immortalized in the *Adventures of Captain Bonneville* (1837) by Washington Irving (1783-1859).

Area (sq mi): 1900.65 (land 1868.48; water 32.18). **Pop per sq mi:** 49.2.

Pop 2005: 91,856. **State rank:** 4. **Pop change:** 2000-20005 +11.3%; 1990-2000 +14.3%. **Pop 2000:** 82,522 (White 90.2%; Black or African American 0.5%; Hispanic or Latino 6.9%; Asian 0.8%; Other 5.9%). **Foreign born:** 3.9%. **Median age:** 31.8.

Income 2000: per capita $18,326; median household $41,805; **Pop below poverty level:** 10.1%. ***Personal per capita income 2000-2003:** $23,652-$26,600.

Unemployment 2004: 3.4%. **Change from 2000:** +0.1%. **Median travel time to work:** 19.6 minutes. **Working outside county of residence:** 10.1%.

Cities with pop over 10,000: Idaho Falls 🏛 (52,148).

BOUNDARY COUNTY

PO Box 419   **Ph:** 208-267-5504
Bonners Ferry, ID 83805   **Fax:** 208-267-7814
www.boundary-idaho.com

On the northern boundary of the ID panhandle; organized Jan 23, 1915 from Kootenai and Bonner counties. **Name Origin:** Because it borders Canada on the north, MT on the east, and WA on the west.

Area (sq mi): 1278.21 (land 1268.81; water 9.4). **Pop per sq mi:** 8.4.

Pop 2005: 10,619. **State rank:** 26. **Pop change:** 2000-20005 +7.6%; 1990-2000 +18.5%. **Pop 2000:** 9,871 (White 93.2%; Black or African American 0.2%; Hispanic or Latino 3.4%; Asian 0.6%; Other 4.1%, including 2% American Indian/Alaska Native). **Foreign born:** 2.9%. **Median age:** 38.3.

Income 2000: per capita $14,636; median household $31,250; **Pop below poverty level:** 15.7%. ***Personal per capita income 2000-2003:** $17,045-$18,542.

Unemployment 2004: 6.9%. **Change from 2000:** -2.2%. **Median travel time to work:** 21.5 minutes. **Working outside county of residence:** 13.6%.

Cities with pop over 10,000: None.

BUTTE COUNTY

248 W Grand Ave PO Box 737   **Ph:** 208-527-3021
Arco, ID 83213   **Fax:** 208-527-3295

In east-central ID, west of Idaho Falls; organized Feb 6, 1917 from Bingham, Blaine, and Jefferson counties. **Name Origin:** For the landmark buttes rising from the Snake River plains.

Area (sq mi): 2233.59 (land 2232.85; water 0.74). **Pop per sq mi:** 1.3.

Pop 2005: 2,808. **State rank:** 42. **Pop change:** 2000-20005 -3.1%; 1990-2000 -0.7%. **Pop 2000:** 2,899 (White 93.3%; Black or African American 0.3%; Hispanic or Latino 4.1%; Asian 0.2%; Other 4.9%). **Foreign born:** 3.9%. **Median age:** 38.8.

Income 2000: per capita $14,948; median household $30,473; **Pop below poverty level:** 18.2%. ***Personal per capita income 2000-2003:** $20,611-$21,430.

Unemployment 2004: 6.4%. **Change from 2000:** +2.5%. **Median travel time to work:** 22.2 minutes. **Working outside county of residence:** 19.8%.

Cities with pop over 10,000: None.

CAMAS COUNTY

PO Box 430   **Ph:** 208-764-2242
Fairfield, ID 83327   **Fax:** 208-764-2349

In south-central ID, east of Boise; organized Feb 6, 1917 from Blaine County. **Name Origin:** From the Chinook name for the camas, an edible root of the lily family.

Area (sq mi): 1079.02 (land 1074.96; water 4.06). **Pop per sq mi:** 1.

Pop 2005: 1,050. **State rank:** 43. **Pop change:** 2000-20005 +6%; 1990-2000 +36.3%. **Pop 2000:** 991 (White 91.8%; Black or African American 1.2%; Hispanic or Latino 5.5%; Asian 0.2%; Other 3.4%). **Foreign born:** 1.8%. **Median age:** 39.7.

Income 2000: per capita $19,550; median household $34,167; **Pop below poverty level:** 8.3%. ***Personal per capita income 2000-2003:** $21,314-$22,010.

Unemployment 2004: 4.1%. **Change from 2000:** -0.9%. **Median travel time to work:** 29 minutes. **Working outside county of residence:** 40.4%.

Cities with pop over 10,000: None.

🏛 *County Seat*

CANYON COUNTY

1115 Albany St   **Ph:** 208-454-7574
Caldwell, ID 83605   **Fax:** 208-454-7525
www.canyoncounty.org

On the southwestern border of ID, west of Boise; established Mar 7, 1891 from Ada County. **Name Origin:** Either for the canyon of the Boise River near Caldwell, or the Snake River canyon, which forms a county boundary.

Area (sq mi): 603.51 (land 589.72; water 13.79). **Pop per sq mi:** 279.1.

Pop 2005: 164,593. **State rank:** 2. **Pop change:** 2000-20005 +25.2%; 1990-2000 +45.9%. **Pop 2000:** 131,441 (White 77.9%; Black or African American 0.3%; Hispanic or Latino 18.6%; Asian 0.8%; Other 15.8%). **Foreign born:** 8.6%. **Median age:** 30.5.

Income 2000: per capita $15,155; median household $35,884; **Pop below poverty level:** 12%. *****Personal per capita income 2000-2003:** $19,712-$19,304.

Unemployment 2004: 5.4%. **Change from 2000:** +0.1%. **Median travel time to work:** 22.3 minutes. **Working outside county of residence:** 34.3%.

Cities with pop over 10,000: Nampa (68,156); Caldwell 🏛 (32,718).

CARIBOU COUNTY

PO Box 775   **Ph:** 208-547-4324
Soda Springs, ID 83276   **Fax:** 208-547-4759

On the southeastern border of ID, east of Pocatello; organized Feb 11, 1919 from Bannock and Oneida counties. **Name Origin:** For 'Caribou (Cariboo)' Fairchild, active in mining in ID; nickname acquired in the Cariboo mine fields of British Columbia, Canada.

Area (sq mi): 1798.62 (land 1766.01; water 32.61). **Pop per sq mi:** 4.

Pop 2005: 7,131. **State rank:** 35. **Pop change:** 2000-20005 -2.4%; 1990-2000 +4.9%. **Pop 2000:** 7,304 (White 94.9%; Black or African American 0.1%; Hispanic or Latino 4%; Asian 0.1%; Other 3.7%). **Foreign born:** 1.8%. **Median age:** 35.

Income 2000: per capita $15,179; median household $37,609; **Pop below poverty level:** 9.6%. *****Personal per capita income 2000-2003:** $20,607-$23,157.

Unemployment 2004: 6.8%. **Change from 2000:** +1%. **Median travel time to work:** 19.1 minutes. **Working outside county of residence:** 10.9%.

Cities with pop over 10,000: None.

CASSIA COUNTY

1459 Overland Ave   **Ph:** 208-878-7302
Burley, ID 83318   **Fax:** 208-878-9109
www.cassiacounty.org

On the central southern border of ID, east of Twin Falls; organized Feb 20, 1879 (prior to statehood) from Oneida County. **Name Origin:** For Cassia Creek (spelled Cassier in 1879), named either from French *cajeaux* 'raft,' for for James John Cazier, member of the Mormon Battalion and a colorful wagon train leader. Locals also believe it is for the cassia plant.

Area (sq mi): 2580.31 (land 2566.45; water 13.86). **Pop per sq mi:** 8.3.

Pop 2005: 21,324. **State rank:** 15. **Pop change:** 2000-20005 -0.4%;

1990-2000 +9.6%. **Pop 2000:** 21,416 (White 79.3%; Black or African American 0.2%; Hispanic or Latino 18.7%; Asian 0.4%; Other 14.9%). **Foreign born:** 7.3%. **Median age:** 31.1.

Income 2000: per capita $14,087; median household $33,322; **Pop below poverty level:** 13.6%. *****Personal per capita income 2000-2003:** $21,576-$23,551.

Unemployment 2004: 6%. **Change from 2000:** +0.5%. **Median travel time to work:** 16.3 minutes. **Working outside county of residence:** 26.6%.

Cities with pop over 10,000: None.

CLARK COUNTY

320 W Main St   **Ph:** 208-374-5402
Dubois, ID 83423   **Fax:** 208-374-5609

On lower northern border of ID, north of Idaho Falls; organized Feb 1, 1919 from Fremont County. **Name Origin:** For Sam K. Clark, an early settler on Medicine Lodge Creek, and first state senator from the county.

Area (sq mi): 1765.21 (land 1764.63; water 0.58). **Pop per sq mi:** 0.5.

Pop 2005: 943. **State rank:** 44. **Pop change:** 2000-20005 -7.7%; 1990-2000 +34.1%. **Pop 2000:** 1,022 (White 63.9%; Black or African American 0.1%; Hispanic or Latino 34.2%; Asian 0.2%; Other 25.6%, including 1% American Indian/Alaska Native). **Foreign born:** 28.2%. **Median age:** 30.7.

Income 2000: per capita $11,141; median household $31,576; **Pop below poverty level:** 19.9%. *****Personal per capita income 2000-2003:** $23,254-$25,311.

Unemployment 2004: 7.2%. **Change from 2000:** +2.8%. **Median travel time to work:** 20.5 minutes. **Working outside county of residence:** 21%.

Cities with pop over 10,000: None.

CLEARWATER COUNTY

PO Box 586   **Ph:** 208-476-3615
Orofino, ID 83544   **Fax:** 208-476-3127
www.clearwatercounty.org

On the eastern border of the ID panhandle, east of Lewiston; organized Feb 27, 1911 from Nez Perce County. **Name Origin:** For the Clearwater River, itself named for the translation of the Nez Perce descriptive name.

Area (sq mi): 2488.1 (land 2461.4; water 26.7). **Pop per sq mi:** 3.4.

Pop 2005: 8,373. **State rank:** 29. **Pop change:** 2000-20005 -6.2%; 1990-2000 +5%. **Pop 2000:** 8,930 (White 93.8%; Black or African American 0.1%; Hispanic or Latino 1.8%; Asian 0.4%; Other 4.7%, including 2% American Indian/Alaska Native). **Foreign born:** 1.2%. **Median age:** 41.7.

Income 2000: per capita $15,463; median household $32,071; **Pop below poverty level:** 13.5%. *****Personal per capita income 2000-2003:** $19,730-$23,130.

Unemployment 2004: 10.1%. **Change from 2000:** -4.8%. **Median travel time to work:** 23.5 minutes. **Working outside county of residence:** 15.2%.

Cities with pop over 10,000: None.

Source: Personal per capita income data are from the Bureau of Economic Analysis; per capita income data are from the Bureau of the Census. See Introduction for explanation of differences.

CUSTER COUNTY

801 Main St
Challis, ID 83226
www.co.custer.id.us

Ph: 208-879-2360
Fax: 208-879-5246

In central ID; organized Jan 8, 1881 (prior to statehood) from Alturas and Lemhi counties. **Name Origin:** For the General Custer mine, named for Gen. George Armstrong Custer (1839-76), U.S. officer and Indian fighter.

Area (sq mi): 4936.79 (land 4925.45; water 11.34). **Pop per sq mi:** 0.8.

Pop 2005: 4,077. **State rank:** 39. **Pop change:** 2000-20005 -6.1%; 1990-2000 +5.1%. **Pop 2000:** 4,342 (White 94.4%; Black or African American 0%; Hispanic or Latino 4.2%; Asian 0%; Other 2.7%). **Foreign born:** 2.3%. **Median age:** 41.2.

Income 2000: per capita $15,783; median household $32,174; **Pop below poverty level:** 14.3%. ***Personal per capita income 2000-2003:** $22,622-$22,928.

Unemployment 2004: 5.7%. **Change from 2000:** -1.9%. **Median travel time to work:** 26.1 minutes. **Working outside county of residence:** 16.3%.

Cities with pop over 10,000: None.

ELMORE COUNTY

150 S 4th East St Suite 3
Mountain Home, ID 83647
www.elmorecounty.org

Ph: 208-587-2129
Fax: 208-587-2159

In southwestern ID, east of Boise; organized Feb 7, 1889 (prior to statehood) from Alturas County. **Name Origin:** For the Ida Elmore Quartz Mine, largest producer of gold and silver during the 1860s.

Area (sq mi): 3100.51 (land 3077.57; water 22.93). **Pop per sq mi:** 9.3.

Pop 2005: 28,634. **State rank:** 12. **Pop change:** 2000-20005 -1.7%; 1990-2000 +37.4%. **Pop 2000:** 29,130 (White 79.7%; Black or African American 3.2%; Hispanic or Latino 12%; Asian 1.7%; Other 9.8%). **Foreign born:** 7.7%. **Median age:** 29.1.

Income 2000: per capita $16,773; median household $35,256; **Pop below poverty level:** 11.2%. ***Personal per capita income 2000-2003:** $20,142-$23,301.

Unemployment 2004: 5.5%. **Change from 2000:** 0.5%. **Median travel time to work:** 19.3 minutes. **Working outside county of residence:** 16.8%.

Cities with pop over 10,000: Mountain Home 🏛 (11,427).

FRANKLIN COUNTY

39 W Oneida St
Preston, ID 83263

Ph: 208-852-1090
Fax: 208-852-1094

On the southern border of ID, southeast of Pocatello; organized Jan 30, 1913 from Oneida County. **Name Origin:** For the first settlement in ID, named for Franklin Dewey Richards (1821-99), a Mormon apostle.

Area (sq mi): 668.36 (land 665.43; water 2.92). **Pop per sq mi:** 18.6.

Pop 2005: 12,371. **State rank:** 23. **Pop change:** 2000-20005 +9.2%; 1990-2000 +22.7%. **Pop 2000:** 11,329 (White 93.7%; Black or African American 0.1%; Hispanic or Latino 5.2%; Asian 0.1%; Other 4.6%). **Foreign born:** 3.4%. **Median age:** 27.7.

Income 2000: per capita $13,702; median household $36,061; **Pop below poverty level:** 7.4%. ***Personal per capita income 2000-2003:** $18,646-$19,551.

Unemployment 2004: 3.9%. **Change from 2000:** +0%. **Median travel time to work:** 23.3 minutes. **Working outside county of residence:** 41.1%.

Cities with pop over 10,000: None.

FREMONT COUNTY

151 W 1st North
Saint Anthony, ID 83445
www.co.fremont.id.us

Ph: 208-624-7332
Fax: 208-624-7335

On the lower northeastern border of ID, northeast of Idaho Falls; organized Mar 4, 1893 from Bingham County. **Name Origin:** For John Charles Fremont (1813-90), soldier and explorer who led five expeditions to the West, U.S. senator from CA (1850-51), and governor of the AZ Territory (1878-81).

Area (sq mi): 1895.59 (land 1866.76; water 28.84). **Pop per sq mi:** 6.6.

Pop 2005: 12,242. **State rank:** 24. **Pop change:** 2000-20005 +3.6%; 1990-2000 +8.1%. **Pop 2000:** 11,819 (White 87.3%; Black or African American 0.2%; Hispanic or Latino 10.6%; Asian 0.4%; Other 8.1%). **Foreign born:** 7.3%. **Median age:** 31.9.

Income 2000: per capita $13,965; median household $33,424; **Pop below poverty level:** 14.2%. ***Personal per capita income 2000-2003:** $18,068-$19,910.

Unemployment 2004: 4.6%. **Change from 2000:** -1.9%. **Median travel time to work:** 22.4 minutes. **Working outside county of residence:** 47.5%.

Cities with pop over 10,000: None.

GEM COUNTY

415 E Main St
Emmett, ID 83617
www.co.gem.id.us

Ph: 208-365-4561
Fax: 208-365-6172

In southwestern ID, north of Boise; organized Mar 19, 1915 from Boise and Canyon counties. **Name Origin:** For the state nickname, 'Gem State,' from the supposed Indian meaning of Idaho 'Gem of the Mountain.'

Area (sq mi): 565.75 (land 562.58; water 3.17). **Pop per sq mi:** 28.9.

Pop 2005: 16,273. **State rank:** 19. **Pop change:** 2000-20005 +7.2%; 1990-2000 +28.2%. **Pop 2000:** 15,181 (White 90.7%; Black or African American 0.1%; Hispanic or Latino 6.9%; Asian 0.4%; Other 5.8%). **Foreign born:** 4.9%. **Median age:** 37.5.

Income 2000: per capita $15,340; median household $34,460; **Pop below poverty level:** 13.1%. ***Personal per capita income 2000-2003:** $19,376-$20,006.

Unemployment 2004: 5.4%. **Change from 2000:** -2.5%. **Median travel time to work:** 26.9 minutes. **Working outside county of residence:** 44.5%.

Cities with pop over 10,000: None.

🏛 *County Seat*

187

GOODING COUNTY

624 Main St   **Ph:** 208-934-4841
Gooding, ID 83330   **Fax:** 208-934-5085
goodingidaho.net

In south-central ID, northwest of Twin Falls; organized Jan 28, 1913 from Lincoln County. **Name Origin:** For Frank Robert Gooding (1859-1928), governor of Idaho (1905-08) and U.S. senator (1921-28).

Area (sq mi): 733.84 (land 730.78; water 3.06). **Pop per sq mi:** 19.8.

Pop 2005: 14,461. **State rank:** 21. **Pop change:** 2000-20005 +2.2%; 1990-2000 +21.7%. **Pop 2000:** 14,155 (White 80.3%; Black or African American 0.2%; Hispanic or Latino 17.1%; Asian 0.2%; Other 11.9%). **Foreign born:** 11.6%. **Median age:** 35.1.

Income 2000: per capita $14,612; median household $31,888; **Pop below poverty level:** 13.8%. ***Personal per capita income 2000-2003:** $23,473-$27,402.

Unemployment 2004: 3.8%. **Change from 2000:** +0.3%. **Median travel time to work:** 20.2 minutes. **Working outside county of residence:** 29.8%.

Cities with pop over 10,000: None.

IDAHO COUNTY

320 W Main St Rm 5   **Ph:** 208-983-2751
Grangeville, ID 83530   **Fax:** 208-983-1458
www.idahocounty.org

At the southern base of the ID panhandle, east and south of Lewiston; original county; organized Feb 4, 1864 (prior to statehood). Originally established in 1861 as the third county of WA Territory, now in ID. **Name Origin:** For the steamer *Idaho*, launched Jun 9, 1860 on the Columbia River to serve miners in the gold rush.

Area (sq mi): 8502.48 (land 8484.88; water 17.59). **Pop per sq mi:** 1.9.

Pop 2005: 15,697. **State rank:** 20. **Pop change:** 2000-20005 +1.2%; 1990-2000 +12.5%. **Pop 2000:** 15,511 (White 93.4%; Black or African American 0.1%; Hispanic or Latino 1.6%; Asian 0.3%; Other 5.5%, including 2.9% American Indian/Alaska Native). **Foreign born:** 1.2%. **Median age:** 42.3.

Income 2000: per capita $14,411; median household $29,515; **Pop below poverty level:** 16.3%. ***Personal per capita income 2000-2003:** $18,972-$20,365.

Unemployment 2004: 7.6%. **Change from 2000:** -1.9%. **Median travel time to work:** 18.4 minutes. **Working outside county of residence:** 15.9%.

Cities with pop over 10,000: None.

JEFFERSON COUNTY

134 N Clark PO Box 275   **Ph:** 208-745-7756
Rigby, ID 83442   **Fax:** 208-745-6636
www.co.jefferson.id.us

In southeastern ID, north of Idaho Falls; organized Feb 18, 1913 from Fremont County. **Name Origin:** For Thomas Jefferson (1743-1826), U.S. patriot and statesman; third U.S. president.

Area (sq mi): 1105.55 (land 1095.08; water 10.47). **Pop per sq mi:** 19.7.

Pop 2005: 21,580. **State rank:** 14. **Pop change:** 2000-20005 +12.7%; 1990-2000 +15.8%. **Pop 2000:** 19,155 (White 88.5%; Black or African American 0.3%; Hispanic or Latino 10%; Asian 0.2%; Other 8.7%). **Foreign born:** 5.9%. **Median age:** 28.8.

Income 2000: per capita $13,838; median household $37,737; **Pop below poverty level:** 10.4%. ***Personal per capita income 2000-2003:** $18,745-$20,470.

Unemployment 2004: 3.7%. **Change from 2000:** +0%. **Median travel time to work:** 25.2 minutes. **Working outside county of residence:** 52.7%.

Cities with pop over 10,000: None.

JEROME COUNTY

300 N Lincoln Ave Rm 301   **Ph:** 208-324-8811
Jerome, ID 83338   **Fax:** 208-324-2719
www.co.jerome.id.us

In south-central ID, north of Twin Falls; organized Feb 18, 1919 from Gooding and Lincoln counties. **Name Origin:** Either for Jerome Hill, a principal figure in the Twin Falls North Side Irrigation Project (1905), or Jerome Kuhn, his son-in-law, or for Jerome Kuhn, Jr., his grandson. All were major figures in the growth of the county.

Area (sq mi): 601.87 (land 599.84; water 2.03). **Pop per sq mi:** 32.7.

Pop 2005: 19,638. **State rank:** 17. **Pop change:** 2000-20005 +7.1%; 1990-2000 +21.2%. **Pop 2000:** 18,342 (White 80.6%; Black or African American 0.2%; Hispanic or Latino 17.2%; Asian 0.3%; Other 12.4%). **Foreign born:** 10.5%. **Median age:** 32.9.

Income 2000: per capita $15,530; median household $34,696; **Pop below poverty level:** 13.9%. ***Personal per capita income 2000-2003:** $21,785-$24,616.

Unemployment 2004: 4.4%. **Change from 2000:** +0.6%. **Median travel time to work:** 19.8 minutes. **Working outside county of residence:** 42.5%.

Cities with pop over 10,000: None.

KOOTENAI COUNTY

PO Box 9000   **Ph:** 208-446-1000
Coeur d'Alene, ID 83816   **Fax:** 208-446-1188
www.co.kootenai.id.us

On the western border of the ID panhandle, east of Spokane, WA; original county; organized Dec 22, 1864 (prior to statehood). **Name Origin:** For the Kootenai (or Kutenai) Indian tribe, whose name means 'water people.'

Area (sq mi): 1315.69 (land 1245.12; water 70.57). **Pop per sq mi:** 102.5.

Pop 2005: 127,668. **State rank:** 3. **Pop change:** 2000-20005 +17.5%; 1990-2000 +55.7%. **Pop 2000:** 108,685 (White 94.4%; Black or African American 0.2%; Hispanic or Latino 2.3%; Asian 0.5%; Other 3.5%, including 1.2% American Indian/Alaska Native). **Foreign born:** 2.4%. **Median age:** 36.1.

Income 2000: per capita $18,430; median household $37,754; **Pop below poverty level:** 10.5%. ***Personal per capita income 2000-2003:** $23,012-$24,805.

*Source: Personal per capita income data are from the Bureau of Economic Analysis; per capita income data are from the Bureau of the Census. See Introduction for explanation of differences.

Kootenai County (cont'd)

Unemployment 2004: 5.5%. **Change from 2000:** -2.1%. **Median travel time to work:** 21.7 minutes. **Working outside county of residence:** 21.5%.

Cities with pop over 10,000: Coeur d'Alene ⛪ (38,388); Post Falls (21,351); Hayden (11,086).

LATAH COUNTY

522 S Adams PO Box 8068
Moscow, ID 83843
www.latah.id.us

Ph: 208-882-8580
Fax: 208-883-7203

On the western border of the ID panhandle, north of Lewiston; organized May 14, 1888 (prior to statehood) from Kootenai County. **Name Origin:** For Latah Creek from a combination of two Nez Perce words, *lakah* 'place of the pines,' and *tah-ol* 'pestle.' The Indians found stones there to grind camas roots and shade in which to work.

Area (sq mi): 1076.89 (land 1076.65; water 0.24). **Pop per sq mi:** 32.2.

Pop 2005: 34,714. **State rank:** 10. **Pop change:** 2000-20005 -0.6%; 1990-2000 +14.1%. **Pop 2000:** 34,935 (White 92.8%; Black or African American 0.6%; Hispanic or Latino 2.1%; Asian 2.1%; Other 3.4%). **Foreign born:** 4.3%. **Median age:** 27.9.

Income 2000: per capita $16,690; median household $32,524; **Pop below poverty level:** 16.7%. ***Personal per capita income 2000-2003:** $21,248-$25,054.

Unemployment 2004: 3.7%. **Change from 2000:** +0.4%. **Median travel time to work:** 17.9 minutes. **Working outside county of residence:** 21.3%.

Cities with pop over 10,000: Moscow ⛪ (21,900).

LEMHI COUNTY

206 Courthouse Dr
Salmon, ID 83467
www.lemhicountyidaho.org

Ph: 208-756-2815
Fax: 208-756-8424

On the central eastern border of ID; organized Mar 3, 1869 (prior to statehood) from Idaho County. **Name Origin:** For Fort Lemhi, a Mormon mission on the Salmon River, named for a character in the Book of Mormon.

Area (sq mi): 4569.5 (land 4564.16; water 5.35). **Pop per sq mi:** 1.7.

Pop 2005: 7,909. **State rank:** 31. **Pop change:** 2000-20005 +1.3%; 1990-2000 +13.1%. **Pop 2000:** 7,806 (White 95.5%; Black or African American 0.1%; Hispanic or Latino 2.2%; Asian 0.2%; Other 3.1%). **Foreign born:** 1.5%. **Median age:** 42.7.

Income 2000: per capita $16,037; median household $30,185; **Pop below poverty level:** 15.3%. ***Personal per capita income 2000-2003:** $19,673-$21,458.

Unemployment 2004: 6.8%. **Change from 2000:** -0.8%. **Median travel time to work:** 17.5 minutes. **Working outside county of residence:** 3.2%.

Cities with pop over 10,000: None.

LEWIS COUNTY

510 Oak St Rm 1
Nezperce, ID 83543
www.lewiscountyid.org

Ph: 208-937-2251
Fax: 208-937-9233

In central-western ID, southeast of Lewiston; organized Mar 3, 1911 from Nez Perce County. **Name Origin:** For Meriwether Lewis (1774-1809), co-leader of the Lewis and Clark expedition (1804-06).

Area (sq mi): 479.81 (land 479.04; water 0.77). **Pop per sq mi:** 7.8.

Pop 2005: 3,750. **State rank:** 40. **Pop change:** 2000-20005 +0.1%; 1990-2000 +6.6%. **Pop 2000:** 3,747 (White 91.5%; Black or African American 0.3%; Hispanic or Latino 1.9%; Asian 0.4%; Other 7%, including 3.8% American Indian/Alaska Native). **Foreign born:** 1.1%. **Median age:** 42.5.

Income 2000: per capita $15,942; median household $31,413; **Pop below poverty level:** 12%. ***Personal per capita income 2000-2003:** $22,829-$23,651.

Unemployment 2004: 3.6%. **Change from 2000:** -3.9%. **Median travel time to work:** 21.3 minutes. **Working outside county of residence:** 38%.

Cities with pop over 10,000: None.

LINCOLN COUNTY

111 W 'B' St Suite C
Shoshone, ID 83352

Ph: 208-886-7641
Fax: 208-886-2798

In south-central ID, north of Twin Falls; organized Mar 18, 1895 from Blaine County. **Name Origin:** For Abraham Lincoln (1809-65), sixteenth U.S. president.

Area (sq mi): 1205.86 (land 1205.53; water 0.33). **Pop per sq mi:** 3.8.

Pop 2005: 4,545. **State rank:** 37. **Pop change:** 2000-20005 +12.4%; 1990-2000 +22.2%. **Pop 2000:** 4,044 (White 83.5%; Black or African American 0.5%; Hispanic or Latino 13.4%; Asian 0.4%; Other 12.5%, including 1.2% American Indian/Alaska Native). **Foreign born:** 10.1%. **Median age:** 34.3.

Income 2000: per capita $14,257; median household $32,484; **Pop below poverty level:** 13.1%. ***Personal per capita income 2000-2003:** $20,143-$21,176.

Unemployment 2004: 5.3%. **Change from 2000:** +1.4%. **Median travel time to work:** 30.4 minutes. **Working outside county of residence:** 46.5%.

Cities with pop over 10,000: None.

MADISON COUNTY

PO Box 389
Rexburg, ID 83440
www.co.madison.id.us

Ph: 208-356-3662
Fax: 208-356-8396

In southeastern ID, northeast of Idaho Falls; organized Feb 18, 1913 from Fremont County. **Name Origin:** For James Madison (1751-1836), fourth U.S. president.

Area (sq mi): 473.36 (land 471.52; water 1.84). **Pop per sq mi:** 65.7.

Pop 2005: 30,975. **State rank:** 11. **Pop change:** 2000-20005 +12.8%; 1990-2000 +16%. **Pop 2000:** 27,467 (White 94.1%; Black or African American 0.2%; Hispanic or Latino 3.9%; Asian 0.6%; Other 3.7%). **Foreign born:** 3.5%. **Median age:** 20.7.

⛪ County Seat

Madison County (cont'd)

Income 2000: per capita $10,956; median household $32,607; **Pop below poverty level:** 30.5%. ***Personal per capita income 2000-2003:** $13,878-$15,371.

Unemployment 2004: 2.7%. **Change from 2000:** +0.7%. **Median travel time to work:** 14.7 minutes. **Working outside county of residence:** 18.5%.

Cities with pop over 10,000: Rexburg 🏛 (24,733).

MINIDOKA COUNTY

PO Box 368   **Ph:** 208-436-7111
Rupert, ID 83350   **Fax:** 208-436-0737
www.minidoka.id.us

In south-central ID, west of Pocatello; organized Jan 28, 1913 from Lincoln County. **Name Origin:** For the first settlement, a railroad siding, from Shoshonean 'broad expanse,' descriptive of the Snake River plain in this area.

Area (sq mi): 762.98 (land 759.62; water 3.36). **Pop per sq mi:** 25.

Pop 2005: 19,014. **State rank:** 18. **Pop change:** 2000-20005 -5.8%; 1990-2000 +4.2%. **Pop 2000:** 20,174 (White 72.1%; Black or African American 0.3%; Hispanic or Latino 25.5%; Asian 0.4%; Other 21.2%). **Foreign born:** 10.9%. **Median age:** 33.5.

Income 2000: per capita $13,813; median household $32,021; **Pop below poverty level:** 14.8%. ***Personal per capita income 2000-2003:** $17,447-$18,544.

Unemployment 2004: 7.9%. **Change from 2000:** +1.5%. **Median travel time to work:** 17.5 minutes. **Working outside county of residence:** 34.7%.

Cities with pop over 10,000: None.

NEZ PERCE COUNTY

1230 Main St PO Box 896   **Ph:** 208-799-3020
Lewiston, ID 83501   **Fax:** 208-799-3070
www.co.nezperce.id.us

On the western border of the ID panhandle; original county; organized Feb 4, 1864 (prior to statehood). It was previously established by WA Territory in 1861. **Name Origin:** From the French name 'pierced nose,' for an Indian tribe that called itself *Chopunnish*. The French term might be better translated as 'mashed' or 'flattened nose.'

Area (sq mi): 856.36 (land 849.08; water 7.28). **Pop per sq mi:** 44.7.

Pop 2005: 37,931. **State rank:** 9. **Pop change:** 2000-20005 +1.4%; 1990-2000 +10.8%. **Pop 2000:** 37,410 (White 90.6%; Black or African American 0.3%; Hispanic or Latino 1.9%; Asian 0.7%; Other 7.5%, including 5.3% American Indian/Alaska Native). **Foreign born:** 1.9%. **Median age:** 38.1.

Income 2000: per capita $18,544; median household $36,282; **Pop below poverty level:** 12.2%. ***Personal per capita income 2000-2003:** $24,899-$26,221.

Unemployment 2004: 4.8%. **Change from 2000:** +0.9%. **Median travel time to work:** 15.9 minutes. **Working outside county of residence:** 14%.

Cities with pop over 10,000: Lewiston 🏛 (31,028).

ONEIDA COUNTY

10 Court St   **Ph:** 208-766-4116
Malad City, ID 83252   **Fax:** 208-766-2990
www.co.oneida.id.us

On the southern border of ID, south of Pocatello; original county; organized Jan 22, 1864 (prior to statehood). **Name Origin:** For Lake Oneida, NY, former home of early settlers, itself named for one of the Five Nations of the Iroquois. Name means 'stone people,' perhaps for their bravery.

Area (sq mi): 1201.61 (land 1200.33; water 1.28). **Pop per sq mi:** 3.5.

Pop 2005: 4,209. **State rank:** 38. **Pop change:** 2000-20005 +2%; 1990-2000 +18.1%. **Pop 2000:** 4,125 (White 96.6%; Black or African American 0.1%; Hispanic or Latino 2.3%; Asian 0.1%; Other 2.3%). **Foreign born:** 2.1%. **Median age:** 36.

Income 2000: per capita $13,829; median household $34,309; **Pop below poverty level:** 10.8%. ***Personal per capita income 2000-2003:** $16,521-$17,701.

Unemployment 2004: 3.1%. **Change from 2000:** -0.5%. **Median travel time to work:** 26.4 minutes. **Working outside county of residence:** 35.2%.

Cities with pop over 10,000: None.

OWYHEE COUNTY

PO Box 128   **Ph:** 208-495-2421
Murphy, ID 83650   **Fax:** 208-495-1173
owyheecounty.net

On the southwestern border of ID, south of Boise; original county; organized Dec 31, 1863 (prior to statehood). **Name Origin:** For the Owyhee River, itself named for a corrupt spelling of Hawaii, in honor of three Hawaiians (Owyhee) who were hired to trade with the Indians; they disappeared and were presumed to have been killed.

Area (sq mi): 7696.71 (land 7677.98; water 18.72). **Pop per sq mi:** 1.4.

Pop 2005: 11,073. **State rank:** 25. **Pop change:** 2000-20005 +4%; 1990-2000 +26.8%. **Pop 2000:** 10,644 (White 71.7%; Black or African American 0.2%; Hispanic or Latino 23.1%; Asian 0.5%; Other 22.5%, including 3.2% American Indian/Alaska Native). **Foreign born:** 11.9%. **Median age:** 32.9.

Income 2000: per capita $13,405; median household $28,339; **Pop below poverty level:** 16.9%. ***Personal per capita income 2000-2003:** $18,376-$19,647.

Unemployment 2004: 2.7%. **Change from 2000:** -1.8%. **Median travel time to work:** 25.6 minutes. **Working outside county of residence:** 51%.

Cities with pop over 10,000: None.

PAYETTE COUNTY

1130 3rd Ave N Rm 104   **Ph:** 208-642-6000
Payette, ID 83661   **Fax:** 208-642-6011
www.payettecounty.org

On western border of ID, northeast of Boise; organized Feb 28, 1917 from Canyon County. **Name Origin:** For the Payette River, which runs diagonally through the county; named for Francis Payette, Canadian fur trapper and explorer.

---

*Source: Personal per capita income data are from the Bureau of Economic Analysis; per capita income data are from the Bureau of the Census. See Introduction for explanation of differences.

Payette County (cont'd)

Area (sq mi): 410.19 (land 407.52; water 2.67). **Pop per sq mi:** 54.5.

Pop 2005: 22,197. **State rank:** 13. **Pop change:** 2000-20005 +7.9%; 1990-2000 +25.2%. **Pop 2000:** 20,578 (White 84.7%; Black or African American 0.1%; Hispanic or Latino 11.9%; Asian 0.9%; Other 8.8%). **Foreign born:** 5.5%. **Median age:** 34.4.

Income 2000: per capita $14,924; median household $33,046; **Pop below poverty level:** 13.2% *Personal per capita income 2000-2003: $18,737-$20,925.

Unemployment 2004: 7.9%. **Change from 2000:** -0.5%. **Median travel time to work:** 20 minutes. **Working outside county of residence:** 49.3%.

Cities with pop over 10,000: None.

POWER COUNTY

543 Bannock Ave   **Ph:** 208-226-7611
American Falls, ID 83211   **Fax:** 208-226-7612
www.co.power.id.us

In southeastern ID, east of Pocatello; organized Jan 30, 1913 from Bingham, Cassia, Oneida, and Blaine counties. **Name Origin:** For the American Falls Canal and Power Company.

Area (sq mi): 1442.6 (land 1405.57; water 37.03). **Pop per sq mi:** 5.5.

Pop 2005: 7,753. **State rank:** 32. **Pop change:** 2000-20005 +2.9%; 1990-2000 +6.4%. **Pop 2000:** 7,538 (White 74.2%; Black or African American 0.1%; Hispanic or Latino 21.7%; Asian 0.3%; Other 15.8%, including 3.3% American Indian/Alaska Native). **Foreign born:** 10.5%. **Median age:** 31.6.

Income 2000: per capita $14,007; median household $32,226; **Pop below poverty level:** 16.1%. *Personal per capita income 2000-2003: $20,635-$19,903.

Unemployment 2004: 6.1%. **Change from 2000:** -1.1%. **Median travel time to work:** 17.6 minutes. **Working outside county of residence:** 30.1%.

Cities with pop over 10,000: None.

SHOSHONE COUNTY

700 Bank St   **Ph:** 208-752-3331
Wallace, ID 83873   **Fax:** 208-753-2711

On the eastern border of the ID panhandle, northeast of Lewiston. The first organized unit of government in ID, it was originally created in 1858 as part of WA Territory, effective in 1861; reorganized Feb 4, 1864 (prior to statehood). **Name Origin:** For the Shonone, one of the major Indian tribes of the northern Rocky Mountain region.

Area (sq mi): 2635.5 (land 2633.91; water 1.59). **Pop per sq mi:** 5.

Pop 2005: 13,157. **State rank:** 22. **Pop change:** 2000-20005 4.5%; 1990-2000 -1.1%. **Pop 2000:** 13,771 (White 94.7%; Black or African American 0.1%; Hispanic or Latino 1.9%; Asian 0.2%; Other 3.8%, including 1.5% American Indian/Alaska Native). **Foreign born:** 2%. **Median age:** 41.8.

Income 2000: per capita $15,934; median household $28,535; **Pop below poverty level:** 16.4%. *Personal per capita income 2000-2003: $19,151-$22,481.

Unemployment 2004: 9.5%. **Change from 2000:** -2.5%. **Median travel time to work:** 21.6 minutes. **Working outside county of residence:** 18.5%.

Cities with pop over 10,000: None.

TETON COUNTY

89 N Main St Suite 1   **Ph:** 208-354-2905
Driggs, ID 83422   **Fax:** 208-354-8410
www.mycommunity.net/TetonCounty.nsf/

On the eastern border of ID, northeast of Idaho Falls; organized Jan 26, 1915 from Madison County. **Name Origin:** For the Teton Mountains.

Area (sq mi): 450.57 (land 450.36; water 0.21). **Pop per sq mi:** 16.6.

Pop 2005: 7,467. **State rank:** 34. **Pop change:** 2000-20005 +24.5%; 1990-2000 +74.4%. **Pop 2000:** 5,999 (White 86.8%; Black or African American 0.2%; Hispanic or Latino 11.8%; Asian 0.2%; Other 8.3%). **Foreign born:** 9.9%. **Median age:** 31.3.

Income 2000: per capita $17,778; median household $41,968; **Pop below poverty level:** 12.9%. *Personal per capita income 2000-2003: $18,628-$20,633.

Unemployment 2004: 2.9%. **Change from 2000:** +0.4%. **Median travel time to work:** 26.9 minutes. **Working outside county of residence:** 40.7%.

Cities with pop over 10,000: None.

TWIN FALLS COUNTY

PO Box 126   **Ph:** 208-736-4004
Twin Falls, ID 83303   **Fax:** 208-736-4182
www.twinfallscounty.org

On the central southern border of ID; organized Feb 21, 1907 from Cassia County. **Name Origin:** For the falls on the Snake River.

Area (sq mi): 1928.47 (land 1925.03; water 3.44). **Pop per sq mi:** 36.1.

Pop 2005: 69,419. **State rank:** 6. **Pop change:** 2000-20005 +8%; 1990-2000 +20%. **Pop 2000:** 64,284 (White 87.7%; Black or African American 0.2%; Hispanic or Latino 9.4%; Asian 0.8%; Other 6.6%). **Foreign born:** 6.4%. **Median age:** 34.9.

Income 2000: per capita $16,678; median household $34,506; **Pop below poverty level:** 12.7%. *Personal per capita income 2000-2003: $21,778-$24,929.

Unemployment 2004: 4.3%. **Change from 2000:** +0.2%. **Median travel time to work:** 16.7 minutes. **Working outside county of residence:** 11.1%.

Cities with pop over 10,000: Twin Falls 🏛 (37,619).

VALLEY COUNTY

PO Box 1350   **Ph:** 208-382-4297
Cascade, ID 83611   **Fax:** 208-382-7107

In west-central ID; organized Feb 26, 1917. **Name Origin:** For Long Valley.

Area (sq mi): 3733.66 (land 3677.82; water 55.84). **Pop per sq mi:** 2.3.

🏛 *County Seat*

Valley County (cont'd)

Pop 2005: 8,332. **State rank:** 30. **Pop change:** 2000-20005 +8.9%; 1990-2000 +25.2%. **Pop 2000:** 7,651 (White 95.8%; Black or African American 0%; Hispanic or Latino 2%; Asian 0.3%; Other 3.2%). **Foreign born:** 1.4%. **Median age:** 43.5.

Income 2000: per capita $19,246; median household $36,927; **Pop below poverty level:** 9.3%. ***Personal per capita income 2000-2003:** $27,783-$29,015.

Unemployment 2004: 6.6%. **Change from 2000:** -1.7%. **Median travel time to work:** 17.2 minutes. **Working outside county of residence:** 11.6%.

Cities with pop over 10,000: None.

WASHINGTON COUNTY

PO Box 670　　　　　　　　**Ph:** 208-414-2092
Weiser, ID 83672　　　　　　**Fax:** 208-414-3925
www.co.washington.id.us

On the central western border of ID, north of Caldwell; organized Feb 20, 1879 (prior to statehood) from Boise County. **Name Origin:** For George Washington (1732-99), American patriot and first U.S. president.

Area (sq mi): 1473.54 (land 1456.32; water 17.23). **Pop per sq mi:** 6.9.

Pop 2005: 10,098. **State rank:** 27. **Pop change:** 2000-20005 +1.2%; 1990-2000 +16.7%. **Pop 2000:** 9,977 (White 83.1%; Black or African American 0.1%; Hispanic or Latino 13.8%; Asian 1%; Other 11.4%). **Foreign born:** 7.1%. **Median age:** 39.2.

Income 2000: per capita $15,464; median household $30,625; **Pop below poverty level:** 13.3%. ***Personal per capita income 2000-2003:** $18,407-$20,224.

Unemployment 2004: 6.7%. **Change from 2000:** -2.1%. **Median travel time to work:** 19.9 minutes. **Working outside county of residence:** 27.1%.

Cities with pop over 10,000: None.

Source: Personal per capita income data are from the Bureau of Economic Analysis; per capita income data are from the Bureau of the Census. See Introduction for explanation of differences.

Illinois

ILLINOIS STATE INFORMATION
www.illinois.gov   **Ph:** 217-782-2000

Area (sq mi): 57,914.38 (land 55,583.58; water 2330.79). **Pop per sq mi:** 229.6.

Pop 2005: 12,763,371. **Pop change:** 2000-20005 +2.8%; 1990-2000 +8.6%. **Pop 2000:** 12,419,293 (White 67.8%; Black or African American 15.1%; Hispanic or Latino 12.3%; Asian 3.4%; Other 7.9%). **Foreign born:** 12.3%. **Median age:** 34.7.

Income 2000: per capita $23,104; median household $46,590; **Pop below poverty level:** 10.7%. ***Personal per capita income 2000-2003:** $32,185-$32,965.

Unemployment 2004: 6.2%. **Change from 2000:** +1.7%. **Median travel time to work:** 28 minutes. **Working outside county of residence:** 25.2%.

ADAMS COUNTY
507 Vermont St   **Ph:** 217-277-2150
Quincy, IL 62301   **Fax:** 217-277-2155
www.co.adams.il.us

On west-central border of IL west of Springfield; organized Jan 13, 1825 from Pike County. Highland County organized from Adams and Marquette counties in 1847 and eliminated in 1848. Marquette County organized in 1843 from Adams County and eliminated in 1847. **Name Origin:** For John Quincy Adams (1767-1848), sixth U.S. president.

Area (sq mi): 871.28 (land 856.63; water 14.64). **Pop per sq mi:** 78.3.

Pop 2005: 67,040. **State rank:** 22. **Pop change:** 2000-20005 -1.8%; 1990-2000 +3.3%. **Pop 2000:** 68,277 (White 94.6%; Black or African American 3.1%; Hispanic or Latino 0.8%; Asian 0.4%; Other 1.5%). **Foreign born:** 0.8%. **Median age:** 38.3.

Income 2000: per capita $17,894; median household $34,784; **Pop below poverty level:** 10%. ***Personal per capita income 2000-2003:** $24,797-$26,515.

Unemployment 2004: 4.7%. **Change from 2000:** +0.4%. **Median travel time to work:** 16.7 minutes. **Working outside county of residence:** 7.4%.

Cities with pop over 10,000: Quincy 🏛 (39,669).

ALEXANDER COUNTY
2000 Washington Ave   **Ph:** 618-734-7000
Cairo, IL 62914   **Fax:** 618-734-7002

On the southwest border southwest of Carbondale; organized Mar 4, 1819 from Johnson County. **Name Origin:** For William M. Alexander, an early settler and IL legislator (1820-24).

Area (sq mi): 252.54 (land 236.38; water 16.16). **Pop per sq mi:** 37.8.

Pop 2005: 8,927. **State rank:** 89. **Pop change:** 2000-20005 -6.9%; 1990-2000 -9.7%. **Pop 2000:** 9,590 (White 62.2%; Black or African American 34.9%; Hispanic or Latino 1.4%; Asian 0.4%; Other 1.7%). **Foreign born:** 0.9%. **Median age:** 38.

Income 2000: per capita $16,084; median household $26,042; **Pop below poverty level:** 26.1%. ***Personal per capita income 2000-2003:** $16,887-$17,525.

Unemployment 2004: 9.7%. **Change from 2000:** +0.8%. **Median travel time to work:** 24.7 minutes. **Working outside county of residence:** 51%.

Cities with pop over 10,000: None.

BOND COUNTY
203 W College Ave   **Ph:** 618-664-0449
Greenville, IL 62246   **Fax:** 618-664-9414

In south-central IL northeast of Belleville; organized Jan 4, 1817 (prior to statehood) from Madison County. **Name Origin:** For Shadrach Bond (1773-1832), IL legislator and first governor (1818-22).

Area (sq mi): 382.67 (land 380.2; water 2.46). **Pop per sq mi:** 47.4.

Pop 2005: 18,027. **State rank:** 63. **Pop change:** 2000-20005 +2.2%; 1990-2000 +17.6%. **Pop 2000:** 17,633 (White 89.8%; Black or African American 7.4%; Hispanic or Latino 1.4%; Asian 0.3%; Other 1.6%). **Foreign born:** 0.8%. **Median age:** 36.8.

Income 2000: per capita $17,947; median household $37,680; **Pop below poverty level:** 9.3%. ***Personal per capita income 2000-2003:** $23,380-$24,306.

Unemployment 2004: 6.7%. **Change from 2000:** +1.7%. **Median travel time to work:** 24.3 minutes. **Working outside county of residence:** 45.6%.

Cities with pop over 10,000: None.

BOONE COUNTY
601 N Main St Suite 201   **Ph:** 815-547-4770
Belvidere, IL 61008   **Fax:** 815-547-3579
www.boonecountyil.org

On the north-central border of IL east of Rockford; organized Mar 4, 1837 from Winnebago County. **Name Origin:** For Daniel Boone (1734-1820), U.S. frontiersman and KY pioneer.

Area (sq mi): 281.94 (land 281.27; water 0.68). **Pop per sq mi:** 179.5.

Boone County (cont'd)

Pop 2005: 50,483. **State rank:** 30. **Pop change:** 2000-20005 +20.8%; 1990-2000 +35.6%. **Pop 2000:** 41,786 (White 85%; Black or African American 0.9%; Hispanic or Latino 12.5%; Asian 0.5%; Other 8.5%). **Foreign born:** 7.5%. **Median age:** 34.5.

Income 2000: per capita $21,590; median household $52,397; **Pop below poverty level:** 7%. *****Personal per capita income 2000-2003:** $27,993-$27,221.

Unemployment 2004: 7.6%. **Change from 2000:** +0.2%. **Median travel time to work:** 28.2 minutes. **Working outside county of residence:** 62.2%.

Cities with pop over 10,000: Belvidere ⛪ (23,797).

BROWN COUNTY

200 Court St Rm 4   **Ph:** 217-773-3421
Mount Sterling, IL 62353   **Fax:** 217-773-2233

In west-central IL east of Quincy; organized Feb 1, 1839 from Schuyler County. **Name Origin:** For Gen. Jacob Jennings Brown (1775-1828), an officer in the War of 1812 and commander of the U.S. Army (1821-28).

Area (sq mi): 307.24 (land 305.65; water 1.59). **Pop per sq mi:** 22.4.

Pop 2005: 6,835. **State rank:** 93. **Pop change:** 2000-20005 -1.7%; 1990-2000 +19.1%. **Pop 2000:** 6,950 (White 77.2%; Black or African American 18.2%; Hispanic or Latino 3.9%; Asian 0.1%; Other 1.4%). **Foreign born:** 1.6%. **Median age:** 35.2.

Income 2000: per capita $14,629; median household $35,445; **Pop below poverty level:** 8.5%. *****Personal per capita income 2000-2003:** $16,187-$18,127.

Unemployment 2004: 4.3%. **Change from 2000:** +1.3%. **Median travel time to work:** 21 minutes. **Working outside county of residence:** 30.7%.

Cities with pop over 10,000: None.

BUREAU COUNTY

700 S Main St   **Ph:** 815-875-2014
Princeton, IL 61356   **Fax:** 815-879-4803
www.bureaucounty-il.com

In north-central IL, east of Moline; organized Feb 28, 1837 from Putnam County. **Name Origin:** Anglicized version of Pierre de Bureo (Buero), a French trader with the Indians.

Area (sq mi): 873.3 (land 868.56; water 4.74). **Pop per sq mi:** 40.7.

Pop 2005: 35,330. **State rank:** 43. **Pop change:** 2000-20005 -0.5%; 1990-2000 -0.5%. **Pop 2000:** 35,503 (White 93.5%; Black or African American 0.3%; Hispanic or Latino 4.9%; Asian 0.5%; Other 2.4%). **Foreign born:** 2.6%. **Median age:** 39.6.

Income 2000: per capita $19,542; median household $40,233; **Pop below poverty level:** 7.3%. *****Personal per capita income 2000-2003:** $25,379-$26,600.

Unemployment 2004: 6.4%. **Change from 2000:** +0.9%. **Median travel time to work:** 20.3 minutes. **Working outside county of residence:** 37.8%.

Cities with pop over 10,000: None.

CALHOUN COUNTY

102 County Rd PO Box 187   **Ph:** 618-576-2351
Hardin, IL 62047   **Fax:** 618-576-2895

On west-central border of IL southwest of Springfield; organized Jan 10, 1825 from Pike County. **Name Origin:** For John Caldwell Calhoun (1782-1850), U.S. statesman and champion of Southern causes.

Area (sq mi): 283.69 (land 253.82; water 29.87). **Pop per sq mi:** 20.3.

Pop 2005: 5,163. **State rank:** 100. **Pop change:** 2000-20005 +1.6%; 1990-2000 -4.5%. **Pop 2000:** 5,084 (White 98.4%; Black or African American 0%; Hispanic or Latino 0.6%; Asian 0.2%; Other 1%). **Foreign born:** 1%. **Median age:** 40.5.

Income 2000: per capita $16,785; median household $34,375; **Pop below poverty level:** 9%. *****Personal per capita income 2000-2003:** $22,381-$22,675.

Unemployment 2004: 7.2%. **Change from 2000:** +1.6%. **Median travel time to work:** 40.4 minutes. **Working outside county of residence:** 52.1%.

Cities with pop over 10,000: None.

CARROLL COUNTY

PO Box 152   **Ph:** 815-244-0221
Mount Carroll, IL 61053   **Fax:** 815-244-3709
www.gocarrollcounty.com

On the northwest border of IL southwest of Rockford; organized Feb 22, 1839 from Jo Daviess County. **Name Origin:** For Charles Carroll (1737-1832), a signer of the Declaration of Independence, U.S. senator from MD (1789-92), and founder of the Baltimore and Ohio Railroad.

Area (sq mi): 465.77 (land 444.21; water 21.56). **Pop per sq mi:** 36.2.

Pop 2005: 16,086. **State rank:** 71. **Pop change:** 2000-20005 -3.5%; 1990-2000 -0.8%. **Pop 2000:** 16,674 (White 95.9%; Black or African American 0.5%; Hispanic or Latino 2%; Asian 0.4%; Other 2%). **Foreign born:** 1.9%. **Median age:** 40.8.

Income 2000: per capita $18,688; median household $37,148; **Pop below poverty level:** 9.6%. *****Personal per capita income 2000-2003:** $24,829-$25,516.

Unemployment 2004: 7.9%. **Change from 2000:** -0.5%. **Median travel time to work:** 23.1 minutes. **Working outside county of residence:** 37.3%.

Cities with pop over 10,000: None.

CASS COUNTY

100 E Springfield St   **Ph:** 217-452-7217
Virginia, IL 62691   **Fax:** 217-452-7219

In west-central IL, northwest of Springfield; organized Mar 3, 1837 from Morgan County. **Name Origin:** For Gen. Lewis Cass (1782-1866), OH legislator, military and civil governor of MI Territory (1913-31), U.S. secretary of war (1831-36), and U.S. secretary of state (1857-60).

Area (sq mi): 383.73 (land 375.9; water 7.83). **Pop per sq mi:** 37.

Source: Personal per capita income data are from the Bureau of Economic Analysis; per capita income data are from the Bureau of the Census. See Introduction for explanation of differences.

Cass County (cont'd)

Pop 2005: 13,898. **State rank:** 82. **Pop change:** 2000-20005 +1.5%; 1990-2000 +1.9%. **Pop 2000:** 13,695 (White 90.1%; Black or African American 0.4%; Hispanic or Latino 8.5%; Asian 0.3%; Other 4.3%). **Foreign born:** 7.8%. **Median age:** 37.2.

Income 2000: per capita $16,532; median household $35,243; **Pop below poverty level:** 12%. *****Personal per capita income 2000-2003:** $23,314-$24,087.

Unemployment 2004: 5.6%. **Change from 2000:** +1.1%. **Median travel time to work:** 22.1 minutes. **Working outside county of residence:** 36.2%.

Cities with pop over 10,000: None.

CHAMPAIGN COUNTY
1776 E Washington St   **Ph:** 217-384-3720
Urbana, IL 61802   **Fax:** 217-384-1241
www.co.champaign.il.us

In east central IL west of Danville; organized Feb 20, 1833 from Vermilion County. **Name Origin:** For the county in OH, from French *campagne* 'field, plain.'

Area (sq mi): 997.53 (land 996.81; water 0.73). **Pop per sq mi:** 185.5.

Pop 2005: 184,905. **State rank:** 11. **Pop change:** 2000-20005 +2.9%; 1990-2000 +3.8%. **Pop 2000:** 179,669 (White 77.4%; Black or African American 11.2%; Hispanic or Latino 2.9%; Asian 6.5%; Other 3.5%). **Foreign born:** 8%. **Median age:** 28.6.

Income 2000: per capita $19,708; median household $37,780; **Pop below poverty level:** 16.1%. *****Personal per capita income 2000-2003:** $25,469-$26,688.

Unemployment 2004: 4.5%. **Change from 2000:** +1.7%. **Median travel time to work:** 16.8 minutes. **Working outside county of residence:** 5.4%.

Cities with pop over 10,000: Champaign (70,306); Urbana ⛪ (39,178); Rantoul (12,604).

CHRISTIAN COUNTY
PO Box 647   **Ph:** 217-824-4969
Taylorville, IL 62568   **Fax:** 217-824-5105

In central IL southwest of Decatur; organized as Dane County Feb 15, 1839 from Sangamon County; name changed Feb 1, 1840. **Name Origin:** For the county in KY, named for Col. William Christian (1743-86), army officer, Indian fighter, and legislator; brother-in-law of Patrick Henry (1736-99).

Area (sq mi): 715.71 (land 709.06; water 6.65). **Pop per sq mi:** 49.6.

Pop 2005: 35,176. **State rank:** 44. **Pop change:** 2000-20005 -0.6%; 1990-2000 +2.8%. **Pop 2000:** 35,372 (White 95.9%; Black or African American 2.1%; Hispanic or Latino 1%; Asian 0.4%; Other 1.2%). **Foreign born:** 1.3%. **Median age:** 38.9.

Income 2000: per capita $17,937; median household $36,561; **Pop below poverty level:** 9.5%. *****Personal per capita income 2000-2003:** $23,752-$24,658.

Unemployment 2004: 6.4%. **Change from 2000:** +1.1%. **Median travel time to work:** 24.9 minutes. **Working outside county of residence:** 40.3%.

Cities with pop over 10,000: Taylorville ⛪ (11,318).

CLARK COUNTY
501 Archer Ave County Courthouse   **Ph:** 217-826-8311
Marshall, IL 62441   **Fax:** 217-826-1931
www.clarkcountyil.org

On the east-central border of IL south of Danville; organized Mar 22, 1819 from Crawford County. **Name Origin:** For Gen. George Rogers Clark (1752-1818), officer in the Revolutionary War and frontiersman in the Northwest Territory.

Area (sq mi): 504.88 (land 501.5; water 3.38). **Pop per sq mi:** 33.9.

Pop 2005: 16,976. **State rank:** 66. **Pop change:** 2000-20005 -0.2%; 1990-2000 +6.8%. **Pop 2000:** 17,008 (White 98.6%; Black or African American 0.2%; Hispanic or Latino 0.3%; Asian 0.1%; Other 0.9%). **Foreign born:** 0.6%. **Median age:** 39.2.

Income 2000: per capita $17,655; median household $35,967; **Pop below poverty level:** 9.2%. *****Personal per capita income 2000-2003:** $21,936-$23,276.

Unemployment 2004: 6.6%. **Change from 2000:** +0.9%. **Median travel time to work:** 22.4 minutes. **Working outside county of residence:** 40.8%.

Cities with pop over 10,000: None.

CLAY COUNTY
PO Box 160   **Ph:** 618-665-3626
Louisville, IL 62858   **Fax:** 618-665-3607

In east-central IL west of Olney; organized Dec 23, 1824 from Lawrence, Wayne, and Fayette counties. **Name Origin:** For Henry Clay (1777-1852), U.S. senator from KY, known as the 'Great Pacificator' for his advocacy of compromise to avert national crises.

Area (sq mi): 469.84 (land 469.25; water 0.59). **Pop per sq mi:** 30.1.

Pop 2005: 14,122. **State rank:** 81. **Pop change:** 2000-20005 -3%; 1990-2000 +0.7%. **Pop 2000:** 14,560 (White 98.2%; Black or African American 0.1%; Hispanic or Latino 0.6%; Asian 0.5%; Other 0.8%). **Foreign born:** 0.7%. **Median age:** 39.7.

Income 2000: per capita $15,771; median household $30,599; **Pop below poverty level:** 11.8%. *****Personal per capita income 2000-2003:** $21,667-$23,148.

Unemployment 2004: 6.7%. **Change from 2000:** -1%. **Median travel time to work:** 19.5 minutes. **Working outside county of residence:** 24.9%.

Cities with pop over 10,000: None.

CLINTON COUNTY
PO Box 308   **Ph:** 618-594-2464
Carlyle, IL 62231   **Fax:** 618-594-0195
www.clintonco.org

In south-central IL, east of Saint Louis, MO; organized Dec 27, 1824 from Washington, Bond, and Fayette counties. **Name Origin:** For DeWitt Clinton (1769-1828), governor of NY (1817-21; 1825-28) and supporter of the Erie Canal.

Area (sq mi): 503.48 (land 474.23; water 29.25). **Pop per sq mi:** 76.1.

Clinton County (cont'd)

Pop 2005: 36,095. **State rank:** 40. **Pop change:** 2000-20005 +1.6%; 1990-2000 +4.7%. **Pop 2000:** 35,535 (White 93.5%; Black or African American 3.9%; Hispanic or Latino 1.6%; Asian 0.3%; Other 1.5%). **Foreign born:** 1.2%. **Median age:** 36.6.

Income 2000: per capita $19,109; median household $44,618; **Pop below poverty level:** 6.4%. ***Personal per capita income 2000-2003:** $26,603-$28,789.

Unemployment 2004: 5.5%. **Change from 2000:** +0.5%. **Median travel time to work:** 25.8 minutes. **Working outside county of residence:** 49.9%.

Cities with pop over 10,000: None.

COLES COUNTY
651 Jackson Ave Rm 122   **Ph:** 217-348-0501
Charleston, IL 61920   **Fax:** 217-348-7337
www.co.coles.il.us

In east-central IL south of Urbana; organized Dec 25, 1830 from Clark and Edgar counties. **Name Origin:** For Edward Coles (1768-1868), humanitarian and IL governor (1822-26).

Area (sq mi): 510.07 (land 508.29; water 1.78). **Pop per sq mi:** 100.5.

Pop 2005: 51,065. **State rank:** 28. **Pop change:** 2000-20005 -4%; 1990-2000 +3%. **Pop 2000:** 53,196 (White 94.6%; Black or African American 2.3%; Hispanic or Latino 1.4%; Asian 0.8%; Other 1.5%). **Foreign born:** 1.6%. **Median age:** 30.8.

Income 2000: per capita $17,370; median household $32,286; **Pop below poverty level:** 17.5%. ***Personal per capita income 2000-2003:** $22,706-$23,795.

Unemployment 2004: 5.7%. **Change from 2000:** +0.4%. **Median travel time to work:** 16.6 minutes. **Working outside county of residence:** 15%.

Cities with pop over 10,000: Charleston 🏛 (20,204); Mattoon (17,671).

COOK COUNTY
118 N Clark St Rm 820   **Ph:** 312-603-4660
Chicago, IL 60602   **Fax:** 312-603-4479
www.co.cook.il.us

On the northeast border of IL bounded on east by the western shore of Lake Michigan; organized Jan 15, 1831 from Putnam County. **Name Origin:** For Daniel Pope Cook (1794-1827), first attorney general of IL and U.S. representative (1819-27).

Area (sq mi): 1635.04 (land 945.68; water 689.36). **Pop per sq mi:** 5608.3.

Pop 2005: 5,303,683. **State rank:** 1. **Pop change:** 2000-20005 -1.4%; 1990-2000 +5.3%. **Pop 2000:** 5,376,741 (White 47.6%; Black or African American 26.1%; Hispanic or Latino 19.9%; Asian 4.8%; Other 12.7%). **Foreign born:** 19.8%. **Median age:** 33.6.

Income 2000: per capita $23,227; median household $45,922; **Pop below poverty level:** 13.5%. ***Personal per capita income 2000-2003:** $33,918-$35,324.

Unemployment 2004: 6.6%. **Change from 2000:** +0.7%. **Median travel time to work:** 32.6 minutes. **Working outside county of residence:** 12.4%.

Cities with pop over 10,000: 79 (see page 34 for cities).

CRAWFORD COUNTY
PO Box 616   **Ph:** 618-546-1212
Robinson, IL 62454   **Fax:** 618-546-0140
www.crawfordcountycentral.com

On the east-central border of IL northeast of Olney; organized Dec 31, 1816 (prior to statehood) from Edwards County. **Name Origin:** For William Harris Crawford (1772-1834), U.S. senator from GA (1807-13), U.S. secretary of war (1815-16), and U.S. secretary of the treasury (1816-25).

Area (sq mi): 445.74 (land 443.53; water 2.2). **Pop per sq mi:** 44.9.

Pop 2005: 19,898. **State rank:** 59. **Pop change:** 2000-20005 -2.7%; 1990-2000 +5.1%. **Pop 2000:** 20,452 (White 92.5%; Black or African American 4.5%; Hispanic or Latino 1.7%; Asian 0.3%; Other 1.5%). **Foreign born:** 1.3%. **Median age:** 38.6.

Income 2000: per capita $16,869; median household $32,531; **Pop below poverty level:** 11.2%. ***Personal per capita income 2000-2003:** $22,158-$23,513.

Unemployment 2004: 6.5%. **Change from 2000:** +0%. **Median travel time to work:** 18.1 minutes. **Working outside county of residence:** 16.9%.

Cities with pop over 10,000: None.

CUMBERLAND COUNTY
140 Courthouse Sq PO Box 146   **Ph:** 217-849-2631
Toledo, IL 62468   **Fax:** 217-849-2968

In east-central IL south of Urbana; organized Mar 2, 1843 from Coles County. **Name Origin:** For the Cumberland Road.

Area (sq mi): 347 (land 346.02; water 0.98). **Pop per sq mi:** 31.7.

Pop 2005: 10,973. **State rank:** 87. **Pop change:** 2000-20005 -2.5%; 1990-2000 +5.5%. **Pop 2000:** 11,253 (White 98.5%; Black or African American 0.1%; Hispanic or Latino 0.6%; Asian 0.2%; Other 0.9%). **Foreign born:** 0.6%. **Median age:** 37.2.

Income 2000: per capita $16,953; median household $36,149; **Pop below poverty level:** 9.5%. ***Personal per capita income 2000-2003:** $22,974-$23,934.

Unemployment 2004: 7.1%. **Change from 2000:** +0.1%. **Median travel time to work:** 26.4 minutes. **Working outside county of residence:** 66%.

Cities with pop over 10,000: None.

DE WITT COUNTY
PO Box 439   **Ph:** 217-935-2119
Clinton, IL 61727   **Fax:** 217-935-4596
www.dewittcountyill.com

In central IL north of Decatur; organized Mar 1, 1839 from McLean and Macon counties. **Name Origin:** For DeWitt Clinton (1769-1828), governor of NY (1817-21; 1825-28) and supporter of the Erie Canal.

Area (sq mi): 405.15 (land 397.58; water 7.58). **Pop per sq mi:** 41.8.

*Source: Personal per capita income data are from the Bureau of Economic Analysis; per capita income data are from the Bureau of the Census.
See Introduction for explanation of differences.

198

De Witt County (cont'd)

Pop 2005: 16,617. **State rank:** 70. **Pop change:** 2000-20005 -1.1%; 1990-2000 +1.7%. **Pop 2000:** 16,798 (White 97.1%; Black or African American 0.5%; Hispanic or Latino 1.3%; Asian 0.3%; Other 1.4%). **Foreign born:** 1.2%. **Median age:** 38.5.

Income 2000: per capita $20,488; median household $41,256; **Pop below poverty level:** 8.2%. ***Personal per capita income 2000-2003: $25,391-$26,513.**

Unemployment 2004: 6.4%. **Change from 2000:** +0.1%. **Median travel time to work:** 21.4 minutes. **Working outside county of residence:** 44.9%.

Cities with pop over 10,000: None.

DEKALB COUNTY

110 E Sycamore St   **Ph:** 815-895-7149
Sycamore, IL 60178   **Fax:** 815-895-7148
www.dekalbcounty.org

In north-central IL, west of Chicago; organized Mar 4, 1837 from Kane County. **Name Origin:** For Johann (1721-80), Baron de Kalb, German-born French soldier who fought with the Americans during the Revolutionary War.

Area (sq mi): 634.97 (land 634.16; water 0.81). **Pop per sq mi:** 154.

Pop 2005: 97,665. **State rank:** 19. **Pop change:** 2000-20005 +9.8%; 1990-2000 +14.2%. **Pop 2000:** 88,969 (White 85.2%; Black or African American 4.6%; Hispanic or Latino 6.6%; Asian 2.3%; Other 4.6%). **Foreign born:** 5.8%. **Median age:** 28.4.

Income 2000: per capita $19,462; median household $45,828; **Pop below poverty level:** 11.4%. ***Personal per capita income 2000-2003: $26,056-$26,016.**

Unemployment 2004: 5.3%. **Change from 2000:** +1%. **Median travel time to work:** 23.8 minutes. **Working outside county of residence:** 35.7%.

Cities with pop over 10,000: DeKalb (41,532); Sycamore 🏛 (14,010).

DOUGLAS COUNTY

401 S Center St PO Box 467   **Ph:** 217-253-2411
Tuscola, IL 61953   **Fax:** 217-253-2233

In east-central IL, east of Decatur; organized Feb 8, 1859 from Coles County. **Name Origin:** For Stephen Arnold Douglas (1813-61), U.S. orator and statesman.

Area (sq mi): 417.42 (land 416.86; water 0.56). **Pop per sq mi:** 47.9.

Pop 2005: 19,950. **State rank:** 58. **Pop change:** 2000-20005 +0.1%; 1990-2000 +2.4%. **Pop 2000:** 19,922 (White 95.3%; Black or African American 0.3%; Hispanic or Latino 3.5%; Asian 0.3%; Other 2.2%). **Foreign born:** 2.5%. **Median age:** 37.4.

Income 2000: per capita $18,474; median household $39,439; **Pop below poverty level:** 6.4%. ***Personal per capita income 2000-2003: $24,412-$25,834.**

Unemployment 2004: 5.4%. **Change from 2000:** +1.5%. **Median travel time to work:** 19.8 minutes. **Working outside county of residence:** 39.8%.

Cities with pop over 10,000: None.

DUPAGE COUNTY

421 N County Farm Rd   **Ph:** 630-407-5500
Wheaton, IL 60187   **Fax:** 630-407-5501
www.dupageco.org

In northeast IL, west of Chicago; organized Feb 9, 1839 from Cook County. **Name Origin:** For the DuPage River, from the French name of a local Indian chief.

Area (sq mi): 336.55 (land 333.61; water 2.95). **Pop per sq mi:** 2785.

Pop 2005: 929,113. **State rank:** 2. **Pop change:** 2000-20005 +2.8%; 1990-2000 +15.7%. **Pop 2000:** 904,161 (White 78.7%; Black or African American 3.1%; Hispanic or Latino 9%; Asian 7.9%; Other 5%). **Foreign born:** 15.3%. **Median age:** 35.2.

Income 2000: per capita $31,315; median household $67,887; **Pop below poverty level:** 3.6%. ***Personal per capita income 2000-2003: $46,233-$44,739.**

Unemployment 2004: 4.9%. **Change from 2000:** +1.1%. **Median travel time to work:** 29 minutes. **Working outside county of residence:** 40.8%.

Cities with pop over 10,000: 24 (see page 34 for cities).

EDGAR COUNTY

115 W Court St Rm J County Courthouse   **Ph:** 217-466-7433
Paris, IL 61944   **Fax:** 217-466-7430
www.edgarcounty-il.gov

On the east-central border of IL south of Danville; organized Jan 3, 1823 from Clark County. **Name Origin:** For John Edgar; pioneer merchant and politician.

Area (sq mi): 624.18 (land 623.55; water 0.63). **Pop per sq mi:** 30.7.

Pop 2005: 19,157. **State rank:** 60. **Pop change:** 2000-20005 -2.8%; 1990-2000 +0.6%. **Pop 2000:** 19,704 (White 96.7%; Black or African American 1.8%; Hispanic or Latino 0.8%; Asian 0.2%; Other 0.9%). **Foreign born:** 0.6%. **Median age:** 39.3.

Income 2000: per capita $17,857; median household $35,203; **Pop below poverty level:** 10.5%. ***Personal per capita income 2000-2003: $23,412-$21,757.**

Unemployment 2004: 5.8%. **Change from 2000:** +1.1%. **Median travel time to work:** 19.8 minutes. **Working outside county of residence:** 29.9%.

Cities with pop over 10,000: None.

EDWARDS COUNTY

50 E Main St   **Ph:** 618-445-2115
Albion, IL 62806   **Fax:** 618-445-4941

In southeastern IL, south of Olney; organized Nov 28, 1814 (prior to statehood) from Madison and Gallatin counties. **Name Origin:** For Ninian Edwards (1775-1833), KY legislator and jurist, and territorial (1809-18) and civil (1826-30) governor of IL.

Area (sq mi): 222.66 (land 222.35; water 0.31). **Pop per sq mi:** 30.5.

Pop 2005: 6,784. **State rank:** 95. **Pop change:** 2000-20005 -2.7%; 1990-2000 -6.3%. **Pop 2000:** 6,971 (White 98.5%; Black or African American 0.1%; Hispanic or Latino 0.5%; Asian 0.4%; Other 0.6%). **Foreign born:** 0.4%. **Median age:** 40.5.

Edwards County (cont'd)

Income 2000: per capita $16,187; median household $31,816; **Pop below poverty level:** 9.8%. ***Personal per capita income 2000-2003:** $22,070-$24,985.

Unemployment 2004: 4.9%. **Change from 2000:** +0%. **Median travel time to work:** 22.5 minutes. **Working outside county of residence:** 35%.

Cities with pop over 10,000: None.

EFFINGHAM COUNTY
PO Box 628   **Ph:** 217-342-6535
Effingham, IL 62401   **Fax:** 217-342-3577
www.co.effingham.il.us

In central IL southeast of Decatur; organized Feb 15, 1831 from Fayette and Crawford counties. **Name Origin:** For either Thomas Howard (1746-91), 3rd Earl of Effingham, who supported the Americans during the Revolutionary War, or Gen. Edward Effingham, who resigned from the British Army rather than fight the colonists.

Area (sq mi): 479.9 (land 478.7; water 1.2). **Pop per sq mi:** 72.2.

Pop 2005: 34,581. **State rank:** 45. **Pop change:** 2000-20005 +0.9%; 1990-2000 +8.1%. **Pop 2000:** 34,264 (White 98.2%; Black or African American 0.2%; Hispanic or Latino 0.7%; Asian 0.3%; Other 0.9%). **Foreign born:** 1%. **Median age:** 35.7.

Income 2000: per capita $18,301; median household $39,379; **Pop below poverty level:** 8.1%. ***Personal per capita income 2000-2003:** $25,054-$26,600.

Unemployment 2004: 6.7%. **Change from 2000:** +1.6%. **Median travel time to work:** 17.4 minutes. **Working outside county of residence:** 10.1%.

Cities with pop over 10,000: Effingham 🏛 (12,413).

FAYETTE COUNTY
PO Box 401   **Ph:** 618-283-5000
Vandalia, IL 62471   **Fax:** 618-283-5004

In south-central IL, northeast of Saint Louis, MO; organized Feb 14, 1821 from Bond, Jefferson, Wayne, and Clark counties. **Name Origin:** For the Marquis de Lafayette (1757-1834), French statesman and soldier who fought with the Americans during the Revolutionary War.

Area (sq mi): 725.36 (land 716.49; water 8.87). **Pop per sq mi:** 30.3.

Pop 2005: 21,713. **State rank:** 57. **Pop change:** 2000-20005 -0.4%; 1990-2000 +4.4%. **Pop 2000:** 21,802 (White 93.5%; Black or African American 4.9%; Hispanic or Latino 0.8%; Asian 0.2%; Other 0.9%). **Foreign born:** 0.4%. **Median age:** 37.5.

Income 2000: per capita $15,357; median household $31,873; **Pop below poverty level:** 12.2%. ***Personal per capita income 2000-2003:** $18,695-$19,368.

Unemployment 2004: 8.1%. **Change from 2000:** +0.8%. **Median travel time to work:** 22.3 minutes. **Working outside county of residence:** 30.2%.

Cities with pop over 10,000: None.

FORD COUNTY
200 W State St Rm 101   **Ph:** 217-379-2721
Paxton, IL 60957   **Fax:** 217-379-3258
fordiroq.prairienet.org/ford.htm

In east-central IL, east of Bloomington; organized Feb 17, 1859 from Vermilion County. **Name Origin:** For Thomas Ford (1800-1850), jurist on the IL Supreme Court (1840) and governor (1842-46).

Area (sq mi): 486.42 (land 485.9; water 0.52). **Pop per sq mi:** 29.1.

Pop 2005: 14,157. **State rank:** 80. **Pop change:** 2000-20005 -0.6%; 1990-2000 -0.2%. **Pop 2000:** 14,241 (White 97.5%; Black or African American 0.2%; Hispanic or Latino 1.2%; Asian 0.3%; Other 1.3%). **Foreign born:** 1.1%. **Median age:** 39.4.

Income 2000: per capita $18,860; median household $38,073; **Pop below poverty level:** 7%. ***Personal per capita income 2000-2003:** $26,774-$27,799.

Unemployment 2004: 5.4%. **Change from 2000:** +0.7%. **Median travel time to work:** 21.2 minutes. **Working outside county of residence:** 42.4%.

Cities with pop over 10,000: None.

FRANKLIN COUNTY
PO Box 607   **Ph:** 618-438-3221
Benton, IL 62812   **Fax:** 618-435-3405

In south-central IL northeast of Carbondale; organized Jan 2, 1818 (prior to statehood) from White and Gallatin counties. **Name Origin:** For Benjamin Franklin (1706-90), U.S. patriot, diplomat, and statesman.

Area (sq mi): 431.4 (land 412.08; water 19.32). **Pop per sq mi:** 96.4.

Pop 2005: 39,723. **State rank:** 36. **Pop change:** 2000-20005 +1.8%; 1990-2000 -3.2%. **Pop 2000:** 39,018 (White 98.2%; Black or African American 0.2%; Hispanic or Latino 0.6%; Asian 0.2%; Other 1%). **Foreign born:** 0.7%. **Median age:** 40.3.

Income 2000: per capita $15,407; median household $28,411; **Pop below poverty level:** 16.2%. ***Personal per capita income 2000-2003:** $19,497-$21,599.

Unemployment 2004: 8.2%. **Change from 2000:** -0.4%. **Median travel time to work:** 23 minutes. **Working outside county of residence:** 41.4%.

Cities with pop over 10,000: None.

FULTON COUNTY
100 N Main St   **Ph:** 309-547-3041
Lewistown, IL 61542   **Fax:** 309-547-3326
www.outfitters.com/illinois/fulton/

In north-central IL, southwest of Peoria; organized Jan 18, 1823 from Pike County. **Name Origin:** For Robert Fulton (1765-1815), builder of the *Clermont*, the first commercially successful steamboat.

Area (sq mi): 882.59 (land 865.62; water 16.97). **Pop per sq mi:** 43.6.

Pop 2005: 37,708. **State rank:** 38. **Pop change:** 2000-20005 -1.4%; 1990-2000 +0.4%. **Pop 2000:** 38,250 (White 94.3%; Black or African American 3.6%; Hispanic or Latino 1.2%; Asian 0.2%; Other 1%). **Foreign born:** 0.8%. **Median age:** 39.2.

---

*Source: Personal per capita income data are from the Bureau of Economic Analysis; per capita income data are from the Bureau of the Census. See Introduction for explanation of differences.

Fulton County (cont'd)

Income 2000: per capita $17,373; median household $33,952; **Pop below poverty level:** 9.9%. ***Personal per capita income 2000-2003:** $22,081-$24,120.

Unemployment 2004: 7%. **Change from 2000:** -1.2%. **Median travel time to work:** 26.8 minutes. **Working outside county of residence:** 42.5%.

Cities with pop over 10,000: Canton (14,933).

GALLATIN COUNTY

PO Box 550   **Ph:** 618-269-3025
Shawneetown, IL 62984   **Fax:** 618-269-3343

On the southeast border of IL; organized Sep 14, 1812 (prior to statehood) from Randolph County. **Name Origin:** For Abraham Alfonse Albert Gallatin (1761-1849), Swiss-born U.S. representative from PA (1795-1801), U.S. secretary of treasury (1801-14), and U.S. minister to France (1815-23) and to Great Britain (1826-27).

Area (sq mi): 328.41 (land 323.73; water 4.68). **Pop per sq mi:** 19.

Pop 2005: 6,152. **State rank:** 97. **Pop change:** 2000-20005 -4.5%; 1990-2000 -6.7%. **Pop 2000:** 6,445 (White 97.9%; Black or African American 0.3%; Hispanic or Latino 0.9%; Asian 0.1%; Other 1.3%). **Foreign born:** 0.4%. **Median age:** 40.7.

Income 2000: per capita $15,575; median household $26,118; **Pop below poverty level:** 20.7%. ***Personal per capita income 2000-2003:** $20,667-$20,478.

Unemployment 2004: 7.6%. **Change from 2000:** +1.6%. **Median travel time to work:** 27.9 minutes. **Working outside county of residence:** 53%.

Cities with pop over 10,000: None.

GREENE COUNTY

519 N Main St   **Ph:** 217-942-5443
Carrollton, IL 62016   **Fax:** 217-942-9323
www.greene-county.com

In west-central IL northwest of Alton; organized Jan 20, 1821 from Madison County. **Name Origin:** For Gen. Nathanael Greene (1742-86), hero of the Revolutionary War, quartermaster general (1778-80), and commander of the Army of the South (1780).

Area (sq mi): 546.34 (land 543.09; water 3.25). **Pop per sq mi:** 26.8.

Pop 2005: 14,581. **State rank:** 78. **Pop change:** 2000-20005 -1.2%; 1990-2000 -3.6%. **Pop 2000:** 14,761 (White 97.8%; Black or African American 0.7%; Hispanic or Latino 0.5%; Asian 0.1%; Other 1%). **Foreign born:** 0.3%. **Median age:** 37.9.

Income 2000: per capita $15,246; median household $31,754; **Pop below poverty level:** 12.4%. ***Personal per capita income 2000-2003:** $18,851-$20,378.

Unemployment 2004: 6.3%. **Change from 2000:** +0.8%. **Median travel time to work:** 29 minutes. **Working outside county of residence:** 50.1%.

Cities with pop over 10,000: None.

GRUNDY COUNTY

PO Box 675   **Ph:** 815-941-3222
Morris, IL 60450   **Fax:** 815-942-2222
www.grundyco.org

In northeast IL, southwest of Chicago, established Feb 17, 1841 from La Salle County. **Name Origin:** For Felix Grundy (1777-1840), chief justice of KY Supreme Court, U.S. senator from TN (1829-38;1839-40), and U.S. Attorney General (1838-39).

Area (sq mi): 430.42 (land 419.9; water 10.52). **Pop per sq mi:** 104.4.

Pop 2005: 43,838. **State rank:** 33. **Pop change:** 2000-20005 +16.8%; 1990-2000 +16.1%. **Pop 2000:** 37,535 (White 94.6%; Black or African American 0.2%; Hispanic or Latino 4.1%; Asian 0.3%; Other 2.4%). **Foreign born:** 2.7%. **Median age:** 36.3.

Income 2000: per capita $22,591; median household $51,719; **Pop below poverty level:** 4.8%. ***Personal per capita income 2000-2003:** $28,936-$29,990.

Unemployment 2004: 7.8%. **Change from 2000:** +1.3%. **Median travel time to work:** 26.4 minutes. **Working outside county of residence:** 51.3%.

Cities with pop over 10,000: Morris 🏛 (12,479).

HAMILTON COUNTY

100 S Jackson St County Courthouse   **Ph:** 618-643-2721
McLeansboro, IL 62859

In southeastern IL northeast of Carbondale; organized Feb 8, 1821 from White County. **Name Origin:** For Alexander Hamilton (1757-1804), first U.S. secretary of the treasury (1789-95).

Area (sq mi): 435.84 (land 435.16; water 0.67). **Pop per sq mi:** 19.1.

Pop 2005: 8,301. **State rank:** 90. **Pop change:** 2000-20005 -3.7%; 1990-2000 +1.4%. **Pop 2000:** 8,621 (White 97.8%; Black or African American 0.7%; Hispanic or Latino 0.6%; Asian 0.1%; Other 0.9%). **Foreign born:** 0.4%. **Median age:** 40.6.

Income 2000: per capita $16,262; median household $30,496; **Pop below poverty level:** 12.9%. ***Personal per capita income 2000-2003:** $19,632-$21,162.

Unemployment 2004: 6.1%. **Change from 2000:** -0.8%. **Median travel time to work:** 26.8 minutes. **Working outside county of residence:** 51%.

Cities with pop over 10,000: None.

HANCOCK COUNTY

PO Box 39   **Ph:** 217-357-3911
Carthage, IL 62321

On the west-central border of IL north of Quincy; organized Jan 13, 1825 from Pike County and unorganized territory. **Name Origin:** For John Hancock (1737-93), noted signer of the Declaration of Independence; governor of MA (1780-85; 1787-93), and statesman.

Area (sq mi): 814.54 (land 794.62; water 19.92). **Pop per sq mi:** 24.1.

Pop 2005: 19,153. **State rank:** 61. **Pop change:** 2000-20005 -4.8%; 1990-2000 -5.9%. **Pop 2000:** 20,121 (White 98.3%; Black or African American 0.2%; Hispanic or Latino 0.5%; Asian 0.2%; Other 0.9%). **Foreign born:** 0.5%. **Median age:** 40.3.

🏛 *County Seat*

Hancock County (cont'd)

Income 2000: per capita $17,478; median household $36,654; **Pop below poverty level:** 8.3%. ***Personal per capita income 2000-2003:** $23,826-$24,545.

Unemployment 2004: 6.5%. **Change from 2000:** +0.3%. **Median travel time to work:** 20.8 minutes. **Working outside county of residence:** 42.7%.

Cities with pop over 10,000: None.

HARDIN COUNTY
PO Box 187   **Ph:** 618-287-2251
Elizabethtown, IL 62931   **Fax:** 618-287-2661
www.hardincountyil.org

On the southeastern border of IL; organized Mar 2, 1839 from Pope County. **Name Origin:** For the county in KY, former home of many settlers.

Area (sq mi): 181.53 (land 178.33; water 3.2). **Pop per sq mi:** 26.5.

Pop 2005: 4,718. **State rank:** 101. **Pop change:** 2000-20005 -1.7%; 1990-2000 -7.5%. **Pop 2000:** 4,800 (White 94.9%; Black or African American 2.8%; Hispanic or Latino 1.1%; Asian 0.5%; Other 1.3%). **Foreign born:** 1.6%. **Median age:** 42.1.

Income 2000: per capita $15,984; median household $27,693; **Pop below poverty level:** 18.6%. ***Personal per capita income 2000-2003:** $18,708-$20,717.

Unemployment 2004: 8.2%. **Change from 2000:** +0.7%. **Median travel time to work:** 24.4 minutes. **Working outside county of residence:** 35.8%.

Cities with pop over 10,000: None.

HENDERSON COUNTY
PO Box 308   **Ph:** 309-867-2911
Oquawka, IL 61469   **Fax:** 309-867-2033
www.outfitters.com/illinois/henderson/

On the northwestern border of IL west of Galesburg; organized Jan 20, 1841 from Warren County. **Name Origin:** For either the county in KY, former home of many settlers, or the Henderson River, which flows through the county.

Area (sq mi): 395.12 (land 378.81; water 16.31). **Pop per sq mi:** 21.

Pop 2005: 7,972. **State rank:** 91. **Pop change:** 2000-20005 -2.9%; 1990-2000 +1.4%. **Pop 2000:** 8,213 (White 97.9%; Black or African American 0.3%; Hispanic or Latino 0.9%; Asian 0.1%; Other 1.1%). **Foreign born:** 0.4%. **Median age:** 41.

Income 2000: per capita $17,456; median household $36,405; **Pop below poverty level:** 9.5%. ***Personal per capita income 2000-2003:** $22,840-$23,782.

Unemployment 2004: 7%. **Change from 2000:** +2.3%. **Median travel time to work:** 25.4 minutes. **Working outside county of residence:** 67.3%.

Cities with pop over 10,000: None.

HENRY COUNTY
307 W Center St   **Ph:** 309-937-3575
Cambridge, IL 61238
www.co.henry.il.us

In northwestern IL, southeast of Davenport; organized Jan 13, 1825 from Fulton County. **Name Origin:** For Patrick Henry (1736-99), patriot, governor of VA (1776-79; 1784-86), and statesman, famous for proclaiming, 'Give me liberty or give me death.'

Area (sq mi): 825.6 (land 823.21; water 2.38). **Pop per sq mi:** 61.5.

Pop 2005: 50,591. **State rank:** 29. **Pop change:** 2000-20005 -0.8%; 1990-2000 -0.3%. **Pop 2000:** 51,020 (White 94.9%; Black or African American 1.1%; Hispanic or Latino 2.9%; Asian 0.2%; Other 2.4%). **Foreign born:** 1.7%. **Median age:** 39.1.

Income 2000: per capita $18,716; median household $39,854; **Pop below poverty level:** 8%. ***Personal per capita income 2000-2003:** $25,527-$26,778.

Unemployment 2004: 5.7%. **Change from 2000:** -0.3%. **Median travel time to work:** 21.8 minutes. **Working outside county of residence:** 42.8%.

Cities with pop over 10,000: Kewanee (12,670).

IROQUOIS COUNTY
1001 E Grant St   **Ph:** 815-432-6960
Watseka, IL 60970   **Fax:** 815-432-3894
fordiroq.prairienet.org/iroquois.htm

On the east-central border of IL, south of Kankakee; organized Feb 26, 1833 from Vermilion County. **Name Origin:** For the Indian tribe, a French transliteration of the Algonquian name 'real adders.'

Area (sq mi): 1118.03 (land 1116.43; water 1.6). **Pop per sq mi:** 27.5.

Pop 2005: 30,677. **State rank:** 49. **Pop change:** 2000-20005 -2.1%; 1990-2000 +1.8%. **Pop 2000:** 31,334 (White 94.4%; Black or African American 0.7%; Hispanic or Latino 3.9%; Asian 0.3%; Other 3.1%). **Foreign born:** 2.4%. **Median age:** 39.6.

Income 2000: per capita $18,435; median household $38,071; **Pop below poverty level:** 8.7%. ***Personal per capita income 2000-2003:** $23,547-$24,407.

Unemployment 2004: 5.7%. **Change from 2000:** -0.7%. **Median travel time to work:** 22.9 minutes. **Working outside county of residence:** 37.5%.

Cities with pop over 10,000: None.

JACKSON COUNTY
1001 Walnut St County Courthouse   **Ph:** 618-687-7360
Murphysboro, IL 62966   **Fax:** 618-687-7359
www.co.jackson.il.us

On the southwest border of IL southeast of Saint Louis, MO; organized Jan 10, 1816 (prior to statehood) from Randolph and Johnson counties. **Name Origin:** For Andrew Jackson (1767-1845), seventh U.S. president.

Area (sq mi): 602.53 (land 588.12; water 14.4). **Pop per sq mi:** 98.5.

Pop 2005: 57,954. **State rank:** 25. **Pop change:** 2000-20005 -2.8%; 1990-2000 -2.4%. **Pop 2000:** 59,612 (White 79.6%; Black or African American 13%; Hispanic or Latino 2.4%; Asian 3%; Other 3.2%). **Foreign born:** 5.2%. **Median age:** 27.5.

Source: Personal per capita income data are from the Bureau of Economic Analysis; per capita income data are from the Bureau of the Census. See Introduction for explanation of differences.

202

Jackson County (cont'd)

Income 2000: per capita $15,755; median household $24,946; **Pop below poverty level:** 25.2%. ***Personal per capita income 2000-2003:** $21,293-$23,620.

Unemployment 2004: 5.5%. **Change from 2000:** +1.9%. **Median travel time to work:** 18.1 minutes. **Working outside county of residence:** 18%.

Cities with pop over 10,000: Carbondale (24,790).

JASPER COUNTY

204 W Washington St Suite 2
Newton, IL 62448

Ph: 618-783-3124
Fax: 618-783-4137

In east-central IL, south of Urbana; organized Feb 15, 1831 from Crawford and Clay counties. **Name Origin:** For Sgt. William Jasper (1750-79), Revolutionary War soldier from SC.

Area (sq mi): 498.02 (land 494.4; water 3.62). **Pop per sq mi:** 20.3.

Pop 2005: 10,020. **State rank:** 88. **Pop change:** 2000-20005 -1%; 1990-2000 -4.6%. **Pop 2000:** 10,117 (White 98.9%; Black or African American 0.1%; Hispanic or Latino 0.5%; Asian 0.2%; Other 0.6%). **Foreign born:** 0.2%. **Median age:** 38.1.

Income 2000: per capita $16,649; median household $34,721; **Pop below poverty level:** 9.9%. ***Personal per capita income 2000-2003:** $22,525-$23,722.

Unemployment 2004: 6.5%. **Change from 2000:** -2.2%. **Median travel time to work:** 19.8 minutes. **Working outside county of residence:** 36.9%.

Cities with pop over 10,000: None.

JEFFERSON COUNTY

100 S 10th St County Courthouse
Mount Vernon, IL 62864

Ph: 618-244-8000
Fax: 618-244-8111

In south-central IL, northeast of Carbondale; organized Mar 26, 1819 from Edwards and White counties. **Name Origin:** For Thomas Jefferson (1743-1826), U.S. patriot and statesman; third U.S. president.

Area (sq mi): 583.71 (land 570.96; water 12.76). **Pop per sq mi:** 70.8.

Pop 2005: 40,434. **State rank:** 34. **Pop change:** 2000-20005 +1%; 1990-2000 +8.2%. **Pop 2000:** 40,045 (White 89.2%; Black or African American 7.8%; Hispanic or Latino 1.3%; Asian 0.5%; Other 1.8%). **Foreign born:** 0.8%. **Median age:** 37.6.

Income 2000: per capita $16,644; median household $33,555; **Pop below poverty level:** 12.3%. ***Personal per capita income 2000-2003:** $21,618-$23,070.

Unemployment 2004: 6.1%. **Change from 2000:** -0.8%. **Median travel time to work:** 20.7 minutes. **Working outside county of residence:** 18%.

Cities with pop over 10,000: Mount Vernon ⚎ (16,337).

JERSEY COUNTY

200 N Lafayette St Suite 1
Jerseyville, IL 62052
www.jerseycounty.org

Ph: 618-498-5571
Fax: 618-498-7721

In west-central IL northwest of Alton; organized Feb 28, 1839 from Greene County. **Name Origin:** For the state of NJ.

Area (sq mi): 377.02 (land 369.16; water 7.86). **Pop per sq mi:** 60.8.

Pop 2005: 22,456. **State rank:** 55. **Pop change:** 2000-20005 +3.6%; 1990-2000 +5.5%. **Pop 2000:** 21,668 (White 97.6%; Black or African American 0.5%; Hispanic or Latino 0.7%; Asian 0.3%; Other 1.1%). **Foreign born:** 1%. **Median age:** 37.3.

Income 2000: per capita $19,581; median household $42,065; **Pop below poverty level:** 7.1%. ***Personal per capita income 2000-2003:** $25,045-$26,363.

Unemployment 2004: 5.9%. **Change from 2000:** +0%. **Median travel time to work:** 28.9 minutes. **Working outside county of residence:** 56.2%.

Cities with pop over 10,000: None.

JO DAVIESS COUNTY

330 N Bench St
Galena, IL 61036
www.jodaviess.org

Ph: 815-777-0161
Fax: 815-777-3688

On the northwestern border of IL; organized Feb 17, 1827 from Mercer, Henry, and Putnam counties. **Name Origin:** For Col. Joseph Hamilton Daviess (1774-1811), VA soldier and jurist who unsuccessfully attempted to indict Aaron Burr (1756-1836) for treason (1807). According to Jacob Piatt Dunn, 'The Colonel's name was Daveiss and he always wrote it that way"; however, the name is sometimes spelled 'Daviess' in biographical entries and in places named for him.

Area (sq mi): 618.72 (land 601.08; water 17.64). **Pop per sq mi:** 37.6.

Pop 2005: 22,580. **State rank:** 54. **Pop change:** 2000-20005 +1.3%; 1990-2000 +2.1%. **Pop 2000:** 22,289 (White 97.5%; Black or African American 0.2%; Hispanic or Latino 1.5%; Asian 0.2%; Other 0.9%). **Foreign born:** 1.7%. **Median age:** 41.6.

Income 2000: per capita $21,497; median household $40,411; **Pop below poverty level:** 6.7%. ***Personal per capita income 2000-2003:** $28,086-$30,401.

Unemployment 2004: 5.5%. **Change from 2000:** -0.1%. **Median travel time to work:** 21 minutes. **Working outside county of residence:** 38.5%.

Cities with pop over 10,000: None.

JOHNSON COUNTY

PO Box 96
Vienna, IL 62995

Ph: 618-658-3611
Fax: 618-658-2908

In south-central IL; organized Sep 14, 1812 (prior to statehood) from Randolph County. **Name Origin:** For Col. Richard Mentor Johnson (1781-1850), officer in War of 1812, U.S. senator from KY (1819-29), and U.S. vice president (1837-41).

Area (sq mi): 348.88 (land 344.63; water 4.25). **Pop per sq mi:** 38.2.

Pop 2005: 13,169. **State rank:** 84. **Pop change:** 2000-20005 +2.3%; 1990-2000 +13.5%. **Pop 2000:** 12,878 (White 81.9%; Black or

Johnson County (cont'd)

African American 14.2%; Hispanic or Latino 2.9%; Asian 0.1%; Other 2.2%). **Foreign born:** 1.5%. **Median age:** 36.7.

Income 2000: per capita $17,990; median household $33,326; **Pop below poverty level:** 11.3%. ***Personal per capita income 2000-2003:** $16,663-$18,323.

Unemployment 2004: 7.4%. **Change from 2000:** +1.9%. **Median travel time to work:** 27.1 minutes. **Working outside county of residence:** 53.6%.

Cities with pop over 10,000: None.

KANE COUNTY

719 Rt 31   **Ph:** 630-232-5950
Geneva, IL 60134   **Fax:** 630-232-5866
www.co.kane.il.us

In northeastern IL, west of Chicago; organized Jan 16, 1836 from La Salle County. **Name Origin:** For Elisha Kent Kane (1796-1835), IL legislator, jurist, and U.S. senator (1825-35).

Area (sq mi): 524.08 (land 520.44; water 3.64). **Pop per sq mi:** 926.4.

Pop 2005: 482,113. **State rank:** 5. **Pop change:** 2000-20005 +19.3%; 1990-2000 +27.3%. **Pop 2000:** 404,119 (White 67.7%; Black or African American 5.8%; Hispanic or Latino 23.7%; Asian 1.8%; Other 13.1%). **Foreign born:** 15.7%. **Median age:** 32.2.

Income 2000: per capita $24,315; median household $59,351; **Pop below poverty level:** 6.7%. ***Personal per capita income 2000-2003:** $30,677-$29,740.

Unemployment 2004: 5.9%. **Change from 2000:** +0.7%. **Median travel time to work:** 27.3 minutes. **Working outside county of residence:** 44.1%.

Cities with pop over 10,000: 7 (see page 34 for cities).

KANKAKEE COUNTY

189 E Court St   **Ph:** 815-937-2990
Kankakee, IL 60901   **Fax:** 815-939-8831
www.co.kankakee.il.us

On the northeastern border of IL, south of Chicago; organized Feb 11, 1853 from Iroquois and Will counties. **Name Origin:** For the Kankakee Indian tribe, possibly from Mohegan 'wolf' or 'wolfplace' but meaning is unclear.

Area (sq mi): 681.44 (land 676.75; water 4.7). **Pop per sq mi:** 159.5.

Pop 2005: 107,972. **State rank:** 18. **Pop change:** 2000-20005 +4%; 1990-2000 +7.9%. **Pop 2000:** 103,833 (White 77.8%; Black or African American 15.5%; Hispanic or Latino 4.8%; Asian 0.7%; Other 4%). **Foreign born:** 3.5%. **Median age:** 35.2.

Income 2000: per capita $19,055; median household $41,532; **Pop below poverty level:** 11.4%. ***Personal per capita income 2000-2003:** $24,744-$25,497.

Unemployment 2004: 7.6%. **Change from 2000:** +1.8%. **Median travel time to work:** 23.6 minutes. **Working outside county of residence:** 21.8%.

Cities with pop over 10,000: Kankakee 🏛 (26,996); Bourbonnais (16,627); Bradley (13,608).

KENDALL COUNTY

111 W Fox St   **Ph:** 630-553-4104
Yorkville, IL 60560   **Fax:** 630-553-4119
www.co.kendall.il.us

In northeastern IL, southwest of Chicago; organized Feb 19, 1841 from La Salle and Kane counties. **Name Origin:** For Amos Kendall (1789-1869), U.S. postmaster general (1835-40) and publisher of the Washington *Evening Star*.

Area (sq mi): 322.67 (land 320.58; water 2.09). **Pop per sq mi:** 248.

Pop 2005: 79,514. **State rank:** 21. **Pop change:** 2000-20005 +45.8%; 1990-2000 +38.4%. **Pop 2000:** 54,544 (White 89.2%; Black or African American 1.3%; Hispanic or Latino 7.5%; Asian 0.9%; Other 4.9%). **Foreign born:** 5.3%. **Median age:** 34.1.

Income 2000: per capita $25,188; median household $64,625; **Pop below poverty level:** 3%. ***Personal per capita income 2000-2003:** $31,144-$30,425.

Unemployment 2004: 5%. **Change from 2000:** +1%. **Median travel time to work:** 29.9 minutes. **Working outside county of residence:** 69%.

Cities with pop over 10,000: Oswego (20,946); Montgomery (10,459).

KNOX COUNTY

200 S Cherry St   **Ph:** 309-345-3860
Galesburg, IL 61401   **Fax:** 309-345-0098
www.knoxcountyil.com

In northwestern IL south of Moline; organized Jan 13, 1825 from Fulton County. **Name Origin:** For Gen. Henry Knox (1750-1806), Revolutionary War officer and first U.S. secretary of war (1785-95).

Area (sq mi): 719.7 (land 716.28; water 3.42). **Pop per sq mi:** 74.4.

Pop 2005: 53,309. **State rank:** 27. **Pop change:** 2000-20005 -4.5%; 1990-2000 -1%. **Pop 2000:** 55,836 (White 88.4%; Black or African American 6.3%; Hispanic or Latino 3.4%; Asian 0.7%; Other 3.2%). **Foreign born:** 1.6%. **Median age:** 39.4.

Income 2000: per capita $17,985; median household $35,407; **Pop below poverty level:** 11.1%. ***Personal per capita income 2000-2003:** $23,108-$24,382.

Unemployment 2004: 8.4%. **Change from 2000:** +2.7%. **Median travel time to work:** 18.2 minutes. **Working outside county of residence:** 14.9%.

Cities with pop over 10,000: Galesburg 🏛 (32,408).

LAKE COUNTY

18 N County St   **Ph:** 847-377-2000
Waukegan, IL 60085
www.co.lake.il.us

On the northeastern border of IL; organized Mar 1, 1839 from McHenry County. **Name Origin:** For Lake Michigan, which forms its eastern boundary.

Area (sq mi): 1367.95 (land 447.56; water 920.39). **Pop per sq mi:** 1570.

Pop 2005: 702,682. **State rank:** 3. **Pop change:** 2000-20005 +9.1%; 1990-2000 +24.8%. **Pop 2000:** 644,356 (White 73.4%; Black or African American 6.9%; Hispanic or Latino 14.4%; Asian 3.9%; Other 9%). **Foreign born:** 14.8%. **Median age:** 33.8.

Source: Personal per capita income data are from the Bureau of Economic Analysis; per capita income data are from the Bureau of the Census. See Introduction for explanation of differences.

Lake County (cont'd)

Income 2000: per capita $32,102; median household $66,973; **Pop below poverty level:** 5.7%. ***Personal per capita income 2000-2003:** $46,204-$45,486.

Unemployment 2004: 5.5%. **Change from 2000:** +0.9%. **Median travel time to work:** 30.1 minutes. **Working outside county of residence:** 33.1%.

Cities with pop over 10,000: 21 (see page 34 for cities).

LASALLE COUNTY

707 E Etna Rd
Ottawa, IL 61350
www.lasallecounty.org

Ph: 815-434-8205
Fax: 815-434-8319

In north-central IL southwest of Chicago; organized Jan 15, 1831 from Putnam and Vermilion counties. **Name Origin:** For Robert Cavelier (1643-87), Sieur de La Salle, French adventurer and explorer who claimed the land west of the Mississippi River for France.

Area (sq mi): 1148.04 (land 1134.92; water 13.12). **Pop per sq mi:** 99.2.

Pop 2005: 112,604. **State rank:** 16. **Pop change:** 2000-20005 +1%; 1990-2000 +4.3%. **Pop 2000:** 111,509 (White 91.9%; Black or African American 1.5%; Hispanic or Latino 5.2%; Asian 0.5%; Other 2.9%). **Foreign born:** 2.7%. **Median age:** 38.1.

Income 2000: per capita $19,185; median household $40,308; **Pop below poverty level:** 9.1%. ***Personal per capita income 2000-2003:** $25,622-$25,493.

Unemployment 2004: 7.5%. **Change from 2000:** +0.9%. **Median travel time to work:** 22.5 minutes. **Working outside county of residence:** 26.7%.

Cities with pop over 10,000: Ottawa 🏛 (18,684); Streator (13,995).

LAWRENCE COUNTY

1100 State St County Courthouse
Lawrenceville, IL 62439
www.lawrencecountyillinois.com

Ph: 618-943-2346
Fax: 618-943-5205

On the east-central border of IL east of Olney; organized Jan 16, 1821 from Crawford and Edwards counties. **Name Origin:** For Capt. James Lawrence (1781-1813), U.S. naval officer in the war with Barbary pirates near Tripoli and commander of the U.S.S. *Chesapeake* in the War of 1812, who said, 'Don't give up the ship!'

Area (sq mi): 373.94 (land 371.98; water 1.96). **Pop per sq mi:** 42.8.

Pop 2005: 15,930. **State rank:** 72. **Pop change:** 2000-20005 +3.1%; 1990-2000 -3.3%. **Pop 2000:** 15,452 (White 97.4%; Black or African American 0.8%; Hispanic or Latino 0.9%; Asian 0.1%; Other 1.1%). **Foreign born:** 0.6%. **Median age:** 40.8.

Income 2000: per capita $17,070; median household $30,361; **Pop below poverty level:** 13.7%. ***Personal per capita income 2000-2003:** $24,696-$23,334.

Unemployment 2004: 6.1%. **Change from 2000:** -0.7%. **Median travel time to work:** 20.3 minutes. **Working outside county of residence:** 36.3%.

Cities with pop over 10,000: None.

LEE COUNTY

112 E 2nd St
Dixon, IL 61021
www.leecountyillinois.com

Ph: 815-288-3309
Fax: 815-288-6492

In north-central IL south of Rockford; organized Feb 27, 1839 from Ogle County. **Name Origin:** For Richard Henry Lee (1732-1794), VA statesman, a signer of the Declaration of Independence, and U.S. senator from VA (1789-92).

Area (sq mi): 729.29 (land 725.36; water 3.92). **Pop per sq mi:** 49.2.

Pop 2005: 35,669. **State rank:** 42. **Pop change:** 2000-20005 -1.1%; 1990-2000 +4.9%. **Pop 2000:** 36,062 (White 90.5%; Black or African American 4.9%; Hispanic or Latino 3.2%; Asian 0.6%; Other 1.8%). **Foreign born:** 1.9%. **Median age:** 37.9.

Income 2000: per capita $18,650; median household $40,967; **Pop below poverty level:** 7.7%. ***Personal per capita income 2000-2003:** $23,134-$24,254.

Unemployment 2004: 5.9%. **Change from 2000:** +0.7%. **Median travel time to work:** 21.8 minutes. **Working outside county of residence:** 36.5%.

Cities with pop over 10,000: Dixon 🏛 (15,452).

LIVINGSTON COUNTY

112 W Madison St
Pontiac, IL 61764
www.livingstoncounty-il.org

Ph: 815-844-2006
Fax: 815-842-1844

In east-central IL, northeast of Peoria, organized Feb 27, 1837 from La Salle and McLean counties. **Name Origin:** For Edward Livingston (1764-1836), NY legislator, LA legislator and U.S. senator (1829-31), and U.S. secretary of state (1831-33).

Area (sq mi): 1045.43 (land 1043.76; water 1.67). **Pop per sq mi:** 37.5.

Pop 2005: 39,186. **State rank:** 37. **Pop change:** 2000-20005 -1.2%; 1990-2000 +1%. **Pop 2000:** 39,678 (White 91.1%; Black or African American 5.2%; Hispanic or Latino 2.7%; Asian 0.3%; Other 2.2%). **Foreign born:** 1.3%. **Median age:** 37.3.

Income 2000: per capita $18,347; median household $41,342; **Pop below poverty level:** 8.8%. ***Personal per capita income 2000-2003:** $25,403-$27,536.

Unemployment 2004: 5.7%. **Change from 2000:** +1.4%. **Median travel time to work:** 20.3 minutes. **Working outside county of residence:** 24.6%.

Cities with pop over 10,000: Pontiac 🏛 (11,409).

LOGAN COUNTY

601 Broadway St Rm 20
Lincoln, IL 62656
www.co.logan.il.us

Ph: 217-732-4148
Fax: 217-732-6064

In central IL, northeast of Springfield; organized Feb 15, 1839 from Sangamon County. **Name Origin:** For Dr. John Logan, an immigrant from Ireland in 1823, IL legislator, and father of John Alexander Logan (1826-86), U.S. general and statesman.

Area (sq mi): 619.01 (land 618.14; water 0.87). **Pop per sq mi:** 49.5.

🏛 *County Seat*

Logan County (cont'd)

Pop 2005: 30,603. **State rank:** 50. **Pop change:** 2000-20005 -1.9%; 1990-2000 +1.3%. **Pop 2000:** 31,183 (White 90.6%; Black or African American 6.6%; Hispanic or Latino 1.6%; Asian 0.5%; Other 1.2%). **Foreign born:** 1.4%. **Median age:** 37.

Income 2000: per capita $17,953; median household $39,389; **Pop below poverty level:** 8.1%. *Personal per capita income 2000-2003: $22,123-$22,142.

Unemployment 2004: 6.2%. **Change from 2000:** +2.1%. **Median travel time to work:** 20.3 minutes. **Working outside county of residence:** 29.8%.

Cities with pop over 10,000: Lincoln ▥ (15,078).

MACON COUNTY
141 S Main St Rm 104 **Ph:** 217-424-1305
Decatur, IL 62523 **Fax:** 217-423-0922

In central IL, east of Springfield, organized Jan 19, 1829 from Shelby County. **Name Origin:** For Nathaniel Macon (1757-1837), NC legislator, U.S. representative (1791-1815), U.S. senator (1815-28), and president of the NC constitutional convention (1835).

Area (sq mi): 585.38 (land 580.52; water 4.86). **Pop per sq mi:** 189.8.

Pop 2005: 110,167. **State rank:** 17. **Pop change:** 2000-20005 - 4%; 1990-2000 -2.1%. **Pop 2000:** 114,706 (White 82.9%; Black or African American 14.1%; Hispanic or Latino 1%; Asian 0.6%; Other 1.9%). **Foreign born:** 1.4%. **Median age:** 38.

Income 2000: per capita $20,067; median household $37,859; **Pop below poverty level:** 12.9%. *Personal per capita income 2000-2003: $27,334-$28,131.

Unemployment 2004: 7.3%. **Change from 2000:** +1%. **Median travel time to work:** 18.2 minutes. **Working outside county of residence:** 9.1%.

Cities with pop over 10,000: Decatur ▥ (78,751).

MACOUPIN COUNTY
PO Box 107 **Ph:** 217-854-3214
Carlinville, IL 62626 **Fax:** 217-854-7347
www.macoupincountyonline.net

In west-central IL, southwest of Springfield, organized Jan 17, 1829 from Madison and Greene counties. **Name Origin:** From an Algonquian Indian word probably meaning 'white potato.'

Area (sq mi): 867.61 (land 863.57; water 4.04). **Pop per sq mi:** 56.9.

Pop 2005: 49,111. **State rank:** 31. **Pop change:** 2000-20005 +0.2%; 1990-2000 +2.8%. **Pop 2000:** 49,019 (White 97.6%; Black or African American 0.8%; Hispanic or Latino 0.6%; Asian 0.2%; Other 0.9%). **Foreign born:** 0.5%. **Median age:** 38.9.

Income 2000: per capita $17,298; median household $36,190; **Pop below poverty level:** 9.4%. *Personal per capita income 2000-2003: $23,997-$25,490.

Unemployment 2004: 6.5%. **Change from 2000:** +0.6%. **Median travel time to work:** 27.1 minutes. **Working outside county of residence:** 49.5%.

Cities with pop over 10,000: None.

MADISON COUNTY
157 N Main St Suite 109 **Ph:** 618-692-6290
Edwardsville, IL 62025 **Fax:** 618-692-8903
www.co.madison.il.us

On the west-central border of IL, north of Saint Louis; organized Sep 14, 1812 (prior to statehood) from Saint Clair County. **Name Origin:** For James Madison (1751-1836), fourth U.S. president.

Area (sq mi): 740.35 (land 725.02; water 15.33). **Pop per sq mi:** 364.6.

Pop 2005: 264,309. **State rank:** 8. **Pop change:** 2000-20005 +2.1%; 1990-2000 +3.9%. **Pop 2000:** 258,941 (White 89.3%; Black or African American 7.3%; Hispanic or Latino 1.5%; Asian 0.6%; Other 1.9%). **Foreign born:** 1.3%. **Median age:** 36.9.

Income 2000: per capita $20,509; median household $41,541; **Pop below poverty level:** 9.8%. *Personal per capita income 2000-2003: $26,400-$28,415.

Unemployment 2004: 6.3%. **Change from 2000:** +0.7%. **Median travel time to work:** 24.3 minutes. **Working outside county of residence:** 38%.

Cities with pop over 10,000: 7 (see page 35 for cities).

MARION COUNTY
PO Box 637 **Ph:** 618-548-3400
Salem, IL 62881 **Fax:** 618-548-2226

In south-central IL west of Olney; organized Jan 24, 1823 from Fayette and Jefferson counties. **Name Origin:** For Gen. Francis Marion (c. 1732-95), SC soldier and legislator, know as 'The Swamp Fox' for his tactics during the Revolutionary War.

Area (sq mi): 575.71 (land 572.26; water 3.44). **Pop per sq mi:** 70.1.

Pop 2005: 40,144. **State rank:** 35. **Pop change:** 2000-20005 -3.7%; 1990-2000 +0.3%. **Pop 2000:** 41,691 (White 93.4%; Black or African American 3.8%; Hispanic or Latino 0.9%; Asian 0.6%; Other 1.5%). **Foreign born:** 0.8%. **Median age:** 38.4.

Income 2000: per capita $17,235; median household $35,227; **Pop below poverty level:** 11.3%. *Personal per capita income 2000-2003: $22,699-$23,920.

Unemployment 2004: 8.6%. **Change from 2000:** -2.2%. **Median travel time to work:** 19.8 minutes. **Working outside county of residence:** 24%.

Cities with pop over 10,000: Centralia (13,775).

MARSHALL COUNTY
PO Box 328 **Ph:** 309-246-6325
Lacon, IL 61540 **Fax:** 309-246-3667
www.co.marshall.il.us

In north-central IL north of Peoria; organized Jan 19, 1839 from Putnam County. **Name Origin:** For John Marshall (1755-1835), American jurist and fourth Chief Justice of the U.S. Supreme Court (1801-35).

Area (sq mi): 398.52 (land 386.06; water 12.45). **Pop per sq mi:** 34.2.

Pop 2005: 13,217. **State rank:** 83. **Pop change:** 2000-20005 +0.3%; 1990-2000 +2.6%. **Pop 2000:** 13,180 (White 97.6%; Black or African American 0.3%; Hispanic or Latino 1%; Asian 0.3%; Other 1.2%). **Foreign born:** 1%. **Median age:** 40.9.

Source: Personal per capita income data are from the Bureau of Economic Analysis; per capita income data are from the Bureau of the Census. See Introduction for explanation of differences.

Marshall County (cont'd)

Income 2000: per capita $19,065; median household $41,576; **Pop below poverty level:** 5.6%. ***Personal per capita income 2000-2003:** $25,864-$26,883.

Unemployment 2004: 5.1%. **Change from 2000:** +0.2%. **Median travel time to work:** 25.3 minutes. **Working outside county of residence:** 51.2%.

Cities with pop over 10,000: None.

MASON COUNTY

PO Box 77   **Ph:** 309-543-6661
Havana, IL 62644   **Fax:** 309-543-2085
www.masoncountyil.org

In central IL southwest of Peoria; organized Jan 20, 1841 from Tazewell County. **Name Origin:** For the county in KY, former home of many of the settlers.

Area (sq mi): 563.37 (land 538.94; water 24.43). **Pop per sq mi:** 29.2.

Pop 2005: 15,741. **State rank:** 74. **Pop change:** 2000-20005 -1.9%; 1990-2000 -1.4%. **Pop 2000:** 16,038 (White 98.5%; Black or African American 0.1%; Hispanic or Latino 0.5%; Asian 0.2%; Other 0.9%). **Foreign born:** 0.4%. **Median age:** 39.5.

Income 2000: per capita $17,357; median household $35,985; **Pop below poverty level:** 9.7%. ***Personal per capita income 2000-2003:** $23,968-$23,808.

Unemployment 2004: 8.2%. **Change from 2000:** +1.5%. **Median travel time to work:** 28.9 minutes. **Working outside county of residence:** 51%.

Cities with pop over 10,000: None.

MASSAC COUNTY

PO Box 429   **Ph:** 618-524-5213
Metropolis, IL 62960   **Fax:** 618-524-8514

On the southern border of IL; organized Feb 8, 1843 from Pope and Johnson counties. **Name Origin:** For Fort Massac, originally named Fort Ascension and then renamed to honor Massiac, a French naval minister. The 'i' was dropped to form the current spelling.

Area (sq mi): 242.12 (land 239.05; water 3.06). **Pop per sq mi:** 64.2.

Pop 2005: 15,348. **State rank:** 75. **Pop change:** 2000-20005 +1.2%; 1990-2000 +2.8%. **Pop 2000:** 15,161 (White 92.1%; Black or African American 5.5%; Hispanic or Latino 0.8%; Asian 0.3%; Other 1.7%). **Foreign born:** 0.4%. **Median age:** 39.6.

Income 2000: per capita $16,334; median household $31,498; **Pop below poverty level:** 13.5%. ***Personal per capita income 2000-2003:** $21,125-$23,174.

Unemployment 2004: 6%. **Change from 2000:** +1.1%. **Median travel time to work:** 21.1 minutes. **Working outside county of residence:** 42.6%.

Cities with pop over 10,000: None.

MCDONOUGH COUNTY

1 Courthouse Sq   **Ph:** 309-833-2474
Macomb, IL 61455   **Fax:** 309-836-3368
www.outfitters.com/illinois/mcdonough/

In west-central IL southwest of Peoria; organized Jan 25, 1826 from Schuyler County. **Name Origin:** For Capt. Thomas McDonough (1783-1825), naval officer in the war against Barbary pirates near Tripoli and in the War of 1812.

Area (sq mi): 590.02 (land 589.27; water 0.75). **Pop per sq mi:** 54.2.

Pop 2005: 31,966. **State rank:** 47. **Pop change:** 2000-20005 -2.9%; 1990-2000 -6.6%. **Pop 2000:** 32,913 (White 92%; Black or African American 3.5%; Hispanic or Latino 1.5%; Asian 2%; Other 1.6%). **Foreign born:** 2.8%. **Median age:** 29.

Income 2000: per capita $15,890; median household $32,141; **Pop below poverty level:** 19.8%. ***Personal per capita income 2000-2003:** $20,780-$21,066.

Unemployment 2004: 5%. **Change from 2000:** +1.9%. **Median travel time to work:** 15.6 minutes. **Working outside county of residence:** 12.2%.

Cities with pop over 10,000: Macomb ⛪ (18,782).

MCHENRY COUNTY

2200 N Seminary Ave   **Ph:** 815-334-4000
Woodstock, IL 60098   **Fax:** 815-334-8727
www.co.mchenry.il.us

On the northern border of IL, northwest of Chicago; organized Jan 16, 1836 from Cook county. **Name Origin:** For Maj. William McHenry (1774-1839), officer in the War of 1812 and the Black Hawk War (1832).

Area (sq mi): 611.13 (land 603.51; water 7.62). **Pop per sq mi:** 503.7.

Pop 2005: 303,990. **State rank:** 6. **Pop change:** 2000-20005 +16.9%; 1990-2000 +41.9%. **Pop 2000:** 260,077 (White 89.6%; Black or African American 0.6%; Hispanic or Latino 7.5%; Asian 1.5%; Other 4.1%). **Foreign born:** 7.2%. **Median age:** 34.2.

Income 2000: per capita $26,476; median household $64,826; **Pop below poverty level:** 3.7%. ***Personal per capita income 2000-2003:** $33,363-$32,959.

Unemployment 2004: 5.2%. **Change from 2000:** +0.6%. **Median travel time to work:** 32.2 minutes. **Working outside county of residence:** 48.9%.

Cities with pop over 10,000: 7 (see page 35 for cities).

MCLEAN COUNTY

115 E Washington St Rm 102   **Ph:** 309-888-5190
Bloomington, IL 61701   **Fax:** 309-888-5932
www.co.mclean.il.us

In central IL, southeast of Peoria; organized Dec 25, 1830 from Tazewell County. **Name Origin:** For John McLean (1791-1830), first U.S. representative from IL (1818-19) and U.S. senator (1824-25;1829-30).

Area (sq mi): 1186.29 (land 1183.53; water 2.76). **Pop per sq mi:** 134.4.

Pop 2005: 159,013. **State rank:** 13. **Pop change:** 2000-20005 +5.7%; 1990-2000 +16.5%. **Pop 2000:** 150,433 (White 87.9%;

Mclean County (cont'd)

Black or African American 6.2%; Hispanic or Latino 2.5%; Asian 2.1%; Other 2.6%). **Foreign born:** 3.3%. **Median age:** 30.5.

Income 2000: per capita $22,227; median household $47,021; **Pop below poverty level:** 9.7%. ***Personal per capita income 2000-2003:** $29,232-$30,511.

Unemployment 2004: 4.5%. **Change from 2000:** +2.1%. **Median travel time to work:** 17 minutes. **Working outside county of residence:** 8.4%.

Cities with pop over 10,000: Bloomington 🏛 (69,282); Normal (49,287).

MENARD COUNTY

PO Box 465   **Ph:** 217-632-2415
Petersburg, IL 62675   **Fax:** 217-632-4301
www.menardil.com

In central IL, north of Springfield; organized Feb 15, 1839 Sangamon County. **Name Origin:** For Lt. Col. Pierre Menard (1766-1844), jurist, first presiding officer of IL Territorial legislature (1812), and first lieutenant governor (1818-22).

Area (sq mi): 315.37 (land 314.25; water 1.13). **Pop per sq mi:** 40.5.

Pop 2005: 12,738. **State rank:** 85. **Pop change:** 2000-20005 +2%; 1990-2000 +11.8%. **Pop 2000:** 12,486 (White 98%; Black or African American 0.4%; Hispanic or Latino 0.8%; Asian 0.2%; Other 0.8%). **Foreign born:** 0.7%. **Median age:** 38.

Income 2000: per capita $21,584; median household $46,596; **Pop below poverty level:** 8.2%. ***Personal per capita income 2000-2003:** $27,163-$27,912.

Unemployment 2004: 5.4%. **Change from 2000:** +1%. **Median travel time to work:** 27.9 minutes. **Working outside county of residence:** 66.7%.

Cities with pop over 10,000: None.

MERCER COUNTY

PO Box 66   **Ph:** 309-582-7021
Aledo, IL 61231   **Fax:** 309-582-7022

On the western border of IL, south of Davenport, IA; organized Jan 13, 1825 from Pike County. **Name Origin:** For Gen. Hugh Mercer (1721-77), Revolutionary War officer and physician.

Area (sq mi): 568.88 (land 561.02; water 7.86). **Pop per sq mi:** 30.1.

Pop 2005: 16,912. **State rank:** 67. **Pop change:** 2000-20005 -0.3%; 1990-2000 -1.9%. **Pop 2000:** 16,957 (White 97.6%; Black or African American 0.3%; Hispanic or Latino 1.3%; Asian 0.2%; Other 1.2%). **Foreign born:** 0.6%. **Median age:** 39.5.

Income 2000: per capita $18,645; median household $40,893; **Pop below poverty level:** 7.8%. ***Personal per capita income 2000-2003:** $24,534-$26,040.

Unemployment 2004: 6.9%. **Change from 2000:** +0.4%. **Median travel time to work:** 27.8 minutes. **Working outside county of residence:** 59.5%.

Cities with pop over 10,000: None.

MONROE COUNTY

100 S Main St   **Ph:** 618-939-8681
Waterloo, IL 62298   **Fax:** 618-939-8639

On the southwest border of IL, south of Saint Louis, MO; organized Jan 6, 1816 (prior to statehood) from Randolph and Saint Clair counties. **Name Origin:** For James Monroe (1758-1831), fifth U.S. president.

Area (sq mi): 397.71 (land 388.29; water 9.42). **Pop per sq mi:** 79.9.

Pop 2005: 31,040. **State rank:** 48. **Pop change:** 2000-20005 +12.4%; 1990-2000 +23.2%. **Pop 2000:** 27,619 (White 98.3%; Black or African American 0.1%; Hispanic or Latino 0.7%; Asian 0.3%; Other 0.9%). **Foreign born:** 0.8%. **Median age:** 37.5.

Income 2000: per capita $22,954; median household $55,320; **Pop below poverty level:** 3.4%. ***Personal per capita income 2000-2003:** $30,775-$31,603.

Unemployment 2004: 4.6%. **Change from 2000:** +0.6%. **Median travel time to work:** 29.4 minutes. **Working outside county of residence:** 62.7%.

Cities with pop over 10,000: None.

MONTGOMERY COUNTY

PO Box 595   **Ph:** 217-532-9530
Hillsboro, IL 62049   **Fax:** 217-532-9581
www.montgomeryco.com

In central IL, south of Springfield; organized Feb 12, 1821 from Bond and Madison counties. **Name Origin:** For Gen. Richard Montgomery (1736-75), American Revolutionary War officer who captured Montreal, Canada.

Area (sq mi): 709.75 (land 703.8; water 5.96). **Pop per sq mi:** 43.2.

Pop 2005: 30,396. **State rank:** 51. **Pop change:** 2000-20005 -0.8%; 1990-2000 -0.2%. **Pop 2000:** 30,652 (White 94.4%; Black or African American 3.7%; Hispanic or Latino 1.1%; Asian 0.2%; Other 1.2%). **Foreign born:** 0.9%. **Median age:** 38.1.

Income 2000: per capita $16,272; median household $33,123; **Pop below poverty level:** 13.4%. ***Personal per capita income 2000-2003:** $21,677-$22,164.

Unemployment 2004: 8.3%. **Change from 2000:** +1.6%. **Median travel time to work:** 24.8 minutes. **Working outside county of residence:** 30.8%.

Cities with pop over 10,000: None.

MORGAN COUNTY

PO Box 1387   **Ph:** 217-243-8581
Jacksonville, IL 62651   **Fax:** 217-243-8368
www.morgancounty-il.com

In west-central IL, west of Springfield; organized Jan 31, 1823 from Sangamon County. **Name Origin:** For Gen. Daniel Morgan (1732-1802), an officer in the Revolutionary War and U.S. representative from VA (1797-99).

Area (sq mi): 572.26 (land 568.76; water 3.51). **Pop per sq mi:** 62.8.

Pop 2005: 35,722. **State rank:** 41. **Pop change:** 2000-20005 -2.4%; 1990-2000 +0.6%. **Pop 2000:** 36,616 (White 91.7%; Black or African American 5.4%; Hispanic or Latino 1.4%; Asian 0.5%; Other 1.9%). **Foreign born:** 1.1%. **Median age:** 37.8.

*Source: Personal per capita income data are from the Bureau of Economic Analysis; per capita income data are from the Bureau of the Census. See Introduction for explanation of differences.

208

Morgan County (cont'd)

Income 2000: per capita $18,205; median household $36,933; **Pop below poverty level:** 9.7%. *****Personal per capita income 2000-2003:** $22,813-$24,134.

Unemployment 2004: 6.4%. **Change from 2000:** +2%. **Median travel time to work:** 19.3 minutes. **Working outside county of residence:** 21.2%.

Cities with pop over 10,000: Jacksonville 🏛 (19,674).

MOULTRIE COUNTY

County Courthouse 10 S Main St Suite 6   **Ph:** 217-728-4389
Sullivan, IL 61951   **Fax:** 217-728-8178

In central IL southwest of Decatur; organized Feb 16, 1843 from Macon and Shelby counties. **Name Origin:** For Gen. William Moultrie (1731-1805), an officer in the Revolutionary War and governor of SC (1785-87; 1792-94).

Area (sq mi): 344.47 (land 335.6; water 8.87). **Pop per sq mi:** 43.2.

Pop 2005: 14,510. **State rank:** 79. **Pop change:** 2000-20005 +1.6%; 1990-2000 +2.6%. **Pop 2000:** 14,287 (White 98.5%; Black or African American 0.2%; Hispanic or Latino 0.5%; Asian 0.1%; Other 0.8%). **Foreign born:** 0.6%. **Median age:** 38.7.

Income 2000: per capita $18,562; median household $40,084; **Pop below poverty level:** 7.8%. *****Personal per capita income 2000-2003:** $23,194-$23,668.

Unemployment 2004: 5.3%. **Change from 2000:** +0.8%. **Median travel time to work:** 21.4 minutes. **Working outside county of residence:** 47.6%.

Cities with pop over 10,000: None.

OGLE COUNTY

PO Box 357   **Ph:** 815-732-3201
Oregon, IL 61061   **Fax:** 815-732-6273
www.oglecounty.org

In north-central IL south of Rockford; organized Jan 16, 1836 from Jo Daviess County. **Name Origin:** For Lt. Joseph Ogle, first Methodist layman in IL and captain of the territorial militia.

Area (sq mi): 763.27 (land 758.83; water 4.43). **Pop per sq mi:** 71.5.

Pop 2005: 54,290. **State rank:** 26. **Pop change:** 2000-20005 +6.4%; 1990-2000 +11%. **Pop 2000:** 51,032 (White 92.2%; Black or African American 0.4%; Hispanic or Latino 6%; Asian 0.4%; Other 3.8%). **Foreign born:** 4.3%. **Median age:** 37.2.

Income 2000: per capita $20,515; median household $45,448; **Pop below poverty level:** 7.1%. *****Personal per capita income 2000-2003:** $25,981-$26,063.

Unemployment 2004: 6.5%. **Change from 2000:** +1.1%. **Median travel time to work:** 22.8 minutes. **Working outside county of residence:** 42.8%.

Cities with pop over 10,000: None.

PEORIA COUNTY

324 Main St Rm 101   **Ph:** 309-672-6059
Peoria, IL 61602   **Fax:** 309-672-6063
www.co.peoria.il.us

In central IL, east of Galesburg; organized Jan 13, 1825 from Fulton County., **Name Origin:** For the Peoria tribe of the Illinois nation; anglicized from French *peourea*, a transliteration of an Illinois word. Meaning of name is in dispute; possibly 'carriers' or 'ones who are carrying packs.'

Area (sq mi): 630.89 (land 619.52; water 11.36). **Pop per sq mi:** 294.3.

Pop 2005: 182,328. **State rank:** 12. **Pop change:** 2000-20005 -0.6%; 1990-2000 +0.3%. **Pop 2000:** 183,433 (White 78.5%; Black or African American 16.1%; Hispanic or Latino 2.1%, Asian 1.7%, Other 2.8%). **Foreign born:** 3.2%. **Median age:** 36.

Income 2000: per capita $21,219; median household $39,978; **Pop below poverty level:** 13.7%. *****Personal per capita income 2000-2003:** $28,151-$29,435.

Unemployment 2004: 6%. **Change from 2000:** +0.9%. **Median travel time to work:** 18.6 minutes. **Working outside county of residence:** 15.2%.

Cities with pop over 10,000: Peoria 🏛 (112,720).

PERRY COUNTY

PO Box 438   **Ph:** 618-357-5116
Pinckneyville, IL 62274   **Fax:** 618-357-3194
www.perrycountyil.org

In south-central IL north of Carbondale; organized Jan 29, 1827 from Randolph and Jackson counties. **Name Origin:** For Oliver Hazard Perry (1785-1819), U.S. naval officer during the War of 1812, famous for the message, 'We have met the enemy and they are ours.'

Area (sq mi): 446.81 (land 440.96; water 5.85). **Pop per sq mi:** 51.7.

Pop 2005: 22,815. **State rank:** 53. **Pop change:** 2000-20005 -1.2%; 1990-2000 +7.9%. **Pop 2000:** 23,094 (White 89%; Black or African American 8%; Hispanic or Latino 1.8%; Asian 0.3%; Other 2.1%). **Foreign born:** 1%. **Median age:** 37.6.

Income 2000: per capita $15,935; median household $33,281; **Pop below poverty level:** 13.2%. *****Personal per capita income 2000-2003:** $17,838-$19,334.

Unemployment 2004: 7.8%. **Change from 2000:** -1%. **Median travel time to work:** 23.4 minutes. **Working outside county of residence:** 40.5%.

Cities with pop over 10,000: None.

PIATT COUNTY

PO Box 558   **Ph:** 217-762-9487
Monticello, IL 61856   **Fax:** 217-762-7563
www.piattcounty.org

In central IL, west of Urbana, organized Jan 27, 1841 from De Wiltt and Macon counties. **Name Origin:** For either James A. Piatt, Sr. (1789-1838), an early settler, or Benjamin Piatt, attorney general of IL Territory (1810-13).

Area (sq mi): 440.33 (land 440.02; water 0.31). **Pop per sq mi:** 37.9.

Pop 2005: 16,680. **State rank:** 69. **Pop change:** 2000-20005 +1.9%; 1990-2000 +5.3%. **Pop 2000:** 16,365 (White 98.3%; Black or African American 0.2%; Hispanic or Latino 0.6%; Asian 0.1%; Other 0.8%). **Foreign born:** 0.6%. **Median age:** 39.6.

🏛 *County Seat*

Piatt County (cont'd)

Income 2000: per capita $21,075; median household $45,752; **Pop below poverty level:** 5%. ***Personal per capita income 2000-2003:** $29,742-$29,878.

Unemployment 2004: 5%. **Change from 2000:** +1.2%. **Median travel time to work:** 23.6 minutes. **Working outside county of residence:** 58.7%.

Cities with pop over 10,000: None.

PIKE COUNTY
100 E Washington St Courthouse   **Ph:** 217-285-6812
Pittsfield, IL 62363   **Fax:** 217-285-5820
www.pikeil.org

On the west-central border of IL, south of Quincy; organized Jan 31, 1821 from Madison, Bond, and Clark counties. **Name Origin:** For Zebulon Montgomery Pike (1779-1813), U.S. army officer and discoverer of Pikes Peak in CO.

Area (sq mi): 848.87 (land 830.3; water 18.57). **Pop per sq mi:** 20.6.

Pop 2005: 17,099. **State rank:** 65. **Pop change:** 2000-20005 -1.6%; 1990-2000 -1.1%. **Pop 2000:** 17,384 (White 97%; Black or African American 1.5%; Hispanic or Latino 0.5%; Asian 0.2%; Other 0.9%). **Foreign born:** 1.1%. **Median age:** 39.8.

Income 2000: per capita $15,946; median household $31,127; **Pop below poverty level:** 12.4%. ***Personal per capita income 2000-2003:** $20,524-$22,676.

Unemployment 2004: 5.8%. **Change from 2000:** +0.1%. **Median travel time to work:** 24.5 minutes. **Working outside county of residence:** 34.5%.

Cities with pop over 10,000: None.

POPE COUNTY
PO Box 216   **Ph:** 618-683-4466
Golconda, IL 62938   **Fax:** 618-683-4466

On the southeastern border of IL; organized Jan 10, 1816 (prior to statehood) from Johnson and Gallatin counties. **Name Origin:** For Nathaniel Pope (1784-1850), first territorial secretary of IL Territory (1809-16) and U.S. district judge for IL (1819-50).

Area (sq mi): 374.64 (land 370.86; water 3.77). **Pop per sq mi:** 11.4.

Pop 2005: 4,211. **State rank:** 102. **Pop change:** 2000-20005 -4.6%; 1990-2000 +0.9%. **Pop 2000:** 4,413 (White 93%; Black or African American 3.8%; Hispanic or Latino 0.9%; Asian 0.3%; Other 2.7%). **Foreign born:** 0.7%. **Median age:** 41.1.

Income 2000: per capita $16,440; median household $30,048; **Pop below poverty level:** 18.2%. ***Personal per capita income 2000-2003:** $18,382-$19,325.

Unemployment 2004: 8.3%. **Change from 2000:** -0.3%. **Median travel time to work:** 30.4 minutes. **Working outside county of residence:** 59.9%.

Cities with pop over 10,000: None.

PULASKI COUNTY
PO Box 118   **Ph:** 618-748-9360
Mound City, IL 62963   **Fax:** 618-748-9305

On the southern border of IL; organized Mar 3, 1843 from Johnson

County. **Name Origin:** For Count Casimir Pulaski (1747-79), Polish soldier who fought for America during the Revolutionary War.

Area (sq mi): 203.33 (land 200.79; water 2.55). **Pop per sq mi:** 33.8.

Pop 2005: 6,794. **State rank:** 94. **Pop change:** 2000-20005 -7.5%; 1990-2000 -2.3%. **Pop 2000:** 7,348 (White 65.9%; Black or African American 31%; Hispanic or Latino 1.5%; Asian 0.9%; Other 1.5%). **Foreign born:** 0.7%. **Median age:** 37.7.

Income 2000: per capita $13,325; median household $25,361; **Pop below poverty level:** 24.7%. ***Personal per capita income 2000-2003:** $16,867-$18,882.

Unemployment 2004: 9.4%. **Change from 2000:** +0%. **Median travel time to work:** 25.8 minutes. **Working outside county of residence:** 54.6%.

Cities with pop over 10,000: None.

PUTNAM COUNTY
PO Box 236   **Ph:** 815-925-7129
Hennepin, IL 61327   **Fax:** 815-925-7549

In north-central IL, northeast of Peoria; organized Jan 13, 1825 from Fulton County. **Name Origin:** For Gen. Israel Putnam (1718-90), Revolutionary War officer and American commander at Battle of Bunker Hill.

Area (sq mi): 172.24 (land 159.8; water 12.45). **Pop per sq mi:** 38.1.

Pop 2005: 6,094. **State rank:** 98. **Pop change:** 2000-20005 +0.1%; 1990-2000 +6.2%. **Pop 2000:** 6,086 (White 95.6%; Black or African American 0.6%; Hispanic or Latino 2.8%; Asian 0.3%; Other 1.4%). **Foreign born:** 1.8%. **Median age:** 39.6.

Income 2000: per capita $19,792; median household $45,492; **Pop below poverty level:** 5.5%. ***Personal per capita income 2000-2003:** $25,003-$26,358.

Unemployment 2004: 6.8%. **Change from 2000:** +0.6%. **Median travel time to work:** 23.8 minutes. **Working outside county of residence:** 60%.

Cities with pop over 10,000: None.

RANDOLPH COUNTY
1 Taylor St   **Ph:** 618-826-2510
Chester, IL 62233   **Fax:** 618-826-3750

On the southwestern border of IL; organized Oct 5, 1795 (prior to statehood) from Saint Clair County. **Name Origin:** For Edmund Jennings Randolph (1753-1813), governor of VA (1786-88), first U.S. Attorney General (1789), and U.S. secretary of state (1794-95).

Area (sq mi): 597.26 (land 578.42; water 18.84). **Pop per sq mi:** 57.3.

Pop 2005: 33,122. **State rank:** 46. **Pop change:** 2000-20005 -2.3%; 1990-2000 -2%. **Pop 2000:** 33,893 (White 88.1%; Black or African American 9.3%; Hispanic or Latino 1.5%; Asian 0.2%; Other 1.8%). **Foreign born:** 0.8%. **Median age:** 37.6.

Income 2000: per capita $17,696; median household $37,013; **Pop below poverty level:** 10%. ***Personal per capita income 2000-2003:** $19,854-$21,169.

Unemployment 2004: 6.1%. **Change from 2000:** +0.4%. **Median travel time to work:** 22.9 minutes. **Working outside county of residence:** 30.7%.

Randolph County (cont'd)

Cities with pop over 10,000: None.

RICHLAND COUNTY
103 W Main St   **Ph:** 618-392-3111
Olney, IL 62450   **Fax:** 618-393-4005

In southeastern IL; organized Feb 24, 1841 from Clay and Lawrence counties. **Name Origin:** For the county in OH.

Area (sq mi): 362.01 (land 360.14; water 1.87). **Pop per sq mi:** 43.9.

Pop 2005: 15,798. **State rank:** 73. **Pop change:** 2000-20005 -2.2%; 1990-2000 -2.4%. **Pop 2000:** 16,149 (White 97.7%; Black or African American 0.3%; Hispanic or Latino 0.8%; Asian 0.6%; Other 0.9%). **Foreign born:** 0.6%. **Median age:** 39.1.

Income 2000: per capita $16,847; median household $31,185; **Pop below poverty level:** 12.9%. *Personal per capita income 2000-2003:** $23,041-$22,919.

Unemployment 2004: 6.6%. **Change from 2000:** -0.2%. **Median travel time to work:** 16.1 minutes. **Working outside county of residence:** 18.7%.

Cities with pop over 10,000: None.

ROCK ISLAND COUNTY
1504 3rd Ave   **Ph:** 309-786-4451
Rock Island, IL 61201
www.co.rock-island.il.us

On the northwestern border of IL; organized Feb 9, 1831 from Jo Daviess County. **Name Origin:** For an island in the Mississippi River near the mouth of the Rock River.

Area (sq mi): 451.16 (land 426.75; water 24.4). **Pop per sq mi:** 346.4.

Pop 2005: 147,808. **State rank:** 14. **Pop change:** 2000-20005 -1%; 1990-2000 +0.4%. **Pop 2000:** 149,374 (White 81.5%; Black or African American 7.5%; Hispanic or Latino 8.6%; Asian 1%; Other 6%). **Foreign born:** 4.6%. **Median age:** 37.8.

Income 2000: per capita $20,164; median household $38,608; **Pop below poverty level:** 10.7%. *Personal per capita income 2000-2003:** $26,716-$27,695.

Unemployment 2004: 5.6%. **Change from 2000:** +0.2%. **Median travel time to work:** 18.7 minutes. **Working outside county of residence:** 24.3%.

Cities with pop over 10,000: Moline (42,927); Rock Island 🏛 (38,807); East Moline (21,114).

SAINT CLAIR COUNTY
10 Public Sq   **Ph:** 618-277-6600
Belleville, IL 62220   **Fax:** 618-277-8783
co.st-clair.il.us

On the west-central border of IL, east of Saint Louis, MO; organized Apr 27, 1790 (prior to statehood) from Northwest Territory. **Name Origin:** For Gen. Arthur Saint Clair (1736?-1818), an officer in the French and Indian War and the Revolutionary War, president of the Continental Congress (1787), and governor of the Northwest Territory (1788-1802).

Area (sq mi): 673.95 (land 663.81; water 10.15). **Pop per sq mi:** 391.8.

Pop 2005: 260,067. **State rank:** 9. **Pop change:** 2000-20005 +1.6%; 1990-2000 -2.6%. **Pop 2000:** 256,082 (White 66.8%; Black or African American 28.8%; Hispanic or Latino 2.2%; Asian 0.9%; Other 2.4%). **Foreign born:** 2.1%. **Median age:** 35.3.

Income 2000: per capita $18,932; median household $39,148; **Pop below poverty level:** 14.5%. *Personal per capita income 2000-2003:** $25,158-$27,324.

Unemployment 2004: 7.1%. **Change from 2000:** +0.9%. **Median travel time to work:** 24.7 minutes. **Working outside county of residence:** 38%.

Cities with pop over 10,000: 6 (see page 35 for cities).

SALINE COUNTY
10 E Poplar St   **Ph:** 618-253-8197
Harrisburg, IL 62946   **Fax:** 618-252-3073

In southeastern IL, east of Carbondale; organized Feb 25, 1847 from Gallatin County. **Name Origin:** For the Saline River, which traverses the county.

Area (sq mi): 386.98 (land 383.31; water 3.67). **Pop per sq mi:** 68.

Pop 2005: 26,072. **State rank:** 52. **Pop change:** 2000-20005 -2.5%; 1990-2000 +0.7%. **Pop 2000:** 26,733 (White 93.6%; Black or African American 4.1%; Hispanic or Latino 1%; Asian 0.2%; Other 1.6%). **Foreign born:** 0.7%. **Median age:** 39.9.

Income 2000: per capita $15,590; median household $28,768; **Pop below poverty level:** 14.2%. *Personal per capita income 2000-2003:** $20,522-$22,123.

Unemployment 2004: 7.3%. **Change from 2000:** +0.2%. **Median travel time to work:** 21.8 minutes. **Working outside county of residence:** 25%.

Cities with pop over 10,000: None.

SANGAMON COUNTY
200 S 9th St   **Ph:** 217-753-6706
Springfield, IL 62701   **Fax:** 217-535-3233
www.co.sangamon.il.us

In central IL, east of Decatur; organized Jan 30, 1821 from Bond and Madison counties. **Name Origin:** For the Sangamon River, which flows through the county; from Ojibway, possibly 'the outlet' or 'the land of plenty to eat.'

Area (sq mi): 877.01 (land 868.18; water 8.82). **Pop per sq mi:** 222.1.

Pop 2005: 192,789. **State rank:** 10. **Pop change:** 2000-20005 +2%; 1990-2000 +5.9%. **Pop 2000:** 188,951 (White 86.8%; Black or African American 9.7%; Hispanic or Latino 1.1%; Asian 1.1%; Other 1.8%). **Foreign born:** 1.9%. **Median age:** 37.3.

Income 2000: per capita $23,173; median household $42,957; **Pop below poverty level:** 9.3%. *Personal per capita income 2000-2003:** $29,914-$31,118.

Unemployment 2004: 5.5%. **Change from 2000:** +1.6%. **Median travel time to work:** 19 minutes. **Working outside county of residence:** 5.3%.

Cities with pop over 10,000: Springfield 🏛 (114,738).

SCHUYLER COUNTY

PO Box 200   **Ph:** 217-322-4734
Rushville, IL 62681   **Fax:** 217-322-6164

In west-central IL, northeast of Quincy; organized Jan 13, 1825 from Pike and Fulton counties. **Name Origin:** For Gen. Philip John Schuyler (1733-1804), an officer in the Revolutionary War, member of the Continental Congress (1775-77; 1778-81), and U.S. senator from NY (1789-91; 1797-98).

Area (sq mi): 441.39 (land 437.31; water 4.07). **Pop per sq mi:** 16.2.

Pop 2005: 7,073. **State rank:** 92. **Pop change:** 2000-20005 -1.6%; 1990-2000 -4.1%. **Pop 2000:** 7,189 (White 98.6%; Black or African American 0.2%; Hispanic or Latino 0.5%; Asian 0.1%; Other 0.9%). **Foreign born:** 0.4%. **Median age:** 40.9.

Income 2000: per capita $17,158; median household $35,233; **Pop below poverty level:** 10.1%. *****Personal per capita income 2000-2003:** $23,017-$25,692.

Unemployment 2004: 5.5%. **Change from 2000:** +1.1%. **Median travel time to work:** 21.8 minutes. **Working outside county of residence:** 47%.

Cities with pop over 10,000: None.

SCOTT COUNTY

County Courthouse 35 E Market St   **Ph:** 217-742-3178
Winchester, IL 62694

In west-central IL, southwest of Springfield; organized Feb 16, 1839 from Morgan County. **Name Origin:** For the county in KY.

Area (sq mi): 252.77 (land 250.92; water 1.85). **Pop per sq mi:** 21.6.

Pop 2005: 5,412. **State rank:** 99. **Pop change:** 2000-20005 -2.3%; 1990-2000 -1.9%. **Pop 2000:** 5,537 (White 99.3%; Black or African American 0%; Hispanic or Latino 0.2%; Asian 0.1%; Other 0.3%). **Foreign born:** 0.5%. **Median age:** 38.8.

Income 2000: per capita $16,998; median household $36,566; **Pop below poverty level:** 9.7%. *****Personal per capita income 2000-2003:** $20,454-$20,583.

Unemployment 2004: 7.1%. **Change from 2000:** +1.7%. **Median travel time to work:** 24.7 minutes. **Working outside county of residence:** 61%.

Cities with pop over 10,000: None.

SHELBY COUNTY

PO Box 230   **Ph:** 217-774-4421
Shelbyville, IL 62565   **Fax:** 217-774-5291

In central IL, south of Decatur; organized Jan 23, 1827 from Fayette County. **Name Origin:** For Gen. Isaac Shelby (1750-1826), officer in the Revolutionary War, NC legislator, and governor of KY (1792-96; 1812-16).

Area (sq mi): 768.05 (land 758.51; water 9.54). **Pop per sq mi:** 29.4.

Pop 2005: 22,322. **State rank:** 56. **Pop change:** 2000-20005 -2.5%; 1990-2000 +2.8%. **Pop 2000:** 22,893 (White 98.6%; Black or African American 0.2%; Hispanic or Latino 0.5%; Asian 0.2%; Other 0.6%). **Foreign born:** 0.4%. **Median age:** 39.3.

Income 2000: per capita $17,313; median household $37,313; **Pop below poverty level:** 9.1%. *****Personal per capita income 2000-2003:** $21,953-$22,027.

Unemployment 2004: 6.4%. **Change from 2000:** +0.3%. **Median travel time to work:** 26.6 minutes. **Working outside county of residence:** 49.7%.

Cities with pop over 10,000: None.

STARK COUNTY

PO Box 97   **Ph:** 309-286-5911
Toulon, IL 61483   **Fax:** 309-286-4039
www.outfitters.com/illinois/stark/

In central IL, north of Peoria; organized Mar 2, 1839 from Knox and Putnam counties. **Name Origin:** For Gen. John Stark (1728-1822), officer in the French and Indian War and the Revolutionary War.

Area (sq mi): 288.21 (land 287.94; water 0.28). **Pop per sq mi:** 21.4.

Pop 2005: 6,169. **State rank:** 96. **Pop change:** 2000-20005 -2.6%; 1990-2000 -3.1%. **Pop 2000:** 6,332 (White 98.1%; Black or African American 0.1%; Hispanic or Latino 0.9%; Asian 0.2%; Other 1.1%). **Foreign born:** 0.4%. **Median age:** 39.9.

Income 2000: per capita $16,767; median household $35,826; **Pop below poverty level:** 8.6%. *****Personal per capita income 2000-2003:** $25,143-$24,934.

Unemployment 2004: 7.1%. **Change from 2000:** -0.9%. **Median travel time to work:** 25.3 minutes. **Working outside county of residence:** 57.6%.

Cities with pop over 10,000: None.

STEPHENSON COUNTY

15 N Galena Ave Suite 1   **Ph:** 815-235-8289
Freeport, IL 61032   **Fax:** 815-235-8378
www.co.stephenson.il.us

Located on northern border of IL; organized on Mar 4, 1837 from Winnebago and Jo Daviess counties. **Name Origin:** For Benjamin Stephenson (?-1821), adjutant general of IL Territory (1813), IL legislator, and prominent banker.

Area (sq mi): 564.72 (land 564.18; water 0.54). **Pop per sq mi:** 85.

Pop 2005: 47,965. **State rank:** 32. **Pop change:** 2000-20005 -2.1%; 1990-2000 +1.9%. **Pop 2000:** 48,979 (White 88.6%; Black or African American 7.7%; Hispanic or Latino 1.5%; Asian 0.7%; Other 2.3%). **Foreign born:** 1.9%. **Median age:** 38.5.

Income 2000: per capita $19,794; median household $40,366; **Pop below poverty level:** 9%. *****Personal per capita income 2000-2003:** $26,800-$28,069.

Unemployment 2004: 7.1%. **Change from 2000:** +0%. **Median travel time to work:** 19.9 minutes. **Working outside county of residence:** 20.4%.

Cities with pop over 10,000: Freeport 🏛 (25,771).

TAZEWELL COUNTY

11 S 4th St   **Ph:** 309-477-2264
Pekin, IL 61554   **Fax:** 309-477-2244
www.tazewell.com

In central IL, south of Peoria; organized Jan 31, 1827 from Fayette County. **Name Origin:** For Littleton Waller Tazewell (1774-1860), VA legislator, U.S. senator (1824-32), and governor (1834-36).

Source: Personal per capita income data are from the Bureau of Economic Analysis; per capita income data are from the Bureau of the Census. See Introduction for explanation of differences.

Tazewell County (cont'd)

Area (sq mi): 657.89 (land 648.86; water 9.03). **Pop per sq mi:** 200.3.

Pop 2005: 129,999. **State rank:** 15. **Pop change:** 2000-20005 +1.2%; 1990-2000 +3.9%. **Pop 2000:** 128,485 (White 96.7%; Black or African American 0.9%; Hispanic or Latino 1%; Asian 0.5%; Other 1.3%). **Foreign born:** 1.1%. **Median age:** 38.1.

Income 2000: per capita $21,511; median household $45,250; **Pop below poverty level:** 6.3%. ***Personal per capita income 2000-2003:** $28,246-$29,584.

Unemployment 2004: 5.7%. **Change from 2000:** +1.2%. **Median travel time to work:** 20.6 minutes. **Working outside county of residence:** 44.9%.

Cities with pop over 10,000: Pekin 🏛 (33,286); East Peoria (22,502); Morton (15,599); Washington (12,394).

UNION COUNTY

309 W Market St Rm 100   **Ph:** 618-833-5711
Jonesboro, IL 62952   **Fax:** 618-833-8712
www.shawneeheartland.com

On the southwest border of IL, south of Carbondale; organized Jan 2, 1818 (prior to statehood) from Johnson County. **Name Origin:** For the temporary union of the Baptists and Dunkards.

Area (sq mi): 422.13 (land 416.16; water 5.97). **Pop per sq mi:** 43.7.

Pop 2005: 18,202. **State rank:** 62. **Pop change:** 2000-20005 -0.5%; 1990-2000 +3.8%. **Pop 2000:** 18,293 (White 95.2%; Black or African American 0.8%; Hispanic or Latino 2.6%; Asian 0.3%; Other 2.6%). **Foreign born:** 1.9%. **Median age:** 40.3.

Income 2000: per capita $16,450; median household $30,994; **Pop below poverty level:** 16.5%. ***Personal per capita income 2000-2003:** $20,195-$21,295.

Unemployment 2004: 7.7%. **Change from 2000:** 2.1%. **Median travel time to work:** 22.9 minutes. **Working outside county of residence:** 36.5%.

Cities with pop over 10,000: None.

VERMILION COUNTY

6 N Vermilion St Courthouse Annex   **Ph:** 217-431-2615
Danville, IL 61832   **Fax:** 217-554-1914
www.co.vermilion.il.us

On the east-central border of IL, east of Urbana; organized Jan 18, 1826 from Edgar County. **Name Origin:** For the Vermilion River, which runs through the county and is colored by the red soil.

Area (sq mi): 902.14 (land 899.08; water 3.06). **Pop per sq mi:** 91.6.

Pop 2005: 82,344. **State rank:** 20. **Pop change:** 2000-20005 -1.9%; 1990-2000 -4.9%. **Pop 2000:** 83,919 (White 84.7%; Black or African American 10.6%; Hispanic or Latino 3%; Asian 0.6%; Other 2.9%). **Foreign born:** 1.7%. **Median age:** 38.

Income 2000: per capita $16,787; median household $34,071; **Pop below poverty level:** 13.3%. ***Personal per capita income 2000-2003:** $21,561-$23,283.

Unemployment 2004: 8.3%. **Change from 2000:** +0.9%. **Median travel time to work:** 20.4 minutes. **Working outside county of residence:** 14%.

Cities with pop over 10,000: Danville 🏛 (33,069).

WABASH COUNTY

PO Box 277   **Ph:** 618-262-4561
Mount Carmel, IL 62863

On the southeastern border of IL, southeast of Olney; organized Dec 27, 1824 from Edwards County. **Name Origin:** For the Wabash River, from Miami Indian *wahba* 'white' and *shik-ki* 'color-bright', usually translated as 'white water.'

Area (sq mi): 227.76 (land 223.47; water 4.29). **Pop per sq mi:** 56.2.

Pop 2005: 12,570. **State rank:** 86. **Pop change:** 2000-20005 -2.8%; 1990-2000 -1.3%. **Pop 2000:** 12,937 (White 97.4%; Black or African American 0.4%; Hispanic or Latino 0.7%; Asian 0.4%; Other 1.3%). **Foreign born:** 0.7%. **Median age:** 39.

Income 2000: per capita $16,747; median household $34,473; **Pop below poverty level:** 14.1%. ***Personal per capita income 2000-2003:** $22,359-$23,460.

Unemployment 2004: 7%. **Change from 2000:** -1.5%. **Median travel time to work:** 22.4 minutes. **Working outside county of residence:** 38.2%.

Cities with pop over 10,000: None.

WARREN COUNTY

100 W Broadway   **Ph:** 309-734-8592
Monmouth, IL 61462   **Fax:** 309-734-7406
www.outfitters.com/illinois/warren/

In northwest IL, west of Galesburg; organized Jan 13, 1825 from Pike County. **Name Origin:** For Gen. Joseph Warren (1741-75), Revolutionary War patriot and member of the Committee of Safety who dispatched Paul Revere (1735-1818) on his famous ride.

Area (sq mi): 543.17 (land 542.52; water 0.65). **Pop per sq mi:** 32.4.

Pop 2005: 17,558. **State rank:** 64. **Pop change:** 2000-20005 -6.3%; 1990-2000 -2.3%. **Pop 2000:** 18,735 (White 94.3%; Black or African American 1.6%; Hispanic or Latino 2.7%; Asian 0.3%; Other 2.5%). **Foreign born:** 1.4%. **Median age:** 37.8.

Income 2000: per capita $16,946; median household $36,224; **Pop below poverty level:** 9.2%. ***Personal per capita income 2000-2003:** $20,343-$21,500.

Unemployment 2004: 6.4%. **Change from 2000:** +2%. **Median travel time to work:** 18.9 minutes. **Working outside county of residence:** 40.5%.

Cities with pop over 10,000: None.

WASHINGTON COUNTY

101 E Saint Louis St County Courthouse   **Ph:** 618-327-8314
Nashville, IL 62263   **Fax:** 618-327-3582

In south-central IL, southeast of Belleville; organized Jan 2, 1818 (prior to statehood) from Saint Clair County. **Name Origin:** For George Washington (1732-99), American patriot and first U.S. president.

Area (sq mi): 564.12 (land 562.61; water 1.51). **Pop per sq mi:** 26.5.

Pop 2005: 14,922. **State rank:** 77. **Pop change:** 2000-20005 -1.5%; 1990-2000 +1.2%. **Pop 2000:** 15,148 (White 98%; Black or African American 0.3%; Hispanic or Latino 0.7%; Asian 0.2%; Other 0.8%). **Foreign born:** 0.6%. **Median age:** 38.8.

🏛 *County Seat*

Washington County (cont'd)

Income 2000: per capita $19,108; median household $40,932; **Pop below poverty level:** 6%. *Personal per capita income 2000-2003: $25,470-$27,347.

Unemployment 2004: 5.1%. **Change from 2000:** +0.9%. **Median travel time to work:** 23.9 minutes. **Working outside county of residence:** 41.7%.

Cities with pop over 10,000: None.

WAYNE COUNTY

PO Box 187   **Ph:** 618-842-5182
Fairfield, IL 62837   **Fax:** 618-842-6427

In southeastern IL, southwest of Olney; organized Mar 26, 1819 from Edwards County. **Name Origin:** For Gen. Anthony Wayne (1745-96), PA soldier and statesman, nicknamed 'Mad Anthony' for his daring during the Revolutionary War.

Area (sq mi): 715.56 (land 713.9; water 1.66). **Pop per sq mi:** 23.5.

Pop 2005: 16,796. **State rank:** 68. **Pop change:** 2000-20005 -2.1%; 1990-2000 -0.5%. **Pop 2000:** 17,151 (White 98.3%; Black or African American 0.2%; Hispanic or Latino 0.6%; Asian 0.3%; Other 0.8%). **Foreign born:** 0.9%. **Median age:** 39.9.

Income 2000: per capita $15,793; median household $30,481; **Pop below poverty level:** 12.4%. *Personal per capita income 2000-2003: $22,287-$23,689.

Unemployment 2004: 5.8%. **Change from 2000:** -0.9%. **Median travel time to work:** 21 minutes. **Working outside county of residence:** 33.9%.

Cities with pop over 10,000: None.

WHITE COUNTY

PO Box 339   **Ph:** 618-382-7211
Carmi, IL 62821   **Fax:** 618-382-2322
www.whitecounty-il.gov

On the southeastern border of IL; organized Dec 9, 1815 (prior to statehood) from Gallatin County. **Name Origin:** For Leonard White, a delegate to the IL Constitutional Convention (1818) and state legislator.

Area (sq mi): 501.7 (land 494.87; water 6.83). **Pop per sq mi:** 30.9.

Pop 2005: 15,284. **State rank:** 76. **Pop change:** 2000-20005 -0.6%; 1990-2000 -7%. **Pop 2000:** 15,371 (White 97.8%; Black or African American 0.3%; Hispanic or Latino 0.7%; Asian 0.2%; Other 1.4%). **Foreign born:** 0.3%. **Median age:** 42.

Income 2000: per capita $16,412; median household $29,601; **Pop below poverty level:** 12.5%. *Personal per capita income 2000-2003: $23,960-$24,575.

Unemployment 2004: 5.2%. **Change from 2000:** -0.1%. **Median travel time to work:** 25.2 minutes. **Working outside county of residence:** 35.9%.

Cities with pop over 10,000: None.

WHITESIDE COUNTY

200 E Knox St   **Ph:** 815-772-5100
Morrison, IL 61270   **Fax:** 815-772-7673
www.whiteside.org

On the northwestern border of IL, northeast of Moline; organized Jan 16, 1836 from Jo Daviess and Henry counties. **Name Origin:** For Gen. Samuel Whiteside, officer in the War of 1812 and the Black Hawk War; IL legislator.

Area (sq mi): 697.01 (land 684.77; water 12.24). **Pop per sq mi:** 87.4.

Pop 2005: 59,863. **State rank:** 24. **Pop change:** 2000-20005 -1.3%; 1990-2000 +0.8%. **Pop 2000:** 60,653 (White 88.9%; Black or African American 1%; Hispanic or Latino 8.8%; Asian 0.4%; Other 5.8%). **Foreign born:** 2.8%. **Median age:** 38.5.

Income 2000: per capita $19,296; median household $40,354; **Pop below poverty level:** 8.5%. *Personal per capita income 2000-2003: $24,617-$24,057.

Unemployment 2004: 6.7%. **Change from 2000:** -0.3%. **Median travel time to work:** 18.5 minutes. **Working outside county of residence:** 27.2%.

Cities with pop over 10,000: Sterling (15,454).

WILL COUNTY

302 N Chicago St   **Ph:** 815-740-4615
Joliet, IL 60432   **Fax:** 815-740-4699
www.willcountyillinois.com

On the northeastern border of IL, south of Chicago; organized Jan 12, 1836 from Cook and Iroquois counties. **Name Origin:** For Dr. Conrad Will (1779-1835), physician and IL legislator.

Area (sq mi): 849.39 (land 836.94; water 12.45). **Pop per sq mi:** 768.1.

Pop 2005: 642,813. **State rank:** 4. **Pop change:** 2000-20005 +28%; 1990-2000 +40.6%. **Pop 2000:** 502,266 (White 77.4%; Black or African American 10.5%; Hispanic or Latino 8.7%; Asian 2.2%; Other 5.4%). **Foreign born:** 7.1%. **Median age:** 33.3.

Income 2000: per capita $24,613; median household $62,238; **Pop below poverty level:** 4.9%. *Personal per capita income 2000-2003: $29,948-$29,312.

Unemployment 2004: 5.9%. **Change from 2000:** +0.7%. **Median travel time to work:** 32 minutes. **Working outside county of residence:** 55.6%.

Cities with pop over 10,000: 11 (see page 35 for cities).

WILLIAMSON COUNTY

200 W Jefferson St   **Ph:** 618-997-1301
Marion, IL 62959   **Fax:** 618-993-2071

In south-central IL, east of Carbondale; organized Feb 28, 1839 from Franklin County. **Name Origin:** For Williamson County, TN, former home of many early settlers.

Area (sq mi): 444.38 (land 423.41; water 20.96). **Pop per sq mi:** 150.2.

Pop 2005: 63,617. **State rank:** 23. **Pop change:** 2000-20005 +3.8%; 1990-2000 +6.2%. **Pop 2000:** 61,296 (White 94.6%; Black or African American 2.5%; Hispanic or Latino 1.2%; Asian 0.5%; Other 1.7%). **Foreign born:** 1.1%. **Median age:** 38.8.

*Source: Personal per capita income data are from the Bureau of Economic Analysis; per capita income data are from the Bureau of the Census. See Introduction for explanation of differences.

Williamson County (cont'd)

Income 2000: per capita $17,779; median household $31,991; **Pop below poverty level:** 14.6%. ***Personal per capita income 2000-2003:** $22,336-$23,898.

Unemployment 2004: 6.6%. **Change from 2000:** +0.9%. **Median travel time to work:** 21.6 minutes. **Working outside county of residence:** 32.2%.

Cities with pop over 10,000: Marion 🏛 (16,853); Herrin (11,503).

WINNEBAGO COUNTY
404 Elm St   **Ph:** 815-987-3050
Rockford, IL 61101   **Fax:** 815-969-0259
www.co.winnebago.il.us

On the northern border of IL; organized Jan 16, 1836 from Jo Daviess County. **Name Origin:** For the Indian tribe of Siouan linguistic stock; their name is thought to mean 'fish eaters.'

Area (sq mi): 519.27 (land 513.74; water 5.54). **Pop per sq mi:** 561.9.

Pop 2005: 288,695. **State rank:** 7. **Pop change:** 2000-20005 +3.7%; 1990-2000 +10.1%. **Pop 2000:** 278,418 (White 79.3%; Black or African American 10.5%; Hispanic or Latino 6.9%; Asian 1.7%; Other 5.3%). **Foreign born:** 6.1%. **Median age:** 35.9.

Income 2000: per capita $21,194; median household $43,886; **Pop below poverty level:** 9.6%. ***Personal per capita income 2000-2003:** $27,038-$27,051.

Unemployment 2004: 7.8%. **Change from 2000:** +1.2%. **Median travel time to work:** 20.8 minutes. **Working outside county of residence:** 13.1%.

Cities with pop over 10,000: Rockford 🏛 (152,452); Loves Park (22,560); Machesney Park (21,415).

WOODFORD COUNTY
115 N Main St Rm 202   **Ph:** 309-467-2822
Eureka, IL 61530   **Fax:** 309-467-7391

In central IL; organized Feb 27, 1841 from Tazewell and McLean counties. **Name Origin:** For Woodford County, KY, former home of many early settlers.

Area (sq mi): 542.74 (land 527.95; water 14.79). **Pop per sq mi:** 70.9.

Pop 2005: 37,448. **State rank:** 39. **Pop change:** 2000-20005 +5.6%; 1990-2000 +8.6%. **Pop 2000:** 35,469 (White 98%; Black or African American 0.3%; Hispanic or Latino 0.7%; Asian 0.3%; Other 0.9%). **Foreign born:** 1%. **Median age:** 37.8.

Income 2000: per capita $21,956; median household $51,394; **Pop below poverty level:** 4.3%. ***Personal per capita income 2000-2003:** $27,347-$28,585.

Unemployment 2004: 4.6%. **Change from 2000:** +1.6%. **Median travel time to work:** 22.2 minutes. **Working outside county of residence:** 56.3%.

Cities with pop over 10,000: None.

🏛 *County Seat*

Indiana

Lake Michigan

MICHIGAN

OHIO

ILLINOIS

KENTUCKY

N

	County boundary
Putnam	County name
⊙	County seat
■	Major city
✪	State capital

0 — 40 mi
0 — 40 km

©Maps.com

Counties and county seats:

Lake — Crown Point
Gary
Porter — Valparaiso
La Porte — La Porte
St. Joseph — South Bend
Elkhart — Goshen
Lagrange — Lagrange
Steuben — Angola
Newton — Kentland
Jasper — Rensselaer
Starke — Knox
Marshall — Plymouth
Kosciusko — Warsaw
Noble — Albion
De Kalb — Auburn
Benton — Fowler
White — Monticello
Pulaski — Winamac
Fulton — Rochester
Whitley — Columbia City
Allen — Fort Wayne
Warren — Williamsport
Tippecanoe — Lafayette
Carroll — Delphi
Cass — Logansport
Miami — Peru
Wabash — Wabash
Huntington — Huntington
Wells — Bluffton
Adams — Decatur
Fountain — Covington
Montgomery — Crawfordsville
Clinton — Frankfort
Howard — Kokomo
Tipton — Tipton
Grant — Marion
Blackford — Hartford City
Jay — Portland
Vermillion — Newport
Parke — Rockville
Putnam — Greencastle
Boone — Lebanon
Hamilton — Noblesville
Madison — Anderson
Delaware — Muncie
Randolph — Winchester
Henry — New Castle
Wayne — Richmond
Hendricks — Danville
Marion — Indianapolis
Hancock — Greenfield
Rush — Rushville
Fayette — Connersville
Union — Liberty
Vigo — Terre Haute
Clay — Brazil
Owen — Spencer
Morgan — Martinsville
Johnson — Franklin
Shelby — Shelbyville
Decatur — Greensburg
Franklin — Brookville
Sullivan — Sullivan
Greene — Bloomfield
Monroe — Bloomington
Brown — Nashville
Bartholomew — Columbus
Ripley — Versailles
Dearborn — Lawrenceburg
Ohio — Rising Sun
Switzerland — Vevay
Jennings — Vernon
Jefferson — Madison
Knox — Vincennes
Daviess — Washington
Martin — Shoals
Lawrence — Bedford
Jackson — Brownstown
Scott — Scottsburg
Gibson — Princeton
Pike — Petersburg
Dubois — Jasper
Orange — Paoli
Washington — Salem
Clark — Jeffersonville
Floyd — New Albany
Crawford — English
Harrison — Corydon
Posey — Mount Vernon
Vanderburgh — Evansville
Warrick — Boonville
Spencer — Rockport
Perry — Cannelton

Indiana

INDIANA STATE INFORMATION
www.in.gov   **Ph:** 317-233-0800

Area (sq mi): 36,417.73 (land 35866.9; water 550.83). **Pop per sq mi:** 174.9.

Pop 2005: 6,271,973. **Pop change:** 2000-20005 +3.1%; 1990-2000 +9.7%. **Pop 2000:** 6,080,485 (White 85.8%; Black or African American 8.4%; Hispanic or Latino 3.5%; Asian 1%; Other 3.1%). **Foreign born:** 3.1%. **Median age:** 35.2.

Income 2000: per capita $20,397; median household $41,567; **Pop below poverty level:** 9.5%. ***Personal per capita income 2000-2003:** $27,132-$28,838.

Unemployment 2004: 5.3%. **Change from 2000:** +2.4%. **Median travel time to work:** 22.6 minutes. **Working outside county of residence:** 29%.

ADAMS COUNTY
PO Box 189   **Ph:** 260-724-5300
Decatur, IN 46733   **Fax:** 260-724-5313
www.co.adams.in.us

On the east-central border of IN, south of Ft. Wayne; organized Jan 23, 1836 from Warren County. **Name Origin:** For John Quincy Adams (1767-1848), sixth U.S. president.

Area (sq mi): 339.93 (land 339.36; water 0.57). **Pop per sq mi:** 99.7.

Pop 2005: 33,849. **State rank:** 46. **Pop change:** 2000-20005 +0.7%; 1990-2000 +8.1%. **Pop 2000:** 33,625 (White 95.8%; Black or African American 0.1%; Hispanic or Latino 3.3%; Asian 0.2%; Other 2.4%). **Foreign born:** 1.1%. **Median age:** 32.9.

Income 2000: per capita $16,704; median household $40,625; **Pop below poverty level:** 9.1%. ***Personal per capita income 2000-2003:** $23,004-$24,114.

Unemployment 2004: 4.1%. **Change from 2000:** -1.4%. **Median travel time to work:** 21.7 minutes. **Working outside county of residence:** 29.1%.

Cities with pop over 10,000: None.

ALLEN COUNTY
715 S Calhoun St
County Courthouse Rm 201   **Ph:** 260-449-7245
Fort Wayne, IN 46802   **Fax:** 260-449-7929
www.co.allen.in.us

On the northeastern border of IN, northeast of Marion; organized Apr 1, 1824 from Indian lands. **Name Origin:** For Col. John Allen (?-1813), KY lawyer and army officer.

Area (sq mi): 660.1 (land 657.25; water 2.85). **Pop per sq mi:** 523.4.

Pop 2005: 344,006. **State rank:** 3. **Pop change:** 2000-20005 +3.7%; 1990-2000 +10.3%. **Pop 2000:** 331,849 (White 81.3%; Black or African American 11.3%; Hispanic or Latino 4.2%; Asian 1.4%; Other 4.2%). **Foreign born:** 4%. **Median age:** 34.1.

Income 2000: per capita $21,544; median household $42,671; **Pop below poverty level:** 9.1%. ***Personal per capita income 2000-2003:** $29,084-$30,509.

Unemployment 2004: 5.2%. **Change from 2000:** +0.6%. **Median travel time to work:** 20.6 minutes. **Working outside county of residence:** 8.9%.

Cities with pop over 10,000: Fort Wayne 🏛 (219,351); New Haven (13,638).

BARTHOLOMEW COUNTY
PO Box 924   **Ph:** 812-379-1600
Columbus, IN 47202   **Fax:** 812-379-1675
www.bartholomewco.com

In south-central IN, south of Indianapolis; organized 1821 from Indian lands. **Name Origin:** For Gen. Joseph Bartholomew (?-1840), officer wounded at the Battle of Tippecanoe (1811) and IN state senator (1821-24).

Area (sq mi): 409.36 (land 406.84; water 2.52). **Pop per sq mi:** 180.8.

Pop 2005: 73,540. **State rank:** 20. **Pop change:** 2000-20005 +2.9%; 1990-2000 +12.2%. **Pop 2000:** 71,435 (White 93%; Black or African American 1.8%; Hispanic or Latino 2.2%; Asian 1.9%; Other 2.1%). **Foreign born:** 3.8%. **Median age:** 36.2.

Income 2000: per capita $21,536; median household $44,184; **Pop below poverty level:** 7.3%. ***Personal per capita income 2000-2003:** $30,448-$30,936.

Unemployment 2004: 4.4%. **Change from 2000:** +0.6%. **Median travel time to work:** 18.9 minutes. **Working outside county of residence:** 14.5%.

Cities with pop over 10,000: Columbus 🏛 (39,251).

BENTON COUNTY
706 E 5th St Suite 37   **Ph:** 765-884-0930
Fowler, IN 47944   **Fax:** 765-884-0322
www.bentoncounty.org

On the northwest border of IN, northwest of Lafayette; organized Feb 18, 1840 from Indian lands. **Name Origin:** For Thomas Hart Benton (1782-1858), U.S. journalist and statesman; nicknamed 'Old Bullion' for championing the use of gold and silver currency rather than paper money.

🏛 *County Seat*

Benton County (cont'd)

Area (sq mi): 406.4 (land 406.31; water 0.09). **Pop per sq mi:** 22.2.

Pop 2005: 9,039. **State rank:** 89. **Pop change:** 2000-20005 -4.1%; 1990-2000 -0.2%. **Pop 2000:** 9,421 (White 96%; Black or African American 0.2%; Hispanic or Latino 2.6%; Asian 0.1%; Other 2.8%). **Foreign born:** 0.8%. **Median age:** 36.7.

Income 2000: per capita $17,220; median household $39,813; **Pop below poverty level:** 5.5%. ***Personal per capita income 2000-2003:** $24,518-$24,549.

Unemployment 2004: 5.3%. **Change from 2000:** +1.8%. **Median travel time to work:** 24.5 minutes. **Working outside county of residence:** 50.2%.

Cities with pop over 10,000: None.

BLACKFORD COUNTY

110 W Washington St   **Ph:** 765-348-1620
Hartford City, IN 47348   **Fax:** 765-348-7222
www.supertiles.com

In east-central IN, north of Muncie; organized Feb 15, 1838 from Jay County. **Name Origin:** For Isaac Newton Blackford (1786-1859), IN legislator and justice of the IN Supreme Court (1817-52).

Area (sq mi): 165.4 (land 165.1; water 0.31). **Pop per sq mi:** 83.9.

Pop 2005: 13,849. **State rank:** 83. **Pop change:** 2000-20005 -1.4%; 1990-2000 -0.1%. **Pop 2000:** 14,048 (White 98%; Black or African American 0.1%; Hispanic or Latino 0.6%; Asian 0.2%; Other 1.3%). **Foreign born:** 0.1%. **Median age:** 38.5.

Income 2000: per capita $16,543; median household $34,760; **Pop below poverty level:** 8.7%. ***Personal per capita income 2000-2003:** $21,128-$22,547.

Unemployment 2004: 7%. **Change from 2000:** +0.1%. **Median travel time to work:** 23.4 minutes. **Working outside county of residence:** 44.4%.

Cities with pop over 10,000: None.

BOONE COUNTY

Courthouse Sq Rm 212   **Ph:** 765-482-3510
Lebanon, IN 46052   **Fax:** 765-485-0150

In central IN, northwest of Indianpolis; organized Jan 29, 1830 from Indian lands. **Name Origin:** For Daniel Boone (1734?-1820), U.S. frontiersman and KY pioneer.

Area (sq mi): 423.28 (land 422.85; water 0.42). **Pop per sq mi:** 123.1.

Pop 2005: 52,061. **State rank:** 27. **Pop change:** 2000-20005 +12.9%; 1990-2000 +20.9%. **Pop 2000:** 46,107 (White 97.3%; Black or African American 0.4%; Hispanic or Latino 1.2%; Asian 0.5%; Other 1.3%). **Foreign born:** 1.5%. **Median age:** 36.9.

Income 2000: per capita $24,182; median household $49,632; **Pop below poverty level:** 5.2%. ***Personal per capita income 2000-2003:** $36,726-$38,791.

Unemployment 2004: 3.8%. **Change from 2000:** +1.5%. **Median travel time to work:** 23 minutes. **Working outside county of residence:** 56.1%.

Cities with pop over 10,000: Lebanon ⌂ (14,560); Zionsville (10,650).

BROWN COUNTY

PO Box 85   **Ph:** 812-988-5510
Nashville, IN 47448   **Fax:** 812-988-5562
www.browncounty.org

In central IN, west of Columbus; organized Feb 4, 1836 from Monroe, Jackson, and Bartholomew counties. **Name Origin:** For Gen. Jacob Jennings Brown (1775-1828), an officer in the War of 1812 and commander of the U.S. Army (1821-28).

Area (sq mi): 316.62 (land 312.26; water 4.36). **Pop per sq mi:** 48.5.

Pop 2005: 15,154. **State rank:** 81. **Pop change:** 2000-20005 +1.3%; 1990-2000 +6.2%. **Pop 2000:** 14,957 (White 97.7%; Black or African American 0.2%; Hispanic or Latino 0.9%; Asian 0.2%; Other 1.4%). **Foreign born:** 1%. **Median age:** 40.8.

Income 2000: per capita $20,548; median household $43,708; **Pop below poverty level:** 8.9%. ***Personal per capita income 2000-2003:** $28,942-$28,068.

Unemployment 2004: 5.2%. **Change from 2000:** +1.7%. **Median travel time to work:** 34.2 minutes. **Working outside county of residence:** 61.9%.

Cities with pop over 10,000: None.

CARROLL COUNTY

101 W Main St   **Ph:** 765-564-4485
Delphi, IN 46923   **Fax:** 765-564-1835
www.carrollnet.org

In west-central IN, west of Kokoma; organized Jan 7, 1828 from Indian lands. **Name Origin:** For Charles Carroll (1737-1832), a signer of the Declaration of Independence, U.S. senator from MD (1789-92), and founder of the Baltimore and Ohio Railroad.

Area (sq mi): 375.05 (land 372.26; water 2.8). **Pop per sq mi:** 54.9.

Pop 2005: 20,426. **State rank:** 73. **Pop change:** 2000-20005 +1.3%; 1990-2000 +7.2%. **Pop 2000:** 20,165 (White 96.3%; Black or African American 0.2%; Hispanic or Latino 2.9%; Asian 0.1%; Other 2.1%). **Foreign born:** 2.2%. **Median age:** 37.2.

Income 2000: per capita $19,436; median household $42,677; **Pop below poverty level:** 6.8%. ***Personal per capita income 2000-2003:** $27,192-$26,695.

Unemployment 2004: 5.6%. **Change from 2000:** +1.7%. **Median travel time to work:** 23.8 minutes. **Working outside county of residence:** 54.1%.

Cities with pop over 10,000: None.

CASS COUNTY

200 Court Pk   **Ph:** 574-753-7740
Logansport, IN 46947   **Fax:** 574-722-1556

In west-central IN, northwest of Kokomo; established Dec 18, 1828 from Indian lands. **Name Origin:** For Gen. Lewis Cass (1782-1866), OH legislator, governor of MI Territory (1813-31), U.S. secretary of war (1831-36), and U.S. secretary of state (1857-60).

Area (sq mi): 414.92 (land 412.87; water 2.06). **Pop per sq mi:** 97.2.

Source: Personal per capita income data are from the Bureau of Economic Analysis; per capita income data are from the Bureau of the Census. See Introduction for explanation of differences.

Cass County (cont'd)

Pop 2005: 40,130. **State rank:** 37. **Pop change:** 2000-20005 -2%; 1990-2000 +6.6%. **Pop 2000:** 40,930 (White 90.2%; Black or African American 1.3%; Hispanic or Latino 7.1%; Asian 0.5%; Other 4.4%). **Foreign born:** 4.3%. **Median age:** 36.7.

Income 2000: per capita $18,892; median household $39,193; **Pop below poverty level:** 7.6%. *Personal per capita income 2000-2003: $24,547-$25,959.

Unemployment 2004: 6.5%. **Change from 2000:** +1.1%. **Median travel time to work:** 20.2 minutes. **Working outside county of residence:** 26.5%.

Cities with pop over 10,000: Logansport ⛪ (19,350).

CLARK COUNTY

501 E Court Ave Rm 137　　　**Ph:** 812-285-6244
Jeffersonville, IN 47130　　　**Fax:** 812-285-6372
www.co.clark.in.us

On the southeast border of IN, north of Louisville, KY; organized Feb 3, 1801 (prior to statehood) from Knox County. **Name Origin:** For Gen. George Rogers Clark (1752-1818), officer in the Revolutionary War and frontiersman in the Northwest Territory.

Area (sq mi): 376.2 (land 375.04; water 1.16). **Pop per sq mi:** 270.9.

Pop 2005: 101,592. **State rank:** 17. **Pop change:** 2000-20005 +5.3%; 1990-2000 +9.9%. **Pop 2000:** 96,472 (White 89.3%; Black or African American 6.6%; Hispanic or Latino 1.9%; Asian 0.6%; Other 2.5%). **Foreign born:** 1.7%. **Median age:** 36.5.

Income 2000: per capita $19,936; median household $40,111; **Pop below poverty level:** 8.1%. *Personal per capita income 2000-2003: $26,353-$28,186.

Unemployment 2004: 5%. **Change from 2000:** +1.2%. **Median travel time to work:** 22.2 minutes. **Working outside county of residence:** 48.9%.

Cities with pop over 10,000: Jeffersonville ⛪ (28,640); Clarksville (21,136).

CLAY COUNTY

609 E National Ave Rm 213　　　**Ph:** 812-448-9024
Brazil, IN 47834　　　**Fax:** 812-446-9602
www.claycountyin.org

In southwest IN, east of Terre Haute; organized Feb 12, 1825 from Indian lands. **Name Origin:** For Henry Clay (1777-1852), U.S. senator from KY, known as the 'Great Pacificator' for his advocacy of compromise to avert national crises.

Area (sq mi): 360.39 (land 357.62; water 2.78). **Pop per sq mi:** 75.9.

Pop 2005: 27,142. **State rank:** 59. **Pop change:** 2000-20005 +2.2%; 1990-2000 +7.5%. **Pop 2000:** 26,556 (White 98%; Black or African American 0.3%; Hispanic or Latino 0.6%; Asian 0.1%; Other 1.1%). **Foreign born:** 0.6%. **Median age:** 37.1.

Income 2000: per capita $16,364; median household $36,865; **Pop below poverty level:** 8.7%. *Personal per capita income 2000-2003: $22,462-$22,589.

Unemployment 2004: 6.4%. **Change from 2000:** +0.3%. **Median travel time to work:** 25.9 minutes. **Working outside county of residence:** 51.4%.

Cities with pop over 10,000: None.

CLINTON COUNTY

265 Courthouse Sq　　　**Ph:** 765-659-6335
Frankfort, IN 46041

In central IN, east of Lafayette; organized Jan 29, 1830 from Indian lands. **Name Origin:** For DeWitt Clinton (1769-1828), governor of NY (1817-21; 1825-28) and supporter of the Erie Canal.

Area (sq mi): 405.28 (land 405.1; water 0.18). **Pop per sq mi:** 84.2.

Pop 2005: 34,091. **State rank:** 45. **Pop change:** 2000-20005 +0.7%; 1990-2000 +9.3%. **Pop 2000:** 33,866 (White 91.7%; Black or African American 0.3%; Hispanic or Latino 7.3%; Asian 0.2%; Other 5.1%). **Foreign born:** 4.8%. **Median age:** 35.6.

Income 2000: per capita $17,862; median household $40,759; **Pop below poverty level:** 8.6%. *Personal per capita income 2000-2003: $21,930-$23,303.

Unemployment 2004: 5.6%. **Change from 2000:** +1.7%. **Median travel time to work:** 19.9 minutes. **Working outside county of residence:** 37.2%.

Cities with pop over 10,000: Frankfort ⛪ (16,441).

CRAWFORD COUNTY

PO Box 375　　　**Ph:** 812-338-2565
English, IN 47118　　　**Fax:** 812-338-2507

On the south-central border of IN; organized Jan 19, 1818 from Harrison County. **Name Origin:** For either Col. William Crawford (1732-82), VA officer in the Revolutionary War, Indian fighter, and surveyor; or William Harris Crawford (1772-1834), senator from GA (1807-13), U.S. secretary of war (1815-16), and U.S. secretary of the treasury (1816-25).

Area (sq mi): 308.85 (land 305.68; water 3.17). **Pop per sq mi:** 36.7.

Pop 2005: 11,216. **State rank:** 86. **Pop change:** 2000-20005 +4.4%; 1990-2000 +8.4%. **Pop 2000:** 10,743 (White 97.9%; Black or African American 0.2%; Hispanic or Latino 0.9%; Asian 0.1%; Other 1.4%). **Foreign born:** 0.3%. **Median age:** 37.3.

Income 2000: per capita $15,926; median household $32,646; **Pop below poverty level:** 16.8%. *Personal per capita income 2000-2003: $19,734-$22,155.

Unemployment 2004: 6.8%. **Change from 2000:** +1.4%. **Median travel time to work:** 35.4 minutes. **Working outside county of residence:** 62.7%.

Cities with pop over 10,000: None.

DAVIESS COUNTY

PO Box 739　　　**Ph:** 812-254-8664
Washington, IN 47501　　　**Fax:** 812-254-8698
www.daviesscounty.org

In southwestern IN, east of Vincennes; established Dec 24, 1816 from Indian lands. **Name Origin:** For Col. Joseph Hamilton Daviess (1774-1811), VA soldier and jurist who unsuccessfully attempted to indict Aaron Burr for treason (1806). According to Jacob Piatt Dunn, 'the Colonel's name was Daveiss and he always wrote it that way"; however, the name is sometimes spelled 'Daviess' in biographical entries and in places named for him.

Area (sq mi): 436.86 (land 430.66; water 6.2). **Pop per sq mi:** 70.7.

⛪ *County Seat*

Daviess County (cont'd)

Pop 2005: 30,466. **State rank:** 54. **Pop change:** 2000-20005 +2.2%; 1990-2000 +8.3%. **Pop 2000:** 29,820 (White 96.6%; Black or African American 0.4%; Hispanic or Latino 2.1%; Asian 0.2%; Other 1.7%). **Foreign born:** 1.9%. **Median age:** 35.5.

Income 2000: per capita $16,015; median household $34,064; **Pop below poverty level:** 13.8%. ***Personal per capita income 2000-2003:** $22,487-$24,088.

Unemployment 2004: 3.9%. **Change from 2000:** -0.1%. **Median travel time to work:** 23.7 minutes. **Working outside county of residence:** 30.8%.

Cities with pop over 10,000: Washington ⛪ (11,304).

DEARBORN COUNTY
215 W High St
Lawrenceburg, IN 47025
www.dearborncounty.org

Ph: 812-537-8877
Fax: 812-532-2021

On the southeastern border of IN, east of Columbus; organized Mar 7, 1803 (prior to statehood). **Name Origin:** For Gen. Henry Dearborn (1751-1829), an officer in the Revolutionary War, MA legislator, U.S. secretary of war (1801-09), and Minister to Portugal (1822-24).

Area (sq mi): 307.05 (land 305.21; water 1.84). **Pop per sq mi:** 160.8.

Pop 2005: 49,082. **State rank:** 28. **Pop change:** 2000-20005 +6.4%; 1990-2000 +18.7%. **Pop 2000:** 46,109 (White 97.7%; Black or African American 0.6%; Hispanic or Latino 0.6%; Asian 0.3%; Other 1.1%). **Foreign born:** 0.8%. **Median age:** 36.2.

Income 2000: per capita $20,431; median household $48,899; **Pop below poverty level:** 6.6%. ***Personal per capita income 2000-2003:** $27,472-$29,279.

Unemployment 2004: 5.2%. **Change from 2000:** +1.7%. **Median travel time to work:** 30.5 minutes. **Working outside county of residence:** 58.1%.

Cities with pop over 10,000: None.

DECATUR COUNTY
150 Courthouse Sq Suite 244
Greensburg, IN 47240
www.decaturcounty.in.gov

Ph: 812-663-8223
Fax: 812-662-6627

In southeast IN, east of Columbus; established Dec 31, 1821 from Indian lands. **Name Origin:** For Stephen Decatur (1779-1820), U.S. naval officer during the War of 1812 and in actions against the Barbary pirates near Tripoli, who said '...may she always be in the right; but our country, right or wrong!'

Area (sq mi): 373.42 (land 372.6; water 0.81). **Pop per sq mi:** 67.6.

Pop 2005: 25,184. **State rank:** 62. **Pop change:** 2000-20005 +2.6%; 1990-2000 +3.8%. **Pop 2000:** 24,555 (White 98.1%; Black or African American 0%; Hispanic or Latino 0.5%; Asian 0.7%; Other 0.7%). **Foreign born:** 1.6%. **Median age:** 35.8.

Income 2000: per capita $18,582; median household $40,401; **Pop below poverty level:** 9.3%. ***Personal per capita income 2000-2003:** $25,266-$26,277.

Unemployment 2004: 5.3%. **Change from 2000:** +2.7%. **Median travel time to work:** 19.9 minutes. **Working outside county of residence:** 25.2%.

Cities with pop over 10,000: Greensburg ⛪ (10,462).

DEKALB COUNTY
PO Box 230
Auburn, IN 46706
www.dekalbnet.org

Ph: 260-925-0912
Fax: 260-925-5126

On the northeastern border of IN, north of Ft. Wayne; established Feb 7, 1835 from Allen Country. **Name Origin:** For Johann (1721-80), Baron de Kalb, German-born French soldier who fought with the Americans during the Revolutionary War.

Area (sq mi): 363.84 (land 362.88; water 0.97). **Pop per sq mi:** 114.8.

Pop 2005: 41,659. **State rank:** 35. **Pop change:** 2000-20005 +3.4%; 1990-2000 +14%. **Pop 2000:** 40,285 (White 96.8%; Black or African American 0.3%; Hispanic or Latino 1.7%; Asian 0.3%; Other 1.6%). **Foreign born:** 0.8%. **Median age:** 34.7.

Income 2000: per capita $19,448; median household $44,909; **Pop below poverty level:** 5.9%. ***Personal per capita income 2000-2003:** $25,441-$26,226.

Unemployment 2004: 5.5%. **Change from 2000:** -0.1%. **Median travel time to work:** 19.3 minutes. **Working outside county of residence:** 33%.

Cities with pop over 10,000: Auburn ⛪ (12,661).

DELAWARE COUNTY
100 W Main St
Muncie, IN 47305
www.co.delaware.in.us

Ph: 765-747-7730
Fax: 765-747-7899

In east-central IN; organized Jan 26, 1827 from Indian lands. **Name Origin:** For the Delaware Indians (also called Leni or Leni-Lenape), in turn named for Thomas West (1577-1618), Lord Delaware (or De La Warr).

Area (sq mi): 395.92 (land 393.29; water 2.63). **Pop per sq mi:** 295.9.

Pop 2005: 116,362. **State rank:** 14. **Pop change:** 2000-20005 -2%; 1990-2000 -0.7%. **Pop 2000:** 118,769 (White 90.1%; Black or African American 6.7%; Hispanic or Latino 1.1%; Asian 0.7%; Other 1.9%). **Foreign born:** 1.5%. **Median age:** 33.8.

Income 2000: per capita $19,233; median household $34,659; **Pop below poverty level:** 15.1%. ***Personal per capita income 2000-2003:** $24,422-$25,905.

Unemployment 2004: 6%. **Change from 2000:** +1.4%. **Median travel time to work:** 19.8 minutes. **Working outside county of residence:** 17.1%.

Cities with pop over 10,000: Muncie ⛪ (67,166).

DUBOIS COUNTY
1 Courthouse Sq
Jasper, IN 47546
www.duboiscounty.org

Ph: 812-481-7035
Fax: 812-481-7044

In south-central IN, northeast of Evansville; established Dec 20, 1817 from Orange and Perry counties. **Name Origin:** For Toussaint

*Source: Personal per capita income data are from the Bureau of Economic Analysis; per capita income data are from the Bureau of the Census. See Introduction for explanation of differences.

220

Dubois County (cont'd)

Dubois, a French immigrant who fought with the Americans at the Battle of Tippecanoe (1811).

Area (sq mi): 435.23 (land 430.09; water 5.14). **Pop per sq mi:** 95.

Pop 2005: 40,858. **State rank:** 36. **Pop change:** 2000-20005 +3%; 1990-2000 +8.4%. **Pop 2000:** 39,674 (White 96.5%; Black or African American 0.1%; Hispanic or Latino 2.8%; Asian 0.2%; Other 2.1%). **Foreign born:** 2.1%. **Median age:** 36.1.

Income 2000: per capita $20,225; median household $44,169; **Pop below poverty level:** 5.3%. ***Personal per capita income 2000-2003:** $29,942-$32,448.

Unemployment 2004: 3.7%. **Change from 2000:** +0.9%. **Median travel time to work:** 17.8 minutes. **Working outside county of residence:** 9.2%.

Cities with pop over 10,000: Jasper 🏛 (13,533).

ELKHART COUNTY

117 N 2nd St Rm 101   **Ph:** 574-535-6409
Goshen, IN 46526
www.elkhartcountygov.org

On the north-central border of IN; organized Jan 29, 1830 from Indian lands. **Name Origin:** For the Elkhart River, named for the Elkhart Indians. Name is probably a translation of either a Potawatomi or Kickapoo term for 'elk's heart', early English spelling was Elksheart.

Area (sq mi): 467.85 (land 463.81; water 4.03). **Pop per sq mi:** 421.2.

Pop 2005: 195,362. **State rank:** 6. **Pop change:** 2000-20005 +6.9%; 1990-2000 +17%. **Pop 2000:** 182,791 (White 83.4%; Black or African American 5.2%; Hispanic or Latino 8.9%; Asian 0.9%; Other 7.5%). **Foreign born:** 7.1%. **Median age:** 33.

Income 2000: per capita $20,250; median household $44,478; **Pop below poverty level:** 7.8%. ***Personal per capita income 2000-2003:** $26,539-$29,315.

Unemployment 2004: 4.2%. **Change from 2000:** -1.2%. **Median travel time to work:** 18.4 minutes. **Working outside county of residence:** 10.7%.

Cities with pop over 10,000: Elkhart (51,878); Goshen 🏛 (30,555).

FAYETTE COUNTY

PO Box 607   **Ph:** 765-825-1813
Connersville, IN 47331   **Fax:** 765-827-4902
www.co.fayette.in.us

In east-central IN, southwest of Richmond; established Dec 28, 1818 from Wayne County. **Name Origin:** For the Marquis de Lafayette (1757-1834), French statesman and soldier who fought with Americans during the Revolutionary War.

Area (sq mi): 215.12 (land 214.96; water 0.16). **Pop per sq mi:** 115.8.

Pop 2005: 24,885. **State rank:** 63. **Pop change:** 2000-20005 -2.7%; 1990-2000 -1.6%. **Pop 2000:** 25,588 (White 96.8%; Black or African American 1.7%; Hispanic or Latino 0.5%; Asian 0.3%; Other 0.9%). **Foreign born:** 0.5%. **Median age:** 38.

Income 2000: per capita $18,624; median household $38,840; **Pop below poverty level:** 7.9%. ***Personal per capita income 2000-2003:** $24,335-$27,172.

Unemployment 2004: 7.9%. **Change from 2000:** -0.9%. **Median travel time to work:** 22.4 minutes. **Working outside county of residence:** 30%.

Cities with pop over 10,000: Connersville 🏛 (14,445).

FLOYD COUNTY

PO Box 1056   **Ph:** 812-948-5415
New Albany, IN 47151   **Fax:** 812-948-4711
www.warrickcounty.gov

On the southeast border of IN, northwest of Louisville, KY; organized Jan 2, 1819 from Harrison and Clark counties. **Name Origin:** According to most sources, for Gen. John Floyd (1783-1837), VA jurist, U.S. congressman from VA (1817-29), and governor (1830-34). Others claim Col. Davis Floyd, an associate of Aaron Burr and an important member of the IN General Assembly.

Area (sq mi): 148.31 (land 148; water 0.31). **Pop per sq mi:** 486.5.

Pop 2005: 71,997. **State rank:** 21. **Pop change:** 2000-20005 +1.7%; 1990-2000 +10%. **Pop 2000:** 70,823 (White 92.7%; Black or African American 4.4%; Hispanic or Latino 1.1%; Asian 0.5%; Other 1.8%). **Foreign born:** 1.2%. **Median age:** 36.8.

Income 2000: per capita $21,852; median household $44,022; **Pop below poverty level:** 8.7%. ***Personal per capita income 2000-2003:** $30,175-$31,848.

Unemployment 2004: 4.9%. **Change from 2000:** +1.7%. **Median travel time to work:** 21.5 minutes. **Working outside county of residence:** 57.9%.

Cities with pop over 10,000: New Albany 🏛 (36,877).

FOUNTAIN COUNTY

PO Box 183   **Ph:** 765-793-2192
Covington, IN 47932   **Fax:** 765-793-5002
www.co.fountain.in.us

On the central western border of IN, north of Terre Haute, established Dec 20, 1825 from Montgomery County. **Name Origin:** For Maj. James Fountain (originally Fontaine) (?-1790), KY army officer killed near Ft. Wayne in the Battle of Maumee.

Area (sq mi): 397.92 (land 395.69; water 2.23). **Pop per sq mi:** 44.1.

Pop 2005: 17,462. **State rank:** 77. **Pop change:** 2000-20005 -2.7%; 1990-2000 +0.8%. **Pop 2000:** 17,954 (White 98%; Black or African American 0.1%; Hispanic or Latino 1.1%; Asian 0.2%; Other 1%). **Foreign born:** 1%. **Median age:** 37.7.

Income 2000: per capita $17,779; median household $38,119; **Pop below poverty level:** 8.5%. ***Personal per capita income 2000-2003:** $23,232-$23,851.

Unemployment 2004: 5.7%. **Change from 2000:** +0.7%. **Median travel time to work:** 25.1 minutes. **Working outside county of residence:** 47.1%.

Cities with pop over 10,000: None.

🏛 *County Seat*

FRANKLIN COUNTY
459 Main St   **Ph:** 765-647-5111
Brookville, IN 47012   **Fax:** 765-647-3224

On southeastern border of IN, south of Richmond; established Nov 27, 1810 (prior to statehood) from Wayne and Ripley counties. **Name Origin:** For Benjamin Franklin (1706-90), patriot, diplomat, and statesman.

Area (sq mi): 391.34 (land 386; water 5.33). **Pop per sq mi:** 59.8.

Pop 2005: 23,085. **State rank:** 66. **Pop change:** 2000-20005 +4.2%; 1990-2000 +13.1%. **Pop 2000:** 22,151 (White 98.7%; Black or African American 0%; Hispanic or Latino 0.5%; Asian 0.2%; Other 0.8%). **Foreign born:** 0.6%. **Median age:** 35.9.

Income 2000: per capita $18,624; median household $43,530; **Pop below poverty level:** 7.1%. ***Personal per capita income 2000-2003:** $25,423-$26,179.

Unemployment 2004: 5.5%. **Change from 2000:** +1.1%. **Median travel time to work:** 29.9 minutes. **Working outside county of residence:** 65.5%.

Cities with pop over 10,000: None.

FULTON COUNTY
815 Main St   **Ph:** 574-223-2911
Rochester, IN 46975   **Fax:** 574-223-8304
www.fultoncounty-in.org

In north-central IN, west of Ft. Wayne; established Feb 7, 1835 from Indian lands. **Name Origin:** For Robert Fulton (1765-1815) builder of the *Clermont*, the first commercially successful steamboat.

Area (sq mi): 371.37 (land 368.51; water 2.87). **Pop per sq mi:** 56.1.

Pop 2005: 20,665. **State rank:** 71. **Pop change:** 2000-20005 +0.8%; 1990-2000 +8.9%. **Pop 2000:** 20,511 (White 95.1%; Black or African American 0.8%; Hispanic or Latino 2.3%; Asian 0.4%; Other 2.7%). **Foreign born:** 2%. **Median age:** 37.9.

Income 2000: per capita $17,950; median household $38,290; **Pop below poverty level:** 7.6%. ***Personal per capita income 2000-2003:** $23,173-$24,209.

Unemployment 2004: 5.6%. **Change from 2000:** -1.9%. **Median travel time to work:** 22.7 minutes. **Working outside county of residence:** 35.9%.

Cities with pop over 10,000: None.

GIBSON COUNTY
PO Box 630   **Ph:** 812-386-8401
Princeton, IN 47670   **Fax:** 812-385-5025

On the southwest border of IN, north of Evansville; organized Mar 9, 1813 (prior to statehood) from Knox County. **Name Origin:** For Gen. John Gibson (1740-1822), an officer in the French and Indian War and the Revolutionary War, jurist, and secretary of IN Territory (1801-16).

Area (sq mi): 499.05 (land 488.78; water 10.27). **Pop per sq mi:** 68.3.

Pop 2005: 33,408. **State rank:** 50. **Pop change:** 2000-20005 +2.8%; 1990-2000 +1.8%. **Pop 2000:** 32,500 (White 96%; Black or African American 1.9%; Hispanic or Latino 0.7%; Asian 0.5%; Other 1.1%). **Foreign born:** 0.9%. **Median age:** 38.

Income 2000: per capita $18,169; median household $37,515; **Pop below poverty level:** 8.2%. ***Personal per capita income 2000-2003:** $23,593-$28,021.

Unemployment 2004: 4.6%. **Change from 2000:** +0.8%. **Median travel time to work:** 23.7 minutes. **Working outside county of residence:** 38.8%.

Cities with pop over 10,000: None.

GRANT COUNTY
101 E 4th St   **Ph:** 765-668-8121
Marion, IN 46952   **Fax:** 765-668-6541
www.grantcounty.net

In central IN, northwest of Muncie; organized Feb 10, 1831 from Delaware County. **Name Origin:** For Samuel and Moses Grant, killed in 1790 in Indian battles in southern IL.

Area (sq mi): 414.83 (land 414.03; water 0.81). **Pop per sq mi:** 170.4.

Pop 2005: 70,557. **State rank:** 22. **Pop change:** 2000-20005 -3.9%; 1990-2000 -1%. **Pop 2000:** 73,403 (White 88%; Black or African American 7.2%; Hispanic or Latino 2.4%; Asian 0.6%; Other 2.9%). **Foreign born:** 1.2%. **Median age:** 37.4.

Income 2000: per capita $18,003; median household $36,162; **Pop below poverty level:** 11.8%. ***Personal per capita income 2000-2003:** $22,401-$25,639.

Unemployment 2004: 8.3%. **Change from 2000:** +1.5%. **Median travel time to work:** 19.5 minutes. **Working outside county of residence:** 16.8%.

Cities with pop over 10,000: Marion 🏛 (30,830).

GREENE COUNTY
PO Box 229   **Ph:** 812-384-8532
Bloomfield, IN 47424   **Fax:** 812-384-8458
www.in-map.net/counties/GREENE/

In southwest IN, southwest of Bloomington; organized Jan 5, 1821 from Knox County. **Name Origin:** For Gen. Nathanael Greene (1742-86), hero of the Revolutionary War, quartermaster general (1778-80), and commander of the army in the South (1780).

Area (sq mi): 545.91 (land 541.73; water 4.18). **Pop per sq mi:** 61.8.

Pop 2005: 33,479. **State rank:** 49. **Pop change:** 2000-20005 +1%; 1990-2000 +9%. **Pop 2000:** 33,157 (White 98.1%; Black or African American 0.1%; Hispanic or Latino 0.8%; Asian 0.2%; Other 1.1%). **Foreign born:** 0.5%. **Median age:** 38.1.

Income 2000: per capita $16,834; median household $33,998; **Pop below poverty level:** 11%. ***Personal per capita income 2000-2003:** $21,076-$22,984.

Unemployment 2004: 5.9%. **Change from 2000:** -2.3%. **Median travel time to work:** 29.7 minutes. **Working outside county of residence:** 51.4%.

Cities with pop over 10,000: None.

HAMILTON COUNTY
1 Hamilton County Sq Suite 106   **Ph:** 317-776-9629
Noblesville, IN 46060   **Fax:** 317-776-9664
www.co.hamilton.in.us

In central IN, north of Indianapolis; organized Jan 8, 1823 from

*Source: Personal per capita income data are from the Bureau of Economic Analysis; per capita income data are from the Bureau of the Census. See Introduction for explanation of differences.

222

Hamilton County (cont'd)

Hancock and Marion counties. **Name Origin:** For Alexander Hamilton (1755-1804), U.S. statesman and first secretary of the treasury (1789-95).

Area (sq mi): 402.73 (land 397.94; water 4.79). **Pop per sq mi:** 604.8.

Pop 2005: 240,685. **State rank:** 5. **Pop change:** 2000-20005 +31.7%; 1990-2000 +67 7% **Pop 2000:** 182,740 (White 93.4%; Black or African American 1.5%; Hispanic or Latino 1.6%; Asian 2.4%; Other 1.6%). **Foreign born:** 4%. **Median age:** 34.1.

Income 2000: per capita $33,109; median household $71,026; **Pop below poverty level:** 2.9%. ***Personal per capita income 2000-2003:** $43,255-$41,746.

Unemployment 2004: 3.1%. **Change from 2000:** +1.1%. **Median travel time to work:** 25.3 minutes. **Working outside county of residence:** 54.2%.

Cities with pop over 10,000: Carmel (58,198); Fishers (54,330); Noblesville 🏛 (35,438); Westfield (11,911).

HANCOCK COUNTY
9 E Main St Rm 201
Greenfield, IN 46140
www.hancockcoingov.org

Ph: 317-462-1109

In central IN, east of Indianapolis; established Jan 26, 1827 from Madison County. **Name Origin:** For John Hancock (1737-93), noted signer of the Declaration of Independence and governor of MA (1780-85;1787-93).

Area (sq mi): 306.73 (land 306.12; water 0.61). **Pop per sq mi:** 206.3.

Pop 2005: 63,138. **State rank:** 25. **Pop change:** 2000-20005 +14%; 1990-2000 +21.7%. **Pop 2000:** 55,391 (White 97.8%; Black or African American 0.1%; Hispanic or Latino 0.9%; Asian 0.4%; Other 1%). **Foreign born:** 0.9%. **Median age:** 37.4.

Income 2000: per capita $24,966; median household $56,416; **Pop below poverty level:** 3%. ***Personal per capita income 2000-2003:** $33,514-$34,016.

Unemployment 2004: 3.8%. **Change from 2000:** +1.1%. **Median travel time to work:** 25.9 minutes. **Working outside county of residence:** 64%.

Cities with pop over 10,000: Greenfield 🏛 (16,048).

HARRISON COUNTY
300 N Capitol Ave
Corydon, IN 47112
www.harrisonchamber.org

Ph: 812-738-8241
Fax: 812-738-0531

On the southern border of IN; organized Oct 11, 1808 (prior to statehood) from Northwest Territory. **Name Origin:** For William Henry Harrison (1773-1841), first territorial governor of IN (1800-11) and ninth U.S. president.

Area (sq mi): 486.88 (land 485.22; water 1.66). **Pop per sq mi:** 75.9.

Pop 2005: 36,827. **State rank:** 43. **Pop change:** 2000-20005 +7.3%; 1990-2000 +14.8%. **Pop 2000:** 34,325 (White 97.6%; Black or African American 0.4%; Hispanic or Latino 1%; Asian 0.2%; Other 1.1%). **Foreign born:** 0.9%. **Median age:** 36.6.

Income 2000: per capita $19,643; median household $43,423; **Pop below poverty level:** 6.4%. ***Personal per capita income 2000-2003:** $25,442-$26,455.

Unemployment 2004: 5.3%. **Change from 2000:** +2%. **Median travel time to work:** 30.5 minutes. **Working outside county of residence:** 56.7%.

Cities with pop over 10,000: None.

HENDRICKS COUNTY
PO Box 599
Danville, IN 46122
www.co.hendricks.in.us

Ph: 317-745-9231
Fax: 317-745-9306

In central IN, west of Indianapolis; established Dec 20, 1823 from Indian lands. **Name Origin:** For William Hendricks (1782-1850), IN legislator, governor (1822-25), and U.S. senator (1825-37).

Area (sq mi): 408.88 (land 408.39; water 0.48). **Pop per sq mi:** 312.2.

Pop 2005: 127,483. **State rank:** 12. **Pop change:** 2000-20005 +22.5%; 1990-2000 +37.5%. **Pop 2000:** 104,093 (White 96%; Black or African American 1.1%; Hispanic or Latino 1.1%; Asian 0.7%; Other 1.6%). **Foreign born:** 1.6%. **Median age:** 35.6.

Income 2000: per capita $23,129; median household $55,208; **Pop below poverty level:** 3.6%. ***Personal per capita income 2000-2003:** $30,755-$30,455.

Unemployment 2004: 3.6%. **Change from 2000:** +1.2%. **Median travel time to work:** 25.6 minutes. **Working outside county of residence:** 63.1%.

Cities with pop over 10,000: Plainfield (22,564); Brownsburg (17,622).

HENRY COUNTY
PO Box B
New Castle, IN 47362

Ph: 765-529-6401
Fax: 765-521-7046

In east-central IN, south of Muncie; established Dec 31, 1821 from Delaware County. **Name Origin:** For Patrick Henry (1736-99), patriot, governor of VA (1776-79; 1784-86), and statesman, famous for proclaiming, 'Give me liberty or give me death.'

Area (sq mi): 394.9 (land 392.93; water 1.97). **Pop per sq mi:** 120.2.

Pop 2005: 47,244. **State rank:** 30. **Pop change:** 2000-20005 -2.6%; 1990-2000 +0.8%. **Pop 2000:** 48,508 (White 97.5%; Black or African American 0.9%; Hispanic or Latino 0.8%; Asian 0.2%; Other 1%). **Foreign born:** 0.5%. **Median age:** 38.7.

Income 2000: per capita $19,355; median household $38,150; **Pop below poverty level:** 7.8%. ***Personal per capita income 2000-2003:** $24,991-$27,428.

Unemployment 2004: 6.9%. **Change from 2000:** +1.8%. **Median travel time to work:** 23.7 minutes. **Working outside county of residence:** 41.4%.

Cities with pop over 10,000: New Castle 🏛 (18,944).

HOWARD COUNTY
PO Box 9004
Kokomo, IN 46904
co.howard.in.us

Ph: 765-456-2204
Fax: 765-456-2267

In central IN, east of Marion; organized as Richardville County

Howard County (cont'd)

Jan 15, 1844 from Indian lands; name changed 1846. **Name Origin:** For Tilghman Ashurst Howard (1797-1844), TN legislator, U.S. representative from IN (1839-40), and charge d'affaires to the Republic of TX (1844).

Area (sq mi): 293.93 (land 293.07; water 0.86). **Pop per sq mi:** 290.

Pop 2005: 84,977. **State rank:** 18. **Pop change:** 2000-20005 +0%; 1990-2000 +5.1%. **Pop 2000:** 84,964 (White 88.7%; Black or African American 6.5%; Hispanic or Latino 2%; Asian 1%; Other 2.7%). **Foreign born:** 1.8%. **Median age:** 37.1.

Income 2000: per capita $22,049; median household $43,487; **Pop below poverty level:** 9.5%. ***Personal per capita income 2000-2003:** $28,659-$31,084.

Unemployment 2004: 6.7%. **Change from 2000:** +0.4%. **Median travel time to work:** 17.4 minutes. **Working outside county of residence:** 10.9%.

Cities with pop over 10,000: Kokomo 🏛 (46,070).

HUNTINGTON COUNTY
201 N Jefferson St
County Courthouse Rm 103   **Ph:** 260-358-4822
Huntington, IN 46750   **Fax:** 260-358-4823
www.huntington.in.us

In northeastern IN, southwest of Ft. Wayne; established Feb 2, 1832 from Grant County. **Name Origin:** For Samuel Huntington (1731-96), a signer of the Declaration of Independence; president of the Continental Congress (1779-81; 1783), chief justice of CT Superior Court (1784), and governor of CT (1786-96).

Area (sq mi): 387.94 (land 382.59; water 5.35). **Pop per sq mi:** 99.9.

Pop 2005: 38,236. **State rank:** 40. **Pop change:** 2000-20005 +0.4%; 1990-2000 +7.5%. **Pop 2000:** 38,075 (White 97.6%; Black or African American 0.2%; Hispanic or Latino 1%; Asian 0.3%; Other 1.4%). **Foreign born:** 0.8%. **Median age:** 36.2.

Income 2000: per capita $19,480; median household $41,620; **Pop below poverty level:** 5.5%. ***Personal per capita income 2000-2003:** $25,303-$25,793.

Unemployment 2004: 5.3%. **Change from 2000:** +0.1%. **Median travel time to work:** 20.4 minutes. **Working outside county of residence:** 36.2%.

Cities with pop over 10,000: Huntington 🏛 (17,040).

JACKSON COUNTY
PO Box 318   **Ph:** 812-358-6116
Brownstown, IN 47220   **Fax:** 812-358-6187

In south-central IN, south of Columbus; established Dec 18, 1815 (prior to statehood) from Washington County. **Name Origin:** For Andrew Jackson (1767-1845), seventh U.S. president.

Area (sq mi): 513.75 (land 509.31; water 4.44). **Pop per sq mi:** 82.9.

Pop 2005: 42,237. **State rank:** 34. **Pop change:** 2000-20005 +2.2%; 1990-2000 +9.6%. **Pop 2000:** 41,335 (White 95.1%; Black or African American 0.5%; Hispanic or Latino 2.7%; Asian 0.8%; Other 2.5%). **Foreign born:** 2.4%. **Median age:** 35.8.

Income 2000: per capita $18,400; median household $39,401; **Pop**

below poverty level: 8.5%. ***Personal per capita income 2000-2003:** $23,173-$25,476.

Unemployment 2004: 4.6%. **Change from 2000:** +0.4%. **Median travel time to work:** 21.4 minutes. **Working outside county of residence:** 22.8%.

Cities with pop over 10,000: Seymour (18,704).

JASPER COUNTY
Courthouse 115 W Washington St Suite 204   **Ph:** 219-866-4926
Rensselaer, IN 47978   **Fax:** 219-866-9450
www.jaspercountyin.com

In northwestern IN, southeast of Gary; established Feb 7,1835 from Indian lands. **Name Origin:** For Sgt. William Jasper (1750-79), Revolutionary War soldier from SC.

Area (sq mi): 561.22 (land 559.87; water 1.36). **Pop per sq mi:** 56.9.

Pop 2005: 31,876. **State rank:** 53. **Pop change:** 2000-20005 +6.1%; 1990-2000 +20.4%. **Pop 2000:** 30,043 (White 96.3%; Black or African American 0.3%; Hispanic or Latino 2.4%; Asian 0.2%; Other 1.5%). **Foreign born:** 1.5%. **Median age:** 35.

Income 2000: per capita $19,012; median household $43,369; **Pop below poverty level:** 6.7%. ***Personal per capita income 2000-2003:** $25,138-$24,792.

Unemployment 2004: 5.7%. **Change from 2000:** +0.2%. **Median travel time to work:** 27.3 minutes. **Working outside county of residence:** 41%.

Cities with pop over 10,000: None.

JAY COUNTY
120 N Court St 2nd Fl   **Ph:** 260-726-6920
Portland, IN 47371   **Fax:** 260-726-6922
www.co.jay.in.us

On central eastern border of IN, northeast of Muncie; established Feb 7, 1835 from Randolph County. **Name Origin:** For John Jay (1745-1829), first Chief Justice of the U.S. Supreme Court (1789-95), and governor of NY (1795-1801).

Area (sq mi): 383.82 (land 383.64; water 0.18). **Pop per sq mi:** 56.3.

Pop 2005: 21,606. **State rank:** 70. **Pop change:** 2000-20005 -0.9%; 1990-2000 +1.4%. **Pop 2000:** 21,806 (White 96.9%; Black or African American 0.3%; Hispanic or Latino 1.8%; Asian 0.3%; Other 1.7%). **Foreign born:** 1.5%. **Median age:** 36.7.

Income 2000: per capita $16,686; median household $35,700; **Pop below poverty level:** 9.1%. ***Personal per capita income 2000-2003:** $20,574-$22,147.

Unemployment 2004: 5.8%. **Change from 2000:** -0.7%. **Median travel time to work:** 22.3 minutes. **Working outside county of residence:** 38.5%.

Cities with pop over 10,000: None.

JEFFERSON COUNTY
300 E Main St Courthouse Rm 203   **Ph:** 812-265-8922
Madison, IN 47250   **Fax:** 812-265-8950
www.madisonindiana.org/govern.html

On southeastern border of IN, southeast of Columbus; established Nov 23, 1810 (prior to statehood) from Indian lands. **Name Origin:**

*Source: Personal per capita income data are from the Bureau of Economic Analysis; per capita income data are from the Bureau of the Census. See Introduction for explanation of differences.

Jefferson County (cont'd)

For Thomas Jefferson (1743-1826), U.S. patriot and statesman; third U.S. president.

Area (sq mi): 362.94 (land 361.37; water 1.58). **Pop per sq mi:** 89.7.

Pop 2005: 32,430. **State rank:** 51. **Pop change:** 2000-20005 +2.3%; 1990-2000 +6.4%. **Pop 2000:** 31,705 (White 95.6%; Black or African American 1.5%, Hispanic or Latino 1%; Asian 0.6%; Other 1.7%). **Foreign born:** 1.2%. **Median age:** 36.6.

Income 2000: per capita $17,412; median household $38,189; **Pop below poverty level:** 9.6%. ***Personal per capita income 2000-2003:** $21,478-$23,983.

Unemployment 2004: 4.6%. **Change from 2000:** -0.1%. **Median travel time to work:** 21.9 minutes. **Working outside county of residence:** 21.8%.

Cities with pop over 10,000: Madison 🏛 (12,335).

JENNINGS COUNTY

PO Box 385   **Ph:** 812-352-3070
Vernon, IN 47282   **Fax:** 812-352-3076
www.jenningsco.org

In southeastern IN, southeast of Columbus; established Dec 27, 1816 from Indian lands. **Name Origin:** For Jonathan Jennings (1784-1834), U.S. representative from IN (1809-16; 1822-31) and first governor (1816-22).

Area (sq mi): 378.35 (land 377.22; water 1.13). **Pop per sq mi:** 75.4.

Pop 2005: 28,427. **State rank:** 55. **Pop change:** 2000-20005 +3.2%; 1990-2000 +16.5%. **Pop 2000:** 27,554 (White 97.1%; Black or African American 0.7%; Hispanic or Latino 0.7%; Asian 0.3%; Other 1.5%). **Foreign born:** 0.7%. **Median age:** 34.6.

Income 2000: per capita $17,059; median household $39,402; **Pop below poverty level:** 9.2%. ***Personal per capita income 2000-2003:** $21,824-$22,910.

Unemployment 2004: 5.8%. **Change from 2000:** +0.9%. **Median travel time to work:** 25.2 minutes. **Working outside county of residence:** 44.3%.

Cities with pop over 10,000: None.

JOHNSON COUNTY

5 E Jefferson St PO Box 368   **Ph:** 317-736-3708
Franklin, IN 46131   **Fax:** 317-736-3749
www.co.johnson.in.us

In central IN, south of Indianapolis; established Dec 31, 1822 from Indian lands. **Name Origin:** For John Johnson, a judge of the first IN supreme court.

Area (sq mi): 321.56 (land 320.19; water 1.36). **Pop per sq mi:** 401.1.

Pop 2005: 128,436. **State rank:** 11. **Pop change:** 2000-20005 +11.5%; 1990-2000 +30.8%. **Pop 2000:** 115,209 (White 96.2%; Black or African American 0.8%; Hispanic or Latino 1.4%; Asian 0.8%; Other 1.4%). **Foreign born:** 1.7%. **Median age:** 34.9.

Income 2000: per capita $22,976; median household $52,693; **Pop below poverty level:** 5.6%. ***Personal per capita income 2000-2003:** $29,768-$29,988.

Unemployment 2004: 4.1%. **Change from 2000:** +1.7%. **Median travel time to work:** 24.7 minutes. **Working outside county of residence:** 58.2%.

Cities with pop over 10,000: Greenwood (40,813); Franklin 🏛 (21,201).

KNOX COUNTY

101 N 7th St   **Ph:** 812-885-2521
Vincennes, IN 47591   **Fax:** 812-895-4929

On the southwest border of IN; organized Jun 20, 1790 (prior to statehood) from Northwest Territory. **Name Origin:** For Gen. Henry Knox (1750-1806), Revolutionary War officer and first U.S. secretary of war (1785-94).

Area (sq mi): 524.06 (land 515.83; water 8.22). **Pop per sq mi:** 74.4.

Pop 2005: 38,366. **State rank:** 38. **Pop change:** 2000-20005 -2.3%; 1990-2000 -1.6%. **Pop 2000:** 39,256 (White 96%; Black or African American 1.9%; Hispanic or Latino 0.8%; Asian 0.5%; Other 1.2%). **Foreign born:** 1.1%. **Median age:** 36.7.

Income 2000: per capita $16,085; median household $31,362; **Pop below poverty level:** 16%. ***Personal per capita income 2000-2003:** $22,828-$25,461.

Unemployment 2004: 4.5%. **Change from 2000:** +1.2%. **Median travel time to work:** 18.3 minutes. **Working outside county of residence:** 16.4%.

Cities with pop over 10,000: Vincennes 🏛 (18,105).

KOSCIUSKO COUNTY

121 N Lake St   **Ph:** 574-372-2334
Warsaw, IN 46580   **Fax:** 574-372-2338
www.kcgov.com

In north-central IN, south of Elkhart; established Feb 7, 1835 from Indian lands. **Name Origin:** For Thaddeus Kosciusko (1746-1817), Polish soldier who fought with the Americans during the Revolutionary War.

Area (sq mi): 554.34 (land 537.5; water 16.84). **Pop per sq mi:** 141.5.

Pop 2005: 76,072. **State rank:** 19. **Pop change:** 2000-20005 +2.7%; 1990-2000 +13.4%. **Pop 2000:** 74,057 (White 92.9%; Black or African American 0.6%; Hispanic or Latino 5%; Asian 0.6%; Other 4.3%). **Foreign born:** 2.9%. **Median age:** 35.1.

Income 2000: per capita $19,806; median household $43,939; **Pop below poverty level:** 6.4%. ***Personal per capita income 2000-2003:** $26,245-$29,279.

Unemployment 2004: 4.1%. **Change from 2000:** -0.6%. **Median travel time to work:** 20 minutes. **Working outside county of residence:** 25.4%.

Cities with pop over 10,000: Warsaw 🏛 (12,672).

LA PORTE COUNTY

813 Lincolnway   **Ph:** 216-326-6808
La Porte, IN 46350   **Fax:** 216-326-5615
www.alco.org

On the northwestern border of IN, west of South Bend; organized Jan 9, 1832 from Indian lands. **Name Origin:** French 'the port' or

La Porte County (cont'd)

'the door,' referring to a natural opening through the forest that served as a gateway to the north.

Area (sq mi): 613.04 (land 598.24; water 14.8). **Pop per sq mi:** 184.7.

Pop 2005: 110,512. **State rank:** 15. **Pop change:** 2000-20005 +0.4%; 1990-2000 +2.8%. **Pop 2000:** 110,106 (White 84.8%; Black or African American 10.1%; Hispanic or Latino 3.1%; Asian 0.5%; Other 3.1%). **Foreign born:** 2.5%. **Median age:** 37.1.

Income 2000: per capita $18,913; median household $41,430; **Pop below poverty level:** 8.7%. ***Personal per capita income 2000-2003:** $24,346-$25,241.

Unemployment 2004: 6%. **Change from 2000:** +1.1%. **Median travel time to work:** 22 minutes. **Working outside county of residence:** 26%.

Cities with pop over 10,000: Michigan City (32,179); La Porte 🏛 (20,982).

LAGRANGE COUNTY

105 N Detroit St   **Ph:** 260-499-6368
LaGrange, IN 46761   **Fax:** 260-463-2187
www.lagrangecounty.com

On the northeastern border of IN, east of Elkhart; organized Feb 2, 1832 from unorganized territory in Elkhart County. **Name Origin:** For the country home near Paris of the Marquis de Lafayette (1757-1834) who fought with the Americans during the Revolutionary War, from French 'the barn.'

Area (sq mi): 386.72 (land 379.56; water 7.15). **Pop per sq mi:** 97.2.

Pop 2005: 36,875. **State rank:** 42. **Pop change:** 2000-20005 +5.6%; 1990-2000 +18.4%. **Pop 2000:** 34,909 (White 95.7%; Black or African American 0.2%; Hispanic or Latino 3.1%; Asian 0.3%; Other 2.7%). **Foreign born:** 2.1%. **Median age:** 29.5.

Income 2000: per capita $16,481; median household $42,848; **Pop below poverty level:** 7.7%. ***Personal per capita income 2000-2003:** $19,562-$20,668.

Unemployment 2004: 4.3%. **Change from 2000:** -1.7%. **Median travel time to work:** 21.4 minutes. **Working outside county of residence:** 38.3%.

Cities with pop over 10,000: None.

LAKE COUNTY

2293 N Main St   **Ph:** 219-755-3440
Crown Point, IN 46307   **Fax:** 219-755-3447
www.lakecountyin.com

In the northwest corner of IN; established Jan 28, 1836 from Porter and Newton counties. **Name Origin:** For its location on the southern shore of Lake Michigan.

Area (sq mi): 626.34 (land 496.98; water 129.36). **Pop per sq mi:** 992.6.

Pop 2005: 493,297. **State rank:** 2. **Pop change:** 2000-20005 +1.8%; 1990-2000 +1.9%. **Pop 2000:** 484,564 (White 60.6%; Black or African American 25.3%; Hispanic or Latino 12.2%; Asian 0.8%; Other 7.2%). **Foreign born:** 5.3%. **Median age:** 35.9.

Income 2000: per capita $19,639; median household $41,829; **Pop below poverty level:** 12.2%. ***Personal per capita income 2000-2003:** $26,318-$27,054.

Unemployment 2004: 6.3%. **Change from 2000:** +0.8%. **Median travel time to work:** 27.1 minutes. **Working outside county of residence:** 27.9%.

Cities with pop over 10,000: 12 (see page 35 for cities).

LAWRENCE COUNTY

916 15th St Rm 31   **Ph:** 812-275-7543
Bedford, IN 47421   **Fax:** 812-277-2024
bedfordonline.com/government/lawrence/

In south-central IN, south of Bloomington; organized Jan 7, 1818 from Orange County. **Name Origin:** For Capt. James Lawrence (1781-1813), U.S. naval officer in the war with Barbary pirates near Trilpoli and commander of the U.S.S. *Chesapeake* in the War of 1812, who said, 'Don't give up the ship!'

Area (sq mi): 452.07 (land 448.83; water 3.24). **Pop per sq mi:** 103.4.

Pop 2005: 46,403. **State rank:** 32. **Pop change:** 2000-20005 +1%; 1990-2000 +7.2%. **Pop 2000:** 45,922 (White 97.4%; Black or African American 0.4%; Hispanic or Latino 0.9%; Asian 0.3%; Other 1.4%). **Foreign born:** 0.9%. **Median age:** 38.2.

Income 2000: per capita $17,653; median household $36,280; **Pop below poverty level:** 9.8%. ***Personal per capita income 2000-2003:** $23,669-$24,858.

Unemployment 2004: 6.9%. **Change from 2000:** -1.2%. **Median travel time to work:** 25.2 minutes. **Working outside county of residence:** 33.7%.

Cities with pop over 10,000: Bedford 🏛 (13,570).

MADISON COUNTY

16 E 9th St   **Ph:** 765-641-9419
Anderson, IN 46016   **Fax:** 765-648-1375
www.madisoncty.com

In central IN, west of Muncie; organized Jan 4, 1823 from Fayette County. **Name Origin:** For James Madison (1751-1836), fourth U.S. president.

Area (sq mi): 452.91 (land 452.13; water 0.78). **Pop per sq mi:** 288.4.

Pop 2005: 130,412. **State rank:** 10. **Pop change:** 2000-20005 -2.2%; 1990-2000 +2.1%. **Pop 2000:** 133,358 (White 89.1%; Black or African American 7.9%; Hispanic or Latino 1.5%; Asian 0.4%; Other 1.8%). **Foreign born:** 1.2%. **Median age:** 37.4.

Income 2000: per capita $20,090; median household $38,925; **Pop below poverty level:** 9.3%. ***Personal per capita income 2000-2003:** $24,791-$27,207.

Unemployment 2004: 5.9%. **Change from 2000:** +1.3%. **Median travel time to work:** 23.3 minutes. **Working outside county of residence:** 32.9%.

Cities with pop over 10,000: Anderson 🏛 (57,942).

MARION COUNTY

200 E Washington St City County
Bldg Rm W122   **Ph:** 317-327-4740
Indianapolis, IN 46204   **Fax:** 317-327-3893
www.indygov.org/county

In central IN, southwest of Muncie; established Dec 31, 1821 from Ohio County. **Name Origin:** For Gen. Francis Marion (c.1732-95), SC soldier and legislator, known as 'The Swamp Fox' for his tactics during the Revolutionary War.

Area (sq mi): 403.04 (land 396.25; water 6.79). **Pop per sq mi:** 2178.3.

Pop 2005: 863,133. **State rank:** 1. **Pop change:** 2000-20005 +0.3%; 1990-2000 +7.9%. **Pop 2000:** 860,454 (White 68.9%; Black or African American 24.2%; Hispanic or Latino 3.9%; Asian 1.4%; Other 3.9%). **Foreign born:** 4.6%. **Median age:** 33.6.

Income 2000: per capita $21,789; median household $40,421; **Pop below poverty level:** 11.4%. ***Personal per capita income 2000-2003:** $30,685-$33,449.

Unemployment 2004: 5.4%. **Change from 2000:** +1.6%. **Median travel time to work:** 23 minutes. **Working outside county of residence:** 13.3%.

Cities with pop over 10,000: Indianapolis 🏛 (784,242); Lawrence (40,878); Beech Grove (14,236); Speedway (12,570).

MARSHALL COUNTY

112 W Jefferson St   **Ph:** 574-935-8510
Plymouth, IN 46563   **Fax:** 574-936-4863
www.co.marshall.in.us

In north-central IN, south of South Bend, established Feb 7, 1835 from Indian lands. **Name Origin:** For John Marshall (1755-1835), fourth Chief Justice of the U.S. Supreme Court (1801-35).

Area (sq mi): 449.92 (land 444.27; water 5.65). **Pop per sq mi:** 105.7.

Pop 2005: 46,945. **State rank:** 31. **Pop change:** 2000-20005 +4%; 1990-2000 +7%. **Pop 2000:** 45,128 (White 92.5%; Black or African American 0.3%; Hispanic or Latino 5.9%; Asian 0.3%; Other 3.8%). **Foreign born:** 4.4%. **Median age:** 35.5.

Income 2000: per capita $18,427; median household $42,581; **Pop below poverty level:** 6.8%. ***Personal per capita income 2000-2003:** $23,977-$25,177.

Unemployment 2004: 5.1%. **Change from 2000:** +0.6%. **Median travel time to work:** 21.8 minutes. **Working outside county of residence:** 31.4%.

Cities with pop over 10,000: Plymouth 🏛 (10,728).

MARTIN COUNTY

PO Box 120   **Ph:** 812-247-3651
Shoals, IN 47581   **Fax:** 812-247-2791

In southwestern IN, southwest of Bloomington; organized Jan 17, 1820 from Indian lands. **Name Origin:** For Maj. John Preston Martin (1811-62), U.S. representative from KY (1845-47).

Area (sq mi): 340.53 (land 336.14; water 4.39). **Pop per sq mi:** 30.9.

Pop 2005: 10,386. **State rank:** 87. **Pop change:** 2000-20005 +0.2%; 1990-2000 +0%. **Pop 2000:** 10,369 (White 98.6%; Black or African

American 0.2%; Hispanic or Latino 0.4%; Asian 0.1%; Other 0.7%). **Foreign born:** 0.3%. **Median age:** 38.5.

Income 2000: per capita $17,054; median household $36,411; **Pop below poverty level:** 11.2%. ***Personal per capita income 2000-2003:** $22,733-$23,336.

Unemployment 2004: 5.2%. **Change from 2000:** +0.1%. **Median travel time to work:** 27.7 minutes. **Working outside county of residence:** 44.3%.

Cities with pop over 10,000: None.

MIAMI COUNTY

PO Box 184   **Ph:** 765-472-3901
Peru, IN 46970   **Fax:** 765-472-1778

In north-central IN, north of Kokomo; established Feb 2, 1832 from Cass County. **Name Origin:** For the Miami Indians, an Algonquin tribe. Origin of the name is uncertain; probably from Ojibway *oumaumeg* 'people of the peninsula' or Delaware *we-mi-u-mik* 'all friends.'

Area (sq mi): 377.36 (land 375.62; water 1.74). **Pop per sq mi:** 94.8.

Pop 2005: 35,620. **State rank:** 44. **Pop change:** 2000-20005 -1.3%; 1990-2000 -2.2%. **Pop 2000:** 36,082 (White 93%; Black or African American 3%; Hispanic or Latino 1.3%; Asian 0.3%; Other 3%, including 1.1% American Indian/Alaska Native). **Foreign born:** 1%. **Median age:** 36.6.

Income 2000: per capita $17,726; median household $39,184; **Pop below poverty level:** 8%. ***Personal per capita income 2000-2003:** $21,697-$22,834.

Unemployment 2004: 6.6%. **Change from 2000:** +0.2%. **Median travel time to work:** 22.1 minutes. **Working outside county of residence:** 41.2%.

Cities with pop over 10,000: Peru 🏛 (12,856).

MONROE COUNTY

301 N College Ave   **Ph:** 812-349-2612
Bloomington, IN 47404   **Fax:** 812-349-2610
www.co.monroe.in.us

In central IN, west of Columbus; organized Jan 14, 1818 from Orange County. **Name Origin:** For James Monroe (1758-1831), fifth U.S. president.

Area (sq mi): 411.32 (land 394.35; water 16.97). **Pop per sq mi:** 307.9.

Pop 2005: 121,407. **State rank:** 13. **Pop change:** 2000-20005 +0.7%; 1990-2000 +10.6%. **Pop 2000:** 120,563 (White 89.8%; Black or African American 3%; Hispanic or Latino 1.9%; Asian 3.4%; Other 2.8%). **Foreign born:** 5.4%. **Median age:** 27.6.

Income 2000: per capita $18,534; median household $33,311; **Pop below poverty level:** 18.9%. ***Personal per capita income 2000-2003:** $23,176-$25,162.

Unemployment 2004: 4.1%. **Change from 2000:** +1%. **Median travel time to work:** 18.2 minutes. **Working outside county of residence:** 10.9%.

Cities with pop over 10,000: Bloomington 🏛 (68,779).

🏛 *County Seat*

MONTGOMERY COUNTY

PO Box 768
Crawfordsville, IN 47933
www.mcedonline.com

Ph: 765-364-6430
Fax: 765-364-6355

In west-central IN, south of Lafayette; organized Mar 1, 1823 from Indian lands. **Name Origin:** For Gen. Richard Montgomery (1738-75), American Revolutionary War officer who captured Montreal, Canada.

Area (sq mi): 505.34 (land 504.51; water 0.83). **Pop per sq mi:** 75.8.

Pop 2005: 38,239. **State rank:** 39. **Pop change:** 2000-20005 +1.6%; 1990-2000 +9.3%. **Pop 2000:** 37,629 (White 96.3%; Black or African American 0.8%; Hispanic or Latino 1.6%; Asian 0.4%; Other 2%). **Foreign born:** 1.5%. **Median age:** 36.6.

Income 2000: per capita $18,938; median household $41,297; **Pop below poverty level:** 8.3%. ***Personal per capita income 2000-2003:** $24,235-$24,908.

Unemployment 2004: 4.3%. **Change from 2000:** +0.4%. **Median travel time to work:** 20.4 minutes. **Working outside county of residence:** 19.8%.

Cities with pop over 10,000: Crawfordsville 🏛 (15,088).

MORGAN COUNTY

PO Box 1556
Martinsville, IN 46151

Ph: 765-342-1025
Fax: 765-342-1111

In central IN, southwest of Indianapolis; organized Feb 15, 1823 from Indian lands. **Name Origin:** For Gen. Daniel Morgan (1736-1802), an officer in the Revolutionary War and U.S. representative from VA (1797-99).

Area (sq mi): 409.39 (land 406.47; water 2.92). **Pop per sq mi:** 171.7.

Pop 2005: 69,778. **State rank:** 23. **Pop change:** 2000-20005 +4.6%; 1990-2000 +19.3%. **Pop 2000:** 66,689 (White 98.1%; Black or African American 0.1%; Hispanic or Latino 0.7%; Asian 0.2%; Other 1.1%). **Foreign born:** 0.9%. **Median age:** 36.

Income 2000: per capita $20,657; median household $47,739; **Pop below poverty level:** 6.6%. ***Personal per capita income 2000-2003:** $26,521-$27,692.

Unemployment 2004: 4.5%. **Change from 2000:** +1.4%. **Median travel time to work:** 28.3 minutes. **Working outside county of residence:** 60.5%.

Cities with pop over 10,000: Martinsville 🏛 (11,739); Mooresville (10,826).

NEWTON COUNTY

PO Box 49
Kentland, IN 47951

Ph: 219-474-6081
Fax: 219-474-5749

In northwestern IN, south of Gary; organized Feb 7, 1857 from Jasper County. **Name Origin:** For Sgt. John Newton (1752-80), a soldier under Gen. Francis Marion (1732?-95) in the Revolutionary War, who saved several colonial patriots from execution by surprising and capturing the British soldiers guarding them.

Area (sq mi): 403.53 (land 401.85; water 1.68). **Pop per sq mi:** 36.

Pop 2005: 14,456. **State rank:** 82. **Pop change:** 2000-20005 -0.8%; 1990-2000 +7.5%. **Pop 2000:** 14,566 (White 95.8%; Black or African American 0.2%; Hispanic or Latino 2.9%; Asian 0.2%; Other 2.3%). **Foreign born:** 2.3%. **Median age:** 37.3.

Income 2000: per capita $17,755; median household $40,944; **Pop below poverty level:** 6.9%. ***Personal per capita income 2000-2003:** $21,675-$21,850.

Unemployment 2004: 5%. **Change from 2000:** -0.2%. **Median travel time to work:** 29.4 minutes. **Working outside county of residence:** 56.2%.

Cities with pop over 10,000: None.

NOBLE COUNTY

101 N Orange St
Albion, IN 46701
www.nobleco.org

Ph: 260-636-2736
Fax: 260-636-4000

In northeastern IN, southeast of Elkhart; established Feb 7, 1835 from Elkhart County. **Name Origin:** For either James Noble (1785-1831), U.S. senator from IN (1816-31), or for Moah Noble, governor of IN (1831-37) when the county was established.

Area (sq mi): 417.61 (land 411.11; water 6.5). **Pop per sq mi:** 115.4.

Pop 2005: 47,448. **State rank:** 29. **Pop change:** 2000-20005 +2.5%; 1990-2000 +22.2%. **Pop 2000:** 46,275 (White 91.2%; Black or African American 0.4%; Hispanic or Latino 7.1%; Asian 0.4%; Other 5.1%). **Foreign born:** 4.9%. **Median age:** 33.3.

Income 2000: per capita $17,896; median household $42,700; **Pop below poverty level:** 7.9%. ***Personal per capita income 2000-2003:** $23,290-$24,189.

Unemployment 2004: 5.8%. **Change from 2000:** -0.9%. **Median travel time to work:** 21.2 minutes. **Working outside county of residence:** 38.4%.

Cities with pop over 10,000: None.

OHIO COUNTY

413 Main St PO Box 185
Rising Sun, IN 47040

Ph: 812-438-2610
Fax: 812-438-1215

On the southestern border of IN, southwest of Cincinnati, OH; organized Jan 4, 1844 from Dearborn County. **Name Origin:** For the Ohio River, which forms the eastern border of the county.

Area (sq mi): 87.47 (land 86.72; water 0.75). **Pop per sq mi:** 67.7.

Pop 2005: 5,874. **State rank:** 92. **Pop change:** 2000-20005 +4.5%; 1990-2000 +5.8%. **Pop 2000:** 5,623 (White 98.4%; Black or African American 0.5%; Hispanic or Latino 0.4%; Asian 0.1%; Other 0.7%). **Foreign born:** 0.1%. **Median age:** 38.4.

Income 2000: per capita $19,627; median household $41,348; **Pop below poverty level:** 7.1%. ***Personal per capita income 2000-2003:** $23,785-$23,175.

Unemployment 2004: 5.4%. **Change from 2000:** +1.9%. **Median travel time to work:** 27.3 minutes. **Working outside county of residence:** 66.3%.

Cities with pop over 10,000: None.

---

*Source: Personal per capita income data are from the Bureau of Economic Analysis; per capita income data are from the Bureau of the Census. See Introduction for explanation of differences.

ORANGE COUNTY

1 Court St   **Ph:** 812-723-2649
Paoli, IN 47454   **Fax:** 812-723-0239
www.co.orange.in.us

In south-central IN, south of Bloomington; established Dec 26, 1815 (prior to statehood) from Crawford and Washington counties. **Name Origin:** For Orange County, NC, former home of many early settlers.

Area (sq mi): 408.2 (land 399.52; water 8.68). **Pop per sq mi:** 49.5.

Pop 2005: 19,770. **State rank:** 74. **Pop change:** 2000-20005 +2.4%; 1990-2000 +4.9%. **Pop 2000:** 19,306 (White 97.5%; Black or African American 0.6%; Hispanic or Latino 0.6%; Asian 0.2%; Other 1.2%). **Foreign born:** 0.8%. **Median age:** 37.5.

Income 2000: per capita $16,717; median household $31,564; **Pop below poverty level:** 12.4%. ***Personal per capita income 2000-2003:** $21,337-$21,516.

Unemployment 2004: 7.3%. **Change from 2000:** -1.8%. **Median travel time to work:** 25.2 minutes. **Working outside county of residence:** 35.7%.

Cities with pop over 10,000: None.

OWEN COUNTY

60 S Main St County Courthouse   **Ph:** 812-829-5000
Spencer, IN 47460   **Fax:** 812-829-5004
www.owencounty.org

In west-central IN, northwest of Bloomington; established Dec 21, 1818 from Indian lands. **Name Origin:** For Col. Abraham Owen (?-1811), killed in the Battle of Tippecanoe.

Area (sq mi): 387.83 (land 385.18; water 2.65). **Pop per sq mi:** 59.3.

Pop 2005: 22,823. **State rank:** 68. **Pop change:** 2000-20005 +4.8%; 1990-2000 +26.1%. **Pop 2000:** 21,786 (White 97.7%; Black or African American 0.3%; Hispanic or Latino 0.8%; Asian 0.2%; Other 1.4%). **Foreign born:** 0.4%. **Median age:** 37.6.

Income 2000: per capita $16,884; median household $36,529; **Pop below poverty level:** 9.4%. ***Personal per capita income 2000-2003:** $21,003-$21,832.

Unemployment 2004: 5.1%. **Change from 2000:** +0.4%. **Median travel time to work:** 33.6 minutes. **Working outside county of residence:** 62%.

Cities with pop over 10,000: None.

PARKE COUNTY

116 W High St Rm 204   **Ph:** 765-569-5132
Rockville, IN 47872   **Fax:** 765-569-4222
www.parkecounty.com

In west-central IN, north of Terre Haute; organized Jan 9, 1821 from Indian lands. **Name Origin:** For Benjamin Parke (1777-1835), attorney general of IN Territory (1804-08), IN legislator, and judge of the U.S. District Court of IN (1817-35).

Area (sq mi): 450.1 (land 444.77; water 5.32). **Pop per sq mi:** 39.

Pop 2005: 17,362. **State rank:** 78. **Pop change:** 2000-20005 +0.7%; 1990-2000 +11.9%. **Pop 2000:** 17,241 (White 96.1%; Black or African American 2.1%; Hispanic or Latino 0.6%; Asian 0.2%; Other 1.1%). **Foreign born:** 0.5%. **Median age:** 38.9.

Income 2000: per capita $16,986; median household $35,724; **Pop below poverty level:** 11.5%. ***Personal per capita income 2000-2003:** $20,431-$21,891.

Unemployment 2004: 6.1%. **Change from 2000:** +1.4%. **Median travel time to work:** 27.5 minutes. **Working outside county of residence:** 51.2%.

Cities with pop over 10,000: None.

PERRY COUNTY

County Courthouse 2219 Payne St   **Ph:** 812-547-3741
Tell City, IN 47586   **Fax:** 812-547-9782
www.perrycountyin.org

On the south-central border of IN; organized Sept 7, 1814 (prior to statehood) from Harrison and Warrick counties. **Name Origin:** For Oliver Hazard Perry (1785-1819), U.S. naval officer during the War of 1812, famous for the message, 'We have met the enemy and they are ours.'

Area (sq mi): 386.34 (land 381.39; water 4.95). **Pop per sq mi:** 49.9.

Pop 2005: 19,032. **State rank:** 75. **Pop change:** 2000-20005 +0.7%; 1990-2000 -1.1%. **Pop 2000:** 18,899 (White 97.1%; Black or African American 1.4%; Hispanic or Latino 0.7%; Asian 0.1%; Other 0.8%). **Foreign born:** 0.4%. **Median age:** 38.

Income 2000: per capita $16,673; median household $36,246; **Pop below poverty level:** 9.4%. ***Personal per capita income 2000-2003:** $22,261-$24,189.

Unemployment 2004: 5.3%. **Change from 2000:** -0.7%. **Median travel time to work:** 24.8 minutes. **Working outside county of residence:** 39.8%.

Cities with pop over 10,000: None.

PIKE COUNTY

801 Main St PO Box 125   **Ph:** 812-354-6025
Petersburg, IN 47567   **Fax:** 812-354-6369
www.pikecountyin.org

In southwestern IN, northeast of Evansville; established Dec 21, 1816 from Indian lands. **Name Origin:** For Zebulon Montgomery Pike (1779-1813), U.S. army officer and discoverer of Pikes Peak in CO.

Area (sq mi): 341.08 (land 336.18; water 4.91). **Pop per sq mi:** 38.

Pop 2005: 12,766. **State rank:** 85. **Pop change:** 2000-20005 -0.6%; 1990-2000 +2.6%. **Pop 2000:** 12,837 (White 98.7%; Black or African American 0.1%; Hispanic or Latino 0.6%; Asian 0.1%; Other 0.6%). **Foreign born:** 0.6%. **Median age:** 38.8.

Income 2000: per capita $16,217; median household $34,759; **Pop below poverty level:** 8%. ***Personal per capita income 2000-2003:** $21,245-$22,507.

Unemployment 2004: 5.3%. **Change from 2000:** +1.2%. **Median travel time to work:** 26.1 minutes. **Working outside county of residence:** 56.1%.

Cities with pop over 10,000: None.

PORTER COUNTY

155 Indiana Ave   **Ph:** 219-465-3445
Valparaiso, IN 46383   **Fax:** 219-465-3592
www.co.porter.in.us

On the northwestern border of IN, east of Gary, bordered on north by Lake Michigan; established Feb 7, 1835 from Indian lands. **Name Origin:** For Commodore David Porter (1780-1843), naval hero in the War of 1812 and U.S. minister to Turkey (1839).

Area (sq mi): 521.61 (land 418.11; water 103.5). **Pop per sq mi:** 377.3.

Pop 2005: 157,772. **State rank:** 8. **Pop change:** 2000-20005 +7.5%; 1990-2000 +13.9%. **Pop 2000:** 146,798 (White 92.2%; Black or African American 0.9%; Hispanic or Latino 4.8%; Asian 0.9%; Other 2.8%). **Foreign born:** 3%. **Median age:** 36.3.

Income 2000: per capita $23,957; median household $53,100; **Pop below poverty level:** 5.9%. ***Personal per capita income 2000-2003:** $30,935-$31,238.

Unemployment 2004: 4.7%. **Change from 2000:** +0.7%. **Median travel time to work:** 25.9 minutes. **Working outside county of residence:** 43.8%.

Cities with pop over 10,000: Portage (35,269); Valparaiso 🏛 (28,750); Chesterton (11,570).

POSEY COUNTY

126 E 3rd St Rm 220   **Ph:** 812-838-1300
Mount Vernon, IN 47620   **Fax:** 812-838-1344
www.poseycounty.org

In the southwestern corner of IN, west of Evansville; organized Sept 7, 1814 (prior to statehood) from Knox County. **Name Origin:** For Gen. Thomas Posey (1750-1818), officer in the American Revolution, LA legislator (1805-06), U.S. senator from LA (1812-13), and IN territorial governor (1813-16).

Area (sq mi): 419.45 (land 408.5; water 10.95). **Pop per sq mi:** 65.7.

Pop 2005: 26,852. **State rank:** 60. **Pop change:** 2000-20005 -0.8%; 1990-2000 +4.2%. **Pop 2000:** 27,061 (White 97.7%; Black or African American 0.9%; Hispanic or Latino 0.4%; Asian 0.2%; Other 1.1%). **Foreign born:** 0.5%. **Median age:** 37.4.

Income 2000: per capita $19,516; median household $44,209; **Pop below poverty level:** 7.4%. ***Personal per capita income 2000-2003:** $27,565-$29,342.

Unemployment 2004: 4.3%. **Change from 2000:** +1.2%. **Median travel time to work:** 23 minutes. **Working outside county of residence:** 50.8%.

Cities with pop over 10,000: None.

PULASKI COUNTY

112 E Main St Rm 230   **Ph:** 574-946-3313
Winamac, IN 46996   **Fax:** 574-946-4953

In northwestern IN, southwest of South Bend; established Feb 7, 1835 from Cass County. **Name Origin:** For Count Casimir Pulaski (1747-79), Polish soldier who fought for America during the Revolutionary War.

Area (sq mi): 434.57 (land 433.68; water 0.89). **Pop per sq mi:** 31.8.

Pop 2005: 13,783. **State rank:** 84. **Pop change:** 2000-20005 +0.2%; 1990-2000 +8.8%. **Pop 2000:** 13,755 (White 96.6%; Black or African American 0.9%; Hispanic or Latino 1.4%; Asian 0.2%; Other 1.3%). **Foreign born:** 0.8%. **Median age:** 37.8.

Income 2000: per capita $16,835; median household $35,422; **Pop below poverty level:** 8.3%. ***Personal per capita income 2000-2003:** $22,456-$23,350.

Unemployment 2004: 5.1%. **Change from 2000:** -1%. **Median travel time to work:** 23.4 minutes. **Working outside county of residence:** 39.1%.

Cities with pop over 10,000: None.

PUTNAM COUNTY

1 Courthouse Sq Rm 20   **Ph:** 765-653-5513
Greencastle, IN 46135   **Fax:** 765-653-5992
www.putnamcountyin.org

In west-central IN, west of Indianapolis; established Dec 31, 1821 from Indian lands. **Name Origin:** For Gen. Israel Putnam (1718-90), Revolutionary War officer and American commander at the Battle of Bunker Hill.

Area (sq mi): 482.58 (land 480.31; water 2.27). **Pop per sq mi:** 76.9.

Pop 2005: 36,957. **State rank:** 41. **Pop change:** 2000-20005 +2.6%; 1990-2000 +18.8%. **Pop 2000:** 36,019 (White 94.3%; Black or African American 2.9%; Hispanic or Latino 1.1%; Asian 0.5%; Other 1.6%). **Foreign born:** 1.1%. **Median age:** 35.1.

Income 2000: per capita $17,163; median household $38,882; **Pop below poverty level:** 8%. ***Personal per capita income 2000-2003:** $22,243-$24,078.

Unemployment 2004: 5.4%. **Change from 2000:** +2.4%. **Median travel time to work:** 25.6 minutes. **Working outside county of residence:** 38%.

Cities with pop over 10,000: Greencastle 🏛 (10,011).

RANDOLPH COUNTY

County Courthouse
100 S Main St PO Box 230   **Ph:** 765-584-7207
Winchester, IN 47394   **Fax:** 765-584-2958
www.randolphcounty.us

On the east-central border of IN, east of Muncie; organized Jan 10, 1818 from Wayne County. **Name Origin:** For either Thomas Randolph (?-1811), attorney-general of IN Territory killed at the Battle of Tippecanoe, or for Randolph County, NC, former home of many early settlers.

Area (sq mi): 453.23 (land 452.83; water 0.39). **Pop per sq mi:** 58.9.

Pop 2005: 26,684. **State rank:** 61. **Pop change:** 2000-20005 -2.6%; 1990-2000 +0.9%. **Pop 2000:** 27,401 (White 97.5%; Black or African American 0.3%; Hispanic or Latino 1.2%; Asian 0.2%; Other 1.5%). **Foreign born:** 0.7%. **Median age:** 38.2.

Income 2000: per capita $16,954; median household $34,544; **Pop below poverty level:** 11.1%. ***Personal per capita income 2000-2003:** $23,087-$23,926.

Unemployment 2004: 6.9%. **Change from 2000:** +0.3%. **Median travel time to work:** 23.3 minutes. **Working outside county of residence:** 45.6%.

Cities with pop over 10,000: None.

*Source: Personal per capita income data are from the Bureau of Economic Analysis; per capita income data are from the Bureau of the Census. See Introduction for explanation of differences.

RIPLEY COUNTY

PO Box 177   **Ph:** 812-689-6115
Versailles, IN 47042   **Fax:** 812-689-6000
www.ripleycounty.com

In southeastern IN, east of Columbus; established Dec 27, 1816 from Indian lands. **Name Origin:** For Gen. Eleazar Wheelock Ripley (1782-1839), officer in the War of 1812, MA legislator, and U.S. representative from LA (1835-39).

Area (sq mi): 447.91 (land 446.36; water 1.55). **Pop per sq mi:** 62.1.

Pop 2005: 27,710. **State rank:** 58. **Pop change:** 2000-20005 +4.5%; 1990-2000 +7.7%. **Pop 2000:** 26,523 (White 97.9%; Black or African American 0%; Hispanic or Latino 0.9%; Asian 0.4%; Other 1.2%). **Foreign born:** 0.7%. **Median age:** 35.7.

Income 2000: per capita $17,559; median household $41,426; **Pop below poverty level:** 7.5%. ***Personal per capita income 2000-2003:** $23,447-$25,030.

Unemployment 2004: 5%. **Change from 2000:** +1.5%. **Median travel time to work:** 26.3 minutes. **Working outside county of residence:** 45.5%.

Cities with pop over 10,000: None.

RUSH COUNTY

101 E 2nd St County Courthouse   **Ph:** 765-932-2077
Rushville, IN 46173   **Fax:** 765-938-1163
www.rushcounty.in.gov

In east-central IN, southeast of Indianapolis; established Dec 31, 1821 from Franklin County. **Name Origin:** For Benjamin Rush (1745-1813), surgeon general in the Continental Army and a signer of the Declaration of Independence.

Area (sq mi): 408.62 (land 408.28; water 0.34). **Pop per sq mi:** 43.7.

Pop 2005: 17,823. **State rank:** 76. **Pop change:** 2000-20005 -2.4%; 1990-2000 +0.7%. **Pop 2000:** 18,261 (White 97.4%; Black or African American 0.6%; Hispanic or Latino 0.5%; Asian 0.5%; Other 1.2%). **Foreign born:** 0.3%. **Median age:** 36.9.

Income 2000: per capita $17,997; median household $38,152; **Pop below poverty level:** 7.3%. ***Personal per capita income 2000-2003:** $24,868-$26,374.

Unemployment 2004: 4.8%. **Change from 2000:** +1.1%. **Median travel time to work:** 25.4 minutes. **Working outside county of residence:** 50.1%.

Cities with pop over 10,000: None.

SAINT JOSEPH COUNTY

101 S Main St   **Ph:** 574-235-9635
South Bend, IN 46601   **Fax:** 574-235-9838
www.stjosephcountyindiana.com

On the central northern border of IN; organized Jan 29, 1830 from Indian lands. **Name Origin:** For the Saint Joseph River, which runs through the county.

Area (sq mi): 460.97 (land 457.34; water 3.63). **Pop per sq mi:** 582.

Pop 2005: 266,160. **State rank:** 4. **Pop change:** 2000-20005 +0.2%; 1990-2000 +7.5%. **Pop 2000:** 265,559 (White 80.5%; Black or African American 11.5%; Hispanic or Latino 4.7%; Asian 1.3%; Other 5%). **Foreign born:** 4.6%. **Median age:** 34.4.

Income 2000: per capita $19,756; median household $40,420; **Pop below poverty level:** 10.4%. ***Personal per capita income 2000-2003:** $26,515-$29,927.

Unemployment 2004: 5%. **Change from 2000:** +0.4%. **Median travel time to work:** 20.2 minutes. **Working outside county of residence:** 16.9%.

Cities with pop over 10,000: South Bend ⚏ (105,494); Mishawaka (48,385).

SCOTT COUNTY

1 E McClain Ave Suite 120   **Ph:** 812-752-4769
Scottsburg, IN 47170   **Fax:** 812-752-5459
www.greatscottindiana.org

On the southeastern border of IN, north of Louisville, KY; organized Jan 12, 1820 from Clark and Jackson counties. **Name Origin:** For Gen. Charles Scott (1739-1813), an officer in the Revolutionary War; governor of KY (1808-12).

Area (sq mi): 192.73 (land 190.39; water 2.34). **Pop per sq mi:** 125.1.

Pop 2005: 23,820. **State rank:** 65. **Pop change:** 2000-20005 +3.7%; 1990-2000 +9.4%. **Pop 2000:** 22,960 (White 98.2%; Black or African American 0%; Hispanic or Latino 1%; Asian 0.2%; Other 1.1%). **Foreign born:** 0.4%. **Median age:** 35.1.

Income 2000: per capita $16,065; median household $34,656; **Pop below poverty level:** 13.1%. ***Personal per capita income 2000-2003:** $21,515-$22,145.

Unemployment 2004: 5.6%. **Change from 2000:** +0.7%. **Median travel time to work:** 25.3 minutes. **Working outside county of residence:** 42.9%.

Cities with pop over 10,000: None.

SHELBY COUNTY

25 W Polk St   **Ph:** 317-392-6330
Shelbyville, IN 46176   **Fax:** 317-392-6393
www.shelbychamber.net

In central IN, southeast of Indianapolis; established Dec 31, 1821 from Indian lands. **Name Origin:** For Gen. Isaac Shelby (1750-1826), officer in the Revolutionary War, NC legislator, and first governor of KY (1792-96; 1812-16).

Area (sq mi): 413.11 (land 412.64; water 0.47). **Pop per sq mi:** 106.1.

Pop 2005: 43,766. **State rank:** 33. **Pop change:** 2000-20005 +0.7%; 1990-2000 +7.8%. **Pop 2000:** 43,445 (White 96.7%; Black or African American 0.8%; Hispanic or Latino 1.1%; Asian 0.6%; Other 1.4%). **Foreign born:** 1.6%. **Median age:** 36.2.

Income 2000: per capita $20,324; median household $43,649; **Pop below poverty level:** 7.6%. ***Personal per capita income 2000-2003:** $26,652-$27,620.

Unemployment 2004: 4.8%. **Change from 2000:** +1.1%. **Median travel time to work:** 21.8 minutes. **Working outside county of residence:** 41.1%.

Cities with pop over 10,000: Shelbyville ⚏ (17,848).

⚏ *County Seat*

SPENCER COUNTY

PO Box 12
Rockport, IN 47635
www.spencerco.org

Ph: 812-649-6027
Fax: 812-649-6030

On the southwestern border of IN, east of Evansville; organized Jan 10, 1818 from Warrick County. **Name Origin:** For Captain Spier (Spear?) Spencer (?-1811), a KY officer killed at the Battle of Tippecanoe.

Area (sq mi): 401.23 (land 398.69; water 2.55). **Pop per sq mi:** 51.5.

Pop 2005: 20,528. **State rank:** 72. **Pop change:** 2000-20005 +0.7%; 1990-2000 +4.6%. **Pop 2000:** 20,391 (White 97.1%; Black or African American 0.6%; Hispanic or Latino 1.5%; Asian 0.2%; Other 1.4%). **Foreign born:** 0.9%. **Median age:** 37.3.

Income 2000: per capita $18,000; median household $42,451; **Pop below poverty level:** 6.9%. ***Personal per capita income 2000-2003:** $23,947-$25,356.

Unemployment 2004: 5.2%. **Change from 2000:** +0.5%. **Median travel time to work:** 28 minutes. **Working outside county of residence:** 53.1%.

Cities with pop over 10,000: None.

STARKE COUNTY

53 E Washington St County Courthouse
Knox, IN 46534

Ph: 574-772-9128
Fax: 574-772-9169

In northwestern IN, southwest of South Bend; established Feb 7, 1835 from Marshall County. **Name Origin:** For Gen. John Stark (1728-1822), an officer in the French and Indian Wars and the American Revolution; no reason known why spelling was altered.

Area (sq mi): 312.31 (land 309.31; water 3). **Pop per sq mi:** 74.1.

Pop 2005: 22,933. **State rank:** 67. **Pop change:** 2000-20005 -2.6%; 1990-2000 +3.6%. **Pop 2000:** 23,556 (White 96.3%; Black or African American 0.2%; Hispanic or Latino 2.2%; Asian 0.2%; Other 1.9%). **Foreign born:** 2.6%. **Median age:** 37.

Income 2000: per capita $16,466; median household $37,243; **Pop below poverty level:** 11.1%. ***Personal per capita income 2000-2003:** $18,704-$20,019.

Unemployment 2004: 6.9%. **Change from 2000:** -0.1%. **Median travel time to work:** 28.9 minutes. **Working outside county of residence:** 52.7%.

Cities with pop over 10,000: None.

STEUBEN COUNTY

55 S Public Sq
Angola, IN 46703
www.co.steuben.in.us

Ph: 260-668-1000
Fax: 260-668-3702

In the northeastern corner of IN; established Feb 7, 1835 from Indian lands. **Name Origin:** For Friedrich Wilhelm, Baron von Steuben (1730-94), Prussian soldier named inspector general of the U.S. Continental Army (1778).

Area (sq mi): 322.48 (land 308.72; water 13.76). **Pop per sq mi:** 109.4.

Pop 2005: 33,773. **State rank:** 48. **Pop change:** 2000-20005 +1.7%; 1990-2000 +21%. **Pop 2000:** 33,214 (White 96.1%; Black or African American 0.4%; Hispanic or Latino 2.1%; Asian 0.4%; Other 2%). **Foreign born:** 1.4%. **Median age:** 35.5.

Income 2000: per capita $20,647; median household $44,089; **Pop below poverty level:** 6.7%. ***Personal per capita income 2000-2003:** $25,494-$25,052.

Unemployment 2004: 5.7%. **Change from 2000:** -0.4%. **Median travel time to work:** 20.9 minutes. **Working outside county of residence:** 29.1%.

Cities with pop over 10,000: None.

SULLIVAN COUNTY

PO Box 370
Sullivan, IN 47882
www.sctb.net

Ph: 812-268-4657
Fax: 812-268-7027

On the west-central border of IN, south of Terre Haute; established Dec 30, 1816 from Knox County. **Name Origin:** For Gen. Daniel Sullivan (?-1779), killed during the Revolutionary War.

Area (sq mi): 454.04 (land 447.2; water 6.85). **Pop per sq mi:** 48.7.

Pop 2005: 21,763. **State rank:** 69. **Pop change:** 2000-20005 +0.1%; 1990-2000 +14.5%. **Pop 2000:** 21,751 (White 93.7%; Black or African American 4.3%; Hispanic or Latino 0.8%; Asian 0.1%; Other 1.4%). **Foreign born:** 0.3%. **Median age:** 37.3.

Income 2000: per capita $16,234; median household $32,976; **Pop below poverty level:** 10.9%. ***Personal per capita income 2000-2003:** $19,463-$20,639.

Unemployment 2004: 7.3%. **Change from 2000:** +1.6%. **Median travel time to work:** 26.8 minutes. **Working outside county of residence:** 51.3%.

Cities with pop over 10,000: None.

SWITZERLAND COUNTY

212 W Main St County Courthouse
Vevay, IN 47043

Ph: 812-427-3302
Fax: 812-427-3179

In the southeastern corner of IN, southeast of Columbus; organized Sept 7, 1814 (prior to statehood) from Indian lands. **Name Origin:** For the European country, named by Swiss settlers.

Area (sq mi): 223.52 (land 221.18; water 2.34). **Pop per sq mi:** 43.9.

Pop 2005: 9,718. **State rank:** 88. **Pop change:** 2000-20005 +7.2%; 1990-2000 +17.1%. **Pop 2000:** 9,065 (White 98.3%; Black or African American 0.2%; Hispanic or Latino 0.9%; Asian 0.1%; Other 0.9%). **Foreign born:** 0.5%. **Median age:** 36.8.

Income 2000: per capita $17,466; median household $37,092; **Pop below poverty level:** 13.9%. ***Personal per capita income 2000-2003:** $21,192-$21,452.

Unemployment 2004: 4.4%. **Change from 2000:** -0.3%. **Median travel time to work:** 33.6 minutes. **Working outside county of residence:** 61.3%.

Cities with pop over 10,000: None.

TIPPECANOE COUNTY

20 N 3rd St
Lafayette, IN 47901
www.county.tippecanoe.in.us

Ph: 765-423-9215
Fax: 765-423-9196

In west-central IN, west of Kokomo; organized Jan 20, 1826 from Montgomery County. **Name Origin:** For the Tippecanoe River, itself named from Potawatomi *quit-te-pe-con-nac* 'buffalo fish,' which were plentiful in the river.

*Source: Personal per capita income data are from the Bureau of Economic Analysis; per capita income data are from the Bureau of the Census. See Introduction for explanation of differences.

Tippecanoe County (cont'd)

Area (sq mi): 503.07 (land 499.79; water 3.28). **Pop per sq mi:** 307.9.

Pop 2005: 153,875. **State rank:** 9. **Pop change:** 2000-20005 +3.3%; 1990-2000 +14.1%. **Pop 2000:** 148,955 (White 86.4%; Black or African American 2.5%; Hispanic or Latino 5.3%; Asian 4.5%; Other 4.2%). **Foreign born:** 8.2%. **Median age:** 27.2.

Income 2000: per capita $19,375; median household $38,052; **Pop below poverty level:** 15.4%. ***Personal per capita income 2000-2003:** $24,232-$25,982.

Unemployment 2004: 4.5%. **Change from 2000:** +1.4%. **Median travel time to work:** 17.3 minutes. **Working outside county of residence:** 7.7%.

Cities with pop over 10,000: Lafayette 🏛 (59,753); West Lafayette (28,609).

TIPTON COUNTY

101 E Jefferson St   **Ph:** 765 675-2794
Tipton, IN 46072   **Fax:** 765-675-3194
www.tiptoncounty.org

In central IN, south of Kokomo; organized Jan 15, 1844 from Hamilton County. **Name Origin:** For Gen. John Tipton (1786-1839), IN legislator (1819-23), and U.S. senator (1832-39).

Area (sq mi): 260.41 (land 260.39; water 0.02). **Pop per sq mi:** 62.9.

Pop 2005: 16,385. **State rank:** 80. **Pop change:** 2000-20005 -1.2%; 1990-2000 +2.8%. **Pop 2000:** 16,577 (White 97.7%; Black or African American 0.1%; Hispanic or Latino 1.2%; Asian 0.3%; Other 1.2%). **Foreign born:** 1%. **Median age:** 38.4.

Income 2000: per capita $21,926; median household $48,546; **Pop below poverty level:** 5.1%. ***Personal per capita income 2000-2003:** $29,830-$31,153.

Unemployment 2004: 5.2%. **Change from 2000:** -0.1%. **Median travel time to work:** 22.1 minutes. **Working outside county of residence:** 55.7%.

Cities with pop over 10,000: None.

UNION COUNTY

26 W Union St   **Ph:** 765-458-6121
Liberty, IN 47353   **Fax:** 765-458-5263

On the southeastern border of IN, south of Richmond; organized Jan 15, 1821 from Wayne County. **Name Origin:** As an expression of belief in the federal union of the states.

Area (sq mi): 165.25 (land 161.55; water 3.7). **Pop per sq mi:** 44.6.

Pop 2005: 7,208. **State rank:** 91. **Pop change:** 2000-20005 -1.9%; 1990-2000 +5.3%. **Pop 2000:** 7,349 (White 98.5%; Black or African American 0.2%; Hispanic or Latino 0.3%; Asian 0.2%; Other 0.9%). **Foreign born:** 0.4%. **Median age:** 36.5.

Income 2000: per capita $19,549; median household $36,672; **Pop below poverty level:** 9.7%. ***Personal per capita income 2000-2003:** $22,537-$24,786.

Unemployment 2004: 5.4%. **Change from 2000:** +0.6%. **Median travel time to work:** 24.6 minutes. **Working outside county of residence:** 63.2%.

Cities with pop over 10,000: None.

VANDERBURGH COUNTY

1 NW ML King Jr Blvd   **Ph:** 812-435-5241
Evansville, IN 47708   **Fax:** 812-435-5963
www.vanderburghgov.org

On the southwestern border of IN; organized Jan 7, 1818 from Indian lands. **Name Origin:** For Henry Vanderburgh, officer in the Revolutionary War and judge of the first court in the IN Territory.

Area (sq mi): 235.74 (land 234.57; water 1.16). **Pop per sq mi:** 738.3.

Pop 2005: 173,187. **State rank:** 7. **Pop change:** 2000-20005 +0.7%; 1990-2000 +4.2%. **Pop 2000:** 171,922 (White 88.7%; Black or African American 8.2%; Hispanic or Latino 1%; Asian 0.8%; Other 1.7%). **Foreign born:** 1.6%. **Median age:** 36.9.

Income 2000: per capita $20,655; median household $36,823; **Pop below poverty level:** 11.2%. ***Personal per capita income 2000-2003:** $28,282-$31,677.

Unemployment 2004: 4.8%. **Change from 2000:** +1.2%. **Median travel time to work:** 19 minutes. **Working outside county of residence:** 10.2%.

Cities with pop over 10,000: Evansville 🏛 (117,156).

VERMILLION COUNTY

PO Box 10   **Ph:** 765-492-3500
Newport, IN 47966   **Fax:** 765-492-5001

On the central western border of IN, north of Terre Haute; organized Jan 2, 1824 from Parke County. **Name Origin:** For the Big Vermilllion River, which runs across the northern part of the county. Shortened French literal transliteration *Vermillion Jaune* 'yellow red' of the Indian name *Osanamon*, suggesting vermilion paint, probably from the soil that colored the river.

Area (sq mi): 259.94 (land 256.89; water 3.05). **Pop per sq mi:** 64.5.

Pop 2005: 16,562. **State rank:** 79. **Pop change:** 2000-20005 -1.3%; 1990-2000 +0.1%. **Pop 2000:** 16,788 (White 98%; Black or African American 0.3%; Hispanic or Latino 0.6%; Asian 0.1%; Other 1.2%). **Foreign born:** 0.8%. **Median age:** 38.9.

Income 2000: per capita $18,579; median household $34,837; **Pop below poverty level:** 9.5%. ***Personal per capita income 2000-2003:** $23,078 $25,313.

Unemployment 2004: 7.9%. **Change from 2000:** +2%. **Median travel time to work:** 22.7 minutes. **Working outside county of residence:** 52.7%.

Cities with pop over 10,000: None.

VIGO COUNTY

PO Box 8449   **Ph:** 812-462-3211
Terre Haute, IN 47808   **Fax:** 812-232-2921
www.vigocountyin.com

On the central western border of IN, northwest of Bloomington; organized Jan 21, 1818 from Indian lands. **Name Origin:** For Giuseppe Maria Francesco Vigo (1747-1836), also known as Col. Francis Vigo, a Mondovian-born fur trader who furnished funds and assistance to Revolutionary soldier George Rogers Clark (1752-1818).

Vigo County (cont'd)

Area (sq mi): 410.47 (land 403.29; water 7.17). **Pop per sq mi:** 254.4.

Pop 2005: 102,592. **State rank:** 16. **Pop change:** 2000-20005 -3.1%; 1990-2000 -0.2%. **Pop 2000:** 105,848 (White 89.9%; Black or African American 6%; Hispanic or Latino 1.2%; Asian 1.2%; Other 2.1%). **Foreign born:** 2%. **Median age:** 34.9.

Income 2000: per capita $17,620; median household $33,184; **Pop below poverty level:** 14.1%. ***Personal per capita income 2000-2003:** $22,364-$24,772.

Unemployment 2004: 7%. **Change from 2000:** +1.6%. **Median travel time to work:** 18.7 minutes. **Working outside county of residence:** 10.4%.

Cities with pop over 10,000: Terre Haute ▥ (57,224).

WABASH COUNTY
69 W Hill St   **Ph:** 260-563-0661
Wabash, IN 46992   **Fax:** 260-569-1352
www.wabashcountycvb.com

In north-central IN, southwest of Ft. Wayne; established Feb 2, 1832 from Huntington County. **Name Origin:** For the Wabash River, which runs across the center of the county itself named from a Miami Indian word probably meaning 'pure white,' referring to a limestone bed in the river.

Area (sq mi): 421.07 (land 413.17; water 7.9). **Pop per sq mi:** 81.9.

Pop 2005: 33,843. **State rank:** 47. **Pop change:** 2000-20005 -3.2%; 1990-2000 -0.3%. **Pop 2000:** 34,960 (White 96.7%; Black or African American 0.4%; Hispanic or Latino 1.2%; Asian 0.4%; Other 1.8%). **Foreign born:** 0.7%. **Median age:** 37.5.

Income 2000: per capita $18,192; median household $40,413; **Pop below poverty level:** 6.9%. ***Personal per capita income 2000-2003:** $24,840-$25,719.

Unemployment 2004: 6.1%. **Change from 2000:** +0.3%. **Median travel time to work:** 19.1 minutes. **Working outside county of residence:** 26.5%.

Cities with pop over 10,000: Wabash ▥ (11,342).

WARREN COUNTY
125 N Monroe St Suite 11   **Ph:** 765-762-3510
Williamsport, IN 47993   **Fax:** 765-762-7251
www.warrenco.net

On the west-central border of IN, southwest of Lafayette; organized Jan 19, 1827 from Indian lands. **Name Origin:** For Dr. Joseph Warren (1741-75), Revolutionary War general and member of the Committee of Safety who dispatched Paul Revere (1735-1818) on his famous ride.

Area (sq mi): 366.6 (land 364.88; water 1.72). **Pop per sq mi:** 24.1.

Pop 2005: 8,785. **State rank:** 90. **Pop change:** 2000-20005 +4.3%; 1990-2000 +3%. **Pop 2000:** 8,419 (White 98.8%; Black or African American 0.1%; Hispanic or Latino 0.4%; Asian 0.2%; Other 0.6%). **Foreign born:** 0.3%. **Median age:** 38.2.

Income 2000: per capita $18,070; median household $41,825; **Pop below poverty level:** 6.5%. ***Personal per capita income 2000-2003:** $22,784-$22,770.

Unemployment 2004: 4.3%. **Change from 2000:** +0.7%. **Median travel time to work:** 24.9 minutes. **Working outside county of residence:** 69%.

Cities with pop over 10,000: None.

WARRICK COUNTY
107 W Locust St Suite 301   **Ph:** 812-897-6120
Boonville, IN 47601   **Fax:** 812-897-6189
www.warrickcounty.gov

On the southwestern border of IN, east of Evansville; organized Mar 9, 1813 (prior to statehood) from Indian lands. **Name Origin:** For Capt. Jacob Warrick (1773-1811), distinguished early settler and officer who died at the Battle of Tippecanoe.

Area (sq mi): 390.86 (land 384.07; water 6.79). **Pop per sq mi:** 146.7.

Pop 2005: 56,362. **State rank:** 26. **Pop change:** 2000-20005 +7.6%; 1990-2000 +16.6%. **Pop 2000:** 52,383 (White 97%; Black or African American 1%; Hispanic or Latino 0.6%; Asian 0.6%; Other 0.8%). **Foreign born:** 1.3%. **Median age:** 37.3.

Income 2000: per capita $21,893; median household $48,814; **Pop below poverty level:** 5.3%. ***Personal per capita income 2000-2003:** $28,480-$30,708.

Unemployment 2004: 4.2%. **Change from 2000:** +1%. **Median travel time to work:** 23.5 minutes. **Working outside county of residence:** 63.7%.

Cities with pop over 10,000: None.

WASHINGTON COUNTY
99 Public Sq Suite 102   **Ph:** 812-883-5748
Salem, IN 47167   **Fax:** 812-883-8108
www.washingtoncountyindiana.com

In south-central IN, northwest of Louisville, KY; established Dec 21, 1813 (prior to statehood) from Indian lands. **Name Origin:** For George Washington (1732-99), American patriot and first U.S. president.

Area (sq mi): 516.53 (land 514.42; water 2.12). **Pop per sq mi:** 54.2.

Pop 2005: 27,885. **State rank:** 57. **Pop change:** 2000-20005 +2.4%; 1990-2000 +14.8%. **Pop 2000:** 27,223 (White 98.3%; Black or African American 0.1%; Hispanic or Latino 0.7%; Asian 0.2%; Other 0.9%). **Foreign born:** 0.5%. **Median age:** 35.8.

Income 2000: per capita $16,748; median household $36,630; **Pop below poverty level:** 10.6%. ***Personal per capita income 2000-2003:** $22,590-$23,035.

Unemployment 2004: 6.3%. **Change from 2000:** -0.6%. **Median travel time to work:** 28.4 minutes. **Working outside county of residence:** 47.8%.

Cities with pop over 10,000: None.

WAYNE COUNTY
401 E Main St   **Ph:** 765-973-9237
Richmond, IN 47374   **Fax:** 765-973-9321
www.co.wayne.in.us

On the central-eastern border of IN, southeast of Muncie; established Nov 27, 1810 (prior to statehood) from Indian lands. **Name**

*Source: Personal per capita income data are from the Bureau of Economic Analysis; per capita income data are from the Bureau of the Census. See Introduction for explanation of differences.

Wayne County (cont'd)

Origin: For Gen. Anthony Wayne (1745-96), PA soldier and statesman, nicknamed 'Mad Anthony' for his daring during the Revolutionary War, but honored here mostly for his defeat of Miami Indian chief Little Turtle (c. 1752-1812) in the Battle of Fallen Timbers (1794).

Area (sq mi): 404.34 (land 403.57; water 0.78). **Pop per sq mi:** 171.4.

Pop 2005: 69,192. **State rank:** 24. **Pop change:** 2000-20005 -2.7%; 1990-2000 -1.2%. **Pop 2000:** 71,097 (White 91.4%; Black or African American 5.1%; Hispanic or Latino 1.4%; Asian 0.5%; Other 2.3%). **Foreign born:** 1.5%. **Median age:** 37.7.

Income 2000: per capita $17,727; median household $34,885; **Pop below poverty level:** 11.4%. ***Personal per capita income 2000-2003:** $24,005-$25,316.

Unemployment 2004: 7%. **Change from 2000:** +1.9%. **Median travel time to work:** 18.4 minutes. **Working outside county of residence:** 13.6%.

Cities with pop over 10,000: Richmond 🏛 (37,943).

WELLS COUNTY

102 W Market St Rm 205   **Ph:** 260-824-6470
Bluffton, IN 46714   **Fax:** 260-824-6475
www.wellscounty.org

In northeastern IN, south of Ft. Wayne; established Feb 7, 1835 from Indian lands. **Name Origin:** For Capt. William Wells (1770?-1812), a white man adopted by Miami Indian Chief Little Turtle (c.1752-1812), who served with the Indians; he returned to the white men and served as Indian agent, then fought the Indians at the Battle of Tippecanoe (1811).

Area (sq mi): 370.41 (land 369.96; water 0.45). **Pop per sq mi:** 75.9.

Pop 2005: 28,085. **State rank:** 56. **Pop change:** 2000-20005 +1.8%; 1990-2000 +6.4%. **Pop 2000:** 27,600 (White 97.4%; Black or African American 0.2%; Hispanic or Latino 1.4%; Asian 0.2%; Other 1.2%). **Foreign born:** 0.8%. **Median age:** 36.8.

Income 2000: per capita $19,158; median household $43,934; **Pop below poverty level:** 5.9%. ***Personal per capita income 2000-2003:** $25,911-$26,226.

Unemployment 2004: 4.9%. **Change from 2000:** +0.6%. **Median travel time to work:** 20.8 minutes. **Working outside county of residence:** 40.4%.

Cities with pop over 10,000: None.

WHITE COUNTY

110 N Main St   **Ph:** 574-583-7032
Monticello, IN 47960   **Fax:** 574-583-1532

In northwestern IN, north of Lafayette; organized Feb 1, 1834 from Carroll County. **Name Origin:** For Col. Isaac White (?-1811), killed at the Battle of Tippecanoe.

Area (sq mi): 508.8 (land 505.24; water 3.56). **Pop per sq mi:** 48.4.

Pop 2005: 24,463. **State rank:** 64. **Pop change:** 2000-20005 -3.2%; 1990-2000 +8.6%. **Pop 2000:** 25,267 (White 93.3%; Black or African American 0.2%; Hispanic or Latino 5.3%; Asian 0.2%; Other 4.4%). **Foreign born:** 3.5%. **Median age:** 37.6.

Income 2000: per capita $18,323; median household $40,707; **Pop below poverty level:** 7%. ***Personal per capita income 2000-2003:** $23,877-$22,828.

Unemployment 2004: 6.6%. **Change from 2000:** +1.4%. **Median travel time to work:** 22.2 minutes. **Working outside county of residence:** 35.8%.

Cities with pop over 10,000: None.

WHITLEY COUNTY

101 W Van Buren St   **Ph:** 260-248-3102
Columbia City, IN 46725   **Fax:** 260-248-3137

In northeastern IN, west of Ft. Wayne, established Feb 7, 1835 from Huntington County. **Name Origin:** For Col. William Whitley (1749-1813), soldier in the War of 1812 who enlisted at the age of 63.

Area (sq mi): 337.9 (land 335.52; water 2.38). **Pop per sq mi:** 96.3.

Pop 2005: 32,323. **State rank:** 52. **Pop change:** 2000-20005 +5.3%; 1990-2000 +11.1%. **Pop 2000:** 30,707 (White 97.8%; Black or African American 0.2%; Hispanic or Latino 0.9%; Asian 0.2%; Other 1.3%). **Foreign born:** 0.8%. **Median age:** 36.9.

Income 2000: per capita $20,519; median household $45,503; **Pop below poverty level:** 4.9%. ***Personal per capita income 2000-2003:** $26,599-$27,153.

Unemployment 2004: 5.6%. **Change from 2000:** +0.3%. **Median travel time to work:** 23.5 minutes. **Working outside county of residence:** 47.5%.

Cities with pop over 10,000: None.

🏛 *County Seat*

Iowa

IOWA STATE INFORMATION

www.iowa.gov   **Ph:** 515-281-5011

Area (sq mi): 56,271.55 (land 55,869.36; water 402.2). **Pop per sq mi:** 53.1.

Pop 2005: 2,966,334. **Pop change:** 2000-20005 +1.4%; 1990-2000 +5.4%. **Pop 2000:** 2,926,324 (White 92.6%; Black or African American 2.1%; Hispanic or Latino 2.8%; Asian 1.3%; Other 2.7%). **Foreign born:** 3.1%. **Median age:** 36.6.

Income 2000: per capita $19,674; median household $39,469; **Pop below poverty level:** 9.1%. ***Personal per capita income 2000-2003:** $26,554-$28,340.

Unemployment 2004: 4.7%. **Change from 2000:** +1.9%. **Median travel time to work:** 18.5 minutes. **Working outside county of residence:** 21.8%.

ADAIR COUNTY

400 Public Sq   **Ph:** 641-743-2546
Greenfield, IA 50849   **Fax:** 641-743-2565

In south-central IA, east of Council Bluffs; established Jan 15, 1851 from Cass County. **Name Origin:** For John Adair (1757-1840), governor of KY (1820-24).

Area (sq mi): 570.31 (land 569.3; water 1). **Pop per sq mi:** 13.8.

Pop 2005: 7,859. **State rank:** 88. **Pop change:** 2000-20005 -4.7%; 1990-2000 -2%. **Pop 2000:** 8,243 (White 98.4%; Black or African American 0.1%; Hispanic or Latino 0.7%; Asian 0.2%; Other 0.8%). **Foreign born:** 0.7%. **Median age:** 41.8.

Income 2000: per capita $17,262; median household $35,179; **Pop below poverty level:** 7.6%. ***Personal per capita income 2000-2003:** $25,043-$26,182.

Unemployment 2004: 4.5%. **Change from 2000:** +2.2%. **Median travel time to work:** 19.9 minutes. **Working outside county of residence:** 34.6%.

Cities with pop over 10,000: None.

ADAMS COUNTY

PO Box 484   **Ph:** 641-322-4711
Corning, IA 50841   **Fax:** 641-322-4523
www.co.adams.ia.us

In southwestern IA, southeast of Council Bluffs; established Jan 15, 1851 from Taylor County. **Name Origin:** For John Adams (1735-1826), second U.S. president.

Area (sq mi): 425.41 (land 423.54; water 1.87). **Pop per sq mi:** 10.1.

Pop 2005: 4,264. **State rank:** 99. **Pop change:** 2000-20005 -4.9%; 1990-2000 -7.9%. **Pop 2000:** 4,482 (White 98.5%; Black or African American 0.1%; Hispanic or Latino 0.6%; Asian 0.2%; Other 0.8%). **Foreign born:** 0.2%. **Median age:** 41.9.

Income 2000: per capita $15,550; median household $30,453; **Pop below poverty level:** 9.3%. ***Personal per capita income 2000-2003:** $23,875-$23,076.

Unemployment 2004: 5.3%. **Change from 2000:** +0.6%. **Median travel time to work:** 19.9 minutes. **Working outside county of residence:** 31.7%.

Cities with pop over 10,000: None.

ALLAMAKEE COUNTY

110 Allamakee St   **Ph:** 563-568-3318
Waukon, IA 52172   **Fax:** 563-568-6353
www.allamakeecounty.com

On the northeastern border of IA; county established Feb 20, 1847 from Clayton County. **Name Origin:** Combined form of an Indian trader's name, Allan Makee.

Area (sq mi): 658.71 (land 639.56; water 19.14). **Pop per sq mi:** 23.

Pop 2005: 14,709. **State rank:** 56. **Pop change:** 2000-20005 +0.2%; 1990-2000 +5.9%. **Pop 2000:** 14,675 (White 95.3%; Black or African American 0.1%; Hispanic or Latino 3.5%; Asian 0.3%; Other 3.7%). **Foreign born:** 5.5%. **Median age:** 39.7.

Income 2000: per capita $16,599; median household $33,967; **Pop below poverty level:** 9.6%. ***Personal per capita income 2000-2003:** $21,999-$23,520.

Unemployment 2004: 6.4%. **Change from 2000:** +1.7%. **Median travel time to work:** 19.3 minutes. **Working outside county of residence:** 24.4%.

Cities with pop over 10,000: None.

APPANOOSE COUNTY

PO Box 400   **Ph:** 641-856-6101
Centerville, IA 52544   **Fax:** 641-856-2282
www.appanoosecounty.net

On the central-southern border of IA; established Feb 17, 1843 (prior to statehood) from Davis County. **Name Origin:** For a respected chief of the Sac and Fox tribes, prominent in IA and KS in the 1830s and 1840s. His name means 'chief when a child; prince.'

Area (sq mi): 516.35 (land 496.25; water 20.1). **Pop per sq mi:** 27.5.

Pop 2005: 13,666. **State rank:** 59. **Pop change:** 2000-20005 -0.4%; 1990-2000 -0.2%. **Pop 2000:** 13,721 (White 97.5%; Black or African

Appanoose County (cont'd)

American 0.4%; Hispanic or Latino 1%; Asian 0.3%; Other 1.2%). **Foreign born:** 1%. **Median age:** 40.6.

Income 2000: per capita $14,644; median household $28,612; **Pop below poverty level:** 14.5%. ***Personal per capita income 2000-2003:** $20,409-$21,654.

Unemployment 2004: 5.9%. **Change from 2000:** +0.9%. **Median travel time to work:** 20.4 minutes. **Working outside county of residence:** 20%.

Cities with pop over 10,000: None.

AUDUBON COUNTY

318 Leroy St No 6   **Ph:** 712-563-4275
Audubon, IA 50025   **Fax:** 712-563-4276
www.auduboncounty.org

In west-central IA, east of Council Bluffs; established Jan 15, 1851 from Cass and Black Hawk counties. **Name Origin:** For John James Audubon (1785-1851), ornithologist and artist.

Area (sq mi): 443.58 (land 443.13; water 0.44). **Pop per sq mi:** 14.6.

Pop 2005: 6,457. **State rank:** 97. **Pop change:** 2000-20005 -5.5%; 1990-2000 -6.9%. **Pop 2000:** 6,830 (White 98.7%; Black or African American 0.1%; Hispanic or Latino 0.5%; Asian 0.2%; Other 0.5%). **Foreign born:** 0.7%. **Median age:** 42.4.

Income 2000: per capita $17,489; median household $32,215; **Pop below poverty level:** 7.7%. ***Personal per capita income 2000-2003:** $24,072-$25,997.

Unemployment 2004: 4.5%. **Change from 2000:** +1.2%. **Median travel time to work:** 18.3 minutes. **Working outside county of residence:** 29.9%.

Cities with pop over 10,000: None.

BENTON COUNTY

PO Box 719   **Ph:** 319-472-2766
Vinton, IA 52349
www.cobentoniaus.com

In east-central IA, west of Grand Rapids; established Dec 21, 1837 (prior to statehood), from Indian lands. **Name Origin:** For Thomas Hart Benton (1782-1858), U.S. journalist and statesman; nicknamed 'Old Bullion' for championing the use of gold and silver currency rather than paper money.

Area (sq mi): 718.45 (land 716.39; water 2.06). **Pop per sq mi:** 37.7.

Pop 2005: 27,000. **State rank:** 23. **Pop change:** 2000-20005 +6.7%; 1990-2000 +12.8%. **Pop 2000:** 25,308 (White 98.4%; Black or African American 0.2%; Hispanic or Latino 0.6%; Asian 0.2%; Other 0.7%). **Foreign born:** 0.6%. **Median age:** 37.2.

Income 2000: per capita $18,891; median household $42,427; **Pop below poverty level:** 6.1%. ***Personal per capita income 2000-2003:** $25,576-$26,450.

Unemployment 2004: 4.9%. **Change from 2000:** +1.3%. **Median travel time to work:** 25 minutes. **Working outside county of residence:** 57.8%.

Cities with pop over 10,000: None.

BLACK HAWK COUNTY

316 E 5th St   **Ph:** 319-833-3012
Waterloo, IA 50703   **Fax:** 319-833-3170
www.co.black-hawk.ia.us

In east-central IA, northwest of Cedar Rapids; established Feb 17, 1843 (prior to statehood) from Delaware County. **Name Origin:** For Black Hawk (1767-1838), famous Indian warrior and chief of the Sac and Fox tribes.

Area (sq mi): 571.91 (land 567.11; water 4.8). **Pop per sq mi:** 222.

Pop 2005: 125,891. **State rank:** 4. **Pop change:** 2000-20005 -1.7%; 1990-2000 +3.4%. **Pop 2000:** 128,012 (White 87.7%; Black or African American 8%; Hispanic or Latino 1.8%; Asian 1%; Other 2.6%). **Foreign born:** 3.7%. **Median age:** 34.4.

Income 2000: per capita $18,885; median household $37,266; **Pop below poverty level:** 13.1%. ***Personal per capita income 2000-2003:** $24,375-$27,531.

Unemployment 2004: 5%. **Change from 2000:** +1.2%. **Median travel time to work:** 15.7 minutes. **Working outside county of residence:** 6.6%.

Cities with pop over 10,000: Waterloo ⚒ (66,767); Cedar Falls (36,343).

BOONE COUNTY

201 State St   **Ph:** 515-433-0500
Boone, IA 50036   **Fax:** 515-432-8102
www.co.boone.ia.us

In central IA, northwest of Des Moines; established Jan 13, 1846 from Polk County. **Name Origin:** For Capt. Nathan Boone (1782-1863), son of Daniel; officer in the U.S. Dragoons and early explorer of IA.

Area (sq mi): 573.51 (land 571.46; water 2.05). **Pop per sq mi:** 46.6.

Pop 2005: 26,602. **State rank:** 24. **Pop change:** 2000-20005 +1.4%; 1990-2000 +4.1%. **Pop 2000:** 26,224 (White 98.1%; Black or African American 0.4%; Hispanic or Latino 0.8%; Asian 0.2%; Other 0.9%). **Foreign born:** 0.8%. **Median age:** 38.6.

Income 2000: per capita $19,943; median household $40,763; **Pop below poverty level:** 7.6%. ***Personal per capita income 2000-2003:** $27,164-$28,880.

Unemployment 2004: 3.8%. **Change from 2000:** +0.9%. **Median travel time to work:** 20.9 minutes. **Working outside county of residence:** 42.1%.

Cities with pop over 10,000: Boone ⚒ (12,856).

BREMER COUNTY

415 E Bremer Ave   **Ph:** 319-352-0130
Waverly, IA 50677   **Fax:** 319-352-0602
www.co.bremer.ia.us

In east-central IA, north of Waterloo; established Apr 29, 1851 from Winnebago Indian Reserve. **Name Origin:** For Frederika Bremer (1801-65), Swedish novelist, traveler, and early feminist.

Area (sq mi): 439.6 (land 437.9; water 1.7). **Pop per sq mi:** 54.1.

Pop 2005: 23,677. **State rank:** 26. **Pop change:** 2000-20005 +1.5%; 1990-2000 +2.2%. **Pop 2000:** 23,325 (White 97.9%; Black or African American 0.5%; Hispanic or Latino 0.6%; Asian 0.5%; Other 0.8%). **Foreign born:** 1.2%. **Median age:** 38.1.

*Source: Personal per capita income data are from the Bureau of Economic Analysis; per capita income data are from the Bureau of the Census. See Introduction for explanation of differences.

238

Bremer County (cont'd)

Income 2000: per capita $19,199; median household $40,826; **Pop below poverty level:** 5.1%. ***Personal per capita income 2000-2003:** $26,264-$27,766.

Unemployment 2004: 4.1%. **Change from 2000:** +1.3%. **Median travel time to work:** 19 minutes. **Working outside county of residence:** 36.8%.

Cities with pop over 10,000: None.

BUCHANAN COUNTY

PO Box 259
Independence, IA 50644
www.buchanancounty.com

Ph: 319-334-2196
Fax: 319-334-7455

In east-central IA, north of Cedar Rapids; established Dec 21, 1837 (prior to statehood), from Delaware County. **Name Origin:** For James Buchanan (1791-1868), fifteenth U.S. president.

Area (sq mi): 573.35 (land 571.26; water 2.09). **Pop per sq mi:** 36.8.

Pop 2005: 21,019. **State rank:** 32. **Pop change:** 2000-20005 -0.4%; 1990-2000 +1.2%. **Pop 2000:** 21,093 (White 98%; Black or African American 0.3%; Hispanic or Latino 0.6%; Asian 0.4%; Other 0.9%). **Foreign born:** 0.9%. **Median age:** 36.4.

Income 2000: per capita $18,405; median household $38,036; **Pop below poverty level:** 9.4%. ***Personal per capita income 2000-2003:** $23,172-$24,056.

Unemployment 2004: 5%. **Change from 2000:** +0.6%. **Median travel time to work:** 23.2 minutes. **Working outside county of residence:** 39.7%.

Cities with pop over 10,000: None.

BUENA VISTA COUNTY

PO Box 1186
Storm Lake, IA 50588
www.co.buena-vista.ia.us

Ph: 712-749-2546
Fax: 712-749-2700

In west-central IA, northest of Fort Dodge; established Jan 15, 1851 from Sac and Clay counties. **Name Origin:** For the Mexican town in Coahuila, site of Gen. Zachary Taylor's (1784-1850; twelfth U.S. president) final victory in the Mexican War (1847); Spanish for 'good view.'

Area (sq mi): 580.07 (land 574.78; water 5.28). **Pop per sq mi:** 35.1.

Pop 2005: 20,151. **State rank:** 36. **Pop change:** 2000-20005 -1.3%; 1990-2000 +2.2%. **Pop 2000:** 20,411 (White 82.1%; Black or African American 0.4%; Hispanic or Latino 12.5%; Asian 4.3%; Other 7.3%). **Foreign born:** 12.4%. **Median age:** 36.4.

Income 2000: per capita $16,042; median household $35,300; **Pop below poverty level:** 10.5%. ***Personal per capita income 2000-2003:** $23,680-$24,288.

Unemployment 2004: 4.2%. **Change from 2000:** +1.7%. **Median travel time to work:** 14.9 minutes. **Working outside county of residence:** 14.5%.

Cities with pop over 10,000: None.

BUTLER COUNTY

428 6th St
Allison, IA 50602
www.butlercoiowa.org

Ph: 319-267-2487
Fax: 319-267-2488

In north-central IA, norhwest of Waterloo; established Jan 15, 1851 from Buchanan and Black Hawk counties. **Name Origin:** For Maj. William Orlando Butler (1791-1880), officer in the War of 1812 and Mexican-American War; U.S. representative from KY (1839-43).

Area (sq mi): 581.56 (land 580.38; water 1.18). **Pop per sq mi:** 26.

Pop 2005: 15,072. **State rank:** 55. **Pop change:** 2000-20005 -1.5%; 1990-2000 -2.7%. **Pop 2000:** 15,305 (White 98.6%; Black or African American 0.1%; Hispanic or Latino 0.6%; Asian 0.2%; Other 0.8%). **Foreign born:** 0.9%. **Median age:** 41.3.

Income 2000: per capita $17,036; median household $35,883; **Pop below poverty level:** 8%. ***Personal per capita income 2000-2003:** $22,996-$23,940.

Unemployment 2004: 4.9%. **Change from 2000:** -0.4%. **Median travel time to work:** 22.3 minutes. **Working outside county of residence:** 51.6%.

Cities with pop over 10,000: None.

CALHOUN COUNTY

416 4th St Suite 5
Rockwell City, IA 50579
www.calhouncountyiowa.com

Ph: 712-297-8122
Fax: 712-297-5082

In central IA, west of Fort Dodge; established as Fox County Jan 15, 1851 from Greene County, name changed Jan 12, 1853. **Name Origin:** For John Caldwell Calhoun (1782-1850), U.S. statesman and proponent of Southern causes.

Area (sq mi): 572.29 (land 570.15; water 2.14). **Pop per sq mi:** 18.3.

Pop 2005: 10,443. **State rank:** 77. **Pop change:** 2000-20005 -6%; 1990-2000 -3.4%. **Pop 2000:** 11,115 (White 97.6%; Black or African American 0.7%; Hispanic or Latino 0.9%; Asian 0.2%; Other 1%). **Foreign born:** 0.5%. **Median age:** 42.4.

Income 2000: per capita $17,498; median household $33,286; **Pop below poverty level:** 10.1%. ***Personal per capita income 2000-2003:** $22,845-$23,743.

Unemployment 2004: 4.5%. **Change from 2000:** +1.2%. **Median travel time to work:** 18.6 minutes. **Working outside county of residence:** 35.2%.

Cities with pop over 10,000: None.

CARROLL COUNTY

114 E 6th St
Carroll, IA 51401
www.co.carroll.ia.us

Ph: 712-792-4923
Fax: 712-792-9423

In west-central IA, west of Ames; established Jan 15, 1851 from Guthrie County. **Name Origin:** For Charles Carroll (1737-1832), a signer of the Declaration of Independence and U.S. senator from MD (1789-92).

Area (sq mi): 570.24 (land 569.31; water 0.92). **Pop per sq mi:** 36.9.

Pop 2005: 21,034. **State rank:** 31. **Pop change:** 2000-20005 -1.8%; 1990-2000 +0%. **Pop 2000:** 21,421 (White 98.6%; Black or African American 0.2%; Hispanic or Latino 0.5%; Asian 0.3%; Other 0.6%). **Foreign born:** 0.6%. **Median age:** 38.7.

Carroll County (cont'd)

Income 2000: per capita $18,595; median household $37,275; **Pop below poverty level:** 6.5%. ***Personal per capita income 2000-2003:** $25,915-$27,449.

Unemployment 2004: 3.2%. **Change from 2000:** +0.6%. **Median travel time to work:** 14.4 minutes. **Working outside county of residence:** 9.5%.

Cities with pop over 10,000: None.

CASS COUNTY

5 W 7th St   **Ph:** 712-243-4570
Atlantic, IA 50022   **Fax:** 712-243-6660
www.casscountyiowa.org

In southwestern IA, east of Council Bluffs; established Jan 15, 1851 from Pottawattamie County. **Name Origin:** For Lewis Cass (1782-1866), OH legislator, governor of MI Territory (1813-31), U.S. secretary of war (1831-36), and U.S. secretary of state (1857-60).

Area (sq mi): 565.01 (land 564.33; water 0.68). **Pop per sq mi:** 25.2.

Pop 2005: 14,219. **State rank:** 58. **Pop change:** 2000-20005 -3.2%; 1990-2000 -2.9%. **Pop 2000:** 14,684 (White 98.5%; Black or African American 0.2%; Hispanic or Latino 0.7%; Asian 0.1%; Other 0.7%). **Foreign born:** 0.8%. **Median age:** 41.6.

Income 2000: per capita $17,067; median household $32,922; **Pop below poverty level:** 11.1%. ***Personal per capita income 2000-2003:** $24,180-$25,026.

Unemployment 2004: 5.2%. **Change from 2000:** +0.7%. **Median travel time to work:** 18.9 minutes. **Working outside county of residence:** 19.3%.

Cities with pop over 10,000: None.

CEDAR COUNTY

400 Cedar St   **Ph:** 563-886-2101
Tipton, IA 52772   **Fax:** 563-886-3594
www.iowacity.com/cedarco/#cedar

In central-eastern IA, east of Iowa City; established Dec 21, 1837 (prior to statehood) from Wisconsin Territory. **Name Origin:** For the Red Cedar River that runs through the county.

Area (sq mi): 581.96 (land 579.52; water 2.44). **Pop per sq mi:** 31.5.

Pop 2005: 18,254. **State rank:** 39. **Pop change:** 2000-20005 +0.4%; 1990-2000 +4.6%. **Pop 2000:** 18,187 (White 97.9%; Black or African American 0.2%; Hispanic or Latino 0.9%; Asian 0.3%; Other 1.1%). **Foreign born:** 0.7%. **Median age:** 39.2.

Income 2000: per capita $19,200; median household $42,198; **Pop below poverty level:** 5.5%. ***Personal per capita income 2000-2003:** $27,245-$28,158.

Unemployment 2004: 4.2%. **Change from 2000:** +1.2%. **Median travel time to work:** 24 minutes. **Working outside county of residence:** 56.9%.

Cities with pop over 10,000: None.

CERRO GORDO COUNTY

220 N Washington Ave   **Ph:** 641-421-3022
Mason City, IA 50401   **Fax:** 641-421-3072
www.co.cerro-gordo.ia.us

In north-central IA, northeast of Fort Dodge; established Jan 15, 1851 from Floyd County. **Name Origin:** For the city in Mexico, site of a Mexican War battle on Apr 18, 1847. Spanish 'fat hill' or 'big hill.'

Area (sq mi): 575.12 (land 568.33; water 6.8). **Pop per sq mi:** 78.6.

Pop 2005: 44,645. **State rank:** 12. **Pop change:** 2000-20005 -3.9%; 1990-2000 -0.6%. **Pop 2000:** 46,447 (White 94.7%; Black or African American 0.8%; Hispanic or Latino 2.8%; Asian 0.7%; Other 2.3%). **Foreign born:** 1.4%. **Median age:** 39.3.

Income 2000: per capita $19,184; median household $35,867; **Pop below poverty level:** 8.5%. ***Personal per capita income 2000-2003:** $26,261-$28,487.

Unemployment 2004: 4.8%. **Change from 2000:** +1.3%. **Median travel time to work:** 15.2 minutes. **Working outside county of residence:** 9%.

Cities with pop over 10,000: Mason City ▥ (28,177).

CHEROKEE COUNTY

520 W Main St PO Box F   **Ph:** 712-225-6744
Cherokee, IA 51012   **Fax:** 712-225-6749
www.cherokeeia.com

In northwestern IA, northeast of Sioux City; established Jan 15, 1851 from Crawford County. **Name Origin:** For the Indian tribe of Iroquoian linguistic stock. Name may derive from Creek *tciloki* 'people of a different speech.'

Area (sq mi): 577.34 (land 577.15; water 0.18). **Pop per sq mi:** 21.2.

Pop 2005: 12,237. **State rank:** 64. **Pop change:** 2000-20005 -6.1%; 1990-2000 -7.5%. **Pop 2000:** 13,035 (White 97.8%; Black or African American 0.3%; Hispanic or Latino 1%; Asian 0.4%; Other 1%). **Foreign born:** 0.9%. **Median age:** 41.7.

Income 2000: per capita $17,934; median household $35,142; **Pop below poverty level:** 7.3%. ***Personal per capita income 2000-2003:** $24,009-$26,541.

Unemployment 2004: 4.8%. **Change from 2000:** +2%. **Median travel time to work:** 16.4 minutes. **Working outside county of residence:** 16.9%.

Cities with pop over 10,000: None.

CHICKASAW COUNTY

PO Box 311   **Ph:** 641-394-2100
New Hampton, IA 50659   **Fax:** 641-394-5541
www.chickasawcoia.org

In northeastern IA, north of Waterloo; established Jan 15, 1851 from Fayette County. **Name Origin:** For the Indian tribe, closely connected with the Choctaw, and of Muskhogean linguistic stock; meaning of name unknown.

Area (sq mi): 505.48 (land 504.64; water 0.84). **Pop per sq mi:** 24.9.

Pop 2005: 12,563. **State rank:** 62. **Pop change:** 2000-20005 -4.1%; 1990-2000 -1.5%. **Pop 2000:** 13,095 (White 98.5%; Black or African American 0.1%; Hispanic or Latino 0.6%; Asian 0.3%; Other 0.9%). **Foreign born:** 0.9%. **Median age:** 39.7.

Source: Personal per capita income data are from the Bureau of Economic Analysis; per capita income data are from the Bureau of the Census. See Introduction for explanation of differences.

240

Chickasaw County (cont'd)

Income 2000: per capita $18,237; median household $37,649; **Pop below poverty level:** 8.3%. ***Personal per capita income 2000-2003:** $24,765-$24,490.

Unemployment 2004: 6.5%. **Change from 2000:** -0.7%. **Median travel time to work:** 20.8 minutes. **Working outside county of residence:** 28.5%.

Cities with pop over 10,000: None.

CLARKE COUNTY

100 S Main St Courthouse   **Ph:** 641-342-6096
Osceola, IA 50213   **Fax:** 641-342-2463
www.clarkecountyia.org

In south-central IA, south of Des Moines, established Jan 13, 1846 from Lucas County. **Name Origin:** For James Clarke (1811-50), publisher of Burlington, IA, *Gazette* (1837), and last governor of IA Territory (1845-46).

Area (sq mi): 431.72 (land 431.12; water 0.6). **Pop per sq mi:** 21.2.

Pop 2005: 9,161. **State rank:** 84. **Pop change:** 2000-20005 +0.3%; 1990-2000 +10.2%. **Pop 2000:** 9,133 (White 94.7%; Black or African American 0.1%; Hispanic or Latino 4%; Asian 0.4%; Other 2.9%). **Foreign born:** 2.5%. **Median age:** 38.6.

Income 2000: per capita $16,409; median household $34,474; **Pop below poverty level:** 8.5%. ***Personal per capita income 2000-2003:** $21,803-$23,297.

Unemployment 2004: 6.8%. **Change from 2000:** +2.6%. **Median travel time to work:** 23.3 minutes. **Working outside county of residence:** 23.3%.

Cities with pop over 10,000: None.

CLAY COUNTY

215 W 4th St   **Ph:** 712-262-4335
Spencer, IA 51301   **Fax:** 712-262-6042
www.co.clay.ia.us

In north-central IA, northwest of Fort Dodge; established Jan 15, 1851 from Indian lands. **Name Origin:** For Lt. Col. Henry Clay, Jr. (1807-47), son of the statesman (1777-1852); killed at the Battle of Buena Vista during the Mexican-American War.

Area (sq mi): 572.51 (land 568.89; water 3.63). **Pop per sq mi:** 29.7.

Pop 2005: 16,897. **State rank:** 43. **Pop change:** 2000-20005 -2.7%; 1990-2000 -1.2%. **Pop 2000:** 17,372 (White 97.3%; Black or African American 0.2%; Hispanic or Latino 1.1%; Asian 0.8%; Other 0.9%). **Foreign born:** 1.8%. **Median age:** 39.4.

Income 2000: per capita $19,451; median household $35,799; **Pop below poverty level:** 8.2%. ***Personal per capita income 2000-2003:** $25,551-$27,970.

Unemployment 2004: 4.3%. **Change from 2000:** +1.3%. **Median travel time to work:** 14.2 minutes. **Working outside county of residence:** 13%.

Cities with pop over 10,000: Spencer 🏛 (11,063).

CLAYTON COUNTY

111 High St NE   **Ph:** 563-245-2204
Elkader, IA 52043   **Fax:** 563-245-1175
www.claytoncountyiowa.net

On northeastern border of IA, north of Dubuque; established Dec 21, 1837 (prior to statehood) from Dubuque County. **Name Origin:** For John Middleton Clayton (1796-1856), U.S. senator from DE and U.S. secretary of state (1849-50).

Area (sq mi): 792.81 (land 778.81; water 14). **Pop per sq mi:** 23.5.

Pop 2005: 18,337. **State rank:** 38. **Pop change:** 2000-20005 -1.8%; 1990-2000 -2%. **Pop 2000:** 18,678 (White 98.4%; Black or African American 0.1%; Hispanic or Latino 0.8%; Asian 0.1%; Other 0.8%). **Foreign born:** 1.2%. **Median age:** 40.2.

Income 2000: per capita $16,930; median household $34,068; **Pop below poverty level:** 8.6%. ***Personal per capita income 2000-2003:** $23,578-$24,581.

Unemployment 2004: 7.3%. **Change from 2000:** +2%. **Median travel time to work:** 20.8 minutes. **Working outside county of residence:** 28.7%.

Cities with pop over 10,000: None.

CLINTON COUNTY

1900 N 3rd St   **Ph:** 563-243-6210
Clinton, IA 52733   **Fax:** 563-243-5869
www.clintoncountyiowa.com

On central eastern border, north of Davenport; established Dec 21,1837 (prior to statehood) from Dubuque County. **Name Origin:** For DeWitt Clinton (1769-1828), governor of NY (1817-23; 1825-28) and supporter of the Erie Canal.

Area (sq mi): 710.19 (land 694.98; water 15.21). **Pop per sq mi:** 71.5.

Pop 2005: 49,717. **State rank:** 11. **Pop change:** 2000-20005 -0.9%; 1990-2000 -1.7%. **Pop 2000:** 50,149 (White 95.2%; Black or African American 1.9%; Hispanic or Latino 1.3%; Asian 0.6%; Other 1.6%). **Foreign born:** 1.4%. **Median age:** 38.2.

Income 2000: per capita $17,724; median household $37,423; **Pop below poverty level:** 10.2%. ***Personal per capita income 2000-2003:** $23,913-$25,483.

Unemployment 2004: 5.7%. **Change from 2000:** +1.1%. **Median travel time to work:** 19.6 minutes. **Working outside county of residence:** 22.9%.

Cities with pop over 10,000: Clinton 🏛 (27,319).

CRAWFORD COUNTY

1202 Broadway   **Ph:** 712-263-2242
Denison, IA 51442   **Fax:** 712-263-5753
www.crawfordcounty.org

In west-central IA, northeast of Council Bluffs; established Jan 15, 1851 from Shelby County. **Name Origin:** For William Harris Crawford (1771-1834), U.S. senator from GA (1807-13), U.S. secretary of war (1815-16), and U.S. secretary of treasury (1816-25).

Area (sq mi): 714.99 (land 714.36; water 0.63). **Pop per sq mi:** 23.6.

Pop 2005: 16,889. **State rank:** 44. **Pop change:** 2000-20005 -0.3%; 1990-2000 +1%. **Pop 2000:** 16,942 (White 89.4%; Black or African

Crawford County (cont'd)

American 0.8%; Hispanic or Latino 8.7%; Asian 0.5%; Other 5.7%). **Foreign born:** 6.1%. **Median age:** 38.2.

Income 2000: per capita $15,851; median household $33,922; **Pop below poverty level:** 11.1%. ***Personal per capita income 2000-2003:** $21,723-$22,868.

Unemployment 2004: 4%. **Change from 2000:** +1.2%. **Median travel time to work:** 16.7 minutes. **Working outside county of residence:** 16.8%.

Cities with pop over 10,000: None.

DALLAS COUNTY
801 Court St
Adel, IA 50003
www.co.dallas.ia.us

Ph: 515-993-5814
Fax: 515-993-4752

In central IA, west of Des Moines; organized 1846 from Polk County. **Name Origin:** For George Mifflin Dallas (1792-1864), U.S. Minister to Great Britain (1856-61).

Area (sq mi): 591.73 (land 586.47; water 5.26). **Pop per sq mi:** 88.3.

Pop 2005: 51,762. **State rank:** 10. **Pop change:** 2000-20005 +27%; 1990-2000 +37%. **Pop 2000:** 40,750 (White 92.4%; Black or African American 0.7%; Hispanic or Latino 5.4%; Asian 0.7%; Other 3.8%). **Foreign born:** 4%. **Median age:** 35.1.

Income 2000: per capita $22,970; median household $48,528; **Pop below poverty level:** 5.6%. ***Personal per capita income 2000-2003:** $30,161-$31,320.

Unemployment 2004: 3.6%. **Change from 2000:** +1.5%. **Median travel time to work:** 22 minutes. **Working outside county of residence:** 62.5%.

Cities with pop over 10,000: None.

DAVIS COUNTY
100 Courthouse Sq
Bloomfield, IA 52537
www.daviscounty.org

Ph: 641-664-2011
Fax: 641-664-2041

On southern border of IA, west of Burlington; established Feb 17, 1843 (prior to statehood) from Van Buren County. **Name Origin:** For Garrett Davis (1801-72), KY legislator and U.S. senator (1861-72).

Area (sq mi): 504.89 (land 503.24; water 1.65). **Pop per sq mi:** 17.2.

Pop 2005: 8,659. **State rank:** 85. **Pop change:** 2000-20005 +1.4%; 1990-2000 +2.8%. **Pop 2000:** 8,541 (White 98%; Black or African American 0.2%; Hispanic or Latino 0.7%; Asian 0.2%; Other 1.2%). **Foreign born:** 0.4%. **Median age:** 38.5.

Income 2000: per capita $15,127; median household $32,864; **Pop below poverty level:** 11.9%. ***Personal per capita income 2000-2003:** $20,457-$20,889.

Unemployment 2004: 5.2%. **Change from 2000:** +1.7%. **Median travel time to work:** 24.9 minutes. **Working outside county of residence:** 37.9%.

Cities with pop over 10,000: None.

DECATUR COUNTY
207 N Main St
Leon, IA 50144

Ph: 641-446-4382
Fax: 641-446-7159

On central southern border of IA, south of Des Moines; organized 1846 from Appanoose County. **Name Origin:** For Stephen Decatur (1779-1820), U.S. naval officer during the War of 1812 and in actions against the Barbary pirates near Tripoli, who said '...may she always be in the right; but our country, right or wrong!'

Area (sq mi): 533.32 (land 531.8; water 1.52). **Pop per sq mi:** 16.2.

Pop 2005: 8,605. **State rank:** 86. **Pop change:** 2000-20005 -1%; 1990-2000 +4.2%. **Pop 2000:** 8,689 (White 95.5%; Black or African American 1%; Hispanic or Latino 1.7%; Asian 0.6%; Other 1.9%). **Foreign born:** 2%. **Median age:** 36.4.

Income 2000: per capita $14,209; median household $27,343; **Pop below poverty level:** 15.5%. ***Personal per capita income 2000-2003:** $18,211-$18,713.

Unemployment 2004: 5.5%. **Change from 2000:** +1.1%. **Median travel time to work:** 22.2 minutes. **Working outside county of residence:** 31.9%.

Cities with pop over 10,000: None.

DELAWARE COUNTY
301 E Main St
Manchester, IA 52057
www.delawarecountyia.com

Ph: 563-927-4942
Fax: 563-927-3074

In eastern IA, west of Dubuque; established Dec 21, 1837 (prior to statehood) from Dubuque County. **Name Origin:** For the state, in appreciation of the services of John Middleton Clayton (1796-1856), U.S. senator from DE (1829-36; 1845-49; 1853-56) and U.S. secretary of state (1849-50).

Area (sq mi): 579.05 (land 577.85; water 1.19). **Pop per sq mi:** 31.2.

Pop 2005: 18,025. **State rank:** 40. **Pop change:** 2000-20005 -2.1%; 1990-2000 +2%. **Pop 2000:** 18,404 (White 98.8%; Black or African American 0.1%; Hispanic or Latino 0.7%; Asian 0.1%; Other 0.5%). **Foreign born:** 0.6%. **Median age:** 37.1.

Income 2000: per capita $17,327; median household $37,168; **Pop below poverty level:** 7.9%. ***Personal per capita income 2000-2003:** $23,424-$24,443.

Unemployment 2004: 5.2%. **Change from 2000:** +0.6%. **Median travel time to work:** 21.3 minutes. **Working outside county of residence:** 34.8%.

Cities with pop over 10,000: None.

DES MOINES COUNTY
PO Box 158
Burlington, IA 52601
www.co.des-moines.ia.us

Ph: 319-753-8272
Fax: 319-753-8253

On southeastern border of IA; established Sep 6, 1834 (prior to statehood) from Wisconsin Territory. **Name Origin:** For the Des Moines River, which runs through the southeastern part of the state. From French *des* 'of the' and *moines*, a form of the Indian tribal name *Moingona* 'river of the mounds.' French name became *Riviere des Moines* 'river of the monks,' because the area was explored by Catholic missionaries. Also spelled De Moin, De Moyen, and Demoine.

*Source: Personal per capita income data are from the Bureau of Economic Analysis; per capita income data are from the Bureau of the Census. See Introduction for explanation of differences.

Des Moines County (cont'd)

Area (sq mi): 429.8 (land 416.15; water 13.65). **Pop per sq mi:** 98.1.

Pop 2005: 40,810. **State rank:** 15. **Pop change:** 2000-20005 -3.6%; 1990-2000 -0.6%. **Pop 2000:** 42,351 (White 92.8%; Black or African American 3.6%; Hispanic or Latino 1.7%; Asian 0.6%; Other 2.1%). **Foreign born:** 1.6%. **Median age:** 38.9.

Income 2000: per capita $19,701; median household $36,790; **Pop below poverty level:** 10.7%. ***Personal per capita income 2000-2003:** $26,021-$27,554.

Unemployment 2004: 6.4%. **Change from 2000:** +1.5%. **Median travel time to work:** 16 minutes. **Working outside county of residence:** 10.4%.

Cities with pop over 10,000: Burlington 🏛 (25,579).

DICKINSON COUNTY

1802 Hill Ave   **Ph:** 712-336-3356
Spirit Lake, IA 51360   **Fax:** 712-336-2677
www.co.dickinson.ia.us

On the northern border of IA; established Jan 15, 1851 from Kossuth County. **Name Origin:** For Daniel Stevens Dickinson (1800-66), U.S. senator from NY (1844-51).

Area (sq mi): 403.69 (land 381.06; water 22.63). **Pop per sq mi:** 43.8.

Pop 2005: 16,687. **State rank:** 45. **Pop change:** 2000-20005 +1.6%; 1990-2000 +10.2%. **Pop 2000:** 16,424 (White 98.4%; Black or African American 0.2%; Hispanic or Latino 0.7%; Asian 0.2%; Other 0.7%). **Foreign born:** 0.7%. **Median age:** 43.3.

Income 2000: per capita $21,929; median household $39,020; **Pop below poverty level:** 6%. ***Personal per capita income 2000-2003:** $29,430-$31,559.

Unemployment 2004: 4.2%. **Change from 2000:** +1.4%. **Median travel time to work:** 15.5 minutes. **Working outside county of residence:** 19.4%.

Cities with pop over 10,000: None.

DUBUQUE COUNTY

720 Central Ave   **Ph:** 563-589-4418
Dubuque, IA 52001
www.dubuquecounty.org

On the eastern border of IA, northeast of Cedar Rapids; established Sep 6, 1834 (prior to statehood) from Wisconsin Territory. The present boundaries were established in 1837. **Name Origin:** For Julien Dubuque (1762-1810), a French-Canadian and the first permanent white settler in Iowa (1785); he negotiated an agreement in 1788 with the Fox Indians so he could work lead mines in the IA region.

Area (sq mi): 616.56 (land 608.16; water 8.41). **Pop per sq mi:** 150.7.

Pop 2005: 91,631. **State rank:** 7. **Pop change:** 2000-20005 +2.8%; 1990-2000 +3.2%. **Pop 2000:** 89,143 (White 96.5%; Black or African American 0.9%; Hispanic or Latino 1.2%; Asian 0.6%; Other 1.5%). **Foreign born:** 1.9%. **Median age:** 36.5.

Income 2000: per capita $19,600; median household $39,582; **Pop below poverty level:** 7.8%. ***Personal per capita income 2000-2003:** $25,691-$27,241.

Unemployment 2004: 4.7%. **Change from 2000:** +0.4%. **Median travel time to work:** 15.5 minutes. **Working outside county of residence:** 6.2%.

Cities with pop over 10,000: Dubuque 🏛 (57,504).

EMMET COUNTY

609 1st Ave N   **Ph:** 712-362-4261
Estherville, IA 51334   **Fax:** 712-362-7454
www.emmetcountyia.com

On central northern border of IA, northwest of Fort Dodge; established Jan 15, 1851 from Kossuth and Dickinson counties. **Name Origin:** For Robert W. Emmet (1778-1803), Irish patriot executed by the English for revolutionary acts. Places were named for him during a time when leaders of rebellions were honored by Americans.

Area (sq mi): 402.38 (land 395.74; water 6.63). **Pop per sq mi:** 26.6.

Pop 2005: 10,534. **State rank:** 76. **Pop change:** 2000-20005 -4.5%; 1990-2000 -4.7%. **Pop 2000:** 11,027 (White 94.5%; Black or African American 0.2%; Hispanic or Latino 4.3%; Asian 0.3%; Other 2.1%). **Foreign born:** 2.3%. **Median age:** 39.6.

Income 2000: per capita $16,619; median household $33,305; **Pop below poverty level:** 8.2%. ***Personal per capita income 2000-2003:** $23,772-$26,382.

Unemployment 2004: 4.8%. **Change from 2000:** +1%. **Median travel time to work:** 16.8 minutes. **Working outside county of residence:** 26.7%.

Cities with pop over 10,000: None.

FAYETTE COUNTY

114 N Vine St   **Ph:** 563-422-5694
West Union, IA 52175   **Fax:** 563-422-3137

In northeastern IA, northeast of Waterloo; established Dec 21, 1837 (prior to statehood) from Clayton County. **Name Origin:** For the Marquis de Lafayette (1757-1834), French statesman and soldier who fought with the Americans during the Revolutionary War.

Area (sq mi): 731.45 (land 730.92; water 0.52). **Pop per sq mi:** 29.1.

Pop 2005: 21,298. **State rank:** 29. **Pop change:** 2000-20005 -3.2%; 1990-2000 +0.8%. **Pop 2000:** 22,008 (White 96.9%; Black or African American 0.5%; Hispanic or Latino 1.5%; Asian 0.4%; Other 1.3%). **Foreign born:** 1.1%. **Median age:** 39.4.

Income 2000: per capita $17,271; median household $32,453; **Pop below poverty level:** 10.8%. ***Personal per capita income 2000-2003:** $21,364-$22,125.

Unemployment 2004: 5.6%. **Change from 2000:** +0.3%. **Median travel time to work:** 18.3 minutes. **Working outside county of residence:** 25.8%.

Cities with pop over 10,000: None.

🏛 *County Seat*

FLOYD COUNTY

101 S Main St   **Ph:** 641-228-7777
Charles City, IA 50616   **Fax:** 641-228-7772
www.floydcoia.org

In north-central IA, northwest of Waterloo; established Jan 15, 1851 from Chickasaw County. **Name Origin:** For Sgt. Charles Floyd (?-1804), a member of the Lewis and Clark expedition (1803-6). He is buried on the banks of the Missouri River; his is the first recorded death and burial of a white man in IA. Some claim for William Floyd (1734-1821), a signer of the Declaration of Independence.

Area (sq mi): 501.31 (land 500.56; water 0.74). **Pop per sq mi:** 32.8.

Pop 2005: 16,443. **State rank:** 46. **Pop change:** 2000-20005 -2.7%; 1990-2000 -0.9%. **Pop 2000:** 16,900 (White 97.4%; Black or African American 0.2%; Hispanic or Latino 1.3%; Asian 0.4%; Other 1.2%). **Foreign born:** 1.1%. **Median age:** 40.3.

Income 2000: per capita $17,091; median household $35,237; **Pop below poverty level:** 9.3%. *****Personal per capita income 2000-2003:** $22,242-$25,125.

Unemployment 2004: 5.3%. **Change from 2000:** +0.4%. **Median travel time to work:** 18.4 minutes. **Working outside county of residence:** 30.5%.

Cities with pop over 10,000: None.

FRANKLIN COUNTY

12 1st Ave NW PO Box 28   **Ph:** 641-456-5626
Hampton, IA 50441   **Fax:** 641-456-5628

In central IA, northwest of Waterloo; established Jan 15, 1851 from Chickasaw County. **Name Origin:** For Benjamin Franklin (1706-90), U.S. patriot, diplomat, and statesman.

Area (sq mi): 583.01 (land 582.44; water 0.57). **Pop per sq mi:** 18.4.

Pop 2005: 10,732. **State rank:** 74. **Pop change:** 2000-20005 +0.3%; 1990-2000 -5.8%. **Pop 2000:** 10,704 (White 93.4%; Black or African American 0.1%; Hispanic or Latino 6%; Asian 0.2%; Other 4.8%). **Foreign born:** 4.4%. **Median age:** 41.3.

Income 2000: per capita $18,767; median household $36,042; **Pop below poverty level:** 8%. *****Personal per capita income 2000-2003:** $25,044-$25,605.

Unemployment 2004: 5%. **Change from 2000:** +1.6%. **Median travel time to work:** 17.2 minutes. **Working outside county of residence:** 31.7%.

Cities with pop over 10,000: None.

FREMONT COUNTY

PO Box 549   **Ph:** 712-374-2232
Sidney, IA 51652   **Fax:** 712-374-3330
www.co.fremont.ia.us

On southwestern border of IA, south of Council Bluffs; established Feb 24, 1847 from Pottawattamie County. **Name Origin:** For John Charles Fremont (1813-90), soldier and explorer who led five expeditions to the West, U.S. senator from CA (1850-51), and governor of the AZ Territory (1878-83).

Area (sq mi): 516.76 (land 511.08; water 5.68). **Pop per sq mi:** 15.2.

Pop 2005: 7,759. **State rank:** 92. **Pop change:** 2000-20005 -3.1%; 1990-2000 -2.6%. **Pop 2000:** 8,010 (White 96.9%; Black or African

American 0%; Hispanic or Latino 2.2%; Asian 0.2%; Other 1.7%). **Foreign born:** 1.7%. **Median age:** 41.2.

Income 2000: per capita $18,081; median household $38,345; **Pop below poverty level:** 9.5%. *****Personal per capita income 2000-2003:** $25,752-$26,965.

Unemployment 2004: 4.3%. **Change from 2000:** +1.7%. **Median travel time to work:** 21.9 minutes. **Working outside county of residence:** 45.2%.

Cities with pop over 10,000: None.

GREENE COUNTY

114 N Chestnut St   **Ph:** 515-386-2516
Jefferson, IA 50129   **Fax:** 515-386-2321
www.jeffersoniowa.com

In central IA, west of Ames; established Jan 15, 1851 from Dallas County. **Name Origin:** For Gen. Nathanael Greene (1742-86), hero of the Revolutionary War, quartermaster general (1778-80), and commander of the Army of the South (1780).

Area (sq mi): 571.13 (land 568.41; water 2.72). **Pop per sq mi:** 17.5.

Pop 2005: 9,963. **State rank:** 79. **Pop change:** 2000-20005 -3.9%; 1990-2000 +3.2%. **Pop 2000:** 10,366 (White 97.4%; Black or African American 0.1%; Hispanic or Latino 1.7%; Asian 0.2%; Other 1.5%). **Foreign born:** 1.2%. **Median age:** 41.

Income 2000: per capita $16,866; median household $33,883; **Pop below poverty level:** 8.1%. *****Personal per capita income 2000-2003:** $22,300-$24,240.

Unemployment 2004: 4.5%. **Change from 2000:** +0.5%. **Median travel time to work:** 19.4 minutes. **Working outside county of residence:** 28.7%.

Cities with pop over 10,000: None.

GRUNDY COUNTY

706 G Ave   **Ph:** 319-824-5229
Grundy Center, IA 50638   **Fax:** 319-824-3447
www.grundycounty.org

In central IA, west of Waterloo; established Jan 15, 1851 from Black Hawk County. **Name Origin:** For Felix Grundy (1777-1840) of KY, U.S. senator from TN (1829-38; 1839-40) and U.S. attorney general (1838-39).

Area (sq mi): 502.55 (land 502.51; water 0.03). **Pop per sq mi:** 24.5.

Pop 2005: 12,329. **State rank:** 63. **Pop change:** 2000-20005 -0.3%; 1990-2000 +2.8%. **Pop 2000:** 12,369 (White 98.6%; Black or African American 0.1%; Hispanic or Latino 0.6%; Asian 0.3%; Other 0.7%). **Foreign born:** 0.8%. **Median age:** 40.8.

Income 2000: per capita $19,142; median household $39,396; **Pop below poverty level:** 4.6%. *****Personal per capita income 2000-2003:** $26,364-$28,571.

Unemployment 2004: 3.8%. **Change from 2000:** +1.5%. **Median travel time to work:** 20.6 minutes. **Working outside county of residence:** 45.8%.

Cities with pop over 10,000: None.

Source: Personal per capita income data are from the Bureau of Economic Analysis; per capita income data are from the Bureau of the Census. See Introduction for explanation of differences.

GUTHRIE COUNTY

200 N 5th St   **Ph:** 641-747-3415
Guthrie Center, IA 50115   **Fax:** 641-747-2420

In west-central IA, west of Des Moines, established Jan 15, 1851 from Jackson County. **Name Origin:** For Capt. Edwin Guthrie (?-1847), army officer from IA killed during the Mexican War.

Area (sq mi): 593.06 (land 590.6; water 2.46). **Pop per sq mi:** 19.6.

Pop 2005: 11,547. **State rank:** 69. **Pop change:** 2000-20005 +1.7%; 1990-2000 +3.8%. **Pop 2000:** 11,353 (White 98%, Black or African American 0.1%; Hispanic or Latino 1.1%; Asian 0.1%; Other 1.1%). **Foreign born:** 1.2%. **Median age:** 41.9.

Income 2000: per capita $19,726; median household $36,495; **Pop below poverty level:** 8%. ***Personal per capita income 2000-2003:** $24,048-$25,412.

Unemployment 2004: 4.6%. **Change from 2000:** +1.6%. **Median travel time to work:** 26.7 minutes. **Working outside county of residence:** 47.2%.

Cities with pop over 10,000: None.

HAMILTON COUNTY

2300 Superior St   **Ph:** 515-832-9510
Webster City, IA 50595   **Fax:** 515-832-9514
www.hamiltoncounty.org

In central IA, north of Ames; established Dec 22, 1856 from Webster County. **Name Origin:** For William H. Hamilton, president of the IA senate (1856-57) at the time the county was established.

Area (sq mi): 577.44 (land 576.68; water 0.76). **Pop per sq mi:** 28.1.

Pop 2005: 16,209. **State rank:** 48. **Pop change:** 2000-20005 -1.4%; 1990-2000 +2.3%. **Pop 2000:** 16,438 (White 96.1%; Black or African American 0.2%; Hispanic or Latino 1.4%; Asian 1.5%; Other 1.6%). **Foreign born:** 2.1%. **Median age:** 39.1.

Income 2000: per capita $18,801; median household $38,658; **Pop below poverty level:** 6.3%. ***Personal per capita income 2000-2003:** $25,959-$26,282.

Unemployment 2004: 4.5%. **Change from 2000:** +1.5%. **Median travel time to work:** 15.9 minutes. **Working outside county of residence:** 24.9%.

Cities with pop over 10,000: None.

HANCOCK COUNTY

PO Box 70   **Ph:** 641-923-2532
Garner, IA 50438   **Fax:** 641-923-3521
www.hancockcountyia.org

In north-central IA, west of Mason City; established Jan 15, 1851 from Wright County. **Name Origin:** For John Hancock (1737-93), noted signer of the Declaration of Independence, governor of MA (1780-85; 1787-93), and statesman.

Area (sq mi): 573.14 (land 571.11; water 2.03). **Pop per sq mi:** 20.6.

Pop 2005: 11,786. **State rank:** 67. **Pop change:** 2000-20005 -2.6%; 1990-2000 -4.3%. **Pop 2000:** 12,100 (White 96.7%; Black or African American 0.1%; Hispanic or Latino 2.5%; Asian 0.3%; Other 1.9%). **Foreign born:** 2.2%. **Median age:** 39.7.

Income 2000: per capita $17,957; median household $37,703; **Pop below poverty level:** 6%. ***Personal per capita income 2000-2003:** $25,926-$28,511.

Unemployment 2004: 3.8%. **Change from 2000:** +1.5%. **Median travel time to work:** 17.6 minutes. **Working outside county of residence:** 35.2%.

Cities with pop over 10,000: None.

HARDIN COUNTY

1215 Edgington Ave County Courthouse   **Ph:** 641-939-8109
Eldora, IA 50627   **Fax:** 641-939-8245
hardincountyonline.com

In central IA, east of Fort Dodge; established Jan 15, 1851 from Black Hawk County. **Name Origin:** For Gen. John J. Hardin (1810-47), officer in the Black Hawk War and U.S. representative from IL (1843-45). He was killed at the Battle of Buena Vista in the Mexican-American War.

Area (sq mi): 569.93 (land 569.26; water 0.68). **Pop per sq mi:** 31.6.

Pop 2005: 18,003. **State rank:** 41. **Pop change:** 2000-20005 -4.3%; 1990-2000 -1.5%. **Pop 2000:** 18,812 (White 96.1%; Black or African American 0.6%; Hispanic or Latino 2.4%; Asian 0.3%; Other 1.8%). **Foreign born:** 1.7%. **Median age:** 40.6.

Income 2000: per capita $17,537; median household $35,429; **Pop below poverty level:** 8%. ***Personal per capita income 2000-2003:** $23,196-$23,865.

Unemployment 2004: 5.6%. **Change from 2000:** +2.2%. **Median travel time to work:** 17.5 minutes. **Working outside county of residence:** 21.8%.

Cities with pop over 10,000: None.

HARRISON COUNTY

111 N 2nd Ave   **Ph:** 712-644-2665
Logan, IA 51546   **Fax:** 712-644-2615
www.harrisoncountyia.org

On central western border of IA, north of Council Bluffs; established Jan 15, 1851 from Pottawattamie County. **Name Origin:** For William Henry Harrison (1773-1841), ninth U.S. president.

Area (sq mi): 700.93 (land 696.72; water 4.2). **Pop per sq mi:** 22.8.

Pop 2005: 15,884. **State rank:** 52. **Pop change:** 2000-20005 +1.4%; 1990-2000 +6.4%. **Pop 2000:** 15,666 (White 98.2%; Black or African American 0.1%; Hispanic or Latino 0.7%; Asian 0.2%; Other 1%). **Foreign born:** 0.8%. **Median age:** 38.9.

Income 2000: per capita $17,662; median household $38,141; **Pop below poverty level:** 7.1%. ***Personal per capita income 2000-2003:** $24,479-$25,043.

Unemployment 2004: 5.4%. **Change from 2000:** +1.6%. **Median travel time to work:** 27.3 minutes. **Working outside county of residence:** 45.4%.

Cities with pop over 10,000: None.

HENRY COUNTY

PO Box 176   **Ph:** 319-385-2632
Mount Pleasant, IA 52641   **Fax:** 319-385-4144
www.co.henry.ia.us

In southeastern IA, west of Burlington; established Dec 7, 1836

🏛 *County Seat*

Henry County (cont'd)

(prior to statehood) from Wisconsin Territory. **Name Origin:** For Col. Henry Dodge (1782-1867), officer in the Black Hawk War; governor of WI Territory (1836-41; 1845-48), and U.S. senator from WI (1848-57).

Area (sq mi): 436.68 (land 434.44; water 2.24). **Pop per sq mi:** 46.6.

Pop 2005: 20,246. **State rank:** 35. **Pop change:** 2000-20005 -0.4%; 1990-2000 +5.8%. **Pop 2000:** 20,336 (White 94.2%; Black or African American 1.5%; Hispanic or Latino 1.3%; Asian 1.9%; Other 1.8%). **Foreign born:** 1.8%. **Median age:** 37.1.

Income 2000: per capita $18,192; median household $39,087; **Pop below poverty level:** 8.8%. ***Personal per capita income 2000-2003:** $23,590-$24,291.

Unemployment 2004: 6.4%. **Change from 2000:** +2.6%. **Median travel time to work:** 17.2 minutes. **Working outside county of residence:** 20.4%.

Cities with pop over 10,000: None.

HOWARD COUNTY
137 N Elm St County Courthouse   **Ph:** 563-547-2661
Cresco, IA 52136   **Fax:** 563-547-3605
www.crescoia.com/howardcounty/index.html

On northern border of IA, north of Waterloo; established Jan 15, 1851 from Chickasaw and Floyd counties. **Name Origin:** For Tilghman Ashurst Howard (1797-1844), TN legislator, U.S. representative from IN (1839-40), and TX patriot.

Area (sq mi): 473.76 (land 473.4; water 0.36). **Pop per sq mi:** 20.5.

Pop 2005: 9,700. **State rank:** 80. **Pop change:** 2000-20005 -2.3%; 1990-2000 +1.3%. **Pop 2000:** 9,932 (White 98.6%; Black or African American 0.1%; Hispanic or Latino 0.6%; Asian 0.2%; Other 0.7%). **Foreign born:** 0.4%. **Median age:** 39.5.

Income 2000: per capita $17,842; median household $34,641; **Pop below poverty level:** 9.3%. ***Personal per capita income 2000-2003:** $23,812-$25,947.

Unemployment 2004: 4.9%. **Change from 2000:** +1.8%. **Median travel time to work:** 19.2 minutes. **Working outside county of residence:** 23.8%.

Cities with pop over 10,000: None.

HUMBOLDT COUNTY
203 Main St   **Ph:** 515-332-1571
Dakota City, IA 50529   **Fax:** 515-332-1738
www.ci.humboldt.ia.us

In north-central IA, north of Fort Dodge; established Jan 15, 1851 from Webster County. **Name Origin:** For Alexander von Humboldt (1769-1859), German explorer and naturalist.

Area (sq mi): 435.73 (land 434.41; water 1.31). **Pop per sq mi:** 23.

Pop 2005: 9,973. **State rank:** 78. **Pop change:** 2000-20005 -3.9%; 1990-2000 -3.5%. **Pop 2000:** 10,381 (White 98.1%; Black or African American 0.1%; Hispanic or Latino 1%; Asian 0.2%; Other 1.1%). **Foreign born:** 1.4%. **Median age:** 41.3.

Income 2000: per capita $18,300; median household $38,201; **Pop below poverty level:** 8.3%. ***Personal per capita income 2000-2003:** $25,311-$26,834.

Unemployment 2004: 4.4%. **Change from 2000:** +1.3%. **Median travel time to work:** 18.8 minutes. **Working outside county of residence:** 27.7%.

Cities with pop over 10,000: None.

IDA COUNTY
401 Moorehead St   **Ph:** 712-364-2626
Ida Grove, IA 51445   **Fax:** 712-364-3929

In western IA, east of Sioux City; established Jan 15, 1851 from Cherokee County. **Name Origin:** For Mt. Ida of Greek myth; either the one in Crete or the one near ancient Troy (in present-day Turkey). The name was suggested by Eliphalet Price to connect the old classic civilization of Europe with the new civilization of the plains. Other sources say the county is named for the first white child born in the community (July 19, 1856), Ida Smith, daughter of Edwin Smith, a trapper.

Area (sq mi): 432.23 (land 431.71; water 0.52). **Pop per sq mi:** 17.1.

Pop 2005: 7,379. **State rank:** 93. **Pop change:** 2000-20005 -5.8%; 1990-2000 -6.3%. **Pop 2000:** 7,837 (White 98.7%; Black or African American 0.1%; Hispanic or Latino 0.5%; Asian 0.2%; Other 0.7%). **Foreign born:** 0.2%. **Median age:** 41.5.

Income 2000: per capita $18,675; median household $34,805; **Pop below poverty level:** 8.8%. ***Personal per capita income 2000-2003:** $23,288-$25,681.

Unemployment 2004: 4.5%. **Change from 2000:** +1.8%. **Median travel time to work:** 15.7 minutes. **Working outside county of residence:** 19.7%.

Cities with pop over 10,000: None.

IOWA COUNTY
PO Box 266   **Ph:** 319-642-3914
Marengo, IA 52301
www.co.iowa.ia.us

In east-central IA, west of Iowa City; established Feb 17, 1843 (prior to statehood) from Washington County. **Name Origin:** For the Iowa River.

Area (sq mi): 587.35 (land 586.45; water 0.9). **Pop per sq mi:** 27.4.

Pop 2005: 16,055. **State rank:** 50. **Pop change:** 2000-20005 +2.5%; 1990-2000 +7.1%. **Pop 2000:** 15,671 (White 98.2%; Black or African American 0.2%; Hispanic or Latino 1%; Asian 0.3%; Other 0.9%). **Foreign born:** 0.8%. **Median age:** 38.8.

Income 2000: per capita $18,884; median household $41,222; **Pop below poverty level:** 5%. ***Personal per capita income 2000-2003:** $28,690-$29,720.

Unemployment 2004: 4.3%. **Change from 2000:** +2.4%. **Median travel time to work:** 21.7 minutes. **Working outside county of residence:** 31.1%.

Cities with pop over 10,000: None.

JACKSON COUNTY
201 W Platt St   **Ph:** 563-652-3144
Maquoketa, IA 52060   **Fax:** 563-652-6975
www.jacksoncountyiowa.com

On central eastern border of IA, south of Dubuque; established

---

*Source: Personal per capita income data are from the Bureau of Economic Analysis; per capita income data are from the Bureau of the Census. See Introduction for explanation of differences.

Jackson County (cont'd)

Dec 21, 1837 (prior to statehood) from Wisconsin Territory. **Name Origin:** For Andrew Jackson (1767-1845), seventh U.S. president.

Area (sq mi): 649.75 (land 636.09; water 13.66). **Pop per sq mi:** 32.

Pop 2005: 20,335. **State rank:** 34. **Pop change:** 2000-20005 +0.2%; 1990-2000 +1.7%. **Pop 2000:** 20,296 (White 98.5%; Black or African American 0.1%; Hispanic or Latino 0.6%; Asian 0.1%; Other 0.8%). **Foreign born:** 0.7%. **Median age:** 39.1.

Income 2000: per capita $17,329; median household $34,529; **Pop below poverty level:** 10.3%. *Personal per capita income 2000-2003:** $22,266-$23,763.

Unemployment 2004: 6%. **Change from 2000:** +0.3%. **Median travel time to work:** 21.9 minutes. **Working outside county of residence:** 36.2%.

Cities with pop over 10,000: None.

JASPER COUNTY

PO Box 944   **Ph:** 641-792-7016
Newton, IA 50208   **Fax:** 641-792-1053
www.co.jasper.ia.us

In central IA, east of Des Moines; established Jan 13, 1846 from Mahaska County. **Name Origin:** For Sgt. Willliam Jasper (1750-79), Revolutionary War soldier from SC.

Area (sq mi): 732.93 (land 729.99; water 2.94). **Pop per sq mi:** 51.6.

Pop 2005: 37,674. **State rank:** 18. **Pop change:** 2000-20005 +1.2%; 1990-2000 +6.9%. **Pop 2000:** 37,213 (White 96.9%; Black or African American 0.8%; Hispanic or Latino 1%; Asian 0.4%; Other 1.2%). **Foreign born:** 1.5%. **Median age:** 38.5.

Income 2000: per capita $19,622; median household $41,683; **Pop below poverty level:** 6.5%. *Personal per capita income 2000-2003:** $25,974-$27,254.

Unemployment 2004: 6.1%. **Change from 2000:** +3.3%. **Median travel time to work:** 19.5 minutes. **Working outside county of residence:** 30.6%.

Cities with pop over 10,000: Newton ⛪ (15,696).

JEFFERSON COUNTY

51 E Briggs Ave   **Ph:** 641-472-2840
Fairfield, IA 52556
www.jeffersoniowa.com

In southeastern IA, east of Ottumwa; established Jan 21, 1839 (prior to statehnood) from Indian lands. **Name Origin:** For Thomas Jefferson (1743-1826), U.S. patriot, statesman, and third U.S. president.

Area (sq mi): 436.72 (land 435.34; water 1.38). **Pop per sq mi:** 36.7.

Pop 2005: 15,972. **State rank:** 51. **Pop change:** 2000-20005 -1.3%; 1990-2000 -0.8%. **Pop 2000:** 16,181 (White 94.7%; Black or African American 0.6%; Hispanic or Latino 1.8%; Asian 1.7%; Other 1.6%). **Foreign born:** 4%. **Median age:** 41.1.

Income 2000: per capita $19,579; median household $33,851; **Pop below poverty level:** 10.9%. *Personal per capita income 2000-2003:** $26,868-$25,829.

Unemployment 2004: 5.6%. **Change from 2000:** +0.5%. **Median travel time to work:** 14.1 minutes. **Working outside county of residence:** 13.3%.

Cities with pop over 10,000: None.

JOHNSON COUNTY

913 S Dubuque St Suite 201   **Ph:** 319-356-6000
Iowa City, IA 52240   **Fax:** 319-356-6036
www.jacksoncountyiowa.com

In east-central IA, south of Cedar Rapids, established Dec 21, 1837 (prior to statehood) from Des Moines County. **Name Origin:** For Col. Richard Mentor Johnson (1780-1850), officer in the War of 1812, U.S. senator from KY (1819-29), and U.S. vice president (1837-41).

Area (sq mi): 623.35 (land 614.48; water 8.87). **Pop per sq mi:** 190.5.

Pop 2005: 117,067. **State rank:** 5. **Pop change:** 2000-20005 +5.5%; 1990-2000 +15.5%. **Pop 2000:** 111,006 (White 88.8%; Black or African American 2.9%; Hispanic or Latino 2.5%; Asian 4.1%; Other 2.8%). **Foreign born:** 6.4%. **Median age:** 28.4.

Income 2000: per capita $22,220; median household $40,060; **Pop below poverty level:** 15%. *Personal per capita income 2000-2003:** $29,216-$31,423.

Unemployment 2004: 3%. **Change from 2000:** +0.6%. **Median travel time to work:** 17.7 minutes. **Working outside county of residence:** 14.1%.

Cities with pop over 10,000: Iowa City ⛪ (63,027); Coralville (17,528).

JONES COUNTY

PO Box 19   **Ph:** 319-462-4341
Anamosa, IA 52205   **Fax:** 319-462-5827
www.co.jones.ia.us

In eastern IA, east of Cedar Rapids, established Dec 21, 1837 (prior to statehood) from Wisconsin Territory. **Name Origin:** For George Wallace Jones (1804-96), surveyor of public lands for WI and IA territories and U.S. senator from IA (1848-59).

Area (sq mi): 576.7 (land 575.31; water 1.39). **Pop per sq mi:** 35.6.

Pop 2005: 20,509. **State rank:** 33. **Pop change:** 2000-20005 +1.4%; 1990-2000 +4%. **Pop 2000:** 20,221 (White 96%; Black or African American 1.8%; Hispanic or Latino 1.1%; Asian 0.2%; Other 1.3%). **Foreign born:** 0.8%. **Median age:** 38.5.

Income 2000: per capita $17,816; median household $37,449; **Pop below poverty level:** 8.6%. *Personal per capita income 2000-2003:** $21,609-$21,713.

Unemployment 2004: 5.4%. **Change from 2000:** +1.4%. **Median travel time to work:** 24.5 minutes. **Working outside county of residence:** 41.3%.

Cities with pop over 10,000: None.

KEOKUK COUNTY

101 S Main St Courthouse   **Ph:** 641-622-2210
Sigourney, IA 52591   **Fax:** 641-622-2171
www.keokukcountyia.com

In south-central IA, north of Ottumwa; established Dec 21, 1837

⛪ *County Seat*

Keokuk County (cont'd)

(prior to statehood) from Washington County. **Name Origin:** For Keokuk (c. 1780-1848), the chief of the Sac and Fox Indians at the time the first settlers arrived. His name was originally *Kiyokaga* 'he who moves around alert.'

Area (sq mi): 579.94 (land 579.19; water 0.75). **Pop per sq mi:** 19.3.

Pop 2005: 11,157. **State rank:** 72. **Pop change:** 2000-20005 -2.1%; 1990-2000 -1.9%. **Pop 2000:** 11,400 (White 98.8%; Black or African American 0.1%; Hispanic or Latino 0.5%; Asian 0.2%; Other 0.7%). **Foreign born:** 0.4%. **Median age:** 40.

Income 2000: per capita $17,120; median household $34,025; **Pop below poverty level:** 10.1%. ***Personal per capita income 2000-2003:** $23,046-$24,572.

Unemployment 2004: 5%. **Change from 2000:** -0.1%. **Median travel time to work:** 25.2 minutes. **Working outside county of residence:** 49.5%.

Cities with pop over 10,000: None.

KOSSUTH COUNTY

114 W State St   **Ph:** 515-295-2718
Algona, IA 50511   **Fax:** 515-295-3071
www.co.kossuth.ia.us

On central northern border of IA, north of Fort Dodge; established Jan 15, 1851 from Webster County. **Name Origin:** For Lajos Kossuth (1802-94), Hungarian resistance leader against Austrian domination who was enthusiastically acclaimed on a visit to the U.S. Named at a time when revolutionaries were celebrated in the U.S.

Area (sq mi): 974.39 (land 973.01; water 1.38). **Pop per sq mi:** 16.6.

Pop 2005: 16,142. **State rank:** 49. **Pop change:** 2000-20005 -5.9%; 1990-2000 -7.7%. **Pop 2000:** 17,163 (White 98.3%; Black or African American 0.1%; Hispanic or Latino 0.8%; Asian 0.3%; Other 0.7%). **Foreign born:** 0.9%. **Median age:** 41.3.

Income 2000: per capita $16,598; median household $34,562; **Pop below poverty level:** 10.2%. ***Personal per capita income 2000-2003:** $24,589-$26,939.

Unemployment 2004: 4.7%. **Change from 2000:** +1.6%. **Median travel time to work:** 16.7 minutes. **Working outside county of residence:** 19.4%.

Cities with pop over 10,000: None.

LEE COUNTY

PO Box 488   **Ph:** 319-372-6557
Fort Madison, IA 52627   **Fax:** 319-372-8200
www.leecounty.org

On southeasternmost border of IA; established Dec 7, 1836 (prior to statehood) from Des Moines County. **Name Origin:** Probably for Albert Miller Lea (1807-90), a surveyor of the Des Moines River who mapped the Iowa District, or for Charles Lee, an official of the New York Land Company, which had extensive landholdings in the area.

Area (sq mi): 538.77 (land 517.39; water 21.37). **Pop per sq mi:** 70.9.

Pop 2005: 36,705. **State rank:** 19. **Pop change:** 2000-20005 -3.5%; 1990-2000 -1.6%. **Pop 2000:** 38,052 (White 93%; Black or African

American 2.8%; Hispanic or Latino 2.4%; Asian 0.4%; Other 2.6%). **Foreign born:** 1.1%. **Median age:** 39.5.

Income 2000: per capita $18,430; median household $36,193; **Pop below poverty level:** 9.7%. ***Personal per capita income 2000-2003:** $23,406-$25,226.

Unemployment 2004: 7.6%. **Change from 2000:** +0.7%. **Median travel time to work:** 16.8 minutes. **Working outside county of residence:** 18.4%.

Cities with pop over 10,000: Fort Madison 🏛 (10,944); Keokuk (10,845).

LINN COUNTY

930 1st St SW   **Ph:** 319-892-5005
Cedar Rapids, IA 52404   **Fax:** 319-892-5009
www.linncounty.org

In east-central IA, north of Iowa City; established Dec 21, 1837 (prior to statehood) from Wisconsin Territory. **Name Origin:** For Lewis Fields Linn (1795-1843), U.S. senator from MO (1833-43).

Area (sq mi): 724.55 (land 717.44; water 7.1). **Pop per sq mi:** 277.2.

Pop 2005: 198,903. **State rank:** 2. **Pop change:** 2000-20005 +3.8%; 1990-2000 +13.6%. **Pop 2000:** 191,701 (White 93.1%; Black or African American 2.6%; Hispanic or Latino 1.4%; Asian 1.4%; Other 2.1%). **Foreign born:** 2.6%. **Median age:** 35.2.

Income 2000: per capita $22,977; median household $46,206; **Pop below poverty level:** 6.5%. ***Personal per capita income 2000-2003:** $31,350-$32,174.

Unemployment 2004: 5.1%. **Change from 2000:** +2.3%. **Median travel time to work:** 17.8 minutes. **Working outside county of residence:** 8.2%.

Cities with pop over 10,000: Cedar Rapids 🏛 (122,206); Marion (29,825).

LOUISA COUNTY

117 S Main St   **Ph:** 319-523-4541
Wapello, IA 52653   **Fax:** 319-523-4542
www.louisacountyiowa.org

On southeastern border of IA, north of Burlington; established Dec 7, 1836 (prior to statehood) from Des Moines County. **Name Origin:** For Louisa Massey, pioneer heroine who shot and wounded her brother's murderer. Some sources claim Louisa, queen of Denmark (1724-51), youngest daughter of George II of England.

Area (sq mi): 417.64 (land 401.92; water 15.73). **Pop per sq mi:** 29.5.

Pop 2005: 11,842. **State rank:** 66. **Pop change:** 2000-20005 -2.8%; 1990-2000 +5.1%. **Pop 2000:** 12,183 (White 86.4%; Black or African American 0.3%; Hispanic or Latino 12.6%; Asian 0.2%; Other 5.7%). **Foreign born:** 6.8%. **Median age:** 35.9.

Income 2000: per capita $17,644; median household $39,086; **Pop below poverty level:** 9.3%. ***Personal per capita income 2000-2003:** $23,284-$24,590.

Unemployment 2004: 4.9%. **Change from 2000:** +1.1%. **Median travel time to work:** 23.5 minutes. **Working outside county of residence:** 53.2%.

Cities with pop over 10,000: None.

Source: Personal per capita income data are from the Bureau of Economic Analysis; per capita income data are from the Bureau of the Census. See Introduction for explanation of differences.

LUCAS COUNTY
916 Braden St
Chariton, IA 50049

Ph: 641-774-4421
Fax: 641-774-8669

In south-central IA, southeast of Des Moines; established Jan 13, 1846 from Monroe County. **Name Origin:** For Col. Robert Lucas (1781-1853), governor of OH (1832-36) and first territorial governor of IA (1838-41).

Area (sq mi). 434.17 (land 430.55; water 3.63) **Pop per sq mi:** 22.5.

Pop 2005: 9,672. **State rank:** 82. **Pop change:** 2000-20005 +2.7%; 1990-2000 +3.9%. **Pop 2000:** 9,422 (White 98%; Black or African American 0.1%; Hispanic or Latino 0.9%; Asian 0.3%; Other 1.1%). **Foreign born:** 0.7%. **Median age:** 39.9.

Income 2000: per capita $15,341; median household $30,876; **Pop below poverty level:** 13.7%. ***Personal per capita income 2000-2003:** $21,664-$21,250.

Unemployment 2004: 5.7%. **Change from 2000:** +2%. **Median travel time to work:** 25.6 minutes. **Working outside county of residence:** 27.1%.

Cities with pop over 10,000: None.

LYON COUNTY
206 S 2nd Ave
Rock Rapids, IA 51246
www.lyoncountyiowa.com

Ph: 712-472-2623
Fax: 712-472-2422

On northwestern border of IA; established as Buncombe County Jan 15, 1851 from Woodbury County; name changed Sep 11, 1862. **Name Origin:** For Gen. Nathaniel Lyon (1818-61), Union commander in the Civil War who helped preserve MO for the Union when it seemed likely to join the Confederacy. He was killed leading the First Iowa Infantry at the Battle of Wilson Creek, MO.

Area (sq mi): 587.63 (land 587.5; water 0.13). **Pop per sq mi:** 20.

Pop 2005: 11,750. **State rank:** 68. **Pop change:** 2000-20005 -0.1%; 1990-2000 -1.6%. **Pop 2000:** 11,763 (White 98.9%; Black or African American 0.1%; Hispanic or Latino 0.4%; Asian 0.2%; Other 0.6%). **Foreign born:** 0.9%. **Median age:** 38.1.

Income 2000: per capita $16,081; median household $36,878; **Pop below poverty level:** 7%. ***Personal per capita income 2000-2003:** $22,458-$22,839.

Unemployment 2004: 3.5%. **Change from 2000:** +0.8%. **Median travel time to work:** 18.4 minutes. **Working outside county of residence:** 37.6%.

Cities with pop over 10,000: None.

MADISON COUNTY
112 N 1st St
Winterset, IA 50273
www.madisoncounty.com

Ph: 515-462-4451
Fax: 515-462-9825

In south-central IA, southwest of Des Moines; established Feb 14, 1844 (prior to statehood) from Polk County. **Name Origin:** For James Madison (1751-1836), fourth U.S. president.

Area (sq mi): 562.3 (land 561.14; water 1.16). **Pop per sq mi:** 27.

Pop 2005: 15,158. **State rank:** 54. **Pop change:** 2000-20005 +8.1%; 1990-2000 +12.3%. **Pop 2000:** 14,019 (White 98.2%; Black or African American 0.1%; Hispanic or Latino 0.7%; Asian 0.2%; Other 1.2%). **Foreign born:** 0.6%. **Median age:** 37.9.

Income 2000: per capita $19,357; median household $41,845; **Pop below poverty level:** 6.7%. ***Personal per capita income 2000-2003:** $24,904-$27,279.

Unemployment 2004: 5.1%. **Change from 2000:** +1.5%. **Median travel time to work:** 27.2 minutes. **Working outside county of residence:** 52.9%.

Cities with pop over 10,000: None.

MAHASKA COUNTY
106 S 1st St Mahaska Courthouse
Oskaloosa, IA 52577
www.mahaskacounty.org

Ph: 641-673-7786
Fax: 641 672-1256

In south-central IA, northwest of Ottumwa; established Feb 17, 1843 (prior to statehood) from Indian lands. **Name Origin:** For Mahaska (1784-1834), a chief of the Iowa tribe, whose name means 'white cloud.' the county seat was named for one of his wives.

Area (sq mi): 573.4 (land 570.87; water 2.53). **Pop per sq mi:** 39.2.

Pop 2005: 22,364. **State rank:** 27. **Pop change:** 2000-20005 +0.1%; 1990-2000 +3.8%. **Pop 2000:** 22,335 (White 96.7%; Black or African American 0.6%; Hispanic or Latino 0.9%; Asian 0.9%; Other 1.3%). **Foreign born:** 1.6%. **Median age:** 37.2.

Income 2000: per capita $18,232; median household $37,314; **Pop below poverty level:** 9.8%. ***Personal per capita income 2000-2003:** $24,650-$25,222.

Unemployment 2004: 4.8%. **Change from 2000:** +1.4%. **Median travel time to work:** 18.9 minutes. **Working outside county of residence:** 37.9%.

Cities with pop over 10,000: Oskaloosa 🏛 (10,945).

MARION COUNTY
PO Box 497
Knoxville, IA 50138
www.redrockarea.com

Ph: 641-828-2207
Fax: 641-828-7580

In south-central IA, southeast of Des Moines; established Jun 10, 1845 (prior to statehood) from Washington County. **Name Origin:** For Gen. Francis Marion (c. 1732-95), SC soldier and legislator, known as 'The Swamp Fox' for his tactics during the Revolutionary War.

Area (sq mi): 570.53 (land 554.21; water 16.32). **Pop per sq mi:** 59.5.

Pop 2005: 32,984. **State rank:** 21. **Pop change:** 2000-20005 +2.9%; 1990-2000 +6.8%. **Pop 2000:** 32,052 (White 96.9%; Black or African American 0.4%; Hispanic or Latino 0.8%; Asian 1%; Other 1%). **Foreign born:** 1.7%. **Median age:** 37.2.

Income 2000: per capita $18,717; median household $42,401; **Pop below poverty level:** 7.6%. ***Personal per capita income 2000-2003:** $26,439-$25,959.

Unemployment 2004: 4.5%. **Change from 2000:** +1.2%. **Median travel time to work:** 19.7 minutes. **Working outside county of residence:** 20.7%.

Cities with pop over 10,000: Pella (10,182).

🏛 *County Seat*

MARSHALL COUNTY

1 E Main St 3rd Fl   **Ph:** 641-754-6355
Marshalltown, IA 50158   **Fax:** 641-754-6349
www.co.marshall.ia.us

In central IA, east of Ames; established Jan 13, 1846 from Jasper County. **Name Origin:** For John Marshall (1755-1835), Chief Justice of the U.S. Supreme Court (1801-35).

Area (sq mi): 573.02 (land 572.32; water 0.7). **Pop per sq mi:** 68.9.

Pop 2005: 39,418. **State rank:** 16. **Pop change:** 2000-20005 +0.3%; 1990-2000 +2.7%. **Pop 2000:** 39,311 (White 88.1%; Black or African American 0.9%; Hispanic or Latino 9%; Asian 0.8%; Other 7.8%). **Foreign born:** 6.6%. **Median age:** 38.6.

Income 2000: per capita $19,176; median household $38,268; **Pop below poverty level:** 10.2%. ***Personal per capita income 2000-2003:** $25,485-$28,048.

Unemployment 2004: 5.6%. **Change from 2000:** +2.7%. **Median travel time to work:** 17.1 minutes. **Working outside county of residence:** 16.3%.

Cities with pop over 10,000: Marshalltown 🏛 (26,057).

MILLS COUNTY

418 Sharp St County Courthouse   **Ph:** 712-527-4880
Glenwood, IA 51534   **Fax:** 712-527-4936
www.millscoia.us

On southwestern border of IA, south of Council Bluffs; established Jan 15, 1851 from Pottawattamie County. **Name Origin:** For Maj. Frederick D. Mills (?-1847), IA officer killed at San Antonio Garita during the Mexican-American War.

Area (sq mi): 439.67 (land 436.53; water 3.13). **Pop per sq mi:** 35.

Pop 2005: 15,284. **State rank:** 53. **Pop change:** 2000-20005 +5.1%; 1990-2000 +10.2%. **Pop 2000:** 14,547 (White 97.2%; Black or African American 0.3%; Hispanic or Latino 1.2%; Asian 0.3%; Other 1.5%). **Foreign born:** 1%. **Median age:** 38.1.

Income 2000: per capita $18,736; median household $42,428; **Pop below poverty level:** 8.3%. ***Personal per capita income 2000-2003:** $28,822-$30,758.

Unemployment 2004: 4.5%. **Change from 2000:** +1.7%. **Median travel time to work:** 23.5 minutes. **Working outside county of residence:** 49.9%.

Cities with pop over 10,000: None.

MITCHELL COUNTY

508 State St   **Ph:** 641-732-3726
Osage, IA 50461   **Fax:** 641-732-3728

On the central northern border of IA, northeast of Mason City; established Jan 15, 1851 from Chickasaw County. **Name Origin:** Named by Irish settlers for John Mitchel (1815-75), Irish journalist and nationalist who was imprisoned for helping to lead revolt against Britain and escaped to the U.S. in 1853.

Area (sq mi): 469.4 (land 468.92; water 0.47). **Pop per sq mi:** 23.3.

Pop 2005: 10,919. **State rank:** 73. **Pop change:** 2000-20005 +0.4%; 1990-2000 -0.5%. **Pop 2000:** 10,874 (White 98.9%; Black or African American 0.2%; Hispanic or Latino 0.6%; Asian 0.2%; Other 0.4%). **Foreign born:** 0.5%. **Median age:** 40.6.

Income 2000: per capita $16,809; median household $34,843; **Pop below poverty level:** 10.7%. ***Personal per capita income 2000-2003:** $23,900-$23,494.

Unemployment 2004: 4%. **Change from 2000:** +1.2%. **Median travel time to work:** 19.3 minutes. **Working outside county of residence:** 26.7%.

Cities with pop over 10,000: None.

MONONA COUNTY

610 Iowa Ave   **Ph:** 712-423-2491
Onawa, IA 51040   **Fax:** 712-423-2744

On central western border of IA, south of Sioux City; established in Jan 15, 1851 from Harrison County. **Name Origin:** Possibly the name of a legendary Indian girl who leaped into the Mississippi River when she believed that her lover had been killed; or the name of an Indian divinity; or Ottawa for 'beautiful land.'

Area (sq mi): 698.85 (land 693.12; water 5.73). **Pop per sq mi:** 13.7.

Pop 2005: 9,520. **State rank:** 83. **Pop change:** 2000-20005 -5%; 1990-2000 -0.1%. **Pop 2000:** 10,020 (White 97.9%; Black or African American 0.1%; Hispanic or Latino 0.7%; Asian 0.1%; Other 1.5%). **Foreign born:** 0.4%. **Median age:** 43.

Income 2000: per capita $17,477; median household $33,235; **Pop below poverty level:** 9.4%. ***Personal per capita income 2000-2003:** $22,767-$23,380.

Unemployment 2004: 6.1%. **Change from 2000:** +2.4%. **Median travel time to work:** 22.8 minutes. **Working outside county of residence:** 30.3%.

Cities with pop over 10,000: None.

MONROE COUNTY

10 Benton Ave E   **Ph:** 641-932-5212
Albia, IA 52531   **Fax:** 641-932-3245

In south-central IA, west of Ottumwa; established as Kishkekosh County Feb 17, 1843 (prior to statehood) from Wapello County. Name changed Jan 19, 1846. **Name Origin:** For James Monroe (1758-1831), fifth U.S. president.

Area (sq mi): 434.11 (land 433.41; water 0.7). **Pop per sq mi:** 18.1.

Pop 2005: 7,835. **State rank:** 89. **Pop change:** 2000-20005 -2.3%; 1990-2000 -1.2%. **Pop 2000:** 8,016 (White 98.1%; Black or African American 0.2%; Hispanic or Latino 0.5%; Asian 0.4%; Other 1%). **Foreign born:** 0.6%. **Median age:** 39.7.

Income 2000: per capita $17,155; median household $34,877; **Pop below poverty level:** 9%. ***Personal per capita income 2000-2003:** $24,683-$24,957.

Unemployment 2004: 6.3%. **Change from 2000:** +2.1%. **Median travel time to work:** 24.4 minutes. **Working outside county of residence:** 41.5%.

Cities with pop over 10,000: None.

MONTGOMERY COUNTY

PO Box 469   **Ph:** 712-623-4986
Red Oak, IA 51566   **Fax:** 712-623-4987

In southwestern IA, southeast of Council Bluffs; established Jan

---

*Source: Personal per capita income data are from the Bureau of Economic Analysis; per capita income data are from the Bureau of the Census. See Introduction for explanation of differences.

Montgomery County (cont'd)

15, 1851 from Polk County. **Name Origin:** For Gen. Richard Montgomery (1736-75), American Revolutionary War officer who captured Montreal, Canada.

Area (sq mi): 424.81 (land 423.88; water 0.93). **Pop per sq mi:** 26.7.

Pop 2005: 11,313. **State rank:** 71. **Pop change:** 2000-20005 -3.9%; 1990-2000 2.5%. **Pop 2000:** 11,771 (White 97.6%; Black or African American 0.1%; Hispanic or Latino 1.3%; Asian 0.2%; Other 1.4%). **Foreign born:** 1.2%. **Median age:** 40.4.

Income 2000: per capita $16,373; median household $33,214; **Pop below poverty level:** 9.1%. ***Personal per capita income 2000-2003:** $24,590-$24,587.

Unemployment 2004: 4.5%. **Change from 2000:** -0.6%. **Median travel time to work:** 17.6 minutes. **Working outside county of residence:** 19%.

Cities with pop over 10,000: None.

MUSCATINE COUNTY
401 E 3rd St
Muscatine, IA 52761
www.co.muscatine.ia.us

Ph: 563-263-5821
Fax: 563-263-7248

On eastern border of IA, west of Davenport; established Dec 7, 1836 (prior to statehood) from Des Moines County. **Name Origin:** Variant name for the Mascouten tribe of the Potawatomic Indians. Meaning of the name is uncertain, but locally believed to be 'burning island.'

Area (sq mi): 449.07 (land 438.67; water 10.4). **Pop per sq mi:** 97.5.

Pop 2005: 42,756. **State rank:** 14. **Pop change:** 2000-20005 +2.5%; 1990-2000 +4.5%. **Pop 2000:** 41,722 (White 85.7%; Black or African American 0.7%; Hispanic or Latino 11.9%; Asian 0.8%; Other 7.8%). **Foreign born:** 5.9%. **Median age:** 36.1.

Income 2000: per capita $19,625; median household $41,803; **Pop below poverty level:** 8.9%. ***Personal per capita income 2000-2003:** $26,023-$28,776.

Unemployment 2004: 4.5%. **Change from 2000:** +0.8%. **Median travel time to work:** 17.3 minutes. **Working outside county of residence:** 19.5%.

Cities with pop over 10,000: Muscatine 🏛 (22,713).

O'BRIEN COUNTY
PO Box 340
Primghar, IA 51245
www.obriencounty.com

Ph: 712-957-3045
Fax: 712-957-3046

In northwestern IA; established Jan 15, 1851 from Cherokee County. **Name Origin:** For William Smith O'Brien (1803-64), leader of the Irish rebellion of 1848.

Area (sq mi): 573.25 (land 573.08; water 0.17). **Pop per sq mi:** 25.2.

Pop 2005: 14,414. **State rank:** 57. **Pop change:** 2000-20005 -4.6%; 1990-2000 -2.2%. **Pop 2000:** 15,102 (White 96.8%; Black or African American 0.3%; Hispanic or Latino 1.8%; Asian 0.5%; Other 1.2%). **Foreign born:** 2%. **Median age:** 40.7.

Income 2000: per capita $17,281; median household $35,758; **Pop below poverty level:** 7.3%. ***Personal per capita income 2000-2003:** $24,453-$26,575.

Unemployment 2004: 4.1%. **Change from 2000:** +1.7%. **Median travel time to work:** 16.9 minutes. **Working outside county of residence:** 26.8%.

Cities with pop over 10,000: None.

OSCEOLA COUNTY
300 7th St
Sibley, IA 51249
www.osceolacountyia.com

Ph: 712-754-2241
Fax: 712-754-3743

On the northwestern border of IA; established Jan 15, 1851 from Woodbury County. **Name Origin:** For Osceola (c. 1804-38), Seminole leader during the early years of the Second Seminole War (1835-37). Name, also spelled *Ashi Vaholo Yahola*, means 'black drink hallower.'

Area (sq mi): 399.48 (land 398.77; water 0.71). **Pop per sq mi:** 16.8.

Pop 2005: 6,694. **State rank:** 94. **Pop change:** 2000-20005 -4.4%; 1990-2000 -3.6%. **Pop 2000:** 7,003 (White 97.3%; Black or African American 0.1%; Hispanic or Latino 1.8%; Asian 0.2%; Other 1.6%). **Foreign born:** 1.2%. **Median age:** 39.7.

Income 2000: per capita $16,463; median household $34,274; **Pop below poverty level:** 7%. ***Personal per capita income 2000-2003:** $22,784-$22,448.

Unemployment 2004: 4.1%. **Change from 2000:** +1%. **Median travel time to work:** 15.6 minutes. **Working outside county of residence:** 32.2%.

Cities with pop over 10,000: None.

PAGE COUNTY
PO Box 263
Clarinda, IA 51632

Ph: 712-542-3214
Fax: 712-542-5460

On southwestern border of IA; established Feb 14, 1847 from Pottawattamie County. **Name Origin:** For Capt. John Page (?-1846), killed at the Battle of Palo Alto during the Mexican-American War.

Area (sq mi): 535.35 (land 534.82; water 0.52). **Pop per sq mi:** 30.4.

Pop 2005: 16,253. **State rank:** 47. **Pop change:** 2000-20005 -4.3%; 1990-2000 +0.6%. **Pop 2000:** 16,976 (White 95.2%; Black or African American 1.7%; Hispanic or Latino 1.6%; Asian 0.5%; Other 1.8%). **Foreign born:** 1%. **Median age:** 40.2.

Income 2000: per capita $16,670; median household $35,466; **Pop below poverty level:** 12.5%. ***Personal per capita income 2000-2003:** $23,185-$24,461.

Unemployment 2004: 4.6%. **Change from 2000:** -0.2%. **Median travel time to work:** 14.8 minutes. **Working outside county of residence:** 21.1%.

Cities with pop over 10,000: None.

PALO ALTO COUNTY
PO Box 387
Emmetsburg, IA 50536

Ph: 712-852-3603
Fax: 712-852-2274

In north-central IA, northwest of Fort Dodge; established Jan 15, 1851 from Kossuth County. **Name Origin:** From Spanish *palo* 'stick,' and *alto* 'tall' or 'high.' For a small town in Texas, the scene of the first battle (1846) of the Mexican War.

Area (sq mi): 569.4 (land 563.83; water 5.57). **Pop per sq mi:** 17.2.

🏛 *County Seat*

Palo Alto County (cont'd)

Pop 2005: 9,697. **State rank:** 81. **Pop change:** 2000-20005 -4.4%; 1990-2000 -4.9%. **Pop 2000:** 10,147 (White 98.1%; Black or African American 0.1%; Hispanic or Latino 0.8%; Asian 0.3%; Other 1%). **Foreign born:** 0.9%. **Median age:** 40.7.

Income 2000: per capita $17,733; median household $32,409; **Pop below poverty level:** 10.6%. ***Personal per capita income 2000-2003:** $22,885-$23,401.

Unemployment 2004: 4.1%. **Change from 2000:** +0.2%. **Median travel time to work:** 15.5 minutes. **Working outside county of residence:** 24.7%.

Cities with pop over 10,000: None.

PLYMOUTH COUNTY

215 4th Ave SE   **Ph:** 712-546-6100
Le Mars, IA 51031   **Fax:** 712-546-5784
www.co.plymouth.ia.us

On northwestern border of IA, north of Sioux City; established Jan 15, 1851 from Woodbury County. **Name Origin:** For Plymouth, Devonshire, England, from which the Mayflower sailed for America in 1620, or to honor Plymouth, MA, the landing site of the pilgrims.

Area (sq mi): 863.96 (land 863.56; water 0.39). **Pop per sq mi:** 28.9.

Pop 2005: 24,958. **State rank:** 25. **Pop change:** 2000-20005 +0.4%; 1990-2000 +6.2%. **Pop 2000:** 24,849 (White 97.4%; Black or African American 0.3%; Hispanic or Latino 1.3%; Asian 0.3%; Other 1.3%). **Foreign born:** 1.2%. **Median age:** 37.8.

Income 2000: per capita $19,442; median household $41,638; **Pop below poverty level:** 6%. ***Personal per capita income 2000-2003:** $26,301-$27,591.

Unemployment 2004: 4.2%. **Change from 2000:** +1.2%. **Median travel time to work:** 19.1 minutes. **Working outside county of residence:** 34.4%.

Cities with pop over 10,000: None.

POCAHONTAS COUNTY

99 Court Sq County Courthouse   **Ph:** 712-335-4208
Pocahontas, IA 50574   **Fax:** 712-335-5045

In north-central IA, northwest of Fort Dodge; established Jan 15, 1851 from Humboldt and Greene counties. **Name Origin:** For Pocahontas (Matoaka c. 1595-1617), daughter of chief Powhatan, who prevented the execution of Capt. John Smith (c. 1580-1631).

Area (sq mi): 579.13 (land 577.7; water 1.42). **Pop per sq mi:** 13.7.

Pop 2005: 7,930. **State rank:** 87. **Pop change:** 2000-20005 -8.5%; 1990-2000 -9.1%. **Pop 2000:** 8,662 (White 98%; Black or African American 0.2%; Hispanic or Latino 0.9%; Asian 0.2%; Other 1.1%). **Foreign born:** 0.9%. **Median age:** 42.5.

Income 2000: per capita $17,006; median household $33,362; **Pop below poverty level:** 9.1%. ***Personal per capita income 2000-2003:** $23,172-$23,790.

Unemployment 2004: 5.6%. **Change from 2000:** +1.8%. **Median travel time to work:** 18.3 minutes. **Working outside county of residence:** 27.6%.

Cities with pop over 10,000: None.

POLK COUNTY

111 Court Ave   **Ph:** 515-286-3000
Des Moines, IA 50309   **Fax:** 515-323-5250
www.co.polk.ia.us

In south-central IA, south of Ames; established Jan 17, 1846 from Indian lands. **Name Origin:** For James Knox Polk (1795-1849), eleventh U.S. president.

Area (sq mi): 591.9 (land 569.35; water 22.55). **Pop per sq mi:** 704.3.

Pop 2005: 401,006. **State rank:** 1. **Pop change:** 2000-20005 +7%; 1990-2000 +14.5%. **Pop 2000:** 374,601 (White 86.4%; Black or African American 4.8%; Hispanic or Latino 4.4%; Asian 2.6%; Other 4.3%). **Foreign born:** 5.9%. **Median age:** 34.4.

Income 2000: per capita $23,654; median household $46,116; **Pop below poverty level:** 7.9%. ***Personal per capita income 2000-2003:** $32,728-$35,014.

Unemployment 2004: 4.8%. **Change from 2000:** +2.2%. **Median travel time to work:** 18.2 minutes. **Working outside county of residence:** 5.9%.

Cities with pop over 10,000: 7 (see page 35 for cities).

POTTAWATTAMIE COUNTY

PO Box 476   **Ph:** 712-328-5604
Council Bluffs, IA 51502
www.pottcounty.com

On southwestern border of IA; established Jan 15, 1848 from Indian lands. **Name Origin:** For the Potawatomie Indian tribe of Algonquian linguistic stock; name means 'people of the place of fire.'

Area (sq mi): 959.94 (land 954.26; water 5.68). **Pop per sq mi:** 94.

Pop 2005: 89,738. **State rank:** 8. **Pop change:** 2000-20005 +2.3%; 1990-2000 +6.1%. **Pop 2000:** 87,704 (White 94.3%; Black or African American 0.8%; Hispanic or Latino 3.3%; Asian 0.5%; Other 2.8%). **Foreign born:** 2%. **Median age:** 36.5.

Income 2000: per capita $19,275; median household $40,089; **Pop below poverty level:** 8.4%. ***Personal per capita income 2000-2003:** $25,564-$27,848.

Unemployment 2004: 5.4%. **Change from 2000:** +2.4%. **Median travel time to work:** 20.2 minutes. **Working outside county of residence:** 44.4%.

Cities with pop over 10,000: Council Bluffs 🏛 (59,347).

POWESHIEK COUNTY

PO Box 218   **Ph:** 641-623-5644
Montezuma, IA 50171   **Fax:** 641-623-5320

In central IA, east of Iowa City; established Feb 17, 1843 (prior to statehood) from Keokuk, Iowa, Johnson, and Mahaska counties. **Name Origin:** For a Sac and Fox chief, properly *Pawishika* 'he who shakes (something off himself).' He was chief during the Black Hawk War (1832); on behalf of his tribe he signed the Treaty of Fort Armstrong at Rock Island, IL.

Area (sq mi): 586.17 (land 585.03; water 1.14). **Pop per sq mi:** 32.3.

Pop 2005: 18,925. **State rank:** 37. **Pop change:** 2000-20005 +0.6%; 1990-2000 -1.1%. **Pop 2000:** 18,815 (White 96.2%; Black or African American 0.5%; Hispanic or Latino 1.2%; Asian 1.1%; Other 1.6%). **Foreign born:** 2.1%. **Median age:** 38.4.

*Source: Personal per capita income data are from the Bureau of Economic Analysis; per capita income data are from the Bureau of the Census. See Introduction for explanation of differences.

Poweshiek County (cont'd)

Income 2000: per capita $18,629; median household $37,836; **Pop below poverty level:** 9.8%. ***Personal per capita income 2000-2003:** $26,847-$28,483.

Unemployment 2004: 5%. **Change from 2000:** +1.4%. **Median travel time to work:** 16.3 minutes. **Working outside county of residence:** 18.9%.

Cities with pop over 10,000: None.

RINGGOLD COUNTY

109 W Madison St   **Ph:** 641-464-3234
Mount Ayr, IA 50854   **Fax:** 641-464-2478
www.ringgoldcounty.us

On central-southern border of IA, southwest of Des Moines; established Feb 24, 1847 from Taylor County. **Name Origin:** For Maj. Samuel Ringgold (1800-1846), officer in the Seminole War and the Mexican-American War, he died at the Battle of Palo Alto.

Area (sq mi): 538.92 (land 537.67; water 1.26). **Pop per sq mi:** 9.8.

Pop 2005: 5,273. **State rank:** 98. **Pop change:** 2000-20005 -3.6%; 1990-2000 +0.9%. **Pop 2000:** 5,469 (White 98.8%; Black or African American 0.1%; Hispanic or Latino 0.2%; Asian 0.2%; Other 0.6%). **Foreign born:** 0.5%. **Median age:** 43.2.

Income 2000: per capita $15,023; median household $29,110; **Pop below poverty level:** 14.3%. ***Personal per capita income 2000-2003:** $20,992-$20,903.

Unemployment 2004: 5.3%. **Change from 2000:** +2.3%. **Median travel time to work:** 22 minutes. **Working outside county of residence:** 26.4%.

Cities with pop over 10,000: None.

SAC COUNTY

PO Box 368   **Ph:** 712-662-7791
Sac City, IA 50583   **Fax:** 712-662-7978
www.saccounty.org

In west-central IA, southwest of Fort Dodge; established Jan 15, 1851 from Greene County. **Name Origin:** An Indian tribal name meaning 'outlet.' Also spelled *Sauk*.

Area (sq mi): 578.38 (land 575.82; water 2.56). **Pop per sq mi:** 18.4.

Pop 2005: 10,621. **State rank:** 75. **Pop change:** 2000-20005 -7.9%; 1990-2000 -6.5%. **Pop 2000:** 11,529 (White 98%; Black or African American 0.3%; Hispanic or Latino 1%; Asian 0.1%; Other 1.1%). **Foreign born:** 1.3%. **Median age:** 42.1.

Income 2000: per capita $16,902; median household $32,874; **Pop below poverty level:** 9.9%. ***Personal per capita income 2000-2003:** $23,010-$24,407.

Unemployment 2004: 4.3%. **Change from 2000:** +1.4%. **Median travel time to work:** 16.8 minutes. **Working outside county of residence:** 31.8%.

Cities with pop over 10,000: None.

SCOTT COUNTY

416 W 4th St   **Ph:** 563-326-8647
Davenport, IA 52801   **Fax:** 563-326-8298
www.co.scott.ia.us

On central eastern border of IA; established Dec 21, 1837 (prior to statehood) from Wisconsin Territory. **Name Origin:** For Gen. Winfield Scott (1786-1866), officer in the War of 1812 and the Mexican-American War; general in chief of the U.S. Army (1841-61).

Area (sq mi): 468.17 (land 457.93; water 10.24). **Pop per sq mi:** 351.6.

Pop 2005: 160,998. **State rank:** 3. **Pop change:** 2000-20005 +1.5%; 1990-2000 +5.1%. **Pop 2000:** 158,668 (White 86.6%; Black or African American 6.1%; Hispanic or Latino 4.1%; Asian 1.6%; Other 3.7%). **Foreign born:** 3.1%. **Median age:** 35.4.

Income 2000: per capita $21,310; median household $42,701; **Pop below poverty level:** 10.5%. ***Personal per capita income 2000-2003:** $28,158-$30,924.

Unemployment 2004: 5.3%. **Change from 2000:** +1.8%. **Median travel time to work:** 18.4 minutes. **Working outside county of residence:** 23.5%.

Cities with pop over 10,000: Davenport 🏛 (98,355); Bettendorf (31,615).

SHELBY COUNTY

PO Box 431   **Ph:** 712-755-5543
Harlan, IA 51537   **Fax:** 712-755-2667
www.shco.org

In western IA, northeast of Council Bluffs; established Jan 15, 1851 from Cass County. **Name Origin:** For Gen. Isaac Shelby (1750-1826), officer in the Revolutionary War, NC legislator, and governor of KY (1792-96; 1812-16).

Area (sq mi): 591.37 (land 590.83; water 0.54). **Pop per sq mi:** 21.4.

Pop 2005: 12,634. **State rank:** 61. **Pop change:** 2000-20005 -4.1%; 1990-2000 -0.4%. **Pop 2000:** 13,173 (White 98.2%; Black or African American 0.1%; Hispanic or Latino 0.7%; Asian 0.3%; Other 1%). **Foreign born:** 0.6%. **Median age:** 40.5.

Income 2000: per capita $16,969; median household $37,442; **Pop below poverty level:** 6%. ***Personal per capita income 2000-2003:** $24,212-$26,073.

Unemployment 2004: 4.1%. **Change from 2000:** +1.4%. **Median travel time to work:** 18.3 minutes. **Working outside county of residence:** 25.9%.

Cities with pop over 10,000: None.

SIOUX COUNTY

PO Box 47   **Ph:** 712-737-2286
Orange City, IA 51041   **Fax:** 712-737-8908
www.siouxcounty.org

On the northwestern border of IA, north of Sioux City, established Jan 13, 1851 from Plymouth County. **Name Origin:** For the Indian tribe, sometimes known as the Dakotas. Name is French form of Ojibway *nadouessioux* 'snakes' or 'enemies.'

Area (sq mi): 768.58 (land 767.88; water 0.7). **Pop per sq mi:** 42.

Sioux County (cont'd)

Pop 2005: 32,277. **State rank:** 22. **Pop change:** 2000-20005 +2.2%; 1990-2000 +5.6%. **Pop 2000:** 31,589 (White 96.2%; Black or African American 0.2%; Hispanic or Latino 2.6%; Asian 0.6%; Other 1.8%). **Foreign born:** 2.9%. **Median age:** 32.8.

Income 2000: per capita $16,532; median household $40,536; **Pop below poverty level:** 6.4%. ***Personal per capita income 2000-2003:** $24,120-$27,222.

Unemployment 2004: 3.1%. **Change from 2000:** +0.4%. **Median travel time to work:** 13 minutes. **Working outside county of residence:** 10.4%.

Cities with pop over 10,000: None.

STORY COUNTY
1315 South B Ave   **Ph:** 515-382-7410
Nevada, IA 50201
www.storycounty.com

In central IA, north of Des Moines; established Jan 13, 1846 from Jasper, Polk, and Boone counties. **Name Origin:** For Joseph Story (1779-1845), MA legislator and associate justice of the Supreme Court (1811-45).

Area (sq mi): 573.7 (land 572.86; water 0.84). **Pop per sq mi:** 139.6.

Pop 2005: 79,952. **State rank:** 9. **Pop change:** 2000-20005 +0%; 1990-2000 +7.7%. **Pop 2000:** 79,981 (White 90.3%; Black or African American 1.8%; Hispanic or Latino 1.5%; Asian 5.1%; Other 1.9%). **Foreign born:** 6.9%. **Median age:** 26.5.

Income 2000: per capita $19,949; median household $40,442; **Pop below poverty level:** 14.1%. ***Personal per capita income 2000-2003:** $25,826-$28,119.

Unemployment 2004: 3.2%. **Change from 2000:** +0.7%. **Median travel time to work:** 16.9 minutes. **Working outside county of residence:** 16.4%.

Cities with pop over 10,000: Ames (52,319).

TAMA COUNTY
PO Box 306   **Ph:** 641-484-3721
Toledo, IA 52342   **Fax:** 641-484-6403
www.tamacounty.org

In central IA, west of Cedar Rapids; established Feb 17, 1843 (prior to statehood) from Boone and Benton counties. **Name Origin:** For either a Fox Indian chief or for the wife of Chief Poweshiek. Meaning is uncertain; has been interpreted as 'beautiful,' 'lovely' or 'pleasant' when referring to a woman, or 'a bear with a voice that makes the rocks tremble' when applied to a man. A nearby Mesquaki Indian suggested that the name derives from *tewaime*, associated with the sound of thunder.

Area (sq mi): 722.37 (land 721.3; water 1.07). **Pop per sq mi:** 24.8.

Pop 2005: 17,919. **State rank:** 42. **Pop change:** 2000-20005 -1%; 1990-2000 +3.9%. **Pop 2000:** 18,103 (White 89.2%; Black or African American 0.3%; Hispanic or Latino 3.8%; Asian 0.2%; Other 9.2%, including 6.1% American Indian/Alaska Native). **Foreign born:** 2%. **Median age:** 39.1.

Income 2000: per capita $17,097; median household $37,419; **Pop below poverty level:** 10.5%. ***Personal per capita income 2000-2003:** $22,308-$23,141.

Unemployment 2004: 6.9%. **Change from 2000:** +3.3%. **Median travel time to work:** 20.7 minutes. **Working outside county of residence:** 38.5%.

Cities with pop over 10,000: None.

TAYLOR COUNTY
405 Jefferson St County Courthouse   **Ph:** 712-523-2095
Bedford, IA 50833   **Fax:** 712-523-2936

On southern border of IA; established Feb 24, 1847 from Page County. **Name Origin:** For Zachary Taylor (1784-1850), twelfth U.S. president.

Area (sq mi): 534.83 (land 533.95; water 0.87). **Pop per sq mi:** 12.4.

Pop 2005: 6,614. **State rank:** 95. **Pop change:** 2000-20005 -4.9%; 1990-2000 -2.2%. **Pop 2000:** 6,958 (White 95.3%; Black or African American 0%; Hispanic or Latino 3.8%; Asian 0.3%; Other 2%). **Foreign born:** 2%. **Median age:** 41.6.

Income 2000: per capita $15,082; median household $31,297; **Pop below poverty level:** 12.1%. ***Personal per capita income 2000-2003:** $20,919-$21,855.

Unemployment 2004: 4.6%. **Change from 2000:** +0.3%. **Median travel time to work:** 20.2 minutes. **Working outside county of residence:** 41%.

Cities with pop over 10,000: None.

UNION COUNTY
300 N Pine St   **Ph:** 641-782-7315
Creston, IA 50801   **Fax:** 641-782-8241
www.unioncountyiowa.org

In south-central IA, southwest of Des Moines; established Jan 15, 1851 from Clarke County. **Name Origin:** Probably for the union of the states.

Area (sq mi): 425.95 (land 424.39; water 1.57). **Pop per sq mi:** 28.2.

Pop 2005: 11,972. **State rank:** 65. **Pop change:** 2000-20005 -2.7%; 1990-2000 -3.5%. **Pop 2000:** 12,309 (White 97.8%; Black or African American 0.2%; Hispanic or Latino 1%; Asian 0.3%; Other 1.1%). **Foreign born:** 0.9%. **Median age:** 40.1.

Income 2000: per capita $16,690; median household $31,905; **Pop below poverty level:** 11.4%. ***Personal per capita income 2000-2003:** $22,033-$23,285.

Unemployment 2004: 5.9%. **Change from 2000:** +2.4%. **Median travel time to work:** 16.4 minutes. **Working outside county of residence:** 14.4%.

Cities with pop over 10,000: None.

VAN BUREN COUNTY
PO Box 475   **Ph:** 319-293-3129
Keosauqua, IA 52565   **Fax:** 319-293-6404
www.800-tourvbc.com

On the southeastern border of IA, west of Burlington; established Dec 7, 1836 (prior to statehood) from Des Moines County. **Name Origin:** For Martin Van Buren (1782-1862), eighth U.S. president.

Area (sq mi): 490.55 (land 484.82; water 5.73). **Pop per sq mi:** 16.1.

Pop 2005: 7,786. **State rank:** 90. **Pop change:** 2000-20005 -0.3%; 1990-2000 +1.7%. **Pop 2000:** 7,809 (White 98.1%; Black or African

*Source: Personal per capita income data are from the Bureau of Economic Analysis; per capita income data are from the Bureau of the Census. See Introduction for explanation of differences.

Van Buren County (cont'd)

American 0.1%; Hispanic or Latino 0.8%; Asian 0.3%; Other 1.1%). **Foreign born:** 0.6%. **Median age:** 40.8.

Income 2000: per capita $15,748; median household $31,094; **Pop below poverty level:** 12.7%. ***Personal per capita income 2000-2003:** $20,125-$20,675.

Unemployment 2004: 5.9%. **Change from 2000:** +1.3%. **Median travel time to work:** 23.9 minutes. **Working outside county of residence:** 39.4%.

Cities with pop over 10,000: None.

WAPELLO COUNTY

101 W 4th St
Ottumwa, IA 52501
www.wapellocounty.org

Ph: 641-683-0060
Fax: 641-683-0064

In south-central IA; established Feb 17, 1843 (prior to statehood) from Indian lands. **Name Origin:** For Wapello (1787-1842), a Fox Indian chief who figured prominently in the signing of several treaties. Variously translated as 'light,' 'dawn,' and 'he of the morning.' It may be just a birth-time designation, for which the last translation would be correct.

Area (sq mi): 435.98 (land 431.81; water 4.17). **Pop per sq mi:** 83.3.

Pop 2005: 35,965. **State rank:** 20. **Pop change:** 2000-20005 -0.2%; 1990-2000 +1%. **Pop 2000:** 36,051 (White 95.3%; Black or African American 0.9%; Hispanic or Latino 2.2%; Asian 0.6%; Other 2.2%). **Foreign born:** 1.9%. **Median age:** 39.2.

Income 2000: per capita $16,500; median household $32,188; **Pop below poverty level:** 13.2%. ***Personal per capita income 2000-2003:** $21,636-$24,663.

Unemployment 2004: 5.9%. **Change from 2000:** +1.3%. **Median travel time to work:** 19.1 minutes. **Working outside county of residence:** 17.4%.

Cities with pop over 10,000: Ottumwa 🏛 (24,680).

WARREN COUNTY

115 N Howard St
Indianola, IA 50125
www.co.warren.ia.us

Ph: 515-961-1033
Fax: 515-961-1071

In south-central IA, south of Des Moines; established Jan 13, 1846 from Polk County. **Name Origin:** For Dr. Joseph Warren (1741-75), Revolutionary War patriot and member of the Committee of Safety who sent Paul Revere (1735-1818) on his famous ride.

Area (sq mi): 573.21 (land 571.64; water 1.56). **Pop per sq mi:** 75.2.

Pop 2005: 42,981. **State rank:** 13. **Pop change:** 2000-20005 +5.7%; 1990-2000 +12.9%. **Pop 2000:** 40,671 (White 97.5%; Black or African American 0.3%; Hispanic or Latino 1.1%; Asian 0.4%; Other 1.3%). **Foreign born:** 1.1%. **Median age:** 36.

Income 2000: per capita $20,558; median household $50,349; **Pop below poverty level:** 5.1%. ***Personal per capita income 2000-2003:** $25,936-$27,957.

Unemployment 2004: 4.2%. **Change from 2000:** +1.9%. **Median travel time to work:** 25.8 minutes. **Working outside county of residence:** 65.5%.

Cities with pop over 10,000: Indianola 🏛 (13,714).

WASHINGTON COUNTY

PO Box 391
Washington, IA 52353
co.washington.ia.us

Ph: 319-653-7741
Fax: 319-653-7787

In southeastern IA, south of Iowa City; established Jan 16, 1837 (prior to statehood) from Wisconsin Territory. **Name Origin:** For George Washington (1732-1799), American patriot and first U.S. president.

Area (sq mi): 570.77 (land 568.71; water 2.06). **Pop per sq mi:** 37.7.

Pop 2005: 21,457. **State rank:** 28. **Pop change:** 2000-20005 +3.8%; 1990-2000 +5.4%. **Pop 2000:** 20,670 (White 96%; Black or African American 0.3%; Hispanic or Latino 2.7%; Asian 0.2%; Other 2.4%). **Foreign born:** 1.5%. **Median age:** 38.8.

Income 2000: per capita $18,221; median household $39,103; **Pop below poverty level:** 7.6%. ***Personal per capita income 2000-2003:** $27,245-$27,407.

Unemployment 2004: 4.2%. **Change from 2000:** +1.5%. **Median travel time to work:** 21.6 minutes. **Working outside county of residence:** 38.2%.

Cities with pop over 10,000: None.

WAYNE COUNTY

PO Box 424
Corydon, IA 50060
www.waynecountyiowa.com

Ph: 641-872-2264
Fax: 641-872-2431

On the central southern border of IA; established Jan 16, 1846 from Appanoose County. **Name Origin:** For Gen. Anthony Wayne (1745-96), PA soldier and statesman, nicknamed 'Mad Anthony' for his daring during the Revolutionary War.

Area (sq mi): 527.08 (land 525.6; water 1.48). **Pop per sq mi:** 12.6.

Pop 2005: 6,601. **State rank:** 96. **Pop change:** 2000-20005 -1.9%; 1990-2000 -4.8%. **Pop 2000:** 6,730 (White 98.3%; Black or African American 0.1%; Hispanic or Latino 0.7%; Asian 0.1%; Other 1%). **Foreign born:** 0.6%. **Median age:** 43.

Income 2000: per capita $15,613; median household $29,380; **Pop below poverty level:** 14%. ***Personal per capita income 2000-2003:** $20,147-$20,242.

Unemployment 2004: 4.7%. **Change from 2000:** +1.3%. **Median travel time to work:** 21.6 minutes. **Working outside county of residence:** 33.3%.

Cities with pop over 10,000: None.

WEBSTER COUNTY

701 Central Ave
Fort Dodge, IA 50501
www.webstercountyia.org

Ph: 515-574-3719
Fax: 515-574-3714

In central IA, northwest of Ames; established Jan 12, 1853 from Yell and Risley counties, both of which were organized in 1851 and abolished in 1853. **Name Origin:** For Daniel Webster (1782-1852), U.S. statesman and orator from MA.

Area (sq mi): 718.05 (land 715.23; water 2.82). **Pop per sq mi:** 54.5.

Pop 2005: 39,003. **State rank:** 17. **Pop change:** 2000-20005 -3.1%; 1990-2000 -0.3%. **Pop 2000:** 40,235 (White 92.4%; Black or African American 3.4%; Hispanic or Latino 2.3%; Asian 0.7%; Other 2.5%). **Foreign born:** 2%. **Median age:** 37.7.

Webster County (cont'd)

Income 2000: per capita $17,857; median household $35,334; **Pop below poverty level:** 10%. ***Personal per capita income 2000-2003:** $23,960-$26,278.

Unemployment 2004: 5.1%. **Change from 2000:** +1.7%. **Median travel time to work:** 16 minutes. **Working outside county of residence:** 13.5%.

Cities with pop over 10,000: Fort Dodge ▥ (25,723).

WINNEBAGO COUNTY

126 S Clark St   **Ph:** 641-585-3412
Forest City, IA 50436

On the central northern border of IA, northwest of Mason City; established Feb 20, 1847 from Kossuth County. **Name Origin:** For the Indian tribe of Siouan linguistic stock; their name is thought to mean 'fish eaters.'

Area (sq mi): 401.57 (land 400.47; water 1.1). **Pop per sq mi:** 28.3.

Pop 2005: 11,351. **State rank:** 70. **Pop change:** 2000-20005 -3.2%; 1990-2000 -3.3%. **Pop 2000:** 11,723 (White 96.4%; Black or African American 0.2%; Hispanic or Latino 2%; Asian 0.7%; Other 1.7%). **Foreign born:** 1.8%. **Median age:** 39.8.

Income 2000: per capita $18,494; median household $38,381; **Pop below poverty level:** 8.4%. ***Personal per capita income 2000-2003:** $21,906-$25,223.

Unemployment 2004: 3.8%. **Change from 2000:** +1%. **Median travel time to work:** 14.8 minutes. **Working outside county of residence:** 21.4%.

Cities with pop over 10,000: None.

WINNESHIEK COUNTY

201 W Main St   **Ph:** 563-382-2469
Decorah, IA 52101   **Fax:** 563-382-0603

On the central northern border of IA, northwest of Mason City; established Feb 20, 1847 from Indian lands. **Name Origin:** For the younger (1812-72?) of two chiefs of the Winnebago tribe with the same name; he took part in the Black Hawk War. Name probably formed from *Winne* for Winnebago and *shiek* 'leader.'

Area (sq mi): 689.88 (land 689.61; water 0.27). **Pop per sq mi:** 30.8.

Pop 2005: 21,234. **State rank:** 30. **Pop change:** 2000-20005 -0.4%; 1990-2000 +2.2%. **Pop 2000:** 21,310 (White 97.4%; Black or African American 0.5%; Hispanic or Latino 0.8%; Asian 0.8%; Other 0.8%). **Foreign born:** 2.1%. **Median age:** 35.7.

Income 2000: per capita $17,047; median household $38,908; **Pop below poverty level:** 8%. ***Personal per capita income 2000-2003:** $24,438-$27,003.

Unemployment 2004: 4.6%. **Change from 2000:** +1.1%. **Median travel time to work:** 15.9 minutes. **Working outside county of residence:** 14.4%.

Cities with pop over 10,000: None.

WOODBURY COUNTY

620 Douglas St   **Ph:** 712-279-6611
Sioux City, IA 51101   **Fax:** 712-279-6021
www.woodbury-ia.com

On the western border of IA; established Jan 15, 1851 from Indian lands. **Name Origin:** For Levi Woodbury (1789-1851), governor of NH (1823-24), U.S. senator (1825-31; 1841-45), U.S. secretary of the navy (1831-34), U.S. secretary of the treasury (1834-41), and U.S. Supreme Court Justice (1845-51).

Area (sq mi): 877.39 (land 872.59; water 4.79). **Pop per sq mi:** 117.6.

Pop 2005: 102,605. **State rank:** 6. **Pop change:** 2000-20005 -1.2%; 1990-2000 +5.7%. **Pop 2000:** 103,877 (White 83.6%; Black or African American 2%; Hispanic or Latino 9.1%; Asian 2.4%; Other 8.1%, including 1.7% American Indian/Alaska Native). **Foreign born:** 7.2%. **Median age:** 34.2.

Income 2000: per capita $18,771; median household $38,509; **Pop below poverty level:** 10.3%. ***Personal per capita income 2000-2003:** $25,545-$26,981.

Unemployment 2004: 5.5%. **Change from 2000:** +2.2%. **Median travel time to work:** 17.6 minutes. **Working outside county of residence:** 21.4%.

Cities with pop over 10,000: Sioux City ▥ (83,680).

WORTH COUNTY

1000 Central Ave   **Ph:** 641-324-2840
Northwood, IA 50459   **Fax:** 641-324-2360
www.worthcounty.org

On the central northern border of IA, north of Mason City; established Jan 15, 1851 from Mitchell County. **Name Origin:** For Gen. William Jenkins Worth (1794-1849), officer in the War of 1812, Seminole War, and Mexican-American War; cited by Congress for bravery.

Area (sq mi): 401.71 (land 400; water 1.71). **Pop per sq mi:** 19.4.

Pop 2005: 7,768. **State rank:** 91. **Pop change:** 2000-20005 -1.8%; 1990-2000 -1%. **Pop 2000:** 7,909 (White 97.3%; Black or African American 0.3%; Hispanic or Latino 1.6%; Asian 0.1%; Other 1.2%). **Foreign born:** 1.1%. **Median age:** 40.7.

Income 2000: per capita $16,952; median household $36,444; **Pop below poverty level:** 8.3%. ***Personal per capita income 2000-2003:** $21,848-$21,463.

Unemployment 2004: 4.5%. **Change from 2000:** +0.9%. **Median travel time to work:** 20 minutes. **Working outside county of residence:** 54.6%.

Cities with pop over 10,000: None.

WRIGHT COUNTY

115 N Main St   **Ph:** 515-532-2771
Clarion, IA 50525   **Fax:** 515-532-2669
www.wrightcounty.org

In north-central IA, northeast of Fort Dodge; established Jan 15, 1851 from Webster County. **Name Origin:** For Joseph Albert Wright (1810-67), IN legislator, governor (1849-57) and U.S. senator (1862-63). Also for Silas Wright (1795-1847), U.S. senator from NY (1833-44) and governor (1844-46).

*Source: Personal per capita income data are from the Bureau of Economic Analysis; per capita income data are from the Bureau of the Census. See Introduction for explanation of differences.

Wright County (cont'd)

Area (sq mi): 582.54 (land 580.72; water 1.82). **Pop per sq mi:** 23.5.

Pop 2005: 13,647. **State rank:** 60. **Pop change:** 2000–20005 -4.8%; 1990-2000 +0.5%. **Pop 2000:** 14,334 (White 94.1%; Black or African American 0.2%; Hispanic or Latino 4.9%; Asian 0.2%; Other 3.7%). **Foreign born:** 3%. **Median age:** 41.4.

Income 2000: per capita $18,347; median household $36,197; **Pop below poverty level:** 7%. *Personal per capita income 2000-2003: $26,882-$28,838.

Unemployment 2004: 5%. **Change from 2000:** +1.8%. **Median travel time to work:** 16 minutes. **Working outside county of residence:** 21.6%.

Cities with pop over 10,000: None.

Kansas

IOWA

MISSOURI

NEBRASKA

COLORADO

OKLAHOMA

Pawnee	County boundary
	County name
⊙	County seat
■	Major city
✚	State capital

Kansas City

Troy
Doniphan

Wyandotte

Olathe
Johnson

Paola
Miami

Linn
Mound City

Bourbon
Fort Scott

Girard
Crawford

Columbus
Cherokee

Hiawatha
Brown

Atchison
Atchison

Leavenworth
Leavenworth

Lawrence
Douglas

Ottawa
Franklin

Garnett
Anderson

Iola
Allen

Erie
Neosho

Labette
Oswego

Seneca
Nemaha

Holton
Jackson

Oskaloosa
Jefferson

Shawnee

Topeka

Osage
Lyndon

Coffey
Burlington

Yates
Center
Woodson

Fredonia
Wilson

Independence
Montgomery

Marysville
Marshall

Westmoreland
Pottawatomie

Alma
Wabaunsee

Lyon
Emporia

Greenwood
Eureka

Howard
Elk

Chautauqua
Sedan

Washington
Washington

Riley
Manhattan

Junction
City
Geary

Morris
Council
Grove

Chase
Cottonwood
Falls

Butler
El Dorado

Winfield
Cowley

Belleville
Republic

Concordia
Cloud

Ottawa
Minneapolis

Clay
Clay
Center

Abilene
Dickinson

Marion
Marion

Harvey
Newton

Sedgwick
Wichita

Sumner
Wellington

Jewell
Mankato

Beloit
Mitchell

Lincoln
Lincoln

Salina
Saline

McPherson
McPherson

Ellsworth
Ellsworth

Lyons
Rice

Reno
Hutchinson

Kingman
Kingman

Harper
Anthony

Smith
Center
Smith

Osborne
Osborne

Russell
Russell

Great
Bend
Barton

Stafford
Saint
John

Pratt
Pratt

Barber
Medicine
Lodge

Phillips
Phillipsburg

Stockton
Rooks

Ellis
Hays

Rush
La Crosse

Pawnee
Larned

Kinsley
Edwards

Kiowa
Greensburg

Comanche
Coldwater

Norton
Norton

Graham
Hill City

Trego
WaKeeney

Ness
Ness
City

Hodgeman
Jetmore

Ford
Dodge City

Clark
Ashland

Oberlin
Decatur

Sheridan
Hoxie

Gove
Gove

Lane
Dighton

Finney
Garden City

Gray
Cimarron

Meade
Meade

Rawlins
Atwood

Thomas
Colby

Logan
Oakley

Scott
Scott
City

Haskell
Sublette

Seward
Liberal

Saint
Francis
Cheyenne

Goodland
Sherman

Wallace
Sharon
Springs

Greeley
Tribune

Wichita
Leoti

Kearny
Lakin

Grant
Ulysses

Stevens
Hugoton

Hamilton
Syracuse

Stanton
Johnson

Morton
Elkhart

0   40 mi

0   40 km

©MAPS.com

Kansas

KANSAS STATE INFORMATION

www.kansas.gov   **Ph:** 785-296-0111

Area (sq mi): 82,276.84 (land 81,814.88; water 461.96). **Pop per sq mi:** 33.5.

Pop 2005: 2,744,687. **Pop change:** 2000-20005 +2.1%; 1990-2000 +8.5%. **Pop 2000:** 2,688,418 (White 83.1%; Black or African American 5.7%; Hispanic or Latino 7%; Asian 1.7%; Other 6.4%). **Foreign born:** 5%. **Median age:** 35.2.

Income 2000: per capita $20,506; median household $40,624; **Pop below poverty level:** 9.9%. ***Personal per capita income 2000-2003:** $27,694-$29,438.

Unemployment 2004: 5.6%. **Change from 2000:** +1.8%. **Median travel time to work:** 19 minutes. **Working outside county of residence:** 22.6%.

ALLEN COUNTY

1 N Washington St   **Ph:** 620-365-1407
Iola, KS 66749   **Fax:** 620-365-1441
www.allencounty.org

In southeastern KS, southeast of Emporia; original county; organized Aug 30, 1855 (prior to statehood). **Name Origin:** For William Allen (1803-79), U.S. senator from OH (1837-49) and governor (1874-76).

Area (sq mi): 505.18 (land 503.01; water 2.18). **Pop per sq mi:** 27.4.

Pop 2005: 13,787. **State rank:** 35. **Pop change:** 2000-20005 -4.2%; 1990-2000 -1.7%. **Pop 2000:** 14,385 (White 94%; Black or African American 1.6%; Hispanic or Latino 1.9%; Asian 0.3%; Other 3.4%). **Foreign born:** 0.9%. **Median age:** 38.8.

Income 2000: per capita $15,640; median household $31,481; **Pop below poverty level:** 14.9%. ***Personal per capita income 2000-2003:** $20,486-$23,097.

Unemployment 2004: 5.7%. **Change from 2000:** -1.7%. **Median travel time to work:** 17.4 minutes. **Working outside county of residence:** 20.3%.

Cities with pop over 10,000: None.

ANDERSON COUNTY

100 E 4th Ave   **Ph:** 785-448-6841
Garnett, KS 66032   **Fax:** 785-448-5621

In eastern KS, southeast of Emporia; original county; organized Aug 25, 1855 (prior to statehood). **Name Origin:** For Joseph C. Anderson, a member of the first KS territorial legislature.

Area (sq mi): 584.29 (land 582.92; water 1.38). **Pop per sq mi:** 14.

Pop 2005: 8,182. **State rank:** 48. **Pop change:** 2000-20005 +0.9%; 1990-2000 +3.9%. **Pop 2000:** 8,110 (White 96.9%; Black or African American 0.3%; Hispanic or Latino 1.1%; Asian 0.2%; Other 1.9%). **Foreign born:** 0.6%. **Median age:** 39.6.

Income 2000: per capita $16,458; median household $33,244; **Pop below poverty level:** 12.8%. ***Personal per capita income 2000-2003:** $20,684-$21,348.

Unemployment 2004: 6%. **Change from 2000:** +0.1%. **Median travel time to work:** 25.5 minutes. **Working outside county of residence:** 39%.

Cities with pop over 10,000: None.

ATCHISON COUNTY

423 N 5th St   **Ph:** 913-367-1653
Atchison, KS 66002   **Fax:** 913-367-0227
www.atchisoncountyks.org

On the northeastern border of KS, northwest of Kansas City; original county; organized Aug 25, 1855 (prior to statehood). **Name Origin:** For the town of Atchison, which was named for David Rice Atchison (1807-86), MO statesman and U.S. senator (1843-55).

Area (sq mi): 435.04 (land 432.34; water 2.7). **Pop per sq mi:** 38.9.

Pop 2005: 16,804. **State rank:** 32. **Pop change:** 2000-20005 +0.2%; 1990-2000 -0.9%. **Pop 2000:** 16,774 (White 90.4%; Black or African American 5.3%; Hispanic or Latino 1.9%; Asian 0.3%; Other 2.8%). **Foreign born:** 0.7%. **Median age:** 36.2.

Income 2000: per capita $15,207; median household $34,355; **Pop below poverty level:** 13.3%. ***Personal per capita income 2000-2003:** $20,466-$21,468.

Unemployment 2004: 5.7%. **Change from 2000:** +0.7%. **Median travel time to work:** 19.4 minutes. **Working outside county of residence:** 22.7%.

Cities with pop over 10,000: Atchison 🏛 (10,185).

BARBER COUNTY

120 E Washington Ave   **Ph:** 620-886-3961
Medicine Lodge, KS 67104   **Fax:** 620-886-5425
www.barbercounty.net

On the central-southern border of KS, southwest of Wichita, organized as Barbour County Feb 26, 1867 from Harper County; spelling changed Mar 1, 1883. **Name Origin:** As a memorial to Thomas W. Barber (?-1855), a Free State martyr, murdered near Lawrence, KS.

Area (sq mi): 1136.21 (land 1134.11; water 2.1). **Pop per sq mi:** 4.4.

Pop 2005: 4,958. **State rank:** 70. **Pop change:** 2000-20005 -6.6%; 1990-2000 -9.7%. **Pop 2000:** 5,307 (White 96.2%; Black or African

Barber County (cont'd)

American 0.4%; Hispanic or Latino 2%; Asian 0.1%; Other 2.5%). **Foreign born:** 0.5%. **Median age:** 42.6.

Income 2000: per capita $16,627; median household $33,407; **Pop below poverty level:** 10.1%. ***Personal per capita income 2000-2003:** $20,117-$24,644.

Unemployment 2004: 3.7%. **Change from 2000:** +0.4%. **Median travel time to work:** 14.3 minutes. **Working outside county of residence:** 14.1%.

Cities with pop over 10,000: None.

BARTON COUNTY

1400 Main St Suite 202   **Ph:** 620-793-1835
Great Bend, KS 67530   **Fax:** 620-793-1990
www.bartoncounty.org

In central KS, southwest of Salina; organized Feb 26, 1867 from Ellsworth County. **Name Origin:** For Clara Barton (1821-1912), Civil War nurse and first president (1881) of the American Red Cross. The only KS county named for a woman.

Area (sq mi): 900.46 (land 894; water 6.46). **Pop per sq mi:** 31.4.

Pop 2005: 28,105. **State rank:** 20. **Pop change:** 2000-20005 -0.4%; 1990-2000 -4%. **Pop 2000:** 28,205 (White 89%; Black or African American 1.1%; Hispanic or Latino 8.3%; Asian 0.2%; Other 5.6%). **Foreign born:** 4.4%. **Median age:** 38.6.

Income 2000: per capita $16,695; median household $32,176; **Pop below poverty level:** 12.9%. ***Personal per capita income 2000-2003:** $24,217-$26,724.

Unemployment 2004: 4.3%. **Change from 2000:** +1.6%. **Median travel time to work:** 16.7 minutes. **Working outside county of residence:** 9%.

Cities with pop over 10,000: Great Bend ⛪ (14,851).

BOURBON COUNTY

210 S National Ave   **Ph:** 620-223-3800
Fort Scott, KS 66701   **Fax:** 620-223-5832
www.bourboncountyks.org

On the southeastern border of KS; original county; organized Aug 25, 1855 (prior to statehood). **Name Origin:** For Bourbon County, KY, former home of Samuel A. Willliams, a member of the first KS legislature.

Area (sq mi): 638.82 (land 637.09; water 1.73). **Pop per sq mi:** 23.5.

Pop 2005: 14,997. **State rank:** 34. **Pop change:** 2000-20005 -2.5%; 1990-2000 +2.8%. **Pop 2000:** 15,379 (White 93.3%; Black or African American 3.1%; Hispanic or Latino 1.3%; Asian 0.4%; Other 2.4%). **Foreign born:** 0.7%. **Median age:** 38.

Income 2000: per capita $16,393; median household $31,199; **Pop below poverty level:** 13.5%. ***Personal per capita income 2000-2003:** $20,662-$23,129.

Unemployment 2004: 5.7%. **Change from 2000:** +1%. **Median travel time to work:** 19.5 minutes. **Working outside county of residence:** 14.5%.

Cities with pop over 10,000: None.

BROWN COUNTY

601 Oregon St   **Ph:** 785-742-2581
Hiawatha, KS 66434   **Fax:** 785-742-7705
www.brown.kansasgov.com

On the northeastern border of KS, west of Saint Joseph; original county; organized Aug 30, 1855 (prior to statehood). **Name Origin:** For either Orville H. Browne, a member of the 1855 KS territorial legislature, or for Albert Gallatin Browne (1813-80), governor of MS (1844-48). The *e* was dropped in 1857 when the county was named.

Area (sq mi): 572.2 (land 570.67; water 1.52). **Pop per sq mi:** 17.9.

Pop 2005: 10,239. **State rank:** 41. **Pop change:** 2000-20005 -4.5%; 1990-2000 -3.6%. **Pop 2000:** 10,724 (White 86.1%; Black or African American 1.6%; Hispanic or Latino 2.3%; Asian 0.2%; Other 11.3%, including 8.8% American Indian/Alaska Native). **Foreign born:** 1.3%. **Median age:** 39.8.

Income 2000: per capita $15,163; median household $31,971; **Pop below poverty level:** 12.9%. ***Personal per capita income 2000-2003:** $22,401-$24,429.

Unemployment 2004: 4.9%. **Change from 2000:** -1.3%. **Median travel time to work:** 17.6 minutes. **Working outside county of residence:** 26.9%.

Cities with pop over 10,000: None.

BUTLER COUNTY

205 W Central Ave   **Ph:** 316-322-4239
El Dorado, KS 67042   **Fax:** 316-321-1011
www.bucoks.com

In east-central KS, east of Wichita; original county, organized Aug 25, 1855 (prior to statehood). **Name Origin:** For Andrew Pickens Butler (1796-1857), SC legislator; jurist, and U.S. senator (1846-57).

Area (sq mi): 1446.42 (land 1427.85; water 18.57). **Pop per sq mi:** 43.7.

Pop 2005: 62,354. **State rank:** 9. **Pop change:** 2000-20005 +4.8%; 1990-2000 +17.6%. **Pop 2000:** 59,482 (White 93.6%; Black or African American 1.4%; Hispanic or Latino 2.2%; Asian 0.4%; Other 3.3%). **Foreign born:** 1.3%. **Median age:** 35.9.

Income 2000: per capita $20,150; median household $45,474; **Pop below poverty level:** 7.3%. ***Personal per capita income 2000-2003:** $26,445-$28,159.

Unemployment 2004: 6.1%. **Change from 2000:** +2.3%. **Median travel time to work:** 22.9 minutes. **Working outside county of residence:** 51.6%.

Cities with pop over 10,000: El Dorado ⛪ (12,717).

CHASE COUNTY

PO Box 529   **Ph:** 620-273-6423
Cottonwood Falls, KS 66845   **Fax:** 620-273-6617
www.chasecountyks.org

In east-central KS, west of Emporia; organized Feb 11, 1859 (prior to statehood) from Butler County. **Name Origin:** For Salmon Portland Chase (1808-73), U.S. senator from OH (1849-53), governor of OH (1855-59), and chief justice of the U.S. Supreme Court (1864-73).

Source: Personal per capita income data are from the Bureau of Economic Analysis; per capita income data are from the Bureau of the Census. See Introduction for explanation of differences.

Chase County (cont'd)

Area (sq mi): 778.01 (land 775.89; water 2.12). **Pop per sq mi:** 4.

Pop 2005: 3,081. **State rank:** 86. **Pop change:** 2000-20005 +1.7%; 1990-2000 +0.3%. **Pop 2000:** 3,030 (White 96%; Black or African American 1%; Hispanic or Latino 1.7%; Asian 0.1%; Other 2%). **Foreign born:** 1.1%. **Median age:** 40.3.

Income 2000. per capita $17,433; median household $32,656; **Pop below poverty level:** 8.6%. ***Personal per capita income 2000-2003:** $27,079-$28,785.

Unemployment 2004: 4.5%. **Change from 2000:** +0.2%. **Median travel time to work:** 25.1 minutes. **Working outside county of residence:** 46.1%.

Cities with pop over 10,000: None.

CHAUTAUQUA COUNTY

215 N Chautauqua St   **Ph:** 620-725-5800
Sedan, KS 67361   **Fax:** 620-725-5801

On the southern border of KS, west of Joplin, MO; organized Mar 3, 1875 (prior to statehood) from Howard County, which was organized in 1855 (named Godfrey and changed to Seward in 1867) and abolished at the time of its division into Chautauqua and Elk counties. **Name Origin:** For Chautauqua County, NY, former home of many settlers.

Area (sq mi): 644.83 (land 641.69; water 3.14). **Pop per sq mi:** 6.4.

Pop 2005: 4,109. **State rank:** 77. **Pop change:** 2000-20005 -5.7%; 1990-2000 -1.1%. **Pop 2000:** 4,359 (White 93%; Black or African American 0.3%; Hispanic or Latino 1.4%; Asian 0.1%; Other 5.7%, including 3.6% American Indian/Alaska Native). **Foreign born:** 0.8%. **Median age:** 44.7.

Income 2000: per capita $16,280; median household $28,717; **Pop below poverty level:** 12.2%. ***Personal per capita income 2000-2003:** $21,131 $23,756.

Unemployment 2004: 5.3%. **Change from 2000:** +0%. **Median travel time to work:** 26.7 minutes. **Working outside county of residence:** 34.6%.

Cities with pop over 10,000: None.

CHEROKEE COUNTY

PO Box 14   **Ph:** 620-429-2042
Columbus, KS 66725   **Fax:** 620-429-1042

On the southeastern border of KS, west of Joplin, MO; organized as McGee County. **Name Origin:** For the Indian tribe of Iroquoian linguistic stock. Name may derive from Creek *tciloki* 'people of a different speech.' Originally for A.M. McGee, a noted proslavery leader.

Area (sq mi): 590.96 (land 587.12; water 3.85). **Pop per sq mi:** 36.7.

Pop 2005: 21,555. **State rank:** 27. **Pop change:** 2000-20005 -4.6%; 1990-2000 +5.8%. **Pop 2000:** 22,605 (White 91.6%; Black or African American 0.6%; Hispanic or Latino 1.3%; Asian 0.2%; Other 6.9%, including 3.5% American Indian/Alaska Native). **Foreign born:** 0.8%. **Median age:** 37.

Income 2000: per capita $14,710; median household $30,505; **Pop below poverty level:** 14.3%. ***Personal per capita income 2000-2003:** $19,866-$22,660.

Unemployment 2004: 7%. **Change from 2000:** +0.2%. **Median travel time to work:** 20 minutes. **Working outside county of residence:** 45.4%.

Cities with pop over 10,000: None.

CHEYENNE COUNTY

PO Box 985   **Ph:** 785-332-8800
Saint Francis, KS 67756 **Fax:** 785-332-8825
www.cheyennecounty.org

On northwestern border of KS; organized Mar 20, 1873 from Kirwin Land District. **Name Origin:** For the Cheyenne Indians, a Dakota tribe of Algonquian linguistic stock; name means 'red talkers.'

Area (sq mi): 1020.84 (land 1019.88; water 0.95). **Pop per sq mi:** 2.9.

Pop 2005: 2,946. **State rank:** 91. **Pop change:** 2000-20005 -6.9%; 1990-2000 -2.4%. **Pop 2000:** 3,165 (White 96.4%; Black or African American 0.1%; Hispanic or Latino 2.6%; Asian 0.3%; Other 1.6%). **Foreign born:** 2.5%. **Median age:** 44.2.

Income 2000: per capita $17,862; median household $30,599; **Pop below poverty level:** 9.4%. ***Personal per capita income 2000-2003:** $21,777-$22,030.

Unemployment 2004: 3.5%. **Change from 2000:** +1.6%. **Median travel time to work:** 14.5 minutes. **Working outside county of residence:** 13.2%.

Cities with pop over 10,000: None.

CLARK COUNTY

913 Highland St   **Ph:** 620-635-2813
Ashland, KS 67831   **Fax:** 620-635-2393

On the central southern border of KS, south of Dodge City; first established Feb 16, 1867; abolished in 1883; recreated in 1885. **Name Origin:** For Capt. Charles F. Clarke (?-1862), Union officer in the Civil War. The *e* was dropped in naming the county.

Area (sq mi): 977.2 (land 974.68; water 2.52). **Pop per sq mi:** 2.3.

Pop 2005: 2,283. **State rank:** 99. **Pop change:** 2000-20005 -4.5%; 1990-2000 -1.2%. **Pop 2000:** 2,390 (White 94.1%; Black or African American 0.3%; Hispanic or Latino 4%; Asian 0.1%; Other 3.9%, including 1.1% American Indian/Alaska Native). **Foreign born:** 2.8%. **Median age:** 42.1.

Income 2000: per capita $17,795; median household $33,857; **Pop below poverty level:** 12.7%. ***Personal per capita income 2000-2003:** $22,470-$25,592.

Unemployment 2004: 3.4%. **Change from 2000:** +1.7%. **Median travel time to work:** 14.1 minutes. **Working outside county of residence:** 22.5%.

Cities with pop over 10,000: None.

CLAY COUNTY

PO Box 98   **Ph:** 785-632-2552
Clay Center, KS 67432   **Fax:** 785-632-5856
www.claycountyks.org

In north-central KS, west of Manhattan; original county, organized Feb 27, 1857 (prior to statehood). **Name Origin:** For Henry Clay (1777-1852), U.S. senator from KY, known as the 'Great Pacificator' for his advocacy of compromise to avert national crises.

Clay County (cont'd)

Area (sq mi): 655.44 (land 643.84; water 11.6). **Pop per sq mi:** 13.4.

Pop 2005: 8,629. **State rank:** 47. **Pop change:** 2000-20005 -2.2%; 1990-2000 -3.7%. **Pop 2000:** 8,822 (White 97.2%; Black or African American 0.6%; Hispanic or Latino 0.8%; Asian 0.1%; Other 1.6%). **Foreign born:** 1%. **Median age:** 41.3.

Income 2000: per capita $17,939; median household $33,965; **Pop below poverty level:** 10.1%. ***Personal per capita income 2000-2003:** $24,574-$26,004.

Unemployment 2004: 4.3%. **Change from 2000:** +0.4%. **Median travel time to work:** 20 minutes. **Working outside county of residence:** 28%.

Cities with pop over 10,000: None.

CLOUD COUNTY

811 Washington St   **Ph:** 785-243-8110
Concordia, KS 66901   **Fax:** 785-243-8123
www.cloudcountyks.org

In north-central KS, north of Salina; organized as Shirley County Feb 27, 1860 (prior to statehood) from unorganized territory; name changed Feb 26, 1867. **Name Origin:** Named by John B. Rupe, a county representative, for William F. Cloud, an officer in the Kansas Volunteers. Originally named as a joke for Jane Shirley, 'a notorious Leavenworth prostitute' known 'to all the boys.'

Area (sq mi): 718.47 (land 715.63; water 2.84). **Pop per sq mi:** 13.6.

Pop 2005: 9,759. **State rank:** 44. **Pop change:** 2000-20005 -5%; 1990-2000 -6.8%. **Pop 2000:** 10,268 (White 98%; Black or African American 0.3%; Hispanic or Latino 0.6%; Asian 0.3%; Other 1.1%). **Foreign born:** 1.4%. **Median age:** 41.4.

Income 2000: per capita $17,536; median household $31,758; **Pop below poverty level:** 10.8%. ***Personal per capita income 2000-2003:** $20,385-$22,805.

Unemployment 2004: 3.7%. **Change from 2000:** +0.3%. **Median travel time to work:** 14.6 minutes. **Working outside county of residence:** 14.1%.

Cities with pop over 10,000: None.

COFFEY COUNTY

110 S 6th St   **Ph:** 620-364-2191
Burlington, KS 66839   **Fax:** 620-364-8975
www.coffeycountyks.org

In eastern KS, east of Emporia; organized Aug 25, 1855 (prior to statehood) from Kiowa County. **Name Origin:** For Col. Asbury M. Coffey, a Confederate officer and settler from MO; first known white man in KS; served as a member of the Bogus Legislature in 1855.

Area (sq mi): 654.57 (land 629.75; water 24.82). **Pop per sq mi:** 13.8.

Pop 2005: 8,683. **State rank:** 46. **Pop change:** 2000-20005 -2.1%; 1990-2000 +5.5%. **Pop 2000:** 8,865 (White 96.3%; Black or African American 0.2%; Hispanic or Latino 1.5%; Asian 0.3%; Other 2.4%). **Foreign born:** 0.8%. **Median age:** 39.2.

Income 2000: per capita $18,337; median household $37,839; **Pop below poverty level:** 6.6%. ***Personal per capita income 2000-2003:** $25,002-$28,275.

Unemployment 2004: 5.4%. **Change from 2000:** -1.1%. **Median travel time to work:** 19.1 minutes. **Working outside county of residence:** 21.7%.

Cities with pop over 10,000: None.

COMANCHE COUNTY

PO Box 776   **Ph:** 620-582-2361
Coldwater, KS 67029   **Fax:** 620-582-2426
www.comanchecounty.com

On the central southern border of KS, southeast of Dodge City; organized Feb 26, 1875 from Kiowa County. **Name Origin:** For the Indian tribe of Shoshoean linguistic stock; the meaning of the name is unknown.

Area (sq mi): 789.7 (land 788.31; water 1.39). **Pop per sq mi:** 2.5.

Pop 2005: 1,935. **State rank:** 102. **Pop change:** 2000-20005 -1.6%; 1990-2000 -15%. **Pop 2000:** 1,967 (White 96.9%; Black or African American 0.1%; Hispanic or Latino 1.8%; Asian 0.1%; Other 2%). **Foreign born:** 1.1%. **Median age:** 46.9.

Income 2000: per capita $17,037; median household $29,415; **Pop below poverty level:** 10.2%. ***Personal per capita income 2000-2003:** $20,895-$23,274.

Unemployment 2004: 2.8%. **Change from 2000:** +1.3%. **Median travel time to work:** 13.5 minutes. **Working outside county of residence:** 14.1%.

Cities with pop over 10,000: None.

COWLEY COUNTY

311 E 9th Ave   **Ph:** 620-221-5400
Winfield, KS 67156   **Fax:** 620-221-5498
www.cowleycounty.org

On the southern border of KS, southeast of Wichita; organized Feb 13, 1867. **Name Origin:** For Lt. Matthew Cowley (?-1864), a Union officer.

Area (sq mi): 1132.6 (land 1126.24; water 6.37). **Pop per sq mi:** 31.3.

Pop 2005: 35,298. **State rank:** 14. **Pop change:** 2000-20005 -2.7%; 1990-2000 -1.7%. **Pop 2000:** 36,291 (White 88.4%; Black or African American 2.7%; Hispanic or Latino 3.6%; Asian 1.5%; Other 5.7%, including 2% American Indian/Alaska Native). **Foreign born:** 2.5%. **Median age:** 37.

Income 2000: per capita $17,509; median household $34,406; **Pop below poverty level:** 12.9%. ***Personal per capita income 2000-2003:** $22,567-$24,430.

Unemployment 2004: 6.2%. **Change from 2000:** +2.1%. **Median travel time to work:** 19.6 minutes. **Working outside county of residence:** 17.4%.

Cities with pop over 10,000: Winfield 🏛 (12,005); Arkansas City (11,753).

---

*Source: Personal per capita income data are from the Bureau of Economic Analysis; per capita income data are from the Bureau of the Census. See Introduction for explanation of differences.

CRAWFORD COUNTY

PO Box 249   **Ph:** 620-724-6115
Girard, KS 66743   **Fax:** 620-724-6007
www.crawfordcountykansas.org

On the southeastern border of KS; organized Feb 13, 1867 from Bourbon and Cherokee counties. **Name Origin:** For Col. Samuel J. Crawford (1835-1913), Union army officer and governor of KS (1865-68); he resigned to command a force to fight Indians.

Area (sq mi): 595.05 (land 592.91; water 2.14). **Pop per sq mi:** 64.5.

Pop 2005: 38,222. **State rank:** 12. **Pop change:** 2000-20005 -0.1%; 1990-2000 +7.5%. **Pop 2000:** 38,242 (White 92.3%; Black or African American 1.8%; Hispanic or Latino 2.4%; Asian 1.1%; Other 3.7%). **Foreign born:** 2.7%. **Median age:** 33.8.

Income 2000: per capita $16,245; median household $29,409; **Pop below poverty level:** 16%. ***Personal per capita income 2000-2003:** $21,116-$23,022.

Unemployment 2004: 6%. **Change from 2000:** +1%. **Median travel time to work:** 16.9 minutes. **Working outside county of residence:** 12.6%.

Cities with pop over 10,000: Pittsburg (19,152).

DECATUR COUNTY

PO Box 28   **Ph:** 785-475-8102
Oberlin, KS 67749   **Fax:** 785-475-8130
www.oberlinkansas.org

On the northwestern border of KS; organized Mar 6, 1873 from Norton County. **Name Origin:** For Stephen F. Decatur (1779-1820), U.S. naval officer during the War of 1812 and in actions against the Barbary pirates near Tripoli, who said '. . . may she always be in the right; but our country, right or wrong.'

Area (sq mi): 894.18 (land 893.55; water 0.63). **Pop per sq mi:** 3.6.

Pop 2005: 3,191. **State rank:** 85. **Pop change:** 2000-20005 -8.1%; 1990-2000 -13.7%. **Pop 2000:** 3,472 (White 97.5%; Black or African American 0.5%; Hispanic or Latino 1%; Asian 0.1%; Other 1.5%). **Foreign born:** 1.2%. **Median age:** 44.3.

Income 2000: per capita $16,348; median household $30,257; **Pop below poverty level:** 11.6%. ***Personal per capita income 2000-2003:** $22,303-$24,121.

Unemployment 2004: 3.4%. **Change from 2000:** +1.1%. **Median travel time to work:** 16.7 minutes. **Working outside county of residence:** 15.4%.

Cities with pop over 10,000: None.

DICKINSON COUNTY

PO Box 248   **Ph:** 785-263-3774
Abilene, KS 67410   **Fax:** 785-263-2045
www.dkcoks.com

In central KS, east of Salina; original county; organized Feb 20, 1855 (prior to statehood). **Name Origin:** For Daniel Stevens Dickinson (1800-66), U.S. senator from NY (1844-51).

Area (sq mi): 852.12 (land 847.92; water 4.2). **Pop per sq mi:** 22.7.

Pop 2005: 19,209. **State rank:** 28. **Pop change:** 2000-20005 -0.7%; 1990-2000 +2%. **Pop 2000:** 19,344 (White 95.2%; Black or African American 0.6%; Hispanic or Latino 2.3%; Asian 0.3%; Other 2.7%). **Foreign born:** 1.7%. **Median age:** 40.

Income 2000: per capita $17,780; median household $35,975; **Pop below poverty level:** 7.5%. ***Personal per capita income 2000-2003:** $23,155-$24,297.

Unemployment 2004: 4.7%. **Change from 2000:** +1.1%. **Median travel time to work:** 21.2 minutes. **Working outside county of residence:** 30.8%.

Cities with pop over 10,000: None.

DONIPHAN COUNTY

PO Box 278   **Ph:** 785-985-3513
Troy, KS 66087   **Fax:** 785-985-3723

On the northeastern border of KS, west of Saint Joseph, MO; original county; organized Aug 25, 1855 (prior to statehood). **Name Origin:** For Alexander Willliam Doniphan (1808-87), MO legislator and officer in the Mexican War.

Area (sq mi): 397.07 (land 392.18; water 4.89). **Pop per sq mi:** 19.9.

Pop 2005: 7,816. **State rank:** 50. **Pop change:** 2000-20005 -5.2%; 1990-2000 +1.4%. **Pop 2000:** 8,249 (White 94.3%; Black or African American 2%; Hispanic or Latino 1.2%; Asian 0.3%; Other 2.9%, including 1.2% American Indian/Alaska Native). **Foreign born:** 0.8%. **Median age:** 36.8.

Income 2000: per capita $14,849; median household $32,537; **Pop below poverty level:** 11.9%. ***Personal per capita income 2000-2003:** $19,704-$20,826.

Unemployment 2004: 7.7%. **Change from 2000:** -2.2%. **Median travel time to work:** 21.5 minutes. **Working outside county of residence:** 50%.

Cities with pop over 10,000: None.

DOUGLAS COUNTY

111 E 11 St   **Ph:** 785-832-5132
Lawrence, KS 66044   **Fax:** 785-832-5174
www.douglas-county.com

In eastern KS, east of Topeka; original county; organized Aug 25, 1855 (prior to statehood). **Name Origin:** For Stephen Arnold Douglas (1813-61), U.S. orator and statesman.

Area (sq mi): 474.47 (land 456.87; water 17.6). **Pop per sq mi:** 225.3.

Pop 2005: 102,914. **State rank:** 5. **Pop change:** 2000-20005 +3%; 1990-2000 +22.2%. **Pop 2000:** 99,962 (White 84.6%; Black or African American 4.2%; Hispanic or Latino 3.3%; Asian 3.1%; Other 6.6%, including 2.6% American Indian/Alaska Native). **Foreign born:** 5.2%. **Median age:** 26.6.

Income 2000: per capita $19,952; median household $37,547; **Pop below poverty level:** 15.9%. ***Personal per capita income 2000-2003:** $24,206-$26,976.

Unemployment 2004: 4.1%. **Change from 2000:** -0.3%. **Median travel time to work:** 19.4 minutes. **Working outside county of residence:** 24%.

Cities with pop over 10,000: Lawrence 🏛 (81,873).

🏛 *County Seat*

EDWARDS COUNTY

312 Massachusetts Ave   **Ph:** 620-659-3000
Kinsley, KS 67547   **Fax:** 620-659-2583
www.edwardscounty.org

In south-central KS, northeast of Dodge City; organized Mar 7, 1874 from Kiowa County. **Name Origin:** For W.C. and R.E. Edwards, prominent early KS settlers.

Area (sq mi): 622.1 (land 622.02; water 0.08). **Pop per sq mi:** 5.3.

Pop 2005: 3,292. **State rank:** 83. **Pop change:** 2000-20005 -4.6%; 1990-2000 -8.9%. **Pop 2000:** 3,449 (White 89%; Black or African American 0.3%; Hispanic or Latino 9.7%; Asian 0.3%; Other 6.9%). **Foreign born:** 6.7%. **Median age:** 41.

Income 2000: per capita $17,586; median household $30,530; **Pop below poverty level:** 10.4%. ***Personal per capita income 2000-2003:** $25,175-$28,515.

Unemployment 2004: 3.6%. **Change from 2000:** +1.7%. **Median travel time to work:** 18.8 minutes. **Working outside county of residence:** 24.6%.

Cities with pop over 10,000: None.

ELK COUNTY

127 N Pine   **Ph:** 620-374-2490
Howard, KS 67349   **Fax:** 620-374-2771
www.elk.kansasgov.com

In southeastern KS, southeast of Wichita; organized Mar 3, 1875 from Howard County, which was organized in 1855 (named Godfrey and changed to Seward in 1867) and abolished at the time of its division into Chautauqua and Elk counties. **Name Origin:** For the large North American deer, the elk or wapiti.

Area (sq mi): 650.36 (land 647.29; water 3.07). **Pop per sq mi:** 4.8.

Pop 2005: 3,075. **State rank:** 87. **Pop change:** 2000-20005 -5.7%; 1990-2000 -2%. **Pop 2000:** 3,261 (White 94.5%; Black or African American 0.2%; Hispanic or Latino 2.2%; Asian 0.2%; Other 4.6%, including 1% American Indian/Alaska Native). **Foreign born:** 0.7%. **Median age:** 46.

Income 2000: per capita $16,066; median household $27,267; **Pop below poverty level:** 13.8%. ***Personal per capita income 2000-2003:** $19,722-$21,214.

Unemployment 2004: 5.4%. **Change from 2000:** +0.5%. **Median travel time to work:** 34 minutes. **Working outside county of residence:** 39.3%.

Cities with pop over 10,000: None.

ELLIS COUNTY

PO Box 720   **Ph:** 785-628-9410
Hays, KS 67601   **Fax:** 785-628-9413
www.ellisco.org

In central KS, west of Salina; organized Feb 26, 1867 from unorganized territory. **Name Origin:** For George Ellis (?-1854) KS infantryman killed during the Civil War.

Area (sq mi): 900.47 (land 899.97; water 0.5). **Pop per sq mi:** 29.7.

Pop 2005: 26,767. **State rank:** 21. **Pop change:** 2000-20005 -2.7%; 1990-2000 +5.8%. **Pop 2000:** 27,507 (White 95.1%; Black or African American 0.7%; Hispanic or Latino 2.4%; Asian 0.8%; Other 2.4%). **Foreign born:** 2.3%. **Median age:** 32.7.

Income 2000: per capita $18,259; median household $32,339; **Pop below poverty level:** 12.9%. ***Personal per capita income 2000-2003:** $24,773-$28,356.

Unemployment 2004: 3.8%. **Change from 2000:** +1.2%. **Median travel time to work:** 13.8 minutes. **Working outside county of residence:** 7.2%.

Cities with pop over 10,000: Hays ⛪ (19,841).

ELLSWORTH COUNTY

210 N Kansas St   **Ph:** 785-472-4161
Ellsworth, KS 67439   **Fax:** 785-472-3818
www.ellsworthcounty.org

In central KS, west of Salina; organized Feb 26, 1867 from Saline County. **Name Origin:** For Lt. Allen Ellsworth, an officer in the Iowa Cavalry, who commanded the fort later named for him.

Area (sq mi): 723.44 (land 715.91; water 7.54). **Pop per sq mi:** 8.9.

Pop 2005: 6,343. **State rank:** 58. **Pop change:** 2000-20005 -2.8%; 1990-2000 -0.9%. **Pop 2000:** 6,525 (White 91.2%; Black or African American 3.6%; Hispanic or Latino 3.6%; Asian 0.2%; Other 2.6%). **Foreign born:** 1.3%. **Median age:** 41.8.

Income 2000: per capita $16,569; median household $35,772; **Pop below poverty level:** 7.2%. ***Personal per capita income 2000-2003:** $21,582-$23,730.

Unemployment 2004: 4.2%. **Change from 2000:** +1.7%. **Median travel time to work:** 17.6 minutes. **Working outside county of residence:** 22.1%.

Cities with pop over 10,000: None.

FINNEY COUNTY

311 N 9th St PO Box M   **Ph:** 620-272-3542
Garden City, KS 67846   **Fax:** 620-272-3599
www.finneycounty.org

In southwestern KS, northwest of Dodge City; organized as Sequoyah County Mar 6, 1873 from Arapahoe and Foote counties; name changed Feb 21, 1883; Garfield County was annexed to Finney County in 1893. **Name Origin:** For David W. Finney, lieutenant governor of KS (1861-65) and KS legislator.

Area (sq mi): 1302.62 (land 1301.77; water 0.84). **Pop per sq mi:** 30.

Pop 2005: 38,988. **State rank:** 11. **Pop change:** 2000-20005 -3.8%; 1990-2000 +22.5%. **Pop 2000:** 40,523 (White 51.4%; Black or African American 1.3%; Hispanic or Latino 43.3%; Asian 2.9%; Other 26.9%, including 1% American Indian/Alaska Native). **Foreign born:** 22.7%. **Median age:** 28.1.

Income 2000: per capita $15,377; median household $38,474; **Pop below poverty level:** 14.2%. ***Personal per capita income 2000-2003:** $20,585-$21,098.

Unemployment 2004: 4.6%. **Change from 2000:** -5%. **Median travel time to work:** 15 minutes. **Working outside county of residence:** 4.7%.

Cities with pop over 10,000: Garden City ⛪ (27,312).

*Source: Personal per capita income data are from the Bureau of Economic Analysis; per capita income data are from the Bureau of the Census. See Introduction for explanation of differences.

FORD COUNTY

100 Gunsmoke St   **Ph:** 620-227-4500
Dodge City, KS 67801   **Fax:** 620-227-4699
www.fordcounty.net

In southwestern KS, southeast of Garden City; organized Feb 26, 1867 from unorganized territory. **Name Origin:** For James Hobart Ford (?-1867), an officer in the Second Colorado cavalry during the Civil War.

Area (sq mi): 1099.29 (land 1098.5; water 0.79). **Pop per sq mi:** 30.7.

Pop 2005: 33,751. **State rank:** 17. **Pop change:** 2000-20005 +4%; 1990-2000 +18.2%. **Pop 2000:** 32,458 (White 57.3%; Black or African American 1.6%; Hispanic or Latino 37.7%; Asian 2.1%; Other 21.5%). **Foreign born:** 22.5%. **Median age:** 29.9.

Income 2000: per capita $15,721; median household $37,860; **Pop below poverty level:** 12.4%. ***Personal per capita income 2000-2003:** $21,443-$22,455.

Unemployment 2004: 3.9%. **Change from 2000:** +1.2%. **Median travel time to work:** 15.1 minutes. **Working outside county of residence:** 6%.

Cities with pop over 10,000: Dodge City ⛪ (25,762)

FRANKLIN COUNTY

315 S Main St   **Ph:** 785-229-3410
Ottawa, KS 66067   **Fax:** 785-229-3419
www.co.franklin.ks.us

In eastern KS, southwest of Olathe; original county; organized Aug 25, 1855 (prior to statehood). **Name Origin:** For Benjamin Franklin (1706-90), U.S. patriot, diplomat, and statesman.

Area (sq mi): 576.65 (land 573.85; water 2.8). **Pop per sq mi:** 45.7.

Pop 2005: 26,247. **State rank:** 22. **Pop change:** 2000-20005 +5.9%; 1990-2000 +12.7%. **Pop 2000:** 24,784 (White 93.6%; Black or African American 1.2%; Hispanic or Latino 2.6%; Asian 0.3%; Other 3.4%). **Foreign born:** 1.3%. **Median age:** 36.

Income 2000: per capita $17,311; median household $39,052; **Pop below poverty level:** 7.7%. ***Personal per capita income 2000-2003:** $23,053-$24,221.

Unemployment 2004: 6.2%. **Change from 2000:** +0.9%. **Median travel time to work:** 25.1 minutes. **Working outside county of residence:** 40.1%.

Cities with pop over 10,000: Ottawa ⛪ (12,499).

GEARY COUNTY

PO Box 927   **Ph:** 785-238-3912
Junction City, KS 66441   **Fax:** 785-238-5419
www.geary.kansasgov.com

In east-central KS, south of Manhattan; organized as Davis County Aug 30, 1855 from Riley county; name changed Mar 7, 1889. **Name Origin:** For John White Geary (1819-73), territorial governor of KS (1856-57) and governor of PA (1867-73). Originally named by the pro-Southern legislature for Jefferson Davis, U.S. secretary of war (1853-57) and later president of the Confederacy.

Area (sq mi): 404.39 (land 384.69; water 19.7). **Pop per sq mi:** 63.9.

Pop 2005: 24,585. **State rank:** 24. **Pop change:** 2000-20005 -12%; 1990-2000 -8.2%. **Pop 2000:** 27,947 (White 61.5%; Black or African American 22%; Hispanic or Latino 8.5%; Asian 3.2%; Other 10.7%). **Foreign born:** 7.3%. **Median age:** 29.1.

Income 2000: per capita $16,199; median household $31,917; **Pop below poverty level:** 12.1%. ***Personal per capita income 2000-2003:** $23,807-$28,063.

Unemployment 2004: 7%. **Change from 2000:** -0.1%. **Median travel time to work:** 17 minutes. **Working outside county of residence:** 40.5%.

Cities with pop over 10,000: Junction City ⛪ (16,806).

GOVE COUNTY

520 Washington St   **Ph:** 785-938-2300
Gove, KS 67736   **Fax:** 785 938-4486

In west-central KS, west of Hays; organized Mar 3, 1868 from Rooks County. **Name Origin:** For Capt. Grenville L. Gove (?-1864), Union army officer from KS.

Area (sq mi): 1071.47 (land 1071.38; water 0.09). **Pop per sq mi:** 2.6.

Pop 2005: 2,763. **State rank:** 93. **Pop change:** 2000-20005 -9.9%; 1990-2000 -5%. **Pop 2000:** 3,068 (White 97.4%; Black or African American 0.1%; Hispanic or Latino 1.3%; Asian 0.1%; Other 1.9%). **Foreign born:** 0.5%. **Median age:** 42.6.

Income 2000: per capita $17,852; median household $33,510; **Pop below poverty level:** 10.3%. ***Personal per capita income 2000-2003:** $24,533-$24,717.

Unemployment 2004: 3.1%. **Change from 2000:** +1.5%. **Median travel time to work:** 14.3 minutes. **Working outside county of residence:** 17.1%.

Cities with pop over 10,000: None.

GRAHAM COUNTY

410 N Pomeroy St   **Ph:** 785-421-3453
Hill City, KS 67642   **Fax:** 785-421-6374

In north-central KS, northwest of Hays; organized Feb 26, 1867 from Rooks County. **Name Origin:** For Capt. John L. Graham (?-1863), a KS infantry officer killed at Chickamauga.

Area (sq mi): 898.67 (land 898.29; water 0.38). **Pop per sq mi:** 3.

Pop 2005: 2,721. **State rank:** 94. **Pop change:** 2000-20005 -7.6%; 1990-2000 -16.9%. **Pop 2000:** 2,946 (White 94.7%; Black or African American 3.2%; Hispanic or Latino 0.8%; Asian 0.3%; Other 1.5%). **Foreign born:** 0.9%. **Median age:** 44.4.

Income 2000: per capita $18,050; median household $31,286; **Pop below poverty level:** 11.5%. ***Personal per capita income 2000-2003:** $26,480-$28,940.

Unemployment 2004: 3.7%. **Change from 2000:** +1.4%. **Median travel time to work:** 16.9 minutes. **Working outside county of residence:** 18.6%.

Cities with pop over 10,000: None.

GRANT COUNTY

108 S Glenn St   **Ph:** 620-356-1335
Ulysses, KS 67880   **Fax:** 620-356-3081
www.grantcoks.org

In southwestern KS; organized Mar 6, 1873 from Finney and

Grant County (cont'd)

Kearny counties. **Name Origin:** For Ulysses Simpson Grant (1822-85), Civil War general and eighteenth U.S. president.

Area (sq mi): 575.04 (land 574.86; water 0.18). **Pop per sq mi:** 13.1.

Pop 2005: 7,530. **State rank:** 52. **Pop change:** 2000-20005 -4.8%; 1990-2000 +10.5%. **Pop 2000:** 7,909 (White 63.5%; Black or African American 0.2%; Hispanic or Latino 34.7%; Asian 0.4%; Other 22.5%). **Foreign born:** 12.3%. **Median age:** 31.4.

Income 2000: per capita $17,072; median household $39,854; **Pop below poverty level:** 10.1%. ***Personal per capita income 2000-2003:** $21,893-$22,538.

Unemployment 2004: 3.9%. **Change from 2000:** +1.2%. **Median travel time to work:** 15.3 minutes. **Working outside county of residence:** 12.2%.

Cities with pop over 10,000: None.

GRAY COUNTY

PO Box 487   **Ph:** 620-855-3618
Cimarron, KS 67835   **Fax:** 620-855-3107

In southwestern KS, west of Dodge City; organized Mar 5, 1887 from Finney and Ford counties. **Name Origin:** For Alfred Gray, teacher, lawyer, and secretary of the KS Board of Agriculture (1873-80).

Area (sq mi): 869.34 (land 868.9; water 0.44). **Pop per sq mi:** 6.7.

Pop 2005: 5,861. **State rank:** 64. **Pop change:** 2000-20005 -0.7%; 1990-2000 +9.4%. **Pop 2000:** 5,904 (White 88.6%; Black or African American 0.2%; Hispanic or Latino 9.8%; Asian 0.1%; Other 7.5%). **Foreign born:** 9.5%. **Median age:** 33.

Income 2000: per capita $18,632; median household $40,000; **Pop below poverty level:** 9.1%. ***Personal per capita income 2000-2003:** $25,086-$25,612.

Unemployment 2004: 3%. **Change from 2000:** +0.7%. **Median travel time to work:** 17.2 minutes. **Working outside county of residence:** 28%.

Cities with pop over 10,000: None.

GREELEY COUNTY

PO Box 277   **Ph:** 620-376-4256
Tribune, KS 67879   **Fax:** 620-376-2294
www.greeleycountygovernment.org

On the central western border of KS; established Mar 6, 1873. **Name Origin:** For Horace Greeley (1811-72), editor of the *New York Tribune* and champion of westward expansion.

Area (sq mi): 778.01 (land 778.01; water 0). **Pop per sq mi:** 1.7.

Pop 2005: 1,349. **State rank:** 105. **Pop change:** 2000-20005 -12.1%; 1990-2000 -13.5%. **Pop 2000:** 1,534 (White 87.2%; Black or African American 0.2%; Hispanic or Latino 11.5%; Asian 0.1%; Other 6.6%). **Foreign born:** 8.5%. **Median age:** 38.6.

Income 2000: per capita $19,974; median household $34,605; **Pop below poverty level:** 11.6%. ***Personal per capita income 2000-2003:** $23,408-$27,006.

Unemployment 2004: 4%. **Change from 2000:** +0.4%. **Median travel time to work:** 15.8 minutes. **Working outside county of residence:** 9.6%.

Cities with pop over 10,000: None.

GREENWOOD COUNTY

311 N Main St   **Ph:** 620-583-8121
Eureka, KS 67045   **Fax:** 620-583-8124

In southeastern KS, east of Wichita; original county; organized Aug 25, 1855 (prior to statehood). **Name Origin:** For Alfred Burton Greenwood (1811-89), U.S. representative from AR (1853-59).

Area (sq mi): 1152.59 (land 1139.67; water 12.92). **Pop per sq mi:** 6.4.

Pop 2005: 7,338. **State rank:** 53. **Pop change:** 2000-20005 -4.4%; 1990-2000 -2.2%. **Pop 2000:** 7,673 (White 95.8%; Black or African American 0.1%; Hispanic or Latino 1.7%; Asian 0.1%; Other 3.2%). **Foreign born:** 1%. **Median age:** 42.6.

Income 2000: per capita $15,976; median household $30,169; **Pop below poverty level:** 12.5%. ***Personal per capita income 2000-2003:** $20,975-$22,051.

Unemployment 2004: 6.2%. **Change from 2000:** +0.6%. **Median travel time to work:** 25.1 minutes. **Working outside county of residence:** 34.3%.

Cities with pop over 10,000: None.

HAMILTON COUNTY

PO Box 1167   **Ph:** 620-384-5629
Syracuse, KS 67878   **Fax:** 620-384-5853

On the western border of KS, west of Garden City; organized Mar 20, 1873 from unorganized territory. **Name Origin:** For Alexander Hamilton (1757-1804), first U.S. secretary of the treasury (1789-95).

Area (sq mi): 997.62 (land 996.49; water 1.13). **Pop per sq mi:** 2.6.

Pop 2005: 2,604. **State rank:** 96. **Pop change:** 2000-20005 -2.5%; 1990-2000 +11.8%. **Pop 2000:** 2,670 (White 77.1%; Black or African American 0.5%; Hispanic or Latino 20.6%; Asian 0.6%; Other 17.3%). **Foreign born:** 13.5%. **Median age:** 37.6.

Income 2000: per capita $16,484; median household $32,033; **Pop below poverty level:** 15.7%. ***Personal per capita income 2000-2003:** $24,587-$28,051.

Unemployment 2004: 3.2%. **Change from 2000:** +1.4%. **Median travel time to work:** 17.3 minutes. **Working outside county of residence:** 9.2%.

Cities with pop over 10,000: None.

HARPER COUNTY

201 N Jennings Ave   **Ph:** 620-842-5555
Anthony, KS 67003   **Fax:** 620-842-3455
www.harpercounty.org

On the central southern border of KS, southwest of Wichita; established Feb 26, 1867 from Kingman County. **Name Origin:** For Sgt. Marion Harper (?-1863), soldier in the Kansas cavalry killed in the Civil War.

Area (sq mi): 802.95 (land 801.44; water 1.51). **Pop per sq mi:** 7.6.

---

*Source: Personal per capita income data are from the Bureau of Economic Analysis; per capita income data are from the Bureau of the Census. See Introduction for explanation of differences.

Harper County (cont'd)

Pop 2005: 6,081. **State rank:** 61. **Pop change:** 2000-20005 -7%; 1990-2000 -8.3%. **Pop 2000:** 6,536 (White 96.7%; Black or African American 0.2%; Hispanic or Latino 1.1%; Asian 0.1%; Other 2.4%). **Foreign born:** 0.4%. **Median age:** 42.9.

Income 2000: per capita $16,368; median household $29,776; **Pop below poverty level:** 11.6%. ***Personal per capita income 2000-2003:** $22,697-$26,256.

Unemployment 2004: 4.2%. **Change from 2000:** +0.7%. **Median travel time to work:** 19.6 minutes. **Working outside county of residence:** 21%.

Cities with pop over 10,000: None.

HARVEY COUNTY
PO Box 687
Newton, KS 67114
www.harveycounty.com

Ph: 316-284-6840
Fax: 316-284-6856

In central KS, east of Hutchinson; organized Feb 29, 1872 from McPherson, Butler, and Sedgwick counties. **Name Origin:** For Capt. James Madison Harvey (1833-94), governor of KS (1869-73) and U.S. senator (1874-77).

Area (sq mi): 540.5 (land 539.33; water 1.17). **Pop per sq mi:** 62.8.

Pop 2005: 33,843. **State rank:** 16. **Pop change:** 2000-20005 +3%; 1990-2000 +5.9%. **Pop 2000:** 32,869 (White 88.1%; Black or African American 1.6%; Hispanic or Latino 8%; Asian 0.5%; Other 6.8%). **Foreign born:** 3.7%. **Median age:** 37.6.

Income 2000: per capita $18,715; median household $40,907; **Pop below poverty level:** 6.4%. ***Personal per capita income 2000-2003:** $25,235-$27,550.

Unemployment 2004: 5%. **Change from 2000:** +1.6%. **Median travel time to work:** 18.2 minutes. **Working outside county of residence:** 32.3%.

Cities with pop over 10,000: Newton 🏛 (18,154).

HASKELL COUNTY
PO Box 518
Sublette, KS 67877
www.haskellcounty.org

Ph: 620-675-2263
Fax: 620-675-2681

In southwestern KS; organized Mar 23, 1887 from Finney County. **Name Origin:** For Dudley Chase Haskell (1842-83), KS legislator and U.S. representative (1877-83).

Area (sq mi): 577.73 (land 577.37; water 0.36). **Pop per sq mi:** 7.3.

Pop 2005: 4,232. **State rank:** 75. **Pop change:** 2000-20005 -1.7%; 1990-2000 +10.8%. **Pop 2000:** 4,307 (White 74%; Black or African American 0.2%; Hispanic or Latino 23.6%; Asian 0.6%; Other 14.1%). **Foreign born:** 13.4%. **Median age:** 30.8.

Income 2000: per capita $17,349; median household $38,634; **Pop below poverty level:** 11.6%. ***Personal per capita income 2000-2003:** $28,754-$31,730.

Unemployment 2004: 3.6%. **Change from 2000:** +1.2%. **Median travel time to work:** 15.6 minutes. **Working outside county of residence:** 22.8%.

Cities with pop over 10,000: None.

HODGEMAN COUNTY
PO Box 247
Jetmore, KS 67854

Ph: 620-357-6421
Fax: 620-357-6161

In southwest-central KS, north of Dodge City; organized Mar 6, 1873 from Indian lands. **Name Origin:** For Capt. Amos Hodgman (?-1863), Civil War officer. The e was mistakenly inserted when the county was named.

Area (sq mi): 860.24 (land 859.92; water 0.32). **Pop per sq mi:** 2.5.

Pop 2005: 2,110. **State rank:** 101. **Pop change:** 2000-20005 +1.2%; 1990-2000 -4.2%. **Pop 2000:** 2,085 (White 95.5%; Black or African American 0.9%; Hispanic or Latino 2.7%; Asian 0%; Other 1.8%). **Foreign born:** 1%. **Median age:** 39.8.

Income 2000: per capita $15,599; median household $35,994; **Pop below poverty level:** 11.5%. ***Personal per capita income 2000-2003:** $24,807-$24,020.

Unemployment 2004: 4.2%. **Change from 2000:** +1.5%. **Median travel time to work:** 15.6 minutes. **Working outside county of residence:** 21.9%.

Cities with pop over 10,000: None.

JACKSON COUNTY
400 New York Ave 2nd Fl
Holton, KS 66436
www.jackson.kansasgov.com

Ph: 785-364-2891
Fax: 785-364-4204

In northeastern KS, north of Topeka; organized as Calhoun County Aug 30, 1855 (prior to statehood); name changed Feb 11, 1859. **Name Origin:** For Andrew Jackson (1767-1845), seventh U.S. president. Originally for John C. Calhoun (1782-1850), U.S. senator from SC.

Area (sq mi): 657.86 (land 655.59; water 2.27). **Pop per sq mi:** 20.6.

Pop 2005: 13,535. **State rank:** 36. **Pop change:** 2000-20005 +6.9%; 1990-2000 +9.8%. **Pop 2000:** 12,657 (White 89.6%; Black or African American 0.5%; Hispanic or Latino 1.5%; Asian 0.2%; Other 9%, including 6.8% American Indian/Alaska Native). **Foreign born:** 0.5%. **Median age:** 37.4.

Income 2000: per capita $18,606; median household $40,451; **Pop below poverty level:** 8.8%. ***Personal per capita income 2000-2003:** $24,422-$26,036.

Unemployment 2004: 6%. **Change from 2000:** +2.3%. **Median travel time to work:** 27.5 minutes. **Working outside county of residence:** 47.3%.

Cities with pop over 10,000: None.

JEFFERSON COUNTY
PO Box 321
Oskaloosa, KS 66066
www.jfcountyks.com

Ph: 785-863-2272
Fax: 785-863-3135

In northeastern KS, east of Topeka; original county; organized Aug 25, 1855 (prior to statehood). **Name Origin:** For Thomas Jefferson (1743-1826), U.S. patriot and statesman; third U.S. president.

Area (sq mi): 556.94 (land 536.11; water 20.83). **Pop per sq mi:** 35.6.

Pop 2005: 19,106. **State rank:** 30. **Pop change:** 2000-20005 +3.7%; 1990-2000 +15.9%. **Pop 2000:** 18,426 (White 96%; Black or African

🏛 *County Seat*

Jefferson County (cont'd)

American 0.4%; Hispanic or Latino 1.3%; Asian 0.2%; Other 2.7%). **Foreign born:** 0.6%. **Median age:** 38.

Income 2000: per capita $19,373; median household $45,535; **Pop below poverty level:** 6.7%. *__Personal per capita income 2000-2003:__ $22,659-$23,555.

Unemployment 2004: 5.7%. **Change from 2000:** +1.3%. **Median travel time to work:** 29.3 minutes. **Working outside county of residence:** 67.4%.

Cities with pop over 10,000: None.

JEWELL COUNTY

307 N Commercial St   **Ph:** 785-378-4020
Mankato, KS 66956   **Fax:** 785-378-4075

On central northern border of KS; organized Feb 26, 1867 from Mitchell County. **Name Origin:** For Lt. Col. Lewis R. Jewell (?-1862), officer in the Kansas cavalry killed during the Civil War.

Area (sq mi): 914.47 (land 909.18; water 5.29). **Pop per sq mi:** 3.7.

Pop 2005: 3,352. **State rank:** 82. **Pop change:** 2000-20005 -11.6%; 1990-2000 -10.8%. **Pop 2000:** 3,791 (White 98.2%; Black or African American 0%; Hispanic or Latino 0.7%; Asian 0.1%; Other 1.1%). **Foreign born:** 0.9%. **Median age:** 46.2.

Income 2000: per capita $16,644; median household $30,538; **Pop below poverty level:** 11.6%. *__Personal per capita income 2000-2003:__ $20,246-$26,682.

Unemployment 2004: 3.1%. **Change from 2000:** +1.4%. **Median travel time to work:** 16.8 minutes. **Working outside county of residence:** 27.3%.

Cities with pop over 10,000: None.

JOHNSON COUNTY

111 S Cherry St Suite 1200   **Ph:** 913-715-0775
Olathe, KS 66061   **Fax:** 913-715-0800
www.jocoks.com

On eastern border of KS, south of Kansas City; original county, organized Aug 25, 1855 (prior to statehood). **Name Origin:** For the Rev. Thomas Johnson (1802-65), assassinated missionary to the Shawnee Indians (1829-58).

Area (sq mi): 480.15 (land 476.78; water 3.37). **Pop per sq mi:** 1062.5.

Pop 2005: 506,562. **State rank:** 1. **Pop change:** 2000-20005 +12.3%; 1990-2000 +27%. **Pop 2000:** 451,086 (White 89%; Black or African American 2.6%; Hispanic or Latino 4%; Asian 2.8%; Other 3.3%). **Foreign born:** 5.7%. **Median age:** 35.2.

Income 2000: per capita $30,919; median household $61,455; **Pop below poverty level:** 3.4%. *__Personal per capita income 2000-2003:__ $44,170-$43,912.

Unemployment 2004: 4.9%. **Change from 2000:** +1.5%. **Median travel time to work:** 20.2 minutes. **Working outside county of residence:** 32%.

Cities with pop over 10,000: 8 (see page 35 for cities).

KEARNY COUNTY

PO Box 86   **Ph:** 620-355-6422
Lakin, KS 67860   **Fax:** 620-355-7382
www.kearnycountykansas.com

In southwestern KS, west of Garden City; organized Mar 6, 1873 from Finney County. **Name Origin:** For Gen. Philip Kearny (1814-62), hero of the Mexican-American War and Civil War.

Area (sq mi): 871.5 (land 871.06; water 0.44). **Pop per sq mi:** 5.2.

Pop 2005: 4,516. **State rank:** 73. **Pop change:** 2000-20005 -0.3%; 1990-2000 +12.5%. **Pop 2000:** 4,531 (White 71.1%; Black or African American 0.6%; Hispanic or Latino 26.6%; Asian 0.3%; Other 18.8%). **Foreign born:** 12.7%. **Median age:** 31.6.

Income 2000: per capita $15,708; median household $40,149; **Pop below poverty level:** 11.7%. *__Personal per capita income 2000-2003:__ $20,084-$20,467.

Unemployment 2004: 4.4%. **Change from 2000:** -0.1%. **Median travel time to work:** 13.9 minutes. **Working outside county of residence:** 29.9%.

Cities with pop over 10,000: None.

KINGMAN COUNTY

130 N Spruce St   **Ph:** 620-532-2521
Kingman, KS 67068   **Fax:** 620-532-2037

In south-central KS, west of Wichita; established Feb 29, 1872 from unorganized territory. **Name Origin:** For Samuel Austin Kingman (1822-?), KY legislator and Chief Justice of the KS Supreme Court (1866-77).

Area (sq mi): 866.7 (land 863.35; water 3.35). **Pop per sq mi:** 9.5.

Pop 2005: 8,165. **State rank:** 49. **Pop change:** 2000-20005 -5.9%; 1990-2000 +4.6%. **Pop 2000:** 8,673 (White 96.5%; Black or African American 0.2%; Hispanic or Latino 1.4%; Asian 0.2%; Other 2.1%). **Foreign born:** 0.3%. **Median age:** 40.2.

Income 2000: per capita $18,533; median household $37,790; **Pop below poverty level:** 10.6%. *__Personal per capita income 2000-2003:__ $21,901-$24,318.

Unemployment 2004: 4.7%. **Change from 2000:** +1.3%. **Median travel time to work:** 25.3 minutes. **Working outside county of residence:** 35.4%.

Cities with pop over 10,000: None.

KIOWA COUNTY

211 E Florida Ave   **Ph:** 620-723-3366
Greensburg, KS 67054   **Fax:** 620-723-3234

In south-central KS, southeast of Dodge City; established Feb 26, 1867 from Comanche and Edwards counties, abolished in 1875, and recreated in 1866 from Comanche and Edwards counties. **Name Origin:** For the Indian tribe of Tanoan linguistic stock; name means 'principal people.'

Area (sq mi): 722.62 (land 722.39; water 0.23). **Pop per sq mi:** 4.1.

Pop 2005: 2,984. **State rank:** 90. **Pop change:** 2000-20005 -9%; 1990-2000 -10.4%. **Pop 2000:** 3,278 (White 96.2%; Black or African American 0.2%; Hispanic or Latino 2%; Asian 0.3%; Other 2.3%). **Foreign born:** 1.9%. **Median age:** 42.1.

*Source: Personal per capita income data are from the Bureau of Economic Analysis; per capita income data are from the Bureau of the Census. See Introduction for explanation of differences.

268

Kiowa County (cont'd)

Income 2000: per capita $17,207; median household $31,576; **Pop below poverty level:** 10.8%. *Personal per capita income 2000-2003: $22,734-$27,590.

Unemployment 2004: 3.5%. **Change from 2000:** +1.4%. **Median travel time to work:** 15.3 minutes. **Working outside county of residence:** 17.5%.

Cities with pop over 10,000: None.

LABETTE COUNTY

PO Box 387   **Ph:** 620-795-2138
Oswego, KS 67356   **Fax:** 620-795-2928
www.labettecounty.com

On the southeastern border of KS, west of Joplin, MO; organized Feb 7, 1867 from Neosho County. **Name Origin:** For the creek, which runs through the county, named La Bette, possibly for a Pierre Labette who lived near the mouth of the stream. An 1836 map names it *La Bete*, French for 'the beast.'

Area (sq mi): 653.3 (land 648.82; water 4.48). **Pop per sq mi:** 34.2.

Pop 2005: 22,169. **State rank:** 26. **Pop change:** 2000-20005 -2.9%; 1990-2000 -3.6%. **Pop 2000:** 22,835 (White 87.8%; Black or African American 4.7%; Hispanic or Latino 3.1%; Asian 0.3%; Other 5.7%, including 1.9% American Indian/Alaska Native). **Foreign born:** 1%. **Median age:** 37.9.

Income 2000: per capita $15,525; median household $30,875; **Pop below poverty level:** 12.7%. *Personal per capita income 2000-2003: $21,051-$22,970.

Unemployment 2004: 6.7%. **Change from 2000:** +1.1%. **Median travel time to work:** 16.8 minutes. **Working outside county of residence:** 15.5%.

Cities with pop over 10,000: Parsons (11,291).

LANE COUNTY

PO Box 788   **Ph:** 620-397-5356
Dighton, KS 67839   **Fax:** 620-397-5419

In west-central KS, northeast of Garden City; organized Mar 6, 1873 from Finney County. **Name Origin:** For Col. James Henry Lane (1814-66), officer in the Mexican-American War, U.S. representative from IN (1853-55), and first U.S. senator from KS (1861-66).

Area (sq mi): 717.43 (land 717.22; water 0.21). **Pop per sq mi:** 2.6.

Pop 2005: 1,894. **State rank:** 103. **Pop change:** 2000-20005 -12.1%; 1990-2000 -9.3%. **Pop 2000:** 2,155 (White 97%; Black or African American 0%; Hispanic or Latino 1.4%; Asian 0.1%; Other 2.1%). **Foreign born:** 0.5%. **Median age:** 41.6.

Income 2000: per capita $18,606; median household $36,047; **Pop below poverty level:** 8.2%. *Personal per capita income 2000-2003: $25,329-$29,002.

Unemployment 2004: 4.2%. **Change from 2000:** +0.3%. **Median travel time to work:** 15.7 minutes. **Working outside county of residence:** 11.5%.

Cities with pop over 10,000: None.

LEAVENWORTH COUNTY

300 Walnut St Suite 106   **Ph:** 913-684-0421
Leavenworth, KS 66048   **Fax:** 913-684-0406
www.leavenworthcounty.org

On the northeastern border of KS, north of Kansas City; original county; organized Aug 25, 1855 (prior to statehood). **Name Origin:** For Fort Leavenworth, the state's first fort, named for Gen. Henry Leavenworth (1783-1834), officer in the War of 1812 who later fought the Indians.

Area (sq mi): 468.33 (land 463.27; water 5.06). **Pop per sq mi:** 157.8.

Pop 2005: 73,113. **State rank:** 6. **Pop change:** 2000-20005 +6.4%; 1990-2000 +6.7%. **Pop 2000:** 68,691 (White 82%; Black or African American 10.4%; Hispanic or Latino 3.8%; Asian 1.1%; Other 4.2%). **Foreign born:** 2.7%. **Median age:** 35.6.

Income 2000: per capita $20,292; median household $48,114; **Pop below poverty level:** 6.7%. *Personal per capita income 2000-2003: $24,572-$26,198.

Unemployment 2004: 6.4%. **Change from 2000:** +1.1%. **Median travel time to work:** 22.4 minutes. **Working outside county of residence:** 38.8%.

Cities with pop over 10,000: Leavenworth (35,290); Lansing (10,117).

LINCOLN COUNTY

216 E Lincoln Ave   **Ph:** 785-524-4757
Lincoln, KS 67455   **Fax:** 785-524-5008

In north-central KS, northwest of Salina; organized Feb 26, 1867 from Ellsworth County. **Name Origin:** For Abraham Lincoln (1809-65), sixteenth U.S. president.

Area (sq mi): 719.94 (land 718.87; water 1.07). **Pop per sq mi:** 4.7.

Pop 2005: 3,411. **State rank:** 80. **Pop change:** 2000-20005 -4.7%; 1990-2000 -2.1%. **Pop 2000:** 3,578 (White 97.6%; Black or African American 0.1%; Hispanic or Latino 1%; Asian 0.1%; Other 1.6%). **Foreign born:** 0.5%. **Median age:** 43.7.

Income 2000: per capita $15,788; median household $30,893; **Pop below poverty level:** 9.7%. *Personal per capita income 2000-2003: $20,282-$21,422.

Unemployment 2004: 4.7%. **Change from 2000:** +1.8%. **Median travel time to work:** 18.1 minutes. **Working outside county of residence:** 26.3%.

Cities with pop over 10,000: None.

LINN COUNTY

PO Box 350   **Ph:** 913-795-2660
Mound City, KS 66056   **Fax:** 913-795-2004
www.linncountyks.com

On the eastern border of KS, south of Kansas City; original county; organized Aug 25, 1855 (prior to statehood). **Name Origin:** For Lewis Fields Linn (1795-1843), U.S. senator from MO (1833-43).

Area (sq mi): 606.29 (land 598.67; water 7.62). **Pop per sq mi:** 16.6.

Pop 2005: 9,914. **State rank:** 42. **Pop change:** 2000-20005 +3.6%; 1990-2000 +15.9%. **Pop 2000:** 9,570 (White 96.9%; Black or African American 0.6%; Hispanic or Latino 0.9%; Asian 0.1%; Other 1.8%). **Foreign born:** 0.3%. **Median age:** 40.8.

Linn County (cont'd)

Income 2000: per capita $17,009; median household $35,906; **Pop below poverty level:** 11%. ***Personal per capita income 2000-2003:** $21,061-$22,278.

Unemployment 2004: 7.6%. **Change from 2000:** -2%. **Median travel time to work:** 34.3 minutes. **Working outside county of residence:** 51.5%.

Cities with pop over 10,000: None.

LOGAN COUNTY

710 W 2nd St   **Ph:** 785-672-4244
Oakley, KS 67748   **Fax:** 785-672-3341

In western KS, northwest of Garden City; organized as Saint John County Mar 4, 1881 from Wallace County; name changed Feb 24, 1887. **Name Origin:** For Gen. John Alexander Logan (1826-86), officer in the Mexican-American War and Civil War, U.S. senator from IL (1871-77; 1879-86).

Area (sq mi): 1073.09 (land 1072.99; water 0.11). **Pop per sq mi:** 2.6.

Pop 2005: 2,794. **State rank:** 92. **Pop change:** 2000-20005 -8.3%; 1990-2000 -1.1%. **Pop 2000:** 3,046 (White 96.2%; Black or African American 0.6%; Hispanic or Latino 1.6%; Asian 0.2%; Other 2.5%). **Foreign born:** 0.6%. **Median age:** 40.7.

Income 2000: per capita $17,294; median household $32,131; **Pop below poverty level:** 7.3%. ***Personal per capita income 2000-2003:** $19,242-$23,392.

Unemployment 2004: 3.6%. **Change from 2000:** +1.1%. **Median travel time to work:** 15.4 minutes. **Working outside county of residence:** 23.9%.

Cities with pop over 10,000: None.

LYON COUNTY

430 Commercial St   **Ph:** 620-341-3243
Emporia, KS 66801   **Fax:** 620-341-3415
www.lyoncounty.org

In east-central KS, northeast of Wichita; established as Breckinridge County Feb 17, 1857 (prior to statehood) from Madison County (which was abolished at the time it was divided between Lyon and Greenwood counties); name changed Feb 5, 1862. **Name Origin:** For Gen. Nathaniel Lyon (1818-61), Union commander in the Civil War who helped preserve MO for the Union when it seemed likely to join the Confederacy.

Area (sq mi): 855.14 (land 850.87; water 4.27). **Pop per sq mi:** 41.9.

Pop 2005: 35,609. **State rank:** 13. **Pop change:** 2000-20005 -0.9%; 1990-2000 +3.5%. **Pop 2000:** 35,935 (White 77.3%; Black or African American 2.3%; Hispanic or Latino 16.7%; Asian 2%; Other 12.5%). **Foreign born:** 9%. **Median age:** 30.9.

Income 2000: per capita $15,724; median household $32,819; **Pop below poverty level:** 14.5%. ***Personal per capita income 2000-2003:** $20,665-$21,980.

Unemployment 2004: 4.7%. **Change from 2000:** -0.1%. **Median travel time to work:** 15.9 minutes. **Working outside county of residence:** 10%.

Cities with pop over 10,000: Emporia 🏛 (26,639).

MARION COUNTY

200 S 3rd Courthouse Sq   **Ph:** 620-382-2185
Marion, KS 66861   **Fax:** 620-382-3420
www.marioncoks.net

In central KS, north of Wichita; established Aug 25, 1855 (prior to statehood) from Chase County. **Name Origin:** For Gen. Francis Marion (c. 1732-95), SC soldier and legislator, known as 'The Swamp Fox' for his tactics during the Revolutionary War.

Area (sq mi): 953.54 (land 943.11; water 10.43). **Pop per sq mi:** 13.7.

Pop 2005: 12,952. **State rank:** 37. **Pop change:** 2000-20005 -3.1%; 1990-2000 +3.7%. **Pop 2000:** 13,361 (White 96%; Black or African American 0.5%; Hispanic or Latino 1.9%; Asian 0.2%; Other 2.2%). **Foreign born:** 1.1%. **Median age:** 41.

Income 2000: per capita $16,100; median household $34,500; **Pop below poverty level:** 8.3%. ***Personal per capita income 2000-2003:** $19,518-$21,454.

Unemployment 2004: 4.3%. **Change from 2000:** +1.7%. **Median travel time to work:** 20.1 minutes. **Working outside county of residence:** 32.1%.

Cities with pop over 10,000: None.

MARSHALL COUNTY

1201 Broadway   **Ph:** 785-562-5361
Marysville, KS 66508   **Fax:** 785-562-5262
www.marshall.kansasgov.com

On the northern border of KS, north of Manhattan; original county; organized Aug 25, 1855 (prior to statehood). **Name Origin:** For Francis J. Marshall, local businessman and member of the first KS territorial legislature. County seat was named for his wife.

Area (sq mi): 904.36 (land 902.53; water 1.83). **Pop per sq mi:** 11.5.

Pop 2005: 10,405. **State rank:** 40. **Pop change:** 2000-20005 -5.1%; 1990-2000 -6.3%. **Pop 2000:** 10,965 (White 97.7%; Black or African American 0.2%; Hispanic or Latino 0.8%; Asian 0.2%; Other 1.5%). **Foreign born:** 1.1%. **Median age:** 41.7.

Income 2000: per capita $17,090; median household $32,089; **Pop below poverty level:** 9.2%. ***Personal per capita income 2000-2003:** $24,834-$27,794.

Unemployment 2004: 3.8%. **Change from 2000:** +0.3%. **Median travel time to work:** 17.3 minutes. **Working outside county of residence:** 12.6%.

Cities with pop over 10,000: None.

MCPHERSON COUNTY

117 N Maple   **Ph:** 620-241-3656
McPherson, KS 67460   **Fax:** 620-241-1168
www.mcphersoncountyks.us

In central KS, north of Hutchinson; organized Feb 26, 1867 from unorganized territory. **Name Origin:** For Gen. James Birdseye McPherson (1828-64), commander of the Union Army of the Tennessee during the Civil War.

Area (sq mi): 901.24 (land 899.71; water 1.52). **Pop per sq mi:** 32.8.

---

*Source: Personal per capita income data are from the Bureau of Economic Analysis; per capita income data are from the Bureau of the Census. See Introduction for explanation of differences.

Mcpherson County (cont'd)

Pop 2005: 29,523. **State rank:** 19. **Pop change:** 2000-20005 -0.1%; 1990-2000 ı8.4%. **Pop 2000:** 29,554 (White 95.6%; Black or African American 0.8%; Hispanic or Latino 1.9%; Asian 0.3%; Other 2.4%). **Foreign born:** 0.6%. **Median age:** 38.1.

Income 2000: per capita $18,921; median household $41,138; **Pop below poverty level:** 6.6%. *Personal per capita income 2000-2003: $25,685-$28,273.

Unemployment 2004: 3.7%. **Change from 2000:** ı0.7%. **Median travel time to work:** 14.6 minutes. **Working outside county of residence:** 15.3%.

Cities with pop over 10,000: McPherson 🏛 (13,681).

MEADE COUNTY

PO Box 278   **Ph:** 620-873-8700
Meade, KS 67864   **Fax:** 620-873-8713

On the southern border of KS, southwest of Dodge City; organized Jan 8, 1873 from unorganized territory. **Name Origin:** For Gen. George Gordon Meade (1815-72), officer in the Mexican American War and Civil War; commander of the Union army that defeated Gen. Robert E. Lee (1807-70) at Gettysburg.

Area (sq mi): 979.66 (land 978.42; water 1.24). **Pop per sq mi:** 4.7.

Pop 2005: 4,625. **State rank:** 71. **Pop change:** 2000-20005 -0.1%; 1990-2000 +9%. **Pop 2000:** 4,631 (White 86.8%; Black or African American 0.4%; Hispanic or Latino 10.9%; Asian 0.2%; Other 8.2%). **Foreign born:** 8.9%. **Median age:** 36.1.

Income 2000: per capita $16,824; median household $36,761; **Pop below poverty level:** 9.3%. *Personal per capita income 2000-2003: $24,161-$24,041.

Unemployment 2004: 3.5%. **Change from 2000:** +1.4%. **Median travel time to work:** 17.7 minutes. **Working outside county of residence:** 26%.

Cities with pop over 10,000: None.

MIAMI COUNTY

201 S Pearl St Suite 102   **Ph:** 913-294-3976
Paola, KS 66071   **Fax:** 913-294-9544
www.miamicountyks.org

On the eastern border of KS, south of Olathe; organized as Lykins County Aug 25, 1855 (prior to statehood); name changed Jun 3, 1861. **Name Origin:** For the Miami Indians, an Algonquin tribe. Origin of name uncertain; probably from Ojibway *oumaumeg* 'people of the peninsula' or from Delaware *we-mi-a-mik* 'all friends.'

Area (sq mi): 590.15 (land 576.72; water 13.43). **Pop per sq mi:** 52.9.

Pop 2005: 30,496. **State rank:** 18. **Pop change:** 2000-20005 +7.6%; 1990-2000 +20.8%. **Pop 2000:** 28,351 (White 95%; Black or African American 1.5%; Hispanic or Latino 1.6%; Asian 0.2%; Other 2.3%). **Foreign born:** 0.6%. **Median age:** 36.7.

Income 2000: per capita $21,408; median household $46,665; **Pop below poverty level:** 5.5%. *Personal per capita income 2000-2003: $26,151-$27,582.

Unemployment 2004: 5.3%. **Change from 2000:** +1.1%. **Median travel time to work:** 28.6 minutes. **Working outside county of residence:** 58.6%.

Cities with pop over 10,000: None.

MITCHELL COUNTY

PO Box 190   **Ph:** 785-738-3652
Beloit, KS 67420   **Fax:** 785-738-5524
www.mcks.org

In north-central KS, northwest of Salina; organized Feb 26, 1867 from Kirwin Land District. **Name Origin:** For Capt. William D. Mitchell (?-1865), Union officer killed at Battle of Monroe's Cross Roads, NC.

Area (sq mi): 718.62 (land 699.82; water 18.8). **Pop per sq mi:** 9.2.

Pop 2005: 6,420. **State rank:** 57. **Pop change:** 2000-20005 -7.4%; 1990-2000 -3.8%. **Pop 2000:** 6,932 (White 97.1%; Black or African American 0.5%; Hispanic or Latino 0.9%; Asian 0.3%; Other 1.5%). **Foreign born:** 0.3%. **Median age:** 41.1.

Income 2000: per capita $17,653; median household $33,385; **Pop below poverty level:** 9.5%. *Personal per capita income 2000-2003: $22,721-$25,447.

Unemployment 2004: 3.7%. **Change from 2000:** +1.3%. **Median travel time to work:** 12.3 minutes. **Working outside county of residence:** 9.2%.

Cities with pop over 10,000: None.

MONTGOMERY COUNTY

PO Box 446   **Ph:** 620-330-1200
Independence, KS 67301   **Fax:** 620-330-1202
www.mgcountyks.org

On the southeastern border of KS, west of Joplin, MO; organized Feb 26, 1867 from Labette County. **Name Origin:** For either James M. Montgomery (1814-71), abolitionist and preacher, a nephew or more distant relative of Gen. Richard Montgomery (1738-75), officer in the American Revolution, or for Gen. Richard Montgomery himself.

Area (sq mi): 651.4 (land 645.2; water 6.19). **Pop per sq mi:** 53.6.

Pop 2005: 34,570. **State rank:** 15. **Pop change:** 2000-20005 -4.6%; 1990-2000 -6.6%. **Pop 2000:** 36,252 (White 84.5%; Black or African American 6.1%; Hispanic or Latino 3.1%; Asian 0.5%; Other 7.6%, including 3.2% American Indian/Alaska Native). **Foreign born:** 1.3%. **Median age:** 39.2.

Income 2000: per capita $16,421; median household $30,997; **Pop below poverty level:** 12.6%. *Personal per capita income 2000-2003: $21,156-$23,527.

Unemployment 2004: 6.8%. **Change from 2000:** +0.3%. **Median travel time to work:** 16.4 minutes. **Working outside county of residence:** 10.8%.

Cities with pop over 10,000: Coffeyville (10,504).

MORRIS COUNTY

501 W Main St   **Ph:** 620-767-5518
Council Grove, KS 66846   **Fax:** 620-767-6861

In east-central KS, northwest of Emporia; organized as Wise County Aug 30, 1855 (prior to statehood) from Madison County;

🏛 *County Seat*

Morris County (cont'd)

name changed Feb 11, 1859. **Name Origin:** For Thomas Morris (1766-1844), opponent of slavery and U.S. senator from OH (1833-39).

Area (sq mi): 702.84 (land 697.38; water 5.46). **Pop per sq mi:** 8.7.

Pop 2005: 6,049. **State rank:** 62. **Pop change:** 2000-20005 -0.9%; 1990-2000 -1.5%. **Pop 2000:** 6,104 (White 96.2%; Black or African American 0.3%; Hispanic or Latino 2.2%; Asian 0.2%; Other 1.9%). **Foreign born:** 1.5%. **Median age:** 42.

Income 2000: per capita $18,491; median household $32,163; **Pop below poverty level:** 9%. ***Personal per capita income 2000-2003:** $21,750-$23,620.

Unemployment 2004: 4.8%. **Change from 2000:** +1.3%. **Median travel time to work:** 21.6 minutes. **Working outside county of residence:** 29.6%.

Cities with pop over 10,000: None.

MORTON COUNTY

PO Box 1116   **Ph:** 620-697-2157
Elkhart, KS 67950   **Fax:** 620-697-2159
www.mtcoks.com

In the southwestern corner of KS; organized Feb 18, 1886 from Stanton County. **Name Origin:** For Oliver Hazard Perry Throck Morton (1823-77), jurist, IN governor (1861-67), and U.S. senator (1867-77).

Area (sq mi): 729.94 (land 729.92; water 0.02). **Pop per sq mi:** 4.4.

Pop 2005: 3,196. **State rank:** 84. **Pop change:** 2000-20005 -8.6%; 1990-2000 +0.5%. **Pop 2000:** 3,496 (White 82.7%; Black or African American 0.2%; Hispanic or Latino 14.1%; Asian 1.1%; Other 10.3%, including 1.1% American Indian/Alaska Native). **Foreign born:** 9.5%. **Median age:** 36.2.

Income 2000: per capita $17,076; median household $37,232; **Pop below poverty level:** 10.5%. ***Personal per capita income 2000-2003:** $21,099-$21,130.

Unemployment 2004: 3.4%. **Change from 2000:** +1%. **Median travel time to work:** 13.7 minutes. **Working outside county of residence:** 15.5%.

Cities with pop over 10,000: None.

NEMAHA COUNTY

PO Box 186   **Ph:** 785-336-3570
Seneca, KS 66538   **Fax:** 785-336-3373

On northern border of KS, west of Saint Joseph, MO; original county; organized Aug 25, 1855 (prior to statehood). **Name Origin:** For the Nemaha River, itself named from the Oto Indian *nimaha* 'muddy water.'

Area (sq mi): 719.4 (land 717.99; water 1.41). **Pop per sq mi:** 14.5.

Pop 2005: 10,443. **State rank:** 39. **Pop change:** 2000-20005 -2.6%; 1990-2000 +2.6%. **Pop 2000:** 10,717 (White 97.9%; Black or African American 0.5%; Hispanic or Latino 0.7%; Asian 0.1%; Other 1.1%). **Foreign born:** 0.4%. **Median age:** 39.1.

Income 2000: per capita $17,121; median household $34,296; **Pop below poverty level:** 9.1%. ***Personal per capita income 2000-2003:** $24,221-$23,937.

Unemployment 2004: 3.7%. **Change from 2000:** +0.4%. **Median travel time to work:** 15.4 minutes. **Working outside county of residence:** 18.1%.

Cities with pop over 10,000: None.

NEOSHO COUNTY

PO Box 138   **Ph:** 620-244-3811
Erie, KS 66733   **Fax:** 620-244-3810

In southeastern KS, west of Pittsburgh; organized as Dorn County Aug 25, 1855 (prior to statehood) from Labette County. **Name Origin:** Osage Indian 'cold, clear water' or 'main river,' unclear which river is referred to.

Area (sq mi): 578.02 (land 571.75; water 6.27). **Pop per sq mi:** 28.9.

Pop 2005: 16,529. **State rank:** 33. **Pop change:** 2000-20005 -2.8%; 1990-2000 -0.2%. **Pop 2000:** 16,997 (White 93.4%; Black or African American 0.9%; Hispanic or Latino 2.9%; Asian 0.3%; Other 4%, including 1% American Indian/Alaska Native). **Foreign born:** 0.7%. **Median age:** 38.4.

Income 2000: per capita $16,539; median household $32,167; **Pop below poverty level:** 13%. ***Personal per capita income 2000-2003:** $20,543-$23,168.

Unemployment 2004: 4.8%. **Change from 2000:** -1%. **Median travel time to work:** 16.3 minutes. **Working outside county of residence:** 20.3%.

Cities with pop over 10,000: None.

NESS COUNTY

202 W Sycamore St   **Ph:** 785-798-2401
Ness City, KS 67560   **Fax:** 785-798-3829

In west-central KS, north of Dodge City; established Feb 26, 1867. **Name Origin:** For Noah V. Ness (?-1864), a corporal in the Kansas cavalry killed in the Civil War, and the only corporal to be so honored in KS.

Area (sq mi): 1075 (land 1074.75; water 0.26). **Pop per sq mi:** 2.8.

Pop 2005: 3,009. **State rank:** 89. **Pop change:** 2000-20005 -12.9%; 1990-2000 -14.4%. **Pop 2000:** 3,454 (White 97.5%; Black or African American 0.1%; Hispanic or Latino 1.5%; Asian 0.1%; Other 1.6%). **Foreign born:** 0.9%. **Median age:** 43.9.

Income 2000: per capita $17,787; median household $32,340; **Pop below poverty level:** 8.7%. ***Personal per capita income 2000-2003:** $26,316-$31,492.

Unemployment 2004: 3.2%. **Change from 2000:** +1.4%. **Median travel time to work:** 16.1 minutes. **Working outside county of residence:** 10%.

Cities with pop over 10,000: None.

NORTON COUNTY

PO Box 70   **Ph:** 785-877-5720
Norton, KS 67654   **Fax:** 785-877-5722

On the central northern border of KS; established as Oro County 1859 (prior to statehood) from unorganized territory; name changed to Norton Feb 26, 1867; changed to Billings Mar 6, 1873; changed back to Norton Feb 19, 1874. **Name Origin:** For Orloff Norton (?-1864), Kansas army officer killed during a skirmish at

Source: Personal per capita income data are from the Bureau of Economic Analysis; per capita income data are from the Bureau of the Census. See Introduction for explanation of differences.

Norton County (cont'd)

Cane Hill, AR. Previously for N. H. Billings, a member of the KS legislature.

Area (sq mi): 881.39 (land 877.84; water 3.55). **Pop per sq mi:** 6.5.

Pop 2005: 5,664. **State rank:** 65. **Pop change:** 2000-20005 -4.9%; 1990-2000 +0.1%. **Pop 2000:** 5,953 (White 92.1%; Black or African American 4%; Hispanic or Latino 2.4%; Asian 0.4%; Other 2.1%). **Foreign born:** 0.6%. **Median age:** 40.1.

Income 2000: per capita $16,835; median household $31,050; **Pop below poverty level:** 10.5%. *Personal per capita income 2000-2003: $21,728-$22,060.

Unemployment 2004: 4.1%. **Change from 2000:** +2.5%. **Median travel time to work:** 12.7 minutes. **Working outside county of residence:** 10.7%.

Cities with pop over 10,000: None.

OSAGE COUNTY

PO Box 226   **Ph:** 785-828-4812
Lyndon, KS 66451   **Fax:** 785-828-4749
www.osage.kansasgov.com

In eastern KS, south of Topeka; original county, organized as Weller County Aug 30, 1855 (prior to statehood); name changed Feb 11, 1859. **Name Origin:** For the Osage Indians, a tribe of Siouan linguistic stock. Name is a corruption of their name in their own language, *Wazhazhe*, meaning unknown.

Area (sq mi): 719.23 (land 703.5; water 15.72). **Pop per sq mi:** 24.4.

Pop 2005: 17,150. **State rank:** 31. **Pop change:** 2000-20005 +2.6%; 1990-2000 +9.6%. **Pop 2000:** 16,712 (White 96.4%; Black or African American 0.2%; Hispanic or Latino 1.5%; Asian 0.2%; Other 2.4%). **Foreign born:** 0.6%. **Median age:** 38.9.

Income 2000: per capita $17,691; median household $37,928; **Pop below poverty level:** 8.4%. *Personal per capita income 2000-2003: $21,617-$22,619.

Unemployment 2004: 6.6%. **Change from 2000:** +1.9%. **Median travel time to work:** 30.1 minutes. **Working outside county of residence:** 60.4%.

Cities with pop over 10,000: None.

OSBORNE COUNTY

PO Box 160   **Ph:** 785-346-2431
Osborne, KS 67473   **Fax:** 785-346-5252
www.osbornecounty.org

In north-central KS, northeast of Hays; organized Feb 26, 1867 from Mitchell County. **Name Origin:** For Vincent B. Osborne (?-1865), Kansas soldier and lawyer. The geodetic center of the U.S. is in this county.

Area (sq mi): 894.28 (land 892.39; water 1.89). **Pop per sq mi:** 4.5.

Pop 2005: 4,050. **State rank:** 78. **Pop change:** 2000-20005 -9%; 1990-2000 -8.5%. **Pop 2000:** 4,452 (White 98.3%; Black or African American 0.1%; Hispanic or Latino 0.4%; Asian 0.2%; Other 1.1%). **Foreign born:** 0.7%. **Median age:** 44.

Income 2000: per capita $16,236; median household $29,145; **Pop below poverty level:** 10.4%. *Personal per capita income 2000-2003: $20,512-$23,517.

Unemployment 2004: 4.1%. **Change from 2000:** +1%. **Median travel time to work:** 15.3 minutes. **Working outside county of residence:** 15.4%.

Cities with pop over 10,000: None.

OTTAWA COUNTY

307 N Concord St Suite 130   **Ph:** 785-392-2279
Minneapolis, KS 67467   **Fax:** 785-392-2011
www.ottawacounty.org

In north-central KS, north of Salina; established Feb 27, 1860 (prior to statehood) from Saline County. **Name Origin:** For the Ottawa Indians of Algonquian linguistic stock. Tribal name derived from *Kadawe* 'to trade,' for their ability as intertribal traders and barterers.

Area (sq mi): 721.9 (land 721.11; water 0.79). **Pop per sq mi:** 8.5.

Pop 2005: 6,123. **State rank:** 60. **Pop change:** 2000-20005 -0.6%; 1990-2000 +9.4%. **Pop 2000:** 6,163 (White 96.9%; Black or African American 0.5%; Hispanic or Latino 1.3%; Asian 0.1%; Other 1.8%). **Foreign born:** 0.7%. **Median age:** 40.1.

Income 2000: per capita $17,663; median household $38,009; **Pop below poverty level:** 8.6%. *Personal per capita income 2000-2003: $22,150-$23,220.

Unemployment 2004: 4.9%. **Change from 2000:** +1.4%. **Median travel time to work:** 23.4 minutes. **Working outside county of residence:** 50.4%.

Cities with pop over 10,000: None.

PAWNEE COUNTY

715 Broadway   **Ph:** 620-285-3721
Larned, KS 67550   **Fax:** 620-285-3802
www.pawneecountykansas.com

In central KS, west of Great Bend; established Feb 26, 1867 from Rush and Stafford counties. **Name Origin:** For an Indian tribe of Caddoan linguistic stock. Name may mean 'horn' for the shape of their hair lock; Osages called them *Pa-in* 'long-haired,' they called themselves 'civilized people.'

Area (sq mi): 754.56 (land 754.17; water 0.38). **Pop per sq mi:** 8.9.

Pop 2005: 6,739. **State rank:** 56. **Pop change:** 2000-20005 -6.8%; 1990-2000 -4.3%. **Pop 2000:** 7,233 (White 88.8%; Black or African American 5%; Hispanic or Latino 4.2%; Asian 0.6%; Other 3.5%, including 1% American Indian/Alaska Native). **Foreign born:** 1.4%. **Median age:** 40.5.

Income 2000: per capita $17,584; median household $35,175; **Pop below poverty level:** 11.8%. *Personal per capita income 2000-2003: $22,611-$23,154.

Unemployment 2004: 3.8%. **Change from 2000:** +2.1%. **Median travel time to work:** 15.3 minutes. **Working outside county of residence:** 16.5%.

Cities with pop over 10,000: None.

PHILLIPS COUNTY

301 State St   **Ph:** 785-543-6825
Phillipsburg, KS 67661   **Fax:** 785-543-6827
www.phillipscounty.org

On the central northern border of KS; established Feb 26, 1867

Phillips County (cont'd)

from Kirwin Land District. **Name Origin:** Either for William A. Phillips (?-1856), a free-state man murdered at Leavenworth by a proslaver, or for a 'gallant private soldier of the Union army.'

Area (sq mi): 894.81 (land 886.23; water 8.58). **Pop per sq mi:** 6.2.

Pop 2005: 5,504. **State rank:** 66. **Pop change:** 2000-20005 -8.3%; 1990-2000 -8.9%. **Pop 2000:** 6,001 (White 97.8%; Black or African American 0.2%; Hispanic or Latino 0.7%; Asian 0.4%; Other 1%). **Foreign born:** 0.4%. **Median age:** 42.5.

Income 2000: per capita $17,121; median household $35,013; **Pop below poverty level:** 10%. ***Personal per capita income 2000-2003:** $24,253-$28,069.

Unemployment 2004: 3.9%. **Change from 2000:** +1.9%. **Median travel time to work:** 13.8 minutes. **Working outside county of residence:** 12.1%.

Cities with pop over 10,000: None.

POTTAWATOMIE COUNTY

PO Box 187   **Ph:** 785-457-3314
Westmoreland, KS 66549   **Fax:** 785-457-3507
www.pottcounty.org

In northeastern KS, east of Manhattan; organized Feb 20, 1857 (prior to statehood) from Indian lands. **Name Origin:** For the Potawatomie Indian tribe of Algonquian linguistic stock. Name means 'people of the place of the fire.'

Area (sq mi): 862.07 (land 844.24; water 17.83). **Pop per sq mi:** 22.7.

Pop 2005: 19,129. **State rank:** 29. **Pop change:** 2000-20005 +5.1%; 1990-2000 +12.9%. **Pop 2000:** 18,209 (White 94.9%; Black or African American 0.7%; Hispanic or Latino 2.3%; Asian 0.3%; Other 2.7%). **Foreign born:** 1%. **Median age:** 35.9.

Income 2000: per capita $17,785; median household $40,176; **Pop below poverty level:** 9.7%. ***Personal per capita income 2000-2003:** $23,927-$26,207.

Unemployment 2004: 4.7%. **Change from 2000:** +1.4%. **Median travel time to work:** 22.1 minutes. **Working outside county of residence:** 46.2%.

Cities with pop over 10,000: None.

PRATT COUNTY

PO Box 885   **Ph:** 620-672-4115
Pratt, KS 67124   **Fax:** 620-672-9541
www.prattcounty.org

In south-central KS, west of Wichita; established Feb 26, 1867. The county was fradulently organized with no bona fide settlers at the time. Official recognition was given in 1879. **Name Origin:** For Lt. Caleb Pratt (?-1861), Union officer killed at battle of Wilson's Creek, MO.

Area (sq mi): 735.76 (land 734.99; water 0.76). **Pop per sq mi:** 12.9.

Pop 2005: 9,496. **State rank:** 45. **Pop change:** 2000-20005 -1.6%; 1990-2000 -0.6%. **Pop 2000:** 9,647 (White 94.3%; Black or African American 1%; Hispanic or Latino 3.1%; Asian 0.5%; Other 3.2%). **Foreign born:** 1.2%. **Median age:** 40.2.

Income 2000: per capita $17,906; median household $35,529; **Pop below poverty level:** 9.4%. ***Personal per capita income 2000-2003:** $24,562-$25,639.

Unemployment 2004: 3.5%. **Change from 2000:** +1.5%. **Median travel time to work:** 13.1 minutes. **Working outside county of residence:** 12.6%.

Cities with pop over 10,000: None.

RAWLINS COUNTY

607 Main St   **Ph:** 785-626-3351
Atwood, KS 67730   **Fax:** 785-626-9019
www.rawlinscounty.info

On the northwestern border of KS; organized Mar 20, 1873 from Kirwin Land District. **Name Origin:** For Gen. John Aaron Rawlins (1831-69), officer in the Civil War and U.S. secretary of war under Grant (1869).

Area (sq mi): 1069.72 (land 1069.62; water 0.11). **Pop per sq mi:** 2.5.

Pop 2005: 2,672. **State rank:** 95. **Pop change:** 2000-20005 -9.9%; 1990-2000 -12.9%. **Pop 2000:** 2,966 (White 98%; Black or African American 0.3%; Hispanic or Latino 0.8%; Asian 0.1%; Other 1.1%). **Foreign born:** 0.4%. **Median age:** 45.4.

Income 2000: per capita $17,161; median household $32,105; **Pop below poverty level:** 12.5%. ***Personal per capita income 2000-2003:** $21,920-$26,811.

Unemployment 2004: 4.3%. **Change from 2000:** +1.8%. **Median travel time to work:** 14.6 minutes. **Working outside county of residence:** 13.7%.

Cities with pop over 10,000: None.

RENO COUNTY

206 W 1st St   **Ph:** 620-694-2934
Hutchinson, KS 67501   **Fax:** 620-694-2534
www.rngov.reno.ks.us

In south-central KS, northwest of Wichita; established Feb 26, 1867 from Sedgwick County. **Name Origin:** For Gen. Jesse Lee Reno (1823-62), officer in the Mexican-American War and the Civil War.

Area (sq mi): 1271.25 (land 1254.42; water 16.84). **Pop per sq mi:** 50.7.

Pop 2005: 63,558. **State rank:** 7. **Pop change:** 2000-20005 -1.9%; 1990-2000 +3.8%. **Pop 2000:** 64,790 (White 89.2%; Black or African American 2.9%; Hispanic or Latino 5.7%; Asian 0.4%; Other 5.1%). **Foreign born:** 2%. **Median age:** 38.2.

Income 2000: per capita $18,520; median household $35,510; **Pop below poverty level:** 10.9%. ***Personal per capita income 2000-2003:** $23,953-$24,982.

Unemployment 2004: 5.3%. **Change from 2000:** +1%. **Median travel time to work:** 17.6 minutes. **Working outside county of residence:** 11.5%.

Cities with pop over 10,000: Hutchinson 🏛 (41,047).

---

*Source: Personal per capita income data are from the Bureau of Economic Analysis; per capita income data are from the Bureau of the Census. See Introduction for explanation of differences.

REPUBLIC COUNTY
1815 M St **Ph:** 785-527-7231
Belleville, KS 66935 **Fax:** 785-527-2668
www.nckcn.com/repco

On the central northern border of KS, north of Salina; established Feb 27, 1860 (prior to statehood) from Washington and Cloud counties. **Name Origin:** For the Republican River, which first enters KS in this county; named for the valley that was home of the Pawnee Republic, a division of the Pawnee Tribe. Also, possibly for the Pawnee Republic.

Area (sq mi): 720.31 (land 716.38; water 3.93). **Pop per sq mi:** 7.2.

Pop 2005: 5,164. **State rank:** 69. **Pop change:** 2000-20005 -11.5%; 1990-2000 -10%. **Pop 2000:** 5,835 (White 98%; Black or African American 0.3%; Hispanic or Latino 0.9%; Asian 0.2%; Other 1%). **Foreign born:** 0.8%. **Median age:** 45.7.

Income 2000: per capita $17,433; median household $30,494; **Pop below poverty level:** 9.1%. ***Personal per capita income 2000-2003:** $20,042-$23,167.

Unemployment 2004: 4.6%. **Change from 2000:** +2.3%. **Median travel time to work:** 16.3 minutes. **Working outside county of residence:** 15.4%.

Cities with pop over 10,000: None.

RICE COUNTY
101 W Commercial St **Ph:** 620-257-2232
Lyons, KS 67554 **Fax:** 620-257-3039
www.ricecounty.us

In central KS, north of Hutchinson; organized Feb 26, 1867 from Reno County. **Name Origin:** For Gen. Samuel Allen Rice (1828-64), attorney and Union officer in the Civil War.

Area (sq mi): 728.3 (land 726.58; water 1.72). **Pop per sq mi:** 14.4.

Pop 2005: 10,452. **State rank:** 38. **Pop change:** 2000-20005 -2.9%; 1990-2000 +1.4%. **Pop 2000:** 10,761 (White 91.4%; Black or African American 1.2%; Hispanic or Latino 5.6%; Asian 0.3%; Other 3.8%). **Foreign born:** 2.2%. **Median age:** 37.6.

Income 2000: per capita $16,064; median household $35,671; **Pop below poverty level:** 10.7%. ***Personal per capita income 2000-2003:** $21,095-$19,776.

Unemployment 2004: 4.6%. **Change from 2000:** +1.1%. **Median travel time to work:** 17.1 minutes. **Working outside county of residence:** 27.5%.

Cities with pop over 10,000: None.

RILEY COUNTY
110 Courthouse Plaza **Ph:** 785-537-6300
Manhattan, KS 66502 **Fax:** 785-537-6394
www.co.riley.ks.us

In east-central KS, northwest of Topeka; organized Aug 25, 1855 (prior to statehood) from Wabaunsee County. **Name Origin:** For Fort Riley, named for Gen. Bennett Riley (1787-1853), professional soldier and territorial governor of CA (1848).

Area (sq mi): 622.11 (land 609.55; water 12.55). **Pop per sq mi:** 103.1.

Pop 2005: 62,826. **State rank:** 8. **Pop change:** 2000-20005 +0%; 1990-2000 -6.4%. **Pop 2000:** 62,843 (White 82.7%; Black or African American 6.9%; Hispanic or Latino 4.6%; Asian 3.2%; Other 5.1%). **Foreign born:** 6.1%. **Median age:** 23.9.

Income 2000: per capita $16,349; median household $32,042; **Pop below poverty level:** 20.6%. ***Personal per capita income 2000-2003:** $22,143-$25,154.

Unemployment 2004: 4.3%. **Change from 2000:** +0.6%. **Median travel time to work:** 14.9 minutes. **Working outside county of residence:** 18.7%.

Cities with pop over 10,000: Manhattan ⬛ (47,916).

ROOKS COUNTY
115 N Walnut St **Ph:** 785-425-6391
Stockton, KS 67669 **Fax:** 785-425-6015
www.rookscounty.net

In north-central KS, north of Hays; established Feb 26, 1867 from Kirwin Land District. **Name Origin:** For John Calvin Rooks (?-1862), soldier who died of wounds received at the Battle of Prairie Grove, AR.

Area (sq mi): 895.36 (land 888.34; water 7.02). **Pop per sq mi:** 6.

Pop 2005: 5,351. **State rank:** 68. **Pop change:** 2000-20005 -5.9%; 1990-2000 -5.9%. **Pop 2000:** 5,685 (White 96.5%; Black or African American 1.1%; Hispanic or Latino 1.1%; Asian 0.2%; Other 1.5%). **Foreign born:** 0.2%. **Median age:** 40.5.

Income 2000: per capita $15,588; median household $30,457; **Pop below poverty level:** 9.8%. ***Personal per capita income 2000-2003:** $21,978-$24,236.

Unemployment 2004: 5.7%. **Change from 2000:** +2.9%. **Median travel time to work:** 15.5 minutes. **Working outside county of residence:** 18.3%.

Cities with pop over 10,000: None.

RUSH COUNTY
PO Box 220 **Ph:** 785-222-2731
La Crosse, KS 67548 **Fax:** 785-222-3559
www.rushcounty.org

In central KS, south of Hays; established Feb 26, 1867 from unorganized territory. **Name Origin:** For Capt. Alexander Rush (?-1864), killed in action at Jenkins Ferry, AR.

Area (sq mi): 718.42 (land 718.21; water 0.21). **Pop per sq mi:** 4.7.

Pop 2005: 3,406. **State rank:** 81. **Pop change:** 2000-20005 -4.1%; 1990-2000 -7.6%. **Pop 2000:** 3,551 (White 97.7%; Black or African American 0.3%; Hispanic or Latino 1%; Asian 0.1%; Other 1.1%). **Foreign born:** 0.5%. **Median age:** 44.6.

Income 2000: per capita $18,033; median household $31,268; **Pop below poverty level:** 9.7%. ***Personal per capita income 2000-2003:** $21,933-$23,787.

Unemployment 2004: 4.2%. **Change from 2000:** +1.9%. **Median travel time to work:** 18 minutes. **Working outside county of residence:** 29.4%.

Cities with pop over 10,000: None.

⬛ *County Seat*

RUSSELL COUNTY
PO Box 113   **Ph:** 785-483-4641
Russell, KS 67665   **Fax:** 785-483-5725
www.russellcounty.org

In central KS, west of Salina; organized Feb 26, 1867 from Ellsworth County. **Name Origin:** For Capt. Avra P. Russell (?-1862), Union army officer who died of wounds received at Prairie Grove, AR.

Area (sq mi): 898.98 (land 884.68; water 14.3). **Pop per sq mi:** 7.7.

Pop 2005: 6,845. **State rank:** 55. **Pop change:** 2000-20005 -7.1%; 1990-2000 -5.9%. **Pop 2000:** 7,370 (White 97%; Black or African American 0.5%; Hispanic or Latino 0.9%; Asian 0.3%; Other 1.6%). **Foreign born:** 0.7%. **Median age:** 44.1.

Income 2000: per capita $17,073; median household $29,284; **Pop below poverty level:** 12%. ***Personal per capita income 2000-2003:** $23,530-$23,339.

Unemployment 2004: 4.7%. **Change from 2000:** +0.2%. **Median travel time to work:** 15.9 minutes. **Working outside county of residence:** 14.2%.

Cities with pop over 10,000: None.

SALINE COUNTY
PO Box 5040   **Ph:** 785-309-5820
Salina, KS 67402   **Fax:** 785-309-5826
www.co.saline.ks.us

In central KS, southwest of Manhattan; original county; organized Feb 15, 1860 (prior to statehood). **Name Origin:** For the Saline River, which flows through the county.

Area (sq mi): 721.28 (land 719.61; water 1.67). **Pop per sq mi:** 74.9.

Pop 2005: 53,919. **State rank:** 10. **Pop change:** 2000-20005 +0.6%; 1990-2000 +8.7%. **Pop 2000:** 53,597 (White 87%; Black or African American 3.1%; Hispanic or Latino 6%; Asian 1.7%; Other 5.9%). **Foreign born:** 4%. **Median age:** 36.1.

Income 2000: per capita $19,073; median household $37,308; **Pop below poverty level:** 8.8%. ***Personal per capita income 2000-2003:** $27,780-$27,579.

Unemployment 2004: 4.8%. **Change from 2000:** +1.3%. **Median travel time to work:** 14.8 minutes. **Working outside county of residence:** 5.3%.

Cities with pop over 10,000: Salina 🏛 (45,988).

SCOTT COUNTY
303 Court St   **Ph:** 620-872-2420
Scott City, KS 67871   **Fax:** 620-872-7145
www.scott.kansasgov.com

In western KS, north of Garden City; organized Mar 20, 1873 from Finney County. **Name Origin:** For Gen. Winfield Scott (1786-1866), officer in the War of 1812 and the Mexican-American War, general in chief of the U.S. Army (1841-61) and commander of the Union armies at the beginning of the Civil War.

Area (sq mi): 717.64 (land 717.52; water 0.12). **Pop per sq mi:** 6.4.

Pop 2005: 4,600. **State rank:** 72. **Pop change:** 2000-20005 -10.2%; 1990-2000 -3.2%. **Pop 2000:** 5,120 (White 92.7%; Black or African American 0.1%; Hispanic or Latino 6.3%; Asian 0.1%; Other 4.3%). **Foreign born:** 2.6%. **Median age:** 39.2.

Income 2000: per capita $20,443; median household $40,534; **Pop below poverty level:** 5.1%. ***Personal per capita income 2000-2003:** $27,062-$29,037.

Unemployment 2004: 3.3%. **Change from 2000:** +1.5%. **Median travel time to work:** 14 minutes. **Working outside county of residence:** 11.1%.

Cities with pop over 10,000: None.

SEDGWICK COUNTY
525 N Main St Rm 211   **Ph:** 316-660-9222
Wichita, KS 67203   **Fax:** 316-383-7961
www.sedgwick.ks.us

In south-central KS, southeast of Hutchinson; organized Feb 26, 1867 from Butler County. **Name Origin:** For Gen. John Sedgwick (1813-64), Indian fighter and Union officer in the Civil War.

Area (sq mi): 1009.41 (land 999.38; water 10.03). **Pop per sq mi:** 466.4.

Pop 2005: 466,061. **State rank:** 2. **Pop change:** 2000-20005 +2.9%; 1990-2000 +12.2%. **Pop 2000:** 452,869 (White 76.4%; Black or African American 9.1%; Hispanic or Latino 8%; Asian 3.3%; Other 8.2%, including 1.1% American Indian/Alaska Native). **Foreign born:** 6.6%. **Median age:** 33.6.

Income 2000: per capita $20,907; median household $42,485; **Pop below poverty level:** 9.5%. ***Personal per capita income 2000-2003:** $28,447-$30,778.

Unemployment 2004: 6.2%. **Change from 2000:** +2%. **Median travel time to work:** 18.7 minutes. **Working outside county of residence:** 3.5%.

Cities with pop over 10,000: Wichita 🏛 (353,823); Derby (20,326).

SEWARD COUNTY
415 N Washington Ave Suite 109   **Ph:** 620-626-3200
Liberal, KS 67901   **Fax:** 620-626-3211
www.seward.kansasgov.com

On the southern border of KS, southwest of Dodge City; organized as Godfrey County Mar 26, 1873 from Indian lands; name changed to Seward Jun 3, 1861; changed to Howard 1867. In 1873 the name Seward was given to a new county in the present location. **Name Origin:** For William Henry Seward (1801-72), U.S. secretary of state (1861-69), renowned for negotiating the purchase of Alaska (1867).

Area (sq mi): 640.51 (land 639.52; water 0.99). **Pop per sq mi:** 36.4.

Pop 2005: 23,274. **State rank:** 25. **Pop change:** 2000-20005 +3.4%; 1990-2000 +20.1%. **Pop 2000:** 22,510 (White 49.4%; Black or African American 3.8%; Hispanic or Latino 42.1%; Asian 2.9%; Other 28%). **Foreign born:** 27.4%. **Median age:** 29.

Income 2000: per capita $15,059; median household $36,752; **Pop below poverty level:** 16.9%. ***Personal per capita income 2000-2003:** $22,085-$21,769.

Unemployment 2004: 4.2%. **Change from 2000:** +0.7%. **Median travel time to work:** 14.8 minutes. **Working outside county of residence:** 9.3%.

Cities with pop over 10,000: Liberal 🏛 (20,218).

---

*Source: Personal per capita income data are from the Bureau of Economic Analysis; per capita income data are from the Bureau of the Census. See Introduction for explanation of differences.

SHAWNEE COUNTY

200 SE 7th St   **Ph:** 785-233-8200
Topeka, KS 66603   **Fax:** 785-291-4912
www.co.shawnee.ks.us

In northeastern KS, west of Lawrence; original county; organized Aug 25, 1855 (prior to statehood). **Name Origin:** For the Indian tribe of Algonquian linguistic stock. Name means 'southerner.'

Area (sq mi): 556.32 (land 549.82; water 6.5). **Pop per sq mi:** 313.5.

Pop 2005: 172,365. **State rank:** 3. **Pop change:** 2000 20005 ₊1.5%; 1990-2000 +5.5%. **Pop 2000:** 169,871 (White 79.9%; Black or African American 9%; Hispanic or Latino 7.3%; Asian 1%; Other 7.1%, including 1.2% American Indian/Alaska Native). **Foreign born:** 2.7%. **Median age:** 37.1.

Income 2000: per capita $20,904; median household $40,988; **Pop below poverty level:** 9.6%. ***Personal per capita income 2000-2003:** $28,049-$29,710.

Unemployment 2004: 6.1%. **Change from 2000:** +2%. **Median travel time to work:** 18 minutes. **Working outside county of residence:** 6.7%.

Cities with pop over 10,000: Topeka 🏛 (121,809).

SHERIDAN COUNTY

PO Box 899   **Ph:** 785-675-3361
Hoxie, KS 67740   **Fax:** 785-675-3487

In northwestern KS, southwest of Norton; organized Mar 20, 1873 from unorganized territory. **Name Origin:** For Gen. Philip Henry Sheridan (1831-88), Union officer during the Civil War and commander in chief of the U.S. army (1883-88).

Area (sq mi): 896.61 (land 896.36; water 0.25). **Pop per sq mi:** 2.9.

Pop 2005: 2,591. **State rank:** 97. **Pop change:** 2000-20005 -7.9%; 1990-2000 -7.6%. **Pop 2000:** 2,813 (White 97.9%; Black or African American 0.1%; Hispanic or Latino 1.5%; Asian 0.1%; Other 1.2%). **Foreign born:** 0.4%. **Median age:** 41.5.

Income 2000: per capita $16,299; median household $33,547; **Pop below poverty level:** 15.7%. ***Personal per capita income 2000-2003:** $23,941-$30,897.

Unemployment 2004: 3.2%. **Change from 2000:** +1.5%. **Median travel time to work:** 12.8 minutes. **Working outside county of residence:** 17.4%.

Cities with pop over 10,000: None.

SHERMAN COUNTY

813 Broadway Rm 102   **Ph:** 785-899-4800
Goodland, KS 67735   **Fax:** 785-899-4844
www.sherman.kansasgov.com

On the northwestern border of KS; organized Mar 20, 1873 from Kirwin Land District. **Name Origin:** For Gen. William Tecumseh Sherman (1820-91), officer in the Mexican-American War and the Civil War, leader of the 'march to the sea' through the Southern states; remembered for the statement 'War is hell.'

Area (sq mi): 1056.01 (land 1055.8; water 0.21). **Pop per sq mi:** 5.8.

Pop 2005: 6,153. **State rank:** 59. **Pop change:** 2000-20005 -9%; 1990-2000 -2.4%. **Pop 2000:** 6,760 (White 90%; Black or African American 0.4%; Hispanic or Latino 8.4%; Asian 0.2%; Other 5.6%). **Foreign born:** 1.8%. **Median age:** 37.8.

Income 2000: per capita $16,761; median household $32,684; **Pop below poverty level:** 12.9%. ***Personal per capita income 2000-2003:** $23,928-$25,232.

Unemployment 2004: 3.4%. **Change from 2000:** +1%. **Median travel time to work:** 13.2 minutes. **Working outside county of residence:** 9.4%.

Cities with pop over 10,000: None.

SMITH COUNTY

218 S Grant St   **Ph:** 785-282-5110
Smith Center, KS 66967   **Fax:** 785-282-5114

On the central northern border of KS; established Feb 26, 1867 from unorganized territory. **Name Origin:** For Maj. J. Nelson Smith (?-1864), Union officer killed at the battle of Little Blue, MO.

Area (sq mi): 896.53 (land 895.43; water 1.1). **Pop per sq mi:** 4.6.

Pop 2005: 4,121. **State rank:** 76. **Pop change:** 2000-20005 -9.1%; 1990-2000 -10.7%. **Pop 2000:** 4,536 (White 98.4%; Black or African American 0.1%; Hispanic or Latino 0.7%; Asian 0%; Other 1%). **Foreign born:** 0.6%. **Median age:** 46.

Income 2000: per capita $14,983; median household $28,486; **Pop below poverty level:** 10.7%. ***Personal per capita income 2000-2003:** $21,863-$24,908.

Unemployment 2004: 3.8%. **Change from 2000:** +1.9%. **Median travel time to work:** 15.4 minutes. **Working outside county of residence:** 15.7%.

Cities with pop over 10,000: None.

STAFFORD COUNTY

209 N Broadway St   **Ph:** 620-549-3509
Saint John, KS 67576   **Fax:** 620-549-3481
www.staffordcounty.org

In south-central KS, west of Hutchinson; established Feb 26, 1867 from unorganized territory. **Name Origin:** For Capt. Lewis Stafford (?-1863), Union army officer killed at Young's Point, LA.

Area (sq mi): 794.72 (land 792.05; water 2.67). **Pop per sq mi:** 5.7.

Pop 2005: 4,488. **State rank:** 74. **Pop change:** 2000-20005 -6.3%; 1990-2000 -10.7%. **Pop 2000:** 4,789 (White 93%; Black or African American 0.1%; Hispanic or Latino 5.4%; Asian 0.1%; Other 4.8%). **Foreign born:** 3.6%. **Median age:** 41.

Income 2000: per capita $16,409; median household $31,107; **Pop below poverty level:** 11.8%. ***Personal per capita income 2000-2003:** $23,608-$25,477.

Unemployment 2004: 4.2%. **Change from 2000:** +1.9%. **Median travel time to work:** 17.8 minutes. **Working outside county of residence:** 26.2%.

Cities with pop over 10,000: None.

STANTON COUNTY

PO Box 190   **Ph:** 620-492-2140
Johnson, KS 67855   **Fax:** 620-492-2688

On the southwestern border of KS, southwest of Garden City; created Mar 6, 1873, later abolished and made part of Hamilton County; in 1887 Stanton County was reorganized from Hamilton County. **Name Origin:** For Edwin McMasters Stanton (1814-69),

Stanton County (cont'd)

U.S. Attorney General (1860-61) and U.S. Secretary of War under Abraham Lincoln and Andrew Johnson (1862-68).

Area (sq mi): 680.06 (land 680; water 0.06). **Pop per sq mi:** 3.3.

Pop 2005: 2,245. **State rank:** 100. **Pop change:** 2000-20005 -6.7%; 1990-2000 +3.1%. **Pop 2000:** 2,406 (White 74%; Black or African American 0.6%; Hispanic or Latino 23.7%; Asian 0.2%; Other 14.8%, including 1.2% American Indian/Alaska Native). **Foreign born:** 12.7%. **Median age:** 33.8.

Income 2000: per capita $18,043; median household $40,172; **Pop below poverty level:** 14.9%. ***Personal per capita income 2000-2003:** $23,618-$24,199.

Unemployment 2004: 3.4%. **Change from 2000:** +1.3%. **Median travel time to work:** 16.2 minutes. **Working outside county of residence:** 18.1%.

Cities with pop over 10,000: None.

STEVENS COUNTY
200 E 6th St   **Ph:** 620-544-2541
Hugoton, KS 67951   **Fax:** 620-544-4094
www.stevenscoks.org

On the southwestern border of KS; organized Mar 6, 1873 from Indian lands. **Name Origin:** For Thaddeus Stevens (1792-1868), U.S. representative from PA (1849-53; 1859-68) who strongly opposed slavery.

Area (sq mi): 727.71 (land 727.53; water 0.18). **Pop per sq mi:** 7.4.

Pop 2005: 5,412. **State rank:** 67. **Pop change:** 2000-20005 -0.9%; 1990-2000 +8.2%. **Pop 2000:** 5,463 (White 75.5%; Black or African American 0.9%; Hispanic or Latino 21.7%; Asian 0.2%; Other 15.8%). **Foreign born:** 12%. **Median age:** 33.6.

Income 2000: per capita $17,814; median household $41,830; **Pop below poverty level:** 10.3%. ***Personal per capita income 2000-2003:** $25,578-$23,673.

Unemployment 2004: 4.2%. **Change from 2000:** +1.4%. **Median travel time to work:** 12.5 minutes. **Working outside county of residence:** 18.2%.

Cities with pop over 10,000: None.

SUMNER COUNTY
501 N Washington Ave   **Ph:** 620-326-3395
Wellington, KS 67152   **Fax:** 620-326-2116
co.sumner.ks.us

On the central southern border of KS, south of Wichita; organized Feb 26, 1867 from Cowley County. **Name Origin:** For Charles Sumner (1811-74), a founder (1848) of the Free-Soil Party and U.S. senator from MA (1851-74); he was physically beaten on the floor of the Senate for his anti-slavery stand.

Area (sq mi): 1184.78 (land 1181.81; water 2.98). **Pop per sq mi:** 21.

Pop 2005: 24,797. **State rank:** 23. **Pop change:** 2000-20005 -4.4%; 1990-2000 +0.4%. **Pop 2000:** 25,946 (White 92.8%; Black or African American 0.7%; Hispanic or Latino 3.6%; Asian 0.2%; Other 4.6%, including 1.1% American Indian/Alaska Native). **Foreign born:** 0.8%. **Median age:** 37.6.

Income 2000: per capita $18,305; median household $39,415; **Pop below poverty level:** 9.5%. ***Personal per capita income 2000-2003:** $23,449-$24,880.

Unemployment 2004: 6.4%. **Change from 2000:** +2.3%. **Median travel time to work:** 22.6 minutes. **Working outside county of residence:** 41.9%.

Cities with pop over 10,000: None.

THOMAS COUNTY
300 N Court Ave   **Ph:** 785-460-4500
Colby, KS 67701   **Fax:** 785-460-4512

In northwestern KS; organized Mar 6, 1873 from Kirwin Land District; reorganized Oct 8, 1895 with territory annexed from Logan County. **Name Origin:** For Gen. George Henry Thomas (1816-70), Union commander of the Army of the Cumberland.

Area (sq mi): 1074.9 (land 1074.78; water 0.11). **Pop per sq mi:** 7.1.

Pop 2005: 7,639. **State rank:** 51. **Pop change:** 2000-20005 -6.6%; 1990-2000 -0.9%. **Pop 2000:** 8,180 (White 96.4%; Black or African American 0.4%; Hispanic or Latino 1.8%; Asian 0.3%; Other 2.2%). **Foreign born:** 0.4%. **Median age:** 35.3.

Income 2000: per capita $19,028; median household $37,034; **Pop below poverty level:** 9.7%. ***Personal per capita income 2000-2003:** $23,220-$26,111.

Unemployment 2004: 3.4%. **Change from 2000:** +1.4%. **Median travel time to work:** 11.7 minutes. **Working outside county of residence:** 9.6%.

Cities with pop over 10,000: None.

TREGO COUNTY
216 N Main St   **Ph:** 785-743-5773
WaKeeney, KS 67672   **Fax:** 785-743-5594

In west-central KS, west of Hays; established Feb 26, 1867. **Name Origin:** For Capt. Edgar P. Trego (?-1863), Union army officer killed at Chickamauga, TN.

Area (sq mi): 899.02 (land 888.29; water 10.73). **Pop per sq mi:** 3.4.

Pop 2005: 3,050. **State rank:** 88. **Pop change:** 2000-20005 -8.1%; 1990-2000 -10.2%. **Pop 2000:** 3,319 (White 97.3%; Black or African American 0.2%; Hispanic or Latino 0.8%; Asian 0.5%; Other 1.7%). **Foreign born:** 0.5%. **Median age:** 43.5.

Income 2000: per capita $16,239; median household $29,677; **Pop below poverty level:** 12.3%. ***Personal per capita income 2000-2003:** $19,397-$20,634.

Unemployment 2004: 3.3%. **Change from 2000:** +1.1%. **Median travel time to work:** 16.4 minutes. **Working outside county of residence:** 23.7%.

Cities with pop over 10,000: None.

UNIFIED GOVERNMENT OF WYANDOTTE COUNTY/ KANSAS CITY
701 N 7th St   **Ph:** 913-573-5260
Kansas City, KS 66101   **Fax:** 913-321-0237
www.wycokck.org

On northeastern border of KS, east of Topeka; original county; organized Jan 29, 1859 (prior to statehood). **Name Origin:** For the

Source: Personal per capita income data are from the Bureau of Economic Analysis; per capita income data are from the Bureau of the Census. See Introduction for explanation of differences.

Wyandotte County/Kansas City (cont'd)

Wyandotte Indians, a tribe of Iroquoian linguistic stock. Name is thought to mean 'islanders' or 'those who live on a peninsula' from their original home on islands in the Saint Lawrence River and on a peninsula.

Area (sq mi): 155.69 (land 151.39; water 4.3). **Pop per sq mi:** 1028.8

Pop 2005: 155,750. **State rank:** 4. **Pop change:** 2000-20005 1.4%; 1990-2000 -2.5%. **Pop 2000:** 157,882 (White 51.6%; Black or African American 28.3%; Hispanic or Latino 16%; Asian 1.6%; Other 11.8%). **Foreign born:** 9.5%. **Median age:** 32.5.

Income 2000: per capita $16,005; median household $33,784; **Pop below poverty level:** 16.5%. ***Personal per capita income 2000-2003:** $19,775-$21,534.

Unemployment 2004: 9.3%. **Change from 2000:** +1%. **Median travel time to work:** 21.5 minutes. **Working outside county of residence:** 52.1%.

Cities with pop over 10,000: Kansas City 🏛 (145,004).

WABAUNSEE COUNTY
215 Kansas Ave PO box 278   **Ph:** 785-765-3414
Alma, KS 66401   **Fax:** 785-765-3704
www.wabaunsee.kansasgov.com

In east-central KS, west of Topeka; organized as Richardson County Aug 30, 1855 (prior to statehood); name changed Feb 11, 1859. **Name Origin:** For Wabaunsee (1760-1845), a Potawatomi chief. Meaning of the name is uncertain: possibly 'dawn of day'; others not sufficiently documented or satisfactory are 'he lives through the winter,' 'daylight,' and 'boggy day.'

Area (sq mi): 799.8 (land 797.38; water 2.41). **Pop per sq mi:** 8.7.

Pop 2005: 6,919. **State rank:** 54. **Pop change:** 2000-20005 +0.5%; 1990-2000 +4.3%. **Pop 2000:** 6,885 (White 96.3%; Black or African American 0.5%; Hispanic or Latino 1.9%; Asian 0.1%; Other 2.2%). **Foreign born:** 0.7%. **Median age:** 39.5.

Income 2000: per capita $17,704; median household $41,710; **Pop below poverty level:** 7.3%. ***Personal per capita income 2000-2003:** $23,541-$24,577.

Unemployment 2004: 4.9%. **Change from 2000:** +1.3%. **Median travel time to work:** 29.4 minutes. **Working outside county of residence:** 64.4%.

Cities with pop over 10,000: None.

WALLACE COUNTY
PO Box 70   **Ph:** 785-852-4282
Sharon Springs, KS 67758   **Fax:** 785-852-4783

On central western border of KS; organized Mar 2, 1868 from Indian lands. **Name Origin:** For Gen. William Harvey Lamb Wallace (?-1862), Union officer in the Civil War who died of wounds received at Shiloh, TN.

Area (sq mi): 914.05 (land 913.99; water 0.05). **Pop per sq mi:** 1.7.

Pop 2005: 1,573. **State rank:** 104. **Pop change:** 2000-20005 -10.1%; 1990-2000 -4%. **Pop 2000:** 1,749 (White 92.8%; Black or African American 0.6%; Hispanic or Latino 4.8%; Asian 0.2%; Other 4.6%). **Foreign born:** 2.2%. **Median age:** 39.5.

Income 2000: per capita $17,016; median household $33,000; **Pop below poverty level:** 16.1%. ***Personal per capita income 2000-2003:** $21,309-$25,809.

Unemployment 2004: 3.2%. **Change from 2000:** +0.2%. **Median travel time to work:** 18.7 minutes. **Working outside county of residence:** 11.7%.

Cities with pop over 10,000: None.

WASHINGTON COUNTY
214 C St   **Ph:** 785-325-2974
Washington, KS 66968   **Fax:** 785-325-2303

On the northern border of KS; northwest of Manhattan; original county; established Feb 20, 1857 (prior to statehood). **Name Origin:** For George Washington (1732-99), American patriot and first U.S. president.

Area (sq mi): 898.84 (land 898.46; water 0.38). **Pop per sq mi:** 6.7.

Pop 2005: 6,009. **State rank:** 63. **Pop change:** 2000-20005 -7.3%; 1990-2000 -8.3%. **Pop 2000:** 6,483 (White 98.4%; Black or African American 0.1%; Hispanic or Latino 0.6%; Asian 0%; Other 0.9%). **Foreign born:** 0.5%. **Median age:** 43.6.

Income 2000: per capita $15,515; median household $29,363; **Pop below poverty level:** 10.1%. ***Personal per capita income 2000-2003:** $20,438-$21,020.

Unemployment 2004: 4%. **Change from 2000:** +0.9%. **Median travel time to work:** 18.6 minutes. **Working outside county of residence:** 27.6%.

Cities with pop over 10,000: None.

WICHITA COUNTY
PO Box 968   **Ph:** 620-375-2731
Leoti, KS 67861   **Fax:** 620-375-4350

In western KS, northwest of Garden City; organized Mar 6, 1873 from Indian lands. **Name Origin:** For the Wichita Indians, one of the more important tribes of Caddoan linguistic stock. Name is translated 'man,' or from Choctaw *owa chito* 'big hunt.'

Area (sq mi): 718.54 (land 718.52; water 0.02). **Pop per sq mi:** 3.2.

Pop 2005: 2,309. **State rank:** 98. **Pop change:** 2000-20005 -8.8%; 1990-2000 -8.2%. **Pop 2000:** 2,531 (White 80%; Black or African American 0.1%; Hispanic or Latino 18.4%; Asian 0.1%; Other 13.6%). **Foreign born:** 8%. **Median age:** 36.7.

Income 2000: per capita $16,720; median household $33,462; **Pop below poverty level:** 14.8%. ***Personal per capita income 2000-2003:** $28,908-$30,226.

Unemployment 2004: 3.6%. **Change from 2000:** +0.4%. **Median travel time to work:** 13 minutes. **Working outside county of residence:** 12.5%.

Cities with pop over 10,000: None.

WILSON COUNTY
615 Madison St   **Ph:** 620-378-2186
Fredonia, KS 66736   **Fax:** 620-378-3841
www.wilson.kansasgov.com

In southeastern KS, south of Iola; original county; organized Aug 25, 1855 (prior to statehood). **Name Origin:** For Hiero T. Wilson (1806-?), army officer, settler, and merchant.

Wilson County (cont'd)

Area (sq mi): 574.97 (land 573.81; water 1.17). **Pop per sq mi:** 17.1.

Pop 2005: 9,834. **State rank:** 43. **Pop change:** 2000-20005 -4.8%; 1990-2000 +0.4%. **Pop 2000:** 10,332 (White 95.9%; Black or African American 0.4%; Hispanic or Latino 1.7%; Asian 0.3%; Other 2.6%). **Foreign born:** 0.6%. **Median age:** 40.6.

Income 2000: per capita $14,910; median household $29,747; **Pop below poverty level:** 11.3%. ***Personal per capita income 2000-2003:** $20,293-$22,014.

Unemployment 2004: 5.2%. **Change from 2000:** -0.2%. **Median travel time to work:** 16.4 minutes. **Working outside county of residence:** 22.1%.

Cities with pop over 10,000: None.

WOODSON COUNTY

105 W Rutledge St   **Ph:** 620-625-2179
Yates Center, KS 66783   **Fax:** 620-625-8670
www.woodsoncounty.net

In southeastern KS, east of Wichita; original county; organized Aug 25, 1855 (prior to statehood). **Name Origin:** For Daniel Woodson, secretary of KS Territory (1854-57).

Area (sq mi): 505.45 (land 500.61; water 4.85). **Pop per sq mi:** 7.1.

Pop 2005: 3,572. **State rank:** 79. **Pop change:** 2000-20005 -5.7%; 1990-2000 -8%. **Pop 2000:** 3,788 (White 96.2%; Black or African American 0.8%; Hispanic or Latino 1.4%; Asian 0.1%; Other 2.2%). **Foreign born:** 0.8%. **Median age:** 44.1.

Income 2000: per capita $14,283; median household $25,335; **Pop below poverty level:** 13.2%. ***Personal per capita income 2000-2003:** $18,386-$18,905.

Unemployment 2004: 7.2%. **Change from 2000:** -0.5%. **Median travel time to work:** 21.7 minutes. **Working outside county of residence:** 40%.

Cities with pop over 10,000: None.

*Source: Personal per capita income data are from the Bureau of Economic Analysis; per capita income data are from the Bureau of the Census. See Introduction for explanation of differences.

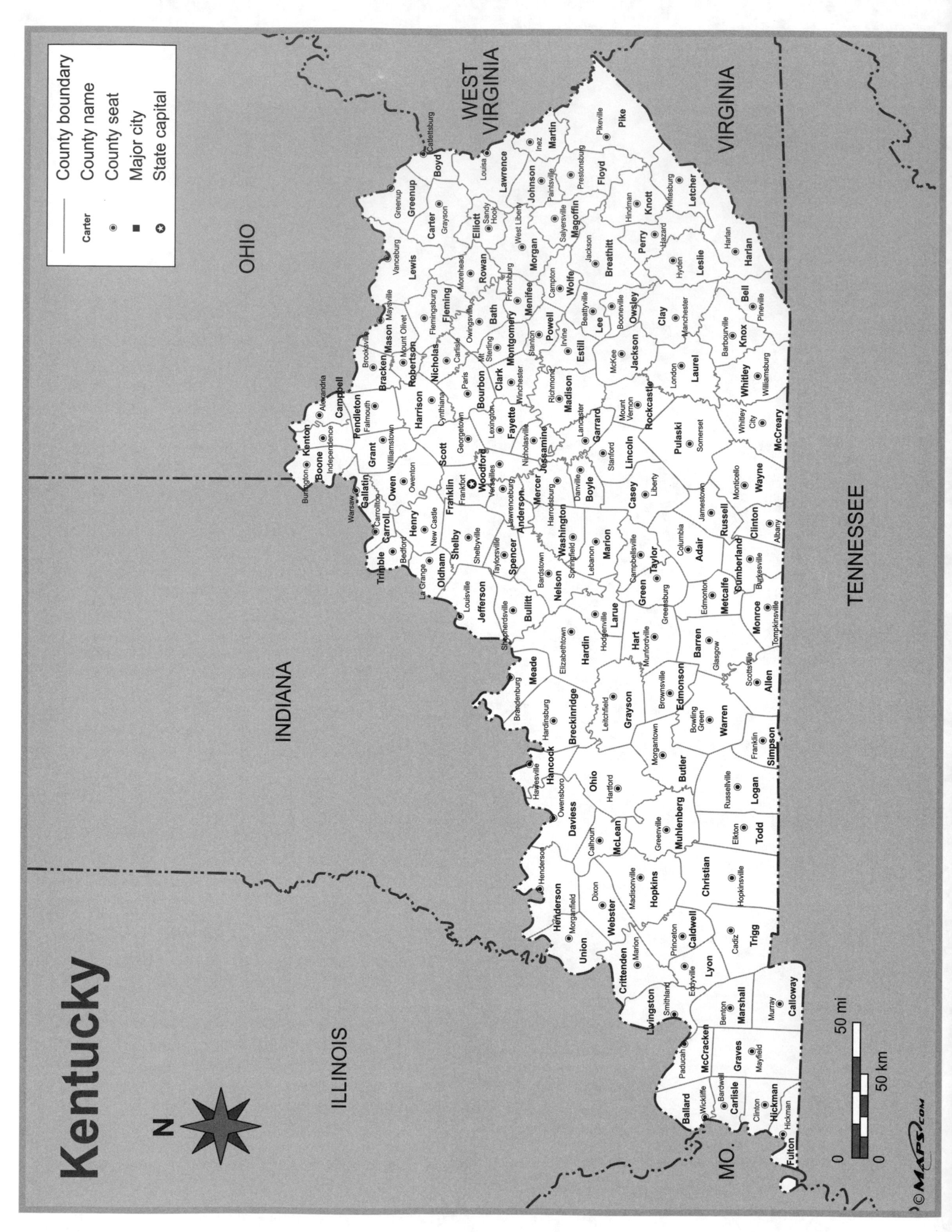

Kentucky

N

County boundary
Carter — County name
County seat ⊙
Major city ■
State capital ✪

OHIO

INDIANA

ILLINOIS

MO.

WEST VIRGINIA

VIRGINIA

TENNESSEE

50 mi
50 km
0
0

Greenup • Greenup
Boyd • Catlettsburg
Louisa • Lawrence
Inez • Martin
Pikeville • Pike
Vanceburg • Lewis
Carter • Grayson
Elliott • Sandy Hook
Johnson • Paintsville
Prestonsburg • Floyd
Whitesburg • Letcher
Mount Olivet • Robertson
Fleming • Flemingsburg
Rowan • Morehead
Morgan • West Liberty
Salyersville • Magoffin
Jackson • Breathitt
Hindman • Knott
Perry • Hazard
Harlan • Harlan
Maysville • Mason
Brooksville • Bracken
Nicholas • Carlisle
Bath • Owingsville
Mt Sterling • Montgomery
Menifee • Frenchburg
Campton • Wolfe
Powell • Stanton
Lee • Beattyville
Booneville • Owsley
Leslie • Hyden
Bell • Pineville
Barbourville • Knox
Alexandria • Campbell
Falmouth • Pendleton
Harrison • Cynthiana
Paris • Bourbon
Georgetown • Scott
Lexington • Fayette
Clark • Winchester
Nicholasville • Jessamine
Richmond • Madison
Estill • Irvine
McKee • Jackson
Clay • Manchester
Mount Vernon • Rockcastle
Laurel • London
Whitley City • Whitley
Williamsburg • Whitley
McCreary
Burlington • Boone
Kenton • Independence
Grant • Williamstown
Owen • Owenton
Warsaw • Gallatin
Carrollton • Carroll
New Castle • Henry
Franklin • Frankfort ✪
Woodford • Versailles
Anderson • Lawrenceburg
Mercer • Harrodsburg
Danville • Boyle
Garrard • Lancaster
Lincoln • Stanford
Casey • Liberty
Pulaski • Somerset
Wayne • Monticello
Clinton • Albany
Jamestown • Russell
Cumberland • Burkesville
Adair • Columbia
Bedford • Trimble
Oldham • La Grange
Shelby • Shelbyville
Spencer • Taylorsville
Jefferson • Louisville
Bullitt • Shepherdsville
Nelson • Bardstown
Washington • Springfield
Marion • Lebanon
Taylor • Campbellsville
Green • Greensburg
Metcalfe • Edmonton
Monroe • Tompkinsville
Meade • Brandenburg
Hardin • Elizabethtown
Breckinridge • Hardinsburg
Grayson • Leitchfield
Hart • Munfordville
Larue • Hodgenville
Barren • Glasgow
Allen • Scottsville
Simpson • Franklin
Warren • Bowling Green
Edmonson • Brownsville
Hancock • Hawesville
Daviess • Owensboro
Ohio • Hartford
McLean • Calhoun
Butler • Morgantown
Muhlenberg • Greenville
Logan • Russellville
Todd • Elkton
Henderson • Henderson
Webster • Dixon
Hopkins • Madisonville
Christian • Hopkinsville
Union • Morganfield
Crittenden • Marion
Caldwell • Princeton
Lyon • Eddyville
Trigg • Cadiz
Livingston • Smithland
Marshall • Benton
Calloway • Murray
Ballard • Wickliffe
Bardwell • Carlisle
McCracken • Paducah
Graves • Mayfield
Hickman • Clinton
Fulton • Hickman

Kentucky

KENTUCKY STATE INFORMATION

www.kentucky.gov   Ph: 502-564-2500

Area (sq mi): 40,409.02 (land 39,728.18; water 680.85). **Pop per sq mi:** 105.

Pop 2005: 4,173,405. **Pop change:** 2000-20005 +3.3%; 1990-2000 +9.7%. **Pop 2000:** 4,041,769 (White 89.3%; Black or African American 7.3%; Hispanic or Latino 1.5%; Asian 0.7%; Other 1.9%). **Foreign born:** 2%. **Median age:** 35.9.

Income 2000: per capita $18,093; median household $33,672; **Pop below poverty level:** 15.8%. ***Personal per capita income 2000-2003:** $24,412-$26,575.

Unemployment 2004: 5.5%. **Change from 2000:** +1.3%. **Median travel time to work:** 23.5 minutes. **Working outside county of residence:** 30.3%.

ADAIR COUNTY
424 Public Sq   Ph: 270-384-2801
Columbia, KY 42728   Fax: 270-384-4805
columbia-adaircounty.com

On central southern border of KY, southeast of Bowling Green; established Dec 11, 1802 from Green County. **Name Origin:** For John Adair (1757-1840), governor of KY (1820-24).

Area (sq mi): 412.23 (land 406.84; water 5.39). **Pop per sq mi:** 43.2.

Pop 2005: 17,573. **State rank:** 62. **Pop change:** 2000-20005 +1.9%; 1990-2000 +12.3%. **Pop 2000:** 17,244 (White 95.5%; Black or African American 2.6%; Hispanic or Latino 0.8%; Asian 0.3%; Other 1.2%). **Foreign born:** 0.6%. **Median age:** 36.9.

Income 2000: per capita $14,931; median household $24,055; **Pop below poverty level:** 24%. ***Personal per capita income 2000-2003:** $18,111-$19,122.

Unemployment 2004: 5%. **Change from 2000:** +0.1%. **Median travel time to work:** 25 minutes. **Working outside county of residence:** 37.7%.

Cities with pop over 10,000: None.

ALLEN COUNTY
201 W Main St Rm 6   Ph: 270-237-3706
Scottsville, KY 42164   Fax: 270-237-9206
www.allencountykentucky.com

On central southern border of KY, southeast of Bowling Green; organized Jan 11, 1815 from Warren and Barren counties. **Name Origin:** For John Allen, army officer killed in IN territory.

Area (sq mi): 352.04 (land 346.12; water 5.92). **Pop per sq mi:** 54.

Pop 2005: 18,706. **State rank:** 59. **Pop change:** 2000-20005 +5.1%; 1990-2000 +21.7%. **Pop 2000:** 17,800 (White 97.2%; Black or African American 1.1%; Hispanic or Latino 0.8%; Asian 0.1%; Other 1.3%). **Foreign born:** 0.8%. **Median age:** 36.2.

Income 2000: per capita $14,506; median household $31,238; **Pop below poverty level:** 17.3%. ***Personal per capita income 2000-2003:** $20,281-$21,960.

Unemployment 2004: 6.2%. **Change from 2000:** -1.1%. **Median travel time to work:** 26.3 minutes. **Working outside county of residence:** 44.6%.

Cities with pop over 10,000: None.

ANDERSON COUNTY
151 S Main St   Ph: 502-839-3041
Lawrenceburg, KY 40342   Fax: 502-839-3043

In north-central KY, west of Lexington; organized Jan 16, 1827 from Franklin, Mercer, and Washington counties. **Name Origin:** For Richard Clough Anderson, Jr. (1788-1826), KY legislator, U.S. representative (1817-21), and U.S. Minister to Colombia (1823).

Area (sq mi): 204.28 (land 202.67; water 1.61). **Pop per sq mi:** 100.6.

Pop 2005: 20,394. **State rank:** 54. **Pop change:** 2000-20005 +6.7%; 1990-2000 +31.2%. **Pop 2000:** 19,111 (White 96%; Black or African American 2.3%; Hispanic or Latino 0.8%; Asian 0.1%; Other 1%). **Foreign born:** 0.9%. **Median age:** 35.5.

Income 2000: per capita $18,621; median household $45,433; **Pop below poverty level:** 7.5%. ***Personal per capita income 2000-2003:** $24,171-$25,114.

Unemployment 2004: 4%. **Change from 2000:** -1.4%. **Median travel time to work:** 26.6 minutes. **Working outside county of residence:** 64.2%.

Cities with pop over 10,000: None.

BALLARD COUNTY
PO Box 145   Ph: 270-335-5168
Wickliffe, KY 42087   Fax: 270-335-3081
www.ballardconet.com

On western border, west of Paducah; organized Feb 15, 1842 from McCracken and Hickman counties. **Name Origin:** For Maj. Bland W. Ballard (1759-1853), professional Indian fighter and scout, army officer, and KY legislator.

Area (sq mi): 273.6 (land 251.16; water 22.44). **Pop per sq mi:** 33.

Pop 2005: 8,277. **State rank:** 107. **Pop change:** 2000-20005 -0.1%; 1990-2000 +4.9%. **Pop 2000:** 8,286 (White 94.9%; Black or African

Ballard County (cont'd)

American 2.9%; Hispanic or Latino 0.6%; Asian 0.2%; Other 1.6%). **Foreign born:** 0.8%. **Median age:** 39.6.

Income 2000: per capita $19,035; median household $32,130; **Pop below poverty level:** 13.6%. ***Personal per capita income 2000-2003:** $26,124-$27,433.

Unemployment 2004: 6.7%. **Change from 2000:** -0.7%. **Median travel time to work:** 23.7 minutes. **Working outside county of residence:** 47.6%.

Cities with pop over 10,000: None.

BARREN COUNTY

117 N Public Sq Suite 1A
Glasgow, KY 42141
www.barrencounty.com

Ph: 270-651-3783
Fax: 270-651-1083

In south-central KY, east of Bowling Green; established Feb 20, 1798 from Warren and Green counties. **Name Origin:** Descriptive of the treeless prairie. It is believed the Indians burned off the growth to facilitate buffalo hunting.

Area (sq mi): 499.93 (land 490.97; water 8.96). **Pop per sq mi:** 81.6.

Pop 2005: 40,073. **State rank:** 24. **Pop change:** 2000-20005 +5.4%; 1990-2000 +11.9%. **Pop 2000:** 38,033 (White 93.8%; Black or African American 4.1%; Hispanic or Latino 0.9%; Asian 0.4%; Other 1.1%). **Foreign born:** 1.2%. **Median age:** 38.

Income 2000: per capita $16,816; median household $31,240; **Pop below poverty level:** 15.6%. ***Personal per capita income 2000-2003:** $22,285-$22,780.

Unemployment 2004: 4.2%. **Change from 2000:** -1.3%. **Median travel time to work:** 19.9 minutes. **Working outside county of residence:** 19.9%.

Cities with pop over 10,000: Glasgow 🏛 (13,829).

BATH COUNTY

PO Box 609
Owingsville, KY 40360

Ph: 606-674-2613
Fax: 606-674-9526

In north-central KY, east of Lexington; organized Jan 15, 1811 from Montgomery County. **Name Origin:** For the hot springs in the area.

Area (sq mi): 283.94 (land 279.46; water 4.48). **Pop per sq mi:** 41.6.

Pop 2005: 11,626. **State rank:** 94. **Pop change:** 2000-20005 +4.9%; 1990-2000 +14.4%. **Pop 2000:** 11,085 (White 96.5%; Black or African American 1.8%; Hispanic or Latino 0.8%; Asian 0%; Other 1.3%). **Foreign born:** 0.7%. **Median age:** 37.4.

Income 2000: per capita $15,326; median household $26,018; **Pop below poverty level:** 21.9%. ***Personal per capita income 2000-2003:** $19,045-$19,266.

Unemployment 2004: 6.6%. **Change from 2000:** -1%. **Median travel time to work:** 28.7 minutes. **Working outside county of residence:** 58.6%.

Cities with pop over 10,000: None.

BELL COUNTY

PO Box 157
Pineville, KY 40977

Ph: 606-337-6143
Fax: 606-337-5415

On southeastern border of KY, west of Harlan; organized as Josh Bell County Feb 28, 1867 from Knox and Harlan counties; name shortened 1872. **Name Origin:** For Joshua Fry Bell (1811-70), KY legislator and U.S. representative (1845-47).

Area (sq mi): 361.35 (land 360.77; water 0.58). **Pop per sq mi:** 82.2.

Pop 2005: 29,665. **State rank:** 36. **Pop change:** 2000-20005 -1.3%; 1990-2000 -4.6%. **Pop 2000:** 30,060 (White 95.6%; Black or African American 2.4%; Hispanic or Latino 0.6%; Asian 0.3%; Other 1.1%). **Foreign born:** 0.7%. **Median age:** 37.

Income 2000: per capita $11,526; median household $19,057; **Pop below poverty level:** 31.1%. ***Personal per capita income 2000-2003:** $16,574-$17,788.

Unemployment 2004: 6.9%. **Change from 2000:** -1.9%. **Median travel time to work:** 24.8 minutes. **Working outside county of residence:** 19.6%.

Cities with pop over 10,000: Middlesborough (10,192).

BOONE COUNTY

2950 E Washington St
Burlington, KY 41005
www.boonecountyky.org

Ph: 859-334-3642
Fax: 859-334-2193

In northwestern KY, southwest of Cincinnati, OH; established Dec 13, 1798 from Campbell County. **Name Origin:** For Daniel Boone (1734?-1820), U.S. frontiersman and KY pioneer.

Area (sq mi): 256.96 (land 246.26; water 10.7). **Pop per sq mi:** 431.5.

Pop 2005: 106,272. **State rank:** 4. **Pop change:** 2000-20005 +23.6%; 1990-2000 +49.3%. **Pop 2000:** 85,991 (White 94%; Black or African American 1.5%; Hispanic or Latino 2%; Asian 1.3%; Other 1.9%). **Foreign born:** 3%. **Median age:** 33.4.

Income 2000: per capita $23,535; median household $53,593; **Pop below poverty level:** 5.6%. ***Personal per capita income 2000-2003:** $29,739-$31,158.

Unemployment 2004: 4.2%. **Change from 2000:** +0.1%. **Median travel time to work:** 24.4 minutes. **Working outside county of residence:** 47%.

Cities with pop over 10,000: Florence (25,449).

BOURBON COUNTY

301 Main St Suite 106
Paris, KY 40361
www.parisky.com

Ph: 859-987-2142
Fax: 859-987-5660

In north-central KY, northeast of Lexington; organized May 1, 1786 (prior to statehood) from Fayette County. **Name Origin:** For the French royal family that ruled in France, Spain, and Naples from the latter 1500s until the 1900s.

Area (sq mi): 291.66 (land 291.43; water 0.23). **Pop per sq mi:** 68.1.

Pop 2005: 19,833. **State rank:** 56. **Pop change:** 2000-20005 +2.4%; 1990-2000 +0.6%. **Pop 2000:** 19,360 (White 89.3%; Black or African American 6.9%; Hispanic or Latino 2.6%; Asian 0.1%; Other 2.5%). **Foreign born:** 2%. **Median age:** 37.6.

*Source: Personal per capita income data are from the Bureau of Economic Analysis; per capita income data are from the Bureau of the Census. See Introduction for explanation of differences.

Bourbon County (cont'd)

Income 2000: per capita $18,335; median household $35,038; **Pop below poverty level:** 14%. ***Personal per capita income 2000-2003:** $28,984-$28,532.

Unemployment 2004: 4.6%. **Change from 2000:** +0.4%. **Median travel time to work:** 25.5 minutes. **Working outside county of residence:** 47.7%.

Cities with pop over 10,000: None.

BOYD COUNTY

PO Box 523   **Ph:** 606-739-5116
Catlettsburg, KY 41129   **Fax:** 606-739-6357

On eastern border of KY; organized Feb 15, 1860 from Carter, Lawrence, and Greenup counties. **Name Origin:** For Linn Boyd (1800-59), KY legislator, U.S. representative (1835-37; 1839-55), and Speaker of the House (1851-55).

Area (sq mi): 161.82 (land 160.17; water 1.65). **Pop per sq mi:** 309.6.

Pop 2005: 49,594. **State rank:** 17. **Pop change:** 2000-20005 -0.3%, 1990-2000 -2.7%. **Pop 2000:** 49,752 (White 95.1%; Black or African American 2.5%; Hispanic or Latino 1.1%; Asian 0.3%; Other 1.2%). **Foreign born:** 1.1%. **Median age:** 39.7.

Income 2000: per capita $18,212; median household $32,749; **Pop below poverty level:** 15.5%. ***Personal per capita income 2000-2003:** $24,190-$27,230.

Unemployment 2004: 6%. **Change from 2000:** -0.6%. **Median travel time to work:** 20.6 minutes. **Working outside county of residence:** 27.7%.

Cities with pop over 10,000: Ashland (21,586).

BOYLE COUNTY

321 W Main St Rm 123   **Ph:** 859-238-1110
Danville, KY 40422   **Fax:** 859-238-1114
www.danville-ky.com

In central KY, southwest of Lexington; organized Feb 15, 1842 from Lincoln and Mercer counties (having the same county seat as the now-abolished Kentucky County, which was organized in 1776 from Fincastle County, VA). **Name Origin:** For John Boyle (1774-1835), KY legislator, U.S. representative (1803-09), and U.S. judge for District of KY (1826-35).

Area (sq mi): 182.99 (land 181.9; water 1.09). **Pop per sq mi:** 155.9.

Pop 2005: 28,363. **State rank:** 39. **Pop change:** 2000-20005 +2.4%; 1990-2000 +8%. **Pop 2000:** 27,697 (White 87%; Black or African American 9.7%; Hispanic or Latino 1.4%; Asian 0.6%; Other 1.9%). **Foreign born:** 1.8%. **Median age:** 36.9.

Income 2000: per capita $18,288; median household $35,241; **Pop below poverty level:** 11.9%. ***Personal per capita income 2000-2003:** $24,001-$25,597.

Unemployment 2004: 6.3%. **Change from 2000:** +1.2%. **Median travel time to work:** 18.7 minutes. **Working outside county of residence:** 26.7%.

Cities with pop over 10,000: Danville 🏛 (15,428).

BRACKEN COUNTY

PO Box 147   **Ph:** 606-735-2952
Brooksville, KY 41004   **Fax:** 606-735-2867

On northeastern border of KY, southeast of Cincinnati, OH; established Dec 14, 1796 from Campbell and Mason counties. **Name Origin:** For two creeks in the county, Big and Little Bracken, named for William Bracken, an early settler.

Area (sq mi): 208.89 (land 203.22; water 5.67). **Pop per sq mi:** 42.7.

Pop 2005: 8,670. **State rank:** 105. **Pop change:** 2000-20005 +4.7%; 1990-2000 +6.6%. **Pop 2000:** 8,279 (White 98.2%; Black or African American 0.6%; Hispanic or Latino 0.5%; Asian 0.1%; Other 0.9%). **Foreign born:** 0.3%. **Median age:** 36.8.

Income 2000: per capita $16,478; median household $34,823; **Pop below poverty level:** 10.8%. ***Personal per capita income 2000-2003:** $21,294-$21,071.

Unemployment 2004: 5.7%. **Change from 2000:** +0.9%. **Median travel time to work:** 37.4 minutes. **Working outside county of residence:** 66.7%.

Cities with pop over 10,000: None.

BREATHITT COUNTY

1137 Main St   **Ph:** 606-666-3810
Jackson, KY 41339   **Fax:** 606-666-3807
www.breathittcounty.com

In southeastern KY; organized Feb 8, 1839 from Estill, Clay, and Perry counties. **Name Origin:** For John Breathitt (1786-1834), KY governor (1832-34).

Area (sq mi): 495.29 (land 495.19; water 0.09). **Pop per sq mi:** 32.2.

Pop 2005: 15,957. **State rank:** 72. **Pop change:** 2000-20005 -0.9%; 1990-2000 +2.5%. **Pop 2000:** 16,100 (White 98.1%; Black or African American 0.4%; Hispanic or Latino 0.7%; Asian 0.3%; Other 0.6%). **Foreign born:** 0.4%. **Median age:** 35.9.

Income 2000: per capita $11,044; median household $19,155; **Pop below poverty level:** 33.2%. ***Personal per capita income 2000-2003:** $16,015-$17,859.

Unemployment 2004: 7.2%. **Change from 2000:** -2.8%. **Median travel time to work:** 33.6 minutes. **Working outside county of residence:** 33.3%.

Cities with pop over 10,000: None.

BRECKINRIDGE COUNTY

PO Box 538   **Ph:** 270-756-2246
Hardinsburg, KY 40143   **Fax:** 270-756-1569
www.breckinridgecounty.net

On western border of KY, southwest of Louisville; established Dec 9, 1799 from Hardin County. **Name Origin:** For John Breckinridge (1760-1806), U.S. senator from KY (1801-05) and U.S. attorney general (1805-06).

Area (sq mi): 585.53 (land 572.41; water 13.12). **Pop per sq mi:** 33.7.

Pop 2005: 19,293. **State rank:** 57. **Pop change:** 2000-20005 +3.5%; 1990-2000 +14.3%. **Pop 2000:** 18,648 (White 95.4%; Black or African American 2.9%; Hispanic or Latino 0.7%; Asian 0.1%; Other 1.2%). **Foreign born:** 0.5%. **Median age:** 38.5.

🏛 *County Seat*

Breckinridge County (cont'd)

Income 2000: per capita $15,402; median household $30,554; **Pop below poverty level:** 15.8%. ***Personal per capita income 2000-2003:** $19,584-$20,886.

Unemployment 2004: 6.1%. **Change from 2000:** -2.3%. **Median travel time to work:** 32.7 minutes. **Working outside county of residence:** 50.6%.

Cities with pop over 10,000: None.

BULLITT COUNTY

149 N Walnut St   **Ph:** 502-543-2513
Shepherdsville, KY 40165   **Fax:** 502-543-9121
www.bullittcounty.org

On western border of KY, south of Louisville; established Dec 13, 1796 from Jefferson and Nelson counties. **Name Origin:** For Alexander Scott Bullitt (1761-1816), first president of the KY senate (1792-99) and first lieutenant-governor (1800-08).

Area (sq mi): 300.2 (land 299.08; water 1.12). **Pop per sq mi:** 228.9.

Pop 2005: 68,474. **State rank:** 11. **Pop change:** 2000-20005 +11.8%; 1990-2000 +28.7%. **Pop 2000:** 61,236 (White 97.7%; Black or African American 0.4%; Hispanic or Latino 0.6%; Asian 0.3%; Other 1.3%). **Foreign born:** 0.6%. **Median age:** 34.5.

Income 2000: per capita $18,339; median household $45,106; **Pop below poverty level:** 7.9%. ***Personal per capita income 2000-2003:** $23,904-$24,674.

Unemployment 2004: 4.8%. **Change from 2000:** +0.6%. **Median travel time to work:** 25.9 minutes. **Working outside county of residence:** 72.5%.

Cities with pop over 10,000: None.

BUTLER COUNTY

PO Box 449   **Ph:** 270-526-5676
Morgantown, KY 42261   **Fax:** 270-526-2658

In western KY, north of Bowling Green; organized Jan 18, 1810 from Logan and Ohio counties. **Name Origin:** For Maj. Gen. Richard Butler (1743-91), officer and Indian commissioner after the American Revolution.

Area (sq mi): 431.52 (land 428.08; water 3.44). **Pop per sq mi:** 31.3.

Pop 2005: 13,414. **State rank:** 86. **Pop change:** 2000-20005 +3.1%; 1990-2000 +15.7%. **Pop 2000:** 13,010 (White 97.5%; Black or African American 0.5%; Hispanic or Latino 1%; Asian 0.2%; Other 1.4%). **Foreign born:** 1.8%. **Median age:** 36.3.

Income 2000: per capita $14,617; median household $29,405; **Pop below poverty level:** 16%. ***Personal per capita income 2000-2003:** $18,405-$18,476.

Unemployment 2004: 6.8%. **Change from 2000:** -0.1%. **Median travel time to work:** 27.7 minutes. **Working outside county of residence:** 39.6%.

Cities with pop over 10,000: None.

CALDWELL COUNTY

100 E Market St Rm 23   **Ph:** 270-365-6754
Princeton, KY 42445   **Fax:** 270-365-7447

In western KY, northwest of Hopkinsville; organized Jan 31, 1809 from Livingston County. **Name Origin:** For Gen. John Caldwell (?-1804), soldier, member of the KY conventions (1787-89), and legislator.

Area (sq mi): 348.18 (land 346.98; water 1.2). **Pop per sq mi:** 37.4.

Pop 2005: 12,973. **State rank:** 88. **Pop change:** 2000-20005 -0.7%; 1990-2000 -1.3%. **Pop 2000:** 13,060 (White 93.7%; Black or African American 4.8%; Hispanic or Latino 0.6%; Asian 0.2%; Other 1.1%). **Foreign born:** 0.5%. **Median age:** 41.2.

Income 2000: per capita $16,264; median household $28,686; **Pop below poverty level:** 15.9%. ***Personal per capita income 2000-2003:** $21,712-$22,960.

Unemployment 2004: 4.8%. **Change from 2000:** -0.2%. **Median travel time to work:** 23.6 minutes. **Working outside county of residence:** 37.2%.

Cities with pop over 10,000: None.

CALLOWAY COUNTY

101 S 5th St 2nd Fl   **Ph:** 270-753-3923
Murray, KY 42071   **Fax:** 270-759-9611

On southwestern border of KY, southeast of Paducah; established Dec 19, 1821 from Hickman County. **Name Origin:** For Col. Richard Calloway (?-1780), one of the founders, with Daniel Boone (1734?-1820) of Boonesborough.

Area (sq mi): 410.79 (land 386.25; water 24.53). **Pop per sq mi:** 90.9.

Pop 2005: 35,122. **State rank:** 30. **Pop change:** 2000-20005 +2.8%; 1990-2000 +11.2%. **Pop 2000:** 34,177 (White 92.7%; Black or African American 3.6%; Hispanic or Latino 1.4%; Asian 1.3%; Other 1.6%). **Foreign born:** 2.7%. **Median age:** 34.5.

Income 2000: per capita $16,566; median household $30,134; **Pop below poverty level:** 16.6%. ***Personal per capita income 2000-2003:** $23,922-$23,729.

Unemployment 2004: 4.9%. **Change from 2000:** -0.3%. **Median travel time to work:** 17.9 minutes. **Working outside county of residence:** 17.5%.

Cities with pop over 10,000: Murray 🏛 (15,270).

CAMPBELL COUNTY

340 York St   **Ph:** 859-292-3845
Newport, KY 41071   **Fax:** 859-292-0615
www.campbellcountyky.org

On northeastern tip of KY, southeast of Cincinnati, OH; established Dec 17, 1794 from Scott, Harrison, and Mason counties. **Name Origin:** Probably for George Washington Campbell (1769-1848), U.S. senator from TN (1811-14; 1815-18).

Area (sq mi): 159.43 (land 151.55; water 7.87). **Pop per sq mi:** 575.7.

Pop 2005: 87,251. **State rank:** 8. **Pop change:** 2000-20005 -1.5%; 1990-2000 +5.7%. **Pop 2000:** 88,616 (White 96.1%; Black or African American 1.6%; Hispanic or Latino 0.9%; Asian 0.5%; Other 1.3%). **Foreign born:** 1.4%. **Median age:** 35.2.

Income 2000: per capita $20,637; median household $41,903; **Pop below poverty level:** 9.3%. ***Personal per capita income 2000-2003:** $26,561-$29,450.

*Source: Personal per capita income data are from the Bureau of Economic Analysis; per capita income data are from the Bureau of the Census. See Introduction for explanation of differences.

Campbell County (cont'd)

Unemployment 2004: 4.7%. **Change from 2000:** +0.3%. **Median travel time to work:** 23.9 minutes. **Working outside county of residence:** 63.9%.

Cities with pop over 10,000: Newport 🏛 (16,086); Fort Thomas (15,733).

CARLISLE COUNTY

PO Box 176	**Ph:** 270-628-3233
Bardwell, KY 42023	**Fax:** 270-628-0191

On western border of KY, southwest of Paducah; organized Apr 3, 1886 from Ballard County. **Name Origin:** For John Griffin Carlisle (1835-1910), KY legislator, U.S. senator (1890-93), and U.S. secretary of the treasury (1893-97).

Area (sq mi): 199.02 (land 192.49; water 6.54). **Pop per sq mi:** 27.7.

Pop 2005: 5,329. **State rank:** 117. **Pop change:** 2000-20005 -0.4%; 1990-2000 +2.2%. **Pop 2000:** 5,351 (White 97.3%; Black or African American 1%; Hispanic or Latino 0.8%; Asian 0.1%; Other 1.2%). **Foreign born:** 0.2%. **Median age:** 39.5.

Income 2000: per capita $16,276; median household $30,087; **Pop below poverty level:** 13.1%. ***Personal per capita income 2000-2003:** $22,586-$23,255.

Unemployment 2004: 7%. **Change from 2000:** +0.9%. **Median travel time to work:** 28.2 minutes. **Working outside county of residence:** 61.9%.

Cities with pop over 10,000: None.

CARROLL COUNTY

440 Main St Courthouse	**Ph:** 502-732-7005
Carrollton, KY 41008	**Fax:** 502-732-7007
www.carrollcountyky.com	

On northwestern border of KY, northeast of Louisville; organized Feb 9, 1838 from Gallatin County. **Name Origin:** For Charles Carroll (1737-1832), signer of the Declaration of Independence, U.S. senator from MD (1789-92), and founder of the Baltimore and Ohio Railroad.

Area (sq mi): 137.27 (land 130.09; water 7.18). **Pop per sq mi:** 80.4.

Pop 2005: 10,454. **State rank:** 98. **Pop change:** 2000-20005 +2.9%; 1990-2000 +9.3%. **Pop 2000:** 10,155 (White 93.4%; Black or African American 1.9%; Hispanic or Latino 3.2%; Asian 0.2%; Other 2.6%). **Foreign born:** 1.9%. **Median age:** 35.9.

Income 2000: per capita $17,057; median household $35,925; **Pop below poverty level:** 14.9%. ***Personal per capita income 2000-2003:** $21,854-$24,786.

Unemployment 2004: 5.2%. **Change from 2000:** -1.8%. **Median travel time to work:** 19.5 minutes. **Working outside county of residence:** 22.2%.

Cities with pop over 10,000: None.

CARTER COUNTY

300 W Main St Rm 232	**Ph:** 606-474-5188
Grayson, KY 41143	**Fax:** 606-474-6883

In northeastern KY, southwest of Ashland; organized Feb 9, 1838 from Greenup and Lawrence counties. **Name Origin:** For Col. William Grayson Carter, a KY state senator.

Area (sq mi): 412.15 (land 410.6; water 1.55). **Pop per sq mi:** 66.5.

Pop 2005: 27,306. **State rank:** 40. **Pop change:** 2000-20005 +1.6%; 1990-2000 +10.5%. **Pop 2000:** 26,889 (White 98.5%; Black or African American 0.1%; Hispanic or Latino 0.6%; Asian 0.1%; Other 0.7%). **Foreign born:** 0.4%. **Median age:** 35.8.

Income 2000: per capita $13,442; median household $26,427; **Pop below poverty level:** 22.3%. ***Personal per capita income 2000-2003:** $16,745-$18,359.

Unemployment 2004: 8.2%. **Change from 2000:** -6.5%. **Median travel time to work:** 32.8 minutes. **Working outside county of residence:** 45%.

Cities with pop over 10,000: None.

CASEY COUNTY

PO Box 306	**Ph:** 606-787-6154
Liberty, KY 42539	**Fax:** 606-787-6154

In south-central KY, southwest of Lexington; established Nov 14, 1806 from Lincoln County. **Name Origin:** For Col. William Casey, a pioneer settler from VA.

Area (sq mi): 445.73 (land 445.61; water 0.12). **Pop per sq mi:** 36.6.

Pop 2005: 16,290. **State rank:** 70. **Pop change:** 2000-20005 +5.5%; 1990-2000 +8.7%. **Pop 2000:** 15,447 (White 97.5%; Black or African American 0.3%; Hispanic or Latino 1.3%; Asian 0.1%; Other 1.4%). **Foreign born:** 1.2%. **Median age:** 37.8.

Income 2000: per capita $12,867; median household $21,580; **Pop below poverty level:** 25.5%. ***Personal per capita income 2000-2003:** $17,422-$18,050.

Unemployment 2004: 5.8%. **Change from 2000:** -2.9%. **Median travel time to work:** 29.5 minutes. **Working outside county of residence:** 45.7%.

Cities with pop over 10,000: None.

CHRISTIAN COUNTY

511 S Main St	**Ph:** 270-887-4105
Hopkinsville, KY 42240	**Fax:** 270-885-5925
www.christiancounty.org	

On southwestern border of KY, west of Bowling Green; established Dec 13, 1796 from Logan County. **Name Origin:** For William Christian (1743-86), attorney and legislator, brother-in-law of Patrick Henry (1736-99).

Area (sq mi): 724.01 (land 721.32; water 2.69). **Pop per sq mi:** 97.2.

Pop 2005: 70,145. **State rank:** 10. **Pop change:** 2000-20005 -2.9%; 1990-2000 +4.8%. **Pop 2000:** 72,265 (White 68.1%; Black or African American 23.7%; Hispanic or Latino 4.8%; Asian 0.9%; Other 5.4%). **Foreign born:** 2.5%. **Median age:** 27.9.

Income 2000: per capita $14,611; median household $31,177; **Pop below poverty level:** 15%. ***Personal per capita income 2000-2003:** $21,110-$24,464.

Unemployment 2004: 6.2%. **Change from 2000:** -1%. **Median travel time to work:** 17.9 minutes. **Working outside county of residence:** 12.5%.

Cities with pop over 10,000: Hopkinsville 🏛 (28,953).

🏛 *County Seat*

CLARK COUNTY
34 S Main St Rm 103   Ph: 859-745-0200
Winchester, KY 40391   Fax: 859-737-5678

In central KY, east of Lexington; established Dec 6, 1792 from Bourbon and Fayette counties. **Name Origin:** For George Rogers Clark (1752-1818), general in the American Revolution and frontiersman in the Northwest Territory.

Area (sq mi): 255.16 (land 254.31; water 0.85). **Pop per sq mi:** 137.2.

Pop 2005: 34,887. **State rank:** 31. **Pop change:** 2000-20005 +5.3%; 1990-2000 +12.4%. **Pop 2000:** 33,144 (White 93%; Black or African American 4.8%; Hispanic or Latino 1.2%; Asian 0.2%; Other 1.4%). **Foreign born:** 1%. **Median age:** 36.8.

Income 2000: per capita $19,170; median household $39,946; **Pop below poverty level:** 10.6%. *****Personal per capita income 2000-2003:** $25,917-$27,682.

Unemployment 2004: 4.9%. **Change from 2000:** -0.6%. **Median travel time to work:** 25.6 minutes. **Working outside county of residence:** 45.2%.

Cities with pop over 10,000: Winchester 🏛 (16,412).

CLAY COUNTY
316 Main St Suite 108   Ph: 606-598-3663
Manchester, KY 40962   Fax: 606-598-4047

In southeastern KY; established Dec 2, 1806 from Madison, Knox, and Floyd counties. **Name Origin:** For Gen. Green Clay (1757-1826), pioneer surveyor, officer in War of 1812, and KY legislator.

Area (sq mi): 471.08 (land 471.01; water 0.07). **Pop per sq mi:** 51.3.

Pop 2005: 24,146. **State rank:** 48. **Pop change:** 2000-20005 -1.7%; 1990-2000 +12.9%. **Pop 2000:** 24,556 (White 93%; Black or African American 4.8%; Hispanic or Latino 1.4%; Asian 0.1%; Other 1.1%). **Foreign born:** 0.7%. **Median age:** 34.6.

Income 2000: per capita $9,716; median household $16,271; **Pop below poverty level:** 39.7%. *****Personal per capita income 2000-2003:** $14,067-$14,871.

Unemployment 2004: 7.6%. **Change from 2000:** +0.8%. **Median travel time to work:** 31.2 minutes. **Working outside county of residence:** 35.8%.

Cities with pop over 10,000: None.

CLINTON COUNTY
County Courthouse 100 S Croff St   Ph: 606-387-5943
Albany, KY 42602   Fax: 606-387-5258

On central southern border of KY; organized Feb 20, 1836 from Wayne and Cumberland counties. **Name Origin:** For De Witt Clinton (1769-1828), governor of NY, and supporter of the Erie Canal.

Area (sq mi): 205.54 (land 197.46; water 8.09). **Pop per sq mi:** 48.4.

Pop 2005: 9,559. **State rank:** 102. **Pop change:** 2000-20005 -0.8%; 1990-2000 +5.5%. **Pop 2000:** 9,634 (White 98.1%; Black or African American 0.1%; Hispanic or Latino 1.2%; Asian 0%; Other 0.7%). **Foreign born:** 0.8%. **Median age:** 39.

Income 2000: per capita $13,286; median household $19,563; **Pop below poverty level:** 25.8%. *****Personal per capita income 2000-2003:** $17,346-$19,602.

Unemployment 2004: 6.5%. **Change from 2000:** +1.4%. **Median travel time to work:** 21 minutes. **Working outside county of residence:** 25.7%.

Cities with pop over 10,000: None.

CRITTENDEN COUNTY
107 S Main St   Ph: 270-965-4200
Marion, KY 42064   Fax: 270-965-4572

On southwestern border of KY, northeast of Paducah; organized Jan 26, 1842 from Livingston County. **Name Origin:** For John Jordan Crittenden (1787-1863), U.S. senator from KY (1817-19; 1835-41; 1842-48; 1855-61), governor (1848-50), and U.S. Attorney General (1841; 1850-53).

Area (sq mi): 370.95 (land 362.14; water 8.81). **Pop per sq mi:** 24.8.

Pop 2005: 8,984. **State rank:** 104. **Pop change:** 2000-20005 -4.3%; 1990-2000 +2%. **Pop 2000:** 9,384 (White 97.9%; Black or African American 0.7%; Hispanic or Latino 0.5%; Asian 0.1%; Other 0.9%). **Foreign born:** 0.4%. **Median age:** 40.1.

Income 2000: per capita $15,262; median household $29,060; **Pop below poverty level:** 19.1%. *****Personal per capita income 2000-2003:** $19,399-$20,523.

Unemployment 2004: 5.7%. **Change from 2000:** -5.1%. **Median travel time to work:** 28.5 minutes. **Working outside county of residence:** 43.3%.

Cities with pop over 10,000: None.

CUMBERLAND COUNTY
601 Courthouse Sq Rm 6   Ph: 270-864-3726
Burkesville, KY 42717   Fax: 270-864-5884

On central southern border of KY; established Dec 14, 1798 from Green County. **Name Origin:** For the Cumberland River that flows through the county.

Area (sq mi): 310.85 (land 305.82; water 5.02). **Pop per sq mi:** 23.4.

Pop 2005: 7,147. **State rank:** 112. **Pop change:** 2000-20005 +0%; 1990-2000 +5.4%. **Pop 2000:** 7,147 (White 95%; Black or African American 3.4%; Hispanic or Latino 0.6%; Asian 0%; Other 1.3%). **Foreign born:** 0.3%. **Median age:** 40.1.

Income 2000: per capita $12,643; median household $21,572; **Pop below poverty level:** 23.8%. *****Personal per capita income 2000-2003:** $16,960-$17,631.

Unemployment 2004: 6.6%. **Change from 2000:** -0.4%. **Median travel time to work:** 24.3 minutes. **Working outside county of residence:** 28%.

Cities with pop over 10,000: None.

DAVIESS COUNTY
PO Box 609   Ph: 270-685-8434
Owensboro, KY 42302   Fax: 270-686-7111
www.daviessky.org

On northwestern border of KY, east of Henderson; organized Jan 14, 1815 from Ohio County. **Name Origin:** For Joseph Hamilton Davies (1774-1811), VA soldier and jurist, unsuccessful in his attempt to indict Aaron Burr (1756-1836) for treason.

Area (sq mi): 476.27 (land 462.39; water 13.88). **Pop per sq mi:** 201.3.

Source: Personal per capita income data are from the Bureau of Economic Analysis; per capita income data are from the Bureau of the Census. See Introduction for explanation of differences.

Daviess County (cont'd)

Pop 2005: 93,060. **State rank:** 7. **Pop change:** 2000-20005 +1.7%; 1990-2000 +5%. **Pop 2000:** 91,545 (White 93.2%; Black or African American 4.3%; Hispanic or Latino 0.9%; Asian 0.4%; Other 1.4%). **Foreign born:** 1%. **Median age:** 36.8.

Income 2000: per capita $18,739; median household $36,813; **Pop below poverty level:** 12.3%. ***Personal per capita income 2000-2003:** $24,635-$26,479.

Unemployment 2004: 5%. **Change from 2000:** -0.4%. **Median travel time to work:** 19.5 minutes. **Working outside county of residence:** 13.8%.

Cities with pop over 10,000: Owensboro ⛪ (54,900).

EDMONSON COUNTY

PO Box 830
Brownsville, KY 42210

Ph: 270-597-2624
Fax: 270-597-9714

In central KY, northeast of Bowling Green; organized 1825 from Hart, Warren, and Grayson counties. **Name Origin:** For Capt. John Edmonson (1764-1813), an American officer in the War of 1812, killed at the Frenchtown Battle on the River Raisin, MI.

Area (sq mi): 308.01 (land 302.62; water 5.39). **Pop per sq mi:** 39.8.

Pop 2005: 12,030. **State rank:** 90. **Pop change:** 2000-20005 +3.3%; 1990-2000 +12.4%. **Pop 2000:** 11,644 (White 98%; Black or African American 0.6%; Hispanic or Latino 0.6%; Asian 0.1%; Other 1%). **Foreign born:** 0.4%. **Median age:** 38.

Income 2000: per capita $14,480; median household $25,413; **Pop below poverty level:** 18.4%. ***Personal per capita income 2000-2003:** $15,827-$17,165.

Unemployment 2004: 5.7%. **Change from 2000:** -0.5%. **Median travel time to work:** 33.9 minutes. **Working outside county of residence:** 65.4%.

Cities with pop over 10,000: None.

ELLIOTT COUNTY

PO Box 788
Sandy Hook, KY 41171

Ph: 606-738-5238
Fax: 606-738-6962

In eastern KY, southwest of Ashland; organized Jan 26, 1869 from Lawrence, Morgan, and Carter counties. **Name Origin:** For John Milton Elliott (1820-79), KY legislator, U.S. representative (1853-59), and justice of the KY Court of Appeals (1876-79). Some claim his father, John Lisle Elliott, a KY legislator.

Area (sq mi): 235.2 (land 233.96; water 1.24). **Pop per sq mi:** 29.5.

Pop 2005: 6,902. **State rank:** 115. **Pop change:** 2000-20005 +2.3%; 1990-2000 +4.5%. **Pop 2000:** 6,748 (White 98.6%; Black or African American 0%; Hispanic or Latino 0.6%; Asian 0%; Other 0.9%). **Foreign born:** 0.2%. **Median age:** 37.

Income 2000: per capita $12,067; median household $21,014; **Pop below poverty level:** 25.9%. ***Personal per capita income 2000-2003:** $13,720-$14,633.

Unemployment 2004: 9.8%. **Change from 2000:** -2.6%. **Median travel time to work:** 48.7 minutes. **Working outside county of residence:** 64.4%.

Cities with pop over 10,000: None.

ESTILL COUNTY

PO Box 59
Irvine, KY 40336
www.estill.net

Ph: 606-723-5156
Fax: 606-723-5108

In east-central KY, southeast of Lexington; organized Jan 27, 1808 from Madison and Clark counties. **Name Origin:** For Capt. James Estill (1750-92), soldier and early pioneer who established Fort Estill in 1781.

Area (sq mi): 255.7 (land 253.93; water 1.70). **Pop per sq mi:** 59.4.

Pop 2005: 15,089. **State rank:** 77. **Pop change:** 2000-20005 -1.4%; 1990-2000 +4.7%. **Pop 2000:** 15,307 (White 98.7%; Black or African American 0.1%; Hispanic or Latino 0.5%; Asian 0%; Other 0.8%). **Foreign born:** 0.3%. **Median age:** 36.7.

Income 2000: per capita $12,285; median household $23,318; **Pop below poverty level:** 26.4%. ***Personal per capita income 2000-2003:** $17,190-$18,133.

Unemployment 2004: 7.3%. **Change from 2000:** +0.5%. **Median travel time to work:** 34.9 minutes. **Working outside county of residence:** 57%.

Cities with pop over 10,000: None.

FLEMING COUNTY

201 Court Sq
Flemingsburg, KY 41041
www.flemingcountyky.org

Ph: 606-845-7571
Fax: 606-845-1312

In northeastern KY, northeast of Lexington; organized Feb 10, 1798 from Mason County. **Name Origin:** For Col. John Fleming (1760-94), early settler and army officer.

Area (sq mi): 351.47 (land 350.84; water 0.62). **Pop per sq mi:** 41.6.

Pop 2005: 14,610. **State rank:** 78. **Pop change:** 2000-20005 +5.9%; 1990-2000 +12.2%. **Pop 2000:** 13,792 (White 96.9%; Black or African American 1.4%; Hispanic or Latino 0.7%; Asian 0.2%; Other 1.1%). **Foreign born:** 0.2%. **Median age:** 36.3.

Income 2000: per capita $14,214; median household $27,990; **Pop below poverty level:** 18.6%. ***Personal per capita income 2000-2003:** $18,663-$18,481.

Unemployment 2004: 5.7%. **Change from 2000:** +0.4%. **Median travel time to work:** 26 minutes. **Working outside county of residence:** 37.2%.

Cities with pop over 10,000: None.

FLOYD COUNTY

PO Box 1089
Prestonsburg, KY 41653
www.floydcountykentucky.com

Ph: 606-886-3816
Fax: 606-886-8089

In southeastern KY; established Dec 13, 1799 from Fleming, Mason, and Montgomery counties. **Name Origin:** For John Floyd (1783-1837), governor of VA (1830-34).

Area (sq mi): 395.46 (land 394.29; water 1.16). **Pop per sq mi:** 107.1.

Pop 2005: 42,218. **State rank:** 22. **Pop change:** 2000-20005 -0.5%; 1990-2000 -2.6%. **Pop 2000:** 42,441 (White 97.3%; Black or African American 1.3%; Hispanic or Latino 0.6%; Asian 0.2%; Other 0.7%). **Foreign born:** 0.6%. **Median age:** 36.7.

Floyd County (cont'd)

Income 2000: per capita $12,442; median household $21,168; **Pop below poverty level:** 30.3%. ***Personal per capita income 2000-2003:** $17,802-$20,290.

Unemployment 2004: 7.1%. **Change from 2000:** +0.7%. **Median travel time to work:** 25.8 minutes. **Working outside county of residence:** 31.3%.

Cities with pop over 10,000: None.

FRANKLIN COUNTY

315 W Main St   **Ph:** 502-875-8702
Frankfort, KY 40602   **Fax:** 502-875-8718

In north-central KY, northwest of Lexington; established Dec 7, 1794 from Woodford, Mercer, and Shelby counties. **Name Origin:** For Benjamin Franklin (1706-90), U.S. patriot, diplomat, and statesman.

Area (sq mi): 212.11 (land 210.46; water 1.65). **Pop per sq mi:** 229.1.

Pop 2005: 48,207. **State rank:** 18. **Pop change:** 2000-20005 +1.1%; 1990-2000 +8.9%. **Pop 2000:** 47,687 (White 87.4%; Black or African American 9.4%; Hispanic or Latino 1.1%; Asian 0.7%; Other 1.9%). **Foreign born:** 1.9%. **Median age:** 37.

Income 2000: per capita $21,229; median household $40,011; **Pop below poverty level:** 10.7%. ***Personal per capita income 2000-2003:** $27,489-$29,387.

Unemployment 2004: 4%. **Change from 2000:** +1.1%. **Median travel time to work:** 18.2 minutes. **Working outside county of residence:** 19.3%.

Cities with pop over 10,000: Frankfort 🏛 (27,281).

FULTON COUNTY

PO Box 126   **Ph:** 270-236-2727
Hickman, KY 42050   **Fax:** 270-236-2522

On southwestern border of KY, southwest of Paducah; organized Jan 15, 1845 from Hickman County. **Name Origin:** For Robert Fulton (1765-1815), builder of the *Clermont*, the first commercially successful steamboat.

Area (sq mi): 230.55 (land 208.95; water 21.6). **Pop per sq mi:** 34.5.

Pop 2005: 7,217. **State rank:** 111. **Pop change:** 2000-20005 -6.9%; 1990-2000 -6.3%. **Pop 2000:** 7,752 (White 74.8%; Black or African American 23.2%; Hispanic or Latino 0.7%; Asian 0.3%; Other 1.3%). **Foreign born:** 0.4%. **Median age:** 38.5.

Income 2000: per capita $14,309; median household $24,382; **Pop below poverty level:** 23.1%. ***Personal per capita income 2000-2003:** $21,588-$23,468.

Unemployment 2004: 9%. **Change from 2000:** +1.8%. **Median travel time to work:** 18.6 minutes. **Working outside county of residence:** 40.2%.

Cities with pop over 10,000: None.

GALLATIN COUNTY

PO Box 1309   **Ph:** 859-567-5411
Warsaw, KY 41095   **Fax:** 859-567-5444
www.gallatincountyky.com

On northwestern border of KY, southwest of Cincinnati, OH; established Dec 4, 1798 from Franklin and Shelby counties. **Name Origin:** For Albert Gallatin (1761-1849), Swiss-born U.S. statesman and diplomat, and U.S. secretary of the treasury (1801-14).

Area (sq mi): 104.67 (land 98.81; water 5.87). **Pop per sq mi:** 82.3.

Pop 2005: 8,134. **State rank:** 109. **Pop change:** 2000-20005 +3.4%; 1990-2000 +45.9%. **Pop 2000:** 7,870 (White 96.1%; Black or African American 1.6%; Hispanic or Latino 1%; Asian 0.2%; Other 1.5%). **Foreign born:** 0.4%. **Median age:** 34.6.

Income 2000: per capita $16,416; median household $36,422; **Pop below poverty level:** 13.4%. ***Personal per capita income 2000-2003:** $20,484-$21,642.

Unemployment 2004: 5.5%. **Change from 2000:** -0.3%. **Median travel time to work:** 30.3 minutes. **Working outside county of residence:** 63.3%.

Cities with pop over 10,000: None.

GARRARD COUNTY

15 Public Sq County Courthouse   **Ph:** 859-792-3071
Lancaster, KY 40444   **Fax:** 859-792-6751

In central KY, south of Lexington; organized Jun 1, 1797 from Madison, Lincoln, and Mercer counties. **Name Origin:** For James Garrard (1749-1822), KY legislator and governor (1796-1804).

Area (sq mi): 233.88 (land 231.21; water 2.67). **Pop per sq mi:** 71.7.

Pop 2005: 16,579. **State rank:** 69. **Pop change:** 2000-20005 +12.1%; 1990-2000 +27.7%. **Pop 2000:** 14,792 (White 95%; Black or African American 3.1%; Hispanic or Latino 1.3%; Asian 0%; Other 1.1%). **Foreign born:** 1.6%. **Median age:** 37.1.

Income 2000: per capita $16,915; median household $34,284; **Pop below poverty level:** 14.7%. ***Personal per capita income 2000-2003:** $20,256-$21,375.

Unemployment 2004: 5.2%. **Change from 2000:** +0.7%. **Median travel time to work:** 31.8 minutes. **Working outside county of residence:** 67.4%.

Cities with pop over 10,000: None.

GRANT COUNTY

107 N Main St   **Ph:** 859-824-3321
Williamstown, KY 41097   **Fax:** 859-824-3367
www.grantco.org

In north-central KY, south of Covington; organized Feb 12, 1820 from Pendleton County. **Name Origin:** For a member of the locally prominent Grant family, which included John Grant (1754-1826), pioneer salt producer; his brother, Samuel (1762-89), surveyor, and another brother, Squire (1769-1833), a surveyor and KY legislator.

Area (sq mi): 260.79 (land 259.93; water 0.86). **Pop per sq mi:** 94.7.

Pop 2005: 24,610. **State rank:** 44. **Pop change:** 2000-20005 +9.9%; 1990-2000 +42.2%. **Pop 2000:** 22,384 (White 97.7%; Black or African American 0.3%; Hispanic or Latino 1%; Asian 0.3%; Other 1.1%). **Foreign born:** 1%. **Median age:** 32.7.

*Source: Personal per capita income data are from the Bureau of Economic Analysis; per capita income data are from the Bureau of the Census. See Introduction for explanation of differences.

Grant County (cont'd)

Income 2000: per capita $16,776; median household $38,438; **Pop below poverty level:** 11.1%. ***Personal per capita income 2000-2003:** $21,150-$21,468.

Unemployment 2004: 5.2%. **Change from 2000:** -1.5%. **Median travel time to work:** 31.5 minutes. **Working outside county of residence:** 59.3%.

Cities with pop over 10,000: None.

GRAVES COUNTY

County Courthouse 101 E South St Suite 2   **Ph:** 270-247-1676
Mayfield, KY 42066   **Fax:** 270-247-1274

On southwestern border of KY, south of Paducah; established Dec 19, 1823 from Hickman County. **Name Origin:** For Col. Benjamin Franklin Graves (1771-1813), an officer during the War of 1812 killed at the Frenchtown Battle on the River Raisin, MI.

Area (sq mi): 556.46 (land 555.59; water 0.87). **Pop per sq mi:** 67.7.

Pop 2005: 37,625. **State rank:** 28. **Pop change:** 2000-20005 +1.6%; 1990-2000 +10.4%. **Pop 2000:** 37,028 (White 91.7%; Black or African American 4.4%; Hispanic or Latino 2.4%; Asian 0.2%; Other 2.6%). **Foreign born:** 2.1%. **Median age:** 38.1.

Income 2000: per capita $16,834; median household $30,874; **Pop below poverty level:** 16.4%. ***Personal per capita income 2000-2003:** $21,282-$21,944.

Unemployment 2004: 7%. **Change from 2000:** -0.3%. **Median travel time to work:** 23.3 minutes. **Working outside county of residence:** 33.7%.

Cities with pop over 10,000: Mayfield 🏛 (10,252).

GRAYSON COUNTY

10 Public Sq   **Ph:** 270-259-3201
Leitchfield, KY 42754   **Fax:** 270-259-9264
www.graysoncountychamber.com

In west-central KY, north of Bowling Green; organized Jan 25, 1810 from Hardin and Ohio counties. **Name Origin:** For Col. Robert Grayson, aide to George Washington (1732-99).

Area (sq mi): 510.85 (land 503.68; water 7.17). **Pop per sq mi:** 50.

Pop 2005: 25,189. **State rank:** 42. **Pop change:** 2000-20005 +4.7%; 1990-2000 +14.3%. **Pop 2000:** 24,053 (White 97.7%; Black or African American 0.5%; Hispanic or Latino 0.8%; Asian 0.1%; Other 1.1%). **Foreign born:** 0.6%. **Median age:** 37.5.

Income 2000: per capita $14,759; median household $27,639; **Pop below poverty level:** 18.1%. ***Personal per capita income 2000-2003:** $18,583-$19,379.

Unemployment 2004: 6.8%. **Change from 2000:** -2%. **Median travel time to work:** 27.3 minutes. **Working outside county of residence:** 26.2%.

Cities with pop over 10,000: None.

GREEN COUNTY

203 W Court St   **Ph:** 270-932-5386
Greensburg, KY 42743   **Fax:** 270-932-6241

In south-central KY, southwest of Lexington; established Dec 20, 1792 from Lincoln and Nelson counties. **Name Origin:** For Gen. Nathanael Greene (1742-86), Revolutionary War officer and quartermaster general (1778-80). The missing *e* not explained.

Area (sq mi): 288.78 (land 288.66; water 0.12). **Pop per sq mi:** 40.1.

Pop 2005: 11,588. **State rank:** 95. **Pop change:** 2000-20005 +0.6%; 1990-2000 +11.1%. **Pop 2000:** 11,518 (White 95.5%; Black or African American 2.6%; Hispanic or Latino 0.9%; Asian 0.1%; Other 1.1%). **Foreign born:** 0.7%. **Median age:** 40.

Income 2000: per capita $16,107; median household $25,463; **Pop below poverty level:** 18.4%. ***Personal per capita income 2000-2003:** $17,280-$18,257.

Unemployment 2004: 5.1%. **Change from 2000:** -2.5%. **Median travel time to work:** 29.9 minutes. **Working outside county of residence:** 47.1%.

Cities with pop over 10,000: None.

GREENUP COUNTY

PO Box 686   **Ph:** 606-473-7394
Greenup, KY 41144   **Fax:** 606-473-5354

In northeastern KY, northwest of Ashland; established Dec 12, 1803 from Mason County. **Name Origin:** For Col. Christopher Greenup (c.1750-1818), U.S. representative from KY (1792-97) and governor (1804-08).

Area (sq mi): 354.51 (land 346.11; water 8.41). **Pop per sq mi:** 107.4.

Pop 2005: 37,184. **State rank:** 29. **Pop change:** 2000-20005 +0.8%; 1990-2000 +0.4%. **Pop 2000:** 36,891 (White 97.7%; Black or African American 0.6%; Hispanic or Latino 0.6%; Asian 0.4%; Other 0.9%). **Foreign born:** 0.6%. **Median age:** 39.2.

Income 2000: per capita $17,137; median household $32,142; **Pop below poverty level:** 14.1%. ***Personal per capita income 2000-2003:** $21,181-$23,482.

Unemployment 2004: 6%. **Change from 2000:** +0%. **Median travel time to work:** 25.3 minutes. **Working outside county of residence:** 57%.

Cities with pop over 10,000: None.

HANCOCK COUNTY

PO Box 146   **Ph:** 270-927-6117
Hawesville, KY 42348   **Fax:** 270-927-8639
www.hancockcounty-ky.com

On northwestern border of KY, east of Owensboro; organized Jan 3, 1829 from Breckinridge, Ohio, and Daviess counties. **Name Origin:** For John Hancock (1737-93), noted signer of the Declaration of Independence, governor of MA (1780-85; 1787-93), and statesman.

Area (sq mi): 198.92 (land 188.8; water 10.12). **Pop per sq mi:** 45.6.

Pop 2005: 8,613. **State rank:** 106. **Pop change:** 2000-20005 +2.6%; 1990-2000 +6.7%. **Pop 2000:** 8,392 (White 97.4%; Black or African American 0.8%; Hispanic or Latino 0.8%; Asian 0.2%; Other 1.1%). **Foreign born:** 0.8%. **Median age:** 35.9.

Income 2000: per capita $16,623; median household $36,914; **Pop below poverty level:** 13.6%. ***Personal per capita income 2000-2003:** $20,524-$21,299.

🏛 *County Seat*

Hancock County (cont'd)

Unemployment 2004: 5.5%. **Change from 2000:** -2%. **Median travel time to work:** 22.8 minutes. **Working outside county of residence:** 41.9%.

Cities with pop over 10,000: None.

HARDIN COUNTY
PO Box 1030   **Ph:** 270-765-2171
Elizabethtown, KY 42702   **Fax:** 270-769-2682
www.hcky.org

In north-central KY, southeast of Louisville; established Dec 15, 1792 from Nelson County. **Name Origin:** For Gen. John Hardin (1753-92), Revolutionary War officer and Indian fighter with George Rogers Clark (1752-1818) in the trans-Ohio campaigns; killed while on a peace mission to the Miami Indians.

Area (sq mi): 629.86 (land 627.98; water 1.88). **Pop per sq mi:** 154.4.

Pop 2005: 96,947. **State rank:** 6. **Pop change:** 2000-20005 +2.9%; 1990-2000 +5.5%. **Pop 2000:** 94,174 (White 80.5%; Black or African American 11.9%; Hispanic or Latino 3.4%; Asian 1.8%; Other 4.3%). **Foreign born:** 4.5%. **Median age:** 33.5.

Income 2000: per capita $17,487; median household $37,744; **Pop below poverty level:** 10%. ***Personal per capita income 2000-2003:** $24,431-$27,808.

Unemployment 2004: 5.3%. **Change from 2000:** -1.1%. **Median travel time to work:** 23 minutes. **Working outside county of residence:** 19.6%.

Cities with pop over 10,000: Elizabethtown 🏛 (23,190); Radcliff (21,617).

HARLAN COUNTY
PO Box 670   **Ph:** 606-573-3636
Harlan, KY 40831   **Fax:** 606-573-0064

On the southeastern border of KY; organized Jan 28, 1819 from Floyd and Knox counties. **Name Origin:** For Maj. Silas Harlan (?-1782), an officer in the Revolutionary War.

Area (sq mi): 467.97 (land 467.2; water 0.78). **Pop per sq mi:** 67.7.

Pop 2005: 31,614. **State rank:** 33. **Pop change:** 2000-20005 -4.8%; 1990-2000 -9.2%. **Pop 2000:** 33,202 (White 95.1%; Black or African American 2.6%; Hispanic or Latino 0.7%; Asian 0.3%; Other 1.6%). **Foreign born:** 0.6%. **Median age:** 37.8.

Income 2000: per capita $11,585; median household $18,665; **Pop below poverty level:** 32.5%. ***Personal per capita income 2000-2003:** $15,948-$17,676.

Unemployment 2004: 7.6%. **Change from 2000:** -1.1%. **Median travel time to work:** 27 minutes. **Working outside county of residence:** 13.3%.

Cities with pop over 10,000: None.

HARRISON COUNTY
313 Oddville Ave   **Ph:** 859-234-7130
Cynthiana, KY 41031   **Fax:** 859-234-8049

In north-central KY, south of Covington; established Dec 21, 1793 from Bourbon and Scott counties. **Name Origin:** For Col. Benjamin Harrison, a Bourbon County representative in the KY legislature when the county was formed in 1793.

Area (sq mi): 309.88 (land 309.68; water 0.2). **Pop per sq mi:** 59.8.

Pop 2005: 18,527. **State rank:** 60. **Pop change:** 2000-20005 +3%; 1990-2000 +10.7%. **Pop 2000:** 17,983 (White 95.2%; Black or African American 2.5%; Hispanic or Latino 1.2%; Asian 0.1%; Other 1.7%). **Foreign born:** 1.2%. **Median age:** 37.1.

Income 2000: per capita $17,478; median household $36,210; **Pop below poverty level:** 12%. ***Personal per capita income 2000-2003:** $22,007-$23,156.

Unemployment 2004: 5.4%. **Change from 2000:** -1.8%. **Median travel time to work:** 26.9 minutes. **Working outside county of residence:** 40.4%.

Cities with pop over 10,000: None.

HART COUNTY
PO Box 277   **Ph:** 270-524-2751
Munfordville, KY 42765   **Fax:** 270-524-0458
www.hartcounty.com

In central KY, northeast of Bowling Green; organized Jan 28, 1819 from Hardin and Barren counties. **Name Origin:** For Nathaniel G.T. Hart (1784-1813), lawyer, merchant, and officer in the War of 1812.

Area (sq mi): 417.91 (land 415.93; water 1.98). **Pop per sq mi:** 44.

Pop 2005: 18,319. **State rank:** 61. **Pop change:** 2000-20005 +5%; 1990-2000 +17.2%. **Pop 2000:** 17,445 (White 92%; Black or African American 6.2%; Hispanic or Latino 0.9%; Asian 0.1%; Other 1.1%). **Foreign born:** 0.6%. **Median age:** 36.9.

Income 2000: per capita $13,495; median household $25,378; **Pop below poverty level:** 22.4%. ***Personal per capita income 2000-2003:** $16,975-$16,941.

Unemployment 2004: 5%. **Change from 2000:** -0.7%. **Median travel time to work:** 26.6 minutes. **Working outside county of residence:** 40.3%.

Cities with pop over 10,000: None.

HENDERSON COUNTY
20 N Main St   **Ph:** 270-826-3906
Henderson, KY 42420   **Fax:** 270-826-9677
www.hendersonky.com

On the northwestern border of KY, west of Owensboro; established Dec 21, 1798 from Christian County. **Name Origin:** For Richard Henderson (1734-85), who backed Daniel Boone's (c.1734-1820) explorations and founded the Transylvania Company.

Area (sq mi): 467.24 (land 440.12; water 27.11). **Pop per sq mi:** 103.5.

Pop 2005: 45,573. **State rank:** 20. **Pop change:** 2000-20005 +1.7%; 1990-2000 +4.1%. **Pop 2000:** 44,829 (White 90.7%; Black or African American 7.1%; Hispanic or Latino 1%; Asian 0.3%; Other 1.5%). **Foreign born:** 1.1%. **Median age:** 37.2.

Income 2000: per capita $18,470; median household $35,892; **Pop below poverty level:** 12.3%. ***Personal per capita income 2000-2003:** $23,974-$26,232.

---

*Source: Personal per capita income data are from the Bureau of Economic Analysis; per capita income data are from the Bureau of the Census. See Introduction for explanation of differences.

Henderson County (cont'd)

Unemployment 2004: 4.5%. **Change from 2000:** -1.2%. **Median travel time to work:** 19.8 minutes. **Working outside county of residence:** 26.3%.

Cities with pop over 10,000: Henderson 🏛 (27,574).

HENRY COUNTY

27 S Property Rd
New Castle, KY 40050
www.henryweb.com

Ph: 502-845-5705
Fax: 502-845-5708

In northwestern KY, northeast of Louisville; established Dec. 14, 1798 from Shelby County. **Name Origin:** For Patrick Henry (1736-99), patriot, governor of VA (1776-79; 1784-86), and statesman, famous for proclaiming, 'Give me liberty or give me death.'

Area (sq mi): 291.11 (land 289.32; water 1.79). **Pop per sq mi:** 55.

Pop 2005: 15,903. **State rank:** 73. **Pop change:** 2000-20005 +5.6%; 1990-2000 +17.4%. **Pop 2000:** 15,060 (White 93.2%; Black or African American 3.3%; Hispanic or Latino 2.3%; Asian 0.3%; Other 2.4%). **Foreign born:** 1.4%. **Median age:** 37.3.

Income 2000: per capita $17,846; median household $37,263; **Pop below poverty level:** 13.7%. ***Personal per capita income 2000-2003:** $23,318-$23,837.

Unemployment 2004: 4.7%. **Change from 2000:** +0.3%. **Median travel time to work:** 30.9 minutes. **Working outside county of residence:** 59.4%.

Cities with pop over 10,000: None.

HICKMAN COUNTY

110 E Clay St County Courthouse
Clinton, KY 42031

Ph: 270-653-2131
Fax: 270-653-4248

On southwestern border of KY, southwest of Paducah; established Dec 19, 1821 from Caldwell and Livingston counties. **Name Origin:** For Capt. Paschal Hickman (?-1813), Army officer. The county comprised the entire KY portion of the Jackson Purchase, bought from the Chickasaw Indians in 1818.

Area (sq mi): 252.94 (land 244.44; water 8.49). **Pop per sq mi:** 20.8.

Pop 2005: 5,075. **State rank:** 118. **Pop change:** 2000-20005 -3.6%; 1990-2000 -5.5%. **Pop 2000:** 5,262 (White 87.7%; Black or African American 9.9%; Hispanic or Latino 1%; Asian 0.1%; Other 1.7%). **Foreign born:** 0.6%. **Median age:** 40.9.

Income 2000: per capita $17,279; median household $31,615; **Pop below poverty level:** 17.4%. ***Personal per capita income 2000-2003:** $30,175-$33,423.

Unemployment 2004: 8.5%. **Change from 2000:** +2.3%. **Median travel time to work:** 24.2 minutes. **Working outside county of residence:** 51.8%.

Cities with pop over 10,000: None.

HOPKINS COUNTY

10 S Main St
Madisonville, KY 42431
www.hopkinscounty.net

Ph: 270-821-7361
Fax: 270-825-5009

In western KY, south of Henderson; established Dec 9, 1806 from

Henderson County. **Name Origin:** For Gen. Samuel Hopkins (1753-1819), officer in the American Revolution and War of 1812, KY legislator, and US. representative (1813-15).

Area (sq mi): 554.23 (land 550.56; water 3.67). **Pop per sq mi:** 84.8.

Pop 2005: 46,705. **State rank:** 19. **Pop change:** 2000-20005 +0.4%; 1990-2000 +0.9%. **Pop 2000:** 46,519 (White 91.5%; Black or African American 6.2%; Hispanic or Latino 0.9%; Asian 0.3%; Other 1.5%). **Foreign born:** 0.6%. **Median age:** 38.3.

Income 2000: per capita $17,382; median household $30,808, **Pop below poverty level:** 16.5%. ***Personal per capita income 2000-2003:** $21,820-$23,368.

Unemployment 2004: 5.3%. **Change from 2000:** -1.7%. **Median travel time to work:** 22 minutes. **Working outside county of residence:** 21%.

Cities with pop over 10,000: Madisonville 🏛 (19,340).

JACKSON COUNTY

PO Box 339
McKee, KY 40447
www.eastky.net/jacksonco/

Ph: 606-287-7800
Fax: 606-287-4505

In south-central KY, southeast of Lexington; organized Feb 2, 1858 from Madison, Owsley, Estill, Laurel, Clay, and Rockcastle counties. **Name Origin:** For Andrew Jackson (1767-1845), seventh U.S. president.

Area (sq mi): 346.57 (land 346.33; water 0.24). **Pop per sq mi:** 39.3.

Pop 2005: 13,618. **State rank:** 84. **Pop change:** 2000-20005 +0.9%; 1990-2000 +12.9%. **Pop 2000:** 13,495 (White 98.7%; Black or African American 0.1%; Hispanic or Latino 0.5%; Asian 0%; Other 0.7%). **Foreign born:** 0.4%. **Median age:** 34.9.

Income 2000: per capita $10,711; median household $20,177; **Pop below poverty level:** 30.2%. ***Personal per capita income 2000-2003:** $14,557-$14,760.

Unemployment 2004: 6.4%. **Change from 2000:** -0.6%. **Median travel time to work:** 35 minutes. **Working outside county of residence:** 39.6%.

Cities with pop over 10,000: None.

JESSAMINE COUNTY

101 N Main St
Nicholasville, KY 40356
www.jessamineco.com

Ph: 859-885-4161
Fax: 859-885-5837

In central KY, south of Lexington; established Dec 19, 1798 from Fayette County. **Name Origin:** For the Jessamine Creek and the jasmine (jessamine) flowers on its banks. The legend that it was named for Jessamine Douglass, daughter of an early settler, is baseless.

Area (sq mi): 174.45 (land 173.13; water 1.32). **Pop per sq mi:** 251.

Pop 2005: 43,463. **State rank:** 21. **Pop change:** 2000-20005 +11.3%; 1990-2000 +28%. **Pop 2000:** 39,041 (White 93.7%; Black or African American 3.1%; Hispanic or Latino 1.3%; Asian 0.6%; Other 1.8%). **Foreign born:** 1.8%. **Median age:** 32.9.

Income 2000: per capita $18,842; median household $40,096; **Pop below poverty level:** 10.5%. ***Personal per capita income 2000-2003:** $25,832-$25,940.

Jessamine County (cont'd)

Unemployment 2004: 4.1%. **Change from 2000:** +1.3%. **Median travel time to work:** 24.1 minutes. **Working outside county of residence:** 53.8%.

Cities with pop over 10,000: Nicholasville 🏛 (22,878).

JOHNSON COUNTY

230 Court St	**Ph:** 606-789-2557
Paintsville, KY 41240	**Fax:** 606-789-2559

In eastern KY, south of Ashland; organized Feb 2, 1843 from Lawrence, Floyd, and Morgan counties. **Name Origin:** For Richard Mentor Johnson (1780-1850), U.S. vice president under Van Buren (1837-41).

Area (sq mi): 263.94 (land 261.54; water 2.4). **Pop per sq mi:** 91.8.

Pop 2005: 24,001. **State rank:** 49. **Pop change:** 2000-20005 +2.4%; 1990-2000 +0.8%. **Pop 2000:** 23,445 (White 98.2%; Black or African American 0.3%; Hispanic or Latino 0.6%; Asian 0.3%; Other 0.8%). **Foreign born:** 0.5%. **Median age:** 37.4.

Income 2000: per capita $14,051; median household $24,911; **Pop below poverty level:** 26.6%. ***Personal per capita income 2000-2003:** $18,380-$20,204.

Unemployment 2004: 6.4%. **Change from 2000:** +0.2%. **Median travel time to work:** 26.2 minutes. **Working outside county of residence:** 33%.

Cities with pop over 10,000: None.

KENTON COUNTY

303 Court St	**Ph:** 859-392-1600
Covington, KY 41011	**Fax:** 859-392-1639
www.kentoncounty.org	

On central northern border of KY, south of Cincinnati, OH; organized Jan 29, 1840 from Campbell County. **Name Origin:** For Simon Kenton (1755-1836), KY scout and Indian fighter.

Area (sq mi): 164.38 (land 161.97; water 2.42). **Pop per sq mi:** 948.7.

Pop 2005: 153,665. **State rank:** 3. **Pop change:** 2000-20005 +1.5%; 1990-2000 +6.6%. **Pop 2000:** 151,464 (White 93.3%; Black or African American 3.8%; Hispanic or Latino 1.1%; Asian 0.6%; Other 1.5%). **Foreign born:** 1.6%. **Median age:** 34.5.

Income 2000: per capita $22,085; median household $43,906; **Pop below poverty level:** 9%. ***Personal per capita income 2000-2003:** $29,194-$32,449.

Unemployment 2004: 4.6%. **Change from 2000:** +0%. **Median travel time to work:** 22.9 minutes. **Working outside county of residence:** 59.6%.

Cities with pop over 10,000: Covington 🏛 (43,010); Independence 🏛 (17,940); Erlanger (16,746).

KNOTT COUNTY

PO Box 446	**Ph:** 606-785-5651
Hindman, KY 41822	**Fax:** 606-785-0996

In southeastern KY; organized May 5, 1884 from Floyd, Letcher, Perry, and Breathitt counties. **Name Origin:** For James Proctor

Knott (1830-1911), KY legislator, U.S. representative (1867-71; 1875-83), and governor (1883-87).

Area (sq mi): 353.01 (land 352.19; water 0.82). **Pop per sq mi:** 49.9.

Pop 2005: 17,561. **State rank:** 63. **Pop change:** 2000-20005 -0.5%; 1990-2000 -1.4%. **Pop 2000:** 17,649 (White 97.8%; Black or African American 0.7%; Hispanic or Latino 0.6%; Asian 0.2%; Other 0.8%). **Foreign born:** 0.4%. **Median age:** 35.9.

Income 2000: per capita $11,297; median household $20,373; **Pop below poverty level:** 31.1%. ***Personal per capita income 2000-2003:** $15,977-$17,092.

Unemployment 2004: 6.1%. **Change from 2000:** +0%. **Median travel time to work:** 29.4 minutes. **Working outside county of residence:** 45.3%.

Cities with pop over 10,000: None.

KNOX COUNTY

PO Box 173	**Ph:** 606-546-8915
Barbourville, KY 40906	**Fax:** 606-546-6196

In southeastern KY, west of Harlan; established Dec 19, 1799 from Lincoln County. **Name Origin:** For Gen. Henry Knox (1750-1806), Revolutionary War officer and first U.S. secretary of war (1785-95).

Area (sq mi): 387.71 (land 387.66; water 0.04). **Pop per sq mi:** 82.7.

Pop 2005: 32,069. **State rank:** 32. **Pop change:** 2000-20005 +0.9%; 1990-2000 +7.1%. **Pop 2000:** 31,795 (White 97.4%; Black or African American 0.8%; Hispanic or Latino 0.6%; Asian 0.2%; Other 1.2%). **Foreign born:** 0.4%. **Median age:** 35.3.

Income 2000: per capita $10,660; median household $18,294; **Pop below poverty level:** 34.8%. ***Personal per capita income 2000-2003:** $16,291-$18,785.

Unemployment 2004: 6.5%. **Change from 2000:** +0.3%. **Median travel time to work:** 24.6 minutes. **Working outside county of residence:** 35.9%.

Cities with pop over 10,000: None.

LARUE COUNTY

209 W High St	**Ph:** 270-358-3544
Hodgenville, KY 42748	**Fax:** 270-358-4528
www.laruecounty.org	

In central western KY, south of Louisville; organized Mar 4, 1843 from Hardin County. **Name Origin:** For John LaRue, maternal grandfather of John LaRue Helm, a KY governor.

Area (sq mi): 263.72 (land 263.2; water 0.53). **Pop per sq mi:** 52.

Pop 2005: 13,699. **State rank:** 82. **Pop change:** 2000-20005 +2.4%; 1990-2000 +14.5%. **Pop 2000:** 13,373 (White 94%; Black or African American 3.5%; Hispanic or Latino 1%; Asian 0.2%; Other 1.6%). **Foreign born:** 0.4%. **Median age:** 38.2.

Income 2000: per capita $15,865; median household $32,056; **Pop below poverty level:** 15.4%. ***Personal per capita income 2000-2003:** $23,634-$24,946.

Unemployment 2004: 5%. **Change from 2000:** +0%. **Median travel time to work:** 27.2 minutes. **Working outside county of residence:** 58%.

Cities with pop over 10,000: None.

---

*Source: Personal per capita income data are from the Bureau of Economic Analysis; per capita income data are from the Bureau of the Census. See Introduction for explanation of differences.

LAUREL COUNTY

101 S Main St Rm 203   **Ph:** 606-864-5158
London, KY 40741   **Fax:** 606-864-7369

In south-central KY; established Dec 12,1825 from Rockcastle, Knox, Clay, and Whitley counties. **Name Origin:** For the Laurel River, named for the abundant mountain laurel (*Kalmia latifolia*) trees on its banks.

Area (sq mi): 443.74 (land 435.67; water 8.07). **Pop per sq mi:** 129.3.

Pop 2005: 56,338. **State rank:** 15. **Pop change:** 2000-20005 +6.9%; 1990-2000 +21.4%. **Pop 2000:** 52,715 (White 97.2%; Black or African American 0.6%; Hispanic or Latino 0.6%; Asian 0.3%; Other 1.4%). **Foreign born:** 0.8%. **Median age:** 35.5.

Income 2000: per capita $14,165; median household $27,015; **Pop below poverty level:** 21.3%. *****Personal per capita income 2000-2003:** $19,925-$20,473.

Unemployment 2004: 5.4%. **Change from 2000:** -0.1%. **Median travel time to work:** 22.5 minutes. **Working outside county of residence:** 23.1%.

Cities with pop over 10,000: None.

LAWRENCE COUNTY

122 S Main Cross St   **Ph:** 606-638-4102
Louisa, KY 41230   **Fax:** 606-638-0638

On eastern border of KY, south of Ashland; established Dec 14, 1821 from Floyd and Greenup counties. **Name Origin:** For Capt. James Lawrence (1781-1813), U.S. Navy commander in the War of 1812 who said, 'Don't give up the ship!'

Area (sq mi): 420.12 (land 418.78; water 1.35). **Pop per sq mi:** 38.6.

Pop 2005: 16,166. **State rank:** 71. **Pop change:** 2000-20005 +3.8%; 1990-2000 +11.2%. **Pop 2000:** 15,569 (White 98.6%; Black or African American 0.1%; Hispanic or Latino 0.4%; Asian 0.1%; Other 1%). **Foreign born:** 0.1%. **Median age:** 36.5.

Income 2000: per capita $12,008; median household $21,610; **Pop below poverty level:** 30.7%. *****Personal per capita income 2000-2003:** $15,307-$16,926.

Unemployment 2004: 7.7%. **Change from 2000:** -2.4%. **Median travel time to work:** 36 minutes. **Working outside county of residence:** 49.3%.

Cities with pop over 10,000: None.

LEE COUNTY

PO Box 551   **Ph:** 606-464-4115
Beattyville, KY 41311   **Fax:** 606-464-4102

In east-central KY, southeast of Lexington; organized Jan 29, 1870 from Owsley, Breathitt, Estill, and Wolfe counties. **Name Origin:** Traditionally for Robert E. Lee (1807-70), American general and commander-in-chief of the Confederate forces during the Civil War. Others claim it was named for Lee County, VA, former home of many early settlers.

Area (sq mi): 211.22 (land 209.86; water 1.36). **Pop per sq mi:** 36.7.

Pop 2005: 7,709. **State rank:** 110. **Pop change:** 2000-20005 -2.6%; 1990-2000 +6.7%. **Pop 2000:** 7,916 (White 94.9%; Black or African American 3.8%; Hispanic or Latino 0.4%; Asian 0.1%; Other 1.1%). **Foreign born:** 0.2%. **Median age:** 37.4.

Income 2000: per capita $13,325; median household $18,544; **Pop below poverty level:** 30.4%. *****Personal per capita income 2000-2003:** $15,244-$16,613.

Unemployment 2004: 7.5%. **Change from 2000:** +0.4%. **Median travel time to work:** 35.4 minutes. **Working outside county of residence:** 41.5%.

Cities with pop over 10,000: None.

LESLIE COUNTY

PO Box 619   **Ph:** 606-672-3200
Hyden, KY 41749   **Fax:** 606-672-7373
www.lesliecounty.net

In southeastern KY; organized Mar 29, 1878 from Clay, Harlan, and Perry counties. **Name Origin:** For Preston Hopkins Leslie (1819-1907), KY legislator and governor (1871-75); territorial governor of MT (1887-89), and U.S. district attorney for MT (1894-98).

Area (sq mi): 404.36 (land 404.03; water 0.33). **Pop per sq mi:** 29.7.

Pop 2005: 11,994. **State rank:** 91. **Pop change:** 2000-20005 -3.3%; 1990-2000 -9.1%. **Pop 2000:** 12,401 (White 98.6%; Black or African American 0.1%; Hispanic or Latino 0.6%; Asian 0.1%; Other 0.6%). **Foreign born:** 0.2%. **Median age:** 36.4.

Income 2000: per capita $10,429; median household $18,546; **Pop below poverty level:** 32.7%. *****Personal per capita income 2000-2003:** $16,476-$17,590.

Unemployment 2004: 8.2%. **Change from 2000:** +3.5%. **Median travel time to work:** 33.5 minutes. **Working outside county of residence:** 40.4%.

Cities with pop over 10,000: None.

LETCHER COUNTY

156 Main St Suite 102   **Ph:** 606-633-2432
Whitesburg, KY 41858   **Fax:** 606-632-9282
www.letchercountykentucky.net

On southeastern border of KY; organized Mar 3, 1842 from Harlan and Perry counties. **Name Origin:** For Robert Perkins Letcher (1788-1861), U.S. representative from KY (1823-33; 1834-35), governor (1840-44), and U.S. Minister to Mexico (1849-52).

Area (sq mi): 339.12 (land 339.04; water 0.07). **Pop per sq mi:** 72.1.

Pop 2005: 24,434. **State rank:** 45. **Pop change:** 2000-20005 -3.3%; 1990-2000 -6.4%. **Pop 2000:** 25,277 (White 98.3%; Black or African American 0.5%; Hispanic or Latino 0.4%; Asian 0.3%; Other 0.5%). **Foreign born:** 0.4%. **Median age:** 37.9.

Income 2000: per capita $11,984; median household $21,110; **Pop below poverty level:** 27.1%. *****Personal per capita income 2000-2003:** $17,177-$19,367.

Unemployment 2004: 7.1%. **Change from 2000:** +0.7%. **Median travel time to work:** 25.9 minutes. **Working outside county of residence:** 27.6%.

Cities with pop over 10,000: None.

LEWIS COUNTY

514 2nd St   **Ph:** 606-796-2722
Vanceburg, KY 41179   **Fax:** 606-796-0822

On northeastern border of KY, west of Ashland; established Dec

Lewis County (cont'd)

2, 1806 from Mason County. **Name Origin:** For Meriwether Lewis (1774-1809), co-leader of the Lewis and Clark Expedition (1804-06).

Area (sq mi): 495.7 (land 484.49; water 11.21). **Pop per sq mi:** 28.6.

Pop 2005: 13,872. **State rank:** 81. **Pop change:** 2000-20005 -1.6%; 1990-2000 +8.2%. **Pop 2000:** 14,092 (White 98.6%; Black or African American 0.2%; Hispanic or Latino 0.4%; Asian 0%; Other 0.8%). **Foreign born:** 0.1%. **Median age:** 35.9.

Income 2000: per capita $12,031; median household $22,208; **Pop below poverty level:** 28.5%. ***Personal per capita income 2000-2003:** $14,269-$15,328.

Unemployment 2004: 8.1%. **Change from 2000:** -4.8%. **Median travel time to work:** 35.7 minutes. **Working outside county of residence:** 57.5%.

Cities with pop over 10,000: None.

LEXINGTON-FAYETTE COUNTY

162 E Main St
Lexington, KY 40507
www.lfucg.com

Ph: 859-253-3344
Fax: 859-231-9619

In central KY, south of Cincinnati, OH; organized May 1, 1780 (prior to statehood) from Kentucky County. In 1974 the county and its seat were combined and given an 'urban-county government.' **Name Origin:** For the Marquis de Lafayette (1757-1834), French statesman and soldier who fought with the Americans during the Revolutionary War.

Area (sq mi): 285.52 (land 284.52; water 1). **Pop per sq mi:** 942.2.

Pop 2005: 268,080. **State rank:** 2. **Pop change:** 2000-20005 +2.9%; 1990-2000 +15.6%. **Pop 2000:** 260,512 (White 79.1%; Black or African American 13.5%; Hispanic or Latino 3.3%; Asian 2.5%; Other 3%). **Foreign born:** 5.9%. **Median age:** 33.

Income 2000: per capita $23,109; median household $39,813; **Pop below poverty level:** 12.9%. ***Personal per capita income 2000-2003:** $31,180-$34,242.

Unemployment 2004: 3.9%. **Change from 2000:** +0.9%. **Median travel time to work:** 19.3 minutes. **Working outside county of residence:** 14%.

Cities with pop over 10,000: Lexington 🏛 (266,358).

LINCOLN COUNTY

102 E Main St County Courthouse
Stanford, KY 40484
www.lincolnky.com

Ph: 606-365-4570
Fax: 606-365-4572

In south-central KY, south of Lexington; organized May 1, 1780 (prior to statehood) from Kentucky County. **Name Origin:** For Gen. Benjamin Lincoln (1733-1810), Revolutionary War officer, U.S. secretary of war (1781-83), and lt. gov. of MA (1788).

Area (sq mi): 336.47 (land 336.26; water 0.21). **Pop per sq mi:** 74.7.

Pop 2005: 25,122. **State rank:** 43. **Pop change:** 2000-20005 +7.5%; 1990-2000 +16.5%. **Pop 2000:** 23,361 (White 95.7%; Black or African American 2.5%; Hispanic or Latino 0.9%; Asian 0.1%; Other 1.2%). **Foreign born:** 0.7%. **Median age:** 36.

Income 2000: per capita $13,602; median household $26,542; **Pop below poverty level:** 21.1%. ***Personal per capita income 2000-2003:** $17,887-$18,690.

Unemployment 2004: 6.8%. **Change from 2000:** +0.3%. **Median travel time to work:** 26.9 minutes. **Working outside county of residence:** 60.1%.

Cities with pop over 10,000: None.

LIVINGSTON COUNTY

335 Court St
Smithland, KY 42081
www.livingstonco.ky.gov

Ph: 270-928-2162
Fax: 270-928-2162

On northwestern border of KY, east of Paducah; established Dec 13, 1798 from Christian County. **Name Origin:** For Robert R. Livingston (1746-1813), NY patriot, statesman, and a drafter of the Declaration of Independence.

Area (sq mi): 342.2 (land 316.08; water 26.12). **Pop per sq mi:** 30.9.

Pop 2005: 9,760. **State rank:** 101. **Pop change:** 2000-20005 -0.4%; 1990-2000 +8.2%. **Pop 2000:** 9,804 (White 98%; Black or African American 0.1%; Hispanic or Latino 0.8%; Asian 0%; Other 1.3%). **Foreign born:** 0.2%. **Median age:** 39.8.

Income 2000: per capita $17,072; median household $31,776; **Pop below poverty level:** 10.3%. ***Personal per capita income 2000-2003:** $21,556-$23,607.

Unemployment 2004: 6%. **Change from 2000:** -1%. **Median travel time to work:** 25.9 minutes. **Working outside county of residence:** 61%.

Cities with pop over 10,000: None.

LOGAN COUNTY

229 W 3rd St PO Box 358
Russellville, KY 42276
www.loganchamber.com

Ph: 270-726-6061
Fax: 270-726-4355

On the southern border of KY, west of Bowling Green; organized Jun 28, 1792 from Lincoln County. **Name Origin:** For Benjamin Logan (c.1743-1802), VA patriot and soldier active in the West during the American Revolution.

Area (sq mi): 557.1 (land 555.68; water 1.41). **Pop per sq mi:** 48.9.

Pop 2005: 27,169. **State rank:** 41. **Pop change:** 2000-20005 +2.2%; 1990-2000 +8.8%. **Pop 2000:** 26,573 (White 90%; Black or African American 7.6%; Hispanic or Latino 1.1%; Asian 0.2%; Other 1.5%). **Foreign born:** 0.8%. **Median age:** 37.

Income 2000: per capita $15,962; median household $32,474; **Pop below poverty level:** 15.5%. ***Personal per capita income 2000-2003:** $21,014-$21,616.

Unemployment 2004: 5.4%. **Change from 2000:** -3.3%. **Median travel time to work:** 23.2 minutes. **Working outside county of residence:** 27%.

Cities with pop over 10,000: None.

LOUISVILLE-JEFFERSON COUNTY

527 W Jefferson St
Louisville, KY 40202
www.louisvilleky.gov

Ph: 502-574-5700
Fax: 502-574-5784

On the northwestern border of KY, west of Lexington; organized

---

*Source: Personal per capita income data are from the Bureau of Economic Analysis; per capita income data are from the Bureau of the Census. See Introduction for explanation of differences.

Louisville-Jefferson County (cont'd)

May 1, 1780 (prior to statehood) from Kentucky County. **Name Origin:** For Thomas Jefferson (1743-1826), U.S. patriot and statesman; third U.S. president.

Area (sq mi): 398.58 (land 385.09; water 13.49). **Pop per sq mi:** 1817.3.

Pop 2005: 699,827. **State rank:** 1. **Pop change:** 2000-20005 +0.9%; 1990-2000 +4.3%. **Pop 2000:** 693,604 (White 76.4%; Black or African American 18.9%; Hispanic or Latino 1.8%; Asian 1.4%; Other 2.3%). **Foreign born:** 3.4%. **Median age:** 36.7.

Income 2000: per capita $22,352; median household $39,457; **Pop below poverty level:** 12.4%. ***Personal per capita income 2000-2003:** $31,504-$36,071.

Unemployment 2004: 5.2%. **Change from 2000:** +0.4%. **Median travel time to work:** 21.9 minutes. **Working outside county of residence:** 7.7%.

Cities with pop over 10,000: Louisville 🏛 (556,332); Jeffersontown (26,232); Saint Matthews (17,374); Shively (15,258); Lyndon (10,270).

LYON COUNTY

PO Box 310	**Ph:** 270-388-2331
Eddyville, KY 42038	**Fax:** 270-388-0634
www.lyoncounty.com	

In western KY, east of Paducah; organized Jan 14, 1854 from Caldwell County. **Name Origin:** For Chittenden Lyon (1787-1842), U.S. representative from KY (1827-35).

Area (sq mi): 256.42 (land 215.7; water 40.71). **Pop per sq mi:** 37.8.

Pop 2005: 8,160. **State rank:** 108. **Pop change:** 2000-20005 +1%; 1990-2000 +22%. **Pop 2000:** 8,080 (White 91.6%; Black or African American 6.7%; Hispanic or Latino 0.7%; Asian 0.2%; Other 1.2%). **Foreign born:** 0.8%. **Median age:** 41.5.

Income 2000: per capita $16,016; median household $31,694; **Pop below poverty level:** 12.7%. ***Personal per capita income 2000-2003:** $18,706-$20,825.

Unemployment 2004: 6.7%. **Change from 2000:** +1.2%. **Median travel time to work:** 22.6 minutes. **Working outside county of residence:** 50.9%.

Cities with pop over 10,000: None.

MADISON COUNTY

101 W Main St	**Ph:** 859-624-4703
Richmond, KY 40475	**Fax:** 859-623-3071

In central KY, southeast of Lexington; established Oct 17, 1785 (prior to statehood) from Lincoln County. **Name Origin:** For James Madison (1751-1836), fourth U.S. president.

Area (sq mi): 443.11 (land 440.68; water 2.42). **Pop per sq mi:** 176.4.

Pop 2005: 77,749. **State rank:** 9. **Pop change:** 2000-20005 +9.7%; 1990-2000 +23.2%. **Pop 2000:** 70,872 (White 92.4%; Black or African American 4.4%; Hispanic or Latino 1%; Asian 0.7%; Other 1.8%). **Foreign born:** 1.5%. **Median age:** 30.7.

Income 2000: per capita $16,790; median household $32,861; **Pop below poverty level:** 16.8%. ***Personal per capita income 2000-2003:** $20,170-$21,726.

Unemployment 2004: 4.7%. **Change from 2000:** +0.4%. **Median travel time to work:** 23.5 minutes. **Working outside county of residence:** 30.2%.

Cities with pop over 10,000: Richmond 🏛 (30,008); Berea (12,738).

MAGOFFIN COUNTY

PO Box 430	**Ph:** 606-349-2313
Salyersville, KY 41465	**Fax:** 606-349-2109

In east-central KY; organized Feb 22, 1860 from Floyd, Johnson, and Morgan counties. **Name Origin:** For Beriah Magoffin (1815-85), KY legislator and governor (1859-62).

Area (sq mi): 309.44 (land 309.44; water 0.01). **Pop per sq mi:** 43.5.

Pop 2005: 13,472. **State rank:** 85. **Pop change:** 2000-20005 +1.1%; 1990-2000 +2%. **Pop 2000:** 13,332 (White 98.9%; Black or African American 0.2%; Hispanic or Latino 0.4%; Asian 0.1%; Other 0.5%). **Foreign born:** 0.2%. **Median age:** 34.3.

Income 2000: per capita $10,685; median household $19,421; **Pop below poverty level:** 36.6%. ***Personal per capita income 2000-2003:** $15,710-$17,255.

Unemployment 2004: 12.6%. **Change from 2000:** +0%. **Median travel time to work:** 38.5 minutes. **Working outside county of residence:** 41.2%.

Cities with pop over 10,000: None.

MARION COUNTY

120 W Main St Suite 3	**Ph:** 270-692-2651
Lebanon, KY 40033	**Fax:** 270-692-9811
www.lebanonky.org	

In west-central KY, southwest of Lexington; organized Jan 25, 1834 from Washington County. **Name Origin:** For Gen. Francis Marion (c.1732-95), SC soldier and legislator, known as 'The Swamp Fox' for his tactics during the Revolutionary War.

Area (sq mi): 346.86 (land 346.39; water 0.47). **Pop per sq mi:** 54.7.

Pop 2005: 18,939. **State rank:** 58. **Pop change:** 2000-20005 +4%; 1990-2000 +10.4%. **Pop 2000:** 18,212 (White 88.8%; Black or African American 9.1%; Hispanic or Latino 0.8%; Asian 0.4%; Other 1.3%). **Foreign born:** 1.2%. **Median age:** 35.4.

Income 2000: per capita $14,472; median household $30,387; **Pop below poverty level:** 18.6%. ***Personal per capita income 2000-2003:** $19,957-$22,624.

Unemployment 2004: 4.9%. **Change from 2000:** -0.7%. **Median travel time to work:** 24.4 minutes. **Working outside county of residence:** 33%.

Cities with pop over 10,000: None.

MARSHALL COUNTY

1101 Main St	**Ph:** 270-527-4740
Benton, KY 42025	**Fax:** 270-527-4738
www.marshallcounty.net	

In western KY, southeast of Paducah; organized Feb 12, 1842 from

🏛 *County Seat*

Marshall County (cont'd)

Calloway County. **Name Origin:** For John Marshall (1755-1835), American jurist; fourth Chief Justice of the U.S. Supreme Court (1801-35).

Area (sq mi): 340.32 (land 304.89; water 35.43). **Pop per sq mi:** 101.6.

Pop 2005: 30,967. **State rank:** 35. **Pop change:** 2000-20005 +2.8%; 1990-2000 +10.7%. **Pop 2000:** 30,125 (White 98.1%; Black or African American 0.1%; Hispanic or Latino 0.8%; Asian 0.1%; Other 1.2%). **Foreign born:** 0.8%. **Median age:** 40.9.

Income 2000: per capita $18,069; median household $35,573; **Pop below poverty level:** 9.5%. ***Personal per capita income 2000-2003:** $24,504-$24,971.

Unemployment 2004: 6.4%. **Change from 2000:** -1%. **Median travel time to work:** 22.3 minutes. **Working outside county of residence:** 39.6%.

Cities with pop over 10,000: None.

MARTIN COUNTY
PO Box 460   **Ph:** 606-298-2810
Inez, KY 41224   **Fax:** 606-298-0143

On the eastern border of KY, south of Ashland; organized May 10, 1870 from Johnson, Pike, Floyd, and Lawrence counties. **Name Origin:** For John Preston Martin (1811-62), KY legislator and U.S. representative (1845-47).

Area (sq mi): 230.81 (land 230.7; water 0.11). **Pop per sq mi:** 52.9.

Pop 2005: 12,215. **State rank:** 89. **Pop change:** 2000-20005 -2.9%; 1990-2000 +0.4%. **Pop 2000:** 12,578 (White 98.7%; Black or African American 0%; Hispanic or Latino 0.6%; Asian 0.1%; Other 0.7%). **Foreign born:** 0.1%. **Median age:** 34.1.

Income 2000: per capita $10,650; median household $18,279; **Pop below poverty level:** 37%. ***Personal per capita income 2000-2003:** $15,884-$18,571.

Unemployment 2004: 7.4%. **Change from 2000:** +1%. **Median travel time to work:** 29.8 minutes. **Working outside county of residence:** 33.2%.

Cities with pop over 10,000: None.

MASON COUNTY
27 W 3rd St PO Box 234   **Ph:** 606-564-3341
Maysville, KY 41056   **Fax:** 606-564-8979
www.masoncounty-ky.com

On the northeastern border of KY, northeast of Lexington; established Nov 5, 1788 (prior to statehood) from Bourbon County. **Name Origin:** For George Mason (1725-92), author of the VA Declaration of Rights (1776), which served as the model for the American Bill of Rights.

Area (sq mi): 246.6 (land 241.11; water 5.49). **Pop per sq mi:** 71.1.

Pop 2005: 17,140. **State rank:** 65. **Pop change:** 2000-20005 +2%; 1990-2000 +0.8%. **Pop 2000:** 16,800 (White 90.5%; Black or African American 7.2%; Hispanic or Latino 1%; Asian 0.4%; Other 1.6%). **Foreign born:** 1.4%. **Median age:** 38.1.

Income 2000: per capita $16,589; median household $30,195; **Pop below poverty level:** 16.8%. ***Personal per capita income 2000-2003:** $21,915-$23,932.

Unemployment 2004: 5.5%. **Change from 2000:** +1.2%. **Median travel time to work:** 21.5 minutes. **Working outside county of residence:** 20.9%.

Cities with pop over 10,000: None.

MCCRACKEN COUNTY
PO Box 609   **Ph:** 270-444-4700
Paducah, KY 42002   **Fax:** 270-444-4704
www.co.mccracken.ky.us

On southwestern border of KY; established Dec 17, 1824 from Hickman County. **Name Origin:** For Capt. Virgil McCracken (?-1813), a soldier killed during the War of 1812 at the Frenchtown Battle on the River Raisin, MI.

Area (sq mi): 268.08 (land 251.02; water 17.05). **Pop per sq mi:** 257.7.

Pop 2005: 64,698. **State rank:** 13. **Pop change:** 2000-20005 -1.2%; 1990-2000 +4.2%. **Pop 2000:** 65,514 (White 86.2%; Black or African American 10.9%; Hispanic or Latino 1.1%; Asian 0.5%; Other 1.9%). **Foreign born:** 0.9%. **Median age:** 39.2.

Income 2000: per capita $19,533; median household $33,865; **Pop below poverty level:** 15.1%. ***Personal per capita income 2000-2003:** $27,761-$30,316.

Unemployment 2004: 5.3%. **Change from 2000:** +0.8%. **Median travel time to work:** 17.8 minutes. **Working outside county of residence:** 16.2%.

Cities with pop over 10,000: Paducah ⛁ (25,545).

MCCREARY COUNTY
PO Box 699   **Ph:** 606-376-2411
Whitley City, KY 42653   **Fax:** 606-376-3898
www.mccrearycounty.com

On the southern border of KY, south of Lexington; organized Mar 12, 1912 from Pulaski, Wayne, and Whitley counties. **Name Origin:** For Lt. Col. James Bennett McCreary (1838-1918), KY legislator, governor (1875-79; 1911-15), and U.S. senator (1903-09).

Area (sq mi): 430.64 (land 427.7; water 2.94). **Pop per sq mi:** 40.3.

Pop 2005: 17,233. **State rank:** 64. **Pop change:** 2000-20005 +0.9%; 1990-2000 +9.5%. **Pop 2000:** 17,080 (White 97.6%; Black or African American 0.6%; Hispanic or Latino 0.6%; Asian 0%; Other 1.3%). **Foreign born:** 0.5%. **Median age:** 34.2.

Income 2000: per capita $9,896; median household $19,348; **Pop below poverty level:** 32.2%. ***Personal per capita income 2000-2003:** $13,655-$15,085.

Unemployment 2004: 7.7%. **Change from 2000:** -4.1%. **Median travel time to work:** 28.2 minutes. **Working outside county of residence:** 36.6%.

Cities with pop over 10,000: None.

MCLEAN COUNTY
PO Box 57   **Ph:** 270-273-3082
Calhoun, KY 42327   **Fax:** 270-273-5084

In western KY, south of Owensboro; organized Feb 6, 1854 from

*Source: Personal per capita income data are from the Bureau of Economic Analysis; per capita income data are from the Bureau of the Census.
See Introduction for explanation of differences.

298

McLean County (cont'd)

Daviess, Ohio, and Muhlenberg counties. **Name Origin:** For Capt. Alney McLean (1779-1841), U.S. representative from KY (1815-17; 1819-21) and district court judge (1821-41).

Area (sq mi): 256.17 (land 254.3; water 1.88). **Pop per sq mi:** 39.

Pop 2005: 9,926. **State rank:** 100. **Pop change:** 2000-20005 -0.1%; 1990-2000 +3.2%. **Pop 2000:** 9,938 (White 98.1%, Black or African American 0.4%; Hispanic or Latino 0.8%; Asian 0%; Other 1%). **Foreign born:** 0.7%. **Median age:** 38.1.

Income 2000: per capita $16,046; median household $29,675; **Pop below poverty level:** 16%. *****Personal per capita income 2000-2003:** $26,903-$25,374.

Unemployment 2004: 6.3%. **Change from 2000:** -0.8%. **Median travel time to work:** 30.1 minutes. **Working outside county of residence:** 61.5%.

Cities with pop over 10,000: None.

MEADE COUNTY

PO Box 614   **Ph:** 270-422-2152
Brandenburg, KY 40108   **Fax:** 270-422-2158
www.meadecountyclerk.ky.gov

On the northwestern border of KY, southwest of Louisville; established Dec 17, 1823 from Breckinridge and Hardin counties. **Name Origin:** For Capt. James Meade (?-1813), an officer in the War of 1812 killed at the Frenchtown Battle on the River Raisin, MI.

Area (sq mi): 324.22 (land 308.51; water 15.71). **Pop per sq mi:** 92.2.

Pop 2005: 28,447. **State rank:** 38. **Pop change:** 2000-20005 +8%; 1990-2000 +9%. **Pop 2000:** 26,349 (White 91.3%; Black or African American 4.1%; Hispanic or Latino 2.2%; Asian 0.5%; Other 2.9%). **Foreign born:** 2%. **Median age:** 32.2.

Income 2000: per capita $16,000; median household $36,966; **Pop below poverty level:** 11.3%. *****Personal per capita income 2000-2003:** $21,355-$22,085.

Unemployment 2004: 5.7%. **Change from 2000:** -0.1%. **Median travel time to work:** 31.1 minutes. **Working outside county of residence:** 65.7%.

Cities with pop over 10,000: None.

MENIFEE COUNTY

PO Box 123   **Ph:** 606-768-3512
Frenchburg, KY 40322   **Fax:** 606-768-6738

In east-central KY, east of Lexington; organized Mar 10, 1869 from Montgomery, Bath, Wolfe, Morgan, and Powell counties. **Name Origin:** For Richard Hickman Menefee (1809-41), KY Commonwealth attorney, legislator, and U.S. representative (1837-39). Spelling evidently changed when county was named.

Area (sq mi): 206.03 (land 203.9; water 2.13). **Pop per sq mi:** 33.4.

Pop 2005: 6,809. **State rank:** 116. **Pop change:** 2000-20005 +3.9%; 1990-2000 +28.8%. **Pop 2000:** 6,556 (White 96.9%; Black or African American 1.4%; Hispanic or Latino 1.1%; Asian 0%; Other 0.9%). **Foreign born:** 0.4%. **Median age:** 36.3.

Income 2000: per capita $11,399; median household $22,064; **Pop below poverty level:** 29.6%. *****Personal per capita income 2000-2003:** $14,590-$15,821.

Unemployment 2004: 6.9%. **Change from 2000:** -1%. **Median travel time to work:** 36.1 minutes. **Working outside county of residence:** 55%.

Cities with pop over 10,000: None.

MERCER COUNTY

PO Box 426   **Ph:** 859-734-6310
Harrodsburg, KY 40330   **Fax:** 859-734-6309
www.merceronline.com/mercer.htm

In central KY, southwest of Lexington; established Oct 17, 1785 (prior to statehood) from Lincoln County. **Name Origin:** For Gen. Hugh Mercer (1721-77), Revolutionary War officer and physician.

Area (sq mi): 253.11 (land 250.92; water 2.2). **Pop per sq mi:** 86.1.

Pop 2005: 21,610. **State rank:** 53. **Pop change:** 2000-20005 +3.8%; 1990-2000 +8.7%. **Pop 2000:** 20,817 (White 93.4%; Black or African American 3.7%; Hispanic or Latino 1.3%; Asian 0.5%; Other 1.8%). **Foreign born:** 1.7%. **Median age:** 38.2.

Income 2000: per capita $17,972; median household $35,555; **Pop below poverty level:** 12.9%. *****Personal per capita income 2000-2003:** $22,966-$23,269.

Unemployment 2004: 5%. **Change from 2000:** -0.3%. **Median travel time to work:** 24 minutes. **Working outside county of residence:** 45.5%.

Cities with pop over 10,000: None.

METCALFE COUNTY

PO Box 25   **Ph:** 270-432-4821
Edmonton, KY 42129   **Fax:** 270-432-5176

In south-central KY, east of Bowling Green; organized Feb 1, 1860 from Adair, Monroe, Cumberland, Barren, and Green counties. **Name Origin:** For Capt. Thomas Metcalfe (1780-1855), KY legislator, governor (1828-32), and U.S. senator (1848-49).

Area (sq mi): 290.96 (land 290.9; water 0.07). **Pop per sq mi:** 35.1.

Pop 2005: 10,197. **State rank:** 99. **Pop change:** 2000-20005 +1.6%; 1990-2000 +12%. **Pop 2000:** 10,037 (White 96.8%; Black or African American 1.6%; Hispanic or Latino 0.5%; Asian 0.1%; Other 0.9%). **Foreign born:** 0.2%. **Median age:** 37.7.

Income 2000: per capita $13,236; median household $23,540; **Pop below poverty level:** 23.6%. *****Personal per capita income 2000-2003:** $17,275-$18,496.

Unemployment 2004: 4.3%. **Change from 2000:** -0.7%. **Median travel time to work:** 26.7 minutes. **Working outside county of residence:** 46.1%.

Cities with pop over 10,000: None.

MONROE COUNTY

200 N Main St Suite D   **Ph:** 270-487-5471
Tompkinsville, KY 42167   **Fax:** 270-487-5976

On southern border of KY, southeast of Bowling Green; organized Jan 19, 1820 from Barren and Cumberland counties. **Name Origin:** For James Monroe (1758-1831), fifth U.S. president.

🏛 *County Seat*

Monroe County (cont'd)

Area (sq mi): 332.11 (land 330.81; water 1.3). **Pop per sq mi:** 35.2.

Pop 2005: 11,660. **State rank:** 93. **Pop change:** 2000-20005 -0.8%; 1990-2000 +3.1%. **Pop 2000:** 11,756 (White 95.1%; Black or African American 2.8%; Hispanic or Latino 1.4%; Asian 0%; Other 1.6%). **Foreign born:** 1.4%. **Median age:** 38.2.

Income 2000: per capita $14,365; median household $22,356; **Pop below poverty level:** 23.4%. ***Personal per capita income 2000-2003:** $18,242-$19,173.

Unemployment 2004: 5.1%. **Change from 2000:** -7.8%. **Median travel time to work:** 23.3 minutes. **Working outside county of residence:** 26.9%.

Cities with pop over 10,000: None.

MONTGOMERY COUNTY

PO Box 414   **Ph:** 859-498-8700
Mount Sterling, KY 40353   **Fax:** 859-498-8729

In central KY, east of Lexington; established May 1, 1797 (prior to statehood) from Clark County. **Name Origin:** For Gen. Richard Montgomery (1736-75), American Revolutionary War officer who captured Montreal, Canada.

Area (sq mi): 198.8 (land 198.59; water 0.21). **Pop per sq mi:** 122.1.

Pop 2005: 24,256. **State rank:** 46. **Pop change:** 2000-20005 +7.5%; 1990-2000 +15.3%. **Pop 2000:** 22,554 (White 94.3%; Black or African American 3.5%; Hispanic or Latino 1.1%; Asian 0.1%; Other 1.3%). **Foreign born:** 0.5%. **Median age:** 36.

Income 2000: per capita $16,701; median household $31,746; **Pop below poverty level:** 15.2%. ***Personal per capita income 2000-2003:** $20,831-$22,115.

Unemployment 2004: 6.2%. **Change from 2000:** -0.2%. **Median travel time to work:** 25.1 minutes. **Working outside county of residence:** 36.9%.

Cities with pop over 10,000: None.

MORGAN COUNTY

PO Box 26   **Ph:** 606-743-3949
West Liberty, KY 41472   **Fax:** 606-743-2111

In eastern KY, east of Lexington; established Dec 7, 1822 from Floyd and Bath counties. **Name Origin:** For Gen. Daniel Morgan (1736-1802), an officer in the Revolutionary War and U.S. representative from VA (1797-99).

Area (sq mi): 383.73 (land 381.26; water 2.47). **Pop per sq mi:** 37.6.

Pop 2005: 14,334. **State rank:** 79. **Pop change:** 2000-20005 +2.8%; 1990-2000 +19.7%. **Pop 2000:** 13,948 (White 94.1%; Black or African American 4.4%; Hispanic or Latino 0.6%; Asian 0.2%; Other 0.9%). **Foreign born:** 0.7%. **Median age:** 35.8.

Income 2000: per capita $12,657; median household $21,869; **Pop below poverty level:** 27.2%. ***Personal per capita income 2000-2003:** $14,047-$15,339.

Unemployment 2004: 8.4%. **Change from 2000:** -1.6%. **Median travel time to work:** 33.2 minutes. **Working outside county of residence:** 34.8%.

Cities with pop over 10,000: None.

MUHLENBERG COUNTY

PO Box 525   **Ph:** 270-338-1441
Greenville, KY 42345   **Fax:** 270-338-1774

In west-central KY, northeast of Hopkinsville; established Dec 14, 1798 from Christian and Logan counties. **Name Origin:** For Gen. John Peter Gabriel Muhlenberg (1746-1807), an officer in the Revolutionary War, Lutheran minister, and U.S. representative from PA (1789-91; 1793-95; 1799-1801).

Area (sq mi): 479.43 (land 474.72; water 4.71). **Pop per sq mi:** 66.5.

Pop 2005: 31,548. **State rank:** 34. **Pop change:** 2000-20005 -0.9%; 1990-2000 +1.7%. **Pop 2000:** 31,839 (White 93.7%; Black or African American 4.6%; Hispanic or Latino 0.7%; Asian 0.1%; Other 1%). **Foreign born:** 0.3%. **Median age:** 38.7.

Income 2000: per capita $14,798; median household $28,566; **Pop below poverty level:** 19.7%. ***Personal per capita income 2000-2003:** $20,203-$20,658.

Unemployment 2004: 7.3%. **Change from 2000:** -3%. **Median travel time to work:** 24.3 minutes. **Working outside county of residence:** 27.1%.

Cities with pop over 10,000: None.

NELSON COUNTY

113 E Steven Foster St   **Ph:** 502-348-1820
Bardstown, KY 40004   **Fax:** 502-348-1822

In west-central KY, southeast of Louisville; established Oct 18, 1784 (prior to statehood) from Jefferson County. **Name Origin:** For Thomas Nelson (1738-89), member of the Continental Congress, a signer of the Declaration of Independence, and governor of VA (1781).

Area (sq mi): 424.07 (land 422.63; water 1.45). **Pop per sq mi:** 97.2.

Pop 2005: 41,088. **State rank:** 23. **Pop change:** 2000-20005 +9.6%; 1990-2000 +26.1%. **Pop 2000:** 37,477 (White 92.3%; Black or African American 5.5%; Hispanic or Latino 1.1%; Asian 0.5%; Other 1.1%). **Foreign born:** 1.2%. **Median age:** 34.9.

Income 2000: per capita $18,120; median household $39,010; **Pop below poverty level:** 12.2%. ***Personal per capita income 2000-2003:** $24,877-$26,906.

Unemployment 2004: 5%. **Change from 2000:** -2%. **Median travel time to work:** 26.5 minutes. **Working outside county of residence:** 36.4%.

Cities with pop over 10,000: Bardstown 🏛 (10,897).

NICHOLAS COUNTY

PO Box 227   **Ph:** 859-289-3730
Carlisle, KY 40311   **Fax:** 859-289-3705
www.carlisle-nicholascounty.org

In north-central KY, northeast of Lexington; established Dec 18, 1799 from Bourbon and Mason counties. **Name Origin:** For Col. George Nicholas (1754-99), officer in the Revolutionary War and first attorney general of KY. He is considered the 'Father of the KY Constitution' for his part in drafting it.

Area (sq mi): 196.85 (land 196.61; water 0.24). **Pop per sq mi:** 35.7.

Pop 2005: 7,027. **State rank:** 114. **Pop change:** 2000-20005 +3.1%; 1990-2000 +1.3%. **Pop 2000:** 6,813 (White 98%; Black or African

*Source: Personal per capita income data are from the Bureau of Economic Analysis; per capita income data are from the Bureau of the Census. See Introduction for explanation of differences.

300

Nicholas County (cont'd)

American 0.8%; Hispanic or Latino 0.5%; Asian 0.1%; Other 0.6%). **Foreign born:** 0.5%. **Median age:** 38.4.

Income 2000: per capita $15,880; median household $29,886; **Pop below poverty level:** 13.2%. ***Personal per capita income 2000-2003:** $21,342-$21,213.

Unemployment 2004: 6%. **Change from 2000:** 2.8%. **Median travel time to work:** 33.8 minutes. **Working outside county of residence:** 64.3%.

Cities with pop over 10,000: None.

OHIO COUNTY

PO Box 85   **Ph:** 270-298-4423
Hartford, KY 42347   **Fax:** 270-298-4425

In west-central KY, south of Owensboro; established Dec 17, 1798 from Hardin County. **Name Origin:** For the Ohio River which originally formed its northern border.

Area (sq mi): 596.73 (land 593.79, water 2.94). **Pop per sq mi** 39.9.

Pop 2005: 23,676. **State rank:** 51. **Pop change:** 2000-20005 +3.3%; 1990-2000 +8.6%. **Pop 2000:** 22,916 (White 97.2%; Black or African American 0.7%; Hispanic or Latino 1%; Asian 0.2%; Other 1.3%). **Foreign born:** 0.7%. **Median age:** 37.5.

Income 2000: per capita $15,317; median household $29,557; **Pop below poverty level:** 17.3%. ***Personal per capita income 2000-2003:** $18,901-$19,956.

Unemployment 2004: 6%. **Change from 2000:** -1.9%. **Median travel time to work:** 28.6 minutes. **Working outside county of residence:** 42.4%.

Cities with pop over 10,000: None.

OLDHAM COUNTY

100 W Jefferson St   **Ph:** 502-222-9311
LaGrange, KY 40031   **Fax:** 502-222-3208
www.oldhamcounty.net

On the northwestern border of KY, north of Louisville; organized Dec 16, 1823 from Jefferson, Shelby, and Henry counties. **Name Origin:** For Col. William Oldham (?-1791), officer in the American Revolution, killed in a battle with Indians.

Area (sq mi): 196.54 (land 189.19; water 7.36). **Pop per sq mi:** 283.

Pop 2005: 53,533. **State rank:** 16. **Pop change:** 2000-20005 +15.9%; 1990-2000 +38.8%. **Pop 2000:** 46,178 (White 92.9%; Black or African American 4.2%; Hispanic or Latino 1.3%; Asian 0.4%; Other 1.8%). **Foreign born:** 1.6%. **Median age:** 36.7.

Income 2000: per capita $25,374; median household $63,229; **Pop below poverty level:** 4.1%. ***Personal per capita income 2000-2003:** $32,342-$33,460.

Unemployment 2004: 3.7%. **Change from 2000:** +1.2%. **Median travel time to work:** 26.1 minutes. **Working outside county of residence:** 66.8%.

Cities with pop over 10,000: None.

OWEN COUNTY

100 N Thomas St   **Ph:** 502-484-3405
Owenton, KY 40359   **Fax:** 502-484-1004
www.owenton.net

In northern KY, northwest of Lexington; organized Feb 6, 1819 from Scott, Gallatin, and Franklin counties. **Name Origin:** For Abraham Owen (?-1811), officer killed at the Battle of Tippecanoe.

Area (sq mi): 354.16 (land 352.14; water 2.02). **Pop per sq mi:** 32.3.

Pop 2005: 11,374. **State rank:** 97. **Pop change:** 2000-20005 +7.8%; 1990-2000 +16.7%. **Pop 2000:** 10,547 (White 96.6%; Black or African American 1.1%; Hispanic or Latino 1%; Asian 0.2%; Other 1.7%). **Foreign born:** 0.7%. **Median age:** 37.5.

Income 2000: per capita $15,521; median household $33,310; **Pop below poverty level:** 15.5%. ***Personal per capita income 2000-2003:** $19,163-$18,804.

Unemployment 2004: 4.8%. **Change from 2000:** +0.6%. **Median travel time to work:** 32.3 minutes. **Working outside county of residence:** 58.2%.

Cities with pop over 10,000: None.

OWSLEY COUNTY

PO Box 500   **Ph:** 606-593-5735
Booneville, KY 41314   **Fax:** 606-593-5737
www.owsleycountykentucky.org

In southeast KY, southeast of Lexington; organized Jan 23, 1843 from Clay, Estill, and Breathitt counties. **Name Origin:** For William Owsley (1782-1862), judge of the KY Court of Appeals, and governor (1844-48).

Area (sq mi): 198.09 (land 198.09; water 0). **Pop per sq mi:** 24.

Pop 2005: 4,746. **State rank:** 119. **Pop change:** 2000-20005 -2.3%; 1990-2000 -3.5%. **Pop 2000:** 4,858 (White 98.5%; Black or African American 0.1%; Hispanic or Latino 0.7%; Asian 0%; Other 0.6%). **Foreign born:** 0.1%. **Median age:** 38.2.

Income 2000: per capita $10,742; median household $15,805; **Pop below poverty level:** 45.4%. ***Personal per capita income 2000-2003:** $16,638-$17,620.

Unemployment 2004: 7.2%. **Change from 2000:** +1.5%. **Median travel time to work:** 28.7 minutes. **Working outside county of residence:** 43.9%.

Cities with pop over 10,000: None.

PENDLETON COUNTY

233 Main St   **Ph:** 859-654-4321
Falmouth, KY 41040   **Fax:** 859-654-5047
www.pendletoncountyky.org

In northern KY, south of Covington; established Dec 4, 1787 from Campbell and Bracken counties. **Name Origin:** For Edmund Pendleton (1721-1803), member of the Continental Congress (1774-75), active in establishment of state of VA, and president of the VA supreme court of appeals (1779-1803).

Area (sq mi): 281.87 (land 280.54; water 1.33). **Pop per sq mi:** 53.9.

Pop 2005: 15,125. **State rank:** 76. **Pop change:** 2000-20005 +5.1%; 1990-2000 +19.6%. **Pop 2000:** 14,390 (White 98.1%; Black or African American 0.5%; Hispanic or Latino 0.7%; Asian 0.1%; Other 1%). **Foreign born:** 0.5%. **Median age:** 34.5.

Pendleton County (cont'd)

Income 2000: per capita $16,551; median household $38,125; **Pop below poverty level:** 11.4%. ***Personal per capita income 2000-2003:** $20,797-$20,801.

Unemployment 2004: 4.7%. **Change from 2000:** -0.6%. **Median travel time to work:** 35.1 minutes. **Working outside county of residence:** 61.6%.

Cities with pop over 10,000: None.

PERRY COUNTY

PO Box 150   **Ph:** 606-436-4614
Hazard, KY 41702   **Fax:** 606-439-0557

In southeastern KY; established Nov 2, 1820 from Clay and Floyd counties. **Name Origin:** For Oliver Hazard Perry (1785-1819), U.S. naval officer during the War of 1812, famous for the message, 'We have met the enemy and they are ours.'

Area (sq mi): 342.64 (land 342.15; water 0.49). **Pop per sq mi:** 86.1.

Pop 2005: 29,452. **State rank:** 37. **Pop change:** 2000-20005 +0.2%; 1990-2000 -2.9%. **Pop 2000:** 29,390 (White 96.9%; Black or African American 1.6%; Hispanic or Latino 0.5%; Asian 0.5%; Other 0.5%). **Foreign born:** 0.6%. **Median age:** 36.3.

Income 2000: per capita $12,224; median household $22,089; **Pop below poverty level:** 29.1%. ***Personal per capita income 2000-2003:** $19,006-$21,062.

Unemployment 2004: 7.6%. **Change from 2000:** +1.5%. **Median travel time to work:** 23.2 minutes. **Working outside county of residence:** 11.1%.

Cities with pop over 10,000: None.

PIKE COUNTY

PO Box 631   **Ph:** 606-432-6240
Pikeville, KY 41502   **Fax:** 606-432-6222

On the central eastern border of KY; established Dec 19, 1821 from Floyd County. **Name Origin:** For Gen. Zebulon Montgomery Pike (1779-1813), U.S. army officer and discoverer of Pikes Peak in CO.

Area (sq mi): 788.84 (land 787.69; water 1.15). **Pop per sq mi:** 85.

Pop 2005: 66,922. **State rank:** 12. **Pop change:** 2000-20005 -2.6%; 1990-2000 -5.3%. **Pop 2000:** 68,736 (White 97.9%; Black or African American 0.5%; Hispanic or Latino 0.7%; Asian 0.4%; Other 0.8%). **Foreign born:** 0.4%. **Median age:** 37.1.

Income 2000: per capita $14,005; median household $23,930; **Pop below poverty level:** 23.4%. ***Personal per capita income 2000-2003:** $19,648-$21,141.

Unemployment 2004: 6.5%. **Change from 2000:** +1.9%. **Median travel time to work:** 27.1 minutes. **Working outside county of residence:** 14.6%.

Cities with pop over 10,000: None.

POWELL COUNTY

PO Box 548   **Ph:** 606-663-6444
Stanton, KY 40380   **Fax:** 606-663-6406

In east-central KY, southeast of Lexington; organized Jan 7, 1852 from Montgomery, Clark, and Estill counties. **Name Origin:** For

Lazarus Whitehead Powell (1812-67), governor of KY (1851-55), U.S. commissioner to UT (1858), and U.S. senator from KY (1859-65).

Area (sq mi): 180.2 (land 180.14; water 0.07). **Pop per sq mi:** 76.

Pop 2005: 13,687. **State rank:** 83. **Pop change:** 2000-20005 +3.4%; 1990-2000 +13.3%. **Pop 2000:** 13,237 (White 98%; Black or African American 0.6%; Hispanic or Latino 0.7%; Asian 0.1%; Other 0.8%). **Foreign born:** 0.2%. **Median age:** 34.8.

Income 2000: per capita $13,060; median household $25,515; **Pop below poverty level:** 23.5%. ***Personal per capita income 2000-2003:** $17,353-$18,627.

Unemployment 2004: 8%. **Change from 2000:** -0.5%. **Median travel time to work:** 28.9 minutes. **Working outside county of residence:** 50.8%.

Cities with pop over 10,000: None.

PULASKI COUNTY

PO Box 724   **Ph:** 606-679-2042
Somerset, KY 42502   **Fax:** 606-678-0073
www.pulaskicountygovt.com

In south-central KY, south of Lexington; established Dec 10, 1798 from Lincoln and Green counties. **Name Origin:** For Count Casimir Pulaski (1747-79), Polish soldier who fought for America during the Revolutionary War.

Area (sq mi): 677.05 (land 661.6; water 15.45). **Pop per sq mi:** 89.5.

Pop 2005: 59,200. **State rank:** 14. **Pop change:** 2000-20005 +5.3%; 1990-2000 +13.6%. **Pop 2000:** 56,217 (White 96.9%; Black or African American 1.1%; Hispanic or Latino 0.8%; Asian 0.4%; Other 1.1%). **Foreign born:** 0.8%. **Median age:** 38.5.

Income 2000: per capita $15,352; median household $27,370; **Pop below poverty level:** 19.1%. ***Personal per capita income 2000-2003:** $20,651-$22,637.

Unemployment 2004: 5.1%. **Change from 2000:** -2.3%. **Median travel time to work:** 22.5 minutes. **Working outside county of residence:** 11.3%.

Cities with pop over 10,000: Somerset ⚒ (11,972).

ROBERTSON COUNTY

PO Box 75   **Ph:** 606-724-5212
Mount Olivet, KY 41064   **Fax:** 606-724-5022
www.robertsoncountyky.com

In north-central KY, southeast of Covington; organized Feb 11, 1867 from Nicholas, Harrison, Bracken, and Mason counties. **Name Origin:** For George Robertson (1790-1874), U.S. representative from KY (1817-21) and chief justice of KY Court of Appeals (1829-34).

Area (sq mi): 100.11 (land 100.07; water 0.04). **Pop per sq mi:** 22.8.

Pop 2005: 2,279. **State rank:** 120. **Pop change:** 2000-20005 +0.6%; 1990-2000 +6.7%. **Pop 2000:** 2,266 (White 98.5%; Black or African American 0%; Hispanic or Latino 0.9%; Asian 0%; Other 1.3%). **Foreign born:** 0.5%. **Median age:** 39.5.

Income 2000: per capita $13,404; median household $30,581; **Pop below poverty level:** 22.2%. ***Personal per capita income 2000-2003:** $18,221-$17,286.

Source: Personal per capita income data are from the Bureau of Economic Analysis; per capita income data are from the Bureau of the Census. See Introduction for explanation of differences.

Robertson County (cont'd)

Unemployment 2004: 5.4%. **Change from 2000:** +0.4%. **Median travel time to work:** 37.8 minutes. **Working outside county of residence:** 61.2%.

Cities with pop over 10,000: None.

ROCKCASTLE COUNTY

205 E Main St Box 6   **Ph:** 606-256-2831
Mount Vernon, KY 40456   **Fax:** 606-256-4302
www.rockcastlecountyky.com

In south-central KY, southeast of Lexington; organized Jan 8, 1810 from Lincoln, Pulaski, Madison, and Knox counties. **Name Origin:** For the Rockcastle River, which flows along the southeastern border of the county; named for the castle-like rock formations along its banks.

Area (sq mi): 318.06 (land 317.53; water 0.54). **Pop per sq mi:** 52.6.

Pop 2005: 16,712. **State rank:** 68. **Pop change:** 2000-20005 +0.8%; 1990-2000 +12%. **Pop 2000:** 16,582 (White 98.3%; Black or African American 0.1%; Hispanic or Latino 0.6%; Asian 0.1%; Other 0.8%). **Foreign born:** 0%. **Median age:** 36.3.

Income 2000: per capita $12,337; median household $23,475; **Pop below poverty level:** 23.1%. ***Personal per capita income 2000-2003:** $15,724-$17,143.

Unemployment 2004: 5.4%. **Change from 2000:** -2.6%. **Median travel time to work:** 28.4 minutes. **Working outside county of residence:** 48.5%.

Cities with pop over 10,000: None.

ROWAN COUNTY

627 E Main St 2nd Fl   **Ph:** 606-784-5212
Morehead, KY 40351   **Fax:** 606-784-2923

In northeastern KY, northeast of Lexington; organized Mar 15, 1856 from Fleming and Morgan counties. **Name Origin:** For John Rowan (1773-1843), judge of the KY Court of Appeals (1819-21) and U.S. senator (1825-31).

Area (sq mi): 286.25 (land 280.82; water 5.43). **Pop per sq mi:** 79.1.

Pop 2005: 22,226. **State rank:** 52. **Pop change:** 2000-20005 +0.6%; 1990-2000 +8.6%. **Pop 2000:** 22,094 (White 95.3%; Black or African American 1.6%; Hispanic or Latino 1.1%; Asian 0.9%; Other 1.6%). **Foreign born:** 1.4%. **Median age:** 29.8.

Income 2000: per capita $13,888; median household $28,055; **Pop below poverty level:** 21.3%. ***Personal per capita income 2000-2003:** $17,227-$20,041.

Unemployment 2004: 4.6%. **Change from 2000:** -1.8%. **Median travel time to work:** 24.4 minutes. **Working outside county of residence:** 23%.

Cities with pop over 10,000: None.

RUSSELL COUNTY

410 Monument Sq Rm 103   **Ph:** 270-343-2125
Jamestown, KY 42629   **Fax:** 270-343-4700
www.russellcountyky.com

In south-central KY, southwest of Lexington; established Dec 14,

1825 from Wayne, Adair, and Cumberland counties. **Name Origin:** For William Russell (1758-1825), VA soldier and statesman; served in legislatures of VA and KY.

Area (sq mi): 282.82 (land 253.53; water 29.29). **Pop per sq mi:** 67.1.

Pop 2005: 17,020. **State rank:** 67. **Pop change:** 2000-20005 +4.3%; 1990-2000 +10.9%. **Pop 2000:** 16,315 (White 97.7%; Black or African American 0.6%; Hispanic or Latino 0.9%; Asian 0.1%; Other 0.9%). **Foreign born:** 1%. **Median age:** 39.9.

Income 2000: per capita $13,183; median household $22,042; **Pop below poverty level:** 24.3%. ***Personal per capita income 2000-2003:** $17,831-$19,201.

Unemployment 2004: 5.7%. **Change from 2000:** -3.1%. **Median travel time to work:** 22.5 minutes. **Working outside county of residence:** 24.8%.

Cities with pop over 10,000: None.

SCOTT COUNTY

101 E Main St   **Ph:** 502-863-7850
Georgetown, KY 40324   **Fax:** 502-863-7852
www.scottky.com

In north-central KY, north of Lexington; organized Jun 22, 1792 from Woodford County. **Name Origin:** For Gen. Charles Scott (1739-1813), career soldier and governor of KY (1808-12).

Area (sq mi): 285.3 (land 284.72; water 0.57). **Pop per sq mi:** 138.3.

Pop 2005: 39,380. **State rank:** 25. **Pop change:** 2000-20005 +19.1%; 1990-2000 +38.5%. **Pop 2000:** 33,061 (White 91.2%; Black or African American 5.4%; Hispanic or Latino 1.6%; Asian 0.5%; Other 2.2%). **Foreign born:** 1.9%. **Median age:** 32.4.

Income 2000: per capita $21,490; median household $47,081; **Pop below poverty level:** 8.8%. ***Personal per capita income 2000-2003:** $29,322-$28,651.

Unemployment 2004: 4.2%. **Change from 2000:** +0.9%. **Median travel time to work:** 21.7 minutes. **Working outside county of residence:** 38.6%.

Cities with pop over 10,000: Georgetown 🏛 (19,732).

SHELBY COUNTY

501 Main St   **Ph:** 502-633-1220
Shelbyville, KY 40065   **Fax:** 502-633-7623
www.shelbyvilleky.com

In northwestern KY, east of Louisville; organized Jun 23, 1792 from Jefferson County. **Name Origin:** For Gen. Isaac Shelby (1750-1826), officer in the Revolutionary War, NC legislator, and governor of KY (1792-96; 1812-16).

Area (sq mi): 385.65 (land 384.19; water 1.46). **Pop per sq mi:** 99.4.

Pop 2005: 38,205. **State rank:** 26. **Pop change:** 2000-20005 +14.6%; 1990-2000 +34.3%. **Pop 2000:** 33,337 (White 84.9%; Black or African American 8.8%; Hispanic or Latino 4.5%; Asian 0.4%; Other 4.1%). **Foreign born:** 3.9%. **Median age:** 35.9.

Income 2000: per capita $20,195; median household $45,534; **Pop below poverty level:** 9.9%. ***Personal per capita income 2000-2003:** $28,598-$28,342.

Shelby County (cont'd)

Unemployment 2004: 4.2%. **Change from 2000:** -0.1%. **Median travel time to work:** 24.7 minutes. **Working outside county of residence:** 44.4%.

Cities with pop over 10,000: Shelbyville ⛪ (10,622).

SIMPSON COUNTY

PO Box 268   **Ph:** 270-586-8161
Franklin, KY 42135   **Fax:** 270-586-6464
www.simpsoncountyclerk.ky.gov

On southern border of KY, south of Bowling Green; organized Jan 28, 1819 from Logan, Warren, and Allen counties. **Name Origin:** For Capt. James Simpson (?-1812), KY legislator, killed in action during the War of 1812.

Area (sq mi): 236.19 (land 236.19; water 0). **Pop per sq mi:** 72.1.

Pop 2005: 17,021. **State rank:** 66. **Pop change:** 2000-20005 +3.8%; 1990-2000 +8.3%. **Pop 2000:** 16,405 (White 87.3%; Black or African American 10.2%; Hispanic or Latino 0.9%; Asian 0.5%; Other 1.5%). **Foreign born:** 1.2%. **Median age:** 35.9.

Income 2000: per capita $17,150; median household $36,432; **Pop below poverty level:** 11.6%. ***Personal per capita income 2000-2003:** $22,560-$24,146.

Unemployment 2004: 4.6%. **Change from 2000:** -1.7%. **Median travel time to work:** 20.6 minutes. **Working outside county of residence:** 30.5%.

Cities with pop over 10,000: None.

SPENCER COUNTY

2 W Main St   **Ph:** 502-477-3215
Taylorsville, KY 40071   **Fax:** 502-477-3216
www.spencercountyky.gov

In northwestern KY, southeast of Louisville; organized Jan 7, 1824 from Nelson, Shelby, and Bullitt counties. **Name Origin:** For Capt. Spier (Spear) Spencer (?-1811), KY officer killed at the Battle of Tippecanoe.

Area (sq mi): 191.8 (land 185.9; water 5.89). **Pop per sq mi:** 84.2.

Pop 2005: 15,651. **State rank:** 74. **Pop change:** 2000-20005 +33%; 1990-2000 +73%. **Pop 2000:** 11,766 (White 96.7%; Black or African American 1.1%; Hispanic or Latino 1.1%; Asian 0.1%; Other 1.3%). **Foreign born:** 1.2%. **Median age:** 35.1.

Income 2000: per capita $19,848; median household $47,042; **Pop below poverty level:** 8.8%. ***Personal per capita income 2000-2003:** $22,033-$21,130.

Unemployment 2004: 4.2%. **Change from 2000:** -1%. **Median travel time to work:** 32.6 minutes. **Working outside county of residence:** 77.9%.

Cities with pop over 10,000: None.

TAYLOR COUNTY

203 N Court St Suite 5   **Ph:** 270-465-6677
Campbellsville, KY 42718 **Fax:** 270-789-1144

In west-central KY, southeast of Bowling Green; organized Jan 13, 1848 from Green County. **Name Origin:** For Zachary Taylor (1784-1850), twelfth U.S. president.

Area (sq mi): 277.05 (land 269.83; water 7.22). **Pop per sq mi:** 88.

Pop 2005: 23,754. **State rank:** 50. **Pop change:** 2000-20005 +3.6%; 1990-2000 +8.4%. **Pop 2000:** 22,927 (White 93.1%; Black or African American 5.1%; Hispanic or Latino 0.8%; Asian 0.2%; Other 1.1%). **Foreign born:** 1.3%. **Median age:** 38.1.

Income 2000: per capita $15,162; median household $28,089; **Pop below poverty level:** 17.5%. ***Personal per capita income 2000-2003:** $19,229-$20,974.

Unemployment 2004: 4.9%. **Change from 2000:** -1.4%. **Median travel time to work:** 22 minutes. **Working outside county of residence:** 23.3%.

Cities with pop over 10,000: Campbellsville ⛪ (10,752).

TODD COUNTY

PO Box 307   **Ph:** 270-265-2363
Elkton, KY 42220   **Fax:** 270-265-2588

On the southern border of KY, east of Hopkinsville; established Dec 30, 1819 from Logan and Christian counties. **Name Origin:** For John Blair Todd (1814-72), governor of the Dakota Territory (1869-71).

Area (sq mi): 376.97 (land 376.35; water 0.62). **Pop per sq mi:** 31.7.

Pop 2005: 11,944. **State rank:** 92. **Pop change:** 2000-20005 -0.2%; 1990-2000 +9.4%. **Pop 2000:** 11,971 (White 88.6%; Black or African American 8.8%; Hispanic or Latino 1.7%; Asian 0.2%; Other 1.8%). **Foreign born:** 1.3%. **Median age:** 35.9.

Income 2000: per capita $15,462; median household $29,718; **Pop below poverty level:** 17.2%. ***Personal per capita income 2000-2003:** $20,604-$20,870.

Unemployment 2004: 4.3%. **Change from 2000:** -5.1%. **Median travel time to work:** 23.4 minutes. **Working outside county of residence:** 43.7%.

Cities with pop over 10,000: None.

TRIGG COUNTY

PO Box 1310   **Ph:** 270-522-6661
Cadiz, KY 42211   **Fax:** 270-522-6662

On the southern border of KY, west of Hopkinsville; organized Jan 27, 1820 from Christian and Caldwell counties. **Name Origin:** For Col. Stephen Trigg (?-1782), an officer killed in action against Indians at Blue Licks.

Area (sq mi): 481.13 (land 443.12; water 38.01). **Pop per sq mi:** 30.1.

Pop 2005: 13,349. **State rank:** 87. **Pop change:** 2000-20005 +6%; 1990-2000 +21.6%. **Pop 2000:** 12,597 (White 87.7%; Black or African American 9.8%; Hispanic or Latino 0.9%; Asian 0.3%; Other 1.6%). **Foreign born:** 0.8%. **Median age:** 40.5.

Income 2000: per capita $17,184; median household $33,002; **Pop below poverty level:** 12.3%. ***Personal per capita income 2000-2003:** $23,307-$26,473.

Unemployment 2004: 5%. **Change from 2000:** -0.7%. **Median travel time to work:** 26.2 minutes. **Working outside county of residence:** 38.4%.

Cities with pop over 10,000: None.

TRIMBLE COUNTY

30 Hwy 42 E   **Ph:** 502-255-7174
Bedford, KY 40006   **Fax:** 502-255-7045
www.trimblecounty.com

On the northwestern border of KY, northeast of Louisville; established Feb 9, 1837 from Gallatin, Oldham, and Henry counties. **Name Origin:** For Robert Trimble (1777-1828), KY jurist and associate justice of the U.S. Supreme Court (1826-28).

Area (sq mi): 156.23 (land 148.85; water 7.38). **Pop per sq mi:** 60.6.

Pop 2005: 9,023. **State rank:** 103. **Pop change:** 2000-20005 +11.1%; 1990-2000 +33.4%. **Pop 2000:** 8,125 (White 97.2%; Black or African American 0.3%; Hispanic or Latino 1.4%; Asian 0.1%; Other 1.8%). **Foreign born:** 1.1%. **Median age:** 35.7.

Income 2000: per capita $16,354; median household $36,192; **Pop below poverty level:** 13.6%. ***Personal per capita income 2000-2003:** $15,843-$16,505.

Unemployment 2004: 5.1%. **Change from 2000:** -2.8%. **Median travel time to work:** 30.7 minutes. **Working outside county of residence:** 76.9%.

Cities with pop over 10,000: None.

UNION COUNTY

PO Box 119   **Ph:** 270-389-1334
Morganfield, KY 42437   **Fax:** 270-389-9135
www.ucky.org/v2/

On northwestern border of KY, southwest of Henderson; organized Jan 15, 1811 from Henderson County. **Name Origin:** Allegedly for the united desire of the residents to form a new county.

Area (sq mi): 363.43 (land 345.1; water 18.33). **Pop per sq mi:** 45.2.

Pop 2005: 15,592. **State rank:** 75. **Pop change:** 2000-20005 -0.3%; 1990-2000 -5.6%. **Pop 2000:** 15,637 (White 84.4%; Black or African American 12.9%; Hispanic or Latino 1.6%; Asian 0.1%; Other 2%). **Foreign born:** 1.4%. **Median age:** 34.5.

Income 2000: per capita $17,465; median household $35,018; **Pop below poverty level:** 17.7%. ***Personal per capita income 2000-2003:** $22,057-$23,839.

Unemployment 2004: 4.9%. **Change from 2000:** -2.1%. **Median travel time to work:** 23.1 minutes. **Working outside county of residence:** 31.4%.

Cities with pop over 10,000: None.

WARREN COUNTY

429 E 10th St Courthouse   **Ph:** 270-842-9416
Bowling Green, KY 42102   **Fax:** 270-842-9416
www.warrencounty.state.ky.us

In southwest KY, northeast of Hopkinsville; established Dec 14, 1796 from Logan County. **Name Origin:** For Gen. Joseph Warren (1741-75), Revolutionary War patriot and member of the Committee of Safety who dispatched Paul Revere (1735-1818) on his famous ride.

Area (sq mi): 547.69 (land 545.21; water 2.48). **Pop per sq mi:** 181.5.

Pop 2005: 98,960. **State rank:** 5. **Pop change:** 2000-20005 +7%; 1990-2000 +20.7%. **Pop 2000:** 92,522 (White 85.8%; Black or

African American 8.6%; Hispanic or Latino 2.7%; Asian 1.4%; Other 3%). **Foreign born:** 4.3%. **Median age:** 32.3.

Income 2000: per capita $18,847; median household $36,151; **Pop below poverty level:** 15.4%. ***Personal per capita income 2000-2003:** $24,463-$26,331.

Unemployment 2004: 4.3%. **Change from 2000:** -0.3%. **Median travel time to work:** 19.6 minutes. **Working outside county of residence:** 11.1%.

Cities with pop over 10,000: Bowling Green 🏛 (51,294).

WASHINGTON COUNTY

PO Box 446   **Ph:** 859-336-5425
Springfield, KY 40069   **Fax:** 859-336-5408

In west-central KY, southwest of Lexington; organized Jun 22, 1792 from Nelson County; the first county formed after KY became a state. **Name Origin:** For George Washington (1732-99), American patriot and first U.S. president.

Area (sq mi): 301.52 (land 300.59; water 0.93). **Pop per sq mi:** 37.9.

Pop 2005: 11,399. **State rank:** 96. **Pop change:** 2000-20005 +4.4%; 1990-2000 +4.5%. **Pop 2000:** 10,916 (White 89.6%; Black or African American 7.5%; Hispanic or Latino 1.6%; Asian 0.3%; Other 1.6%). **Foreign born:** 0.7%. **Median age:** 37.1.

Income 2000: per capita $15,722; median household $33,136; **Pop below poverty level:** 13.5%. ***Personal per capita income 2000-2003:** $20,590-$21,708.

Unemployment 2004: 5.1%. **Change from 2000:** -1.1%. **Median travel time to work:** 25.9 minutes. **Working outside county of residence:** 42.7%.

Cities with pop over 10,000: None.

WAYNE COUNTY

PO Box 565   **Ph:** 606-348-6661
Monticello, KY 42633   **Fax:** 606-348-8303
www.monticellokychamber.com

On the southern border of KY, south of Lexington; established Dec 18, 1800 from Pulaski and Cumberland counties. **Name Origin:** For Gen. Anthony Wayne (1745-96), PA soldier and statesman, nicknamed 'Mad Anthony' for his daring during the Revolutionary War.

Area (sq mi): 484.2 (land 459.4; water 24.8). **Pop per sq mi:** 44.3.

Pop 2005: 20,352. **State rank:** 55. **Pop change:** 2000-20005 +2.2%; 1990-2000 +14.1%. **Pop 2000:** 19,923 (White 96.2%; Black or African American 1.5%; Hispanic or Latino 1.5%; Asian 0.1%; Other 1.5%). **Foreign born:** 1.3%. **Median age:** 36.6.

Income 2000: per capita $12,601; median household $20,863; **Pop below poverty level:** 29.4%. ***Personal per capita income 2000-2003:** $15,863-$17,748.

Unemployment 2004: 5.3%. **Change from 2000:** -3.6%. **Median travel time to work:** 22.2 minutes. **Working outside county of residence:** 22.4%.

Cities with pop over 10,000: None.

WEBSTER COUNTY

PO Box 155   **Ph:** 270-639-5042
Dixon, KY 42409   **Fax:** 270-639-7009
www.webstercountyky.com

In western KY, south of Henderson; organized Feb 29, 1860 from Hopkins, Union, and Henderson counties. **Name Origin:** For Daniel Webster (1782-1852), U.S. statesman and orator from MA.

Area (sq mi): 335.68 (land 334.75; water 0.93). **Pop per sq mi:** 42.3.

Pop 2005: 14,161. **State rank:** 80. **Pop change:** 2000-20005 +0.3%; 1990-2000 +1.2%. **Pop 2000:** 14,120 (White 92.7%; Black or African American 4.7%; Hispanic or Latino 1.9%; Asian 0.1%; Other 1.7%). **Foreign born:** 1.9%. **Median age:** 37.8.

Income 2000: per capita $15,657; median household $31,529; **Pop below poverty level:** 15.4%. ***Personal per capita income 2000-2003:** $24,591-$26,485.

Unemployment 2004: 4.3%. **Change from 2000:** -2.7%. **Median travel time to work:** 26.4 minutes. **Working outside county of residence:** 52.1%.

Cities with pop over 10,000: None.

WHITLEY COUNTY

PO Box 8   **Ph:** 606-549-6002
Williamsburg, KY 40769   **Fax:** 606-549-2790

On the southeastern border of KY; organized Jan 17, 1818 from Knox County. **Name Origin:** For William Whitley (1749-1813), soldier believed by some to be the one who killed Shawnee Chief Tecumseh (1768-1813).

Area (sq mi): 445.15 (land 440.15; water 4.99). **Pop per sq mi:** 86.4.

Pop 2005: 38,029. **State rank:** 27. **Pop change:** 2000-20005 +6%; 1990-2000 +7.6%. **Pop 2000:** 35,865 (White 97.8%; Black or African American 0.3%; Hispanic or Latino 0.7%; Asian 0.2%; Other 1.1%). **Foreign born:** 0.7%. **Median age:** 35.4.

Income 2000: per capita $12,777; median household $22,075; **Pop below poverty level:** 26.4%. ***Personal per capita income 2000-2003:** $18,248-$19,372.

Unemployment 2004: 5.5%. **Change from 2000:** -0.7%. **Median travel time to work:** 25.1 minutes. **Working outside county of residence:** 29.4%.

Cities with pop over 10,000: None.

WOLFE COUNTY

PO Box 400   **Ph:** 606-668-3515
Campton, KY 41301   **Fax:** 606-668-3492

In eastern KY, southeast of Lexington; organized Mar 5, 1860 from Breathitt, Morgan, Powell, and Owsley counties. **Name Origin:** For Nathaniel Wolfe (1810-65), KY legislator (1853-55; 1859-63).

Area (sq mi): 222.86 (land 222.78; water 0.08). **Pop per sq mi:** 31.7.

Pop 2005: 7,070. **State rank:** 113. **Pop change:** 2000-20005 +0.1%; 1990-2000 +8.6%. **Pop 2000:** 7,065 (White 98.8%; Black or African American 0.2%; Hispanic or Latino 0.5%; Asian 0%; Other 0.5%). **Foreign born:** 0.7%. **Median age:** 36.4.

Income 2000: per capita $10,321; median household $19,310; **Pop below poverty level:** 35.9%. ***Personal per capita income 2000-2003:** $15,400-$16,523.

Unemployment 2004: 9.4%. **Change from 2000:** +0%. **Median travel time to work:** 33.8 minutes. **Working outside county of residence:** 51.5%.

Cities with pop over 10,000: None.

WOODFORD COUNTY

103 S Main St County Courthouse   **Ph:** 859-873-3421
Versailles, KY 40383   **Fax:** 859-873-0196
www.woodfordchamber-ky.com

In central KY, west of Lexington; established Nov 12, 1788 (prior to statehood) from Fayette County; the last county formed while KY was still part of VA. **Name Origin:** For William Woodford (1735-1780), Revolutionary War general

Area (sq mi): 191.98 (land 190.68; water 1.3). **Pop per sq mi:** 127.2.

Pop 2005: 24,246. **State rank:** 47. **Pop change:** 2000-20005 +4.5%; 1990-2000 +16.3%. **Pop 2000:** 23,208 (White 90.2%; Black or African American 5.4%; Hispanic or Latino 3%; Asian 0.3%; Other 2.1%). **Foreign born:** 2.7%. **Median age:** 37.1.

Income 2000: per capita $22,839; median household $49,491; **Pop below poverty level:** 7.3%. ***Personal per capita income 2000-2003:** $35,913-$33,830.

Unemployment 2004: 3.6%. **Change from 2000:** +0.2%. **Median travel time to work:** 21.4 minutes. **Working outside county of residence:** 54.8%.

Cities with pop over 10,000: None.

Source: Personal per capita income data are from the Bureau of Economic Analysis; per capita income data are from the Bureau of the Census. See Introduction for explanation of differences.

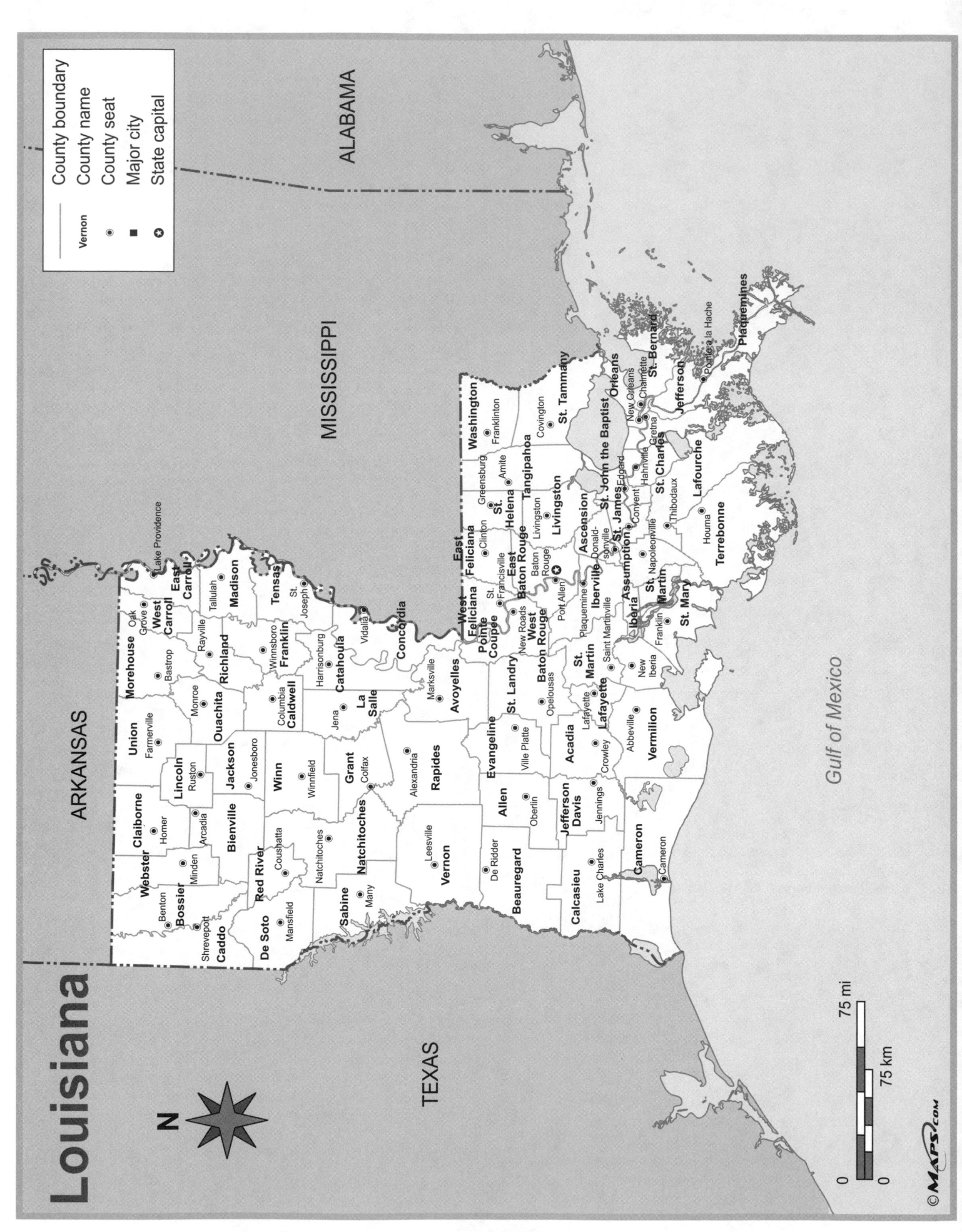

Louisiana

N

TEXAS

ARKANSAS

MISSISSIPPI

ALABAMA

Gulf of Mexico

County boundary
Vernon County name
⊙ County seat
■ Major city
✪ State capital

0 — 75 km
0 — 75 mi

©MAPS.com

Caddo · Shreveport
Bossier · Benton
De Soto · Mansfield
Webster · Minden
Claiborne · Homer
Bienville · Arcadia
Red River · Coushatta
Natchitoches · Natchitoches
Sabine · Many
Union · Farmerville
Lincoln · Ruston
Jackson · Jonesboro
Winn · Winnfield
Grant · Colfax
Vernon · Leesville
Beauregard · De Ridder
Allen · Oberlin
Calcasieu · Lake Charles
Cameron · Cameron
Jefferson Davis · Jennings
Morehouse · Bastrop
Ouachita · Monroe
Richland · Rayville
Franklin · Winnsboro
Caldwell · Columbia
La Salle · Jena
Rapides · Alexandria
Evangeline · Ville Platte
Acadia · Crowley
Vermilion · Abbeville
West Carroll · Oak Grove
East Carroll · Lake Providence
Madison · Tallulah
Tensas · St. Joseph
Catahoula · Harrisonburg
Concordia · Vidalia
Avoyelles · Marksville
St. Landry · Opelousas
Lafayette · Lafayette
Iberia · New Iberia
St. Martin · Saint Martinville
St. Mary · Franklin
Pointe Coupee · New Roads
West Feliciana · St. Francisville
West Baton Rouge · Port Allen
East Baton Rouge · Baton Rouge
East Feliciana · Clinton
St. Helena · Greensburg
Washington · Franklinton
Tangipahoa · Amite
Livingston · Livingston
Ascension · Donaldsonville
Iberville · Plaquemine
Assumption · Napoleonville
St. James · Convent
St. John the Baptist · Edgard
St. Charles · Hahnville
Lafourche · Thibodaux
Terrebonne · Houma
St. Tammany · Covington
Orleans · New Orleans
Jefferson · Gretna
St. Bernard · Chalmette
Plaquemines · Pointe a la Hache

Louisiana

LOUISIANA STATE INFORMATION

www.louisiana.gov   **Ph:** 225-342-6600

Area (sq mi): 51839.7 (land 43,561.85; water 8277.85). **Pop per sq mi:** 103.8.

Pop 2005: 4,523,628. **Pop change:** 2000-20005 +1.2%; 1990-2000 +5.9%. **Pop 2000:** 4,468,976 (White 62.5%; Black or African American 32.5%; Hispanic or Latino 2.4%; Asian 1.2%; Other 2.4%). **Foreign born:** 2.6%. **Median age:** 34.

Income 2000: per capita $16,912; median household $32,566; **Pop below poverty level:** 19.6%. *Personal per capita income 2000-2003: $23,078-$26,312.

Unemployment 2004: 5.7%. **Change from 2000:** +0.7%. **Median travel time to work:** 25.7 minutes. **Working outside county of residence:** 28.7%.

ACADIA PARISH

N Parkson Court Cir 3rd Fl   **Ph:** 337-788-8800
Crowley, LA 70526   **Fax:** 337-788-2421
www.acadiaparishpolicejury.org

In south-central LA, west of Lafayette; organized 1886 from Saint Landry Parish. **Name Origin:** French *Acadie,* an area in northeastern Canada and ME, former home of present-day Cajuns, descendants of Frence settlers displaced by English troops. Their journey is subject of Henry Wadsworth Longfellow's (1807-82) poem, 'Evangeline.'

Area (sq mi): 657.62 (land 655.28; water 2.33). **Pop per sq mi:** 90.9.

Pop 2005: 59,552. **State rank:** 19. **Pop change:** 2000-20005 +1.2%; 1990-2000 +5.3%. **Pop 2000:** 58,861 (White 80.1%; Black or African American 18.2%; Hispanic or Latino 0.9%; Asian 0.2%; Other 0.9%). **Foreign born:** 0.4%. **Median age:** 33.7.

Income 2000: per capita $13,424; median household $26,684; **Pop below poverty level:** 24.5%. *Personal per capita income 2000-2003: $18,513-$21,683.

Unemployment 2004: 5.8%. **Change from 2000:** -0.3%. **Median travel time to work:** 29.9 minutes. **Working outside county of residence:** 43.4%.

Cities with pop over 10,000: Crowley 🏛 (13,797).

ALLEN PARISH

PO Drawer G   **Ph:** 337-639-4396
Oberlin, LA 70655   **Fax:** 337-639-4326
www.allenparish.com

In south-central LA, northeast of Lake Charles; established Jun 12, 1912 from Calcasieu Parish. **Name Origin:** For Henry Watkins Allen (1820-66), Confederate general and governor of LA (1864-65).

Area (sq mi): 765.67 (land 764.5; water 1.17). **Pop per sq mi:** 33.1.

Pop 2005: 25,270. **State rank:** 38. **Pop change:** 2000-20005 -0.7%; 1990-2000 +19.9%. **Pop 2000:** 25,440 (White 68.1%; Black or African American 24.6%; Hispanic or Latino 4.5%; Asian 0.6%; Other 2.9%, including 1.7% American Indian/Alaska Native). **Foreign born:** 0.6%. **Median age:** 34.8.

Income 2000: per capita $13,101; median household $27,777; **Pop below poverty level:** 19.9%. *Personal per capita income 2000-2003: $15,494-$17,932.

Unemployment 2004: 8.3%. **Change from 2000:** +1.6%. **Median travel time to work:** 27.8 minutes. **Working outside county of residence:** 30.4%.

Cities with pop over 10,000: None.

ASCENSION PARISH

PO Box 1659   **Ph:** 225-621-5709
Gonzales, LA 70707   **Fax:** 225-621-5704
www.ascensionparish.net

In eastern LA, southeast of Baton Rouge; organized Mar 31, 1807 (prior to statehood) from Acadia Parish. **Name Origin:** For the Feast of the Ascension of Jesus Christ usually observed by Christians of the fortieth day after Easter.

Area (sq mi): 302.88 (land 291.53; water 11.35). **Pop per sq mi:** 310.4.

Pop 2005: 90,501. **State rank:** 15. **Pop change:** 2000-20005 +18.1%; 1990-2000 +31.6%. **Pop 2000:** 76,627 (White 76.2%; Black or African American 20.3%; Hispanic or Latino 2.5%; Asian 0.3%; Other 2%). **Foreign born:** 1.8%. **Median age:** 32.

Income 2000: per capita $17,858; median household $44,288; **Pop below poverty level:** 12.9%. *Personal per capita income 2000-2003: $23,788-$26,441.

Unemployment 2004: 6.3%. **Change from 2000:** -0.2%. **Median travel time to work:** 26.3 minutes. **Working outside county of residence:** 48.6%.

Cities with pop over 10,000: None.

ASSUMPTION PARISH

PO Box 249   **Ph:** 985-369-6653
Napoleonville, LA 70390   **Fax:** 985-369-2032
www.assumptionla.com/ala/

In southeastern LA, south of Baton Rouge; organized Mar 31, 1807 (prior to statehood) from Lafourche Parish. **Name Origin:** For the

Assumption Parish (cont'd)

Feast of the Assumption of the Virgin Mary observed by Christians on August 15.

Area (sq mi): 364.55 (land 338.68; water 25.87). **Pop per sq mi:** 68.5.

Pop 2005: 23,196. **State rank:** 40. **Pop change:** 2000-20005 -0.8%; 1990-2000 +2.8%. **Pop 2000:** 23,388 (White 66.6%; Black or African American 31.5%; Hispanic or Latino 1.2%; Asian 0.2%; Other 1.1%). **Foreign born:** 0.8%. **Median age:** 34.2.

Income 2000: per capita $14,008; median household $31,168; **Pop below poverty level:** 21.8%. ***Personal per capita income 2000-2003:** $19,163-$25,903.

Unemployment 2004: 8.4%. **Change from 2000:** +0.4%. **Median travel time to work:** 29.1 minutes. **Working outside county of residence:** 64.2%.

Cities with pop over 10,000: None.

AVOYELLES PARISH

312 N Main St Courthouse Bldg Suite D   **Ph:** 318-253-9208
Marksville, LA 71351   **Fax:** 318-253-4614

In east-central LA, east of Alexandria; original Parish; organized Mar 31, 1807 (prior to statehood). **Name Origin:** For the Indian tribe. The name probably means 'flint people.'

Area (sq mi): 865.67 (land 832.44; water 33.24). **Pop per sq mi:** 50.6.

Pop 2005: 42,098. **State rank:** 28. **Pop change:** 2000-20005 +1.5%; 1990-2000 +5.9%. **Pop 2000:** 41,481 (White 67.9%; Black or African American 29.5%; Hispanic or Latino 1%; Asian 0.2%; Other 1.9%, including 1% American Indian/Alaska Native). **Foreign born:** 0.5%. **Median age:** 35.2.

Income 2000: per capita $12,146; median household $23,851; **Pop below poverty level:** 25.9%. ***Personal per capita income 2000-2003:** $16,478-$18,810.

Unemployment 2004: 8.1%. **Change from 2000:** -0.2%. **Median travel time to work:** 31.8 minutes. **Working outside county of residence:** 29.4%.

Cities with pop over 10,000: None.

BEAUREGARD PARISH

PO Box 100   **Ph:** 337-463-8595
DeRidder, LA 70634   **Fax:** 337-462-3916

On southwestern border of LA, north of Lake Charles; organized Jun 12, 1912 from Calcasieu Parish. **Name Origin:** For Pierre Gustave Toutant Beauregard (1818-93), superintendent at West Point who resigned to join the Confederate army (1861); he was the general who directed the bombardment of Fort Sumter and battles of Bull Run and Shiloh.

Area (sq mi): 1165.99 (land 1160.09; water 5.9). **Pop per sq mi:** 29.8.

Pop 2005: 34,562. **State rank:** 32. **Pop change:** 2000-20005 +4.8%; 1990-2000 +9.7%. **Pop 2000:** 32,986 (White 83.4%; Black or African American 12.9%; Hispanic or Latino 1.4%; Asian 0.6%; Other 2.2%). **Foreign born:** 1.1%. **Median age:** 35.5.

Income 2000: per capita $15,514; median household $32,582; **Pop below poverty level:** 15.6%. ***Personal per capita income 2000-2003:** $18,825-$20,670.

Unemployment 2004: 6.5%. **Change from 2000:** -0.9%. **Median travel time to work:** 31.4 minutes. **Working outside county of residence:** 42.1%.

Cities with pop over 10,000: None.

BIENVILLE PARISH

100 Courthouse Dr Rm 100   **Ph:** 318-263-2123
Arcadia, LA 71001   **Fax:** 318-263-7426
www.bienvilleparish.org

In north-central LA, southeast of Shreveport; organized Mar 14, 1848 from Claiborne Parish. **Name Origin:** For Jean Baptiste Le Moyne, Sieur de Bienville (1680-1765?), founder of New Orleans (1718) and governor of the French colony of Louisiana (1701-13; 1718-26; 1733-43).

Area (sq mi): 821.77 (land 810.64; water 11.13). **Pop per sq mi:** 18.7.

Pop 2005: 15,176. **State rank:** 53. **Pop change:** 2000-20005 -3.7%; 1990-2000 -1.4%. **Pop 2000:** 15,752 (White 54.6%; Black or African American 43.8%; Hispanic or Latino 0.9%; Asian 0.2%; Other 1.2%). **Foreign born:** 0.4%. **Median age:** 38.

Income 2000: per capita $12,471; median household $23,663; **Pop below poverty level:** 26.1%. ***Personal per capita income 2000-2003:** $17,628-$20,362.

Unemployment 2004: 8.4%. **Change from 2000:** -2.7%. **Median travel time to work:** 32.9 minutes. **Working outside county of residence:** 53.2%.

Cities with pop over 10,000: None.

BOSSIER PARISH

204 Burt Blvd 2nd Fl   **Ph:** 318-965-2336
Benton, LA 71006   **Fax:** 318-965-2713
www.mybossier.com

On the northwestern border of panhandle of LA, north of Shreveport; organized Feb 24, 1843 from Claiborne Parish. **Name Origin:** For Pierre Evariste Jean Baptiste Bossier (1797-1844), LA legislator and U.S. representative (1843-44).

Area (sq mi): 866.93 (land 839.25; water 27.68). **Pop per sq mi:** 125.8.

Pop 2005: 105,541. **State rank:** 13. **Pop change:** 2000-20005 +7.4%; 1990-2000 +14.2%. **Pop 2000:** 98,310 (White 72.9%; Black or African American 20.8%; Hispanic or Latino 3.1%; Asian 1.3%; Other 3.3%). **Foreign born:** 2.5%. **Median age:** 33.8.

Income 2000: per capita $18,119; median household $39,203; **Pop below poverty level:** 13.7%. ***Personal per capita income 2000-2003:** $22,662-$25,608.

Unemployment 2004: 5.4%. **Change from 2000:** -0.1%. **Median travel time to work:** 22.4 minutes. **Working outside county of residence:** 45%.

Cities with pop over 10,000: Bossier City (59,611).

Source: Personal per capita income data are from the Bureau of Economic Analysis; per capita income data are from the Bureau of the Census. See Introduction for explanation of differences.

CADDO PARISH

505 Travis St 8th Fl   **Ph:** 318-226-6900
Shreveport, LA 71101   **Fax:** 318-429-7630
www.caddo.org

On northwestern border of panhandle of LA; organized Jan 18, 1838 from Natchitoches Parish. **Name Origin:** For name of a group of tribes of Caddoan linguistic stock. Derived from one of the tribal groups, the Kadohadacho ('real chiefs') Confederacy.

Area (sq mi): 936.9 (land 881.99; water 54.91). **Pop per sq mi:** 284.9.

Pop 2005: 251,309. **State rank:** 4. **Pop change:** 2000-20005 -0.3%; 1990-2000 +1.6%. **Pop 2000:** 252,161 (White 52.2%; Black or African American 44.6%; Hispanic or Latino 1.5%; Asian 0.7%; Other 1.8%). **Foreign born:** 1.5%. **Median age:** 35.1.

Income 2000: per capita $17,839; median household $31,467; **Pop below poverty level:** 21.1%. ***Personal per capita income 2000-2003:** $25,131-$28,884.

Unemployment 2004: 6.2%. **Change from 2000:** -0.2%. **Median travel time to work:** 21 minutes. **Working outside county of residence:** 16.8%.

Cities with pop over 10,000: Shreveport 🏛 (198,675).

CALCASIEU PARISH

PO Box 1030   **Ph:** 337-437-3550
Lake Charles, LA 70602   **Fax:** 337-437-3350
www.cppj.net

On southwestern border of LA; organized Mar 24, 1840 from Saint Landry Parish. **Name Origin:** Said to be from Atakapan 'crying eagle,' the name of an Indian chief.

Area (sq mi): 1094.34 (land 1071.12; water 23.22). **Pop per sq mi:** 173.1.

Pop 2005: 185,419. **State rank:** 7. **Pop change:** 2000-20005 +1%; 1990-2000 +9.2%. **Pop 2000:** 183,577 (White 72.8%; Black or African American 24%; Hispanic or Latino 1.3%; Asian 0.6%; Other 1.7%). **Foreign born:** 1.4%. **Median age:** 34.5.

Income 2000: per capita $17,710; median household $35,372; **Pop below poverty level:** 15.4%. ***Personal per capita income 2000-2003:** $22,525-$26,389.

Unemployment 2004: 5.6%. **Change from 2000:** -0.5%. **Median travel time to work:** 20.4 minutes. **Working outside county of residence:** 6.4%.

Cities with pop over 10,000: Lake Charles 🏛 (70,819); Sulphur (19,747).

CALDWELL PARISH

PO Box 1737   **Ph:** 318-649-2681
Columbia, LA 71418   **Fax:** 318-649-5930

In north-central LA, south of Monroe; organized Mar 6, 1838 from Catahoula and Ouachita parishes. **Name Origin:** For Matthew Caldwell, a pioneer from NC.

Area (sq mi): 540.72 (land 529.42; water 11.3). **Pop per sq mi:** 20.

Pop 2005: 10,563. **State rank:** 58. **Pop change:** 2000-20005 +0%; 1990-2000 +7.6%. **Pop 2000:** 10,560 (White 79.5%; Black or African American 17.9%; Hispanic or Latino 1.5%; Asian 0.1%; Other 1.6%). **Foreign born:** 0.6%. **Median age:** 36.7.

Income 2000: per capita $13,884; median household $26,972; **Pop below poverty level:** 21.2%. ***Personal per capita income 2000-2003:** $17,145-$19,104.

Unemployment 2004: 8.4%. **Change from 2000:** -0.8%. **Median travel time to work:** 36.8 minutes. **Working outside county of residence:** 43.3%.

Cities with pop over 10,000: None.

CAMERON PARISH

PO Box 549   **Ph:** 337-775-5316
Cameron, LA 70631   **Fax:** 337-775-7172
www.cameronparish.net

On the southwestern border of LA, south of Lake Charles; organized Mar 15, 1870 from Calcasieu and Vermilion parishes. **Name Origin:** For Robert Alexander Cameron, a Confederate soldier active in LA politics after the Civil War; or possibly for Simon Cameron (1799-1889), U.S. senator from PA (1845-49; 1857-61; 1867-77) and secretary of war (1861-62).

Area (sq mi): 1931.6 (land 1312.96; water 618.63). **Pop per sq mi:** 7.3.

Pop 2005: 9,558. **State rank:** 61. **Pop change:** 2000-20005 -4.3%; 1990-2000 +7.9%. **Pop 2000:** 9,991 (White 92.5%; Black or African American 3.9%; Hispanic or Latino 2.2%; Asian 0.4%; Other 2%). **Foreign born:** 1.6%. **Median age:** 35.

Income 2000: per capita $15,348; median household $34,232; **Pop below poverty level:** 12.3%. ***Personal per capita income 2000-2003:** $17,930-$19,127.

Unemployment 2004: 5.2%. **Change from 2000:** -0.7%. **Median travel time to work:** 26.3 minutes. **Working outside county of residence:** 41.1%.

Cities with pop over 10,000: None.

CATAHOULA PARISH

PO Box 654   **Ph:** 318-744-5497
Harrisonburg, LA 71340   **Fax:** 318-744-5488

In northeastern LA, northeast of Alexandria; organized Mar 23, 1808 (prior to statehood) from Rapides Parish. **Name Origin:** From an Indian name of uncertain origin. Three derivations have been suggested: for the Etacoulow River 'River of the Great Spirit,' now called Little River, which runs through the parish; from Choctaw *okkattahoola* 'beautiful white water,' or Choctaw-French combination 'lake people.'

Area (sq mi): 739.43 (land 703.65; water 35.78). **Pop per sq mi:** 14.8.

Pop 2005: 10,447. **State rank:** 59. **Pop change:** 2000-20005 -4.3%; 1990-2000 -1.3%. **Pop 2000:** 10,920 (White 71.3%; Black or African American 27.1%; Hispanic or Latino 0.9%; Asian 0.1%; Other 1%). **Foreign born:** 0.1%. **Median age:** 36.7.

Income 2000: per capita $12,608; median household $22,528; **Pop below poverty level:** 28.1%. ***Personal per capita income 2000-2003:** $16,747-$19,922.

Unemployment 2004: 8.1%. **Change from 2000:** -3%. **Median travel time to work:** 38.3 minutes. **Working outside county of residence:** 40.3%.

Cities with pop over 10,000: None.

🏛 County Seat

CLAIBORNE PARISH

512 E Main St PO Box 330
Homer, LA 71040
www.claiborneone.org

Ph: 318-927-9601
Fax: 318-927-2345

On the central northern border of the LA panhandle, northeast of Shreveport; organized Mar 13, 1828 from Natchitoches Parish. **Name Origin:** For William Charles Cole Claiborne (1775-1817), governor of the Mississippi Territory (1801-05), of the Orleans Territory (1804-12), and of LA (1812-16).

Area (sq mi): 767.55 (land 754.65; water 12.9). **Pop per sq mi:** 21.6.

Pop 2005: 16,309. **State rank:** 50. **Pop change:** 2000-20005 -3.2%; 1990-2000 -3.2%. **Pop 2000:** 16,851 (White 51.5%; Black or African American 47.4%; Hispanic or Latino 0.8%; Asian 0.1%; Other 0.7%). **Foreign born:** 0.4%. **Median age:** 37.7.

Income 2000: per capita $13,825; median household $25,344; **Pop below poverty level:** 26.5%. *****Personal per capita income 2000-2003:** $17,661-$21,157.

Unemployment 2004: 6.7%. **Change from 2000:** -1.4%. **Median travel time to work:** 25.9 minutes. **Working outside county of residence:** 35.6%.

Cities with pop over 10,000: None.

CONCORDIA PARISH

PO Box 790
Vidalia, LA 71373

Ph: 318-336-4204
Fax: 318-336-8777

On the central eastern border of LA, west of Natchez, MS; original colony, organized Apr 10, 1807 (prior to statehood). **Name Origin:** For either Concordia, the Roman goddess of peace and harmony, or a Latinized form of *concord* 'harmony.'

Area (sq mi): 748.68 (land 695.91; water 52.77). **Pop per sq mi:** 27.7.

Pop 2005: 19,273. **State rank:** 49. **Pop change:** 2000-20005 -4.8%; 1990-2000 -2.8%. **Pop 2000:** 20,247 (White 60.1%; Black or African American 37.7%; Hispanic or Latino 1.5%; Asian 0.2%; Other 1.3%). **Foreign born:** 1.3%. **Median age:** 36.9.

Income 2000: per capita $11,966; median household $22,742; **Pop below poverty level:** 29.1%. *****Personal per capita income 2000-2003:** $16,050-$19,698.

Unemployment 2004: 10.3%. **Change from 2000:** -2.5%. **Median travel time to work:** 26.5 minutes. **Working outside county of residence:** 42.4%.

Cities with pop over 10,000: None.

DESOTO PARISH

PO Box 1206
Mansfield, LA 71052

Ph: 318-872-3110
Fax: 318-872-4202

On the western border, south of Shreveport; organized Apr 1, 1843 from Natchitoches Parish. **Name Origin:** For Hernando de Soto (c.1500-42), Spanish explorer of southern U.S.

Area (sq mi): 894.49 (land 877.2; water 17.29). **Pop per sq mi:** 30.1.

Pop 2005: 26,383. **State rank:** 37. **Pop change:** 2000-20005 +3.5%; 1990-2000 +0.6%. **Pop 2000:** 25,494 (White 55.3%; Black or African American 42.2%; Hispanic or Latino 1.6%; Asian 0.1%; Other 1.8%). **Foreign born:** 1%. **Median age:** 36.3.

Income 2000: per capita $13,606; median household $28,252; **Pop below poverty level:** 25.1%. *****Personal per capita income 2000-2003:** $19,463-$21,701.

Unemployment 2004: 7.4%. **Change from 2000:** -2.1%. **Median travel time to work:** 30.1 minutes. **Working outside county of residence:** 51.1%.

Cities with pop over 10,000: None.

EAST BATON ROUGE PARISH

1755 Florida St
Baton Rouge, LA 70802
www.brgov.com

Ph: 225-389-3129
Fax: 225-389-3118

In eastern LA, northwest of New Orleans; organized 1810 (prior to statehood) from Spanish West Florida. **Name Origin:** For its location. The city and the parish share a joint mayor-council form of government.

Area (sq mi): 470.54 (land 455.43; water 15.11). **Pop per sq mi:** 903.4.

Pop 2005: 411,417. **State rank:** 3. **Pop change:** 2000-20005 -0.3%; 1990-2000 +8.6%. **Pop 2000:** 412,852 (White 55.1%; Black or African American 40.1%; Hispanic or Latino 1.8%; Asian 2.1%; Other 1.6%). **Foreign born:** 3.7%. **Median age:** 31.5.

Income 2000: per capita $19,790; median household $37,224; **Pop below poverty level:** 17.9%. *****Personal per capita income 2000-2003:** $26,633-$29,786.

Unemployment 2004: 5.6%. **Change from 2000:** +0.6%. **Median travel time to work:** 23.2 minutes. **Working outside county of residence:** 11.5%.

Cities with pop over 10,000: Baton Rouge ⚒ (224,097); Baker (13,386); Zachary (12,070).

EAST CARROLL PARISH

400 1st St
Lake Providence, LA 71254
www.eastcarroll.net/home.htm

Ph: 318-559-2399
Fax: 318-559-0037

On the northeastern border of the LA panhandle; organized Mar 28, 1877 from Carroll Parish. **Name Origin:** From the division of Carroll Parish into two parishes, East and West. Originally for Charles Carroll (1737-1832), signer of the Declaration of Independence and U.S. senator from MD (1789-92).

Area (sq mi): 442.45 (land 421.44; water 21.01). **Pop per sq mi:** 20.8.

Pop 2005: 8,756. **State rank:** 63. **Pop change:** 2000-20005 -7.1%; 1990-2000 -3%. **Pop 2000:** 9,421 (White 31.1%; Black or African American 67.3%; Hispanic or Latino 1.2%; Asian 0.3%; Other 0.9%). **Foreign born:** 0.9%. **Median age:** 30.9.

Income 2000: per capita $9,629; median household $20,723; **Pop below poverty level:** 40.5%. *****Personal per capita income 2000-2003:** $14,232-$18,302.

Unemployment 2004: 13.7%. **Change from 2000:** -4.9%. **Median travel time to work:** 20.4 minutes. **Working outside county of residence:** 26.5%.

Cities with pop over 10,000: None.

Source: Personal per capita income data are from the Bureau of Economic Analysis; per capita income data are from the Bureau of the Census.
See Introduction for explanation of differences.

EAST FELICIANA PARISH

PO Box 599
Clinton, LA 70722
www.felicianatourism.org

Ph: 225-683-5145
Fax: 225-683-3556

On the northeastern border of LA, north of Baton Rouge; organized Feb 17, 1824 from Feliciana Parish. **Name Origin:** From the division of Feliciana Parish into two parishes: East and West. Name is Spanish for 'happiness,' or possibly for Felicite, the wife of a colonial governor.

Area (sq mi): 455.69 (land 453.4; water 2.29). **Pop per sq mi:** 45.9.

Pop 2005: 20,823. **State rank:** 45. **Pop change:** 2000-20005 -2.5%; 1990-2000 +11.2%. **Pop 2000:** 21,360 (White 51.4%; Black or African American 47.1%; Hispanic or Latino 0.7%; Asian 0.2%; Other 0.9%). **Foreign born:** 0.6%. **Median age:** 35.8.

Income 2000: per capita $15,428; median household $31,631; **Pop below poverty level:** 23%. ***Personal per capita income 2000-2003:** $19,522-$21,590.

Unemployment 2004: 7.1%. **Change from 2000:** +0.5%. **Median travel time to work:** 32.4 minutes. **Working outside county of residence:** 55.4%.

Cities with pop over 10,000: None.

EVANGELINE PARISH

PO Drawer 347
Ville Platte, LA 70586
www.evangelinetourism.com

Ph: 337-363-5671
Fax: 337-363-5780

In south-central LA, northwest of Lafayette; established Jun 15, 1910 from Saint Landry Parish. **Name Origin:** For the heroine of Henry Wadsworth Longfellow's (1807-82) poem of the same name.

Area (sq mi): 679.61 (land 664.27; water 15.34). **Pop per sq mi:** 53.5.

Pop 2005: 35,540. **State rank:** 31. **Pop change:** 2000-20005 +0.3%; 1990-2000 +6.5%. **Pop 2000:** 35,434 (White 69.8%; Black or African American 28.6%; Hispanic or Latino 1%; Asian 0.1%; Other 0.9%). **Foreign born:** 0.6%. **Median age:** 33.7.

Income 2000: per capita $11,432; median household $20,532; **Pop below poverty level:** 32.2%. ***Personal per capita income 2000-2003:** $15,846-$18,058.

Unemployment 2004: 6.9%. **Change from 2000:** +0.3%. **Median travel time to work:** 32.7 minutes. **Working outside county of residence:** 36.2%.

Cities with pop over 10,000: None.

FRANKLIN PARISH

PO Box 1564
Winnsboro, LA 71295

Ph: 318-435-5133
Fax: 318-435-5134

In northeastern LA, southeast of Monroe; organized Mar 1, 1843 from Catahoula, Ouachita, and Madison parishes. **Name Origin:** For Benjamin Franklin (1706-90), U.S. patriot, diplomat, and statesman.

Area (sq mi): 635.43 (land 623.61; water 11.82). **Pop per sq mi:** 32.7.

Pop 2005: 20,380. **State rank:** 47. **Pop change:** 2000-20005 -4.2%; 1990-2000 -5%. **Pop 2000:** 21,263 (White 66.8%; Black or African

American 31.6%; Hispanic or Latino 0.8%; Asian 0.2%; Other 1%). **Foreign born:** 0.6%. **Median age:** 35.9.

Income 2000: per capita $12,675; median household $22,964; **Pop below poverty level:** 28.4%. ***Personal per capita income 2000-2003:** $16,437-$19,145.

Unemployment 2004: 9.2%. **Change from 2000:** -0.7%. **Median travel time to work:** 32.5 minutes. **Working outside county of residence:** 27.4%.

Cities with pop over 10,000: None.

GRANT PARISH

PO Box 263
Colfax, LA 71417

Ph: 318-627-3246
Fax: 318-627-3201

In central LA, north of Alexandria; organized Mar 4, 1869 from Rapides and Winn parishes. **Name Origin:** For Ulysses S. Grant (1822-85), Civil War general and eighteenth U.S. president.

Area (sq mi): 664.56 (land 645.11; water 19.45). **Pop per sq mi:** 30.2.

Pop 2005: 19,503. **State rank:** 48. **Pop change:** 2000-20005 +4.3%; 1990-2000 +6.7%. **Pop 2000:** 18,698 (White 84.8%; Black or African American 11.9%; Hispanic or Latino 1.1%; Asian 0.1%; Other 2.6%). **Foreign born:** 0.5%. **Median age:** 35.5.

Income 2000: per capita $14,410; median household $29,622; **Pop below poverty level:** 21.5%. ***Personal per capita income 2000-2003:** $17,664-$20,175.

Unemployment 2004: 6.8%. **Change from 2000:** -2.6%. **Median travel time to work:** 38.6 minutes. **Working outside county of residence:** 65.7%.

Cities with pop over 10,000: None.

IBERIA PARISH

PO Box 12010
New Iberia, LA 70562
www.iberiaparishgovernment.com

Ph: 337-365-7282
Fax: 337-365-0737

On the central southern border of LA, southeast of Lafayette; organized Oct 30, 1868 from Saint Martin and Saint Mary parishes. **Name Origin:** For the European peninsula containing present-day Spain and Portugal.

Area (sq mi): 1030.86 (land 575.13; water 455.73). **Pop per sq mi:** 129.3.

Pop 2005: 74,388. **State rank:** 17. **Pop change:** 2000-20005 +1.5%; 1990-2000 +7.3%. **Pop 2000:** 73,266 (White 64.3%; Black or African American 30.8%; Hispanic or Latino 1.5%; Asian 1.9%; Other 2.1%). **Foreign born:** 2%. **Median age:** 33.3.

Income 2000: per capita $14,145; median household $31,204; **Pop below poverty level:** 23.6%. ***Personal per capita income 2000-2003:** $20,018-$23,533.

Unemployment 2004: 6.2%. **Change from 2000:** +0.5%. **Median travel time to work:** 24 minutes. **Working outside county of residence:** 27%.

Cities with pop over 10,000: New Iberia 🏛 (32,499).

🏛 County Seat

IBERVILLE PARISH
PO Box 423   **Ph:** 225-687-5160
Plaquemine, LA 70765   **Fax:** 225-687-5260
www.ibervilleparish.com

In south-central LA, west of Baton Rouge; organized 1807 (prior to statehood). **Name Origin:** For Pierre le Moyne, Sieur d'Iberville (1661-1706), French-Canadian naval officer who explored the Mississippi River delta and founded French colonies at present-day Biloxi and Mobile; governor of LA (1703).

Area (sq mi): 652.84 (land 618.64; water 34.2). **Pop per sq mi:** 52.4.

Pop 2005: 32,386. **State rank:** 33. **Pop change:** 2000-20005 -2.8%; 1990-2000 +7.3%. **Pop 2000:** 33,320 (White 48.6%; Black or African American 49.7%; Hispanic or Latino 1%; Asian 0.3%; Other 0.8%). **Foreign born:** 0.7%. **Median age:** 34.4.

Income 2000: per capita $13,272; median household $29,039; **Pop below poverty level:** 23.1%. ***Personal per capita income 2000-2003:** $18,446-$21,498.

Unemployment 2004: 8.9%. **Change from 2000:** +0.3%. **Median travel time to work:** 26.6 minutes. **Working outside county of residence:** 45.3%.

Cities with pop over 10,000: None.

JACKSON PARISH
PO Box 730   **Ph:** 318-259-2424
Jonesboro, LA 71251   **Fax:** 318-395-0386
www.jacksonparishpolicejury.org

In north-central LA, southwest of Monroe; organized Feb 27, 1845 from Claiborne, Ouachita, and Union parishes. **Name Origin:** For Andrew Jackson (1767-1845), seventh U.S. president.

Area (sq mi): 580.34 (land 569.75; water 10.59). **Pop per sq mi:** 26.6.

Pop 2005: 15,135. **State rank:** 54. **Pop change:** 2000-20005 -1.7%; 1990-2000 -2%. **Pop 2000:** 15,397 (White 70.7%; Black or African American 27.9%; Hispanic or Latino 0.6%; Asian 0.2%; Other 0.9%). **Foreign born:** 0.4%. **Median age:** 37.6.

Income 2000: per capita $15,354; median household $28,352; **Pop below poverty level:** 19.8%. ***Personal per capita income 2000-2003:** $22,404-$24,577.

Unemployment 2004: 6.5%. **Change from 2000:** -2.5%. **Median travel time to work:** 24.5 minutes. **Working outside county of residence:** 51.1%.

Cities with pop over 10,000: None.

JEFFERSON DAVIS PARISH
PO Box 799   **Ph:** 337-824-8340
Jennings, LA 70546
www.jeffdavis.org

In southwestern LA, east of Lake Charles; organized Jun 12, 1912 from Calcasieu Parish. **Name Origin:** For Jefferson Davis (1808-89), president of the Confederate States of America (1862-65).

Area (sq mi): 658.58 (land 652.31; water 6.26). **Pop per sq mi:** 47.9.

Pop 2005: 31,272. **State rank:** 34. **Pop change:** 2000-20005 -0.5%; 1990-2000 +2.3%. **Pop 2000:** 31,435 (White 80%; Black or African American 17.8%; Hispanic or Latino 1%; Asian 0.2%; Other 1.4%). **Foreign born:** 0.6%. **Median age:** 34.5.

Income 2000: per capita $13,398; median household $27,736; **Pop below poverty level:** 20.9%. ***Personal per capita income 2000-2003:** $16,811-$19,715.

Unemployment 2004: 5.2%. **Change from 2000:** -1.6%. **Median travel time to work:** 30.8 minutes. **Working outside county of residence:** 45.3%.

Cities with pop over 10,000: Jennings ⚖ (10,674).

JEFFERSON PARISH
200 Durbigny St   **Ph:** 504-364-2600
Gretna, LA 70053
www.jeffparish.net

In southeastern LA bordered on the north by Lake Pontchartrain and on the south by the Gulf of Mexico; organized Feb 11, 1825 from Orleans Parish. **Name Origin:** For Thomas Jefferson (1743-1826), U.S. patriot and statesman; third U.S. president.

Area (sq mi): 642.41 (land 306.52; water 335.89). **Pop per sq mi:** 1477.3.

Pop 2005: 452,824. **State rank:** 2. **Pop change:** 2000-20005 -0.6%; 1990-2000 +1.6%. **Pop 2000:** 455,466 (White 65.4%; Black or African American 22.9%; Hispanic or Latino 7.1%; Asian 3.1%; Other 4.1%). **Foreign born:** 7.5%. **Median age:** 35.9.

Income 2000: per capita $19,953; median household $38,435; **Pop below poverty level:** 13.7%. ***Personal per capita income 2000-2003:** $27,742-$31,585.

Unemployment 2004: 4.3%. **Change from 2000:** +0%. **Median travel time to work:** 25 minutes. **Working outside county of residence:** 35.2%.

Cities with pop over 10,000: Kenner (70,252); Gretna ⚖ (17,178); Westwego (10,537).

LAFAYETTE CONSOLIDATED GOVERNMENT
PO Box 2009   **Ph:** 337-233-0150
Lafayette, LA 70502   **Fax:** 337-291-6392
www.lafayettegov.org

In south-central LA, west of Baton Rouge; organized Jan 17, 1823 from Attakapas and Saint Martin parishes. **Name Origin:** For the Mauquis de Lafayette (1757-1834), French statesman and soldier who fought with the Americans during the Revolutionary War.

Area (sq mi): 270.29 (land 269.83; water 0.46). **Pop per sq mi:** 731.5.

Pop 2005: 197,390. **State rank:** 6. **Pop change:** 2000-20005 +3.6%; 1990-2000 +15.6%. **Pop 2000:** 190,503 (White 72.3%; Black or African American 23.8%; Hispanic or Latino 1.7%; Asian 1.1%; Other 1.7%). **Foreign born:** 2.5%. **Median age:** 32.4.

Income 2000: per capita $19,371; median household $36,518; **Pop below poverty level:** 15.7%. ***Personal per capita income 2000-2003:** $27,368-$29,879.

Unemployment 2004: 4.5%. **Change from 2000:** +0.6%. **Median travel time to work:** 23.8 minutes. **Working outside county of residence:** 13.8%.

Cities with pop over 10,000: Lafayette ⚖ (111,966).

Source: Personal per capita income data are from the Bureau of Economic Analysis; per capita income data are from the Bureau of the Census. See Introduction for explanation of differences.

LAFOURCHE PARISH

PO Box 5548　　　　　　　　**Ph:** 985-446-8427
Thibodaux, LA 70302　　　　**Fax:** 985-446-8459
www.lapage.com/parishes/lafou.htm

In southeastern LA, southwest of New Orleans; organized 1807 (prior to statehood). **Name Origin:** For Bayou Lafourche, which runs the length of the county; from French 'the fork.'

Area (sq mi): 1472.19 (land 1084.68; water 387.51). **Pop per sq mi:** 85.

Pop 2005: 92,179. **State rank:** 14. **Pop change:** 2000-20005 +2.5%; 1990-2000 +4.8%. **Pop 2000:** 89,974 (White 82.2%; Black or African American 12.6%; Hispanic or Latino 1.4%; Asian 0.7%; Other 3.9%, including 2.3% American Indian/Alaska Native). **Foreign born:** 1.5%. **Median age:** 34.1.

Income 2000: per capita $15,809; median household $34,910; **Pop below poverty level:** 16.5%. ***Personal per capita income 2000-2003:** $22,539-$26,847.

Unemployment 2004: 5%. **Change from 2000:** +1.2%. **Median travel time to work:** 26.8 minutes. **Working outside county of residence:** 35%.

Cities with pop over 10,000: Thibodaux ⛪ (14,501).

LASALLE PARISH

PO Box 1288　　　　　　　　**Ph:** 318-992-2101
Jena, LA 71342　　　　　　　**Fax:** 318-992-2103

In east-central LA, northeast of Alexandria; organized Jul 3, 1908 from Catahoula Parish. **Name Origin:** For Robert Cavelier (1643-87), Sieur de La Salle, French adventurer and explorer who claimed the land west of the Mississippi River for France.

Area (sq mi): 662.36 (land 623.83; water 38.54). **Pop per sq mi:** 22.5.

Pop 2005: 14,040. **State rank:** 55. **Pop change:** 2000-20005 -1.7%; 1990-2000 +4.5%. **Pop 2000:** 14,282 (White 85.6%; Black or African American 12.2%; Hispanic or Latino 0.8%; Asian 0.2%; Other 1.4%). **Foreign born:** 0.6%. **Median age:** 36.4.

Income 2000: per capita $14,033; median household $28,189; **Pop below poverty level:** 18.7%. ***Personal per capita income 2000-2003:** $16,521-$19,082.

Unemployment 2004: 6.2%. **Change from 2000:** 1%. **Median travel time to work:** 36.3 minutes. **Working outside county of residence:** 30.4%.

Cities with pop over 10,000: None.

LINCOLN PARISH

100 W Texas Ave　　　　　　**Ph:** 318-251-5150
Ruston, LA 71270　　　　　　**Fax:** 318-251-5149
www.lincolnparish.org

In north-central LA, west of Monroe; organized Feb 27, 1873 from Bienville, Jackson, and Union parishes. **Name Origin:** For Abraham Lincoln (1809-65), sixteenth U.S. president.

Area (sq mi): 472.27 (land 471.38; water 0.89). **Pop per sq mi:** 89.3.

Pop 2005: 42,108. **State rank:** 27. **Pop change:** 2000-20005 -0.9%; 1990-2000 +1.8%. **Pop 2000:** 42,509 (White 56.9%; Black or African American 39.8%; Hispanic or Latino 1.2%; Asian 1.3%; Other 1.5%). **Foreign born:** 2.1%. **Median age:** 26.5.

Income 2000: per capita $14,313; median household $26,977; **Pop below poverty level:** 26.5%. ***Personal per capita income 2000-2003:** $19,645-$22,158.

Unemployment 2004: 6%. **Change from 2000:** +1.4%. **Median travel time to work:** 18.6 minutes. **Working outside county of residence:** 19.6%.

Cities with pop over 10,000: Ruston ⛪ (20,665).

LIVINGSTON PARISH

PO Box 427　　　　　　　　　**Ph:** 225-686-2266
Livingston, LA 70754　　　　**Fax:** 225-686-7079
www.lapage.com/parishes/livin.htm

On eastern border of LA, east of Baton Rouge; organized Feb 10, 1832 from Saint Helena Parish. **Name Origin:** For Robert R. Livingston (1746-1813), NY patriot, statesman, and a drafter of the Declaration of Independence.

Area (sq mi): 702.84 (land 648.02; water 54.82). **Pop per sq mi:** 168.5.

Pop 2005: 109,206. **State rank:** 10. **Pop change:** 2000-20005 +18.9%; 1990-2000 +30.2%. **Pop 2000:** 91,814 (White 93.5%; Black or African American 4.2%; Hispanic or Latino 1.1%; Asian 0.2%; Other 1.3%). **Foreign born:** 0.8%. **Median age:** 32.8.

Income 2000: per capita $16,282; median household $38,887; **Pop below poverty level:** 11.4%. ***Personal per capita income 2000-2003:** $21,169-$22,181.

Unemployment 2004: 6.3%. **Change from 2000:** +0.2%. **Median travel time to work:** 33.1 minutes. **Working outside county of residence:** 69%.

Cities with pop over 10,000: Denham Springs (10,106).

MADISON PARISH

PO Box 1710　　　　　　　　**Ph:** 318-574-0655
Tallulah, LA 71282　　　　　**Fax:** 318-574-3961

On the northeastern border of LA, west of Vicksburg, MS; organized Jan 19, 1838 from Concordia Parish. **Name Origin:** For James Madison (1751-1836), fourth U.S. president.

Area (sq mi): 650.53 (land 624.09; water 26.45). **Pop per sq mi:** 20.

Pop 2005: 12,457. **State rank:** 56. **Pop change:** 2000-20005 -9.3%; 1990-2000 +10.2%. **Pop 2000:** 13,728 (White 37.1%; Black or African American 60.3%; Hispanic or Latino 2.1%; Asian 0.2%; Other 1.6%). **Foreign born:** 0.5%. **Median age:** 29.8.

Income 2000: per capita $10,114; median household $20,509; **Pop below poverty level:** 36.7%. ***Personal per capita income 2000-2003:** $13,988-$18,549.

Unemployment 2004: 10%. **Change from 2000:** -1.5%. **Median travel time to work:** 22.5 minutes. **Working outside county of residence:** 30.7%.

Cities with pop over 10,000: None.

MOREHOUSE PARISH

PO Box 1543　　　　　　　　**Ph:** 318-281-3343
Bastrop, LA 71221　　　　　**Fax:** 318-281-3775

On the northern border of the LA panhandle, northeast of Monroe; organized Mar 25, 1844 from Ouachita Territory. **Name Origin:**

Morehouse Parish (cont'd)

For Abraham Morehouse (?-1813), colonizer and representative to the legislature of the Territory of Orleans.

Area (sq mi): 805.2 (land 794.25; water 10.95). **Pop per sq mi:** 37.8.

Pop 2005: 29,989. **State rank:** 35. **Pop change:** 2000-20005 -3.3%; 1990-2000 -2.9%. **Pop 2000:** 31,021 (White 55.5%; Black or African American 43.4%; Hispanic or Latino 0.7%; Asian 0.2%; Other 0.6%). **Foreign born:** 0.4%. **Median age:** 35.6.

Income 2000: per capita $13,197; median household $25,124; **Pop below poverty level:** 26.8%. ***Personal per capita income 2000-2003:** $18,214-$21,001.

Unemployment 2004: 9.9%. **Change from 2000:** -2.3%. **Median travel time to work:** 24.9 minutes. **Working outside county of residence:** 33.1%.

Cities with pop over 10,000: Bastrop 🏛 (12,661).

NATCHITOCHES PARISH

PO Box 799   **Ph:** 318-352-2714
Natchitoches, LA 71458   **Fax:** 318-357-2208
nppj.org

In west-central LA, northwest of Alexandria; organized 1807 (prior to statehood). **Name Origin:** For the Indian tribe, from a Caddoan word translated variously as 'chinquapin eaters,' 'chestnut eaters,' 'pawpaw eaters,' or 'pawpaws.'

Area (sq mi): 1299.3 (land 1255.45; water 43.85). **Pop per sq mi:** 30.7.

Pop 2005: 38,541. **State rank:** 30. **Pop change:** 2000-20005 -1.4%; 1990-2000 +6.5%. **Pop 2000:** 39,080 (White 57.2%; Black or African American 38.4%; Hispanic or Latino 1.4%; Asian 0.4%; Other 3.3%, including 1.1% American Indian/Alaska Native). **Foreign born:** 1.5%. **Median age:** 30.2.

Income 2000: per capita $13,743; median household $25,722; **Pop below poverty level:** 26.5%. ***Personal per capita income 2000-2003:** $18,004-$21,698.

Unemployment 2004: 6.4%. **Change from 2000:** -0.3%. **Median travel time to work:** 24.8 minutes. **Working outside county of residence:** 17.5%.

Cities with pop over 10,000: Natchitoches 🏛 (17,916).

ORLEANS PARISH

1300 Perdido St Rm 9-E-06   **Ph:** 504-658-4000
New Orleans, LA 70112   **Fax:** 504-658-8647
www.neworleans.com

In southeastern LA, southeast of Baton Rouge; organized 1807 (prior to statehood). **Name Origin:** For the city of France, former home of many early settlers.

Area (sq mi): 350.21 (land 180.56; water 169.66). **Pop per sq mi:** 2519.2.

Pop 2005: 454,863. **State rank:** 1. **Pop change:** 2000-20005 -6.2%; 1990-2000 -2.5%. **Pop 2000:** 484,674 (White 26.6%; Black or African American 67.3%; Hispanic or Latino 3.1%; Asian 2.3%; Other 2.4%). **Foreign born:** 4.2%. **Median age:** 33.1.

Income 2000: per capita $17,258; median household $27,133; **Pop below poverty level:** 27.9%. ***Personal per capita income 2000-2003:** $25,523-$30,152.

Unemployment 2004: 5.2%. **Change from 2000:** -0.7%. **Median travel time to work:** 25.7 minutes. **Working outside county of residence:** 21.8%.

Cities with pop over 10,000: New Orleans 🏛 (462,269).

OUACHITA PARISH

PO Box 1862   **Ph:** 318-327-1444
Monroe, LA 71210   **Fax:** 318-327-1462

In north-central LA; organized 1807 (prior to statehood). **Name Origin:** For the Ouachita River, which runs through the parish; named for an Indian tribe of the Natchitoches Confederacy; meaning of the name is unclear.

Area (sq mi): 632.7 (land 610.53; water 22.17). **Pop per sq mi:** 242.8.

Pop 2005: 148,237. **State rank:** 8. **Pop change:** 2000-20005 +0.7%; 1990-2000 +3.6%. **Pop 2000:** 147,250 (White 63.8%; Black or African American 33.6%; Hispanic or Latino 1.2%; Asian 0.6%; Other 1.2%). **Foreign born:** 1%. **Median age:** 32.3.

Income 2000: per capita $17,084; median household $32,047; **Pop below poverty level:** 20.7%. ***Personal per capita income 2000-2003:** $23,107-$26,237.

Unemployment 2004: 5.6%. **Change from 2000:** +0.1%. **Median travel time to work:** 20.4 minutes. **Working outside county of residence:** 7.5%.

Cities with pop over 10,000: Monroe 🏛 (52,141); West Monroe (12,990).

PLAQUEMINES PARISH

301 Main St   **Ph:** 504-392-4969
Belle Chasse, LA 70037   **Fax:** 504-297-5195
www.plaqueminesparish.com

On southeastern border of LA, south of New Orleans; organized Mar 31, 1807 (prior to statehood) from Orleans Parish. **Name Origin:** A French rendering of Illinois Indian *piakimin* 'persimmon' for the many trees.

Area (sq mi): 2428.54 (land 844.56; water 1583.98). **Pop per sq mi:** 34.3.

Pop 2005: 28,995. **State rank:** 36. **Pop change:** 2000-20005 +8.4%; 1990-2000 +4.6%. **Pop 2000:** 26,757 (White 68.8%; Black or African American 23.4%; Hispanic or Latino 1.6%; Asian 2.6%; Other 4.2%, including 2.1% American Indian/Alaska Native). **Foreign born:** 2.8%. **Median age:** 33.7.

Income 2000: per capita $15,937; median household $38,173; **Pop below poverty level:** 18%. ***Personal per capita income 2000-2003:** $20,981-$23,793.

Unemployment 2004: 4.7%. **Change from 2000:** -0.4%. **Median travel time to work:** 26.4 minutes. **Working outside county of residence:** 36.4%.

Cities with pop over 10,000: None.

---

*Source: Personal per capita income data are from the Bureau of Economic Analysis; per capita income data are from the Bureau of the Census. See Introduction for explanation of differences.

POINTE COUPEE PARISH

PO Box 86
New Roads, LA 70760
www.pcpolicejury.org

Ph: 225-638-9596
Fax: 225-638-9590

In south-central LA, northwest of Baton Rouge; organized 1807 (prior to statehood). **Name Origin:** From French 'cut-off point,' descriptive of a point where the Mississippi River cut a new channel.

Area (sq mi): 590.68 (land 557.34; water 33.34). **Pop per sq mi:** 40.1.

Pop 2005: 22,377. **State rank:** 42. **Pop change:** 2000-20005 -1.7%; 1990-2000 +1%. **Pop 2000:** 22,763 (White 60.3%; Black or African American 37.8%; Hispanic or Latino 1.1%; Asian 0.3%; Other 1.1%). **Foreign born:** 0.9%. **Median age:** 36.7.

Income 2000: per capita $15,387; median household $30,618; **Pop below poverty level:** 23.1%. ***Personal per capita income 2000-2003:** $20,484-$22,783.

Unemployment 2004: 7.5%. **Change from 2000:** -1.2%. **Median travel time to work:** 31.2 minutes. **Working outside county of residence:** 45.4%.

Cities with pop over 10,000: None.

RAPIDES PARISH

PO Box 952
Alexandria, LA 71309
www.rppj.com

Ph: 318-473 8153
Fax: 318-473-4667

In central LA; organized 1807 (prior to statehood). **Name Origin:** French for the 'rapids,' on the Red River, which runs through the parish.

Area (sq mi): 1361.96 (land 1322.54; water 39.42). **Pop per sq mi:** 97.1.

Pop 2005: 128,462. **State rank:** 9. **Pop change:** 2000-20005 +1.7%; 1990-2000 -4%. **Pop 2000:** 126,337 (White 65.7%; Black or African American 30.4%; Hispanic or Latino 1.4%; Asian 0.9%; Other 2.1%). **Foreign born:** 1.6%. **Median age:** 35.5.

Income 2000: per capita $16,088; median household $29,856; **Pop below poverty level:** 20.5%. ***Personal per capita income 2000-2003:** $23,627-$26,934.

Unemployment 2004: 5.6%. **Change from 2000:** -0.4%. **Median travel time to work:** 23.6 minutes. **Working outside county of residence:** 8.8%.

Cities with pop over 10,000: Alexandria ⚏ (45,971); Pineville (13,784).

RED RIVER PARISH

PO Box 485
Coushatta, LA 71019

Ph: 318-932-6741
Fax: 318-932-3126

In west-central LA, southeast of Shreveport; organized 1871 from Caddo, Bossier, Bienville, Natchitoches, and De Soto parishes. **Name Origin:** For the river, which runs through the county.

Area (sq mi): 402.08 (land 389.29; water 12.79). **Pop per sq mi:** 24.3.

Pop 2005: 9,465. **State rank:** 62. **Pop change:** 2000-20005 -1.6%; 1990-2000 +2.5%. **Pop 2000:** 9,622 (White 57.6%; Black or African American 40.9%; Hispanic or Latino 1%; Asian 0.1%; Other 1.1%). **Foreign born:** 0.4%. **Median age:** 34.6.

Income 2000: per capita $12,119; median household $23,153; **Pop below poverty level:** 29.9%. ***Personal per capita income 2000-2003:** $16,393-$18,618.

Unemployment 2004: 9.8%. **Change from 2000:** -0.8%. **Median travel time to work:** 31 minutes. **Working outside county of residence:** 38.6%.

Cities with pop over 10,000: None.

RICHLAND PARISH

708 Julia St
Rayville, LA 71269

Ph: 318-728-2061
Fax: 318-728-7004

In northeastern LA, east of Monroe; organized Mar 11, 1852 from Ouachita, Carroll, Franklin, and Morehouse parishes. **Name Origin:** Descriptive of the fertile soil.

Area (sq mi): 564.51 (land 558.45; water 6.05). **Pop per sq mi:** 36.8.

Pop 2005: 20,526. **State rank:** 46. **Pop change:** 2000-20005 -2.2%; 1990-2000 +1.7%. **Pop 2000:** 20,981 (White 60.4%; Black or African American 38%; Hispanic or Latino 1.1%; Asian 0.2%; Other 0.8%). **Foreign born:** 0.5%. **Median age:** 35.8.

Income 2000: per capita $12,479; median household $23,668; **Pop below poverty level:** 27.9%. ***Personal per capita income 2000-2003:** $17,888-$19,725.

Unemployment 2004: 8.2%. **Change from 2000:** -2.3%. **Median travel time to work:** 27.3 minutes. **Working outside county of residence:** 42%.

Cities with pop over 10,000: None.

SABINE PARISH

400 S Capitol St
Many, LA 71449
www.sabineparish.com

Ph: 318-256-6223
Fax: 318-256-9037

On the western border of LA, south of Shreveport; organized Mar 7, 1843 from Natchitoches Parish. **Name Origin:** For the Sabine River, which forms the parish's western border.

Area (sq mi): 1011.51 (land 865.27; water 146.25). **Pop per sq mi:** 27.5.

Pop 2005: 23,786. **State rank:** 39. **Pop change:** 2000-20005 +1.4%; 1990-2000 +3.6%. **Pop 2000:** 23,459 (White 71.3%; Black or African American 16.9%; Hispanic or Latino 2.7%; Asian 0.1%; Other 10.3%, including 7.8% American Indian/Alaska Native). **Foreign born:** 1%. **Median age:** 38.2.

Income 2000: per capita $15,199; median household $26,655; **Pop below poverty level:** 21.5%. ***Personal per capita income 2000-2003:** $17,588-$19,960.

Unemployment 2004: 6.1%. **Change from 2000:** -1.1%. **Median travel time to work:** 35.4 minutes. **Working outside county of residence:** 30.9%.

Cities with pop over 10,000: None.

SAINT BERNARD PARISH

8201 W Judge Perez Dr
Chalmette, LA 70043
www.st-bernard.la.us

Ph: 504-277-6371
Fax: 504-278-4329

On the northeastern border of LA, east of New Orleans; organized

Saint Bernard Parish (cont'd)

Mar 31, 1807 (prior to statehood) from Orleans Parish. **Name Origin:** For Don Bernardo de Galvez (1746-86), Spanish colonial governor who supplied American forces during the American Revolution.

Area (sq mi): 1793.75 (land 465.04; water 1328.71). **Pop per sq mi:** 140.6.

Pop 2005: 65,364. **State rank:** 18. **Pop change:** 2000-20005 -2.8%; 1990-2000 +0.9%. **Pop 2000:** 67,229 (White 84.4%; Black or African American 7.6%; Hispanic or Latino 5.1%; Asian 1.3%; Other 2.7%). **Foreign born:** 3%. **Median age:** 36.6.

Income 2000: per capita $16,718; median household $35,939; **Pop below poverty level:** 13.1%. ***Personal per capita income 2000-2003:** $21,635-$25,046.

Unemployment 2004: 4.8%. **Change from 2000:** -1.1%. **Median travel time to work:** 29.3 minutes. **Working outside county of residence:** 58.7%.

Cities with pop over 10,000: None.

SAINT CHARLES PARISH
15045 River Rd   **Ph:** 985-783-5000
Hahnville, LA 70057   **Fax:** 985-783-2067
www.st-charles.la.us

In southeastern LA, southwest of New Orleans; organized Mar 31, 1807 (prior to statehood) from German Coast Parish. **Name Origin:** For Saint Charles Borromeo (1538-84), founder of the order of the Oblates of Saint Ambrose.

Area (sq mi): 410.16 (land 283.64; water 126.52). **Pop per sq mi:** 178.5.

Pop 2005: 50,633. **State rank:** 22. **Pop change:** 2000-20005 +5.3%; 1990-2000 +13.3%. **Pop 2000:** 48,072 (White 70.5%; Black or African American 25.2%; Hispanic or Latino 2.8%; Asian 0.6%; Other 1.8%). **Foreign born:** 2.5%. **Median age:** 34.2.

Income 2000: per capita $19,054; median household $45,139; **Pop below poverty level:** 11.4%. ***Personal per capita income 2000-2003:** $24,210-$26,470.

Unemployment 2004: 4.5%. **Change from 2000:** -1.1%. **Median travel time to work:** 26.5 minutes. **Working outside county of residence:** 54.5%.

Cities with pop over 10,000: None.

SAINT HELENA PARISH
PO Box 308   **Ph:** 225-222-4514
Greensburg, LA 70441   **Fax:** 225-222-3443

On the northern border of LA, northeast of Baton Rouge; organized Oct 27, 1810 (prior to statehood) from Feliciana Parish. **Name Origin:** For Saint Helena (c.250-330), mother of Constantine the Great.

Area (sq mi): 409.46 (land 408.36; water 1.09). **Pop per sq mi:** 25.1.

Pop 2005: 10,259. **State rank:** 60. **Pop change:** 2000-20005 -2.5%; 1990-2000 +6.6%. **Pop 2000:** 10,525 (White 46.2%; Black or African American 52.4%; Hispanic or Latino 1%; Asian 0.1%; Other 0.9%). **Foreign born:** 0.3%. **Median age:** 35.

Income 2000: per capita $12,318; median household $24,970; **Pop below poverty level:** 26.8%. ***Personal per capita income 2000-2003:** $16,389-$19,985.

Unemployment 2004: 6.6%. **Change from 2000:** -0.1%. **Median travel time to work:** 35.7 minutes. **Working outside county of residence:** 67.1%.

Cities with pop over 10,000: None.

SAINT JAMES PARISH
PO Box 63   **Ph:** 225-562-2270
Convent, LA 70723   **Fax:** 225-562-2383
www.stjamesla.com

In southeastern LA, southeast of Baton Rouge; original parish, organized Mar 31, 1807 (prior to statehood). **Name Origin:** For James the Apostle, disciple of Jesus Christ.

Area (sq mi): 257.79 (land 246.13; water 11.66). **Pop per sq mi:** 85.9.

Pop 2005: 21,150. **State rank:** 44. **Pop change:** 2000-20005 -0.3%; 1990-2000 +1.6%. **Pop 2000:** 21,216 (White 49.7%; Black or African American 49.4%; Hispanic or Latino 0.6%; Asian 0%; Other 0.6%). **Foreign born:** 0.2%. **Median age:** 34.

Income 2000: per capita $14,381; median household $35,277; **Pop below poverty level:** 20.7%. ***Personal per capita income 2000-2003:** $18,507-$21,487.

Unemployment 2004: 9.8%. **Change from 2000:** -1.7%. **Median travel time to work:** 25.4 minutes. **Working outside county of residence:** 47.3%.

Cities with pop over 10,000: None.

SAINT JOHN THE BAPTIST PARISH
1801 W Airline Hwy   **Ph:** 985-652-9569
LaPlace, LA 70068   **Fax:** 985-652-4131
www.sjbparish.com

On the southeastern border of LA, west of New Orleans; organized Mar 31, 1807 (prior to statehood) from German Coast Parish. **Name Origin:** For the saint who baptized Jesus, his cousin.

Area (sq mi): 347.84 (land 218.9; water 128.94). **Pop per sq mi:** 211.9.

Pop 2005: 46,393. **State rank:** 25. **Pop change:** 2000-20005 +7.8%; 1990-2000 +7.6%. **Pop 2000:** 43,044 (White 51%; Black or African American 44.8%; Hispanic or Latino 2.9%; Asian 0.5%; Other 2.2%). **Foreign born:** 2.3%. **Median age:** 32.

Income 2000: per capita $15,445; median household $39,456; **Pop below poverty level:** 16.7%. ***Personal per capita income 2000-2003:** $19,721-$22,592.

Unemployment 2004: 5.9%. **Change from 2000:** -2.3%. **Median travel time to work:** 27.8 minutes. **Working outside county of residence:** 57.7%.

Cities with pop over 10,000: None.

SAINT LANDRY PARISH
118 S Court St Suite 109   **Ph:** 337-942-5606
Opelousas, LA 70571   **Fax:** 337-948-7265
www.stlandry.org

In south-central LA, north of Lafayette; organized Mar 31, 1807

*Source: Personal per capita income data are from the Bureau of Economic Analysis; per capita income data are from the Bureau of the Census. See Introduction for explanation of differences.

318

Saint Landry Parish (cont'd)

(prior to statehood) from Opelousas Parish. **Name Origin:** For Saint Landry (or Landri or Landericus; ?-656), bishop of Paris (650-656).

Area (sq mi): 938.83 (land 928.65; water 10.18). **Pop per sq mi:** 96.8.

Pop 2005: 89,937. **State rank:** 16. **Pop change:** 2000-20005 +2.6%; 1990-2000 +9.2%. **Pop 2000:** 87,700 (White 56.1%; Black or African American 42.1%; Hispanic or Latino 0.9%; Asian 0.2%; Other 1.1%). **Foreign born:** 0.5%. **Median age:** 34.6.

Income 2000: per capita $12,042; median household $22,855; **Pop below poverty level:** 29.3%. ***Personal per capita income 2000-2003:** $17,464-$19,517.

Unemployment 2004: 6.6%. **Change from 2000:** -0.9%. **Median travel time to work:** 28.6 minutes. **Working outside county of residence:** 38.8%.

Cities with pop over 10,000: Opelousas 🏛 (22,865); Eunice (11,569).

SAINT MARTIN PARISH

PO Box 308   **Ph:** 337-394-2210
Saint Martinville, LA 70582   **Fax:** 337-394-7772
stmartinparish-la.org

In south-central LA, east of Lafayette; organized 1815 from Attakapas County. **Name Origin:** For Saint Martin (c.315-399), bishop of Tours.

Area (sq mi): 816.46 (land 739.85; water 76.6). **Pop per sq mi:** 68.2.

Pop 2005: 50,434. **State rank:** 23. **Pop change:** 2000-20005 +3.8%; 1990-2000 +10.5%. **Pop 2000:** 48,583 (White 65.5%; Black or African American 32%; Hispanic or Latino 0.8%; Asian 0.9%; Other 1.2%). **Foreign born:** 0.9%. **Median age:** 33.4.

Income 2000: per capita $13,619; median household $30,701; **Pop below poverty level:** 21.5%. ***Personal per capita income 2000-2003:** $17,101-$19,252.

Unemployment 2004: 5.6%. **Change from 2000:** -2.4%. **Median travel time to work:** 30 minutes. **Working outside county of residence:** 58%.

Cities with pop over 10,000: None.

SAINT MARY PARISH

PO Box 1231   **Ph:** 337-828-4100
Franklin, LA 70538   **Fax:** 337-828-2509
www.parish.st-mary.la.us

On the central southern border of LA, southeast of New Iberia; organized Apr 17, 1811 (prior to statehood) from Attakapas Parish. **Name Origin:** For the Virgin Mary, the mother of Jesus.

Area (sq mi): 1118.83 (land 612.79; water 506.04). **Pop per sq mi:** 83.9.

Pop 2005: 51,416. **State rank:** 21. **Pop change:** 2000-20005 -3.9%; 1990-2000 -7.9%. **Pop 2000:** 53,500 (White 61.8%; Black or African American 31.8%; Hispanic or Latino 2.2%; Asian 1.6%; Other 3.8%, including 1.4% American Indian/Alaska Native). **Foreign born:** 2%. **Median age:** 34.3.

Income 2000: per capita $13,399; median household $28,072; **Pop below poverty level:** 23.6%. ***Personal per capita income 2000-2003:** $21,067-$25,026.

Unemployment 2004: 8.6%. **Change from 2000:** +0.1%. **Median travel time to work:** 18.8 minutes. **Working outside county of residence:** 12.5%.

Cities with pop over 10,000: Morgan City (12,153).

SAINT TAMMANY PARISH

701 N Columbia St   **Ph:** 985-809-8700
Covington, LA 70433
www.stpgov.org

On the southeastern border of LA, east of Baton Rouge; organized Oct 27, 1810 (prior to statehood) from Feliciana Parish. **Name Origin:** For a celebrated Delaware Indian chief who lived in the 1600s; from *Tamanend*, possibly 'friendly' or 'affable.' His admirers claimed him as their 'patron saint' during the American Revolution.

Area (sq mi): 1124.08 (land 854.15; water 269.93). **Pop per sq mi:** 257.9.

Pop 2005: 220,295. **State rank:** 5. **Pop change:** 2000-20005 +15.2%; 1990-2000 +32.4%. **Pop 2000:** 191,268 (White 85.3%; Black or African American 9.9%; Hispanic or Latino 2.5%; Asian 0.7%; Other 2.3%). **Foreign born:** 2.4%. **Median age:** 36.3.

Income 2000: per capita $22,514; median household $47,883; **Pop below poverty level:** 9.7%. ***Personal per capita income 2000-2003:** $29,220-$31,639.

Unemployment 2004: 3.6%. **Change from 2000:** -0.7%. **Median travel time to work:** 32.1 minutes. **Working outside county of residence:** 39.5%.

Cities with pop over 10,000: Slidell (26,845); Mandeville (11,511).

TANGIPAHOA PARISH

PO Box 215   **Ph:** 985-748-3211
Amite, LA 70422   **Fax:** 985-748-7576
www.tangipahoa.org

On the northern border of LA, east of Baton Rouge; organized Mar 6, 1869 from Livingston, Saint Tammany, Saint Helena, and Washington parishes. **Name Origin:** For the Indian tribe, which has since disappeared. The name is probably from Choctaw *tanchapi* 'cornstalk' or 'cob,' and *ayua* 'gather': 'corn gatherers.'

Area (sq mi): 823.12 (land 790.24; water 32.88). **Pop per sq mi:** 134.8.

Pop 2005: 106,502. **State rank:** 12. **Pop change:** 2000-20005 +5.9%; 1990-2000 +17.4%. **Pop 2000:** 100,588 (White 68.9%; Black or African American 28.4%; Hispanic or Latino 1.5%; Asian 0.4%; Other 1.5%). **Foreign born:** 0.8%. **Median age:** 32.3.

Income 2000: per capita $14,461; median household $29,412; **Pop below poverty level:** 22.7%. ***Personal per capita income 2000-2003:** $19,071-$21,789.

Unemployment 2004: 6.8%. **Change from 2000:** -1.7%. **Median travel time to work:** 29.5 minutes. **Working outside county of residence:** 31.1%.

Cities with pop over 10,000: Hammond (18,044).

🏛 *County Seat*

TENSAS PARISH

PO Box 78   **Ph:** 318-766-3921
Saint Joseph, LA 71366   **Fax:** 318-766-3926

On the northeastern border of LA, north of Natchez, MS; organized Mar 17, 1843 from Concordia Parish. **Name Origin:** For the Taensa Indian tribe, which lived in the area. The origin and meaning of the name have been lost.

Area (sq mi): 641.2 (land 602.48; water 38.72). **Pop per sq mi:** 10.2.

Pop 2005: 6,125. **State rank:** 64. **Pop change:** 2000-20005 -7.4%; 1990-2000 -6.8%. **Pop 2000:** 6,618 (White 42.9%; Black or African American 55.4%; Hispanic or Latino 1.3%; Asian 0.1%; Other 1%). **Foreign born:** 1.2%. **Median age:** 37.3.

Income 2000: per capita $12,622; median household $19,799; **Pop below poverty level:** 36.3%. ***Personal per capita income 2000-2003:** $18,045-$22,516.

Unemployment 2004: 8.7%. **Change from 2000:** -0.3%. **Median travel time to work:** 26.6 minutes. **Working outside county of residence:** 24.6%.

Cities with pop over 10,000: None.

TERREBONNE PARISH

PO Box 1569   **Ph:** 985-872-0466
Houma, LA 70361   **Fax:** 985-868-5143
www.terrebonneparish.com

On the southern border of LA, southwest of New Orleans; organized Mar 22, 1822 from Lafourche Parish. **Name Origin:** From the French for 'good land.'

Area (sq mi): 2079.9 (land 1254.93; water 824.97). **Pop per sq mi:** 85.7.

Pop 2005: 107,491. **State rank:** 11. **Pop change:** 2000-20005 +2.9%; 1990-2000 +7.8%. **Pop 2000:** 104,503 (White 73.2%; Black or African American 17.8%; Hispanic or Latino 1.6%; Asian 0.8%; Other 7.3%, including 5.3% American Indian/Alaska Native). **Foreign born:** 1.5%. **Median age:** 33.

Income 2000: per capita $16,051; median household $35,235; **Pop below poverty level:** 19.1%. ***Personal per capita income 2000-2003:** $20,763-$23,851.

Unemployment 2004: 5.2%. **Change from 2000:** +1.4%. **Median travel time to work:** 25.2 minutes. **Working outside county of residence:** 17.1%.

Cities with pop over 10,000: Houma 🏛 (32,022).

UNION PARISH

100 E Bayou St Suite 105   **Ph:** 318-368-3055
Farmerville, LA 71241   **Fax:** 318-368-3861

On the central northern border of the LA panhandle, north of Monroe; organized Mar 13, 1839 from Ouachita Parish. **Name Origin:** For the union of the United States.

Area (sq mi): 905.28 (land 877.6; water 27.68). **Pop per sq mi:** 26.1.

Pop 2005: 22,901. **State rank:** 41. **Pop change:** 2000-20005 +0.4%; 1990-2000 +10.2%. **Pop 2000:** 22,803 (White 69.2%; Black or African American 27.9%; Hispanic or Latino 2%; Asian 0.3%; Other 2%). **Foreign born:** 1.2%. **Median age:** 37.3.

Income 2000: per capita $14,819; median household $29,061; **Pop below poverty level:** 18.6%. ***Personal per capita income 2000-2003:** $19,170-$22,276.

Unemployment 2004: 6.4%. **Change from 2000:** +0.5%. **Median travel time to work:** 30.8 minutes. **Working outside county of residence:** 52%.

Cities with pop over 10,000: None.

VERMILION PARISH

County Courthouse 100 N State St Suite 101 **Ph:** 337-898-1992
Abbeville, LA 70510   **Fax:** 337-898-9803
www.vermilion.org

On the central southern border of LA, south of Lafayette; organized Mar 25, 1844 from Lafayette Parish. **Name Origin:** For the red clay soil.

Area (sq mi): 1538.31 (land 1173.78; water 364.53). **Pop per sq mi:** 47.

Pop 2005: 55,195. **State rank:** 20. **Pop change:** 2000-20005 +2.6%; 1990-2000 +7.5%. **Pop 2000:** 53,807 (White 81.8%; Black or African American 14.2%; Hispanic or Latino 1.4%; Asian 1.8%; Other 1.4%). **Foreign born:** 2%. **Median age:** 35.1.

Income 2000: per capita $14,201; median household $29,500; **Pop below poverty level:** 22.1%. ***Personal per capita income 2000-2003:** $18,726-$20,786.

Unemployment 2004: 5.9%. **Change from 2000:** -0.5%. **Median travel time to work:** 29.4 minutes. **Working outside county of residence:** 40.2%.

Cities with pop over 10,000: Abbeville 🏛 (11,683).

VERNON PARISH

215 S 4th St   **Ph:** 337-238-1384
Leesville, LA 71446   **Fax:** 337-238-9902

On the central western border of LA, southwest of Alexandria; organized Mar 30, 1871 from Natchitoches, Rapides, and Sabine parishes. **Name Origin:** For Mount Vernon, the home of George Washington (1732-99) in VA.

Area (sq mi): 1341.51 (land 1328.41; water 13.1). **Pop per sq mi:** 36.7.

Pop 2005: 48,745. **State rank:** 24. **Pop change:** 2000-20005 -7.2%; 1990-2000 -15.2%. **Pop 2000:** 52,531 (White 71.4%; Black or African American 17.1%; Hispanic or Latino 5.9%; Asian 1.6%; Other 7.7%, including 1.5% American Indian/Alaska Native). **Foreign born:** 4.1%. **Median age:** 28.3.

Income 2000: per capita $14,036; median household $31,216; **Pop below poverty level:** 15.3%. ***Personal per capita income 2000-2003:** $20,100-$24,888.

Unemployment 2004: 5.9%. **Change from 2000:** -0.3%. **Median travel time to work:** 24 minutes. **Working outside county of residence:** 18.7%.

Cities with pop over 10,000: None.

WASHINGTON PARISH

909 Pearl St   **Ph:** 985-839-7825
Franklinton, LA 70438   **Fax:** 985-839-7828

On the northeastern border of LA, northeast of Baton Rouge;

---

*Source: Personal per capita income data are from the Bureau of Economic Analysis; per capita income data are from the Bureau of the Census.
See Introduction for explanation of differences.

Washington Parish (cont'd)

organized Mar 6, 1819 from Saint Tammany Parish. **Name Origin:** For George Washington (1732-99), American patriot and first U.S. president.

Area (sq mi): 675.97 (land 669.57; water 6.4). **Pop per sq mi:** 66.6.

Pop 2005: 44,623. **State rank:** 26. **Pop change:** 2000-20005 +1.6%; 1990-2000 +1.7%. **Pop 2000.** 43,926 (White 66.0%; Black or African American 31.5%; Hispanic or Latino 0.8%; Asian 0.2%; Other 0.8%). **Foreign born:** 0.4%. **Median age:** 36.1.

Income 2000: per capita $12,915; median household $24,264; **Pop below poverty level:** 24.7%. *Personal per capita income 2000-2003: $17,336-$19,809.

Unemployment 2004: 7.4%. **Change from 2000:** -1%. **Median travel time to work:** 32.6 minutes. **Working outside county of residence:** 31%.

Cities with pop over 10,000: Bogalusa (12,908).

WEBSTER PARISH

PO Box 370   **Ph:** 318-371-0366
Minden, LA 71058   **Fax:** 318-371-0226
www.wppj.org

On the northwestern border of the LA panhandle, northeast of Shreveport; organized Feb 27, 1871 from Bossier, Claiborne, and Bienville parishes. **Name Origin:** For Daniel Webster (1782-1852), U.S. statesman and orator from MA.

Area (sq mi): 615.07 (land 595.22; water 19.85). **Pop per sq mi:** 69.5.

Pop 2005: 41,356. **State rank:** 29. **Pop change:** 2000-20005 -1.1%; 1990-2000 -0.4%. **Pop 2000:** 41,831 (White 65.1%; Black or African American 32.8%; Hispanic or Latino 0.9%; Asian 0.2%; Other 1.4%). **Foreign born:** 0.7%. **Median age:** 38.1.

Income 2000: per capita $15,203; median household $28,408; **Pop below poverty level:** 20.2%. *Personal per capita income 2000-2003: $19,964-$22,382.

Unemployment 2004: 6.9%. **Change from 2000:** -1.5%. **Median travel time to work:** 26.7 minutes. **Working outside county of residence:** 35.2%.

Cities with pop over 10,000: Minden 🏛 (13,281).

WEST BATON ROUGE PARISH

PO Box 757   **Ph:** 225-383-4755
Port Allen, LA 70767   **Fax:** 225-387-0218
www.wbrcouncil.org

In east-central LA, west of Baton Rouge; organized Mar 31, 1807 (prior to statehood) from Baton Rouge Parish. **Name Origin:** From the division of Baton Rouge Parish into two parishes: East and West.

Area (sq mi): 203.62 (land 191.2; water 12.42). **Pop per sq mi:** 113.1.

Pop 2005: 21,634. **State rank:** 43. **Pop change:** 2000-20005 +0.2%; 1990-2000 +11.2%. **Pop 2000:** 21,601 (White 62%; Black or African American 35.5%; Hispanic or Latino 1.4%; Asian 0.2%; Other 1.5%). **Foreign born:** 0.9%. **Median age:** 34.

Income 2000: per capita $15,773; median household $37,117; **Pop below poverty level:** 17%. *Personal per capita income 2000-2003: $23,131-$24,586.

Unemployment 2004: 6.7%. **Change from 2000:** +1%. **Median travel time to work:** 21.2 minutes. **Working outside county of residence:** 62.5%.

Cities with pop over 10,000: None.

WEST CARROLL PARISH

PO Box 1078   **Ph:** 318-428-3281
Oak Grove, LA 71263   **Fax:** 318-428-9896

On the northeastern border of the LA panhandle, northeast of Monroe; organized Mar 28, 1877 from Carroll Parish. **Name Origin:** From the division of Carroll Parish into two parishes: East and West.

Area (sq mi): 360.32 (land 359.4; water 0.92). **Pop per sq mi:** 32.8.

Pop 2005: 11,806. **State rank:** 57. **Pop change:** 2000-20005 -4.1%; 1990-2000 +1.8%. **Pop 2000:** 12,314 (White 79.1%; Black or African American 18.9%; Hispanic or Latino 1.3%; Asian 0.1%; Other 1.1%). **Foreign born:** 0.3%. **Median age:** 37.2.

Income 2000: per capita $12,302; median household $24,637; **Pop below poverty level:** 23.4%. *Personal per capita income 2000-2003: $15,632-$18,231.

Unemployment 2004: 13%. **Change from 2000:** -2%. **Median travel time to work:** 26.5 minutes. **Working outside county of residence:** 39.5%.

Cities with pop over 10,000: None.

WEST FELICIANA PARISH

PO Box 1921   **Ph:** 225-635-3864
Saint Francisville, LA 70775   **Fax:** 225-635-3705

On the northern border of LA, northwest of Baton Rouge; organized Feb 17, 1824 from Feliciana Parish. **Name Origin:** From the divison of Feliciana Parish into two parishes: East and West.

Area (sq mi): 426.01 (land 406; water 20.01). **Pop per sq mi:** 37.4.

Pop 2005: 15,199. **State rank:** 52. **Pop change:** 2000-20005 +0.6%; 1990-2000 +17%. **Pop 2000:** 15,111 (White 48.1%; Black or African American 50.5%; Hispanic or Latino 1%; Asian 0.2%; Other 0.6%). **Foreign born:** 0.5%. **Median age:** 36.6.

Income 2000: per capita $16,201; median household $39,667; **Pop below poverty level:** 19.9%. *Personal per capita income 2000-2003: $16,062-$17,183.

Unemployment 2004: 6.9%. **Change from 2000:** +0.6%. **Median travel time to work:** 28.4 minutes. **Working outside county of residence:** 41.5%.

Cities with pop over 10,000: None.

WINN PARISH

PO Box 951   **Ph:** 318-628-5824
Winnfield, LA 71483   **Fax:** 318-628-7336

In north-central LA, southwest of Monroe; organized 1852 from Natchitoches, Catahoula, and Rapides parishes. **Name Origin:** For Walter O. Winn, a prominent lawyer and citizen.

Area (sq mi): 956.91 (land 950.49; water 6.43). **Pop per sq mi:** 16.8.

🏛 *County Seat*

321

Winn Parish (cont'd)

Pop 2005: 15,968. **State rank:** 51. **Pop change:** 2000-20005 -5.5%; 1990-2000 +3.8%. **Pop 2000:** 16,894 (White 65.7%; Black or African American 32%; Hispanic or Latino 0.9%; Asian 0.2%; Other 1.6%). **Foreign born:** 0.5%. **Median age:** 36.2.

Income 2000: per capita $11,794; median household $25,462; **Pop below poverty level:** 21.5%. ***Personal per capita income 2000-2003:** $15,393-$18,243.

Unemployment 2004: 6.8%. **Change from 2000:** -0.4%. **Median travel time to work:** 28.3 minutes. **Working outside county of residence:** 25.7%.

Cities with pop over 10,000: None.

*Source: Personal per capita income data are from the Bureau of Economic Analysis; per capita income data are from the Bureau of the Census. See Introduction for explanation of differences.

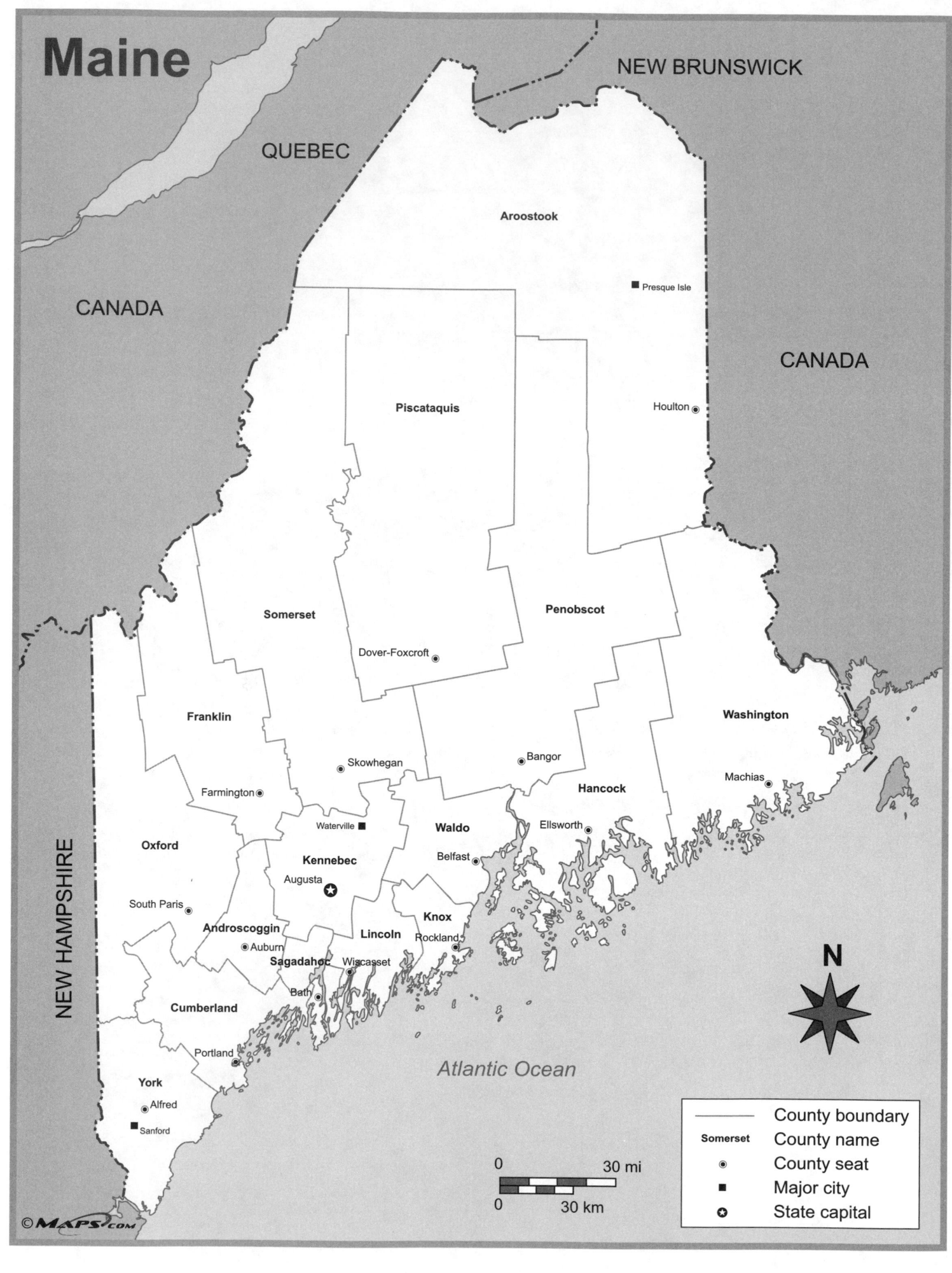

Maine

QUEBEC

NEW BRUNSWICK

CANADA

CANADA

Aroostook

■ Presque Isle

Piscataquis

Houlton ⊙

Somerset

Dover-Foxcroft ⊙

Penobscot

Franklin

Washington

Skowhegan ⊙

Bangor ⊙

Machias ⊙

Farmington ⊙

Hancock

NEW HAMPSHIRE

Oxford

Waterville ■

Waldo

Ellsworth ⊙

Kennebec

Belfast ⊙

Augusta ✪

South Paris ⊙

Knox

Androscoggin

Lincoln

Rockland ⊙

⊙ Auburn

Sagadahoc

Wiscasset ⊙

Bath ⊙

Cumberland

Portland ⊙

Atlantic Ocean

N

York

⊙ Alfred

■ Sanford

© Maps.com

	County boundary
Somerset	County name
⊙	County seat
■	Major city
✪	State capital

0   30 mi

0   30 km

Maine

MAINE STATE INFORMATION

www.maine.gov   **Ph:** 207-624-9494

Area (sq mi): 35,384.65 (land 30,861.55; water 4523.1). **Pop per sq mi:** 42.8.

Pop 2005: 1,321,505. **Pop change:** 2000-20005 +3.7%; 1990-2000 +3.8%. **Pop 2000:** 1,274,923 (White 96.5%; Black or African American 0.5%; Hispanic or Latino 0.7%; Asian 0.7%; Other 1.8%). **Foreign born:** 2.9%. **Median age:** 38.6.

Income 2000: per capita $19,533; median household $37,240; **Pop below poverty level:** 10.9%. *****Personal per capita income 2000-2003:** $25,969-$29,164.

Unemployment 2004: 4.6%. **Change from 2000:** ⌐1.3%. **Median travel time to work:** 22.7 minutes. **Working outside county of residence:** 21.9%.

ANDROSCOGGIN COUNTY

2 Turner St   **Ph:** 207-784-8390
Auburn, ME 04210   **Fax:** 207-782-5367
www.androscoggincounty.com

In southern ME, southwest of Augusta; organized Mar 18, 1854 from Cumberland, Oxford, and Kennebec counties. **Name Origin:** For the river, from an Abnaki Indian name meaning either 'place where fish are cured,' 'fishing place for alewives.' or 'fish spearing.'

Area (sq mi): 497.23 (land 470.27; water 26.95). **Pop per sq mi:** 229.7.

Pop 2005: 108,039. **State rank:** 5. **Pop change:** 2000-20005 +4.1%; 1990-2000 -1.4%. **Pop 2000:** 103,793 (White 96.4%; Black or African American 0.7%; Hispanic or Latino 1%; Asian 0.6%; Other 1.8%). **Foreign born:** 2.6%. **Median age:** 37.2.

Income 2000: per capita $18,734; median household $35,793; **Pop below poverty level:** 11.1%. *****Personal per capita income 2000-2003:** $24,377-$28,166.

Unemployment 2004: 4.5%. **Change from 2000:** +0.4%. **Median travel time to work:** 23.3 minutes. **Working outside county of residence:** 26%.

Cities with pop over 10,000: Lewiston (35,776); Auburn 🏛 (23,551).

AROOSTOOK COUNTY

144 Sweden St Suite 101   **Ph:** 207-498-8125
Caribou, ME 04736
www.aroostook.me.us

In northern ME, bordered on west and northwest by Quebec, Canada, and on the northeast and east by New Brunswick, Canada. Organized Mar 16, 1839 from Washington and Penobscot counties. **Name Origin:** For the Aroostook River, which runs through the county; from Micmac Indian 'clear river.'

Area (sq mi): 6828.79 (land 6671.54; water 157.25). **Pop per sq mi:** 11.

Pop 2005: 73,240. **State rank:** 6. **Pop change:** 2000-20005 -0.9%; 1990-2000 -15%. **Pop 2000:** 73,938 (White 96.4%; Black or African American 0.4%; Hispanic or Latino 0.6%; Asian 0.5%; Other 2.4%, including 1.4% American Indian/Alaska Native). **Foreign born:** 5.8%. **Median age:** 40.7.

Income 2000: per capita $15,033; median household $28,837; **Pop below poverty level:** 14.3%. *****Personal per capita income 2000-2003:** $20,837-$24,742.

Unemployment 2004: 6.2%. **Change from 2000:** +1.8%. **Median travel time to work:** 18.3 minutes. **Working outside county of residence:** 3.9%.

Cities with pop over 10,000: None.

CUMBERLAND COUNTY

142 Federal St Rm 102   **Ph:** 207-871-8380
Portland, ME 04101   **Fax:** 207-871-8292
www.cumberlandcounty.org

In southern ME, south of Lewiston; organized May 28, 1760 (prior to statehood) from York County. **Name Origin:** For William Augustus, Duke of Cumberland (1721-65), British general and second son of King George II (1683-1760).

Area (sq mi): 1216.89 (land 835.51; water 381.38). **Pop per sq mi:** 329.1.

Pop 2005: 274,950. **State rank:** 1. **Pop change:** 2000-20005 +3.5%; 1990-2000 +9.2%. **Pop 2000:** 265,612 (White 95.2%; Black or African American 1.1%; Hispanic or Latino 1%; Asian 1.4%; Other 1.7%). **Foreign born:** 3.8%. **Median age:** 37.6.

Income 2000: per capita $23,949; median household $44,048; **Pop below poverty level:** 7.9%. *****Personal per capita income 2000-2003:** $31,861-$35,962.

Unemployment 2004: 3.3%. **Change from 2000:** +1%. **Median travel time to work:** 22 minutes. **Working outside county of residence:** 11.3%.

Cities with pop over 10,000: Portland 🏛 (63,905); South Portland (23,513); Westbrook (16,004).

🏛 *County Seat*

FRANKLIN COUNTY

140 Main St   **Ph:** 207-778-6614
Farmington, ME 04938   **Fax:** 207-778-5899
www.franklincountymaine.com

On northwestern border of ME, northwest of Augusta; organized Mar 20, 1838 from Cumberland County. **Name Origin:** For Benjamin Franklin (1706-90), U.S. patriot, diplomat, and statesman.

Area (sq mi): 1744.31 (land 1697.81; water 46.5). **Pop per sq mi:** 17.5.

Pop 2005: 29,704. **State rank:** 15. **Pop change:** 2000-20005 +0.8%; 1990-2000 +1.6%. **Pop 2000:** 29,467 (White 97.6%; Black or African American 0.2%; Hispanic or Latino 0.5%; Asian 0.4%; Other 1.4%). **Foreign born:** 1.6%. **Median age:** 38.2.

Income 2000: per capita $15,796; median household $31,459; **Pop below poverty level:** 14.6%. ***Personal per capita income 2000-2003:** $21,321-$23,942.

Unemployment 2004: 5.6%. **Change from 2000:** -0.8%. **Median travel time to work:** 23.2 minutes. **Working outside county of residence:** 21.3%.

Cities with pop over 10,000: None.

HANCOCK COUNTY

50 State St Suite 7   **Ph:** 207-667-9542
Ellsworth, ME 04605   **Fax:** 207-667-1412
www.co.hancock.me.us

In eastern ME, on the Atlantic Coast; organized Jun 25, 1789 (prior to statehood) from Lincoln County. **Name Origin:** For John Hancock (1737-93), president of the Continental Congress (1775-77), noted signer of the Declaration of Independence, and governor of MA (1780-85; 1787-93).

Area (sq mi): 2351.03 (land 1587.7; water 763.33). **Pop per sq mi:** 33.8.

Pop 2005: 53,660. **State rank:** 8. **Pop change:** 2000-20005 +3.6%; 1990-2000 +10.3%. **Pop 2000:** 51,791 (White 97.2%; Black or African American 0.3%; Hispanic or Latino 0.6%; Asian 0.4%; Other 1.7%). **Foreign born:** 2.3%. **Median age:** 40.7.

Income 2000: per capita $19,809; median household $35,811; **Pop below poverty level:** 10.2%. ***Personal per capita income 2000-2003:** $27,503-$29,798.

Unemployment 2004: 5.1%. **Change from 2000:** +0.6%. **Median travel time to work:** 22.4 minutes. **Working outside county of residence:** 13.1%.

Cities with pop over 10,000: None.

KENNEBEC COUNTY

125 State St   **Ph:** 207-622-0971
Augusta, ME 04330   **Fax:** 207-623-4083
www.kennebeccounty.org

In south-central ME, southwest of Bangor; organized Feb 20, 1799 (prior to statehood) from Lincoln County. **Name Origin:** For part of the Kennebec River; from an Abnaki Indian word probably meaning 'long, quiet water.'

Area (sq mi): 951.18 (land 867.58; water 83.6). **Pop per sq mi:** 139.5.

Pop 2005: 120,986. **State rank:** 4. **Pop change:** 2000-20005 +3.3%; 1990-2000 +1%. **Pop 2000:** 117,114 (White 97%; Black or African American 0.3%; Hispanic or Latino 0.7%; Asian 0.6%; Other 1.6%). **Foreign born:** 2.2%. **Median age:** 38.7.

Income 2000: per capita $18,520; median household $36,498; **Pop below poverty level:** 11.1%. ***Personal per capita income 2000-2003:** $25,430-$28,421.

Unemployment 2004: 4.8%. **Change from 2000:** +0.8%. **Median travel time to work:** 22.6 minutes. **Working outside county of residence:** 19.6%.

Cities with pop over 10,000: Augusta 🏛 (18,631); Waterville (15,897).

KNOX COUNTY

62 Union St   **Ph:** 207-594-0420
Rockland, ME 04841   **Fax:** 207-594-0445
knoxcounty.midcoast.com

On Atlantic coast of ME, east of Augusta; organized Mar 9, 1860 from Lincoln and Waldo counties. **Name Origin:** For Gen. Henry Knox (1750-1806), officer in the Revolutionary War, and first U.S. secretary of war (1785-95).

Area (sq mi): 1142.1 (land 365.67; water 776.43). **Pop per sq mi:** 112.7.

Pop 2005: 41,219. **State rank:** 10. **Pop change:** 2000-20005 +4%; 1990-2000 +9.1%. **Pop 2000:** 39,618 (White 97.9%; Black or African American 0.2%; Hispanic or Latino 0.6%; Asian 0.4%; Other 1.1%). **Foreign born:** 2.1%. **Median age:** 41.4.

Income 2000: per capita $19,981; median household $36,774; **Pop below poverty level:** 10.1%. ***Personal per capita income 2000-2003:** $26,264-$31,114.

Unemployment 2004: 3.6%. **Change from 2000:** +0.7%. **Median travel time to work:** 18.9 minutes. **Working outside county of residence:** 13.9%.

Cities with pop over 10,000: None.

LINCOLN COUNTY

PO Box 249   **Ph:** 207-882-6311
Wiscasset, ME 04578   **Fax:** 207-882-4320
www.co.lincoln.me.us

On Atlantic coast of ME, south of Augusta; organized May 28, 1760 (prior to statehood) from York County. **Name Origin:** For either Enoch Lincoln (1788-1829), governor of ME (1827-29), or for Gen. Benjamin Lincoln (1733-1810), officer in the Revolutionary War, U.S. secretary of war (1781-83), and lt. gov. of MA (1788).

Area (sq mi): 699.81 (land 455.99; water 243.82). **Pop per sq mi:** 77.3.

Pop 2005: 35,240. **State rank:** 13. **Pop change:** 2000-20005 +4.8%; 1990-2000 +10.7%. **Pop 2000:** 33,616 (White 98.1%; Black or African American 0.2%; Hispanic or Latino 0.5%; Asian 0.4%; Other 1%). **Foreign born:** 2%. **Median age:** 42.6.

Income 2000: per capita $20,760; median household $38,686; **Pop below poverty level:** 10.1%. ***Personal per capita income 2000-2003:** $26,810-$29,955.

*Source: Personal per capita income data are from the Bureau of Economic Analysis; per capita income data are from the Bureau of the Census.
See Introduction for explanation of differences.*

Lincoln County (cont'd)

Unemployment 2004: 3.8%. **Change from 2000:** +0.9%. **Median travel time to work:** 23.4 minutes. **Working outside county of residence:** 35.2%.

Cities with pop over 10,000: None.

OXFORD COUNTY

PO Box 179   **Ph:** 207-743-6359
South Paris, ME 04281   **Fax:** 207-743-1545
www.oxfordcounty.org

On western border of ME and NH, west of Lewiston; organized Mar 4, 1805 (prior to starthood) from York and Cumberland counties. **Name Origin:** For Oxford, MA; named by David Leonard, an early settler who came from there.

Area (sq mi): 2175.26 (land 2078; water 97.26). **Pop per sq mi:** 27.3.

Pop 2005: 56,628. **State rank:** 7. **Pop change:** 2000-20005 +3.4%; 1990-2000 +4.1%. **Pop 2000:** 54,755 (White 97.9%; Black or African American 0.2%; Hispanic or Latino 0.5%; Asian 0.4%; Other 1.2%). **Foreign born:** 1.8%. **Median age:** 40.2.

Income 2000: per capita $16,945; median household $33,435; **Pop below poverty level:** 11.8%. ***Personal per capita income 2000-2003:** $21,427-$24,166.

Unemployment 2004: 5.6%. **Change from 2000:** -0.4%. **Median travel time to work:** 25.9 minutes. **Working outside county of residence:** 32.6%.

Cities with pop over 10,000: None.

PENOBSCOT COUNTY

97 Hammond St   **Ph:** 207-942-8535
Bangor, ME 04401   **Fax:** 207-945-6027

In east-central ME; organized Feb 15, 1816 (prior to statehood) from Hancock County. **Name Origin:** For the Penobscot River, which flows through the county; from an Indian word *penobskeag* 'rocky place' or 'river of rocks.'

Area (sq mi): 3556.14 (land 3395.73; water 160.41). **Pop per sq mi:** 43.3.

Pop 2005: 147,068. **State rank:** 3. **Pop change:** 2000-20005 +1.5%; 1990-2000 -1.1%. **Pop 2000:** 144,919 (White 96.2%; Black or African American 0.5%; Hispanic or Latino 0.6%; Asian 0.7%; Other 2.2%, including 1% American Indian/Alaska Native). **Foreign born:** 2.5%. **Median age:** 37.2.

Income 2000: per capita $17,801; median household $34,274; **Pop below poverty level:** 13.7%. ***Personal per capita income 2000-2003:** $23,622-$26,780.

Unemployment 2004: 5.4%. **Change from 2000:** +1.3%. **Median travel time to work:** 20.7 minutes. **Working outside county of residence:** 8.5%.

Cities with pop over 10,000: Bangor ⚖ (31,595).

PISCATAQUIS COUNTY

159 E Main St   **Ph:** 207-564-2161
Dover-Foxcroft, ME 04426   **Fax:** 207-564-3022
www.pcedc.org

In central ME, north of Bangor; organized 1838 from Penobscot

and Somerset counties. **Name Origin:** For the Piscataquis River, which runs through it; from an Abnaki Indian word probably meaning 'divided tidal river.'

Area (sq mi): 4377.36 (land 3966.22; water 411.14). **Pop per sq mi:** 4.5.

Pop 2005: 17,674. **State rank:** 16. **Pop change:** 2000-20005 +2.5%; 1990-2000 -7.6%. **Pop 2000:** 17,235 (White 97.5%; Black or African American 0.2%; Hispanic or Latino 0.5%; Asian 0.3%; Other 1.6%). **Foreign born:** 1.9%. **Median age:** 42.1.

Income 2000: per capita $14,374; median household $28,250; **Pop below poverty level:** 14.8%. ***Personal per capita income 2000-2003:** $20,700-$23,392.

Unemployment 2004: 6.8%. **Change from 2000:** +0.1%. **Median travel time to work:** 22.1 minutes. **Working outside county of residence:** 24.6%.

Cities with pop over 10,000: None.

SAGADAHOC COUNTY

PO Box 246   **Ph:** 207-443-8200
Bath, ME 04530   **Fax:** 207-443-8213

On Atlantic coast of ME, east of Portland; organized Apr 4, 1854 from Lincoln County. **Name Origin:** From an Abnaki Indian word probably meaning 'land of the mouth,' or 'mouth of the river,' for its location at the confluence of the Androscoggin and Kennebec rivers where they meet the Atlantic.

Area (sq mi): 370.19 (land 253.9; water 116.29). **Pop per sq mi:** 145.6.

Pop 2005: 36,962. **State rank:** 12. **Pop change:** 2000-20005 +5%; 1990-2000 +5%. **Pop 2000:** 35,214 (White 95.9%; Black or African American 0.9%; Hispanic or Latino 1.1%; Asian 0.6%; Other 2%). **Foreign born:** 2.4%. **Median age:** 38.

Income 2000: per capita $20,378; median household $41,908; **Pop below poverty level:** 8.6%. ***Personal per capita income 2000-2003:** $26,044-$28,854.

Unemployment 2004: 3.6%. **Change from 2000:** +0.4%. **Median travel time to work:** 22.5 minutes. **Working outside county of residence:** 52.8%.

Cities with pop over 10,000: None.

SOMERSET COUNTY

County Courthouse   **Ph:** 207-474-9861
Skowhegan, ME 04976   **Fax:** 207-474-7405
www.somersetcountymaine.org

In west-central ME and north to the border with Quebec, Canada; organized Mar 1, 1809 (prior to statehood) from Kennebec County. **Name Origin:** For Somerset county in England.

Area (sq mi): 4095.37 (land 3926.5; water 168.87). **Pop per sq mi:** 13.2.

Pop 2005: 51,667. **State rank:** 9. **Pop change:** 2000-20005 +1.5%; 1990-2000 +2.3%. **Pop 2000:** 50,888 (White 97.7%; Black or African American 0.2%; Hispanic or Latino 0.5%; Asian 0.3%; Other 1.4%). **Foreign born:** 1.7%. **Median age:** 38.9.

Income 2000: per capita $15,474; median household $30,731; **Pop below poverty level:** 14.9%. ***Personal per capita income 2000-2003:** $21,403-$23,524.

⚖ *County Seat*

Somerset County (cont'd)

Unemployment 2004: 7.4%. **Change from 2000:** -0.2%. **Median travel time to work:** 24.2 minutes. **Working outside county of residence:** 34.4%.

Cities with pop over 10,000: None.

WALDO COUNTY

PO Box D   **Ph:** 207-338-1710
Belfast, ME 04915   **Fax:** 207-338-6360
www.waldocountyme.gov

On central Atlantic coast of ME, southwest of Bangor; organized Feb 7, 1827 from Hancock County. **Name Origin:** For Gen. Samuel Waldo (1695-1759), an officer in the French and Indian Wars, and promoter of settlement in the area that became Maine.

Area (sq mi): 852.74 (land 729.73; water 123.01). **Pop per sq mi:** 53.

Pop 2005: 38,705. **State rank:** 11. **Pop change:** 2000-20005 +6.7%; 1990-2000 +9.9%. **Pop 2000:** 36,280 (White 97.5%; Black or African American 0.2%; Hispanic or Latino 0.6%; Asian 0.2%; Other 1.7%). **Foreign born:** 1.7%. **Median age:** 39.3.

Income 2000: per capita $17,438; median household $33,986; **Pop below poverty level:** 13.9%. ***Personal per capita income 2000-2003:** $21,974-$24,552.

Unemployment 2004: 5%. **Change from 2000:** +1%. **Median travel time to work:** 26.4 minutes. **Working outside county of residence:** 39.5%.

Cities with pop over 10,000: None.

WASHINGTON COUNTY

PO Box 297   **Ph:** 207-255-3127
Machias, ME 04654   **Fax:** 207-255-3313

On Atlantic coast in extreme eastern ME, east of Bangor; organized Jun 25, 1789 (prior to statehood) from Lincoln County. **Name Origin:** For George Washington (1732-99), American patriot and first U.S. president.

Area (sq mi): 3254.91 (land 2568.48; water 686.44). **Pop per sq mi:** 13.

Pop 2005: 33,448. **State rank:** 14. **Pop change:** 2000-20005 -1.5%; 1990-2000 -3.9%. **Pop 2000:** 33,941 (White 93.2%; Black or African American 0.3%; Hispanic or Latino 0.8%; Asian 0.3%; Other 5.9%, including 4.4% American Indian/Alaska Native). **Foreign born:** 4.1%. **Median age:** 40.5.

Income 2000: per capita $14,119; median household $25,869; **Pop below poverty level:** 19%. ***Personal per capita income 2000-2003:** $20,536-$23,508.

Unemployment 2004: 7.5%. **Change from 2000:** -0.6%. **Median travel time to work:** 19.2 minutes. **Working outside county of residence:** 8.4%.

Cities with pop over 10,000: None.

YORK COUNTY

45 Kennebunk Rd PO Box 399   **Ph:** 207-324-1571
Alfred, ME 04002   **Fax:** 207-324-9494
www.co.york.me.us

At southwestern tip of ME along Atlantic coast and NH border, southwest of Portland; original county (formerly Yorkshire County, MA), organized Nov 20, 1652 (prior to statehood). **Name Origin:** For James, Duke of York and Albany (1633-1701), later James II of England.

Area (sq mi): 1271.34 (land 990.92; water 280.43). **Pop per sq mi:** 204.2.

Pop 2005: 202,315. **State rank:** 2. **Pop change:** 2000-20005 +8.3%; 1990-2000 +13.5%. **Pop 2000:** 186,742 (White 97.1%; Black or African American 0.4%; Hispanic or Latino 0.7%; Asian 0.7%; Other 1.2%). **Foreign born:** 2.8%. **Median age:** 38.5.

Income 2000: per capita $21,225; median household $43,630; **Pop below poverty level:** 8.2%. ***Personal per capita income 2000-2003:** $27,556-$29,584.

Unemployment 2004: 3.9%. **Change from 2000:** +0.3%. **Median travel time to work:** 25.8 minutes. **Working outside county of residence:** 41.2%.

Cities with pop over 10,000: Biddeford (21,842); Saco (18,090).

---

*Source: Personal per capita income data are from the Bureau of Economic Analysis; per capita income data are from the Bureau of the Census. See Introduction for explanation of differences.

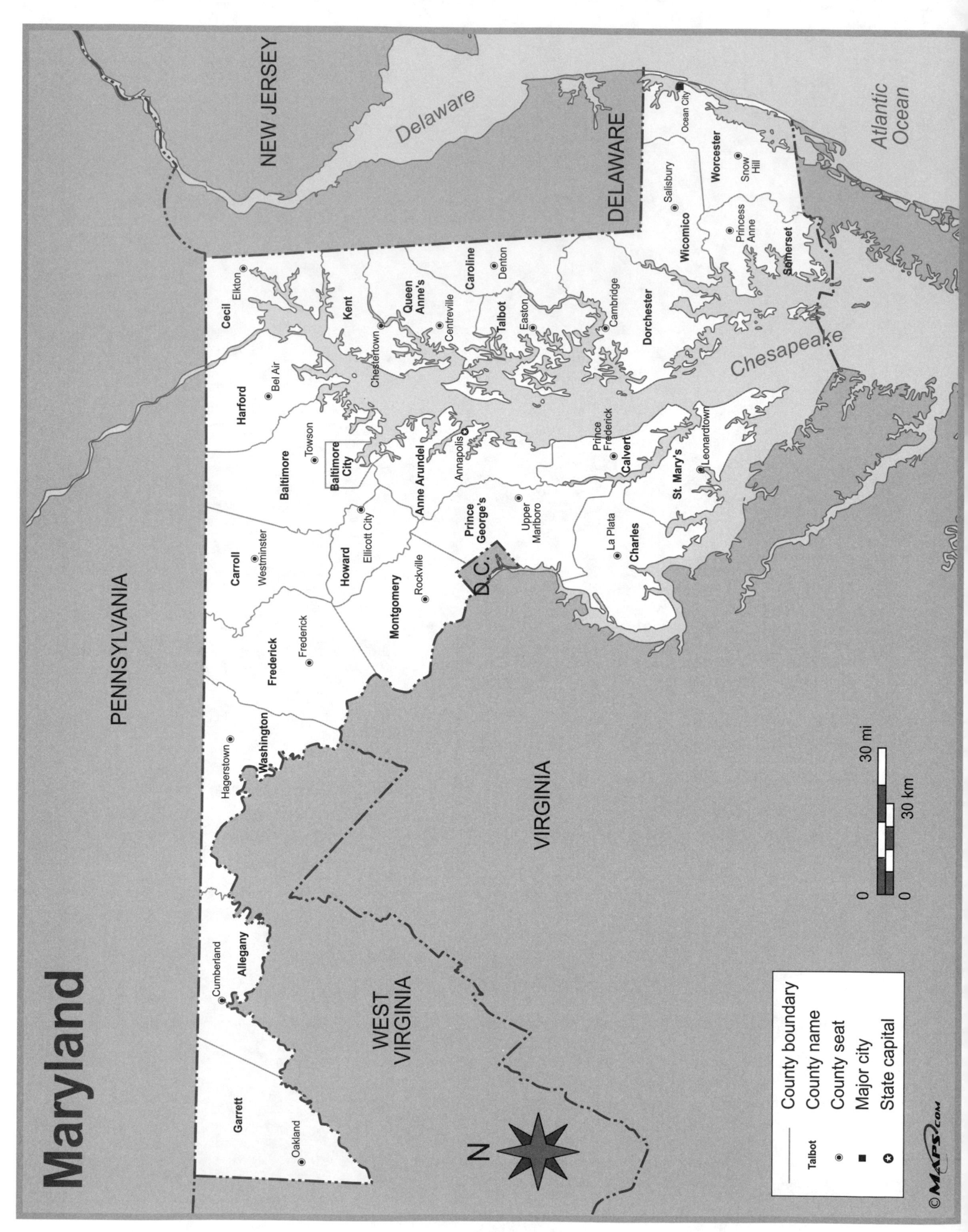

Maryland

PENNSYLVANIA

NEW JERSEY

Delaware

DELAWARE

WEST VIRGINIA

VIRGINIA

Atlantic Ocean

Chesapeake

Garrett

Oakland

Allegany

Cumberland

Washington

Hagerstown

Frederick

Frederick

Carroll

Westminster

Baltimore

Towson

Baltimore City

Harford

Bel Air

Cecil

Elkton

Kent

Chestertown

Howard

Ellicott City

Montgomery

Rockville

D.C.

Anne Arundel

Annapolis

Queen Anne's

Centreville

Caroline

Denton

Talbot

Easton

Prince George's

Upper Marlboro

Charles

La Plata

Calvert

Prince Frederick

St. Mary's

Leonardtown

Dorchester

Cambridge

Wicomico

Salisbury

Worcester

Snow Hill

Princess Anne

Somerset

Ocean City

N

© MAPS.com

Talbot	County boundary
	County name
⊙	County seat
■	Major city
✪	State capital

30 mi

0

30 km

0

Maryland

MARYLAND STATE INFORMATION
www.maryland.gov **Ph:** 410-974-3901

Area (sq mi): 12,406.68 (land 9773.82; water 2632.86). **Pop per sq mi:** 573.

Pop 2005: 5,600,388. **Pop change:** 2000-20005 +5.7%; 1990-2000 +10.8%. **Pop 2000:** 5,296,486 (White 62.1%; Black or African American 27.9%; Hispanic or Latino 4.3%; Asian 4%; Other 4.1%). **Foreign born:** 9.8%. **Median age:** 36.

Income 2000: per capita $25,614; median household $52,868; **Pop below poverty level:** 8.5%. ***Personal per capita income 2000-2003:** $34,257-$37,446.

Unemployment 2004: 4.3%. **Change from 2000:** +0.7%. **Median travel time to work:** 31.2 minutes. **Working outside county of residence:** 46.5%.

ALLEGANY COUNTY
701 Kelly Rd **Ph:** 301-777-5911
Cumberland, MD 21502 **Fax:** 301-777-5819
www.allconet.org

On northwestern border of panhandle of MD; organized Dec 25, 1789 from Washington County. **Name Origin:** For the Allegheny Mountains (using a variant spelling), which cross through the county.

Area (sq mi): 429.82 (land 425.42; water 4.4). **Pop per sq mi:** 173.1.

Pop 2005: 73,639. **State rank:** 16. **Pop change:** 2000-20005 -1.7%; 1990-2000 +0%. **Pop 2000:** 74,930 (White 92.5%; Black or African American 5.3%; Hispanic or Latino 0.8%; Asian 0.5%; Other 1.1%). **Foreign born:** 1.2%. **Median age:** 39.1.

Income 2000: per capita $16,780; median household $30,821; **Pop below poverty level:** 14.8%. ***Personal per capita income 2000-2003:** $20,810-$23,462.

Unemployment 2004: 6.4%. **Change from 2000:** -1.2%. **Median travel time to work:** 22.6 minutes. **Working outside county of residence:** 14.9%.

Cities with pop over 10,000: Cumberland 🏛 (20,957).

ANNE ARUNDEL COUNTY
44 Calvert St **Ph:** 410-222-7000
Annapolis, MD 21401
www.co.anne-arundel.md.us

In east-central MD, south of Baltimore; original county, organized 1650. **Name Origin:** For Anne Arundel, daughter of Lord Thomas Arundell of Wardour and wife of Cecilius Calvert, Lord Baltimore (1605-75).

Area (sq mi): 587.9 (land 415.94; water 171.96). **Pop per sq mi:** 1228.2.

Pop 2005: 510,878. **State rank:** 5. **Pop change:** 2000-20005 +4.3%; 1990-2000 +14.6%. **Pop 2000:** 489,656 (White 79.8%; Black or African American 13.6%; Hispanic or Latino 2.6%; Asian 2.3%; Other 3%). **Foreign born:** 4.7%. **Median age:** 36.

Income 2000: per capita $27,578; median household $61,768; **Pop below poverty level:** 5.1%. ***Personal per capita income 2000-2003:** $36,466-$40,463.

Unemployment 2004: 3.6%. **Change from 2000:** +0.4%. **Median travel time to work:** 28.9 minutes. **Working outside county of residence:** 43.7%.

Cities with pop over 10,000: Annapolis 🏛 (36,217).

BALTIMORE COUNTY
401 Bosley Ave **Ph:** 410-887-2697
Towson, MD 21204 **Fax:** 410-887-3062
www.co.ba.md.us

On central northern border of MD, north of Annapolis; original county, legal origin not known, but was in existence by Jan 12, 1659. Baltimore City was made independent of the county in 1851. **Name Origin:** For the barony of Baltimore in Ireland, source of the hereditary title Lord Baltimore of the Calvert family, proprietors of the colony of MD.

Area (sq mi): 682.03 (land 598.59; water 83.44). **Pop per sq mi:** 1313.3.

Pop 2005: 786,113. **State rank:** 3. **Pop change:** 2000-20005 +4.2%; 1990-2000 +9%. **Pop 2000:** 754,292 (White 73.4%; Black or African American 20.1%; Hispanic or Latino 1.8%; Asian 3.2%; Other 2.3%). **Foreign born:** 7.1%. **Median age:** 37.7.

Income 2000: per capita $26,167; median household $50,667; **Pop below poverty level:** 6.5%. ***Personal per capita income 2000-2003:** $35,824-$39,478.

Unemployment 2004: 4.4%. **Change from 2000:** +0%. **Median travel time to work:** 27.6 minutes. **Working outside county of residence:** 47.3%.

Cities with pop over 10,000: None.

BALTIMORE (INDEPENDENT CITY)
100 N Holliday St **Ph:** 410-396-3100
Baltimore, MD 21202 **Fax:** 410-396-9568
www.ci.baltimore.md.us

In northern MD on Patapsco River, upper Chesapeake Bay, 41 mi. northeast of Washington, DC. Founded 1729; incorporated 1796.

🏛 *County Seat*

Baltimore (Independent City) (cont'd)

Distinct from and independent of Baltimore County since 1851, with the same political power as a county. Major East Coast port. Headquarters of McCormick & Co, world's largest producer of spices and seasonings. Other industries include steel, chemicals, and manufacture of radar and other electronic equipment. Site of Johns Hopkins University. Site of Fort McHenry, whose bombardment by the British in 1814 inspired Francis Scott Key (1779-1843) to write The Star-Spangled Banner. **Name Origin:** For the barony of Baltimore in Ireland, source of the hereditary title Lord Baltimore of the Calvert family, proprietors of the colony of MD.

Area (sq mi): 92.08 (land 80.8; water 11.27). **Pop per sq mi:** 7869.

Pop 2005: 635,815. **State rank:** 4. **Pop change:** 2000-20005 -2.4%; 1990-2000 -11.5%. **Pop 2000:** 651,154 (White 31%; Black or African American 64.3%; Hispanic or Latino 1.7%; Asian 1.5%; Other 2.5%). **Foreign born:** 4.6%. **Median age:** 35.

Income 2000: per capita $16,978; median household $30,078; **Pop below poverty level:** 22.9%. ***Personal per capita income 2000-2003:** $24,789-$27,828.

Unemployment 2004: 7.4%. **Change from 2000:** +3%. **Median travel time to work:** 31.1 minutes. **Working outside county of residence:** 38.1%.

Cities with pop over 10,000: None.

CALVERT COUNTY
175 Main St   **Ph:** 410-535-1600
Prince Frederick, MD 20678   **Fax:** 410-535-9572
www.co.cal.md.us

In south-central MD, south of Annapolis; original county, organized as Patuxent County in 1654; name changed in 1658. **Name Origin:** For the family name of the Lords Baltimore, proprietors of MD.

Area (sq mi): 345.09 (land 215.17; water 129.91). **Pop per sq mi:** 408.6.

Pop 2005: 87,925. **State rank:** 15. **Pop change:** 2000-20005 +17.9%; 1990-2000 +45.1%. **Pop 2000:** 74,563 (White 83%; Black or African American 13.1%; Hispanic or Latino 1.5%; Asian 0.9%; Other 2.1%). **Foreign born:** 2.2%. **Median age:** 35.9.

Income 2000: per capita $25,410; median household $65,945; **Pop below poverty level:** 4.4%. ***Personal per capita income 2000-2003:** $31,285-$33,665.

Unemployment 2004: 3.3%. **Change from 2000:** +0.8%. **Median travel time to work:** 39.8 minutes. **Working outside county of residence:** 60.6%.

Cities with pop over 10,000: None.

CAROLINE COUNTY
109 Market St   **Ph:** 410-479-0660
Denton, MD 21629   **Fax:** 410-479-4060
www.carolinemd.org

On eastern border of MD, southwest of Dover, DE; organized Jun 15, 1773 (prior to statehood) from Dorchester and Queen Anne's counties. **Name Origin:** For Caroline Calvert Eden, sister of Frederick Calvert, 6th Baron Baltimore and the last proprietor of MD.

Area (sq mi): 326.06 (land 320.14; water 5.92). **Pop per sq mi:** 99.4.

Pop 2005: 31,822. **State rank:** 20. **Pop change:** 2000-20005 +6.9%; 1990-2000 +10.1%. **Pop 2000:** 29,772 (White 80.7%; Black or African American 14.8%; Hispanic or Latino 2.7%; Asian 0.5%; Other 3%). **Foreign born:** 2.5%. **Median age:** 37.

Income 2000: per capita $17,275; median household $38,832; **Pop below poverty level:** 11.7%. ***Personal per capita income 2000-2003:** $21,734-$23,186.

Unemployment 2004: 4%. **Change from 2000:** -1.1%. **Median travel time to work:** 30.4 minutes. **Working outside county of residence:** 55.9%.

Cities with pop over 10,000: None.

CARROLL COUNTY
225 N Center St Rm 300   **Ph:** 410-386-2400
Westminster, MD 21157   **Fax:** 410-386-2485
www.ccgov.carr.org

On central northern border of MD, northwest of Baltimore; organized Jun 19, 1836 from Baltimore and Frederick counties. **Name Origin:** For Charles Carroll (1737-1832), signer of the Declaration of Independence, U.S. senator from MD, and founder of the Baltimore and Ohio Railroad.

Area (sq mi): 452.4 (land 449.13; water 3.27). **Pop per sq mi:** 375.3.

Pop 2005: 168,541. **State rank:** 9. **Pop change:** 2000-20005 +11.7%; 1990-2000 +22.3%. **Pop 2000:** 150,897 (White 95.1%; Black or African American 2.3%; Hispanic or Latino 1%; Asian 0.8%; Other 1.2%). **Foreign born:** 2%. **Median age:** 36.9.

Income 2000: per capita $23,829; median household $60,021; **Pop below poverty level:** 3.8%. ***Personal per capita income 2000-2003:** $32,373-$35,259.

Unemployment 2004: 3.3%. **Change from 2000:** +0.5%. **Median travel time to work:** 34.1 minutes. **Working outside county of residence:** 55.1%.

Cities with pop over 10,000: Westminster 🏛 (17,562).

CECIL COUNTY
129 E Main St Rm 108   **Ph:** 410-996-5375
Elkton, MD 21921   **Fax:** 410-392-6032
www.ccgov.org

On northeastern border of MD, west of Wilmington, DE; organized 1674 from Baltimore and Kent counties. **Name Origin:** For Cecilius Calvert, 2nd Lord Baltimore (1605-75), founder and first proprietor of the colony of MD, though he never visited it.

Area (sq mi): 417.88 (land 348.13; water 69.75). **Pop per sq mi:** 280.9.

Pop 2005: 97,796. **State rank:** 12. **Pop change:** 2000-20005 +13.8%; 1990-2000 +20.5%. **Pop 2000:** 85,951 (White 92.5%; Black or African American 3.9%; Hispanic or Latino 1.5%; Asian 0.7%; Other 2%). **Foreign born:** 1.8%. **Median age:** 35.5.

Income 2000: per capita $21,384; median household $50,510; **Pop below poverty level:** 7.2%. ***Personal per capita income 2000-2003:** $28,240-$30,201.

Unemployment 2004: 4.3%. **Change from 2000:** -1.4%. **Median travel time to work:** 28.2 minutes. **Working outside county of residence:** 56.1%.

*Source: Personal per capita income data are from the Bureau of Economic Analysis; per capita income data are from the Bureau of the Census. See Introduction for explanation of differences.

Cecil County (cont'd)

Cities with pop over 10,000: Elkton ⛫ (14,067).

CHARLES COUNTY

PO Box 2150   **Ph:** 301-645-0600
La Plata, MD 20646   **Fax:** 301-645-0560
www.charlescounty.org

In southwestern MD, south of Alexandria, VA; original county, organized 1658. **Name Origin:** For Charles Calvert, 3rd Baron Baltimore (1637-1715), second proprietor of the colony of MD; the son of Cecilius Calvert (1606-75) and Anne Arundell.

Area (sq mi): 643.22 (land 461; water 182.22). **Pop per sq mi:** 301.1.

Pop 2005: 138,822. **State rank:** 11. **Pop change:** 2000-20005 +15.2%; 1990-2000 +19.2%. **Pop 2000:** 120,546 (White 67.3%; Black or African American 26.1%; Hispanic or Latino 2.3%; Asian 1.8%; Other 3.7%). **Foreign born:** 2.9%. **Median age:** 34.6.

Income 2000: per capita $24,285; median household $62,199; **Pop below poverty level:** 5.5%. ***Personal per capita income 2000-2003:** $30,753-$33,226.

Unemployment 2004: 3.4%. **Change from 2000:** +0.8%. **Median travel time to work:** 39.3 minutes. **Working outside county of residence:** 59.8%.

Cities with pop over 10,000: None.

DORCHESTER COUNTY

501 Court Ln   **Ph:** 410-228-1700
Cambridge, MD 21613   **Fax:** 410-228-9641
www.commissioners.net

In south-central MD, west of Salisbury; original county whose legal origin is unknown, but it was in existence by Feb 16,1668-69. **Name Origin:** For Richard Sackville II, 5th Earl of Dorset (1622-77), friend of the Calvert family.

Area (sq mi): 982.92 (land 557.54; water 425.38). **Pop per sq mi:** 56.3.

Pop 2005: 31,401. **State rank:** 21. **Pop change:** 2000-20005 +2.4%; 1990-2000 +1.4%. **Pop 2000:** 30,674 (White 68.8%; Black or African American 28.4%; Hispanic or Latino 1.3%; Asian 0.7%; Other 1.5%). **Foreign born:** 2%. **Median age:** 40.7.

Income 2000: per capita $18,929; median household $34,077; **Pop below poverty level:** 13.8%. ***Personal per capita income 2000-2003:** $23,526-$25,843.

Unemployment 2004: 5.6%. **Change from 2000:** -3.7%. **Median travel time to work:** 25.2 minutes. **Working outside county of residence:** 32.8%.

Cities with pop over 10,000: Cambridge ⛫ (10,826).

FREDERICK COUNTY

12 E Church St   **Ph:** 301-694-1100
Frederick, MD 21701   **Fax:** 301-694-1849
www.co.frederick.md.us

On northwestern border of MD, southeast of Hagerstown; organized Jun 10, 1748 from Baltimore and Prince George's counties. **Name Origin:** For Frederick Calvert, 6th Baron Baltimore (1731-71), fifth and last proprietor of the colony of MD.

Area (sq mi): 667.34 (land 662.88; water 4.46). **Pop per sq mi:** 332.9.

Pop 2005: 220,701. **State rank:** 8. **Pop change:** 2000-20005 +13%; 1990-2000 +30%. **Pop 2000:** 195,277 (White 88.1%; Black or African American 6.4%; Hispanic or Latino 2.4%; Asian 1.7%; Other 2.6%). **Foreign born:** 4%. **Median age:** 35.6.

Income 2000: per capita $25,404; median household $60,276; **Pop below poverty level:** 4.5%. ***Personal per capita income 2000-2003:** $32,695-$35,423.

Unemployment 2004: 3.2%. **Change from 2000:** +0.4%. **Median travel time to work:** 31.9 minutes. **Working outside county of residence:** 41.1%.

Cities with pop over 10,000: Frederick ⛫ (57,009).

GARRETT COUNTY

203 S 4th St Rm 207   **Ph:** 301-334-8970
Oakland, MD 21550   **Fax:** 301-334-5000
www.garrettcounty.org

On northwestern border of the panhandle of MD, west of Cumberland; organized Apr 1, 1872 from Allegany County; the last county to be formed in MD. **Name Origin:** For John Work Garrett (1820-84), president of the Baltimore and Ohio railroad (1858-84).

Area (sq mi): 655.9 (land 647.96; water 7.94). **Pop per sq mi:** 46.2.

Pop 2005: 29,909. **State rank:** 22. **Pop change:** 2000-20005 +0.2%; 1990-2000 +6.1%. **Pop 2000:** 29,846 (White 98.4%; Black or African American 0.4%; Hispanic or Latino 0.4%; Asian 0.2%; Other 0.6%). **Foreign born:** 0.8%. **Median age:** 38.3.

Income 2000: per capita $16,219; median household $32,238; **Pop below poverty level:** 13.3%. ***Personal per capita income 2000-2003:** $22,126 $24,176.

Unemployment 2004: 4.9%. **Change from 2000:** -2.8%. **Median travel time to work:** 24.8 minutes. **Working outside county of residence:** 27.2%.

Cities with pop over 10,000: None.

HARFORD COUNTY

220 S Main St   **Ph:** 410-838-6000
Bel Air, MD 21014   **Fax:** 410-638-1387
www.co.ha.md.us

On northern border of MD, northeast of Baltimore; organized 1773 (prior to statehood) from Baltimore County. **Name Origin:** For Henry Hartford (c. 1759-1834), an illegitimate son of Frederick Calvert (1731-71), 6th Lord Baltimore, and the last proprietor of the colony of MD.

Area (sq mi): 526.72 (land 440.35; water 86.37). **Pop per sq mi:** 543.3.

Pop 2005: 239,259. **State rank:** 7. **Pop change:** 2000-20005 +9.5%; 1990-2000 +20%. **Pop 2000:** 218,590 (White 85.8%; Black or African American 9.3%; Hispanic or Latino 1.9%; Asian 1.5%; Other 2.5%). **Foreign born:** 3.4%. **Median age:** 36.2.

Income 2000: per capita $24,232; median household $57,234; **Pop below poverty level:** 4.9%. ***Personal per capita income 2000-2003:** $31,318-$34,553.

Harford County (cont'd)

Unemployment 2004: 3.9%. **Change from 2000:** +0%. **Median travel time to work:** 31.6 minutes. **Working outside county of residence:** 48.1%.

Cities with pop over 10,000: Aberdeen (14,204); Havre de Grace (11,605).

HOWARD COUNTY

3430 Courthouse Dr	**Ph:** 410-313-2011
Ellicott City, MD 21043	**Fax:** 410-313-3051
www.co.ho.md.us	

In north-central MD, west of Baltimore; organized as Howard District in1838 from Anne Arundel County; formed as county May 13, 1851. **Name Origin:** For John Eager Howard (1752-1827), member of the Continental Congress (1784-88), MD governor (1788-91), and U.S. senator (1796-1803).

Area (sq mi): 253.55 (land 252.04; water 1.51). **Pop per sq mi:** 1069.1.

Pop 2005: 269,457. **State rank:** 6. **Pop change:** 2000-20005 +8.7%; 1990-2000 +32.3%. **Pop 2000:** 247,842 (White 72.6%; Black or African American 14.4%; Hispanic or Latino 3%; Asian 7.7%; Other 3.5%). **Foreign born:** 11.3%. **Median age:** 35.5.

Income 2000: per capita $32,402; median household $74,167; **Pop below poverty level:** 3.9%. ***Personal per capita income 2000-2003:** $43,647-$46,281.

Unemployment 2004: 3.1%. **Change from 2000:** +0.5%. **Median travel time to work:** 30.2 minutes. **Working outside county of residence:** 62%.

Cities with pop over 10,000: Baltimore 🏛 (636,251).

KENT COUNTY

400 High St	**Ph:** 410-778-7435
Chestertown, MD 21620	**Fax:** 410-778-7482
www.kentcounty.com	

On northeastern border of MD, northwest of Dover, MD; original county, organized Dec 16, 1642. **Name Origin:** For the county in England.

Area (sq mi): 414.31 (land 279.43; water 134.87). **Pop per sq mi:** 71.2.

Pop 2005: 19,899. **State rank:** 24. **Pop change:** 2000-20005 +3.7%; 1990-2000 +7.6%. **Pop 2000:** 19,197 (White 78.4%; Black or African American 17.4%; Hispanic or Latino 2.8%; Asian 0.5%; Other 2.3%). **Foreign born:** 2.9%. **Median age:** 41.3.

Income 2000: per capita $21,573; median household $39,869; **Pop below poverty level:** 13%. ***Personal per capita income 2000-2003:** $30,260-$34,261.

Unemployment 2004: 4%. **Change from 2000:** -0.1%. **Median travel time to work:** 24.6 minutes. **Working outside county of residence:** 28%.

Cities with pop over 10,000: None.

MONTGOMERY COUNTY

101 Monroe St	**Ph:** 240-777-2500
Rockville, MD 20850	**Fax:** 240-777-2517
www.montgomerycountymd.gov	

On central western border of MD, north of Washington, D.C.; organized Sept 6, 1776 (prior to statehood) from Frederick County. Added territory (Takoma Park city) from Prince George's County effective July 1, 1997. **Name Origin:** For Gen. Richard Montgomery (1736-75), an officer in the Revolutionary War.

Area (sq mi): 507.14 (land 495.52; water 11.63). **Pop per sq mi:** 1871.9.

Pop 2005: 927,583. **State rank:** 1. **Pop change:** 2000-20005 +6.2%; 1990-2000 +15.4%. **Pop 2000:** 873,341 (White 59.5%; Black or African American 15.1%; Hispanic or Latino 11.5%; Asian 11.3%; Other 8.7%). **Foreign born:** 26.7%. **Median age:** 36.8.

Income 2000: per capita $35,684; median household $71,551; **Pop below poverty level:** 5.4%. ***Personal per capita income 2000-2003:** $49,647-$52,854.

Unemployment 2004: 3.1%. **Change from 2000:** +0.8%. **Median travel time to work:** 32.8 minutes. **Working outside county of residence:** 41.3%.

Cities with pop over 10,000: Gaithersburg (58,091); Rockville 🏛 (57,100); Takoma Park (17,591).

PRINCE GEORGE'S COUNTY

14741 Governor Oden Bowie Dr	**Ph:** 301-952-3600
Upper Marlboro, MD 20772	**Fax:** 301-952-4862
www.goprincegeorgescounty.com	

In central MD, east of Washington, D.C.; organized May 20, 1695 from Charles and Calvert counties. Lost territory (Takoma Park city) to Montgomery County effective July 1, 1997. **Name Origin:** For Prince George of Denmark (1653-1708), husband of Queen Anne of England (1665-1714).

Area (sq mi): 498.45 (land 485.43; water 13.01). **Pop per sq mi:** 1743.

Pop 2005: 846,123. **State rank:** 2. **Pop change:** 2000-20005 +5.6%; 1990-2000 +9.9%. **Pop 2000:** 801,515 (White 24.3%; Black or African American 62.7%; Hispanic or Latino 7.1%; Asian 3.9%; Other 6.4%). **Foreign born:** 13.8%. **Median age:** 33.3.

Income 2000: per capita $23,360; median household $55,256; **Pop below poverty level:** 7.7%. ***Personal per capita income 2000-2003:** $28,865-$31,936.

Unemployment 2004: 4.6%. **Change from 2000:** +0.5%. **Median travel time to work:** 35.9 minutes. **Working outside county of residence:** 60.8%.

Cities with pop over 10,000: 6 (see page 35 for cities).

QUEEN ANNE'S COUNTY

107 N Liberty St	**Ph:** 410-758-4098
Centreville, MD 21617	**Fax:** 410-758-1170
www.qac.org	

On eastern border of MD, west of Dover, DE; organized 1706 from Talbot County. **Name Origin:** For Anne (1665-1714), queen of Great Britain and Ireland (1702-14).

Area (sq mi): 509.79 (land 372.21; water 137.58). **Pop per sq mi:** 122.5.

---

*Source: Personal per capita income data are from the Bureau of Economic Analysis; per capita income data are from the Bureau of the Census. See Introduction for explanation of differences.

Queen Anne's County (cont'd)

Pop 2005: 45,612. **State rank:** 18. **Pop change:** 2000-20005 +12.4%; 1990-2000 +19.5%. **Pop 2000:** 40,563 (White 88.4%; Black or African American 8.8%; Hispanic or Latino 1.1%; Asian 0.6%; Other 1.5%). **Foreign born:** 2.4%. **Median age:** 38.8.

Income 2000: per capita $26,364; median household $57,037; **Pop below poverty level:** 6.3%. ***Personal per capita income 2000-2003:** $34,087-$35,436.

Unemployment 2004: 3.4%. **Change from 2000:** +0.1%. **Median travel time to work:** 33.6 minutes. **Working outside county of residence:** 59.8%.

Cities with pop over 10,000: None.

SAINT MARY'S COUNTY

PO Box 676   **Ph:** 301-475-4567
Leonardtown, MD 20650   **Fax:** 301-475-4470
www.co.saint-marys.md.us

On southern border of MD, bounded by the Potomac River on the west, the Patuxent River on the east, and Chesapeake Bay on the south; the first original county, organized 1637. **Name Origin:** For Mary, the mother of Jesus Christ. The ships Ark and Dove, carrying colonists, landed on Saint Clement's Island on Mar 25, 1634, the Feast of the Annunciation of Mary.

Area (sq mi): 764.5 (land 361.25; water 403.25). **Pop per sq mi:** 267.2.

Pop 2005: 96,518. **State rank:** 13. **Pop change:** 2000-20005 +12%; 1990-2000 +13.5%. **Pop 2000:** 86,211 (White 80.4%; Black or African American 13.9%; Hispanic or Latino 2%; Asian 1.8%; Other 2.7%). **Foreign born:** 2.8%. **Median age:** 34.2.

Income 2000: per capita $22,662; median household $54,706; **Pop below poverty level:** 7.2%. ***Personal per capita income 2000-2003:** $29,021-$31,140.

Unemployment 2004: 3.3%. **Change from 2000:** +0.5%. **Median travel time to work:** 29.2 minutes. **Working outside county of residence:** 25.7%.

Cities with pop over 10,000: None.

SOMERSET COUNTY

11916 Somerset Ave Rm 111   **Ph:** 410-651-0320
Princess Anne, MD 21853   **Fax:** 410-651-0366
www.visitsomerset.com

On southern border of MD, southwest of Salisbury; original county; organized Aug 22, 1666. **Name Origin:** For Mary Somerset, sister-in-law of Cecilius Calvert (1605-75), 2nd Lord Baltimore.

Area (sq mi): 610.78 (land 327.21; water 283.56). **Pop per sq mi:** 79.

Pop 2005: 25,845. **State rank:** 23. **Pop change:** 2000-20005 +4.4%; 1990-2000 +5.6%. **Pop 2000:** 24,747 (White 55.8%; Black or African American 41.1%; Hispanic or Latino 1.3%; Asian 0.5%; Other 2.1%). **Foreign born:** 2.5%. **Median age:** 36.5.

Income 2000: per capita $15,965; median household $29,903; **Pop below poverty level:** 20.1%. ***Personal per capita income 2000-2003:** $18,400-$20,528.

Unemployment 2004: 6.3%. **Change from 2000:** -1.2%. **Median travel time to work:** 25.1 minutes. **Working outside county of residence:** 42.2%.

Cities with pop over 10,000: None.

TALBOT COUNTY

11 N Washington St County Courthouse   **Ph:** 410-770-8010
Easton, MD 21601   **Fax:** 410-770-8007
www.co.talbot.md.us

In east-central MD, southeast of Annapolis; in existence by Feb 18, 1661-62, organized from Kent County. **Name Origin:** For Grace Talbot, daughter of George Calvert (1580?-1632), 1st Lord Baltimore, and sister of Cecilius Calvert, first proprietor of the colony of MD.

Area (sq mi): 476.77 (land 269.14; water 207.64). **Pop per sq mi:** 132.6.

Pop 2005: 35,683. **State rank:** 19. **Pop change:** 2000-20005 +5.5%; 1990-2000 +10.7%. **Pop 2000:** 33,812 (White 81.2%; Black or African American 15.4%; Hispanic or Latino 1.8%; Asian 0.8%; Other 1.9%). **Foreign born:** 3.3%. **Median age:** 43.3.

Income 2000: per capita $28,164; median household $43,532; **Pop below poverty level:** 8.3%. ***Personal per capita income 2000-2003:** $37,961-$44,321.

Unemployment 2004: 3.5%. **Change from 2000:** +0.4%. **Median travel time to work:** 22.4 minutes. **Working outside county of residence:** 23.9%.

Cities with pop over 10,000: Easton 🏛 (12,845).

WASHINGTON COUNTY

100 W Washington St   **Ph:** 240-313-2200
Hagerstown, MD 21740   **Fax:** 240-313-2201
www.washco-md.net/

On central northern border of MD; organized Sept 6, 1776 from Frederick County. **Name Origin:** For George Washington (1732-99), American patriot and first U.S. president.

Area (sq mi): 467.55 (land 458.14; water 9.41). **Pop per sq mi:** 309.7.

Pop 2005: 141,895. **State rank:** 10. **Pop change:** 2000-20005 +7.6%; 1990-2000 +8.7%. **Pop 2000:** 131,923 (White 89.1%; Black or African American 7.8%; Hispanic or Latino 1.2%; Asian 0.8%; Other 1.7%). **Foreign born:** 1.9%. **Median age:** 37.4.

Income 2000: per capita $20,062; median household $40,617; **Pop below poverty level:** 9.5%. ***Personal per capita income 2000-2003:** $25,148-$27,848.

Unemployment 2004: 4.4%. **Change from 2000:** +0.3%. **Median travel time to work:** 25.1 minutes. **Working outside county of residence:** 27%.

Cities with pop over 10,000: Hagerstown 🏛 (37,536).

WICOMICO COUNTY

125 N Division St   **Ph:** 410-548-4801
Salisbury, MD 21803   **Fax:** 410-548-4803
www.wicomicocounty.org

In southeastern MD, north of Princess Anne; organized Aug 17, 1867 from Somerset and Worcester counties. **Name Origin:** For

🏛 County Seat

Wicomico County (cont'd)

the Wicomico River, which flows through it. Possibly for a Nanticoke Indian village near its banks named *wicko-mekee*, possibly 'where houses are being built,' or 'pleasant place of dwelling.'

Area (sq mi): 399.79 (land 377.17; water 22.62). **Pop per sq mi:** 239.7.

Pop 2005: 90,402. **State rank:** 14. **Pop change:** 2000-20005 +6.8%; 1990-2000 +13.9%. **Pop 2000:** 84,644 (White 71.5%; Black or African American 23.3%; Hispanic or Latino 2.2%; Asian 1.7%; Other 2.3%). **Foreign born:** 3.9%. **Median age:** 35.8.

Income 2000: per capita $19,171; median household $39,035; **Pop below poverty level:** 12.8%. ***Personal per capita income 2000-2003:** $24,120-$26,885.

Unemployment 2004: 4.3%. **Change from 2000:** -1.1%. **Median travel time to work:** 20.9 minutes. **Working outside county of residence:** 21.7%.

Cities with pop over 10,000: Salisbury 🏛 (26,148).

WORCESTER COUNTY

1 W Market St Rm 1103
Snow Hill, MD 21863
www.co.worcester.md.us

Ph: 410-632-1194
Fax: 410-632-3131

On southeastern border of MD, on Atlantic Ocean; organized Oct 29, 1742 from Somerset County. **Name Origin:** For Edward Somerset, Earl of Worcester (c.1601-67), son-in-law of George Calvert (1580?-1632).

Area (sq mi): 694.73 (land 473.24; water 221.49). **Pop per sq mi:** 103.

Pop 2005: 48,750. **State rank:** 17. **Pop change:** 2000-20005 +4.7%; 1990-2000 +32.9%. **Pop 2000:** 46,543 (White 80.4%; Black or African American 16.7%; Hispanic or Latino 1.3%; Asian 0.6%; Other 1.6%). **Foreign born:** 2.7%. **Median age:** 43.

Income 2000: per capita $22,505; median household $40,650; **Pop below poverty level:** 9.6%. ***Personal per capita income 2000-2003:** $27,782-$30,653.

Unemployment 2004: 6.4%. **Change from 2000:** -3.5%. **Median travel time to work:** 23.3 minutes. **Working outside county of residence:** 27%.

Cities with pop over 10,000: None.

---

*Source: Personal per capita income data are from the Bureau of Economic Analysis; per capita income data are from the Bureau of the Census. See Introduction for explanation of differences.

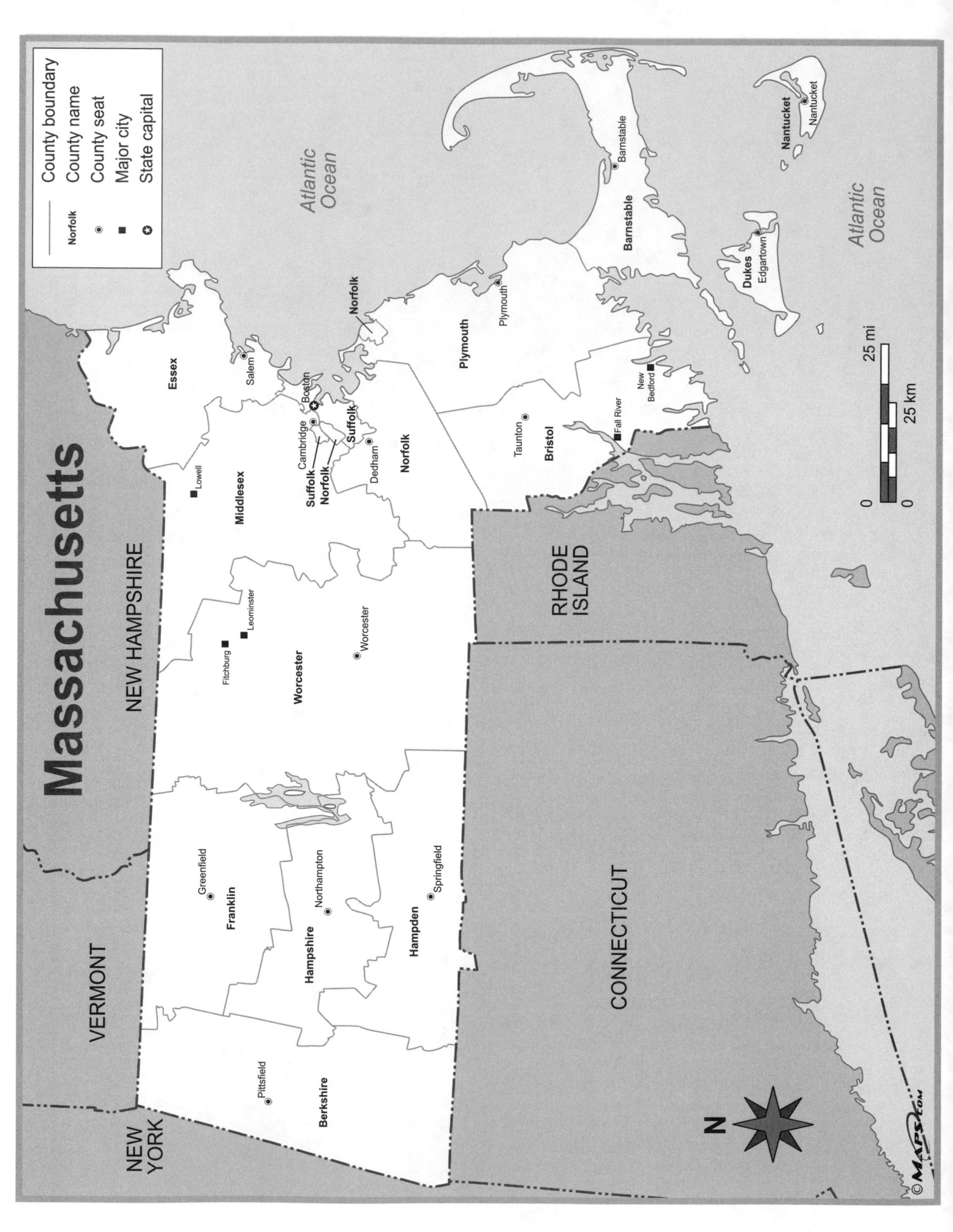

Massachusetts

Massachusetts

MASSACHUSETTS STATE INFORMATION
www.mass.gov   **Ph:** 866-888-2808

Area (sq mi): 10,554.57 (land 7840.02; water 2714.55). **Pop per sq mi:** 816.2.

Pop 2005: 6,398,743. **Pop change:** 2000-20005 +0.8%; 1990-2000 +5.5%. **Pop 2000:** 6,349,097 (White 81.9%; Black or African American 5.4%; Hispanic or Latino 6.8%; Asian 3.8%; Other 6.2%). **Foreign born:** 12.2%. **Median age:** 36.5.

Income 2000: per capita $25,952; median household $50,502; **Pop below poverty level:** 9.3%. ***Personal per capita income 2000-2003:** $37,756-$39,504.

Unemployment 2004: 5.2%. **Change from 2000:** +2.5%. **Median travel time to work:** 27 minutes. **Working outside county of residence:** 33.4%.

BARNSTABLE COUNTY
3195 Main St   **Ph:** 508-362-2511
Barnstable, MA 02630   **Fax:** 508-362-4136
www.tsic.com

Coextensive with Cape Cod, in southeastern MA; organized Jun 2, 1685 from Old Plymouth Colony. **Name Origin:** For Barnstaple, Devonshire, England. Original meaning was 'Bearda's staple or post,' or 'post to which a warship was moored.' Folk etymology changed it to -*stable*.

Area (sq mi): 1305.62 (land 395.51; water 910.1). **Pop per sq mi:** 572.7.

Pop 2005: 226,514. **State rank:** 9. **Pop change:** 2000-20005 +1.9%; 1990-2000 +19.1%. **Pop 2000:** 222,230 (White 93.4%; Black or African American 1.8%; Hispanic or Latino 1.3%; Asian 0.6%; Other 3.4%). **Foreign born:** 4.9%. **Median age:** 44.6.

Income 2000: per capita $25,318; median household $45,933; **Pop below poverty level:** 6.9%. ***Personal per capita income 2000-2003:** $35,747-$38,638.

Unemployment 2004: 4.8%. **Change from 2000:** +0.9%. **Median travel time to work:** 24.1 minutes. **Working outside county of residence:** 14.6%.

Cities with pop over 10,000: Barnstable 🏛 (48,535).

BERKSHIRE COUNTY
76 East St   **Ph:** 413-499-1940
Pittsfield, MA 01201   **Fax:** 413-499-7990

On western border of MA, bordered on north by VT, by NY on west, and by CT on south; organized April 21, 1761 from Hampshire County. **Name Origin:** For the county in England.

Area (sq mi): 946.27 (land 931.32; water 14.95). **Pop per sq mi:** 141.6.

Pop 2005: 131,868. **State rank:** 11. **Pop change:** 2000-20005 2.3%; 1990-2000 -3.2%. **Pop 2000:** 134,953 (White 94.1%; Black or African American 2%; Hispanic or Latino 1.7%; Asian 1%; Other 1.9%). **Foreign born:** 3.7%. **Median age:** 40.5.

Income 2000: per capita $21,807; median household $39,047; **Pop below poverty level:** 9.5%. ***Personal per capita income 2000-2003:** $30,278-$32,796.

Unemployment 2004: 4.6%. **Change from 2000:** +0.9%. **Median travel time to work:** 19.2 minutes. **Working outside county of residence:** 7.3%.

Cities with pop over 10,000: Pittsfield 🏛 (44,285); North Adams (14,167).

BRISTOL COUNTY
9 Court St   **Ph:** 508-824-9681
Taunton, MA 02780   **Fax:** 508-821-3101

On southwestern border of MA with RI; organized Jun 2, 1685 from Old Plymouth Colony. **Name Origin:** For Bristol, Gloucestershire and Somerset, England.

Area (sq mi): 691.19 (land 556; water 135.19). **Pop per sq mi:** 982.6.

Pop 2005: 546,331. **State rank:** 6. **Pop change:** 2000-20005 +2.2%; 1990-2000 +5.6%. **Pop 2000:** 534,678 (White 89.4%; Black or African American 2%; Hispanic or Latino 3.6%; Asian 1.3%; Other 5.6%). **Foreign born:** 11.7%. **Median age:** 36.7.

Income 2000: per capita $20,978; median household $43,496; **Pop below poverty level:** 10%. ***Personal per capita income 2000-2003:** $28,500-$31,161.

Unemployment 2004: 6.1%. **Change from 2000:** +1.3%. **Median travel time to work:** 25.6 minutes. **Working outside county of residence:** 36.4%.

Cities with pop over 10,000: New Bedford (93,979); Fall River (92,526); Taunton 🏛 (56,648); Attleboro (43,506).

DUKES COUNTY
PO Box 190   **Ph:** 508 696 3840
Edgartown, MA 02539   **Fax:** 508-696-3841
www.dukescounty.org

Southeast of New Bedford; includes islands of Martha's Vineyard, Chappaquiddick, Elizabeth, and Noman's Land. Organized Jun 22, 1695 from Martha's Vineyard. **Name Origin:** For James II (1633-1701), Duke of York and Albany, administrator of the colonies at the time of naming.

🏛 *County Seat*

Dukes County (cont'd)

Area (sq mi): 490.95 (land 103.78; water 387.18). **Pop per sq mi:** 150.2.

Pop 2005: 15,592. **State rank:** 13. **Pop change:** 2000-20005 +4%; 1990-2000 +28.8%. **Pop 2000:** 14,987 (White 90%; Black or African American 2.4%; Hispanic or Latino 1%; Asian 0.5%; Other 6.5%, including 1.7% American Indian/Alaska Native). **Foreign born:** 6.3%. **Median age:** 40.7.

Income 2000: per capita $26,472; median household $45,559; **Pop below poverty level:** 7.3%. ***Personal per capita income 2000-2003:** $35,462-$40,723.

Unemployment 2004: 3.9%. **Change from 2000:** +0.6%. **Median travel time to work:** 16.5 minutes. **Working outside county of residence:** 4.4%.

Cities with pop over 10,000: None.

ESSEX COUNTY
36 Federal St   **Ph:** 978-741-0200
County Administration Bldg 1st Fl
Salem, MA 01970

On northeastern border of MA, north of Boston; original county, organized May 10, 1643. **Name Origin:** For the county of Essex, England.

Area (sq mi): 828.53 (land 500.67; water 327.86). **Pop per sq mi:** 1474.6.

Pop 2005: 738,301. **State rank:** 3. **Pop change:** 2000-20005 +2.1%; 1990-2000 +8%. **Pop 2000:** 723,419 (White 83.1%; Black or African American 2.6%; Hispanic or Latino 11%; Asian 2.3%; Other 8.5%). **Foreign born:** 11.3%. **Median age:** 37.5.

Income 2000: per capita $26,358; median household $51,576; **Pop below poverty level:** 8.9%. ***Personal per capita income 2000-2003:** $37,626-$38,536.

Unemployment 2004: 5.7%. **Change from 2000:** +1.6%. **Median travel time to work:** 27.1 minutes. **Working outside county of residence:** 34.3%.

Cities with pop over 10,000: 9 (see page 35 for cities).

FRANKLIN COUNTY
425 Main St PO Box 1573   **Ph:** 413-774-5535
Greenfield, MA 01302   **Fax:** 413-774-4770
www.co.franklin.ma.us

On northern border of MA, north of Northampton; organized Jun 24, 1811 from Hampshire County. **Name Origin:** For Benjamin Franklin (1706-90), U.S. patriot, diplomat, and statesman.

Area (sq mi): 724.74 (land 702.03; water 22.71). **Pop per sq mi:** 103.

Pop 2005: 72,334. **State rank:** 12. **Pop change:** 2000-20005 +1.1%; 1990-2000 +2.1%. **Pop 2000:** 71,535 (White 94.4%; Black or African American 0.9%; Hispanic or Latino 2%; Asian 1%; Other 2.6%). **Foreign born:** 3.6%. **Median age:** 39.5.

Income 2000: per capita $20,672; median household $40,768; **Pop below poverty level:** 9.4%. ***Personal per capita income 2000-2003:** $28,277-$30,032.

Unemployment 2004: 4.2%. **Change from 2000:** +1%. **Median travel time to work:** 23.7 minutes. **Working outside county of residence:** 37.5%.

Cities with pop over 10,000: None.

HAMPDEN COUNTY
50 State St   **Ph:** 413-748-8600
Springfield, MA 01102

On southern border of MA, south of Northampton; organized Feb 25, 1812 from Hampshire County. **Name Origin:** For John Hampden (1594-1643), English statesman influential in the establishment of Puritan colonies in North America.

Area (sq mi): 634.12 (land 618.4; water 15.71). **Pop per sq mi:** 746.4.

Pop 2005: 461,591. **State rank:** 8. **Pop change:** 2000-20005 +1.2%; 1990-2000 +0%. **Pop 2000:** 456,228 (White 74.4%; Black or African American 8.1%; Hispanic or Latino 15.2%; Asian 1.3%; Other 11.5%). **Foreign born:** 7.2%. **Median age:** 36.4.

Income 2000: per capita $19,541; median household $39,718; **Pop below poverty level:** 14.7%. ***Personal per capita income 2000-2003:** $27,527-$29,515.

Unemployment 2004: 6.1%. **Change from 2000:** +1.8%. **Median travel time to work:** 21.8 minutes. **Working outside county of residence:** 18.2%.

Cities with pop over 10,000: 6 (see page 35 for cities).

HAMPSHIRE COUNTY
99 Main St Rm 205   **Ph:** 413-584-0557
Northampton, MA 01060   **Fax:** 413-584-1465

In west-central MA, north of Springfield, organized May 7, 1662 from Middlesex County. **Name Origin:** Named by Capt. John Mason (1586-1635) for the county of Hampshire, England.

Area (sq mi): 545.44 (land 529.03; water 16.41). **Pop per sq mi:** 289.8.

Pop 2005: 153,339. **State rank:** 10. **Pop change:** 2000-20005 +0.7%; 1990-2000 +3.9%. **Pop 2000:** 152,251 (White 89.5%; Black or African American 2%; Hispanic or Latino 3.4%; Asian 3.4%; Other 3.6%). **Foreign born:** 6.6%. **Median age:** 34.4.

Income 2000: per capita $21,685; median household $46,098; **Pop below poverty level:** 9.4%. ***Personal per capita income 2000-2003:** $27,395-$28,903.

Unemployment 2004: 3.8%. **Change from 2000:** +1.3%. **Median travel time to work:** 21.9 minutes. **Working outside county of residence:** 36.5%.

Cities with pop over 10,000: Northampton ⌂ (28,930); Easthampton (16,089).

MIDDLESEX COUNTY
40 Thorndike St   **Ph:** 617-494-4300
Cambridge, MA 02141   **Fax:** 617-494-9129

In northern MA, west and northwest of Boston; bounded on north by NH and on the south by Massachusetts Bay. Original county, organized May 10, 1643. **Name Origin:** For an ancient county in England, most of which became part of Greater London in 1965.

*Source: Personal per capita income data are from the Bureau of Economic Analysis; per capita income data are from the Bureau of the Census. See Introduction for explanation of differences.

Middlesex County (cont'd)

Area (sq mi): 847.54 (land 823.46; water 24.08). **Pop per sq mi:** 1771.8.

Pop 2005: 1,459,011. **State rank:** 1. **Pop change:** 2000-20005 - 0.4%; 1990-2000 +4.8%. **Pop 2000:** 1,465,396 (White 83.6%; Black or African American 3.4%; Hispanic or Latino 4.6%; Asian 6.3%; Other 4.5%). **Foreign born:** 15.2%. **Median age:** 36.4.

Income 2000: per capita $31,199; median household $60,821; **Pop below poverty level:** 6.5%. ***Personal per capita income 2000-2003:** $46,347-$47,451.

Unemployment 2004: 4.4%. **Change from 2000:** +1.3%. **Median travel time to work:** 27.4 minutes. **Working outside county of residence:** 31.3%.

Cities with pop over 10,000: 12 (see page 35 for cities).

NANTUCKET COUNTY

16 Broad St	**Ph:** 508-228-7216
Nantucket, MA 02554	**Fax:** 508-325-5313

Coextensive with Nantucket Island, south of Cape Cod, MA; original county, organized Jun 22, 1695. **Name Origin:** From an Indian word of uncertain meaning. An early map marks the island as *Natocok*, which may mean 'far away.' Others suggest the root *Nantuck* means 'the sandy, sterile soil tempted no one.'

Area (sq mi): 303.64 (land 47.81; water 255.83). **Pop per sq mi:** 212.7.

Pop 2005: 10,168. **State rank:** 14. **Pop change:** 2000-20005 +6.8%; 1990-2000 +58.4%. **Pop 2000:** 9,520 (White 86.9%; Black or African American 8.3%; Hispanic or Latino 2.2%; Asian 0.6%; Other 3.2%). **Foreign born:** 8%. **Median age:** 36.7.

Income 2000: per capita $31,314; median household $55,522; **Pop below poverty level:** 7.5%. ***Personal per capita income 2000-2003:** $45,100-$49,361.

Unemployment 2004: 2.5%. **Change from 2000:** +1%. **Median travel time to work:** 9.5 minutes. **Working outside county of residence:** 1.6%.

Cities with pop over 10,000: None.

NORFOLK COUNTY

614 High St	**Ph:** 781-461-6105
Dedham, MA 02026	**Fax:** 781-326-6480
www.norfolkcounty.org	

In eastern MA, south of Boston; organized Mar 26, 1793 from Suffolk County. **Name Origin:** For the county in England.

Area (sq mi): 443.94 (land 399.58; water 44.35). **Pop per sq mi:** 1635.7.

Pop 2005: 653,595. **State rank:** 5. **Pop change:** 2000-20005 +0.5%; 1990-2000 +5.6%. **Pop 2000:** 650,308 (White 87.9%; Black or African American 3.2%; Hispanic or Latino 1.8%; Asian 5.5%; Other 2.3%). **Foreign born:** 11.8%. **Median age:** 38.1.

Income 2000: per capita $32,484; median household $63,432; **Pop below poverty level:** 4.6%. ***Personal per capita income 2000-2003:** $46,824-$48,238.

Unemployment 2004: 4.5%. **Change from 2000:** +1.7%. **Median travel time to work:** 30 minutes. **Working outside county of residence:** 53.2%.

Cities with pop over 10,000: Quincy (89,909); Franklin (30,192).

PLYMOUTH COUNTY

Court St	**Ph:** 508-747-6911
Plymouth, MA 02360	**Fax:** 508-830-0676
www.seeplymouth.com	

In southeastern MA, northeast of New Bedford; organized Jun 2, 1685 from Old Plymouth Colony. **Name Origin:** For Plymouth, Devonshire, England, from which the *Mayflower* sailed for America.

Area (sq mi): 1093.39 (land 660.85; water 432.54). **Pop per sq mi:** 745.1.

Pop 2005: 492,409. **State rank:** 7. **Pop change:** 2000-20005 +4.1%; 1990-2000 +8.6%. **Pop 2000:** 472,822 (White 87.6%; Black or African American 4.6%; Hispanic or Latino 2.4%; Asian 0.9%; Other 5.8%). **Foreign born:** 6.3%. **Median age:** 36.8.

Income 2000: per capita $24,789; median household $55,615; **Pop below poverty level:** 6.6%. ***Personal per capita income 2000-2003:** $34,588-$36,755.

Unemployment 2004: 5.1%. **Change from 2000:** +1.6%. **Median travel time to work:** 32.3 minutes. **Working outside county of residence:** 48.2%.

Cities with pop over 10,000: Brockton (95,009).

SUFFOLK COUNTY

3 Pemberton Sq Government Center	**Ph:** 617-725-8787
Boston, MA 02108	

In eastern MA, on Massachusetts Bay; original county, organized May 10, 1643. **Name Origin:** For the county in England.

Area (sq mi): 120.19 (land 58.52; water 61.68). **Pop per sq mi:** 11,183.

Pop 2005: 654,428. **State rank:** 4. **Pop change:** 2000-20005 -5.1%; 1990-2000 +3.9%. **Pop 2000:** 689,807 (White 52.1%; Black or African American 22.2%; Hispanic or Latino 15.5%; Asian 7%; Other 13.1%). **Foreign born:** 25.5%. **Median age:** 31.7.

Income 2000: per capita $22,766; median household $39,355; **Pop below poverty level:** 19%. ***Personal per capita income 2000-2003:** $38,140-$42,215.

Unemployment 2004: 5.7%. **Change from 2000:** +1.6%. **Median travel time to work:** 29 minutes. **Working outside county of residence:** 32.7%.

Cities with pop over 10,000: Boston 🏛 (569,165); Revere (46,169); Chelsea (33,227).

WORCESTER COUNTY

2 Main St County Courthouse	**Ph:** 508-798-7717
Worcester, MA 01608	**Fax:** 508-798-7746

In central MA, having its northern border with NH, its southern border with CT; organized Apr 2, 1731 from Middlesex and Suffolk counties. **Name Origin:** For either the town of Worcester or the county of Worcestershire, both in England.

🏛 *County Seat*

Worcester County (cont'd)

Area (sq mi): 1579.02 (land 1513.06; water 65.95). **Pop per sq mi:** 517.7.

Pop 2005: 783,262. **State rank:** 2. **Pop change:** 2000-20005 +4.3%; 1990-2000 +5.8%. **Pop 2000:** 750,963 (White 86.5%; Black or African American 2.7%; Hispanic or Latino 6.8%; Asian 2.6%; Other 5%). **Foreign born:** 7.9%. **Median age:** 36.3.

Income 2000: per capita $22,983; median household $47,874; **Pop below poverty level:** 9.2%. ***Personal per capita income 2000-2003:** $32,600-$33,479.

Unemployment 2004: 5.5%. **Change from 2000:** +1.4%. **Median travel time to work:** 25.8 minutes. **Working outside county of residence:** 26%.

Cities with pop over 10,000: Worcester 🏛 (175,966); Leominster (41,911); Fitchburg (39,910); Gardner (20,967).

*Source: Personal per capita income data are from the Bureau of Economic Analysis; per capita income data are from the Bureau of the Census.
See Introduction for explanation of differences.*

342

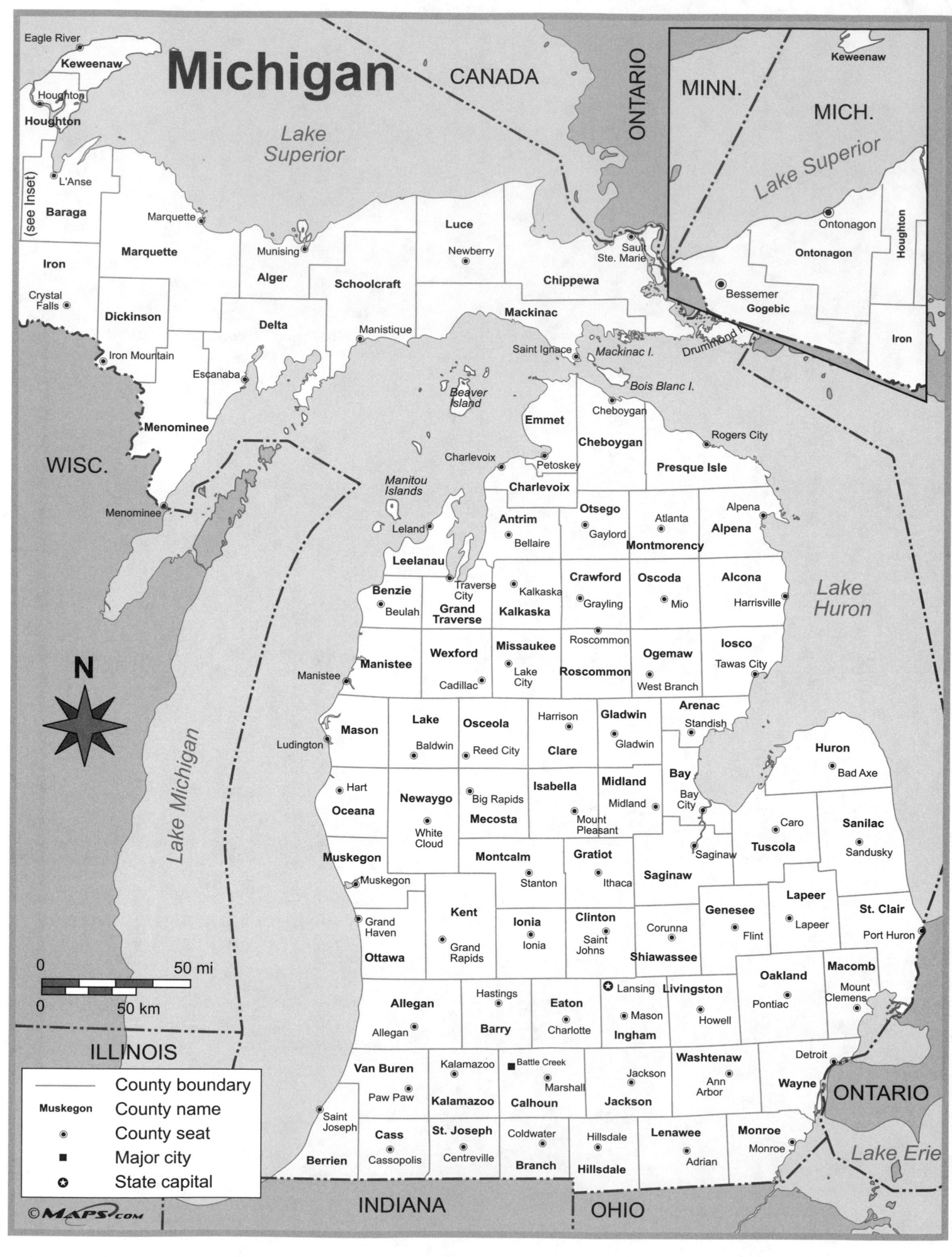

Michigan

CANADA

ONTARIO

MINN.

MICH.

Lake Superior

Lake Superior

Keweenaw

Eagle River
Keweenaw
Houghton
Houghton

L'Anse
Baraga

Iron

Crystal Falls

Marquette
Marquette

Munising
Alger

Dickinson
Iron Mountain

Escanaba
Delta

Schoolcraft
Manistique

Menominee

WISC.

Menominee

Luce
Newberry

Chippewa

Mackinac
Sault Ste. Marie

Ontonagon
Ontonagon

Houghton

Bessemer
Gogebic

Iron

Mackinac I.
Saint Ignace
Beaver Island
Bois Blanc I.
Drummond I.

ONTARIO

N

Lake Michigan

Manitou Islands
Leland

Leelanau

Benzie
Beulah

Manistee
Manistee

Emmet
Cheboygan

Cheboygan

Charlevoix
Petoskey
Charlevoix

Rogers City
Presque Isle

Antrim
Bellaire

Traverse City
Grand Traverse

Otsego
Gaylord

Atlanta
Montmorency

Alpena
Alpena

Kalkaska
Kalkaska

Crawford
Grayling

Oscoda
Mio

Alcona
Harrisville

Wexford
Cadillac

Missaukee
Lake City

Roscommon
Roscommon

Ogemaw
West Branch

Iosco
Tawas City

Lake Huron

Mason
Ludington

Lake
Baldwin

Osceola
Reed City

Harrison
Clare

Gladwin
Gladwin

Arenac
Standish

Oceana
Hart

Newaygo
White Cloud

Big Rapids
Mecosta

Isabella
Mount Pleasant

Midland
Midland

Bay
Bay City

Saginaw

Huron
Bad Axe

Caro
Tuscola

Sanilac
Sandusky

Muskegon
Muskegon

Montcalm
Stanton

Gratiot
Ithaca

Saginaw

Genesee
Flint

Lapeer
Lapeer

St. Clair
Port Huron

Ottawa
Grand Haven

Kent
Grand Rapids

Ionia
Ionia

Clinton
Saint Johns

Corunna
Shiawassee

Oakland
Pontiac

Macomb
Mount Clemens

Allegan
Allegan

Hastings

Barry

Eaton
Charlotte

Lansing ✪ **Livingston**
Mason
Ingham
Howell

Detroit
Wayne

ONTARIO

Lake Erie

Van Buren
Paw Paw

Kalamazoo
Kalamazoo

Battle Creek ■
Marshall
Calhoun

Jackson
Jackson

Washtenaw
Ann Arbor

Saint Joseph

Berrien

Cass
Cassopolis

St. Joseph
Centreville

Coldwater
Branch

Hillsdale
Hillsdale

Lenawee
Adrian

Monroe
Monroe

ILLINOIS

INDIANA

OHIO

——	County boundary
Muskegon	County name
⊙	County seat
■	Major city
✪	State capital

©MAPS.com

0 ——— 50 mi
0 ——— 50 km

Michigan

MICHIGAN STATE INFORMATION

www.michigan.gov **Ph:** 517-373-1837

Area (sq mi): 96,716.11 (land 56,803.82; water 39,912.28). **Pop per sq mi:** 178.2.

Pop 2005: 10,120,860. **Pop change:** 2000-20005 +1.8%; 1990-2000 +6.9%. **Pop 2000:** 9,938,444 (White 78.6%; Black or African American 14.2%; Hispanic or Latino 3.3%; Asian 1.8%; Other 3.8%). **Foreign born:** 5.3%. **Median age:** 35.5.

Income 2000: per capita $22,168; median household $44,667; **Pop below poverty level:** 10.5%. ***Personal per capita income 2000-2003:** $29,552-$31,178.

Unemployment 2004: 7%. **Change from 2000:** +3.3%. **Median travel time to work:** 24.1 minutes. **Working outside county of residence:** 29.1%.

ALCONA COUNTY

PO Box 308 **Ph:** 989-724-5374
Harrisville, MI 48740 **Fax:** 989-724-5838

On the northeastern coast of MI on Lake Huron; established as Neewaygo County Apr 1, 1840 from Alpena County; name changed Mar 8, 1843. **Name Origin:** A local coinage, said to mean 'beautiful plains.'

Area (sq mi): 1790.54 (land 674.43; water 1116.1). **Pop per sq mi:** 17.3.

Pop 2005: 11,653. **State rank:** 74. **Pop change:** 2000-20005 -0.6%; 1990-2000 +15.5%. **Pop 2000:** 11,719 (White 97.4%; Black or African American 0.2%; Hispanic or Latino 0.7%; Asian 0.2%; Other 1.6%). **Foreign born:** 1.5%. **Median age:** 49.

Income 2000: per capita $17,653; median household $31,362; **Pop below poverty level:** 12.6%. ***Personal per capita income 2000-2003:** $20,195-$21,109.

Unemployment 2004: 11%. **Change from 2000:** +0.8%. **Median travel time to work:** 27.5 minutes. **Working outside county of residence:** 50.4%.

Cities with pop over 10,000: None.

ALGER COUNTY

PO Box 538 **Ph:** 906-387-2076
Munising, MI 49862 **Fax:** 906-387-2156

On the north-central coast of the Upper Peninsula of MI, on Lake Superior, established Mar 17, 1885, from Schoolcraft County. **Name Origin:** For Gen. Russell Alexander Alger (1836-1907), governor of MI (1885-87), U.S. secretary of war (1897-99), and U.S. senator from MI (1902-07).

Area (sq mi): 5049.08 (land 917.83; water 4131.25). **Pop per sq mi:** 10.5.

Pop 2005: 9,662. **State rank:** 77. **Pop change:** 2000-20005 -2%; 1990-2000 +9.9%. **Pop 2000:** 9,862 (White 87.5%; Black or African American 6.1%; Hispanic or Latino 1%; Asian 0.3%; Other 5.7%, including 3.3% American Indian/Alaska Native). **Foreign born:** 1%. **Median age:** 41.2.

Income 2000: per capita $18,210; median household $35,892; **Pop below poverty level:** 10.3%. ***Personal per capita income 2000-2003:** $18,683-$19,648.

Unemployment 2004: 7.9%. **Change from 2000:** +1.9%. **Median travel time to work:** 19.8 minutes. **Working outside county of residence:** 16.3%.

Cities with pop over 10,000: None.

ALLEGAN COUNTY

113 Chestnut St **Ph:** 269-673-0450
Allegan, MI 49010 **Fax:** 269-673-0298
www.allegancounty.org

On the southwestern coast of MI, bordered on the west by Lake Michigan; established Mar 2, 1831 (prior to statehood) from Kalamazoo County. **Name Origin:** Named for the Allegan (Alleghen) Indian tribe by Henry Rowe Schoolcraft (1793-1864), explorer, MI legislator, author, and superintendent of Indian Affairs for MI (1836-41).

Area (sq mi): 1833.3 (land 827.46; water 1005.83). **Pop per sq mi:** 136.8.

Pop 2005: 113,174. **State rank:** 18. **Pop change:** 2000-20005 +7.1%; 1990-2000 +16.7%. **Pop 2000:** 105,665 (White 91%; Black or African American 1.3%; Hispanic or Latino 5.7%; Asian 0.6%; Other 4.6%). **Foreign born:** 2.9%. **Median age:** 35.2.

Income 2000: per capita $19,918; median household $45,813; **Pop below poverty level:** 7.3%. ***Personal per capita income 2000-2003:** $26,396-$26,190.

Unemployment 2004: 6.6%. **Change from 2000:** +2%. **Median travel time to work:** 23.4 minutes. **Working outside county of residence:** 50.2%.

Cities with pop over 10,000: None.

ALPENA COUNTY

720 W Chisholm St **Ph:** 989-356-0930
Alpena, MI 49707 **Fax:** 989-354-9648
www.alpenacounty.org

On the northeastern coast of MI, bordered on the east by Lake

Alpena County (cont'd)

Huron; established as Anamickee County Apr 1, 1840 from Presque Isle County; name changed Mar 8, 1843. **Name Origin:** From an Indian word probably meaning 'partridge' or 'partridge country.' Originally named for the Chippewa chief.

Area (sq mi): 1695 (land 574.15; water 1120.85). **Pop per sq mi:** 53.

Pop 2005: 30,428. **State rank:** 49. **Pop change:** 2000-20005 -2.8%; 1990-2000 +2.3%. **Pop 2000:** 31,314 (White 97.8%; Black or African American 0.2%; Hispanic or Latino 0.6%; Asian 0.3%; Other 1.2%). **Foreign born:** 1.2%. **Median age:** 40.4.

Income 2000: per capita $17,566; median household $34,177; **Pop below poverty level:** 10.5%. ***Personal per capita income 2000-2003:** $23,335-$24,814.

Unemployment 2004: 8.5%. **Change from 2000:** -0.2%. **Median travel time to work:** 17 minutes. **Working outside county of residence:** 7.3%.

Cities with pop over 10,000: Alpena 🏛 (10,939).

ANTRIM COUNTY

PO Box 520   **Ph:** 231-533-6353
Bellaire, MI 49615   **Fax:** 231-533-6935
www.antrimcounty.org

On the northwest coast of MI; established as Meegisee County Apr 1, 1840 from Mackinac County; name changed Mar 8, 1843. **Name Origin:** For the county in Ireland.

Area (sq mi): 601.9 (land 476.94; water 124.97). **Pop per sq mi:** 51.2.

Pop 2005: 24,422. **State rank:** 61. **Pop change:** 2000-20005 +5.7%; 1990-2000 +27.1%. **Pop 2000:** 23,110 (White 96.2%; Black or African American 0.2%; Hispanic or Latino 1.2%; Asian 0.2%; Other 2.7%, including 1.1% American Indian/Alaska Native). **Foreign born:** 1.5%. **Median age:** 41.1.

Income 2000: per capita $19,485; median household $38,107; **Pop below poverty level:** 9%. ***Personal per capita income 2000-2003:** $24,431-$26,042.

Unemployment 2004: 7.9%. **Change from 2000:** +0.4%. **Median travel time to work:** 23 minutes. **Working outside county of residence:** 41.8%.

Cities with pop over 10,000: None.

ARENAC COUNTY

PO Box 747   **Ph:** 989-846-4626
Standish, MI 48658
www.arenaccountygov.com

On the east coast of MI on Saginaw Bay; established Mar 2, 1831 (prior to statehood). **Name Origin:** Name coined by Henry Rowe Schoolcraft (1793-1864), author, explorer, MI legislator, and superintendent of Indian Affairs for MI (1836-41), meaning 'sandy place' from Spanish *arena* 'sand' and *-ac* 'place of.'

Area (sq mi): 680.81 (land 366.84; water 313.97). **Pop per sq mi:** 46.8.

Pop 2005: 17,154. **State rank:** 67. **Pop change:** 2000-20005 -0.7%; 1990-2000 +15.7%. **Pop 2000:** 17,269 (White 94.4%; Black or

African American 1.8%; Hispanic or Latino 1.4%; Asian 0.3%; Other 2.4%). **Foreign born:** 1.1%. **Median age:** 40.1.

Income 2000: per capita $16,300; median household $32,805; **Pop below poverty level:** 13.9%. ***Personal per capita income 2000-2003:** $20,513-$21,655.

Unemployment 2004: 9.9%. **Change from 2000:** +0.8%. **Median travel time to work:** 28.3 minutes. **Working outside county of residence:** 42.8%.

Cities with pop over 10,000: None.

BARAGA COUNTY

16 N 3rd St   **Ph:** 906-524-6183
L'Anse, MI 49946   **Fax:** 906-524-6186

On the north coast of the Upper Peninsula of MI on Keweenaw Bay; established Feb 19, 1875 from Houghton County. **Name Origin:** For the Rev. Frederic Baraga (1797-1868), Slovenian-born Roman Catholic missionary to the Ojibways who became a bishop in 1853. He established schools for the Chippewa and Ottawa (1830-68).

Area (sq mi): 1068.85 (land 904; water 164.85). **Pop per sq mi:** 9.7.

Pop 2005: 8,746. **State rank:** 80. **Pop change:** 2000-20005 +0%; 1990-2000 +10%. **Pop 2000:** 8,746 (White 78.3%; Black or African American 5%; Hispanic or Latino 0.9%; Asian 0.3%; Other 16.1%, including 12% American Indian/Alaska Native). **Foreign born:** 0.8%. **Median age:** 39.

Income 2000: per capita $15,860; median household $33,673; **Pop below poverty level:** 11.1%. ***Personal per capita income 2000-2003:** $18,915-$19,229.

Unemployment 2004: 11.6%. **Change from 2000:** +2.1%. **Median travel time to work:** 17.8 minutes. **Working outside county of residence:** 12.2%.

Cities with pop over 10,000: None.

BARRY COUNTY

220 W State St   **Ph:** 269-948-4810
Hastings, MI 49058   **Fax:** 269-945-0209
www.barrycounty.org

In southwestern MI, northeast of Kalamazoo; established Oct 29, 1829 (prior to statehood) from Eaton County. **Name Origin:** For William Taylor Barry (1784-1835), KY legislator, U.S. senator (1814-16), and U.S. Postmaster General (1829-35).

Area (sq mi): 576.9 (land 556.14; water 20.77). **Pop per sq mi:** 107.7.

Pop 2005: 59,892. **State rank:** 33. **Pop change:** 2000-20005 +5.5%; 1990-2000 +13.4%. **Pop 2000:** 56,755 (White 96.5%; Black or African American 0.2%; Hispanic or Latino 1.5%; Asian 0.3%; Other 2.1%). **Foreign born:** 0.8%. **Median age:** 36.9.

Income 2000: per capita $20,636; median household $46,820; **Pop below poverty level:** 5.5%. ***Personal per capita income 2000-2003:** $27,664-$28,153.

Unemployment 2004: 5.9%. **Change from 2000:** +1.6%. **Median travel time to work:** 26.9 minutes. **Working outside county of residence:** 59.2%.

Cities with pop over 10,000: None.

---

*Source: Personal per capita income data are from the Bureau of Economic Analysis; per capita income data are from the Bureau of the Census. See Introduction for explanation of differences.

BAY COUNTY

515 Center Ave Suite 101 **Ph:** 989-895-4280
Bay City, MI 48708 **Fax:** 989-895-4284
www.co.bay.mi.us

On the east coast of MI, north of Saginaw; established Feb 27, 1857 from Saginaw and Midland counties. **Name Origin:** For its location at the head of Saginaw Bay.

Area (sq mi): 630.91 (land 444.25; water 186.66). **Pop per sq mi:** 245.4.

Pop 2005: 109,029. **State rank:** 19. **Pop change:** 2000-20005 -1%; 1990-2000 -1.4%. **Pop 2000:** 110,157 (White 92.7%; Black or African American 1.3%; Hispanic or Latino 3.9%; Asian 0.5%; Other 3.2%). **Foreign born:** 1.4%. **Median age:** 38.4.

Income 2000: per capita $19,698; median household $38,646; **Pop below poverty level:** 9.7%. ***Personal per capita income 2000-2003:** $25,949-$26,726.

Unemployment 2004: 7.6%. **Change from 2000:** +2%. **Median travel time to work:** 21.8 minutes. **Working outside county of residence:** 35.6%.

Cities with pop over 10,000: Bay City 🏛 (35,317).

BENZIE COUNTY

PO Box 377 **Ph:** 231-882-9671
Beulah, MI 49617 **Fax:** 231-882-5941

On the northwestern coast of MI, bordered on west by Lake Michigan; established Feb 27, 1863 from Manistee and Grand Traverse counties. **Name Origin:** Origin uncertain; perhaps a variant of the French name for the Betsie river, *Aux Bec Scies* 'sawbill' a species of duck. Americans corrupted it to *Betsie*, then to *Benzie* for the county.

Area (sq mi): 859.64 (land 321.31; water 538.32). **Pop per sq mi:** 54.9.

Pop 2005: 17,644. **State rank:** 65. **Pop change:** 2000-20005 +10.3%; 1990-2000 +31.1%. **Pop 2000:** 15,998 (White 95.4%; Black or African American 0.3%; Hispanic or Latino 1.5%; Asian 0.2%; Other 3.2%, including 1.6% American Indian/Alaska Native). **Foreign born:** 1.7%. **Median age:** 40.8.

Income 2000: per capita $18,524; median household $37,350; **Pop below poverty level:** 7%. ***Personal per capita income 2000-2003:** $23,648-$24,747.

Unemployment 2004: 7.5%. **Change from 2000:** +0.8%. **Median travel time to work:** 25.4 minutes. **Working outside county of residence:** 48.2%.

Cities with pop over 10,000: None.

BERRIEN COUNTY

811 Port St **Ph:** 269-983-7111
Saint Joseph, MI 49085 **Fax:** 269-982-8642
www.berriencounty.org

In the southwestern corner of MI, bordered on west by Lake Michigan; established Oct 29, 1829 (prior to statehood) from Indian lands. **Name Origin:** For Col. John Macpherson Berrien (1781-1856), U.S. senator from GA (1825-29; 1841-52) and U.S. attorney general (1829-31).

Area (sq mi): 1581.38 (land 571; water 1010.39). **Pop per sq mi:** 284.8.

Pop 2005: 162,611. **State rank:** 15. **Pop change:** 2000-20005 +0.1%; 1990-2000 +0.7%. **Pop 2000:** 162,453 (White 78.1%; Black or African American 15.9%; Hispanic or Latino 3%; Asian 1.1%; Other 3.1%). **Foreign born:** 4.9%. **Median age:** 37.4.

Income 2000: per capita $19,952; median household $38,567; **Pop below poverty level:** 12.7%. ***Personal per capita income 2000-2003:** $26,072-$27,572.

Unemployment 2004: 7.8%. **Change from 2000:** +2.1%. **Median travel time to work:** 20 minutes. **Working outside county of residence:** 18.6%.

Cities with pop over 10,000: Niles (11,876); Benton Harbor (10,851).

BRANCH COUNTY

31 Division St **Ph:** 517-279-4301
Coldwater, MI 49036 **Fax:** 517-278-4130
www.co.branch.mi.us

On the south-central border of MI; established Oct 29, 1829 (prior to statehood) from Saint Joseph County. **Name Origin:** For John Branch (1782-1863), NC governor (1817-20), U.S. secretary of the navy (1829-31), and governor of FL Territory (1844-45).

Area (sq mi): 519.49 (land 507.41; water 12.08). **Pop per sq mi:** 91.6.

Pop 2005: 46,460. **State rank:** 38. **Pop change:** 2000-20005 +1.5%; 1990-2000 +10.3%. **Pop 2000:** 45,787 (White 92%; Black or African American 2.6%; Hispanic or Latino 3%; Asian 0.4%; Other 3.6%). **Foreign born:** 2.6%. **Median age:** 36.7.

Income 2000: per capita $17,552; median household $38,760; **Pop below poverty level:** 9.3%. ***Personal per capita income 2000-2003:** $20,985-$22,318.

Unemployment 2004: 7.1%. **Change from 2000:** +1.4%. **Median travel time to work:** 21.6 minutes. **Working outside county of residence:** 29.2%.

Cities with pop over 10,000: Coldwater 🏛 (10,821).

CALHOUN COUNTY

315 W Green St **Ph:** 269-781-0730
Marshall, MI 49068 **Fax:** 269-781-0721
www.calhouncountymi.org

In south-central MI, east of Kalamazoo; established Oct. 29, 1829 (prior to statehood) from Indian lands. **Name Origin:** For John Caldwell Calhoun (1782-1850), U.S. statesman and proponent of Southern causes.

Area (sq mi): 718.44 (land 708.72; water 9.72). **Pop per sq mi:** 196.4.

Pop 2005: 139,191. **State rank:** 17. **Pop change:** 2000-20005 +0.9%; 1990-2000 +1.5%. **Pop 2000:** 137,985 (White 82.4%; Black or African American 10.9%; Hispanic or Latino 3.2%; Asian 1.1%; Other 4%). **Foreign born:** 2.4%. **Median age:** 36.4.

Income 2000: per capita $19,230; median household $38,918; **Pop below poverty level:** 11.3%. ***Personal per capita income 2000-2003:** $25,138-$26,778.

Unemployment 2004: 7%. **Change from 2000:** +1.6%. **Median travel time to work:** 20.1 minutes. **Working outside county of residence:** 17%.

Calhoun County (cont'd)

Cities with pop over 10,000: Battle Creek (53,399).

CASS COUNTY

PO Box 132   **Ph:** 269-445-3701
Cassopolis, MI 49031   **Fax:** 269-445-5018
casscountymi.org

On the southwestern border of MI, southwest of Kalamazoo; established Oct 29, 1829 (prior to statehood) from Indian lands. **Name Origin:** For Gen. Lewis Cass (1782-1866), OH legislator, governor of MI Territory (1813-31), U.S. secretary of war (1831-36), and U.S. secretary of state (1857-60).

Area (sq mi): 508.46 (land 492.18; water 16.29). **Pop per sq mi:** 105.6.

Pop 2005: 51,996. **State rank:** 35. **Pop change:** 2000-20005 +1.7%; 1990-2000 +3.3%. **Pop 2000:** 51,104 (White 88.2%; Black or African American 6.1%; Hispanic or Latino 2.4%; Asian 0.5%; Other 4.1%). **Foreign born:** 1.9%. **Median age:** 38.5.

Income 2000: per capita $19,474; median household $41,264; **Pop below poverty level:** 9.9%. ***Personal per capita income 2000-2003:** $24,733-$26,429.

Unemployment 2004: 4.7%. **Change from 2000:** -0.5%. **Median travel time to work:** 24.2 minutes. **Working outside county of residence:** 61.4%.

Cities with pop over 10,000: None.

CHARLEVOIX COUNTY

203 Antrim St   **Ph:** 231-547-7200
Charlevoix, MI 49720   **Fax:** 231-547-7217
www.charlevoixcounty.org

On the northwestern coast of MI, bordered on west by Lake Michigan; established as Reshkauko County Apr 1, 1840; name changed Mar 8, 1843. **Name Origin:** For Pierre Francois Xavier de Charlevoix (1682-1761), French Jesuit explorer and writer who traveled from the Great Lakes down the Illinois and Mississippi rivers to New Orleans (1720-22).

Area (sq mi): 1390.76 (land 416.84; water 973.92). **Pop per sq mi:** 64.1.

Pop 2005: 26,722. **State rank:** 56. **Pop change:** 2000-20005 +2.4%; 1990-2000 +21.5%. **Pop 2000:** 26,090 (White 95.8%; Black or African American 0.2%; Hispanic or Latino 1%; Asian 0.2%; Other 3.2%, including 1.5% American Indian/Alaska Native). **Foreign born:** 1.4%. **Median age:** 39.1.

Income 2000: per capita $20,130; median household $39,788; **Pop below poverty level:** 8%. ***Personal per capita income 2000-2003:** $26,070-$28,506.

Unemployment 2004: 7.8%. **Change from 2000:** +1%. **Median travel time to work:** 19.8 minutes. **Working outside county of residence:** 26.5%.

Cities with pop over 10,000: None.

CHEBOYGAN COUNTY

PO Box 70   **Ph:** 231-627-8808
Cheboygan, MI 49721   **Fax:** 231-627-8453
www.cheboygancounty.net

On the north coast of MI; established Apr 1, 1840 from Antrim County. **Name Origin:** For the Cheboygan River; the name is Algonquian but the meaning is in dispute.

Area (sq mi): 885.23 (land 715.6; water 169.63). **Pop per sq mi:** 38.4.

Pop 2005: 27,463. **State rank:** 53. **Pop change:** 2000-20005 +3.8%; 1990-2000 +23.6%. **Pop 2000:** 26,448 (White 94.3%; Black or African American 0.2%; Hispanic or Latino 0.8%; Asian 0.2%; Other 4.6%, including 2.5% American Indian/Alaska Native). **Foreign born:** 1.2%. **Median age:** 41.3.

Income 2000: per capita $18,088; median household $33,417; **Pop below poverty level:** 12.2%. ***Personal per capita income 2000-2003:** $21,468-$22,995.

Unemployment 2004: 9.6%. **Change from 2000:** -1.6%. **Median travel time to work:** 23 minutes. **Working outside county of residence:** 29.7%.

Cities with pop over 10,000: None.

CHIPPEWA COUNTY

319 Court St   **Ph:** 906-635-6300
Sault Sainte Marie, MI 49783   **Fax:** 906-635-6851
users.lighthouse.net/chippewa/

On the northeast coast of the Upper Peninsula of MI on Whitefish Bay; established Dec 22, 1826 (prior to statehood) from Mackinac County. **Name Origin:** For the Ojibway Indians of Algonquian linguistic stock. The name means 'puckered' and probably refers to the seam in their moccasins.

Area (sq mi): 2697.98 (land 1561.06; water 1136.92). **Pop per sq mi:** 24.8.

Pop 2005: 38,780. **State rank:** 42. **Pop change:** 2000-20005 +0.6%; 1990-2000 +11.4%. **Pop 2000:** 38,543 (White 75.2%; Black or African American 5.5%; Hispanic or Latino 1.6%; Asian 0.5%; Other 18.1%, including 13.3% American Indian/Alaska Native). **Foreign born:** 3%. **Median age:** 36.2.

Income 2000: per capita $15,858; median household $34,464; **Pop below poverty level:** 12.8%. ***Personal per capita income 2000-2003:** $18,620-$19,682.

Unemployment 2004: 9%. **Change from 2000:** +1.2%. **Median travel time to work:** 17.7 minutes. **Working outside county of residence:** 5.7%.

Cities with pop over 10,000: Sault Sainte Marie 🏛 (14,157).

CLARE COUNTY

225 W Main St   **Ph:** 989-539-7131
Harrison, MI 48625   **Fax:** 989-539-6616
clarecountyinternet.com

In central MI, northwest of Midland; established as Kaykakee County Apr 1, 1840 from Isabella County; name changed Mar 8, 1843. **Name Origin:** For the county in Ireland. Originally for the Indian chief, Kaykakee 'pigeon hawk' who had signed the Treaty of 1826.

---

*Source: Personal per capita income data are from the Bureau of Economic Analysis; per capita income data are from the Bureau of the Census. See Introduction for explanation of differences.

Clare County (cont'd)

Area (sq mi): 575.22 (land 566.8; water 8.42). **Pop per sq mi:** 55.8.

Pop 2005: 31,653. **State rank:** 48. **Pop change:** 2000-20005 +1.3%; 1990-2000 +25.2%. **Pop 2000:** 31,252 (White 96.7%; Black or African American 0.3%; Hispanic or Latino 1.1%; Asian 0.3%; Other 2%). **Foreign born:** 1.1%. **Median age:** 40.5.

Income 2000: per capita $15,922; median household $28,845; **Pop below poverty level:** 16%. ***Personal per capita income 2000-2003:** $19,084-$20,523.

Unemployment 2004: 9.7%. **Change from 2000:** +0.8%. **Median travel time to work:** 28.3 minutes. **Working outside county of residence:** 42.6%.

Cities with pop over 10,000: None.

CLINTON COUNTY

PO Box 69   **Ph:** 989-224-5140
Saint Johns, MI 48879   **Fax:** 989-224-5102
www.clinton-county.org

In central MI, north of Lansing; established Mar 2, 1831 (prior to statehood) from Shiawassee County. **Name Origin:** For DeWitt Clinton (1769-1828), governor of NY (1817-21; 1825-28) and supporter of the Erie Canal.

Area (sq mi): 574.57 (land 571.46; water 3.12). **Pop per sq mi:** 121.3.

Pop 2005: 69,329. **State rank:** 27. **Pop change:** 2000-20005 +7.1%; 1990-2000 +11.9%. **Pop 2000:** 64,753 (White 94.8%; Black or African American 0.6%; Hispanic or Latino 2.6%; Asian 0.5%; Other 2.4%). **Foreign born:** 1.2%. **Median age:** 36.7.

Income 2000: per capita $22,913; median household $52,806; **Pop below poverty level:** 4.6%. ***Personal per capita income 2000-2003:** $28,659-$28,464.

Unemployment 2004: 5.3%. **Change from 2000:** +2.5%. **Median travel time to work:** 24.2 minutes. **Working outside county of residence:** 65.6%.

Cities with pop over 10,000: None.

CRAWFORD COUNTY

200 W Michigan Ave   **Ph:** 989-344-3206
Grayling, MI 49738   **Fax:** 989-344-3223
www.crawfordco.org

In north-central MI; established Apr 1, 1840 as Shawano County; name changed Mar 8, 1843. **Name Origin:** For Col. William Crawford (1732-82), VA officer in the Revolutionary War, Indian fighter, and surveyor.

Area (sq mi): 563.37 (land 558.12; water 5.25). **Pop per sq mi:** 27.

Pop 2005: 15,074. **State rank:** 70. **Pop change:** 2000-20005 +5.6%; 1990-2000 +16.4%. **Pop 2000:** 14,273 (White 95.7%; Black or African American 1.5%; Hispanic or Latino 1%; Asian 0.3%; Other 1.9%). **Foreign born:** 1.3%. **Median age:** 40.6.

Income 2000: per capita $16,903; median household $33,364; **Pop below poverty level:** 12.7%. ***Personal per capita income 2000-2003:** $19,683-$20,135.

Unemployment 2004: 7.5%. **Change from 2000:** +0.7%. **Median travel time to work:** 21.3 minutes. **Working outside county of residence:** 35.7%.

Cities with pop over 10,000: None.

DELTA COUNTY

310 Ludington St   **Ph:** 906-789-5105
Escanaba, MI 49829   **Fax:** 906-789-5196
www.deltami.org

On the Upper Peninsula of MI on Green Bay; established Mar 9, 1843 from Schoolcraft County. **Name Origin:** For the Greek letter, which the shape of the county resembles.

Area (sq mi): 1991.58 (land 1170.03; water 821.56). **Pop per sq mi:** 32.8.

Pop 2005: 38,347. **State rank:** 43. **Pop change:** 2000-20005 -0.4%; 1990-2000 +2%. **Pop 2000:** 38,520 (White 95.5%; Black or African American 0.1%; Hispanic or Latino 0.5%; Asian 0.3%; Other 3.7%, including 2.2% American Indian/Alaska Native). **Foreign born:** 1%. **Median age:** 40.4.

Income 2000: per capita $18,667; median household $35,511; **Pop below poverty level:** 9.5%. ***Personal per capita income 2000-2003:** $23,121-$24,704.

Unemployment 2004: 7.9%. **Change from 2000:** +0.6%. **Median travel time to work:** 18.8 minutes. **Working outside county of residence:** 11.9%.

Cities with pop over 10,000: Escanaba 🏛 (12,752).

DICKINSON COUNTY

PO Box 609   **Ph:** 906-774-0988
Iron Mountain, MI 49801   **Fax:** 906-774-4660
www.dickinsoncountymi.org

On the south-central border of the Upper Peninsula of MI, south of Ishpeming; established May 21, 1891 from Marquette County. **Name Origin:** For Donald McDonald Dickinson (1846-1917), U.S. postmaster-general (1887-89).

Area (sq mi): 777.12 (land 766.34; water 10.78). **Pop per sq mi:** 36.6.

Pop 2005: 28,032. **State rank:** 52. **Pop change:** 2000-20005 +2%; 1990-2000 +2.4%. **Pop 2000:** 27,472 (White 97.5%; Black or African American 0.1%; Hispanic or Latino 0.7%; Asian 0.4%; Other 1.4%). **Foreign born:** 1.1%. **Median age:** 40.

Income 2000: per capita $18,516; median household $34,825; **Pop below poverty level:** 9.1%. ***Personal per capita income 2000-2003:** $25,257-$27,727.

Unemployment 2004: 6.4%. **Change from 2000:** +1.3%. **Median travel time to work:** 15.7 minutes. **Working outside county of residence:** 9.6%.

Cities with pop over 10,000: None.

EATON COUNTY

1045 Independence Blvd   **Ph:** 517-543-7500
Charlotte, MI 48813   **Fax:** 517-541-0666
www.co.eaton.mi.us

In south-central MI, east of Lansing; established Oct 29, 1829. **Name Origin:** For John Henry Eaton (1790-1856), U.S. senator

Eaton County (cont'd)

from TN (1818-29), U.S. secretary of War (1829-31), and governor of FL Territory (1834-36).

Area (sq mi): 579.02 (land 576.41; water 2.61). **Pop per sq mi:** 186.3.

Pop 2005: 107,394. **State rank:** 20. **Pop change:** 2000-20005 +3.6%; 1990-2000 +11.6%. **Pop 2000:** 103,655 (White 88.7%; Black or African American 5.3%; Hispanic or Latino 3.2%; Asian 1.1%; Other 3.3%). **Foreign born:** 2.2%. **Median age:** 36.4.

Income 2000: per capita $22,411; median household $49,588; **Pop below poverty level:** 5.8%. ***Personal per capita income 2000-2003:** $26,982-$28,399.

Unemployment 2004: 5.4%. **Change from 2000:** +2.2%. **Median travel time to work:** 22.4 minutes. **Working outside county of residence:** 55.5%.

Cities with pop over 10,000: None.

EMMET COUNTY

200 Division St   **Ph:** 231-348-1744
Petoskey, MI 49770   **Fax:** 231-348-0602
www.co.emmet.mi.us

On the northwest coast of MI, bordered on west by Lake Michigan; established as Tonedagana County Apr 1, 1840 from Mackinac County; name changed Mar 8, 1843. **Name Origin:** For Robert W. Emmet (1778-1803), Irish rebel executed by the British; named for him during a time when rebel leaders were honored by Americans.

Area (sq mi): 882.26 (land 467.82; water 414.44). **Pop per sq mi:** 71.8.

Pop 2005: 33,580. **State rank:** 46. **Pop change:** 2000-20005 +6.8%; 1990-2000 +25.5%. **Pop 2000:** 31,437 (White 93.8%; Black or African American 0.5%; Hispanic or Latino 0.9%; Asian 0.4%; Other 4.8%, including 3.1% American Indian/Alaska Native). **Foreign born:** 1.7%. **Median age:** 38.9.

Income 2000: per capita $21,070; median household $40,222; **Pop below poverty level:** 7.4%. ***Personal per capita income 2000-2003:** $27,459-$30,467.

Unemployment 2004: 8.1%. **Change from 2000:** +1%. **Median travel time to work:** 19.1 minutes. **Working outside county of residence:** 12.8%.

Cities with pop over 10,000: None.

GENESEE COUNTY

900 S Saginaw St Rm 202   **Ph:** 810-257-3282
Flint, MI 48502   **Fax:** 810-257-3464
www.co.genesee.mi.us

In east-central MI, northeast of Lansing; organized Mar 28, 1835 (prior to statehood) from Oakland County. **Name Origin:** For Genesee County, NY, former home of many early settlers; from Iroquoian 'beautiful valley.'

Area (sq mi): 649.34 (land 639.64; water 9.7). **Pop per sq mi:** 694.

Pop 2005: 443,883. **State rank:** 5. **Pop change:** 2000-20005 +1.8%; 1990-2000 +1.3%. **Pop 2000:** 436,141 (White 74.1%; Black or African American 20.4%; Hispanic or Latino 2.3%; Asian 0.8%; Other 3.6%). **Foreign born:** 2.1%. **Median age:** 35.

Income 2000: per capita $20,883; median household $41,951; **Pop below poverty level:** 13.1%. ***Personal per capita income 2000-2003:** $26,430-$27,521.

Unemployment 2004: 8.3%. **Change from 2000:** +0.7%. **Median travel time to work:** 25.6 minutes. **Working outside county of residence:** 22.7%.

Cities with pop over 10,000: Flint ⚒ (119,716); Burton (30,926); Fenton (11,911).

GLADWIN COUNTY

401 W Cedar Ave   **Ph:** 989-426-7351
Gladwin, MI 48624   **Fax:** 989-426-6917
www.gladwinco.com

In east-central MI, north of Midland; established Mar 2, 1831 (prior to statehood) from unorganized territory. **Name Origin:** For Gen. Henry Gladwin (1729-91), British soldier during the French and Indian War and defender of Detroit against Chief Pontiac.

Area (sq mi): 516.43 (land 506.8; water 9.63). **Pop per sq mi:** 53.7.

Pop 2005: 27,209. **State rank:** 54. **Pop change:** 2000-20005 +4.6%; 1990-2000 +18.8%. **Pop 2000:** 26,023 (White 97.1%; Black or African American 0.1%; Hispanic or Latino 1%; Asian 0.3%; Other 2%). **Foreign born:** 1.3%. **Median age:** 42.3.

Income 2000: per capita $16,614; median household $32,019; **Pop below poverty level:** 13.8%. ***Personal per capita income 2000-2003:** $19,933-$21,263.

Unemployment 2004: 10.4%. **Change from 2000:** +1.8%. **Median travel time to work:** 29.5 minutes. **Working outside county of residence:** 44.8%.

Cities with pop over 10,000: None.

GOGEBIC COUNTY

200 N Moore St   **Ph:** 906-663-4518
Bessemer, MI 49911   **Fax:** 906-663-4660
www.gogebic.org

On the southwest border of the Upper Peninsula of MI; organized Feb 7, 1887 from Ontonagon County. **Name Origin:** From Ojibway *agogebic*, of uncertain origin, though *bic* translates to 'lake'; also possibly 'trembling ground.'

Area (sq mi): 1476.43 (land 1101.86; water 374.57). **Pop per sq mi:** 15.3.

Pop 2005: 16,861. **State rank:** 68. **Pop change:** 2000-20005 -2.9%; 1990-2000 -3.8%. **Pop 2000:** 17,370 (White 93.8%; Black or African American 1.8%; Hispanic or Latino 0.9%; Asian 0.2%; Other 3.7%, including 2.2% American Indian/Alaska Native). **Foreign born:** 1.3%. **Median age:** 42.9.

Income 2000: per capita $16,169; median household $27,405; **Pop below poverty level:** 14.4%. ***Personal per capita income 2000-2003:** $20,035-$20,985.

Unemployment 2004: 7.9%. **Change from 2000:** +0.6%. **Median travel time to work:** 17.3 minutes. **Working outside county of residence:** 21.2%.

Cities with pop over 10,000: None.

*Source: Personal per capita income data are from the Bureau of Economic Analysis; per capita income data are from the Bureau of the Census. See Introduction for explanation of differences.

350

GRAND TRAVERSE COUNTY

400 Boardman Ave   **Ph:** 231-922-4760
Traverse City, MI 49684   **Fax:** 231-922-4658
www.grandtraverse.org

On the northwest coast of MI on Grand Traverse Bay; organized as Omeena County Apr 1, 1840; name changed Apr 17, 1851. **Name Origin:** From French *Le Grand Traverse* 'the long crossing,' for the trail across the foot of Traverse Bay.

Area (sq mi): 601.13 (land 465.07; water 136.06). **Pop per sq mi:** 180.6.

Pop 2005: 83,971. **State rank:** 24. **Pop change:** 2000-20005 +8.1%; 1990-2000 +20.8%. **Pop 2000:** 77,654 (White 95.6%; Black or African American 0.4%; Hispanic or Latino 1.5%; Asian 0.5%; Other 2.5%). **Foreign born:** 2.1%. **Median age:** 37.7.

Income 2000: per capita $22,111; median household $43,169; **Pop below poverty level:** 5.9%. *****Personal per capita income 2000-2003:** $28,912-$29,662.

Unemployment 2004: 6.4%. **Change from 2000:** +1.4%. **Median travel time to work:** 20.5 minutes. **Working outside county of residence:** 11.3%.

Cities with pop over 10,000: Traverse City ⛪ (14,508).

GRATIOT COUNTY

County Courthouse
214 E Center St PO Box 437   **Ph:** 989-875-5215
Ithaca, MI 48847   **Fax:** 989-875-5284
www.gratiotcounty.org

In central MI, north of Lansing; established Mar 2, 1831 from Saginaw County. **Name Origin:** For Gen. Charles Gratiot (1786-1855), U.S. army officer who built Ft. Gratiot at Port Huron (1814); chief engineer of U.S. Army (1828-38).

Area (sq mi): 571.61 (land 570.13; water 1.48). **Pop per sq mi:** 74.3.

Pop 2005: 42,345. **State rank:** 41. **Pop change:** 2000-20005 +0.1%; 1990-2000 +8.5%. **Pop 2000:** 42,285 (White 89.9%; Black or African American 3.7%; Hispanic or Latino 4.4%; Asian 0.3%; Other 3.9%). **Foreign born:** 1.2%. **Median age:** 35.6.

Income 2000: per capita $17,118; median household $37,262; **Pop below poverty level:** 10.3%. *****Personal per capita income 2000-2003:** $20,048-$22,287.

Unemployment 2004: 8%. **Change from 2000:** +2.5%. **Median travel time to work:** 22.7 minutes. **Working outside county of residence:** 30.7%.

Cities with pop over 10,000: None.

HILLSDALE COUNTY

29 N Howell St   **Ph:** 517-437-3391
Hillsdale, MI 49242   **Fax:** 517-437-3392
www.co.hillsdale.mi.us

On the south-central border of MI, southeast of Kalamazoo; established Oct 29, 1829 (prior to statehood) from Lenawee County. **Name Origin:** For its topography of hills and dales.

Area (sq mi): 607.14 (land 598.84; water 8.3). **Pop per sq mi:** 78.6.

Pop 2005: 47,066. **State rank:** 37. **Pop change:** 2000-20005 +1.2%; 1990-2000 +7.1%. **Pop 2000:** 46,527 (White 96.8%; Black or African American 0.4%; Hispanic or Latino 1.2%; Asian 0.3%; Other 1.7%). **Foreign born:** 1.1%. **Median age:** 36.5.

Income 2000: per capita $18,255; median household $40,396; **Pop below poverty level:** 8.2%. *****Personal per capita income 2000-2003:** $22,740-$23,742.

Unemployment 2004: 8.4%. **Change from 2000:** +1.9%. **Median travel time to work:** 23.6 minutes. **Working outside county of residence:** 31.5%.

Cities with pop over 10,000: None.

HOUGHTON COUNTY

401 E Houghton Ave   **Ph:** 906-482-1150
Houghton, MI 49931   **Fax:** 906-483-0364
www.houghtoncounty.net

On the northwest coast of the Upper Peninsula of MI; organized Mar 19, 1845 from Marquette, Schoolcraft, and Ontonagon counties. **Name Origin:** For Douglas Houghton (1809-45), professor and pioneer state geologist (1834-41).

Area (sq mi): 1501.56 (land 1011.72; water 489.84). **Pop per sq mi:** 35.3.

Pop 2005: 35,705. **State rank:** 44. **Pop change:** 2000-20005 -0.9%; 1990-2000 +1.6%. **Pop 2000:** 36,016 (White 95.1%; Black or African American 0.9%; Hispanic or Latino 0.7%; Asian 1.8%; Other 1.7%). **Foreign born:** 2.7%. **Median age:** 34.

Income 2000: per capita $15,078; median household $28,817; **Pop below poverty level:** 16.8%. *****Personal per capita income 2000-2003:** $19,436-$20,747.

Unemployment 2004: 6.4%. **Change from 2000:** +0.5%. **Median travel time to work:** 15.6 minutes. **Working outside county of residence:** 7.1%.

Cities with pop over 10,000: None.

HURON COUNTY

250 E Huron Ave Rm 305   **Ph:** 989-269-8242
Bad Axe, MI 48413   **Fax:** 989-269-6152
www.huroncounty.com

On the east coast of MI on Saginaw Bay; organized Apr 1, 1840 from Sanilac and Tuscola counties. **Name Origin:** For the Huron Indians (later known as Wyandots), a tribe of Iroquoian linguistic stock; from a French word for 'rough,' probably because they were formidable opponents.

Area (sq mi): 2136.47 (land 836.52; water 1299.95). **Pop per sq mi:** 41.4.

Pop 2005: 34,640. **State rank:** 45. **Pop change:** 2000-20005 -4%; 1990-2000 +3.2%. **Pop 2000:** 36,079 (White 96.8%; Black or African American 0.2%; Hispanic or Latino 1.6%; Asian 0.4%; Other 1.4%). **Foreign born:** 1.4%. **Median age:** 41.2.

Income 2000: per capita $17,851; median household $35,315; **Pop below poverty level:** 10.2%. *****Personal per capita income 2000-2003:** $24,811-$26,175.

Unemployment 2004: 8.8%. **Change from 2000:** +0.6%. **Median travel time to work:** 20.6 minutes. **Working outside county of residence:** 14%.

Huron County (cont'd)

Cities with pop over 10,000: None.

INGHAM COUNTY

315 S Jefferson St   **Ph:** 517-676-7204
Mason, MI 48854   **Fax:** 517-676-7254
www.ingham.org

In south-central MI; established Oct 29, 1829 (prior to statehood) from unorganized territory. **Name Origin:** For Samuel Delucenna Ingham (1779-1860), U.S. representative from PA (1813-18; 1822-29) and U.S. secretary of the treasury (1829-31).

Area (sq mi): 560.94 (land 559.19; water 1.75). **Pop per sq mi:** 498.2.

Pop 2005: 278,592. **State rank:** 7. **Pop change:** 2000-20005 -0.3%; 1990-2000 -0.9%. **Pop 2000:** 279,320 (White 76.9%; Black or African American 10.9%; Hispanic or Latino 5.8%; Asian 3.7%; Other 6%). **Foreign born:** 6.3%. **Median age:** 30.4.

Income 2000: per capita $21,079; median household $40,774; **Pop below poverty level:** 14.6%. ***Personal per capita income 2000-2003:** $26,483-$28,825.

Unemployment 2004: 6.3%. **Change from 2000:** +2.7%. **Median travel time to work:** 20.1 minutes. **Working outside county of residence:** 19.6%.

Cities with pop over 10,000: Lansing ⚖ (116,941); East Lansing (46,678).

IONIA COUNTY

100 Main St   **Ph:** 616-527-5322
Ionia, MI 48846   **Fax:** 616-527-8201
www.ioniacounty.org

In central MI, east of Grand Rapids; established Mar 2, 1831 (prior to statehood) from unorganized territory. **Name Origin:** For the ancient province in Greece.

Area (sq mi): 580.23 (land 573.21; water 7.02). **Pop per sq mi:** 112.7.

Pop 2005: 64,608. **State rank:** 30. **Pop change:** 2000-20005 +5%; 1990-2000 +7.9%. **Pop 2000:** 61,518 (White 90.6%; Black or African American 4.6%; Hispanic or Latino 2.8%; Asian 0.3%; Other 3.1%). **Foreign born:** 1.2%. **Median age:** 32.9.

Income 2000: per capita $17,451; median household $43,074; **Pop below poverty level:** 8.7%. ***Personal per capita income 2000-2003:** $20,941-$22,319.

Unemployment 2004: 8.1%. **Change from 2000:** +2.4%. **Median travel time to work:** 27.6 minutes. **Working outside county of residence:** 51.8%.

Cities with pop over 10,000: Ionia ⚖ (12,359).

IOSCO COUNTY

PO Box 778   **Ph:** 989-362-4212
Tawas City, MI 48764   **Fax:** 989-984-1002
iosco.m33access.com

On the east-central coast of MI bordered on east by Lake Huron;

organized as Kanotin County Apr 1, 1840 from unorganized territory; name changed Mar 8, 1843. **Name Origin:** From an Indian word meaning 'shining water' or 'water of light.'

Area (sq mi): 1890.77 (land 549.11; water 1341.66). **Pop per sq mi:** 49.2.

Pop 2005: 26,992. **State rank:** 55. **Pop change:** 2000-20005 -1.3%; 1990-2000 -9.5%. **Pop 2000:** 27,339 (White 96.3%; Black or African American 0.4%; Hispanic or Latino 1%; Asian 0.5%; Other 2.3%). **Foreign born:** 1.3%. **Median age:** 44.2.

Income 2000: per capita $17,115; median household $31,321; **Pop below poverty level:** 12.7%. ***Personal per capita income 2000-2003:** $19,900-$20,740.

Unemployment 2004: 9.7%. **Change from 2000:** -0.9%. **Median travel time to work:** 21.8 minutes. **Working outside county of residence:** 15.2%.

Cities with pop over 10,000: None.

IRON COUNTY

2 S 6th St   **Ph:** 906-875-3221
Crystal Falls, MI 49920   **Fax:** 906-875-6775
www.iron.org

On the southwest border of the Upper Peninsula of MI; established Apr 3, 1885 from Marquette and Menominee counties. **Name Origin:** For the iron mines in the area.

Area (sq mi): 1211.02 (land 1166.36; water 44.67). **Pop per sq mi:** 10.5.

Pop 2005: 12,299. **State rank:** 72. **Pop change:** 2000-20005 -6.4%; 1990-2000 -0.3%. **Pop 2000:** 13,138 (White 95.9%; Black or African American 1.1%; Hispanic or Latino 0.6%; Asian 0.2%; Other 2.4%, including 1% American Indian/Alaska Native). **Foreign born:** 1.1%. **Median age:** 45.4.

Income 2000: per capita $16,506; median household $28,560; **Pop below poverty level:** 11.3%. ***Personal per capita income 2000-2003:** $20,344-$22,822.

Unemployment 2004: 7.5%. **Change from 2000:** +1%. **Median travel time to work:** 20.2 minutes. **Working outside county of residence:** 17.4%.

Cities with pop over 10,000: None.

ISABELLA COUNTY

200 N Main St   **Ph:** 989-772-0911
Mount Pleasant, MI 48858   **Fax:** 989-773-7431
www.isabellacounty.org

In central MI, west of Midland; organized Mar 2, 1831 (prior to statehood) from unorganized territory. **Name Origin:** For Isabella (1451-1504), queen of Spain who financed Christopher Columbus's expeditions.

Area (sq mi): 577.75 (land 574.27; water 3.48). **Pop per sq mi:** 114.3.

Pop 2005: 65,618. **State rank:** 28. **Pop change:** 2000-20005 +3.6%; 1990-2000 +16%. **Pop 2000:** 63,351 (White 90.4%; Black or African American 1.9%; Hispanic or Latino 2.2%; Asian 1.4%; Other 5.2%, including 2.8% American Indian/Alaska Native). **Foreign born:** 2.3%. **Median age:** 25.1.

---

*Source: Personal per capita income data are from the Bureau of Economic Analysis; per capita income data are from the Bureau of the Census. See Introduction for explanation of differences.

Isabella County (cont'd)

Income 2000: per capita $16,242; median household $34,262; **Pop below poverty level:** 20.4%. ***Personal per capita income 2000-2003:** $20,538-$22,111.

Unemployment 2004: 4.9%. **Change from 2000:** +1.6%. **Median travel time to work:** 18.2 minutes. **Working outside county of residence:** 20.6%.

Cities with pop over 10,000: Mount Pleasant 🏛 (25,651).

JACKSON COUNTY

312 S Jackson St 1st Fl   **Ph:** 517-788-4265
Jackson, MI 49201   **Fax:** 517-788-4601
www.co.jackson.mi.us

In south-central MI, west of Ann Arbor, established Oct 29, 1829 (prior to statehood) from Washtenaw County. **Name Origin:** For Andrew Jackson (1767-1845), seventh U.S. president.

Area (sq mi): 723.76 (land 706.6; water 17.17). **Pop per sq mi:** 231.6.

Pop 2005: 163,629. **State rank:** 14. **Pop change:** 2000-20005 +3.3%; 1990-2000 +5.8%. **Pop 2000:** 158,422 (White 87.4%; Black or African American 7.9%; Hispanic or Latino 2.2%; Asian 0.5%; Other 2.9%). **Foreign born:** 1.7%. **Median age:** 36.6.

Income 2000: per capita $20,171; median household $43,171; **Pop below poverty level:** 9%. ***Personal per capita income 2000-2003:** $24,984-$25,712.

Unemployment 2004: 7.6%. **Change from 2000:** +2.3%. **Median travel time to work:** 23.1 minutes. **Working outside county of residence:** 24.1%.

Cities with pop over 10,000: Jackson 🏛 (35,133).

KALAMAZOO COUNTY

201 W Kalamazoo Ave   **Ph:** 269-383-8840
Kalamazoo, MI 49007   **Fax:** 269-384-8143
www.kalcounty.com

In southwest MI, south of Grand Rapids; organized Oct 29, 1829 (prior to statehood) from Saint Joseph County. **Name Origin:** From Algonquian, *ke-kala-mazoo*, meaning uncertain, interpreted as connected with 'smoke,' 'beautiful water,' 'otters,' or 'boiling water.'

Area (sq mi): 580.18 (land 561.86; water 18.32). **Pop per sq mi:** 428.1.

Pop 2005: 240,536. **State rank:** 9. **Pop change:** 2000-20005 +0.8%; 1990-2000 +6.8%. **Pop 2000:** 238,603 (White 83.5%; Black or African American 9.7%; Hispanic or Latino 2.6%; Asian 1.8%; Other 3.9%). **Foreign born:** 4%. **Median age:** 32.7.

Income 2000: per capita $21,739; median household $42,022; **Pop below poverty level:** 12%. ***Personal per capita income 2000-2003:** $27,813-$30,429.

Unemployment 2004: 5.8%. **Change from 2000:** +1.6%. **Median travel time to work:** 19.7 minutes. **Working outside county of residence:** 14.3%.

Cities with pop over 10,000: Kalamazoo 🏛 (73,960); Portage (45,210).

KALKASKA COUNTY

PO Box 10   **Ph:** 231-258-3300
Kalkaska, MI 49646   **Fax:** 231-258-3337
www.kalkaskami.com

In north-central MI, east of Traverse City; established as Wabassee County Apr 1, 1840 from Crawford County; name changed Mar 8, 1843. **Name Origin:** From an Indian word of uncertain origin and meaning, although some sources suggest that it is from a Chippewa word meaning 'burned over.'

Area (sq mi): 570.76 (land 561.02; water 9.75). **Pop per sq mi:** 30.7.

Pop 2005: 17,239. **State rank:** 66. **Pop change:** 2000-20005 +4%; 1990-2000 +22.8%. **Pop 2000:** 16,571 (White 96.9%; Black or African American 0.2%; Hispanic or Latino 0.9%; Asian 0.2%; Other 2%). **Foreign born:** 0.8%. **Median age:** 38.

Income 2000: per capita $16,309; median household $36,072; **Pop below poverty level:** 10.5%. ***Personal per capita income 2000-2003:** $18,350-$18,881.

Unemployment 2004: 7.7%. **Change from 2000:** -1.4%. **Median travel time to work:** 28.2 minutes. **Working outside county of residence:** 52%.

Cities with pop over 10,000: None.

KENT COUNTY

300 Monroe Ave NW   **Ph:** 616-336-3550
Grand Rapids, MI 49503   **Fax:** 616-336-2885
www.accesskent.com

In west-central MI, east of Muskegon; established Mar 2, 1831 (prior to statehood) from unorganized territory. **Name Origin:** For James Kent (1763-1847), chief justice of the NY supreme court (1804-14).

Area (sq mi): 872.18 (land 856.17; water 16.01). **Pop per sq mi:** 696.9.

Pop 2005: 596,666. **State rank:** 4. **Pop change:** 2000-20005 +3.9%; 1990-2000 +14.7%. **Pop 2000:** 574,335 (White 80.3%; Black or African American 8.9%; Hispanic or Latino 7%; Asian 1.9%; Other 6.1%). **Foreign born:** 6.6%. **Median age:** 32.5.

Income 2000: per capita $21,629; median household $45,980; **Pop below poverty level:** 8.9%. ***Personal per capita income 2000-2003:** $29,392-$30,624.

Unemployment 2004: 6.9%. **Change from 2000:** +1.9%. **Median travel time to work:** 20.7 minutes. **Working outside county of residence:** 9%.

Cities with pop over 10,000: 6 (see page 35 for cities).

KEWEENAW COUNTY

5095 Forest St   **Ph:** 906-337-2229
Eagle River, MI 49950   **Fax:** 906-337-2795
www.keweenaw.org

On northernmost tip of the Upper Peninsula of MI on Lake Superior; organized Mar 11, 1861 from Houghton County. **Name Origin:** From Ojibway (or Potawatomi), probably 'to cross a point,' or 'portage,' variant of Kewaunee.

Area (sq mi): 5965.96 (land 540.97; water 5424.98). **Pop per sq mi:** 4.1.

🏛 *County Seat*

Keweenaw County (cont'd)

Pop 2005: 2,195. **State rank:** 83. **Pop change:** 2000-20005 -4.6%; 1990-2000 +35.3%. **Pop 2000:** 2,301 (White 94.6%; Black or African American 3.5%; Hispanic or Latino 0.8%; Asian 0.1%; Other 1.4%). **Foreign born:** 1%. **Median age:** 44.9.

Income 2000: per capita $16,769; median household $28,140; **Pop below poverty level:** 12.7%. *Personal per capita income 2000-2003:** $20,900-$22,422.

Unemployment 2004: 11.9%. **Change from 2000:** +2%. **Median travel time to work:** 21.3 minutes. **Working outside county of residence:** 61.3%.

Cities with pop over 10,000: None.

LAKE COUNTY

800 10th St Suite 200   **Ph:** 231-745-2725
Baldwin, MI 49304   **Fax:** 231-745-8632
www.lakecountymichigan.com

In west-central MI, north of Grand Rapids; established as Aishcum County Apr 1, 1840; name changed Mar 8, 1843. **Name Origin:** Possibly for Lake Michigan.

Area (sq mi): 574.6 (land 567.44; water 7.17). **Pop per sq mi:** 21.3.

Pop 2005: 12,069. **State rank:** 73. **Pop change:** 2000-20005 +6.5%; 1990-2000 +32%. **Pop 2000:** 11,333 (White 83.9%; Black or African American 11.2%; Hispanic or Latino 1.7%; Asian 0.2%; Other 4%, including 1% American Indian/Alaska Native). **Foreign born:** 1%. **Median age:** 43.1.

Income 2000: per capita $14,457; median household $26,622; **Pop below poverty level:** 19.4%. *Personal per capita income 2000-2003:** $18,596-$20,246.

Unemployment 2004: 10.5%. **Change from 2000:** +1.3%. **Median travel time to work:** 30.6 minutes. **Working outside county of residence:** 57.3%.

Cities with pop over 10,000: None.

LAPEER COUNTY

255 Clay St   **Ph:** 810-667-0356
Lapeer, MI 48446   **Fax:** 810-667-0362
www.county.lapeer.org

In east-central MI, east of Flint; established Sept 10, 1822 (prior to statehood) from Oakland and Saint Clair counties. **Name Origin:** From the local spelling of French *la pierre* 'the stone' or 'flint', probably a transliteration of an Indian name for the Flint River, for its rocky bed.

Area (sq mi): 663.08 (land 654.2; water 8.88). **Pop per sq mi:** 142.7.

Pop 2005: 93,361. **State rank:** 22. **Pop change:** 2000-20005 +6.2%; 1990-2000 +17.6%. **Pop 2000:** 87,904 (White 94.4%; Black or African American 0.8%; Hispanic or Latino 3.1%; Asian 0.4%; Other 2.7%). **Foreign born:** 2.2%. **Median age:** 35.9.

Income 2000: per capita $21,462; median household $51,717; **Pop below poverty level:** 5.4%. *Personal per capita income 2000-2003:** $28,089-$27,928.

Unemployment 2004: 7.7%. **Change from 2000:** +1%. **Median travel time to work:** 35.3 minutes. **Working outside county of residence:** 54.2%.

Cities with pop over 10,000: None.

LEELANAU COUNTY

PO Box 467   **Ph:** 231-256-9824
Leland, MI 49654   **Fax:** 231-256-8295
www.leelanaucounty.com

On the northwest coast of MI, bordered on the west by Lake Michigan; established Apr 1, 1840. **Name Origin:** For an Indian maid, supposedly, whose name means 'delight of life.' Named at the suggestion of Henry Rowe Schoolcraft (1793-1864), author, explorer, MI legislator, and superintendent of Indian Affairs for MI (1836-41).

Area (sq mi): 2532.38 (land 348.47; water 2183.91). **Pop per sq mi:** 63.6.

Pop 2005: 22,157. **State rank:** 63. **Pop change:** 2000-20005 +4.9%; 1990-2000 +27.8%. **Pop 2000:** 21,119 (White 92%; Black or African American 0.2%; Hispanic or Latino 3.3%; Asian 0.2%; Other 6%, including 3.7% American Indian/Alaska Native). **Foreign born:** 2.2%. **Median age:** 42.6.

Income 2000: per capita $24,686; median household $47,062; **Pop below poverty level:** 5.4%. *Personal per capita income 2000-2003:** $27,981-$31,599.

Unemployment 2004: 5.3%. **Change from 2000:** +1.9%. **Median travel time to work:** 22.6 minutes. **Working outside county of residence:** 47.6%.

Cities with pop over 10,000: None.

LENAWEE COUNTY

425 N Main St   **Ph:** 517-264-4606
Adrian, MI 49221   **Fax:** 517-264-4790
www.lenawee.mi.us

On the southern border of MI, southwest of Ann Arbor; established Sep 10, 1822 (prior to statehood) from Indian lands. **Name Origin:** Origin uncertain; perhaps from an Indian word meaning 'man'.

Area (sq mi): 761.31 (land 750.5; water 10.81). **Pop per sq mi:** 136.

Pop 2005: 102,033. **State rank:** 21. **Pop change:** 2000-20005 +3.2%; 1990-2000 +8.1%. **Pop 2000:** 98,890 (White 89.2%; Black or African American 2.1%; Hispanic or Latino 7%; Asian 0.5%; Other 4.9%). **Foreign born:** 1.6%. **Median age:** 36.4.

Income 2000: per capita $20,186; median household $45,739; **Pop below poverty level:** 6.7%. *Personal per capita income 2000-2003:** $25,998-$28,452.

Unemployment 2004: 7.4%. **Change from 2000:** +1.9%. **Median travel time to work:** 25 minutes. **Working outside county of residence:** 32.2%.

Cities with pop over 10,000: Adrian 🏛 (21,977).

LIVINGSTON COUNTY

200 E Grand River Ave   **Ph:** 517-546-0500
Howell, MI 48843   **Fax:** 517-546-4354
www.co.livingston.mi.us

In south-central MI, southwest of Flint; established Mar 21, 1833 (prior to statehood) from Shiawassee County. **Name Origin:** For Edward Livingston (1764-1836), NY legislator, LA legislator and U.S. senator (1829-31), and U.S. secretary of state (1831-33).

Source: Personal per capita income data are from the Bureau of Economic Analysis; per capita income data are from the Bureau of the Census. See Introduction for explanation of differences.

Livingston County (cont'd)

Area (sq mi): 585.43 (land 568.4; water 17.03). **Pop per sq mi:** 319.3.

Pop 2005: 181,517. **State rank:** 11. **Pop change:** 2000-20005 +15.7%; 1990-2000 +35.7%. **Pop 2000:** 156,951 (White 96.3%; Black or African American 0.5%; Hispanic or Latino 1.2%; Asian 0.6%; Other 1.8%). **Foreign born:** 3%. **Median age:** 36.2.

Income 2000: per capita $28,069; median household $67,400; **Pop below poverty level:** 3.4%. *Personal per capita income 2000-2003:** $35,804-$35,869.

Unemployment 2004: 4.8%. **Change from 2000:** +1.7%. **Median travel time to work:** 31 minutes. **Working outside county of residence:** 57.5%.

Cities with pop over 10,000: None.

LUCE COUNTY
407 W Harrie St   **Ph:** 906-293-5521
Newberry, MI 49868   **Fax:** 906-293-0050

On the northern coast of the Upper Peninsula of MI on Lake Superior; established Mar 1, 1887 from Chippewa County. **Name Origin:** For Cyrus Gray Luce (1824-1905), MI legislator, member of MI Constitutional Convention (1867), and governor (1887-96).

Area (sq mi): 1911.89 (land 903.08; water 1008.8). **Pop per sq mi:** 7.5.

Pop 2005: 6,789. **State rank:** 82. **Pop change:** 2000-20005 -3.3%; 1990-2000 +21.9%. **Pop 2000:** 7,024 (White 82.4%; Black or African American 7.5%; Hispanic or Latino 1.8%; Asian 0.4%; Other 9.2%, including 5.5% American Indian/Alaska Native). **Foreign born:** 1.1%. **Median age:** 38.6.

Income 2000: per capita $16,828; median household $32,031; **Pop below poverty level:** 14.9%. *Personal per capita income 2000-2003:** $17,184-$18,829.

Unemployment 2004: 7.5%. **Change from 2000:** +0.6%. **Median travel time to work:** 18.5 minutes. **Working outside county of residence:** 12.6%.

Cities with pop over 10,000: None.

MACKINAC COUNTY
100 S Marley St   **Ph:** 906-643-7300
Saint Ignace, MI 49781   **Fax:** 906-643-7302
www.mackinaccounty.net

On the southeast coast of the Upper Peninsula of MI bordering Lakes Michigan and Huron; original county; established as Michilimackinac County Oct 26, 1818 (prior to statehood); name changed Mar 9, 1843. **Name Origin:** For Mackinac Island, from Ojibway *Michilimackinak* 'island of the large turtle.'

Area (sq mi): 2100.55 (land 1021.58; water 1078.96). **Pop per sq mi:** 11.1.

Pop 2005: 11,331. **State rank:** 75. **Pop change:** 2000-20005 -5.1%; 1990-2000 +11.9%. **Pop 2000:** 11,943 (White 79.6%; Black or African American 0.2%; Hispanic or Latino 0.9%; Asian 0.3%; Other 19.4%, including 14.2% American Indian/Alaska Native). **Foreign born:** 1.2%. **Median age:** 42.8.

Income 2000: per capita $17,777; median household $33,356; **Pop below poverty level:** 10.5%. *Personal per capita income 2000-2003:** $24,560-$25,663.

Unemployment 2004: 10%. **Change from 2000:** +0.7%. **Median travel time to work:** 22.5 minutes. **Working outside county of residence:** 24.4%.

Cities with pop over 10,000: None.

MACOMB COUNTY
40 N Main St 1st Fl   **Ph:** 586-469-5120
Mount Clemens, MI 48043
macombcountymi.gov

On the southeast coast of MI, north of Detroit; original county; established Jan 15, 1818 (prior to statehood). **Name Origin:** For Alexander Macomb (1782-1841), officer in the War of 1812 and commanding general of the U.S. Army (1835-41).

Area (sq mi): 569.78 (land 480.44; water 89.34). **Pop per sq mi:** 1726.4.

Pop 2005: 829,453. **State rank:** 3. **Pop change:** 2000-20005 +5.2%; 1990-2000 +9.9%. **Pop 2000:** 788,149 (White 91.6%; Black or African American 2.7%; Hispanic or Latino 1.6%; Asian 2.1%; Other 2.5%). **Foreign born:** 8.8%. **Median age:** 36.9.

Income 2000: per capita $24,446; median household $52,102; **Pop below poverty level:** 5.6%. *Personal per capita income 2000-2003:** $32,944-$34,206.

Unemployment 2004: 6.7%. **Change from 2000:** +1.7%. **Median travel time to work:** 26.2 minutes. **Working outside county of residence:** 41.4%.

Cities with pop over 10,000: 8 (see page 35 for cities).

MANISTEE COUNTY
415 3rd St   **Ph:** 231-723-3331
Manistee, MI 49660   **Fax:** 231-723-1492
www.manisteecounty.net

On the northwest coast of MI, bordered on west by Lake Michigan; established Apr 1, 1840. **Name Origin:** For the Manistee River, which runs through it; from an Ojibway word possibly meaning 'sound of the winds,' 'lost river,' 'spirit of the woods,' 'crooked river,' or 'red river.'

Area (sq mi): 1280.77 (land 543.61; water 737.16). **Pop per sq mi:** 46.4.

Pop 2005: 25,226. **State rank:** 58. **Pop change:** 2000-20005 +2.8%; 1990-2000 +15.3%. **Pop 2000:** 24,527 (White 92.9%; Black or African American 1.6%; Hispanic or Latino 2.6%; Asian 0.3%; Other 3.8%, including 1.3% American Indian/Alaska Native). **Foreign born:** 1.3%. **Median age:** 41.5.

Income 2000: per capita $17,204; median household $34,208; **Pop below poverty level:** 10.3%. *Personal per capita income 2000-2003:** $21,881-$22,775.

Unemployment 2004: 8.7%. **Change from 2000:** +1.6%. **Median travel time to work:** 20.9 minutes. **Working outside county of residence:** 20.8%.

Cities with pop over 10,000: None.

MARQUETTE COUNTY

234 W Baraga Ave
Marquette, MI 49855
www.co.marquette.mi.us

Ph: 906-225-8330
Fax: 906-228-1572

On the north coast of the Upper Peninsula of MI on Lake Superior; organized Mar 9, 1843 from Schoolcraft County. **Name Origin:** For Jacques Marquette (1637-75), known as Pere Marquette, French Jesuit missionary and explorer with Louis Joliet (1645-1700).

Area (sq mi): 3425.17 (land 1821.05; water 1604.12). **Pop per sq mi:** 35.6.

Pop 2005: 64,760. **State rank:** 29. **Pop change:** 2000-20005 +0.2%; 1990-2000 -8.8%. **Pop 2000:** 64,634 (White 94.7%; Black or African American 1.3%; Hispanic or Latino 0.7%; Asian 0.5%; Other 3%, including 1.5% American Indian/Alaska Native). **Foreign born:** 1.4%. **Median age:** 37.5.

Income 2000: per capita $18,070; median household $35,548; **Pop below poverty level:** 10.9%. ***Personal per capita income 2000-2003:** $22,315-$24,191.

Unemployment 2004: 6.1%. **Change from 2000:** +0.1%. **Median travel time to work:** 17.7 minutes. **Working outside county of residence:** 4.4%.

Cities with pop over 10,000: Marquette ⛪ (20,664).

MASON COUNTY

304 E Ludington Ave
Ludington, MI 49431

Ph: 231-843-8202
Fax: 231-843-1972

On the west-central coast of MI bordered on west by Lake Michigan; established as Notiopekago County Apr 1, 1840 from Ionia County; name changed Mar 8, 1843. **Name Origin:** For Stevens Thomson Mason (1811-43), secretary and acting governor of MI Territory (1831-35) and first state governor (1835-38).

Area (sq mi): 1241.86 (land 495.17; water 746.7). **Pop per sq mi:** 58.5.

Pop 2005: 28,986. **State rank:** 50. **Pop change:** 2000-20005 +2.5%; 1990-2000 +10.7%. **Pop 2000:** 28,274 (White 94%; Black or African American 0.7%; Hispanic or Latino 3%; Asian 0.3%; Other 3.1%). **Foreign born:** 1.6%. **Median age:** 40.4.

Income 2000: per capita $17,713; median household $34,704; **Pop below poverty level:** 11%. ***Personal per capita income 2000-2003:** $22,678-$24,117.

Unemployment 2004: 9.5%. **Change from 2000:** -1.9%. **Median travel time to work:** 18.9 minutes. **Working outside county of residence:** 15.3%.

Cities with pop over 10,000: None.

MECOSTA COUNTY

400 Elm St
Big Rapids, MI 49307
www.co.mecosta.mi.us

Ph: 231-592-0787
Fax: 231-592-0193

In central MI, northeast of Grand Rapids; established Apr 1, 1840 from Newaygo and Osceola counties. **Name Origin:** For the Potawatomi chief whose name means 'bear cub.'

Area (sq mi): 571.1 (land 555.69; water 15.41). **Pop per sq mi:** 76.3.

Pop 2005: 42,391. **State rank:** 40. **Pop change:** 2000-20005 +4.5%; 1990-2000 +8.7%. **Pop 2000:** 40,553 (White 91.9%; Black or African American 3.6%; Hispanic or Latino 1.3%; Asian 0.9%; Other 2.8%). **Foreign born:** 1.9%. **Median age:** 31.9.

Income 2000: per capita $16,372; median household $33,849; **Pop below poverty level:** 16.1%. ***Personal per capita income 2000-2003:** $18,548-$20,049.

Unemployment 2004: 7.2%. **Change from 2000:** +1.9%. **Median travel time to work:** 24.4 minutes. **Working outside county of residence:** 31%.

Cities with pop over 10,000: Big Rapids ⛪ (10,852).

MENOMINEE COUNTY

839 10th Ave
Menominee, MI 49858
www.menomineecounty.com

Ph: 906-863-9968
Fax: 906-863-8839

On the south-central coast of the Upper Peninsula of MI on Green Bay; established as Bleecker County Mar 19, 1863 from Marquette County; name changed Mar 19, 1863. **Name Origin:** For the Menominee Indians, a tribe of Algonquian linguistic stock; name means 'wild rice people.'

Area (sq mi): 1337.99 (land 1043.52; water 294.47). **Pop per sq mi:** 24.

Pop 2005: 24,996. **State rank:** 59. **Pop change:** 2000-20005 -1.3%; 1990-2000 +1.6%. **Pop 2000:** 25,326 (White 95.8%; Black or African American 0.1%; Hispanic or Latino 0.8%; Asian 0.2%; Other 3.5%, including 2.3% American Indian/Alaska Native). **Foreign born:** 0.9%. **Median age:** 40.4.

Income 2000: per capita $16,909; median household $32,888; **Pop below poverty level:** 11.5%. ***Personal per capita income 2000-2003:** $21,945-$22,558.

Unemployment 2004: 5.8%. **Change from 2000:** -0.8%. **Median travel time to work:** 19.7 minutes. **Working outside county of residence:** 40%.

Cities with pop over 10,000: None.

MIDLAND COUNTY

220 W Ellsworth St
Midland, MI 48640
www.co.midland.mi.us

Ph: 989-832-6739
Fax: 989-832-6680

In central MI, east of Bay City; established Mar 2, 1831 (prior to statehood) from Saginaw County. **Name Origin:** For its location in the geographic center of the state.

Area (sq mi): 527.89 (land 521.19; water 6.7). **Pop per sq mi:** 161.3.

Pop 2005: 84,064. **State rank:** 23. **Pop change:** 2000-20005 +1.4%; 1990-2000 +9.5%. **Pop 2000:** 82,874 (White 94.5%; Black or African American 1%; Hispanic or Latino 1.6%; Asian 1.5%; Other 1.9%). **Foreign born:** 3.2%. **Median age:** 36.3.

Income 2000: per capita $23,383; median household $45,674; **Pop below poverty level:** 8.4%. ***Personal per capita income 2000-2003:** $31,586-$32,821.

Unemployment 2004: 6.5%. **Change from 2000:** +2.5%. **Median travel time to work:** 21.1 minutes. **Working outside county of residence:** 27.1%.

Cities with pop over 10,000: Midland ⛪ (42,145).

---

*Source: Personal per capita income data are from the Bureau of Economic Analysis; per capita income data are from the Bureau of the Census. See Introduction for explanation of differences.

MISSAUKEE COUNTY

PO Box 800   **Ph:** 231-839-4967
Lake City, MI 49651   **Fax:** 231-839-3684
www.missaukee.org

In north-central MI, east of Cadillac; established Apr 1, 1840 from unorganized territory. **Name Origin:** For an Ottawa chief.

Area (sq mi): 573.82 (land 566.75; water 7.08). **Pop per sq mi:** 27.

Pop 2005: 15,299. **State rank:** 69. **Pop change:** 2000-20005 +5.7%; 1990-2000 +19.2%. **Pop 2000:** 14,478 (White 96.9%; Black or African American 0.2%; Hispanic or Latino 1.2%; Asian 0.2%; Other 2.1%). **Foreign born:** 1%. **Median age:** 37.7.

Income 2000: per capita $16,072; median household $35,224; **Pop below poverty level:** 10.7%. ***Personal per capita income 2000-2003:** $19,296-$19,043.

Unemployment 2004: 7.9%. **Change from 2000:** -0.1%. **Median travel time to work:** 24.8 minutes. **Working outside county of residence:** 56.1%.

Cities with pop over 10,000: None.

MONROE COUNTY

106 E 1st St   **Ph:** 734-240-7020
Monroe, MI 48161   **Fax:** 734-240-7045
www.co.monroe.mi.us

In the southeast corner of MI bordered on east by Lake Erie; original county; established Jul 14, 1817 (prior to statehood). **Name Origin:** For James Monroe (1758-1831), fifth U.S. president.

Area (sq mi): 680.03 (land 551.1; water 128.93). **Pop per sq mi:** 279.3.

Pop 2005: 153,935. **State rank:** 16. **Pop change:** 2000-20005 +5.5%; 1990-2000 +9.2%. **Pop 2000:** 145,945 (White 94.1%; Black or African American 1.9%; Hispanic or Latino 2.1%; Asian 0.5%; Other 2.2%). **Foreign born:** 1.9%. **Median age:** 36.

Income 2000: per capita $22,458; median household $51,743; **Pop below poverty level:** 7%. ***Personal per capita income 2000-2003:** $29,223-$29,914.

Unemployment 2004: 6.3%. **Change from 2000:** +2%. **Median travel time to work:** 24 minutes. **Working outside county of residence:** 48.9%.

Cities with pop over 10,000: Monroe 🏛 (21,690).

MONTCALM COUNTY

PO Box 368   **Ph:** 989-831-7339
Stanton, MI 48888   **Fax:** 989-831-7474

In central MI, northeast of Grand Rapids; established Mar 2, 1831 (prior to statehood) from Isabella County. **Name Origin:** For Louis Joseph de Montcalm (1712-59), commander of French troops against the British in Canada.

Area (sq mi): 720.98 (land 708.04; water 12.94). **Pop per sq mi:** 90.2.

Pop 2005: 63,893. **State rank:** 31. **Pop change:** 2000-20005 +4.3%; 1990-2000 +15.5%. **Pop 2000:** 61,266 (White 93.5%; Black or African American 2.2%; Hispanic or Latino 2.3%; Asian 0.3%; Other 2.7%). **Foreign born:** 1.1%. **Median age:** 35.6.

Income 2000: per capita $16,183; median household $37,218; **Pop below poverty level:** 10.9%. ***Personal per capita income 2000-2003:** $18,950-$20,604.

Unemployment 2004: 8.1%. **Change from 2000:** +0.3%. **Median travel time to work:** 28.2 minutes. **Working outside county of residence:** 42.3%.

Cities with pop over 10,000: None.

MONTMORENCY COUNTY

PO Box 789   **Ph:** 989-785-8013
Atlanta, MI 49709   **Fax:** 989-785-8014

In northeast MI, west of Alpena; established as Chenoquet County Apr 1, 1840 from Alpena County; name changed Mar 8, 1843. **Name Origin:** For Count Raymond de Montmorency (1806-89), a French officer who helped the colonies against England during the Revolutionary War.

Area (sq mi): 562.44 (land 547.63; water 14.81). **Pop per sq mi:** 19.1.

Pop 2005: 10,445. **State rank:** 76. **Pop change:** 2000-20005 +1.3%; 1990-2000 +15.4%. **Pop 2000:** 10,315 (White 97.9%; Black or African American 0.2%; Hispanic or Latino 0.6%; Asian 0.1%; Other 1.3%). **Foreign born:** 1.3%. **Median age:** 47.

Income 2000: per capita $16,493; median household $30,005; **Pop below poverty level:** 12.8%. ***Personal per capita income 2000-2003:** $18,142-$19,641.

Unemployment 2004: 12%. **Change from 2000:** -0.8%. **Median travel time to work:** 24.7 minutes. **Working outside county of residence:** 35%.

Cities with pop over 10,000: None.

MUSKEGON COUNTY

990 Terrace St   **Ph:** 231-724-6211
Muskegon, MI 49442   **Fax:** 231-724-6673
www.co.muskegon.mi.us

On the west-central coast of MI, bordered on west by Lake Michigan; established Jan 7, 1859 from Newaygo County. **Name Origin:** For the Muskegon River, from an Ojibway word meaning 'marshy river.'

Area (sq mi): 1459.3 (land 509.12; water 950.18). **Pop per sq mi:** 344.8.

Pop 2005: 175,554. **State rank:** 12. **Pop change:** 2000-20005 +3.1%; 1990-2000 +7.1%. **Pop 2000:** 170,200 (White 79.5%; Black or African American 14.2%; Hispanic or Latino 3.5%; Asian 0.4%; Other 4.1%). **Foreign born:** 1.9%. **Median age:** 35.5.

Income 2000: per capita $17,967; median household $38,008; **Pop below poverty level:** 11.4%. ***Personal per capita income 2000-2003:** $23,122-$24,468.

Unemployment 2004: 7.9%. **Change from 2000:** +1%. **Median travel time to work:** 20.8 minutes. **Working outside county of residence:** 25.1%.

Cities with pop over 10,000: Muskegon 🏛 (39,954); Norton Shores (23,287); Muskegon Heights (11,807).

🏛 *County Seat*

NEWAYGO COUNTY

1087 Newell St   **Ph:** 231-689-7200
White Cloud, MI 49349   **Fax:** 231-689-7205
www.countyofnewaygo.com

In west-central MI, north of Grand Rapids; established Apr 1, 1840 from unorganized territory. **Name Origin:** For the Ojibway Indian chief, signer of the Saginaw Treaty of 1819.

Area (sq mi): 861.39 (land 842.37; water 19.03). **Pop per sq mi:** 59.4.

Pop 2005: 50,019. **State rank:** 36. **Pop change:** 2000-20005 +4.5%; 1990-2000 +25.3%. **Pop 2000:** 47,874 (White 93%; Black or African American 1.1%; Hispanic or Latino 3.9%; Asian 0.3%; Other 3.7%). **Foreign born:** 1.8%. **Median age:** 36.4.

Income 2000: per capita $16,976; median household $37,130; **Pop below poverty level:** 11.6%. ***Personal per capita income 2000-2003:** $21,123-$22,123.

Unemployment 2004: 8.1%. **Change from 2000:** -0.1%. **Median travel time to work:** 31 minutes. **Working outside county of residence:** 47%.

Cities with pop over 10,000: None.

OAKLAND COUNTY

1200 N Telegraph Rd   **Ph:** 248-858-0582
Pontiac, MI 48341   **Fax:** 248-452-9221
www.co.oakland.mi.us

In southeast MI, northwest of Detroit; original county; established Jan 12, 1819 (prior to statehood). **Name Origin:** For the abundant oak trees in the area.

Area (sq mi): 908 (land 872.51; water 35.49). **Pop per sq mi:** 1391.8.

Pop 2005: 1,214,361. **State rank:** 2. **Pop change:** 2000-20005 +1.7%; 1990-2000 +10.2%. **Pop 2000:** 1,194,156 (White 81.4%; Black or African American 10.1%; Hispanic or Latino 2.4%; Asian 4.1%; Other 3%). **Foreign born:** 10%. **Median age:** 36.7.

Income 2000: per capita $32,534; median household $61,907; **Pop below poverty level:** 5.5%. ***Personal per capita income 2000-2003:** $47,079-$49,048.

Unemployment 2004: 5.6%. **Change from 2000:** +1.7%. **Median travel time to work:** 26.5 minutes. **Working outside county of residence:** 28.9%.

Cities with pop over 10,000: 20 (see page 35 for cities).

OCEANA COUNTY

100 State St Suite 1   **Ph:** 231-873-4328
Hart, MI 49420   **Fax:** 231-873-1391
www.oceana.mi.us

On the west-central coast of MI, bordered on west by Lake Michigan; established Mar 2, 1831 (prior to statehood) from Newaygo County. **Name Origin:** For its long shoreline on the 'fresh water ocean' of Lake Michigan.

Area (sq mi): 1306.73 (land 540.46; water 766.27). **Pop per sq mi:** 52.7.

Pop 2005: 28,473. **State rank:** 51. **Pop change:** 2000-20005 +6%; 1990-2000 +19.7%. **Pop 2000:** 26,873 (White 85.8%; Black or African American 0.3%; Hispanic or Latino 11.6%; Asian 0.2%;

Other 9%, including 1% American Indian/Alaska Native). **Foreign born:** 4.4%. **Median age:** 36.9.

Income 2000: per capita $15,878; median household $35,307; **Pop below poverty level:** 14.7%. ***Personal per capita income 2000-2003:** $19,234-$21,995.

Unemployment 2004: 8.9%. **Change from 2000:** +0.7%. **Median travel time to work:** 24.4 minutes. **Working outside county of residence:** 44.6%.

Cities with pop over 10,000: None.

OGEMAW COUNTY

806 W Houghton Ave   **Ph:** 989-345-0215
West Branch, MI 48661   **Fax:** 989-345-7223

In northeast MI, north of Bay City; established Apr 1, 1840. **Name Origin:** The Chippewa word for 'chief.'

Area (sq mi): 574.63 (land 564.3; water 10.33). **Pop per sq mi:** 38.8.

Pop 2005: 21,905. **State rank:** 64. **Pop change:** 2000-20005 +1.2%; 1990-2000 +15.9%. **Pop 2000:** 21,645 (White 96.6%; Black or African American 0.1%; Hispanic or Latino 1.2%; Asian 0.4%; Other 1.9%). **Foreign born:** 1.3%. **Median age:** 42.3.

Income 2000: per capita $15,768; median household $30,474; **Pop below poverty level:** 14%. ***Personal per capita income 2000-2003:** $18,035-$19,662.

Unemployment 2004: 8.6%. **Change from 2000:** +0.3%. **Median travel time to work:** 24.8 minutes. **Working outside county of residence:** 25.6%.

Cities with pop over 10,000: None.

ONTONAGON COUNTY

725 Greenland Rd   **Ph:** 906-884-4255
Ontonagon, MI 49953   **Fax:** 906-884-2916
www.ontonagonmi.com

On the northwest coast of the Upper Peninsula of MI; established Mar 9, 1843 from Michilimacknac and Chippewa counties. **Name Origin:** For the Ontonagon River, which runs through it; from Ojibway *onagan* 'dish' or 'bowl,' from the shape of the river's mouth.

Area (sq mi): 3741.45 (land 1311.53; water 2429.92). **Pop per sq mi:** 5.6.

Pop 2005: 7,363. **State rank:** 81. **Pop change:** 2000-20005 -5.8%; 1990-2000 -11.7%. **Pop 2000:** 7,818 (White 96.8%; Black or African American 0%; Hispanic or Latino 0.7%; Asian 0.2%; Other 2.6%, including 1% American Indian/Alaska Native). **Foreign born:** 1.4%. **Median age:** 45.9.

Income 2000: per capita $16,695; median household $29,552; **Pop below poverty level:** 10.4%. ***Personal per capita income 2000-2003:** $20,890-$22,264.

Unemployment 2004: 7.7%. **Change from 2000:** -1.5%. **Median travel time to work:** 21.7 minutes. **Working outside county of residence:** 24%.

Cities with pop over 10,000: None.

*Source: Personal per capita income data are from the Bureau of Economic Analysis; per capita income data are from the Bureau of the Census. See Introduction for explanation of differences.

OSCEOLA COUNTY

301 W Upton Ave **Ph:** 231-832-3261
Reed City, MI 49677 **Fax:** 231-832-6149
www.osceola-county.org

In central MI, south of Cadillac; established as Unwattin County Apr 1, 1840; name changed Mar 8, 1843. **Name Origin:** For the Seminole chief (c. 1804-38) who led the second Seminole War against the U.S.

Area (sq mi): 573.1 (land 565.98; water 7.12). **Pop per sq mi:** 42.

Pop 2005: 23,750. **State rank:** 62. **Pop change:** 2000-20005 +2.4%; 1990-2000 +15.1%. **Pop 2000:** 23,197 (White 96.8%; Black or African American 0.3%; Hispanic or Latino 1%; Asian 0.2%; Other 1.9%). **Foreign born:** 1.2%. **Median age:** 37.6.

Income 2000: per capita $15,632; median household $34,102; **Pop below poverty level:** 12.7%. ***Personal per capita income 2000-2003:** $19,446-$20,947.

Unemployment 2004: 8.7%. **Change from 2000:** +0.7%. **Median travel time to work:** 23.2 minutes. **Working outside county of residence:** 39.3%.

Cities with pop over 10,000: None.

OSCODA COUNTY

PO Box 399 **Ph:** 989-826-1109
Mio, MI 48647 **Fax:** 989-826-1136

In northeast MI, southwest of Alpena; established Apr 1, 1840 from unorganized territory. **Name Origin:** 'Pebbly prairie' from *ossin* 'stone' and *muskoda* 'prairie,' coined by Henry Rowe Schoolcraft (1793-1864), author, explorer, MI legislator, and superintendent of Indian Affairs for MI (1836-41).

Area (sq mi): 571.57 (land 565; water 6.57). **Pop per sq mi:** 16.5.

Pop 2005: 9,298. **State rank:** 78. **Pop change:** 2000-20005 -1.3%; 1990-2000 +20.1%. **Pop 2000:** 9,418 (White 97.3%; Black or African American 0.1%; Hispanic or Latino 0.9%; Asian 0.1%; Other 2%). **Foreign born:** 1.5%. **Median age:** 43.7.

Income 2000: per capita $15,697; median household $28,228; **Pop below poverty level:** 14.6%. ***Personal per capita income 2000-2003:** $15,552-$16,674.

Unemployment 2004: 11.1%. **Change from 2000:** +0.1%. **Median travel time to work:** 23.5 minutes. **Working outside county of residence:** 30.2%.

Cities with pop over 10,000: None.

OTSEGO COUNTY

225 W Main St **Ph:** 989-732-6484
Gaylord, MI 49735 **Fax:** 989-732-1562
www.otsegocountymi.gov

In north-central MI, southeast of Petoskey; established as Okkuddo County Apr 1, 1840; name changed Mar 8, 1843. **Name Origin:** Probably for Otsego County, NY, home of some early settlers; from Iroquoian 'rock site' or 'place of the rock.'

Area (sq mi): 525.98 (land 514.54; water 11.44). **Pop per sq mi:** 47.9.

Pop 2005: 24,665. **State rank:** 60. **Pop change:** 2000-20005 +5.9%; 1990-2000 +29.8%. **Pop 2000:** 23,301 (White 97%; Black or African

American 0.2%; Hispanic or Latino 0.8%; Asian 0.3%; Other 2%). **Foreign born:** 1.6%. **Median age:** 37.7.

Income 2000: per capita $19,810; median household $40,876; **Pop below poverty level:** 6.8%. ***Personal per capita income 2000-2003:** $24,365-$24,465.

Unemployment 2004: 7.7%. **Change from 2000:** +1.5%. **Median travel time to work:** 18.4 minutes. **Working outside county of residence:** 12.9%.

Cities with pop over 10,000: None.

OTTAWA COUNTY

414 Washington St **Ph:** 616-846-8312
Grand Haven, MI 49417 **Fax:** 616-846-8138
www.co.ottawa.mi.us

On the west-central coast of MI bordered on west by Lake Michigan; established Mar 2, 1831 (prior to statehood). **Name Origin:** For the Ottawa Indians, a tribe of Algonquian linguistic stock whose name is derived from *adawe* 'to trade.'

Area (sq mi): 1631.97 (land 565.65; water 1066.32). **Pop per sq mi:** 451.5.

Pop 2005: 255,406. **State rank:** 8. **Pop change:** 2000-20005 +7.2%; 1990-2000 +26.9%. **Pop 2000:** 238,314 (White 88.6%; Black or African American 1%; Hispanic or Latino 7%; Asian 2.1%; Other 5.4%). **Foreign born:** 4.9%. **Median age:** 32.3.

Income 2000: per capita $21,676; median household $52,347; **Pop below poverty level:** 5.5%. ***Personal per capita income 2000-2003:** $27,881-$28,570.

Unemployment 2004: 5.6%. **Change from 2000:** +1.3%. **Median travel time to work:** 19.4 minutes. **Working outside county of residence:** 37.6%.

Cities with pop over 10,000: Holland (34,606); Grand Haven 🏛 (10,733).

PRESQUE ISLE COUNTY

PO Box 110 **Ph:** 989-734-3288
Rogers City, MI 49779 **Fax:** 989-734-7635

On the northeast coast of MI, bordered on east by Lake Huron; established Apr 1, 1840 from unorganized territory. **Name Origin:** French 'almost an island,' i.e., a peninsula.

Area (sq mi): 2572.75 (land 660.07; water 1912.68). **Pop per sq mi:** 21.7.

Pop 2005: 14,330. **State rank:** 71. **Pop change:** 2000-20005 -0.6%; 1990-2000 +4.9%. **Pop 2000:** 14,411 (White 97.7%; Black or African American 0.3%; Hispanic or Latino 0.5%; Asian 0.2%; Other 1.5%). **Foreign born:** 1.2%. **Median age:** 45.1.

Income 2000: per capita $17,363; median household $31,656; **Pop below poverty level:** 10.3%. ***Personal per capita income 2000-2003:** $20,105-$21,454.

Unemployment 2004: 11.1%. **Change from 2000:** +0%. **Median travel time to work:** 23.9 minutes. **Working outside county of residence:** 34.9%.

Cities with pop over 10,000: None.

ROSCOMMON COUNTY

500 Lake St   **Ph:** 989-275-5923
Roscommon, MI 48653   **Fax:** 989-275-8640
www.roscommoncounty.net

In central MI, east of Cadillac; established as Mikenauk County Apr 1, 1840; name changed Mar 8, 1843. **Name Origin:** For the county in Ireland.

Area (sq mi): 579.84 (land 521.4; water 58.44). **Pop per sq mi:** 50.

Pop 2005: 26,079. **State rank:** 57. **Pop change:** 2000-20005 +2.4%; 1990-2000 +28.8%. **Pop 2000:** 25,469 (White 97.4%; Black or African American 0.3%; Hispanic or Latino 0.8%; Asian 0.2%; Other 1.4%). **Foreign born:** 1.7%. **Median age:** 47.2.

Income 2000: per capita $17,837; median household $30,029; **Pop below poverty level:** 12.4%. ***Personal per capita income 2000-2003:** $19,765-$20,872.

Unemployment 2004: 8.4%. **Change from 2000:** +0.8%. **Median travel time to work:** 24.2 minutes. **Working outside county of residence:** 29.6%.

Cities with pop over 10,000: None.

SAGINAW COUNTY

111 S Michigan Ave   **Ph:** 989-790-5251
Saginaw, MI 48602   **Fax:** 989-790-5254
www.saginawcounty.com

In central MI, northwest of Flint; established Sep 10, 1822 (prior to statehood) from unorganized territory. **Name Origin:** For the Saginaw River, which runs through it; from Ojibway 'the place of the Sac [Indians].'

Area (sq mi): 815.78 (land 808.93; water 6.85). **Pop per sq mi:** 257.6.

Pop 2005: 208,356. **State rank:** 10. **Pop change:** 2000-20005 -0.8%; 1990-2000 -0.9%. **Pop 2000:** 210,039 (White 72.4%; Black or African American 18.6%; Hispanic or Latino 6.7%; Asian 0.8%; Other 5.3%). **Foreign born:** 2%. **Median age:** 36.3.

Income 2000: per capita $19,438; median household $38,637; **Pop below poverty level:** 13.9%. ***Personal per capita income 2000-2003:** $25,596-$26,454.

Unemployment 2004: 8.7%. **Change from 2000:** +2.8%. **Median travel time to work:** 21.6 minutes. **Working outside county of residence:** 18.4%.

Cities with pop over 10,000: Saginaw 🏛 (59,045).

SAINT CLAIR COUNTY

201 McMorran Blvd   **Ph:** 810-985-2200
Port Huron, MI 48060   **Fax:** 810-985-4796
www.stclaircounty.org

On the southeast coast of Michigan, northeast of Detroit, bordered on east by the Saint Clair River, original county, established Mar 28, 1820 (prior to statehood). **Name Origin:** For Gen. Arthur Saint Clair (1736?-1818), an officer in the French and Indian War and the Revolutionary War, president of the Continental Congress (1787), and governor of the Northwest Territory (1788-1802).

Area (sq mi): 836.63 (land 724.37; water 112.26). **Pop per sq mi:** 236.7.

Pop 2005: 171,426. **State rank:** 13. **Pop change:** 2000-20005 +4.4%; 1990-2000 +12.8%. **Pop 2000:** 164,235 (White 93.7%; Black or African American 2.1%; Hispanic or Latino 2.2%; Asian 0.4%; Other 2.5%). **Foreign born:** 2.7%. **Median age:** 36.4.

Income 2000: per capita $21,582; median household $46,313; **Pop below poverty level:** 7.8%. ***Personal per capita income 2000-2003:** $27,833-$28,646.

Unemployment 2004: 7.7%. **Change from 2000:** +0.8%. **Median travel time to work:** 28.7 minutes. **Working outside county of residence:** 36.8%.

Cities with pop over 10,000: Port Huron 🏛 (31,710).

SAINT JOSEPH COUNTY

PO Box 189   **Ph:** 269-467-5602
Centreville, MI 49032   **Fax:** 269-467-5628
www.stjosephcountymi.org

On the southern border of MI, south of Kalamazoo; established Oct 29, 1829 (prior to statehood) from Indian lands. **Name Origin:** For the spouse of the Virgin Mary.

Area (sq mi): 521.15 (land 503.72; water 17.43). **Pop per sq mi:** 125.

Pop 2005: 62,984. **State rank:** 32. **Pop change:** 2000-20005 +0.9%; 1990-2000 +6%. **Pop 2000:** 62,422 (White 91.3%; Black or African American 2.6%; Hispanic or Latino 4%; Asian 0.6%; Other 3.4%). **Foreign born:** 3.4%. **Median age:** 35.6.

Income 2000: per capita $18,247; median household $40,355; **Pop below poverty level:** 11.3%. ***Personal per capita income 2000-2003:** $23,098-$24,496.

Unemployment 2004: 6.8%. **Change from 2000:** +0%. **Median travel time to work:** 20.8 minutes. **Working outside county of residence:** 28.7%.

Cities with pop over 10,000: Sturgis (11,120).

SANILAC COUNTY

60 W Sanilac Ave Rm 203   **Ph:** 810-648-3212
Sandusky, MI 48471   **Fax:** 810-648-5466
www.sanilaccounty.net

On the east-central coast of MI bordered on the east by Lake Huron; established Sep 10, 1822 (prior to statehood). **Name Origin:** For the Wyandot chief who is the main character in Henry Whiting's poem 'Sannilac.' The name was spelled with only one 'n' in the proclamation by Gov. Lewis Cass (1782-1866) that announced the formation of the county.

Area (sq mi): 1590.22 (land 963.8; water 626.42). **Pop per sq mi:** 46.4.

Pop 2005: 44,752. **State rank:** 39. **Pop change:** 2000-20005 +0.5%; 1990-2000 +11.6%. **Pop 2000:** 44,547 (White 95.4%; Black or African American 0.3%; Hispanic or Latino 2.8%; Asian 0.3%; Other 2.6%). **Foreign born:** 1.6%. **Median age:** 37.8.

Income 2000: per capita $17,089; median household $36,870; **Pop below poverty level:** 10.4%. ***Personal per capita income 2000-2003:** $23,350-$24,811.

Unemployment 2004: 9.3%. **Change from 2000:** +1%. **Median travel time to work:** 28.1 minutes. **Working outside county of residence:** 35.4%.

Cities with pop over 10,000: None.

---

*Source: Personal per capita income data are from the Bureau of Economic Analysis; per capita income data are from the Bureau of the Census. See Introduction for explanation of differences.

SCHOOLCRAFT COUNTY

300 Walnut St Rm 164   **Ph:** 906-341-3618
Manistique, MI 49854   **Fax:** 906-341-5680

On the south-central coast of the Upper Peninsula of MI, on Lake Michigan; established Mar 9, 1843 from Michilimackinac and Chippewa counties. **Name Origin:** For Henry Rowe Schoolcraft (1793-1864), explorer, MI legislator, author, and superintendent of Indian Affairs for MI (1836-41).

Area (sq mi): 1883.69 (land 1178.11; water 705.58). **Pop per sq mi:** 7.5.

Pop 2005: 8,819. **State rank:** 79. **Pop change:** 2000-20005 -0.9%; 1990-2000 +7.2%. **Pop 2000:** 8,903 (White 88.1%; Black or African American 1.6%; Hispanic or Latino 0.9%; Asian 0.4%; Other 9.3%, including 6.1% American Indian/Alaska Native). **Foreign born:** 1%. **Median age:** 41.4.

Income 2000: per capita $17,137; median household $31,140; **Pop below poverty level:** 12.2%. ***Personal per capita income 2000-2003:** $20,337-$21,899.

Unemployment 2004: 11%. **Change from 2000:** +2%. **Median travel time to work:** 20.8 minutes. **Working outside county of residence:** 14.2%.

Cities with pop over 10,000: None.

SHIAWASSEE COUNTY

208 N Shiawassee St   **Ph:** 989-743-2242
Corunna, MI 48817   **Fax:** 989-743-2241
www.co.shiawassee.mi.us

In south-central MI, west of Flint; established Sep 10, 1822 (prior to statehood) from Indian lands. **Name Origin:** For the Shiawassee River, which runs through it; from Algonquian 'the water straight ahead' or 'river that twists about.'

Area (sq mi): 540.73 (land 538.73; water 2). **Pop per sq mi:** 135.4.

Pop 2005: 72,945. **State rank:** 26. **Pop change:** 2000-20005 +1.8%; 1990-2000 +2.7%. **Pop 2000:** 71,687 (White 96.3%; Black or African American 0.2%; Hispanic or Latino 1.8%; Asian 0.3%; Other 2.2%). **Foreign born:** 1.2%. **Median age:** 36.4.

Income 2000: per capita $19,229; median household $42,553; **Pop below poverty level:** 7.8%. ***Personal per capita income 2000-2003:** $23,145-$24,020.

Unemployment 2004: 8%. **Change from 2000:** +2%. **Median travel time to work:** 27.6 minutes. **Working outside county of residence:** 50.4%.

Cities with pop over 10,000: Owosso (15,532).

TUSCOLA COUNTY

440 N State St   **Ph:** 989-672-3780
Caro, MI 48723   **Fax:** 989-672-4266
www.tuscolacounty.org

In east MI, northeast of Flint; established Apr 1, 1840 from Sanilac County. **Name Origin:** Name coined by Henry Rowe Schoolcraft (1793-1864), author, explorer, MI legislator, and superintendent of Indian Affairs for MI (1836-41); means either 'warrior prairie' or 'level lands.'

Area (sq mi): 913.82 (land 812.43; water 101.39). **Pop per sq mi:** 71.9.

Pop 2005: 58,428. **State rank:** 34. **Pop change:** 2000-20005 +0.3%; 1990-2000 +5%. **Pop 2000:** 58,266 (White 94.7%; Black or African American 1.1%; Hispanic or Latino 2.3%; Asian 0.3%; Other 2.6%). **Foreign born:** 1.1%. **Median age:** 37.

Income 2000: per capita $17,985; median household $40,174; **Pop below poverty level:** 8.2%. ***Personal per capita income 2000-2003:** $21,477-$21,985.

Unemployment 2004: 8.9%. **Change from 2000:** +1%. **Median travel time to work:** 30.3 minutes. **Working outside county of residence:** 50.8%.

Cities with pop over 10,000: None.

VAN BUREN COUNTY

212 E Paw Paw St Suite 101   **Ph:** 269-657-8218
Paw Paw, MI 49079   **Fax:** 269-657-8298
www.vbco.org

On the southwest coast of MI, bordered on west by Lake Michigan; established Oct 29, 1829 (prior to statehood) from unorganized territory. **Name Origin:** For Martin Van Buren (1782-1862), eighth U.S. president.

Area (sq mi): 1090.19 (land 610.86; water 479.33). **Pop per sq mi:** 129.

Pop 2005: 78,812. **State rank:** 25. **Pop change:** 2000-20005 +3.3%; 1990-2000 +8.9%. **Pop 2000:** 76,263 (White 84.5%; Black or African American 5.2%; Hispanic or Latino 7.4%; Asian 0.3%; Other 6.5%). **Foreign born:** 3.5%. **Median age:** 36.6.

Income 2000: per capita $17,878; median household $39,365; **Pop below poverty level:** 11.1%. ***Personal per capita income 2000-2003:** $22,032-$24,362.

Unemployment 2004: 7.4%. **Change from 2000:** +1.4%. **Median travel time to work:** 23.6 minutes. **Working outside county of residence:** 50%.

Cities with pop over 10,000: None.

WASHTENAW COUNTY

PO Box 8645   **Ph:** 734-222-6850
Ann Arbor, MI 48107   **Fax:** 734-222-6715
www.ewashtenaw.org

In southeast MI, west of Detroit; original county; established Sept 10, 1822 (prior to statehood). **Name Origin:** For the small stream running through the county; from an Ojibway word meaning 'on the river' or 'far off.'

Area (sq mi): 722.53 (land 709.94; water 12.59). **Pop per sq mi:** 481.5.

Pop 2005: 341,847. **State rank:** 6. **Pop change:** 2000-20005 +5.9%; 1990-2000 +14.1%. **Pop 2000:** 322,895 (White 75.9%; Black or African American 12.3%; Hispanic or Latino 2.7%; Asian 6.3%; Other 4%). **Foreign born:** 10.3%. **Median age:** 31.3.

Income 2000: per capita $27,173; median household $51,990; **Pop below poverty level:** 11.1%. ***Personal per capita income 2000-2003:** $35,594-$38,323.

Unemployment 2004: 4.3%. **Change from 2000:** +1.9%. **Median travel time to work:** 22.2 minutes. **Working outside county of residence:** 23.3%.

⚏ County Seat

Washtenaw County (cont'd)

Cities with pop over 10,000: Ann Arbor 🏛 (113,567); Ypsilanti (22,214).

WAYNE COUNTY

211 Coleman A Young Municipal Center   **Ph:** 313-224-6262
Detroit, MI 48226   **Fax:** 313-224-5364
www.co.wayne.mi.us

In southeastern MI bordered on the east by the Detroit River and Lake Saint Clair; original colony; established Nov 21, 1815 (prior to statehood). **Name Origin:** For Gen. Anthony Wayne (1745-96), PA soldier and statesman, nicknamed 'Mad Anthony' for his daring during the Revolutionary War.

Area (sq mi): 672.2 (land 614.15; water 58.05). **Pop per sq mi:** 3253.6.

Pop 2005: 1,998,217. **State rank:** 1. **Pop change:** 2000-20005 -3.1%; 1990-2000 -2.4%. **Pop 2000:** 2,061,162 (White 49.9%; Black or African American 42.2%; Hispanic or Latino 3.7%; Asian 1.7%; Other 4.5%). **Foreign born:** 6.7%. **Median age:** 34.

Income 2000: per capita $20,058; median household $40,776; **Pop below poverty level:** 16.4%. ***Personal per capita income 2000-2003:** $27,514-$29,879.

Unemployment 2004: 8.6%. **Change from 2000:** +2.8%. **Median travel time to work:** 25.8 minutes. **Working outside county of residence:** 25.3%.

Cities with pop over 10,000: 24 (see page 36 for cities).

WEXFORD COUNTY

437 E Division St   **Ph:** 231-779-9453
Cadillac, MI 49601   **Fax:** 231-779-0292
www.wexfordcounty.org

In northwest MI, south of Traverse City; established as Kautawaubet County Apr 1, 1840 from unorganized territory; name changed Mar 8, 1843. **Name Origin:** For the county in Ireland.

Area (sq mi): 575.84 (land 565.49; water 10.35). **Pop per sq mi:** 56.4.

Pop 2005: 31,876. **State rank:** 47. **Pop change:** 2000-20005 +4.6%; 1990-2000 +15.6%. **Pop 2000:** 30,484 (White 96.7%; Black or African American 0.2%; Hispanic or Latino 1%; Asian 0.4%; Other 2%). **Foreign born:** 1.8%. **Median age:** 37.3.

Income 2000: per capita $17,144; median household $35,363; **Pop below poverty level:** 10.3%. ***Personal per capita income 2000-2003:** $22,167-$22,781.

Unemployment 2004: 8.4%. **Change from 2000:** -1.8%. **Median travel time to work:** 20.9 minutes. **Working outside county of residence:** 19.9%.

Cities with pop over 10,000: Cadillac 🏛 (10,135).

*Source: Personal per capita income data are from the Bureau of Economic Analysis; per capita income data are from the Bureau of the Census.
See Introduction for explanation of differences.*

Minnesota

MANITOBA

CANADA

ONTARIO

N

Lake of the Woods

MICH.

Lake Superior

WISCONSIN

NORTH DAKOTA

SOUTH DAKOTA

IOWA

Hallock
Kittson

Roseau
Roseau

Baudette
Lake of the Woods

International Falls

Marshall
Warren

Koochiching

St. Louis

Cook
Grand Marais

Thief River Falls
Pennington

Beltrami

Lake

Red Lake Falls
Red Lake

Crookston
Polk

Clear-water
Bagley

Bemidji

Norman
Ada

Mahnomen
Mahnomen

Hubbard
Park Rapids

Walker

Itasca

Grand Rapids

Two Harbors

Clay
Moorhead

Becker
Detroit Lakes

Cass

Aitkin
Aitkin

Duluth

Carlton
Carlton

Wilkin
Breckenridge

Otter Tail
Fergus Falls

Wadena
Wadena

Crow Wing
Brainerd

Pine

Elbow Lake

Todd

Morrison
Little Falls

Mille Lacs

Pine City

Grant
Wheaton

Douglas
Alexandria

Long Prairie

Milaca

Kanabec
Mora

Traverse

Morris

Glenwood

Benton
Foley

Cambridge

Big Stone

Stevens

Pope

Stearns
Saint Cloud

Sherburne

Isanti

Chisago
Center City

Ortonville

Benson

Elk River

Anoka

Swift

Kandiyohi

Litchfield

Buffalo

Anoka

Lac Qui Parle

Madison

Chippewa
Montevideo

Willmar

Meeker

Wright

Ramsey
Stillwater

Granite Falls

Olivia

McLeod
Glencoe

Hennepin
Minneapolis

Saint Paul

Washington

Yellow Medicine

Renville

Carver
Chaska

Shakopee

Hastings

Lyon
Marshall

Redwood Falls

Sibley
Gaylord

Scott

Dakota

Ivanhoe

Lincoln

Redwood

Nicollet

New Ulm

Saint Peter

Le Center

Le Sueur

Rice
Faribault

Goodhue
Red Wing

Wabasha

Brown

Mankato

Waseca

Blue Earth

Pipestone

Murray
Slayton

Cotton-wood
Windom

Saint James

Watonwan

Waseca

Owatonna

Steele

Mantorville

Dodge

Rochester

Olmsted

Wabasha

Winona
Winona

Pipestone

Rock
Luverne

Nobles
Worthington

Jackson
Jackson

Martin
Fairmont

Faribault
Blue Earth

Freeborn
Albert Lea

Austin
Mower

Fillmore
Preston

Houston
Caledonia

	County boundary
Murray	County name
•	County seat
■	Major city
✪	State capital

0   50 mi

0   50 km

©MAPS.com

Minnesota

MINNESOTA STATE INFORMATION

www.state.mn.us   **Ph:** 651-296-6013

Area (sq mi): 86,938.87 (land 79,610.08; water 7328.79). **Pop per sq mi:** 64.5.

Pop 2005: 5,132,799. **Pop change:** 2000-20005 +4.3%; 1990-2000 +12.4%. **Pop 2000:** 4,919,479 (White 88.2%; Black or African American 3.5%; Hispanic or Latino 2.9%; Asian 2.9%; Other 4.1%, including 1.1% American Indian/Alaska Native). **Foreign born:** 5.3%. **Median age:** 35.4.

Income 2000: per capita $23,198; median household $47,111; **Pop below poverty level:** 7.9%. *****Personal per capita income 2000-2003:** $32,017-$34,031.

Unemployment 2004: 4.6%. **Change from 2000:** +1.5%. **Median travel time to work:** 21.9 minutes. **Working outside county of residence:** 33.7%.

AITKIN COUNTY

209 2nd St NW   **Ph:** 218-927-7350
Aitkin, MN 56431   **Fax:** 218-927-4535
www.co.aitkin.mn.us

In east-central MN, west of Duluth; established May 23, 1857 (prior to statehood) from Cass and Itasca counties. **Name Origin:** For William Alexander Aitkin (c. 1787-1851), a local fur trader.

Area (sq mi): 1995.31 (land 1819.3; water 176.01). **Pop per sq mi:** 8.9.

Pop 2005: 16,174. **State rank:** 55. **Pop change:** 2000-20005 +5.7%; 1990-2000 +23.1%. **Pop 2000:** 15,301 (White 96.1%; Black or African American 0.2%; Hispanic or Latino 0.6%; Asian 0.2%; Other 3.2%, including 2.3% American Indian/Alaska Native). **Foreign born:** 0.9%. **Median age:** 46.5.

Income 2000: per capita $17,848; median household $31,139; **Pop below poverty level:** 11.6%. *****Personal per capita income 2000-2003:** $21,331-$23,176.

Unemployment 2004: 6.7%. **Change from 2000:** -0.8%. **Median travel time to work:** 25.2 minutes. **Working outside county of residence:** 34.9%.

Cities with pop over 10,000: None.

ANOKA COUNTY

325 E Main St   **Ph:** 763-422-7350
Anoka, MN 55303   **Fax:** 763-422-6919
www.co.anoka.mn.us

In east-central MN, north of Minneapolis; established May 23, 1857 (prior to statehood) from Hennepin County; annexed Manomin County in 1869. **Name Origin:** For the town of the same name; from Siouan 'the other side' or 'both sides'; the town is on both sides of the Rum River.

Area (sq mi): 446.26 (land 423.61; water 22.65). **Pop per sq mi:** 764.8.

Pop 2005: 323,996. **State rank:** 4. **Pop change:** 2000-20005 +8.7%; 1990-2000 +22.3%. **Pop 2000:** 298,084 (White 92.8%; Black or African American 1.6%; Hispanic or Latino 1.7%; Asian 1.7%; Other 3%). **Foreign born:** 3.6%. **Median age:** 33.7.

Income 2000: per capita $23,297; median household $57,754; **Pop below poverty level:** 4.2%. *****Personal per capita income 2000-2003:** $30,770-$32,620.

Unemployment 2004: 4.5%. **Change from 2000:** +1.2%. **Median travel time to work:** 27.3 minutes. **Working outside county of residence:** 59%.

Cities with pop over 10,000: 10 (see page 36 for cities).

BECKER COUNTY

913 Lake Ave   **Ph:** 218-846-7301
Detroit Lakes, MN 56502   **Fax:** 218-846-7257
www.co.becker.mn.us

In west-central MN, east of Fargo, ND; established Mar 18, 1858 from Indian lands. **Name Origin:** For Gen. George Loomis Becker (1829-1904), lawyer, MN legislator, and land commissioner of the Saint Paul and Pacific Railroad.

Area (sq mi): 1445.11 (land 1310.42; water 134.69). **Pop per sq mi:** 24.3.

Pop 2005: 31,868. **State rank:** 33. **Pop change:** 2000-20005 +6.2%; 1990-2000 +7.6%. **Pop 2000:** 30,000 (White 89%; Black or African American 0.2%; Hispanic or Latino 0.8%; Asian 0.4%; Other 10%, including 7.5% American Indian/Alaska Native). **Foreign born:** 1%. **Median age:** 39.4.

Income 2000: per capita $17,085; median household $34,797; **Pop below poverty level:** 12.2%. *****Personal per capita income 2000-2003:** $24,160-$26,540.

Unemployment 2004: 5.6%. **Change from 2000:** -0.5%. **Median travel time to work:** 23.1 minutes. **Working outside county of residence:** 24.8%.

Cities with pop over 10,000: None.

BELTRAMI COUNTY

619 Beltrami Ave NW Courthouse   **Ph:** 218-333-4120
Bemidji, MN 56601   **Fax:** 218-333-4209
www.co.beltrami.mn.us

In north-central MN, east of Grand Forks, ND; established Feb 28, 1866 from unorganized territory. **Name Origin:** For Giacomo Constantino Beltrami (1779-1855), an Italian who, under the anglicized name James Constantine, explored the sources of the Mississippi River and wrote *A Pilgrimage in Europe and America, Leading to the Discovery of the Sources of the Mississippi and Bloody River*.

Area (sq mi): 3055.59 (land 2505.27; water 550.32). **Pop per sq mi:** 17.1.

Pop 2005: 42,871. **State rank:** 22. **Pop change:** 2000-20005 +8.1%; 1990-2000 +15.3%. **Pop 2000:** 39,650 (White 76.3%; Black or African American 0.4%; Hispanic or Latino 1%; Asian 0.6%; Other 22.4%, including 20.4% American Indian/Alaska Native). **Foreign born:** 1.8%. **Median age:** 31.5.

Income 2000: per capita $15,497; median household $33,392; **Pop below poverty level:** 17.6%. ***Personal per capita income 2000-2003:** $21,524-$24,157.

Unemployment 2004: 5.7%. **Change from 2000:** +0.8%. **Median travel time to work:** 19.4 minutes. **Working outside county of residence:** 12.2%.

Cities with pop over 10,000: Bemidji ⬛ (13,016).

BENTON COUNTY

615 Hwy 23 PO Box 189   **Ph:** 320-968-5205
Foley, MN 56329   **Fax:** 320-968-5353
www.co.benton.mn.us

In east-central MN, northeast of Saint Cloud; original county; established Oct 27, 1849 (prior to statehood). **Name Origin:** For Thomas Hart Benton (1782-1858), U.S. journalist and statesman; nicknamed 'Old Bullion' for championing the use of gold and silver currency rather than paper money.

Area (sq mi): 413 (land 408.28; water 4.72). **Pop per sq mi:** 94.3.

Pop 2005: 38,505. **State rank:** 25. **Pop change:** 2000-20005 +12.5%; 1990-2000 +13.4%. **Pop 2000:** 34,226 (White 95.7%; Black or African American 0.8%; Hispanic or Latino 0.9%; Asian 1.1%; Other 1.8%). **Foreign born:** 2.1%. **Median age:** 31.9.

Income 2000: per capita $19,008; median household $41,968; **Pop below poverty level:** 7.1%. ***Personal per capita income 2000-2003:** $24,991-$27,420.

Unemployment 2004: 5.2%. **Change from 2000:** +0.8%. **Median travel time to work:** 21.1 minutes. **Working outside county of residence:** 61.4%.

Cities with pop over 10,000: Saint Cloud ⬛ (64,337); Sauk Rapids (11,381).

BIG STONE COUNTY

20 SE 2nd St   **Ph:** 320-839-2537
Ortonville, MN 56278   **Fax:** 320-839-2537
www.bigstonecounty.org

On central western border of MN; established Feb 20, 1862 from Pierce County (which was abolished the same year). **Name Origin:** For Big Stone Lake in the western part of the county.

Area (sq mi): 527.88 (land 496.95; water 30.93). **Pop per sq mi:** 11.

Pop 2005: 5,481. **State rank:** 81. **Pop change:** 2000-20005 -5.8%; 1990-2000 -7.4%. **Pop 2000:** 5,820 (White 98.3%; Black or African American 0.2%; Hispanic or Latino 0.3%; Asian 0.4%; Other 0.9%). **Foreign born:** 0.8%. **Median age:** 43.6.

Income 2000: per capita $15,708; median household $30,721; **Pop below poverty level:** 12%. ***Personal per capita income 2000-2003:** $22,328-$24,959.

Unemployment 2004: 4.8%. **Change from 2000:** +0.6%. **Median travel time to work:** 15.7 minutes. **Working outside county of residence:** 24.9%.

Cities with pop over 10,000: None.

BLUE EARTH COUNTY

204 S 5th St   **Ph:** 507-389-8100
Mankato, MN 56002   **Fax:** 507-389-8437
www.co.blue-earth.mn.us

In south-central MN, west of Rochester; established Mar 5, 1853 (prior to statehood) from unorganized territory. **Name Origin:** For the Blue Earth River, which runs through it; a transliteration of the Nankato name for the color of the earth in the river, used as a pigment by the Sisseton Sioux.

Area (sq mi): 765.9 (land 752.36; water 13.54). **Pop per sq mi:** 77.1.

Pop 2005: 58,030. **State rank:** 15. **Pop change:** 2000-20005 +3.7%; 1990-2000 +3.5%. **Pop 2000:** 55,941 (White 94.1%; Black or African American 1.2%; Hispanic or Latino 1.8%; Asian 1.8%; Other 2.1%). **Foreign born:** 2.9%. **Median age:** 29.9.

Income 2000: per capita $18,712; median household $38,940; **Pop below poverty level:** 12.9%. ***Personal per capita income 2000-2003:** $25,910-$28,491.

Unemployment 2004: 3.9%. **Change from 2000:** +1.2%. **Median travel time to work:** 17 minutes. **Working outside county of residence:** 23.2%.

Cities with pop over 10,000: Mankato ⬛ (34,463); North Mankato (12,134).

BROWN COUNTY

14 S State St PO Box 248   **Ph:** 507-233-6600
New Ulm, MN 56073   **Fax:** 507-359-1430
www.co.brown.mn.us

In south-central MN, west of Mankato; established Feb 20, 1855 (prior to statehood) from Nicollet County. **Name Origin:** For Joseph Renshaw Brown (1805-70), a trader with the Sioux Indians, publisher, and MN legislator.

Area (sq mi): 618.6 (land 610.86; water 7.74). **Pop per sq mi:** 43.4.

Pop 2005: 26,534. **State rank:** 39. **Pop change:** 2000-20005 -1.4%; 1990-2000 -0.3%. **Pop 2000:** 26,911 (White 96.9%; Black or African American 0.1%; Hispanic or Latino 2%; Asian 0.4%; Other 1.6%). **Foreign born:** 1.3%. **Median age:** 38.4.

Income 2000: per capita $19,535; median household $39,800; **Pop below poverty level:** 6.4%. ***Personal per capita income 2000-2003:** $25,597-$28,072.

Unemployment 2004: 4.8%. **Change from 2000:** +0.5%. **Median travel time to work:** 14.5 minutes. **Working outside county of residence:** 10.4%.

Source: Personal per capita income data are from the Bureau of Economic Analysis; per capita income data are from the Bureau of the Census. See Introduction for explanation of differences.

Brown County (cont'd)

Cities with pop over 10,000: New Ulm 🏛 (13,705).

CARLTON COUNTY

PO Box 190
Carlton, MN 55718
www.co.carlton.mn.us

Ph: 218-384-4281
Fax: 218-384-9182

On central-eastern border of MN, south of Duluth; established May 23, 1857 (prior to statehood) from Pine County. **Name Origin:** For Reuben B. Carlton (1812-62), farmer and blacksmith for Ojibway Indians and MN state legislator.

Area (sq mi): 875.23 (land 860.33; water 14.9). **Pop per sq mi:** 39.5.

Pop 2005: 34,026. **State rank:** 30. **Pop change:** 2000-20005 +7.4%; 1990-2000 +8.2%. **Pop 2000:** 31,671 (White 91.3%; Black or African American 1%; Hispanic or Latino 0.8%; Asian 0.4%; Other 6.9%, including 5.2% American Indian/Alaska Native). **Foreign born:** 1.6%. **Median age:** 38.4.

Income 2000: per capita $18,073; median household $40,021; **Pop below poverty level:** 7.9%. ***Personal per capita income 2000-2003:** $23,911-$25,272.

Unemployment 2004: 6.3%. **Change from 2000:** +0.5%. **Median travel time to work:** 21.2 minutes. **Working outside county of residence:** 31.9%.

Cities with pop over 10,000: Cloquet (11,463).

CARVER COUNTY

606 E 4th St
Chaska, MN 55318
www.co.carver.mn.us

Ph: 952-361-1500
Fax: 952-361-1491

In south-central MN, east of Minneapolis, established Feb 20, 1855 (prior to statehood) from Hennepin County. **Name Origin:** For Capt. Jonathan Carver (1710-80), an officer in the French and Indian War, explorer, and author.

Area (sq mi): 376.15 (land 357.04; water 19.11). **Pop per sq mi:** 237.7.

Pop 2005: 84,864. **State rank:** 11. **Pop change:** 2000-20005 +20.9%; 1990-2000 +46.5%. **Pop 2000:** 70,205 (White 94.4%; Black or African American 0.6%; Hispanic or Latino 2.6%; Asian 1.6%; Other 1.9%). **Foreign born:** 3.4%. **Median age:** 33.9.

Income 2000: per capita $28,486; median household $65,540; **Pop below poverty level:** 3.5%. ***Personal per capita income 2000-2003:** $38,913-$40,807.

Unemployment 2004: 3.9%. **Change from 2000:** +0.9%. **Median travel time to work:** 25.6 minutes. **Working outside county of residence:** 60.9%.

Cities with pop over 10,000: Chanhassen (22,977); Chaska 🏛 (21,694).

CASS COUNTY

PO Box 3000
Walker, MN 56484
www.co.cass.mn.us

Ph: 218-547-7200
Fax: 218-547-1904

In central MN, northwest of Duluth; original county; established Mar 31, 1851 (prior to statehood). **Name Origin:** For Gen. Lewis Cass (1782-1866), OH legislator, governor of MI Territory (1813-31), U.S. secretary of war (1831-36), and U.S. secretary of state (1857-60). Formerly called Van Buren.

Area (sq mi): 2414.21 (land 2017.6; water 396.61). **Pop per sq mi:** 14.3.

Pop 2005: 28,910. **State rank:** 36. **Pop change:** 2000-20005 +6.5%; 1990-2000 +24.6%. **Pop 2000:** 27,150 (White 86.1%; Black or African American 0.1%; Hispanic or Latino 0.8%; Asian 0.3%; Other 13.1%, including 11.5% American Indian/Alaska Native). **Foreign born:** 0.8%. **Median age:** 42.2.

Income 2000: per capita $17,189; median household $34,332; **Pop below poverty level:** 13.6%. ***Personal per capita income 2000-2003:** $24,455-$26,631.

Unemployment 2004: 7%. **Change from 2000:** +0.8%. **Median travel time to work:** 21.9 minutes. **Working outside county of residence:** 39.9%.

Cities with pop over 10,000: None.

CHIPPEWA COUNTY

629 N 11th St
Montevideo, MN 56265
www.co.chippewa.mn.us

Ph: 320-269-7447
Fax: 320-269-7412

In west-central MN, southwest of Saint Cloud; established Feb 20, 1862 from Pierce County, which was abolished in 1862. **Name Origin:** For the Chippewa (more properly Ojibway) Indians, a tribe of Algonquian linguistic stock. The name probably means 'puckered,' and refers to the seam in their moccasins.

Area (sq mi): 587.83 (land 582.8; water 5.02). **Pop per sq mi:** 22.

Pop 2005: 12,802. **State rank:** 62. **Pop change:** 2000-20005 -2.2%; 1990-2000 -1.1%. **Pop 2000:** 13,088 (White 95.9%; Black or African American 0.2%; Hispanic or Latino 1.9%; Asian 0.3%; Other 2.7%, including 1% American Indian/Alaska Native). **Foreign born:** 1.4%. **Median age:** 40.5.

Income 2000: per capita $18,039; median household $35,582; **Pop below poverty level:** 8.6%. ***Personal per capita income 2000-2003:** $24,695-$27,429.

Unemployment 2004: 4.9%. **Change from 2000:** -0.8%. **Median travel time to work:** 15.3 minutes. **Working outside county of residence:** 25.7%.

Cities with pop over 10,000: None.

CHISAGO COUNTY

313 N Main St Rm 174
Center City, MN 55012
www.co.chisago.mn.us

Ph: 651-213-1300
Fax: 651-213-0359

On the central eastern border of MN, northeast of Minneapolis; established Sep 1, 1851 (prior to statehood) from Washington County. **Name Origin:** For Chisago Lake, largest in the county; from Ojibway *kichi* 'large' and *saga* 'fair' or 'beautiful.' The first syllable was omitted and a clerical error changed *a* to *o*.

Area (sq mi): 442.49 (land 417.63; water 24.86). **Pop per sq mi:** 118.3.

Pop 2005: 49,400. **State rank:** 18. **Pop change:** 2000-20005 +20.2%; 1990-2000 +34.7%. **Pop 2000:** 41,101 (White 96.4%;

Chisago County (cont'd)

Black or African American 0.5%; Hispanic or Latino 1.2%; Asian 0.7%; Other 1.6%). **Foreign born:** 1.2%. **Median age:** 34.3.

Income 2000: per capita $21,013; median household $52,012; **Pop below poverty level:** 5.1%. ***Personal per capita income 2000-2003:** $27,827-$28,448.

Unemployment 2004: 5.3%. **Change from 2000:** +0.6%. **Median travel time to work:** 31.9 minutes. **Working outside county of residence:** 65.8%.

Cities with pop over 10,000: North Branch (10,016).

CLAY COUNTY

PO Box 280   **Ph:** 218-299-5002
Moorhead, MN 56560   **Fax:** 218-299-5195
www.co.clay.mn.us

On the central western border of MN; established as Breckenridge County Mar 9, 1862; name changed later in 1862. **Name Origin:** For Henry Clay (1777-1852), U.S. senator from KY, known as the 'Great Pacificator' for his advocacy of compromise to avert national crises.

Area (sq mi): 1052.74 (land 1045.24; water 7.49). **Pop per sq mi:** 51.5.

Pop 2005: 53,838. **State rank:** 17. **Pop change:** 2000-20005 +5.1%; 1990-2000 +1.6%. **Pop 2000:** 51,229 (White 92.4%; Black or African American 0.5%; Hispanic or Latino 3.7%; Asian 0.9%; Other 4.6%, including 1.4% American Indian/Alaska Native). **Foreign born:** 2.6%. **Median age:** 32.3.

Income 2000: per capita $17,557; median household $37,889; **Pop below poverty level:** 13.2%. ***Personal per capita income 2000-2003:** $22,877-$25,311.

Unemployment 2004: 3.6%. **Change from 2000:** +0.9%. **Median travel time to work:** 17.4 minutes. **Working outside county of residence:** 53.1%.

Cities with pop over 10,000: Moorhead 🏛 (33,390).

CLEARWATER COUNTY

213 Main Ave N   **Ph:** 218-694-6520
Bagley, MN 56621   **Fax:** 218-694-6244
www.co.clearwater.mn.us

In north-central MN, east of Grand Forks, ND; established Dec 2, 1902 from Beltrami County. **Name Origin:** For Clearwater River and Lake, which are partly within the county.

Area (sq mi): 1029.79 (land 994.71; water 35.08). **Pop per sq mi:** 8.5.

Pop 2005: 8,476. **State rank:** 75. **Pop change:** 2000-20005 +0.6%; 1990-2000 +1.4%. **Pop 2000:** 8,423 (White 89.1%; Black or African American 0.2%; Hispanic or Latino 0.8%; Asian 0.2%; Other 10.3%, including 8.6% American Indian/Alaska Native). **Foreign born:** 0.9%. **Median age:** 39.7.

Income 2000: per capita $15,694; median household $30,517; **Pop below poverty level:** 15.1%. ***Personal per capita income 2000-2003:** $20,837-$21,374.

Unemployment 2004: 10.9%. **Change from 2000:** -0.7%. **Median travel time to work:** 23.9 minutes. **Working outside county of residence:** 32%.

Cities with pop over 10,000: None.

COOK COUNTY

411 E 2nd St   **Ph:** 218-387-3610
Grand Marais, MN 55604   **Fax:** 218-387-3007
www.co.cook.mn.us

On the northeastern border of MN; established Mar 9, 1874 from Lake County. **Name Origin:** For Maj. Michael Cook (1828-64), an officer in the Civil War and MN legislator. Some claim John Cook (?-1872), killed by Ojibway Indians.

Area (sq mi): 3339.72 (land 1450.6; water 1889.11). **Pop per sq mi:** 3.7.

Pop 2005: 5,367. **State rank:** 82. **Pop change:** 2000-20005 +3.9%; 1990-2000 +33.6%. **Pop 2000:** 5,168 (White 89.2%; Black or African American 0.3%; Hispanic or Latino 0.8%; Asian 0.3%; Other 10%, including 7.6% American Indian/Alaska Native). **Foreign born:** 2.7%. **Median age:** 44.

Income 2000: per capita $21,775; median household $36,640; **Pop below poverty level:** 10.1%. ***Personal per capita income 2000-2003:** $26,661-$29,301.

Unemployment 2004: 4.6%. **Change from 2000:** +0%. **Median travel time to work:** 18.2 minutes. **Working outside county of residence:** 4.6%.

Cities with pop over 10,000: None.

COTTONWOOD COUNTY

900 3rd Ave   **Ph:** 507-831-1905
Windom, MN 56101   **Fax:** 507-831-4553
www.co.cottonwood.mn.us

In southwestern MN, southwest of Mankato; established May 23, 1857 (prior to statehood) from Brown County. **Name Origin:** For the Cottonwood River, which runs through the county; itself named for the poplar trees along its banks, which have cotton-like tufts on the seeds.

Area (sq mi): 648.91 (land 639.99; water 8.91). **Pop per sq mi:** 18.5.

Pop 2005: 11,834. **State rank:** 63. **Pop change:** 2000-20005 -2.7%; 1990-2000 -4.2%. **Pop 2000:** 12,167 (White 94.6%; Black or African American 0.3%; Hispanic or Latino 2.2%; Asian 1.6%; Other 2.7%). **Foreign born:** 2.2%. **Median age:** 41.7.

Income 2000: per capita $16,647; median household $31,943; **Pop below poverty level:** 11.7%. ***Personal per capita income 2000-2003:** $23,248-$26,097.

Unemployment 2004: 4.7%. **Change from 2000:** +0.8%. **Median travel time to work:** 14 minutes. **Working outside county of residence:** 16.8%.

Cities with pop over 10,000: None.

CROW WING COUNTY

326 Laurel St   **Ph:** 218-824-1000
Brainerd, MN 56401   **Fax:** 218-824-1046
www.co.crow-wing.mn.us

In central MN, north of Saint Cloud; established May 23, 1857

---

*Source: Personal per capita income data are from the Bureau of Economic Analysis; per capita income data are from the Bureau of the Census. See Introduction for explanation of differences.

Crow Wing County (cont'd)

(prior to statehood) from Cass and Aitkin counties. **Name Origin:** For the Crow Wing river, which forms the southwestern border of the county; the Ojibway called the river *Kagiwigwan* or *Gagagiw-gwuni* 'crow wing' or 'raven feather.'

Area (sq mi): 1156.56 (land 996.57; water 160). **Pop per sq mi:** 60.1.

Pop 2005: 59,917. **State rank:** 14. **Pop change:** 2000-2005 +8.7%; 1990-2000 +24.5%. **Pop 2000:** 55,099 (White 97.2%; Black or African American 0.3%; Hispanic or Latino 0.7%; Asian 0.3%; Other 1.8%). **Foreign born:** 1.2%. **Median age:** 39.4.

Income 2000: per capita $19,174; median household $37,589; **Pop below poverty level:** 9.8%. ***Personal per capita income 2000-2003:** $23,527-$24,763.

Unemployment 2004: 5.2%. **Change from 2000:** +0.6%. **Median travel time to work:** 20.5 minutes. **Working outside county of residence:** 13%.

Cities with pop over 10,000: Brainerd ⚏ (13,746).

DAKOTA COUNTY
1560 Hwy 55   **Ph:** 651-438-8100
Hastings, MN 55033   **Fax:** 651-438-4405
www.co.dakota.mn.us

On the southeastern border of MN, south of Saint Paul; original county; established Oct 27, 1849 (prior to statehood); originally spelled Dakotah. **Name Origin:** For the Dakota (also known as Sioux) Indians of Siouan linguistic stock.

Area (sq mi): 586.33 (land 569.58; water 16.75). **Pop per sq mi:** 673.5.

Pop 2005: 383,592. **State rank:** 3. **Pop change:** 2000-2005 +7.8%; 1990-2000 +29.3%. **Pop 2000:** 355,904 (White 90%; Black or African American 2.3%; Hispanic or Latino 2.9%; Asian 2.9%; Other 3.5%). **Foreign born:** 5.1%. **Median age:** 33.7.

Income 2000: per capita $27,008; median household $61,863; **Pop below poverty level:** 3.6%. ***Personal per capita income 2000-2003:** $36,576-$38,272.

Unemployment 2004: 4.1%. **Change from 2000:** +1.3%. **Median travel time to work:** 22.8 minutes. **Working outside county of residence:** 54.2%.

Cities with pop over 10,000: 11 (see page 36 for cities).

DODGE COUNTY
22 6th St E   **Ph:** 507-635-6239
Mantorville, MN 55955   **Fax:** 507-635-6265
www.co.dodge.mn.us

In southeastern MN, west of Rochester; established Feb 20, 1855 (prior to statehood) from Olmstead County. **Name Origin:** For Gen. Henry Dodge (1782-1867), officer in the War of 1812 and the Black Hawk War, governor of WI Territory (1836-41; 1845-48), and U.S. senator (1848-57); also for his son, Augustus Caesar Dodge (1812-83), U.S. senator from IA (1848-55) and U.S. Minister to Spain (1855-59).

Area (sq mi): 439.63 (land 439.5; water 0.12). **Pop per sq mi:** 44.6.

Pop 2005: 19,595. **State rank:** 49. **Pop change:** 2000-2005 +10.5%; 1990-2000 +12.7%. **Pop 2000:** 17,731 (White 95.7%;

Black or African American 0.2%; Hispanic or Latino 3%; Asian 0.4%; Other 2.8%). **Foreign born:** 2.5%. **Median age:** 34.8.

Income 2000: per capita $19,259; median household $47,437; **Pop below poverty level:** 5.8%. ***Personal per capita income 2000-2003:** $26,420-$29,501.

Unemployment 2004: 4.3%. **Change from 2000:** +0.3%. **Median travel time to work:** 22.6 minutes. **Working outside county of residence:** 55.8%.

Cities with pop over 10,000: None.

DOUGLAS COUNTY
305 8th Ave W   **Ph:** 320-762-3877
Alexandria, MN 56308   **Fax:** 320-762-2389
www.co.douglas.mn.us

In west-central MN, northwest of Saint Cloud; established Mar 8, 1858 from Todd County. **Name Origin:** For Stephen Arnold Douglas (1813-61), U.S. orator and statesman.

Area (sq mi): 719.94 (land 634.32; water 85.62). **Pop per sq mi:** 55.4.

Pop 2005: 35,138. **State rank:** 29. **Pop change:** 2000-2005 +7.1%; 1990-2000 +14.5%. **Pop 2000:** 32,821 (White 98.2%; Black or African American 0.2%; Hispanic or Latino 0.6%; Asian 0.4%; Other 0.9%). **Foreign born:** 0.9%. **Median age:** 39.7.

Income 2000: per capita $18,850; median household $37,703; **Pop below poverty level:** 8.5%. ***Personal per capita income 2000-2003:** $25,218-$27,431.

Unemployment 2004: 3.7%. **Change from 2000:** +0%. **Median travel time to work:** 17.2 minutes. **Working outside county of residence:** 11.4%.

Cities with pop over 10,000: Alexandria ⚏ (10,231).

FARIBAULT COUNTY
415 N Main St   **Ph:** 507-526-6277
Blue Earth, MN 56013   **Fax:** 507-526-3054
www.co.faribault.mn.us

On the central southern border of MN, south of Mankato; established Feb 20, 1855 (prior to statehood) from Blue Earth County. **Name Origin:** For Jean Baptiste Faribault (1774-1860), a French-Canadian fur trader in the Northwest Territory who had great influence with the Sioux.

Area (sq mi): 721.61 (land 713.63; water 7.98). **Pop per sq mi:** 21.7.

Pop 2005: 15,506. **State rank:** 57. **Pop change:** 2000-2005 -4.2%; 1990-2000 -4.5%. **Pop 2000:** 16,181 (White 95.2%; Black or African American 0.2%; Hispanic or Latino 3.5%; Asian 0.4%; Other 2.3%). **Foreign born:** 1.6%. **Median age:** 42.4.

Income 2000: per capita $17,193; median household $34,440; **Pop below poverty level:** 8.6%. ***Personal per capita income 2000-2003:** $23,573-$26,609.

Unemployment 2004: 5.6%. **Change from 2000:** +1.3%. **Median travel time to work:** 19.4 minutes. **Working outside county of residence:** 22.8%.

Cities with pop over 10,000: None.

FILLMORE COUNTY

101 Fillmore St   **Ph:** 507-765-3356
Preston, MN 55965   **Fax:** 507-765-4571
www.co.fillmore.mn.us

On the southeastern border of MN, southeast of Rochester; original county; established Mar 5, 1853 (prior to statehood). **Name Origin:** For Millard Fillmore (1800-74), thirteenth U.S. president.

Area (sq mi): 862.15 (land 861.25; water 0.9). **Pop per sq mi:** 24.8.

Pop 2005: 21,368. **State rank:** 45. **Pop change:** 2000-20005 +1.2%; 1990-2000 +1.7%. **Pop 2000:** 21,122 (White 98.6%; Black or African American 0.2%; Hispanic or Latino 0.5%; Asian 0.1%; Other 0.8%). **Foreign born:** 0.8%. **Median age:** 39.8.

Income 2000: per capita $17,067; median household $36,651; **Pop below poverty level:** 10.1%. ***Personal per capita income 2000-2003:** $23,559-$25,790.

Unemployment 2004: 4.9%. **Change from 2000:** +0.8%. **Median travel time to work:** 25 minutes. **Working outside county of residence:** 37%.

Cities with pop over 10,000: None.

FREEBORN COUNTY

411 S Broadway   **Ph:** 507-377-5116
Albert Lea, MN 56007   **Fax:** 507-377-5109
www.co.freeborn.mn.us

On the southern border of MN, southwest of Rochester; established Feb 20, 1855 (prior to statehood) from Blue Earth and Rice counties. **Name Origin:** For William Freeborn (1816-1900), MN territorial legislator (1854-57)

Area (sq mi): 722.63 (land 707.64; water 14.99). **Pop per sq mi:** 45.1.

Pop 2005: 31,946. **State rank:** 32. **Pop change:** 2000-20005 -2%; 1990-2000 -1.4%. **Pop 2000:** 32,584 (White 92.3%; Black or African American 0.2%; Hispanic or Latino 6.3%; Asian 0.5%; Other 4%). **Foreign born:** 3.1%. **Median age:** 40.4.

Income 2000: per capita $18,325; median household $36,964; **Pop below poverty level:** 8.4%. ***Personal per capita income 2000-2003:** $23,968-$25,606.

Unemployment 2004: 5.2%. **Change from 2000:** +0.7%. **Median travel time to work:** 18.1 minutes. **Working outside county of residence:** 22.3%.

Cities with pop over 10,000: Albert Lea ⚒ (17,819).

GOODHUE COUNTY

454 W 6th St   **Ph:** 651-267-4800
Red Wing, MN 55066   **Fax:** 651-267-4986
www.co.goodhue.mn.us

In southeastern MN, southeast of Saint Paul; established Mar 5, 1853 (prior to statehood) from Wabasha County. **Name Origin:** For James Madison Goodhue (1810-52), lawyer and prominent editor of the first newspaper in the MN Territory.

Area (sq mi): 780.44 (land 758.27; water 22.17). **Pop per sq mi:** 60.1.

Pop 2005: 45,585. **State rank:** 20. **Pop change:** 2000-20005 +3.3%; 1990-2000 +8.4%. **Pop 2000:** 44,127 (White 96.1%; Black or African American 0.6%; Hispanic or Latino 1.1%; Asian 0.6%; Other 2.2%, including 1% American Indian/Alaska Native). **Foreign born:** 1.2%. **Median age:** 38.1.

Income 2000: per capita $21,934; median household $46,972; **Pop below poverty level:** 5.7%. ***Personal per capita income 2000-2003:** $27,648-$30,266.

Unemployment 2004: 4.8%. **Change from 2000:** +1.3%. **Median travel time to work:** 21.3 minutes. **Working outside county of residence:** 32.6%.

Cities with pop over 10,000: Red Wing ⚒ (15,907).

GRANT COUNTY

PO Box 1007 County Courthouse   **Ph:** 218-685-4825
Elbow Lake, MN 56531   **Fax:** 218-685-5349
www.co.grant.mn.us

In west-central MN, southeast of Fargo, ND; established Mar 6, 1868 from Stearns County. **Name Origin:** For Ulysses S. Grant (1822-85), Civil War general and eighteenth U.S. president.

Area (sq mi): 575.18 (land 546.41; water 28.77). **Pop per sq mi:** 11.2.

Pop 2005: 6,114. **State rank:** 79. **Pop change:** 2000-20005 -2.8%; 1990-2000 +0.7%. **Pop 2000:** 6,289 (White 98.1%; Black or African American 0.2%; Hispanic or Latino 0.5%; Asian 0.2%; Other 1.3%). **Foreign born:** 0.7%. **Median age:** 42.5.

Income 2000: per capita $17,131; median household $33,775; **Pop below poverty level:** 8.4%. ***Personal per capita income 2000-2003:** $24,509-$24,943.

Unemployment 2004: 5.7%. **Change from 2000:** -1.1%. **Median travel time to work:** 19 minutes. **Working outside county of residence:** 30.3%.

Cities with pop over 10,000: None.

HENNEPIN COUNTY

300 S 6th St   **Ph:** 612-348-3000
Minneapolis, MN 55487
www.co.hennepin.mn.us

In east-central MN, west of Saint Paul; original county; established Mar 6, 1852 (prior to statehood). **Name Origin:** For Louis Hennepin (1640-1701), Franciscan missionary and explorer (with La Salle) who named the Falls of Saint Anthony in the Mississippi River at present-day Minneapolis.

Area (sq mi): 606.38 (land 556.62; water 49.77). **Pop per sq mi:** 2011.

Pop 2005: 1,119,364. **State rank:** 1. **Pop change:** 2000-20005 +0.3%; 1990-2000 +8.1%. **Pop 2000:** 1,116,200 (White 78.9%; Black or African American 9%; Hispanic or Latino 4.1%; Asian 4.8%; Other 5.7%, including 1% American Indian/Alaska Native). **Foreign born:** 9.9%. **Median age:** 34.9.

Income 2000: per capita $28,789; median household $51,711; **Pop below poverty level:** 8.3%. ***Personal per capita income 2000-2003:** $43,075-$44,924.

Unemployment 2004: 4.5%. **Change from 2000:** +1.3%. **Median travel time to work:** 22.2 minutes. **Working outside county of residence:** 16.9%.

Cities with pop over 10,000: 17 (see page 36 for cities).

*Source: Personal per capita income data are from the Bureau of Economic Analysis; per capita income data are from the Bureau of the Census. See Introduction for explanation of differences.

HOUSTON COUNTY

304 S Marshall St   **Ph:** 507-725-5806
Caledonia, MN 55921   **Fax:** 507-725-5550
www.geocities.com/houstoncountymn/HC.html

In the southeastern corner of MN, southeast of Rochester; established Feb 23, 1854 (prior to statehood) from Fillmore County. **Name Origin:** For Samuel Houston (1793-1863), governor of TN (1827-29), president of the Republic of Texas (1836-38; 1841-44), U.S. senator from TX (1846-59), and TX governor (1859-61).

Area (sq mi): 568.91 (land 558.41; water 10.5). **Pop per sq mi:** 35.7.

Pop 2005: 19,941. **State rank:** 48. **Pop change:** 2000-20005 +1.1%; 1990-2000 +6.6%. **Pop 2000:** 19,718 (White 98.1%; Black or African American 0.3%; Hispanic or Latino 0.6%; Asian 0.4%; Other 0.8%). **Foreign born:** 1.1%. **Median age:** 38.8.

Income 2000: per capita $18,826; median household $40,680; **Pop below poverty level:** 6.5%. ***Personal per capita income 2000-2003:** $25,942-$28,035.

Unemployment 2004: 5.1%. **Change from 2000:** +1.3%. **Median travel time to work:** 20.7 minutes. **Working outside county of residence:** 50.5%.

Cities with pop over 10,000: None.

HUBBARD COUNTY

301 Court Ave County Courthouse   **Ph:** 218-732-3196
Park Rapids, MN 56470   **Fax:** 218-732-3645
www.co.hubbard.mn.us

In north-central MN, northeast of Fargo, ND; established Feb 26, 1883 from Cass County. **Name Origin:** For Gen. Lucius Frederick Hubbard (1836-1913), an officer in the Civil War and the Spanish-American War, MN legislator and governor (1882-87).

Area (sq mi): 999.39 (land 922.46; water 76.93). **Pop per sq mi:** 20.4.

Pop 2005: 18,861. **State rank:** 51. **Pop change:** 2000-20005 +2.6%; 1990-2000 +23%. **Pop 2000:** 18,376 (White 95.9%; Black or African American 0.2%; Hispanic or Latino 0.7%; Asian 0.3%; Other 3.2%, including 2.1% American Indian/Alaska Native). **Foreign born:** 1.1%. **Median age:** 41.8.

Income 2000: per capita $18,115; median household $35,321; **Pop below poverty level:** 9.7%. ***Personal per capita income 2000-2003:** $21,184-$23,514.

Unemployment 2004: 5.8%. **Change from 2000:** +0.3%. **Median travel time to work:** 20.7 minutes. **Working outside county of residence:** 38%.

Cities with pop over 10,000: None.

ISANTI COUNTY

555 18th Ave SW   **Ph:** 763-689-3859
Cambridge, MN 55008   **Fax:** 763-689-8226
www.co.isanti.mn.us

In central-eastern MN, north of Minneapolis; established Feb 13, 1857 (prior to statehood) from Anoka County. **Name Origin:** For the Izaty or Santee Indians, a tribe of the Dakotas who inhabited the area. Also spelled *Issati*. The name means 'knife' or perhaps 'ones who make knives.'

Area (sq mi): 451.87 (land 439.07; water 12.81). **Pop per sq mi:** 85.8.

Pop 2005: 37,664. **State rank:** 26. **Pop change:** 2000-20005 +20.4%; 1990-2000 +20.7%. **Pop 2000:** 31,287 (White 97.1%; Black or African American 0.3%; Hispanic or Latino 0.8%; Asian 0.4%; Other 1.7%). **Foreign born:** 1.3%. **Median age:** 35.7.

Income 2000: per capita $20,348; median household $50,127; **Pop below poverty level:** 5.7%. ***Personal per capita income 2000-2003:** $26,311-$27,323.

Unemployment 2004: 5.2%. **Change from 2000:** +0.5%. **Median travel time to work:** 32.6 minutes. **Working outside county of residence:** 60.4%.

Cities with pop over 10,000: None.

ITASCA COUNTY

123 NE 4th St   **Ph:** 218-327-2847
Grand Rapids, MN 55744   **Fax:** 218-327-2848
www.co.itasca.mn.us

In north-central MN, west of Hibbing; original county; established Oct 27, 1850 (prior to statehood). **Name Origin:** For Itasca Lake; name coined by explorer and ethnologist Henry Rowe Schoolcraft (1793-1864), who thought the lake was the 'true source' of the Mississippi River. From Latin: the last part of *veritas* 'truth' and first part of *caput* 'head.'

Area (sq mi): 2927.78 (land 2665.06; water 262.72). **Pop per sq mi:** 16.7.

Pop 2005: 44,384. **State rank:** 21. **Pop change:** 2000-20005 +0.9%; 1990-2000 +7.7%. **Pop 2000:** 43,992 (White 94.3%; Black or African American 0.2%; Hispanic or Latino 0.6%; Asian 0.3%; Other 4.9%, including 3.4% American Indian/Alaska Native). **Foreign born:** 1.3%. **Median age:** 41.1.

Income 2000: per capita $17,717; median household $36,234; **Pop below poverty level:** 10.6%. ***Personal per capita income 2000-2003:** $22,204-$24,048.

Unemployment 2004: 7.3%. **Change from 2000:** +0.2%. **Median travel time to work:** 22 minutes. **Working outside county of residence:** 15.6%.

Cities with pop over 10,000: None.

JACKSON COUNTY

PO Box 226   **Ph:** 507-847-2763
Jackson, MN 56143   **Fax:** 507-847-4718
www.co.jackson.mn.us

On southern border of MN, southwest of Mankato; established May 23, 1857 (prior to statehood) from unorganized lands. **Name Origin:** For Henry Jackson (1811-57), an early merchant in Saint Paul (1842), first postmaster (1846-49), and territorial legislator. There is also a debatable claim that the county was named for Andrew Jackson.

Area (sq mi): 719.46 (land 701.69; water 17.76). **Pop per sq mi:** 15.9.

Pop 2005: 11,182. **State rank:** 67. **Pop change:** 2000-20005 -0.8%; 1990-2000 -3.5%. **Pop 2000:** 11,268 (White 96.2%; Black or African American 0.1%; Hispanic or Latino 1.9%; Asian 1.4%; Other 1.5%). **Foreign born:** 1.5%. **Median age:** 40.8.

Income 2000: per capita $17,499; median household $36,746; **Pop below poverty level:** 8.6%. ***Personal per capita income 2000-2003:** $22,761-$26,262.

Jackson County (cont'd)

Unemployment 2004: 3.6%. **Change from 2000:** +0.3%. **Median travel time to work:** 15.7 minutes. **Working outside county of residence:** 29.1%.

Cities with pop over 10,000: None.

KANABEC COUNTY
18 N Vine St   **Ph:** 320-679-6466
Mora, MN 55051   **Fax:** 320-679-6431
www.kanabeccounty.org

In east-central MN, north of Minneapolis; established Mar 13, 1858 from Pine County. **Name Origin:** For the meandering Snake River, which flows through the county; from the Ojibway word for 'snake.'

Area (sq mi): 533.38 (land 524.93; water 8.45). **Pop per sq mi:** 30.9.

Pop 2005: 16,215. **State rank:** 54. **Pop change:** 2000-20005 +8.1%; 1990-2000 +17.1%. **Pop 2000:** 14,996 (White 96.6%; Black or African American 0.2%; Hispanic or Latino 0.9%; Asian 0.4%; Other 2.1%). **Foreign born:** 0.9%. **Median age:** 38.

Income 2000: per capita $17,741; median household $38,520; **Pop below poverty level:** 9.5%. ***Personal per capita income 2000-2003:** $21,673-$22,553.

Unemployment 2004: 7.5%. **Change from 2000:** -0.7%. **Median travel time to work:** 31.3 minutes. **Working outside county of residence:** 46.3%.

Cities with pop over 10,000: None.

KANDIYOHI COUNTY
PO Box 936   **Ph:** 320-231-6202
Willmar, MN 56201   **Fax:** 320-231-6263
www.co.kandiyohi.mn.us

In south-central MN, west of Minneapollis; established Mar 20, 1858 from Meeker County, annexed Monongalia County in Nov 1870. **Name Origin:** From Siouan 'place where the buffalo fish arrive,' the Indian name for several lakes at the source of the Crow River where the fish *Ictiobus cyprinella, I. urus* and *I. bubalus* go to spawn.

Area (sq mi): 861.97 (land 796.06; water 65.92). **Pop per sq mi:** 51.8.

Pop 2005: 41,199. **State rank:** 23. **Pop change:** 2000-20005 +0%; 1990-2000 +6.3%. **Pop 2000:** 41,203 (White 90.3%; Black or African American 0.5%; Hispanic or Latino 8%; Asian 0.4%; Other 5.5%). **Foreign born:** 3.8%. **Median age:** 36.9.

Income 2000: per capita $19,627; median household $39,772; **Pop below poverty level:** 9.2%. ***Personal per capita income 2000-2003:** $26,778-$29,101.

Unemployment 2004: 4.5%. **Change from 2000:** +0.8%. **Median travel time to work:** 17.9 minutes. **Working outside county of residence:** 11.6%.

Cities with pop over 10,000: Willmar 🏛 (18,205).

KITTSON COUNTY
410 5th St S Suite 214   **Ph:** 218-843-2655
Hallock, MN 56728   **Fax:** 218-843-2656
www.visitnwminnesota.com/Kittson.htm

In the northwestern corner of MN, north of Grand Forks, ND; established as Pembina County Apr 24, 1879 from unorganized lands; name changed Mar 9, 1878. **Name Origin:** For Norman Wolfred Kittson (1814-88), fur trader, territorial legislator (1851-55), and mayor of Saint Paul (1858).

Area (sq mi): 1103.51 (land 1097.08; water 6.43). **Pop per sq mi:** 4.4.

Pop 2005: 4,792. **State rank:** 84. **Pop change:** 2000-20005 -9.3%; 1990-2000 -8.4%. **Pop 2000:** 5,285 (White 97.3%; Black or African American 0.2%; Hispanic or Latino 1.3%; Asian 0.2%; Other 1.6%). **Foreign born:** 2%. **Median age:** 42.4.

Income 2000: per capita $16,525; median household $32,515; **Pop below poverty level:** 10.2%. ***Personal per capita income 2000-2003:** $25,329-$29,479.

Unemployment 2004: 6.6%. **Change from 2000:** +0.4%. **Median travel time to work:** 19.5 minutes. **Working outside county of residence:** 27.5%.

Cities with pop over 10,000: None.

KOOCHICHING COUNTY
715 4th St   **Ph:** 218-283-1152
International Falls, MN 56649   **Fax:** 218-283-1151
www.co.koochiching.mn.us

On the central-northern border of MN; established Dec 19, 1906 from Itasca County. **Name Origin:** Origin uncertain, but evidence points to a Cree Indian word meaning 'rainy lake,' descriptive of the mists from the nearby International Falls on Rainy River.

Area (sq mi): 3154.32 (land 3102.36; water 51.96). **Pop per sq mi:** 4.5.

Pop 2005: 13,907. **State rank:** 59. **Pop change:** 2000-20005 -3.1%; 1990-2000 -11.9%. **Pop 2000:** 14,355 (White 95.7%; Black or African American 0.2%; Hispanic or Latino 0.6%; Asian 0.2%; Other 3.6%, including 2.2% American Indian/Alaska Native). **Foreign born:** 5.9%. **Median age:** 41.5.

Income 2000: per capita $19,167; median household $36,262; **Pop below poverty level:** 12.1%. ***Personal per capita income 2000-2003:** $24,491-$27,706.

Unemployment 2004: 6.2%. **Change from 2000:** +0.1%. **Median travel time to work:** 15.5 minutes. **Working outside county of residence:** 7.4%.

Cities with pop over 10,000: None.

LAC QUI PARLE COUNTY
600 6th St   **Ph:** 320-598-7444
Madison, MN 56256   **Fax:** 320-598-3125
www.ci.madison.mn.us/

On the southwestern border of MN; organized 1863 north of the Minnesota River, disestablished in 1868, then recreated Mar 6, 1871 south of the river. **Name Origin:** French 'talking lake,' probably a transliteration of Siouan *mde*'lake,' *iye* 'speaks,' and *dan*, a diminutive suffix. Origin uncertain, but possibly for echoes reflected from surrounding cliffs.

Area (sq mi): 778.05 (land 764.87; water 13.19). **Pop per sq mi:** 9.9.

Pop 2005: 7,604. **State rank:** 76. **Pop change:** 2000-20005 -5.7%; 1990-2000 -9.6%. **Pop 2000:** 8,067 (White 98.7%; Black or African

*Source: Personal per capita income data are from the Bureau of Economic Analysis; per capita income data are from the Bureau of the Census. See Introduction for explanation of differences.

372

Lac Qui Parle County (cont'd)

American 0.2%; Hispanic or Latino 0.3%; Asian 0.3%; Other 0.7%). **Foreign born:** 1%. **Median age:** 43.4.

Income 2000: per capita $17,399; median household $32,626; **Pop below poverty level:** 8.5%. ***Personal per capita income 2000-2003:** $23,584-$23,817.

Unemployment 2004: 4.3%. **Change from 2000:** +0%. **Median travel time to work:** 17.5 minutes. **Working outside county of residence:** 26.6%.

Cities with pop over 10,000: None.

LAKE COUNTY

601 3rd Ave	**Ph:** 218-834-8300
Two Harbors, MN 55616	**Fax:** 218-834-8360
www.lakecnty.com	

On the northeastern border of MN, northeast of Duluth; established Mar 1, 1856 (prior to statehood); name changed from Doty County. **Name Origin:** For Lake Superior, which forms its eastern border.

Area (sq mi): 2990.82 (land 2099.16; water 891.66). **Pop per sq mi:** 5.3.

Pop 2005: 11,156. **State rank:** 68. **Pop change:** 2000-20005 +0.9%; 1990-2000 +6.2%. **Pop 2000:** 11,058 (White 97.7%; Black or African American 0.1%; Hispanic or Latino 0.6%; Asian 0.2%; Other 1.7%). **Foreign born:** 1.7%. **Median age:** 42.9.

Income 2000: per capita $19,761; median household $40,402; **Pop below poverty level:** 7.4%. ***Personal per capita income 2000-2003:** $24,288-$29,664.

Unemployment 2004: 4.7%. **Change from 2000:** -0.5%. **Median travel time to work:** 21.4 minutes. **Working outside county of residence:** 27.8%.

Cities with pop over 10,000: None.

LAKE OF THE WOODS COUNTY

PO Box 808	**Ph:** 218-634-2836
Baudette, MN 56623	**Fax:** 218-634-2509
www.co.lake-of-the-woods.mn.us	

On the central northern border of MN; established Nov 28, 1922 from Beltrami County; the latest county formed. **Name Origin:** For the Lake of the Woods in Canada, which forms its northern border.

Area (sq mi): 1775.05 (land 1296.7; water 478.35). **Pop per sq mi:** 3.4.

Pop 2005: 4,421. **State rank:** 85. **Pop change:** 2000-20005 -2.2%; 1990-2000 +10.9%. **Pop 2000:** 4,522 (White 96.7%; Black or African American 0.3%; Hispanic or Latino 0.6%; Asian 0.2%; Other 2.2%, including 1.1% American Indian/Alaska Native). **Foreign born:** 2.9%. **Median age:** 41.6.

Income 2000: per capita $16,976; median household $32,861; **Pop below poverty level:** 9.8%. ***Personal per capita income 2000-2003:** $19,908-$22,920.

Unemployment 2004: 4.7%. **Change from 2000:** +0.2%. **Median travel time to work:** 17.4 minutes. **Working outside county of residence:** 18.7%.

Cities with pop over 10,000: None.

LE SUEUR COUNTY

88 South Pk	**Ph:** 507-357-2251
Le Center, MN 56057	**Fax:** 507-357-6433
www.co.le-sueur.mn.us	

In south-central MN, north of Mankato; established Mar 5, 1853 (prior to statehood) from unorganized lands. **Name Origin:** For Pierre Charles Le Sueur (1657-1702?), French-Canadian fur trader and explorer of the upper Mississippi River and its tributaries.

Area (sq mi): 473.86 (land 448.5; water 25.36). **Pop per sq mi:** 61.3.

Pop 2005: 27,490. **State rank:** 38. **Pop change:** 2000-20005 +8.1%; 1990-2000 +9.4%. **Pop 2000:** 25,426 (White 94.8%; Black or African American 0.1%; Hispanic or Latino 3.9%; Asian 0.3%; Other 3%). **Foreign born:** 1.8%. **Median age:** 37.3.

Income 2000: per capita $20,151; median household $45,933; **Pop below poverty level:** 6.9%. ***Personal per capita income 2000-2003:** $27,532-$27,459.

Unemployment 2004: 5.6%. **Change from 2000:** +0.9%. **Median travel time to work:** 22.5 minutes. **Working outside county of residence:** 53.1%.

Cities with pop over 10,000: None.

LINCOLN COUNTY

319 N Rebecca St	**Ph:** 507-694-1529
Ivanhoe, MN 56142	**Fax:** 507-694-1198
www.co.lincoln.mn.us	

On the southwestern border of MN; established Mar 1, 1866 from Lyon County. **Name Origin:** For Abraham Lincoln (1809-65), sixteenth U.S. president.

Area (sq mi): 548.44 (land 537.03; water 11.41). **Pop per sq mi:** 11.3.

Pop 2005: 6,050. **State rank:** 80. **Pop change:** 2000-20005 -5.9%; 1990-2000 -6.7%. **Pop 2000:** 6,429 (White 98.4%; Black or African American 0%; Hispanic or Latino 0.9%; Asian 0.2%; Other 0.9%). **Foreign born:** 0.7%. **Median age:** 43.

Income 2000: per capita $16,009; median household $31,607; **Pop below poverty level:** 9.7%. ***Personal per capita income 2000-2003:** $22,451-$24,697.

Unemployment 2004: 4%. **Change from 2000:** +0.3%. **Median travel time to work:** 18.3 minutes. **Working outside county of residence:** 36.7%.

Cities with pop over 10,000: None.

LYON COUNTY

607 W Main St	**Ph:** 507-537-6728
Marshall, MN 56258	**Fax:** 507-537-6091
www.lyonco.org	

In southwestern MN; established Mar 6, 1868 from Yellow Medicine County. **Name Origin:** For Gen. Nathaniel Lyon (1818-61), officer in the Seminole War and the Mexican-American War; as a Union commander in the Civil War, he helped preserve MO for the Union.

Area (sq mi): 721.46 (land 714.17; water 7.29). **Pop per sq mi:** 34.3.

Pop 2005: 24,472. **State rank:** 42. **Pop change:** 2000-20005 -3.7%; 1990-2000 +2.6%. **Pop 2000:** 25,425 (White 91.8%; Black or African American 1.5%; Hispanic or Latino 4%; Asian 1.7%; Other 3.2%). **Foreign born:** 4.5%. **Median age:** 34.

Lyon County (cont'd)

Income 2000: per capita $18,013; median household $38,996; **Pop below poverty level:** 10.1%. ***Personal per capita income 2000-2003:** $25,956-$27,958.

Unemployment 2004: 3.9%. **Change from 2000:** +0.2%. **Median travel time to work:** 13.5 minutes. **Working outside county of residence:** 5.8%.

Cities with pop over 10,000: Marshall 🏛 (12,409).

MAHNOMEN COUNTY
PO Box 379   **Ph:** 218-935-5669
Mahnomen, MN 56557   **Fax:** 218-935-5946

In west-central MN, northeast of Fargo, ND; established Dec 27, 1906 from Norman County. **Name Origin:** The Ojibway word meaning 'wild rice,' which grows abundantly in the region.

Area (sq mi): 582.99 (land 556.14; water 26.85). **Pop per sq mi:** 9.2.

Pop 2005: 5,113. **State rank:** 83. **Pop change:** 2000-20005 -1.5%; 1990-2000 +2.9%. **Pop 2000:** 5,190 (White 62.7%; Black or African American 0.1%; Hispanic or Latino 0.9%; Asian 0.1%; Other 37%, including 28.6% American Indian/Alaska Native). **Foreign born:** 1.3%. **Median age:** 38.2.

Income 2000: per capita $13,438; median household $30,053; **Pop below poverty level:** 16.7%. ***Personal per capita income 2000-2003:** $19,949-$22,331.

Unemployment 2004: 5.9%. **Change from 2000:** -1.4%. **Median travel time to work:** 21.5 minutes. **Working outside county of residence:** 20.5%.

Cities with pop over 10,000: None.

MARSHALL COUNTY
208 E Colvin Ave   **Ph:** 218-745-4851
Warren, MN 56762   **Fax:** 218-745-5089
www.visitnwminnesota.com/Marshall.htm

In northwestern MN, north of Grand Forks, ND; established Feb 25, 1879 from Kittson County. **Name Origin:** For Gen. William Rainey Marshall (1825-96), MN businessman and governor (1866-70).

Area (sq mi): 1812.79 (land 1772.24; water 40.55). **Pop per sq mi:** 5.6.

Pop 2005: 9,965. **State rank:** 70. **Pop change:** 2000-20005 -1.9%; 1990-2000 -7.6%. **Pop 2000:** 10,155 (White 96%; Black or African American 0.1%; Hispanic or Latino 2.9%; Asian 0.2%; Other 2.5%). **Foreign born:** 1.9%. **Median age:** 40.5.

Income 2000: per capita $16,317; median household $34,804; **Pop below poverty level:** 9.8%. ***Personal per capita income 2000-2003:** $24,922-$28,589.

Unemployment 2004: 7.5%. **Change from 2000:** -1.3%. **Median travel time to work:** 23.2 minutes. **Working outside county of residence:** 43.8%.

Cities with pop over 10,000: None.

MARTIN COUNTY
201 Lake Ave Suite 201   **Ph:** 507-238-3211
Fairmont, MN 56031   **Fax:** 507-238-3259
www.co.martin.mn.us

On the central southern border of MN, southwest of Mankato; established May 23, 1857 (prior to statehood) from Faribault County. **Name Origin:** Either for Henry Martin (1829-1908), CT speculator with large holdings in the area, or for Morgan Lewis Martin (1805-87), U.S. representative from WI Territory who introduced the bill for the organization of the Territory of MN.

Area (sq mi): 729.56 (land 709.34; water 20.21). **Pop per sq mi:** 29.6.

Pop 2005: 21,002. **State rank:** 46. **Pop change:** 2000-20005 -3.7%; 1990-2000 -4.9%. **Pop 2000:** 21,802 (White 96.8%; Black or African American 0.3%; Hispanic or Latino 1.9%; Asian 0.4%; Other 2.1%). **Foreign born:** 1.4%. **Median age:** 41.5.

Income 2000: per capita $18,529; median household $34,810; **Pop below poverty level:** 10.5%. ***Personal per capita income 2000-2003:** $26,117-$29,634.

Unemployment 2004: 4.8%. **Change from 2000:** +0.7%. **Median travel time to work:** 15.8 minutes. **Working outside county of residence:** 15.3%.

Cities with pop over 10,000: Fairmont 🏛 (10,548).

MCLEOD COUNTY
830 11th St E Suite 106   **Ph:** 320-864-1281
Glencoe, MN 55336   **Fax:** 320-864-5905
www.co.mcleod.mn.us

In south-central MN, west of Minneapolis; established Mar 1, 1856 (prior to statehood) from Carver County. **Name Origin:** For Martin McLeod (1813-60), fur trader, MN territorial legislator (1849-53), and a founder of Glencoe.

Area (sq mi): 505.67 (land 491.91; water 13.76). **Pop per sq mi:** 74.5.

Pop 2005: 36,636. **State rank:** 27. **Pop change:** 2000-20005 +5%; 1990-2000 +9%. **Pop 2000:** 34,898 (White 94.9%; Black or African American 0.2%; Hispanic or Latino 3.6%; Asian 0.6%; Other 2.7%). **Foreign born:** 2.2%. **Median age:** 35.6.

Income 2000: per capita $20,137; median household $45,953; **Pop below poverty level:** 4.8%. ***Personal per capita income 2000-2003:** $26,676-$27,779.

Unemployment 2004: 4.6%. **Change from 2000:** +0.8%. **Median travel time to work:** 20.1 minutes. **Working outside county of residence:** 25%.

Cities with pop over 10,000: Hutchinson (13,521).

MEEKER COUNTY
325 N Sibley Ave   **Ph:** 320-693-5230
Litchfield, MN 55355   **Fax:** 320-693-5254
www.co.meeker.mn.us

In south-central MN, northwest of Minneapolis; established Feb 23, 1856 (prior to statehood) from Wright County. **Name Origin:** For Bradley B. Meeker (1813-73), associate justice of the MN supreme court (1849-53).

Area (sq mi): 645.08 (land 608.54; water 36.54). **Pop per sq mi:** 38.4.

**Source: Personal per capita income data are from the Bureau of Economic Analysis; per capita income data are from the Bureau of the Census.
See Introduction for explanation of differences.*

374

Meeker County (cont'd)

Pop 2005: 23,371. **State rank:** 43. **Pop change:** 2000-20005 +3.2%; 1990-2000 +8.6%. **Pop 2000:** 22,644 (White 96.7%; Black or African American 0.2%; Hispanic or Latino 2.2%; Asian 0.4%; Other 2.1%). **Foreign born:** 0.8%. **Median age:** 38.3.

Income 2000: per capita $18,628; median household $40,908; **Pop below poverty level:** 7.1%. ***Personal per capita income 2000-2003:** $23,274-$24,808.

Unemployment 2004: 5.5%. **Change from 2000:** -1.1%. **Median travel time to work:** 23.8 minutes. **Working outside county of residence:** 44%.

Cities with pop over 10,000: None.

MILLE LACS COUNTY

635 2nd St SE　　　　　　　　　**Ph:** 320-983-8313
Milaca, MN 56353　　　　　　　　**Fax:** 320-983-8384
www.co.mille-lacs.mn.us

In east-central MN, northeast of Saint Cloud; established May 23, 1857 (prior to statehood) from Kanabec County. **Name Origin:** For Mille Lacs Lake in the northern part of the county; French 'thousand lakes.'

Area (sq mi): 681.77 (land 574.47; water 107.3). **Pop per sq mi:** 44.7.

Pop 2005: 25,680. **State rank:** 40. **Pop change:** 2000-20005 +15%; 1990-2000 +19.6%. **Pop 2000:** 22,330 (White 93%; Black or African American 0.3%; Hispanic or Latino 1%; Asian 0.2%; Other 6%, including 4.7% American Indian/Alaska Native). **Foreign born:** 1.1%. **Median age:** 38.

Income 2000: per capita $17,656; median household $36,977; **Pop below poverty level:** 9.6%. ***Personal per capita income 2000-2003:** $21,919-$22,486.

Unemployment 2004: 7%. **Change from 2000:** +0%. **Median travel time to work:** 27.1 minutes. **Working outside county of residence:** 40.2%.

Cities with pop over 10,000: None.

MORRISON COUNTY

213 SE 1st Ave　　　　　　　　　**Ph:** 320-632-0293
Little Falls, MN 56345　　　　　　**Fax:** 320-632-0294
www.co.morrison.mn.us

In central MN, north of Saint Cloud; established Feb 25, 1856 (prior to statehood) from Benton and Stearns counties. **Name Origin:** For the Morrison brothers; William (1785-1866), fur trader and explorer, and Allen (1803-77), fur trader and representative in the first territorial legislature.

Area (sq mi): 1153.32 (land 1124.5; water 28.82). **Pop per sq mi:** 29.2.

Pop 2005: 32,788. **State rank:** 31. **Pop change:** 2000-20005 +3.4%; 1990-2000 +7.1%. **Pop 2000:** 31,712 (White 98.1%; Black or African American 0.2%; Hispanic or Latino 0.6%; Asian 0.3%; Other 1%). **Foreign born:** 1%. **Median age:** 36.9.

Income 2000: per capita $16,566; median household $37,047; **Pop below poverty level:** 11.1%. ***Personal per capita income 2000-2003:** $21,241-$22,479.

Unemployment 2004: 5.8%. **Change from 2000:** -1%. **Median travel time to work:** 24.6 minutes. **Working outside county of residence:** 32.5%.

Cities with pop over 10,000: None.

MOWER COUNTY

201 1st St NE　　　　　　　　　**Ph:** 507-437-9535
Austin, MN 55912　　　　　　　　**Fax:** 507-437-9471
www.co.mower.mn.us

On the southeastern border of MN, south of Rochester; established Feb 20, 1855 (prior to statehood) from Fillmore County. **Name Origin:** For John Mower (1815-79), MN territorial and state legislator (1854-55; 1874-75).

Area (sq mi): 711.71 (land 711.5; water 0.21). **Pop per sq mi:** 54.5.

Pop 2005: 38,799. **State rank:** 24. **Pop change:** 2000-20005 +0.5%; 1990-2000 +3.3%. **Pop 2000:** 38,603 (White 93%; Black or African American 0.6%; Hispanic or Latino 4.3%; Asian 1.5%; Other 3.3%). **Foreign born:** 3.6%. **Median age:** 38.9.

Income 2000: per capita $19,795; median household $36,654; **Pop below poverty level:** 9.2%. ***Personal per capita income 2000-2003:** $25,299-$27,807.

Unemployment 2004: 4.4%. **Change from 2000:** +1.4%. **Median travel time to work:** 18.7 minutes. **Working outside county of residence:** 22.7%.

Cities with pop over 10,000: Austin 🏛 (23,507).

MURRAY COUNTY

2500 28th St　　　　　　　　　**Ph:** 507-836-6148
Slayton, MN 56172　　　　　　　**Fax:** 507-836-8904
www.murray-countymn.com

In southwestern MN, southwest of Mankato; established May 23, 1857 from Lyon County. **Name Origin:** For William Pitt Murray (1825-1910), MN legislator and Saint Paul city attorney (1876-89).

Area (sq mi): 719.52 (land 704.43; water 15.09). **Pop per sq mi:** 12.6.

Pop 2005: 8,852. **State rank:** 74. **Pop change:** 2000-20005 -3.4%; 1990-2000 -5.1%. **Pop 2000:** 9,165 (White 97.4%; Black or African American 0.1%; Hispanic or Latino 1.5%; Asian 0.2%; Other 1.3%). **Foreign born:** 1.4%. **Median age:** 42.4.

Income 2000: per capita $17,936; median household $34,966; **Pop below poverty level:** 8.3%. ***Personal per capita income 2000-2003:** $23,722-$25,890.

Unemployment 2004: 4.3%. **Change from 2000:** -0.7%. **Median travel time to work:** 20.1 minutes. **Working outside county of residence:** 32.6%.

Cities with pop over 10,000: None.

NICOLLET COUNTY

501 S Minnesota Ave　　　　　　**Ph:** 507-931-6800
Saint Peter, MN 56082　　　　　**Fax:** 507-931-9220
www.co.nicollet.mn.us

In south-central MN, northwest of Mankato; established Mar 5, 1853 (prior to statehood) from unorganized lands. **Name Origin:** For Joseph Nicholas Nicollet (1786-1843), French explorer who

🏛 County Seat

Nicollet County (cont'd)

mapped area of MN, ND and SD; author of *Map of the Hydrographical Basin of the Upper Mississippi River.*

Area (sq mi): 466.95 (land 452.29; water 14.65). **Pop per sq mi:** 68.2.

Pop 2005: 30,848. **State rank:** 35. **Pop change:** 2000-20005 +3.6%; 1990-2000 +6%. **Pop 2000:** 29,771 (White 95.4%; Black or African American 0.8%; Hispanic or Latino 1.8%; Asian 1.1%; Other 1.7%). **Foreign born:** 2.7%. **Median age:** 32.6.

Income 2000: per capita $20,517; median household $46,170; **Pop below poverty level:** 7.5%. ***Personal per capita income 2000-2003:** $26,543-$27,360.

Unemployment 2004: 3.6%. **Change from 2000:** +1%. **Median travel time to work:** 15.1 minutes. **Working outside county of residence:** 48.8%.

Cities with pop over 10,000: Saint Peter ⚏ (10,358).

NOBLES COUNTY
1530 Airport Rd   **Ph:** 507-372-8263
Worthington, MN 56187   **Fax:** 507-372-4994
www.co.nobles.mn.us

On the southwestern border of MN, southwest of Mankato; established May 23, 1857 (prior to statehood) from Jackson County. **Name Origin:** For William H. Nobles (1816-76), MN Territory legislator (1854;1856); discovered Nobles Pass through the Rocky Mountains.

Area (sq mi): 722.33 (land 715.39; water 6.94). **Pop per sq mi:** 28.7.

Pop 2005: 20,508. **State rank:** 47. **Pop change:** 2000-20005 -1.6%; 1990-2000 +3.7%. **Pop 2000:** 20,832 (White 82.7%; Black or African American 1.1%; Hispanic or Latino 11.2%; Asian 4%; Other 8.4%). **Foreign born:** 9%. **Median age:** 37.5.

Income 2000: per capita $16,987; median household $35,684; **Pop below poverty level:** 11.7%. ***Personal per capita income 2000-2003:** $23,188-$26,127.

Unemployment 2004: 3.9%. **Change from 2000:** +0.3%. **Median travel time to work:** 15.8 minutes. **Working outside county of residence:** 13.8%.

Cities with pop over 10,000: Worthington ⚏ (11,087).

NORMAN COUNTY
16 3rd Ave E PO Box 146   **Ph:** 218-784-5481
Ada, MN 56510   **Fax:** 218-784-2399
www.co.norman.mn.us

On the northwestern border of MN, north of Fargo, ND; established Feb 17, 1881 from Polk County. **Name Origin:** For the many Norwegians, known locally as Normans (Norsemen), living in the area and serving in the state legislature when the county was formed.

Area (sq mi): 876.82 (land 876.27; water 0.55). **Pop per sq mi:** 8.

Pop 2005: 7,003. **State rank:** 77. **Pop change:** 2000-20005 -5.9%; 1990-2000 -6.7%. **Pop 2000:** 7,442 (White 93.5%; Black or African American 0.1%; Hispanic or Latino 3.1%; Asian 0.3%; Other 4.2%, including 1.7% American Indian/Alaska Native). **Foreign born:** 1.9%. **Median age:** 40.9.

Income 2000: per capita $15,895; median household $32,535; **Pop below poverty level:** 10.3%. ***Personal per capita income 2000-2003:** $24,012-$27,973.

Unemployment 2004: 5%. **Change from 2000:** +0.3%. **Median travel time to work:** 20.9 minutes. **Working outside county of residence:** 30.4%.

Cities with pop over 10,000: None.

OLMSTED COUNTY
151 4th St SE   **Ph:** 507-285-8115
Rochester, MN 55904   **Fax:** 507-287-2693
www.olmstedcounty.com

In southeastern MN, southeast of Mankato; established Feb 20, 1855 (prior to statehood) from unorganized lands. **Name Origin:** For David Olmsted (1822-61), president of the first MN territorial legislature (1849-50) and first mayor of Saint Paul. Some claim S. Baldwin Olmstead (1810-78), a member of the territorial council (1854-55) when the county was formed.

Area (sq mi): 654.5 (land 653.01; water 1.49). **Pop per sq mi:** 207.

Pop 2005: 135,189. **State rank:** 8. **Pop change:** 2000-20005 +8.8%; 1990-2000 +16.7%. **Pop 2000:** 124,277 (White 89%; Black or African American 2.7%; Hispanic or Latino 2.4%; Asian 4.3%; Other 2.7%). **Foreign born:** 7.9%. **Median age:** 35.

Income 2000: per capita $24,939; median household $51,316; **Pop below poverty level:** 6.4%. ***Personal per capita income 2000-2003:** $32,555-$37,124.

Unemployment 2004: 4%. **Change from 2000:** +1.5%. **Median travel time to work:** 16.3 minutes. **Working outside county of residence:** 5.5%.

Cities with pop over 10,000: Rochester ⚏ (93,284).

OTTER TAIL COUNTY
121 W Junius Ave Suite 310   **Ph:** 218-998-8000
Fergus Falls, MN 56537   **Fax:** 218-998-8438
www.co.ottertail.mn.us

In west-central MN, southeast of Fargo, ND; established Mar 18, 1858 from Pembina and Cass counties. **Name Origin:** For Otter Tail lake and river. The lake was named by the Ojibway *nigigwanowe* 'otter tail,' referring to the shape of the lake.

Area (sq mi): 2224.91 (land 1979.71; water 245.2). **Pop per sq mi:** 29.1.

Pop 2005: 57,658. **State rank:** 16. **Pop change:** 2000-20005 +0.9%; 1990-2000 +12.7%. **Pop 2000:** 57,159 (White 96.5%; Black or African American 0.3%; Hispanic or Latino 1.7%; Asian 0.4%; Other 2.1%). **Foreign born:** 2%. **Median age:** 41.1.

Income 2000: per capita $18,014; median household $35,395; **Pop below poverty level:** 10.1%. ***Personal per capita income 2000-2003:** $22,928-$25,198.

Unemployment 2004: 5.3%. **Change from 2000:** +0.7%. **Median travel time to work:** 19.4 minutes. **Working outside county of residence:** 18.8%.

Cities with pop over 10,000: Fergus Falls ⚏ (13,715).

*Source: Personal per capita income data are from the Bureau of Economic Analysis; per capita income data are from the Bureau of the Census. See Introduction for explanation of differences.

376

PENNINGTON COUNTY

County Courthouse 101 Main Ave N
Thief River Falls, MN 56701
www.visitnwminnesota.com/Pennington.htm

Ph: 218-683-7000
Fax: 218-683-7026

In northwestern MN, east of Grand Forks, ND; established Nov 23, 1910 from Red Lake County. **Name Origin:** For Edmund Pennington (1848-1926), president of the Saint Paul and Sault Sainte Marie Railroad.

Area (sq mi): 618.34 (land 616.54; water 1.8). **Pop per sq mi:** 22.1.

Pop 2005: 13,608. **State rank:** 61. **Pop change:** 2000-20005 +0.2%; 1990-2000 +2.1%. **Pop 2000:** 13,584 (White 96.4%; Black or African American 0.2%; Hispanic or Latino 1.2%; Asian 0.6%; Other 2.1%). **Foreign born:** 1.6%. **Median age:** 37.9.

Income 2000: per capita $17,346; median household $34,216; **Pop below poverty level:** 11.1%. *Personal per capita income 2000-2003: $26,315-$30,022.

Unemployment 2004: 6.5%. **Change from 2000:** +1.4%. **Median travel time to work:** 14.9 minutes. **Working outside county of residence:** 9%.

Cities with pop over 10,000: None.

PINE COUNTY

315 Main St S Suite 9
Pine City, MN 55063
www.pinecounty.org

Ph: 320-629-5634
Fax: 320-629-5762

On the central eastern border of MN, northeast of Saint Paul; established Mar 1, 1856 (prior to statehood) from unorganized lands; annexed Buchanan County in 1861. **Name Origin:** For the extensive forests of red (Norway) and white pine, and possibly for the Pine lakes and river in the county.

Area (sq mi): 1434.57 (land 1411.04; water 23.52). **Pop per sq mi:** 20.2.

Pop 2005: 28,485. **State rank:** 37. **Pop change:** 2000-20005 +7.4%; 1990-2000 +24.8%. **Pop 2000:** 26,530 (White 93.1%; Black or African American 1.3%; Hispanic or Latino 1.8%; Asian 0.3%; Other 4%, including 2.7% American Indian/Alaska Native). **Foreign born:** 1.1%. **Median age:** 38.4.

Income 2000: per capita $17,445; median household $37,379; **Pop below poverty level:** 11.3%. *Personal per capita income 2000-2003: $20,757-$22,718.

Unemployment 2004: 6.6%. **Change from 2000:** -1.4%. **Median travel time to work:** 30.2 minutes. **Working outside county of residence:** 39.6%.

Cities with pop over 10,000: None.

PIPESTONE COUNTY

416 S Hiawatha Ave
Pipestone, MN 56164
www.mncounties.org/pipestone/

Ph: 507 825-6740
Fax: 507-825-6741

On the southwestern border of MN; established mistakenly as Rock County May 23, 1857 (prior to statehood) from Murray County; name changed Feb 20, 1862. **Name Origin:** For the red stone (catlinite) quarried by Indians to make pipe bowls.

Area (sq mi): 466.15 (land 465.89; water 0.26). **Pop per sq mi:** 20.2.

Pop 2005: 9,421. **State rank:** 73. **Pop change:** 2000-20005 -4.8%; 1990-2000 -5.7%. **Pop 2000:** 9,895 (White 96.4%; Black or African American 0.2%; Hispanic or Latino 0.7%; Asian 0.5%; Other 2.7%, including 1.5% American Indian/Alaska Native). **Foreign born:** 1.4%. **Median age:** 40.2.

Income 2000: per capita $16,450; median household $31,909; **Pop below poverty level:** 9.5%. *Personal per capita income 2000-2003: $23,856-$28,096.

Unemployment 2004: 4.2%. **Change from 2000:** +0.8%. **Median travel time to work:** 15.2 minutes. **Working outside county of residence:** 18.4%.

Cities with pop over 10,000: None.

POLK COUNTY

612 N Broadway Suite 301
Crookston, MN 56716
www.co.polk.mn.us

Ph: 218-281-2332
Fax: 218-281-2204

In northwestern MN, east of Grand Forks, ND; established Jul 20, 1858 from Indian lands. **Name Origin:** For James Knox Polk (1795-1849), eleventh U.S. president.

Area (sq mi): 1997.81 (land 1970.37; water 27.44) **Pop per sq mi:** 15.8.

Pop 2005: 31,133. **State rank:** 34. **Pop change:** 2000-20005 -0.8%; 1990-2000 -3.5%. **Pop 2000:** 31,369 (White 92.4%; Black or African American 0.3%; Hispanic or Latino 4.8%; Asian 0.3%; Other 5.2%, including 1.3% American Indian/Alaska Native). **Foreign born:** 2.2%. **Median age:** 38.2.

Income 2000: per capita $17,279; median household $35,105; **Pop below poverty level:** 10.9%. *Personal per capita income 2000-2003: $23,007-$25,738.

Unemployment 2004: 5.2%. **Change from 2000:** +0.9%. **Median travel time to work:** 16.5 minutes. **Working outside county of residence:** 30.4%.

Cities with pop over 10,000: None.

POPE COUNTY

130 E Minnesota Ave
Glenwood, MN 56334
www.mncounties.org/pope/

Ph: 320-634-5705
Fax: 320-634-3087

In west-central MN, west of Saint Cloud; established Feb 20, 1862 from Pierce County, which was abolished the same year. **Name Origin:** For explorer Gen. John Pope (1822-92), career army officer in the Mexican-American War and the Civil War.

Area (sq mi): 717.29 (land 670.14; water 47.15). **Pop per sq mi:** 16.8.

Pop 2005: 11,252. **State rank:** 65. **Pop change:** 2000-20005 +0.1%; 1990-2000 +4.6%. **Pop 2000:** 11,236 (White 98.6%; Black or African American 0.2%; Hispanic or Latino 0.5%; Asian 0.1%; Other 0.9%). **Foreign born:** 0.9%. **Median age:** 42.1.

Income 2000: per capita $19,032; median household $35,633; **Pop below poverty level:** 8.8%. *Personal per capita income 2000-2003: $23,368-$27,733.

Unemployment 2004: 4%. **Change from 2000:** +0%. **Median travel time to work:** 18 minutes. **Working outside county of residence:** 32.1%.

Pope County (cont'd)

Cities with pop over 10,000: None.

RAMSEY COUNTY

15 W Kellogg Blvd Rm 250   **Ph:** 651-266-8000
Saint Paul, MN 55102   **Fax:** 651-266-8039
www.co.ramsey.mn.us

In east-central MN, west of Minneapolis; original county; established Oct 27, 1849 (prior to statehood). **Name Origin:** For Alexander Ramsey (1815-1903), PA legislator, first MN territorial governor (1849-53), state governor (1860-63), U.S. senator (1863-75), and U.S. secretary of war (1879-81).

Area (sq mi): 170.13 (land 155.78; water 14.36). **Pop per sq mi:** 3177.

Pop 2005: 494,920. **State rank:** 2. **Pop change:** 2000-20005 -3.2%; 1990-2000 +5.2%. **Pop 2000:** 511,035 (White 75.3%; Black or African American 7.6%; Hispanic or Latino 5.3%; Asian 8.8%; Other 6.3%). **Foreign born:** 10.6%. **Median age:** 33.7.

Income 2000: per capita $23,536; median household $45,722; **Pop below poverty level:** 10.6%. ***Personal per capita income 2000-2003:** $33,394-$36,760.

Unemployment 2004: 4.7%. **Change from 2000:** +1.4%. **Median travel time to work:** 21.2 minutes. **Working outside county of residence:** 41.5%.

Cities with pop over 10,000: 9 (see page 36 for cities).

RED LAKE COUNTY

PO Box 367   **Ph:** 218-253-2598
Red Lake Falls, MN 56750   **Fax:** 218-253-4894
www.prairieagcomm.com/redlakecounty/index.cfm

In northwestern MN, southeast of Grand Forks, ND; established Dec 24, 1896 from Polk County. **Name Origin:** For the Red Lake River, which flows through it; from a translation of the Ojibway word meaning 'red', referring to the color of the lake when the setting sun is reflected in it.

Area (sq mi): 432.51 (land 432.43; water 0.08). **Pop per sq mi:** 10.

Pop 2005: 4,317. **State rank:** 86. **Pop change:** 2000-20005 +0.4%; 1990-2000 -5%. **Pop 2000:** 4,299 (White 97.3%; Black or African American 0.2%; Hispanic or Latino 0.3%; Asian 0.1%; Other 2.2%, including 1.8% American Indian/Alaska Native). **Foreign born:** 1.1%. **Median age:** 40.4.

Income 2000: per capita $15,372; median household $32,052; **Pop below poverty level:** 10.8%. ***Personal per capita income 2000-2003:** $21,941-$22,918.

Unemployment 2004: 7.6%. **Change from 2000:** -2%. **Median travel time to work:** 21.2 minutes. **Working outside county of residence:** 43.6%.

Cities with pop over 10,000: None.

REDWOOD COUNTY

PO Box 130 3rd & Jefferson Courthouse Sq   **Ph:** 507-637-4013
Redwood Falls, MN 56283   **Fax:** 507-637-4072
www.mncounties2.org/redwood/

In southwestern MN, northwest of Mankato; established Feb 6, 1862 from Brown County. **Name Origin:** For the Redwood River, which flows through it; from a Dakota phrase *chan sha ayapi* 'wood-red-on the river,' which may refer to the red bark taken from a shrub, which the Indians dried and mixed with smoking tobacco; the red cedar trees lining the banks; or spots of red paint found on trees, marking an ancient trail for a war party.

Area (sq mi): 881.24 (land 879.73; water 1.51). **Pop per sq mi:** 18.2.

Pop 2005: 16,022. **State rank:** 56. **Pop change:** 2000-20005 -4.7%; 1990-2000 -2.5%. **Pop 2000:** 16,815 (White 94.4%; Black or African American 0.1%; Hispanic or Latino 1.1%; Asian 0.3%; Other 4.6%, including 3.2% American Indian/Alaska Native). **Foreign born:** 0.7%. **Median age:** 39.5.

Income 2000: per capita $18,903; median household $37,352; **Pop below poverty level:** 7.7%. ***Personal per capita income 2000-2003:** $23,849-$25,029.

Unemployment 2004: 4.5%. **Change from 2000:** +0.4%. **Median travel time to work:** 16.4 minutes. **Working outside county of residence:** 18.4%.

Cities with pop over 10,000: None.

RENVILLE COUNTY

500 E DePue Ave 3rd Fl   **Ph:** 320-523-3680
Olivia, MN 56277   **Fax:** 320-523-3689
www.co.renville.mn.us

In south-central MN, southwest of Minneapolis; established Feb 20, 1855 (prior to statehood) from unorganized lands. **Name Origin:** For Joseph Renville (1779?-1846), captain in the British Army during the War of 1812, fur trader, and assistant to missionaries to the Sioux.

Area (sq mi): 987.22 (land 982.92; water 4.3). **Pop per sq mi:** 17.1.

Pop 2005: 16,764. **State rank:** 52. **Pop change:** 2000-20005 -2.3%; 1990-2000 -2.9%. **Pop 2000:** 17,154 (White 93.8%; Black or African American 0.1%; Hispanic or Latino 5.1%; Asian 0.2%; Other 4%). **Foreign born:** 2.1%. **Median age:** 39.7.

Income 2000: per capita $17,770; median household $37,652; **Pop below poverty level:** 8.8%. ***Personal per capita income 2000-2003:** $23,486-$24,454.

Unemployment 2004: 5.9%. **Change from 2000:** -0.1%. **Median travel time to work:** 18.8 minutes. **Working outside county of residence:** 30%.

Cities with pop over 10,000: None.

RICE COUNTY

320 NW 3rd St   **Ph:** 507-332-6101
Faribault, MN 55021   **Fax:** 507-332-5999
www.co.rice.mn.us

In south-central MN, south of Minneapolis; established Mar 5, 1853 (prior to statehood) from Nobles County. **Name Origin:** For Henry Mower Rice (1817-94), MN territorial delegate to Congress (1853-57) and one of its first two U.S. senators (1858-63).

Area (sq mi): 516.13 (land 497.57; water 18.56). **Pop per sq mi:** 122.5.

Pop 2005: 60,949. **State rank:** 13. **Pop change:** 2000-20005 +7.6%; 1990-2000 +15.2%. **Pop 2000:** 56,665 (White 90.5%; Black or

*Source: Personal per capita income data are from the Bureau of Economic Analysis; per capita income data are from the Bureau of the Census. See Introduction for explanation of differences.

378

Rice County (cont'd)

African American 1.3%; Hispanic or Latino 5.5%; Asian 1.5%; Other 3.6%). **Foreign born:** 4.8%. **Median age:** 32.9.

Income 2000: per capita $19,695; median household $48,651; **Pop below poverty level:** 6.9%. ***Personal per capita income 2000-2003:** $23,985-$25,171.

Unemployment 2004: 4.7%. **Change from 2000:** +1%. **Median travel time to work:** 20.2 minutes. **Working outside county of residence:** 29.3%.

Cities with pop over 10,000: Faribault 🏛 (21,924); Northfield (18,567).

ROCK COUNTY

204 E Brown St   **Ph:** 507-283-5020
Luverne, MN 56156   **Fax:** 507-283-5017
www.co.rock.mn.us

In the southwestern corner of MN; established mistakenly as Pipestone County May 23, 1857 (prior to statehood) from Nobles County; name changed Feb 20, 1862. **Name Origin:** For the Rock River, which runs through the county; named for the outcrop of quartzite about 3 sq. mi. in area and rising 175 ft. above this prairie region; now called 'the Mound.'

Area (sq mi): 482.84 (land 482.61; water 0.23). **Pop per sq mi:** 19.7.

Pop 2005: 9,520. **State rank:** 72. **Pop change:** 2000-20005 -2.1%; 1990-2000 -0.9%. **Pop 2000:** 9,721 (White 96.7%; Black or African American 0.5%; Hispanic or Latino 1.3%; Asian 0.6%; Other 1.5%). **Foreign born:** 1.1%. **Median age:** 39.9.

Income 2000: per capita $17,411; median household $38,102; **Pop below poverty level:** 8%. ***Personal per capita income 2000-2003:** $24,574-$26,735.

Unemployment 2004: 3.3%. **Change from 2000:** +0.9%. **Median travel time to work:** 19 minutes. **Working outside county of residence:** 31.2%.

Cities with pop over 10,000: None.

ROSEAU COUNTY

606 5th Ave SW Rm 20   **Ph:** 218-463-2541
Roseau, MN 56751   **Fax:** 218-463-1889
www.visitnwminnesota.com/Roseau.htm

On the northern border of MN, northeast of Grand Forks, ND; established Dec 31, 1894 from Kittson County. **Name Origin:** For Roseau lake and river, both in the northern part of the county; from French 'reed,' from a translation of an Ojibway word that refers to the coarse grass (Phragmites communis) growing along the banks.

Area (sq mi): 1678.33 (land 1662.51; water 15.82). **Pop per sq mi:** 9.9.

Pop 2005: 16,495. **State rank:** 53. **Pop change:** 2000-20005 +1%; 1990-2000 +8.7%. **Pop 2000:** 16,338 (White 95.6%; Black or African American 0.1%; Hispanic or Latino 0.4%; Asian 1.7%; Other 2.2%, including 1.4% American Indian/Alaska Native). **Foreign born:** 2.8%. **Median age:** 35.3.

Income 2000: per capita $17,053; median household $39,852; **Pop below poverty level:** 6.6%. ***Personal per capita income 2000-2003:** $26,188-$28,821.

Unemployment 2004: 4.6%. **Change from 2000:** +0.6%. **Median travel time to work:** 17.5 minutes. **Working outside county of residence:** 4.8%.

Cities with pop over 10,000: None.

SAINT LOUIS COUNTY

100 North 5th Ave W Rm 214   **Ph:** 218-726-2380
Duluth, MN 55802   **Fax:** 218-725-5060
www.co.st-louis.mn.us

On the northeastern border of MN, bordered on the southeast by Lake Superior; established Mar 3, 1855 (prior to statehood) from Lake County (then called Doty County). **Name Origin:** For the Saint Louis River, which flows through the county; itself named for Louis IX of France (1215-70), who participated in the Sixth Crusade (1248-54) and was canonized in 1297.

Area (sq mi): 6859.91 (land 6225.16; water 634.75). **Pop per sq mi:** 31.7.

Pop 2005: 197,179. **State rank:** 6. **Pop change:** 2000-20005 -1.7%; 1990-2000 +1.2%. **Pop 2000:** 200,528 (White 94.4%; Black or African American 0.8%; Hispanic or Latino 0.8%; Asian 0.7%; Other 3.5%, including 2% American Indian/Alaska Native). **Foreign born:** 1.9%. **Median age:** 39.

Income 2000: per capita $18,982; median household $36,306; **Pop below poverty level:** 12.1%. ***Personal per capita income 2000-2003:** $26,246-$28,235.

Unemployment 2004: 5.8%. **Change from 2000:** +0.3%. **Median travel time to work:** 19.4 minutes. **Working outside county of residence:** 9.2%.

Cities with pop over 10,000: Duluth 🏛 (85,556); Hibbing (16,706).

SCOTT COUNTY

200 4th Ave W   **Ph:** 952-445-7750
Shakopee, MN 55379   **Fax:** 952-496-8257
www.co.scott.mn.us

In south-central MN, south of Minneapolis; established Mar 5, 1853 (prior to statehood) from Dakota County. **Name Origin:** For Gen. Winfield Scott (1786-1866), officer in the War of 1812 and the Mexican-American War; general in chief of the U.S. Army (1841-61) and commander of the Union armies at the beginning of the Civil War.

Area (sq mi): 368.56 (land 356.68; water 11.88). **Pop per sq mi:** 335.9.

Pop 2005: 119,825. **State rank:** 9. **Pop change:** 2000-20005 +33.9%; 1990-2000 +54.7%. **Pop 2000:** 89,498 (White 92.4%; Black or African American 0.9%; Hispanic or Latino 2.7%; Asian 2.2%; Other 3.2%). **Foreign born:** 4%. **Median age:** 32.7.

Income 2000: per capita $26,418; median household $66,612; **Pop below poverty level:** 3.4%. ***Personal per capita income 2000-2003:** $33,713-$32,870.

Unemployment 2004: 3.8%. **Change from 2000:** +0.4%. **Median travel time to work:** 24.3 minutes. **Working outside county of residence:** 64.9%.

Cities with pop over 10,000: Shakopee 🏛 (29,321); Savage (25,714); Prior Lake (21,286).

🏛 *County Seat*

SHERBURNE COUNTY

13880 Hwy 10   **Ph:** 763-241-2800
Elk River, MN 55330   **Fax:** 763-241-2816
www.co.sherburne.mn.us

In east-central MN, southeast of Saint Cloud; established Feb 25, 1856 (prior to statehood) from Anoka County. **Name Origin:** For Moses Sherburne (1808-68), associate justice of the MN Territory supreme court (1853-57) and active in the formation of the state.

Area (sq mi): 451 (land 436.3; water 14.7). **Pop per sq mi:** 187.4.

Pop 2005: 81,752. **State rank:** 12. **Pop change:** 2000-20005 +26.9%; 1990-2000 +53.6%. **Pop 2000:** 64,417 (White 96.1%; Black or African American 0.9%; Hispanic or Latino 1.1%; Asian 0.6%; Other 1.7%). **Foreign born:** 1.5%. **Median age:** 31.4.

Income 2000: per capita $21,322; median household $57,014; **Pop below poverty level:** 4.4%. ***Personal per capita income 2000-2003:** $25,590-$26,084.

Unemployment 2004: 4.9%. **Change from 2000:** +0.9%. **Median travel time to work:** 29.9 minutes. **Working outside county of residence:** 67.8%.

Cities with pop over 10,000: Elk River 🏛 (20,224).

SIBLEY COUNTY

400 Court St   **Ph:** 507-237-4051
Gaylord, MN 55334   **Fax:** 507-237-4062
www.co.sibley.mn.us

In south-central MN, southwest of Minneapolis; established Mar 5, 1853 (prior to statehood) from unorganized lands. **Name Origin:** For Henry Hastings Sibley (1811-91), delegate to the U.S. Congress from WI territory (1848-49) and from MN Territory (1849-53), and first governor of MN (1858-60).

Area (sq mi): 600.41 (land 588.65; water 11.76). **Pop per sq mi:** 25.9.

Pop 2005: 15,237. **State rank:** 58. **Pop change:** 2000-20005 -0.8%; 1990-2000 +6.9%. **Pop 2000:** 15,356 (White 93.4%; Black or African American 0.1%; Hispanic or Latino 5.4%; Asian 0.3%; Other 4%). **Foreign born:** 2.6%. **Median age:** 37.3.

Income 2000: per capita $18,004; median household $41,458; **Pop below poverty level:** 8.1%. ***Personal per capita income 2000-2003:** $21,985-$23,922.

Unemployment 2004: 5%. **Change from 2000:** -0.1%. **Median travel time to work:** 24.1 minutes. **Working outside county of residence:** 49.5%.

Cities with pop over 10,000: None.

STEARNS COUNTY

705 Courthouse Sq Rm 121   **Ph:** 320-656-3601
Saint Cloud, MN 56303   **Fax:** 320-656-6393
www.co.stearns.mn.us

In central MN, northwest of Minneapolis; established Feb 20, 1855 (prior to statehood) from unorganized lands. **Name Origin:** For Charles Thomas Stearns (1807-98), territorial legislator (1854-55). In the original bill, the county was to be named for Isaac Ingalls Stevens (1818-62), first territorial governor of WA and surveyor for the Northern Pacific Railway, but apparently a clerical error was made and allowed to stand.

Area (sq mi): 1389.93 (land 1344.52; water 45.41). **Pop per sq mi:** 106.1.

Pop 2005: 142,654. **State rank:** 7. **Pop change:** 2000-20005 +7.1%; 1990-2000 +12.1%. **Pop 2000:** 133,166 (White 95.2%; Black or African American 0.8%; Hispanic or Latino 1.4%; Asian 1.6%; Other 1.6%). **Foreign born:** 2.4%. **Median age:** 31.6.

Income 2000: per capita $19,211; median household $42,426; **Pop below poverty level:** 8.7%. ***Personal per capita income 2000-2003:** $25,138-$27,399.

Unemployment 2004: 4.5%. **Change from 2000:** +0.5%. **Median travel time to work:** 19.3 minutes. **Working outside county of residence:** 19.4%.

Cities with pop over 10,000: Sartell (12,303).

STEELE COUNTY

111 E Main St   **Ph:** 507-444-7700
Owatonna, MN 55060   **Fax:** 507-444-7491
www.co.steele.mn.us

In southeastern MN, west of Rochester; established Feb 20, 1855 (prior to statehood) from unorganized territory. **Name Origin:** For Franklin Steele (1813-80), prominent civic leader and member of the first board of regents of the University of Minnesota.

Area (sq mi): 432.16 (land 429.55; water 2.62). **Pop per sq mi:** 83.2.

Pop 2005: 35,755. **State rank:** 28. **Pop change:** 2000-20005 +6.2%; 1990-2000 +9.6%. **Pop 2000:** 33,680 (White 93.3%; Black or African American 1.1%; Hispanic or Latino 3.8%; Asian 0.8%; Other 2.8%). **Foreign born:** 3.5%. **Median age:** 35.7.

Income 2000: per capita $20,328; median household $46,106; **Pop below poverty level:** 6.2%. ***Personal per capita income 2000-2003:** $27,189-$25,872.

Unemployment 2004: 4.6%. **Change from 2000:** +0.8%. **Median travel time to work:** 16.3 minutes. **Working outside county of residence:** 16.9%.

Cities with pop over 10,000: Owatonna 🏛 (23,707).

STEVENS COUNTY

PO Box 530   **Ph:** 320-589-7287
Morris, MN 56267   **Fax:** 320-589-7288
www.co.stevens.mn.us

In west-central MN, west of Saint Cloud; established Feb 20, 1862 from Pierce County, which was abolished the same year. **Name Origin:** For Gen. Isaac Ingalls Stevens (1818-62), an officer in the Mexican-American War and the Civil War, first governor of WA Territory (1853-57) and surveyor for the Northern Pacific Railway.

Area (sq mi): 575.24 (land 562.06; water 13.17). **Pop per sq mi:** 17.5.

Pop 2005: 9,826. **State rank:** 71. **Pop change:** 2000-20005 -2.3%; 1990-2000 -5.5%. **Pop 2000:** 10,053 (White 95.8%; Black or African American 0.9%; Hispanic or Latino 0.9%; Asian 0.9%; Other 2.1%). **Foreign born:** 1.7%. **Median age:** 33.9.

Income 2000: per capita $17,569; median household $37,267; **Pop below poverty level:** 13.6%. ***Personal per capita income 2000-2003:** $24,697-$27,138.

---

*Source: Personal per capita income data are from the Bureau of Economic Analysis; per capita income data are from the Bureau of the Census. See Introduction for explanation of differences.

Stevens County (cont'd)

Unemployment 2004: 3.8%. **Change from 2000:** +1%. **Median travel time to work:** 13 minutes. **Working outside county of residence:** 11.1%.

Cities with pop over 10,000: None.

SWIFT COUNTY
PO Box 110
Benson, MN 56215
www.swiftcounty.com

Ph: 320-843-2744
Fax: 320-843-4124

In west-central MN, southwest of Saint Cloud; established Feb 18, 1870 from Chippewa County. **Name Origin:** For Henry Adoniram Swift (1823-69), MN legislator and governor (1863-64).

Area (sq mi): 752.35 (land 743.53; water 8.82). **Pop per sq mi:** 15.2.

Pop 2005: 11,324. **State rank:** 64. **Pop change:** 2000-20005 -5.3%; 1990-2000 +11.5%. **Pop 2000:** 11,956 (White 89.7%; Black or African American 2.7%; Hispanic or Latino 2.7%; Asian 1.4%; Other 5.2%, including 1.5% Native Hawaiian/Other Pacific Islander). **Foreign born:** 1.2%. **Median age:** 39.3.

Income 2000: per capita $16,360; median household $34,820; **Pop below poverty level:** 8.4%. ***Personal per capita income 2000-2003:** $20,163-$20,893.

Unemployment 2004: 5.1%. **Change from 2000:** +0.7%. **Median travel time to work:** 17.2 minutes. **Working outside county of residence:** 23.7%.

Cities with pop over 10,000: None.

TODD COUNTY
221 1st Ave S Suite 200
Long Prairie, MN 56347
www.co.todd.mn.us

Ph: 320-732-4469
Fax: 320-732-4001

In central MN, northwest of Saint Cloud; established Feb 20, 1855 (prior to statehood) from Stearns County. **Name Origin:** For John Blair Smith Todd (1814-72), army officer in the Seminole Wars, the Mexican-American War, and the Civil War; delegate to Congress for Dakota (1861-65), and Dakota Territory lawyer and legislator.

Area (sq mi): 979.34 (land 942.02; water 37.32). **Pop per sq mi:** 26.1.

Pop 2005: 24,603. **State rank:** 41. **Pop change:** 2000-20005 +0.7%; 1990-2000 +4.5%. **Pop 2000:** 24,426 (White 96.6%; Black or African American 0.1%; Hispanic or Latino 1.9%; Asian 0.3%; Other 2%). **Foreign born:** 1.8%. **Median age:** 38.5.

Income 2000: per capita $15,658; median household $32,281; **Pop below poverty level:** 12.9%. ***Personal per capita income 2000-2003:** $19,618-$20,810.

Unemployment 2004: 5.2%. **Change from 2000:** -0.9%. **Median travel time to work:** 23.2 minutes. **Working outside county of residence:** 40.7%.

Cities with pop over 10,000: None.

TRAVERSE COUNTY
PO Box 428
Wheaton, MN 56296

Ph: 320-563-4242
Fax: 320-563-4424

On the central western border of MN, south of Fargo, ND; established Feb 20, 1862 from Wilkin County (then called Toombs County). **Name Origin:** For Lake Traverse on the southwestern border of the county; from the French *lac travers*, a translation of the Siouan name *Mdehdakinyan* 'lake lying crosswise' [to Big Stone and Lac Qui Parle lakes].

Area (sq mi): 585.96 (land 574.09; water 11.87). **Pop per sq mi:** 6.6.

Pop 2005: 3,810. **State rank:** 87. **Pop change:** 2000-20005 -7.8%; 1990-2000 -7.4%. **Pop 2000:** 4,134 (White 95.5%; Black or African American 0%; Hispanic or Latino 1.2%; Asian 0.3%; Other 3.3%, including 2.8% American Indian/Alaska Native). **Foreign born:** 0.7%. **Median age:** 42.9.

Income 2000: per capita $16,378; median household $30,617; **Pop below poverty level:** 12%. ***Personal per capita income 2000-2003:** $22,460-$23,325.

Unemployment 2004: 4.2%. **Change from 2000:** -1.1%. **Median travel time to work:** 13.2 minutes. **Working outside county of residence:** 20.5%.

Cities with pop over 10,000: None.

WABASHA COUNTY
625 Jefferson Ave
Wabasha, MN 55981
www.co.wabasha.mn.us

Ph: 651-565-2048
Fax: 651-565-2774

On the southeastern border of MN, north of Rochester; original county; established Oct 27, 1849 (prior to statehood); originally spelled Wabashaw. **Name Origin:** The name of hereditary Sioux chiefs. The name of the chiefs has been transliterated as *Wapashaw* and is said to mean 'red leaf,' 'red hat,' or 'red battle-standard.' The origin of the latter is probably a decoration or red uniform given by the British to one of the chiefs.

Area (sq mi): 549.83 (land 525.01; water 24.82). **Pop per sq mi:** 42.3.

Pop 2005: 22,200. **State rank:** 44. **Pop change:** 2000-20005 +2.7%; 1990-2000 +9.5%. **Pop 2000:** 21,610 (White 97%; Black or African American 0.2%; Hispanic or Latino 1.7%; Asian 0.4%; Other 1.3%). **Foreign born:** 2%. **Median age:** 38.

Income 2000: per capita $19,664; median household $42,117; **Pop below poverty level:** 6%. ***Personal per capita income 2000-2003:** $26,146-$28,624.

Unemployment 2004: 4.4%. **Change from 2000:** +1%. **Median travel time to work:** 23.7 minutes. **Working outside county of residence:** 43.5%.

Cities with pop over 10,000: None.

WADENA COUNTY
415 S Jefferson St
Wadena, MN 56482
www.co.wadena.mn.us

Ph: 218-631-7634
Fax: 218-631-7635

In central MN, northwest of Saint Cloud; established Jun 11, 1858 from Cass and Todd counties. **Name Origin:** For the Wadena trading post on the trail from Crow Wing to Otter Tail City; from an archaic Ojibway word meaning 'a little round hill,' possibly a reference to the Crow Wing bluffs, but also a common Ojibway personal name.

Area (sq mi): 543 (land 535.02; water 7.98). **Pop per sq mi:** 25.5.

Wadena County (cont'd)

Pop 2005: 13,650. **State rank:** 60. **Pop change:** 2000-20005 -0.5%; 1990-2000 +4.2%. **Pop 2000:** 13,713 (White 97.3%; Black or African American 0.5%; Hispanic or Latino 0.9%; Asian 0.2%; Other 1.5%). **Foreign born:** 1%. **Median age:** 39.9.

Income 2000: per capita $15,146; median household $30,651; **Pop below poverty level:** 14.1%. *Personal per capita income 2000-2003:** $19,375-$21,244.

Unemployment 2004: 6.3%. **Change from 2000:** +0.6%. **Median travel time to work:** 19.3 minutes. **Working outside county of residence:** 25%.

Cities with pop over 10,000: None.

WASECA COUNTY

307 N State St   **Ph:** 507-835-0610
Waseca, MN 56093   **Fax:** 507-835-0633
www.co.waseca.mn.us

In south-central MN, southeast of Mankato; established Feb 27, 1857 (prior to statehood) from Steele County. **Name Origin:** From Dakota 'rich,' referring either to provisions or the fertile soil.

Area (sq mi): 432.81 (land 423.25; water 9.56). **Pop per sq mi:** 45.7.

Pop 2005: 19,330. **State rank:** 50. **Pop change:** 2000-20005 -1%; 1990-2000 +8%. **Pop 2000:** 19,526 (White 93.2%; Black or African American 2.3%; Hispanic or Latino 2.9%; Asian 0.5%; Other 2.6%). **Foreign born:** 1.3%. **Median age:** 36.3.

Income 2000: per capita $18,631; median household $42,440; **Pop below poverty level:** 6.5%. *Personal per capita income 2000-2003:** $23,400-$25,516.

Unemployment 2004: 4.6%. **Change from 2000:** +0.6%. **Median travel time to work:** 17.6 minutes. **Working outside county of residence:** 30.3%.

Cities with pop over 10,000: None.

WASHINGTON COUNTY

14949 62nd St N   **Ph:** 651-430-6001
Stillwater, MN 55082   **Fax:** 651-430-6017
www.co.washington.mn.us

On the central eastern border of MN, east of Saint Paul; original county; established Oct 27, 1849 (prior to statehood). **Name Origin:** For George Washington (1732-99), American patriot and first U.S. president.

Area (sq mi): 423.16 (land 391.7; water 31.46). **Pop per sq mi:** 562.7.

Pop 2005: 220,426. **State rank:** 5. **Pop change:** 2000-20005 +9.6%; 1990-2000 +37.9%. **Pop 2000:** 201,130 (White 92.5%; Black or African American 1.8%; Hispanic or Latino 1.9%; Asian 2.1%; Other 2.4%). **Foreign born:** 3.4%. **Median age:** 35.1.

Income 2000: per capita $28,148; median household $66,305; **Pop below poverty level:** 2.9%. *Personal per capita income 2000-2003:** $36,432-$38,787.

Unemployment 2004: 4%. **Change from 2000:** +1.4%. **Median travel time to work:** 24.6 minutes. **Working outside county of residence:** 66.4%.

Cities with pop over 10,000: Woodbury (50,020); Cottage Grove (32,146); Oakdale (27,571); Stillwater 🏛 (17,171); Forest Lake (16,948).

WATONWAN COUNTY

710 7th Ave S   **Ph:** 507-375-1236
Saint James, MN 56081   **Fax:** 507-375-5010
www.extension.umn.edu/county/watonwan/

In south-central MN, southwest of Mankato; established Feb 25, 1860 from Brown County. **Name Origin:** For the Watonwan River, whose head steams flow through the county; probably from a Dakota word meaning 'where fish bait can be found' or 'where fish abound.'

Area (sq mi): 439.92 (land 434.51; water 5.4). **Pop per sq mi:** 25.9.

Pop 2005: 11,234. **State rank:** 66. **Pop change:** 2000-20005 -5.4%; 1990-2000 +1.7%. **Pop 2000:** 11,876 (White 82.9%; Black or African American 0.4%; Hispanic or Latino 15.2%; Asian 0.9%; Other 10.2%). **Foreign born:** 8%. **Median age:** 38.6.

Income 2000: per capita $16,413; median household $35,441; **Pop below poverty level:** 9.8%. *Personal per capita income 2000-2003:** $22,854-$26,406.

Unemployment 2004: 4.6%. **Change from 2000:** +1%. **Median travel time to work:** 17.7 minutes. **Working outside county of residence:** 25.3%.

Cities with pop over 10,000: None.

WILKIN COUNTY

PO Box 219   **Ph:** 218-643-7172
Breckenridge, MN 56520   **Fax:** 218-643-7167
www.co.wilkin.mn.us

On the central western border of MN, south of Fargo, ND; established Mar 8, 1858 from Cass County; name changed from Toombs County to Andy Johnson County in 1863 and from Andy Johnson County to present name Mar 6, 1868. **Name Origin:** For Col. Alexander Wilkin (1820-64), an officer in the Union army killed at the Battle of Tupelo. Originally for Robert Toombs (1810-85), U.S. senator from GA (1853-61), who became the Confederate secretary of state and thus angered the local residents. Changed to honor the seventeenth U.S. president, Andrew Johnson (1808-75), but his subsequent political stands also angered them.

Area (sq mi): 751.63 (land 751.43; water 0.2). **Pop per sq mi:** 9.1.

Pop 2005: 6,802. **State rank:** 78. **Pop change:** 2000-20005 -4.7%; 1990-2000 -5%. **Pop 2000:** 7,138 (White 96.8%; Black or African American 0.2%; Hispanic or Latino 1.5%; Asian 0.2%; Other 1.9%). **Foreign born:** 0.7%. **Median age:** 38.1.

Income 2000: per capita $16,873; median household $38,093; **Pop below poverty level:** 8.1%. *Personal per capita income 2000-2003:** $22,580-$25,736.

Unemployment 2004: 3.9%. **Change from 2000:** +0.5%. **Median travel time to work:** 18.3 minutes. **Working outside county of residence:** 54.1%.

Cities with pop over 10,000: None.

Source: Personal per capita income data are from the Bureau of Economic Analysis; per capita income data are from the Bureau of the Census. See Introduction for explanation of differences.

WINONA COUNTY
177 Main St   **Ph:** 507-457-6350
Winona, MN 55987   **Fax:** 507-454-9365
www.co.winona.mn.us/

On the southeastern border of MN, east of Rochester; established Feb 23, 1854 (prior to statehood) from unorganized lands. **Name Origin:** For the town that became the county seat, which was named for a Dakota Indian woman active in the removal of the Winnebagos from IA to MN. Name was also popularized by H.L. Gordon's poem, 'Winona' (1881).

Area (sq mi): 641.59 (land 626.3; water 15.29). **Pop per sq mi:** 78.7.

Pop 2005: 49,276. **State rank:** 19. **Pop change:** 2000-20005 -1.4%; 1990-2000 +4.5%. **Pop 2000:** 49,985 (White 95.1%; Black or African American 0.8%; Hispanic or Latino 1.4%; Asian 1.9%; Other 1.5%). **Foreign born:** 2.7%. **Median age:** 32.8.

Income 2000: per capita $18,077; median household $38,700; **Pop below poverty level:** 12%. ***Personal per capita income 2000-2003:** $24,277-$26,281.

Unemployment 2004: 4.4%. **Change from 2000:** +0.9%. **Median travel time to work:** 17 minutes. **Working outside county of residence:** 16.7%.

Cities with pop over 10,000: Winona ⛪ (26,451).

WRIGHT COUNTY
10 2nd St NW Rm 201   **Ph:** 763-682-7539
Buffalo, MN 55313   **Fax:** 763-682-7300
www.co.wright.mn.us

In east-central MN, northwest of Minneapolis; established Feb 20, 1855 (prior to statehood). **Name Origin:** For Silas Wright (1795-1847), NY governor (1845-47) and friend of a member of the county organization committee; his name was chosen 'as a compromise after a somewhat animated discussion.'

Area (sq mi): 714.39 (land 660.75; water 53.63). **Pop per sq mi:** 167.6.

Pop 2005: 110,730. **State rank:** 10. **Pop change:** 2000-20005 +23.1%; 1990-2000 +31%. **Pop 2000:** 89,986 (White 97.2%; Black or African American 0.3%; Hispanic or Latino 1.1%; Asian 0.4%; Other 1.5%). **Foreign born:** 1.1%. **Median age:** 33.1.

Income 2000: per capita $21,844; median household $53,945; **Pop below poverty level:** 4.7%. ***Personal per capita income 2000-2003:** $27,635-$29,039.

Unemployment 2004: 4.9%. **Change from 2000:** +0.9%. **Median travel time to work:** 29.1 minutes. **Working outside county of residence:** 57.2%.

Cities with pop over 10,000: Saint Michael (13,505); Buffalo ⛪ (12,801); Monticello (10,412); Otsego (10,057).

YELLOW MEDICINE COUNTY
415 9th Ave   **Ph:** 320-564-3325
Granite Falls, MN 56241   **Fax:** 320-564-4435
www.yellowmedicine.govoffice.com

On the southwestern border of MN; established Mar 6, 1871 from Redwood County. **Name Origin:** For the Yellow Medicine River, which flows through it; from a translation of the Siouan name for moonseed, *Menispermum canadense*, a medicinal plant that grows abundantly in the area.

Area (sq mi): 763.39 (land 757.96; water 5.43). **Pop per sq mi:** 13.8.

Pop 2005: 10,449. **State rank:** 69. **Pop change:** 2000-20005 -5.7%; 1990-2000 -5.2%. **Pop 2000:** 11,080 (White 95.4%; Black or African American 0.1%; Hispanic or Latino 1.8%; Asian 0.2%; Other 3.6%, including 2% American Indian/Alaska Native). **Foreign born:** 1.2%. **Median age:** 40.4.

Income 2000: per capita $17,120; median household $34,393; **Pop below poverty level:** 10.4%. ***Personal per capita income 2000-2003:** $22,871-$24,149.

Unemployment 2004: 5.1%. **Change from 2000:** -1%. **Median travel time to work:** 16.8 minutes. **Working outside county of residence:** 34.7%.

Cities with pop over 10,000: None.

Mississippi

TENNESSEE

ARKANSAS

ALABAMA

LOUISIANA

Gulf of Mexico

N

0   50 mi
0   50 km

County boundary
Jasper   County name
⊙   County seat
■   Major city
✪   State capital

©MAPS.com

De Soto · Hernando
Marshall · Holly Springs
Benton · Ashland
Corinth · **Alcorn** · Iuka
Tunica · Tunica
Tate · Senatobia
Ripley · **Tippah** · **Tishomingo**
Booneville · **Prentiss**
Union · New Albany
Sardis · **Panola** · Batesville
Oxford · **Lafayette**
Pontotoc · **Pontotoc**
Lee · Tupelo
Fulton · **Itawamba**
Coahoma · Clarksdale
Marks · **Quitman**
Water Valley · **Yalobusha** · Coffeeville
Calhoun · Pittsboro
Okolona · **Monroe**
Houston · **Chickasaw** · Aberdeen
Sumner · Charleston · **Tallahatchie**
Grenada · **Grenada**
Clay · West Point
Rosedale · **Bolivar** · Cleveland
Leflore · Greenwood
Montgomery · Winona
Walthall
Starkville · Columbus
Webster · **Choctaw** · Ackerman
Oktibbeha · **Lowndes**
Sunflower · Indianola
Carrollton · **Carroll** · Vaiden
Greenville · **Washington** · **Humphreys** · Belzoni
Holmes · Lexington
Attala · Kosciusko
Louisville · **Winston** · Macon · **Noxubee**
Sharkey · Rolling Fork
Mayersville · Yazoo City
Leake · Carthage
Neshoba · Philadelphia
De Kalb · **Kemper**
Issaquena · **Yazoo**
Canton · **Madison**
Warren · Vicksburg
Hinds · Jackson · Raymond
Brandon · **Rankin**
Scott · Forest
Decatur · **Newton**
Lauderdale · Meridian
Jasper · Paulding
Raleigh · Quitman · **Clarke**
Claiborne · Port Gibson
Copiah · Hazlehurst
Mendenhall · **Simpson**
Smith · Bay Springs
Fayette · **Jefferson**
Brookhaven
Lawrence · **Jefferson Davis** · Prentiss
Covington · Collins
Laurel · Ellisville
Wayne · Waynesboro
Natchez · **Adams**
Meadville · **Franklin** · **Lincoln**
Monticello · **Jones**
Wilkinson · Woodville
Amite · Liberty
Pike · Magnolia
Walthall · Tylertown
Marion · Columbia
Lamar · Pervis
Forrest · Hattiesburg
Perry · New Augusta
Greene · Leakesville
Lucedale · **George**
Poplarville
Pearl River · **Stone** · Wiggins
Hancock · Gulfport · Biloxi · Bay Saint Louis
Harrison · **Jackson** · Pascagoula

Mississippi

MISSISSIPPI STATE INFORMATION
www.mississippi.gov   **Ph:** 601-359-1000

Area (sq mi): 48,430.19 (land 46,906.96; water 1523.24). **Pop per sq mi:** 62.3.

Pop 2005: 2,921,088. **Pop change:** 2000-20005 +2.7%; 1990-2000 +10.5%. **Pop 2000:** 2,844,658 (White 60.7%; Black or African American 36.3%; Hispanic or Latino 1.4%; Asian 0.7%; Other 1.6%). **Foreign born:** 1.4%. **Median age:** 33.8.

Income 2000: per capita $15,853; median household $31,330; **Pop below poverty level:** 19.9%. ***Personal per capita income 2000-2003:** $21,005-$23,466.

Unemployment 2004: 6.3%. **Change from 2000:** +0.6%. **Median travel time to work:** 24.6 minutes. **Working outside county of residence:** 31.9%.

ADAMS COUNTY
PO Box 1006   **Ph:** 601-446-6684
Natchez, MS 39121   **Fax:** 601-445-7913

On the southwestern border of MS; organized Apr 2, 1799 (prior to statehood) from Natchez District. **Name Origin:** For John Adams (1735-1826), second U.S. president.

Area (sq mi): 486.25 (land 460.26; water 25.99). **Pop per sq mi:** 69.7.

Pop 2005: 32,099. **State rank:** 28. **Pop change:** 2000-20005 -6.5%; 1990-2000 -2.9%. **Pop 2000:** 34,340 (White 45.7%; Black or African American 52.8%; Hispanic or Latino 0.8%; Asian 0.2%; Other 0.9%). **Foreign born:** 1.4%. **Median age:** 38.1.

Income 2000: per capita $15,778; median household $25,234; **Pop below poverty level:** 25.9%. ***Personal per capita income 2000-2003:** $21,250-$22,517.

Unemployment 2004: 7.7%. **Change from 2000:** +0.8%. **Median travel time to work:** 21.9 minutes. **Working outside county of residence:** 15.2%.

Cities with pop over 10,000: Natchez ⛪ (17,272).

ALCORN COUNTY
305 S Fulton Dr   **Ph:** 662-286-7700
Corinth, MS 38834   **Fax:** 662-286-7773

On the northeastern border of MS, southeast of Memphis, TN; organized Apr 15, 1870 from Tippah, Tishomingo, and Wilkinson counties. **Name Origin:** For James Lusk Alcorn (1816-94), MS governor (1870-71) and U.S. senator (1871-77).

Area (sq mi): 401.35 (land 399.89; water 1.46). **Pop per sq mi:** 88.3.

Pop 2005: 35,306. **State rank:** 25. **Pop change:** 2000-20005 +2.2%; 1990-2000 +8.9%. **Pop 2000:** 34,558 (White 86.7%; Black or African American 11.1%; Hispanic or Latino 1.3%; Asian 0.2%; Other 1.4%). **Foreign born:** 1%. **Median age:** 37.6.

Income 2000: per capita $15,418; median household $29,041; **Pop below poverty level:** 16.6%. ***Personal per capita income 2000-2003:** $19,688-$21,126.

Unemployment 2004: 6.6%. **Change from 2000:** +1.1%. **Median travel time to work:** 20.8 minutes. **Working outside county of residence:** 20.9%.

Cities with pop over 10,000: Corinth ⛪ (14,222).

AMITE COUNTY
PO Box 680   **Ph:** 601-657-8022
Liberty, MS 39645   **Fax:** 601-657-8288

On the southwestern border of MS, southeast of Natchez; organized Feb 24, 1809 (prior to statehood) from Wilkinson County. **Name Origin:** Adapted from *amitie*, the French word for 'friendship.'

Area (sq mi): 731.64 (land 729.6; water 2.04). **Pop per sq mi:** 18.4.

Pop 2005: 13,435. **State rank:** 62. **Pop change:** 2000-20005 -1.2%; 1990-2000 +2%. **Pop 2000:** 13,599 (White 56.2%; Black or African American 42.7%; Hispanic or Latino 0.8%; Asian 0.1%; Other 0.8%). **Foreign born:** 0.4%. **Median age:** 38.3.

Income 2000: per capita $14,048; median household $26,033; **Pop below poverty level:** 22.6%. ***Personal per capita income 2000-2003:** $17,420-$19,172.

Unemployment 2004: 6.4%. **Change from 2000:** +2.3%. **Median travel time to work:** 36.1 minutes. **Working outside county of residence:** 56.8%.

Cities with pop over 10,000: None.

ATTALA COUNTY
230 W Washington St   **Ph:** 662-289-2921
Kosciusko, MS 39090   **Fax:** 662-289-7662

In central MS, southwest of Columbus; organized Dec 23, 1833 from Choctaw cession. **Name Origin:** Either from Cherokee *otale* 'mountain,' or *Attala*, an Indian heroine.

Area (sq mi): 737.1 (land 735.13; water 1.97). **Pop per sq mi:** 26.6.

Pop 2005: 19,552. **State rank:** 51. **Pop change:** 2000-20005 -0.6%; 1990-2000 +6.4%. **Pop 2000:** 19,661 (White 57.8%; Black or African American 40%; Hispanic or Latino 1.4%; Asian 0.3%; Other 1.4%). **Foreign born:** 0.8%. **Median age:** 37.3.

⛪ *County Seat*

385

Attala County (cont'd)

Income 2000: per capita $13,782; median household $24,794; **Pop below poverty level:** 21.8%. ***Personal per capita income 2000-2003:** $17,502-$21,054.

Unemployment 2004: 7.7%. **Change from 2000:** -0.3%. **Median travel time to work:** 28.6 minutes. **Working outside county of residence:** 27.2%.

Cities with pop over 10,000: None.

BENTON COUNTY

PO Box 218   **Ph:** 662-224-6300
Ashland, MS 38603   **Fax:** 662-224-6303

On the central northern border of MS, southeast of Memphis, TN; organized Jul 21, 1870 from Marshall and Tippah counties. **Name Origin:** For Thomas Hart Benton (1782-1858), U.S. journalist and statesman; nicknamed 'Old Bullion' for championing the use of gold and silver currency rather than paper money.

Area (sq mi): 408.65 (land 406.79; water 1.86). **Pop per sq mi:** 19.3.

Pop 2005: 7,852. **State rank:** 80. **Pop change:** 2000-20005 -2.2%; 1990-2000 -0.2%. **Pop 2000:** 8,026 (White 61.5%; Black or African American 36.8%; Hispanic or Latino 1%; Asian 0%; Other 1.5%). **Foreign born:** 0.7%. **Median age:** 35.6.

Income 2000: per capita $12,212; median household $24,149; **Pop below poverty level:** 23.2%. ***Personal per capita income 2000-2003:** $15,538-$17,191.

Unemployment 2004: 9.2%. **Change from 2000:** +2.9%. **Median travel time to work:** 32.9 minutes. **Working outside county of residence:** 62.7%.

Cities with pop over 10,000: None.

BOLIVAR COUNTY

200 Court St PO Box 698   **Ph:** 662-846-5877
Cleveland, MS 38732   **Fax:** 662-846-5880
www.co.bolivar.ms.us

On the northwestern border of MS, north of Greenville; organized Feb 9, 1836 from Choctaw cession. **Name Origin:** For Simon Bolivar (1783-1830), Venezuelan leader of South American revolt against Spanish rule; known as 'the Liberator' and 'George Washington to South America.'

Area (sq mi): 905.76 (land 876.28; water 29.47). **Pop per sq mi:** 44.1.

Pop 2005: 38,641. **State rank:** 20. **Pop change:** 2000-20005 -4.9%; 1990-2000 -3%. **Pop 2000:** 40,633 (White 32.9%; Black or African American 65.1%; Hispanic or Latino 1.2%; Asian 0.5%; Other 1.2%). **Foreign born:** 0.5%. **Median age:** 29.8.

Income 2000: per capita $12,088; median household $23,428; **Pop below poverty level:** 33.3%. ***Personal per capita income 2000-2003:** $17,048-$19,165.

Unemployment 2004: 8.2%. **Change from 2000:** +0.9%. **Median travel time to work:** 19.7 minutes. **Working outside county of residence:** 19.8%.

Cities with pop over 10,000: Cleveland 🏛 (12,897).

CALHOUN COUNTY

PO Box 8   **Ph:** 662-412-3117
Pittsboro, MS 38951   **Fax:** 662-412-3128

In north-central MS, northwest of Columbus; organized Mar 8, 1852 from Chickasaw, Lafayette, and Yalobusha counties. **Name Origin:** For John Caldwell Calhoun (1782-1850), U.S. statesman and champion of Southern causes.

Area (sq mi): 587.97 (land 586.54; water 1.43). **Pop per sq mi:** 25.

Pop 2005: 14,652. **State rank:** 59. **Pop change:** 2000-20005 -2.8%; 1990-2000 +1.1%. **Pop 2000:** 15,069 (White 68.6%; Black or African American 28.7%; Hispanic or Latino 2.1%; Asian 0.1%; Other 1.8%). **Foreign born:** 1.6%. **Median age:** 37.4.

Income 2000: per capita $15,106; median household $27,113; **Pop below poverty level:** 18.1%. ***Personal per capita income 2000-2003:** $19,479-$22,619.

Unemployment 2004: 6.7%. **Change from 2000:** -3.7%. **Median travel time to work:** 24.9 minutes. **Working outside county of residence:** 36%.

Cities with pop over 10,000: None.

CARROLL COUNTY

PO Box 60   **Ph:** 662-237-9274
Carrollton, MS 38917   **Fax:** 662-237-9642

In north-central MS, east of Greenville; organized Dec 23, 1833 from Choctaw cession. **Name Origin:** For Charles Carroll (1737-1832), signer of the Declaration of Independence, U.S. senator from MD (1789-92), and founder of the Baltimore and Ohio Railroad.

Area (sq mi): 634.54 (land 627.73; water 6.81). **Pop per sq mi:** 16.6.

Pop 2005: 10,397. **State rank:** 71. **Pop change:** 2000-20005 -3.5%; 1990-2000 +16.6%. **Pop 2000:** 10,769 (White 62.3%; Black or African American 36.6%; Hispanic or Latino 0.7%; Asian 0.2%; Other 0.6%). **Foreign born:** 0.8%. **Median age:** 38.1.

Income 2000: per capita $15,744; median household $28,878; **Pop below poverty level:** 16%. ***Personal per capita income 2000-2003:** $18,010-$20,699.

Unemployment 2004: 6%. **Change from 2000:** -0.9%. **Median travel time to work:** 30.9 minutes. **Working outside county of residence:** 76%.

Cities with pop over 10,000: None.

CHICKASAW COUNTY

County Courthouse 1 Pinson Sq   **Ph:** 662-456-2513
Houston, MS 38851   **Fax:** 662-456-5295

In east-central MS, northwest of Columbus; organized Feb 9, 1836 from Chickasaw cession of 1832. **Name Origin:** For the Indian tribe, closely connected with the Choctaw, of Muskhogean linguistic stock; meaning of name unknown.

Area (sq mi): 504.27 (land 501.56; water 2.71). **Pop per sq mi:** 38.2.

Pop 2005: 19,184. **State rank:** 53. **Pop change:** 2000-20005 -1.3%; 1990-2000 +7.5%. **Pop 2000:** 19,440 (White 56%; Black or African American 41.3%; Hispanic or Latino 2.3%; Asian 0.2%; Other 1.7%). **Foreign born:** 1.3%. **Median age:** 34.4.

Source: Personal per capita income data are from the Bureau of Economic Analysis; per capita income data are from the Bureau of the Census. See Introduction for explanation of differences.

Chickasaw County (cont'd)

Income 2000: per capita $13,279; median household $26,364; **Pop below poverty level:** 20%. ***Personal per capita income 2000-2003:** $18,148-$20,232.

Unemployment 2004: 8.1%. **Change from 2000:** -6.4%. **Median travel time to work:** 23.3 minutes. **Working outside county of residence:** 38.5%.

Cities with pop over 10,000: None.

CHOCTAW COUNTY

PO Box 250   **Ph:** 662-285-6329
Ackerman, MS 39735   **Fax:** 662-285-3444

In east-central MS, west of Columbus; organized Dec 23, 1833 from Chickasaw cession of 1832. **Name Origin:** For the Indian tribe of Muskhogean linguistic stock; meaning of name unknown.

Area (sq mi): 419.81 (land 419.1; water 0.71). **Pop per sq mi:** 22.8.

Pop 2005: 9,572. **State rank:** 76. **Pop change:** 2000-20005 -1.9%; 1990-2000 +7.6%. **Pop 2000:** 9,758 (White 67.8%; Black or African American 30.7%; Hispanic or Latino 0.8%; Asian 0.1%; Other 1.1%). **Foreign born:** 0.3%. **Median age:** 36.9.

Income 2000: per capita $13,474; median household $27,020; **Pop below poverty level:** 24.7%. ***Personal per capita income 2000-2003:** $14,352-$16,219.

Unemployment 2004: 8.2%. **Change from 2000:** -3.8%. **Median travel time to work:** 26.9 minutes. **Working outside county of residence:** 52.5%.

Cities with pop over 10,000: None.

CLAIBORNE COUNTY

410 Market St   **Ph:** 601-437-5841
Port Gibson, MS 39150   **Fax:** 601-437-4543

On the southwestern border of MS, south of Vicksburg; organized Jan 27, 1802 (prior to statehood) from Jefferson County. **Name Origin:** For William Charles Cole Claiborne (1775-1817), governor of the Mississippi Territory (1801-05), of the Orleans Territory (1804-12), and of LA (1812-16).

Area (sq mi): 501.36 (land 486.77; water 14.59). **Pop per sq mi:** 23.6.

Pop 2005: 11,492. **State rank:** 69. **Pop change:** 2000-20005 -2.9%; 1990-2000 +4.1%. **Pop 2000:** 11,831 (White 15.1%; Black or African American 84.1%; Hispanic or Latino 0.8%; Asian 0.1%; Other 0.6%). **Foreign born:** 0.6%. **Median age:** 25.6.

Income 2000: per capita $11,244; median household $22,615; **Pop below poverty level:** 32.4%. ***Personal per capita income 2000-2003:** $15,143-$17,028.

Unemployment 2004: 10.1%. **Change from 2000:** +0.7%. **Median travel time to work:** 30.7 minutes. **Working outside county of residence:** 43.4%.

Cities with pop over 10,000: None.

CLARKE COUNTY

PO Box 689   **Ph:** 601-776-2126
Quitman, MS 39355   **Fax:** 601-776-2756

On the central eastern border of MS, south of Meridian; organized Dec 10, 1812 (prior to statehood) from Choctaw cession. **Name Origin:** For Joshua G. Clarke, first chancellor of MS.

Area (sq mi): 693.41 (land 691.27; water 2.14). **Pop per sq mi:** 25.6.

Pop 2005: 17,670. **State rank:** 55. **Pop change:** 2000-20005 -1.6%; 1990-2000 +3.7%. **Pop 2000:** 17,955 (White 64.1%; Black or African American 34.8%; Hispanic or Latino 0.7%; Asian 0.1%; Other 0.6%). **Foreign born:** 0.3%. **Median age:** 36.8.

Income 2000: per capita $14,288; median household $26,610; **Pop below poverty level:** 23%. ***Personal per capita income 2000-2003:** $17,446-$18,676.

Unemployment 2004: 7.6%. **Change from 2000:** -1.8%. **Median travel time to work:** 31.3 minutes. **Working outside county of residence:** 43.7%.

Cities with pop over 10,000: None.

CLAY COUNTY

PO Box 815   **Ph:** 662-494-3124
West Point, MS 39773   **Fax:** 662-492-4059

In east-central MS, northwest of Columbus; established as Colfax County May 12, 1871 from Chickasaw, Oktibbeha, and Lowndes counties; name changed Apr 10, 1876. **Name Origin:** For Henry Clay (1777-1852), U.S. senator from KY, known as the 'Great Pacificator' for his advocacy of compromise to avert national crises.

Area (sq mi): 416.02 (land 408.56; water 7.46). **Pop per sq mi:** 51.9.

Pop 2005: 21,223. **State rank:** 46. **Pop change:** 2000-20005 -3.4%; 1990-2000 +4.1%. **Pop 2000:** 21,979 (White 42.5%; Black or African American 56.3%; Hispanic or Latino 0.9%; Asian 0.2%; Other 0.7%). **Foreign born:** 0.5%. **Median age:** 33.9.

Income 2000: per capita $14,512; median household $27,372; **Pop below poverty level:** 23.5%. ***Personal per capita income 2000-2003:** $19,372-$21,241.

Unemployment 2004: 9.3%. **Change from 2000:** -1%. **Median travel time to work:** 21.7 minutes. **Working outside county of residence:** 28.5%.

Cities with pop over 10,000: West Point 🏛 (11,809).

COAHOMA COUNTY

PO Box 98   **Ph:** 662-624-3000
Clarksdale, MS 38614   **Fax:** 662-624-3040

On the northwestern border of MS, north of Greenville; organized Feb 9, 1836 from Chickasaw cession of 1836. **Name Origin:** For Sweet Coahoma, known also as Coahoma Sheriff, daughter of the last Choctaw in the area. The name means 'red panther.'

Area (sq mi): 583.14 (land 554.15; water 28.99). **Pop per sq mi:** 52.3.

Pop 2005: 29,002. **State rank:** 31. **Pop change:** 2000-20005 -5.3%; 1990-2000 -3.3%. **Pop 2000:** 30,622 (White 29.1%; Black or African American 69.2%; Hispanic or Latino 0.9%; Asian 0.5%; Other 1%). **Foreign born:** 0.9%. **Median age:** 30.5.

Income 2000: per capita $12,558; median household $22,338; **Pop below poverty level:** 35.9%. ***Personal per capita income 2000-2003:** $19,703-$22,728.

Coahoma County (cont'd)

Unemployment 2004: 9.2%. **Change from 2000:** +0.9%. **Median travel time to work:** 24 minutes. **Working outside county of residence:** 21.9%.

Cities with pop over 10,000: Clarksdale ⚖ (19,467).

COPIAH COUNTY
PO Box 507   **Ph:** 601-894-3021
Hazlehurst, MS 39083   **Fax:** 601-894-4081
www.copiahcounty.org

In southwestern MS, southwest of Jackson; organized Jan 21, 1823 from Hinds County. **Name Origin:** From an Indian word, said to mean 'panther,' but uncertain. It is believed locally to mean 'clear water.'

Area (sq mi): 779.38 (land 776.6; water 2.78). **Pop per sq mi:** 37.6.

Pop 2005: 29,164. **State rank:** 30. **Pop change:** 2000-20005 +1.4%; 1990-2000 +4.2%. **Pop 2000:** 28,757 (White 47.4%; Black or African American 51%; Hispanic or Latino 1.2%; Asian 0.2%; Other 1.1%). **Foreign born:** 0.8%. **Median age:** 34.

Income 2000: per capita $12,408; median household $26,358; **Pop below poverty level:** 25.1%. ***Personal per capita income 2000-2003:** $17,059-$18,965.

Unemployment 2004: 7%. **Change from 2000:** +0.8%. **Median travel time to work:** 29.3 minutes. **Working outside county of residence:** 48%.

Cities with pop over 10,000: None.

COVINGTON COUNTY
PO Box 1679   **Ph:** 601-765-4242
Collins, MS 39428   **Fax:** 601-765-5016

In south-central MS, west of Laurel; organized Feb 5, 1819 from Lawrence and Wayne counties. **Name Origin:** For Leonard Wales Covington (1768-1813), general in the War of 1812.

Area (sq mi): 414.94 (land 413.79; water 1.15). **Pop per sq mi:** 49.

Pop 2005: 20,273. **State rank:** 49. **Pop change:** 2000-20005 +4.5%; 1990-2000 +17.4%. **Pop 2000:** 19,407 (White 63.1%; Black or African American 35.6%; Hispanic or Latino 0.8%; Asian 0.1%; Other 0.9%). **Foreign born:** 0.6%. **Median age:** 33.8.

Income 2000: per capita $14,506; median household $26,669; **Pop below poverty level:** 23.5%. ***Personal per capita income 2000-2003:** $16,571-$18,596.

Unemployment 2004: 5.4%. **Change from 2000:** +0.9%. **Median travel time to work:** 29.5 minutes. **Working outside county of residence:** 46.6%.

Cities with pop over 10,000: None.

DESOTO COUNTY
365 Losher St   **Ph:** 662-429-1460
Hernando, MS 38632   **Fax:** 662-429-4116
www.desotoms.com

In the northwestern corner of MS, south of Memphis, TN; organized Feb 9, 1836 from Indian lands. **Name Origin:** For Hernando De Soto (c.1500-42), Spanish explorer of southern U.S.

Area (sq mi): 496.77 (land 477.86; water 18.91). **Pop per sq mi:** 286.7.

Pop 2005: 137,004. **State rank:** 3. **Pop change:** 2000-20005 +27.8%; 1990-2000 +57.9%. **Pop 2000:** 107,199 (White 84.7%; Black or African American 11.4%; Hispanic or Latino 2.3%; Asian 0.6%; Other 2.2%). **Foreign born:** 1.9%. **Median age:** 33.7.

Income 2000: per capita $20,468; median household $48,206; **Pop below poverty level:** 7.1%. ***Personal per capita income 2000-2003:** $26,070-$28,713.

Unemployment 2004: 3.5%. **Change from 2000:** +0.8%. **Median travel time to work:** 25.8 minutes. **Working outside county of residence:** 64.1%.

Cities with pop over 10,000: Southaven (36,244); Olive Branch (26,516); Horn Lake (21,764).

FORREST COUNTY
630 N Main St   **Ph:** 601-582-3213
Hattiesburg, MS 39401   **Fax:** 601-545-6065
www.co.forrest.ms.us

In southeastern MS, southwest of Laurel; organized Apr 19, 1906 from Perry County. **Name Origin:** For Nathan Bedford Forrest (1821-77), Confederate general often quoted as saying 'Get there fustest with the mostest.'

Area (sq mi): 470.17 (land 466.58; water 3.59). **Pop per sq mi:** 160.9.

Pop 2005: 75,095. **State rank:** 9. **Pop change:** 2000-20005 +3.4%; 1990-2000 +6.3%. **Pop 2000:** 72,604 (White 63.7%; Black or African American 33.6%; Hispanic or Latino 1.3%; Asian 0.7%; Other 1.4%). **Foreign born:** 2%. **Median age:** 29.7.

Income 2000: per capita $15,160; median household $27,420; **Pop below poverty level:** 22.5%. ***Personal per capita income 2000-2003:** $21,337-$24,803.

Unemployment 2004: 5.5%. **Change from 2000:** +2.1%. **Median travel time to work:** 21.6 minutes. **Working outside county of residence:** 25.5%.

Cities with pop over 10,000: Hattiesburg ⚖ (46,442).

FRANKLIN COUNTY
PO Box 297   **Ph:** 601-384-2330
Meadville, MS 39653   **Fax:** 601-384-5864
www.franklincountyms.com

In southwestern MS, east of Natchez; organized Dec 21, 1809 (prior to statehood) from Adams County. **Name Origin:** For Benjamin Franklin (1706-90), patriot, diplomat, and statesman.

Area (sq mi): 566.74 (land 564.6; water 2.14). **Pop per sq mi:** 14.9.

Pop 2005: 8,411. **State rank:** 79. **Pop change:** 2000-20005 -0.4%; 1990-2000 +0.8%. **Pop 2000:** 8,448 (White 62.6%; Black or African American 36.3%; Hispanic or Latino 0.5%; Asian 0.1%; Other 0.8%). **Foreign born:** 0.3%. **Median age:** 37.

Income 2000: per capita $13,643; median household $24,885; **Pop below poverty level:** 24.1%. ***Personal per capita income 2000-2003:** $15,217-$17,522.

Unemployment 2004: 7.7%. **Change from 2000:** -0.5%. **Median travel time to work:** 32.7 minutes. **Working outside county of residence:** 46.7%.

**Source: Personal per capita income data are from the Bureau of Economic Analysis; per capita income data are from the Bureau of the Census.
See Introduction for explanation of differences.*

388

Franklin County (cont'd)

Cities with pop over 10,000: None.

GEORGE COUNTY

355 Cox St Suite A
Lucedale, MS 39452

Ph: 601-947-4801
Fax: 601-947-1300

On the southeastern border of MS, north of Pascagoula, organized Mar 16, 1810 (prior to statehood) from Greene and Jackson counties. **Name Origin:** For Gen. James Zachariah George (1826-97), Confederate army officer and U.S. senator from MS (1881-97).

Area (sq mi): 483.63 (land 478.29; water 5.34). **Pop per sq mi:** 44.4.

Pop 2005: 21,259. **State rank:** 45. **Pop change:** 2000-20005 +11%; 1990-2000 +14.8%. **Pop 2000:** 19,144 (White 88.7%; Black or African American 8.8%; Hispanic or Latino 1.6%; Asian 0.2%; Other 1.6%). **Foreign born:** 1.3%. **Median age:** 33.3.

Income 2000: per capita $14,337; median household $34,730; **Pop below poverty level:** 16.7%. ***Personal per capita income 2000-2003:** $18,745-$19,725.

Unemployment 2004: 8.9%. **Change from 2000:** -0.3%. **Median travel time to work:** 36.6 minutes. **Working outside county of residence:** 52.6%.

Cities with pop over 10,000: None.

GREENE COUNTY

PO Box 610
Leakesville, MS 39451

Ph: 601-394-2377
Fax: 601-394-4445

On the southeastern border of MS, east of Hattiesburg; organized Dec 9, 1811 (prior to statehood) from Amite, Franklin, and Wayne counties. **Name Origin:** For Gen. Nathanael Greene (1742-86), hero of the Revolutionary War, quartermaster general (1778-80), and commander of the Army of the South (1780).

Area (sq mi): 718.69 (land 712.82; water 5.87). **Pop per sq mi:** 18.5.

Pop 2005: 13,183. **State rank:** 64. **Pop change:** 2000-20005 -0.9%; 1990-2000 +30.1%. **Pop 2000:** 13,299 (White 72.5%; Black or African American 26.2%; Hispanic or Latino 0.8%; Asian 0.1%; Other 0.9%). **Foreign born:** 0.3%. **Median age:** 32.4.

Income 2000: per capita $11,868; median household $28,336; **Pop below poverty level:** 19.6%. ***Personal per capita income 2000-2003:** $13,624-$15,672.

Unemployment 2004: 9.1%. **Change from 2000:** +0.5%. **Median travel time to work:** 42.1 minutes. **Working outside county of residence:** 62.6%.

Cities with pop over 10,000: None.

GRENADA COUNTY

PO Drawer 1208
Grenada, MS 38902

Ph: 662-226-1821
Fax: 662-227-2860

In north-central MS, northwest of Columbus; organized May 9, 1870 from Carroll and Tallahatchie counties. **Name Origin:** Believed to have been named for the island in the West Indies, chosen when the towns of Pittsburg and Tullohoma united after some years of rivalry. There is also a theory that it is a form of Granada, Spain.

Area (sq mi): 449.38 (land 421.79; water 27.58). **Pop per sq mi:** 54.2.

Pop 2005: 22,861. **State rank:** 41. **Pop change:** 2000-20005 -1.7%; 1990-2000 +7.9%. **Pop 2000:** 23,263 (White 57.7%; Black or African American 40.9%; Hispanic or Latino 0.6%; Asian 0.3%; Other 0.7%). **Foreign born:** 1%. **Median age:** 35.7.

Income 2000: per capita $13,786; median household $27,385; **Pop below poverty level:** 20.9%. ***Personal per capita income 2000-2003:** $19,868-$22,356.

Unemployment 2004: 6.4%. **Change from 2000:** -0.5%. **Median travel time to work:** 20.1 minutes. **Working outside county of residence:** 13.7%.

Cities with pop over 10,000: Grenada ⚖ (14,492).

HANCOCK COUNTY

PO Box 550
Bay Saint Louis, MS 39520
www.hancockcountyms.org

Ph: 228-467-5404
Fax: 228-467-3159

In the southwestern corner of MS, west of Gulfport; organized Dec 18, 1812 (prior to statehood) from Mobile District. **Name Origin:** For John Hancock (1737-93), noted signer of the Declaration of Independence, governor of MA (1780-85; 1787-93), and statesman.

Area (sq mi): 552.53 (land 476.88; water 75.65). **Pop per sq mi:** 98.

Pop 2005: 46,711. **State rank:** 15. **Pop change:** 2000-20005 +8.7%; 1990-2000 +35.3%. **Pop 2000:** 42,967 (White 88.9%; Black or African American 6.8%; Hispanic or Latino 1.8%; Asian 0.9%; Other 2%). **Foreign born:** 1.4%. **Median age:** 38.5.

Income 2000: per capita $17,748; median household $35,202; **Pop below poverty level:** 14.4%. ***Personal per capita income 2000-2003:** $21,451-$23,990.

Unemployment 2004: 4.9%. **Change from 2000:** +1.6%. **Median travel time to work:** 32.5 minutes. **Working outside county of residence:** 40.9%.

Cities with pop over 10,000: None.

HARRISON COUNTY

PO Drawer CC
Gulfport, MS 39502
www.co.harrison.ms.us

Ph: 228-865-4036
Fax: 228-868-1480

On the southern border of MS, west of Pascagoula; organized Feb 5, 1841 from Hancock and Jackson counties. **Name Origin:** For William Henry Harrison (1773-1841), ninth U.S. president.

Area (sq mi): 976.15 (land 580.98; water 395.17). **Pop per sq mi:** 333.6.

Pop 2005: 193,810. **State rank:** 2. **Pop change:** 2000-20005 +2.2%; 1990-2000 +14.7%. **Pop 2000:** 189,601 (White 71.8%; Black or African American 21.1%; Hispanic or Latino 2.6%; Asian 2.6%; Other 3.2%). **Foreign born:** 3.6%. **Median age:** 33.9.

Income 2000: per capita $18,024; median household $35,624; **Pop below poverty level:** 14.6%. ***Personal per capita income 2000-2003:** $24,418-$26,673.

Unemployment 2004: 5.2%. **Change from 2000:** +1.4%. **Median travel time to work:** 21.8 minutes. **Working outside county of residence:** 11%.

Cities with pop over 10,000: Gulfport ⚖ (71,851); Biloxi (50,115); Long Beach (17,258).

⚖ *County Seat*

HINDS COUNTY

316 S President St   **Ph:** 601-968-6501
Jackson, MS 39205   **Fax:** 601-968-6794
www.co.hinds.ms.us

In west-central MS, east of Vicksburg; organized Feb 12, 1821 from Choctaw cession. **Name Origin:** For Gen. Thomas Hinds (1780-1840), officer during the War of 1812 and U.S. representative from MS (1828-31).

Area (sq mi): 877.35 (land 869.18; water 8.16). **Pop per sq mi:** 286.9.

Pop 2005: 249,345. **State rank:** 1. **Pop change:** 2000-20005 -0.6%; 1990-2000 -1.4%. **Pop 2000:** 250,800 (White 37%; Black or African American 61.1%; Hispanic or Latino 0.8%; Asian 0.6%; Other 0.9%). **Foreign born:** 1.1%. **Median age:** 31.9.

Income 2000: per capita $17,785; median household $33,991; **Pop below poverty level:** 19.9%. ***Personal per capita income 2000-2003:** $24,779-$27,468.

Unemployment 2004: 5.7%. **Change from 2000:** +1.5%. **Median travel time to work:** 21.6 minutes. **Working outside county of residence:** 20.8%.

Cities with pop over 10,000: Jackson 🏛 (179,298); Clinton (24,392).

HOLMES COUNTY

PO Box 239   **Ph:** 662-834-2508
Lexington, MS 39095   **Fax:** 662-834-3020

In central MS, north of Jackson; organized Feb 19, 1833 from Yazoo County. **Name Origin:** For David Holmes (1769-1832), U.S. representative from VA (1797-1809), MS territorial governor (1809-17), state governor (1817-20; 1826), and U.S. senator (1820-25).

Area (sq mi): 764.18 (land 756; water 8.18). **Pop per sq mi:** 27.9.

Pop 2005: 21,099. **State rank:** 48. **Pop change:** 2000-20005 -2.4%; 1990-2000 +0%. **Pop 2000:** 21,609 (White 20.3%; Black or African American 78.7%; Hispanic or Latino 0.9%; Asian 0.2%; Other 0.7%). **Foreign born:** 0.3%. **Median age:** 29.7.

Income 2000: per capita $10,683; median household $17,235; **Pop below poverty level:** 41.1%. ***Personal per capita income 2000-2003:** $13,829-$16,468.

Unemployment 2004: 10.7%. **Change from 2000:** -7.3%. **Median travel time to work:** 29.1 minutes. **Working outside county of residence:** 38.1%.

Cities with pop over 10,000: None.

HUMPHREYS COUNTY

102 Castleman St PO Box 547   **Ph:** 662-247-1740
Belzoni, MS 39038   **Fax:** 662-247-0101

In west-central MS, southeast of Greenville; organized Mar 28, 1918 from Holmes, Washington, Yazoo, and Sunflower counties. **Name Origin:** For Benjamin Grubb Humphreys (1808-82), general in the Confederate army, MS legislator, and governor (1865-66).

Area (sq mi): 431.16 (land 418.09; water 13.07). **Pop per sq mi:** 25.2.

Pop 2005: 10,527. **State rank:** 70. **Pop change:** 2000-20005 -6.1%; 1990-2000 -7.6%. **Pop 2000:** 11,206 (White 26.8%; Black or African

American 71.5%; Hispanic or Latino 1.5%; Asian 0.3%; Other 1%). **Foreign born:** 0.8%. **Median age:** 30.5.

Income 2000: per capita $10,926; median household $20,566; **Pop below poverty level:** 38.2%. ***Personal per capita income 2000-2003:** $17,837-$19,090.

Unemployment 2004: 8.4%. **Change from 2000:** -4.4%. **Median travel time to work:** 19.6 minutes. **Working outside county of residence:** 20.6%.

Cities with pop over 10,000: None.

ISSAQUENA COUNTY

PO Box 27   **Ph:** 662-873-2761
Mayersville, MS 39113   **Fax:** 662-873-2061

On the central western border of MS, north of Vicksburg; organized Jan 23, 1844 from Washington County. **Name Origin:** From the Choctaw word probably meaning 'deer's head.'

Area (sq mi): 441.36 (land 413.06; water 28.3). **Pop per sq mi:** 4.6.

Pop 2005: 1,909. **State rank:** 82. **Pop change:** 2000-20005 -16.1%; 1990-2000 +19.1%. **Pop 2000:** 2,274 (White 36.1%; Black or African American 62.8%; Hispanic or Latino 0.4%; Asian 0%; Other 0.9%). **Foreign born:** 0.2%. **Median age:** 33.1.

Income 2000: per capita $10,581; median household $19,936; **Pop below poverty level:** 33.2%. ***Personal per capita income 2000-2003:** $11,383-$15,833.

Unemployment 2004: 9.7%. **Change from 2000:** -8%. **Median travel time to work:** 23.4 minutes. **Working outside county of residence:** 66.6%.

Cities with pop over 10,000: None.

ITAWAMBA COUNTY

PO Box 776   **Ph:** 662-862-3421
Fulton, MS 38843   **Fax:** 662-862-3421
www.itawamba.com

On the northeastern border of MS, north of Columbus; organized Feb 9, 1836 from Indian lands. **Name Origin:** For the personal name of an Indian chief; meaning uncertain.

Area (sq mi): 540.42 (land 532.31; water 8.11). **Pop per sq mi:** 43.9.

Pop 2005: 23,359. **State rank:** 40. **Pop change:** 2000-20005 +2.6%; 1990-2000 +13.8%. **Pop 2000:** 22,770 (White 92%; Black or African American 6.5%; Hispanic or Latino 1%; Asian 0.2%; Other 0.8%). **Foreign born:** 0.6%. **Median age:** 36.2.

Income 2000: per capita $14,956; median household $31,156; **Pop below poverty level:** 14%. ***Personal per capita income 2000-2003:** $19,415-$22,111.

Unemployment 2004: 5.8%. **Change from 2000:** +1.1%. **Median travel time to work:** 27.2 minutes. **Working outside county of residence:** 58.1%.

Cities with pop over 10,000: None.

JACKSON COUNTY

PO Box 998   **Ph:** 228-769-3089
Pascagoula, MS 39568   **Fax:** 228-769-3348
www.co.jackson.ms.us

In the southeastern corner of MS, east of Biloxi; organized Dec

*Source: Personal per capita income data are from the Bureau of Economic Analysis; per capita income data are from the Bureau of the Census. See Introduction for explanation of differences.

Jackson County (cont'd)

18, 1812 (prior to statehood) from Mobile District. **Name Origin:** For Andrew Jackson (1767-1845), seventh U.S. president.

Area (sq mi): 1043.3 (land 726.9; water 316.4). **Pop per sq mi:** 187.

Pop 2005: 135,940. **State rank:** 4. **Pop change:** 2000-20005 +3.4%; 1990-2000 +14%. **Pop 2000:** 131,420 (White 74.2%; Black or African American 20.9%; Hispanic or Latino 2.1%, Asian 1.0%, Other 2.1%). **Foreign born:** 2.7%. **Median age:** 34.7.

Income 2000: per capita $17,768; median household $39,118; **Pop below poverty level:** 12.7%. ***Personal per capita income 2000-2003:** $22,315-$25,046.

Unemployment 2004: 5.8%. **Change from 2000:** +1%. **Median travel time to work:** 23.7 minutes. **Working outside county of residence:** 29.5%.

Cities with pop over 10,000: Pascagoula 🏛 (25,873); Ocean Springs (17,698); Gautier (16,853); Moss Point (15,318).

JASPER COUNTY

PO Box 1047   **Ph:** 601-764-3368
Bay Springs, MS 39422   **Fax:** 601-764-3999

In east-central MS, north of Laurel; organized Dec 23, 1833 from Indian lands. **Name Origin:** For Sgt. William Jasper (1750-79), American Revolutionary War soldier from SC.

Area (sq mi): 677.44 (land 676; water 1.44). **Pop per sq mi:** 26.9.

Pop 2005: 18,162. **State rank:** 54. **Pop change:** 2000-20005 +0.1%; 1990-2000 +6%. **Pop 2000:** 18,149 (White 46.2%; Black or African American 52.9%; Hispanic or Latino 0.6%; Asian 0.1%; Other 0.6%). **Foreign born:** 0.3%. **Median age:** 35.1.

Income 2000: per capita $12,889; median household $24,441; **Pop below poverty level:** 22.7%. ***Personal per capita income 2000-2003:** $16,657-$19,077.

Unemployment 2004: 7.8%. **Change from 2000:** +3%. **Median travel time to work:** 27.8 minutes. **Working outside county of residence:** 50.2%.

Cities with pop over 10,000: None.

JEFFERSON COUNTY

PO Box 145   **Ph:** 601-786-3021
Fayette, MS 39069   **Fax:** 601-786-6009

On the southwestern border of MS, north of Natchez; organized Apr 2, 1799 (prior to statehood) from Pickering County. **Name Origin:** For Thomas Jefferson (1743-1826), U.S. patriot and statesman; third U.S. president.

Area (sq mi): 527.19 (land 519.39; water 7.81). **Pop per sq mi:** 18.2.

Pop 2005: 9,432. **State rank:** 78. **Pop change:** 2000-20005 -3.2%; 1990-2000 +12.6%. **Pop 2000:** 9,740 (White 13%; Black or African American 86.5%; Hispanic or Latino 0.7%; Asian 0.1%; Other 0.3%). **Foreign born:** 0.3%. **Median age:** 32.4.

Income 2000: per capita $9,709; median household $18,447; **Pop below poverty level:** 36%. ***Personal per capita income 2000-2003:** $11,639-$13,608.

Unemployment 2004: 13.2%. **Change from 2000:** -4.1%. **Median travel time to work:** 33 minutes. **Working outside county of residence:** 52.2%.

Cities with pop over 10,000: None.

JEFFERSON DAVIS COUNTY

PO Box 1137   **Ph:** 601-792-4204
Prentiss, MS 39474   **Fax:** 601-792-2894

In south-central MS, northwest of Hattiesburg, organized Mar 31, 1906 from Covington and Lawrence counties. **Name Origin:** For Jefferson Davis (1808-89), president of the Confederate States of America (1862-65).

Area (sq mi): 409.1 (land 408.41; water 0.7). **Pop per sq mi:** 32.2.

Pop 2005: 13,158. **State rank:** 65. **Pop change:** 2000-20005 -5.8%; 1990-2000 -0.6%. **Pop 2000:** 13,962 (White 41.4%; Black or African American 57.4%; Hispanic or Latino 0.8%; Asian 0.2%; Other 0.8%). **Foreign born:** 0.3%. **Median age:** 35.

Income 2000: per capita $11,974; median household $21,834; **Pop below poverty level:** 28.2%. ***Personal per capita income 2000-2003:** $15,241-$17,781.

Unemployment 2004: 8.1%. **Change from 2000:** -2.5%. **Median travel time to work:** 37.2 minutes. **Working outside county of residence:** 59.2%.

Cities with pop over 10,000: None.

JONES COUNTY

PO Box 1468   **Ph:** 601-428-0527
Laurel, MS 39441   **Fax:** 601-428-3610
www.edajones.com

In east-central MS, north of Hattiesburg; organized Jan 24, 1826 from Covington and Wayne counties. **Name Origin:** For John Paul Jones (1747-92), commander of the *Bonhomme Richard* in its victory over the British ship *Serapis* during the American Revolution. He later served as an admiral in the Russian Navy.

Area (sq mi): 699.73 (land 693.82; water 5.91). **Pop per sq mi:** 95.4.

Pop 2005: 66,160. **State rank:** 10. **Pop change:** 2000-20005 +1.9%; 1990-2000 +4.7%. **Pop 2000:** 64,958 (White 70.7%; Black or African American 26.3%; Hispanic or Latino 2%; Asian 0.3%; Other 2.3%). **Foreign born:** 2%. **Median age:** 35.8.

Income 2000: per capita $14,820; median household $28,786; **Pop below poverty level:** 19.8%. ***Personal per capita income 2000-2003:** $21,078-$24,030.

Unemployment 2004: 5.2%. **Change from 2000:** +1.9%. **Median travel time to work:** 22.7 minutes. **Working outside county of residence:** 19.1%.

Cities with pop over 10,000: Laurel 🏛 (18,186).

KEMPER COUNTY

PO Box 188   **Ph:** 601-743-2460
De Kalb, MS 39328   **Fax:** 601-743-2789

On the central eastern border of MS, north of Meridian; organized Dec 23, 1833 from Indian lands. **Name Origin:** For Reuben Kemper (?-1827), hero of the Florida and Mexican Wars.

Area (sq mi): 767 (land 766.13; water 0.87). **Pop per sq mi:** 13.4.

🏛 *County Seat*

Kemper County (cont'd)

Pop 2005: 10,246. **State rank:** 74. **Pop change:** 2000-20005 -2%; 1990-2000 +0.9%. **Pop 2000:** 10,453 (White 38.9%; Black or African American 58.1%; Hispanic or Latino 0.7%; Asian 0.1%; Other 2.8%, including 2.1% American Indian/Alaska Native). **Foreign born:** 0.4%. **Median age:** 35.2.

Income 2000: per capita $11,985; median household $23,998; **Pop below poverty level:** 26%. ***Personal per capita income 2000-2003:** $16,685-$17,711.

Unemployment 2004: 8.4%. **Change from 2000:** -0.5%. **Median travel time to work:** 33.5 minutes. **Working outside county of residence:** 60.5%.

Cities with pop over 10,000: None.

LAFAYETTE COUNTY

PO Box 1240   **Ph:** 662-234-7563
Oxford, MS 38655   **Fax:** 662-234-5038
www.oxfordms.com

In north-central MS, southeast of Memphis, TN; organized Feb 9, 1836 from Chickasaw cession of 1832. **Name Origin:** For the Marquis de Lafayette (1757-1834), French statesman and soldier who fought with Ameicans during the Revolutionary War.

Area (sq mi): 679.29 (land 631.11; water 48.17). **Pop per sq mi:** 64.7.

Pop 2005: 40,842. **State rank:** 18. **Pop change:** 2000-20005 +5.4%; 1990-2000 +21.7%. **Pop 2000:** 38,744 (White 71.3%; Black or African American 25%; Hispanic or Latino 1.1%; Asian 1.7%; Other 1.4%). **Foreign born:** 2.4%. **Median age:** 26.9.

Income 2000: per capita $16,406; median household $28,517; **Pop below poverty level:** 21.3%. ***Personal per capita income 2000-2003:** $20,693-$23,927.

Unemployment 2004: 4.8%. **Change from 2000:** +2.6%. **Median travel time to work:** 19 minutes. **Working outside county of residence:** 16.3%.

Cities with pop over 10,000: Oxford 🏛 (13,301).

LAMAR COUNTY

PO Box 247   **Ph:** 601-794-8504
Purvis, MS 39475   **Fax:** 601-794-3903
www.lamarcounty.com

In south-central MS, west of Hattiesburg; organized Feb 19, 1904 from Marion and Pearl River counties. **Name Origin:** For Lucius Quintus Cincinnatus Lamar (1825-93), U.S. statesman and a justice of the U.S. Supreme Court (1888-93).

Area (sq mi): 500.49 (land 497.07; water 3.42). **Pop per sq mi:** 89.8.

Pop 2005: 44,616. **State rank:** 16. **Pop change:** 2000-20005 +14.2%; 1990-2000 +28.4%. **Pop 2000:** 39,070 (White 84.7%; Black or African American 12.9%; Hispanic or Latino 1.1%; Asian 0.7%; Other 1.1%). **Foreign born:** 1.1%. **Median age:** 32.6.

Income 2000: per capita $18,849; median household $37,628; **Pop below poverty level:** 13.3%. ***Personal per capita income 2000-2003:** $20,909-$23,453.

Unemployment 2004: 4.1%. **Change from 2000:** +1.5%. **Median travel time to work:** 25.1 minutes. **Working outside county of residence:** 60.3%.

Cities with pop over 10,000: None.

LAUDERDALE COUNTY

PO Box 1587   **Ph:** 601-482-9714
Meridian, MS 39302   **Fax:** 601-486-4943
www.lauderdalecounty.org

On the central eastern border of MS, south of Columbus; organized Dec 23, 1833 from Choctaw cession. **Name Origin:** For Col. James Lauderdale (?-1814), soldier killed at the Battle of New Orleans during the War of 1812.

Area (sq mi): 715.28 (land 703.51; water 11.77). **Pop per sq mi:** 109.8.

Pop 2005: 77,218. **State rank:** 8. **Pop change:** 2000-20005 -1.2%; 1990-2000 +3.4%. **Pop 2000:** 78,161 (White 59.6%; Black or African American 38.2%; Hispanic or Latino 1.1%; Asian 0.5%; Other 1.1%). **Foreign born:** 0.7%. **Median age:** 35.

Income 2000: per capita $16,026; median household $30,768; **Pop below poverty level:** 20.8%. ***Personal per capita income 2000-2003:** $22,463-$25,011.

Unemployment 2004: 6.5%. **Change from 2000:** +1.3%. **Median travel time to work:** 21.3 minutes. **Working outside county of residence:** 8.2%.

Cities with pop over 10,000: Meridian 🏛 (38,833).

LAWRENCE COUNTY

PO Box 821   **Ph:** 601-587-7162
Monticello, MS 39654   **Fax:** 601-587-0767
www.lawrencecounty.org

In south-central MS, south of Jackson; organized Dec 22, 1814 (prior to statehood) from Marion County. **Name Origin:** For Capt. James Lawrence (1781-1813), U.S. Navy commander in War of 1812 who said, 'Don't give up the ship!'

Area (sq mi): 435.73 (land 430.63; water 5.11). **Pop per sq mi:** 31.4.

Pop 2005: 13,502. **State rank:** 61. **Pop change:** 2000-20005 +1.8%; 1990-2000 +6.4%. **Pop 2000:** 13,258 (White 66.6%; Black or African American 32.1%; Hispanic or Latino 0.7%; Asian 0.3%; Other 0.7%). **Foreign born:** 0.6%. **Median age:** 35.8.

Income 2000: per capita $14,469; median household $28,495; **Pop below poverty level:** 19.6%. ***Personal per capita income 2000-2003:** $20,603-$21,956.

Unemployment 2004: 6.7%. **Change from 2000:** -2.6%. **Median travel time to work:** 36.7 minutes. **Working outside county of residence:** 48.8%.

Cities with pop over 10,000: None.

LEAKE COUNTY

PO Box 72   **Ph:** 601-267-7372
Carthage, MS 39051   **Fax:** 601-267-6137
www.leakems.com

In central MS, northeast of Jackson; organized Dec 23, 1833 from

---

*Source: Personal per capita income data are from the Bureau of Economic Analysis; per capita income data are from the Bureau of the Census. See Introduction for explanation of differences.

Leake County (cont'd)

Choctaw cession of 1830. **Name Origin:** For Walter Leake (1762-1825), VA legislator, judge of the MS Territory (1807), U.S. senator from MS (1817-20), and governor (1822-25).

Area (sq mi): 585.39 (land 582.71; water 2.68). **Pop per sq mi:** 38.5.

Pop 2005: 22,453. **State rank:** 42. **Pop change:** 2000-20005 +7.2%; 1990-2000 +13.6%. **Pop 2000:** 20,940 (White 55.5%; Black or African American 37.4%; Hispanic or Latino 2.1%; Asian 0.1%; Other 6.3%, including 4.6% American Indian/Alaska Native). **Foreign born:** 1.4%. **Median age:** 34.8.

Income 2000: per capita $13,365; median household $27,055; **Pop below poverty level:** 23.3%. ***Personal per capita income 2000-2003:** $18,415-$20,578.

Unemployment 2004: 6.1%. **Change from 2000:** +0.7%. **Median travel time to work:** 32.6 minutes. **Working outside county of residence:** 39%.

Cities with pop over 10,000: None.

LEE COUNTY

PO Box 7127   **Ph:** 662-841-9100
Tupelo, MS 38802   **Fax:** 662-680-6091
www.leecoms.com

In northeastern MS, north of Columbus; organized Oct 26, 1866 from Itawamba and Pontotoc counties. **Name Origin:** For Robert E. Lee (1807-70), American general and commander in chief of the Confederate forces during the Civil War.

Area (sq mi): 453.14 (land 449.59; water 3.55). **Pop per sq mi:** 175.3.

Pop 2005: 78,793. **State rank:** 7. **Pop change:** 2000-20005 +4%; 1990-2000 +15.5%. **Pop 2000:** 75,755 (White 73.1%; Black or African American 24.5%; Hispanic or Latino 1.2%; Asian 0.5%; Other 1.2%). **Foreign born:** 1.1%. **Median age:** 34.6.

Income 2000: per capita $18,956; median household $36,165; **Pop below poverty level:** 13.4%. ***Personal per capita income 2000-2003:** $25,227-$27,941.

Unemployment 2004: 5.5%. **Change from 2000:** +1%. **Median travel time to work:** 19.3 minutes. **Working outside county of residence:** 12%.

Cities with pop over 10,000: Tupelo 🏛 (35,418).

LEFLORE COUNTY

306 W Market St   **Ph:** 662-453-1435
Greenwood, MS 38930   **Fax:** 662-455-1278

In west-central MS, northeast of Greenville; organized Mar 15, 1871 from Carroll and Sunflower counties. **Name Origin:** For Greenwood LeFlore (1800-65), leader of a prominent Choctaw family of French ancestry, landowner, and legislator.

Area (sq mi): 606.35 (land 591.93; water 14.42). **Pop per sq mi:** 61.5.

Pop 2005: 36,431. **State rank:** 22. **Pop change:** 2000-20005 -4%; 1990-2000 +1.6%. **Pop 2000:** 37,947 (White 29.6%; Black or African American 67.7%; Hispanic or Latino 1.9%; Asian 0.6%; Other 1.6%). **Foreign born:** 1.1%. **Median age:** 30.1.

Income 2000: per capita $12,553; median household $21,518; **Pop below poverty level:** 34.8%. ***Personal per capita income 2000-2003:** $17,765-$20,642.

Unemployment 2004: 9.3%. **Change from 2000:** -0.7%. **Median travel time to work:** 18 minutes. **Working outside county of residence:** 9.9%.

Cities with pop over 10,000: Greenwood 🏛 (17,439).

LINCOLN COUNTY

PO Box 555   **Ph:** 601-835-3479
Brookhaven, MS 39602   **Fax:** 601-835-3423
www.co.lincoln.ms.us

In southwestern MS, east of Natchez; organized Apr 7, 1870 from Amite, Pike, Lawrence, and Franklin counties. **Name Origin:** For Abraham Lincoln (1809-65), sixteenth U.S. president.

Area (sq mi): 588.17 (land 585.71; water 2.47). **Pop per sq mi:** 57.9.

Pop 2005: 33,906. **State rank:** 26. **Pop change:** 2000-20005 +2.2%; 1990-2000 +9.5%. **Pop 2000:** 33,166 (White 68.9%; Black or African American 29.7%; Hispanic or Latino 0.7%; Asian 0.2%; Other 0.8%). **Foreign born:** 0.6%. **Median age:** 35.8.

Income 2000: per capita $13,961; median household $27,279; **Pop below poverty level:** 19.2%. ***Personal per capita income 2000-2003:** $19,685-$22,192.

Unemployment 2004: 6.1%. **Change from 2000:** +1.2%. **Median travel time to work:** 30.5 minutes. **Working outside county of residence:** 28.9%.

Cities with pop over 10,000: None.

LOWNDES COUNTY

505 2nd Ave N   **Ph:** 662-329-5888
Columbus, MS 39701   **Fax:** 662-329-5881

On the central eastern border of MS, north of Meridian; organized Jan 30, 1830 from Monroe County. **Name Origin:** For William Jones Lowndes (1782-1822), SC legislator and U.S. representative (1811-22).

Area (sq mi): 516.45 (land 502.3; water 14.15). **Pop per sq mi:** 119.2.

Pop 2005: 59,895. **State rank:** 11. **Pop change:** 2000-20005 -2.7%; 1990-2000 +3.8%. **Pop 2000:** 61,586 (White 56%; Black or African American 41.6%; Hispanic or Latino 1.1%; Asian 0.5%; Other 1.5%). **Foreign born:** 1.3%. **Median age:** 32.7.

Income 2000: per capita $16,514; median household $32,123; **Pop below poverty level:** 21.3%. ***Personal per capita income 2000-2003:** $21,194-$23,061.

Unemployment 2004: 6.8%. **Change from 2000:** -0.4%. **Median travel time to work:** 21.1 minutes. **Working outside county of residence:** 13.5%.

Cities with pop over 10,000: Columbus 🏛 (24,791).

MADISON COUNTY

PO Box 404   **Ph:** 601-859-1177
Canton, MS 39046   **Fax:** 601-859-5875
www.madison-co.com

In central MS, north of Jackson; organized Jan 29, 1828 from

Madison County (cont'd)

Yazoo County. **Name Origin:** For James Madison (1751-1836), fourth U.S. president.

Area (sq mi): 741.97 (land 717.11; water 24.86). **Pop per sq mi:** 117.5.

Pop 2005: 84,286. **State rank:** 6. **Pop change:** 2000-20005 +12.9%; 1990-2000 +38.8%. **Pop 2000:** 74,674 (White 59.7%; Black or African American 37.5%; Hispanic or Latino 1%; Asian 1.3%; Other 0.9%). **Foreign born:** 1.7%. **Median age:** 33.4.

Income 2000: per capita $23,469; median household $46,970; **Pop below poverty level:** 14%. ***Personal per capita income 2000-2003:** $31,706-$36,451.

Unemployment 2004: 4.7%. **Change from 2000:** +1.5%. **Median travel time to work:** 24.5 minutes. **Working outside county of residence:** 57.2%.

Cities with pop over 10,000: Ridgeland (21,577); Madison (16,462); Canton ⛪ (12,826).

MARION COUNTY
250 Broad St Suite 2   **Ph:** 601-736-2691
Columbia, MS 39429   **Fax:** 601-444-0206

On the central southern border of MS, west of Hattiesburg; organized Dec 9, 1811 (prior to statehood) from Amite, Wayne, and Franklin counties. **Name Origin:** For Gen. Francis Marion (c.1732-95), SC soldier and legislator, known as 'The Swamp Fox' for his tactics during the Revolutionary War.

Area (sq mi): 548.58 (land 542.34; water 6.24). **Pop per sq mi:** 46.5.

Pop 2005: 25,235. **State rank:** 39. **Pop change:** 2000-20005 -1.4%; 1990-2000 +0.2%. **Pop 2000:** 25,595 (White 66.7%; Black or African American 31.9%; Hispanic or Latino 0.6%; Asian 0.2%; Other 0.9%). **Foreign born:** 0.8%. **Median age:** 35.1.

Income 2000: per capita $12,301; median household $24,555; **Pop below poverty level:** 24.8%. ***Personal per capita income 2000-2003:** $17,067-$19,898.

Unemployment 2004: 6.7%. **Change from 2000:** +1.4%. **Median travel time to work:** 34.8 minutes. **Working outside county of residence:** 29.2%.

Cities with pop over 10,000: None.

MARSHALL COUNTY
PO Box 219   **Ph:** 662-252-4431
Holly Springs, MS 38635   **Fax:** 662-252-0004

On central northern border of MS, southeast of Memphis, TN; organized Feb 9, 1836 from Indian lands. **Name Origin:** For John Marshall (1755-1835), American jurist; fourth Chief Justice of the U.S. Supreme Court (1801-35).

Area (sq mi): 709.8 (land 706.33; water 3.47). **Pop per sq mi:** 50.5.

Pop 2005: 35,659. **State rank:** 23. **Pop change:** 2000-20005 +1.9%; 1990-2000 +15.3%. **Pop 2000:** 34,993 (White 47.9%; Black or African American 50.4%; Hispanic or Latino 1.2%; Asian 0.1%; Other 1.2%). **Foreign born:** 1%. **Median age:** 33.9.

Income 2000: per capita $14,028; median household $28,756; **Pop below poverty level:** 21.9%. ***Personal per capita income 2000-2003:** $17,397-$19,224.

Unemployment 2004: 7.6%. **Change from 2000:** -0.1%. **Median travel time to work:** 30.8 minutes. **Working outside county of residence:** 61.5%.

Cities with pop over 10,000: None.

MONROE COUNTY
PO Box 578   **Ph:** 662-369-8143
Aberdeen, MS 39730   **Fax:** 662-369-7928
www.gomonroe.org

On the central eastern border of MS, north of Columbus; organized Feb 9, 1821 from Chickasaw cession of 1821. **Name Origin:** For James Monroe (1758-1831), fifth U.S. president.

Area (sq mi): 772.04 (land 764.17; water 7.87). **Pop per sq mi:** 49.3.

Pop 2005: 37,704. **State rank:** 21. **Pop change:** 2000-20005 -0.8%; 1990-2000 +3.9%. **Pop 2000:** 38,014 (White 68%; Black or African American 30.8%; Hispanic or Latino 0.7%; Asian 0.2%; Other 0.7%). **Foreign born:** 0.6%. **Median age:** 35.7.

Income 2000: per capita $14,072; median household $30,307; **Pop below poverty level:** 17.2%. ***Personal per capita income 2000-2003:** $19,398-$20,994.

Unemployment 2004: 7.6%. **Change from 2000:** -3.1%. **Median travel time to work:** 25.7 minutes. **Working outside county of residence:** 38.5%.

Cities with pop over 10,000: None.

MONTGOMERY COUNTY
PO Box 71   **Ph:** 662-283-2333
Winona, MS 38967   **Fax:** 662-283-2233

In central MS, west of Columbus; organized May 13, 1871 from Carroll and Choctaw counties. **Name Origin:** For Gen. Richard Montgomery (1736-75), American Revolutionary War officer who captured Montreal, Canada.

Area (sq mi): 407.86 (land 406.85; water 1.02). **Pop per sq mi:** 29.1.

Pop 2005: 11,829. **State rank:** 68. **Pop change:** 2000-20005 -3%; 1990-2000 -1.6%. **Pop 2000:** 12,189 (White 53.9%; Black or African American 45%; Hispanic or Latino 0.8%; Asian 0.3%; Other 0.6%). **Foreign born:** 0.2%. **Median age:** 37.3.

Income 2000: per capita $14,040; median household $25,270; **Pop below poverty level:** 24.3%. ***Personal per capita income 2000-2003:** $17,623-$20,377.

Unemployment 2004: 8.1%. **Change from 2000:** -1.5%. **Median travel time to work:** 25.4 minutes. **Working outside county of residence:** 42.1%.

Cities with pop over 10,000: None.

NESHOBA COUNTY
401 Beacon St Suite 107   **Ph:** 601-656-3581
Philadelphia, MS 39350   **Fax:** 601-656-5915
www.neshoba.org

In east-central MS, northwest of Meridian; organized Dec 23, 1833 from Choctaw cession in 1830. **Name Origin:** Choctaw, probably 'wolf,' but debatable.

Area (sq mi): 571.64 (land 570; water 1.64). **Pop per sq mi:** 52.5.

---

*Source: Personal per capita income data are from the Bureau of Economic Analysis; per capita income data are from the Bureau of the Census.
See Introduction for explanation of differences.

Neshoba County (cont'd)

Pop 2005: 29,905. **State rank:** 29. **Pop change:** 2000-20005 +4.3%; 1990-2000 +15.7%. **Pop 2000:** 28,684 (White 64.9%; Black or African American 19.3%; Hispanic or Latino 1.2%; Asian 0.2%; Other 14.9%, including 13.8% American Indian/Alaska Native). **Foreign born:** 0.8%. **Median age:** 34.7.

Income 2000: per capita $14,964; median household $28,300; **Pop below poverty level:** 21%. *Personal per capita income 2000-2003: $20,438-$25,687.

Unemployment 2004: 5.7%. **Change from 2000:** +0.9%. **Median travel time to work:** 24.1 minutes. **Working outside county of residence:** 24.6%.

Cities with pop over 10,000: None.

NEWTON COUNTY

PO Box 447   **Ph:** 601-635-2368
Decatur, MS 39327   **Fax:** 601-635-3210

In east-central MS, west of Meridian; organized Feb 25, 1836 from Neshoba County. **Name Origin:** For Sir Isaac Newton (1642-1727), English mathematician and natural philosopher, formulator of the law of gravitation.

Area (sq mi): 579.58 (land 578.03; water 1.55). **Pop per sq mi:** 38.7.

Pop 2005: 22,366. **State rank:** 43. **Pop change:** 2000-20005 +2.4%; 1990-2000 +7.6%. **Pop 2000:** 21,838 (White 64.5%; Black or African American 30.4%; Hispanic or Latino 0.9%; Asian 0.2%; Other 4.4%, including 3.7% American Indian/Alaska Native). **Foreign born:** 0.5%. **Median age:** 35.1.

Income 2000: per capita $14,008; median household $28,735; **Pop below poverty level:** 19.9%. *Personal per capita income 2000-2003: $19,256-$22,003.

Unemployment 2004: 5.4%. **Change from 2000:** -0.3%. **Median travel time to work:** 24.1 minutes. **Working outside county of residence:** 36.9%.

Cities with pop over 10,000: None.

NOXUBEE COUNTY

PO Box 147   **Ph:** 662-726-4243
Macon, MS 39341   **Fax:** 662-726-2272
www.noxubeecounty.org

On the central eastern border of MS, south of Columbus; organized Dec 23, 1833 for Choctaw cession in 1830. **Name Origin:** For the Noxubee River, which runs through it; from Choctaw probably 'stinking water.'

Area (sq mi): 700.05 (land 694.79; water 5.26). **Pop per sq mi:** 17.6.

Pop 2005: 12,202. **State rank:** 66. **Pop change:** 2000-20005 -2.8%; 1990-2000 -0.4%. **Pop 2000:** 12,548 (White 29.2%; Black or African American 69.3%; Hispanic or Latino 1.1%; Asian 0.1%; Other 1.2%). **Foreign born:** 1%. **Median age:** 32.3.

Income 2000: per capita $12,018; median household $22,330; **Pop below poverty level:** 32.8%. *Personal per capita income 2000-2003: $16,100-$17,847.

Unemployment 2004: 11.9%. **Change from 2000:** +0.6%. **Median travel time to work:** 23.3 minutes. **Working outside county of residence:** 27.3%.

Cities with pop over 10,000: None.

OKTIBBEHA COUNTY

101 E Main St   **Ph:** 662-323-5834
Starkville, MS 39759   **Fax:** 662-338-1064
www.gtpdd.com/counties/oktibbeha/

In east-central MS, west of Columbus; organized Dec 23, 1833 from Choctaw cession 1830. **Name Origin:** For Choctaw, locally believed to mean 'pure water.'

Area (sq mi): 461.9 (land 457.71; water 4.19). **Pop per sq mi:** 90.1.

Pop 2005: 41,247. **State rank:** 17. **Pop change:** 2000-20005 -3.9%; 1990-2000 +11.8%. **Pop 2000:** 42,902 (White 58.2%; Black or African American 37.4%; Hispanic or Latino 1.1%; Asian 2.5%; Other 1.4%). **Foreign born:** 3.3%. **Median age:** 24.8.

Income 2000: per capita $14,998; median household $24,899; **Pop below poverty level:** 28.2%. *Personal per capita income 2000-2003: $18,858-$22,500.

Unemployment 2004: 5.5%. **Change from 2000:** +2.4%. **Median travel time to work:** 17.5 minutes. **Working outside county of residence:** 18.1%.

Cities with pop over 10,000: Starkville 🏛 (21,964).

PANOLA COUNTY

151 Public Sq   **Ph:** 662-563-6205
Batesville, MS 38606   **Fax:** 662-563-6277

In northwestern MS, south of Memphis, TN; organized Feb 9, 1836 from Indian lands. **Name Origin:** From the Choctaw word probably meaning 'cotton.'

Area (sq mi): 705.13 (land 684.2; water 20.94). **Pop per sq mi:** 51.6.

Pop 2005: 35,331. **State rank:** 24. **Pop change:** 2000-20005 +3.1%; 1990-2000 +14.3%. **Pop 2000:** 34,274 (White 50.2%; Black or African American 48.4%; Hispanic or Latino 1.1%; Asian 0.2%; Other 1%). **Foreign born:** 0.6%. **Median age:** 33.

Income 2000: per capita $13,075; median household $26,785; **Pop below poverty level:** 25.3%. *Personal per capita income 2000-2003: $17,186-$19,173.

Unemployment 2004: 8.9%. **Change from 2000:** -1.3%. **Median travel time to work:** 27.2 minutes. **Working outside county of residence:** 35.2%.

Cities with pop over 10,000: None.

PEARL RIVER COUNTY

PO Box 431   **Ph:** 601-403-2300
Poplarville, MS 39470   **Fax:** 601-795-3093
www.pearlrivercounty.net

In south-central MS, northwest of Biloxi; organized Feb 22, 1890 from Hancock and Marion counties. **Name Origin:** For the river, which flows through the county.

Area (sq mi): 818.93 (land 811.33; water 7.6). **Pop per sq mi:** 64.9.

Pop 2005: 52,659. **State rank:** 13. **Pop change:** 2000-20005 +8.3%; 1990-2000 +25.6%. **Pop 2000:** 48,621 (White 84.7%; Black or African American 12.2%; Hispanic or Latino 1.4%; Asian 0.3%; Other 1.9%). **Foreign born:** 1.2%. **Median age:** 35.9.

🏛 *County Seat*

Pearl River County (cont'd)

Income 2000: per capita $15,160; median household $30,912; **Pop below poverty level:** 18.4%. ***Personal per capita income 2000-2003:** $17,855-$19,540.

Unemployment 2004: 5.3%. **Change from 2000:** +1.9%. **Median travel time to work:** 36.4 minutes. **Working outside county of residence:** 48.2%.

Cities with pop over 10,000: Picayune (10,750).

PERRY COUNTY
PO Box 198   **Ph:** 601-964-8398
New Augusta, MS 39462   **Fax:** 601-964-8746

In southeastern MS, southeast of Hattiesburg; organized Feb 3, 1820 from Greene County. **Name Origin:** For Oliver Hazard Perry (1785-1819), U.S. naval officer during the War of 1812, famous for the message, 'We have met the enemy and they are ours.'

Area (sq mi): 650.2 (land 647.18; water 3.02). **Pop per sq mi:** 18.8.

Pop 2005: 12,160. **State rank:** 67. **Pop change:** 2000-20005 +0.2%; 1990-2000 +11.7%. **Pop 2000:** 12,138 (White 75.7%; Black or African American 22.6%; Hispanic or Latino 1%; Asian 0.1%; Other 1.1%). **Foreign born:** 0.5%. **Median age:** 33.5.

Income 2000: per capita $12,837; median household $27,189; **Pop below poverty level:** 22%. ***Personal per capita income 2000-2003:** $14,738-$16,786.

Unemployment 2004: 7.3%. **Change from 2000:** +0.5%. **Median travel time to work:** 36.1 minutes. **Working outside county of residence:** 57.7%.

Cities with pop over 10,000: None.

PIKE COUNTY
PO Box 309   **Ph:** 601-783-3363
Magnolia, MS 39652   **Fax:** 601-783-5982
www.co.pike.ms.us

On the central southern border of MS; organized Dec 9, 1815 (prior to statehood) from Marion County. **Name Origin:** For Zebulon Montgomery Pike (1779-1813), U.S. army officer and discoverer of Pikes Peak in CO.

Area (sq mi): 410.78 (land 408.89; water 1.89). **Pop per sq mi:** 96.4.

Pop 2005: 39,426. **State rank:** 19. **Pop change:** 2000-20005 +1.2%; 1990-2000 +5.6%. **Pop 2000:** 38,940 (White 51%; Black or African American 47.5%; Hispanic or Latino 0.7%; Asian 0.3%; Other 0.9%). **Foreign born:** 0.9%. **Median age:** 35.2.

Income 2000: per capita $14,040; median household $24,562; **Pop below poverty level:** 25.3%. ***Personal per capita income 2000-2003:** $18,298-$20,439.

Unemployment 2004: 7%. **Change from 2000:** +1.1%. **Median travel time to work:** 26.4 minutes. **Working outside county of residence:** 19.9%.

Cities with pop over 10,000: McComb (13,213).

PONTOTOC COUNTY
PO Box 209   **Ph:** 662-489-3900
Pontotoc, MS 38863   **Fax:** 662-489-3940

In north-central MS, northwest of Columbus; organized Feb 9,

1836 from Chickasaw cession. **Name Origin:** From the Chickasaw term probably meaning 'cattails growing on the prairie.'

Area (sq mi): 500.99 (land 497.35; water 3.64). **Pop per sq mi:** 56.7.

Pop 2005: 28,208. **State rank:** 33. **Pop change:** 2000-20005 +5.5%; 1990-2000 +20.2%. **Pop 2000:** 26,726 (White 83.6%; Black or African American 14%; Hispanic or Latino 1.8%; Asian 0.1%; Other 1.5%). **Foreign born:** 1.1%. **Median age:** 34.8.

Income 2000: per capita $15,658; median household $32,055; **Pop below poverty level:** 13.8%. ***Personal per capita income 2000-2003:** $18,640-$20,497.

Unemployment 2004: 5%. **Change from 2000:** -0.1%. **Median travel time to work:** 23.3 minutes. **Working outside county of residence:** 40.2%.

Cities with pop over 10,000: None.

PRENTISS COUNTY
PO Box 477   **Ph:** 662-728-8151
Booneville, MS 38829   **Fax:** 662-728-2007

In northeastern MS, south of Corinth; organized Apr 15, 1870 from Tishomingo County. **Name Origin:** For Seargeant Smith Prentiss (1808-50), MS legislator and U.S. representative (1838-39).

Area (sq mi): 418.24 (land 414.93; water 3.32). **Pop per sq mi:** 61.7.

Pop 2005: 25,593. **State rank:** 38. **Pop change:** 2000-20005 +0.1%; 1990-2000 +9.8%. **Pop 2000:** 25,556 (White 85.5%; Black or African American 12.9%; Hispanic or Latino 0.7%; Asian 0.2%; Other 1.1%). **Foreign born:** 0.4%. **Median age:** 35.

Income 2000: per capita $14,131; median household $28,446; **Pop below poverty level:** 16.5%. ***Personal per capita income 2000-2003:** $16,446-$18,511.

Unemployment 2004: 6.9%. **Change from 2000:** +2.2%. **Median travel time to work:** 22.8 minutes. **Working outside county of residence:** 36.9%.

Cities with pop over 10,000: None.

QUITMAN COUNTY
230 Chestnut St County Courthouse   **Ph:** 662-326-2661
Marks, MS 38646   **Fax:** 662-326-8004

In northwestern MS, southwest of Memphis, TN; organized Feb 1, 1877 from Panola and Coahoma counties. **Name Origin:** For John Anthony Quitman (1799-1858), tenth and sixteenth governor of MS (1835-36; 1850-51) and U.S. representative (1855-58).

Area (sq mi): 406.49 (land 404.84; water 1.66). **Pop per sq mi:** 23.5.

Pop 2005: 9,512. **State rank:** 77. **Pop change:** 2000-20005 -6%; 1990-2000 -3.6%. **Pop 2000:** 10,117 (White 30.3%; Black or African American 68.6%; Hispanic or Latino 0.5%; Asian 0.2%; Other 0.7%). **Foreign born:** 0.2%. **Median age:** 31.8.

Income 2000: per capita $10,817; median household $20,636; **Pop below poverty level:** 33.1%. ***Personal per capita income 2000-2003:** $14,717-$17,933.

Unemployment 2004: 9.6%. **Change from 2000:** -2%. **Median travel time to work:** 27.8 minutes. **Working outside county of residence:** 50.1%.

Cities with pop over 10,000: None.

*Source: Personal per capita income data are from the Bureau of Economic Analysis; per capita income data are from the Bureau of the Census. See Introduction for explanation of differences.

RANKIN COUNTY

PO Box 1599   **Ph:** 601-825-1466
Brandon, MS 39043   **Fax:** 601-825-1465
www.rankincounty.org

In central MS, east of Jackson; organized Feb 4, 1828 from Hinds County. **Name Origin:** For Christopher Rankin (1788-1826), MS legislator and U.S. representative (1819-26).

Area (sq mi). 806.09 (land 774.52; water 31.57). **Pop per sq mi:** 170.2.

Pop 2005: 131,841. **State rank:** 5. **Pop change:** 2000-20005 +14.3%; 1990-2000 +32.3%. **Pop 2000:** 115,327 (White 80.3%; Black or African American 17.1%; Hispanic or Latino 1.3%; Asian 0.7%; Other 1.2%). **Foreign born:** 1.6%. **Median age:** 34.6.

Income 2000: per capita $20,412; median household $44,946; **Pop below poverty level:** 9.5%. ***Personal per capita income 2000-2003:** $26,512-$27,729.

Unemployment 2004: 4%. **Change from 2000:** +1.5%. **Median travel time to work:** 25.5 minutes. **Working outside county of residence:** 52.5%.

Cities with pop over 10,000: Pearl (23,039); Brandon 🏛 (18,631).

SCOTT COUNTY

PO Box 630   **Ph:** 601-469-1922
Forest, MS 39074   **Fax:** 601-469-5180

In central MS, east of Jackson; organized Dec 23, 1833 from Choctaw cession in 1832. **Name Origin:** For Abram M. Scott (?-1833), governor of MS (1832-33).

Area (sq mi): 610.38 (land 609.08; water 1.3). **Pop per sq mi:** 47.2.

Pop 2005: 28,739. **State rank:** 32. **Pop change:** 2000-20005 +1.1%; 1990-2000 +17.8%. **Pop 2000:** 28,423 (White 54.7%; Black or African American 38.9%; Hispanic or Latino 5.8%; Asian 0.2%; Other 3.7%). **Foreign born:** 4.2%. **Median age:** 33.8.

Income 2000: per capita $14,013; median household $26,686; **Pop below poverty level:** 20.7%. ***Personal per capita income 2000-2003:** $18,126-$20,225.

Unemployment 2004: 5.1%. **Change from 2000:** +0.6%. **Median travel time to work:** 27.2 minutes. **Working outside county of residence:** 28.7%.

Cities with pop over 10,000: None.

SHARKEY COUNTY

PO Box 218   **Ph:** 662-873-2755
Rolling Fork, MS 39159   **Fax:** 662-873-6045

In central western MS, north of Vicksburg; organized Mar 29, 1876 from Warren, Washington, and Issaquena counties. **Name Origin:** For William Lewis Sharkey (1798-1873), MS legislator, circuit court judge (1832), and provisional governor (1865).

Area (sq mi): 434.88 (land 427.71; water 7.17). **Pop per sq mi:** 14.

Pop 2005: 5,967. **State rank:** 81. **Pop change:** 2000-20005 -9.3%; 1990-2000 -6.9%. **Pop 2000:** 6,580 (White 29%; Black or African American 69.3%; Hispanic or Latino 1.3%; Asian 0.3%; Other 1.1%). **Foreign born:** 0.4%. **Median age:** 30.8.

Income 2000: per capita $11,396; median household $22,285; **Pop below poverty level:** 38.3%. ***Personal per capita income 2000-2003:** $15,377-$18,498.

Unemployment 2004: 9.9%. **Change from 2000:** -3.1%. **Median travel time to work:** 24.2 minutes. **Working outside county of residence:** 31.7%.

Cities with pop over 10,000: None.

SIMPSON COUNTY

PO Box 367   **Ph:** 601-847-2626
Mendenhall, MS 39114   **Fax:** 601-847-7004

In south-central MS, south of Jackson; organized Jan 23, 1824 from Copiah County. **Name Origin:** For Josiah Simpson, a judge in the Mississippi Territory.

Area (sq mi): 590.53 (land 588.73; water 1.8). **Pop per sq mi:** 47.5.

Pop 2005: 27,944. **State rank:** 35. **Pop change:** 2000-20005 +1.1%; 1990-2000 +15.4%. **Pop 2000:** 27,639 (White 64%; Black or African American 34.3%; Hispanic or Latino 1.2%; Asian 0.1%; Other 1.2%). **Foreign born:** 0.9%. **Median age:** 35.

Income 2000: per capita $13,344; median household $28,343; **Pop below poverty level:** 21.6%. ***Personal per capita income 2000-2003:** $18,285-$21,582.

Unemployment 2004: 5.3%. **Change from 2000:** +1%. **Median travel time to work:** 32.8 minutes. **Working outside county of residence:** 49.1%.

Cities with pop over 10,000: None.

SMITH COUNTY

PO Box 517   **Ph:** 601-782-4751
Raleigh, MS 39153   **Fax:** 601-782-4007

In east-central MS, southeast of Jackson; organized Dec 23, 1833 from Indian lands. **Name Origin:** For a David Smith; other information has been lost.

Area (sq mi): 637.27 (land 635.89; water 1.38). **Pop per sq mi:** 25.3.

Pop 2005: 16,058. **State rank:** 56. **Pop change:** 2000-20005 -0.8%; 1990-2000 +9.4%. **Pop 2000:** 16,182 (White 75.8%; Black or African American 23.1%; Hispanic or Latino 0.6%; Asian 0.1%; Other 0.7%). **Foreign born:** 0.5%. **Median age:** 35.6.

Income 2000: per capita $14,752; median household $30,840; **Pop below poverty level:** 16.9%. ***Personal per capita income 2000-2003:** $19,681-$22,783.

Unemployment 2004: 5.4%. **Change from 2000:** +0.1%. **Median travel time to work:** 29.7 minutes. **Working outside county of residence:** 50.8%.

Cities with pop over 10,000: None.

STONE COUNTY

PO Drawer 7   **Ph:** 601-928-5266
Wiggins, MS 39577   **Fax:** 601-928-6464
www.stonecounty.com

In southeastern MS, north of Gulfport; organized Apr 3, 1916 from Harrison County. **Name Origin:** For Col. John Marshall Stone (1830-1900), acting governor (1876-82) and governor (1890-96).

Area (sq mi): 448.07 (land 445.37; water 2.71). **Pop per sq mi:** 33.4.

Stone County (cont'd)

Pop 2005: 14,862. **State rank:** 58. **Pop change:** 2000-20005 +9.1%; 1990-2000 +26.7%. **Pop 2000:** 13,622 (White 78.7%; Black or African American 19.2%; Hispanic or Latino 1.2%; Asian 0.2%; Other 1.2%). **Foreign born:** 1%. **Median age:** 33.6.

Income 2000: per capita $14,693; median household $30,495; **Pop below poverty level:** 17.5%. ***Personal per capita income 2000-2003:** $19,474-$22,053.

Unemployment 2004: 5.4%. **Change from 2000:** -0.1%. **Median travel time to work:** 33 minutes. **Working outside county of residence:** 42.7%.

Cities with pop over 10,000: None.

SUNFLOWER COUNTY
PO Box 988   **Ph:** 662-887-4703
Indianola, MS 38751   **Fax:** 662-887-7054

In west-central MS, northeast of Greenville; organized Feb 15, 1844 from Bolivar County. **Name Origin:** For the Sunflower River, which runs through the county.

Area (sq mi): 707.22 (land 693.79; water 13.43). **Pop per sq mi:** 46.6.

Pop 2005: 32,311. **State rank:** 27. **Pop change:** 2000-20005 -6%; 1990-2000 +4.6%. **Pop 2000:** 34,369 (White 28.5%; Black or African American 69.9%; Hispanic or Latino 1.3%; Asian 0.4%; Other 0.9%). **Foreign born:** 0.6%. **Median age:** 30.2.

Income 2000: per capita $11,365; median household $24,970; **Pop below poverty level:** 30%. ***Personal per capita income 2000-2003:** $15,670-$16,375.

Unemployment 2004: 9.1%. **Change from 2000:** -3.6%. **Median travel time to work:** 20.6 minutes. **Working outside county of residence:** 22.7%.

Cities with pop over 10,000: Indianola 🏛 (11,449).

TALLAHATCHIE COUNTY
PO Box 350   **Ph:** 662-647-5551
Charleston, MS 38921   **Fax:** 662-647-8490

In north-central MS, northeast of Greenville; organized Dec 23, 1833 from Indian lands. **Name Origin:** For the Tallahatchie River, which runs through it; possibly from Cree *talwa* 'town,' and *hachi* 'river': 'river town.'

Area (sq mi): 652.08 (land 643.92; water 8.16). **Pop per sq mi:** 22.

Pop 2005: 14,191. **State rank:** 60. **Pop change:** 2000-20005 -4.8%; 1990-2000 -2%. **Pop 2000:** 14,903 (White 39.4%; Black or African American 59.4%; Hispanic or Latino 0.9%; Asian 0.4%; Other 0.6%). **Foreign born:** 0.5%. **Median age:** 33.3.

Income 2000: per capita $10,749; median household $22,229; **Pop below poverty level:** 32.2%. ***Personal per capita income 2000-2003:** $15,381-$18,958.

Unemployment 2004: 9.5%. **Change from 2000:** -2.7%. **Median travel time to work:** 30.5 minutes. **Working outside county of residence:** 51.9%.

Cities with pop over 10,000: None.

TATE COUNTY
PO Box 309   **Ph:** 662-562-5661
Senatobia, MS 38668   **Fax:** 662-560-6205

In northwestern MS, south of Memphis, TN; organized Apr 15, 1873 from DeSoto, Marshall, and Tunica counties. **Name Origin:** Named by T.S. Tate, an early settler, for his family.

Area (sq mi): 410.95 (land 404.48; water 6.47). **Pop per sq mi:** 65.6.

Pop 2005: 26,548. **State rank:** 37. **Pop change:** 2000-20005 +4.6%; 1990-2000 +18.4%. **Pop 2000:** 25,370 (White 67.4%; Black or African American 31%; Hispanic or Latino 0.9%; Asian 0.1%; Other 1%). **Foreign born:** 0.2%. **Median age:** 34.2.

Income 2000: per capita $16,154; median household $35,836; **Pop below poverty level:** 13.5%. ***Personal per capita income 2000-2003:** $21,049-$22,818.

Unemployment 2004: 6%. **Change from 2000:** +1.2%. **Median travel time to work:** 31.1 minutes. **Working outside county of residence:** 50%.

Cities with pop over 10,000: None.

TIPPAH COUNTY
101 Spring St   **Ph:** 662-837-7374
Ripley, MS 38663   **Fax:** 662-837-7148
www.tippahcounty.ripley.ms

On the northern border of MS; organized Feb 9, 1836 from Chickasaw cession. **Name Origin:** For the wife of a Chickasaw chief; name is thought to mean 'cut-off.'

Area (sq mi): 459.97 (land 457.91; water 2.07). **Pop per sq mi:** 46.3.

Pop 2005: 21,212. **State rank:** 47. **Pop change:** 2000-20005 +1.9%; 1990-2000 +6.7%. **Pop 2000:** 20,826 (White 81.1%; Black or African American 15.9%; Hispanic or Latino 2.1%; Asian 0.1%; Other 2.1%). **Foreign born:** 1.9%. **Median age:** 35.9.

Income 2000: per capita $14,041; median household $29,300; **Pop below poverty level:** 16.9%. ***Personal per capita income 2000-2003:** $19,284-$20,356.

Unemployment 2004: 6.9%. **Change from 2000:** +0.9%. **Median travel time to work:** 25.3 minutes. **Working outside county of residence:** 35.3%.

Cities with pop over 10,000: None.

TISHOMINGO COUNTY
1008 Battleground Dr   **Ph:** 662-423-7010
Iuka, MS 38852   **Fax:** 662-423-7005
www.tunicacounty.com

On northeastern corner of MS; organized Feb 9, 1836 from Chickasaw cession, divided in 1870 into Alcorn, Prentiss, and Tishomingo counties. **Name Origin:** For Tishomingo (1733?-1837?), last full-blooded war chief of the Chickasaw Indians. Name means 'assistant chief': at this time he was the principal leader next to Ishtehotopa, the Chickasaw king.

Area (sq mi): 444.54 (land 424.12; water 20.41). **Pop per sq mi:** 45.3.

Pop 2005: 19,202. **State rank:** 52. **Pop change:** 2000-20005 +0.2%; 1990-2000 +8.4%. **Pop 2000:** 19,163 (White 94.3%; Black or African American 3.1%; Hispanic or Latino 1.8%; Asian 0.1%; Other 1.9%). **Foreign born:** 1%. **Median age:** 39.1.

*Source: Personal per capita income data are from the Bureau of Economic Analysis; per capita income data are from the Bureau of the Census.
See Introduction for explanation of differences.

Tishomingo County (cont'd)

Income 2000: per capita $15,395; median household $28,315; **Pop below poverty level:** 14.1%. ***Personal per capita income 2000-2003:** $18,125-$19,236.

Unemployment 2004: 7.8%. **Change from 2000:** +0.4%. **Median travel time to work:** 24.9 minutes. **Working outside county of residence:** 40%

Cities with pop over 10,000: None.

TUNICA COUNTY
PO Box 217   **Ph:** 662-363-2451
Tunica, MS 38676   **Fax:** 662-357-5934
www.tunicacounty.com

On the northwestern border of MS, southwest of Memphis, TN; organized Feb 9, 1836 by the Treaty of Pontotoc from Chickasaw cession of 1832. **Name Origin:** For a tribe of Tunican linguistic stock located on the lower Yazoo River in MS. Their name probably means 'the people' or 'those who are the people.'

Area (sq mi): 480.78 (land 454.81; water 25.97). **Pop per sq mi:** 22.7.

Pop 2005: 10,321. **State rank:** 72. **Pop change:** 2000-20005 +11.9%; 1990-2000 +13%. **Pop 2000:** 9,227 (White 26.9%; Black or African American 70.2%; Hispanic or Latino 2.5%; Asian 0.4%; Other 1.9%). **Foreign born:** 0.9%. **Median age:** 30.6.

Income 2000: per capita $11,978; median household $23,270; **Pop below poverty level:** 33.1%. ***Personal per capita income 2000-2003:** $17,327-$19,325.

Unemployment 2004: 8.6%. **Change from 2000:** +3.1%. **Median travel time to work:** 19.7 minutes. **Working outside county of residence:** 11.9%.

Cities with pop over 10,000: None.

UNION COUNTY
PO Box 847   **Ph:** 662-534-1900
New Albany, MS 38652   **Fax:** 662-534-1907
www.ucda-newalbany.com

In north-central MS, northwest of Tupelo; organized Jul 7, 1870 from Pontotoc and Tippah counties. **Name Origin:** Possibly for its establishment from parts of two counties or for the union of the north and south following the Civil War.

Area (sq mi): 416.87 (land 415.43; water 1.44). **Pop per sq mi:** 64.5.

Pop 2005: 26,784. **State rank:** 36. **Pop change:** 2000-20005 +5.6%; 1990-2000 +14.8%. **Pop 2000:** 25,362 (White 82.7%; Black or African American 14.9%; Hispanic or Latino 1.6%; Asian 0.2%; Other 1.4%). **Foreign born:** 1.8%. **Median age:** 35.6.

Income 2000: per capita $15,700; median household $32,682; **Pop below poverty level:** 12.6%. ***Personal per capita income 2000-2003:** $19,539-$20,980.

Unemployment 2004: 6.1%. **Change from 2000:** +1.9%. **Median travel time to work:** 22.4 minutes. **Working outside county of residence:** 41.5%.

Cities with pop over 10,000: None.

WALTHALL COUNTY
PO Box 351   **Ph:** 601-876-4947
Tylertown, MS 39667   **Fax:** 601-876-6026
www.walthallcountychamber.org

On the central southern border of MS, west of Hattiesburg; organized Mar 16, 1910 from Marion and Pike counties. **Name Origin:** For Gen. Edward Cary Walthall (1831-98), Confederate army officer and U.S. senator from MS (1885-86; 1895-98).

Area (sq mi): 404.44 (land 403.82; water 0.62). **Pop per sq mi:** 38.3.

Pop 2005: 15,460. **State rank:** 57. **Pop change:** 2000-20005 +2%; 1990-2000 +5.6%. **Pop 2000:** 15,156 (White 54.2%; Black or African American 44.1%; Hispanic or Latino 1.3%; Asian 0.2%; Other 1.1%). **Foreign born:** 0.5%. **Median age:** 35.1.

Income 2000: per capita $12,563; median household $22,945; **Pop below poverty level:** 27.8%. ***Personal per capita income 2000-2003:** $15,864-$17,308.

Unemployment 2004: 6.6%. **Change from 2000:** -0.1%. **Median travel time to work:** 32.6 minutes. **Working outside county of residence:** 47.3%.

Cities with pop over 10,000: None.

WARREN COUNTY
PO Box 351   **Ph:** 601-636-4415
Vicksburg, MS 39181   **Fax:** 601-630-8016
www.co.warren.ms.us

On the central western border of MS, west of Jackson; organized Dec 22, 1809 (prior to statehood) from Natchez District. **Name Origin:** For Gen. Joseph Warren (1741-75), Revolutionary War patriot and member of the Committee of Safety who dispatched Paul Revere (1735-1818) on his famous ride.

Area (sq mi): 618.76 (land 586.61; water 32.15). **Pop per sq mi:** 83.8.

Pop 2005: 49,131. **State rank:** 14. **Pop change:** 2000-20005 -1%; 1990-2000 +3.7%. **Pop 2000:** 49,644 (White 54.5%; Black or African American 43.2%; Hispanic or Latino 1%; Asian 0.6%; Other 1.2%). **Foreign born:** 1.2%. **Median age:** 34.8.

Income 2000: per capita $17,527; median household $35,056; **Pop below poverty level:** 18.7%. ***Personal per capita income 2000-2003:** $25,029-$28,149.

Unemployment 2004: 6%. **Change from 2000:** +2%. **Median travel time to work:** 21 minutes. **Working outside county of residence:** 12.8%.

Cities with pop over 10,000: Vicksburg ⌂ (25,776).

WASHINGTON COUNTY
PO Box 309   **Ph:** 662-332-1595
Greenville, MS 38702   **Fax:** 662-334-2725
www.thedelta.org

On the central western border of MS, north of Vicksburg; organized Jan 29, 1827 from Warren and Yazoo counties. **Name Origin:** For George Washington (1732-99), American patriot and first U.S. president.

Area (sq mi): 761.26 (land 723.99; water 37.27). **Pop per sq mi:** 81.8.

Washington County (cont'd)

Pop 2005: 59,220. **State rank:** 12. **Pop change:** 2000-20005 -6%; 1990-2000 -7.3%. **Pop 2000:** 62,977 (White 33.7%; Black or African American 64.6%; Hispanic or Latino 0.8%; Asian 0.5%; Other 0.9%). **Foreign born:** 0.8%. **Median age:** 31.5.

Income 2000: per capita $13,430; median household $25,757; **Pop below poverty level:** 29.2%. *Personal per capita income 2000-2003: $18,568-$20,183.

Unemployment 2004: 9.7%. **Change from 2000:** -1.5%. **Median travel time to work:** 17.2 minutes. **Working outside county of residence:** 7.4%.

Cities with pop over 10,000: Greenville 🏛 (38,979).

WAYNE COUNTY

609 Azalea Dr County Courthouse   **Ph:** 601-735-2873
Waynesboro, MS 39367   **Fax:** 601-735-6224
www.wayneco.com

On the central eastern border of MS, east of Laurel; organized Dec 21, 1809 (prior to statehood) from Washington County. **Name Origin:** For Gen. Anthony Wayne (1745-96), PA soldier and statesman, nicknamed 'Mad Anthony' for his daring during the Revolutionary War.

Area (sq mi): 813.5 (land 810.32; water 3.18). **Pop per sq mi:** 26.3.

Pop 2005: 21,291. **State rank:** 44. **Pop change:** 2000-20005 +0.4%; 1990-2000 +8.7%. **Pop 2000:** 21,216 (White 61.1%; Black or African American 38%; Hispanic or Latino 0.6%; Asian 0.2%; Other 0.5%). **Foreign born:** 0.3%. **Median age:** 33.8.

Income 2000: per capita $12,757; median household $25,918; **Pop below poverty level:** 25.4%. *Personal per capita income 2000-2003: $16,763-$18,926.

Unemployment 2004: 6.9%. **Change from 2000:** -0.7%. **Median travel time to work:** 30.8 minutes. **Working outside county of residence:** 33.2%.

Cities with pop over 10,000: None.

WEBSTER COUNTY

PO Box 398   **Ph:** 662-258-4131
Walthall, MS 39771   **Fax:** 662-258-6657
www.webstercountyms.com/county/

In east-central MS, west of Columbus; organized as Sumner County Apr 6, 1874 from Montgomery County; name changed Jan 20, 1882. Originally named for an early settler. **Name Origin:** For Daniel Webster (1782-1852), U.S. statesman and orator from MA.

Area (sq mi): 423.34 (land 422.49; water 0.85). **Pop per sq mi:** 23.9.

Pop 2005: 10,092. **State rank:** 75. **Pop change:** 2000-20005 -2%; 1990-2000 +0.7%. **Pop 2000:** 10,294 (White 76.9%; Black or African American 20.9%; Hispanic or Latino 1.7%; Asian 0.2%; Other 1.3%). **Foreign born:** 0.5%. **Median age:** 37.3.

Income 2000: per capita $14,109; median household $28,834; **Pop below poverty level:** 18.7%. *Personal per capita income 2000-2003: $18,117-$17,961.

Unemployment 2004: 8.4%. **Change from 2000:** -2.5%. **Median travel time to work:** 28.8 minutes. **Working outside county of residence:** 40.1%.

Cities with pop over 10,000: None.

WILKINSON COUNTY

PO Box 516   **Ph:** 601-888-4381
Woodville, MS 39669   **Fax:** 601-888-6776

On the southwestern border of MS, south of Natchez; organized Jan 30, 1802 (prior to statehood) from Adams County. **Name Origin:** For James Wilkinson (1757-1825), officer under Washington, negotiator for the Louisiana Purchase, and first governor of the Louisiana Territory.

Area (sq mi): 687.66 (land 676.7; water 10.95). **Pop per sq mi:** 15.2.

Pop 2005: 10,269. **State rank:** 73. **Pop change:** 2000-20005 -0.4%; 1990-2000 +6.6%. **Pop 2000:** 10,312 (White 31.1%; Black or African American 68.2%; Hispanic or Latino 0.4%; Asian 0%; Other 0.6%). **Foreign born:** 0.1%. **Median age:** 35.

Income 2000: per capita $10,868; median household $18,929; **Pop below poverty level:** 37.7%. *Personal per capita income 2000-2003: $14,290-$16,515.

Unemployment 2004: 8.7%. **Change from 2000:** +0%. **Median travel time to work:** 34.1 minutes. **Working outside county of residence:** 44.3%.

Cities with pop over 10,000: None.

WINSTON COUNTY

PO Box 69   **Ph:** 662-773-3631
Louisville, MS 39339   **Fax:** 662-773-8814
www.winstoncounty.com

In east-central MS, northwest of Meridian; organized Dec 23, 1833 from Indian lands. **Name Origin:** For Louis Winston (?-1824), judge on the MS supreme court (1821).

Area (sq mi): 610.11 (land 606.97; water 3.14). **Pop per sq mi:** 32.7.

Pop 2005: 19,870. **State rank:** 50. **Pop change:** 2000-20005 -1.4%; 1990-2000 +3.7%. **Pop 2000:** 20,160 (White 54.7%; Black or African American 43.2%; Hispanic or Latino 1.2%; Asian 0.1%; Other 1.5%). **Foreign born:** 1.1%. **Median age:** 36.3.

Income 2000: per capita $14,548; median household $28,256; **Pop below poverty level:** 23.7%. *Personal per capita income 2000-2003: $18,088-$19,091.

Unemployment 2004: 7.7%. **Change from 2000:** -5.5%. **Median travel time to work:** 26.1 minutes. **Working outside county of residence:** 29.7%.

Cities with pop over 10,000: None.

YALOBUSHA COUNTY

PO Box 664   **Ph:** 662-473-5024
Water Valley, MS 38965   **Fax:** 662-473-3622

In north-central MS; organized Dec 23, 1833 from Choctaw cession in 1830. **Name Origin:** For the Yalobusha River, which flows through a nearby county; from Choctaw, probably 'tadpole-place.'

Area (sq mi): 495 (land 467.12; water 27.88). **Pop per sq mi:** 28.7.

Pop 2005: 13,417. **State rank:** 63. **Pop change:** 2000-20005 +2.8%; 1990-2000 +8.5%. **Pop 2000:** 13,051 (White 60%; Black or African American 38.7%; Hispanic or Latino 1%; Asian 0.1%; Other 0.8%). **Foreign born:** 0.4%. **Median age:** 37.7.

Source: Personal per capita income data are from the Bureau of Economic Analysis; per capita income data are from the Bureau of the Census. See Introduction for explanation of differences.

Yalobusha County (cont'd)

Income 2000: per capita $14,953; median household $26,315; **Pop below poverty level:** 21.8%. ***Personal per capita income 2000-2003:** $18,640-$21,061.

Unemployment 2004: 8.7%. **Change from 2000:** +1.2%. **Median travel time to work:** 26 minutes. **Working outside county of residence:** 18.3%.

Cities with pop over 10,000: None.

YAZOO COUNTY
211 E Broadway   **Ph:** 662-746-2661
Yazoo City, MS 39194   **Fax:** 662-746 3893
www.yazoo.org

In west-central MS, north of Jackson; organized 1823 from Hinds County. **Name Origin:** For the Yazoo River, which forms its western border; named for the Indian tribe that inhabited the lower part of the river. The meaning and origin of the name are unknown.

Area (sq mi): 934.12 (land 919.48; water 14.64). **Pop per sq mi:** 30.7.

Pop 2005: 28,195. **State rank:** 34. **Pop change:** 2000-20005 +0.2%; 1990-2000 +10.4%. **Pop 2000:** 28,149 (White 41.1%; Black or African American 54%; Hispanic or Latino 4.4%; Asian 0.4%; Other 0.9%). **Foreign born:** 3.9%. **Median age:** 33.7.

Income 2000: per capita $12,062; median household $24,795; **Pop below poverty level:** 31.9%. ***Personal per capita income 2000-2003:** $17,898-$19,707.

Unemployment 2004: 8.5%. **Change from 2000:** +0.5%. **Median travel time to work:** 26.3 minutes. **Working outside county of residence:** 31.2%.

Cities with pop over 10,000: Yazoo City 🏛 (11,936).

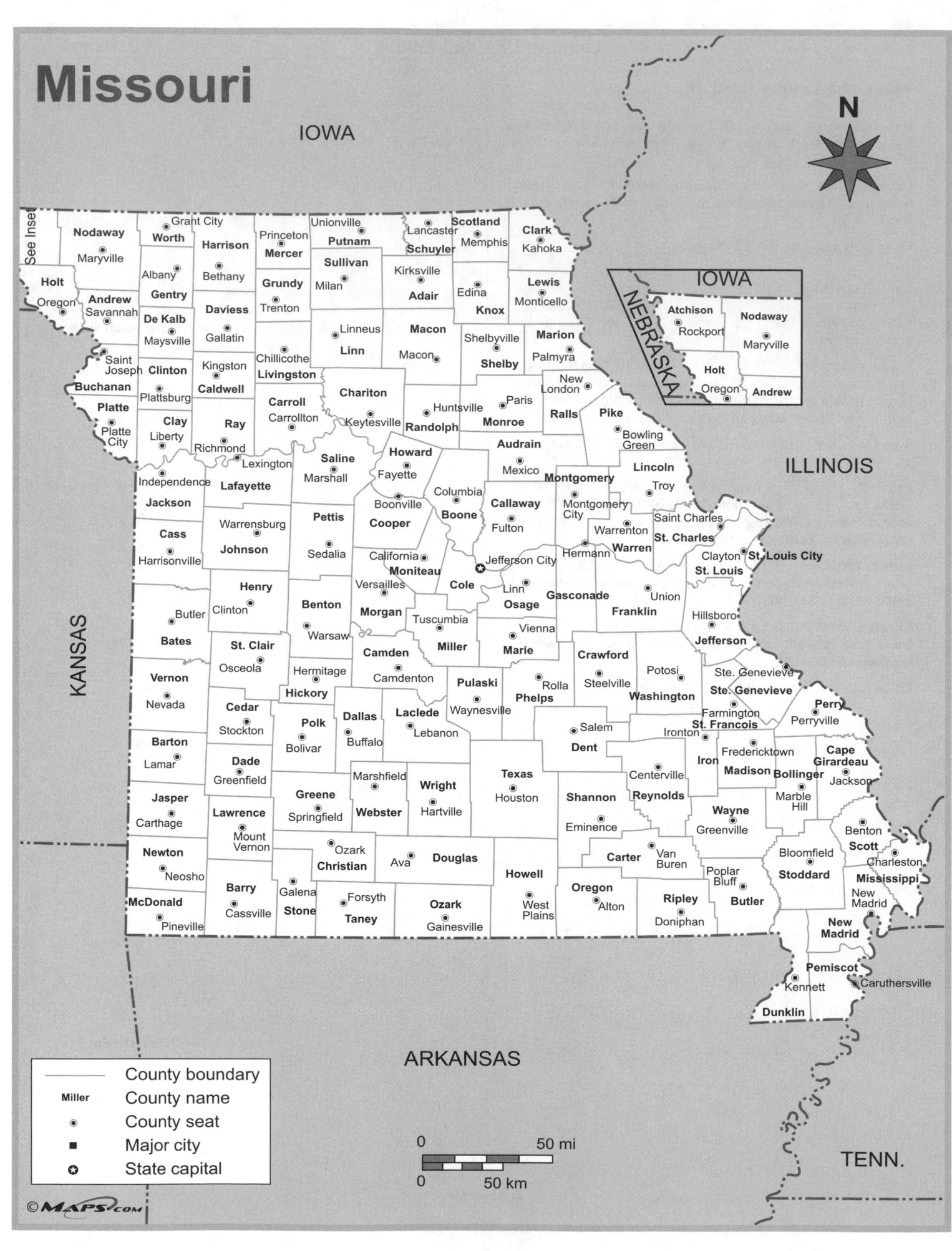

Missouri

IOWA

N

ILLINOIS

KANSAS

IOWA (inset)
NEBRASKA
Atchison • Rockport
Nodaway • Maryville
Holt • Oregon
Andrew

Nodaway • Maryville
Worth Grant City
Harrison Bethany
Princeton
Mercer
Putnam Unionville
Lancaster • **Scotland** Memphis
Schuyler
Clark Kahoka

Holt Oregon
Andrew Savannah
Albany **Gentry**
De Kalb Maysville
Daviess Gallatin
Grundy Trenton Milan **Sullivan**
Schuyler Kirksville
Adair
Edina **Knox**
Lewis Monticello

Saint Joseph
Buchanan
Clinton Plattsburg
Kingston **Caldwell**
Livingston Chillicothe
Linneus **Linn**
Macon Macon
Shelbyville **Shelby**
Marion Palmyra
New London

Platte
Clay Liberty
Ray Richmond
Carroll Carrollton
Chariton Keytesville
Huntsville **Randolph**
Paris **Monroe**
Ralls
Pike Bowling Green

Platte City
Independence
Jackson
Lexington **Lafayette**
Saline Marshall
Howard Fayette
Columbia **Boone**
Audrain Mexico
Montgomery
Montgomery City
Lincoln Troy
Saint Charles

Cass Harrisonville
Warrensburg
Johnson
Pettis Sedalia
Cooper Boonville
California
Jefferson City
Callaway Fulton
Warrenton **Warren**
Hermann
St. Charles
Clayton **St. Louis City**
St. Louis

Henry Clinton
Benton Warsaw
Morgan Versailles
Moniteau
Cole ✪
Linn **Osage**
Gasconade Union
Franklin
Hillsboro

Bates
Butler
St. Clair Osceola
Hickory Hermitage
Camden Camdenton
Tuscumbia **Miller**
Marie Vienna
Crawford
Potosi
Jefferson
Ste. Genevieve

Vernon Nevada
Cedar Stockton
Polk Bolivar
Dallas Buffalo
Laclede Lebanon
Pulaski Waynesville
Phelps Rolla
Steelville
Washington
Ste. Genevieve
Perry

Barton Lamar
Dade Greenfield
Marshfield
Wright Hartville
Texas Houston
Salem
Dent
Ironton **Iron**
Centerville
Madison Fredericktown
Bollinger Marble Hill
Cape Girardeau Jackson

Jasper Carthage
Lawrence Mount Vernon
Greene Springfield
Webster
Shannon Eminence
Reynolds
St. Francois
Farmington
Wayne Greenville
Benton **Scott**

Newton Neosho
Ozark **Christian**
Ava **Douglas**
Howell
Carter Van Buren
Bloomfield
Stoddard
Charleston
Mississippi New Madrid

McDonald Pineville
Barry Cassville
Galena **Stone**
Forsyth
Taney
Ozark Gainesville
West Plains
Oregon Alton
Ripley Doniphan
Poplar Bluff
Butler
New Madrid

Dunklin Kennett
Pemiscot Caruthersville

ARKANSAS

TENN.

0 — 50 mi
0 — 50 km

— County boundary
Miller County name
⊙ County seat
■ Major city
✪ State capital

©MAPS.com

Missouri

MISSOURI STATE INFORMATION

www.missouri.gov   **Ph:** 573-751-2000

Area (sq mi): 69,704.31 (land 68,885.93; water 818.39). **Pop per sq mi:** 84.2.

Pop 2005: 5,800,310. **Pop change:** 2000-20005 +3.7%; 1990-2000 +9.3%. **Pop 2000:** 5,595,211 (White 83.8%; Black or African American 11.2%; Hispanic or Latino 2.1%; Asian 1.1%; Other 2.8%). **Foreign born:** 2.7%. **Median age:** 36.1.

Income 2000: per capita $19,936; median household $37,934; **Pop below poverty level:** 11.7%. ***Personal per capita income 2000-2003:** $27,241-$29,464.

Unemployment 2004: 5.8%. **Change from 2000:** +2.5%. **Median travel time to work:** 23.8 minutes. **Working outside county of residence:** 33.4%.

ADAIR COUNTY

106 W Washington St County Courthouse   **Ph:** 660-665-3350
Kirksville, MO 63501   **Fax:** 660-785-3233

In north-central MO; organized Jan 29, 1841 from Macon County. **Name Origin:** For John Adair (1757-1840), governor of KY (1820-24).

Area (sq mi): 569.32 (land 567; water 2.31). **Pop per sq mi:** 43.2.

Pop 2005: 24,509. **State rank:** 45. **Pop change:** 2000-20005 -1.9%; 1990-2000 +1.6%. **Pop 2000:** 24,977 (White 95%; Black or African American 1.2%; Hispanic or Latino 1.3%; Asian 1.4%; Other 1.6%). **Foreign born:** 2%. **Median age:** 27.9.

Income 2000: per capita $15,484; median household $26,677; **Pop below poverty level:** 23.3%. ***Personal per capita income 2000-2003:** $19,746-$21,015.

Unemployment 2004: 4.8%. **Change from 2000:** +1.3%. **Median travel time to work:** 14.7 minutes. **Working outside county of residence:** 9.5%.

Cities with pop over 10,000: Kirksville ⚖ (17,057).

ANDREW COUNTY

PO Box 206   **Ph:** 816-324-3624
Savannah, MO 64485   **Fax:** 816-324-6154

On northwestern border of MO, north of Saint Joseph; organized Jan 29, 1841 from Platte Purchase. **Name Origin:** For either Andrew Jackson, seventh U.S. president, or Andrew Jackson Davis, a distinguished lawyer from Saint Louis.

Area (sq mi): 436.5 (land 435.18; water 1.32). **Pop per sq mi:** 38.8.

Pop 2005: 16,899. **State rank:** 65. **Pop change:** 2000-20005 +2.5%; 1990-2000 +12.7%. **Pop 2000:** 16,492 (White 97.8%; Black or African American 0.4%; Hispanic or Latino 0.8%; Asian 0.2%; Other 1%). **Foreign born:** 0.6%. **Median age:** 37.8.

Income 2000: per capita $19,375; median household $40,688; **Pop below poverty level:** 8.2%. ***Personal per capita income 2000-2003:** $25,099-$26,321.

Unemployment 2004: 5%. **Change from 2000:** +0.4%. **Median travel time to work:** 25.2 minutes. **Working outside county of residence:** 72.7%.

Cities with pop over 10,000: None.

ATCHISON COUNTY

PO Box 280   **Ph:** 660-744-2707
Rock Port, MO 64482 **Fax:** 660-744-5705

At the northwestern tip of MO, northwest of Saint Joseph; established Feb 3, 1843 from Holt County. **Name Origin:** For David Rice Atchison (1807-86), MO statesman and U.S. senator (1843-55)

Area (sq mi): 547.36 (land 544.72; water 2.64). **Pop per sq mi:** 11.5.

Pop 2005: 6,246. **State rank:** 107. **Pop change:** 2000-20005 -2.9%; 1990-2000 -13.8%. **Pop 2000:** 6,430 (White 96.6%; Black or African American 2.1%; Hispanic or Latino 0.7%; Asian 0.1%; Other 0.8%). **Foreign born:** 0.3%. **Median age:** 41.7.

Income 2000: per capita $16,956; median household $30,959; **Pop below poverty level:** 11.6%. ***Personal per capita income 2000-2003:** $24,196-$25,585.

Unemployment 2004: 4.5%. **Change from 2000:** +1.4%. **Median travel time to work:** 18.9 minutes. **Working outside county of residence:** 27.2%.

Cities with pop over 10,000: None.

AUDRAIN COUNTY

101 N Jefferson St Rm 101   **Ph:** 573-473-5820
Mexico, MO 65265   **Fax:** 573-581-2380
www.audraincounty.org

In east-central MO, northeast of Columbia; established Jan 12, 1831 from Pike, Callaway, and Ralls counties. **Name Origin:** For James H. Audrain (1782-1831), MO legislator.

Area (sq mi): 696.79 (land 693.1; water 3.69). **Pop per sq mi:** 37.2.

Pop 2005: 25,759. **State rank:** 41. **Pop change:** 2000-20005 -0.4%; 1990-2000 +9.6%. **Pop 2000:** 25,853 (White 90.6%; Black or African American 7.2%; Hispanic or Latino 0.7%; Asian 0.3%; Other 1.4%). **Foreign born:** 0.7%. **Median age:** 38.

⚖ *County Seat*

Audrain County (cont'd)

Income 2000: per capita $16,441; median household $32,057; **Pop below poverty level:** 14.8%. ***Personal per capita income 2000-2003:** $22,327-$22,026.

Unemployment 2004: 5.9%. **Change from 2000:** +1.9%. **Median travel time to work:** 18.3 minutes. **Working outside county of residence:** 20.1%.

Cities with pop over 10,000: Mexico ⚒ (10,965).

BARRY COUNTY

700 Main St Suite 2   **Ph:** 417-847-2561
Cassville, MO 65625   **Fax:** 417-847-5311

On the southwestern border of MO, southwest of Springfield; organized Jan 5, 1835 from Greene County. **Name Origin:** For William Taylor Barry (1784-1835), KY legislator, U.S. senator (1814-16), and U.S. Postmaster General (1829-35).

Area (sq mi): 790.89 (land 779.06; water 11.83). **Pop per sq mi:** 45.7.

Pop 2005: 35,599. **State rank:** 31. **Pop change:** 2000-20005 +4.7%; 1990-2000 +23.5%. **Pop 2000:** 34,010 (White 92.6%; Black or African American 0.1%; Hispanic or Latino 5%; Asian 0.3%; Other 5.6%). **Foreign born:** 3.5%. **Median age:** 38.2.

Income 2000: per capita $14,980; median household $28,906; **Pop below poverty level:** 16.6%. ***Personal per capita income 2000-2003:** $20,527-$21,819.

Unemployment 2004: 5.1%. **Change from 2000:** +0.5%. **Median travel time to work:** 23.2 minutes. **Working outside county of residence:** 26.1%.

Cities with pop over 10,000: None.

BARTON COUNTY

1004 Gulf St   **Ph:** 417-682-3529
Lamar, MO 64759   **Fax:** 417-682-4100
www.bartoncounty.com

On the southwestern border of MO, north of Joplin; organized Dec 12, 1855 from Jasper County. **Name Origin:** For David Barton (1788-1837), MO jurist, legislator, and U.S. senator (1821-31).

Area (sq mi): 596.72 (land 594.25; water 2.47). **Pop per sq mi:** 22.

Pop 2005: 13,057. **State rank:** 79. **Pop change:** 2000-20005 +4.1%; 1990-2000 +10.9%. **Pop 2000:** 12,541 (White 96.3%; Black or African American 0.3%; Hispanic or Latino 0.9%; Asian 0.3%; Other 2.4%). **Foreign born:** 0.7%. **Median age:** 37.3.

Income 2000: per capita $13,987; median household $29,275; **Pop below poverty level:** 13%. ***Personal per capita income 2000-2003:** $19,869-$21,703.

Unemployment 2004: 5%. **Change from 2000:** +1.5%. **Median travel time to work:** 19.1 minutes. **Working outside county of residence:** 23.7%.

Cities with pop over 10,000: None.

BATES COUNTY

1 N Delaware St   **Ph:** 660-679-3371
Butler, MO 64730   **Fax:** 660-679-9922
www.batescounty.net

On the central western border of MO, south of Kansas City; organized Jan 29, 1841 from Cooper County. **Name Origin:** For Frederick Bates (1777-1825), secretary of LA Territory (1806), governor of MO Territory (1809-10), and state governor (1824-25).

Area (sq mi): 851.37 (land 848.47; water 2.9). **Pop per sq mi:** 20.1.

Pop 2005: 17,027. **State rank:** 64. **Pop change:** 2000-20005 +2.2%; 1990-2000 +10.8%. **Pop 2000:** 16,653 (White 96.8%; Black or African American 0.6%; Hispanic or Latino 1.1%; Asian 0.2%; Other 1.9%). **Foreign born:** 0.9%. **Median age:** 38.4.

Income 2000: per capita $15,477; median household $30,731; **Pop below poverty level:** 14.5%. ***Personal per capita income 2000-2003:** $21,190-$23,378.

Unemployment 2004: 6.9%. **Change from 2000:** +0.8%. **Median travel time to work:** 31.8 minutes. **Working outside county of residence:** 43.8%.

Cities with pop over 10,000: None.

BENTON COUNTY

PO Box 1238   **Ph:** 660-438-7326
Warsaw, MO 65355   **Fax:** 660-438-3275

In west-central MO, southwest of Jefferson City; organized Jan 3, 1835 from Cooper County. **Name Origin:** For Thomas Hart Benton (1782-1858), U.S. journalist and statesman; nicknamed 'Old Bullion' for championing the use of gold and silver currency rather than paper money.

Area (sq mi): 752.48 (land 705.51; water 46.97). **Pop per sq mi:** 26.7.

Pop 2005: 18,854. **State rank:** 57. **Pop change:** 2000-20005 +9.7%; 1990-2000 +24%. **Pop 2000:** 17,180 (White 97.3%; Black or African American 0.1%; Hispanic or Latino 0.9%; Asian 0.1%; Other 1.7%). **Foreign born:** 0.7%. **Median age:** 46.3.

Income 2000: per capita $15,457; median household $26,646; **Pop below poverty level:** 15.7%. ***Personal per capita income 2000-2003:** $18,773-$20,543.

Unemployment 2004: 6.1%. **Change from 2000:** -1.9%. **Median travel time to work:** 27.2 minutes. **Working outside county of residence:** 39%.

Cities with pop over 10,000: None.

BOLLINGER COUNTY

PO Box 110   **Ph:** 573-238-1900
Marble Hill, MO 63764   **Fax:** 573-238-4511

In southeastern MO, west of Cape Girardeau; organized Mar 1, 1851 from Cape Girardeau, Madison, Stoddard, and Wayne counties. **Name Origin:** For Col. George Frederick Bollinger (1770-1842), who led German settlers into MO in 1800.

Area (sq mi): 621.2 (land 620.74; water 0.46). **Pop per sq mi:** 19.9.

Pop 2005: 12,325. **State rank:** 81. **Pop change:** 2000-20005 +2.5%; 1990-2000 +13.3%. **Pop 2000:** 12,029 (White 97.4%; Black or African American 0.2%; Hispanic or Latino 0.6%; Asian 0.2%; Other 1.7%). **Foreign born:** 0.4%. **Median age:** 37.9.

*Source: Personal per capita income data are from the Bureau of Economic Analysis; per capita income data are from the Bureau of the Census.
See Introduction for explanation of differences.

404

Bollinger County (cont'd)

Income 2000: per capita $13,641; median household $30,462; **Pop below poverty level:** 13.8%. *Personal per capita income 2000-2003: $17,551-$19,190.

Unemployment 2004: 5.9%. **Change from 2000:** -1.3%. **Median travel time to work:** 33.8 minutes. **Working outside county of residence:** 61.7%.

Cities with pop over 10,000: None.

BOONE COUNTY

801 E Walnut St
Columbia, MO 65201
www.co.boone.mo.us

Ph: 573-886-4295
Fax: 573-886-4300

In central MO, north of Jefferson City; organized Nov 16, 1820 (prior to statehood) from Howard County. **Name Origin:** For Daniel Boone (1734?-1820), U.S. frontiersman and KY pioneer.

Area (sq mi): 691.31 (land 685.43; water 5.88). **Pop per sq mi:** 209.1.

Pop 2005: 143,326. **State rank:** 8. **Pop change:** 2000-20005 +5.8%; 1990-2000 +20.5%. **Pop 2000:** 135,454 (White 84.4%; Black or African American 8.5%; Hispanic or Latino 1.8%; Asian 3%; Other 3%). **Foreign born:** 4.5%. **Median age:** 29.5.

Income 2000: per capita $19,844; median household $37,485; **Pop below poverty level:** 14.5%. *Personal per capita income 2000-2003: $26,686-$27,991.

Unemployment 2004: 3.7%. **Change from 2000:** +1.9%. **Median travel time to work:** 17.8 minutes. **Working outside county of residence:** 9.2%.

Cities with pop over 10,000: Columbia 🏛 (89,593).

BUCHANAN COUNTY

411 Jules St
Saint Joseph, MO 64501
www.co.buchanan.mo.us

Ph: 816-271-1411
Fax: 816-271-1535

On the northwestern border of MO, northwest of Kansas City; organized Dec 31, 1838 from Platte Purchase. **Name Origin:** For James Buchanan (1791-1868), fifteenth U.S. president.

Area (sq mi): 414.57 (land 409.73; water 4.84). **Pop per sq mi:** 207.2.

Pop 2005: 84,904. **State rank:** 12. **Pop change:** 2000-20005 -1.3%; 1990-2000 +3.5%. **Pop 2000:** 85,998 (White 91.2%; Black or African American 4.4%; Hispanic or Latino 2.4%; Asian 0.4%; Other 2.4%). **Foreign born:** 1.1%. **Median age:** 36.1.

Income 2000: per capita $17,882; median household $34,704; **Pop below poverty level:** 12.2%. *Personal per capita income 2000-2003: $23,887-$25,919.

Unemployment 2004: 6%. **Change from 2000:** +0.7%. **Median travel time to work:** 18.3 minutes. **Working outside county of residence:** 15%.

Cities with pop over 10,000: Saint Joseph 🏛 (72,628).

BUTLER COUNTY

100 N Main St Courthouse Rm 202
Poplar Bluff, MO 63901

Ph: 573-686-8050
Fax: 573-686-8066

On the southeastern border of MO, southwest of Cape Girardeau; organized Feb 27, 1849 from Wayne County. **Name Origin:** For Maj. William Orlando Butler (1791-1880), officer in the War of 1812 and Mexican- American War, U.S. representative from KY (1839-43).

Area (sq mi): 698.97 (land 697.54; water 1.43). **Pop per sq mi:** 59.3.

Pop 2005: 41,338. **State rank:** 25. **Pop change:** 2000-20005 +1.2%; 1990-2000 +5.4%. **Pop 2000:** 40,867 (White 91.6%; Black or African American 5.2%; Hispanic or Latino 1%; Asian 0.4%; Other 2.3%). **Foreign born:** 1.4%. **Median age:** 38.7.

Income 2000: per capita $15,721; median household $27,228; **Pop below poverty level:** 18.6%. *Personal per capita income 2000-2003: $21,834-$24,618.

Unemployment 2004: 5.5%. **Change from 2000:** -0.5%. **Median travel time to work:** 19.4 minutes. **Working outside county of residence:** 11.1%.

Cities with pop over 10,000: Poplar Bluff 🏛 (16,678).

CALDWELL COUNTY

PO Box 67
Kingston, MO 64650

Ph: 816-586-2571
Fax: 816-586-3600

In northwestern MO, east of Saint Joseph; organized Dec 29, 1836 from Ray County. **Name Origin:** For Matthew Caldwell, an officer of the KY Volunteers in the War of 1812, or for Gen. John Caldwell (?-1804), KY Indian fighter and legislator.

Area (sq mi): 429.72 (land 429.34; water 0.38). **Pop per sq mi:** 21.7.

Pop 2005: 9,307. **State rank:** 94. **Pop change:** 2000-20005 +3.8%; 1990-2000 +7%. **Pop 2000:** 8,969 (White 98%; Black or African American 0.1%; Hispanic or Latino 0.7%; Asian 0.1%; Other 1.2%). **Foreign born:** 0.4%. **Median age:** 38.8.

Income 2000: per capita $15,343; median household $31,240; **Pop below poverty level:** 11.9%. *Personal per capita income 2000-2003: $22,454-$23,208.

Unemployment 2004: 5.8%. **Change from 2000:** -0.3%. **Median travel time to work:** 33.4 minutes. **Working outside county of residence:** 62.4%.

Cities with pop over 10,000: None.

CALLAWAY COUNTY

10 E 5th St
Fulton, MO 65251
callaway.county.missouri.org

Ph: 573-642-0730
Fax: 573-642-7181

In east-central MO, east of Columbia; organized Nov 25, 1820 (prior to statehood) from Howard, Boone, and Montgomery counties. **Name Origin:** For Capt. James Callaway (1783-1815), grandson of Daniel Boone, killed in a battle with Indians.

Area (sq mi): 847.03 (land 838.84; water 8.19). **Pop per sq mi:** 50.7.

Pop 2005: 42,541. **State rank:** 23. **Pop change:** 2000-20005 +4.4%; 1990-2000 +24.3%. **Pop 2000:** 40,766 (White 91.2%; Black or African American 5.7%; Hispanic or Latino 0.9%; Asian 0.5%; Other 2%). **Foreign born:** 1.1%. **Median age:** 34.7.

🏛 *County Seat*

Callaway County (cont'd)

Income 2000: per capita $17,005; median household $39,110; **Pop below poverty level:** 8.5%. ***Personal per capita income 2000-2003:** $20,685-$21,562.

Unemployment 2004: 4.6%. **Change from 2000:** +1.1%. **Median travel time to work:** 23.1 minutes. **Working outside county of residence:** 48.5%.

Cities with pop over 10,000: Fulton 🏛 (11,879).

CAMDEN COUNTY

| 1 Court Cir Suite 2 | **Ph:** 573-346-4440 |
| Camdenton, MO 65020 | **Fax:** 573-346-5181 |

www.camdenmo.org

In central MO, southwest of Jefferson City; organized Jan 29, 1841 as Kinderhook County from Pulaski, Morgan, and Benton counties; name changed Feb 23, 1843. **Name Origin:** For Charles Pratt (1714-94), 1st Earl of Camden, English statesman who supported the American colonies before the Revolutionary War.

Area (sq mi): 708.86 (land 655.14; water 53.71). **Pop per sq mi:** 60.2.

Pop 2005: 39,432. **State rank:** 28. **Pop change:** 2000-20005 +6.4%; 1990-2000 +34.8%. **Pop 2000:** 37,051 (White 97%; Black or African American 0.3%; Hispanic or Latino 0.9%; Asian 0.3%; Other 1.7%). **Foreign born:** 1.4%. **Median age:** 45.2.

Income 2000: per capita $20,197; median household $35,840; **Pop below poverty level:** 11.4%. ***Personal per capita income 2000-2003:** $24,688-$26,822.

Unemployment 2004: 5.6%. **Change from 2000:** -0.4%. **Median travel time to work:** 23.3 minutes. **Working outside county of residence:** 24.3%.

Cities with pop over 10,000: None.

CAPE GIRARDEAU COUNTY

| 1 Barton Sq | **Ph:** 573-243-3547 |
| Jackson, MO 63755 | **Fax:** 573-204-2418 |

www.showme.net/CapeCounty/

On the southeastern border of MO, original county; organized Oct 1, 1812 (prior to statehood). **Name Origin:** For Jean Girardot, a French naval officer stationed at Kaskaskia, IL (1704-20), later a trading-post operator. No explanation for the spelling variance.

Area (sq mi): 586.29 (land 578.62; water 7.67). **Pop per sq mi:** 123.

Pop 2005: 71,161. **State rank:** 15. **Pop change:** 2000-20005 +3.6%; 1990-2000 +11.5%. **Pop 2000:** 68,693 (White 91.6%; Black or African American 5.3%; Hispanic or Latino 0.9%; Asian 0.7%; Other 1.8%). **Foreign born:** 1.3%. **Median age:** 35.2.

Income 2000: per capita $18,593; median household $36,458; **Pop below poverty level:** 11.1%. ***Personal per capita income 2000-2003:** $25,278-$27,895.

Unemployment 2004: 4.6%. **Change from 2000:** +0.7%. **Median travel time to work:** 18.6 minutes. **Working outside county of residence:** 9.8%.

Cities with pop over 10,000: Cape Girardeau (35,993); Jackson 🏛 (12,751).

CARROLL COUNTY

| 8 S Main St Suite 6 | **Ph:** 660-542-0615 |
| Carrollton, MO 64633 | **Fax:** 660-542-0621 |

In north-central MO, northeast of Kansas City; organized Jan 2, 1833 from Ray County. **Name Origin:** For Charles Carroll (1737-1832), a signer of the Declaration of Independence, U.S. senator from MD (1789-92), and founder of the Baltimore and Ohio Railroad.

Area (sq mi): 702.3 (land 694.72; water 7.57). **Pop per sq mi:** 14.7.

Pop 2005: 10,193. **State rank:** 87. **Pop change:** 2000-20005 -0.9%; 1990-2000 -4.3%. **Pop 2000:** 10,285 (White 96.4%; Black or African American 1.7%; Hispanic or Latino 0.7%; Asian 0.1%; Other 1.2%). **Foreign born:** 0.4%. **Median age:** 40.

Income 2000: per capita $15,522; median household $30,643; **Pop below poverty level:** 13.7%. ***Personal per capita income 2000-2003:** $20,790-$22,543.

Unemployment 2004: 5.6%. **Change from 2000:** +0.7%. **Median travel time to work:** 26.5 minutes. **Working outside county of residence:** 33.2%.

Cities with pop over 10,000: None.

CARTER COUNTY

| 105 Main St | **Ph:** 573-323-4527 |
| Van Buren, MO 63965 | **Fax:** 573-323-4527 |

In southeastern MO, southwest of Cape Girardeau; organized Mar 10, 1859 from Ripley, Reynolds, Shannon, and Oregon counties. **Name Origin:** For Zimri A. Carter, a settler from SC in 1812.

Area (sq mi): 509.02 (land 507.58; water 1.44). **Pop per sq mi:** 11.6.

Pop 2005: 5,910. **State rank:** 108. **Pop change:** 2000-20005 -0.5%; 1990-2000 +7.7%. **Pop 2000:** 5,941 (White 95.7%; Black or African American 0.1%; Hispanic or Latino 1.2%; Asian 0.1%; Other 3.1%, including 1.3% American Indian/Alaska Native). **Foreign born:** 0.3%. **Median age:** 38.9.

Income 2000: per capita $13,349; median household $22,863; **Pop below poverty level:** 25.2%. ***Personal per capita income 2000-2003:** $17,603-$19,864.

Unemployment 2004: 6.7%. **Change from 2000:** +0.2%. **Median travel time to work:** 28.1 minutes. **Working outside county of residence:** 37.2%.

Cities with pop over 10,000: None.

CASS COUNTY

| 2501 W Wall St | **Ph:** 816-380-8100 |
| Harrisonville, MO 64701 | **Fax:** 816-380-8101 |

www.casscounty.com

On the central western border of MO, south of Kansas City; organized as Van Buren County Mar 3, 1835 from Jackson County; name changed in 1849. **Name Origin:** For Gen. Lewis Cass (1782-1866), OH legislator, governor of MI Territory (1813-31), U.S. secretary of war (1831-36), and U.S. secretary of state (1857-60).

Area (sq mi): 702.67 (land 698.99; water 3.68). **Pop per sq mi:** 134.8.

Pop 2005: 94,232. **State rank:** 11. **Pop change:** 2000-20005 +14.8%; 1990-2000 +28.7%. **Pop 2000:** 82,092 (White 94.1%;

*Source: Personal per capita income data are from the Bureau of Economic Analysis; per capita income data are from the Bureau of the Census. See Introduction for explanation of differences.

406

Cass County (cont'd)

Black or African American 1.4%; Hispanic or Latino 2.2%; Asian 0.5%; Other 2.5%). **Foreign born:** 1.6%. **Median age:** 35.8.

Income 2000: per capita $21,073; median household $49,562; **Pop below poverty level:** 5.8%. ***Personal per capita income 2000-2003:** $26,608-$28,032.

Unemployment 2004: 5.4%. **Change from 2000:** +1.8%. **Median travel time to work:** 29.2 minutes. **Working outside county of residence:** 64.1%.

Cities with pop over 10,000: Belton (23,793); Raymore (14,414).

CEDAR COUNTY

113 South St PO Box 126	**Ph:** 417-276-6700
Stockton, MO 65785	**Fax:** 417-276-3461

In southwestern MO, northwest of Springfield; organized Feb 14, 1845 from Dade and Saint Clair counties. **Name Origin:** For the many cedar trees found by early settlers.

Area (sq mi): 498.51 (land 475.93; water 22.57). **Pop per sq mi:** 29.8.

Pop 2005: 14,160. **State rank:** 72. **Pop change:** 2000-20005 +3.1%; 1990-2000 +13.6%. **Pop 2000:** 13,733 (White 96%; Black or African American 0.3%; Hispanic or Latino 1.1%; Asian 0.5%; Other 2.6%). **Foreign born:** 1.3%. **Median age:** 42.2.

Income 2000: per capita $14,356; median household $26,694; **Pop below poverty level:** 17.4%. ***Personal per capita income 2000-2003:** $17,624-$19,925.

Unemployment 2004: 6.1%. **Change from 2000:** +1.1%. **Median travel time to work:** 24.7 minutes. **Working outside county of residence:** 33.1%.

Cities with pop over 10,000: None.

CHARITON COUNTY

306 S Cherry St	**Ph:** 660-288-3273
Keytesville, MO 65261	**Fax:** 660-288-3403

In north-central MO, northwest of Columbia; organized Nov 16, 1820 (prior to statehood) from Howard County. **Name Origin:** For a French fur trader, probably Jean Chariton, who was also called Joseph or John Chorette. During the 1700s he established a trading post on the north bank of the Missouri River in what is now IA.

Area (sq mi): 768.25 (land 755.87; water 12.38). **Pop per sq mi:** 10.7.

Pop 2005: 8,124. **State rank:** 99. **Pop change:** 2000-20005 -3.7%; 1990-2000 -8.3%. **Pop 2000:** 8,438 (White 95.6%; Black or African American 3.2%; Hispanic or Latino 0.6%; Asian 0.1%; Other 0.7%). **Foreign born:** 0.6%. **Median age:** 42.5.

Income 2000: per capita $15,515; median household $32,285; **Pop below poverty level:** 11.6%. ***Personal per capita income 2000-2003:** $22,262-$24,087.

Unemployment 2004: 5.8%. **Change from 2000:** -0.9%. **Median travel time to work:** 23.4 minutes. **Working outside county of residence:** 41.6%.

Cities with pop over 10,000: None.

CHRISTIAN COUNTY

100 W Church St Rm 206	**Ph:** 417-581-6360
Ozark, MO 65721	**Fax:** 417-581-8331
www.christiancountymo.gov	

In southwestern MO, south of Springfield; organized Mar 8, 1859 from Taney, Greene, and Webster counties. **Name Origin:** For Col. William Christian (1743-86), army officer, Indian fighter, and legislator; brother-in-law of Revolutionary leader Patrick Henry (1736-99).

Area (sq mi): 564.05 (land 563.16; water 0.89). **Pop per sq mi:** 119.4.

Pop 2005: 67,266. **State rank:** 16. **Pop change:** 2000-20005 +23.9%; 1990-2000 +66.3%. **Pop 2000:** 54,285 (White 96.5%; Black or African American 0.3%; Hispanic or Latino 1.3%; Asian 0.3%; Other 2.1%). **Foreign born:** 0.9%. **Median age:** 34.5.

Income 2000: per capita $18,422; median household $38,085; **Pop below poverty level:** 9.1%. ***Personal per capita income 2000-2003:** $22,808-$23,634.

Unemployment 2004: 4.3%. **Change from 2000:** +0.4%. **Median travel time to work:** 25.1 minutes. **Working outside county of residence:** 64.3%.

Cities with pop over 10,000: Springfield 🏛 (150,704); Nixa (14,617); Ozark 🏛 (14,457).

CLARK COUNTY

111 E Court St	**Ph:** 660-727-3283
Kahoka, MO 63445	**Fax:** 660-727-1051

On the northeastern tip of MO; organized Dec 16, 1836 from Lewis County. **Name Origin:** For William Clark (1770-1838), explorer and co-leader of the Lewis and Clark Expedition (1803-06).

Area (sq mi): 511.9 (land 507.31; water 4.59). **Pop per sq mi:** 14.4.

Pop 2005: 7,323. **State rank:** 102. **Pop change:** 2000-20005 -1.3%; 1990-2000 -1.7%. **Pop 2000:** 7,416 (White 98.4%; Black or African American 0.1%; Hispanic or Latino 0.7%; Asian 0.1%; Other 1%). **Foreign born:** 0.2%. **Median age:** 39.2.

Income 2000: per capita $15,988; median household $29,457; **Pop below poverty level:** 14.1%. ***Personal per capita income 2000-2003:** $20,326-$21,629.

Unemployment 2004: 6.4%. **Change from 2000:** -0.9%. **Median travel time to work:** 28.1 minutes. **Working outside county of residence:** 51.3%.

Cities with pop over 10,000: None.

CLAY COUNTY

1 Courthouse Sq	**Ph:** 816-792-7733
Liberty, MO 64068	**Fax:** 816-792-7777
www.claycogov.com	

In west-central MO, north of Kansas City; organized Jun 2, 1822 from Ray County. **Name Origin:** For Henry Clay (1777-1852), U.S. senator from KY, known as the 'Great Pacificator' for his advocacy of compromise to avert national crises.

Area (sq mi): 408.86 (land 396.35; water 12.52). **Pop per sq mi:** 509.8.

Pop 2005: 202,078. **State rank:** 7. **Pop change:** 2000-20005 +9.8%; 1990-2000 +19.9%. **Pop 2000:** 184,006 (White 90.5%; Black or

Clay County (cont'd)

African American 2.7%; Hispanic or Latino 3.6%; Asian 1.3%; Other 3.6%). **Foreign born:** 2.9%. **Median age:** 35.

Income 2000: per capita $23,144; median household $48,347; **Pop below poverty level:** 5.5%. ***Personal per capita income 2000-2003:** $30,074-$32,285.

Unemployment 2004: 4.8%. **Change from 2000:** +1.7%. **Median travel time to work:** 22.4 minutes. **Working outside county of residence:** 51.3%.

Cities with pop over 10,000: Liberty ⛪ (28,528); Gladstone (27,182); Excelsior Springs (11,324).

CLINTON COUNTY

PO Box 245   **Ph:** 816-539-3713
Plattsburg, MO 64477   **Fax:** 816-539-3072

In west-central MO, north of Kansas City; organized Jan 2, 1833 from Clay and Ray counties. **Name Origin:** For DeWitt Clinton (1769-1828), governor of NY (1817-21; 1825-28) and supporter of the Erie Canal.

Area (sq mi): 423.47 (land 418.76; water 4.71). **Pop per sq mi:** 49.5.

Pop 2005: 20,715. **State rank:** 53. **Pop change:** 2000-20005 +9.1%; 1990-2000 +14.4%. **Pop 2000:** 18,979 (White 95.8%; Black or African American 1.5%; Hispanic or Latino 1.1%; Asian 0.2%; Other 1.7%). **Foreign born:** 0.5%. **Median age:** 37.7.

Income 2000: per capita $19,056; median household $41,629; **Pop below poverty level:** 9.3%. ***Personal per capita income 2000-2003:** $24,362-$25,403.

Unemployment 2004: 5.6%. **Change from 2000:** +1.9%. **Median travel time to work:** 30 minutes. **Working outside county of residence:** 66.4%.

Cities with pop over 10,000: None.

COLE COUNTY

311 E High St   **Ph:** 573-634-9106
Jefferson City, MO 65101   **Fax:** 573-681-9678
www.colecounty.org

In central MO, south of Columbia; organized Nov 16, 1820 (prior to statehood) from Cooper county. **Name Origin:** For Capt. Stephen Cole (?-1822), an Indian fighter.

Area (sq mi): 399.08 (land 391.44; water 7.64). **Pop per sq mi:** 185.9.

Pop 2005: 72,757. **State rank:** 14. **Pop change:** 2000-20005 +1.9%; 1990-2000 +12.3%. **Pop 2000:** 71,397 (White 86.4%; Black or African American 9.9%; Hispanic or Latino 1.3%; Asian 0.9%; Other 2%). **Foreign born:** 2.2%. **Median age:** 35.5.

Income 2000: per capita $20,739; median household $42,924; **Pop below poverty level:** 8.7%. ***Personal per capita income 2000-2003:** $27,805-$32,120.

Unemployment 2004: 3.9%. **Change from 2000:** +1%. **Median travel time to work:** 17.4 minutes. **Working outside county of residence:** 9.5%.

Cities with pop over 10,000: Jefferson City ⛪ (38,671).

COOPER COUNTY

200 Main St   **Ph:** 660-882-2114
Boonville, MO 65233   **Fax:** 660-882-5645

In central MO, west of Columbia; organized Dec 17, 1818 (prior to statehood) from Howard County. **Name Origin:** For Sarshel Cooper (?-1814), an early settler.

Area (sq mi): 570.22 (land 565.03; water 5.19). **Pop per sq mi:** 30.6.

Pop 2005: 17,294. **State rank:** 63. **Pop change:** 2000-20005 +3.7%; 1990-2000 +12.4%. **Pop 2000:** 16,670 (White 88.6%; Black or African American 9%; Hispanic or Latino 0.9%; Asian 0.2%; Other 1.8%). **Foreign born:** 0.6%. **Median age:** 35.2.

Income 2000: per capita $15,648; median household $35,313; **Pop below poverty level:** 10.7%. ***Personal per capita income 2000-2003:** $20,513-$21,989.

Unemployment 2004: 4.9%. **Change from 2000:** +0.1%. **Median travel time to work:** 22.4 minutes. **Working outside county of residence:** 38%.

Cities with pop over 10,000: None.

CRAWFORD COUNTY

302 Main St   **Ph:** 573-775-2376
Steelville, MO 65565   **Fax:** 573-775-3066

In east-central MO, southwest of Saint Louis; organized Jan 23, 1829 from Gasconade County. **Name Origin:** For William Harris Crawford (1772-1834), U.S. senator from GA (1807-13), U.S. Secretary of War (1815-16), and U.S. Secretary of Treasury (1816-25).

Area (sq mi): 743.79 (land 742.52; water 1.27). **Pop per sq mi:** 32.2.

Pop 2005: 23,932. **State rank:** 48. **Pop change:** 2000-20005 +4.9%; 1990-2000 +18.9%. **Pop 2000:** 22,804 (White 97.7%; Black or African American 0.1%; Hispanic or Latino 0.8%; Asian 0.1%; Other 1.4%). **Foreign born:** 1.2%. **Median age:** 37.9.

Income 2000: per capita $14,825; median household $30,860; **Pop below poverty level:** 16.3%. ***Personal per capita income 2000-2003:** $20,899-$23,604.

Unemployment 2004: 6.4%. **Change from 2000:** +0%. **Median travel time to work:** 29.2 minutes. **Working outside county of residence:** 43.5%.

Cities with pop over 10,000: None.

DADE COUNTY

300 W Water St   **Ph:** 417-637-2724
Greenfield, MO 65661   **Fax:** 417-637-1006

In southwestern MO, northwest of Springfield; organized Jan 29, 1841 from Polk and Barry counties. **Name Origin:** For Francis Langhorne Dade (1793-1835), officer killed in the Seminole War (1835-42).

Area (sq mi): 506.3 (land 490.34; water 15.96). **Pop per sq mi:** 16.

Pop 2005: 7,830. **State rank:** 101. **Pop change:** 2000-20005 -1.2%; 1990-2000 +6.4%. **Pop 2000:** 7,923 (White 96.8%; Black or African American 0.3%; Hispanic or Latino 0.8%; Asian 0.1%; Other 2.2%). **Foreign born:** 1%. **Median age:** 41.7.

Income 2000: per capita $14,254; median household $29,097; **Pop below poverty level:** 13.4%. ***Personal per capita income 2000-2003:** $19,191-$22,003.

*Source: Personal per capita income data are from the Bureau of Economic Analysis; per capita income data are from the Bureau of the Census.
See Introduction for explanation of differences.

Dade County (cont'd)

Unemployment 2004: 5.1%. **Change from 2000:** +0.6%. **Median travel time to work:** 27.8 minutes. **Working outside county of residence:** 43.5%.

Cities with pop over 10,000: None.

DALLAS COUNTY

102 S Cedar St   **Ph:** 417-345-2632
Buffalo, MO 65622   **Fax:** 417-345-5321

In south-central MO, northeast of Springfield; organized as Niangua County Jan 29, 1841 from Polk County; name changed Dec 16, 1844. **Name Origin:** For George Mifflin Dallas (1792-1864), U.S. senator from PA (1831-33), U.S. vice president (1845-49), and U.S. Minister to Russia (1837-39) and Great Britain (1856-61).

Area (sq mi): 542.83 (land 541.54; water 1.29). **Pop per sq mi:** 30.4.

Pop 2005: 16,437. **State rank:** 66. **Pop change:** 2000-20005 +5%; 1990-2000 +23.8%. **Pop 2000:** 15,661 (White 96.8%; Black or African American 0.1%; Hispanic or Latino 0.9%; Asian 0.1%; Other 2.4%). **Foreign born:** 0.5%. **Median age:** 37.9.

Income 2000: per capita $15,106; median household $27,346; **Pop below poverty level:** 17.9%. ***Personal per capita income 2000-2003:** $19,241-$21,692.

Unemployment 2004: 5.7%. **Change from 2000:** -1.3%. **Median travel time to work:** 32 minutes. **Working outside county of residence:** 53.2%.

Cities with pop over 10,000: None.

DAVIESS COUNTY

102 N Main St   **Ph:** 660-663-2641
Gallatin, MO 64640   **Fax:** 660-663-3376

In north-central MO, northeast of Saint Joseph; organized Dec 29, 1836 from Ray County. **Name Origin:** For Col. Joseph Hamilton Daviess (1774-1811), VA soldier and jurist who unsuccessfully attempted to indict Aaron Burr for treason (1806). According to Jacob Piatt Dunn, 'The Colonel's name was Daveiss and he always wrote it that way", however, the name is sometimes spelled 'Daviess' in biographical entries and in places named for him.

Area (sq mi): 569.07 (land 566.97; water 2.11). **Pop per sq mi:** 14.3.

Pop 2005: 8,121. **State rank:** 100. **Pop change:** 2000-20005 +1.3%; 1990-2000 +1.9%. **Pop 2000:** 8,016 (White 98.3%; Black or African American 0%; Hispanic or Latino 0.7%; Asian 0.1%; Other 1.2%). **Foreign born:** 0.2%. **Median age:** 38.9.

Income 2000: per capita $15,953; median household $30,855; **Pop below poverty level:** 15.2%. ***Personal per capita income 2000-2003:** $20,889-$21,082.

Unemployment 2004: 5.2%. **Change from 2000:** +0.1%. **Median travel time to work:** 29.2 minutes. **Working outside county of residence:** 48.6%.

Cities with pop over 10,000: None.

DEKALB COUNTY

PO Box 248   **Ph:** 816-449-5402
Maysville, MO 64469   **Fax:** 816-449-2440

In northwestern MO, east of Saint Joseph; organized Feb 25, 1845 from Clinton County. **Name Origin:** For Johann, Baron de Kalb (1721-1780), German-born French soldier who fought with the Americans during the Revolutionary War.

Area (sq mi): 425.77 (land 424.2; water 1.57). **Pop per sq mi:** 29.1.

Pop 2005: 12,342. **State rank:** 80. **Pop change:** 2000-20005 +6.4%; 1990-2000 +16.4%. **Pop 2000:** 11,597 (White 88.4%; Black or African American 8.9%; Hispanic or Latino 1.1%; Asian 0.2%; Other 1.9%). **Foreign born:** 1%. **Median age:** 37.7.

Income 2000: per capita $12,687; median household $31,654; **Pop below poverty level:** 10.8%. ***Personal per capita income 2000-2003:** $13,913-$14,577.

Unemployment 2004: 5.5%. **Change from 2000:** +2.7%. **Median travel time to work:** 26.8 minutes. **Working outside county of residence:** 56.3%.

Cities with pop over 10,000: None.

DENT COUNTY

400 N Main St   **Ph:** 573-729-4144
Salem, MO 65560   **Fax:** 573-729-6106
www.salemmissouri.com/government.html

In south-central MO, northwest of Cape Girardeau; organized Feb 10, 1851 from Shannon and Crawford counties. **Name Origin:** For Lewis Dent (1808-80), landowner and MO legislator.

Area (sq mi): 754.51 (land 753.54; water 0.97). **Pop per sq mi:** 20.

Pop 2005: 15,083. **State rank:** 70. **Pop change:** 2000-20005 +1%; 1990-2000 +8.9%. **Pop 2000:** 14,927 (White 96.6%; Black or African American 0.4%; Hispanic or Latino 0.8%; Asian 0.2%; Other 2.3%). **Foreign born:** 0.6%. **Median age:** 39.6.

Income 2000: per capita $14,463; median household $27,193; **Pop below poverty level:** 17.2%. ***Personal per capita income 2000-2003:** $19,330-$20,208.

Unemployment 2004: 6.6%. **Change from 2000:** -2.2%. **Median travel time to work:** 24.4 minutes. **Working outside county of residence:** 27.4%.

Cities with pop over 10,000: None.

DOUGLAS COUNTY

283 SE 2nd Ave   **Ph:** 417-683-4714
Ava, MO 65608   **Fax:** 417-683-1017

In south-central MO, southeast of Springfield; organized Oct 29, 1857 from Ozark County. **Name Origin:** For Stephen Arnold Douglas (1813-61), U.S. orator and statesman.

Area (sq mi): 814.6 (land 814.53; water 0.07). **Pop per sq mi:** 16.7.

Pop 2005: 13,594. **State rank:** 75. **Pop change:** 2000-20005 +3.9%; 1990-2000 +10.2%. **Pop 2000:** 13,084 (White 96.4%; Black or African American 0.1%; Hispanic or Latino 0.8%; Asian 0.2%; Other 2.8%). **Foreign born:** 0.9%. **Median age:** 40.1.

Income 2000: per capita $13,785; median household $25,918; **Pop below poverty level:** 17.5%. ***Personal per capita income 2000-2003:** $16,729-$18,187.

Unemployment 2004: 5.9%. **Change from 2000:** -4.2%. **Median travel time to work:** 31 minutes. **Working outside county of residence:** 42.8%.

Cities with pop over 10,000: None.

DUNKLIN COUNTY

Courthouse Sq PO Box 188   **Ph:** 573-888-1374
Kennett, MO 63857   **Fax:** 573-888-2832

On the southern border of MO, southwest of Cape Girardeau; organized Feb 14, 1845 from Stoddard County. **Name Origin:** For Daniel Dunklin (1790-1844), governor of MO (1833-36) and surveyor-general of MO, IL, and AR.

Area (sq mi): 547.11 (land 545.62; water 1.49). **Pop per sq mi:** 59.6.

Pop 2005: 32,545. **State rank:** 35. **Pop change:** 2000-20005 -1.8%; 1990-2000 +0.1%. **Pop 2000:** 33,155 (White 87.4%; Black or African American 8.7%; Hispanic or Latino 2.5%; Asian 0.3%; Other 2.4%). **Foreign born:** 1.5%. **Median age:** 37.8.

Income 2000: per capita $13,561; median household $24,878; **Pop below poverty level:** 24.5%. ***Personal per capita income 2000-2003:** $19,444-$22,451.

Unemployment 2004: 7.5%. **Change from 2000:** +0.2%. **Median travel time to work:** 20.7 minutes. **Working outside county of residence:** 28.9%.

Cities with pop over 10,000: Kennett 🏛 (11,005).

FRANKLIN COUNTY

300 E Main St Rm 201   **Ph:** 636-583-6355
Union, MO 63084   **Fax:** 636-583-7320
www.franklinmo.org

In central-eastern MO, west of Saint Louis; organized Dec 11, 1818 (prior to statehood) from Saint Louis County. **Name Origin:** For Benjamin Franklin (1706-90), U.S. patriot, diplomat, and statesman.

Area (sq mi): 930.65 (land 922.81; water 7.84). **Pop per sq mi:** 107.4.

Pop 2005: 99,090. **State rank:** 10. **Pop change:** 2000-20005 +5.6%; 1990-2000 +16.4%. **Pop 2000:** 93,807 (White 97%; Black or African American 0.9%; Hispanic or Latino 0.7%; Asian 0.3%; Other 1.3%). **Foreign born:** 0.8%. **Median age:** 35.8.

Income 2000: per capita $19,705; median household $43,474; **Pop below poverty level:** 7%. ***Personal per capita income 2000-2003:** $25,729-$27,728.

Unemployment 2004: 5.7%. **Change from 2000:** +0.2%. **Median travel time to work:** 29.2 minutes. **Working outside county of residence:** 40.1%.

Cities with pop over 10,000: Washington (13,955).

GASCONADE COUNTY

119 E 1st St Rm 2   **Ph:** 573-486-5427
Hermann, MO 65041   **Fax:** 573-486-8893
www.gscnd.com

In east-central MO, west of Saint Louis; organized Nov 25, 1820 (prior to statehood) from Franklin County. **Name Origin:** For the Gasconade River, which runs through it. It is believed that French residents of Saint Louis gave this name to the river and general area for the bragging of the inhabitants when they went to Saint Louis; an allusion to the residents of the French province of Gascony, supposed to be boastful.

Area (sq mi): 526.09 (land 520.67; water 5.43). **Pop per sq mi:** 30.2.

Pop 2005: 15,745. **State rank:** 67. **Pop change:** 2000-20005 +2.6%; 1990-2000 +9.5%. **Pop 2000:** 15,342 (White 98.4%; Black or African American 0.1%; Hispanic or Latino 0.4%; Asian 0.2%; Other 1%). **Foreign born:** 0.5%. **Median age:** 40.3.

Income 2000: per capita $17,319; median household $35,047; **Pop below poverty level:** 9.5%. ***Personal per capita income 2000-2003:** $22,444-$23,237.

Unemployment 2004: 6.1%. **Change from 2000:** +0.8%. **Median travel time to work:** 29.1 minutes. **Working outside county of residence:** 37.7%.

Cities with pop over 10,000: None.

GENTRY COUNTY

200 W Clay St   **Ph:** 660-726-3618
Albany, MO 64402   **Fax:** 660-726-4102

In northwestern MO, northeast of Saint Joseph; established Feb 12, 1841 from Clinton County. **Name Origin:** For Richard Gentry (1788-1837), officer in the Black Hawk War who died fighting the Seminoles in Florida.

Area (sq mi): 491.81 (land 491.52; water 0.29). **Pop per sq mi:** 13.3.

Pop 2005: 6,555. **State rank:** 106. **Pop change:** 2000-20005 -4.5%; 1990-2000 +0.2%. **Pop 2000:** 6,861 (White 98%; Black or African American 0.1%; Hispanic or Latino 0.6%; Asian 0.2%; Other 1.2%). **Foreign born:** 0.6%. **Median age:** 40.2.

Income 2000: per capita $15,879; median household $28,750; **Pop below poverty level:** 12%. ***Personal per capita income 2000-2003:** $21,145-$23,234.

Unemployment 2004: 4.6%. **Change from 2000:** +0.7%. **Median travel time to work:** 24.4 minutes. **Working outside county of residence:** 33.4%.

Cities with pop over 10,000: None.

GREENE COUNTY

940 N Boonville Ave   **Ph:** 417-868-4055
Springfield, MO 65802   **Fax:** 417-868-4170
www.greenecountymo.org

In south-central MO, northeast of Joplin; organized Jan 2, 1833 from Wayne and Crawford counties. **Name Origin:** For Gen. Nathanael Greene (1742-1786), hero of the Revolutionary War, quartermaster general (1778-80), and commander of the Army of the South.

Area (sq mi): 677.8 (land 674.97; water 2.82). **Pop per sq mi:** 371.5.

Pop 2005: 250,784. **State rank:** 5. **Pop change:** 2000-20005 +4.3%; 1990-2000 +15.6%. **Pop 2000:** 240,391 (White 92.5%; Black or African American 2.3%; Hispanic or Latino 1.8%; Asian 1.1%; Other 3.2%). **Foreign born:** 1.9%. **Median age:** 35.1.

Income 2000: per capita $19,185; median household $34,157; **Pop below poverty level:** 12.1%. ***Personal per capita income 2000-2003:** $25,732-$28,847.

Unemployment 2004: 4.5%. **Change from 2000:** +1.2%. **Median travel time to work:** 19.2 minutes. **Working outside county of residence:** 7%.

Cities with pop over 10,000: None.

*Source: Personal per capita income data are from the Bureau of Economic Analysis; per capita income data are from the Bureau of the Census. See Introduction for explanation of differences.

GRUNDY COUNTY

700 Main St   **Ph:** 660-359-6305
Trenton, MO 64683   **Fax:** 660-359-6786

In north-central MO, northeast of Saint Joseph; organized Jan 29, 1841 from Livingston and Ray counties. **Name Origin:** For Felix Grundy (1777-1840), chief justice of KY supreme court, U.S. senator from TN (1829-38; 1839-40), and U.S. Attorney General (1838-39).

Area (sq mi): 437.98 (land 435.82; water 2.16). **Pop per sq mi:** 23.7.

Pop 2005: 10,327. **State rank:** 85. **Pop change:** 2000-20005 -1%; 1990-2000 -1%. **Pop 2000:** 10,432 (White 96.7%; Black or African American 0.4%; Hispanic or Latino 1.6%; Asian 0.2%; Other 1.8%). **Foreign born:** 1.4%. **Median age:** 41.3.

Income 2000: per capita $15,432; median household $27,333; **Pop below poverty level:** 15.8%. ***Personal per capita income 2000-2003:** $20,651-$21,117.

Unemployment 2004: 5.7%. **Change from 2000:** +1.7%. **Median travel time to work:** 19.6 minutes. **Working outside county of residence:** 23.9%.

Cities with pop over 10,000: None.

HARRISON COUNTY

PO Box 525   **Ph:** 660-425-6424
Bethany, MO 64424   **Fax:** 660-425-3772

On the central northern border of MO, northeast of Saint Joseph; organized Feb 14, 1845 from Daviess and Ray counties. **Name Origin:** For Albert Galliton Harrison (1800-39), U.S. representative from MO (1835-39).

Area (sq mi): 726.45 (land 725.13; water 1.32). **Pop per sq mi:** 12.2.

Pop 2005: 8,876. **State rank:** 97. **Pop change:** 2000-20005 +0.3%; 1990-2000 +4.5%. **Pop 2000:** 8,850 (White 97.8%; Black or African American 0.1%; Hispanic or Latino 1%; Asian 0.1%; Other 1.4%). **Foreign born:** 1%. **Median age:** 41.7.

Income 2000: per capita $14,192; median household $28,707; **Pop below poverty level:** 13.5%. ***Personal per capita income 2000-2003:** $19,582-$19,782.

Unemployment 2004: 5.2%. **Change from 2000:** +1.9%. **Median travel time to work:** 22.4 minutes. **Working outside county of residence:** 24.3%.

Cities with pop over 10,000: None.

HENRY COUNTY

100 W Franklin St   **Ph:** 660-885-7204
Clinton, MO 64735   **Fax:** 660-890-2693

In west-central MO, southeast of Kansas City; organized as Rives County Dec 13, 1834 from Lafayette County; name changed Feb 15, 1841. **Name Origin:** For Patrick Henry (1736-99), patriot, governor of VA (1776-79; 1784-86), and statesman, famous for proclaiming 'Give me liberty or give me death.'

Area (sq mi): 732.55 (land 702.48; water 30.07). **Pop per sq mi:** 32.1.

Pop 2005: 22,577. **State rank:** 51. **Pop change:** 2000-20005 +2.6%; 1990-2000 +9.7%. **Pop 2000:** 21,997 (White 96.2%; Black or African American 1%; Hispanic or Latino 0.9%; Asian 0.2%; Other 2.1%). **Foreign born:** 0.8%. **Median age:** 40.

Income 2000: per capita $16,468; median household $30,949; **Pop below poverty level:** 14.3%. ***Personal per capita income 2000-2003:** $21,813-$23,092.

Unemployment 2004: 6.7%. **Change from 2000:** +0.9%. **Median travel time to work:** 25.4 minutes. **Working outside county of residence:** 27.7%.

Cities with pop over 10,000: None.

HICKORY COUNTY

PO Box 3   **Ph:** 417-745-6450
Hermitage, MO 65668   **Fax:** 417-745-6057

In west-central MO, north of Springfield; organized Feb 14, 1845 from Benton and Polk counties. **Name Origin:** For 'Old Hickory,' the nickname of Andrew Jackson (1767-1845), seventh U.S. president.

Area (sq mi): 411.74 (land 398.63; water 13.11). **Pop per sq mi:** 23.3.

Pop 2005: 9,271. **State rank:** 95. **Pop change:** 2000-20005 +3.7%; 1990-2000 +21.9%. **Pop 2000:** 8,940 (White 97%; Black or African American 0.1%; Hispanic or Latino 0.8%; Asian 0.1%; Other 2.3%). **Foreign born:** 1%. **Median age:** 49.7.

Income 2000: per capita $13,536; median household $25,346; **Pop below poverty level:** 19.7%. ***Personal per capita income 2000-2003:** $16,321-$17,562.

Unemployment 2004: 8.2%. **Change from 2000:** -0.5%. **Median travel time to work:** 33.2 minutes. **Working outside county of residence:** 51.4%.

Cities with pop over 10,000: None.

HOLT COUNTY

PO Box 437   **Ph:** 660-446-3303
Oregon, MO 64473   **Fax:** 660-446-3353

On northwestern border of MO, northwest of Saint Joseph; organized as Nodaway County Jan 29, 1841 from Platte Purchase; name changed Feb 15, 1841. **Name Origin:** For David Rice Holt (1803-40), MO legislator.

Area (sq mi): 469.05 (land 461.87; water 7.18). **Pop per sq mi:** 11.

Pop 2005: 5,081. **State rank:** 110. **Pop change:** 2000-20005 -5%; 1990-2000 -11.3%. **Pop 2000:** 5,351 (White 98.2%; Black or African American 0.1%; Hispanic or Latino 0.4%; Asian 0.1%; Other 1.3%). **Foreign born:** 0.4%. **Median age:** 41.8.

Income 2000: per capita $15,876; median household $29,461; **Pop below poverty level:** 13%. ***Personal per capita income 2000-2003:** $22,221-$23,600.

Unemployment 2004: 4.9%. **Change from 2000:** +0.6%. **Median travel time to work:** 23.1 minutes. **Working outside county of residence:** 35.2%.

Cities with pop over 10,000: None.

HOWARD COUNTY

1 Courthouse Sq   **Ph:** 660-248-2284
Fayette, MO 65248   **Fax:** 660-248-1075

In north-central MO, northwest of Columbia; organized Jan 13, 1816 (prior to statehood) from Saint Louis and Saint Charles

Howard County (cont'd)

counties. **Name Origin:** For Gen. Benjamin Howard (1760-1814), KY legislator and U.S. representative (1807-10), governor of LA Territory (1810-12), and commander of the Eighth Military Department, territory west of the Mississippi River.

Area (sq mi): 470.55 (land 465.74; water 4.82). **Pop per sq mi:** 21.4.

Pop 2005: 9,957. **State rank:** 89. **Pop change:** 2000-20005 -2.5%; 1990-2000 +6%. **Pop 2000:** 10,212 (White 90.7%; Black or African American 6.8%; Hispanic or Latino 0.9%; Asian 0.1%; Other 1.9%). **Foreign born:** 1%. **Median age:** 36.7.

Income 2000: per capita $15,198; median household $31,614; **Pop below poverty level:** 11.6%. ***Personal per capita income 2000-2003:** $21,912-$23,319.

Unemployment 2004: 4.6%. **Change from 2000:** -0.3%. **Median travel time to work:** 25.3 minutes. **Working outside county of residence:** 51.5%.

Cities with pop over 10,000: None.

HOWELL COUNTY

1 Courthouse   **Ph:** 417-256-2591
West Plains, MO 65775   **Fax:** 417-256-2512
www.howellcounty.net

On the central southern border of MO; organized Mar 2, 1857 from Oregon County. **Name Origin:** For Thomas Jefferson Howell, MO legislator; or for James Howell, a prominent citizen; or for Josiah Howell.

Area (sq mi): 928.33 (land 927.74; water 0.59). **Pop per sq mi:** 41.4.

Pop 2005: 38,400. **State rank:** 29. **Pop change:** 2000-20005 +3.1%; 1990-2000 +18.4%. **Pop 2000:** 37,238 (White 95.7%; Black or African American 0.3%; Hispanic or Latino 1.2%; Asian 0.4%; Other 2.9%, including 1% American Indian/Alaska Native). **Foreign born:** 1.3%. **Median age:** 38.2.

Income 2000: per capita $13,959; median household $25,628; **Pop below poverty level:** 18.7%. ***Personal per capita income 2000-2003:** $18,301-$20,763.

Unemployment 2004: 5.4%. **Change from 2000:** +0.6%. **Median travel time to work:** 20.1 minutes. **Working outside county of residence:** 10%.

Cities with pop over 10,000: West Plains 🏛 (11,112).

IRON COUNTY

25 S Main St   **Ph:** 573-546-2912
Ironton, MO 63650   **Fax:** 573-546-6499
www.ironcounty.org

In southeastern MO, northwest of Cape Girardeau; organized Feb 17, 1857 from Madison, Saint Francois, Wayne, Washington, and Reynolds counties. **Name Origin:** For the rich iron deposits.

Area (sq mi): 552.05 (land 551.34; water 0.71). **Pop per sq mi:** 18.6.

Pop 2005: 10,273. **State rank:** 86. **Pop change:** 2000-20005 -4%; 1990-2000 -0.3%. **Pop 2000:** 10,697 (White 96.4%; Black or African American 1.6%; Hispanic or Latino 0.6%; Asian 0.1%; Other 1.5%). **Foreign born:** 0.4%. **Median age:** 39.7.

Income 2000: per capita $14,227; median household $26,080; **Pop below poverty level:** 19%. ***Personal per capita income 2000-2003:** $18,056-$20,417.

Unemployment 2004: 8.5%. **Change from 2000:** +0.5%. **Median travel time to work:** 28.1 minutes. **Working outside county of residence:** 41.4%.

Cities with pop over 10,000: None.

JACKSON COUNTY

415 E 12th St   **Ph:** 816-881-3000
Kansas City, MO 64106   **Fax:** 816-881-3133
www.co.jackson.mo.us

On central western border of MO; organized Dec 15, 1826 from Lafayette County. **Name Origin:** For Andrew Jackson (1767-1845), seventh U.S. president.

Area (sq mi): 616.41 (land 604.84; water 11.57). **Pop per sq mi:** 1096.1.

Pop 2005: 662,959. **State rank:** 2. **Pop change:** 2000-20005 +1.2%; 1990-2000 +3.4%. **Pop 2000:** 654,880 (White 67.7%; Black or African American 23.3%; Hispanic or Latino 5.4%; Asian 1.3%; Other 5.4%). **Foreign born:** 4.3%. **Median age:** 35.2.

Income 2000: per capita $20,788; median household $39,277; **Pop below poverty level:** 11.9%. ***Personal per capita income 2000-2003:** $29,319-$31,966.

Unemployment 2004: 6.8%. **Change from 2000:** +1.9%. **Median travel time to work:** 23.6 minutes. **Working outside county of residence:** 24.9%.

Cities with pop over 10,000: 6 (see page 36 for cities).

JASPER COUNTY

302 S Main St Rm 102   **Ph:** 417-358-0416
Carthage, MO 64836   **Fax:** 417-358-0415
www.jaspercounty.org

On the southwestern border of MO, west of Springfield; organized Jan 29, 1841 from Barry County. **Name Origin:** For Sgt. William Jasper (1750-79), Revolutionary War soldier from SC.

Area (sq mi): 641.32 (land 639.73; water 1.59). **Pop per sq mi:** 172.9.

Pop 2005: 110,624. **State rank:** 9. **Pop change:** 2000-20005 +5.7%; 1990-2000 +15.7%. **Pop 2000:** 104,686 (White 91.1%; Black or African American 1.5%; Hispanic or Latino 3.5%; Asian 0.7%; Other 5.2%, including 1.3% American Indian/Alaska Native). **Foreign born:** 2.6%. **Median age:** 34.9.

Income 2000: per capita $16,227; median household $31,323; **Pop below poverty level:** 14.5%. ***Personal per capita income 2000-2003:** $22,796-$24,176.

Unemployment 2004: 5.1%. **Change from 2000:** +1%. **Median travel time to work:** 17.8 minutes. **Working outside county of residence:** 17.3%.

Cities with pop over 10,000: Joplin (46,830); Carthage 🏛 (13,003); Webb City (10,553).

---

*Source: Personal per capita income data are from the Bureau of Economic Analysis; per capita income data are from the Bureau of the Census. See Introduction for explanation of differences.

JEFFERSON COUNTY

PO Box 100
Hillsboro, MO 63050
www.jeffcomo.org

Ph: 636-797-5478
Fax: 636-797-5360

On the central eastern border of MO, south of Saint Louis; organized Dec 8, 1818 (prior to statehood) from Saint Genevieve and Saint Louis counties. **Name Origin:** For Thomas Jefferson (1743-1826), U.S. patriot and statesman, third U.S. president.

Area (sq mi): 664.09 (land 656.8; water 7.29) **Pop per sq mi:** 325.3.

Pop 2005: 213,669. **State rank:** 6. **Pop change:** 2000-20005 +7.9%; 1990-2000 +15.6%. **Pop 2000:** 198,099 (White 96.8%; Black or African American 0.7%; Hispanic or Latino 1%; Asian 0.4%; Other 1.4%). **Foreign born:** 1%. **Median age:** 34.9.

Income 2000: per capita $19,435; median household $46,338; **Pop below poverty level:** 6.8%. ***Personal per capita income 2000-2003:** $24,539-$26,352.

Unemployment 2004: 5.5%. **Change from 2000:** +0.7%. **Median travel time to work:** 31.1 minutes. **Working outside county of residence:** 65%.

Cities with pop over 10,000: Arnold (20,146); Festus (10,438).

JOHNSON COUNTY

300 N Holden St County Courthouse
Warrensburg, MO 64093
www.jaspercounty.org

Ph: 660-747-6161
Fax: 660-747-9332

In west-central MO, southeast of Kansas City; organized Dec 13, 1834 from Lafayette County. **Name Origin:** For Col. Richard Mentor Johnson (1781-1850), officer in the War of 1812, U.S. senator from KY (1819-29), and U.S. vice president under Van Buren (1837-41).

Area (sq mi): 833.03 (land 830.44; water 2.59). **Pop per sq mi:** 61.2.

Pop 2005: 50,784. **State rank:** 19. **Pop change:** 2000-20005 +5.2%; 1990-2000 +13.5%. **Pop 2000:** 48,258 (White 88.7%; Black or African American 4.3%; Hispanic or Latino 2.9%; Asian 1.4%; Other 4.1%). **Foreign born:** 3%. **Median age:** 28.5.

Income 2000: per capita $16,037; median household $35,391; **Pop below poverty level:** 14.9%. ***Personal per capita income 2000-2003:** $20,031-$22,213.

Unemployment 2004: 5%. **Change from 2000:** +1.4%. **Median travel time to work:** 22.5 minutes. **Working outside county of residence:** 31%.

Cities with pop over 10,000: Warrensburg ▥ (17,452).

KNOX COUNTY

107 N 4th St
Edina, MO 63537

Ph: 660-397-2184
Fax: 660-397-3331

In northeastern MO, north of Columbia; organized Feb 14, 1845 from Scotland County. **Name Origin:** For Gen. Henry Knox (1750-1806), Revolutionary War officer and first U.S. Secretary of War (1785-95).

Area (sq mi): 506.77 (land 505.71; water 1.07). **Pop per sq mi:** 8.2.

Pop 2005: 4,171. **State rank:** 113. **Pop change:** 2000-20005 -4.4%; 1990-2000 -2.7%. **Pop 2000:** 4,361 (White 98.1%; Black or African American 0.1%; Hispanic or Latino 0.6%; Asian 0.1%; Other 1.3%). **Foreign born:** 0.3%. **Median age:** 41.6.

Income 2000: per capita $13,075; median household $27,124; **Pop below poverty level:** 18%. ***Personal per capita income 2000-2003:** $20,490-$22,343.

Unemployment 2004: 4.1%. **Change from 2000:** -0.4%. **Median travel time to work:** 23.4 minutes. **Working outside county of residence:** 35.3%.

Cities with pop over 10,000: None.

LACLEDE COUNTY

200 N Adams Ave
Lebanon, MO 65536
www.lacledecountymissouri.org

Ph: 417-532-5471
Fax: 417-588-9288

In south-central MO, northeast of Springfield; organized Feb 24, 1849 from Pulaski, Wright, and Camden counties. **Name Origin:** For Pierre Laclede Liguest (1724-78), French fur trader who established the site of Saint Louis (Dec 1763).

Area (sq mi): 768 (land 765.85; water 2.14). **Pop per sq mi:** 45.

Pop 2005: 34,492. **State rank:** 33. **Pop change:** 2000-20005 +6.1%; 1990-2000 +19.7%. **Pop 2000:** 32,513 (White 96.3%; Black or African American 0.4%; Hispanic or Latino 1.2%; Asian 0.3%; Other 2.2%). **Foreign born:** 0.9%. **Median age:** 36.6.

Income 2000: per capita $15,572; median household $29,562; **Pop below poverty level:** 14.3%. ***Personal per capita income 2000-2003:** $19,410-$21,156.

Unemployment 2004: 7.4%. **Change from 2000:** +0.9%. **Median travel time to work:** 20.7 minutes. **Working outside county of residence:** 16.3%.

Cities with pop over 10,000: Lebanon ▥ (12,865).

LAFAYETTE COUNTY

1001 Main St
Lexington, MO 64067
www.historiclexington.com/LafayetteOfficials.html

Ph: 660-259-4315
Fax: 660-259-6109

In west-central MO, east of Kansas City; organized as Lillard County Nov 16, 1820 (prior to statehood) from Cooper County; name changed Feb 16, 1825. **Name Origin:** For Marquis de Lafayette (1757-1834), French statesman and soldier who fought with the Americans during the Revolutionary War.

Area (sq mi): 638.86 (land 629.31; water 9.55). **Pop per sq mi:** 52.6.

Pop 2005: 33,108. **State rank:** 34. **Pop change:** 2000-20005 +0.4%; 1990-2000 +6%. **Pop 2000:** 32,960 (White 94.9%; Black or African American 2.3%; Hispanic or Latino 1.2%; Asian 0.2%; Other 1.9%). **Foreign born:** 0.7%. **Median age:** 37.9.

Income 2000: per capita $18,493; median household $38,235; **Pop below poverty level:** 8.8%. ***Personal per capita income 2000-2003:** $24,647-$26,518.

Unemployment 2004: 5.6%. **Change from 2000:** +1.2%. **Median travel time to work:** 28.3 minutes. **Working outside county of residence:** 49.8%.

Cities with pop over 10,000: None.

LAWRENCE COUNTY

1 Courthouse Sq Suite 101
Mount Vernon, MO 65712

Ph: 417-466-2638
Fax: 417-466-4348

In southwestern MO, west of Springfield; organized Feb 14, 1845

Lawrence County (cont'd)

from Dade and Barry counties. **Name Origin:** For Capt. James Lawrence (1781-1813), U.S. naval officer in the war with Barbary pirates near Tripoli and commander of the U.S.S. Chesapeake in the War of 1812, who said, 'Don't give up the ship!'

Area (sq mi): 613.38 (land 613.08; water 0.3). **Pop per sq mi:** 60.6.

Pop 2005: 37,127. **State rank:** 30. **Pop change:** 2000-20005 +5.5%; 1990-2000 +16.4%. **Pop 2000:** 35,204 (White 94.3%; Black or African American 0.3%; Hispanic or Latino 3.4%; Asian 0.2%; Other 3.9%). **Foreign born:** 2.3%. **Median age:** 36.9.

Income 2000: per capita $15,399; median household $31,239; **Pop below poverty level:** 14.1%. ***Personal per capita income 2000-2003:** $18,728-$19,725.

Unemployment 2004: 4.8%. **Change from 2000:** -0.1%. **Median travel time to work:** 23.6 minutes. **Working outside county of residence:** 47%.

Cities with pop over 10,000: None.

LEWIS COUNTY
100 Lafayette St   **Ph:** 573-767-5205
Monticello, MO 63457   **Fax:** 573-767-8245

On the northeastern border of MO, northeast of Columbia; organized Jan 2, 1833 from Marion County. **Name Origin:** For Meriwether Lewis (1774-1809), co-leader of the Lewis and Clark Expedition (1804-06).

Area (sq mi): 510.85 (land 505.01; water 5.85). **Pop per sq mi:** 20.2.

Pop 2005: 10,186. **State rank:** 88. **Pop change:** 2000-20005 -2.9%; 1990-2000 +2.6%. **Pop 2000:** 10,494 (White 95.6%; Black or African American 2.5%; Hispanic or Latino 0.7%; Asian 0.2%; Other 1.3%). **Foreign born:** 0.6%. **Median age:** 36.

Income 2000: per capita $14,746; median household $30,651; **Pop below poverty level:** 16.1%. ***Personal per capita income 2000-2003:** $17,969-$19,851.

Unemployment 2004: 4.9%. **Change from 2000:** +0.8%. **Median travel time to work:** 22.9 minutes. **Working outside county of residence:** 43.2%.

Cities with pop over 10,000: None.

LINCOLN COUNTY
201 Main St   **Ph:** 636-528-6300
Troy, MO 63379   **Fax:** 636-528-5528
www.lcmo.us

On the central eastern border of MO, north of Saint Louis; organized Dec 14, 1818 (prior to statehood) from Saint Charles County. **Name Origin:** For Gen. Benjamin Lincoln (1733-1810), Revolutionary War officer, U.S. Secretary of War (1781-83), and Lt. Gov. of MA (1788).

Area (sq mi): 640.41 (land 630.49; water 9.92). **Pop per sq mi:** 75.7.

Pop 2005: 47,727. **State rank:** 20. **Pop change:** 2000-20005 +22.6%; 1990-2000 +34.8%. **Pop 2000:** 38,944 (White 95.5%; Black or African American 1.7%; Hispanic or Latino 1.1%; Asian 0.2%; Other 1.9%). **Foreign born:** 0.6%. **Median age:** 34.5.

Income 2000: per capita $17,149; median household $42,592; **Pop below poverty level:** 8.3%. ***Personal per capita income 2000-2003:** $22,501-$23,946.

Unemployment 2004: 5.5%. **Change from 2000:** +0.4%. **Median travel time to work:** 31.3 minutes. **Working outside county of residence:** 54.8%.

Cities with pop over 10,000: None.

LINN COUNTY
108 N High St   **Ph:** 660-895-5417
Linneus, MO 64653   **Fax:** 660-895-5527

In north-central MO, east of Saint Joseph; organized Jan 6, 1837 from Chariton County. **Name Origin:** For Lewis Fields Linn (1795-1843), U.S. senator from MO (1833-43).

Area (sq mi): 621.46 (land 620.35; water 1.11). **Pop per sq mi:** 21.2.

Pop 2005: 13,133. **State rank:** 77. **Pop change:** 2000-20005 -4.5%; 1990-2000 -0.9%. **Pop 2000:** 13,754 (White 97.5%; Black or African American 0.6%; Hispanic or Latino 0.8%; Asian 0.1%; Other 1.4%). **Foreign born:** 0.6%. **Median age:** 40.3.

Income 2000: per capita $15,378; median household $28,242; **Pop below poverty level:** 14.9%. ***Personal per capita income 2000-2003:** $21,153-$22,824.

Unemployment 2004: 7.4%. **Change from 2000:** -1.8%. **Median travel time to work:** 20.8 minutes. **Working outside county of residence:** 20.8%.

Cities with pop over 10,000: None.

LIVINGSTON COUNTY
700 Webster St   **Ph:** 660-646-2293
Chillicothe, MO 64601   **Fax:** 660-646-6139

In north-central MO, east of Saint Joseph; organized Jan 6, 1837 from Carroll County. **Name Origin:** For Edward Livingston (1764-1836), NY legislator, LA legislator and U.S. senator (1829-31), and U.S. Secretary of State (1831-33).

Area (sq mi): 538.48 (land 534.52; water 3.95). **Pop per sq mi:** 26.7.

Pop 2005: 14,291. **State rank:** 71. **Pop change:** 2000-20005 -1.8%; 1990-2000 -0.2%. **Pop 2000:** 14,558 (White 95.6%; Black or African American 2.3%; Hispanic or Latino 0.6%; Asian 0.3%; Other 1.4%). **Foreign born:** 0.4%. **Median age:** 39.7.

Income 2000: per capita $16,685; median household $32,290; **Pop below poverty level:** 12.4%. ***Personal per capita income 2000-2003:** $24,285-$24,368.

Unemployment 2004: 5.2%. **Change from 2000:** +1.6%. **Median travel time to work:** 18.2 minutes. **Working outside county of residence:** 14.1%.

Cities with pop over 10,000: None.

MACON COUNTY
PO Box 96   **Ph:** 660-385-2913
Macon, MO 63552   **Fax:** 660-385-7203
www.maconcounty.org

In north-central MO, northwest of Columbia; organized Jan 6, 1837 from Randolph and Chariton counties. **Name Origin:** For

*Source: Personal per capita income data are from the Bureau of Economic Analysis; per capita income data are from the Bureau of the Census. See Introduction for explanation of differences.

Macon County (cont'd)

Nathaniel Macon (1757-1837), Revolutionary War soldier, NC legislator, U.S. representative (1791-1815), U.S. senator (1815-28), and president of the NC constitutional convention (1835).

Area (sq mi): 812.53 (land 803.77; water 8.76). **Pop per sq mi:** 19.4.

Pop 2005: 15,600. **State rank:** 68. **Pop change:** 2000-20005 -1%; 1990-2000 -2.7%. **Pop 2000:** 15,762 (White 95.6%; Black or African American 2.2%; Hispanic or Latino 0.8%; Asian 0.2%; Other 1.4%). **Foreign born:** 0.3%. **Median age:** 40.1.

Income 2000: per capita $16,189; median household $30,195; **Pop below poverty level:** 12.5%. ***Personal per capita income 2000-2003:** $20,873-$22,455.

Unemployment 2004: 5.4%. **Change from 2000:** -4.9%. **Median travel time to work:** 21.3 minutes. **Working outside county of residence:** 28%.

Cities with pop over 10,000: None.

MADISON COUNTY

1 Courthouse Sq
Fredericktown, MO 63645

Ph: 573-783-2176
Fax: 573-783-5351

In southeastern MO, northwest of Cape Girardeau; organized Dec 14, 1818 (prior to statehood) from Sainte Genevieve and Cape Girardeau counties. **Name Origin:** For James Madison (1751-1836), fourth U.S. president.

Area (sq mi): 497.6 (land 496.73; water 0.87). **Pop per sq mi:** 24.5.

Pop 2005: 12,151. **State rank:** 83. **Pop change:** 2000-20005 +3%; 1990-2000 +6%. **Pop 2000:** 11,800 (White 97.9%; Black or African American 0.1%; Hispanic or Latino 0.6%; Asian 0.3%; Other 1.3%). **Foreign born:** 0.8%. **Median age:** 39.1.

Income 2000: per capita $13,215; median household $25,601; **Pop below poverty level:** 17.2%. ***Personal per capita income 2000-2003:** $17,261-$19,309.

Unemployment 2004: 6.4%. **Change from 2000:** -1.9%. **Median travel time to work:** 29.5 minutes. **Working outside county of residence:** 40.5%.

Cities with pop over 10,000: None.

MARIES COUNTY

211 4th St
Vienna, MO 65582

Ph: 573-422-3388
Fax: 573-422-3269

In east-central MO, southwest of Saint Louis; established Mar 2, 1855 from Osage and Pulaski counties. **Name Origin:** For the Maries River, which runs through it; a corruption of French *marais* 'swamp.'

Area (sq mi): 529.97 (land 527.73; water 2.25). **Pop per sq mi:** 17.

Pop 2005: 8,989. **State rank:** 96. **Pop change:** 2000-20005 +1%; 1990-2000 +11.6%. **Pop 2000:** 8,903 (White 96.7%; Black or African American 0.3%; Hispanic or Latino 1.2%; Asian 0.1%; Other 2.1%). **Foreign born:** 0.8%. **Median age:** 38.5.

Income 2000: per capita $15,662; median household $31,925; **Pop below poverty level:** 13.1%. ***Personal per capita income 2000-2003:** $19,498-$22,182.

Unemployment 2004: 5.1%. **Change from 2000:** +0%. **Median travel time to work:** 33.7 minutes. **Working outside county of residence:** 65.5%.

Cities with pop over 10,000: None.

MARION COUNTY

100 S Main St
Palmyra, MO 63461

Ph: 573-769-2549
Fax: 573-769-4312

On the northeastern border of MO, north of Saint Louis; established Dec 14, 1822 from Ralls County. **Name Origin:** For Gen. Francis Marion (c. 1732-95), SC soldier and legislator, known as 'The Swamp Fox' for his tactics in the Carolina swamps during the Revolutionary War.

Area (sq mi): 444.05 (land 438.07; water 5.97). **Pop per sq mi:** 64.8.

Pop 2005: 28,375. **State rank:** 40. **Pop change:** 2000-20005 +0.3%; 1990-2000 +2.2%. **Pop 2000:** 28,289 (White 92.7%; Black or African American 4.6%; Hispanic or Latino 0.9%; Asian 0.3%; Other 1.9%). **Foreign born:** 0.8%. **Median age:** 37.1.

Income 2000: per capita $16,964; median household $31,774; **Pop below poverty level:** 12.1%. ***Personal per capita income 2000-2003:** $22,287-$24,069.

Unemployment 2004: 5.7%. **Change from 2000:** +0.2%. **Median travel time to work:** 16.7 minutes. **Working outside county of residence:** 24.2%.

Cities with pop over 10,000: Hannibal (17,719).

MCDONALD COUNTY

602 Main St
Pineville, MO 64856

Ph: 417-223-4717
Fax: 417-223-7519

In southwestern corner of MO, south of Joplin; organized Mar 3, 1849 from Newton County. **Name Origin:** For Sgt. Alexander McDonald, a soldier in the American Revolution.

Area (sq mi): 539.7 (land 539.51; water 0.19). **Pop per sq mi:** 42.3.

Pop 2005: 22,844. **State rank:** 50. **Pop change:** 2000-20005 +5.4%; 1990-2000 +28%. **Pop 2000:** 21,681 (White 84.6%; Black or African American 0.2%; Hispanic or Latino 9.4%; Asian 0.1%; Other 10%, including 2.9% American Indian/Alaska Native). **Foreign born:** 5.6%. **Median age:** 34.3.

Income 2000: per capita $13,175; median household $27,010; **Pop below poverty level:** 20.7%. ***Personal per capita income 2000-2003:** $17,395-$20,395.

Unemployment 2004: 4.9%. **Change from 2000:** -0.3%. **Median travel time to work:** 27.3 minutes. **Working outside county of residence:** 48.4%.

Cities with pop over 10,000: None.

MERCER COUNTY

802 Main St County Courthouse
Princeton, MO 64673

Ph: 660-748-3425
Fax: 660-748-3180

On the central northern border of MO, northeast of Saint Joseph; organized Feb 14, 1845 from Grundy and Livingston counties. **Name Origin:** For Lt. Col. John Francis Mercer (1759-1821), officer in the Revolutionary War, MD legislator, and governor of MD (1801-13); or possibly for Gen. Hugh Mercer (1721-77), Revolutionary War officer and physician.

Mercer County (cont'd)

Area (sq mi): 455.18 (land 454.18; water 1). **Pop per sq mi:** 7.9.

Pop 2005: 3,595. **State rank:** 114. **Pop change:** 2000-20005 -4.3%; 1990-2000 +0.9%. **Pop 2000:** 3,757 (White 98.6%; Black or African American 0.2%; Hispanic or Latino 0.3%; Asian 0%; Other 1.2%). **Foreign born:** 0.4%. **Median age:** 42.4.

Income 2000: per capita $15,140; median household $29,640; **Pop below poverty level:** 13.3%. ***Personal per capita income 2000-2003:** $22,865-$19,936.

Unemployment 2004: 5.2%. **Change from 2000:** +1.6%. **Median travel time to work:** 24.8 minutes. **Working outside county of residence:** 31.5%.

Cities with pop over 10,000: None.

MILLER COUNTY
PO Box 12   **Ph:** 573-369-1900
Tuscumbia, MO 65082   **Fax:** 573-369-2910

In central MO, south of Jefferson City; organized Feb 6, 1837 from Cole and Pulaski counties. **Name Origin:** For Col. John Miller (1781-1846), officer in the War of 1812, governor of MO (1825-32), and U.S. representative (1837-43).

Area (sq mi): 599.94 (land 592.26; water 7.69). **Pop per sq mi:** 41.7.

Pop 2005: 24,712. **State rank:** 43. **Pop change:** 2000-20005 +4.9%; 1990-2000 +13.8%. **Pop 2000:** 23,564 (White 97.3%; Black or African American 0.3%; Hispanic or Latino 1%; Asian 0.1%; Other 1.6%). **Foreign born:** 0.7%. **Median age:** 37.2.

Income 2000: per capita $15,144; median household $30,977; **Pop below poverty level:** 14.2%. ***Personal per capita income 2000-2003:** $18,378-$19,832.

Unemployment 2004: 6.4%. **Change from 2000:** -0.2%. **Median travel time to work:** 25 minutes. **Working outside county of residence:** 42.6%.

Cities with pop over 10,000: None.

MISSISSIPPI COUNTY
200 n Main St   **Ph:** 573-683-2146
Charleston, MO 63834   **Fax:** 573-683-6071
www.misscomo.net

On the southeastern border of MO, south of Cape Girardeau; established Feb 14, 1845 from Scott County. **Name Origin:** For its location on the Mississippi River.

Area (sq mi): 428.91 (land 413.16; water 15.75). **Pop per sq mi:** 32.9.

Pop 2005: 13,599. **State rank:** 74. **Pop change:** 2000-20005 +1.3%; 1990-2000 -7%. **Pop 2000:** 13,427 (White 77.5%; Black or African American 20.5%; Hispanic or Latino 1%; Asian 0.1%; Other 1.4%). **Foreign born:** 0.5%. **Median age:** 37.3.

Income 2000: per capita $13,038; median household $23,012; **Pop below poverty level:** 23.7%. ***Personal per capita income 2000-2003:** $18,895-$21,132.

Unemployment 2004: 7.5%. **Change from 2000:** -1.6%. **Median travel time to work:** 19.7 minutes. **Working outside county of residence:** 35.3%.

Cities with pop over 10,000: None.

MONITEAU COUNTY
200 E Main St   **Ph:** 573-796-4661
California, MO 65018   **Fax:** 573-796-3082

In central MO, west of Jefferson City; organized Feb 14, 1845 from Cole and Morgan counties, annexed small part of Morgan County in 1881. **Name Origin:** A French transliteration of an Algonquian word meaning 'God spirit' or 'great spirit.'

Area (sq mi): 418.85 (land 416.52; water 2.33). **Pop per sq mi:** 36.2.

Pop 2005: 15,084. **State rank:** 69. **Pop change:** 2000-20005 +1.7%; 1990-2000 +20.6%. **Pop 2000:** 14,827 (White 91.4%; Black or African American 3.8%; Hispanic or Latino 2.9%; Asian 0.3%; Other 3.2%). **Foreign born:** 1.6%. **Median age:** 35.9.

Income 2000: per capita $16,609; median household $37,168; **Pop below poverty level:** 9.9%. ***Personal per capita income 2000-2003:** $20,702-$21,973.

Unemployment 2004: 4.7%. **Change from 2000:** +0.6%. **Median travel time to work:** 24.4 minutes. **Working outside county of residence:** 46.5%.

Cities with pop over 10,000: None.

MONROE COUNTY
300 N Main St Rm 204   **Ph:** 660-327-5106
Paris, MO 65275   **Fax:** 660-327-1019

In northeastern MO, northeast of Columbia; organized Jan 6, 1831 from Ralls County. **Name Origin:** For James Monroe (1758-1831), fifth U.S. president.

Area (sq mi): 670.23 (land 645.98; water 24.24). **Pop per sq mi:** 14.5.

Pop 2005: 9,379. **State rank:** 93. **Pop change:** 2000-20005 +0.7%; 1990-2000 +2.3%. **Pop 2000:** 9,311 (White 94.2%; Black or African American 3.8%; Hispanic or Latino 0.6%; Asian 0.1%; Other 1.4%). **Foreign born:** 0.5%. **Median age:** 39.4.

Income 2000: per capita $14,695; median household $30,871; **Pop below poverty level:** 11.9%. ***Personal per capita income 2000-2003:** $20,689-$20,756.

Unemployment 2004: 6%. **Change from 2000:** -1.4%. **Median travel time to work:** 25.1 minutes. **Working outside county of residence:** 45.8%.

Cities with pop over 10,000: None.

MONTGOMERY COUNTY
211 E 3rd St   **Ph:** 573-564-3357
Montgomery City, MO 63361   **Fax:** 573-564-8088
www.montgomerycountymo.org

In east-central MO, northwest of Saint Louis; organized Dec 14, 1818 (prior to statehood) from Saint Charles County. **Name Origin:** For Gen. Richard Montgomery (1736-75), American Revolutionary War officer who captured Montreal, Canada.

Area (sq mi): 540.34 (land 537.46; water 2.88). **Pop per sq mi:** 22.6.

Pop 2005: 12,166. **State rank:** 82. **Pop change:** 2000-20005 +0.2%; 1990-2000 +6.9%. **Pop 2000:** 12,136 (White 95.6%; Black or African American 2%; Hispanic or Latino 0.8%; Asian 0.3%; Other 1.7%). **Foreign born:** 1.2%. **Median age:** 39.4.

*Source: Personal per capita income data are from the Bureau of Economic Analysis; per capita income data are from the Bureau of the Census. See Introduction for explanation of differences.

Montgomery County (cont'd)

Income 2000: per capita $15,092; median household $32,772; **Pop below poverty level:** 11.8%. ***Personal per capita income 2000-2003:** $21,781-$23,808.

Unemployment 2004: 6.3%. **Change from 2000:** +0.4%. **Median travel time to work:** 27.7 minutes. **Working outside county of residence:** 44.5%.

Cities with pop over 10,000: None.

MORGAN COUNTY
100 E Newton St   **Ph:** 573-378-5436
Versailles, MO 65084   **Fax:** 573-378-5991

In central MO, west of Jefferson City; organized Jan 5, 1833 from Cooper County. **Name Origin:** For Gen. Daniel Morgan (1736-1802), an officer in the Revolutionary War and U.S. representative from VA (1797-99).

Area (sq mi): 613.89 (land 597.41; water 16.48). **Pop per sq mi:** 34.2.

Pop 2005: 20,436. **State rank:** 55. **Pop change:** 2000-20005 +5.8%; 1990-2000 +24%. **Pop 2000:** 19,309 (White 96.8%; Black or African American 0.5%; Hispanic or Latino 0.8%; Asian 0.1%; Other 2%). **Foreign born:** 1%. **Median age:** 42.6.

Income 2000: per capita $15,950; median household $30,659; **Pop below poverty level:** 16.2%. ***Personal per capita income 2000-2003:** $19,008-$21,368.

Unemployment 2004: 6.4%. **Change from 2000:** -0.6%. **Median travel time to work:** 25.3 minutes. **Working outside county of residence:** 38.9%.

Cities with pop over 10,000: None.

NEW MADRID COUNTY
450 Main St   **Ph:** 573-748-2524
New Madrid, MO 63869   **Fax:** 573-748-9269

On the southeastern border of MO, south of Cape Girardeau; original county; organized Oct 1, 1812 (prior to statehood). **Name Origin:** For the city, named for the capital of Spain. Originally called *Nuevo Madrid* by Col. George Morgan, who founded the city in 1788.

Area (sq mi): 698.02 (land 678.01; water 20.01). **Pop per sq mi:** 27.4.

Pop 2005: 18,566. **State rank:** 60. **Pop change:** 2000-20005 -6%; 1990-2000 -5.6%. **Pop 2000:** 19,760 (White 82.7%; Black or African American 15.4%; Hispanic or Latino 0.9%; Asian 0.1%; Other 1.3%). **Foreign born:** 0.3%. **Median age:** 37.4.

Income 2000: per capita $14,204; median household $26,826; **Pop below poverty level:** 22.1%. ***Personal per capita income 2000-2003:** $20,110-$22,680.

Unemployment 2004: 8.5%. **Change from 2000:** +0.6%. **Median travel time to work:** 18.1 minutes. **Working outside county of residence:** 33.6%.

Cities with pop over 10,000: None.

NEWTON COUNTY
101 S Wood St   **Ph:** 417-451-8220
Neosho, MO 64850   **Fax:** 417-451-7434

On the southwestern border of MO, south of Joplin; organized Dec 30, 1838 from Barry County. **Name Origin:** For Sgt. John Newton (1752-80); soldier under Gen. Francis Marion in the Revolutionary War, who saved several colonial patriots from execution by surprising and capturing the British soldiers guarding them.

Area (sq mi): 626.66 (land 626.42; water 0.24). **Pop per sq mi:** 88.7.

Pop 2005: 55,554. **State rank:** 18. **Pop change:** 2000-20005 +5.5%; 1990-2000 +18.4%. **Pop 2000:** 52,636 (White 92.4%; Black or African American 0.6%; Hispanic or Latino 2.2%; Asian 0.3%; Other 5.8%, including 2.2% American Indian/Alaska Native). **Foreign born:** 1.4%. **Median age:** 37.1.

Income 2000: per capita $17,502; median household $35,041; **Pop below poverty level:** 11.6%. ***Personal per capita income 2000-2003:** $21,617-$23,489.

Unemployment 2004: 5.3%. **Change from 2000:** +0.2%. **Median travel time to work:** 21.8 minutes. **Working outside county of residence:** 42.4%.

Cities with pop over 10,000: Neosho 🏛 (10,061).

NODAWAY COUNTY
PO Box 218   **Ph:** 660-582-2251
Maryville, MO 64468   **Fax:** 660-582-5282

On the northwestern border of MO, north of Saint Joseph; established Jan 29, 1841 from Andrew County. **Name Origin:** A Potawatomi Indian word whose meaning is unclear, possibly 'placid.'

Area (sq mi): 877.75 (land 876.62; water 1.13). **Pop per sq mi:** 24.8.

Pop 2005: 21,710. **State rank:** 52. **Pop change:** 2000-20005 -0.9%; 1990-2000 +0.9%. **Pop 2000:** 21,912 (White 96.1%; Black or African American 1.3%; Hispanic or Latino 0.7%; Asian 0.9%; Other 1.1%). **Foreign born:** 1.4%. **Median age:** 30.2.

Income 2000: per capita $15,384; median household $31,781; **Pop below poverty level:** 16.5%. ***Personal per capita income 2000-2003:** $19,021-$20,914.

Unemployment 2004: 3.7%. **Change from 2000:** +1.8%. **Median travel time to work:** 16.3 minutes. **Working outside county of residence:** 11.9%.

Cities with pop over 10,000: Maryville 🏛 (10,511).

OREGON COUNTY
PO Box 324   **Ph:** 417-778-7475
Alton, MO 65606   **Fax:** 417-778-7488

On the central southern border of MO, southwest of Cape Giradeau; organized Feb 14, 1845 from Ripley County. **Name Origin:** For OR Territory, named during the dispute with Great Britain over its possession.

Area (sq mi): 791.59 (land 791.4; water 0.18). **Pop per sq mi:** 13.1.

Pop 2005: 10,403. **State rank:** 84. **Pop change:** 2000-20005 +0.6%; 1990-2000 +9.2%. **Pop 2000:** 10,344 (White 93.7%; Black or African American 0.1%; Hispanic or Latino 1.1%; Asian 0.1%; Other 5.2%, including 2.9% American Indian/Alaska Native). **Foreign born:** 0.7%. **Median age:** 41.

🏛 *County Seat*

Oregon County (cont'd)

Income 2000: per capita $12,812; median household $22,359; **Pop below poverty level:** 22%. ***Personal per capita income 2000-2003:** $15,450-$17,523.

Unemployment 2004: 5.6%. **Change from 2000:** +1.2%. **Median travel time to work:** 27.9 minutes. **Working outside county of residence:** 36.1%.

Cities with pop over 10,000: None.

OSAGE COUNTY

106 E Main St   **Ph:** 573-897-2139
Linn, MO 65051   **Fax:** 573-897-4741
www.osagecountymo.com

In east-central MO, west of Saint Louis; organized Jan 29, 1841 from Gasconade County. **Name Origin:** For the Osage Indians, a tribe of Siouan linguistic stock. Name is a corruption of their name in their language, *Wazhazhe*, meaning unknown.

Area (sq mi): 613.41 (land 606.11; water 7.3). **Pop per sq mi:** 22.2.

Pop 2005: 13,485. **State rank:** 76. **Pop change:** 2000-20005 +3.2%; 1990-2000 +8.7%. **Pop 2000:** 13,062 (White 98.2%; Black or African American 0.2%; Hispanic or Latino 0.6%; Asian 0.1%; Other 1.1%). **Foreign born:** 0.5%. **Median age:** 36.1.

Income 2000: per capita $17,245; median household $39,565; **Pop below poverty level:** 8.3%. ***Personal per capita income 2000-2003:** $23,243-$25,374.

Unemployment 2004: 4.6%. **Change from 2000:** -0.5%. **Median travel time to work:** 28 minutes. **Working outside county of residence:** 58.7%.

Cities with pop over 10,000: None.

OZARK COUNTY

PO Box 416   **Ph:** 417-679-3516
Gainesville, MO 65655   **Fax:** 417-679-3209

On the central southern border of MO, southeast of Springfield; organized Jan 29, 1841 from Taney County. **Name Origin:** For the Ozark Mountains, whose name derives from the anglicized phonetic spelling of French *aux arcs* or *aux Arks* 'in the country of the Arkansas Indians.'

Area (sq mi): 755.07 (land 742.15; water 12.92). **Pop per sq mi:** 12.8.

Pop 2005: 9,490. **State rank:** 92. **Pop change:** 2000-20005 -0.5%; 1990-2000 +11%. **Pop 2000:** 9,542 (White 96.9%; Black or African American 0.1%; Hispanic or Latino 0.9%; Asian 0.1%; Other 2.2%). **Foreign born:** 1%. **Median age:** 43.6.

Income 2000: per capita $14,133; median household $25,861; **Pop below poverty level:** 21.6%. ***Personal per capita income 2000-2003:** $16,231-$17,797.

Unemployment 2004: 6%. **Change from 2000:** +0.1%. **Median travel time to work:** 29.5 minutes. **Working outside county of residence:** 43.4%.

Cities with pop over 10,000: None.

PEMISCOT COUNTY

610 Ward Ave   **Ph:** 573-333-4203
Caruthersville, MO 63830   **Fax:** 573-333-0440

On southeastern tip of MO, south of Cape Girardeau; organized Feb 19, 1851 from New Madrid County. **Name Origin:** From an Indian name of uncertain origin and meaning 'at the long place,' 'running beside,' and 'liquid mud' have been suggested.

Area (sq mi): 512.41 (land 493.08; water 19.33). **Pop per sq mi:** 39.4.

Pop 2005: 19,412. **State rank:** 56. **Pop change:** 2000-20005 -3.2%; 1990-2000 -8.5%. **Pop 2000:** 20,047 (White 71.1%; Black or African American 26.2%; Hispanic or Latino 1.6%; Asian 0.3%; Other 1.7%). **Foreign born:** 0.9%. **Median age:** 34.4.

Income 2000: per capita $12,968; median household $21,911; **Pop below poverty level:** 30.4%. ***Personal per capita income 2000-2003:** $19,419-$22,228.

Unemployment 2004: 9%. **Change from 2000:** -0.4%. **Median travel time to work:** 18.3 minutes. **Working outside county of residence:** 31.2%.

Cities with pop over 10,000: None.

PERRY COUNTY

321 N Main St Suite 2   **Ph:** 573-547-4242
Perryville, MO 63775   **Fax:** 573-547-7367
www.perryvillemo.com/county/

On the southeastern border of MO, north of Cape Girardeau; organized Nov 16, 1820 (prior to statehood) from Sainte Genevieve County. **Name Origin:** For Oliver Hazard Perry (1785-1819), U.S. naval officer who won the Battle of Lake Erie during the War of 1812, famous for the message, 'We have met the enemy and they are ours.'

Area (sq mi): 484.28 (land 474.67; water 9.61). **Pop per sq mi:** 39.1.

Pop 2005: 18,571. **State rank:** 59. **Pop change:** 2000-20005 +2.4%; 1990-2000 +8.9%. **Pop 2000:** 18,132 (White 97.8%; Black or African American 0.2%; Hispanic or Latino 0.5%; Asian 0.6%; Other 0.9%). **Foreign born:** 1.1%. **Median age:** 36.8.

Income 2000: per capita $16,554; median household $36,632; **Pop below poverty level:** 9%. ***Personal per capita income 2000-2003:** $21,299-$22,918.

Unemployment 2004: 4.1%. **Change from 2000:** +0.6%. **Median travel time to work:** 22.3 minutes. **Working outside county of residence:** 23.3%.

Cities with pop over 10,000: None.

PETTIS COUNTY

415 S Ohio St   **Ph:** 660-826-5395
Sedalia, MO 65301   **Fax:** 660-829-0717

In west-central MO, southwest of Columbia; organized Jan 26, 1833 from Saline and Cooper counties. **Name Origin:** For Spencer Darwin Pettis (1802-31), U.S. representative from MO (1829-31) killed in a duel with Maj. Thomas Biddle.

Area (sq mi): 686.34 (land 684.82; water 1.52). **Pop per sq mi:** 58.6.

Pop 2005: 40,121. **State rank:** 27. **Pop change:** 2000-20005 +1.8%; 1990-2000 +11.2%. **Pop 2000:** 39,403 (White 90.9%; Black or

Source: Personal per capita income data are from the Bureau of Economic Analysis; per capita income data are from the Bureau of the Census. See Introduction for explanation of differences.

418

Pettis County (cont'd)

African American 3%; Hispanic or Latino 3.9%; Asian 0.4%; Other 4.6%). **Foreign born:** 2.9%. **Median age:** 36.4.

Income 2000: per capita $16,251; median household $31,822; **Pop below poverty level:** 12.8%. ***Personal per capita income 2000-2003:** $22,849-$24,813.

Unemployment 2004: 6%. **Change from 2000:** -0.2%. **Median travel time to work:** 18.9 minutes. **Working outside county of residence:** 13.8%.

Cities with pop over 10,000: Sedalia ⛪ (20,196).

PHELPS COUNTY

200 N Main St   **Ph:** 573-364-1891
Rolla, MO 65401   **Fax:** 573-458-6119
www.phelpscounty.org

In south-central MO, southwest of Saint Louis; organized Nov 13, 1857 from Crawford County. **Name Origin:** For John Smith Phelps (1814-86), MO legislator, U.S. representative (1845-63), and governor (1876-80)

Area (sq mi): 674.28 (land 672.85; water 1.43). **Pop per sq mi:** 62.6.

Pop 2005: 42,125. **State rank:** 24. **Pop change:** 2000-20005 +5.8%; 1990-2000 +13%. **Pop 2000:** 39,825 (White 92.6%; Black or African American 1.5%; Hispanic or Latino 1.2%; Asian 2.4%; Other 3%). **Foreign born:** 4%. **Median age:** 34.9.

Income 2000: per capita $16,084; median household $29,378; **Pop below poverty level:** 16.4%. ***Personal per capita income 2000-2003:** $21,348-$24,052.

Unemployment 2004: 4.5%. **Change from 2000:** +1%. **Median travel time to work:** 19.1 minutes. **Working outside county of residence:** 15.5%.

Cities with pop over 10,000: Rolla ⛪ (17,411).

PIKE COUNTY

115 W Main St   **Ph:** 573-324-2412
Bowling Green, MO 63334   **Fax:** 573-324-5154
www.pikecountytourism.com

On the central eastern border of MO, north of Saint Louis; organized Dec 14, 1818 (prior to statehood) from Saint Charles County. **Name Origin:** For Zebulon Montgomery Pike (1779-1813), U.S. army officer and discoverer of Pikes Peak, CO.

Area (sq mi): 684.81 (land 672.82; water 11.99). **Pop per sq mi:** 27.9.

Pop 2005: 18,762. **State rank:** 58. **Pop change:** 2000-20005 +2.2%; 1990-2000 +14.9%. **Pop 2000:** 18,351 (White 87.8%; Black or African American 9.2%; Hispanic or Latino 1.6%; Asian 0.2%; Other 2.1%). **Foreign born:** 1.6%. **Median age:** 37.7.

Income 2000: per capita $14,462; median household $32,373; **Pop below poverty level:** 15.5%. ***Personal per capita income 2000-2003:** $19,180-$20,338.

Unemployment 2004: 5.5%. **Change from 2000:** -0.1%. **Median travel time to work:** 24.6 minutes. **Working outside county of residence:** 30.7%.

Cities with pop over 10,000: None.

PLATTE COUNTY

415 3rd St   **Ph:** 816-858-2232
Platte City, MO 64079   **Fax:** 816-858-3363
www.co.platte.mo.us

On the northwestern border of MO, northwest of Kansas City; organized Dec 31, 1838 from Platte Purchase. **Name Origin:** For the Platte River, which runs through it; French 'flat' or 'still.'

Area (sq mi): 427.22 (land 420.33; water 6.89). **Pop per sq mi:** 195.3.

Pop 2005: 82,085. **State rank:** 13. **Pop change:** 2000-20005 +11.3%; 1990-2000 +27.5%. **Pop 2000:** 73,781 (White 89.8%; Black or African American 3.5%; Hispanic or Latino 3%; Asian 1.5%; Other 3.6%). **Foreign born:** 3.7%. **Median age:** 35.9.

Income 2000: per capita $26,356; median household $55,849; **Pop below poverty level:** 4.8%. ***Personal per capita income 2000-2003:** $33,156-$35,174.

Unemployment 2004: 4.4%. **Change from 2000:** +1.6%. **Median travel time to work:** 23 minutes. **Working outside county of residence:** 60.3%.

Cities with pop over 10,000: None.

POLK COUNTY

102 E Broadway   **Ph:** 417 326-4031
Bolivar, MO 65613   **Fax:** 417-326-3525
www.polkcountymo.org

In south-central MO, north of Springfield; organized Jan 5, 1835 from Greene and Laclede counties. **Name Origin:** For James Knox Polk (1795-1849), eleventh U.S. president.

Area (sq mi): 642.46 (land 637.2; water 5.26). **Pop per sq mi:** 45.3.

Pop 2005: 28,892. **State rank:** 38. **Pop change:** 2000-20005 +7%; 1990-2000 +23.7%. **Pop 2000:** 26,992 (White 96.4%; Black or African American 0.5%; Hispanic or Latino 1.3%; Asian 0.2%; Other 2.1%). **Foreign born:** 1.5%. **Median age:** 35.

Income 2000: per capita $13,645; median household $29,656; **Pop below poverty level:** 16.3%. ***Personal per capita income 2000-2003:** $17,742-$19,595.

Unemployment 2004: 5%. **Change from 2000:** +0.7%. **Median travel time to work:** 25.3 minutes. **Working outside county of residence:** 37.5%.

Cities with pop over 10,000: None.

PULASKI COUNTY

301 Historic 66 E Suite 101   **Ph:** 573-774-4701
Waynesville, MO 65583   **Fax:** 573-774-5601
www.visitpulaskicounty.org

In south-central MO, northeast of Springfield; organized Jan 19, 1833 from Crawford County. **Name Origin:** For Count Casimir Pulaski (1747-79), Polish soldier who fought for America during the Revolutionary War.

Area (sq mi): 551.41 (land 547.02; water 4.39). **Pop per sq mi:** 80.8.

Pop 2005: 44,187. **State rank:** 21. **Pop change:** 2000-20005 +7.3%; 1990-2000 -0.3%. **Pop 2000:** 41,165 (White 75.8%; Black or African American 12%; Hispanic or Latino 5.8%; Asian 2.3%; Other 7.4%, including 1% American Indian/Alaska Native). **Foreign born:** 4.8%. **Median age:** 28.5.

⛪ *County Seat*

Pulaski County (cont'd)

Income 2000: per capita $14,586; median household $34,247; **Pop below poverty level:** 10.3%. ***Personal per capita income 2000-2003:** $22,756-$24,327.

Unemployment 2004: 5.4%. **Change from 2000:** -0.9%. **Median travel time to work:** 18.8 minutes. **Working outside county of residence:** 13.3%.

Cities with pop over 10,000: None.

PUTNAM COUNTY

Rm 204 County Courthouse   **Ph:** 660-947-2674
Unionville, MO 63565   **Fax:** 660-947-4214

On the central northern border of MO; established Feb 22, 1843 from Adair, Sullivan, and Linn counties, annexed Dodge County in 1853. **Name Origin:** For Gen. Israel Putnam (1718-90), Revolutionary War officer and American commander at the Battle of Bunker Hill.

Area (sq mi): 519.66 (land 517.9; water 1.76). **Pop per sq mi:** 10.

Pop 2005: 5,168. **State rank:** 109. **Pop change:** 2000-20005 -1.1%; 1990-2000 +2.8%. **Pop 2000:** 5,223 (White 98.7%; Black or African American 0.1%; Hispanic or Latino 0.6%; Asian 0.1%; Other 0.7%). **Foreign born:** 0.5%. **Median age:** 41.9.

Income 2000: per capita $14,647; median household $26,282; **Pop below poverty level:** 16%. ***Personal per capita income 2000-2003:** $17,687-$19,304.

Unemployment 2004: 4.9%. **Change from 2000:** +0.9%. **Median travel time to work:** 26.7 minutes. **Working outside county of residence:** 37.6%.

Cities with pop over 10,000: None.

RALLS COUNTY

311 S Main St   **Ph:** 573-985-7111
New London, MO 63459   **Fax:** 573-985-6100

On northeastern border of MO; northeast of Columbia; organized Nov 16, 1820 (prior to statehood) from Pike County. **Name Origin:** For Daniel Ralls (1785-1820) a MO legislator who died the year the county was formed.

Area (sq mi): 483.82 (land 471; water 12.82). **Pop per sq mi:** 20.7.

Pop 2005: 9,761. **State rank:** 90. **Pop change:** 2000-20005 +1.4%; 1990-2000 +13.6%. **Pop 2000:** 9,626 (White 97.6%; Black or African American 1.1%; Hispanic or Latino 0.4%; Asian 0.1%; Other 0.8%). **Foreign born:** 0.3%. **Median age:** 39.3.

Income 2000: per capita $16,456; median household $37,094; **Pop below poverty level:** 8.7%. ***Personal per capita income 2000-2003:** $21,976-$22,341.

Unemployment 2004: 6%. **Change from 2000:** +0.3%. **Median travel time to work:** 21.5 minutes. **Working outside county of residence:** 60.3%.

Cities with pop over 10,000: None.

RANDOLPH COUNTY

110 S Main St   **Ph:** 660-277-4717
Huntsville, MO 65259   **Fax:** 660-277-3246
www.randolphcountymo.com

In north-central MO, north of Columbia; organized Jan 22, 1829 from Chariton and Ralls counties. **Name Origin:** For John Randolph (1773-1833), VA statesman and U.S. Minister to Russia (1830).

Area (sq mi): 487.65 (land 482.32; water 5.33). **Pop per sq mi:** 52.5.

Pop 2005: 25,336. **State rank:** 42. **Pop change:** 2000-20005 +2.7%; 1990-2000 +1.2%. **Pop 2000:** 24,663 (White 89.9%; Black or African American 7%; Hispanic or Latino 1.1%; Asian 0.4%; Other 2%). **Foreign born:** 1.3%. **Median age:** 37.2.

Income 2000: per capita $15,010; median household $31,464; **Pop below poverty level:** 12.5%. ***Personal per capita income 2000-2003:** $20,010-$22,154.

Unemployment 2004: 5.5%. **Change from 2000:** -0.5%. **Median travel time to work:** 21.1 minutes. **Working outside county of residence:** 22.7%.

Cities with pop over 10,000: Moberly (13,745).

RAY COUNTY

100 W Main St County Courthouse   **Ph:** 816-776-4502
Richmond, MO 64085   **Fax:** 816-776-4512

In west-central MO, northeast of Kansas City; organized Nov 16, 1820 (prior to statehood) from Howard County. **Name Origin:** For John Ray, a MO legislator when the county was named.

Area (sq mi): 573.57 (land 569.47; water 4.11). **Pop per sq mi:** 42.3.

Pop 2005: 24,101. **State rank:** 46. **Pop change:** 2000-20005 +3.2%; 1990-2000 +6.3%. **Pop 2000:** 23,354 (White 95.8%; Black or African American 1.5%; Hispanic or Latino 1.1%; Asian 0.2%; Other 1.9%). **Foreign born:** 0.4%. **Median age:** 37.1.

Income 2000: per capita $18,685; median household $41,886; **Pop below poverty level:** 6.8%. ***Personal per capita income 2000-2003:** $23,813-$25,286.

Unemployment 2004: 6.1%. **Change from 2000:** +1.8%. **Median travel time to work:** 32.7 minutes. **Working outside county of residence:** 64.1%.

Cities with pop over 10,000: None.

REYNOLDS COUNTY

Hwy 21 & Courthouse Sq PO Box 10   **Ph:** 573-648-2494
Centerville, MO 63633   **Fax:** 573-648-2449

In southeastern MO, west of Cape Girardeau; organized Feb 25, 1845 from Shannon County. **Name Origin:** For Thomas Reynolds (1796-1844), IL legislator, MO legislator, and governor (1840-440.

Area (sq mi): 814.41 (land 811.2; water 3.21). **Pop per sq mi:** 8.1.

Pop 2005: 6,585. **State rank:** 105. **Pop change:** 2000-20005 -1.6%; 1990-2000 +0.4%. **Pop 2000:** 6,689 (White 95.2%; Black or African American 0.5%; Hispanic or Latino 0.8%; Asian 0.2%; Other 3.6%, including 1.3% American Indian/Alaska Native). **Foreign born:** 0.4%. **Median age:** 40.7.

Income 2000: per capita $13,065; median household $25,867; **Pop below poverty level:** 20.1%. ***Personal per capita income 2000-2003:** $17,610-$19,337.

Source: Personal per capita income data are from the Bureau of Economic Analysis; per capita income data are from the Bureau of the Census. See Introduction for explanation of differences.

Reynolds County (cont'd)

Unemployment 2004: 8.4%. **Change from 2000:** -0.8%. **Median travel time to work:** 28 minutes. **Working outside county of residence:** 26.4%.

Cities with pop over 10,000: None.

RIPLEY COUNTY

County Courthouse 100 Courthouse Sq   **Ph:** 573-996-3215
Doniphan, MO 63935   **Fax:** 573-996-9774
www.ripleycountymissouri.org/ripley.asp

On the southeastern border of MO, southwest of Cape Girardeau; organized Jan 5, 1833 from Wayne County. **Name Origin:** For Gen. Eleazar Wheelock Ripley (1782-1839), officer in the War of 1812, MA legislator, and U.S. representative from LA (1835-39).

Area (sq mi): 631.66 (land 629.47; water 2.2). **Pop per sq mi:** 22.

Pop 2005: 13,851. **State rank:** 73. **Pop change:** 2000-20005 +2.5%; 1990-2000 +9.8%. **Pop 2000:** 13,509 (White 96.4%; Black or African American 0%; Hispanic or Latino 1%; Asian 0.2%; Other 2.6%, including 1.3% American Indian/Alaska Native). **Foreign born:** 1.1%. **Median age:** 39.4.

Income 2000: per capita $12,889; median household $22,761; **Pop below poverty level:** 22%. ***Personal per capita income 2000-2003:** $16,383-$18,719.

Unemployment 2004: 6.3%. **Change from 2000:** -1.1%. **Median travel time to work:** 25.4 minutes. **Working outside county of residence:** 39.3%.

Cities with pop over 10,000: None.

SAINT CHARLES COUNTY

201 N 2nd St   **Ph:** 636-949-7550
Saint Charles, MO 63301   **Fax:** 636-949-7552
www.saintcharlescounty.org

On central eastern border of MO, north of Saint Louis; original county; organized Oct 1, 1812 (prior to statehood). **Name Origin:** For Saint Carlo Borromeo (1538-84), archbishop of Milan and founder of the religious order of the Oblates of Saint Ambrose.

Area (sq mi): 592.35 (land 560.42; water 31.93). **Pop per sq mi:** 588.7.

Pop 2005: 329,940. **State rank:** 4. **Pop change:** 2000-20005 +16.2%; 1990-2000 +33.3%. **Pop 2000:** 283,883 (White 93.8%; Black or African American 2.7%; Hispanic or Latino 1.5%; Asian 0.9%; Other 1.8%). **Foreign born:** 2.1%. **Median age:** 34.3.

Income 2000: per capita $23,592; median household $57,258; **Pop below poverty level:** 4%. ***Personal per capita income 2000-2003:** $29,794-$31,587.

Unemployment 2004: 4.3%. **Change from 2000:** +1%. **Median travel time to work:** 26.4 minutes. **Working outside county of residence:** 53%.

Cities with pop over 10,000: 6 (see page 36 for cities).

SAINT CLAIR COUNTY

655 2nd St   **Ph:** 417-646-2315
Osceola, MO 64776   **Fax:** 417-646-8080

In west-central MO, northwest of Springfield; organized Jan 29,

1841 from Rives County. **Name Origin:** For Gen. Arthur Saint Clair (1736?-1818), an officer in the French and Indian War and the Revolutionary War, president of the Continental Congress (1787), and governor of the Northwest Territory (1788-1802).

Area (sq mi): 701.9 (land 676.66; water 25.25). **Pop per sq mi:** 14.3.

Pop 2005: 9,686. **State rank:** 91. **Pop change:** 2000-20005 +0.4%; 1990-2000 +14.1%. **Pop 2000:** 9,652 (White 96.7%; Black or African American 0.2%; Hispanic or Latino 1%; Asian 0.1%; Other 2.2%). **Foreign born:** 0.7%. **Median age:** 43.9.

Income 2000: per capita $14,025; median household $25,321; **Pop below poverty level:** 19.6%. ***Personal per capita income 2000-2003:** $17,294-$19,861.

Unemployment 2004: 6.5%. **Change from 2000:** +0.9%. **Median travel time to work:** 32.3 minutes. **Working outside county of residence:** 46.6%.

Cities with pop over 10,000: None.

SAINT FRANCOIS COUNTY

1 N Washington St Rm 206   **Ph:** 573-756-5411
Farmington, MO 63640   **Fax:** 573-431-6967

In southeastern MO, south of Saint Louis; established Dec 19, 1821 from Sainte Genevieve, Jefferson, and Washington counties. **Name Origin:** For the Saint Francois Mountains, part of which are in the county; French for Saint Francis.

Area (sq mi): 452.4 (land 449.46; water 2.94). **Pop per sq mi:** 137.2.

Pop 2005: 61,661. **State rank:** 17. **Pop change:** 2000-20005 +10.8%; 1990-2000 +13.8%. **Pop 2000:** 55,641 (White 95.7%; Black or African American 2%; Hispanic or Latino 0.8%; Asian 0.3%; Other 1.5%). **Foreign born:** 0.9%. **Median age:** 37.2.

Income 2000: per capita $15,273; median household $31,199; **Pop below poverty level:** 14.9%. ***Personal per capita income 2000-2003:** $19,819-$21,391.

Unemployment 2004: 6.9%. **Change from 2000:** -0.4%. **Median travel time to work:** 27.6 minutes. **Working outside county of residence:** 27.9%.

Cities with pop over 10,000: Farmington ⛪ (14,807).

SAINT LOUIS COUNTY

41 S Central Ave   **Ph:** 314-615-5432
Clayton, MO 63105   **Fax:** 314-615-7890
www.stlouisco.com

On the central-eastern border of MO on the Mississippi River, 11 mi. below its confluence with the Missouri River. Organized 1812; original county. **Name Origin:** For Louis IX (1214-70), crusader king of France, canonized in 1297.

Area (sq mi): 523.69 (land 507.81; water 15.89). **Pop per sq mi:** 1978.4.

Pop 2005: 1,004,666. **State rank:** 1. **Pop change:** 2000-20005 -1.1%; 1990-2000 +2.3%. **Pop 2000:** 1,016,315 (White 76%; Black or African American 19%; Hispanic or Latino 1.4%; Asian 2.2%; Other 2%). **Foreign born:** 4.2%. **Median age:** 37.5.

Income 2000: per capita $27,595; median household $50,532; **Pop below poverty level:** 6.9%. ***Personal per capita income 2000-2003:** $39,987-$43,225.

⛪ County Seat

Saint Louis County (cont'd)

Unemployment 2004: 5.4%. **Change from 2000:** +1.5%. **Median travel time to work:** 24 minutes. **Working outside county of residence:** 28%.

Cities with pop over 10,000: 19 (see page 36 for cities).

SAINT LOUIS (INDEPENDENT CITY)

1200 Market St	**Ph:** 314-622-3201
Saint Louis, MO 63103	**Fax:** 314-622-4061
stlouis.missouri.org	

On the central-eastern border of MO on the Mississippi River, 11 mi. below its confluence with the Missouri River. In 1763 site was selected by Pierre Laclede Liguest (1724?-78), partner in Maxent, Laclede and Company; settled 1764; chartered as city 1822. Busiest inland port on the Mississippi River; in early 1800s known as the 'Gateway to the West.' Manufacturing city (transportation equipment, automobile production); home of Anheuser-Busch, largest beer-producer in U.S. **Name Origin:** For Louis IX (1214-70), crusader king of France, canonized in 1297.

Area (sq mi): 66.15 (land 61.92; water 4.23). **Pop per sq mi:** 5561.4.

Pop 2005: 344,362. **State rank:** 3. **Pop change:** 2000-20005 -1.1%; 1990-2000 -12.2%. **Pop 2000:** 348,189 (White 42.9%; Black or African American 51.2%; Hispanic or Latino 2%; Asian 2%; Other 3%). **Foreign born:** 5.6%. **Median age:** 33.7.

Income 2000: per capita $16,108; median household $27,156; **Pop below poverty level:** 24.6%. ***Personal per capita income 2000-2003:** $24,685-$27,236.

Unemployment 2004: 9.1%. **Change from 2000:** +0.9%. **Median travel time to work:** 25.1 minutes. **Working outside county of residence:** 41.4%.

Cities with pop over 10,000: Saint Louis (343,279).

SAINTE GENEVIEVE COUNTY

55 S 3rd St	**Ph:** 573-883-5589
Sainte Genevieve, MO 63670	**Fax:** 573-883-5312

On southeastern border of MO, south of Saint Louis; original county; organized Oct 1, 1812 (prior to statehood). **Name Origin:** For the city, the oldest white settlement in MO; itself named for Sainte Genevieve (c. 422-c. 500), French nun and patron saint of Paris.

Area (sq mi): 508.94 (land 502.39; water 6.55). **Pop per sq mi:** 36.2.

Pop 2005: 18,198. **State rank:** 62. **Pop change:** 2000-20005 +2%; 1990-2000 +11.3%. **Pop 2000:** 17,842 (White 97.5%; Black or African American 0.7%; Hispanic or Latino 0.7%; Asian 0.2%; Other 1.1%). **Foreign born:** 0.6%. **Median age:** 37.7.

Income 2000: per capita $17,283; median household $39,200; **Pop below poverty level:** 8.2%. ***Personal per capita income 2000-2003:** $22,119-$23,254.

Unemployment 2004: 5.6%. **Change from 2000:** +0.4%. **Median travel time to work:** 25.9 minutes. **Working outside county of residence:** 41%.

Cities with pop over 10,000: None.

SALINE COUNTY

101 E Arrow St County Courthouse	**Ph:** 660-886-3331
Marshall, MO 65340	**Fax:** 660-886-2644

In central MO, east of Kansas City; organized Nov 25, 1820 (prior to statehood) from Cooper County. **Name Origin:** French 'salt spring' or 'lick.'

Area (sq mi): 764.59 (land 755.55; water 9.04). **Pop per sq mi:** 30.5.

Pop 2005: 23,075. **State rank:** 49. **Pop change:** 2000-20005 -2.9%; 1990-2000 +1%. **Pop 2000:** 23,756 (White 88.1%; Black or African American 5.4%; Hispanic or Latino 4.4%; Asian 0.4%; Other 4.2%). **Foreign born:** 3.5%. **Median age:** 37.2.

Income 2000: per capita $16,132; median household $32,743; **Pop below poverty level:** 13.2%. ***Personal per capita income 2000-2003:** $22,528-$25,592.

Unemployment 2004: 5.3%. **Change from 2000:** +0.1%. **Median travel time to work:** 17.1 minutes. **Working outside county of residence:** 14.8%.

Cities with pop over 10,000: Marshall 🏛 (12,103).

SCHUYLER COUNTY

PO Box 187	**Ph:** 660-457-3842
Lancaster, MO 63548	**Fax:** 660-457-3016

On the northeastern border of MO; organized Feb 14, 1845 from Adair County. **Name Origin:** For Gen. Philip John Schuyler (1733-1804), an officer in the Revolutionary War, member of the Continental Congress (1775-77; 1778-81), and U.S. senator from NY (1789-91; 1797-98).

Area (sq mi): 308.16 (land 307.87; water 0.29). **Pop per sq mi:** 14.

Pop 2005: 4,308. **State rank:** 112. **Pop change:** 2000-20005 +3.3%; 1990-2000 -1.6%. **Pop 2000:** 4,170 (White 98%; Black or African American 0%; Hispanic or Latino 0.6%; Asian 0.2%; Other 1.3%). **Foreign born:** 0.4%. **Median age:** 40.8.

Income 2000: per capita $15,850; median household $27,385; **Pop below poverty level:** 17%. ***Personal per capita income 2000-2003:** $17,969-$20,263.

Unemployment 2004: 6.3%. **Change from 2000:** +1%. **Median travel time to work:** 25 minutes. **Working outside county of residence:** 51.4%.

Cities with pop over 10,000: None.

SCOTLAND COUNTY

County Courthouse	
117 S Market St Suite 100	**Ph:** 660-465-7027
Memphis, MO 63555	**Fax:** 660-465-7785
www.scotlandcounty.net	

On the northeastern border of MO; organized Jan 29, 1841 from Clark, Lewis and Shelby counties. **Name Origin:** For the country, the former home of early settlers.

Area (sq mi): 439.25 (land 438.47; water 0.79). **Pop per sq mi:** 11.2.

Pop 2005: 4,928. **State rank:** 111. **Pop change:** 2000-20005 -1.1%; 1990-2000 +3.3%. **Pop 2000:** 4,983 (White 98.1%; Black or African American 0.2%; Hispanic or Latino 0.8%; Asian 0.1%; Other 0.9%). **Foreign born:** 0.3%. **Median age:** 37.4.

Source: Personal per capita income data are from the Bureau of Economic Analysis; per capita income data are from the Bureau of the Census. See Introduction for explanation of differences.

Scotland County (cont'd)

Income 2000: per capita $14,474; median household $27,409; **Pop below poverty level:** 16.8%. ***Personal per capita income 2000-2003:** $19,740-$21,113.

Unemployment 2004: 4.1%. **Change from 2000:** -0.2%. **Median travel time to work:** 21.9 minutes. **Working outside county of residence:** 28.6%.

Cities with pop over 10,000: None.

SCOTT COUNTY

131 S Winchester St
Benton, MO 63736

Ph: 573-545-3549
Fax: 573-545-3540

On the southeastern border of MO, south of Cape Girardeau; established Dec 28,1821 from New Madrid County. **Name Origin:** For John Scott (1785-1861), lawyer and U.S. representative from MO (1821-27).

Area (sq mi): 426.04 (land 421.01; water 5.03). **Pop per sq mi:** 97.7.

Pop 2005: 41,143. **State rank:** 26. **Pop change:** 2000-20005 +1.8%; 1990-2000 +2.7%. **Pop 2000:** 40,422 (White 87.1%; Black or African American 10.5%; Hispanic or Latino 1.1%; Asian 0.2%; Other 1.6%). **Foreign born:** 0.6%. **Median age:** 36.

Income 2000: per capita $15,620; median household $31,352; **Pop below poverty level:** 16.1%. ***Personal per capita income 2000-2003:** $21,906-$24,083.

Unemployment 2004: 6.1%. **Change from 2000:** +0.2%. **Median travel time to work:** 19.1 minutes. **Working outside county of residence:** 37.2%.

Cities with pop over 10,000: Sikeston (17,057).

SHANNON COUNTY

111 N Main St
Eminence, MO 65466

Ph: 573-226-3414
Fax: 573-226-5321

In south-central MO, east of Springfield; organized Jan 29, 1841 from Ripley County. **Name Origin:** For George F. 'Peg-leg' Shannon (1785-1836), a member of the Lewis and Clark expedition.

Area (sq mi): 1003.99 (land 1003.83; water 0.15). **Pop per sq mi:** 8.3.

Pop 2005: 8,367. **State rank:** 98. **Pop change:** 2000-20005 +0.5%; 1990-2000 +9.3%. **Pop 2000:** 8,324 (White 94.5%; Black or African American 0.2%; Hispanic or Latino 0.9%; Asian 0%; Other 4.7%, including 1.8% American Indian/Alaska Native). **Foreign born:** 0.5%. **Median age:** 38.8.

Income 2000: per capita $11,492; median household $20,878; **Pop below poverty level:** 26.9%. ***Personal per capita income 2000-2003:** $15,675-$17,191.

Unemployment 2004: 8.6%. **Change from 2000:** +2%. **Median travel time to work:** 26.1 minutes. **Working outside county of residence:** 37.2%.

Cities with pop over 10,000: None.

SHELBY COUNTY

100 E Main St
Shelbyville, MO 63469

Ph: 573-633-2181
Fax: 573-633-1004

In northeastern MO, northeast of Columbia; organized Jan 2, 1835

from Marion County. **Name Origin:** For Gen. Isaac Shelby (1750-1826), officer in the Revolutionary War, NC legislator, and governor of KY (1792-96; 1812-16).

Area (sq mi): 502.43 (land 500.93; water 1.49). **Pop per sq mi:** 13.5.

Pop 2005: 6,744. **State rank:** 104. **Pop change:** 2000-20005 -0.8%; 1990-2000 -2.1%. **Pop 2000:** 6,799 (White 97.5%; Black or African American 1%; Hispanic or Latino 0.6%; Asian 0.1%; Other 1.1%). **Foreign born:** 0.8%. **Median age:** 40.4.

Income 2000: per capita $15,632; median household $29,448; **Pop below poverty level:** 16.3%. ***Personal per capita income 2000-2003:** $23,817-$22,837.

Unemployment 2004: 5.9%. **Change from 2000:** -0.9%. **Median travel time to work:** 20.5 minutes. **Working outside county of residence:** 28.5%.

Cities with pop over 10,000: None.

STODDARD COUNTY

316 S Prairie St
Bloomfield, MO 63825

Ph: 573-568-3339
Fax: 573-568-2194

In southeastern MO, southwest of Cape Girardeau; organized Jun 21, 1835 from Cape Girardeau County. **Name Origin:** For Capt. Amos Stoddard (1762-1813), an officer in the Revolutionary War and acting governor of LA Territory (1804-05).

Area (sq mi): 828.94 (land 827.12; water 1.82). **Pop per sq mi:** 35.9.

Pop 2005: 29,714. **State rank:** 37. **Pop change:** 2000-20005 +0%; 1990-2000 +2.8%. **Pop 2000:** 29,705 (White 96.9%; Black or African American 0.9%; Hispanic or Latino 0.8%; Asian 0.1%; Other 1.6%). **Foreign born:** 0.5%. **Median age:** 39.1.

Income 2000: per capita $14,656; median household $26,987; **Pop below poverty level:** 16.5%. ***Personal per capita income 2000-2003:** $19,994-$23,206.

Unemployment 2004: 6%. **Change from 2000:** -1%. **Median travel time to work:** 21.1 minutes. **Working outside county of residence:** 29.5%.

Cities with pop over 10,000: None.

STONE COUNTY

108 4th St
Galena, MO 65656
www.stoneco-mo.us

Ph: 417-357-6127
Fax: 417-357-6861

On the southwestern border of MO, south of Springfield; organized Feb 10, 1851 from Taney County. **Name Origin:** For either William Stone, a prominent judge, or John W. Stone, an early settler.

Area (sq mi): 510.91 (land 463.22; water 47.68). **Pop per sq mi:** 66.8.

Pop 2005: 30,931. **State rank:** 36. **Pop change:** 2000-20005 +7.9%; 1990-2000 +50.2%. **Pop 2000:** 28,658 (White 97%; Black or African American 0.1%; Hispanic or Latino 1%; Asian 0.2%; Other 2.1%). **Foreign born:** 1.1%. **Median age:** 44.1.

Income 2000: per capita $18,036; median household $32,637; **Pop below poverty level:** 12.8%. ***Personal per capita income 2000-2003:** $22,104-$24,503.

Stone County (cont'd)

Unemployment 2004: 8.4%. **Change from 2000:** -1.5%. **Median travel time to work:** 30.1 minutes. **Working outside county of residence:** 54%.

Cities with pop over 10,000: None.

SULLIVAN COUNTY

109 N Main St	**Ph:** 660-265-3786
Milan, MO 63556	**Fax:** 660-265-3724

In north-central MO; organized Feb 14, 1845 from Linn County. **Name Origin:** For either James Sullivan, a prominent local resident, or for Sullivan County, TN, which was named for Gen. John Sullivan (1740-95), Revolutionary War officer, member of the Continental Congress, chief executive and governor (1786-87, 1789) of NH.

Area (sq mi): 651.43 (land 650.95; water 0.48). **Pop per sq mi:** 10.6.

Pop 2005: 6,907. **State rank:** 103. **Pop change:** 2000-20005 -4.3%; 1990-2000 +14.1%. **Pop 2000:** 7,219 (White 90.2%; Black or African American 0.1%; Hispanic or Latino 8.8%; Asian 0.1%; Other 4.7%). **Foreign born:** 5.8%. **Median age:** 38.9.

Income 2000: per capita $13,392; median household $26,107; **Pop below poverty level:** 16.5%. ***Personal per capita income 2000-2003:** $22,116-$20,855.

Unemployment 2004: 6.7%. **Change from 2000:** +3.1%. **Median travel time to work:** 21.2 minutes. **Working outside county of residence:** 21.7%.

Cities with pop over 10,000: None.

TANEY COUNTY

266-A Main St	**Ph:** 417-546-7200
Forsyth, MO 65653	**Fax:** 417-546-2519
www.co.taney.mo.us	

On southwestern border of MO, south of Springfield; organized Jan 6, 1837 from Greene County. **Name Origin:** For Roger Brooke Taney (1777-1864), Chief Justice of the U.S. Supreme Court (1836-64), who wrote the decision in the Dred Scott Case.

Area (sq mi): 651.48 (land 632.36; water 19.12). **Pop per sq mi:** 68.

Pop 2005: 42,985. **State rank:** 22. **Pop change:** 2000-20005 +8.3%; 1990-2000 +55.3%. **Pop 2000:** 39,703 (White 94.8%; Black or African American 0.3%; Hispanic or Latino 2.4%; Asian 0.3%; Other 3.1%). **Foreign born:** 2%. **Median age:** 38.8.

Income 2000: per capita $17,267; median household $30,898; **Pop below poverty level:** 12.4%. ***Personal per capita income 2000-2003:** $22,377-$23,509.

Unemployment 2004: 9%. **Change from 2000:** +1.1%. **Median travel time to work:** 21.7 minutes. **Working outside county of residence:** 9.1%.

Cities with pop over 10,000: None.

TEXAS COUNTY

210 N Grand Ave	**Ph:** 417-967-2112
Houston, MO 65483	**Fax:** 417-967-3837

In south-central MO, east of Springfield; organized as Ashley County Feb 17, 1843 from Shannon and Wright counties; name changed Feb 14, 1845. **Name Origin:** Probably in honor of the admission of the state of TX.

Area (sq mi): 1179.24 (land 1178.54; water 0.7). **Pop per sq mi:** 20.9.

Pop 2005: 24,614. **State rank:** 44. **Pop change:** 2000-20005 +7%; 1990-2000 +7.1%. **Pop 2000:** 23,003 (White 95.8%; Black or African American 0.2%; Hispanic or Latino 1%; Asian 0.3%; Other 3%, including 1% American Indian/Alaska Native). **Foreign born:** 0.8%. **Median age:** 40.4.

Income 2000: per capita $13,799; median household $24,545; **Pop below poverty level:** 21.4%. ***Personal per capita income 2000-2003:** $16,276-$17,107.

Unemployment 2004: 6.9%. **Change from 2000:** -0.2%. **Median travel time to work:** 27.2 minutes. **Working outside county of residence:** 31.8%.

Cities with pop over 10,000: None.

VERNON COUNTY

100 W Cherry St	**Ph:** 417-448-2500
Nevada, MO 64772	**Fax:** 417-667-6035
www.vernoncountymo.org	

On central western border of MO, north of Joplin; organized Feb 17, 1851 from Bates County. **Name Origin:** For Col. Miles Vernon (1786-1866), veteran of the Battle of New Orleans and MO legislator.

Area (sq mi): 837.04 (land 833.95; water 3.09). **Pop per sq mi:** 24.5.

Pop 2005: 20,441. **State rank:** 54. **Pop change:** 2000-20005 -0.1%; 1990-2000 +7.4%. **Pop 2000:** 20,454 (White 96.5%; Black or African American 0.6%; Hispanic or Latino 0.8%; Asian 0.3%; Other 2.1%). **Foreign born:** 1.3%. **Median age:** 37.1.

Income 2000: per capita $15,047; median household $30,021; **Pop below poverty level:** 14.9%. ***Personal per capita income 2000-2003:** $20,826-$22,475.

Unemployment 2004: 5.3%. **Change from 2000:** +1.5%. **Median travel time to work:** 20.9 minutes. **Working outside county of residence:** 21.3%.

Cities with pop over 10,000: None.

WARREN COUNTY

104 W Main St	**Ph:** 636-456-3331
Warrenton, MO 63383	**Fax:** 636-456-1801
www.co.warren.mo.us	

In east-central MO, west of Saint Louis; organized Jan 5, 1833 from Montgomery County. **Name Origin:** For Gen. Joseph Warren (1741-75), Revolutionary War patriot and member of the Committee of Safety who dispatched Paul Revere (1735-1818) on his famous ride (1775).

Area (sq mi): 437.74 (land 431.31; water 6.43). **Pop per sq mi:** 66.7.

Pop 2005: 28,764. **State rank:** 39. **Pop change:** 2000-20005 +17.3%; 1990-2000 +25.6%. **Pop 2000:** 24,525 (White 95.1%; Black or African American 1.9%; Hispanic or Latino 1.3%; Asian 0.2%; Other 1.8%). **Foreign born:** 1.5%. **Median age:** 37.4.

*Source: Personal per capita income data are from the Bureau of Economic Analysis; per capita income data are from the Bureau of the Census. See Introduction for explanation of differences.

Warren County (cont'd)

Income 2000: per capita $19,690; median household $41,016; **Pop below poverty level:** 8.6%. ***Personal per capita income 2000-2003:** $24,062-$25,656.

Unemployment 2004: 5.3%. **Change from 2000:** +0.2%. **Median travel time to work:** 29.4 minutes. **Working outside county of residence:** 56.8%.

Cities with pop over 10,000: None.

WASHINGTON COUNTY

102 N Missouri St
Potosi, MO 63664

Ph: 573-438-4901
Fax: 573-438-4038

In east-central MO, southwest of Saint Louis; organized Aug 21, 1813 (prior to statehood) from Sainte Genevieve County. **Name Origin:** For George Washington (1732-99), American patriot and first U.S. president.

Area (sq mi): 762.46 (land 759.59; water 2.87). **Pop per sq mi:** 31.6.

Pop 2005: 24,032. **State rank:** 47. **Pop change:** 2000-20005 +2.9%; 1990-2000 +14.5%. **Pop 2000:** 23,344 (White 94.9%; Black or African American 2.5%; Hispanic or Latino 0.7%; Asian 0.1%; Other 2%). **Foreign born:** 0.7%. **Median age:** 35.2.

Income 2000: per capita $12,934; median household $27,112; **Pop below poverty level:** 20.8%. ***Personal per capita income 2000-2003:** $16,207-$18,174.

Unemployment 2004: 8.4%. **Change from 2000:** -0.3%. **Median travel time to work:** 36.5 minutes. **Working outside county of residence:** 51.6%.

Cities with pop over 10,000: None.

WAYNE COUNTY

109 Walnut St County Courthouse
Greenville, MO 63944

Ph: 573-224-3011
Fax: 573-224-5609

In southeastern MO, southwest of Cape Giradeau; organized Dec 11, 1818 (prior to statehood) from Cape Girardeau and Lawrence counties. **Name Origin:** For Gen. Anthony Wayne (1745-96), PA soldier and statesman, nicknamed 'Mad Anthony' for his daring during the Revolutionary War.

Area (sq mi): 774.09 (land 761.03; water 13.05). **Pop per sq mi:** 17.2.

Pop 2005: 13,097. **State rank:** 78. **Pop change:** 2000-20005 -1.2%; 1990-2000 +14.9%. **Pop 2000:** 13,259 (White 97.3%; Black or African American 0.2%; Hispanic or Latino 0.5%; Asian 0.1%; Other 2.1%). **Foreign born:** 0.3%. **Median age:** 42.5.

Income 2000: per capita $13,434; median household $24,007; **Pop below poverty level:** 21.9%. ***Personal per capita income 2000-2003:** $16,313-$18,649.

Unemployment 2004: 7.4%. **Change from 2000:** -4.2%. **Median travel time to work:** 33.3 minutes. **Working outside county of residence:** 42.9%.

Cities with pop over 10,000: None.

WEBSTER COUNTY

101 S Crittenden St County
Courthouse Rm 12
Marshfield, MO 65706

Ph: 417-468-2223
Fax: 417-468-5307

In south-central MO, east of Springfield; organized Mar 3, 1855 from Greene County. **Name Origin:** For Daniel Webster (1782-1852), U.S. statesman and orator from MA.

Area (sq mi): 593.69 (land 593.32; water 0.37). **Pop per sq mi:** 58.6.

Pop 2005: 34,745. **State rank:** 32. **Pop change:** 2000-20005 +11.9%; 1990-2000 +30.7%. **Pop 2000:** 31,045 (White 95.4%; Black or African American 1.2%; Hispanic or Latino 1.3%; Asian 0.3%; Other 2.4%). **Foreign born:** 0.8%. **Median age:** 34.6.

Income 2000: per capita $14,502; median household $31,929; **Pop below poverty level:** 14.8%. ***Personal per capita income 2000-2003:** $18,066-$19,249.

Unemployment 2004: 4.7%. **Change from 2000:** +0.3%. **Median travel time to work:** 29 minutes. **Working outside county of residence:** 55.5%.

Cities with pop over 10,000: None.

WORTH COUNTY

PO Box 450
Grant City, MO 64456

Ph: 660-564-2219
Fax: 660-564-2432

On the northwestern border of MO, northeast of Saint Joseph; organized Feb 8, 1861 from Gentry County. **Name Origin:** For Gen. William Jenkins Worth (1794-1849), officer in the War of 1812, Seminole War, and the Mexican-American War; cited by Congress for bravery.

Area (sq mi): 266.75 (land 266.52; water 0.23). **Pop per sq mi:** 8.2.

Pop 2005: 2,174. **State rank:** 115. **Pop change:** 2000-20005 -8.7%; 1990-2000 -2.4%. **Pop 2000:** 2,382 (White 98.7%; Black or African American 0.2%; Hispanic or Latino 0.3%; Asian 0.1%; Other 0.7%). **Foreign born:** 0.2%. **Median age:** 41.9.

Income 2000: per capita $14,367; median household $27,471; **Pop below poverty level:** 14.3%. ***Personal per capita income 2000-2003:** $17,522-$19,559.

Unemployment 2004: 4.4%. **Change from 2000:** -0.6%. **Median travel time to work:** 24.7 minutes. **Working outside county of residence:** 38.6%.

Cities with pop over 10,000: None.

WRIGHT COUNTY

125 Court Sq
Hartville, MO 65667
www.wrightcountymo.com

Ph: 417-741-6661
Fax: 417-741-6142

In south-central MO, east of Springfield; organized Jan 29, 1841 from Pulaski County. **Name Origin:** For Silas Wright (1795-1847), NY governor (1844-46), U.S. representative, and senator (1833-45).

Area (sq mi): 683.18 (land 682.13; water 1.05). **Pop per sq mi:** 26.8.

Pop 2005: 18,306. **State rank:** 61. **Pop change:** 2000-20005 +2%; 1990-2000 +7.1%. **Pop 2000:** 17,955 (White 97.1%; Black or African American 0.3%; Hispanic or Latino 0.8%; Asian 0.1%; Other 2%). **Foreign born:** 0.9%. **Median age:** 37.7.

Wright County (cont'd)

Income 2000: per capita $13,135; median household $24,691; **Pop below poverty level:** 21.7%. ***Personal per capita income 2000-2003:** $16,759-$17,559.

Unemployment 2004: 6.7%. **Change from 2000:** -2.6%. **Median travel time to work:** 26.6 minutes. **Working outside county of residence:** 35.4%.

Cities with pop over 10,000: None.

*Source: Personal per capita income data are from the Bureau of Economic Analysis; per capita income data are from the Bureau of the Census.
See Introduction for explanation of differences.

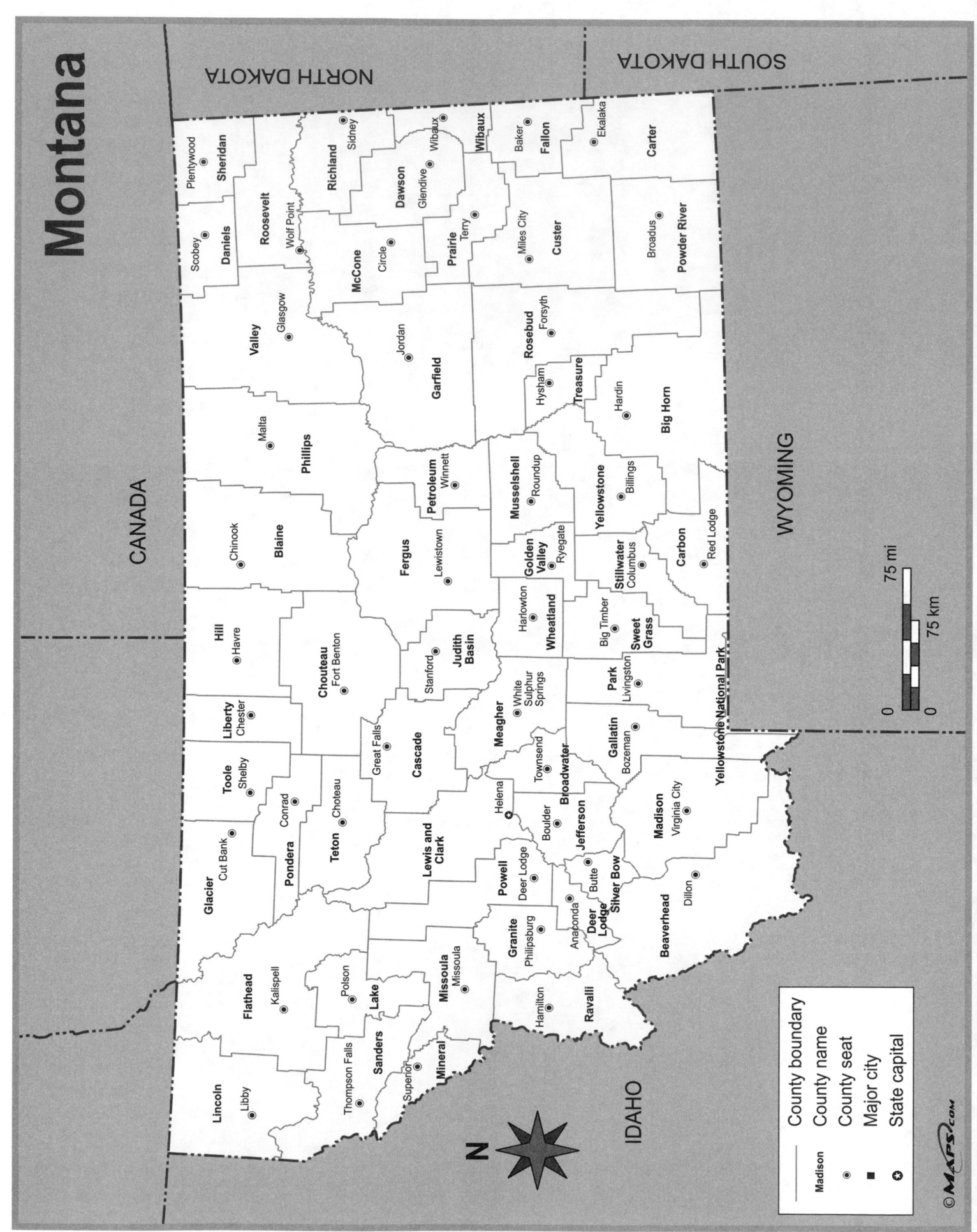

Montana

CANADA

NORTH DAKOTA

SOUTH DAKOTA

WYOMING

IDAHO

Plentywood • Sheridan

Scobey • Daniels

Sidney •

Richland

Wibaux • Wibaux

Baker • Fallon

Ekalaka •

Carter

Roosevelt
Wolf Point •

Dawson
Glendive •

McCone
Circle •

Prairie
Terry •

Miles City •
Custer

Broadus •
Powder River

Valley
Glasgow •

Garfield
Jordan •

Rosebud
Forsyth •

Treasure
Hysham •

Hardin •
Big Horn

Phillips
Malta •

Petroleum
Winnett •

Musselshell
Roundup •

Yellowstone
Billings •

Blaine
Chinook •

Fergus
Lewistown •

Golden
Valley
Ryegate •

Stillwater
Columbus •

Carbon
Red Lodge •

Hill
Havre •

Chouteau
Fort Benton •

Judith
Basin
Stanford •

Harlowton •
Wheatland

Big Timber •
Sweet
Grass

Liberty
Chester •

Cascade
Great Falls •

Meagher
White
Sulphur
Springs •

Park
Livingston •

Toole
Shelby •

Pondera
Conrad •

Teton
Choteau •

Lewis and
Clark

Helena ✪

Broadwater
Townsend •

Boulder •

Gallatin
Bozeman •

Glacier
Cut Bank •

Powell
Deer Lodge •

Jefferson

Madison
Virginia City •

Yellowstone National Park

Flathead
Kalispell •

Lake
Polson •

Missoula
Missoula •

Granite
Philipsburg •

Anaconda •
Deer
Lodge

Butte •
Silver Bow

Beaverhead
Dillon •

Lincoln
Libby •

Sanders
Thompson Falls •

Mineral
Superior •

Ravalli
Hamilton •

N

Legend

Madison — County name

—— County boundary

⊙ County seat

■ Major city

✪ State capital

0 75 mi

0 75 km

©MAPS.com

Montana

MONTANA STATE INFORMATION
www.mt.gov   **Ph:** 406-444-2511

Area (sq mi): 14,7042.4 (land 145,552.43; water 1489.96). **Pop per sq mi:** 6.4.

Pop 2005: 935,670. **Pop change:** 2000-20005 +3.7%; 1990-2000 +12.9%. **Pop 2000:** 902,195 (White 89.5%; Black or African American 0.3%; Hispanic or Latino 2%; Asian 0.5%; Other 8.6%, including 6.2% American Indian/Alaska Native). **Foreign born:** 1.8%. **Median age:** 37.5.

Income 2000: per capita $17,151; median household $33,024; **Pop below poverty level:** 14.6%. ***Personal per capita income 2000-2003:** $22,929-$25,406.

Unemployment 2004: 4.3%. **Change from 2000:** -0.5%. **Median travel time to work:** 17.7 minutes. **Working outside county of residence:** 8.3%.

ANACONDA-DEER LODGE COUNTY
800 Main St   **Ph:** 406-563-4060
Anaconda, MT 59711   **Fax:** 406-563-4001
www.anacondamt.org

In southwestern MT, west of Butte; original county; organized Feb 2, 1865 (prior to statehood). **Name Origin:** Descriptive of the area where deer came to the salt licks.

Area (sq mi): 741.16 (land 736.98; water 4.19). **Pop per sq mi:** 12.1.

Pop 2005: 8,948. **State rank:** 23. **Pop change:** 2000-20005 -5%; 1990-2000 -8.4%. **Pop 2000:** 9,417 (White 94.7%; Black or African American 0.2%; Hispanic or Latino 1.6%; Asian 0.4%; Other 3.6%, including 1.8% American Indian/Alaska Native). **Foreign born:** 1.4%. **Median age:** 42.3.

Income 2000: per capita $15,580; median household $26,305; **Pop below poverty level:** 15.8%. ***Personal per capita income 2000-2003:** $20,020-$21,417.

Unemployment 2004: 6.3%. **Change from 2000:** -0.5%. **Median travel time to work:** 21.1 minutes. **Working outside county of residence:** 26.7%.

Cities with pop over 10,000: None.

BEAVERHEAD COUNTY
2 S Pacific St   **Ph:** 406-683-5245
Dillon, MT 59725   **Fax:** 406-683-3769
www.beaverhead.com

On the southwestern border of MT, south of Butte; original county; organized Feb 2, 1865 (prior to statehood); annexed part of Madison

County in 1911. **Name Origin:** For the Beaverhead River, which contains a rock formation that the Indians thought resembled a beaver's head.

Area (sq mi): 5572.04 (land 5542.31; water 29.73). **Pop per sq mi:** 1.6.

Pop 2005: 8,773. **State rank:** 24. **Pop change:** 2000-20005 -4.7%; 1990-2000 +9.2%. **Pop 2000:** 9,202 (White 94.4%; Black or African American 0.2%; Hispanic or Latino 2.7%; Asian 0.2%; Other 3.8%, including 1.5% American Indian/Alaska Native). **Foreign born:** 1.6%. **Median age:** 37.6.

Income 2000: per capita $15,621; median household $28,962; **Pop below poverty level:** 17.1%. ***Personal per capita income 2000-2003:** $21,418-$24,204.

Unemployment 2004: 3.6%. **Change from 2000:** +0.3%. **Median travel time to work:** 14.4 minutes. **Working outside county of residence:** 6.3%.

Cities with pop over 10,000: None.

BIG HORN COUNTY
121 W 3rd St   **Ph:** 406-665-9735
Hardin, MT 59034   **Fax:** 406-665 9738

On the central southern border of MT, south of Billings; organized Jan 13, 1913 from Rosebud and Yellowstone counties. **Name Origin:** For the Big Horn and Little Big Horn rivers that flow through it; the rivers named for the great droves of bighorn sheep on the hillsides.

Area (sq mi): 5014.65 (land 4994.81; water 19.84). **Pop per sq mi:** 2.6.

Pop 2005: 13,149. **State rank:** 14. **Pop change:** 2000-20005 +3.8%; 1990-2000 +11.8%. **Pop 2000:** 12,671 (White 35.2%; Black or African American 0%; Hispanic or Latino 3.7%; Asian 0.2%; Other 63.2%, including 59.7% American Indian/Alaska Native). **Foreign born:** 0.8%. **Median age:** 29.8.

Income 2000: per capita $10,792; median household $27,684; **Pop below poverty level:** 29.2%. ***Personal per capita income 2000-2003:** $15,940-$17,063.

Unemployment 2004: 9%. **Change from 2000:** -7.8%. **Median travel time to work:** 20.8 minutes. **Working outside county of residence:** 14%.

Cities with pop over 10,000: None.

BLAINE COUNTY
400 Ohio St   **Ph:** 406-357-3250
Chinook, MT 59523   **Fax:** 406-357-2199

On the central northern border of MT, northeast of Great Falls;

Blaine County (cont'd)

organized Feb 29, 1912 from Chouteau County. **Name Origin:** For James Gillespie Blaine (1830-93), U.S. representative from ME (1863-76), U.S. senator (1876-81), and U.S. secretary of state (1881; 1889-92).

Area (sq mi): 4238.92 (land 4226.18; water 12.74). **Pop per sq mi:** 1.6.

Pop 2005: 6,629. **State rank:** 30. **Pop change:** 2000-20005 -5.4%; 1990-2000 +4.2%. **Pop 2000:** 7,009 (White 52.4%; Black or African American 0.2%; Hispanic or Latino 1%; Asian 0.1%; Other 47.1%, including 45.4% American Indian/Alaska Native). **Foreign born:** 1.4%. **Median age:** 34.4.

Income 2000: per capita $12,101; median household $25,247; **Pop below poverty level:** 28.1%. ***Personal per capita income 2000-2003:** $15,946-$16,136.

Unemployment 2004: 4.6%. **Change from 2000:** -1%. **Median travel time to work:** 16.1 minutes. **Working outside county of residence:** 8.7%.

Cities with pop over 10,000: None.

BROADWATER COUNTY

515 Broadway　　　　　　　**Ph:** 406-266-3443
Townsend, MT 59644　　　　**Fax:** 406-266-3674

In west-central MT, east of Helena; organized Feb 9, 1895 from Jefferson and Meagher counties. **Name Origin:** For Col. Charles A. Broadwater (1840-92), miner, businessman, president of the Montana Central Railroad, and local resort proprietor.

Area (sq mi): 1238.94 (land 1191.35; water 47.59). **Pop per sq mi:** 3.8.

Pop 2005: 4,517. **State rank:** 35. **Pop change:** 2000-20005 +3%; 1990-2000 +32.2%. **Pop 2000:** 4,385 (White 96.1%; Black or African American 0.3%; Hispanic or Latino 1.3%; Asian 0.1%; Other 2.6%, including 1.2% American Indian/Alaska Native). **Foreign born:** 1.4%. **Median age:** 41.3.

Income 2000: per capita $16,237; median household $32,689; **Pop below poverty level:** 10.8%. ***Personal per capita income 2000-2003:** $19,326-$20,787.

Unemployment 2004: 4%. **Change from 2000:** -0.3%. **Median travel time to work:** 22.7 minutes. **Working outside county of residence:** 30%.

Cities with pop over 10,000: None.

BUTTE-SILVER BOW COUNTY

155 W Granite St　　　　　　**Ph:** 406-497-6200
Butte, MT 59703　　　　　　**Fax:** 406-497-6328
www.co.silverbow.mt.us

In southwestern MT, southwest of Helena; organized Feb 16, 1881 (prior to statehood) from Deer Lodge County. **Name Origin:** For Silver Bow Creek, which runs through the county; named by prospectors who saw the sun shining 'like a silver bow' on its waters.

Area (sq mi): 718.97 (land 718.31; water 0.66). **Pop per sq mi:** 45.9.

Pop 2005: 32,982. **State rank:** 8. **Pop change:** 2000-20005 -4.7%; 1990-2000 +2%. **Pop 2000:** 34,606 (White 93.7%; Black or African American 0.2%; Hispanic or Latino 2.7%; Asian 0.4%; Other 4.1%, including 2% American Indian/Alaska Native). **Foreign born:** 1.6%. **Median age:** 38.9.

Income 2000: per capita $17,009; median household $30,402; **Pop below poverty level:** 14.9%. ***Personal per capita income 2000-2003:** $22,691-$26,522.

Unemployment 2004: 4.8%. **Change from 2000:** -0.3%. **Median travel time to work:** 14.3 minutes. **Working outside county of residence:** 7%.

Cities with pop over 10,000: Butte ⚒ (32,393).

CARBON COUNTY

17 W 11th St　　　　　　　　**Ph:** 406-446-1220
Red Lodge, MT 59068　　　　**Fax:** 406-446-2640
www.co.carbon.mt.us/gp/

On the central southern border of MT, southwest of Billings; organized Mar 4, 1895 from Park and Yellowstone counties. **Name Origin:** For the abundant coal deposits within its borders.

Area (sq mi): 2062.19 (land 2047.99; water 14.2). **Pop per sq mi:** 4.8.

Pop 2005: 9,902. **State rank:** 20. **Pop change:** 2000-20005 +3.7%; 1990-2000 +18.2%. **Pop 2000:** 9,552 (White 96.2%; Black or African American 0.3%; Hispanic or Latino 1.8%; Asian 0.4%; Other 2.3%). **Foreign born:** 1.6%. **Median age:** 41.9.

Income 2000: per capita $17,204; median household $32,139; **Pop below poverty level:** 11.6%. ***Personal per capita income 2000-2003:** $24,050-$25,518.

Unemployment 2004: 3.9%. **Change from 2000:** -0.7%. **Median travel time to work:** 28.1 minutes. **Working outside county of residence:** 32.4%.

Cities with pop over 10,000: None.

CARTER COUNTY

214 Park St　　　　　　　　**Ph:** 406-775-8749
Ekalaka, MT 59324　　　　　**Fax:** 406-775-8750
www.cartercountymt.com

In the southeastern corner of MT; organized Feb 22, 1917 from Fallon County. **Name Origin:** For Thomas Henry Carter (1854-1911), first U.S. senator from MT (1895-1901; 1905-11).

Area (sq mi): 3348.29 (land 3339.57; water 8.73). **Pop per sq mi:** 0.4.

Pop 2005: 1,320. **State rank:** 50. **Pop change:** 2000-20005 -2.9%; 1990-2000 -9.5%. **Pop 2000:** 1,360 (White 98.5%; Black or African American 0.1%; Hispanic or Latino 0.6%; Asian 0.1%; Other 1.2%). **Foreign born:** 1%. **Median age:** 41.8.

Income 2000: per capita $13,280; median household $26,313; **Pop below poverty level:** 18.1%. ***Personal per capita income 2000-2003:** $18,686-$17,727.

Unemployment 2004: 2.9%. **Change from 2000:** +0.6%. **Median travel time to work:** 22.5 minutes. **Working outside county of residence:** 9.7%.

Cities with pop over 10,000: None.

---

*Source: Personal per capita income data are from the Bureau of Economic Analysis; per capita income data are from the Bureau of the Census. See Introduction for explanation of differences.

CASCADE COUNTY

121 4th St N
Suite 10B, MT 59401
www.co.cascade.mt.us

Ph: 406-454-6800
Fax: 406-454-6703

In central MT, northeast of Helena; organized Sep 12, 1887 (prior to statehood) from Chouteau and Meagher counties. **Name Origin:** For the falls in the Missouri River, which runs through the northern part of the county.

Area (sq mi): 2711.65 (land 2697.9; water 13.75). **Pop per sq mi:** 29.5.

Pop 2005: 79,569. **State rank:** 4. **Pop change:** 2000-20005 -1%; 1990-2000 +3.4%. **Pop 2000:** 80,357 (White 89.5%; Black or African American 1.1%; Hispanic or Latino 2.4%; Asian 0.8%; Other 7.4%, including 4.2% American Indian/Alaska Native). **Foreign born:** 2.4%. **Median age:** 36.7.

Income 2000: per capita $17,566; median household $32,971; **Pop below poverty level:** 13.5%. ***Personal per capita income 2000-2003:** $24,528-$27,523.

Unemployment 2004: 4.2%. **Change from 2000:** -0.3%. **Median travel time to work:** 15.9 minutes. **Working outside county of residence:** 2.8%.

Cities with pop over 10,000: Great Falls 🏛 (56,503).

CHOUTEAU COUNTY

1308 Franklin St
Fort Benton, MT 59442
www.co.chouteau.mt.us

Ph: 406-622-5151
Fax: 406-622-3012

In north-central MT, north of Great Falls; original county; organized Feb 2, 1865 (prior to statehood). **Name Origin:** For the Chouteau family, whose members included Auguste (1749-1829) and Pierre (1758-1849), fur traders.

Area (sq mi): 3997 (land 3973.24; water 23.76). **Pop per sq mi:** 1.4.

Pop 2005: 5,463. **State rank:** 33. **Pop change:** 2000-20005 -8.5%; 1990-2000 +9.5%. **Pop 2000:** 5,970 (White 83.9%; Black or African American 0.1%; Hispanic or Latino 0.7%; Asian 0.2%; Other 15.6%, including 14.6% American Indian/Alaska Native). **Foreign born:** 1.9%. **Median age:** 39.3.

Income 2000: per capita $14,851; median household $29,150; **Pop below poverty level:** 20.5%. ***Personal per capita income 2000-2003:** $19,984-$22,541.

Unemployment 2004: 3.3%. **Change from 2000:** +0.2%. **Median travel time to work:** 19.7 minutes. **Working outside county of residence:** 20.6%.

Cities with pop over 10,000: None.

CUSTER COUNTY

1010 Main St
Miles City, MT 59301
www.co.chouteau.mt.us

Ph: 406-874-3343
Fax: 406-874-3452

In southeastern MT; original county; organized as Big Horn County Feb 2, 1865 (prior to statehood); name changed Feb 16, 1877. **Name Origin:** For Gen. George Armstrong Custer (1839-76), U.S. army officer defeated at the Battle of Little Bighorn (1876).

Area (sq mi): 3793.22 (land 3783.13; water 10.09). **Pop per sq mi:** 3.

Pop 2005: 11,267. **State rank:** 16. **Pop change:** 2000-20005 -3.7%; 1990-2000 +0%. **Pop 2000:** 11,696 (White 96%; Black or African American 0.1%; Hispanic or Latino 1.5%; Asian 0.3%; Other 2.7%, including 1.3% American Indian/Alaska Native). **Foreign born:** 1.4%. **Median age:** 39.3.

Income 2000: per capita $15,876; median household $30,000; **Pop below poverty level:** 15.1%. ***Personal per capita income 2000-2003:** $21,738-$23,428.

Unemployment 2004: 4%. **Change from 2000:** +0.3%. **Median travel time to work:** 11.9 minutes. **Working outside county of residence:** 4.5%.

Cities with pop over 10,000: None.

DANIELS COUNTY

213 Main St
Scobey, MT 59263
www.scobey.org

Ph: 406-487-5561
Fax: 406-487-5583

On the northeastern border of MT; organized Aug 30, 1920 from Sheridan and Valley counties. **Name Origin:** For Mansfield A. Daniels, an early rancher and storekeeper.

Area (sq mi): 1426.52 (land 1426.09; water 0.43). **Pop per sq mi:** 1.3.

Pop 2005: 1,836. **State rank:** 47. **Pop change:** 2000-20005 -9%; 1990-2000 -11%. **Pop 2000:** 2,017 (White 95.7%; Black or African American 0%; Hispanic or Latino 1.6%; Asian 0.2%; Other 3.7%, including 1.3% American Indian/Alaska Native). **Foreign born:** 4.7%. **Median age:** 47.

Income 2000: per capita $16,055; median household $27,306; **Pop below poverty level:** 16.9%. ***Personal per capita income 2000-2003:** $27,908-$26,351.

Unemployment 2004: 3.9%. **Change from 2000:** +1.1%. **Median travel time to work:** 12.5 minutes. **Working outside county of residence:** 5.3%.

Cities with pop over 10,000: None.

DAWSON COUNTY

207 W Bell St
Glendive, MT 59330
www.dawsoncountymontana.org

Ph: 406-377-3058
Fax: 406-377-1717

In central eastern MT; original county, organized Jan 15, 1869 (prior to statehood). **Name Origin:** For Maj. Andrew Dawson, commander of Fort Benton for the American Fur Company.

Area (sq mi): 2383.13 (land 2373.14; water 9.99). **Pop per sq mi:** 3.7.

Pop 2005: 8,688. **State rank:** 25. **Pop change:** 2000-20005 -4.1%; 1990-2000 -4.7%. **Pop 2000:** 9,059 (White 97%; Black or African American 0.3%; Hispanic or Latino 0.9%; Asian 0.1%; Other 2.1%, including 1.2% American Indian/Alaska Native). **Foreign born:** 1.1%. **Median age:** 41.

Income 2000: per capita $15,368; median household $31,393; **Pop below poverty level:** 14.9%. ***Personal per capita income 2000-2003:** $20,473-$22,590.

Unemployment 2004: 4%. **Change from 2000:** +1.3%. **Median travel time to work:** 13.1 minutes. **Working outside county of residence:** 5.4%.

Dawson County (cont'd)

Cities with pop over 10,000: None.

FALLON COUNTY

10 W Fallon St   **Ph:** 406-778-7114
Baker, MT 59313   **Fax:** 406-778-2815

On southeastern border of MT; organized Dec 9, 1913 from Custer County. **Name Origin:** For Benjamin O'Fallon (1793-1842), army officer, Indian agent, and nephew of the explorer William Clark (1770-1838).

Area (sq mi): 1623.02 (land 1620.33; water 2.69). **Pop per sq mi:** 1.7.

Pop 2005: 2,717. **State rank:** 42. **Pop change:** 2000-20005 -4.2%; 1990-2000 -8.6%. **Pop 2000:** 2,837 (White 98.3%; Black or African American 0.1%; Hispanic or Latino 0.4%; Asian 0.4%; Other 0.9%). **Foreign born:** 1%. **Median age:** 41.1.

Income 2000: per capita $16,014; median household $29,944; **Pop below poverty level:** 12.5%. ***Personal per capita income 2000-2003:** $20,605-$23,523.

Unemployment 2004: 2.8%. **Change from 2000:** +0.2%. **Median travel time to work:** 14.9 minutes. **Working outside county of residence:** 8.8%.

Cities with pop over 10,000: None.

FERGUS COUNTY

712 W Main St   **Ph:** 406-538-5119
Lewistown, MT 59457   **Fax:** 406-538-9023
www.co.fergus.mt.us

In central MT, northwest of Billings; organized Mar 12, 1885 (prior to statehood) from Meagher County. Its county seat is in the exact center of MT. **Name Origin:** For James Fergus (1813-97), cattleman, miner, and a MT territorial legislator.

Area (sq mi): 4350.36 (land 4339.17; water 11.2). **Pop per sq mi:** 2.7.

Pop 2005: 11,551. **State rank:** 15. **Pop change:** 2000-20005 -2.9%; 1990-2000 -1.6%. **Pop 2000:** 11,893 (White 96.7%; Black or African American 0.1%; Hispanic or Latino 0.8%; Asian 0.2%; Other 2.7%, including 1.2% American Indian/Alaska Native). **Foreign born:** 1%. **Median age:** 42.4.

Income 2000: per capita $15,808; median household $30,409; **Pop below poverty level:** 15.4%. ***Personal per capita income 2000-2003:** $21,348-$23,052.

Unemployment 2004: 5%. **Change from 2000:** -0.8%. **Median travel time to work:** 16.4 minutes. **Working outside county of residence:** 3.8%.

Cities with pop over 10,000: None.

FLATHEAD COUNTY

800 S Main St   **Ph:** 406-758-5503
Kalispell, MT 59901   **Fax:** 406-758-5861
www.co.flathead.mt.us

On the northwestern border of MT, north of Missoula; organized Feb 6, 1893 from Missoula County; annexed part of Deer Lodge County before 1900. **Name Origin:** For the Salish or Flathead

Indians of the Catawba group; there is no evidence that they flattened the heads of their infants, as some other tribes did. It has been suggested the name comes from their home at the 'flat' head of the Columbia River rather than in the deep canyons below.

Area (sq mi): 5256.45 (land 5098.34; water 158.11). **Pop per sq mi:** 16.3.

Pop 2005: 83,172. **State rank:** 3. **Pop change:** 2000-20005 +11.7%; 1990-2000 +25.8%. **Pop 2000:** 74,471 (White 95.4%; Black or African American 0.2%; Hispanic or Latino 1.4%; Asian 0.5%; Other 3.1%, including 1.1% American Indian/Alaska Native). **Foreign born:** 2.1%. **Median age:** 39.

Income 2000: per capita $18,112; median household $34,466; **Pop below poverty level:** 13%. ***Personal per capita income 2000-2003:** $24,001-$25,981.

Unemployment 2004: 5.4%. **Change from 2000:** -0.5%. **Median travel time to work:** 19 minutes. **Working outside county of residence:** 3.2%.

Cities with pop over 10,000: Kalispell ⛪ (17,381).

GALLATIN COUNTY

311 W Main St Rm 203   **Ph:** 406-582-3050
Bozeman, MT 59715   **Fax:** 406-582-3068
www.co.gallatin.mt.us

On the southwestern border of MT, east of Butte; original county; organized Feb 2, 1865 (prior to statehood). Annexed populated portion of deleted Yellowstone National Park (county equivalent) effective November 7, 1997. **Name Origin:** For the Gallatin River, which flows through the county; itself named by Lewis and Clark in 1805 for Abraham Alfonse Albert Gallatin (1761-1849), U.S. secretary of the treasury (1802-14) at the time.

Area (sq mi): 2631.84 (land 2605.84; water 26). **Pop per sq mi:** 30.

Pop 2005: 78,210. **State rank:** 5. **Pop change:** 2000-20005 +15.3%; 1990-2000 +34.4%. **Pop 2000:** 67,831 (White 95.3%; Black or African American 0.2%; Hispanic or Latino 1.5%; Asian 0.9%; Other 2.7%). **Foreign born:** 2.7%. **Median age:** 30.7.

Income 2000: per capita $19,074; median household $38,120; **Pop below poverty level:** 12.8%. ***Personal per capita income 2000-2003:** $24,885-$27,211.

Unemployment 2004: 3.3%. **Change from 2000:** +0.8%. **Median travel time to work:** 17 minutes. **Working outside county of residence:** 4.2%.

Cities with pop over 10,000: Bozeman ⛪ (32,414).

GARFIELD COUNTY

352 Leavitt St   **Ph:** 406-557-6254
Jordan, MT 59337   **Fax:** 406-557-2567
www.garfieldcounty.com

In east-central MT, northeast of Billings; organized Feb 7, 1919 from Valley and McCone counties. **Name Origin:** For James Abram Garfield (1831-81), twentieth U.S. president.

Area (sq mi): 4847.54 (land 4668.06; water 179.48). **Pop per sq mi:** 0.3.

Pop 2005: 1,199. **State rank:** 51. **Pop change:** 2000-20005 -6.3%; 1990-2000 -19.5%. **Pop 2000:** 1,279 (White 98.8%; Black or African

---

*Source: Personal per capita income data are from the Bureau of Economic Analysis; per capita income data are from the Bureau of the Census. See Introduction for explanation of differences.

Garfield County (cont'd)

American 0.1%; Hispanic or Latino 0.4%; Asian 0.1%; Other 0.7%). **Foreign born:** 1.1%. **Median age:** 41.6.

Income 2000: per capita $13,930; median household $25,917; **Pop below poverty level:** 21.5%. ***Personal per capita income 2000-2003:** $20,067-$23,094.

Unemployment 2004: 0.5%. **Change from 2000:** 1.3%. **Median travel time to work:** 13.2 minutes. **Working outside county of residence:** 4.3%.

Cities with pop over 10,000: None.

GLACIER COUNTY

512 E Main St   **Ph:** 406-873-5063
Cut Bank, MT 59427   **Fax:** 406-873-2125
www.glaciercountymt.org

On the northwestern border of MT, northwest of Great Falls, bordering Alberta province, Canada and Glacier National Park; organized Feb 17, 1919 from Flathead and Teton counties. **Name Origin:** For Glacier National Park on the county's western border.

Area (sq mi): 3037.11 (land 2994.72; water 42.39). **Pop per sq mi:** 4.5.

Pop 2005: 13,552. **State rank:** 13. **Pop change:** 2000-20005 +2.3%; 1990-2000 +9.3%. **Pop 2000:** 13,247 (White 35.3%; Black or African American 0.1%; Hispanic or Latino 1.2%; Asian 0.1%; Other 64.5%, including 61.8% American Indian/Alaska Native). **Foreign born:** 2.1%. **Median age:** 30.6.

Income 2000: per capita $11,597; median household $27,921; **Pop below poverty level:** 27.3%. ***Personal per capita income 2000-2003:** $16,378-$18,549.

Unemployment 2004: 8%. **Change from 2000:** -3.1%. **Median travel time to work:** 14.9 minutes. **Working outside county of residence:** 4.6%.

Cities with pop over 10,000: None.

GOLDEN VALLEY COUNTY

107 Kemp St   **Ph:** 406-568-2231
Ryegate, MT 59074   **Fax:** 406-568-2598
www.co.golden-valley.mt.us

In south-central MT, northwest of Billings; organized Oct 4, 1920 from Musselshell and Sweet Grass counties. **Name Origin:** For the rich soil and plentiful streams.

Area (sq mi): 1176.4 (land 1175.3; water 1.1). **Pop per sq mi:** 1.

Pop 2005: 1,159. **State rank:** 52. **Pop change:** 2000-20005 +11.2%; 1990-2000 +14.3%. **Pop 2000:** 1,042 (White 97.9%; Black or African American 0%; Hispanic or Latino 1.2%; Asian 0.1%; Other 0.8%). **Foreign born:** 2.6%. **Median age:** 41.5.

Income 2000: per capita $13,573; median household $27,308; **Pop below poverty level:** 25.8%. ***Personal per capita income 2000-2003:** $18,444-$17,735.

Unemployment 2004: 5.5%. **Change from 2000:** +0.8%. **Median travel time to work:** 29.2 minutes. **Working outside county of residence:** 26.8%.

Cities with pop over 10,000: None.

GRANITE COUNTY

220 N Sansome St PO Box 925   **Ph:** 406-859-3771
Philipsburg, MT 59858   **Fax:** 406-859-3817
www.co.granite.mt.us

In west-central MT, northwest of Butte; organized Mar 2, 1893 from Deer Lodge County. **Name Origin:** For the Granite Mountain Silver Mine, itself named for the granite rock within the mine.

Area (sq mi): 1733.11 (land 1727.44; water 5.67). **Pop per sq mi:** 1.7.

Pop 2005: 2,965. **State rank:** 41. **Pop change:** 2000-20005 +4.8%; 1990-2000 +11.1%. **Pop 2000:** 2,830 (White 95.3%; Black or African American 0%; Hispanic or Latino 1.3%; Asian 0.1%; Other 3.6%, including 1.3% American Indian/Alaska Native). **Foreign born:** 1%. **Median age:** 42.8.

Income 2000: per capita $16,636; median household $27,813; **Pop below poverty level:** 16.8%. ***Personal per capita income 2000-2003:** $19,317-$22,194.

Unemployment 2004: 5.2%. **Change from 2000:** -2.5%. **Median travel time to work:** 26.4 minutes. **Working outside county of residence:** 26.3%.

Cities with pop over 10,000: None.

HILL COUNTY

315 4th St   **Ph:** 406-265-5481
Havre, MT 59501   **Fax:** 406-265-3693
co.hill.mt.us

On the central northern border of MT, northeast of Great Falls; organized Feb 28, 1912 from Chouteau County. **Name Origin:** For James Jerome Hill (1838-1916), president and developer of the Great Northern Railroad.

Area (sq mi): 2916.05 (land 2896.36; water 19.69). **Pop per sq mi:** 5.6.

Pop 2005: 16,304. **State rank:** 11. **Pop change:** 2000-20005 -2.2%; 1990-2000 -5.6%. **Pop 2000:** 16,673 (White 79.1%; Black or African American 0.1%; Hispanic or Latino 1.2%; Asian 0.4%; Other 20%, including 17.3% American Indian/Alaska Native). **Foreign born:** 2%. **Median age:** 34.5.

Income 2000: per capita $14,935; median household $30,781; **Pop below poverty level:** 18.4%. ***Personal per capita income 2000-2003:** $22,404-$24,624.

Unemployment 2004: 4.4%. **Change from 2000:** +0.3%. **Median travel time to work:** 12.5 minutes. **Working outside county of residence:** 4.9%.

Cities with pop over 10,000: None.

JEFFERSON COUNTY

PO Box H   **Ph:** 406-225-4020
Boulder, MT 59632   **Fax:** 406-225-4149
www.co.jefferson.mt.us

In west-central MT, east of Butte; original county, organized Feb 2, 1865 (prior to statehood). **Name Origin:** For the Jefferson River, which forms part of the county's southern border; itself named by Lewis and Clark for Thomas Jefferson (1743-1826), third U.S. president.

Area (sq mi): 1658.83 (land 1656.64; water 2.19). **Pop per sq mi:** 6.7.

Jefferson County (cont'd)

Pop 2005: 11,170. **State rank:** 17. **Pop change:** 2000-20005 +11.2%; 1990-2000 +26.6%. **Pop 2000:** 10,049 (White 95.2%; Black or African American 0.1%; Hispanic or Latino 1.5%; Asian 0.4%; Other 3.5%, including 1.3% American Indian/Alaska Native). **Foreign born:** 1%. **Median age:** 40.2.

Income 2000: per capita $18,250; median household $41,506; **Pop below poverty level:** 9%. *****Personal per capita income 2000-2003:** $24,989-$26,489.

Unemployment 2004: 4.2%. **Change from 2000:** -0.2%. **Median travel time to work:** 22.4 minutes. **Working outside county of residence:** 61.2%.

Cities with pop over 10,000: None.

JUDITH BASIN COUNTY
11 3rd St NW　　　　　　　　　　**Ph:** 406-566-2277
Stanford, MT 59479　　　　　　　**Fax:** 406-566-2211

In central MT, southeast of Great Falls; organized Dec 10, 1920 from Fergus and Cascade counties. **Name Origin:** For the basin of the Judith River, which flows through the county; named by Meriwether Lewis (1774-1809) for his cousin, Judith Hancock, who later married Lt. William Clark (1770-1838).

Area (sq mi): 1870.71 (land 1869.85; water 0.86). **Pop per sq mi:** 1.2.

Pop 2005: 2,198. **State rank:** 43. **Pop change:** 2000-20005 -5.6%; 1990-2000 +2.1%. **Pop 2000:** 2,329 (White 98.2%; Black or African American 0%; Hispanic or Latino 0.6%; Asian 0.1%; Other 1.2%). **Foreign born:** 1.4%. **Median age:** 42.

Income 2000: per capita $14,291; median household $29,241; **Pop below poverty level:** 21.1%. *****Personal per capita income 2000-2003:** $18,601-$18,980.

Unemployment 2004: 4.1%. **Change from 2000:** +0.4%. **Median travel time to work:** 17.5 minutes. **Working outside county of residence:** 21.8%.

Cities with pop over 10,000: None.

LAKE COUNTY
106 4th Ave E　　　　　　　　　　**Ph:** 406-883-7208
Polson, MT 59860　　　　　　　　**Fax:** 406-883-7283
www.lakecounty-mt.org

In northwestern MT, north of Missoula; organized May 11, 1923 from Flathead and Missoula counties. **Name Origin:** For Flathead Lake, which comprises most of the northern part of the county.

Area (sq mi): 1653.72 (land 1493.77; water 159.95). **Pop per sq mi:** 18.9.

Pop 2005: 28,297. **State rank:** 9. **Pop change:** 2000-20005 +6.8%; 1990-2000 +26%. **Pop 2000:** 26,507 (White 70.6%; Black or African American 0.1%; Hispanic or Latino 2.5%; Asian 0.3%; Other 28.2%, including 23.8% American Indian/Alaska Native). **Foreign born:** 1.6%. **Median age:** 38.2.

Income 2000: per capita $15,173; median household $28,740; **Pop below poverty level:** 18.7%. *****Personal per capita income 2000-2003:** $18,291-$19,399.

Unemployment 2004: 5.8%. **Change from 2000:** -2.8%. **Median travel time to work:** 18.4 minutes. **Working outside county of residence:** 16.3%.

Cities with pop over 10,000: None.

LEWIS & CLARK COUNTY
316 N Park Ave　　　　　　　　　**Ph:** 406-447-8200
Helena, MT 59623　　　　　　　　**Fax:** 406-447-8370
www.co.lewis-clark.mt.us

In west-central MT in the Helena metro area. **Name Origin:** For the Lewis & Clark Expedition.

Area (sq mi): 3497.56 (land 3460.96; water 36.6). **Pop per sq mi:** 16.9.

Pop 2005: 58,449. **State rank:** 6. **Pop change:** 2000-20005 +4.9%; 1990-2000 +17.3%. **Pop 2000:** 55,716 (White 94.4%; Black or African American 0.2%; Hispanic or Latino 1.5%; Asian 0.5%; Other 4.1%, including 2% American Indian/Alaska Native). **Foreign born:** 1.6%. **Median age:** 38.

Income 2000: per capita $18,763; median household $37,360; **Pop below poverty level:** 10.9%. *****Personal per capita income 2000-2003:** $25,489-$28,079.

Unemployment 2004: 3.9%. **Change from 2000:** -0.4%. **Median travel time to work:** 16.7 minutes. **Working outside county of residence:** 4.4%.

Cities with pop over 10,000: Helena 🏛 (27,196).

LIBERTY COUNTY
111 1st St E　　　　　　　　　　**Ph:** 406-759-5365
Chester, MT 59522　　　　　　　**Fax:** 406-759-5395
www.co.lewis-clark.mt.us

On the central northern border of MT, north of Great Falls; organized Feb 11, 1920 from Chouteau and Hill counties. **Name Origin:** For the inhabitants' 'freedom' from Hill County.

Area (sq mi): 1447.19 (land 1429.76; water 17.44). **Pop per sq mi:** 1.4.

Pop 2005: 2,003. **State rank:** 45. **Pop change:** 2000-20005 -7.2%; 1990-2000 -6%. **Pop 2000:** 2,158 (White 99.1%; Black or African American 0%; Hispanic or Latino 0.2%; Asian 0.3%; Other 0.5%). **Foreign born:** 1.4%. **Median age:** 41.5.

Income 2000: per capita $14,882; median household $30,284; **Pop below poverty level:** 20.3%. *****Personal per capita income 2000-2003:** $20,142-$22,741.

Unemployment 2004: 4%. **Change from 2000:** +1.1%. **Median travel time to work:** 16.1 minutes. **Working outside county of residence:** 9%.

Cities with pop over 10,000: None.

LINCOLN COUNTY
512 California Ave　　　　　　　**Ph:** 406-293-7781
Libby, MT 59923　　　　　　　　**Fax:** 406-293-8577
www.lincolncountymt.us/

On the northwestern corner of MT; organized Mar 9, 1909 from Flathead County. **Name Origin:** For Abraham Lincoln (1809-65), sixteenth U.S. president.

Source: Personal per capita income data are from the Bureau of Economic Analysis; per capita income data are from the Bureau of the Census. See Introduction for explanation of differences.

434

Lincoln County (cont'd)

Area (sq mi): 3675.11 (land 3612.67; water 62.44). **Pop per sq mi:** 5.3.

Pop 2005: 19,193. **State rank:** 10. **Pop change:** 2000-20005 +1.9%; 1990-2000 +7.8%. **Pop 2000:** 18,837 (White 95.1%; Black or African American 0.1%; Hispanic or Latino 1.4%; Asian 0.3%; Other 3.5%, including 1.2% American Indian/Alaska Native). **Foreign born:** 1.4%. **Median age:** 42.1.

Income 2000: per capita $13,923; median household $26,754; **Pop below poverty level:** 19.2%. ***Personal per capita income 2000-2003:** $17,783-$19,832.

Unemployment 2004: 9.7%. **Change from 2000:** -1.6%. **Median travel time to work:** 17.6 minutes. **Working outside county of residence:** 8.1%.

Cities with pop over 10,000: None.

MADISON COUNTY

100 Wallace St　　　　　　**Ph:** 406-843-4230
Virginia City, MT 59755　　**Fax:** 406-843-5207

In southwestern MT, southeast of Butte; original county; organized Feb 2, 1865 (prior to statehood). **Name Origin:** For the Madison River, which flows through the county; itself named by Lewis and Clark for James Madison (1751-1836), then secretary of state (1801-09), later fourth U.S. president.

Area (sq mi): 3602.85 (land 3586.54; water 16.31). **Pop per sq mi:** 2.

Pop 2005: 7,274. **State rank:** 27. **Pop change:** 2000-20005 +6.2%; 1990-2000 +14.4%. **Pop 2000:** 6,851 (White 96%; Black or African American 0%; Hispanic or Latino 1.9%; Asian 0.3%; Other 2.7%). **Foreign born:** 1.4%. **Median age:** 43.4.

Income 2000: per capita $16,944; median household $30,233; **Pop below poverty level:** 12.1%. ***Personal per capita income 2000-2003:** $19,702-$21,468.

Unemployment 2004: 3.8%. **Change from 2000:** +0.4%. **Median travel time to work:** 22.4 minutes. **Working outside county of residence:** 18%.

Cities with pop over 10,000: None.

MCCONE COUNTY

1004 C Ave　　　　　　　**Ph:** 406-485-3505
Circle, MT 59215　　　　**Fax:** 406-485-2689
circle-montana.com

In east-central MT; organized Feb 20, 1919 from Dawson and Richland counties. **Name Origin:** For George McCone, a MT state legislator.

Area (sq mi): 2682.77 (land 2642.53; water 40.25). **Pop per sq mi:** 0.7.

Pop 2005: 1,805. **State rank:** 48. **Pop change:** 2000-20005 -8.7%; 1990-2000 -13.1%. **Pop 2000:** 1,977 (White 96.3%; Black or African American 0.3%; Hispanic or Latino 1%; Asian 0.3%; Other 2.5%, including 1.1% American Indian/Alaska Native). **Foreign born:** 0.7%. **Median age:** 42.4.

Income 2000: per capita $15,162; median household $29,718; **Pop below poverty level:** 16.8%. ***Personal per capita income 2000-2003:** $19,905-$20,469.

Unemployment 2004: 2.8%. **Change from 2000:** +0.5%. **Median travel time to work:** 15.1 minutes. **Working outside county of residence:** 19.6%.

Cities with pop over 10,000: None.

MEAGHER COUNTY

15 W Main St　　　　　　**Ph:** 406-547-3612
White Sulphur Springs, MT 59645　　**Fax:** 406 547 3388

In central MT, east of Helena; original county; organized Nov 16, 1867 (prior to statehood) from Chouteau and Gallatin counties; annexed part of Fergus County in 1911. **Name Origin:** For Thomas Francis Meagher (1823-67), Irish revolutionary tried for sedition and banished to Tasmania. He escaped to New York Cilty, where he practiced law. He became a brigadier general in the Civil War and led the 'Irish Brigade.' He was acting governor of MT Territory (1865-66).

Area (sq mi): 2394.83 (land 2391.82; water 3.02). **Pop per sq mi:** 0.8.

Pop 2005: 1,999. **State rank:** 46. **Pop change:** 2000-20005 +3.5%; 1990-2000 +6.2%. **Pop 2000:** 1,932 (White 96.8%; Black or African American 0%; Hispanic or Latino 1.5%; Asian 0.2%; Other 2.7%, including 1% American Indian/Alaska Native). **Foreign born:** 1.8%. **Median age:** 42.8.

Income 2000: per capita $15,019; median household $29,375; **Pop below poverty level:** 18.9%. ***Personal per capita income 2000-2003:** $19,893-$20,640.

Unemployment 2004: 5.4%. **Change from 2000:** -0.5%. **Median travel time to work:** 16.6 minutes. **Working outside county of residence:** 11.1%.

Cities with pop over 10,000: None.

MINERAL COUNTY

300 River St　　　　　　**Ph:** 406-822-3520
Superior, MT 59872　　　**Fax:** 406-822-3579
www.co.mineral.mt.us

On the central western border of MT, west of Missoula; organized Aug 7, 1914 from Missoula County. **Name Origin:** For its many mines.

Area (sq mi): 1223.38 (land 1219.82; water 3.56). **Pop per sq mi:** 3.3.

Pop 2005: 4,014. **State rank:** 38. **Pop change:** 2000-20005 +3.3%; 1990-2000 +17.2%. **Pop 2000:** 3,884 (White 93.6%; Black or African American 0.2%; Hispanic or Latino 1.6%; Asian 0.5%; Other 4.7%, including 1.9% American Indian/Alaska Native). **Foreign born:** 1.5%. **Median age:** 41.1.

Income 2000: per capita $15,166; median household $27,143; **Pop below poverty level:** 15.8%. ***Personal per capita income 2000-2003:** $17,036-$20,588.

Unemployment 2004: 6%. **Change from 2000:** -2.2%. **Median travel time to work:** 22.6 minutes. **Working outside county of residence:** 25.1%.

Cities with pop over 10,000: None.

MISSOULA COUNTY

200 W Broadway St   **Ph:** 406-523-4780
Missoula, MT 59802   **Fax:** 406-258-4899
www.co.missoula.mt.us

In west-central MT; original county; organized Feb 2, 1865 (prior to statehood). **Name Origin:** From a Salish (Flathead) Indian word whose meaning is in dispute; possibly 'feared water,' 'at the stream of surprise and ambush,' or 'river of awe'; believed to refer to Hell Gate Canyon where Blackfeet Indians ambushed the Salish.

Area (sq mi): 2618.34 (land 2597.97; water 20.37). **Pop per sq mi:** 38.5.

Pop 2005: 100,086. **State rank:** 2. **Pop change:** 2000-20005 +4.5%; 1990-2000 +21.8%. **Pop 2000:** 95,802 (White 93.1%; Black or African American 0.3%; Hispanic or Latino 1.6%; Asian 1%; Other 4.7%, including 2.3% American Indian/Alaska Native). **Foreign born:** 2.3%. **Median age:** 33.2.

Income 2000: per capita $17,808; median household $34,454; **Pop below poverty level:** 14.8%. *****Personal per capita income 2000-2003:** $24,383-$27,997.

Unemployment 2004: 4%. **Change from 2000:** +0.4%. **Median travel time to work:** 17.5 minutes. **Working outside county of residence:** 4.6%.

Cities with pop over 10,000: Missoula 🏛 (61,790).

MUSSELSHELL COUNTY

506 Main St   **Ph:** 406-323-1104
Roundup, MT 59072   **Fax:** 406-323-3303

In south-central MT, north of Billings; organized Feb 11, 1911 from Fergus, Yellowstone, and Meagher counties. **Name Origin:** For the Musselshell River, which forms part of the county's eastern border, the river was named for the mussel shells found on its banks.

Area (sq mi): 1870.91 (land 1867.15; water 3.76). **Pop per sq mi:** 2.4.

Pop 2005: 4,497. **State rank:** 36. **Pop change:** 2000-20005 +0%; 1990-2000 +9.5%. **Pop 2000:** 4,497 (White 95.9%; Black or African American 0.1%; Hispanic or Latino 1.6%; Asian 0.2%; Other 2.9%, including 1.3% American Indian/Alaska Native). **Foreign born:** 2%. **Median age:** 43.2.

Income 2000: per capita $15,389; median household $25,527; **Pop below poverty level:** 19.9%. *****Personal per capita income 2000-2003:** $15,674-$17,703.

Unemployment 2004: 5.8%. **Change from 2000:** -0.8%. **Median travel time to work:** 25 minutes. **Working outside county of residence:** 22.2%.

Cities with pop over 10,000: None.

PARK COUNTY

414 E Callender St   **Ph:** 406-222-4110
Livingston, MT 59047
www.parkcounty.org

On the southern border of MT, east of Bozeman; organized Feb 23, 1887 (prior to statehood) from Gallatin County. Annexed unpopulated portion of deleted Yellowstone National Park (county equivalent) effective November 7, 1997. **Name Origin:** For Yellowstone National Park, which is on the county's southern border.

Area (sq mi): 2813.59 (land 2802.41; water 11.18). **Pop per sq mi:** 5.7.

Pop 2005: 15,968. **State rank:** 12. **Pop change:** 2000-20005 +1.7%; 1990-2000 +7.8%. **Pop 2000:** 15,694 (White 95.5%; Black or African American 0.4%; Hispanic or Latino 1.8%; Asian 0.4%; Other 2.6%). **Foreign born:** 2.7%. **Median age:** 40.6.

Income 2000: per capita $17,704; median household $31,739; **Pop below poverty level:** 11.4%. *****Personal per capita income 2000-2003:** $21,093-$22,894.

Unemployment 2004: 4.4%. **Change from 2000:** -0.3%. **Median travel time to work:** 21.3 minutes. **Working outside county of residence:** 20.8%.

Cities with pop over 10,000: None.

PETROLEUM COUNTY

201 E Main St   **Ph:** 406-429-5311
Winnett, MT 59087   **Fax:** 406-429-6328

In central MT, north of Billings; organized Feb 22, 1925 from Fergus County. **Name Origin:** For the petroleum production in the Cat Creek fields.

Area (sq mi): 1674.01 (land 1653.9; water 20.11). **Pop per sq mi:** 0.3.

Pop 2005: 470. **State rank:** 56. **Pop change:** 2000-20005 -4.7%; 1990-2000 -5%. **Pop 2000:** 493 (White 98.2%; Black or African American 0%; Hispanic or Latino 1.2%; Asian 0%; Other 0.8%). **Foreign born:** 0.6%. **Median age:** 41.1.

Income 2000: per capita $15,986; median household $24,107; **Pop below poverty level:** 23.2%. *****Personal per capita income 2000-2003:** $15,388-$18,442.

Unemployment 2004: 5%. **Change from 2000:** +2.6%. **Median travel time to work:** 11.7 minutes. **Working outside county of residence:** 12.7%.

Cities with pop over 10,000: None.

PHILLIPS COUNTY

314 S 2nd Ave W PO Box 360   **Ph:** 406-654-2423
Malta, MT 59538   **Fax:** 406-654-2429

On central northern border of MT; organized Feb 5, 1915 from Blaine and Valley counties. **Name Origin:** For Benjamin D. Phillips, a local landowner and prominent citizen.

Area (sq mi): 5212.17 (land 5139.57; water 72.6). **Pop per sq mi:** 0.8.

Pop 2005: 4,179. **State rank:** 37. **Pop change:** 2000-20005 -9.2%; 1990-2000 -10.9%. **Pop 2000:** 4,601 (White 88.8%; Black or African American 0.2%; Hispanic or Latino 1.2%; Asian 0.3%; Other 10.1%, including 7.6% American Indian/Alaska Native). **Foreign born:** 1%. **Median age:** 40.8.

Income 2000: per capita $15,058; median household $28,702; **Pop below poverty level:** 18.3%. *****Personal per capita income 2000-2003:** $18,726-$20,306.

Unemployment 2004: 4.5%. **Change from 2000:** +0.1%. **Median travel time to work:** 14.3 minutes. **Working outside county of residence:** 6.1%.

Cities with pop over 10,000: None.

Source: Personal per capita income data are from the Bureau of Economic Analysis; per capita income data are from the Bureau of the Census. See Introduction for explanation of differences.

PONDERA COUNTY

20 4th Ave SW   **Ph:** 406-271-4000
Conrad, MT 59425   **Fax:** 406-271-4070
www.ponderacountymontana.org

In northwest-central MT, northwest of Great Falls; organized Feb 17, 1919 from Chouteau and Teton counties. **Name Origin:** From French #it1pend d'oreille 'hanging ear,' first applied to a lake in ID, thought to resemble an earlobe. To avoid confusion with the lake and town, name was changed to Pondera.

Area (sq mi): 1639.85 (land 1624.7; water 15.16). **Pop per sq mi:** 3.7.

Pop 2005: 6,087. **State rank:** 32. **Pop change:** 2000-20005 -5.2%; 1990-2000 -0.1%. **Pop 2000:** 6,424 (White 83.2%; Black or African American 0.1%; Hispanic or Latino 0.8%; Asian 0.1%; Other 16.1%, including 14.5% American Indian/Alaska Native). **Foreign born:** 1.6%. **Median age:** 38.6.

Income 2000: per capita $14,276; median household $30,464; **Pop below poverty level:** 18.8%. ***Personal per capita income 2000-2003:** $20,283-$21,847.

Unemployment 2004: 5.4%. **Change from 2000:** +1.2%. **Median travel time to work:** 15.8 minutes. **Working outside county of residence:** 14.6%.

Cities with pop over 10,000: None.

POWDER RIVER COUNTY

PO Box 270   **Ph:** 406-436-2657
Broadus, MT 59317   **Fax:** 406-436-2151

On the southeastern border of MT, southeast of Billings; organized Mar 7, 1919 from Custer County. **Name Origin:** For the river, which runs diagonally through the county; the river's name comes either from the fine black sand resembling gunpowder that is found along its banks, or from an incident when a group of soldiers were attacked by Indians, and one yelled 'hide the powder!'

Area (sq mi): 3297.94 (land 3297.18; water 0.76). **Pop per sq mi:** 0.5.

Pop 2005: 1,705. **State rank:** 49. **Pop change:** 2000-20005 -8.2%; 1990-2000 -11.1%. **Pop 2000:** 1,858 (White 97%; Black or African American 0%; Hispanic or Latino 0.6%; Asian 0.1%; Other 2.5%, including 1.8% American Indian/Alaska Native). **Foreign born:** 0.6%. **Median age:** 42.1.

Income 2000: per capita $15,351; median household $28,398; **Pop below poverty level:** 12.9%. ***Personal per capita income 2000-2003:** $17,629-$18,947.

Unemployment 2004: 4%. **Change from 2000:** +2.1%. **Median travel time to work:** 13.2 minutes. **Working outside county of residence:** 12.8%.

Cities with pop over 10,000: None.

POWELL COUNTY

409 Missouri Ave   **Ph:** 406-846 3680
Deer Lodge, MT 59722   **Fax:** 406-846-2784
www.powellcountymontana.com

In west-central MT, west of Helena; organized Jan 31, 1901 from Deer Lodge County. **Name Origin:** For John Wesley Powell (1834-1902), geologist and explorer of the Grand Canyon (1870), director of the U.S. Geological Survey, and first head of the U.S. Bureau of Reclamation.

Area (sq mi): 2332.68 (land 2325.94; water 6.74). **Pop per sq mi:** 3.

Pop 2005: 6,999. **State rank:** 29. **Pop change:** 2000-20005 -2.5%; 1990-2000 +8.5%. **Pop 2000:** 7,180 (White 91.5%; Black or African American 0.5%; Hispanic or Latino 1.9%; Asian 0.4%; Other 6.5%, including 3.5% American Indian/Alaska Native). **Foreign born:** 0.6%. **Median age:** 39.7.

Income 2000: per capita $13,816; median household $30,625; **Pop below poverty level:** 12.6%. ***Personal per capita income 2000-2003:** $17,613-$18,746.

Unemployment 2004: 6.2%. **Change from 2000:** +1.4%. **Median travel time to work:** 22.3 minutes. **Working outside county of residence:** 21.2%.

Cities with pop over 10,000: None.

PRAIRIE COUNTY

217 W Park St   **Ph:** 406-635-5575
Terry, MT 59349   **Fax:** 406-635-5576

In east-central MT, north of Miles City; organized Feb 5, 1915 from Custer, Dawson, and Fallon counties. **Name Origin:** For the topography of most of the eastern half of the state.

Area (sq mi): 1742.56 (land 1736.55; water 6). **Pop per sq mi:** 0.6.

Pop 2005: 1,105. **State rank:** 53. **Pop change:** 2000-20005 -7.8%; 1990-2000 -13.3%. **Pop 2000:** 1,199 (White 97.7%; Black or African American 0%; Hispanic or Latino 0.7%; Asian 0.2%; Other 1.9%). **Foreign born:** 1.2%. **Median age:** 48.9.

Income 2000: per capita $14,422; median household $25,451; **Pop below poverty level:** 17.2%. ***Personal per capita income 2000-2003:** $21,253-$22,284.

Unemployment 2004: 4.8%. **Change from 2000:** +0.2%. **Median travel time to work:** 13.6 minutes. **Working outside county of residence:** 16.3%.

Cities with pop over 10,000: None.

RAVALLI COUNTY

215 S 4th St Suite C   **Ph:** 406-375-6212
Hamilton, MT 59840   **Fax:** 406-375-6326
www.co.ravalli.mt.us

On the central western border of MT, west of Butte; organized Feb 16, 1893 from Missoula County. **Name Origin:** For Father Anthony Ravalli (1812-84), Jesuit missionary to the Salish (Flathead) Indians at Saint Mary's Mission, Stevensville, MT, the first white settlement in MT.

Area (sq mi): 2400.32 (land 2394.21; water 6.11). **Pop per sq mi:** 16.7.

Pop 2005: 39,940. **State rank:** 7. **Pop change:** 2000-20005 +10.7%; 1990-2000 +44.2%. **Pop 2000:** 36,070 (White 95.5%; Black or African American 0.1%; Hispanic or Latino 1.9%; Asian 0.3%; Other 2.8%). **Foreign born:** 1.7%. **Median age:** 41.1.

Income 2000: per capita $17,935; median household $31,992; **Pop below poverty level:** 13.8%. ***Personal per capita income 2000-2003:** $20,188-$22,041.

⛪ *County Seat*

Ravalli County (cont'd)

Unemployment 2004: 5.2%. **Change from 2000:** +0.6%. **Median travel time to work:** 23 minutes. **Working outside county of residence:** 23.4%.

Cities with pop over 10,000: None.

RICHLAND COUNTY

201 W Main St   **Ph:** 406-433-1708
Sidney, MT 59270   **Fax:** 406-482-3731
www.richland.org

On the northeastern border of MT; organized May 27, 1914 from Dawson County. **Name Origin:** Promotional, to attract new visitors.

Area (sq mi): 2103.02 (land 2084.09; water 18.93). **Pop per sq mi:** 4.4.

Pop 2005: 9,096. **State rank:** 22. **Pop change:** 2000-20005 -5.9%; 1990-2000 -9.8%. **Pop 2000:** 9,667 (White 95.4%; Black or African American 0.1%; Hispanic or Latino 2.2%; Asian 0.2%; Other 3.1%, including 1.5% American Indian/Alaska Native). **Foreign born:** 1.4%. **Median age:** 39.2.

Income 2000: per capita $16,006; median household $32,110; **Pop below poverty level:** 12.2%. ***Personal per capita income 2000-2003:** $21,480-$23,777.

Unemployment 2004: 3.6%. **Change from 2000:** -1.3%. **Median travel time to work:** 13.5 minutes. **Working outside county of residence:** 7.8%.

Cities with pop over 10,000: None.

ROOSEVELT COUNTY

400 2nd Ave S   **Ph:** 406-653-6250
Wolf Point, MT 59201   **Fax:** 406-653-6289

On the northeastern border of MT; organized Feb 18, 1919 from Sheridan County. **Name Origin:** For Theodore Roosevelt (1858-1919), twenty-sixth U.S. president.

Area (sq mi): 2369.65 (land 2355.6; water 14.05). **Pop per sq mi:** 4.5.

Pop 2005: 10,524. **State rank:** 19. **Pop change:** 2000-20005 -0.9%; 1990-2000 -3.4%. **Pop 2000:** 10,620 (White 40.8%; Black or African American 0%; Hispanic or Latino 1.2%; Asian 0.4%; Other 58.6%, including 55.8% American Indian/Alaska Native). **Foreign born:** 0.9%. **Median age:** 32.3.

Income 2000: per capita $11,347; median household $24,834; **Pop below poverty level:** 32.4%. ***Personal per capita income 2000-2003:** $17,989-$19,188.

Unemployment 2004: 6.4%. **Change from 2000:** -0.8%. **Median travel time to work:** 11.7 minutes. **Working outside county of residence:** 8.1%.

Cities with pop over 10,000: None.

ROSEBUD COUNTY

1200 Main St   **Ph:** 406-346-2251
Forsyth, MT 59327   **Fax:** 406-356-7551

In south-central MT, east of Billling; organized Feb 11, 1901 from Custer County. **Name Origin:** For Rosebud Creek, which runs

through the county; named for the profusion of wild roses along its banks.

Area (sq mi): 5026.94 (land 5012.37; water 14.57). **Pop per sq mi:** 1.8.

Pop 2005: 9,212. **State rank:** 21. **Pop change:** 2000-20005 -1.8%; 1990-2000 -10.7%. **Pop 2000:** 9,383 (White 63.5%; Black or African American 0.2%; Hispanic or Latino 2.3%; Asian 0.3%; Other 35.1%, including 32.4% American Indian/Alaska Native). **Foreign born:** 1.1%. **Median age:** 34.5.

Income 2000: per capita $15,032; median household $35,898; **Pop below poverty level:** 22.4%. ***Personal per capita income 2000-2003:** $21,654-$24,473.

Unemployment 2004: 5.3%. **Change from 2000:** -1.8%. **Median travel time to work:** 16 minutes. **Working outside county of residence:** 6.1%.

Cities with pop over 10,000: None.

SANDERS COUNTY

111 Main St   **Ph:** 406-827-6942
Thompson Falls, MT 59873   **Fax:** 406-827-4388
www.co.sanders.mt.us

On the northwestern border of MT, northwest of Missoula; organized Feb 5, 1907 from Missoula County. **Name Origin:** For Wilbur Fisk Sanders (1834-1905), officer in the Civil War and U.S. senator from MT (1890-93).

Area (sq mi): 2790.03 (land 2762.17; water 27.86). **Pop per sq mi:** 4.

Pop 2005: 11,057. **State rank:** 18. **Pop change:** 2000-20005 +8.1%; 1990-2000 +18%. **Pop 2000:** 10,227 (White 90.9%; Black or African American 0.1%; Hispanic or Latino 1.6%; Asian 0.3%; Other 7.6%, including 4.7% American Indian/Alaska Native). **Foreign born:** 2%. **Median age:** 44.2.

Income 2000: per capita $14,593; median household $26,852; **Pop below poverty level:** 17.2%. ***Personal per capita income 2000-2003:** $16,941-$18,888.

Unemployment 2004: 6.6%. **Change from 2000:** -1.7%. **Median travel time to work:** 22.3 minutes. **Working outside county of residence:** 14.5%.

Cities with pop over 10,000: None.

SHERIDAN COUNTY

100 W Laurel Ave   **Ph:** 406-765-2310
Plentywood, MT 59254   **Fax:** 406-765-2609
www.co.sheridan.mt.us

In the northeastern corner of MT; organized Mar 4, 1913 from Valley County. **Name Origin:** For Gen. Philip Henry Sheridan (1831-88), Union officer during the Civil War and commander in chief of the U.S. army (1883-88).

Area (sq mi): 1706.3 (land 1676.58; water 29.73). **Pop per sq mi:** 2.1.

Pop 2005: 3,524. **State rank:** 40. **Pop change:** 2000-20005 -14.2%; 1990-2000 -13.3%. **Pop 2000:** 4,105 (White 96.4%; Black or African American 0.1%; Hispanic or Latino 1.1%; Asian 0.3%; Other 2.6%, including 1.2% American Indian/Alaska Native). **Foreign born:** 1.9%. **Median age:** 45.1.

*Source: Personal per capita income data are from the Bureau of Economic Analysis; per capita income data are from the Bureau of the Census. See Introduction for explanation of differences.

Sheridan County (cont'd)

Income 2000: per capita $16,038; median household $29,518; **Pop below poverty level:** 14.7%. *Personal per capita income 2000-2003: $23,991-$24,882.

Unemployment 2004: 3.8%. **Change from 2000:** +0.6%. **Median travel time to work:** 12.8 minutes. **Working outside county of residence:** 4.9%.

Cities with pop over 10,000: None.

STILLWATER COUNTY

400 3rd Ave N   **Ph:** 406 322 8000
Columbus, MT 59019   **Fax:** 406-322-8007
www.co.stillwater.mt.us

In south-central MT, west of Billlings; organized Mar 24, 1913 from Carbon, Sweet Grass, and Yellowstone counties. **Name Origin:** For the Stillwater River, which runs through the county.

Area (sq mi): 1804.61 (land 1795.09; water 9.52). **Pop per sq mi:** 4.7.

Pop 2005: 8,493. **State rank:** 26. **Pop change:** 2000-20005 +3.6%; 1990-2000 +25.4%. **Pop 2000:** 8,195 (White 95.9%; Black or African American 0.1%; Hispanic or Latino 2%; Asian 0.2%; Other 2.8%). **Foreign born:** 1.5%. **Median age:** 40.8.

Income 2000: per capita $18,468; median household $39,205; **Pop below poverty level:** 9.8%. *Personal per capita income 2000-2003: $24,559-$26,712.

Unemployment 2004: 3.6%. **Change from 2000:** +0.5%. **Median travel time to work:** 28.5 minutes. **Working outside county of residence:** 26.9%.

Cities with pop over 10,000: None.

SWEET GRASS COUNTY

200 W 1st Ave   **Ph:** 406-932-5152
Big Timber, MT 59011   **Fax:** 406-932-5177
www.co.sweetgrass.mt.us

In south-central MT, west of Billings; organized Mar 5, 1895 from Meagher, Park, and Yellowstone counties. **Name Origin:** For the abundant fragrant grass of the genus *Glyceria*, at the suggestion of Mrs. Paul Van Cleve, Sr.

Area (sq mi): 1862 (land 1855.08; water 6.92). **Pop per sq mi:** 2.

Pop 2005: 3,672. **State rank:** 39. **Pop change:** 2000-20005 +1.7%; 1990-2000 +14.4%. **Pop 2000:** 3,609 (White 96.1%; Black or African American 0.1%; Hispanic or Latino 1.5%; Asian 0.3%; Other 2.6%). **Foreign born:** 1.7%. **Median age:** 41.2.

Income 2000: per capita $17,880; median household $32,422; **Pop below poverty level:** 11.4%. *Personal per capita income 2000-2003: $19,819-$22,039.

Unemployment 2004: 2.1%. **Change from 2000:** -0.5%. **Median travel time to work:** 20.8 minutes. **Working outside county of residence:** 11.7%.

Cities with pop over 10,000: None.

TETON COUNTY

1 S Main St   **Ph:** 406-466-2151
Choteau, MT 59422   **Fax:** 406-466-2138
www.tetoncomt.org

In west-central MT, northwest of Great Falls; organized Feb 7, 1893 from Chouteau County. **Name Origin:** For the Teton River and Teton Peak in the Teton Mountains or for the Teton Indian tribe.

Area (sq mi): 2292.58 (land 2272.61; water 19.97). **Pop per sq mi:** 2.7.

Pop 2005: 6,240. **State rank:** 31. **Pop change:** 2000-20005 -3.2%; 1990-2000 +2.8%. **Pop 2000:** 6,445 (White 95.6%; Black or African American 0.2%; Hispanic or Latino 1.1%; Asian 0.1%; Other 3.4%, including 1.5% American Indian/Alaska Native). **Foreign born:** 1.5%. **Median age:** 40.

Income 2000: per capita $14,635; median household $30,197; **Pop below poverty level:** 16.6%. *Personal per capita income 2000-2003: $20,864-$22,735.

Unemployment 2004: 3.9%. **Change from 2000:** +0.4%. **Median travel time to work:** 19.2 minutes. **Working outside county of residence:** 21.1%.

Cities with pop over 10,000: None.

TOOLE COUNTY

226 1st St S   **Ph:** 406-424-8310
Shelby, MT 59474   **Fax:** 406-424-8301

On the central northern border of MT, north of Great Falls; organized May 7, 1914 from Hill and Teton counties. **Name Origin:** For Joseph Kemp Toole (1851-1929), governor of MT (1889-93; 1901-08).

Area (sq mi): 1945.86 (land 1910.95; water 34.91). **Pop per sq mi:** 2.6.

Pop 2005: 5,031. **State rank:** 34. **Pop change:** 2000-20005 -4.5%; 1990-2000 +4.4%. **Pop 2000:** 5,267 (White 93.3%; Black or African American 0.2%; Hispanic or Latino 1.2%; Asian 0.3%; Other 5.6%, including 3.2% American Indian/Alaska Native). **Foreign born:** 3.6%. **Median age:** 39.1.

Income 2000: per capita $14,731; median household $30,169; **Pop below poverty level:** 12.9%. *Personal per capita income 2000-2003: $21,331-$22,853.

Unemployment 2004: 3.3%. **Change from 2000:** +0.6%. **Median travel time to work:** 14.2 minutes. **Working outside county of residence:** 10%.

Cities with pop over 10,000: None.

TREASURE COUNTY

PO Box 392   **Ph:** 406-342-5547
Hysham, MT 59038   **Fax:** 406-342-5445

In south-central MT, northeast of Billings; organized Feb 7, 1919 from Rosebud County. **Name Origin:** For the nickname of MT, the 'Treasure State.'

Area (sq mi): 984.11 (land 978.86; water 5.24). **Pop per sq mi:** 0.7.

Pop 2005: 689. **State rank:** 55. **Pop change:** 2000-20005 -20%; 1990-2000 -1.5%. **Pop 2000:** 861 (White 95.6%; Black or African American 0.1%; Hispanic or Latino 1.5%; Asian 0.3%; Other 3.1%,

Treasure County (cont'd)

including 1.6% American Indian/Alaska Native). **Foreign born:** 0.8%. **Median age:** 41.8.

Income 2000: per capita $14,392; median household $29,830; **Pop below poverty level:** 14.7%. ***Personal per capita income 2000-2003:** $17,179-$18,272.

Unemployment 2004: 4.3%. **Change from 2000:** +1.1%. **Median travel time to work:** 18.3 minutes. **Working outside county of residence:** 19.8%.

Cities with pop over 10,000: None.

VALLEY COUNTY

501 Court Sq Box 2   **Ph:** 406-228-6220
Glasgow, MT 59230   **Fax:** 406-228-9027

On the northern border of MT with the province of Saskatchewan, Canada; organized Feb 6, 1893 from Dawson County. **Name Origin:** For the Milk and Missouri river valleys.

Area (sq mi): 5061.98 (land 4921; water 140.98). **Pop per sq mi:** 1.5.

Pop 2005: 7,143. **State rank:** 28. **Pop change:** 2000-20005 -6.9%; 1990-2000 -6.8%. **Pop 2000:** 7,675 (White 87.8%; Black or African American 0.1%; Hispanic or Latino 0.8%; Asian 0.2%; Other 11.5%, including 9.4% American Indian/Alaska Native). **Foreign born:** 1.1%. **Median age:** 41.7.

Income 2000: per capita $16,246; median household $30,979; **Pop below poverty level:** 13.5%. ***Personal per capita income 2000-2003:** $24,166-$26,760.

Unemployment 2004: 4.2%. **Change from 2000:** +0.7%. **Median travel time to work:** 12.6 minutes. **Working outside county of residence:** 6.4%.

Cities with pop over 10,000: None.

WHEATLAND COUNTY

201 A Ave NW   **Ph:** 406-632-4891
Harlowton, MT 59036   **Fax:** 406-632-4880

In south-central MT, northwest of Billlings; organized Feb 22, 1917 from Meagher and Sweet Grass counties. **Name Origin:** For the major crop in the area.

Area (sq mi): 1428.29 (land 1423.09; water 5.19). **Pop per sq mi:** 1.4.

Pop 2005: 2,037. **State rank:** 44. **Pop change:** 2000-20005 -9.8%; 1990-2000 +0.6%. **Pop 2000:** 2,259 (White 96.4%; Black or African American 0.1%; Hispanic or Latino 1.1%; Asian 0.2%; Other 2.7%). **Foreign born:** 2.9%. **Median age:** 41.4.

Income 2000: per capita $11,954; median household $24,492; **Pop below poverty level:** 20.4%. ***Personal per capita income 2000-2003:** $15,842-$17,337.

Unemployment 2004: 4.5%. **Change from 2000:** +1%. **Median travel time to work:** 18.8 minutes. **Working outside county of residence:** 14.7%.

Cities with pop over 10,000: None.

WIBAUX COUNTY

200 S Wibaux St   **Ph:** 406-796-2484
Wibaux, MT 59353

On the central eastern border of MT; organized Aug 17, 1914 from Dawson, Fallon, and Richland counties. **Name Origin:** For Pierre Wibaux, a Huguenot immigrant who owned one of the largest herds of cattle in MT.

Area (sq mi): 890.09 (land 889.31; water 0.78). **Pop per sq mi:** 1.1.

Pop 2005: 951. **State rank:** 54. **Pop change:** 2000-20005 -11%; 1990-2000 -10.3%. **Pop 2000:** 1,068 (White 97.8%; Black or African American 0.2%; Hispanic or Latino 0.4%; Asian 0.2%; Other 1.6%). **Foreign born:** 1.4%. **Median age:** 42.3.

Income 2000: per capita $16,121; median household $28,224; **Pop below poverty level:** 15.3%. ***Personal per capita income 2000-2003:** $18,483-$20,760.

Unemployment 2004: 3.5%. **Change from 2000:** +0.9%. **Median travel time to work:** 19.5 minutes. **Working outside county of residence:** 28.4%.

Cities with pop over 10,000: None.

YELLOWSTONE COUNTY

217 N 27th St Rm 401   **Ph:** 406-256-2785
Billings, MT 59101   **Fax:** 406-256-2736
www.co.yellowstone.mt.us

In south-central MT; organized Feb 26, 1883 from Custer County. **Name Origin:** For the Yellowstone River, which flows through the county.

Area (sq mi): 2649.05 (land 2635.15; water 13.9). **Pop per sq mi:** 51.9.

Pop 2005: 136,691. **State rank:** 1. **Pop change:** 2000-20005 +5.7%; 1990-2000 +14%. **Pop 2000:** 129,352 (White 91%; Black or African American 0.4%; Hispanic or Latino 3.7%; Asian 0.5%; Other 6.3%, including 3.1% American Indian/Alaska Native). **Foreign born:** 1.4%. **Median age:** 36.9.

Income 2000: per capita $19,303; median household $36,727; **Pop below poverty level:** 11.1%. ***Personal per capita income 2000-2003:** $26,404-$29,421.

Unemployment 2004: 3.5%. **Change from 2000:** +0.2%. **Median travel time to work:** 17.9 minutes. **Working outside county of residence:** 3.3%.

Cities with pop over 10,000: Billings 🏛 (96,977).

---

*Source: Personal per capita income data are from the Bureau of Economic Analysis; per capita income data are from the Bureau of the Census. See Introduction for explanation of differences.

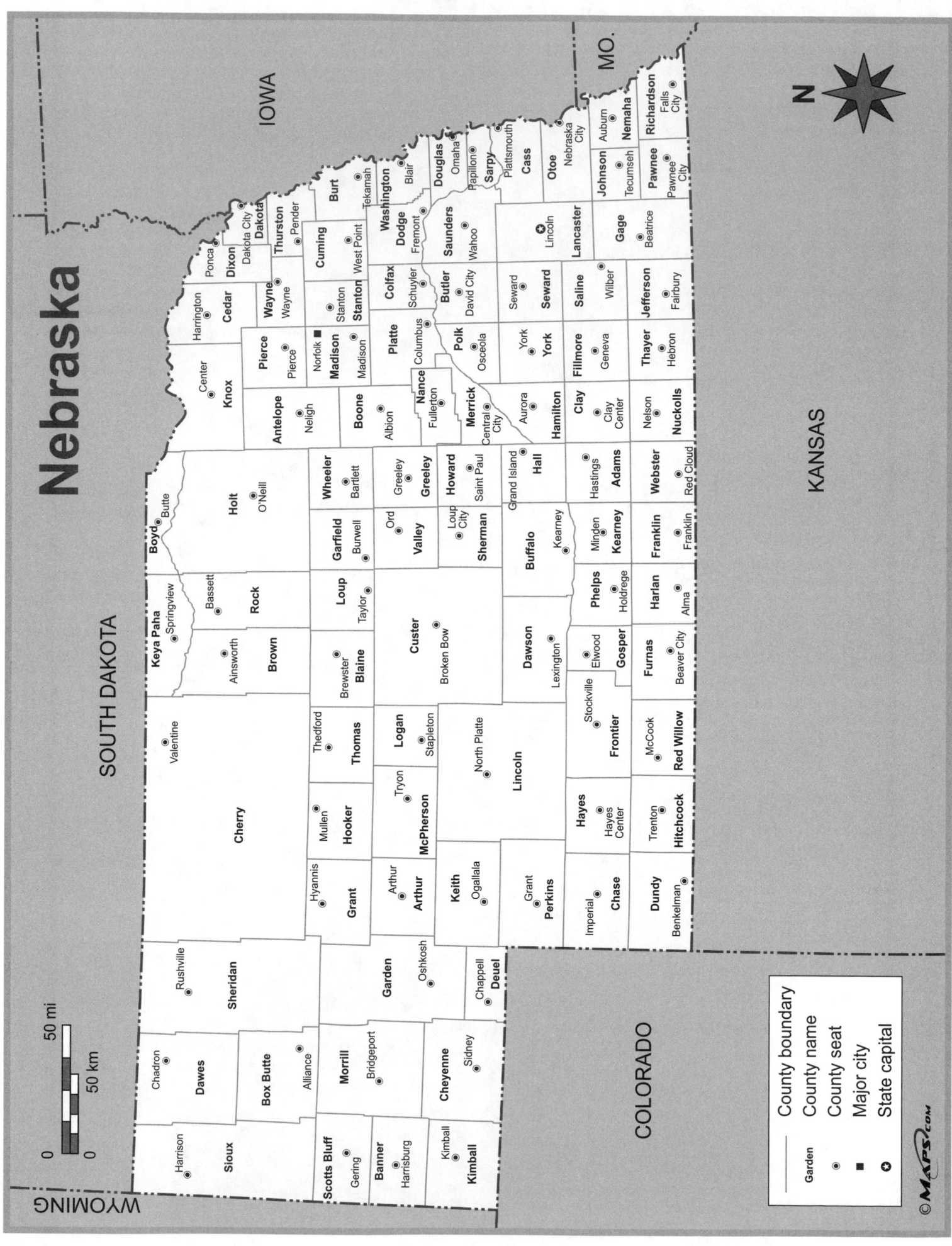

Nebraska

NEBRASKA STATE INFORMATION

www.nebraska.gov   **Ph:** 402-471-2311

Area (sq mi): 77,353.73 (land 76,872.41; water 481.31). **Pop per sq mi:** 22.9.

Pop 2005: 1,758,787. **Pop change:** 2000-20005 +2.8%; 1990-2000 +8.4%. **Pop 2000:** 1,711,263 (White 87.3%; Black or African American 4%; Hispanic or Latino 5.5%; Asian 1.3%; Other 5.1%). **Foreign born:** 4.4%. **Median age:** 35.3.

Income 2000: per capita $19,613; median household $39,250; **Pop below poverty level:** 9.7%. *Personal per capita income 2000-2003: $27,625-$30,179.

Unemployment 2004: 3.9%. **Change from 2000:** +1.1%. **Median travel time to work:** 18 minutes. **Working outside county of residence:** 19.4%.

ADAMS COUNTY

PO Box 2067   **Ph:** 402-461-7104
Hastings, NE 68902   **Fax:** 402-461-7185
www.adamscounty.org

In south-central NE, south of Grand Island; organized Feb 16, 1867 from Clay County. **Name Origin:** For John Adams (1735-1826), second U.S. president.

Area (sq mi): 564.16 (land 563.41; water 0.76). **Pop per sq mi:** 58.7.

Pop 2005: 33,070. **State rank:** 10. **Pop change:** 2000-20005 +6.2%; 1990-2000 +5.2%. **Pop 2000:** 31,151 (White 92.2%; Black or African American 0.6%; Hispanic or Latino 4.6%; Asian 1.6%; Other 3.2%). **Foreign born:** 4.4%. **Median age:** 36.5.

Income 2000: per capita $18,308; median household $37,160; **Pop below poverty level:** 9.3%. *Personal per capita income 2000-2003: $23,928-$25,815.

Unemployment 2004: 3.7%. **Change from 2000:** +0.9%. **Median travel time to work:** 15.5 minutes. **Working outside county of residence:** 10.3%.

Cities with pop over 10,000: Hastings ⚖ (23,404).

ANTELOPE COUNTY

501 Main St   **Ph:** 402-887-4410
Neligh, NE 68756   **Fax:** 402-887-4719
www.co.antelope.ne.us

In east-central NE, southwest of Sioux City, IA; organized Jun 15, 1871 from Pierce County. **Name Origin:** The bill for establishment of the county was introduced by Leander Gerrard who once shot an antelope for food while on the trail of Indians.

Area (sq mi): 858.43 (land 857.06; water 1.37). **Pop per sq mi:** 8.2.

Pop 2005: 7,004. **State rank:** 43. **Pop change:** 2000-20005 -6%; 1990-2000 -6.4%. **Pop 2000:** 7,452 (White 98.5%; Black or African American 0.1%; Hispanic or Latino 0.7%; Asian 0.1%; Other 1.1%). **Foreign born:** 0.4%. **Median age:** 40.6.

Income 2000: per capita $14,601; median household $30,114; **Pop below poverty level:** 13.6%. *Personal per capita income 2000-2003: $23,062-$27,068.

Unemployment 2004: 3.3%. **Change from 2000:** -0.5%. **Median travel time to work:** 18.6 minutes. **Working outside county of residence:** 25%.

Cities with pop over 10,000: None.

ARTHUR COUNTY

PO Box 126   **Ph:** 308-764-2203
Arthur, NE 69121   **Fax:** 308-764-2216

In west-central NE, northwest of North Platte; county approved Mar 31, 1887 from unattached lands; formed Jun 7, 1913. **Name Origin:** For Chester A. Arthur (1830-86), twenty-first U.S. presidesnt.

Area (sq mi): 718.32 (land 715.37; water 2.95). **Pop per sq mi:** 0.5.

Pop 2005: 378. **State rank:** 93. **Pop change:** 2000-20005 -14.9%; 1990-2000 -3.9%. **Pop 2000:** 444 (White 95.7%; Black or African American 0%; Hispanic or Latino 1.4%; Asian 0.7%; Other 2.9%). **Foreign born:** 0.7%. **Median age:** 40.3.

Income 2000: per capita $15,810; median household $27,375; **Pop below poverty level:** 13.8%. *Personal per capita income 2000-2003: $8,939-$17,461.

Unemployment 2004: 3.7%. **Change from 2000:** +0.3%. **Median travel time to work:** 18.7 minutes. **Working outside county of residence:** 30.3%.

Cities with pop over 10,000: None.

BANNER COUNTY

204 State St PO Box 67   **Ph:** 308-436-5265
Harrisburg, NE 69345   **Fax:** 308-436-4180
www.co.banner.ne.us

On the southwestern border of NE, south of Scottsbluff; organized Nov 6, 1888 from Cheyenne County. **Name Origin:** Named by the citizens who wanted the county to be the 'banner county' of the state.

Area (sq mi): 746.37 (land 746.22; water 0.15). **Pop per sq mi:** 1.

Pop 2005: 733. **State rank:** 87. **Pop change:** 2000-20005 -10.5%; 1990-2000 -3.9%. **Pop 2000:** 819 (White 93.9%; Black or African

Banner County (cont'd)

American 0.1%; Hispanic or Latino 5.6%; Asian 0.1%; Other 3.9%). **Foreign born:** 0.9%. **Median age:** 39.9.

Income 2000: per capita $17,149; median household $31,339; **Pop below poverty level:** 13.6%. ***Personal per capita income 2000-2003:** $17,362-$24,318.

Unemployment 2004: 3.3%. **Change from 2000:** +1.6%. **Median travel time to work:** 24.1 minutes. **Working outside county of residence:** 47.2%.

Cities with pop over 10,000: None.

BLAINE COUNTY

Lincoln Ave Bldg 1   **Ph:** 308-547-2222
Brewster, NE 68821   **Fax:** 308-547-2228
www.blainecounty.ne.gov

In central NE, northeast of North Platte; organized Mar 5, 1885 from Custer County. **Name Origin:** For James Gillespie Blaine (1830-93), U.S. representative from ME (1863-76), U.S. senator (1876-81), and U.S. secretary of state (1881; 1889-92).

Area (sq mi): 714.34 (land 710.74; water 3.59). **Pop per sq mi:** 0.7.

Pop 2005: 484. **State rank:** 92. **Pop change:** 2000-20005 -17%; 1990-2000 -13.6%. **Pop 2000:** 583 (White 98.8%; Black or African American 0%; Hispanic or Latino 0.2%; Asian 0%; Other 1%). **Foreign born:** 0.3%. **Median age:** 39.8.

Income 2000: per capita $12,323; median household $25,278; **Pop below poverty level:** 19.4%. ***Personal per capita income 2000-2003:** $9,624-$16,698.

Unemployment 2004: 3.2%. **Change from 2000:** +1.6%. **Median travel time to work:** 20.9 minutes. **Working outside county of residence:** 19.6%.

Cities with pop over 10,000: None.

BOONE COUNTY

222 S 4th St   **Ph:** 402-395-2055
Albion, NE 68620
www.co.boone.ne.us

In east-central NE, northeast of Grand Island; organized Mar 28, 1871 from Platte County. **Name Origin:** For Daniel Boone (1734?-1820), U.S. frontiersman and KY pioneer.

Area (sq mi): 687.25 (land 686.69; water 0.56). **Pop per sq mi:** 8.4.

Pop 2005: 5,772. **State rank:** 52. **Pop change:** 2000-20005 -7.8%; 1990-2000 -6.1%. **Pop 2000:** 6,259 (White 98.8%; Black or African American 0%; Hispanic or Latino 0.9%; Asian 0%; Other 0.6%). **Foreign born:** 0.9%. **Median age:** 39.9.

Income 2000: per capita $15,831; median household $31,444; **Pop below poverty level:** 10.4%. ***Personal per capita income 2000-2003:** $21,928-$26,033.

Unemployment 2004: 3.2%. **Change from 2000:** -0.3%. **Median travel time to work:** 16.4 minutes. **Working outside county of residence:** 21.4%.

Cities with pop over 10,000: None.

BOX BUTTE COUNTY

PO Box 678   **Ph:** 308-762-6565
Alliance, NE 69301   **Fax:** 308-762-2867
www.co.box-butte.ne.us

In northwestern NE, northeast of Scottsbluff; organized Nov 2, 1886 from Dawes County. **Name Origin:** Descriptive of the rectangular-shaped butte near Alliance.

Area (sq mi): 1077.84 (land 1075.29; water 2.54). **Pop per sq mi:** 10.6.

Pop 2005: 11,374. **State rank:** 23. **Pop change:** 2000-20005 -6.4%; 1990-2000 -7.4%. **Pop 2000:** 12,158 (White 87.7%; Black or African American 0.4%; Hispanic or Latino 7.6%; Asian 0.5%; Other 8.3%, including 2.7% American Indian/Alaska Native). **Foreign born:** 3.1%. **Median age:** 38.2.

Income 2000: per capita $18,407; median household $39,366; **Pop below poverty level:** 10.7%. ***Personal per capita income 2000-2003:** $25,195-$26,905.

Unemployment 2004: 4%. **Change from 2000:** -0.4%. **Median travel time to work:** 14.5 minutes. **Working outside county of residence:** 3%.

Cities with pop over 10,000: None.

BOYD COUNTY

PO Box 26   **Ph:** 402-775-2391
Butte, NE 68722   **Fax:** 402-775-2146

On the northern border of NE; organized Mar 20, 1891 from Holt County. **Name Origin:** For James E. Boyd (1834-1906), NE governor (1891; 1892-93).

Area (sq mi): 544.59 (land 540.05; water 4.54). **Pop per sq mi:** 4.2.

Pop 2005: 2,261. **State rank:** 74. **Pop change:** 2000-20005 -7.3%; 1990-2000 -14%. **Pop 2000:** 2,438 (White 98.8%; Black or African American 0%; Hispanic or Latino 0.1%; Asian 0.2%; Other 1%). **Foreign born:** 0.4%. **Median age:** 43.8.

Income 2000: per capita $13,840; median household $26,075; **Pop below poverty level:** 15.2%. ***Personal per capita income 2000-2003:** $16,711-$21,257.

Unemployment 2004: 2.9%. **Change from 2000:** -0.9%. **Median travel time to work:** 15.2 minutes. **Working outside county of residence:** 17.6%.

Cities with pop over 10,000: None.

BROWN COUNTY

148 W 4th St   **Ph:** 402-387-2705
Ainsworth, NE 69210   **Fax:** 402-387-0918
www.co.brown.ne.us

In north-central NE; organized Feb 19, 1883 from unorganized territory. **Name Origin:** Possibly for two state legislators named Brown who sponsored the bill for organization of the county.

Area (sq mi): 1225.08 (land 1221.28; water 3.8). **Pop per sq mi:** 2.7.

Pop 2005: 3,328. **State rank:** 67. **Pop change:** 2000-20005 -5.6%; 1990-2000 -3.6%. **Pop 2000:** 3,525 (White 98.1%; Black or African American 0%; Hispanic or Latino 0.8%; Asian 0.3%; Other 1%). **Foreign born:** 0.7%. **Median age:** 43.1.

*Source: Personal per capita income data are from the Bureau of Economic Analysis; per capita income data are from the Bureau of the Census. See Introduction for explanation of differences.

Brown County (cont'd)

Income 2000: per capita $15,924; median household $28,356; **Pop below poverty level:** 11.1%. ***Personal per capita income 2000-2003:** $20,120-$24,899.

Unemployment 2004: 3.2%. **Change from 2000:** -0.2%. **Median travel time to work:** 13.4 minutes. **Working outside county of residence:** 9.3%.

Cities with pop over 10,000: None.

BUFFALO COUNTY

PO Box 1270　　　　　　　　**Ph:** 308-236-1226
Kearney, NE 68848　　　　　　**Fax:** 308-233-3649
www.buffalogov.org

In south-central NE, west of Grand Island; original county; organized Mar 14, 1855 (prior to statehood); not officially recognized until Jan 20, 1870. **Name Origin:** For the former feeding grounds of the buffalo.

Area (sq mi): 975.27 (land 967.99; water 7.28). **Pop per sq mi:** 45.

Pop 2005: 43,572. **State rank:** 5. **Pop change:** 2000-20005 +3.1%; 1990-2000 +12.9%. **Pop 2000:** 42,259 (White 93%; Black or African American 0.5%; Hispanic or Latino 4.7%; Asian 0.7%; Other 3.5%). **Foreign born:** 2.6%. **Median age:** 30.

Income 2000: per capita $17,510; median household $36,782; **Pop below poverty level:** 11.2%. ***Personal per capita income 2000-2003:** $23,091-$26,694.

Unemployment 2004: 2.8%. **Change from 2000:** -0.2%. **Median travel time to work:** 15.6 minutes. **Working outside county of residence:** 8.8%.

Cities with pop over 10,000: Kearney 🏛 (28,640).

BURT COUNTY

PO Box 87　　　　　　　　　**Ph:** 402-374-2955
Tekamah, NE 68061　　　　　　**Fax:** 402-374-2956
www.burtcounty.ne.gov

On the central eastern border of NE, north of Omaha; original county; organized Feb 18, 1855 (prior to statehood). **Name Origin:** For Francis Burt (1807-54), SC legislator, editor, and first territorial governor of NE (1854).

Area (sq mi): 497.1 (land 492.77; water 4.33). **Pop per sq mi:** 15.1.

Pop 2005: 7,455. **State rank:** 41. **Pop change:** 2000-20005 -4.3%; 1990-2000 -1%. **Pop 2000:** 7,791 (White 96.8%; Black or African American 0.2%; Hispanic or Latino 1.3%; Asian 0.2%; Other 2%, including 1.1% American Indian/Alaska Native). **Foreign born:** 1.1%. **Median age:** 42.2.

Income 2000: per capita $16,654; median household $33,954; **Pop below poverty level:** 8.9%. ***Personal per capita income 2000-2003:** $23,001-$25,791.

Unemployment 2004: 5%. **Change from 2000:** +0.7%. **Median travel time to work:** 22.9 minutes. **Working outside county of residence:** 38.5%.

Cities with pop over 10,000: None.

BUTLER COUNTY

PO Box 289　　　　　　　　**Ph:** 402-367-7430
David City, NE 68632　　　　　**Fax:** 402-367-3329
www.co.butler.ne.us

In east-central NE, west of Omaha; organized Jun 26, 1856 from unorganized territory. **Name Origin:** For David Butler (1829-91), first governor of NE (1867-71).

Area (sq mi): 584.41 (land 583.59; water 0.82). **Pop per sq mi:** 14.9.

Pop 2005: 8,720. **State rank:** 35. **Pop change:** 2000-20005 -0.5%; 1990-2000 +1.9%. **Pop 2000:** 8,767 (White 97.6%; Black or African American 0.1%; Hispanic or Latino 1.7%; Asian 0.1%; Other 1.4%). **Foreign born:** 0.9%. **Median age:** 38.8.

Income 2000: per capita $16,394; median household $36,331; **Pop below poverty level:** 8.2%. ***Personal per capita income 2000-2003:** $22,915-$24,710.

Unemployment 2004: 4%. **Change from 2000:** +0.5%. **Median travel time to work:** 23.9 minutes. **Working outside county of residence:** 43.2%.

Cities with pop over 10,000: None.

CASS COUNTY

346 Main St　　　　　　　　**Ph:** 402-296-9300
Plattsmouth, NE 68048　　　　**Fax:** 402-296-9332
www.cassne.org

On the southeastern border of NE, northeast of Lincoln; original county; organized Mar 7, 1855 (prior to statehood). **Name Origin:** For Gen. Lewis Cass (1782-1866), OH legislator, military and civil governor of MI Territory (1813-31), U.S. secretary of war (1831-36), and U.S. secretary of state (1857-60).

Area (sq mi): 566.21 (land 559.18; water 7.03). **Pop per sq mi:** 46.

Pop 2005: 25,734. **State rank:** 12. **Pop change:** 2000-20005 +5.8%; 1990-2000 +14.1%. **Pop 2000:** 24,334 (White 96.9%; Black or African American 0.2%; Hispanic or Latino 1.5%; Asian 0.3%; Other 1.6%). **Foreign born:** 1.2%. **Median age:** 36.9.

Income 2000: per capita $20,156; median household $46,515; **Pop below poverty level:** 5.2%. ***Personal per capita income 2000-2003:** $27,465-$29,966.

Unemployment 2004: 4.1%. **Change from 2000:** +1%. **Median travel time to work:** 27 minutes. **Working outside county of residence:** 66.2%.

Cities with pop over 10,000: None.

CEDAR COUNTY

101 S Broadway　　　　　　　**Ph:** 402-254-7411
Hartington, NE 68739　　　　　**Fax:** 402-254-7410
www.co.cedar.ne.us

On the northeastern border of NE, west of Sioux City, IA; original county; organized Feb 12, 1855 (prior to statehood). **Name Origin:** For the cedar trees that are abundant locally.

Area (sq mi): 745.81 (land 740.23; water 5.59). **Pop per sq mi:** 12.2.

Pop 2005: 9,066. **State rank:** 32. **Pop change:** 2000-20005 -5.7%; 1990-2000 -5.1%. **Pop 2000:** 9,615 (White 98.9%; Black or African American 0.1%; Hispanic or Latino 0.4%; Asian 0%; Other 0.8%). **Foreign born:** 0.4%. **Median age:** 38.8.

Cedar County (cont'd)

Income 2000: per capita $15,514; median household $33,435; **Pop below poverty level:** 9.1%. ***Personal per capita income 2000-2003:** $23,488-$27,774.

Unemployment 2004: 2.8%. **Change from 2000:** +0.3%. **Median travel time to work:** 17.5 minutes. **Working outside county of residence:** 32.7%.

Cities with pop over 10,000: None.

CHASE COUNTY

PO Box 1299   **Ph:** 308-882-5266
Imperial, NE 69033   **Fax:** 308-882-7552
www.co.chase.ne.us

On the southwestern border of NE, southwest of North Platte; organized Apr 24, 1886 from Keith County. **Name Origin:** For Champion S. Chase (?-1898), mayor of Omaha, NE, and first attorney general of NE.

Area (sq mi): 897.63 (land 894.5; water 3.14). **Pop per sq mi:** 4.3.

Pop 2005: 3,866. **State rank:** 61. **Pop change:** 2000-20005 -5%; 1990-2000 -7.1%. **Pop 2000:** 4,068 (White 95.9%; Black or African American 0.2%; Hispanic or Latino 3.4%; Asian 0.2%; Other 1.8%). **Foreign born:** 1.4%. **Median age:** 42.1.

Income 2000: per capita $17,490; median household $32,351; **Pop below poverty level:** 9.6%. ***Personal per capita income 2000-2003:** $24,412-$26,598.

Unemployment 2004: 2.7%. **Change from 2000:** +0.5%. **Median travel time to work:** 12.9 minutes. **Working outside county of residence:** 8%.

Cities with pop over 10,000: None.

CHERRY COUNTY

PO Box 120   **Ph:** 402-376-2771
Valentine, NE 69201   **Fax:** 402-376-3095
www.co.cherry.ne.us

On the central northern border of NE; organized Feb 23, 1883 from unorganized territory. Claims to be the largest county in the U.S. **Name Origin:** For Lt. Samuel A. Cherry (?-1881), an army officer.

Area (sq mi): 6009.54 (land 5960.52; water 49.02). **Pop per sq mi:** 1.

Pop 2005: 6,098. **State rank:** 51. **Pop change:** 2000-20005 -0.8%; 1990-2000 -2.5%. **Pop 2000:** 6,148 (White 93.8%; Black or African American 0.1%; Hispanic or Latino 0.9%; Asian 0.4%; Other 5.3%, including 3.3% American Indian/Alaska Native). **Foreign born:** 0.7%. **Median age:** 39.4.

Income 2000: per capita $15,943; median household $29,268; **Pop below poverty level:** 12.3%. ***Personal per capita income 2000-2003:** $20,722-$24,787.

Unemployment 2004: 2.4%. **Change from 2000:** +0.6%. **Median travel time to work:** 12.4 minutes. **Working outside county of residence:** 10%.

Cities with pop over 10,000: None.

CHEYENNE COUNTY

PO Box 217   **Ph:** 308-254-2141
Sidney, NE 69162   **Fax:** 308-254-5049
www.co.cheyenne.ne.us

On the southwestern border of NE, west of North Platte; organized Jun 6, 1871 from Lincoln County. **Name Origin:** For the Cheyenne Indians who once lived in the area.

Area (sq mi): 1196.45 (land 1196.34; water 0.11). **Pop per sq mi:** 8.4.

Pop 2005: 9,993. **State rank:** 27. **Pop change:** 2000-20005 +1.7%; 1990-2000 +3.5%. **Pop 2000:** 9,830 (White 93.9%; Black or African American 0.1%; Hispanic or Latino 4.5%; Asian 0.4%; Other 3.2%). **Foreign born:** 0.9%. **Median age:** 38.7.

Income 2000: per capita $17,437; median household $33,438; **Pop below poverty level:** 10%. ***Personal per capita income 2000-2003:** $23,993-$30,125.

Unemployment 2004: 3%. **Change from 2000:** +0.9%. **Median travel time to work:** 15.5 minutes. **Working outside county of residence:** 5%.

Cities with pop over 10,000: None.

CLAY COUNTY

111 W Fairfield St PO Box 67   **Ph:** 402-762-3463
Clay Center, NE 68933   **Fax:** 402-762-3506
www.claycounty.ne.gov

In south-central NE, southeast of Grand Island; original county, organized Mar 7, 1855 (prior to statehood). According to Thorndale and Dollarhide's *Map Guide to the U.S. Federal Censuses, 1790-1920*, area originally called Clay County is now part of Lancaster and Gage counties, while present-day Clay county occupies area which was unattached in 1860. **Name Origin:** For Henry Clay (1777-1852), U.S. senator from KY, known as the 'Great Pacificator' for his advocacy of compromise to avert national crises.

Area (sq mi): 573.53 (land 573.03; water 0.49). **Pop per sq mi:** 11.7.

Pop 2005: 6,733. **State rank:** 46. **Pop change:** 2000-20005 -4.3%; 1990-2000 -1.2%. **Pop 2000:** 7,039 (White 95.6%; Black or African American 0.2%; Hispanic or Latino 3.5%; Asian 0.3%; Other 1.9%). **Foreign born:** 2.6%. **Median age:** 39.9.

Income 2000: per capita $16,870; median household $34,259; **Pop below poverty level:** 10.4%. ***Personal per capita income 2000-2003:** $24,777-$26,428.

Unemployment 2004: 3.3%. **Change from 2000:** +0.6%. **Median travel time to work:** 19.9 minutes. **Working outside county of residence:** 37.5%.

Cities with pop over 10,000: None.

COLFAX COUNTY

411 E 11th St   **Ph:** 402-352-8504
Schuyler, NE 68661   **Fax:** 402-352-8515
www.colfaxcounty.ne.gov

In east-central NE, northwest of Omaha; organized Feb 15, 1869 from Platte County. **Name Origin:** For Schuyler Colfax (1823-85), U.S. vice president under Ulysses S. Grant (1869-73).

Area (sq mi): 418.58 (land 413.14; water 5.44). **Pop per sq mi:** 25.3.

*Source: Personal per capita income data are from the Bureau of Economic Analysis; per capita income data are from the Bureau of the Census.
See Introduction for explanation of differences.*

446

Colfax County (cont'd)

Pop 2005: 10,433. **State rank:** 26. **Pop change:** 2000-20005 -0.1%; 1990-2000 +14.2%. **Pop 2000:** 10,441 (White 73%; Black or African American 0.1%; Hispanic or Latino 26.2%; Asian 0.2%; Other 17.9%). **Foreign born:** 18.2%. **Median age:** 35.

Income 2000: per capita $15,148; median household $35,849; **Pop below poverty level:** 10.8%. **Personal per capita income 2000 2003:** $23,930-$26,506.

Unemployment 2004: 3.1%. **Change from 2000:** +0.6%. **Median travel time to work:** 18.6 minutes. **Working outside county of residence:** 29.8%.

Cities with pop over 10,000: None.

CUMING COUNTY

200 S Lincoln St PO Box 290   **Ph:** 402-372-6002
West Point, NE 68788   **Fax:** 402-372-6013
www.co.cuming.ne.us

In east-central NE; northwest of Omaha; organized Mar 16, 1855 from Burt County. **Name Origin:** For Thomas B. Cuming (?-1858), acting governor of NE Territory (1854-55; 1857-58).

Area (sq mi): 574.54 (land 572; water 2.54). **Pop per sq mi:** 16.9.

Pop 2005: 9,688. **State rank:** 28. **Pop change:** 2000-20005 -5%; 1990-2000 +0.9%. **Pop 2000:** 10,203 (White 93.6%; Black or African American 0.1%; Hispanic or Latino 5.5%; Asian 0.2%; Other 3.8%). **Foreign born:** 3.8%. **Median age:** 39.2.

Income 2000: per capita $16,443; median household $33,186; **Pop below poverty level:** 9%. **Personal per capita income 2000-2003:** $28,366-$33,379.

Unemployment 2004: 2.8%. **Change from 2000:** +0.7%. **Median travel time to work:** 15.5 minutes. **Working outside county of residence:** 19.1%.

Cities with pop over 10,000: None.

CUSTER COUNTY

431 S 10th St   **Ph:** 308-872-5701
Broken Bow, NE 68822   **Fax:** 308-872-2811
www.co.custer.ne.us

In south-central NE, east of North Platte; organized as Kountze County Feb 17, 1877 from unorganized territory. **Name Origin:** For Gen. George Armstrong Custer (1839-76), U.S. army officer and Indian fighter.

Area (sq mi): 2576.08 (land 2575.71; water 0.37). **Pop per sq mi:** 4.4.

Pop 2005: 11,410. **State rank:** 22. **Pop change:** 2000-20005 -3.2%; 1990-2000 -3.9%. **Pop 2000:** 11,793 (White 98%; Black or African American 0.1%; Hispanic or Latino 0.9%; Asian 0.2%; Other 1.2%). **Foreign born:** 0.4%. **Median age:** 41.3.

Income 2000: per capita $16,171; median household $30,677; **Pop below poverty level:** 12.4%. **Personal per capita income 2000-2003:** $22,855-$28,329.

Unemployment 2004: 2.9%. **Change from 2000:** +1%. **Median travel time to work:** 17.7 minutes. **Working outside county of residence:** 11.1%.

Cities with pop over 10,000: None.

DAKOTA COUNTY

1601 Broadway   **Ph:** 402-987-2126
Dakota City, NE 68731   **Fax:** 402-494-9228
www.dakotacountyne.org

On the northeastern border of NE, south of Sioux City, IA; original county, organized Mar 7, 1855. **Name Origin:** For the Dakota (also called the Sioux) Indian tribe.

Area (sq mi): 267.39 (land 263.8; water 3.6). **Pop per sq mi:** 77.1.

Pop 2005: 20,349. **State rank:** 16. **Pop change:** 2000-20005 +0.5%; 1990-2000 +21%. **Pop 2000:** 20,253 (White 70.9%; Black or African American 0.6%; Hispanic or Latino 22.6%; Asian 3.1%; Other 17.5%, including 1.9% American Indian/Alaska Native). **Foreign born:** 15.6%. **Median age:** 31.4.

Income 2000: per capita $16,125; median household $38,834; **Pop below poverty level:** 11.4%. **Personal per capita income 2000-2003:** $21,260-$22,022.

Unemployment 2004: 4.5%. **Change from 2000:** +1.7%. **Median travel time to work:** 17.3 minutes. **Working outside county of residence:** 49%.

Cities with pop over 10,000: South Sioux City (12,142).

DAWES COUNTY

451 Main St   **Ph:** 308-432-0100
Chadron, NE 69337   **Fax:** 308-432-5179
www.co.dawes.ne.us

On the northwestern border of NE, northeast of Scottsbluff; organized Feb 19, 1885 from Sioux County. **Name Origin:** For James William Dawes (1845-87), governor of NE (1883-87).

Area (sq mi): 1400.86 (land 1396.24; water 4.62). **Pop per sq mi:** 6.2.

Pop 2005: 8,636. **State rank:** 36. **Pop change:** 2000-20005 -4.7%; 1990-2000 +0.4%. **Pop 2000:** 9,060 (White 92.4%; Black or African American 0.8%; Hispanic or Latino 2.4%; Asian 0.3%; Other 5.6%, including 2.9% American Indian/Alaska Native). **Foreign born:** 2.2%. **Median age:** 30.6.

Income 2000: per capita $16,353; median household $29,476; **Pop below poverty level:** 18.9%. **Personal per capita income 2000-2003:** $17,926-$20,328.

Unemployment 2004: 3.1%. **Change from 2000:** -0.8%. **Median travel time to work:** 13.3 minutes. **Working outside county of residence:** 9.3%.

Cities with pop over 10,000: None.

DAWSON COUNTY

PO Box 370   **Ph:** 308-324-2127
Lexington, NE 68850   **Fax:** 308-324-6106
www.dawsoncountyne.net

In south-central NE, west of Grand Island; organized Jan 11, 1860 from Buffalo County. **Name Origin:** For Jacob Dawson, first postmaster of Lancaster (now Lincoln).

Area (sq mi): 1019.3 (land 1012.92; water 6.37). **Pop per sq mi:** 24.3.

Pop 2005: 24,617. **State rank:** 13. **Pop change:** 2000-20005 +1%; 1990-2000 +22.2%. **Pop 2000:** 24,365 (White 72.8%; Black or

Dawson County (cont'd)

African American 0.3%; Hispanic or Latino 25.4%; Asian 0.7%; Other 16.7%). **Foreign born:** 15.9%. **Median age:** 34.3.

Income 2000: per capita $15,973; median household $36,132; **Pop below poverty level:** 10.8%. ***Personal per capita income 2000-2003:** $21,883-$23,630.

Unemployment 2004: 4.1%. **Change from 2000:** +0.9%. **Median travel time to work:** 14 minutes. **Working outside county of residence:** 9.9%.

Cities with pop over 10,000: Lexington ⛪ (10,056).

DEUEL COUNTY
PO Box 327   **Ph:** 308-874-3308
Chappell, NE 69129   **Fax:** 308-874-3472
www.co.deuel.ne.us

On the southern border of NE, west of North Platte; organized Jan 1889 from Cheyenne County. **Name Origin:** For Henry (or Harry) Porter Deuel (1836-1914), an early settler of Omaha and later a local railroad official.

Area (sq mi): 440.79 (land 439.89; water 0.9). **Pop per sq mi:** 4.6.

Pop 2005: 2,004. **State rank:** 77. **Pop change:** 2000-20005 -4.5%; 1990-2000 -6.2%. **Pop 2000:** 2,098 (White 96%; Black or African American 0%; Hispanic or Latino 2.7%; Asian 0.4%; Other 2.2%). **Foreign born:** 0.9%. **Median age:** 43.5.

Income 2000: per capita $17,891; median household $32,981; **Pop below poverty level:** 9.1%. ***Personal per capita income 2000-2003:** $20,737-$26,226.

Unemployment 2004: 2.7%. **Change from 2000:** -0.1%. **Median travel time to work:** 18 minutes. **Working outside county of residence:** 31.6%.

Cities with pop over 10,000: None.

DIXON COUNTY
PO Box 395   **Ph:** 402-755-2881
Ponca, NE 68770   **Fax:** 402-755-2632
www.co.dixon.ne.us

On the northeastern border of NE, west of Sioux City, IA; original county, organized Dec 1858 (prior to statehood) from Dakota County. **Name Origin:** For an early settler.

Area (sq mi): 482.72 (land 476.39; water 6.33). **Pop per sq mi:** 12.9.

Pop 2005: 6,155. **State rank:** 50. **Pop change:** 2000-20005 -2.9%; 1990-2000 +3.2%. **Pop 2000:** 6,339 (White 93.5%; Black or African American 0%; Hispanic or Latino 5.5%; Asian 0.3%; Other 5.1%). **Foreign born:** 3.4%. **Median age:** 38.7.

Income 2000: per capita $15,350; median household $34,201; **Pop below poverty level:** 10%. ***Personal per capita income 2000-2003:** $25,039-$29,658.

Unemployment 2004: 3.6%. **Change from 2000:** +0.7%. **Median travel time to work:** 22.8 minutes. **Working outside county of residence:** 49.6%.

Cities with pop over 10,000: None.

DODGE COUNTY
435 N Park Ave Rm 102   **Ph:** 402-727-2767
Fremont, NE 68025   **Fax:** 402-727-2764
www.dodgecounty.ne.gov

In east-central NE, northwest of Omaha; original county, organized Mar 6, 1855 (prior to statehood). **Name Origin:** For Augustus Caesar Dodge (1812-83), son of Henry Dodge. First U.S. senator from IA (1848-55) and an active supporter of the Kansas-Nebraska bill.

Area (sq mi): 543.92 (land 534.39; water 9.53). **Pop per sq mi:** 67.5.

Pop 2005: 36,078. **State rank:** 7. **Pop change:** 2000-20005 -0.2%; 1990-2000 +4.8%. **Pop 2000:** 36,160 (White 94.3%; Black or African American 0.4%; Hispanic or Latino 3.9%; Asian 0.5%; Other 3.2%). **Foreign born:** 2.8%. **Median age:** 37.9.

Income 2000: per capita $17,757; median household $37,188; **Pop below poverty level:** 8.6%. ***Personal per capita income 2000-2003:** $24,961-$26,384.

Unemployment 2004: 4.5%. **Change from 2000:** +0.9%. **Median travel time to work:** 19.7 minutes. **Working outside county of residence:** 26.4%.

Cities with pop over 10,000: Fremont ⛪ (25,272).

DOUGLAS COUNTY
1819 Farnam St   **Ph:** 402-444-6762
Omaha, NE 68183   **Fax:** 402-444-6456
www.co.douglas.ne.us

On the eastern border of NE, west of Council Bluffs, IA; original county; organized 1854 (prior to statehood). **Name Origin:** For Stephen Arnold Douglas (1813-61), U.S. orator and statesman.

Area (sq mi): 339.6 (land 330.98; water 8.62). **Pop per sq mi:** 1471.2.

Pop 2005: 486,929. **State rank:** 1. **Pop change:** 2000-20005 +5%; 1990-2000 +11.3%. **Pop 2000:** 463,585 (White 78.2%; Black or African American 11.5%; Hispanic or Latino 6.7%; Asian 1.7%; Other 5.9%). **Foreign born:** 5.9%. **Median age:** 33.6.

Income 2000: per capita $22,879; median household $43,209; **Pop below poverty level:** 9.8%. ***Personal per capita income 2000-2003:** $34,714-$36,672.

Unemployment 2004: 4.5%. **Change from 2000:** +1.1%. **Median travel time to work:** 18.6 minutes. **Working outside county of residence:** 9.8%.

Cities with pop over 10,000: None.

DUNDY COUNTY
PO Box 506   **Ph:** 308-423-2058
Benkelman, NE 69021
www.co.dundy.ne.us

On the southern border of NE, west of McCook; organized Feb 27, 1873 from unorganized territory. **Name Origin:** For Elmer S. Dundy (1830-96), NE territorial legislator and jurist of the U.S. circuit court.

Area (sq mi): 920.79 (land 919.86; water 0.93). **Pop per sq mi:** 2.3.

Pop 2005: 2,133. **State rank:** 75. **Pop change:** 2000-20005 -6.9%; 1990-2000 -11.2%. **Pop 2000:** 2,292 (White 94.7%; Black or African

*Source: Personal per capita income data are from the Bureau of Economic Analysis; per capita income data are from the Bureau of the Census. See Introduction for explanation of differences.

448

Dundy County (cont'd)

American 0%; Hispanic or Latino 3.2%; Asian 0.5%; Other 2.5%).
Foreign born: 1.9%. **Median age:** 43.5.

Income 2000: per capita $15,786; median household $27,010; **Pop
below poverty level:** 13.6%. ***Personal per capita income 2000-
2003:** $26,958-$30,600.

Unemployment 2004: 3.5%. **Change from 2000:** +1.5%. **Median
travel time to work:** 14.4 minutes. **Working outside county of
residence:** 15.5%.

Cities with pop over 10,000: None.

FILLMORE COUNTY

PO Box 307   **Ph:** 402-759-4931
Geneva, NE 68361   **Fax:** 402-759-4307
www.fillmorecounty.org

In southeastern NE, southwest of Lincoln; established Jan 26, 1856
from unorganized territory, organized 1871. **Name Origin:** For
Millard Fillmore (1800-74), thirteenth U.S. president.

Area (sq mi): 576.62 (land 576.46; water 0.16). **Pop per sq mi:** 11.1.

Pop 2005: 6,385. **State rank:** 49. **Pop change:** 2000-20005 -3.8%;
1990-2000 -6.6%. **Pop 2000:** 6,634 (White 97.1%; Black or African
American 0.2%; Hispanic or Latino 1.7%; Asian 0.1%; Other 1.9%).
Foreign born: 0.8%. **Median age:** 41.4.

Income 2000: per capita $17,465; median household $35,162; **Pop
below poverty level:** 7.8%. ***Personal per capita income 2000-
2003:** $26,226-$28,974.

Unemployment 2004: 3.4%. **Change from 2000:** +0.7%. **Median
travel time to work:** 15.7 minutes. **Working outside county of
residence:** 23.2%.

Cities with pop over 10,000: None.

FRANKLIN COUNTY

PO Box 146   **Ph:** 308-425-6202
Franklin, NE 68939   **Fax:** 308-425-6093

On central southern border of NE, southwest of Grand Island;
organized Mar 9, 1871 from Kearney County. **Name Origin:** For
Benjamin Franklin (1706-90), U.S. patriot, diplomat, and
statesman.

Area (sq mi): 576.11 (land 575.92; water 0.19). **Pop per sq mi:** 5.9.

Pop 2005: 3,421. **State rank:** 66. **Pop change:** 2000-20005 -4.3%;
1990-2000 -9.2%. **Pop 2000:** 3,574 (White 98.7%; Black or African
American 0%; Hispanic or Latino 0.6%; Asian 0.1%; Other 0.7%).
Foreign born: 0.6%. **Median age:** 42.8.

Income 2000: per capita $15,390; median household $29,304; **Pop
below poverty level:** 13.2%. ***Personal per capita income 2000-
2003:** $21,850-$25,610.

Unemployment 2004: 3.1%. **Change from 2000:** +0.6%. **Median
travel time to work:** 20.9 minutes. **Working outside county of
residence:** 32.8%.

Cities with pop over 10,000: None.

FRONTIER COUNTY

PO Box 40   **Ph:** 308-367-8641
Stockville, NE 69042   **Fax:** 308-367-8730
www.co.frontier.ne.us

In south-central NE, south of North Platter; organized Jan 17,
1872 from unorganized territory. **Name Origin:** For its location
on the NE frontier at the time of naming.

Area (sq mi): 980.06 (land 974.55; water 5.51). **Pop per sq mi:** 2.9.

Pop 2005: 2,795. **State rank:** 72. **Pop change:** 2000-20005 -9.8%;
1990-2000 -0.1%. **Pop 2000:** 3,099 (White 98%; Black or African
American 0.1%; Hispanic or Latino 1%; Asian 0.3%; Other 1.4%).
Foreign born: 1%. **Median age:** 38.5.

Income 2000: per capita $16,648; median household $33,038; **Pop
below poverty level:** 12.2%. ***Personal per capita income 2000-
2003:** $19,807-$26,001.

Unemployment 2004: 2.8%. **Change from 2000:** +0.7%. **Median
travel time to work:** 18 minutes. **Working outside county of residence:** 28.7%.

Cities with pop over 10,000: None.

FURNAS COUNTY

PO Box 387   **Ph:** 308-268-4145
Beaver City, NE 68926   **Fax:** 308-268-3205

On the central southern border of NE, east of McCook; organized
Feb 27, 1873 from unorganized territory. **Name Origin:** For Col.
Robert Wilkinson Furnas (1824-1905), an officer in the Civil War
and governor of NE (1873-75).

Area (sq mi): 720.51 (land 718.09; water 2.42). **Pop per sq mi:** 7.

Pop 2005: 5,019. **State rank:** 57. **Pop change:** 2000-20005 -5.7%;
1990-2000 -4.1%. **Pop 2000:** 5,324 (White 97.6%; Black or African
American 0.1%; Hispanic or Latino 1.1%; Asian 0.2%; Other 1.5%).
Foreign born: 0.3%. **Median age:** 43.5.

Income 2000: per capita $17,223; median household $30,498; **Pop
below poverty level:** 10.6%. ***Personal per capita income 2000-
2003:** $22,332-$24,627.

Unemployment 2004: 3.2%. **Change from 2000:** +1.3%. **Median
travel time to work:** 15.7 minutes. **Working outside county of
residence:** 21.2%.

Cities with pop over 10,000: None.

GAGE COUNTY

PO Box 429   **Ph:** 402-223-1300
Beatrice, NE 68310   **Fax:** 402-223-1371
www.co.gage.ne.us

On the southern border of NE, south of Lincoln; original county;
organized Mar 16, 1855 (prior to statehood). **Name Origin:** For
William D. Gage (1803-85). Methodist minister and a local official.

Area (sq mi): 859.94 (land 855.29; water 4.65). **Pop per sq mi:** 27.2.

Pop 2005: 23,306. **State rank:** 14. **Pop change:** 2000-20005 +1.4%;
1990-2000 +0.9%. **Pop 2000:** 22,993 (White 97.2%; Black or African American 0.3%; Hispanic or Latino 0.9%; Asian 0.3%; Other
1.7%). **Foreign born:** 0.7%. **Median age:** 39.9.

Gage County (cont'd)

Income 2000: per capita $17,190; median household $34,908; **Pop below poverty level:** 8.7%. ***Personal per capita income 2000-2003:** $25,444-$27,857.

Unemployment 2004: 4.2%. **Change from 2000:** +1.5%. **Median travel time to work:** 18.6 minutes. **Working outside county of residence:** 20.4%.

Cities with pop over 10,000: Beatrice 🏛 (12,963).

GARDEN COUNTY

PO Box 486   **Ph:** 308-772-3924
Oshkosh, NE 69154   **Fax:** 308-772-0124
www.co.garden.ne.us

In west-central NE, southeast of Scottsbluff; organized Nov 2, 1909 from Devel County. **Name Origin:** Named by John T. and William R. Twiford, the developers who thought it would become the 'garden spot of the west.'

Area (sq mi): 1731 (land 1704.4; water 26.6). **Pop per sq mi:** 1.2.

Pop 2005: 1,997. **State rank:** 78. **Pop change:** 2000-20005 -12.9%; 1990-2000 -6.8%. **Pop 2000:** 2,292 (White 97.3%; Black or African American 0.1%; Hispanic or Latino 1.4%; Asian 0.3%; Other 1.3%). **Foreign born:** 0.9%. **Median age:** 45.6.

Income 2000: per capita $15,414; median household $26,458; **Pop below poverty level:** 14.8%. ***Personal per capita income 2000-2003:** $19,657-$25,644.

Unemployment 2004: 3.5%. **Change from 2000:** +0.4%. **Median travel time to work:** 14.1 minutes. **Working outside county of residence:** 13.5%.

Cities with pop over 10,000: None.

GARFIELD COUNTY

PO Box 218   **Ph:** 308-346-4161
Burwell, NE 68823
www.garfieldcounty.ne.gov

In east-central NE, northwest of Grand Island; organized Nov 8, 1881 from Wheeler County. **Name Origin:** For James Abram Garfield (1831-81), twentieth U.S. president.

Area (sq mi): 571.34 (land 570.03; water 1.31). **Pop per sq mi:** 3.2.

Pop 2005: 1,816. **State rank:** 79. **Pop change:** 2000-20005 -4.5%; 1990-2000 -11.2%. **Pop 2000:** 1,902 (White 98.2%; Black or African American 0%; Hispanic or Latino 1%; Asian 0.1%; Other 1.2%). **Foreign born:** 0.7%. **Median age:** 45.9.

Income 2000: per capita $14,368; median household $27,407; **Pop below poverty level:** 12.6%. ***Personal per capita income 2000-2003:** $23,584-$26,715.

Unemployment 2004: 3.1%. **Change from 2000:** +1.3%. **Median travel time to work:** 16.5 minutes. **Working outside county of residence:** 18.1%.

Cities with pop over 10,000: None.

GOSPER COUNTY

507 Smith Ave PO Box 136   **Ph:** 308-785-2611
Elwood, NE 68937   **Fax:** 308-785-2300
www.co.gosper.ne.us

In south-central NE, organized Aug 29, 1873 from unorganized territory. **Name Origin:** For John J. Gosper, NE secretary of state (1873-75).

Area (sq mi): 462.74 (land 458.18; water 4.57). **Pop per sq mi:** 4.4.

Pop 2005: 2,020. **State rank:** 76. **Pop change:** 2000-20005 -5.7%; 1990-2000 +11.2%. **Pop 2000:** 2,143 (White 98%; Black or African American 0%; Hispanic or Latino 1.3%; Asian 0.2%; Other 0.9%). **Foreign born:** 0.5%. **Median age:** 43.4.

Income 2000: per capita $17,957; median household $36,827; **Pop below poverty level:** 7.9%. ***Personal per capita income 2000-2003:** $23,211-$27,305.

Unemployment 2004: 3.7%. **Change from 2000:** +1.5%. **Median travel time to work:** 18.7 minutes. **Working outside county of residence:** 51.6%.

Cities with pop over 10,000: None.

GRANT COUNTY

105 E Harrison St PO Box 139   **Ph:** 308-458-2488
Hyannis, NE 69350   **Fax:** 308-458-2780

In west-central NE, northwest of North Platte; organized Mar 31, 1888 from unorganized territory. In 1870 a 'paper' county called Grant covered parts of present-day Lincoln, Frontier, Red Willow, Furnas, Gosper, Dawson, Hayes, and Hitchcock counties, much of which was known as Shorter County in 1860. **Name Origin:** For Ulysses Simpson Grant (1822-85), Civil War general and eighteenth U.S. president.

Area (sq mi): 783.23 (land 776.22; water 7). **Pop per sq mi:** 0.9.

Pop 2005: 670. **State rank:** 89. **Pop change:** 2000-20005 -10.3%; 1990-2000 -2.9%. **Pop 2000:** 747 (White 98.3%; Black or African American 0%; Hispanic or Latino 1.3%; Asian 0.3%; Other 0.9%). **Foreign born:** 1.1%. **Median age:** 39.9.

Income 2000: per capita $14,815; median household $34,821; **Pop below poverty level:** 9.7%. ***Personal per capita income 2000-2003:** $9,669-$13,705.

Unemployment 2004: 2.3%. **Change from 2000:** +0.6%. **Median travel time to work:** 18.7 minutes. **Working outside county of residence:** 10.5%.

Cities with pop over 10,000: None.

GREELEY COUNTY

PO Box 287   **Ph:** 308-428-3625
Greeley, NE 68842   **Fax:** 308-428-3022

In east-central NE, north of Grand Island; organized Mar 1, 1871 from Boone County. **Name Origin:** For Horace Greeley (1811-72), editor who championed westward expansion.

Area (sq mi): 570.71 (land 569.85; water 0.85). **Pop per sq mi:** 4.4.

Pop 2005: 2,512. **State rank:** 73. **Pop change:** 2000-20005 -7.4%; 1990-2000 -9.7%. **Pop 2000:** 2,714 (White 97.9%; Black or African American 0.7%; Hispanic or Latino 0.8%; Asian 0.1%; Other 1.4%). **Foreign born:** 0.7%. **Median age:** 41.7.

---

*Source: Personal per capita income data are from the Bureau of Economic Analysis; per capita income data are from the Bureau of the Census. See Introduction for explanation of differences.

Greeley County (cont'd)

Income 2000: per capita $13,731; median household $28,375; **Pop below poverty level:** 14.6%. ***Personal per capita income 2000-2003:** $20,637-$26,559.

Unemployment 2004: 3.6%. **Change from 2000:** +0.6%. **Median travel time to work:** 18.6 minutes. **Working outside county of residence:** 24.5%.

Cities with pop over 10,000: None.

HALL COUNTY
121 S Pine St   **Ph:** 308-385-5080
Grand Island, NE 68801   **Fax:** 308-385-5184
www.hcgi.org

In south-central NE, west of Lincoln; original county; organized Nov 4, 1858 (prior to statehood). **Name Origin:** For Augustus Hall (1814-61), U.S. representative from IA (1855-57) and chief justice of NE Territory (1858-61).

Area (sq mi): 552.22 (land 546.4; water 5.83). **Pop per sq mi:** 100.8.

Pop 2005: 55,104. **State rank:** 4. **Pop change:** 2000-20005 +2.9%; 1990-2000 +9.4%. **Pop 2000:** 53,534 (White 83.7%; Black or African American 0.4%; Hispanic or Latino 14%; Asian 1.1%; Other 9.8%). **Foreign born:** 8.3%. **Median age:** 35.6.

Income 2000: per capita $17,386; median household $36,972; **Pop below poverty level:** 12%. ***Personal per capita income 2000-2003:** $24,843-$27,837.

Unemployment 2004: 4.7%. **Change from 2000:** +1.8%. **Median travel time to work:** 15.2 minutes. **Working outside county of residence:** 8.8%.

Cities with pop over 10,000: Grand Island 🏛 (44,287).

HAMILTON COUNTY
1111 13th St Suite 1   **Ph:** 402-694-3443
Aurora, NE 68818   **Fax:** 402-694-2397
www.co.hamilton.ne.us

In south-central NE, east of Grand Island; organized Feb 16, 1867 from York County. **Name Origin:** For Alexander Hamilton (1757-1804), first U.S. secretary of treasury (1789-95).

Area (sq mi): 546.77 (land 543.68; water 3.09). **Pop per sq mi:** 17.6.

Pop 2005: 9,568. **State rank:** 29. **Pop change:** 2000-20005 +1.8%; 1990-2000 +6.1%. **Pop 2000:** 9,403 (White 98%; Black or African American 0.2%; Hispanic or Latino 1.1%; Asian 0.2%; Other 1.2%). **Foreign born:** 0.4%. **Median age:** 38.1.

Income 2000: per capita $17,590; median household $40,277; **Pop below poverty level:** 7.5%. ***Personal per capita income 2000-2003:** $22,728-$25,254.

Unemployment 2004: 3%. **Change from 2000:** +1.1%. **Median travel time to work:** 17.3 minutes. **Working outside county of residence:** 35.3%.

Cities with pop over 10,000: None.

HARLAN COUNTY
PO Box 698   **Ph:** 308-928-2173
Alma, NE 68920   **Fax:** 308-928-2079

On the central southern border of NE, southwest of Kearney; organized Jun 3, 1871 from Lincoln County. **Name Origin:** For either Thomas Harlan, a local official, or for his uncle, James Harlan (1820-99), U.S. senator from IA (1855-65; 1867-73) and U.S. secretary of the interior (1865-66).

Area (sq mi): 574.18 (land 552.78; water 21.4). **Pop per sq mi:** 6.3.

Pop 2005: 3,462. **State rank:** 65. **Pop change:** 2000-20005 -8.6%; 1990-2000 -0.6%. **Pop 2000:** 3,786 (White 98.5%; Black or African American 0.1%; Hispanic or Latino 0.8%; Asian 0.1%; Other 0.9%). **Foreign born:** 0.3%. **Median age:** 44.5.

Income 2000: per capita $15,618; median household $30,679; **Pop below poverty level:** 10.1%. ***Personal per capita income 2000-2003:** $21,003-$25,176.

Unemployment 2004: 3.1%. **Change from 2000:** +0.7%. **Median travel time to work:** 17.5 minutes. **Working outside county of residence:** 31.9%.

Cities with pop over 10,000: None.

HAYES COUNTY
PO Box 370   **Ph:** 308-286-3413
Hayes Center, NE 69033   **Fax:** 308-286-3208
www.geocities.com/hayes_county/

In south-central NE, southwest of North Platte; organized Feb 19, 1877 from unorganized territory. **Name Origin:** For Rutherford Birchard Hayes (1822-93), nineteenth U.S. president.

Area (sq mi): 713.33 (land 713.11; water 0.22). **Pop per sq mi:** 1.4.

Pop 2005: 1,027. **State rank:** 82. **Pop change:** 2000-20005 -3.8%; 1990-2000 -12.6%. **Pop 2000:** 1,068 (White 96.4%; Black or African American 0.2%; Hispanic or Latino 2.5%; Asian 0.3%; Other 2.4%). **Foreign born:** 2%. **Median age:** 42.5.

Income 2000: per capita $14,099; median household $26,667; **Pop below poverty level:** 18.4%. ***Personal per capita income 2000-2003:** $16,839-$21,899.

Unemployment 2004: 3.4%. **Change from 2000:** +1%. **Median travel time to work:** 17.4 minutes. **Working outside county of residence:** 26.3%.

Cities with pop over 10,000: None.

HITCHCOCK COUNTY
PO Box 248   **Ph:** 308-334-5646
Trenton, NE 69044   **Fax:** 308-334-5398
www.co.hitchcock.ne.us

On the central southern border of NE, south of North Platte; organized Feb 27, 1873 from unorganized territory. **Name Origin:** For Phineas Warrener Hitchcock (1831-81), U.S. senator from NE (1871-77).

Area (sq mi): 718.57 (land 710.03; water 8.54). **Pop per sq mi:** 4.2.

Pop 2005: 2,970. **State rank:** 70. **Pop change:** 2000-20005 -4.5%; 1990-2000 -17%. **Pop 2000:** 3,111 (White 97.4%; Black or African American 0.1%; Hispanic or Latino 1.4%; Asian 0.1%; Other 1.4%). **Foreign born:** 1.2%. **Median age:** 43.6.

Income 2000: per capita $14,804; median household $28,287; **Pop below poverty level:** 14.9%. ***Personal per capita income 2000-2003:** $16,666-$20,374.

Hitchcock County (cont'd)

Unemployment 2004: 3.8%. **Change from 2000:** +0.7%. **Median travel time to work:** 20.7 minutes. **Working outside county of residence:** 38.9%.

Cities with pop over 10,000: None.

HOLT COUNTY

PO Box 329   **Ph:** 402-336-1762
O'Neill, NE 68763   **Fax:** 402-336-1762
www.co.holt.ne.us

In north-central NE; organized Jan 9, 1862 from Elkhorn County. **Name Origin:** For Joseph Holt (1807-94), U.S. Postmaster General (1859-61); secretary of war (1861), and judge advocate general for the U.S. army (1862-75).

Area (sq mi): 2417.65 (land 2412.66; water 4.99). **Pop per sq mi:** 4.5.

Pop 2005: 10,784. **State rank:** 25. **Pop change:** 2000-20005 -6.6%; 1990-2000 -8.3%. **Pop 2000:** 11,551 (White 98.5%; Black or African American 0%; Hispanic or Latino 0.7%; Asian 0.2%; Other 1%). **Foreign born:** 0.8%. **Median age:** 40.5.

Income 2000: per capita $15,256; median household $30,738; **Pop below poverty level:** 13%. ***Personal per capita income 2000-2003:** $22,208-$26,698.

Unemployment 2004: 3%. **Change from 2000:** +0%. **Median travel time to work:** 15.5 minutes. **Working outside county of residence:** 6.5%.

Cities with pop over 10,000: None.

HOOKER COUNTY

PO Box 184   **Ph:** 308-546-2244
Mullen, NE 69152   **Fax:** 308-546-2490
www.co.hooker.ne.us

In west-central NE, northwest of North Platte; organized Mar 29, 1889 from unorganized territory. **Name Origin:** For Joseph Hooker (1814-79), famous Union general during the Civil War.

Area (sq mi): 721.51 (land 721.17; water 0.34). **Pop per sq mi:** 1.

Pop 2005: 744. **State rank:** 85. **Pop change:** 2000-20005 -5%; 1990-2000 -1.3%. **Pop 2000:** 783 (White 97.8%; Black or African American 0%; Hispanic or Latino 1%; Asian 0.1%; Other 1.1%). **Foreign born:** 0%. **Median age:** 45.3.

Income 2000: per capita $15,513; median household $27,868; **Pop below poverty level:** 6.9%. ***Personal per capita income 2000-2003:** $13,222-$19,567.

Unemployment 2004: 3.3%. **Change from 2000:** +0.2%. **Median travel time to work:** 15 minutes. **Working outside county of residence:** 13.9%.

Cities with pop over 10,000: None.

HOWARD COUNTY

PO Box 25   **Ph:** 308-754-4343
Saint Paul, NE 68873   **Fax:** 308-754-4125
www.howardcounty.ne.gov

In east-central NE, north of Grand Island; organized Mar 1, 1871 from Hall County. **Name Origin:** For Gen. Oliver Otis Howard (1830-1909), Union officer in the Seminole War and the Civil War; president of Howard University (1869-73). Others believe it was for Howard Paul, son of an early settler, whose family founded Saint Paul, the county seat.

Area (sq mi): 575.74 (land 569.47; water 6.27). **Pop per sq mi:** 11.8.

Pop 2005: 6,708. **State rank:** 47. **Pop change:** 2000-20005 +2.1%; 1990-2000 +8.5%. **Pop 2000:** 6,567 (White 98%; Black or African American 0.3%; Hispanic or Latino 1%; Asian 0.1%; Other 0.8%). **Foreign born:** 0.8%. **Median age:** 38.1.

Income 2000: per capita $15,535; median household $33,305; **Pop below poverty level:** 11.7%. ***Personal per capita income 2000-2003:** $21,496-$25,053.

Unemployment 2004: 4%. **Change from 2000:** +1.2%. **Median travel time to work:** 22.2 minutes. **Working outside county of residence:** 47.5%.

Cities with pop over 10,000: None.

JEFFERSON COUNTY

411 4th St   **Ph:** 402-729-2323
Fairbury, NE 68352   **Fax:** 402-729-2016
www.co.jefferson.ne.us

On the southern border of NE, southwest of Lincoln. Organized 1864; combined with Jones County 1867; both counties dissolved 1871 and eastern part (Jones County) named Jefferson. Original Jones County probably established Jan 26, 1856. Jefferson County attached to Gage County for judicial purposes between 1857 and 1864. **Name Origin:** For Thomas Jefferson (1743-1826), U.S. patriot and statesman; third U.S. president.

Area (sq mi): 575.5 (land 573.01; water 2.48). **Pop per sq mi:** 13.8.

Pop 2005: 7,925. **State rank:** 39. **Pop change:** 2000-20005 -4.9%; 1990-2000 -4.9%. **Pop 2000:** 8,333 (White 97.7%; Black or African American 0.1%; Hispanic or Latino 1.3%; Asian 0.2%; Other 1.3%). **Foreign born:** 0.4%. **Median age:** 42.9.

Income 2000: per capita $18,380; median household $32,629; **Pop below poverty level:** 8.9%. ***Personal per capita income 2000-2003:** $22,708-$25,493.

Unemployment 2004: 4.1%. **Change from 2000:** -0.6%. **Median travel time to work:** 18.6 minutes. **Working outside county of residence:** 26%.

Cities with pop over 10,000: None.

JOHNSON COUNTY

PO Box 416   **Ph:** 402-335-6300
Tecumseh, NE 68450   **Fax:** 402-335-6311
www.co.johnson.ne.us

In southeastern NE, southeast of Lincoln; original county; organized Mar 2, 1855 (prior to statehood). **Name Origin:** For Col. Richard Mentor Johnson (1781-1850), officer in the War of 1812, U.S. senator from KY (1819-29), and U.S. vice president under Van Buren (1837-41).

Area (sq mi): 376.82 (land 376.13; water 0.69). **Pop per sq mi:** 12.5.

Pop 2005: 4,695. **State rank:** 59. **Pop change:** 2000-20005 +4.6%; 1990-2000 -4%. **Pop 2000:** 4,488 (White 92.8%; Black or African

*Source: Personal per capita income data are from the Bureau of Economic Analysis; per capita income data are from the Bureau of the Census. See Introduction for explanation of differences.

452

Johnson County (cont'd)

American 0.1%; Hispanic or Latino 2.9%; Asian 2.7%; Other 3.7%). **Foreign born:** 4.3%. **Median age:** 42.4.

Income 2000: per capita $16,437; median household $32,460; **Pop below poverty level:** 8.9%. ***Personal per capita income 2000-2003:** $21,352-$27,471.

Unemployment 2004: 3.2%. **Change from 2000:** +0%. **Median travel time to work:** 24 minutes. **Working outside county of residence:** 40.6%.

Cities with pop over 10,000: None.

KEARNEY COUNTY
PO Box 339   **Ph:** 308-832-2723
Minden, NE 68959   **Fax:** 308-832-2729
www.kearneycounty.ne.gov

In south-central NE, southwest of Grand Island; original county; organized Jan 10, 1860 (prior to statehood). **Name Origin:** For Fort Kearny, itself named for Gen. Stephen Watts Kearny (1794-1848), officer in the War of 1812 and the Mexican-American War. The e in the last syllable was added in 1857, reason unknown.

Area (sq mi): 516.13 (land 516.03; water 0.11). **Pop per sq mi:** 13.1.

Pop 2005: 6,774. **State rank:** 45. **Pop change:** 2000-20005 -1.6%; 1990-2000 +3.8%. **Pop 2000:** 6,882 (White 96.8%; Black or African American 0.2%; Hispanic or Latino 2.3%; Asian 0.2%; Other 1.8%). **Foreign born:** 1.6%. **Median age:** 38.7.

Income 2000: per capita $18,118; median household $39,247; **Pop below poverty level:** 8.5%. ***Personal per capita income 2000-2003:** $26,171-$29,842.

Unemployment 2004: 2.8%. **Change from 2000:** +0.5%. **Median travel time to work:** 18.5 minutes. **Working outside county of residence:** 44.1%.

Cities with pop over 10,000: None.

KEITH COUNTY
PO Box 149   **Ph:** 308-284-4726
Ogallala, NE 69153   **Fax:** 308-284-6277
www.co.keith.ne.us

In west-central NE, west of North Platte; organized May 3, 1873 from Lincoln County. **Name Origin:** For either Morrill C. Keith, the grandfather of NE governor Keith Morrill (1917-19), or John Keith, a prominent citizen of North Platte.

Area (sq mi): 1109.77 (land 1061.26; water 48.51). **Pop per sq mi:** 7.8.

Pop 2005: 8,330. **State rank:** 37. **Pop change:** 2000-20005 -6.1%; 1990-2000 +3.4%. **Pop 2000:** 8,875 (White 94.5%; Black or African American 0.1%; Hispanic or Latino 4.2%; Asian 0.2%; Other 3%). **Foreign born:** 1.7%. **Median age:** 41.1.

Income 2000: per capita $17,421; median household $32,325; **Pop below poverty level:** 9.3%. ***Personal per capita income 2000-2003:** $21,256-$23,138.

Unemployment 2004: 3.3%. **Change from 2000:** +0.4%. **Median travel time to work:** 16.4 minutes. **Working outside county of residence:** 13.5%.

Cities with pop over 10,000: None.

KEYA PAHA COUNTY
PO Box 349   **Ph:** 402-497-3791
Springview, NE 68778   **Fax:** 402-497-3799
www.co.keya-paha.ne.us

On the central northern border of NE; organized Nov 4, 1884 from Brown County. **Name Origin:** For the Keya Paha River, which flows through the northeastern part of the county. From Dakota Indian keya 'turtle' and paha 'hill,' for a turtle-shaped hill.

Area (sq mi): 774.17 (land 773.29; water 0.89). **Pop per sq mi:** 1.2.

Pop 2005: 902. **State rank:** 83. **Pop change:** 2000-20005 -8.2%; 1990-2000 -4.5%. **Pop 2000:** 983 (White 95.7%; Black or African American 0%; Hispanic or Latino 3.9%; Asian 0%; Other 0.6%). **Foreign born:** 2.2%. **Median age:** 41.9.

Income 2000: per capita $11,860; median household $24,911; **Pop below poverty level:** 26.9%. ***Personal per capita income 2000-2003:** $15,423-$23,932.

Unemployment 2004: 3%. **Change from 2000:** +1.7%. **Median travel time to work:** 18.2 minutes. **Working outside county of residence:** 24.1%.

Cities with pop over 10,000: None.

KIMBALL COUNTY
114 E 3rd St   **Ph:** 308-235-2241
Kimball, NE 69145   **Fax:** 308-235-3654
www.co.kimball.ne.us

In the southwestern corner of NE, south of Scottsbluff; organized Nov 6, 1888 from Cheyenne County. **Name Origin:** For Thomas Lord Kimball (1831-99), vice president of the Union Pacific Railroad.

Area (sq mi): 952.31 (land 951.72; water 0.58). **Pop per sq mi:** 4.

Pop 2005: 3,782. **State rank:** 62. **Pop change:** 2000-20005 -7.5%; 1990-2000 -0.5%. **Pop 2000:** 4,089 (White 94.5%; Black or African American 0.2%; Hispanic or Latino 3.3%; Asian 0.1%; Other 2.7%). **Foreign born:** 0.7%. **Median age:** 42.8.

Income 2000: per capita $17,525; median household $30,586; **Pop below poverty level:** 11.1%. ***Personal per capita income 2000-2003:** $22,878-$25,053.

Unemployment 2004: 2.8%. **Change from 2000:** +0.6%. **Median travel time to work:** 15.7 minutes. **Working outside county of residence:** 14.9%.

Cities with pop over 10,000: None.

KNOX COUNTY
PO Box 166   **Ph:** 402-288-5604
Center, NE 68724   **Fax:** 402-288-5605
www.co.knox.ne.us

On the northeastern border of NE, northwest of Sioux City, IA. Original county; organized as L'Eau Qui Court County, Feb 10, 1857 (prior to statehood); name changed to Emmett County; then to present name Feb 21, 1873. **Name Origin:** For Gen. Henry Knox (1750-1806), Revolutionary War officer and first U.S. secretary of war (1785-95).

Area (sq mi): 1139.65 (land 1108.12; water 31.53). **Pop per sq mi:** 8.

Pop 2005: 8,916. **State rank:** 33. **Pop change:** 2000-20005 -4.9%; 1990-2000 -1.7%. **Pop 2000:** 9,374 (White 91.3%; Black or African

Knox County (cont'd)

American 0.1%; Hispanic or Latino 0.9%; Asian 0.2%; Other 8%, including 7.1% American Indian/Alaska Native). **Foreign born:** 1%. **Median age:** 43.

Income 2000: per capita $13,971; median household $27,564; **Pop below poverty level:** 15.6%. ***Personal per capita income 2000-2003:** $20,152-$24,721.

Unemployment 2004: 3.4%. **Change from 2000:** -0.2%. **Median travel time to work:** 17.3 minutes. **Working outside county of residence:** 22.2%.

Cities with pop over 10,000: None.

LANCASTER COUNTY
555 S 10th St Rm 108 **Ph:** 402-441-7481
Lincoln, NE 68508   **Fax:** 402-441-8728
www.lancaster.ne.gov

In southeastern NE, southwest of Omaha; original county, organized Mar 6, 1855 (prior to statehood). **Name Origin:** For Lancaster County, PA, former home of many settlers.

Area (sq mi): 846.71 (land 838.88; water 7.83). **Pop per sq mi:** 315.7.

Pop 2005: 264,814. **State rank:** 2. **Pop change:** 2000-20005 +5.8%; 1990-2000 +17.2%. **Pop 2000:** 250,291 (White 88.7%; Black or African American 2.8%; Hispanic or Latino 3.4%; Asian 2.9%; Other 4.3%). **Foreign born:** 5.4%. **Median age:** 32.

Income 2000: per capita $21,265; median household $41,850; **Pop below poverty level:** 9.5%. ***Personal per capita income 2000-2003:** $29,231-$30,978.

Unemployment 2004: 3.4%. **Change from 2000:** +0.6%. **Median travel time to work:** 17.8 minutes. **Working outside county of residence:** 5.8%.

Cities with pop over 10,000: Lincoln 🏛 (236,146).

LINCOLN COUNTY
301 N Jeffers St   **Ph:** 308-534-4350
North Platte, NE 69101 **Fax:** 308-535-3527
www.co.lincoln.ne.us

In south-central NE, north of McCook; organized as Shorter County Jan 7, 1860 (prior to statehood) from unorganized territory (contained the 'paper' counties of Grant and Jackson in 1870); name changed 1866. **Name Origin:** For Abraham Lincoln (1809-65), sixteenth U.S. president.

Area (sq mi): 2575.1 (land 2563.98; water 11.12). **Pop per sq mi:** 13.9.

Pop 2005: 35,636. **State rank:** 8. **Pop change:** 2000-20005 +2.9%; 1990-2000 +6.5%. **Pop 2000:** 34,632 (White 92.6%; Black or African American 0.5%; Hispanic or Latino 5.4%; Asian 0.4%; Other 4.4%). **Foreign born:** 1.2%. **Median age:** 37.8.

Income 2000: per capita $18,696; median household $36,568; **Pop below poverty level:** 9.7%. ***Personal per capita income 2000-2003:** $23,823-$26,519.

Unemployment 2004: 3.4%. **Change from 2000:** -0.1%. **Median travel time to work:** 16 minutes. **Working outside county of residence:** 4.8%.

Cities with pop over 10,000: North Platte 🏛 (23,944).

LOGAN COUNTY
317 Main St PO Box 8 **Ph:** 308-636-2311
Stapleton, NE 69163
www.co.logan.ne.us

In central NE, north of North Platte; organized Feb 24, 1885 from Custer County. **Name Origin:** For Gen. John Alexander Logan (1826-86), officer in the Mexican-American War and Civil War; U.S. senator from IL (1871-77; 1879-86).

Area (sq mi): 571.15 (land 570.68; water 0.46). **Pop per sq mi:** 1.3.

Pop 2005: 740. **State rank:** 86. **Pop change:** 2000-20005 -4.4%; 1990-2000 -11.8%. **Pop 2000:** 774 (White 97.7%; Black or African American 0.1%; Hispanic or Latino 0.9%; Asian 0%; Other 1.3%, including 1% American Indian/Alaska Native). **Foreign born:** 0.3%. **Median age:** 41.8.

Income 2000: per capita $14,937; median household $33,125; **Pop below poverty level:** 10.5%. ***Personal per capita income 2000-2003:** $19,018-$23,261.

Unemployment 2004: 2.9%. **Change from 2000:** +0.6%. **Median travel time to work:** 24.1 minutes. **Working outside county of residence:** 38.9%.

Cities with pop over 10,000: None.

LOUP COUNTY
408 4th St   **Ph:** 308-942-3135
Taylor, NE 68879 **Fax:** 308-942-3103
www.co.loup.ne.us

In central NE, northeast of North Platte; organized as Taylor County Mar 6, 1855 from unorganized territory (prior to statehood); name changed Jul 23, 1883. **Name Origin:** For the Loup River, which flows through the county; itself named for the Pawnee Loup Indians. Name is French translation of Pawnee *skidi* 'wolf.'

Area (sq mi): 571.02 (land 569.71; water 1.31). **Pop per sq mi:** 1.2.

Pop 2005: 686. **State rank:** 88. **Pop change:** 2000-20005 -3.7%; 1990-2000 +4.2%. **Pop 2000:** 712 (White 97.8%; Black or African American 0%; Hispanic or Latino 1.7%; Asian 0.1%; Other 1%). **Foreign born:** 1%. **Median age:** 42.9.

Income 2000: per capita $12,427; median household $26,250; **Pop below poverty level:** 17.7%. ***Personal per capita income 2000-2003:** $7,459-$12,819.

Unemployment 2004: 3.5%. **Change from 2000:** +1.6%. **Median travel time to work:** 24.6 minutes. **Working outside county of residence:** 29.7%.

Cities with pop over 10,000: None.

MADISON COUNTY
PO Box 290   **Ph:** 402-454-3311
Madison, NE 68748 **Fax:** 402-454-6682
www.co.madison.ne.us

In east-central NE, northwest of Omaha; organized Dec 1867 from Platte County. **Name Origin:** For either James Madison (1751-1836), fourth U.S. president, or for Madison County, WI, former home of early German settlers.

Area (sq mi): 575.05 (land 572.57; water 2.49). **Pop per sq mi:** 62.

*Source: Personal per capita income data are from the Bureau of Economic Analysis; per capita income data are from the Bureau of the Census. See Introduction for explanation of differences.

454

Madison County (cont'd)

Pop 2005: 35,488. **State rank:** 9. **Pop change:** 2000-20005 +0.7%; 1990-2000 +7.9%. **Pop 2000:** 35,226 (White 88.3%; Black or African American 0.9%; Hispanic or Latino 8.6%; Asian 0.4%; Other 7.3%, including 1.2% American Indian/Alaska Native). **Foreign born:** 5.5%. **Median age:** 35.

Income 2000: per capita $16,804; median household $35,807; **Pop below poverty level:** 11.2%. ***Personal per capita income 2000-2003:** $23,658-$26,420.

Unemployment 2004: 3.8%. **Change from 2000:** +0.2%. **Median travel time to work:** 13.7 minutes. **Working outside county of residence:** 9.1%.

Cities with pop over 10,000: Norfolk (24,072).

MCPHERSON COUNTY

PO Box 122   **Ph:** 308-587-2363
Tryon, NE 69167

In central NE, north of North Platte; boundaries set Mar 31, 1887 from Lincoln and Keith counties. **Name Origin:** For Gen. James Birdseye McPherson (1828-64), commander of the Union army in Tennessee during the Civil War.

Area (sq mi): 860.02 (land 858.98; water 1.04). **Pop per sq mi:** 0.6.

Pop 2005: 507. **State rank:** 91. **Pop change:** 2000-20005 -4.9%; 1990-2000 -2.4%. **Pop 2000:** 533 (White 97.2%; Black or African American 0%; Hispanic or Latino 1.5%; Asian 0.4%; Other 1.7%). **Foreign born:** 0%. **Median age:** 40.6.

Income 2000: per capita $13,055; median household $25,750; **Pop below poverty level:** 16.2%. ***Personal per capita income 2000-2003:** $11,657-$16,735.

Unemployment 2004: 1.6%. **Change from 2000:** +0.6%. **Median travel time to work:** 28.9 minutes. **Working outside county of residence:** 30.5%.

Cities with pop over 10,000: None.

MERRICK COUNTY

PO Box 27   **Ph:** 308-946-2881
Central City, NE 68826   **Fax:** 308-946-2332

In east-central NE, northeast of Grand Island; original county; organized Nov 4, 1858 (prior to statehood). **Name Origin:** For Elvira Merrick De Puy, wife of Rep. Henry W. De Puy, who introduced the bill for the county's establishment.

Area (sq mi): 494.72 (land 484.88; water 9.85). **Pop per sq mi:** 16.6.

Pop 2005: 8,066. **State rank:** 38. **Pop change:** 2000-20005 -1.7%; 1990-2000 +2%. **Pop 2000:** 8,204 (White 97.2%; Black or African American 0.2%; Hispanic or Latino 2%; Asian 0.2%; Other 1.3%). **Foreign born:** 1%. **Median age:** 39.2.

Income 2000: per capita $15,958; median household $34,961; **Pop below poverty level:** 8.9%. ***Personal per capita income 2000-2003:** $22,739-$26,110.

Unemployment 2004: 4%. **Change from 2000:** +1.5%. **Median travel time to work:** 20.7 minutes. **Working outside county of residence:** 45.1%.

Cities with pop over 10,000: None.

MORRILL COUNTY

PO Box 610   **Ph:** 308-262-0860
Bridgeport, NE 69336   **Fax:** 308-262-1469
www.co.morrill.ne.us

In western NE, east of Scottsbluff; organized Nov 3, 1908 from Cheyenne County. **Name Origin:** For Charles Henry Morrill, regent of the University of Nebraska (1890-1903).

Area (sq mi): 1429.81 (land 1423.75; water 6.06). **Pop per sq mi:** 3.6.

Pop 2005: 5,165. **State rank:** 56. **Pop change:** 2000-20005 -5.1%; 1990-2000 +0.3%. **Pop 2000:** 5,440 (White 88.6%; Black or African American 0.1%; Hispanic or Latino 10.1%; Asian 0.2%; Other 6%). **Foreign born:** 3.8%. **Median age:** 39.5.

Income 2000: per capita $14,725; median household $30,235; **Pop below poverty level:** 14.7%. ***Personal per capita income 2000-2003:** $18,905-$22,832.

Unemployment 2004: 3.3%. **Change from 2000:** +0.5%. **Median travel time to work:** 20.7 minutes. **Working outside county of residence:** 29.4%.

Cities with pop over 10,000: None.

NANCE COUNTY

209 Esther St PO Box 338   **Ph:** 308-536-2331
Fullerton, NE 68638   **Fax:** 308-536-2742
www.co.nance.ne.us

In east-central NE, northeast of Grand Island; organized Feb 4, 1879 from Merrick County, encompassing the entire former Pawnee Reservation. **Name Origin:** For Albinus Nance (1848-1911), governor of NE (1879-83).

Area (sq mi): 448.04 (land 441.32; water 6.73). **Pop per sq mi:** 8.3.

Pop 2005: 3,666. **State rank:** 64. **Pop change:** 2000-20005 -9.2%; 1990-2000 -5.5%. **Pop 2000:** 4,038 (White 97.9%; Black or African American 0%; Hispanic or Latino 1.1%; Asian 0%; Other 1.5%). **Foreign born:** 0.8%. **Median age:** 40.1.

Income 2000: per capita $16,886; median household $31,267; **Pop below poverty level:** 13.1%. ***Personal per capita income 2000-2003:** $19,751-$24,446.

Unemployment 2004: 4.4%. **Change from 2000:** +0.3%. **Median travel time to work:** 21.2 minutes. **Working outside county of residence:** 39.9%.

Cities with pop over 10,000: None.

NEMAHA COUNTY

1824 'N' St   **Ph:** 402-274-4285
Auburn, NE 68305   **Fax:** 402-274-4389
www.visitnemahacounty.org

On the southeastern border of NE, southeast of Lincoln; original county, organized Mar 7, 1855 (prior to statehood). **Name Origin:** For the Nemaha River, which flows through the county; itself named from the Otoe Indian word *nimaha* 'murky water.'

Area (sq mi): 411.89 (land 409.3; water 2.58). **Pop per sq mi:** 17.

Pop 2005: 6,965. **State rank:** 44. **Pop change:** 2000-20005 -8.1%; 1990-2000 -5.1%. **Pop 2000:** 7,576 (White 97.1%; Black or African American 0.4%; Hispanic or Latino 1%; Asian 0.6%; Other 1.4%). **Foreign born:** 0.8%. **Median age:** 39.4.

Nemaha County (cont'd)

Income 2000: per capita $17,004; median household $32,588; **Pop below poverty level:** 12.6%. ***Personal per capita income 2000-2003:** $26,524-$29,625.

Unemployment 2004: 4.3%. **Change from 2000:** +0.8%. **Median travel time to work:** 17 minutes. **Working outside county of residence:** 18.8%.

Cities with pop over 10,000: None.

NUCKOLLS COUNTY

PO Box 366
Nelson, NE 68961
www.nuckollscounty.ne.gov

Ph: 402-225-4361
Fax: 402-225-4301

On the southern border of NE, southeast of Grand Island; organized Jun 27, 1871 from unorganized territory; a county originally named Nuckolls is now Thayer County. **Name Origin:** For Stephen Friel Nuckolls (1825-79), pioneer, NE territorial legislator (1859), and U.S. representative from WY (1869-71).

Area (sq mi): 575.96 (land 575.3; water 0.66). **Pop per sq mi:** 8.2.

Pop 2005: 4,739. **State rank:** 58. **Pop change:** 2000-20005 -6.3%; 1990-2000 -12.6%. **Pop 2000:** 5,057 (White 98.5%; Black or African American 0%; Hispanic or Latino 1%; Asian 0.2%; Other 0.9%). **Foreign born:** 0.6%. **Median age:** 44.1.

Income 2000: per capita $15,608; median household $28,958; **Pop below poverty level:** 11.2%. ***Personal per capita income 2000-2003:** $21,010-$24,974.

Unemployment 2004: 3.1%. **Change from 2000:** +0.6%. **Median travel time to work:** 16.8 minutes. **Working outside county of residence:** 25.5%.

Cities with pop over 10,000: None.

OTOE COUNTY

1021 Central Ave Rm 103
Nebraska City, NE 68410
www.co.otoe.ne.us

Ph: 402-873-9500
Fax: 402-873-9506

On the southeastern border of NE, southeast of Lincoln; original county; organized Mar 2, 1855 (prior to statehood). **Name Origin:** For the Indian tribe of Siouan linguistic stock; meaning uncertain, but said to be 'lechers,' either as 'lovers' or in the pejorative sense. The name seems to be a shortened version of a Siouan or possibly French name.

Area (sq mi): 619.09 (land 615.69; water 3.4). **Pop per sq mi:** 25.2.

Pop 2005: 15,509. **State rank:** 19. **Pop change:** 2000-20005 +0.7%; 1990-2000 +8%. **Pop 2000:** 15,396 (White 96.3%; Black or African American 0.3%; Hispanic or Latino 2.4%; Asian 0.2%; Other 1.9%). **Foreign born:** 1.4%. **Median age:** 39.5.

Income 2000: per capita $17,752; median household $37,302; **Pop below poverty level:** 8.1%. ***Personal per capita income 2000-2003:** $23,458-$25,588.

Unemployment 2004: 3.9%. **Change from 2000:** +0.5%. **Median travel time to work:** 20.3 minutes. **Working outside county of residence:** 31.8%.

Cities with pop over 10,000: None.

PAWNEE COUNTY

625 6th St
Pawnee City, NE 68420
www.co.pawnee.ne.us

Ph: 402-852-2962
Fax: 402-852-2963

In southeastern NE, southeast of Lincoln; original county; organized Mar 6, 1855 (prior to statehood). **Name Origin:** For the Indian tribe of Caddoan linguistic stock. The name may mean 'horn,' for the shape of their forelock; they called themselves 'civilized people.'

Area (sq mi): 432.95 (land 431.57; water 1.38). **Pop per sq mi:** 6.7.

Pop 2005: 2,878. **State rank:** 71. **Pop change:** 2000-20005 -6.8%; 1990-2000 -6.9%. **Pop 2000:** 3,087 (White 98.5%; Black or African American 0%; Hispanic or Latino 0.7%; Asian 0.3%; Other 0.8%). **Foreign born:** 0.4%. **Median age:** 45.9.

Income 2000: per capita $16,687; median household $29,000; **Pop below poverty level:** 11%. ***Personal per capita income 2000-2003:** $23,714-$27,583.

Unemployment 2004: 3.6%. **Change from 2000:** +0.7%. **Median travel time to work:** 21.8 minutes. **Working outside county of residence:** 32.4%.

Cities with pop over 10,000: None.

PERKINS COUNTY

PO Box 156
Grant, NE 69140
www.co.perkins.ne.us

Ph: 308-352-4643
Fax: 308-352-2455

In west-central NE, west of North Platte; organized Nov 8, 1887 from Keith County. **Name Origin:** For Charles Elliott Perkins (1807-1907), president of the Chicago, Burlington, and Quincy Railroad. Locally it is also said to be for Joseph Perkins, an early resident.

Area (sq mi): 884.27 (land 883.18; water 1.1). **Pop per sq mi:** 3.5.

Pop 2005: 3,057. **State rank:** 69. **Pop change:** 2000-20005 -4.5%; 1990-2000 -5%. **Pop 2000:** 3,200 (White 96.6%; Black or African American 0%; Hispanic or Latino 2.3%; Asian 0.2%; Other 2%). **Foreign born:** 1.4%. **Median age:** 40.7.

Income 2000: per capita $17,830; median household $34,205; **Pop below poverty level:** 13.6%. ***Personal per capita income 2000-2003:** $23,935-$29,599.

Unemployment 2004: 2.4%. **Change from 2000:** +0.5%. **Median travel time to work:** 15.1 minutes. **Working outside county of residence:** 17.1%.

Cities with pop over 10,000: None.

PHELPS COUNTY

PO Box 404
Holdrege, NE 68949
www.phelpsgov.org

Ph: 308-995-4469
Fax: 308-995-4368

In south-central NE, southwest of Grand Island; organized Feb 11, 1873 from unorganized territory. **Name Origin:** For Capt. William Phelps (1808-?), an early settler and former Missouri River steamboat captain.

Area (sq mi): 540.6 (land 539.97; water 0.64). **Pop per sq mi:** 17.5.

Pop 2005: 9,449. **State rank:** 30. **Pop change:** 2000-20005 -3.1%; 1990-2000 +0.3%. **Pop 2000:** 9,747 (White 96.6%; Black or African

---

*Source: Personal per capita income data are from the Bureau of Economic Analysis; per capita income data are from the Bureau of the Census.
See Introduction for explanation of differences.

Phelps County (cont'd)

American 0.1%; Hispanic or Latino 2.3%; Asian 0.3%; Other 1.8%). **Foreign born:** 0.8%. **Median age:** 39.4.

Income 2000: per capita $19,044; median household $37,319; **Pop below poverty level:** 8.9%. ***Personal per capita income 2000-2003:** $26,868-$30,309.

Unemployment 2004: 3.1%. **Change from 2000:** +0.8%. **Median travel time to work:** 15.5 minutes. **Working outside county of residence:** 15%.

Cities with pop over 10,000: None.

PIERCE COUNTY
111 W Court St Rm 1   **Ph:** 402-329-4225
Pierce, NE 68767   **Fax:** 402-329-6439
www.co.pierce.ne.us

In northeast NE, southwest of Sioux City, IA; organized Jan 26, 1856 from Madison County. **Name Origin:** For Franklin Pierce (1804-69), fourteenth U.S. president.

Area (sq mi): 575.27 (land 573.93; water 1.34). **Pop per sq mi:** 13.2.

Pop 2005: 7,600. **State rank:** 40. **Pop change:** 2000-20005 -3.3%; 1990-2000 +0.4%. **Pop 2000:** 7,857 (White 98.2%; Black or African American 0.1%; Hispanic or Latino 0.7%; Asian 0.2%; Other 1.1%). **Foreign born:** 0.8%. **Median age:** 37.9.

Income 2000: per capita $15,980; median household $32,239; **Pop below poverty level:** 11.8%. ***Personal per capita income 2000-2003:** $21,182-$25,181.

Unemployment 2004: 3.3%. **Change from 2000:** +0.3%. **Median travel time to work:** 19.7 minutes. **Working outside county of residence:** 46%.

Cities with pop over 10,000: None.

PLATTE COUNTY
2610 14th St   **Ph:** 402-563-4904
Columbus, NE 68601   **Fax:** 402-564-4164
www.plattecounty.net

In east-central NE, northwest of Omaha; original county; organized as Loup County Jan 26, 1856 (prior to statehood); name changed 1859. **Name Origin:** For the Platte River, which forms part of its southern border; from French for 'flat' or 'still.'

Area (sq mi): 689.08 (land 678.07; water 11.01). **Pop per sq mi:** 46.1.

Pop 2005: 31,262. **State rank:** 11. **Pop change:** 2000-20005 -1.3%; 1990-2000 +6.2%. **Pop 2000:** 31,662 (White 92%; Black or African American 0.4%; Hispanic or Latino 6.5%; Asian 0.4%; Other 5%). **Foreign born:** 4.1%. **Median age:** 35.8.

Income 2000: per capita $18,064; median household $39,359; **Pop below poverty level:** 7.7%. ***Personal per capita income 2000-2003:** $24,586-$26,568.

Unemployment 2004: 4.2%. **Change from 2000:** +0.5%. **Median travel time to work:** 14.3 minutes. **Working outside county of residence:** 8.6%.

Cities with pop over 10,000: Columbus ⚎ (20,881).

POLK COUNTY
PO Box 276   **Ph:** 402-747-5431
Osceola, NE 68651   **Fax:** 402-747-2656
www.polkcounty.ne.gov

In east-central NE, west of Omaha; boundaries established Jan 26, 1856 (prior to statehood) from Butler County. **Name Origin:** For James Knox Polk (1795-1849), eleventh U.S. president.

Area (sq mi): 440.72 (land 438.84; water 1.88). **Pop per sq mi:** 12.4.

Pop 2005: 5,421. **State rank:** 55. **Pop change:** 2000-20005 -3.9%; 1990-2000 -0.6%. **Pop 2000:** 5,639 (White 98.3%; Black or African American 0%; Hispanic or Latino 1.1%; Asian 0.1%; Other 1%). **Foreign born:** 0.8%. **Median age:** 41.6.

Income 2000: per capita $17,934; median household $37,819; **Pop below poverty level:** 5.8%. ***Personal per capita income 2000-2003:** $23,973-$27,905.

Unemployment 2004: 3.3%. **Change from 2000:** +0.4%. **Median travel time to work:** 19.8 minutes. **Working outside county of residence:** 41.8%.

Cities with pop over 10,000: None.

RED WILLOW COUNTY
502 Norris Ave   **Ph:** 308-345-1552
McCook, NE 69001   **Fax:** 308-345-4460
www.co.red-willow.ne.us

On the central southern border of NE, south of North Platte; organized Feb 27, 1873 from unorganized territory. **Name Origin:** For Red Willow Creek, which runs through the county; a mistranslation of the Dakota term for 'Red Dogwood Creek,' for the trees that grow there.

Area (sq mi): 718.06 (land 716.65; water 1.4). **Pop per sq mi:** 15.4.

Pop 2005: 11,060. **State rank:** 24. **Pop change:** 2000-20005 -3.4%; 1990-2000 -2.2%. **Pop 2000:** 11,448 (White 96.3%; Black or African American 0.2%; Hispanic or Latino 2.5%; Asian 0.2%; Other 2.1%). **Foreign born:** 1.2%. **Median age:** 39.9.

Income 2000: per capita $16,303; median household $32,293; **Pop below poverty level:** 9.6%. ***Personal per capita income 2000-2003:** $22,817-$25,910.

Unemployment 2004: 3.3%. **Change from 2000:** +1.1%. **Median travel time to work:** 12 minutes. **Working outside county of residence:** 7.9%.

Cities with pop over 10,000: None.

RICHARDSON COUNTY
1700 Stone St   **Ph:** 402-245-2911
Falls City, NE 68355   **Fax:** 402-245-2946
www.co.richardson.ne.us

In the southeastern corner of NE, southeast of Lincoln; original county; organized Mar 7, 1855 (prior to statehood). **Name Origin:** For Maj. William A. Richardson (1811-75), officer in the Mexican-American War, U.S. senator from IL (1863-65), and governor of NE Territory (1858).

Area (sq mi): 555.95 (land 553.26; water 2.7). **Pop per sq mi:** 15.8.

Pop 2005: 8,732. **State rank:** 34. **Pop change:** 2000-20005 -8.4%; 1990-2000 -4.1%. **Pop 2000:** 9,531 (White 95.1%; Black or African American 0.2%; Hispanic or Latino 1%; Asian 0.1%; Other 4%,

⚎ *County Seat*

Richardson County (cont'd)

including 2.3% American Indian/Alaska Native). **Foreign born:** 1.2%. **Median age:** 41.4.

Income 2000: per capita $16,460; median household $29,884; **Pop below poverty level:** 10.1%. ***Personal per capita income 2000-2003:** $22,920-$25,501.

Unemployment 2004: 4.8%. **Change from 2000:** -0.5%. **Median travel time to work:** 19.5 minutes. **Working outside county of residence:** 28.1%.

Cities with pop over 10,000: None.

ROCK COUNTY

400 State St   **Ph:** 402-684-3933
Bassett, NE 68714   **Fax:** 402-684-2741
www.co.rock.ne.us

In north-central NE; organized Nov 6, 1888 from Brown County. **Name Origin:** For the rocky soil.

Area (sq mi): 1011.85 (land 1008.46; water 3.4). **Pop per sq mi:** 1.6.

Pop 2005: 1,567. **State rank:** 80. **Pop change:** 2000-20005 -10.8%; 1990-2000 -13%. **Pop 2000:** 1,756 (White 98.8%; Black or African American 0%; Hispanic or Latino 0.5%; Asian 0.2%; Other 0.9%). **Foreign born:** 0.3%. **Median age:** 43.5.

Income 2000: per capita $14,350; median household $25,795; **Pop below poverty level:** 21.8%. ***Personal per capita income 2000-2003:** $18,430-$24,422.

Unemployment 2004: 3.3%. **Change from 2000:** -0.5%. **Median travel time to work:** 15.2 minutes. **Working outside county of residence:** 15.8%.

Cities with pop over 10,000: None.

SALINE COUNTY

215 S Court ST   **Ph:** 402-821-2374
Wilber, NE 68465   **Fax:** 402-821-3381
www.co.saline.ne.us

In southeastern NE, southwest of Lincoln; organized Feb 18, 1867 from Gage and Lancaster counties. **Name Origin:** In the unfounded belief that extensive salt springs or deposits could be found within its boundaries.

Area (sq mi): 576.06 (land 575.34; water 0.73). **Pop per sq mi:** 24.7.

Pop 2005: 14,195. **State rank:** 21. **Pop change:** 2000-20005 +2.5%; 1990-2000 +8.9%. **Pop 2000:** 13,843 (White 90.3%; Black or African American 0.4%; Hispanic or Latino 6.6%; Asian 1.7%; Other 4.9%). **Foreign born:** 6%. **Median age:** 36.4.

Income 2000: per capita $16,287; median household $35,914; **Pop below poverty level:** 9.4%. ***Personal per capita income 2000-2003:** $21,995-$25,689.

Unemployment 2004: 3.2%. **Change from 2000:** +0.4%. **Median travel time to work:** 19.2 minutes. **Working outside county of residence:** 27.7%.

Cities with pop over 10,000: None.

SARPY COUNTY

1210 Golden Gate Dr Suite 1118   **Ph:** 402-593-2105
Papillion, NE 68046   **Fax:** 402-593-4360
www.co.sarpy.ne.us

On the central eastern border of NE, south of Omaha; organized Feb 7, 1857 from Douglas County. **Name Origin:** For Col. Peter A. Sarpy (1805-65), an early settler, trader and quartermaster for NE volunteer regiment (1855).

Area (sq mi): 247.28 (land 240.52; water 6.76). **Pop per sq mi:** 579.5.

Pop 2005: 139,371. **State rank:** 3. **Pop change:** 2000-20005 +13.7%; 1990-2000 +19.5%. **Pop 2000:** 122,595 (White 87.1%; Black or African American 4.4%; Hispanic or Latino 4.4%; Asian 1.9%; Other 4.6%). **Foreign born:** 3.7%. **Median age:** 31.5.

Income 2000: per capita $21,985; median household $53,804; **Pop below poverty level:** 4.2%. ***Personal per capita income 2000-2003:** $26,980-$29,286.

Unemployment 2004: 3.3%. **Change from 2000:** +0.8%. **Median travel time to work:** 19.4 minutes. **Working outside county of residence:** 59.4%.

Cities with pop over 10,000: Omaha 🏛 (409,416); Bellevue (47,347); Papillion 🏛 (19,497); La Vista (14,685).

SAUNDERS COUNTY

PO Box 61   **Ph:** 402-443-8101
Wahoo, NE 68066   **Fax:** 402-443-5010
www.co.saunders.ne.us

In east-central NE, west of Omaha; organized as Calhoun County Jan 26, 1856 (prior to statehood); name changed Jan 8, 1862. **Name Origin:** For Alvin Saunders (1817-99), NE Territory governor (1861-67) and U.S. senator from NE (1877-83).

Area (sq mi): 758.82 (land 753.9; water 4.92). **Pop per sq mi:** 27.1.

Pop 2005: 20,458. **State rank:** 15. **Pop change:** 2000-20005 +3.2%; 1990-2000 +8.4%. **Pop 2000:** 19,830 (White 97.9%; Black or African American 0.1%; Hispanic or Latino 1%; Asian 0.2%; Other 1.1%). **Foreign born:** 1.2%. **Median age:** 38.

Income 2000: per capita $18,392; median household $42,173; **Pop below poverty level:** 6.6%. ***Personal per capita income 2000-2003:** $25,760-$28,263.

Unemployment 2004: 3.6%. **Change from 2000:** +0.3%. **Median travel time to work:** 24.2 minutes. **Working outside county of residence:** 57%.

Cities with pop over 10,000: None.

SCOTTS BLUFF COUNTY

1825 10th St   **Ph:** 308-436-6600
Gering, NE 69341   **Fax:** 308-436-3178
www.scottsbluffcounty.org

On western border of NE; organized Nov 6, 1888 from Cheyenne County. **Name Origin:** For the prominent bluff on the North Platte River, named for Hiram Scott, a member of the Bonneville expedition of 1832, who died there.

Area (sq mi): 745.5 (land 739.27; water 6.22). **Pop per sq mi:** 49.7.

Source: Personal per capita income data are from the Bureau of Economic Analysis; per capita income data are from the Bureau of the Census. See Introduction for explanation of differences.

Scotts Bluff County (cont'd)

Pop 2005: 36,752. **State rank:** 6. **Pop change:** 2000-20005 -0.5%; 1990-2000 +2.6%. **Pop 2000:** 36,951 (White 79.7%; Black or African American 0.3%; Hispanic or Latino 17.2%; Asian 0.6%; Other 11.5%, including 1.9% American Indian/Alaska Native). **Foreign born:** 4.1%. **Median age:** 38.4.

Income 2000: per capita $17,355; median household $32,016; **Pop below poverty level:** 14.5%. ***Personal per capita income 2000-2003:** $23,788-$25,335.

Unemployment 2004: 4.3%. **Change from 2000:** +0.3%. **Median travel time to work:** 14.9 minutes. **Working outside county of residence:** 5%.

Cities with pop over 10,000: Scottsbluff (14,767).

SEWARD COUNTY
PO Box 190   **Ph:** 402-643-2883
Seward, NE 68434   **Fax:** 402-643-9243
connectseward.org/cgov/

In east-central NE, west of Lincoln; organized as Greene County Jan 26, 1856 (prior to statehood) from Lancaster County; name changed Jan 3, 1862 when Gen. Greene of Missouri joined the Confederacy. **Name Origin:** For William Henry Seward (1801-72), U.S. secretary of state (1861-69) who negotiated the purchase of Alaska (1867).

Area (sq mi): 575.73 (land 574.75; water 0.97). **Pop per sq mi:** 29.1.

Pop 2005: 16,739. **State rank:** 18. **Pop change:** 2000-20005 +1.5%; 1990-2000 +6.8%. **Pop 2000:** 16,496 (White 97.5%; Black or African American 0.3%; Hispanic or Latino 1.1%; Asian 0.3%; Other 1.3%). **Foreign born:** 1.7%. **Median age:** 35.7.

Income 2000: per capita $18,379; median household $42,700; **Pop below poverty level:** 7%. ***Personal per capita income 2000-2003:** $26,224-$28,928.

Unemployment 2004: 2.9%. **Change from 2000:** -0.3%. **Median travel time to work:** 19.9 minutes. **Working outside county of residence:** 38.3%.

Cities with pop over 10,000: None.

SHERIDAN COUNTY
301 E 2nd St PO Box 39   **Ph:** 308-327-5650
Rushville, NE 69360   **Fax:** 308-327-5624

On the northern border of NE, northeast of Scottsbluff; organized Feb 25, 1885 from Sioux County. **Name Origin:** For Gen. Philip Henry Sheridan (1831-88), Union officer during the Civil War and commander in chief of the U.S. army (1883-88).

Area (sq mi): 2469.99 (land 2441.04; water 28.95). **Pop per sq mi:** 2.3.

Pop 2005: 5,668. **State rank:** 53. **Pop change:** 2000-20005 -8.6%; 1990-2000 -8.2%. **Pop 2000:** 6,198 (White 87.6%; Black or African American 0.1%; Hispanic or Latino 1.5%; Asian 0.1%; Other 11.6%, including 9.2% American Indian/Alaska Native). **Foreign born:** 0.7%. **Median age:** 42.

Income 2000: per capita $14,844; median household $29,484; **Pop below poverty level:** 13.2%. ***Personal per capita income 2000-2003:** $19,444-$22,671.

Unemployment 2004: 2.7%. **Change from 2000:** +0%. **Median travel time to work:** 17.3 minutes. **Working outside county of residence:** 17.9%.

Cities with pop over 10,000: None.

SHERMAN COUNTY
PO Box 456   **Ph:** 308-745-1513
Loup City, NE 68853   **Fax:** 308-745-1820
www.co.sherman.ne.us

In central NE, northwest of Grand Island; organized Mar 1, 1871 from Buffalo County. **Name Origin:** For Gen. William Tecumseh Sherman (1820-91), officer in the Mexican-American War and the Civil War, remembered for his 'march to the sea' through the South.

Area (sq mi): 571.63 (land 565.84; water 5.78). **Pop per sq mi:** 5.5.

Pop 2005: 3,112. **State rank:** 68. **Pop change:** 2000-20005 -6.2%; 1990-2000 -10.8%. **Pop 2000:** 3,318 (White 98%; Black or African American 0.1%; Hispanic or Latino 1%; Asian 0.2%; Other 1.1%). **Foreign born:** 0.4%. **Median age:** 43.3.

Income 2000: per capita $14,064; median household $28,646; **Pop below poverty level:** 12.9%. ***Personal per capita income 2000-2003:** $17,381-$23,380.

Unemployment 2004: 3.3%. **Change from 2000:** +0.6%. **Median travel time to work:** 24.7 minutes. **Working outside county of residence:** 34.4%.

Cities with pop over 10,000: None.

SIOUX COUNTY
PO Box 158   **Ph:** 308-668-2443
Harrison, NE 69346   **Fax:** 308-668-2443
www.co.sioux.ne.us

On the northwestern border of NE, north of Scottsbluff; organized Feb 19, 1877 from unorganized territory. **Name Origin:** For the Sioux Indian tribe, also known as the Dakotas.

Area (sq mi): 2067.32 (land 2066.59; water 0.73). **Pop per sq mi:** 0.7.

Pop 2005: 1,458. **State rank:** 81. **Pop change:** 2000-20005 -1.2%; 1990-2000 -4.8%. **Pop 2000:** 1,475 (White 96.5%; Black or African American 0%; Hispanic or Latino 2.3%; Asian 0.2%; Other 2.2%). **Foreign born:** 1.3%. **Median age:** 41.5.

Income 2000: per capita $15,999; median household $29,851; **Pop below poverty level:** 15.4%. ***Personal per capita income 2000-2003:** $12,327-$19,291.

Unemployment 2004: 2.6%. **Change from 2000:** +1.3%. **Median travel time to work:** 23 minutes. **Working outside county of residence:** 42.1%.

Cities with pop over 10,000: None.

STANTON COUNTY
PO Box 347   **Ph:** 402-439-2222
Stanton, NE 68779   **Fax:** 402-439-2200
www.co.stanton.ne.us

In east-central NE, west of Norfolk; organized Jan 10, 1862 from Dodge County; previously called Izard County. **Name Origin:** For

Stanton County (cont'd)

Edwin McMasters Stanton (1814-69), U.S. secretary of war under Abraham Lincoln and Andrew Johnson (1862-68).

Area (sq mi): 431.06 (land 429.83; water 1.23). **Pop per sq mi:** 15.2.

Pop 2005: 6,534. **State rank:** 48. **Pop change:** 2000-20005 +1.2%; 1990-2000 +3.4%. **Pop 2000:** 6,455 (White 96%; Black or African American 0.4%; Hispanic or Latino 2.3%; Asian 0.1%; Other 2.8%). **Foreign born:** 1.2%. **Median age:** 35.9.

Income 2000: per capita $15,511; median household $36,676; **Pop below poverty level:** 6.8%. ***Personal per capita income 2000-2003:** $21,326-$24,220.

Unemployment 2004: 3%. **Change from 2000:** +0.1%. **Median travel time to work:** 19.1 minutes. **Working outside county of residence:** 62.6%.

Cities with pop over 10,000: None.

THAYER COUNTY
PO Box 208   **Ph:** 402-768-6126
Hebron, NE 68370   **Fax:** 402-768-2129
www.thayercounty.ne.gov

On the southern border of NE, southwest of Lincoln; organized as Jefferson County 1867; name changed 1871. **Name Origin:** For Gen. John Milton Thayer (1820-1906), an officer in the Civil War, U.S. senator from NE (1867-71), and governor (1887-92).

Area (sq mi): 575.3 (land 574.55; water 0.75). **Pop per sq mi:** 9.5.

Pop 2005: 5,436. **State rank:** 54. **Pop change:** 2000-20005 -10.2%; 1990-2000 -8.7%. **Pop 2000:** 6,055 (White 98.1%; Black or African American 0%; Hispanic or Latino 1%; Asian 0.1%; Other 1.2%). **Foreign born:** 0.8%. **Median age:** 44.1.

Income 2000: per capita $17,043; median household $30,740; **Pop below poverty level:** 10.7%. ***Personal per capita income 2000-2003:** $23,541-$29,383.

Unemployment 2004: 3.1%. **Change from 2000:** +0.5%. **Median travel time to work:** 14.4 minutes. **Working outside county of residence:** 16.3%.

Cities with pop over 10,000: None.

THOMAS COUNTY
PO Box 226   **Ph:** 308-645-2261
Thedford, NE 69166   **Fax:** 308-645-2623

In central NE, north of North Platte; organized Mar 31, 1887 from Blaine County. **Name Origin:** For Gen. George Henry Thomas (1816-70), Union commander of the Army of the Cumberland.

Area (sq mi): 713.65 (land 712.86; water 0.79). **Pop per sq mi:** 0.9.

Pop 2005: 623. **State rank:** 90. **Pop change:** 2000-20005 -14.5%; 1990-2000 -14.3%. **Pop 2000:** 729 (White 98.8%; Black or African American 0%; Hispanic or Latino 0.8%; Asian 0%; Other 0.6%). **Foreign born:** 1.6%. **Median age:** 44.2.

Income 2000: per capita $15,335; median household $27,292; **Pop below poverty level:** 14.3%. ***Personal per capita income 2000-2003:** $15,293-$21,370.

Unemployment 2004: 3%. **Change from 2000:** -2.7%. **Median travel time to work:** 15.1 minutes. **Working outside county of residence:** 23.6%.

Cities with pop over 10,000: None.

THURSTON COUNTY
PO Box G   **Ph:** 402-385-2343
Pender, NE 68047   **Fax:** 402-385-3544

On the northeastern border of NE, south of Sioux City, IA; organized as Blackbird County Mar 7, 1865 from Burt County; name changed in 1889. **Name Origin:** For John Mellen Thurston (1847-1916), U.S. senator from NE (1895-1901), active in establishing the county. Originally named for either Chief Blackbird of the Omaha Indians, or Black Bird, for their mythological Thunder Bird.

Area (sq mi): 396.25 (land 393.81; water 2.44). **Pop per sq mi:** 18.7.

Pop 2005: 7,365. **State rank:** 42. **Pop change:** 2000-20005 +2.7%; 1990-2000 +3.4%. **Pop 2000:** 7,171 (White 45.5%; Black or African American 0.2%; Hispanic or Latino 2.4%; Asian 0.1%; Other 54%, including 52% American Indian/Alaska Native). **Foreign born:** 1.6%. **Median age:** 29.8.

Income 2000: per capita $10,951; median household $28,170; **Pop below poverty level:** 25.6%. ***Personal per capita income 2000-2003:** $17,567-$21,640.

Unemployment 2004: 7.7%. **Change from 2000:** +0.2%. **Median travel time to work:** 18.6 minutes. **Working outside county of residence:** 32.2%.

Cities with pop over 10,000: None.

VALLEY COUNTY
125 S 15th St   **Ph:** 308-728-3700
Ord, NE 68862   **Fax:** 308-728-7725
www.co.valley.ne.us

In central NE, northwest of Grand Island; organized Mar 1, 1871 from unorganized territory. **Name Origin:** For the North Loup River valley, which comprises the county.

Area (sq mi): 570.51 (land 568.11; water 2.41). **Pop per sq mi:** 7.7.

Pop 2005: 4,402. **State rank:** 60. **Pop change:** 2000-20005 -5.3%; 1990-2000 -10.1%. **Pop 2000:** 4,647 (White 97.5%; Black or African American 0.2%; Hispanic or Latino 1.6%; Asian 0.1%; Other 1.6%). **Foreign born:** 1.1%. **Median age:** 43.5.

Income 2000: per capita $14,996; median household $27,926; **Pop below poverty level:** 12.8%. ***Personal per capita income 2000-2003:** $19,861-$24,201.

Unemployment 2004: 3.1%. **Change from 2000:** +0.3%. **Median travel time to work:** 15.1 minutes. **Working outside county of residence:** 14.2%.

Cities with pop over 10,000: None.

WASHINGTON COUNTY
PO Box 466   **Ph:** 402-426-6822
Blair, NE 68008   **Fax:** 402-426-6825

On the central eastern border of NE, north of Omaha; original county; organized Feb 22, 1855 (prior to statehood). **Name Origin:** For George Washington (1732-99), American patriot and first U.S. president.

Source: Personal per capita income data are from the Bureau of Economic Analysis; per capita income data are from the Bureau of the Census. See Introduction for explanation of differences.

Washington County (cont'd)

Area (sq mi): 393.76 (land 390.49; water 3.27). **Pop per sq mi:** 50.6.

Pop 2005: 19,772. **State rank:** 17. **Pop change:** 2000-20005 +5.3%; 1990-2000 +13.1%. **Pop 2000:** 18,780 (White 97.5%; Black or African American 0.3%; Hispanic or Latino 1.1%; Asian 0.3%; Other 1.2%). **Foreign born:** 1.6%. **Median age:** 37.1.

Income 2000: per capita $21,055; median household $48,500; **Pop below poverty level:** 6%. ***Personal per capita income 2000-2003:** $28,958-$30,551.

Unemployment 2004: 3.2%. **Change from 2000:** +0.6%. **Median travel time to work:** 22.8 minutes. **Working outside county of residence:** 52.6%.

Cities with pop over 10,000: None.

WAYNE COUNTY

PO Box 248   **Ph:** 402-375-2288
Wayne, NE 68787   **Fax:** 402-375-4137
county.waynene.org

In northeastern NE, southwest of Sioux City, IA; organized 1870 from Thurston County. **Name Origin:** For Gen. Anthony Wayne (1745-96), PA soldier and statesman, nicknamed 'Mad Anthony' for his daring during the Revolutionary War.

Area (sq mi): 443.48 (land 443.43; water 0.05). **Pop per sq mi:** 20.8.

Pop 2005: 9,211. **State rank:** 31. **Pop change:** 2000-20005 -6.5%; 1990-2000 +5.2%. **Pop 2000:** 9,851 (White 96.2%; Black or African American 0.9%; Hispanic or Latino 1.5%; Asian 0.3%; Other 1.9%). **Foreign born:** 1.7%. **Median age:** 27.9.

Income 2000: per capita $14,644; median household $32,366; **Pop below poverty level:** 14.5%. ***Personal per capita income 2000-2003:** $20,433-$24,941.

Unemployment 2004: 2.9%. **Change from 2000:** -0.5%. **Median travel time to work:** 15.5 minutes. **Working outside county of residence:** 32.1%.

Cities with pop over 10,000: None.

WEBSTER COUNTY

PO Box 250   **Ph:** 402-746-2716
Red Cloud, NE 68970   **Fax:** 402-746-2710
www.co.webster.ne.us

On the central southern border of NE, south of Grand Island; organized Feb 16, 1867 (prior to statehood) from unorganized territory. **Name Origin:** For Daniel Webster (1782-1852), U.S. statesman and orator from MA.

Area (sq mi): 575.02 (land 574.89; water 0.13). **Pop per sq mi:** 6.5.

Pop 2005: 3,762. **State rank:** 63. **Pop change:** 2000-20005 -7.4%; 1990-2000 -5.1%. **Pop 2000:** 4,061 (White 97.8%; Black or African American 0.1%; Hispanic or Latino 0.5%; Asian 0.5%; Other 1.3%). **Foreign born:** 1.3%. **Median age:** 44.2.

Income 2000: per capita $16,802; median household $30,026; **Pop below poverty level:** 11.2%. ***Personal per capita income 2000-2003:** $22,849-$28,827.

Unemployment 2004: 4%. **Change from 2000:** +1.5%. **Median travel time to work:** 20.7 minutes. **Working outside county of residence:** 34%.

Cities with pop over 10,000: None.

WHEELER COUNTY

PO Box 127   **Ph:** 308-654-3235
Bartlett, NE 68622   **Fax:** 308-654-3470

In north-central NE, north of Grand Island; organized Feb 17, 1877 from Boone County. **Name Origin:** For Daniel H. Wheeler (1834-?), a state official.

Area (sq mi): 575.57 (land 575.17, water 0.41). **Pop per sq mi:** 1.4.

Pop 2005: 820. **State rank:** 84. **Pop change:** 2000-20005 -7.4%; 1990-2000 -6.5%. **Pop 2000:** 886 (White 99.1%; Black or African American 0%; Hispanic or Latino 0.6%; Asian 0%; Other 0.9%). **Foreign born:** 0%. **Median age:** 40.4.

Income 2000: per capita $14,355; median household $26,771; **Pop below poverty level:** 20.9%. ***Personal per capita income 2000-2003:** $23,688-$35,867.

Unemployment 2004: 2.6%. **Change from 2000:** -0.3%. **Median travel time to work:** 18.3 minutes. **Working outside county of residence:** 16.3%.

Cities with pop over 10,000: None.

YORK COUNTY

510 Lincoln Ave   **Ph:** 402-362-7759
York, NE 68467   **Fax:** 402-362-7558
www.yorkcounty.ne.gov

In south-central NE, west of Lincoln; original county; boundaries defined Mar 13, 1855 (prior to statehood). **Name Origin:** Either for York, England, named by Alfred D. Jones. Or for York County, PA, former home of early settlers.

Area (sq mi): 576.02 (land 575.66; water 0.36). **Pop per sq mi:** 25.

Pop 2005: 14,397. **State rank:** 20. **Pop change:** 2000-20005 -1.4%; 1990-2000 +1.2%. **Pop 2000:** 14,598 (White 96.3%; Black or African American 1%; Hispanic or Latino 1.4%; Asian 0.5%; Other 1.8%). **Foreign born:** 1.7%. **Median age:** 38.8.

Income 2000: per capita $17,670; median household $37,093; **Pop below poverty level:** 8.5%. ***Personal per capita income 2000-2003:** $25,429-$29,783.

Unemployment 2004: 3.1%. **Change from 2000:** +1.1%. **Median travel time to work:** 13.1 minutes. **Working outside county of residence:** 10.9%.

Cities with pop over 10,000: None.

Nevada

OREGON IDAHO

UTAH

Humboldt

Elko

● Winnemucca

● Elko

Washoe

Pershing

● Lovelock

Lander

Eureka

● Reno

Churchill

● Austin

White Pine

● Fallon

Eureka

Storey

● Ely

● Virginia City

● Eureka

Carson City

★ Carson City

● Minden

Douglas ● Yerington

Lyon

Mineral

● Hawthorne

● Tonopah

● Pioche

Nye

Esmeralda

Lincoln

● Goldfield

CALIFORNIA

Clark

● Las Vegas

ARIZONA

N

County boundary
Eureka   County name
●   County seat
■   Major city
✪   State capital

0   100 mi
0   100 km

© MAPS.com

Nevada

NEVADA STATE INFORMATION

www.nv.gov   **Ph:** 775-687-5000

Area (sq mi): 110,560.71 (land 109,825.99; water 734.71). **Pop per sq mi:** 22.

Pop 2005: 2,414,807. **Pop change:** 2000-20005 +20.8%; 1990-2000 +66.3%. **Pop 2000:** 1,998,257 (White 65.2%; Black or African American 6.8%; Hispanic or Latino 19.7%; Asian 4.5%; Other 13.5%, including 1.3% American Indian/Alaska Native). **Foreign born:** 15.8%. **Median age:** 35.

Income 2000: per capita $21,989; median household $44,581; **Pop below poverty level:** 10.5%. *****Personal per capita income 2000-2003:** $30,437-$31,910.

Unemployment 2004: 4.6%. **Change from 2000:** +0.1%. **Median travel time to work:** 23.3 minutes. **Working outside county of residence:** 5.2%.

CARSON CITY (INDEPENDENT CITY)

201 N Carson St   **Ph:** 775-887-2100
Carson City, NV 89701   **Fax:** 775-887-2286
www.carson-city.nv.us

In western NV near the Carson River and Lake Tahoe, 28 mi. south of Reno. Laid out 1858 by Maj. William M. Omsby; county seat since 1861; independent city 1969; state capital. City government consolidated with county. **Name Origin:** For frontiersman Christopher 'Kit' Carson (1809-68). Previously called Eagle Station.

Area (sq mi): 155.66 (land 143.35; water 12.31). **Pop per sq mi:** 391.1.

Pop 2005: 56,062. **State rank:** 3. **Pop change:** 2000-20005 +6.9%; 1990-2000 +29.7%. **Pop 2000:** 52,457 (White 78.5%; Black or African American 1.8%; Hispanic or Latino 14.2%; Asian 1.8%; Other 11.1%, including 2.4% American Indian/Alaska Native). **Foreign born:** 9.9%. **Median age:** 38.7.

Income 2000: per capita $20,943; median household $41,809; **Pop below poverty level:** 10%. *****Personal per capita income 2000-2003:** $32,043-$32,872.

Unemployment 2004: 5%. **Change from 2000:** -0.5%. **Median travel time to work:** 17.7 minutes. **Working outside county of residence:** 24.1%.

Cities with pop over 10,000: Carson City ⛪ (55,974).

CHURCHILL COUNTY

155 N Taylor St Suite 153   **Ph:** 775-423-5136
Fallon, NV 89406   **Fax:** 775-423-0717
www.churchillcounty.org

In west-central NV, east of Reno; original county, organized Nov 25, 1861 (prior to statehood). **Name Origin:** For Fort Churchill, which was named for either Charles C. Churchill, an officer of the Third U.S. Artillery Regiment, or possibly Gen. Sylvester Churchill (1783-1862), an officer in the War of 1812 and the Mexican-American War.

Area (sq mi): 5023.38 (land 4929.08; water 94.3). **Pop per sq mi:** 5.

Pop 2005: 24,556. **State rank:** 8. **Pop change:** 2000-20005 +2.4%; 1990-2000 +33.7%. **Pop 2000:** 23,982 (White 79.9%; Black or African American 1.6%; Hispanic or Latino 8.7%; Asian 2.7%; Other 11.5%, including 4.8% American Indian/Alaska Native). **Foreign born:** 6%. **Median age:** 34.7.

Income 2000: per capita $19,264; median household $40,808; **Pop below poverty level:** 8.7%. *****Personal per capita income 2000-2003:** $25,053-$28,517.

Unemployment 2004: 4.4%. **Change from 2000:** -4.3%. **Median travel time to work:** 20.7 minutes. **Working outside county of residence:** 15.6%.

Cities with pop over 10,000: None.

CLARK COUNTY

200 S 3rd St   **Ph:** 702-455-4277
Las Vegas, NV 89155   **Fax:** 702-386-9104
www.co.clark.nv.us

In the southeastern corner of NV; organized Feb 5, 1908 from Lincoln County. **Name Origin:** For William Andrews Clark (1839-1925), U.S. senator from MT (1899-1900; 1901-07).

Area (sq mi): 8090.66 (land 7910.34; water 180.32). **Pop per sq mi:** 216.2.

Pop 2005: 1,710,551. **State rank:** 1. **Pop change:** 2000-20005 +24.3%; 1990-2000 +85.5%. **Pop 2000:** 1,375,765 (White 60.2%; Black or African American 9.1%; Hispanic or Latino 22%; Asian 5.3%; Other 14.1%). **Foreign born:** 18%. **Median age:** 34.4.

Income 2000: per capita $21,785; median household $44,616; **Pop below poverty level:** 10.8%. *****Personal per capita income 2000-2003:** $29,600-$30,961.

Unemployment 2004: 4.4%. **Change from 2000:** -1.1%. **Median travel time to work:** 24.3 minutes. **Working outside county of residence:** 1.7%.

Cities with pop over 10,000: Las Vegas ⛪ (534,847); Henderson

Clark County (cont'd)

(224,829); North Las Vegas (158,748); Boulder City (15,246); Mesquite (12,631).

DOUGLAS COUNTY
PO Box 218   **Ph:** 775-782-9020
Minden, NV 89423   **Fax:** 775-782-9016
www.co.douglas.nv.us

On the southwestern border of NV, south of Reno; original county; organized Nov 25, 1861 (prior to statehood). **Name Origin:** For Stephen Arnold Douglas (1813-61), U.S. orator and statesman.

Area (sq mi): 737.65 (land 709.85; water 27.8). **Pop per sq mi:** 66.2.

Pop 2005: 47,017. **State rank:** 5. **Pop change:** 2000-20005 +14%; 1990-2000 +49.3%. **Pop 2000:** 41,259 (White 87.8%; Black or African American 0.3%; Hispanic or Latino 7.4%; Asian 1.3%; Other 6.6%, including 1.7% American Indian/Alaska Native). **Foreign born:** 5.7%. **Median age:** 41.7.

Income 2000: per capita $27,288; median household $51,849; **Pop below poverty level:** 7.3%. ***Personal per capita income 2000-2003:** $39,539-$41,048.

Unemployment 2004: 4.2%. **Change from 2000:** -0.6%. **Median travel time to work:** 23.5 minutes. **Working outside county of residence:** 34.3%.

Cities with pop over 10,000: None.

ELKO COUNTY
569 Court St   **Ph:** 775-738-5398
Elko, NV 89801   **Fax:** 775-753-8535
www.elkocountynv.net

On the northeastern border of NV; organized Mar 5, 1869 from Lander County. **Name Origin:** For the town; meaning of name is undetermined, possibly *elk* plus *-o*, a typical railroad name. It has been suggested that the town was named for elk (the animal) or that the word is an Indian term meaning 'first white woman.'

Area (sq mi): 17,202.94 (land 17,179.03; water 23.91). **Pop per sq mi:** 2.7.

Pop 2005: 45,570. **State rank:** 6. **Pop change:** 2000-20005 +0.6%; 1990-2000 +35.1%. **Pop 2000:** 45,291 (White 72.4%; Black or African American 0.6%; Hispanic or Latino 19.7%; Asian 0.7%; Other 16.7%, including 5.3% American Indian/Alaska Native). **Foreign born:** 10.2%. **Median age:** 31.2.

Income 2000: per capita $18,482; median household $48,383; **Pop below poverty level:** 8.9%. ***Personal per capita income 2000-2003:** $24,610-$26,227.

Unemployment 2004: 4.1%. **Change from 2000:** -1.9%. **Median travel time to work:** 25.2 minutes. **Working outside county of residence:** 11.4%.

Cities with pop over 10,000: Elko 🏛 (16,230).

ESMERALDA COUNTY
PO Box 547   **Ph:** 775-485-6367
Goldfield, NV 89013   **Fax:** 775-485-6376
www.governet.net/NV/CO/ESM/home.cfm

On the central southern border of NV with CA; original county; organized Nov 25, 1861 (prior to statehood). **Name Origin:** For the Esmeralda Mining District, from Spanish 'emerald,' for the stones found there.

Area (sq mi): 3589 (land 3588.5; water 0.5). **Pop per sq mi:** 0.2.

Pop 2005: 787. **State rank:** 17. **Pop change:** 2000-20005 -18.9%; 1990-2000 -27.8%. **Pop 2000:** 971 (White 80.4%; Black or African American 0.1%; Hispanic or Latino 10.2%; Asian 0%; Other 17.8%, including 5.1% American Indian/Alaska Native). **Foreign born:** 6.5%. **Median age:** 45.1.

Income 2000: per capita $18,971; median household $33,203; **Pop below poverty level:** 15.3%. ***Personal per capita income 2000-2003:** $24,411-$29,435.

Unemployment 2004: 5.3%. **Change from 2000:** -2.9%. **Median travel time to work:** 21.9 minutes. **Working outside county of residence:** 29.6%.

Cities with pop over 10,000: None.

EUREKA COUNTY
PO Box 677   **Ph:** 775-237-5262
Eureka, NV 89316   **Fax:** 775-237-6015
www.co.eureka.nv.us

In east-central NV; organized Mar 1, 1873 from Lander County. **Name Origin:** For the Eureka Mining District, from Greek 'I have found it.'

Area (sq mi): 4179.96 (land 4175.68; water 4.28). **Pop per sq mi:** 0.3.

Pop 2005: 1,428. **State rank:** 16. **Pop change:** 2000-20005 -13.5%; 1990-2000 +6.7%. **Pop 2000:** 1,651 (White 84.9%; Black or African American 0.4%; Hispanic or Latino 9.6%; Asian 0.8%; Other 9.6%, including 1.6% American Indian/Alaska Native). **Foreign born:** 7.8%. **Median age:** 38.3.

Income 2000: per capita $18,629; median household $41,417; **Pop below poverty level:** 12.6%. ***Personal per capita income 2000-2003:** $23,284-$25,830.

Unemployment 2004: 4.2%. **Change from 2000:** +0.6%. **Median travel time to work:** 18.2 minutes. **Working outside county of residence:** 11.5%.

Cities with pop over 10,000: None.

HUMBOLDT COUNTY
50 W 5th St County Courthouse Rm 205   **Ph:** 775-623-6300
Winnemucca, NV 89445   **Fax:** 775-623-6302
www.hcnv.us

On the northern border of NV; original county; organized Nov 25, 1861 (prior to statehood). **Name Origin:** For the Little Humboldt River, which runs through the county; named for Alexander von Humboldt (1769-1859), German explorer and naturalist.

Area (sq mi): 9657.87 (land 9647.91; water 9.96). **Pop per sq mi:** 1.8.

Pop 2005: 17,129. **State rank:** 9. **Pop change:** 2000-20005 +6.4%; 1990-2000 +25.4%. **Pop 2000:** 16,106 (White 74.4%; Black or African American 0.5%; Hispanic or Latino 18.9%; Asian 0.6%; Other 15.7%, including 4% American Indian/Alaska Native). **Foreign born:** 10.4%. **Median age:** 33.4.

Source: Personal per capita income data are from the Bureau of Economic Analysis; per capita income data are from the Bureau of the Census. See Introduction for explanation of differences.

464

Humboldt County (cont'd)

Income 2000: per capita $19,539; median household $47,147; **Pop below poverty level:** 9.7%. ***Personal per capita income 2000-2003:** $24,700-$23,975.

Unemployment 2004: 4.1%. **Change from 2000:** -2%. **Median travel time to work:** 26.2 minutes. **Working outside county of residence:** 8.2%.

Cities with pop over 10,000: None.

LANDER COUNTY

315 S Humboldt St
Battle Mountain, NV 89820
www.landercounty.org

Ph: 775-635-5738
Fax: 775-635-5761

In central NV; organized Dec 19, 1862 (prior to statehood). Originally encompassed a third of the state and was called 'Great East' and later 'mother of counties.' **Name Origin:** For Gen. Frederick William Lander (1822-62), Union army officer, surveyor, and Indian agent.

Area (sq mi): 5519.47 (land 5493.63; water 25.84). **Pop per sq mi:** 0.9.

Pop 2005: 5,114. **State rank:** 12. **Pop change:** 2000-20005 -11.7%; 1990-2000 -7.5%. **Pop 2000:** 5,794 (White 75.7%; Black or African American 0.2%; Hispanic or Latino 18.5%; Asian 0.3%; Other 15%, including 4% American Indian/Alaska Native). **Foreign born:** 9.6%. **Median age:** 34.1.

Income 2000: per capita $16,998; median household $46,067; **Pop below poverty level:** 12.5%. ***Personal per capita income 2000-2003:** $25,522-$26,588.

Unemployment 2004: 4.7%. **Change from 2000:** -4.9%. **Median travel time to work:** 23.6 minutes. **Working outside county of residence:** 25.1%.

Cities with pop over 10,000: None.

LINCOLN COUNTY

PO Box 90
Pioche, NV 89043
www.co.lincoln.nv.us

Ph: 775-962-5390
Fax: 775-962-5180

On the southeast border of NV, north of Las Vegas; organized Feb 25, 1866. **Name Origin:** For Abraham Lincoln (1809-65), sixteenth U.S.president.

Area (sq mi): 10,636.77 (land 10,633.61; water 3.17). **Pop per sq mi:** 0.4.

Pop 2005: 4,391. **State rank:** 14. **Pop change:** 2000-20005 +5.4%; 1990-2000 +10.3%. **Pop 2000:** 4,165 (White 89.1%; Black or African American 1.8%; Hispanic or Latino 5.3%; Asian 0.3%; Other 6.4%, including 1.8% American Indian/Alaska Native). **Foreign born:** 3.5%. **Median age:** 38.8.

Income 2000: per capita $17,326; median household $31,979; **Pop below poverty level:** 16.5%. ***Personal per capita income 2000-2003:** $18,561-$20,641.

Unemployment 2004: 5.4%. **Change from 2000:** -1.8%. **Median travel time to work:** 20.2 minutes. **Working outside county of residence:** 10.3%.

Cities with pop over 10,000: None.

LYON COUNTY

27 S Main St
Yerington, NV 89447
www.lyon-county.org

Ph: 775-463-6503
Fax: 775-463-6533

In southwestern NV, southeast of Reno; original county; organized Nov 25, 1861 (prior to statehood). **Name Origin:** For either Gen. Nathaniel Lyon (1818-61), an officer in the Seminole War, Mexican-American War, and Civil War, or for Capt. Robert Lyon, a hero of the Indian Wars.

Area (sq mi): 2016.4 (land 1993.69; water 22.71). **Pop per sq mi:** 23.8.

Pop 2005: 47,515. **State rank:** 4. **Pop change:** 2000-20005 +37.7%; 1990-2000 +72.5%. **Pop 2000:** 34,501 (White 83.4%; Black or African American 0.7%; Hispanic or Latino 11%; Asian 0.6%; Other 10%, including 2.4% American Indian/Alaska Native). **Foreign born:** 6%. **Median age:** 38.2.

Income 2000: per capita $18,543; median household $40,699; **Pop below poverty level:** 10.4%. ***Personal per capita income 2000-2003:** $22,965-$23,264.

Unemployment 2004: 5.2%. **Change from 2000:** -2%. **Median travel time to work:** 28 minutes. **Working outside county of residence:** 48%.

Cities with pop over 10,000: Fernley (10,505).

MINERAL COUNTY

PO Box 1450
Hawthorne, NV 89415

Ph: 775-945-2446
Fax: 775-945-0706

On the southwestern border of NV with CA, southeast of Reno; organized Feb 10, 1911 from Esmeralda County. **Name Origin:** For the profusion of various minerals in the area.

Area (sq mi): 3812.97 (land 3756.4; water 56.56). **Pop per sq mi:** 1.3.

Pop 2005: 4,910. **State rank:** 13. **Pop change:** 2000-20005 -3.2%; 1990-2000 -21.7%. **Pop 2000:** 5,071 (White 70.1%; Black or African American 4.8%; Hispanic or Latino 8.4%; Asian 0.8%; Other 20.6%, including 15.4% American Indian/Alaska Native). **Foreign born:** 2.4%. **Median age:** 42.9.

Income 2000: per capita $16,952; median household $32,891; **Pop below poverty level:** 15.2%. ***Personal per capita income 2000-2003:** $24,287-$24,254.

Unemployment 2004: 5.4%. **Change from 2000:** -3.2%. **Median travel time to work:** 16.9 minutes. **Working outside county of residence:** 11.2%.

Cities with pop over 10,000: None.

NYE COUNTY

PO Box 1031
Tonopah, NV 89049
www.co.nye.nv.us

Ph: 775-482-8127
Fax: 775-482-8133

In south-central NV; organized Feb 16, 1864 from Esmeralda County; largest county in NV. **Name Origin:** For James Warren Nye (1814-76), NY statesman, governor of NV Territory (1861-64), and U.S. senator from NV (1864-73).

Area (sq mi): 18,158.73 (land 18,146.66; water 12.07). **Pop per sq mi:** 2.2.

Nye County (cont'd)

Pop 2005: 40,477. **State rank:** 7. **Pop change:** 2000-20005 +24.6%; 1990-2000 +82.7%. **Pop 2000:** 32,485 (White 84.7%; Black or African American 1.2%; Hispanic or Latino 8.4%; Asian 0.8%; Other 8.4%, including 2% American Indian/Alaska Native). **Foreign born:** 5%. **Median age:** 42.9.

Income 2000: per capita $17,962; median household $36,024; **Pop below poverty level:** 10.7%. ***Personal per capita income 2000-2003:** $24,201-$25,752.

Unemployment 2004: 5.7%. **Change from 2000:** -0.9%. **Median travel time to work:** 28.6 minutes. **Working outside county of residence:** 24.1%.

Cities with pop over 10,000: None.

PERSHING COUNTY
PO Box 820   **Ph:** 775-273-2208
Lovelock, NV 89419   **Fax:** 775-273-3015
www.pershingcounty.net

In west-central NV northeast of Reno; organized Mar 18, 1919 from Humboldt County. **Name Origin:** For Gen. John Joseph 'Black Jack' Pershing (1860-1948), an officer who served in Cuba, the Philippines, and Manchuria; commander in chief of the American Expeditionary Force (1917-18) during WWI, and U.S. army chief of staff (1921-24).

Area (sq mi): 6067.55 (land 6036.56; water 30.99). **Pop per sq mi:** 1.1.

Pop 2005: 6,360. **State rank:** 11. **Pop change:** 2000-20005 -5%; 1990-2000 +54.4%. **Pop 2000:** 6,693 (White 69.7%; Black or African American 5.3%; Hispanic or Latino 19.3%; Asian 0.6%; Other 16.3%, including 3.4% American Indian/Alaska Native). **Foreign born:** 7%. **Median age:** 34.4.

Income 2000: per capita $16,589; median household $40,670; **Pop below poverty level:** 11.4%. ***Personal per capita income 2000-2003:** $16,892-$16,737.

Unemployment 2004: 4.7%. **Change from 2000:** +0%. **Median travel time to work:** 22.8 minutes. **Working outside county of residence:** 25.6%.

Cities with pop over 10,000: None.

STOREY COUNTY
Drawer D   **Ph:** 775-847-0968
Virginia City, NV 89440   **Fax:** 775-847-0949

In southwestern NV, east of Reno; original county; organized Nov 25, 1861 (prior to statehood). **Name Origin:** For Capt. Edward Faris Storey (?-1860), army officer killed by Paiute Indians at Pyramid Lake.

Area (sq mi): 263.8 (land 263.45; water 0.34). **Pop per sq mi:** 15.5.

Pop 2005: 4,074. **State rank:** 15. **Pop change:** 2000-20005 +19.9%; 1990-2000 +34.6%. **Pop 2000:** 3,399 (White 90%; Black or African American 0.3%; Hispanic or Latino 5.1%; Asian 1%; Other 5.6%, including 1.4% American Indian/Alaska Native). **Foreign born:** 2.2%. **Median age:** 44.5.

Income 2000: per capita $23,642; median household $45,490; **Pop below poverty level:** 5.8%. ***Personal per capita income 2000-2003:** $28,266-$29,105.

Unemployment 2004: 3.4%. **Change from 2000:** -0.5%. **Median travel time to work:** 29.4 minutes. **Working outside county of residence:** 80.7%.

Cities with pop over 10,000: None.

WASHOE COUNTY
PO Box 30083   **Ph:** 775-328-3260
Reno, NV 89520   **Fax:** 775-328-3582
www.co.washoe.nv.us

On the western border of NV; original county; organized Nov 25, 1861 (prior to statehood); in 1883 annexed Roop County (called Lake County until 1862), which was also an original county. **Name Origin:** For the Washo or Washiu Indian tribe in northwestern NV and adjacent areas of CA. Their name has been translated as 'person,' 'tall bunch grass,' and 'rye grass.' The first seems most probable.

Area (sq mi): 6551.32 (land 6342.27; water 209.05). **Pop per sq mi:** 61.5.

Pop 2005: 389,872. **State rank:** 2. **Pop change:** 2000-20005 +14.8%; 1990-2000 +33.3%. **Pop 2000:** 339,486 (White 73%; Black or African American 2.1%; Hispanic or Latino 16.6%; Asian 4.3%; Other 13.3%, including 1.8% American Indian/Alaska Native). **Foreign born:** 14.1%. **Median age:** 35.6.

Income 2000: per capita $24,277; median household $45,815; **Pop below poverty level:** 10%. ***Personal per capita income 2000-2003:** $36,100-$38,241.

Unemployment 2004: 4%. **Change from 2000:** -0.1%. **Median travel time to work:** 19.2 minutes. **Working outside county of residence:** 4.3%.

Cities with pop over 10,000: Reno 🏛 (197,963); Sparks (81,014).

WHITE PINE COUNTY
801 Clark St Suite 4   **Ph:** 775-289-2341
Ely, NV 89301   **Fax:** 775-289-2544
www.co.white-pine.nv.us

On the central eastern border of NV; organized Mar 2, 1869 from Lander County. **Name Origin:** For the White Pine Mining District, itself named for the area's many pine trees.

Area (sq mi): 8896.6 (land 8875.98; water 20.62). **Pop per sq mi:** 1.

Pop 2005: 8,994. **State rank:** 10. **Pop change:** 2000-20005 -2%; 1990-2000 -0.9%. **Pop 2000:** 9,181 (White 79.5%; Black or African American 4.1%; Hispanic or Latino 11%; Asian 0.8%; Other 8.7%, including 3.3% American Indian/Alaska Native). **Foreign born:** 2.9%. **Median age:** 37.7.

Income 2000: per capita $18,309; median household $36,688; **Pop below poverty level:** 11%. ***Personal per capita income 2000-2003:** $24,293-$26,429.

Unemployment 2004: 4%. **Change from 2000:** -0.5%. **Median travel time to work:** 18.3 minutes. **Working outside county of residence:** 7.6%.

Cities with pop over 10,000: None.

Source: Personal per capita income data are from the Bureau of Economic Analysis; per capita income data are from the Bureau of the Census. See Introduction for explanation of differences.

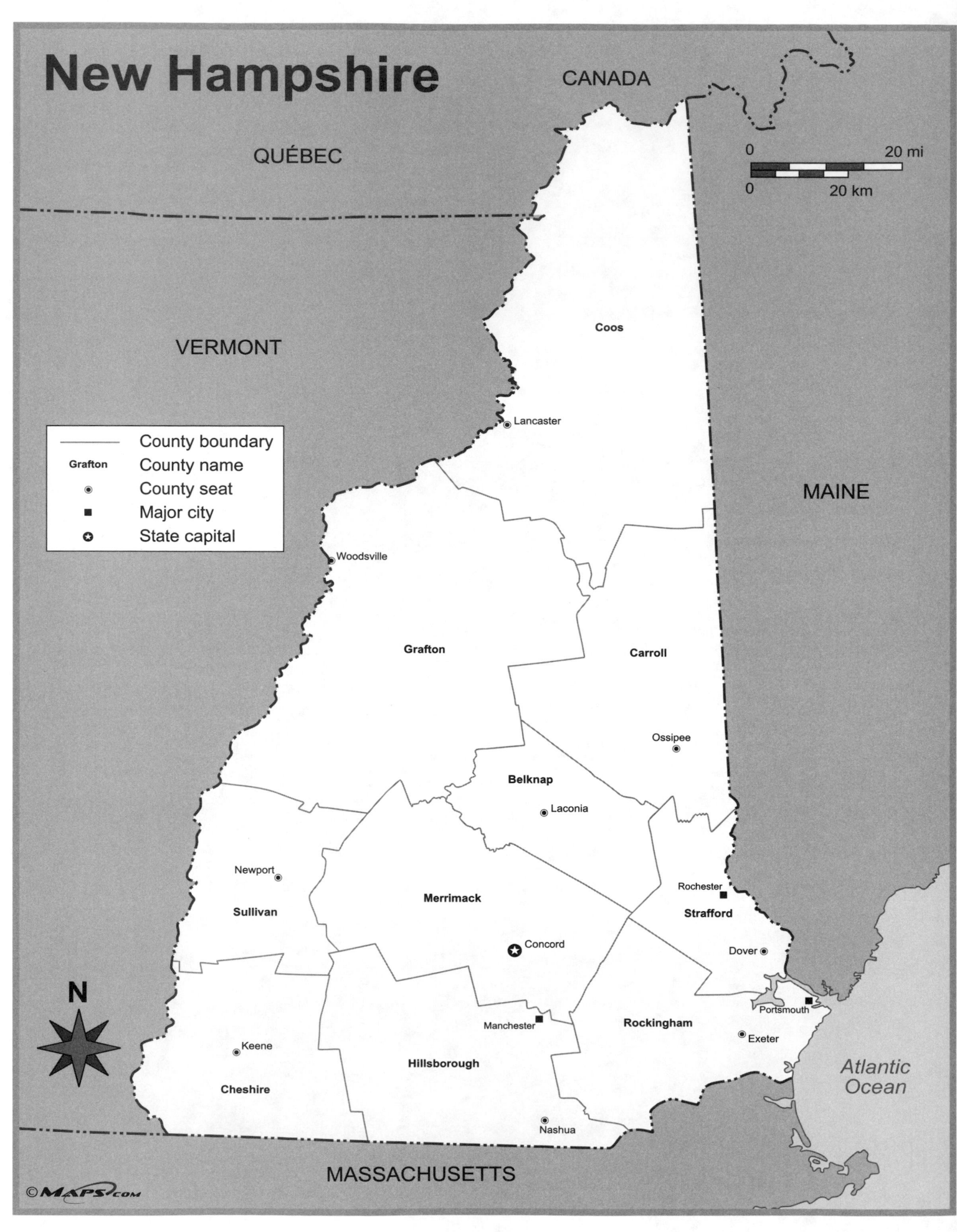

New Hampshire

QUÉBEC

CANADA

VERMONT

MAINE

Coos

● Lancaster

County boundary
Grafton — County name
◉ County seat
■ Major city
✪ State capital

Woodsville ●

Grafton

Carroll

Ossipee ◉

Belknap

● Laconia

Newport ◉

Merrimack

Rochester ■

Sullivan

Strafford

✪ Concord

Dover ◉

N

Manchester ■

Rockingham

Keene ●

Portsmouth ■

Exeter ◉

Cheshire

Atlantic Ocean

Nashua ●

MASSACHUSETTS

©MAPS.com

New Hampshire

NEW HAMPSHIRE STATE INFORMATION
www.nh.gov   Ph: 603-271-1110

Area (sq mi): 9349.94 (land 8968.1; water 381.84). **Pop per sq mi:** 146.1.

Pop 2005: 1,309,940. **Pop change:** 2000-20005 +6%; 1990-2000 +11.4%. **Pop 2000:** 1,235,786 (White 95.1%; Black or African American 0.7%; Hispanic or Latino 1.7%; Asian 1.3%; Other 1.9%). **Foreign born:** 4.4%. **Median age:** 37.1.

Income 2000: per capita $23,844; median household $49,467; **Pop below poverty level:** 6.5%. *Personal per capita income 2000-2003: $33,396-$35,140.

Unemployment 2004: 3.9%. **Change from 2000:** +1.2%. **Median travel time to work:** 25.3 minutes. **Working outside county of residence:** 33.3%.

BELKNAP COUNTY
34 County Dr   Ph: 603-527-5400
Laconia, NH 03246   Fax: 603-527-5409
www.belknapcounty.org

In east-central NH, north of Concord; organized Dec 22, 1840 from Strafford County. **Name Origin:** For Jeremy Belknap (1744-98), clergyman and historian, author of *History of New Hampshire* (1784-92) and *American Biography* (1794-98).

Area (sq mi): 468.55 (land 401.29; water 67.26). **Pop per sq mi:** 153.4.

Pop 2005: 61,547. **State rank:** 7. **Pop change:** 2000-20005 +9.3%; 1990-2000 +14.4%. **Pop 2000:** 56,325 (White 97.1%; Black or African American 0.3%; Hispanic or Latino 0.7%; Asian 0.6%; Other 1.6%). **Foreign born:** 2.5%. **Median age:** 40.1.

Income 2000: per capita $22,758; median household $43,605; **Pop below poverty level:** 6.1%. *Personal per capita income 2000-2003: $30,081-$32,513.

Unemployment 2004: 3.4%. **Change from 2000:** +0.4%. **Median travel time to work:** 24.8 minutes. **Working outside county of residence:** 32.6%.

Cities with pop over 10,000: Laconia 🏛 (17,133).

CARROLL COUNTY
PO Box 152   Ph: 603-539-2428
Ossipee, NH 03864   Fax: 603-539-4287

On central eastern border of NH, north of Laconia; organized Dec 22, 1840 from Strafford, Coos, and Grafton counties. **Name Origin:**

For Charles Carroll (1737-1832), signer of the Declaration of Independence, U.S. senator from MD, and founder of the Baltimore and Ohio Railroad.

Area (sq mi): 992.24 (land 933.8; water 58.44). **Pop per sq mi:** 50.8.

Pop 2005: 47,439. **State rank:** 8. **Pop change:** 2000-20005 +8.6%; 1990-2000 +23.3%. **Pop 2000:** 43,666 (White 97.9%; Black or African American 0.2%; Hispanic or Latino 0.5%; Asian 0.4%; Other 1.3%). **Foreign born:** 2.4%. **Median age:** 42.5.

Income 2000: per capita $21,931; median household $39,990; **Pop below poverty level:** 7.9%. *Personal per capita income 2000-2003: $30,424-$33,228.

Unemployment 2004: 3.1%. **Change from 2000:** +0%. **Median travel time to work:** 26 minutes. **Working outside county of residence:** 23.9%.

Cities with pop over 10,000: None.

CHESHIRE COUNTY
12 Court St   Ph: 603-352-6902
Keene, NH 03431
www.co.cheshire.nh.us

In southwestern corner of NH, west of Manchester;original county, organized Apr 29, 1769. **Name Origin:** For Cheshire county in England, site of one of the estates of the Wentworths; named by NH Gov. John Wentworth (1737-1820) on its establishment.

Area (sq mi): 729.15 (land 707.4; water 21.75). **Pop per sq mi:** 109.3.

Pop 2005: 77,287. **State rank:** 6. **Pop change:** 2000-20005 +4.7%; 1990-2000 +5.3%. **Pop 2000:** 73,825 (White 97.3%; Black or African American 0.4%; Hispanic or Latino 0.7%; Asian 0.5%; Other 1.4%). **Foreign born:** 2.2%. **Median age:** 37.6.

Income 2000: per capita $20,685; median household $42,382; **Pop below poverty level:** 8%. *Personal per capita income 2000-2003: $28,214-$30,506.

Unemployment 2004: 3.3%. **Change from 2000:** +0.1%. **Median travel time to work:** 22.3 minutes. **Working outside county of residence:** 23.2%.

Cities with pop over 10,000: Keene 🏛 (22,955).

COOS COUNTY
55 School St Suite 301   Ph: 603-788-4900
Lancaster, NH 03584

In northern NH; organized Dec 24, 1803 from Grafton County. **Name Origin:** From the Pennacook Indian word *cohos* 'pine tree' or 'place where pines grow.'

🏛 *County Seat*

Coos County (cont'd)

Area (sq mi): 1831.44 (land 1800.39; water 31.06). **Pop per sq mi:** 18.7.

Pop 2005: 33,655. **State rank:** 10. **Pop change:** 2000-20005 +1.6%; 1990-2000 -4.9%. **Pop 2000:** 33,111 (White 97.7%; Black or African American 0.1%; Hispanic or Latino 0.6%; Asian 0.4%; Other 1.5%). **Foreign born:** 4%. **Median age:** 41.5.

Income 2000: per capita $17,218; median household $33,593; **Pop below poverty level:** 10%. ***Personal per capita income 2000-2003:** $25,244-$27,077.

Unemployment 2004: 4.5%. **Change from 2000:** -1%. **Median travel time to work:** 19.3 minutes. **Working outside county of residence:** 17.3%.

Cities with pop over 10,000: Berlin (10,484).

GRAFTON COUNTY

3855 Dartmouth College Hwy Box 1   **Ph:** 603-787-6941
North Haverhill, NH 03774   **Fax:** 603-787-2345
www.graftoncountynh.us

On central western border of NH; original county, organized Apr 29, 1769. **Name Origin:** For Augustus Henry Fitzroy (1735-1811), 3rd Duke of Grafton, an English parliamentarian who supported American colonial interests.

Area (sq mi): 1750.08 (land 1713.33; water 36.75). **Pop per sq mi:** 49.4.

Pop 2005: 84,708. **State rank:** 5. **Pop change:** 2000-20005 +3.6%; 1990-2000 +9.1%. **Pop 2000:** 81,743 (White 95.1%; Black or African American 0.5%; Hispanic or Latino 1.1%; Asian 1.7%; Other 2%). **Foreign born:** 3.9%. **Median age:** 37.

Income 2000: per capita $22,227; median household $41,962; **Pop below poverty level:** 8.6%. ***Personal per capita income 2000-2003:** $31,348-$35,241.

Unemployment 2004: 2.7%. **Change from 2000:** +0.6%. **Median travel time to work:** 21.3 minutes. **Working outside county of residence:** 18.1%.

Cities with pop over 10,000: Lebanon (12,655).

HILLSBOROUGH COUNTY

329 Mast Rd   **Ph:** 603-627-5600
Golfstown, NH 03045   **Fax:** 603-627-5603
www.hillsboroughcountynh.org

On central southern border of NH, south of Concord; original county, organized Apr 29, 1769. **Name Origin:** For Wills Hill (1718-93), 1st Earl of Hillsborough, English secretary of state for the colonies (1768-72). Also spelled *Hillsboro*. Some also note that one of the original grantees of land was Col. John Hill of MA.

Area (sq mi): 892.2 (land 876.36; water 15.84). **Pop per sq mi:** 457.9.

Pop 2005: 401,291. **State rank:** 1. **Pop change:** 2000-20005 +5.4%; 1990-2000 +13.3%. **Pop 2000:** 380,841 (White 92.3%; Black or African American 1.3%; Hispanic or Latino 3.2%; Asian 2%; Other 2.7%). **Foreign born:** 6.8%. **Median age:** 35.9.

Income 2000: per capita $25,198; median household $53,384; **Pop below poverty level:** 6.3%. ***Personal per capita income 2000-2003:** $36,011-$36,858.

Unemployment 2004: 3.9%. **Change from 2000:** +0.1%. **Median travel time to work:** 25.5 minutes. **Working outside county of residence:** 28.4%.

Cities with pop over 10,000: Manchester (109,310); Nashua 🏛 (87,411).

MERRIMACK COUNTY

4 Court St Suite 2   **Ph:** 603-228-0331
Concord, NH 03301   **Fax:** 603-224-2665
www.ci.concord.nh.us

In south-central NH, north of Manchester; organized Jul 1, 1823 from Rickingham and Hillsborough counties. **Name Origin:** For the Merrimack River, which bisects the county.

Area (sq mi): 956.49 (land 934.43; water 22.06). **Pop per sq mi:** 157.2.

Pop 2005: 146,881. **State rank:** 3. **Pop change:** 2000-20005 +7.8%; 1990-2000 +13.5%. **Pop 2000:** 136,225 (White 96.4%; Black or African American 0.5%; Hispanic or Latino 1%; Asian 0.9%; Other 1.4%). **Foreign born:** 3.2%. **Median age:** 37.7.

Income 2000: per capita $23,208; median household $48,522; **Pop below poverty level:** 5.9%. ***Personal per capita income 2000-2003:** $30,907-$32,633.

Unemployment 2004: 3.1%. **Change from 2000:** +0.4%. **Median travel time to work:** 24.3 minutes. **Working outside county of residence:** 31%.

Cities with pop over 10,000: Concord 🏛 (42,345).

ROCKINGHAM COUNTY

PO Box 1258   **Ph:** 603-642-5256
Kingston, NH 03848
www.co.rockingham.nh.us

On southeastern border of NH, southeast of Concord; original county, organized Apr 29, 1769. **Name Origin:** For Charles Watson-Wentworth, Marquis of Rockingham (1730-82), British statesman, prime minister, and cousin of the NH Wentworths, largely responsible for repeal of the Stamp Act.

Area (sq mi): 793.96 (land 694.96; water 99). **Pop per sq mi:** 424.6.

Pop 2005: 295,076. **State rank:** 2. **Pop change:** 2000-20005 +6.4%; 1990-2000 +12.8%. **Pop 2000:** 277,359 (White 96.1%; Black or African American 0.6%; Hispanic or Latino 1.2%; Asian 1.1%; Other 1.5%). **Foreign born:** 3.7%. **Median age:** 37.2.

Income 2000: per capita $26,656; median household $58,150; **Pop below poverty level:** 4.5%. ***Personal per capita income 2000-2003:** $38,478-$40,103.

Unemployment 2004: 4.6%. **Change from 2000:** +0.3%. **Median travel time to work:** 28.6 minutes. **Working outside county of residence:** 47.1%.

Cities with pop over 10,000: Portsmouth (20,786).

*Source: Personal per capita income data are from the Bureau of Economic Analysis; per capita income data are from the Bureau of the Census. See Introduction for explanation of differences.

STRAFFORD COUNTY

259 County Farm Rd   **Ph:** 603-742-1458
Dover, NH 03820   **Fax:** 603-743-4407
www.co.strafford.nh.us

On southeastern border of NH, south of Portsmouth; original county, organized Apr 29, 1769. **Name Origin:** For William Wentworth (1722-91), 4th Earl of Strafford, cousin of John Wentworth (1737-1820), governor of NH at the time of its establishment.

Area (sq mi): 383.91 (land 368.76; water 15.15). **Pop per sq mi** 322.7.

Pop 2005: 119,015. **State rank:** 4. **Pop change:** 2000-20005 +6%; 1990-2000 +7.7%. **Pop 2000:** 112,233 (White 95.7%; Black or African American 0.6%; Hispanic or Latino 1%; Asian 1.4%; Other 1.6%). **Foreign born:** 3.4%. **Median age:** 34.4.

Income 2000: per capita $20,479; median household $44,803; **Pop below poverty level:** 9.2%. *Personal per capita income 2000-2003:** $27,141-$29,079.

Unemployment 2004: 3.4%. **Change from 2000:** +0.3%. **Median travel time to work:** 24.1 minutes. **Working outside county of residence:** 41.2%.

Cities with pop over 10,000: Rochester (29,757); Dover ⛪ (28,495); Somersworth (11,736).

SULLIVAN COUNTY

14 Main St   **Ph:** 603-863-2560
Newport, NH 03773   **Fax:** 603-863-9314
www.sullivancountynh.gov

On southwestern border of NH, north of Keene; organized Jul 5, 1827 from Cheshire County. **Name Origin:** For Gen. John Sullivan (1740-95), officer in the Revolutionary War, member of the Continental Congress, chief executive of NH (1786-87), and governor (1789).

Area (sq mi): 551.92 (land 537.38; water 14.54). **Pop per sq mi:** 80.1.

Pop 2005: 43,041. **State rank:** 9. **Pop change:** 2000-20005 +6.4%; 1990-2000 +4.8%. **Pop 2000:** 40,458 (White 97.6%; Black or African American 0.2%; Hispanic or Latino 0.5%; Asian 0.4%; Other 1.3%). **Foreign born:** 2.9%. **Median age:** 40.

Income 2000: per capita $21,319; median household $40,938; **Pop below poverty level:** 8.5%. *Personal per capita income 2000-2003:** $27,663-$30,688.

Unemployment 2004: 3.2%. **Change from 2000:** +1%. **Median travel time to work:** 23.2 minutes. **Working outside county of residence:** 37.4%.

Cities with pop over 10,000: Claremont (13,344).

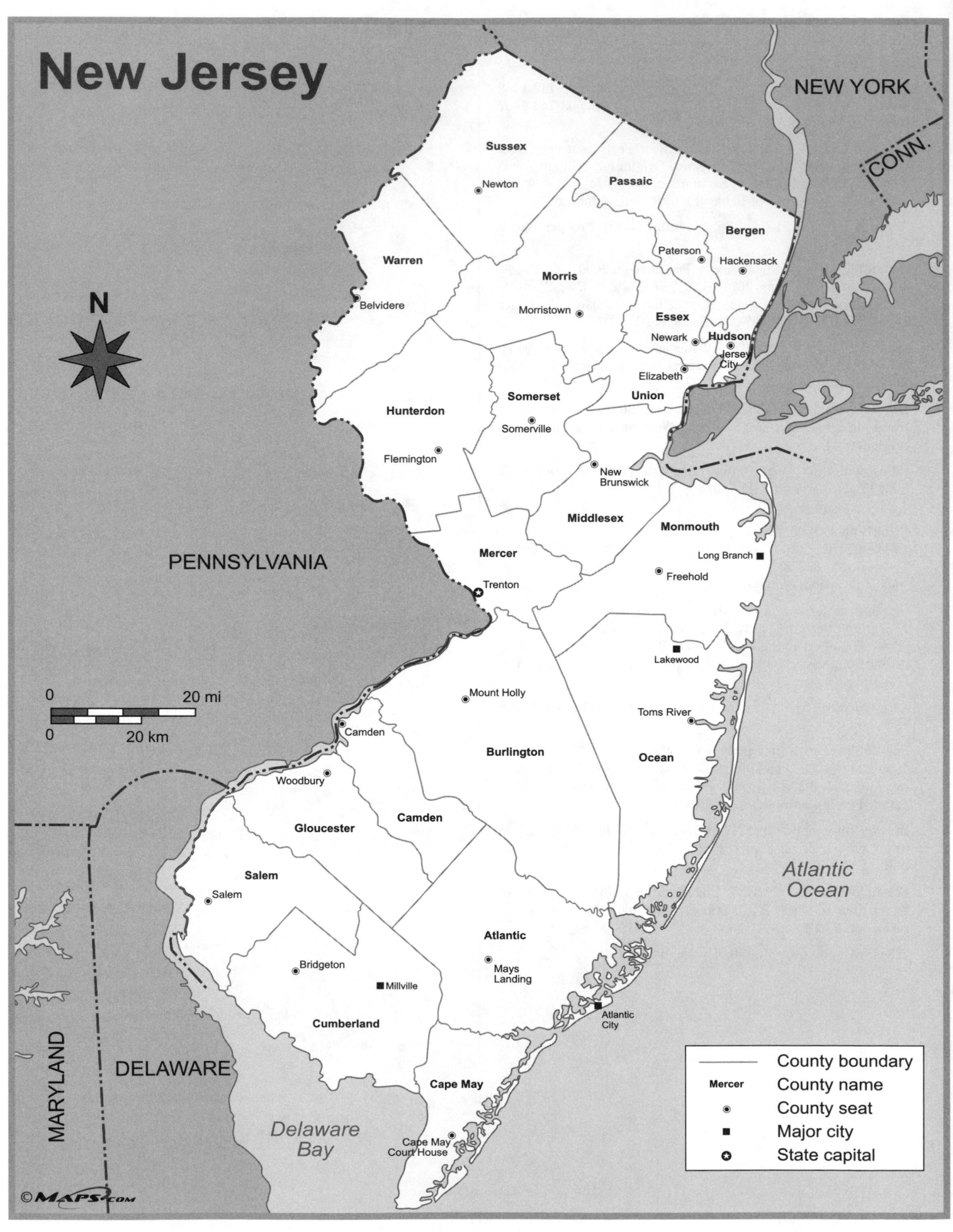

New Jersey

NEW YORK

CONN.

N

PENNSYLVANIA

Sussex
· Newton

Passaic

Warren

Morris

Bergen
Paterson · · Hackensack

· Belvidere

· Morristown

Essex

Newark · · **Hudson**
· Jersey
City

Hunterdon

Somerset

· Elizabeth

Union

· Somerville

· Flemington

· New
Brunswick

Middlesex

Monmouth
Long Branch ■

Mercer

· Freehold

· Trenton

Lakewood ■

· Mount Holly

Toms River ·

Camden ·

Burlington

Ocean

Woodbury ·

Gloucester

Camden

Salem

Salem ·

Atlantic

· Atlantic
· Mays
Landing

Bridgeton ·

■ Millville

■ Atlantic
City

Cumberland

MARYLAND

DELAWARE

Cape May

Cape May ·
Court House

*Delaware
Bay*

*Atlantic
Ocean*

© MAPS.com

	County boundary
Mercer	County name
·	County seat
■	Major city
✪	State capital

0 20 mi
0 20 km

New Jersey

NEW JERSEY STATE INFORMATION
www.newjersey.gov   **Ph:** 609-292-2121

Area (sq mi): 8721.3 (land 7417.34; water 1303.96). **Pop per sq mi:** 1175.3.

Pop 2005: 8,717,925. **Pop change:** 2000-20005 +3.6%; 1990-2000 +8.9%. **Pop 2000:** 8,414,350 (White 66%; Black or African American 13.6%; Hispanic or Latino 13.3%; Asian 5.7%; Other 8.1%). **Foreign born:** 17.5%. **Median age:** 36.7.

Income 2000: per capita $27,006; median household $55,146; **Pop below poverty level:** 8.5%. *Personal per capita income 2000-2003: $38,365-$39,577.

Unemployment 2004: 4.9%. **Change from 2000:** +1.2%. **Median travel time to work:** 30 minutes. **Working outside county of residence:** 45.2%.

ATLANTIC COUNTY
5901 E Main St   **Ph:** 609-641-7867
Mays Landing, NJ 08330   **Fax:** 609-625-4738
www.aclink.org

In southern NJ on Atlantic coast, east of Vineland; organized Feb 7, 1837 from Gloucester County. **Name Origin:** For the Atlantic Ocean.

Area (sq mi): 671.45 (land 561.07; water 110.37). **Pop per sq mi:** 483.

Pop 2005: 271,015. **State rank:** 15. **Pop change:** 2000-20005 +7.3%; 1990-2000 +12.6%. **Pop 2000:** 252,552 (White 63.9%; Black or African American 17.6%; Hispanic or Latino 12.2%; Asian 5.1%; Other 9%). **Foreign born:** 11.8%. **Median age:** 37.

Income 2000: per capita $21,034; median household $43,933; **Pop below poverty level:** 10.5%. *Personal per capita income 2000-2003: $31,510-$31,749.

Unemployment 2004: 5.6%. **Change from 2000:** +0.2%. **Median travel time to work:** 23.7 minutes. **Working outside county of residence:** 14.8%.

Cities with pop over 10,000: 6 (see page 36 for cities).

BERGEN COUNTY
1 Bergen County Plaza Rm 580   **Ph:** 201-336-7300
Hackensack, NJ 07601   **Fax:** 201-336-7304
www.co.bergen.nj.us

In northeastern NJ bordering on NY, north of Jersey City; original county, organized Mar 7, 1683. **Name Origin:** Named by early Dutch settlers for the town of Bergen-op-zoom, North Brabant, Netherlands.

Area (sq mi): 246.8 (land 234.17; water 12.63). **Pop per sq mi:** 3854.3.

Pop 2005: 902,561. **State rank:** 1. **Pop change:** 2000-20005 +2.1%; 1990-2000 +7.1%. **Pop 2000:** 884,118 (White 72.3%; Black or African American 5.3%; Hispanic or Latino 10.3%; Asian 10.7%; Other 5.7%). **Foreign born:** 25.1%. **Median age:** 39.1.

Income 2000: per capita $33,638; median household $65,241; **Pop below poverty level:** 5%. *Personal per capita income 2000-2003: $51,227-$51,758.

Unemployment 2004: 4.2%. **Change from 2000:** +0.6%. **Median travel time to work:** 29.7 minutes. **Working outside county of residence:** 42.4%.

Cities with pop over 10,000: 30 (see page 36 for cities).

BURLINGTON COUNTY
49 Rancocas Rd   **Ph:** 609-265-5122
Mount Holly, NJ 08060   **Fax:** 609-265-0696
www.co.burlington.nj.us

In central NJ, east of Philadelphia, original county, organzed May 17, 1694. **Name Origin:** For Bridlington, Yorkshire, England. The alternate spelling reflects the pronunciation used in England.

Area (sq mi): 819.43 (land 804.57; water 14.86). **Pop per sq mi:** 560.2.

Pop 2005: 450,743. **State rank:** 11. **Pop change:** 2000-20005 +6.5%; 1990-2000 +7.2%. **Pop 2000:** 423,394 (White 76.3%; Black or African American 15.1%; Hispanic or Latino 4.2%; Asian 2.7%; Other 3.8%). **Foreign born:** 6.3%. **Median age:** 37.1.

Income 2000: per capita $26,339; median household $58,608; **Pop below poverty level:** 4.7%. *Personal per capita income 2000-2003: $35,044-$37,105.

Unemployment 2004: 4.2%. **Change from 2000:** +1%. **Median travel time to work:** 28.2 minutes. **Working outside county of residence:** 43.9%.

Cities with pop over 10,000: None.

CAMDEN COUNTY
520 Market St Rm 102   **Ph:** 856-225-5300
Camden, NJ 08102   **Fax:** 856-225-5316
www.co.camden.nj.us

On central western border of NJ, east of Philadelphia, organized Mar 13, 1844 from Gloucester County. **Name Origin:** For the city of Camden.

Area (sq mi): 227.58 (land 222.3; water 5.28). **Pop per sq mi:** 2331.3.

🏛 *County Seat*

Camden County (cont'd)

Pop 2005: 518,249. **State rank:** 8. **Pop change:** 2000-20005 +1.8%; 1990-2000 +1.2%. **Pop 2000:** 508,932 (White 67.8%; Black or African American 18.1%; Hispanic or Latino 9.7%; Asian 3.7%; Other 7.3%). **Foreign born:** 6.9%. **Median age:** 35.8.

Income 2000: per capita $22,354; median household $48,097; **Pop below poverty level:** 10.4%. ***Personal per capita income 2000-2003:** $29,417-$32,449.

Unemployment 2004: 5.4%. **Change from 2000:** +1.3%. **Median travel time to work:** 27.9 minutes. **Working outside county of residence:** 46.3%.

Cities with pop over 10,000: 7 (see page 36 for cities).

CAPE MAY COUNTY

7 N Main St PO Box 5000   **Ph:** 609-465-1010
Cape May Court House, NJ 08210   **Fax:** 609-465-8625
www.capemaycountygov.net

On southern tip of NJ, south of Atlantic City; organized Nov 12, 1692 from Cumberland County. **Name Origin:** For the cape, whose name commemorates Cornelis Jacobsen Mey, Dutch captain who explored the Atlantic coast of North America from Long Island to Cape May in 1612-14.

Area (sq mi): 620.28 (land 255.19; water 365.09). **Pop per sq mi:** 389.1.

Pop 2005: 99,286. **State rank:** 20. **Pop change:** 2000-20005 -3%; 1990-2000 +7.6%. **Pop 2000:** 102,326 (White 90%; Black or African American 5.1%; Hispanic or Latino 3.3%; Asian 0.6%; Other 2.7%). **Foreign born:** 3.2%. **Median age:** 42.3.

Income 2000: per capita $24,172; median household $41,591; **Pop below poverty level:** 8.6%. ***Personal per capita income 2000-2003:** $31,662-$34,386.

Unemployment 2004: 6.9%. **Change from 2000:** -1.3%. **Median travel time to work:** 23.2 minutes. **Working outside county of residence:** 27.8%.

Cities with pop over 10,000: Ocean City (15,506).

CUMBERLAND COUNTY

60 W Broad St   **Ph:** 856-451-8000
Bridgeton, NJ 08302   **Fax:** 856-455-1410
www.co.cumberland.nj.us

In southern NJ, on Delaware Bay; organized Jan 19, 1748 from Salem County. **Name Origin:** For William Augustus, Duke of Cumberland (1721-65), British general and second son of King George II (1683-1760).

Area (sq mi): 676.59 (land 489.3; water 187.29). **Pop per sq mi:** 313.2.

Pop 2005: 153,252. **State rank:** 16. **Pop change:** 2000-20005 +4.7%; 1990-2000 +6.1%. **Pop 2000:** 146,438 (White 58.4%; Black or African American 20.2%; Hispanic or Latino 19%; Asian 1%; Other 13.1%, including 1% American Indian/Alaska Native). **Foreign born:** 6.2%. **Median age:** 35.6.

Income 2000: per capita $17,376; median household $39,150; **Pop below poverty level:** 15%. ***Personal per capita income 2000-2003:** $23,365-$26,012.

Unemployment 2004: 6.6%. **Change from 2000:** -0.9%. **Median travel time to work:** 23.1 minutes. **Working outside county of residence:** 23.6%.

Cities with pop over 10,000: Vineland (58,009); Millville (27,611); Bridgeton 🏛 (22,727).

ESSEX COUNTY

465 ML King Jr Blvd Rm 245   **Ph:** 973-621-4920
Newark, NJ 07102   **Fax:** 973-621-2537
www.co.essex.nj.us

In northeastern NJ, west of New York City; original county, organized Mar 7, 1683. **Name Origin:** For the county of Essex, England.

Area (sq mi): 129.56 (land 126.27; water 3.29). **Pop per sq mi:** 6264.8.

Pop 2005: 791,057. **State rank:** 2. **Pop change:** 2000-20005 -0.3%; 1990-2000 +2%. **Pop 2000:** 793,633 (White 37.6%; Black or African American 41.2%; Hispanic or Latino 15.4%; Asian 3.7%; Other 10.6%). **Foreign born:** 21.2%. **Median age:** 34.7.

Income 2000: per capita $24,943; median household $44,944; **Pop below poverty level:** 15.6%. ***Personal per capita income 2000-2003:** $37,034-$37,963.

Unemployment 2004: 5.9%. **Change from 2000:** +0.5%. **Median travel time to work:** 31.2 minutes. **Working outside county of residence:** 46.6%.

Cities with pop over 10,000: Newark 🏛 (280,451); East Orange (68,930).

GLOUCESTER COUNTY

1 N Broad St Rm 101   **Ph:** 856-853-3237
Woodbury, NJ 08096   **Fax:** 856-853-3327
www.co.gloucester.nj.us

In southwestern NJ, southeast of Philadelphia; original county, organized May 26, 1686. **Name Origin:** For Henry, Duke of Gloucester (1639-60), third son of Charles I (1600-49), king of England.

Area (sq mi): 336.92 (land 324.72; water 12.2). **Pop per sq mi:** 852.8.

Pop 2005: 276,910. **State rank:** 14. **Pop change:** 2000-20005 +8.7%; 1990-2000 +10.7%. **Pop 2000:** 254,673 (White 85.7%; Black or African American 9.1%; Hispanic or Latino 2.6%; Asian 1.5%; Other 2.4%). **Foreign born:** 3.4%. **Median age:** 36.1.

Income 2000: per capita $22,708; median household $54,273; **Pop below poverty level:** 6.2%. ***Personal per capita income 2000-2003:** $28,134-$31,056.

Unemployment 2004: 4.8%. **Change from 2000:** +0.9%. **Median travel time to work:** 28 minutes. **Working outside county of residence:** 53.6%.

Cities with pop over 10,000: Glassboro (19,177); Woodbury 🏛 (10,437).

HUDSON COUNTY

583 Newark Ave Brennan Courthouse   **Ph:** 201-795-6112
Jersey City, NJ 07306   **Fax:** 201-795-2581
www.hudsoncountynj.org

In northeastern NJ, across the Hudson River from New York City;

*Source: Personal per capita income data are from the Bureau of Economic Analysis; per capita income data are from the Bureau of the Census. See Introduction for explanation of differences.

Hudson County (cont'd)

organized Feb 22, 1840 from Bergen County. **Name Origin:** For the Hudson River.

Area (sq mi): 62.43 (land 46.69; water 15.74). **Pop per sq mi:** 12926.1.

Pop 2005: 603,521. **State rank:** 5. **Pop change:** 2000-20005 -0.9%; 1990-2000 +10.1%. **Pop 2000:** 608,975 (White 35.3%; Black or African American 13.5%; Hispanic or Latino 39.8%; Asian 9.4%; Other 21.6%). **Foreign born:** 38.5%. **Median age:** 33.6.

Income 2000: per capita $21,154; median household $40,293; **Pop below poverty level:** 15.5%. ***Personal per capita income 2000-2003:** $28,932-$30,447.

Unemployment 2004: 6.1%. **Change from 2000:** -0.1%. **Median travel time to work:** 32.6 minutes. **Working outside county of residence:** 54.1%.

Cities with pop over 10,000: 9 (see page 36 for cities).

HUNTERDON COUNTY

71 Main St
Flemington, NJ 08822
www.co.hunterdon.nj.us

Ph: 908-788-1221
Fax: 908-782-4068

In central NJ along the Delaware River, northwest of Trenton; organized Mar 13, 1714 from Burlington County. **Name Origin:** For Robert Hunter (?-1734), colonial governor of New York and East and West Jersey (1710-19).

Area (sq mi): 437.76 (land 429.94; water 7.82). **Pop per sq mi:** 303.3.

Pop 2005: 130,404. **State rank:** 18. **Pop change:** 2000-20005 +6.9%; 1990-2000 +13.2%. **Pop 2000:** 121,989 (White 92.2%; Black or African American 2.2%; Hispanic or Latino 2.8%; Asian 1.9%; Other 1.9%). **Foreign born:** 6.3%. **Median age:** 38.8.

Income 2000: per capita $36,370; median household $79,888; **Pop below poverty level:** 2.6%. ***Personal per capita income 2000-2003:** $52,836-$55,196.

Unemployment 2004: 3.2%. **Change from 2000:** +1.1%. **Median travel time to work:** 33.5 minutes. **Working outside county of residence:** 58.7%.

Cities with pop over 10,000: None.

MERCER COUNTY

PO Box 8068
Trenton, NJ 08650
www.mercercounty.org

Ph: 609-989-6470
Fax: 609-989-1111

In central NJ along the Delaware River, northeast of Philadelphia; organized Feb 22, 1838 from Hunterdon and Middlesex counties. **Name Origin:** For Gen. Hugh Mercer (1721-77), Revolutionary War officer and physician.

Area (sq mi): 228.84 (land 225.93; water 2.91). **Pop per sq mi:** 1621.1.

Pop 2005: 366,256. **State rank:** 12. **Pop change:** 2000-20005 +4.4%; 1990-2000 +7.7%. **Pop 2000:** 350,761 (White 64.2%; Black or African American 19.8%; Hispanic or Latino 9.7%; Asian 4.9%; Other 6.8%). **Foreign born:** 13.9%. **Median age:** 36.

Income 2000: per capita $27,914; median household $56,613; **Pop below poverty level:** 8.6%. ***Personal per capita income 2000-2003:** $39,456-$41,499.

Unemployment 2004: 4.2%. **Change from 2000:** +0.8%. **Median travel time to work:** 27.1 minutes. **Working outside county of residence:** 31.1%.

Cities with pop over 10,000: Trenton 🏛 (85,379); Princeton (13,590).

MIDDLESEX COUNTY

75 Bayard St
New Brunswick, NJ 08903
co.middlesex.nj.us

Ph: 732-745-3828
Fax: 732-745-3642

In northern NJ, southwest of Newark; original county, organized Mar 1, 1683. **Name Origin:** For the ancient county in England (most of which is now part of Greater London).

Area (sq mi): 322.51 (land 309.72; water 12.79). **Pop per sq mi:** 2549.1.

Pop 2005: 789,516. **State rank:** 3. **Pop change:** 2000-20005 +5.2%; 1990-2000 +11.7%. **Pop 2000:** 750,162 (White 61.9%; Black or African American 9.1%; Hispanic or Latino 13.6%; Asian 13.9%; Other 8.5%). **Foreign born:** 24.2%. **Median age:** 35.7.

Income 2000: per capita $26,535; median household $61,446; **Pop below poverty level:** 6.6%. ***Personal per capita income 2000-2003:** $36,487-$38,096.

Unemployment 2004: 4.5%. **Change from 2000:** +0.8%. **Median travel time to work:** 31.5 minutes. **Working outside county of residence:** 44.4%.

Cities with pop over 10,000: 9 (see page 37 for cities).

MONMOUTH COUNTY

Market Yard
Freehold, NJ 07728
www.co.monmouth.nj.us

Ph: 732-431-7324
Fax: 732-409-7566

In central NJ on Lower New York Bay and the Atlantic Ocean, south of Jersey City; original county, organized Mar 7, 1683. **Name Origin:** For Monmouthshire, a county in England.

Area (sq mi): 665.12 (land 471.94; water 193.18). **Pop per sq mi:** 1347.5.

Pop 2005: 635,952. **State rank:** 4. **Pop change:** 2000-20005 +3.4%; 1990-2000 +11.2%. **Pop 2000:** 615,301 (White 80.6%; Black or African American 8.1%; Hispanic or Latino 6.2%; Asian 4%; Other 3.5%). **Foreign born:** 10.4%. **Median age:** 37.7.

Income 2000: per capita $31,149; median household $64,271; **Pop below poverty level:** 6.3%. ***Personal per capita income 2000-2003:** $42,635-$43,427.

Unemployment 2004: 4.4%. **Change from 2000:** +0.8%. **Median travel time to work:** 34.8 minutes. **Working outside county of residence:** 40%.

Cities with pop over 10,000: 7 (see page 37 for cities).

MORRIS COUNTY

PO Box 315   **Ph:** 973-285-6120
Morristown, NJ 07963   **Fax:** 973-285-5231
www.co.morris.nj.us

In north-central NJ, west of Newark; organized Mar 15, 1739 from Hunterdon County. **Name Origin:** For Lewis Morris (1671-1746), chief justice of the superior court of NY and NJ (1692) and first governor the colony of NJ (1738-46).

Area (sq mi): 481.29 (land 468.99; water 12.29). **Pop per sq mi:** 1046.1.

Pop 2005: 490,593. **State rank:** 10. **Pop change:** 2000-20005 +4.3%; 1990-2000 +11.6%. **Pop 2000:** 470,212 (White 82%; Black or African American 2.8%; Hispanic or Latino 7.8%; Asian 6.3%; Other 3.7%). **Foreign born:** 15.4%. **Median age:** 37.8.

Income 2000: per capita $36,964; median household $77,340; **Pop below poverty level:** 3.9%. ***Personal per capita income 2000-2003:** $56,163-$55,796.

Unemployment 2004: 3.5%. **Change from 2000:** +0.6%. **Median travel time to work:** 29.4 minutes. **Working outside county of residence:** 42.2%.

Cities with pop over 10,000: 7 (see page 37 for cities).

OCEAN COUNTY

118 Washington St   **Ph:** 732-929-2018
Toms River, NJ 08753   **Fax:** 732-349-4334
www.co.ocean.nj.us

In central NJ, north of Atlantic City; organized Feb 15, 1850 from Monmouth County. **Name Origin:** For its location on the Atlantic coast.

Area (sq mi): 915.88 (land 636.28; water 279.6). **Pop per sq mi:** 877.5.

Pop 2005: 558,341. **State rank:** 6. **Pop change:** 2000-20005 +9.3%; 1990-2000 +17.9%. **Pop 2000:** 510,916 (White 89.9%; Black or African American 3%; Hispanic or Latino 5%; Asian 1.3%; Other 2.6%). **Foreign born:** 6.5%. **Median age:** 41.

Income 2000: per capita $23,054; median household $46,443; **Pop below poverty level:** 7%. ***Personal per capita income 2000-2003:** $30,332-$31,782.

Unemployment 2004: 4.9%. **Change from 2000:** +0.8%. **Median travel time to work:** 32.4 minutes. **Working outside county of residence:** 42.3%.

Cities with pop over 10,000: None.

PASSAIC COUNTY

401 Grand St   **Ph:** 973-225-3632
Paterson, NJ 07505   **Fax:** 973-754-1920
www.passaiccountynj.org

In northern NJ on the NY border, northwest of Newark; organized Feb 7, 1837 from Bergen and Sussex counties. **Name Origin:** For the Passaic River; its name is from a Delaware Indian term *passaic* or *passajeek*, variously translated as 'peace' or 'valley.'

Area (sq mi): 197.05 (land 185.29; water 11.76). **Pop per sq mi:** 2693.4.

Pop 2005: 499,060. **State rank:** 9. **Pop change:** 2000-20005 +2%; 1990-2000 +7.9%. **Pop 2000:** 489,049 (White 51.5%; Black or

African American 13.2%; Hispanic or Latino 30%; Asian 3.7%; Other 20.6%). **Foreign born:** 26.6%. **Median age:** 34.8.

Income 2000: per capita $21,370; median household $49,210; **Pop below poverty level:** 12.3%. ***Personal per capita income 2000-2003:** $30,452-$32,003.

Unemployment 2004: 6.1%. **Change from 2000:** +0.4%. **Median travel time to work:** 26.4 minutes. **Working outside county of residence:** 54.5%.

Cities with pop over 10,000: 9 (see page 37 for cities).

SALEM COUNTY

PO Box 18   **Ph:** 856-935-7510
Salem, NJ 08079   **Fax:** 856-935-8882
www.salemco.org

In southwestern NJ along Delaware River, east of Wilmington, DE; original county, organized May 17, 1694. **Name Origin:** Anglicization of Hebrew *shalom* 'peace.'

Area (sq mi): 372.57 (land 337.88; water 34.69). **Pop per sq mi:** 196.4.

Pop 2005: 66,346. **State rank:** 21. **Pop change:** 2000-20005 +3.2%; 1990-2000 -1.5%. **Pop 2000:** 64,285 (White 79.6%; Black or African American 14.8%; Hispanic or Latino 3.9%; Asian 0.6%; Other 3.5%). **Foreign born:** 2.5%. **Median age:** 38.

Income 2000: per capita $20,874; median household $45,573; **Pop below poverty level:** 9.5%. ***Personal per capita income 2000-2003:** $27,665-$29,568.

Unemployment 2004: 5.2%. **Change from 2000:** +0.6%. **Median travel time to work:** 24.6 minutes. **Working outside county of residence:** 50.4%.

Cities with pop over 10,000: None.

SOMERSET COUNTY

20 Grove St   **Ph:** 908-231-7006
Somerville, NJ 08876   **Fax:** 908-253-8853
www.co.somerset.nj.us

In north-central NJ, southwest of Newark, organized May 14, 1688 from Middlesex County. **Name Origin:** For Somersetshire, the county in England.

Area (sq mi): 305.05 (land 304.69; water 0.36). **Pop per sq mi:** 1049.9.

Pop 2005: 319,900. **State rank:** 13. **Pop change:** 2000-20005 +7.5%; 1990-2000 +23.8%. **Pop 2000:** 297,490 (White 74.1%; Black or African American 7.5%; Hispanic or Latino 8.7%; Asian 8.4%; Other 4.6%). **Foreign born:** 18.1%. **Median age:** 37.2.

Income 2000: per capita $37,970; median household $76,933; **Pop below poverty level:** 3.8%. ***Personal per capita income 2000-2003:** $57,249-$55,443.

Unemployment 2004: 3.6%. **Change from 2000:** +0.9%. **Median travel time to work:** 30.1 minutes. **Working outside county of residence:** 56.1%.

Cities with pop over 10,000: North Plainfield (21,135); Somerville 🏭 (12,434); Manville (10,416); Bound Brook (10,174).

---

*Source: Personal per capita income data are from the Bureau of Economic Analysis; per capita income data are from the Bureau of the Census. See Introduction for explanation of differences.

SUSSEX COUNTY

4 Park Pl   **Ph:** 973-579-0900
Newton, NJ 07860   **Fax:** 973-383-7493
www.sussex.nj.us

In northwestern NJ on border with PA and NY, northwest of Newark; organized May 16, 1753 from Morris County. **Name Origin:** For the county of Sussex, England.

Area (sq mi): 535.99 (land 521.26; water 14.73). **Pop per sq mi:** 293.8.

Pop 2005: 153,130. **State rank:** 17. **Pop change:** 2000-20005 +6.2%; 1990-2000 +10.1%. **Pop 2000:** 144,166 (White 93.4%; Black or African American 1%; Hispanic or Latino 3.3%; Asian 1.2%; Other 1.9%). **Foreign born:** 5.7%. **Median age:** 37.1.

Income 2000: per capita $26,992; median household $65,266; **Pop below poverty level:** 4%. ***Personal per capita income 2000-2003:** $36,972-$38,196.

Unemployment 2004: 4.1%. **Change from 2000:** +0.5%. **Median travel time to work:** 38.3 minutes. **Working outside county of residence:** 59.2%.

Cities with pop over 10,000: Hopatcong (16,035).

UNION COUNTY

2 Broad St Rm 115   **Ph:** 908-527-4999
Elizabeth, NJ 07207   **Fax:** 908-558-2589
www.unioncountynj.org

In northeastern NJ, south of Newark; organized Mar 19, 1857 from Essex County. **Name Origin:** As an expression of belief in the federal union of the states; also in the hope that citizens of Elizabeth and Newark would settle their differences.

Area (sq mi): 105.46 (land 103.29; water 2.17). **Pop per sq mi:** 5145.3.

Pop 2005: 531,457. **State rank:** 7. **Pop change:** 2000-20005 +1.7%; 1990-2000 +5.8%. **Pop 2000:** 522,541 (White 54.2%; Black or African American 20.8%; Hispanic or Latino 19.7%; Asian 3.8%; Other 9.8%). **Foreign born:** 25.1%. **Median age:** 36.6.

Income 2000: per capita $26,992; median household $55,339; **Pop below poverty level:** 8.4%. ***Personal per capita income 2000-2003:** $39,649-$40,181.

Unemployment 2004: 5.1%. **Change from 2000:** +0.6%. **Median travel time to work:** 28.7 minutes. **Working outside county of residence:** 52.5%.

Cities with pop over 10,000: 9 (see page 37 for cities).

WARREN COUNTY

413 2nd St   **Ph:** 908-475-6211
Belvidere, NJ 07823   **Fax:** 908-475-6208
www.co.warren.nj.us

On northwestern border of NJ, east of Easton, PA; organized Nov 20, 1824 from Sussex County. **Name Origin:** For Joseph Warren (1741-75), the Revolutionary War patriot and member of the Continental Congress who dispatched Paul Revere (1735-1818) on his famous ride.

Area (sq mi): 362.75 (land 357.87; water 4.89). **Pop per sq mi:** 308.4.

Pop 2005: 110,376. **State rank:** 19. **Pop change:** 2000-20005 +7.8%; 1990-2000 +11.8%. **Pop 2000:** 102,437 (White 92.2%; Black or African American 1.9%; Hispanic or Latino 3.7%; Asian 1.2%; Other 2.3%). **Foreign born:** 5.8%. **Median age:** 37.6.

Income 2000: per capita $25,728; median household $56,100; **Pop below poverty level:** 5.4%. ***Personal per capita income 2000-2003:** $32,681-$33,579.

Unemployment 2004: 4.2%. **Change from 2000:** +0.6%. **Median travel time to work:** 33.3 minutes. **Working outside county of residence:** 58.2%.

Cities with pop over 10,000: Phillipsburg (15,070).

🏛 *County Seat*

New Mexico

NEW MEXICO STATE INFORMATION

www.state.nm.us **Ph:** 505-476-2200

Area (sq mi): 121,589.48 (land 121,355.53; water 233.96). **Pop per sq mi:** 15.9.

Pop 2005: 1,928,384. **Pop change:** 2000-20005 +6%; 1990-2000 +20.1%. **Pop 2000:** 1,819,046 (White 44.7%; Black or African American 1.9%; Hispanic or Latino 42.1%; Asian 1.1%; Other 30.2%, including 9.5% American Indian/Alaska Native). **Foreign born:** 8.2%. **Median age:** 34.6.

Income 2000: per capita $17,261; median household $34,133; **Pop below poverty level:** 18.4%. ***Personal per capita income 2000-2003:** $22,135-$24,995.

Unemployment 2004: 5.7%. **Change from 2000:** +0.7%. **Median travel time to work:** 21.9 minutes. **Working outside county of residence:** 15.4%.

BERNALILLO COUNTY

1 Civic Plaza NW 10th Fl **Ph:** 505-768-4240
Albuquerque, NM 87102 **Fax:** 505 768 4329
www.bernco.gov

In west-central NM, southwest of Santa Fe, original county; organized Jan 8, 1852 (prior to statehood); annexed Santa Ana County 1876. **Name Origin:** Spanish for 'little Bernal,' possibly for a young member of the Gonzales-Bernal family who lived in the area as early as 1680. It may also have been named for Fray Juan Bernal, a friend of one of the community leaders.

Area (sq mi): 1168.65 (land 1166.03; water 2.62). **Pop per sq mi:** 517.6.

Pop 2005: 603,562. **State rank:** 1. **Pop change:** 2000-20005 +8.4%; 1990-2000 +15.8%. **Pop 2000:** 556,678 (White 48.3%; Black or African American 2.8%; Hispanic or Latino 42%; Asian 1.9%; Other 24.6%, including 4.2% American Indian/Alaska Native). **Foreign born:** 8.6%. **Median age:** 35.

Income 2000: per capita $20,790; median household $38,788; **Pop below poverty level:** 13.7%. ***Personal per capita income 2000-2003:** $27,046-$30,064.

Unemployment 2004: 5.1%. **Change from 2000:** +1.6%. **Median travel time to work:** 21.3 minutes. **Working outside county of residence:** 6.8%.

Cities with pop over 10,000: Albuquerque ⛪ (484,246).

CATRON COUNTY

100 Main St **Ph:** 505-533-6423
Reserve, NM 87830 **Fax:** 505-533-6433
www.mylocalgov.com/catroncountynm/Index.asp

On the central western border of NM, southwest of Albuquerque; organized Feb 25, 1921 from Socorro County. **Name Origin:** For Thomas Benton Catron (1840-1921), Confederate officer during the Civil War and U.S. senator from NM (1912-17).

Area (sq mi): 6929.03 (land 6927.81; water 1.22). **Pop per sq mi:** 0.5.

Pop 2005: 3,409. **State rank:** 31. **Pop change:** 2000-20005 -3.8%; 1990-2000 +38.2%. **Pop 2000:** 3,543 (White 75.8%; Black or African American 0.3%; Hispanic or Latino 19.2%; Asian 0.7%; Other 11.3%, including 2.2% American Indian/Alaska Native). **Foreign born:** 1.6%. **Median age:** 47.8.

Income 2000: per capita $13,951; median household $23,892; **Pop below poverty level:** 24.5%. ***Personal per capita income 2000-2003:** $14,377-$16,303.

Unemployment 2004: 7.5%. **Change from 2000:** +0.7%. **Median travel time to work:** 25 minutes. **Working outside county of residence:** 16.7%.

Cities with pop over 10,000: None.

CHAVES COUNTY

PO Box 580 **Ph:** 505-624-6614
Roswell, NM 88202 **Fax:** 505-624-6523
www.co.chaves.nm.us

In southeastern NM, northeast of Las Cruces; organized Feb 24, 1889 from Lincoln County (prior to statehood). **Name Origin:** For Lt. Col. Jose Francisco Chaves (1833-1904), an officer during the Civil War and U.S. representative from NM (1865-67; 1869-71).

Area (sq mi): 6075.07 (land 6070.86; water 4.21). **Pop per sq mi:** 10.2.

Pop 2005: 61,860. **State rank:** 9. **Pop change:** 2000-20005 +0.8%; 1990-2000 +6.1%. **Pop 2000:** 61,382 (White 52.1%; Black or African American 2%; Hispanic or Latino 43.8%; Asian 0.5%; Other 25.5%, including 1.1% American Indian/Alaska Native). **Foreign born:** 11.2%. **Median age:** 35.2.

Income 2000: per capita $14,990; median household $28,513; **Pop below poverty level:** 21.3%. ***Personal per capita income 2000-2003:** $19,007-$21,714.

Unemployment 2004: 6.9%. **Change from 2000:** +1.1%. **Median travel time to work:** 17.1 minutes. **Working outside county of residence:** 5.5%.

Cities with pop over 10,000: Roswell ⛪ (45,074).

⛪ County Seat

CIBOLA COUNTY

515 W High Ave   **Ph:** 505-287-9431
Grants, NM 87020   **Fax:** 505-285-2562
www.grants.org

On the central western border of NM, west of Albuquerque; organized Jun 19, 1981 from Valencia County. **Name Origin:** For the Cibola National Forest, part of which is within the county. Origin and meaning of name unknown; possibly a transliteration of Zuni Indian *shiwina*, the name for their tribal range; or possibly from Isleta Indian *sibulada* 'buffalo.'

Area (sq mi): 4541.71 (land 4539.21; water 2.5). **Pop per sq mi:** 6.1.

Pop 2005: 27,620. **State rank:** 17. **Pop change:** 2000-20005 +7.9%; 1990-2000 +7.6%. **Pop 2000:** 25,595 (White 24.7%; Black or African American 1%; Hispanic or Latino 33.4%; Asian 0.4%; Other 59%, including 40.3% American Indian/Alaska Native). **Foreign born:** 2.3%. **Median age:** 33.1.

Income 2000: per capita $11,731; median household $27,774; **Pop below poverty level:** 24.8%. ***Personal per capita income 2000-2003:** $14,935-$16,926.

Unemployment 2004: 5.9%. **Change from 2000:** +0.3%. **Median travel time to work:** 23.5 minutes. **Working outside county of residence:** 22.1%.

Cities with pop over 10,000: None.

COLFAX COUNTY

230 N 3rd St   **Ph:** 505-445-5551
Raton, NM 87740   **Fax:** 505-445-4031

On the northern border of NM, northeast of Santa Fe; organized Jan 25, 1869 from Mora County (prior to statehood). **Name Origin:** For Schuyler Colfax (1823-85), U.S. vice president under Ulysses S. Grant (1869-73).

Area (sq mi): 3768.05 (land 3756.79; water 11.26). **Pop per sq mi:** 3.7.

Pop 2005: 13,755. **State rank:** 24. **Pop change:** 2000-20005 -3.1%; 1990-2000 +9.8%. **Pop 2000:** 14,189 (White 49.9%; Black or African American 0.3%; Hispanic or Latino 47.5%; Asian 0.3%; Other 17.9%, including 1.5% American Indian/Alaska Native). **Foreign born:** 2.2%. **Median age:** 40.8.

Income 2000: per capita $16,418; median household $30,744; **Pop below poverty level:** 14.8%. ***Personal per capita income 2000-2003:** $19,881-$22,496.

Unemployment 2004: 5.9%. **Change from 2000:** +0.8%. **Median travel time to work:** 16.5 minutes. **Working outside county of residence:** 6.4%.

Cities with pop over 10,000: None.

CURRY COUNTY

700 N Main St Suite 7   **Ph:** 505-763-5591
Clovis, NM 88101   **Fax:** 505-763-4232
www.currycounty.org

On the central eastern border of NM, southeast of Albuquerque; organized Feb 25, 1909 from Quay and Roosevelt counties (prior to statehood). **Name Origin:** For Capt. George Curry (1863-1947), an officer in the Spanish-American War, NM territorial governor (1907-11), and U.S. representative (1912-13).

Area (sq mi): 1407.67 (land 1405.95; water 1.72). **Pop per sq mi:** 32.6.

Pop 2005: 45,846. **State rank:** 12. **Pop change:** 2000-20005 +1.8%; 1990-2000 +6.7%. **Pop 2000:** 45,044 (White 58.7%; Black or African American 6.9%; Hispanic or Latino 30.4%; Asian 1.8%; Other 18.9%, including 1% American Indian/Alaska Native). **Foreign born:** 5.9%. **Median age:** 30.8.

Income 2000: per capita $15,049; median household $28,917; **Pop below poverty level:** 19%. ***Personal per capita income 2000-2003:** $20,620-$24,721.

Unemployment 2004: 4.6%. **Change from 2000:** +1.4%. **Median travel time to work:** 15.6 minutes. **Working outside county of residence:** 8.9%.

Cities with pop over 10,000: Clovis ▥ (33,063).

DE BACA COUNTY

548 E Ave C   **Ph:** 505-355-2601
Fort Sumner, NM 88119   **Fax:** 505-355-2441

In east-central NM, west of Clovis; organized Feb 28, 1917 from Chaves, Guadalupe, and Roosevelt counties. **Name Origin:** For Ezequiel Cabeza de Baca (1864-1917), lt. governor (1911-16) and governor (1917) who died after six weeks in office.

Area (sq mi): 2333.83 (land 2324.87; water 8.96). **Pop per sq mi:** 0.9.

Pop 2005: 2,016. **State rank:** 32. **Pop change:** 2000-20005 -10%; 1990-2000 -0.5%. **Pop 2000:** 2,240 (White 62.8%; Black or African American 0%; Hispanic or Latino 35.3%; Asian 0.2%; Other 15.6%). **Foreign born:** 3.7%. **Median age:** 43.8.

Income 2000: per capita $14,065; median household $25,441; **Pop below poverty level:** 17.7%. ***Personal per capita income 2000-2003:** $17,591-$21,449.

Unemployment 2004: 6.8%. **Change from 2000:** +2.1%. **Median travel time to work:** 16.8 minutes. **Working outside county of residence:** 12.1%.

Cities with pop over 10,000: None.

DOÑA ANA COUNTY

180 W Amador Ave   **Ph:** 505-647-7200
Las Cruces, NM 88001   **Fax:** 505-647-7302
www.co.dona-ana.nm.us

On the central southern border of NM, south of Albuquerque; original county; organized Jan 9, 1852 (prior to statehood); annexed Arizona County 1861. **Name Origin:** For either Dona Ana Robledo, a woman famous for charity in the 1600s, or for Dona Ana Maria Nina de Cordova, a girl captured during an Apache raid and never seen again.

Area (sq mi): 3814.62 (land 3807.18; water 7.44). **Pop per sq mi:** 49.8.

Pop 2005: 189,444. **State rank:** 2. **Pop change:** 2000-20005 +8.5%; 1990-2000 +28.9%. **Pop 2000:** 174,682 (White 32.5%; Black or African American 1.6%; Hispanic or Latino 63.4%; Asian 0.8%; Other 29.9%, including 1.5% American Indian/Alaska Native). **Foreign born:** 18.7%. **Median age:** 30.2.

*Source: Personal per capita income data are from the Bureau of Economic Analysis; per capita income data are from the Bureau of the Census. See Introduction for explanation of differences.

Doña Ana County (cont'd)

Income 2000: per capita $13,999; median household $29,808; **Pop below poverty level:** 25.4%. ***Personal per capita income 2000-2003:** $17,829-$20,756.

Unemployment 2004: 6.4%. **Change from 2000:** -0.3%. **Median travel time to work:** 21.3 minutes. **Working outside county of residence:** 18.5%.

Cities with pop over 10,000: Las Cruces ⚎ (79,524); Sunland Park (13,934).

EDDY COUNTY

101 W Greene St Suite 225
Carlsbad, NM 88220
www.carlsbadnm.com/ecourt

Ph: 505-887-9511
Fax: 505-887-1039

On the southern border of NM, east of Las Cruces; organized Feb 25, 1889 from Lincoln County (prior to statehood). **Name Origin:** For Charles B. Eddy, rancher, promoter of the Carlsbad Irrigation Project, and railroad builder.

Area (sq mi): 4197.57 (land 4182.02; water 15.55). **Pop per sq mi:** 12.3.

Pop 2005: 51,437. **State rank:** 11. **Pop change:** 2000-20005 -0.4%; 1990-2000 +6.3%. **Pop 2000:** 51,658 (White 57.7%; Black or African American 1.6%; Hispanic or Latino 38.8%; Asian 0.4%; Other 21.7%, including 1.3% American Indian/Alaska Native). **Foreign born:** 5.3%. **Median age:** 36.4.

Income 2000: per capita $15,823; median household $31,998; **Pop below poverty level:** 17.2%. ***Personal per capita income 2000-2003:** $20,594-$24,628.

Unemployment 2004: 5.8%. **Change from 2000:** +0.7%. **Median travel time to work:** 18.3 minutes. **Working outside county of residence:** 4.7%.

Cities with pop over 10,000: Carlsbad ⚎ (25,417); Artesia (10,553).

GRANT COUNTY

PO Box 898
Silver City, NM 88062
www.grantcountynm.com

Ph: 505-574-0000

On the western border of NM, northwest of Las Cruces; organized Jan 30, 1868 from Socorro County (prior to statehood). **Name Origin:** For Ulysses Simpson Grant (1822-85), Civil War general and eighteenth U.S. president.

Area (sq mi): 3967.5 (land 3965.88; water 1.62). **Pop per sq mi:** 7.5.

Pop 2005: 29,747. **State rank:** 15. **Pop change:** 2000-20005 -4%; 1990-2000 +12%. **Pop 2000:** 31,002 (White 48.5%; Black or African American 0.5%; Hispanic or Latino 48.8%; Asian 0.3%; Other 23.5%, including 1.4% American Indian/Alaska Native). **Foreign born:** 3.3%. **Median age:** 38.8.

Income 2000: per capita $14,597; median household $29,134; **Pop below poverty level:** 18.7%. ***Personal per capita income 2000-2003:** $18,702-$19,190.

Unemployment 2004: 8.8%. **Change from 2000:** +2%. **Median travel time to work:** 19.1 minutes. **Working outside county of residence:** 4.8%.

Cities with pop over 10,000: None.

GUADALUPE COUNTY

420 Parker Ave Suite 1
Santa Rosa, NM 88435

Ph: 505-472-3791
Fax: 505-472-4791

In east-central NM, east of Albuquerque; organized Feb 26, 1891 from Lincoln and San Miguel counties (prior to statehood). **Name Origin:** For Our Lady of Guadalupe, patron saint of Mexico.

Area (sq mi): 3031.58 (land 3030.37; water 1.2). **Pop per sq mi:** 1.4.

Pop 2005: 4,369. **State rank:** 29. **Pop change:** 2000-20005 -6.6%; 1990-2000 +12.6%. **Pop 2000:** 4,680 (White 15.5%; Black or African American 1.3%; Hispanic or Latino 81.2%; Asian 0.5%; Other 44%, including 1.1% American Indian/Alaska Native). **Foreign born:** 4%. **Median age:** 37.5.

Income 2000: per capita $11,241; median household $24,783; **Pop below poverty level:** 21.6%. ***Personal per capita income 2000-2003:** $13,351-$14,455.

Unemployment 2004: 7.4%. **Change from 2000:** -1.3%. **Median travel time to work:** 17.6 minutes. **Working outside county of residence:** 10.9%.

Cities with pop over 10,000: None.

HARDING COUNTY

35 Pine St
Mosquero, NM 87733
www.hardingcounty.org

Ph: 505-673-2301
Fax: 505-673-2922

In northeastern NM, northeast of Santa Fe; organized Mar 4, 1921 from Mora and Union counties. **Name Origin:** For Warren Gamaliel Harding (1865-1923), twenty-ninth U.S. president.

Area (sq mi): 2125.95 (land 2125.34; water 0.61). **Pop per sq mi:** 0.3.

Pop 2005: 740. **State rank:** 33. **Pop change:** 2000-20005 -8.6%; 1990-2000 -17.9%. **Pop 2000:** 810 (White 52.8%; Black or African American 0.4%; Hispanic or Latino 44.9%; Asian 0%; Other 15.3%, including 1.4% American Indian/Alaska Native). **Foreign born:** 2.5%. **Median age:** 48.7.

Income 2000: per capita $16,240; median household $26,111; **Pop below poverty level:** 16.3%. ***Personal per capita income 2000-2003:** $18,350-$18,632.

Unemployment 2004: 4.5%. **Change from 2000:** +1.2%. **Median travel time to work:** 21.1 minutes. **Working outside county of residence:** 13.3%.

Cities with pop over 10,000: None.

HIDALGO COUNTY

300 Shakespeare St
Lordsburg, NM 88045

Ph: 505-542-9213
Fax: 505-542-3193

In the southwestern corner of NM, southwest of Las Cruces; organized Feb 25, 1919 from Grant County. **Name Origin:** Probably for the Treaty of Guadalupe Hidalgo, which ended the Mexican War; others claim for Miguel Hidalgo y Costilla (1753-1811), leader of the Mexican war for independence from Spain.

Area (sq mi): 3445.91 (land 3445.63; water 0.28). **Pop per sq mi:** 1.5.

Pop 2005: 5,139. **State rank:** 27. **Pop change:** 2000-20005 -13.4%; 1990-2000 -0.4%. **Pop 2000:** 5,932 (White 42.7%; Black or African

Hidalgo County (cont'd)

American 0.4%; Hispanic or Latino 56%; Asian 0.3%; Other 15.6%). **Foreign born:** 11.1%. **Median age:** 34.8.

Income 2000: per capita $12,431; median household $24,819; **Pop below poverty level:** 27.3%. ***Personal per capita income 2000-2003:** $15,868-$17,370.

Unemployment 2004: 6.3%. **Change from 2000:** -2.4%. **Median travel time to work:** 22.6 minutes. **Working outside county of residence:** 19.5%.

Cities with pop over 10,000: None.

LEA COUNTY
100 N Main St Suite 11   **Ph:** 505-396-8521
Lovington, NM 88260   **Fax:** 505-396-5684
www.leacounty.net

In the southeastern corner of NM, east of Roswell; organized Mar 7, 1917 from Chaves and Eddy counties. **Name Origin:** For Gen. Joseph C. Lea (?-1904), Confederate officer in the Civil War, 'father of [the town of] Roswell,' and founder of the New Mexico Military Institute there.

Area (sq mi): 4394.02 (land 4392.96; water 1.06). **Pop per sq mi:** 12.9.

Pop 2005: 56,719. **State rank:** 10. **Pop change:** 2000-20005 +2.2%; 1990-2000 -0.5%. **Pop 2000:** 55,511 (White 54%; Black or African American 4.4%; Hispanic or Latino 39.6%; Asian 0.4%; Other 28.1%, including 1% American Indian/Alaska Native). **Foreign born:** 11.3%. **Median age:** 33.1.

Income 2000: per capita $14,184; median household $29,799; **Pop below poverty level:** 21.1%. ***Personal per capita income 2000-2003:** $19,993-$22,544.

Unemployment 2004: 5.1%. **Change from 2000:** +1.9%. **Median travel time to work:** 18.7 minutes. **Working outside county of residence:** 6.4%.

Cities with pop over 10,000: Hobbs (28,708).

LINCOLN COUNTY
300 Central Ave PO Box 338   **Ph:** 505-648-2394
Carrizozo, NM 88301   **Fax:** 505-648-2576
www.lincolncountynm.net

In south-central NM, west of Roswell; organized Jan 16, 1869 (prior to statehood). **Name Origin:** For Abraham Lincoln (1809-65), sixteenth U.S. president.

Area (sq mi): 4831.25 (land 4830.97; water 0.28). **Pop per sq mi:** 4.3.

Pop 2005: 21,007. **State rank:** 19. **Pop change:** 2000-20005 +8.2%; 1990-2000 +58.9%. **Pop 2000:** 19,411 (White 70.9%; Black or African American 0.4%; Hispanic or Latino 25.6%; Asian 0.3%; Other 15.9%, including 2% American Indian/Alaska Native). **Foreign born:** 6.1%. **Median age:** 43.8.

Income 2000: per capita $19,338; median household $33,886; **Pop below poverty level:** 14.9%. ***Personal per capita income 2000-2003:** $18,999-$20,976.

Unemployment 2004: 4.1%. **Change from 2000:** +0%. **Median travel time to work:** 20.9 minutes. **Working outside county of residence:** 11.3%.

Cities with pop over 10,000: None.

LOS ALAMOS COUNTY
2300 Trinity Dr Rm 230   **Ph:** 505-662-8080
Los Alamos, NM 87544   **Fax:** 505-662-8079
www.lac-nm.us

In north-central NM, northwest of Santa Fe; organized Mar 16, 1949 from Sandoval and Santa Fe counties. Site of the Manhattan Project that produced the first atomic bomb. **Name Origin:** For its county seat, itself named for the Los Alamos School for Boys, established 1925 by Ashley Pond; form Spanish 'poplars' or 'cottonwoods.'

Area (sq mi): 109.35 (land 109.35; water 0). **Pop per sq mi:** 172.1.

Pop 2005: 18,822. **State rank:** 20. **Pop change:** 2000-20005 +2.6%; 1990-2000 +1.3%. **Pop 2000:** 18,343 (White 82.1%; Black or African American 0.4%; Hispanic or Latino 11.7%; Asian 3.8%; Other 5.6%). **Foreign born:** 6.7%. **Median age:** 40.8.

Income 2000: per capita $34,646; median household $78,993; **Pop below poverty level:** 2.9%. ***Personal per capita income 2000-2003:** $41,687-$48,541.

Unemployment 2004: 2.8%. **Change from 2000:** +1.8%. **Median travel time to work:** 15.2 minutes. **Working outside county of residence:** 3.6%.

Cities with pop over 10,000: None.

LUNA COUNTY
110 N Gold St   **Ph:** 505-546-0491
Deming, NM 88031   **Fax:** 505-544-4187
www.lunacountynm.com

On the southern border of NM, west of Las Cruces; organized Mar 16, 1901 from Dona Ana and Grant counties (prior to statehood). **Name Origin:** For Don Salomon Luna, a sheep rancher and a leader of the Republican party in the state.

Area (sq mi): 2965.28 (land 2965.09; water 0.19). **Pop per sq mi:** 8.9.

Pop 2005: 26,498. **State rank:** 18. **Pop change:** 2000-20005 +5.9%; 1990-2000 +38.1%. **Pop 2000:** 25,016 (White 39.7%; Black or African American 0.9%; Hispanic or Latino 57.7%; Asian 0.3%; Other 24.4%, including 1.1% American Indian/Alaska Native). **Foreign born:** 19.5%. **Median age:** 36.7.

Income 2000: per capita $11,218; median household $20,784; **Pop below poverty level:** 32.9%. ***Personal per capita income 2000-2003:** $14,594-$17,145.

Unemployment 2004: 15.7%. **Change from 2000:** -8%. **Median travel time to work:** 17.9 minutes. **Working outside county of residence:** 10.5%.

Cities with pop over 10,000: Deming ⚖ (14,647).

MCKINLEY COUNTY
207 W Hill Ave   **Ph:** 505-863-6866
Gallup, NM 87301   **Fax:** 505-863-1419
www.co.mckinley.nm.us

On the northwestern border of NM, west of Santa Fe; organized

*Source: Personal per capita income data are from the Bureau of Economic Analysis; per capita income data are from the Bureau of the Census. See Introduction for explanation of differences.

482

McKinley County (cont'd)

Feb 23, 1899 from Bernalillo, Valencia, and San Juan counties. **Name Origin:** For William McKinley (1843-1901), twenty-fifth U.S. president.

Area (sq mi): 5455.22 (land 5448.72; water 6.49). **Pop per sq mi:** 13.2.

Pop 2005: 71,918. **State rank:** 6. **Pop change:** 2000-20005 -3.9%; 1990-2000 +23.3%. **Pop 2000:** 74,798 (White 11.9%; Black or African American 0.4%; Hispanic or Latino 12.4%; Asian 0.5%; Other 82.7%, including 74.7% American Indian/Alaska Native). **Foreign born:** 1.8%. **Median age:** 26.9.

Income 2000: per capita $9,872; median household $25,005; **Pop below poverty level:** 36.1%. ***Personal per capita income 2000-2003:** $13,549-$16,437.

Unemployment 2004: 7.6%. **Change from 2000:** +1.5%. **Median travel time to work:** 24.2 minutes. **Working outside county of residence:** 14.6%.

Cities with pop over 10,000: Gallup ⚒ (19,715).

MORA COUNTY
518 Mile Marker 29 PO Box 360   **Ph:** 505-387-2448
Mora, NM 87732   **Fax:** 505-387-9023

In east-central NM, northeast of Santa Fe; organized Feb 1, 1860 from San Miguel County (prior to statehood). **Name Origin:** Either from personal and family names of early settlers, such as Mora Pineda and Garcia de la Mora, or possibly from the Spanish word meaning 'blackberry' or 'mulberry,' referring to the abundance of fruit locally.

Area (sq mi): 1933.48 (land 1931.1; water 2.38). **Pop per sq mi:** 2.6.

Pop 2005: 5,107. **State rank:** 28. **Pop change:** 2000-20005 -1.4%; 1990-2000 +21.5%. **Pop 2000:** 5,180 (White 16.9%; Black or African American 0.1%; Hispanic or Latino 81.6%; Asian 0.1%; Other 40.9%, including 1.1% American Indian/Alaska Native). **Foreign born:** 1.7%. **Median age:** 39.6.

Income 2000: per capita $12,340; median household $24,518; **Pop below poverty level:** 25.4%. ***Personal per capita income 2000-2003:** $13,378-$15,867.

Unemployment 2004: 11.2%. **Change from 2000:** -1%. **Median travel time to work:** 35.1 minutes. **Working outside county of residence:** 45.3%.

Cities with pop over 10,000: None.

OTERO COUNTY
1000 New York Ave Rm 101   **Ph:** 505-437-7427
Alamogordo, NM 88310   **Fax:** 505-443-2904
www.co.otero.nm.us

On the central southern border of NM, east of Las Cruces; organized Jan 30, 1899 from Dona Ana and Lincoln counties. **Name Origin:** For Miguel Antonio Otero (1859-1944), territorial governor of New Mexico (1896-1906).

Area (sq mi): 6627.43 (land 6626.5; water 0.93). **Pop per sq mi:** 9.6.

Pop 2005: 63,538. **State rank:** 8. **Pop change:** 2000-20005 +2%; 1990-2000 +20%. **Pop 2000:** 62,298 (White 55.7%; Black or African American 3.9%; Hispanic or Latino 32.2%; Asian 1.2%; Other 21.2%, including 5.8% American Indian/Alaska Native). **Foreign born:** 11.1%. **Median age:** 33.8.

Income 2000: per capita $14,345; median household $30,861; **Pop below poverty level:** 19.3%. ***Personal per capita income 2000-2003:** $16,929-$19,831.

Unemployment 2004: 5.4%. **Change from 2000:** +0%. **Median travel time to work:** 20.9 minutes. **Working outside county of residence:** 12.6%.

Cities with pop over 10,000: Alamogordo ⚒ (36,211).

QUAY COUNTY
300 S 3rd St   **Ph:** 505-461-2112
Tucumcari, NM 88401   **Fax:** 505-461-6208
www.tucumcarinm.com

On the central eastern border of NM; organized Jan 28, 1903 (prior to statehood). **Name Origin:** For Lt. Col. Matthew S. Quay (1833-1904), U.S. senator from PA (1887-99; 1901-04) who was active in establishing the area.

Area (sq mi): 2881.8 (land 2874.93; water 6.87). **Pop per sq mi:** 3.2.

Pop 2005: 9,259. **State rank:** 26. **Pop change:** 2000-20005 -8.8%; 1990-2000 -6.2%. **Pop 2000:** 10,155 (White 58.6%; Black or African American 0.8%; Hispanic or Latino 38%; Asian 0.8%; Other 16.2%, including 1.3% American Indian/Alaska Native). **Foreign born:** 3.4%. **Median age:** 41.5.

Income 2000: per capita $14,938; median household $24,894; **Pop below poverty level:** 20.9%. ***Personal per capita income 2000-2003:** $18,924-$19,812.

Unemployment 2004: 6.3%. **Change from 2000:** +1.9%. **Median travel time to work:** 15.1 minutes. **Working outside county of residence:** 8.4%.

Cities with pop over 10,000: None.

RIO ARRIBA COUNTY
PO Box 127   **Ph:** 505-588-7255
Tierra Amarilla, NM 87575   **Fax:** 505-588-7418

On the central northern border of NM, northwest of Santa Fe; original county; organized Jan 9, 1852 (prior to statehood). **Name Origin:** Spanish 'upper river,' the Spanish designation for the upper Rio Grande in NM.

Area (sq mi): 5896.1 (land 5857.63; water 38.47). **Pop per sq mi:** 7.

Pop 2005: 40,828. **State rank:** 13. **Pop change:** 2000-20005 -0.9%; 1990-2000 +19.9%. **Pop 2000:** 41,190 (White 13.6%; Black or African American 0.3%; Hispanic or Latino 72.9%; Asian 0.1%; Other 42.9%, including 13.9% American Indian/Alaska Native). **Foreign born:** 3.7%. **Median age:** 34.5.

Income 2000: per capita $14,263; median household $29,429; **Pop below poverty level:** 20.3%. ***Personal per capita income 2000-2003:** $17,035-$20,720.

Unemployment 2004: 6.6%. **Change from 2000:** +0%. **Median travel time to work:** 28.1 minutes. **Working outside county of residence:** 44.2%.

Cities with pop over 10,000: None.

⚒ *County Seat*

ROOSEVELT COUNTY

County Courthouse 109 W 1st St
Portales, NM 88130
www.rooseveltcounty.com

Ph: 505-356-8562
Fax: 505-356-3560

On the central eastern border of NM, south of Clovis; organized Feb 28, 1903 from Chaves and Guadalupe counties (prior to statehood). **Name Origin:** For Theodore Roosevelt (1858-1919), twenty-sixth U.S. president.

Area (sq mi): 2454.87 (land 2448.5; water 6.37). **Pop per sq mi:** 7.4.

Pop 2005: 18,238. **State rank:** 21. **Pop change:** 2000-20005 +1.2%; 1990-2000 +7.9%. **Pop 2000:** 18,018 (White 62.7%; Black or African American 1.7%; Hispanic or Latino 33.3%; Asian 0.6%; Other 23.7%, including 1.1% American Indian/Alaska Native). **Foreign born:** 6.2%. **Median age:** 29.5.

Income 2000: per capita $14,185; median household $26,586; **Pop below poverty level:** 22.7%. ***Personal per capita income 2000-2003:** $19,131-$23,484.

Unemployment 2004: 3.9%. **Change from 2000:** +1.1%. **Median travel time to work:** 16.7 minutes. **Working outside county of residence:** 20.6%.

Cities with pop over 10,000: Portales 🏛 (11,214).

SAN JUAN COUNTY

100 S Oliver Dr
Aztec, NM 87410
www.co.san-juan.nm.us

Ph: 505-334-9471
Fax: 505-334-3635

On the northwestern border of NM; organized Jan 24, 1887 from Rio Arriba County (prior to statehood). **Name Origin:** For the San Juan River, which flows through the county; Spanish for Saint John (the Baptist).

Area (sq mi): 5538.36 (land 5514.02; water 24.35). **Pop per sq mi:** 22.9.

Pop 2005: 126,208. **State rank:** 4. **Pop change:** 2000-20005 +10.9%; 1990-2000 +24.2%. **Pop 2000:** 113,801 (White 46.5%; Black or African American 0.4%; Hispanic or Latino 15%; Asian 0.3%; Other 46.5%, including 36.9% American Indian/Alaska Native). **Foreign born:** 2.4%. **Median age:** 31.

Income 2000: per capita $14,282; median household $33,762; **Pop below poverty level:** 21.5%. ***Personal per capita income 2000-2003:** $18,969-$21,124.

Unemployment 2004: 6.1%. **Change from 2000:** +0%. **Median travel time to work:** 23.8 minutes. **Working outside county of residence:** 6.6%.

Cities with pop over 10,000: Farmington (42,421).

SAN MIGUEL COUNTY

County Courthouse
500 W National St Suite 100
Las Vegas, NM 87701
www.smcounty.net

Ph: 505-425-9333
Fax: 505-425-7019

In east-central NM, east of Santa Fe; original county; organized Jan 9, 1852 (prior to statehood). **Name Origin:** For the town of San Miguel del Bado, Spanish 'Saint Michael of the ford,' a river crossing on the Pecos River on the Old Santa Fe Trail.

Area (sq mi): 4735.63 (land 4717.04; water 18.59). **Pop per sq mi:** 6.3.

Pop 2005: 29,530. **State rank:** 16. **Pop change:** 2000-20005 -2%; 1990-2000 +17%. **Pop 2000:** 30,126 (White 18.9%; Black or African American 0.8%; Hispanic or Latino 78%; Asian 0.5%; Other 42.4%, including 1.8% American Indian/Alaska Native). **Foreign born:** 2.5%. **Median age:** 35.1.

Income 2000: per capita $13,268; median household $26,524; **Pop below poverty level:** 24.4%. ***Personal per capita income 2000-2003:** $16,489-$19,956.

Unemployment 2004: 6.8%. **Change from 2000:** +0.4%. **Median travel time to work:** 23.6 minutes. **Working outside county of residence:** 25.6%.

Cities with pop over 10,000: Las Vegas 🏛 (14,031).

SANDOVAL COUNTY

711 Camino del Pueblo
Bernalillo, NM 87004
www.sandovalcounty.com

Ph: 505-867-7572
Fax: 505-771-8610

In north-central NM, west of Santa Fe; organized Mar 10, 1903 from Rio Arriba County (prior to statehood). **Name Origin:** For the Sandoval family, descendants of Juan de Dios Sandoval Martinez, who came to the area in 1692.

Area (sq mi): 3714.32 (land 3709.34; water 4.98). **Pop per sq mi:** 29.

Pop 2005: 107,460. **State rank:** 5. **Pop change:** 2000-20005 +19.5%; 1990-2000 +42%. **Pop 2000:** 89,908 (White 50.3%; Black or African American 1.7%; Hispanic or Latino 29.4%; Asian 1%; Other 32.3%, including 16.3% American Indian/Alaska Native). **Foreign born:** 4.3%. **Median age:** 35.1.

Income 2000: per capita $19,174; median household $44,949; **Pop below poverty level:** 12.1%. ***Personal per capita income 2000-2003:** $23,932-$25,523.

Unemployment 2004: 5.5%. **Change from 2000:** +1.6%. **Median travel time to work:** 28.1 minutes. **Working outside county of residence:** 59.3%.

Cities with pop over 10,000: Rio Rancho (61,953).

SANTA FE COUNTY

102 Grant Ave
Santa Fe, NM 87504
www.co.santa-fe.nm.us

Ph: 505-986-6200
Fax: 505-995-2740

In north-central NM, northeast of Albuquerque; original county; organized Jan 9, 1852 (prior to statehood). **Name Origin:** For the capital of NM and the county seat; Spanish 'Holy Faith.'

Area (sq mi): 1910.79 (land 1909.19; water 1.6). **Pop per sq mi:** 73.8.

Pop 2005: 140,855. **State rank:** 3. **Pop change:** 2000-20005 +8.9%; 1990-2000 +30.7%. **Pop 2000:** 129,292 (White 45.5%; Black or African American 0.6%; Hispanic or Latino 49%; Asian 0.9%; Other 25%, including 3.1% American Indian/Alaska Native). **Foreign born:** 10.1%. **Median age:** 37.9.

Income 2000: per capita $23,594; median household $42,207; **Pop below poverty level:** 12%. ***Personal per capita income 2000-2003:** $29,627-$32,378.

Unemployment 2004: 4.3%. **Change from 2000:** +1.7%. **Median travel time to work:** 22.1 minutes. **Working outside county of residence:** 16.8%.

*Source: Personal per capita income data are from the Bureau of Economic Analysis; per capita income data are from the Bureau of the Census. See Introduction for explanation of differences.

Santa Fe County (cont'd)

Cities with pop over 10,000: Santa Fe 🏛 (68,041).

SIERRA COUNTY

100 N Date St   **Ph:** 505-894-6215
Truth or Consequences, NM 87901   **Fax:** 505-894-9548
www.truthorconsequencesnm.net

In west-central NM, northwest of Las Cruces; organized Apr 3, 1884 from Socorro County (prior to statehood). **Name Origin:** For the Sierra de los Caballos Range, Spanish 'saw' for the shape of the mountains, thus 'saw-toothed mountain of the horses.' The county may have been named for the Sierra family, whose members included Nicholas de la Sierra.

Area (sq mi): 4236.3 (land 4180.23; water 56.07). **Pop per sq mi:** 3.1.

Pop 2005: 12,815. **State rank:** 25. **Pop change:** 2000-20005 -3.4%; 1990-2000 +33.9%. **Pop 2000:** 13,270 (White 70.5%; Black or African American 0.5%; Hispanic or Latino 26.3%; Asian 0.3%; Other 12.4%, including 1.5% American Indian/Alaska Native). **Foreign born:** 6.6%. **Median age:** 48.9.

Income 2000: per capita $15,023; median household $24,152; **Pop below poverty level:** 20.9%. ***Personal per capita income 2000-2003:** $17,168-$18,295.

Unemployment 2004: 5.6%. **Change from 2000:** +1.8%. **Median travel time to work:** 20.1 minutes. **Working outside county of residence:** 9.3%.

Cities with pop over 10,000: None.

SOCORRO COUNTY

210 Park St   **Ph:** 505-835-0589
Socorro, NM 87801   **Fax:** 505-835-4629
www.socorro-nm.com

In west-central NM, south of Albuquerque; original county; organized Jul 1850 (prior to statehood). **Name Origin:** Name given to the Piro Indian pueblo of Teypana in 1598 by Juan de Onate (1550?-1630) because 'they gave us much corn.' Spanish 'aid, help, succor, assistance.'

Area (sq mi): 6648.71 (land 6646.4; water 2.31). **Pop per sq mi:** 2.7.

Pop 2005: 18,148. **State rank:** 22. **Pop change:** 2000-20005 +0.4%; 1990-2000 +22.4%. **Pop 2000:** 18,078 (White 37.6%; Black or African American 0.6%; Hispanic or Latino 48.7%; Asian 1.1%; Other 35.4%, including 10.9% American Indian/Alaska Native). **Foreign born:** 6.4%. **Median age:** 32.4.

Income 2000: per capita $12,826; median household $23,439; **Pop below poverty level:** 31.7%. ***Personal per capita income 2000-2003:** $15,424-$18,695.

Unemployment 2004: 5.1%. **Change from 2000:** -1%. **Median travel time to work:** 20.9 minutes. **Working outside county of residence:** 17.7%.

Cities with pop over 10,000: None.

TAOS COUNTY

105 Albright St Suite A   **Ph:** 505-737-6300
Taos, NM 87571   **Fax:** 505-751-8637
www.taoscounty.org

On the central northern border of NM; north of Santa Fe; original county; organized Jan 9, 1852 (prior to statehood). **Name Origin:** A Spanish transliteration for a town of the Tewa Pueblos, located in what is now Taos County. From either *tuota* 'red willow place,' or *tuatah* 'at the village.'

Area (sq mi): 2204.62 (land 2203.17; water 1.45). **Pop per sq mi:** 14.4.

Pop 2005: 31,722. **State rank:** 14. **Pop change:** 2000-20005 +5.8%; 1990-2000 +29.7%. **Pop 2000:** 29,979 (White 33.8%; Black or African American 0.4%; Hispanic or Latino 57.9%; Asian 0.4%; Other 35.5%, including 6.6% American Indian/Alaska Native). **Foreign born:** 4.1%. **Median age:** 39.5.

Income 2000: per capita $16,103; median household $26,762; **Pop below poverty level:** 20.9%. ***Personal per capita income 2000-2003:** $18,006-$21,694.

Unemployment 2004: 7.4%. **Change from 2000:** -2.3%. **Median travel time to work:** 21.5 minutes. **Working outside county of residence:** 9%.

Cities with pop over 10,000: None.

TORRANCE COUNTY

205 9th & Allen St PO Box 767   **Ph:** 505-384-2221
Estancia, NM 87016   **Fax:** 505-384-4080
www.torrancecountynm.org

In central NM, southeast of Albuquerque; organized Mar 16, 1903 (prior to statehood). **Name Origin:** For the town of Torrance, itself named for Francis J. Torrance, a New Mexico Central Railroad promoter.

Area (sq mi): 3345.81 (land 3344.81; water 1). **Pop per sq mi:** 5.2.

Pop 2005: 17,501. **State rank:** 23. **Pop change:** 2000-20005 +3.5%; 1990-2000 +64.4%. **Pop 2000:** 16,911 (White 57.2%; Black or African American 1.7%; Hispanic or Latino 37.2%; Asian 0.3%; Other 24.1%, including 2.1% American Indian/Alaska Native). **Foreign born:** 4.2%. **Median age:** 34.8.

Income 2000: per capita $14,134; median household $30,446; **Pop below poverty level:** 19%. ***Personal per capita income 2000-2003:** $17,631-$20,190.

Unemployment 2004: 5.8%. **Change from 2000:** +1.2%. **Median travel time to work:** 36.3 minutes. **Working outside county of residence:** 48.7%.

Cities with pop over 10,000: None.

UNION COUNTY

200 Court St   **Ph:** 505-374-9491
Clayton, NM 88415   **Fax:** 505-374-9442
www.claytonnewmexico.org

In the northeastern corner of NM; organized Feb 13, 1893 from Colfax, Mora, and San Miguel counties (prior to statehood). **Name Origin:** For the union of the three counties.

Area (sq mi): 3830.79 (land 3830; water 0.79). **Pop per sq mi:** 1.

Union County (cont'd)

Pop 2005: 3,850. **State rank:** 30. **Pop change:** 2000-20005 -7.8%; 1990-2000 +1.2%. **Pop 2000:** 4,174 (White 62.7%; Black or African American 0%; Hispanic or Latino 35.1%; Asian 0.3%; Other 19.3%, including 1% American Indian/Alaska Native). **Foreign born:** 2.2%. **Median age:** 39.9.

Income 2000: per capita $14,700; median household $28,080; **Pop below poverty level:** 18.1%. ***Personal per capita income 2000-2003:** $23,859-$26,372.

Unemployment 2004: 3.9%. **Change from 2000:** +1.4%. **Median travel time to work:** 20 minutes. **Working outside county of residence:** 15.1%.

Cities with pop over 10,000: None.

VALENCIA COUNTY

444 Luna Ave   **Ph:** 505-866-2073
Los Lunas, NM 87031   **Fax:** 505-866-2023
www.co.valencia.nm.us

In west-central NM, south of Albuquerque; original county; organized Jan 9, 1852 (prior to statehood). **Name Origin:** Either for the town, itself named for Juan de Valencia, a seventeenth-century Spanish settler, or for the seventeenth-century home of Francisco de Valencia, a Spanish official.

Area (sq mi): 1068.21 (land 1067.63; water 0.58). **Pop per sq mi:** 65.

Pop 2005: 69,417. **State rank:** 7. **Pop change:** 2000-20005 +4.9%; 1990-2000 +46.2%. **Pop 2000:** 66,152 (White 39.4%; Black or African American 1.3%; Hispanic or Latino 55%; Asian 0.4%; Other 31.9%, including 3.3% American Indian/Alaska Native). **Foreign born:** 6.4%. **Median age:** 33.8.

Income 2000: per capita $14,747; median household $34,099; **Pop below poverty level:** 16.8%. ***Personal per capita income 2000-2003:** $20,511-$21,756.

Unemployment 2004: 5.7%. **Change from 2000:** +1.6%. **Median travel time to work:** 30.7 minutes. **Working outside county of residence:** 53.9%.

Cities with pop over 10,000: Los Lunas 🏛 (11,748).

*Source: Personal per capita income data are from the Bureau of Economic Analysis; per capita income data are from the Bureau of the Census. See Introduction for explanation of differences.

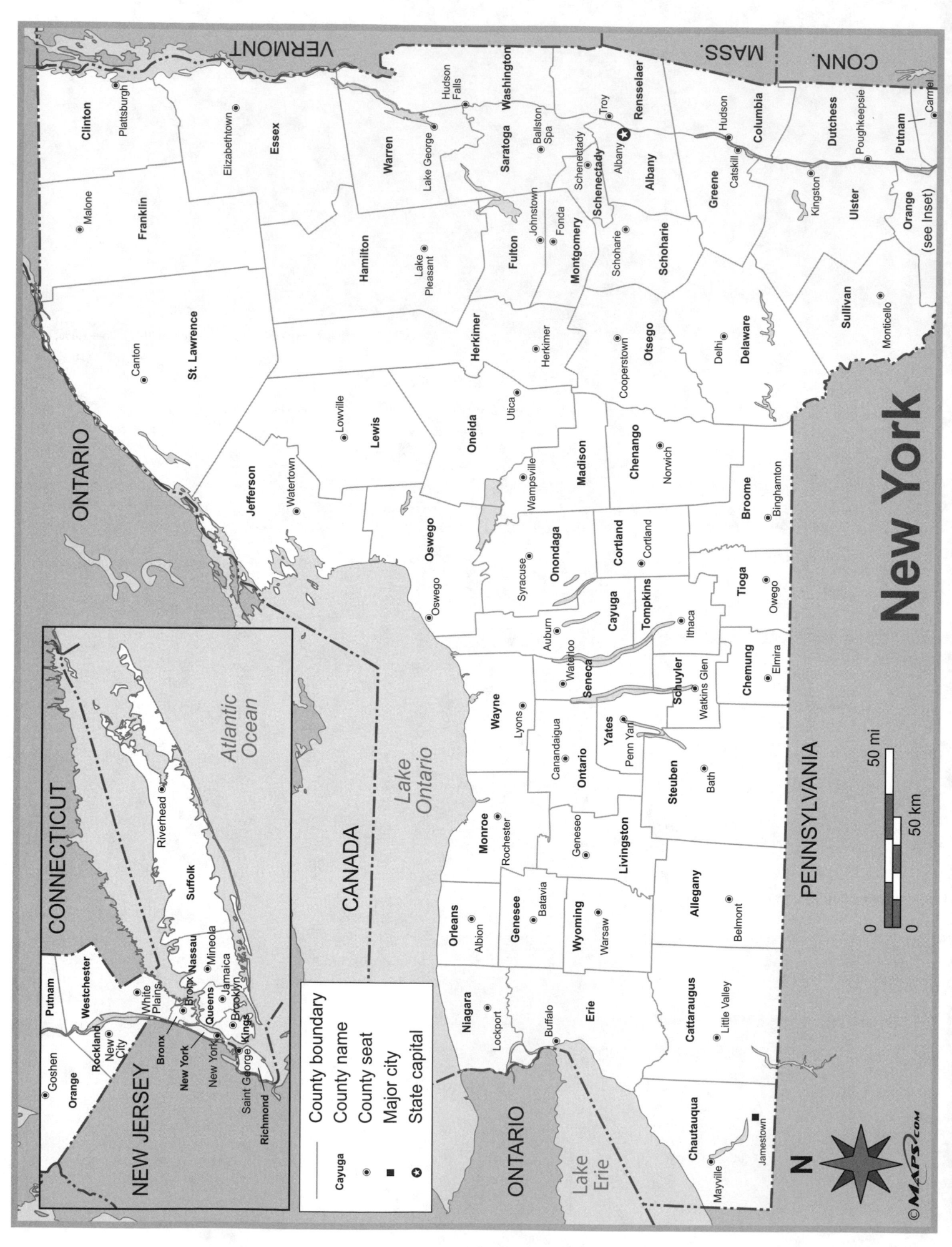

New York

VERMONT

MASS.

CONN.

ONTARIO

PENNSYLVANIA

CANADA

NEW JERSEY

CONNECTICUT

ONTARIO

Lake Ontario

Lake Erie

Atlantic Ocean

Counties and County Seats

Clinton — Plattsburgh
Essex — Elizabethtown
Franklin — Malone
St. Lawrence — Canton
Warren — Lake George
Hamilton — Lake Pleasant
Hudson Falls
Washington
Saratoga — Ballston Spa
Schenectady — Schenectady
Fulton — Johnstown, Fonda
Montgomery
Rensselaer — Troy
Albany — Albany
Schoharie — Schoharie
Greene — Catskill
Columbia — Hudson
Dutchess — Poughkeepsie
Putnam — Carmel
Ulster — Kingston
Orange (see Inset)
Sullivan — Monticello
Delaware — Delhi
Otsego — Cooperstown
Herkimer — Herkimer
Lewis — Lowville
Jefferson — Watertown
Oneida — Utica
Madison — Wampsville
Chenango — Norwich
Broome — Binghamton
Oswego — Oswego
Onondaga — Syracuse
Cortland — Cortland
Tioga — Owego
Cayuga — Auburn
Seneca — Waterloo
Tompkins — Ithaca
Schuyler — Watkins Glen
Chemung — Elmira
Wayne — Lyons
Ontario — Canandaigua
Yates — Penn Yan
Steuben — Bath
Monroe — Rochester
Livingston — Geneseo
Orleans — Albion
Genesee — Batavia
Wyoming — Warsaw
Allegany — Belmont
Niagara — Lockport
Erie — Buffalo
Cattaraugus — Little Valley
Chautauqua — Mayville, Jamestown

Inset
Suffolk — Riverhead
Nassau — Mineola
Westchester — White Plains
Putnam
Rockland — New City
Orange — Goshen
Bronx — Bronx
Queens — Jamaica
Kings — Brooklyn
New York — New York
Richmond — Saint George

Legend

— County boundary
Cayuga — County name
◉ County seat
■ Major city
✪ State capital

0 — 50 mi
0 — 50 km

N

©MAPS.com

New York

NEW YORK STATE INFORMATION
www.state.ny.us   Ph: 518-474-2121

Area (sq mi): 54,556 (land 47,213.79; water 7342.22). **Pop per sq mi:** 407.8.

Pop 2005: 19,254,630. **Pop change:** 2000-20005 +1.5%; 1990-2000 +5.5%. **Pop 2000:** 18,976,457 (White 62%; Black or African American 15.9%; Hispanic or Latino 15.1%; Asian 5.5%; Other 10.6%). **Foreign born:** 20.4%. **Median age:** 35.9.

Income 2000: per capita $23,389; median household $43,393; **Pop below poverty level:** 14.6%. ***Personal per capita income 2000-2003:** $34,897-$36,112.

Unemployment 2004: 5.8%. **Change from 2000:** +1.3%. **Median travel time to work:** 31.7 minutes. **Working outside county of residence:** 35.4%.

ALBANY COUNTY
112 State St Rm 200   Ph: 518-447-7040
Albany, NY 12207   Fax: 518-447-5589
www.albanycounty.com

In east-central NY, southeast of Schenectady; original county, organized Nov 1, 1683. **Name Origin:** For James Stuart, Duke of York and Albany (1633-1701), who later became James II, king of England.

Area (sq mi): 533.21 (land 523.45; water 9.76). **Pop per sq mi:** 568.2.

Pop 2005: 297,414. **State rank:** 13. **Pop change:** 2000-20005 +1%; 1990-2000 +0.7%. **Pop 2000:** 294,565 (White 81.8%; Black or African American 11.1%; Hispanic or Latino 3.1%; Asian 2.7%; Other 3%). **Foreign born:** 6.5%. **Median age:** 36.8.

Income 2000: per capita $23,345; median household $42,935; **Pop below poverty level:** 10.6%. ***Personal per capita income 2000-2003:** $33,302-$35,383.

Unemployment 2004: 4.1%. **Change from 2000:** +1.5%. **Median travel time to work:** 20.3 minutes. **Working outside county of residence:** 17%.

Cities with pop over 10,000: Albany ⚓ (94,226); Cohoes (15,211).

ALLEGANY COUNTY
7 Court St County Courthouse   Ph: 585-268-9270
Belmont, NY 14813   Fax: 585-268-9659
www.alleganyco.com

In southwestern NY, southeast of Buffalo; organized Apr 7, 1806 from Genesee County. **Name Origin:** For the Allegheny River, with a variant spelling.

Area (sq mi): 1034.42 (land 1030.22; water 4.2). **Pop per sq mi:** 49.1.

Pop 2005: 50,602. **State rank:** 49. **Pop change:** 2000-20005 +1.4%; 1990-2000 -1.1%. **Pop 2000:** 49,927 (White 96.6%; Black or African American 0.7%; Hispanic or Latino 0.9%; Asian 0.7%; Other 1.6%). **Foreign born:** 1.8%. **Median age:** 35.

Income 2000: per capita $14,975; median household $32,106; **Pop below poverty level:** 15.5%. ***Personal per capita income 2000-2003:** $19,160-$19,660.

Unemployment 2004: 6.1%. **Change from 2000:** +0.4%. **Median travel time to work:** 21.8 minutes. **Working outside county of residence:** 29.7%.

Cities with pop over 10,000: None.

BRONX COUNTY
851 Grand Concourse Suite 301   Ph: 718-590-3500
Bronx, NY 10451   Fax: 718-590-3537
www.nyc.gov

Established Apr 19, 1912 from New York County. The county is coterminous with the borough of the Bronx, part of New York City. The only borough of New York City that is not on an island. **Name Origin:** For Jonas Bronck or Bronk (?-1643), the first European settler north of the Harlem River. His farm was called 'Broncksland.' the borough is usually called 'The Bronx.'

Area (sq mi): 57.43 (land 42.03; water 15.4). **Pop per sq mi:** 32300.5.

Pop 2005: 1,357,589. **State rank:** 5. **Pop change:** 2000-20005 +1.9%; 1990-2000 +10.7%. **Pop 2000:** 1,332,650 (White 14.5%; Black or African American 35.6%; Hispanic or Latino 48.4%; Asian 3%; Other 31.5%). **Foreign born:** 29%. **Median age:** 31.2.

Income 2000: per capita $13,959; median household $27,611; **Pop below poverty level:** 30.7%. ***Personal per capita income 2000-2003:** $19,343-$21,611.

Unemployment 2004: 9.1%. **Change from 2000:** +1.7%. **Median travel time to work:** 43 minutes. **Working outside county of residence:** 59.3%.

Cities with pop over 10,000: Part of New York City.

BROOME COUNTY
PO Box 2062   Ph: 607-778-2451
Binghamton, NY 13902   Fax: 607-778-2243
www.gobroomecounty.com

On central southern border of NY, southeast of Ithaca; organized Mar 28, 1806 from Tioga County. **Name Origin:** For John Broome

Broome County (cont'd)

(1738-1810), member of the NY constitutional convention (1777) and lieutenant governor (1804-10).

Area (sq mi): 715.46 (land 706.82; water 8.64). **Pop per sq mi:** 278.6.

Pop 2005: 196,947. **State rank:** 19. **Pop change:** 2000-20005 - 1.8%; 1990-2000 -5.5%. **Pop 2000:** 200,536 (White 90.4%; Black or African American 3.3%; Hispanic or Latino 2%; Asian 2.8%; Other 2.6%). **Foreign born:** 5.3%. **Median age:** 38.2.

Income 2000: per capita $19,168; median household $35,347; **Pop below poverty level:** 12.8%. ***Personal per capita income 2000-2003:** $25,343-$26,059.

Unemployment 2004: 5.4%. **Change from 2000:** +1.2%. **Median travel time to work:** 18.9 minutes. **Working outside county of residence:** 8.5%.

Cities with pop over 10,000: Binghamton 🏛 (45,864); Johnson City (15,084); Endicott (12,749).

CATTARAUGUS COUNTY
303 Court St   **Ph:** 716-938-9111
Little Valley, NY 14755   **Fax:** 716-938-6009
www.co.cattaraugus.ny.us

On southwestern border of NY, south of Buffalo; organized Mar 11, 1808 from Genesee County. **Name Origin:** For the Cattaraugus Creek, which forms its northern border; probably from Seneca 'bad smelling shore.'

Area (sq mi): 1322.25 (land 1309.85; water 12.4). **Pop per sq mi:** 63.

Pop 2005: 82,502. **State rank:** 33. **Pop change:** 2000-20005 -1.7%; 1990-2000 -0.3%. **Pop 2000:** 83,955 (White 94%; Black or African American 1.1%; Hispanic or Latino 0.9%; Asian 0.5%; Other 3.8%, including 2.6% American Indian/Alaska Native). **Foreign born:** 1.4%. **Median age:** 37.4.

Income 2000: per capita $15,959; median household $33,404; **Pop below poverty level:** 13.7%. ***Personal per capita income 2000-2003:** $20,936-$24,100.

Unemployment 2004: 6%. **Change from 2000:** -0.7%. **Median travel time to work:** 21.7 minutes. **Working outside county of residence:** 28.8%.

Cities with pop over 10,000: Olean (14,972).

CAYUGA COUNTY
160 Genesee St   **Ph:** 315-253-1271
Auburn, NY 13021   **Fax:** 315-253-1673
www.co.cayuga.ny.us

On central northern border of NY, east of Rochester; organized Mar 8, 1799 from Onondaga County. **Name Origin:** For the Cayuga Indians, one of the Five Nations of the Iroquois.

Area (sq mi): 863.64 (land 693.18; water 170.46). **Pop per sq mi:** 117.5.

Pop 2005: 81,454. **State rank:** 35. **Pop change:** 2000-20005 -0.6%; 1990-2000 -0.4%. **Pop 2000:** 81,963 (White 92.4%; Black or African American 4%; Hispanic or Latino 2%; Asian 0.4%; Other 2.2%). **Foreign born:** 2.3%. **Median age:** 37.3.

Income 2000: per capita $18,003; median household $37,487; **Pop below poverty level:** 11.1%. ***Personal per capita income 2000-2003:** $22,697-$24,951.

Unemployment 2004: 5.2%. **Change from 2000:** +0.3%. **Median travel time to work:** 22 minutes. **Working outside county of residence:** 36.6%.

Cities with pop over 10,000: Auburn 🏛 (28,080).

CHAUTAUQUA COUNTY
3 N Erie St Gerace Office Bldg   **Ph:** 716-753-4211
Mayville, NY 14757   **Fax:** 716-753-4756
www.chautco.com

In southwestern corner of NY, southwest of Buffalo; organized Mar 11, 1808 from Genesee County. **Name Origin:** For Lake Chautauqua, which is in the middle of the county; its name is a contraction of Seneca Indian words of uncertain origin and meaning; possibly 'where the fish was taken out.'

Area (sq mi): 1500.02 (land 1062.05; water 437.97). **Pop per sq mi:** 128.4.

Pop 2005: 136,409. **State rank:** 23. **Pop change:** 2000-20005 - 2.4%; 1990-2000 -1.5%. **Pop 2000:** 139,750 (White 91.9%; Black or African American 2.2%; Hispanic or Latino 4.2%; Asian 0.4%; Other 3.3%). **Foreign born:** 1.9%. **Median age:** 37.9.

Income 2000: per capita $16,840; median household $33,458; **Pop below poverty level:** 13.8%. ***Personal per capita income 2000-2003:** $21,384-$22,347.

Unemployment 2004: 5.5%. **Change from 2000:** +0.1%. **Median travel time to work:** 18.4 minutes. **Working outside county of residence:** 10.7%.

Cities with pop over 10,000: Jamestown (30,695); Dunkirk (12,627); Fredonia (10,705).

CHEMUNG COUNTY
PO Box 588   **Ph:** 607-737-2920
Elmira, NY 14902   **Fax:** 607-737-2897
www.chemungcounty.com

On central southern border of NY, southwest of Syracuse; organized Mar 29, 1836 from Tioga County. **Name Origin:** For a former Seneca village near the town of Chemung. The name means 'big horn.'

Area (sq mi): 410.79 (land 408.17; water 2.62). **Pop per sq mi:** 219.3.

Pop 2005: 89,512. **State rank:** 32. **Pop change:** 2000-20005 -1.7%; 1990-2000 -4.3%. **Pop 2000:** 91,070 (White 90.2%; Black or African American 5.8%; Hispanic or Latino 1.8%; Asian 0.8%; Other 2.3%). **Foreign born:** 2.2%. **Median age:** 37.9.

Income 2000: per capita $18,264; median household $36,415; **Pop below poverty level:** 13%. ***Personal per capita income 2000-2003:** $24,350-$24,349.

Unemployment 2004: 6.1%. **Change from 2000:** +0.8%. **Median travel time to work:** 19.3 minutes. **Working outside county of residence:** 18.9%.

Cities with pop over 10,000: Elmira 🏛 (30,073).

---

*Source: Personal per capita income data are from the Bureau of Economic Analysis; per capita income data are from the Bureau of the Census. See Introduction for explanation of differences.

CHENANGO COUNTY

5 Court St   **Ph:** 607-337-1450
Norwich, NY 13815   **Fax:** 607-337-1455
www.co.chenango.ny.us

In south-central NY, southeast of Ithaca; organized Mar 15, 1798 from Herkimer and Tioga counties. **Name Origin:** From an Onondaga Indian word probably meaning 'bull thistle.'

Area (sq mi): 898.7 (land 894.36; water 4.34). **Pop per sq mi:** 57.9.

Pop 2005: 51,755. **State rank:** 46. **Pop change:** 2000-20005 +0.7%; 1990-2000 -0.7%. **Pop 2000:** 51,401 (White 96.9%; Black or African American 0.8%; Hispanic or Latino 1.1%; Asian 0.3%; Other 1.2%). **Foreign born:** 1.7%. **Median age:** 38.4.

Income 2000: per capita $16,427; median household $33,679; **Pop below poverty level:** 14.4%. ***Personal per capita income 2000-2003:** $21,334-$22,975.

Unemployment 2004: 5.6%. **Change from 2000:** +0.5%. **Median travel time to work:** 26.3 minutes. **Working outside county of residence:** 32.3%.

Cities with pop over 10,000: None.

CLINTON COUNTY

137 Margaret St Suite 208   **Ph:** 518-565-4600
Plattsburgh, NY 12901   **Fax:** 518-565-4616
www.co.clinton.ny.us

In northeastern corner of NY, northwest of Burlington, VT; organized Mar 7, 1788 (prior to statehood) from Washington County. **Name Origin:** For George Clinton (1739-1812), first governor of NY (1777-95).

Area (sq mi): 1117.61 (land 1038.95; water 78.67). **Pop per sq mi:** 79.

Pop 2005: 82,047. **State rank:** 34. **Pop change:** 2000-20005 +2.7%; 1990-2000 -7.1%. **Pop 2000:** 79,894 (White 92.3%; Black or African American 3.6%; Hispanic or Latino 2.5%; Asian 0.7%; Other 2.4%). **Foreign born:** 4.5%. **Median age:** 35.7.

Income 2000: per capita $17,946; median household $37,028; **Pop below poverty level:** 13.9%. ***Personal per capita income 2000-2003:** $22,534-$24,473.

Unemployment 2004: 6%. **Change from 2000:** +1.8%. **Median travel time to work:** 20.2 minutes. **Working outside county of residence:** 8.6%.

Cities with pop over 10,000: Plattsburgh ⚒ (19,218).

COLUMBIA COUNTY

560 Warren St   **Ph:** 518-828-3339
Hudson, NY 12534
www.govt.co.columbia.ny.us

On central eastern border of NY, southeast of Albany; organized Apr 4, 1786 (prior to statehood) from Albany County. **Name Origin:** Feminine form of Columbus, a poetic and honorific reference to Christopher Columbus (1451-1506) and America.

Area (sq mi): 648.27 (land 635.73; water 12.54). **Pop per sq mi:** 100.1.

Pop 2005: 63,622. **State rank:** 41. **Pop change:** 2000-20005 +0.8%; 1990-2000 +0.2%. **Pop 2000:** 63,094 (White 90.9%; Black or African American 4.5%; Hispanic or Latino 2.5%; Asian 0.8%; Other 2.5%). **Foreign born:** 4.4%. **Median age:** 40.5.

Income 2000: per capita $22,265; median household $41,915; **Pop below poverty level:** 9%. ***Personal per capita income 2000-2003:** $28,579-$28,452.

Unemployment 2004: 4.3%. **Change from 2000:** +1.6%. **Median travel time to work:** 26.1 minutes. **Working outside county of residence:** 36.8%.

Cities with pop over 10,000: None.

CORTLAND COUNTY

46 Greenbush St Suite 101   **Ph:** 607-753-5021
Cortland, NY 13045   **Fax:** 607-753-5378
www.cortland-co.org

In south-central NY, south of Syracuse; organized Apr 8, 1808 from Onondaga County. **Name Origin:** For Pierre Van Cortland, Jr. (1762-1848), NY legislator, U.S. representative (1811-13), and banker.

Area (sq mi): 501.52 (land 499.65; water 1.87). **Pop per sq mi:** 97.3.

Pop 2005: 48,622. **State rank:** 52. **Pop change:** 2000-20005 +0%; 1990-2000 -0.7%. **Pop 2000:** 48,599 (White 96.2%; Black or African American 0.9%; Hispanic or Latino 1.2%; Asian 0.4%; Other 1.8%). **Foreign born:** 2.2%. **Median age:** 34.2.

Income 2000: per capita $16,622; median household $34,364; **Pop below poverty level:** 15.5%. ***Personal per capita income 2000-2003:** $22,043-$22,629.

Unemployment 2004: 6%. **Change from 2000:** +0%. **Median travel time to work:** 21.1 minutes. **Working outside county of residence:** 28.1%.

Cities with pop over 10,000: Cortland ⚒ (18,713).

DELAWARE COUNTY

PO Box 426   **Ph:** 607-746-2123
Delhi, NY 13753   **Fax:** 607-746-6924
www.co.delaware.ny.us

In south-central NY, east of Binghamton; organized Mar 10, 1797 from Ulster and Otsego counties. **Name Origin:** For the Delaware River, whose two main branches flow through the county.

Area (sq mi): 1468.04 (land 1446.37; water 21.67). **Pop per sq mi:** 32.9.

Pop 2005: 47,534. **State rank:** 53. **Pop change:** 2000-20005 -1.1%; 1990-2000 +1.8%. **Pop 2000:** 48,055 (White 95.1%; Black or African American 1.2%; Hispanic or Latino 2%; Asian 0.5%; Other 1.8%). **Foreign born:** 3.4%. **Median age:** 41.4.

Income 2000: per capita $17,357; median household $32,461; **Pop below poverty level:** 12.9%. ***Personal per capita income 2000-2003:** $21,810-$23,260.

Unemployment 2004: 4.4%. **Change from 2000:** +0.1%. **Median travel time to work:** 24 minutes. **Working outside county of residence:** 29%.

Cities with pop over 10,000: None.

⚒ *County Seat*

491

DUTCHESS COUNTY

22 Market St
Poughkeepsie, NY 12601   **Ph:** 845-486-2120
www.co.dutchess.ny.us

In southeastern NY, north of NYC, original county, organized Nov 1, 1683. **Name Origin:** For Mary (1658-1718), Duchess of York, wife of James, Duke of York and Albany, later James II, king of England; spelling is 17th-century variant of *duchess*.

Area (sq mi): 825.38 (land 801.59; water 23.78). **Pop per sq mi:** 367.8.

Pop 2005: 294,849. **State rank:** 14. **Pop change:** 2000-20005 +5.2%; 1990-2000 +8%. **Pop 2000:** 280,150 (White 80.3%; Black or African American 9.3%; Hispanic or Latino 6.4%; Asian 2.5%; Other 4.5%). **Foreign born:** 8.4%. **Median age:** 36.7.

Income 2000: per capita $23,940; median household $53,086; **Pop below poverty level:** 7.5%. *****Personal per capita income 2000-2003:** $31,535-$32,635.

Unemployment 2004: 4.2%. **Change from 2000:** +1%. **Median travel time to work:** 29.8 minutes. **Working outside county of residence:** 30.7%.

Cities with pop over 10,000: Poughkeepsie 🏛 (30,348); Beacon (14,762).

ERIE COUNTY

25 Delaware Ave   **Ph:** 716-858-8785
Buffalo, NY 14202   **Fax:** 716-858-6550
www.erie.gov

On central western border of NY on Lake Erie, south of Niagara Falls; organized Apr 2, 1821 from Niagara County. **Name Origin:** For the Erie Indian tribe of Iroquoian linguistic stock, who lived along the southern shore of Lake Erie.

Area (sq mi): 1226.89 (land 1044.21; water 182.68). **Pop per sq mi:** 891.3.

Pop 2005: 930,703. **State rank:** 8. **Pop change:** 2000-20005 -2.1%; 1990-2000 -1.9%. **Pop 2000:** 950,265 (White 80.8%; Black or African American 13%; Hispanic or Latino 3.3%; Asian 1.5%; Other 3.3%). **Foreign born:** 4.5%. **Median age:** 38.

Income 2000: per capita $20,357; median household $38,567; **Pop below poverty level:** 12.2%. *****Personal per capita income 2000-2003:** $27,836-$29,868.

Unemployment 2004: 5.7%. **Change from 2000:** +0.6%. **Median travel time to work:** 21.3 minutes. **Working outside county of residence:** 5.9%.

Cities with pop over 10,000: 6 (see page 37 for cities).

ESSEX COUNTY

7559 Court St   **Ph:** 518-873-3600
Elizabethtown, NY 12932   **Fax:** 518-873-3548
www.co.essex.ny.us

On northeastern border of NY, southwest of Burlington, VT; organized Mar 1, 1799 from Clinton County. **Name Origin:** For the county of Essex, England.

Area (sq mi): 1916.5 (land 1796.8; water 119.7). **Pop per sq mi:** 21.5.

Pop 2005: 38,676. **State rank:** 56. **Pop change:** 2000-20005 -0.5%; 1990-2000 +4.6%. **Pop 2000:** 38,851 (White 93.6%; Black or African American 2.8%; Hispanic or Latino 2.2%; Asian 0.4%; Other 2%). **Foreign born:** 3.4%. **Median age:** 39.4.

Income 2000: per capita $18,194; median household $34,823; **Pop below poverty level:** 11.6%. *****Personal per capita income 2000-2003:** $22,206-$23,406.

Unemployment 2004: 5.5%. **Change from 2000:** +0.2%. **Median travel time to work:** 20.7 minutes. **Working outside county of residence:** 25.6%.

Cities with pop over 10,000: None.

FRANKLIN COUNTY

355 W Main St PO Box 70   **Ph:** 518-481-1681
Malone, NY 12953   **Fax:** 518-483-9143
www.adirondacklakes.org

On northeastern border of NY, south of Montreal, prov. of Quebec, Canada; organized Mar 11, 1808 from Clinton County. **Name Origin:** For Benjamin Franklin (1706-90), U.S. patriot, diplomat, and statesman.

Area (sq mi): 1697.44 (land 1631.49; water 65.95). **Pop per sq mi:** 31.3.

Pop 2005: 51,033. **State rank:** 48. **Pop change:** 2000-20005 -0.2%; 1990-2000 +9.9%. **Pop 2000:** 51,134 (White 82.6%; Black or African American 6.6%; Hispanic or Latino 4%; Asian 0.4%; Other 9%, including 6.2% American Indian/Alaska Native). **Foreign born:** 3.7%. **Median age:** 36.3.

Income 2000: per capita $15,888; median household $31,517; **Pop below poverty level:** 14.6%. *****Personal per capita income 2000-2003:** $18,816-$20,115.

Unemployment 2004: 6.5%. **Change from 2000:** -0.5%. **Median travel time to work:** 19.1 minutes. **Working outside county of residence:** 19.5%.

Cities with pop over 10,000: None.

FULTON COUNTY

223 W Main St   **Ph:** 518-736-5555
Johnstown, NY 12095   **Fax:** 518-762-3839
www.fultoncountyny.org

In east-central NY, east of Utica; organized Apr 18, 1838 from Montgomery County. **Name Origin:** For Robert Fulton (1765-1815), developer of the *Clermont*, the first commercially successful steamboat.

Area (sq mi): 532.9 (land 496.17; water 36.73). **Pop per sq mi:** 112.1.

Pop 2005: 55,625. **State rank:** 45. **Pop change:** 2000-20005 +1%; 1990-2000 +1.6%. **Pop 2000:** 55,073 (White 95.1%; Black or African American 1.8%; Hispanic or Latino 1.6%; Asian 0.5%; Other 1.7%). **Foreign born:** 1.9%. **Median age:** 38.6.

Income 2000: per capita $16,844; median household $33,663; **Pop below poverty level:** 12.5%. *****Personal per capita income 2000-2003:** $24,088-$25,109.

Unemployment 2004: 5.7%. **Change from 2000:** +0.9%. **Median travel time to work:** 22.4 minutes. **Working outside county of residence:** 34.6%.

Source: Personal per capita income data are from the Bureau of Economic Analysis; per capita income data are from the Bureau of the Census. See Introduction for explanation of differences.

Fulton County (cont'd)

Cities with pop over 10,000: Gloversville (15,277).

GENESEE COUNTY

7 Main St
Batavia, NY 14020
www.co.genesee.ny.us

Ph: 585-344-2550
Fax: 585-344-8582

In northwestern NY, southeast of Rochester; organized Mar 30, 1802 from Ontario County. **Name Origin:** From the Iroquoian word probably meaning 'beautiful valley.'

Area (sq mi): 495.33 (land 494.11; water 1.22). **Pop per sq mi:** 119.9.

Pop 2005: 59,257. **State rank:** 44. **Pop change:** 2000-20005 -1.8%; 1990-2000 +0.5%. **Pop 2000:** 60,370 (White 94.1%; Black or African American 2.1%; Hispanic or Latino 1.5%; Asian 0.5%; Other 2.7%). **Foreign born:** 2.2%. **Median age:** 37.4.

Income 2000: per capita $18,498; median household $40,542; **Pop below poverty level:** 7.6%. ***Personal per capita income 2000-2003:** $23,792-$25,307.

Unemployment 2004: 5.6%. **Change from 2000:** +0.6%. **Median travel time to work:** 22.4 minutes. **Working outside county of residence:** 39.2%.

Cities with pop over 10,000: Batavia 🏛 (15,830).

GREENE COUNTY

411 Main St
Catskill, NY 12414
www.greene-ny.com

Ph: 518-943-2050
Fax: 518-719-3284

In southeastern NY, southwest of Albany; organized Mar 25, 1800 from Albany and Ulster counties. **Name Origin:** For Gen,. Nathanael Greene (1742-86), hero of the Revolutionary War; quartermaster general (1778-80).

Area (sq mi): 658.13 (land 647.75; water 10.38). **Pop per sq mi:** 76.7.

Pop 2005: 49,682. **State rank:** 50. **Pop change:** 2000-20005 +3.1%; 1990-2000 +7.7%. **Pop 2000:** 48,195 (White 88.5%; Black or African American 5.5%; Hispanic or Latino 4.3%; Asian 0.5%; Other 3.2%). **Foreign born:** 6.4%. **Median age:** 39.1.

Income 2000: per capita $18,931; median household $36,493; **Pop below poverty level:** 12.2%. ***Personal per capita income 2000-2003:** $23,549-$26,264.

Unemployment 2004: 5.2%. **Change from 2000:** +0.8%. **Median travel time to work:** 29.1 minutes. **Working outside county of residence:** 42.3%.

Cities with pop over 10,000: None.

HAMILTON COUNTY

PO Box 204 Rt 8
Lake Pleasant, NY 12108
hamiltoncounty.com

Ph: 518-548-7111
Fax: 518-548-9740

In north-central NY, northeast of Utica; organized Apr 12, 1816 from Montgomery County. **Name Origin:** For Alexander Hamilton (1757-1804), first U.S. secretary of the treasury (1789-95).

Area (sq mi): 1807.81 (land 1720.39; water 87.41). **Pop per sq mi:** 3.

Pop 2005: 5,228. **State rank:** 62. **Pop change:** 2000-20005 -2.8%; 1990-2000 +1.9%. **Pop 2000:** 5,379 (White 97.1%; Black or African American 0.4%; Hispanic or Latino 1.1%; Asian 0.1%; Other 1.8%). **Foreign born:** 1.5%. **Median age:** 45.4.

Income 2000: per capita $18,643; median household $32,287; **Pop below poverty level:** 10.4%. ***Personal per capita income 2000-2003:** $23,315-$25,768.

Unemployment 2004: 5.7%. **Change from 2000:** +0.3%. **Median travel time to work:** 22.8 minutes. **Working outside county of residence:** 31.6%.

Cities with pop over 10,000: None.

HERKIMER COUNTY

109 Mary St Suite 1111
Herkimer, NY 13350
www.herkimercounty.org

Ph: 315-867-1129
Fax: 315-866-4396

In north-central NY, east of Utica; organized Feb 16, 1791 from Montgomery County. **Name Origin:** For Gen. Nicholas Herkimer (1728-77), Revolutionary War officer and patriot, fatally wounded at the Battle of Oriskany. An earlier name was German Flats, for German settlers.

Area (sq mi): 1458.35 (land 1411.25; water 47.1). **Pop per sq mi:** 45.2.

Pop 2005: 63,780. **State rank:** 40. **Pop change:** 2000-20005 -1%; 1990-2000 -2.1%. **Pop 2000:** 64,427 (White 97.3%; Black or African American 0.5%; Hispanic or Latino 0.9%; Asian 0.4%; Other 1.2%). **Foreign born:** 2%. **Median age:** 39.

Income 2000: per capita $16,141; median household $32,924; **Pop below poverty level:** 12.5%. ***Personal per capita income 2000-2003:** $21,390-$22,641.

Unemployment 2004: 5.7%. **Change from 2000:** +1%. **Median travel time to work:** 21.9 minutes. **Working outside county of residence:** 41.4%.

Cities with pop over 10,000: None.

JEFFERSON COUNTY

175 Arsenal St
Watertown, NY 13601
www.co.jefferson.ny.us

Ph: 315-785-3081
Fax: 315-785-5145

On central western border of NY on Lake Ontario; organized Mar 28, 1805 from Oneida County. **Name Origin:** For Thomas Jefferson (1743-1826), U.S. patriot and statesman; third U.S. president.

Area (sq mi): 1857.08 (land 1272.2; water 584.88). **Pop per sq mi:** 91.5.

Pop 2005: 116,384. **State rank:** 25. **Pop change:** 2000-20005 +4.2%; 1990-2000 +0.7%. **Pop 2000:** 111,738 (White 87.2%; Black or African American 5.8%; Hispanic or Latino 4.2%; Asian 0.9%; Other 4.5%). **Foreign born:** 3.7%. **Median age:** 32.5.

Income 2000: per capita $16,202; median household $34,006; **Pop below poverty level:** 13.3%. ***Personal per capita income 2000-2003:** $22,889-$24,958.

Unemployment 2004: 6.9%. **Change from 2000:** -1.2%. **Median travel time to work:** 18.4 minutes. **Working outside county of residence:** 6.8%.

Cities with pop over 10,000: Watertown 🏛 (26,240).

🏛 *County Seat*

KINGS COUNTY

360 Adams St   **Ph:** 718-643-7037
Brooklyn, NY 11201   **Fax:** 718-643-8187
www.nyc.gov

On the southwestern end of Long Island, east of Manhattan Island; original county, organized Nov 1, 1683. The county is coterminous with the borough of Brooklyn, part of New York City. **Name Origin:** For Charles II (1630-85), king of England.

Area (sq mi): 96.9 (land 70.61; water 26.29). **Pop per sq mi:** 35210.8.

Pop 2005: 2,486,235. **State rank:** 1. **Pop change:** 2000-20005 +0.8%; 1990-2000 +7.2%. **Pop 2000:** 2,465,326 (White 34.7%; Black or African American 36.4%; Hispanic or Latino 19.8%; Asian 7.5%; Other 14.9%). **Foreign born:** 37.8%. **Median age:** 33.1.

Income 2000: per capita $16,775; median household $32,135; **Pop below poverty level:** 25.1%. ***Personal per capita income 2000-2003:** $24,514-$25,934.

Unemployment 2004: 7.7%. **Change from 2000:** +1%. **Median travel time to work:** 43.2 minutes. **Working outside county of residence:** 52.1%.

Cities with pop over 10,000: Part of New York City.

LEWIS COUNTY

PO Box 232   **Ph:** 315-376-5333
Lowville, NY 13367   **Fax:** 315-376-3768
lewiscountyny.org

In north-central NY, east of Syracuse; organized Mar 28, 1805 from Oneida County. **Name Origin:** For Morgan Lewis (1754-1844), officer in the Revolutionary War and the War of 1812, NY legislator, and governor (1804-07).

Area (sq mi): 1289.89 (land 1275.42; water 14.47). **Pop per sq mi:** 20.8.

Pop 2005: 26,571. **State rank:** 59. **Pop change:** 2000-20005 -1.4%; 1990-2000 +0.6%. **Pop 2000:** 26,944 (White 97.8%; Black or African American 0.4%; Hispanic or Latino 0.6%; Asian 0.2%; Other 1.3%). **Foreign born:** 1.1%. **Median age:** 36.8.

Income 2000: per capita $14,971; median household $34,361; **Pop below poverty level:** 13.2%. ***Personal per capita income 2000-2003:** $19,615-$20,608.

Unemployment 2004: 6.7%. **Change from 2000:** -1.9%. **Median travel time to work:** 21 minutes. **Working outside county of residence:** 33.5%.

Cities with pop over 10,000: None.

LIVINGSTON COUNTY

6 Court St Rm 201   **Ph:** 585-243-7010
Geneseo, NY 14454
www.co.livingston.state.ny.us

In western NY, south of Rochester; organized Feb 23, 1821 from Genesee and Ontario counties. **Name Origin:** For Robert R. Livingston (1746-1813), NY patriot, statesman, and a drafter of the Declaration of Independence.

Area (sq mi): 640.44 (land 632.13; water 8.32). **Pop per sq mi:** 101.6.

Pop 2005: 64,205. **State rank:** 39. **Pop change:** 2000-20005 -0.2%; 1990-2000 +3.1%. **Pop 2000:** 64,328 (White 92.9%; Black or African American 3%; Hispanic or Latino 2.3%; Asian 0.8%; Other 2.1%). **Foreign born:** 2.6%. **Median age:** 35.3.

Income 2000: per capita $18,062; median household $42,066; **Pop below poverty level:** 10.4%. ***Personal per capita income 2000-2003:** $22,911-$23,814.

Unemployment 2004: 5.9%. **Change from 2000:** +1.3%. **Median travel time to work:** 25.3 minutes. **Working outside county of residence:** 47.9%.

Cities with pop over 10,000: None.

MADISON COUNTY

PO Box 668   **Ph:** 315-366-2261
Wampsville, NY 13163   **Fax:** 315-366-2615
www.madisoncounty.org

In central NY, east of Syracuse; organized Mar 21, 1806 from Chenango County. **Name Origin:** For James Madison (1751-1836), U.S. secretary of state at the time of the county's creation, later fourth U.S. president.

Area (sq mi): 661.54 (land 655.86; water 5.69). **Pop per sq mi:** 107.2.

Pop 2005: 70,337. **State rank:** 37. **Pop change:** 2000-20005 +1.3%; 1990-2000 +0.5%. **Pop 2000:** 69,441 (White 95.9%; Black or African American 1.3%; Hispanic or Latino 1.1%; Asian 0.6%; Other 1.6%). **Foreign born:** 2.2%. **Median age:** 36.1.

Income 2000: per capita $19,105; median household $40,184; **Pop below poverty level:** 9.8%. ***Personal per capita income 2000-2003:** $25,163-$25,839.

Unemployment 2004: 5.6%. **Change from 2000:** +0.6%. **Median travel time to work:** 22.6 minutes. **Working outside county of residence:** 49.4%.

Cities with pop over 10,000: Oneida (10,977).

MONROE COUNTY

39 W Main St Rm 101   **Ph:** 585-428-5151
Rochester, NY 14614   **Fax:** 585-428-5447
www.monroecounty.gov

On northwestern border of NY on Lake Ontario; organized Feb 23, 1821 from Genesee and Ontario counties. **Name Origin:** For James Monroe (1758-1831), fifth U.S. president, in office at the time of the county's creation.

Area (sq mi): 1365.61 (land 659.29; water 706.31). **Pop per sq mi:** 1112.4.

Pop 2005: 733,366. **State rank:** 9. **Pop change:** 2000-20005 -0.3%; 1990-2000 +3%. **Pop 2000:** 735,343 (White 77.1%; Black or African American 13.7%; Hispanic or Latino 5.3%; Asian 2.4%; Other 4.6%). **Foreign born:** 7.3%. **Median age:** 36.1.

Income 2000: per capita $22,821; median household $44,891; **Pop below poverty level:** 11.2%. ***Personal per capita income 2000-2003:** $31,134-$33,272.

Unemployment 2004: 5.2%. **Change from 2000:** +0.8%. **Median travel time to work:** 19.6 minutes. **Working outside county of residence:** 4.8%.

Cities with pop over 10,000: Rochester ▥ (212,481).

---

*Source: Personal per capita income data are from the Bureau of Economic Analysis; per capita income data are from the Bureau of the Census. See Introduction for explanation of differences.

MONTGOMERY COUNTY

PO Box 1500   **Ph:** 518-853-3834
Fonda, NY 12068   **Fax:** 518-853-8220
www.co.montgomery.ny.us

In south-central NY, northwest of Albany; organized as Tryon County Mar 12, 1772 (prior to statehood) from Albany County; name changed Apr 2, 1784. **Name Origin:** For Gen. Richard Montgomery (1736-75), Revolutionary War officer

Area (sq mi): 410.32 (land 404.82; water 5.51). **Pop per sq mi:** 121.

Pop 2005: 48,968. **State rank:** 51. **Pop change:** 2000-20005 -1.5%; 1990-2000 -4.4%. **Pop 2000:** 49,708 (White 90.7%; Black or African American 1.2%; Hispanic or Latino 6.9%; Asian 0.5%; Other 3.4%). **Foreign born:** 3.2%. **Median age:** 39.7.

Income 2000: per capita $17,005; median household $32,128; **Pop below poverty level:** 12%. ***Personal per capita income 2000-2003:** $24,019-$26,087.

Unemployment 2004: 5.9%. **Change from 2000:** +0.2%. **Median travel time to work:** 23.3 minutes. **Working outside county of residence:** 37.8%.

Cities with pop over 10,000: Amsterdam (17,928).

NASSAU COUNTY

240 Old Country Rd   **Ph:** 516-571-2664
Mineola, NY 11501   **Fax:** 516-742-4099
www.nassaucountyny.gov

On the western end of Long Island, east of Manhattan Island; organized Apr 27, 1898 from Queens County. **Name Origin:** For the duchy in Germany associated with the House of Orange, hence with William, Prince of Orange (1650-1702), later William III, King of England.

Area (sq mi): 453.08 (land 286.69; water 166.39). **Pop per sq mi:** 4650.1.

Pop 2005: 1,333,137. **State rank:** 6. **Pop change:** 2000-20005 -0.1%; 1990-2000 +3.7%. **Pop 2000:** 1,334,544 (White 74%; Black or African American 10.1%; Hispanic or Latino 10%; Asian 4.7%; Other 5.9%). **Foreign born:** 17.9%. **Median age:** 38.5.

Income 2000: per capita $32,151; median household $72,030; **Pop below poverty level:** 5.2%. ***Personal per capita income 2000-2003:** $47,445-$50,242.

Unemployment 2004: 4.5%. **Change from 2000:** +1.4%. **Median travel time to work:** 34.3 minutes. **Working outside county of residence:** 41.9%.

Cities with pop over 10,000: 13 (see page 37 for cities).

NEW YORK COUNTY

60 Centre St   **Ph:** 646-386-5955
New York, NY 10007   **Fax:** 212-374-5790
www.nyc.gov

Primarily on Manhattan Island at the southeastern tip of NY, west of Long Island; original county, organized Nov 1, 1683. The county is coterminous with the borough of Manhattan, part of New York City. **Name Origin:** Named in 1664 when Col. Richard Nicolls seized the Dutch territories for King Charles II of England, who granted them to his brother, James (1633-1701), Duke of York and Albany, later James II, King of England. Lands east of the Hudson River were called Yorkshire, later New York. Called Nieuw Amsterdam by the Dutch.

Area (sq mi): 33.77 (land 22.96; water 10.81). **Pop per sq mi:** 69390.2.

Pop 2005: 1,593,200. **State rank:** 3. **Pop change:** 2000-20005 +3.6%; 1990-2000 +3.3%. **Pop 2000:** 1,537,195 (White 45.8%; Black or African American 17.4%; Hispanic or Latino 27.2%; Asian 9.4%; Other 18.8%). **Foreign born:** 29.4%. **Median age:** 35.7.

Income 2000: per capita $42,922; median household $47,030; **Pop below poverty level:** 20%. ***Personal per capita income 2000-2003:** $85,829-$84,044.

Unemployment 2004: 6.2%. **Change from 2000:** +0.2%. **Median travel time to work:** 30.5 minutes. **Working outside county of residence:** 16.2%.

Cities with pop over 10,000: Part of New York City.

NIAGARA COUNTY

PO Box 461   **Ph:** 716-439-7022
Lockport, NY 14095   **Fax:** 716-439-7066
www.niagaracounty.com

In northwestern corner of NY on Lake Ontario; organized Mar 11, 1808 from Genesee County. **Name Origin:** For the Niagara River, which forms its western border.

Area (sq mi): 1139.83 (land 522.95; water 616.89). **Pop per sq mi:** 415.

Pop 2005: 217,008. **State rank:** 17. **Pop change:** 2000-20005 -1.3%; 1990-2000 -0.4%. **Pop 2000:** 219,846 (White 90%; Black or African American 6.1%; Hispanic or Latino 1.3%; Asian 0.6%; Other 2.5%). **Foreign born:** 3.9%. **Median age:** 38.2.

Income 2000: per capita $19,219; median household $38,136; **Pop below poverty level:** 10.6%. ***Personal per capita income 2000-2003:** $24,499-$26,033.

Unemployment 2004: 6.2%. **Change from 2000:** -0.4%. **Median travel time to work:** 20.1 minutes. **Working outside county of residence:** 33.8%.

Cities with pop over 10,000: Niagara Falls (53,708); North Tonawanda (32,188); Lockport ⚏ (21,504).

ONEIDA COUNTY

800 Park Ave   **Ph:** 315-798-5776
Utica, NY 13501   **Fax:** 315-798-6440
www.oneidacounty.org

In central NY, northeast of Syracuse; organized May 15, 1798 from Herkimer County. **Name Origin:** For the Oneida Indian tribe of Iroquoian linguistic stock; one of the Five Nations of the Iroquois. The name probably means 'stone people,' perhaps in praise of their bravery.

Area (sq mi): 1257.11 (land 1212.7; water 44.41). **Pop per sq mi:** 193.

Pop 2005: 234,105. **State rank:** 16. **Pop change:** 2000-20005 -0.6%; 1990-2000 -6.1%. **Pop 2000:** 235,469 (White 88.6%; Black or African American 5.7%; Hispanic or Latino 3.2%; Asian 1.2%; Other 2.8%). **Foreign born:** 5.2%. **Median age:** 38.2.

⚏ *County Seat*

Oneida County (cont'd)

Income 2000: per capita $18,516; median household $35,909; **Pop below poverty level:** 13%. ***Personal per capita income 2000-2003:** $24,099-$25,126.

Unemployment 2004: 5.2%. **Change from 2000:** +0.6%. **Median travel time to work:** 20.1 minutes. **Working outside county of residence:** 11.7%.

Cities with pop over 10,000: Utica 🏛 (59,684); Rome (34,551).

ONONDAGA COUNTY

401 Montgomery St Rm 200   **Ph:** 315-435-2226
Syracuse, NY 13202   **Fax:** 315-435-3455
www.ongov.net

In north-central NY, southwest of Rome; organized Mar 5, 1794. **Name Origin:** For the lake, named for the Onondaga Indian tribe, one of the Five Nations of the Iroquois; name probably means 'hill people.'

Area (sq mi): 805.69 (land 780.29; water 25.4). **Pop per sq mi:** 587.

Pop 2005: 458,053. **State rank:** 11. **Pop change:** 2000-20005 -0.1%; 1990-2000 -2.3%. **Pop 2000:** 458,336 (White 83.7%; Black or African American 9.4%; Hispanic or Latino 2.4%; Asian 2.1%; Other 3.8%). **Foreign born:** 5.7%. **Median age:** 36.3.

Income 2000: per capita $21,336; median household $40,847; **Pop below poverty level:** 12.2%. ***Personal per capita income 2000-2003:** $28,737-$30,372.

Unemployment 2004: 5.1%. **Change from 2000:** +0.9%. **Median travel time to work:** 19.3 minutes. **Working outside county of residence:** 5.9%.

Cities with pop over 10,000: Syracuse 🏛 (143,101).

ONTARIO COUNTY

20 Ontario St   **Ph:** 585-396-4200
Canandaigua, NY 14424   **Fax:** 585-393-2951
www.co.ontario.ny.us

In west-central NY, southeast of Rochester, organized Jan 27, 1789 from Montgomery County. **Name Origin:** For Lake Ontario.

Area (sq mi): 662.43 (land 644.38; water 18.05). **Pop per sq mi:** 162.1.

Pop 2005: 104,461. **State rank:** 27. **Pop change:** 2000-20005 +4.2%; 1990-2000 +5.4%. **Pop 2000:** 100,224 (White 94%; Black or African American 2.1%; Hispanic or Latino 2.1%; Asian 0.7%; Other 2.2%). **Foreign born:** 2.7%. **Median age:** 37.9.

Income 2000: per capita $21,533; median household $44,579; **Pop below poverty level:** 7.3%. ***Personal per capita income 2000-2003:** $28,151-$28,798.

Unemployment 2004: 5%. **Change from 2000:** +0.7%. **Median travel time to work:** 23.2 minutes. **Working outside county of residence:** 38.2%.

Cities with pop over 10,000: Geneva (13,558); Canandaigua 🏛 (11,363).

ORANGE COUNTY

255 Main St   **Ph:** 845-291-2700
Goshen, NY 10924   **Fax:** 845-291-2724
www.co.orange.ny.us

In southeastern NY, southwest of Poughkeepsie; original county, organized Nov 1, 1683. **Name Origin:** For William of Orange (1650-1702), later William III, king of England.

Area (sq mi): 838.55 (land 816.34; water 22.21). **Pop per sq mi:** 456.8.

Pop 2005: 372,893. **State rank:** 12. **Pop change:** 2000-20005 +9.2%; 1990-2000 +11%. **Pop 2000:** 341,367 (White 77.6%; Black or African American 8.1%; Hispanic or Latino 11.6%; Asian 1.5%; Other 6.7%). **Foreign born:** 8.4%. **Median age:** 34.7.

Income 2000: per capita $21,597; median household $52,058; **Pop below poverty level:** 10.5%. ***Personal per capita income 2000-2003:** $27,749-$28,903.

Unemployment 2004: 4.6%. **Change from 2000:** +1%. **Median travel time to work:** 32.5 minutes. **Working outside county of residence:** 34.5%.

Cities with pop over 10,000: Newburgh (28,551); Middletown (26,117); Kiryas Joel (17,651).

ORLEANS COUNTY

3 S Main St   **Ph:** 585-589-5334
Albion, NY 14411   **Fax:** 585-589-0181
www.orleansny.com

On northwestern border of NY, on Lake Ontario, west of Rochester; organized Nov 12, 1824 from Genesee County. **Name Origin:** For the French city of Orleans

Area (sq mi): 817.47 (land 391.4; water 426.07). **Pop per sq mi:** 110.9.

Pop 2005: 43,387. **State rank:** 54. **Pop change:** 2000-20005 -1.8%; 1990-2000 +5.6%. **Pop 2000:** 44,171 (White 87.3%; Black or African American 7.3%; Hispanic or Latino 3.9%; Asian 0.3%; Other 3.2%). **Foreign born:** 2.7%. **Median age:** 36.2.

Income 2000: per capita $16,457; median household $37,972; **Pop below poverty level:** 10.8%. ***Personal per capita income 2000-2003:** $20,388-$21,119.

Unemployment 2004: 6.5%. **Change from 2000:** +1%. **Median travel time to work:** 25.7 minutes. **Working outside county of residence:** 49%.

Cities with pop over 10,000: None.

OSWEGO COUNTY

46 E Bridge St   **Ph:** 315-349-8385
Oswego, NY 13126   **Fax:** 315-349-8383
www.co.oswego.ny.us/

In northwestern NY on Lake Ontario, north of Syracuse; organized Mar 1, 1816 from Oneida and Onondage counties. **Name Origin:** For the Oswego River, which runs through its western part; from Iroquoian *osh-we-go*, probably 'outpouring,' in reference to the mouth of the Oswego River where it empties into Lake Ontario, also translated 'the place where the valley widens.'

Area (sq mi): 1312.18 (land 953.3; water 358.88). **Pop per sq mi:** 129.4.

*Source: Personal per capita income data are from the Bureau of Economic Analysis; per capita income data are from the Bureau of the Census. See Introduction for explanation of differences.

Oswego County (cont'd)

Pop 2005: 123,373. **State rank:** 24. **Pop change:** 2000-20005 +0.8%; 1990-2000 +0.5%. **Pop 2000:** 122,377 (White 96.5%; Black or African American 0.6%; Hispanic or Latino 1.3%; Asian 0.4%; Other 1.8%). **Foreign born:** 1.6%. **Median age:** 35.

Income 2000: per capita $16,853; median household $36,598; **Pop below poverty level:** 14%. *Personal per capita income 2000-2003: $21,578-$22,679.

Unemployment 2004: 6.9%. **Change from 2000:** +0.4%. **Median travel time to work:** 24.4 minutes. **Working outside county of residence:** 41%.

Cities with pop over 10,000: Oswego ⛪ (18,407), Fulton (11,643).

OTSEGO COUNTY
PO Box 710   **Ph:** 607-547-4275
Cooperstown, NY 13326   **Fax:** 607-547-7544
www.otsegocounty.com

In south-central NY, south of Utica; organized Feb 16, 1791 from Montgomery County. **Name Origin:** Iroquoian 'rock site' or 'place of the rock.'

Area (sq mi): 1015.1 (land 1002.8; water 12.31). **Pop per sq mi:** 62.6.

Pop 2005: 62,746. **State rank:** 43. **Pop change:** 2000-20005 +1.7%; 1990-2000 +1.9%. **Pop 2000:** 61,676 (White 94.6%; Black or African American 1.7%; Hispanic or Latino 1.9%; Asian 0.6%; Other 1.8%). **Foreign born:** 2.3%. **Median age:** 37.1.

Income 2000: per capita $16,806; median household $33,444; **Pop below poverty level:** 14.9%. *Personal per capita income 2000-2003: $21,857-$22,679.

Unemployment 2004: 4.6%. **Change from 2000:** +0.3%. **Median travel time to work:** 22.4 minutes. **Working outside county of residence:** 23.1%.

Cities with pop over 10,000: Oneonta (13,099).

PUTNAM COUNTY
40 Gleneida Ave   **Ph:** 845-225-3641
Carmel, NY 10512   **Fax:** 845-228-0231
www.putnamcountyny.com

In southeastern NY, southeast of Poughkeepsie; organized Jun 12, 1812 from Dutchess County. **Name Origin:** For Israel Putnam (1718-90), MA general and American commander at the Battle of Bunker Hill.

Area (sq mi): 246.25 (land 231.28; water 14.97). **Pop per sq mi:** 434.6.

Pop 2005: 100,507. **State rank:** 28. **Pop change:** 2000-20005 +5%; 1990-2000 +14.1%. **Pop 2000:** 95,745 (White 89.8%; Black or African American 1.6%; Hispanic or Latino 6.2%; Asian 1.2%; Other 3.2%). **Foreign born:** 8.8%. **Median age:** 37.4.

Income 2000: per capita $30,127; median household $72,279; **Pop below poverty level:** 4.4%. *Personal per capita income 2000-2003: $38,879-$39,410.

Unemployment 2004: 3.9%. **Change from 2000:** +1.2%. **Median travel time to work:** 38.4 minutes. **Working outside county of residence:** 71.5%.

Cities with pop over 10,000: None.

QUEENS COUNTY
120-55 Queens Blvd   **Ph:** 718-286-3000
Kew Gardens, NY 11424
www.nyc.gov

In western end of Long Island, east of Brooklyn; original county, organized Nov 1, 1683. The county is coterminous with the borough of Queens, part of New York City. Includes the following areas; Astoria, Bay Ridge, Flushing, Forest Hills, Howard Beach, Jackson Heights, and Ozone Park. **Name Origin:** For Queen Catharine of Braganza (1638-1705), wife of King Charles II of England.

Area (sq mi): 178.28 (land 109.24; water 69.04). **Pop per sq mi:** 20,520.

Pop 2005: 2,241,600. **State rank:** 2. **Pop change:** 2000-20005 +0.5%; 1990-2000 +14.2%. **Pop 2000:** 2,229,379 (White 32.9%; Black or African American 20%; Hispanic or Latino 25%; Asian 17.6%; Other 18.4%). **Foreign born:** 46.1%. **Median age:** 35.4.

Income 2000: per capita $19,222; median household $42,439; **Pop below poverty level:** 14.6%. *Personal per capita income 2000-2003: $27,921-$29,227.

Unemployment 2004: 6.4%. **Change from 2000:** +1.3%. **Median travel time to work:** 42.2 minutes. **Working outside county of residence:** 60.5%.

Cities with pop over 10,000: Part of New York City.

RENSSELAER COUNTY
1600 7th Ave   **Ph:** 518-270-2900
Troy, NY 12180   **Fax:** 518-270-2961
www.rensco.com

On central eastern border of NY, east of Albany; organized Feb 7, 1791 from Albany County. **Name Origin:** For Kiliaen Van Rensselaer (1595-1644), one of the early patrons of the Dutch New Netherlands territories and a founder of the Dutch West India Company. Much of the territory of the county had been granted him by patent in 1630.

Area (sq mi): 665.39 (land 653.96; water 11.43). **Pop per sq mi:** 237.4.

Pop 2005: 155,251. **State rank:** 21. **Pop change:** 2000-20005 +1.8%; 1990-2000 -1.2%. **Pop 2000:** 152,538 (White 90.2%; Black or African American 4.7%; Hispanic or Latino 2.1%; Asian 1.7%; Other 2.4%). **Foreign born:** 3.7%. **Median age:** 36.7.

Income 2000: per capita $21,095; median household $42,905; **Pop below poverty level:** 9.5%. *Personal per capita income 2000-2003: $27,337-$29,022.

Unemployment 2004: 4.6%. **Change from 2000:** +0.8%. **Median travel time to work:** 23.7 minutes. **Working outside county of residence:** 55.8%.

Cities with pop over 10,000: Troy ⛪ (48,162).

RICHMOND COUNTY
130 Stuyvesant Pl   **Ph:** 718-390-5393
Staten Island, NY 10301   **Fax:** 718-390-5269
www.nyc.gov

Coterminous with Staten Island in New York Bay between Long

Richmond County (cont'd)

Island and New Jersey; original county, organized Nov 1, 1683. The county is coterminous with the borough of Staten Island, part of New York City. **Name Origin:** For Charles Lennox (1672-1723), first Duke of Richmond, son of King Charles II of England (1630-85).

Area (sq mi): 102.5 (land 58.48; water 44.02). **Pop per sq mi:** 7944.1.

Pop 2005: 464,573. **State rank:** 10. **Pop change:** 2000-20005 +4.7%; 1990-2000 +17.1%. **Pop 2000:** 443,728 (White 71.3%; Black or African American 9.7%; Hispanic or Latino 12.1%; Asian 5.7%; Other 7%). **Foreign born:** 16.4%. **Median age:** 35.9.

Income 2000: per capita $23,905; median household $55,039; **Pop below poverty level:** 10%. ***Personal per capita income 2000-2003:** $34,184-$35,443.

Unemployment 2004: 6.3%. **Change from 2000:** +1.5%. **Median travel time to work:** 43.9 minutes. **Working outside county of residence:** 54.9%.

Cities with pop over 10,000: Part of New York City.

ROCKLAND COUNTY

11 New Hempstead Rd   **Ph:** 845-638-5100
New City, NY 10956   **Fax:** 845-638-5675
www.co.rockland.ny.us

In southeastern NY, northwest of NYC; organized Feb 23, 1798 from Orange County. **Name Origin:** For the rugged land and the Palisades on the Hudson River, which form its eastern border.

Area (sq mi): 199.34 (land 174.22; water 25.12). **Pop per sq mi:** 1681.3.

Pop 2005: 292,916. **State rank:** 15. **Pop change:** 2000-20005 +2.1%; 1990-2000 +8%. **Pop 2000:** 286,753 (White 71.7%; Black or African American 11%; Hispanic or Latino 10.2%; Asian 5.5%; Other 6.6%). **Foreign born:** 19.1%. **Median age:** 36.2.

Income 2000: per capita $28,082; median household $67,971; **Pop below poverty level:** 9.5%. ***Personal per capita income 2000-2003:** $41,138-$41,661.

Unemployment 2004: 4.4%. **Change from 2000:** +1.3%. **Median travel time to work:** 32.6 minutes. **Working outside county of residence:** 45.6%.

Cities with pop over 10,000: Spring Valley (25,542); Suffern (10,984); West Haverstraw (10,314); Haverstraw (10,136).

SAINT LAWRENCE COUNTY

48 Court St   **Ph:** 315-379-2237
Canton, NY 13617   **Fax:** 315-379-2302
www.co.st-lawrence.ny.us

On northwestern border of NY, north of Watertown; organized Mar 3, 1802 from Clinton, Montgomery, and Herkimer counties. **Name Origin:** For the Saint Lawrence River, which forms its western boundary.

Area (sq mi): 2821.48 (land 2685.6; water 135.88). **Pop per sq mi:** 41.5.

Pop 2005: 111,380. **State rank:** 26. **Pop change:** 2000-20005 - 0.5%; 1990-2000 +0%. **Pop 2000:** 111,931 (White 93.6%; Black

or African American 2.4%; Hispanic or Latino 1.8%; Asian 0.7%; Other 2.4%). **Foreign born:** 3.4%. **Median age:** 35.4.

Income 2000: per capita $15,728; median household $32,356; **Pop below poverty level:** 16.9%. ***Personal per capita income 2000-2003:** $19,893-$20,731.

Unemployment 2004: 6.9%. **Change from 2000:** -0.7%. **Median travel time to work:** 20.2 minutes. **Working outside county of residence:** 7.8%.

Cities with pop over 10,000: Ogdensburg (11,486); Massena (10,911).

SARATOGA COUNTY

40 McMaster St   **Ph:** 518-885-5381
Ballston Spa, NY 12020   **Fax:** 518-884-4726
www.co.saratoga.ny.us

In east-central NY, north of Albany; organized Feb 7, 1791 from Albany County. **Name Origin:** Of Indian origin; possibly from Mohawk word meaning 'springs from the hillside', or from Iroquois for 'beaver place.'

Area (sq mi): 843.71 (land 811.84; water 31.87). **Pop per sq mi:** 264.7.

Pop 2005: 214,859. **State rank:** 18. **Pop change:** 2000-20005 +7.1%; 1990-2000 +10.7%. **Pop 2000:** 200,635 (White 95.1%; Black or African American 1.4%; Hispanic or Latino 1.4%; Asian 1%; Other 1.6%). **Foreign born:** 3.1%. **Median age:** 36.9.

Income 2000: per capita $23,945; median household $49,460; **Pop below poverty level:** 5.7%. ***Personal per capita income 2000-2003:** $30,649-$31,689.

Unemployment 2004: 3.8%. **Change from 2000:** +0.8%. **Median travel time to work:** 25 minutes. **Working outside county of residence:** 50.5%.

Cities with pop over 10,000: Saratoga Springs (27,686).

SCHENECTADY COUNTY

620 State St   **Ph:** 518-388-4222
Schenectady, NY 12305   **Fax:** 518-388-4224
www.schenectadycounty.com

In east-central NY, northwest of Albany; organized Mar 7, 1809 from Albany County. **Name Origin:** For the city, its county seat.

Area (sq mi): 209.62 (land 206.1; water 3.52). **Pop per sq mi:** 723.3.

Pop 2005: 149,078. **State rank:** 22. **Pop change:** 2000-20005 +1.7%; 1990-2000 -1.8%. **Pop 2000:** 146,555 (White 86.3%; Black or African American 6.8%; Hispanic or Latino 3.2%; Asian 2%; Other 3.4%). **Foreign born:** 5.3%. **Median age:** 38.6.

Income 2000: per capita $21,992; median household $41,739; **Pop below poverty level:** 10.9%. ***Personal per capita income 2000-2003:** $29,184-$31,695.

Unemployment 2004: 4.4%. **Change from 2000:** +1.4%. **Median travel time to work:** 21.8 minutes. **Working outside county of residence:** 43.9%.

Cities with pop over 10,000: Schenectady 🏛 (61,125).

*Source: Personal per capita income data are from the Bureau of Economic Analysis; per capita income data are from the Bureau of the Census. See Introduction for explanation of differences.

498

SCHOHARIE COUNTY
284 Main St
Schoharie, NY 12157
www.schohariecounty-ny.gov

Ph: 518-295-8347
Fax: 518-295-8482

In south-central NY, west of Albany; organized Apr 6, 1795 from Albany and Otsego counties. **Name Origin:** For the Schoharie Creek, which runs through it; from Iroquoian for 'driftwood.' Variants include *skoharie, towasschoher, shoary, skohary,* and *schughhorre.*

Area (sq mi): 626.36 (land 622.02; water 4.34). **Pop per sq mi:** 51.9.

Pop 2005: 32,277. **State rank:** 58. **Pop change:** 2000-20005 +2.2%; 1990-2000 -0.9%. **Pop 2000:** 31,582 (White 95.3%; Black or African American 1.3%; Hispanic or Latino 1.9%; Asian 0.4%; Other 1.7%). **Foreign born:** 2.4%. **Median age:** 38.

Income 2000: per capita $17,778; median household $36,585; **Pop below poverty level:** 11.4%. ***Personal per capita income 2000-2003:** $23,343-$23,633.

Unemployment 2004: 5.4%. **Change from 2000:** +1.2%. **Median travel time to work:** 28.5 minutes. **Working outside county of residence:** 40.5%.

Cities with pop over 10,000: None.

SCHUYLER COUNTY
105 9th St
Watkins Glen, NY 14891
www.schuylercounty.us

Ph: 607-535-8133
Fax: 607-535-8130

In north-central NY, southeast of Rochester; organized Apr 17, 1854 from Tompkins, Steuben, and Chemung counties. **Name Origin:** For Gen. Philip John Schuyler (1733-1804), an officer in the Revolutionary War, NY legislator, and U.S. senator (1789-91; 1797-98).

Area (sq mi): 342.22 (land 328.71; water 13.51). **Pop per sq mi:** 58.8.

Pop 2005: 19,342. **State rank:** 61. **Pop change:** 2000-20005 +0.6%; 1990-2000 +3%. **Pop 2000:** 19,224 (White 95.8%; Black or African American 1.5%; Hispanic or Latino 1.2%; Asian 0.3%; Other 1.8%). **Foreign born:** 1.2%. **Median age:** 38.8.

Income 2000: per capita $17,039; median household $36,010; **Pop below poverty level:** 11.8%. ***Personal per capita income 2000-2003:** $21,710-$22,379.

Unemployment 2004: 5.9%. **Change from 2000:** -0.8%. **Median travel time to work:** 25.4 minutes. **Working outside county of residence:** 54.8%.

Cities with pop over 10,000: None.

SENECA COUNTY
1 DiPronio Dr
Waterloo, NY 13165
www.co.seneca.ny.us

Ph: 315-539-1770
Fax: 315-539-3789

In north-central NY, southeast of Rochester; organized Mar 24, 1804 from Cayuga County. **Name Origin:** For the Seneca Indians, one of the Five Nations of the Iroquois.

Area (sq mi): 390.51 (land 324.91; water 65.6). **Pop per sq mi:** 107.3.

Pop 2005: 34,855. **State rank:** 57. **Pop change:** 2000-20005 +4.5%; 1990-2000 -1%. **Pop 2000:** 33,342 (White 94%; Black or African American 2.3%; Hispanic or Latino 2%; Asian 0.7%; Other 2%). **Foreign born:** 2.4%. **Median age:** 38.2.

Income 2000: per capita $17,630; median household $37,140; **Pop below poverty level:** 11.5%. ***Personal per capita income 2000-2003:** $23,206-$24,080.

Unemployment 2004: 5.3%. **Change from 2000:** +0.9%. **Median travel time to work:** 22.5 minutes. **Working outside county of residence:** 43.8%.

Cities with pop over 10,000: None.

STEUBEN COUNTY
3 E Pulteny Sq
Bath, NY 14810
www.steubencony.org

Ph: 607-776-9631
Fax: 607-664-2158

On central southern border of NY, south of Rochester; organized Mar 17, 1796 from Ontario County. **Name Origin:** For Baron Friedrich Wilhelm von Steuben (1730-94), Prussian soldier and inspector general of the Continental Army during the American Revolution.

Area (sq mi): 1404.1 (land 1392.64; water 11.45). **Pop per sq mi:** 70.8.

Pop 2005: 98,632. **State rank:** 30. **Pop change:** 2000-20005 -0.1%; 1990-2000 -0.4%. **Pop 2000:** 98,726 (White 95.9%; Black or African American 1.4%; Hispanic or Latino 0.8%; Asian 0.9%; Other 1.3%). **Foreign born:** 1.9%. **Median age:** 38.2.

Income 2000: per capita $18,197; median household $35,479; **Pop below poverty level:** 13.2%. ***Personal per capita income 2000-2003:** $28,765-$25,919.

Unemployment 2004: 6.4%. **Change from 2000:** +0.7%. **Median travel time to work:** 21.6 minutes. **Working outside county of residence:** 22.1%.

Cities with pop over 10,000: Corning (10,608).

SUFFOLK COUNTY
310 Center Dr
Riverhead, NY 11901
www.co.suffolk.ny.us

Ph: 631-852-2000
Fax: 631-852-2004

On eastern end of Long Island, NY; original county, organized Nov 1, 1683. **Name Origin:** For Suffolk County, England.

Area (sq mi): 2373.07 (land 912.2; water 1460.87). **Pop per sq mi:** 1616.9.

Pop 2005: 1,474,927. **State rank:** 4. **Pop change:** 2000-20005 +3.9%; 1990-2000 +7.4%. **Pop 2000:** 1,419,369 (White 78.8%; Black or African American 6.9%; Hispanic or Latino 10.5%; Asian 2.4%; Other 6.1%). **Foreign born:** 11.2%. **Median age:** 36.5.

Income 2000: per capita $26,577; median household $65,288; **Pop below poverty level:** 6%. ***Personal per capita income 2000-2003:** $37,136-$37,901.

Unemployment 2004: 4.7%. **Change from 2000:** +1.2%. **Median travel time to work:** 31.8 minutes. **Working outside county of residence:** 26.6%.

Cities with pop over 10,000: Lindenhurst (28,426); Babylon (12,736); Patchogue (12,026); Lake Grove (10,646).

County Seat

SULLIVAN COUNTY

100 North St   **Ph:** 845-794-3000
Monticello, NY 12701   **Fax:** 845-794-6928
www.co.sullivan.ny.us

In south-central NY, west of Poughkeepsie; organized Mar 27, 1809 from Ulster County. **Name Origin:** For Gen. John Sullivan (1740-95), Revolutionary War officer, member of the Continental Congress (1780-81), and president of NH (1786, 1787, 1789).

Area (sq mi): 996.85 (land 969.71; water 27.14). **Pop per sq mi:** 78.9.

Pop 2005: 76,539. **State rank:** 36. **Pop change:** 2000-20005 +3.5%; 1990-2000 +6.8%. **Pop 2000:** 73,966 (White 80.1%; Black or African American 8.5%; Hispanic or Latino 9.2%; Asian 1.1%; Other 5.1%). **Foreign born:** 7.9%. **Median age:** 38.8.

Income 2000: per capita $18,892; median household $36,998; **Pop below poverty level:** 16.3%. *Personal per capita income 2000-2003: $25,663-$27,247.

Unemployment 2004: 5.3%. **Change from 2000:** +0.4%. **Median travel time to work:** 29.3 minutes. **Working outside county of residence:** 32.6%.

Cities with pop over 10,000: None.

TIOGA COUNTY

PO Box 307   **Ph:** 607-687-8660
Owego, NY 13827   **Fax:** 607-687-8686
www.tiogacountyny.com

On central southern border of NY, south of Ithaca; organized Feb 16, 1791 from Montgomery County. **Name Origin:** For the Iroquoian town on the Susquehanna River near Athens, PA, just south of the county line; from Iroquoian probably meaning 'place between two points' or 'at the forks.'

Area (sq mi): 522.91 (land 518.69; water 4.21). **Pop per sq mi:** 99.2.

Pop 2005: 51,475. **State rank:** 47. **Pop change:** 2000-20005 -0.6%; 1990-2000 -1.1%. **Pop 2000:** 51,784 (White 96.9%; Black or African American 0.5%; Hispanic or Latino 1%; Asian 0.6%; Other 1.3%). **Foreign born:** 1.7%. **Median age:** 38.

Income 2000: per capita $18,673; median household $40,266; **Pop below poverty level:** 8.4%. *Personal per capita income 2000-2003: $23,947-$24,547.

Unemployment 2004: 5.2%. **Change from 2000:** +1%. **Median travel time to work:** 24.8 minutes. **Working outside county of residence:** 59%.

Cities with pop over 10,000: None.

TOMPKINS COUNTY

320 N Tioga St   **Ph:** 607-274-5431
Ithaca, NY 14850   **Fax:** 607-274-5445
www.co.tompkins.ny.us

In south-central NY, northeast of Elmira; organized Apr 7, 1817 from Cayuga and Seneca counties. **Name Origin:** For Daniel D. Tompkins (1774-1825), associate justice of the NY supreme court (1804-07), governor (1807-17) and U.S. vice president (1817-25).

Area (sq mi): 491.63 (land 476.05; water 15.57). **Pop per sq mi:** 210.1.

Pop 2005: 100,018. **State rank:** 29. **Pop change:** 2000-20005 +3.6%; 1990-2000 +2.6%. **Pop 2000:** 96,501 (White 83.8%; Black or African American 3.6%; Hispanic or Latino 3.1%; Asian 7.2%; Other 3.7%). **Foreign born:** 10.5%. **Median age:** 28.6.

Income 2000: per capita $19,659; median household $37,272; **Pop below poverty level:** 17.6%. *Personal per capita income 2000-2003: $24,038-$26,042.

Unemployment 2004: 3.6%. **Change from 2000:** +1%. **Median travel time to work:** 17.8 minutes. **Working outside county of residence:** 8.6%.

Cities with pop over 10,000: Ithaca 🏛 (29,952).

ULSTER COUNTY

PO Box 1800   **Ph:** 845-340-3288
Kingston, NY 12402   **Fax:** 845-340-3299
www.co.ulster.ny.us

In southeastern NY, west of Poughkeepsie; original county, organized Nov 1, 1683. **Name Origin:** For Ulster, Ireland, the earldom of the Duke of York, specifically honoring James Stuart (1633-1701), later James II, king of England.

Area (sq mi): 1160.76 (land 1126.48; water 34.28). **Pop per sq mi:** 162.2.

Pop 2005: 182,693. **State rank:** 20. **Pop change:** 2000-20005 +2.8%; 1990-2000 +7.5%. **Pop 2000:** 177,749 (White 85.5%; Black or African American 5.4%; Hispanic or Latino 6.2%; Asian 1.2%; Other 4.5%). **Foreign born:** 5.9%. **Median age:** 38.2.

Income 2000: per capita $20,846; median household $42,551; **Pop below poverty level:** 11.4%. *Personal per capita income 2000-2003: $25,550-$26,871.

Unemployment 2004: 4.8%. **Change from 2000:** +1.3%. **Median travel time to work:** 26.9 minutes. **Working outside county of residence:** 33.5%.

Cities with pop over 10,000: Kingston 🏛 (23,219).

WARREN COUNTY

1340 State Rt 9   **Ph:** 518-761-6429
Lake George, NY 12845   **Fax:** 518-761-6551
www.co.warren.ny.us

In northeastern NY, north of Saratoga; organized Mar 12, 1813 from Washington County. **Name Origin:** For Joseph Warren (1741-75), Revolutionary War patriot and member of the Continental Congress who dispatched Paul Revere (1735-1818) on his famous ride.

Area (sq mi): 931.66 (land 869.29; water 62.37). **Pop per sq mi:** 75.4.

Pop 2005: 65,548. **State rank:** 38. **Pop change:** 2000-20005 +3.5%; 1990-2000 +6.9%. **Pop 2000:** 63,303 (White 96.8%; Black or African American 0.6%; Hispanic or Latino 1%; Asian 0.5%; Other 1.3%). **Foreign born:** 2.4%. **Median age:** 39.

Income 2000: per capita $20,727; median household $39,198; **Pop below poverty level:** 9.7%. *Personal per capita income 2000-2003: $26,921-$28,384.

Unemployment 2004: 4.9%. **Change from 2000:** +0.1%. **Median travel time to work:** 21.4 minutes. **Working outside county of residence:** 27.5%.

Source: Personal per capita income data are from the Bureau of Economic Analysis; per capita income data are from the Bureau of the Census. See Introduction for explanation of differences.

Warren County (cont'd)

Cities with pop over 10,000: Glens Falls (14,166).

WASHINGTON COUNTY

383 Broadway Bldg A   **Ph:** 518-746-2170
Fort Edward, NY 12828   **Fax:** 518-746-2177
www.co.washington.ny.us

On central eastern border of NY, east of Glens Falls; organized as Charlotte County Mar 12, 1772 (prior to statehood) from Albany County. **Name Origin:** For George Washington (1732-99), American patriot and first U.S. president. Name changed Apr 2, 1784 from Charlotte, which had been given to honor the wife of King George III of England (1738-1820).

Area (sq mi): 845.84 (land 835.44; water 10.4). **Pop per sq mi:** 75.4.

Pop 2005: 63,024. **State rank:** 42. **Pop change:** 2000-20005 +3.2%; 1990-2000 +2.9%. **Pop 2000:** 61,042 (White 94%; Black or African American 2.9%; Hispanic or Latino 2%; Asian 0.3%; Other 1.8%). **Foreign born:** 1.9%. **Median age:** 37.5.

Income 2000: per capita $17,958; median household $37,668; **Pop below poverty level:** 9.4%. ***Personal per capita income 2000-2003:** $21,365-$22,031.

Unemployment 2004: 4.7%. **Change from 2000:** +0.8%. **Median travel time to work:** 24.4 minutes. **Working outside county of residence:** 50.5%.

Cities with pop over 10,000: None.

WAYNE COUNTY

26 Church St   **Ph:** 315-946-5400
Lyons, NY 14489   **Fax:** 315-946-5407
www.co.wayne.ny.us

On central western border of NY on Lake Ontario, east of Rochester; organized Apr 11, 1823 from Ontario and Seneca counties. **Name Origin:** For Gen. Anthony Wayne (1745-1796), PA soldier and statesman, nicknamed 'Mad Anthony' for his daring during the American Revolution.

Area (sq mi): 1384.14 (land 604.21; water 779.93). **Pop per sq mi:** 154.9.

Pop 2005: 93,609. **State rank:** 31. **Pop change:** 2000-20005 -0.2%; 1990-2000 +5.2%. **Pop 2000:** 93,765 (White 92.5%; Black or African American 3.2%; Hispanic or Latino 2.4%; Asian 0.5%; Other 2.5%). **Foreign born:** 2.3%. **Median age:** 36.9.

Income 2000: per capita $19,258; median household $44,157; **Pop below poverty level:** 8.6%. ***Personal per capita income 2000-2003:** $25,035-$25,806.

Unemployment 2004: 5.6%. **Change from 2000:** +0.3%. **Median travel time to work:** 24.6 minutes. **Working outside county of residence:** 47.6%.

Cities with pop over 10,000: None.

WESTCHESTER COUNTY

110 Dr ML King Jr Blvd   **Ph:** 914-995-3080
White Plains, NY 10601
www.co.westchester.ny.us

In southwestern NY, north of New York City; original county, organized Nov 1, 1683. **Name Origin:** For the town and county of Chester in England.

Area (sq mi): 500.08 (land 432.82; water 67.26). **Pop per sq mi:** 2173.7.

Pop 2005: 940,807. **State rank:** 7. **Pop change:** 2000-20005 +1.9%; 1990-2000 +5.6%. **Pop 2000:** 923,459 (White 64.1%; Black or African American 14.2%; Hispanic or Latino 15.6%; Asian 4.5%; Other 9.9%) **Foreign born:** 22.2%. **Median age:** 37.6.

Income 2000: per capita $36,726; median household $63,582; **Pop below poverty level:** 8.8%. ***Personal per capita income 2000-2003:** $55,066-$55,557.

Unemployment 2004: 4.5%. **Change from 2000:** +1%. **Median travel time to work:** 32.7 minutes. **Working outside county of residence:** 37.1%.

Cities with pop over 10,000: 14 (see page 37 for cities).

WYOMING COUNTY

143 N Main St   **Ph:** 585-786-8810
Warsaw, NY 14569   **Fax:** 585-786-3703
www.wyomingco.net

In northwestern NY, southeast of Buffalo, organized May 19, 1841 from Genesee County. **Name Origin:** From an Indian word *maughwauwame* 'large meadows,' originally applied to a valley in northeastern PA, but made famous in the popular poem 'Gertrude of Wyoming,' published in 1809 by British poet Thomas Campbell (1777-1844).

Area (sq mi): 596.44 (land 592.91; water 3.53). **Pop per sq mi:** 72.

Pop 2005: 42,693. **State rank:** 55. **Pop change:** 2000-20005 -1.7%; 1990-2000 +2.2%. **Pop 2000:** 43,424 (White 90.6%; Black or African American 5.5%; Hispanic or Latino 2.9%; Asian 0.4%; Other 2.3%). **Foreign born:** 2.3%. **Median age:** 36.7.

Income 2000: per capita $17,248; median household $39,895; **Pop below poverty level:** 8.4%. ***Personal per capita income 2000-2003:** $19,758-$21,963.

Unemployment 2004: 6.3%. **Change from 2000:** +0.9%. **Median travel time to work:** 25.6 minutes. **Working outside county of residence:** 45.7%.

Cities with pop over 10,000: None.

YATES COUNTY

417 Liberty St   **Ph:** 315-536-5120
Penn Yan, NY 14527   **Fax:** 315-536-5545
www.yatescounty.org

In northwestern NY, southeast of Rochester; organized Feb 5, 1823 from Ontario County. **Name Origin:** For Joseph Christopher Yates (1768-1837), NY supreme court justice (1808-22) and governor (1823-24) at the time of the county's creation.

Area (sq mi): 375.76 (land 338.24; water 37.52). **Pop per sq mi:** 73.2.

Pop 2005: 24,756. **State rank:** 60. **Pop change:** 2000-20005 +0.5%; 1990-2000 +7.9%. **Pop 2000:** 24,621 (White 97.4%; Black or African American 0.6%; Hispanic or Latino 0.9%; Asian 0.3%; Other 1.2%). **Foreign born:** 2.3%. **Median age:** 37.9.

🏛 County Seat

Yates County (cont'd)

Income 2000: per capita $16,781; median household $34,640; **Pop below poverty level:** 13.1%. ***Personal per capita income 2000-2003:** $20,404-$20,686.

Unemployment 2004: 4.6%. **Change from 2000:** +1.1%. **Median travel time to work:** 23.6 minutes. **Working outside county of residence:** 40.8%.

Cities with pop over 10,000: None.

*Source: Personal per capita income data are from the Bureau of Economic Analysis; per capita income data are from the Bureau of the Census. See Introduction for explanation of differences.

502

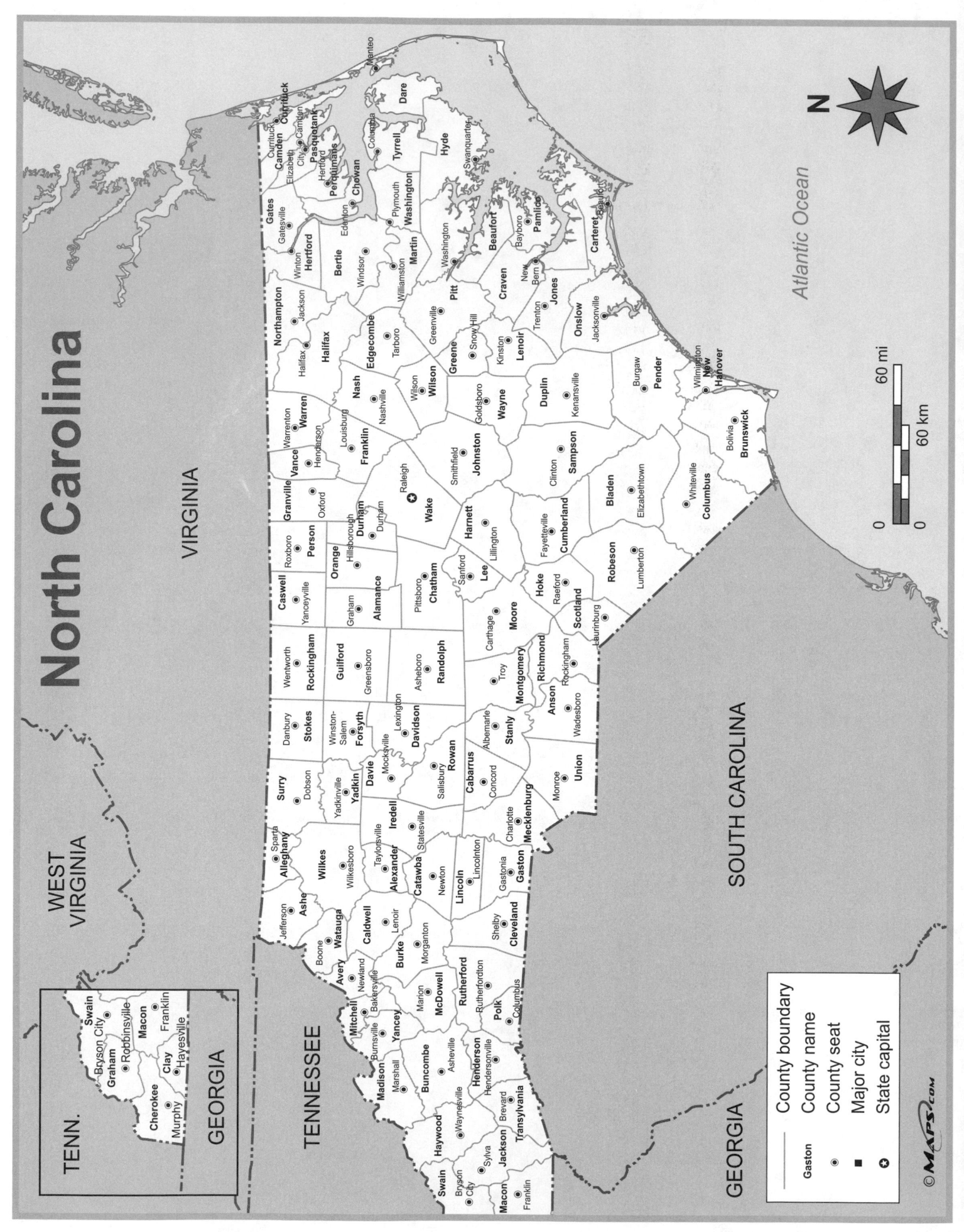

North Carolina

North Carolina

NORTH CAROLINA STATE INFORMATION
www.ncgov.com **Ph:** 919-733-1110

Area (sq mi): 53,818.51 (land 48,710.88; water 5107.63). **Pop per sq mi:** 178.3.

Pop 2005: 8,683,242. **Pop change:** 2000-20005 +7.9%; 1990-2000 +21.4%. **Pop 2000:** 8,049,313 (White 70.2%; Black or African American 21.6%; Hispanic or Latino 4.7%; Asian 1.4%; Other 4.8%, including 1.2% American Indian/Alaska Native). **Foreign born:** 5.3%. **Median age:** 35.3.

Income 2000: per capita $20,307; median household $39,184; **Pop below poverty level:** 12.3%. ***Personal per capita income 2000-2003:** $27,068 $28,071.

Unemployment 2004: 5.5%. **Change from 2000:** +1.8%. **Median travel time to work:** 24 minutes. **Working outside county of residence:** 26.4%.

ALAMANCE COUNTY
124 W Elm St **Ph:** 336-228-1312
Graham, NC 27253 **Fax:** 336-570-6788
www.alamance-nc.com

In north-central NC, west of Durham; organized Jan 29, 1849 from Orange County. **Name Origin:** For Great Alamance Creek, which flows through the county, from an Indian word of uncertain meaning; or for the Battle of Alamance (May 6, 1771).

Area (sq mi): 434.77 (land 429.99; water 4.78). **Pop per sq mi:** 326.8.

Pop 2005: 140,533. **State rank:** 18. **Pop change:** 2000-20005 +7.4%; 1990-2000 +20.9%. **Pop 2000:** 130,800 (White 72.5%; Black or African American 18.8%; Hispanic or Latino 6.8%; Asian 0.9%; Other 4.8%). **Foreign born:** 6.3%. **Median age:** 36.3.

Income 2000: per capita $19,391; median household $39,168; **Pop below poverty level:** 11.1%. ***Personal per capita income 2000-2003:** $26,097-$26,030.

Unemployment 2004: 6.2%. **Change from 2000:** +0.5%. **Median travel time to work:** 21.6 minutes. **Working outside county of residence:** 25.1%.

Cities with pop over 10,000: Burlington (46,645); Graham 🏛 (13,494).

ALEXANDER COUNTY
621 Liledoun Rd **Ph:** 828-632-9332
Taylorsville, NC 28681 **Fax:** 828-632-0059
www.co.alexander.nc.us

In west-central NC, northwest of Charlotte; established Jan 15, 1847 from Iredell, Caldwell, and Wilks counties. **Name Origin:** For William Julius Alexander (1797-1857), NC legislator.

Area (sq mi): 263.14 (land 260.18; water 2.95). **Pop per sq mi:** 136.4.

Pop 2005: 35,492. **State rank:** 65. **Pop change:** 2000-20005 +5.6%; 1990-2000 +22%. **Pop 2000:** 33,603 (White 91%; Black or African American 4.6%; Hispanic or Latino 2.5%; Asian 1%; Other 2.2%). **Foreign born:** 2.4%. **Median age:** 36.6.

Income 2000: per capita $18,507; median household $38,684; **Pop below poverty level:** 8.5%. ***Personal per capita income 2000-2003:** $24,246-$24,486.

Unemployment 2004: 6%. **Change from 2000:** -0.2%. **Median travel time to work:** 22.9 minutes. **Working outside county of residence:** 49.2%.

Cities with pop over 10,000: None.

ALLEGHANY COUNTY
PO Box 61 **Ph:** 336-372-8949
Sparta, NC 28675 **Fax:** 336-372-4899
www.alleghanycounty-nc.gov

On the northwestern border of NC, northwest of Winston-Salem; organized 1859 from Ashe County. **Name Origin:** For the Allegheny River, with a variant spelling.

Area (sq mi): 235.52 (land 234.65; water 0.87). **Pop per sq mi:** 46.5.

Pop 2005: 10,900. **State rank:** 94. **Pop change:** 2000-20005 +2.1%; 1990-2000 +11.3%. **Pop 2000:** 10,677 (White 93%; Black or African American 1.2%; Hispanic or Latino 5%; Asian 0.2%; Other 3%). **Foreign born:** 4.1%. **Median age:** 43.

Income 2000: per capita $17,691; median household $29,244; **Pop below poverty level:** 17.2%. ***Personal per capita income 2000-2003:** $24,833-$24,023.

Unemployment 2004: 6.3%. **Change from 2000:** -2.2%. **Median travel time to work:** 24.1 minutes. **Working outside county of residence:** 22.5%.

Cities with pop over 10,000: None.

ANSON COUNTY
114 N Green St Courthouse Rm 30 **Ph:** 704-694-2796
Wadesboro, NC 28170 **Fax:** 704-694-7015
www.co.anson.nc.us

On the central-southern border of NC, southeast of Charlotte; organized Mar 17, 1749 (prior to statehood) from Bladen County. **Name Origin:** For George, Lord Anson (1697-1762), British admiral assigned to protect the Carolina coast from pirates.

🏛 *County Seat*

Anson County (cont'd)

Area (sq mi): 537.13 (land 531.57; water 5.56). **Pop per sq mi:** 48.

Pop 2005: 25,499. **State rank:** 73. **Pop change:** 2000-20005 +0.9%; 1990-2000 +7.7%. **Pop 2000:** 25,275 (White 49.2%; Black or African American 48.6%; Hispanic or Latino 0.8%; Asian 0.6%; Other 1.2%). **Foreign born:** 0.7%. **Median age:** 36.6.

Income 2000: per capita $14,853; median household $29,849; **Pop below poverty level:** 17.8%. ***Personal per capita income 2000-2003:** $21,033-$21,274.

Unemployment 2004: 8.7%. **Change from 2000:** -1.7%. **Median travel time to work:** 27.5 minutes. **Working outside county of residence:** 40.5%.

Cities with pop over 10,000: None.

ASHE COUNTY
150 Government Cir Suite 3100   **Ph:** 336-246-5641
Jefferson, NC 28640   **Fax:** 336-246-4276
www.ashechamber.com

In the northwest corner of NC; organized Nov 18, 1799 from Wilkes County. **Name Origin:** For Samuel Ashe (1725-1813), NC legislator, chief justice of NC (1777-95), and governor (1795-98).

Area (sq mi): 426.78 (land 426.13; water 0.65). **Pop per sq mi:** 59.5.

Pop 2005: 25,347. **State rank:** 74. **Pop change:** 2000-20005 +3.9%; 1990-2000 +9.8%. **Pop 2000:** 24,384 (White 96.1%; Black or African American 0.7%; Hispanic or Latino 2.4%; Asian 0.2%; Other 2%). **Foreign born:** 1.9%. **Median age:** 42.1.

Income 2000: per capita $16,429; median household $28,824; **Pop below poverty level:** 13.5%. ***Personal per capita income 2000-2003:** $23,200-$23,702.

Unemployment 2004: 5.5%. **Change from 2000:** -3.8%. **Median travel time to work:** 26.6 minutes. **Working outside county of residence:** 25.2%.

Cities with pop over 10,000: None.

AVERY COUNTY
PO Box 115   **Ph:** 828-733-2900
Newland, NC 28657   **Fax:** 828-733-8410
www.averycounty.com

On the northwestern border of NC, northeast of Asheville; organized Feb 23, 1911 from Mitchell, Caldwell, and Watauga counties. **Name Origin:** For Col. Waightstill Avery (1745-1821), Revolutionary War officer, NC legislator, and attorney general (1777-79).

Area (sq mi): 247.21 (land 247; water 0.2). **Pop per sq mi:** 71.4.

Pop 2005: 17,641. **State rank:** 86. **Pop change:** 2000-20005 +2.8%; 1990-2000 +15.5%. **Pop 2000:** 17,167 (White 93%; Black or African American 3.5%; Hispanic or Latino 2.4%; Asian 0.2%; Other 2.3%). **Foreign born:** 2.6%. **Median age:** 38.4.

Income 2000: per capita $15,176; median household $30,627; **Pop below poverty level:** 15.3%. ***Personal per capita income 2000-2003:** $23,164-$23,431.

Unemployment 2004: 4.9%. **Change from 2000:** +0.3%. **Median travel time to work:** 22.9 minutes. **Working outside county of residence:** 29%.

Cities with pop over 10,000: None.

BEAUFORT COUNTY
121 W 3rd St   **Ph:** 252-946-0079
Washington, NC 27889   **Fax:** 252-946-7722
www.co.beaufort.nc.us

On central eastern border of NC, east of Goldsboro; organized as Pamptecough Precinct Dec 3, 1705 (prior to statehood) from Bath County, which was organized in 1696 and abolished in 1739; name changed about 1712. **Name Origin:** For Henry Somerset (1684-1714), Duke of Beaufort, a Lord Proprietor of the colony of SC. Originally for the Pamptecough (Pamlico) River.

Area (sq mi): 958.69 (land 827.97; water 130.72). **Pop per sq mi:** 55.6.

Pop 2005: 46,018. **State rank:** 54. **Pop change:** 2000-20005 +2.4%; 1990-2000 +6.3%. **Pop 2000:** 44,958 (White 66.8%; Black or African American 29%; Hispanic or Latino 3.2%; Asian 0.2%; Other 2.3%). **Foreign born:** 2.6%. **Median age:** 40.2.

Income 2000: per capita $16,722; median household $31,066; **Pop below poverty level:** 19.5%. ***Personal per capita income 2000-2003:** $22,439-$23,324.

Unemployment 2004: 7.1%. **Change from 2000:** -2.5%. **Median travel time to work:** 25.4 minutes. **Working outside county of residence:** 23.7%.

Cities with pop over 10,000: None.

BERTIE COUNTY
106 Dundee St PO Box 530   **Ph:** 252-794-5300
Windsor, NC 27983   **Fax:** 252-794-5327
www.co.bertie.nc.us

In northeastern NC, east of Rocky Mount; organized 1722 (prior to statehood) from Chowan County. **Name Origin:** For James (1673-1735) and Henry (1675-1735) Bertie, brothers who were Lords Proprietor of the colony of North Carolina.

Area (sq mi): 741.22 (land 699.19; water 42.03). **Pop per sq mi:** 27.9.

Pop 2005: 19,480. **State rank:** 83. **Pop change:** 2000-20005 -1.5%; 1990-2000 -3%. **Pop 2000:** 19,773 (White 36%; Black or African American 62.3%; Hispanic or Latino 1%; Asian 0.1%; Other 1.2%). **Foreign born:** 0.7%. **Median age:** 38.6.

Income 2000: per capita $14,096; median household $25,177; **Pop below poverty level:** 23.5%. ***Personal per capita income 2000-2003:** $19,856-$20,845.

Unemployment 2004: 8.1%. **Change from 2000:** -0.5%. **Median travel time to work:** 28.5 minutes. **Working outside county of residence:** 41.4%.

Cities with pop over 10,000: None.

BLADEN COUNTY
166 E Broad St Rm 105   **Ph:** 910-862-6700
Elizabethtown, NC 28337   **Fax:** 910-862-6767
www.bladeninfo.org

In south-central NC, southeast of Fayetteville; organized 1734 (prior to statehood) from New Hanover County. **Name Origin:** For Martin Bladen (1680-1746), English soldier and commissioner of trade and plantations (1717-46).

*Source: Personal per capita income data are from the Bureau of Economic Analysis; per capita income data are from the Bureau of the Census. See Introduction for explanation of differences.

Bladen County (cont'd)

Area (sq mi): 887.13 (land 874.94; water 12.19). **Pop per sq mi:** 37.6.

Pop 2005: 32,938. **State rank:** 68. **Pop change:** 2000-20005 +2%; 1990-2000 +12.6%. **Pop 2000:** 32,278 (White 55.9%; Black or African American 37.9%; Hispanic or Latino 3.7%; Asian 0.1%; Other 4.7%, including 2% American Indian/Alaska Native). **Foreign born:** 2.3%. **Median age:** 37.9.

Income 2000: per capita $14,735; median household $26,877; **Pop below poverty level:** 21%. ***Personal per capita income 2000-2003:** $21,083-$21,244.

Unemployment 2004: 7.3%. **Change from 2000:** -0.1%. **Median travel time to work:** 26.9 minutes. **Working outside county of residence:** 35.3%.

Cities with pop over 10,000: None.

BRUNSWICK COUNTY

PO Box 249   **Ph:** 910-253-2000
Bolivia, NC 28422   **Fax:** 910-253-2022
www.brunsco.net

On the southeastern border of NC, west of Wilmington; organized 1764 (prior to statehood) from New Hanover and Bladen counties. **Name Origin:** For the German city and duchy; the Duke of Brunswick was one of the titles of the British royal house of Hanover.

Area (sq mi): 1050.01 (land 854.79; water 195.21). **Pop per sq mi:** 104.3.

Pop 2005: 89,162. **State rank:** 31. **Pop change:** 2000-20005 +21.9%; 1990-2000 +43.5%. **Pop 2000:** 73,143 (White 81.1%; Black or African American 14.4%; Hispanic or Latino 2.7%; Asian 0.3%; Other 3%). **Foreign born:** 2.9%. **Median age:** 42.2.

Income 2000: per capita $19,857; median household $35,888; **Pop below poverty level:** 12.6%. ***Personal per capita income 2000-2003:** $22,411-$24,095.

Unemployment 2004: 5.2%. **Change from 2000:** -0.2%. **Median travel time to work:** 24.6 minutes. **Working outside county of residence:** 34%.

Cities with pop over 10,000: None.

BUNCOMBE COUNTY

205 College St Suite 300   **Ph:** 828-250-4100
Asheville, NC 28801   **Fax:** 828-250-6077
www.buncombecounty.org

In southwestern NC; organized Dec 5, 1791 from Burke and Rutherford counties (in 1812 annexed Walton County, which was formed in 1803 from Indian lands). **Name Origin:** For Col. Edward Buncombe (1742-78), a NC officer in the Revolutionary War who died while a prisoner of the British.

Area (sq mi): 659.8 (land 655.99; water 3.81). **Pop per sq mi:** 333.7.

Pop 2005: 218,876. **State rank:** 7. **Pop change:** 2000-20005 +6.1%; 1990-2000 +18%. **Pop 2000:** 206,330 (White 87.6%; Black or African American 7.5%; Hispanic or Latino 2.8%; Asian 0.7%; Other 2.7%). **Foreign born:** 3.9%. **Median age:** 38.9.

Income 2000: per capita $20,384; median household $36,666; **Pop below poverty level:** 11.4%. ***Personal per capita income 2000-2003:** $26,692-$27,681.

Unemployment 2004: 4.2%. **Change from 2000:** +0.6%. **Median travel time to work:** 21.1 minutes. **Working outside county of residence:** 10.6%.

Cities with pop over 10,000: Asheville ⚏ (70,400).

BURKE COUNTY

PO Box 219   **Ph:** 828-439-4340
Morganton, NC 28680   **Fax:** 828-438-2782
www.co.burke.nc.us

In southwestern NC, northeast of Asheville; organized Apr 8, 1777 (prior to statehood) from Rowan County. **Name Origin:** For Dr. Thomas Burke (1747-83), member of the Continental Congress (1776-81) and NC governor (1781-82).

Area (sq mi): 514.89 (land 506.72; water 8.17). **Pop per sq mi:** 176.4.

Pop 2005: 89,399. **State rank:** 30. **Pop change:** 2000-20005 +0.3%; 1990-2000 +17.7%. **Pop 2000:** 89,148 (White 84.9%; Black or African American 6.7%; Hispanic or Latino 3.6%; Asian 3.5%; Other 3.8%). **Foreign born:** 4.8%. **Median age:** 36.9.

Income 2000: per capita $17,397; median household $35,629; **Pop below poverty level:** 10.7%. ***Personal per capita income 2000-2003:** $22,957-$23,401.

Unemployment 2004: 6.7%. **Change from 2000:** +0.1%. **Median travel time to work:** 21 minutes. **Working outside county of residence:** 31%.

Cities with pop over 10,000: Morganton ⚏ (17,176).

CABARRUS COUNTY

65 Church St SE   **Ph:** 704-920-2100
Concord, NC 28025   **Fax:** 704-920-2820
www.cabarruscounty.us

In west-central NC, northeast of Charlotte; organized Nov 15, 1791 from Mecklenburg County. **Name Origin:** For Stephen Cabarrus (1754-1808), NC legislator and speaker of the NC House of Commons.

Area (sq mi): 364.98 (land 364.39; water 0.59). **Pop per sq mi:** 412.3.

Pop 2005: 150,244. **State rank:** 14. **Pop change:** 2000-20005 +14.6%; 1990-2000 +32.5%. **Pop 2000:** 131,063 (White 80.9%; Black or African American 12.2%; Hispanic or Latino 5.1%; Asian 0.9%; Other 3.6%). **Foreign born:** 4.7%. **Median age:** 35.4.

Income 2000: per capita $21,121; median household $46,140; **Pop below poverty level:** 7.1%. ***Personal per capita income 2000-2003:** $29,273-$29,842.

Unemployment 2004: 6.1%. **Change from 2000:** +1.3%. **Median travel time to work:** 27 minutes. **Working outside county of residence:** 46.9%.

Cities with pop over 10,000: Concord ⚏ (59,960); Kannapolis (38,547).

⚏ *County Seat*

CALDWELL COUNTY

PO Box 2200   **Ph:** 828-757-1300
Lenoir, NC 28645   **Fax:** 828-757-1295
www.co.caldwell.nc.us

In northwestern NC, northwest of Charlotte; organized Jan 11, 1841 from Burke and Wilkes counties. **Name Origin:** For Joseph Caldwell (1773-1835), first president of the University of North Carolina (1804-12; 1817-35).

Area (sq mi): 474.29 (land 471.6; water 2.7). **Pop per sq mi:** 167.8.

Pop 2005: 79,122. **State rank:** 33. **Pop change:** 2000-20005 +2.2%; 1990-2000 +9.5%. **Pop 2000:** 77,415 (White 90.8%; Black or African American 5.5%; Hispanic or Latino 2.5%; Asian 0.4%; Other 2.4%). **Foreign born:** 1.9%. **Median age:** 37.5.

Income 2000: per capita $17,353; median household $35,739; **Pop below poverty level:** 10.7%. ***Personal per capita income 2000-2003:** $23,896-$25,247.

Unemployment 2004: 7.4%. **Change from 2000:** +0.7%. **Median travel time to work:** 21.6 minutes. **Working outside county of residence:** 30.9%.

Cities with pop over 10,000: Lenoir 🏛 (17,943).

CAMDEN COUNTY

PO Box 190   **Ph:** 252-335-4691
Camden, NC 27921   **Fax:** 252-333-1603
www.camdencountync.gov

On northeastern border of NC, east of Elizabeth City; organized Apr 8, 1777 (prior to statehood) from Pasquotank County. **Name Origin:** For Charles Pratt (1716-94), Earl of Camden, English jurist and political leader who supported the American colonies before the Revolutionary War.

Area (sq mi): 305.7 (land 240.68; water 65.02). **Pop per sq mi:** 37.3.

Pop 2005: 8,967. **State rank:** 97. **Pop change:** 2000-20005 +30.2%; 1990-2000 +16.6%. **Pop 2000:** 6,885 (White 80.1%; Black or African American 17.3%; Hispanic or Latino 0.7%; Asian 0.6%; Other 1.5%). **Foreign born:** 0.7%. **Median age:** 39.1.

Income 2000: per capita $18,681; median household $39,493; **Pop below poverty level:** 10.1%. ***Personal per capita income 2000-2003:** $25,394-$25,886.

Unemployment 2004: 3.7%. **Change from 2000:** +0.4%. **Median travel time to work:** 32.4 minutes. **Working outside county of residence:** 76.3%.

Cities with pop over 10,000: None.

CARTERET COUNTY

Courthouse Sq   **Ph:** 252-728-8450
Beaufort, NC 28516   **Fax:** 252-728-2092
www.co.carteret.nc.us

On the central eastern shore of NC, east of Jacksonville; organized 1722 (prior to statehood) from Craven County. **Name Origin:** For John Carteret (1690-1763), later Earl Granville, a lord proprietor of the Carolinas.

Area (sq mi): 1340.53 (land 519.84; water 820.68). **Pop per sq mi:** 120.3.

Pop 2005: 62,525. **State rank:** 40. **Pop change:** 2000-20005 +5.3%; 1990-2000 +13%. **Pop 2000:** 59,383 (White 89.3%; Black or African American 7%; Hispanic or Latino 1.7%; Asian 0.5%; Other 2.2%). **Foreign born:** 2%. **Median age:** 42.3.

Income 2000: per capita $21,260; median household $38,344; **Pop below poverty level:** 10.7%. ***Personal per capita income 2000-2003:** $25,757-$28,239.

Unemployment 2004: 4.7%. **Change from 2000:** -0.2%. **Median travel time to work:** 23 minutes. **Working outside county of residence:** 25.3%.

Cities with pop over 10,000: None.

CASWELL COUNTY

PO Box 790   **Ph:** 336-694-4171
Yanceyville, NC 27379   **Fax:** 336-694-7338
www.caswellcountync.gov

On the central northern border of NC, northwest of Durham; organized Apr 8, 1777 (prior to statehood) from Orange County. **Name Origin:** For Gen. Richard Caswell (1729-89), Revolutionary War officer; first and fifth governor of NC (1775-79; 1784-87).

Area (sq mi): 428.43 (land 424.67; water 3.76). **Pop per sq mi:** 55.6.

Pop 2005: 23,608. **State rank:** 76. **Pop change:** 2000-20005 +0.5%; 1990-2000 +13.6%. **Pop 2000:** 23,501 (White 60.6%; Black or African American 36.5%; Hispanic or Latino 1.8%; Asian 0.2%; Other 2.3%). **Foreign born:** 1.6%. **Median age:** 38.2.

Income 2000: per capita $16,470; median household $35,018; **Pop below poverty level:** 14.4%. ***Personal per capita income 2000-2003:** $21,635-$21,200.

Unemployment 2004: 8.1%. **Change from 2000:** +2.7%. **Median travel time to work:** 30.6 minutes. **Working outside county of residence:** 72.8%.

Cities with pop over 10,000: None.

CATAWBA COUNTY

PO Box 389   **Ph:** 828-465-8201
Newton, NC 28658   **Fax:** 828-465-8392
www.co.catawba.nc.us

In west-central NC, northwest of Charlotte; organized Dec 12, 1842 from Lincoln County. **Name Origin:** For the Catawba Indians of Siouan linguistic stock who lived in the area and were recognized as the most powerful tribe; origin of name unknown.

Area (sq mi): 413.51 (land 399.97; water 13.54). **Pop per sq mi:** 379.1.

Pop 2005: 151,641. **State rank:** 13. **Pop change:** 2000-20005 +7%; 1990-2000 +19.7%. **Pop 2000:** 141,685 (White 82.1%; Black or African American 8.4%; Hispanic or Latino 5.6%; Asian 2.9%; Other 3.8%). **Foreign born:** 6.5%. **Median age:** 36.1.

Income 2000: per capita $20,358; median household $40,536; **Pop below poverty level:** 9.1%. ***Personal per capita income 2000-2003:** $27,478-$26,483.

Unemployment 2004: 6.6%. **Change from 2000:** -0.1%. **Median travel time to work:** 20.7 minutes. **Working outside county of residence:** 15.6%.

Cities with pop over 10,000: Hickory (40,112); Newton 🏛 (12,881).

---

*Source: Personal per capita income data are from the Bureau of Economic Analysis; per capita income data are from the Bureau of the Census. See Introduction for explanation of differences.

CHATHAM COUNTY

PO Box 369
Pittsboro, NC 27312
www.co.chatham.nc.us

Ph: 919-542-3240
Fax: 919-542-1402

In north-central NC, southwest of Durham; established Apr 1, 1771 (prior to statehood) from Orange County. **Name Origin:** For William Pitt (the Elder; 1708-78), 1st Earl of Chatham, known as 'the Great Commoner,' for his support of the American colonies before the Revolutionary War.

Area (sq mi): 709.05 (land 682.85; water 26.19). **Pop per sq mi:** 84.9.

Pop 2005: 58,002. **State rank:** 42. **Pop change:** 2000-20005 +17.6%; 1990-2000 +27.3%. **Pop 2000:** 49,329 (White 71.6%; Black or African American 17.1%; Hispanic or Latino 9.6%; Asian 0.6%; Other 7.3%). **Foreign born:** 8.7%. **Median age:** 38.8.

Income 2000: per capita $23,355; median household $42,851; **Pop below poverty level:** 9.7%. ***Personal per capita income 2000-2003:** $34,233-$32,236.

Unemployment 2004: 3.8%. **Change from 2000:** +0.6%. **Median travel time to work:** 27.3 minutes. **Working outside county of residence:** 55.3%.

Cities with pop over 10,000: None.

CHEROKEE COUNTY

75 Peachtree St
Murphy, NC 28906
www.cherokeecounty-nc.org

Ph: 828-837-5527
Fax: 828-837-9684

In the southwestern corner of NC, southwest of Asheville; organized Jan 4, 1839 from Macon County. **Name Origin:** For the Indian tribe of Iroquoian linguistic stock. Name may derive from Creek *tciloki* 'people of a different speech.'

Area (sq mi): 466.68 (land 455.19; water 11.49). **Pop per sq mi:** 56.7.

Pop 2005: 25,796. **State rank:** 72. **Pop change:** 2000-20005 +6.2%; 1990-2000 +20.5%. **Pop 2000:** 24,298 (White 94.1%; Black or African American 1.6%; Hispanic or Latino 1.2%; Asian 0.3%; Other 3.2%, including 1.6% American Indian/Alaska Native). **Foreign born:** 1.2%. **Median age:** 44.

Income 2000: per capita $15,814; median household $27,992; **Pop below poverty level:** 15.3%. ***Personal per capita income 2000-2003:** $18,572-$19,290.

Unemployment 2004: 5.9%. **Change from 2000:** -2.2%. **Median travel time to work:** 24.1 minutes. **Working outside county of residence:** 18.7%.

Cities with pop over 10,000: None.

CHOWAN COUNTY

115 E King St PO Box 1030
Edenton, NC 27932
www.chowancounty-nc.gov

Ph: 252-482-8431
Fax: 252-482-0126

In northeastern NC on Albemarle Sound; organized as Shaftsbury Precinct of Albemarle County in 1668 (prior to statehood); name changed about 1681. **Name Origin:** For the Chowan River, which forms its western border; itself named for the Chowanoc, an Algonquian Indian tribe, probably 'those in the south.' Originally for

Anthony Ashley Cooper (1621-83), Earl of Shaftsbury, an original lord proprietor of Carolina.

Area (sq mi): 233.31 (land 172.64; water 60.67). **Pop per sq mi:** 84.2.

Pop 2005: 14,528. **State rank:** 88. **Pop change:** 2000-20005 +0%; 1990-2000 +7.6%. **Pop 2000:** 14,526 (White 59.9%; Black or African American 37.5%; Hispanic or Latino 1.5%; Asian 0.3%; Other 1.6%). **Foreign born:** 0.9%. **Median age:** 39.8.

Income 2000: per capita $15,027; median household $30,928; **Pop below poverty level:** 17.6%. ***Personal per capita income 2000-2003:** $23,122-$24,682.

Unemployment 2004: 4.8%. **Change from 2000:** -0.3%. **Median travel time to work:** 27.4 minutes. **Working outside county of residence:** 28.4%.

Cities with pop over 10,000: None.

CLAY COUNTY

PO Box 506
Hayesville, NC 28904
www.main.nc.us/clay/

Ph: 828-389-8334
Fax: 828-389-3329

On the southwestern border of NC, southwest of Asheville; organized Feb 20, 1861 from Cherokee County. **Name Origin:** For Henry Clay (1777-1852), U.S. senator from KY, known as the 'Great Pacificator' for his advocacy of compromise to avert national crises.

Area (sq mi): 220.6 (land 214.7; water 5.89). **Pop per sq mi:** 45.5.

Pop 2005: 9,765. **State rank:** 96. **Pop change:** 2000-20005 +11.3%; 1990-2000 +22.6%. **Pop 2000:** 8,775 (White 97.3%; Black or African American 0.8%; Hispanic or Latino 0.8%; Asian 0.1%; Other 1.1%). **Foreign born:** 1.2%. **Median age:** 46.7.

Income 2000: per capita $18,221; median household $31,397; **Pop below poverty level:** 11.4%. ***Personal per capita income 2000-2003:** $21,164-$21,580.

Unemployment 2004: 3.8%. **Change from 2000:** -0.2%. **Median travel time to work:** 26.2 minutes. **Working outside county of residence:** 48.4%.

Cities with pop over 10,000: None.

CLEVELAND COUNTY

PO Box 1210
Shelby, NC 28151
www.clevelandcounty.com

Ph: 704-484-4800
Fax: 704-484-4930

On the southern border of NC, west of Charlotte; organized as Cleaveland County Jan 11, 1841 from Rutherford and Lincoln counties. Present spelling adopted in 1887. **Name Origin:** For Col. Benjamin Cleaveland (1738-1806), a hero of the Battle of King's Mountain (1780).

Area (sq mi): 468.6 (land 464.63; water 3.97). **Pop per sq mi:** 211.5.

Pop 2005: 98,288. **State rank:** 25. **Pop change:** 2000-20005 +2.1%; 1990-2000 +13.7%. **Pop 2000:** 96,287 (White 76.2%; Black or African American 20.9%; Hispanic or Latino 1.5%; Asian 0.7%; Other 1.6%). **Foreign born:** 1.7%. **Median age:** 36.5.

Income 2000: per capita $17,395; median household $35,283; **Pop below poverty level:** 13.3%. ***Personal per capita income 2000-2003:** $22,888-$23,505.

Cleveland County (cont'd)

Unemployment 2004: 7.6%. **Change from 2000:** -3.8%. **Median travel time to work:** 23.5 minutes. **Working outside county of residence:** 32.8%.

Cities with pop over 10,000: Shelby 🏛 (21,275); Kings Mountain (10,634).

COLUMBUS COUNTY

PO Box 1587   **Ph:** 910-641-3000
Whiteville, NC 28472   **Fax:** 910-641-3027
www.columbusco.org

On southeastern border of NC, west of Wilmington; organized Dec 15, 1808 from Bladen and Brunswick counties. **Name Origin:** For explorer Christopher Columbus (1451-1506).

Area (sq mi): 953.6 (land 936.8; water 16.8). **Pop per sq mi:** 58.4.

Pop 2005: 54,746. **State rank:** 47. **Pop change:** 2000-20005 +0%; 1990-2000 +10.4%. **Pop 2000:** 54,749 (White 62.8%; Black or African American 30.9%; Hispanic or Latino 2.3%; Asian 0.2%; Other 5.4%, including 3.1% American Indian/Alaska Native). **Foreign born:** 1.4%. **Median age:** 36.9.

Income 2000: per capita $14,415; median household $26,805; **Pop below poverty level:** 22.7%. ***Personal per capita income 2000-2003:** $22,044-$22,746.

Unemployment 2004: 6.6%. **Change from 2000:** -2.9%. **Median travel time to work:** 27.1 minutes. **Working outside county of residence:** 28.1%.

Cities with pop over 10,000: None.

CRAVEN COUNTY

406 Craven St   **Ph:** 252-636-6600
New Bern, NC 28560   **Fax:** 252-637-0526
www.co.craven.nc.us

In central eastern NC, northeast of Jacksonville; organized Dec 3, 1705 (prior to statehood) as Archdale Precinct of Bath District, although there is evidence that an Archdale County had existed since 1696. Name changed 1712. **Name Origin:** Probably for William (1668-1711), 2nd Earl of Craven, who died the year before the name changed. Others claim the 1st Earl (1606-97), an original lord proprietor of Carolina, or the 3rd Earl, one of the proprietors when the name was changed. Originally named for John Archdale (1642?-1717), a lord proprietor and governor of Carolina (1694-96).

Area (sq mi): 774.14 (land 708.43; water 65.72). **Pop per sq mi:** 128.2.

Pop 2005: 90,795. **State rank:** 29. **Pop change:** 2000-20005 -0.7%; 1990-2000 +12%. **Pop 2000:** 91,436 (White 68.3%; Black or African American 25.1%; Hispanic or Latino 4%; Asian 1%; Other 4%). **Foreign born:** 3.4%. **Median age:** 34.4.

Income 2000: per capita $18,423; median household $35,966; **Pop below poverty level:** 13.1%. ***Personal per capita income 2000-2003:** $25,856-$28,097.

Unemployment 2004: 5.1%. **Change from 2000:** -0.2%. **Median travel time to work:** 20.6 minutes. **Working outside county of residence:** 14.1%.

Cities with pop over 10,000: New Bern 🏛 (23,368); Havelock (22,369).

CUMBERLAND COUNTY

PO Box 1829   **Ph:** 910-678-7700
Fayetteville, NC 28302   **Fax:** 910-678-7717
www.co.cumberland.nc.us

In south-central NC, south of Durham; organized Feb 19, 1754 (prior to statehood) from Bladen County. **Name Origin:** For William Augustus (1721-65), Duke of Cumberland, British general and second son of George II.

Area (sq mi): 658.46 (land 652.72; water 5.74). **Pop per sq mi:** 466.5.

Pop 2005: 304,520. **State rank:** 5. **Pop change:** 2000-20005 +0.5%; 1990-2000 +10.3%. **Pop 2000:** 302,963 (White 52.6%; Black or African American 34.9%; Hispanic or Latino 6.9%; Asian 1.9%; Other 8%, including 1.5% American Indian/Alaska Native). **Foreign born:** 5.3%. **Median age:** 29.6.

Income 2000: per capita $17,376; median household $37,466; **Pop below poverty level:** 12.8%. ***Personal per capita income 2000-2003:** $23,901-$27,257.

Unemployment 2004: 5.6%. **Change from 2000:** +0.2%. **Median travel time to work:** 21.9 minutes. **Working outside county of residence:** 9.5%.

Cities with pop over 10,000: Fayetteville 🏛 (125,241); Hope Mills (12,529).

CURRITUCK COUNTY

153 Courthouse Rd PO Box 39   **Ph:** 252-232-2075
Currituck, NC 27929   **Fax:** 252-232-3551
www.co.currituck.nc.us

On the northeastern shore of NC, east of Elizabeth City; organized by 1668 (prior to statehood) as a precinct of Albemarle District. **Name Origin:** From an obscure Indian name, said to mean 'wild geese.'

Area (sq mi): 525.65 (land 261.7; water 263.95). **Pop per sq mi:** 88.3.

Pop 2005: 23,112. **State rank:** 78. **Pop change:** 2000-20005 +27.1%; 1990-2000 +32.4%. **Pop 2000:** 18,190 (White 89.5%; Black or African American 7.2%; Hispanic or Latino 1.4%; Asian 0.4%; Other 2%). **Foreign born:** 1.4%. **Median age:** 38.3.

Income 2000: per capita $19,908; median household $40,822; **Pop below poverty level:** 10.7%. ***Personal per capita income 2000-2003:** $25,521-$26,574.

Unemployment 2004: 2.9%. **Change from 2000:** +0.1%. **Median travel time to work:** 35 minutes. **Working outside county of residence:** 66.5%.

Cities with pop over 10,000: None.

DARE COUNTY

PO Box 1000   **Ph:** 252-475-5800
Manteo, NC 27954   **Fax:** 252-473-1817
www.co.dare.nc.us

On the central eastern shore of NC on Pamlico Sound, east of Greenville; organized Feb 2, 1870 from Tyrrell, Hyde, and Currituck counties. **Name Origin:** For Virginia Dare, born (Aug 18, 1587) on Roanoke Island in the county, the first child of English parents to be born in the Americas.

---

*Source: Personal per capita income data are from the Bureau of Economic Analysis; per capita income data are from the Bureau of the Census. See Introduction for explanation of differences.

Dare County (cont'd)

Area (sq mi): 1561.51 (land 383.58; water 1177.93). **Pop per sq mi:** 88.4.

Pop 2005: 33,903. **State rank:** 67. **Pop change:** 2000-20005 +13.1%; 1990-2000 +31.7%. **Pop 2000:** 29,967 (White 93.5%; Black or African American 2.7%; Hispanic or Latino 2.2%; Asian 0.4%; Other 2.2%). **Foreign born:** 2.5%. **Median age:** 40.4.

Income 2000: per capita $23,614; median household $42,411; **Pop below poverty level:** 8%. ***Personal per capita income 2000-2003:** $26,852-$29,466.

Unemployment 2004: 4.5%. **Change from 2000:** -1.9%. **Median travel time to work:** 19.9 minutes. **Working outside county of residence:** 10%.

Cities with pop over 10,000: None.

DAVIDSON COUNTY

PO Box 1067   **Ph:** 336-242-2200
Lexington, NC 27293   **Fax:** 336-248-8440
www.co.davidson.nc.us/dcinfo.htm

In west-central NC, south of Winston-Salem; organized 1822 from Rowan County. **Name Origin:** For Gen. William Lee Davidson (1746-81), army officer killed during the Revolutionary War.

Area (sq mi): 566.77 (land 552.15; water 14.62). **Pop per sq mi:** 280.

Pop 2005: 154,623. **State rank:** 11. **Pop change:** 2000-20005 +5%; 1990-2000 +16.2%. **Pop 2000:** 147,246 (White 85.7%; Black or African American 9.1%; Hispanic or Latino 3.2%; Asian 0.8%; Other 3%). **Foreign born:** 3.6%. **Median age:** 37.1.

Income 2000: per capita $18,703; median household $38,640; **Pop below poverty level:** 10.1%. ***Personal per capita income 2000-2003:** $26,718-$26,036.

Unemployment 2004: 6.5%. **Change from 2000:** +0.2%. **Median travel time to work:** 22.8 minutes. **Working outside county of residence:** 44.3%.

Cities with pop over 10,000: Thomasville (25,752); Lexington 🏛 (20,472).

DAVIE COUNTY

123 S Main St   **Ph:** 336-751-5513
Mocksville, NC 27028   **Fax:** 336-751-7408
www.co.davie.nc.us

In west-central NC, southwest of Winston-Salem; organized 1836 from Rowan County. **Name Origin:** For Gen. William Richardson Davie (1756-1820), Revolutionary War hero, NC governor (1798-99), and a founder of the University of NC.

Area (sq mi): 266.89 (land 265.18; water 1.7). **Pop per sq mi:** 147.6.

Pop 2005: 39,136. **State rank:** 60. **Pop change:** 2000-20005 +12.3%; 1990-2000 +25%. **Pop 2000:** 34,835 (White 88.5%; Black or African American 6.8%; Hispanic or Latino 3.5%; Asian 0.3%; Other 2.4%). **Foreign born:** 3.4%. **Median age:** 38.4.

Income 2000: per capita $21,359; median household $40,174; **Pop below poverty level:** 8.6%. ***Personal per capita income 2000-2003:** $29,271-$29,174.

Unemployment 2004: 4.9%. **Change from 2000:** -0.2%. **Median travel time to work:** 23.9 minutes. **Working outside county of residence:** 53.6%.

Cities with pop over 10,000: None.

DUPLIN COUNTY

PO Box 189   **Ph:** 910-296-1686
Kenansville, NC 28349   **Fax:** 910-296-2310
www.duplincounty.org

In southeastern NC, south of Goldsboro; organized 1750 (prior to statehood) from New Hanover County. **Name Origin:** For Thomas Hay (1710-87), Lord Duplin, member of the Board of Trade and Plantations.

Area (sq mi): 819.11 (land 817.73; water 1.38). **Pop per sq mi:** 63.6.

Pop 2005: 51,985. **State rank:** 51. **Pop change:** 2000-20005 +6%; 1990-2000 +22.7%. **Pop 2000:** 49,063 (White 55.2%; Black or African American 28.9%; Hispanic or Latino 15.1%; Asian 0.2%; Other 12.3%). **Foreign born:** 11.3%. **Median age:** 34.9.

Income 2000: per capita $14,499; median household $29,890; **Pop below poverty level:** 19.4%. ***Personal per capita income 2000-2003:** $20,901-$20,827.

Unemployment 2004: 5.8%. **Change from 2000:** -0.4%. **Median travel time to work:** 26.6 minutes. **Working outside county of residence:** 32.3%.

Cities with pop over 10,000: None.

DURHAM COUNTY

200 E Main St   **Ph:** 919-560-0000
Durham, NC 27701   **Fax:** 919-560-0020
www.co.durham.nc.us

In north-central NC, northwest of Raleigh; organized Feb 28, 1881 from Orange and Wake counties. **Name Origin:** For the city of Durham, the county seat.

Area (sq mi): 297.79 (land 290.32; water 7.47). **Pop per sq mi:** 835.6.

Pop 2005: 242,582. **State rank:** 6. **Pop change:** 2000-20005 +8.6%; 1990-2000 +22.8%. **Pop 2000:** 223,314 (White 48.1%; Black or African American 39.5%; Hispanic or Latino 7.6%; Asian 3.3%; Other 6.3%). **Foreign born:** 10.9%. **Median age:** 32.2.

Income 2000: per capita $23,156; median household $43,337; **Pop below poverty level:** 13.4%. ***Personal per capita income 2000-2003:** $30,677-$31,129.

Unemployment 2004: 4.5%. **Change from 2000:** +0.7%. **Median travel time to work:** 21.2 minutes. **Working outside county of residence:** 25.1%.

Cities with pop over 10,000: Durham 🏛 (201,726).

EDGECOMBE COUNTY

PO Box 10   **Ph:** 252-641-7833
Tarboro, NC 27886   **Fax:** 252-641-0456
www.edgecombecountync.gov

In east-central NC, northeast of Goldsboro; organized Apr 4, 1741 (prior to statehood) from Bertie County, although deeds began in 1732. **Name Origin:** For Richard Edgecumbe (1680-1758), later

Edgecombe County (cont'd)

1st Baron Edgecumbe, English statesman. Present spelling is now accepted.

Area (sq mi): 506.58 (land 505.03; water 1.55). **Pop per sq mi:** 107.2.

Pop 2005: 54,129. **State rank:** 49. **Pop change:** 2000-20005 -2.7%; 1990-2000 -1.7%. **Pop 2000:** 55,606 (White 39.3%; Black or African American 57.5%; Hispanic or Latino 2.8%; Asian 0.1%; Other 2.4%). **Foreign born:** 2.1%. **Median age:** 36.2.

Income 2000: per capita $14,435; median household $30,983; **Pop below poverty level:** 19.6%. ***Personal per capita income 2000-2003:** $21,804-$22,328.

Unemployment 2004: 8.8%. **Change from 2000:** -0.8%. **Median travel time to work:** 21 minutes. **Working outside county of residence:** 43.9%.

Cities with pop over 10,000: Rocky Mount (56,351); Tarboro 🏛 (10,583).

FORSYTH COUNTY

PO Box 20099   **Ph:** 336-761-2250
Winston-Salem, NC 27120   **Fax:** 336-761-2018
www.co.forsyth.nc.us

In north-central NC, west of Greensboro; organized Jan 6, 1849 from Stokes County. **Name Origin:** For Col. Benjamin Forsyth (c.1760-1814), NC legislator and army officer killed during the War of 1812.

Area (sq mi): 412.92 (land 409.6; water 3.32). **Pop per sq mi:** 795.8.

Pop 2005: 325,967. **State rank:** 4. **Pop change:** 2000-20005 +6.5%; 1990-2000 +15.1%. **Pop 2000:** 306,067 (White 66.1%; Black or African American 25.6%; Hispanic or Latino 6.4%; Asian 1%; Other 4.9%). **Foreign born:** 6.5%. **Median age:** 36.

Income 2000: per capita $23,023; median household $42,097; **Pop below poverty level:** 11%. ***Personal per capita income 2000-2003:** $31,013-$32,067.

Unemployment 2004: 5%. **Change from 2000:** +0.8%. **Median travel time to work:** 21.2 minutes. **Working outside county of residence:** 19.3%.

Cities with pop over 10,000: Winston-Salem 🏛 (191,523); Kernersville (20,486); Clemmons (16,276).

FRANKLIN COUNTY

113 Market St   **Ph:** 919-496-5994
Louisburg, NC 27549   **Fax:** 919-496-2683
www.co.franklin.nc.us

In north-central NC, northeast of Raleigh; organized 1779 (prior to statehood) from Bute County, which was discontinued at that time. **Name Origin:** For Benjamin Franklin (1706-90), U.S. patriot, diplomat, and statesman.

Area (sq mi): 494.59 (land 492.02; water 2.57). **Pop per sq mi:** 110.6.

Pop 2005: 54,429. **State rank:** 48. **Pop change:** 2000-20005 +15.2%; 1990-2000 +29.8%. **Pop 2000:** 47,260 (White 64.2%; Black or African American 30%; Hispanic or Latino 4.4%; Asian 0.3%; Other 3.6%). **Foreign born:** 3.6%. **Median age:** 35.8.

Income 2000: per capita $17,562; median household $38,968; **Pop below poverty level:** 12.6%. ***Personal per capita income 2000-2003:** $24,324-$24,264.

Unemployment 2004: 5.1%. **Change from 2000:** +0.7%. **Median travel time to work:** 33.2 minutes. **Working outside county of residence:** 65.1%.

Cities with pop over 10,000: None.

GASTON COUNTY

PO Box 1578   **Ph:** 704-866-3100
Gastonia, NC 28053   **Fax:** 704-866-3147
www.co.gaston.nc.us

On the southern central border of NC, west of Charlotte; organized Dec 21, 1846 from Lincoln County. **Name Origin:** For William Gaston (1778-1844), NC legislator, U.S. representative (1813-17), and judge of the NC Supreme Court (1833-44).

Area (sq mi): 363.54 (land 356.21; water 7.33). **Pop per sq mi:** 550.6.

Pop 2005: 196,137. **State rank:** 8. **Pop change:** 2000-20005 +3%; 1990-2000 +8.7%. **Pop 2000:** 190,365 (White 81.4%; Black or African American 13.9%; Hispanic or Latino 3%; Asian 1%; Other 2.2%). **Foreign born:** 3.3%. **Median age:** 36.2.

Income 2000: per capita $19,225; median household $39,482; **Pop below poverty level:** 10.9%. ***Personal per capita income 2000-2003:** $26,359-$27,649.

Unemployment 2004: 6.4%. **Change from 2000:** -1.7%. **Median travel time to work:** 24.6 minutes. **Working outside county of residence:** 37%.

Cities with pop over 10,000: Gastonia 🏛 (68,292).

GATES COUNTY

PO Box 148   **Ph:** 252-357-1240
Gatesville, NC 27938   **Fax:** 252-357-0073
www.albemarle-nc.com/gates/

On the northeastern border of NC, northwest of Elizabeth City; organized 1779 (prior to statehood) from Chowan, Hertford, and Perquimans counties. **Name Origin:** For Gen. Horatio Gates (1728?-1806), Continental Army officer who defeated John Burgoyne (1722-92) at the Battle of Satatoga (1777).

Area (sq mi): 345.6 (land 340.61; water 5). **Pop per sq mi:** 33.

Pop 2005: 11,224. **State rank:** 93. **Pop change:** 2000-20005 +6.7%; 1990-2000 +13%. **Pop 2000:** 10,516 (White 58.5%; Black or African American 39.2%; Hispanic or Latino 0.8%; Asian 0.2%; Other 1.4%). **Foreign born:** 1.1%. **Median age:** 38.1.

Income 2000: per capita $15,963; median household $35,647; **Pop below poverty level:** 17%. ***Personal per capita income 2000-2003:** $19,515-$20,336.

Unemployment 2004: 4.1%. **Change from 2000:** +0.6%. **Median travel time to work:** 37.7 minutes. **Working outside county of residence:** 65.3%.

Cities with pop over 10,000: None.

*Source: Personal per capita income data are from the Bureau of Economic Analysis; per capita income data are from the Bureau of the Census. See Introduction for explanation of differences.

GRAHAM COUNTY

12 N Main St   **Ph:** 828-479-7973
Robbinsville, NC 28771   **Fax:** 828-479-6417
main.nc.us/graham/

On the southwestern border of NC, southwest of Asheville; organized Jan 30, 1872 from Cherokee County. **Name Origin:** For William Alexander Graham (1804-75), U.S. senator from NC (1840-43), governor (1845-49), and U.S. secretary of the navy (1850-52).

Area (sq mi): 301.6 (land 292.07; water 9.53). **Pop per sq mi:** 27.7.

Pop 2005: 8,085. **State rank:** 98. **Pop change:** 2000-20005 +1.2%; 1990-2000 +11.1%. **Pop 2000:** 7,993 (White 91.4%; Black or African American 0.2%; Hispanic or Latino 0.8%; Asian 0.2%; Other 7.7%, including 6.8% American Indian/Alaska Native). **Foreign born:** 1.3%. **Median age:** 41.5.

Income 2000: per capita $14,237; median household $26,645; **Pop below poverty level:** 19.5%. ***Personal per capita income 2000-2003:** $19,589-$21,508.

Unemployment 2004: 8.2%. **Change from 2000:** -1.1%. **Median travel time to work:** 27.9 minutes. **Working outside county of residence:** 24.4%.

Cities with pop over 10,000: None.

GRANVILLE COUNTY

PO Box 906   **Ph:** 919-693-4761
Oxford, NC 27565   **Fax:** 919-690-1766
www.granvillecounty.org

On the central northern border of NC, north of Raleigh; organized Jun 28, 1746 (prior to statehood) from Edgecombe County. **Name Origin:** For John Carteret (1690-1763), Earl Granville, a lord proprietor who owned the district in which the new county was located.

Area (sq mi): 536.56 (land 531.12; water 5.45). **Pop per sq mi:** 101.1.

Pop 2005: 53,674. **State rank:** 50. **Pop change:** 2000-20005 +10.7%; 1990-2000 +26.5%. **Pop 2000:** 48,498 (White 59.3%; Black or African American 34.9%; Hispanic or Latino 4%; Asian 0.4%; Other 4%). **Foreign born:** 4%. **Median age:** 36.2.

Income 2000: per capita $17,118; median household $39,965; **Pop below poverty level:** 11.7%. ***Personal per capita income 2000-2003:** $22,352-$21,433.

Unemployment 2004: 6.8%. **Change from 2000:** +0.8%. **Median travel time to work:** 27.4 minutes. **Working outside county of residence:** 46.5%.

Cities with pop over 10,000: None.

GREENE COUNTY

PO Box 675   **Ph:** 252-747-3505
Snow Hill, NC 28580   **Fax:** 252-747-2700
www.co.greene.nc.us

In east-central NC, northeast of Goldsboro; organized Nov 18, 1799 when Glasgow County was renamed Greene. **Name Origin:** For Gen. Nathanael Greene (1742-86), hero of the Revolutionary War, quartermaster general (1778-80), and commander of the Army of the South (1780). Originally for James Glasgow, NC secretary of state (1777-98), who became involved in land frauds.

Area (sq mi): 265.89 (land 265.4; water 0.49). **Pop per sq mi:** 75.5.

Pop 2005: 20,026. **State rank:** 81. **Pop change:** 2000-20005 +5.5%; 1990-2000 +23.3%. **Pop 2000:** 18,974 (White 50.1%; Black or African American 41.2%; Hispanic or Latino 8%; Asian 0.1%; Other 6.8%). **Foreign born:** 4.9%. **Median age:** 35.5.

Income 2000: per capita $15,452; median household $32,074; **Pop below poverty level:** 20.2%. ***Personal per capita income 2000-2003:** $21,185-$21,033.

Unemployment 2004: 6.2%. **Change from 2000:** -0.1%. **Median travel time to work:** 27.6 minutes. **Working outside county of residence:** 64.1%.

Cities with pop over 10,000: None.

GUILFORD COUNTY

PO Box 3427   **Ph:** 336-641-3383
Greensboro, NC 27402   **Fax:** 336-641-6833
www.co.guilford.nc.us

In north-central NC, east of Winston-Salem; organized 1771 (prior to statehood) from Rowan and Orange counties. **Name Origin:** For Francis North (1704-90), 1st Earl of Guilford and father of Frederick, Lord North (1732-92), who was the prime minister of England at the time of the American Revolution.

Area (sq mi): 657.7 (land 649.42; water 8.28). **Pop per sq mi:** 682.9.

Pop 2005: 443,519. **State rank:** 3. **Pop change:** 2000-20005 +5.3%; 1990-2000 +21.2%. **Pop 2000:** 421,048 (White 62.9%; Black or African American 29.3%; Hispanic or Latino 3.8%; Asian 2.4%; Other 3.8%). **Foreign born:** 6.5%. **Median age:** 34.9.

Income 2000: per capita $23,340; median household $42,618; **Pop below poverty level:** 10.6%. ***Personal per capita income 2000-2003:** $30,782-$31,786.

Unemployment 2004: 5.4%. **Change from 2000:** +0.6%. **Median travel time to work:** 21.4 minutes. **Working outside county of residence:** 12.2%.

Cities with pop over 10,000: Greensboro 🏛 (231,543); High Point (92,857).

HALIFAX COUNTY

PO Box 38   **Ph:** 252-583-1131
Halifax, NC 27839   **Fax:** 252-583-9921
www.halifaxnc.com

On the central northern border of NC, north of Rocky Mount; organized 1758 (prior to statehood) from Edgecombe County. **Name Origin:** For George Montagu (1716-71), second Earl of Halifax, president of the English Board of Trade, called the 'Father of the Colonies' for his strong support of trade with them.

Area (sq mi): 731.35 (land 725.36; water 5.99). **Pop per sq mi:** 77.2.

Pop 2005: 56,023. **State rank:** 45. **Pop change:** 2000-20005 -2.3%; 1990-2000 +3.3%. **Pop 2000:** 57,370 (White 42.3%; Black or African American 52.6%; Hispanic or Latino 1%; Asian 0.5%; Other 4.3%, including 3.1% American Indian/Alaska Native). **Foreign born:** 1.1%. **Median age:** 37.2.

Income 2000: per capita $13,810; median household $26,459; **Pop below poverty level:** 23.9%. ***Personal per capita income 2000-2003:** $19,775-$20,313.

🏛 *County Seat*

Halifax County (cont'd)

Unemployment 2004: 8.1%. **Change from 2000:** -3%. **Median travel time to work:** 24.2 minutes. **Working outside county of residence:** 29.5%.

Cities with pop over 10,000: Roanoke Rapids (16,397).

HARNETT COUNTY
PO Box 759   **Ph:** 910-893-7555
Lillington, NC 27546   **Fax:** 910-814-2662
www.harnett.org

In central NC, north of Fayetteville; organized Feb 7, 1855 from Cumberland County. **Name Origin:** For Cornelius Harnett (1723-81), patriot and member of the Continental Congress (1777-80).

Area (sq mi): 601.3 (land 595.01; water 6.29). **Pop per sq mi:** 174.3.

Pop 2005: 103,692. **State rank:** 24. **Pop change:** 2000-20005 +13.9%; 1990-2000 +34.2%. **Pop 2000:** 91,025 (White 68.9%; Black or African American 22.5%; Hispanic or Latino 5.9%; Asian 0.6%; Other 5.8%). **Foreign born:** 4.6%. **Median age:** 32.5.

Income 2000: per capita $16,775; median household $35,105; **Pop below poverty level:** 14.9%. ***Personal per capita income 2000-2003:** $21,616-$22,837.

Unemployment 2004: 5.2%. **Change from 2000:** -1.7%. **Median travel time to work:** 29.2 minutes. **Working outside county of residence:** 60.8%.

Cities with pop over 10,000: None.

HAYWOOD COUNTY
215 N Main St   **Ph:** 828-452-6625
Waynesville, NC 28786   **Fax:** 828-452-6715
www.gov.co.haywood.nc.us

On the southwestern border of NC, west of Asheville; organized Dec 15, 1808 from Buncombe County. **Name Origin:** For John Haywood (1755-1827), NC state treasurer (1787-1827).

Area (sq mi): 554.62 (land 553.66; water 0.96). **Pop per sq mi:** 102.

Pop 2005: 56,482. **State rank:** 44. **Pop change:** 2000-20005 +4.5%; 1990-2000 +15.1%. **Pop 2000:** 54,033 (White 96%; Black or African American 1.3%; Hispanic or Latino 1.4%; Asian 0.2%; Other 1.6%). **Foreign born:** 1.6%. **Median age:** 42.3.

Income 2000: per capita $18,554; median household $33,922; **Pop below poverty level:** 11.5%. ***Personal per capita income 2000-2003:** $23,319-$24,324.

Unemployment 2004: 4.5%. **Change from 2000:** -1.2%. **Median travel time to work:** 22.7 minutes. **Working outside county of residence:** 27.2%.

Cities with pop over 10,000: None.

HENDERSON COUNTY
100 N King St   **Ph:** 828-697-4808
Hendersonville, NC 28792   **Fax:** 828-692-9855
www.hendersoncountync.org

On the southwestern border of NC, south of Asheville; organized Dec 15, 1838 from Buncombe County. **Name Origin:** For Leonard Henderson (1772-1833), judge of the NC Supreme Court (1818-29) and chief justice (1829-33).

Area (sq mi): 375.04 (land 374; water 1.04). **Pop per sq mi:** 259.9.

Pop 2005: 97,217. **State rank:** 26. **Pop change:** 2000-20005 +9%; 1990-2000 +28.7%. **Pop 2000:** 89,173 (White 89.8%; Black or African American 3.1%; Hispanic or Latino 5.5%; Asian 0.6%; Other 3.8%). **Foreign born:** 5.9%. **Median age:** 42.7.

Income 2000: per capita $21,110; median household $38,109; **Pop below poverty level:** 9.7%. ***Personal per capita income 2000-2003:** $27,754-$28,286.

Unemployment 2004: 4.1%. **Change from 2000:** +0.7%. **Median travel time to work:** 22.2 minutes. **Working outside county of residence:** 25.9%.

Cities with pop over 10,000: Hendersonville 🏛 (11,232).

HERTFORD COUNTY
PO Box 86   **Ph:** 252-358-7845
Winton, NC 27986   **Fax:** 252-358-0793
www.co.hertford.nc.us

On the northeastern border of NC, northeast of Rocky Mount; organized 1759 (prior to statehood) from Chowan, Bertie, and Northampton counties. **Name Origin:** For Francis Seymour Conway (1719-94), Earl (later Marquis) of Hertford, British statesman.

Area (sq mi): 360.42 (land 353.26; water 7.16). **Pop per sq mi:** 66.7.

Pop 2005: 23,574. **State rank:** 77. **Pop change:** 2000-20005 +4.3%; 1990-2000 +0.3%. **Pop 2000:** 22,601 (White 37.1%; Black or African American 59.6%; Hispanic or Latino 1.6%; Asian 0.3%; Other 2.7%, including 1.2% American Indian/Alaska Native). **Foreign born:** 1.2%. **Median age:** 39.2.

Income 2000: per capita $15,641; median household $26,422; **Pop below poverty level:** 18.3%. ***Personal per capita income 2000-2003:** $19,022-$20,006.

Unemployment 2004: 5.9%. **Change from 2000:** -1.2%. **Median travel time to work:** 25.1 minutes. **Working outside county of residence:** 31.9%.

Cities with pop over 10,000: None.

HOKE COUNTY
PO Box 210   **Ph:** 910-875-8751
Raeford, NC 28376   **Fax:** 910-875-9222
www.hoke-raeford.com

In south-central NC, west of Fayetteville; organized Feb 7, 1911 from Cumberland and Robeson counties. **Name Origin:** For Gen. Robert F. Hoke (1837-1912), a Confederate Army officer and railway president.

Area (sq mi): 392.34 (land 391.21; water 1.12). **Pop per sq mi:** 104.8.

Pop 2005: 41,016. **State rank:** 59. **Pop change:** 2000-20005 +21.9%; 1990-2000 +47.2%. **Pop 2000:** 33,646 (White 41.6%; Black or African American 37.6%; Hispanic or Latino 7.2%; Asian 0.8%; Other 17%, including 11.4% American Indian/Alaska Native). **Foreign born:** 5.8%. **Median age:** 30.

Income 2000: per capita $13,635; median household $33,230; **Pop below poverty level:** 17.7%. ***Personal per capita income 2000-2003:** $17,271-$17,611.

---

*Source: Personal per capita income data are from the Bureau of Economic Analysis; per capita income data are from the Bureau of the Census. See Introduction for explanation of differences.

Hoke County (cont'd)

Unemployment 2004: 6%. Change from 2000: -2.1%. Median travel time to work: 26.4 minutes. Working outside county of residence: 64.1%.

Cities with pop over 10,000: None.

HYDE COUNTY

PO Box 188   Ph: 252-926-4178
Swanquarter, NC 27885   Fax: 252-926-3701
www.hydecounty.org

On the central eastern shore of NC on Pamlico Sound, northeast of Jacksonville; organized Dec 3, 1705 (prior to statehood) as Wickham Precinct of Bath District; name changed in 1712. Name Origin: Either for Edward Hyde (1661-1723), 3rd Earl of Clarendon, a colonial governor of NJ and NY (1701-08); or for Edward Hyde (1650-1712), deputy governor, acting governor, and governor of NC (1709-12). Originally for the manor home of the Archdale family in Buckinghamshire, England.

Area (sq mi): 1424 (land 612.8; water 811.2). Pop per sq mi: 8.8.

Pop 2005: 5,413. State rank: 99. Pop change: 2000-20005 -7.1%; 1990-2000 +7.7%. Pop 2000: 5,826 (White 61.6%; Black or African American 35.1%; Hispanic or Latino 2.2%; Asian 0.4%; Other 1.9%). Foreign born: 2.3%. Median age: 39.7.

Income 2000: per capita $13,164; median household $28,444; Pop below poverty level: 15.4%. *Personal per capita income 2000-2003: $19,037-$20,564.

Unemployment 2004: 6.9%. Change from 2000: +0.1%. Median travel time to work: 21.5 minutes. Working outside county of residence: 12.6%.

Cities with pop over 10,000: None.

IREDELL COUNTY

200 S Center St PO Box 788   Ph: 704-878-3000
Statesville, NC 28687   Fax: 704-878-5355
www.co.iredell.nc.us

In west-central NC, north of Charlotte; organized Nov 3, 1788 (prior to statehood) from Rowan County. Name Origin: For James Iredell (1751-99), NC attorney general (1779), delegate to the Constitutional Convention of 1788, and associate justice of the U.S. Supreme Court (1790-99).

Area (sq mi): 597.01 (land 575.57; water 21.44). Pop per sq mi: 244.8.

Pop 2005: 140,924. State rank: 17. Pop change: 2000-20005 +14.9%; 1990-2000 +32%. Pop 2000: 122,660 (White 80.7%; Black or African American 13.7%; Hispanic or Latino 3.4%; Asian 1.3%; Other 2.9%). Foreign born: 3.6%. Median age: 36.5.

Income 2000: per capita $21,148; median household $41,920; Pop below poverty level: 8.2%. *Personal per capita income 2000-2003: $26,911-$27,137.

Unemployment 2004: 5.4%. Change from 2000: -0.3%. Median travel time to work: 24.5 minutes. Working outside county of residence: 30.6%.

Cities with pop over 10,000: Statesville 🏛 (24,489); Mooresville (20,122).

JACKSON COUNTY

401 Grindstaff Cove Rd   Ph: 828-586-4055
Sylva, NC 28779   Fax: 828-586-7528
www.jacksonnc.org

On the southwestern border of NC, southwest of Asheville; organized Jan 29, 1851 from Haywood and Macon counties. Name Origin: For Andrew Jackson (1767-1845), seventh U.S. president.

Area (sq mi): 494.5 (land 490.71; water 3.79). Pop per sq mi: 72.1.

Pop 2005: 35,368. State rank: 66. Pop change: 2000-20005 +6.8%; 1990-2000 +23.4%. Pop 2000: 33,121 (White 84.8%; Black or African American 1.7%; Hispanic or Latino 1.7%; Asian 0.5%; Other 12.1%, including 10.2% American Indian/Alaska Native). Foreign born: 1.7%. Median age: 36.2.

Income 2000: per capita $17,582; median household $32,552; Pop below poverty level: 15.1%. *Personal per capita income 2000-2003: $21,049-$22,506.

Unemployment 2004: 4%. Change from 2000: +0.1%. Median travel time to work: 20.6 minutes. Working outside county of residence: 25.7%.

Cities with pop over 10,000: None.

JOHNSTON COUNTY

PO Box 297   Ph: 919-934-3191
Smithfield, NC 27577   Fax: 919-934-5857
www.co.johnston.nc.us

In east-central NC, southeast of Raleigh; organized 1746 (prior to statehood) from Craven County. Name Origin: For Gabriel Johnston (1699-1752), colonial governor of NC (1734-52).

Area (sq mi): 795.79 (land 791.85; water 3.94). Pop per sq mi: 184.9.

Pop 2005: 146,437. State rank: 15. Pop change: 2000-20005 +20.1%; 1990-2000 +50%. Pop 2000: 121,965 (White 75.3%; Black or African American 15.7%; Hispanic or Latino 7.7%; Asian 0.3%; Other 5.9%). Foreign born: 5.9%. Median age: 34.2.

Income 2000: per capita $18,788; median household $40,872; Pop below poverty level: 12.8%. *Personal per capita income 2000-2003: $25,441-$25,790.

Unemployment 2004: 4.4%. Change from 2000: +0.9%. Median travel time to work: 31.3 minutes. Working outside county of residence: 54%.

Cities with pop over 10,000: Clayton (12,173); Smithfield 🏛 (11,702).

JONES COUNTY

PO Box 280   Ph: 252-448-7351
Trenton, NC 28585   Fax: 252-448-1607
www.co.jones.nc.us

In southeastern NC, north of Jacksonville; organized 1778 (prior to statehood) from Craven County. Name Origin: For Willie Jones (1740-1801), American Revolutionary leader and member of the Continental Congress (1780-81); he later opposed the adoption of the Constitution.

Area (sq mi): 473.32 (land 471.88; water 1.44). Pop per sq mi: 21.9.

Pop 2005: 10,311. State rank: 95. Pop change: 2000-20005 -0.7%; 1990-2000 +10.3%. Pop 2000: 10,381 (White 60.3%; Black or

Jones County (cont'd)

African American 35.9%; Hispanic or Latino 2.7%; Asian 0.2%; Other 3%). **Foreign born:** 2.1%. **Median age:** 39.1.

Income 2000: per capita $15,916; median household $30,882; **Pop below poverty level:** 16.9%. ***Personal per capita income 2000-2003:** $20,211-$22,322.

Unemployment 2004: 4.9%. **Change from 2000:** -0.6%. **Median travel time to work:** 29.7 minutes. **Working outside county of residence:** 72.5%.

Cities with pop over 10,000: None.

LEE COUNTY

PO Box 4209   **Ph:** 919-708-4400
Sanford, NC 27331   **Fax:** 919-775-3483
www.leecountync.com

In central NC, southwest of Raleigh; organized Mar 6, 1907 from Chatham and Moore counties. **Name Origin:** For Robert E. Lee (1807-70), American general and commander in chief of the Confederate forces during the Civil War.

Area (sq mi): 259.33 (land 257.26; water 2.07). **Pop per sq mi:** 216.5.

Pop 2005: 55,704. **State rank:** 46. **Pop change:** 2000-20005 +13.6%; 1990-2000 +18.5%. **Pop 2000:** 49,040 (White 66.2%; Black or African American 20.5%; Hispanic or Latino 11.7%; Asian 0.7%; Other 8.8%). **Foreign born:** 9.5%. **Median age:** 35.9.

Income 2000: per capita $19,147; median household $38,900; **Pop below poverty level:** 12.8%. ***Personal per capita income 2000-2003:** $25,155-$27,669.

Unemployment 2004: 5.8%. **Change from 2000:** -0.3%. **Median travel time to work:** 24.1 minutes. **Working outside county of residence:** 28.4%.

Cities with pop over 10,000: Sanford ⛪ (23,469).

LENOIR COUNTY

PO Box 3289   **Ph:** 252-559-6450
Kinston, NC 28502   **Fax:** 252-559-6454
www.co.lenoir.nc.us

In east-central NC, southeast of Goldsboro; organized Dec 5, 1791 from Dobbs County, when Dobbs County was dissolved and divided between Glasgow and Lenoir counties. **Name Origin:** For Gen. William Lenoir (1751-1839), one of the heros of the Battle of Kings Mountain (1780) during the American Revolution and first president of the board of the University of NC.

Area (sq mi): 402.09 (land 399.85; water 2.24). **Pop per sq mi:** 145.

Pop 2005: 57,961. **State rank:** 43. **Pop change:** 2000-20005 -2.8%; 1990-2000 +4.1%. **Pop 2000:** 59,648 (White 55.5%; Black or African American 40.4%; Hispanic or Latino 3.2%; Asian 0.3%; Other 2.9%). **Foreign born:** 2.7%. **Median age:** 38.1.

Income 2000: per capita $16,744; median household $31,191; **Pop below poverty level:** 16.6%. ***Personal per capita income 2000-2003:** $23,583-$24,149.

Unemployment 2004: 6.2%. **Change from 2000:** -1.9%. **Median travel time to work:** 23.8 minutes. **Working outside county of residence:** 20.3%.

Cities with pop over 10,000: Kinston ⛪ (22,917).

LINCOLN COUNTY

115 W Main St   **Ph:** 704-736-8471
Lincolnton, NC 28092   **Fax:** 704-736-8718
www.co.lincoln.nc.us

In southwestern NC, northwest of Charlotte; organized 1779 (prior to statehood) from Tyron County, which was organized in 1768 and abolished in 1779. **Name Origin:** For Gen. Benjamin Lincoln (1733-1810), Revolutionary War officer, U.S. secretary of war (1781-83), and lt. gov. of MA (1788).

Area (sq mi): 307.03 (land 298.79; water 8.24). **Pop per sq mi:** 233.8.

Pop 2005: 69,851. **State rank:** 36. **Pop change:** 2000-20005 +9.5%; 1990-2000 +26.8%. **Pop 2000:** 63,780 (White 86.7%; Black or African American 6.4%; Hispanic or Latino 5.7%; Asian 0.3%; Other 3%). **Foreign born:** 4.8%. **Median age:** 36.4.

Income 2000: per capita $18,877; median household $41,421; **Pop below poverty level:** 9.2%. ***Personal per capita income 2000-2003:** $23,312-$23,998.

Unemployment 2004: 6.2%. **Change from 2000:** -1.4%. **Median travel time to work:** 27.1 minutes. **Working outside county of residence:** 52.1%.

Cities with pop over 10,000: Lincolnton ⛪ (10,194).

MACON COUNTY

5 W Main St   **Ph:** 828-349-2025
Franklin, NC 28734   **Fax:** 828-349-2400
www.maconnc.org

On the southwestern border of NC, southwest of Asheville; organized 1828 from Haywood County. **Name Origin:** For Nathaniel Macon (1757-1837), U.S. representative from NC (1791-1815), U.S. senator (1815-28), and president of the NC constitutional convention (1835).

Area (sq mi): 519.47 (land 516.47; water 3). **Pop per sq mi:** 62.2.

Pop 2005: 32,148. **State rank:** 69. **Pop change:** 2000-20005 +7.8%; 1990-2000 +26.9%. **Pop 2000:** 29,811 (White 96%; Black or African American 1.2%; Hispanic or Latino 1.5%; Asian 0.4%; Other 1.2%). **Foreign born:** 2.6%. **Median age:** 45.2.

Income 2000: per capita $18,642; median household $32,139; **Pop below poverty level:** 12.6%. ***Personal per capita income 2000-2003:** $22,966-$23,755.

Unemployment 2004: 4.6%. **Change from 2000:** +0.8%. **Median travel time to work:** 20 minutes. **Working outside county of residence:** 16.9%.

Cities with pop over 10,000: None.

MADISON COUNTY

PO Box 579   **Ph:** 828-649-2531
Marshall, NC 28753   **Fax:** 828-649-2829
www.main.nc.us/madison/

On the southwestern border of NC, north of Asheville; organized Jan 27, 1851 from Yancey and Buncombe counties. **Name Origin:** For James Madison (1751-1836), fourth U.S. president.

Area (sq mi): 451.59 (land 449.42; water 2.17). **Pop per sq mi:** 45.1.

---

*Source: Personal per capita income data are from the Bureau of Economic Analysis; per capita income data are from the Bureau of the Census. See Introduction for explanation of differences.

Madison County (cont'd)

Pop 2005: 20,256. **State rank:** 80. **Pop change:** 2000-20005 +3.2%; 1990-2000 +15.8%. **Pop 2000:** 19,635 (White 96.8%; Black or African American 0.8%; Hispanic or Latino 1.4%; Asian 0.2%; Other 1.3%). **Foreign born:** 1.7%. **Median age:** 39.3.

Income 2000: per capita $16,076; median household $30,985; **Pop below poverty level.** 15.4%. ***Personal per capita income 2000-2003:** $20,787-$21,609.

Unemployment 2004: 5.2%. **Change from 2000:** +0%. **Median travel time to work:** 30.1 minutes. **Working outside county of residence:** 54.2%.

Cities with pop over 10,000: None.

MARTIN COUNTY
PO Box 807   **Ph:** 252-792-2515
Williamston, NC 27892   **Fax:** 252-792-6668
www.martincountyncgov.com

In east central NC, northeast of Greenville; organized Mar 2, 1774 (prior to statehood) from Tyrell and Halifax counties. **Name Origin:** For Josiah Martin (1737-86), the last royal governor of NC (1771-75). The name was reinforced by the popularity of Alexander Martin, NC governor (1782-85; 1789-92).

Area (sq mi): 461.49 (land 461.17; water 0.32). **Pop per sq mi:** 53.4.

Pop 2005: 24,643. **State rank:** 75. **Pop change:** 2000-20005 -3.7%; 1990-2000 +2.1%. **Pop 2000:** 25,593 (White 51.8%; Black or African American 45.4%; Hispanic or Latino 2.1%; Asian 0.2%; Other 1.8%). **Foreign born:** 1.5%. **Median age:** 38.7.

Income 2000: per capita $15,102; median household $28,793; **Pop below poverty level:** 20.2%. ***Personal per capita income 2000-2003:** $20,547-$22,227.

Unemployment 2004: 7%. **Change from 2000:** -1.2%. **Median travel time to work:** 24.3 minutes. **Working outside county of residence:** 41.7%.

Cities with pop over 10,000: None.

MCDOWELL COUNTY
60 E Court St   **Ph:** 828-652-7121
Marion, NC 28752   **Fax:** 828-659-3484
www.mcdowellgov.com

In southwestern NC, east of Asheville; organized Dec 19, 1842 from Burke and Rutherford counties. **Name Origin:** For Maj. Joseph McDowell (1756-1801), a hero of the Battle of Kings Mountain (1780) during the Revolutionary War and U.S. representative from NC (1797-99).

Area (sq mi): 446.41 (land 441.68; water 4.73). **Pop per sq mi:** 97.8.

Pop 2005: 43,201. **State rank:** 57. **Pop change:** 2000-20005 +2.5%; 1990-2000 +18.1%. **Pop 2000:** 42,151 (White 91%; Black or African American 4.2%; Hispanic or Latino 2.9%; Asian 0.9%; Other 2.7%). **Foreign born:** 2.7%. **Median age:** 38.

Income 2000: per capita $16,109; median household $32,396; **Pop below poverty level:** 11.6%. ***Personal per capita income 2000-2003:** $21,049-$21,021.

Unemployment 2004: 6.7%. **Change from 2000:** -1.3%. **Median travel time to work:** 25.3 minutes. **Working outside county of residence:** 25.3%.

Cities with pop over 10,000: None.

MECKLENBURG COUNTY
600 E 4th St 11th Fl
Charlotte-Mecklenburg Govt Center   **Ph:** 704-336-2472
Charlotte, NC 28202   **Fax:** 704-336-5887
www.co.mecklenburg.nc.us

On the central southern border of NC, east of Gastonia; organized Nov 3, 1762 (prior to statehood) from Anson County. **Name Origin:** For Mecklenburg-Strelitz, home of Princess Charlotte Sophia (1744-1818), wife of King George III (1738-1820) of England

Area (sq mi): 546.22 (land 526.28; water 19.94). **Pop per sq mi:** 1513.2.

Pop 2005: 796,372. **State rank:** 1. **Pop change:** 2000-20005 +14.5%; 1990-2000 +36%. **Pop 2000:** 695,454 (White 61.1%; Black or African American 27.9%; Hispanic or Latino 6.5%; Asian 3.1%; Other 4.9%). **Foreign born:** 9.8%. **Median age:** 33.1.

Income 2000: per capita $27,352; median household $50,579; **Pop below poverty level:** 9.2%. ***Personal per capita income 2000-2003:** $37,274-$38,376.

Unemployment 2004: 5.1%. **Change from 2000:** +1%. **Median travel time to work:** 26 minutes. **Working outside county of residence:** 9.2%.

Cities with pop over 10,000: Charlotte 🏛 (594,359); Huntersville (34,332); Cornelius (17,875); Mint Hill (17,480).

MITCHELL COUNTY
PO Box 409   **Ph:** 828-688-2434
Bakersville, NC 28705   **Fax:** 828-688-4443
www.mitchellcounty.org

On the southwestern border of NC, northeast of Asheville; organized Feb 16, 1861 from Burke, Caldwell, Yancey, McDowell, and Watauga counties. **Name Origin:** For Elisha Mitchell (1793-1857), a professor at the University of North Carolina who was killed while exploring what is now called Mt. Mitchell.

Area (sq ml): 222.14 (land 221.43; water 0.71). **Pop per sq mi:** 71.3.

Pop 2005: 15,784. **State rank:** 87. **Pop change:** 2000-20005 +0.6%; 1990-2000 +8.7%. **Pop 2000:** 15,687 (White 97%; Black or African American 0.2%; Hispanic or Latino 2%; Asian 0.2%; Other 1.7%). **Foreign born:** 1.5%. **Median age:** 42.

Income 2000: per capita $15,933; median household $30,508; **Pop below poverty level:** 13.8%. ***Personal per capita income 2000-2003:** $19,658-$19,875.

Unemployment 2004: 7.4%. **Change from 2000:** -2.8%. **Median travel time to work:** 24.9 minutes. **Working outside county of residence:** 30.5%.

Cities with pop over 10,000: None.

MONTGOMERY COUNTY
PO Box 527   **Ph:** 910-576-4211
Troy, NC 27371   **Fax:** 910-576-5020
www.montgomery-county.com

In south-central NC, east of Charlotte; organized 1779 (prior to

Montgomery County (cont'd)

statehood) from Anson County. **Name Origin:** For Gen. Richard Montgomery (1736-75), American Revolutionary War officer who captured Montreal, Canada.

Area (sq mi): 501.64 (land 491.6; water 10.04). **Pop per sq mi:** 55.6.

Pop 2005: 27,322. **State rank:** 71. **Pop change:** 2000-20005 +1.9%; 1990-2000 +14.9%. **Pop 2000:** 26,822 (White 65.3%; Black or African American 21.8%; Hispanic or Latino 10.4%; Asian 1.6%; Other 7.4%). **Foreign born:** 8%. **Median age:** 36.7.

Income 2000: per capita $16,504; median household $32,903; **Pop below poverty level:** 15.4%. ***Personal per capita income 2000-2003:** $21,767-$22,174.

Unemployment 2004: 7.3%. **Change from 2000:** +0.1%. **Median travel time to work:** 24.5 minutes. **Working outside county of residence:** 29.6%.

Cities with pop over 10,000: None.

MOORE COUNTY

PO Box 905   **Ph:** 910-947-6363
Carthage, NC 28327   **Fax:** 910-947-1874
www.co.moore.nc.us

In south-central NC, northwest of Fayetteville; organized Apr 18, 1784 (prior to statehood) from Cumberland County. **Name Origin:** For Capt. Alfred Moore (1755-1810), Revolutionary War officer, attorney general of NC (1782), and associate justice of the U.S. Supreme Court (1799-1804).

Area (sq mi): 705.67 (land 697.74; water 7.94). **Pop per sq mi:** 117.1.

Pop 2005: 81,685. **State rank:** 32. **Pop change:** 2000-20005 +9.2%; 1990-2000 +26.7%. **Pop 2000:** 74,769 (White 78.7%; Black or African American 15.5%; Hispanic or Latino 4%; Asian 0.4%; Other 3.9%). **Foreign born:** 4.2%. **Median age:** 41.8.

Income 2000: per capita $23,377; median household $41,240; **Pop below poverty level:** 11.4%. ***Personal per capita income 2000-2003:** $31,535-$32,038.

Unemployment 2004: 5.5%. **Change from 2000:** +0.5%. **Median travel time to work:** 22.8 minutes. **Working outside county of residence:** 23.9%.

Cities with pop over 10,000: Southern Pines (11,556); Pinehurst (10,998).

NASH COUNTY

120 W Washington St Suite 3072   **Ph:** 252-459-9800
Nashville, NC 27856   **Fax:** 252-459-9817
www.co.nash.nc.us

In east-central NC, northeast of Raleigh; organized Nov 15, 1777 (prior to statehood) from Edgecombe County. **Name Origin:** For Gen. Francis Nash (1742-77), Revolutionary War officer and NC legislator.

Area (sq mi): 542.69 (land 540.27; water 2.42). **Pop per sq mi:** 169.1.

Pop 2005: 91,378. **State rank:** 28. **Pop change:** 2000-20005 +4.5%; 1990-2000 +14%. **Pop 2000:** 87,420 (White 61%; Black or African

American 33.9%; Hispanic or Latino 3.4%; Asian 0.6%; Other 3.6%). **Foreign born:** 3%. **Median age:** 36.5.

Income 2000: per capita $18,863; median household $37,147; **Pop below poverty level:** 13.4%. ***Personal per capita income 2000-2003:** $25,255-$26,602.

Unemployment 2004: 6.5%. **Change from 2000:** -0.1%. **Median travel time to work:** 22.7 minutes. **Working outside county of residence:** 31.4%.

Cities with pop over 10,000: None.

NEW HANOVER COUNTY

320 Chestnut St Rm 502   **Ph:** 910-341-7184
Wilmington, NC 28401   **Fax:** 910-341-4027
www.co.new-hanover.nc.us

On the southeastern shore of NC, southwest of Jacksonville; organized Nov 27, 1729 from Craven County. **Name Origin:** For the British royal house of Hanover, which began with George I (1660-1727), Duke of Hannover. Anglicized to Hanover.

Area (sq mi): 327.92 (land 198.93; water 128.98). **Pop per sq mi:** 902.6.

Pop 2005: 179,553. **State rank:** 9. **Pop change:** 2000-20005 +12%; 1990-2000 +33.3%. **Pop 2000:** 160,307 (White 78.9%; Black or African American 17%; Hispanic or Latino 2%; Asian 0.8%; Other 2.4%). **Foreign born:** 3.2%. **Median age:** 36.3.

Income 2000: per capita $23,123; median household $40,172; **Pop below poverty level:** 13.1%. ***Personal per capita income 2000-2003:** $28,558-$29,607.

Unemployment 2004: 4.4%. **Change from 2000:** -0.3%. **Median travel time to work:** 20.7 minutes. **Working outside county of residence:** 9.7%.

Cities with pop over 10,000: Wilmington 🏛 (93,292).

NORTHAMPTON COUNTY

PO Box 808   **Ph:** 252-534-2501
Jackson, NC 27845   **Fax:** 252-534-1166
www.northamptonnc.com

On the northern border of NC, northeast of Rocky Mount; organized 1741 from Bertie County. **Name Origin:** For Northampton, England, or the British earl of Northampton.

Area (sq mi): 550.61 (land 536.48; water 14.13). **Pop per sq mi:** 40.

Pop 2005: 21,483. **State rank:** 79. **Pop change:** 2000-20005 -2.7%; 1990-2000 +6.2%. **Pop 2000:** 22,086 (White 39%; Black or African American 59.4%; Hispanic or Latino 0.7%; Asian 0.1%; Other 1.4%). **Foreign born:** 0.7%. **Median age:** 40.

Income 2000: per capita $15,413; median household $26,652; **Pop below poverty level:** 21.3%. ***Personal per capita income 2000-2003:** $20,749-$22,572.

Unemployment 2004: 7.4%. **Change from 2000:** -2.1%. **Median travel time to work:** 27.2 minutes. **Working outside county of residence:** 58%.

Cities with pop over 10,000: None.

*Source: Personal per capita income data are from the Bureau of Economic Analysis; per capita income data are from the Bureau of the Census.
See Introduction for explanation of differences.

518

ONSLOW COUNTY

118 Old Bridge St
Jacksonville, NC 28540
www.co.onslow.nc.us

Ph: 910-347-4717
Fax: 910-455-7878

On the southeastern shore of NC, northeast of Wilmington; organized 1734 (prior to statehood) from New Hanover County. **Name Origin:** For Arthur Onslow (1691-1768), speaker of the House of Commons in England (1728-61).

Area (sq mi): 908.56 (land 766.82; water 141.74). **Pop per sq mi:** 198.8.

Pop 2005: 152,440. **State rank:** 12. **Pop change:** 2000-20005 +1.4%; 1990-2000 +0.3%. **Pop 2000:** 150,355 (White 69.6%; Black or African American 18.5%; Hispanic or Latino 7.2%; Asian 1.7%; Other 7.7%). **Foreign born:** 4.1%. **Median age:** 25.

Income 2000: per capita $14,853; median household $33,756; **Pop below poverty level:** 12.9%. ***Personal per capita income 2000-2003:** $22,900-$26,487.

Unemployment 2004: 5.5%. **Change from 2000:** +1%. **Median travel time to work:** 21.2 minutes. **Working outside county of residence:** 12.1%.

Cities with pop over 10,000: Jacksonville 🏛 (72,335).

ORANGE COUNTY

106 E Margaret Ln
Hillsborough, NC 27278
www.co.orange.nc.us

Ph: 919-732-8181
Fax: 919-644-3043

In north-central NC, west of Durham; organized Mar 31, 1753 (prior to statehood) from Bladen, Granville, and Johnston counties. **Name Origin:** Said to be for William III of the House of Orange, but when the county was formed, William V (1748-1806) was Stadholder; it seems more likely to be named for the latter (grandson of George II of England) than for the former, who had been dead for fifty years.

Area (sq mi): 401.21 (land 399.84; water 1.37). **Pop per sq mi:** 296.1.

Pop 2005: 118,386. **State rank:** 22. **Pop change:** 2000-20005 +0.1%; 1990-2000 +26%. **Pop 2000:** 118,227 (White 75.8%; Black or African American 13.8%; Hispanic or Latino 4.5%; Asian 4.1%; Other 4.1%). **Foreign born:** 9.1%. **Median age:** 30.4.

Income 2000: per capita $24,873; median household $42,372; **Pop below poverty level:** 14.1%. ***Personal per capita income 2000-2003:** $30,914-$34,182.

Unemployment 2004: 3.8%. **Change from 2000:** +1.6%. **Median travel time to work:** 22 minutes. **Working outside county of residence:** 42.4%.

Cities with pop over 10,000: Chapel Hill (49,368); Carrboro (16,429).

PAMLICO COUNTY

PO Box 776
Bayboro, NC 28515
www.co.pamlico.nc.us

Ph: 252-745-3133
Fax: 252-745-5514

On the central eastern shore of NC on Pamlico Sound, east of New Bern; organized Feb 8, 1872 from Craven and Beaufort counties. **Name Origin:** For Pamlico Sound.

Area (sq mi): 566.23 (land 336.94; water 229.29). **Pop per sq mi:** 37.8.

Pop 2005: 12,735. **State rank:** 91. **Pop change:** 2000-20005 -1.5%; 1990-2000 +13.7%. **Pop 2000:** 12,934 (White 72.6%; Black or African American 24.6%; Hispanic or Latino 1.3%; Asian 0.4%; Other 1.8%). **Foreign born:** 1.8%. **Median age:** 42.9.

Income 2000: per capita $18,005; median household $34,084; **Pop below poverty level:** 15.3%. ***Personal per capita income 2000-2003:** $23,144-$24,751.

Unemployment 2004: 4.8%. **Change from 2000:** +0.3%. **Median travel time to work:** 28.9 minutes. **Working outside county of residence:** 48.1%.

Cities with pop over 10,000: None.

PASQUOTANK COUNTY

PO Box 39
Elizabeth City, NC 27907
www.co.pasquotank.nc.us

Ph: 252-335-0865
Fax: 252-335-0866

On the northeastern border of NC, on Albemarle Sound; organized 1668 (prior to statehood) as a precinct of Albemarle County. **Name Origin:** For the Pasquotank River, which forms its eastern border; from the Indian word *pask-etan-ki* 'where the current [of the stream] divides or forks.'

Area (sq mi): 289.44 (land 226.88; water 62.56). **Pop per sq mi:** 168.7.

Pop 2005: 38,270. **State rank:** 61. **Pop change:** 2000-20005 +9.7%; 1990-2000 +11.5%. **Pop 2000:** 34,897 (White 56.4%; Black or African American 40%; Hispanic or Latino 1.2%; Asian 0.9%; Other 2.2%). **Foreign born:** 2.3%. **Median age:** 35.9.

Income 2000: per capita $14,815; median household $30,444; **Pop below poverty level:** 18.4%. ***Personal per capita income 2000-2003:** $20,815-$22,266.

Unemployment 2004: 4.6%. **Change from 2000:** +0.1%. **Median travel time to work:** 22.8 minutes. **Working outside county of residence:** 22.9%.

Cities with pop over 10,000: Elizabeth City 🏛 (17,811).

PENDER COUNTY

PO Box 5
Burgaw, NC 28425
www.pender-county.com

Ph: 910-259-1200
Fax: 910-259-1402

On the southeastern shore of NC, north of Wilmington; organized Feb 16, 1875 from New Hanover County. **Name Origin:** For Gen. William Dorsey Pender (1834-63), officer in the Confederate Army killed at the Battle of Gettysburg.

Area (sq mi): 932.64 (land 870.67; water 61.97). **Pop per sq mi:** 53.3.

Pop 2005: 46,429. **State rank:** 53. **Pop change:** 2000-20005 +13%; 1990-2000 +42.4%. **Pop 2000:** 41,082 (White 71.7%; Black or African American 23.6%; Hispanic or Latino 3.6%; Asian 0.2%; Other 3.4%). **Foreign born:** 3.6%. **Median age:** 38.8.

Income 2000: per capita $17,882; median household $35,902; **Pop below poverty level:** 13.6%. ***Personal per capita income 2000-2003:** $21,242-$21,489.

Pender County (cont'd)

Unemployment 2004: 4.8%. **Change from 2000:** -1.3%. **Median travel time to work:** 29.2 minutes. **Working outside county of residence:** 61.8%.

Cities with pop over 10,000: None.

PERQUIMANS COUNTY
PO Box 45   **Ph:** 252-426-8484
Hertford, NC 27944   **Fax:** 252-426-4034
www.co.perquimans.nc.us

In northeastern NC on Albemarle Sound, west of Elizabeth City; organized 1679 (prior to statehood) as Berkeley Precinct of Albemarle County. **Name Origin:** For the Perquimans River, which runs through it, named for the Indian tribe who once lived along its banks.

Area (sq mi): 328.93 (land 247.17; water 81.76). **Pop per sq mi:** 48.9.

Pop 2005: 12,080. **State rank:** 92. **Pop change:** 2000-20005 +6.3%; 1990-2000 +8.8%. **Pop 2000:** 11,368 (White 70.5%; Black or African American 28%; Hispanic or Latino 0.6%; Asian 0.2%; Other 0.9%). **Foreign born:** 0.7%. **Median age:** 42.2.

Income 2000: per capita $15,728; median household $29,538; **Pop below poverty level:** 17.9%. ***Personal per capita income 2000-2003:** $20,342-$21,968.

Unemployment 2004: 4.7%. **Change from 2000:** -0.2%. **Median travel time to work:** 33.1 minutes. **Working outside county of residence:** 62.2%.

Cities with pop over 10,000: None.

PERSON COUNTY
304 S Morgan St Rm 212   **Ph:** 336-597-1720
Roxboro, NC 27573   **Fax:** 336-599-1609
www.personcounty.net

On the central northern border of NC, north of Durham; organized Dec 5, 1791 from Caswell County. **Name Origin:** For Gen. Thomas Person (1733-1800), Revolutionary War officer and NC legislator.

Area (sq mi): 404.09 (land 392.31; water 11.78). **Pop per sq mi:** 94.9.

Pop 2005: 37,217. **State rank:** 63. **Pop change:** 2000-20005 +4.5%; 1990-2000 +18%. **Pop 2000:** 35,623 (White 68.1%; Black or African American 28.2%; Hispanic or Latino 2.1%; Asian 0.1%; Other 2.9%). **Foreign born:** 1.3%. **Median age:** 38.

Income 2000: per capita $18,709; median household $37,159; **Pop below poverty level:** 12%. ***Personal per capita income 2000-2003:** $23,034-$23,824.

Unemployment 2004: 6.6%. **Change from 2000:** -1.3%. **Median travel time to work:** 29.7 minutes. **Working outside county of residence:** 41.9%.

Cities with pop over 10,000: None.

PITT COUNTY
1717 W 5th St   **Ph:** 252-902-2951
Greenville, NC 27834   **Fax:** 252-830-6311
www.pittcountync.gov

In east-central NC, northeast of Goldsboro; organized Apr 24, 1760 (prior to statehood) from Beaufort County. **Name Origin:** For William Pitt (1708-78), 1st Earl of Chatham, known as 'the Great Commoner' for his support of the American colonies before the Revolutionary War.

Area (sq mi): 654.77 (land 651.58; water 3.19). **Pop per sq mi:** 218.8.

Pop 2005: 142,570. **State rank:** 16. **Pop change:** 2000-20005 +6.6%; 1990-2000 +24%. **Pop 2000:** 133,798 (White 61%; Black or African American 33.6%; Hispanic or Latino 3.2%; Asian 1.1%; Other 3.2%). **Foreign born:** 3.6%. **Median age:** 30.4.

Income 2000: per capita $18,243; median household $32,868; **Pop below poverty level:** 20.3%. ***Personal per capita income 2000-2003:** $24,331-$25,746.

Unemployment 2004: 5.7%. **Change from 2000:** -0.4%. **Median travel time to work:** 20.7 minutes. **Working outside county of residence:** 14.1%.

Cities with pop over 10,000: Greenville ⛭ (68,687).

POLK COUNTY
40 Courthouse Sq   **Ph:** 828-894-3301
Columbus, NC 28722   **Fax:** 828-894-2263
www.co.polk.nc.us

On the southwestern border, southeast of Asheville; organized 1855 from Rutherford and Henderson counties. **Name Origin:** For Col. William Polk (1785-1834), an officer in the American Revolution, NC legislator, and supervisor of internal revenue (1791-1808).

Area (sq mi): 238.6 (land 237.85; water 0.75). **Pop per sq mi:** 80.4.

Pop 2005: 19,134. **State rank:** 84. **Pop change:** 2000-20005 +4.4%; 1990-2000 +27.1%. **Pop 2000:** 18,324 (White 90.1%; Black or African American 5.9%; Hispanic or Latino 3%; Asian 0.2%; Other 1.6%). **Foreign born:** 3.7%. **Median age:** 44.9.

Income 2000: per capita $19,804; median household $36,259; **Pop below poverty level:** 10.1%. ***Personal per capita income 2000-2003:** $30,769-$32,290.

Unemployment 2004: 4.3%. **Change from 2000:** +0.8%. **Median travel time to work:** 26.2 minutes. **Working outside county of residence:** 49.7%.

Cities with pop over 10,000: None.

RANDOLPH COUNTY
PO Box 4728   **Ph:** 336-318-6300
Asheboro, NC 27204   **Fax:** 336-318-6853
www.co.randolph.nc.us

In west-central NC, south of Greensboro; organized 1779 (prior to statehood) from Guilford County. **Name Origin:** For Peyton Randolph (1721?-75), member of the VA House of Burgesses (1748-49; 1752-75) and speaker (1766-75); president of the Continental Congress (1774-75).

Area (sq mi): 789.93 (land 787.36; water 2.57). **Pop per sq mi:** 175.7.

Pop 2005: 138,367. **State rank:** 19. **Pop change:** 2000-20005 +6.1%; 1990-2000 +22.4%. **Pop 2000:** 130,454 (White 86%; Black or African American 5.6%; Hispanic or Latino 6.6%; Asian 0.6%; Other 4.5%). **Foreign born:** 5.7%. **Median age:** 36.2.

Source: Personal per capita income data are from the Bureau of Economic Analysis; per capita income data are from the Bureau of the Census. See Introduction for explanation of differences.

Randolph County (cont'd)

Income 2000: per capita $18,236; median household $38,348; **Pop below poverty level:** 9.1%. ***Personal per capita income 2000-2003:** $23,592-$23,651.

Unemployment 2004: 5.1%. **Change from 2000:** -0.3%. **Median travel time to work:** 23.6 minutes. **Working outside county of residence:** 41.3%.

Cities with pop over 10,000: Asheboro ⛫ (23,215).

RICHMOND COUNTY
125 S Hancock St   **Ph:** 910-997-8211
Rockingham, NC 28379   **Fax:** 910-997-8208
www.co.richmond.nc.us

On the southern border of NC, west of Fayetteville; organized Oct 18, 1779 (prior to statehood) from Anson County. **Name Origin:** For Charles Lennox (1735-1806), third Duke of Richmond, British secretary of state who denounced British policy toward American colonies.

Area (sq mi): 479.58 (land 473.98; water 5.6). **Pop per sq mi:** 98.7.

Pop 2005: 46,781. **State rank:** 52. **Pop change:** 2000-20005 +0.5%; 1990-2000 +4.6%. **Pop 2000:** 46,564 (White 63.4%; Black or African American 30.5%; Hispanic or Latino 2.8%; Asian 0.7%; Other 4%, including 1.7% American Indian/Alaska Native). **Foreign born:** 2.2%. **Median age:** 35.5.

Income 2000: per capita $14,485; median household $28,830; **Pop below poverty level:** 19.6%. ***Personal per capita income 2000-2003:** $20,222-$20,974.

Unemployment 2004: 8.3%. **Change from 2000:** -1.4%. **Median travel time to work:** 21.6 minutes. **Working outside county of residence:** 25.5%.

Cities with pop over 10,000: None.

ROBESON COUNTY
701 N Elm St   **Ph:** 910-671-3022
Lumberton, NC 28358   **Fax:** 910-671-3010
www.co.robeson.nc.us

On southern border of NC, south of Fayetteville; organized 1786 from Bladen County (prior to statehood). **Name Origin:** For Col. Thomas Robeson (1740-85), an officer in the American Revolution.

Area (sq mi): 951.03 (land 948.84; water 2.19). **Pop per sq mi:** 134.5.

Pop 2005: 127,586. **State rank:** 21. **Pop change:** 2000-20005 +3.4%; 1990-2000 +17.3%. **Pop 2000:** 123,339 (White 30.8%; Black or African American 25.1%; Hispanic or Latino 4.9%; Asian 0.3%; Other 41.8%, including 38% American Indian/Alaska Native). **Foreign born:** 4.2%. **Median age:** 32.

Income 2000: per capita $13,224; median household $28,202; **Pop below poverty level:** 22.8%. ***Personal per capita income 2000-2003:** $17,932-$18,659.

Unemployment 2004: 7.5%. **Change from 2000:** -4%. **Median travel time to work:** 28.1 minutes. **Working outside county of residence:** 28.1%.

Cities with pop over 10,000: Lumberton ⛫ (21,314).

ROCKINGHAM COUNTY
PO Box 206   **Ph:** 336-342-8101
Wentworth, NC 27375   **Fax:** 336-342-8105
www.co.rockingham.nc.us

On the central northern border of NC, north of Greensboro; organized Nov 19, 1785 (prior to statehood) from Guilford County. **Name Origin:** For Charles Watson Wentworth (1730-82), second Marquis of Rockingham, prime minister of England (1765-66; 1782), and supporter of independence for American colonies.

Area (sq mi): 572.33 (land 566.44; water 5.9). **Pop per sq mi:** 163.5.

Pop 2005: 92,614. **State rank:** 27. **Pop change:** 2000-20005 +0.7%; 1990-2000 +6.8%. **Pop 2000:** 91,928 (White 76.2%; Black or African American 19.6%; Hispanic or Latino 3.1%; Asian 0.3%; Other 2.8%). **Foreign born:** 2.7%. **Median age:** 38.5.

Income 2000: per capita $17,120; median household $33,784; **Pop below poverty level:** 12.8%. ***Personal per capita income 2000-2003:** $22,227-$23,309.

Unemployment 2004: 7.4%. **Change from 2000:** +0%. **Median travel time to work:** 26.1 minutes. **Working outside county of residence:** 38.7%.

Cities with pop over 10,000: Eden (15,754); Reidsville (14,780).

ROWAN COUNTY
130 W Innes St   **Ph:** 704-636-0361
Salisbury, NC 28144   **Fax:** 704-638-3092
www.co.rowan.nc.us

In west-central NC, southwest of Winston-Salem; organized Mar 27, 1753 (prior to statehood) from Anson County. **Name Origin:** For Matthew Rowan (?-1760), NC legislator, justice of the peace, and acting governor when the county was established.

Area (sq mi): 523.86 (land 511.31; water 12.55). **Pop per sq mi:** 264.2.

Pop 2005: 135,099. **State rank:** 20. **Pop change:** 2000-20005 +3.7%; 1990-2000 +17.8%. **Pop 2000:** 130,340 (White 78.1%; Black or African American 15.8%; Hispanic or Latino 4.1%; Asian 0.8%; Other 3.3%). **Foreign born:** 3.7%. **Median age:** 36.4.

Income 2000: per capita $18,071; median household $37,494; **Pop below poverty level:** 10.6%. ***Personal per capita income 2000-2003:** $24,154-$25,326.

Unemployment 2004: 7.2%. **Change from 2000:** +0.6%. **Median travel time to work:** 23.3 minutes. **Working outside county of residence:** 32.5%.

Cities with pop over 10,000: Salisbury ⛫ (26,519).

RUTHERFORD COUNTY
289 N Main St   **Ph:** 828-287-6060
Rutherfordton, NC 28139   **Fax:** 828-287-6262
www.rutherfordgov.org

On the southwestern border of NC, southeast of Asheville; organized Apr 14, 1779 (prior to statehood) from Burke and Tryon counties, the latter organized in 1768 and abolished in 1779. **Name Origin:** For Gen. Griffith Rutherford (1731-1800), Indian fighter, member of the Provincial Congress, and Revolutionary War officer.

Area (sq mi): 565.9 (land 564.12; water 1.78). **Pop per sq mi:** 113.

⛫ *County Seat*

Rutherford County (cont'd)

Pop 2005: 63,771. **State rank:** 38. **Pop change:** 2000-20005 +1.4%; 1990-2000 +10.5%. **Pop 2000:** 62,899 (White 85.8%; Black or African American 11.2%; Hispanic or Latino 1.8%; Asian 0.3%; Other 1.6%). **Foreign born:** 1.4%. **Median age:** 38.3.

Income 2000: per capita $16,270; median household $31,122; **Pop below poverty level:** 13.9%. *Personal per capita income 2000-2003:* $21,300-$22,778.

Unemployment 2004: 9.3%. **Change from 2000:** +0.9%. **Median travel time to work:** 22.1 minutes. **Working outside county of residence:** 21.2%.

Cities with pop over 10,000: None.

SAMPSON COUNTY
435 Rowan Rd   **Ph:** 910-592-6308
Clinton, NC 28328   **Fax:** 910-592-1945
www.sampsonnc.com

In south-central NC, east of Fayetteville; organized Apr 18, 1784 (prior to statehood) from Duplin County. **Name Origin:** For Col. John Sampson (?-1784), advisor to Josiah Martin, the last royal governor.

Area (sq mi): 947.45 (land 945.45; water 2.01). **Pop per sq mi:** 66.7.

Pop 2005: 63,063. **State rank:** 39. **Pop change:** 2000-20005 +4.8%; 1990-2000 +27.2%. **Pop 2000:** 60,161 (White 56.8%; Black or African American 29.9%; Hispanic or Latino 10.8%; Asian 0.3%; Other 10%, including 1.8% American Indian/Alaska Native). **Foreign born:** 7.1%. **Median age:** 35.

Income 2000: per capita $14,976; median household $31,793; **Pop below poverty level:** 17.6%. *Personal per capita income 2000-2003:* $20,480-$21,447.

Unemployment 2004: 5%. **Change from 2000:** -2.2%. **Median travel time to work:** 25.1 minutes. **Working outside county of residence:** 36.8%.

Cities with pop over 10,000: None.

SCOTLAND COUNTY
PO Box 489   **Ph:** 910-277-2406
Laurinburg, NC 28353   **Fax:** 910-277-2411
www.scotlandcounty.org

On the southern border of NC, southwest of Fayetteville; organized Feb 20, 1899 from Richmond County. **Name Origin:** For the country, former home of many early settlers.

Area (sq mi): 320.64 (land 319.14; water 1.5). **Pop per sq mi:** 116.5.

Pop 2005: 37,180. **State rank:** 64. **Pop change:** 2000-20005 +3.3%; 1990-2000 +6.6%. **Pop 2000:** 35,998 (White 51.1%; Black or African American 37.3%; Hispanic or Latino 1.2%; Asian 0.5%; Other 10.7%, including 8.9% American Indian/Alaska Native). **Foreign born:** 1.3%. **Median age:** 34.6.

Income 2000: per capita $15,693; median household $31,010; **Pop below poverty level:** 20.6%. *Personal per capita income 2000-2003:* $20,540-$21,529.

Unemployment 2004: 10.9%. **Change from 2000:** +0.8%. **Median travel time to work:** 22.4 minutes. **Working outside county of residence:** 25.9%.

Cities with pop over 10,000: Laurinburg 🏛 (15,792).

STANLY COUNTY
201 S 2nd St   **Ph:** 704-986-3600
Albemarle, NC 28001   **Fax:** 704-983-3133
www.co.stanly.nc.us

In west-central NC, northeast of Charlotte; organized Jan 11, 1841 from Montgomery County. **Name Origin:** For John Stanly (1774-1834), NC legislator and U.S. representative (1801-03; 1809-11).

Area (sq mi): 404.26 (land 395.06; water 9.2). **Pop per sq mi:** 149.3.

Pop 2005: 58,964. **State rank:** 41. **Pop change:** 2000-20005 +1.5%; 1990-2000 +12.2%. **Pop 2000:** 58,100 (White 83.7%; Black or African American 11.5%; Hispanic or Latino 2.1%; Asian 1.8%; Other 2%). **Foreign born:** 2.6%. **Median age:** 36.9.

Income 2000: per capita $17,825; median household $36,898; **Pop below poverty level:** 10.7%. *Personal per capita income 2000-2003:* $23,132-$23,354.

Unemployment 2004: 6.2%. **Change from 2000:** -2.1%. **Median travel time to work:** 25.3 minutes. **Working outside county of residence:** 31.8%.

Cities with pop over 10,000: Albemarle 🏛 (15,390).

STOKES COUNTY
PO Box 250   **Ph:** 336-593-9173
Danbury, NC 27016   **Fax:** 336-593-5459
www.co.stokes.nc.us

On the northern border of NC, north of Winston-Salem; organized Nov 2, 1798 from Surry County. **Name Origin:** For Col. John Stokes (1756-90), hero of the American Revolution, NC legislator, and district judge (1783).

Area (sq mi): 455.89 (land 451.84; water 4.05). **Pop per sq mi:** 101.5.

Pop 2005: 45,858. **State rank:** 55. **Pop change:** 2000-20005 +2.6%; 1990-2000 +20.1%. **Pop 2000:** 44,711 (White 92.5%; Black or African American 4.7%; Hispanic or Latino 1.9%; Asian 0.2%; Other 1.7%). **Foreign born:** 1.5%. **Median age:** 37.2.

Income 2000: per capita $18,130; median household $38,808; **Pop below poverty level:** 9.1%. *Personal per capita income 2000-2003:* $22,810-$23,581.

Unemployment 2004: 5.3%. **Change from 2000:** +0.3%. **Median travel time to work:** 30.7 minutes. **Working outside county of residence:** 70.8%.

Cities with pop over 10,000: None.

SURRY COUNTY
202 Kapp St   **Ph:** 336-386-3700
Dobson, NC 27017   **Fax:** 336-386-9879
www.co.surry.nc.us

On the northwestern border of NC, northwest of Winston-Salem; organized 1771 (prior to statehood) from Rowan County. **Name Origin:** For Surrey County in England, home of then-incumbent governor, William Tryon. Possibly influenced by similarity to *Saura*, the local Indian tribe. Spelling the name without the 'e' seems to have been a common colonial practice.

Source: Personal per capita income data are from the Bureau of Economic Analysis; per capita income data are from the Bureau of the Census. See Introduction for explanation of differences.

Surry County (cont'd)

Area (sq mi): 537.79 (land 536.52; water 1.27). **Pop per sq mi:** 135.3.

Pop 2005: 72,601. **State rank:** 35. **Pop change:** 2000-20005 +1.9%; 1990-2000 +15.4%. **Pop 2000:** 71,219 (White 88%; Black or African American 4.2%; Hispanic or Latino 6.5%; Asian 0.6%; Other 4.8%). **Foreign born:** 5.3%. **Median age:** 38.

Income 2000: per capita $17,722; median household $33,046; **Pop below poverty level:** 12.4%. ***Personal per capita income 2000-2003:** $23,504-$24,051.

Unemployment 2004: 6.2%. **Change from 2000:** -0.3%. **Median travel time to work:** 25.5 minutes. **Working outside county of residence:** 25.8%.

Cities with pop over 10,000: None.

SWAIN COUNTY

PO Box 1397   **Ph:** 828-488-2288
Bryson City, NC 28713   **Fax:** 828-488-9360
www.swaincounty.org

On the southwestern border of NC, west of Asheville; organized Feb 24, 1871 from Jackson and Macon counties. **Name Origin:** For David Lowrie Swain (1801-68), NC governor (1832-35) and president of the University of NC (1835-68).

Area (sq mi): 540.64 (land 528.1; water 12.54). **Pop per sq mi:** 24.9.

Pop 2005: 13,167. **State rank:** 90. **Pop change:** 2000-20005 +1.5%; 1990-2000 +15.1%. **Pop 2000:** 12,968 (White 65.9%; Black or African American 1.7%; Hispanic or Latino 1.5%; Asian 0.2%; Other 31.8%, including 29% American Indian/Alaska Native). **Foreign born:** 1%. **Median age:** 38.8.

Income 2000: per capita $14,647; median household $28,608; **Pop below poverty level:** 18.3%. ***Personal per capita income 2000-2003:** $17,369-$19,813.

Unemployment 2004: 7.1%. **Change from 2000:** -4.1%. **Median travel time to work:** 20.8 minutes. **Working outside county of residence:** 28.5%.

Cities with pop over 10,000: None.

TRANSYLVANIA COUNTY

28 E Main St   **Ph:** 828-884-3100
Brevard, NC 28712   **Fax:** 828-884-3119
www.transylvaniacounty.org

On the southwestern border of NC, southwest of Asheville; organized Feb 15, 1861 from Jacksonville and Henderson counties. **Name Origin:** From Latin *trans* plus *sylva* 'across the woods.' The name may also echo that of the province of Transylvania, now in Rumania, but more probably it is literary or promotional name.

Area (sq mi): 380.56 (land 378.39; water 2.17). **Pop per sq mi:** 78.3.

Pop 2005: 29,626. **State rank:** 70. **Pop change:** 2000-20005 +1%; 1990-2000 +14.9%. **Pop 2000:** 29,334 (White 93.1%; Black or African American 4.2%; Hispanic or Latino 1%; Asian 0.4%; Other 1.7%). **Foreign born:** 2.3%. **Median age:** 43.9.

Income 2000: per capita $20,767; median household $38,587; **Pop below poverty level:** 9.5%. ***Personal per capita income 2000-2003:** $26,234-$25,280.

Unemployment 2004: 7%. **Change from 2000:** +2.3%. **Median travel time to work:** 22.1 minutes. **Working outside county of residence:** 21.6%.

Cities with pop over 10,000: None.

TYRRELL COUNTY

108 S Water St PO Box 449   **Ph:** 252-796-1371
Columbia, NC 27925   **Fax:** 252-796-1188
albemarle-nc.com/columbia/

In northeastern NC, on Albemarle Sound, south of Elizabeth City; organized 1729 (prior to statehood) from Chowan, Bertie, Currituck, and Pasquotank counties. **Name Origin:** For John Tyrrell (1685-1729), a lord proprietor of NC.

Area (sq mi): 600.3 (land 389.91; water 210.39). **Pop per sq mi:** 10.7.

Pop 2005: 4,157. **State rank:** 100. **Pop change:** 2000-20005 +0.2%; 1990-2000 +7.6%. **Pop 2000:** 4,149 (White 55.5%; Black or African American 39.4%; Hispanic or Latino 3.6%; Asian 0.7%; Other 3.3%). **Foreign born:** 4%. **Median age:** 38.7.

Income 2000: per capita $13,326; median household $25,684; **Pop below poverty level:** 23.3%. ***Personal per capita income 2000-2003:** $17,567-$19,082.

Unemployment 2004: 7.1%. **Change from 2000:** -1.7%. **Median travel time to work:** 32.5 minutes. **Working outside county of residence:** 39.8%.

Cities with pop over 10,000: None.

UNION COUNTY

500 N Main St Rm 921   **Ph:** 704-283-3672
Monroe, NC 28112   **Fax:** 704-282-0121
www.co.union.nc.us

On the southern border of NC, southeast of Charlotte; organized Dec 19, 1842 from Mecklenburg and Anson counties. **Name Origin:** A compromise to a disagreement between Whigs and Democrats as to whether it should be named for Clay or Jackson; county was also a union of parts of two other counties.

Area (sq mi): 639.59 (land 637.37; water 2.22). **Pop per sq mi:** 255.6.

Pop 2005: 162,929. **State rank:** 10. **Pop change:** 2000-20005 +31.7%; 1990-2000 +46.9%. **Pop 2000:** 123,677 (White 79.7%; Black or African American 12.5%; Hispanic or Latino 6.2%; Asian 0.6%; Other 4%). **Foreign born:** 5.7%. **Median age:** 34.

Income 2000: per capita $21,978; median household $50,638; **Pop below poverty level:** 8.1%. ***Personal per capita income 2000-2003:** $26,171-$26,778.

Unemployment 2004: 4.6%. **Change from 2000:** +0.8%. **Median travel time to work:** 29 minutes. **Working outside county of residence:** 46.7%.

Cities with pop over 10,000: Monroe 🏛 (28,422); Matthews (23,897); Indian Trail (15,610).

🏛 *County Seat*

VANCE COUNTY
122 Young St Suite F   Ph: 212-738-2110
Henderson, NC 27536
www.vancecounty.org

On the central northern border of NC, northeast of Raleigh; organized Mar 5, 1881 from Franklin, Granville, and Warren counties. **Name Origin:** For Zebulon Baird Vance (1830-94), U.S. representative from NC (1858-61), governor (1862-65; 1877-79), and U.S. senator (1879-94).

Area (sq mi): 269.82 (land 253.52; water 16.31). **Pop per sq mi:** 172.7.

Pop 2005: 43,771. **State rank:** 56. **Pop change:** 2000-20005 +1.9%; 1990-2000 +10.4%. **Pop 2000:** 42,954 (White 46.3%; Black or African American 48.3%; Hispanic or Latino 4.6%; Asian 0.4%; Other 3%). **Foreign born:** 3.4%. **Median age:** 35.

Income 2000: per capita $15,897; median household $31,301; **Pop below poverty level:** 20.5%. ***Personal per capita income 2000-2003:** $20,973-$21,594.

Unemployment 2004: 10%. **Change from 2000:** -0.3%. **Median travel time to work:** 23.6 minutes. **Working outside county of residence:** 29.9%.

Cities with pop over 10,000: Henderson ⛪ (16,243).

WAKE COUNTY
PO Box 550 Suite 1100   Ph: 919-856-6160
Raleigh, NC 27602   Fax: 919-856-6168
www.wakegov.com

In north-central NC, east of Durham; organized 1771 (prior to statehood) from Cumberland, Johnston, and Orange counties. **Name Origin:** For Margaret Wake (1733-1819), wife of Gov. William Tryon (1729-88).

Area (sq mi): 857.26 (land 831.92; water 25.33). **Pop per sq mi:** 900.1.

Pop 2005: 748,815. **State rank:** 2. **Pop change:** 2000-20005 +19.3%; 1990-2000 +48.3%. **Pop 2000:** 627,846 (White 69.9%; Black or African American 19.7%; Hispanic or Latino 5.4%; Asian 3.4%; Other 4.4%). **Foreign born:** 9.7%. **Median age:** 32.9.

Income 2000: per capita $27,004; median household $54,988; **Pop below poverty level:** 7.8%. ***Personal per capita income 2000-2003:** $35,955-$35,864.

Unemployment 2004: 4.3%. **Change from 2000:** +1%. **Median travel time to work:** 24.7 minutes. **Working outside county of residence:** 19.5%.

Cities with pop over 10,000: 8 (see page 37 for cities).

WARREN COUNTY
PO Box 709   Ph: 252-257-3261
Warrenton, NC 27589   Fax: 252-257-5529
www.warrencountync.org

On the central northern border of NC, northeast of Raleigh; organized Apr 14, 1779 (prior to statehood) from Bute County, which was discontinued at that time. **Name Origin:** For Gen. Joseph Warren (1741-75), Revolutionary War patriot and member of the Committee of Safety who dispatched Paul Revere (1735-1818) on his famous ride.

Area (sq mi): 443.8 (land 428.7; water 15.09). **Pop per sq mi:** 46.

Pop 2005: 19,729. **State rank:** 82. **Pop change:** 2000-20005 -1.2%; 1990-2000 +15.7%. **Pop 2000:** 19,972 (White 38.5%; Black or African American 54.5%; Hispanic or Latino 1.6%; Asian 0.1%; Other 6.5%, including 4.8% American Indian/Alaska Native). **Foreign born:** 2.3%. **Median age:** 39.7.

Income 2000: per capita $14,716; median household $28,351; **Pop below poverty level:** 19.4%. ***Personal per capita income 2000-2003:** $17,231-$17,971.

Unemployment 2004: 7.6%. **Change from 2000:** -2.7%. **Median travel time to work:** 30.4 minutes. **Working outside county of residence:** 55.1%.

Cities with pop over 10,000: None.

WASHINGTON COUNTY
PO Box 1007   Ph: 252-793-5823
Plymouth, NC 27962   Fax: 252-793-1183
www.washingtoncountygov.com

In east-central NC, on Albemarle Sound, southwest of Elizabeth City; organized 1799 from Tyrrell County. **Name Origin:** For George Washington (1732-99), American patriot and first U.S. president.

Area (sq mi): 424.39 (land 348.46; water 75.93). **Pop per sq mi:** 38.1.

Pop 2005: 13,282. **State rank:** 89. **Pop change:** 2000-20005 -3.2%; 1990-2000 -2%. **Pop 2000:** 13,723 (White 47.8%; Black or African American 48.9%; Hispanic or Latino 2.3%; Asian 0.3%; Other 2.5%). **Foreign born:** 1.4%. **Median age:** 39.2.

Income 2000: per capita $14,994; median household $28,865; **Pop below poverty level:** 21.8%. ***Personal per capita income 2000-2003:** $20,198-$21,239.

Unemployment 2004: 7.4%. **Change from 2000:** +0.3%. **Median travel time to work:** 28.3 minutes. **Working outside county of residence:** 32.6%.

Cities with pop over 10,000: None.

WATAUGA COUNTY
842 W King St Courthouse   Ph: 828-265-8000
Boone, NC 28607   Fax: 828-264-3230
www.wataugacounty.org

On the northeastern border of NC, northeast of Asheville; organized Jan 27, 1849 from Ashe, Caldwell, Wilkes, and Yancey counties. **Name Origin:** For the Watauga River, which runs through the county; from the Indian word probably meaning 'beautiful water.'

Area (sq mi): 312.73 (land 312.51; water 0.22). **Pop per sq mi:** 135.9.

Pop 2005: 42,472. **State rank:** 58. **Pop change:** 2000-20005 -0.5%; 1990-2000 +15.5%. **Pop 2000:** 42,695 (White 95.4%; Black or African American 1.6%; Hispanic or Latino 1.5%; Asian 0.6%; Other 1.4%). **Foreign born:** 1.9%. **Median age:** 29.9.

Income 2000: per capita $17,258; median household $32,611; **Pop below poverty level:** 17.9%. ***Personal per capita income 2000-2003:** $22,467-$24,472.

*Source: Personal per capita income data are from the Bureau of Economic Analysis; per capita income data are from the Bureau of the Census. See Introduction for explanation of differences.

Watauga County (cont'd)

Unemployment 2004: 3.5%. **Change from 2000:** +1.4%. **Median travel time to work:** 20.4 minutes. **Working outside county of residence:** 13.8%.

Cities with pop over 10,000: Boone ⛪ (13,286).

WAYNE COUNTY
PO Box 227   **Ph:** 919-731-1435
Goldsboro, NC 27533   **Fax:** 919-731-1446
www.waynegov.com

In east-central NC, southeast of Raleigh; organized Oct 18, 1779 (prior to statehood) from Dobbs County. **Name Origin:** For Gen. Anthony Wayne (1745-96), PA soldier and statesman, nicknamed 'Mad Anthony' for his daring during the Revolutionary War.

Area (sq mi): 556.69 (land 552.57; water 4.12). **Pop per sq mi:** 207.1.

Pop 2005: 114,448. **State rank:** 23. **Pop change:** 2000-20005 +1%; 1990-2000 +8.3%. **Pop 2000:** 113,329 (White 59.8%; Black or African American 33%; Hispanic or Latino 4.9%; Asian 1%; Other 4.8%). **Foreign born:** 4.2%. **Median age:** 34.8.

Income 2000: per capita $17,010; median household $33,942; **Pop below poverty level:** 13.8%. ***Personal per capita income 2000-2003:** $22,089-$23,584.

Unemployment 2004: 5.4%. **Change from 2000:** +0%. **Median travel time to work:** 21.5 minutes. **Working outside county of residence:** 18.5%.

Cities with pop over 10,000: Goldsboro ⛪ (38,774).

WILKES COUNTY
110 North St   **Ph:** 336-651-7345
Wilkesboro, NC 28697   **Fax:** 336-651-7546
www.wilkescounty.net

In northwestern NC, northwest of Winston-Salem; organized Nov 15, 1777 (prior to statehood) from Surry County. **Name Origin:** For John Wilkes (1727-97), English political leader who supported American rights at the time of the Revolutionary War.

Area (sq mi): 759.93 (land 757.19; water 2.74). **Pop per sq mi:** 89.

Pop 2005: 67,390. **State rank:** 37. **Pop change:** 2000-20005 +2.7%; 1990-2000 +10.5%. **Pop 2000:** 65,632 (White 91.4%; Black or African American 4.2%; Hispanic or Latino 3.4%; Asian 0.3%; Other 2.5%). **Foreign born:** 3%. **Median age:** 38.5.

Income 2000: per capita $17,516; median household $34,258; **Pop below poverty level:** 11.9%. ***Personal per capita income 2000-2003:** $23,625-$24,633.

Unemployment 2004: 6.2%. **Change from 2000:** +0.5%. **Median travel time to work:** 24 minutes. **Working outside county of residence:** 21.8%.

Cities with pop over 10,000: None.

WILSON COUNTY
PO Box 1728   **Ph:** 252-399-2810
Wilson, NC 27894   **Fax:** 252-237-4341
www.wilson-co.com

In east-central NC, north of Goldsboro; organized Feb 13, 1855 from Edgecombe, Johnston, Wayne, and Nash counties. **Name Origin:** For Louis Dicken Wilson (1789-1847), member of the NC General Assembly and an officer in the Mexican war.

Area (sq mi): 374.26 (land 371.09; water 3.17). **Pop per sq mi:** 205.6.

Pop 2005: 76,281. **State rank:** 34. **Pop change:** 2000-20005 +3.3%; 1990-2000 +11.7%. **Pop 2000:** 73,814 (White 53.5%; Black or African American 39.3%; Hispanic or Latino 6%; Asian 0.4%; Other 4.4%). **Foreign born:** 4.9%. **Median age:** 36.2.

Income 2000: per capita $17,102; median household $33,116; **Pop below poverty level:** 18.5%. ***Personal per capita income 2000-2003:** $23,408-$25,121.

Unemployment 2004: 8.3%. **Change from 2000:** +0%. **Median travel time to work:** 21 minutes. **Working outside county of residence:** 20.2%.

Cities with pop over 10,000: Wilson ⛪ (46,507).

YADKIN COUNTY
PO Box 146   **Ph:** 336-679-4200
Yadkinville, NC 27055   **Fax:** 336-679-6005
www.yadkincounty.gov

In north-central NC, west of Winston-Salem; organized Dec 28, 1850 from Surry County. **Name Origin:** For the Yadkin River, which runs through it; meaning of the name is unknown.

Area (sq mi): 337.49 (land 335.55; water 1.94). **Pop per sq mi:** 112.3.

Pop 2005: 37,668. **State rank:** 62. **Pop change:** 2000-20005 +3.6%; 1990-2000 +19.2%. **Pop 2000:** 36,348 (White 89.3%; Black or African American 3.4%; Hispanic or Latino 6.5%; Asian 0.2%; Other 3.9%). **Foreign born:** 4.4%. **Median age:** 37.6.

Income 2000: per capita $18,576; median household $36,660; **Pop below poverty level:** 10%. ***Personal per capita income 2000-2003:** $23,110-$23,863.

Unemployment 2004: 5.2%. **Change from 2000:** +0.3%. **Median travel time to work:** 27.5 minutes. **Working outside county of residence:** 56.1%.

Cities with pop over 10,000: None.

YANCEY COUNTY
110 Town Square Rm 11   **Ph:** 828-682-3971
Burnsville, NC 28714   **Fax:** 828-682-4301
www.main.nc.us/yancey/

On the northwestern border of NC, northeast of Asheville; organized 1833 from Buncombe and Burke counties. **Name Origin:** For Bartlett Yancey (1785-1828), U.S. representative from NC (1813-17) and presiding officer of the state senate (1817-27).

Area (sq mi): 313.11 (land 312.45; water 0.65). **Pop per sq mi:** 58.3.

Pop 2005: 18,201. **State rank:** 85. **Pop change:** 2000-20005 +2.4%; 1990-2000 +15.3%. **Pop 2000:** 17,774 (White 95.8%; Black or African American 0.6%; Hispanic or Latino 2.7%; Asian 0.1%; Other 1.3%). **Foreign born:** 2.8%. **Median age:** 41.9.

⛪ *County Seat*

Yancey County (cont'd)

Income 2000: per capita $16,335; median household $29,674; **Pop below poverty level:** 15.8%. ***Personal per capita income 2000-2003:** $19,998-$19,730.

Unemployment 2004: 6.8%. **Change from 2000:** -5.9%. **Median travel time to work:** 27 minutes. **Working outside county of residence:** 34.5%.

Cities with pop over 10,000: None.

Source: Personal per capita income data are from the Bureau of Economic Analysis; per capita income data are from the Bureau of the Census. See Introduction for explanation of differences.

526

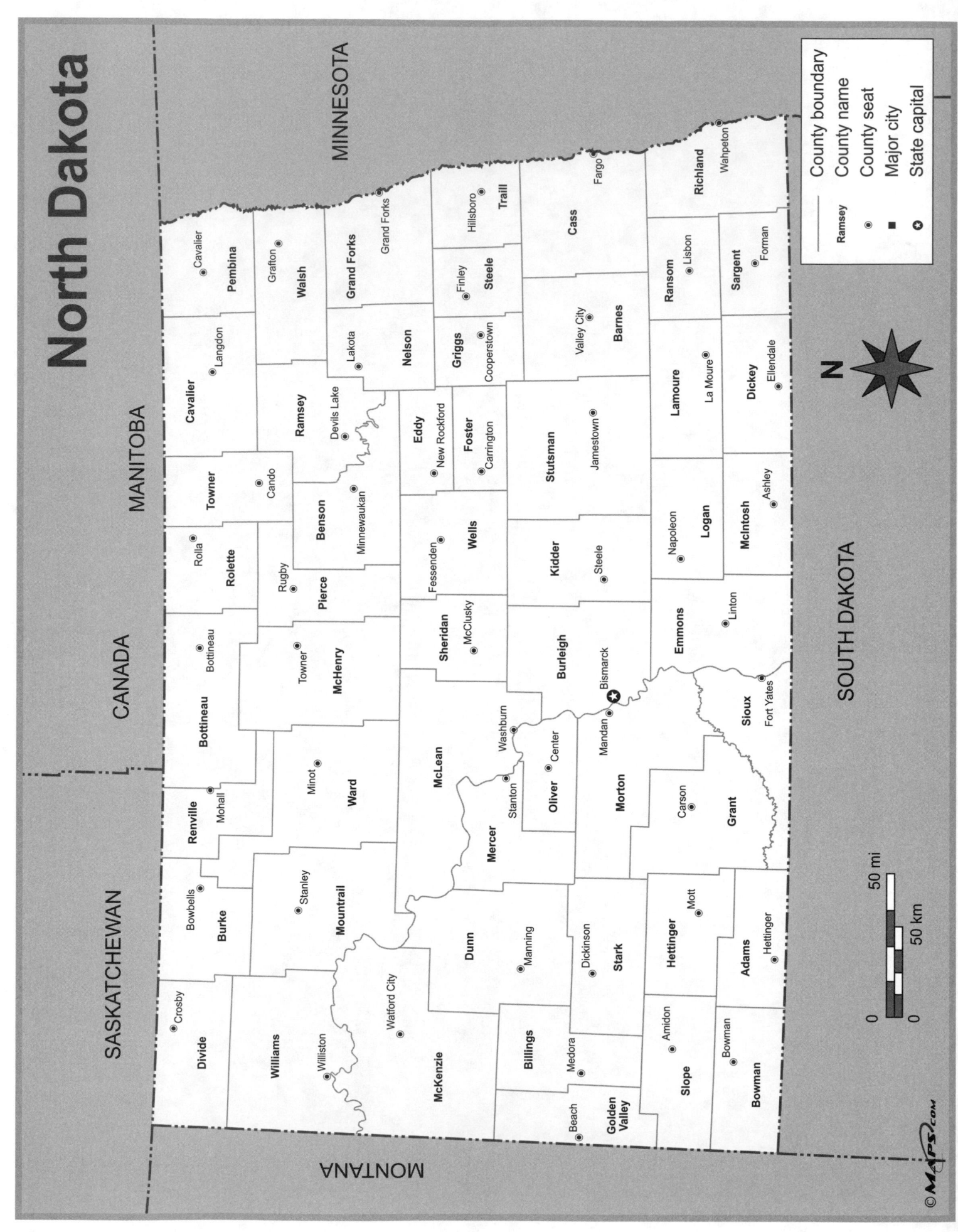

North Dakota

North Dakota

NORTH DAKOTA STATE INFORMATION

www.nd.gov   **Ph:** 701-328-2000

Area (sq mi): 70,699.79 (land 68,975.93; water 1723.86). **Pop per sq mi:** 9.2.

Pop 2005: 636,677. **Pop change:** 2000-20005 -0.9%; 1990-2000 +0.5%. **Pop 2000:** 642,200 (White 91.7%; Black or African American 0.6%; Hispanic or Latino 1.2%; Asian 0.6%; Other 6.5%, including 4.9% American Indian/Alaska Native). **Foreign born:** 1.9%. **Median age:** 36.2.

Income 2000: per capita $17,769; median household $34,604; **Pop below poverty level:** 11.9%. ***Personal per capita income 2000-2003:** $25,106-$28,922.

Unemployment 2004: 3.5%. **Change from 2000:** +0.6%. **Median travel time to work:** 15.8 minutes. **Working outside county of residence:** 13.4%.

ADAMS COUNTY

602 Adams Ave PO Box 469   **Ph:** 701-567-2460
Hettinger, ND 58639   **Fax:** 701-567-2910
www.hettingernd.com

On the southwestern border of ND, south of Dickinson; organized Apr 24, 1907 from Hettinger County. **Name Origin:** For John Quincy Adams (1848-1919), land and townsite agent for the Chicago, Milwaukee and Saint Paul Railway whose main line to the Pacific coast was built through the area (1906-07). Adams was distantly related to the president of the same name.

Area (sq mi): 988.84 (land 987.91; water 0.92). **Pop per sq mi:** 2.5.

Pop 2005: 2,433. **State rank:** 43. **Pop change:** 2000-20005 -6.2%; 1990-2000 -18.3%. **Pop 2000:** 2,593 (White 98.3%; Black or African American 0.5%; Hispanic or Latino 0.3%; Asian 0.2%; Other 0.7%). **Foreign born:** 1.5%. **Median age:** 45.6.

Income 2000: per capita $18,425; median household $29,079; **Pop below poverty level:** 10.4%. ***Personal per capita income 2000-2003:** $22,213-$23,596.

Unemployment 2004: 2.5%. **Change from 2000:** +0.5%. **Median travel time to work:** 12.6 minutes. **Working outside county of residence:** 13.6%.

Cities with pop over 10,000: None.

BARNES COUNTY

230 4th St NW Rm 202   **Ph:** 701-845-8500
Valley City, ND 58072   **Fax:** 701-845-8548
www.co.barnes.nd.us

In southeastern ND, west of Fargo; organized as Burbank County by the 1872-1873 territorial legislature (prior to statehood) from Cass County; renamed Jan 14, 1875. **Name Origin:** For Alanson H. Barnes (1818-90), judge of the federal district court (1872-81). Originally for John A. Burbank (1827-1905), governor of Dakota Territory (1869-73).

Area (sq mi): 1513.23 (land 1491.65; water 21.58). **Pop per sq mi:** 7.4.

Pop 2005: 11,075. **State rank:** 13. **Pop change:** 2000-20005 -5.9%; 1990-2000 -6.1%. **Pop 2000:** 11,775 (White 97.5%; Black or African American 0.5%; Hispanic or Latino 0.5%; Asian 0.2%; Other 1.5%). **Foreign born:** 0.9%. **Median age:** 40.6.

Income 2000: per capita $16,566; median household $31,166; **Pop below poverty level:** 10.8%. ***Personal per capita income 2000-2003:** $23,763-$27,976.

Unemployment 2004: 3.3%. **Change from 2000:** +0.7%. **Median travel time to work:** 15.7 minutes. **Working outside county of residence:** 15.6%.

Cities with pop over 10,000: None.

BENSON COUNTY

PO Box 213   **Ph:** 701-473-5345
Minnewaukan, ND 58351   **Fax:** 701-473-5571

In east-central ND, east of Minot; organized Mar 9, 1883 (prior to statehood) from Ramsey County. **Name Origin:** For Bertil W. Benson, a Dakota Territory legislator at the time the county was organized.

Area (sq mi): 1439.27 (land 1380.6; water 58.68). **Pop per sq mi:** 5.1.

Pop 2005: 6,999. **State rank:** 18. **Pop change:** 2000-20005 +0.5%; 1990-2000 -3.3%. **Pop 2000:** 6,964 (White 50.7%; Black or African American 0.1%; Hispanic or Latino 0.8%; Asian 0%; Other 49%, including 48% American Indian/Alaska Native). **Foreign born:** 0.5%. **Median age:** 31.4.

Income 2000: per capita $11,509; median household $26,688; **Pop below poverty level:** 29.1%. ***Personal per capita income 2000-2003:** $16,870-$21,935.

Unemployment 2004: 5%. **Change from 2000:** -2.5%. **Median travel time to work:** 18.4 minutes. **Working outside county of residence:** 23.1%.

Cities with pop over 10,000: None.

BILLINGS COUNTY

PO Box 138   **Ph:** 701-623-4491
Medora, ND 58645   **Fax:** 701-623-4896

In southwestern ND, west of Dickinson; organized Feb 10, 1879

Billings County (cont'd)

(prior to statehood) from unorganized territory. **Name Origin:** For Frederick K. Billings (1823-90), president of the Northern Pacific Railroad (1879-81).

Area (sq mi): 1153.4 (land 1151.41; water 1.99). **Pop per sq mi:** 0.7.

Pop 2005: 813. **State rank:** 52. **Pop change:** 2000-20005 -8.4%; 1990-2000 -19.9%. **Pop 2000:** 888 (White 98.4%; Black or African American 0%; Hispanic or Latino 0.3%; Asian 0%; Other 1.2%). **Foreign born:** 1%. **Median age:** 41.9.

Income 2000: per capita $16,186; median household $32,667; **Pop below poverty level:** 12.8%. ***Personal per capita income 2000-2003:** $18,289-$22,245.

Unemployment 2004: 2.6%. **Change from 2000:** -1.3%. **Median travel time to work:** 22.3 minutes. **Working outside county of residence:** 32.3%.

Cities with pop over 10,000: None.

BOTTINEAU COUNTY
314 W 5th St   **Ph:** 701-228-3983
Bottineau, ND 58318   **Fax:** 701-228-2336
www.bottineau.com

On the central northern border of ND, northeast of Minot; organized Jan 4, 1873 (prior to statehood) from unorganized territory. **Name Origin:** For Pierre Bottineau (c. 1814-95), a French-Canadian frontiersman, guide, and land speculator.

Area (sq mi): 1697.74 (land 1668.59; water 29.16). **Pop per sq mi:** 4.

Pop 2005: 6,741. **State rank:** 19. **Pop change:** 2000-20005 -5.7%; 1990-2000 -10.8%. **Pop 2000:** 7,149 (White 97%; Black or African American 0.2%; Hispanic or Latino 0.5%; Asian 0.2%; Other 2.4%, including 1.5% American Indian/Alaska Native). **Foreign born:** 2.1%. **Median age:** 43.4.

Income 2000: per capita $16,227; median household $29,853; **Pop below poverty level:** 10.7%. ***Personal per capita income 2000-2003:** $26,312-$30,957.

Unemployment 2004: 4%. **Change from 2000:** +0.9%. **Median travel time to work:** 17.9 minutes. **Working outside county of residence:** 20.6%.

Cities with pop over 10,000: None.

BOWMAN COUNTY
PO Box 379   **Ph:** 701-523-3450
Bowman, ND 58623   **Fax:** 701-523-5443
www.bowmannd.com

In the southwestern corner of ND; organized Mar 8, 1883 (prior to statehood) from Billings County. Eliminated in 1903 for lack of settlement; reestablished Jun 10, 1907. **Name Origin:** Possibly for Edward M. Bowman, a Dakota Territory representative. Another source says that William Bowman was the territorial legislator, and Edward M. Bowman was an official of the Milwaukee Road Railroad that ran through the county.

Area (sq mi): 1166.99 (land 1162.05; water 4.95). **Pop per sq mi:** 2.6.

Pop 2005: 3,048. **State rank:** 35. **Pop change:** 2000-20005 -6%; 1990-2000 -9.8%. **Pop 2000:** 3,242 (White 98.6%; Black or African

American 0%; Hispanic or Latino 0.7%; Asian 0%; Other 1%). **Foreign born:** 0.4%. **Median age:** 43.

Income 2000: per capita $17,662; median household $31,906; **Pop below poverty level:** 8.2%. ***Personal per capita income 2000-2003:** $23,601-$29,290.

Unemployment 2004: 2.4%. **Change from 2000:** +0.5%. **Median travel time to work:** 12.9 minutes. **Working outside county of residence:** 9.1%.

Cities with pop over 10,000: None.

BURKE COUNTY
PO Box 219   **Ph:** 701-377-2718
Bowbells, ND 58721   **Fax:** 701-377-2020
www.burkecountynd.com

On the northwestern border of ND, northwest of Minot; organized Jul 12, 1910 from Ward County. **Name Origin:** For John Burke (1859-1937), ND governor (1907-13), treasurer of the U.S. (1913-21), and justice of ND Supreme Court (1925-37).

Area (sq mi): 1129.26 (land 1103.53; water 25.73). **Pop per sq mi:** 1.8.

Pop 2005: 2,032. **State rank:** 47. **Pop change:** 2000-20005 -9.4%; 1990-2000 -25.3%. **Pop 2000:** 2,242 (White 99%; Black or African American 0.1%; Hispanic or Latino 0.4%; Asian 0.1%; Other 0.4%). **Foreign born:** 1.5%. **Median age:** 47.5.

Income 2000: per capita $14,026; median household $25,330; **Pop below poverty level:** 15.4%. ***Personal per capita income 2000-2003:** $26,499-$28,934.

Unemployment 2004: 3.3%. **Change from 2000:** +0.8%. **Median travel time to work:** 18.5 minutes. **Working outside county of residence:** 21.8%.

Cities with pop over 10,000: None.

BURLEIGH COUNTY
PO Box 1055   **Ph:** 701-222-6761
Bismarck, ND 58502   **Fax:** 701-221-3756
www.co.burleigh.nd.us

In south-central ND; organized Jan 4, 1873 (prior to statehood) from Buffalo County, which was discontinued. **Name Origin:** For Walter Atwood Burleigh (1820-96), attorney, physician, Dakota Territory delegate to Congress (1865-69), and legislator.

Area (sq mi): 1668.04 (land 1633.09; water 34.95). **Pop per sq mi:** 45.2.

Pop 2005: 73,818. **State rank:** 2. **Pop change:** 2000-20005 +6.3%; 1990-2000 +15.4%. **Pop 2000:** 69,416 (White 94.6%; Black or African American 0.3%; Hispanic or Latino 0.7%; Asian 0.4%; Other 4.3%, including 3.3% American Indian/Alaska Native). **Foreign born:** 1.5%. **Median age:** 35.9.

Income 2000: per capita $20,436; median household $41,309; **Pop below poverty level:** 7.8%. ***Personal per capita income 2000-2003:** $26,981-$31,327.

Unemployment 2004: 2.8%. **Change from 2000:** +0.6%. **Median travel time to work:** 15.1 minutes. **Working outside county of residence:** 10.5%.

Cities with pop over 10,000: Bismarck 🏛 (56,619).

---

*Source: Personal per capita income data are from the Bureau of Economic Analysis; per capita income data are from the Bureau of the Census. See Introduction for explanation of differences.

CASS COUNTY

PO Box 2806
Fargo, ND 58108
www.co.cass.nd.us

Ph: 701-241-5601
Fax: 701-241-5728

On the southeastern border of ND, south of Grand Forks; original county; organized Jan 4, 1873 (prior to statehood). **Name Origin:** For George W. Cass (1810-88), president of the Northern Pacific Railroad (1856).

Area (sq mi): 1767.91 (land 1765.23; water 2.68). **Pop per sq mi:** 74.2.

Pop 2005: 131,019. **State rank:** 1. **Pop change:** 2000-20005 +6.4%; 1990-2000 +19.7%. **Pop 2000:** 123,138 (White 94.4%; Black or African American 0.8%; Hispanic or Latino 1.2%; Asian 1.3%; Other 2.8%, including 1.1% American Indian/Alaska Native). **Foreign born:** 3.2%. **Median age:** 31.3.

Income 2000: per capita $20,889; median household $38,147; **Pop below poverty level:** 10.1%. ***Personal per capita income 2000-2003:** $29,561-$33,063.

Unemployment 2004: 2.6%. **Change from 2000:** +1.1%. **Median travel time to work:** 15.7 minutes. **Working outside county of residence:** 10.8%.

Cities with pop over 10,000: Fargo 🏛 (91,048); West Fargo (17,581).

CAVALIER COUNTY

901 3rd St Suite 15
Langdon, ND 58249
www.ccjda.org

Ph: 701-256-2229
Fax: 701-256-2566

On the northeastern border of ND, northwest of Grand Forks; organized Jan 4, 1873 (prior to statehood) from Pembina County. **Name Origin:** For either Charles T. Cavileer (1818-1902), an early white settler and public official (with the spelling changed to seem French); or Rene Robert Cavalier, Sieur de la Salle (1643-87), the explorer.

Area (sq mi): 1510.14 (land 1488.46; water 21.68). **Pop per sq mi:** 2.9.

Pop 2005: 4,330. **State rank:** 27. **Pop change:** 2000-20005 -10.4%; 1990-2000 -20.3%. **Pop 2000:** 4,831 (White 97.7%; Black or African American 0.1%; Hispanic or Latino 0.6%; Asian 0.1%; Other 1.6%). **Foreign born:** 2.5%. **Median age:** 45.2.

Income 2000: per capita $15,817; median household $31,868; **Pop below poverty level:** 11.5%. ***Personal per capita income 2000-2003:** $30,155-$35,934.

Unemployment 2004: 3.7%. **Change from 2000:** +0.8%. **Median travel time to work:** 12.7 minutes. **Working outside county of residence:** 11.4%.

Cities with pop over 10,000: None.

DICKEY COUNTY

PO Box 215
Ellendale, ND 58436

Ph: 701-349-3249
Fax: 701-349-4639

On the southern border of ND, southwest of Fargo; organized Mar 5, 1881 (prior to statehood) from La Moure County. **Name Origin:** For either Alfred M. Dickey (1846-1901), a homesteader in the county and lt. governor of ND (1889-90), or for George H. Dickey (1858-1923), an attorney and ND legislator.

Area (sq mi): 1141.66 (land 1131; water 10.66). **Pop per sq mi:** 4.9.

Pop 2005: 5,487. **State rank:** 24. **Pop change:** 2000-20005 -4.7%; 1990-2000 -5.7%. **Pop 2000:** 5,757 (White 97%; Black or African American 0.1%; Hispanic or Latino 1.4%; Asian 0.5%; Other 1.6%). **Foreign born:** 1.6%. **Median age:** 40.7.

Income 2000: per capita $15,846; median household $29,231; **Pop below poverty level:** 14.8%. ***Personal per capita income 2000-2003:** $25,110-$28,470.

Unemployment 2004: 2.6%. **Change from 2000:** +0.4%. **Median travel time to work:** 15 minutes. **Working outside county of residence:** 12.6%.

Cities with pop over 10,000: None.

DIVIDE COUNTY

PO Box 68
Crosby, ND 58730

Ph: 701-965-6831
Fax: 701-965-6943

In the northwestern corner of ND; organized Dec 9, 1910 from Williams County. **Name Origin:** For the division of Williams County to form it, or possibly for the mountains that divide the county.

Area (sq mi): 1294.18 (land 1259.53; water 34.65). **Pop per sq mi:** 1.7.

Pop 2005: 2,149. **State rank:** 45. **Pop change:** 2000-20005 -5.9%; 1990-2000 -21.2%. **Pop 2000:** 2,283 (White 98.6%; Black or African American 0%; Hispanic or Latino 0.6%; Asian 0.5%; Other 0.5%). **Foreign born:** 2.4%. **Median age:** 49.

Income 2000: per capita $16,225; median household $30,089; **Pop below poverty level:** 14.6%. ***Personal per capita income 2000-2003:** $24,368-$25,707.

Unemployment 2004: 3.1%. **Change from 2000:** +1.2%. **Median travel time to work:** 13.4 minutes. **Working outside county of residence:** 11%.

Cities with pop over 10,000: None.

DUNN COUNTY

PO Box 105
Manning, ND 58642

Ph: 701-573-4448
Fax: 701-573-4323

In west-central ND, north of Dickinson; organized Mar 9, 1883 (prior to statehood) from Howard County, which was discontinued. **Name Origin:** For John P. Dunn (1839-1917), early settler and mayor of Bismarck, ND.

Area (sq mi): 2082.25 (land 2009.6; water 72.65). **Pop per sq mi:** 1.7.

Pop 2005: 3,442. **State rank:** 33. **Pop change:** 2000-20005 -4.4%; 1990-2000 -10.1%. **Pop 2000:** 3,600 (White 86.1%; Black or African American 0%; Hispanic or Latino 0.8%; Asian 0.1%; Other 13.3%, including 12.4% American Indian/Alaska Native). **Foreign born:** 0.7%. **Median age:** 40.9.

Income 2000: per capita $14,624; median household $30,015; **Pop below poverty level:** 17.5%. ***Personal per capita income 2000-2003:** $20,600-$21,527.

Unemployment 2004: 3.6%. **Change from 2000:** +0%. **Median travel time to work:** 19.2 minutes. **Working outside county of residence:** 26.8%.

Cities with pop over 10,000: None.

🏛 *County Seat*

EDDY COUNTY

524 Central Ave   **Ph:** 701-947-2434
New Rockford, ND 58356   **Fax:** 701-947-2067

In east-central ND, west of Grand Forks; organized Mar 9, 1885 (prior to statehood) from Foster County. **Name Origin:** For Ezra B. Eddy (1830-85), founder of the First National Bank of Fargo.

Area (sq mi): 644.23 (land 630.12; water 14.11). **Pop per sq mi:** 4.2.

Pop 2005: 2,626. **State rank:** 37. **Pop change:** 2000-20005 -4.8%; 1990-2000 -6.6%. **Pop 2000:** 2,757 (White 96.1%; Black or African American 0.1%; Hispanic or Latino 0.6%; Asian 0.1%; Other 3.5%, including 2.4% American Indian/Alaska Native). **Foreign born:** 0.4%. **Median age:** 43.8.

Income 2000: per capita $15,941; median household $28,642; **Pop below poverty level:** 9.7%. ***Personal per capita income 2000-2003:** $21,026-$27,015.

Unemployment 2004: 4.8%. **Change from 2000:** +0%. **Median travel time to work:** 16.6 minutes. **Working outside county of residence:** 27.4%.

Cities with pop over 10,000: None.

EMMONS COUNTY

PO Box 129   **Ph:** 701-254-4807
Linton, ND 58552   **Fax:** 701-254-4012

On the central southern border of ND, southeast of Bismarck; organized Feb 10, 1879 (prior to statehood) from unorganized territory. **Name Origin:** For James A. Emmons (1845-1919), steamboat captain, early settler, and merchant.

Area (sq mi): 1554.72 (land 1509.88; water 44.83). **Pop per sq mi:** 2.5.

Pop 2005: 3,845. **State rank:** 31. **Pop change:** 2000-20005 -11.2%; 1990-2000 -10.3%. **Pop 2000:** 4,331 (White 98.3%; Black or African American 0%; Hispanic or Latino 1.2%; Asian 0.2%; Other 0.7%). **Foreign born:** 0.5%. **Median age:** 44.5.

Income 2000: per capita $14,604; median household $26,119; **Pop below poverty level:** 20.1%. ***Personal per capita income 2000-2003:** $21,646-$23,875.

Unemployment 2004: 5.5%. **Change from 2000:** +0.9%. **Median travel time to work:** 17.6 minutes. **Working outside county of residence:** 11.3%.

Cities with pop over 10,000: None.

FOSTER COUNTY

PO Box 257   **Ph:** 701-652-1001
Carrington, ND 58421   **Fax:** 701-652-2173
www.fostercounty.com

In east-central ND, southwest of Grand Forks; organized Jan 4, 1873 (prior to statehood) from Pembina County. **Name Origin:** For either James S. Foster, commissioner of immigration, or possibly his brother, George I. Foster. Both were prominent in Dakota territorial affairs.

Area (sq mi): 646.72 (land 635.2; water 11.52). **Pop per sq mi:** 5.6.

Pop 2005: 3,580. **State rank:** 32. **Pop change:** 2000-20005 -4.8%; 1990-2000 -5.6%. **Pop 2000:** 3,759 (White 98.9%; Black or African American 0.1%; Hispanic or Latino 0.2%; Asian 0%; Other 0.9%). **Foreign born:** 1.5%. **Median age:** 40.5.

Income 2000: per capita $17,928; median household $32,019; **Pop below poverty level:** 9.3%. ***Personal per capita income 2000-2003:** $25,152-$30,017.

Unemployment 2004: 3.2%. **Change from 2000:** +0.4%. **Median travel time to work:** 12.3 minutes. **Working outside county of residence:** 13.8%.

Cities with pop over 10,000: None.

GOLDEN VALLEY COUNTY

150 1st Ave SE PO Box 9   **Ph:** 701-872-3713
Beach, ND 58621
www.beachnd.com

On the southwestern border of ND, west of Dickinson; organized Nov 11, 1912 from Billings County. **Name Origin:** Descriptive, or for the Golden Valley Land and Cattle Company.

Area (sq mi): 1002.36 (land 1001.99; water 0.37). **Pop per sq mi:** 1.7.

Pop 2005: 1,739. **State rank:** 50. **Pop change:** 2000-20005 -9.6%; 1990-2000 -8.7%. **Pop 2000:** 1,924 (White 97.2%; Black or African American 0%; Hispanic or Latino 1%; Asian 0.1%; Other 2.1%). **Foreign born:** 0.5%. **Median age:** 41.2.

Income 2000: per capita $14,173; median household $29,967; **Pop below poverty level:** 15.3%. ***Personal per capita income 2000-2003:** $18,337-$20,568.

Unemployment 2004: 3%. **Change from 2000:** +0.9%. **Median travel time to work:** 14.1 minutes. **Working outside county of residence:** 11.3%.

Cities with pop over 10,000: None.

GRAND FORKS COUNTY

124 S 4th St   **Ph:** 701-787-2715
Grand Forks, ND 58201   **Fax:** 701-787-2716
www.grandforkscountygov.com

On the central border of ND; organized Jan 4, 1873 (prior to statehood) from Pembina County. **Name Origin:** For the village of Grand Forks, itself named for the forks of the Red River of the North and Red Lake River.

Area (sq mi): 1439.83 (land 1437.81; water 2.02). **Pop per sq mi:** 45.9.

Pop 2005: 65,940. **State rank:** 3. **Pop change:** 2000-20005 -0.3%; 1990-2000 -6.5%. **Pop 2000:** 66,109 (White 92%; Black or African American 1.4%; Hispanic or Latino 2.1%; Asian 1%; Other 4.7%, including 2.3% American Indian/Alaska Native). **Foreign born:** 3.2%. **Median age:** 29.2.

Income 2000: per capita $17,868; median household $35,785; **Pop below poverty level:** 12.3%. ***Personal per capita income 2000-2003:** $24,092-$28,364.

Unemployment 2004: 3%. **Change from 2000:** +0.3%. **Median travel time to work:** 14.5 minutes. **Working outside county of residence:** 9.1%.

Cities with pop over 10,000: Grand Forks 🏛 (48,984).

---

*Source: Personal per capita income data are from the Bureau of Economic Analysis; per capita income data are from the Bureau of the Census. See Introduction for explanation of differences.

GRANT COUNTY

102 2nd Ave   **Ph:** 701-622-3615
Carson, ND 58529   **Fax:** 701-622-3717

In south-central ND, southwest of Bismarck; organized Nov 25, 1916 from Morton County. **Name Origin:** For Ulysses Simpson Grant (1822-85), Civil War general and eighteenth U.S. president.

Area (sq mi): 1665.92 (land 1659.46; water 6.46). **Pop per sq mi:** 1.6.

Pop 2005: 2,615. **State rank:** 38. **Pop change:** 2000-20005 -8%; 1990-2000 -19.9%. **Pop 2000:** 2,841 (White 96.7%; Black or African American 0%; Hispanic or Latino 0.6%; Asian 0.4%; Other 2.8%, including 1.7% American Indian/Alaska Native). **Foreign born:** 1.3%. **Median age:** 46.5.

Income 2000: per capita $14,616; median household $23,165; **Pop below poverty level:** 20.3%. ***Personal per capita income 2000-2003:** $20,843-$21,840.

Unemployment 2004: 3.6%. **Change from 2000:** +0.9%. **Median travel time to work:** 20.7 minutes. **Working outside county of residence:** 16.8%.

Cities with pop over 10,000: None.

GRIGGS COUNTY

PO Box 326   **Ph:** 701-797-2772
Cooperstown, ND 58425   **Fax:** 701-797-3587
www.cooperstownnd.com

In east-central ND, southwest of Grand Forks; organized Feb 18, 1881 (prior to statehood) from Foster County. **Name Origin:** For Alexander Griggs (1838-1903), a Red River pilot known as 'Captain,' closely identified with the earliest navigation on the Red River.

Area (sq mi): 716.17 (land 708.5; water 7.67). **Pop per sq mi:** 3.5.

Pop 2005: 2,497. **State rank:** 40. **Pop change:** 2000-20005 -9.3%; 1990-2000 -16.6%. **Pop 2000:** 2,754 (White 99.1%; Black or African American 0%; Hispanic or Latino 0.4%; Asian 0.1%; Other 0.5%). **Foreign born:** 1%. **Median age:** 45.8.

Income 2000: per capita $16,131; median household $29,572; **Pop below poverty level:** 10.1%. ***Personal per capita income 2000-2003:** $26,069-$31,198.

Unemployment 2004: 2.4%. **Change from 2000:** +0.7%. **Median travel time to work:** 14.4 minutes. **Working outside county of residence:** 12.7%.

Cities with pop over 10,000: None.

HETTINGER COUNTY

PO Box 668   **Ph:** 701-824-2645
Mott, ND 58646   **Fax:** 701-824-2717
www.hettingercounty.org

In southwestern ND, south of Dickinson; organized Mar 9, 1883 (prior to statehood) from Stark County. **Name Origin:** For Mathias K. Hettinger of IL; named by his son-in-law, Erastus A. Williams, a ND territorial legislator and county founder.

Area (sq mi): 1133.7 (land 1132.25; water 1.45). **Pop per sq mi:** 2.2.

Pop 2005: 2,486. **State rank:** 41. **Pop change:** 2000-20005 -8.4%; 1990-2000 -21.2%. **Pop 2000:** 2,715 (White 98.7%; Black or African American 0.1%; Hispanic or Latino 0.2%; Asian 0.1%; Other 0.9%). **Foreign born:** 0.1%. **Median age:** 46.2.

Income 2000: per capita $15,555; median household $29,209; **Pop below poverty level:** 14.8%. ***Personal per capita income 2000-2003:** $27,499-$26,971.

Unemployment 2004: 3.3%. **Change from 2000:** +1.1%. **Median travel time to work:** 17.5 minutes. **Working outside county of residence:** 15.1%.

Cities with pop over 10,000: None.

KIDDER COUNTY

120 E Broadway Kidder County Courthouse   **Ph:** 701-475-2632
Steele, ND 58482   **Fax:** 701-475-2202

In central ND, east of Bismarck; organized Jan 4, 1873 (prior to statehood) from Buffalo County, which was discontinued. **Name Origin:** For Jefferson Parrish Kidder (1815-83), VT legislator and lieutenant governor, MN legislator (1863-64), and associate justice of the Dakota territorial supreme court (1865-76; 1879-83).

Area (sq mi): 1433.21 (land 1350.79; water 82.42). **Pop per sq mi:** 1.8.

Pop 2005: 2,481. **State rank:** 42. **Pop change:** 2000-20005 -9.9%; 1990-2000 -17.4%. **Pop 2000:** 2,753 (White 98.9%; Black or African American 0.2%; Hispanic or Latino 0.6%; Asian 0.1%; Other 0.2%). **Foreign born:** 0.9%. **Median age:** 44.5.

Income 2000: per capita $14,270; median household $25,389; **Pop below poverty level:** 19.8%. ***Personal per capita income 2000-2003:** $21,598-$24,124.

Unemployment 2004: 5.9%. **Change from 2000:** +0.6%. **Median travel time to work:** 22.7 minutes. **Working outside county of residence:** 17.2%.

Cities with pop over 10,000: None.

LAMOURE COUNTY

PO Box 128   **Ph:** 701-883-5301
La Moure, ND 58458   **Fax:** 701-883-4240
lamoco.drtel.net

In southeastern ND, southwest of Fargo; organized Jan 4, 1873 (prior to statehood) from Pembina County. **Name Origin:** For Judson LaMoure (1839-1918), pioneer, legislator, and commissioner of Dakota Territory (1890).

Area (sq mi): 1150.81 (land 1147.18; water 3.63). **Pop per sq mi:** 3.8.

Pop 2005: 4,384. **State rank:** 26. **Pop change:** 2000-20005 -6.7%; 1990-2000 -12.7%. **Pop 2000:** 4,701 (White 98.9%; Black or African American 0%; Hispanic or Latino 0.6%; Asian 0.1%; Other 0.6%). **Foreign born:** 0.8%. **Median age:** 43.3.

Income 2000: per capita $17,059; median household $29,707; **Pop below poverty level:** 14.7%. ***Personal per capita income 2000-2003:** $26,074-$28,745.

Unemployment 2004: 3.4%. **Change from 2000:** +0.5%. **Median travel time to work:** 17.2 minutes. **Working outside county of residence:** 21.1%.

Cities with pop over 10,000: None.

🏛 *County Seat*

LOGAN COUNTY

301 Broadway St
Napoleon, ND 58561
www.napoleonnd.com

Ph: 701-754-2751
Fax: 701-754-2270

In south-central ND, southeast of Bismarck; organized Jan 4, 1873 (prior to statehood) from Buffalo County, which was discontinued. **Name Origin:** For Gen. John Alexander Logan (1826-86), officer in the Mexican-American War and Civil War; U.S. senator from IL (1871-77; 1879-86).

Area (sq mi): 1011.07 (land 992.64; water 18.43). **Pop per sq mi:** 2.1.

Pop 2005: 2,059. **State rank:** 46. **Pop change:** 2000-20005 -10.8%; 1990-2000 -18.9%. **Pop 2000:** 2,308 (White 98.6%; Black or African American 0.1%; Hispanic or Latino 0.7%; Asian 0.2%; Other 0.5%). **Foreign born:** 0.6%. **Median age:** 46.4.

Income 2000: per capita $16,947; median household $27,986; **Pop below poverty level:** 15.1%. *Personal per capita income 2000-2003: $26,155-$30,219.

Unemployment 2004: 4%. **Change from 2000:** +1.8%. **Median travel time to work:** 20.4 minutes. **Working outside county of residence:** 18.8%.

Cities with pop over 10,000: None.

MCHENRY COUNTY

PO Box 117
Towner, ND 58788

Ph: 701-537-5729
Fax: 701-537-5969

In north-central ND, east of Minot; organized Jan 4, 1873 (prior to statehood) from Buffalo County, which was discontinued. **Name Origin:** For James McHenry, an early settler of Vermillion, SD.

Area (sq mi): 1911.71 (land 1874.09; water 37.62). **Pop per sq mi:** 2.9.

Pop 2005: 5,511. **State rank:** 23. **Pop change:** 2000-20005 -8%; 1990-2000 -8.3%. **Pop 2000:** 5,987 (White 98.5%; Black or African American 0.1%; Hispanic or Latino 0.4%; Asian 0%; Other 1.2%). **Foreign born:** 1%. **Median age:** 43.

Income 2000: per capita $15,140; median household $27,274; **Pop below poverty level:** 15.8%. *Personal per capita income 2000-2003: $19,888-$23,368.

Unemployment 2004: 5.8%. **Change from 2000:** +0.8%. **Median travel time to work:** 24.6 minutes. **Working outside county of residence:** 40.1%.

Cities with pop over 10,000: None.

MCINTOSH COUNTY

PO Box 179
Ashley, ND 58413

Ph: 701-288-3450
Fax: 701-288-3671

On the central southern border of ND, southeast of Bismarck; organized Mar 9, 1883 (prior to statehood) from Logan County. **Name Origin:** For either John J. McIntosh, a state legislator, or for Edward H. McIntosh (1922-1901), a Dakota territorial legislator.

Area (sq mi): 995.04 (land 975.19; water 19.84). **Pop per sq mi:** 3.1.

Pop 2005: 3,013. **State rank:** 36. **Pop change:** 2000-20005 -11.1%; 1990-2000 -15.7%. **Pop 2000:** 3,390 (White 98.2%; Black or African American 0%; Hispanic or Latino 0.8%; Asian 0.3%; Other 0.8%). **Foreign born:** 0.8%. **Median age:** 51.

Income 2000: per capita $15,018; median household $26,389; **Pop below poverty level:** 15.4%. *Personal per capita income 2000-2003: $25,266-$27,538.

Unemployment 2004: 2.7%. **Change from 2000:** +0.5%. **Median travel time to work:** 13.7 minutes. **Working outside county of residence:** 9%.

Cities with pop over 10,000: None.

MCKENZIE COUNTY

PO Box 524
Watford City, ND 58854
www.4eyes.net

Ph: 701-444-3452
Fax: 701-444-3916

On the central western border of ND, southwest of Minot; organized Mar 9, 1883 (prior to statehood) from Howard County; which was discontinued. McKenzie County eliminated in 1891 for lack of settlement; present county formed 1905. **Name Origin:** For Alexander McKenzie (1851-1922), sheriff of Burleigh County and a powerful political leader.

Area (sq mi): 2860.89 (land 2742.02; water 118.87). **Pop per sq mi:** 2.

Pop 2005: 5,594. **State rank:** 22. **Pop change:** 2000-20005 -2.5%; 1990-2000 -10.1%. **Pop 2000:** 5,737 (White 77%; Black or African American 0.1%; Hispanic or Latino 1%; Asian 0.1%; Other 22.5%, including 21.2% American Indian/Alaska Native). **Foreign born:** 1.4%. **Median age:** 39.5.

Income 2000: per capita $14,732; median household $29,342; **Pop below poverty level:** 17.2%. *Personal per capita income 2000-2003: $21,645-$23,900.

Unemployment 2004: 3.5%. **Change from 2000:** +0.9%. **Median travel time to work:** 19.8 minutes. **Working outside county of residence:** 18.6%.

Cities with pop over 10,000: None.

MCLEAN COUNTY

PO Box 1108
Washburn, ND 58577
www.visitmcleancounty.com

Ph: 701-462-8541
Fax: 701-462-8212

In west-central ND, northwest of Bismarck; organized Mar 8, 1883 (prior to statehood) from Stevens County. **Name Origin:** For John A. McLean (1849-1916), first mayor of Bismarck, ND.

Area (sq mi): 2328.17 (land 2109.95; water 218.21). **Pop per sq mi:** 4.1.

Pop 2005: 8,604. **State rank:** 14. **Pop change:** 2000-20005 -7.6%; 1990-2000 -11%. **Pop 2000:** 9,311 (White 92.3%; Black or African American 0%; Hispanic or Latino 0.9%; Asian 0.1%; Other 7.3%, including 5.9% American Indian/Alaska Native). **Foreign born:** 0.9%. **Median age:** 44.1.

Income 2000: per capita $16,220; median household $32,337; **Pop below poverty level:** 13.5%. *Personal per capita income 2000-2003: $22,966-$28,396.

Unemployment 2004: 5.6%. **Change from 2000:** -0.3%. **Median travel time to work:** 22.1 minutes. **Working outside county of residence:** 24.9%.

Cities with pop over 10,000: None.

Source: Personal per capita income data are from the Bureau of Economic Analysis; per capita income data are from the Bureau of the Census. See Introduction for explanation of differences.

MERCER COUNTY

PO Box 39
Stanton, ND 58571
www.mercercountynd.com

Ph: 701-745-3262
Fax: 701-745-3710

In west-central ND, northwest of Bismarck; organized Jan 14, 1875 (prior to statehood) from original territory. **Name Origin:** For William Henry Harrison Mercer (1884-1901), an early rancher.

Area (sq mi): 1112.42 (land 1045.49; water 66.93). **Pop per sq mi:** 8.

Pop 2005: 8,364. **State rank:** 15. **Pop change:** 2000-20005 -3.2%; 1990-2000 -11.9%. **Pop 2000:** 8,644 (White 95.8%; Black or African American 0%; Hispanic or Latino 0.4%; Asian 0.3%; Other 3.7%, including 2% American Indian/Alaska Native). **Foreign born:** 1.5%. **Median age:** 40.1.

Income 2000: per capita $18,256; median household $42,269; **Pop below poverty level:** 7.5%. ***Personal per capita income 2000-2003:** $26,310-$29,832.

Unemployment 2004: 4.6%. **Change from 2000:** -0.5%. **Median travel time to work:** 14.8 minutes. **Working outside county of residence:** 8.5%.

Cities with pop over 10,000: None.

MORTON COUNTY

210 2nd Ave NW
Mandan, ND 58554
www.co.morton.nd.us

Ph: 701-667-3300
Fax: 701-667-3453

In south-central ND, west of Bismarck; organized Jan 8, 1873 (prior to statehood) from original territory. **Name Origin:** For Oliver Hazard Perry Throck Morton (1823-77), jurist, IN governor (1861-67), and U.S. senator (1867-77).

Area (sq mi): 1945.28 (land 1926.27; water 19.01). **Pop per sq mi:** 13.3.

Pop 2005: 25,528. **State rank:** 5. **Pop change:** 2000-20005 +0.9%; 1990-2000 +6.8%. **Pop 2000:** 25,303 (White 95.5%; Black or African American 0.2%; Hispanic or Latino 0.6%; Asian 0.3%; Other 3.8%, including 2.4% American Indian/Alaska Native). **Foreign born:** 0.9%. **Median age:** 37.4.

Income 2000: per capita $17,202; median household $37,028; **Pop below poverty level:** 9.6%. ***Personal per capita income 2000-2003:** $22,072-$24,821.

Unemployment 2004: 3.6%. **Change from 2000:** +0.3%. **Median travel time to work:** 19.1 minutes. **Working outside county of residence:** 52.3%.

Cities with pop over 10,000: Mandan 🏛 (16,969).

MOUNTRAIL COUNTY

PO Box 69
Stanley, ND 58784

Ph: 701-628-2915
Fax: 701-628-3975

In north-central ND, west of Minot; organized as Mountraille County Jan 4, 1873 (prior to statehood) from Ward County. Eliminated in 1891; reestablished with present spelling Jan 25, 1909. **Name Origin:** For 'Savage' Joseph Mountraille, prominent voyageur who carried the mail.

Area (sq mi): 1941.08 (land 1823.93; water 117.15). **Pop per sq mi:** 3.6.

Pop 2005: 6,513. **State rank:** 20. **Pop change:** 2000-20005 -1.8%; 1990-2000 -5.6%. **Pop 2000:** 6,631 (White 65.7%; Black or African American 0.1%; Hispanic or Latino 1.3%; Asian 0.2%; Other 33.7%, including 30% American Indian/Alaska Native). **Foreign born:** 1.2%. **Median age:** 39.6.

Income 2000: per capita $13,422; median household $27,098; **Pop below poverty level:** 19.3%. ***Personal per capita income 2000-2003:** $23,356-$25,624.

Unemployment 2004: 5.3%. **Change from 2000:** +0.6%. **Median travel time to work:** 16.5 minutes. **Working outside county of residence:** 21.7%.

Cities with pop over 10,000: None.

NELSON COUNTY

210 B Ave W Suite 203
Lakota, ND 58344

Ph: 701-247-2462
Fax: 701-247-2412

In east-central ND, west of Grand Forks; organized Mar 9, 1883 (prior to statehood) from Foster and Grand Forks counties. **Name Origin:** For Nelson E. Nelson (1830-1913), a ND legislator at the time.

Area (sq mi): 1008.74 (land 981.62; water 27.12). **Pop per sq mi:** 3.5.

Pop 2005: 3,424. **State rank:** 34. **Pop change:** 2000-20005 -7.8%; 1990-2000 -15.8%. **Pop 2000:** 3,715 (White 98.5%; Black or African American 0.1%; Hispanic or Latino 0.2%; Asian 0.3%; Other 1%). **Foreign born:** 1.7%. **Median age:** 47.2.

Income 2000: per capita $16,320; median household $28,892; **Pop below poverty level:** 10.3%. ***Personal per capita income 2000-2003:** $21,828-$28,571.

Unemployment 2004: 3.7%. **Change from 2000:** -0.3%. **Median travel time to work:** 21.8 minutes. **Working outside county of residence:** 24.2%.

Cities with pop over 10,000: None.

OLIVER COUNTY

PO Box 125
Center, ND 58530

Ph: 701-794-8777
Fax: 701-794-3476

In south-central ND, northwest of Bismarck; organized Mar 12, 1885 (prior to statehood) from Mercer County. **Name Origin:** For Harry S. Oliver (1855-1909), a Dakota Territory legislator.

Area (sq mi): 731.19 (land 723.52; water 7.67). **Pop per sq mi:** 2.5.

Pop 2005: 1,813. **State rank:** 49. **Pop change:** 2000-20005 -12.2%; 1990-2000 -13.3%. **Pop 2000:** 2,065 (White 97.1%; Black or African American 0.1%; Hispanic or Latino 0.6%; Asian 0.1%; Other 2.2%, including 1.3% American Indian/Alaska Native). **Foreign born:** 0.3%. **Median age:** 42.

Income 2000: per capita $16,271; median household $36,650; **Pop below poverty level:** 14.9%. ***Personal per capita income 2000-2003:** $21,688-$25,196.

Unemployment 2004: 3.8%. **Change from 2000:** -1.1%. **Median travel time to work:** 23.1 minutes. **Working outside county of residence:** 39.6%.

Cities with pop over 10,000: None.

🏛 *County Seat*

PEMBINA COUNTY

301 Dakota St W Suite 6   **Ph:** 701-265-4275
Cavalier, ND 58220   **Fax:** 701-265-4876
pembinacountynd.gov

In the northeast corner of ND; organized Jan 9, 1867 (prior to statehood) from Indian lands. **Name Origin:** From Ojibway Indian *anepeminan* 'high bush cranberries,' which grew abundantly in the area.

Area (sq mi): 1121.74 (land 1118.75; water 2.99). **Pop per sq mi:** 7.2.

Pop 2005: 8,038. **State rank:** 17. **Pop change:** 2000-20005 -6.4%; 1990-2000 -7.1%. **Pop 2000:** 8,585 (White 93.9%; Black or African American 0.2%; Hispanic or Latino 3.1%; Asian 0.2%; Other 4.1%, including 1.4% American Indian/Alaska Native). **Foreign born:** 3.8%. **Median age:** 41.6.

Income 2000: per capita $18,692; median household $36,430; **Pop below poverty level:** 9.2%. ***Personal per capita income 2000-2003:** $29,233-$30,600.

Unemployment 2004: 8.1%. **Change from 2000:** +3%. **Median travel time to work:** 16.6 minutes. **Working outside county of residence:** 15.8%.

Cities with pop over 10,000: None.

PIERCE COUNTY

240 SE 2nd St PO Box 258   **Ph:** 701-776-6161
Rugby, ND 58368   **Fax:** 701-776-5707

In north-central ND, east of Minot; organized Mar 11, 1887 (prior to statehood) from parts of Rolette, Bottineau, and McHenry counties and all of De Smet County; annexed part of Church County in 1891. **Name Origin:** For Lt. Col. Gilbert Ashville Pierce (1839-1901), officer in the Civil War, governor of Dakota Territory (1884-87), and U.S. senator from ND (1889-91).

Area (sq mi): 1082.16 (land 1017.82; water 64.34). **Pop per sq mi:** 4.2.

Pop 2005: 4,291. **State rank:** 28. **Pop change:** 2000-20005 -8.2%; 1990-2000 -7.5%. **Pop 2000:** 4,675 (White 98.1%; Black or African American 0.1%; Hispanic or Latino 0.6%; Asian 0.3%; Other 1.1%). **Foreign born:** 1.2%. **Median age:** 42.9.

Income 2000: per capita $14,055; median household $26,524; **Pop below poverty level:** 12.5%. ***Personal per capita income 2000-2003:** $21,969-$23,799.

Unemployment 2004: 4.7%. **Change from 2000:** +1.4%. **Median travel time to work:** 14.8 minutes. **Working outside county of residence:** 11.4%.

Cities with pop over 10,000: None.

RAMSEY COUNTY

524 4th Ave Rm 4   **Ph:** 701-662-7006
Devils Lake, ND 58301   **Fax:** 701-662-7063
www.co.ramsey.nd.us

In east-central ND, northwest of Grand Forks; organized Jan 4, 1873 (prior to statehood) from Pembina County. **Name Origin:** For Alexander Ramsey (1815-1903), first governor of MN Territory, U.S. senator from MN (1863-75), and U.S. secretary of war (1879-81).

Area (sq mi): 1300.88 (land 1184.85; water 116.04). **Pop per sq mi:** 9.6.

Pop 2005: 11,429. **State rank:** 12. **Pop change:** 2000-20005 -5.3%; 1990-2000 -4.8%. **Pop 2000:** 12,066 (White 92.1%; Black or African American 0.2%; Hispanic or Latino 0.5%; Asian 0.3%; Other 7.2%, including 5.4% American Indian/Alaska Native). **Foreign born:** 1.5%. **Median age:** 39.5.

Income 2000: per capita $18,060; median household $35,600; **Pop below poverty level:** 12.6%. ***Personal per capita income 2000-2003:** $23,306-$27,168.

Unemployment 2004: 4.1%. **Change from 2000:** +0.8%. **Median travel time to work:** 13.9 minutes. **Working outside county of residence:** 10.3%.

Cities with pop over 10,000: None.

RANSOM COUNTY

PO Box 626   **Ph:** 701-683-5823
Lisbon, ND 58054   **Fax:** 701-683-5826

In southeastern ND, southwest of Fargo; organized Jan 4, 1873 (prior to statehood) from Pembina County. **Name Origin:** For Fort Ransom, built in 1867 and named for Gen. Thomas E.G. Ransom (1834-64), a Union officer from IL.

Area (sq mi): 864.13 (land 862.75; water 1.38). **Pop per sq mi:** 6.7.

Pop 2005: 5,810. **State rank:** 21. **Pop change:** 2000-20005 -1.4%; 1990-2000 -0.5%. **Pop 2000:** 5,890 (White 97.6%; Black or African American 0.2%; Hispanic or Latino 0.8%; Asian 0.3%; Other 1.6%). **Foreign born:** 0.9%. **Median age:** 40.7.

Income 2000: per capita $18,219; median household $37,672; **Pop below poverty level:** 8.8%. ***Personal per capita income 2000-2003:** $24,693-$27,485.

Unemployment 2004: 2.9%. **Change from 2000:** +0.8%. **Median travel time to work:** 15.1 minutes. **Working outside county of residence:** 23.6%.

Cities with pop over 10,000: None.

RENVILLE COUNTY

205 Main St E   **Ph:** 701-756-6398
Mohall, ND 58761   **Fax:** 701-756-6398
www.renvillecounty.org

On the central northern border of ND, northwest of Minot; organized Jan 4, 1873 (prior to statehood) from Pembina County. Dissolved in 1891 for lack of settlement; present county created Jul 23, 1910. **Name Origin:** For Gabriel Renville, an early settler and trader.

Area (sq mi): 892.03 (land 874.77; water 17.27). **Pop per sq mi:** 2.8.

Pop 2005: 2,422. **State rank:** 44. **Pop change:** 2000-20005 -7.2%; 1990-2000 -17.4%. **Pop 2000:** 2,610 (White 97.1%; Black or African American 0.2%; Hispanic or Latino 0.7%; Asian 0.5%; Other 1.6%). **Foreign born:** 1.5%. **Median age:** 43.6.

Income 2000: per capita $16,478; median household $30,746; **Pop below poverty level:** 11%. ***Personal per capita income 2000-2003:** $26,723-$33,720.

Unemployment 2004: 2.9%. **Change from 2000:** +1%. **Median travel time to work:** 19.1 minutes. **Working outside county of residence:** 29.8%.

*Source: Personal per capita income data are from the Bureau of Economic Analysis; per capita income data are from the Bureau of the Census. See Introduction for explanation of differences.

Renville County (cont'd)

Cities with pop over 10,000: None.

RICHLAND COUNTY

418 2nd Ave N   **Ph:** 701-671-1524
Wahpeton, ND 58075   **Fax:** 701-671-1512
www.mylocalgov.com/richlandcountynd/

In the southeastern corner of ND, south of Fargo; original county; organized Jan 4, 1873 (prior to statehood). **Name Origin:** For Morgan T. Rich (1832-98), settler and founder of the city of Wahpeton.

Area (sq mi): 1445.73 (land 1436.71; water 9.02). **Pop per sq mi:** 12.1.

Pop 2005: 17,340. **State rank:** 9. **Pop change:** 2000-20005 -3.7%; 1990-2000 -0.8%. **Pop 2000:** 17,998 (White 96.3%; Black or African American 0.3%; Hispanic or Latino 0.7%; Asian 0.2%; Other 2.5%, including 1.7% American Indian/Alaska Native). **Foreign born:** 1.1%. **Median age:** 35.4.

Income 2000: per capita $16,339; median household $36,098; **Pop below poverty level:** 10.4%. ***Personal per capita income 2000-2003:** $23,946-$25,883.

Unemployment 2004: 3.3%. **Change from 2000:** +0.4%. **Median travel time to work:** 18.8 minutes. **Working outside county of residence:** 24.4%.

Cities with pop over 10,000: None.

ROLETTE COUNTY

102 2nd Ave PO Box 460   **Ph:** 701-477-3816
Rolla, ND 58367   **Fax:** 701-477-8594
www.rolettecounty.com

On the central northern border of ND, northeast of Minot; organized Jan 4, 1873 (prior to statehood) from Buffalo County, which was discontinued. **Name Origin:** For Joseph Rolette (1820-71), pioneer and fur trader who opened a post for the American Fur Co.

Area (sq mi): 939.33 (land 902.45; water 36.88). **Pop per sq mi:** 15.4.

Pop 2005: 13,864. **State rank:** 10. **Pop change:** 2000-20005 +1.4%; 1990-2000 +7.1%. **Pop 2000:** 13,674 (White 25%; Black or African American 0.1%; Hispanic or Latino 0.8%; Asian 0.1%; Other 74.7%, including 73% American Indian/Alaska Native). **Foreign born:** 1.3%. **Median age:** 28.9.

Income 2000: per capita $10,873; median household $26,232; **Pop below poverty level:** 31%. ***Personal per capita income 2000-2003:** $17,365-$20,157.

Unemployment 2004: 9.6%. **Change from 2000:** -1.1%. **Median travel time to work:** 15.8 minutes. **Working outside county of residence:** 5%.

Cities with pop over 10,000: None.

SARGENT COUNTY

PO Box 176   **Ph:** 701-724-6241
Forman, ND 58032   **Fax:** 701-724-6244
mylocalgov.com/SargentCountyND/

On the southeastern border of ND, southwest of Fargo; organized Mar 3, 1883 (prior to statehood) from Ransom County. **Name Origin:** For Gen. Homer E. Sargent, superintendent of the Northern Pacific Railroad Company and developer of the Red River Valley.

Area (sq mi): 867.09 (land 858.75; water 8.34). **Pop per sq mi:** 4.8.

Pop 2005: 4,150. **State rank:** 30. **Pop change:** 2000-20005 -4.9%; 1990-2000 -4%. **Pop 2000:** 4,366 (White 98%; Black or African American 0%; Hispanic or Latino 0.7%; Asian 0%; Other 1.7%). **Foreign born:** 0.5%. **Median age:** 40.3.

Income 2000: per capita $18,689; median household $37,213; **Pop below poverty level:** 8.2%. ***Personal per capita income 2000-2003:** $29,992-$31,290.

Unemployment 2004: 3%. **Change from 2000:** +0.2%. **Median travel time to work:** 16.7 minutes. **Working outside county of residence:** 17.8%.

Cities with pop over 10,000: None.

SHERIDAN COUNTY

PO Box 409   **Ph:** 701-363-2207
McClusky, ND 58463   **Fax:** 701-363-2953
mylocalgov.com/SheridanCountyND/

In central ND, northeast of Bismarck; organized Nov 1908 (prior to statehood) from McLean County. **Name Origin:** For Gen. Philip Henry Sheridan (1831-88), Union officer during the Civil War and commander in chief of the U.S. Army (1883-88).

Area (sq mi): 1005.78 (land 971.75; water 34.02). **Pop per sq mi:** 1.5.

Pop 2005: 1,430. **State rank:** 51. **Pop change:** 2000-20005 -16.4%; 1990-2000 -20.4%. **Pop 2000:** 1,710 (White 98.9%; Black or African American 0.1%; Hispanic or Latino 0.4%; Asian 0%; Other 0.7%). **Foreign born:** 1.1%. **Median age:** 48.1.

Income 2000: per capita $13,283; median household $24,450; **Pop below poverty level:** 21%. ***Personal per capita income 2000-2003:** $18,711-$25,691.

Unemployment 2004: 6.3%. **Change from 2000:** +0.1%. **Median travel time to work:** 19.1 minutes. **Working outside county of residence:** 21.4%.

Cities with pop over 10,000: None.

SIOUX COUNTY

PO Box L   **Ph:** 701-854-3481
Fort Yates, ND 58538   **Fax:** 701-854-3854

On the central southern border of ND, south of Bismarck; organized Sep 3, 1914 from the Standing Rock Indian Reservation. **Name Origin:** For the Sioux Indians, sometimes known as the Dakotas.

Area (sq mi): 1128.3 (land 1094.12; water 34.18). **Pop per sq mi:** 3.8.

Pop 2005: 4,182. **State rank:** 29. **Pop change:** 2000-20005 +3.4%; 1990-2000 +7.5%. **Pop 2000:** 4,044 (White 14.3%; Black or African American 0%; Hispanic or Latino 1.6%; Asian 0%; Other 85.6%, including 84.6% American Indian/Alaska Native). **Foreign born:** 0.8%. **Median age:** 23.9.

Income 2000: per capita $7,731; median household $22,483; **Pop below poverty level:** 39.2%. ***Personal per capita income 2000-2003:** $13,506-$15,468.

Sioux County (cont'd)

Unemployment 2004: 6.9%. **Change from 2000:** +1.5%. **Median travel time to work:** 16.5 minutes. **Working outside county of residence:** 10.1%.

Cities with pop over 10,000: None.

SLOPE COUNTY

PO Box JJ   **Ph:** 701-879-6275
Amidon, ND 58620   **Fax:** 701-879-6278

On the southwestern border of ND, southwest of Dickinson; organized Jan 14, 1915 from Billings County. **Name Origin:** For the Missouri Slope, a popular name for western ND, especially the area west of the Missouri River.

Area (sq mi): 1219.22 (land 1217.94; water 1.28). **Pop per sq mi:** 0.6.

Pop 2005: 709. **State rank:** 53. **Pop change:** 2000-20005 -7.6%; 1990-2000 -15.4%. **Pop 2000:** 767 (White 99.6%; Black or African American 0%; Hispanic or Latino 0.1%; Asian 0%; Other 0.2%). **Foreign born:** 0.3%. **Median age:** 42.5.

Income 2000: per capita $14,513; median household $24,667; **Pop below poverty level:** 16.9%. ***Personal per capita income 2000-2003:** $25,344-$22,862.

Unemployment 2004: 2.9%. **Change from 2000:** +0.7%. **Median travel time to work:** 16.7 minutes. **Working outside county of residence:** 26.5%.

Cities with pop over 10,000: None.

STARK COUNTY

PO Box 130   **Ph:** 701-456-7630
Dickinson, ND 58602   **Fax:** 701-456-7634

In southwestern ND, west of Bismarck; organized Feb 10, 1879 (prior to statehood) from unorganized territory. **Name Origin:** For George Stark, vice president of the Northern Pacific Railroad Co.

Area (sq mi): 1340.46 (land 1338.16; water 2.3). **Pop per sq mi:** 16.5.

Pop 2005: 22,073. **State rank:** 6. **Pop change:** 2000-20005 -2.5%; 1990-2000 -0.9%. **Pop 2000:** 22,636 (White 96.8%; Black or African American 0.2%; Hispanic or Latino 1%; Asian 0.2%; Other 2%). **Foreign born:** 0.8%. **Median age:** 36.9.

Income 2000: per capita $15,929; median household $32,526; **Pop below poverty level:** 12.3%. ***Personal per capita income 2000-2003:** $22,128-$26,020.

Unemployment 2004: 3.2%. **Change from 2000:** +0.4%. **Median travel time to work:** 14.1 minutes. **Working outside county of residence:** 5.9%.

Cities with pop over 10,000: Dickinson ⏚ (15,686).

STEELE COUNTY

PO Box 296   **Ph:** 701-524-2152
Finley, ND 58230   **Fax:** 701-524-1325

In east-central ND, southwest of Grand Forks; organized Mar 8, 1883 (prior to statehood) from Traill County. **Name Origin:** For Edward H. Steele (1846-99), an officer of the Red River Land Co., which figured prominently in the establishment of the county.

Area (sq mi): 715.49 (land 712.36; water 3.13). **Pop per sq mi:** 2.8.

Pop 2005: 2,007. **State rank:** 48. **Pop change:** 2000-20005 -11.1%; 1990-2000 -6.7%. **Pop 2000:** 2,258 (White 98.3%; Black or African American 0%; Hispanic or Latino 0.2%; Asian 0%; Other 1.6%). **Foreign born:** 0.3%. **Median age:** 41.4.

Income 2000: per capita $17,601; median household $35,757; **Pop below poverty level:** 7.1%. ***Personal per capita income 2000-2003:** $26,478-$32,021.

Unemployment 2004: 2.3%. **Change from 2000:** +1.1%. **Median travel time to work:** 19.3 minutes. **Working outside county of residence:** 32.4%.

Cities with pop over 10,000: None.

STUTSMAN COUNTY

511 2nd Ave SE   **Ph:** 701-252-9035
Jamestown, ND 58401   **Fax:** 701-251-6325
www.co.stutsman.nd.us

In south-central ND, west of Fargo; organized Jan 4, 1873 (prior to statehood) from Pembina County. **Name Origin:** For Enos Stutsman (1926-74), member of the Dakota Council and a special agent of the U.S. Treasury Dept.

Area (sq mi): 2298.26 (land 2221.4; water 76.86). **Pop per sq mi:** 9.4.

Pop 2005: 20,835. **State rank:** 7. **Pop change:** 2000-20005 -4.9%; 1990-2000 -1.5%. **Pop 2000:** 21,908 (White 97%; Black or African American 0.3%; Hispanic or Latino 0.9%; Asian 0.4%; Other 1.7%). **Foreign born:** 1%. **Median age:** 39.6.

Income 2000: per capita $17,706; median household $33,848; **Pop below poverty level:** 10.4%. ***Personal per capita income 2000-2003:** $23,682-$27,014.

Unemployment 2004: 3.3%. **Change from 2000:** +1.2%. **Median travel time to work:** 13.9 minutes. **Working outside county of residence:** 4.7%.

Cities with pop over 10,000: Jamestown ⏚ (14,925).

TOWNER COUNTY

PO Box 517   **Ph:** 701-968-4340
Cando, ND 58324   **Fax:** 701-968-4344
www.mylocalgov.com/townercountynd/

On the central northern border of ND; organized Mar 8, 1883 (prior to statehood) from Rolette County. **Name Origin:** For Oscar M. Towner (1842-97), Dakota Territory legislator.

Area (sq mi): 1041.56 (land 1024.55; water 17). **Pop per sq mi:** 2.5.

Pop 2005: 2,544. **State rank:** 39. **Pop change:** 2000-20005 -11.5%; 1990-2000 -20.7%. **Pop 2000:** 2,876 (White 97.3%; Black or African American 0.1%; Hispanic or Latino 0.2%; Asian 0.1%; Other 2.6%, including 2.1% American Indian/Alaska Native). **Foreign born:** 0.8%. **Median age:** 44.

Income 2000: per capita $17,605; median household $32,740; **Pop below poverty level:** 8.9%. ***Personal per capita income 2000-2003:** $25,992-$33,740.

Unemployment 2004: 4.3%. **Change from 2000:** +1.6%. **Median travel time to work:** 15.8 minutes. **Working outside county of residence:** 17%.

Source: Personal per capita income data are from the Bureau of Economic Analysis; per capita income data are from the Bureau of the Census. See Introduction for explanation of differences.

Towner County (cont'd)

Cities with pop over 10,000: None.

TRAILL COUNTY

114 W Caledonia Ave   **Ph:** 701-636-4454
Hillsboro, ND 58045   **Fax:** 701-636-4457
mylocalgov.com/traillcountynd

On the central eastern border of ND, south of Grand Forks; organized Jan 12, 1875 (prior to statehood) from Grand Forks County. **Name Origin:** For Walter J.S. Traill (1847-1933) of the Hudson Bay Company; he was a founder of the county.

Area (sq mi): 862.53 (land 861.89; water 0.65). **Pop per sq mi:** 9.7.

Pop 2005: 8,321. **State rank:** 16. **Pop change:** 2000-20005 -1.8%; 1990-2000 -3.1%. **Pop 2000:** 8,477 (White 96.4%; Black or African American 0.1%; Hispanic or Latino 2.2%; Asian 0.2%; Other 2.4%). **Foreign born:** 1.4%. **Median age:** 39.

Income 2000: per capita $18,014; median household $37,445; **Pop below poverty level:** 9.2%. **Personal per capita income 2000-2003:* $25,145-$28,089.

Unemployment 2004: 3.7%. **Change from 2000:** +0.5%. **Median travel time to work:** 17.5 minutes. **Working outside county of residence:** 28.3%.

Cities with pop over 10,000: None.

WALSH COUNTY

600 Cooper Ave   **Ph:** 701-352-2851
Grafton, ND 58237   **Fax:** 701-352-3340
mylocalgov.com/WalshCountyND/

On the northeastern border of ND, north of Grand Forks; organized Feb 18, 1881 (prior to statehood) from Grand Forks and Pembina counties. **Name Origin:** For George H. Walsh (1868-1913), newspaper publisher and member of the ND legislative council (1881, 1883, 1885, 1889).

Area (sq mi): 1294.11 (land 1281.74; water 12.36). **Pop per sq mi:** 9.1.

Pop 2005: 11,607. **State rank:** 11. **Pop change:** 2000-20005 -6.3%; 1990-2000 -10.5%. **Pop 2000:** 12,389 (White 92.3%; Black or African American 0.3%; Hispanic or Latino 5.7%; Asian 0.2%; Other 4.6%, including 1% American Indian/Alaska Native). **Foreign born:** 1.9%. **Median age:** 40.9.

Income 2000: per capita $16,496; median household $33,845; **Pop below poverty level:** 10.9%. **Personal per capita income 2000-2003:* $24,483-$27,152.

Unemployment 2004: 4.7%. **Change from 2000:** +1.1%. **Median travel time to work:** 17.5 minutes. **Working outside county of residence:** 14.6%.

Cities with pop over 10,000: None.

WARD COUNTY

PO Box 5005   **Ph:** 701-857-6600
Minot, ND 58702   **Fax:** 701-857-6623
www.co.ward.nd.us

In north-central ND; organized Apr 14, 1885 (prior to statehood) from Renville County. **Name Origin:** For either J.P. Ward or Mark Ward (1844-1902), or both, members of the Dakota Territory legislature in 1885 when the county was formed.

Area (sq mi): 2056.25 (land 2012.88; water 43.36). **Pop per sq mi:** 27.7.

Pop 2005: 55,767. **State rank:** 4. **Pop change:** 2000-20005 -5.2%; 1990-2000 +1.5%. **Pop 2000:** 58,795 (White 91.5%; Black or African American 2.2%; Hispanic or Latino 1.9%; Asian 0.8%; Other 4.0%, including 2.1% American Indian/Alaska Native). **Foreign born:** 2.1%. **Median age:** 32.4.

Income 2000: per capita $16,926; median household $33,670; **Pop below poverty level:** 10.8%. **Personal per capita income 2000-2003:* $25,041-$30,100.

Unemployment 2004: 3.7%. **Change from 2000:** +0.8%. **Median travel time to work:** 14.5 minutes. **Working outside county of residence:** 4.3%.

Cities with pop over 10,000: Minot ⚒ (35,149).

WELLS COUNTY

PO Box 155   **Ph:** 701-547-3122
Fessenden, ND 58438   **Fax:** 701-547-3840
mylocalgov.com/wellscountynd/

In central ND, northeast of Bismarck; organized as Gingras County Jan 4, 1873 (prior to statehood) from Sheridan County; name changed Feb 26, 1881. **Name Origin:** For Edward Payson Wells (1847-1936), ND territorial legislator (1881), banker, and developer of the James River valley.

Area (sq mi): 1290.62 (land 1271.28; water 19.34). **Pop per sq mi:** 3.6.

Pop 2005: 4,574. **State rank:** 25. **Pop change:** 2000-20005 -10.3%; 1990-2000 -13%. **Pop 2000:** 5,102 (White 98.9%; Black or African American 0.1%; Hispanic or Latino 0.3%; Asian 0.2%; Other 0.5%). **Foreign born:** 0.8%. **Median age:** 45.2.

Income 2000: per capita $17,932; median household $31,894; **Pop below poverty level:** 13.5%. **Personal per capita income 2000-2003:* $22,589-$30,066.

Unemployment 2004: 4.7%. **Change from 2000:** +1.3%. **Median travel time to work:** 17 minutes. **Working outside county of residence:** 14.3%.

Cities with pop over 10,000: None.

WILLIAMS COUNTY

PO Box 2047   **Ph:** 701-577-4540
Williston, ND 58802   **Fax:** 701-577-4535
www.williamsnd.com

On the northwestern border of ND, west of Minot; established Jan 8, 1873 by absorbing both Buford and Flannery counties. Originally located south of the Missouri River, near present-day Dunn and Mercer counties; established in present location in 1892. **Name Origin:** For Erastus A. Williams (1850-1930), Dakota Territory legislator, ND surveyor general, and a founder of Hettinger County.

Area (sq mi): 2147.97 (land 2070.46; water 77.51). **Pop per sq mi:** 9.3.

Pop 2005: 19,282. **State rank:** 8. **Pop change:** 2000-20005 -2.4%; 1990-2000 -6.5%. **Pop 2000:** 19,761 (White 92.3%; Black or African American 0.1%; Hispanic or Latino 0.9%; Asian 0.2%; Other 6.7%,

⚒ *County Seat*

Williams County (cont'd)

including 4.4% American Indian/Alaska Native). **Foreign born:** 1.2%. **Median age:** 39.8.

Income 2000: per capita $16,763; median household $31,491; **Pop below poverty level:** 11.9%. ***Personal per capita income 2000-2003:** $22,628-$26,869.

Unemployment 2004: 2.7%. **Change from 2000:** +0%. **Median travel time to work:** 15.1 minutes. **Working outside county of residence:** 4.8%.

Cities with pop over 10,000: Williston ⏛ (12,191).

*Source: Personal per capita income data are from the Bureau of Economic Analysis; per capita income data are from the Bureau of the Census. See Introduction for explanation of differences.

540

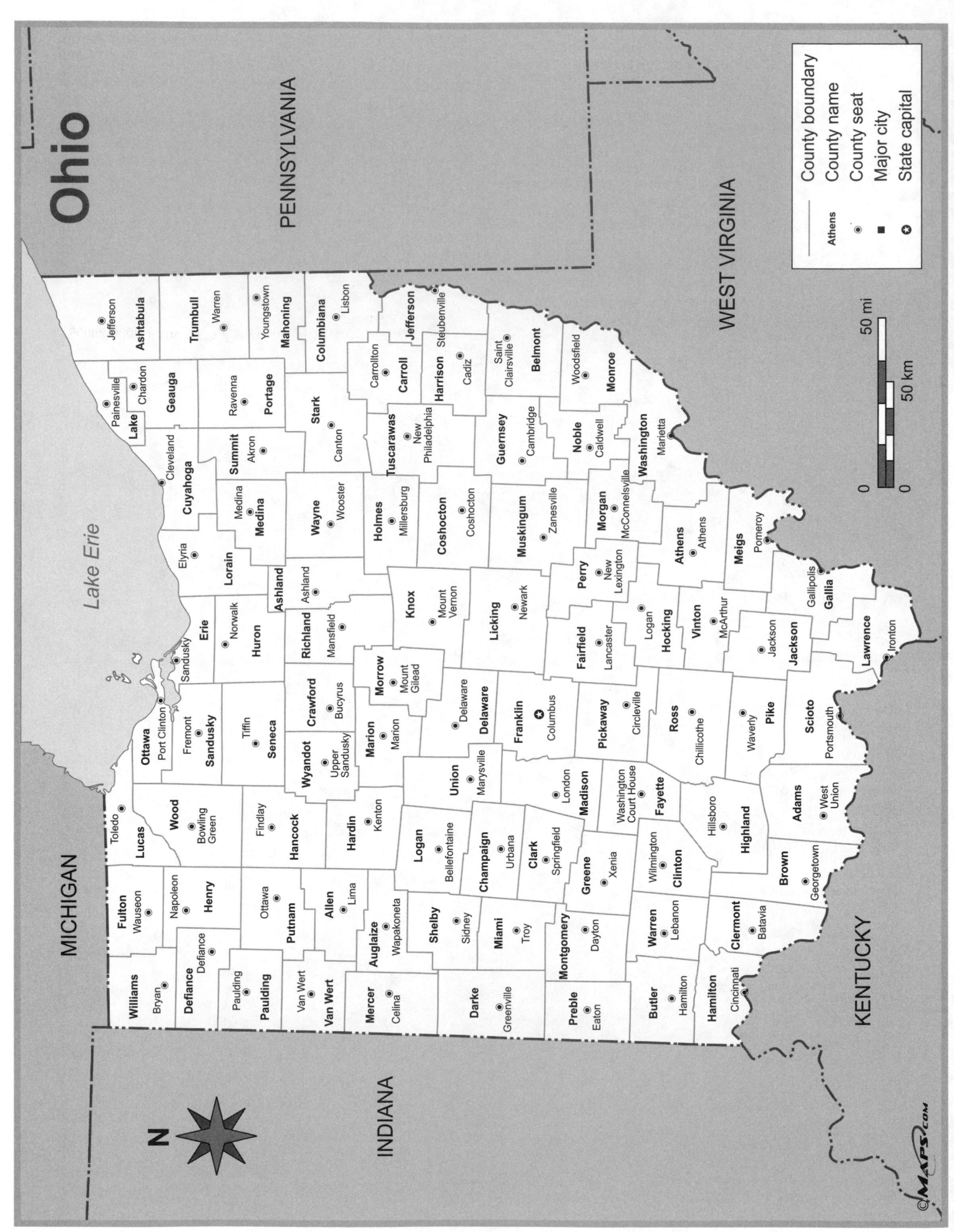

Ohio

OHIO STATE INFORMATION

www.ohio.gov   Ph: 614-466-2000

Area (sq mi): 44824.9 (land 40,948.38; water 3876.53). **Pop per sq mi:** 280.

Pop 2005: 11,464,042. **Pop change:** 2000-20005 +1%; 1990-2000 +4.7%. **Pop 2000:** 11,353,140 (White 84%; Black or African American 11.5%; Hispanic or Latino 1.9%; Asian 1.2%; Other 2.4%). **Foreign born:** 3%. **Median age:** 36.2.

Income 2000: per capita $21,003; median household $40,956; **Pop below poverty level:** 10.6%. ***Personal per capita income 2000-2003:** $28,207-$30,129.

Unemployment 2004: 6.2%. **Change from 2000:** +2.2%. **Median travel time to work:** 22.9 minutes. **Working outside county of residence:** 27.1%.

ADAMS COUNTY

110 W Main St Rm 25 County Courthouse   **Ph:** 937-544-2011
West Union, OH 45693   **Fax:** 937-544-8911
www.adamscountytravel.org

On the south-central border of OH; original county; organized Jul 10, 1797 (prior to statehood). **Name Origin:** For John Adams (1735-1826), second U.S. president.

Area (sq mi): 585.79 (land 583.91; water 1.88). **Pop per sq mi:** 48.7.

Pop 2005: 28,454. **State rank:** 78. **Pop change:** 2000-20005 +4.1%; 1990-2000 +7.7%. **Pop 2000:** 27,330 (White 97.3%; Black or African American 0.2%; Hispanic or Latino 0.6%; Asian 0.1%; Other 1.9%). **Foreign born:** 0.2%. **Median age:** 36.3.

Income 2000: per capita $14,515; median household $29,315; **Pop below poverty level:** 17.4%. ***Personal per capita income 2000-2003:** $19,595-$19,722.

Unemployment 2004: 9.3%. **Change from 2000:** +0%. **Median travel time to work:** 36.8 minutes. **Working outside county of residence:** 40.1%.

Cities with pop over 10,000: None.

ALLEN COUNTY

301 N Main St   **Ph:** 419-228-3700
Lima, OH 45801   **Fax:** 419-222-8427
www.allencountyohio.com

In west-central OH, north of Dayton; organized Feb 12, 1820 from Mercer County. **Name Origin:** For Ethan Allen (1738-89), leader of the Green Mountain Boys of VT in the Revolutionary War.

Area (sq mi): 406.88 (land 404.43; water 2.46). **Pop per sq mi:** 262.7.

Pop 2005: 106,234. **State rank:** 26. **Pop change:** 2000-20005 -2.1%; 1990-2000 -1.2%. **Pop 2000:** 108,473 (White 84.2%; Black or African American 12.2%; Hispanic or Latino 1.4%; Asian 0.6%; Other 2.3%). **Foreign born:** 1%. **Median age:** 36.3.

Income 2000: per capita $17,511; median household $37,048; **Pop below poverty level:** 12.1%. ***Personal per capita income 2000-2003:** $24,256-$27,411.

Unemployment 2004: 6.6%. **Change from 2000:** +1.5%. **Median travel time to work:** 18.4 minutes. **Working outside county of residence:** 15.7%.

Cities with pop over 10,000: Lima ⛫ (39,333).

ASHLAND COUNTY

142 W 2nd St   **Ph:** 419-289-0000
Ashland, OH 44805   **Fax:** 419-282-4240
www.ashlandcounty.org

In north-central OH, southwest of Akron; organized Feb 24, 1846 from the counties of Huron (Ruggles twp), Lorain (Sullivan and Trop twps), Richland (Vermillion, Montgomery, Orange, Green, Hanover, and parts of Monroe, Mifflin, and Clear Fork twps), and Wayne (Jackson, Perry, Mohican, and Lake twps). **Name Origin:** Named in 1822 for the home of Henry Clay (1777-1852) at Lexington, KY.

Area (sq mi): 426.85 (land 424.37; water 2.47). **Pop per sq mi:** 127.5.

Pop 2005: 54,123. **State rank:** 46. **Pop change:** 2000-20005 +3%; 1990-2000 +10.6%. **Pop 2000:** 52,523 (White 97.1%; Black or African American 0.8%; Hispanic or Latino 0.6%; Asian 0.5%; Other 1.1%). **Foreign born:** 1.1%. **Median age:** 36.3.

Income 2000: per capita $17,308; median household $39,179; **Pop below poverty level:** 9.5%. ***Personal per capita income 2000-2003:** $22,358-$23,315.

Unemployment 2004: 6.8%. **Change from 2000:** +2.2%. **Median travel time to work:** 20.3 minutes. **Working outside county of residence:** 32.2%.

Cities with pop over 10,000: Ashland ⛫ (21,627).

ASHTABULA COUNTY

25 W Jefferson St   **Ph:** 440-576-3637
Jefferson, OH 44047   **Fax:** 440-576-2819
www.co.ashtabula.oh.us

In the northeastern corner of OH, bordered on north by Lake Erie;

Ashtabula County (cont'd)

organized Jun 7, 1807 from Trumbull County. **Name Origin:** For the Ashtabula River, which runs through the northeastern part of the county; from an Algonquian name thought to mean 'fish river' or 'there are always enough moving,' possibly referring to the fish.

Area (sq mi): 1368.47 (land 702.44; water 666.03). **Pop per sq mi:** 146.9.

Pop 2005: 103,221. **State rank:** 27. **Pop change:** 2000-20005 +0.5%; 1990-2000 +2.9%. **Pop 2000:** 102,728 (White 92.9%; Black or African American 3.2%; Hispanic or Latino 2.2%; Asian 0.3%; Other 2.5%). **Foreign born:** 1.6%. **Median age:** 37.6.

Income 2000: per capita $16,814; median household $35,607; **Pop below poverty level:** 12.1%. ***Personal per capita income 2000-2003:** $22,424-$23,965.

Unemployment 2004: 7.3%. **Change from 2000:** +0.8%. **Median travel time to work:** 23.9 minutes. **Working outside county of residence:** 27.9%.

Cities with pop over 10,000: Ashtabula (20,353); Conneaut (12,693).

ATHENS COUNTY

PO Box 290   **Ph:** 740-592-3242
Athens, OH 45701   **Fax:** 740-592-3282
www.athenscountygovernment.com

In southeastern OH, southeast of Columbus; organized Mar 1, 1805 from Washington County. **Name Origin:** For Athens, Greece.

Area (sq mi): 508.54 (land 506.76; water 1.78). **Pop per sq mi:** 122.5.

Pop 2005: 62,062. **State rank:** 41. **Pop change:** 2000-20005 -0.3%; 1990-2000 +4.5%. **Pop 2000:** 62,223 (White 92.8%; Black or African American 2.4%; Hispanic or Latino 1%; Asian 1.9%; Other 2.3%). **Foreign born:** 3.3%. **Median age:** 25.7.

Income 2000: per capita $14,171; median household $27,322; **Pop below poverty level:** 27.4%. ***Personal per capita income 2000-2003:** $17,876-$20,293.

Unemployment 2004: 6.2%. **Change from 2000:** +2.4%. **Median travel time to work:** 21.7 minutes. **Working outside county of residence:** 16.8%.

Cities with pop over 10,000: Athens 🏛 (21,824).

AUGLAIZE COUNTY

201 Willipie St Suite 211   **Ph:** 419-738-4219
Wapakoneta, OH 45895   **Fax:** 419-738-7953
www.auglaizecounty.org

In west-central OH, south of Lima; organized Feb 14, 1848 from Allen and Mercer counties. **Name Origin:** For the Auglaize River, which traverses it; from French 'at the stream' or 'at the lick,' with possible reference to a salt lick; or from an Indian word meaning 'fallen timbers.'

Area (sq mi): 401.72 (land 401.25; water 0.47). **Pop per sq mi:** 117.7.

Pop 2005: 47,242. **State rank:** 50. **Pop change:** 2000-20005 +1.4%; 1990-2000 +4.5%. **Pop 2000:** 46,611 (White 97.7%; Black or African American 0.2%; Hispanic or Latino 0.7%; Asian 0.4%; Other 1.2%). **Foreign born:** 1.1%. **Median age:** 36.5.

Income 2000: per capita $19,593; median household $43,367; **Pop below poverty level:** 6.2%. ***Personal per capita income 2000-2003:** $28,002-$28,789.

Unemployment 2004: 5.1%. **Change from 2000:** +0.7%. **Median travel time to work:** 18.1 minutes. **Working outside county of residence:** 39.3%.

Cities with pop over 10,000: None.

BELMONT COUNTY

101 W Main St Courthouse   **Ph:** 740-695-2121
Saint Clairsville, OH 43950   **Fax:** 740-695-5305
www.belmontcountyohio.org

On the central eastern border of OH, west of Wheeling, WV; organized Sept 7, 1801 (prior to statehood) from Jefferson County. **Name Origin:** French 'beautiful mountain.'

Area (sq mi): 541.39 (land 537.35; water 4.04). **Pop per sq mi:** 128.8.

Pop 2005: 69,228. **State rank:** 37. **Pop change:** 2000-20005 -1.4%; 1990-2000 -1.2%. **Pop 2000:** 70,226 (White 94.7%; Black or African American 3.6%; Hispanic or Latino 0.4%; Asian 0.3%; Other 1.1%). **Foreign born:** 1%. **Median age:** 40.9.

Income 2000: per capita $16,221; median household $29,714; **Pop below poverty level:** 14.6%. ***Personal per capita income 2000-2003:** $21,592-$24,152.

Unemployment 2004: 6.7%. **Change from 2000:** +2.6%. **Median travel time to work:** 23.5 minutes. **Working outside county of residence:** 36%.

Cities with pop over 10,000: None.

BROWN COUNTY

800 Mount Orab Pike Suite 101   **Ph:** 937-378-3956
Georgetown, OH 45121   **Fax:** 937-378-6324
www.county.brown.oh.us

On the southwestern border of OH, east of Cincinnati; organized Mar 1, 1818 from Adams and Clermont counties. **Name Origin:** For Gen. Jacob Jennings Brown (1775-1828), an officer in the War of 1812 and commander of the U.S. Army (1821-28).

Area (sq mi): 495.22 (land 491.76; water 3.46). **Pop per sq mi:** 90.3.

Pop 2005: 44,398. **State rank:** 54. **Pop change:** 2000-20005 +5%; 1990-2000 +20.9%. **Pop 2000:** 42,285 (White 97.8%; Black or African American 0.9%; Hispanic or Latino 0.4%; Asian 0.1%; Other 0.9%). **Foreign born:** 0.4%. **Median age:** 35.4.

Income 2000: per capita $17,100; median household $38,303; **Pop below poverty level:** 11.6%. ***Personal per capita income 2000-2003:** $21,940-$23,740.

Unemployment 2004: 6.9%. **Change from 2000:** +0.5%. **Median travel time to work:** 35 minutes. **Working outside county of residence:** 63.8%.

Cities with pop over 10,000: None.

---

*Source: Personal per capita income data are from the Bureau of Economic Analysis; per capita income data are from the Bureau of the Census. See Introduction for explanation of differences.

BUTLER COUNTY

315 High St   **Ph:** 513-887-3278
Hamilton, OH 45011   **Fax:** 513-887-3966
www.butlercountyohio.org

On the southwestern border of OH, north of Cincinnati; organized May 1, 1803 from Hamilton County. **Name Origin:** For Maj. Gen. Richard Butler (1743-91), an officer in the Revolutionary War, PA legislator, and Indian commissioner.

Area (sq mi): 470.2 (land 467.27, water 2.93). **Pop per sq mi:** 749.9.

Pop 2005: 350,412. **State rank:** 8. **Pop change:** 2000-20005 +5.3%; 1990-2000 +14.2%. **Pop 2000:** 332,807 (White 90.5%; Black or African American 5.3%; Hispanic or Latino 1.4%; Asian 1.5%; Other 1.9%). **Foreign born:** 2.7%. **Median age:** 34.2.

Income 2000: per capita $22,076; median household $47,885; **Pop below poverty level:** 8.7%. ***Personal per capita income 2000-2003:** $28,609-$29,864.

Unemployment 2004: 5.4%. **Change from 2000:** +2.2%. **Median travel time to work:** 23 minutes. **Working outside county of residence:** 43.6%.

Cities with pop over 10,000: Hamilton 🏛 (60,996); Middletown (51,804); Fairfield (42,379); Oxford (22,317); Trenton (10,294).

CARROLL COUNTY

119 S Lisbon St Suite 201   **Ph:** 330-627-4869
Carrollton, OH 44615   **Fax:** 330-627-6656
www.carrollcountyohio.net

In east-central OH, southeast of Canton; organized Jan 1, 1833 from Columbiana, Stark, Harrison, and Jefferson counties. **Name Origin:** For Charles Carroll (1737-1832), a signer of the Declaration of Independence, U.S. senator from MD (1789-92), and founder of the Baltimore and Ohio Railroad.

Area (sq mi): 399.01 (land 394.67; water 4.33). **Pop per sq mi:** 74.5.

Pop 2005: 29,388. **State rank:** 75. **Pop change:** 2000-20005 +1.9%; 1990-2000 +8.7%. **Pop 2000:** 28,836 (White 97.8%; Black or African American 0.5%; Hispanic or Latino 0.5%; Asian 0.1%; Other 1.1%). **Foreign born:** 0.6%. **Median age:** 38.8.

Income 2000: per capita $16,701; median household $35,509; **Pop below poverty level:** 11.4%. ***Personal per capita income 2000-2003:** $21,985-$22,518.

Unemployment 2004: 7.2%. **Change from 2000:** +2.5%. **Median travel time to work:** 27.5 minutes. **Working outside county of residence:** 57%.

Cities with pop over 10,000: None.

CHAMPAIGN COUNTY

1512 S US Hwy 68   **Ph:** 937-484-1611
Urbana, OH 43078   **Fax:** 937-484-1609
www.co.champaign.oh.us

In west-central OH, west of Columbus; organized Mar 1, 1805 from Greene and Franklin counties. **Name Origin:** Variation of French *campagne* 'field' or 'plain,' referring to the flatness of the county.

Area (sq mi): 429.71 (land 428.56; water 1.15). **Pop per sq mi:** 92.6.

Pop 2005: 39,698. **State rank:** 64. **Pop change:** 2000-20005 +2.1%; 1990-2000 +8%. **Pop 2000:** 38,890 (White 95.3%; Black or African American 2.3%; Hispanic or Latino 0.7%; Asian 0.3%; Other 1.7%). **Foreign born:** 0.7%. **Median age:** 37.

Income 2000: per capita $19,542; median household $43,139; **Pop below poverty level:** 7.6%. ***Personal per capita income 2000-2003:** $25,511-$26,787.

Unemployment 2004: 6%. **Change from 2000:** +1.4%. **Median travel time to work:** 25 minutes. **Working outside county of residence:** 53.1%.

Cities with pop over 10,000: Urbana 🏛 (11,615).

CLARK COUNTY

101 N Limestone St   **Ph:** 937-328-2458
Springfield, OH 45502   **Fax:** 937-328-2436
www.co.clark.oh.us

In west-central OH, west of Columbus; organized Mar 1, 1817 from Champaign, Madison and Greene counties. **Name Origin:** For Gen. George Rogers Clark (1752-1818), officer in the Revolutionary War and frontiersman in the Northwest Territory.

Area (sq mi): 403.56 (land 399.86; water 3.7). **Pop per sq mi:** 356.1.

Pop 2005: 142,376. **State rank:** 20. **Pop change:** 2000-20005 -1.6%; 1990-2000 -1.9%. **Pop 2000:** 144,742 (White 87.6%; Black or African American 8.9%; Hispanic or Latino 1.2%; Asian 0.5%; Other 2.4%). **Foreign born:** 1.2%. **Median age:** 37.6.

Income 2000: per capita $19,501; median household $40,340; **Pop below poverty level:** 10.7%. ***Personal per capita income 2000-2003:** $25,821-$27,246.

Unemployment 2004: 6.8%. **Change from 2000:** +1.5%. **Median travel time to work:** 21.6 minutes. **Working outside county of residence:** 31.5%.

Cities with pop over 10,000: Springfield 🏛 (63,609).

CLERMONT COUNTY

101 E Main St   **Ph:** 513-732-7300
Batavia, OH 45103   **Fax:** 513-732-7826
www.co.clermont.oh.us

On the southwestern border of OH, east of Cincinnati; original county; organized Dec 6, 1800 (prior to statehood). **Name Origin:** For the province in France, former home of some early settlers; French 'clear mountain.'

Area (sq mi): 457.67 (land 451.99; water 5.68). **Pop per sq mi:** 421.7.

Pop 2005: 190,589. **State rank:** 14. **Pop change:** 2000-20005 +7.1%; 1990-2000 +18.5%. **Pop 2000:** 177,977 (White 96.6%; Black or African American 0.9%; Hispanic or Latino 0.9%; Asian 0.6%; Other 1.4%). **Foreign born:** 1.6%. **Median age:** 34.8.

Income 2000: per capita $22,370; median household $49,386; **Pop below poverty level:** 7.1%. ***Personal per capita income 2000-2003:** $28,977-$30,720.

Unemployment 2004: 5.4%. **Change from 2000:** +1.5%. **Median travel time to work:** 28.2 minutes. **Working outside county of residence:** 59.9%.

Cities with pop over 10,000: None.

🏛 *County Seat*

CLINTON COUNTY

46 S South St   **Ph:** 937-382-2103
Wilmington, OH 45177   **Fax:** 937-383-2884
www.co.clinton.oh.us

In southwestern OH, northeast of Cincinnati; organized Mar 1, 1810 from Highland County. **Name Origin:** For George Clinton (1739-1812), first governor of NY and vice president of the U.S. (1805-12).

Area (sq mi): 412.29 (land 410.88; water 1.41). **Pop per sq mi:** 103.6.

Pop 2005: 42,570. **State rank:** 57. **Pop change:** 2000-20005 +5%; 1990-2000 +14.5%. **Pop 2000:** 40,543 (White 95.6%; Black or African American 2.2%; Hispanic or Latino 0.7%; Asian 0.4%; Other 1.5%). **Foreign born:** 1%. **Median age:** 35.3.

Income 2000: per capita $18,462; median household $40,467; **Pop below poverty level:** 8.6%. ***Personal per capita income 2000-2003:** $25,944-$26,505.

Unemployment 2004: 5.9%. **Change from 2000:** +3%. **Median travel time to work:** 23.8 minutes. **Working outside county of residence:** 30.4%.

Cities with pop over 10,000: Wilmington 🏛 (12,356).

COLUMBIANA COUNTY

105 S Market St   **Ph:** 330-424-7777
Lisbon, OH 44432   **Fax:** 330-424-3960
www.columbianacounty.org

On the northeastern border of OH, east of Canton; organized May 1, 1803 from Jefferson and Washington counties. **Name Origin:** A variation of Columbus or Columbia, for Christopher Columbus (1451-1506). The ending '-iana' may be the feminine form, which was considered appropriate for place names, or it may refer to an unidentified person named Anne or Anna.

Area (sq mi): 535.18 (land 532.46; water 2.73). **Pop per sq mi:** 208.3.

Pop 2005: 110,928. **State rank:** 25. **Pop change:** 2000-20005 -1%; 1990-2000 +3.5%. **Pop 2000:** 112,075 (White 95.5%; Black or African American 2.2%; Hispanic or Latino 1.2%; Asian 0.2%; Other 1.1%). **Foreign born:** 1.4%. **Median age:** 38.5.

Income 2000: per capita $16,655; median household $34,226; **Pop below poverty level:** 11.5%. ***Personal per capita income 2000-2003:** $21,931-$23,377.

Unemployment 2004: 7.3%. **Change from 2000:** +1.8%. **Median travel time to work:** 22.7 minutes. **Working outside county of residence:** 39.5%.

Cities with pop over 10,000: East Liverpool (12,539); Salem (12,063).

COSHOCTON COUNTY

349 1/2 Main St   **Ph:** 740-622-1753
Coshocton, OH 43812   **Fax:** 740-622-4917
www.co.coshocton.oh.us

In central OH, southwest of Canton; organized Jan 31, 1810 from Muskingum County. **Name Origin:** From Delaware Indian *goschachgunk*, thought to mean 'union of waters,' referring to the confluence of the Tuscarawas and Muskingum rivers; 'crossing' or 'ford,' or 'black bear town.'

Area (sq mi): 567.58 (land 564.07; water 3.51). **Pop per sq mi:** 65.5.

Pop 2005: 36,945. **State rank:** 67. **Pop change:** 2000-20005 +0.8%; 1990-2000 +3.5%. **Pop 2000:** 36,655 (White 97%; Black or African American 1.1%; Hispanic or Latino 0.6%; Asian 0.3%; Other 1.2%). **Foreign born:** 1%. **Median age:** 37.8.

Income 2000: per capita $16,364; median household $34,701; **Pop below poverty level:** 9.1%. ***Personal per capita income 2000-2003:** $23,203-$23,193.

Unemployment 2004: 8.8%. **Change from 2000:** +2.8%. **Median travel time to work:** 22.4 minutes. **Working outside county of residence:** 27.2%.

Cities with pop over 10,000: Coshocton 🏛 (11,650).

CRAWFORD COUNTY

112 E Mansfield St   **Ph:** 419-562-5876
Bucyrus, OH 44820   **Fax:** 419-562-3491
www.crawford-co.org

In north-central OH, north of Columbus; organized Apr 1, 1820 from Old Indian Territory. **Name Origin:** For Col. William Crawford (1732-82), VA officer in the Revolutionary War, Indian fighter, and surveyor.

Area (sq mi): 402.83 (land 402.11; water 0.72). **Pop per sq mi:** 113.8.

Pop 2005: 45,774. **State rank:** 52. **Pop change:** 2000-20005 -2.5%; 1990-2000 -1.9%. **Pop 2000:** 46,966 (White 97.5%; Black or African American 0.6%; Hispanic or Latino 0.8%; Asian 0.3%; Other 1%). **Foreign born:** 0.5%. **Median age:** 38.2.

Income 2000: per capita $17,466; median household $36,227; **Pop below poverty level:** 10.4%. ***Personal per capita income 2000-2003:** $23,092-$24,768.

Unemployment 2004: 7.6%. **Change from 2000:** +0.7%. **Median travel time to work:** 20 minutes. **Working outside county of residence:** 34.4%.

Cities with pop over 10,000: Bucyrus 🏛 (12,949); Galion (11,423).

CUYAHOGA COUNTY

1219 Ontario St   **Ph:** 216-443-7010
Cleveland, OH 44113   **Fax:** 216-443-5091
www.cuyahogacounty.us

On the northeastern border of OH, bordered on north by Lake Erie; organized Jun 7, 1808 from Geauga County. **Name Origin:** For the Cuyahoga River, which runs through it; from an Indian word, exact origin uncertain. Possibly from *Cayahaga* 'crooked,' or *Cuyahoganuk* 'lake river,' or the Iroquoian word for 'river.'

Area (sq mi): 1245.56 (land 458.49; water 787.07). **Pop per sq mi:** 2912.4.

Pop 2005: 1,335,317. **State rank:** 1. **Pop change:** 2000-20005 -4.2%; 1990-2000 -1.3%. **Pop 2000:** 1,393,978 (White 65.9%; Black or African American 27.4%; Hispanic or Latino 3.4%; Asian 1.8%; Other 3.4%). **Foreign born:** 6.4%. **Median age:** 37.3.

Income 2000: per capita $22,272; median household $39,168; **Pop below poverty level:** 13.1%. ***Personal per capita income 2000-2003:** $32,523-$34,439.

*Source: Personal per capita income data are from the Bureau of Economic Analysis; per capita income data are from the Bureau of the Census. See Introduction for explanation of differences.

Cuyahoga County (cont'd)

Unemployment 2004: 6.2%. **Change from 2000:** +1.6%. **Median travel time to work:** 24.4 minutes. **Working outside county of residence:** 9.1%.

Cities with pop over 10,000: 34 (see page 37 for cities).

DARKE COUNTY

504 S Broadway St   **Ph:** 937-547-7370
Greenville, OH 45331   **Fax:** 937-547-7367
www.co.darke.oh.us

On the central western border of OH, northwest of Dayton; organized Jan 3, 1809 from Miami County. **Name Origin:** For Gen. William Darke (1736-1801), an officer in the French and Indian War and the Revolutionary War.

Area (sq mi): 600.29 (land 599.8; water 0.49). **Pop per sq mi:** 88.3.

Pop 2005: 52,983. **State rank:** 48. **Pop change:** 2000-20005 -0.6%; 1990-2000 -0.6%. **Pop 2000:** 53,309 (White 97.6%; Black or African American 0.4%; Hispanic or Latino 0.9%; Asian 0.2%; Other 1.2%). **Foreign born:** 0.7%. **Median age:** 37.4.

Income 2000: per capita $18,670; median household $39,307; **Pop below poverty level:** 8%. ***Personal per capita income 2000-2003:** $25,566-$27,487.

Unemployment 2004: 6%. **Change from 2000:** +1.8%. **Median travel time to work:** 22.8 minutes. **Working outside county of residence:** 36.8%.

Cities with pop over 10,000: Greenville ⚏ (13,267).

DEFIANCE COUNTY

500 Court St Suite A   **Ph:** 419-782-4761
Defiance, OH 43512   **Fax:** 419-782-8449
www.defiance-county.com/

On the northwestern border of OH; organized Apr 7, 1845 from Williams, Henry, and Paulding counties. **Name Origin:** For Fort Defiance, built here 1794 by Gen. 'Mad Anthony' Wayne (1745-96), and which he described as being so strong that he 'defied hell and all her emissaries...' to take it.

Area (sq mi): 414.19 (land 411.16; water 3.03). **Pop per sq mi:** 95.1.

Pop 2005: 39,112. **State rank:** 65. **Pop change:** 2000-20005 -1%; 1990-2000 +0.4%. **Pop 2000:** 39,500 (White 89.8%; Black or African American 1.8%; Hispanic or Latino 7.2%; Asian 0.4%; Other 5.3%). **Foreign born:** 1.5%. **Median age:** 36.5.

Income 2000: per capita $19,667; median household $44,938; **Pop below poverty level:** 5.6%. ***Personal per capita income 2000-2003:** $25,996-$27,599.

Unemployment 2004: 6.1%. **Change from 2000:** +1%. **Median travel time to work:** 19.2 minutes. **Working outside county of residence:** 33.4%.

Cities with pop over 10,000: Defiance ⚏ (16,076).

DELAWARE COUNTY

101 N Sandusky St   **Ph:** 740-833-2100
Delaware, OH 43015   **Fax:** 740-833-2099
www.co.delaware.oh.us

In central OH, north of Columbus; organized Apr 1, 1808 from Franklin County. **Name Origin:** For the Delaware Indians (also called Leni-Lenape), named for the Delaware Bay.

Area (sq mi): 455.97 (land 442.41; water 13.56). **Pop per sq mi:** 339.7.

Pop 2005: 150,268. **State rank:** 19. **Pop change:** 2000-20005 +36.6%; 1990-2000 +64.3%. **Pop 2000:** 109,989 (White 93.6%; Black or African American 2.5%; Hispanic or Latino 1%; Asian 1.5%; Other 1.6%). **Foreign born:** 2.6%. **Median age:** 35.3.

Income 2000: per capita $31,600; median household $67,258; **Pop below poverty level:** 3.8%. ***Personal per capita income 2000-2003:** $41,937-$38,940.

Unemployment 2004: 4%. **Change from 2000:** +1.8%. **Median travel time to work:** 26.5 minutes. **Working outside county of residence:** 63.5%.

Cities with pop over 10,000: Delaware ⚏ (30,012).

ERIE COUNTY

323 Columbus Ave   **Ph:** 419-627-7705
Sandusky, OH 44870   **Fax:** 419-624-6873
www.erie-county-ohio.net

On the north-central coast of OH, bordered on north by Lake Erie; organized Mar 15, 1838 from Huron and Sandusky counties. **Name Origin:** For Lake Erie.

Area (sq mi): 626.15 (land 254.88; water 371.27). **Pop per sq mi:** 308.6.

Pop 2005: 78,665. **State rank:** 32. **Pop change:** 2000-20005 -1.1%; 1990-2000 +3.6%. **Pop 2000:** 79,551 (White 87.4%; Black or African American 8.6%; Hispanic or Latino 2.1%; Asian 0.4%; Other 2.3%). **Foreign born:** 1.5%. **Median age:** 39.5.

Income 2000: per capita $21,530; median household $42,746; **Pop below poverty level:** 8.3%. ***Personal per capita income 2000-2003:** $28,645-$32,050.

Unemployment 2004: 6.3%. **Change from 2000:** +1.6%. **Median travel time to work:** 18.8 minutes. **Working outside county of residence:** 25.3%.

Cities with pop over 10,000: Sandusky ⚏ (26,977); Vermilion (10,971).

FAIRFIELD COUNTY

210 E Main St   **Ph:** 740-687-7190
Lancaster, OH 43130   **Fax:** 740-687-6048
www.co.fairfield.oh.us

In central OH, southeast of Columbus; organized Dec 9, 1800 (prior to statehood) from Franklin County. **Name Origin:** Descriptive name for the rich farmland in the area.

Area (sq mi): 508.6 (land 505.11; water 3.49). **Pop per sq mi:** 274.

Pop 2005: 138,423. **State rank:** 21. **Pop change:** 2000-20005 +12.8%; 1990-2000 +18.7%. **Pop 2000:** 122,759 (White 94.7%; Black or African American 2.7%; Hispanic or Latino 0.8%; Asian 0.7%; Other 1.4%). **Foreign born:** 1.3%. **Median age:** 36.2.

Income 2000: per capita $21,671; median household $47,962; **Pop below poverty level:** 5.9%. ***Personal per capita income 2000-2003:** $28,088-$29,079.

⚏ *County Seat*

Fairfield County (cont'd)

Unemployment 2004: 5.4%. **Change from 2000:** +2.6%. **Median travel time to work:** 27.7 minutes. **Working outside county of residence:** 55.8%.

Cities with pop over 10,000: Lancaster 🏛 (35,933); Pickerington (14,968).

FAYETTE COUNTY

133 S Main St Suite 401	**Ph:** 740-335-0720
Washington Court House, OH 43160	**Fax:** 740-333-3530
www.fayette-co-oh.com	

In central OH, east of Dayton; organized Mar 1, 1810 from Ross and Highland counties. **Name Origin:** For the Marquis de Lafayette (1757-1834), French statesman and soldier who fought with the Americans during the Revolutionary War.

Area (sq mi): 407.08 (land 406.58; water 0.5). **Pop per sq mi:** 69.4.

Pop 2005: 28,199. **State rank:** 79. **Pop change:** 2000-20005 -0.8%; 1990-2000 +3.5%. **Pop 2000:** 28,433 (White 95%; Black or African American 2.1%; Hispanic or Latino 1.2%; Asian 0.5%; Other 2%). **Foreign born:** 0.9%. **Median age:** 37.5.

Income 2000: per capita $18,063; median household $36,735; **Pop below poverty level:** 10.1%. ***Personal per capita income 2000-2003:** $22,412-$26,414.

Unemployment 2004: 5.7%. **Change from 2000:** +2.1%. **Median travel time to work:** 24.4 minutes. **Working outside county of residence:** 35.1%.

Cities with pop over 10,000: Washington Court House 🏛 (13,302).

FRANKLIN COUNTY

369 S High St 3rd Fl	**Ph:** 614-462-3650
Columbus, OH 43215	**Fax:** 614-462-4325
www.co.franklin.oh.us	

In central OH; organized Apr 30, 1803 from Ross County. **Name Origin:** For Benjamin Franklin (1706-90), author, inventor, founder of the Philadelphia Library, scientist, and statesman.

Area (sq mi): 543.32 (land 539.87; water 3.45). **Pop per sq mi:** 2020.4.

Pop 2005: 1,090,771. **State rank:** 2. **Pop change:** 2000-20005 +2%; 1990-2000 +11.2%. **Pop 2000:** 1,068,978 (White 74.4%; Black or African American 17.9%; Hispanic or Latino 2.3%; Asian 3.1%; Other 3.5%). **Foreign born:** 6%. **Median age:** 32.5.

Income 2000: per capita $23,059; median household $42,734; **Pop below poverty level:** 11.6%. ***Personal per capita income 2000-2003:** $31,540-$34,471.

Unemployment 2004: 5.4%. **Change from 2000:** +2.6%. **Median travel time to work:** 21.9 minutes. **Working outside county of residence:** 7.3%.

Cities with pop over 10,000: 11 (see page 37 for cities).

FULTON COUNTY

152 S Fulton St Suite 270	**Ph:** 419-337-9255
Wauseon, OH 43567	**Fax:** 419-337-9285
www.fultoncountyoh.com	

On the northwestern border of OH, west of Toledo; organized Apr 1, 1850 from Lucas, Henry, and Williams counties. **Name Origin:** For Robert Fulton (1765-1815), builder of the *Clermont*, the first commercially successful steamboat.

Area (sq mi): 407.32 (land 406.78; water 0.54). **Pop per sq mi:** 105.6.

Pop 2005: 42,955. **State rank:** 55. **Pop change:** 2000-20005 +2.1%; 1990-2000 +9.3%. **Pop 2000:** 42,084 (White 92.7%; Black or African American 0.2%; Hispanic or Latino 5.8%; Asian 0.4%; Other 3.7%). **Foreign born:** 1.3%. **Median age:** 36.1.

Income 2000: per capita $18,999; median household $44,074; **Pop below poverty level:** 5.4%. ***Personal per capita income 2000-2003:** $26,776-$28,860.

Unemployment 2004: 6.3%. **Change from 2000:** +2%. **Median travel time to work:** 21.3 minutes. **Working outside county of residence:** 39%.

Cities with pop over 10,000: None.

GALLIA COUNTY

18 Locust St	**Ph:** 740-446-4374
Gallipolis, OH 45631	**Fax:** 740-446-4804
www.galliacounty.org	

On the southeastern border of OH; organized Apr 30, 1803 from Washington County. **Name Origin:** For Gaul, the Latin name for France, chosen by French colonists.

Area (sq mi): 471.13 (land 468.78; water 2.36). **Pop per sq mi:** 66.9.

Pop 2005: 31,362. **State rank:** 73. **Pop change:** 2000-20005 +0.9%; 1990-2000 +0.4%. **Pop 2000:** 31,069 (White 94.8%; Black or African American 2.7%; Hispanic or Latino 0.6%; Asian 0.4%; Other 1.6%). **Foreign born:** 0.8%. **Median age:** 37.4.

Income 2000: per capita $15,183; median household $30,191; **Pop below poverty level:** 18.1%. ***Personal per capita income 2000-2003:** $22,103-$24,357.

Unemployment 2004: 8.1%. **Change from 2000:** +2.5%. **Median travel time to work:** 28.1 minutes. **Working outside county of residence:** 25.2%.

Cities with pop over 10,000: None.

GEAUGA COUNTY

470 Center St Bldg 4	**Ph:** 440-285-2222
Chardon, OH 44024	**Fax:** 440-286-9177
www.co.geauga.oh.us	

In northeastern OH, east of Cleveland; organized Mar 1, 1806 from Trumbull County. **Name Origin:** Meaning of name is unclear; possibly from Iroquoian *sheauga* 'raccoon,' or for an Indian chief.

Area (sq mi): 408.29 (land 403.66; water 4.63). **Pop per sq mi:** 235.9.

Pop 2005: 95,218. **State rank:** 29. **Pop change:** 2000-20005 +4.8%; 1990-2000 +12%. **Pop 2000:** 90,895 (White 97%; Black or African American 1.2%; Hispanic or Latino 0.6%; Asian 0.4%; Other 0.9%). **Foreign born:** 2.8%. **Median age:** 38.7.

Income 2000: per capita $27,944; median household $60,200; **Pop below poverty level:** 4.6%. ***Personal per capita income 2000-2003:** $37,229-$38,403.

Source: Personal per capita income data are from the Bureau of Economic Analysis; per capita income data are from the Bureau of the Census. See Introduction for explanation of differences.

548

Geauga County (cont'd)

Unemployment 2004: 4.7%. Change from 2000: +1.5%. Median travel time to work: 27 minutes. Working outside county of residence: 57.2%.

Cities with pop over 10,000: None.

GREENE COUNTY

35 Green St   Ph: 937-562-5006
Xenia, OH 45385   Fax: 937-562-5331
www.co.greene.oh.us

In west-central OH, east of Dayton; organized May 1, 1803 from Hamilton and Ross counties. Name Origin: For Gen. Nathanael Greene (1742-86), hero of the Revolutionary War, quartermaster general (1778-80), and commander of the Army of the South (1780).

Area (sq mi): 416.21 (land 414.88; water 1.34). Pop per sq mi: 366.4.

Pop 2005: 151,996. State rank: 18. Pop change: 2000-20005 +2.8%; 1990-2000 +8.2%. Pop 2000: 147,886 (White 88.5%; Black or African American 6.4%; Hispanic or Latino 1.2%; Asian 2%; Other 2.4%). Foreign born: 3.4%. Median age: 35.6.

Income 2000: per capita $23,057; median household $48,656; Pop below poverty level: 8.5%. *Personal per capita income 2000-2003: $28,833-$31,014.

Unemployment 2004: 5.5%. Change from 2000: +2.1%. Median travel time to work: 20.3 minutes. Working outside county of residence: 44.5%.

Cities with pop over 10,000: Fairborn (32,411); Xenia 🏛 (23,768); Riverside (22,869).

GUERNSEY COUNTY

627 Wheeling Ave Suite 53   Ph: 740-432-9200
Cambridge, OH 43725   Fax: 740-432-9359
www.guernseycounty.org

In east-central OH, south of Canton; organized Mar 1, 1810 from Belmont County. Name Origin: For the British Island in the English Channel.

Area (sq mi): 528.29 (land 521.9; water 6.39). Pop per sq mi: 78.8.

Pop 2005: 41,123. State rank: 63. Pop change: 2000-20005 +0.8%; 1990-2000 +4.5%. Pop 2000: 40,792 (White 95.9%; Black or African American 1.5%; Hispanic or Latino 0.6%; Asian 0.3%; Other 1.9%). Foreign born: 1.1%. Median age: 37.7.

Income 2000: per capita $15,542; median household $30,110; Pop below poverty level: 16%. *Personal per capita income 2000-2003: $19,830-$22,140.

Unemployment 2004: 7.9%. Change from 2000: +2%. Median travel time to work: 23.7 minutes. Working outside county of residence: 26.4%.

Cities with pop over 10,000: Cambridge 🏛 (11,657).

HAMILTON COUNTY

138 E Court St Rm 603   Ph: 513-946-4400
Cincinnati, OH 45202   Fax: 513-946-4444
www.hamilton-co.org

In the southwest corner of OH; original county; organized Jan 2,

1790 (prior to statehood). Name Origin: For Alexander Hamilton (1757-1804), first U.S. secretary of the treasury (1789-95).

Area (sq mi): 412.78 (land 407.36; water 5.42). Pop per sq mi: 1980.2.

Pop 2005: 806,652. State rank: 3. Pop change: 2000-20005 -4.6%; 1990-2000 -2.4%. Pop 2000: 845,303 (White 72.4%; Black or African American 23.4%; Hispanic or Latino 1.1%; Asian 1.6%; Other 2%). Foreign born: 3.4%. Median age: 35.5.

Income 2000: per capita $24,053; median household $40,964; Pop below poverty level: 11.8%. *Personal per capita income 2000-2003: $33,565-$37,436.

Unemployment 2004: 5.6%. Change from 2000: +2%. Median travel time to work: 23 minutes. Working outside county of residence: 15.6%.

Cities with pop over 10,000: 8 (see page 37 for cities).

HANCOCK COUNTY

300 S Main St   Ph: 419-424-7037
Findlay, OH 45840   Fax: 419-424-7801
www.co.hancock.oh.us

In north-central OH, south of Toledo; organized Apr 1, 1820 from Indian lands. Name Origin: For John Hancock (1737-93), noted signer of the Declaration of Independence, governor of MA (1780-85; 1787-93), and statesman.

Area (sq mi): 533.6 (land 531.35; water 2.24). Pop per sq mi: 138.3.

Pop 2005: 73,503. State rank: 35. Pop change: 2000-20005 +3.1%; 1990-2000 +8.8%. Pop 2000: 71,295 (White 93.6%; Black or African American 1.1%; Hispanic or Latino 3.1%; Asian 1.2%; Other 2.5%). Foreign born: 2%. Median age: 36.

Income 2000: per capita $20,991; median household $43,856; Pop below poverty level: 7.5%. *Personal per capita income 2000-2003: $28,419-$30,043.

Unemployment 2004: 5.1%. Change from 2000: +1.9%. Median travel time to work: 17.5 minutes. Working outside county of residence: 18.7%.

Cities with pop over 10,000: Findlay 🏛 (40,175).

HARDIN COUNTY

1 Courthouse Sq Suite 100   Ph: 419-674-2205
Kenton, OH 43326   Fax: 419-674-2272
www.co.hardin.oh.us

In west-central OH, northwest of Columbus; organized Apr 1, 1820 from Indian lands. Name Origin: For Gen. John Hardin (1753-92), Revolutionary War officer and Indian fighter with George Rogers Clark (1752-1818) in the trans-Ohio campaigns; killed while on a peace mission to the Miami Indians.

Area (sq mi): 470.54 (land 470.29; water 0.25). Pop per sq mi: 68.1.

Pop 2005: 32,032. State rank: 72. Pop change: 2000-20005 +0.3%; 1990-2000 +2.7%. Pop 2000: 31,945 (White 97.1%; Black or African American 0.7%; Hispanic or Latino 0.8%; Asian 0.4%; Other 1.3%). Foreign born: 1%. Median age: 33.3.

Income 2000: per capita $16,200; median household $34,440; Pop below poverty level: 13.2%. *Personal per capita income 2000-2003: $20,872-$22,388.

🏛 County Seat

Hardin County (cont'd)

Unemployment 2004: 6.2%. **Change from 2000:** +1.6%. **Median travel time to work:** 21.8 minutes. **Working outside county of residence:** 38.3%.

Cities with pop over 10,000: None.

HARRISON COUNTY

100 W Market St   **Ph:** 740-942-8861
Cadiz, OH 43907   **Fax:** 740-942-8860
www.harrisoncountyohio.org

In east-central OH, southeast of Canton; organized Feb 1, 1813 from Jefferson and Tuscarawas counties. **Name Origin:** For William Henry Harrison (1773-1841), ninth U.S. president.

Area (sq mi): 410.79 (land 403.53; water 7.26). **Pop per sq mi:** 39.5.

Pop 2005: 15,920. **State rank:** 84. **Pop change:** 2000-20005 +0.4%; 1990-2000 -1.4%. **Pop 2000:** 15,856 (White 96.3%; Black or African American 2.2%; Hispanic or Latino 0.4%; Asian 0.1%; Other 1.2%). **Foreign born:** 0.5%. **Median age:** 41.1.

Income 2000: per capita $16,479; median household $30,318; **Pop below poverty level:** 13.3%. ***Personal per capita income 2000-2003:** $21,210-$22,218.

Unemployment 2004: 7%. **Change from 2000:** +2.3%. **Median travel time to work:** 28.8 minutes. **Working outside county of residence:** 52.4%.

Cities with pop over 10,000: None.

HENRY COUNTY

1853 Oakwood Ave   **Ph:** 419-592-4876
Napoleon, OH 43545
www.henrycountyohio.com

In northwestern OH, southwest of Toledo; organized Feb 12, 1820 from Wood County. **Name Origin:** For Patrick Henry (1736-99), patriot, governor of VA (1776-79; 1784-86), and statesman, famous for proclaiming, 'Give me liberty or give me death.'

Area (sq mi): 419.98 (land 416.5; water 3.47). **Pop per sq mi:** 70.7.

Pop 2005: 29,453. **State rank:** 74. **Pop change:** 2000-20005 +0.8%; 1990-2000 +0.4%. **Pop 2000:** 29,210 (White 93%; Black or African American 0.6%; Hispanic or Latino 5.4%; Asian 0.4%; Other 3.7%). **Foreign born:** 1.3%. **Median age:** 36.5.

Income 2000: per capita $18,667; median household $42,657; **Pop below poverty level:** 7%. ***Personal per capita income 2000-2003:** $25,581-$26,713.

Unemployment 2004: 6.3%. **Change from 2000:** +1.2%. **Median travel time to work:** 21.4 minutes. **Working outside county of residence:** 43%.

Cities with pop over 10,000: None.

HIGHLAND COUNTY

114 Governor Foraker Pl   **Ph:** 937-393-1911
Hillsboro, OH 45133   **Fax:** 937-393-5850
www.highland-co.com

In southwest OH; organized May 1, 1805 from Ross, Adams, and Clermont counties. **Name Origin:** For the terrain.

Area (sq mi): 557.84 (land 553.28; water 4.56). **Pop per sq mi:** 77.4.

Pop 2005: 42,818. **State rank:** 56. **Pop change:** 2000-20005 +4.8%; 1990-2000 +14.4%. **Pop 2000:** 40,875 (White 96.6%; Black or African American 1.5%; Hispanic or Latino 0.5%; Asian 0.3%; Other 1.3%). **Foreign born:** 0.6%. **Median age:** 36.1.

Income 2000: per capita $16,521; median household $35,313; **Pop below poverty level:** 11.8%. ***Personal per capita income 2000-2003:** $20,575-$22,643.

Unemployment 2004: 6.2%. **Change from 2000:** +0.9%. **Median travel time to work:** 29.3 minutes. **Working outside county of residence:** 43.2%.

Cities with pop over 10,000: None.

HOCKING COUNTY

1 E Main St   **Ph:** 740-385-5195
Logan, OH 43138   **Fax:** 740-385-1105
www.co.hocking.oh.us

In central OH, southeast of Columbus; organized Jan 3, 1818 from Athens and Ross counties. **Name Origin:** For the Hocking River, which runs through it; from an anglicized Algonquian word whose meaning is uncertain, perhaps referred to cleared fields.

Area (sq mi): 423.6 (land 422.75; water 0.85). **Pop per sq mi:** 68.6.

Pop 2005: 29,009. **State rank:** 77. **Pop change:** 2000-20005 +2.7%; 1990-2000 +10.6%. **Pop 2000:** 28,241 (White 97.2%; Black or African American 0.9%; Hispanic or Latino 0.4%; Asian 0.1%; Other 1.5%). **Foreign born:** 0.6%. **Median age:** 37.7.

Income 2000: per capita $16,095; median household $34,261; **Pop below poverty level:** 13.5%. ***Personal per capita income 2000-2003:** $20,229-$21,762.

Unemployment 2004: 7.7%. **Change from 2000:** +1.1%. **Median travel time to work:** 35.9 minutes. **Working outside county of residence:** 51.4%.

Cities with pop over 10,000: None.

HOLMES COUNTY

2 Court St   **Ph:** 330-674-0286
Millersburg, OH 44654   **Fax:** 330-674-0566
www.holmescounty.com/gov

In central OH, southwest of Canton; organized Jan 20, 1824 from Coshocton County. **Name Origin:** For Maj. Andrew Hunter Holmes (?-1814), officer in the War of 1812.

Area (sq mi): 424.02 (land 422.99; water 1.03). **Pop per sq mi:** 98.3.

Pop 2005: 41,567. **State rank:** 60. **Pop change:** 2000-20005 +6.7%; 1990-2000 +18.6%. **Pop 2000:** 38,943 (White 98.4%; Black or African American 0.3%; Hispanic or Latino 0.7%; Asian 0.1%; Other 0.6%). **Foreign born:** 0.7%. **Median age:** 28.

Income 2000: per capita $14,197; median household $36,944; **Pop below poverty level:** 12.9%. ***Personal per capita income 2000-2003:** $18,094-$20,069.

Unemployment 2004: 4.2%. **Change from 2000:** +1.6%. **Median travel time to work:** 21.6 minutes. **Working outside county of residence:** 26.1%.

Cities with pop over 10,000: None.

---

*Source: Personal per capita income data are from the Bureau of Economic Analysis; per capita income data are from the Bureau of the Census. See Introduction for explanation of differences.

HURON COUNTY

County Courthouse 2 E Main St 2nd Fl   **Ph:** 419-668-5113
Norwalk, OH 44857   **Fax:** 419-663-4048
www.hccommissioners.com

In north-central OH, west of Akron; organized Feb 7, 1809 from Indian lands. **Name Origin:** For the Huron Indians, a tribe of Iroquoian linguistic stock, later known as the Wyandot. Name from a French word for 'rough,' with a derogatory suffix, -on, probably indicating that they were formidable opponents.

Area (sq mi): 494.52 (land 492.69; water 1.83). **Pop per sq mi:** 122.6.

Pop 2005: 60,385. **State rank:** 43. **Pop change:** 2000-20005 +1.5%; 1990-2000 +5.8%. **Pop 2000:** 59,487 (White 94.2%; Black or African American 1%; Hispanic or Latino 3.6%; Asian 0.3%; Other 2.8%). **Foreign born:** 1.9%. **Median age:** 34.9.

Income 2000: per capita $18,133; median household $40,558; **Pop below poverty level:** 8.5%. ***Personal per capita income 2000-2003:** $24,169-$24,495.

Unemployment 2004: 7.8%. **Change from 2000:** +0.6%. **Median travel time to work:** 20.2 minutes. **Working outside county of residence:** 33.6%.

Cities with pop over 10,000: Norwalk 🏛 (16,457).

JACKSON COUNTY

275 Portsmouth St   **Ph:** 740-286-3301
Jackson, OH 45640   **Fax:** 740-286-4061

In south-central OH; organized Mar 1, 1816 from Pike County. **Name Origin:** For Andrew Jackson (1767-1845), seventh U.S. president.

Area (sq mi): 421.5 (land 420.28; water 1.22). **Pop per sq mi:** 79.8.

Pop 2005: 33,526. **State rank:** 71. **Pop change:** 2000-20005 +2.7%; 1990-2000 +8%. **Pop 2000:** 32,641 (White 97.5%; Black or African American 0.6%; Hispanic or Latino 0.6%; Asian 0.2%; Other 1.3%). **Foreign born:** 1.1%. **Median age:** 36.3.

Income 2000: per capita $14,789; median household $30,661; **Pop below poverty level:** 16.5%. ***Personal per capita income 2000-2003:** $19,362-$20,705.

Unemployment 2004: 8.4%. **Change from 2000:** +1.2%. **Median travel time to work:** 28.3 minutes. **Working outside county of residence:** 32.5%.

Cities with pop over 10,000: None.

JEFFERSON COUNTY

301 Market St Courthouse   **Ph:** 740-283-8500
Steubenville, OH 43952   **Fax:** 740-283-8599
www.jeffersoncountyoh.com

On east-central border of OH, southeast of Canton; original county; organized Jul 27, 1797 (prior to statehood). **Name Origin:** For Thomas Jefferson (1743-1826), U.S. patriot and statesman; third U.S. president.

Area (sq mi): 410.87 (land 409.61; water 1.27). **Pop per sq mi:** 172.4.

Pop 2005: 70,599. **State rank:** 36. **Pop change:** 2000-20005 -4.5%; 1990-2000 -8%. **Pop 2000:** 73,894 (White 92.1%; Black or African American 5.7%; Hispanic or Latino 0.6%; Asian 0.3%; Other 1.5%). **Foreign born:** 1.3%. **Median age:** 41.6.

Income 2000: per capita $16,476; median household $30,853; **Pop below poverty level:** 15.1%. ***Personal per capita income 2000-2003:** $22,145-$24,417.

Unemployment 2004: 8%. **Change from 2000:** +2.7%. **Median travel time to work:** 22.2 minutes. **Working outside county of residence:** 31.3%.

Cities with pop over 10,000: Steubenville 🏛 (19,512).

KNOX COUNTY

117 E High St Suite 161   **Ph:** 740-393-6703
Mount Vernon, OH 43050   **Fax:** 740-393-6705
www.knoxcountyohio.org

In central OH, northeast of Columbus; organized Mar 1, 1808 from Fairfield County. **Name Origin:** For Gen. Henry Knox (1750-1806), Revolutionary War officer and first U.S. secretary of war (1785-95).

Area (sq mi): 529.53 (land 527.12; water 2.41). **Pop per sq mi:** 110.8.

Pop 2005: 58,398. **State rank:** 44. **Pop change:** 2000-20005 +7.2%; 1990-2000 +14.8%. **Pop 2000:** 54,500 (White 97.2%; Black or African American 0.7%; Hispanic or Latino 0.7%; Asian 0.3%; Other 1.3%). **Foreign born:** 1%. **Median age:** 36.5.

Income 2000: per capita $17,695; median household $38,877; **Pop below poverty level:** 10.1%. ***Personal per capita income 2000-2003:** $23,197-$24,932.

Unemployment 2004: 5.6%. **Change from 2000:** +1.9%. **Median travel time to work:** 25.8 minutes. **Working outside county of residence:** 29.5%.

Cities with pop over 10,000: Mount Vernon 🏛 (16,019).

LAKE COUNTY

25 N Park Pl   **Ph:** 440-350-2500
Painesville, OH 44077
www.lakecountyohio.org

On the northeastern border of OH, bounded on the north by Lake Erie, organized Mar 6, 1840 from Geauga and Cuyahoga counties. **Name Origin:** For its location on Lake Erie.

Area (sq mi): 978.87 (land 228.21; water 750.65). **Pop per sq mi:** 1018.6.

Pop 2005: 232,466. **State rank:** 11. **Pop change:** 2000-20005 +2.2%; 1990-2000 +5.6%. **Pop 2000:** 227,511 (White 94.4%; Black or African American 2%; Hispanic or Latino 1.7%; Asian 0.9%; Other 1.7%). **Foreign born:** 4.3%. **Median age:** 38.6.

Income 2000: per capita $23,160; median household $48,763; **Pop below poverty level:** 5.1%. ***Personal per capita income 2000-2003:** $30,495-$31,501.

Unemployment 2004: 5.4%. **Change from 2000:** +1.2%. **Median travel time to work:** 22.9 minutes. **Working outside county of residence:** 37.6%.

Cities with pop over 10,000: 6 (see page 37 for cities).

🏛 *County Seat*

LAWRENCE COUNTY

PO Box 208   **Ph:** 740-533-4355
Ironton, OH 45638   **Fax:** 740-533-4383
www.lawrencecountyohio.org

On the southeastern border of OH; organized Dec 21, 1815 from Gallia County. **Name Origin:** For Capt. James Lawrence (1781-1813), U.S. naval officer in the war with Barbary pirates near Tripoli and commander of the U.S.S. *Chesapeake* in the War of 1812, who said, 'Don't give up the ship!'

Area (sq mi): 457.28 (land 454.96; water 2.32). **Pop per sq mi:** 138.7.

Pop 2005: 63,112. **State rank:** 39. **Pop change:** 2000-20005 +1.3%; 1990-2000 +0.8%. **Pop 2000:** 62,319 (White 96.1%; Black or African American 2.1%; Hispanic or Latino 0.6%; Asian 0.2%; Other 1.2%). **Foreign born:** 0.5%. **Median age:** 37.6.

Income 2000: per capita $14,678; median household $29,127; **Pop below poverty level:** 18.9%. ***Personal per capita income 2000-2003:** $19,192-$21,017.

Unemployment 2004: 6.2%. **Change from 2000:** +1%. **Median travel time to work:** 24.1 minutes. **Working outside county of residence:** 58%.

Cities with pop over 10,000: Ironton 🏛 (11,337).

LICKING COUNTY

20 S 2nd St   **Ph:** 740-670-5110
Newark, OH 43055   **Fax:** 740-670-5119
www.lcounty.com

In central OH, east of Columbus; organized Mar 1, 1808 from Fairfield County. **Name Origin:** For the salt licks in the area.

Area (sq mi): 688.38 (land 686.5; water 1.88). **Pop per sq mi:** 225.5.

Pop 2005: 154,806. **State rank:** 17. **Pop change:** 2000-20005 +6.4%; 1990-2000 +13.4%. **Pop 2000:** 145,491 (White 95.2%; Black or African American 2.1%; Hispanic or Latino 0.8%; Asian 0.6%; Other 1.7%). **Foreign born:** 1.1%. **Median age:** 36.6.

Income 2000: per capita $20,581; median household $44,124; **Pop below poverty level:** 7.5%. ***Personal per capita income 2000-2003:** $26,820-$28,510.

Unemployment 2004: 6%. **Change from 2000:** +2.4%. **Median travel time to work:** 24.8 minutes. **Working outside county of residence:** 40.4%.

Cities with pop over 10,000: Newark 🏛 (46,745); Pataskala (12,348).

LOGAN COUNTY

117 E Columbus St   **Ph:** 937-599-7283
Bellefontaine, OH 43311   **Fax:** 937-599-7268
www.co.logan.oh.us

In west-central OH, northwest of Columbus; organized Mar 1, 1817 from Champaign County. **Name Origin:** For Gen. Benjamin Logan (c. 1743-1802), VA patriot and soldier active in the West during the Revolutionary War.

Area (sq mi): 466.78 (land 458.44; water 8.34). **Pop per sq mi:** 101.6.

Pop 2005: 46,580. **State rank:** 51. **Pop change:** 2000-20005 +1.2%; 1990-2000 +8.7%. **Pop 2000:** 46,005 (White 95.7%; Black or African American 1.7%; Hispanic or Latino 0.7%; Asian 0.4%; Other 1.7%). **Foreign born:** 1.1%. **Median age:** 36.9.

Income 2000: per capita $18,984; median household $41,479; **Pop below poverty level:** 9.3%. ***Personal per capita income 2000-2003:** $25,774-$28,471.

Unemployment 2004: 5.5%. **Change from 2000:** +2.5%. **Median travel time to work:** 22 minutes. **Working outside county of residence:** 31.2%.

Cities with pop over 10,000: Bellefontaine 🏛 (13,034).

LORAIN COUNTY

225 Court St   **Ph:** 440-329-5536
Elyria, OH 44035   **Fax:** 440-329-5404
www.loraincounty.us

On the northern coast of OH, bordered on the north by Lake Erie; organized Dec 26, 1822 from Huron, Cuyahoga, and Medina counties. **Name Origin:** For the province of Lorraine, France, former home of early settlers.

Area (sq mi): 923.02 (land 492.5; water 430.52). **Pop per sq mi:** 601.6.

Pop 2005: 296,307. **State rank:** 9. **Pop change:** 2000-20005 +4.1%; 1990-2000 +5%. **Pop 2000:** 284,664 (White 82.4%; Black or African American 8.5%; Hispanic or Latino 6.9%; Asian 0.6%; Other 5.4%). **Foreign born:** 2.6%. **Median age:** 36.5.

Income 2000: per capita $21,054; median household $45,042; **Pop below poverty level:** 9%. ***Personal per capita income 2000-2003:** $26,808-$27,995.

Unemployment 2004: 5.8%. **Change from 2000:** +0.2%. **Median travel time to work:** 22.8 minutes. **Working outside county of residence:** 33.2%.

Cities with pop over 10,000: 6 (see page 38 for cities).

LUCAS COUNTY

1 Government Center Suite 800   **Ph:** 419-213-4500
Toledo, OH 43604   **Fax:** 419-213-4532
www.co.lucas.oh.us

On the northwest coast of OH, bordered on the north by Lake Erie, organized Jun 20, 1835 from Wood County. **Name Origin:** For Col. Robert Lucas (1781-1853), governor of OH (1832-36) and first territorial governor of IA (1838-41).

Area (sq mi): 595.88 (land 340.46; water 255.42). **Pop per sq mi:** 1316.5.

Pop 2005: 448,229. **State rank:** 6. **Pop change:** 2000-20005 -1.5%; 1990-2000 -1.6%. **Pop 2000:** 455,054 (White 75.4%; Black or African American 17%; Hispanic or Latino 4.5%; Asian 1.2%; Other 4.4%). **Foreign born:** 3.2%. **Median age:** 35.

Income 2000: per capita $20,518; median household $38,004; **Pop below poverty level:** 13.9%. ***Personal per capita income 2000-2003:** $27,853-$30,171.

Unemployment 2004: 7.4%. **Change from 2000:** +2.4%. **Median travel time to work:** 20.5 minutes. **Working outside county of residence:** 15.5%.

Lucas County (cont'd)

Cities with pop over 10,000: Toledo 🏛 (304,973); Oregon (19,269); Sylvania (18,905); Maumee (14,472).

MADISON COUNTY

PO Box 618
London, OH 43140
www.co.madison.oh.us

Ph: 740-852-2972
Fax: 740-845-1660

In west-central OH, west of Columbus; organized Mar 1, 1810 from Fayette County. **Name Origin:** For James Madison (1751-1836), fourth U.S. president.

Area (sq mi): 466.18 (land 465.44; water 0.74). **Pop per sq mi:** 88.7.

Pop 2005: 41,295. **State rank:** 61. **Pop change:** 2000-20005 +2.7%; 1990-2000 +8.5%. **Pop 2000:** 40,213 (White 91.4%; Black or African American 6.2%; Hispanic or Latino 0.7%; Asian 0.4%; Other 1.5%). **Foreign born:** 1.1%. **Median age:** 35.8.

Income 2000: per capita $18,721; median household $44,212; **Pop below poverty level:** 7.8%. ***Personal per capita income 2000-2003:** $23,788-$26,131.

Unemployment 2004: 5.9%. **Change from 2000:** +3.3%. **Median travel time to work:** 25.8 minutes. **Working outside county of residence:** 57.5%.

Cities with pop over 10,000: None.

MAHONING COUNTY

120 Market St
Youngstown, OH 44503
www.mahoningcountyoh.gov

Ph: 330-740-2104
Fax: 330-740-2105

On the northeastern border of OH, northeast of Canton; organized Feb 16, 1846 from Columbiana and Trumbull counties. **Name Origin:** From Delaware Indian *mahanoi* or *m'hoani* 'salt lick,' also spelled *Mahanoy*.

Area (sq mi): 423.38 (land 415.25; water 8.14). **Pop per sq mi:** 612.3.

Pop 2005: 254,274. **State rank:** 10. **Pop change:** 2000-20005 - 1.3%; 1990-2000 -2.7%. **Pop 2000:** 257,555 (White 79.6%; Black or African American 15.9%; Hispanic or Latino 3%; Asian 0.5%; Other 2.6%). **Foreign born:** 2.4%. **Median age:** 39.7.

Income 2000: per capita $18,818; median household $35,248; **Pop below poverty level:** 12.5%. ***Personal per capita income 2000-2003:** $24,780-$27,047.

Unemployment 2004: 7.4%. **Change from 2000:** +1.5%. **Median travel time to work:** 21.5 minutes. **Working outside county of residence:** 29.7%.

Cities with pop over 10,000: Youngstown 🏛 (77,713); Struthers (11,321).

MARION COUNTY

100 N Main St
Marion, OH 43302
www.co.marion.oh.us

Ph: 740-223-4270
Fax: 740-223-4279

In central OH, north of Columbus; organized Apr 1, 1820 from Crawford County. **Name Origin:** For Gen. Francis Marion (c. 1732-95), SC soldier and legislator, known as 'The Swamp Fox' for his tactics in the Carolina swamps during the Revolutionary War.

Area (sq mi): 404.15 (land 403.84; water 0.3). **Pop per sq mi:** 163.3.

Pop 2005: 65,932. **State rank:** 38. **Pop change:** 2000-20005 -0.4%; 1990-2000 +3%. **Pop 2000:** 66,217 (White 91.5%; Black or African American 5.7%; Hispanic or Latino 1.1%; Asian 0.5%; Other 1.6%). **Foreign born:** 1.1%. **Median age:** 37.2.

Income 2000: per capita $18,255; median household $38,709; **Pop below poverty level:** 9.7%. ***Personal per capita income 2000-2003:** $22,530-$24,858.

Unemployment 2004: 6.6%. **Change from 2000:** +2.2%. **Median travel time to work:** 21.5 minutes. **Working outside county of residence:** 22.1%.

Cities with pop over 10,000: Marion 🏛 (37,136).

MEDINA COUNTY

93 Public Sq
Medina, OH 44256
www.co.medina.oh.us

Ph: 330-725-9722

In north-central OH, northwest of Akron; organized Feb 18, 1812 from Portage County. **Name Origin:** Named for the city in Saudi Arabia to which Muhammad (c. 570-632), founder of Islam, fled from Mecca in 622.

Area (sq mi): 423.11 (land 421.55; water 1.57). **Pop per sq mi:** 396.2.

Pop 2005: 167,010. **State rank:** 15. **Pop change:** 2000-20005 +10.5%; 1990-2000 +23.5%. **Pop 2000:** 151,095 (White 96.6%; Black or African American 0.9%; Hispanic or Latino 0.9%; Asian 0.6%; Other 1.2%). **Foreign born:** 3%. **Median age:** 36.6.

Income 2000: per capita $24,251; median household $55,811; **Pop below poverty level:** 4.6%. ***Personal per capita income 2000-2003:** $30,761-$31,494.

Unemployment 2004: 4.9%. **Change from 2000:** +1%. **Median travel time to work:** 26.4 minutes. **Working outside county of residence:** 53.4%.

Cities with pop over 10,000: Brunswick (34,929); Medina 🏛 (26,564); Wadsworth (19,707).

MEIGS COUNTY

PO Box 151
Pomeroy, OH 45769
www.meigscountyohio.com

Ph: 740-992-5290
Fax: 740-992-4429

On the southeastern border of OH; organized Jan 21, 1819 from Gallia and Athens counties. **Name Origin:** For Return Jonathan Meigs (1764-1824), OH governor (1810-14) and U.S. Postmaster General (1814-23).

Area (sq mi): 432.38 (land 429.42; water 2.95). **Pop per sq mi:** 54.1.

Pop 2005: 23,232. **State rank:** 81. **Pop change:** 2000-20005 +0.7%; 1990-2000 +0.4%. **Pop 2000:** 23,072 (White 97.4%; Black or African American 0.7%; Hispanic or Latino 0.6%; Asian 0.1%; Other 1.5%). **Foreign born:** 0.2%. **Median age:** 38.6.

Income 2000: per capita $13,848; median household $27,287; **Pop below poverty level:** 19.8%. ***Personal per capita income 2000-2003:** $19,765-$18,931.

🏛 *County Seat*

Meigs County (cont'd)

Unemployment 2004: 10.8%. **Change from 2000:** +2.1%. **Median travel time to work:** 31.8 minutes. **Working outside county of residence:** 51.7%.

Cities with pop over 10,000: None.

MERCER COUNTY

220 W Livingston St Rm A201   **Ph:** 419-586-3178
Celina, OH 45822   **Fax:** 419-586-1699
www.mercercountyohio.org

On the central-western border of OH, southwest of Lima; organized Feb 12, 1820 from Darke County. **Name Origin:** For Gen. Hugh Mercer (1721-77), Revolutionary War officer and physician.

Area (sq mi): 473.29 (land 463.27; water 10.03). **Pop per sq mi:** 88.9.

Pop 2005: 41,202. **State rank:** 62. **Pop change:** 2000-20005 +0.7%; 1990-2000 +3.8%. **Pop 2000:** 40,924 (White 97.8%; Black or African American 0.1%; Hispanic or Latino 1.1%; Asian 0.3%; Other 1.2%). **Foreign born:** 0.8%. **Median age:** 35.7.

Income 2000: per capita $18,531; median household $42,742; **Pop below poverty level:** 6.4%. ***Personal per capita income 2000-2003:** $25,435-$27,948.

Unemployment 2004: 4.5%. **Change from 2000:** -1.3%. **Median travel time to work:** 19.9 minutes. **Working outside county of residence:** 34.1%.

Cities with pop over 10,000: Celina 🏛 (10,268).

MIAMI COUNTY

201 W Main St   **Ph:** 937-440-5900
Troy, OH 45373
www.co.miami.oh.us

In west-central OH, north of Dayton; organized Mar 1, 1807 from Montgomery County. **Name Origin:** For the Miami Indians, an Algonquin Indian tribe. Origin of the name uncertain, probably from Ojibway *oumaumeg* 'people of the peninsula,' or from Delaware *we-mi-a-mik* 'all friends.'

Area (sq mi): 409.22 (land 407.04; water 2.18). **Pop per sq mi:** 249.7.

Pop 2005: 101,619. **State rank:** 28. **Pop change:** 2000-20005 +2.8%; 1990-2000 +6.1%. **Pop 2000:** 98,868 (White 95.3%; Black or African American 2%; Hispanic or Latino 0.7%; Asian 0.8%; Other 1.5%). **Foreign born:** 1.5%. **Median age:** 37.7.

Income 2000: per capita $21,669; median household $44,109; **Pop below poverty level:** 6.7%. ***Personal per capita income 2000-2003:** $27,876-$29,193.

Unemployment 2004: 5.7%. **Change from 2000:** +1.4%. **Median travel time to work:** 20.1 minutes. **Working outside county of residence:** 37.4%.

Cities with pop over 10,000: Troy 🏛 (22,183); Piqua (20,774).

MONROE COUNTY

101 N Main St Rm 35   **Ph:** 740-472-5181
Woodsfield, OH 43793   **Fax:** 740-472-2526
www.monroecountyohio.net

On the central-eastern border of OH; organized Jan 29, 1813 from Belmont, Washington, and Guernsey counties. **Name Origin:** For James Monroe (1758-1831), fifth U.S. president.

Area (sq mi): 457.46 (land 455.54; water 1.92). **Pop per sq mi:** 32.3.

Pop 2005: 14,698. **State rank:** 86. **Pop change:** 2000-20005 -3.2%; 1990-2000 -2%. **Pop 2000:** 15,180 (White 98.4%; Black or African American 0.3%; Hispanic or Latino 0.4%; Asian 0.1%; Other 1%). **Foreign born:** 0.3%. **Median age:** 40.8.

Income 2000: per capita $15,096; median household $30,467; **Pop below poverty level:** 13.9%. ***Personal per capita income 2000-2003:** $18,995-$21,277.

Unemployment 2004: 10.1%. **Change from 2000:** +3.5%. **Median travel time to work:** 30.8 minutes. **Working outside county of residence:** 38.5%.

Cities with pop over 10,000: None.

MONTGOMERY COUNTY

451 W 3rd St   **Ph:** 937-496-7591
Dayton, OH 45422   **Fax:** 937-496-7627
www.co.montgomery.oh.us

In west-central OH, north of Cincinnati; organized Mar 24, 1803 from Hamilton and Ross counties. **Name Origin:** For Gen. Richard Montgomery (1736-75), American Revolutionary War officer who captured Montreal, Canada.

Area (sq mi): 464.34 (land 461.68; water 2.67). **Pop per sq mi:** 1185.7.

Pop 2005: 547,435. **State rank:** 4. **Pop change:** 2000-20005 -2.1%; 1990-2000 -2.6%. **Pop 2000:** 559,062 (White 75.9%; Black or African American 19.9%; Hispanic or Latino 1.3%; Asian 1.3%; Other 2.2%). **Foreign born:** 2.5%. **Median age:** 36.4.

Income 2000: per capita $21,743; median household $40,156; **Pop below poverty level:** 11.3%. ***Personal per capita income 2000-2003:** $28,948-$31,476.

Unemployment 2004: 6.5%. **Change from 2000:** +2.2%. **Median travel time to work:** 21.2 minutes. **Working outside county of residence:** 18.6%.

Cities with pop over 10,000: 11 (see page 38 for cities).

MORGAN COUNTY

19 E Main St   **Ph:** 740-962-4752
McConnelsville, OH 43756   **Fax:** 740-962-4522
www.morgancounty.org

In east-central OH, southeast of Columbus; organized Dec 29, 1817 from Washington County. **Name Origin:** For Gen. Daniel Morgan (1736-1802), an officer in the Revolutionary War and U.S. representative from VA (1797-99).

Area (sq mi): 421.86 (land 417.66; water 4.2). **Pop per sq mi:** 35.8.

Pop 2005: 14,958. **State rank:** 85. **Pop change:** 2000-20005 +0.4%; 1990-2000 +5%. **Pop 2000:** 14,897 (White 93.4%; Black or African American 3.4%; Hispanic or Latino 0.4%; Asian 0.1%; Other 2.8%). **Foreign born:** 0.5%. **Median age:** 38.9.

Income 2000: per capita $13,967; median household $28,868; **Pop below poverty level:** 18.4%. ***Personal per capita income 2000-2003:** $19,413-$20,150.

---

*Source: Personal per capita income data are from the Bureau of Economic Analysis; per capita income data are from the Bureau of the Census. See Introduction for explanation of differences.

Morgan County (cont'd)

Unemployment 2004: 10.4%. **Change from 2000:** -4.6%. **Median travel time to work:** 36.2 minutes. **Working outside county of residence:** 47%.

Cities with pop over 10,000: None.

MORROW COUNTY

48 E High St   **Ph:** 419-947-4085
Mount Gilead, OH 43338   **Fax:** 419-947-1860
www.co.morrow.oh.us

In central OH, north of Columbus; organized Mar 1, 1848 from Knox, Marion, Delaware, and Richland counties. **Name Origin:** For Jeremiah Morrow (1771-1852), OH legislator, U.S. senator (1813-19), and governor (1822-36).

Area (sq mi): 407.36 (land 406.22; water 1.13). **Pop per sq mi:** 84.5.

Pop 2005: 34,322. **State rank:** 70. **Pop change:** 2000-20005 +8.5%; 1990-2000 +14%. **Pop 2000:** 31,628 (White 98%; Black or African American 0.3%; Hispanic or Latino 0.6%; Asian 0.1%; Other 1.2%). **Foreign born:** 0.5%. **Median age:** 36.5.

Income 2000: per capita $17,830; median household $40,882; **Pop below poverty level:** 9%. ***Personal per capita income 2000-2003:** $21,727-$23,641.

Unemployment 2004: 6%. **Change from 2000:** +0%. **Median travel time to work:** 30.4 minutes. **Working outside county of residence:** 67%.

Cities with pop over 10,000: None.

MUSKINGUM COUNTY

401 Main St   **Ph:** 740-455-7104
Zanesville, OH 43701
www.muskingumcounty.org

In central OH, east of Columbus; organized Mar 1, 1804 from Washington and Fairfield counties. **Name Origin:** For the Muskingum River, which flows through it; from Algonquian but the meaning is uncertain, possibly 'by the river.'

Area (sq mi): 672.59 (land 664.63; water 7.97). **Pop per sq mi:** 128.8.

Pop 2005: 85,579. **State rank:** 31. **Pop change:** 2000-20005 +1.2%; 1990-2000 +3.1%. **Pop 2000:** 84,585 (White 93.5%; Black or African American 4%; Hispanic or Latino 0.5%; Asian 0.3%; Other 1.8%). **Foreign born:** 0.7%. **Median age:** 36.5.

Income 2000: per capita $17,533; median household $35,185; **Pop below poverty level:** 12.9%. ***Personal per capita income 2000-2003:** $23,350-$24,821.

Unemployment 2004: 8.2%. **Change from 2000:** +2.3%. **Median travel time to work:** 24.2 minutes. **Working outside county of residence:** 20.9%.

Cities with pop over 10,000: Zanesville 🏛 (25,324).

NOBLE COUNTY

County Courthouse Rm 210   **Ph:** 740-732-2969
Caldwell, OH 43724   **Fax:** 740-732-5702
www.noblecountyohio.com

In east-central OH, south of Canton; organized Apr 1, 1851 from Monroe, Morgan, Guernsey, and Washington counties. **Name Origin:** For James and Warren P. Noble, early settlers.

Area (sq mi): 404.59 (land 399; water 5.59). **Pop per sq mi:** 35.5.

Pop 2005: 14,156. **State rank:** 87. **Pop change:** 2000-20005 +0.7%; 1990-2000 +24%. **Pop 2000:** 14,058 (White 92.2%; Black or African American 6.7%; Hispanic or Latino 0.4%; Asian 0.1%; Other 0.7%). **Foreign born:** 0.6%. **Median age:** 35.5.

Income 2000: per capita $14,100; median household $32,940; **Pop below poverty level:** 11.4%. ***Personal per capita income 2000-2003:** $15,674-$16,872.

Unemployment 2004: 8.5%. **Change from 2000:** +2.9%. **Median travel time to work:** 26.7 minutes. **Working outside county of residence:** 45.3%.

Cities with pop over 10,000: None.

OTTAWA COUNTY

315 Madison St   **Ph:** 419-734-6710
Port Clinton, OH 43452   **Fax:** 419-734-6898
www.co.ottawa.oh.us

On the northern coast of OH, bordered on the north by Lake Erie; organized Mar 6, 1840 from Erie, Sandusky, and Lucas counties. **Name Origin:** For the Ottawa Indians, a tribe of Algonquian linguistic stock. Tribal name is derived from *adawe* 'to trade,' for their ability as intertribal traders and barterers.

Area (sq mi): 585.12 (land 254.95; water 330.17). **Pop per sq mi:** 163.1.

Pop 2005: 41,583. **State rank:** 59. **Pop change:** 2000-20005 +1.5%; 1990-2000 +2.4%. **Pop 2000:** 40,985 (White 94.6%; Black or African American 0.6%; Hispanic or Latino 3.7%; Asian 0.2%; Other 2.5%). **Foreign born:** 1.1%. **Median age:** 41.

Income 2000: per capita $21,973; median household $44,224; **Pop below poverty level:** 5.9%. ***Personal per capita income 2000-2003:** $29,101-$31,451.

Unemployment 2004: 8.1%. **Change from 2000:** +2.4%. **Median travel time to work:** 22.5 minutes. **Working outside county of residence:** 43.8%.

Cities with pop over 10,000: None.

PAULDING COUNTY

County Courthouse 115 N Williams St
Rm 104   **Ph:** 419-399-8210
Paulding, OH 45879   **Fax:** 419-399-8248

On the northwest coast of OH; organized Feb 12, 1820 from Indian lands. **Name Origin:** For John Paulding (1758-1818) of Peekskill, NY, one of the captors (1780) of British spy John Andre (1750-80) during the Revolutionary War.

Area (sq mi): 418.9 (land 416.26; water 2.64). **Pop per sq mi:** 46.9.

Pop 2005: 19,537. **State rank:** 83. **Pop change:** 2000-20005 -3.7%; 1990-2000 -1%. **Pop 2000:** 20,293 (White 94.7%; Black or African American 1%; Hispanic or Latino 3%; Asian 0.2%; Other 3%). **Foreign born:** 0.6%. **Median age:** 36.5.

Income 2000: per capita $18,062; median household $40,327; **Pop below poverty level:** 7.7%. ***Personal per capita income 2000-2003:** $22,512-$23,133.

Paulding County (cont'd)

Unemployment 2004: 5.9%. Change from 2000: +0.7%. Median travel time to work: 24.6 minutes. Working outside county of residence: 52.9%.

Cities with pop over 10,000: None.

PERRY COUNTY

121 W Brown St PO Box 248   Ph: 740-342-2045
New Lexington, OH 43764   Fax: 740-342-5505
www.perrycountyohiocofc.com

In central OH, southeast of Columbus; organized Mar 1, 1818 from Washington, Fairfield, and Muskingum counties. Name Origin: For Oliver Hazard Perry (1785-1819), U.S. naval officer during the War of 1812, famous for the message, 'We have met the enemy and they are ours.'

Area (sq mi): 412.59 (land 409.78; water 2.82). Pop per sq mi: 86.

Pop 2005: 35,246. State rank: 68. Pop change: 2000-20005 +3.4%; 1990-2000 +8%. Pop 2000: 34,078 (White 98.2%; Black or African American 0.2%; Hispanic or Latino 0.4%; Asian 0.1%; Other 1.2%). Foreign born: 0.6%. Median age: 35.

Income 2000: per capita $15,674; median household $34,383; Pop below poverty level: 11.8%. *Personal per capita income 2000-2003: $18,400-$19,569.

Unemployment 2004: 8.8%. Change from 2000: +1.6%. Median travel time to work: 33.5 minutes. Working outside county of residence: 58.4%.

Cities with pop over 10,000: None.

PICKAWAY COUNTY

139 W Franklin St   Ph: 740-474-6093
Circleville, OH 43113   Fax: 740-474-8988
www.pickaway.org

In central OH, south of Columbus; organized Jan 12, 1810 from Ross, Fairfield, and Franklin counties. Name Origin: A folk etymological form of *Piqua*, believed to be the name of the Shawnee subtribe to which Tecumseh (1768-1813) belonged. Name is thought to mean 'ashes,' referring to the myth that the first man of their tribe rose out of ashes.

Area (sq mi): 506.79 (land 501.91; water 4.88). Pop per sq mi: 105.6.

Pop 2005: 52,989. State rank: 47. Pop change: 2000-20005 +0.5%; 1990-2000 +9.3%. Pop 2000: 52,727 (White 91.5%; Black or African American 6.4%; Hispanic or Latino 0.6%; Asian 0.2%; Other 1.4%). Foreign born: 0.7%. Median age: 36.

Income 2000: per capita $17,478; median household $42,832; Pop below poverty level: 9.5%. *Personal per capita income 2000-2003: $21,802-$23,096.

Unemployment 2004: 7.4%. Change from 2000: +3.9%. Median travel time to work: 26.7 minutes. Working outside county of residence: 55.4%.

Cities with pop over 10,000: Circleville ⛪ (13,365).

PIKE COUNTY

100 E 2nd St   Ph: 740-947-2715
Waverly, OH 45690   Fax: 740-947-1729
www.piketravel.com

In south-central OH, south of Columbus; organized Jan 4, 1815 from Ross, Highland, and Scioto counties. Name Origin: For Gen. Zebulon Montgomery Pike (1779-1813), U.S. army officer and discoverer of Pikes Peak, CO.

Area (sq mi): 443.94 (land 441.49; water 2.46). Pop per sq mi: 63.8.

Pop 2005: 28,146. State rank: 80. Pop change: 2000-20005 +1.6%; 1990-2000 +14.2%. Pop 2000: 27,695 (White 96.3%; Black or African American 0.9%; Hispanic or Latino 0.6%; Asian 0.2%; Other 2.2%). Foreign born: 0.6%. Median age: 35.3.

Income 2000: per capita $16,093; median household $31,649; Pop below poverty level: 18.6%. *Personal per capita income 2000-2003: $19,714-$20,901.

Unemployment 2004: 10.2%. Change from 2000: +2.2%. Median travel time to work: 29.6 minutes. Working outside county of residence: 34.7%.

Cities with pop over 10,000: None.

PORTAGE COUNTY

449 S Meridian St   Ph: 330-297-3600
Ravenna, OH 44266   Fax: 330-297-3610
www.co.portage.oh.us

In northeastern OH, east of Akron; organized Jun 7, 1807 from Trumbull and Jackson counties. Name Origin: For the portage of canoes or other craft between the Cuyahoga and Manhoning rivers.

Area (sq mi): 507.11 (land 492.39; water 14.72). Pop per sq mi: 316.1.

Pop 2005: 155,631. State rank: 16. Pop change: 2000-20005 +2.3%; 1990-2000 +6.6%. Pop 2000: 152,061 (White 93.9%; Black or African American 3.2%; Hispanic or Latino 0.7%; Asian 0.8%; Other 1.6%). Foreign born: 2%. Median age: 34.4.

Income 2000: per capita $20,428; median household $44,347; Pop below poverty level: 9.3%. *Personal per capita income 2000-2003: $26,245-$27,735.

Unemployment 2004: 5.8%. Change from 2000: +1.7%. Median travel time to work: 25.1 minutes. Working outside county of residence: 49.6%.

Cities with pop over 10,000: Kent (27,601); Aurora (14,357); Streetsboro (13,900); Ravenna ⛪ (11,503).

PREBLE COUNTY

101 E Main St   Ph: 937-456-8143
Eaton, OH 45320   Fax: 937-456-8114
www.prebco.org

On the southwestern border of OH, west of Dayton; organized Mar 1, 1808 from Montgomery and Butler counties. Name Origin: For Capt. Edward Preble (1761-1807), commander of the U.S.S. *Constitution*, which bombarded Tripoli in 1804 during the war against the Barbary pirates.

Area (sq mi): 426.33 (land 424.8; water 1.52). Pop per sq mi: 100.1.

*Source: Personal per capita income data are from the Bureau of Economic Analysis; per capita income data are from the Bureau of the Census. See Introduction for explanation of differences.

Preble County (cont'd)

Pop 2005: 42,527. **State rank:** 58. **Pop change:** 2000-20005 +0.4%; 1990-2000 +5.5%. **Pop 2000:** 42,337 (White 98.2%; Black or African American 0.3%; Hispanic or Latino 0.4%; Asian 0.3%; Other 0.9%). **Foreign born:** 0.6%. **Median age:** 37.5.

Income 2000: per capita $18,444; median household $42,093; **Pop below poverty level:** 6.1% ***Personal per capita income 2000-2003:** $23,867 $24,015.

Unemployment 2004: 6.1%. **Change from 2000:** +1.7%. **Median travel time to work:** 26.7 minutes. **Working outside county of residence:** 54.1%.

Cities with pop over 10,000: None.

PUTNAM COUNTY

245 E Main St Suite 101   **Ph:** 419-523-3656
Ottawa, OH 45875   **Fax:** 419-523-9213
www.putnamcountyohio.com

In northwestern OH, north of Lima; organized Apr 1, 1820 from Indian Territory. **Name Origin:** For Gen. Israel Putnam, (1718-90), Revolutionary War officer and American commander at the Battle of Bunker Hill.

Area (sq mi): 484.23 (land 483.87; water 0.36). **Pop per sq mi:** 72.2.

Pop 2005: 34,928. **State rank:** 69. **Pop change:** 2000-20005 +0.6%; 1990-2000 +2.7%. **Pop 2000:** 34,726 (White 94.8%; Black or African American 0.2%; Hispanic or Latino 4.4%; Asian 0.2%; Other 3.4%). **Foreign born:** 0.7%. **Median age:** 35.

Income 2000: per capita $18,680; median household $46,426; **Pop below poverty level:** 5.6%. ***Personal per capita income 2000-2003:** $25,997-$27,820.

Unemployment 2004: 6.7%. **Change from 2000:** +2.7%. **Median travel time to work:** 21.1 minutes. **Working outside county of residence:** 42.8%.

Cities with pop over 10,000: None.

RICHLAND COUNTY

50 Park Ave E   **Ph:** 419-774-5549
Mansfield, OH 44902   **Fax:** 419-774-5547
www.richlandcountyohio.org

In north-central OH, west of Canton; organized Mar 1, 1808 from Knox County. **Name Origin:** For the fertile soil in the area.

Area (sq mi): 500.33 (land 496.88; water 3.45). **Pop per sq mi:** 257.5.

Pop 2005: 127,949. **State rank:** 22. **Pop change:** 2000-20005 -0.7%; 1990-2000 +2.2%. **Pop 2000:** 128,852 (White 87.6%; Black or African American 9.4%; Hispanic or Latino 0.9%; Asian 0.5%; Other 1.9%). **Foreign born:** 1.8%. **Median age:** 37.7.

Income 2000: per capita $18,582; median household $37,397; **Pop below poverty level:** 10.6%. ***Personal per capita income 2000-2003:** $23,479-$26,232.

Unemployment 2004: 7.2%. **Change from 2000:** +2%. **Median travel time to work:** 20.2 minutes. **Working outside county of residence:** 16.4%.

Cities with pop over 10,000: Mansfield 🏛 (50,557).

ROSS COUNTY

2 N Paint St Suite B   **Ph:** 740-702-3010
Chillicothe, OH 45601   **Fax:** 740-702-3018
www.co.ross.oh.us

In south-central OH, south of Columbus; original county; organized Aug 20, 1798 (prior to statehood). **Name Origin:** For James Ross (1762-1847), U.S. senator from PA (1794-1803).

Area (sq mi): 692.96 (land 688.41; water 4.55). **Pop per sq mi:** 109.2.

Pop 2005: 75,197. **State rank:** 34. **Pop change:** 2000-20005 +2.5%; 1990-2000 +5.8%. **Pop 2000:** 73,345 (White 91.3%; Black or African American 6.2%; Hispanic or Latino 0.6%; Asian 0.4%; Other 1.7%). **Foreign born:** 0.7%. **Median age:** 36.9.

Income 2000: per capita $17,569; median household $37,117; **Pop below poverty level:** 12%. ***Personal per capita income 2000-2003:** $22,219-$23,554.

Unemployment 2004: 7.7%. **Change from 2000:** +2.6%. **Median travel time to work:** 25.9 minutes. **Working outside county of residence:** 29.6%.

Cities with pop over 10,000: Chillicothe 🏛 (22,039).

SANDUSKY COUNTY

622 Croghan St   **Ph:** 419-334-6100
Fremont, OH 43420   **Fax:** 419-334-6104
www.sandusky-county.org

In north-central OH, southeast of Toledo; organized Feb 12, 1820 from Huron County. **Name Origin:** For the Sandusky River, which flows through it. From a Wyandot word, now lost, which seems to have meant 'cold water' or 'pure water.'

Area (sq mi): 417.77 (land 409.18; water 8.59). **Pop per sq mi:** 150.7.

Pop 2005: 61,676. **State rank:** 42. **Pop change:** 2000-20005 -0.2%; 1990-2000 -0.3%. **Pop 2000:** 61,792 (White 89%; Black or African American 2.7%; Hispanic or Latino 7%; Asian 0.3%; Other 1.8%). **Foreign born:** 1.3%. **Median age:** 37.3.

Income 2000: per capita $19,239; median household $40,584; **Pop below poverty level:** 7.5%. ***Personal per capita income 2000-2003:** $23,923-$25,827.

Unemployment 2004: 6.5%. **Change from 2000:** +1.4%. **Median travel time to work:** 19.4 minutes. **Working outside county of residence:** 31.1%.

Cities with pop over 10,000: Fremont 🏛 (17,181).

SCIOTO COUNTY

602 7th St Rm 205   **Ph:** 740-355-8218
Portsmouth, OH 45662   **Fax:** 740-354-2057
www.sciotocountyohio.com

On the southern border of OH; organized May 1, 1803 from Indian Territory. **Name Origin:** For the Scioto River, which flows through it; from an Iroquoian word of uncertain meaning, said by some scholars to be Wyandot 'deer.'

Area (sq mi): 616.07 (land 612.27; water 3.8). **Pop per sq mi:** 125.

Pop 2005: 76,561. **State rank:** 33. **Pop change:** 2000-20005 -3.3%; 1990-2000 -1.4%. **Pop 2000:** 79,195 (White 94.5%; Black or African

Scioto County (cont'd)

American 2.7%; Hispanic or Latino 0.6%; Asian 0.2%; Other 2.1%). **Foreign born:** 0.6%. **Median age:** 36.7.

Income 2000: per capita $15,408; median household $28,008; **Pop below poverty level:** 19.3%. ***Personal per capita income 2000-2003:** $19,714-$21,536.

Unemployment 2004: 9%. **Change from 2000:** +2%. **Median travel time to work:** 26 minutes. **Working outside county of residence:** 22.7%.

Cities with pop over 10,000: Portsmouth 🏛 (20,100).

SENECA COUNTY

81 Jefferson St   **Ph:** 419-447-4550
Tiffin, OH 44883   **Fax:** 419-447-0556
www.senecacounty.com

In north-central OH, southeast of Toledo; organized Feb 12, 1820 from Sandusky County. **Name Origin:** For the Seneca Indians, one of the Five Nations of the Iroquois; name probably means 'stony area.'

Area (sq mi): 552.37 (land 550.59; water 1.78). **Pop per sq mi:** 104.4.

Pop 2005: 57,483. **State rank:** 45. **Pop change:** 2000-20005 -2%; 1990-2000 -1.8%. **Pop 2000:** 58,683 (White 93.4%; Black or African American 1.8%; Hispanic or Latino 3.4%; Asian 0.4%; Other 2.8%). **Foreign born:** 1.2%. **Median age:** 36.3.

Income 2000: per capita $17,027; median household $38,037; **Pop below poverty level:** 9%. ***Personal per capita income 2000-2003:** $23,095-$25,047.

Unemployment 2004: 6.7%. **Change from 2000:** +0.9%. **Median travel time to work:** 20.5 minutes. **Working outside county of residence:** 37.2%.

Cities with pop over 10,000: Tiffin 🏛 (17,509); Fostoria (13,611).

SHELBY COUNTY

129 E Court St Suite 100   **Ph:** 937-498-7226
Sidney, OH 45365   **Fax:** 937-498-1293
www.co.shelby.oh.us

In west-central OH, north of Dayton; organized Jan 7, 1819 from Miami County. **Name Origin:** For Gen. Isaac Shelby (1750-1826), officer in the Revolutionary War, NC legislator, and governor of KY (1792-96; 1812-16).

Area (sq mi): 411.03 (land 409.27; water 1.76). **Pop per sq mi:** 119.1.

Pop 2005: 48,736. **State rank:** 49. **Pop change:** 2000-20005 +1.7%; 1990-2000 +6.7%. **Pop 2000:** 47,910 (White 95.5%; Black or African American 1.5%; Hispanic or Latino 0.8%; Asian 1%; Other 1.5%). **Foreign born:** 1.4%. **Median age:** 34.8.

Income 2000: per capita $20,255; median household $44,507; **Pop below poverty level:** 6.7%. ***Personal per capita income 2000-2003:** $26,478-$28,807.

Unemployment 2004: 5.1%. **Change from 2000:** +1%. **Median travel time to work:** 17.4 minutes. **Working outside county of residence:** 22.9%.

Cities with pop over 10,000: Sidney 🏛 (20,149).

STARK COUNTY

225 4th St NE   **Ph:** 330-451-7432
Canton, OH 44702   **Fax:** 330-451-7190
www.co.stark.oh.us

In northeastern OH, south of Akron; organized Feb 13, 1808 from Indian Territory. **Name Origin:** For Gen. John Stark (1728-1822), officer in the French and Indian War and the Revolutionary War.

Area (sq mi): 580.91 (land 576.14; water 4.77). **Pop per sq mi:** 660.6.

Pop 2005: 380,608. **State rank:** 7. **Pop change:** 2000-20005 +0.7%; 1990-2000 +2.9%. **Pop 2000:** 378,098 (White 89.7%; Black or African American 7.2%; Hispanic or Latino 0.9%; Asian 0.5%; Other 1.9%). **Foreign born:** 1.8%. **Median age:** 38.2.

Income 2000: per capita $20,417; median household $39,824; **Pop below poverty level:** 9.2%. ***Personal per capita income 2000-2003:** $26,746-$27,642.

Unemployment 2004: 6.6%. **Change from 2000:** +2.6%. **Median travel time to work:** 21.3 minutes. **Working outside county of residence:** 20.7%.

Cities with pop over 10,000: Canton 🏛 (79,905); Massillon (32,055); Alliance (23,268); North Canton (16,796).

SUMMIT COUNTY

175 S Main St   **Ph:** 330-643-2500
Akron, OH 44308   **Fax:** 330-643-2507
www.co.summit.oh.us

In northeastern OH, south of Cleveland; organized Mar 3, 1840 from Portage, Medina, and Stark counties. **Name Origin:** From the Greek 'summit,' because the highest point on the Ohio Canal is at the county seat, Akron.

Area (sq mi): 420.06 (land 412.72; water 7.34). **Pop per sq mi:** 1324.4.

Pop 2005: 546,604. **State rank:** 5. **Pop change:** 2000-20005 +0.7%; 1990-2000 +5.4%. **Pop 2000:** 542,899 (White 83%; Black or African American 13.2%; Hispanic or Latino 0.9%; Asian 1.4%; Other 1.9%). **Foreign born:** 3.3%. **Median age:** 37.2.

Income 2000: per capita $22,842; median household $42,304; **Pop below poverty level:** 9.9%. ***Personal per capita income 2000-2003:** $30,527-$31,765.

Unemployment 2004: 6.1%. **Change from 2000:** +1.8%. **Median travel time to work:** 22.4 minutes. **Working outside county of residence:** 25%.

Cities with pop over 10,000: 10 (see page 38 for cities).

TRUMBULL COUNTY

160 High St NW 5th Fl Administration Bldg **Ph:** 330-675-2451
Warren, OH 44481   **Fax:** 330-675-2462
www.co.trumbull.oh.us

On the northeastern border of OH; organized Jul 10, 1800 from Jefferson County (prior to statehood). **Name Origin:** For Jonathan Trumbull (1740-1809), aide-de-camp to Gen. George Washington (1780-83), governor of CT (1798-1809), and son of the colonial governor of the same name.

Area (sq mi): 634.72 (land 616.48; water 18.24). **Pop per sq mi:** 355.7.

---

*Source: Personal per capita income data are from the Bureau of Economic Analysis; per capita income data are from the Bureau of the Census. See Introduction for explanation of differences.

Trumbull County (cont'd)

Pop 2005: 219,296. **State rank:** 12. **Pop change:** 2000-20005 -2.6%; 1990-2000 -1.2%. **Pop 2000:** 225,116 (White 89.7%; Black or African American 7.9%; Hispanic or Latino 0.8%; Asian 0.5%; Other 1.4%). **Foreign born:** 1.8%. **Median age:** 39.

Income 2000: per capita $19,188; median household $38,298; **Pop below poverty level:** 10.3%. *Personal per capita income 2000 2003:** $24,975-$26,163.

Unemployment 2004: 7.5%. **Change from 2000:** +1.2%. **Median travel time to work:** 21 minutes. **Working outside county of residence:** 27.1%.

Cities with pop over 10,000: Warren ⚒ (46,235); Niles (20,194); Girard (10,594).

TUSCARAWAS COUNTY

125 E High Ave Rm 230	**Ph:** 330-365-3243
New Philadelphia, OH 44663	**Fax:** 330-343-4682
www.co.tuscarawas.oh.us	

In east-central OH, south of Canton; organized Mar 15, 1808 from Jefferson County. **Name Origin:** For the Tuscarawas River, which flows through it; from an Indian word thought to mean 'open mouth.'

Area (sq mi): 571.48 (land 567.58; water 3.91). **Pop per sq mi:** 162.

Pop 2005: 91,944. **State rank:** 30. **Pop change:** 2000-20005 +1.1%; 1990-2000 +8.1%. **Pop 2000:** 90,914 (White 97.4%; Black or African American 0.7%; Hispanic or Latino 0.7%; Asian 0.2%; Other 1.1%). **Foreign born:** 0.9%. **Median age:** 37.9.

Income 2000: per capita $17,276; median household $35,489; **Pop below poverty level:** 9.4%. *Personal per capita income 2000-2003:** $22,435-$23,777.

Unemployment 2004: 6%. **Change from 2000:** +1.3%. **Median travel time to work:** 21.6 minutes. **Working outside county of residence:** 26.8%.

Cities with pop over 10,000: New Philadelphia ⚒ (17,470); Dover (12,498).

UNION COUNTY

233 W 6th St	**Ph:** 937-645-3012
Marysville, OH 43040	**Fax:** 937-645-3002
www.co.union.oh.us	

In central OH, northwest of Columbus; organized Apr 1, 1820 from Franklin, Madison, and Logan counties. **Name Origin:** For the union of parts of four counties.

Area (sq mi): 436.98 (land 436.65; water 0.33). **Pop per sq mi:** 104.8.

Pop 2005: 45,751. **State rank:** 53. **Pop change:** 2000-20005 +11.8%; 1990-2000 +28%. **Pop 2000:** 40,909 (White 94.8%; Black or African American 2.8%; Hispanic or Latino 0.8%; Asian 0.5%; Other 1.4%). **Foreign born:** 1%. **Median age:** 34.5.

Income 2000: per capita $20,577; median household $51,743; **Pop below poverty level:** 4.6%. *Personal per capita income 2000-2003:** $26,725-$28,421.

Unemployment 2004: 4.9%. **Change from 2000:** +2.2%. **Median travel time to work:** 23 minutes. **Working outside county of residence:** 42.7%.

Cities with pop over 10,000: Marysville ⚒ (16,787).

VAN WERT COUNTY

114 E Main St	**Ph:** 419-238-6159
Van Wert, OH 45891	**Fax:** 419-238-4528
vanwertcounty.org	

On the western border of OH, west of Lima; organized Apr 1, 1820 from Indian Territory. **Name Origin:** For Isaac Van Wert (?-1828), a captor of John Andre (1750-80), a British spy, during the Revolutionary War.

Area (sq mi): 410.49 (land 410.09; water 0.4). **Pop per sq mi:** 71.1.

Pop 2005: 29,154. **State rank:** 76. **Pop change:** 2000-20005 -1.7%; 1990-2000 -2.6%. **Pop 2000:** 29,659 (White 96.7%; Black or African American 0.7%; Hispanic or Latino 1.6%; Asian 0.2%; Other 1.7%). **Foreign born:** 0.7%. **Median age:** 37.6.

Income 2000: per capita $18,293; median household $39,497; **Pop below poverty level:** 5.5%. *Personal per capita income 2000-2003:** $24,661-$25,191.

Unemployment 2004: 5.4%. **Change from 2000:** -0.2%. **Median travel time to work:** 19 minutes. **Working outside county of residence:** 34.5%.

Cities with pop over 10,000: Van Wert ⚒ (10,533).

VINTON COUNTY

100 E Main St County Courthouse	**Ph:** 740-596-4571
McArthur, OH 45651	**Fax:** 740-596-4571
www.vintoncounty.com	

In south-central OH; organized Mar 23, 1850 from Gallia, Athens, Ross, Hocking, Meigs, and Jackson counties. **Name Origin:** For Samuel Finley Vinton (1792-1862), U.S. representative from OH (1823-37; 1843-51).

Area (sq mi): 414.96 (land 414.08; water 0.88). **Pop per sq mi:** 32.4.

Pop 2005: 13,429. **State rank:** 88. **Pop change:** 2000-20005 +4.9%; 1990-2000 +15.4%. **Pop 2000:** 12,806 (White 97.8%; Black or African American 0.4%; Hispanic or Latino 0.5%; Asian 0.1%; Other 1.6%). **Foreign born:** 0.3%. **Median age:** 35.5.

Income 2000: per capita $13,731; median household $29,465; **Pop below poverty level:** 20%. *Personal per capita income 2000-2003:** $17,211-$18,452.

Unemployment 2004: 8.6%. **Change from 2000:** -3.1%. **Median travel time to work:** 37 minutes. **Working outside county of residence:** 59.7%.

Cities with pop over 10,000: None.

WARREN COUNTY

550 Justice Dr	**Ph:** 513-695-1370
Lebanon, OH 45036	**Fax:** 513-695-2990
www.co.warren.oh.us	

In southwestern OH, northeast of Cincinnati; organized Mar 24, 1803 from Hamilton County. **Name Origin:** For Gen. Joseph Warren (1741-75), Revolutionary War patriot and member of the Committee of Safety, who dispatched Paul Revere (1735-1818) on his famous ride.

⚒ *County Seat*

Warren County (cont'd)

Area (sq mi): 407.14 (land 399.63; water 7.51). **Pop per sq mi:** 492.

Pop 2005: 196,622. **State rank:** 13. **Pop change:** 2000-20005 +24.1%; 1990-2000 +39%. **Pop 2000:** 158,383 (White 94%; Black or African American 2.7%; Hispanic or Latino 1%; Asian 1.3%; Other 1.3%). **Foreign born:** 2.3%. **Median age:** 35.2.

Income 2000: per capita $25,517; median household $57,952; **Pop below poverty level:** 4.2%. ***Personal per capita income 2000-2003:** $30,767-$32,075.

Unemployment 2004: 4.7%. **Change from 2000:** +1.4%. **Median travel time to work:** 24.1 minutes. **Working outside county of residence:** 61.5%.

Cities with pop over 10,000: Mason (27,958); Lebanon 🏛 (19,370); Springboro (15,780); Franklin (12,246).

WASHINGTON COUNTY

205 Putnam St   **Ph:** 740-373-6623
Marietta, OH 45750   **Fax:** 740-373-2085
www.co.washington.oh.us

On the southeastern border of OH; original county; organized Jul 27, 1788 (prior to statehood). **Name Origin:** For George Washington (1732-99), American patriot and first U.S. president.

Area (sq mi): 640.15 (land 635.15; water 5). **Pop per sq mi:** 97.9.

Pop 2005: 62,210. **State rank:** 40. **Pop change:** 2000-20005 -1.6%; 1990-2000 +1.6%. **Pop 2000:** 63,251 (White 96.9%; Black or African American 0.9%; Hispanic or Latino 0.5%; Asian 0.4%; Other 1.2%). **Foreign born:** 0.6%. **Median age:** 39.1.

Income 2000: per capita $18,082; median household $34,275; **Pop below poverty level:** 11.4%. ***Personal per capita income 2000-2003:** $22,736-$24,929.

Unemployment 2004: 6.3%. **Change from 2000:** +2.5%. **Median travel time to work:** 22.5 minutes. **Working outside county of residence:** 29.2%.

Cities with pop over 10,000: Marietta 🏛 (14,295).

WAYNE COUNTY

428 W Liberty St   **Ph:** 330-287-5400
Wooster, OH 44691   **Fax:** 330-287-5407
www.wayneohio.org

In north-central OH, west of Canton; original county; organized Aug 15, 1796 (prior to statehood). **Name Origin:** For Gen. Anthony Wayne (1745-96), PA soldier and statesman, nicknamed 'Mad Anthony' for his daring during the Revolutionary War.

Area (sq mi): 556.31 (land 555.36; water 0.96). **Pop per sq mi:** 204.7.

Pop 2005: 113,697. **State rank:** 24. **Pop change:** 2000-20005 +1.9%; 1990-2000 +10%. **Pop 2000:** 111,564 (White 96%; Black or African American 1.6%; Hispanic or Latino 0.8%; Asian 0.7%; Other 1.2%). **Foreign born:** 1.7%. **Median age:** 35.4.

Income 2000: per capita $18,330; median household $41,538; **Pop below poverty level:** 8%. ***Personal per capita income 2000-2003:** $23,954-$25,771.

Unemployment 2004: 5.3%. **Change from 2000:** +1.4%. **Median travel time to work:** 19.4 minutes. **Working outside county of residence:** 27.1%.

Cities with pop over 10,000: Wooster 🏛 (25,605).

WILLIAMS COUNTY

1 Courthouse Sq   **Ph:** 419-636-2059
Bryan, OH 43506   **Fax:** 419-636-0643
www.co.williams.oh.us

In the northwestern corner of OH; organized Feb 12, 1820 from Henry County. **Name Origin:** For David Williams, a captor of British spy John Andre (1750-80), in the Revolutionary War.

Area (sq mi): 423.05 (land 421.74; water 1.31). **Pop per sq mi:** 91.7.

Pop 2005: 38,688. **State rank:** 66. **Pop change:** 2000-20005 -1.3%; 1990-2000 +6%. **Pop 2000:** 39,188 (White 95.3%; Black or African American 0.7%; Hispanic or Latino 2.7%; Asian 0.5%; Other 2.2%). **Foreign born:** 1%. **Median age:** 36.9.

Income 2000: per capita $18,441; median household $40,735; **Pop below poverty level:** 6%. ***Personal per capita income 2000-2003:** $24,831-$26,173.

Unemployment 2004: 6.4%. **Change from 2000:** +0.6%. **Median travel time to work:** 18 minutes. **Working outside county of residence:** 23.7%.

Cities with pop over 10,000: None.

WOOD COUNTY

1 Courthouse Sq PO Box 829   **Ph:** 419-354-9280
Bowling Green, OH 43402   **Fax:** 419-354-9241
www.co.wood.oh.us

In west-central OH, south of Toledo; organized Feb 12, 1820 from Indian lands. **Name Origin:** For Capt. Eleazer Derby Wood (1783-1814), an officer in the War of 1812 and builder of Fort Meigs.

Area (sq mi): 620.54 (land 617.32; water 3.22). **Pop per sq mi:** 200.8.

Pop 2005: 123,929. **State rank:** 23. **Pop change:** 2000-20005 +2.4%; 1990-2000 +6.9%. **Pop 2000:** 121,065 (White 93.3%; Black or African American 1.3%; Hispanic or Latino 3.3%; Asian 1%; Other 2.9%). **Foreign born:** 2.4%. **Median age:** 32.6.

Income 2000: per capita $21,284; median household $44,442; **Pop below poverty level:** 9.6%. ***Personal per capita income 2000-2003:** $27,345-$29,073.

Unemployment 2004: 5.7%. **Change from 2000:** +2.2%. **Median travel time to work:** 20.1 minutes. **Working outside county of residence:** 44.3%.

Cities with pop over 10,000: Bowling Green 🏛 (29,454); Perrysburg (16,947).

WYANDOT COUNTY

109 S Sandusky Ave County Courthouse **Ph:** 419-294-1432
Upper Sandusky, OH 43351   **Fax:** 419-294-6414
www.co.wyandot.oh.us

In west-central OH; organized Feb 3, 1845 from Marion, Crawford, Hardin, and Hancock counties. **Name Origin:** For the Wyandot Indians, a tribe of Iroquoian linguistic stock. Name is thought to mean 'islanders' or 'those who live on a peninsula,' from their

*Source: Personal per capita income data are from the Bureau of Economic Analysis; per capita income data are from the Bureau of the Census.
See Introduction for explanation of differences.

Wyandot County (cont'd)

original home on island in the Saint Lawrence River and on a peninsula. Also spelled *Wyandotte*.

Area (sq mi): 407.62 (land 405.61; water 2.01). **Pop per sq mi:** 56.2.

Pop 2005: 22,813. **State rank:** 82. **Pop change:** 2000-20005 -0.4%; 1990-2000 +2.9%. **Pop 2000:** 22,908 (White 97.3%; Black or African American 0.1%; Hispanic or Latino 1.5%; Asian 0.5%; Other 1.4%). **Foreign born:** 0.8%. **Median age:** 37.4.

Income 2000: per capita $17,170; median household $38,839; **Pop below poverty level:** 5.5%. ***Personal per capita income 2000-2003:** $23,582-$26,271.

Unemployment 2004: 5.6%. **Change from 2000:** +1.2%. **Median travel time to work:** 20 minutes. **Working outside county of residence:** 33.6%.

Cities with pop over 10,000: None.

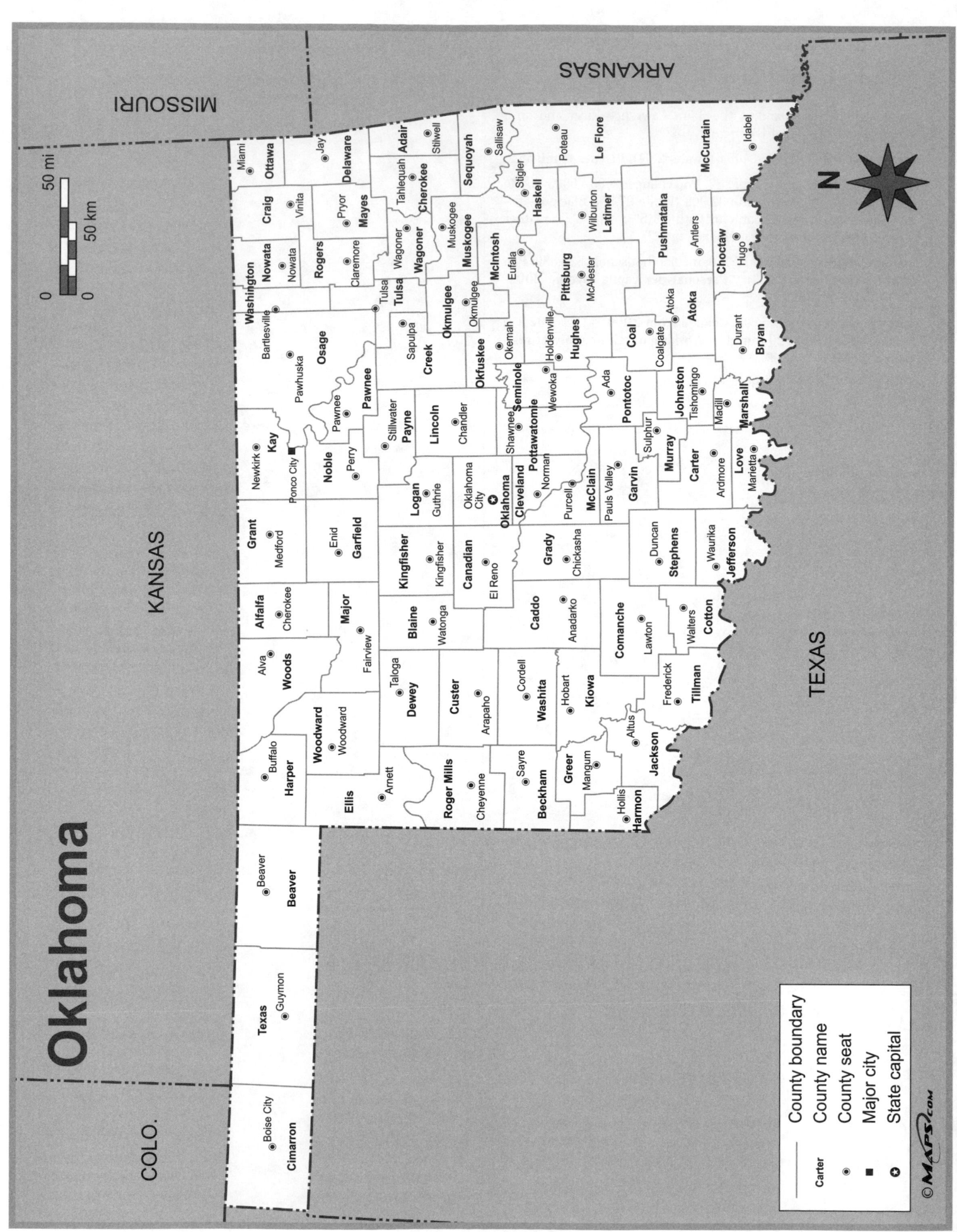

Oklahoma

Oklahoma

OKLAHOMA STATE INFORMATION

www.ok.gov   **Ph:** 405-521-2011

Area (sq mi): 69,898.19 (land 68,667.06; water 1231.13). **Pop per sq mi:** 51.7.

Pop 2005: 3,547,884. **Pop change:** 2000-20005 +2.8%; 1990-2000 +9.7%. **Pop 2000:** 3,450,654 (White 74.1%; Black or African American 7.6%; Hispanic or Latino 5.2%; Asian 1.4%; Other 14.9%, including 7.9% American Indian/Alaska Native). **Foreign born:** 3.8%. **Median age:** 35.5.

Income 2000: per capita $17,646; median household $33,400; **Pop below poverty level:** 14.7%. ***Personal per capita income 2000-2003:** $24,407-$26,719.

Unemployment 2004: 4.9%. **Change from 2000:** +1.8%. **Median travel time to work:** 21.7 minutes. **Working outside county of residence:** 23.8%.

ADAIR COUNTY

PO Box 169   **Ph:** 918-696-7198
Stilwell, OK 74960   **Fax:** 918-696-2603

On the central eastern border of OK, east of Tulsa; organized Jul 16, 1907 from Cherokee lands. **Name Origin:** For either John Lynch Adair (1828-96) or members of a well-known Cherokee family.

Area (sq mi): 577.03 (land 575.67; water 1.36). **Pop per sq mi:** 38.2.

Pop 2005: 21,988. **State rank:** 38. **Pop change:** 2000-20005 +4.5%; 1990-2000 +14.2%. **Pop 2000:** 21,038 (White 47.7%; Black or African American 0.2%; Hispanic or Latino 3.1%; Asian 0.1%; Other 51.2%, including 42.5% American Indian/Alaska Native). **Foreign born:** 1.4%. **Median age:** 33.2.

Income 2000: per capita $11,185; median household $24,881; **Pop below poverty level:** 23.2%. ***Personal per capita income 2000-2003:** $15,720-$18,787.

Unemployment 2004: 6.2%. **Change from 2000:** +1.4%. **Median travel time to work:** 25.8 minutes. **Working outside county of residence:** 36%.

Cities with pop over 10,000: None.

ALFALFA COUNTY

300 S Grand Ave   **Ph:** 580-596-3158
Cherokee, OK 73728

On the central northern border of OK, northwest of Enid; organized Nov 16, 1907 from Woods County. **Name Origin:** For William Henry 'Alfalfa Bill' Murray (1869-1956), U.S. representative from OK (1913-17) and governor (1931-35).

Area (sq mi): 881.44 (land 866.65; water 14.79). **Pop per sq mi:** 6.6.

Pop 2005: 5,725. **State rank:** 69. **Pop change:** 2000-20005 -6.2%; 1990-2000 -4.8%. **Pop 2000:** 6,105 (White 88.4%; Black or African American 4.2%; Hispanic or Latino 2.9%; Asian 0.1%; Other 6.2%, including 2.7% American Indian/Alaska Native). **Foreign born:** 0.7%. **Median age:** 42.3.

Income 2000: per capita $14,704; median household $30,259; **Pop below poverty level:** 13.7%. ***Personal per capita income 2000-2003:** $20,302-$24,166.

Unemployment 2004: 3.6%. **Change from 2000:** +2.2%. **Median travel time to work:** 18.1 minutes. **Working outside county of residence:** 26.1%.

Cities with pop over 10,000: None.

ATOKA COUNTY

200 E Court St   **Ph:** 580-889-2643
Atoka, OK 74525   **Fax:** 580-889-2608
www.atokacity.org

In south-central OK, southwest of McAlester; organized as Shappaway County Nov 16, 1907 from Choctaw lands. **Name Origin:** For Capt. Atoka, the Choctaw athlete who led a band of his people to OK during their removal from MS and AL. Originally for another noted Choctaw leader.

Area (sq mi): 990 (land 978.29; water 11.71). **Pop per sq mi:** 14.8.

Pop 2005: 14,456. **State rank:** 47. **Pop change:** 2000-20005 +4.2%; 1990-2000 +8.6%. **Pop 2000:** 13,879 (White 75.4%; Black or African American 5.9%; Hispanic or Latino 1.4%; Asian 0.2%; Other 18.1%, including 11.4% American Indian/Alaska Native). **Foreign born:** 0.3%. **Median age:** 38.3.

Income 2000: per capita $12,919; median household $24,752; **Pop below poverty level:** 19.8%. ***Personal per capita income 2000-2003:** $15,655-$17,953.

Unemployment 2004: 6.1%. **Change from 2000:** +2.1%. **Median travel time to work:** 29.5 minutes. **Working outside county of residence:** 31%.

Cities with pop over 10,000: None.

BEAVER COUNTY

PO Box 338   **Ph:** 580-625-3151
Beaver, OK 73932   **Fax:** 580-625-3430

In the OK panhandle; original county; organized 1890 (prior to statehood) and comprising the entire panhandle. Present Beaver County was organized Nov 16, 1907 from the eastern third of the original county. **Name Origin:** For the Beaver River, which runs across the county.

Beaver County (cont'd)

Area (sq mi): 1817.58 (land 1814.36; water 3.22). **Pop per sq mi:** 3.

Pop 2005: 5,379. **State rank:** 70. **Pop change:** 2000-20005 -8.2%; 1990-2000 -2.8%. **Pop 2000:** 5,857 (White 86.6%; Black or African American 0.3%; Hispanic or Latino 10.8%; Asian 0.1%; Other 6.9%, including 1.2% American Indian/Alaska Native). **Foreign born:** 5.5%. **Median age:** 39.3.

Income 2000: per capita $17,905; median household $36,715; **Pop below poverty level:** 11.7%. ***Personal per capita income 2000-2003:** $22,637-$25,002.

Unemployment 2004: 3.4%. **Change from 2000:** +0.7%. **Median travel time to work:** 21.1 minutes. **Working outside county of residence:** 36.9%.

Cities with pop over 10,000: None.

BECKHAM COUNTY

PO Box 67   **Ph:** 580-928-2457
Sayre, OK 73662   **Fax:** 580-928-2467

On the southwestern border of OK; organized Nov 16, 1907 from Greer and Roger Mills counties. **Name Origin:** For John Crepps Wickliffe Beckham (1869-1940), KY governor (1900-07) and U.S. senator (1915-21).

Area (sq mi): 904.14 (land 901.83; water 2.31). **Pop per sq mi:** 20.9.

Pop 2005: 18,880. **State rank:** 42. **Pop change:** 2000-20005 -4.6%; 1990-2000 +5.2%. **Pop 2000:** 19,799 (White 84.7%; Black or African American 5.5%; Hispanic or Latino 5.4%; Asian 0.4%; Other 7%, including 2.6% American Indian/Alaska Native). **Foreign born:** 1.6%. **Median age:** 36.6.

Income 2000: per capita $14,488; median household $27,402; **Pop below poverty level:** 18.2%. ***Personal per capita income 2000-2003:** $17,942-$21,198.

Unemployment 2004: 3.4%. **Change from 2000:** +0.7%. **Median travel time to work:** 18.4 minutes. **Working outside county of residence:** 12%.

Cities with pop over 10,000: Elk City (10,442).

BLAINE COUNTY

212 N Weigle   **Ph:** 580-623-5890
Watonga, OK 73772
www.watonga.com

In west-central OK, northwest of Oklahoma City; original county; organized as 'C' County in 1890; renamed in Nov 1892 (prior to statehood). **Name Origin:** For James Gillespie Blaine (1830-93), U.S. representative from ME (1863-76), U.S. senator (1876-81), and U.S. secretary of state (1881; 1889-92).

Area (sq mi): 938.88 (land 928.43; water 10.45). **Pop per sq mi:** 13.9.

Pop 2005: 12,859. **State rank:** 51. **Pop change:** 2000-20005 +7.4%; 1990-2000 +4.4%. **Pop 2000:** 11,976 (White 73.7%; Black or African American 6.7%; Hispanic or Latino 6.6%; Asian 0.7%; Other 16.4%, including 8.7% American Indian/Alaska Native). **Foreign born:** 3.5%. **Median age:** 37.6.

Income 2000: per capita $13,546; median household $28,356; **Pop below poverty level:** 16.9%. ***Personal per capita income 2000-2003:** $17,937-$21,210.

Unemployment 2004: 4.3%. **Change from 2000:** -0.4%. **Median travel time to work:** 19.1 minutes. **Working outside county of residence:** 20.7%.

Cities with pop over 10,000: None.

BRYAN COUNTY

PO Box 1789   **Ph:** 580-924-2202
Durant, OK 74702   **Fax:** 580-924-2289

On the central southern border of OK; organized Nov 16, 1907 from Chickasaw lands. **Name Origin:** For William Jennings Bryan (1860-1925), U.S. representative from NE (1891-95), U.S. secretary of state (1913-15), and prosecuter in John Scopes' (1900-70) trial for teaching the theory of evolution (1925).

Area (sq mi): 943.43 (land 908.8; water 34.63). **Pop per sq mi:** 41.6.

Pop 2005: 37,815. **State rank:** 26. **Pop change:** 2000-20005 +3.5%; 1990-2000 +13.9%. **Pop 2000:** 36,534 (White 78.9%; Black or African American 1.4%; Hispanic or Latino 2.6%; Asian 0.4%; Other 18.1%, including 12.2% American Indian/Alaska Native). **Foreign born:** 1.4%. **Median age:** 35.8.

Income 2000: per capita $14,217; median household $27,888; **Pop below poverty level:** 18.4%. ***Personal per capita income 2000-2003:** $18,964-$21,544.

Unemployment 2004: 3.9%. **Change from 2000:** +1%. **Median travel time to work:** 23.7 minutes. **Working outside county of residence:** 33.2%.

Cities with pop over 10,000: Durant 🏛 (14,780).

CADDO COUNTY

SW 2nd & Oklahoma PO Box 68   **Ph:** 405-247-6609
Anadarko, OK 73005   **Fax:** 405-247-6510

In west-central OK, west of Oklahoma City; original county; organized Aug 6, 1901 (prior to statehood). **Name Origin:** Name applied to a group of tribes of Caddoan linguistic stock, from Caddo Indian *kaadi* 'life' or 'chiefs.'

Area (sq mi): 1290.31 (land 1278.33; water 11.98). **Pop per sq mi:** 23.6.

Pop 2005: 30,229. **State rank:** 32. **Pop change:** 2000-20005 +0.3%; 1990-2000 +2%. **Pop 2000:** 30,150 (White 64.1%; Black or African American 2.9%; Hispanic or Latino 6.3%; Asian 0.2%; Other 31.4%, including 24.3% American Indian/Alaska Native). **Foreign born:** 2.2%. **Median age:** 36.

Income 2000: per capita $13,298; median household $27,347; **Pop below poverty level:** 21.7%. ***Personal per capita income 2000-2003:** $17,702-$20,009.

Unemployment 2004: 5.6%. **Change from 2000:** +0.2%. **Median travel time to work:** 23.6 minutes. **Working outside county of residence:** 31.8%.

Cities with pop over 10,000: None.

*Source: Personal per capita income data are from the Bureau of Economic Analysis; per capita income data are from the Bureau of the Census. See Introduction for explanation of differences.

CANADIAN COUNTY

201 N Choctaw St   **Ph:** 405-262-1070
El Reno, OK 73036   **Fax:** 405-422-2411
www.canadiancounty.org

In central OK, west of Oklahoma City; original county; organized 1890 (prior to statehood). **Name Origin:** For the Canadian River, which runs through it; known to the Osage as *Ne-sout-che-bra-ra*, probably named in honor of their homelands by French-Canadian explorers or traders.

Area (sq mi): 905.17 (land 899.71; water 5.45). **Pop per sq mi:** 109.7.

Pop 2005: 98,701. **State rank:** 5. **Pop change:** 2000-20005 +12.5%; 1990-2000 +17.9%. **Pop 2000:** 87,697 (White 85%; Black or African American 2.2%; Hispanic or Latino 3.9%; Asian 2.4%; Other 8.4%, including 4.3% American Indian/Alaska Native). **Foreign born:** 3.2%. **Median age:** 35.4.

Income 2000: per capita $19,691; median household $45,439; **Pop below poverty level:** 7.9%. ***Personal per capita income 2000-2003:** $25,055-$26,929.

Unemployment 2004: 3.9%. **Change from 2000:** +0.8%. **Median travel time to work:** 22.9 minutes. **Working outside county of residence:** 63.4%.

Cities with pop over 10,000: Yukon (21,596); El Reno ♨ (15,952); Mustang (15,168).

CARTER COUNTY

PO Box 1236   **Ph:** 580-223-8162
Ardmore, OK 73402   **Fax:** 580-221-5508
www.brightok.net/cartercounty/

In south-central OK, southeast of Lawton; organized Nov 16, 1907 from Chickasaw lands. **Name Origin:** For Charles David Carter (1868-1929), U.S. representative from OK (1907-27); or possibly for Benjamin Wisnor Carter, a Cherokee Indian, soldier in the Confederate army, and OK territorial judge.

Area (sq mi): 833.72 (land 823.79; water 9.93). **Pop per sq mi:** 57.2.

Pop 2005: 47,125. **State rank:** 16. **Pop change:** 2000-20005 +3.3%; 1990-2000 +6.3%. **Pop 2000:** 45,621 (White 76.8%; Black or African American 7.6%; Hispanic or Latino 2.8%; Asian 0.6%; Other 13.8%, including 8.3% American Indian/Alaska Native). **Foreign born:** 1.3%. **Median age:** 38.

Income 2000: per capita $15,511; median household $29,405; **Pop below poverty level:** 16.6%. ***Personal per capita income 2000-2003:** $23,386-$23,587.

Unemployment 2004: 4.6%. **Change from 2000:** +0.4%. **Median travel time to work:** 23.7 minutes. **Working outside county of residence:** 10.2%.

Cities with pop over 10,000: Ardmore ♨ (24,341).

CHEROKEE COUNTY

213 W Delaware St Rm 200   **Ph:** 918-456-3171
Tahlequah, OK 74464   **Fax:** 918-458-6508

In central-eastern OK, southeast of Tulsa; organized Nov 16, 1907 from Indian lands. **Name Origin:** For the Cherokee Nation, a tribe of Iroquoian linguistic stock. Name may derive from Creek *tciloki* 'people of a different speech.'

Area (sq mi): 776.4 (land 751.04; water 25.37). **Pop per sq mi:** 59.5.

Pop 2005: 44,671. **State rank:** 19. **Pop change:** 2000-20005 +5.1%; 1990-2000 +24.9%. **Pop 2000:** 42,521 (White 55.2%; Black or African American 1.2%; Hispanic or Latino 4.1%; Asian 0.3%; Other 42.1%, including 32.4% American Indian/Alaska Native). **Foreign born:** 2.6%. **Median age:** 32.3.

Income 2000: per capita $13,436; median household $26,536; **Pop below poverty level:** 22.9% ***Personal per capita income 2000-2003:** $16,752 $19,625.

Unemployment 2004: 4.5%. **Change from 2000:** +1.4%. **Median travel time to work:** 24.6 minutes. **Working outside county of residence:** 27.8%.

Cities with pop over 10,000: Tahlequah ♨ (15,710).

CHOCTAW COUNTY

300 E Duke St   **Ph:** 580-326-3778
Hugo, OK 74743   **Fax:** 580-326-6787

On the southeastern border of OK; organized Nov 16, 1907 from Choctaw lands. **Name Origin:** For the Choctaw Nation, an Indian tribe of Muskhogean linguistic stock. Meaning of the name is unknown.

Area (sq mi): 800.68 (land 773.93; water 26.75). **Pop per sq mi:** 19.8.

Pop 2005: 15,297. **State rank:** 44. **Pop change:** 2000-20005 -0.3%; 1990-2000 +0.3%. **Pop 2000:** 15,342 (White 67.8%; Black or African American 10.9%; Hispanic or Latino 1.6%; Asian 0.2%; Other 20.4%, including 15% American Indian/Alaska Native). **Foreign born:** 0.5%. **Median age:** 38.7.

Income 2000: per capita $12,296; median household $22,743; **Pop below poverty level:** 24.3%. ***Personal per capita income 2000-2003:** $15,892-$19,258.

Unemployment 2004: 6.9%. **Change from 2000:** +0.2%. **Median travel time to work:** 24.9 minutes. **Working outside county of residence:** 27.4%.

Cities with pop over 10,000: None.

CIMARRON COUNTY

Courthouse Sq PO Box 145   **Ph:** 580-544-2251
Boise City, OK 73933   **Fax:** 580-544-2251
www.ccccok.org

In the OK panhandle; organized Nov 16, 1907 from Beaver County. **Name Origin:** For the Cimarron River, which flows across the northern part of the county. Meaning and application of the term are uncertain. The river may have been called in Spanish *el rio de los carneros cimarron* 'River of the Wild Sheep'; or it is possibly a Mexican-Apache word meaning 'wanderer.'

Area (sq mi): 1841.17 (land 1835.04; water 6.13). **Pop per sq mi:** 1.5.

Pop 2005: 2,833. **State rank:** 77. **Pop change:** 2000-20005 -10%; 1990-2000 -4.6%. **Pop 2000:** 3,148 (White 81%; Black or African American 0.6%; Hispanic or Latino 15.4%; Asian 0.2%; Other 13.4%, including 1% American Indian/Alaska Native). **Foreign born:** 10.3%. **Median age:** 39.3.

♨ *County Seat*

Cimarron County (cont'd)

Income 2000: per capita $15,744; median household $30,625; **Pop below poverty level:** 17.6%. *Personal per capita income 2000-2003: $21,499-$21,325.

Unemployment 2004: 3%. **Change from 2000:** +0.7%. **Median travel time to work:** 14.8 minutes. **Working outside county of residence:** 14%.

Cities with pop over 10,000: None.

CLEVELAND COUNTY

641 E Robinson St Rm 300   **Ph:** 405-366-0240
Norman, OK 73071   **Fax:** 405-366-0229

In central OK, south of Oklahoma City; original county; organized 1890 (prior to statehood) from Cherokee lands. **Name Origin:** For Grover Cleveland (1837-1908), twenty-second and twenty-fourth U.S. president.

Area (sq mi): 558.34 (land 536.11; water 22.23). **Pop per sq mi:** 419.5.

Pop 2005: 224,898. **State rank:** 3. **Pop change:** 2000-20005 +8.1%; 1990-2000 +19.4%. **Pop 2000:** 208,016 (White 81.5%; Black or African American 3.6%; Hispanic or Latino 4%; Asian 2.8%; Other 10%, including 4.4% American Indian/Alaska Native). **Foreign born:** 4.4%. **Median age:** 32.2.

Income 2000: per capita $20,114; median household $41,846; **Pop below poverty level:** 10.6%. *Personal per capita income 2000-2003: $25,136-$27,440.

Unemployment 2004: 3.6%. **Change from 2000:** +0.4%. **Median travel time to work:** 22.3 minutes. **Working outside county of residence:** 49.4%.

Cities with pop over 10,000: Norman 🏛 (100,923).

COAL COUNTY

4 N Main St   **Ph:** 580-927-3122
Coalgate, OK 74538   **Fax:** 580-927-4003

In south-central OK, southeast of Ada; organized Nov 16, 1907 from Tobucksy County. **Name Origin:** For the chief economic product of the county.

Area (sq mi): 521.3 (land 518.22; water 3.07). **Pop per sq mi:** 11.1.

Pop 2005: 5,743. **State rank:** 68. **Pop change:** 2000-20005 -4.8%; 1990-2000 +4.3%. **Pop 2000:** 6,031 (White 74.5%; Black or African American 0.4%; Hispanic or Latino 2.1%; Asian 0.3%; Other 24.1%, including 17.3% American Indian/Alaska Native). **Foreign born:** 1.6%. **Median age:** 38.1.

Income 2000: per capita $12,013; median household $23,705; **Pop below poverty level:** 23.1%. *Personal per capita income 2000-2003: $14,947-$16,777.

Unemployment 2004: 10.3%. **Change from 2000:** +3.5%. **Median travel time to work:** 24.3 minutes. **Working outside county of residence:** 41.3%.

Cities with pop over 10,000: None.

COMANCHE COUNTY

315 SW 5th St Suite 304   **Ph:** 580-355-5214
Lawton, OK 73501
www.comanchecounty.us

In south-central OK, southwest of Oklahoma City; organized Nov 16, 1907 from Cherokee lands. **Name Origin:** For the Comanche Indians of Shoshonean linguistic stock; name is believed to derive from Spanish *camino ancho* 'broad trail.'

Area (sq mi): 1083.82 (land 1069.35; water 14.48). **Pop per sq mi:** 105.1.

Pop 2005: 112,429. **State rank:** 4. **Pop change:** 2000-20005 -2.2%; 1990-2000 +3.1%. **Pop 2000:** 114,996 (White 62%; Black or African American 19%; Hispanic or Latino 8.4%; Asian 2.1%; Other 13.7%, including 5.1% American Indian/Alaska Native). **Foreign born:** 5.4%. **Median age:** 30.1.

Income 2000: per capita $15,728; median household $33,867; **Pop below poverty level:** 15.6%. *Personal per capita income 2000-2003: $21,397-$25,545.

Unemployment 2004: 4.5%. **Change from 2000:** +1.2%. **Median travel time to work:** 16.9 minutes. **Working outside county of residence:** 5.8%.

Cities with pop over 10,000: Lawton 🏛 (88,214).

COTTON COUNTY

301 N Broadway   **Ph:** 580-875-3026
Walters, OK 73572   **Fax:** 580-875-3756

On the southern border of OK, south of Lawton; organized Aug 28, 1912 from Comanche County. **Name Origin:** For the principal agricultural product of the county.

Area (sq mi): 641.94 (land 636.64; water 5.31). **Pop per sq mi:** 10.3.

Pop 2005: 6,589. **State rank:** 65. **Pop change:** 2000-20005 -0.4%; 1990-2000 -0.6%. **Pop 2000:** 6,614 (White 82.8%; Black or African American 2.9%; Hispanic or Latino 4.9%; Asian 0.1%; Other 12.3%, including 7.4% American Indian/Alaska Native). **Foreign born:** 1.5%. **Median age:** 38.6.

Income 2000: per capita $14,626; median household $27,210; **Pop below poverty level:** 18.2%. *Personal per capita income 2000-2003: $20,639-$23,164.

Unemployment 2004: 3.9%. **Change from 2000:** -0.2%. **Median travel time to work:** 25.3 minutes. **Working outside county of residence:** 50.9%.

Cities with pop over 10,000: None.

CRAIG COUNTY

PO Box 397   **Ph:** 918-256-2507
Vinita, OK 74301   **Fax:** 918-256-3617

On the northeastern border of OK, northeast of Tulsa; organized Nov 16, 1907 from Cherokee lands. **Name Origin:** For Granville Craig, a prominent Cherokee citizen.

Area (sq mi): 762.71 (land 761.03; water 1.68). **Pop per sq mi:** 19.8.

Pop 2005: 15,078. **State rank:** 45. **Pop change:** 2000-20005 +0.9%; 1990-2000 +6%. **Pop 2000:** 14,950 (White 68.1%; Black or African American 3.1%; Hispanic or Latino 1.2%; Asian 0.2%; Other 28.2%, including 16.3% American Indian/Alaska Native). **Foreign born:** 0.5%. **Median age:** 39.3.

Source: Personal per capita income data are from the Bureau of Economic Analysis; per capita income data are from the Bureau of the Census.
See Introduction for explanation of differences.

Craig County (cont'd)

Income 2000: per capita $16,539; median household $30,997; **Pop below poverty level:** 13.7%. *****Personal per capita income 2000-2003:** $19,858-$22,740.

Unemployment 2004: 4.8%. **Change from 2000:** +1.2%. **Median travel time to work:** 23.2 minutes. **Working outside county of residence:** 33.4%.

Cities with pop over 10,000: None.

CREEK COUNTY

317 E Lee St Rm 100   **Ph:** 918-224-4084
Sapulpa, OK 74066

In east-central OK, southwest of Tulsa; organized Nov 16, 1907 from Cherokee lands. **Name Origin:** For the Creek Nation, a loose confederation of southeastern tribes of Muskhogean linguistic stock. The name is from 'Ochese Creek Indians.' applied to them by settlers in what is now TN. They were probably the Yuchi.

Area (sq mi): 969.77 (land 955.53; water 14.23). **Pop per sq mi:** 71.9.

Pop 2005: 68,708. **State rank:** 9. **Pop change:** 2000-20005 +2%; 1990-2000 +10.6%. **Pop 2000:** 67,367 (White 81.4%; Black or African American 2.6%; Hispanic or Latino 1.9%; Asian 0.3%; Other 14.9%, including 9.1% American Indian/Alaska Native). **Foreign born:** 0.7%. **Median age:** 36.9.

Income 2000: per capita $16,191; median household $33,168; **Pop below poverty level:** 13.5%. *****Personal per capita income 2000-2003:** $21,036-$22,212.

Unemployment 2004: 5.7%. **Change from 2000:** +2%. **Median travel time to work:** 26 minutes. **Working outside county of residence:** 55.1%.

Cities with pop over 10,000: Sapulpa 🏛 (19,803).

CUSTER COUNTY

Broadway & B St   **Ph:** 580-323-1221
Arapaho, OK 73620

In west-central OK, west of Oklahoma City; original county; organized 1891 (prior to statehood). **Name Origin:** For Gen. George Armstrong Custer (1839-76), U.S. army officer and Indian fighter.

Area (sq mi): 1002 (land 986.51; water 15.49). **Pop per sq mi:** 25.6.

Pop 2005: 25,208. **State rank:** 36. **Pop change:** 2000-20005 -3.6%; 1990-2000 -2.8%. **Pop 2000:** 26,142 (White 79.3%; Black or African American 2.9%; Hispanic or Latino 9%; Asian 0.9%; Other 14.8%, including 5.8% American Indian/Alaska Native). **Foreign born:** 3.4%. **Median age:** 32.7.

Income 2000: per capita $15,584; median household $28,524; **Pop below poverty level:** 18.5%. *****Personal per capita income 2000-2003:** $20,424-$22,534.

Unemployment 2004: 3.3%. **Change from 2000:** -0.1%. **Median travel time to work:** 15.7 minutes. **Working outside county of residence:** 16.3%.

Cities with pop over 10,000: None.

DELAWARE COUNTY

PO Box 309   **Ph:** 918-253-4520
Jay, OK 74346   **Fax:** 918-253-8352

On the northeastern border of OK, northeast of Tulsa; organized Nov 16, 1907 from Cherokee lands. **Name Origin:** For the Indian tribe, also known as Leni or Leni-Lenape, named for Thomas West (1577-1618), Lord Delaware (or De La Warr).

Area (sq mi): 792.33 (land 740.65; water 51.68). **Pop per sq mi:** 52.9.

Pop 2005: 39,146. **State rank:** 25. **Pop change:** 2000-20005 +5.6%; 1990-2000 +32.1%. **Pop 2000:** 37,077 (White 69.4%; Black or African American 0.1%; Hispanic or Latino 1.8%; Asian 0.2%; Other 29.4%, including 22.3% American Indian/Alaska Native). **Foreign born:** 1.3%. **Median age:** 40.8.

Income 2000: per capita $15,424; median household $27,996; **Pop below poverty level:** 18.3%. *****Personal per capita income 2000-2003:** $20,552-$23,243.

Unemployment 2004: 4.9%. **Change from 2000:** +1.3%. **Median travel time to work:** 25.5 minutes. **Working outside county of residence:** 46.8%.

Cities with pop over 10,000: None.

DEWEY COUNTY

Broadway & Ruble PO Box 368   **Ph:** 580-328-5361
Taloga, OK 73667

In west-central OK, southwest of Enid; original county; organized 1892 (prior to statehood). **Name Origin:** For George Dewey (1837-1917), who captured Manila (1898) during the Spanish-American War and was given the rank of Admiral of the Navy.

Area (sq mi): 1008.26 (land 1000.13; water 8.13). **Pop per sq mi:** 4.6.

Pop 2005: 4,568. **State rank:** 72. **Pop change:** 2000-20005 -3.7%; 1990-2000 -14.6%. **Pop 2000:** 4,743 (White 90.6%; Black or African American 0.1%; Hispanic or Latino 2.7%; Asian 0.1%; Other 7.6%, including 4.6% American Indian/Alaska Native). **Foreign born:** 1.3%. **Median age:** 43.

Income 2000: per capita $15,806; median household $28,172; **Pop below poverty level:** 15%. *****Personal per capita income 2000-2003:** $20,877-$25,171.

Unemployment 2004: 3%. **Change from 2000:** +0.3%. **Median travel time to work:** 22.9 minutes. **Working outside county of residence:** 31.3%.

Cities with pop over 10,000: None.

ELLIS COUNTY

PO Box 197   **Ph:** 580-885-7301
Arnett, OK 73832   **Fax:** 580-885-7258

On the western border of OK, below the panhandle; organized Nov 16, 1907 from Day (which had been the northern part of Roger Mills County and was now abolished) and Woodward counties. **Name Origin:** For Albert H. Ellis, an OK constitutional convention delegate in 1907.

Area (sq mi): 1231.84 (land 1229.14; water 2.7). **Pop per sq mi:** 3.2.

Pop 2005: 3,963. **State rank:** 73. **Pop change:** 2000-20005 -2.7%; 1990-2000 -9.4%. **Pop 2000:** 4,075 (White 94.8%; Black or African

Ellis County (cont'd)

American 0%; Hispanic or Latino 2.6%; Asian 0.1%; Other 3.5%, including 1.2% American Indian/Alaska Native). **Foreign born:** 0.8%. **Median age:** 45.3.

Income 2000: per capita $16,472; median household $27,951; **Pop below poverty level:** 12.5%. ***Personal per capita income 2000-2003:** $21,340-$25,323.

Unemployment 2004: 2.6%. **Change from 2000:** -0.5%. **Median travel time to work:** 18.7 minutes. **Working outside county of residence:** 31.4%.

Cities with pop over 10,000: None.

GARFIELD COUNTY

114 W Broadway   **Ph:** 580-237-0225
Enid, OK 73701   **Fax:** 580-249-5951

In north-central OK, southwest of Ponca City; original county; organized 1895 (prior to statehood). **Name Origin:** For James Abram Garfield (1831-81), twentieth U.S. president.

Area (sq mi): 1059.94 (land 1058.39; water 1.55). **Pop per sq mi:** 53.8.

Pop 2005: 56,958. **State rank:** 12. **Pop change:** 2000-20005 -1.5%; 1990-2000 +1.9%. **Pop 2000:** 57,813 (White 86.9%; Black or African American 3.3%; Hispanic or Latino 4.1%; Asian 0.8%; Other 7.2%, including 2.1% American Indian/Alaska Native). **Foreign born:** 2.7%. **Median age:** 37.7.

Income 2000: per capita $17,457; median household $33,006; **Pop below poverty level:** 13.9%. ***Personal per capita income 2000-2003:** $23,904-$26,067.

Unemployment 2004: 3.6%. **Change from 2000:** +0.7%. **Median travel time to work:** 17.7 minutes. **Working outside county of residence:** 6.6%.

Cities with pop over 10,000: Enid 🏛 (46,626).

GARVIN COUNTY

201 W Grant St   **Ph:** 405-238-2772
Pauls Valley, OK 73075   **Fax:** 405-238-6283

In south-central OK, east of Ada; organized Nov 16, 1907 from Chickasaw lands. **Name Origin:** For Samuel J. Garvin, a leader of the Chickasaw Nation.

Area (sq mi): 813.66 (land 807.49; water 6.18). **Pop per sq mi:** 33.7.

Pop 2005: 27,228. **State rank:** 34. **Pop change:** 2000-20005 +0.1%; 1990-2000 +2.3%. **Pop 2000:** 27,210 (White 83.4%; Black or African American 2.6%; Hispanic or Latino 3.4%; Asian 0.2%; Other 12.2%, including 7.4% American Indian/Alaska Native). **Foreign born:** 1.6%. **Median age:** 39.

Income 2000: per capita $14,856; median household $28,070; **Pop below poverty level:** 15.9%. ***Personal per capita income 2000-2003:** $20,578-$23,058.

Unemployment 2004: 4.1%. **Change from 2000:** +0%. **Median travel time to work:** 23.4 minutes. **Working outside county of residence:** 25.1%.

Cities with pop over 10,000: None.

GRADY COUNTY

326 Choctaw St   **Ph:** 405-224-7388
Chickasha, OK 73018   **Fax:** 405-222-4506
www.gradycountyok.com

In south-central OK, southwest of Oklahoma City; organized Nov 16, 1907 from Caddo and Comanche counties. **Name Origin:** For Henry Woodfin Grady (1850-89), orator and editor of the *Atlanta Constitution* newspaper, whose writings and ideas helped alleviate the post-Civil War depression of the South.

Area (sq mi): 1105.3 (land 1100.96; water 4.34). **Pop per sq mi:** 44.8.

Pop 2005: 49,369. **State rank:** 14. **Pop change:** 2000-20005 +8.5%; 1990-2000 +9%. **Pop 2000:** 45,516 (White 86.1%; Black or African American 3.1%; Hispanic or Latino 2.9%; Asian 0.3%; Other 9.2%, including 4.8% American Indian/Alaska Native). **Foreign born:** 1.1%. **Median age:** 36.5.

Income 2000: per capita $15,846; median household $32,625; **Pop below poverty level:** 13.9%. ***Personal per capita income 2000-2003:** $20,357-$22,956.

Unemployment 2004: 4.4%. **Change from 2000:** +0.8%. **Median travel time to work:** 26.9 minutes. **Working outside county of residence:** 41.7%.

Cities with pop over 10,000: Chickasha 🏛 (16,463).

GRANT COUNTY

112 E Guthrie St PO Box 167   **Ph:** 580-395-2274
Medford, OK 73759   **Fax:** 580-395-2086

On the central northern border of OK, north of Enid; original county; organized 1895 (prior to statehood). **Name Origin:** For Ulysses S. Grant (1822-85), Civil War general and eighteenth U.S. president.

Area (sq mi): 1003.61 (land 1000.56; water 3.05). **Pop per sq mi:** 4.8.

Pop 2005: 4,779. **State rank:** 71. **Pop change:** 2000-20005 -7.1%; 1990-2000 -9.6%. **Pop 2000:** 5,144 (White 94.3%; Black or African American 0.1%; Hispanic or Latino 1.8%; Asian 0.1%; Other 4.4%, including 2.4% American Indian/Alaska Native). **Foreign born:** 0.9%. **Median age:** 41.4.

Income 2000: per capita $15,709; median household $28,977; **Pop below poverty level:** 13.7%. ***Personal per capita income 2000-2003:** $23,064-$28,198.

Unemployment 2004: 3.5%. **Change from 2000:** +0.8%. **Median travel time to work:** 21.1 minutes. **Working outside county of residence:** 33.5%.

Cities with pop over 10,000: None.

GREER COUNTY

PO Box 207   **Ph:** 580-782-3664
Mangum, OK 73554   **Fax:** 580-782-3803
www.greercounty-ok.com

In southwestern OK, northwest of Lawton; original county; organized 1890 (prior to statehood). **Name Origin:** For John A. Greer, a lieutenant governor of TX.

Area (sq mi): 643.66 (land 639.36; water 4.3). **Pop per sq mi:** 9.2.

*Source: Personal per capita income data are from the Bureau of Economic Analysis; per capita income data are from the Bureau of the Census. See Introduction for explanation of differences.

Greer County (cont'd)

Pop 2005: 5,901. **State rank:** 67. **Pop change:** 2000-20005 -2.6%; 1990-2000 -7.6%. **Pop 2000:** 6,061 (White 78.7%; Black or African American 8.8%; Hispanic or Latino 7.4%; Asian 0.3%; Other 9.5%, including 2.5% American Indian/Alaska Native). **Foreign born:** 1.5%. **Median age:** 40.

Income 2000: per capita $14,053; median household $25,793; **Pop below poverty level:** 19.6%. *Personal per capita income 2000-2003: $21,311-$22,841.

Unemployment 2004: 6.1%. **Change from 2000:** +3%. **Median travel time to work:** 17.8 minutes. **Working outside county of residence:** 30.1%.

Cities with pop over 10,000: None.

HARMON COUNTY

114 W Hollis St   **Ph:** 580-688-3658
Hollis, OK 73550   **Fax:** 580-688-9784

On the southwestern border of OK, west of Lawton; organized May 22, 1909 from Greer County. **Name Origin:** For Judson C. Harmon (1846-1927), U.S. Attorney General (1895-97) and governor of OH (1908-13).

Area (sq mi): 538.56 (land 537.82; water 0.74). **Pop per sq mi:** 5.6.

Pop 2005: 3,030. **State rank:** 76. **Pop change:** 2000-20005 -7.7%; 1990-2000 -13.4%. **Pop 2000:** 3,283 (White 65.8%; Black or African American 9.8%; Hispanic or Latino 22.8%; Asian 0.2%; Other 17.3%, including 1.1% American Indian/Alaska Native). **Foreign born:** 3%. **Median age:** 39.9.

Income 2000: per capita $13,464; median household $22,365; **Pop below poverty level:** 29.7%. *Personal per capita income 2000-2003: $18,353-$22,222.

Unemployment 2004: 3.4%. **Change from 2000:** -0.5%. **Median travel time to work:** 14.6 minutes. **Working outside county of residence:** 20.8%.

Cities with pop over 10,000: None.

HARPER COUNTY

PO Box 369   **Ph:** 580-735-2130
Buffalo, OK 73834   **Fax:** 580-735-6034

On the northwestern border of OK, at eastern end of panhandle; organized Nov 16, 1905 from Woodward County. **Name Origin:** For Oscar G. Harper, an official at the OK constitutional convention (1906-07).

Area (sq mi): 1040.96 (land 1039; water 1.96). **Pop per sq mi:** 3.2.

Pop 2005: 3,313. **State rank:** 74. **Pop change:** 2000-20005 -7%; 1990-2000 -12.3%. **Pop 2000:** 3,562 (White 92.9%; Black or African American 0%; Hispanic or Latino 5.6%; Asian 0.1%; Other 4%). **Foreign born:** 3.5%. **Median age:** 43.1.

Income 2000: per capita $18,011; median household $33,705; **Pop below poverty level:** 10.2%. *Personal per capita income 2000-2003: $26,095-$32,247.

Unemployment 2004: 3%. **Change from 2000:** +0.2%. **Median travel time to work:** 18.9 minutes. **Working outside county of residence:** 20.6%.

Cities with pop over 10,000: None.

HASKELL COUNTY

202 E Main St   **Ph:** 918-967-2884
Stigler, OK 74462   **Fax:** 918-967-2885

In east-central OK, south of Muskogee; organized Nov 16, 1907 from Choctaw lands. **Name Origin:** For Charles Nathaniel Haskell (1860-1933), member of the OK Constitutional Convention (1906-07) and first governor (1907-11).

Area (sq mi): 625.27 (land 577.03; water 48.24). **Pop per sq mi:** 21.1.

Pop 2005: 12,183. **State rank:** 52. **Pop change:** 2000-20005 +3.3%; 1990-2000 +7.8%. **Pop 2000:** 11,792 (White 77.5%; Black or African American 0.6%; Hispanic or Latino 1.5%; Asian 0.3%; Other 20.8%, including 14.6% American Indian/Alaska Native). **Foreign born:** 0.8%. **Median age:** 38.6.

Income 2000: per capita $13,775; median household $24,553; **Pop below poverty level:** 20.5%. *Personal per capita income 2000-2003: $18,575-$21,424.

Unemployment 2004: 5.3%. **Change from 2000:** +0.6%. **Median travel time to work:** 28.7 minutes. **Working outside county of residence:** 33.4%.

Cities with pop over 10,000: None.

HUGHES COUNTY

200 N Broadway St Suite 7   **Ph:** 405-379-2746
Holdenville, OK 74848   **Fax:** 405-379-6739

In east-central OK, northeast of Ada; organized Nov 16, 1907 from Creek lands. **Name Origin:** For William C. Hughes, delegate to the OK Constitutional Convention (1906-07).

Area (sq mi): 814.64 (land 806.73; water 7.9). **Pop per sq mi:** 17.1.

Pop 2005: 13,835. **State rank:** 49. **Pop change:** 2000-20005 -2.3%; 1990-2000 +8.7%. **Pop 2000:** 14,154 (White 71.8%; Black or African American 4.5%; Hispanic or Latino 2.5%; Asian 0.2%; Other 22.6%, including 16.2% American Indian/Alaska Native). **Foreign born:** 1.1%. **Median age:** 39.3.

Income 2000: per capita $12,687; median household $22,621; **Pop below poverty level:** 21.9%. *Personal per capita income 2000-2003: $16,131-$18,370.

Unemployment 2004: 8.4%. **Change from 2000:** +3.4%. **Median travel time to work:** 25 minutes. **Working outside county of residence:** 38%.

Cities with pop over 10,000: None.

JACKSON COUNTY

PO Box 515   **Ph:** 580-482-4070
Altus, OK 73522   **Fax:** 580-482-4472
www.intplsrv.net/jacksoncounty/

On the southwestern border of OK, west of Lawton; organized Nov 16, 1907 from Greer County. **Name Origin:** For Gen. Thomas J. 'Stonewall' Jackson (1824-63), Confederate officer who stood firm against the enemy 'like a stonewall.' Some claim Andrew Jackson (1767-1845), seventh U.S. president.

Area (sq mi): 804.15 (land 802.68; water 1.47). **Pop per sq mi:** 33.

Pop 2005: 26,518. **State rank:** 35. **Pop change:** 2000-20005 -6.8%; 1990-2000 -1.1%. **Pop 2000:** 28,439 (White 71.5%; Black or African American 8%; Hispanic or Latino 15.6%; Asian 1.2%; Other 14.6%,

Jackson County (cont'd)

including 1.7% American Indian/Alaska Native). **Foreign born:** 4.7%. **Median age:** 33.

Income 2000: per capita $15,454; median household $30,737; **Pop below poverty level:** 16.2%. ***Personal per capita income 2000-2003:** $20,966-$25,038.

Unemployment 2004: 4%. **Change from 2000:** +1.2%. **Median travel time to work:** 14.4 minutes. **Working outside county of residence:** 6.1%.

Cities with pop over 10,000: Altus ⛫ (20,393).

JEFFERSON COUNTY
220 N Main St Rm 103   **Ph:** 580-228-2029
Waurika, OK 73573   **Fax:** 580-228-3608

On the central southern border of OK, southeast of Lawton; organized Nov 16, 1907 from Comanche County. **Name Origin:** For Thomas Jefferson (1743-1826), U.S. patriot and statesman; third U.S. president.

Area (sq mi): 773.83 (land 758.75; water 15.07). **Pop per sq mi:** 8.5.

Pop 2005: 6,461. **State rank:** 66. **Pop change:** 2000-20005 -5.2%; 1990-2000 -2.7%. **Pop 2000:** 6,818 (White 83.7%; Black or African American 0.7%; Hispanic or Latino 7%; Asian 1.1%; Other 11%, including 5.2% American Indian/Alaska Native). **Foreign born:** 3.6%. **Median age:** 40.4.

Income 2000: per capita $12,899; median household $23,674; **Pop below poverty level:** 19.2%. ***Personal per capita income 2000-2003:** $17,698-$19,464.

Unemployment 2004: 5.8%. **Change from 2000:** +2.1%. **Median travel time to work:** 27.5 minutes. **Working outside county of residence:** 35.6%.

Cities with pop over 10,000: None.

JOHNSTON COUNTY
403 W Main St   **Ph:** 580-371-3058
Tishomingo, OK 73460   **Fax:** 580-371-2174

In south-central OK, south of Ada; organized Nov 16, 1907 from Chickasaw lands. **Name Origin:** For Douglas H. Johnston (1856-1939), last governor for the Chickasaw nation, who remained in office until his death.

Area (sq mi): 658.29 (land 644.5; water 13.78). **Pop per sq mi:** 15.9.

Pop 2005: 10,259. **State rank:** 59. **Pop change:** 2000-20005 -2.4%; 1990-2000 +4.8%. **Pop 2000:** 10,513 (White 75.4%; Black or African American 1.7%; Hispanic or Latino 2.5%; Asian 0.3%; Other 21.9%, including 15.3% American Indian/Alaska Native). **Foreign born:** 0.8%. **Median age:** 38.

Income 2000: per capita $13,747; median household $24,592; **Pop below poverty level:** 22%. ***Personal per capita income 2000-2003:** $16,147-$19,333.

Unemployment 2004: 5.7%. **Change from 2000:** +0.7%. **Median travel time to work:** 24.9 minutes. **Working outside county of residence:** 41.3%.

Cities with pop over 10,000: None.

KAY COUNTY
201 S Main St   **Ph:** 580-362-2537
Newkirk, OK 74647   **Fax:** 580-362-3300
www.courthouse.kay.ok.us/home.html

On the central northern border of OK, northeast of Enid; original county; organized as 'K' County 1895 (prior to statehood). **Name Origin:** For the letter *K*. The first seven counties of OK were originally numbered. The next fifteen were lettered (A-Q, except I and J). All later received names except 'K' County, which became Kay.

Area (sq mi): 945.12 (land 918.7; water 26.42). **Pop per sq mi:** 50.6.

Pop 2005: 46,480. **State rank:** 17. **Pop change:** 2000-20005 -3.3%; 1990-2000 +0%. **Pop 2000:** 48,080 (White 82.5%; Black or African American 1.8%; Hispanic or Latino 4.3%; Asian 0.5%; Other 13.5%, including 7.5% American Indian/Alaska Native). **Foreign born:** 2.3%. **Median age:** 38.1.

Income 2000: per capita $16,643; median household $30,762; **Pop below poverty level:** 16%. ***Personal per capita income 2000-2003:** $22,844-$25,126.

Unemployment 2004: 6%. **Change from 2000:** +1%. **Median travel time to work:** 16.1 minutes. **Working outside county of residence:** 8.3%.

Cities with pop over 10,000: Ponca City (25,224).

KINGFISHER COUNTY
101 S Main St Rm 3   **Ph:** 405-375-3887
Kingfisher, OK 73750   **Fax:** 405-375-6033
www.kingfisherco.com

In central OK, northwest of Oklahoma City; original county; organized 1890 (prior to statehood). **Name Origin:** For Kingfisher Creek, which runs through the county; itself named for King David Fisher (1819-63), who ran a stage and trading station on the Chisholm Trail.

Area (sq mi): 905.96 (land 903; water 2.96). **Pop per sq mi:** 15.8.

Pop 2005: 14,302. **State rank:** 48. **Pop change:** 2000-20005 +2.7%; 1990-2000 +5.4%. **Pop 2000:** 13,926 (White 86.1%; Black or African American 1.6%; Hispanic or Latino 6.9%; Asian 0.2%; Other 10%, including 3% American Indian/Alaska Native). **Foreign born:** 4.1%. **Median age:** 38.

Income 2000: per capita $18,167; median household $36,676; **Pop below poverty level:** 10.8%. ***Personal per capita income 2000-2003:** $24,200-$27,503.

Unemployment 2004: 3.3%. **Change from 2000:** +0.7%. **Median travel time to work:** 22.5 minutes. **Working outside county of residence:** 29.1%.

Cities with pop over 10,000: None.

KIOWA COUNTY
PO Box 73   **Ph:** 580-726-5286
Hobart, OK 73651   **Fax:** 580-726-6033

In southwestern OK, northwest of Lawton; original county; organized 1891 (prior to statehood); re-formed from part of the original county in 1901. **Name Origin:** For the Indian tribe of Tanoan linguistic stock; name means 'principal people.'

Area (sq mi): 1030.66 (land 1014.56; water 16.1). **Pop per sq mi:** 9.7.

Source: Personal per capita income data are from the Bureau of Economic Analysis; per capita income data are from the Bureau of the Census. See Introduction for explanation of differences.

Kiowa County (cont'd)

Pop 2005: 9,848. **State rank:** 60. **Pop change:** 2000-20005 -3.7%; 1990-2000 -9.9%. **Pop 2000:** 10,227 (White 80.5%; Black or African American 4.7%; Hispanic or Latino 6.7%; Asian 0.3%; Other 11.5%, including 6.3% American Indian/Alaska Native). **Foreign born:** 1%. **Median age:** 40.9.

Income 2000: per capita $14,231; median household $26,053; **Pop below poverty level:** 19.3%. ***Personal per capita income 2000-2003:** $19,540-$22,643.

Unemployment 2004: 4.5%. **Change from 2000:** +1.4%. **Median travel time to work:** 18.3 minutes. **Working outside county of residence:** 26.9%.

Cities with pop over 10,000: None.

LATIMER COUNTY

109 N Central St	**Ph:** 918-465-2021
Wilburton, OK 74578	**Fax:** 918-465-3736

In east-central OK, east of McAlester; organized Nov 16, 1907 from Choctaw lands. **Name Origin:** For James S. Latimer, member of the OK Constitutional Convention (1906-07).

Area (sq mi): 729.12 (land 722.17; water 6.95). **Pop per sq mi:** 14.7.

Pop 2005: 10,635. **State rank:** 58. **Pop change:** 2000-20005 -0.5%; 1990-2000 +3.5%. **Pop 2000:** 10,692 (White 72.5%; Black or African American 1%; Hispanic or Latino 1.5%; Asian 0.2%; Other 25.8%, including 19.4% American Indian/Alaska Native). **Foreign born:** 1.3%. **Median age:** 36.8.

Income 2000: per capita $12,842; median household $23,962; **Pop below poverty level:** 22.7%. ***Personal per capita income 2000-2003:** $18,971-$21,849.

Unemployment 2004: 5.6%. **Change from 2000:** +0.5%. **Median travel time to work:** 22.1 minutes. **Working outside county of residence:** 35.4%.

Cities with pop over 10,000: None.

LEFLORE COUNTY

PO Box 218	**Ph:** 918-647-5738
Poteau, OK 74953	**Fax:** 918-647-8930

On the eastern border of OK, east of McAlester; organized Nov 16, 1907 from Choctaw lands. **Name Origin:** For Greenwood LeFlore (1800-65), leader of a prominent Choctaw family of French ancestry, a landowner, and MS state legislator. He remained in MS when most of the tribe were moved to OK.

Area (sq mi): 1608.03 (land 1585.82; water 22.2). **Pop per sq mi:** 31.2.

Pop 2005: 49,528. **State rank:** 13. **Pop change:** 2000-20005 +2.9%; 1990-2000 +11.2%. **Pop 2000:** 48,109 (White 78.4%; Black or African American 2.2%; Hispanic or Latino 3.8%; Asian 0.2%; Other 17.1%, including 10.7% American Indian/Alaska Native). **Foreign born:** 2.5%. **Median age:** 36.1.

Income 2000: per capita $13,737; median household $27,278; **Pop below poverty level:** 19.1%. ***Personal per capita income 2000-2003:** $18,404-$20,832.

Unemployment 2004: 5.5%. **Change from 2000:** -0.3%. **Median travel time to work:** 23.6 minutes. **Working outside county of residence:** 36.2%.

Cities with pop over 10,000: None.

LINCOLN COUNTY

811 Manuel St Suite 5	**Ph:** 405-258-1264
Chandler, OK 74834	**Fax:** 405-258-0430

In east central OK, northeast of Oklahoma City; original county; organized Oct 1, 1891 (prior to statehood). **Name Origin:** For Abraham Lincoln (1809-65), sixteenth U.S. president.

Area (sq mi): 965.62 (land 957.74; water 7.88). **Pop per sq mi:** 33.7.

Pop 2005: 32,311. **State rank:** 31. **Pop change:** 2000-20005 +0.7%; 1990-2000 +9.8%. **Pop 2000:** 32,080 (White 85.7%; Black or African American 2.5%; Hispanic or Latino 1.5%; Asian 0.2%; Other 10.8%, including 6.6% American Indian/Alaska Native). **Foreign born:** 0.8%. **Median age:** 37.5.

Income 2000: per capita $14,890; median household $31,187; **Pop below poverty level:** 14.5%. ***Personal per capita income 2000-2003:** $18,997-$20,648.

Unemployment 2004: 4.9%. **Change from 2000:** +0.5%. **Median travel time to work:** 31 minutes. **Working outside county of residence:** 55.6%.

Cities with pop over 10,000: None.

LOGAN COUNTY

301 E Harrison Ave Suite 102	**Ph:** 405-282-0266
Guthrie, OK 73044	**Fax:** 405-282-0267

In north-central OK, north of Oklahoma City; original county; organized as County No. 1 in 1891 (prior to statehood). **Name Origin:** For Gen. John Alexander Logan (1826-86), Civil War officer, U.S. senator from IL (1871-77; 1879-86), and national commander of the Grand Army of the Republic.

Area (sq mi): 748.92 (land 744.45; water 4.46). **Pop per sq mi:** 49.6.

Pop 2005: 36,894. **State rank:** 27. **Pop change:** 2000-20005 +8.8%; 1990-2000 +16.9%. **Pop 2000:** 33,924 (White 80.3%; Black or African American 11%; Hispanic or Latino 2.9%; Asian 0.3%; Other 7%, including 2.9% American Indian/Alaska Native). **Foreign born:** 1.5%. **Median age:** 36.1.

Income 2000: per capita $17,872; median household $36,784; **Pop below poverty level:** 12.9%. ***Personal per capita income 2000-2003:** $22,427-$26,236.

Unemployment 2004: 3.9%. **Change from 2000:** +0.8%. **Median travel time to work:** 28.5 minutes. **Working outside county of residence:** 61.9%.

Cities with pop over 10,000: Guthrie ⛪ (10,505).

LOVE COUNTY

405 W Main St Suite 203	**Ph:** 580-276-3059
Marietta, OK 73448	

On the central southern border of OK; organized Nov 16, 1907 from Chickasaw lands. **Name Origin:** For a prominent Chickasaw family whose best-known member was Overton Love, a prominent judge of the Chickasaws.

Love County (cont'd)

Area (sq mi): 531.94 (land 515.38; water 16.56). **Pop per sq mi:** 17.7.

Pop 2005: 9,126. **State rank:** 61. **Pop change:** 2000-20005 +3.3%; 1990-2000 +8.3%. **Pop 2000:** 8,831 (White 81.3%; Black or African American 2.2%; Hispanic or Latino 7%; Asian 0.3%; Other 13.4%, including 6.4% American Indian/Alaska Native). **Foreign born:** 3.2%. **Median age:** 39.4.

Income 2000: per capita $16,648; median household $32,558; **Pop below poverty level:** 11.8%. ***Personal per capita income 2000-2003:** $18,504-$21,697.

Unemployment 2004: 6%. **Change from 2000:** +1.3%. **Median travel time to work:** 26.8 minutes. **Working outside county of residence:** 48.7%.

Cities with pop over 10,000: None.

MAJOR COUNTY

500 E Broadway   **Ph:** 580-227-4732
Fairview, OK 73737   **Fax:** 580-227-2736

In north-central OK, west of Enid; organized Nov 16, 1907 from Woods County. **Name Origin:** For John C. Major, member of the OK Constitutional Convention (1906-07).

Area (sq mi): 957.87 (land 956.76; water 1.11). **Pop per sq mi:** 7.7.

Pop 2005: 7,364. **State rank:** 64. **Pop change:** 2000-20005 -2.4%; 1990-2000 -6.3%. **Pop 2000:** 7,545 (White 93.8%; Black or African American 0.2%; Hispanic or Latino 4%; Asian 0.1%; Other 4.7%). **Foreign born:** 2.1%. **Median age:** 41.6.

Income 2000: per capita $17,272; median household $30,949; **Pop below poverty level:** 12%. ***Personal per capita income 2000-2003:** $21,386-$23,862.

Unemployment 2004: 3%. **Change from 2000:** +0.4%. **Median travel time to work:** 20.1 minutes. **Working outside county of residence:** 28.8%.

Cities with pop over 10,000: None.

MARSHALL COUNTY

1 County Courthouse Rm 106   **Ph:** 580-795-3165
Madill, OK 73446   **Fax:** 580-795-3165

On the central southern border of OK; organized Nov 16, 1907 from Chickasaw lands. **Name Origin:** For the maiden name of the mother of George A. Hendshaw, a member of the OK Constitutional Convention (1906-07).

Area (sq mi): 426.95 (land 371.11; water 55.84). **Pop per sq mi:** 39.

Pop 2005: 14,461. **State rank:** 46. **Pop change:** 2000-20005 +9.7%; 1990-2000 +21.7%. **Pop 2000:** 13,184 (White 76.5%; Black or African American 1.8%; Hispanic or Latino 8.6%; Asian 0.2%; Other 20%, including 9.1% American Indian/Alaska Native). **Foreign born:** 5%. **Median age:** 41.3.

Income 2000: per capita $14,982; median household $26,437; **Pop below poverty level:** 17.9%. ***Personal per capita income 2000-2003:** $18,227-$20,483.

Unemployment 2004: 4.6%. **Change from 2000:** +0.4%. **Median travel time to work:** 23.6 minutes. **Working outside county of residence:** 30.6%.

Cities with pop over 10,000: None.

MAYES COUNTY

1 Court Pl Suite 120   **Ph:** 918-825-2426
Pryor, OK 74361   **Fax:** 918-825-3803

In northeastern OK, east of Tulsa; organized Nov 16, 1907 from Indian lands. **Name Origin:** For Chief Samuel Houston Mayes (1845-1927), principal leader of the Cherokee Nation, also a prominent merchant and rancher.

Area (sq mi): 683.51 (land 656.14; water 27.37). **Pop per sq mi:** 60.2.

Pop 2005: 39,471. **State rank:** 24. **Pop change:** 2000-20005 +2.9%; 1990-2000 +15%. **Pop 2000:** 38,369 (White 71.3%; Black or African American 0.3%; Hispanic or Latino 1.9%; Asian 0.3%; Other 27.2%, including 19.1% American Indian/Alaska Native). **Foreign born:** 1%. **Median age:** 37.2.

Income 2000: per capita $15,350; median household $31,125; **Pop below poverty level:** 14.3%. ***Personal per capita income 2000-2003:** $19,944-$21,249.

Unemployment 2004: 5.9%. **Change from 2000:** +1%. **Median travel time to work:** 25.7 minutes. **Working outside county of residence:** 29.5%.

Cities with pop over 10,000: None.

MCCLAIN COUNTY

121 N 2nd St Suite 303   **Ph:** 405-527-3360
Purcell, OK 73080

In south-central OK, south of Oklahoma City; organized Nov 16, 1907 from Chickasaw lands. **Name Origin:** For Charles M. McClain, a member of the OK Constitutional Convention (1906-07).

Area (sq mi): 580.13 (land 569.67; water 10.46). **Pop per sq mi:** 52.8.

Pop 2005: 30,096. **State rank:** 33. **Pop change:** 2000-20005 +8.5%; 1990-2000 +21.7%. **Pop 2000:** 27,740 (White 85.3%; Black or African American 0.7%; Hispanic or Latino 4.9%; Asian 0.2%; Other 11.8%, including 5.6% American Indian/Alaska Native). **Foreign born:** 2.6%. **Median age:** 36.9.

Income 2000: per capita $18,158; median household $37,275; **Pop below poverty level:** 10.5%. ***Personal per capita income 2000-2003:** $22,057-$24,062.

Unemployment 2004: 4.3%. **Change from 2000:** +0.4%. **Median travel time to work:** 27.3 minutes. **Working outside county of residence:** 63.9%.

Cities with pop over 10,000: None.

MCCURTAIN COUNTY

108 N Central St   **Ph:** 580-286-2370
Idabel, OK 74745   **Fax:** 580-286-1040

In the southeastern corner of OK; organized Nov 16, 1907 from Choctaw lands. **Name Origin:** For a prominent Choctaw family, of which the father and his three sons each served as chief of the Choctaw Nation.

Area (sq mi): 1901.32 (land 1852.26; water 49.07). **Pop per sq mi:** 18.4.

---

*Source: Personal per capita income data are from the Bureau of Economic Analysis; per capita income data are from the Bureau of the Census.
See Introduction for explanation of differences.

McCurtain County (cont'd)

Pop 2005: 33,992. **State rank:** 29. **Pop change:** 2000-20005 -1.2%; 1990-2000 +2.9%. **Pop 2000:** 34,402 (White 69.5%; Black or African American 9.3%; Hispanic or Latino 3.1%; Asian 0.2%; Other 19.9%, including 13.6% American Indian/Alaska Native). **Foreign born:** 1.8%. **Median age:** 36.

Income 2000: per capita $13,603; median household $24,162; **Pop below poverty level:** 24.7%. ***Personal per capita income 2000-2003:** $18,540-$20,531.

Unemployment 2004: 7.6%. **Change from 2000:** +1.3%. **Median travel time to work:** 23.7 minutes. **Working outside county of residence:** 11.1%.

Cities with pop over 10,000: None.

MCINTOSH COUNTY
PO Box 110   **Ph:** 918-689-2741
Eufaula, OK 74432   **Fax:** 918-689-3385

In east-central OK, southwest of Muskogee; organized Nov 16, 1907 from Indian lands. **Name Origin:** For a prominent Creek family, which included a number of prominent tribal chiefs.

Area (sq mi): 712.48 (land 620.01; water 92.48). **Pop per sq mi:** 32.2.

Pop 2005: 19,965. **State rank:** 40. **Pop change:** 2000-20005 +2.6%; 1990-2000 +16%. **Pop 2000:** 19,456 (White 72%; Black or African American 4.1%; Hispanic or Latino 1.3%; Asian 0.1%; Other 23.1%, including 16.2% American Indian/Alaska Native). **Foreign born:** 0.5%. **Median age:** 44.1.

Income 2000: per capita $16,410; median household $25,964; **Pop below poverty level:** 18.2%. ***Personal per capita income 2000-2003:** $18,237-$19,937.

Unemployment 2004: 6.9%. **Change from 2000:** +1.1%. **Median travel time to work:** 27.5 minutes. **Working outside county of residence:** 43.1%.

Cities with pop over 10,000: None.

MURRAY COUNTY
PO Box 240   **Ph:** 580-622-3777
Sulphur, OK 73086   **Fax:** 580-622-6209

In south-central OK, north of Ardmore; organized Nov 16, 1907 from Chickasaw lands. **Name Origin:** For William Henry 'Alfalfa Bill' Murray (1869-1956), U.S. representative from OK (1913-17) and governor (1931-35).

Area (sq mi): 424.92 (land 418.25; water 6.67). **Pop per sq mi:** 30.8.

Pop 2005: 12,880. **State rank:** 50. **Pop change:** 2000-20005 +2%; 1990-2000 +4.8%. **Pop 2000:** 12,623 (White 79.2%; Black or African American 1.9%; Hispanic or Latino 3.1%; Asian 0.3%; Other 17.1%, including 11.6% American Indian/Alaska Native). **Foreign born:** 2.8%. **Median age:** 39.8.

Income 2000: per capita $16,084; median household $30,294; **Pop below poverty level:** 14.1%. ***Personal per capita income 2000-2003:** $18,343-$20,426.

Unemployment 2004: 4.4%. **Change from 2000:** -0.5%. **Median travel time to work:** 21 minutes. **Working outside county of residence:** 30.5%.

Cities with pop over 10,000: None.

MUSKOGEE COUNTY
PO Box 1008   **Ph:** 918-682-7781
Muskogee, OK 74402   **Fax:** 918-682-8803

In east-cental OK, southeast of Tulsa; organized Nov 16, 1907 from Cherokee lands. **Name Origin:** For the Muscogee Creek Indians, a tribe of Muskhogean linguistic stock.

Area (sq mi): 838.99 (land 813.85; water 25.14). **Pop per sq mi:** 86.8.

Pop 2005: 70,607. **State rank:** 7. **Pop change:** 2000-20005 +1.7%; 1990-2000 +2%. **Pop 2000:** 69,451 (White 62.8%; Black or African American 13.2%; Hispanic or Latino 2.7%; Asian 0.6%; Other 22.5%, including 14.9% American Indian/Alaska Native). **Foreign born:** 1.8%. **Median age:** 37.

Income 2000: per capita $14,828; median household $28,438; **Pop below poverty level:** 17.9%. ***Personal per capita income 2000-2003:** $19,910-$22,012.

Unemployment 2004: 6.9%. **Change from 2000:** +2.6%. **Median travel time to work:** 21.7 minutes. **Working outside county of residence:** 17.1%.

Cities with pop over 10,000: Muskogee 🏛 (38,846).

NOBLE COUNTY
300 Courthouse Dr Rm 11   **Ph:** 580-336-2141
Perry, OK 73077   **Fax:** 580-336-2481

In north-central OK, east of Enid; organized as County 'P' 1897 (prior to statehood) from Indian lands. **Name Origin:** For Gen. John Willock Noble (1831-1912), U.S. district attorney for the eastern district of MO (1867) and U.S. secretary of the interior (1889-93).

Area (sq mi): 742.44 (land 731.9; water 10.54). **Pop per sq mi:** 15.3.

Pop 2005: 11,211. **State rank:** 56. **Pop change:** 2000-20005 -1.8%; 1990-2000 +3.3%. **Pop 2000:** 11,411 (White 85.8%; Black or African American 1.6%; Hispanic or Latino 1.8%; Asian 0.3%; Other 11.6%, including 7.6% American Indian/Alaska Native). **Foreign born:** 1.1%. **Median age:** 38.3.

Income 2000: per capita $17,022; median household $33,968; **Pop below poverty level:** 12.8%. ***Personal per capita income 2000-2003:** $22,146-$22,438.

Unemployment 2004: 4.1%. **Change from 2000:** -0.4%. **Median travel time to work:** 19 minutes. **Working outside county of residence:** 27.8%.

Cities with pop over 10,000: None.

NOWATA COUNTY
229 N Maple St   **Ph:** 918-273-0175
Nowata, OK 74048   **Fax:** 918-273-1936

On the northeastern border of OK, northeast of Tulsa; organized Nov 16, 1907 from Cherokee lands. **Name Origin:** For the town of Nowata.

Area (sq mi): 580.87 (land 564.95; water 15.92). **Pop per sq mi:** 19.2.

Pop 2005: 10,864. **State rank:** 57. **Pop change:** 2000-20005 +2.8%;

Nowata County (cont'd)

1990-2000 +5.8%. **Pop 2000:** 10,569 (White 71.9%; Black or African American 2.5%; Hispanic or Latino 1.2%; Asian 0.1%; Other 25.1%, including 16.6% American Indian/Alaska Native). **Foreign born:** 0.2%. **Median age:** 39.

Income 2000: per capita $14,244; median household $29,470; **Pop below poverty level:** 14.1%. ***Personal per capita income 2000-2003:** $17,410-$18,158.

Unemployment 2004: 5.5%. **Change from 2000:** -0.3%. **Median travel time to work:** 26.7 minutes. **Working outside county of residence:** 54.5%.

Cities with pop over 10,000: None.

OKFUSKEE COUNTY

PO Box 26   **Ph:** 918-623-0939
Okemah, OK 74859   **Fax:** 918-623-0635

In east-central OK, east of Oklahoma City; organized Nov 16, 1907 from Creek lands. **Name Origin:** For a Creek town in Cleburne County, AL, probably transferred by the Creek Indians; name possibly means 'point between streams' or 'promontory.'

Area (sq mi): 628.91 (land 624.76; water 4.15). **Pop per sq mi:** 18.3.

Pop 2005: 11,434. **State rank:** 55. **Pop change:** 2000-20005 -3.2%; 1990-2000 +2.3%. **Pop 2000:** 11,814 (White 64.9%; Black or African American 10.4%; Hispanic or Latino 1.6%; Asian 0.1%; Other 24.1%, including 18.2% American Indian/Alaska Native). **Foreign born:** 1.7%. **Median age:** 38.6.

Income 2000: per capita $12,746; median household $24,324; **Pop below poverty level:** 23%. ***Personal per capita income 2000-2003:** $15,119-$17,206.

Unemployment 2004: 8.8%. **Change from 2000:** +4.1%. **Median travel time to work:** 27.1 minutes. **Working outside county of residence:** 39.7%.

Cities with pop over 10,000: None.

OKLAHOMA COUNTY

320 Robert S Kerr Ave   **Ph:** 405-270-0082
Oklahoma City, OK 73102
www.oklahomacounty.org

In central OK, north of Norman; original county; organized 1891 (prior to statehood). **Name Origin:** For Oklahoma City.

Area (sq mi): 718.31 (land 709.09; water 9.22). **Pop per sq mi:** 965.4.

Pop 2005: 684,543. **State rank:** 1. **Pop change:** 2000-20005 +3.6%; 1990-2000 +10.1%. **Pop 2000:** 660,448 (White 67.1%; Black or African American 15%; Hispanic or Latino 8.7%; Asian 2.8%; Other 11.8%, including 3.4% American Indian/Alaska Native). **Foreign born:** 7.2%. **Median age:** 34.2.

Income 2000: per capita $19,551; median household $35,063; **Pop below poverty level:** 15.3%. ***Personal per capita income 2000-2003:** $28,309-$30,891.

Unemployment 2004: 4.8%. **Change from 2000:** +0.7%. **Median travel time to work:** 20.9 minutes. **Working outside county of residence:** 7.2%.

Cities with pop over 10,000: 7 (see page 38 for cities).

OKMULGEE COUNTY

PO Box 904   **Ph:** 918-756-0788
Okmulgee, OK 74447   **Fax:** 918-758-1261

In east-central OK, south of Tulsa; organized Nov 16, 1907 from Creek lands. **Name Origin:** For a Creek town in Russell County, AL; from *oki mulgi* 'boiling waters,' probably referring to a spring.

Area (sq mi): 702.32 (land 696.97; water 5.34). **Pop per sq mi:** 57.

Pop 2005: 39,732. **State rank:** 23. **Pop change:** 2000-20005 +0.1%; 1990-2000 +8.8%. **Pop 2000:** 39,685 (White 69%; Black or African American 10.2%; Hispanic or Latino 1.9%; Asian 0.2%; Other 19.8%, including 12.8% American Indian/Alaska Native). **Foreign born:** 0.7%. **Median age:** 36.9.

Income 2000: per capita $14,065; median household $27,652; **Pop below poverty level:** 18.9%. ***Personal per capita income 2000-2003:** $17,397-$19,418.

Unemployment 2004: 7.1%. **Change from 2000:** +0.3%. **Median travel time to work:** 27.3 minutes. **Working outside county of residence:** 37.9%.

Cities with pop over 10,000: Okmulgee 🏛 (12,854).

OSAGE COUNTY

PO Box 87   **Ph:** 918-287-3136
Pawhuska, OK 74056   **Fax:** 918-287-4979

On the central northern border of OK, northeast of Tulsa; organized Nov 16, 1907 from Osage Indian lands. **Name Origin:** For the Osage Indian tribe of Siouan linguistic stock from the area near the Osage River. The name is a French corruption of their tribal name, *Washazhe*, meaning unknown.

Area (sq mi): 2303.8 (land 2250.8; water 53). **Pop per sq mi:** 20.2.

Pop 2005: 45,416. **State rank:** 18. **Pop change:** 2000-20005 +2.2%; 1990-2000 +6.7%. **Pop 2000:** 44,437 (White 66.1%; Black or African American 10.8%; Hispanic or Latino 2.1%; Asian 0.2%; Other 21.8%, including 14.4% American Indian/Alaska Native). **Foreign born:** 1%. **Median age:** 38.1.

Income 2000: per capita $17,014; median household $34,477; **Pop below poverty level:** 13.2%. ***Personal per capita income 2000-2003:** $20,681-$22,724.

Unemployment 2004: 5.2%. **Change from 2000:** +1.7%. **Median travel time to work:** 25.3 minutes. **Working outside county of residence:** 65.6%.

Cities with pop over 10,000: None.

OTTAWA COUNTY

102 E Central Ave Suite 203   **Ph:** 918-542-3332
Miami, OK 74354   **Fax:** 918-542-8260

On the northeastern border of OK, northeast of Tulsa; organized Nov 16, 1907 from Indian lands. **Name Origin:** For the Ottawa Indians, a tribe of Algonquian linguistic stock whose earliest known location was along the northern shore of Georgian Bay, Ont., Canada. The name is derived from Algonquian *adawe*, probably 'to trade.'

Area (sq mi): 484.73 (land 471.32; water 13.41). **Pop per sq mi:** 69.7.

*Source: Personal per capita income data are from the Bureau of Economic Analysis; per capita income data are from the Bureau of the Census. See Introduction for explanation of differences.

Ottawa County (cont'd)

Pop 2005: 32,866. **State rank:** 30. **Pop change:** 2000-20005 -1%; 1990-2000 +8.6%. **Pop 2000:** 33,194 (White 72.9%; Black or African American 0.6%; Hispanic or Latino 3.2%; Asian 0.3%; Other 24.9%, including 16.5% American Indian/Alaska Native). **Foreign born:** 1.7%. **Median age:** 37.3.

Income 2000: per capita $14,478; median household $27,507; **Pop below poverty level:** 16.6%. ***Personal per capita income 2000-2003:** $18,682-$20,784.

Unemployment 2004: 5.8%. **Change from 2000:** -1.5%. **Median travel time to work:** 21.1 minutes. **Working outside county of residence:** 28.9%.

Cities with pop over 10,000: Miami 🏛 (13,464).

PAWNEE COUNTY

500 Harrison St Rm 203   **Ph:** 918-762-3741
Pawnee, OK 74058   **Fax:** 918-762-3714
www.cityofpawnee.com/cofc/

In north-central OK, northwest of Tulsa; organized as County 'Q' in 1892 (prior to statehood) from Indian lands. **Name Origin:** For the Pawnee Indian tribe of Caddoan linguistic stock. The name may mean 'horn,' for the shape in which they wore their hair lock. The Osages called them *Pa-in* 'long haired'; they called themselves 'civilized people.'

Area (sq mi): 594.87 (land 569.44; water 25.43). **Pop per sq mi:** 29.6.

Pop 2005: 16,860. **State rank:** 43. **Pop change:** 2000-20005 +1.5%; 1990-2000 +6.7%. **Pop 2000:** 16,612 (White 81.7%; Black or African American 0.7%; Hispanic or Latino 1.2%; Asian 0.2%; Other 16.7%, including 12.1% American Indian/Alaska Native). **Foreign born:** 0.6%. **Median age:** 38.5.

Income 2000: per capita $15,261; median household $31,661; **Pop below poverty level:** 13%. ***Personal per capita income 2000-2003:** $19,880-$21,405.

Unemployment 2004: 5.8%. **Change from 2000:** +0.9%. **Median travel time to work:** 30.6 minutes. **Working outside county of residence:** 60.9%.

Cities with pop over 10,000: None.

PAYNE COUNTY

315 W 6th St Suite 202   **Ph:** 405-747-8310
Stillwater, OK 74074   **Fax:** 405-747-8304
www.paynecounty.org

In north-central OK, west of Tulsa; original county; organized 1890 (prior to statehood), known as 'Old Oklahoma.' **Name Origin:** For David L. Payne (1836-84), active in the Oklahoma Boomer (land development) movement.

Area (sq mi): 697.13 (land 686.34; water 10.79). **Pop per sq mi:** 100.8.

Pop 2005: 69,151. **State rank:** 8. **Pop change:** 2000-20005 +1.4%; 1990-2000 +10.9%. **Pop 2000:** 68,190 (White 83.3%; Black or African American 3.6%; Hispanic or Latino 2.1%; Asian 3%; Other 9%, including 4.6% American Indian/Alaska Native). **Foreign born:** 4.6%. **Median age:** 27.6.

Income 2000: per capita $15,983; median household $28,733; **Pop below poverty level:** 20.3%. ***Personal per capita income 2000-2003:** $21,042-$22,433.

Unemployment 2004: 3.8%. **Change from 2000:** +2.3%. **Median travel time to work:** 16.8 minutes. **Working outside county of residence:** 11.9%.

Cities with pop over 10,000: Stillwater 🏛 (40,731).

PITTSBURG COUNTY

115 E Carl Albert Pkwy Suite 1A   **Ph:** 918-423-6865
McAlester, OK 74501   **Fax:** 918-423-7304

In east-central OK, southwest of Muskogee; organized Nov 16, 1907 from Tobucksy County. **Name Origin:** For Pittsburgh, PA.

Area (sq mi): 1377.85 (land 1305.94; water 71.91). **Pop per sq mi:** 34.2.

Pop 2005: 44,641. **State rank:** 20. **Pop change:** 2000-20005 +1.6%; 1990-2000 +8.3%. **Pop 2000:** 43,953 (White 76.3%; Black or African American 4%; Hispanic or Latino 2.1%; Asian 0.3%; Other 18.5%, including 12.5% American Indian/Alaska Native). **Foreign born:** 1.1%. **Median age:** 39.4.

Income 2000: per capita $15,494; median household $28,679; **Pop below poverty level:** 17.2%. ***Personal per capita income 2000-2003:** $19,015-$21,723.

Unemployment 2004: 5.4%. **Change from 2000:** +1.2%. **Median travel time to work:** 20.6 minutes. **Working outside county of residence:** 10.9%.

Cities with pop over 10,000: McAlester 🏛 (17,783).

PONTOTOC COUNTY

100 W 13th St   **Ph:** 580-332-1425
Ada, OK 74820

In south-central OK, southeast of Oklahoma City; organized Nov 16, 1907 from Choctaw lands. **Name Origin:** Of Chickasaw origin; the name of a chief, said to mean 'cattails growing on the prairie.'

Area (sq mi): 725.45 (land 719.64; water 5.82). **Pop per sq mi:** 49.1.

Pop 2005: 35,346. **State rank:** 28. **Pop change:** 2000-20005 +0.6%; 1990-2000 +3%. **Pop 2000:** 35,143 (White 74.8%; Black or African American 2.1%; Hispanic or Latino 2.3%; Asian 0.5%; Other 21.7%, including 15.5% American Indian/Alaska Native). **Foreign born:** 1.2%. **Median age:** 35.7.

Income 2000: per capita $14,664; median household $26,955; **Pop below poverty level:** 16.5%. ***Personal per capita income 2000-2003:** $20,719-$22,422.

Unemployment 2004: 5.8%. **Change from 2000:** +1.9%. **Median travel time to work:** 18 minutes. **Working outside county of residence:** 9.8%.

Cities with pop over 10,000: Ada 🏛 (15,840).

POTTAWATOMIE COUNTY

325 N Broadway   **Ph:** 405-273-8222
Shawnee, OK 74801   **Fax:** 405-275-6898

In central OK, southeast of Oklahoma City; original county; organized as County 'B' in 1891 (prior to statehood); name changed

Pottawatomie County (cont'd)

in 1892. **Name Origin:** For the Potawatomie Indian tribe of Algonquian linguistic stock. The name probably means 'people of the place of the fire.'

Area (sq mi): 793.26 (land 787.7; water 5.57). **Pop per sq mi:** 86.7.

Pop 2005: 68,272. **State rank:** 10. **Pop change:** 2000-20005 +4.2%; 1990-2000 +11.5%. **Pop 2000:** 65,521 (White 78.8%; Black or African American 2.9%; Hispanic or Latino 2.4%; Asian 0.6%; Other 16.6%, including 11.2% American Indian/Alaska Native). **Foreign born:** 1.1%. **Median age:** 35.5.

Income 2000: per capita $15,972; median household $31,573; **Pop below poverty level:** 14.6%. ***Personal per capita income 2000-2003:** $20,214-$22,563.

Unemployment 2004: 5.4%. **Change from 2000:** +0.2%. **Median travel time to work:** 25 minutes. **Working outside county of residence:** 34.2%.

Cities with pop over 10,000: Shawnee ⛪ (29,746).

PUSHMATAHA COUNTY

304 SW 'B' St   **Ph:** 580-298-2512
Antlers, OK 74523   **Fax:** 580-298-5299

In southeastern OK, southeast of McAlester; organized Nov 16, 1907 from Indian lands. **Name Origin:** For the Pushmataha district of the Choctaw Nation, named for the noted Choctaw chief (c.1765-1824) who served with Andrew Jackson (1767-1845) and is buried in the Congressional Cemetery. The name may mean 'ready to be a sapling,' ie., now grown to be a young man; or 'qualified sapling,' indicating a rank to which he belonged.

Area (sq mi): 1422.78 (land 1397.31; water 25.47). **Pop per sq mi:** 8.4.

Pop 2005: 11,693. **State rank:** 53. **Pop change:** 2000-20005 +0.2%; 1990-2000 +6.1%. **Pop 2000:** 11,667 (White 77.1%; Black or African American 0.8%; Hispanic or Latino 1.6%; Asian 0.1%; Other 21.2%, including 15.6% American Indian/Alaska Native). **Foreign born:** 0.5%. **Median age:** 40.1.

Income 2000: per capita $12,864; median household $22,127; **Pop below poverty level:** 23.2%. ***Personal per capita income 2000-2003:** $15,415-$18,528.

Unemployment 2004: 6.2%. **Change from 2000:** -0.4%. **Median travel time to work:** 26.8 minutes. **Working outside county of residence:** 26.9%.

Cities with pop over 10,000: None.

ROGER MILLS COUNTY

PO Box 708   **Ph:** 580-497-3365
Cheyenne, OK 73628   **Fax:** 580-497-3199

On the central western border of OK; original county; organized as County 'F' Apr 19, 1892; name changed Nov 1892; annexed part of Day County when the latter was abolished in 1907. **Name Origin:** For Col. Roger Quarles Mills (1832-1911), U.S. representative from TX (1873-92) and U.S. senator (1892-99).

Area (sq mi): 1146.46 (land 1141.87; water 4.58). **Pop per sq mi:** 2.9.

Pop 2005: 3,311. **State rank:** 75. **Pop change:** 2000-20005 -3.6%; 1990-2000 -17.1%. **Pop 2000:** 3,436 (White 90.2%; Black or African American 0.3%; Hispanic or Latino 2.6%; Asian 0.1%; Other 7.9%, including 5.5% American Indian/Alaska Native). **Foreign born:** 0.7%. **Median age:** 41.7.

Income 2000: per capita $16,821; median household $30,078; **Pop below poverty level:** 16.3%. ***Personal per capita income 2000-2003:** $20,663-$24,599.

Unemployment 2004: 2.6%. **Change from 2000:** +0.7%. **Median travel time to work:** 24.7 minutes. **Working outside county of residence:** 28.6%.

Cities with pop over 10,000: None.

ROGERS COUNTY

219 S Missouri St   **Ph:** 918-341-2518
Claremore, OK 74017   **Fax:** 918-341-4529
www.rogerscounty.org

In northeastern OK, east of Tulsa; organized Nov 16, 1907 from Cherokee lands. **Name Origin:** For Clement V. Rogers, member of the OK Constitutional Convention (1906-07) and father of the humorist Will Rogers (1879-1935).

Area (sq mi): 711.44 (land 674.95; water 36.49). **Pop per sq mi:** 119.6.

Pop 2005: 80,757. **State rank:** 6. **Pop change:** 2000-20005 +14.3%; 1990-2000 +28%. **Pop 2000:** 70,641 (White 79%; Black or African American 0.7%; Hispanic or Latino 1.8%; Asian 0.3%; Other 19.1%, including 12.1% American Indian/Alaska Native). **Foreign born:** 1.3%. **Median age:** 36.2.

Income 2000: per capita $19,073; median household $44,471; **Pop below poverty level:** 8.6%. ***Personal per capita income 2000-2003:** $24,245-$24,703.

Unemployment 2004: 4.4%. **Change from 2000:** +1.4%. **Median travel time to work:** 25.4 minutes. **Working outside county of residence:** 56%.

Cities with pop over 10,000: Claremore ⛪ (16,994).

SEMINOLE COUNTY

PO Box 1180   **Ph:** 405-257-2501
Wewoka, OK 74884   **Fax:** 405-257-6422

In central OK, east of Shawnee; organized Nov 16, 1907 from Seminole lands. **Name Origin:** For the Seminole Indians, a Muskhogean tribe from FL, forced to move to OK at the conclusion of the Seminole War (1835-42). The name is from Creek, probably 'the separate ones.'

Area (sq mi): 640.57 (land 632.51; water 8.06). **Pop per sq mi:** 39.2.

Pop 2005: 24,770. **State rank:** 37. **Pop change:** 2000-20005 -0.5%; 1990-2000 -2%. **Pop 2000:** 24,894 (White 69.9%; Black or African American 5.6%; Hispanic or Latino 2.2%; Asian 0.2%; Other 23.4%, including 17.4% American Indian/Alaska Native). **Foreign born:** 1%. **Median age:** 38.1.

Income 2000: per capita $13,956; median household $25,568; **Pop below poverty level:** 20.8%. ***Personal per capita income 2000-2003:** $17,162-$19,699.

---

*Source: Personal per capita income data are from the Bureau of Economic Analysis; per capita income data are from the Bureau of the Census. See Introduction for explanation of differences.

Seminole County (cont'd)

Unemployment 2004: 9.8%. **Change from 2000:** +4.1%. **Median travel time to work:** 23.7 minutes. **Working outside county of residence:** 32.5%.

Cities with pop over 10,000: None.

SEQUOYAH COUNTY

120 E Chickasaw Ave
Sallisaw, OK 74955

Ph: 918-775-4516
Fax: 918-775-1218

On central eastern border of OK, west of Fort Smith, AR; organized Nov 16, 1907 from Cherokee lands. **Name Origin:** From the Sequoyah District of the Cherokee Nation, named for the Indian chief Sequoyah (c.1773-1843), who invented the Cherokee alphabet. He was also called George Guess.

Area (sq mi): 714.88 (land 673.82; water 41.06). **Pop per sq mi:** 60.7.

Pop 2005: 40,868. **State rank:** 22. **Pop change:** 2000-20005 +4.9%; 1990-2000 +15.2%. **Pop 2000:** 38,972 (White 67.4%; Black or African American 1.9%; Hispanic or Latino 2%; Asian 0.2%; Other 29.7%, including 19.6% American Indian/Alaska Native). **Foreign born:** 0.7%. **Median age:** 36.4.

Income 2000: per capita $13,405; median household $27,615; **Pop below poverty level:** 19.8%. ***Personal per capita income 2000-2003:** $18,712-$19,977.

Unemployment 2004: 6%. **Change from 2000:** +0.7%. **Median travel time to work:** 27.4 minutes. **Working outside county of residence:** 44%.

Cities with pop over 10,000: None.

STEPHENS COUNTY

101 S 11th St
Duncan, OK 73533

Ph: 580-255-4193
Fax: 580-255-1771

In south-central OK, east of Lawton; organized Nov 16, 1907 from Comanche County. **Name Origin:** For John Hall Stephens (1847-1924), U.S. representative from TX (1897-1917) and strong advocate for OK statehood.

Area (sq mi): 891.12 (land 874.04; water 17.08). **Pop per sq mi:** 49.1.

Pop 2005: 42,946. **State rank:** 21. **Pop change:** 2000-20005 -0.5%; 1990-2000 +2.1%. **Pop 2000:** 43,182 (White 86.2%; Black or African American 2.2%; Hispanic or Latino 4%; Asian 0.3%; Other 9%, including 4.9% American Indian/Alaska Native). **Foreign born:** 1.8%. **Median age:** 40.1.

Income 2000: per capita $16,357; median household $30,709; **Pop below poverty level:** 14.6%. ***Personal per capita income 2000-2003:** $21,882-$24,034.

Unemployment 2004: 4.5%. **Change from 2000:** +1.1%. **Median travel time to work:** 21.2 minutes. **Working outside county of residence:** 15.9%.

Cities with pop over 10,000: Duncan ⛪ (22,207).

TEXAS COUNTY

319 N Main St
Guymon, OK 73942
www.txcountyok.com

Ph: 580-338-3233
Fax: 580-338-4311

In the central OK panhandle; organized Nov 16, 1907 from part of the old Beaver County. **Name Origin:** For the state.

Area (sq mi): 2048.81 (land 2037.16; water 11.66). **Pop per sq mi:** 9.9.

Pop 2005: 20,112. **State rank:** 39. **Pop change:** 2000-20005 +0%; 1990-2000 +22.5%. **Pop 2000:** 20,107 (White 66.7%; Black or African American 0.7%; Hispanic or Latino 29.9%; Asian 0.6%; Other 22%, including 1.2% American Indian/Alaska Native). **Foreign born:** 16.9%. **Median age:** 30.4.

Income 2000: per capita $15,692; median household $35,872; **Pop below poverty level:** 14.1%. ***Personal per capita income 2000-2003:** $28,238-$25,220.

Unemployment 2004: 3.4%. **Change from 2000:** +1.4%. **Median travel time to work:** 16.6 minutes. **Working outside county of residence:** 14.6%.

Cities with pop over 10,000: Guymon ⛪ (10,730).

TILLMAN COUNTY

201 N Main St
Frederick, OK 73542

Ph: 580-335-3421
Fax: 580-335-3795

On the southwestern border of OK, southwest of Lawton; organized Nov 16, 1907 from Comanche County. **Name Origin:** For Benjamin Ryan Tillman (1847-1918), governor of SC (1890-94) and U.S. senator from SC (1895-1918), who was active in the formation of the state of OK.

Area (sq mi): 879.21 (land 871.97; water 7.25). **Pop per sq mi:** 9.8.

Pop 2005: 8,513. **State rank:** 63. **Pop change:** 2000-20005 -8.3%; 1990-2000 -10.6%. **Pop 2000:** 9,287 (White 68.5%; Black or African American 9%; Hispanic or Latino 17.7%; Asian 0.3%; Other 16.4%, including 2.7% American Indian/Alaska Native). **Foreign born:** 4.3%. **Median age:** 38.9.

Income 2000: per capita $14,270; median household $24,828; **Pop below poverty level:** 21.9%. ***Personal per capita income 2000-2003:** $16,589-$19,534.

Unemployment 2004: 4.7%. **Change from 2000:** +0%. **Median travel time to work:** 20.9 minutes. **Working outside county of residence:** 24.9%.

Cities with pop over 10,000: None.

TULSA COUNTY

500 S Denver Ave Suite 120
Tulsa, OK 74103
www.tulsacounty.org

Ph: 918-596-5801
Fax: 918-596-5819

In northeastern OK, northwest of Muskogee; organized Nov 16, 1907 from Creek lands. **Name Origin:** For Tulsa, a town at the time.

Area (sq mi): 587.02 (land 570.3; water 16.72). **Pop per sq mi:** 1003.1.

Pop 2005: 572,059. **State rank:** 2. **Pop change:** 2000-20005 +1.6%; 1990-2000 +11.9%. **Pop 2000:** 563,299 (White 72.5%; Black or African American 10.9%; Hispanic or Latino 6%; Asian 1.6%; Other

⛪ County Seat

Tulsa County (cont'd)

12.4%, including 5.2% American Indian/Alaska Native). **Foreign born:** 5.4%. **Median age:** 34.4.

Income 2000: per capita $21,115; median household $38,213; **Pop below poverty level:** 11.6%. ***Personal per capita income 2000-2003:** $33,111-$35,470.

Unemployment 2004: 4.8%. **Change from 2000:** +1.4%. **Median travel time to work:** 19.7 minutes. **Working outside county of residence:** 5.8%.

Cities with pop over 10,000: 6 (see page 38 for cities).

WAGONER COUNTY

PO Box 156   **Ph:** 918-485-6171
Wagoner, OK 74477   **Fax:** 918-485-7709

In east-central OK, north of Muskogee; organized Nov 16, 1907 from Creek lands. **Name Origin:** For the city of Wagoner.

Area (sq mi): 590.99 (land 562.91; water 28.07). **Pop per sq mi:** 114.

Pop 2005: 64,183. **State rank:** 11. **Pop change:** 2000-20005 +11.6%; 1990-2000 +20.1%. **Pop 2000:** 57,491 (White 78.9%; Black or African American 3.8%; Hispanic or Latino 2.5%; Asian 0.5%; Other 15.7%, including 9.4% American Indian/Alaska Native). **Foreign born:** 1.8%. **Median age:** 36.2.

Income 2000: per capita $18,272; median household $41,744; **Pop below poverty level:** 8.9%. ***Personal per capita income 2000-2003:** $21,137-$22,232.

Unemployment 2004: 4.6%. **Change from 2000:** +1.6%. **Median travel time to work:** 26.6 minutes. **Working outside county of residence:** 75.5%.

Cities with pop over 10,000: None.

WASHINGTON COUNTY

400 S Johnstone Ave Rm 100   **Ph:** 918-337-2840
Bartlesville, OK 74003   **Fax:** 918-337-2894
www.co.washington.ok.us

On the northern border of OK, north of Tulsa; organized Nov 16, 1907 from Cherokee lands. **Name Origin:** For George Washington (1732-99), American patriot and first U.S. president.

Area (sq mi): 424.15 (land 416.82; water 7.34). **Pop per sq mi:** 117.9.

Pop 2005: 49,149. **State rank:** 15. **Pop change:** 2000-20005 +0.3%; 1990-2000 +1.9%. **Pop 2000:** 48,996 (White 79.9%; Black or African American 2.5%; Hispanic or Latino 2.6%; Asian 0.7%; Other 15.6%, including 8.6% American Indian/Alaska Native). **Foreign born:** 2%. **Median age:** 40.1.

Income 2000: per capita $20,250; median household $35,816; **Pop below poverty level:** 11.9%. ***Personal per capita income 2000-2003:** $27,985-$29,984.

Unemployment 2004: 4.9%. **Change from 2000:** +1.6%. **Median travel time to work:** 20.1 minutes. **Working outside county of residence:** 21.4%.

Cities with pop over 10,000: Bartlesville 🏛 (34,638).

WASHITA COUNTY

PO Box 380   **Ph:** 580-832-2284
Cordell, OK 73632   **Fax:** 580-832-3526

In west-central OK, southwest of Oklahoma City; organized as County 'H' in 1892 (prior to statehood) from Indian lands; name changed later. **Name Origin:** For the Washita River, which runs through it. Name is believed to be from Choctaw *owa* and *chita* 'big hunt.'

Area (sq mi): 1009.07 (land 1003.35; water 5.73). **Pop per sq mi:** 11.4.

Pop 2005: 11,471. **State rank:** 54. **Pop change:** 2000-20005 -0.3%; 1990-2000 +0.6%. **Pop 2000:** 11,508 (White 90.4%; Black or African American 0.4%; Hispanic or Latino 4.5%; Asian 0.3%; Other 7%, including 3% American Indian/Alaska Native). **Foreign born:** 1.6%. **Median age:** 39.2.

Income 2000: per capita $15,528; median household $29,563; **Pop below poverty level:** 15.5%. ***Personal per capita income 2000-2003:** $16,933-$20,470.

Unemployment 2004: 3.2%. **Change from 2000:** +0.2%. **Median travel time to work:** 21.2 minutes. **Working outside county of residence:** 42.3%.

Cities with pop over 10,000: None.

WOODS COUNTY

407 Government St   **Ph:** 580-327-2126
Alva, OK 73717   **Fax:** 580-327-1219

On the northern border of OK, northwest of Enid; original county; organized as County 'M' in 1893 (prior to statehood); name changed later; re-formed Nov 16, 1907. **Name Origin:** For Lt. Col. Samuel N. Wood (?-1814), career army officer killed in the war of 1812. The letter *s* was a clerical error allowed to stand.

Area (sq mi): 1290.07 (land 1286.57; water 3.51). **Pop per sq mi:** 6.6.

Pop 2005: 8,546. **State rank:** 62. **Pop change:** 2000-20005 -6%; 1990-2000 -0.2%. **Pop 2000:** 9,089 (White 91.9%; Black or African American 2.4%; Hispanic or Latino 2.4%; Asian 0.5%; Other 3.7%, including 1.6% American Indian/Alaska Native). **Foreign born:** 0.9%. **Median age:** 37.8.

Income 2000: per capita $17,487; median household $28,927; **Pop below poverty level:** 15%. ***Personal per capita income 2000-2003:** $20,490-$25,515.

Unemployment 2004: 6.9%. **Change from 2000:** +5.4%. **Median travel time to work:** 12.6 minutes. **Working outside county of residence:** 11.3%.

Cities with pop over 10,000: None.

WOODWARD COUNTY

1600 Main St Suite 9   **Ph:** 580-256-8097
Woodward, OK 73801   **Fax:** 580-254-6840

In northwestern OK, west of Enid; organized as County 'N' in 1893 from Indian lands; re-formed Nov 16, 1907. **Name Origin:** For the railroad station, itself named for Brinton W. Woodward, a director of the Santa Fe Railroad.

Area (sq mi): 1246.01 (land 1242.3; water 3.71). **Pop per sq mi:** 15.4.

*Source: Personal per capita income data are from the Bureau of Economic Analysis; per capita income data are from the Bureau of the Census. See Introduction for explanation of differences.

Woodward County (cont'd)

Pop 2005: 19,088. **State rank:** 41. **Pop change:** 2000-20005 +3.3%; 1990-2000 -2.6%. **Pop 2000:** 18,486 (White 90.3%; Black or African American 1.1%; Hispanic or Latino 4.8%; Asian 0.5%; Other 6.2%, including 2.1% American Indian/Alaska Native). **Foreign born:** 2.5%. **Median age:** 37.4.

Income 2000: per capita $16,734; median household $33,581; **Pop below poverty level:** 12.5%. ***Personal per capita income 2000-2003:** $19,877-$21,581.

Unemployment 2004: 3.6%. **Change from 2000:** +0.5%. **Median travel time to work:** 19.8 minutes. **Working outside county of residence:** 9.6%.

Cities with pop over 10,000: Woodward ⚒ (11,864).

Oregon

OREGON STATE INFORMATION

www.oregon.gov

Area (sq mi): 98,380.64 (land 95,996.79; water 2383.85). **Pop per sq mi:** 37.9.

Pop 2005: 3,641,056. **Pop change:** 2000-20005 +6.4%; 1990-2000 +20.4%. **Pop 2000:** 3,421,399 (White 83.5%; Black or African American 1.6%; Hispanic or Latino 8%; Asian 3%; Other 8.8%, including 1.3% American Indian/Alaska Native). **Foreign born:** 8.5%. **Median age:** 36.3.

Income 2000: per capita $20,940; median household $40,916; **Pop below poverty level:** 11.6%. ***Personal per capita income 2000-2003:** $28,097-$28,734.

Unemployment 2004: 7.3%. **Change from 2000:** +2.2%. **Median travel time to work:** 22.2 minutes. **Working outside county of residence:** 22.5%.

BAKER COUNTY

| 1995 3rd St Suite 150 | **Ph:** 541-523-8207 |
| Baker City, OR 97814 | **Fax:** 541-523-8240 |

www.bakercounty.org

On the northeastern border of OR; organized Sep 22, 1862 from Wasco County. **Name Origin:** For Col. Edward Dickinson Baker (1811-61), officer in the Civil War, U.S. representative from IL (1845-47; 1849-51), and U.S. senator from OR (1860-61).

Area (sq mi): 3088.43 (land 3068.12; water 20.32). **Pop per sq mi:** 5.3.

Pop 2005: 16,287. **State rank:** 28. **Pop change:** 2000-20005 -2.7%; 1990-2000 +9.3%. **Pop 2000:** 16,741 (White 94.6%; Black or African American 0.2%; Hispanic or Latino 2.3%; Asian 0.4%; Other 3.7%, including 1.1% American Indian/Alaska Native). **Foreign born:** 1.8%. **Median age:** 42.7.

Income 2000: per capita $15,612; median household $30,367; **Pop below poverty level:** 14.7%. ***Personal per capita income 2000-2003:** $20,317-$21,185.

Unemployment 2004: 9.1%. **Change from 2000:** +0.3%. **Median travel time to work:** 17 minutes. **Working outside county of residence:** 8.3%.

Cities with pop over 10,000: None.

BENTON COUNTY

| 408 SW Monroe Ave Suite 111 | **Ph:** 541-766-6800 |
| Corvallis, OR 97339 | **Fax:** 541-766-6893 |

www.co.benton.or.us

In west-central OR, north of Eugene; original county; organized

Dec 23, 1847 (prior to statehood). **Name Origin:** For Thomas Hart Benton (1782-1858), U.S. journalist and statesman; nicknamed 'Old Bullion' for championing the use of gold and silver currency rather than paper money.

Area (sq mi): 678.97 (land 676.46; water 2.51). **Pop per sq mi:** 116.3.

Pop 2005: 78,640. **State rank:** 12. **Pop change:** 2000-20005 +0.6%; 1990-2000 +10.4%. **Pop 2000:** 78,153 (White 86.8%; Black or African American 0.8%; Hispanic or Latino 4.7%; Asian 4.5%; Other 5.5%). **Foreign born:** 7.6%. **Median age:** 31.1.

Income 2000: per capita $21,868; median household $41,897; **Pop below poverty level:** 14.6%. ***Personal per capita income 2000-2003:** $28,923-$30,436.

Unemployment 2004: 5.4%. **Change from 2000:** +2.4%. **Median travel time to work:** 17.8 minutes. **Working outside county of residence:** 20.6%.

Cities with pop over 10,000: Corvallis 🏛 (50,380).

CLACKAMAS COUNTY

| 2051 Kaen Rd | **Ph:** 503-655-8551 |
| Oregon City, OR 97045 | **Fax:** 503-650-5688 |

www.co.clackamas.or.us

In northern OR, south of Portland; original county; organized Jul 5, 1843 (prior to statehood). **Name Origin:** For the Clackamas tribe of Chinook Indians; meaning of name is unknown.

Area (sq mi): 1879.01 (land 1868.17; water 10.83). **Pop per sq mi:** 197.2.

Pop 2005: 368,470. **State rank:** 3. **Pop change:** 2000-20005 +8.9%; 1990-2000 +21.4%. **Pop 2000:** 338,391 (White 89.1%; Black or African American 0.7%; Hispanic or Latino 4.9%; Asian 2.5%; Other 5.7%). **Foreign born:** 7.1%. **Median age:** 37.5.

Income 2000: per capita $25,973; median household $52,080; **Pop below poverty level:** 6.6%. ***Personal per capita income 2000-2003:** $36,557-$34,900.

Unemployment 2004: 6.8%. **Change from 2000:** +2.3%. **Median travel time to work:** 26.2 minutes. **Working outside county of residence:** 50.9%.

Cities with pop over 10,000: 7 (see page 38 for cities).

CLATSOP COUNTY

| 820 Exchange St 2nd Fl | **Ph:** 503-325-8511 |
| Astoria, OR 97103 | **Fax:** 503-325-9307 |

www.co.clatsop.or.us

In the northwestern corner of OR; original county; organized Jun

Clatsop County (cont'd)

22, 1844 (prior to statehood) from the Tuality district. **Name Origin:** For the Clatsop Indian tribe of Chinook Indians, whose name means 'dried salmon.'

Area (sq mi): 1084.75 (land 827.23; water 257.52). **Pop per sq mi:** 44.5.

Pop 2005: 36,798. **State rank:** 19. **Pop change:** 2000-20005 +3.3%; 1990-2000 +7%. **Pop 2000:** 35,630 (White 90.8%; Black or African American 0.5%; Hispanic or Latino 4.5%; Asian 1.2%; Other 5.1%, including 1% American Indian/Alaska Native). **Foreign born:** 4.2%. **Median age:** 40.

Income 2000: per capita $19,515; median household $36,301; **Pop below poverty level:** 13.2%. ***Personal per capita income 2000-2003:** $24,214-$25,801.

Unemployment 2004: 6.9%. **Change from 2000:** +1.7%. **Median travel time to work:** 19.5 minutes. **Working outside county of residence:** 8.7%.

Cities with pop over 10,000: None.

COLUMBIA COUNTY

County Courthouse 230 Strand St   **Ph:** 503-397-3796
Saint Helens, OR 97051   **Fax:** 503-397-7266
www.co.columbia.or.us

On the northwestern border of OR, northwest of Portland; organized Jan 16, 1854 (prior to statehood) from Washington County. **Name Origin:** For the Columbia River, which forms its northern and eastern borders.

Area (sq mi): 688.33 (land 656.72; water 31.61). **Pop per sq mi:** 73.2.

Pop 2005: 48,065. **State rank:** 17. **Pop change:** 2000-20005 +10.3%; 1990-2000 +16%. **Pop 2000:** 43,560 (White 93.1%; Black or African American 0.2%; Hispanic or Latino 2.5%; Asian 0.6%; Other 4.7%, including 1.3% American Indian/Alaska Native). **Foreign born:** 1.8%. **Median age:** 37.7.

Income 2000: per capita $20,078; median household $45,797; **Pop below poverty level:** 9.1%. ***Personal per capita income 2000-2003:** $26,750-$26,488.

Unemployment 2004: 9.2%. **Change from 2000:** +1.4%. **Median travel time to work:** 29.3 minutes. **Working outside county of residence:** 50.3%.

Cities with pop over 10,000: Saint Helens 🏛 (11,432).

COOS COUNTY

250 N Baxter St   **Ph:** 541-396-3121
Coquille, OR 97423   **Fax:** 541-396-4861
www.co.coos.or.us

On the southwestern coast of OR, southwest of Eugene; organized Dec 22, 1853 (prior to statehood) from Umpqua and Jackson counties. **Name Origin:** For the Coos Bay Indian tribe, the name being interpreted as either 'take' or 'place of pines.'

Area (sq mi): 1806.38 (land 1600.48; water 205.9). **Pop per sq mi:** 40.4.

Pop 2005: 64,711. **State rank:** 16. **Pop change:** 2000-20005 +3.1%; 1990-2000 +4.2%. **Pop 2000:** 62,779 (White 90.2%; Black or African American 0.3%; Hispanic or Latino 3.4%; Asian 0.9%; Other 6.9%, including 2.4% American Indian/Alaska Native). **Foreign born:** 2.7%. **Median age:** 43.1.

Income 2000: per capita $17,547; median household $31,542; **Pop below poverty level:** 15%. ***Personal per capita income 2000-2003:** $21,959-$24,380.

Unemployment 2004: 9.1%. **Change from 2000:** +0.9%. **Median travel time to work:** 19.9 minutes. **Working outside county of residence:** 4.9%.

Cities with pop over 10,000: Coos Bay (15,565).

CROOK COUNTY

300 NE 3rd St Rm 23   **Ph:** 541-447-6553
Prineville, OR 97754   **Fax:** 541-416-2145
www.co.crook.or.us

In central OR; organized Oct 24, 1882 from Wasco and Grant counties. **Name Origin:** For Gen. George Crook (1829-90), army officer in the OR Territory (1852-60).

Area (sq mi): 2987.41 (land 2979.38; water 8.03). **Pop per sq mi:** 7.4.

Pop 2005: 22,067. **State rank:** 25. **Pop change:** 2000-20005 +15%; 1990-2000 +35.9%. **Pop 2000:** 19,182 (White 91.4%; Black or African American 0%; Hispanic or Latino 5.6%; Asian 0.4%; Other 6.5%, including 1.3% American Indian/Alaska Native). **Foreign born:** 3.3%. **Median age:** 38.6.

Income 2000: per capita $16,899; median household $35,186; **Pop below poverty level:** 11.3%. ***Personal per capita income 2000-2003:** $20,359-$21,381.

Unemployment 2004: 8.2%. **Change from 2000:** -1.5%. **Median travel time to work:** 18.7 minutes. **Working outside county of residence:** 19.6%.

Cities with pop over 10,000: None.

CURRY COUNTY

29821 Ellensburg Ave   **Ph:** 541-247-3295
Gold Beach, OR 97444   **Fax:** 541-247-6440
www.co.curry.or.us

On the southwestern coast of OR; organized Dec 18, 1855 (prior to statehood) from Coos County. **Name Origin:** For George Law Curry (1820-78), governor of OR Territory (1853-59).

Area (sq mi): 1988.57 (land 1627.38; water 361.19). **Pop per sq mi:** 13.8.

Pop 2005: 22,427. **State rank:** 24. **Pop change:** 2000-20005 +6.1%; 1990-2000 +9.4%. **Pop 2000:** 21,137 (White 90.9%; Black or African American 0.2%; Hispanic or Latino 3.6%; Asian 0.7%; Other 6.2%, including 2.1% American Indian/Alaska Native). **Foreign born:** 3.7%. **Median age:** 48.8.

Income 2000: per capita $18,138; median household $30,117; **Pop below poverty level:** 12.2%. ***Personal per capita income 2000-2003:** $23,650-$24,228.

Unemployment 2004: 7.3%. **Change from 2000:** +1.3%. **Median travel time to work:** 14.4 minutes. **Working outside county of residence:** 9%.

*Source: Personal per capita income data are from the Bureau of Economic Analysis; per capita income data are from the Bureau of the Census.
See Introduction for explanation of differences.

Curry County (cont'd)

Cities with pop over 10,000: None.

DESCHUTES COUNTY

1300 NW Wall St Suite 200　　　　**Ph:** 541-388-6570
Bend, OR 97701　　　　　　　　**Fax:** 541-385-3202
www.co.deschutes.or.us

In central OR, east of Eugene; organized Dec 13, 1916 from Crook County. **Name Origin:** For the Deschutes River, which traverses the county; from French '[river] of the falls.'

Area (sq mi): 3054.77 (land 3018.15; water 36.61). **Pop per sq mi:** 46.8.

Pop 2005: 141,382. **State rank:** 7. **Pop change:** 2000-20005 +22.5%; 1990-2000 +53.9%. **Pop 2000:** 115,367 (White 92.9%; Black or African American 0.2%; Hispanic or Latino 3.7%; Asian 0.7%; Other 4.3%). **Foreign born:** 2.8%. **Median age:** 38.3.

Income 2000: per capita $21,767; median household $41,847; **Pop below poverty level:** 9.3%. ***Personal per capita income 2000-2003:** $26,926-$27,880.

Unemployment 2004: 6.7%. **Change from 2000:** +0.3%. **Median travel time to work:** 18.7 minutes. **Working outside county of residence:** 5.8%.

Cities with pop over 10,000: Bend ⛪ (62,937); Redmond (18,017).

DOUGLAS COUNTY

1036 SE Douglas St　　　　　　**Ph:** 541-440-4323
Roseburg, OR 97470　　　　　**Fax:** 541-440-4408
www.co.douglas.or.us

In southwestern OR, south of Eugene; organized Jan 7, 1852 (prior to statehood) from Umpqua County, which was organized in 1851 and whose remnant, after Coos County was broken off in 1855, was annexed to Douglas County in 1862. **Name Origin:** For Stephen Arnold Douglas (1813-61), U.S. orator and statesman.

Area (sq mi): 5133.83 (land 5036.62; water 97.21). **Pop per sq mi:** 20.7.

Pop 2005: 104,202. **State rank:** 9. **Pop change:** 2000-20005 +3.8%; 1990-2000 +6.1%. **Pop 2000:** 100,399 (White 91.9%; Black or African American 0.2%; Hispanic or Latino 3.3%; Asian 0.6%; Other 5.3%, including 1.5% American Indian/Alaska Native). **Foreign born:** 2.1%. **Median age:** 41.2.

Income 2000: per capita $16,581; median household $33,223; **Pop below poverty level:** 13.1%. ***Personal per capita income 2000-2003:** $22,650-$24,357.

Unemployment 2004: 9.4%. **Change from 2000:** +0.4%. **Median travel time to work:** 20 minutes. **Working outside county of residence:** 6.1%.

Cities with pop over 10,000: Roseburg ⛪ (20,447).

GILLIAM COUNTY

221 S Oregon St　　　　　　　**Ph:** 541-384-2311
Condon, OR 97823　　　　　　**Fax:** 541-384-2166

On the central northern border of OR; organized Feb 25, 1885 from Wasco County. **Name Origin:** For Col. Cornelius Gilliam

(1798-1848), veteran of Indian wars and former county official in MT.

Area (sq mi): 1222.84 (land 1204.07; water 18.77). **Pop per sq mi:** 1.5.

Pop 2005: 1,794. **State rank:** 34. **Pop change:** 2000-20005 -6.3%; 1990-2000 +11.5%. **Pop 2000:** 1,915 (White 96%; Black or African American 0.2%; Hispanic or Latino 1.8%; Asian 0.2%; Other 2.8%). **Foreign born:** 1.7%. **Median age:** 42.8.

Income 2000: per capita $17,659; median household $33,611; **Pop below poverty level:** 9.1%. ***Personal per capita income 2000-2003:** $18,851-$20,832.

Unemployment 2004: 6.2%. **Change from 2000:** +0.4%. **Median travel time to work:** 18.1 minutes. **Working outside county of residence:** 11.3%.

Cities with pop over 10,000: None.

GRANT COUNTY

201 S Humbolt St Suite 290　　　**Ph:** 541-575-1675
Canyon City, OR 97820　　　　**Fax:** 541-575-2248
www.grantcounty.cc

In northeastern OR; organized Oct 14, 1864. **Name Origin:** For Ulysses Simpson Grant (1822-85), Civil War general and eighteenth U.S. president.

Area (sq mi): 4529.32 (land 4528.6; water 0.71). **Pop per sq mi:** 1.6.

Pop 2005: 7,297. **State rank:** 31. **Pop change:** 2000-20005 -8%; 1990-2000 +1%. **Pop 2000:** 7,935 (White 94.6%; Black or African American 0.1%; Hispanic or Latino 2.1%; Asian 0.2%; Other 4%, including 1.6% American Indian/Alaska Native). **Foreign born:** 1.4%. **Median age:** 41.7.

Income 2000: per capita $16,794; median household $32,560; **Pop below poverty level:** 13.7%. ***Personal per capita income 2000-2003:** $21,358-$23,828.

Unemployment 2004: 10.2%. **Change from 2000:** -0.1%. **Median travel time to work:** 18.7 minutes. **Working outside county of residence:** 5.9%.

Cities with pop over 10,000: None.

HARNEY COUNTY

450 N Buena Vista Ave　　　　**Ph:** 541-573-6641
Burns, OR 97720　　　　　　**Fax:** 541-573-8370
www.co.harney.or.us

In southeastern OR; organized Feb 25, 1889 from Grant County. **Name Origin:** For Gen. William Selby Harney (1800-89), officer in the Black Hawk War, Seminole War, and Mexican-American War; commander of department of OR who was instrumental in opening eastern OR for settlement.

Area (sq mi): 10,226.49 (land 10,134.33; water 92.16). **Pop per sq mi:** 0.7.

Pop 2005: 6,898. **State rank:** 33. **Pop change:** 2000-20005 -9.3%; 1990-2000 +7.8%. **Pop 2000:** 7,609 (White 89.7%; Black or African American 0.1%; Hispanic or Latino 4.2%; Asian 0.5%; Other 7.5%, including 4% American Indian/Alaska Native). **Foreign born:** 2.1%. **Median age:** 39.8.

Harney County (cont'd)

Income 2000: per capita $16,159; median household $30,957; **Pop below poverty level:** 11.8%. ***Personal per capita income 2000-2003:** $21,140-$22,823.

Unemployment 2004: 9.9%. **Change from 2000:** -4.2%. **Median travel time to work:** 14.8 minutes. **Working outside county of residence:** 2.4%.

Cities with pop over 10,000: None.

HOOD RIVER COUNTY

601 State St   **Ph:** 541-386-3970
Hood River, OR 97031   **Fax:** 541-386-9392
www.co.hood-river.or.us

On northwestern border of OR, east of Portland; organized Jun 23, 1908 from Wasco County. **Name Origin:** For the river and the town; the river was named for either Samuel Hood (1724-1816), or for Arthur William Acland Hood (1824-1901), admirals in the British Navy.

Area (sq mi): 533.56 (land 522.35; water 11.21). **Pop per sq mi:** 40.7.

Pop 2005: 21,284. **State rank:** 26. **Pop change:** 2000-20005 +4.3%; 1990-2000 +20.8%. **Pop 2000:** 20,411 (White 70.7%; Black or African American 0.6%; Hispanic or Latino 25%; Asian 1.5%; Other 19.1%, including 1.1% American Indian/Alaska Native). **Foreign born:** 16.4%. **Median age:** 35.3.

Income 2000: per capita $17,877; median household $38,326; **Pop below poverty level:** 14.2%. ***Personal per capita income 2000-2003:** $22,815-$23,676.

Unemployment 2004: 7.5%. **Change from 2000:** -1.7%. **Median travel time to work:** 19.1 minutes. **Working outside county of residence:** 16.2%.

Cities with pop over 10,000: None.

JACKSON COUNTY

10 S Oakdale Ave Rm 214 Courthouse   **Ph:** 541-774-6035
Medford, OR 97501   **Fax:** 541-774-6455
www.co.jackson.or.us

On the southwestern border of OR; organized Jan 12, 1852 (prior to statehood) from the original Yamhill and Champoeg districts. **Name Origin:** For Andrew Jackson (1767-1845), seventh U.S. president.

Area (sq mi): 2801.77 (land 2785.19; water 16.57). **Pop per sq mi:** 70.1.

Pop 2005: 195,322. **State rank:** 6. **Pop change:** 2000-20005 +7.8%; 1990-2000 +23.8%. **Pop 2000:** 181,269 (White 88.7%; Black or African American 0.4%; Hispanic or Latino 6.7%; Asian 0.9%; Other 7.1%, including 1.1% American Indian/Alaska Native). **Foreign born:** 4.9%. **Median age:** 39.2.

Income 2000: per capita $19,498; median household $36,461; **Pop below poverty level:** 12.5%. ***Personal per capita income 2000-2003:** $24,914-$26,617.

Unemployment 2004: 7.1%. **Change from 2000:** +0.8%. **Median travel time to work:** 18.9 minutes. **Working outside county of residence:** 5.2%.

Cities with pop over 10,000: Medford 🏛 (68,099); Ashland (20,755); Central Point (15,152).

JEFFERSON COUNTY

66 SE 'D' St Suite C   **Ph:** 541-475-4451
Madras, OR 97741   **Fax:** 541-325-5018

In north-central OR; organized Dec 12, 1914 from Crook County. **Name Origin:** For Mount Jefferson on the county's western border, itself named for Thomas Jefferson (1743-1826), third U.S. president.

Area (sq mi): 1791.17 (land 1780.78; water 10.38). **Pop per sq mi:** 11.3.

Pop 2005: 20,100. **State rank:** 27. **Pop change:** 2000-20005 +5.7%; 1990-2000 +39%. **Pop 2000:** 19,009 (White 64.9%; Black or African American 0.3%; Hispanic or Latino 17.7%; Asian 0.3%; Other 30.4%, including 15.7% American Indian/Alaska Native). **Foreign born:** 9.9%. **Median age:** 34.8.

Income 2000: per capita $15,675; median household $35,853; **Pop below poverty level:** 14.6%. ***Personal per capita income 2000-2003:** $19,841-$20,670.

Unemployment 2004: 6.6%. **Change from 2000:** -1%. **Median travel time to work:** 20.9 minutes. **Working outside county of residence:** 24.4%.

Cities with pop over 10,000: None.

JOSEPHINE COUNTY

500 NW 6th St   **Ph:** 541-474-5240
Grants Pass, OR 97526   **Fax:** 541-474-5246
www.co.josephine.or.us

On the southwestern border of OR, west of Jackson; organized Jan 22, 1856 from Jackson County. **Name Origin:** For either Josephine Rollins (1835-c.1911), daughter of the leader of a wagon train bound for California and first white woman to settle in the county, or for Josephine Creek, which was also named in her honor.

Area (sq mi): 1641.63 (land 1639.59; water 2.04). **Pop per sq mi:** 49.3.

Pop 2005: 80,761. **State rank:** 11. **Pop change:** 2000-20005 +6.6%; 1990-2000 +20.9%. **Pop 2000:** 75,726 (White 91.4%; Black or African American 0.3%; Hispanic or Latino 4.3%; Asian 0.6%; Other 5.3%, including 1.3% American Indian/Alaska Native). **Foreign born:** 3.1%. **Median age:** 43.1.

Income 2000: per capita $17,234; median household $31,229; **Pop below poverty level:** 15%. ***Personal per capita income 2000-2003:** $21,434-$22,506.

Unemployment 2004: 8.2%. **Change from 2000:** -0.3%. **Median travel time to work:** 20 minutes. **Working outside county of residence:** 14.9%.

Cities with pop over 10,000: Grants Pass 🏛 (27,195).

KLAMATH COUNTY

305 Main St   **Ph:** 541-883-5134
Klamath Falls, OR 97601   **Fax:** 541-883-5165
www.co.klamath.or.us

On central southern border of OR; organized Oct 17, 1882 from Lake County. **Name Origin:** For the Klamath Indians; the name

Source: Personal per capita income data are from the Bureau of Economic Analysis; per capita income data are from the Bureau of the Census. See Introduction for explanation of differences.

Klamath County (cont'd)

is probably from Chinook *tlamatl*, their name for the sister tribe of the Modocs; the meaning is unknown. Also spelled *Claminitt* and *Clammittee*.

Area (sq mi): 6135.75 (land 5944.19; water 191.56). **Pop per sq mi:** 11.1.

Pop 2005: 66,192. **State rank:** 15. **Pop change:** 2000-20005 +3.0%; 1990-2000 +10.5%. **Pop 2000:** 63,775 (White 84.1%; Black or African American 0.6%; Hispanic or Latino 7.8%; Asian 0.8%; Other 11.2%, including 4.2% American Indian/Alaska Native). **Foreign born:** 4.8%. **Median age:** 38.2.

Income 2000: per capita $16,719; median household $31,537; **Pop below poverty level:** 16.8%. ***Personal per capita income 2000-2003:** $21,305-$23,216.

Unemployment 2004: 9.5%. **Change from 2000:** +0%. **Median travel time to work:** 17.2 minutes. **Working outside county of residence:** 4%.

Cities with pop over 10,000: Klamath Falls ⚖ (19,694).

LAKE COUNTY
513 Center St
Lakeview, OR 97630
www.lakecountyor.org

Ph: 541-947-6006
Fax: 541-947-6015

On central southern border of OR; organized Oct 24, 1874 from Jackson County. **Name Origin:** For the many lakes in the area.

Area (sq mi): 8358.47 (land 8135.75; water 222.71). **Pop per sq mi:** 0.9.

Pop 2005: 7,313. **State rank:** 30. **Pop change:** 2000-20005 -1.5%; 1990-2000 +3.3%. **Pop 2000:** 7,422 (White 89.2%; Black or African American 0.1%; Hispanic or Latino 5.4%; Asian 0.7%; Other 8.2%, including 2.4% American Indian/Alaska Native). **Foreign born:** 3.4%. **Median age:** 42.7.

Income 2000: per capita $16,136; median household $29,506; **Pop below poverty level:** 16.1%. ***Personal per capita income 2000-2003:** $21,334-$22,300.

Unemployment 2004: 9.9%. **Change from 2000:** -0.5%. **Median travel time to work:** 16.1 minutes. **Working outside county of residence:** 5.7%.

Cities with pop over 10,000: None.

LANE COUNTY
125 E 8th Ave
Eugene, OR 97401
www.co.lane.or.us

Ph: 541-682-4203
Fax: 541-682-4616

On central-western coast of OR; organized Jan 28, 1851 (prior to statehood) from Linn and Benton counties. **Name Origin:** For Gen. Joseph Lane (1801-81). OR territorial governor (1849-50; 1853) and first U.S. senator from OR (1859-61).

Area (sq mi): 4721.79 (land 4554; water 167.79). **Pop per sq mi:** 73.6.

Pop 2005: 335,180. **State rank:** 4. **Pop change:** 2000-20005 +3.8%; 1990-2000 +14.2%. **Pop 2000:** 322,959 (White 88.6%; Black or African American 0.8%; Hispanic or Latino 4.6%; Asian 2%; Other

6.5%, including 1.1% American Indian/Alaska Native). **Foreign born:** 4.9%. **Median age:** 36.6.

Income 2000: per capita $19,681; median household $36,942; **Pop below poverty level:** 14.4%. ***Personal per capita income 2000-2003:** $25,500-$26,344.

Unemployment 2004: 7.4%. **Change from 2000:** +0.6%. **Median travel time to work:** 19.9 minutes. **Working outside county of residence:** 4.1%.

Cities with pop over 10,000: Eugene ⚖ (142,681); Springfield (55,048).

LINCOLN COUNTY
225 W Olive St Rm 201
Newport, OR 97365
www.co.lincoln.or.us

Ph: 541-265-4121
Fax: 541-265-4114

On central western coast of OR; organized Feb 20, 1893 from Benton and Polk counties. **Name Origin:** For Abraham Lincoln (1809-65), sixteenth U.S. president.

Area (sq mi): 1193.79 (land 979.57; water 214.23). **Pop per sq mi:** 47.

Pop 2005: 45,994. **State rank:** 18. **Pop change:** 2000-20005 +3.4%; 1990-2000 +14.4%. **Pop 2000:** 44,479 (White 88.3%; Black or African American 0.3%; Hispanic or Latino 4.8%; Asian 0.9%; Other 8.2%, including 3.1% American Indian/Alaska Native). **Foreign born:** 4.2%. **Median age:** 44.1.

Income 2000: per capita $18,692; median household $32,769; **Pop below poverty level:** 13.9%. ***Personal per capita income 2000-2003:** $24,441-$26,672.

Unemployment 2004: 8.3%. **Change from 2000:** +1.4%. **Median travel time to work:** 20.5 minutes. **Working outside county of residence:** 7.4%.

Cities with pop over 10,000: None.

LINN COUNTY
300 4th Ave SW
Albany, OR 97321
www.co.linn.or.us

Ph: 541-967-3831
Fax: 541-926-5109

In northwest OR, northeast of Eugene; original county; organized 1847 (prior to statehood). **Name Origin:** For Lewis Fields Linn (1795-1843), physician and U.S. senator from MO (1833-43); author of the Donation Land Law, which gave free land in the west to settlers.

Area (sq mi): 2310.15 (land 2292.18; water 17.97). **Pop per sq mi:** 47.5.

Pop 2005: 108,914. **State rank:** 8. **Pop change:** 2000-20005 +5.7%; 1990-2000 +13%. **Pop 2000:** 103,069 (White 91.2%; Black or African American 0.3%; Hispanic or Latino 4.4%; Asian 0.8%; Other 5.7%, including 1.3% American Indian/Alaska Native). **Foreign born:** 3.5%. **Median age:** 37.4.

Income 2000: per capita $17,633; median household $37,518; **Pop below poverty level:** 11.4%. ***Personal per capita income 2000-2003:** $22,590-$23,734.

Unemployment 2004: 9.3%. **Change from 2000:** +1%. **Median travel time to work:** 22.2 minutes. **Working outside county of residence:** 28.4%.

⚖ *County Seat*

Linn County (cont'd)

Cities with pop over 10,000: Albany ⚖ (43,889); Lebanon (13,515).

MALHEUR COUNTY

251 B St W   **Ph:** 541-473-5151
Vale, OR 97918   **Fax:** 541-473-5523
www.malheurco.org

On eastern border of OR; organized Feb 17, 1887 from Baker county. **Name Origin:** For the Malheur River, which flows through it; from French 'misfortune', given to the river by trappers who were attacked by Indians and lost all their furs.

Area (sq mi): 9929.99 (land 9887.09; water 42.9). **Pop per sq mi:** 3.2.

Pop 2005: 31,330. **State rank:** 20. **Pop change:** 2000-20005 -0.9%; 1990-2000 +21.4%. **Pop 2000:** 31,615 (White 68.8%; Black or African American 1.2%; Hispanic or Latino 25.6%; Asian 2%; Other 21.1%, including 1% American Indian/Alaska Native). **Foreign born:** 8.2%. **Median age:** 34.

Income 2000: per capita $13,895; median household $30,241; **Pop below poverty level:** 18.6%. ***Personal per capita income 2000-2003:** $19,025-$18,857.

Unemployment 2004: 10.1%. **Change from 2000:** +1.1%. **Median travel time to work:** 17.7 minutes. **Working outside county of residence:** 15.8%.

Cities with pop over 10,000: Ontario (11,152).

MARION COUNTY

100 High St NE Rm 1331   **Ph:** 503-588-5225
Salem, OR 97301   **Fax:** 503-373-4408
www.co.marion.or.us

In northwest OR, south of Portland; original county; organized as Champoick County Jul 5, 1843 (prior to statehood); name changed 1849. **Name Origin:** For Gen. Francis Marion (c. 1732-95), SC soldier and legislator, known as 'The Swamp Fox' for his tactics during the Revolutionary War.

Area (sq mi): 1194.13 (land 1183.95; water 10.18). **Pop per sq mi:** 257.8.

Pop 2005: 305,265. **State rank:** 5. **Pop change:** 2000-20005 +7.2%; 1990-2000 +24.7%. **Pop 2000:** 284,834 (White 76.5%; Black or African American 0.9%; Hispanic or Latino 17.1%; Asian 1.8%; Other 15.8%, including 1.4% American Indian/Alaska Native). **Foreign born:** 12.6%. **Median age:** 33.7.

Income 2000: per capita $18,408; median household $40,314; **Pop below poverty level:** 13.5%. ***Personal per capita income 2000-2003:** $24,439-$24,955.

Unemployment 2004: 7.6%. **Change from 2000:** +1.2%. **Median travel time to work:** 23.5 minutes. **Working outside county of residence:** 19.9%.

Cities with pop over 10,000: Salem ⚖ (146,120); Keizer (34,414); Woodburn (22,147).

MORROW COUNTY

100 Court St   **Ph:** 541-676-9061
Heppner, OR 97836   **Fax:** 541-676-9876
morrowcountyoregon.com

On central northern border of OR; organized Feb 16, 1885 from Umatilla County. **Name Origin:** For Jackson L. Morrow (1827-99), member of the first state legislature.

Area (sq mi): 2048.53 (land 2032.38; water 16.15). **Pop per sq mi:** 5.7.

Pop 2005: 11,666. **State rank:** 29. **Pop change:** 2000-20005 +6.1%; 1990-2000 +44.2%. **Pop 2000:** 10,995 (White 72%; Black or African American 0.1%; Hispanic or Latino 24.4%; Asian 0.4%; Other 23.1%, including 1.4% American Indian/Alaska Native). **Foreign born:** 14.5%. **Median age:** 33.3.

Income 2000: per capita $15,802; median household $37,521; **Pop below poverty level:** 14.8%. ***Personal per capita income 2000-2003:** $20,457-$22,891.

Unemployment 2004: 8.2%. **Change from 2000:** -2.6%. **Median travel time to work:** 23 minutes. **Working outside county of residence:** 35.3%.

Cities with pop over 10,000: None.

MULTNOMAH COUNTY

1021 SW 4th Ave   **Ph:** 503-988-3957
Portland, OR 97204   **Fax:** 503-988-5773
www.co.multnomah.or.us

On central northern border of OR; organized Dec 22, 1854 (prior to statehood) from Clackamas and Washington counties. The smallest county in OR by size and largest by population. **Name Origin:** For the Multnomah Indian village on Sauvie Island; Lewis and Clark applied the name to all local Indians. From *nemathlonamaq*, probably meaning 'downriver.'

Area (sq mi): 465.65 (land 435.23; water 30.42). **Pop per sq mi:** 1546.1.

Pop 2005: 672,906. **State rank:** 1. **Pop change:** 2000-20005 +1.9%; 1990-2000 +13.1%. **Pop 2000:** 660,486 (White 76.5%; Black or African American 5.7%; Hispanic or Latino 7.5%; Asian 5.7%; Other 9.5%, including 1% American Indian/Alaska Native). **Foreign born:** 12.7%. **Median age:** 34.9.

Income 2000: per capita $22,606; median household $41,278; **Pop below poverty level:** 12.7%. ***Personal per capita income 2000-2003:** $32,328-$34,017.

Unemployment 2004: 7.6%. **Change from 2000:** +1.3%. **Median travel time to work:** 23.8 minutes. **Working outside county of residence:** 21.6%.

Cities with pop over 10,000: Portland ⚖ (533,492); Gresham (95,376); Troutdale (14,711).

POLK COUNTY

850 Main St   **Ph:** 503-623-9217
Dallas, OR 97338   **Fax:** 503-623-0717
www.co.polk.or.us

In northwest OR, west of Salem; original county; organized Dec 22, 1845 (prior to statehood) from the Yamhill district. **Name Origin:** For James Knox Polk (1795-1849), eleventh U.S. president.

---

*Source: Personal per capita income data are from the Bureau of Economic Analysis; per capita income data are from the Bureau of the Census. See Introduction for explanation of differences.

Polk County (cont'd)

Area (sq mi): 744.15 (land 741.03; water 3.12). **Pop per sq mi:** 94.9.

Pop 2005: 70,295. **State rank:** 14. **Pop change:** 2000-20005 +12.7%; 1990-2000 +25.9%. **Pop 2000:** 62,380 (White 85.6%; Black or African American 0.4%; Hispanic or Latino 8.8%; Asian 1.1%; Other 9.2%, including 1.8% American Indian/Alaska Native). **Foreign born:** 6.5%. **Median age:** 36.5.

Income 2000: per capita $19,282; median household $42,311; **Pop below poverty level:** 11.5%. ***Personal per capita income 2000-2003:** $24,497-$25,083.

Unemployment 2004: 6.6%. **Change from 2000:** +0.9%. **Median travel time to work:** 23.4 minutes. **Working outside county of residence:** 56.2%.

Cities with pop over 10,000: Dallas ⚏ (13,461).

SHERMAN COUNTY
500 Court St   **Ph:** 541-565-3606
Moro, OR 97039   **Fax:** 541-565-3312
www.sherman-county.com

On central northern border of OR; organized Feb 25, 1889 from Wasco County. **Name Origin:** For Gen. William Tecumseh Sherman (1820-91), officer in the Mexican-American War and the Civil War, remembered for his 'march to the sea' through the South.

Area (sq mi): 831.2 (land 823.21; water 8). **Pop per sq mi:** 2.1.

Pop 2005: 1,749. **State rank:** 35. **Pop change:** 2000-20005 -9.6%; 1990-2000 +0.8%. **Pop 2000:** 1,934 (White 92.1%; Black or African American 0.2%; Hispanic or Latino 4.9%; Asian 0.5%; Other 5.8%, including 1.4% American Indian/Alaska Native). **Foreign born:** 2.5%. **Median age:** 41.8.

Income 2000: per capita $17,448; median household $35,142; **Pop below poverty level:** 14.6%. ***Personal per capita income 2000-2003:** $19,055-$18,985.

Unemployment 2004: 9.7%. **Change from 2000:** -1.3%. **Median travel time to work:** 20.6 minutes. **Working outside county of residence:** 25.1%.

Cities with pop over 10,000: None.

TILLAMOOK COUNTY
201 Laurel Ave   **Ph:** 503-842-3403
Tillamook, OR 97141   **Fax:** 503-842-1384
www.co.tillamook.or.us

On the northwestern coast of OR, west of Portland; organized Dec 15, 1853 (prior to statehood) from Clatsop and Yamhill counties. **Name Origin:** For the Tillamook Indians, from Chinook 'people of Nekelim,' because the tribe lived on the Nehalem and Salmon rivers.

Area (sq mi): 1332.78 (land 1102.15; water 230.63). **Pop per sq mi:** 22.9.

Pop 2005: 25,277. **State rank:** 21. **Pop change:** 2000-20005 +4.2%; 1990-2000 +12.5%. **Pop 2000:** 24,262 (White 91%; Black or African American 0.2%; Hispanic or Latino 5.1%; Asian 0.6%; Other 5.3%, including 1.2% American Indian/Alaska Native). **Foreign born:** 4.2%. **Median age:** 43.5.

Income 2000: per capita $19,052; median household $34,269; **Pop below poverty level:** 11.4%. ***Personal per capita income 2000-2003:** $23,739-$25,210.

Unemployment 2004: 7.1%. **Change from 2000:** +1.6%. **Median travel time to work:** 20.7 minutes. **Working outside county of residence:** 11.7%.

Cities with pop over 10,000: None.

UMATILLA COUNTY
216 SE 4th St   **Ph:** 541-278-6236
Pendleton, OR 97801   **Fax:** 541-278-6345
www.co.umatilla.or.us

On northeastern border of OR; organized Sep 27, 1862 from Wasco County. **Name Origin:** For the Umatilla River, which runs through the county; the river is itself named for the Umatilla Indian tribe. The meaning of the name is disputed: possibly 'water rippling over sand.'

Area (sq mi): 3231.25 (land 3215.26; water 15.99). **Pop per sq mi:** 23.

Pop 2005: 73,878. **State rank:** 13. **Pop change:** 2000-20005 +4.7%; 1990-2000 +19.1%. **Pop 2000:** 70,548 (White 77.5%; Black or African American 0.8%; Hispanic or Latino 16.1%; Asian 0.8%; Other 16.5%, including 3.4% American Indian/Alaska Native). **Foreign born:** 8.4%. **Median age:** 34.6.

Income 2000: per capita $16,410; median household $36,249; **Pop below poverty level:** 12.7%. ***Personal per capita income 2000-2003:** $21,421-$23,011.

Unemployment 2004: 8.2%. **Change from 2000:** +1%. **Median travel time to work:** 17 minutes. **Working outside county of residence:** 12.3%.

Cities with pop over 10,000: Pendleton ⚏ (16,605); Hermiston (14,439).

UNION COUNTY
1106 K Ave   **Ph:** 541-963-1001
La Grande, OR 97850   **Fax:** 541-963-1079
www.union-county.org

In northeastern OR; organized Oct 14, 1864 from Baker County. **Name Origin:** For the town of Union, named in 1862 in support of the Union forces in the Civil War.

Area (sq mi): 2038.55 (land 2036.55; water 2). **Pop per sq mi:** 12.

Pop 2005: 24,540. **State rank:** 22. **Pop change:** 2000-20005 +0%; 1990-2000 +3.9%. **Pop 2000:** 24,530 (White 93.1%; Black or African American 0.5%; Hispanic or Latino 2.4%; Asian 0.9%; Other 4.3%). **Foreign born:** 2.7%. **Median age:** 37.7.

Income 2000: per capita $16,907; median household $33,738; **Pop below poverty level:** 13.8%. ***Personal per capita income 2000-2003:** $22,771-$24,463.

Unemployment 2004: 7.4%. **Change from 2000:** +1.6%. **Median travel time to work:** 16.3 minutes. **Working outside county of residence:** 6.2%.

Cities with pop over 10,000: La Grande ⚏ (12,371).

⚏ *County Seat*

587

WALLOWA COUNTY

101 S River St Rm 100   **Ph:** 541-426-4543
Enterprise, OR 97828   **Fax:** 541-426-5901
www.co.wallowa.or.us

On northeastern border of OR; organized Feb 11, 1887 from Union County. **Name Origin:** A Nez Perce word for the 'tripod' used to support netting to catch fish.

Area (sq mi): 3151.69 (land 3145.34; water 6.36). **Pop per sq mi:** 2.2.

Pop 2005: 7,014. **State rank:** 32. **Pop change:** 2000-20005 -2.9%; 1990-2000 +4.6%. **Pop 2000:** 7,226 (White 95.7%; Black or African American 0%; Hispanic or Latino 1.7%; Asian 0.2%; Other 3.2%). **Foreign born:** 0.8%. **Median age:** 44.4.

Income 2000: per capita $17,276; median household $32,129; **Pop below poverty level:** 14%. ***Personal per capita income 2000-2003:** $21,891-$23,319.

Unemployment 2004: 9.1%. **Change from 2000:** -1.7%. **Median travel time to work:** 17.5 minutes. **Working outside county of residence:** 4.9%.

Cities with pop over 10,000: None.

WASCO COUNTY

511 Washington St   **Ph:** 541-506-2500
The Dalles, OR 97058   **Fax:** 541-298-3607
www.co.wasco.or.us

On the central northern border of OR; organized Jan 11, 1854 (prior to statehood), from the original Champoeg district; it covered all of Oregon east of the Cascade Range, most of Idaho, and parts of MT and WY. **Name Origin:** For the Wasco or Wascopam Indian tribe of Chinookan linguistic stock; the name means 'cup' or 'bowl.'

Area (sq mi): 2395.32 (land 2381.05; water 14.28). **Pop per sq mi:** 9.9.

Pop 2005: 23,593. **State rank:** 23. **Pop change:** 2000-20005 -0.8%; 1990-2000 +9.7%. **Pop 2000:** 23,791 (White 83.9%; Black or African American 0.3%; Hispanic or Latino 9.3%; Asian 0.8%; Other 12.3%, including 3.8% American Indian/Alaska Native). **Foreign born:** 6.2%. **Median age:** 39.9.

Income 2000: per capita $17,195; median household $35,959; **Pop below poverty level:** 12.9%. ***Personal per capita income 2000-2003:** $23,663-$23,516.

Unemployment 2004: 8.9%. **Change from 2000:** -1.2%. **Median travel time to work:** 18.6 minutes. **Working outside county of residence:** 18.7%.

Cities with pop over 10,000: City of The Dalles (11,948).

WASHINGTON COUNTY

155 N 1st Ave Rm 340   **Ph:** 503-846-8747
Hillsboro, OR 97124   **Fax:** 503-846-8636
www.co.washington.or.us

In northwest OR, west of Portland; original county; organized as Tuality County Jul 5, 1843 (prior to statehood); name changed Sep 3, 1849. **Name Origin:** For George Washington (1732-99), American patriot and first U.S. president.

Area (sq mi): 726.38 (land 723.75; water 2.63). **Pop per sq mi:** 690.6.

Pop 2005: 499,794. **State rank:** 2. **Pop change:** 2000-20005 +12.2%; 1990-2000 +42.9%. **Pop 2000:** 445,342 (White 77.7%; Black or African American 1.1%; Hispanic or Latino 11.2%; Asian 6.7%; Other 10.1%). **Foreign born:** 14.2%. **Median age:** 33.

Income 2000: per capita $24,969; median household $52,122; **Pop below poverty level:** 7.4%. ***Personal per capita income 2000-2003:** $33,178-$31,675.

Unemployment 2004: 6.3%. **Change from 2000:** +1%. **Median travel time to work:** 23.7 minutes. **Working outside county of residence:** 32.2%.

Cities with pop over 10,000: 7 (see page 38 for cities).

WHEELER COUNTY

701 Adams St   **Ph:** 541-763-2400
Fossil, OR 97830   **Fax:** 541-763-2026
www.wheelercounty-oregon.com

In north-central OR; organized Feb 17, 1899 from Crook, Gilliam, and Grant counties. **Name Origin:** For Henry H. Wheeler (1826-1915), who operated the first stage line through the county and later became a prominent rancher in the area.

Area (sq mi): 1715.46 (land 1714.92; water 0.55). **Pop per sq mi:** 0.8.

Pop 2005: 1,455. **State rank:** 36. **Pop change:** 2000-20005 -5.9%; 1990-2000 +10.8%. **Pop 2000:** 1,547 (White 92.5%; Black or African American 0.1%; Hispanic or Latino 5.1%; Asian 0.3%; Other 6.3%). **Foreign born:** 2.1%. **Median age:** 48.1.

Income 2000: per capita $15,884; median household $28,750; **Pop below poverty level:** 15.6%. ***Personal per capita income 2000-2003:** $19,318-$21,372.

Unemployment 2004: 7.9%. **Change from 2000:** -1.4%. **Median travel time to work:** 30.8 minutes. **Working outside county of residence:** 20.4%.

Cities with pop over 10,000: None.

YAMHILL COUNTY

535 NE 5th St   **Ph:** 503-434-7518
McMinnville, OR 97128   **Fax:** 503-434-7520
www.co.yamhill.or.us

In northwest OR, southwest of Portland; original county; organized 1843 (prior to statehood). **Name Origin:** For the Yamhela or Yamhill Indian tribe; meaning of name is unknown.

Area (sq mi): 718.36 (land 715.56; water 2.79). **Pop per sq mi:** 128.8.

Pop 2005: 92,196. **State rank:** 10. **Pop change:** 2000-20005 +8.5%; 1990-2000 +29.7%. **Pop 2000:** 84,992 (White 84.3%; Black or African American 0.8%; Hispanic or Latino 10.6%; Asian 1.1%; Other 9.1%, including 1.5% American Indian/Alaska Native). **Foreign born:** 7.6%. **Median age:** 34.1.

*Source: Personal per capita income data are from the Bureau of Economic Analysis; per capita income data are from the Bureau of the Census. See Introduction for explanation of differences.

Yamhill County (cont'd)

Income 2000: per capita $18,951; median household $44,111; **Pop below poverty level:** 9.2%. ***Personal per capita income 2000-2003:** $24,363-$25,479.

Unemployment 2004: 7.4%. **Change from 2000:** +1.5%. **Median travel time to work:** 24.8 minutes. **Working outside county of residence:** 36.3%

Cities with pop over 10,000: McMinnville 🏛 (28,973); Newberg (20,280).

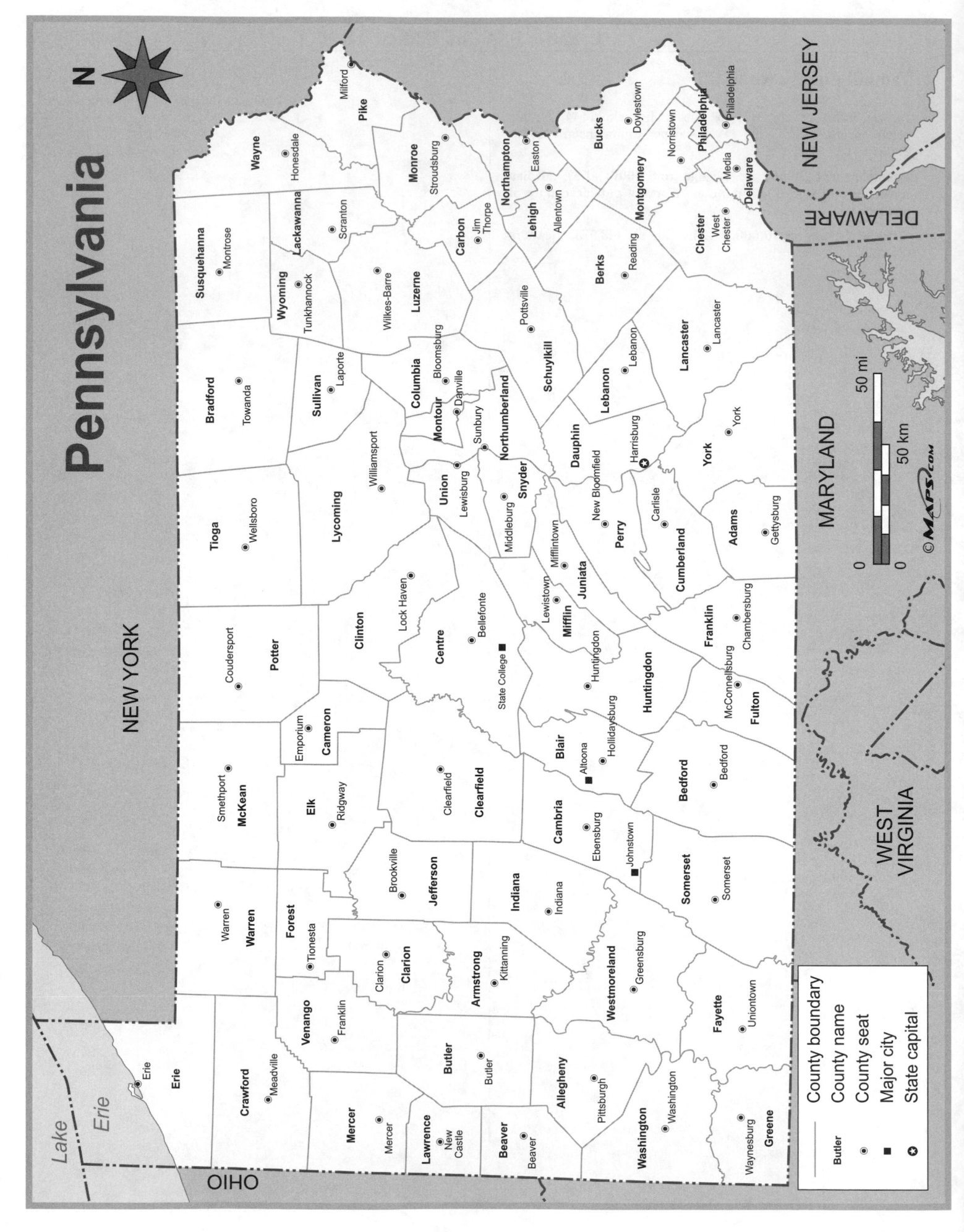

Pennsylvania

PENNSYLVANIA STATE INFORMATION
www.state.pa.us   **Ph:** 717-787-2121

Area (sq mi): 46,055.24 (land 44,816.61; water 1238.63). **Pop per sq mi:** 277.3.

Pop 2005: 12,429,616. **Pop change:** 2000-20005 +1.2%; 1990-2000 +3.4%. **Pop 2000:** 12,281,054 (White 84.1%; Black or African American 10%; Hispanic or Latino 3.2%; Asian 1.8%; Other 2.8%). **Foreign born:** 4.1%. **Median age:** 38.

Income 2000: per capita $20,880; median household $40,106; **Pop below poverty level:** 11%. *Personal per capita income 2000-2003: $29,695-$31,911.

Unemployment 2004: 5.4%. **Change from 2000:** +1.2%. **Median travel time to work:** 25.2 minutes. **Working outside county of residence:** 27.6%.

ADAMS COUNTY
111-117 Baltimore St   **Ph:** 717-334-6781
Gettysburg, PA 17325   **Fax:** 717-334-2091
www.adamscounty.us

On central southern border of PA, southwest of Harrisburg; organized Jan 22, 1800 from York County. **Name Origin:** For John Adams (1735-1826), second U.S. president.

Area (sq mi): 521.52 (land 520.01; water 1.51). **Pop per sq mi:** 191.8.

Pop 2005: 99,749. **State rank:** 31. **Pop change:** 2000-20005 +9.3%; 1990-2000 +16.6%. **Pop 2000:** 91,292 (White 93.7%; Black or African American 1.2%; Hispanic or Latino 3.6%; Asian 0.5%; Other 2.9%). **Foreign born:** 3.4%. **Median age:** 37.

Income 2000: per capita $18,577; median household $42,704; **Pop below poverty level:** 7.1%. *Personal per capita income 2000-2003: $25,193-$27,110.

Unemployment 2004: 4%. **Change from 2000:** -0.1%. **Median travel time to work:** 25.1 minutes. **Working outside county of residence:** 46.1%.

Cities with pop over 10,000: None.

ALLEGHENY COUNTY
436 Grant St County Courthouse Rm 119   **Ph:** 412-350-5300
Pittsburgh, PA 15219   **Fax:** 412-350-3581
info.co.allegheny.pa.us

In southwestern PA; organized Sep 24, 1788 from Westmoreland and Washington counties. **Name Origin:** For the Allegheny River.

Area (sq mi): 744.71 (land 730.17; water 14.54). **Pop per sq mi:** 1692.5.

Pop 2005: 1,235,841. **State rank:** 2. **Pop change:** 2000-20005 -3.6%; 1990-2000 -4.1%. **Pop 2000:** 1,281,666 (White 83.8%; Black or African American 12.4%; Hispanic or Latino 0.9%; Asian 1.7%; Other 1.5%). **Foreign born:** 3.8%. **Median age:** 39.6.

Income 2000: per capita $22,491; median household $38,329; **Pop below poverty level:** 11.2%. *Personal per capita income 2000-2003: $34,613-$37,475.

Unemployment 2004: 5.4%. **Change from 2000:** +1.6%. **Median travel time to work:** 25.3 minutes. **Working outside county of residence:** 7.8%.

Cities with pop over 10,000: 11 (see page 38 for cities).

ARMSTRONG COUNTY
450 E Market St Courthouse Complex   **Ph:** 724-543-2500
Kittanning, PA 16201   **Fax:** 724-548-3285
www.armstrongcounty.com

In central portion of western PA, northeast of Pittsburgh; organized Mar 12, 1800 from Allegheny, Lycoming, and Westmoreland counties. **Name Origin:** For John Armstrong (1758-1843), officer in the Revolutionary War and the War of 1812, U.S. senator from NY (1800-02; 1803-04), and U.S. secretary of war (1813-14).

Area (sq mi): 664.44 (land 653.93; water 10.51). **Pop per sq mi:** 107.9.

Pop 2005: 70,586. **State rank:** 38. **Pop change:** 2000-20005 -2.5%; 1990-2000 -1.5%. **Pop 2000:** 72,392 (White 98%; Black or African American 0.8%; Hispanic or Latino 0.4%; Asian 0.1%; Other 0.7%). **Foreign born:** 0.7%. **Median age:** 40.4.

Income 2000: per capita $15,709; median household $31,557; **Pop below poverty level:** 11.7%. *Personal per capita income 2000-2003: $23,071-$25,903.

Unemployment 2004: 7.2%. **Change from 2000:** -0.1%. **Median travel time to work:** 26.9 minutes. **Working outside county of residence:** 45.4%.

Cities with pop over 10,000: None.

BEAVER COUNTY
810 3rd St Courthouse   **Ph:** 724-728-3934
Beaver, PA 15009   **Fax:** 724-728-0725
www.co.beaver.pa.us

On central western border of PA, northwest of Pittsburgh; organized Mar 12, 1800 from Allegheny and Washington counties. **Name Origin:** For the Beaver River, which traverses it.

Beaver County (cont'd)

Area (sq mi): 443.9 (land 434.21; water 9.69). **Pop per sq mi:** 408.5.

Pop 2005: 177,377. **State rank:** 20. **Pop change:** 2000-20005 - 2.2%; 1990-2000 -2.5%. **Pop 2000:** 181,412 (White 92.1%; Black or African American 6%; Hispanic or Latino 0.7%; Asian 0.3%; Other 1.2%). **Foreign born:** 1.7%. **Median age:** 40.7.

Income 2000: per capita $18,402; median household $36,995; **Pop below poverty level:** 9.4%. ***Personal per capita income 2000-2003:** $24,812-$26,472.

Unemployment 2004: 5.9%. **Change from 2000:** +1%. **Median travel time to work:** 24.5 minutes. **Working outside county of residence:** 42%.

Cities with pop over 10,000: Aliquippa (11,270).

BEDFORD COUNTY

211 S Juliana St	**Ph:** 814-623-4807
Bedford, PA 15522	**Fax:** 814-623-0991
bedford.sapdc.org	

On southern border with MD, southeast of Johnstown; organized May 9, 1771 (prior to statehood) from Cumberland County. **Name Origin:** For Fort Bedford, which became the site of the county seat of Bedford. The fort was named in 1759 to honor England's Duke of Bedford.

Area (sq mi): 1017.4 (land 1014.51; water 2.89). **Pop per sq mi:** 49.4.

Pop 2005: 50,091. **State rank:** 45. **Pop change:** 2000-20005 +0.2%; 1990-2000 +4.3%. **Pop 2000:** 49,984 (White 98.2%; Black or African American 0.4%; Hispanic or Latino 0.5%; Asian 0.3%; Other 0.8%). **Foreign born:** 0.6%. **Median age:** 39.5.

Income 2000: per capita $16,316; median household $32,731; **Pop below poverty level:** 10.3%. ***Personal per capita income 2000-2003:** $20,949-$22,319.

Unemployment 2004: 7.9%. **Change from 2000:** +0.5%. **Median travel time to work:** 27.9 minutes. **Working outside county of residence:** 30.2%.

Cities with pop over 10,000: None.

BERKS COUNTY

633 Court St 4th Fl	**Ph:** 610-478-6550
Reading, PA 19601	**Fax:** 610-478-6570
www.co.berks.pa.us	

In southeastern PA, southwest of Allentown; established Mar 11, 1752 from Chester, Lancaster, and Philadelphia counties. **Name Origin:** The shortened form for Berkshire, England, which also has a Reading as its county seat; site of large land holdings of the Penn family.

Area (sq mi): 865.67 (land 858.88; water 6.79). **Pop per sq mi:** 461.4.

Pop 2005: 396,314. **State rank:** 9. **Pop change:** 2000-20005 +6.1%; 1990-2000 +11%. **Pop 2000:** 373,638 (White 84.8%; Black or African American 3.7%; Hispanic or Latino 9.7%; Asian 1%; Other 7.1%). **Foreign born:** 4.3%. **Median age:** 37.4.

Income 2000: per capita $21,232; median household $44,714; **Pop below poverty level:** 9.4%. ***Personal per capita income 2000-2003:** $28,776-$29,790.

Unemployment 2004: 5.3%. **Change from 2000:** +0.4%. **Median travel time to work:** 22.3 minutes. **Working outside county of residence:** 20.8%.

Cities with pop over 10,000: Reading 🏛 (80,727); Wyomissing (11,142).

BLAIR COUNTY

423 Allegheny St Suite 142	**Ph:** 814-693-3030
Hollidaysburg, PA 16648	**Fax:** 814-693-3033
www.blairco.org	

In western PA, east of Johnstown; organized Feb 26, 1846 from Huntingdon and Bedford counties. **Name Origin:** For John Blair, PA legislator and prominent citizen. The only county in PA named for a local citizen.

Area (sq mi): 527.11 (land 525.8; water 1.31). **Pop per sq mi:** 241.1.

Pop 2005: 126,795. **State rank:** 27. **Pop change:** 2000-20005 - 1.8%; 1990-2000 -1.1%. **Pop 2000:** 129,144 (White 97.3%; Black or African American 1.2%; Hispanic or Latino 0.5%; Asian 0.4%; Other 0.8%). **Foreign born:** 1%. **Median age:** 39.5.

Income 2000: per capita $16,743; median household $32,861; **Pop below poverty level:** 12.6%. ***Personal per capita income 2000-2003:** $23,689-$25,478.

Unemployment 2004: 5.5%. **Change from 2000:** -0.4%. **Median travel time to work:** 20.2 minutes. **Working outside county of residence:** 10.8%.

Cities with pop over 10,000: Altoona (47,832).

BRADFORD COUNTY

301 Main St Courthouse	**Ph:** 570-265-1727
Towanda, PA 18848	**Fax:** 570-265-1729
www.bradfordcountypa.org	

On northern border of PA, northwest of Scranton; organized as Ontario County Feb 10, 1810 from Luzerne and Lycoming counties. **Name Origin:** For William Bradford (1755-95), associate justice of the PA supreme court (1791) and U.S. attorney general (1794-95). Name changed Mar 24, 1812 from Ontario (named for the lake).

Area (sq mi): 1161.03 (land 1150.67; water 10.37). **Pop per sq mi:** 54.3.

Pop 2005: 62,537. **State rank:** 40. **Pop change:** 2000-20005 -0.4%; 1990-2000 +2.9%. **Pop 2000:** 62,761 (White 97.5%; Black or African American 0.4%; Hispanic or Latino 0.6%; Asian 0.5%; Other 1.2%). **Foreign born:** 1%. **Median age:** 38.9.

Income 2000: per capita $17,148; median household $35,038; **Pop below poverty level:** 11.8%. ***Personal per capita income 2000-2003:** $21,752-$23,995.

Unemployment 2004: 5.4%. **Change from 2000:** -0.3%. **Median travel time to work:** 22.6 minutes. **Working outside county of residence:** 23.7%.

Cities with pop over 10,000: None.

---

*Source: Personal per capita income data are from the Bureau of Economic Analysis; per capita income data are from the Bureau of the Census. See Introduction for explanation of differences.

BUCKS COUNTY

55 E Court St   **Ph:** 215-348-6000
Doylestown, PA 18901   **Fax:** 215-348-6571
www.buckscounty.org

On southeastern border of PA, north of Philadelphia; original county, organized as Buckingham County Mar 10, 1682. **Name Origin:** Shortened from the original name, Buckingham, for the English county of Buckinghamshire (also called Bucks), home of the Penn family and of many original settlers.

Area (sq mi): 622.11 (land 607.38; water 14.74). **Pop per sq mi:** 1023.

Pop 2005: 621,342. **State rank:** 4. **Pop change:** 2000-20005 +4%; 1990-2000 +10.4%. **Pop 2000:** 597,635 (White 91.1%; Black or African American 3.3%; Hispanic or Latino 2.3%; Asian 2.3%; Other 1.9%). **Foreign born:** 5.9%. **Median age:** 37.7.

Income 2000: per capita $27,430; median household $59,727; **Pop below poverty level:** 4.5%. ***Personal per capita income 2000-2003:** $38,236-$40,450.

Unemployment 2004: 4.7%. **Change from 2000:** +0.9%. **Median travel time to work:** 28.6 minutes. **Working outside county of residence:** 44.6%.

Cities with pop over 10,000: None.

BUTLER COUNTY

290 S Main St PO Box 1208   **Ph:** 724-284-5233
Butler, PA 16003   **Fax:** 724-284-5244
www.co.butler.pa.us

In central portion of western PA, north of Pittsburgh; organized Mar 12, 1800 from Allegheny County. **Name Origin:** For Maj. Gen. Richard Butler (1743-91), officer and Indian commissioner after the American Revolution.

Area (sq mi): 794.79 (land 788.53; water 6.26). **Pop per sq mi:** 230.9.

Pop 2005: 182,087. **State rank:** 19. **Pop change:** 2000-20005 +4.6%; 1990-2000 +14.5%. **Pop 2000:** 174,083 (White 97.4%; Black or African American 0.8%; Hispanic or Latino 0.6%; Asian 0.6%; Other 0.8%). **Foreign born:** 1.4%. **Median age:** 37.6.

Income 2000: per capita $20,794; median household $42,308; **Pop below poverty level:** 9.1%. ***Personal per capita income 2000-2003:** $28,798-$30,055.

Unemployment 2004: 5.6%. **Change from 2000:** +1.3%. **Median travel time to work:** 25.3 minutes. **Working outside county of residence:** 36.4%.

Cities with pop over 10,000: Butler 🏛 (14,626).

CAMBRIA COUNTY

200 S Center St   **Ph:** 814-472-6176
Ebensburg, PA 15931   **Fax:** 814-472-6940
www.co.cambria.pa.us

In western PA, west of Altoona; organized Mar 26, 1804 from Somerset, Bedford, and Huntingdon counties. **Name Origin:** For Cambria township in Somerset County. Cambria is an ancient, poetic name for Wales, from Welsh *cymy* or *cumbri* 'brotherhood' or 'fraternity.'

Area (sq mi): 693.43 (land 688.02; water 5.41). **Pop per sq mi:** 215.2.

Pop 2005: 148,073. **State rank:** 22. **Pop change:** 2000-20005 -3%; 1990-2000 -6.4%. **Pop 2000:** 152,598 (White 95.2%; Black or African American 2.8%; Hispanic or Latino 0.9%; Asian 0.4%; Other 0.9%). **Foreign born:** 1.3%. **Median age:** 41.2.

Income 2000: per capita $16,058; median household $30,179; **Pop below poverty level:** 12.5%. ***Personal per capita income 2000-2003:** $22,420-$24,368.

Unemployment 2004: 7%. **Change from 2000:** +0.2%. **Median travel time to work:** 21.9 minutes. **Working outside county of residence:** 20.1%.

Cities with pop over 10,000: Johnstown (22,772).

CAMERON COUNTY

20 E 5th St   **Ph:** 814-486-2315
Emporium, PA 15834   **Fax:** 814-486-3176
www.cameroncountypa.com

In north-west central PA, west of Williamsport; organized Mar 29, 1860 from Clinton, Elk, McKean, and Potter counties. **Name Origin:** For Simon Cameron (1799-1889), U.S. senator from PA (1845-49; 1857-61; 1867-77), U.S. secretary of war (1861-62), and U.S. Minister to Russia (1862).

Area (sq mi): 398.6 (land 397.16; water 1.44). **Pop per sq mi:** 14.2.

Pop 2005: 5,639. **State rank:** 67. **Pop change:** 2000-20005 -5.6%; 1990-2000 +1%. **Pop 2000:** 5,974 (White 98.5%; Black or African American 0.4%; Hispanic or Latino 0.6%; Asian 0.1%; Other 0.8%). **Foreign born:** 0.6%. **Median age:** 41.3.

Income 2000: per capita $15,968; median household $32,212; **Pop below poverty level:** 9.4%. ***Personal per capita income 2000-2003:** $23,205-$24,229.

Unemployment 2004: 7.3%. **Change from 2000:** -2.8%. **Median travel time to work:** 15.4 minutes. **Working outside county of residence:** 15.4%.

Cities with pop over 10,000: None.

CARBON COUNTY

2 Hazard Sq   **Ph:** 570-325-3611
Jim Thorpe, PA 18229   **Fax:** 570-325-3622
www.carboncounty.com

In eastern PA, south of Scranton; organized Mar 13, 1843 from Northampton and Monroe counties. **Name Origin:** For its rich deposits of anthracite coal.

Area (sq mi): 387.23 (land 381.04; water 6.2). **Pop per sq mi:** 162.6.

Pop 2005: 61,959. **State rank:** 41. **Pop change:** 2000-20005 +5.4%; 1990-2000 +3.4%. **Pop 2000:** 58,802 (White 96.9%; Black or African American 0.6%; Hispanic or Latino 1.5%; Asian 0.3%; Other 1.3%). **Foreign born:** 1.8%. **Median age:** 40.6.

Income 2000: per capita $17,064; median household $35,113; **Pop below poverty level:** 9.5%. ***Personal per capita income 2000-2003:** $24,194-$26,372.

Unemployment 2004: 6.5%. **Change from 2000:** +0.4%. **Median travel time to work:** 29.2 minutes. **Working outside county of residence:** 52.3%.

Cities with pop over 10,000: None.

🏛 *County Seat*

CENTRE COUNTY

420 Holmes St Willowbank Office Bldg   **Ph:** 814-355-6700
Bellefonte, PA 16823   **Fax:** 814-355-6980
www.co.centre.pa.us

In central PA, southwest of Williamsport; organized Feb 13, 1800 from Lycoming, Mifflin, Northumberland, and Huntingdon counties. **Name Origin:** For its location in the geographic center of the state, with the British spelling of the time.

Area (sq mi): 1111.85 (land 1107.53; water 4.32). **Pop per sq mi:** 126.9.

Pop 2005: 140,561. **State rank:** 25. **Pop change:** 2000-20005 +3.5%; 1990-2000 +9.7%. **Pop 2000:** 135,758 (White 90.6%; Black or African American 2.6%; Hispanic or Latino 1.7%; Asian 4%; Other 2%). **Foreign born:** 5.8%. **Median age:** 28.7.

Income 2000: per capita $18,020; median household $36,165; **Pop below poverty level:** 18.8%. ***Personal per capita income 2000-2003:** $24,048-$25,776.

Unemployment 2004: 4.4%. **Change from 2000:** +1.5%. **Median travel time to work:** 19.6 minutes. **Working outside county of residence:** 8.4%.

Cities with pop over 10,000: State College (39,311).

CHESTER COUNTY

2 N High St Suite 512 PO Box 2748   **Ph:** 610-344-6100
West Chester, PA 19380   **Fax:** 610-344-5995
dsf.chesco.org

On southeastern border of PA, west of Philadelphia; original county, organized as Upland County Mar 10, 1682; name changed soon after. **Name Origin:** For Chester, Cheshire, England, home of many settlers brought to America by William Penn (1644-1718).

Area (sq mi): 759.81 (land 755.97; water 3.84). **Pop per sq mi:** 627.

Pop 2005: 474,027. **State rank:** 7. **Pop change:** 2000-20005 +9.3%; 1990-2000 +15.2%. **Pop 2000:** 433,501 (White 87.2%; Black or African American 6.2%; Hispanic or Latino 3.7%; Asian 2%; Other 2.5%). **Foreign born:** 5.5%. **Median age:** 36.9.

Income 2000: per capita $31,627; median household $65,295; **Pop below poverty level:** 5.2%. ***Personal per capita income 2000-2003:** $46,453-$47,480.

Unemployment 2004: 3.8%. **Change from 2000:** +0.8%. **Median travel time to work:** 27.5 minutes. **Working outside county of residence:** 36.9%.

Cities with pop over 10,000: West Chester ⛪ (17,701); Phoenixville (14,976); Coatesville (11,386).

CLARION COUNTY

421 Main St Courthouse   **Ph:** 814-226-1119
Clarion, PA 16214   **Fax:** 814-227-2501
www.co.clarion.pa.us

In central portion of western PA, northeast of Pittsburgh; organized Mar 11, 1839 from Venango and Armstrong counties. **Name Origin:** For the Clarion River, which flows through it. The rippling waters of the river sounded 'like the notes of a distant clarion' to Daniel Stanard, one of the state surveyors.

Area (sq mi): 608.95 (land 602.44; water 6.51). **Pop per sq mi:** 67.4.

Pop 2005: 40,589. **State rank:** 55. **Pop change:** 2000-20005 -2.8%; 1990-2000 +0.2%. **Pop 2000:** 41,765 (White 97.8%; Black or African American 0.8%; Hispanic or Latino 0.4%; Asian 0.3%; Other 0.7%). **Foreign born:** 1%. **Median age:** 36.3.

Income 2000: per capita $15,243; median household $30,770; **Pop below poverty level:** 15.4%. ***Personal per capita income 2000-2003:** $21,966-$24,319.

Unemployment 2004: 5.7%. **Change from 2000:** +1%. **Median travel time to work:** 22.9 minutes. **Working outside county of residence:** 26.3%.

Cities with pop over 10,000: None.

CLEARFIELD COUNTY

230 E Market St   **Ph:** 814-765-2641
Clearfield, PA 16830   **Fax:** 814-765-2640
www.clearfieldco.org

In west-central PA, north of Altoona; organized Mar 26, 1804 from Lycoming and Huntingdon counties. Functioned as part of Centre County in early years; first county commissioners elected 1812, courts established 1822. **Name Origin:** For Clearfield Creek, which runs through a part of the county where buffalo had cleared the undergrowth.

Area (sq mi): 1153.8 (land 1147.32; water 6.49). **Pop per sq mi:** 72.2.

Pop 2005: 82,783. **State rank:** 36. **Pop change:** 2000-20005 -0.7%; 1990-2000 +6.8%. **Pop 2000:** 83,382 (White 97.1%; Black or African American 1.5%; Hispanic or Latino 0.6%; Asian 0.3%; Other 0.9%). **Foreign born:** 0.7%. **Median age:** 39.3.

Income 2000: per capita $16,010; median household $31,357; **Pop below poverty level:** 12.5%. ***Personal per capita income 2000-2003:** $21,583-$23,476.

Unemployment 2004: 7.1%. **Change from 2000:** -1.2%. **Median travel time to work:** 24.3 minutes. **Working outside county of residence:** 28.2%.

Cities with pop over 10,000: None.

CLINTON COUNTY

232 E Main St 3rd Fl   **Ph:** 570-893-4000
Lock Haven, PA 17745   **Fax:** 570-893-4041
www.clintoncountypa.com

In north-central PA, west of Williamsport; organized Jun 21, 1839 from Lycoming and Centre counties. **Name Origin:** Most likely for DeWitt Clinton (1769-1828), governor of NY, and supporter of the Erie Canal. The name may have been a substitute to the originally proposed name, Eagle, to thwart political opponents of county formation.

Area (sq mi): 898.09 (land 890.87; water 7.23). **Pop per sq mi:** 42.

Pop 2005: 37,439. **State rank:** 58. **Pop change:** 2000-20005 -1.3%; 1990-2000 +2%. **Pop 2000:** 37,914 (White 97.9%; Black or African American 0.5%; Hispanic or Latino 0.5%; Asian 0.4%; Other 0.7%). **Foreign born:** 0.9%. **Median age:** 37.8.

Income 2000: per capita $15,750; median household $31,064; **Pop below poverty level:** 14.2%. ***Personal per capita income 2000-2003:** $20,862-$22,790.

*Source: Personal per capita income data are from the Bureau of Economic Analysis; per capita income data are from the Bureau of the Census. See Introduction for explanation of differences.

Clinton County (cont'd)

Unemployment 2004: 6.7%. **Change from 2000:** +0.1%. **Median travel time to work:** 23.5 minutes. **Working outside county of residence:** 33.5%.

Cities with pop over 10,000: None.

COLUMBIA COUNTY
35 W Main St   **Ph:** 570-389-5600
Bloomsburg, PA 17815   **Fax:** 570-784-0257
www.columbiapa.org

In east-central PA, southwest of Scranton; organized Mar 22, 1813 from Northumberland County. **Name Origin:** Feminine form of Columbus, a poetic and honorific reference to Christopher Columbus (1451-1506) and America.

Area (sq mi): 489.79 (land 485.55; water 4.24). **Pop per sq mi:** 133.7.

Pop 2005: 64,939. **State rank:** 39. **Pop change:** 2000-20005 +1.2%; 1990-2000 +1.5%. **Pop 2000:** 64,151 (White 97.1%; Black or African American 0.8%; Hispanic or Latino 0.9%; Asian 0.5%; Other 1%). **Foreign born:** 1.4%. **Median age:** 37.5.

Income 2000: per capita $16,973; median household $34,094; **Pop below poverty level:** 13.1%. ***Personal per capita income 2000-2003:** $22,648-$25,264.

Unemployment 2004: 6.6%. **Change from 2000:** +1.1%. **Median travel time to work:** 21.1 minutes. **Working outside county of residence:** 24.6%.

Cities with pop over 10,000: Bloomsburg 🏛 (12,805); Berwick (10,493).

CRAWFORD COUNTY
903 Diamond Pk   **Ph:** 814-333-7400
Meadville, PA 16335   **Fax:** 814-337-0457
www.co.crawford.pa.us

On northwest border of PA, south of Erie; organized Mar 12, 1800 from Allegheny County. **Name Origin:** For Col. William Crawford (1732-82), surveyor, army officer, and Indian fighter.

Area (sq mi): 1037.74 (land 1012.72; water 25.01). **Pop per sq mi:** 88.3.

Pop 2005: 89,442. **State rank:** 34. **Pop change:** 2000-20005 -1%; 1990-2000 +4.9%. **Pop 2000:** 90,366 (White 96.6%; Black or African American 1.6%; Hispanic or Latino 0.6%; Asian 0.3%; Other 1.1%). **Foreign born:** 1.1%. **Median age:** 38.1.

Income 2000: per capita $16,870; median household $33,560; **Pop below poverty level:** 12.8%. ***Personal per capita income 2000-2003:** $22,820-$22,753.

Unemployment 2004: 6.7%. **Change from 2000:** -0.4%. **Median travel time to work:** 21.5 minutes. **Working outside county of residence:** 22.4%.

Cities with pop over 10,000: Meadville 🏛 (13,360).

CUMBERLAND COUNTY
1 Courthouse Sq   **Ph:** 717-240-6150
Carlisle, PA 17013   **Fax:** 717-240-6448
www.ccpa.net/cumberland/

In south-central PA, west of Harrisburg; organized Jan 27, 1750 from Lancaster County. **Name Origin:** For William Augustus, Duke of Cumberland (1721-65), British general and second son of George II (1683-1760).

Area (sq mi): 551.14 (land 550.17; water 0.98). **Pop per sq mi:** 405.5.

Pop 2005: 223,089. **State rank:** 16. **Pop change:** 2000-20005 +4.4%; 1990-2000 +9.4%. **Pop 2000:** 213,674 (White 93.6%; Black or African American 2.4%; Hispanic or Latino 1.3%; Asian 1.7%; Other 1.5%) **Foreign born:** 3.2%. **Median age:** 38.1.

Income 2000: per capita $23,610; median household $46,707; **Pop below poverty level:** 6.6%. ***Personal per capita income 2000-2003:** $31,090-$33,370.

Unemployment 2004: 3.9%. **Change from 2000:** +0.8%. **Median travel time to work:** 20.5 minutes. **Working outside county of residence:** 31%.

Cities with pop over 10,000: Carlisle 🏛 (18,074).

DAUPHIN COUNTY
2 S 2nd St   **Ph:** 717-780-6300
Harrisburg, PA 17101   **Fax:** 717-255-2684
www.dauphincounty.org

In south central PA, northwest of Lancaster; organized Mar 4, 1785 from Lancaster County. **Name Origin:** To honor France, ally of the American states in the Revolutionary War, by use of the hereditary title of the eldest son of the king of France, dauphin. Louis Joseph (1781-89), son of Louis XVI (1754-93) and Marie Antoinette (1755-93), was *dauphin* at the time the county was established.

Area (sq mi): 557.53 (land 525.29; water 32.24). **Pop per sq mi:** 483.5.

Pop 2005: 253,995. **State rank:** 15. **Pop change:** 2000-20005 +0.9%; 1990-2000 +5.9%. **Pop 2000:** 251,798 (White 75.6%; Black or African American 16.9%; Hispanic or Latino 4.1%; Asian 2%; Other 4.1%). **Foreign born:** 4.1%. **Median age:** 37.9.

Income 2000: per capita $22,134; median household $41,507; **Pop below poverty level:** 9.7%. ***Personal per capita income 2000-2003:** $29,473-$32,953.

Unemployment 2004: 4.9%. **Change from 2000:** +1.2%. **Median travel time to work:** 21.1 minutes. **Working outside county of residence:** 22.5%.

Cities with pop over 10,000: Harrisburg 🏛 (47,635).

DELAWARE COUNTY
201 W Front St Government Center Bldg   **Ph:** 610-891-4000
Media, PA 19063   **Fax:** 610-891-0647
www.co.delaware.pa.us

On southeastern border of PA, west of Philadelphia; organized Sept 6, 1789 from Chester County. **Name Origin:** For the Delaware River, which forms its southeastern border.

Area (sq mi): 190.74 (land 184.21; water 6.53). **Pop per sq mi:** 3016.4.

Pop 2005: 555,648. **State rank:** 5. **Pop change:** 2000-20005 +0.9%; 1990-2000 +0.6%. **Pop 2000:** 550,864 (White 79.6%; Black or African American 14.5%; Hispanic or Latino 1.5%; Asian 3.3%; Other 1.9%). **Foreign born:** 6.7%. **Median age:** 37.4.

🏛 *County Seat*

Delaware County (cont'd)

Income 2000: per capita $25,040; median household $50,092; **Pop below poverty level:** 8%. ***Personal per capita income 2000-2003:** $36,813-$38,813.

Unemployment 2004: 5.2%. **Change from 2000:** +1.3%. **Median travel time to work:** 27.1 minutes. **Working outside county of residence:** 45.7%.

Cities with pop over 10,000: Chester (36,922); Yeadon (11,535); Lansdowne (10,827); Darby (10,085).

ELK COUNTY

PO Box 448   **Ph:** 814-776-1161
Ridgway, PA 15853   **Fax:** 814-776-5379
www.co.elk.pa.us

In west-central PA, west of Williamsport; organized Apr 18, 1843 from Jefferson, Clearfield, and McKean counties. **Name Origin:** For the North American elk, once common in the county.

Area (sq mi): 832.23 (land 828.65; water 3.58). **Pop per sq mi:** 40.5.

Pop 2005: 33,577. **State rank:** 59. **Pop change:** 2000-20005 -4.4%; 1990-2000 +0.7%. **Pop 2000:** 35,112 (White 98.7%; Black or African American 0.1%; Hispanic or Latino 0.4%; Asian 0.3%; Other 0.5%). **Foreign born:** 1.1%. **Median age:** 39.4.

Income 2000: per capita $18,174; median household $37,550; **Pop below poverty level:** 7%. ***Personal per capita income 2000-2003:** $25,701-$27,492.

Unemployment 2004: 5.8%. **Change from 2000:** -3.2%. **Median travel time to work:** 16.8 minutes. **Working outside county of residence:** 10.4%.

Cities with pop over 10,000: Saint Marys (14,081).

ERIE COUNTY

140 W 6th St Rm 116   **Ph:** 814-451-6303
Erie, PA 16501   **Fax:** 814-451-6350
www.eriecountygov.org

At northwestern corner of PA, along southern shore of Lake Erie; organized Mar 12, 1800 from Allegheny County. **Name Origin:** For Lake Erie, which forms its northern border.

Area (sq mi): 1558.4 (land 801.95; water 756.46). **Pop per sq mi:** 349.7.

Pop 2005: 280,446. **State rank:** 14. **Pop change:** 2000-20005 -0.1%; 1990-2000 +1.9%. **Pop 2000:** 280,843 (White 89.8%; Black or African American 6.1%; Hispanic or Latino 2.2%; Asian 0.7%; Other 2.3%). **Foreign born:** 2.7%. **Median age:** 36.2.

Income 2000: per capita $17,932; median household $36,627; **Pop below poverty level:** 12%. ***Personal per capita income 2000-2003:** $24,538-$25,505.

Unemployment 2004: 6.3%. **Change from 2000:** +0.5%. **Median travel time to work:** 18.5 minutes. **Working outside county of residence:** 3.8%.

Cities with pop over 10,000: Erie 🏛 (103,925).

FAYETTE COUNTY

61 E Main St   **Ph:** 724-430-1201
Uniontown, PA 15401   **Fax:** 724-430-1265
www.fayettepa.org

On southern border of western PA, southeast of Pittsburgh; organized Sep 26, 1783 from Westmoreland County. **Name Origin:** For the Marquis de Lafayette or La Fayette (1757-1834), French statesman and soldier who fought with the Americans during the Revolutionary War.

Area (sq mi): 798 (land 790.14; water 7.86). **Pop per sq mi:** 185.

Pop 2005: 146,142. **State rank:** 24. **Pop change:** 2000-20005 -1.7%; 1990-2000 +2.3%. **Pop 2000:** 148,644 (White 95%; Black or African American 3.5%; Hispanic or Latino 0.4%; Asian 0.2%; Other 0.9%). **Foreign born:** 0.6%. **Median age:** 40.2.

Income 2000: per capita $15,274; median household $27,451; **Pop below poverty level:** 18%. ***Personal per capita income 2000-2003:** $21,984-$24,540.

Unemployment 2004: 7.8%. **Change from 2000:** +0.9%. **Median travel time to work:** 26.5 minutes. **Working outside county of residence:** 38%.

Cities with pop over 10,000: Uniontown 🏛 (12,065).

FOREST COUNTY

526 Elm St Suite 3   **Ph:** 814-755-3537
Tionesta, PA 16353   **Fax:** 814-755-8837
www.co.forest.pa.us

In north-western PA, east of Oil City; organized Apr 11, 1848 from Jefferson County. **Name Origin:** Named by Cyrus Blood (1795-?), pioneer settler, because the county was virgin forestland.

Area (sq mi): 431.4 (land 428.12; water 3.28). **Pop per sq mi:** 13.4.

Pop 2005: 5,739. **State rank:** 66. **Pop change:** 2000-20005 +16%; 1990-2000 +3%. **Pop 2000:** 4,946 (White 95.4%; Black or African American 2.2%; Hispanic or Latino 1.2%; Asian 0.1%; Other 1.7%). **Foreign born:** 0.6%. **Median age:** 44.2.

Income 2000: per capita $14,341; median household $27,581; **Pop below poverty level:** 16.4%. ***Personal per capita income 2000-2003:** $20,710-$23,374.

Unemployment 2004: 10.1%. **Change from 2000:** -5.1%. **Median travel time to work:** 24.4 minutes. **Working outside county of residence:** 42.6%.

Cities with pop over 10,000: None.

FRANKLIN COUNTY

14 N Main St   **Ph:** 717-261-3810
Chambersburg, PA 17201   **Fax:** 717-267-3438
www.co.franklin.pa.us

On central southern border of PA, southwest of Harrisburg; organized Sep 9, 1784 from Cumberland County. **Name Origin:** For Benjamin Franklin (1706-90), U.S. patriot, diplomat, and statesman.

Area (sq mi): 772.63 (land 771.92; water 0.71). **Pop per sq mi:** 178.

Pop 2005: 137,409. **State rank:** 26. **Pop change:** 2000-20005 +6.3%; 1990-2000 +6.8%. **Pop 2000:** 129,313 (White 94.5%; Black or African American 2.3%; Hispanic or Latino 1.8%; Asian 0.6%; Other 1.7%). **Foreign born:** 2%. **Median age:** 38.3.

*Source: Personal per capita income data are from the Bureau of Economic Analysis; per capita income data are from the Bureau of the Census. See Introduction for explanation of differences.

Franklin County (cont'd)

Income 2000: per capita $19,339; median household $40,476; **Pop below poverty level:** 7.6%. ***Personal per capita income 2000-2003:** $24,885-$26,565.

Unemployment 2004: 3.8%. **Change from 2000:** -1%. **Median travel time to work:** 23 minutes. **Working outside county of residence:** 28.2%.

Cities with pop over 10,000: Chambersburg ⛪ (18,026).

FULTON COUNTY

116 W Market St Suite 203   **Ph:** 717-485-3691
McConnellsburg, PA 17233   **Fax:** 717-485-9411
fulton.sapdc.org

On central southern border of PA, southeast of Altoona; organized Apr 19, 1851 from Bedford County. **Name Origin:** For Robert Fulton (1765-1815), developer of the *Clermont*, the first commercially successful steamboat.

Area (sq mi): 438.03 (land 437.57; water 0.46). **Pop per sq mi:** 33.5.

Pop 2005: 14,673. **State rank:** 64. **Pop change:** 2000-20005 +2.9%; 1990-2000 +3.1%. **Pop 2000:** 14,261 (White 98%; Black or African American 0.7%; Hispanic or Latino 0.4%; Asian 0.1%; Other 0.9%). **Foreign born:** 0.7%. **Median age:** 38.2.

Income 2000: per capita $16,409; median household $34,882; **Pop below poverty level:** 10.8%. ***Personal per capita income 2000-2003:** $23,300-$24,939.

Unemployment 2004: 5%. **Change from 2000:** -2.4%. **Median travel time to work:** 31.5 minutes. **Working outside county of residence:** 45.4%.

Cities with pop over 10,000: None.

GREENE COUNTY

93 E High St   **Ph:** 724-852-5210
Waynesburg, PA 15370   **Fax:** 724-852-5327
www.co.greene.pa.us

At southwestern corner of PA, south of Pittsburgh; organized Feb 9, 1796 from Washington County. **Name Origin:** For Gen. Nathanael Greene (1742-86), hero of the Revolutionary War; quartermaster general (1778-80).

Area (sq mi): 577.95 (land 575.86; water 2.09). **Pop per sq mi:** 69.1.

Pop 2005: 39,808. **State rank:** 56. **Pop change:** 2000-20005 -2.1%; 1990-2000 +2.8%. **Pop 2000:** 40,672 (White 94.3%; Black or African American 3.9%; Hispanic or Latino 0.9%; Asian 0.2%; Other 0.8%). **Foreign born:** 0.7%. **Median age:** 38.2.

Income 2000: per capita $14,959; median household $30,352; **Pop below poverty level:** 15.9%. ***Personal per capita income 2000-2003:** $20,027-$21,539.

Unemployment 2004: 6.7%. **Change from 2000:** +1%. **Median travel time to work:** 28.3 minutes. **Working outside county of residence:** 37.2%.

Cities with pop over 10,000: None.

HUNTINGDON COUNTY

223 Penn St County Courthouse   **Ph:** 814-643-3091
Huntingdon, PA 16652   **Fax:** 814-643-8152
www.huntingdoncounty.net

In south-central PA, east of Altoona; organized Sep 20, 1787 from Bedford County. **Name Origin:** For the county seat.

Area (sq mi): 889.03 (land 874.05; water 14.98). **Pop per sq mi:** 52.6.

Pop 2005: 45,947. **State rank:** 47. **Pop change:** 2000-20005 +0.8%; 1990-2000 +3.2%. **Pop 2000:** 45,586 (White 92.8%; Black or African American 5.1%; Hispanic or Latino 1.1%; Asian 0.2%; Other 1.3%). **Foreign born:** 0.7%. **Median age:** 37.7.

Income 2000: per capita $15,379; median household $33,313; **Pop below poverty level:** 11.3%. ***Personal per capita income 2000-2003:** $19,402-$20,539.

Unemployment 2004: 7.1%. **Change from 2000:** -2.2%. **Median travel time to work:** 28.9 minutes. **Working outside county of residence:** 35.7%.

Cities with pop over 10,000: None.

INDIANA COUNTY

825 Philadelphia St Courthouse   **Ph:** 724-465-3805
Indiana, PA 15701   **Fax:** 724-465-3953
www.indianacounty.org

In central porton of western PA, northeast of Pittsburgh; organized Mar 30, 1803 from Westmoreland and Lycoming territories. **Name Origin:** For the Indiana Territory, which had been formed as part of the Northwest Territory in 1800.

Area (sq mi): 834.29 (land 829.27; water 5.02). **Pop per sq mi:** 107.

Pop 2005: 88,703. **State rank:** 35. **Pop change:** 2000-20005 -1%; 1990-2000 -0.4%. **Pop 2000:** 89,605 (White 96.5%; Black or African American 1.6%; Hispanic or Latino 0.5%; Asian 0.7%; Other 0.9%). **Foreign born:** 1.6%. **Median age:** 36.2.

Income 2000: per capita $15,312; median household $30,233; **Pop below poverty level:** 17.3%. ***Personal per capita income 2000-2003:** $22,398-$24,267.

Unemployment 2004: 6.3%. **Change from 2000:** +0.3%. **Median travel time to work:** 23.8 minutes. **Working outside county of residence:** 24.3%.

Cities with pop over 10,000: Indiana ⛪ (14,925).

JEFFERSON COUNTY

155 Main St Jefferson Pl   **Ph:** 814-849-1653
Brookville, PA 15825   **Fax:** 814-849-4084
www.jeffersoncountypa.com

In central portion of western PA, northeast of Pittsburgh; organized Mar 26, 1804 from Lycoming County. **Name Origin:** For Thomas Jefferson (1743-1826), U.S. patriot and statesman; third U.S. president.

Area (sq mi): 656.87 (land 655.48; water 1.39). **Pop per sq mi:** 69.8.

Pop 2005: 45,759. **State rank:** 48. **Pop change:** 2000-20005 -0.4%; 1990-2000 -0.3%. **Pop 2000:** 45,932 (White 98.7%; Black or African American 0.1%; Hispanic or Latino 0.4%; Asian 0.2%; Other 0.8%). **Foreign born:** 0.6%. **Median age:** 39.8.

Jefferson County (cont'd)

Income 2000: per capita $16,186; median household $31,722; **Pop below poverty level:** 11.8%. ***Personal per capita income 2000-2003:** $22,056-$23,628.

Unemployment 2004: 6.2%. **Change from 2000:** -0.9%. **Median travel time to work:** 22.3 minutes. **Working outside county of residence:** 32.9%.

Cities with pop over 10,000: None.

JUNIATA COUNTY

PO Box 68   **Ph:** 717-436-7715
Mifflintown, PA 17059   **Fax:** 717-436-7734
www.co.juniata.pa.us

In central PA, northwest of Harrisburg; organized Mar 2, 1831 from Mifflin County. **Name Origin:** For the Juniata River, which flows through it; it is named for an Indian word of uncertain origin.

Area (sq mi): 393.57 (land 391.59; water 1.98). **Pop per sq mi:** 60.

Pop 2005: 23,507. **State rank:** 61. **Pop change:** 2000-20005 +3%; 1990-2000 +10.6%. **Pop 2000:** 22,821 (White 97.3%; Black or African American 0.4%; Hispanic or Latino 1.6%; Asian 0.2%; Other 1.3%). **Foreign born:** 1%. **Median age:** 37.7.

Income 2000: per capita $16,142; median household $34,698; **Pop below poverty level:** 9.5%. ***Personal per capita income 2000-2003:** $21,798-$24,426.

Unemployment 2004: 4.7%. **Change from 2000:** -0.5%. **Median travel time to work:** 32.6 minutes. **Working outside county of residence:** 44.8%.

Cities with pop over 10,000: None.

LACKAWANNA COUNTY

200 N Washington Ave   **Ph:** 570-963-6723
Scranton, PA 18503   **Fax:** 570-963-6387
www.lackawannacounty.org

In northeastern PA, northeast of Wilkes-Barre. Organized Aug 13, 1878 from Luzerne County, the last PA county to be created. **Name Origin:** For the Lackawanna River, which runs through it. From a Delaware Indian word probably meaning 'the stream that forks.'

Area (sq mi): 464.51 (land 458.63; water 5.88). **Pop per sq mi:** 456.8.

Pop 2005: 209,525. **State rank:** 17. **Pop change:** 2000-20005 -1.8%; 1990-2000 -2.6%. **Pop 2000:** 213,295 (White 95.9%; Black or African American 1.3%; Hispanic or Latino 1.4%; Asian 0.8%; Other 1.3%). **Foreign born:** 2.3%. **Median age:** 40.3.

Income 2000: per capita $18,710; median household $34,438; **Pop below poverty level:** 10.6%. ***Personal per capita income 2000-2003:** $27,029-$28,986.

Unemployment 2004: 6%. **Change from 2000:** +0.6%. **Median travel time to work:** 19.8 minutes. **Working outside county of residence:** 15.9%.

Cities with pop over 10,000: Scranton ⛪ (73,928); Dunmore (13,672).

LANCASTER COUNTY

50 N Duke St   **Ph:** 717-299-8000
Lancaster, PA 17602   **Fax:** 717-293-7208
www.co.lancaster.pa.us

In southeastern PA, southeast of Harrisburg; organized May 10, 1729 from Chester County. **Name Origin:** For Lancaster, Lancashire, England, former home of John Wright, a prime figure in the formation of the county.

Area (sq mi): 983.81 (land 949.06; water 34.75). **Pop per sq mi:** 516.9.

Pop 2005: 490,562. **State rank:** 6. **Pop change:** 2000-20005 +4.2%; 1990-2000 +11.3%. **Pop 2000:** 470,658 (White 89.3%; Black or African American 2.8%; Hispanic or Latino 5.7%; Asian 1.4%; Other 4.3%). **Foreign born:** 3.2%. **Median age:** 36.1.

Income 2000: per capita $20,398; median household $45,507; **Pop below poverty level:** 7.8%. ***Personal per capita income 2000-2003:** $28,765-$29,654.

Unemployment 2004: 4%. **Change from 2000:** +0.8%. **Median travel time to work:** 21.7 minutes. **Working outside county of residence:** 13%.

Cities with pop over 10,000: Lancaster ⛪ (55,182); Ephrata (13,180); Elizabethtown (11,920); Columbia (10,159).

LAWRENCE COUNTY

County Courthouse 430 Court St   **Ph:** 724-658-2541
New Castle, PA 16101   **Fax:** 724-652-9646
www.co.lawrence.pa.us

On central-western border of PA, northwest of Pittsburgh; organized Mar 20, 1849 from Beaver and Mercer counties. **Name Origin:** For the *Lawrence*, the flagship of American commander Oliver Hazard Perry (1785-1819) in the Battle of Lake Erie (1813).

Area (sq mi): 362.76 (land 360.46; water 2.3). **Pop per sq mi:** 257.5.

Pop 2005: 92,809. **State rank:** 32. **Pop change:** 2000-20005 -1.9%; 1990-2000 -1.7%. **Pop 2000:** 94,643 (White 94.6%; Black or African American 3.6%; Hispanic or Latino 0.6%; Asian 0.3%; Other 1.1%). **Foreign born:** 1.3%. **Median age:** 40.5.

Income 2000: per capita $16,835; median household $33,152; **Pop below poverty level:** 12.1%. ***Personal per capita income 2000-2003:** $22,687-$24,188.

Unemployment 2004: 6.4%. **Change from 2000:** +0.2%. **Median travel time to work:** 21.3 minutes. **Working outside county of residence:** 31.6%.

Cities with pop over 10,000: New Castle ⛪ (25,308).

LEBANON COUNTY

400 S 8th St   **Ph:** 717-274-2801
Lebanon, PA 17042   **Fax:** 717-274-8094
dsf.pacounties.org/lebanon/

In east-central PA, east of Harrisburg; organized Feb 16, 1815 from Dauphin and Lancaster counties. **Name Origin:** For Lebanon Township, from which the county was formed.

Area (sq mi): 362.6 (land 361.86; water 0.74). **Pop per sq mi:** 347.

Pop 2005: 125,578. **State rank:** 28. **Pop change:** 2000-20005 +4.4%; 1990-2000 +5.8%. **Pop 2000:** 120,327 (White 92.3%; Black

*Source: Personal per capita income data are from the Bureau of Economic Analysis; per capita income data are from the Bureau of the Census. See Introduction for explanation of differences.

598

Lebanon County (cont'd)

or African American 1.3%; Hispanic or Latino 5%; Asian 0.9%; Other 3.3%). **Foreign born:** 2.4%. **Median age:** 38.7.

Income 2000: per capita $19,773; median household $40,838; **Pop below poverty level:** 7.5%. *****Personal per capita income 2000-2003:** $26,366-$28,315.

Unemployment 2004: 4.1%. **Change from 2000.** –1%. **Median travel time to work:** 21.8 minutes. **Working outside county of residence:** 37.6%.

Cities with pop over 10,000: Lebanon ⚖ (23,925).

LEHIGH COUNTY

455 W Hamilton St   **Ph:** 610-782-3148
Allentown, PA 18101   **Fax:** 610-770-3840
www.lehighcounty.org

In mideastern PA, northeast of Reading; organized Mar 6, 1812 from Northampton County. **Name Origin:** For the Lehigh River, which forms most of its eastern border. From Algonquian *lechauwekink* 'where there are forks'; shortened by Germans to *Lecha*, then anglicized.

Area (sq mi): 348.34 (land 346.66; water 1.68). **Pop per sq mi:** 953.2.

Pop 2005: 330,433. **State rank:** 11. **Pop change:** 2000-20005 +5.9%; 1990-2000 +7.2%. **Pop 2000:** 312,090 (White 83.2%; Black or African American 3.6%; Hispanic or Latino 10.2%; Asian 2.1%; Other 7.3%). **Foreign born:** 6.2%. **Median age:** 38.3.

Income 2000: per capita $21,897; median household $43,449; **Pop below poverty level:** 9.3%. *****Personal per capita income 2000-2003:** $31,050-$33,040.

Unemployment 2004: 5.4%. **Change from 2000:** +1.2%. **Median travel time to work:** 22.1 minutes. **Working outside county of residence:** 25.4%.

Cities with pop over 10,000: Allentown ⚖ (106,732); Emmaus (11,325).

LUZERNE COUNTY

200 N River St   **Ph:** 570-825-1500
Wilkes-Barre, PA 18711   **Fax:** 570-825-9343
www.luzernecounty.org

In north-central PA, southwest of Scranton; organized Sep 25, 1786 from Northumberland County. **Name Origin:** For Anne Cesar, Chevalier de la Luzerne (1741-91), French diplomat who helped negotiate the termination of the American Revolution.

Area (sq mi): 907.13 (land 890.81; water 16.32). **Pop per sq mi:** 351.2.

Pop 2005: 312,861. **State rank:** 12. **Pop change:** 2000-20005 -2%; 1990-2000 -2.7%. **Pop 2000:** 319,250 (White 96%; Black or African American 1.7%; Hispanic or Latino 1.2%; Asian 0.6%; Other 1.1%). **Foreign born:** 1.9%. **Median age:** 40.8.

Income 2000: per capita $18,228; median household $33,771; **Pop below poverty level:** 11.1%. *****Personal per capita income 2000-2003:** $25,891-$28,026.

Unemployment 2004: 6.8%. **Change from 2000:** +1.3%. **Median travel time to work:** 21.2 minutes. **Working outside county of residence:** 14.5%.

Cities with pop over 10,000: Wilkes-Barre ⚖ (41,559); Hazleton (22,319); Kingston (13,284); Nanticoke (10,471).

LYCOMING COUNTY

48 W 3rd St   **Ph:** 570-327-2256
Williamsport, PA 17701   **Fax:** 570-327-2505
www.lyco.org

In north-central PA, west of Wilkes-Barre; organized Apr 13, 1795 from Northumberland County. **Name Origin:** For Lycoming Creek, which runs through it and had for many years been the dividing line between settled and disputed Indian lands. From Delaware Indian word probably meaning 'sandy or gravel-bed creek.'

Area (sq mi): 1243.77 (land 1234.85; water 8.91). **Pop per sq mi:** 95.9.

Pop 2005: 118,395. **State rank:** 30. **Pop change:** 2000-20005 -1.4%; 1990-2000 +1.1%. **Pop 2000:** 120,044 (White 93.6%; Black or African American 4.3%; Hispanic or Latino 0.7%; Asian 0.4%; Other 1.4%). **Foreign born:** 1.2%. **Median age:** 38.4.

Income 2000: per capita $17,224; median household $34,016; **Pop below poverty level:** 11.5%. *****Personal per capita income 2000-2003:** $23,026-$26,039.

Unemployment 2004: 6.2%. **Change from 2000:** +0.4%. **Median travel time to work:** 19.6 minutes. **Working outside county of residence:** 12.4%.

Cities with pop over 10,000: Williamsport ⚖ (30,175).

MCKEAN COUNTY

PO Box 1507   **Ph:** 814-887-5571
Smethport, PA 16749   **Fax:** 814-887-2242
www.mckeancountypa.org

On northern border of western PA. Organized Mar 26, 1804 from Lycoming County, but administered through Centre County until 1814, then Potter and Lycoming counties; fully organized in 1826. **Name Origin:** For Thomas McKean (1734-1817), signer of the Declaration of Independence, chief justice of PA (1777-79), and governor (1799-1808).

Area (sq mi): 984.17 (land 981.57; water 2.6). **Pop per sq mi:** 45.2.

Pop 2005: 44,370. **State rank:** 50. **Pop change:** 2000-20005 -3.4%; 1990-2000 -2.5%. **Pop 2000:** 45,936 (White 96%; Black or African American 1.9%; Hispanic or Latino 1.1%; Asian 0.3%; Other 1.3%). **Foreign born:** 1.4%. **Median age:** 38.7.

Income 2000: per capita $16,777; median household $33,040; **Pop below poverty level:** 13.1%. *****Personal per capita income 2000-2003:** $24,630-$25,516.

Unemployment 2004: 6.2%. **Change from 2000:** +0.3%. **Median travel time to work:** 20.1 minutes. **Working outside county of residence:** 18.4%.

Cities with pop over 10,000: None.

⚖ *County Seat*

MERCER COUNTY

Mercer County Courthouse Rm 103　　**Ph:** 724-662-3800
Mercer, PA 16137　　**Fax:** 724-662-1530
www.merlink.org/mcjac/governmt.htm

On central-western border of PA, north of New Castle; organized Mar 12, 1800 from Allegheny County. **Name Origin:** For Gen. Hugh Mercer (1721-77), Revolutionary War officer and physician.

Area (sq mi): 682.57 (land 671.82; water 10.76). **Pop per sq mi:** 178.

Pop 2005: 119,598. **State rank:** 29. **Pop change:** 2000-20005 - 0.6%; 1990-2000 -0.6%. **Pop 2000:** 120,293 (White 92.7%; Black or African American 5.3%; Hispanic or Latino 0.7%; Asian 0.4%; Other 1.2%). **Foreign born:** 1.6%. **Median age:** 39.6.

Income 2000: per capita $17,636; median household $34,666; **Pop below poverty level:** 11.5%. ***Personal per capita income 2000-2003:** $23,432-$25,292.

Unemployment 2004: 6.5%. **Change from 2000:** +1.4%. **Median travel time to work:** 19.6 minutes. **Working outside county of residence:** 21.1%.

Cities with pop over 10,000: Hermitage (16,549); Sharon (15,652).

MIFFLIN COUNTY

20 N Wayne St　　**Ph:** 717-248-6733
Lewistown, PA 17044　　**Fax:** 717-248-3695
www.co.mifflin.pa.us

In central PA, east of Altoona; organized Sep 19, 1789 from Cumberland and Northumberland counties. **Name Origin:** For Gen. Thomas Mifflin (1744-1800), member of the Continental Congress (1774-76; 1782-84), PA legislator, and longest-serving governor of PA (1788-99).

Area (sq mi): 414.6 (land 411.86; water 2.75). **Pop per sq mi:** 112.3.

Pop 2005: 46,235. **State rank:** 46. **Pop change:** 2000-20005 -0.5%; 1990-2000 +0.6%. **Pop 2000:** 46,486 (White 98.2%; Black or African American 0.5%; Hispanic or Latino 0.6%; Asian 0.3%; Other 0.7%). **Foreign born:** 0.8%. **Median age:** 38.8.

Income 2000: per capita $15,553; median household $32,175; **Pop below poverty level:** 12.5%. ***Personal per capita income 2000-2003:** $20,460-$22,158.

Unemployment 2004: 6.8%. **Change from 2000:** -0.2%. **Median travel time to work:** 22.1 minutes. **Working outside county of residence:** 21.6%.

Cities with pop over 10,000: None.

MONROE COUNTY

County Courthouse Sq　　**Ph:** 570-420-3400
Stroudsburg, PA 18360　　**Fax:** 570-420-3458
www.co.monroe.pa.us

On central eastern border of PA, southeast of Scranton; organized Apr 1, 1836 from Northampton and Pike counties. **Name Origin:** For James Monroe (1758-1831), fifth U.S. president.

Area (sq mi): 617.42 (land 608.5; water 8.92). **Pop per sq mi:** 268.3.

Pop 2005: 163,234. **State rank:** 21. **Pop change:** 2000-20005 +17.7%; 1990-2000 +44.9%. **Pop 2000:** 138,687 (White 84.8%; Black or African American 6%; Hispanic or Latino 6.6%; Asian 1.1%; Other 4.6%). **Foreign born:** 5.8%. **Median age:** 37.2.

Income 2000: per capita $20,011; median household $46,257; **Pop below poverty level:** 9%. ***Personal per capita income 2000-2003:** $24,440-$25,536.

Unemployment 2004: 5.7%. **Change from 2000:** -0.2%. **Median travel time to work:** 36.7 minutes. **Working outside county of residence:** 36%.

Cities with pop over 10,000: East Stroudsburg (10,404).

MONTGOMERY COUNTY

PO Box 311　　**Ph:** 610-278-3346
Norristown, PA 19404　　**Fax:** 610-278-5188
www.montcopa.org

In southeastern PA, northwest of Philadelphia; organized Sep 10, 1784 from old Philadelphia County. **Name Origin:** For Gen. Richard Montgomery (1736-1775), Revolutionary War officer and hero.

Area (sq mi): 487.45 (land 483.12; water 4.33). **Pop per sq mi:** 1606.

Pop 2005: 775,883. **State rank:** 3. **Pop change:** 2000-20005 +3.4%; 1990-2000 +10.6%. **Pop 2000:** 750,097 (White 85.3%; Black or African American 7.5%; Hispanic or Latino 2%; Asian 4%; Other 2%). **Foreign born:** 7%. **Median age:** 38.2.

Income 2000: per capita $30,898; median household $60,829; **Pop below poverty level:** 4.4%. ***Personal per capita income 2000-2003:** $45,989-$49,429.

Unemployment 2004: 4.3%. **Change from 2000:** +0.8%. **Median travel time to work:** 26.5 minutes. **Working outside county of residence:** 35.3%.

Cities with pop over 10,000: Norristown 🏛 (30,873); Pottstown (21,665); Lansdale (16,014).

MONTOUR COUNTY

29 Mill St　　**Ph:** 570-271-3012
Danville, PA 17821　　**Fax:** 570-271-3071
www.montourco.org

In central PA, southeast of Williamsport; organized May 3, 1850 from Columbia County. **Name Origin:** For Madame Montour (c. 1682-1752), an early PA settler. Of French-Canadian and Indian stock, she was captured and adopted at age ten by an Iroquois tribe. She later used her background as an Indian interpreter and greatly influenced Indian affairs in PA and NY.

Area (sq mi): 132.3 (land 130.75; water 1.55). **Pop per sq mi:** 137.9.

Pop 2005: 18,032. **State rank:** 62. **Pop change:** 2000-20005 -1.1%; 1990-2000 +2.8%. **Pop 2000:** 18,236 (White 96.2%; Black or African American 1%; Hispanic or Latino 0.9%; Asian 1.3%; Other 1.1%). **Foreign born:** 2.2%. **Median age:** 39.8.

Income 2000: per capita $19,302; median household $38,075; **Pop below poverty level:** 8.7%. ***Personal per capita income 2000-2003:** $26,046-$29,871.

Unemployment 2004: 5.2%. **Change from 2000:** +1.7%. **Median travel time to work:** 19.7 minutes. **Working outside county of residence:** 41.4%.

Cities with pop over 10,000: None.

*Source: Personal per capita income data are from the Bureau of Economic Analysis; per capita income data are from the Bureau of the Census. See Introduction for explanation of differences.

NORTHAMPTON COUNTY

669 Washington St   **Ph:** 610-559-6700
Easton, PA 18042   **Fax:** 610-559-6702
www.northamptoncounty.org

On central eastern border of PA, east of Allentown; organized Mar 11, 1752 from Bucks County. **Name Origin:** For Northamptonshire, England, home of Thomas Penn's father-in-law, Thomas Fermor, the Earl of Pomfret.

Area (sq mi): 377.36 (land 373.8; water 3.56). **Pop per sq mi:** 769.8.

Pop 2005: 287,767. **State rank:** 13. **Pop change:** 2000-20005 +7.8%; 1990-2000 +8.1%. **Pop 2000:** 267,066 (White 88.2%; Black or African American 2.8%; Hispanic or Latino 6.7%; Asian 1.4%; Other 4.7%). **Foreign born:** 4.6%. **Median age:** 38.5.

Income 2000: per capita $21,399; median household $45,234; **Pop below poverty level:** 7.9%. ***Personal per capita income 2000-2003:** $28,867-$30,589.

Unemployment 2004: 5.4%. **Change from 2000:** +1.3%. **Median travel time to work:** 24.2 minutes. **Working outside county of residence:** 45.5%.

Cities with pop over 10,000: Bethlehem (72,441); Easton 🏛 (26,267).

NORTHUMBERLAND COUNTY

201 Market St Rt 7   **Ph:** 570-988-4151
Sunbury, PA 17801
www.northumberlandco.org

In central PA, southeast of Williamsport; organized Mar 21, 1772 from Lancaster, Bedford, Berks, Northampton, and Cumberland counties. **Name Origin:** For the county of Northumberland in England.

Area (sq mi): 477.38 (land 459.91; water 17.47). **Pop per sq mi:** 201.4.

Pop 2005: 92,610. **State rank:** 33. **Pop change:** 2000-20005 -2.1%; 1990-2000 -2.3%. **Pop 2000:** 94,556 (White 96.6%; Black or African American 1.5%; Hispanic or Latino 1.1%; Asian 0.2%; Other 1.2%). **Foreign born:** 1.1%. **Median age:** 40.8.

Income 2000: per capita $16,489; median household $31,314; **Pop below poverty level:** 11.9%. ***Personal per capita income 2000-2003:** $22,388-$25,002.

Unemployment 2004: 6.6%. **Change from 2000:** +1.1%. **Median travel time to work:** 23.4 minutes. **Working outside county of residence:** 42%.

Cities with pop over 10,000: Sunbury 🏛 (10,171).

PERRY COUNTY

25 W Main St PO Box 37   **Ph:** 717-582-2131
New Bloomfield, PA 17068   **Fax:** 717-582-5162
www.perryco.org

In south-central PA, northwest of Harrisburg; organized Mar 22, 1820 from Cumberland County. **Name Origin:** For Oliver Hazard Perry (1785-1819), U.S. naval officer during the War of 1812, famous for the message, 'We have met the enemy and they are ours.'

Area (sq mi): 555.77 (land 553.52; water 2.25). **Pop per sq mi:** 80.8.

Pop 2005: 44,728. **State rank:** 49. **Pop change:** 2000-20005 +2.6%; 1990-2000 +5.9%. **Pop 2000:** 43,602 (White 98.1%; Black or African American 0.4%; Hispanic or Latino 0.7%; Asian 0.1%; Other 0.8%). **Foreign born:** 0.9%. **Median age:** 37.5.

Income 2000: per capita $18,551; median household $41,909; **Pop below poverty level:** 7.7%. ***Personal per capita income 2000-2003:** $24,507-$26,070.

Unemployment 2004: 5%. **Change from 2000:** +0.9%. **Median travel time to work:** 34.7 minutes. **Working outside county of residence:** 68.5%.

Cities with pop over 10,000: None.

PHILADELPHIA COUNTY

City Hall Broad & Market St   **Ph:** 215-686-1776
Philadelphia, PA 19107   **Fax:** 215-567-7380
www.phila.gov

On southeastern border of PA, southwest of Trenton, NJ; original county, organized Mar 10, 1682. The county is coterminous with the city. **Name Origin:** Named by William Penn (1644-1718) for either Philadelphia, an ancient biblical city of Lydia, in western Asia Minor, seat of one of the seven early Christian churches, or the abstract Greek noun *philadelphia* 'brotherly love.'

Area (sq mi): 142.64 (land 135.09; water 7.55). **Pop per sq mi:** 10831.9.

Pop 2005: 1,463,281. **State rank:** 1. **Pop change:** 2000-20005 -3.6%; 1990-2000 -4.3%. **Pop 2000:** 1,517,550 (White 42.5%; Black or African American 43.2%; Hispanic or Latino 8.5%; Asian 4.5%; Other 7.3%). **Foreign born:** 9%. **Median age:** 34.2.

Income 2000: per capita $16,509; median household $30,746; **Pop below poverty level:** 22.9%. ***Personal per capita income 2000-2003:** $24,572-$28,194.

Unemployment 2004: 7.5%. **Change from 2000:** +1.1%. **Median travel time to work:** 32 minutes. **Working outside county of residence:** 24.6%.

Cities with pop over 10,000: Philadelphia 🏛 (147,015).

PIKE COUNTY

506 Broad St   **Ph:** 570-296-7613
Milford, PA 18337   **Fax:** 570-296-6055
www.pikepa.org

On northeastern border of PA, east of Scranton; organized Mar 26, 1814 from Wayne County. **Name Origin:** For Gen. Zebulon Montgomery Pike (1779-1813), U.S. army officer and discoverer of Pikes Peak, CO.

Area (sq mi): 566.64 (land 546.81; water 19.83). **Pop per sq mi:** 103.

Pop 2005: 56,337. **State rank:** 42. **Pop change:** 2000-20005 +21.7%; 1990-2000 +65.6%. **Pop 2000:** 46,302 (White 89.8%; Black or African American 3.3%; Hispanic or Latino 5%; Asian 0.6%; Other 3%). **Foreign born:** 5%. **Median age:** 39.6.

Income 2000: per capita $20,315; median household $44,608; **Pop below poverty level:** 6.9%. ***Personal per capita income 2000-2003:** $24,005-$25,056.

Unemployment 2004: 5.8%. **Change from 2000:** +1%. **Median travel time to work:** 46 minutes. **Working outside county of residence:** 71.7%.

Pike County (cont'd)

Cities with pop over 10,000: None.

POTTER COUNTY

1 E 2nd St Rm 22
Coudersport, PA 16915
www.pottercountypa.net

Ph: 814-274-8290
Fax: 814-274-8284

On central northern border of PA; organized Mar 26, 1804 from Lycoming County. **Name Origin:** For Gen. James Potter (1729-89), hero of the Revolutionary War.

Area (sq mi): 1081.42 (land 1081.17; water 0.25). **Pop per sq mi:** 16.5.

Pop 2005: 17,834. **State rank:** 63. **Pop change:** 2000-20005 -1.4%; 1990-2000 +8.2%. **Pop 2000:** 18,080 (White 97.7%; Black or African American 0.3%; Hispanic or Latino 0.6%; Asian 0.5%; Other 1.1%). **Foreign born:** 1.1%. **Median age:** 39.1.

Income 2000: per capita $16,070; median household $32,253; **Pop below poverty level:** 12.7%. ***Personal per capita income 2000-2003:** $24,118-$24,412.

Unemployment 2004: 6.8%. **Change from 2000:** +2.2%. **Median travel time to work:** 23.2 minutes. **Working outside county of residence:** 25.9%.

Cities with pop over 10,000: None.

SCHUYLKILL COUNTY

401 N 2nd St
Pottsville, PA 17901
www.co.schuylkill.pa.us

Ph: 570-628-1200
Fax: 570-628-1210

In east-central PA, west of Allentown; organized Mar 1, 1811 from Berks and Northampton counties. **Name Origin:** For the Schuylkill River, which traverses it; from Dutch *schuy* 'hidden,' and *kill* 'stream'.

Area (sq mi): 782.61 (land 778.36; water 4.25). **Pop per sq mi:** 189.4.

Pop 2005: 147,447. **State rank:** 23. **Pop change:** 2000-20005 -1.9%; 1990-2000 -1.5%. **Pop 2000:** 150,336 (White 96%; Black or African American 2.1%; Hispanic or Latino 1.1%; Asian 0.4%; Other 0.9%). **Foreign born:** 1%. **Median age:** 40.9.

Income 2000: per capita $17,230; median household $32,699; **Pop below poverty level:** 9.5%. ***Personal per capita income 2000-2003:** $22,879-$24,756.

Unemployment 2004: 7%. **Change from 2000:** +0%. **Median travel time to work:** 24.9 minutes. **Working outside county of residence:** 29.9%.

Cities with pop over 10,000: Pottsville ⛪ (14,881).

SNYDER COUNTY

9 W Market St
Middleburg, PA 17842
www.snydercounty.org

Ph: 570-837-4207
Fax: 570-837-4282

In central PA, south of Williamsport; organized Mar 2, 1855 from Union County. **Name Origin:** For Simon Snyder (1759-1819), member of the PA assembly (1797-1807), speaker of the house (1802-07), and governor (1808-17).

Area (sq mi): 332.16 (land 331.2; water 0.95). **Pop per sq mi:** 115.4.

Pop 2005: 38,207. **State rank:** 57. **Pop change:** 2000-20005 +1.8%; 1990-2000 +2.4%. **Pop 2000:** 37,546 (White 97.4%; Black or African American 0.8%; Hispanic or Latino 1%; Asian 0.4%; Other 0.8%). **Foreign born:** 0.9%. **Median age:** 36.7.

Income 2000: per capita $16,756; median household $35,981; **Pop below poverty level:** 9.9%. ***Personal per capita income 2000-2003:** $25,041-$25,863.

Unemployment 2004: 4.8%. **Change from 2000:** +1%. **Median travel time to work:** 22 minutes. **Working outside county of residence:** 31.3%.

Cities with pop over 10,000: None.

SOMERSET COUNTY

300 N Center Ave
Somerset, PA 15501
www.co.somerset.pa.us

Ph: 814-445-1400
Fax: 814-445-1447

On the southern border of western PA, south of Johnstown; organized Apr 17, 1795 from Bedford County. **Name Origin:** For Somersetshire, England.

Area (sq mi): 1081.17 (land 1074.66; water 6.51). **Pop per sq mi:** 73.4.

Pop 2005: 78,907. **State rank:** 37. **Pop change:** 2000-20005 -1.4%; 1990-2000 +2.3%. **Pop 2000:** 80,023 (White 97.1%; Black or African American 1.6%; Hispanic or Latino 0.7%; Asian 0.2%; Other 0.8%). **Foreign born:** 0.7%. **Median age:** 40.2.

Income 2000: per capita $15,178; median household $30,911; **Pop below poverty level:** 11.8%. ***Personal per capita income 2000-2003:** $20,892-$22,125.

Unemployment 2004: 6.5%. **Change from 2000:** +0.1%. **Median travel time to work:** 22.9 minutes. **Working outside county of residence:** 26.9%.

Cities with pop over 10,000: None.

SULLIVAN COUNTY

PO Box 157 Main & Muncy Sts
Laporte, PA 18626
www.sullivancounty-pa.us

Ph: 570-946-5201
Fax: 570-946-4421

In north-central PA, west of Scranton; organized Mar 15, 1847 from Lycoming County. **Name Origin:** For Gen. John Sullivan (1740-95), Revolutionary War officer, member of the Continental Congress (1774-75), and chief executive of NH (1786-88; 1789-90). He led the punitive expedition against the Iroquois Indians (1779) who had caused the Wyoming Massacre.

Area (sq mi): 452.35 (land 449.94; water 2.41). **Pop per sq mi:** 14.2.

Pop 2005: 6,391. **State rank:** 65. **Pop change:** 2000-20005 -2.5%; 1990-2000 +7.4%. **Pop 2000:** 6,556 (White 95.2%; Black or African American 2.2%; Hispanic or Latino 1.1%; Asian 0.2%; Other 2.2%). **Foreign born:** 0.8%. **Median age:** 43.

Income 2000: per capita $16,438; median household $30,279; **Pop below poverty level:** 14.5%. ***Personal per capita income 2000-2003:** $21,839-$23,647.

Unemployment 2004: 5.9%. **Change from 2000:** -0.3%. **Median travel time to work:** 25.3 minutes. **Working outside county of residence:** 36.4%.

**Source: Personal per capita income data are from the Bureau of Economic Analysis; per capita income data are from the Bureau of the Census.
See Introduction for explanation of differences.*

Sullivan County (cont'd)

Cities with pop over 10,000: None.

SUSQUEHANNA COUNTY

11 Maple St   **Ph:** 570-278-4600
Montrose, PA 18801   **Fax:** 570-278-9268
www.susquehanna.pa.us

On northern border of eastern PA, north of Scranton, organized Feb 21, 1810 from Luzerne County. **Name Origin:** For the Susquehanna River, which runs through it.

Area (sq mi): 832.4 (land 822.86; water 9.54). **Pop per sq mi:** 51.2.

Pop 2005: 42,124. **State rank:** 52. **Pop change:** 2000-20005 -0.3%; 1990-2000 +4.6%. **Pop 2000:** 42,238 (White 98.1%; Black or African American 0.3%; Hispanic or Latino 0.7%; Asian 0.2%; Other 0.9%). **Foreign born:** 1.3%. **Median age:** 39.5.

Income 2000: per capita $16,435; median household $33,622; **Pop below poverty level:** 12.3%. ***Personal per capita income 2000-2003:** $23,433-$23,650.

Unemployment 2004: 5.8%. **Change from 2000:** -1.1%. **Median travel time to work:** 26.2 minutes. **Working outside county of residence:** 51.8%.

Cities with pop over 10,000: None.

TIOGA COUNTY

118 Main St   **Ph:** 570-723-8191
Wellsboro, PA 16901
www.visittiogapa.com

On central northern border of PA, north of Williamsport; organized Mar 26, 1804 from Lycoming County. **Name Origin:** For the Tioga River, which flows through it; from Iroquoian for 'place between two points' or 'at the forks,' for the Indian town on the Susquehanna River near Athens, PA; the town was called *Diahoga* or *Tioga*.

Area (sq mi): 1137.3 (land 1133.73; water 3.58). **Pop per sq mi:** 36.7.

Pop 2005: 41,649. **State rank:** 54. **Pop change:** 2000-20005 +0.7%; 1990-2000 +0.6%. **Pop 2000:** 41,373 (White 97.8%; Black or African American 0.6%; Hispanic or Latino 0.5%; Asian 0.3%; Other 0.9%). **Foreign born:** 1.1%. **Median age:** 38.5.

Income 2000: per capita $15,549; median household $32,020; **Pop below poverty level:** 13.5%. ***Personal per capita income 2000-2003:** $20,492-$21,277.

Unemployment 2004: 5.9%. **Change from 2000:** -1%. **Median travel time to work:** 23.1 minutes. **Working outside county of residence:** 24.2%.

Cities with pop over 10,000: None.

UNION COUNTY

103 S 2nd St   **Ph:** 570-524-8600
Lewisburg, PA 17837   **Fax:** 570-524-8635
www.unionco.org

In central PA, south of Williamsport; organized Mar 22, 1813 from Northumberland County. **Name Origin:** As an expression of belief in the federal union of the states.

Area (sq mi): 317.12 (land 316.73; water 0.39). **Pop per sq mi:** 136.2.

Pop 2005: 43,131. **State rank:** 51. **Pop change:** 2000-20005 +3.6%; 1990-2000 +15.1%. **Pop 2000:** 41,624 (White 87.6%; Black or African American 6.9%; Hispanic or Latino 3.9%; Asian 1.1%; Other 2%). **Foreign born:** 3.7%. **Median age:** 35.8.

Income 2000: per capita $17,918; median household $40,336; **Pop below poverty level:** 8.8%. ***Personal per capita income 2000-2003:** $21,919-$23,056.

Unemployment 2004: 5.4%. **Change from 2000:** +1.9%. **Median travel time to work:** 20 minutes. **Working outside county of residence:** 34.3%.

Cities with pop over 10,000: None.

VENANGO COUNTY

Courthouse Annex 1174 Elk St   **Ph:** 814-432-9510
Franklin, PA 16323   **Fax:** 814-432-3149
www.co.venango.pa.us

In northwestern PA, southeast of Erie; organized Mar 12, 1800 from Allegheny and Lycoming counties. **Name Origin:** For the Venango River (now called French Creek), which flows through it; from an Indian term of uncertain origin, possibly from *innungah* 'a figure carved on a tree.'

Area (sq mi): 683.02 (land 675.04; water 7.98). **Pop per sq mi:** 82.9.

Pop 2005: 55,928. **State rank:** 43. **Pop change:** 2000-20005 -2.8%; 1990-2000 -3.1%. **Pop 2000:** 57,565 (White 97.3%; Black or African American 1.1%; Hispanic or Latino 0.5%; Asian 0.2%; Other 1.1%). **Foreign born:** 0.6%. **Median age:** 40.2.

Income 2000: per capita $16,252; median household $32,257; **Pop below poverty level:** 13.4%. ***Personal per capita income 2000-2003:** $23,317-$24,548.

Unemployment 2004: 6.3%. **Change from 2000:** +0.9%. **Median travel time to work:** 21.2 minutes. **Working outside county of residence:** 22.9%.

Cities with pop over 10,000: Oil City (11,060).

WARREN COUNTY

204 4th Ave   **Ph:** 814-728-3400
Warren, PA 16365   **Fax:** 814-728-3479
www.warren-county.net

On northern border of western PA, southeast of Erie; organized Mar 12, 1800 from Allegheny and Lycoming counties. **Name Origin:** For Gen. Joseph Warren (1741-75), Revolutionary War patriot and member of the Continental Congress who dispatched Paul Revere (1735-1818) on his famous ride.

Area (sq mi): 897.81 (land 883.45; water 14.36). **Pop per sq mi:** 47.6.

Pop 2005: 42,033. **State rank:** 53. **Pop change:** 2000-20005 -4.2%; 1990-2000 -2.6%. **Pop 2000:** 43,863 (White 98.4%; Black or African American 0.2%; Hispanic or Latino 0.3%; Asian 0.3%; Other 0.8%). **Foreign born:** 0.9%. **Median age:** 40.5.

Income 2000: per capita $17,862; median household $36,083; **Pop below poverty level:** 9.9%. ***Personal per capita income 2000-2003:** $23,473-$24,584.

Warren County (cont'd)

Unemployment 2004: 5.9%. **Change from 2000:** +0.8%. **Median travel time to work:** 19.6 minutes. **Working outside county of residence:** 18.5%.

Cities with pop over 10,000: None.

WASHINGTON COUNTY

1 S Main St Suite 1005   **Ph:** 724-228-6787
Washington, PA 15301
www.co.washington.pa.us

On western border of PA, southwest of Pittsburgh; organized Mar 28, 1781 from Westmoreland County. **Name Origin:** For George Washington (1732-99), commander-in-chief of the Revolutionary forces at the time the country was formed; later the first U.S. president.

Area (sq mi): 860.95 (land 857.09; water 3.86). **Pop per sq mi:** 240.8.

Pop 2005: 206,406. **State rank:** 18. **Pop change:** 2000-20005 +1.7%; 1990-2000 -0.8%. **Pop 2000:** 202,897 (White 94.9%; Black or African American 3.3%; Hispanic or Latino 0.6%; Asian 0.4%; Other 1.1%). **Foreign born:** 1.2%. **Median age:** 40.8.

Income 2000: per capita $19,935; median household $37,607; **Pop below poverty level:** 9.8%. ***Personal per capita income 2000-2003:** $27,859-$30,035.

Unemployment 2004: 5.9%. **Change from 2000:** +0.9%. **Median travel time to work:** 25.6 minutes. **Working outside county of residence:** 40.5%.

Cities with pop over 10,000: Washington 🏛 (14,849).

WAYNE COUNTY

925 Court St   **Ph:** 570-253-5970
Honesdale, PA 18431   **Fax:** 570-253-5432
www.co.wayne.pa.us

At the northeastern corner of PA, east of Scranton; organized Mar 21, 1798 from Northampton County. **Name Origin:** For Gen. Anthony Wayne (1745-1796), PA soldier and statesman, nicknamed 'Mad Anthony' for his daring during the Revolutionary War.

Area (sq mi): 750.54 (land 729.22; water 21.32). **Pop per sq mi:** 68.7.

Pop 2005: 50,113. **State rank:** 44. **Pop change:** 2000-20005 +5%; 1990-2000 +19.5%. **Pop 2000:** 47,722 (White 95.7%; Black or African American 1.6%; Hispanic or Latino 1.7%; Asian 0.4%; Other 1.2%). **Foreign born:** 3%. **Median age:** 40.8.

Income 2000: per capita $16,977; median household $34,082; **Pop below poverty level:** 11.3%. ***Personal per capita income 2000-2003:** $23,094-$25,084.

Unemployment 2004: 5.2%. **Change from 2000:** -0.3%. **Median travel time to work:** 26.3 minutes. **Working outside county of residence:** 36.4%.

Cities with pop over 10,000: None.

WESTMORELAND COUNTY

2 N Main St Courthouse Sq Suite 101   **Ph:** 724-830-3100
Greensburg, PA 15601   **Fax:** 724-830-3029
www.co.westmoreland.pa.us

In southwestern PA, east of Pittsburgh; organized Feb 26, 1773 (prior to statehood) from Bedford County. **Name Origin:** For the former county of Westmorland in northwest England, with spelling change.

Area (sq mi): 1036.34 (land 1025.48; water 10.86). **Pop per sq mi:** 358.5.

Pop 2005: 367,635. **State rank:** 10. **Pop change:** 2000-20005 -0.6%; 1990-2000 -0.1%. **Pop 2000:** 369,993 (White 96.2%; Black or African American 2%; Hispanic or Latino 0.5%; Asian 0.5%; Other 0.8%). **Foreign born:** 1.4%. **Median age:** 41.3.

Income 2000: per capita $19,674; median household $37,106; **Pop below poverty level:** 8.6%. ***Personal per capita income 2000-2003:** $26,906-$28,803.

Unemployment 2004: 6.1%. **Change from 2000:** +1.2%. **Median travel time to work:** 25.4 minutes. **Working outside county of residence:** 35.8%.

Cities with pop over 10,000: Murrysville (19,407); Greensburg 🏛 (15,579); New Kensington (14,245); Lower Burrell (12,521); Jeannette (10,309).

WYOMING COUNTY

1 Courthouse Sq   **Ph:** 570-836-3200
Tunkhannock, PA 18657   **Fax:** 570-836-7244
www.pacounties.org/wyoming

In northeastern PA, west of Scranton; organized Apr 4, 1842 from Luzerne County. **Name Origin:** For the Wyoming Valley, the northern extent of which is in the county.

Area (sq mi): 404.79 (land 397.2; water 7.59). **Pop per sq mi:** 70.9.

Pop 2005: 28,160. **State rank:** 60. **Pop change:** 2000-20005 +0.3%; 1990-2000 +0%. **Pop 2000:** 28,080 (White 97.8%; Black or African American 0.5%; Hispanic or Latino 0.7%; Asian 0.3%; Other 0.9%). **Foreign born:** 1.2%. **Median age:** 37.8.

Income 2000: per capita $17,452; median household $36,365; **Pop below poverty level:** 10.2%. ***Personal per capita income 2000-2003:** $22,798-$24,055.

Unemployment 2004: 6.2%. **Change from 2000:** +1.6%. **Median travel time to work:** 26.2 minutes. **Working outside county of residence:** 48.7%.

Cities with pop over 10,000: None.

YORK COUNTY

45 N George St   **Ph:** 717-771-9612
York, PA 17401   **Fax:** 717-771-9096
www.york-county.org

On southeastern border of PA, south of Harrisburg; organized Aug 19, 1749 from Lancaster County. **Name Origin:** For York and Yorkshire, England, and for James, Duke of York and Albany (1633-1701), later James II, king of England. Name perhaps suggested by its proximity to Lancaster County; the houses of York and Lancaster are linked in English history.

Area (sq mi): 910.25 (land 904.45; water 5.8). **Pop per sq mi:** 452.

*Source: Personal per capita income data are from the Bureau of Economic Analysis; per capita income data are from the Bureau of the Census. See Introduction for explanation of differences.

York County (cont'd)

Pop 2005: 408,801. **State rank:** 8. **Pop change:** 2000-20005 +7.1%; 1990-2000 +12.4%. **Pop 2000:** 381,751 (White 91.5%; Black or African American 3.7%; Hispanic or Latino 3%; Asian 0.9%; Other 2.7%). **Foreign born:** 2.2%. **Median age:** 37.8.

Income 2000: per capita $21,086; median household $45,268; **Pop below poverty level:** 6.7%. *Personal per capita income 2000-2003:** $28,788-$29,181.

Unemployment 2004: 4.6%. **Change from 2000:** +0.1%. **Median travel time to work:** 23.9 minutes. **Working outside county of residence:** 26.4%.

Cities with pop over 10,000: York ▥ (40,043); Hanover (14,916).

Rhode Island

MASSACHUSETTS

■ Woonsocket

Providence

◉ Providence ✪

CONNECTICUT

Bristol

Bristol ◉

Kent

East Greenwich ◉

Newport

Washington

West Kingston ◉

Newport ◉

N

NEW YORK

Atlantic Ocean

	County boundary
◉	**Kent** County name
◉	County seat
■	Major city
✪	State capital

Rhode Island

RHODE ISLAND STATE INFORMATION

www.ri.gov   **Ph:** 401-222-2000

Area (sq mi): 1545.05 (land 1044.93; water 500.12). **Pop per sq mi:** 1029.9.

Pop 2005: 1,076,189. **Pop change:** 2000-20005 +2.7%; 1990-2000 +4.5%. **Pop 2000:** 1,048,319 (White 81.9%; Black or African American 4.5%; Hispanic or Latino 8.7%; Asian 2.3%; Other 8.3%). **Foreign born:** 11.4%. **Median age:** 36.7.

Income 2000: per capita $21,688; median household $42,090; **Pop below poverty level:** 11.9%. ***Personal per capita income 2000-2003:** $29,214-$32,038.

Unemployment 2004: 5.2%. **Change from 2000:** +1%. **Median travel time to work:** 22.5 minutes. **Working outside county of residence:** 35.3%.

BRISTOL COUNTY

10 Court St   **Ph:** 401-253-7000
Bristol, RI 02809   **Fax:** 401-253-3080

Largely peninsular area in eastern RI, south of Providence; organized Feb 17, 1747 from Newport County. **Name Origin:** For Bristol, England.

Area (sq mi): 44.71 (land 24.68; water 20.03). **Pop per sq mi:** 2137.1.

Pop 2005: 52,743. **State rank:** 5. **Pop change:** 2000-20005 +4.1%; 1990-2000 +3.7%. **Pop 2000:** 50,648 (White 96.1%; Black or African American 0.7%; Hispanic or Latino 1.1%; Asian 1%; Other 1.5%). **Foreign born:** 10%. **Median age:** 39.3.

Income 2000: per capita $26,503; median household $50,737; **Pop below poverty level:** 6.3%. ***Personal per capita income 2000-2003:** $36,289-$38,771.

Unemployment 2004: 4.4%. **Change from 2000:** +1%. **Median travel time to work:** 23.4 minutes. **Working outside county of residence:** 60%.

Cities with pop over 10,000: None.

KENT COUNTY

222 Quaker Ln Suite 6   **Ph:** 401-822-1311
Warwick, RI 02886

In central RI, south of Cranston; organized Jun 11, 1750 from Washington County. **Name Origin:** For the county in England.

Area (sq mi): 188.1 (land 170.17; water 17.92). **Pop per sq mi:** 1008.3.

Pop 2005: 171,590. **State rank:** 2. **Pop change:** 2000-20005 +2.7%; 1990-2000 +3.7%. **Pop 2000:** 167,090 (White 94.6%; Black or African American 0.9%; Hispanic or Latino 1.7%; Asian 1.3%; Other 2.1%). **Foreign born:** 4.9%. **Median age:** 38.9.

Income 2000: per capita $23,833; median household $47,617; **Pop below poverty level:** 6.6%. ***Personal per capita income 2000-2003:** $30,862-$33,908.

Unemployment 2004: 4.9%. **Change from 2000:** +0.6%. **Median travel time to work:** 22.8 minutes. **Working outside county of residence:** 50.9%.

Cities with pop over 10,000: Warwick 🏛 (87,683).

NEWPORT COUNTY

45 Washington Sq   **Ph:** 401-841-8330
Newport, RI 02840   **Fax:** 401-846-1673

In southeastern RI, comprising the islands in Narragansett Bay and mainland along the eastern border of RI, south of Fall River, MA. Original county, organized as Rhode Island County Jun 22, 1703; name changed Jun 16, 1729. **Name Origin:** Descriptive, or possibly recalling Newport, Monmouthshire, England.

Area (sq mi): 313.64 (land 104.05; water 209.59). **Pop per sq mi:** 804.8.

Pop 2005: 83,740. **State rank:** 4. **Pop change:** 2000-20005 -2%; 1990-2000 -2%. **Pop 2000:** 85,433 (White 90.1%; Black or African American 3.7%; Hispanic or Latino 2.8%; Asian 1.2%; Other 3.6%). **Foreign born:** 4.9%. **Median age:** 38.6.

Income 2000: per capita $26,779; median household $50,448; **Pop below poverty level:** 7.1%. ***Personal per capita income 2000-2003:** $35,159-$37,851.

Unemployment 2004: 4.6%. **Change from 2000:** +0.8%. **Median travel time to work:** 21.7 minutes. **Working outside county of residence:** 31.2%.

Cities with pop over 10,000: Newport 🏛 (25,879).

PROVIDENCE COUNTY

1 Dorrance Plaza   **Ph:** 401-458-5400
Providence, RI 02903

In northern RI; original county, organized as the County of Providence Plantations Jun 22, 1703; name modified Jun 16, 1729. **Name Origin:** For the city, its county seat.

Area (sq mi): 435.82 (land 413.27; water 22.56). **Pop per sq mi:** 1547.8.

Pop 2005: 639,653. **State rank:** 1. **Pop change:** 2000-20005 +2.9%; 1990-2000 +4.2%. **Pop 2000:** 621,602 (White 73.8%; Black or

Providence County (cont'd)

African American 6.5%; Hispanic or Latino 13.4%; Asian 2.9%; Other 12.2%). **Foreign born:** 15.6%. **Median age:** 35.4.

Income 2000: per capita $19,255; median household $36,950; **Pop below poverty level:** 15.5%. ***Personal per capita income 2000-2003:** $26,670-$29,505.

Unemployment 2004: 5.6%. **Change from 2000:** +0.2%. **Median travel time to work:** 22 minutes. **Working outside county of residence:** 26.6%.

Cities with pop over 10,000: 6 (see page 38 for cities).

WASHINGTON COUNTY

4800 Tower Hill Rd	**Ph:** 401-782-4121
Wakefield, RI 02879	**Fax:** 401-782-4190

In southwestern RI; incorporated as King's County Jun 16, 1729 from Newport County. **Name Origin:** For George Washingtron (1732-99), American patriot and first U.S. president. Name changed from King's County on Oct 29, 1781. Originally called the Narragansett Country; changed to King's Province on Mar 20, 1654.

Area (sq mi): 562.77 (land 332.75; water 230.02). **Pop per sq mi:** 386.1.

Pop 2005: 128,463. **State rank:** 3. **Pop change:** 2000-20005 +4%; 1990-2000 +12.3%. **Pop 2000:** 123,546 (White 94%; Black or African American 0.9%; Hispanic or Latino 1.4%; Asian 1.5%; Other 2.8%). **Foreign born:** 4.2%. **Median age:** 37.4.

Income 2000: per capita $25,530; median household $53,103; **Pop below poverty level:** 7.3%. ***Personal per capita income 2000-2003:** $32,767-$35,564.

Unemployment 2004: 4.2%. **Change from 2000:** +0.9%. **Median travel time to work:** 24.7 minutes. **Working outside county of residence:** 46.2%.

Cities with pop over 10,000: None.

*Source: Personal per capita income data are from the Bureau of Economic Analysis; per capita income data are from the Bureau of the Census. See Introduction for explanation of differences.

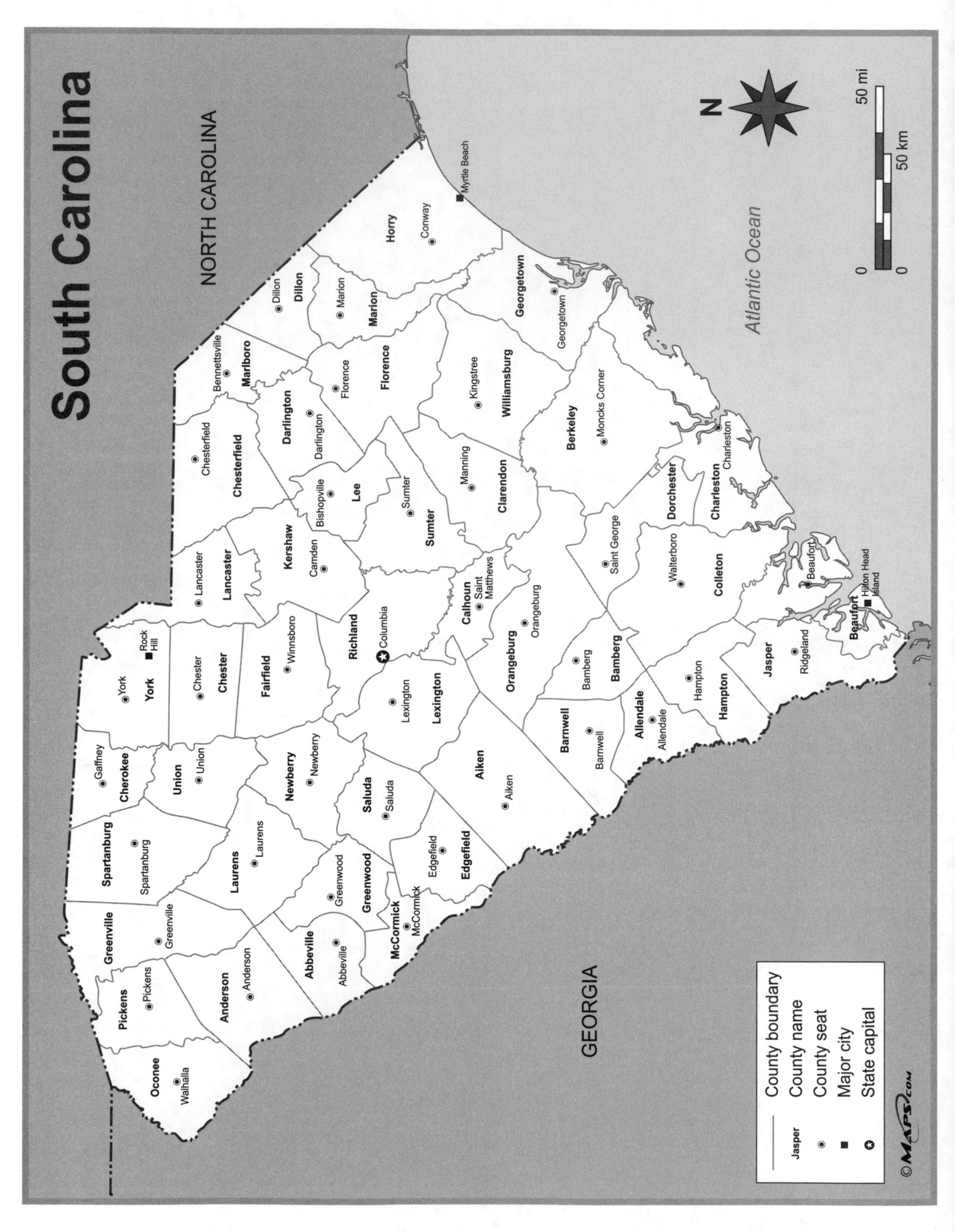

South Carolina

South Carolina

SOUTH CAROLINA STATE INFORMATION

www.sc.gov **Ph:** 803-896-0000

Area (sq mi): 32020.2 (land 30,109.47; water 1910.73). **Pop per sq mi:** 141.3.

Pop 2005: 4,255,083. **Pop change:** 2000-20005 +6.1%; 1990-2000 +15.1%. **Pop 2000:** 4,012,012 (White 66.1%; Black or African American 29.5%; Hispanic or Latino 2.4%; Asian 0.9%; Other 2.3%). **Foreign born:** 2.9%. **Median age:** 35.4.

Income 2000: per capita $18,795; median household $37,082; **Pop below poverty level:** 14.1%. *Personal per capita income 2000-2003:** $24,424-$26,144.

Unemployment 2004: 6.8%. **Change from 2000:** +3.2%. **Median travel time to work:** 24.3 minutes. **Working outside county of residence:** 27.6%.

ABBEVILLE COUNTY

Courthouse PO Box 99 **Ph:** 864-366-5312
Abbeville, SC 29620 **Fax:** 864-366-4595
www.sccounties.org/counties/Abbeville.htm

On northwestern coast of SC, south of Greenville; established Mar 12, 1785 from Ninety Six District. (In 1868 all districts were re-named counties.) **Name Origin:** For the city in Somme, France.

Area (sq mi): 511.05 (land 508.03; water 3.02). **Pop per sq mi:** 51.4.

Pop 2005: 26,133. **State rank:** 35. **Pop change:** 2000-20005 -0.1%; 1990-2000 +9.7%. **Pop 2000:** 26,167 (White 68%; Black or African American 30.3%; Hispanic or Latino 0.8%; Asian 0.2%; Other 1.1%). **Foreign born:** 1%. **Median age:** 36.9.

Income 2000: per capita $15,370; median household $32,635; **Pop below poverty level:** 13.7%. *Personal per capita income 2000-2003:** $22,966-$20,289.

Unemployment 2004: 8.2%. **Change from 2000:** +0.2%. **Median travel time to work:** 25.4 minutes. **Working outside county of residence:** 48%.

Cities with pop over 10,000: None.

AIKEN COUNTY

828 Richland Ave W **Ph:** 803-642-2012
Aiken, SC 29801 **Fax:** 803-642-2124
www.aikencounty.net

On the central western border of SC, east of Augusta, GA; organized Mar 10, 1871 from Edgefield, Barnwell, Lexington, and Orangeburg counties. **Name Origin:** For William Aiken (1806-87), SC governor (1844-46).

Area (sq mi): 1080.46 (land 1072.66; water 7.79). **Pop per sq mi:** 140.

Pop 2005: 150,181. **State rank:** 10. **Pop change:** 2000-20005 +5.4%; 1990-2000 +17.9%. **Pop 2000:** 142,552 (White 70.4%; Black or African American 25.6%; Hispanic or Latino 2.1%; Asian 0.6%; Other 2.4%). **Foreign born:** 2.3%. **Median age:** 36.4.

Income 2000: per capita $18,772; median household $37,889; **Pop below poverty level:** 13.8%. *Personal per capita income 2000-2003:** $24,832-$27,350.

Unemployment 2004: 5.8%. **Change from 2000:** +0%. **Median travel time to work:** 24.8 minutes. **Working outside county of residence:** 29.6%.

Cities with pop over 10,000: Aiken 🏛 (27,299); North Augusta (19,095).

ALLENDALE COUNTY

PO Box 190 **Ph:** 803-584-3438
Allendale, SC 29810 **Fax:** 803-584-7042
www.allendalecounty.com

On southwestern border of SC, south of Augusta, GA; organized Feb 6, 1919 from Barnwell and Hampton counties. **Name Origin:** For the county seat.

Area (sq mi): 412.58 (land 408.2; water 4.38). **Pop per sq mi:** 26.7.

Pop 2005: 10,917. **State rank:** 45. **Pop change:** 2000-20005 -2.6%; 1990-2000 -4.4%. **Pop 2000:** 11,211 (White 27%; Black or African American 71%; Hispanic or Latino 1.6%; Asian 0.1%; Other 1.5%). **Foreign born:** 1.4%. **Median age:** 35.1.

Income 2000: per capita $11,293; median household $20,898; **Pop below poverty level:** 34.5%. *Personal per capita income 2000-2003:** $16,246-$17,221.

Unemployment 2004: 9.8%. **Change from 2000:** +5.2%. **Median travel time to work:** 26.7 minutes. **Working outside county of residence:** 35.9%.

Cities with pop over 10,000: None.

ANDERSON COUNTY

100 S Main St **Ph:** 864-260-4000
Anderson, SC 29624 **Fax:** 864-260-4106
www.andersoncountysc.org

On the northwestern border of SC, southwest of Greenville; organized Dec 20, 1826 from Old Pendleton District, which was abolished at that time. **Name Origin:** For Gen. Robert Anderson (?-1813), a SC officer in the American Revolution.

🏛 *County Seat*

Anderson County (cont'd)

Area (sq mi): 757.45 (land 718.02; water 39.43). **Pop per sq mi:** 244.4.

Pop 2005: 175,514. **State rank:** 8. **Pop change:** 2000-20005 +5.9%; 1990-2000 +14.1%. **Pop 2000:** 165,740 (White 80.9%; Black or African American 16.6%; Hispanic or Latino 1.1%; Asian 0.4%; Other 1.4%). **Foreign born:** 1.5%. **Median age:** 37.3.

Income 2000: per capita $18,365; median household $36,807; **Pop below poverty level:** 12%. *Personal per capita income 2000-2003: $24,272-$25,946.

Unemployment 2004: 7.1%. **Change from 2000:** +1.5%. **Median travel time to work:** 23.7 minutes. **Working outside county of residence:** 31.5%.

Cities with pop over 10,000: Anderson 🏛 (25,715).

BAMBERG COUNTY

PO Box 150   **Ph:** 803-245-3025
Bamberg, SC 29003   **Fax:** 803-245-3088
bambergsc.com

In south-central SC, south of Columbia; organized Feb 25, 1897 from Barnwell County. **Name Origin:** For the Bamberg family, original settlers of the county seat.

Area (sq mi): 395.47 (land 393.25; water 2.22). **Pop per sq mi:** 40.4.

Pop 2005: 15,880. **State rank:** 43. **Pop change:** 2000-20005 -4.7%; 1990-2000 -1.4%. **Pop 2000:** 16,658 (White 36.3%; Black or African American 62.5%; Hispanic or Latino 0.7%; Asian 0.2%; Other 0.8%). **Foreign born:** 0.9%. **Median age:** 35.2.

Income 2000: per capita $12,584; median household $24,007; **Pop below poverty level:** 27.8%. *Personal per capita income 2000-2003: $17,395-$19,051.

Unemployment 2004: 7.3%. **Change from 2000:** +1.3%. **Median travel time to work:** 26 minutes. **Working outside county of residence:** 43.1%.

Cities with pop over 10,000: None.

BARNWELL COUNTY

PO Box 723   **Ph:** 803-541-1020
Barnwell, SC 29812   **Fax:** 803-541-1025
www.barnwellcountysc.com

On the central western border of SC, south of Augusta, GA; organized as Winston District in 1798 from Orangeburg District. **Name Origin:** For John (1748-99) and Robert (1761-1814) Barnwell, legislators.

Area (sq mi): 557.25 (land 548.41; water 8.84). **Pop per sq mi:** 42.6.

Pop 2005: 23,345. **State rank:** 38. **Pop change:** 2000-20005 -0.6%; 1990-2000 +15.7%. **Pop 2000:** 23,478 (White 54.8%; Black or African American 42.6%; Hispanic or Latino 1.4%; Asian 0.4%; Other 1.8%). **Foreign born:** 0.6%. **Median age:** 35.5.

Income 2000: per capita $15,870; median household $28,591; **Pop below poverty level:** 20.9%. *Personal per capita income 2000-2003: $22,216-$19,296.

Unemployment 2004: 9.6%. **Change from 2000:** +1.6%. **Median travel time to work:** 27.9 minutes. **Working outside county of residence:** 34.9%.

Cities with pop over 10,000: None.

BEAUFORT COUNTY

102 Ribaut Rd   **Ph:** 843-470-5218
Beaufort, SC 29902   **Fax:** 843-470-5248
www.co.beaufort.sc.us

On southern border of SC, southwest of Charleston; original county; organized 1768 (prior to statehood). **Name Origin:** For the town.

Area (sq mi): 922.88 (land 586.86; water 336.03). **Pop per sq mi:** 234.9.

Pop 2005: 137,849. **State rank:** 11. **Pop change:** 2000-20005 +14%; 1990-2000 +39.9%. **Pop 2000:** 120,937 (White 67.4%; Black or African American 24%; Hispanic or Latino 6.8%; Asian 0.8%; Other 4.6%). **Foreign born:** 6.3%. **Median age:** 35.8.

Income 2000: per capita $25,377; median household $46,992; **Pop below poverty level:** 10.7%. *Personal per capita income 2000-2003: $32,456-$34,814.

Unemployment 2004: 4.7%. **Change from 2000:** +2.1%. **Median travel time to work:** 23.3 minutes. **Working outside county of residence:** 5.7%.

Cities with pop over 10,000: Hilton Head Island (34,371); Beaufort 🏛 (12,289).

BERKELEY COUNTY

PO Box 219   **Ph:** 843-719-4403
Moncks Corner, SC 29461   **Fax:** 843-719-4511
www.co.berkeley.sc.us

On southeastern border of SC, north of Charleston; organized Jan 31, 1882 from Charleston County. **Name Origin:** For John Berkeley (1607-78), one of eight original lords proprietor of Carolina, and for his brother Sir William Berkeley (1610-77), governor of VA (1642-49; 1660-77).

Area (sq mi): 1228.07 (land 1097.72; water 130.35). **Pop per sq mi:** 138.2.

Pop 2005: 151,673. **State rank:** 9. **Pop change:** 2000-20005 +6.3%; 1990-2000 +10.8%. **Pop 2000:** 142,651 (White 66.8%; Black or African American 26.6%; Hispanic or Latino 2.8%; Asian 1.9%; Other 3.5%). **Foreign born:** 3.1%. **Median age:** 32.

Income 2000: per capita $16,879; median household $39,908; **Pop below poverty level:** 11.8%. *Personal per capita income 2000-2003: $20,156-$23,441.

Unemployment 2004: 5.5%. **Change from 2000:** +1.5%. **Median travel time to work:** 26.5 minutes. **Working outside county of residence:** 54.9%.

Cities with pop over 10,000: Goose Creek (32,250).

CALHOUN COUNTY

102 Courthouse Dr Suite 108
Courthouse Annex   **Ph:** 803-874-2435
Saint Matthews, SC 29135   **Fax:** 803-874-1242

In central SC, south of Columbia; organized Feb 14, 1908 from Lexington and Orangeburg counties. **Name Origin:** For John Caldwell Calhoun (1782-1850), U.S. statesman and champion of Southern causes.

*Source: Personal per capita income data are from the Bureau of Economic Analysis; per capita income data are from the Bureau of the Census. See Introduction for explanation of differences.

Calhoun County (cont'd)

Area (sq mi): 392.34 (land 380.22; water 12.11). **Pop per sq mi:** 39.7.

Pop 2005: 15,100. **State rank:** 44. **Pop change:** 2000-20005 -0.6%; 1990-2000 +19.1%. **Pop 2000:** 15,185 (White 49.5%; Black or African American 48.7%; Hispanic or Latino 1.4%; Asian 0.1%; Other 1.1%). **Foreign born:** 1%. **Median age:** 38.9.

Income 2000: per capita $17,446; median household $32,736; **Pop below poverty level:** 16.2%. ***Personal per capita income 2000-2003:** $22,217-$24,831.

Unemployment 2004: 6.6%. **Change from 2000:** -0.7%. **Median travel time to work:** 29.9 minutes. **Working outside county of residence:** 67.9%.

Cities with pop over 10,000: None.

CHARLESTON COUNTY

4045 Bridge View   **Ph:** 843-958-4030
Charleston, SC 29405   **Fax:** 843-958-4035
www.charlestoncounty.org

On the southeastern border of SC; original district; organized Mar 12, 1785 (prior to statehood). **Name Origin:** For Charles II (1630-85), king of Great Britian, with whose help the American colonies grew vigorously.

Area (sq mi): 1358.11 (land 918.51; water 439.61). **Pop per sq mi:** 359.7.

Pop 2005: 330,368. **State rank:** 3. **Pop change:** 2000-20005 +6.6%; 1990-2000 +5.1%. **Pop 2000:** 309,969 (White 60.8%; Black or African American 34.5%; Hispanic or Latino 2.4%; Asian 1.1%; Other 2.6%). **Foreign born:** 3.6%. **Median age:** 34.5.

Income 2000: per capita $21,393; median household $37,810; **Pop below poverty level:** 16.4%. ***Personal per capita income 2000-2003:** $28,722-$30,951.

Unemployment 2004: 5.4%. **Change from 2000:** +1.8%. **Median travel time to work:** 22.6 minutes. **Working outside county of residence:** 10.4%.

Cities with pop over 10,000: Charleston 🏛 (104,883); North Charleston (84,271); Mount Pleasant (56,350); Hanahan (13,376).

CHEROKEE COUNTY

210 N Limestone St   **Ph:** 864-487-2562
Gaffney, SC 29340   **Fax:** 864-487-2594
www.cherokeecounty-sc.org

On the central northern border of SC, east of Spartanburg; organized Feb 25, 1897 from Union, Spartanburg, and York counties. **Name Origin:** For the Indian tribe of Iroquoian linguistic stock. Name may derive from Creek *tciloki* 'people of a different speech.'

Area (sq mi): 397.28 (land 392.69; water 4.59). **Pop per sq mi:** 137.1.

Pop 2005: 53,844. **State rank:** 24. **Pop change:** 2000-20005 +2.5%; 1990-2000 +18%. **Pop 2000:** 52,537 (White 76.2%; Black or African American 20.6%; Hispanic or Latino 2.1%; Asian 0.3%; Other 2.2%). **Foreign born:** 1.3%. **Median age:** 35.3.

Income 2000: per capita $16,421; median household $33,787; **Pop below poverty level:** 13.9%. ***Personal per capita income 2000-2003:** $20,314-$21,492.

Unemployment 2004: 8.9%. **Change from 2000:** +1.2%. **Median travel time to work:** 23 minutes. **Working outside county of residence:** 30.2%.

Cities with pop over 10,000: Gaffney 🏛 (12,969).

CHESTER COUNTY

PO Box 580   **Ph:** 803-385-2605
Chester, SC 29706   **Fax:** 803-581-7975
www.chesterchamber.com

In north-central SC, south of Rock Hill; organized Mar 12, 1785 from Camden District. **Name Origin:** For Chester, PA.

Area (sq mi): 586.16 (land 580.52; water 5.64). **Pop per sq mi:** 57.2.

Pop 2005: 33,228. **State rank:** 31. **Pop change:** 2000-20005 -2.5%; 1990-2000 +5.9%. **Pop 2000:** 34,068 (White 59.6%; Black or African American 38.7%; Hispanic or Latino 0.7%; Asian 0.3%; Other 1.1%). **Foreign born:** 0.8%. **Median age:** 36.

Income 2000: per capita $14,709; median household $32,425; **Pop below poverty level:** 15.3%. ***Personal per capita income 2000-2003:** $19,941-$22,139.

Unemployment 2004: 10.1%. **Change from 2000:** -0.2%. **Median travel time to work:** 27.8 minutes. **Working outside county of residence:** 43.9%.

Cities with pop over 10,000: None.

CHESTERFIELD COUNTY

PO Box 529   **Ph:** 843-623-2574
Chesterfield, SC 29709   **Fax:** 843-623-6944
www.chesterfield.k12.sc.us

On northeastern border of SC, northwest of Florence; organized 1798 from Cheraws District. **Name Origin:** For Philip Dormer Stanhope (1694-1773), 4th Earl of Chesterfield, English statesman and writer.

Area (sq mi): 805.78 (land 798.6; water 7.18). **Pop per sq mi:** 54.4.

Pop 2005: 43,435. **State rank:** 25. **Pop change:** 2000-20005 +1.6%; 1990-2000 +10.9%. **Pop 2000:** 42,768 (White 63.5%; Black or African American 33.2%; Hispanic or Latino 2.3%; Asian 0.3%; Other 2.1%). **Foreign born:** 1.6%. **Median age:** 35.7.

Income 2000: per capita $14,233; median household $29,483; **Pop below poverty level:** 20.3%. ***Personal per capita income 2000-2003:** $19,558-$20,981.

Unemployment 2004: 10.1%. **Change from 2000:** +1.3%. **Median travel time to work:** 25.7 minutes. **Working outside county of residence:** 33.2%.

Cities with pop over 10,000: None.

CLARENDON COUNTY

3 W Key St   **Ph:** 803-435-8424
Manning, SC 29102   **Fax:** 803-435-8258
www.clarendoncounty.com

In central SC, south of Sumter; organized 1855 from Sumter District. **Name Origin:** For Edward Hyde (1661-1724), 3rd Earl of Clarendon, colonial governor of NY and NJ (1702-08).

Clarendon County (cont'd)

Area (sq mi): 695.66 (land 607.21; water 88.46). **Pop per sq mi:** 54.9.

Pop 2005: 33,363. **State rank:** 30. **Pop change:** 2000-20005 +2.6%; 1990-2000 +14.2%. **Pop 2000:** 32,502 (White 44.5%; Black or African American 53.1%; Hispanic or Latino 1.7%; Asian 0.3%; Other 1.6%). **Foreign born:** 1.3%. **Median age:** 37.

Income 2000: per capita $13,998; median household $27,131; **Pop below poverty level:** 23.1%. *Personal per capita income 2000-2003: $17,902-$19,630.

Unemployment 2004: 8.8%. **Change from 2000:** -0.1%. **Median travel time to work:** 26.1 minutes. **Working outside county of residence:** 44.3%.

Cities with pop over 10,000: None.

COLLETON COUNTY

PO Box 157   **Ph:** 843-549-1725
Walterboro, SC 29488   **Fax:** 843-549-7215
www.colletoncounty.org

In south-central SC, west of Charleston; organized 1798 from part of the Province of Carolina. **Name Origin:** For Sir John Colleton, an original lord proprietor.

Area (sq mi): 1133.21 (land 1056.36; water 76.86). **Pop per sq mi:** 37.5.

Pop 2005: 39,605. **State rank:** 26. **Pop change:** 2000-20005 +3.5%; 1990-2000 +11.3%. **Pop 2000:** 38,264 (White 55.1%; Black or African American 42.2%; Hispanic or Latino 1.4%; Asian 0.3%; Other 2%). **Foreign born:** 1.2%. **Median age:** 36.5.

Income 2000: per capita $14,831; median household $29,733; **Pop below poverty level:** 21.1%. *Personal per capita income 2000-2003: $19,103-$20,416.

Unemployment 2004: 7.3%. **Change from 2000:** +2.2%. **Median travel time to work:** 32.7 minutes. **Working outside county of residence:** 35%.

Cities with pop over 10,000: None.

DARLINGTON COUNTY

PO Box 1177   **Ph:** 843-398-4330
Darlington, SC 29540   **Fax:** 843-393-6871
www.darcosc.com

In northeastern SC, north of Florence; established Mar 12, 1785 from Cheraws District. **Name Origin:** Traditionally for Darlington, Durham, England, but possibly for a Col. Darlington of the Revolutionary War.

Area (sq mi): 566.78 (land 561.14; water 5.63). **Pop per sq mi:** 120.

Pop 2005: 67,346. **State rank:** 20. **Pop change:** 2000-20005 -0.1%; 1990-2000 +9%. **Pop 2000:** 67,394 (White 56.6%; Black or African American 41.7%; Hispanic or Latino 1%; Asian 0.2%; Other 1.1%). **Foreign born:** 0.9%. **Median age:** 36.

Income 2000: per capita $16,283; median household $31,087; **Pop below poverty level:** 20.3%. *Personal per capita income 2000-2003: $22,115-$23,797.

Unemployment 2004: 8%. **Change from 2000:** +0.6%. **Median travel time to work:** 22.7 minutes. **Working outside county of residence:** 37.6%.

Cities with pop over 10,000: None.

DILLON COUNTY

PO Box 449   **Ph:** 843-774-1400
Dillon, SC 29536   **Fax:** 843-774-1443
www.dilloncounty.org

On the northeastern border of PA, northeast of Florence; organized Feb 5, 1910 from Marion County. **Name Origin:** For the county seat.

Area (sq mi): 406.54 (land 404.84; water 1.7). **Pop per sq mi:** 76.5.

Pop 2005: 30,974. **State rank:** 32. **Pop change:** 2000-20005 +0.8%; 1990-2000 +5.5%. **Pop 2000:** 30,722 (White 49.8%; Black or African American 45.3%; Hispanic or Latino 1.8%; Asian 0.3%; Other 3.9%, including 2.2% American Indian/Alaska Native). **Foreign born:** 1%. **Median age:** 34.2.

Income 2000: per capita $13,272; median household $26,630; **Pop below poverty level:** 24.2%. *Personal per capita income 2000-2003: $17,965-$19,378.

Unemployment 2004: 9.7%. **Change from 2000:** -2.8%. **Median travel time to work:** 28.5 minutes. **Working outside county of residence:** 32.5%.

Cities with pop over 10,000: None.

DORCHESTER COUNTY

101 Ridge St   **Ph:** 843-563-0121
Saint George, SC 29477   **Fax:** 843-563-0178
www.dorchestercounty.net

In south-central SC, northwest of Charleston; organized Feb 25, 1897 from Colleton and Berkeley counties. **Name Origin:** For the town in SC, named for Dorchester, MA, former home of the town founders.

Area (sq mi): 576.69 (land 574.73; water 1.96). **Pop per sq mi:** 196.4.

Pop 2005: 112,858. **State rank:** 14. **Pop change:** 2000-20005 +17.1%; 1990-2000 +16.1%. **Pop 2000:** 96,413 (White 70.1%; Black or African American 25.1%; Hispanic or Latino 1.8%; Asian 1.1%; Other 2.8%). **Foreign born:** 2.8%. **Median age:** 34.7.

Income 2000: per capita $18,840; median household $43,316; **Pop below poverty level:** 9.7%. *Personal per capita income 2000-2003: $21,968-$24,226.

Unemployment 2004: 4.9%. **Change from 2000:** +0.8%. **Median travel time to work:** 28 minutes. **Working outside county of residence:** 62.6%.

Cities with pop over 10,000: Summerville (34,241).

EDGEFIELD COUNTY

129 Courthouse Sq Suite 205   **Ph:** 803-637-4080
Edgefield, SC 29824   **Fax:** 803-637-4007
www.edgefieldcounty.sc.gov

On the central western border of SC, north of Augusta, GA; established Mar 12, 1785 from Ninety Six District. **Name Origin:** Said to be so named because the old district of Edgefield was bordered

Source: Personal per capita income data are from the Bureau of Economic Analysis; per capita income data are from the Bureau of the Census.
See Introduction for explanation of differences.

614

Edgefield County (cont'd)

by the Savannah River and by Indian lands, and thus was the edge of SC.

Area (sq mi): 506.54 (land 501.89; water 4.64). **Pop per sq mi:** 50.9.

Pop 2005: 25,528. **State rank:** 36. **Pop change:** 2000-20005 +3.8%; 1990-2000 +33.9%. **Pop 2000:** 24,595 (White 55.5%; Black or African American 41.5%; Hispanic or Latino 2%; Asian 0.2%; Other 1.4%). **Foreign born:** 1.3%. **Median age:** 35.6.

Income 2000: per capita $15,415; median household $35,146; **Pop below poverty level:** 15.5%. ***Personal per capita income 2000-2003:** $18,921-$20,345.

Unemployment 2004: 6%. **Change from 2000:** +1.2%. **Median travel time to work:** 27.1 minutes. **Working outside county of residence:** 58.3%.

Cities with pop over 10,000: None.

FAIRFIELD COUNTY
PO Drawer 60   **Ph:** 803-635-1415
Winnsboro, SC 29180   **Fax:** 803-635-5060
www.fairfieldchamber.org

In north-central SC, north of Columbia; established Mar 12, 1785 from Camden District. **Name Origin:** From Lord Cornwallis' (1738-1805) exclamation when his army first camped there, 'What fair fields!'

Area (sq mi): 709.93 (land 686.59; water 23.34). **Pop per sq mi:** 35.

Pop 2005: 24,047. **State rank:** 37. **Pop change:** 2000-20005 +2.5%; 1990-2000 +5.2%. **Pop 2000:** 23,454 (White 39.2%; Black or African American 59.1%; Hispanic or Latino 1.1%; Asian 0.2%; Other 1.2%). **Foreign born:** 0.5%. **Median age:** 36.9.

Income 2000: per capita $14,911; median household $30,376; **Pop below poverty level:** 19.6%. ***Personal per capita income 2000-2003:** $20,045-$21,645.

Unemployment 2004: 8%. **Change from 2000:** -4.6%. **Median travel time to work:** 28.3 minutes. **Working outside county of residence:** 50.4%.

Cities with pop over 10,000: None.

FLORENCE COUNTY
180 N Irby   **Ph:** 843-665-3031
Florence, SC 29501   **Fax:** 843-665-3097
www.florenceco.org

In east-central SC, east of Sumter; organized Dec 22, 1888 from Marion, Darlington, Williamsburg, and Clarendon counties. **Name Origin:** For Florence Harllee, daughter of Gen. William Harllee, first president of the Wilmington and Manchester Railroad Co.

Area (sq mi): 803.74 (land 799.84; water 3.9). **Pop per sq mi:** 163.9.

Pop 2005: 131,097. **State rank:** 12. **Pop change:** 2000-20005 +4.2%; 1990-2000 +10%. **Pop 2000:** 125,761 (White 58.2%; Black or African American 39.3%; Hispanic or Latino 1.1%; Asian 0.7%; Other 1.3%). **Foreign born:** 1.8%. **Median age:** 35.5.

Income 2000: per capita $17,876; median household $35,144; **Pop below poverty level:** 16.4%. ***Personal per capita income 2000-2003:** $23,795-$26,088.

Unemployment 2004: 8.2%. **Change from 2000:** +2.4%. **Median travel time to work:** 24 minutes. **Working outside county of residence:** 16.5%.

Cities with pop over 10,000: Florence ⚒ (30,883).

GEORGETOWN COUNTY
PO Drawer 421270   **Ph:** 843-545-3063
Georgetown, SC 29442   **Fax:** 843-545-3202
www.georgetowncountysc.org

On the central eastern border of SC, northeast of Charleston; original district; organized 1768 (prior to statehood). **Name Origin:** For the county seat.

Area (sq mi): 1035 (land 814.83; water 220.16). **Pop per sq mi:** 74.8.

Pop 2005: 60,983. **State rank:** 22. **Pop change:** 2000-20005 +9.3%; 1990-2000 +20.5%. **Pop 2000:** 55,797 (White 59.2%; Black or African American 38.6%; Hispanic or Latino 1.6%; Asian 0.2%; Other 1.4%). **Foreign born:** 2.2%. **Median age:** 39.1.

Income 2000: per capita $19,805; median household $35,312; **Pop below poverty level:** 17.1%. ***Personal per capita income 2000-2003:** $24,253-$26,614.

Unemployment 2004: 9.4%. **Change from 2000:** -0.3%. **Median travel time to work:** 26 minutes. **Working outside county of residence:** 26.1%.

Cities with pop over 10,000: None.

GREENVILLE COUNTY
305 E North St Courthouse Suite 224   **Ph:** 864-467-8551
Greenville, SC 29601   **Fax:** 864-467-8540
www.greenvillecounty.org

On the northwestern border of SC, west of Spartanburg; organized Mar 22, 1786 from Ninety Six District. **Name Origin:** Either for Gen. Nathanael Greene (1742-86), Revolutionary War hero, or for Isaac Green (1762-1831), pioneer and owner of the mill around which the town of Greenville grew.

Area (sq mi): 794.96 (land 790.08; water 4.88). **Pop per sq mi:** 515.6.

Pop 2005: 407,383. **State rank:** 1. **Pop change:** 2000-20005 +7.3%; 1990-2000 +18.6%. **Pop 2000:** 379,616 (White 75.5%; Black or African American 18.3%; Hispanic or Latino 3.8%; Asian 1.4%; Other 2.7%). **Foreign born:** 4.9%. **Median age:** 35.5.

Income 2000: per capita $22,081; median household $41,149; **Pop below poverty level:** 10.5%. ***Personal per capita income 2000-2003:** $29,689-$30,037.

Unemployment 2004: 5.9%. **Change from 2000:** +2.7%. **Median travel time to work:** 21.6 minutes. **Working outside county of residence:** 12.7%.

Cities with pop over 10,000: Greenville ⚒ (56,291); Greer (20,416); Mauldin (18,604); Simpsonville (14,924).

GREENWOOD COUNTY
600 Monument St Box P-103   **Ph:** 864-942-8500
Greenwood, SC 29646   **Fax:** 864-942-8566
www.co.greenwood.sc.us

In west-central SC, south of Spartanburg; organized June 3, 1897

⚒ *County Seat*

Greenwood County (cont'd)

from Abbeville and Edgefield counties. **Name Origin:** For the county seat.

Area (sq mi): 462.94 (land 455.52; water 7.42). **Pop per sq mi:** 149.2.

Pop 2005: 67,979. **State rank:** 19. **Pop change:** 2000-20005 +2.6%; 1990-2000 +11.3%. **Pop 2000:** 66,271 (White 64.1%; Black or African American 31.7%; Hispanic or Latino 2.9%; Asian 0.7%; Other 1.9%). **Foreign born:** 2.8%. **Median age:** 35.2.

Income 2000: per capita $17,446; median household $34,702; **Pop below poverty level:** 14.2%. *Personal per capita income 2000-2003: $23,092-$23,922.

Unemployment 2004: 8.9%. **Change from 2000:** +0.7%. **Median travel time to work:** 20.2 minutes. **Working outside county of residence:** 14%.

Cities with pop over 10,000: Greenwood 🏛 (22,242).

HAMPTON COUNTY

201 Jackson Ave W   **Ph:** 803-943-7561
Hampton, SC 29924   **Fax:** 803-943-7502
www.hamptoncountysc.org

On the southwestern border of SC, west of Charleston; organized Feb 18, 1875 from Old Beaufort County. **Name Origin:** For Gen. Wade Hampton (1818-1902), SC governor (1876-79), U.S. senator (1858-62; 1878-91), and U.S. railroad commissioner.

Area (sq mi): 562.63 (land 559.78; water 2.85). **Pop per sq mi:** 38.1.

Pop 2005: 21,329. **State rank:** 40. **Pop change:** 2000-20005 -0.3%; 1990-2000 +17.6%. **Pop 2000:** 21,386 (White 41.3%; Black or African American 55.7%; Hispanic or Latino 2.6%; Asian 0.2%; Other 1.2%). **Foreign born:** 0.7%. **Median age:** 34.8.

Income 2000: per capita $13,129; median household $28,771; **Pop below poverty level:** 21.8%. *Personal per capita income 2000-2003: $18,548-$19,855.

Unemployment 2004: 9.3%. **Change from 2000:** +2.5%. **Median travel time to work:** 33.1 minutes. **Working outside county of residence:** 37.8%.

Cities with pop over 10,000: None.

HORRY COUNTY

PO Box 677   **Ph:** 843-915-5080
Conway, SC 29528   **Fax:** 843-915-6081
www.horrycounty.org

On the central eastern border of SC, southeast of Florence; organized Dec 19, 1801 from All Saints Parish. **Name Origin:** For Gen. Peter Horry (1743-1815), officer in the Revolutionary War and prominent citizen. Referred to by inhabitants as 'The Independent Republic of Horry.'

Area (sq mi): 1254.96 (land 1133.68; water 121.28). **Pop per sq mi:** 200.2.

Pop 2005: 226,992. **State rank:** 6. **Pop change:** 2000-20005 +15.4%; 1990-2000 +36.5%. **Pop 2000:** 196,629 (White 79.9%; Black or African American 15.5%; Hispanic or Latino 2.6%; Asian 0.8%; Other 2.8%). **Foreign born:** 4%. **Median age:** 38.3.

Income 2000: per capita $19,949; median household $36,470; **Pop below poverty level:** 12%. *Personal per capita income 2000-2003: $23,933-$25,266.

Unemployment 2004: 5.7%. **Change from 2000:** +1%. **Median travel time to work:** 23.7 minutes. **Working outside county of residence:** 9.4%.

Cities with pop over 10,000: Myrtle Beach (25,410); Conway 🏛 (13,293); North Myrtle Beach (13,160).

JASPER COUNTY

PO Box 248   **Ph:** 843-726-7710
Ridgeland, SC 29936   **Fax:** 843-726-7782
www.jaspersc.org

On the southwestern border of SC, west of Beaufort; organized Jan 30, 1912 from Beaufort and Hampton counties. **Name Origin:** For Sgt. William Jasper (1750-79), American Revolutionary War soldier from SC.

Area (sq mi): 699.79 (land 656.12; water 43.67). **Pop per sq mi:** 32.6.

Pop 2005: 21,398. **State rank:** 39. **Pop change:** 2000-20005 +3.5%; 1990-2000 +33.5%. **Pop 2000:** 20,678 (White 40.5%; Black or African American 52.7%; Hispanic or Latino 5.8%; Asian 0.4%; Other 4.5%). **Foreign born:** 5.4%. **Median age:** 33.8.

Income 2000: per capita $14,161; median household $30,727; **Pop below poverty level:** 20.7%. *Personal per capita income 2000-2003: $17,683-$19,338.

Unemployment 2004: 5.5%. **Change from 2000:** +1.6%. **Median travel time to work:** 34.2 minutes. **Working outside county of residence:** 56.1%.

Cities with pop over 10,000: None.

KERSHAW COUNTY

1121 Broad St Rm 202   **Ph:** 803-425-1500
Camden, SC 29020   **Fax:** 803-425-6044
www.kershawcountysc.org

In north-central SC, northeast of Columbia; organized 1798 from old Craven County. **Name Origin:** For Col. Joseph Kershaw, SC army officer during the Revolutionary War and SC legislator.

Area (sq mi): 740.25 (land 726.26; water 14). **Pop per sq mi:** 77.8.

Pop 2005: 56,486. **State rank:** 23. **Pop change:** 2000-20005 +7.3%; 1990-2000 +20.8%. **Pop 2000:** 52,647 (White 70.7%; Black or African American 26.3%; Hispanic or Latino 1.7%; Asian 0.3%; Other 1.7%). **Foreign born:** 1.7%. **Median age:** 37.4.

Income 2000: per capita $18,360; median household $38,804; **Pop below poverty level:** 12.8%. *Personal per capita income 2000-2003: $23,355-$26,159.

Unemployment 2004: 6.2%. **Change from 2000:** -0.2%. **Median travel time to work:** 27.9 minutes. **Working outside county of residence:** 45.1%.

Cities with pop over 10,000: None.

Source: Personal per capita income data are from the Bureau of Economic Analysis; per capita income data are from the Bureau of the Census. See Introduction for explanation of differences.

LANCASTER COUNTY

PO Box 1809   **Ph:** 803-285-1581
Lancaster, SC 29721   **Fax:** 803-416-9388
www.lancastercountysc.net

On the central border of SC, northeast of Columbia; established Mar 12, 1785 from Camden District. **Name Origin:** For Lancaster, PA, home of many early settlers.

Area (sq mi): 555.29 (land 548.99; water 6.3). **Pop per sq mi:** 115.

Pop 2005: 63,113. **State rank:** 21. **Pop change:** 2000-20005 +2.9%; 1990-2000 +12.5%. **Pop 2000:** 61,351 (White 70.5%; Black or African American 26.9%; Hispanic or Latino 1.6%; Asian 0.3%; Other 1.8%). **Foreign born:** 1.3%. **Median age:** 35.9.

Income 2000: per capita $16,276; median household $34,688; **Pop below poverty level:** 12.8%. ***Personal per capita income 2000-2003:** $20,591-$21,269.

Unemployment 2004: 8.9%. **Change from 2000:** +2.8%. **Median travel time to work:** 27 minutes. **Working outside county of residence:** 39.7%.

Cities with pop over 10,000: None.

LAURENS COUNTY

PO Box 287   **Ph:** 864-984-3538
Laurens, SC 29360   **Fax:** 864-984-3726
www.laurenscountysc.org

In west-central SC, south of Spartanburg; established Mar 12, 1785 from Ninety Six District. **Name Origin:** For Henry Laurens (1724-92), president of the Continental Congress (1777-78).

Area (sq mi): 723.98 (land 715.11; water 8.87). **Pop per sq mi:** 98.3.

Pop 2005: 70,293. **State rank:** 17. **Pop change:** 2000-20005 +1%; 1990-2000 +19.8%. **Pop 2000:** 69,567 (White 71%; Black or African American 26.2%; Hispanic or Latino 1.9%; Asian 0.1%; Other 2.2%). **Foreign born:** 1.6%. **Median age:** 36.2.

Income 2000: per capita $15,761; median household $33,933; **Pop below poverty level:** 14.3%. ***Personal per capita income 2000-2003:** $20,391-$21,422.

Unemployment 2004: 7.1%. **Change from 2000:** -1.4%. **Median travel time to work:** 23.6 minutes. **Working outside county of residence:** 43.8%.

Cities with pop over 10,000: None.

LEE COUNTY

PO Box 387   **Ph:** 803-484-5341
Bishopville, SC 29010   **Fax:** 803-484-1632

In north-central SC, north of Sumter; organized Feb 25, 1902 from Darlington, Sumter, and Kershaw counties. **Name Origin:** For Robert E. Lee (1807-70), American general and commander of the Confederate forces during the Civil War.

Area (sq mi): 411.3 (land 410.3; water 1). **Pop per sq mi:** 50.3.

Pop 2005: 20,638. **State rank:** 41. **Pop change:** 2000-20005 +2.6%; 1990-2000 +9.1%. **Pop 2000:** 20,119 (White 34.6%; Black or African American 63.6%; Hispanic or Latino 1.3%; Asian 0.2%; Other 1.2%). **Foreign born:** 2.1%. **Median age:** 35.7.

Income 2000: per capita $13,896; median household $26,907; **Pop below poverty level:** 21.8%. ***Personal per capita income 2000-2003:** $17,225-$18,643.

Unemployment 2004: 8.6%. **Change from 2000:** +0.4%. **Median travel time to work:** 29.7 minutes. **Working outside county of residence:** 57.3%.

Cities with pop over 10,000: None.

LEXINGTON COUNTY

205 E Main St County Courthouse   **Ph:** 803-785-8212
Lexington, SC 29072   **Fax:** 803-785-8314
www.co.lexington.sc.us

In west-central SC, west of Columbia; organized Mar 12, 1785 from Orangeburg District. **Name Origin:** For the Battle of Lexington, the first conflict in the Revolutionary War.

Area (sq mi): 757.88 (land 699.25; water 58.63). **Pop per sq mi:** 336.5.

Pop 2005: 235,272. **State rank:** 5. **Pop change:** 2000-20005 +8.9%; 1990-2000 +28.9%. **Pop 2000:** 216,014 (White 83.2%; Black or African American 12.6%; Hispanic or Latino 1.9%; Asian 1%; Other 2.1%). **Foreign born:** 2.9%. **Median age:** 35.7.

Income 2000: per capita $21,063; median household $44,659; **Pop below poverty level:** 9%. ***Personal per capita income 2000-2003:** $28,902-$30,048.

Unemployment 2004: 4.9%. **Change from 2000:** +2.1%. **Median travel time to work:** 26 minutes. **Working outside county of residence:** 46%.

Cities with pop over 10,000: West Columbia (13,029); Lexington 🏛 (12,610); Cayce (12,418).

MARION COUNTY

PO Box 183   **Ph:** 843-423-3904
Marion, SC 29571   **Fax:** 843-423-8306
www.co.marion.sc.us

In east-central SC, east of Florence; organized as Liberty County in 1798; name changed 1800. **Name Origin:** For Gen. Francis Marion (c.1732-95), SC soldier and legislator, known as 'The Swamp Fox' for his tactics during the Revolutionary War.

Area (sq mi): 494.09 (land 489.06; water 5.03). **Pop per sq mi:** 71.4.

Pop 2005: 34,904. **State rank:** 29. **Pop change:** 2000-20005 -1.6%; 1990-2000 +4.6%. **Pop 2000:** 35,466 (White 41.1%; Black or African American 56.3%; Hispanic or Latino 1.8%; Asian 0.3%; Other 1.7%). **Foreign born:** 1.4%. **Median age:** 35.1.

Income 2000: per capita $13,878; median household $26,526; **Pop below poverty level:** 23.2%. ***Personal per capita income 2000-2003:** $17,948-$20,048.

Unemployment 2004: 13.6%. **Change from 2000:** -3.7%. **Median travel time to work:** 24.7 minutes. **Working outside county of residence:** 28%.

Cities with pop over 10,000: None.

🏛 *County Seat*

MARLBORO COUNTY

PO Box 419
Bennettsville, SC 29512
www.marlborocounty.sc.gov

Ph: 843-479-5600
Fax: 843-479-5639

On northeastern border of SC, north of Florence; organized 1798 from Cheraws District. **Name Origin:** For John Churchill (1650-1722), Duke of Marlborough.

Area (sq mi): 485.28 (land 479.71; water 5.57). **Pop per sq mi:** 58.4.

Pop 2005: 28,021. **State rank:** 34. **Pop change:** 2000-20005 -2.8%; 1990-2000 -1.8%. **Pop 2000:** 28,818 (White 44.3%; Black or African American 50.7%; Hispanic or Latino 0.7%; Asian 0.2%; Other 4.5%, including 3.4% American Indian/Alaska Native). **Foreign born:** 0.6%. **Median age:** 35.4.

Income 2000: per capita $13,385; median household $26,598; **Pop below poverty level:** 21.7%. ***Personal per capita income 2000-2003:** $16,841-$18,676.

Unemployment 2004: 13.1%. **Change from 2000:** -0.3%. **Median travel time to work:** 24 minutes. **Working outside county of residence:** 40.8%.

Cities with pop over 10,000: None.

MCCORMICK COUNTY

133 S Mine St Rm 102
McCormick, SC 29835
www.mccormickcountysc.com

Ph: 864-465-2195
Fax: 864-465-0071

On the central western border of SC, northwest of Augusta, GA; established Feb 19, 1916 from Edgefield, Greenwood, and Abbeville counties. **Name Origin:** For Cyrus Hall McCormick (1809-84), inventor of farm implements and local landowner.

Area (sq mi): 393.85 (land 359.56; water 34.29). **Pop per sq mi:** 28.1.

Pop 2005: 10,108. **State rank:** 46. **Pop change:** 2000-20005 +1.5%; 1990-2000 +12.3%. **Pop 2000:** 9,958 (White 44.4%; Black or African American 53.9%; Hispanic or Latino 0.9%; Asian 0.3%; Other 1.1%). **Foreign born:** 0.6%. **Median age:** 41.1.

Income 2000: per capita $14,770; median household $31,577; **Pop below poverty level:** 17.9%. ***Personal per capita income 2000-2003:** $17,308-$18,338.

Unemployment 2004: 10.9%. **Change from 2000:** +0%. **Median travel time to work:** 33.8 minutes. **Working outside county of residence:** 52.2%.

Cities with pop over 10,000: None.

NEWBERRY COUNTY

1226 College St PO Drawer 10
Newberry, SC 29108
www.newberrycounty.net

Ph: 803-321-2110
Fax: 803-321-2111

In north-central SC, northwest of Columbia; organized 1789 from Ninety Six District. **Name Origin:** Origin is uncertain, but believed to be for Capt. John Newberry of Gen. Thomas Sumter's (1734-1832) Revolutionary War troops.

Area (sq mi): 647.28 (land 630.77; water 16.51). **Pop per sq mi:** 59.1.

Pop 2005: 37,250. **State rank:** 27. **Pop change:** 2000-20005 +3.2%; 1990-2000 +8.9%. **Pop 2000:** 36,108 (White 61.7%; Black or African American 33.1%; Hispanic or Latino 4.2%; Asian 0.3%; Other 2.6%). **Foreign born:** 3.5%. **Median age:** 37.1.

Income 2000: per capita $16,045; median household $32,867; **Pop below poverty level:** 17%. ***Personal per capita income 2000-2003:** $20,545-$21,933.

Unemployment 2004: 7.1%. **Change from 2000:** +0.3%. **Median travel time to work:** 25.3 minutes. **Working outside county of residence:** 34.9%.

Cities with pop over 10,000: Newberry 🏛 (10,700).

OCONEE COUNTY

415 S Pine St
Walhalla, SC 29691
www.oconeesc.com

Ph: 864-638-4242
Fax: 864-638-4241

On the northwestern border of SC, west of Greenville; organized Jan 29, 1868 from Pickens County. **Name Origin:** For an Indian word of uncertain meaning. Possibly refers to the mythical Cherokee snake dragon, or to mean 'water eyes of the hills' or 'beautiful springs.'

Area (sq mi): 673.58 (land 625.41; water 48.17). **Pop per sq mi:** 111.3.

Pop 2005: 69,577. **State rank:** 18. **Pop change:** 2000-20005 +5.1%; 1990-2000 +15.2%. **Pop 2000:** 66,215 (White 88%; Black or African American 8.4%; Hispanic or Latino 2.4%; Asian 0.4%; Other 2.1%). **Foreign born:** 2.4%. **Median age:** 39.5.

Income 2000: per capita $18,965; median household $36,666; **Pop below poverty level:** 10.8%. ***Personal per capita income 2000-2003:** $24,108-$26,201.

Unemployment 2004: 7.4%. **Change from 2000:** +1.2%. **Median travel time to work:** 23.3 minutes. **Working outside county of residence:** 30.2%.

Cities with pop over 10,000: None.

ORANGEBURG COUNTY

PO Drawer 9000
Orangeburg, SC 29116
www.orangeburgcounty.org

Ph: 803-533-6243
Fax: 803-534-3848

In south-central SC, south of Columbia; original district; organized 1768 (prior to statehood). **Name Origin:** For Prince William IV of Orange (1738-1820), who later became King George III of England.

Area (sq mi): 1128.09 (land 1106.16; water 21.93). **Pop per sq mi:** 83.3.

Pop 2005: 92,167. **State rank:** 16. **Pop change:** 2000-20005 +0.6%; 1990-2000 +8%. **Pop 2000:** 91,582 (White 36.8%; Black or African American 60.9%; Hispanic or Latino 1%; Asian 0.4%; Other 1.6%). **Foreign born:** 1%. **Median age:** 35.3.

Income 2000: per capita $15,057; median household $29,567; **Pop below poverty level:** 21.4%. ***Personal per capita income 2000-2003:** $19,711-$22,325.

Unemployment 2004: 9.4%. **Change from 2000:** -1.7%. **Median travel time to work:** 26.5 minutes. **Working outside county of residence:** 23.1%.

Cities with pop over 10,000: Orangeburg 🏛 (12,895).

*Source: Personal per capita income data are from the Bureau of Economic Analysis; per capita income data are from the Bureau of the Census. See Introduction for explanation of differences.

PICKENS COUNTY

PO Box 215
Pickens, SC 29671
www.co.pickens.sc.us

Ph: 864-898-5866
Fax: 864-898-5863

On the northeastern border of SC, west of Greenville; organized Dec 20, 1826 from Pendleton District, which was abolished at that time. **Name Origin:** For Gen. Andrew Pickens (1739-1817), Revolutionary War hero and U.S. representative from SC (1793-95).

Area (sq mi): 511.85 (land 496.89; water 14.96). **Pop per sq mi:** 228.6.

Pop 2005: 113,575. **State rank:** 13. **Pop change:** 2000-20005 +2.5%; 1990-2000 +18%. **Pop 2000:** 110,757 (White 89.3%; Black or African American 6.8%; Hispanic or Latino 1.7%; Asian 1.2%; Other 1.8%). **Foreign born:** 2.9%. **Median age:** 32.7.

Income 2000: per capita $17,434; median household $36,214; **Pop below poverty level:** 13.7%. ***Personal per capita income 2000-2003:** $21,069-$23,593.

Unemployment 2004: 6.8%. **Change from 2000:** +1.8%. **Median travel time to work:** 24 minutes. **Working outside county of residence:** 44.5%.

Cities with pop over 10,000: Easley (18,643); Clemson (12,074).

RICHLAND COUNTY

2020 Hampton St
Columbia, SC 29204
www.richlandonline.com

Ph: 803-576-2050
Fax: 803-576-2137

In north-central SC, west of Sumter; established Mar 12, 1785. **Name Origin:** For the fertile farmland along its rivers.

Area (sq mi): 771.72 (land 756.41; water 15.3). **Pop per sq mi:** 449.6.

Pop 2005: 340,078. **State rank:** 2. **Pop change:** 2000-20005 +6.1%; 1990-2000 +12.2%. **Pop 2000:** 320,677 (White 49.2%; Black or African American 45.2%; Hispanic or Latino 2.7%; Asian 1.7%; Other 2.8%). **Foreign born:** 3.9%. **Median age:** 32.6.

Income 2000: per capita $20,794; median household $39,961; **Pop below poverty level:** 13.7%. ***Personal per capita income 2000-2003:** $27,118-$28,966.

Unemployment 2004: 6%. **Change from 2000:** +2.5%. **Median travel time to work:** 21.7 minutes. **Working outside county of residence:** 17.3%.

Cities with pop over 10,000: Columbia 🏛 (116,331); Irmo (11,181); Forest Acres (10,127).

SALUDA COUNTY

100 E Church St Suite 6
Saluda, SC 29138
www.saludacounty.sc.gov

Ph: 864-445-3303
Fax: 864-445-3772

In west-central SC, west of Columbia; organized 1895 from Edgefield County. **Name Origin:** For the Saluda River, which forms its northern border, itself named perhaps from Cherokee *selu* 'corn,' for the corn-growing area, with ending *tah* 'river': 'corn river.'

Area (sq mi): 461.78 (land 452.48; water 9.3). **Pop per sq mi:** 41.8.

Pop 2005: 18,895. **State rank:** 42. **Pop change:** 2000-20005 -1.5%; 1990-2000 +17.3%. **Pop 2000:** 19,181 (White 62.2%; Black or

African American 30%; Hispanic or Latino 7.3%; Asian 0%; Other 4.1%). **Foreign born:** 5.9%. **Median age:** 37.

Income 2000: per capita $16,328; median household $35,774; **Pop below poverty level:** 15.6%. ***Personal per capita income 2000-2003:** $20,990-$22,910.

Unemployment 2004: 7.5%. **Change from 2000:** +2.2%. **Median travel time to work:** 32.1 minutes. **Working outside county of residence:** 55.7%.

Cities with pop over 10,000: None.

SPARTANBURG COUNTY

180 Magnolia St
Spartanburg, SC 29306
www.spartanburgcounty.org

Ph: 864-596-2591
Fax: 864-596-2239

On the central northern border of SC, east of Greenville; established Mar 12, 1785 from Ninety Six District. **Name Origin:** For the Spartan Regiment of SC militia, which distinguished itself in the Revolutionary War.

Area (sq mi): 819.14 (land 810.93; water 8.22). **Pop per sq mi:** 329.

Pop 2005: 266,809. **State rank:** 4. **Pop change:** 2000-20005 +5.1%; 1990-2000 +11.9%. **Pop 2000:** 253,791 (White 74%; Black or African American 20.8%; Hispanic or Latino 2.8%; Asian 1.5%; Other 2.6%). **Foreign born:** 3.7%. **Median age:** 36.1.

Income 2000: per capita $18,738; median household $37,579; **Pop below poverty level:** 12.3%. ***Personal per capita income 2000-2003:** $24,327-$25,773.

Unemployment 2004: 7.6%. **Change from 2000:** +2.4%. **Median travel time to work:** 22.5 minutes. **Working outside county of residence:** 18.4%.

Cities with pop over 10,000: Spartanburg 🏛 (38,599).

SUMTER COUNTY

141 N Main St
Sumter, SC 29150
www.sumtercountysc.org

Ph: 803-436-2227
Fax: 803-436-2223

In east-central SC, east of Columbia; organized 1798 from Camden District. **Name Origin:** For Gen. Thomas Sumter (1734-1832), American Revolutionary officer nicknamed the 'Gamecock of the Revolution,' U.S. representative from GA (1789-93; 1797-1801), and U.S. senator (1801-10).

Area (sq mi): 682.03 (land 665.41; water 16.63). **Pop per sq mi:** 158.6.

Pop 2005: 105,517. **State rank:** 15. **Pop change:** 2000-20005 +0.8%; 1990-2000 +2%. **Pop 2000:** 104,646 (White 49.4%; Black or African American 46.7%; Hispanic or Latino 1.8%; Asian 0.9%; Other 2.4%). **Foreign born:** 2.1%. **Median age:** 33.4.

Income 2000: per capita $15,657; median household $33,278; **Pop below poverty level:** 16.2%. ***Personal per capita income 2000-2003:** $20,535-$22,390.

Unemployment 2004: 8.1%. **Change from 2000:** +0.9%. **Median travel time to work:** 21.5 minutes. **Working outside county of residence:** 15.8%.

Cities with pop over 10,000: Sumter 🏛 (39,671).

🏛 *County Seat*

UNION COUNTY

PO Box 703   **Ph:** 864-429-1630
Union, SC 29379   **Fax:** 864-429-1715
www.countyofunion.com

In north-central SC, southeast of Spartanburg; organized 1798 from Ninety Six District. **Name Origin:** For the old Union Church, erected in 1765 for use by many different denominations.

Area (sq mi): 515.92 (land 514.12; water 1.8). **Pop per sq mi:** 55.5.

Pop 2005: 28,539. **State rank:** 33. **Pop change:** 2000-20005 -4.5%; 1990-2000 -1.5%. **Pop 2000:** 29,881 (White 67.5%; Black or African American 31%; Hispanic or Latino 0.7%; Asian 0.2%; Other 0.9%). **Foreign born:** 0.6%. **Median age:** 38.6.

Income 2000: per capita $15,877; median household $31,441; **Pop below poverty level:** 14.3%. ***Personal per capita income 2000-2003:** $20,178-$22,644.

Unemployment 2004: 12.4%. **Change from 2000:** +1.5%. **Median travel time to work:** 27 minutes. **Working outside county of residence:** 37.3%.

Cities with pop over 10,000: None.

WILLIAMSBURG COUNTY

147 W Main St   **Ph:** 843-355-9321
Kingstree, SC 29556   **Fax:** 843-355-2106
www.williamsburgsc.com

In east-central SC, north of Charleston; organized 1804 from Georgetown District. **Name Origin:** For William III (1650-1702), king of England with Queen Mary (1689-1702).

Area (sq mi): 936.92 (land 933.9; water 3.02). **Pop per sq mi:** 37.9.

Pop 2005: 35,395. **State rank:** 28. **Pop change:** 2000-20005 -4.9%; 1990-2000 +1.1%. **Pop 2000:** 37,217 (White 32.5%; Black or African American 66.3%; Hispanic or Latino 0.7%; Asian 0.2%; Other 0.9%). **Foreign born:** 0.5%. **Median age:** 35.5.

Income 2000: per capita $12,794; median household $24,214; **Pop below poverty level:** 27.9%. ***Personal per capita income 2000-2003:** $16,074-$18,298.

Unemployment 2004: 12%. **Change from 2000:** -2.6%. **Median travel time to work:** 31.5 minutes. **Working outside county of residence:** 40.9%.

Cities with pop over 10,000: None.

YORK COUNTY

2 S Congress St PO Box 649   **Ph:** 803-684-8507
York, SC 29745   **Fax:** 803-684-8575
www.yorkcountygov.com

On central northern border of SC, north of Columbia; organized 1798 from Camden District. **Name Origin:** For York, PA, former home of many early settlers. Formerly called *New Acquisition*.

Area (sq mi): 695.72 (land 682.45; water 13.27). **Pop per sq mi:** 278.6.

Pop 2005: 190,097. **State rank:** 7. **Pop change:** 2000-20005 +15.5%; 1990-2000 +25.2%. **Pop 2000:** 164,614 (White 76.4%; Black or African American 19.2%; Hispanic or Latino 2%; Asian 0.9%; Other 2.7%). **Foreign born:** 2.4%. **Median age:** 34.9.

Income 2000: per capita $20,536; median household $44,539; **Pop below poverty level:** 10%. ***Personal per capita income 2000-2003:** $25,942-$27,407.

Unemployment 2004: 7.1%. **Change from 2000:** +2%. **Median travel time to work:** 27.2 minutes. **Working outside county of residence:** 40.1%.

Cities with pop over 10,000: Rock Hill (57,902).

---

*Source: Personal per capita income data are from the Bureau of Economic Analysis; per capita income data are from the Bureau of the Census. See Introduction for explanation of differences.

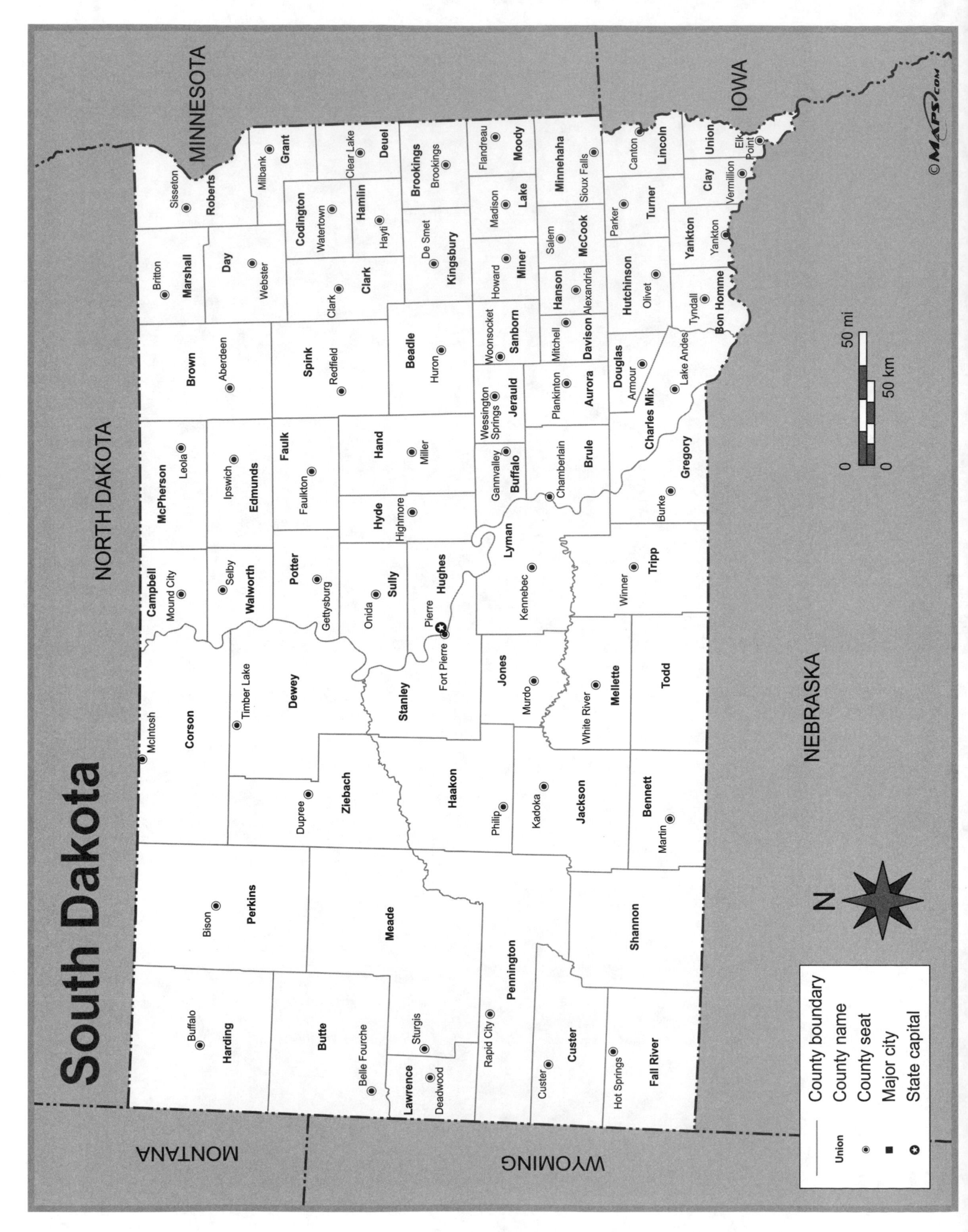

South Dakota

SOUTH DAKOTA STATE INFORMATION

www.state.sd.us **Ph:** 605-773-3011

Area (sq mi): 77,116.49 (land 75,884.64; water 1231.85). **Pop per sq mi:** 10.2.

Pop 2005: 775,933. **Pop change:** 2000-20005 +2.8%; 1990-2000 +8.5%. **Pop 2000:** 754,844 (White 88%; Black or African American 0.6%; Hispanic or Latino 1.4%; Asian 0.6%; Other 10.1%, including 8.3% American Indian/Alaska Native). **Foreign born:** 1.8%. **Median age:** 35.6.

Income 2000: per capita $17,562; median household $35,282; **Pop below poverty level:** 13.2%. ***Personal per capita income 2000-2003:** $25,720-$28,856.

Unemployment 2004: 3.8%. **Change from 2000:** +1.1%. **Median travel time to work:** 16.6 minutes. **Working outside county of residence:** 16.3%.

AURORA COUNTY

PO Box 366 **Ph:** 605-942-7165
Plankinton, SD 57368 **Fax:** 605-942-7170

In south-central SD, west of Sioux Falls; created Feb 22, 1879 and organized 1882 (prior to statehood) from land that had been parts of Hanson County (what was later Davison, Jerauld and Cragin counties). **Name Origin:** For the Roman goddess of dawn.

Area (sq mi): 712.53 (land 708.18; water 4.35). **Pop per sq mi:** 4.1.

Pop 2005: 2,901. **State rank:** 49. **Pop change:** 2000-20005 -5.1%; 1990-2000 -2.5%. **Pop 2000:** 3,058 (White 95.1%; Black or African American 0.3%; Hispanic or Latino 2.1%; Asian 0.1%; Other 3.9%, including 1.9% American Indian/Alaska Native). **Foreign born:** 1.5%. **Median age:** 40.6.

Income 2000: per capita $13,887; median household $29,783; **Pop below poverty level:** 11.4%. ***Personal per capita income 2000-2003:** $23,417-$28,178.

Unemployment 2004: 3.6%. **Change from 2000:** +1.2%. **Median travel time to work:** 19.3 minutes. **Working outside county of residence:** 30.1%.

Cities with pop over 10,000: None.

BEADLE COUNTY

PO Box 1358 **Ph:** 605-353-7165
Huron, SD 57350 **Fax:** 605-353-0118
www.beadlecounty.org

In east-central SD, northwest of Sioux Falls; created Feb 22, 1879 (prior to statehood) from Spink and Clark counties. **Name Origin:**

For Gen. William Henry Harrison Beadle (1838-1915), officer in the Civil War, surveyor general of the Dakota Territory (1869-73), and educator.

Area (sq mi): 1264.82 (land 1258.7; water 6.13). **Pop per sq mi:** 12.6.

Pop 2005: 15,896. **State rank:** 12. **Pop change:** 2000-20005 -6.6%; 1990-2000 -6.7%. **Pop 2000:** 17,023 (White 96.4%; Black or African American 0.7%; Hispanic or Latino 0.9%; Asian 0.3%; Other 2%). **Foreign born:** 1.2%. **Median age:** 40.1.

Income 2000: per capita $17,832; median household $30,510; **Pop below poverty level:** 11.9%. ***Personal per capita income 2000-2003:** $26,892-$29,645.

Unemployment 2004: 3.8%. **Change from 2000:** +0.1%. **Median travel time to work:** 14.6 minutes. **Working outside county of residence:** 7.4%.

Cities with pop over 10,000: Huron 🏛 (11,198).

BENNETT COUNTY

PO Box 281 **Ph:** 605-685-6969
Martin, SD 57551 **Fax:** 605-685-1075

On the central southern border of SD, southeast of Rapid City; created Mar 9, 1909 from Indian lands. **Name Origin:** For either John E. Bennett, SD supreme court judge, or jointly for John E. Bennett and Granville G. Bennett, IL legislator and federally appointed judge in Dakota Territory.

Area (sq mi): 1190.59 (land 1185.29; water 5.3). **Pop per sq mi:** 3.

Pop 2005: 3,585. **State rank:** 45. **Pop change:** 2000-20005 +0.3%; 1990-2000 +11.5%. **Pop 2000:** 3,574 (White 40.5%; Black or African American 0.3%; Hispanic or Latino 2%; Asian 0.1%; Other 58.8%, including 52.1% American Indian/Alaska Native). **Foreign born:** 0.4%. **Median age:** 29.2.

Income 2000: per capita $10,106; median household $25,313; **Pop below poverty level:** 39.2%. ***Personal per capita income 2000-2003:** $18,211-$19,963.

Unemployment 2004: 4%. **Change from 2000:** -1.9%. **Median travel time to work:** 17.3 minutes. **Working outside county of residence:** 18.6%.

Cities with pop over 10,000: None.

BON HOMME COUNTY

300 W 18th Ave **Ph:** 605-589-4215
Tyndall, SD 57066 **Fax:** 605-589-4245

On the southeastern border of SD, west of Sioux Falls; original

Bon Homme County (cont'd)

county; organized Apr 5, 1862 (prior to statehood) from unorganized territory. **Name Origin:** For a village, which was named for a nearby large island in the Missouri River; mentioned in Lewis and Clark's journals. French 'good man,' name used by fourteenth-century French aristocracy for peasants.

Area (sq mi): 581.32 (land 563.34; water 17.98). **Pop per sq mi:** 12.6.

Pop 2005: 7,087. **State rank:** 26. **Pop change:** 2000-20005 -2.4%; 1990-2000 +2.4%. **Pop 2000:** 7,260 (White 95.3%; Black or African American 0.6%; Hispanic or Latino 0.6%; Asian 0.1%; Other 3.8%, including 3% American Indian/Alaska Native). **Foreign born:** 0.7%. **Median age:** 40.3.

Income 2000: per capita $13,892; median household $30,644; **Pop below poverty level:** 12.9%. ***Personal per capita income 2000-2003:** $21,934-$24,706.

Unemployment 2004: 3.3%. **Change from 2000:** +0.3%. **Median travel time to work:** 18 minutes. **Working outside county of residence:** 25.9%.

Cities with pop over 10,000: None.

BROOKINGS COUNTY

314 6th Ave   **Ph:** 605-692-6284
Brookings, SD 57006   **Fax:** 605-696-8211
www.brookingscountysd.gov

On the central eastern border of SD, north of Sioux Falls; created Apr 5, 1862 (prior to statehood) from unorganized territory. **Name Origin:** For Wilmot W. Brookings (1833-85), prominent legislator and associate justice on the Dakota Territory supreme court (1869-73). He promoted the Southern Dakota Railway, and 'Judge Brookings' was the name of the first locomotive to enter what is now SD.

Area (sq mi): 804.76 (land 794.46; water 10.3). **Pop per sq mi:** 35.4.

Pop 2005: 28,121. **State rank:** 5. **Pop change:** 2000-20005 -0.4%; 1990-2000 +12%. **Pop 2000:** 28,220 (White 95.9%; Black or African American 0.3%; Hispanic or Latino 0.9%; Asian 1.3%; Other 1.9%). **Foreign born:** 2.3%. **Median age:** 26.6.

Income 2000: per capita $17,586; median household $35,438; **Pop below poverty level:** 14%. ***Personal per capita income 2000-2003:** $23,825-$25,666.

Unemployment 2004: 2.8%. **Change from 2000:** +0.9%. **Median travel time to work:** 14.1 minutes. **Working outside county of residence:** 11.7%.

Cities with pop over 10,000: Brookings 🏛 (18,705).

BROWN COUNTY

25 Market St Suite 1   **Ph:** 605-626-7110
Aberdeen, SD 57401   **Fax:** 605-626-4010
www.brown.sd.us

On the northeastern border of SD; created Feb 22, 1879 (prior to statehood) from Beadle County. **Name Origin:** For Alfred Brown (1836-?), member of the Dakota Territory legislature instrumental in consolidating the then existing counties, which earned him the nickname 'Consolidation Brown.'

Area (sq mi): 1731.21 (land 1713.07; water 18.14). **Pop per sq mi:** 20.3.

Pop 2005: 34,706. **State rank:** 3. **Pop change:** 2000-20005 -2.1%; 1990-2000 -0.3%. **Pop 2000:** 35,460 (White 95.1%; Black or African American 0.3%; Hispanic or Latino 0.7%; Asian 0.4%; Other 3.9%, including 2.7% American Indian/Alaska Native). **Foreign born:** 0.6%. **Median age:** 37.2.

Income 2000: per capita $18,464; median household $35,017; **Pop below poverty level:** 9.9%. ***Personal per capita income 2000-2003:** $27,927-$33,540.

Unemployment 2004: 3.1%. **Change from 2000:** +0.2%. **Median travel time to work:** 12.6 minutes. **Working outside county of residence:** 3.5%.

Cities with pop over 10,000: Aberdeen 🏛 (24,196).

BRULE COUNTY

300 S Courtland St Suite 111   **Ph:** 605-734-4580
Chamberlain, SD 57325   **Fax:** 605-734-4582
bruleco.tripod.com

In south-central SD, west of Sioux Falls; created Jan 14, 1875 (prior to statehood) from Buffalo County. **Name Origin:** For the Brule tribe of Sioux Indians. French 'burned,' partial transliteration of *sicangu* 'burned thighs,' a name derisively given to a group of Sioux who tried to raid the Pawnees, who set the plains on fire. Many of the unsuccessful raiders were badly burned but escaped.

Area (sq mi): 846.49 (land 818.96; water 27.54). **Pop per sq mi:** 6.3.

Pop 2005: 5,187. **State rank:** 36. **Pop change:** 2000-20005 -3.3%; 1990-2000 -2.2%. **Pop 2000:** 5,364 (White 89.6%; Black or African American 0.3%; Hispanic or Latino 0.5%; Asian 0.5%; Other 9.4%, including 8.3% American Indian/Alaska Native). **Foreign born:** 0.4%. **Median age:** 36.9.

Income 2000: per capita $14,874; median household $32,370; **Pop below poverty level:** 14.3%. ***Personal per capita income 2000-2003:** $22,303-$25,191.

Unemployment 2004: 2.8%. **Change from 2000:** -0.5%. **Median travel time to work:** 16.5 minutes. **Working outside county of residence:** 18.1%.

Cities with pop over 10,000: None.

BUFFALO COUNTY

PO Box 148   **Ph:** 605-293-3234
Gann Valley, SD 57341   **Fax:** 605-293-3240

In south-central SD, southeast of Pierre; organized 1871 (prior to statehood) from territorial country. **Name Origin:** For the once-plentiful herds of buffalo.

Area (sq mi): 487.43 (land 470.59; water 16.83). **Pop per sq mi:** 4.5.

Pop 2005: 2,100. **State rank:** 59. **Pop change:** 2000-20005 +3.3%; 1990-2000 +15.5%. **Pop 2000:** 2,032 (White 16.3%; Black or African American 0.1%; Hispanic or Latino 0.9%; Asian 0%; Other 83.6%, including 81.6% American Indian/Alaska Native). **Foreign born:** 0.4%. **Median age:** 23.4.

Income 2000: per capita $5,213; median household $12,692; **Pop below poverty level:** 56.9%. ***Personal per capita income 2000-2003:** $12,097-$14,649.

Unemployment 2004: 10.2%. **Change from 2000:** +1.8%. **Median travel time to work:** 16 minutes. **Working outside county of residence:** 22.3%.

Buffalo County (cont'd)

Cities with pop over 10,000: None.

BUTTE COUNTY

PO Box 250   **Ph:** 605-892-2516
Belle Fourche, SD 57717   **Fax:** 605-892-2836

On the central western border of SD, organized Mar 2, 1883 (prior to statehood) from Harding County. **Name Origin:** For nearby buttes (flat-topped mounds or mountains).

Area (sq mi): 2266.36 (land 2248.51; water 17.84). **Pop per sq mi:** 4.1.

Pop 2005: 9,326. **State rank:** 19. **Pop change:** 2000-20005 +2.6%; 1990-2000 +14.9%. **Pop 2000:** 9,094 (White 94.1%; Black or African American 0.1%; Hispanic or Latino 2.9%; Asian 0.2%; Other 4.1%, including 1.6% American Indian/Alaska Native). **Foreign born:** 1.2%. **Median age:** 38.

Income 2000: per capita $13,997; median household $29,040; **Pop below poverty level:** 12.8%. ***Personal per capita income 2000-2003:** $19,403-$21,736.

Unemployment 2004: 3.4%. **Change from 2000:** -0.6%. **Median travel time to work:** 18.6 minutes. **Working outside county of residence:** 29.5%.

Cities with pop over 10,000: None.

CAMPBELL COUNTY

PO Box 146   **Ph:** 605-955-3536
Mound City, SD 57646   **Fax:** 605-955-5303

On the central northern border of SD, northwest of Aberdeen; created Jan 8, 1873 (prior to statehood) from Buffalo County. **Name Origin:** For Norman B. Campbell, Dakota Territory legislator (1872-73).

Area (sq mi): 771.34 (land 735.79; water 35.54). **Pop per sq mi:** 2.1.

Pop 2005: 1,565. **State rank:** 63. **Pop change:** 2000-20005 -12.2%; 1990-2000 -9.3%. **Pop 2000:** 1,782 (White 99.1%; Black or African American 0%; Hispanic or Latino 0.2%; Asian 0.1%; Other 0.6%). **Foreign born:** 0.4%. **Median age:** 41.9.

Income 2000: per capita $14,117; median household $28,793; **Pop below poverty level:** 14.1%. ***Personal per capita income 2000-2003:** $25,625-$24,642.

Unemployment 2004: 3.7%. **Change from 2000:** -3.1%. **Median travel time to work:** 18.3 minutes. **Working outside county of residence:** 22.6%.

Cities with pop over 10,000: None.

CHARLES MIX COUNTY

PO Box 490   **Ph:** 605-487-7131
Lake Andes, SD 57356   **Fax:** 605-487-7221

On the southeastern border of SD, southwest of Sioux Falls; original county; created May 8, 1862 (prior to statehood). **Name Origin:** For either Charles E. Mix, a commissioner of Indian affairs, or Charles H. Mix, a scout during the Civil War.

Area (sq mi): 1150.19 (land 1097.57; water 52.61). **Pop per sq mi:** 8.4.

Pop 2005: 9,194. **State rank:** 20. **Pop change:** 2000-20005 -1.7%; 1990-2000 +2.4%. **Pop 2000:** 9,350 (White 69.2%; Black or African American 0.1%; Hispanic or Latino 1.9%; Asian 0.1%; Other 30.2%, including 28.3% American Indian/Alaska Native). **Foreign born:** 0.8%. **Median age:** 35.7.

Income 2000: per capita $11,502; median household $26,060; **Pop below poverty level:** 26.9%. ***Personal per capita income 2000-2003:** $21,782-$24,634.

Unemployment 2004: 4%. **Change from 2000:** +0.7%. **Median travel time to work:** 13.7 minutes. **Working outside county of residence:** 7.5%.

Cities with pop over 10,000: None.

CLARK COUNTY

200 N Commercial St   **Ph:** 605-532-5921
Clark, SD 57225   **Fax:** 605-532-5931

In east-central SD, southeast of Aberdeen; created Jan 8, 1873 (prior to statehood) from Hanson County. **Name Origin:** For Newton Clark, pioneer schoolteacher and Dakota territorial legislator.

Area (sq mi): 967.79 (land 957.92; water 9.87). **Pop per sq mi:** 4.

Pop 2005: 3,799. **State rank:** 43. **Pop change:** 2000-20005 -8.3%; 1990-2000 -5.9%. **Pop 2000:** 4,143 (White 98.5%; Black or African American 0.1%; Hispanic or Latino 0.5%; Asian 0.1%; Other 1.2%). **Foreign born:** 0.8%. **Median age:** 41.6.

Income 2000: per capita $15,597; median household $30,208; **Pop below poverty level:** 14.8%. ***Personal per capita income 2000-2003:** $26,126-$27,009.

Unemployment 2004: 4.2%. **Change from 2000:** -3.1%. **Median travel time to work:** 18.8 minutes. **Working outside county of residence:** 20.4%.

Cities with pop over 10,000: None.

CLAY COUNTY

211 W Main St Suite 200   **Ph:** 605-677-7120
Vermillion, SD 57069   **Fax:** 605-677-7104
www.claycountysd.org

In southeastern SD, south of Sioux Falls; original county; organized Apr 5, 1862 (prior to statehood) from unorganized territory. **Name Origin:** For Henry Clay (1777-1852), U.S. senator from KY, known as the 'Great Pacificator' for his advocacy of compromise to avert national crises.

Area (sq mi): 416.7 (land 411.6; water 5.1). **Pop per sq mi:** 31.6.

Pop 2005: 12,995. **State rank:** 15. **Pop change:** 2000-20005 -4%; 1990-2000 +2.7%. **Pop 2000:** 13,537 (White 92.3%; Black or African American 1%; Hispanic or Latino 0.9%; Asian 2%; Other 4.3%, including 2.7% American Indian/Alaska Native). **Foreign born:** 2.6%. **Median age:** 24.9.

Income 2000: per capita $14,452; median household $27,535; **Pop below poverty level:** 21.2%. ***Personal per capita income 2000-2003:** $23,090-$25,570.

Unemployment 2004: 3.2%. **Change from 2000:** +1.9%. **Median travel time to work:** 16.3 minutes. **Working outside county of residence:** 25.6%.

Cities with pop over 10,000: None.

CODINGTON COUNTY

PO Box 1054
Watertown, SD 57201
www.codington.org

Ph: 605-882-5095
Fax: 605-882-5384

In east-central SD, southeast of Aberdeen; organized Aug 7, 1878 (prior to statehood) from Indian lands. **Name Origin:** For the Rev. G.S.S. Codington, clergyman and Dakota Territory legislator.

Area (sq mi): 717.08 (land 687.67; water 29.41). **Pop per sq mi:** 37.8.

Pop 2005: 26,010. **State rank:** 6. **Pop change:** 2000-20005 +0.4%; 1990-2000 +14.1%. **Pop 2000:** 25,897 (White 96.3%; Black or African American 0.1%; Hispanic or Latino 1.1%; Asian 0.3%; Other 2.8%, including 1.4% American Indian/Alaska Native). **Foreign born:** 1.2%. **Median age:** 35.3.

Income 2000: per capita $18,761; median household $36,257; **Pop below poverty level:** 9%. ***Personal per capita income 2000-2003:** $26,121-$29,001.

Unemployment 2004: 3.5%. **Change from 2000:** -1.1%. **Median travel time to work:** 14.3 minutes. **Working outside county of residence:** 5.4%.

Cities with pop over 10,000: Watertown 🏛 (20,207).

CORSON COUNTY

PO Box 175
McIntosh, SD 57641

Ph: 605-273-4201
Fax: 605-273-4597

On the central northern border of SD; organized Mar 2, 1909 from Dewey County. **Name Origin:** For Dighton Corson (1827-1915), WI legislator, a framer of the SD constitution, and SD Supreme Court Justice (1889-1913).

Area (sq mi): 2529.42 (land 2472.93; water 56.48). **Pop per sq mi:** 1.8.

Pop 2005: 4,366. **State rank:** 38. **Pop change:** 2000-20005 +4.4%; 1990-2000 -0.3%. **Pop 2000:** 4,181 (White 37.1%; Black or African American 0.1%; Hispanic or Latino 2.1%; Asian 0%; Other 62.7%, including 60.8% American Indian/Alaska Native). **Foreign born:** 0.3%. **Median age:** 28.3.

Income 2000: per capita $8,615; median household $20,654; **Pop below poverty level:** 41%. ***Personal per capita income 2000-2003:** $16,501-$18,505.

Unemployment 2004: 6.2%. **Change from 2000:** -2.1%. **Median travel time to work:** 20.9 minutes. **Working outside county of residence:** 29.8%.

Cities with pop over 10,000: None.

CUSTER COUNTY

RR 1 Box 101
Custer, SD 57730
www.custercountysd.com

Ph: 605-673-8100

On the southwestern border of SD, south of Rapid City; created Jan 11, 1875 (prior to statehood) from Indian lands. **Name Origin:** For Gen. George Armstrong Custer (1839-76), U.S. soldier and Indian fighter.

Area (sq mi): 1559.14 (land 1557.69; water 1.45). **Pop per sq mi:** 5.1.

Pop 2005: 7,904. **State rank:** 22. **Pop change:** 2000-20005 +8.6%; 1990-2000 +17.7%. **Pop 2000:** 7,275 (White 93.4%; Black or African American 0.3%; Hispanic or Latino 1.5%; Asian 0.2%; Other 5.4%, including 3.1% American Indian/Alaska Native). **Foreign born:** 1.1%. **Median age:** 43.2.

Income 2000: per capita $17,945; median household $36,303; **Pop below poverty level:** 9.4%. ***Personal per capita income 2000-2003:** $22,095-$25,947.

Unemployment 2004: 3.6%. **Change from 2000:** -0.2%. **Median travel time to work:** 21.9 minutes. **Working outside county of residence:** 34.9%.

Cities with pop over 10,000: None.

DAVISON COUNTY

200 E 4th Ave
Mitchell, SD 57301
www.davisoncounty.org

Ph: 605-995-8105
Fax: 605-995-8112

In southeastern SD, west of Sioux Falls; created Jan 8, 1873 (prior to statehood) from Hanson County. **Name Origin:** For Henry C. Davison, prominent merchant and homesteader.

Area (sq mi): 436.78 (land 435.44; water 1.34). **Pop per sq mi:** 43.1.

Pop 2005: 18,777. **State rank:** 10. **Pop change:** 2000-20005 +0.2%; 1990-2000 +7.1%. **Pop 2000:** 18,741 (White 96%; Black or African American 0.3%; Hispanic or Latino 0.7%; Asian 0.4%; Other 3.1%, including 2% American Indian/Alaska Native). **Foreign born:** 1%. **Median age:** 36.

Income 2000: per capita $17,879; median household $33,476; **Pop below poverty level:** 11.5%. ***Personal per capita income 2000-2003:** $27,111-$31,965.

Unemployment 2004: 2.9%. **Change from 2000:** +0.6%. **Median travel time to work:** 14 minutes. **Working outside county of residence:** 6.1%.

Cities with pop over 10,000: Mitchell 🏛 (14,887).

DAY COUNTY

711 W 1st St
Webster, SD 57274

Ph: 605-345-3771
Fax: 605-345-3818

In northeastern SD, east of Aberdeen; created Feb 22, 1879 (prior to statehood) from Clark County. **Name Origin:** For Merritt H. Day (1844-1900), Dakota Territory legislator.

Area (sq mi): 1091.21 (land 1028.57; water 62.63). **Pop per sq mi:** 5.6.

Pop 2005: 5,757. **State rank:** 32. **Pop change:** 2000-20005 -8.1%; 1990-2000 -10.2%. **Pop 2000:** 6,267 (White 91.2%; Black or African American 0.1%; Hispanic or Latino 0.4%; Asian 0.1%; Other 8.5%, including 7.4% American Indian/Alaska Native). **Foreign born:** 0.9%. **Median age:** 42.9.

Income 2000: per capita $15,856; median household $30,227; **Pop below poverty level:** 14.3%. ***Personal per capita income 2000-2003:** $22,748-$26,102.

Unemployment 2004: 6.1%. **Change from 2000:** -0.4%. **Median travel time to work:** 17.7 minutes. **Working outside county of residence:** 17.7%.

Cities with pop over 10,000: None.

*Source: Personal per capita income data are from the Bureau of Economic Analysis; per capita income data are from the Bureau of the Census. See Introduction for explanation of differences.

DEUEL COUNTY

PO Box 308
Clear Lake, SD 57226
www.deuelcountysd.com

Ph: 605-874-2120
Fax: 605-874-2916

On central eastern border of SD, north of Sioux Falls; created Apr 5, 1862 (prior to statehood) from Brookings County. **Name Origin:** For Jacob S. Deuel (1830-?), sawmill owner and a member of the first Territorial legislature (1862-63).

Area (sq mi): 636.72 (land 623.55; water 13.17). **Pop per sq mi:** 6.9.

Pop 2005: 4,296. **State rank:** 39. **Pop change:** 2000-20005 -4.5%; 1990-2000 -0.5%. **Pop 2000:** 4,498 (White 97.9%; Black or African American 0.1%; Hispanic or Latino 0.8%; Asian 0.2%; Other 1.2%). **Foreign born:** 0.7%. **Median age:** 40.8.

Income 2000: per capita $15,977; median household $31,788; **Pop below poverty level:** 10.3%. ***Personal per capita income 2000-2003:** $25,159-$28,423.

Unemployment 2004: 4.3%. **Change from 2000:** -0.8%. **Median travel time to work:** 20.5 minutes. **Working outside county of residence:** 34.7%.

Cities with pop over 10,000: None.

DEWEY COUNTY

PO Box 277
Timber Lake, SD 57656

Ph: 605-865-3672
Fax: 605-865-3691

In north-central SD, north of Pierre; created as Rusk County in 1883 (prior to statehood); organized 1909 from Indian lands. **Name Origin:** For William Pitt Dewey (?-1900), surveyor general of the Dakota Territory (1873-77).

Area (sq mi): 2445.67 (land 2302.64; water 143.03). **Pop per sq mi:** 2.7.

Pop 2005: 6,161. **State rank:** 29. **Pop change:** 2000-20005 +3.2%; 1990-2000 +8.1%. **Pop 2000:** 5,972 (White 24.1%; Black or African American 0%; Hispanic or Latino 0.9%; Asian 0.1%; Other 75.8%, including 74.2% American Indian/Alaska Native). **Foreign born:** 0.6%. **Median age:** 26.5.

Income 2000: per capita $9,251; median household $23,272; **Pop below poverty level:** 33.6%. ***Personal per capita income 2000-2003:** $16,272-$18,070.

Unemployment 2004: 8.4%. **Change from 2000:** -7.7%. **Median travel time to work:** 17.2 minutes. **Working outside county of residence:** 8.3%.

Cities with pop over 10,000: None.

DOUGLAS COUNTY

PO Box 36
Armour, SD 57313

Ph: 605-724-2585
Fax: 605-724-2508

In south-central SD, southwest of Sioux Falls; created Jan 8, 1873 (prior to statehood) from Charles Mix County. **Name Origin:** For Stephen Arnold Douglas (1813-61), U.S. orator and statesman.

Area (sq mi): 434.13 (land 433.53; water 0.6). **Pop per sq mi:** 7.6.

Pop 2005: 3,309. **State rank:** 46. **Pop change:** 2000-20005 -4.3%; 1990-2000 -7.7%. **Pop 2000:** 3,458 (White 97.9%; Black or African American 0.1%; Hispanic or Latino 0.4%; Asian 0.1%; Other 1.7%, including 1% American Indian/Alaska Native). **Foreign born:** 0.4%. **Median age:** 41.8.

Income 2000: per capita $13,827; median household $28,478; **Pop below poverty level:** 14.6%. ***Personal per capita income 2000-2003:** $23,634-$25,487.

Unemployment 2004: 2.8%. **Change from 2000:** +0.4%. **Median travel time to work:** 14.6 minutes. **Working outside county of residence:** 19.8%.

Cities with pop over 10,000: None.

EDMUNDS COUNTY

PO Box 384
Ipswich, SD 57451

Ph: 605-426-6671
Fax: 605-426-6323

In north-central SD, west of Aberdeen; created Jan 8, 1873 (prior to statehood) from Buffalo County. **Name Origin:** For Newton Edmunds (1819-1908), governor of Dakota Territory (1863-66).

Area (sq mi): 1151.16 (land 1145.58; water 5.58). **Pop per sq mi:** 3.6.

Pop 2005: 4,112. **State rank:** 41. **Pop change:** 2000-20005 -5.8%; 1990-2000 +0.3%. **Pop 2000:** 4,367 (White 98.9%; Black or African American 0.1%; Hispanic or Latino 0.5%; Asian 0.1%; Other 0.6%). **Foreign born:** 1%. **Median age:** 41.6.

Income 2000: per capita $16,149; median household $32,205; **Pop below poverty level:** 13.8%. ***Personal per capita income 2000-2003:** $27,888-$33,059.

Unemployment 2004: 3.3%. **Change from 2000:** +1.1%. **Median travel time to work:** 17.2 minutes. **Working outside county of residence:** 31.8%.

Cities with pop over 10,000: None.

FALL RIVER COUNTY

906 N River St
Hot Springs, SD 57747

Ph: 605-745-5132
Fax: 605-745-6835

On the southwestern border of SD, south of Rapid City; organized Mar 6, 1883 (prior to statehood) from Custer County. Seat of government for Shannon County. **Name Origin:** For the Fall River, which flows through the county. Literal translation of the Indian name.

Area (sq mi): 1749.14 (land 1739.86; water 9.28). **Pop per sq mi:** 4.2.

Pop 2005: 7,355. **State rank:** 25. **Pop change:** 2000-20005 -1.3%; 1990-2000 +1.4%. **Pop 2000:** 7,453 (White 89.3%; Black or African American 0.3%; Hispanic or Latino 1.7%; Asian 0.2%; Other 9%, including 6.1% American Indian/Alaska Native). **Foreign born:** 0.6%. **Median age:** 45.5.

Income 2000: per capita $17,048; median household $29,631; **Pop below poverty level:** 13.6%. ***Personal per capita income 2000-2003:** $21,438-$23,488.

Unemployment 2004: 4%. **Change from 2000:** -0.1%. **Median travel time to work:** 19.8 minutes. **Working outside county of residence:** 13.5%.

Cities with pop over 10,000: None.

FAULK COUNTY

PO Box 309
Faulkton, SD 57438

Ph: 605-598-6224

In north-central SD, southwest of Aberdeen; created Jan 8, 1873

Faulk County (cont'd)

(prior to statehood) from Buffalo County and unorganized territory. **Name Origin:** For Andrew Jackson Faulk (1814-98), a governor of Dakota Territory.

Area (sq mi): 1005.69 (land 1000.14; water 5.55). **Pop per sq mi:** 2.4.

Pop 2005: 2,386. **State rank:** 56. **Pop change:** 2000-20005 -9.6%; 1990-2000 -3.8%. **Pop 2000:** 2,640 (White 99.2%; Black or African American 0.1%; Hispanic or Latino 0.2%; Asian 0%; Other 0.5%). **Foreign born:** 2%. **Median age:** 41.5.

Income 2000: per capita $14,660; median household $30,237; **Pop below poverty level:** 18.1%. ***Personal per capita income 2000-2003:** $26,662-$26,489.

Unemployment 2004: 3.1%. **Change from 2000:** +0.4%. **Median travel time to work:** 14.8 minutes. **Working outside county of residence:** 14.7%.

Cities with pop over 10,000: None.

GRANT COUNTY

210 E 5th Ave   **Ph:** 605-432-6711
Milbank, SD 57252   **Fax:** 605-432-9004

On the northeastern border of SD, northeast of Watertown; organized Jun 12, 1878 (prior to statehood) from Codington and Deuel counties. **Name Origin:** For Ulysses Simpson Grant (1822-85), Civil War general and eighteenth U.S. president.

Area (sq mi): 687.91 (land 682.51; water 5.4). **Pop per sq mi:** 10.8.

Pop 2005: 7,384. **State rank:** 24. **Pop change:** 2000-20005 -5.9%; 1990-2000 -6.3%. **Pop 2000:** 7,847 (White 98.5%; Black or African American 0%; Hispanic or Latino 0.5%; Asian 0.2%; Other 1.1%). **Foreign born:** 1.1%. **Median age:** 40.3.

Income 2000: per capita $16,543; median household $33,088; **Pop below poverty level:** 9.9%. ***Personal per capita income 2000-2003:** $24,838-$27,697.

Unemployment 2004: 4.3%. **Change from 2000:** -0.2%. **Median travel time to work:** 14.3 minutes. **Working outside county of residence:** 15.7%.

Cities with pop over 10,000: None.

GREGORY COUNTY

PO Box 430   **Ph:** 605-775-2665
Burke, SD 57523   **Fax:** 605-775-2965

On the central southern border of SD, east of Winner; created May 8, 1862 (prior to statehood) from Yankton County. **Name Origin:** For John Shaw Gregory (1831-?), Indian agent and Dakota territorial legislator (1862-64).

Area (sq mi): 1053.45 (land 1015.93; water 37.51). **Pop per sq mi:** 4.2.

Pop 2005: 4,290. **State rank:** 40. **Pop change:** 2000-20005 -10.5%; 1990-2000 -10.6%. **Pop 2000:** 4,792 (White 92.5%; Black or African American 0%; Hispanic or Latino 0.9%; Asian 0.2%; Other 6.6%, including 5.6% American Indian/Alaska Native). **Foreign born:** 0.7%. **Median age:** 44.3.

Income 2000: per capita $13,656; median household $22,732; **Pop below poverty level:** 20.1%. ***Personal per capita income 2000-2003:** $22,093-$27,393.

Unemployment 2004: 3.3%. **Change from 2000:** -0.4%. **Median travel time to work:** 13.7 minutes. **Working outside county of residence:** 10.8%.

Cities with pop over 10,000: None.

HAAKON COUNTY

PO Box 698   **Ph:** 605-859-2800
Philip, SD 57567

In west-central SD, west of Pierre; created Nov, 1914 from Stanley County. **Name Origin:** For Haakon VII (1872-1957), king of Norway; the name was suggested by Hugh J. McMahon, an Irish immigrant who wished to gain the votes of the Norwegian immigrants in favor of the division of Stanley County into two new counties.

Area (sq mi): 1827.22 (land 1812.97; water 14.26). **Pop per sq mi:** 1.1.

Pop 2005: 1,912. **State rank:** 61. **Pop change:** 2000-20005 -12.9%; 1990-2000 -16.3%. **Pop 2000:** 2,196 (White 95.9%; Black or African American 0%; Hispanic or Latino 0.6%; Asian 0.1%; Other 3.5%, including 2.5% American Indian/Alaska Native). **Foreign born:** 1%. **Median age:** 41.3.

Income 2000: per capita $16,780; median household $29,894; **Pop below poverty level:** 13.9%. ***Personal per capita income 2000-2003:** $28,118-$33,230.

Unemployment 2004: 2.6%. **Change from 2000:** +0%. **Median travel time to work:** 14.2 minutes. **Working outside county of residence:** 7.4%.

Cities with pop over 10,000: None.

HAMLIN COUNTY

PO Box 256   **Ph:** 605-783-3751
Hayti, SD 57243   **Fax:** 605-783-2157

In east-central SD, northwest of Sioux Falls; created Jan 8, 1873 (prior to statehood) from Deuel County. **Name Origin:** For Hannibal Hamlin (1809-91), governor of ME (1857), U.S. senator from ME (1848-67; 1857-61; 1869-81), and vice president (1861-65) under Lincoln.

Area (sq mi): 537.96 (land 506.86; water 31.1). **Pop per sq mi:** 11.3.

Pop 2005: 5,707. **State rank:** 33. **Pop change:** 2000-20005 +3%; 1990-2000 +11.4%. **Pop 2000:** 5,540 (White 98%; Black or African American 0.1%; Hispanic or Latino 0.6%; Asian 0.2%; Other 1.2%). **Foreign born:** 0.8%. **Median age:** 38.

Income 2000: per capita $16,982; median household $33,851; **Pop below poverty level:** 12.1%. ***Personal per capita income 2000-2003:** $22,028-$23,660.

Unemployment 2004: 3.7%. **Change from 2000:** -0.5%. **Median travel time to work:** 22.3 minutes. **Working outside county of residence:** 46.6%.

Cities with pop over 10,000: None.

*Source: Personal per capita income data are from the Bureau of Economic Analysis; per capita income data are from the Bureau of the Census. See Introduction for explanation of differences.

HAND COUNTY

415 W 1st Ave **Ph:** 605-853-3337
Miller, SD 57362 **Fax:** 605-853-3779

In east-central SD, southwest of Aberdeen; created 1873 (prior to statehood) from Buffalo County. **Name Origin:** For George H. Hand (1837-91), secretary of Dakota Territory (1874-83).

Area (sq mi): 1440.21 (land 1436.58; water 3.63). **Pop per sq mi:** 2.3.

Pop 2005: 3,307. **State rank:** 47. **Pop change:** 2000-20005 -11.6%; 1990-2000 -12.4%. **Pop 2000:** 3,741 (White 99.1%; Black or African American 0%; Hispanic or Latino 0.3%; Asian 0.1%; Other 0.5%). **Foreign born:** 1%. **Median age:** 43.6.

Income 2000: per capita $18,735; median household $32,377; **Pop below poverty level:** 9.2%. ***Personal per capita income 2000-2003:** $25,220-$27,600.

Unemployment 2004: 3%. **Change from 2000:** +0.8%. **Median travel time to work:** 16.2 minutes. **Working outside county of residence:** 14.4%.

Cities with pop over 10,000: None.

HANSON COUNTY

PO Box 127 **Ph:** 605-239-4446
Alexandria, SD 57311 **Fax:** 605-239-9446

In southeastern SD, west of Sioux Falls; organized Jan 13, 1871 (prior to statehood) from Buffalo and Deuel counties. **Name Origin:** For Maj. Joseph R. Hanson (1837-1917), Dakota Territory legislator and Indian affairs official.

Area (sq mi): 435.64 (land 434.76; water 0.87). **Pop per sq mi:** 8.6.

Pop 2005: 3,747. **State rank:** 44. **Pop change:** 2000-20005 +19.4%; 1990-2000 +4.8%. **Pop 2000:** 3,139 (White 99.5%; Black or African American 0%; Hispanic or Latino 0.1%; Asian 0.1%; Other 0.3%). **Foreign born:** 0.5%. **Median age:** 36.

Income 2000: per capita $14,778; median household $33,049; **Pop below poverty level:** 16.6%. ***Personal per capita income 2000-2003:** $21,479-$23,395.

Unemployment 2004: 2.8%. **Change from 2000:** +0.5%. **Median travel time to work:** 23.6 minutes. **Working outside county of residence:** 59.2%.

Cities with pop over 10,000: None.

HARDING COUNTY

410 Ramsland St PO Box 534 **Ph:** 605-375-3351
Buffalo, SD 57720 **Fax:** 605-375-3432

On the northwest border of SD; organized Feb 26, 1909 from Butte County. **Name Origin:** For J.A. Harding, a Dakota Territory legislator.

Area (sq mi): 2677.58 (land 2670.5; water 7.08). **Pop per sq mi:** 0.5.

Pop 2005: 1,218. **State rank:** 65. **Pop change:** 2000-20005 -10%; 1990-2000 -18.9%. **Pop 2000:** 1,353 (White 96.6%; Black or African American 0.3%; Hispanic or Latino 1.6%; Asian 0.6%; Other 1.5%). **Foreign born:** 0.5%. **Median age:** 37.6.

Income 2000: per capita $12,794; median household $25,000; **Pop below poverty level:** 21.1%. ***Personal per capita income 2000-2003:** $19,059-$21,300.

Unemployment 2004: 3.2%. **Change from 2000:** +0%. **Median travel time to work:** 18.3 minutes. **Working outside county of residence:** 10.2%.

Cities with pop over 10,000: None.

HUGHES COUNTY

PO Box 1238 **Ph:** 605-773-3713
Pierre, SD 57501

In central SD, east of Pierre; organized Nov 26, 1880 (prior to statehood) from Buffalo County. **Name Origin:** For Alexander Hughes, Dakota Territory legislator.

Area (sq mi): 800.29 (land 740.92; water 59.37). **Pop per sq mi:** 22.8.

Pop 2005: 16,875. **State rank:** 11. **Pop change:** 2000-20005 +2.4%; 1990-2000 +11.2%. **Pop 2000:** 16,481 (White 88.4%; Black or African American 0.2%; Hispanic or Latino 1.2%; Asian 0.4%; Other 10.5%, including 8.7% American Indian/Alaska Native). **Foreign born:** 1.3%. **Median age:** 37.5.

Income 2000: per capita $20,689; median household $42,970; **Pop below poverty level:** 8%. ***Personal per capita income 2000-2003:** $26,736-$30,047.

Unemployment 2004: 2.8%. **Change from 2000:** +0.5%. **Median travel time to work:** 11.3 minutes. **Working outside county of residence:** 7.5%.

Cities with pop over 10,000: Pierre 🏛 (13,983).

HUTCHINSON COUNTY

140 Euclid St Rm 36 **Ph:** 605-387-4215
Olivet, SD 57052 **Fax:** 605-387-4208

In southeastern SD, southwest of Sioux Falls; created May 8, 1862 (prior to statehood) from unorganized territory. **Name Origin:** For John S. Hutchinson (1821-?), secretary of the Dakota Territory (1861-65), during which time he was frequently acting governor; member of the Hutchinson family singing and bell-ringing group, famous during the mid-1850's.

Area (sq mi): 814.37 (land 812.82; water 1.55). **Pop per sq mi:** 9.3.

Pop 2005: 7,581. **State rank:** 23. **Pop change:** 2000-20005 -6.1%; 1990-2000 -2.3%. **Pop 2000:** 8,075 (White 98.4%; Black or African American 0.1%; Hispanic or Latino 0.5%; Asian 0.1%; Other 1.1%). **Foreign born:** 0.7%. **Median age:** 43.1.

Income 2000: per capita $15,922; median household $30,026; **Pop below poverty level:** 13%. ***Personal per capita income 2000-2003:** $24,655-$28,552.

Unemployment 2004: 3.5%. **Change from 2000:** +0.5%. **Median travel time to work:** 17.3 minutes. **Working outside county of residence:** 23%.

Cities with pop over 10,000: None.

HYDE COUNTY

PO Box 306 **Ph:** 605-852-2512
Highmore, SD 57345 **Fax:** 605-852-2767

In central SD, east of Pierre; created Jan 8, 1873 (prior to statehood) from Buffalo County. **Name Origin:** For James Hyde (1842-1902), Civil War prisoner of war at Andersonville and Dakota territorial legislator.

🏛 *County Seat*

Hyde County (cont'd)

Area (sq mi): 866.59 (land 860.97; water 5.62). **Pop per sq mi:** 1.9.

Pop 2005: 1,614. **State rank:** 62. **Pop change:** 2000-20005 -3.4%; 1990-2000 -1.5%. **Pop 2000:** 1,671 (White 90.9%; Black or African American 0.1%; Hispanic or Latino 0.5%; Asian 0%; Other 8.8%, including 8% American Indian/Alaska Native). **Foreign born:** 0.3%. **Median age:** 42.2.

Income 2000: per capita $16,356; median household $31,103; **Pop below poverty level:** 12.3%. ***Personal per capita income 2000-2003:** $22,366-$24,987.

Unemployment 2004: 3.3%. **Change from 2000:** +0.7%. **Median travel time to work:** 13.6 minutes. **Working outside county of residence:** 10.3%.

Cities with pop over 10,000: None.

JACKSON COUNTY

PO Box 128   **Ph:** 605-837-2121
Kadoka, SD 57543   **Fax:** 605-837-2120

In south-central SD, southwest of Pierre; created Nov, 1914 from Stanley County. In 1976 annexed Washabaugh County, which was organized 1883 from Indian lands and continued as an Indian reservation. An original Jackson County, formed in 1883, gradually disappeared as parts of its territory joined other counties. **Name Origin:** For John R. Jackson, Dakota Territory legislator when the original Jackson county was formed in 1883. A claim has been made for Andrew Jackson, but seems to be unjustified.

Area (sq mi): 1871.24 (land 1869.13; water 2.12). **Pop per sq mi:** 1.5.

Pop 2005: 2,858. **State rank:** 50. **Pop change:** 2000-20005 -2.5%; 1990-2000 +4.2%. **Pop 2000:** 2,930 (White 50%; Black or African American 0%; Hispanic or Latino 0.4%; Asian 0%; Other 49.7%, including 47.8% American Indian/Alaska Native). **Foreign born:** 0.9%. **Median age:** 30.6.

Income 2000: per capita $9,981; median household $23,945; **Pop below poverty level:** 36.5%. ***Personal per capita income 2000-2003:** $15,879-$15,786.

Unemployment 2004: 5.9%. **Change from 2000:** -1.1%. **Median travel time to work:** 16.9 minutes. **Working outside county of residence:** 17.2%.

Cities with pop over 10,000: None.

JERAULD COUNTY

PO Box 435   **Ph:** 605-539-1202
Wessington Springs, SD 57382   **Fax:** 605-539-1203

In south-central SD, northwest of Sioux Falls; organized Mar 9, 1883 (prior to statehood) from Aurora County. **Name Origin:** For H.A. Jerauld, Dakota Territory legislator when the county was formed.

Area (sq mi): 532.63 (land 529.91; water 2.72). **Pop per sq mi:** 4.

Pop 2005: 2,136. **State rank:** 58. **Pop change:** 2000-20005 -6.9%; 1990-2000 -5.4%. **Pop 2000:** 2,295 (White 98.7%; Black or African American 0%; Hispanic or Latino 0.3%; Asian 0.1%; Other 0.9%). **Foreign born:** 0.3%. **Median age:** 46.3.

Income 2000: per capita $16,856; median household $30,690; **Pop below poverty level:** 20.6%. ***Personal per capita income 2000-2003:** $27,507-$30,154.

Unemployment 2004: 2.9%. **Change from 2000:** +0.5%. **Median travel time to work:** 18 minutes. **Working outside county of residence:** 21.9%.

Cities with pop over 10,000: None.

JONES COUNTY

PO Box 448   **Ph:** 605-669-2361
Murdo, SD 57559   **Fax:** 605-669-2641

In south-central SD, south of Pierre; organized Jan 16, 1917 from Lyman County. **Name Origin:** For Jones County, IA, former home of some settlers.

Area (sq mi): 971.66 (land 970.52; water 1.14). **Pop per sq mi:** 1.1.

Pop 2005: 1,033. **State rank:** 66. **Pop change:** 2000-20005 -13.4%; 1990-2000 -9.9%. **Pop 2000:** 1,193 (White 95.6%; Black or African American 0%; Hispanic or Latino 0.3%; Asian 0%; Other 4.2%, including 2.4% American Indian/Alaska Native). **Foreign born:** 0%. **Median age:** 41.1.

Income 2000: per capita $15,896; median household $30,288; **Pop below poverty level:** 15.8%. ***Personal per capita income 2000-2003:** $25,223-$31,369.

Unemployment 2004: 2.3%. **Change from 2000:** +0.8%. **Median travel time to work:** 14.3 minutes. **Working outside county of residence:** 11.6%.

Cities with pop over 10,000: None.

KINGSBURY COUNTY

PO Box 176   **Ph:** 605-854-3811
De Smet, SD 57231   **Fax:** 605-854-9080

In east-central SD, northwest of Sioux Falls; created Jan 8, 1873 (prior to statehood) from Hanson County. **Name Origin:** For George Washington Kingsbury (1837-1925) and T.A. Kingsbury, brothers prominent in territorial affairs and members of several Territorial legislatures. George was a newspaper publisher and author of *History of Dakota Territory*.

Area (sq mi): 863.67 (land 838.37; water 25.3). **Pop per sq mi:** 6.6.

Pop 2005: 5,532. **State rank:** 34. **Pop change:** 2000-20005 -4.9%; 1990-2000 -1.9%. **Pop 2000:** 5,815 (White 98.1%; Black or African American 0.1%; Hispanic or Latino 0.7%; Asian 0.3%; Other 1.1%). **Foreign born:** 0.6%. **Median age:** 42.7.

Income 2000: per capita $16,522; median household $31,262; **Pop below poverty level:** 10%. ***Personal per capita income 2000-2003:** $25,765-$29,990.

Unemployment 2004: 3.7%. **Change from 2000:** -0.2%. **Median travel time to work:** 19 minutes. **Working outside county of residence:** 28.2%.

Cities with pop over 10,000: None.

LAKE COUNTY

200 E Center St   **Ph:** 605-256-5644
Madison, SD 57042   **Fax:** 605-256-5012

In east-central SD, northwest of Sioux Falls; organized Jan 8, 1873

*Source: Personal per capita income data are from the Bureau of Economic Analysis; per capita income data are from the Bureau of the Census.
See Introduction for explanation of differences.

630

Lake County (cont'd)

(prior to statehood) from Brookings and Hanson counties. **Name Origin:** For the area's numerous lakes.

Area (sq mi): 575.06 (land 563.23; water 11.83). **Pop per sq mi:** 19.6.

Pop 2005: 11,039. **State rank:** 16. **Pop change:** 2000-20005 -2.1%; 1990-2000 +6.9%. **Pop 2000:** 11,276 (White 97.4%; Black or African American 0.2%; Hispanic or Latino 0.8%; Asian 0.5%; Other 1.5%). **Foreign born:** 0.9%. **Median age:** 36.5.

Income 2000: per capita $16,446; median household $34,087; **Pop below poverty level:** 9.7%. ***Personal per capita income 2000-2003:** $24,339-$27,528.

Unemployment 2004: 3.5%. **Change from 2000:** +0.2%. **Median travel time to work:** 15.8 minutes. **Working outside county of residence:** 19.9%.

Cities with pop over 10,000: None.

LAWRENCE COUNTY
90 Sherman St   **Ph:** 605-578-1941
Deadwood, SD 57732   **Fax:** 605-578-1065
www.lawrence.sd.us

On the central western border of SD, northwest of Rapid City; created Jan 11, 1875 (prior to statehood) from unorganized territory. **Name Origin:** For John Lawrence, Dakota Territory legislator and first treasurer of the county.

Area (sq mi): 800.31 (land 800.04; water 0.28). **Pop per sq mi:** 28.

Pop 2005: 22,395. **State rank:** 8. **Pop change:** 2000-20005 +2.7%; 1990-2000 +5.6%. **Pop 2000:** 21,802 (White 94.6%; Black or African American 0.2%; Hispanic or Latino 1.8%; Asian 0.3%; Other 3.7%, including 2.2% American Indian/Alaska Native). **Foreign born:** 1.2%. **Median age:** 37.2.

Income 2000: per capita $17,195; median household $31,755; **Pop below poverty level:** 14.8%. ***Personal per capita income 2000-2003:** $22,139-$26,199.

Unemployment 2004: 3.3%. **Change from 2000:** +0.2%. **Median travel time to work:** 17.7 minutes. **Working outside county of residence:** 17.8%.

Cities with pop over 10,000: None.

LINCOLN COUNTY
100 E 5th St   **Ph:** 605-764-2581
Canton, SD 57013   **Fax:** 605-764-5932

On the southeastern border of SD, south of Sioux Falls; created Dec 30, 1867 (prior to statehood) from Minnehaha County. **Name Origin:** For Abraham Lincoln (1809-65), sixteenth U.S. president.

Area (sq mi): 578.59 (land 578.09; water 0.5). **Pop per sq mi:** 57.7.

Pop 2005: 33,381. **State rank:** 4. **Pop change:** 2000-20005 +38.3%; 1990-2000 +56.4%. **Pop 2000:** 24,131 (White 97.3%; Black or African American 0.3%; Hispanic or Latino 0.7%; Asian 0.5%; Other 1.6%). **Foreign born:** 1.1%. **Median age:** 34.

Income 2000: per capita $22,304; median household $48,338; **Pop below poverty level:** 4.4%. ***Personal per capita income 2000-2003:** $28,375-$30,544.

Unemployment 2004: 2.4%. **Change from 2000:** +0.5%. **Median travel time to work:** 20.7 minutes. **Working outside county of residence:** 71.4%.

Cities with pop over 10,000: None.

LYMAN COUNTY
PO Box 38   **Ph:** 605-869-2247
Kennebec, SD 57544   **Fax:** 605-869-2203

In south-central SD, southeast of Pierre; created Jan 8, 1873 (prior to statehood) from unorganized territory. **Name Origin:** For W.P. Lyman, member of the Dakota territorial legislature and first settler in Yankton County.

Area (sq mi): 1707.06 (land 1639.96; water 67.1). **Pop per sq mi:** 2.4.

Pop 2005: 3,919. **State rank:** 42. **Pop change:** 2000-20005 +0.6%; 1990-2000 +7.1%. **Pop 2000:** 3,895 (White 64.5%; Black or African American 0.1%; Hispanic or Latino 0.5%; Asian 0.2%; Other 35%, including 33.3% American Indian/Alaska Native). **Foreign born:** 0.6%. **Median age:** 34.5.

Income 2000: per capita $13,862; median household $28,509; **Pop below poverty level:** 24.3%. ***Personal per capita income 2000-2003:** $20,603-$22,974.

Unemployment 2004: 4.7%. **Change from 2000:** -0.2%. **Median travel time to work:** 19.4 minutes. **Working outside county of residence:** 26.1%.

Cities with pop over 10,000: None.

MARSHALL COUNTY
PO Box 130   **Ph:** 605-448-5213
Britton, SD 57430   **Fax:** 605-448-5213

On the northeastern border of SD, northeast of Aberdeen; organized Mar 10, 1885 (prior to statehood) from Day County. **Name Origin:** For Marshall Vincent of NY, an early homesteader and one of the first Marshall County commissioners.

Area (sq mi): 885.63 (land 837.71; water 47.92). **Pop per sq mi:** 5.3.

Pop 2005: 4,418. **State rank:** 37. **Pop change:** 2000-20005 -3.5%; 1990-2000 -5.5%. **Pop 2000:** 4,576 (White 92.2%; Black or African American 0.1%; Hispanic or Latino 0.8%; Asian 0.1%; Other 7.2%, including 6.3% American Indian/Alaska Native). **Foreign born:** 0.7%. **Median age:** 41.6.

Income 2000: per capita $15,462; median household $30,567; **Pop below poverty level:** 13.9%. ***Personal per capita income 2000-2003:** $24,070-$27,819.

Unemployment 2004: 4.7%. **Change from 2000:** -2.6%. **Median travel time to work:** 16.8 minutes. **Working outside county of residence:** 17.5%.

Cities with pop over 10,000: None.

MCCOOK COUNTY
PO Box 504   **Ph:** 605-425-2781
Salem, SD 57058   **Fax:** 605-425-3144

In southeastern SD, west of Sioux Falls; created Jan 8, 1873 (prior to statehood) from Hanson County. **Name Origin:** For Edwin S. McCook (1837-73), secretary of the Dakota Territory, killed in a political dispute.

County Seat

Mccook County (cont'd)

Area (sq mi): 577.16 (land 574.52; water 2.64). **Pop per sq mi:** 10.3.

Pop 2005: 5,930. **State rank:** 31. **Pop change:** 2000-20005 +1.7%; 1990-2000 +2.5%. **Pop 2000:** 5,832 (White 98.3%; Black or African American 0.1%; Hispanic or Latino 0.8%; Asian 0.2%; Other 1%). **Foreign born:** 0.7%. **Median age:** 38.6.

Income 2000: per capita $16,374; median household $35,396; **Pop below poverty level:** 8.1%. ***Personal per capita income 2000-2003:** $28,323-$28,127.

Unemployment 2004: 3.2%. **Change from 2000:** -0.6%. **Median travel time to work:** 25 minutes. **Working outside county of residence:** 41.9%.

Cities with pop over 10,000: None.

MCPHERSON COUNTY

PO Box 248   **Ph:** 605-439-3361
Leola, SD 57456   **Fax:** 605-439-3394

On the central northern border of SD, northwest of Aberdeen; created Jan 8, 1873 (prior to statehood) from Buffalo County. **Name Origin:** For Gen. James Birdseye McPherson (1828-64), commander of the Union Army of the Tennessee during the Civil War.

Area (sq mi): 1151.85 (land 1136.94; water 14.91). **Pop per sq mi:** 2.3.

Pop 2005: 2,617. **State rank:** 53. **Pop change:** 2000-20005 -9.9%; 1990-2000 -10%. **Pop 2000:** 2,904 (White 99.2%; Black or African American 0%; Hispanic or Latino 0.2%; Asian 0.1%; Other 0.5%). **Foreign born:** 0.8%. **Median age:** 47.6.

Income 2000: per capita $12,748; median household $22,380; **Pop below poverty level:** 22.6%. ***Personal per capita income 2000-2003:** $21,769-$23,951.

Unemployment 2004: 4.2%. **Change from 2000:** +1.9%. **Median travel time to work:** 16.4 minutes. **Working outside county of residence:** 16.1%.

Cities with pop over 10,000: None.

MEADE COUNTY

PO Box 939   **Ph:** 605-347-4411
Sturgis, SD 57785   **Fax:** 605-347-3526
www.meadecounty.org

In west-central SD, north of Rapid City; created Feb 7, 1889 from Lawrence County. **Name Origin:** For Fort Meade, named for Gen. George Gordon Meade (1815-72), officer in the Mexican-American War and the Civil War, Union commander who defeated Gen. Lee at Gettysburg.

Area (sq mi): 3482.46 (land 3470.63; water 11.82). **Pop per sq mi:** 7.1.

Pop 2005: 24,623. **State rank:** 7. **Pop change:** 2000-20005 +1.5%; 1990-2000 +10.9%. **Pop 2000:** 24,253 (White 91.6%; Black or African American 1.5%; Hispanic or Latino 2.1%; Asian 0.6%; Other 5.2%, including 2% American Indian/Alaska Native). **Foreign born:** 1.4%. **Median age:** 33.4.

Income 2000: per capita $17,680; median household $36,992; **Pop below poverty level:** 9.4%. ***Personal per capita income 2000-2003:** $23,511-$29,732.

Unemployment 2004: 3.4%. **Change from 2000:** +0.2%. **Median travel time to work:** 18 minutes. **Working outside county of residence:** 54.1%.

Cities with pop over 10,000: None.

MELLETTE COUNTY

PO Box 257   **Ph:** 605-259-3230
White River, SD 57579   **Fax:** 605-259-3030

In south-central SD, south of Pierre; organized May 25, 1911 from Tripp County. **Name Origin:** For Arthur C. Mellette (1842-96), first governor of SD (1889-93).

Area (sq mi): 1309.75 (land 1306.49; water 3.26). **Pop per sq mi:** 1.6.

Pop 2005: 2,088. **State rank:** 60. **Pop change:** 2000-20005 +0.2%; 1990-2000 -2.5%. **Pop 2000:** 2,083 (White 44.5%; Black or African American 0%; Hispanic or Latino 1.7%; Asian 0.1%; Other 55.1%, including 52.4% American Indian/Alaska Native). **Foreign born:** 0.4%. **Median age:** 32.1.

Income 2000: per capita $10,362; median household $23,219; **Pop below poverty level:** 35.8%. ***Personal per capita income 2000-2003:** $15,359-$16,725.

Unemployment 2004: 5.7%. **Change from 2000:** -0.8%. **Median travel time to work:** 21.3 minutes. **Working outside county of residence:** 27.6%.

Cities with pop over 10,000: None.

MINER COUNTY

PO Box 265   **Ph:** 605-772-4612
Howard, SD 57349   **Fax:** 605-772-4412
www.howardsd.com

In east-central SD, northwest of Sioux Falls; created Jan 8, 1873 (prior to statehood) from Hanson County. **Name Origin:** For Capt. Nelson Miner (1827-79) and Ephraim Miner (1833-?), members of the Dakota Territory legislature when the county was formed.

Area (sq mi): 571.99 (land 570.34; water 1.65). **Pop per sq mi:** 4.5.

Pop 2005: 2,584. **State rank:** 54. **Pop change:** 2000-20005 -10.4%; 1990-2000 -11.9%. **Pop 2000:** 2,884 (White 98.2%; Black or African American 0.5%; Hispanic or Latino 0.6%; Asian 0.1%; Other 0.6%). **Foreign born:** 0.4%. **Median age:** 42.5.

Income 2000: per capita $15,155; median household $29,519; **Pop below poverty level:** 11.8%. ***Personal per capita income 2000-2003:** $23,394-$24,557.

Unemployment 2004: 4.3%. **Change from 2000:** -1.5%. **Median travel time to work:** 17.4 minutes. **Working outside county of residence:** 20.8%.

Cities with pop over 10,000: None.

MINNEHAHA COUNTY

415 N Dakota Ave   **Ph:** 605-367-4206
Sioux Falls, SD 57104   **Fax:** 605-367-8314
www.minnehahacounty.org

On the southeastern border of SD; original county; organized Apr 5, 1862 (prior to statehood) from Big Sioux, a territorial county. **Name Origin:** Siouan, literally 'waterfall,' popularly 'laughing water.'

*Source: Personal per capita income data are from the Bureau of Economic Analysis; per capita income data are from the Bureau of the Census. See Introduction for explanation of differences.

Minnehaha County (cont'd)

Area (sq mi): 813.69 (land 809.67; water 4.01). **Pop per sq mi:** 197.7.

Pop 2005: 160,087. **State rank:** 1. **Pop change:** 2000-20005 +8%; 1990-2000 +19.8%. **Pop 2000:** 148,281 (White 92.1%; Black or African American 1.5%; Hispanic or Latino 2.1%; Asian 1%; Other 4.6%, including 1.9% American Indian/Alaska Native) **Foreign born:** 4.1%. **Median age:** 33.5.

Income 2000: per capita $20,713; median household $42,566; **Pop below poverty level:** 7.5%. ***Personal per capita income 2000-2003:** $30,504-$34,083.

Unemployment 2004: 3.3%. **Change from 2000:** +1%. **Median travel time to work:** 16.8 minutes. **Working outside county of residence:** 4.7%.

Cities with pop over 10,000: Sioux Falls ⌂ (136,695).

MOODY COUNTY

101 E Pipestone Ave   **Ph:** 605-997-3181
Flandreau, SD 57028   **Fax:** 605-997-3861

On the central eastern border of SD, north of Sioux Falls; organized Jan 8, 1873 (prior to statehood) from Brookings and Minnehaha counties. **Name Origin:** For Col. Gideon Curtis Moody (1832-1906), officer in the Civil War, Dakota Territory legislator, and one of the first two U.S. senators from SD (1889-91).

Area (sq mi): 521.1 (land 519.67; water 1.43). **Pop per sq mi:** 12.8.

Pop 2005: 6,637. **State rank:** 28. **Pop change:** 2000-20005 +0.6%; 1990-2000 +1.4%. **Pop 2000:** 6,595 (White 84.5%; Black or African American 0.3%; Hispanic or Latino 0.8%; Asian 0.6%; Other 14.3%, including 12% American Indian/Alaska Native). **Foreign born:** 1.4%. **Median age:** 37.

Income 2000: per capita $16,541; median household $35,467; **Pop below poverty level:** 9.6%. ***Personal per capita income 2000-2003:** $26,153-$28,675.

Unemployment 2004: 4.9%. **Change from 2000:** -2%. **Median travel time to work:** 21.3 minutes. **Working outside county of residence:** 41.4%.

Cities with pop over 10,000: None.

PENNINGTON COUNTY

315 Saint Joseph St   **Ph:** 605-394-2171
Rapid City, SD 57701   **Fax:** 605-394-6833
www.co.pennington.sd.us

On the southwestern border of SD; created Jan 11, 1875 (prior to statehood) from unorganized territory. **Name Origin:** For John L. Pennington, Dakota Territory governor (1874-78).

Area (sq mi): 2784.31 (land 2776.15; water 8.16). **Pop per sq mi:** 33.7.

Pop 2005: 93,580. **State rank:** 2. **Pop change:** 2000-20005 +5.7%; 1990-2000 +8.9%. **Pop 2000:** 88,565 (White 85.6%; Black or African American 0.9%; Hispanic or Latino 2.6%; Asian 0.9%; Other 11.6%, including 8.1% American Indian/Alaska Native). **Foreign born:** 2.1%. **Median age:** 35.

Income 2000: per capita $18,938; median household $37,485; **Pop below poverty level:** 11.5%. ***Personal per capita income 2000-2003:** $26,452-$29,160.

Unemployment 2004: 3.3%. **Change from 2000:** +0.2%. **Median travel time to work:** 17.3 minutes. **Working outside county of residence:** 4.9%.

Cities with pop over 10,000: Rapid City ⌂ (61,459).

PERKINS COUNTY

PO Box 426   **Ph:** 605-244-5626
Bison, SD 57620   **Fax:** 605-244-7110

On the northwestern border of SD; organized Feb 26, 1909 from Harding and Butte counties. **Name Origin:** For Henry E.Perkins, state senator who helped pass the act that established the county.

Area (sq mi): 2890.71 (land 2871.62; water 19.09). **Pop per sq mi:** 1.1.

Pop 2005: 3,023. **State rank:** 48. **Pop change:** 2000-20005 -10.1%; 1990-2000 -14.5%. **Pop 2000:** 3,363 (White 96.5%; Black or African American 0.1%; Hispanic or Latino 0.7%; Asian 0.2%; Other 2.9%, including 1.6% American Indian/Alaska Native). **Foreign born:** 1.3%. **Median age:** 43.1.

Income 2000: per capita $15,734; median household $27,750; **Pop below poverty level:** 16.9%. ***Personal per capita income 2000-2003:** $22,658-$24,912.

Unemployment 2004: 3.5%. **Change from 2000:** +0.8%. **Median travel time to work:** 13.6 minutes. **Working outside county of residence:** 6.6%.

Cities with pop over 10,000: None.

POTTER COUNTY

201 S Exene St PO Box 67   **Ph:** 605-765-9472
Gettysburg, SD 57442   **Fax:** 605-765-9670

In north-central SD, northeast of Pierre; created as Ashmore County Jan 14, 1875 (prior to statehood) from Buffalo County; name changed 1877. **Name Origin:** For Dr. Joel A. Potter, legislator and steward of the State Hospital for the Insane, Yankton. Originally named for Samuel Ashmore, legislator (1872-73).

Area (sq mi): 898.43 (land 866.49; water 31.94). **Pop per sq mi:** 2.7.

Pop 2005: 2,351. **State rank:** 57. **Pop change:** 2000-20005 -12.7%; 1990-2000 -15.6%. **Pop 2000:** 2,693 (White 98%; Black or African American 0%; Hispanic or Latino 0.2%; Asian 0.2%; Other 1.7%). **Foreign born:** 0.5%. **Median age:** 45.8.

Income 2000: per capita $17,417; median household $30,086; **Pop below poverty level:** 12.6%. ***Personal per capita income 2000-2003:** $30,247-$33,394.

Unemployment 2004: 3.4%. **Change from 2000:** -0.2%. **Median travel time to work:** 15.8 minutes. **Working outside county of residence:** 8.6%.

Cities with pop over 10,000: None.

ROBERTS COUNTY

411 2nd Ave E   **Ph:** 605-698-7336
Sisseton, SD 57262   **Fax:** 605-698-4277

On the northeastern border of SD, east of Aberdeen; organized

⌂ *County Seat*

Roberts County (cont'd)

Mar 8, 1883 (prior to statehood) from Grant County. **Name Origin:** Most likely for S.G. Roberts, a publisher and a member of the Dakota territorial legislature when the county was established.

Area (sq mi): 1135.35 (land 1101.28; water 34.08). **Pop per sq mi:** 9.1.

Pop 2005: 10,044. **State rank:** 17. **Pop change:** 2000-20005 +0.3%; 1990-2000 +1%. **Pop 2000:** 10,016 (White 68.1%; Black or African American 0.1%; Hispanic or Latino 0.6%; Asian 0.2%; Other 31.4%, including 29.9% American Indian/Alaska Native). **Foreign born:** 0.8%. **Median age:** 37.1.

Income 2000: per capita $13,428; median household $28,322; **Pop below poverty level:** 22.1%. ***Personal per capita income 2000-2003:** $20,666-$22,379.

Unemployment 2004: 5%. **Change from 2000:** -0.5%. **Median travel time to work:** 16.5 minutes. **Working outside county of residence:** 27%.

Cities with pop over 10,000: None.

SANBORN COUNTY
PO Box 56   **Ph:** 605-796-4515
Woonsocket, SD 57385   **Fax:** 605-796-4502

In south-central SD, northwest of Sioux Falls; organized Mar 9, 1883 (prior to statehood) from Miner County. **Name Origin:** For George W. Sanborn, a Milwaukee Railroad official.

Area (sq mi): 570.21 (land 569.01; water 1.2). **Pop per sq mi:** 4.5.

Pop 2005: 2,541. **State rank:** 55. **Pop change:** 2000-20005 -5%; 1990-2000 -5.6%. **Pop 2000:** 2,675 (White 98%; Black or African American 0%; Hispanic or Latino 1%; Asian 0.4%; Other 0.7%). **Foreign born:** 0.6%. **Median age:** 40.8.

Income 2000: per capita $18,301; median household $33,375; **Pop below poverty level:** 14.9%. ***Personal per capita income 2000-2003:** $28,817-$34,788.

Unemployment 2004: 3.2%. **Change from 2000:** -0.2%. **Median travel time to work:** 20.8 minutes. **Working outside county of residence:** 38.1%.

Cities with pop over 10,000: None.

SHANNON COUNTY
906 N River St   **Ph:** 605-745-5131
Hot Springs, SD 57747   **Fax:** 605-745-5688

On the southwestern border of SD, southeast of Rapid City; created Jan 11, 1875 (prior to statehood) from territorial county. Unorganized; attached to Fall River County for government purposes. County seat is in Fall River County. **Name Origin:** For Peter C. Shannon (1821-?), chief justice of the Dakota Territory Supreme Court (1873-82).

Area (sq mi): 2096.65 (land 2093.88; water 2.77). **Pop per sq mi:** 6.5.

Pop 2005: 13,657. **State rank:** 13. **Pop change:** 2000-20005 +9.6%; 1990-2000 +25.9%. **Pop 2000:** 12,466 (White 4.4%; Black or African American 0.1%; Hispanic or Latino 1.4%; Asian 0%; Other 95.3%, including 94.2% American Indian/Alaska Native). **Foreign born:** 0.6%. **Median age:** 20.6.

Income 2000: per capita $6,286; median household $20,916; **Pop below poverty level:** 52.3%. ***Personal per capita income 2000-2003:** $12,205-$14,106.

Unemployment 2004: 9.1%. **Change from 2000:** -3.5%. **Median travel time to work:** 17.2 minutes. **Working outside county of residence:** 8%.

Cities with pop over 10,000: None.

SPINK COUNTY
210 E 7th Ave   **Ph:** 605-472-1825
Redfield, SD 57469   **Fax:** 605-472-2410

In east-central SD, south of Aberdeen; created Jan 8, 1873 (prior to statehood) from Hanson and Walworth counties. **Name Origin:** For Solomon Lewis Spink (1831-81), Dakota Territory secretary and territorial delegate to Congress (1869-71).

Area (sq mi): 1510.05 (land 1503.87; water 6.18). **Pop per sq mi:** 4.6.

Pop 2005: 6,899. **State rank:** 27. **Pop change:** 2000-20005 -7.4%; 1990-2000 -6.6%. **Pop 2000:** 7,454 (White 97.3%; Black or African American 0.2%; Hispanic or Latino 0.4%; Asian 0.1%; Other 2.1%, including 1.5% American Indian/Alaska Native). **Foreign born:** 0.6%. **Median age:** 39.9.

Income 2000: per capita $15,728; median household $31,717; **Pop below poverty level:** 12.8%. ***Personal per capita income 2000-2003:** $27,509-$30,325.

Unemployment 2004: 3.6%. **Change from 2000:** +0%. **Median travel time to work:** 15.5 minutes. **Working outside county of residence:** 14.8%.

Cities with pop over 10,000: None.

STANLEY COUNTY
PO Box 595   **Ph:** 605-223-7780
Fort Pierre, SD 57532   **Fax:** 605-223-7791

In central SD, created Jan 8, 1873 (prior to statehood) from unorganized territory. **Name Origin:** For Gen. David Sloane Stanley (1829-1902), army officer; after retirement, he served as director of the U.S. Soldiers' Home in Washington, D.C.

Area (sq mi): 1516.99 (land 1443.28; water 73.71). **Pop per sq mi:** 2.

Pop 2005: 2,829. **State rank:** 51. **Pop change:** 2000-20005 +2.1%; 1990-2000 +13%. **Pop 2000:** 2,772 (White 92.9%; Black or African American 0.2%; Hispanic or Latino 0.4%; Asian 0.3%; Other 6.4%, including 4.9% American Indian/Alaska Native). **Foreign born:** 0.7%. **Median age:** 37.6.

Income 2000: per capita $20,300; median household $41,170; **Pop below poverty level:** 8.7%. ***Personal per capita income 2000-2003:** $27,076-$31,618.

Unemployment 2004: 2.7%. **Change from 2000:** -0.1%. **Median travel time to work:** 13.4 minutes. **Working outside county of residence:** 63.7%.

Cities with pop over 10,000: None.

*Source: Personal per capita income data are from the Bureau of Economic Analysis; per capita income data are from the Bureau of the Census. See Introduction for explanation of differences.

SULLY COUNTY

PO Box 188   **Ph:** 605-258-2535
Onida, SD 57564   **Fax:** 605-258-2270

In central SD, north of Pierre; created Jan 8, 1873 (prior to statehood) from Potter County. **Name Origin:** For Fort Sully, which was named for Gen. Alfred Sully (1821-79), its builder and commander, famous as an Indian fighter and cited several times for bravery during the Civil War.

Area (sq mi): 1070.36 (land 1006.9; water 63.46). **Pop per sq mi:** 1.4.

Pop 2005: 1,430. **State rank:** 64. **Pop change:** 2000-20005 -8.1%; 1990-2000 -2.1%. **Pop 2000:** 1,556 (White 97.4%; Black or African American 0%; Hispanic or Latino 0.8%; Asian 0.1%; Other 2.1%). **Foreign born:** 0.8%. **Median age:** 40.

Income 2000: per capita $17,407; median household $32,500; **Pop below poverty level:** 12.1%. ***Personal per capita income 2000-2003:** $37,981-$42,668.

Unemployment 2004: 2.2%. **Change from 2000:** -0.2%. **Median travel time to work:** 17.3 minutes. **Working outside county of residence:** 23.1%.

Cities with pop over 10,000: None.

TODD COUNTY

200 E 3rd St   **Ph:** 605-842-3727
Winner, SD 57580   **Fax:** 605-842-1116

On the central southern border of SD, south of Pierre; created Mar 9, 1909 from Indian lands. Unorganized; attached to Tripp County for governmental purposes. County seat is in Tripp County. **Name Origin:** For Gen. John Blair Smith Todd (1814-72), officer in the Seminole War and the Mexican-American War, U.S. congressional delegate from the Dakota Territory (1862-65), and territorial legislator (1866-67).

Area (sq mi): 1390.9 (land 1388.12; water 2.78). **Pop per sq mi:** 7.1.

Pop 2005: 9,882. **State rank:** 18. **Pop change:** 2000-20005 +9.2%; 1990-2000 +8.4%. **Pop 2000:** 9,050 (White 12.5%; Black or African American 0.1%; Hispanic or Latino 1.5%; Asian 0.1%; Other 87.2%, including 85.6% American Indian/Alaska Native). **Foreign born:** 0.6%. **Median age:** 21.7.

Income 2000: per capita $7,714; median household $20,035; **Pop below poverty level:** 48.3%. ***Personal per capita income 2000-2003:** $13,038-$13,505.

Unemployment 2004: 5.9%. **Change from 2000:** -2.4%. **Median travel time to work:** 18.6 minutes. **Working outside county of residence:** 10.4%.

Cities with pop over 10,000: None.

TRIPP COUNTY

200 E 3rd St   **Ph:** 605-842-2266
Winner, SD 57580   **Fax:** 605-842-2267

On the central southern border of SD, southeast of Pierre; created Jan 8, 1873 (prior to statehood) from unorganized territory. Seat of government for Todd County. **Name Origin:** For Bartlett Tripp (1842-1911), promoter of SD's statehood, U.S. minister to Austria-Hungary (1893), chief justice of the Dakota Territory (1886-89), and trustee of Yankton College.

Area (sq mi): 1617.4 (land 1613.52; water 3.88). **Pop per sq mi:** 3.8.

Pop 2005: 6,065. **State rank:** 30. **Pop change:** 2000-20005 -5.7%; 1990-2000 -7.1%. **Pop 2000:** 6,430 (White 87.2%; Black or African American 0%; Hispanic or Latino 0.9%; Asian 0.1%; Other 12.5%, including 11.2% American Indian/Alaska Native). **Foreign born:** 0.4%. **Median age:** 39.5.

Income 2000: per capita $13,776; median household $28,333; **Pop below poverty level:** 19.0%. ***Personal per capita income 2000-2003:** $21,670-$25,354.

Unemployment 2004: 3.4%. **Change from 2000:** +0.3%. **Median travel time to work:** 13.9 minutes. **Working outside county of residence:** 5.7%.

Cities with pop over 10,000: None.

TURNER COUNTY

PO Box 446   **Ph:** 605-297-3115
Parker, SD 57053   **Fax:** 605-297-2115

In southeastern SD, southwest of Sioux Falls; organized Jan 13, 1871 (prior to statehood) from Lincoln County and part of the now defunct Jayne County. **Name Origin:** For John W. Turner (1800-83), member of the Dakota Territory legislature (1865-66; 1872) and a superintendent of public instruction.

Area (sq mi): 617.45 (land 616.82; water 0.63). **Pop per sq mi:** 13.8.

Pop 2005: 8,520. **State rank:** 21. **Pop change:** 2000-20005 -3.7%; 1990-2000 +3.2%. **Pop 2000:** 8,849 (White 98.6%; Black or African American 0.1%; Hispanic or Latino 0.4%; Asian 0.2%; Other 0.8%). **Foreign born:** 0.5%. **Median age:** 40.5.

Income 2000: per capita $17,343; median household $36,059; **Pop below poverty level:** 7.2%. ***Personal per capita income 2000-2003:** $27,209-$30,190.

Unemployment 2004: 3.7%. **Change from 2000:** +0.4%. **Median travel time to work:** 24.4 minutes. **Working outside county of residence:** 46.9%.

Cities with pop over 10,000: None.

UNION COUNTY

209 E Main St Suite 230   **Ph:** 605-356-2132
Elk Point, SD 57025   **Fax:** 605-356-3687

In southeastern SD, south of Sioux Falls; organized as Cole County Apr 10, 1862 (prior to statehood) from unorganized territory; name changed 1864. **Name Origin:** For support of the Union in the Civil War. Originally for Austin Cole, member of the first Territorial legislature.

Area (sq mi): 467.08 (land 460.38; water 6.7). **Pop per sq mi:** 29.2.

Pop 2005: 13,462. **State rank:** 14. **Pop change:** 2000-20005 +7%; 1990-2000 +23.5%. **Pop 2000:** 12,584 (White 96%; Black or African American 0.3%; Hispanic or Latino 1.3%; Asian 1.3%; Other 1.5%). **Foreign born:** 2.4%. **Median age:** 36.9.

Income 2000: per capita $24,355; median household $44,790; **Pop below poverty level:** 5.5%. ***Personal per capita income 2000-2003:** $37,299-$38,855.

Unemployment 2004: 4.5%. **Change from 2000:** +0.4%. **Median travel time to work:** 17.9 minutes. **Working outside county of residence:** 43.6%.

Union County (cont'd)

Cities with pop over 10,000: None.

WALWORTH COUNTY

PO Box 199　　　　　　　　　**Ph:** 605-649-7878
Selby, SD 57472　　　　　　　**Fax:** 605-649-7867

In north-central SD, west of Aberdeen; created Jan 8, 1873 (prior to statehood) from territorial county. **Name Origin:** For Walworth County, WI, former home of early settlers.

Area (sq mi): 744.22 (land 707.81; water 36.41). **Pop per sq mi:** 7.8.

Pop 2005: 5,494. **State rank:** 35. **Pop change:** 2000-20005 -8%; 1990-2000 -1.9%. **Pop 2000:** 5,974 (White 86.3%; Black or African American 0%; Hispanic or Latino 0.6%; Asian 0.2%; Other 13.3%, including 11.8% American Indian/Alaska Native). **Foreign born:** 0.7%. **Median age:** 42.8.

Income 2000: per capita $15,492; median household $27,834; **Pop below poverty level:** 18.2%. ***Personal per capita income 2000-2003:** $22,220-$24,367.

Unemployment 2004: 5.2%. **Change from 2000:** +1.8%. **Median travel time to work:** 12.7 minutes. **Working outside county of residence:** 9.6%.

Cities with pop over 10,000: None.

YANKTON COUNTY

410 Walnut St　　　　　　　　**Ph:** 605-668-3080
Yankton, SD 57078　　　　　　**Fax:** 605-668-5411
www.co.yankton.sd.us

On the southeastern border of SD, southwest of Sioux Falls; original county; organized Apr 5, 1862 (prior to statehood) from territorial county. **Name Origin:** For the city of Yankton.

Area (sq mi): 532.62 (land 521.55; water 11.07). **Pop per sq mi:** 41.6.

Pop 2005: 21,718. **State rank:** 9. **Pop change:** 2000-20005 +0.3%; 1990-2000 +12.5%. **Pop 2000:** 21,652 (White 94.1%; Black or African American 1.2%; Hispanic or Latino 1.8%; Asian 0.4%; Other 3.2%, including 1.6% American Indian/Alaska Native). **Foreign born:** 1.5%. **Median age:** 37.

Income 2000: per capita $17,312; median household $35,374; **Pop below poverty level:** 9.6%. ***Personal per capita income 2000-2003:** $24,617-$26,551.

Unemployment 2004: 3.3%. **Change from 2000:** +0%. **Median travel time to work:** 14.4 minutes. **Working outside county of residence:** 9.4%.

Cities with pop over 10,000: Yankton 🏛 (13,491).

ZIEBACH COUNTY

PO Box 68　　　　　　　　　　**Ph:** 605-365-5157
Dupree, SD 57623　　　　　　　**Fax:** 605-365-5204

In west-central SD, northwest of Pierre; organized Feb 1, 1911 from Pennington County. **Name Origin:** For Frank M. Ziebach (1830-1929), publisher of the *Weekly Dakotian*.

Area (sq mi): 1971.05 (land 1962.33; water 8.72). **Pop per sq mi:** 1.3.

Pop 2005: 2,631. **State rank:** 52. **Pop change:** 2000-20005 +4.4%; 1990-2000 +13.5%. **Pop 2000:** 2,519 (White 26.4%; Black or African American 0%; Hispanic or Latino 1%; Asian 0.1%; Other 73.5%, including 72.3% American Indian/Alaska Native). **Foreign born:** 0.4%. **Median age:** 23.8.

Income 2000: per capita $7,463; median household $18,063; **Pop below poverty level:** 49.9%. ***Personal per capita income 2000-2003:** $11,581-$11,264.

Unemployment 2004: 7%. **Change from 2000:** -7.4%. **Median travel time to work:** 19.7 minutes. **Working outside county of residence:** 34.5%.

Cities with pop over 10,000: None.

*Source: Personal per capita income data are from the Bureau of Economic Analysis; per capita income data are from the Bureau of the Census. See Introduction for explanation of differences.

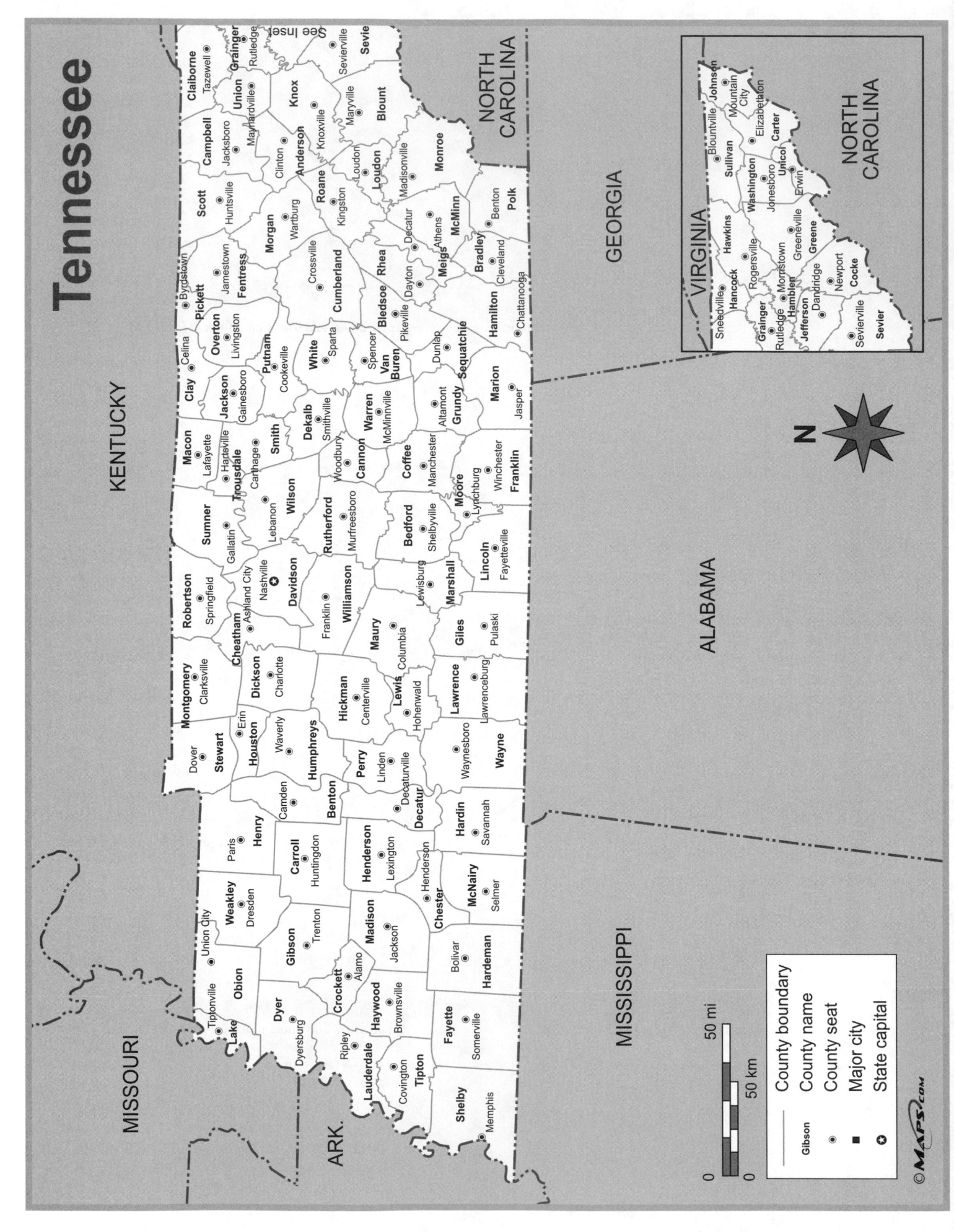

Tennessee

KENTUCKY

MISSOURI

ARK.

MISSISSIPPI

ALABAMA

GEORGIA

NORTH CAROLINA

VIRGINIA

See Inset

N

County boundary
Gibson — County name
⊙ County seat
■ Major city
✪ State capital

0 50 mi
0 50 km

©MAPS.com

Claiborne — Tazewell
Grainger — Rutledge
Sevier — Sevierville
Union — Maynardville
Knox — Knoxville
Blount — Maryville
Campbell — Jacksboro
Anderson — Clinton
Loudon — Loudon
Monroe — Madisonville
Scott — Huntsville
Morgan — Wartburg
Roane — Kingston
Polk — Benton
McMinn — Athens
Bradley — Cleveland
Hamilton — Chattanooga
Fentress — Jamestown
Cumberland — Crossville
Rhea — Dayton
Meigs — Decatur
Sequatchie — Dunlap
Marion — Jasper
Pickett — Byrdstown
Overton — Livingston
Putnam — Cookeville
White — Sparta
Van Buren — Spencer
Bledsoe — Pikeville
Grundy — Altamont
Clay — Celina
Jackson — Gainesboro
Smith — Carthage
Dekalb — Smithville
Warren — McMinnville
Coffee — Manchester
Franklin — Winchester
Macon — Lafayette
Trousdale — Hartsville
Cannon — Woodbury
Moore — Lynchburg
Sumner — Gallatin
Wilson — Lebanon
Rutherford — Murfreesboro
Bedford — Shelbyville
Lincoln — Fayetteville
Robertson — Springfield
Davidson — Nashville
Williamson — Franklin
Marshall — Lewisburg
Cheatham — Ashland City
Maury — Columbia
Giles — Pulaski
Montgomery — Clarksville
Dickson — Charlotte
Lewis — Hohenwald
Lawrence — Lawrenceburg
Hickman — Centerville
Stewart — Dover
Houston — Erin
Humphreys — Waverly
Perry — Linden
Wayne — Waynesboro
Benton — Camden
Decatur — Decaturville
Hardin — Savannah
Henry — Paris
Carroll — Huntingdon
Henderson — Lexington
Weakley — Dresden
Gibson — Trenton
Madison — Jackson
Chester — Henderson
McNairy — Selmer
Obion — Union City
Dyer — Dyersburg
Crockett — Alamo
Haywood — Brownsville
Hardeman — Bolivar
Lake — Tiptonville
Lauderdale — Ripley
Tipton — Covington
Fayette — Somerville
Shelby — Memphis

VIRGINIA

NORTH CAROLINA

Johnson — Mountain City
Sullivan — Blountville
Carter — Elizabethton
Unicoi — Erwin
Washington — Jonesboro
Hawkins — Rogersville
Greene — Greeneville
Hancock — Sneedville
Grainger — Rutledge
Hamblen — Morristown
Jefferson — Dandridge
Cocke — Newport
Sevier — Sevierville

Tennessee

TENNESSEE STATE INFORMATION

www.tennessee.gov   **Ph:** 615-741-3011

Area (sq mi): 42,143.27 (land 41,217.12; water 926.15). **Pop per sq mi:** 144.7.

Pop 2005: 5,962,959. **Pop change:** 2000-20005 +4.8%; 1990-2000 +16.7%. **Pop 2000:** 5,689,283 (White 79.2%; Black or African American 16.4%; Hispanic or Latino 2.2%; Asian 1%; Other 2.4%). **Foreign born:** 2.8%. **Median age:** 35.9.

Income 2000: per capita $19,393; median household $36,360; **Pop below poverty level:** 13.5%. *Personal per capita income 2000-2003:** $26,097-$28,641.

Unemployment 2004: 5.5%. **Change from 2000:** +1.5%. **Median travel time to work:** 24.5 minutes. **Working outside county of residence:** 26.6%.

ANDERSON COUNTY

100 N Main St Rm 111   **Ph:** 865-457-5400
Clinton, TN 37716   **Fax:** 865-259-0116
www.andersoncountychamber.org

In northeastern TN, west of Knoxville; organized Nov 6, 1801 from Knox and Grainger counties. **Name Origin:** For Maj. Joseph Anderson (1757-1837), U.S. senator from TN (1797-1815) and first comptroller of the U.S. Treasury (1815-36).

Area (sq mi): 344.82 (land 337.51; water 7.31). **Pop per sq mi:** 214.6.

Pop 2005: 72,430. **State rank:** 17. **Pop change:** 2000-20005 +1.5%; 1990-2000 +4.5%. **Pop 2000:** 71,330 (White 92.7%; Black or African American 3.9%; Hispanic or Latino 1.1%; Asian 0.8%; Other 1.9%). **Foreign born:** 1.9%. **Median age:** 39.9.

Income 2000: per capita $19,009; median household $35,483; **Pop below poverty level:** 13.1%. *Personal per capita income 2000-2003:** $25,035-$27,668.

Unemployment 2004: 4.9%. **Change from 2000:** +0.9%. **Median travel time to work:** 22.9 minutes. **Working outside county of residence:** 34.7%.

Cities with pop over 10,000: Oak Ridge (27,298).

BEDFORD COUNTY

104 Northside Sq   **Ph:** 931-684-1921
Shelbyville, TN 37160   **Fax:** 931-685-9590
www.shelbyvilletn.com

In south-central TN, south of Murfreesboro; organized Dec 3, 1807 from Rutherford County and Indian lands. **Name Origin:** For Lt. Col. Thomas Bedford, an army officer.

Area (sq mi): 474.83 (land 473.67; water 1.17). **Pop per sq mi:** 89.1.

Pop 2005: 42,204. **State rank:** 34. **Pop change:** 2000-20005 +12.3%; 1990-2000 +23.6%. **Pop 2000:** 37,586 (White 82.6%; Black or African American 8.5%; Hispanic or Latino 7.5%; Asian 0.5%; Other 4.3%). **Foreign born:** 6.4%. **Median age:** 34.9.

Income 2000: per capita $16,698; median household $36,729; **Pop below poverty level:** 13.1%. *Personal per capita income 2000-2003:** $23,202-$24,685.

Unemployment 2004: 5.4%. **Change from 2000:** -0.4%. **Median travel time to work:** 34.1 minutes. **Working outside county of residence:** 29.7%.

Cities with pop over 10,000: Shelbyville 🏛 (17,981).

BENTON COUNTY

1 E Court Sq Rm 102   **Ph:** 731-584-6011
Camden, TN 38320   **Fax:** 731-584-4640

In northwestern TN, west of Nashville; organized 1835 from Henry and Humphreys counties. **Name Origin:** For David Benton, an 'old and respectable citizen of said county.'

Area (sq mi): 436.2 (land 394.84; water 41.37). **Pop per sq mi:** 41.7.

Pop 2005: 16,467. **State rank:** 74. **Pop change:** 2000-20005 -0.4%; 1990-2000 +13.9%. **Pop 2000:** 16,537 (White 95.7%; Black or African American 2.1%; Hispanic or Latino 0.9%; Asian 0.2%; Other 1.2%). **Foreign born:** 0.7%. **Median age:** 41.6.

Income 2000: per capita $14,646; median household $28,679; **Pop below poverty level:** 15.6%. *Personal per capita income 2000-2003:** $19,801-$20,612.

Unemployment 2004: 8.4%. **Change from 2000:** +1.1%. **Median travel time to work:** 27.1 minutes. **Working outside county of residence:** 39.1%.

Cities with pop over 10,000: None.

BLEDSOE COUNTY

104 N Frazier St   **Ph:** 423-447-6855
Pikeville, TN 37367   **Fax:** 423-447-7265

In east-central TN, north of Chattanooga; organized Nov 30, 1807 from Roane County and Indian lands. **Name Origin:** For either Anthony Bledsoe (1733-88), member of the VA legislature, active in establishing TN as a state; or for Maj. Abraham Bledsoe, an officer in the Revolutionary War.

Area (sq mi): 406.71 (land 406.32; water 0.4). **Pop per sq mi:** 31.8.

Pop 2005: 12,928. **State rank:** 81. **Pop change:** 2000-20005 +4.5%; 1990-2000 +27.9%. **Pop 2000:** 12,367 (White 93.7%; Black or

Bledsoe County (cont'd)

African American 3.7%; Hispanic or Latino 1.1%; Asian 0.1%; Other 1.7%). **Foreign born:** 0.4%. **Median age:** 37.4.

Income 2000: per capita $13,889; median household $28,982; **Pop below poverty level:** 18.1%. ***Personal per capita income 2000-2003:** $17,743-$20,251.

Unemployment 2004: 7.4%. **Change from 2000:** +2.3%. **Median travel time to work:** 33 minutes. **Working outside county of residence:** 52.5%.

Cities with pop over 10,000: None.

BLOUNT COUNTY
341 Court St
Maryville, TN 37804   **Ph:** 865-273-5700
www.blounttn.org   **Fax:** 865-273-5705

On southeastern border of TN, south of Knoxville; organized Jul 11, 1795 (prior to statehood) from Knox County. **Name Origin:** For William Blount (1749-1800), territorial governor of TN (1790-96) and U.S. senator from TN (1796-97).

Area (sq mi): 566.65 (land 558.56; water 8.08). **Pop per sq mi:** 206.8.

Pop 2005: 115,535. **State rank:** 10. **Pop change:** 2000-20005 +9.2%; 1990-2000 +23.1%. **Pop 2000:** 105,823 (White 94.1%; Black or African American 2.9%; Hispanic or Latino 1.1%; Asian 0.7%; Other 1.6%). **Foreign born:** 1.5%. **Median age:** 38.4.

Income 2000: per capita $19,416; median household $37,862; **Pop below poverty level:** 9.7%. ***Personal per capita income 2000-2003:** $23,947-$26,253.

Unemployment 2004: 4.2%. **Change from 2000:** +0.2%. **Median travel time to work:** 24 minutes. **Working outside county of residence:** 36.5%.

Cities with pop over 10,000: Maryville ⛪ (25,569).

BRADLEY COUNTY
155 N Ocoee St
Cleveland, TN 37311   **Ph:** 423-728-7226
www.bradleyco.net   **Fax:** 423-478-8845

On the southwestern border of TN, east of Chattanooga; organized Feb 10, 1836 from Indian lands. **Name Origin:** For Lt. Col. Edward Bradley (?-1829), an officer in the War of 1812 and the Southern Indian wars.

Area (sq mi): 331.5 (land 328.72; water 2.78). **Pop per sq mi:** 280.2.

Pop 2005: 92,092. **State rank:** 14. **Pop change:** 2000-20005 +4.7%; 1990-2000 +19.3%. **Pop 2000:** 87,965 (White 92%; Black or African American 4%; Hispanic or Latino 2.1%; Asian 0.6%; Other 2.5%). **Foreign born:** 2.2%. **Median age:** 35.5.

Income 2000: per capita $18,108; median household $35,034; **Pop below poverty level:** 12.2%. ***Personal per capita income 2000-2003:** $22,726-$25,933.

Unemployment 2004: 5.1%. **Change from 2000:** +1.3%. **Median travel time to work:** 20.7 minutes. **Working outside county of residence:** 23.3%.

Cities with pop over 10,000: Cleveland ⛪ (37,746).

CAMPBELL COUNTY
195 Kentucky St Suite 2
Jacksboro, TN 37757   **Ph:** 423-562-4985
co.campbell.tn.us   **Fax:** 423-566-3852

On the central northern border of TN, north of Oak Ridge; organized Sep 11, 1806 from Anderson and Claiborne counties. **Name Origin:** For George Washington Campbell (1769-1848), U.S. senator from TN (1811-14; 1815-18), U.S. secretary of the treasury (1814), and ambassador to Russia (1818-20). Others claim Arthur Campbell, a negotiator with the Indians.

Area (sq mi): 498.25 (land 480.07; water 18.19). **Pop per sq mi:** 84.8.

Pop 2005: 40,686. **State rank:** 37. **Pop change:** 2000-20005 +2.1%; 1990-2000 +13.6%. **Pop 2000:** 39,854 (White 97.6%; Black or African American 0.3%; Hispanic or Latino 0.7%; Asian 0.2%; Other 1.4%). **Foreign born:** 0.8%. **Median age:** 38.3.

Income 2000: per capita $13,301; median household $25,285; **Pop below poverty level:** 22.8%. ***Personal per capita income 2000-2003:** $17,793-$21,186.

Unemployment 2004: 6%. **Change from 2000:** +0.2%. **Median travel time to work:** 30.8 minutes. **Working outside county of residence:** 39.5%.

Cities with pop over 10,000: None.

CANNON COUNTY
1 County Courthouse Public Sq   **Ph:** 615-563-4278
Woodbury, TN 37190   **Fax:** 615-563-1289

In central TN, southeast of Nashville; organized Jan 31, 1836 from Rutherford, Warren, and Smith counties. **Name Origin:** For Col. Newton Cannon (1781-1842), U.S. representative from TN (1814-17; 1819-23) and governor (1836-39).

Area (sq mi): 265.71 (land 265.64; water 0.06). **Pop per sq mi:** 50.2.

Pop 2005: 13,337. **State rank:** 79. **Pop change:** 2000-20005 +4%; 1990-2000 +22.5%. **Pop 2000:** 12,826 (White 96.1%; Black or African American 1.5%; Hispanic or Latino 1.2%; Asian 0.1%; Other 1.5%). **Foreign born:** 0.8%. **Median age:** 36.8.

Income 2000: per capita $16,405; median household $32,809; **Pop below poverty level:** 12.8%. ***Personal per capita income 2000-2003:** $22,026-$24,986.

Unemployment 2004: 4.5%. **Change from 2000:** -0.4%. **Median travel time to work:** 32.7 minutes. **Working outside county of residence:** 62.9%.

Cities with pop over 10,000: None.

CARROLL COUNTY
625 High St Suite 103   **Ph:** 731-986-1961
Huntingdon, TN 38344   **Fax:** 731-986-1978
www.carrollcounty-tn-chamber.com

In western TN, northeast of Jackson; organized Nov 7, 1821 from Western District (Indian lands). **Name Origin:** For Gen. William Carroll (1788-1844), officer in the Battle of New Orleans (1815) and TN governor (1821-27; 1829-35).

Area (sq mi): 599.86 (land 599.02; water 0.84). **Pop per sq mi:** 48.6.

Pop 2005: 29,121. **State rank:** 50. **Pop change:** 2000-20005 -1.2%; 1990-2000 +7.1%. **Pop 2000:** 29,475 (White 87%; Black or African

*Source: Personal per capita income data are from the Bureau of Economic Analysis; per capita income data are from the Bureau of the Census. See Introduction for explanation of differences.

Carroll County (cont'd)

American 10.3%; Hispanic or Latino 1.3%; Asian 0.2%; Other 1.8%). **Foreign born:** 1.1%. **Median age:** 39.

Income 2000: per capita $16,251; median household $30,463; **Pop below poverty level:** 13.9%. ***Personal per capita income 2000-2003:** $20,942-$22,821.

Unemployment 2004: 8.2%. **Change from 2000:** -1.3%. **Median travel time to work:** 24.1 minutes. **Working outside county of residence:** 44.2%.

Cities with pop over 10,000: None.

CARTER COUNTY

801 E Elk Ave Courthouse Bldg   **Ph:** 423-542-1814
Elizabethton, TN 37643   **Fax:** 423-547-1502
www.tourelizabethton.com

On the northeastern border of TN, east of Johnson City; organized as Carteret County Apr 9, 1796 from Washington County; name changed later. **Name Origin:** For Col. Landon Carter (1760-1800), officer in the Revolutionary and Indian wars; officeholder in NC, the territories, and in TN, whose statehood he advocated.

Area (sq mi): 347.62 (land 341.05; water 6.57). **Pop per sq mi:** 172.6.

Pop 2005: 58,865. **State rank:** 22. **Pop change:** 2000-20005 +3.7%; 1990-2000 +10.2%. **Pop 2000:** 56,742 (White 96.9%; Black or African American 1%; Hispanic or Latino 0.9%; Asian 0.3%; Other 1.3%). **Foreign born:** 0.8%. **Median age:** 38.5.

Income 2000: per capita $14,678; median household $27,371; **Pop below poverty level:** 16.9%. ***Personal per capita income 2000-2003:** $18,691-$20,197.

Unemployment 2004: 5.8%. **Change from 2000:** +1%. **Median travel time to work:** 24.1 minutes. **Working outside county of residence:** 56.5%.

Cities with pop over 10,000: Elizabethton 🏛 (13,993).

CHEATHAM COUNTY

100 Public Sq Suite 105   **Ph:** 615-792-4316
Ashland City, TN 37015   **Fax:** 615-792-2001
www.cheathamcounty.net

In west-central TN, northwest of Nashville; organized Feb 28, 1856 from Dickson, Montgomery, Davidson, and Robertson counties. **Name Origin:** Probably for Edwin S. Cheatham, speaker of the TN senate when county was formed. Others claim Gen. Benjamin F. Cheatham (1820-86), an officer in the Mexican-American War and for the Confederacy; or Nathaniel Cheatham.

Area (sq mi): 307.13 (land 302.66; water 4.47). **Pop per sq mi:** 127.5.

Pop 2005: 38,603. **State rank:** 39. **Pop change:** 2000-20005 +7.5%; 1990-2000 +32.3%. **Pop 2000:** 35,912 (White 96.1%; Black or African American 1.5%; Hispanic or Latino 1.2%; Asian 0.2%; Other 1.5%). **Foreign born:** 1.1%. **Median age:** 35.3.

Income 2000: per capita $18,882; median household $45,836; **Pop below poverty level:** 7.4%. ***Personal per capita income 2000-2003:** $24,870-$26,888.

Unemployment 2004: 4.3%. **Change from 2000:** +1.5%. **Median travel time to work:** 32.9 minutes. **Working outside county of residence:** 72.6%.

Cities with pop over 10,000: None.

CHESTER COUNTY

PO Box 205   **Ph:** 731-989-2233
Henderson, TN 38040   **Fax:** 731-989-9602

In southwestern TN, southeast of Jackson; organized Mar 4, 1879 from Hardeman, Madison, McNairy, and Henderson counties. **Name Origin:** For Col. Robert I. Chester (1793-c.1860), officer in the Republic of Texas army and TN state legislator.

Area (sq mi): 288.74 (land 288.52, water 0.22). **Pop per sq mi:** 55.3.

Pop 2005: 15,941. **State rank:** 76. **Pop change:** 2000-20005 +2.6%; 1990-2000 +21.2%. **Pop 2000:** 15,540 (White 87.6%; Black or African American 10%; Hispanic or Latino 1%; Asian 0.2%; Other 1.6%). **Foreign born:** 0.5%. **Median age:** 34.1.

Income 2000: per capita $15,756; median household $34,349; **Pop below poverty level:** 14.4%. ***Personal per capita income 2000-2003:** $19,889-$21,681.

Unemployment 2004: 5.7%. **Change from 2000:** +1.6%. **Median travel time to work:** 26.1 minutes. **Working outside county of residence:** 54.2%.

Cities with pop over 10,000: None.

CLAIBORNE COUNTY

1740 Main St   **Ph:** 423-626-3284
Tazewell, TN 37879   **Fax:** 423-626-3604
www.claibornecounty.com

On central northern border of TN, north of Knoxville; organized Oct 29, 1801 from Grainger and Hawkins counties. **Name Origin:** For William Charles Coles Claiborne (1775-1817), governor of the Mississippi Territory (1801-05), of the Orleans Territory (1804-12), and of LA (1812-16), and U.S. representative from TN (1797-1801).

Area (sq mi): 441.55 (land 434.28; water 7.27). **Pop per sq mi:** 71.5.

Pop 2005: 31,033. **State rank:** 47. **Pop change:** 2000-20005 +3.9%; 1990-2000 +14.3%. **Pop 2000:** 29,862 (White 97.4%; Black or African American 0.8%; Hispanic or Latino 0.6%; Asian 0.3%; Other 1.1%). **Foreign born:** 0.9%. **Median age:** 37.4.

Income 2000: per capita $13,032; median household $25,782; **Pop below poverty level:** 22.6%. ***Personal per capita income 2000-2003:** $19,155-$21,037.

Unemployment 2004: 5.5%. **Change from 2000:** +0.5%. **Median travel time to work:** 27.7 minutes. **Working outside county of residence:** 35.5%.

Cities with pop over 10,000: None.

CLAY COUNTY

PO Box 387   **Ph:** 931-243-2161
Celina, TN 38551   **Fax:** 931-243-2436
www.dalehollowlake.org/county.htm

On the central northern border of TN, northeast of Nashville; organized Jun 24, 1870 from Jackson and Overton counties. **Name Origin:** For Henry Clay (1777-1852), U.S. senator from KY, known

🏛 County Seat

Clay County (cont'd)

as the 'Great Pacificator' for his advocacy of compromise to avert national crises.

Area (sq mi): 259.25 (land 236.11; water 23.14). **Pop per sq mi:** 33.8.

Pop 2005: 7,992. **State rank:** 87. **Pop change:** 2000-20005 +0.2%; 1990-2000 +10.2%. **Pop 2000:** 7,976 (White 96.1%; Black or African American 1.4%; Hispanic or Latino 1.4%; Asian 0.1%; Other 1.6%). **Foreign born:** 1.1%. **Median age:** 39.9.

Income 2000: per capita $13,320; median household $23,958; **Pop below poverty level:** 19.1%. ***Personal per capita income 2000-2003:** $18,141-$19,576.

Unemployment 2004: 9.1%. **Change from 2000:** -0.9%. **Median travel time to work:** 29 minutes. **Working outside county of residence:** 40.6%.

Cities with pop over 10,000: None.

COCKE COUNTY

360 E Main St Room 146 Courthouse Annex   **Ph:** 423-623-8791
Newport, TN 37821   **Fax:** 423-623-8792
www.cockecounty.com

On the central eastern border of TN, east of Knoxville; organized Aug 9, 1797 from Jefferson County. **Name Origin:** For William Cocke (1747-1828), explorer with Daniel Boone (c.1734-1820), TN legislator and judge, and U.S. senator (1796-97; 1799-1805).

Area (sq mi): 443.15 (land 434.4; water 8.75). **Pop per sq mi:** 80.4.

Pop 2005: 34,929. **State rank:** 41. **Pop change:** 2000-20005 +4.1%; 1990-2000 +15.2%. **Pop 2000:** 33,565 (White 95.5%; Black or African American 2%; Hispanic or Latino 1.1%; Asian 0.2%; Other 1.7%). **Foreign born:** 0.8%. **Median age:** 38.6.

Income 2000: per capita $13,881; median household $25,553; **Pop below poverty level:** 22.5%. ***Personal per capita income 2000-2003:** $17,955-$18,816.

Unemployment 2004: 8.1%. **Change from 2000:** +0.7%. **Median travel time to work:** 28.5 minutes. **Working outside county of residence:** 40.3%.

Cities with pop over 10,000: None.

COFFEE COUNTY

1327 McArthur Dr Suite 1   **Ph:** 931-723-5106
Manchester, TN 37355   **Fax:** 931-723-8248
www.coffeecountytn.org

In south-central TN, southeast of Murfreesboro; organized Jan 8, 1836 from Franklin, Warren, and Bedford counties. **Name Origin:** For Gen. John Coffee (1772-1833), officer in the War of 1812 who later oversaw the removal of the Choctaws and Chickasaws to OK Territory.

Area (sq mi): 434.46 (land 428.84; water 5.62). **Pop per sq mi:** 118.6.

Pop 2005: 50,869. **State rank:** 28. **Pop change:** 2000-20005 +5.9%; 1990-2000 +19%. **Pop 2000:** 48,014 (White 92.3%; Black or African American 3.6%; Hispanic or Latino 2.2%; Asian 0.7%; Other 2.2%). **Foreign born:** 2.3%. **Median age:** 37.5.

Income 2000: per capita $18,137; median household $34,898; **Pop below poverty level:** 14.3%. ***Personal per capita income 2000-2003:** $23,095-$26,560.

Unemployment 2004: 4.8%. **Change from 2000:** +0.4%. **Median travel time to work:** 22.4 minutes. **Working outside county of residence:** 24.2%.

Cities with pop over 10,000: Tullahoma (18,677).

CROCKETT COUNTY

1 S Bellis St Suite 3   **Ph:** 731-696-5460
Alamo, TN 38001   **Fax:** 731-696-4101

In central-western TN, northwest of Jackson; established Dec 20, 1845 from Dyer, Madison, Gibson, and Haywood counties. **Name Origin:** For David 'Davy' Crockett (1786-1836), soldier, scout, and U.S. representative from TN (1827-31; 1833-35), killed at the Alamo.

Area (sq mi): 265.47 (land 265.27; water 0.21). **Pop per sq mi:** 55.

Pop 2005: 14,595. **State rank:** 78. **Pop change:** 2000-20005 +0.4%; 1990-2000 +8.6%. **Pop 2000:** 14,532 (White 79.5%; Black or African American 14.4%; Hispanic or Latino 5.5%; Asian 0.1%; Other 3.6%). **Foreign born:** 3.9%. **Median age:** 37.4.

Income 2000: per capita $14,600; median household $30,015; **Pop below poverty level:** 16.9%. ***Personal per capita income 2000-2003:** $22,688-$23,887.

Unemployment 2004: 7.9%. **Change from 2000:** +2.3%. **Median travel time to work:** 20.9 minutes. **Working outside county of residence:** 43.4%.

Cities with pop over 10,000: None.

CUMBERLAND COUNTY

2 N Main St Suite 206   **Ph:** 931-484-6442
Crossville, TN 38555   **Fax:** 931-484-6440
www.crossville-chamber.com

In east-central TN, west of Oak Ridge; organized Nov 16, 1855 from Bledsoe, Morgan, Roane, White, Putnam, Rhea, Van Buren, and Fentress counties. **Name Origin:** For William Augustus, Duke of Cumberland (1721-65), British general and second son of George II of England.

Area (sq mi): 684.95 (land 681.61; water 3.34). **Pop per sq mi:** 75.3.

Pop 2005: 51,346. **State rank:** 26. **Pop change:** 2000-20005 +9.7%; 1990-2000 +34.7%. **Pop 2000:** 46,802 (White 97.4%; Black or African American 0.1%; Hispanic or Latino 1.2%; Asian 0.2%; Other 1.6%). **Foreign born:** 1.9%. **Median age:** 42.5.

Income 2000: per capita $16,808; median household $30,901; **Pop below poverty level:** 14.7%. ***Personal per capita income 2000-2003:** $21,744-$23,191.

Unemployment 2004: 6.1%. **Change from 2000:** -0.3%. **Median travel time to work:** 23 minutes. **Working outside county of residence:** 16.9%.

Cities with pop over 10,000: None.

*Source: Personal per capita income data are from the Bureau of Economic Analysis; per capita income data are from the Bureau of the Census. See Introduction for explanation of differences.

DAVIDSON COUNTY

205 Metro Courthouse   **Ph:** 615-862-6770
Nashville, TN 37201   **Fax:** 615-862-6774
www.nashville.gov

In west-central TN, northwest of Murfreesboro; organized Apr 18, 1783 (prior to statehood) from Washington County. **Name Origin:** For Gen. William Lee Davidson (1746-81), officer killed during the Revolutionary War.

Area (sq mi): 526.11 (land 502.26; water 23.85). **Pop per sq mi:** 1145.3.

Pop 2005: 575,261. **State rank:** 2. **Pop change:** 2000-20005 +0.9%; 1990-2000 +11.6%. **Pop 2000:** 569,891 (White 65.1%; Black or African American 25.9%; Hispanic or Latino 4.6%; Asian 2.3%; Other 4.8%). **Foreign born:** 6.9%. **Median age:** 34.1.

Income 2000: per capita $23,069; median household $39,797; **Pop below poverty level:** 13%. ***Personal per capita income 2000-2003:** $33,388-$38,056.

Unemployment 2004: 4.4%. **Change from 2000:** +1.3%. **Median travel time to work:** 23.3 minutes. **Working outside county of residence:** 13%.

Cities with pop over 10,000: Nashville 🏛 (546,719); Goodlettsville (15,111).

DECATUR COUNTY

PO Box 488   **Ph:** 731-852-2131
Decaturville, TN 38329   **Fax:** 731-852-2130
www.decaturcountytn.org

In western TN, southeast of Jackson; organized Nov 1845 from Perry County. **Name Origin:** For Stephen Decatur (1779-1820), U.S. naval officer during the War of 1812 and in actions against the Barbary pirates near Tripoli, who said, '. . . may she always be in the right; but our country, right or wrong.'

Area (sq mi): 344.91 (land 333.9; water 11.01). **Pop per sq mi:** 35.

Pop 2005: 11,686. **State rank:** 83. **Pop change:** 2000-20005 -0.4%; 1990-2000 +12%. **Pop 2000:** 11,731 (White 93.4%; Black or African American 3.5%; Hispanic or Latino 2%; Asian 0.2%; Other 2.2%). **Foreign born:** 1.7%. **Median age:** 41.2.

Income 2000: per capita $17,285; median household $28,741; **Pop below poverty level:** 16%. ***Personal per capita income 2000-2003:** $20,184-$22,491.

Unemployment 2004: 7.2%. **Change from 2000:** -0.8%. **Median travel time to work:** 25.7 minutes. **Working outside county of residence:** 34.3%.

Cities with pop over 10,000: None.

DEKALB COUNTY

1 Public Sq Rm 205   **Ph:** 615-597-5177
Smithville, TN 37166   **Fax:** 615-597-1404
www.smithvilletn.com

In east-central TN, southeast of Nashville; organized 1837 from Cannon, Warren, White, Wilson, and Jackson counties. **Name Origin:** For Johann, Baron de Kalb (1721-80), German-born French soldier who fought with the Americans during the Revolutionary War.

Area (sq mi): 328.98 (land 304.57; water 24.41). **Pop per sq mi:** 59.9.

Pop 2005: 18,254. **State rank:** 68. **Pop change:** 2000-20005 +4.8%; 1990-2000 +21.3%. **Pop 2000:** 17,423 (White 93.8%; Black or African American 1.4%; Hispanic or Latino 3.6%; Asian 0.1%; Other 2.8%). **Foreign born:** 2.7%. **Median age:** 37.7.

Income 2000: per capita $17,217; median household $30,359; **Pop below poverty level:** 17%. ***Personal per capita income 2000-2003:** $20,038-$23,655.

Unemployment 2004: 5.1%. **Change from 2000:** 0.3%. **Median travel time to work:** 24.3 minutes. **Working outside county of residence:** 33.6%.

Cities with pop over 10,000: None.

DICKSON COUNTY

PO Box 267   **Ph:** 615-789-7003
Charlotte, TN 37036   **Fax:** 615-789-6075
www.dicksoncounty.net

In west-central TN, west of Nashville; organized Oct 25, 1803 from Montgomery and Robertson counties. **Name Origin:** For William Dickson (1770-1816), physician, TN legislator, and U.S. representative (1801-07).

Area (sq mi): 491.28 (land 489.87; water 1.42). **Pop per sq mi:** 93.7.

Pop 2005: 45,894. **State rank:** 31. **Pop change:** 2000-20005 +6.3%; 1990-2000 +23.1%. **Pop 2000:** 43,156 (White 92.7%; Black or African American 4.6%; Hispanic or Latino 1.1%; Asian 0.3%; Other 1.9%). **Foreign born:** 0.7%. **Median age:** 35.7.

Income 2000: per capita $18,043; median household $39,056; **Pop below poverty level:** 10.2%. ***Personal per capita income 2000-2003:** $23,531-$23,877.

Unemployment 2004: 4.9%. **Change from 2000:** +0.7%. **Median travel time to work:** 30.5 minutes. **Working outside county of residence:** 42.2%.

Cities with pop over 10,000: Dickson (12,760).

DYER COUNTY

PO Box 1360   **Ph:** 731-286-7814
Dyersburg, TN 38025   **Fax:** 731-288-7719
www.co.dyer.tn.us

On northwestern border of TN, northwest of Jackson; organized Oct 16, 1823 from Western District (Indian lands). **Name Origin:** For Robert H. Dyer, a prominent fighter in the Indian wars.

Area (sq mi): 526.48 (land 510.5; water 15.98). **Pop per sq mi:** 74.1.

Pop 2005: 37,829. **State rank:** 40. **Pop change:** 2000-20005 +1.5%; 1990-2000 +7%. **Pop 2000:** 37,279 (White 84.8%; Black or African American 12.9%; Hispanic or Latino 1.2%; Asian 0.3%; Other 1.3%). **Foreign born:** 1.3%. **Median age:** 36.5.

Income 2000: per capita $16,451; median household $32,788; **Pop below poverty level:** 15.9%. ***Personal per capita income 2000-2003:** $22,372-$25,047.

Unemployment 2004: 6%. **Change from 2000:** -1.2%. **Median travel time to work:** 19.1 minutes. **Working outside county of residence:** 17.3%.

Cities with pop over 10,000: Dyersburg 🏛 (17,406).

🏛 *County Seat*

FAYETTE COUNTY

PO Box 218   **Ph:** 901-465-5213
Somerville, TN 38068   **Fax:** 901-465-5293
www.fayettecountychamber.com

On the southwestern border of TN, east of Memphis; organized Sep 29, 1824 from Shelby and Hardeman counties. **Name Origin:** For the Marquis de Lafayette (1757-1834), French statesman and soldier who fought with the Americans during the Revolutionary War.

Area (sq mi): 706.23 (land 704.5; water 1.73). **Pop per sq mi:** 48.9.

Pop 2005: 34,458. **State rank:** 42. **Pop change:** 2000-20005 +19.6%; 1990-2000 +12.7%. **Pop 2000:** 28,806 (White 62%; Black or African American 35.9%; Hispanic or Latino 1%; Asian 0.2%; Other 1.4%). **Foreign born:** 0.7%. **Median age:** 38.1.

Income 2000: per capita $17,969; median household $40,279; **Pop below poverty level:** 14.3%. ***Personal per capita income 2000-2003:** $25,292-$28,355.

Unemployment 2004: 6.2%. **Change from 2000:** +0.7%. **Median travel time to work:** 35.4 minutes. **Working outside county of residence:** 67.3%.

Cities with pop over 10,000: None.

FENTRESS COUNTY

PO Box 823   **Ph:** 931-879-8014
Jamestown, TN 38556   **Fax:** 931-879-8438
www.jamestowntn.org

In north-central TN, northwest of Oak Ridge; organized Nov 28, 1823 from Overton, White, and Morgan counties. **Name Origin:** For James Fentress, speaker of the TN House of Representatives.

Area (sq mi): 498.97 (land 498.64; water 0.33). **Pop per sq mi:** 34.4.

Pop 2005: 17,159. **State rank:** 72. **Pop change:** 2000-20005 +3.2%; 1990-2000 +13.3%. **Pop 2000:** 16,625 (White 98.8%; Black or African American 0.1%; Hispanic or Latino 0.5%; Asian 0.1%; Other 0.6%). **Foreign born:** 0.4%. **Median age:** 38.

Income 2000: per capita $12,999; median household $23,238; **Pop below poverty level:** 23.1%. ***Personal per capita income 2000-2003:** $18,598-$20,325.

Unemployment 2004: 6.7%. **Change from 2000:** -4.3%. **Median travel time to work:** 29.5 minutes. **Working outside county of residence:** 31.4%.

Cities with pop over 10,000: None.

FRANKLIN COUNTY

1 S Jefferson St   **Ph:** 931-967-2541
Winchester, TN 37398   **Fax:** 931-962-3394
www.franklincountychamber.com

On the central southern border of TN, west of Chattanooga; organized Dec 3, 1807 from Rutherford County and Indian lands. **Name Origin:** For Benjamin Franklin (1706-90), U.S. patriot, diplomat, and statesman.

Area (sq mi): 575.77 (land 554.52; water 21.25). **Pop per sq mi:** 73.9.

Pop 2005: 41,003. **State rank:** 36. **Pop change:** 2000-20005 +4.4%; 1990-2000 +13.1%. **Pop 2000:** 39,270 (White 91.4%; Black or African American 5.5%; Hispanic or Latino 1.6%; Asian 0.4%; Other 1.9%). **Foreign born:** 1.4%. **Median age:** 38.1.

Income 2000: per capita $17,987; median household $36,044; **Pop below poverty level:** 13.2%. ***Personal per capita income 2000-2003:** $21,016-$22,571.

Unemployment 2004: 5.2%. **Change from 2000:** +1.4%. **Median travel time to work:** 24.1 minutes. **Working outside county of residence:** 40.2%.

Cities with pop over 10,000: None.

GIBSON COUNTY

1 Court Sq Suite 100   **Ph:** 731-855-7642
Trenton, TN 38382   **Fax:** 731-855-7643
www.gibsoncountytn.com

In northwestern TN, north of Jackson; organized Oct 21, 1823 from Western District (Indian lands). **Name Origin:** For Maj. John Gibson, an officer in Gen. Andrew Jackson's (1767-1845) Natchez expedition (1812-13).

Area (sq mi): 603.59 (land 602.67; water 0.92). **Pop per sq mi:** 79.9.

Pop 2005: 48,148. **State rank:** 30. **Pop change:** 2000-20005 +0%; 1990-2000 +4%. **Pop 2000:** 48,152 (White 78.2%; Black or African American 19.7%; Hispanic or Latino 1.1%; Asian 0.1%; Other 1.5%). **Foreign born:** 0.8%. **Median age:** 38.8.

Income 2000: per capita $16,320; median household $31,105; **Pop below poverty level:** 12.8%. ***Personal per capita income 2000-2003:** $22,333-$24,629.

Unemployment 2004: 8.1%. **Change from 2000:** -1.5%. **Median travel time to work:** 22.1 minutes. **Working outside county of residence:** 33.7%.

Cities with pop over 10,000: None.

GILES COUNTY

1 Public Sq   **Ph:** 931-363-1509
Pulaski, TN 38478   **Fax:** 931-424-4795
www.gilescounty-tn.us

On the central southern border of TN, south of Columbia; organized Nov 14, 1809 from Maury County. **Name Origin:** For William Branch Giles (1762-1830), U.S. senator from VA (1804-15) and governor (1827-30).

Area (sq mi): 611.17 (land 610.93; water 0.25). **Pop per sq mi:** 48.

Pop 2005: 29,297. **State rank:** 49. **Pop change:** 2000-20005 -0.5%; 1990-2000 +14.4%. **Pop 2000:** 29,447 (White 85.9%; Black or African American 11.8%; Hispanic or Latino 0.9%; Asian 0.3%; Other 1.4%). **Foreign born:** 0.9%. **Median age:** 38.

Income 2000: per capita $17,543; median household $34,824; **Pop below poverty level:** 11.7%. ***Personal per capita income 2000-2003:** $22,940-$24,280.

Unemployment 2004: 7.3%. **Change from 2000:** +1.2%. **Median travel time to work:** 25.1 minutes. **Working outside county of residence:** 28.9%.

Cities with pop over 10,000: None.

---

*Source: Personal per capita income data are from the Bureau of Economic Analysis; per capita income data are from the Bureau of the Census. See Introduction for explanation of differences.

GRAINGER COUNTY

Hwy 11 W PO Box 126 Courthouse Sq **Ph:** 865-828-3513
Rutledge, TN 37861 **Fax:** 865-828-4284
www.graingertn.com

In northeastern TN, northeast of Knoxville; organized Apr 22, 1796 from Hawkins County. **Name Origin:** For Mary Grainger Blount, wife of William Blount (1749-1800), governor (1790-95) of the territory south of the Ohio River, present-day TN.

Area (sq mi): 302.44 (land 280.33; water 22.11). **Pop per sq mi:** 79.5.

Pop 2005: 22,283. **State rank:** 60. **Pop change:** 2000-20005 +7.9%; 1990-2000 +20.8%. **Pop 2000:** 20,659 (White 97.7%; Black or African American 0.3%; Hispanic or Latino 1.1%; Asian 0.1%; Other 1.2%). **Foreign born:** 1.1%. **Median age:** 37.7.

Income 2000: per capita $14,505; median household $27,997; **Pop below poverty level:** 18.7%. ***Personal per capita income 2000-2003:** $18,947-$19,897.

Unemployment 2004: 6.1%. **Change from 2000:** +0.4%. **Median travel time to work:** 29.1 minutes. **Working outside county of residence:** 65.5%.

Cities with pop over 10,000: None.

GREENE COUNTY

204 N Cutler St Suite 200 **Ph:** 423-798-1708
Greeneville, TN 37745 **Fax:** 423-798-1822
www.greenecountypartnership.com

On the northeastern border of TN, west of Johnson City; organized Apr 18, 1783 (prior to statehood) from Washington County. **Name Origin:** For Gen. Nathanael Greene (1742-86), hero of the Revolutionary War, quartermaster general (1778-80), and commander of the Army of the South (1780).

Area (sq mi): 624.11 (land 621.69; water 2.42). **Pop per sq mi:** 105.1.

Pop 2005: 65,318. **State rank:** 19. **Pop change:** 2000-20005 +3.8%; 1990-2000 +12.6%. **Pop 2000:** 62,909 (White 95.9%; Black or African American 2.1%; Hispanic or Latino 1%; Asian 0.3%; Other 1.2%). **Foreign born:** 1.3%. **Median age:** 38.9.

Income 2000: per capita $15,746; median household $30,382; **Pop below poverty level:** 14.5%. ***Personal per capita income 2000-2003:** $22,749-$26,610.

Unemployment 2004: 7.7%. **Change from 2000:** +0.5%. **Median travel time to work:** 22.4 minutes. **Working outside county of residence:** 15%.

Cities with pop over 10,000: Greeneville 🏛 (15,302).

GRUNDY COUNTY

PO Box 177 **Ph:** 931-692-3718
Altamont, TN 37301 **Fax:** 931-692-3721

In east-central TN, northeast of Chattanooga; organized Jan 29, 1844 from Franklin and Warren counties. **Name Origin:** For Felix Grundy (1777-1840), U.S. representative from TN (1811-15) who played a leading part in bringing on and sustaining the War of 1812.

Area (sq mi): 361.14 (land 360.56; water 0.58). **Pop per sq mi:** 40.5.

Pop 2005: 14,608. **State rank:** 77. **Pop change:** 2000-20005 +1.9%; 1990-2000 +7.3%. **Pop 2000:** 14,332 (White 97.8%; Black or African American 0.1%; Hispanic or Latino 1%; Asian 0.2%; Other 1.3%). **Foreign born:** 0.7%. **Median age:** 36.6.

Income 2000: per capita $12,039; median household $22,959; **Pop below poverty level:** 25.8%. ***Personal per capita income 2000-2003:** $17,585-$20,007.

Unemployment 2004: 6.3%. **Change from 2000:** +0.3%. **Median travel time to work:** 32.2 minutes. **Working outside county of residence:** 50.4%.

Cities with pop over 10,000: None.

HAMBLEN COUNTY

511 W 2nd North St **Ph:** 423-586-1993
Morristown, TN 37814 **Fax:** 423-318-2508
www.hamblencountygovernment.us

In northeastern TN, northeast of Knoxville; organized Jun 8, 1870 from Grainger, Hawkins, and Jefferson counties. **Name Origin:** For Hezekiah Hamblen (1775-1854?), member of the Hawkins County court.

Area (sq mi): 175.77 (land 161.03; water 14.74). **Pop per sq mi:** 372.

Pop 2005: 59,898. **State rank:** 21. **Pop change:** 2000-20005 +3%; 1990-2000 +15.2%. **Pop 2000:** 58,128 (White 88.5%; Black or African American 4.1%; Hispanic or Latino 5.7%; Asian 0.6%; Other 4.6%). **Foreign born:** 5.3%. **Median age:** 37.1.

Income 2000: per capita $17,743; median household $32,350; **Pop below poverty level:** 14.4%. ***Personal per capita income 2000-2003:** $22,628-$25,395.

Unemployment 2004: 5.6%. **Change from 2000:** -0.6%. **Median travel time to work:** 19.6 minutes. **Working outside county of residence:** 18.5%.

Cities with pop over 10,000: Morristown 🏛 (25,462).

HAMILTON COUNTY

County Courthouse Rm 201 **Ph:** 423-209-6500
Chattanooga, TN 37402 **Fax:** 423-209-6501
www.hamiltontn.gov

On the southeastern border of TN, west of Cleveland; organized Oct 25, 1819 from Rhea County and Indian lands, and in January 1920 annexed James County, which was organized 1871 from Hamilton and Bradley counties. **Name Origin:** For Alexander Hamilton (1757-1804), first U.S. secretary of the treasury (1789-95).

Area (sq mi): 575.72 (land 542.44; water 33.28). **Pop per sq mi:** 573.2.

Pop 2005: 310,935. **State rank:** 4. **Pop change:** 2000-20005 +1%; 1990-2000 +7.8%. **Pop 2000:** 307,896 (White 75.5%; Black or African American 20.1%; Hispanic or Latino 1.8%; Asian 1.3%; Other 2.3%). **Foreign born:** 3%. **Median age:** 37.4.

Income 2000: per capita $21,593; median household $38,930; **Pop below poverty level:** 12.1%. ***Personal per capita income 2000-2003:** $29,822-$32,365.

Unemployment 2004: 4.6%. **Change from 2000:** +1.6%. **Median travel time to work:** 22.6 minutes. **Working outside county of residence:** 9%.

Hamilton County (cont'd)

Cities with pop over 10,000: Chattanooga 🏛 (154,853); East Ridge (20,010); Soddy-Daisy (11,970); Red Bank (11,865).

HANCOCK COUNTY

418 Harrison St Suite 96   **Ph:** 423-733-2519
Sneedville, TN 37869   **Fax:** 423-733-4509

On the northeastern border of TN, west of Kingsport; organized Jan 7, 1844 from Claiborne and Hawkins counties. **Name Origin:** For John Hancock (1737-93), noted signer of the Declaration of Independence, governor of MA (1780-85; 1787-93), and statesman.

Area (sq mi): 223.5 (land 222.29; water 1.21). **Pop per sq mi:** 30.2.

Pop 2005: 6,704. **State rank:** 92. **Pop change:** 2000-20005 -1.2%; 1990-2000 +0.7%. **Pop 2000:** 6,786 (White 97.6%; Black or African American 0.5%; Hispanic or Latino 0.4%; Asian 0.1%; Other 1.4%). **Foreign born:** 0.3%. **Median age:** 39.2.

Income 2000: per capita $11,986; median household $19,760; **Pop below poverty level:** 29.4%. ***Personal per capita income 2000-2003:** $13,904-$14,610.

Unemployment 2004: 9.8%. **Change from 2000:** +2.4%. **Median travel time to work:** 32.7 minutes. **Working outside county of residence:** 40.7%.

Cities with pop over 10,000: None.

HARDEMAN COUNTY

100 N Main St   **Ph:** 731-658-3541
Bolivar, TN 38008   **Fax:** 731-658-3482
www.hardemancotn.org

On the southwestern border of TN, south of Jackson; organized Oct 16, 1823 from Hardin County and Western District (Indian lands). **Name Origin:** For Col. Thomas Jones Hardeman (1788-1854), TN officer in the War of 1812, later a Texas patriot and legislator.

Area (sq mi): 670.39 (land 667.55; water 2.84). **Pop per sq mi:** 42.2.

Pop 2005: 28,170. **State rank:** 52. **Pop change:** 2000-20005 +0.2%; 1990-2000 +20.2%. **Pop 2000:** 28,105 (White 56.9%; Black or African American 41%; Hispanic or Latino 1%; Asian 0.3%; Other 1.4%). **Foreign born:** 0.7%. **Median age:** 36.

Income 2000: per capita $13,349; median household $29,111; **Pop below poverty level:** 19.7%. ***Personal per capita income 2000-2003:** $16,627-$18,884.

Unemployment 2004: 8.2%. **Change from 2000:** -0.7%. **Median travel time to work:** 29.4 minutes. **Working outside county of residence:** 34.7%.

Cities with pop over 10,000: None.

HARDIN COUNTY

465 Main St Courthouse   **Ph:** 731-925-3921
Savannah, TN 38372   **Fax:** 731-926-4313
www.tourhardincounty.org

On the southwestern border of TN, southeast of Jackson; organized Nov 13, 1819 from Western District (Indian lands). **Name Origin:** For Joseph Hardin, a soldier in the Revolutionary War and a TN legislator.

Area (sq mi): 596.31 (land 577.86; water 18.45). **Pop per sq mi:** 44.9.

Pop 2005: 25,930. **State rank:** 56. **Pop change:** 2000-20005 +1.4%; 1990-2000 +13%. **Pop 2000:** 25,578 (White 94.2%; Black or African American 3.7%; Hispanic or Latino 1%; Asian 0.2%; Other 1.2%). **Foreign born:** 0.7%. **Median age:** 39.8.

Income 2000: per capita $15,598; median household $27,819; **Pop below poverty level:** 18.8%. ***Personal per capita income 2000-2003:** $20,972-$22,421.

Unemployment 2004: 7.6%. **Change from 2000:** +1.6%. **Median travel time to work:** 24 minutes. **Working outside county of residence:** 30.6%.

Cities with pop over 10,000: None.

HAWKINS COUNTY

110 E Main St   **Ph:** 423-272-7002
Rogersville, TN 37857   **Fax:** 423-272-5801
www.hawkinscounty.org

On the northeastern border of TN, west of Kingsport; organized Nov 18, 1786 (prior to statehood) from Sullivan County. **Name Origin:** For Benjamin Hawkins (1754-1816), French interpreter for George Washington (1732-99), member of the Continental Congress (1781-84; 1786-87), U.S. senator from NC (1789-95), and Indian agent for all tribes south of the Ohio River.

Area (sq mi): 499.63 (land 486.66; water 12.97). **Pop per sq mi:** 115.5.

Pop 2005: 56,196. **State rank:** 23. **Pop change:** 2000-20005 +4.9%; 1990-2000 +20.2%. **Pop 2000:** 53,563 (White 96.7%; Black or African American 1.5%; Hispanic or Latino 0.8%; Asian 0.2%; Other 1%). **Foreign born:** 0.7%. **Median age:** 37.8.

Income 2000: per capita $16,073; median household $31,300; **Pop below poverty level:** 15.8%. ***Personal per capita income 2000-2003:** $20,248-$22,029.

Unemployment 2004: 6.1%. **Change from 2000:** +0.5%. **Median travel time to work:** 24.7 minutes. **Working outside county of residence:** 48.4%.

Cities with pop over 10,000: None.

HAYWOOD COUNTY

1 N Washington St   **Ph:** 731-772-1432
Brownsville, TN 38012   **Fax:** 731-772-3864

In southwestern TN, west of Jackson; organized Nov 3, 1823 from Western District (Indian lands). **Name Origin:** For John Haywood (1753-1826), NC attorney-general (1791-94) and TN supreme court judge (1816-26).

Area (sq mi): 534.15 (land 533.2; water 0.95). **Pop per sq mi:** 36.9.

Pop 2005: 19,656. **State rank:** 65. **Pop change:** 2000-20005 -0.7%; 1990-2000 +1.9%. **Pop 2000:** 19,797 (White 45.9%; Black or African American 51%; Hispanic or Latino 2.6%; Asian 0.1%; Other 2.2%). **Foreign born:** 1.7%. **Median age:** 35.3.

Income 2000: per capita $14,669; median household $27,671; **Pop below poverty level:** 19.5%. ***Personal per capita income 2000-2003:** $20,148-$21,792.

---

*Source: Personal per capita income data are from the Bureau of Economic Analysis; per capita income data are from the Bureau of the Census. See Introduction for explanation of differences.

Haywood County (cont'd)

Unemployment 2004: 8.6%. **Change from 2000:** -0.7%. **Median travel time to work:** 24 minutes. **Working outside county of residence:** 40%.

Cities with pop over 10,000: Brownsville 🏛 (10,705).

HENDERSON COUNTY
17 Monroe Ave Suite 2   **Ph:** 731-968-2856
Lexington, TN 38351   **Fax:** 731-968-6644

In western TN, east of Jackson; organized Nov 7, 1821 from Western District (Indian lands). **Name Origin:** For James Henderson, an officer under the command of Andrew Jackson (1767-1845) in the War of 1812.

Area (sq mi): 525.91 (land 520.02; water 5.89). **Pop per sq mi:** 50.8.

Pop 2005: 26,425. **State rank:** 55. **Pop change:** 2000-20005 +3.5%; 1990-2000 +16.8%. **Pop 2000:** 25,522 (White 89.9%; Black or African American 8%; Hispanic or Latino 1%; Asian 0.1%; Other 1.3%). **Foreign born:** 0.7%. **Median age:** 37.3.

Income 2000: per capita $17,019; median household $32,057; **Pop below poverty level:** 12.4%. ***Personal per capita income 2000-2003:** $21,583-$23,081.

Unemployment 2004: 6.9%. **Change from 2000:** +0.1%. **Median travel time to work:** 24.6 minutes. **Working outside county of residence:** 32.4%.

Cities with pop over 10,000: None.

HENRY COUNTY
101 W Washington St Suite 100 PO Box 24   **Ph:** 731-642-2412
Paris, TN 38242   **Fax:** 731-644-0947
www.henryco.com

On northwestern border of TN, southwest of Clarksville; organized Nov 7, 1821 from Western District (Indian lands). **Name Origin:** For Patrick Henry (1736-99), patriot, governor of VA (1776-79; 1784-86), and statesman, famous for declaring, 'Give me liberty or give me death.'

Area (sq mi): 593.45 (land 561.68; water 31.77). **Pop per sq mi:** 56.1.

Pop 2005: 31,511. **State rank:** 46. **Pop change:** 2000-20005 +1.3%; 1990-2000 +11.6%. **Pop 2000:** 31,115 (White 88.7%; Black or African American 9%; Hispanic or Latino 1%; Asian 0.3%; Other 1.5%). **Foreign born:** 1%. **Median age:** 40.9.

Income 2000: per capita $15,855; median household $30,169; **Pop below poverty level:** 14.3%. ***Personal per capita income 2000-2003:** $22,041-$22,962.

Unemployment 2004: 8%. **Change from 2000:** +1.6%. **Median travel time to work:** 19.9 minutes. **Working outside county of residence:** 19.4%.

Cities with pop over 10,000: None.

HICKMAN COUNTY
101 S Public Sq   **Ph:** 931-729-2621
Centerville, TN 37033   **Fax:** 931-729-9951
www.hickmanco.com

In west-central TN, southwest of Nashville; organized Dec 3, 1807

from Dickson County. **Name Origin:** For Edwin Hickman (?-1791), American explorer killed by Indians.

Area (sq mi): 612.7 (land 612.52; water 0.18). **Pop per sq mi:** 38.8.

Pop 2005: 23,793. **State rank:** 59. **Pop change:** 2000-20005 +6.7%; 1990-2000 +33.1%. **Pop 2000:** 22,295 (White 93.1%; Black or African American 4.5%; Hispanic or Latino 1%; Asian 0.1%; Other 1.7%). **Foreign born:** 0.8%. **Median age:** 36.3.

Income 2000: per capita $14,446; median household $31,013; **Pop below poverty level:** 14.3%. ***Personal per capita income 2000-2003:** $17,540-$18,318.

Unemployment 2004: 5.8%. **Change from 2000:** +0.2%. **Median travel time to work:** 36.7 minutes. **Working outside county of residence:** 59.6%.

Cities with pop over 10,000: None.

HOUSTON COUNTY
PO Box 388   **Ph:** 931-289-4165
Erin, TN 37061   **Fax:** 931-289-2603

In west-central TN, southwest of Clarksville; organized Jan 23, 1871 from Dickson, Montgomery, Stewart, and Humphreys counties. **Name Origin:** For Samuel Houston (1793-1863), governor of TN (1827-29), president of the Republic of Texas (1836-38; 1841-44), U.S. senator from TX (1846-59), and governor (1859-61).

Area (sq mi): 206.92 (land 200.21; water 6.71). **Pop per sq mi:** 39.9.

Pop 2005: 7,988. **State rank:** 88. **Pop change:** 2000-20005 -1.2%; 1990-2000 +15.2%. **Pop 2000:** 8,088 (White 94.1%; Black or African American 3.3%; Hispanic or Latino 1.2%; Asian 0.1%; Other 2.1%). **Foreign born:** 1.6%. **Median age:** 39.5.

Income 2000: per capita $15,614; median household $29,968; **Pop below poverty level:** 18.1%. ***Personal per capita income 2000-2003:** $19,071-$21,563.

Unemployment 2004: 8%. **Change from 2000:** -2.4%. **Median travel time to work:** 32 minutes. **Working outside county of residence:** 58%.

Cities with pop over 10,000: None.

HUMPHREYS COUNTY
Courthouse Annex Rm 1   **Ph:** 931-296-7795
Waverly, TN 37185   **Fax:** 931-296-5011

In west-central TN, west of Nashville; organized Oct 19, 1809 from Stewart County. **Name Origin:** For Parry Wayne Humphreys (1780-1839), TN superior court judge (1807-13; 1818-36) and U.S. representative (1813-15).

Area (sq mi): 556.72 (land 532.22; water 24.5). **Pop per sq mi:** 34.2.

Pop 2005: 18,212. **State rank:** 69. **Pop change:** 2000-20005 +1.6%; 1990-2000 +13.5%. **Pop 2000:** 17,929 (White 95%; Black or African American 2.9%; Hispanic or Latino 0.8%; Asian 0.3%; Other 1.3%). **Foreign born:** 0.9%. **Median age:** 39.

Income 2000: per capita $17,757; median household $35,786; **Pop below poverty level:** 10.8%. ***Personal per capita income 2000-2003:** $21,898-$22,728.

Unemployment 2004: 7.3%. **Change from 2000:** -0.2%. **Median travel time to work:** 29.8 minutes. **Working outside county of residence:** 33.6%.

Humphreys County (cont'd)

Cities with pop over 10,000: None.

JACKSON COUNTY

PO Box 617
Gainesboro, TN 38562
www.jacksonco.com

Ph: 931-268-9888
Fax: 931-268-9060

In north-central TN, northeast of Nashville; organized Nov 6, 1801 from Smith County and Indian lands. **Name Origin:** For Andrew Jackson (1767-1845), seventh U.S. president.

Area (sq mi): 319.56 (land 308.88; water 10.67). **Pop per sq mi:** 35.8.

Pop 2005: 11,072. **State rank:** 86. **Pop change:** 2000-20005 +0.8%; 1990-2000 +18.1%. **Pop 2000:** 10,984 (White 98%; Black or African American 0.1%; Hispanic or Latino 0.8%; Asian 0.1%; Other 1.1%). **Foreign born:** 1.6%. **Median age:** 39.8.

Income 2000: per capita $15,020; median household $26,502; **Pop below poverty level:** 18.1%. ***Personal per capita income 2000-2003:** $18,477-$21,776.

Unemployment 2004: 6.7%. **Change from 2000:** +0.2%. **Median travel time to work:** 29.7 minutes. **Working outside county of residence:** 56.5%.

Cities with pop over 10,000: None.

JEFFERSON COUNTY

214 W Main St
Dandridge, TN 37725
www.jefferson-tn-chamber.org

Ph: 865-397-2935
Fax: 865-397-3839

In northeastern TN, east of Knoxville; organized Jun 11, 1792 (prior to statehood) from Greene and Hawkins counties. **Name Origin:** For Thomas Jefferson (1743-1826), U.S. patriot and statesman; third U.S. president.

Area (sq mi): 314.33 (land 273.81; water 40.51). **Pop per sq mi:** 176.7.

Pop 2005: 48,394. **State rank:** 29. **Pop change:** 2000-20005 +9.3%; 1990-2000 +34.2%. **Pop 2000:** 44,294 (White 95.1%; Black or African American 2.3%; Hispanic or Latino 1.3%; Asian 0.3%; Other 1.7%). **Foreign born:** 1.5%. **Median age:** 36.5.

Income 2000: per capita $16,841; median household $32,824; **Pop below poverty level:** 13.4%. ***Personal per capita income 2000-2003:** $20,424-$22,448.

Unemployment 2004: 6.1%. **Change from 2000:** +1.2%. **Median travel time to work:** 26.4 minutes. **Working outside county of residence:** 55.4%.

Cities with pop over 10,000: None.

JOHNSON COUNTY

222 Main St
Mountain City, TN 37683
www.johnsoncountytn.org

Ph: 423-727-9633
Fax: 423-727-7047

On the northeastern border of TN, east of Kingsport; organized Jan 2, 1836 from Carter County. **Name Origin:** For Cave Johnson (1793-1866), U.S. representative from TN (1829-37; 1839-45) and U.S. postmaster general (1845-49).

Area (sq mi): 302.73 (land 298.47; water 4.26). **Pop per sq mi:** 60.7.

Pop 2005: 18,116. **State rank:** 70. **Pop change:** 2000-20005 +3.5%; 1990-2000 +27.1%. **Pop 2000:** 17,499 (White 95.8%; Black or African American 2.4%; Hispanic or Latino 0.9%; Asian 0.1%; Other 1%). **Foreign born:** 0.6%. **Median age:** 40.

Income 2000: per capita $13,388; median household $23,067; **Pop below poverty level:** 22.6%. ***Personal per capita income 2000-2003:** $15,206-$15,904.

Unemployment 2004: 7.6%. **Change from 2000:** -1%. **Median travel time to work:** 32 minutes. **Working outside county of residence:** 36.5%.

Cities with pop over 10,000: None.

KNOX COUNTY

City-County Bldg 400 Main St Suite 603
Knoxville, TN 37902
www.knoxcounty.org

Ph: 865-215-2534
Fax: 865-215-2038

In central eastern TN, east of Oak Ridge; organized Jun 11, 1792 (prior to statehood) from Greene and Hawkins counties. **Name Origin:** For Gen. Henry Knox (1750-1806), Revolutionary War officer and first U.S. secretary of war (1785-95).

Area (sq mi): 525.78 (land 508.46; water 17.32). **Pop per sq mi:** 796.5.

Pop 2005: 404,972. **State rank:** 3. **Pop change:** 2000-20005 +6%; 1990-2000 +13.8%. **Pop 2000:** 382,032 (White 87.4%; Black or African American 8.6%; Hispanic or Latino 1.3%; Asian 1.3%; Other 2%). **Foreign born:** 2.5%. **Median age:** 36.

Income 2000: per capita $21,875; median household $37,454; **Pop below poverty level:** 12.6%. ***Personal per capita income 2000-2003:** $28,554-$30,901.

Unemployment 2004: 3.9%. **Change from 2000:** +1.4%. **Median travel time to work:** 22.2 minutes. **Working outside county of residence:** 14.4%.

Cities with pop over 10,000: Knoxville ⬛ (178,118); Farragut (18,985).

LAKE COUNTY

116 S Court St
Tiptonville, TN 38079

Ph: 731-253-7582
Fax: 731-253-6815

On the northern border of TN; organized Jun 24, 1870 from Obion County. **Name Origin:** For Reelfoot Lake, on its eastern border. The lake formed in 1811 and 1812, when earthquakes caused the Mississippi River to flow backward.

Area (sq mi): 193.79 (land 163.42; water 30.38). **Pop per sq mi:** 46.4.

Pop 2005: 7,583. **State rank:** 90. **Pop change:** 2000-20005 -4.7%; 1990-2000 +11.6%. **Pop 2000:** 7,954 (White 66.2%; Black or African American 31.2%; Hispanic or Latino 1.4%; Asian 0.1%; Other 2%). **Foreign born:** 0.5%. **Median age:** 35.8.

Income 2000: per capita $10,794; median household $21,995; **Pop below poverty level:** 23.6%. ***Personal per capita income 2000-2003:** $12,955-$14,930.

Unemployment 2004: 6.5%. **Change from 2000:** +0.9%. **Median travel time to work:** 20.4 minutes. **Working outside county of residence:** 32.6%.

*Source: Personal per capita income data are from the Bureau of Economic Analysis; per capita income data are from the Bureau of the Census. See Introduction for explanation of differences.

Lake County (cont'd)

Cities with pop over 10,000: None.

LAUDERDALE COUNTY

100 Court Sq	**Ph:** 731-635-2561
Ripley, TN 38063	**Fax:** 731-635-9682

On central western border of TN, northeast of Memphis; organized Nov 24, 1835 from Dyer, Tipton, and Haywood counties. **Name Origin:** For Col. James Lauderdale (?-1814), a soldier killed at the Battle of New Orleans during the War of 1812.

Area (sq mi): 507.14 (land 470.45; water 36.69). **Pop per sq mi:** 57.

Pop 2005: 26,795. **State rank:** 54. **Pop change:** 2000-20005 -1.1%; 1990-2000 +15.4%. **Pop 2000:** 27,101 (White 63.4%; Black or African American 34.1%; Hispanic or Latino 1.2%; Asian 0.2%; Other 1.9%). **Foreign born:** 0.7%. **Median age:** 34.9.

Income 2000: per capita $13,682; median household $29,751; **Pop below poverty level:** 19.2%. ***Personal per capita income 2000-2003:** $17,486-$18,985.

Unemployment 2004: 10.1%. **Change from 2000:** +0.2%. **Median travel time to work:** 23.6 minutes. **Working outside county of residence:** 32.1%.

Cities with pop over 10,000: None.

LAWRENCE COUNTY

240 W Gaines St	**Ph:** 931-762-7700
Lawrenceburg, TN 38464	**Fax:** 931-766-2291
www.co.lawrence.tn.us	

On the central southern border of TN, southwest of Nashville; organized Oct 21, 1817 from Hickman and Maury counties. **Name Origin:** For Capt. James Lawrence (1781-1813), U.S. Navy commander in the War of 1812 who said, 'Don't give up the ship!'

Area (sq mi): 617.91 (land 617.17; water 0.74). **Pop per sq mi:** 66.6.

Pop 2005: 41,101. **State rank:** 35. **Pop change:** 2000-20005 +2.9%; 1990-2000 +13.1%. **Pop 2000:** 39,926 (White 96.3%; Black or African American 1.5%; Hispanic or Latino 1%; Asian 0.2%; Other 1.4%). **Foreign born:** 0.9%. **Median age:** 36.2.

Income 2000: per capita $15,848; median household $30,498; **Pop below poverty level:** 14.6%. ***Personal per capita income 2000-2003:** $20,232-$21,818.

Unemployment 2004: 8.7%. **Change from 2000:** -2.3%. **Median travel time to work:** 24.2 minutes. **Working outside county of residence:** 23.4%.

Cities with pop over 10,000: Lawrenceburg ⚖ (10,865).

LEWIS COUNTY

110 N Park St Rm 108	**Ph:** 931-796-3378
Hohenwald, TN 38462	**Fax:** 931-796-6010
www.lewisedc.org	

In west-central TN, southwest of Nashville; organized Dec 21, 1843 from Hickman, Maury, Wayne, and Lawrence counties. **Name Origin:** For Meriwether Lewis (1774-1809), co-leader of the Lewis and Clark Expedition (1804-06).

Area (sq mi): 282.48 (land 282.09; water 0.38). **Pop per sq mi:** 40.5.

Pop 2005: 11,435. **State rank:** 85. **Pop change:** 2000-20005 +0.6%; 1990-2000 +22.9%. **Pop 2000:** 11,367 (White 96.2%; Black or African American 1.5%; Hispanic or Latino 1.2%; Asian 0.2%; Other 1.3%). **Foreign born:** 1%. **Median age:** 37.3.

Income 2000: per capita $14,664; median household $30,444; **Pop below poverty level:** 13.4%. ***Personal per capita income 2000-2003:** $17,536-$10,054.

Unemployment 2004: 7.1%. **Change from 2000:** -2.4%. **Median travel time to work:** 28.5 minutes. **Working outside county of residence:** 45.5%.

Cities with pop over 10,000: None.

LINCOLN COUNTY

112 Main St S	**Ph:** 931-433-2454
Fayetteville, TN 37334	**Fax:** 931-433-9304
www.vallnet.com/lincolncounty	

On the central southern border of TN, west of Chattanooga; organized Nov 14, 1809 from Bedford County. **Name Origin:** For Gen. Benjamin Lincoln (1733-1810), Revolutionary War officer, U.S. secretary of war (1781-83), and lt. gov. of MA (1788).

Area (sq mi): 570.63 (land 570.23; water 0.39). **Pop per sq mi:** 56.8.

Pop 2005: 32,392. **State rank:** 44. **Pop change:** 2000-20005 +3.4%; 1990-2000 +11.3%. **Pop 2000:** 31,340 (White 89.6%; Black or African American 7.4%; Hispanic or Latino 1%; Asian 0.3%; Other 2%). **Foreign born:** 0.9%. **Median age:** 38.9.

Income 2000: per capita $18,837; median household $33,434; **Pop below poverty level:** 13.6%. ***Personal per capita income 2000-2003:** $21,937-$24,248.

Unemployment 2004: 5.3%. **Change from 2000:** +0.7%. **Median travel time to work:** 27.9 minutes. **Working outside county of residence:** 39%.

Cities with pop over 10,000: None.

LOUDON COUNTY

101 Mulberry St Suite 200	**Ph:** 865-458-2726
Loudon, TN 37774	**Fax:** 865-458-9891
www.loudoncounty.org	

In east-central TN, south of Oak Ridge; organized as Christiana Sumner County Jun 2, 1870 from Blount, Monroe, McMinn, and Roane counties; name changed Jul 7, 1870. **Name Origin:** For John Campbell (1705-82), 4th Earl of Loudoun, commander of British forces during the French and Indian Wars.

Area (sq mi): 247.31 (land 228.88; water 18.43). **Pop per sq mi:** 189.6.

Pop 2005: 43,387. **State rank:** 32. **Pop change:** 2000-20005 +11%; 1990-2000 +25.1%. **Pop 2000:** 39,086 (White 95.2%; Black or African American 1.1%; Hispanic or Latino 2.3%; Asian 0.2%; Other 2.7%). **Foreign born:** 1.8%. **Median age:** 41.

Income 2000: per capita $21,061; median household $40,401; **Pop below poverty level:** 10%. ***Personal per capita income 2000-2003:** $25,400-$27,515.

Unemployment 2004: 4.4%. **Change from 2000:** +0.9%. **Median travel time to work:** 24.8 minutes. **Working outside county of residence:** 49.3%.

⚖ *County Seat*

Loudon County (cont'd)

Cities with pop over 10,000: None.

MACON COUNTY

County Courthouse Rm 104   **Ph:** 615-666-2333
Lafayette, TN 37083   **Fax:** 615-666-2202
www.maconcountytn.com

On central northern border of TN, northeast of Nashville; organized 1842 from Smith and Sumner counties. **Name Origin:** For Nathaniel Macon (1757-1837), NC legislator, U.S. representative (1791-1815), U.S. senator (1815-28), and president of the NC constitutional convention (1835).

Area (sq mi): 307.19 (land 307.13; water 0.06). **Pop per sq mi:** 70.2.

Pop 2005: 21,549. **State rank:** 62. **Pop change:** 2000-20005 +5.7%; 1990-2000 +28.2%. **Pop 2000:** 20,386 (White 97%; Black or African American 0.2%; Hispanic or Latino 1.7%; Asian 0.2%; Other 1.7%). **Foreign born:** 1.8%. **Median age:** 35.5.

Income 2000: per capita $15,286; median household $29,867; **Pop below poverty level:** 15.1%. ***Personal per capita income 2000-2003:** $20,923-$21,152.

Unemployment 2004: 5.3%. **Change from 2000:** -1.9%. **Median travel time to work:** 31.1 minutes. **Working outside county of residence:** 43.9%.

Cities with pop over 10,000: None.

MADISON COUNTY

100 E Main St Rm 105   **Ph:** 731-423-6022
Jackson, TN 38301   **Fax:** 731-424-4903
www.co.madison.tn.us

In western TN, northeast of Memphis; organized Nov 7, 1821 from Western District (Indian lands). **Name Origin:** For James Madison (1751-1836), fourth U.S. president.

Area (sq mi): 558.63 (land 557; water 1.63). **Pop per sq mi:** 170.4.

Pop 2005: 94,916. **State rank:** 13. **Pop change:** 2000-20005 +3.4%; 1990-2000 +17.8%. **Pop 2000:** 91,837 (White 64.4%; Black or African American 32.5%; Hispanic or Latino 1.7%; Asian 0.6%; Other 1.8%). **Foreign born:** 2.3%. **Median age:** 34.7.

Income 2000: per capita $19,389; median household $36,982; **Pop below poverty level:** 14%. ***Personal per capita income 2000-2003:** $25,587-$27,414.

Unemployment 2004: 5.6%. **Change from 2000:** +0.9%. **Median travel time to work:** 19 minutes. **Working outside county of residence:** 11.4%.

Cities with pop over 10,000: Jackson 🏛 (61,772).

MARION COUNTY

24 Courthouse Sq   **Ph:** 423-942-2515
Jasper, TN 37347   **Fax:** 423-942-0815
www.marioncountychamber.com

On the southeastern border of TN, west of Chattanooga; organized Nov 20, 1817 from Western District (Indian lands). **Name Origin:** For Gen. Francis Marion (c.1732-95), SC soldier and legislator, known as 'The Swamp Fox' for his tactics during the Revolutionary War.

Area (sq mi): 512.32 (land 498.36; water 13.96). **Pop per sq mi:** 55.7.

Pop 2005: 27,757. **State rank:** 53. **Pop change:** 2000-20005 -0.1%; 1990-2000 +11.7%. **Pop 2000:** 27,776 (White 93.9%; Black or African American 4.1%; Hispanic or Latino 0.7%; Asian 0.2%; Other 1.4%). **Foreign born:** 0.5%. **Median age:** 38.2.

Income 2000: per capita $16,419; median household $31,419; **Pop below poverty level:** 14.1%. ***Personal per capita income 2000-2003:** $21,848-$22,512.

Unemployment 2004: 6.3%. **Change from 2000:** +1.2%. **Median travel time to work:** 29.2 minutes. **Working outside county of residence:** 52.4%.

Cities with pop over 10,000: None.

MARSHALL COUNTY

1107 Courthouse Annex   **Ph:** 931-359-1072
Lewisburg, TN 37091   **Fax:** 931-359-0559
www.marshallcountytn.com

In south-central TN, south of Nashville; organized Feb 20, 1836 from Giles, Bedford, Lincoln, and Maury counties. **Name Origin:** For John Marshall (1755-1835), American jurist; fourth Chief Justice of the U.S. Supreme Court (1801-35).

Area (sq mi): 376.1 (land 375.36; water 0.75). **Pop per sq mi:** 75.6.

Pop 2005: 28,372. **State rank:** 51. **Pop change:** 2000-20005 +6%; 1990-2000 +24.3%. **Pop 2000:** 26,767 (White 88.1%; Black or African American 7.8%; Hispanic or Latino 2.9%; Asian 0.3%; Other 2.5%). **Foreign born:** 1.4%. **Median age:** 36.3.

Income 2000: per capita $17,749; median household $38,457; **Pop below poverty level:** 10%. ***Personal per capita income 2000-2003:** $24,530-$24,726.

Unemployment 2004: 7%. **Change from 2000:** +0.9%. **Median travel time to work:** 25.3 minutes. **Working outside county of residence:** 32.3%.

Cities with pop over 10,000: Lewisburg 🏛 (10,782).

MAURY COUNTY

10 Public Sq   **Ph:** 931-381-3690
Columbia, TN 38401   **Fax:** 931-381-1016
www.mauryalliance.com

In west-central TN, southwest of Nashville; organized Nov 16, 1807 from Williamson County and Indian lands. **Name Origin:** For a prominent local family, whose members included Abram Maury (1801-48), U.S. representative from TN (1835-39).

Area (sq mi): 615.52 (land 612.86; water 2.66). **Pop per sq mi:** 124.5.

Pop 2005: 76,292. **State rank:** 16. **Pop change:** 2000-20005 +9.8%; 1990-2000 +26.8%. **Pop 2000:** 69,498 (White 81%; Black or African American 14.3%; Hispanic or Latino 3.3%; Asian 0.3%; Other 3%). **Foreign born:** 2.1%. **Median age:** 36.3.

Income 2000: per capita $19,365; median household $41,591; **Pop below poverty level:** 10.9%. ***Personal per capita income 2000-2003:** $26,482-$28,810.

Unemployment 2004: 5.4%. **Change from 2000:** +1.5%. **Median travel time to work:** 26 minutes. **Working outside county of residence:** 30%.

---

*Source: Personal per capita income data are from the Bureau of Economic Analysis; per capita income data are from the Bureau of the Census. See Introduction for explanation of differences.

Maury County (cont'd)

Cities with pop over 10,000: Columbia 🏛 (33,599); Spring Hill (14,431).

MCMINN COUNTY

5 S Hill St Suite A
Athens, TN 37303
www.mcminnco.org

Ph: 423-745-4440
Fax: 423-744-1657

In southeastern TN, northeast of Chattanooga; organized Nov 13, 1819 from Cherokee Indian lands. **Name Origin:** For Joseph McMinn (1785-1824), governor of TN (1817-21), known as 'the Quaker governor.'

Area (sq mi): 432.22 (land 430.28; water 1.94). **Pop per sq mi:** 119.3.

Pop 2005: 51,327. **State rank:** 27. **Pop change:** 2000-20005 +4.7%; 1990-2000 +15.6%. **Pop 2000:** 49,015 (White 91.9%; Black or African American 4.5%; Hispanic or Latino 1.8%; Asian 0.7%; Other 2.1%). **Foreign born:** 1.3%. **Median age:** 37.9.

Income 2000: per capita $16,725; median household $31,919; **Pop below poverty level:** 14.5%. *Personal per capita income 2000-2003: $20,520-$21,800.

Unemployment 2004: 6.5%. **Change from 2000:** -1.2%. **Median travel time to work:** 23.1 minutes. **Working outside county of residence:** 27.7%.

Cities with pop over 10,000: Athens 🏛 (13,719).

MCNAIRY COUNTY

County Courthouse Rm 102
Selmer, TN 38375
www.mcnairy.com

Ph: 731-645-3511
Fax: 731-646-1414

On the southwestern border of TN, southeast of Jackson; organized Oct 8, 1823 from Hardin County. **Name Origin:** For John McNairy, a judge in U.S. District Court for TN (1797).

Area (sq mi): 560.84 (land 560.04; water 0.79). **Pop per sq mi:** 45.1.

Pop 2005: 25,285. **State rank:** 57. **Pop change:** 2000-20005 +2.6%; 1990-2000 +10%. **Pop 2000:** 24,653 (White 91.6%; Black or African American 6.2%; Hispanic or Latino 0.9%; Asian 0.1%; Other 1.4%). **Foreign born:** 0.9%. **Median age:** 39.1.

Income 2000: per capita $16,385; median household $30,154; **Pop below poverty level:** 15.9%. *Personal per capita income 2000-2003: $21,207-$23,607.

Unemployment 2004: 6.1%. **Change from 2000:** -0.3%. **Median travel time to work:** 26 minutes. **Working outside county of residence:** 41.8%.

Cities with pop over 10,000: None.

MEIGS COUNTY

PO Box 218
Decatur, TN 37322
www.meigscountytnchamber.org

Ph: 423-334-5747

In southeastern TN, northeast of Chattanooga; organized Jan 20, 1836 from Hamilton, McMinn, Rhea, and Roane counties. **Name Origin:** For Return Jonathan Meigs (1764-1824), U.S. senator from OH (1808-1810), OH governor (1810-14), and U.S. postmaster general (1814-23).

Area (sq mi): 216.78 (land 194.86; water 21.92). **Pop per sq mi:** 59.8.

Pop 2005: 11,657. **State rank:** 84. **Pop change:** 2000-20005 +5.2%; 1990-2000 +38%. **Pop 2000:** 11,086 (White 97.3%; Black or African American 1.2%; Hispanic or Latino 0.6%; Asian 0.2%; Other 0.9%). **Foreign born:** 0.6%. **Median age:** 36.7.

Income 2000: per capita $14,551; median household $29,354; **Pop below poverty level:** 18.3%. *Personal per capita income 2000-2003: $18,085-$19,967.

Unemployment 2004: 7.4%. **Change from 2000:** +0.1%. **Median travel time to work:** 33.7 minutes. **Working outside county of residence:** 67.1%.

Cities with pop over 10,000: None.

MONROE COUNTY

103 College St
Madisonville, TN 37354
www.monroegovernment.org

Ph: 423-442-2220
Fax: 423-442-9542

On southeastern border of TN, northeast of Chattanooga; organized Nov 13, 1819 from Roane County (Hiwassee Purchase, Indian lands). **Name Origin:** For James Monroe (1758-1831), fifth U.S. president.

Area (sq mi): 652.58 (land 634.91; water 17.67). **Pop per sq mi:** 68.

Pop 2005: 43,185. **State rank:** 33. **Pop change:** 2000-20005 +10.8%; 1990-2000 +27.6%. **Pop 2000:** 38,961 (White 94.1%; Black or African American 2.3%; Hispanic or Latino 1.8%; Asian 0.4%; Other 2.6%). **Foreign born:** 1.2%. **Median age:** 36.8.

Income 2000: per capita $14,951; median household $30,337; **Pop below poverty level:** 15.5%. *Personal per capita income 2000-2003: $17,456-$19,668.

Unemployment 2004: 6.4%. **Change from 2000:** -0.8%. **Median travel time to work:** 26 minutes. **Working outside county of residence:** 35.4%.

Cities with pop over 10,000: None.

MONTGOMERY COUNTY

PO Box 687
Clarksville, TN 37041
www.montgomerycountytn.org

Ph: 931-648-5711
Fax: 931-553-5160

On central northern border of TN, northwest of Nashville; organized Apr 9, 1796 by the division between Montgomery and Robertson counties of Tennessee County, which had been organized in 1788 from Davidson County and was then abolished. **Name Origin:** For John Montgomery (1748-94), explorer of Cumberland County (1771) and Indian fighter.

Area (sq mi): 543.84 (land 539.28; water 4.57). **Pop per sq mi:** 273.

Pop 2005: 147,202. **State rank:** 8. **Pop change:** 2000-20005 +9.2%; 1990-2000 +34.1%. **Pop 2000:** 134,768 (White 70.9%; Black or African American 19.2%; Hispanic or Latino 5.2%; Asian 1.8%; Other 5.8%). **Foreign born:** 4.4%. **Median age:** 30.

Income 2000: per capita $17,265; median household $38,981; **Pop below poverty level:** 10%. *Personal per capita income 2000-2003: $23,992-$27,405.

Montgomery County (cont'd)

Unemployment 2004: 4.8%. **Change from 2000:** +1.1%. **Median travel time to work:** 25.5 minutes. **Working outside county of residence:** 38.2%.

Cities with pop over 10,000: Clarksville 🏛 (108,972).

MOORE COUNTY
PO Box 206   **Ph:** 931-759-7346
Lynchburg, TN 37352   **Fax:** 931-759-6394
www.lynchburgtenn.com

In south-central TN, south of Murfreesboro; organized Dec 14, 1871 from Bedford, Franklin, Lincoln, and Coffee counties. **Name Origin:** For Gen. William Moore, TN officer in the War of 1812 and later a TN legislator.

Area (sq mi): 130.38 (land 129.18; water 1.21). **Pop per sq mi:** 46.6.

Pop 2005: 6,024. **State rank:** 93. **Pop change:** 2000-20005 +4.9%; 1990-2000 +21.6%. **Pop 2000:** 5,740 (White 95.6%; Black or African American 2.7%; Hispanic or Latino 0.8%; Asian 0.1%; Other 1.3%). **Foreign born:** 1%. **Median age:** 39.7.

Income 2000: per capita $19,040; median household $36,591; **Pop below poverty level:** 9.6%. *Personal per capita income 2000-2003:** $20,562-$23,166.

Unemployment 2004: 4.4%. **Change from 2000:** +1.2%. **Median travel time to work:** 22.3 minutes. **Working outside county of residence:** 64.5%.

Cities with pop over 10,000: None.

MORGAN COUNTY
415 Kingston St   **Ph:** 423-346-3480
Wartburg, TN 37887   **Fax:** 423-346-4161

In east-central TN, west of Oak Ridge; organized 1817 from Roane County, and in 1903 annexed part of Anderson County. **Name Origin:** For Gen. Daniel Morgan (1736-1802), an officer in the Revolutionary War and U.S. representative from VA (1797-99).

Area (sq mi): 522.4 (land 522.04; water 0.35). **Pop per sq mi:** 38.6.

Pop 2005: 20,157. **State rank:** 64. **Pop change:** 2000-20005 +2%; 1990-2000 +14.2%. **Pop 2000:** 19,757 (White 96.2%; Black or African American 2.2%; Hispanic or Latino 0.6%; Asian 0.1%; Other 0.9%). **Foreign born:** 0.4%. **Median age:** 36.5.

Income 2000: per capita $12,925; median household $27,712; **Pop below poverty level:** 16%. *Personal per capita income 2000-2003:** $17,194-$17,455.

Unemployment 2004: 7.9%. **Change from 2000:** +1.7%. **Median travel time to work:** 34.8 minutes. **Working outside county of residence:** 60.9%.

Cities with pop over 10,000: None.

OBION COUNTY
2 Bill Burnett Cir   **Ph:** 731-885-3831
Union City, TN 38261   **Fax:** 731-885-0287
www.obioncountytennessee.com

On the northwestern border of TN; organized Oct 24, 1823 from Western District (Indian lands). **Name Origin:** For the Obion River, which runs through it; from an Indian word meaning either 'many forks or branches,' as of a river, or possibly a personal name.

Area (sq mi): 555.35 (land 544.91; water 10.43). **Pop per sq mi:** 59.1.

Pop 2005: 32,213. **State rank:** 45. **Pop change:** 2000-20005 -0.7%; 1990-2000 +2.3%. **Pop 2000:** 32,450 (White 87.3%; Black or African American 9.8%; Hispanic or Latino 1.9%; Asian 0.2%; Other 1.7%). **Foreign born:** 1.3%. **Median age:** 38.7.

Income 2000: per capita $17,409; median household $32,764; **Pop below poverty level:** 13.3%. *Personal per capita income 2000-2003:** $24,338-$24,889.

Unemployment 2004: 6.5%. **Change from 2000:** +2.2%. **Median travel time to work:** 18.3 minutes. **Working outside county of residence:** 24.8%.

Cities with pop over 10,000: Union City 🏛 (10,824).

OVERTON COUNTY
317 University St Courthouse Annex Suite 22 **Ph:** 931-823-2631
Livingston, TN 38570   **Fax:** 931-823-7036

In north-central TN, northwest of Oak Ridge; organized Sep 11, 1806 from Jackson County and Indian lands. **Name Origin:** For John Overton (1766-1833), founder (with Andrew Jackson, 1767-1845) of Memphis, TN (1819); judge in the TN superior and supreme courts (1804-16).

Area (sq mi): 434.82 (land 433.38; water 1.43). **Pop per sq mi:** 47.4.

Pop 2005: 20,523. **State rank:** 63. **Pop change:** 2000-20005 +2%; 1990-2000 +14.1%. **Pop 2000:** 20,118 (White 98.2%; Black or African American 0.3%; Hispanic or Latino 0.7%; Asian 0.1%; Other 1%). **Foreign born:** 0.5%. **Median age:** 38.8.

Income 2000: per capita $13,910; median household $26,915; **Pop below poverty level:** 16%. *Personal per capita income 2000-2003:** $18,372-$20,593.

Unemployment 2004: 5.6%. **Change from 2000:** -0.8%. **Median travel time to work:** 26.1 minutes. **Working outside county of residence:** 46.8%.

Cities with pop over 10,000: None.

PERRY COUNTY
PO Box 16   **Ph:** 931-589-2216
Linden, TN 37096   **Fax:** 931-589-2215
www.perrycountytennessee.com

In west-central TN, east of Jackson; established Nov 14, 1821 from Hickman and Humphreys counties. **Name Origin:** For Oliver Hazard Perry (1785-1819), U.S. naval officer during the War of 1812, famous for the message, 'We have met the enemy and they are ours.'

Area (sq mi): 422.9 (land 414.89; water 8). **Pop per sq mi:** 18.3.

Pop 2005: 7,574. **State rank:** 91. **Pop change:** 2000-20005 -0.7%; 1990-2000 +15.4%. **Pop 2000:** 7,631 (White 96.1%; Black or African American 1.7%; Hispanic or Latino 0.8%; Asian 0.1%; Other 1.5%). **Foreign born:** 0.5%. **Median age:** 39.8.

Income 2000: per capita $16,969; median household $28,061; **Pop below poverty level:** 15.4%. *Personal per capita income 2000-2003:** $21,665-$21,727.

Source: Personal per capita income data are from the Bureau of Economic Analysis; per capita income data are from the Bureau of the Census. See Introduction for explanation of differences.

Perry County (cont'd)

Unemployment 2004: 6.7%. **Change from 2000:** -0.5%. **Median travel time to work:** 27.9 minutes. **Working outside county of residence:** 28.4%.

Cities with pop over 10,000: None.

PICKETT COUNTY

1 Courthouse Sq Suite 201   **Ph:** 931-864-3879
Byrdstown, TN 38549   **Fax:** 931-864-7885
www.dalehollow.com/government.htm

In east-central TN, northwest of Oak Ridge; organized Feb 27, 1879 from Fentress and Overton counties. **Name Origin:** For H.L. Pickett, a TN legislator instrumental in forming the county.

Area (sq mi): 174.58 (land 162.92; water 11.66). **Pop per sq mi:** 29.6.

Pop 2005: 4,821. **State rank:** 95. **Pop change:** 2000-20005 -2.5%; 1990-2000 +8.7%. **Pop 2000:** 4,945 (White 98.5%; Black or African American 0.1%; Hispanic or Latino 0.8%; Asian 0%; Other 0.7%). **Foreign born:** 0.3%. **Median age:** 41.6.

Income 2000: per capita $14,681; median household $24,673; **Pop below poverty level:** 15.6%. ***Personal per capita income 2000-2003:** $17,494-$17,563.

Unemployment 2004: 8.6%. **Change from 2000:** -0.5%. **Median travel time to work:** 25.1 minutes. **Working outside county of residence:** 38.1%.

Cities with pop over 10,000: None.

POLK COUNTY

6239 Hwy 411   **Ph:** 423-338-4524
Benton, TN 37307   **Fax:** 423-338-8611
www.ocoeetn.org

On the southeastern border of TN, east of Chattanooga; organized Nov 28, 1839 from Bradley and McMinn counties. **Name Origin:** For James Knox Polk (1795-1849), eleventh U.S. president.

Area (sq mi): 442.35 (land 435.05; water 7.3). **Pop per sq mi:** 36.6.

Pop 2005: 15,944. **State rank:** 75. **Pop change:** 2000-20005 -0.7%; 1990-2000 +17.6%. **Pop 2000:** 16,050 (White 97.8%; Black or African American 0.1%; Hispanic or Latino 0.7%; Asian 0.1%; Other 1.4%). **Foreign born:** 0.8%. **Median age:** 38.6.

Income 2000: per capita $16,025; median household $29,643; **Pop below poverty level:** 13%. ***Personal per capita income 2000-2003:** $20,396-$21,141.

Unemployment 2004: 5.7%. **Change from 2000:** +0.7%. **Median travel time to work:** 30.1 minutes. **Working outside county of residence:** 70.4%.

Cities with pop over 10,000: None.

PUTNAM COUNTY

29 N Washington Ave   **Ph:** 931-526-7106
Cookeville, TN 38501   **Fax:** 931-372-8201
www.putnamcountytn.gov

In north-central TN, east of Nashville; organized Feb 2, 1842 from Smith, White, DeKalb, Overton, and Jackson counties. **Name Origin:** For Gen. Israel Putnam (1718-90), Revolutionary War officer and American commander at the Battle of Bunker Hill.

Area (sq mi): 402.56 (land 401.05; water 1.5). **Pop per sq mi:** 166.

Pop 2005: 66,580. **State rank:** 18. **Pop change:** 2000-20005 +6.8%; 1990-2000 +21.3%. **Pop 2000:** 62,315 (White 93.2%; Black or African American 1.7%; Hispanic or Latino 3%; Asian 0.9%; Other 2.8%). **Foreign born:** 3.4%. **Median age:** 34.4.

Income 2000: per capita $16,927; median household $30,914; **Pop below poverty level:** 16.4%. ***Personal per capita income 2000-2003:** $22,875-$24,827.

Unemployment 2004: 4.5%. **Change from 2000:** +0%. **Median travel time to work:** 19.6 minutes. **Working outside county of residence:** 14.8%.

Cities with pop over 10,000: Cookeville 🏛 (27,648).

RHEA COUNTY

375 Church St Suite 101   **Ph:** 423-775-7808
Dayton, TN 37321   **Fax:** 423-775-7898
www.rheacountyetc.com

In east-central TN, northeast of Chattanooga; organized Nov 30, 1807 from Roane County. **Name Origin:** For John Rhea (1753-1832), U.S. representative from TN (1803-15; 1817-23).

Area (sq mi): 336.39 (land 315.94; water 20.45). **Pop per sq mi:** 94.7.

Pop 2005: 29,918. **State rank:** 48. **Pop change:** 2000-20005 +5.3%; 1990-2000 +16.7%. **Pop 2000:** 28,400 (White 94.6%; Black or African American 2%; Hispanic or Latino 1.7%; Asian 0.3%; Other 2.3%). **Foreign born:** 1.3%. **Median age:** 37.2.

Income 2000: per capita $15,672; median household $30,418; **Pop below poverty level:** 14.7%. ***Personal per capita income 2000-2003:** $19,624-$21,097.

Unemployment 2004: 6.3%. **Change from 2000:** +0.3%. **Median travel time to work:** 24.4 minutes. **Working outside county of residence:** 25.5%.

Cities with pop over 10,000: None.

ROANE COUNTY

200 E Race St   **Ph:** 865-376-5556
Kingston, TN 37763   **Fax:** 865-717-4121
www.roanealliance.org

In east-central TN, southwest of Oak Ridge; organized Nov 6, 1801 from Knox County and Indian lands. **Name Origin:** For Archibald Roane (1759-1819), governor of TN (1801-03) and judge of the TN supreme court (1815-19).

Area (sq mi): 394.98 (land 360.98; water 34). **Pop per sq mi:** 146.5.

Pop 2005: 52,889. **State rank:** 25. **Pop change:** 2000-20005 +1.9%; 1990-2000 +9.9%. **Pop 2000:** 51,910 (White 94.8%; Black or African American 2.7%; Hispanic or Latino 0.7%; Asian 0.4%; Other 1.6%). **Foreign born:** 1.2%. **Median age:** 40.7.

Income 2000: per capita $18,456; median household $33,226; **Pop below poverty level:** 13.9%. ***Personal per capita income 2000-2003:** $22,339-$25,332.

Roane County (cont'd)

Unemployment 2004: 5.8%. **Change from 2000:** +1.3%. **Median travel time to work:** 26 minutes. **Working outside county of residence:** 49.7%.

Cities with pop over 10,000: None.

ROBERTSON COUNTY

511 S Brown St   **Ph:** 615-384-5895
Springfield, TN 37172   **Fax:** 615-384-2218
www.robertsoncountytn.org

On the central northern border of TN, north of Nashville; organized Apr 9, 1796 by the division between Montgomery and Robertson counties of Tennessee County, which had been organized in 1788 from Davidson County and was then abolished. **Name Origin:** For Gen. James Robertson (1742-1814), office in the Revolutionary War; called 'Father of Tennessee' for his active support of statehood, and founder of present-day Nashville (1780).

Area (sq mi): 476.67 (land 476.47; water 0.2). **Pop per sq mi:** 126.7.

Pop 2005: 60,379. **State rank:** 20. **Pop change:** 2000-20005 +10.9%; 1990-2000 +31.2%. **Pop 2000:** 54,433 (White 87.5%; Black or African American 8.6%; Hispanic or Latino 2.7%; Asian 0.3%; Other 1.9%). **Foreign born:** 2.5%. **Median age:** 35.4.

Income 2000: per capita $19,054; median household $43,174; **Pop below poverty level:** 9%. ***Personal per capita income 2000-2003:** $25,333-$26,958.

Unemployment 2004: 4.6%. **Change from 2000:** +0.5%. **Median travel time to work:** 29.3 minutes. **Working outside county of residence:** 56.4%.

Cities with pop over 10,000: Springfield 🏛 (15,683).

RUTHERFORD COUNTY

319 N Maple St   **Ph:** 615-898-7799
Murfreesboro, TN 37130   **Fax:** 615-898-7830
www.rutherfordcounty.org

In central TN, southeast of Nashville; organized Oct 25, 1803 from Davidson, Williamson, and Wilson counties. **Name Origin:** For Gen. Griffith Rutherford (1731-1800), Revolutionary War hero, NC legislator (1784), and president of the TN legislative council (1796).

Area (sq mi): 623.94 (land 618.91; water 5.03). **Pop per sq mi:** 352.7.

Pop 2005: 218,292. **State rank:** 5. **Pop change:** 2000-20005 +19.9%; 1990-2000 +53.5%. **Pop 2000:** 182,023 (White 84.5%; Black or African American 9.5%; Hispanic or Latino 2.8%; Asian 1.9%; Other 2.8%). **Foreign born:** 3.6%. **Median age:** 31.2.

Income 2000: per capita $19,938; median household $46,312; **Pop below poverty level:** 9%. ***Personal per capita income 2000-2003:** $26,624-$27,910.

Unemployment 2004: 3.9%. **Change from 2000:** +0.3%. **Median travel time to work:** 26.8 minutes. **Working outside county of residence:** 37.5%.

Cities with pop over 10,000: Murfreesboro 🏛 (81,511); Smyrna (31,925); La Vergne (24,811).

SCOTT COUNTY

283 Court St   **Ph:** 423-663-2588
Huntsville, TN 37756   **Fax:** 423-663-3969
www.scottcounty.com

On the central northern border of TN, northwest of Oak Ridge; established Dec 17, 1839 from Fentriss, Morgan, Anderson, and Campbell counties. **Name Origin:** For Winfield Scott (1786-1866), general in chief of the U.S. Army (1841) and commander of the Union armies at the beginning of the Civil War.

Area (sq mi): 533.22 (land 532.09; water 1.13). **Pop per sq mi:** 41.1.

Pop 2005: 21,868. **State rank:** 61. **Pop change:** 2000-20005 +3.5%; 1990-2000 +15.1%. **Pop 2000:** 21,127 (White 98.1%; Black or African American 0.1%; Hispanic or Latino 0.6%; Asian 0.1%; Other 1.2%). **Foreign born:** 0.4%. **Median age:** 34.7.

Income 2000: per capita $12,927; median household $24,093; **Pop below poverty level:** 20.2%. ***Personal per capita income 2000-2003:** $16,805-$17,456.

Unemployment 2004: 7.4%. **Change from 2000:** +0.1%. **Median travel time to work:** 27.2 minutes. **Working outside county of residence:** 20%.

Cities with pop over 10,000: None.

SEQUATCHIE COUNTY

307 Cherry St E Rm 6   **Ph:** 423-949-2522
Dunlap, TN 37327   **Fax:** 423-949-6316
www.sequatchie.com

In southeastern TN, northwest of Chattanooga; organized Dec 9, 1857 from Hamilton County (and previously from Bledsoe, Marion, and Grundy counties). **Name Origin:** For the Sequatchie River, which runs through it; name is Cherokee, probably for 'hog river.'

Area (sq mi): 266.02 (land 265.85; water 0.18). **Pop per sq mi:** 47.7.

Pop 2005: 12,691. **State rank:** 82. **Pop change:** 2000-20005 +11.6%; 1990-2000 +28.3%. **Pop 2000:** 11,370 (White 98%; Black or African American 0.2%; Hispanic or Latino 0.8%; Asian 0.1%; Other 1%). **Foreign born:** 1.2%. **Median age:** 36.7.

Income 2000: per capita $16,468; median household $30,959; **Pop below poverty level:** 16.5%. ***Personal per capita income 2000-2003:** $19,176-$21,039.

Unemployment 2004: 5.4%. **Change from 2000:** +0.4%. **Median travel time to work:** 27.7 minutes. **Working outside county of residence:** 50.4%.

Cities with pop over 10,000: None.

SEVIER COUNTY

125 Court Ave Suite 202 E   **Ph:** 865-453-5502
Sevierville, TN 37862   **Fax:** 865-453-6830
www.seviercountytn.org

On the central eastern border of TN, southeast of Knoxville; organized Sep 27, 1794 (prior to statehood) from Jefferson County. **Name Origin:** For John Sevier (1745-1815), only governor of Franklin (original name of the state; 1785-88), then governor of TN (1796-81; 1803-09), and U.S. representative (1811-15).

Area (sq mi): 597.73 (land 592.29; water 5.45). **Pop per sq mi:** 133.9.

*Source: Personal per capita income data are from the Bureau of Economic Analysis; per capita income data are from the Bureau of the Census. See Introduction for explanation of differences.

654

Sevier County (cont'd)

Pop 2005: 79,282. **State rank:** 15. **Pop change:** 2000-20005 +11.4%; 1990-2000 +39.4%. **Pop 2000:** 71,170 (White 96.5%; Black or African American 0.6%; Hispanic or Latino 1.2%; Asian 0.6%; Other 1.6%). **Foreign born:** 1.6%. **Median age:** 38.1.

Income 2000: per capita $18,064; median household $34,719; **Pop below poverty level:** 10.7%. ***Personal per capita income 2000 2003:** $22,374-$25,822.

Unemployment 2004: 6.2%. **Change from 2000:** +0.3%. **Median travel time to work:** 25.3 minutes. **Working outside county of residence:** 26.2%.

Cities with pop over 10,000: Sevierville ⚏ (14,101).

SHELBY COUNTY

160 N Main St Suite 450   **Ph:** 901-545-4301
Memphis, TN 38103   **Fax:** 901-545-4283
www.co.shelby.tn.us

On the southwest border of TN; organized Nov 24, 1819 from Hardin County. **Name Origin:** For Gen. Isaac Shelby (1750-1826), officer in the Revolutionary War, NC legislator, and governor of KY (1792-96; 1812-16).

Area (sq mi): 783.63 (land 754.53; water 29.1). **Pop per sq mi:** 1204.8.

Pop 2005: 909,035. **State rank:** 1. **Pop change:** 2000-20005 +1.3%; 1990-2000 +8.6%. **Pop 2000:** 897,472 (White 46.2%; Black or African American 48.6%; Hispanic or Latino 2.6%; Asian 1.6%; Other 2.4%). **Foreign born:** 3.8%. **Median age:** 32.9.

Income 2000: per capita $20,856; median household $39,593; **Pop below poverty level:** 16%. ***Personal per capita income 2000-2003:** $30,496-$34,087.

Unemployment 2004: 6.2%. **Change from 2000:** +2%. **Median travel time to work:** 23.7 minutes. **Working outside county of residence:** 4.8%.

Cities with pop over 10,000: Memphis ⚏ (671,929); Bartlett (42,865); Germantown (37,555); Collierville (36,562); Millington (10,399).

SMITH COUNTY

122 Turner High Cir   **Ph:** 615-735-9833
Carthage, TN 37030   **Fax:** 615-735-8252
www.smithcountychamber.org

In north-central TN, northeast of Nashville; organized Oct 26, 1799 from Indian lands. **Name Origin:** For Col. Daniel Smith (1748-1818), officer in the Revolutionary War, member of the first TN Constitutional Convention (1796), and U.S. senator from TN (1798-99; 1805-09).

Area (sq mi): 325.35 (land 314.41; water 10.94). **Pop per sq mi:** 59.3.

Pop 2005: 18,647. **State rank:** 67. **Pop change:** 2000-20005 +5.3%; 1990-2000 +25.2%. **Pop 2000:** 17,712 (White 94.9%; Black or African American 2.5%; Hispanic or Latino 1.1%; Asian 0.2%; Other 1.9%). **Foreign born:** 0.9%. **Median age:** 36.8.

Income 2000: per capita $17,473; median household $35,625; **Pop below poverty level:** 12.2%. ***Personal per capita income 2000-2003:** $22,478-$23,678.

Unemployment 2004: 6.4%. **Change from 2000:** +1.5%. **Median travel time to work:** 29.9 minutes. **Working outside county of residence:** 39.7%.

Cities with pop over 10,000: None.

STEWART COUNTY

PO Box 67   **Ph:** 931-232-7616
Dover, TN 37058   **Fax:** 931-232-4934
www.3tewartcountygovernment.com

On the central northern border of TN, west of Clarksville; organized Nov 1, 1803 from Montgomery County. **Name Origin:** For Duncan Stewart, Revolutionary War veteran and early settler.

Area (sq mi): 493.2 (land 458.48; water 34.72). **Pop per sq mi:** 28.3.

Pop 2005: 12,969. **State rank:** 80. **Pop change:** 2000-20005 +4.8%; 1990-2000 +30.5%. **Pop 2000:** 12,370 (White 94.6%; Black or African American 1.3%; Hispanic or Latino 1%; Asian 1.5%; Other 1.9%). **Foreign born:** 1.7%. **Median age:** 38.7.

Income 2000: per capita $16,302; median household $32,316; **Pop below poverty level:** 12.4%. ***Personal per capita income 2000-2003:** $19,301-$20,536.

Unemployment 2004: 6.7%. **Change from 2000:** -0.5%. **Median travel time to work:** 37.2 minutes. **Working outside county of residence:** 57.4%.

Cities with pop over 10,000: None.

SULLIVAN COUNTY

3258 Hwy 126   **Ph:** 423-323-6428
Blountville, TN 37617   **Fax:** 423-279-2725
www.sullivancounty.org

On the northeastern border of TN, north of Johnson City; organized Oct 18, 1779 (prior to statehood) from Washington County. **Name Origin:** For Gen. John Sullivan (1740-95), officer in the Revolutionary War, member of the Continental Congress (1774-75; 1780-81), and governor of NH (1786-87; 1789).

Area (sq mi): 429.69 (land 413.02; water 16.67). **Pop per sq mi:** 369.8.

Pop 2005: 152,716. **State rank:** 7. **Pop change:** 2000-20005 -0.2%; 1990-2000 +6.6%. **Pop 2000:** 153,048 (White 96.1%; Black or African American 1.9%; Hispanic or Latino 0.7%; Asian 0.4%; Other 1.1%). **Foreign born:** 1.3%. **Median age:** 40.1.

Income 2000: per capita $19,202; median household $33,529; **Pop below poverty level:** 12.9%. ***Personal per capita income 2000-2003:** $24,528-$27,232.

Unemployment 2004: 5.6%. **Change from 2000:** +1.7%. **Median travel time to work:** 21.3 minutes. **Working outside county of residence:** 28.3%.

Cities with pop over 10,000: Kingsport (44,070); Bristol (24,933).

SUMNER COUNTY

355 N Belvedere Dr   **Ph:** 615-452-4063
Gallatin, TN 37066   **Fax:** 615-452-9371
www.sumnertn.org

On the central northern border of TN, northeast of Nashville; organized Nov 18, 1786 (prior to statehood) from Davidson County (NC), becoming part of the Territory South of the River Ohio

⚏ *County Seat*

Sumner County (cont'd)

(popularly called the Southwest Territory) from its creation in May 1790 until it became the state of TN in 1796. **Name Origin:** For Gen. Jethro Sumner (1733-85), officer in the Revolutionary War who was active in promoting TN statehood.

Area (sq mi): 543.12 (land 529.3; water 13.81). **Pop per sq mi:** 274.

Pop 2005: 145,009. **State rank:** 9. **Pop change:** 2000-20005 +11.2%; 1990-2000 +26.3%. **Pop 2000:** 130,449 (White 90.6%; Black or African American 5.8%; Hispanic or Latino 1.8%; Asian 0.7%; Other 2.1%). **Foreign born:** 2.4%. **Median age:** 36.1.

Income 2000: per capita $21,164; median household $46,030; **Pop below poverty level:** 8.1%. ***Personal per capita income 2000-2003:** $27,061-$28,544.

Unemployment 2004: 4.2%. **Change from 2000:** -0.3%. **Median travel time to work:** 27.2 minutes. **Working outside county of residence:** 50.7%.

Cities with pop over 10,000: Hendersonville (43,866); Gallatin 🏛 (25,653); Portland (10,087).

TIPTON COUNTY
PO Box 528   **Ph:** 901-476-0207
Covington, TN 38019   **Fax:** 901-476-0227
tiptonco.com

On the southwest border of TN, northeast of Memphis; organized Oct 29, 1823 from Western District (Indian lands). **Name Origin:** For Jacob Tipton (?-1791), soldier killed in a battle with Indians.

Area (sq mi): 474.72 (land 459.37; water 15.35). **Pop per sq mi:** 121.9.

Pop 2005: 55,998. **State rank:** 24. **Pop change:** 2000-20005 +9.2%; 1990-2000 +36.5%. **Pop 2000:** 51,271 (White 77.2%; Black or African American 19.9%; Hispanic or Latino 1.2%; Asian 0.4%; Other 1.9%). **Foreign born:** 0.8%. **Median age:** 34.4.

Income 2000: per capita $17,952; median household $41,856; **Pop below poverty level:** 12.1%. ***Personal per capita income 2000-2003:** $22,946-$23,787.

Unemployment 2004: 6.3%. **Change from 2000:** +1.3%. **Median travel time to work:** 31.7 minutes. **Working outside county of residence:** 58.6%.

Cities with pop over 10,000: None.

TROUSDALE COUNTY
200 E Main St Rm 2   **Ph:** 615-374-2906
Hartsville, TN 37074   **Fax:** 615-374-1100

In north-central TN, northeast of Nashville; organized Jan 21, 1870 from Macon, Smith, Wilson, and Sumner counties. **Name Origin:** For Gen. William Trousdale (1790-1872), TN legislator, governor (1849-51), and U.S. minister to Brazil (1852-57).

Area (sq mi): 116.64 (land 114.24; water 2.4). **Pop per sq mi:** 67.2.

Pop 2005: 7,677. **State rank:** 89. **Pop change:** 2000-20005 +5.8%; 1990-2000 +22.6%. **Pop 2000:** 7,259 (White 86.1%; Black or African American 11.4%; Hispanic or Latino 1.5%; Asian 0.1%; Other 1.9%). **Foreign born:** 1.7%. **Median age:** 38.1.

Income 2000: per capita $15,838; median household $32,212; **Pop below poverty level:** 13.4%. ***Personal per capita income 2000-2003:** $20,432-$21,146.

Unemployment 2004: 5.5%. **Change from 2000:** -4.5%. **Median travel time to work:** 32.7 minutes. **Working outside county of residence:** 63%.

Cities with pop over 10,000: None.

UNICOI COUNTY
100 Main St   **Ph:** 423-743-9391
Erwin, TN 37650   **Fax:** 423-743-8007
www.unicoicounty.org

On the northeastern border of TN, south of Johnson City; organized Mar 23, 1875 from Washington and Carter counties. **Name Origin:** For Unicoi Creek, which runs through it, or a variant form of Cherokee *unaka* 'white,' referring to the color of the rocks in the Unaka Mountains.

Area (sq mi): 186.49 (land 186.14; water 0.35). **Pop per sq mi:** 94.4.

Pop 2005: 17,572. **State rank:** 71. **Pop change:** 2000-20005 -0.5%; 1990-2000 +6.8%. **Pop 2000:** 17,667 (White 97.1%; Black or African American 0.1%; Hispanic or Latino 1.9%; Asian 0.1%; Other 1.8%). **Foreign born:** 1.4%. **Median age:** 41.5.

Income 2000: per capita $15,612; median household $29,863; **Pop below poverty level:** 13.1%. ***Personal per capita income 2000-2003:** $21,623-$23,272.

Unemployment 2004: 6.3%. **Change from 2000:** +0.4%. **Median travel time to work:** 21.2 minutes. **Working outside county of residence:** 45.9%.

Cities with pop over 10,000: None.

UNION COUNTY
901 Main St Suite 119   **Ph:** 865-992-8043
Maynardville, TN 37807   **Fax:** 865-992-4992
www.unioncountytn.org

In north-central TN, north of Knoxville; organized 1850 from Anderson, Campbell, Grainger, Claiborne, and Knox counties. **Name Origin:** In honor of the strong sentiment of people in the area in favor of the preservation of the Union.

Area (sq mi): 247.13 (land 223.56; water 23.57). **Pop per sq mi:** 85.3.

Pop 2005: 19,076. **State rank:** 66. **Pop change:** 2000-20005 +7.1%; 1990-2000 +30%. **Pop 2000:** 17,808 (White 97.9%; Black or African American 0.1%; Hispanic or Latino 0.8%; Asian 0.2%; Other 1.3%). **Foreign born:** 0.3%. **Median age:** 35.8.

Income 2000: per capita $13,375; median household $27,335; **Pop below poverty level:** 19.6%. ***Personal per capita income 2000-2003:** $17,492-$17,802.

Unemployment 2004: 4.9%. **Change from 2000:** +1.1%. **Median travel time to work:** 31.5 minutes. **Working outside county of residence:** 64.8%.

Cities with pop over 10,000: None.

Source: Personal per capita income data are from the Bureau of Economic Analysis; per capita income data are from the Bureau of the Census. See Introduction for explanation of differences.

VAN BUREN COUNTY

PO Box 827   **Ph:** 931-946-2121
Spencer, TN 38585   **Fax:** 931-946-7572

In east-central TN, northwest of Chattanooga; organized Jan 3, 1840 from Bledsoe, Warren, and White counties. **Name Origin:** For Martin Van Buren (1782-1862), eighth U.S. president.

Area (sq mi): 274.59 (land 273.46; water 1.14). **Pop per sq mi:** 20.

Pop 2005: 5,470. **State rank:** 94. **Pop change:** 2000-20005 -0.7%; 1990-2000 +13.7%. **Pop 2000:** 5,508 (White 98.7%; Black or African American 0.1%; Hispanic or Latino 0.3%; Asian 0.1%; Other 0.8%). **Foreign born:** 0.2%. **Median age:** 38.7.

Income 2000: per capita $17,497; median household $28,165; **Pop below poverty level:** 15.2%. ***Personal per capita income 2000-2003:** $18,598-$21,530.

Unemployment 2004: 6.4%. **Change from 2000:** -1.2%. **Median travel time to work:** 29.9 minutes. **Working outside county of residence:** 57.7%.

Cities with pop over 10,000: None.

WARREN COUNTY

201 Locust St Suite 2P   **Ph:** 931-473-2623
McMinnville, TN 37110   **Fax:** 931-473-8622
www.warrentn.com

In east-central TN, northwest of Chattanooga; organized Nov 26, 1807 from White, Jackson, and Smith counties, and Indian lands. **Name Origin:** For Gen. Joseph Warren (1741-75), Revolutionary War patriot and member of the Committee of Safety who dispatched Paul Revere (1735-1818) on his famous ride.

Area (sq mi): 434.08 (land 432.69; water 1.4). **Pop per sq mi:** 91.9.

Pop 2005: 39,753. **State rank:** 38. **Pop change:** 2000-20005 +3.9%; 1990-2000 +16%. **Pop 2000:** 38,276 (White 90.6%; Black or African American 3.2%; Hispanic or Latino 4.9%; Asian 0.4%; Other 4.7%). **Foreign born:** 3.7%. **Median age:** 36.6.

Income 2000: per capita $15,759; median household $30,920; **Pop below poverty level:** 16.6%. ***Personal per capita income 2000-2003:** $21,378-$23,455.

Unemployment 2004: 5.3%. **Change from 2000:** -1.9%. **Median travel time to work:** 23.4 minutes. **Working outside county of residence:** 17.7%.

Cities with pop over 10,000: McMinnville 🏛 (13,108).

WASHINGTON COUNTY

100 E Main St   **Ph:** 423-753-1621
Jonesborough, TN 37659   **Fax:** 423-753-4716
www.washingtoncountytn.com

In northeastern TN, south of Kingsport; original county; organized Nov 15, 1777 (prior to statehood). **Name Origin:** For George Washington (1732-99), American patriot and first U.S. president.

Area (sq mi): 329.8 (land 326.31; water 3.49). **Pop per sq mi:** 344.8.

Pop 2005: 112,507. **State rank:** 11. **Pop change:** 2000-20005 +5%; 1990-2000 +16.1%. **Pop 2000:** 107,198 (White 92.9%; Black or African American 3.8%; Hispanic or Latino 1.4%; Asian 0.7%; Other 1.7%). **Foreign born:** 1.9%. **Median age:** 37.1.

Income 2000: per capita $19,085; median household $33,116; **Pop below poverty level:** 13.9%. ***Personal per capita income 2000-2003:** $22,786-$24,886.

Unemployment 2004: 5%. **Change from 2000:** +0.4%. **Median travel time to work:** 20.6 minutes. **Working outside county of residence:** 26.2%.

Cities with pop over 10,000: Johnson City (57,812).

WAYNE COUNTY

PO Box 848   **Ph:** 931-722-3653
Waynesboro, TN 38485   **Fax:** 931-722-5994
www.waynecountytn.org

On the central southern border of TN, southeast of Jackson; organized Nov 24, 1817 from Hickman and Humphreys counties. **Name Origin:** For Gen. Anthony Wayne (1745-96), PA soldier and statesman, nicknamed 'Mad Anthony' for his daring during the Revolutionary War.

Area (sq mi): 735.59 (land 733.96; water 1.63). **Pop per sq mi:** 23.

Pop 2005: 16,909. **State rank:** 73. **Pop change:** 2000-20005 +0.4%; 1990-2000 +20.9%. **Pop 2000:** 16,842 (White 91.3%; Black or African American 6.8%; Hispanic or Latino 0.8%; Asian 0.2%; Other 1%). **Foreign born:** 0.4%. **Median age:** 37.3.

Income 2000: per capita $14,472; median household $26,576; **Pop below poverty level:** 16.3%. ***Personal per capita income 2000-2003:** $14,943-$16,699.

Unemployment 2004: 8.7%. **Change from 2000:** -1.1%. **Median travel time to work:** 31.3 minutes. **Working outside county of residence:** 36.3%.

Cities with pop over 10,000: None.

WEAKLEY COUNTY

PO Box 587   **Ph:** 731-364-2285
Dresden, TN 38225   **Fax:** 731-364-5236
www.weakleycountytn.gov

On northwestern border of TN, north of Jackson; organized Oct 21, 1823 from Western District (Indian lands). **Name Origin:** For Robert Weakley (1764-1845), U.S. representative from TN (1809-11), TN legislator, and member of the TN Constitutional Convention (1834).

Area (sq mi): 581.81 (land 580.19; water 1.62). **Pop per sq mi:** 58.1.

Pop 2005: 33,732. **State rank:** 43. **Pop change:** 2000-20005 -3.3%; 1990-2000 +9.1%. **Pop 2000:** 34,895 (White 89.7%; Black or African American 6.9%; Hispanic or Latino 1.2%; Asian 1.3%; Other 1.4%). **Foreign born:** 2%. **Median age:** 34.8.

Income 2000: per capita $15,408; median household $30,008; **Pop below poverty level:** 16%. ***Personal per capita income 2000-2003:** $20,530-$22,154.

Unemployment 2004: 7.4%. **Change from 2000:** +1.5%. **Median travel time to work:** 20.2 minutes. **Working outside county of residence:** 29.8%.

Cities with pop over 10,000: Martin (10,098).

🏛 *County Seat*

WHITE COUNTY

County Courthouse Rm 205   **Ph:** 931-836-3203
Sparta, TN 38583   **Fax:** 931-836-3204
www.sparta-chamber.net

In east-central TN, west of Oak Ridge; organized Sep 11, 1806 from Jackson and Smith counties. **Name Origin:** For Col. John White (?-1782), an officer in the American Revolution who was an early settler in the area.

Area (sq mi): 379.39 (land 376.58; water 2.8). **Pop per sq mi:** 64.4.

Pop 2005: 24,253. **State rank:** 58. **Pop change:** 2000-20005 +5%; 1990-2000 +15%. **Pop 2000:** 23,102 (White 96.1%; Black or African American 1.6%; Hispanic or Latino 1%; Asian 0.2%; Other 1.6%). **Foreign born:** 0.8%. **Median age:** 38.8.

Income 2000: per capita $14,791; median household $29,383; **Pop below poverty level:** 14.3%. ***Personal per capita income 2000-2003:** $18,902-$19,698.

Unemployment 2004: 6%. **Change from 2000:** +0.3%. **Median travel time to work:** 22.4 minutes. **Working outside county of residence:** 33%.

Cities with pop over 10,000: None.

WILLIAMSON COUNTY

1320 W Main St PO Box 624   **Ph:** 615-790-5712
Franklin, TN 37065   **Fax:** 615-790-5610
www.williamson-tn.org

In west-central TN, south of Nashville; organized Oct 26, 1799 from Davidson County. **Name Origin:** For Hugh Williamson (1735-1819), member of the Continental Congress (1782-85; 1787; 1788) and U.S. representative from NC (1789-93).

Area (sq mi): 583.62 (land 582.68; water 0.94). **Pop per sq mi:** 263.6.

Pop 2005: 153,595. **State rank:** 6. **Pop change:** 2000-20005 +21.3%; 1990-2000 +56.3%. **Pop 2000:** 126,638 (White 90.2%; Black or African American 5.2%; Hispanic or Latino 2.5%; Asian 1.3%; Other 2%). **Foreign born:** 3.9%. **Median age:** 36.2.

Income 2000: per capita $32,496; median household $69,104; **Pop below poverty level:** 4.7%. ***Personal per capita income 2000-2003:** $40,660-$42,694.

Unemployment 2004: 3.3%. **Change from 2000:** +1.1%. **Median travel time to work:** 26.3 minutes. **Working outside county of residence:** 49.2%.

Cities with pop over 10,000: Franklin ▥ (48,191); Brentwood (30,586).

WILSON COUNTY

PO Box 950   **Ph:** 615-444-0314
Lebanon, TN 37088   **Fax:** 615-443-2615
www.wilsoncountytn.com

In north-central TN, east of Nashville; organized Oct 26, 1799 from Sumner County. **Name Origin:** For David Wilson (?-1804), an officer in the Revolutionary War; he later presided over the General Assembly of the Territory South of Ohio River during which the state of TN was organized.

Area (sq mi): 583.2 (land 570.57; water 12.63). **Pop per sq mi:** 176.2.

Pop 2005: 100,508. **State rank:** 12. **Pop change:** 2000-20005 +13.2%; 1990-2000 +31.2%. **Pop 2000:** 88,809 (White 90.8%; Black or African American 6.3%; Hispanic or Latino 1.3%; Asian 0.5%; Other 1.7%). **Foreign born:** 1.4%. **Median age:** 36.3.

Income 2000: per capita $22,739; median household $50,140; **Pop below poverty level:** 6.7%. ***Personal per capita income 2000-2003:** $29,934-$31,376.

Unemployment 2004: 4.3%. **Change from 2000:** +0.8%. **Median travel time to work:** 29.2 minutes. **Working outside county of residence:** 56.1%.

Cities with pop over 10,000: Lebanon ▥ (22,452); Mount Juliet (17,296).

*Source: Personal per capita income data are from the Bureau of Economic Analysis; per capita income data are from the Bureau of the Census. See Introduction for explanation of differences.

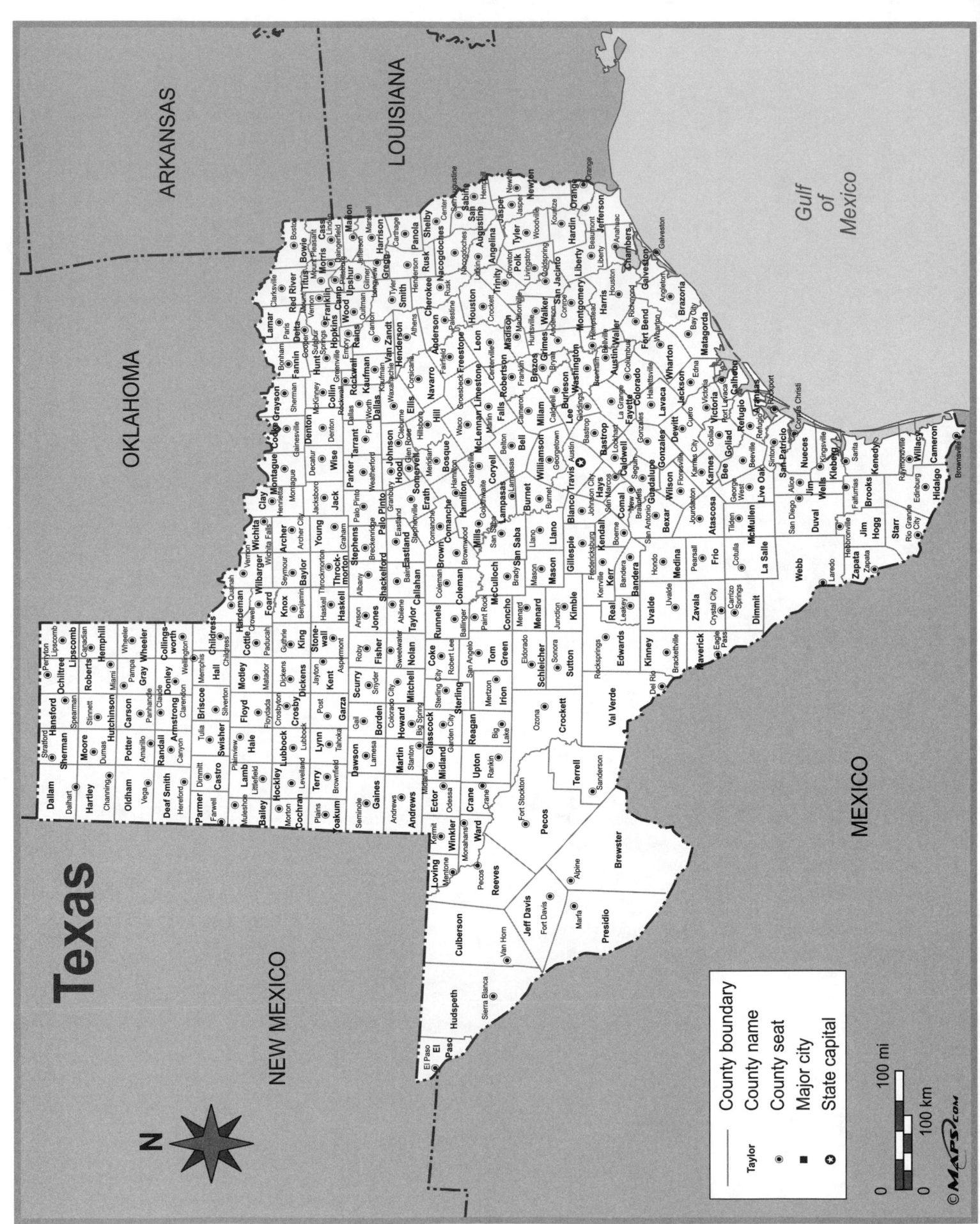

Texas

TEXAS STATE INFORMATION

www.texas.gov **Ph:** 512-463-4630

Area (sq mi): 268,580.82 (land 261,797.12; water 6783.7). **Pop per sq mi:** 87.3.

Pop 2005: 22,859,968. **Pop change:** 2000-20005 +9.6%; 1990-2000 +22.8%. **Pop 2000:** 20,851,820 (White 52.4%; Black or African American 11.5%; Hispanic or Latino 32%; Asian 2.7%; Other 14.9%). **Foreign born:** 13.9%. **Median age:** 32.3.

Income 2000: per capita $19,617; median household $39,927; **Pop below poverty level:** 15.4%. *Personal per capita income 2000-2003: $28,313-$29,074.

Unemployment 2004: 6%. **Change from 2000:** +1.6%. **Median travel time to work:** 25.4 minutes. **Working outside county of residence:** 21.4%.

ANDERSON COUNTY

500 N Church St **Ph:** 903-723-7432
Palestine, TX 75801 **Fax:** 903-723-4625
www.co.anderson.tx.us

In east-central TX, southeast of Dallas; organized Mar 24, 1846 from Houston County. **Name Origin:** For Kenneth Lewis Anderson (1805-45), TX legislator and vice president of the Republic of TX (1844).

Area (sq mi): 1077.95 (land 1070.79; water 7.16). **Pop per sq mi:** 52.7.

Pop 2005: 56,408. **State rank:** 56. **Pop change:** 2000-20005 +2.4%; 1990-2000 +14.8%. **Pop 2000:** 55,109 (White 63.1%; Black or African American 23.5%; Hispanic or Latino 12.2%; Asian 0.4%; Other 9.6%). **Foreign born:** 3.2%. **Median age:** 35.8.

Income 2000: per capita $13,838; median household $31,957; **Pop below poverty level:** 16.5%. *Personal per capita income 2000-2003: $17,667-$18,779.

Unemployment 2004: 7.2%. **Change from 2000:** +3.2%. **Median travel time to work:** 22.8 minutes. **Working outside county of residence:** 17%.

Cities with pop over 10,000: Palestine 🏛 (17,869).

ANDREWS COUNTY

215 NW 1st St Annex Bldg **Ph:** 432-524-1426
Andrews, TX 79714
www.co.andrews.tx.us

On the southwest border of the TX panhandle, north of Odessa; organized Aug 21, 1876 from Bexar County. **Name Origin:** For

Richard 'Big Dick' Andrews (1814-35), the first TX soldier killed in the Texas revolution.

Area (sq mi): 1500.99 (land 1500.64; water 0.36). **Pop per sq mi:** 8.5.

Pop 2005: 12,748. **State rank:** 152. **Pop change:** 2000-20005 -2%; 1990-2000 -9.3%. **Pop 2000:** 13,004 (White 56.3%; Black or African American 1.6%; Hispanic or Latino 40%; Asian 0.7%; Other 20.6%). **Foreign born:** 10.6%. **Median age:** 34.1.

Income 2000: per capita $15,916; median household $34,036; **Pop below poverty level:** 16.4%. *Personal per capita income 2000-2003: $20,460-$22,762.

Unemployment 2004: 5.1%. **Change from 2000:** +1.2%. **Median travel time to work:** 20.6 minutes. **Working outside county of residence:** 22.8%.

Cities with pop over 10,000: None.

ANGELINA COUNTY

PO Box 908 **Ph:** 936-634-8339
Lufkin, TX 75902 **Fax:** 936-634-8460
www.angelinacounty.net

In eastern TX, south of Nacogdoches; organized Apr 22, 1846 from Nacogdoches County. **Name Origin:** For the Angelina River, which forms its eastern border; Spanish diminutive for 'angel.'

Area (sq mi): 864.45 (land 801.56; water 62.89). **Pop per sq mi:** 101.7.

Pop 2005: 81,557. **State rank:** 44. **Pop change:** 2000-20005 +1.8%; 1990-2000 +14.7%. **Pop 2000:** 80,130 (White 69.4%; Black or African American 14.7%; Hispanic or Latino 14.3%; Asian 0.7%; Other 9.5%). **Foreign born:** 6.9%. **Median age:** 34.2.

Income 2000: per capita $15,876; median household $33,806; **Pop below poverty level:** 15.8%. *Personal per capita income 2000-2003: $22,398-$25,576.

Unemployment 2004: 6.6%. **Change from 2000:** +0.8%. **Median travel time to work:** 19.6 minutes. **Working outside county of residence:** 9.6%.

Cities with pop over 10,000: Lufkin 🏛 (33,500).

ARANSAS COUNTY

301 N Live Oak St **Ph:** 361-790-0122
Rockport, TX 78382 **Fax:** 361-790-0119
www.aransascounty.org

On the southeastern coast of TX, northeast of Corpus Christi; organized Sep 18, 1871 from Refugio County. **Name Origin:** For

🏛 *County Seat*

Aransas County (cont'd)

Aransas Bay, on its eastern border; itself named for the Aransas River, which empties into the bay.

Area (sq mi): 527.95 (land 251.86; water 276.09). **Pop per sq mi:** 97.8.

Pop 2005: 24,640. **State rank:** 102. **Pop change:** 2000-20005 +9.5%; 1990-2000 +25.7%. **Pop 2000:** 22,497 (White 73.8%; Black or African American 1.4%; Hispanic or Latino 20.3%; Asian 2.8%; Other 8.3%). **Foreign born:** 5.7%. **Median age:** 42.7.

Income 2000: per capita $18,560; median household $30,702; **Pop below poverty level:** 19.9%. ***Personal per capita income 2000-2003:** $24,116-$25,394.

Unemployment 2004: 8.4%. **Change from 2000:** +2.6%. **Median travel time to work:** 24 minutes. **Working outside county of residence:** 38%.

Cities with pop over 10,000: None.

ARCHER COUNTY

PO Box 815   **Ph:** 940-574-4615
Archer City, TX 76351   **Fax:** 940-574-2432
www.co.archer.tx.us

On the central northern border of TX, northwest of Ft. Worth; organized Jan 22, 1858 from Fannin County. **Name Origin:** For Dr. Branch Tanner Archer (1790-1856), TX legislator (1836) and secretary of war (1836-42).

Area (sq mi): 925.78 (land 909.7; water 16.09). **Pop per sq mi:** 10.

Pop 2005: 9,095. **State rank:** 172. **Pop change:** 2000-20005 +2.7%; 1990-2000 +11%. **Pop 2000:** 8,854 (White 93.3%; Black or African American 0.1%; Hispanic or Latino 4.9%; Asian 0.1%; Other 4.2%). **Foreign born:** 2.3%. **Median age:** 38.1.

Income 2000: per capita $19,300; median household $38,514; **Pop below poverty level:** 9%. ***Personal per capita income 2000-2003:** $25,317-$27,167.

Unemployment 2004: 3.7%. **Change from 2000:** +1.3%. **Median travel time to work:** 23.6 minutes. **Working outside county of residence:** 63.8%.

Cities with pop over 10,000: None.

ARMSTRONG COUNTY

PO Box 309   **Ph:** 806-226-2081
Claude, TX 79019   **Fax:** 806-226-5301
www.co.armstrong.tx.us

In north-central TX panhandle, southeast of Amarillo; organized Aug 21, 1876 from Bexar County. **Name Origin:** For the Armstrong family, early settlers.

Area (sq mi): 913.81 (land 913.63; water 0.18). **Pop per sq mi:** 2.4.

Pop 2005: 2,173. **State rank:** 235. **Pop change:** 2000-20005 +1.2%; 1990-2000 +6.3%. **Pop 2000:** 2,148 (White 93.5%; Black or African American 0.3%; Hispanic or Latino 5.4%; Asian 0%; Other 4.3%). **Foreign born:** 0.9%. **Median age:** 40.7.

Income 2000: per capita $17,151; median household $38,194; **Pop below poverty level:** 10.6%. ***Personal per capita income 2000-2003:** $22,446-$27,144.

Unemployment 2004: 4.2%. **Change from 2000:** +2.9%. **Median travel time to work:** 24.9 minutes. **Working outside county of residence:** 55.1%.

Cities with pop over 10,000: None.

ATASCOSA COUNTY

1 Courthouse Circle Dr Suite 102   **Ph:** 830-767-2511
Jourdanton, TX 78026   **Fax:** 830-769-1021
www.co.atascosa.tx.us

In south-central TX, south of San Antonio; organized Jan 25, 1856 from Bexar County. **Name Origin:** For the Atascosa River, which runs through it; from Spanish 'wet' or 'swampy.'

Area (sq mi): 1235.61 (land 1232.12; water 3.49). **Pop per sq mi:** 35.1.

Pop 2005: 43,226. **State rank:** 68. **Pop change:** 2000-20005 +11.9%; 1990-2000 +26.5%. **Pop 2000:** 38,628 (White 39.6%; Black or African American 0.6%; Hispanic or Latino 58.6%; Asian 0.3%; Other 25.9%). **Foreign born:** 5.1%. **Median age:** 32.3.

Income 2000: per capita $14,276; median household $33,081; **Pop below poverty level:** 20.2%. ***Personal per capita income 2000-2003:** $19,087-$19,770.

Unemployment 2004: 5.7%. **Change from 2000:** +1.5%. **Median travel time to work:** 33 minutes. **Working outside county of residence:** 51.9%.

Cities with pop over 10,000: None.

AUSTIN COUNTY

1 E Main St   **Ph:** 979-865-5911
Bellville, TX 77418   **Fax:** 979-865-8786
www.austincounty.com

In eastern TX, west of Houston; original county; organized Mar 17, 1836 (prior to statehood) from Old Mexican Municipality. **Name Origin:** For Stephen Fuller Austin (1793-1836), MO territorial legislator (1814-20), AR jurist (1820), surveyor and explorer of TX (1822), and secretary of state of the Republic of TX (1836).

Area (sq mi): 656.37 (land 652.59; water 3.78). **Pop per sq mi:** 40.

Pop 2005: 26,123. **State rank:** 98. **Pop change:** 2000-20005 +10.7%; 1990-2000 +18.9%. **Pop 2000:** 23,590 (White 71.9%; Black or African American 10.6%; Hispanic or Latino 16.1%; Asian 0.3%; Other 8.9%). **Foreign born:** 7.3%. **Median age:** 37.6.

Income 2000: per capita $18,140; median household $38,615; **Pop below poverty level:** 12.1%. ***Personal per capita income 2000-2003:** $26,497-$27,493.

Unemployment 2004: 5.4%. **Change from 2000:** +2.6%. **Median travel time to work:** 29 minutes. **Working outside county of residence:** 47.2%.

Cities with pop over 10,000: None.

BAILEY COUNTY

300 S 1st St   **Ph:** 806-272-3044
Muleshoe, TX 79347   **Fax:** 806-272-3538
www.co.bailey.tx.us

On the central western border of TX panhandle, northwest of Lubbock; organized Aug 21, 1876 from Bexar County. **Name Origin:**

Source: Personal per capita income data are from the Bureau of Economic Analysis; per capita income data are from the Bureau of the Census. See Introduction for explanation of differences.

Bailey County (cont'd)

For Pvt. Peter James Bailey (1812-36), killed at the Battle of the Alamo.

Area (sq mi): 827.38 (land 826.69; water 0.68). **Pop per sq mi:** 8.1.

Pop 2005: 6,726. **State rank:** 189. **Pop change:** 2000-20005 +2%; 1990-2000 -6.7%. **Pop 2000:** 6,594 (White 50.3%; Black or African American 1.3%, Hispanic or Latino 47.3%, Asian 0.1%, Other 32%). **Foreign born:** 13.1%. **Median age:** 34.9.

Income 2000: per capita $12,979; median household $27,901; **Pop below poverty level:** 16.7%. ***Personal per capita income 2000-2003:** $21,343-$22,498.

Unemployment 2004: 5.6%. **Change from 2000:** +0.5%. **Median travel time to work:** 19.1 minutes. **Working outside county of residence:** 21.6%.

Cities with pop over 10,000: None.

BANDERA COUNTY

500 Main St PO Box 823   **Ph:** 830-796-3332
Bandera, TX 78003   **Fax:** 830-796-8323
www.banderacounty.org

In south-central TX, northwest of San Antonio; organized Jan 26, 1856 from Uvalde County. **Name Origin:** From the Spanish for 'flag'; reason unknown.

Area (sq mi): 797.54 (land 791.73; water 5.81). **Pop per sq mi:** 25.2.

Pop 2005: 19,988. **State rank:** 117. **Pop change:** 2000-20005 +13.3%; 1990-2000 +67.1%. **Pop 2000:** 17,645 (White 84.1%; Black or African American 0.3%; Hispanic or Latino 13.5%; Asian 0.3%; Other 5.5%). **Foreign born:** 3.9%. **Median age:** 41.3.

Income 2000: per capita $19,635; median household $39,013; **Pop below poverty level:** 10.8%. ***Personal per capita income 2000-2003:** $25,771-$24,905.

Unemployment 2004: 4.9%. **Change from 2000:** +2.2%. **Median travel time to work:** 34.3 minutes. **Working outside county of residence:** 58%.

Cities with pop over 10,000: None.

BASTROP COUNTY

804 Pecan St   **Ph:** 512-332-7244
Bastrop, TX 78602   **Fax:** 512-332-7249
www.bastropcounty.com

In east-central TX, southeast of Austin; organized Mar 17, 1836 (prior to statehood) from Old Mexican Municipality. **Name Origin:** For Felipe Enrique Neri (?-1828), Baron de Bastrop, who established a colony of Germans in TX (1823); first commissioner of Austin's colony (1824).

Area (sq mi): 895.92 (land 888.35; water 7.57). **Pop per sq mi:** 78.7.

Pop 2005: 69,932. **State rank:** 48. **Pop change:** 2000-20005 +21.1%; 1990-2000 +50.9%. **Pop 2000:** 57,733 (White 65.4%; Black or African American 8.8%; Hispanic or Latino 24%; Asian 0.5%; Other 10.6%). **Foreign born:** 8.1%. **Median age:** 35.4.

Income 2000: per capita $18,146; median household $43,578; **Pop below poverty level:** 11.6%. ***Personal per capita income 2000-2003:** $22,415-$21,692.

Unemployment 2004: 5.6%. **Change from 2000:** +1.6%. **Median travel time to work:** 37.1 minutes. **Working outside county of residence:** 59.3%.

Cities with pop over 10,000: None.

BAYLOR COUNTY

PO Box 689   **Ph:** 940-889-3322
Seymour, TX 76380

In north-central TX, southwest of Wichita Falls; organized Feb 1, 1858 from Fannin County. **Name Origin:** For Henry Weidner Baylor (1818-53), a physician in the Texas Rangers during the Mexican War.

Area (sq mi): 901.01 (land 870.77; water 30.24). **Pop per sq mi:** 4.4.

Pop 2005: 3,843. **State rank:** 213. **Pop change:** 2000-20005 -6.1%; 1990-2000 -6.7%. **Pop 2000:** 4,093 (White 85.8%; Black or African American 3.3%; Hispanic or Latino 9.3%; Asian 0.5%; Other 5.1%). **Foreign born:** 2%. **Median age:** 44.8.

Income 2000: per capita $16,384; median household $24,627; **Pop below poverty level:** 16.1%. ***Personal per capita income 2000-2003:** $20,107-$21,911.

Unemployment 2004: 5.3%. **Change from 2000:** +1.1%. **Median travel time to work:** 17.9 minutes. **Working outside county of residence:** 25.5%.

Cities with pop over 10,000: None.

BEE COUNTY

105 W Corpus Christi St Rm 103   **Ph:** 361-362-3245
Beeville, TX 78102   **Fax:** 361-362-3247
www.co.bee.tx.us

In southeastern TX, northwest of Corpus Christi; organized Dec 8, 1857 from Goliad and Refugio counties. **Name Origin:** For Barnard E. Bee (1787-1853), TX soldier, statesman, and Minister from TX to the U.S. (1838-41) who opposed the annexation of TX.

Area (sq mi): 880.31 (land 880.14; water 0.17). **Pop per sq mi:** 37.3.

Pop 2005: 32,873. **State rank:** 87. **Pop change:** 2000-20005 +1.6%; 1990-2000 +28.7%. **Pop 2000:** 32,359 (White 35.1%; Black or African American 9.9%; Hispanic or Latino 53.9%; Asian 0.5%; Other 21.7%). **Foreign born:** 2%. **Median age:** 31.8.

Income 2000: per capita $10,625; median household $28,392; **Pop below poverty level:** 24%. ***Personal per capita income 2000-2003:** $14,973-$15,695.

Unemployment 2004: 7.9%. **Change from 2000:** +2.9%. **Median travel time to work:** 24.2 minutes. **Working outside county of residence:** 23.2%.

Cities with pop over 10,000: Beeville ⚏ (13,586).

BELL COUNTY

PO Box 480   **Ph:** 254-933-5160
Belton, TX 76513   **Fax:** 254-933-5176
www.bellcountytx.com

In south-central TX, northeast of Austin; organized Jan 22, 1850 from Bexar County. **Name Origin:** For Peter Hansborough Bell (1812-98), governor of TX (1849-53) and U.S. representative from TX (1853-57).

Bell County (cont'd)

Area (sq mi): 1087.93 (land 1059.72; water 28.21). **Pop per sq mi:** 241.6.

Pop 2005: 256,057. **State rank:** 17. **Pop change:** 2000-20005 +7.6%; 1990-2000 +24.5%. **Pop 2000:** 237,974 (White 57.3%; Black or African American 20.4%; Hispanic or Latino 16.7%; Asian 2.6%; Other 13.6%). **Foreign born:** 7.3%. **Median age:** 29.2.

Income 2000: per capita $17,219; median household $36,872; **Pop below poverty level:** 12.1%. ***Personal per capita income 2000-2003:** $23,776-$26,412.

Unemployment 2004: 5.6%. **Change from 2000:** +1.4%. **Median travel time to work:** 21.1 minutes. **Working outside county of residence:** 11.1%.

Cities with pop over 10,000: Killeen (96,943); Temple (54,505); Harker Heights (20,255); Belton ⬛ (14,838).

BEXAR COUNTY

100 Dolorosa St	**Ph:** 210-335-2011
San Antonio, TX 78205	**Fax:** 210-335-2252
www.bexar.org	

In south-central TX, southwest of Austin; original county, established Mar 17, 1836 (prior to statehood) from Old Mexican Municipality. **Name Origin:** For the Presidio of San Antonio de Bexas (later known as the Alamo), named for the second son of the Duke of Bexar, of the Spanish royal family. Alternate spelling of *Bejar*.

Area (sq mi): 1256.66 (land 1246.82; water 9.84). **Pop per sq mi:** 1217.8.

Pop 2005: 1,518,370. **State rank:** 4. **Pop change:** 2000-20005 +9%; 1990-2000 +17.5%. **Pop 2000:** 1,392,931 (White 35.6%; Black or African American 7.2%; Hispanic or Latino 54.3%; Asian 1.6%; Other 22.3%). **Foreign born:** 10.9%. **Median age:** 32.1.

Income 2000: per capita $18,363; median household $38,328; **Pop below poverty level:** 15.9%. ***Personal per capita income 2000-2003:** $27,322-$27,810.

Unemployment 2004: 5.8%. **Change from 2000:** +1.7%. **Median travel time to work:** 24 minutes. **Working outside county of residence:** 4.3%.

Cities with pop over 10,000: San Antonio ⬛ (123,624); Universal City (15,821); Converse (12,014); Live Oak (10,023).

BLANCO COUNTY

101 E Pecan Dr Po Box 65	**Ph:** 830-868-7357
Johnson City, TX 78636	**Fax:** 830-868-7788
www.co.blanco.tx.us	

In south-central TX, west of Austin; organized Feb 12, 1858 from Gillespie and Comal counties. **Name Origin:** For the Blanco River, which runs through the south of the county; Spanish 'white'; origin uncertain.

Area (sq mi): 713.41 (land 711.24; water 2.16). **Pop per sq mi:** 12.8.

Pop 2005: 9,110. **State rank:** 171. **Pop change:** 2000-20005 +8.2%; 1990-2000 +41%. **Pop 2000:** 8,418 (White 82.1%; Black or African American 0.7%; Hispanic or Latino 15.3%; Asian 0.2%; Other 8.1%). **Foreign born:** 5%. **Median age:** 41.2.

Income 2000: per capita $19,721; median household $39,369; **Pop below poverty level:** 11.2%. ***Personal per capita income 2000-2003:** $25,302-$27,473.

Unemployment 2004: 4.3%. **Change from 2000:** +1.6%. **Median travel time to work:** 31.4 minutes. **Working outside county of residence:** 44%.

Cities with pop over 10,000: None.

BORDEN COUNTY

Po Box 156	**Ph:** 806-756-4391
Gail, TX 79738	**Fax:** 806-756-4405
www.co.borden.tx.us	

In south-central TX panhandle, southeast of Lubbock; organized Aug 21, 1876 from Bexar County. **Name Origin:** For Gail Borden, Jr. (1801-74), surveyor of Austin's colony (1830), publisher, and inventor of food products, including condensed milk.

Area (sq mi): 906.04 (land 898.8; water 7.24). **Pop per sq mi:** 0.7.

Pop 2005: 648. **State rank:** 251. **Pop change:** 2000-20005 -11.1%; 1990-2000 -8.8%. **Pop 2000:** 729 (White 85.6%; Black or African American 0.1%; Hispanic or Latino 11.9%; Asian 0%; Other 9.3%). **Foreign born:** 4.5%. **Median age:** 40.5.

Income 2000: per capita $18,364; median household $29,205; **Pop below poverty level:** 14%. ***Personal per capita income 2000-2003:** $17,792-$26,651.

Unemployment 2004: 3.7%. **Change from 2000:** +1.7%. **Median travel time to work:** 21.4 minutes. **Working outside county of residence:** 47.4%.

Cities with pop over 10,000: None.

BOSQUE COUNTY

PO Box 617	**Ph:** 254-435-2201
Meridian, TX 76665	**Fax:** 254-435-2152
users.htcomp.net/bosque	

In central TX, northwest of Waco; organized Feb 14, 1854 from McLennan County. **Name Origin:** For the N. Bosque River, which runs through it; Spanish 'woods, forest.'

Area (sq mi): 1002.63 (land 989.18; water 13.46). **Pop per sq mi:** 18.3.

Pop 2005: 18,053. **State rank:** 127. **Pop change:** 2000-20005 +4.9%; 1990-2000 +13.7%. **Pop 2000:** 17,204 (White 84.3%; Black or African American 1.9%; Hispanic or Latino 12.2%; Asian 0.1%; Other 7.2%). **Foreign born:** 4.4%. **Median age:** 41.7.

Income 2000: per capita $17,455; median household $34,181; **Pop below poverty level:** 12.7%. ***Personal per capita income 2000-2003:** $21,276-$22,310.

Unemployment 2004: 5.6%. **Change from 2000:** +1.2%. **Median travel time to work:** 31 minutes. **Working outside county of residence:** 44.2%.

Cities with pop over 10,000: None.

BOWIE COUNTY

710 James Bowie Dr	**Ph:** 903-628-2571
New Boston, TX 75570	**Fax:** 903-628-6729
www.co.bowie.tx.us	

On the northeastern border of TX, northwest of Shreveport, LA;

*Source: Personal per capita income data are from the Bureau of Economic Analysis; per capita income data are from the Bureau of the Census. See Introduction for explanation of differences.

Bowie County (cont'd)

organized 1840 (prior to statehood) from Red River County. **Name Origin:** For Col. James A. Bowie (1795-1836), pioneer and officer in the Texas Revolution, killled at the Alamo. The bowie knife is named for him.

Area (sq mi): 922.77 (land 887.87; water 34.9). **Pop per sq mi:** 102.1.

Pop 2005: 90,643. **State rank:** 39. **Pop change:** 2000-20005 +1.5%; 1990-2000 +9.4%. **Pop 2000:** 89,306 (White 70.2%; Black or African American 23.4%; Hispanic or Latino 4.5%; Asian 0.4%; Other 2.8%). **Foreign born:** 1.5%. **Median age:** 36.3.

Income 2000: per capita $17,357; median household $33,001; **Pop below poverty level:** 17.7%. ***Personal per capita income 2000-2003:** $22,795-$24,540.

Unemployment 2004: 6.2%. **Change from 2000:** +1.6%. **Median travel time to work:** 19.9 minutes. **Working outside county of residence:** 20.2%.

Cities with pop over 10,000: Texarkana (35,492).

BRAZORIA COUNTY

111 E Locust St Suite 200   **Ph:** 979-849-5711
Angleton, TX 77515   **Fax:** 979-864-1358
www.brazoria-county.com

On central eastern border of TX, south of Houston; original county; organized Mar 17, 1836 (prior to statehood) from Old Mexican Municipality. **Name Origin:** For the Brazos River, which forms its northern border; a Latinized form of Spanish *brazos* 'arms' or 'forks' as the forks of a river.

Area (sq mi): 1597.44 (land 1386.4; water 211.04). **Pop per sq mi:** 200.9.

Pop 2005: 278,484. **State rank:** 15. **Pop change:** 2000-20005 +15.2%; 1990-2000 +26.1%. **Pop 2000:** 241,767 (White 65.4%; Black or African American 8.5%; Hispanic or Latino 22.8%; Asian 2%; Other 12.3%). **Foreign born:** 8.5%. **Median age:** 34.

Income 2000: per capita $20,021; median household $48,632; **Pop below poverty level:** 10.2%. ***Personal per capita income 2000-2003:** $27,022-$27,985.

Unemployment 2004: 7%. **Change from 2000:** +1.1%. **Median travel time to work:** 28 minutes. **Working outside county of residence:** 40.3%.

Cities with pop over 10,000: 6 (see page 38 for cities).

BRAZOS COUNTY

300 E 26th St Suite 120   **Ph:** 979-361-4135
Bryan, TX 77803   **Fax:** 979-361-4125
www.co.brazos.tx.us

In east-central TX, northwest of Houston; organized Jan 30, 1841 (prior to statehood) from Washington County. **Name Origin:** For the Brazos River, which forms its western border; Spanish 'arms' or 'forks' as forks in a river.

Area (sq mi): 590.29 (land 585.78; water 4.51). **Pop per sq mi:** 266.8.

Pop 2005: 156,305. **State rank:** 23. **Pop change:** 2000-20005 +2.6%; 1990-2000 +25.1%. **Pop 2000:** 152,415 (White 66%; Black

or African American 10.7%; Hispanic or Latino 17.9%; Asian 4%; Other 10.9%). **Foreign born:** 10.3%. **Median age:** 23.6.

Income 2000: per capita $16,212; median household $29,104; **Pop below poverty level:** 26.9%. ***Personal per capita income 2000-2003:** $19,709-$21,741.

Unemployment 2004: 4.3%. **Change from 2000:** +2.7%. **Median travel time to work:** 16.7 minutes. **Working outside county of residence:** 7%.

Cities with pop over 10,000: College Station (72,186); Bryan 🏛 (66,316).

BREWSTER COUNTY

201 W Ave E   **Ph:** 432-837-3366
Alpine, TX 79830   **Fax:** 432-837-6217
www.co.brewster.tx.us

On southwestern border of TX, southwest of Odessa; organized Feb 2, 1887 from Presidio County. **Name Origin:** For Henry Percy Brewster (1816-84), TX soldier, secretary to Sam Houston (1836), and attorney general of TX (1847-49).

Area (sq mi): 6192.78 (land 6192.61; water 0.18). **Pop per sq mi:** 1.5.

Pop 2005: 9,079. **State rank:** 173. **Pop change:** 2000-20005 +2.4%; 1990-2000 +2.1%. **Pop 2000:** 8,866 (White 53.1%; Black or African American 1.2%; Hispanic or Latino 43.6%; Asian 0.4%; Other 17.3%). **Foreign born:** 6.9%. **Median age:** 36.2.

Income 2000: per capita $15,183; median household $27,386; **Pop below poverty level:** 18.2%. ***Personal per capita income 2000-2003:** $21,674-$23,440.

Unemployment 2004: 4.2%. **Change from 2000:** +2%. **Median travel time to work:** 12.6 minutes. **Working outside county of residence:** 8.4%.

Cities with pop over 10,000: None.

BRISCOE COUNTY

PO Box 555   **Ph:** 806-823-2134
Silverton, TX 79257   **Fax:** 806-823-2359
www.co.briscoe.tx.us

In the central TX panhandle, southeast of Amarillo; organized Aug 21, 1876 from Bexar County. **Name Origin:** For Capt. Andrew Briscoe (1810-49), Republic of TX officer, signer of the TX Declaration of Independence (1836), and chief justice of Harrisburg, TX (1836-39).

Area (sq mi): 901.59 (land 900.25; water 1.33). **Pop per sq mi:** 1.8.

Pop 2005: 1,644. **State rank:** 240. **Pop change:** 2000-20005 -8.2%; 1990-2000 -9.2%. **Pop 2000:** 1,790 (White 73.7%; Black or African American 2.3%; Hispanic or Latino 22.7%; Asian 0.1%; Other 14.4%). **Foreign born:** 4.9%. **Median age:** 39.9.

Income 2000: per capita $14,218; median household $29,917; **Pop below poverty level:** 16%. ***Personal per capita income 2000-2003:** $20,669-$21,626.

Unemployment 2004: 6.1%. **Change from 2000:** +3.4%. **Median travel time to work:** 18.8 minutes. **Working outside county of residence:** 29.4%.

Cities with pop over 10,000: None.

🏛 *County Seat*

BROOKS COUNTY
PO Box 427
Falfurrias, TX 78355

Ph: 361-325-5604
Fax: 361-325-4944

In southeastern TX, southwest of Corpus Christi; organized Mar 11, 1911 from Starr and Zapata counties. **Name Origin:** For James Abijah Brooks (1855-1944), TX legislator, ranger (1882-1906), and judge of Brooks County (1911-39).

Area (sq mi): 943.61 (land 943.28; water 0.33). **Pop per sq mi:** 8.1.

Pop 2005: 7,687. **State rank:** 181. **Pop change:** 2000-20005 -3.6%; 1990-2000 -2.8%. **Pop 2000:** 7,976 (White 7.9%; Black or African American 0.2%; Hispanic or Latino 91.6%; Asian 0.1%; Other 24%). **Foreign born:** 6.1%. **Median age:** 34.4.

Income 2000: per capita $10,234; median household $18,622; **Pop below poverty level:** 40.2%. ***Personal per capita income 2000-2003:** $14,876-$16,573.

Unemployment 2004: 7.9%. **Change from 2000:** +2.2%. **Median travel time to work:** 18.3 minutes. **Working outside county of residence:** 23.1%.

Cities with pop over 10,000: None.

BROWN COUNTY
200 S Broadway
Brownwood, TX 76801

Ph: 325-643-2594

In central TX, southeast of Abilene; organized Aug 27, 1856 from Caldwell County. **Name Origin:** For Henry Stevenson Brown (1793-1834), Republic of TX soldier and delegate to the TX convention (1832-33).

Area (sq mi): 956.94 (land 943.85; water 13.08). **Pop per sq mi:** 41.

Pop 2005: 38,664. **State rank:** 75. **Pop change:** 2000-20005 +2.6%; 1990-2000 +9.6%. **Pop 2000:** 37,674 (White 79%; Black or African American 4%; Hispanic or Latino 15.4%; Asian 0.4%; Other 8.3%). **Foreign born:** 3.1%. **Median age:** 37.2.

Income 2000: per capita $15,624; median household $30,974; **Pop below poverty level:** 17.2%. ***Personal per capita income 2000-2003:** $20,305-$21,376.

Unemployment 2004: 5.5%. **Change from 2000:** +1.8%. **Median travel time to work:** 19.5 minutes. **Working outside county of residence:** 7.6%.

Cities with pop over 10,000: Brownwood ⚖ (19,467).

BURLESON COUNTY
100 W Buck St Suite 203
Caldwell, TX 77836
www.co.burleson.tx.us

Ph: 979-567-2329
Fax: 979-567-2376

In east-central TX, northeast of Austin; organized Mar 24, 1846 from Milam and Washington counties. **Name Origin:** For Gen. Edward Burleston (1798-1852), senator in the first TX congress (1836), vice president of the Republic of TX (1841), and TX legislator.

Area (sq mi): 677.78 (land 665.54; water 12.24). **Pop per sq mi:** 25.9.

Pop 2005: 17,238. **State rank:** 130. **Pop change:** 2000-20005 +4.7%; 1990-2000 +20.9%. **Pop 2000:** 16,470 (White 69%; Black or African American 15.1%; Hispanic or Latino 14.6%; Asian 0.2%; Other 10.7%). **Foreign born:** 3%. **Median age:** 37.9.

Income 2000: per capita $16,616; median household $33,026; **Pop below poverty level:** 17.2%. ***Personal per capita income 2000-2003:** $21,126-$22,116.

Unemployment 2004: 5.5%. **Change from 2000:** +2.6%. **Median travel time to work:** 28.3 minutes. **Working outside county of residence:** 52.9%.

Cities with pop over 10,000: None.

BURNET COUNTY
220 S Pierce St
Burnet, TX 78611
www.burnetcountytexas.org

Ph: 512-756-5420
Fax: 512-756-5410

In central TX, northwest of Austin; organized Feb 5, 1852 from Travis County. **Name Origin:** For David Gouverneur Burnet (1778-1870), president of the Republic of TX (1836) and vice president (1838-41).

Area (sq mi): 1020.96 (land 996.04; water 24.93). **Pop per sq mi:** 41.8.

Pop 2005: 41,676. **State rank:** 70. **Pop change:** 2000-20005 +22%; 1990-2000 +50.6%. **Pop 2000:** 34,147 (White 82%; Black or African American 1.5%; Hispanic or Latino 14.8%; Asian 0.3%; Other 8.6%). **Foreign born:** 5.4%. **Median age:** 40.2.

Income 2000: per capita $18,850; median household $37,921; **Pop below poverty level:** 10.9%. ***Personal per capita income 2000-2003:** $24,319-$26,099.

Unemployment 2004: 4.6%. **Change from 2000:** +0.9%. **Median travel time to work:** 28.8 minutes. **Working outside county of residence:** 35.1%.

Cities with pop over 10,000: None.

CALDWELL COUNTY
110 S Main St
Lockhart, TX 78644
www.co.caldwell.tx.us

Ph: 512-398-1824
Fax: 512-398-1816

In east-central TX, south of Austin; organized Mar 6, 1848 from Gonzales County. **Name Origin:** For Matthew 'Old Paint' Caldwell (1798-1842), TX ranger, soldier, and a signer of the TX Declaration of Independence (1836).

Area (sq mi): 547.41 (land 545.73; water 1.69). **Pop per sq mi:** 66.9.

Pop 2005: 36,523. **State rank:** 79. **Pop change:** 2000-20005 +13.4%; 1990-2000 +22%. **Pop 2000:** 32,194 (White 49.5%; Black or African American 8.5%; Hispanic or Latino 40.4%; Asian 0.3%; Other 21%). **Foreign born:** 5.1%. **Median age:** 34.4.

Income 2000: per capita $15,099; median household $36,573; **Pop below poverty level:** 13.1%. ***Personal per capita income 2000-2003:** $19,778-$20,175.

Unemployment 2004: 6.3%. **Change from 2000:** +2.1%. **Median travel time to work:** 31.4 minutes. **Working outside county of residence:** 62.8%.

Cities with pop over 10,000: Lockhart ⚖ (13,523).

*Source: Personal per capita income data are from the Bureau of Economic Analysis; per capita income data are from the Bureau of the Census. See Introduction for explanation of differences.

CALHOUN COUNTY
211 S Ann St   **Ph:** 361-553-4411
Port Lavaca, TX 77979   **Fax:** 361-553-4420
www.tisd.net/~calhoun/

On the central eastern coast of TX, northeast of Corpus Christi; organized Apr 4, 1846 from Victoria County. **Name Origin:** For John Caldwell Calhoun (1782-1850), U.S. statesman and champion of Southern causes.

Area (sq mi): 1032.16 (land 512.31; water 519.84). **Pop per sq mi:** 40.2.

Pop 2005: 20,606. **State rank:** 113. **Pop change:** 2000-20005 -0.2%; 1990-2000 +8.4%. **Pop 2000:** 20,647 (White 52.2%; Black or African American 2.6%; Hispanic or Latino 40.9%; Asian 3.3%; Other 16.1%). **Foreign born:** 8.5%. **Median age:** 35.3.

Income 2000: per capita $17,125; median household $35,849; **Pop below poverty level:** 16.4%. ***Personal per capita income 2000-2003:** $21,048-$22,351.

Unemployment 2004: 7.5%. **Change from 2000:** -0.4%. **Median travel time to work:** 19.6 minutes. **Working outside county of residence:** 16.3%.

Cities with pop over 10,000: Port Lavaca ⛪ (11,759).

CALLAHAN COUNTY
100 W 4th St   **Ph:** 325-854-1155
Baird, TX 79504   **Fax:** 325-854-1227
www.co.callahan.tx.us

In north-central TX, east of Abilene; established Apr 1, 1858 from Milam and Travis counties. **Name Origin:** For James Hughes Callahan (1814-1856), soldier and Texas ranger; killed by Indians.

Area (sq mi): 901.26 (land 898.62; water 2.64). **Pop per sq mi:** 15.

Pop 2005: 13,516. **State rank:** 148. **Pop change:** 2000-20005 +4.7%; 1990-2000 +8.8%. **Pop 2000:** 12,905 (White 91.6%; Black or African American 0.2%; Hispanic or Latino 6.3%; Asian 0.3%; Other 4.7%). **Foreign born:** 1.4%. **Median age:** 39.8.

Income 2000: per capita $15,204; median household $32,463; **Pop below poverty level:** 12.2%. ***Personal per capita income 2000-2003:** $20,541-$22,145.

Unemployment 2004: 4.7%. **Change from 2000:** +1%. **Median travel time to work:** 24.3 minutes. **Working outside county of residence:** 62.3%.

Cities with pop over 10,000: None.

CAMERON COUNTY
964 E Harrison St   **Ph:** 956-544-0815
Brownsville, TX 78520   **Fax:** 956-544-0813
www.co.cameron.tx.us

On the southeastern coast of TX, east of McAllen; organized Feb 12, 1848 from Nueces County. **Name Origin:** For Capt. Ewin Cameron (1811-43), a Republic of TX soldier, executed by the Mexicans.

Area (sq mi): 1276.33 (land 905.76; water 370.58). **Pop per sq mi:** 417.7.

Pop 2005: 378,311. **State rank:** 11. **Pop change:** 2000-20005 +12.9%; 1990-2000 +28.9%. **Pop 2000:** 335,227 (White 14.5%; Black or African American 0.5%; Hispanic or Latino 84.3%; Asian 0.5%; Other 18.7%). **Foreign born:** 25.6%. **Median age:** 29.

Income 2000: per capita $10,960; median household $26,155; **Pop below poverty level:** 33.1%. ***Personal per capita income 2000-2003:** $14,913-$16,308.

Unemployment 2004: 8.8%. **Change from 2000:** -0.4%. **Median travel time to work:** 20.7 minutes. **Working outside county of residence:** 8.8%.

Cities with pop over 10,000: Brownsville ⛪ (161,225); Harlingen (61,509), San Benito (24,387).

CAMP COUNTY
126 Church St   **Ph:** 903-856-2731
Pittsburg, TX 75686   **Fax:** 903-856-2309
www.co.camp.tx.us

In northeastern TX, southwest of Texarkana; organized Apr 6, 1874 from Upshur County. **Name Origin:** For Col. John Lafayette Camp (1828-91), officer in the Confederate army, TX legislator (1874), and district judge (1878).

Area (sq mi): 203.2 (land 197.51; water 5.69). **Pop per sq mi:** 62.

Pop 2005: 12,238. **State rank:** 155. **Pop change:** 2000-20005 +6%; 1990-2000 +16.6%. **Pop 2000:** 11,549 (White 65%; Black or African American 19.2%; Hispanic or Latino 14.8%; Asian 0.2%; Other 11.1%). **Foreign born:** 9.9%. **Median age:** 36.9.

Income 2000: per capita $16,500; median household $31,164; **Pop below poverty level:** 20.9%. ***Personal per capita income 2000-2003:** $24,893-$26,725.

Unemployment 2004: 5.7%. **Change from 2000:** +0.5%. **Median travel time to work:** 22.1 minutes. **Working outside county of residence:** 40.6%.

Cities with pop over 10,000: None.

CARSON COUNTY
PO Box 487   **Ph:** 806-537-3873
Panhandle, TX 79068   **Fax:** 806-537-3623
www.co.carson.tx.us

In the north-central TX panhandle, east of Amarillo; organized Aug 21, 1876 from Bexar County. **Name Origin:** For Samuel Price Carson (1798-1838), signer of the TX Declaration of Independence (1836) and secretary of state of the Republic of TX (1836-38).

Area (sq mi): 924.1 (land 923.19; water 0.91). **Pop per sq mi:** 7.1.

Pop 2005: 6,586. **State rank:** 192. **Pop change:** 2000-20005 +1.1%; 1990-2000 -0.9%. **Pop 2000:** 6,516 (White 90.6%; Black or African American 0.6%; Hispanic or Latino 7%; Asian 0.1%; Other 5.4%, including 1% American Indian/Alaska Native). **Foreign born:** 2.7%. **Median age:** 38.9.

Income 2000: per capita $19,368; median household $40,285; **Pop below poverty level:** 7.3%. ***Personal per capita income 2000-2003:** $26,917-$24,829.

Unemployment 2004: 4.2%. **Change from 2000:** +1.4%. **Median travel time to work:** 21.4 minutes. **Working outside county of residence:** 57.4%.

Cities with pop over 10,000: None.

⛪ *County Seat*

CASS COUNTY

PO Box 449   **Ph:** 903-756-5071
Linden, TX 75563   **Fax:** 903-756-8057
www.co.cass.tx.us

On northeastern border of TX, south of Texarkana. The area now called Cass Co. has had five names and boundaries: (1) 1924-36, under Mexican rule, part of Paschal Co.; (2) 1836-41 part of Red River Co.; (3) 1841-46 part of Bowie Co.; (4) 1846-60 Cass Co. included Marion Co.; (5) name changed in 1861 to Davis to honor Jeff Davis; name changed back in 1871. **Name Origin:** For Gen. Lewis Cass (1782-1866), OH legislator, military and civil governor of MI Territory (1813-30), U.S. secretary of war (1831-36), and U.S. secretary of state (1857-60).

Area (sq mi): 960.35 (land 937.35; water 22.99). **Pop per sq mi:** 32.2.

Pop 2005: 30,155. **State rank:** 91. **Pop change:** 2000-20005 -0.9%; 1990-2000 +1.5%. **Pop 2000:** 30,438 (White 77.3%; Black or African American 19.5%; Hispanic or Latino 1.7%; Asian 0.1%; Other 2.2%). **Foreign born:** 1.1%. **Median age:** 40.

Income 2000: per capita $15,777; median household $28,441; **Pop below poverty level:** 17.7%. ***Personal per capita income 2000-2003:** $20,991-$22,234.

Unemployment 2004: 7.2%. **Change from 2000:** +1.2%. **Median travel time to work:** 27.1 minutes. **Working outside county of residence:** 39.9%.

Cities with pop over 10,000: None.

CASTRO COUNTY

100 E Bedford St   **Ph:** 806-647-3338
Dimmitt, TX 79027   **Fax:** 806-647-5438
www.co.castro.tx.us

In the west-central panhandle, southwest of Amarillo; organized Aug 21, 1876 from Wheeler County. **Name Origin:** For Henri Castro (1786-1865), who established a colony in the Republic of TX (1842). Consul general of TX to France (1842).

Area (sq mi): 899.32 (land 898.31; water 1). **Pop per sq mi:** 8.5.

Pop 2005: 7,640. **State rank:** 183. **Pop change:** 2000-20005 -7.8%; 1990-2000 -8.7%. **Pop 2000:** 8,285 (White 45.4%; Black or African American 2.3%; Hispanic or Latino 51.6%; Asian 0%; Other 22.4%, including 1.2% American Indian/Alaska Native). **Foreign born:** 12.1%. **Median age:** 32.3.

Income 2000: per capita $14,457; median household $30,619; **Pop below poverty level:** 19%. ***Personal per capita income 2000-2003:** $29,328-$42,430.

Unemployment 2004: 5.5%. **Change from 2000:** +1.4%. **Median travel time to work:** 15.5 minutes. **Working outside county of residence:** 23.6%.

Cities with pop over 10,000: None.

CHAMBERS COUNTY

404 Washington Ave   **Ph:** 409-267-8309
Anahuac, TX 77514   **Fax:** 409-267-8315
www.co.chambers.tx.us

On the central eastern coast of TX, east of Houston; organized Feb 12, 1858 from Jefferson and Liberty counties. **Name Origin:** For Gen. Thomas Jefferson Chambers (1802-65), surveyor general of TX (1829), attorney, and member of secession convention (1861).

Area (sq mi): 871.99 (land 599.31; water 272.68). **Pop per sq mi:** 47.4.

Pop 2005: 28,411. **State rank:** 94. **Pop change:** 2000-20005 +9.1%; 1990-2000 +29.6%. **Pop 2000:** 26,031 (White 77.6%; Black or African American 9.8%; Hispanic or Latino 10.8%; Asian 0.7%; Other 7.7%). **Foreign born:** 5.1%. **Median age:** 35.1.

Income 2000: per capita $19,863; median household $47,964; **Pop below poverty level:** 11%. ***Personal per capita income 2000-2003:** $27,629-$28,470.

Unemployment 2004: 5.9%. **Change from 2000:** +1.4%. **Median travel time to work:** 25.7 minutes. **Working outside county of residence:** 60.2%.

Cities with pop over 10,000: None.

CHEROKEE COUNTY

PO Box 420   **Ph:** 903-683-2350
Rusk, TX 75785   **Fax:** 903-683-5931
www.co.cherokee.tx.us

In northeastern TX, south of Tyler; organized Apr 11, 1846 from Nacogdoches County. **Name Origin:** For the Indian tribe of Iroquoian linguistic stock. Name may derive from Creek *tciloki* 'people of a different speech.'

Area (sq mi): 1061.93 (land 1052.22; water 9.72). **Pop per sq mi:** 46.1.

Pop 2005: 48,464. **State rank:** 62. **Pop change:** 2000-20005 +3.9%; 1990-2000 +13.7%. **Pop 2000:** 46,659 (White 69.3%; Black or African American 16%; Hispanic or Latino 13.2%; Asian 0.4%; Other 9.3%). **Foreign born:** 7.9%. **Median age:** 36.

Income 2000: per capita $13,980; median household $29,313; **Pop below poverty level:** 17.9%. ***Personal per capita income 2000-2003:** $22,165-$24,341.

Unemployment 2004: 5.6%. **Change from 2000:** +1.3%. **Median travel time to work:** 23.8 minutes. **Working outside county of residence:** 26.7%.

Cities with pop over 10,000: Jacksonville (14,138).

CHILDRESS COUNTY

Courthouse Box 4   **Ph:** 940-937-6143
Childress, TX 79201   **Fax:** 940-937-3479
www.co.childress.tx.us

On the southeastern border of TX panhandle, northeast of Lubbock; established Aug 21, 1876 from Bexar and Fannin counties. **Name Origin:** For George Campbell Childress (1804-41), one of the drafters of the Texas Declaration of Independence.

Area (sq mi): 713.61 (land 710.34; water 3.27). **Pop per sq mi:** 10.8.

Pop 2005: 7,676. **State rank:** 182. **Pop change:** 2000-20005 -0.2%; 1990-2000 +29.1%. **Pop 2000:** 7,688 (White 64%; Black or African American 14.1%; Hispanic or Latino 20.5%; Asian 0.3%; Other 17.9%). **Foreign born:** 4.7%. **Median age:** 36.6.

Income 2000: per capita $12,452; median household $27,457; **Pop below poverty level:** 17.6%. ***Personal per capita income 2000-2003:** $15,378-$16,747.

*Source: Personal per capita income data are from the Bureau of Economic Analysis; per capita income data are from the Bureau of the Census. See Introduction for explanation of differences.

Childress County (cont'd)

Unemployment 2004: 5.7%. **Change from 2000:** +2.8%. **Median travel time to work:** 10.8 minutes. **Working outside county of residence:** 7.7%.

Cities with pop over 10,000: None.

CLAY COUNTY
PO Box 548   **Ph:** 940-538-4631
Henrietta, TX 76365   **Fax:** 940-538-5597
www.co.clay.tx.us

On the central northern border of TX, east of Wichita Falls; organized Dec 24, 1857 from Cooke County. **Name Origin:** For Henry Clay (1777-1852), U.S. senator from KY, known as the 'Great Pacificator' for his advocacy of compromise to avert national crises.

Area (sq mi): 1116.17 (land 1097.82; water 18.36). **Pop per sq mi:** 10.3.

Pop 2005: 11,287. **State rank:** 160. **Pop change:** 2000-20005 +2.6%; 1990-2000 +9.8%. **Pop 2000:** 11,006 (White 93.7%; Black or African American 0.4%; Hispanic or Latino 3.7%; Asian 0.1%; Other 4.1%, Including 1% American Indian/Alaska Native). **Foreign born:** 1.4%. **Median age:** 40.2.

Income 2000: per capita $16,361; median household $35,738; **Pop below poverty level:** 10.3%. ***Personal per capita income 2000-2003:** $21,173-$24,088.

Unemployment 2004: 4%. **Change from 2000:** +1.6%. **Median travel time to work:** 26.6 minutes. **Working outside county of residence:** 64.6%.

Cities with pop over 10,000: None.

COCHRAN COUNTY
County Courthouse Rm 102   **Ph:** 806-266-5450
Morton, TX 79346   **Fax:** 806-266-9027
www.co.cochran.tx.us

On the central western border of TX panhandle, west of Lubbock; organized Aug 21, 1876 from Bexar County. **Name Origin:** For Robert Cochran (?-1836), a soldier killed at the Alamo.

Area (sq mi): 775.31 (land 775.22; water 0.09). **Pop per sq mi:** 4.2.

Pop 2005: 3,289. **State rank:** 222. **Pop change:** 2000-20005 -11.8%; 1990-2000 -14.8%. **Pop 2000:** 3,730 (White 50%; Black or African American 4.5%; Hispanic or Latino 44.1%; Asian 0.2%; Other 30.7%). **Foreign born:** 9.8%. **Median age:** 35.1.

Income 2000: per capita $13,125; median household $27,525; **Pop below poverty level:** 27%. ***Personal per capita income 2000-2003:** $20,347-$23,034.

Unemployment 2004: 7.3%. **Change from 2000:** +0.8%. **Median travel time to work:** 18.5 minutes. **Working outside county of residence:** 27.7%.

Cities with pop over 10,000: None.

COKE COUNTY
PO Box 150   **Ph:** 325-453-2631
Robert Lee, TX 76945   **Fax:** 325-453-2650
www.co.coke.tx.us

In central TX, southwest of Abilene; organized Mar 13, 1889 from Tom Green County. **Name Origin:** For Capt. Richard Coke (1829-97), Confederate Army officer, TX governor (1874-76), and U.S. senator (1876-94).

Area (sq mi): 927.97 (land 898.81; water 29.17). **Pop per sq mi:** 4.

Pop 2005: 3,612. **State rank:** 218. **Pop change:** 2000-20005 -6.5%; 1990-2000 +12.9%. **Pop 2000:** 3,864 (White 79.7%; Black or African American 1.9%; Hispanic or Latino 16.9%; Asian 0.1%; Other 0.1%). **Foreign born:** 2.8%. **Median age:** 43.3.

Income 2000: per capita $16,734; median household $29,085; **Pop below poverty level:** 13%. ***Personal per capita income 2000-2003:** $18,319-$19,023.

Unemployment 2004: 5.5%. **Change from 2000:** +3.6%. **Median travel time to work:** 23.8 minutes. **Working outside county of residence:** 37.1%.

Cities with pop over 10,000: None.

COLEMAN COUNTY
PO Box 591   **Ph:** 325-625-2889
Coleman, TX 76834
www.co.coleman.tx.us

In central TX, southeast of Abilene; organized Feb 1, 1858 from Travis County. **Name Origin:** For Col. Robert M. Coleman (1799-1837), one of the signers of the TX Declaration of Independence.

Area (sq mi): 1281.45 (land 1260.2; water 21.25). **Pop per sq mi:** 6.9.

Pop 2005: 8,665. **State rank:** 176. **Pop change:** 2000-20005 -6.2%; 1990-2000 -4.9%. **Pop 2000:** 9,235 (White 82.3%; Black or African American 2.2%; Hispanic or Latino 14%; Asian 0.2%; Other 9%). **Foreign born:** 3.4%. **Median age:** 43.

Income 2000: per capita $14,911; median household $25,658; **Pop below poverty level:** 19.9%. ***Personal per capita income 2000-2003:** $20,062-$20,875.

Unemployment 2004: 5.7%. **Change from 2000:** +0.9%. **Median travel time to work:** 23.3 minutes. **Working outside county of residence:** 23.6%.

Cities with pop over 10,000: None.

COLLIN COUNTY
200 S McDonald St Suite 120   **Ph:** 972-548-4134
McKinney, TX 75069   **Fax:** 972-547-5731
www.co.collin.tx.us

In east-central TX, north of Dallas; organized Apr 3, 1846 from Fannin County. **Name Origin:** For Collin McKinney (1766-1861), Republic of TX legislator and a noted signer of the TX Declaration of Independence (1836).

Area (sq mi): 885.85 (land 847.56; water 38.29). **Pop per sq mi:** 778.1.

Pop 2005: 659,457. **State rank:** 8. **Pop change:** 2000-20005 +34.1%; 1990-2000 +86.2%. **Pop 2000:** 491,675 (White 76.1%; Black or African American 4.8%; Hispanic or Latino 10.3%; Asian 6.9%; Other 6.9%). **Foreign born:** 13.3%. **Median age:** 32.9.

Income 2000: per capita $33,345; median household $70,835; **Pop below poverty level:** 4.9%. ***Personal per capita income 2000-2003:** $45,404-$39,941.

Collin County (cont'd)

Unemployment 2004: 4.8%. **Change from 2000:** +0.7%. **Median travel time to work:** 28.4 minutes. **Working outside county of residence:** 51.3%.

Cities with pop over 10,000: 6 (see page 38 for cities).

COLLINGSWORTH COUNTY

800 West Ave County Courthouse Box 10   **Ph:** 806-447-2408
Wellington, TX 79095   **Fax:** 806-447-2409
www.co.collingsworth.tx.us

On the southeastern border of TX panhandle, southwest of Amarillo; organized Aug 21, 1876 from Bexar and Fannin counties. **Name Origin:** For Maj. James T. Collinsworth (1806-38), aide to Gen. Sam Houston (1793-1863), Republic of TX senator (1836), and first chief justice (1837). Clerical spelling error was allowed to stand.

Area (sq mi): 919.44 (land 918.8; water 0.64). **Pop per sq mi:** 3.2.

Pop 2005: 2,968. **State rank:** 229. **Pop change:** 2000-20005 -7.4%; 1990-2000 -10.3%. **Pop 2000:** 3,206 (White 71.4%; Black or African American 5.3%; Hispanic or Latino 20.4%; Asian 0.2%; Other 14.7%, including 1.6% American Indian/Alaska Native). **Foreign born:** 4.3%. **Median age:** 40.6.

Income 2000: per capita $15,318; median household $25,438; **Pop below poverty level:** 18.7%. *****Personal per capita income 2000-2003:** $22,905-$28,636.

Unemployment 2004: 5.1%. **Change from 2000:** +4%. **Median travel time to work:** 14.8 minutes. **Working outside county of residence:** 20.5%.

Cities with pop over 10,000: None.

COLORADO COUNTY

PO Box 68   **Ph:** 979-732-2155
Columbus, TX 78934   **Fax:** 979-732-8852
www.co.colorado.tx.us

In east-central TX, west of Houston; original county; organized Mar 17, 1836 (prior to statehood) from Old Mexican Municipality. **Name Origin:** For the Colorado River, which flows through it; Spanish 'reddish brown' for the color of its waters from the soil and rocks on its banks.

Area (sq mi): 973.59 (land 962.95; water 10.64). **Pop per sq mi:** 21.5.

Pop 2005: 20,736. **State rank:** 111. **Pop change:** 2000-20005 +1.7%; 1990-2000 +10.9%. **Pop 2000:** 20,390 (White 64.6%; Black or African American 14.8%; Hispanic or Latino 19.7%; Asian 0.2%; Other 12.2%). **Foreign born:** 7.9%. **Median age:** 39.3.

Income 2000: per capita $16,910; median household $32,425; **Pop below poverty level:** 16.2%. *****Personal per capita income 2000-2003:** $23,550-$24,243.

Unemployment 2004: 5.1%. **Change from 2000:** +1.3%. **Median travel time to work:** 26.2 minutes. **Working outside county of residence:** 28.8%.

Cities with pop over 10,000: None.

COMAL COUNTY

150 N Seguin St   **Ph:** 830-620-5513
New Braunfels, TX 78130   **Fax:** 830-620-3410
www.co.comal.tx.us

In south-central TX, north of San Antonio; organized Mar 24, 1846 from Bexar and Gonzales counties. **Name Origin:** From Spanish 'basin,' descriptive of an area drained by a stream.

Area (sq mi): 574.59 (land 561.45; water 13.15). **Pop per sq mi:** 171.

Pop 2005: 96,018. **State rank:** 38. **Pop change:** 2000-20005 +23.1%; 1990-2000 +50.5%. **Pop 2000:** 78,021 (White 74.8%; Black or African American 0.9%; Hispanic or Latino 22.6%; Asian 0.5%; Other 9.5%). **Foreign born:** 4.8%. **Median age:** 39.

Income 2000: per capita $21,914; median household $46,147; **Pop below poverty level:** 8.6%. *****Personal per capita income 2000-2003:** $29,133-$29,486.

Unemployment 2004: 5.1%. **Change from 2000:** +1.6%. **Median travel time to work:** 28.2 minutes. **Working outside county of residence:** 45.9%.

Cities with pop over 10,000: New Braunfels 🏛 (44,931).

COMANCHE COUNTY

County Courthouse 101 W Central Ave   **Ph:** 325-356-2655
Comanche, TX 76442   **Fax:** 325-356-5764

In central TX, southeast of Abilene; organized Jan 25, 1856 from Bosque and Coryell counties. **Name Origin:** For an Indian tribe of Shoshonean linguistic stock; the meaning of the name is unknown.

Area (sq mi): 947.67 (land 937.69; water 9.98). **Pop per sq mi:** 14.6.

Pop 2005: 13,709. **State rank:** 146. **Pop change:** 2000-20005 -2.3%; 1990-2000 +4.8%. **Pop 2000:** 14,026 (White 77.3%; Black or African American 0.4%; Hispanic or Latino 20.9%; Asian 0.1%; Other 12.1%). **Foreign born:** 7.1%. **Median age:** 40.3.

Income 2000: per capita $14,677; median household $28,422; **Pop below poverty level:** 17.3%. *****Personal per capita income 2000-2003:** $20,535-$23,477.

Unemployment 2004: 5%. **Change from 2000:** +2.3%. **Median travel time to work:** 22.2 minutes. **Working outside county of residence:** 29.7%.

Cities with pop over 10,000: None.

CONCHO COUNTY

PO Box 98   **Ph:** 325-732-4322
Paint Rock, TX 76866   **Fax:** 325-732-2040
www.co.concho.tx.us

In central TX, east of San Angelo; organized Feb 1, 1858 from Bexar County. **Name Origin:** For the Concho River, which runs through it; from the Indian tribal name.

Area (sq mi): 993.69 (land 991.45; water 2.23). **Pop per sq mi:** 3.8.

Pop 2005: 3,735. **State rank:** 216. **Pop change:** 2000-20005 -5.8%; 1990-2000 +30.3%. **Pop 2000:** 3,966 (White 57.1%; Black or African American 1%; Hispanic or Latino 41.3%; Asian 0.1%; Other 10.7%). **Foreign born:** 2.8%. **Median age:** 36.

Income 2000: per capita $15,727; median household $31,313; **Pop below poverty level:** 11.9%. *****Personal per capita income 2000-2003:** $14,520-$16,529.

*Source: Personal per capita income data are from the Bureau of Economic Analysis; per capita income data are from the Bureau of the Census. See Introduction for explanation of differences.

670

Concho County (cont'd)

Unemployment 2004: 6.4%. **Change from 2000:** +4.5%. **Median travel time to work:** 20.6 minutes. **Working outside county of residence:** 29%.

Cities with pop over 10,000: None.

COOKE COUNTY

100 S Dixon St   **Ph:** 940-668-5420
Gainesville, TX 76240   **Fax:** 940-668-5440
www.co.cooke.tx.us

On the central northern border of TX, north of Fort Worth; organized Mar 20, 1848 from Fannin County. **Name Origin:** For Capt. William G. Cooke (1808-47), officer in the Texas War for Independence and quartermaster general (1839).

Area (sq mi): 898.81 (land 873.64; water 25.17). **Pop per sq mi:** 44.5.

Pop 2005: 38,847. **State rank:** 74. **Pop change:** 2000-20005 +6.8%; 1990-2000 +18.1%. **Pop 2000:** 36,363 (White 84.8%; Black or African American 3.1%; Hispanic or Latino 10%; Asian 0.3%; Other 7.8%, including 1% American Indian/Alaska Native). **Foreign born:** 5.5%. **Median age:** 36.7.

Income 2000: per capita $17,889; median household $37,649; **Pop below poverty level:** 14.1%. ***Personal per capita income 2000-2003:** $24,160-$25,560.

Unemployment 2004: 4.9%. **Change from 2000:** +0.2%. **Median travel time to work:** 25.7 minutes. **Working outside county of residence:** 33.7%.

Cities with pop over 10,000: Gainesville ⛪ (16,361).

CORYELL COUNTY

620 E Main St PO Box 237   **Ph:** 254-865-5911
Gatesville, TX 76528   **Fax:** 254-865-8631
www.co.coryell.tx.us

In east-central TX, west of Waco; organized Feb 4, 1854 from Bell and McLennan counties. **Name Origin:** For James Coryell (1801-37), a Texas ranger killed by Indians.

Area (sq mi): 1056.73 (land 1051.76; water 4.97). **Pop per sq mi:** 72.1.

Pop 2005: 75,802. **State rank:** 46. **Pop change:** 2000-20005 +1.1%; 1990-2000 +16.8%. **Pop 2000:** 74,978 (White 60.5%; Black or African American 21.8%; Hispanic or Latino 12.6%; Asian 1.8%; Other 11.2%). **Foreign born:** 5.3%. **Median age:** 27.8.

Income 2000: per capita $14,410; median household $35,999; **Pop below poverty level:** 9.5%. ***Personal per capita income 2000-2003:** $18,268-$20,389.

Unemployment 2004: 6.8%. **Change from 2000:** +1.9%. **Median travel time to work:** 21 minutes. **Working outside county of residence:** 69.7%.

Cities with pop over 10,000: Copperas Cove (29,997); Gatesville ⛪ (15,732).

COTTLE COUNTY

PO Box 717   **Ph:** 806-492-3823
Paducah, TX 79248   **Fax:** 806-492-2625
www.co.cottle.tx.us

In the southeastern TX panhandle, west of Wichita Falls; organized 1892 from Childress County (other sources say organized Aug 21, 1876; first federal census: 1880). **Name Origin:** For Pvt. George Washington Cottle (1798-1836), killed at the Alamo.

Area (sq mi): 901.59 (land 901.18; water 0.42). **Pop per sq mi:** 1.9.

Pop 2005: 1,746. **State rank:** 239. **Pop change:** 2000-20005 -8.3%; 1990-2000 -15.3%. **Pop 2000:** 1,904 (White 70.8%; Black or African American 9.9%; Hispanic or Latino 18.9%; Asian 0%; Other 8.7%). **Foreign born:** 3.6%. **Median age:** 43.9.

Income 2000: per capita $16,212; median household $25,446; **Pop below poverty level:** 18.4%. ***Personal per capita income 2000-2003:** $22,579-$27,814.

Unemployment 2004: 5.5%. **Change from 2000:** +0.5%. **Median travel time to work:** 18.8 minutes. **Working outside county of residence:** 22.5%.

Cities with pop over 10,000: None.

CRANE COUNTY

201 W 6th St   **Ph:** 432-558-3581
Crane, TX 79731   **Fax:** 432-558-1185
www.co.crane.tx.us

In west-central TX, south of Odessa; organized 1927 from Ector County (other sources say organized Feb 26, 1887 from Tom Green County; first federal census: 1890). **Name Origin:** For William Carey Crane (1816-85), Baptist minister and president of Baylor University (1863-85).

Area (sq mi): 785.59 (land 785.56; water 0.03). **Pop per sq mi:** 4.9.

Pop 2005: 3,837. **State rank:** 214. **Pop change:** 2000-20005 -4%; 1990-2000 -14.1%. **Pop 2000:** 3,996 (White 52.1%; Black or African American 2.9%; Hispanic or Latino 43.9%; Asian 0.4%; Other 23.1%, including 1% American Indian/Alaska Native). **Foreign born:** 14.4%. **Median age:** 34.2.

Income 2000: per capita $15,374; median household $32,194; **Pop below poverty level:** 13.4%. ***Personal per capita income 2000-2003:** $19,199-$20,241.

Unemployment 2004: 6.5%. **Change from 2000:** +0.5%. **Median travel time to work:** 18 minutes. **Working outside county of residence:** 23.4%.

Cities with pop over 10,000: None.

CROCKETT COUNTY

PO Box C   **Ph:** 325-392-2022
Ozona, TX 76943   **Fax:** 325-392-3742
www.co.crockett.tx.us

In west-central TX, southwest of San Angelo; organized Jan 22, 1875 from Bexar County. **Name Origin:** For David 'Davy' Crockett (1786-1836), frontiersman, U.S. representative from TN (1827-31; 1833-35), fighter for TX independence killed at the Alamo.

Area (sq mi): 2807.43 (land 2807.42; water 0.01). **Pop per sq mi:** 1.4.

⛪ *County Seat*

Crockett County (cont'd)

Pop 2005: 3,934. **State rank:** 210. **Pop change:** 2000-20005 -4%; 1990-2000 +0.5%. **Pop 2000:** 4,099 (White 43.7%; Black or African American 0.7%; Hispanic or Latino 54.7%; Asian 0.3%; Other 22.7%). **Foreign born:** 10.5%. **Median age:** 37.2.

Income 2000: per capita $14,414; median household $29,355; **Pop below poverty level:** 19.4%. ***Personal per capita income 2000-2003:** $17,191-$18,122.

Unemployment 2004: 4.1%. **Change from 2000:** +1.5%. **Median travel time to work:** 18.4 minutes. **Working outside county of residence:** 13.2%.

Cities with pop over 10,000: None.

CROSBY COUNTY

201 W Aspen St Suite 102   **Ph:** 806-675-2334
Crosbyton, TX 79322
www.co.crosby.tx.us

In the south-central TX panhandle, east of Lubbock; organized Aug 21, 1876 from Baylor County (other sources say organized from Garza County). **Name Origin:** For Stephen F. Crosby (1800-69), chief clerk in TX land office (1853-57; 1859-67).

Area (sq mi): 901.69 (land 899.51; water 2.17). **Pop per sq mi:** 7.4.

Pop 2005: 6,686. **State rank:** 191. **Pop change:** 2000-20005 -5.5%; 1990-2000 -3.2%. **Pop 2000:** 7,072 (White 46.7%; Black or African American 3.9%; Hispanic or Latino 48.9%; Asian 0%; Other 32.3%). **Foreign born:** 3.9%. **Median age:** 34.3.

Income 2000: per capita $14,445; median household $25,769; **Pop below poverty level:** 28.1%. ***Personal per capita income 2000-2003:** $21,594-$25,215.

Unemployment 2004: 6.3%. **Change from 2000:** +0.6%. **Median travel time to work:** 20.7 minutes. **Working outside county of residence:** 35.5%.

Cities with pop over 10,000: None.

CULBERSON COUNTY

300 La Caverna St   **Ph:** 432-283-2058
Van Horn, TX 79855   **Fax:** 432-283-9234
www.co.culberson.tx.us

On the northwestern border of TX, east of El Paso; organized Mar 10, 1911 from El Paso County. **Name Origin:** For Col. David Browning Culberson (1830-1903), Confederate army officer, TX legislator, and U.S. representative (1875-97).

Area (sq mi): 3812.71 (land 3812.46; water 0.25). **Pop per sq mi:** 0.7.

Pop 2005: 2,627. **State rank:** 232. **Pop change:** 2000-20005 -11.7%; 1990-2000 -12.7%. **Pop 2000:** 2,975 (White 24.6%; Black or African American 0.7%; Hispanic or Latino 72.2%; Asian 0.6%; Other 29.8%). **Foreign born:** 15.6%. **Median age:** 32.8.

Income 2000: per capita $11,493; median household $25,882; **Pop below poverty level:** 25.1%. ***Personal per capita income 2000-2003:** $13,913-$15,522.

Unemployment 2004: 5.7%. **Change from 2000:** -1.9%. **Median travel time to work:** 13.1 minutes. **Working outside county of residence:** 8.6%.

Cities with pop over 10,000: None.

DALLAM COUNTY

PO Box 1352   **Ph:** 806-244-4751
Dalhart, TX 79022   **Fax:** 806-244-3751
www.dallam.org/county/

On the northwestern border of TX panhandle, northwest of Amarillo; organized Aug 21, 1876 from Bexar County. **Name Origin:** For James Wilmer Dallam (1818-47), Texas legal writer.

Area (sq mi): 1505.26 (land 1504.69; water 0.56). **Pop per sq mi:** 4.1.

Pop 2005: 6,174. **State rank:** 194. **Pop change:** 2000-20005 -0.8%; 1990-2000 +13.9%. **Pop 2000:** 6,222 (White 68.4%; Black or African American 1.6%; Hispanic or Latino 28.4%; Asian 0.2%; Other 15.5%). **Foreign born:** 7.9%. **Median age:** 31.4.

Income 2000: per capita $13,653; median household $27,946; **Pop below poverty level:** 14.1%. ***Personal per capita income 2000-2003:** $30,285-$28,615.

Unemployment 2004: 4%. **Change from 2000:** +1.8%. **Median travel time to work:** 15.8 minutes. **Working outside county of residence:** 23.6%.

Cities with pop over 10,000: None.

DALLAS COUNTY

411 Elm St   **Ph:** 214-653-7361
Dallas, TX 75202   **Fax:** 214-653-7057
www.dallascounty.org

In northeastern TX, east of Fort Worth; organized 1846 from Nacogdoches County. **Name Origin:** Traditionally believed to be for George Mifflin Dallas (1792-1864), PA statesman, U.S. vice president (1845-49), and U.S. Minister to Great Britian (1856-61). County historians believe it unlikely that the city founders would honor a vice president when they had several friends so named, especially Joseph Dallas, an old friend from AK.

Area (sq mi): 908.56 (land 879.6; water 28.96). **Pop per sq mi:** 2621.

Pop 2005: 2,305,454. **State rank:** 2. **Pop change:** 2000-20005 +3.9%; 1990-2000 +19.8%. **Pop 2000:** 2,218,899 (White 44.3%; Black or African American 20.3%; Hispanic or Latino 29.9%; Asian 4%; Other 17.4%). **Foreign born:** 20.9%. **Median age:** 31.1.

Income 2000: per capita $22,603; median household $43,324; **Pop below poverty level:** 13.4%. ***Personal per capita income 2000-2003:** $36,047-$36,617.

Unemployment 2004: 6.8%. **Change from 2000:** +1.5%. **Median travel time to work:** 26.9 minutes. **Working outside county of residence:** 12.8%.

Cities with pop over 10,000: 19 (see page 38 for cities).

DAWSON COUNTY

PO Box 1268   **Ph:** 806-872-3778
Lamesa, TX 79331   **Fax:** 806-872-2473
www.co.dawson.tx.us

In the southwestern TX panhandle, south of Lubbock; organized Feb 1, 1858 from Bexar County. **Name Origin:** For Nicholas Mosby Dawson (1808-42), Republic of TX army officer killed in action.

Area (sq mi): 902.12 (land 902.06; water 0.06). **Pop per sq mi:** 15.8.

*Source: Personal per capita income data are from the Bureau of Economic Analysis; per capita income data are from the Bureau of the Census. See Introduction for explanation of differences.

Dawson County (cont'd)

Pop 2005: 14,256. **State rank:** 144. **Pop change:** 2000-20005 - 4.9%; 1990-2000 +4.4%. **Pop 2000:** 14,985 (White 42.4%; Black or African American 8.7%; Hispanic or Latino 48.2%; Asian 0.2%; Other 18.7%). **Foreign born:** 4.2%. **Median age:** 35.6.

Income 2000: per capita $15,011; median household $28,211; **Pop below poverty level:** 19.7%. ***Personal per capita income 2000-2003:** $18,054-$20,042.

Unemployment 2004: 7.4%. **Change from 2000:** +2.7%. **Median travel time to work:** 14.3 minutes. **Working outside county of residence:** 10.4%.

Cities with pop over 10,000: None.

DEAF SMITH COUNTY

235 E 3rd St Rm 203   **Ph:** 806-363-7077
Hereford, TX 79045   **Fax:** 806-363-7023
www.co.deaf-smith.tx.us

On the northeastern border of TX panhandle, southwest of Amarillo; organized Aug 21, 1876 from Bexar County. **Name Origin:** For Erastus 'Deaf' Smith (1787-1837), Republic of Texas scout and soldier.

Area (sq mi): 1498.26 (land 1497.34; water 0.92). **Pop per sq mi:** 12.4.

Pop 2005: 18,538. **State rank:** 124. **Pop change:** 2000-20005 - 0.1%; 1990-2000 -3.1%. **Pop 2000:** 18,561 (White 40.4%; Black or African American 1.5%; Hispanic or Latino 57.4%; Asian 0.3%; Other 25.9%). **Foreign born:** 11.6%. **Median age:** 30.6.

Income 2000: per capita $13,119; median household $29,601; **Pop below poverty level:** 20.6%. ***Personal per capita income 2000-2003:** $24,387-$23,286.

Unemployment 2004: 5.7%. **Change from 2000:** +0.7%. **Median travel time to work:** 19.4 minutes. **Working outside county of residence:** 16.8%.

Cities with pop over 10,000: Hereford ⬛ (14,458).

DELTA COUNTY

90 Texas Hwy 24 S   **Ph:** 903-395-4118
Cooper, TX 75432   **Fax:** 903-395-4455

In northeastern TX, northeast of Dallas; organized Jul 29, 1870 from Lamar County. **Name Origin:** For its triangular shape, like the Greek letter *delta*.

Area (sq mi): 277.92 (land 277.08; water 0.84). **Pop per sq mi:** 19.8.

Pop 2005: 5,480. **State rank:** 198. **Pop change:** 2000-20005 +2.9%; 1990-2000 +9.7%. **Pop 2000:** 5,327 (White 86.7%; Black or African American 8.3%; Hispanic or Latino 3.1%; Asian 0.1%; Other 3.7%). **Foreign born:** 0.5%. **Median age:** 38.8.

Income 2000: per capita $15,080; median household $29,094; **Pop below poverty level:** 17.6%. ***Personal per capita income 2000-2003:** $18,997-$20,091.

Unemployment 2004: 7.3%. **Change from 2000:** +2.7%. **Median travel time to work:** 27.7 minutes. **Working outside county of residence:** 59.6%.

Cities with pop over 10,000: None.

DENTON COUNTY

1450 E McKinney   **Ph:** 940-349-2012
Denton, TX 76209   **Fax:** 940-349-2019
www.co.denton.tx.us

In north-central TX, north of Fort Worth; organized Apr 11, 1846 from Fannin County. **Name Origin:** For John B. Denton (1806-41), an officer killed by Indians.

Area (sq mi): 957.88 (land 888.54; water 69.34). **Pop per sq mi:** 624.2.

Pop 2005: 554,642. **State rank:** 9. **Pop change:** 2000-20005 +28.1%; 1990-2000 +58.3%. **Pop 2000:** 432,976 (White 76%; Black or African American 5.9%; Hispanic or Latino 12.2%; Asian 4%; Other 8.5%). **Foreign born:** 9.4%. **Median age:** 31.

Income 2000: per capita $26,895; median household $58,216; **Pop below poverty level:** 6.6%. ***Personal per capita income 2000-2003:** $33,059-$31,841.

Unemployment 2004: 4.4%. **Change from 2000:** +1.4%. **Median travel time to work:** 28.2 minutes. **Working outside county of residence:** 56%.

Cities with pop over 10,000: 6 (see page 38 for cities).

DEWITT COUNTY

307 N Gonzales St   **Ph:** 361-275-3724
Cuero, TX 77954   **Fax:** 361-275-8994
www.co.dewitt.tx.us

In east-central TX, southeast of San Antonio; organized Mar 24, 1846 from Goliad, Gonzales, and Victoria counties. **Name Origin:** For Green C. De Witt (1787-1835), an early colonizer in Mexican Texas.

Area (sq mi): 910.47 (land 909.18; water 1.29). **Pop per sq mi:** 22.6.

Pop 2005: 20,507. **State rank:** 114. **Pop change:** 2000-20005 +2.5%; 1990-2000 +6.2%. **Pop 2000:** 20,013 (White 60.8%; Black or African American 11%; Hispanic or Latino 27.2%; Asian 0.2%; Other 12.3%). **Foreign born:** 2.6%. **Median age:** 40.1.

Income 2000: per capita $14,780; median household $28,714; **Pop below poverty level:** 19.6%. ***Personal per capita income 2000-2003:** $20,456-$21,399.

Unemployment 2004: 5.5%. **Change from 2000:** +1.9%. **Median travel time to work:** 26.3 minutes. **Working outside county of residence:** 28.7%.

Cities with pop over 10,000: None.

DICKENS COUNTY

PO Box 120   **Ph:** 806-623-5531
Dickens, TX 79229   **Fax:** 806-623-5319

In the southeastern TX panhandle, east of Lubbock; organized Aug 21, 1876 from Bexar County. **Name Origin:** For J. Dickens (?-1836), killed at the Alamo.

Area (sq mi): 905.21 (land 904.21; water 1). **Pop per sq mi:** 2.9.

Pop 2005: 2,646. **State rank:** 231. **Pop change:** 2000-20005 -4.2%; 1990-2000 +7.4%. **Pop 2000:** 2,762 (White 67.2%; Black or African American 8.2%; Hispanic or Latino 23.9%; Asian 0.1%; Other 14.1%). **Foreign born:** 2%. **Median age:** 39.2.

Dickens County (cont'd)

Income 2000: per capita $13,156; median household $25,898; **Pop below poverty level:** 17.4%. ***Personal per capita income 2000-2003:** $16,407-$16,250.

Unemployment 2004: 6.1%. **Change from 2000:** +3%. **Median travel time to work:** 20.5 minutes. **Working outside county of residence:** 19.1%.

Cities with pop over 10,000: None.

DIMMIT COUNTY
103 N 5th St　　　　　　　　**Ph:** 830-876-2323
Carrizo Springs, TX 78834　　**Fax:** 830-876-5036
www.dimmitcountytx.com

On the southwestern border of TX, northwest of Laredo; organized Feb 1, 1858 from Bexar and Maverick counties. **Name Origin:** For Capt. Philip Dimmit (1801-41), Republic of TX officer.

Area (sq mi): 1334.48 (land 1330.91; water 3.57). **Pop per sq mi:** 7.8.

Pop 2005: 10,395. **State rank:** 164. **Pop change:** 2000-20005 +1.4%; 1990-2000 -1.8%. **Pop 2000:** 10,248 (White 13.2%; Black or African American 0.9%; Hispanic or Latino 85%; Asian 0.7%; Other 21.5%). **Foreign born:** 7.6%. **Median age:** 31.6.

Income 2000: per capita $9,765; median household $21,917; **Pop below poverty level:** 33.2%. ***Personal per capita income 2000-2003:** $13,262-$16,333.

Unemployment 2004: 9.2%. **Change from 2000:** -0.5%. **Median travel time to work:** 21.2 minutes. **Working outside county of residence:** 20.3%.

Cities with pop over 10,000: None.

DONLEY COUNTY
PO Box U　　　　　　　　**Ph:** 806-874-3436
Clarendon, TX 79226　　**Fax:** 806-874-3351
www.donleytx.com

In the east-central TX panhandle, southeast of Amarillo; organized Aug 21, 1876 from Jack [sic] County. **Name Origin:** For Stockton P. Donley (1821-71), Confederate army officer and member of the supreme court of TX (1866).

Area (sq mi): 933.05 (land 929.77; water 3.28). **Pop per sq mi:** 4.2.

Pop 2005: 3,889. **State rank:** 211. **Pop change:** 2000-20005 +1.6%; 1990-2000 +3.6%. **Pop 2000:** 3,828 (White 88.1%; Black or African American 3.9%; Hispanic or Latino 6.3%; Asian 0.1%; Other 4.5%). **Foreign born:** 1.6%. **Median age:** 42.8.

Income 2000: per capita $15,958; median household $29,006; **Pop below poverty level:** 15.9%. ***Personal per capita income 2000-2003:** $21,549-$22,466.

Unemployment 2004: 5%. **Change from 2000:** +2.4%. **Median travel time to work:** 23.5 minutes. **Working outside county of residence:** 27.8%.

Cities with pop over 10,000: None.

DUVAL COUNTY
PO Box 248　　　　　　　　**Ph:** 361-279-6274
San Diego, TX 78384

In southern TX, west of Corpus Christi; organized Feb 1, 1858 from Live Oak, Starr, and Nueces counties. **Name Origin:** For Capt. Burr H. Duval (1809-36), an officer killed at Goliad during the Texas Revolution.

Area (sq mi): 1795.67 (land 1792.71; water 2.97). **Pop per sq mi:** 7.

Pop 2005: 12,578. **State rank:** 153. **Pop change:** 2000-20005 -4.1%; 1990-2000 +1.6%. **Pop 2000:** 13,120 (White 11.1%; Black or African American 0.5%; Hispanic or Latino 88%; Asian 0.1%; Other 19.1%). **Foreign born:** 3.4%. **Median age:** 33.8.

Income 2000: per capita $11,324; median household $22,416; **Pop below poverty level:** 27.2%. ***Personal per capita income 2000-2003:** $15,499-$18,330.

Unemployment 2004: 7.4%. **Change from 2000:** +0.2%. **Median travel time to work:** 26.5 minutes. **Working outside county of residence:** 37.7%.

Cities with pop over 10,000: None.

EASTLAND COUNTY
PO Box 110　　　　　　　　**Ph:** 254-629-1583
Eastland, TX 76448　　　　**Fax:** 254-629-8125
county.eastlandcountytexas.com

In north-central TX, east of Abilene; organized Feb 1, 1858 from Bosque, Coryell, and Travis counties. **Name Origin:** For William Mosby Eastland (1806-43), Texas Revolutionary officer executed by Mexican Gen. Antonio Lopez de Santa Anna (1794-1876).

Area (sq mi): 931.9 (land 926.01; water 5.89). **Pop per sq mi:** 19.9.

Pop 2005: 18,393. **State rank:** 125. **Pop change:** 2000-20005 +0.5%; 1990-2000 -1%. **Pop 2000:** 18,297 (White 85.7%; Black or African American 2.2%; Hispanic or Latino 10.8%; Asian 0.2%; Other 6.6%). **Foreign born:** 4%. **Median age:** 41.3.

Income 2000: per capita $14,870; median household $26,832; **Pop below poverty level:** 16.8%. ***Personal per capita income 2000-2003:** $21,368-$23,504.

Unemployment 2004: 5.4%. **Change from 2000:** +1.8%. **Median travel time to work:** 19.7 minutes. **Working outside county of residence:** 17.7%.

Cities with pop over 10,000: None.

ECTOR COUNTY
300 N Grant Ave Rm 111　　**Ph:** 432-498-4130
Odessa, TX 79761　　　　　**Fax:** 432-498-4177
www.co.ector.tx.us

In the southwestern TX panhandle, west of Midland; organized Feb 26, 1887 from Tom Green County. **Name Origin:** For Gen. Matthew Duncan Ector (1822-79), TX legislator and jurist.

Area (sq mi): 901.68 (land 901.06; water 0.62). **Pop per sq mi:** 139.1.

Pop 2005: 125,339. **State rank:** 27. **Pop change:** 2000-20005 +3.5%; 1990-2000 +1.8%. **Pop 2000:** 121,123 (White 51.3%; Black or African American 4.6%; Hispanic or Latino 42.4%; Asian 0.6%; Other 21%). **Foreign born:** 10.6%. **Median age:** 32.

*Source: Personal per capita income data are from the Bureau of Economic Analysis; per capita income data are from the Bureau of the Census. See Introduction for explanation of differences.

Ector County (cont'd)

Income 2000: per capita $15,031; median household $31,152; **Pop below poverty level:** 18.7%. ***Personal per capita income 2000-2003:** $21,093-$22,665.

Unemployment 2004: 6%. **Change from 2000:** +0.8%. **Median travel time to work:** 18.6 minutes. **Working outside county of residence:** 14.6%.

Cities with pop over 10,000: Odessa 🏛 (92,844).

EDWARDS COUNTY

PO Box 184   **Ph:** 830-683-2235
Rocksprings, TX 78880   **Fax:** 830-683-5376

In southwestern TX, northeast of Del Rio; organized Feb 1, 1858 from Bexar County. **Name Origin:** For Hayden Edwards (1771-1849), founder of a colony at Nacogdoches in Mexican TX (1825).

Area (sq mi): 2119.95 (land 2119.75; water 0.19). **Pop per sq mi:** 0.9.

Pop 2005: 1,987. **State rank:** 237. **Pop change:** 2000-20005 -8.1%; 1990-2000 -4.6%. **Pop 2000:** 2,162 (White 53.7%; Black or African American 0.8%; Hispanic or Latino 45.1%; Asian 0.1%; Other 15.8%). **Foreign born:** 10.8%. **Median age:** 39.

Income 2000: per capita $12,691; median household $25,298; **Pop below poverty level:** 31.6%. ***Personal per capita income 2000-2003:** $14,604-$19,338.

Unemployment 2004: 4.3%. **Change from 2000:** -0.3%. **Median travel time to work:** 23.4 minutes. **Working outside county of residence:** 23.9%.

Cities with pop over 10,000: None.

EL PASO COUNTY

500 E San Antonio Ave   **Ph:** 915-546-2000
El Paso, TX 79901   **Fax:** 915-546-2012
www.co.el-paso.tx.us

On the northwestern border of TX, north of Cuidad Juarez, Mexico; organized Jan 3, 1850 from Bexar County. **Name Origin:** For the city, itself from Spanish for 'the ford,' for a major crossing of the Rio Grande River, or 'the pass' for El Paso del Norte 'the north pass' through either the Sierra Madre or the Franklin mountains: the city lies in a valley between them.

Area (sq mi): 1014.68 (land 1013.11; water 1.57). **Pop per sq mi:** 712.3.

Pop 2005: 721,598. **State rank:** 6. **Pop change:** 2000-20005 +6.2%; 1990-2000 +14.9%. **Pop 2000:** 679,622 (White 17%; Black or African American 3.1%; Hispanic or Latino 78.2%; Asian 1%; Other 22%). **Foreign born:** 27.4%. **Median age:** 30.

Income 2000: per capita $13,421; median household $31,051; **Pop below poverty level:** 23.8%. ***Personal per capita income 2000-2003:** $18,562-$20,875.

Unemployment 2004: 7.8%. **Change from 2000:** -0.4%. **Median travel time to work:** 22.7 minutes. **Working outside county of residence:** 4.8%.

Cities with pop over 10,000: El Paso 🏛 (592,099); Socorro (28,029).

ELLIS COUNTY

1201 N Hwy 77 Suite B   **Ph:** 972-825-5071
Waxahachie, TX 75165   **Fax:** 972-923-5010
www.co.ellis.tx.us

In east-central TX, south of Dallas; organized Dec 20, 1849 from Navarro County. **Name Origin:** Named by Gen. Edward H. Tarrant (1796-1858) for his friend, Richard Ellis (1781-1846), AL jurist and legislator, and member of the Constitutional Congress that declared TX independent from Mexico in 1836.

Area (sq mi): 951.66 (land 939.91; water 11.75). **Pop per sq mi:** 142.

Pop 2005: 133,474. **State rank:** 25. **Pop change:** 2000-20005 +19.9%; 1990-2000 +30.8%. **Pop 2000:** 111,360 (White 71.3%; Black or African American 8.6%; Hispanic or Latino 18.4%; Asian 0.4%; Other 10.4%). **Foreign born:** 7.1%. **Median age:** 33.2.

Income 2000: per capita $20,212; median household $50,350; **Pop below poverty level:** 8.6%. ***Personal per capita income 2000-2003:** $26,750-$26,881.

Unemployment 2004: 5.6%. **Change from 2000:** +1.4%. **Median travel time to work:** 30.3 minutes. **Working outside county of residence:** 51.4%.

Cities with pop over 10,000: Waxahachie 🏛 (24,654); Ennis (18,551); Midlothian (11,599).

ERATH COUNTY

100 W Washington St County Courthouse   **Ph:** 254-965-1482
Stephenville, TX 76401   **Fax:** 254-965-5732
www.co.erath.tx.us

In north-central TX, southwest of Fort Worth; organized Jan 25, 1856 from Bosque and Coryell counties. **Name Origin:** For George Bernard Erath (1813-91), Indian fighter, Texas Ranger, and legislator.

Area (sq mi): 1089.8 (land 1086.33; water 3.47). **Pop per sq mi:** 31.4.

Pop 2005: 34,076. **State rank:** 84. **Pop change:** 2000-20005 +3.3%; 1990-2000 +17.9%. **Pop 2000:** 33,001 (White 82.6%; Black or African American 0.8%; Hispanic or Latino 15%; Asian 0.4%; Other 9.1%). **Foreign born:** 7.3%. **Median age:** 31.4.

Income 2000: per capita $16,655; median household $30,708; **Pop below poverty level:** 16%. ***Personal per capita income 2000-2003:** $22,227-$23,332.

Unemployment 2004: 4.2%. **Change from 2000:** +1.9%. **Median travel time to work:** 20.1 minutes. **Working outside county of residence:** 17.4%.

Cities with pop over 10,000: Stephenville 🏛 (15,416).

FALLS COUNTY

PO Box 458   **Ph:** 254-883-1408
Marlin, TX 76661   **Fax:** 254-883-1406

In east-central TX, southeast of Waco; organized Jan 28, 1850 from Limestone and Milam counties. **Name Origin:** For the rapids on the Brazos River, which traverses the county.

Area (sq mi): 773.81 (land 769.09; water 4.72). **Pop per sq mi:** 22.9.

Pop 2005: 17,646. **State rank:** 129. **Pop change:** 2000-20005 -5%; 1990-2000 +4.9%. **Pop 2000:** 18,576 (White 55.8%; Black or

Falls County (cont'd)

African American 27.5%; Hispanic or Latino 15.8%; Asian 0.1%; Other 10.9%). **Foreign born:** 4.6%. **Median age:** 36.5.

Income 2000: per capita $14,311; median household $26,589; **Pop below poverty level:** 22.6%. ***Personal per capita income 2000-2003:** $17,133-$19,304.

Unemployment 2004: 6.5%. **Change from 2000:** +2.6%. **Median travel time to work:** 25 minutes. **Working outside county of residence:** 45.3%.

Cities with pop over 10,000: None.

FANNIN COUNTY
101 Sam Rayburn Dr
County Courthouse Suite 102   **Ph:** 903-583-7486
Bonham, TX 75418   **Fax:** 903-583-7811
www.co.fannin.tx.us

On the northeastern border of TX, northeast of Dallas; organized Dec 14, 1837 from Red River County. **Name Origin:** For James Walker Fannin (1809-36), GA soldier killed in action in the TX War of Independence.

Area (sq mi): 899.16 (land 891.45; water 7.71). **Pop per sq mi:** 37.2.

Pop 2005: 33,142. **State rank:** 86. **Pop change:** 2000-20005 +6.1%; 1990-2000 +26%. **Pop 2000:** 31,242 (White 84.2%; Black or African American 8%; Hispanic or Latino 5.6%; Asian 0.3%; Other 5.2%). **Foreign born:** 3.1%. **Median age:** 38.

Income 2000: per capita $16,066; median household $34,501; **Pop below poverty level:** 13.9%. ***Personal per capita income 2000-2003:** $19,922-$20,683.

Unemployment 2004: 6.9%. **Change from 2000:** +0.5%. **Median travel time to work:** 29.6 minutes. **Working outside county of residence:** 40.2%.

Cities with pop over 10,000: Bonham 🏛 (10,439).

FAYETTE COUNTY
PO Box 59   **Ph:** 979-968-3251
La Grange, TX 78945   **Fax:** 979-968-8531
www.co.fayette.tx.us

In east-central TX, southeast of Austin; organized Dec 14, 1837 from Bastrop and Colorado counties. **Name Origin:** For the Marquis de Lafayette (1757-1834), French statesman and soldier who fought with the Americans during the Revolutionary War.

Area (sq mi): 959.84 (land 950.03; water 9.81). **Pop per sq mi:** 23.7.

Pop 2005: 22,537. **State rank:** 108. **Pop change:** 2000-20005 +3.4%; 1990-2000 +8.5%. **Pop 2000:** 21,804 (White 79.2%; Black or African American 7%; Hispanic or Latino 12.8%; Asian 0.2%; Other 8.3%). **Foreign born:** 5.6%. **Median age:** 42.6.

Income 2000: per capita $18,888; median household $34,526; **Pop below poverty level:** 11.4%. ***Personal per capita income 2000-2003:** $25,697-$28,200.

Unemployment 2004: 4%. **Change from 2000:** +1.7%. **Median travel time to work:** 23.3 minutes. **Working outside county of residence:** 25.9%.

Cities with pop over 10,000: None.

FISHER COUNTY
PO Box 368   **Ph:** 325-776-2401
Roby, TX 79543   **Fax:** 325-776-3274
www.co.fisher.tx.us

In north-central TX, northwest of Abilene; organized Aug 21, 1876 from Bexar County. **Name Origin:** For Samuel Rhoads Fisher (1794-1839), signer of the TX Declaration of Independence (1836) and secretary of the TX Navy.

Area (sq mi): 901.74 (land 901.16; water 0.58). **Pop per sq mi:** 4.5.

Pop 2005: 4,089. **State rank:** 209. **Pop change:** 2000-20005 -5.9%; 1990-2000 -10.3%. **Pop 2000:** 4,344 (White 74.8%; Black or African American 2.8%; Hispanic or Latino 21.4%; Asian 0.1%; Other 13.4%). **Foreign born:** 2.3%. **Median age:** 42.9.

Income 2000: per capita $15,120; median household $27,659; **Pop below poverty level:** 17.5%. ***Personal per capita income 2000-2003:** $17,798-$23,033.

Unemployment 2004: 5%. **Change from 2000:** +1.8%. **Median travel time to work:** 20.2 minutes. **Working outside county of residence:** 35.8%.

Cities with pop over 10,000: None.

FLOYD COUNTY
100 Main St Courthouse Rm 101   **Ph:** 806-983-4900
Floydada, TX 79235   **Fax:** 806-983-4909

In the central TX panhandle, northeast of Lubbock; organized Aug 21, 1876 from Bexar County. **Name Origin:** For Dolfin Ward Floyd (1807-36), killed at the Alamo.

Area (sq mi): 992.51 (land 992.19; water 0.32). **Pop per sq mi:** 7.2.

Pop 2005: 7,174. **State rank:** 187. **Pop change:** 2000-20005 -7.7%; 1990-2000 -8.5%. **Pop 2000:** 7,771 (White 49.9%; Black or African American 3.4%; Hispanic or Latino 45.9%; Asian 0.2%; Other 22.4%). **Foreign born:** 5.9%. **Median age:** 34.8.

Income 2000: per capita $14,206; median household $26,851; **Pop below poverty level:** 21.5%. ***Personal per capita income 2000-2003:** $24,170-$24,973.

Unemployment 2004: 6.9%. **Change from 2000:** -0.3%. **Median travel time to work:** 16.5 minutes. **Working outside county of residence:** 24.8%.

Cities with pop over 10,000: None.

FOARD COUNTY
PO Box 539   **Ph:** 940-684-1365
Crowell, TX 79227   **Fax:** 940-684-1947

In north-central TX, west of Wichita Falls; organized Mar 3, 1891 from Knox and King counties. **Name Origin:** For Maj. Robert J. Foard (1831-98), Confederate army officer and attorney.

Area (sq mi): 707.69 (land 706.68; water 1.01). **Pop per sq mi:** 2.1.

Pop 2005: 1,518. **State rank:** 242. **Pop change:** 2000-20005 -6.4%; 1990-2000 -9.6%. **Pop 2000:** 1,622 (White 78.7%; Black or African American 3.3%; Hispanic or Latino 16.3%; Asian 0.2%; Other 12.3%). **Foreign born:** 1.6%. **Median age:** 41.7.

Income 2000: per capita $14,799; median household $25,813; **Pop below poverty level:** 14.3%. ***Personal per capita income 2000-2003:** $20,992-$23,440.

*Source: Personal per capita income data are from the Bureau of Economic Analysis; per capita income data are from the Bureau of the Census. See Introduction for explanation of differences.

676

Foard County (cont'd)

Unemployment 2004: 6.2%. Change from 2000: +3.4%. Median travel time to work: 16.8 minutes. Working outside county of residence: 27.7%.

Cities with pop over 10,000: None.

FORT BEND COUNTY

301 Jackson St Suite 101   Ph: 281-341-8685
Richmond, TX 77469   Fax: 281-341-8669
www.co.fort-bend.tx.us

In east-central TX, southwest of Houston; organized Dec 29, 1837 from Austin County. Name Origin: For the fort built at a bend in the Brazos River, on the western border of the county.

Area (sq mi): 886.05 (land 874.64; water 11.41). Pop per sq mi: 530.1.

Pop 2005: 463,650. State rank: 10. Pop change: 2000-20005 +30.8%; 1990-2000 +57.2%. Pop 2000: 354,452 (White 46.2%; Black or African American 19.8%; Hispanic or Latino 21.1%; Asian 11.2%; Other 12%). Foreign born: 18.3%. Median age: 33.3.

Income 2000: per capita $24,985; median household $63,831; Pop below poverty level: 7.1%. *Personal per capita income 2000-2003: $33,672-$32,887.

Unemployment 2004: 5.3%. Change from 2000: +2.2%. Median travel time to work: 32.3 minutes. Working outside county of residence: 63.4%.

Cities with pop over 10,000: Sugar Land (73,721); Missouri City (66,587); Rosenberg (29,470); Stafford (18,794); Richmond (13,001).

FRANKLIN COUNTY

PO Box 68   Ph: 903-537-4252
Mount Vernon, TX 75457
www.co.franklin.tx.us

In northeastern TX, southwest of Texarkana; organized Mar 6, 1875 from Titus County. Name Origin: For Capt. Benjamin Cromwell Franklin (1805-73), an officer in the Republic of Texas army and a jurist.

Area (sq mi): 294.77 (land 285.66; water 9.12). Pop per sq mi: 35.7.

Pop 2005: 10,200. State rank: 166. Pop change: 2000-20005 +7.8%; 1990-2000 +21.2%. Pop 2000: 9,458 (White 85.9%; Black or African American 3.9%; Hispanic or Latino 8.9%; Asian 0.2%; Other 6.6%). Foreign born: 5.4%. Median age: 40.3.

Income 2000: per capita $17,563; median household $31,955; Pop below poverty level: 15.6%. *Personal per capita income 2000-2003: $23,243-$25,944.

Unemployment 2004: 4.4%. Change from 2000: +1.6%. Median travel time to work: 22.8 minutes. Working outside county of residence: 46.7%.

Cities with pop over 10,000: None.

FREESTONE COUNTY

PO Box 1010   Ph: 903-389-2635
Fairfield, TX 75840   Fax: 903-389-6533

In east-central TX, northeast of Waco; organized Sep 6, 1850 from

Limestone County. Name Origin: Either for freestone water, which contains little or no dissolved substances, such as calcium, or for any stone that can be cut easily and without splitting.

Area (sq mi): 892.13 (land 877.43; water 14.7). Pop per sq mi: 21.4.

Pop 2005: 18,800. State rank: 123. Pop change: 2000-20005 +5.2%; 1990-2000 +13%. Pop 2000: 17,867 (White 71.8%; Black or African American 18.9%; Hispanic or Latino 8.2%; Asian 0.3%; Other 5.3%). Foreign born: 3.1%. Median age: 37.8.

Income 2000: per capita $16,338; median household $31,283; Pop below poverty level: 14.2%. *Personal per capita income 2000-2003: $18,417-$19,903.

Unemployment 2004: 4.8%. Change from 2000: +1.2%. Median travel time to work: 23.8 minutes. Working outside county of residence: 37%.

Cities with pop over 10,000: None.

FRIO COUNTY

500 E San Antonio St Rm 6   Ph: 830-334-2214
Pearsall, TX 78061   Fax: 830-334-0021
www.co.frio.tx.us

In southern TX, southwest of San Antonio; organized Feb 1, 1858 from Bexar and Uvalde counties. Name Origin: For the Frio River, which runs through it; Spanish 'cold.'

Area (sq mi): 1134.28 (land 1133.02; water 1.26). Pop per sq mi: 14.5.

Pop 2005: 16,387. State rank: 132. Pop change: 2000-20005 +0.8%; 1990-2000 +20.6%. Pop 2000: 16,252 (White 20.6%; Black or African American 4.9%; Hispanic or Latino 73.8%; Asian 0.4%; Other 22.9%). Foreign born: 5.8%. Median age: 30.7.

Income 2000: per capita $16,069; median household $24,504; Pop below poverty level: 29%. *Personal per capita income 2000-2003: $14,880-$16,532.

Unemployment 2004: 7.4%. Change from 2000: +0.3%. Median travel time to work: 26.4 minutes. Working outside county of residence: 23.4%.

Cities with pop over 10,000: None.

GAINES COUNTY

101 S Main St Rm 107   Ph: 432-758-4003
Seminole, TX 79360   Fax: 432-758-1442
www.gainescountyonline.us

On the southwestern border of TX panhandle, north of Odessa; organized Aug 21, 1876 from Bexar County. Name Origin: For James Gaines (1776-1850), signer of the TX Declaration of Independence (1836) and TX legislator (1838-42).

Area (sq mi): 1502.84 (land 1502.35; water 0.49). Pop per sq mi: 9.8.

Pop 2005: 14,712. State rank: 139. Pop change: 2000-20005 +1.7%; 1990-2000 +2.4%. Pop 2000: 14,467 (White 60.8%; Black or African American 2.3%; Hispanic or Latino 35.8%; Asian 0.2%; Other 17.4%). Foreign born: 18.9%. Median age: 29.7.

Income 2000: per capita $13,088; median household $30,432; Pop below poverty level: 21.7%. *Personal per capita income 2000-2003: $18,763-$23,506.

Gaines County (cont'd)

Unemployment 2004: 5.5%. **Change from 2000:** +1%. **Median travel time to work:** 17.4 minutes. **Working outside county of residence:** 19.4%.

Cities with pop over 10,000: None.

GALVESTON COUNTY

722 Moody St   **Ph:** 409-766-2200
Galveston, TX 77550   **Fax:** 409-770-5133
www.co.galveston.tx.us

On the central-eastern coast of TX, south of Houston; organized May 15, 1838 (prior to statehood) from Brazoria County. **Name Origin:** For Bernardo de Galvez (1746-86), Spanish colonial leader active in the Spanish possessions along the Gulf of Mexico. Form of the name is anglicized.

Area (sq mi): 872.93 (land 398.47; water 474.46). **Pop per sq mi:** 696.6.

Pop 2005: 277,563. **State rank:** 16. **Pop change:** 2000-20005 +11%; 1990-2000 +15.1%. **Pop 2000:** 250,158 (White 63.1%; Black or African American 15.4%; Hispanic or Latino 18%; Asian 2.1%; Other 9.8%). **Foreign born:** 8.3%. **Median age:** 35.9.

Income 2000: per capita $21,568; median household $42,419; **Pop below poverty level:** 13.2%. ***Personal per capita income 2000-2003:** $29,450-$30,762.

Unemployment 2004: 7%. **Change from 2000:** +1%. **Median travel time to work:** 26 minutes. **Working outside county of residence:** 39.3%.

Cities with pop over 10,000: 7 (see page 38 for cities).

GARZA COUNTY

PO Box 366   **Ph:** 806-495-4430
Post, TX 79356   **Fax:** 806-495-4431
www.garzacounty.net

In south-central TX panhandle, southeast of Lubbock; organized Aug 21, 1876 from Bexar County. **Name Origin:** For Geronimo Garza, a colonizer who founded San Antonio.

Area (sq mi): 896.19 (land 895.56; water 0.63). **Pop per sq mi:** 5.6.

Pop 2005: 5,002. **State rank:** 203. **Pop change:** 2000-20005 +2.7%; 1990-2000 -5.3%. **Pop 2000:** 4,872 (White 56.7%; Black or African American 4.8%; Hispanic or Latino 37.2%; Asian 0.1%; Other 20.3%). **Foreign born:** 6.3%. **Median age:** 35.1.

Income 2000: per capita $12,704; median household $27,206; **Pop below poverty level:** 22.3%. ***Personal per capita income 2000-2003:** $19,723-$20,197.

Unemployment 2004: 5.3%. **Change from 2000:** +2.8%. **Median travel time to work:** 16.9 minutes. **Working outside county of residence:** 19.4%.

Cities with pop over 10,000: None.

GILLESPIE COUNTY

101 W Main St Unit 13   **Ph:** 830-997-6515
Fredericksburg, TX 78624 **Fax:** 830-997-9958
www.gillespiecounty.org

In central TX, west of Austin; established Feb 23, 1848 from Bexar County. **Name Origin:** For Robert Addison Gillespie (?-1846), Texas Ranger killed during the Mexican War.

Area (sq mi): 1061.48 (land 1061.06; water 0.42). **Pop per sq mi:** 21.8.

Pop 2005: 23,088. **State rank:** 104. **Pop change:** 2000-20005 +10.9%; 1990-2000 +21%. **Pop 2000:** 20,814 (White 82.8%; Black or African American 0.2%; Hispanic or Latino 15.9%; Asian 0.2%; Other 6.8%). **Foreign born:** 7%. **Median age:** 46.3.

Income 2000: per capita $20,423; median household $38,109; **Pop below poverty level:** 10.2%. ***Personal per capita income 2000-2003:** $25,462-$27,424.

Unemployment 2004: 3.4%. **Change from 2000:** +1.5%. **Median travel time to work:** 21.8 minutes. **Working outside county of residence:** 17.8%.

Cities with pop over 10,000: Fredericksburg ⛪ (10,087).

GLASSCOCK COUNTY

117 E Currie St   **Ph:** 432-354-2371
Garden City, TX 79739
www.co.glasscock.tx.us

In west-central TX, east of Midland; organized Apr 4, 1887 from Tom Green County. **Name Origin:** For George Washington Glasscock (1810-79), a miller at Austin, TX, and TX legislator.

Area (sq mi): 900.93 (land 900.75; water 0.19). **Pop per sq mi:** 1.5.

Pop 2005: 1,327. **State rank:** 244. **Pop change:** 2000-20005 -5.6%; 1990-2000 -2.8%. **Pop 2000:** 1,406 (White 67.9%; Black or African American 0.5%; Hispanic or Latino 29.9%; Asian 0%; Other 21.9%). **Foreign born:** 14.1%. **Median age:** 33.5.

Income 2000: per capita $18,279; median household $35,655; **Pop below poverty level:** 14.7%. ***Personal per capita income 2000-2003:** $18,126-$25,526.

Unemployment 2004: 4.1%. **Change from 2000:** +1.1%. **Median travel time to work:** 19.6 minutes. **Working outside county of residence:** 33.3%.

Cities with pop over 10,000: None.

GOLIAD COUNTY

127 N Courthouse Sq   **Ph:** 361-645-3294
Goliad, TX 77963   **Fax:** 361-645-3858
www.goliadcogovt.org

In southeastern TX, north of Corpus Christi; original county; organized Mar 17, 1836 (prior to statehood) from Old Mexican Municipality. **Name Origin:** Probably originally of biblical origin from *Goliath*; also believed to be an anagram from *Hidalgo* (minus the silent h), referring to Miguel Hidalgo y Costilla (1753-1811), the first promotor of Mexican independence from Spain. Applied to a presidio by the 1829 Congress of Coahuila and Texas.

Area (sq mi): 859.35 (land 853.52; water 5.83). **Pop per sq mi:** 8.3.

Pop 2005: 7,102. **State rank:** 188. **Pop change:** 2000-20005 +2.5%; 1990-2000 +15.9%. **Pop 2000:** 6,928 (White 59.4%; Black or African American 4.8%; Hispanic or Latino 35.2%; Asian 0.2%; Other 12.2%). **Foreign born:** 2.8%. **Median age:** 40.2.

Income 2000: per capita $17,126; median household $34,201; **Pop below poverty level:** 16.4%. ***Personal per capita income 2000-2003:** $20,555-$21,737.

*Source: Personal per capita income data are from the Bureau of Economic Analysis; per capita income data are from the Bureau of the Census. See Introduction for explanation of differences.

Goliad County (cont'd)

Unemployment 2004: 5.7%. **Change from 2000:** +1.9%. **Median travel time to work:** 30.9 minutes. **Working outside county of residence:** 45.7%.

Cities with pop over 10,000: None.

GONZALES COUNTY
1709 Sarah Dewitt Dr
Gonzales, TX 78629
www.co.gonzales.tx.us

Ph: 830-672-2801
Fax: 830 672 2636

In east-central TX, east of San Antonio; original county; organized Mar 17, 1836 (prior to statehood) from Old Mexican Municipality. **Name Origin:** For Col. Rafael Gonzales (1789-1857), provisional governor of Coahuila and TX (1824-26).

Area (sq mi): 1069.82 (land 1067.75; water 2.07). **Pop per sq mi:** 18.3.

Pop 2005: 19,587. **State rank:** 121. **Pop change:** 2000-20005 +5.1%; 1990-2000 +8.3%. **Pop 2000:** 18,628 (White 51.2%; Black or African American 8.4%; Hispanic or Latino 39.6%; Asian 0.3%; Other 19.1%). **Foreign born:** 11%. **Median age:** 36.3.

Income 2000: per capita $14,269; median household $28,368; **Pop below poverty level:** 18.6%. ***Personal per capita income 2000-2003:** $22,573-$25,014.

Unemployment 2004: 4.7%. **Change from 2000:** +1.6%. **Median travel time to work:** 24 minutes. **Working outside county of residence:** 25.2%.

Cities with pop over 10,000: None.

GRAY COUNTY
PO Box 1902
Pampa, TX 79066
www.co.gray.tx.us

Ph: 806-669-8004
Fax: 806-669-8054

In northeastern TX panhandle, east of Amarillo; organized Aug 21, 1876 from Bexar County. **Name Origin:** For Capt. Peter W. Gray (1819-74), an officer in the TX army, TX legislator and justice of the TX supreme court (1874).

Area (sq mi): 929.25 (land 928.28; water 0.97). **Pop per sq mi:** 23.1.

Pop 2005: 21,479. **State rank:** 110. **Pop change:** 2000-20005 -5.6%; 1990-2000 -5.1%. **Pop 2000:** 22,744 (White 78.3%; Black or African American 5.8%; Hispanic or Latino 13%; Asian 0.4%; Other 11.5%). **Foreign born:** 4.3%. **Median age:** 38.9.

Income 2000: per capita $16,702; median household $31,368; **Pop below poverty level:** 13.8%. ***Personal per capita income 2000-2003:** $24,589-$26,765.

Unemployment 2004: 5.4%. **Change from 2000:** +1.9%. **Median travel time to work:** 16.6 minutes. **Working outside county of residence:** 13.5%.

Cities with pop over 10,000: Pampa ⚏ (16,702).

GRAYSON COUNTY
100 W Houston St
Sherman, TX 75090
www.co.grayson.tx.us

Ph: 903-813-4207
Fax: 903-868-9691

On the northeastern border of TX, north of Dallas; organized Mar 17, 1846 from Fannin County. **Name Origin:** For Peter William Grayson (1788-1838), Republic of TX attorney general (1836) who was nominated for presidency of the Republic of Sam Houston (1793-1863), first president of the Republic of TX.

Area (sq mi): 979.19 (land 933.51; water 45.68). **Pop per sq mi:** 125.2.

Pop 2005: 116,834. **State rank:** 32. **Pop change:** 2000-20005 +5.6%; 1990-2000 +16.4%. **Pop 2000:** 110,595 (White 84%; Black or African American 5.9%; Hispanic or Latino 6.8%; Asian 0.6%; Other 6.3%, including 1.3% American Indian/Alaska Native). **Foreign born:** 3.9%. **Median age:** 37.2.

Income 2000: per capita $18,862; median household $37,178; **Pop below poverty level:** 11.3%. ***Personal per capita income 2000-2003:** $23,046-$23,424.

Unemployment 2004: 6.2%. **Change from 2000:** +0.8%. **Median travel time to work:** 24.9 minutes. **Working outside county of residence:** 21%.

Cities with pop over 10,000: Sherman ⚏ (36,578); Denison (23,379).

GREGG COUNTY
PO Box 3049
Longview, TX 75606
www.co.gregg.tx.us

Ph: 903-236-8430
Fax: 903-237-2574

In northeastern TX, northeast of Tyler; organized Apr 12, 1873 from Rusk and Upshur counties. **Name Origin:** For Gen. John Gregg (1828-64), officer in the Confederate Army.

Area (sq mi): 276.37 (land 274.03; water 2.34). **Pop per sq mi:** 422.

Pop 2005: 115,649. **State rank:** 33. **Pop change:** 2000-20005 +3.8%; 1990-2000 +6.1%. **Pop 2000:** 111,379 (White 69%; Black or African American 19.9%; Hispanic or Latino 9.1%; Asian 0.7%; Other 6.6%). **Foreign born:** 5.4%. **Median age:** 35.

Income 2000: per capita $18,449; median household $35,006; **Pop below poverty level:** 15.1%. ***Personal per capita income 2000-2003:** $27,206-$29,092.

Unemployment 2004: 6.1%. **Change from 2000:** +0.7%. **Median travel time to work:** 19.5 minutes. **Working outside county of residence:** 14.6%.

Cities with pop over 10,000: Longview ⚏ (75,306); Kilgore (11,619).

GRIMES COUNTY
PO Box 209
Anderson, TX 77830
www.co.grimes.tx.us

Ph: 936-873-2662
Fax: 936-873-2056

In east-central TX, east of Austin; organized Apr 6, 1846 from Montgomery County. **Name Origin:** For Jesse Grimes (1788-1866), signer of the TX Declaration of Independence (1836) and legislator (1836-37; 1841-45).

Area (sq mi): 801.16 (land 793.6; water 7.56). **Pop per sq mi:** 31.7.

Pop 2005: 25,192. **State rank:** 100. **Pop change:** 2000-20005 +7%; 1990-2000 +25.1%. **Pop 2000:** 23,552 (White 62.7%; Black or African American 20%; Hispanic or Latino 16.1%; Asian 0.3%; Other 7.8%). **Foreign born:** 5%. **Median age:** 38.1.

⚏ *County Seat*

Grimes County (cont'd)

Income 2000: per capita $14,368; median household $32,280; **Pop below poverty level:** 16.6%. ***Personal per capita income 2000-2003:** $17,852-$18,712.

Unemployment 2004: 7.1%. **Change from 2000:** +1.8%. **Median travel time to work:** 32.4 minutes. **Working outside county of residence:** 44.7%.

Cities with pop over 10,000: None.

GUADALUPE COUNTY

PO Box 990   **Ph:** 830-303-4188
Seguin, TX 78156   **Fax:** 830-401-0300
www.co.guadalupe.tx.us

In south-central TX, east of San Antonio; organized Mar 30, 1846 from Bexar and Gonzales counties. **Name Origin:** For the Guadalupe River, which traverses the county; named for Our Lady of Guadalupe, the patron saint of Mexico.

Area (sq mi): 714.17 (land 711.14; water 3.03). **Pop per sq mi:** 144.9.

Pop 2005: 103,032. **State rank:** 36. **Pop change:** 2000-20005 +15.7%; 1990-2000 +37.2%. **Pop 2000:** 89,023 (White 59.4%; Black or African American 5%; Hispanic or Latino 33.2%; Asian 0.9%; Other 16.5%). **Foreign born:** 6.5%. **Median age:** 34.9.

Income 2000: per capita $18,430; median household $43,949; **Pop below poverty level:** 9.8%. ***Personal per capita income 2000-2003:** $23,107-$25,302.

Unemployment 2004: 4.8%. **Change from 2000:** +1.8%. **Median travel time to work:** 24.8 minutes. **Working outside county of residence:** 57.9%.

Cities with pop over 10,000: Schertz (24,975); Seguin ⛪ (24,212).

HALE COUNTY

500 Broadway St Suite 140   **Ph:** 806-291-5261
Plainview, TX 79072   **Fax:** 806-291-9810
www.texasonline.net/halecounty/

In west-central TX panhandle, north of Lubbock; organized Aug 21, 1876 from Bexar County. **Name Origin:** For Lt. John C. Hale (?-1836), a TX officer killed in the battle of San Jacinto.

Area (sq mi): 1004.77 (land 1004.65; water 0.12). **Pop per sq mi:** 36.1.

Pop 2005: 36,233. **State rank:** 80. **Pop change:** 2000-20005 -1%; 1990-2000 +5.6%. **Pop 2000:** 36,602 (White 45.2%; Black or African American 5.8%; Hispanic or Latino 47.9%; Asian 0.3%; Other 27.1%). **Foreign born:** 8.2%. **Median age:** 31.4.

Income 2000: per capita $13,655; median household $31,280; **Pop below poverty level:** 18%. ***Personal per capita income 2000-2003:** $20,690-$22,848.

Unemployment 2004: 6.2%. **Change from 2000:** +1.4%. **Median travel time to work:** 15.4 minutes. **Working outside county of residence:** 13.9%.

Cities with pop over 10,000: Plainview ⛪ (21,995).

HALL COUNTY

512 Main St County Courthouse   **Ph:** 806-259-2627
Memphis, TX 79245   **Fax:** 806-259-5078
www.co.hall.tx.us

In east-central TX panhandle, northeast of Lubbock; organized Aug 21, 1876 from Bexar County. **Name Origin:** For Gen. Warren D. C. Hall (1788-1867), TX Republic officer and secretary of war.

Area (sq mi): 904.08 (land 903.09; water 0.99). **Pop per sq mi:** 4.1.

Pop 2005: 3,700. **State rank:** 217. **Pop change:** 2000-20005 -2.2%; 1990-2000 -3.1%. **Pop 2000:** 3,782 (White 63.4%; Black or African American 8.2%; Hispanic or Latino 27.5%; Asian 0.2%; Other 19.6%). **Foreign born:** 9.1%. **Median age:** 40.2.

Income 2000: per capita $13,210; median household $23,016; **Pop below poverty level:** 26.3%. ***Personal per capita income 2000-2003:** $15,901-$19,392.

Unemployment 2004: 6.6%. **Change from 2000:** +2.4%. **Median travel time to work:** 17 minutes. **Working outside county of residence:** 19.5%.

Cities with pop over 10,000: None.

HAMILTON COUNTY

County Courthouse   **Ph:** 254-386-3518
Hamilton, TX 76531   **Fax:** 254-386-8727
www.co.hamilton.tx.us

In central TX, northwest of Waco; created Jan 22, 1858 and organized Jun 2, 1858, being part of the Milam Land District of TX and developed from parts of Bosque, Lampasas, and Comanche counties. **Name Origin:** For Gen. James Hamilton, Jr. (1786-1857), U.S. representative from SC (1822-29), governor (1830-32), and legislator who championed the cause of TX independence and settled there (1855).

Area (sq mi): 836.38 (land 835.71; water 0.67). **Pop per sq mi:** 9.7.

Pop 2005: 8,105. **State rank:** 177. **Pop change:** 2000-20005 -1.5%; 1990-2000 +6.4%. **Pop 2000:** 8,229 (White 91.1%; Black or African American 0.1%; Hispanic or Latino 7.4%; Asian 0.1%; Other 5.8%). **Foreign born:** 3.7%. **Median age:** 43.1.

Income 2000: per capita $16,800; median household $31,150; **Pop below poverty level:** 14.2%. ***Personal per capita income 2000-2003:** $22,734-$23,763.

Unemployment 2004: 4.4%. **Change from 2000:** +2%. **Median travel time to work:** 23.9 minutes. **Working outside county of residence:** 31.7%.

Cities with pop over 10,000: None.

HANSFORD COUNTY

15 NW Court   **Ph:** 806-659-4110
Spearman, TX 79081   **Fax:** 806-659-4168
www.co.hansford.tx.us

In north-central TX panhandle, northeast of Amarillo; organized Aug 21, 1876 from Bexar County. **Name Origin:** For Gen. John M. Hansford (?-1844), TX district court judge (1840-42) and attorney general of TX.

Area (sq mi): 920.4 (land 919.8; water 0.6). **Pop per sq mi:** 5.7.

Pop 2005: 5,230. **State rank:** 201. **Pop change:** 2000-20005 -2.6%; 1990-2000 -8.2%. **Pop 2000:** 5,369 (White 67.1%; Black or African

Source: Personal per capita income data are from the Bureau of Economic Analysis; per capita income data are from the Bureau of the Census. See Introduction for explanation of differences.

Hansford County (cont'd)

American 0%; Hispanic or Latino 31.5%; Asian 0.2%; Other 19.8%). **Foreign born:** 15.6%. **Median age:** 36.5.

Income 2000: per capita $17,408; median household $35,438; **Pop below poverty level:** 16.4%. ***Personal per capita income 2000-2003:** $33,530-$34,080.

Unemployment 2004: 3.9%. **Change from 2000:** +1.7%. **Median travel time to work:** 15.9 minutes. **Working outside county of residence:** 15.7%.

Cities with pop over 10,000: None.

HARDEMAN COUNTY

PO Box 30   **Ph:** 940-663-2901
Quanah, TX 79252

On the central northern border of TX, northwest of Wichita Falls; organized Feb 1, 1858 from Fannin County. **Name Origin:** For Lt. Bailey Hardeman (1795 1836), signer of the TX Declaration of Independence (1836) and secretary of the treasury of the TX Republic.

Area (sq mi): 697 (land 695.38; water 1.62). **Pop per sq mi:** 6.2.

Pop 2005: 4,291. **State rank:** 207. **Pop change:** 2000-20005 -9.2%; 1990-2000 -10.6%. **Pop 2000:** 4,724 (White 79%; Black or African American 4.8%; Hispanic or Latino 14.5%; Asian 0.3%; Other 9.5%). **Foreign born:** 2.5%. **Median age:** 41.2.

Income 2000: per capita $16,824; median household $28,312; **Pop below poverty level:** 17.8%. ***Personal per capita income 2000-2003:** $20,498-$23,313.

Unemployment 2004: 5.5%. **Change from 2000:** +2%. **Median travel time to work:** 15.7 minutes. **Working outside county of residence:** 27.7%.

Cities with pop over 10,000: None.

HARDIN COUNTY

300 Monroe St Suite B-110   **Ph:** 409-246-5185
Kountze, TX 77625
www.co.hardin.tx.us

In east-central TX, north of Beaumont; organized Jan 22, 1858 from Jefferson and Liberty counties. **Name Origin:** For William Hardin (1801-39), primary judge of Liberty, TX (1834).

Area (sq mi): 897.37 (land 894.33; water 3.04). **Pop per sq mi:** 57.

Pop 2005: 50,976. **State rank:** 59. **Pop change:** 2000-20005 +6%; 1990-2000 +16.3%. **Pop 2000:** 48,073 (White 89.3%; Black or African American 6.9%; Hispanic or Latino 2.5%; Asian 0.2%; Other 1.9%). **Foreign born:** 1.3%. **Median age:** 36.

Income 2000: per capita $17,962; median household $37,612; **Pop below poverty level:** 11.2%. ***Personal per capita income 2000-2003:** $22,683-$24,753.

Unemployment 2004: 7.5%. **Change from 2000:** +0.7%. **Median travel time to work:** 29.7 minutes. **Working outside county of residence:** 59.8%.

Cities with pop over 10,000: Beaumont 🏛 (112,294).

HARRIS COUNTY

1001 Preston St 4th Fl   **Ph:** 713-755-5000
Houston, TX 77002
www.co.harris.tx.us

In east-central TX, north of Galveston; organized as Harrrisburg County Mar 17, 1836 (prior to statehood) from Austin and Liberty counties (Old Mexican Municipality); name changed Dec 28, 1839. **Name Origin:** For John Richardson Harris (1790-1829), trading post owner who ran steamboats between Texas and New Orleans.

Area (sq mi): 1777.69 (land 1728.83; water 48.87). **Pop per sq mi:** 2136.2.

Pop 2005: 3,693,050. **State rank:** 1. **Pop change:** 2000-20005 +8.6%; 1990-2000 +20.7%. **Pop 2000:** 3,400,578 (White 42.1%; Black or African American 18.5%; Hispanic or Latino 32.9%; Asian 5.1%; Other 17.7%). **Foreign born:** 22.2%. **Median age:** 31.2.

Income 2000: per capita $21,435; median household $42,598; **Pop below poverty level:** 15%. ***Personal per capita income 2000-2003:** $35,607-$36,314.

Unemployment 2004: 6.4%. **Change from 2000:** +1.9%. **Median travel time to work:** 28.1 minutes. **Working outside county of residence:** 6.5%.

Cities with pop over 10,000: 13 (see page 39 for cities).

HARRISON COUNTY

PO Box 1365   **Ph:** 903-935-8403
Marshall, TX 75671
www.co.harrison.tx.us

On the northeastern border of TX, west of Shreveport, LA; organized Jan 28, 1839 (prior to statehood) from Shelby County. **Name Origin:** For Jonas Harrison (1777-1837), a pioneer lawyer from Shelby County.

Area (sq mi): 915.09 (land 898.71; water 16.38). **Pop per sq mi:** 70.6.

Pop 2005: 63,459. **State rank:** 50. **Pop change:** 2000-20005 +2.2%; 1990-2000 +8%. **Pop 2000:** 62,110 (White 69.3%; Black or African American 24%; Hispanic or Latino 5.3%; Asian 0.3%; Other 4.3%). **Foreign born:** 3.3%. **Median age:** 36.1.

Income 2000: per capita $16,702; median household $33,520; **Pop below poverty level:** 16.7%. ***Personal per capita income 2000-2003:** $21,560-$24,053.

Unemployment 2004: 5.8%. **Change from 2000:** +0.2%. **Median travel time to work:** 23 minutes. **Working outside county of residence:** 39.9%.

Cities with pop over 10,000: Marshall 🏛 (23,671).

HARTLEY COUNTY

PO Box Q   **Ph:** 806-235-3582
Channing, TX 79018   **Fax:** 806-235-2316
www.co.hartley.tx.us

On the northwestern border of TX panhandle, northwest of Amarillo; organized Aug 21, 1876 from Bexar County. **Name Origin:** For Oliver Cromwell Hartley (1823-59), TX attorney, legislator, and legal scholar.

Area (sq mi): 1463.2 (land 1462.25; water 0.95). **Pop per sq mi:** 3.7.

🏛 *County Seat*

Hartley County (cont'd)

Pop 2005: 5,450. **State rank:** 199. **Pop change:** 2000-20005 -1.6%; 1990-2000 +52.4%. **Pop 2000:** 5,537 (White 77.1%; Black or African American 8.1%; Hispanic or Latino 13.7%; Asian 0.3%; Other 10.5%). **Foreign born:** 2.6%. **Median age:** 39.6.

Income 2000: per capita $18,067; median household $46,327; **Pop below poverty level:** 6.6%. ***Personal per capita income 2000-2003:** $27,972-$29,735.

Unemployment 2004: 4.1%. **Change from 2000:** +2.9%. **Median travel time to work:** 13.4 minutes. **Working outside county of residence:** 56.1%.

Cities with pop over 10,000: None.

HASKELL COUNTY

PO Box 725   **Ph:** 940-864-2451
Haskell, TX 79521   **Fax:** 940-864-6164
www.co.haskell.tx.us

In north-central TX, north of Abilene; organized Feb 1, 1858 from Fannin and Milam counties. **Name Origin:** For Charles Ready Haskell (1817-36), Republic of Texas soldier killed in battle.

Area (sq mi): 910.25 (land 902.97; water 7.29). **Pop per sq mi:** 6.1.

Pop 2005: 5,541. **State rank:** 197. **Pop change:** 2000-20005 -9.1%; 1990-2000 -10.7%. **Pop 2000:** 6,093 (White 75.5%; Black or African American 2.8%; Hispanic or Latino 20.5%; Asian 0.1%; Other 14.3%). **Foreign born:** 3.6%. **Median age:** 43.9.

Income 2000: per capita $14,918; median household $23,690; **Pop below poverty level:** 22.8%. ***Personal per capita income 2000-2003:** $19,040-$23,940.

Unemployment 2004: 4.6%. **Change from 2000:** +1.7%. **Median travel time to work:** 19.4 minutes. **Working outside county of residence:** 26.7%.

Cities with pop over 10,000: None.

HAYS COUNTY

110 E Martin Luther King St   **Ph:** 512-393-7738
San Marcos, TX 78666   **Fax:** 512-393-7735
www.co.hays.tx.us

In south-central TX, southwest of Austin; organized Mar 1, 1848 from Travis County. **Name Origin:** For Capt. John Coffee Hays (1817-83), Texas Ranger, officer in the Mexican War, sheriff of San Francisco County, CA (1849-53), and surveyor general of CA (1859).

Area (sq mi): 679.79 (land 677.87; water 1.92). **Pop per sq mi:** 183.6.

Pop 2005: 124,432. **State rank:** 29. **Pop change:** 2000-20005 +27.5%; 1990-2000 +48.7%. **Pop 2000:** 97,589 (White 64.5%; Black or African American 3.7%; Hispanic or Latino 29.6%; Asian 0.8%; Other 16.7%). **Foreign born:** 5.6%. **Median age:** 28.4.

Income 2000: per capita $19,931; median household $45,006; **Pop below poverty level:** 14.3%. ***Personal per capita income 2000-2003:** $23,462-$23,341.

Unemployment 2004: 4.9%. **Change from 2000:** +1.6%. **Median travel time to work:** 28 minutes. **Working outside county of residence:** 49.5%.

Cities with pop over 10,000: San Marcos ⛪ (44,628); Kyle (14,053).

HEMPHILL COUNTY

PO Box 867   **Ph:** 806-323-6212
Canadian, TX 79014

On the northeastern border of TX panhandle, northeast of Amarillo; organized Aug 21, 1876 from Bexar County. **Name Origin:** For Gen. John Hemphill (1803-62), chief justice of the TX supreme court (1846-58) and U.S. senator (1859-61).

Area (sq mi): 912.06 (land 909.68; water 2.38). **Pop per sq mi:** 3.8.

Pop 2005: 3,422. **State rank:** 219. **Pop change:** 2000-20005 +2.1%; 1990-2000 -9.9%. **Pop 2000:** 3,351 (White 81.2%; Black or African American 1.6%; Hispanic or Latino 15.6%; Asian 0.3%; Other 10.5%). **Foreign born:** 6.5%. **Median age:** 38.6.

Income 2000: per capita $16,929; median household $35,456; **Pop below poverty level:** 12.6%. ***Personal per capita income 2000-2003:** $33,584-$37,096.

Unemployment 2004: 3.3%. **Change from 2000:** +1.6%. **Median travel time to work:** 18.1 minutes. **Working outside county of residence:** 15.8%.

Cities with pop over 10,000: None.

HENDERSON COUNTY

Courthouse Sq Rm 107   **Ph:** 903-675-6140
Athens, TX 75751   **Fax:** 903-675-6105
www.co.henderson.tx.us/

In northeastern TX, southwest of Tyler; organized Apr 27, 1846 from Houston County. **Name Origin:** For Gen. James Pinckney Henderson (1808-58), TX minister to the U.S. (1844), first governor of the state of TX (1846-47), and U.S. senator (1857-58).

Area (sq mi): 949 (land 874.24; water 74.76). **Pop per sq mi:** 91.5.

Pop 2005: 80,017. **State rank:** 45. **Pop change:** 2000-20005 +9.2%; 1990-2000 +25.2%. **Pop 2000:** 73,277 (White 84.8%; Black or African American 6.6%; Hispanic or Latino 6.9%; Asian 0.3%; Other 4.5%). **Foreign born:** 3.8%. **Median age:** 40.2.

Income 2000: per capita $17,772; median household $32,533; **Pop below poverty level:** 15.1%. ***Personal per capita income 2000-2003:** $22,790-$23,218.

Unemployment 2004: 6%. **Change from 2000:** +2.2%. **Median travel time to work:** 35.4 minutes. **Working outside county of residence:** 45.3%.

Cities with pop over 10,000: Athens ⛪ (12,364).

HIDALGO COUNTY

PO Box 58   **Ph:** 956-318-2100
Edinburg, TX 78540   **Fax:** 956-318-2105
www.co.hidalgo.tx.us

On the southern border of TX, west of Harlingen; organized Jan 24, 1852 from Cameron County. **Name Origin:** Either for Guadalupe Hidalgo, D.F., Mexico, or possibly in honor of Miguel Hidalgo y Costilla (1753-1811), Mexican priest and hero of the Mexican war for Independence from Spain. Spanish 'nobleman.'

Area (sq mi): 1582.66 (land 1569.75; water 12.92). **Pop per sq mi:** 432.1.

Source: Personal per capita income data are from the Bureau of Economic Analysis; per capita income data are from the Bureau of the Census. See Introduction for explanation of differences.

Hidalgo County (cont'd)

Pop 2005: 678,275. **State rank:** 7. **Pop change:** 2000-20005 +19.1%; 1990-2000 +48.5%. **Pop 2000:** 569,463 (White 10.4%; Black or African American 0.5%; Hispanic or Latino 88.3%; Asian 0.6%; Other 21.1%). **Foreign born:** 29.5%. **Median age:** 27.2.

Income 2000: per capita $9,899; median household $24,863; **Pop below poverty level:** 35.0%. ***Personal per capita income 2000-2003:** $13,576-$15,184.

Unemployment 2004: 9.1%. **Change from 2000:** -4%. **Median travel time to work:** 20.9 minutes. **Working outside county of residence:** 7.8%.

Cities with pop over 10,000: 10 (see page 39 for cities).

HILL COUNTY

PO Box 398   **Ph:** 254-582-4030
Hillsboro, TX 76645   **Fax:** 254-582-4003
www.co.hill.tx.us

In north-central TX, south of Fort Worth; organized Feb 7, 1853 from Navarro County. **Name Origin:** For George Washington Hill (1814-60), secretary of war and navy under Republic of TX presidents Sam Houston (1793-1863) and Anson Jones (1798-1858).

Area (sq mi): 985.65 (land 962.36; water 23.29). **Pop per sq mi:** 36.8.

Pop 2005: 35,424. **State rank:** 82. **Pop change:** 2000-20005 +9.6%; 1990-2000 +19.1%. **Pop 2000:** 32,321 (White 77.6%; Black or African American 7.4%; Hispanic or Latino 13.5%; Asian 0.3%; Other 8.1%). **Foreign born:** 5.9%. **Median age:** 38.3.

Income 2000: per capita $15,514; median household $31,600; **Pop below poverty level:** 15.7%. ***Personal per capita income 2000-2003:** $20,006-$21,616.

Unemployment 2004: 6.4%. **Change from 2000:** +1.3%. **Median travel time to work:** 29.4 minutes. **Working outside county of residence:** 36.8%.

Cities with pop over 10,000: None.

HOCKLEY COUNTY

802 Houston St Suite 213   **Ph:** 806-894-4404
Levelland, TX 79336
www.co.hockley.tx.us

In southwestern TX panhandle, west of Lubbock; organized 1921 (other sources say organized Aug 21, 1876; first federal census: 1880 with no population). **Name Origin:** For Gen. George Washington Hockley (1802-54), Republic of Texas officer and secretary of war (1838; 1841).

Area (sq mi): 908.55 (land 908.28; water 0.27). **Pop per sq mi:** 25.1.

Pop 2005: 22,787. **State rank:** 106. **Pop change:** 2000-20005 +0.3%; 1990-2000 -6.1%. **Pop 2000:** 22,716 (White 57.9%; Black or African American 3.7%; Hispanic or Latino 37.2%; Asian 0.1%; Other 21.7%). **Foreign born:** 5.2%. **Median age:** 33.3.

Income 2000: per capita $15,022; median household $31,085; **Pop below poverty level:** 18.9%. ***Personal per capita income 2000-2003:** $20,466-$22,687.

Unemployment 2004: 4.7%. **Change from 2000:** +1.3%. **Median travel time to work:** 22.4 minutes. **Working outside county of residence:** 33.1%.

Cities with pop over 10,000: Levelland ▦ (12,771).

HOOD COUNTY

PO Box 339   **Ph:** 817-579-3222
Granbury, TX 76048   **Fax:** 817-579-3227
www.co.hood.tx.us

In north-central TX, southwest of Fort Worth; organized Nov 3, 1865 from Johnson County. **Name Origin:** For Gen. John Bell Hood (1831-79), commander of TX troops in the Confederate army and later commander of the Confederate Army of TN.

Area (sq mi): 436.8 (land 421.61; water 15.19). **Pop per sq mi:** 113.7.

Pop 2005: 47,930. **State rank:** 64. **Pop change:** 2000-20005 +16.6%; 1990-2000 +41.8%. **Pop 2000:** 41,100 (White 90.5%; Black or African American 0.3%; Hispanic or Latino 7.2%; Asian 0.3%; Other 4.5%). **Foreign born:** 3.3%. **Median age:** 41.5.

Income 2000: per capita $22,261; median household $43,668; **Pop below poverty level:** 8.5%. ***Personal per capita income 2000-2003:** $27,699-$28,503.

Unemployment 2004: 5.5%. **Change from 2000:** +1.3%. **Median travel time to work:** 34.1 minutes. **Working outside county of residence:** 45.3%.

Cities with pop over 10,000: None.

HOPKINS COUNTY

PO Box 288   **Ph:** 903-438-4074
Sulphur Springs, TX 75483   **Fax:** 903-438-4110
www.hopkinscountytx.org

In northeastern TX, northeast of Dallas; organized Mar 25, 1846 from Lamar and Nacogdoches counties. **Name Origin:** For the pioneer family headed by Henry Harrison Hopkins and James Elliott Hopkins.

Area (sq mi): 792.74 (land 782.4; water 10.35). **Pop per sq mi:** 42.7.

Pop 2005: 33,381. **State rank:** 85. **Pop change:** 2000-20005 +4.4%; 1990-2000 +10.8%. **Pop 2000:** 31,960 (White 81.2%; Black or African American 8%; Hispanic or Latino 9.3%; Asian 0.2%; Other 6.8%). **Foreign born:** 5.6%. **Median age:** 36.9.

Income 2000: per capita $17,182; median household $32,136; **Pop below poverty level:** 14.6%. ***Personal per capita income 2000-2003:** $22,531-$22,987.

Unemployment 2004: 5.3%. **Change from 2000:** +1.1%. **Median travel time to work:** 22.6 minutes. **Working outside county of residence:** 24.6%.

Cities with pop over 10,000: Sulphur Springs ▦ (15,081).

▦ *County Seat*

HOUSTON COUNTY

PO Box 370   **Ph:** 936-544-3256
Crockett, TX 75835   **Fax:** 936-544-1954
www.co.houston.tx.us

In east-central TX, west of Lufkin; organized 1837 from Nacogdoches County (prior to statehood). **Name Origin:** For Samuel Houston (1793-1863), governor of TN (1827-29), president of the Republic of Texas (1836-38; 1841-44); U.S. senator from TX (1846-59) and TX governor (1859-61).

Area (sq mi): 1236.83 (land 1230.89; water 5.94). **Pop per sq mi:** 18.9.

Pop 2005: 23,218. **State rank:** 103. **Pop change:** 2000-20005 +0.1%; 1990-2000 +8.5%. **Pop 2000:** 23,185 (White 63.7%; Black or African American 27.9%; Hispanic or Latino 7.5%; Asian 0.2%; Other 3.4%). **Foreign born:** 3%. **Median age:** 40.3.

Income 2000: per capita $14,525; median household $28,119; **Pop below poverty level:** 21%. ***Personal per capita income 2000-2003:** $22,238-$23,121.

Unemployment 2004: 6.8%. **Change from 2000:** +3.1%. **Median travel time to work:** 23.9 minutes. **Working outside county of residence:** 20.9%.

Cities with pop over 10,000: None.

HOWARD COUNTY

300 Main St   **Ph:** 432-264-2213
Big Spring, TX 79720   **Fax:** 432-264-2215
www.co.howard.tx.us

In south-central TX panhandle, west of Abilene; organized Aug 21, 1876 from Bexar County. **Name Origin:** For Volney Erskine Howard (1809-89), MS legislator, U.S. representative from TX (1849-53), and judge of CA superior court (1878-79).

Area (sq mi): 904.19 (land 902.84; water 1.36). **Pop per sq mi:** 36.

Pop 2005: 32,522. **State rank:** 88. **Pop change:** 2000-20005 -3.3%; 1990-2000 +4%. **Pop 2000:** 33,627 (White 56.8%; Black or African American 4.1%; Hispanic or Latino 37.5%; Asian 0.6%; Other 15.1%). **Foreign born:** 6%. **Median age:** 36.4.

Income 2000: per capita $15,027; median household $30,805; **Pop below poverty level:** 18.6%. ***Personal per capita income 2000-2003:** $20,011-$21,925.

Unemployment 2004: 6%. **Change from 2000:** +2.1%. **Median travel time to work:** 17.3 minutes. **Working outside county of residence:** 8.6%.

Cities with pop over 10,000: Big Spring 🏛 (24,524).

HUDSPETH COUNTY

PO Box 58   **Ph:** 915-369-2301
Sierra Blanca, TX 79851   **Fax:** 915-369-2407

In western TX, east of El Paso; organized Feb 16, 1917 from El Paso County. **Name Origin:** For Claude Benton Hudspeth (1877-1941), TX legislator (1902-18) and U.S. representative (1919-31).

Area (sq mi): 4571.93 (land 4571; water 0.93). **Pop per sq mi:** 0.7.

Pop 2005: 3,295. **State rank:** 221. **Pop change:** 2000-20005 -1.5%; 1990-2000 +14.7%. **Pop 2000:** 3,344 (White 23%; Black or African American 0.3%; Hispanic or Latino 75%; Asian 0.2%; Other 12.3%,

including 1.4% American Indian/Alaska Native). **Foreign born:** 33.2%. **Median age:** 30.2.

Income 2000: per capita $9,549; median household $21,045; **Pop below poverty level:** 35.8%. ***Personal per capita income 2000-2003:** $14,137-$16,482.

Unemployment 2004: 7%. **Change from 2000:** +2.7%. **Median travel time to work:** 17 minutes. **Working outside county of residence:** 24.8%.

Cities with pop over 10,000: None.

HUNT COUNTY

PO Box 1316   **Ph:** 903-408-4130
Greenville, TX 75403   **Fax:** 903-408-4287
www.huntcounty.net

In east-central TX, northeast of Dallas; organized Apr 11, 1846 from Fannin and Nacogdoches counties. **Name Origin:** For Gen. Menucan Hunt (1807-56), Republic of TX officer and statesman.

Area (sq mi): 882.02 (land 841.16; water 40.87). **Pop per sq mi:** 98.1.

Pop 2005: 82,543. **State rank:** 43. **Pop change:** 2000-20005 +7.8%; 1990-2000 +19%. **Pop 2000:** 76,596 (White 79.9%; Black or African American 9.5%; Hispanic or Latino 8.3%; Asian 0.5%; Other 6.4%). **Foreign born:** 4.7%. **Median age:** 35.5.

Income 2000: per capita $17,554; median household $36,752; **Pop below poverty level:** 12.8%. ***Personal per capita income 2000-2003:** $22,944-$24,318.

Unemployment 2004: 6.1%. **Change from 2000:** +1.2%. **Median travel time to work:** 30.1 minutes. **Working outside county of residence:** 38%.

Cities with pop over 10,000: Greenville 🏛 (25,149).

HUTCHINSON COUNTY

PO Box 1186   **Ph:** 806-878-4002
Stinnett, TX 79083
www.co.hutchinson.tx.us

In north-central TX panhandle, northeast of Amarillo; organized Aug 21, 1876 from Bexar County. **Name Origin:** For Anderson Hutchinson (1798-1853), Republic of TX district judge.

Area (sq mi): 894.95 (land 887.37; water 7.58). **Pop per sq mi:** 25.3.

Pop 2005: 22,484. **State rank:** 109. **Pop change:** 2000-20005 -5.8%; 1990-2000 -7.1%. **Pop 2000:** 23,857 (White 80.1%; Black or African American 2.4%; Hispanic or Latino 14.7%; Asian 0.3%; Other 10.3%, including 1.4% American Indian/Alaska Native). **Foreign born:** 5.8%. **Median age:** 37.5.

Income 2000: per capita $17,317; median household $36,588; **Pop below poverty level:** 11.1%. ***Personal per capita income 2000-2003:** $23,405-$26,554.

Unemployment 2004: 6.5%. **Change from 2000:** +2.3%. **Median travel time to work:** 19.3 minutes. **Working outside county of residence:** 15.6%.

Cities with pop over 10,000: Borger (13,400).

Source: Personal per capita income data are from the Bureau of Economic Analysis; per capita income data are from the Bureau of the Census. See Introduction for explanation of differences.

IRION COUNTY

PO Box 736
Mertzon, TX 76941
www.co.irion.tx.us

Ph: 325-835-2421
Fax: 325-835-2008

In central TX, west of San Angelo; organized Mar 7, 1889 from Tom Green County. **Name Origin:** For Robert Anderson Irion (1806-61), senator in first TX congress (1836-37) and secretary of state of the Republic (1837-38).

Area (sq mi): 1051.59 (land 1051.48; water 0.11). **Pop per sq mi:** 1.7.

Pop 2005: 1,756. **State rank:** 238. **Pop change:** 2000-20005 -0.8%; 1990-2000 +8.7%. **Pop 2000:** 1,771 (White 74.6%; Black or African American 0.4%; Hispanic or Latino 24.6%; Asian 0%; Other 8.9%). **Foreign born:** 3.5%. **Median age:** 39.9.

Income 2000: per capita $20,515; median household $37,500; **Pop below poverty level:** 8.4%. ***Personal per capita income 2000-2003:** $22,984-$23,303.

Unemployment 2004: 4.3%. **Change from 2000:** +2%. **Median travel time to work:** 25.9 minutes. **Working outside county of residence:** 46.6%.

Cities with pop over 10,000: None.

JACK COUNTY

100 Main St
Jacksboro, TX 76458

Ph: 940-567-2111
Fax: 940-567-6641

In north-central TX, northwest of Fort Worth; organized July 4, 1857 from Cooke County. **Name Origin:** For the Jack brothers, William Houston (1806-44) and Patrick Churchill (1808-44), both TX statesman and legislators.

Area (sq mi): 920.11 (land 916.61; water 3.5). **Pop per sq mi:** 9.9.

Pop 2005: 9,064. **State rank:** 174. **Pop change:** 2000-20005 +3.4%; 1990-2000 +25.5%. **Pop 2000:** 8,763 (White 85.2%; Black or African American 5.5%; Hispanic or Latino 7.9%; Asian 0.3%; Other 5.5%). **Foreign born:** 2.8%. **Median age:** 37.

Income 2000: per capita $15,210; median household $32,500; **Pop below poverty level:** 12.9%. ***Personal per capita income 2000-2003:** $18,488-$19,453.

Unemployment 2004: 4.9%. **Change from 2000:** +1.7%. **Median travel time to work:** 28.1 minutes. **Working outside county of residence:** 37.2%.

Cities with pop over 10,000: None.

JACKSON COUNTY

115 W Main St Rm 101
Edna, TX 77957
www.co.jackson.tx.us

Ph: 361-782-3563

On the central eastern coast of TX, east of Victoria; original county; organized Mar 17, 1836 (prior to statehood) from Old Mexican Municipality. **Name Origin:** For Andrew Jackson (1767-1845), seventh U.S. president.

Area (sq mi): 857.03 (land 829.49; water 27.54). **Pop per sq mi:** 17.3.

Pop 2005: 14,339. **State rank:** 142. **Pop change:** 2000-20005 -0.4%; 1990-2000 +10.4%. **Pop 2000:** 14,391 (White 66.3%; Black

or African American 7.6%; Hispanic or Latino 24.7%; Asian 0.4%; Other 15.5%). **Foreign born:** 4.8%. **Median age:** 37.3.

Income 2000: per capita $16,693; median household $35,254; **Pop below poverty level:** 14.7%. ***Personal per capita income 2000-2003:** $22,896-$22,394.

Unemployment 2004: 5.9%. **Change from 2000:** +2.6%. **Median travel time to work:** 23.6 minutes. **Working outside county of residence:** 36.2%.

Cities with pop over 10,000: None.

JASPER COUNTY

P121 N Austin St Rm 103
Jasper, TX 75951
www.co.jasper.tx.us

Ph: 409-384-2632
Fax: 409-384-7198

In east-central TX, north of Beaumont; original county; organized Mar 17, 1836 (prior to statehood) from Old Mexican Municipality. **Name Origin:** For Sgt. William Jasper (1750-79), American Revolutionary War soldier from SC.

Area (sq mi): 969.62 (land 937.4; water 32.22). **Pop per sq mi:** 38.

Pop 2005: 35,587. **State rank:** 81. **Pop change:** 2000-20005 +0%; 1990-2000 +14.5%. **Pop 2000:** 35,604 (White 76.7%; Black or African American 17.8%; Hispanic or Latino 3.9%; Asian 0.3%; Other 3.6%). **Foreign born:** 2.2%. **Median age:** 37.3.

Income 2000: per capita $15,636; median household $30,902; **Pop below poverty level:** 18.1%. ***Personal per capita income 2000-2003:** $20,970-$21,873.

Unemployment 2004: 9.1%. **Change from 2000:** -2.3%. **Median travel time to work:** 28.1 minutes. **Working outside county of residence:** 35.2%.

Cities with pop over 10,000: None.

JEFF DAVIS COUNTY

100 Woodward Ave
Fort Davis, TX 79734
www.co.jeff-davis.tx.us

Ph: 432-426-3251
Fax: 432-426-3760

In western TX, southwest of Odessa; organized Mar 15, 1887 from Presidio County. **Name Origin:** For Jefferson Davis (1808-89), president of the Confederate States of America (1862-65).

Area (sq mi): 2264.6 (land 2264.43; water 0.18). **Pop per sq mi:** 1.

Pop 2005: 2,306. **State rank:** 233. **Pop change:** 2000-20005 +4.5%; 1990-2000 +13.4%. **Pop 2000:** 2,207 (White 62.3%; Black or African American 0.9%; Hispanic or Latino 35.5%; Asian 0.1%; Other 8.5%). **Foreign born:** 10.9%. **Median age:** 42.5.

Income 2000: per capita $18,846; median household $32,212; **Pop below poverty level:** 15%. ***Personal per capita income 2000-2003:** $17,081-$20,154.

Unemployment 2004: 3.6%. **Change from 2000:** +1.8%. **Median travel time to work:** 24.1 minutes. **Working outside county of residence:** 28.3%.

Cities with pop over 10,000: None.

JEFFERSON COUNTY

114 Pearl St   **Ph:** 409-835-8475
Beaumont, TX 77701   **Fax:** 409-839-2394
www.co.jefferson.tx.us

On the northeastern coast of TX, east of Houston; original county; organized Mar 17, 1836 (prior to statehood) from Old Mexican Municipality. **Name Origin:** For Jefferson Beaumont, an early settler.

Area (sq mi): 1111.26 (land 903.55; water 207.71). **Pop per sq mi:** 274.

Pop 2005: 247,571. **State rank:** 19. **Pop change:** 2000-20005 -1.8%; 1990-2000 +5.3%. **Pop 2000:** 252,051 (White 51.8%; Black or African American 33.7%; Hispanic or Latino 10.5%; Asian 2.9%; Other 6.1%). **Foreign born:** 6.2%. **Median age:** 35.3.

Income 2000: per capita $17,571; median household $34,706; **Pop below poverty level:** 17.4%. ***Personal per capita income 2000-2003:** $24,335-$27,108.

Unemployment 2004: 8.4%. **Change from 2000:** +0.5%. **Median travel time to work:** 20.3 minutes. **Working outside county of residence:** 9.2%.

Cities with pop over 10,000: Port Arthur (56,727); Nederland (16,837); Groves (15,147); Port Neches (13,224).

JIM HOGG COUNTY

PO Box 878   **Ph:** 361-527-4031
Hebbronville, TX 78361   **Fax:** 361-527-5843
www.co.jim-hogg.tx.us

In southern TX, southeast of Laredo; organized Mar 31, 1913 from Brooks and Duval counties. **Name Origin:** For James Stephen Hogg (1851-1906), newspaper publisher, attorney general of TX (1886-90), and governor (1891-95).

Area (sq mi): 1136.16 (land 1136.11; water 0.05). **Pop per sq mi:** 4.4.

Pop 2005: 5,029. **State rank:** 202. **Pop change:** 2000-20005 -4.8%; 1990-2000 +3.4%. **Pop 2000:** 5,281 (White 9%; Black or African American 0.5%; Hispanic or Latino 90%; Asian 0.2%; Other 18.9%). **Foreign born:** 5.1%. **Median age:** 33.9.

Income 2000: per capita $12,185; median household $25,833; **Pop below poverty level:** 25.9%. ***Personal per capita income 2000-2003:** $17,360-$21,259.

Unemployment 2004: 5.1%. **Change from 2000:** +0.6%. **Median travel time to work:** 23.2 minutes. **Working outside county of residence:** 25.2%.

Cities with pop over 10,000: None.

JIM WELLS COUNTY

PO Box 1459   **Ph:** 361-668-5702
Alice, TX 78333
www.co.jim-wells.tx.us

In southeastern TX, west of Corpus Christi; organized Mar 25, 1911 from Nueces County. **Name Origin:** For James B. Wells, a jurist.

Area (sq mi): 868.22 (land 864.52; water 3.71). **Pop per sq mi:** 47.4.

Pop 2005: 40,951. **State rank:** 72. **Pop change:** 2000-20005 +4.1%; 1990-2000 +4.4%. **Pop 2000:** 39,326 (White 22.9%; Black or African American 0.6%; Hispanic or Latino 75.7%; Asian 0.4%; Other 21%). **Foreign born:** 3.6%. **Median age:** 32.8.

Income 2000: per capita $12,252; median household $28,843; **Pop below poverty level:** 24.1%. ***Personal per capita income 2000-2003:** $18,653-$21,149.

Unemployment 2004: 6.6%. **Change from 2000:** +0.9%. **Median travel time to work:** 25.1 minutes. **Working outside county of residence:** 27.8%.

Cities with pop over 10,000: Alice ⚖ (19,445).

JOHNSON COUNTY

PO Box 662   **Ph:** 817-556-6323
Cleburne, TX 76033   **Fax:** 817-556-6327
www.johnsoncountytx.org

In north-central TX, south of Fort Worth; organized Feb 13, 1854 from McLennan and Navarro counties. **Name Origin:** For Middleton Tate Johnson (1810-66), AL legislator, Texas Ranger, and legislator.

Area (sq mi): 734.46 (land 729.42; water 5.03). **Pop per sq mi:** 200.7.

Pop 2005: 146,376. **State rank:** 24. **Pop change:** 2000-20005 +15.4%; 1990-2000 +30.5%. **Pop 2000:** 126,811 (White 83.2%; Black or African American 2.5%; Hispanic or Latino 12.1%; Asian 0.5%; Other 6.9%). **Foreign born:** 5.2%. **Median age:** 34.3.

Income 2000: per capita $18,400; median household $44,621; **Pop below poverty level:** 8.8%. ***Personal per capita income 2000-2003:** $24,117-$24,728.

Unemployment 2004: 5.9%. **Change from 2000:** +1.8%. **Median travel time to work:** 31.8 minutes. **Working outside county of residence:** 57.6%.

Cities with pop over 10,000: Cleburne ⚖ (28,803); Burleson (27,932).

JONES COUNTY

PO Box 552   **Ph:** 325-823-3762
Anson, TX 79501   **Fax:** 325-823-4223
www.co.jones.tx.us

In north-central TX, north of Abilene; established Feb 1, 1858 from Bexar and Bosque counties. **Name Origin:** For Anson Jones (1798-1858), secretary of state of the Republic of TX (1841-44) and president of the Republic (1844-46).

Area (sq mi): 937.13 (land 930.99; water 6.14). **Pop per sq mi:** 21.2.

Pop 2005: 19,736. **State rank:** 118. **Pop change:** 2000-20005 -5%; 1990-2000 +26%. **Pop 2000:** 20,785 (White 66.2%; Black or African American 11.5%; Hispanic or Latino 20.9%; Asian 0.5%; Other 9.3%). **Foreign born:** 1.6%. **Median age:** 36.

Income 2000: per capita $13,656; median household $29,572; **Pop below poverty level:** 16.8%. ***Personal per capita income 2000-2003:** $16,211-$18,214.

Unemployment 2004: 6.1%. **Change from 2000:** +3.3%. **Median travel time to work:** 21.3 minutes. **Working outside county of residence:** 48%.

Cities with pop over 10,000: None.

---

*Source: Personal per capita income data are from the Bureau of Economic Analysis; per capita income data are from the Bureau of the Census. See Introduction for explanation of differences.

KARNES COUNTY

101 N Panna Maria Ave Suite 9   **Ph:** 830-780-3938
Karnes City, TX 78118   **Fax:** 830-780-4576
www.co.karnes.tx.us

In south-central TX, southeast of San Antonio; organized Feb 4, 1854 from Goliad County. **Name Origin:** For Capt. Henry Wax Karnes (1812-40), TX Republic officer and military scout.

Area (sq mi): 753.58 (land 750.32; water 3.27). **Pop per sq mi:** 20.5

Pop 2005: 15,351. **State rank:** 137. **Pop change:** 2000-20005 -0.6%; 1990-2000 +24%. **Pop 2000:** 15,446 (White 40.8%; Black or African American 10.8%; Hispanic or Latino 47.4%; Asian 0.4%; Other 20.3%). **Foreign born:** 3.7%. **Median age:** 34.1.

Income 2000: per capita $13,603; median household $26,526; **Pop below poverty level:** 21.9%. ***Personal per capita income 2000-2003:** $15,056-$16,234.

Unemployment 2004: 6.9%. **Change from 2000:** +3.1%. **Median travel time to work:** 27.4 minutes. **Working outside county of residence:** 27.8%.

Cities with pop over 10,000: None.

KAUFMAN COUNTY

100 W Mulberry St   **Ph:** 972-932-4331
Kaufman, TX 75142   **Fax:** 972-932-8018
www.kaufmancounty.net

In northeastern TX, east of Dallas; organized Feb 26, 1848 from Henderson County. **Name Origin:** For David Spangler Kaufman (1813-51), Republic of TX legislator (1839-45) and U.S. representative (1846-51).

Area (sq mi): 806.81 (land 786.04; water 20.76). **Pop per sq mi:** 113.4.

Pop 2005: 89,129. **State rank:** 40. **Pop change:** 2000-20005 +25%; 1990-2000 +36.6%. **Pop 2000:** 71,313 (White 76.3%; Black or African American 10.5%; Hispanic or Latino 11.1%; Asian 0.5%; Other 7.9%). **Foreign born:** 5.7%. **Median age:** 34.9.

Income 2000: per capita $18,827; median household $44,783; **Pop below poverty level:** 10.5%. ***Personal per capita income 2000-2003:** $25,212-$24,720.

Unemployment 2004: 6.6%. **Change from 2000:** +1%. **Median travel time to work:** 35.6 minutes. **Working outside county of residence:** 57.2%.

Cities with pop over 10,000: Terrell (16,914).

KENDALL COUNTY

201 E San Antonio St   **Ph:** 830-249-9343
Boerne, TX 78006   **Fax:** 830-249-1763
www.co.kendall.tx.us

In south-central TX, northwest of San Antonio; organized Jan 10, 1862 from Kerr and Blanco counties. **Name Origin:** For George Wilkins Kendall (1809-67), a founder of the New Orleans *Picayune* and Republic of TX army officer.

Area (sq mi): 663.04 (land 662.44; water 0.6). **Pop per sq mi:** 43.2.

Pop 2005: 28,607. **State rank:** 93. **Pop change:** 2000-20005 +20.5%; 1990-2000 +62.7%. **Pop 2000:** 23,743 (White 80.5%; Black or African American 0.3%; Hispanic or Latino 17.9%; Asian 0.2%; Other 6.5%). **Foreign born:** 5.6%. **Median age:** 39.3.

Income 2000: per capita $24,619; median household $49,521; **Pop below poverty level:** 10.5%. ***Personal per capita income 2000-2003:** $30,712-$33,056.

Unemployment 2004: 4.5%. **Change from 2000:** +2.2%. **Median travel time to work:** 29 minutes. **Working outside county of residence:** 52.5%.

Cities with pop over 10,000: None.

KENEDY COUNTY

PO Box 227   **Ph:** 361-294-5220
Sarita, TX 78385   **Fax:** 361-294-5218

On the southeastern coast of TX, south of Corpus Christi; organized as Willacy County 1911 from Hidalgo and Cameron counties; name changed Apr 2, 1921, at which time a new Willacy County was created from Cameron and Hidalgo counties plus a 1.4 mile strip of Old Willacy. **Name Origin:** For Capt. Mifflin Kenedy (1818-95), commercial navigator of the Rio Grande, half-owner of the King ranch (1860-68), and part-owner of the TX narrow gauge railroad (1876-81).

Area (sq mi): 1945.6 (land 1456.77; water 488.83). **Pop per sq mi:** 0.3.

Pop 2005: 417. **State rank:** 252. **Pop change:** 2000-20005 +0.7%; 1990-2000 -10%. **Pop 2000:** 414 (White 20.3%; Black or African American 0.7%; Hispanic or Latino 79%; Asian 0.5%; Other 34.3%). **Foreign born:** 13.3%. **Median age:** 34.2.

Income 2000: per capita $17,959; median household $25,000; **Pop below poverty level:** 15.3%. ***Personal per capita income 2000-2003:** $25,504-$28,792.

Unemployment 2004: 4.7%. **Change from 2000:** +2.9%. **Median travel time to work:** 18.1 minutes. **Working outside county of residence:** 30.5%.

Cities with pop over 10,000: None.

KENT COUNTY

PO Box 9   **Ph:** 806-237-3881
Jayton, TX 79528   **Fax:** 806-237-2632
www.co.kent.tx.us

In southern TX panhandle, northwest of Abilene; organized Aug 21, 1876 from Bexar County. **Name Origin:** For Andrew Kent (1798-1836), TX soldier killed at the Alamo.

Area (sq mi): 902.91 (land 902.33; water 0.58). **Pop per sq mi:** 0.9.

Pop 2005: 782. **State rank:** 250. **Pop change:** 2000-20005 -9%; 1990-2000 -15%. **Pop 2000:** 859 (White 90.5%; Black or African American 0.2%; Hispanic or Latino 9.1%; Asian 0%; Other 4.2%). **Foreign born:** 1.7%. **Median age:** 47.1.

Income 2000: per capita $17,626; median household $30,433; **Pop below poverty level:** 10.4%. ***Personal per capita income 2000-2003:** $19,759-$23,755.

Unemployment 2004: 4.3%. **Change from 2000:** +2.3%. **Median travel time to work:** 19.7 minutes. **Working outside county of residence:** 17.9%.

Cities with pop over 10,000: None.

KERR COUNTY

700 Main St Rm 122   **Ph:** 830-792-2255
Kerrville, TX 78028   **Fax:** 830-792-2274
www.kerrcounty.org

In central TX, northwest of San Antonio; organized Jan 26, 1856 from Bexar County. **Name Origin:** For James Kerr (1790-1850), member of the TX constitutional convention (1836) and TX congress.

Area (sq mi): 1107.66 (land 1106.12; water 1.54). **Pop per sq mi:** 42.

Pop 2005: 46,496. **State rank:** 67. **Pop change:** 2000-20005 +6.5%; 1990-2000 +20.2%. **Pop 2000:** 43,653 (White 77.4%; Black or African American 1.8%; Hispanic or Latino 19.1%; Asian 0.5%; Other 8.9%). **Foreign born:** 6.6%. **Median age:** 43.8.

Income 2000: per capita $19,767; median household $34,283; **Pop below poverty level:** 14.5%. ***Personal per capita income 2000-2003:** $26,414-$29,250.

Unemployment 2004: 4.5%. **Change from 2000:** +1.9%. **Median travel time to work:** 18.3 minutes. **Working outside county of residence:** 10.7%.

Cities with pop over 10,000: Kerrville ⚒ (21,477).

KIMBLE COUNTY

501 Main St Courthouse   **Ph:** 325-446-3353
Junction, TX 76849   **Fax:** 325-446-2986
www.co.kimble.tx.us

In central TX, southeast of San Angelo; organized Jan 22, 1858 from Bexar County. **Name Origin:** For George C. Kimble (1810-36), a TX officer killed at the Alamo. Name is variously spelled *Kimball* and *Kimbell*.

Area (sq mi): 1250.92 (land 1250.7; water 0.23). **Pop per sq mi:** 3.7.

Pop 2005: 4,591. **State rank:** 205. **Pop change:** 2000-20005 +2.8%; 1990-2000 +8.4%. **Pop 2000:** 4,468 (White 77.9%; Black or African American 0.1%; Hispanic or Latino 20.7%; Asian 0.4%; Other 9.1%). **Foreign born:** 5.5%. **Median age:** 43.1.

Income 2000: per capita $17,127; median household $29,396; **Pop below poverty level:** 18.8%. ***Personal per capita income 2000-2003:** $17,523-$18,889.

Unemployment 2004: 4.2%. **Change from 2000:** +2.5%. **Median travel time to work:** 21.5 minutes. **Working outside county of residence:** 12.2%.

Cities with pop over 10,000: None.

KING COUNTY

PO Box 135   **Ph:** 806-596-4412
Guthrie, TX 79236   **Fax:** 806-596-4664

In southeastern TX panhandle, east of Lubbock; established Aug 21, 1876 from Fannin County. **Name Origin:** For William King (1812-26), a soldier killed at the Alamo.

Area (sq mi): 913.33 (land 912.29; water 1.04). **Pop per sq mi:** 0.3.

Pop 2005: 307. **State rank:** 253. **Pop change:** 2000-20005 -13.8%; 1990-2000 +0.6%. **Pop 2000:** 356 (White 88.5%; Black or African American 0%; Hispanic or Latino 9.6%; Asian 0%; Other 5.9%, including 1.1% American Indian/Alaska Native). **Foreign born:** 2.2%. **Median age:** 37.

Income 2000: per capita $12,321; median household $35,625; **Pop below poverty level:** 20.7%. ***Personal per capita income 2000-2003:** $20,664-$25,090.

Unemployment 2004: 2.7%. **Change from 2000:** -1.1%. **Median travel time to work:** 14.4 minutes. **Working outside county of residence:** 31.1%.

Cities with pop over 10,000: None.

KINNEY COUNTY

PO Box 9   **Ph:** 830-563-2521
Brackettville, TX 78832   **Fax:** 830-563-2644
www.co.kinney.tx.us

On southwestern border of TX, east of Del Rio; organized 1876 from Bexar County. **Name Origin:** For H.L. Kinney, a TX legislator.

Area (sq mi): 1365.31 (land 1363.44; water 1.87). **Pop per sq mi:** 2.4.

Pop 2005: 3,327. **State rank:** 220. **Pop change:** 2000-20005 -1.5%; 1990-2000 +8.3%. **Pop 2000:** 3,379 (White 47%; Black or African American 1.7%; Hispanic or Latino 50.5%; Asian 0.1%; Other 22.3%). **Foreign born:** 11.7%. **Median age:** 43.2.

Income 2000: per capita $15,350; median household $28,320; **Pop below poverty level:** 24%. ***Personal per capita income 2000-2003:** $16,614-$19,419.

Unemployment 2004: 6.3%. **Change from 2000:** +0%. **Median travel time to work:** 22.2 minutes. **Working outside county of residence:** 27.8%.

Cities with pop over 10,000: None.

KLEBERG COUNTY

PO Box 1327   **Ph:** 361-595-8548
Kingsville, TX 78364   **Fax:** 361-593-1355
www.co.kleberg.tx.us

On the southeastern coast of TX, south of Corpus Christi; organized Feb 27, 1913 from Nueces County. **Name Origin:** For Robert Justice Kleberg (1803-88), German immigrant, Republic of TX soldier, and jurist.

Area (sq mi): 1090.29 (land 870.97; water 219.32). **Pop per sq mi:** 35.3.

Pop 2005: 30,757. **State rank:** 90. **Pop change:** 2000-20005 -2.5%; 1990-2000 +4.2%. **Pop 2000:** 31,549 (White 28.5%; Black or African American 3.7%; Hispanic or Latino 65.4%; Asian 1.5%; Other 22.9%). **Foreign born:** 6.5%. **Median age:** 29.2.

Income 2000: per capita $13,542; median household $29,313; **Pop below poverty level:** 26.7%. ***Personal per capita income 2000-2003:** $18,001-$21,157.

Unemployment 2004: 5.9%. **Change from 2000:** +1.1%. **Median travel time to work:** 19 minutes. **Working outside county of residence:** 21.9%.

Cities with pop over 10,000: Kingsville ⚒ (25,257).

KNOX COUNTY

PO Box 196   **Ph:** 940-459-2441
Benjamin, TX 79505   **Fax:** 940-459-2005
www.knoxcountytexas.com

In north-central TX, southwest of Wichita Falls; organized Feb 1,

Source: Personal per capita income data are from the Bureau of Economic Analysis; per capita income data are from the Bureau of the Census. See Introduction for explanation of differences.

688

Knox County (cont'd)

1858 from Fannin County. **Name Origin:** For Gen. Henry Knox (1750-1806), Revolutionary War officer and first U.S. secretary of war (1785-95).

Area (sq mi): 855.43 (land 849; water 6.43). **Pop per sq mi:** 4.5.

Pop 2005: 3,781. **State rank:** 215. **Pop change:** 2000-20005 -11.1%; 1990-2000 -12.1%. **Pop 2000:** 4,253 (White 66.5%; Black or African American 6.9%; Hispanic or Latino 25.1%; Asian 0.2%; Other 18.6%, including 1.1% American Indian/Alaska Native). **Foreign born:** 6.7%. **Median age:** 40.5.

Income 2000: per capita $13,443; median household $25,453; **Pop below poverty level:** 22.9%. ***Personal per capita income 2000-2003:** $18,195-$22,275.

Unemployment 2004: 5.4%. **Change from 2000:** +2.1%. **Median travel time to work:** 16.3 minutes. **Working outside county of residence:** 17.8%.

Cities with pop over 10,000: None.

LA SALLE COUNTY

PO Box 340   **Ph:** 830-879-3033
Cotulla, TX 78014   **Fax:** 830-879-2933
www.lasallecountytx.org

In southern TX, northeast of Laredo; organized Feb 1, 1858 from Bexar and Webb counties. **Name Origin:** For Robert Cavelier (1643-87), Sieur de La Salle, French adventurer and explorer who claimed the land west of the Mississippi River for France.

Area (sq mi): 1494.23 (land 1488.85; water 5.38). **Pop per sq mi:** 4.

Pop 2005: 6,016. **State rank:** 196. **Pop change:** 2000-20005 +2.6%; 1990-2000 +11.6%. **Pop 2000:** 5,866 (White 19%; Black or African American 3.5%; Hispanic or Latino 77.1%; Asian 0.3%; Other 14.6%). **Foreign born:** 4%. **Median age:** 33.

Income 2000: per capita $9,692; median household $21,857; **Pop below poverty level:** 29.8%. ***Personal per capita income 2000-2003:** $14,182-$15,917.

Unemployment 2004: 6.9%. **Change from 2000:** +0.7%. **Median travel time to work:** 28.8 minutes. **Working outside county of residence:** 28.2%.

Cities with pop over 10,000: None.

LAMAR COUNTY

119 N Main St Rm 109   **Ph:** 903-737-2420
Paris, TX 75460   **Fax:** 903-782-1000
66.165.115.117

On the northeastern border of TX, northwest of Texarkana; organized Dec 17, 1840 from Red River County. **Name Origin:** For Mirabeau Buonaparte Lamar (1798-1859), Republic of TX attorney general, secretary of war, vice president (1836-38), and president (1838-41).

Area (sq mi): 932.47 (land 916.81; water 15.66). **Pop per sq mi:** 54.1.

Pop 2005: 49,644. **State rank:** 60. **Pop change:** 2000-20005 +2.4%; 1990-2000 +10.4%. **Pop 2000:** 48,499 (White 80.7%; Black or African American 13.5%; Hispanic or Latino 3.3%; Asian 0.4%;

Other 3.7%, including 1.1% American Indian/Alaska Native). **Foreign born:** 2.1%. **Median age:** 36.9.

Income 2000: per capita $17,000; median household $31,609; **Pop below poverty level:** 16.4%. ***Personal per capita income 2000-2003:** $22,201-$22,562.

Unemployment 2004: 6.5%. **Change from 2000:** -0.1%. **Median travel time to work:** 20.1 minutes. **Working outside county of residence.** 10.4%.

Cities with pop over 10,000: Paris 🏛 (26,578).

LAMB COUNTY

100 6th St Rm 103   **Ph:** 806-385-4222
Littlefield, TX 79339   **Fax:** 806-385-6485

In west-central TX panhandle, northwest of Lubbock; organized Aug 21, 1876 from Bexar County. **Name Origin:** For Lt. George A. Lamb (?-1836), Republic of TX army officer killed at the Battle of San Jacinto.

Area (sq mi): 1017.73 (land 1016.21; water 1.52). **Pop per sq mi:** 14.2.

Pop 2005: 14,467. **State rank:** 140. **Pop change:** 2000-20005 -1.6%; 1990-2000 -2.4%. **Pop 2000:** 14,709 (White 51.3%; Black or African American 4.3%; Hispanic or Latino 43.5%; Asian 0.1%; Other 19.5%). **Foreign born:** 6.3%. **Median age:** 36.2.

Income 2000: per capita $15,169; median household $27,898; **Pop below poverty level:** 20.9%. ***Personal per capita income 2000-2003:** $20,110-$21,190.

Unemployment 2004: 5.9%. **Change from 2000:** -0.8%. **Median travel time to work:** 17.9 minutes. **Working outside county of residence:** 21%.

Cities with pop over 10,000: None.

LAMPASAS COUNTY

409 Pecan St   **Ph:** 512-556-8271
Lampasas, TX 76550
www.co.lampasas.tx.us

In central TX, southwest of Waco; organized Feb 1, 1856 from Bell and Travis counties. **Name Origin:** From a Spanish term meaning 'water lily.'

Area (sq mi): 713.96 (land 712.04; water 1.92). **Pop per sq mi:** 27.6.

Pop 2005: 19,669. **State rank:** 120. **Pop change:** 2000-20005 +10.7%; 1990-2000 +31.4%. **Pop 2000:** 17,762 (White 79.5%; Black or African American 3.1%; Hispanic or Latino 15.1%; Asian 0.8%; Other 9.4%). **Foreign born:** 6%. **Median age:** 36.9.

Income 2000: per capita $17,184; median household $36,176; **Pop below poverty level:** 14.1%. ***Personal per capita income 2000-2003:** $22,844-$23,446.

Unemployment 2004: 4.5%. **Change from 2000:** +1.4%. **Median travel time to work:** 25.8 minutes. **Working outside county of residence:** 50.7%.

Cities with pop over 10,000: None.

🏛 *County Seat*

LAVACA COUNTY

109 N La Grange St   **Ph:** 361-798-3612
Hallettsville, TX 77964   **Fax:** 361-798-1610
www.co.lavaca.tx.us

In southeastern TX, east of San Antonio; organized Apr 6, 1846 from Colorado, Victoria, and Jackson counties. **Name Origin:** For the Lavaca River; Spanish translation of original French *la vache* 'the cow,' for the buffalo in the area, which La Salle thought resembled cows.

Area (sq mi): 970.35 (land 969.9; water 0.45). **Pop per sq mi:** 19.5.

Pop 2005: 18,925. **State rank:** 122. **Pop change:** 2000-20005 -1.5%; 1990-2000 +2.8%. **Pop 2000:** 19,210 (White 81.1%; Black or African American 6.8%; Hispanic or Latino 11.4%; Asian 0.2%; Other 6.1%). **Foreign born:** 2.5%. **Median age:** 41.9.

Income 2000: per capita $16,398; median household $29,132; **Pop below poverty level:** 13.2%. ***Personal per capita income 2000-2003:** $22,388-$24,656.

Unemployment 2004: 3.6%. **Change from 2000:** +2%. **Median travel time to work:** 22 minutes. **Working outside county of residence:** 31.8%.

Cities with pop over 10,000: None.

LEE COUNTY

PO Box 419   **Ph:** 979-542-3684
Giddings, TX 78942   **Fax:** 979-542-2623
www.co.lee.tx.us

In east-central TX, east of Austin; organized Apr 14, 1874 from Bastrop, Burleson, Washington, and Fayette counties. **Name Origin:** For Robert E. Lee (1807-70), American general and commander in chief of the Confederate forces during the Civil War.

Area (sq mi): 634.03 (land 628.5; water 5.53). **Pop per sq mi:** 26.3.

Pop 2005: 16,526. **State rank:** 131. **Pop change:** 2000-20005 +5.6%; 1990-2000 +21.8%. **Pop 2000:** 15,657 (White 68.5%; Black or African American 12.1%; Hispanic or Latino 18.2%; Asian 0.2%; Other 11.1%). **Foreign born:** 6.1%. **Median age:** 35.6.

Income 2000: per capita $17,163; median household $36,280; **Pop below poverty level:** 11.9%. ***Personal per capita income 2000-2003:** $22,229-$23,017.

Unemployment 2004: 4.5%. **Change from 2000:** +0.7%. **Median travel time to work:** 30 minutes. **Working outside county of residence:** 37.4%.

Cities with pop over 10,000: None.

LEON COUNTY

PO Box 98   **Ph:** 903-536-2352
Centerville, TX 75833
www.co.leon.tx.us

In east-central TX, southeast of Waco; organized Mar 17, 1846 from Robertson County. **Name Origin:** For a Martin de Leon, or for Leon Prairie where a 'lion' was killed.

Area (sq mi): 1080.38 (land 1072.04; water 8.34). **Pop per sq mi:** 15.2.

Pop 2005: 16,344. **State rank:** 133. **Pop change:** 2000-20005 +6.6%; 1990-2000 +21.1%. **Pop 2000:** 15,335 (White 80.6%; Black

or African American 10.4%; Hispanic or Latino 7.9%; Asian 0.2%; Other 5.9%). **Foreign born:** 4.2%. **Median age:** 42.1.

Income 2000: per capita $17,599; median household $30,981; **Pop below poverty level:** 15.6%. ***Personal per capita income 2000-2003:** $22,049-$22,850.

Unemployment 2004: 6%. **Change from 2000:** +1.3%. **Median travel time to work:** 28 minutes. **Working outside county of residence:** 30%.

Cities with pop over 10,000: None.

LIBERTY COUNTY

1923 Sam Houston St   **Ph:** 936-336-4600
Liberty, TX 77575   **Fax:** 936-336-4640
www.co.liberty.tx.us

In east-central TX, northeast of Houston; organized Mar 17, 1836 from Bexar County. **Name Origin:** Honoring TX independence (1836).

Area (sq mi): 1176.22 (land 1159.68; water 16.54). **Pop per sq mi:** 64.8.

Pop 2005: 75,141. **State rank:** 47. **Pop change:** 2000-20005 +7.1%; 1990-2000 +33.1%. **Pop 2000:** 70,154 (White 74.5%; Black or African American 12.8%; Hispanic or Latino 10.9%; Asian 0.3%; Other 7.9%). **Foreign born:** 5.1%. **Median age:** 34.

Income 2000: per capita $15,539; median household $38,361; **Pop below poverty level:** 14.3%. ***Personal per capita income 2000-2003:** $21,083-$23,358.

Unemployment 2004: 9%. **Change from 2000:** +2.6%. **Median travel time to work:** 36.8 minutes. **Working outside county of residence:** 53.5%.

Cities with pop over 10,000: None.

LIMESTONE COUNTY

PO Box 350   **Ph:** 254-729-5504
Groesbeck, TX 76642   **Fax:** 254-729-2951
www.co.limestone.tx.us

In east-central TX, east of Waco; organized Apr 11, 1846 from Robertson County. **Name Origin:** For Lake Limestone.

Area (sq mi): 933.15 (land 908.88; water 24.27). **Pop per sq mi:** 25.

Pop 2005: 22,763. **State rank:** 107. **Pop change:** 2000-20005 +3.2%; 1990-2000 +5.3%. **Pop 2000:** 22,051 (White 66.7%; Black or African American 19.1%; Hispanic or Latino 13%; Asian 0.1%; Other 10.1%). **Foreign born:** 5.5%. **Median age:** 37.4.

Income 2000: per capita $14,352; median household $29,366; **Pop below poverty level:** 17.8%. ***Personal per capita income 2000-2003:** $19,061-$21,737.

Unemployment 2004: 5.3%. **Change from 2000:** +1.8%. **Median travel time to work:** 21.5 minutes. **Working outside county of residence:** 26.9%.

Cities with pop over 10,000: None.

LIPSCOMB COUNTY

1 Courthouse Sq PO Box 70   **Ph:** 806-862-3091
Lipscomb, TX 79056   **Fax:** 806-862-3004
www.co.lipscomb.tx.us

On the northeastern border of TX panhandle; organized Aug 21,

*Source: Personal per capita income data are from the Bureau of Economic Analysis; per capita income data are from the Bureau of the Census.
See Introduction for explanation of differences.

690

Lipscomb County (cont'd)

1876 from Bexar County. **Name Origin:** For Abner S. Lipscomb (1789-1858), AL legislator, secretary of state for the Republic of TX (1839-40), and associate justice of the TX supreme court (1846-58).

Area (sq mi): 932.22 (land 932.11; water 0.11). **Pop per sq mi:** 3.3.

Pop 2005: 3,101. **State rank:** 224. **Pop change:** 2000-20005 +1.4%; 1990-2000 -2.7%. **Pop 2000:** 3,057 (White 76.7%; Black or African American 0.5%; Hispanic or Latino 20.7%; Asian 0.1%; Other 16.6%, including 1.4% American Indian/Alaska Native). **Foreign born:** 11.7%. **Median age:** 39.5.

Income 2000: per capita $16,328; median household $31,964; **Pop below poverty level:** 16.7%. ***Personal per capita income 2000-2003:** $25,125-$27,963.

Unemployment 2004: 3.6%. **Change from 2000:** +1.6%. **Median travel time to work:** 19.6 minutes. **Working outside county of residence:** 29.4%.

Cities with pop over 10,000: None.

LIVE OAK COUNTY

PO Box 280   **Ph:** 361-449-2733
George West, TX 78022
www.co.live-oak.tx.us

In southern TX, northwest of Corpus Christi; organized Feb 2, 1856 from Nueces County. **Name Origin:** For the indigenous live oak trees, *Quercus virginiana* and *Q. chrysolepsis*.

Area (sq mi): 1078.83 (land 1036.3; water 42.53). **Pop per sq mi:** 11.3.

Pop 2005: 11,717. **State rank:** 157. **Pop change:** 2000-20005 -4.8%; 1990-2000 +28.8%. **Pop 2000:** 12,309 (White 58.5%; Black or African American 2.4%; Hispanic or Latino 38%; Asian 0.2%; Other 10%). **Foreign born:** 2.3%. **Median age:** 39.2.

Income 2000: per capita $15,886; median household $32,057; **Pop below poverty level:** 16.5%. ***Personal per capita income 2000-2003:** $16,754-$18,905.

Unemployment 2004: 5.3%. **Change from 2000:** +2.8%. **Median travel time to work:** 27.2 minutes. **Working outside county of residence:** 32.7%.

Cities with pop over 10,000: Corpus Christi 🏛 (281,196).

LLANO COUNTY

PO Box 40   **Ph:** 325-247-4455
Llano, TX 78643   **Fax:** 325-247-2406
www.co.llano.tx.us

In central TX, northwest of Austin; organized Feb 1, 1856 from Bexar County. **Name Origin:** For the Llano River, which flows through the county; from its Spanish name, *el rio de los llanos* 'the river of the plains.'

Area (sq mi): 966.18 (land 934.76; water 31.41). **Pop per sq mi:** 19.5.

Pop 2005: 18,236. **State rank:** 126. **Pop change:** 2000-20005 +7%; 1990-2000 +46.5%. **Pop 2000:** 17,044 (White 93.1%; Black or African American 0.3%; Hispanic or Latino 5.1%; Asian 0.4%; Other 3%). **Foreign born:** 2%. **Median age:** 53.

Income 2000: per capita $23,547; median household $34,830; **Pop below poverty level:** 10.3%. ***Personal per capita income 2000-2003:** $23,161-$23,622.

Unemployment 2004: 5.4%. **Change from 2000:** +2.2%. **Median travel time to work:** 27.8 minutes. **Working outside county of residence:** 38.1%.

Cities with pop over 10,000: None.

LOVING COUNTY

100 Bell St PO Box 194   **Ph:** 432-377-2441
Mentone, TX 79754   **Fax:** 432-377-2701
www.co.loving.tx.us

On the northwestern border of TX, west of Odessa; organized Feb 26, 1887 from Tom Green County. **Name Origin:** For Oliver Loving, pioneer and rancher.

Area (sq mi): 676.85 (land 673.08; water 3.77). **Pop per sq mi:** 0.1.

Pop 2005: 62. **State rank:** 254. **Pop change:** 2000-20005 -7.5%; 1990-2000 -37.4%. **Pop 2000:** 67 (White 89.6%; Black or African American 0%; Hispanic or Latino 10.4%; Asian 0%; Other 10.5%). **Foreign born:** 0%. **Median age:** 45.8.

Income 2000: per capita $24,084; median household $40,000; **Pop below poverty level:** 0%. ***Personal per capita income 2000-2003:** $71,723-$72,063.

Unemployment 2004: 6.4%. **Change from 2000:** -1.5%. **Median travel time to work:** 14.6 minutes. **Working outside county of residence:** 18.4%.

Cities with pop over 10,000: None.

LUBBOCK COUNTY

904 Broadway St Rm 207   **Ph:** 806-775-1043
Lubbock, TX 79401
www.co.lubbock.tx.us

In south-central TX panhandle, north of Midland; organized 1891 from Baylor County (other sources say organized Aug 21, 1876; first federal census: 1880). **Name Origin:** For Col. Thomas S. Lubbock, signer of the TX Declaration of Independence and an organizer of the Texas Rangers.

Area (sq mi): 900.7 (land 899.49; water 1.2). **Pop per sq mi:** 280.5.

Pop 2005: 252,284. **State rank:** 18. **Pop change:** 2000-20005 +4%; 1990-2000 +9%. **Pop 2000:** 242,628 (White 62.5%; Black or African American 7.7%; Hispanic or Latino 27.5%; Asian 1.3%; Other 16.7%). **Foreign born:** 3.3%. **Median age:** 30.5.

Income 2000: per capita $17,323; median household $32,198; **Pop below poverty level:** 17.8%. ***Personal per capita income 2000-2003:** $24,306-$25,081.

Unemployment 2004: 4.6%. **Change from 2000:** +2%. **Median travel time to work:** 17.1 minutes. **Working outside county of residence:** 4.2%.

Cities with pop over 10,000: Lubbock 🏛 (207,852).

LYNN COUNTY

PO Box 937   **Ph:** 806-561-4750
Tahoka, TX 79373   **Fax:** 806-561-4988
www.co.lynn.tx.us

In southwestern TX panhandle, south of Lubbock; organized Aug

Lynn County (cont'd)

21, 1876 from Bexar County. **Name Origin:** For W. Linn (?-1836), a soldier killed at the Alamo.

Area (sq mi): 893.46 (land 891.88; water 1.58). **Pop per sq mi:** 7.

Pop 2005: 6,237. **State rank:** 193. **Pop change:** 2000-20005 -4.8%; 1990-2000 -3.1%. **Pop 2000:** 6,550 (White 51.6%; Black or African American 2.8%; Hispanic or Latino 44.6%; Asian 0.2%; Other 21.4%, including 1% American Indian/Alaska Native). **Foreign born:** 5%. **Median age:** 35.2.

Income 2000: per capita $14,090; median household $26,694; **Pop below poverty level:** 22.6%. ***Personal per capita income 2000-2003:** $18,510-$25,386.

Unemployment 2004: 6.1%. **Change from 2000:** +1.1%. **Median travel time to work:** 19.6 minutes. **Working outside county of residence:** 35.6%.

Cities with pop over 10,000: None.

MADISON COUNTY

101 W Main St Rm 102   **Ph:** 936-348-2638
Madisonville, TX 77864   **Fax:** 936-348-5858
www.co.madison.tx.us

In east-central TX, northeast of Austin; organized 1854 from Montgomery, Walker, Grimes, and Leon counties. **Name Origin:** For James Madison (1751-1836), fourth U.S. president.

Area (sq mi): 472.44 (land 469.65; water 2.8). **Pop per sq mi:** 28.

Pop 2005: 13,167. **State rank:** 150. **Pop change:** 2000-20005 +1.8%; 1990-2000 +18.4%. **Pop 2000:** 12,940 (White 60.3%; Black or African American 22.9%; Hispanic or Latino 15.8%; Asian 0.4%; Other 9.9%). **Foreign born:** 4.8%. **Median age:** 33.4.

Income 2000: per capita $14,056; median household $29,418; **Pop below poverty level:** 15.8%. ***Personal per capita income 2000-2003:** $18,606-$21,322.

Unemployment 2004: 6.2%. **Change from 2000:** +3.5%. **Median travel time to work:** 26 minutes. **Working outside county of residence:** 32.8%.

Cities with pop over 10,000: None.

MARION COUNTY

PO Box 763   **Ph:** 903-665-3971
Jefferson, TX 75657   **Fax:** 903-665-8732
www.co.marion.tx.us

On the northeastern border of TX, north of Marshall; organized Feb 8, 1860 from Cass and Harrison counties. **Name Origin:** For Gen. Francis Marion (c.1732-95), SC soldier and legislator, known as 'The Swamp Fox' for his tactics during the Revolutionary War.

Area (sq mi): 420.36 (land 381.21; water 39.15). **Pop per sq mi:** 28.7.

Pop 2005: 10,952. **State rank:** 162. **Pop change:** 2000-20005 +0.1%; 1990-2000 +9.6%. **Pop 2000:** 10,941 (White 71.5%; Black or African American 23.9%; Hispanic or Latino 2.4%; Asian 0.2%; Other 3.1%). **Foreign born:** 0.9%. **Median age:** 43.3.

Income 2000: per capita $14,535; median household $25,347; **Pop below poverty level:** 22.4%. ***Personal per capita income 2000-2003:** $16,840-$18,242.

Unemployment 2004: 6.3%. **Change from 2000:** -1.6%. **Median travel time to work:** 32.9 minutes. **Working outside county of residence:** 57.8%.

Cities with pop over 10,000: None.

MARTIN COUNTY

301 N Saint Peter St   **Ph:** 432-756-3412
Stanton, TX 79782   **Fax:** 432-607-2212

In southwestern TX panhandle, north of Midland; organized Aug 21, 1876 from Bexar County. **Name Origin:** For Wyly Martin, active in achieving TX statehood.

Area (sq mi): 915.62 (land 914.78; water 0.84). **Pop per sq mi:** 4.8.

Pop 2005: 4,391. **State rank:** 206. **Pop change:** 2000-20005 -7.5%; 1990-2000 -4.2%. **Pop 2000:** 4,746 (White 56.8%; Black or African American 1.6%; Hispanic or Latino 40.6%; Asian 0.2%; Other 19.3%). **Foreign born:** 8.1%. **Median age:** 32.5.

Income 2000: per capita $15,647; median household $31,836; **Pop below poverty level:** 18.7%. ***Personal per capita income 2000-2003:** $17,721-$23,513.

Unemployment 2004: 5.3%. **Change from 2000:** +1.2%. **Median travel time to work:** 19.3 minutes. **Working outside county of residence:** 35.6%.

Cities with pop over 10,000: None.

MASON COUNTY

PO Box 702   **Ph:** 325-347-5253
Mason, TX 76856   **Fax:** 325-347-6868
www.co.mason.tx.us

In central TX, northwest of Austin; organized Jan 22, 1858 from Bexar County. **Name Origin:** For Lt. George (G.T.) Mason, army officer who chose locations for forts along the Rio Grande.

Area (sq mi): 932.18 (land 932.07; water 0.11). **Pop per sq mi:** 4.2.

Pop 2005: 3,880. **State rank:** 212. **Pop change:** 2000-20005 +3.8%; 1990-2000 +9.2%. **Pop 2000:** 3,738 (White 77.9%; Black or African American 0.1%; Hispanic or Latino 20.9%; Asian 0.1%; Other 8.2%). **Foreign born:** 4.7%. **Median age:** 46.7.

Income 2000: per capita $20,931; median household $30,921; **Pop below poverty level:** 13.2%. ***Personal per capita income 2000-2003:** $18,952-$22,303.

Unemployment 2004: 3.5%. **Change from 2000:** +1.9%. **Median travel time to work:** 18.7 minutes. **Working outside county of residence:** 20.7%.

Cities with pop over 10,000: None.

MATAGORDA COUNTY

1700 7th St Rm 202   **Ph:** 979-244-7680
Bay City, TX 77414   **Fax:** 979-244-7688
www.co.matagorda.tx.us

On the central east coast of TX, southwest of Houston; original county; organized Mar 17, 1836 (prior to statehood) from Old Mexican Municipality. **Name Origin:** For Matagorda Island; Spanish 'thicket' or 'rough area.'

Area (sq mi): 1612.19 (land 1114.46; water 497.73). **Pop per sq mi:** 34.

---

*Source: Personal per capita income data are from the Bureau of Economic Analysis; per capita income data are from the Bureau of the Census. See Introduction for explanation of differences.

Matagorda County (cont'd)

Pop 2005: 37,849. **State rank:** 77. **Pop change:** 2000-20005 -0.3%; 1990-2000 +2.8%. **Pop 2000:** 37,957 (White 52.4%; Black or African American 12.7%; Hispanic or Latino 31.3%; Asian 2.4%; Other 17.1%). **Foreign born:** 9.9%. **Median age:** 34.8.

Income 2000: per capita $15,709; median household $32,174; **Pop below poverty level.** 10.5%. ***Personal per capita income 2000-2003:** $20,549-$21,377.

Unemployment 2004: 9.7%. **Change from 2000:** -1.1%. **Median travel time to work:** 23.9 minutes. **Working outside county of residence:** 24.2%.

Cities with pop over 10,000: Bay City 🏛 (18,381).

MAVERICK COUNTY

PO Box 4050   **Ph:** 830-773-2829
Eagle Pass, TX 78853   **Fax:** 830-752-4479
www.maverickcounty.org

On the southwestern border of TX, southeast of Del Rio; organized Feb 2, 1856 from Kenedy County. **Name Origin:** For Samuel Augustus Maverick (1803-70), Republic of TX patriot, rancher, and legislator. Many of his cattle went unbranded and were stolen, thus the word 'maverick' to describe a stray animal or a person with no attachment to a place or group.

Area (sq mi): 1291.74 (land 1280.08; water 11.66). **Pop per sq mi:** 40.

Pop 2005: 51,181. **State rank:** 58. **Pop change:** 2000-20005 +8.2%; 1990-2000 +30%. **Pop 2000:** 47,297 (White 3.4%; Black or African American 0.3%; Hispanic or Latino 95%; Asian 0.4%; Other 28.3%, including 1.3% American Indian/Alaska Native). **Foreign born:** 37.8%. **Median age:** 27.8.

Income 2000: per capita $8,758; median household $21,232; **Pop below poverty level:** 34.8%. ***Personal per capita income 2000-2003:** $11,509-$12,774.

Unemployment 2004: 15.2%. **Change from 2000:** -8.1%. **Median travel time to work:** 20.2 minutes. **Working outside county of residence:** 13%.

Cities with pop over 10,000: Eagle Pass 🏛 (24,847).

MCCULLOCH COUNTY

199 County Courthouse Sq   **Ph:** 325-597-0733
Brady, TX 76825   **Fax:** 325-597-1731
www.co.mcculloch.tx.us

In central TX, east of San Angelo; organized Aug 27, 1856 from Bexar County. **Name Origin:** For Gen. Benjamin McCulloch (1811-62), Republic of TX soldier, U.S. marshall (1853), and Confederate army officer.

Area (sq mi): 1073.35 (land 1069.31; water 4.05). **Pop per sq mi:** 7.4.

Pop 2005: 7,956. **State rank:** 178. **Pop change:** 2000-20005 -3%; 1990-2000 -6.5%. **Pop 2000:** 8,205 (White 70.6%; Black or African American 1.6%; Hispanic or Latino 27%; Asian 0.2%; Other 13.6%). **Foreign born:** 3.2%. **Median age:** 40.4.

Income 2000: per capita $14,579; median household $25,705; **Pop below poverty level:** 22.5%. ***Personal per capita income 2000-2003:** $20,804-$24,140.

Unemployment 2004: 6.4%. **Change from 2000:** +0.6%. **Median travel time to work:** 20.3 minutes. **Working outside county of residence:** 12.7%.

Cities with pop over 10,000: None.

MCLENNAN COUNTY

PO Box 1727   **Ph:** 254-757-5078
Waco, TX 76703   **Fax:** 254-757-5146
www.co.mclennan.tx.us

In east-central TX, south of Fort Worth; organized Jan 22, 1850 from Milam, Robertson, and Navarro counties. **Name Origin:** For Neil McLennan (1777-1867), surveyor and pioneer.

Area (sq mi): 1060.23 (land 1041.88; water 18.34). **Pop per sq mi:** 215.6.

Pop 2005: 224,668. **State rank:** 21. **Pop change:** 2000-20005 +5.2%; 1990-2000 +12.9%. **Pop 2000:** 213,517 (White 64.6%; Black or African American 15.2%; Hispanic or Latino 17.9%; Asian 1.1%; Other 11.5%). **Foreign born:** 6.1%. **Median age:** 31.9.

Income 2000: per capita $17,174; median household $33,560; **Pop below poverty level:** 17.6%. ***Personal per capita income 2000-2003:** $22,716-$24,007.

Unemployment 2004: 5.3%. **Change from 2000:** +1.4%. **Median travel time to work:** 20 minutes. **Working outside county of residence:** 6.8%.

Cities with pop over 10,000: Waco 🏛 (118,093); Hewitt (12,679).

MCMULLEN COUNTY

PO Box 235   **Ph:** 361-274-3215
Tilden, TX 78072   **Fax:** 361-274-3858

In south-central TX, south of San Antonio; organized Feb 1, 1858 from Bexar and Live Oak counties. **Name Origin:** For John McMullen, an early settler.

Area (sq mi): 1142.6 (land 1113; water 29.6). **Pop per sq mi:** 0.8.

Pop 2005: 883. **State rank:** 248. **Pop change:** 2000-20005 +3.8%; 1990-2000 +4.2%. **Pop 2000:** 851 (White 65.3%; Black or African American 1.2%; Hispanic or Latino 33.1%; Asian 0%; Other 10.4%). **Foreign born:** 4.2%. **Median age:** 43.1.

Income 2000: per capita $22,258; median household $32,500; **Pop below poverty level:** 20.7%. ***Personal per capita income 2000-2003:** $26,458-$27,519.

Unemployment 2004: 4.4%. **Change from 2000:** +1.3%. **Median travel time to work:** 19.7 minutes. **Working outside county of residence:** 30%.

Cities with pop over 10,000: None.

MEDINA COUNTY

1100 16th St Rm 109   **Ph:** 830-741-6001
Hondo, TX 78861   **Fax:** 830-741-6015

In south-central TX, west of San Antonio; organized Feb 12, 1848 from Bexar County. **Name Origin:** For the Medina River and Lake, in the northern part of the county. Possibly named for a member of Alonzo de Leon's expedition into TX (1689): either Pedro Medina, an engineer, or Nicolas de Medina, a sergeant major.

Area (sq mi): 1334.53 (land 1327.76; water 6.77). **Pop per sq mi:** 32.4.

Medina County (cont'd)

Pop 2005: 43,027. **State rank:** 69. **Pop change:** 2000-20005 +9.5%; 1990-2000 +43.9%. **Pop 2000:** 39,304 (White 50.7%; Black or African American 2.2%; Hispanic or Latino 45.5%; Asian 0.3%; Other 18.1%). **Foreign born:** 4.1%. **Median age:** 34.4.

Income 2000: per capita $15,210; median household $36,063; **Pop below poverty level:** 15.4%. ***Personal per capita income 2000-2003:** $19,693-$21,147.

Unemployment 2004: 5.5%. **Change from 2000:** +1.2%. **Median travel time to work:** 30.5 minutes. **Working outside county of residence:** 51%.

Cities with pop over 10,000: None.

MENARD COUNTY

PO Box 1038   **Ph:** 325-396-4682
Menard, TX 76859   **Fax:** 325-396-2047

In central TX, southeast of San Angelo; organized Jan 22, 1858 from Bexar County. **Name Origin:** For Michel Branaman Menard (1803-56), signer of the TX Declaration of Independence (1836), Republic of TX legislator (1840-42), and founder of Galveston.

Area (sq mi): 902.25 (land 901.91; water 0.34). **Pop per sq mi:** 2.4.

Pop 2005: 2,201. **State rank:** 234. **Pop change:** 2000-20005 -6.7%; 1990-2000 +4.8%. **Pop 2000:** 2,360 (White 66.4%; Black or African American 0.5%; Hispanic or Latino 31.7%; Asian 0.3%; Other 11.5%). **Foreign born:** 4.8%. **Median age:** 44.1.

Income 2000: per capita $15,987; median household $24,762; **Pop below poverty level:** 25.8%. ***Personal per capita income 2000-2003:** $15,839-$18,436.

Unemployment 2004: 5.6%. **Change from 2000:** +1.6%. **Median travel time to work:** 21.1 minutes. **Working outside county of residence:** 26%.

Cities with pop over 10,000: None.

MIDLAND COUNTY

200 W Wall Suite 105   **Ph:** 432-688-4401
Midland, TX 79701   **Fax:** 432-688-4925
www.co.midland.tx.us

In west-central TX, east of Odessa; organized Mar 4, 1885 from Tom Green County. **Name Origin:** For its location midpoint on the railway between Fort Worth and El Paso.

Area (sq mi): 901.97 (land 900.25; water 1.72). **Pop per sq mi:** 134.8.

Pop 2005: 121,371. **State rank:** 30. **Pop change:** 2000-20005 +4.6%; 1990-2000 +8.8%. **Pop 2000:** 116,009 (White 62.1%; Black or African American 7%; Hispanic or Latino 29%; Asian 0.9%; Other 14.7%). **Foreign born:** 7.6%. **Median age:** 34.1.

Income 2000: per capita $20,369; median household $39,082; **Pop below poverty level:** 12.9%. ***Personal per capita income 2000-2003:** $35,419-$33,578.

Unemployment 2004: 4.5%. **Change from 2000:** +1.1%. **Median travel time to work:** 18.5 minutes. **Working outside county of residence:** 13.4%.

Cities with pop over 10,000: Midland 🏛 (98,082).

MILAM COUNTY

107 W Main St   **Ph:** 254-697-7049
Cameron, TX 76520   **Fax:** 254-697-7055
www.co.milam.tx.us

In east-central TX, northeast of Austin; original county; organized Mar 17, 1836 (prior to statehood) from Old Mexican Municipality. **Name Origin:** For Benjamin Rush Milam (?-1836), Republic of TX army officer.

Area (sq mi): 1021.67 (land 1016.71; water 4.95). **Pop per sq mi:** 24.9.

Pop 2005: 25,354. **State rank:** 99. **Pop change:** 2000-20005 +4.6%; 1990-2000 +5.6%. **Pop 2000:** 24,238 (White 69.2%; Black or African American 11%; Hispanic or Latino 18.6%; Asian 0.2%; Other 9.8%). **Foreign born:** 5.6%. **Median age:** 38.

Income 2000: per capita $16,920; median household $33,186; **Pop below poverty level:** 15.9%. ***Personal per capita income 2000-2003:** $22,380-$21,546.

Unemployment 2004: 5.9%. **Change from 2000:** +1.5%. **Median travel time to work:** 27.1 minutes. **Working outside county of residence:** 33.2%.

Cities with pop over 10,000: None.

MILLS COUNTY

PO Box 646   **Ph:** 325-648-2711
Goldthwaite, TX 76844   **Fax:** 325-648-3251
www.co.mills.tx.us

In central TX, west of Waco; organized Mar 15, 1887 from Brown, Comanche, Lampasas, and Hamilton counties. **Name Origin:** For John T. Mills, Republic of TX district judge.

Area (sq mi): 749.89 (land 748.11; water 1.78). **Pop per sq mi:** 7.

Pop 2005: 5,237. **State rank:** 200. **Pop change:** 2000-20005 +1.7%; 1990-2000 +13.7%. **Pop 2000:** 5,151 (White 84.8%; Black or African American 1.3%; Hispanic or Latino 13%; Asian 0.1%; Other 9.4%). **Foreign born:** 4.4%. **Median age:** 44.4.

Income 2000: per capita $15,915; median household $30,579; **Pop below poverty level:** 18.4%. ***Personal per capita income 2000-2003:** $21,023-$22,728.

Unemployment 2004: 4%. **Change from 2000:** +2.6%. **Median travel time to work:** 23.7 minutes. **Working outside county of residence:** 28.3%.

Cities with pop over 10,000: None.

MITCHELL COUNTY

349 Oak St Rm 103   **Ph:** 325-728-3481
Colorado City, TX 79512   **Fax:** 325-728-5322

In north-central TX, west of Abilene; organized Aug 21, 1876 from Bexar County. **Name Origin:** For Asa (1795-1865) and Eli (n.d.) Mitchell, early settlers of Austin's colony.

Area (sq mi): 915.9 (land 910.04; water 5.86). **Pop per sq mi:** 10.3.

Pop 2005: 9,413. **State rank:** 169. **Pop change:** 2000-20005 -2.9%; 1990-2000 +21%. **Pop 2000:** 9,698 (White 55.1%; Black or African American 12.8%; Hispanic or Latino 31%; Asian 0.4%; Other 12.3%). **Foreign born:** 2.8%. **Median age:** 38.6.

*Source: Personal per capita income data are from the Bureau of Economic Analysis; per capita income data are from the Bureau of the Census. See Introduction for explanation of differences.

Mitchell County (cont'd)

Income 2000: per capita $14,043; median household $25,399; **Pop below poverty level:** 17.7%. ***Personal per capita income 2000-2003:** $14,568-$16,270.

Unemployment 2004: 7.2%. **Change from 2000:** +3.4%. **Median travel time to work:** 18.4 minutes. **Working outside county of residence:** 25.1%

Cities with pop over 10,000: None.

MONTAGUE COUNTY

PO Box 77   **Ph:** 940-894-2461
Montague, TX 76251   **Fax:** 940-894-3110
www.co.montague.tx.us

On the central northern border of TX, southeast of Wichita Falls; organized Dec 24, 1857 from Cooke County. **Name Origin:** For Daniel Montague (1798-1876), surveyor and veteran of the Mexican War.

Area (sq mi): 938.44 (land 930.66; water 7.78). **Pop per sq mi:** 21.1.

Pop 2005: 19,677. **State rank:** 119. **Pop change:** 2000-20005 +2.9%; 1990-2000 +10.7%. **Pop 2000:** 19,117 (White 92.7%; Black or African American 0.2%; Hispanic or Latino 5.4%; Asian 0.3%; Other 3.5%). **Foreign born:** 2.4%. **Median age:** 41.3.

Income 2000: per capita $17,115; median household $31,048; **Pop below poverty level:** 14%. ***Personal per capita income 2000-2003:** $22,367-$22,983.

Unemployment 2004: 5.2%. **Change from 2000:** +0.7%. **Median travel time to work:** 30.2 minutes. **Working outside county of residence:** 35.9%.

Cities with pop over 10,000: None.

MONTGOMERY COUNTY

PO Box 959   **Ph:** 936-539-7885
Conroe, TX 77305   **Fax:** 936-760-6990
www.co.montgomery.tx.us

In east-central TX, north of Houston; organized Dec 14, 1837 from Washington County. **Name Origin:** For Gen. Richard Montgomery (1736-75), American Revolutionary War officer who captured Montreal, Canada.

Area (sq mi): 1076.81 (land 1044.03; water 32.78). **Pop per sq mi:** 362.1.

Pop 2005: 378,033. **State rank:** 12. **Pop change:** 2000-20005 +28.7%; 1990-2000 +61.2%. **Pop 2000:** 293,768 (White 81.4%; Black or African American 3.5%; Hispanic or Latino 12.6%; Asian 1.1%; Other 7.2%). **Foreign born:** 8.6%. **Median age:** 34.4.

Income 2000: per capita $24,544; median household $50,864; **Pop below poverty level:** 9.4%. ***Personal per capita income 2000-2003:** $32,989-$32,068.

Unemployment 2004: 5.1%. **Change from 2000:** +1.8%. **Median travel time to work:** 32.9 minutes. **Working outside county of residence:** 48.7%.

Cities with pop over 10,000: Conroe 🏛 (43,402).

MOORE COUNTY

715 S Dumas Ave Rm 105   **Ph:** 806-935-6164
Dumas, TX 79029   **Fax:** 806-935-9004
www.co.moore.tx.us

In north-central TX panhandle, north of Amarillo; organized Aug 21, 1876 from Bexar County. **Name Origin:** For Edwin Ward Moore (1810-60), a Republic of TX naval officer.

Area (sq mi): 909.61 (land 899.66; water 9.95). **Pop per sq mi:** 22.6.

Pop 2005: 20,348. **State rank:** 116. **Pop change:** 2000-20005 +1.1%; 1990-2000 +12.6%. **Pop 2000:** 20,121 (White 49.9%; Black or African American 0.7%; Hispanic or Latino 47.5%; Asian 0.9%; Other 34.5%). **Foreign born:** 20.9%. **Median age:** 30.4.

Income 2000: per capita $15,214; median household $34,852; **Pop below poverty level:** 13.5%. ***Personal per capita income 2000-2003:** $21,460-$23,835.

Unemployment 2004: 4.6%. **Change from 2000:** +1.8%. **Median travel time to work:** 17.7 minutes. **Working outside county of residence:** 9.6%.

Cities with pop over 10,000: Dumas 🏛 (13,819).

MORRIS COUNTY

500 Broadnax St   **Ph:** 903-645-3911
Daingerfield, TX 75638   **Fax:** 903-645-5729
www.co.morris.tx.us

In northeastern TX, north of Tyler; organized Mar 6, 1875 from Titus County. **Name Origin:** For W.W. Morris, thrown off a stagecoach because he was unruly and drunk. He stayed, founded a settlement called Morristown, and became a prominent east TX attorney.

Area (sq mi): 258.64 (land 254.51; water 4.13). **Pop per sq mi:** 50.8.

Pop 2005: 12,936. **State rank:** 151. **Pop change:** 2000-20005 -0.9%; 1990-2000 -1.2%. **Pop 2000:** 13,048 (White 70.6%; Black or African American 24.1%; Hispanic or Latino 3.7%; Asian 0.2%; Other 4%). **Foreign born:** 2%. **Median age:** 40.2.

Income 2000: per capita $15,612; median household $29,011; **Pop below poverty level:** 18.3%. ***Personal per capita income 2000-2003:** $22,032-$23,145.

Unemployment 2004: 7.7%. **Change from 2000:** +0.9%. **Median travel time to work:** 23.9 minutes. **Working outside county of residence:** 45.8%.

Cities with pop over 10,000: None.

MOTLEY COUNTY

PO Box 660   **Ph:** 806-347-2621
Matador, TX 79244   **Fax:** 806-347-2220
www.co.motley.tx.us

In east-central TX panhandle, northeast of Lubbock; organized Aug 21, 1876 from Bexar County. **Name Origin:** For Junius William Mottley (1812-36), signer of the TX Declaration of Independence (1836) who was killed at the Battle of San Jacinto. Clerical spelling error was allowed to stand.

Area (sq mi): 989.81 (land 989.38; water 0.43). **Pop per sq mi:** 1.3.

Pop 2005: 1,299. **State rank:** 246. **Pop change:** 2000-20005 -8.9%; 1990-2000 -6.9%. **Pop 2000:** 1,426 (White 82.2%; Black or African

Motley County (cont'd)

American 3.5%; Hispanic or Latino 12.1%; Asian 0.1%; Other 8.9%). **Foreign born:** 3.3%. **Median age:** 44.4.

Income 2000: per capita $16,584; median household $28,348; **Pop below poverty level:** 19.4%. ***Personal per capita income 2000-2003:** $16,447-$20,647.

Unemployment 2004: 4.7%. **Change from 2000:** +3%. **Median travel time to work:** 18.2 minutes. **Working outside county of residence:** 21.6%.

Cities with pop over 10,000: None.

NACOGDOCHES COUNTY

101 W Main St Rm 205   **Ph:** 936-560-7733
Nacogdoches, TX 75961   **Fax:** 936-559-5926
www.co.nacogdoche

In northeastern TX, northwest of Beaumont; original county; organized Mar 17, 1836 (prior to statehood) from Old Mexican Municipality. **Name Origin:** For an Indian tribe of Caddoan linguistic stock, a member of the Hasianai Confederacy.

Area (sq mi): 981.33 (land 946.77; water 34.56). **Pop per sq mi:** 63.9.

Pop 2005: 60,468. **State rank:** 54. **Pop change:** 2000-20005 +2.1%; 1990-2000 +8.1%. **Pop 2000:** 59,203 (White 70.3%; Black or African American 16.7%; Hispanic or Latino 11.2%; Asian 0.7%; Other 7.6%). **Foreign born:** 6.2%. **Median age:** 29.7.

Income 2000: per capita $15,437; median household $28,301; **Pop below poverty level:** 23.3%. ***Personal per capita income 2000-2003:** $19,486-$21,057.

Unemployment 2004: 5.4%. **Change from 2000:** +1.9%. **Median travel time to work:** 19.5 minutes. **Working outside county of residence:** 14.1%.

Cities with pop over 10,000: Nacogdoches 🏛 (30,647).

NAVARRO COUNTY

PO Box 423   **Ph:** 903-654-3036
Corsicana, TX 75151   **Fax:** 903-654-3097
www.co.navarro.tx.us

In east-central TX, south of Dallas; organized Apr 25, 1846 from Robertson County. **Name Origin:** For Juan Jose Antonio Navarro (1795-1870), Republic of TX patriot active in promoting statehood.

Area (sq mi): 1086.17 (land 1007.66; water 78.51). **Pop per sq mi:** 48.3.

Pop 2005: 48,687. **State rank:** 61. **Pop change:** 2000-20005 +7.9%; 1990-2000 +13%. **Pop 2000:** 45,124 (White 65.6%; Black or African American 16.8%; Hispanic or Latino 15.8%; Asian 0.5%; Other 11.9%). **Foreign born:** 9.1%. **Median age:** 35.2.

Income 2000: per capita $15,266; median household $31,268; **Pop below poverty level:** 18.2%. ***Personal per capita income 2000-2003:** $20,835-$21,463.

Unemployment 2004: 6.5%. **Change from 2000:** +1.5%. **Median travel time to work:** 26.4 minutes. **Working outside county of residence:** 24%.

Cities with pop over 10,000: Corsicana 🏛 (25,858).

NEWTON COUNTY

110 Court St   **Ph:** 409-379-5341
Newton, TX 75966   **Fax:** 409-379-9049
www.co.newton.tx.us

On the central eastern border of TX, northeast of Beaumont; organized Apr 22, 1846 from Jasper County. **Name Origin:** For Sgt. John Newton (1752-80), a soldier under Gen. Francis Marion (1732?-95) in the Revolutionary War, who saved several colonial patriots from execution by surprising and capturing the British soldiers guarding them.

Area (sq mi): 939.51 (land 932.69; water 6.82). **Pop per sq mi:** 15.3.

Pop 2005: 14,309. **State rank:** 143. **Pop change:** 2000-20005 -5.1%; 1990-2000 +11.1%. **Pop 2000:** 15,072 (White 74%; Black or African American 20.7%; Hispanic or Latino 3.8%; Asian 0.3%; Other 3.2%). **Foreign born:** 0.9%. **Median age:** 36.9.

Income 2000: per capita $13,381; median household $28,500; **Pop below poverty level:** 19.1%. ***Personal per capita income 2000-2003:** $15,173-$17,360.

Unemployment 2004: 11.2%. **Change from 2000:** -1.4%. **Median travel time to work:** 37.6 minutes. **Working outside county of residence:** 61.6%.

Cities with pop over 10,000: None.

NOLAN COUNTY

100 E 3rd St Suite 108   **Ph:** 325-235-2462
Sweetwater, TX 79556   **Fax:** 325-236-9416
www.co.nolan.tx.us

In north-central TX, west of Abilene; organized Aug 21, 1876 from Bexar County. **Name Origin:** For Philip Nolan (1771-1801), an American agitator in Spanish-held TX, killed by Spanish soldiers.

Area (sq mi): 913.93 (land 911.98; water 1.94). **Pop per sq mi:** 16.3.

Pop 2005: 14,878. **State rank:** 138. **Pop change:** 2000-20005 -5.8%; 1990-2000 -4.8%. **Pop 2000:** 15,802 (White 66.3%; Black or African American 4.7%; Hispanic or Latino 28%; Asian 0.2%; Other 16.7%). **Foreign born:** 4.2%. **Median age:** 37.4.

Income 2000: per capita $14,077; median household $26,209; **Pop below poverty level:** 21.7%. ***Personal per capita income 2000-2003:** $20,036-$21,683.

Unemployment 2004: 5.7%. **Change from 2000:** +0.8%. **Median travel time to work:** 16.4 minutes. **Working outside county of residence:** 12.1%.

Cities with pop over 10,000: Sweetwater 🏛 (10,882).

NUECES COUNTY

901 Leopard St Suite 201   **Ph:** 361-888-0580
Corpus Christi, TX 78401 **Fax:** 361-888-0329
www.co.nueces.tx.us

On the southeastern coast of TX, north of Brownsville; organized Apr 18, 1846 from San Patricio County. **Name Origin:** For the Nueces River, which forms part of its eastern border; Spanish 'nuts,' for the abundant pecan trees.

Area (sq mi): 1166.42 (land 835.82; water 330.6). **Pop per sq mi:** 382.5.

Pop 2005: 319,704. **State rank:** 14. **Pop change:** 2000-20005 +1.9%; 1990-2000 +7.7%. **Pop 2000:** 313,645 (White 37.7%; Black

*Source: Personal per capita income data are from the Bureau of Economic Analysis; per capita income data are from the Bureau of the Census.
See Introduction for explanation of differences.*

696

Nueces County (cont'd)

or African American 4.2%; Hispanic or Latino 55.8%; Asian 1.2%; Other 22.5%). **Foreign born:** 6.5%. **Median age:** 33.3.

Income 2000: per capita $17,036; median household $35,959; **Pop below poverty level:** 18.2%. ***Personal per capita income 2000-2003:** $23,925-$26,368.

Unemployment 2004: 6.3%. **Change from 2000:** +0.6%. **Median travel time to work:** 20.2 minutes. **Working outside county of residence:** 7.3%.

Cities with pop over 10,000: Robstown (12,614).

OCHILTREE COUNTY

511 S Main St   **Ph:** 806-435-8039
Perryton, TX 79070   **Fax:** 806-435-2081
www.co.ochiltree.tx.us

On the northeastern border of TX panhandle, northeast of Amarillo; organized Aug, 1876 from Bexar County. **Name Origin:** For Col. William Beck Ochiltree (1811-67), Republic of TX secretary of the treasury (1844), TX legislator (1855), delegate to the TX Constitutional Convention (1861), and Confederate officer.

Area (sq mi): 918.07 (land 917.56; water 0.51). **Pop per sq mi:** 10.2.

Pop 2005: 9,385. **State rank:** 170. **Pop change:** 2000-20005 +4.2%; 1990-2000 -1.3%. **Pop 2000:** 9,006 (White 66.3%; Black or African American 0.1%; Hispanic or Latino 31.8%; Asian 0.4%; Other 13.2%). **Foreign born:** 16.1%. **Median age:** 33.7.

Income 2000: per capita $16,707; median household $38,013; **Pop below poverty level:** 13%. ***Personal per capita income 2000-2003:** $28,097-$28,814.

Unemployment 2004: 3.7%. **Change from 2000:** +1.4%. **Median travel time to work:** 19.2 minutes. **Working outside county of residence:** 11.5%.

Cities with pop over 10,000: None.

OLDHAM COUNTY

PO Box 360   **Ph:** 806-267-2667
Vega, TX 79092   **Fax:** 806-267-2671
www.co.oldham.tx.us

On the northwestern border of TX panhandle, west of Amarillo; organized Aug 21, 1876 from Bexar County. **Name Origin:** For Williamson Simpson Oldham (1813-68), AR legislator, member of the TX secession convention (1861), and TX senator to the Confederate Congress.

Area (sq mi): 1501.42 (land 1500.63; water 0.79). **Pop per sq mi:** 1.4.

Pop 2005: 2,118. **State rank:** 236. **Pop change:** 2000-20005 -3.1%; 1990-2000 -4.1%. **Pop 2000:** 2,185 (White 84.8%; Black or African American 1.9%; Hispanic or Latino 11%; Asian 0.4%; Other 7.1%, including 1.3% American Indian/Alaska Native). **Foreign born:** 5.4%. **Median age:** 32.9.

Income 2000: per capita $14,806; median household $33,713; **Pop below poverty level:** 19.8%. ***Personal per capita income 2000-2003:** $23,086-$22,661.

Unemployment 2004: 4.5%. **Change from 2000:** +3.1%. **Median travel time to work:** 20.2 minutes. **Working outside county of residence:** 23.6%.

Cities with pop over 10,000: None.

ORANGE COUNTY

801 Division St   **Ph:** 409-883-7740
Orange, TX 77631   **Fax:** 409-882-7012
www.co.orange.tx.us

On the central eastern border of TX, east of Beaumont; organized Feb 5, 1852 from Jefferson County. **Name Origin:** For the orange groves in the region.

Area (sq mi): 379.54 (land 356.4; water 23.14). **Pop per sq mi:** 238.4.

Pop 2005: 84,983. **State rank:** 42. **Pop change:** 2000-20005 +0%; 1990-2000 +5.5%. **Pop 2000:** 84,966 (White 85.9%; Black or African American 8.4%; Hispanic or Latino 3.6%; Asian 0.8%; Other 2.9%). **Foreign born:** 2.1%. **Median age:** 36.1.

Income 2000: per capita $17,554; median household $37,586; **Pop below poverty level:** 13.8%. ***Personal per capita income 2000-2003:** $22,985-$25,302.

Unemployment 2004: 9%. **Change from 2000:** -0.8%. **Median travel time to work:** 22.1 minutes. **Working outside county of residence:** 43.5%.

Cities with pop over 10,000: Orange 🏛 (18,140); Vidor (11,293).

PALO PINTO COUNTY

PO Box 219   **Ph:** 940-659-1277
Palo Pinto, TX 76484
www.co.palo-pinto.tx.us

In north-central TX, west of Fort Worth; organized Aug 27, 1856 from Navarro County. **Name Origin:** From Spanish for 'painted tree,' but connotation is unclear.

Area (sq mi): 985.5 (land 952.93; water 32.57). **Pop per sq mi:** 28.8.

Pop 2005: 27,478. **State rank:** 95. **Pop change:** 2000-20005 +1.7%; 1990-2000 +7.9%. **Pop 2000:** 27,026 (White 82%; Black or African American 2.3%; Hispanic or Latino 13.6%; Asian 0.5%; Other 9%). **Foreign born:** 4.4%. **Median age:** 38.3.

Income 2000: per capita $15,454; median household $31,203; **Pop below poverty level:** 15.9%. ***Personal per capita income 2000-2003:** $21,616-$23,409.

Unemployment 2004: 5.5%. **Change from 2000:** +1.1%. **Median travel time to work:** 24.9 minutes. **Working outside county of residence:** 35.1%.

Cities with pop over 10,000: Mineral Wells (16,854).

PANOLA COUNTY

110 Sycamore St Rm 201   **Ph:** 903 693 0302
Carthage, TX 75633   **Fax:** 903-693-2726
www.carthagetexas.com

On northeastern border of TX, southwest of Shreveport, LA; organized Mar 30, 1846 from Harrison and Shelby counties. **Name Origin:** For Choctaw word for 'cotton,' but connotation is unclear.

Area (sq mi): 821.34 (land 800.92; water 20.42). **Pop per sq mi:** 28.7.

Panola County (cont'd)

Pop 2005: 22,997. **State rank:** 105. **Pop change:** 2000-20005 +1.1%; 1990-2000 +3.3%. **Pop 2000:** 22,756 (White 77.5%; Black or African American 17.7%; Hispanic or Latino 3.5%; Asian 0.2%; Other 3.4%). **Foreign born:** 2.9%. **Median age:** 38.8.

Income 2000: per capita $15,439; median household $31,909; **Pop below poverty level:** 14.1%. ***Personal per capita income 2000-2003:** $21,417-$22,906.

Unemployment 2004: 5.8%. **Change from 2000:** -1%. **Median travel time to work:** 25.9 minutes. **Working outside county of residence:** 33.2%.

Cities with pop over 10,000: None.

PARKER COUNTY

PO Box 819   **Ph:** 817-594-7461
Weatherford, TX 76086   **Fax:** 817-594-9540
www.co.parker.tx.us

In north-central TX, west of Fort Worth; organized Dec 12, 1855 from Bosque and Navarro counties. **Name Origin:** For Isaac Parker (1793-1883), Republic of TX patriot and legislator.

Area (sq mi): 910.09 (land 903.51; water 6.58). **Pop per sq mi:** 113.8.

Pop 2005: 102,801. **State rank:** 37. **Pop change:** 2000-20005 +16.2%; 1990-2000 +36.6%. **Pop 2000:** 88,495 (White 89.2%; Black or African American 1.8%; Hispanic or Latino 7%; Asian 0.3%; Other 5.3%). **Foreign born:** 2.6%. **Median age:** 36.5.

Income 2000: per capita $20,305; median household $45,497; **Pop below poverty level:** 8.3%. ***Personal per capita income 2000-2003:** $28,548-$27,782.

Unemployment 2004: 5.1%. **Change from 2000:** +1.9%. **Median travel time to work:** 32.8 minutes. **Working outside county of residence:** 59.4%.

Cities with pop over 10,000: Weatherford ⚒ (22,343).

PARMER COUNTY

PO Box 356   **Ph:** 806-481-3691
Farwell, TX 79325
www.co.parmer.tx.us

On the central western border of TX panhandle, southwest of Amarillo; organized Aug 21, 1876 from Bexar County. **Name Origin:** For Martin Parmer (1778-1850), Republic of TX legislator, signer of the TX Declaration of Independence (1836), and chief justice of Jasper County (1839-40).

Area (sq mi): 885.17 (land 881.66; water 3.51). **Pop per sq mi:** 11.1.

Pop 2005: 9,754. **State rank:** 167. **Pop change:** 2000-20005 -2.6%; 1990-2000 +1.6%. **Pop 2000:** 10,016 (White 48.7%; Black or African American 1%; Hispanic or Latino 49.2%; Asian 0.3%; Other 32.6%). **Foreign born:** 20.1%. **Median age:** 32.1.

Income 2000: per capita $14,184; median household $30,813; **Pop below poverty level:** 17%. ***Personal per capita income 2000-2003:** $25,592-$24,264.

Unemployment 2004: 4.8%. **Change from 2000:** +1.7%. **Median travel time to work:** 16.4 minutes. **Working outside county of residence:** 17.6%.

Cities with pop over 10,000: None.

PECOS COUNTY

103 W Callaghan St   **Ph:** 432-336-7555
Fort Stockton, TX 79735   **Fax:** 432-336-7557
www.co.pecos.tx.us

In west-central TX, south of Odessa; organized May 3, 1871 from Presidio County. **Name Origin:** For the Pecos River, which forms its northeastern border. Believed to be the name of an Indian tribe now lost or unidentified, and to be a Spanish translation of a Keresan word meaning 'watering place.'

Area (sq mi): 4764.73 (land 4763.66; water 1.07). **Pop per sq mi:** 3.3.

Pop 2005: 15,859. **State rank:** 136. **Pop change:** 2000-20005 -5.7%; 1990-2000 +14.5%. **Pop 2000:** 16,809 (White 33.4%; Black or African American 4.4%; Hispanic or Latino 61.1%; Asian 0.5%; Other 19.2%). **Foreign born:** 13.5%. **Median age:** 31.2.

Income 2000: per capita $12,212; median household $28,033; **Pop below poverty level:** 20.4%. ***Personal per capita income 2000-2003:** $13,953-$15,955.

Unemployment 2004: 6.2%. **Change from 2000:** +1.2%. **Median travel time to work:** 17.6 minutes. **Working outside county of residence:** 9.7%.

Cities with pop over 10,000: None.

POLK COUNTY

PO Drawer 2119   **Ph:** 936-327-6804
Livingston, TX 77351   **Fax:** 936-327-6874
www.co.polk.tx.us

In eastern TX, northwest of Beaumont; organized Mar 30, 1846 from Liberty County. **Name Origin:** For James Knox Polk (1795-1849), eleventh U.S. president.

Area (sq mi): 1109.81 (land 1057.26; water 52.55). **Pop per sq mi:** 44.1.

Pop 2005: 46,640. **State rank:** 66. **Pop change:** 2000-20005 +13.4%; 1990-2000 +34%. **Pop 2000:** 41,133 (White 74.7%; Black or African American 13.2%; Hispanic or Latino 9.4%; Asian 0.4%; Other 6.7%, including 1.7% American Indian/Alaska Native). **Foreign born:** 4.3%. **Median age:** 39.3.

Income 2000: per capita $15,834; median household $30,495; **Pop below poverty level:** 17.4%. ***Personal per capita income 2000-2003:** $24,294-$25,174.

Unemployment 2004: 6.9%. **Change from 2000:** +1.8%. **Median travel time to work:** 30.9 minutes. **Working outside county of residence:** 30.7%.

Cities with pop over 10,000: None.

POTTER COUNTY

PO Box 9638   **Ph:** 806-379-2275
Amarillo, TX 79105   **Fax:** 806-379-2296
www.co.potter.tx.us

In north-central TX panhandle, north of Lubbock; organized Aug 21, 1876 from Bexar County. **Name Origin:** For Robert Potter (1800-42), NC legislator (1826; 1828), U.S. representative from NC (1829-31), Republic of TX official and naval officer.

**Source: Personal per capita income data are from the Bureau of Economic Analysis; per capita income data are from the Bureau of the Census.
See Introduction for explanation of differences.*

Potter County (cont'd)

Area (sq mi): 921.98 (land 909.24; water 12.74). **Pop per sq mi:** 131.8.

Pop 2005: 119,852. **State rank:** 31. **Pop change:** 2000-20005 +5.6%; 1990-2000 +16%. **Pop 2000:** 113,546 (White 57.7%; Black or African American 10%; Hispanic or Latino 28.1%; Asian 2.5%; Other 18.9%). **Foreign born:** 9.4% **Median age:** 32.1.

Income 2000: per capita $14,947; median household $29,492; **Pop below poverty level:** 19.2%. *****Personal per capita income 2000-2003:** $23,837-$24,110.

Unemployment 2004: 5.6%. **Change from 2000:** +0.5%. **Median travel time to work:** 17.9 minutes. **Working outside county of residence:** 20.9%.

Cities with pop over 10,000: Amarillo 🏛 (180,791).

PRESIDIO COUNTY

320 N Highland Ave   **Ph:** 432-729-4812
Marfa, TX 79843   **Fax:** 432-729-4313
www.co.presidio.tx.us

On the central western border of TX, southeast of El Paso; organized Jan 3, 1850 from Bexar County. **Name Origin:** From Spanish for 'garrisoned fortress.'

Area (sq mi): 3856.26 (land 3855.51; water 0.75). **Pop per sq mi:** 2.

Pop 2005: 7,722. **State rank:** 180. **Pop change:** 2000-20005 +5.7%; 1990-2000 +10%. **Pop 2000:** 7,304 (White 14.8%; Black or African American 0.3%; Hispanic or Latino 84.4%; Asian 0.1%; Other 14.7%). **Foreign born:** 35.8%. **Median age:** 32.8.

Income 2000: per capita $9,558; median household $19,860; **Pop below poverty level:** 36.4%. *****Personal per capita income 2000-2003:** $13,446-$14,465.

Unemployment 2004: 14.5%. **Change from 2000:** -9%. **Median travel time to work:** 17.3 minutes. **Working outside county of residence:** 18.5%.

Cities with pop over 10,000: None.

RAINS COUNTY

PO Box 187   **Ph:** 903-474-9999
Emory, TX 75440   **Fax:** 903-474-9390
www.co.rains.tx.us

In northeastern TX, east of Dallas; organized Jun 9, 1870 from Hopkins, Wood, and Hunt counties. **Name Origin:** For Emory Rains (1800-78), Republic of TX legislator and surveyor.

Area (sq mi): 258.87 (land 232.05; water 26.82). **Pop per sq mi:** 48.7.

Pop 2005: 11,305. **State rank:** 159. **Pop change:** 2000-20005 +23.7%; 1990-2000 +36.1%. **Pop 2000:** 9,139 (White 89.5%; Black or African American 2.9%; Hispanic or Latino 5.5%; Asian 0.3%; Other 4.7%). **Foreign born:** 2.5%. **Median age:** 41.

Income 2000: per capita $16,442; median household $33,712; **Pop below poverty level:** 14.9%. *****Personal per capita income 2000-2003:** $19,722-$18,896.

Unemployment 2004: 5.7%. **Change from 2000:** +1.3%. **Median travel time to work:** 36.9 minutes. **Working outside county of residence:** 59.1%.

Cities with pop over 10,000: None.

RANDALL COUNTY

PO Box 660   **Ph:** 806-468-5505
Canyon, TX 79015   **Fax:** 806-468-5509
www.randallcounty.org

In north-central TX panhandle, south of Amarillo; organized Aug 21, 1876 from Bexar County. **Name Origin:** For Gen. Horace Randal (1833-64), Confederate army officer. Misspelling allowed to stand.

Area (sq mi): 922.42 (land 914.43; water 7.99). **Pop per sq mi:** 120.4.

Pop 2005: 110,053. **State rank:** 34. **Pop change:** 2000-20005 +5.5%; 1990-2000 +16.3%. **Pop 2000:** 104,312 (White 85.7%; Black or African American 1.5%; Hispanic or Latino 10.3%; Asian 1%; Other 6.9%). **Foreign born:** 2.6%. **Median age:** 34.9.

Income 2000: per capita $21,840; median household $42,712; **Pop below poverty level:** 8.1%. *****Personal per capita income 2000-2003:** $25,126-$26,835.

Unemployment 2004: 3.2%. **Change from 2000:** +2%. **Median travel time to work:** 18.7 minutes. **Working outside county of residence:** 60%.

Cities with pop over 10,000: Canyon 🏛 (13,060).

REAGAN COUNTY

PO Box 100   **Ph:** 325-884-2442
Big Lake, TX 76932   **Fax:** 325-884-1503

In central TX, west of San Angelo; organized Mar 7, 1903 from Tom Green County. **Name Origin:** For Col. John Henninger Reagan (1818-1905), postmaster general and acting secretary of the treasury of the Confederacy (1861-64), U.S. representative from TX (1875-87), and U.S. senator from TX (1887-91).

Area (sq mi): 1175.98 (land 1175.3; water 0.68). **Pop per sq mi:** 2.5.

Pop 2005: 2,995. **State rank:** 228. **Pop change:** 2000-20005 -10%; 1990-2000 -26.3%. **Pop 2000:** 3,326 (White 46.5%; Black or African American 3%; Hispanic or Latino 49.5%; Asian 0.3%; Other 32.1%). **Foreign born:** 16.4%. **Median age:** 32.4.

Income 2000: per capita $13,174; median household $33,231; **Pop below poverty level:** 11.8%. *****Personal per capita income 2000-2003:** $16,599-$19,928.

Unemployment 2004: 4.4%. **Change from 2000:** +1.4%. **Median travel time to work:** 18.8 minutes. **Working outside county of residence:** 13%.

Cities with pop over 10,000: None.

REAL COUNTY

PO Box 750   **Ph:** 830-232-5202
Leakey, TX 78873   **Fax:** 830-232-6888
www.co.real.tx.us

In south-central TX, northwest of San Antonio; organized Apr 3, 1913 from Bandera and Kerr counties. **Name Origin:** For Julius Real (1860-1944), county jurist and TX legislator (1910-14; 1924-28).

Area (sq mi): 700.04 (land 699.91; water 0.13). **Pop per sq mi:** 4.3.

Cities with pop over 10,000: None.

Real County (cont'd)

Pop 2005: 3,031. **State rank:** 226. **Pop change:** 2000-20005 -0.5%; 1990-2000 +26.3%. **Pop 2000:** 3,047 (White 75.7%; Black or African American 0.2%; Hispanic or Latino 22.6%; Asian 0.2%; Other 8.1%). **Foreign born:** 4%. **Median age:** 44.6.

Income 2000: per capita $14,321; median household $25,118; **Pop below poverty level:** 21.2%. ***Personal per capita income 2000-2003:** $18,234-$19,414.

Unemployment 2004: 5%. **Change from 2000:** +1.2%. **Median travel time to work:** 21.8 minutes. **Working outside county of residence:** 28.3%.

Cities with pop over 10,000: None.

RED RIVER COUNTY

200 N Walnut St   **Ph:** 903-427-2401
Clarksville, TX 75426   **Fax:** 903-427-5510
www.co.red-river.tx.us

On the northeastern border of TX, west of Texarkana; original county; organized 1836 (prior to statehood) from Old Mexican Municipality. **Name Origin:** For the Red River, which forms its northern border.

Area (sq mi): 1057.61 (land 1050.18; water 7.43). **Pop per sq mi:** 12.9.

Pop 2005: 13,575. **State rank:** 147. **Pop change:** 2000-20005 -5.2%; 1990-2000 +0%. **Pop 2000:** 14,314 (White 75.9%; Black or African American 17.8%; Hispanic or Latino 4.7%; Asian 0.1%; Other 4.1%). **Foreign born:** 2.5%. **Median age:** 40.4.

Income 2000: per capita $15,058; median household $27,558; **Pop below poverty level:** 17.3%. ***Personal per capita income 2000-2003:** $18,204-$19,796.

Unemployment 2004: 6.9%. **Change from 2000:** -3.6%. **Median travel time to work:** 27.5 minutes. **Working outside county of residence:** 35.6%.

Cities with pop over 10,000: None.

REEVES COUNTY

100 E 4th St   **Ph:** 432-445-5467
Pecos, TX 79772   **Fax:** 432-445-3997

In western TX, southwest of Odessa; established Apr 14, 1883 from Pecos County. **Name Origin:** For Col. George R. Reeves (1826-82), TX legislator (1855-61), Confederate army officer, and Speaker of the House (1881-82).

Area (sq mi): 2641.95 (land 2635.88; water 6.07). **Pop per sq mi:** 4.4.

Pop 2005: 11,638. **State rank:** 158. **Pop change:** 2000-20005 -11.4%; 1990-2000 -17.1%. **Pop 2000:** 13,137 (White 23.8%; Black or African American 2.1%; Hispanic or Latino 73.4%; Asian 0.4%; Other 18.2%). **Foreign born:** 14.7%. **Median age:** 32.1.

Income 2000: per capita $10,811; median household $23,306; **Pop below poverty level:** 28.9%. ***Personal per capita income 2000-2003:** $15,832-$16,372.

Unemployment 2004: 9.4%. **Change from 2000:** +2.6%. **Median travel time to work:** 17.5 minutes. **Working outside county of residence:** 11.4%.

Cities with pop over 10,000: None.

REFUGIO COUNTY

808 Commerce St PO Box 704   **Ph:** 361-526-2233
Refugio, TX 78377   **Fax:** 361-526-1325
www.co.refugio.tx.us

On the southeastern coast of TX, north of Corpus Christi; original county; organized Mar 17, 1836 (prior to statehood) from Old Mexican Municipality. **Name Origin:** For the mission established there, 'Our Lady of Refuge,' honoring the Virgin Mary.

Area (sq mi): 818.64 (land 770.21; water 48.43). **Pop per sq mi:** 9.9.

Pop 2005: 7,639. **State rank:** 184. **Pop change:** 2000-20005 -2.4%; 1990-2000 -1.9%. **Pop 2000:** 7,828 (White 47.3%; Black or African American 6.8%; Hispanic or Latino 44.6%; Asian 0.3%; Other 12.8%). **Foreign born:** 2.6%. **Median age:** 38.6.

Income 2000: per capita $15,481; median household $29,986; **Pop below poverty level:** 17.8%. ***Personal per capita income 2000-2003:** $25,779-$26,411.

Unemployment 2004: 5.4%. **Change from 2000:** +0.8%. **Median travel time to work:** 22.5 minutes. **Working outside county of residence:** 29.1%.

Cities with pop over 10,000: None.

ROBERTS COUNTY

PO Box 477   **Ph:** 806-868-2341
Miami, TX 79059   **Fax:** 806-868-3381
www.co.roberts.tx.us

In the TX panhandle, northeast of Amarillo; organized Aug 21, 1876 from Bexar County. **Name Origin:** For both Lt. John S. Roberts (1796-1871), a signer of the TX Declaration of Independence, and Oran Milo Roberts, TX governor (1879-83).

Area (sq mi): 924.19 (land 924.09; water 0.1). **Pop per sq mi:** 0.9.

Pop 2005: 820. **State rank:** 249. **Pop change:** 2000-20005 -7.6%; 1990-2000 -13.5%. **Pop 2000:** 887 (White 95.8%; Black or African American 0.3%; Hispanic or Latino 3.2%; Asian 0.1%; Other 3.1%). **Foreign born:** 0.5%. **Median age:** 42.

Income 2000: per capita $20,923; median household $44,792; **Pop below poverty level:** 7.2%. ***Personal per capita income 2000-2003:** $23,305-$25,623.

Unemployment 2004: 4%. **Change from 2000:** +2.5%. **Median travel time to work:** 27.2 minutes. **Working outside county of residence:** 53.7%.

Cities with pop over 10,000: None.

ROBERTSON COUNTY

PO Box 1029   **Ph:** 979-828-4130
Franklin, TX 77856   **Fax:** 979-828-1260
www.co.robertson.tx.us

In east-central TX, southeast of Waco; organized Dec 14, 1837 (prior to statehood) from Bexar County. **Name Origin:** For Gen. Sterling Clark Robertson (1785-1842), officer in the Battle of New Orleans (1815), signer of the TX Declaration of Independence (1836), and Republic of TX legislator (1836; 1840).

Area (sq mi): 865.67 (land 854.56; water 11.11). **Pop per sq mi:** 18.9.

Source: Personal per capita income data are from the Bureau of Economic Analysis; per capita income data are from the Bureau of the Census. See Introduction for explanation of differences.

Robertson County (cont'd)

Pop 2005: 16,192. **State rank:** 135. **Pop change:** 2000-20005 +1.2%; 1990-2000 +3.2%. **Pop 2000:** 16,000 (White 59.9%; Black or African American 24.2%; Hispanic or Latino 14.7%; Asian 0.2%; Other 9.5%). **Foreign born:** 3.3%. **Median age:** 37.6.

Income 2000: per capita $14,714; median household $28,886; **Pop below poverty level:** 20.6%. ***Personal per capita income 2000-2003:** $19,790-$22,778.

Unemployment 2004: 5.8%. **Change from 2000:** +0.8%. **Median travel time to work:** 29.1 minutes. **Working outside county of residence:** 51.4%.

Cities with pop over 10,000: None.

ROCKWALL COUNTY
1101 Ridge Rd Suite 101   **Ph:** 972-882-0220
Rockwall, TX 75087   **Fax:** 972-882-0229
www.rockwallcountytexas.com

In northeastern TX, east of Dallas; organized May 1, 1873 from Kaufman County. The smallest county in Texas, covering 147 square miles. **Name Origin:** For a subterranean wall or dike that thrusts up in various parts of the county. It is unclear whether the wall is a geological formation or man-made.

Area (sq mi): 148.7 (land 128.79; water 19.91). **Pop per sq mi:** 488.7.

Pop 2005: 62,944. **State rank:** 51. **Pop change:** 2000-20005 +46.1%; 1990-2000 +68.3%. **Pop 2000:** 43,080 (White 83.1%; Black or African American 3.2%; Hispanic or Latino 11.1%; Asian 1.3%; Other 6.3%). **Foreign born:** 7.8%. **Median age:** 35.3.

Income 2000: per capita $28,573; median household $65,164; **Pop below poverty level:** 4.7%. ***Personal per capita income 2000-2003:** $36,935-$34,135.

Unemployment 2004: 4.9%. **Change from 2000:** +1.2%. **Median travel time to work:** 32 minutes. **Working outside county of residence:** 66.1%.

Cities with pop over 10,000: Rockwall 🏛 (26,696).

RUNNELS COUNTY
PO Box 189   **Ph:** 325-365-2720
Ballinger, TX 76821   **Fax:** 325-365-3408
www.co.runnels.tx.us

In central TX, northeast of San Angelo; organized Feb 1, 1858 from Coleman County. **Name Origin:** For Hardin Richard Runnels (1820-73), TX legislator (1847-53) and governor (1857-59).

Area (sq mi): 1057.13 (land 1050.73; water 6.4). **Pop per sq mi:** 10.4.

Pop 2005: 10,974. **State rank:** 161. **Pop change:** 2000-20005 -4.5%; 1990-2000 +1.8%. **Pop 2000:** 11,495 (White 67.8%; Black or African American 1.4%; Hispanic or Latino 29.3%; Asian 0.3%; Other 16.8%). **Foreign born:** 4.5%. **Median age:** 39.4.

Income 2000: per capita $13,577; median household $27,806; **Pop below poverty level:** 19.2%. ***Personal per capita income 2000-2003:** $18,751-$20,362.

Unemployment 2004: 5.2%. **Change from 2000:** +1.4%. **Median travel time to work:** 18.8 minutes. **Working outside county of residence:** 21.9%.

Cities with pop over 10,000: None.

RUSK COUNTY
115 N Main St Suite 206   **Ph:** 903-657-0330
Henderson, TX 75652
www.co.rusk.tx.us

In northeastern TX, east of Tyler; organized Jan 16, 1843 from Nacogdoches County. **Name Origin:** For Gen. Thomas Jefferson Rusk (1803-57), chief justice of the Republic of TX supreme court (1838-42), signer of the TX Declaration of Independence (1836), and U.S. senator (1846-57).

Area (sq mi): 938.62 (land 923.55; water 15.07). **Pop per sq mi:** 51.9.

Pop 2005: 47,971. **State rank:** 63. **Pop change:** 2000-20005 |1.3%; 1990-2000 +8.3%. **Pop 2000:** 47,372 (White 71.2%; Black or African American 19.2%; Hispanic or Latino 8.4%; Asian 0.2%; Other 5.6%). **Foreign born:** 4.4%. **Median age:** 38.1.

Income 2000: per capita $16,674; median household $32,898; **Pop below poverty level:** 14.6%. ***Personal per capita income 2000-2003:** $21,044-$22,698.

Unemployment 2004: 6%. **Change from 2000:** +1.6%. **Median travel time to work:** 23.7 minutes. **Working outside county of residence:** 44.7%.

Cities with pop over 10,000: Henderson 🏛 (11,417).

SABINE COUNTY
PO Box 580   **Ph:** 409-787-3786
Hemphill, TX 75948   **Fax:** 409-787-2044
www.sabinecountytexas.com

On the northeastern border of TX, east of Lufkin; original county; organized Mar 17, 1836 (prior to statehood) from Old Mexican Municipality. **Name Origin:** For the Sabine River, which forms its eastern border. French form of Spanish *sabinas* 'red cedar trees' that grow along the banks.

Area (sq mi): 576.61 (land 490.27; water 86.34). **Pop per sq mi:** 21.2.

Pop 2005: 10,416. **State rank:** 163. **Pop change:** 2000-20005 -0.5%; 1990-2000 +9.2%. **Pop 2000:** 10,469 (White 87.1%; Black or African American 9.9%; Hispanic or Latino 1.8%; Asian 0.1%; Other 2.1%). **Foreign born:** 1.1%. **Median age:** 47.

Income 2000: per capita $15,821; median household $27,198; **Pop below poverty level:** 15.9%. ***Personal per capita income 2000-2003:** $21,098-$22,222.

Unemployment 2004: 11.1%. **Change from 2000:** +1.2%. **Median travel time to work:** 28.5 minutes. **Working outside county of residence:** 33.2%.

Cities with pop over 10,000: None.

SAN AUGUSTINE COUNTY
Courthouse Rm 106   **Ph:** 936-275-2452
San Augustine, TX 75972   **Fax:** 936-275-9579
www.co.san-augustine.tx.us

On central east border of TX, north of Beaumont; original county;

San Augustine County (cont'd)

organized Mar 17, 1836 (prior to statehood) from Old Mexican Municipality. **Name Origin:** For the Presidio de San Augustin de Ahumada (Fort of Saint Augustine of Ahumada), Mission Nuestra Senora de los Dolores de los Ais (Mission of Our Lady of Sorrows of the Ais), which was established on Ayish Bayou by the Marquis de San Miguel de Ahuayo in 1721.

Area (sq mi): 592.21 (land 527.87; water 64.34). **Pop per sq mi:** 16.9.

Pop 2005: 8,907. **State rank:** 175. **Pop change:** 2000-20005 -0.4%; 1990-2000 +11.8%. **Pop 2000:** 8,946 (White 67.8%; Black or African American 27.9%; Hispanic or Latino 3.6%; Asian 0.2%; Other 2.5%). **Foreign born:** 2%. **Median age:** 42.1.

Income 2000: per capita $15,548; median household $27,025; **Pop below poverty level:** 21.2%. ***Personal per capita income 2000-2003:** $18,797-$20,603.

Unemployment 2004: 7%. **Change from 2000:** +1.5%. **Median travel time to work:** 32 minutes. **Working outside county of residence:** 42.2%.

Cities with pop over 10,000: None.

SAN JACINTO COUNTY

1 State Hwy 150 Rm 2   **Ph:** 936-653-2324
Coldspring, TX 77331   **Fax:** 936-653-8312
www.co.san-jacinto.tx.us

In east-central TX, northwest of Beaumont; organized Aug 13, 1870 from Liberty County. **Name Origin:** For the San Jacinto River, which runs through the county; site of the battle that eventually won Texan independence from Mexico (1836). Spanish 'Saint Hyacinth' for the many water lilies.

Area (sq mi): 627.9 (land 570.65; water 57.25). **Pop per sq mi:** 43.5.

Pop 2005: 24,801. **State rank:** 101. **Pop change:** 2000-20005 +11.5%; 1990-2000 +35.9%. **Pop 2000:** 22,246 (White 80.8%; Black or African American 12.6%; Hispanic or Latino 4.9%; Asian 0.3%; Other 3.5%). **Foreign born:** 2.5%. **Median age:** 40.

Income 2000: per capita $16,144; median household $32,220; **Pop below poverty level:** 18.8%. ***Personal per capita income 2000-2003:** $19,965-$20,589.

Unemployment 2004: 6.6%. **Change from 2000:** +2.6%. **Median travel time to work:** 42.2 minutes. **Working outside county of residence:** 72%.

Cities with pop over 10,000: None.

SAN PATRICIO COUNTY

PO Box 578   **Ph:** 361-364-6290
Sinton, TX 78387   **Fax:** 361-364-6112
www.co.san-patricio.tx.us

On the southeastern coast of TX, north of Corpus Christi; original county; organized Mar 17, 1836 (prior to statehood) from Old Mexican Municipality. **Name Origin:** From the Spanish for 'Saint Patrick,' the patron saint of Ireland.

Area (sq mi): 707.06 (land 691.65; water 15.41). **Pop per sq mi:** 100.1.

Pop 2005: 69,209. **State rank:** 49. **Pop change:** 2000-20005 +3.1%; 1990-2000 +14.3%. **Pop 2000:** 67,138 (White 45.8%; Black or African American 2.8%; Hispanic or Latino 49.4%; Asian 0.6%; Other 19.7%). **Foreign born:** 3.3%. **Median age:** 32.

Income 2000: per capita $15,425; median household $34,836; **Pop below poverty level:** 18%. ***Personal per capita income 2000-2003:** $19,405-$22,669.

Unemployment 2004: 7.9%. **Change from 2000:** +2.1%. **Median travel time to work:** 23.3 minutes. **Working outside county of residence:** 43.2%.

Cities with pop over 10,000: Portland (15,584).

SAN SABA COUNTY

500 E Wallace St County Courthouse   **Ph:** 325-372-3614
San Saba, TX 76877
www.sansabacounty.org

In central TX, southeast of San Angelo; organized Feb 1, 1856 from Bexar County. **Name Origin:** For the San Saba River, which flows through it; Spanish contraction of *San Sabado* 'Holy Saturday,' named for the day before Easter when Spanish explorers discovered it.

Area (sq mi): 1138.25 (land 1134.47; water 3.78). **Pop per sq mi:** 5.4.

Pop 2005: 6,076. **State rank:** 195. **Pop change:** 2000-20005 -1.8%; 1990-2000 +14.5%. **Pop 2000:** 6,186 (White 74.7%; Black or African American 2.7%; Hispanic or Latino 21.5%; Asian 0.1%; Other 12.7%, including 1.1% American Indian/Alaska Native). **Foreign born:** 5.5%. **Median age:** 39.4.

Income 2000: per capita $15,309; median household $30,104; **Pop below poverty level:** 16.6%. ***Personal per capita income 2000-2003:** $19,458-$21,005.

Unemployment 2004: 4.9%. **Change from 2000:** +2%. **Median travel time to work:** 24.8 minutes. **Working outside county of residence:** 22.3%.

Cities with pop over 10,000: None.

SCHLEICHER COUNTY

PO Drawer 580   **Ph:** 325-853-2833
Eldorado, TX 76936   **Fax:** 325-853-2768
www.co.schleicher.tx.us

In west-central TX, south of San Angelo; organized Apr 1, 1887 from Crockett County. **Name Origin:** For Capt. Gustave Schleicher (1823-79), TX legislator (1853-54; 1859-61), Confederate army officer, and U.S. representative (1875-79).

Area (sq mi): 1310.65 (land 1310.61; water 0.04). **Pop per sq mi:** 2.1.

Pop 2005: 2,742. **State rank:** 230. **Pop change:** 2000-20005 -6.6%; 1990-2000 -1.8%. **Pop 2000:** 2,935 (White 54.3%; Black or African American 1.5%; Hispanic or Latino 43.5%; Asian 0.2%; Other 21.7%). **Foreign born:** 13.9%. **Median age:** 38.8.

Income 2000: per capita $15,969; median household $29,746; **Pop below poverty level:** 21.5%. ***Personal per capita income 2000-2003:** $17,371-$19,210.

---

*Source: Personal per capita income data are from the Bureau of Economic Analysis; per capita income data are from the Bureau of the Census.
See Introduction for explanation of differences.

Schleicher County (cont'd)

Unemployment 2004: 3.9%. **Change from 2000:** +1.6%. **Median travel time to work:** 21.6 minutes. **Working outside county of residence:** 25.3%.

Cities with pop over 10,000: None.

SCURRY COUNTY
1806 25th St Suite 300
Snyder, TX 79549
www.co.scurry.tx.us

Ph: 325-573-5332
Fax: 325-573-7396

In south-central TX panhandle, northwest of Abilene; organized Aug 21, 1876 from Bexar County. **Name Origin:** Either for Gen. William Read Scurry (1821-64), Republic of TX legislator and jurist, publisher of the *Austin State Gazette* and Confederate army officer; or for Gen. Richardson Scurry (1811-62), TX legislator (1842-44) and U.S. representative (1851-53).

Area (sq mi): 907.53 (land 902.5; water 5.03). **Pop per sq mi:** 18.

Pop 2005: 16,217. **State rank:** 134. **Pop change:** 2000-20005 -0.9%; 1990-2000 -12.2%. **Pop 2000:** 16,361 (White 65.2%; Black or African American 6.1%; Hispanic or Latino 27.8%; Asian 0.2%; Other 12.4%). **Foreign born:** 3.1%. **Median age:** 37.

Income 2000: per capita $15,871; median household $31,646; **Pop below poverty level:** 16%. ***Personal per capita income 2000-2003:** $20,532-$22,575.

Unemployment 2004: 5.5%. **Change from 2000:** +0.5%. **Median travel time to work:** 16 minutes. **Working outside county of residence:** 11.2%.

Cities with pop over 10,000: Snyder 🏛 (10,542).

SHACKELFORD COUNTY
PO Box 247
Albany, TX 76430
www.co.shackelford.tx.us

Ph: 325-762-2232
Fax: 325-762-2830

In north-central TX, northeast of Abilene; organized Feb 1, 1858 from Bosque County. **Name Origin:** For John Shackelford (1790-1857), AL physician and legislator (1822-24) who fought for TX independence then returned to AL to practice medicine.

Area (sq mi): 915.54 (land 913.95; water 1.59). **Pop per sq mi:** 3.5.

Pop 2005: 3,167. **State rank:** 223. **Pop change:** 2000-20005 -4.1%; 1990-2000 -0.4%. **Pop 2000:** 3,302 (White 91.3%; Black or African American 0.5%; Hispanic or Latino 7.6%; Asian 0%; Other 5.2%). **Foreign born:** 2.9%. **Median age:** 40.1.

Income 2000: per capita $16,341; median household $30,479; **Pop below poverty level:** 13.6%. ***Personal per capita income 2000-2003:** $25,235-$26,260.

Unemployment 2004: 3.2%. **Change from 2000:** +1%. **Median travel time to work:** 25.4 minutes. **Working outside county of residence:** 37.4%.

Cities with pop over 10,000: None.

SHELBY COUNTY
PO Box 1987
Center, TX 75935
www.co.shelby.tx.us

Ph: 936-598-6361
Fax: 936-598-3701

On the northeastern border of TX, northeast of Lufkin; original county; organized Mar 17, 1836 (prior to statehood) from Old Mexican Municipality. **Name Origin:** For Gen. Isaac Shelby (1750-1826), officer in the Revolutionary War, NC legislator, and governor of KY (1792-96; 1812-16).

Area (sq mi): 834.53 (land 794.11; water 40.43). **Pop per sq mi:** 33.2.

Pop 2005: 26,346. **State rank:** 97. **Pop change:** 2000-20005 +4.4%; 1990-2000 +14.5%. **Pop 2000:** 25,224 (White 69.6%; Black or African American 19.4%; Hispanic or Latino 9.9%; Asian 0.2%; Other 7.7%). **Foreign born:** 6.6%. **Median age:** 36.9.

Income 2000: per capita $15,186; median household $29,112; **Pop below poverty level:** 19.4%. ***Personal per capita income 2000-2003:** $21,274-$22,640.

Unemployment 2004: 6.3%. **Change from 2000:** +0.3%. **Median travel time to work:** 24.9 minutes. **Working outside county of residence:** 23.7%.

Cities with pop over 10,000: None.

SHERMAN COUNTY
PO Box 270
Stratford, TX 79084
www.co.sherman.tx.us

Ph: 806-366-2371
Fax: 806-396-5670

In north-central TX panhandle, north of Amarillo; organized Aug 21, 1876 from Bexar County. **Name Origin:** For Gen. Sidney Sherman (1805-73), officer in the Republic of TX army, TX legislator (1842; 1852-53), and organizer of the first railroad in TX.

Area (sq mi): 923.2 (land 923.03; water 0.16). **Pop per sq mi:** 3.3.

Pop 2005: 3,002. **State rank:** 227. **Pop change:** 2000-20005 -5.8%; 1990-2000 +11.5%. **Pop 2000:** 3,186 (White 71%; Black or African American 0.5%; Hispanic or Latino 27.4%; Asian 0%; Other 17%). **Foreign born:** 12.4%. **Median age:** 34.4.

Income 2000: per capita $17,210; median household $33,179; **Pop below poverty level:** 16.1%. ***Personal per capita income 2000-2003:** $43,549-$43,316.

Unemployment 2004: 3.8%. **Change from 2000:** +2.3%. **Median travel time to work:** 19.1 minutes. **Working outside county of residence:** 35.2%.

Cities with pop over 10,000: None.

SMITH COUNTY
PO Box 1018
Tyler, TX 75710
www.smith-county.com

Ph: 903-535-0630
Fax: 903-535-0684

In northeastern TX, southeast of Dallas; organized Apr 11, 1846 from Nacogdoches County. **Name Origin:** For Gen. James Smith (1792-1855), officer in the War of 1812 and the war of TX independence; TX legislator (1846-47).

Area (sq mi): 949.45 (land 928.38; water 21.06). **Pop per sq mi:** 205.3.

Pop 2005: 190,594. **State rank:** 22. **Pop change:** 2000-20005 +9.1%; 1990-2000 +15.5%. **Pop 2000:** 174,706 (White 67.9%; Black or African American 19.1%; Hispanic or Latino 11.2%; Asian 0.7%; Other 7.5%). **Foreign born:** 6.6%. **Median age:** 35.5.

🏛 *County Seat*

Smith County (cont'd)

Income 2000: per capita $19,072; median household $37,148; **Pop below poverty level:** 13.8%. ***Personal per capita income 2000-2003:** $28,055-$28,441.

Unemployment 2004: 5.3%. **Change from 2000:** +1.2%. **Median travel time to work:** 22.2 minutes. **Working outside county of residence:** 9.9%.

Cities with pop over 10,000: Tyler ⛪ (89,552).

SOMERVELL COUNTY

PO Box 1098   **Ph:** 254-897-4427
Glen Rose, TX 76043   **Fax:** 254-897-3233
www.glenrose.org

In north-central TX, southwest of Fort Worth; organized Mar 13, 1875 from Hood County. **Name Origin:** For Gen. Alexander Somervell (1796-1854), Republic of TX secretary of war (1836), legislator (1836-38), and collector of customs (1842-45).

Area (sq mi): 191.9 (land 187.17; water 4.73). **Pop per sq mi:** 40.5.

Pop 2005: 7,578. **State rank:** 185. **Pop change:** 2000-20005 +11.3%; 1990-2000 +27%. **Pop 2000:** 6,809 (White 84.6%; Black or African American 0.3%; Hispanic or Latino 13.4%; Asian 0.3%; Other 7.3%). **Foreign born:** 5.7%. **Median age:** 36.8.

Income 2000: per capita $18,367; median household $39,404; **Pop below poverty level:** 8.6%. ***Personal per capita income 2000-2003:** $24,464-$25,808.

Unemployment 2004: 5%. **Change from 2000:** -1.5%. **Median travel time to work:** 27.1 minutes. **Working outside county of residence:** 32.6%.

Cities with pop over 10,000: None.

STARR COUNTY

County Courthouse Rm 201   **Ph:** 956-487-2954
Rio Grande City, TX 78582   **Fax:** 956-487-6227

On the southwestern border of TX, west of McAllen; organized Feb 10, 1848 from Nueces County. **Name Origin:** For James Harper Starr (1809-90), physician; an official in the Republic of Texas government.

Area (sq mi): 1229.28 (land 1223.02; water 6.26). **Pop per sq mi:** 49.8.

Pop 2005: 60,941. **State rank:** 53. **Pop change:** 2000-20005 +13.7%; 1990-2000 +32.3%. **Pop 2000:** 53,597 (White 2%; Black or African American 0.1%; Hispanic or Latino 97.5%; Asian 0.3%; Other 11.6%). **Foreign born:** 36.9%. **Median age:** 26.1.

Income 2000: per capita $7,069; median household $16,504; **Pop below poverty level:** 50.9%. ***Personal per capita income 2000-2003:** $9,558-$10,805.

Unemployment 2004: 14.6%. **Change from 2000:** -5.4%. **Median travel time to work:** 21.4 minutes. **Working outside county of residence:** 19.6%.

Cities with pop over 10,000: Rio Grande City ⛪ (13,403); Roma (10,698).

STEPHENS COUNTY

200 W Walker St   **Ph:** 254-559-3700
Breckenridge, TX 76424   **Fax:** 254-559-9645
www.co.stephens.tx.us

In north-central TX, northeast of Abilene; established as Buchanan County Jan 22, 1858 from Bosque County; organized Sep 20, 1860. **Name Origin:** For Alexander Hamilton Stephens (1812-83), GA legislator, vice president of the Confederate government (1861), and governor of GA (1882-83).

Area (sq mi): 921.48 (land 894.64; water 26.84). **Pop per sq mi:** 10.7.

Pop 2005: 9,561. **State rank:** 168. **Pop change:** 2000-20005 -1.2%; 1990-2000 +7.4%. **Pop 2000:** 9,674 (White 81.3%; Black or African American 2.9%; Hispanic or Latino 14.7%; Asian 0.3%; Other 9.9%). **Foreign born:** 6.6%. **Median age:** 38.9.

Income 2000: per capita $15,475; median household $29,583; **Pop below poverty level:** 15.6%. ***Personal per capita income 2000-2003:** $20,751-$21,933.

Unemployment 2004: 5.2%. **Change from 2000:** +2%. **Median travel time to work:** 18.7 minutes. **Working outside county of residence:** 18.4%.

Cities with pop over 10,000: None.

STERLING COUNTY

PO Box 55   **Ph:** 325-378-5191
Sterling City, TX 76951   **Fax:** 325-378-2266
www.co.sterling.tx.us

In central TX, northwest of San Angelo; organized Mar 4, 1891 from Tom Green County. **Name Origin:** For W.S. Sterling (?-1881), Indian fighter, rancher, and buffalo hunter.

Area (sq mi): 923.49 (land 923.36; water 0.13). **Pop per sq mi:** 1.4.

Pop 2005: 1,303. **State rank:** 245. **Pop change:** 2000-20005 -6.5%; 1990-2000 -3.1%. **Pop 2000:** 1,393 (White 68.6%; Black or African American 0.1%; Hispanic or Latino 31%; Asian 0%; Other 14.2%). **Foreign born:** 9.2%. **Median age:** 37.9.

Income 2000: per capita $16,972; median household $35,129; **Pop below poverty level:** 16.8%. ***Personal per capita income 2000-2003:** $16,026-$19,506.

Unemployment 2004: 3.4%. **Change from 2000:** -0.4%. **Median travel time to work:** 24.8 minutes. **Working outside county of residence:** 23.5%.

Cities with pop over 10,000: None.

STONEWALL COUNTY

PO Drawer P   **Ph:** 940-989-2272
Aspermont, TX 79502   **Fax:** 940-989-2715

In north-central TX, northwest of Abilene; organized Aug 21, 1876 from Fannin County. **Name Origin:** For Gen. Thomas Jonathan 'Stonewall' Jackson (1824-63), Confederate army officer; he earned his nickname from his stand at Bull Run.

Area (sq mi): 920.23 (land 918.67; water 1.56). **Pop per sq mi:** 1.5.

Pop 2005: 1,372. **State rank:** 243. **Pop change:** 2000-20005 -19%; 1990-2000 -15.9%. **Pop 2000:** 1,693 (White 83.4%; Black or African American 3%; Hispanic or Latino 11.8%; Asian 0.4%; Other 8.5%). **Foreign born:** 2%. **Median age:** 43.7.

---

*Source: Personal per capita income data are from the Bureau of Economic Analysis; per capita income data are from the Bureau of the Census. See Introduction for explanation of differences.

Stonewall County (cont'd)

Income 2000: per capita $16,094; median household $27,935; **Pop below poverty level:** 19.3%. ***Personal per capita income 2000-2003:** $22,454-$27,238.

Unemployment 2004: 4.7%. **Change from 2000:** +0%. **Median travel time to work:** 17.8 minutes. **Working outside county of residence:** 15.8%.

Cities with pop over 10,000: None.

SUTTON COUNTY

300 E Oak St Suite 3   **Ph:** 325-387-3815
Sonora, TX 76950   **Fax:** 325-387-6028
www.co.sutton.tx.us

In central TX, south of San Angelo; organized Apr 1, 1887 from Wood County. **Name Origin:** For Lt. Col. John S. Sutton (1821-62), Confederate army officer from TX.

Area (sq mi): 1454.4 (land 1453.76; water 0.63). **Pop per sq mi:** 2.9.

Pop 2005: 4,212. **State rank:** 208. **Pop change:** 2000-20005 +3.3%; 1990-2000 -1.4%. **Pop 2000:** 4,077 (White 47.4%; Black or African American 0.2%; Hispanic or Latino 51.7%; Asian 0.2%; Other 24.3%). **Foreign born:** 13%. **Median age:** 36.5.

Income 2000: per capita $17,105; median household $34,385; **Pop below poverty level:** 18%. ***Personal per capita income 2000-2003:** $19,403-$22,686.

Unemployment 2004: 3.1%. **Change from 2000:** +0.3%. **Median travel time to work:** 16.2 minutes. **Working outside county of residence:** 9.1%.

Cities with pop over 10,000: None.

SWISHER COUNTY

County Courthouse 119 S Maxwell St   **Ph:** 806-995-3294
Tulia, TX 79088   **Fax:** 806-995-4121
www.co.swisher.tx.us

In central TX panhandle, south of Amarillo; organized Aug 21, 1876 from Bexar County. **Name Origin:** For James Gibson Swisher (1795-1864), Republic of TX soldier and a signer of the TX Declaration of Independence (1836).

Area (sq mi): 900.68 (land 900.43; water 0.25). **Pop per sq mi:** 8.7.

Pop 2005: 7,828. **State rank:** 179. **Pop change:** 2000-20005 -6.6%; 1990-2000 +3%. **Pop 2000:** 8,378 (White 57.9%; Black or African American 5.8%; Hispanic or Latino 35.2%; Asian 0.2%; Other 22.2%). **Foreign born:** 4.9%. **Median age:** 34.6.

Income 2000: per capita $14,326; median household $29,846; **Pop below poverty level:** 17.4%. ***Personal per capita income 2000-2003:** $24,683-$28,611.

Unemployment 2004: 5.8%. **Change from 2000:** +2%. **Median travel time to work:** 17 minutes. **Working outside county of residence:** 27.1%.

Cities with pop over 10,000: None.

TARRANT COUNTY

100 W Weatherford St   **Ph:** 817-884-1195
Fort Worth, TX 76196   **Fax:** 817-884-3295
www.tarrantcounty.com

In north-central TX, west of Dallas; organized Dec 20, 1849 from Navarro County. **Name Origin:** For Gen. Edward H. Tarrant (1796-1858), TX Ranger, legislator, and delegate to the TX Constitutional Convention (1845).

Area (sq mi): 897.48 (land 863.42; water 34.06). **Pop per sq mi:** 1876.8.

Pop 2005: 1,620,479. **State rank:** 3. **Pop change:** 2000-20005 +12%; 1990-2000 +23.6%. **Pop 2000:** 1,446,219 (White 61.9%; Black or African American 12.8%; Hispanic or Latino 19.7%; Asian 3.6%; Other 12.4%). **Foreign born:** 12.7%. **Median age:** 32.3.

Income 2000: per capita $22,548; median household $46,179; **Pop below poverty level:** 10.6%. ***Personal per capita income 2000-2003:** $30,299-$31,054.

Unemployment 2004: 5.7%. **Change from 2000:** +1.5%. **Median travel time to work:** 25.8 minutes. **Working outside county of residence:** 24%.

Cities with pop over 10,000: 18 (see page 39 for cities).

TAYLOR COUNTY

300 Oak St   **Ph:** 325-674-1202
Abilene, TX 79602   **Fax:** 325-674-1279
www.taylorcountytexas.org

In central TX, northeast of San Angelo; organized Feb 1, 1858 from Bexar County. **Name Origin:** Either for three Taylor brothers who died at the Alamo, or for Edward Taylor, an early settler of Sterling Clark Robertson's colony (1785-1842).

Area (sq mi): 919.25 (land 915.63; water 3.63). **Pop per sq mi:** 136.6.

Pop 2005: 125,039. **State rank:** 28. **Pop change:** 2000-20005 -1.2%; 1990-2000 +5.8%. **Pop 2000:** 126,555 (White 72.7%; Black or African American 6.7%; Hispanic or Latino 17.6%; Asian 1.2%; Other 11.4%). **Foreign born:** 4%. **Median age:** 32.2.

Income 2000: per capita $17,176; median household $34,035; **Pop below poverty level:** 14.5%. ***Personal per capita income 2000-2003:** $25,932-$26,120.

Unemployment 2004: 4.7%. **Change from 2000:** +0.8%. **Median travel time to work:** 16.4 minutes. **Working outside county of residence:** 6.5%.

Cities with pop over 10,000: Abilene 🏛 (114,807).

TERRELL COUNTY

108 Hackberry St   **Ph:** 432-345-2391
Sanderson, TX 79848   **Fax:** 432-345-2274
www.co.terrell.tx.us

On the southwestern border of TX, northwest of Del Rio; organized Apr 8, 1905 from Pecos County. **Name Origin:** For Gen. Alexander Watkins Terrell (1827-1912), TX judicial district judge (1857-62), legislator (1875-82), and U.S. Minister Plenipotentiary to Turkey (1893-97).

Area (sq mi): 2357.75 (land 2357.72; water 0.03). **Pop per sq mi:** 0.4.

Terrell County (cont'd)

Pop 2005: 996. **State rank:** 247. **Pop change:** 2000-20005 -7.9%; 1990-2000 -23.3%. **Pop 2000:** 1,081 (White 48.9%; Black or African American 0%; Hispanic or Latino 48.6%; Asian 0.6%; Other 11%, including 1.7% American Indian/Alaska Native). **Foreign born:** 9.9%. **Median age:** 42.

Income 2000: per capita $13,721; median household $24,219; **Pop below poverty level:** 25.2%. ***Personal per capita income 2000-2003:** $24,892-$27,007.

Unemployment 2004: 5.6%. **Change from 2000:** +2.6%. **Median travel time to work:** 17.7 minutes. **Working outside county of residence:** 15.4%.

Cities with pop over 10,000: None.

TERRY COUNTY
500 W Main St Rm 105   **Ph:** 806-637-8551
Brownfield, TX 79316   **Fax:** 806-637-4874
www.co.terry.tx.us

In southwestern TX panhandle, southwest of Lubbock; organized Aug 21, 1876 from Bexar County. **Name Origin:** For Col. Benjamin Franklin Terry (1821-61), a Confederate army officer.

Area (sq mi): 890.93 (land 889.88; water 1.06). **Pop per sq mi:** 14.

Pop 2005: 12,419. **State rank:** 154. **Pop change:** 2000-20005 -2.7%; 1990-2000 -3.5%. **Pop 2000:** 12,761 (White 49.8%; Black or African American 5%; Hispanic or Latino 44.1%; Asian 0.2%; Other 18.2%). **Foreign born:** 7.2%. **Median age:** 35.

Income 2000: per capita $13,860; median household $28,090; **Pop below poverty level:** 23.3%. ***Personal per capita income 2000-2003:** $20,907-$23,782.

Unemployment 2004: 6.6%. **Change from 2000:** +0.6%. **Median travel time to work:** 18.2 minutes. **Working outside county of residence:** 22.8%.

Cities with pop over 10,000: None.

THROCKMORTON COUNTY
PO Box 309   **Ph:** 940-849-2501
Throckmorton, TX 76483   **Fax:** 940-849-3220
www.co.throckmorton.tx.us

In north-central TX, northeast of Abilene; organized Jan 13, 1858 from Bosque County. **Name Origin:** For William Edward Throckmorton (1795-1843), father of Gov. James Webb Throckmorton.

Area (sq mi): 915.47 (land 912.34; water 3.13). **Pop per sq mi:** 1.8.

Pop 2005: 1,618. **State rank:** 241. **Pop change:** 2000-20005 -12.5%; 1990-2000 -1.6%. **Pop 2000:** 1,850 (White 89.5%; Black or African American 0.1%; Hispanic or Latino 9.4%; Asian 0.1%; Other 7.8%). **Foreign born:** 1.6%. **Median age:** 41.8.

Income 2000: per capita $17,719; median household $28,277; **Pop below poverty level:** 13.5%. ***Personal per capita income 2000-2003:** $24,142-$27,078.

Unemployment 2004: 4%. **Change from 2000:** +1.9%. **Median travel time to work:** 19.7 minutes. **Working outside county of residence:** 29%.

Cities with pop over 10,000: None.

TITUS COUNTY
100 W 1st Suite 204   **Ph:** 903-577-6796
Mount Pleasant, TX 75455   **Fax:** 903-572-5078
www.co.titus.tx.us

In northeastern TX, southwest of Texarkana; organized May 11, 1846 from Red River County. **Name Origin:** For Andrew Jackson Titus (1823-55), early settler and TX legislator (1851-52).

Area (sq mi): 425.69 (land 410.54; water 15.15). **Pop per sq mi:** 71.7.

Pop 2005: 29,445. **State rank:** 92. **Pop change:** 2000-20005 +4.7%; 1990-2000 +17.1%. **Pop 2000:** 28,118 (White 59.7%; Black or African American 10.7%; Hispanic or Latino 28.3%; Asian 0.4%; Other 18.7%). **Foreign born:** 17.4%. **Median age:** 31.8.

Income 2000: per capita $15,501; median household $32,452; **Pop below poverty level:** 18.5%. ***Personal per capita income 2000-2003:** $20,732-$23,126.

Unemployment 2004: 5.2%. **Change from 2000:** +1.1%. **Median travel time to work:** 19.2 minutes. **Working outside county of residence:** 16.1%.

Cities with pop over 10,000: Mount Pleasant ⛪ (14,610).

TOM GREEN COUNTY
124 W Beauregard Ave   **Ph:** 325-659-6553
San Angelo, TX 76903   **Fax:** 325-659-3251
www.co.tom-green.tx.us/county/index.html

In central TX, southwest of Abilene; organized Mar 13, 1874 from Bexar County. **Name Origin:** For Gen. Thomas Green (1814-64), officer in the War for Texas Independence and the Mexican-American War; Confederate Army officer.

Area (sq mi): 1540.54 (land 1522.1; water 18.44). **Pop per sq mi:** 68.1.

Pop 2005: 103,611. **State rank:** 35. **Pop change:** 2000-20005 -0.4%; 1990-2000 +5.6%. **Pop 2000:** 104,010 (White 63%; Black or African American 4.1%; Hispanic or Latino 30.7%; Asian 0.9%; Other 16%). **Foreign born:** 5.9%. **Median age:** 33.8.

Income 2000: per capita $17,325; median household $33,148; **Pop below poverty level:** 15.2%. ***Personal per capita income 2000-2003:** $23,869-$25,851.

Unemployment 2004: 4.9%. **Change from 2000:** +2.1%. **Median travel time to work:** 17.8 minutes. **Working outside county of residence:** 4.8%.

Cities with pop over 10,000: San Angelo ⛪ (88,112).

TRAVIS COUNTY
314 W 11th St   **Ph:** 512-854-9343
Austin, TX 78701   **Fax:** 512-854-9542
www.co.travis.tx.us

In east-central TX, northeast of San Antonio; organized Jan 25, 1840 (prior to statehood) from Bastrop County. **Name Origin:** For Lt. Col. William Barret Travis (1809-36), an officer in the Republic of TX cavalry, killed at the Alamo.

Area (sq mi): 1022.08 (land 989.3; water 32.77). **Pop per sq mi:** 897.8.

Pop 2005: 888,185. **State rank:** 5. **Pop change:** 2000-20005 +9.3%; 1990-2000 +40.9%. **Pop 2000:** 812,280 (White 56.4%; Black or

Source: Personal per capita income data are from the Bureau of Economic Analysis; per capita income data are from the Bureau of the Census. See Introduction for explanation of differences.

706

Travis County (cont'd)

African American 9.3%; Hispanic or Latino 28.2%; Asian 4.5%; Other 18.2%). **Foreign born:** 15.1%. **Median age:** 30.4.

Income 2000: per capita $25,883; median household $46,761; **Pop below poverty level:** 12.5%. ***Personal per capita income 2000-2003:** $35,214-$34,439.

Unemployment 2004: 5.2%. **Change from 2000:** +1.1%. **Median travel time to work:** 23.6 minutes. **Working outside county of residence:** 8.6%.

Cities with pop over 10,000: Austin 🏛 (681,804); Pflugerville (25,911); Leander (15,874).

TRINITY COUNTY

PO Box 456   **Ph:** 936-642-1208
Groveton, TX 75845   **Fax:** 936-642-3004
www.co.trinity.tx.us

In east central TX, southwest of Lufkin; organized Feb 11, 1850 from Houston County. **Name Origin:** For the Trinity River, which forms its southern border; itself probably named for the feast of the Holy Trinity.

Area (sq mi): 714 (land 692.84; water 21.16). **Pop per sq mi:** 20.7.

Pop 2005: 14,363. **State rank:** 141. **Pop change:** 2000-20005 +4.2%; 1990-2000 +20.4%. **Pop 2000:** 13,779 (White 81.9%; Black or African American 11.9%; Hispanic or Latino 4.8%; Asian 0.2%; Other 4.1%). **Foreign born:** 2.7%. **Median age:** 43.3.

Income 2000: per capita $15,472; median household $27,070; **Pop below poverty level:** 17.6%. ***Personal per capita income 2000-2003:** $18,721-$20,538.

Unemployment 2004: 6.9%. **Change from 2000:** +1.9%. **Median travel time to work:** 31.1 minutes. **Working outside county of residence:** 53.4%.

Cities with pop over 10,000: None.

TYLER COUNTY

100 Bluff St Rm 110   **Ph:** 409-283-2281
Woodville, TX 75979   **Fax:** 409-283-6305
www.co.tyler.tx.us

In east-central TX, north of Beaumont; organized Apr 3, 1846 from Liberty County. **Name Origin:** For John Tyler (1790-1862), tenth U.S. president.

Area (sq mi): 935.71 (land 922.9; water 12.81). **Pop per sq mi:** 22.3.

Pop 2005: 20,617. **State rank:** 112. **Pop change:** 2000-20005 -1.2%; 1990-2000 +25.4%. **Pop 2000:** 20,871 (White 82.8%; Black or African American 12%; Hispanic or Latino 3.6%; Asian 0.2%; Other 4%). **Foreign born:** 1.2%. **Median age:** 38.9.

Income 2000: per capita $15,367; median household $29,808; **Pop below poverty level:** 15.8%. ***Personal per capita income 2000-2003:** $18,152-$20,521.

Unemployment 2004: 8.2%. **Change from 2000:** -0.1%. **Median travel time to work:** 34.5 minutes. **Working outside county of residence:** 44.1%.

Cities with pop over 10,000: None.

UPSHUR COUNTY

PO Box 730   **Ph:** 903-843-4015
Gilmer, TX 75644   **Fax:** 903-843-5492
www.countyofupshur.com

In northeastern TX, northeast of Tyler; organized Jul 13, 1846 from Harrison and Nacogdoches counties. **Name Origin:** For Abel Parker Upshur (1791-1844), judge in VA courts (1826-41), U.S. secretary of the navy (1841-43), and U.S. secretary of state (1843-44).

Area (sq mi): 592.67 (land 587.64; water 5.02). **Pop per sq mi:** 64.5.

Pop 2005: 37,881. **State rank:** 76. **Pop change:** 2000-20005 +7.3%; 1990-2000 +12.5%. **Pop 2000:** 35,291 (White 84.2%; Black or African American 10.1%; Hispanic or Latino 4%; Asian 0.2%; Other 4%). **Foreign born:** 2%. **Median age:** 37.7.

Income 2000: per capita $16,358; median household $33,347; **Pop below poverty level:** 14.9%. ***Personal per capita income 2000-2003:** $21,214-$21,810.

Unemployment 2004: 5.8%. **Change from 2000:** +0.9%. **Median travel time to work:** 27.8 minutes. **Working outside county of residence:** 61.1%.

Cities with pop over 10,000: None.

UPTON COUNTY

205 E 10th St   **Ph:** 432-693-2861
Rankin, TX 79778   **Fax:** 432-693-2129
www.co.upton.tx.us

In west-central TX, south of Midland; organized Feb 26, 1887 from Tom Green County. **Name Origin:** For Lt. Col. John Cunningham Upton (1823-62), Confederate army officer.

Area (sq mi): 1241.83 (land 1241.68; water 0.16). **Pop per sq mi:** 2.5.

Pop 2005: 3,056. **State rank:** 225. **Pop change:** 2000-20005 -10.2%; 1990-2000 -23.5%. **Pop 2000:** 3,404 (White 54.5%; Black or African American 1.6%; Hispanic or Latino 42.6%; Asian 0%; Other 20.6%, including 1.2% American Indian/Alaska Native). **Foreign born:** 11.2%. **Median age:** 38.1.

Income 2000: per capita $14,274; median household $28,977; **Pop below poverty level:** 19.9%. ***Personal per capita income 2000-2003:** $19,114-$21,824.

Unemployment 2004: 5.2%. **Change from 2000:** +1.1%. **Median travel time to work:** 21 minutes. **Working outside county of residence:** 24.9%.

Cities with pop over 10,000: None.

UVALDE COUNTY

PO Box 284   **Ph:** 830-278-6614
Uvalde, TX 78802   **Fax:** 830-278-8692
www.uvaldecounty.com

In south-central TX, east of Del Rio; organized Feb 8, 1850 from Bexar County. **Name Origin:** For Juan de Ugalde, Mexican army officer, civil and military governor of Coahuila and TX (1777); Indian fighter. The present spelling is a corruption of his name.

Area (sq mi): 1558.6 (land 1556.55; water 2.06). **Pop per sq mi:** 17.3.

Uvalde County (cont'd)

Pop 2005: 26,955. **State rank:** 96. **Pop change:** 2000-20005 +4%; 1990-2000 +11.1%. **Pop 2000:** 25,926 (White 32.7%; Black or African American 0.4%; Hispanic or Latino 65.9%; Asian 0.4%; Other 23.7%). **Foreign born:** 11.2%. **Median age:** 32.2.

Income 2000: per capita $12,557; median household $27,164; **Pop below poverty level:** 24.3%. *Personal per capita income 2000-2003:** $18,669-$20,381.

Unemployment 2004: 7.1%. **Change from 2000:** -0.5%. **Median travel time to work:** 19.8 minutes. **Working outside county of residence:** 11.9%.

Cities with pop over 10,000: Uvalde 🏛 (16,233).

VAL VERDE COUNTY

PO Box 1267   **Ph:** 830-774-7564
Del Rio, TX 78841   **Fax:** 830-774-7608

On the southwestern border of TX, northwest of Laredo; organized Feb 20, 1885 from Kinney and Pecos counties. **Name Origin:** A shortening of the Spanish *valle verde* 'green valley.'

Area (sq mi): 3232.4 (land 3170.38; water 62.02). **Pop per sq mi:** 15.

Pop 2005: 47,596. **State rank:** 65. **Pop change:** 2000-20005 +6.1%; 1990-2000 +15.8%. **Pop 2000:** 44,856 (White 21.7%; Black or African American 1.5%; Hispanic or Latino 75.5%; Asian 0.6%; Other 21.6%). **Foreign born:** 23.4%. **Median age:** 30.8.

Income 2000: per capita $12,096; median household $28,376; **Pop below poverty level:** 26.1%. *Personal per capita income 2000-2003:** $16,797-$18,894.

Unemployment 2004: 7.4%. **Change from 2000:** +1.2%. **Median travel time to work:** 17.6 minutes. **Working outside county of residence:** 8.8%.

Cities with pop over 10,000: Del Rio 🏛 (35,816).

VAN ZANDT COUNTY

121 E Dallas St Rm 202   **Ph:** 903-567-6503
Canton, TX 75103   **Fax:** 903-567-6722
www.vanzandtcounty.org

In northeastern TX, east of Dallas; organized Mar 20, 1848 from Henderson County. **Name Origin:** For Isaac Van Zandt (1813-47), Republic of TX legislator (1840-42).

Area (sq mi): 859.48 (land 848.64; water 10.84). **Pop per sq mi:** 61.9.

Pop 2005: 52,491. **State rank:** 57. **Pop change:** 2000-20005 +9%; 1990-2000 +26.9%. **Pop 2000:** 48,140 (White 88.5%; Black or African American 2.9%; Hispanic or Latino 6.6%; Asian 0.2%; Other 4.9%). **Foreign born:** 3.6%. **Median age:** 39.5.

Income 2000: per capita $16,930; median household $35,029; **Pop below poverty level:** 13.3%. *Personal per capita income 2000-2003:** $23,525-$24,604.

Unemployment 2004: 5.3%. **Change from 2000:** +1.6%. **Median travel time to work:** 37.3 minutes. **Working outside county of residence:** 54.4%.

Cities with pop over 10,000: None.

VICTORIA COUNTY

PO Box 1968   **Ph:** 361-575-1478
Victoria, TX 77902   **Fax:** 361-575-6276
www.victoriacountytx.org

In south-central TX, northeast of Corpus Christi; original county; organized Mar 17, 1836 (prior to statehood) from Old Mexican Municipality. **Name Origin:** For Juan Manuel Felix Fernandez, called Guadelupe Victoria (1789-1843), first president of the Republic of Mexico (1824).

Area (sq mi): 888.73 (land 882.5; water 6.23). **Pop per sq mi:** 97.1.

Pop 2005: 85,648. **State rank:** 41. **Pop change:** 2000-20005 +1.9%; 1990-2000 +13.1%. **Pop 2000:** 84,088 (White 52.9%; Black or African American 6.3%; Hispanic or Latino 39.2%; Asian 0.8%; Other 18.6%). **Foreign born:** 4.3%. **Median age:** 34.2.

Income 2000: per capita $18,379; median household $38,732; **Pop below poverty level:** 12.9%. *Personal per capita income 2000-2003:** $26,552-$27,015.

Unemployment 2004: 5.4%. **Change from 2000:** +1.4%. **Median travel time to work:** 21.4 minutes. **Working outside county of residence:** 15.1%.

Cities with pop over 10,000: Victoria 🏛 (61,677).

WALKER COUNTY

PO Box 1207   **Ph:** 936-436-4933
Huntsville, TX 77342   **Fax:** 936-436-4930
www.co.walker.tx.us

In east-central TX, northwest of Houston; organized Apr 6, 1846 from Montgomery County. **Name Origin:** Either for Robert James Walker (1801-69), U.S. senator who introduced the resolution to annex TX to the U.S., or for Samuel Hamilton Walker (1809-47), a Mexican War casualty.

Area (sq mi): 801.44 (land 787.45; water 13.99). **Pop per sq mi:** 79.7.

Pop 2005: 62,735. **State rank:** 52. **Pop change:** 2000-20005 +1.6%; 1990-2000 +21.3%. **Pop 2000:** 61,758 (White 60.1%; Black or African American 23.9%; Hispanic or Latino 14.1%; Asian 0.8%; Other 6.3%). **Foreign born:** 4.5%. **Median age:** 31.

Income 2000: per capita $14,508; median household $31,468; **Pop below poverty level:** 18.4%. *Personal per capita income 2000-2003:** $16,982-$17,839.

Unemployment 2004: 5.7%. **Change from 2000:** +3%. **Median travel time to work:** 22.7 minutes. **Working outside county of residence:** 22.2%.

Cities with pop over 10,000: Huntsville 🏛 (35,840).

WALLER COUNTY

836 Austin St   **Ph:** 979-826-3357
Hempstead, TX 77445   **Fax:** 979-826-8317
www.wallercounty.org

In east-central TX, west of Houston; organized Apr 28, 1873 from Austin County. **Name Origin:** For Edwin Waller (1800-83), signer of the TX declaration of independence (1836) and chief justice of Austin County (1844-56).

Area (sq mi): 518.49 (land 513.63; water 4.87). **Pop per sq mi:** 67.8.

*Source: Personal per capita income data are from the Bureau of Economic Analysis; per capita income data are from the Bureau of the Census. See Introduction for explanation of differences.

708

Waller County (cont'd)

Pop 2005: 34,821. **State rank:** 83. **Pop change:** 2000-20005 +6.6%; 1990-2000 +39.6%. **Pop 2000:** 32,663 (White 49.9%; Black or African American 29.2%; Hispanic or Latino 19.4%; Asian 0.4%; Other 12.6%). **Foreign born:** 9.4%. **Median age:** 30.1.

Income 2000: per capita $16,338; median household $38,136; **Pop below poverty level:** 16% *Personal per capita income 2000-2003:** $19,851-$23,244.

Unemployment 2004: 6.4%. **Change from 2000:** +1.8%. **Median travel time to work:** 32.3 minutes. **Working outside county of residence:** 59%.

Cities with pop over 10,000: None.

WARD COUNTY

County Courthouse 400 S Allen St Suite 101 **Ph:** 432-943-3294
Monahans, TX 79756   **Fax:** 432-943-6054
www.co.ward.tx.us

In west-central TX, southwest of Odessa; organized 1891 from Tom Green County (other sources say organized Feb 26, 1887; first federal census: 1890). **Name Origin:** For Thomas William 'Peg Leg' Ward (1807-72), soldier in the TX war of independence, mayor of Austin (1840; 1857; 1865), and U.S. consul to Panama (1840; 1853; 1865).

Area (sq mi): 835.74 (land 835.49; water 0.25). **Pop per sq mi:** 12.3.

Pop 2005: 10,237. **State rank:** 165. **Pop change:** 2000-20005 -6.2%; 1990-2000 -16.8%. **Pop 2000:** 10,909 (White 52.2%; Black or African American 4.6%; Hispanic or Latino 42%; Asian 0.3%; Other 15.3%). **Foreign born:** 6.6%. **Median age:** 36.

Income 2000: per capita $14,393; median household $29,386; **Pop below poverty level:** 17.9%. *Personal per capita income 2000-2003:** $18,774-$20,727.

Unemployment 2004: 7%. **Change from 2000:** +0.8%. **Median travel time to work:** 19.3 minutes. **Working outside county of residence:** 26%.

Cities with pop over 10,000: None.

WASHINGTON COUNTY

100 E Main St Suite 102   **Ph:** 979-277-6200
Brenham, TX 77833   **Fax:** 979-277-6278
www.co.washington.tx.us

In east-central TX, northwest of Houston; organized Mar 17, 1836 (prior to statehood) from Texas Municipality. **Name Origin:** For George Washington (1732-99), American patriot and first U.S. president.

Area (sq mi): 621.35 (land 609.22; water 12.13). **Pop per sq mi:** 51.7.

Pop 2005: 31,521. **State rank:** 89. **Pop change:** 2000-20005 +3.8%; 1990-2000 +16.1%. **Pop 2000:** 30,373 (White 70.8%; Black or African American 18.7%; Hispanic or Latino 8.7%; Asian 1.2%; Other 5.5%). **Foreign born:** 5.4%. **Median age:** 37.4.

Income 2000: per capita $17,384; median household $36,760; **Pop below poverty level:** 12.9%. *Personal per capita income 2000-2003:** $27,826-$28,747.

Unemployment 2004: 4.9%. **Change from 2000:** +2.9%. **Median travel time to work:** 19.4 minutes. **Working outside county of residence:** 16.5%.

Cities with pop over 10,000: Brenham ⌂ (14,044).

WEBB COUNTY

1000 Houston County Courthouse   **Ph:** 956-721-2500
Laredo, TX 78040   **Fax:** 956-726-6906
www.webbcounty.com

On the southwestern border of TX, west of Corpus Christi; organized Jan 28, 1848 from Bexar County. **Name Origin:** For James Webb (1792-1856), Republic of TX Attorney General (1839-41), legislator (1841-44), and judge (1854-56).

Area (sq mi): 3375.53 (land 3356.83; water 18.69). **Pop per sq mi:** 66.9.

Pop 2005: 224,695. **State rank:** 20. **Pop change:** 2000-20005 +16.4%; 1990-2000 +44.9%. **Pop 2000:** 193,117 (White 4.9%; Black or African American 0.4%; Hispanic or Latino 94.3%; Asian 0.4%; Other 17%). **Foreign born:** 29%. **Median age:** 26.5.

Income 2000: per capita $10,759; median household $28,100; **Pop below poverty level:** 31.2%. *Personal per capita income 2000-2003:** $15,070-$17,060.

Unemployment 2004: 6.8%. **Change from 2000:** -0.3%. **Median travel time to work:** 21.7 minutes. **Working outside county of residence:** 3.2%.

Cities with pop over 10,000: Laredo ⌂ (203,212).

WHARTON COUNTY

PO Box 69   **Ph:** 979-532-2381
Wharton, TX 77488   **Fax:** 979-532-8426
www.co.wharton.tx.us

In east-central TX, southwest of Houston; organized Apr 3, 1846 from Colorado and Jackson counties. **Name Origin:** For William Harris Wharton (1802-39), Republic of TX soldier, minister to the U.S. (1836), and legislator (1838).

Area (sq mi): 1094.43 (land 1090.13; water 4.29). **Pop per sq mi:** 38.1.

Pop 2005: 41,554. **State rank:** 71. **Pop change:** 2000-20005 +0.9%; 1990-2000 +3.1%. **Pop 2000:** 41,188 (White 53%; Black or African American 15%; Hispanic or Latino 31.3%; Asian 0.3%; Other 15.7%). **Foreign born:** 6.6%. **Median age:** 35.3.

Income 2000: per capita $15,388; median household $32,208; **Pop below poverty level:** 16.5%. *Personal per capita income 2000-2003:** $22,216-$24,197.

Unemployment 2004: 5.9%. **Change from 2000:** +1.1%. **Median travel time to work:** 23.8 minutes. **Working outside county of residence:** 26.5%.

Cities with pop over 10,000: El Campo (10,928).

WHEELER COUNTY

PO Box 465   **Ph:** 806-826-5544
Wheeler, TX 79096   **Fax:** 806-826-3282
www.co.wheeler.tx.us

On northeastern border of TX panhandle, east of Amarillo; organized Aug 21, 1876 from Bexar County. **Name Origin:** For Royal Tyler Wheeler (1810-64), prominent TX judge.

⌂ *County Seat*

Wheeler County (cont'd)

Area (sq mi): 915.34 (land 914.26; water 1.08). **Pop per sq mi:** 5.2.

Pop 2005: 4,799. **State rank:** 204. **Pop change:** 2000-20005 -9.2%; 1990-2000 -10.1%. **Pop 2000:** 5,284 (White 83%; Black or African American 2.8%; Hispanic or Latino 12.6%; Asian 0.5%; Other 8.8%). **Foreign born:** 5.4%. **Median age:** 42.5.

Income 2000: per capita $16,083; median household $31,029; **Pop below poverty level:** 13%. ***Personal per capita income 2000-2003:** $29,824-$34,441.

Unemployment 2004: 4.1%. **Change from 2000:** +1.1%. **Median travel time to work:** 17.9 minutes. **Working outside county of residence:** 18.6%.

Cities with pop over 10,000: None.

WICHITA COUNTY

PO Box 1679   **Ph:** 940-766-8144
Wichita Falls, TX 76307   **Fax:** 940-716-8554
www.co.wichita.tx.us

On the central northern border of TX, northwest of Fort Worth; organized Feb 1, 1858 from Fannin County. **Name Origin:** For the Wichita River, which traverses its northern border; itself named for one of the more important tribes of Caddoan linguistic stock. The name is translated as 'man,' or as taken from Choctaw *owa chito* 'big hunt.'

Area (sq mi): 633.01 (land 627.66; water 5.35). **Pop per sq mi:** 200.6.

Pop 2005: 125,894. **State rank:** 26. **Pop change:** 2000-20005 -4.4%; 1990-2000 +7.6%. **Pop 2000:** 131,664 (White 73.3%; Black or African American 10.2%; Hispanic or Latino 12.2%; Asian 1.8%; Other 9.2%). **Foreign born:** 5.1%. **Median age:** 33.2.

Income 2000: per capita $16,965; median household $33,780; **Pop below poverty level:** 13.2%. ***Personal per capita income 2000-2003:** $24,745-$27,527.

Unemployment 2004: 5.4%. **Change from 2000:** +1.8%. **Median travel time to work:** 17 minutes. **Working outside county of residence:** 4%.

Cities with pop over 10,000: Wichita Falls ⚒ (100,929); Burkburnett (10,513).

WILBARGER COUNTY

1700 Wilbarger St County Courthouse Rm 15 **Ph:** 940-552-5486
Vernon, TX 76384
www.co.wilbarger.tx.us

In north-central TX, west of Wichita Falls; organized Feb 1, 1858 from Bexar County. **Name Origin:** For Josiah Pugh Wilbarger (1801-45), a surveyor, and Mathias Wilbarger, brothers who settled in Austin's colony.

Area (sq mi): 978.1 (land 971.06; water 7.03). **Pop per sq mi:** 14.3.

Pop 2005: 13,896. **State rank:** 145. **Pop change:** 2000-20005 -5.3%; 1990-2000 -2.9%. **Pop 2000:** 14,676 (White 68.7%; Black or African American 8.9%; Hispanic or Latino 20.5%; Asian 0.6%; Other 12.3%). **Foreign born:** 4.2%. **Median age:** 36.3.

Income 2000: per capita $16,520; median household $29,500; **Pop below poverty level:** 13.1%. ***Personal per capita income 2000-2003:** $22,174-$24,247.

Unemployment 2004: 5.4%. **Change from 2000:** +3%. **Median travel time to work:** 12.5 minutes. **Working outside county of residence:** 8.2%.

Cities with pop over 10,000: Vernon ⚒ (11,165).

WILLACY COUNTY

540 W Hidalgo St 1st Fl   **Ph:** 956-689-2710
Raymondville, TX 78580   **Fax:** 956-689-0937

On the southeastern coast of TX, north of Brownsville; organized 1921 from Cameron and Hidalgo counties plus a 1.4-mile strip of a former Willacy County, which was renamed Kenedy County at the same time that the new county was created. **Name Origin:** For John G. Willacy (1850-1943), TX legislator (1899-1914).

Area (sq mi): 784.23 (land 596.68; water 187.55). **Pop per sq mi:** 34.2.

Pop 2005: 20,382. **State rank:** 115. **Pop change:** 2000-20005 +1.5%; 1990-2000 +13.4%. **Pop 2000:** 20,082 (White 11.7%; Black or African American 2.2%; Hispanic or Latino 85.7%; Asian 0.1%; Other 27.3%). **Foreign born:** 13.3%. **Median age:** 29.8.

Income 2000: per capita $9,421; median household $22,114; **Pop below poverty level:** 33.2%. ***Personal per capita income 2000-2003:** $13,554-$16,397.

Unemployment 2004: 11.9%. **Change from 2000:** -4.5%. **Median travel time to work:** 22.1 minutes. **Working outside county of residence:** 36.9%.

Cities with pop over 10,000: None.

WILLIAMSON COUNTY

405 ML King St   **Ph:** 512-930-4300
Georgetown, TX 78626   **Fax:** 512-943-1616
www.co.williamson.tx.us

In central TX, north of Austin; organized Mar 13, 1848 from Milam County. **Name Origin:** For Maj. Robert McAlpin 'Three Legged Willie' Williamson (1806-59), Republic of TX army officer, editor, and legislator.

Area (sq mi): 1134.74 (land 1122.77; water 11.97). **Pop per sq mi:** 297.

Pop 2005: 333,457. **State rank:** 13. **Pop change:** 2000-20005 +33.4%; 1990-2000 +79.1%. **Pop 2000:** 249,967 (White 73.5%; Black or African American 5.1%; Hispanic or Latino 17.2%; Asian 2.6%; Other 9.9%). **Foreign born:** 7.4%. **Median age:** 32.3.

Income 2000: per capita $24,547; median household $60,642; **Pop below poverty level:** 4.8%. ***Personal per capita income 2000-2003:** $31,449-$28,178.

Unemployment 2004: 4.4%. **Change from 2000:** +1.1%. **Median travel time to work:** 28 minutes. **Working outside county of residence:** 55.7%.

Cities with pop over 10,000: Round Rock (82,040); Cedar Park (45,360); Georgetown ⚒ (36,462); Taylor (14,636).

*Source: Personal per capita income data are from the Bureau of Economic Analysis; per capita income data are from the Bureau of the Census. See Introduction for explanation of differences.

WILSON COUNTY

PO Box 27   **Ph:** 830-393-7308
Floresville, TX 78114   **Fax:** 830-393-7334

In south-central TX, southeast of San Antonio; organized Feb 13, 1860 from Bexar County. **Name Origin:** For James Charles Wilson (1816-61), Republic of TX soldier and legislator (1851-52).

Area (sq mi): 808.57 (land 806.99; water 1.58). **Pop per sq mi:** 46.5.

Pop 2005: 37,529. **State rank:** 78. **Pop change:** 2000-20005 +15.8%; 1990-2000 +43.1%. **Pop 2000:** 32,408 (White 60.9%; Black or African American 1.2%; Hispanic or Latino 36.5%; Asian 0.3%; Other 17.2%). **Foreign born:** 3.3%. **Median age:** 35.9.

Income 2000: per capita $17,253; median household $40,006; **Pop below poverty level:** 11.3%. ***Personal per capita income 2000-2003:** $21,965-$23,512.

Unemployment 2004: 5%. **Change from 2000:** +1.9%. **Median travel time to work:** 35.8 minutes. **Working outside county of residence:** 66.9%.

Cities with pop over 10,000: None.

WINKLER COUNTY

100 E Winkler ST   **Ph:** 432-586-3401
Kermit, TX 79745
www.co.wichita.tx.us

In western TX, west of Odessa; organized Feb 26, 1887 from Tom Green County. **Name Origin:** For Lt. Col. Clinton McKamy Winkler (1827-82), TX legislator (1848), officer in the Confederate army, and civil appeals court judge (1876-82).

Area (sq mi): 841.24 (land 841.05; water 0.19). **Pop per sq mi:** 8.

Pop 2005: 6,690. **State rank:** 190. **Pop change:** 2000-20005 -6.7%; 1990-2000 -16.8%. **Pop 2000:** 7,173 (White 53.3%; Black or African American 1.9%; Hispanic or Latino 44%; Asian 0.2%; Other 23.1%). **Foreign born:** 14.3%. **Median age:** 35.2.

Income 2000: per capita $13,725; median household $30,591; **Pop below poverty level:** 18.7%. ***Personal per capita income 2000-2003:** $18,703-$20,814.

Unemployment 2004: 6.7%. **Change from 2000:** +0.8%. **Median travel time to work:** 24.5 minutes. **Working outside county of residence:** 24.3%.

Cities with pop over 10,000: None.

WISE COUNTY

PO Box 359   **Ph:** 940-627-3351
Decatur, TX 76234   **Fax:** 940-627-2138
www.co.wise.tx.us

In north-central TX, northwest of Fort Worth; organized Jan 23, 1856 from Cooke County. **Name Origin:** For Maj. Gen. Henry Alexander Wise (1806-76), governor of VA (1856-60), and an officer in the Confederate army.

Area (sq mi): 922.77 (land 904.61; water 18.17). **Pop per sq mi:** 62.7.

Pop 2005: 56,696. **State rank:** 55. **Pop change:** 2000-20005 +16.2%; 1990-2000 +40.7%. **Pop 2000:** 48,793 (White 86.1%; Black or African American 1.2%; Hispanic or Latino 10.8%; Asian 0.2%; Other 7.5%). **Foreign born:** 5.1%. **Median age:** 35.5.

Income 2000: per capita $17,729; median household $41,933; **Pop below poverty level:** 9.9%. ***Personal per capita income 2000-2003:** $21,769-$22,898.

Unemployment 2004: 5.1%. **Change from 2000:** +1.7%. **Median travel time to work:** 33.3 minutes. **Working outside county of residence:** 49.2%.

Cities with pop over 10,000: None.

WOOD COUNTY

PO Box 1796   **Ph:** 903-763-2711
Quitman, TX 75783   **Fax:** 903-763-2902
www.co.wood.tx.us

In northeastern TX, east of Dallas; organized Feb 5, 1850 from Van Zandt County. **Name Origin:** For George Tyler Wood (1795-1856), TX legislator (1846) and governor of TX (1847-49).

Area (sq mi): 695.8 (land 650.22; water 45.58). **Pop per sq mi:** 62.8.

Pop 2005: 40,855. **State rank:** 73. **Pop change:** 2000-20005 +11.2%; 1990-2000 +25.1%. **Pop 2000:** 36,752 (White 86.7%; Black or African American 6.1%; Hispanic or Latino 5.7%; Asian 0.2%; Other 4.6%). **Foreign born:** 3.8%. **Median age:** 43.

Income 2000: per capita $17,702; median household $32,885; **Pop below poverty level:** 14.3%. ***Personal per capita income 2000-2003:** $19,899-$20,804.

Unemployment 2004: 5.8%. **Change from 2000:** +0.9%. **Median travel time to work:** 28.4 minutes. **Working outside county of residence:** 39.9%.

Cities with pop over 10,000: None.

YOAKUM COUNTY

PO Box 309   **Ph:** 806-456-2721
Plains, TX 79355   **Fax:** 806-456-2258
www.co.yoakum.tx.us

On southwestern border of TX panhandle, southwest of Lubbock; created Aug 21, 1876 from Bexar County; organized 1907. **Name Origin:** For Col. Henderson King Yoakum (1810-56), army officer in Indian and Mexican wars, and trustee of Austin College (1849-56).

Area (sq mi): 799.76 (land 799.75; water 0.01). **Pop per sq mi:** 9.3.

Pop 2005: 7,408. **State rank:** 186. **Pop change:** 2000-20005 +1.2%; 1990-2000 -16.7%. **Pop 2000:** 7,322 (White 51.8%; Black or African American 1.4%; Hispanic or Latino 45.9%; Asian 0.1%; Other 27.9%). **Foreign born:** 16.6%. **Median age:** 34.1.

Income 2000: per capita $14,504; median household $32,672; **Pop below poverty level:** 19.6%. ***Personal per capita income 2000-2003:** $20,330-$24,514.

Unemployment 2004: 5.3%. **Change from 2000:** +0.7%. **Median travel time to work:** 15.9 minutes. **Working outside county of residence:** 15.6%.

Cities with pop over 10,000: None.

YOUNG COUNTY

516 4th St Rm 104   **Ph:** 940-549-8432
Graham, TX 76450   **Fax:** 940-521-0305

In north-central TX, south of Wichita Falls; organized Feb 2, 1856

Young County (cont'd)

from Bosque County. **Name Origin:** For William Cocke Young (1812-62), TX sheriff and district attorney, U.S. marshal in IL (1851), and Confederate army officer (1861).

Area (sq mi): 930.84 (land 922.33; water 8.51). **Pop per sq mi:** 19.5.

Pop 2005: 18,000. **State rank:** 128. **Pop change:** 2000-20005 +0.3%; 1990-2000 -1%. **Pop 2000:** 17,943 (White 86.5%; Black or African American 1.2%; Hispanic or Latino 10.6%; Asian 0.3%; Other 7.5%). **Foreign born:** 3.7%. **Median age:** 40.7.

Income 2000: per capita $16,710; median household $30,499; **Pop below poverty level:** 15.7%. ***Personal per capita income 2000-2003:** $25,271-$25,322.

Unemployment 2004: 5.2%. **Change from 2000:** +0.3%. **Median travel time to work:** 18.1 minutes. **Working outside county of residence:** 12.4%.

Cities with pop over 10,000: None.

ZAPATA COUNTY

PO Box 789   **Ph:** 956-765-9915
Zapata, TX 78076   **Fax:** 956-765-9933
www.zapatausa.com

On the southwestern border of TX, southeast of Laredo; organized Jan 22, 1858 from Starr and Webb counties. **Name Origin:** For Col. Antonio Zapata (?-1840), an officer in the Mexican army and a rancher.

Area (sq mi): 1058.1 (land 996.76; water 61.34). **Pop per sq mi:** 13.4.

Pop 2005: 13,373. **State rank:** 149. **Pop change:** 2000-20005 +9.8%; 1990-2000 +31.3%. **Pop 2000:** 12,182 (White 14.5%; Black or African American 0.4%; Hispanic or Latino 84.8%; Asian 0.2%; Other 15.2%). **Foreign born:** 24.1%. **Median age:** 30.7.

Income 2000: per capita $10,486; median household $24,635; **Pop below poverty level:** 35.8%. ***Personal per capita income 2000-2003:** $12,210-$13,847.

Unemployment 2004: 7.2%. **Change from 2000:** +0.4%. **Median travel time to work:** 22.6 minutes. **Working outside county of residence:** 13.7%.

Cities with pop over 10,000: None.

ZAVALA COUNTY

200 E Uvalde St County Courthouse   **Ph:** 830-374-2331
Crystal City, TX 78839   **Fax:** 830-374-5955
www.co.zavala.tx.us

In southern TX, southwest of Del Rio; organized Feb 1, 1858 from Uvalde and Maverick counties. **Name Origin:** For Manuel Lorenzo Justiniano de Zavala (1789-1836), a governor of the state of Mexico, vice president of the Repubic of TX, and a signer of the Texas Declaration of Independence (1836).

Area (sq mi): 1301.72 (land 1298.48; water 3.24). **Pop per sq mi:** 9.1.

Pop 2005: 11,796. **State rank:** 156. **Pop change:** 2000-20005 +1.7%; 1990-2000 -4.6%. **Pop 2000:** 11,600 (White 8%; Black or African American 0.5%; Hispanic or Latino 91.2%; Asian 0.1%; Other 34.4%). **Foreign born:** 13.8%. **Median age:** 29.

Income 2000: per capita $10,034; median household $16,844; **Pop below poverty level:** 41.8%. ***Personal per capita income 2000-2003:** $10,873-$13,304.

Unemployment 2004: 12.9%. **Change from 2000:** -2.9%. **Median travel time to work:** 18.1 minutes. **Working outside county of residence:** 31%.

Cities with pop over 10,000: None.

---

*Source: Personal per capita income data are from the Bureau of Economic Analysis; per capita income data are from the Bureau of the Census. See Introduction for explanation of differences.

Utah

N

IDAHO

WYOMING

Box Elder

Logan

Randolph

Cache

Rich

Brigham City

Weber

Ogden

Morgan

Morgan

Davis

Coalville

Manila

Farmington

Summit

Daggett

Salt Lake City

Salt Lake

Heber City

Duchesne

Vernal

Tooele

Tooele

Wasatch

Duchesne

Provo

Uintah

Utah

Juab

Nephi

Carbon

Price

Sanpete

Manti

Castle Dale

Millard

Emery

Grand

Fillmore

Richfield

Sevier

Moab

Beaver

Piute

Loa

Wayne

Beaver

Junction

Iron

Parowan

Panguitch

Garfield

Monticello

Cedar City

San Juan

Washington

Kane

Saint George

Kanab

NEVADA

COLORADO

ARIZONA

N.M

0 — 50 mi

0 — 50 km

©MAPS.com

Utah

UTAH STATE INFORMATION

www.utah.gov   **Ph:** 801-538-3000

Area (sq mi): 84,898.83 (land 82,143.65; water 2755.18). **Pop per sq mi:** 30.1.

Pop 2005: 2,469,585. **Pop change:** 2000-20005 +10.6%; 1990-2000 +29.6%. **Pop 2000:** 2,233,169 (White 85.3%; Black or African American 0.8%; Hispanic or Latino 9%; Asian 1.7%; Other 8.3%, including 1.3% American Indian/Alaska Native). **Foreign born:** 7.1%. **Median age:** 27.1.

Income 2000: per capita $18,185; median household $45,726; **Pop below poverty level:** 9.4%. ***Personal per capita income 2000-2003:** $23,878-$25,407.

Unemployment 2004: 5%. **Change from 2000:** +1.6%. **Median travel time to work:** 21.3 minutes. **Working outside county of residence:** 16.6%.

BEAVER COUNTY

105 E Center St   **Ph:** 435-438-6463
Beaver, UT 84713   **Fax:** 435-438-6462
www.beaver.state.ut.us

On the southwestern border of UT; organized Jan 5, 1856 (prior to statehood) from Iron County. **Name Origin:** For the beaver once plentiful in the area.

Area (sq mi): 2592.28 (land 2589.95; water 2.33). **Pop per sq mi:** 2.4.

Pop 2005: 6,204. **State rank:** 23. **Pop change:** 2000-20005 +3.3%; 1990-2000 +26%. **Pop 2000:** 6,005 (White 91.4%; Black or African American 0.3%; Hispanic or Latino 5.5%; Asian 0.6%; Other 5.9%). **Foreign born:** 4.4%. **Median age:** 30.8.

Income 2000: per capita $14,957; median household $34,544; **Pop below poverty level:** 8.3%. ***Personal per capita income 2000-2003:** $21,231-$23,597.

Unemployment 2004: 4.8%. **Change from 2000:** +0.6%. **Median travel time to work:** 17.1 minutes. **Working outside county of residence:** 8.2%.

Cities with pop over 10,000: None.

BOX ELDER COUNTY

01 S Main St   **Ph:** 435-734-3300
Brigham City, UT 84302   **Fax:** 435-723-7562
www.boxeldercounty.org

On the northwestern border of UT, west of Ogden; organized Jan 5, 1856 (prior to statehood) from Weber County. **Name Origin:**

For the abundant box elder trees in the area. It is more commonly known as the North American maple tree *Acer negundo*.

Area (sq mi): 6729.03 (land 5723.34; water 1005.69). **Pop per sq mi:** 8.1.

Pop 2005: 46,440. **State rank:** 8. **Pop change:** 2000-20005 +8.6%; 1990-2000 +17.2%. **Pop 2000:** 42,745 (White 90.6%; Black or African American 0.2%; Hispanic or Latino 6.5%; Asian 1%; Other 6%). **Foreign born:** 3%. **Median age:** 28.

Income 2000: per capita $15,625; median household $44,630; **Pop below poverty level:** 7.1%. ***Personal per capita income 2000-2003:** $20,351-$21,911.

Unemployment 2004: 5.3%. **Change from 2000:** -0.3%. **Median travel time to work:** 21.6 minutes. **Working outside county of residence:** 24.7%.

Cities with pop over 10,000: Brigham City 🏛 (17,149).

CACHE COUNTY

179 N Main St Suite 102   **Ph:** 435-716-7150
Logan, UT 84321   **Fax:** 435-752-3597
www.cachecounty.org

On the central northern border of UT, northeast of Ogden; organized Jan 5, 1856 (prior to statehood) from unorganized territory. **Name Origin:** For Cache Valley, from the French for 'hiding place,' because early trappers or hunters stored furs and supplies in the valley.

Area (sq mi): 1173.07 (land 1164.52; water 8.55). **Pop per sq mi:** 84.2.

Pop 2005: 98,055. **State rank:** 6. **Pop change:** 2000-20005 +7.3%; 1990-2000 +30.2%. **Pop 2000:** 91,391 (White 89.7%; Black or African American 0.4%; Hispanic or Latino 6.3%; Asian 2%; Other 5.4%). **Foreign born:** 6.7%. **Median age:** 23.9.

Income 2000: per capita $15,094; median household $39,730; **Pop below poverty level:** 13.5%. ***Personal per capita income 2000-2003:** $18,762-$20,353.

Unemployment 2004: 3.9%. **Change from 2000:** +0.7%. **Median travel time to work:** 16.8 minutes. **Working outside county of residence:** 10.3%.

Cities with pop over 10,000: Logan 🏛 (45,517).

CARBON COUNTY

120 E Main St   **Ph:** 435-636-3200
Price, UT 84501   **Fax:** 435-636-3210
www.co.carbon.ut.us

In east-central UT, southeast of Provo; organized 1894 (prior to

Carbon County (cont'd)

statehood) from Emery County. **Name Origin:** For the abundant coal deposits within its borders.

Area (sq mi): 1484.57 (land 1478.46; water 6.12). **Pop per sq mi:** 13.1.

Pop 2005: 19,437. **State rank:** 13. **Pop change:** 2000-20005 -4.8%; 1990-2000 +1%. **Pop 2000:** 20,422 (White 86.5%; Black or African American 0.3%; Hispanic or Latino 10.3%; Asian 0.3%; Other 8.3%, including 1.1% American Indian/Alaska Native). **Foreign born:** 2%. **Median age:** 33.6.

Income 2000: per capita $15,325; median household $34,036; **Pop below poverty level:** 13.4%. ***Personal per capita income 2000-2003:** $21,355-$22,914.

Unemployment 2004: 7.2%. **Change from 2000:** +0.9%. **Median travel time to work:** 16.4 minutes. **Working outside county of residence:** 11.5%.

Cities with pop over 10,000: None.

DAGGETT COUNTY
95 N & 100 W PO Box 219   **Ph:** 435-784-3154
Manila, UT 84046   **Fax:** 435-784-3335
www.dsdf.org/county

On the northeastern border of UT; organized Jan 7, 1918 from Uintah County. **Name Origin:** For Ellsworth Daggett (1845-1923), mining engineer and first surveyor-general of UT.

Area (sq mi): 723.06 (land 698.36; water 24.71). **Pop per sq mi:** 1.4.

Pop 2005: 943. **State rank:** 29. **Pop change:** 2000-20005 +2.4%; 1990-2000 +33.5%. **Pop 2000:** 921 (White 92.6%; Black or African American 0.7%; Hispanic or Latino 5.1%; Asian 0.1%; Other 4.7%). **Foreign born:** 2.7%. **Median age:** 39.2.

Income 2000: per capita $15,511; median household $30,833; **Pop below poverty level:** 5.5%. ***Personal per capita income 2000-2003:** $15,201-$18,161.

Unemployment 2004: 5.4%. **Change from 2000:** +0.8%. **Median travel time to work:** 21.5 minutes. **Working outside county of residence:** 21.2%.

Cities with pop over 10,000: None.

DAVIS COUNTY
PO Box 618   **Ph:** 801-451-3324
Farmington, UT 84025   **Fax:** 801-451-3421
www.co.davis.ut.us

In north-central UT, north of Salt Lake City; original county; organized Oct 5, 1850 (prior to statehood). **Name Origin:** For Daniel C. Davis (1804-50), commander of 'The Mormon Volunteers.'

Area (sq mi): 633.7 (land 304.48; water 329.22). **Pop per sq mi:** 880.8.

Pop 2005: 268,187. **State rank:** 3. **Pop change:** 2000-20005 +12.2%; 1990-2000 +27.2%. **Pop 2000:** 238,994 (White 89.8%; Black or African American 1.1%; Hispanic or Latino 5.4%; Asian 1.5%; Other 5.2%). **Foreign born:** 3.6%. **Median age:** 26.8.

Income 2000: per capita $19,506; median household $53,726; **Pop below poverty level:** 5.1%. ***Personal per capita income 2000-2003:** $25,066-$26,265.

Unemployment 2004: 4.9%. **Change from 2000:** +1.1%. **Median travel time to work:** 22.4 minutes. **Working outside county of residence:** 45.7%.

Cities with pop over 10,000: 8 (see page 39 for cities).

DUCHESNE COUNTY
734 N Center St   **Ph:** 435-738-1101
Duchesne, UT 84021   **Fax:** 435-738-5522
www.duchesnegov.net

In north-central UT, east of Provo; organized Aug 13, 1914 from Wasatch County. **Name Origin:** For the Duchesne River, which flows through the county. Origin of name unknown. Possibly for Rose Du Chesne (1769-1852), founder of the Society of the Sacred Heart in America; for a fur trapper of that name; or for Fort Duquesne, PA.

Area (sq mi): 3255.97 (land 3238.05; water 17.92). **Pop per sq mi:** 4.7.

Pop 2005: 15,354. **State rank:** 16. **Pop change:** 2000-20005 +6.8%; 1990-2000 +13.6%. **Pop 2000:** 14,371 (White 88.8%; Black or African American 0.1%; Hispanic or Latino 3.5%; Asian 0.2%; Other 9.6%, including 5.4% American Indian/Alaska Native). **Foreign born:** 1.3%. **Median age:** 28.3.

Income 2000: per capita $12,326; median household $31,298; **Pop below poverty level:** 16.8%. ***Personal per capita income 2000-2003:** $18,981-$21,091.

Unemployment 2004: 6%. **Change from 2000:** -0.2%. **Median travel time to work:** 22.4 minutes. **Working outside county of residence:** 20.8%.

Cities with pop over 10,000: None.

EMERY COUNTY
95 E Main   **Ph:** 435-381-5106
Castle Dale, UT 84513   **Fax:** 435-381-5183
www.co.emery.ut.us

In east-central UT; organized Feb 12, 1880 (prior to statehood) from Sanpete and Sevier counties. **Name Origin:** For George W. Emery, a territorial governor (1875-80).

Area (sq mi): 4461.54 (land 4451.85; water 9.69). **Pop per sq mi:** 2.4.

Pop 2005: 10,711. **State rank:** 19. **Pop change:** 2000-20005 -1.4%; 1990-2000 +5.1%. **Pop 2000:** 10,860 (White 92.5%; Black or African American 0.2%; Hispanic or Latino 5.2%; Asian 0.3%; Other 3.9%). **Foreign born:** 2.5%. **Median age:** 30.1.

Income 2000: per capita $14,243; median household $39,850; **Pop below poverty level:** 11.5%. ***Personal per capita income 2000-2003:** $17,987-$19,098.

Unemployment 2004: 7.4%. **Change from 2000:** -2.2%. **Median travel time to work:** 21 minutes. **Working outside county of residence:** 25%.

Cities with pop over 10,000: None.

*Source: Personal per capita income data are from the Bureau of Economic Analysis; per capita income data are from the Bureau of the Census. See Introduction for explanation of differences.

GARFIELD COUNTY

55 S Main St   **Ph:** 435-676-8826
Panguitch, UT 84759   **Fax:** 435-676-8239
www.utahreach.org/garfield/

In south-central UT; organized Mar 9, 1882 (prior to statehood) from Iron County. **Name Origin:** For James Abram Garfield (1831-81), twentieth U.S. president.

Area (sq mi): 5208.2 (land 5174.22; water 33.98). **Pop per sq mi:** 0.9.

Pop 2005: 4,470. **State rank:** 25. **Pop change:** 2000-20005 -5.6%; 1990-2000 +19%. **Pop 2000:** 4,735 (White 93.8%; Black or African American 0.2%; Hispanic or Latino 2.9%; Asian 0.4%; Other 4.4%, including 1.8% American Indian/Alaska Native). **Foreign born:** 0.8%. **Median age:** 33.8.

Income 2000: per capita $13,439; median household $35,180; **Pop below poverty level:** 8.1%. *Personal per capita income 2000-2003:** $18,319-$20,295.

Unemployment 2004: 8.5%. **Change from 2000:** -0.7%. **Median travel time to work:** 13.9 minutes. **Working outside county of residence:** 10.4%.

Cities with pop over 10,000: None.

GRAND COUNTY

125 E Center St   **Ph:** 435-259-1321
Moab, UT 84532   **Fax:** 435-259-2959
www.grandcountyutah.net

On the central eastern border of UT; organized Mar 13, 1890 (prior to statehood). **Name Origin:** For the Grand River, which flows through the county; the river was renamed the Colorado in 1921.

Area (sq mi): 3694.08 (land 3681.56; water 12.52). **Pop per sq mi:** 2.4.

Pop 2005: 8,743. **State rank:** 21. **Pop change:** 2000-20005 +3%; 1990-2000 +28.2%. **Pop 2000:** 8,485 (White 89.2%; Black or African American 0.2%; Hispanic or Latino 5.6%; Asian 0.2%; Other 6.9%, including 3.9% American Indian/Alaska Native). **Foreign born:** 3%. **Median age:** 36.9.

Income 2000: per capita $17,356; median household $32,387; **Pop below poverty level:** 14.8%. *Personal per capita income 2000-2003:** $20,181-$20,634.

Unemployment 2004: 7.7%. **Change from 2000:** +1%. **Median travel time to work:** 15 minutes. **Working outside county of residence:** 6.5%.

Cities with pop over 10,000: None.

IRON COUNTY

68 S 100 East   **Ph:** 435-477-3375
Parowan, UT 84761   **Fax:** 435-477-8847
www.ironcounty.net

On the southwestern border of UT; organized as Little Salt Lake County in 1850 (prior to statehood) from unorganized territory; name changed later that year. **Name Origin:** For the county's iron ore deposits and mines.

Area (sq mi): 3301.84 (land 3297.98; water 3.87). **Pop per sq mi:** 11.6.

Pop 2005: 38,311. **State rank:** 9. **Pop change:** 2000-20005 +13.4%; 1990-2000 +62.5%. **Pop 2000:** 33,779 (White 91.3%; Black or African American 0.4%; Hispanic or Latino 4.1%; Asian 0.7%; Other 6%, including 2.2% American Indian/Alaska Native). **Foreign born:** 2.9%. **Median age:** 24.2.

Income 2000: per capita $13,568; median household $33,114; **Pop below poverty level:** 19.2%. *Personal per capita income 2000-2003:** $16,389-$18,908.

Unemployment 2004: 4.9%. **Change from 2000:** +0.3%. **Median travel time to work:** 15 minutes. **Working outside county of residence:** 9%.

Cities with pop over 10,000: Cedar City (22,224).

JUAB COUNTY

160 N Main St   **Ph:** 435-623-3410
Nephi, UT 84648   **Fax:** 435-623-5936
www.co.juab.ut.us

On the central western border of UT, southwest of Provo; original county; organized Mar 3, 1852 (prior to statehood). **Name Origin:** From the Juab Valley, named by the local Indians, the Uabs, Yuabs, or Yoabs of the Piute tribe. Meaning is either 'flat, level plain,' or possibly 'thirsty plain.'

Area (sq mi): 3406.28 (land 3391.74; water 14.54). **Pop per sq mi:** 2.7.

Pop 2005: 9,113. **State rank:** 20. **Pop change:** 2000-20005 +10.6%; 1990-2000 +41.6%. **Pop 2000:** 8,238 (White 95.2%; Black or African American 0.1%; Hispanic or Latino 2.6%; Asian 0.3%; Other 2.9%, including 1% American Indian/Alaska Native). **Foreign born:** 1.4%. **Median age:** 26.5.

Income 2000: per capita $12,790; median household $38,139; **Pop below poverty level:** 10.4%. *Personal per capita income 2000-2003:** $18,028-$18,448.

Unemployment 2004: 6.2%. **Change from 2000:** +1.2%. **Median travel time to work:** 23.1 minutes. **Working outside county of residence:** 40.3%.

Cities with pop over 10,000: None.

KANE COUNTY

76 N Main St   **Ph:** 435-644-2458
Kanab, UT 84741   **Fax:** 435-644-2052
www.kaneutah.com

On the central southern border of UT; organized Jan 16, 1864 (prior to statehood) from Washington County. **Name Origin:** For Gen. Thomas Leiper Kane (1822-83), Union army officer and friend to the Mormons who acted as an intermediary in the so-called Mormon War of 1858.

Area (sq mi): 4108.42 (land 3991.96; water 116.46). **Pop per sq mi:** 1.6.

Pop 2005: 6,202. **State rank:** 24. **Pop change:** 2000-20005 +2.6%; 1990-2000 +17%. **Pop 2000:** 6,046 (White 94.7%; Black or African American 0%; Hispanic or Latino 2.3%; Asian 0.2%; Other 3.7%, including 1.6% American Indian/Alaska Native). **Foreign born:** 2.9%. **Median age:** 39.1.

Income 2000: per capita $15,455; median household $34,247; **Pop below poverty level:** 7.9%. *Personal per capita income 2000-2003:** $21,637-$24,237.

Kane County (cont'd)

Unemployment 2004: 5.7%. **Change from 2000:** +2.2%. **Median travel time to work:** 18.9 minutes. **Working outside county of residence:** 28.8%.

Cities with pop over 10,000: None.

MILLARD COUNTY

765 S Hwy 99 Suite 6   **Ph:** 435-743-6223
Fillmore, UT 84631   **Fax:** 435-743-6923
www.millardcounty.com

On the central western border of UT, southwest of Provo; organized Oct 4, 1851 (prior to statehood) from Juab County. **Name Origin:** For Millard Fillmore (1800-74), 13th U.S. president, who signed the act creating the Territory of Utah and appointed Brigham Young (1801-77) the first governor.

Area (sq mi): 6828.01 (land 6589.13; water 238.87). **Pop per sq mi:** 1.9.

Pop 2005: 12,284. **State rank:** 18. **Pop change:** 2000-20005 -1%; 1990-2000 +9.5%. **Pop 2000:** 12,405 (White 90%; Black or African American 0.1%; Hispanic or Latino 7.2%; Asian 0.5%; Other 5.5%, including 1.3% American Indian/Alaska Native). **Foreign born:** 5.1%. **Median age:** 29.9.

Income 2000: per capita $13,408; median household $36,178; **Pop below poverty level:** 13.1%. ***Personal per capita income 2000-2003:** $17,379-$20,698.

Unemployment 2004: 5.2%. **Change from 2000:** +0.3%. **Median travel time to work:** 19 minutes. **Working outside county of residence:** 7.5%.

Cities with pop over 10,000: None.

MORGAN COUNTY

PO Box 886   **Ph:** 801-845-4011
Morgan, UT 84050   **Fax:** 801-829-6176
www.morgan-county.net

In north-central UT, east of Bountiful; organized Jan 17, 1862 (prior to statehood) from Davis and Summit counties. **Name Origin:** For Jedediah Morgan Grant (1816-56), prominent Mormon churchman.

Area (sq mi): 610.79 (land 609.13; water 1.66). **Pop per sq mi:** 13.

Pop 2005: 7,906. **State rank:** 22. **Pop change:** 2000-20005 +10.9%; 1990-2000 +29%. **Pop 2000:** 7,129 (White 97.3%; Black or African American 0%; Hispanic or Latino 1.4%; Asian 0.2%; Other 1.7%). **Foreign born:** 2.7%. **Median age:** 28.5.

Income 2000: per capita $17,684; median household $50,273; **Pop below poverty level:** 5.2%. ***Personal per capita income 2000-2003:** $21,746-$22,414.

Unemployment 2004: 4.9%. **Change from 2000:** +1.3%. **Median travel time to work:** 26.3 minutes. **Working outside county of residence:** 61.6%.

Cities with pop over 10,000: None.

PIUTE COUNTY

550 N Main St   **Ph:** 435-577-2840
Junction, UT 84740   **Fax:** 435-577-2433
www.millardcounty.com

In south-central UT; organized Jan 16, 1865 (prior to statehood) from Beaver County. **Name Origin:** For the sub-tribe of the Ute Indians. The name means 'water Ute.'

Area (sq mi): 765.76 (land 757.81; water 7.95). **Pop per sq mi:** 1.8.

Pop 2005: 1,365. **State rank:** 28. **Pop change:** 2000-20005 -4.9%; 1990-2000 +12.4%. **Pop 2000:** 1,435 (White 93.3%; Black or African American 0.1%; Hispanic or Latino 4.5%; Asian 0.2%; Other 4.1%, including 1.2% American Indian/Alaska Native). **Foreign born:** 2%. **Median age:** 38.9.

Income 2000: per capita $12,697; median household $29,625; **Pop below poverty level:** 16.2%. ***Personal per capita income 2000-2003:** $15,522-$19,001.

Unemployment 2004: 4.5%. **Change from 2000:** -3.2%. **Median travel time to work:** 26.3 minutes. **Working outside county of residence:** 30.8%.

Cities with pop over 10,000: None.

RICH COUNTY

20 S Main St   **Ph:** 435-793-2415
Randolph, UT 84064   **Fax:** 435-793-2410
utahreach.org/rich/

On the northern border of UT, northeast of Ogden; original county. Created as Richland in 1863; organized and name changed Jan 16, 1864 (prior to statehood). **Name Origin:** For Charles Coulson Rich, a Mormon apostle.

Area (sq mi): 1086.29 (land 1028.53; water 57.76). **Pop per sq mi:** 2.

Pop 2005: 2,051. **State rank:** 27. **Pop change:** 2000-20005 +4.6%; 1990-2000 +13.7%. **Pop 2000:** 1,961 (White 97.3%; Black or African American 0%; Hispanic or Latino 1.8%; Asian 0.4%; Other 1.5%). **Foreign born:** 1.9%. **Median age:** 34.3.

Income 2000: per capita $16,267; median household $39,766; **Pop below poverty level:** 10.2%. ***Personal per capita income 2000-2003:** $20,810-$23,235.

Unemployment 2004: 3.4%. **Change from 2000:** -0.5%. **Median travel time to work:** 29 minutes. **Working outside county of residence:** 35.3%.

Cities with pop over 10,000: None.

SALT LAKE COUNTY

2001 S State St Suite S2200   **Ph:** 801-468-3000
Salt Lake City, UT 84190   **Fax:** 801-468-3440
www.co.slc.ut.us

In north-central UT, on the eastern shore of Great Salt Lake; original county. Organized as Great Salt Lake County in 1849 (prior to statehood); name changed Jan 29, 1868. **Name Origin:** For the Great Salt Lake.

Area (sq mi): 807.78 (land 737.38; water 70.4). **Pop per sq mi:** 1285.9.

Pop 2005: 948,172. **State rank:** 1. **Pop change:** 2000-20005 +5.5%; 1990-2000 +23.8%. **Pop 2000:** 898,387 (White 80.9%; Black or African American 1.1%; Hispanic or Latino 11.9%; Asian 2.6%;

Source: Personal per capita income data are from the Bureau of Economic Analysis; per capita income data are from the Bureau of the Census. See Introduction for explanation of differences.

Salt Lake County (cont'd)

Other 10.1%, including 1.2% Native Hawaiian/Other Pacific Islander). **Foreign born:** 10.4%. **Median age:** 28.9.

Income 2000: per capita $20,190; median household $48,373; **Pop below poverty level:** 8%. ***Personal per capita income 2000-2003:** $27,674-$29,699.

Unemployment 2004: 5.4%. **Change from 2000:** +1.1%. **Median travel time to work:** 22.5 minutes. **Working outside county of residence:** 6.2%.

Cities with pop over 10,000: 12 (see page 39 for cities).

SAN JUAN COUNTY

117 S Main St   **Ph:** 435-587-3223
Monticello, UT 84535   **Fax:** 435-587-2425
www.sanjuancounty.org

On the southeastern border of UT; organized Feb 17, 1880 (prior to statehood) from Kane, Iron, Sevier, and Piute counties. **Name Origin:** For the San Juan River, which runs through the county; Spanish 'Saint John.' The origin of th river's name is in dispute.

Area (sq mi): 7933.09 (land 7820.18; water 112.91). **Pop per sq mi:** 1.8.

Pop 2005: 14,104. **State rank:** 17. **Pop change:** 2000-20005 -2.1%; 1990-2000 +14.2%. **Pop 2000:** 14,413 (White 39.6%; Black or African American 0.1%; Hispanic or Latino 3.7%; Asian 0.2%; Other 58.9%, including 55.7% American Indian/Alaska Native). **Foreign born:** 0.9%. **Median age:** 25.5.

Income 2000: per capita $10,229; median household $28,137; **Pop below poverty level:** 31.4%. ***Personal per capita income 2000-2003:** $12,881-$14,363.

Unemployment 2004: 10%. **Change from 2000:** +0.9%. **Median travel time to work:** 21.4 minutes. **Working outside county of residence:** 20.3%.

Cities with pop over 10,000: None.

SANPETE COUNTY

160 N Main St   **Ph:** 435-835-2131
Manti, UT 84642   **Fax:** 435-835-2135
utahreach.org/sanpete/govt/index.htm

In central UT, south of Provo; original county; organized 1850 (prior to statehood). **Name Origin:** Corruption of *San Pitch*, name of the Ute Indian chieftain whose people lived in the region.

Area (sq mi): 1602.66 (land 1588.11; water 14.55). **Pop per sq mi:** 15.1.

Pop 2005: 24,044. **State rank:** 12. **Pop change:** 2000-20005 +5.6%; 1990-2000 +40%. **Pop 2000:** 22,763 (White 90.5%; Black or African American 0.3%; Hispanic or Latino 6.6%; Asian 0.5%; Other 6.9%). **Foreign born:** 4.8%. **Median age:** 25.3.

Income 2000: per capita $12,442; median household $33,042; **Pop below poverty level:** 15.9%. ***Personal per capita income 2000-2003:** $15,142-$16,275.

Unemployment 2004: 6.5%. **Change from 2000:** +0.8%. **Median travel time to work:** 22.4 minutes. **Working outside county of residence:** 20.3%.

Cities with pop over 10,000: None.

SEVIER COUNTY

250 N Main St   **Ph:** 435-896-9262
Richfield, UT 84701   **Fax:** 435-896-8888
www.sevierutah.net

In south-central UT; organized Jan 16, 1865 (prior to statehood) from Sanpete County. **Name Origin:** For the Sevier River, which runs through the county. Anglicization of Spanish *Rio Severo* 'violent river.'

Area (sq mi): 1918.28 (land 1910.25; water 8.03). **Pop per sq mi:** 10.1.

Pop 2005: 19,386. **State rank:** 14. **Pop change:** 2000-20005 +2.9%; 1990-2000 +22.1%. **Pop 2000:** 18,842 (White 94.2%; Black or African American 0.3%; Hispanic or Latino 2.6%; Asian 0.3%; Other 3.9%, including 2% American Indian/Alaska Native). **Foreign born:** 1.3%. **Median age:** 30.3.

Income 2000: per capita $14,180; median household $35,822; **Pop below poverty level:** 10.8%. ***Personal per capita income 2000-2003:** $17,685-$18,782.

Unemployment 2004: 5.4%. **Change from 2000:** +0.8%. **Median travel time to work:** 17.6 minutes. **Working outside county of residence:** 9.8%.

Cities with pop over 10,000: None.

SUMMIT COUNTY

60 N Main St   **Ph:** 435-336-3203
Coalville, UT 84017   **Fax:** 435-336-3030
www.co.summit.ut.us

On the central northern border of UT, east of Salt Lake City; organized Jan 13, 1854 (prior to statehood) from Green River Valley. **Name Origin:** For its location on the divide between the Colorado River Valley and the Salt Lake Valley.

Area (sq mi): 1882.05 (land 1871.05; water 11). **Pop per sq mi:** 18.7.

Pop 2005: 35,001. **State rank:** 10. **Pop change:** 2000-20005 +17.7%; 1990-2000 +91.6%. **Pop 2000:** 29,736 (White 89.5%; Black or African American 0.2%; Hispanic or Latino 8.1%; Asian 1%; Other 6.9%). **Foreign born:** 7.7%. **Median age:** 33.3.

Income 2000: per capita $33,767; median household $64,962; **Pop below poverty level:** 5.4%. ***Personal per capita income 2000-2003:** $44,545-$45,500.

Unemployment 2004: 5.3%. **Change from 2000:** -0.5%. **Median travel time to work:** 24.8 minutes. **Working outside county of residence:** 35.6%.

Cities with pop over 10,000: None.

TOOELE COUNTY

47 S Main St   **Ph:** 435-843-3140
Tooele, UT 84074   **Fax:** 435-882-7317
www.co.tooele.ut.us

On the northwestern border of UT, west of Salt Lake City; original county. Organized as Tuilla County Jan 31, 1850 (prior to statehood); includes Shambip County, which was abolished in 1862. Spelling was changed Mar 1852. **Name Origin:** Possibly for Tuilla, a Goshute Indian chief, or for the bulrushes (tules) in the swamps, or for Mat Tooele, an Austrian village.

Area (sq mi): 7287.12 (land 6930.35; water 356.76). **Pop per sq mi:** 7.4.

Tooele County (cont'd)

Pop 2005: 51,311. **State rank:** 7. **Pop change:** 2000-20005 +26%; 1990-2000 +53.1%. **Pop 2000:** 40,735 (White 84.7%; Black or African American 1.3%; Hispanic or Latino 10.3%; Asian 0.6%; Other 9%, including 1.7% American Indian/Alaska Native). **Foreign born:** 3.7%. **Median age:** 27.1.

Income 2000: per capita $16,321; median household $45,773; **Pop below poverty level:** 6.7%. ***Personal per capita income 2000-2003:** $19,680-$20,359.

Unemployment 2004: 5.4%. **Change from 2000:** -2%. **Median travel time to work:** 32.1 minutes. **Working outside county of residence:** 45.5%.

Cities with pop over 10,000: Tooele 🏛 (27,903).

UINTAH COUNTY
147 E Main St   **Ph:** 435-781-0770
Vernal, UT 84078   **Fax:** 435-781-6701
www.co.uintah.ut.us

On the northeastern border of UT; original county; organized Jan 31, 1850 (prior to statehood). **Name Origin:** For a subtribe of the Utes; named said to mean 'pineland.'

Area (sq mi): 4498.98 (land 4477.07; water 21.91). **Pop per sq mi:** 6.

Pop 2005: 26,995. **State rank:** 11. **Pop change:** 2000-20005 +7%; 1990-2000 +13.6%. **Pop 2000:** 25,224 (White 85.9%; Black or African American 0.1%; Hispanic or Latino 3.5%; Asian 0.2%; Other 11.9%, including 9.4% American Indian/Alaska Native). **Foreign born:** 1.4%. **Median age:** 29.

Income 2000: per capita $13,571; median household $34,518; **Pop below poverty level:** 14.5%. ***Personal per capita income 2000-2003:** $16,924-$19,396.

Unemployment 2004: 5.4%. **Change from 2000:** +0.8%. **Median travel time to work:** 19.5 minutes. **Working outside county of residence:** 12.2%.

Cities with pop over 10,000: None.

UTAH COUNTY
100 E Center St Suite 2300   **Ph:** 801-851-8136
Provo, UT 84606   **Fax:** 801-851-8146
www.co.utah.ut.us

In north-central UT, south of Salt Lake City; original county; organized Jan 31, 1850 (prior to statehood); includes Cedar County; which was abolished in 1862. **Name Origin:** For the Ute Indians. *Ute* or *Eutaw* is variously defined as 'in the tops of the mountains,' 'high up,' 'the hill dwellers,' 'the land of the sun,' or 'the land of plenty.'

Area (sq mi): 2140.98 (land 1998.33; water 142.64). **Pop per sq mi:** 222.1.

Pop 2005: 443,738. **State rank:** 2. **Pop change:** 2000-20005 +20.4%; 1990-2000 +39.8%. **Pop 2000:** 368,536 (White 89.2%; Black or African American 0.3%; Hispanic or Latino 7%; Asian 1.1%; Other 6.3%). **Foreign born:** 6.3%. **Median age:** 23.3.

Income 2000: per capita $15,557; median household $45,833; **Pop below poverty level:** 12%. ***Personal per capita income 2000-2003:** $19,641-$20,506.

Unemployment 2004: 4.8%. **Change from 2000:** +1%. **Median travel time to work:** 18.8 minutes. **Working outside county of residence:** 13.9%.

Cities with pop over 10,000: 9 (see page 39 for cities).

WASATCH COUNTY
25 N Main St   **Ph:** 435-654-3211
Heber City, UT 84032   **Fax:** 435-654-9924
www.co.wasatch.ut.us

In east-central UT, east of Provo; organized Jan 17, 1862 (prior to statehood) from Summit County. **Name Origin:** For the Wasatch Mountains, a Ute word meaning 'mountain pass' or 'low place in a high mountain,' referring to the place where the Weber River cuts through.

Area (sq mi): 1209.17 (land 1177.39; water 31.78). **Pop per sq mi:** 16.1.

Pop 2005: 18,974. **State rank:** 15. **Pop change:** 2000-20005 +24.7%; 1990-2000 +50.8%. **Pop 2000:** 15,215 (White 93.3%; Black or African American 0.2%; Hispanic or Latino 5.1%; Asian 0.3%; Other 3.9%). **Foreign born:** 4.2%. **Median age:** 29.5.

Income 2000: per capita $19,869; median household $49,612; **Pop below poverty level:** 5.2%. ***Personal per capita income 2000-2003:** $20,818-$21,719.

Unemployment 2004: 5.4%. **Change from 2000:** -0.1%. **Median travel time to work:** 25.3 minutes. **Working outside county of residence:** 43.8%.

Cities with pop over 10,000: None.

WASHINGTON COUNTY
197 E Tabernacle St   **Ph:** 435-634-5700
Saint George, UT 84770   **Fax:** 435-634-5753
www.washco.state.ut.us

On the southwestern border of UT; organized Mar 2, 1852 (prior to statehood) from unorganized territory. **Name Origin:** For George Washington (1732-1799), American patriot and first U.S. president.

Area (sq mi): 2429.91 (land 2426.62; water 3.28). **Pop per sq mi:** 49.

Pop 2005: 118,885. **State rank:** 5. **Pop change:** 2000-20005 +31.6%; 1990-2000 +86.1%. **Pop 2000:** 90,354 (White 91.1%; Black or African American 0.2%; Hispanic or Latino 5.2%; Asian 0.4%; Other 5.7%, including 1.5% American Indian/Alaska Native). **Foreign born:** 4.1%. **Median age:** 31.

Income 2000: per capita $15,873; median household $37,212; **Pop below poverty level:** 11.2%. ***Personal per capita income 2000-2003:** $19,202-$20,084.

Unemployment 2004: 4.4%. **Change from 2000:** +0.6%. **Median travel time to work:** 17.2 minutes. **Working outside county of residence:** 6.7%.

Cities with pop over 10,000: Saint George 🏛 (59,780); Washington (11,521).

WAYNE COUNTY
18 S Main St   **Ph:** 435-836-2765
Loa, UT 84747   **Fax:** 435-836-2479
www.waynecnty.com

In south-central UT; organized Mar 10, 1892 (prior to statehood)

---

*Source: Personal per capita income data are from the Bureau of Economic Analysis; per capita income data are from the Bureau of the Census. See Introduction for explanation of differences.

Wayne County (cont'd)

from Piute County. **Name Origin:** Named by Willis Robinson, a delegate to the state constitutional convention, for his deceased son, Wayne.

Area (sq mi): 2466.47 (land 2460.32; water 6.15). **Pop per sq mi:** 1.

Pop 2005: 2,450. **State rank:** 26. **Pop change:** 2000-20005 -2.4%; 1990-2000 +15.3%. **Pop 2000.** 2,509 (White 96%; Black or African American 0.2%, Hispanic or Latino 2%; Asian 0.1%; Other 2.5%). **Foreign born:** 1.7%. **Median age:** 34.1.

Income 2000: per capita $15,392; median household $32,000; **Pop below poverty level:** 15.4%. ***Personal per capita income 2000-2003:** $18,292-$19,869.

Unemployment 2004: 7%. **Change from 2000:** +1.7%. **Median travel time to work:** 19.5 minutes. **Working outside county of residence:** 12.4%.

Cities with pop over 10,000: None.

WEBER COUNTY

2380 Washington Blvd Suite 350   **Ph:** 801-399-8454
Ogden, UT 84401   **Fax:** 801-399-8314
www.co.weber.ut.us

In north-central UT, north of Salt Lake City; original county; organized Jan 31, 1850 (prior to statehood). **Name Origin:** For the Weber River, which runs through the county. The river is itself named for John H. Weber (?-1859), a Dutch sea captain and trapper who traveled west with Gen. Ashby and was killed near the river, or for another trapper named Weber.

Area (sq mi): 659.46 (land 575.54; water 83.93). **Pop per sq mi:** 366.2.

Pop 2005: 210,749. **State rank:** 4. **Pop change:** 2000-20005 +7.2%; 1990-2000 +24.1%. **Pop 2000:** 196,533 (White 82.8%; Black or African American 1.4%; Hispanic or Latino 12.6%; Asian 1.3%; Other 9.7%). **Foreign born:** 6.4%. **Median age:** 29.3.

Income 2000: per capita $18,246; median household $44,014; **Pop below poverty level:** 9.3%. ***Personal per capita income 2000-2003:** $23,260-$25,075.

Unemployment 2004: 5.8%. **Change from 2000:** +0.8%. **Median travel time to work:** 21.6 minutes. **Working outside county of residence:** 29.2%.

Cities with pop over 10,000: Ogden 🏛 (78,519); Roy (35,308); North Ogden (16,328); South Ogden (15,130).

🏛 *County Seat*

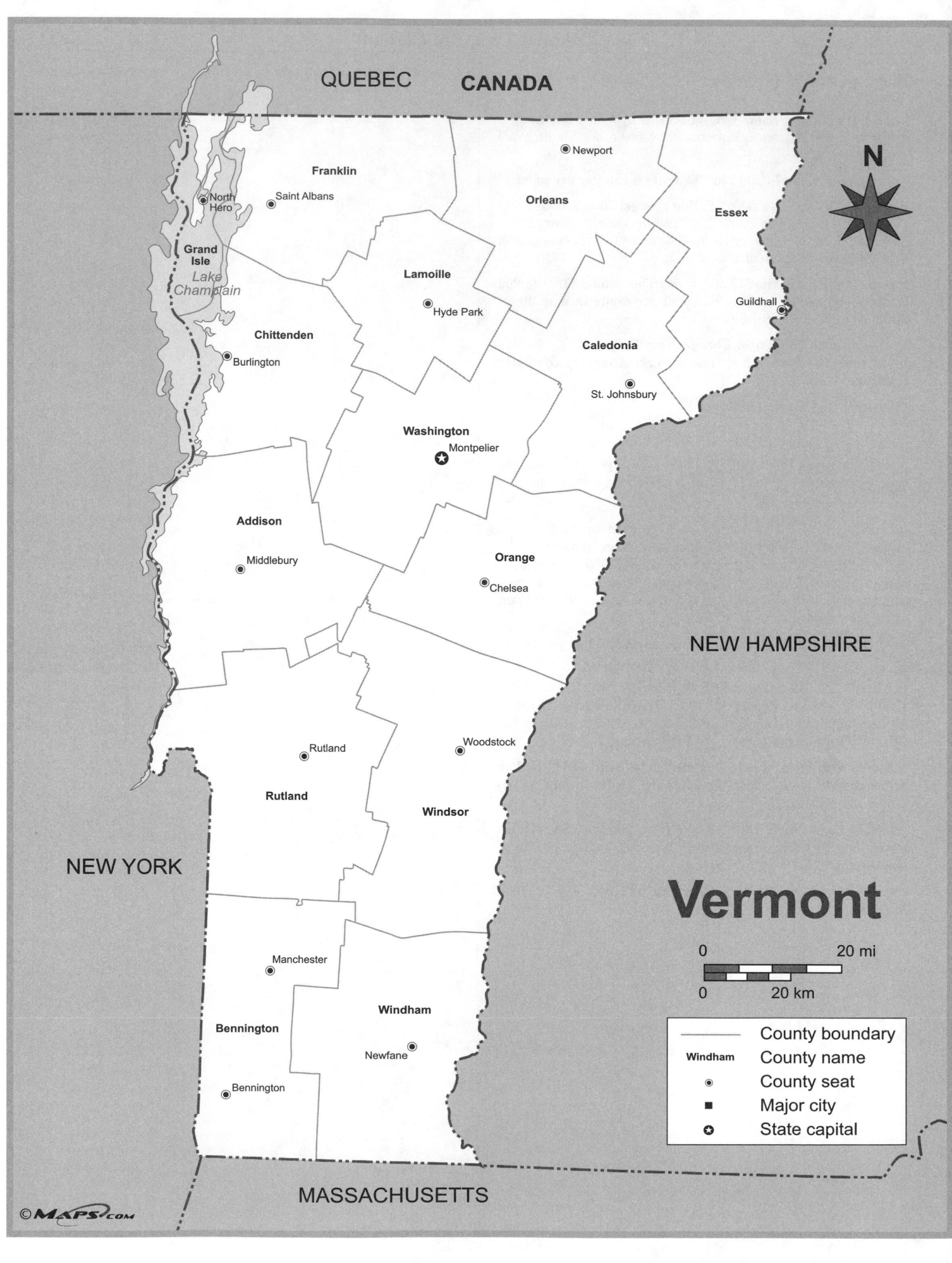

Vermont

VERMONT STATE INFORMATION

www.vermont.gov   **Ph:** 802-828-1110

Area (sq mi): 9614.26 (land 9249.56; water 364.7). **Pop per sq mi:** 67.4.

Pop 2005: 623,050. **Pop change:** 2000-20005 +2.3%; 1990-2000 +8.2%. **Pop 2000:** 608,827 (White 96.2%; Black or African American 0.5%; Hispanic or Latino 0.9%; Asian 0.9%; Other 1.8%). **Foreign born:** 3.8%. **Median age:** 37.7.

Income 2000: per capita $20,625; median household $40,856; **Pop below poverty level:** 9.4%. ***Personal per capita income 2000-2003:** $27,680-$30,888.

Unemployment 2004: 3.7%. **Change from 2000:** +1%. **Median travel time to work:** 21.6 minutes. **Working outside county of residence:** 21.5%.

ADDISON COUNTY

7 Mahady Ct   **Ph:** 802-388-7741
Middlebury, VT 05753   **Fax:** 802-388-4621
www.addisoncountychamber.com

On central western border of VT, west of Barre; organized Oct 18, 1785 (prior to statehood) from Rutland County. **Name Origin:** For the town of Addison.

Area (sq mi): 808.3 (land 770.18; water 38.12). **Pop per sq mi:** 48.

Pop 2005: 36,965. **State rank:** 8. **Pop change:** 2000-20005 +2.8%; 1990-2000 +9.2%. **Pop 2000:** 35,974 (White 96.2%; Black or African American 0.5%; Hispanic or Latino 1.1%; Asian 0.7%; Other 1.9%). **Foreign born:** 3.5%. **Median age:** 36.1.

Income 2000: per capita $19,539; median household $43,142; **Pop below poverty level:** 8.6%. ***Personal per capita income 2000-2003:** $25,549-$28,788.

Unemployment 2004: 3.5%. **Change from 2000:** +0.2%. **Median travel time to work:** 23.2 minutes. **Working outside county of residence:** 29.4%.

Cities with pop over 10,000: None.

BENNINGTON COUNTY

PO Box 4157   **Ph:** 802-447-2700
Bennington, VT 05201   **Fax:** 802-447-2703
www.bennington.com

On the southwestern border of VT, south of Rutland. Oldest county, organized Feb 11, 1779 (prior to statehood). **Name Origin:** For the town, its county seat.

Area (sq mi): 677.67 (land 676.27; water 1.4). **Pop per sq mi:** 54.7.

Pop 2005: 36,999. **State rank:** 7. **Pop change:** 2000-20005 +0%; 1990-2000 +3.2%. **Pop 2000:** 36,994 (White 97.1%; Black or African American 0.4%; Hispanic or Latino 0.9%; Asian 0.6%; Other 1.2%). **Foreign born:** 2.7%. **Median age:** 40.3.

Income 2000: per capita $21,193; median household $39,926; **Pop below poverty level:** 10%. ***Personal per capita income 2000-2003:** $29,191-$32,793.

Unemployment 2004: 3.8%. **Change from 2000:** -0.8%. **Median travel time to work:** 19.1 minutes. **Working outside county of residence:** 17.4%.

Cities with pop over 10,000: None.

CALEDONIA COUNTY

1126 Main St   **Ph:** 802-748-6600
Saint Johnsbury, VT 05819   **Fax:** 802-748-6603

In northeastern VT, east of Montpelier; organized Nov 5, 1792 from Chittenden and Orange counties. **Name Origin:** For the ancient name of Scotland; name given by the many Scots who had settled in this part of the state.

Area (sq mi): 657.52 (land 650.59; water 6.94). **Pop per sq mi:** 46.8.

Pop 2005: 30,440. **State rank:** 9. **Pop change:** 2000-20005 +2.5%; 1990-2000 +6.7%. **Pop 2000:** 29,702 (White 97%; Black or African American 0.3%; Hispanic or Latino 0.7%; Asian 0.4%; Other 1.8%). **Foreign born:** 2.5%. **Median age:** 38.5.

Income 2000: per capita $16,976; median household $34,800; **Pop below poverty level:** 12.3%. ***Personal per capita income 2000-2003:** $23,310-$25,873.

Unemployment 2004: 4.1%. **Change from 2000:** -1.1%. **Median travel time to work:** 22.2 minutes. **Working outside county of residence:** 25.2%.

Cities with pop over 10,000: None.

CHITTENDEN COUNTY

PO Box 187   **Ph:** 802-863-3467
Burlington, VT 05402

In northwestern VT, west of Montpelier, organized Oct 22, 1787 (prior to statehood) from Addison County. **Name Origin:** For Thomas Chittenden (1730-97), first governor of the republic of VT (1778-89; 1790-91), and of the state (1791-97).

Area (sq mi): 619.64 (land 539.04; water 80.6). **Pop per sq mi:** 277.6.

Pop 2005: 149,613. **State rank:** 1. **Pop change:** 2000-20005 +2.1%; 1990-2000 +11.2%. **Pop 2000:** 146,571 (White 94.4%; Black or

Chittenden County (cont'd)

African American 0.9%; Hispanic or Latino 1.1%; Asian 2%; Other 1.9%). **Foreign born:** 5.9%. **Median age:** 34.2.

Income 2000: per capita $23,501; median household $47,673; **Pop below poverty level:** 8.8%. *Personal per capita income 2000-2003:* $32,241-$35,899.

Unemployment 2004: 3.2%. **Change from 2000:** +0.8%. **Median travel time to work:** 19.7 minutes. **Working outside county of residence:** 7%.

Cities with pop over 10,000: Burlington ⛪ (38,934); South Burlington (16,460).

ESSEX COUNTY

PO Box 75   **Ph:** 802-676-3910
Guildhall, VT 05905   **Fax:** 802-676-3463

At the northeastern corner of VT; organized Nov 5, 1792 from Chittenden and Orange counties. **Name Origin:** For the county of Essex, England; many early residents had ancestors originally from there.

Area (sq mi): 673.75 (land 665.2; water 8.56). **Pop per sq mi:** 9.9.

Pop 2005: 6,602. **State rank:** 14. **Pop change:** 2000-20005 +2.2%; 1990-2000 +0.8%. **Pop 2000:** 6,459 (White 96.3%; Black or African American 0.2%; Hispanic or Latino 0.5%; Asian 0.3%; Other 2.9%). **Foreign born:** 5.5%. **Median age:** 39.

Income 2000: per capita $14,388; median household $30,490; **Pop below poverty level:** 13.7%. *Personal per capita income 2000-2003:* $18,777-$19,126.

Unemployment 2004: 3.9%. **Change from 2000:** -2.7%. **Median travel time to work:** 22 minutes. **Working outside county of residence:** 58.7%.

Cities with pop over 10,000: None.

FRANKLIN COUNTY

PO Box 808   **Ph:** 802-524-3863
Saint Albans, VT 05478
www.stalbanschamber.com

At the northwestern corner of VT, north of Burlington; organized Nov 5, 1792 from Chittenden County. **Name Origin:** For Benjamin Franklin (1706-90), U.S. patriot, diplomat, and statesman.

Area (sq mi): 692.02 (land 637.07; water 54.95). **Pop per sq mi:** 75.2.

Pop 2005: 47,914. **State rank:** 5. **Pop change:** 2000-20005 +5.5%; 1990-2000 +13.6%. **Pop 2000:** 45,417 (White 95.6%; Black or African American 0.3%; Hispanic or Latino 0.6%; Asian 0.3%; Other 3.3%, including 1.5% American Indian/Alaska Native). **Foreign born:** 3.7%. **Median age:** 35.7.

Income 2000: per capita $17,816; median household $41,659; **Pop below poverty level:** 9%. *Personal per capita income 2000-2003:* $23,929-$26,184.

Unemployment 2004: 4.1%. **Change from 2000:** -0.1%. **Median travel time to work:** 25.6 minutes. **Working outside county of residence:** 36.1%.

Cities with pop over 10,000: None.

GRAND ISLE COUNTY

9 Hyde Rd PO Box 49   **Ph:** 802-372-8830
Grand Isle, VT 05458   **Fax:** 802-372-8815

Islands and peninsula in Lake Champlain, in northwestern VT; organized Nov 9, 1802 from Franklin and Chittenden counties. **Name Origin:** For the largest of the islands comprising the county. Often referred to as 'The Islands.'

Area (sq mi): 194.67 (land 82.62; water 112.06). **Pop per sq mi:** 93.2.

Pop 2005: 7,703. **State rank:** 13. **Pop change:** 2000-20005 +11.6%; 1990-2000 +29.8%. **Pop 2000:** 6,901 (White 97.1%; Black or African American 0.1%; Hispanic or Latino 0.4%; Asian 0.2%; Other 2.2%). **Foreign born:** 4.2%. **Median age:** 40.1.

Income 2000: per capita $22,207; median household $43,033; **Pop below poverty level:** 7.6%. *Personal per capita income 2000-2003:* $28,279-$30,418.

Unemployment 2004: 4.8%. **Change from 2000:** -0.3%. **Median travel time to work:** 33.4 minutes. **Working outside county of residence:** 68.2%.

Cities with pop over 10,000: None.

LAMOILLE COUNTY

PO Box 490   **Ph:** 802-888-2207
Hyde Park, VT 05655
www.lamoilleeconomy.org

In north-central VT, north of Montpelier; organized Oct 26, 1835 from Orleans, Franklin, Washington, and Chittenden counties. **Name Origin:** For the Lamoille River, which runs through it; a corruption of French *la mouette* 'the seagull,' the name given to the river by Champlain. The 1744 Charlevois map of discoveries in America showed the river as *La Mouelle* owing to an engraver's neglecting to cross the *tt*s; with spelling variations.

Area (sq mi): 463.75 (land 460.97; water 2.78). **Pop per sq mi:** 53.1.

Pop 2005: 24,495. **State rank:** 12. **Pop change:** 2000-20005 +5.4%; 1990-2000 +17.7%. **Pop 2000:** 23,233 (White 96.8%; Black or African American 0.3%; Hispanic or Latino 0.8%; Asian 0.4%; Other 1.9%). **Foreign born:** 3.8%. **Median age:** 36.5.

Income 2000: per capita $20,972; median household $39,356; **Pop below poverty level:** 9.6%. *Personal per capita income 2000-2003:* $25,832-$29,733.

Unemployment 2004: 4%. **Change from 2000:** -0.9%. **Median travel time to work:** 25.7 minutes. **Working outside county of residence:** 28.6%.

Cities with pop over 10,000: None.

ORANGE COUNTY

5 Court St   **Ph:** 802-685-4610
Chelsea, VT 05038   **Fax:** 802-685-3246

On the central eastern border of VT, south of Montpelier; organized Feb 22, 1781 (prior to statehood) from the former Cumberland County. **Name Origin:** For William of Orange (1650-1702), later William III, king of England (1689-1702).

Area (sq mi): 691.74 (land 688.56; water 3.18). **Pop per sq mi:** 42.5.

---

*Source: Personal per capita income data are from the Bureau of Economic Analysis; per capita income data are from the Bureau of the Census. See Introduction for explanation of differences.

Orange County (cont'd)

Pop 2005: 29,287. **State rank:** 10. **Pop change:** 2000-20005 +3.8%; 1990-2000 +7.9%. **Pop 2000:** 28,226 (White 97.5%; Black or African American 0.2%; Hispanic or Latino 0.6%; Asian 0.4%; Other 1.4%). **Foreign born:** 1.8%. **Median age:** 38.6.

Income 2000: per capita $18,784; median household $39,855; **Pop below poverty level.** 9.1%. ***Personal per capita income 2000 2003:** $23,437-$26,441.

Unemployment 2004: 3.4%. **Change from 2000:** +0.7%. **Median travel time to work:** 25.3 minutes. **Working outside county of residence:** 53.3%.

Cities with pop over 10,000: None.

ORLEANS COUNTY

247 Main St   **Ph:** 802-334-3344
Newport, VT 05855   **Fax:** 802-334-3385

On the central northern border of VT; organized Nov 5, 1792 from Chittenden and Orange counties. **Name Origin:** Probably for Louis Philippe Joseph (1747-93), Duke of Orleans, a friend of Marquis de Lafayette (1757-1834) and supporter of the American Revolution.

Area (sq mi): 721.14 (land 697.7; water 23.44). **Pop per sq mi:** 39.6.

Pop 2005: 27,640. **State rank:** 11. **Pop change:** 2000-20005 +5.2%; 1990-2000 +9.2%. **Pop 2000:** 26,277 (White 96.7%; Black or African American 0.4%; Hispanic or Latino 0.7%; Asian 0.3%; Other 2.2%). **Foreign born:** 5.5%. **Median age:** 39.3.

Income 2000: per capita $16,518; median household $31,084; **Pop below poverty level:** 14.1%. ***Personal per capita income 2000-2003:** $21,988-$25,017.

Unemployment 2004: 5%. **Change from 2000:** -2.1%. **Median travel time to work:** 21.5 minutes. **Working outside county of residence:** 15.5%.

Cities with pop over 10,000: None.

RUTLAND COUNTY

83 Center St Suite 3   **Ph:** 802-775-4394
Rutland, VT 05701   **Fax:** 802-775-2291
www.rutlandvermont.com

On the central western border of VT, south of Middlebury; organized Feb 22, 1781 (prior to statehood) from Bennington County. **Name Origin:** For the town, its county seat.

Area (sq mi): 944.77 (land 932.53; water 12.24). **Pop per sq mi:** 68.4.

Pop 2005: 63,743. **State rank:** 2. **Pop change:** 2000-20005 +0.5%; 1990-2000 +2%. **Pop 2000:** 63,400 (White 97.7%; Black or African American 0.3%; Hispanic or Latino 0.7%; Asian 0.4%; Other 1.1%). **Foreign born:** 2%. **Median age:** 39.5.

Income 2000: per capita $18,874; median household $36,743; **Pop below poverty level:** 10.9%. ***Personal per capita income 2000-2003:** $25,987-$29,475.

Unemployment 2004: 4%. **Change from 2000:** -0.1%. **Median travel time to work:** 20.6 minutes. **Working outside county of residence:** 13.6%.

Cities with pop over 10,000: Rutland 🏛 (17,080).

WASHINGTON COUNTY

65 State St   **Ph:** 802-828-2091
Montpelier, VT 05602

In north-central VT, east of Burlington; organized as Jefferson County Nov 1, 1810 from Addison, Caledonia, Chittenden, and Orange counties. **Name Origin:** For George Washington (1732-99), U.S. patriot and first U.S. president. Originally named Jefferson; changed Nov 8, 1814, by newly elected Federalist majority in VT legislature.

Area (sq mi): 695.43 (land 689.17; water 6.26). **Pop per sq mi:** 86.3.

Pop 2005: 59,478. **State rank:** 3. **Pop change:** 2000-20005 +2.5%; 1990-2000 +5.7%. **Pop 2000:** 58,039 (White 96.1%; Black or African American 0.5%; Hispanic or Latino 1.3%; Asian 0.6%; Other 1.9%). **Foreign born:** 3.6%. **Median age:** 38.5.

Income 2000: per capita $21,113; median household $40,972; **Pop below poverty level:** 8%. ***Personal per capita income 2000-2003:** $28,394-$31,971.

Unemployment 2004: 4.1%. **Change from 2000:** +0.3%. **Median travel time to work:** 21.8 minutes. **Working outside county of residence:** 17.9%.

Cities with pop over 10,000: None.

WINDHAM COUNTY

PO Box 207   **Ph:** 802-365-7979
Newfane, VT 05345   **Fax:** 802-365-4360

At the southeastern corner of VT; organized Feb 11, 1781 (prior to statehood) from the former Cumberland County. **Name Origin:** For Windham, CT, former home of early settlers.

Area (sq mi): 798.12 (land 788.72; water 9.4). **Pop per sq mi:** 56.

Pop 2005: 44,143. **State rank:** 6. **Pop change:** 2000-20005 -0.2%; 1990-2000 +6.3%. **Pop 2000:** 44,216 (White 96%; Black or African American 0.5%; Hispanic or Latino 1.1%; Asian 0.8%; Other 1.9%). **Foreign born:** 3.1%. **Median age:** 40.

Income 2000: per capita $20,533; median household $38,204; **Pop below poverty level:** 9.4%. ***Personal per capita income 2000-2003:** $27,937-$31,023.

Unemployment 2004: 3.4%. **Change from 2000:** +0.1%. **Median travel time to work:** 20.5 minutes. **Working outside county of residence:** 17.7%.

Cities with pop over 10,000: None.

WINDSOR COUNTY

PO Box 458   **Ph:** 802-457-2121
Woodstock, VT 05091   **Fax:** 802-457-3446

On the central eastern border of VT, east of Rutland; organized Feb 22, 1781 (prior to statehood) from the former Cumberland County. **Name Origin:** For the English town of Windsor.

Area (sq mi): 975.74 (land 970.96; water 4.78). **Pop per sq mi:** 59.8.

Pop 2005: 58,028. **State rank:** 4. **Pop change:** 2000-20005 +1.1%; 1990-2000 +6.2%. **Pop 2000:** 57,418 (White 97.1%; Black or African American 0.3%; Hispanic or Latino 0.8%; Asian 0.6%; Other 1.2%). **Foreign born:** 3%. **Median age:** 41.3.

Windsor County (cont'd)

Income 2000: per capita $22,369; median household $40,688; **Pop below poverty level:** 7.7%. ***Personal per capita income 2000-2003:** $28,944-$31,765.

Unemployment 2004: 3.2%. **Change from 2000:** +0.4%. **Median travel time to work:** 21.3 minutes. **Working outside county of residence:** 34.8%.

Cities with pop over 10,000: None.

*Source: Personal per capita income data are from the Bureau of Economic Analysis; per capita income data are from the Bureau of the Census. See Introduction for explanation of differences.

726

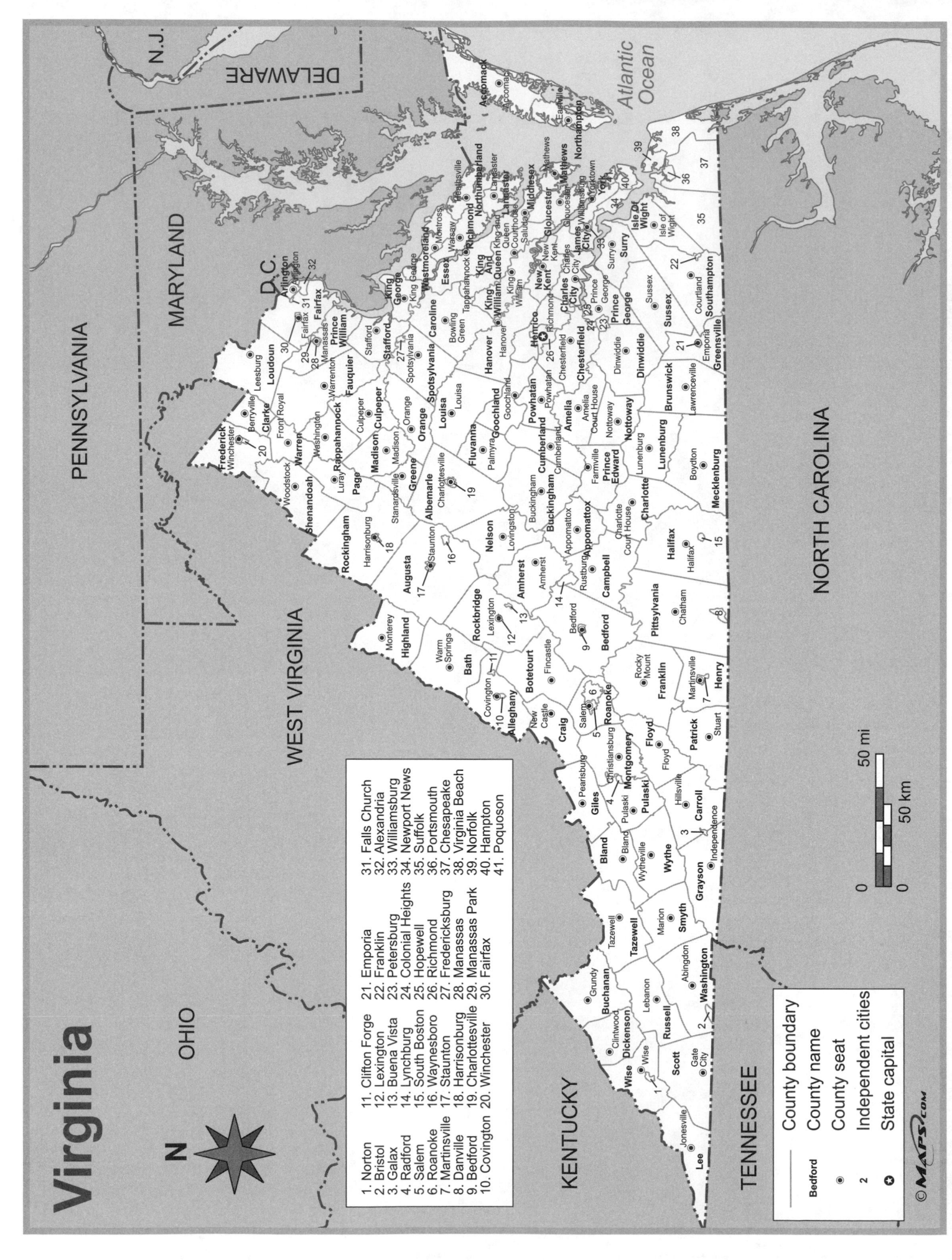

Virginia

N

OHIO

KENTUCKY

TENNESSEE

PENNSYLVANIA

MARYLAND

WEST VIRGINIA

NORTH CAROLINA

N.J.

DELAWARE

D.C.

Atlantic Ocean

1. Norton
2. Bristol
3. Galax
4. Radford
5. Salem
6. Roanoke
7. Martinsville
8. Danville
9. Bedford
10. Covington
11. Clifton Forge
12. Lexington
13. Buena Vista
14. Lynchburg
15. South Boston
16. Waynesboro
17. Staunton
18. Harrisonburg
19. Charlottesville
20. Winchester
21. Emporia
22. Franklin
23. Petersburg
24. Colonial Heights
25. Hopewell
26. Richmond
27. Fredericksburg
28. Manassas
29. Manassas Park
30. Winchester
31. Falls Church
32. Alexandria
33. Williamsburg
34. Newport News
35. Suffolk
36. Portsmouth
37. Chesapeake
38. Virginia Beach
39. Norfolk
40. Hampton
41. Poquoson

Bedford — County name
● County seat
2 Independent cities
✪ State capital
— County boundary

0   50 mi
0   50 km

©MAPS.com

Virginia

VIRGINIA STATE INFORMATION

www.virginia.gov   **Ph:** 804-786-0000

Area (sq mi): 42774.2 (land 39,594.07; water 3180.13). **Pop per sq mi:** 191.1.

Pop 2005: 7,567,465. **Pop change:** 2000-20005 +6.9%; 1990-2000 +14.4%. **Pop 2000:** 7,078,515 (White 70.2%; Black or African American 19.6%; Hispanic or Latino 4.7%; Asian 3.7%; Other 4.4%). **Foreign born:** 8.1%. **Median age:** 35.7.

Income 2000: per capita $23,975; median household $46,677; **Pop below poverty level:** 9.6%. *Personal per capita income 2000-2003: $31,087-$33,730.

Unemployment 2004: 3.7%. **Change from 2000:** +1.4%. **Median travel time to work:** 27 minutes. **Working outside county of residence:** 51.8%.

ACCOMACK COUNTY

PO Box 388   **Ph:** 757-787-5700
Accomac, VA 23301   **Fax:** 757-787-2468
www.co.accomack.va.us

On the southern Delmarva peninsula, off the east coast of VA; organized 1663 from Northampton County. **Name Origin:** For a subtribe of the Powhatans; name is said to mean 'across the water,' since they lived across Chesapeake Bay from their kinsmen. The county retains the spelling closer to the Indian word *accawmacke*.

Area (sq mi): 1310.05 (land 455.24; water 854.8). **Pop per sq mi:** 86.6.

Pop 2005: 39,424. **State rank:** 42. **Pop change:** 2000-20005 +2.9%; 1990-2000 +20.8%. **Pop 2000:** 38,305 (White 61.9%; Black or African American 31.6%; Hispanic or Latino 5.4%; Asian 0.2%; Other 4.9%). **Foreign born:** 4.2%. **Median age:** 39.4.

Income 2000: per capita $16,309; median household $30,250; **Pop below poverty level:** 18%. *Personal per capita income 2000-2003: $18,314-$20,776.

Unemployment 2004: 4.3%. **Change from 2000:** +0%. **Median travel time to work:** 23 minutes. **Working outside county of residence:** 21.1%.

Cities with pop over 10,000: None.

ALBEMARLE COUNTY

401 McIntire Rd   **Ph:** 434-296-5841
Charlottesville, VA 22902   **Fax:** 434-296-5800
www.albemarle.org

In central VA, northeast of Lynchburg; organized May 6, 1744 from Goochland County. **Name Origin:** For William Anne Keppel (1702-54), 2nd Earl of Albemarle, absentee governor of the colony of VA (1737-54).

Area (sq mi): 726.18 (land 722.61; water 3.58). **Pop per sq mi:** 125.5.

Pop 2005: 90,717. **State rank:** 19. **Pop change:** 2000-20005 +14.5%; 1990-2000 +16.5%. **Pop 2000:** 79,236 (White 83.6%; Black or African American 9.7%; Hispanic or Latino 2.6%; Asian 2.9%; Other 2.4%). **Foreign born:** 7.3%. **Median age:** 37.4.

Income 2000: per capita $28,852; median household $50,749; **Pop below poverty level:** 6.7%. *Personal per capita income 2000-2003: $33,393-$35,303 (includes Albemarle County & Charlottesville).

Unemployment 2004: 2.5%. **Change from 2000:** +0.7%. **Median travel time to work:** 22.3 minutes. **Working outside county of residence:** 45.2%.

Cities with pop over 10,000: Charlottesville 🏛 (36,605).

ALEXANDRIA (INDEPENDENT CITY)

301 King St Suite 2300   **Ph:** 703-838-4500
Alexandria, VA 22314   **Fax:** 703-838-6433
ci.alexandria.va.us

On the Potomac River, immediately south of Washington, D.C. Established 1749; incorporated as a town in 1779; as a city in 1852. **Name Origin:** For colonial settler John Alexander, who came to the area in 1669. Formerly known as Hunting Creek Warehouse and Belhaven.

Area (sq mi): 15.41 (land 15.18; water 0.23). **Pop per sq mi:** 8915.5.

Pop 2005: 135,337. **State rank:** 13. **Pop change:** 2000-20005 +5.5%; 1990-2000 +15.4%. **Pop 2000:** 128,283 (White 53.7%; Black or African American 22.5%; Hispanic or Latino 14.7%; Asian 5.7%; Other 12.1%). **Foreign born:** 25.4%. **Median age:** 34.4.

Income 2000: per capita $37,645; median household $56,054; **Pop below poverty level:** 8.9%. *Personal per capita income 2000-2003: $48,106-$55,690.

Unemployment 2004: 2.9%. **Change from 2000:** +0.1%. **Median travel time to work:** 29.7 minutes. **Working outside county of residence:** 74.8%.

Cities with pop over 10,000: Alexandria 🏛 (128,206).

ALLEGHANY COUNTY

9212 Winterberry Ave Suite C   **Ph:** 540-863-6600
Covington, VA 24426   **Fax:** 540-863-6606
www.co.alleghany.va.us

On the central western border of VA, north of Roanoke; organized

🏛 *County Seat*

729

Alleghany County (cont'd)

1822 from Bath and Botetourt counties, VA, and Monroe County (now WV). **Name Origin:** Probably for the Allegheny River, with a variant spelling.

Area (sq mi): 445.67 (land 444.63; water 1.04). **Pop per sq mi:** 37.6.

Pop 2005: 16,715. **State rank:** 88. **Pop change:** 2000-20005 +29.3%; 1990-2000 -1.9%. **Pop 2000:** 12,926 (White 96.1%; Black or African American 2.5%; Hispanic or Latino 0.4%; Asian 0.2%; Other 0.9%). **Foreign born:** 0.9%. **Median age:** 41.1.

Income 2000: per capita $19,635; median household $38,545; **Pop below poverty level:** 7.1%. ***Personal per capita income 2000-2003:** $22,387-$23,950 (includes Alleghany County & Covington).

Unemployment 2004: 4.7%. **Change from 2000:** +0.9%. **Median travel time to work:** 24.6 minutes. **Working outside county of residence:** 42.8%.

Cities with pop over 10,000: None.

AMELIA COUNTY
PO Box A   **Ph:** 804-561-3039
Amelia Court House, VA 23002   **Fax:** 804-561-6039
www.ameliacova.us

In south-central VA, southwest of Richmond; organized Feb 1, 1734 from Brunswick and Prince George counties. **Name Origin:** For Amelia Sophia (1711-86), second daughter of George II (1683-1760) of England.

Area (sq mi): 358.54 (land 356.8; water 1.74). **Pop per sq mi:** 34.4.

Pop 2005: 12,273. **State rank:** 106. **Pop change:** 2000-20005 +7.7%; 1990-2000 +29.7%. **Pop 2000:** 11,400 (White 70.2%; Black or African American 28.1%; Hispanic or Latino 0.8%; Asian 0.2%; Other 1.2%). **Foreign born:** 0.7%. **Median age:** 38.5.

Income 2000: per capita $18,858; median household $40,252; **Pop below poverty level:** 8.4%. ***Personal per capita income 2000-2003:** $23,048-$25,330.

Unemployment 2004: 3.5%. **Change from 2000:** +0.7%. **Median travel time to work:** 41.5 minutes. **Working outside county of residence:** 66.5%.

Cities with pop over 10,000: None.

AMHERST COUNTY
153 Washington St   **Ph:** 434-946-9400
Amherst, VA 24521   **Fax:** 434-946-9370
www.countyofamherst.com

In west-central VA, north of Lynchburg; organized 1761 from Albemarle County. **Name Origin:** For Lord Jeffery Amherst (1717-97), commander of British forces in North America during the French and Indian Wars.

Area (sq mi): 478.78 (land 475.18; water 3.6). **Pop per sq mi:** 67.6.

Pop 2005: 32,134. **State rank:** 54. **Pop change:** 2000-20005 +0.8%; 1990-2000 +11.6%. **Pop 2000:** 31,894 (White 77.3%; Black or African American 19.8%; Hispanic or Latino 1%; Asian 0.4%; Other 2.1%). **Foreign born:** 1.2%. **Median age:** 38.

Income 2000: per capita $16,952; median household $37,393; **Pop below poverty level:** 10.7%. ***Personal per capita income 2000-2003:** $20,957-$22,055.

Unemployment 2004: 4.4%. **Change from 2000:** +0.6%. **Median travel time to work:** 23.6 minutes. **Working outside county of residence:** 53.7%.

Cities with pop over 10,000: None.

APPOMATTOX COUNTY
297 Court St   **Ph:** 434-352-5275
Appomattox, VA 24522   **Fax:** 434-352-2781
www.appomattox.com

In south-central VA, east of Lynchburg; organized 1845 from Buckingham, Campbell, Charlotte, and Prince Edward counties. **Name Origin:** For the Appomattox River, which runs through the county; origin of name is obscure: 'tobacco plant country' and 'curving tidal estuary' have been suggested. Apumetec is mentioned as an Indian queen in John Smith's (c.1580-1631) *The Generall Historie of Virginia, New-England, & the Summer Isles* (1624).

Area (sq mi): 334.73 (land 333.69; water 1.05). **Pop per sq mi:** 41.9.

Pop 2005: 13,967. **State rank:** 100. **Pop change:** 2000-20005 +1.9%; 1990-2000 +11.4%. **Pop 2000:** 13,705 (White 75.7%; Black or African American 22.9%; Hispanic or Latino 0.5%; Asian 0.2%; Other 1%). **Foreign born:** 1.4%. **Median age:** 39.1.

Income 2000: per capita $18,086; median household $36,507; **Pop below poverty level:** 11.4%. ***Personal per capita income 2000-2003:** $23,502-$24,059.

Unemployment 2004: 4.4%. **Change from 2000:** -2.3%. **Median travel time to work:** 29 minutes. **Working outside county of residence:** 57.9%.

Cities with pop over 10,000: None.

ARLINGTON COUNTY
2100 Clarendon Blvd Suite 300   **Ph:** 703-228-3130
Arlington, VA 22201   **Fax:** 703-228-7430
www.co.arlington.va.us

On the northeastern border of VA, west of Washington, D.C. Established 1801 as Alexandria County of the Dist. of Columbia; in 1846 county was returned to VA; renamed March 16, 1920. Arlington functions politically as a county in VA. **Name Origin:** For the home of George Washington Parke Custis (1781-1857), grandson of Martha Washington (1732-1802), named for the 1st Earl of Arlington, Henry Bennet (1618-85) who shared Charles II's (1630-85) grant of the colony of VA. It was later the home of Gen. Robert E. Lee (1807-70).

Area (sq mi): 25.96 (land 25.87; water 0.09). **Pop per sq mi:** 7575.

Pop 2005: 195,965. **State rank:** 9. **Pop change:** 2000-20005 +3.4%; 1990-2000 +10.8%. **Pop 2000:** 189,453 (White 60.4%; Black or African American 9.3%; Hispanic or Latino 18.6%; Asian 8.6%; Other 13%). **Foreign born:** 27.8%. **Median age:** 34.

Income 2000: per capita $37,706; median household $63,001; **Pop below poverty level:** 7.8%. ***Personal per capita income 2000-2003:** $49,555-$56,888.

Unemployment 2004: 2.6%. **Change from 2000:** +0.3%. **Median travel time to work:** 27.3 minutes. **Working outside county of residence:** 70.4%.

Cities with pop over 10,000: Arlington 🏛 (186,117).

---

*Source: Personal per capita income data are from the Bureau of Economic Analysis; per capita income data are from the Bureau of the Census. See Introduction for explanation of differences.

AUGUSTA COUNTY

18 Government Center Ln   **Ph:** 540-245-5600
Verona, VA 24482   **Fax:** 540-245-5621
www.co.augusta.va.us

On the northwestern border of VA, west of Charlottesville; organized Aug 1, 1738 from Orange County. Part annexed to Waynesboro (independent) city effective July 1, 1994. **Name Origin:** For Princess Augusta of Saxe-Gotha (1719?-72), mother of George III of England.

Area (sq mi): 970.93 (land 970.36; water 0.57). **Pop per sq mi:** 71.9.

Pop 2005: 69,725. **State rank:** 24. **Pop change:** 2000-20005 +6.3%; 1990-2000 +20%. **Pop 2000:** 65,615 (White 94.4%; Black or African American 3.6%; Hispanic or Latino 0.9%; Asian 0.3%; Other 1.1%). **Foreign born:** 1.4%. **Median age:** 39.

Income 2000: per capita $19,744; median household $43,045; **Pop below poverty level:** 5.8%. ***Personal per capita income 2000-2003:** $24,053-$25,847 (includes Augusta County, Staunton & Waynesboro).

Unemployment 2004: 2.9%. **Change from 2000:** +0.1%. **Median travel time to work:** 23.7 minutes. **Working outside county of residence:** 50.5%.

Cities with pop over 10,000: None.

BATH COUNTY

PO Box 309   **Ph:** 540-839-7221
Warm Springs, VA 24484   **Fax:** 540-839-7222
www.bathcountyva.org

On the central western border of VA, west of Charlottesville; organized Dec 14, 1790 from Augusta and Botetourt counties, VA, and Greenbrier County (now WV). **Name Origin:** For the city in England, which was also famed for its hot springs.

Area (sq mi): 534.56 (land 531.86; water 2.7). **Pop per sq mi:** 9.3.

Pop 2005: 4,937. **State rank:** 132. **Pop change:** 2000-20005 -2.2%; 1990-2000 +5.2%. **Pop 2000:** 5,048 (White 92%; Black or African American 6.3%; Hispanic or Latino 0.4%; Asian 0.4%; Other 1.1%). **Foreign born:** 4.3%. **Median age:** 41.8.

Income 2000: per capita $23,092; median household $35,013; **Pop below poverty level:** 7.8%. ***Personal per capita income 2000-2003:** $25,799-$28,193.

Unemployment 2004: 3.5%. **Change from 2000:** -1.1%. **Median travel time to work:** 24.4 minutes. **Working outside county of residence:** 28.6%.

Cities with pop over 10,000: None.

BEDFORD COUNTY

122 E Main St Suite 202   **Ph:** 540-586-7601
Bedford, VA 24523   **Fax:** 540-586-0406
www.co.bedford.va.us

In west-central VA, west of Lynchburg; organized 1753 from Albemarle and Lunenburg counties. Part annexed to Bedford (independent) city effective July 1, 1993. **Name Origin:** For John Russell (1710-71), 4th Duke of Bedford, British statesman who negotiated the treaty that ended the French and Indian Wars.

Area (sq mi): 769.25 (land 754.5; water 14.75). **Pop per sq mi:** 86.5.

Pop 2005: 65,286. **State rank:** 27. **Pop change:** 2000-20005 +8.1%; 1990-2000 +32.2%. **Pop 2000:** 60,371 (White 91.7%; Black or African American 6.2%; Hispanic or Latino 0.7%; Asian 0.4%; Other 1.1%). **Foreign born:** 1.8%. **Median age:** 39.7.

Income 2000: per capita $21,582; median household $43,136; **Pop below poverty level:** 7.1%. ***Personal per capita income 2000-2003:** $27,904-$30,051 (includes Bedford County & Bedford City).

Unemployment 2004: 3.6%. **Change from 2000:** +0.1%. **Median travel time to work:** 27.8 minutes. **Working outside county of residence:** 77.5%.

Cities with pop over 10,000: None.

BEDFORD (INDEPENDENT CITY)

215 E Main St   **Ph:** 540-587-6001
Bedford, VA 24523   **Fax:** 540-586-7134
www.ci.bedford.va.us

In south-central VA, between Roanoke and Lynchburg. Serves as county seat for Bedford County. Annexed part of Bedford County effective July 1, 1993. **Name Origin:** Incorporated as the town of Liberty in 1839; name changed to Bedford City in 1890 for John Russell (1710-71), the fourth Duke of Bedford; shortened to Bedford in 1912. Incorporated as a city in 1969.

Area (sq mi): 6.9 (land 6.89; water 0.01). **Pop per sq mi:** 901.5.

Pop 2005: 6,211. **State rank:** 128. **Pop change:** 2000-20005 -1.4%; 1990-2000 +3.7%. **Pop 2000:** 6,299 (White 74.7%; Black or African American 22.4%; Hispanic or Latino 0.9%; Asian 0.6%; Other 1.7%). **Foreign born:** 1.6%. **Median age:** 40.9.

Income 2000: per capita $15,423; median household $28,792; **Pop below poverty level:** 19.7%. ***Personal per capita income 2000-2003:** $27,904-$30,051 (includes Bedford County & Bedford City).

Unemployment 2004: 4.6%. **Change from 2000:** +1.1%. **Median travel time to work:** 20 minutes. **Working outside county of residence:** 44.4%.

Cities with pop over 10,000: None.

BLAND COUNTY

PO Box 295   **Ph:** 276-688-4562
Bland, VA 24315   **Fax:** 276-688-2438
www.bland.org

On the southwestern border of VA, west of Roanoke; organized Mar 30, 1861 from Giles, Tazewell, and Wythe counties. **Name Origin:** For Richard Bland (1710-76), member of the VA House of Burgesses (1745-75) and the Continental Congress (1774-75).

Area (sq mi): 358.73 (land 358.67; water 0.06). **Pop per sq mi:** 19.4.

Pop 2005: 6,943. **State rank:** 123. **Pop change:** 2000-20005 +1%; 1990-2000 +5.5%. **Pop 2000:** 6,871 (White 94.5%; Black or African American 4.2%; Hispanic or Latino 0.5%; Asian 0.1%; Other 0.9%). **Foreign born:** 0.8%. **Median age:** 40.3.

Income 2000: per capita $17,744; median household $30,397; **Pop below poverty level:** 12.4%. ***Personal per capita income 2000-2003:** $17,721-$19,687.

Unemployment 2004: 4.3%. **Change from 2000:** -1.6%. **Median travel time to work:** 33.4 minutes. **Working outside county of residence:** 54.7%.

Cities with pop over 10,000: None.

🏛 County Seat

BOTETOURT COUNTY

1 W Main St 1st Fl   **Ph:** 540-473-8220
Fincastle, VA 24090
www.co.botetourt.va.us

In west-central VA, north of Roanoke; organized Nov 7, 1769 from Augusta County. **Name Origin:** For Norborne Berkeley, Baron de Botetourt, the penultimate English governor of VA (1769-70).

Area (sq mi): 545.94 (land 542.66; water 3.28). **Pop per sq mi:** 59.

Pop 2005: 32,027. **State rank:** 55. **Pop change:** 2000-20005 +5%; 1990-2000 +22%. **Pop 2000:** 30,496 (White 94.5%; Black or African American 3.5%; Hispanic or Latino 0.6%; Asian 0.5%; Other 1.1%). **Foreign born:** 0.9%. **Median age:** 40.7.

Income 2000: per capita $22,218; median household $48,731; **Pop below poverty level:** 5.2%. ***Personal per capita income 2000-2003:** $28,840-$29,593.

Unemployment 2004: 3.1%. **Change from 2000:** +0.7%. **Median travel time to work:** 26.7 minutes. **Working outside county of residence:** 65.4%.

Cities with pop over 10,000: None.

BRISTOL (INDEPENDENT CITY)

497 Cumberland St Rm 210   **Ph:** 276-645-7321
Bristol, VA 24201   **Fax:** 276-821-6097
www.bristolva.org

In southwestern VA on the Tennessee border. **Name Origin:** Established in 1850 as Goodson, for Samuel Goodson, the founder; incorporated as a town in 1856. Incorporated as a city and renamed Bristol in 1890 for the contiguous town in TN of the same name.

Area (sq mi): 13.16 (land 12.9; water 0.27). **Pop per sq mi:** 1343.8.

Pop 2005: 17,335. **State rank:** 85. **Pop change:** 2000-20005 -0.2%; 1990-2000 -5.7%. **Pop 2000:** 17,367 (White 91.9%; Black or African American 5.6%; Hispanic or Latino 1%; Asian 0.4%; Other 1.5%). **Foreign born:** 1.4%. **Median age:** 41.3.

Income 2000: per capita $17,311; median household $27,389; **Pop below poverty level:** 16.2%. ***Personal per capita income 2000-2003:** $23,044-$25,307 (includes Washington County & Bristol).

Unemployment 2004: 6.1%. **Change from 2000:** +2.1%. **Median travel time to work:** 18 minutes. **Working outside county of residence:** 53.6%.

Cities with pop over 10,000: Bristol 🏛 (17,308).

BRUNSWICK COUNTY

216 N Main St   **Ph:** 434-848-2215
Lawrenceville, VA 23868   **Fax:** 434-848-4307
www.tourbrunswick.org

On the central southern border of VA, southwest of Richmond; organized Nov 2, 1720 from Prince George, Isle of Wight, and Surry counties (prior to statehood). **Name Origin:** For the Royal House of Brunswick, one of the titles of the British royal house of Hanover (the latter was changed to Windsor during World War I to sound less German).

Area (sq mi): 569.37 (land 566.14; water 3.23). **Pop per sq mi:** 31.7.

Pop 2005: 17,920. **State rank:** 81. **Pop change:** 2000-20005 -2.7%; 1990-2000 +15.2%. **Pop 2000:** 18,419 (White 41.4%; Black or

African American 56.9%; Hispanic or Latino 1.3%; Asian 0.2%; Other 0.9%). **Foreign born:** 0.7%. **Median age:** 38.1.

Income 2000: per capita $14,890; median household $31,288; **Pop below poverty level:** 16.5%. ***Personal per capita income 2000-2003:** $17,328-$18,802.

Unemployment 2004: 7.2%. **Change from 2000:** +1.9%. **Median travel time to work:** 30.8 minutes. **Working outside county of residence:** 50.2%.

Cities with pop over 10,000: None.

BUCHANAN COUNTY

PO Box 950   **Ph:** 276-935-6500
Grundy, VA 24614   **Fax:** 276-935-4479

On the southwestern border of VA, north of Bristol, TN; organized Feb 13, 1858 from Tazewell and Russell counties. **Name Origin:** For James Buchanan (1791-1868), fifteenth U.S. president.

Area (sq mi): 503.88 (land 503.88; water 0). **Pop per sq mi:** 49.1.

Pop 2005: 24,755. **State rank:** 65. **Pop change:** 2000-20005 -8.2%; 1990-2000 -13.9%. **Pop 2000:** 26,978 (White 96.4%; Black or African American 2.6%; Hispanic or Latino 0.5%; Asian 0.1%; Other 0.5%). **Foreign born:** 0.3%. **Median age:** 38.8.

Income 2000: per capita $12,788; median household $22,213; **Pop below poverty level:** 23.2%. ***Personal per capita income 2000-2003:** $19,475-$21,612.

Unemployment 2004: 6.1%. **Change from 2000:** -1.6%. **Median travel time to work:** 33.4 minutes. **Working outside county of residence:** 28.5%.

Cities with pop over 10,000: None.

BUCKINGHAM COUNTY

PO Box 252   **Ph:** 434-969-4242
Buckingham, VA 23921   **Fax:** 434-969-1638

In south-central VA, east of Lynchburg; organized 1761 from Albemarle County. **Name Origin:** Either for the town in Buckinghamshire, England, or the dukedom held by George Villiers and his son, George.

Area (sq mi): 583.56 (land 580.86; water 2.7). **Pop per sq mi:** 27.6.

Pop 2005: 16,058. **State rank:** 92. **Pop change:** 2000-20005 +2.8%; 1990-2000 +21.4%. **Pop 2000:** 15,623 (White 58.8%; Black or African American 39.1%; Hispanic or Latino 0.8%; Asian 0.2%; Other 1.7%). **Foreign born:** 0.8%. **Median age:** 38.2.

Income 2000: per capita $13,669; median household $29,882; **Pop below poverty level:** 20%. ***Personal per capita income 2000-2003:** $16,403-$18,060.

Unemployment 2004: 4.4%. **Change from 2000:** +1.8%. **Median travel time to work:** 38.8 minutes. **Working outside county of residence:** 55.5%.

Cities with pop over 10,000: None.

BUENA VISTA (INDEPENDENT CITY)

2039 Sycamore Ave   **Ph:** 540-261-8611
Buena Vista, VA 24416   **Fax:** 540-261-8727
www.buenavistavirginia.org

In south-central VA, north of Lynchburg. Established 1889; incorporated as a town in 1890, and as a city in 1892. **Name Origin:**

**Source: Personal per capita income data are from the Bureau of Economic Analysis; per capita income data are from the Bureau of the Census.
See Introduction for explanation of differences.*

732

Buena Vista (Independent City) (cont'd)

The town was built on the site of an abandoned iron furnace, dubbed Buena Vista, because it supplied cannonballs used in the Battle of Buena Vista in the Mexican-American War.

Area (sq mi): 6.83 (land 6.83; water 0). **Pop per sq mi:** 942.5.

Pop 2005: 6,437. **State rank:** 127. **Pop change:** 2000-20005 +1.4%; 1990-2000 -0.9%. **Pop 2000:** 6,349 (White 92.8%; Black or African American 4.8%; Hispanic or Latino 1%; Asian 0.4%; Other 1.2%). **Foreign born:** 0.5%. **Median age:** 37.9.

Income 2000: per capita $16,377; median household $32,410; **Pop below poverty level:** 10.4%. ***Personal per capita income 2000-2003:** $21,778-$23,612 (includes Rockbridge County, Buena Vista & Lexington).

Unemployment 2004: 3.7%. **Change from 2000:** +0.4%. **Median travel time to work:** 19.6 minutes. **Working outside county of residence:** 62.4%.

Cities with pop over 10,000: None.

CAMPBELL COUNTY

732 Village Hwy   **Ph:** 434-332-9517
Rustburg, VA 24588   **Fax:** 434-332-9518
www.co.campbell.va.us

In south-central VA, south of Lynchburg; organized Nov 5, 1781 from Bedford County. **Name Origin:** For Gen. William Campbell (1745-81), officer in the American Revolution.

Area (sq mi): 507.26 (land 504.48; water 2.78). **Pop per sq mi:** 103.7.

Pop 2005: 52,339. **State rank:** 33. **Pop change:** 2000-20005 +2.5%; 1990-2000 +7.4%. **Pop 2000:** 51,078 (White 82.8%; Black or African American 14.7%; Hispanic or Latino 0.8%; Asian 0.6%; Other 1.4%). **Foreign born:** 1.1%. **Median age:** 38.3.

Income 2000: per capita $18,134; median household $37,280; **Pop below poverty level:** 10.6%. ***Personal per capita income 2000-2003:** $23,783-$25,297 (includes Campbell County & Lynchburg).

Unemployment 2004: 4.2%. **Change from 2000:** -0.8%. **Median travel time to work:** 23.5 minutes. **Working outside county of residence:** 62.2%.

Cities with pop over 10,000: None.

CAROLINE COUNTY

PO Box 447   **Ph:** 804-633-5380
Bowling Green, VA 22427   **Fax:** 804-633-4970
www.co.caroline.va.us

In east-central VA, north of Richmond; organized Feb 1, 1727 from Essex, King and Queen, and King William counties. **Name Origin:** For Princess Wilhelmina Carolina of Anspach (1683-1737), wife of George II of England.

Area (sq mi): 538.89 (land 532.52; water 6.36). **Pop per sq mi:** 48.

Pop 2005: 25,563. **State rank:** 62. **Pop change:** 2000-20005 +15.6%; 1990-2000 +15.1%. **Pop 2000:** 22,121 (White 62%; Black or African American 34.4%; Hispanic or Latino 1.3%; Asian 0.4%; Other 2.7%). **Foreign born:** 1.7%. **Median age:** 37.7.

Income 2000: per capita $18,342; median household $39,845; **Pop below poverty level:** 9.4%. ***Personal per capita income 2000-2003:** $23,819-$25,539.

Unemployment 2004: 3.9%. **Change from 2000:** +0.8%. **Median travel time to work:** 37.7 minutes. **Working outside county of residence:** 67.6%.

Cities with pop over 10,000: None.

CARROLL COUNTY

605-1 Pine St PO Box 218   **Ph:** 276-730-3070
Hillsville, VA 24343   **Fax:** 276-730-3071
www.chillsnet.org

On the southwestern border of VA, southwest of Roanoke; organized Jan 17, 1842 from Grayson County. **Name Origin:** For Charles Carroll (1737-1832), signer of the Declaration of Independence, U.S. senator from MD (1789-92), and founder of the Baltimore and Ohio Railroad.

Area (sq mi): 477.64 (land 476.34; water 1.3). **Pop per sq mi:** 61.8.

Pop 2005: 29,438. **State rank:** 58. **Pop change:** 2000-20005 +0.7%; 1990-2000 +10%. **Pop 2000:** 29,245 (White 97.2%; Black or African American 0.4%; Hispanic or Latino 1.6%; Asian 0.1%; Other 1.4%). **Foreign born:** 0.9%. **Median age:** 40.7.

Income 2000: per capita $16,475; median household $30,597; **Pop below poverty level:** 12.5%. ***Personal per capita income 2000-2003:** $20,000-$21,476 (includes Carroll County & Galax).

Unemployment 2004: 4.8%. **Change from 2000:** -6.1%. **Median travel time to work:** 26.5 minutes. **Working outside county of residence:** 49.4%.

Cities with pop over 10,000: None.

CHARLES CITY COUNTY

PO Box 128   **Ph:** 804-829-9201
Charles City, VA 23030   **Fax:** 804-829-5819

In east-central VA, west of Williamsburg; original county; organized 1634. Birthplace of two U.S. presidents: William Henry Harrison (1773-1841) and John Tyler (1790-1862). **Name Origin:** For Charles I (1600-49), king of Great Britain.

Area (sq mi): 204.22 (land 182.76; water 21.46). **Pop per sq mi:** 39.

Pop 2005: 7,119. **State rank:** 121. **Pop change:** 2000-20005 +2.8%; 1990-2000 +10.3%. **Pop 2000:** 6,926 (White 35.4%; Black or African American 54.9%; Hispanic or Latino 0.6%; Asian 0.1%; Other 9.4%, including 7.8% American Indian/Alaska Native). **Foreign born:** 1.3%. **Median age:** 39.9.

Income 2000: per capita $19,182; median household $42,745; **Pop below poverty level:** 10.6%. ***Personal per capita income 2000-2003:** $23,360-$26,065.

Unemployment 2004: 4.9%. **Change from 2000:** -1.2%. **Median travel time to work:** 34.6 minutes. **Working outside county of residence:** 77.6%.

Cities with pop over 10,000: None.

CHARLOTTE COUNTY

125 David Bruce Ave   **Ph:** 434-542-5147
Charlotte Court House, VA 23923   **Fax:** 434-542-4336
www.co.charlotte.va.us

In south-central VA, southeast of Lynchburg; organized Mar 1, 1765 from Lunenburg County. **Name Origin:** For Charlotte Sophia, Princess of Mecklenburg-Strelitz (1744-1818) wife of George III (1738-1820) of England.

Area (sq mi): 477.44 (land 474.99; water 2.45). **Pop per sq mi:** 26.1.

Pop 2005: 12,404. **State rank:** 105. **Pop change:** 2000-20005 -0.5%; 1990-2000 +6.7%. **Pop 2000:** 12,472 (White 64.6%; Black or African American 32.9%; Hispanic or Latino 1.7%; Asian 0.2%; Other 1.4%). **Foreign born:** 0.8%. **Median age:** 40.

Income 2000: per capita $14,717; median household $28,929; **Pop below poverty level:** 18.1%. ***Personal per capita income 2000-2003:** $19,506-$20,792.

Unemployment 2004: 5.7%. **Change from 2000:** +1.5%. **Median travel time to work:** 31.3 minutes. **Working outside county of residence:** 52.1%.

Cities with pop over 10,000: None.

CHARLOTTESVILLE (INDEPENDENT CITY)

605 E Main St   **Ph:** 434-970-3101
Charlottesville, VA 22902   **Fax:** 434-970-3890
www.charlottesville.org

In central VA, 70 mi. northwest of Richmond. Established 1762; incorporated as a town in 1802; as a city in 1888. Site of University of VA. Serves as county seat for Albemarle County. **Name Origin:** For Princess Charlotte Sophia of Mecklenberg-Stelitz (1744-1818), wife of King George III (1738-1820) of Great Britian.

Area (sq mi): 10.26 (land 10.26; water 0). **Pop per sq mi:** 3941.2.

Pop 2005: 40,437. **State rank:** 41. **Pop change:** 2000-20005 -10.2%; 1990-2000 +11.7%. **Pop 2000:** 45,049 (White 68.4%; Black or African American 22.2%; Hispanic or Latino 2.4%; Asian 4.9%; Other 3.2%). **Foreign born:** 6.9%. **Median age:** 25.6.

Income 2000: per capita $16,973; median household $31,007; **Pop below poverty level:** 25.9%. ***Personal per capita income 2000-2003:** $33,393-$35,303 (includes Albemarle County & Charlottesville).

Unemployment 2004: 4.7%. **Change from 2000:** +2.1%. **Median travel time to work:** 16.6 minutes. **Working outside county of residence:** 44.7%.

Cities with pop over 10,000: None.

CHESAPEAKE (INDEPENDENT CITY)

306 Cedar Rd   **Ph:** 757-382-6151
Chesapeake, VA 23322   **Fax:** 757-382-6678
www.chesapeake.va.us

In southeastern VA, southeast of Norfolk. Formed in 1963 by merger of Norfolk County and the former city of South Norfolk, both of which then became extinct. **Name Origin:** For Chesapeake Bay.

Area (sq mi): 350.9 (land 340.72; water 10.18). **Pop per sq mi:** 642.7.

Pop 2005: 218,968. **State rank:** 8. **Pop change:** 2000-20005 +9.9%; 1990-2000 +31.1%. **Pop 2000:** 199,184 (White 65.9%; Black or African American 28.5%; Hispanic or Latino 2%; Asian 1.8%; Other 2.8%). **Foreign born:** 3%. **Median age:** 34.7.

Income 2000: per capita $20,949; median household $50,743; **Pop below poverty level:** 7.3%. ***Personal per capita income 2000-2003:** $26,849-$30,401.

Unemployment 2004: 3.7%. **Change from 2000:** +0.8%. **Median travel time to work:** 25.1 minutes. **Working outside county of residence:** 60.1%.

Cities with pop over 10,000: Chesapeake 🏛 (214,725).

CHESTERFIELD COUNTY

PO Box 70   **Ph:** 804-748-1201
Chesterfield, VA 23832   **Fax:** 804-751-4993
www.co.chesterfield.va.us

In east-central VA, south of Richmond; organized May 1, 1749 from Henrico County. **Name Origin:** For Philip Dormer Stanhope (1694-1773), 4th Earl of Chesterfield, English statesman and writer.

Area (sq mi): 436.99 (land 425.75; water 11.23). **Pop per sq mi:** 678.5.

Pop 2005: 288,876. **State rank:** 4. **Pop change:** 2000-20005 +11.1%; 1990-2000 +24.2%. **Pop 2000:** 259,903 (White 75.4%; Black or African American 17.8%; Hispanic or Latino 2.9%; Asian 2.4%; Other 3%). **Foreign born:** 5.2%. **Median age:** 35.7.

Income 2000: per capita $25,286; median household $58,537; **Pop below poverty level:** 4.5%. ***Personal per capita income 2000-2003:** $32,221-$34,428.

Unemployment 2004: 3.2%. **Change from 2000:** +0.7%. **Median travel time to work:** 26.1 minutes. **Working outside county of residence:** 54.2%.

Cities with pop over 10,000: None.

CLARKE COUNTY

102 N Church St   **Ph:** 540-955-5100
Berryville, VA 22611   **Fax:** 540-955-4002
www.co.clarke.va.us

On northern border of VA, northwest of Arlington; organized Mar 8, 1836 from Frederick and Warren counties. **Name Origin:** Alternate spelling for George Rogers Clark (1752-1818), a general in the American Revolution and frontiersman in the Northwest Territory.

Area (sq mi): 178.19 (land 176.62; water 1.57). **Pop per sq mi:** 80.4.

Pop 2005: 14,205. **State rank:** 99. **Pop change:** 2000-20005 +12.3%; 1990-2000 +4.6%. **Pop 2000:** 12,652 (White 90.3%; Black or African American 6.7%; Hispanic or Latino 1.5%; Asian 0.5%; Other 1.7%). **Foreign born:** 2.5%. **Median age:** 40.6.

Income 2000: per capita $24,844; median household $51,601; **Pop below poverty level:** 6.6%. ***Personal per capita income 2000-2003:** $30,985-$30,962.

Unemployment 2004: 2.7%. **Change from 2000:** +0.9%. **Median travel time to work:** 32.4 minutes. **Working outside county of residence:** 63.6%.

Cities with pop over 10,000: None.

---

*Source: Personal per capita income data are from the Bureau of Economic Analysis; per capita income data are from the Bureau of the Census. See Introduction for explanation of differences.

COLONIAL HEIGHTS (INDEPENDENT CITY)

PO Box 3401
Colonial Heights, VA 23834
www.colonial-heights.com

Ph: 804-520-9265
Fax: 804-520-9207

In southeastern VA on the heights overlooking the Appomattox River. Established 1910; incorporated as a town in 1926; as a city in 1948. **Name Origin:** For the Marquis de Lafayette's (1757-1834) artillery, known as the Colonials, which he placed here to shell British positions in Petersburg during the American Revolution.

Area (sq mi): 7.79 (land 7.48; water 0.31). **Pop per sq mi:** 2348.5.

Pop 2005: 17,567. **State rank:** 83. **Pop change:** 2000-20005 +4%; 1990-2000 +5.2%. **Pop 2000:** 16,897 (White 88.3%; Black or African American 6.3%; Hispanic or Latino 1.6%; Asian 2.7%; Other 1.9%). **Foreign born:** 4.9%. **Median age:** 39.9.

Income 2000: per capita $23,659; median household $43,224; **Pop below poverty level:** 5.5%. ***Personal per capita income 2000-2003:** $24,506-$26,729 (includes Dinwiddie County, Colonial Heights & Petersburg).

Unemployment 2004: 3.9%. **Change from 2000:** +0.4%. **Median travel time to work:** 20.7 minutes. **Working outside county of residence:** 74.1%.

Cities with pop over 10,000: Colonial Heights 🏛 (17,511).

COVINGTON (INDEPENDENT CITY)

333 W Locust St
Covington, VA 24426
www.covington.va.us

Ph: 540-965-6300
Fax: 540-965-6303

In south-central VA, north of Roanoke. Established 1818; incorporated as a town in 1833, as a city in 1953. Serves as county seat for Alleghany County. **Name Origin:** For Peter Covington, an early settler.

Area (sq mi): 5.67 (land 5.67; water 0). **Pop per sq mi:** 1094.4.

Pop 2005: 6,205. **State rank:** 129. **Pop change:** 2000-20005 -1.6%; 1990-2000 -9.8%. **Pop 2000:** 6,303 (White 83.6%; Black or African American 13.1%; Hispanic or Latino 0.6%; Asian 0.7%; Other 2.1%). **Foreign born:** 2.3%. **Median age:** 40.5.

Income 2000: per capita $16,758; median household $30,325; **Pop below poverty level:** 12.9%. ***Personal per capita income 2000-2003:** $22,387-$23,950 (includes Alleghany County & Covington).

Unemployment 2004: 5.6%. **Change from 2000:** +0.2%. **Median travel time to work:** 19.2 minutes. **Working outside county of residence:** 77.2%.

Cities with pop over 10,000: None.

CRAIG COUNTY

303 Main St
New Castle, VA 24127
www.co.craig.va.us

Ph: 540-864-6141
Fax: 540-864-7471

On the central western border of VA, west of Roanoke; organized Mar 21, 1851 from Botetourt, Roanoke, Giles, and Monroe counties. **Name Origin:** For Robert Craig (1792-1852), U.S. representative from VA (1829-33; 1835-41).

Area (sq mi): 330.61 (land 330.61; water 0). **Pop per sq mi:** 15.6.

Pop 2005: 5,154. **State rank:** 131. **Pop change:** 2000-20005 +1.2%; 1990-2000 +16.4%. **Pop 2000:** 5,091 (White 98.7%; Black or African American 0.2%; Hispanic or Latino 0.3%; Asian 0.2%; Other 0.7%). **Foreign born:** 0.3%. **Median age:** 39.6.

Income 2000: per capita $17,322; median household $37,314; **Pop below poverty level:** 10.3%. ***Personal per capita income 2000-2003:** $21,737-$23,428.

Unemployment 2004: 3.8%. **Change from 2000:** +0.5%. **Median travel time to work:** 34.7 minutes. **Working outside county of residence:** 76.2%.

Cities with pop over 10,000: None.

CULPEPER COUNTY

302 N Main St
Culpeper, VA 22701
www.culpepercounty.gov

Ph: 540-727-3427
Fax: 540-727-3460

In north-central VA, northeast of Charlottesville; organized Mar 23, 1748 from Orange County. **Name Origin:** For Sir Thomas Culpeper (1635-89), colonial governor of VA. Also spelled Culpepper or Colepeper.

Area (sq mi): 382.28 (land 381; water 1.27). **Pop per sq mi:** 111.6.

Pop 2005: 42,530. **State rank:** 38. **Pop change:** 2000-20005 +24.1%; 1990-2000 +23.3%. **Pop 2000:** 34,262 (White 77.1%; Black or African American 18.2%; Hispanic or Latino 2.5%; Asian 0.7%; Other 2.8%). **Foreign born:** 3.5%. **Median age:** 36.5.

Income 2000: per capita $20,162; median household $45,290; **Pop below poverty level:** 9.2%. ***Personal per capita income 2000-2003:** $26,360-$27,864.

Unemployment 2004: 3.2%. **Change from 2000:** +1.1%. **Median travel time to work:** 37.9 minutes. **Working outside county of residence:** 46.1%.

Cities with pop over 10,000: Culpeper 🏛 (11,070).

CUMBERLAND COUNTY

1 Courthouse Cir
Cumberland, VA 23040
www.cumberlandcounty.virginia.gov

Ph: 804-492-4280
Fax: 804-492-3342

In south-central VA, west of Richmond; organized 1749 from Goochland County. **Name Origin:** For William Augustus, Duke of Cumberland (1721-65), British general and second son of George II (1683-1760) of England.

Area (sq mi): 299.73 (land 298.45; water 1.28). **Pop per sq mi:** 31.4.

Pop 2005: 9,378. **State rank:** 116. **Pop change:** 2000-20005 +4%; 1990-2000 +15.2%. **Pop 2000:** 9,017 (White 59.7%; Black or African American 37.4%; Hispanic or Latino 1.7%; Asian 0.4%; Other 1.9%). **Foreign born:** 1.3%. **Median age:** 38.4.

Income 2000: per capita $15,103; median household $31,816; **Pop below poverty level:** 15.1%. ***Personal per capita income 2000-2003:** $19,629-$20,847.

Unemployment 2004: 3.9%. **Change from 2000:** +1.6%. **Median travel time to work:** 36.9 minutes. **Working outside county of residence:** 70.6%.

Cities with pop over 10,000: None.

🏛 *County Seat*

735

DANVILLE (INDEPENDENT CITY)

401 Patton St   **Ph:** 434-799-5168
Danville, VA 24544   **Fax:** 434-799-6502
www.ci.danville.va.us

In southern VA on the Dan River, just north of the NC border. Established 1793; incorporated as a town in 1830; as a city in 1890. **Name Origin:** For its location on the Dan River.

Area (sq mi): 43.94 (land 43.06; water 0.88). **Pop per sq mi:** 1071.6.

Pop 2005: 46,143. **State rank:** 36. **Pop change:** 2000-20005 -4.7%; 1990-2000 -8.8%. **Pop 2000:** 48,411 (White 53.3%; Black or African American 44.1%; Hispanic or Latino 1.3%; Asian 0.6%; Other 1.5%). **Foreign born:** 1.4%. **Median age:** 40.5.

Income 2000: per capita $17,151; median household $26,900; **Pop below poverty level:** 20%. ***Personal per capita income 2000-2003:** $21,486-$23,310 (includes Pittsylvania County & Danville).

Unemployment 2004: 9.2%. **Change from 2000:** +0.6%. **Median travel time to work:** 18.7 minutes. **Working outside county of residence:** 24.1%.

Cities with pop over 10,000: Danville ⛪ (46,371).

DICKENSON COUNTY

PO Box 190   **Ph:** 276-926-1616
Clintwood, VA 24228   **Fax:** 276-926-6465
www.dickensonctyva.com

On the southwestern border of VA, north of Bristol, TN; organized Mar 3, 1880 from Buchanan, Russell, and Wise counties. **Name Origin:** For William J. Dickenson (1828-1907), lawyer and legislator.

Area (sq mi): 333.63 (land 331.71; water 1.91). **Pop per sq mi:** 49.

Pop 2005: 16,243. **State rank:** 90. **Pop change:** 2000-20005 -0.9%; 1990-2000 -7%. **Pop 2000:** 16,395 (White 98.6%; Black or African American 0.4%; Hispanic or Latino 0.4%; Asian 0.1%; Other 0.6%). **Foreign born:** 0.2%. **Median age:** 39.7.

Income 2000: per capita $12,822; median household $23,431; **Pop below poverty level:** 21.3%. ***Personal per capita income 2000-2003:** $17,231-$18,299.

Unemployment 2004: 6.2%. **Change from 2000:** -10.7%. **Median travel time to work:** 35.8 minutes. **Working outside county of residence:** 45.2%.

Cities with pop over 10,000: None.

DINWIDDIE COUNTY

PO Drawer 70   **Ph:** 804-469-4500
Dinwiddie, VA 23841   **Fax:** 804-469-4503
www.dinwiddieva.us

In southeastern VA, south of Richmond; organized Feb 27, 1752 from Prince George County. **Name Origin:** For Robert Dinwiddie (1693-1770), lieutenant governor of VA (1751-58).

Area (sq mi): 506.98 (land 503.67; water 3.31). **Pop per sq mi:** 50.4.

Pop 2005: 25,391. **State rank:** 63. **Pop change:** 2000-20005 +3.5%; 1990-2000 +17%. **Pop 2000:** 24,533 (White 64.1%; Black or African American 33.7%; Hispanic or Latino 1%; Asian 0.3%; Other 1.4%). **Foreign born:** 1.4%. **Median age:** 38.5.

Income 2000: per capita $19,122; median household $41,582; **Pop below poverty level:** 9.3%. ***Personal per capita income 2000-2003:** $24,506-$26,729 (includes Dinwiddie County, Colonial Heights & Petersburg).

Unemployment 2004: 3.8%. **Change from 2000:** +0.9%. **Median travel time to work:** 30.8 minutes. **Working outside county of residence:** 68.3%.

Cities with pop over 10,000: None.

EMPORIA (INDEPENDENT CITY)

201 S Main St   **Ph:** 434-634-3332
Emporia, VA 23847   **Fax:** 434-634-0003
www.ci.emporia.va.us

In southeastern VA, southwest of Norfolk. Incorporated in 1887 from the merger of Hicksford and Belfield. Charter revoked in 1888; reincorporated in 1892; became a city in 1967. Serves as county seat for Greensville County. **Name Origin:** Named in 1887 to indicate that it was to be a center of trade.

Area (sq mi): 6.97 (land 6.89; water 0.07). **Pop per sq mi:** 810.9.

Pop 2005: 5,587. **State rank:** 130. **Pop change:** 2000-20005 -1.4%; 1990-2000 +6.8%. **Pop 2000:** 5,665 (White 41.3%; Black or African American 56.2%; Hispanic or Latino 1.5%; Asian 0.5%; Other 0.9%). **Foreign born:** 3.2%. **Median age:** 38.8.

Income 2000: per capita $15,377; median household $30,333; **Pop below poverty level:** 16%. ***Personal per capita income 2000-2003:** $17,388-$18,312 (includes Greensville County & Emporia).

Unemployment 2004: 7.4%. **Change from 2000:** +3%. **Median travel time to work:** 19.6 minutes. **Working outside county of residence:** 55.6%.

Cities with pop over 10,000: None.

ESSEX COUNTY

PO Box 445   **Ph:** 804-443-3541
Tappahannock, VA 22560   **Fax:** 804-445-1216
www.essex-virginia.org

In east-central VA, on west bank of the Rappahannock River; organized Apr 16, 1692 from Old Rappahannock County, which was organized 1656 from Lancaster County and abolished in 1692. **Name Origin:** For the county of Essex, England.

Area (sq mi): 285.91 (land 257.77; water 28.14). **Pop per sq mi:** 40.7.

Pop 2005: 10,492. **State rank:** 115. **Pop change:** 2000-20005 +5%; 1990-2000 +15%. **Pop 2000:** 9,989 (White 57.7%; Black or African American 39%; Hispanic or Latino 0.7%; Asian 0.8%; Other 2.2%). **Foreign born:** 1.4%. **Median age:** 40.3.

Income 2000: per capita $17,994; median household $37,395; **Pop below poverty level:** 11.2%. ***Personal per capita income 2000-2003:** $22,334-$23,441.

Unemployment 2004: 4.2%. **Change from 2000:** -0.4%. **Median travel time to work:** 33.5 minutes. **Working outside county of residence:** 47.5%.

Cities with pop over 10,000: None.

---

*Source: Personal per capita income data are from the Bureau of Economic Analysis; per capita income data are from the Bureau of the Census. See Introduction for explanation of differences.

FAIRFAX COUNTY

12000 Government Ctr Pkwy   **Ph:** 703-324-2531
Fairfax, VA 22035   **Fax:** 703-324-3956
www.co.fairfax.va.us

On the northeastern border of VA, west of Washington, D.C.; organized May 6, 1742 from Prince William County. Parts annexed to Fairfax (independent) city effective December 31, 1991 and January 1, 1994. **Name Origin:** For Thomas, 6th Baron Fairfax of Cameron (1692-1780), inheritor of the 'Fairfax Proprietary,' vast estates in northern VA; the colonies' only resident peer.

Area (sq mi): 406.61 (land 395.04; water 11.57). **Pop per sq mi:** 2547.9.

Pop 2005: 1,006,529. **State rank:** 1. **Pop change:** 2000-20005 +3.8%; 1990-2000 +18.5%. **Pop 2000:** 969,749 (White 64.4%; Black or African American 8.6%; Hispanic or Latino 11%; Asian 13%; Other 8.6%). **Foreign born:** 24.5%. **Median age:** 35.9.

Income 2000: per capita $36,888; median household $81,050; **Pop below poverty level:** 4.5%. ***Personal per capita income 2000-2003:** $50,035-$53,984 (includes Fairfax County, Fairfax City & Falls Church).

Unemployment 2004: 2.7%. **Change from 2000:** +0.4%. **Median travel time to work:** 30.7 minutes. **Working outside county of residence:** 47.3%.

Cities with pop over 10,000: Fairfax ⚏ (22,062); Herndon (21,666); Vienna (14,850).

FAIRFAX (INDEPENDENT CITY)

10455 Armstrong St   **Ph:** 703-385-7936
Fairfax, VA 22030   **Fax:** 703-385-7811
www.co.fairfax.va.us

In northeastern VA, west of Washington, D.C. Incorporated as a town in 1874; as a city in 1961. Site of George Mason University. Serves as county seat for Fairfax County. Annexed parts of Fairfax County effective December 31, 1991 and January 1, 1994. **Name Origin:** Established in 1805 as Providence. After the former town of Fairfax (now Culpepper, in Culpepper County), named for Thomas, Lord Fairfax (1692-1780), one of the early great landowners, changed its name in 1859, Providence renamed itself Fairfax.

Area (sq mi): 6.31 (land 6.31; water 0). **Pop per sq mi:** 3480.7.

Pop 2005: 21,963. **State rank:** 73. **Pop change:** 2000-20005 +2.2%; 1990-2000 +9.6%. **Pop 2000:** 21,498 (White 66.7%; Black or African American 5.1%; Hispanic or Latino 13.6%; Asian 12.2%; Other 9.9%). **Foreign born:** 25.4%. **Median age:** 37.

Income 2000: per capita $31,247; median household $67,642; **Pop below poverty level:** 5.7%. ***Personal per capita income 2000-2003:** $50,035-$53,984 (includes Fairfax County, Fairfax City & Falls Church).

Unemployment 2004: 2.7%. **Change from 2000:** +2%. **Median travel time to work:** 30.1 minutes. **Working outside county of residence:** 77.1%.

Cities with pop over 10,000: None.

FALLS CHURCH (INDEPENDENT CITY)

300 Park Ave   **Ph:** 703-248-5001
Falls Church, VA 22046   **Fax:** 703-248-5146
www.ci.falls-church.va.us

In northeastern VA, west of Washington, D.C., near the Little Falls of the Potomac River. Established in 1850, incorporated as a town in 1875; as a city in 1948. **Name Origin:** For an Anglican church, so named for its location near the falls, built in the area about 1769.

Area (sq mi): 1.99 (land 1.99; water 0). **Pop per sq mi:** 5417.6.

Pop 2005: 10,781. **State rank:** 113. **Pop change:** 2000-20005 +3.9%; 1990-2000 +8.3%. **Pop 2000:** 10,377 (White 79.6%; Black or African American 3.3%; Hispanic or Latino 8.4%; Asian 6.5%; Other 5.2%). **Foreign born:** 16.1%. **Median age:** 39.7.

Income 2000: per capita $41,051; median household $74,924; **Pop below poverty level:** 4.2%. ***Personal per capita income 2000-2003:** $50,035-$53,984 (includes Fairfax County, Fairfax City & Falls Church).

Unemployment 2004: 3.2%. **Change from 2000:** +0.6%. **Median travel time to work:** 26.4 minutes. **Working outside county of residence:** 84.1%.

Cities with pop over 10,000: Falls Church ⚏ (10,781).

FAUQUIER COUNTY

10 Hotel St   **Ph:** 540-347-8680
Warrenton, VA 20186   **Fax:** 540-349-2331
www.fauquiercounty.gov

In north-central VA, west of Alexandria; organized May 1, 1759 from Prince William County. **Name Origin:** For Francis Fauquier (1704-68), lieutenant governor of the colony of VA (1758-68).

Area (sq mi): 651.42 (land 649.7; water 1.72). **Pop per sq mi:** 100.

Pop 2005: 64,997. **State rank:** 28. **Pop change:** 2000-20005 +17.9%; 1990-2000 +13.1%. **Pop 2000:** 55,139 (White 87.2%; Black or African American 8.8%; Hispanic or Latino 2%; Asian 0.6%; Other 2.2%). **Foreign born:** 3.6%. **Median age:** 37.8.

Income 2000: per capita $28,757; median household $61,999; **Pop below poverty level:** 5.4%. ***Personal per capita income 2000-2003:** $38,946-$41,207.

Unemployment 2004: 2.6%. **Change from 2000:** +0.9%. **Median travel time to work:** 36.8 minutes. **Working outside county of residence:** 58.1%.

Cities with pop over 10,000: None.

FLOYD COUNTY

120 W Oxford St   **Ph:** 540-745-9300
Floyd, VA 24091   **Fax:** 540-745-9305
www.fin.org

In southwestern VA, southwest of Roanoke; organized Jan 15, 1831 from Montgomery and Franklin counties. **Name Origin:** For Gen. John Floyd (1783-1837), U.S. representative (1817-29) and governor of VA (1830-34).

Area (sq mi): 381.23 (land 381.22; water 0.01). **Pop per sq mi:** 38.4.

Pop 2005: 14,649. **State rank:** 97. **Pop change:** 2000-20005 +5.6%; 1990-2000 +15.6%. **Pop 2000:** 13,874 (White 95.7%; Black or African American 2%; Hispanic or Latino 1.3%; Asian 0.1%; Other 1.2%). **Foreign born:** 1.5%. **Median age:** 40.5.

Floyd County (cont'd)

Income 2000: per capita $16,345; median household $31,585; **Pop below poverty level:** 11.7%. ***Personal per capita income 2000-2003:** $20,145-$21,375.

Unemployment 2004: 3.8%. **Change from 2000:** -0.7%. **Median travel time to work:** 33.6 minutes. **Working outside county of residence:** 57%.

Cities with pop over 10,000: None.

FLUVANNA COUNTY

132 Main St   **Ph:** 434-591-1910
Palmyra, VA 22963   **Fax:** 434-591-1911
www.co.fluvanna.va.us

In central VA, southeast of Charlottesville; organized May 5, 1777 from Albemarle County. **Name Origin:** For the name by which the upper James River was known until the Civil War; from Latin *fluvius* 'river,' and *anna* for Queen Anne (1665-1714) of England.

Area (sq mi): 290.21 (land 287.37; water 2.84). **Pop per sq mi:** 86.1.

Pop 2005: 24,751. **State rank:** 66. **Pop change:** 2000-20005 +23.5%; 1990-2000 +61.3%. **Pop 2000:** 20,047 (White 78.8%; Black or African American 18.4%; Hispanic or Latino 1.2%; Asian 0.4%; Other 1.7%). **Foreign born:** 2.3%. **Median age:** 38.3.

Income 2000: per capita $20,338; median household $46,372; **Pop below poverty level:** 5.9%. ***Personal per capita income 2000-2003:** $23,232-$24,515.

Unemployment 2004: 2.8%. **Change from 2000:** +0.7%. **Median travel time to work:** 32.5 minutes. **Working outside county of residence:** 72.1%.

Cities with pop over 10,000: None.

FRANKLIN COUNTY

40 E Court St   **Ph:** 540-483-3030
Rocky Mount, VA 24151   **Fax:** 540-483-3035
www.franklincountyva.org

In southwestern VA, south of Roanoke; organized Oct 17, 1785 from Bedford, Henry, and Patrick counties. **Name Origin:** For Benjamin Franklin (1706-90), U.S. patriot, diplomat, and statesman.

Area (sq mi): 711.56 (land 692.08; water 19.48). **Pop per sq mi:** 72.7.

Pop 2005: 50,345. **State rank:** 35. **Pop change:** 2000-20005 +6.5%; 1990-2000 +19.6%. **Pop 2000:** 47,286 (White 88.3%; Black or African American 9.3%; Hispanic or Latino 1.2%; Asian 0.4%; Other 1.3%). **Foreign born:** 1.4%. **Median age:** 39.7.

Income 2000: per capita $19,605; median household $38,056; **Pop below poverty level:** 9.7%. ***Personal per capita income 2000-2003:** $23,436-$25,249.

Unemployment 2004: 3.7%. **Change from 2000:** -1%. **Median travel time to work:** 29.1 minutes. **Working outside county of residence:** 41.3%.

Cities with pop over 10,000: None.

FRANKLIN (INDEPENDENT CITY)

120 Pretlow St   **Ph:** 757-562-8559
Franklin, VA 23851   **Fax:** 757-562-8561
www.ci.franklin.va.us

In southeastern VA, southwest of Norfolk. Incorporated as a town in 1876; as a city in 1961. Annexed part of Southampton County effective December 31, 1995. **Name Origin:** Origin unclear: possibly for patriot and statesman Benjamin Franklin (1707-90) or for a local storekeeper named Franklin. One story has it that the name originated from the exclamation of a railroad section foreman who, upon driving a spike while working here, said, 'This shall be Franklin!'

Area (sq mi): 8.4 (land 8.35; water 0.05). **Pop per sq mi:** 1029.2.

Pop 2005: 8,594. **State rank:** 119. **Pop change:** 2000-20005 +3%; 1990-2000 +6.1%. **Pop 2000:** 8,346 (White 45.5%; Black or African American 52.3%; Hispanic or Latino 0.6%; Asian 0.8%; Other 1.1%). **Foreign born:** 0.7%. **Median age:** 39.9.

Income 2000: per capita $18,573; median household $31,687; **Pop below poverty level:** 19.8%. ***Personal per capita income 2000-2003:** $23,046-$24,646 (includes Southampton County & Franklin).

Unemployment 2004: 5%. **Change from 2000:** +0.5%. **Median travel time to work:** 20.9 minutes. **Working outside county of residence:** 52.3%.

Cities with pop over 10,000: None.

FREDERICK COUNTY

107 N Kent St   **Ph:** 540-665-5600
Winchester, VA 22601   **Fax:** 540-667-0370
www.co.frederick.va.us

On the northern border of VA; organized Aug 1, 1738 from Orange County. **Name Origin:** For Frederick Louis (1707-51), Prince of Wales, son of George II (1683-1760) and father of George III (1738-1820) of England.

Area (sq mi): 415.62 (land 414.63; water 1). **Pop per sq mi:** 166.7.

Pop 2005: 69,123. **State rank:** 25. **Pop change:** 2000-20005 +16.7%; 1990-2000 +29.5%. **Pop 2000:** 59,209 (White 94%; Black or African American 2.6%; Hispanic or Latino 1.7%; Asian 0.7%; Other 1.8%). **Foreign born:** 2.4%. **Median age:** 36.7.

Income 2000: per capita $21,080; median household $46,941; **Pop below poverty level:** 6.4%. ***Personal per capita income 2000-2003:** $27,238-$28,791 (includes Frederick County & Winchester).

Unemployment 2004: 2.8%. **Change from 2000:** +0.2%. **Median travel time to work:** 27.3 minutes. **Working outside county of residence:** 58%.

Cities with pop over 10,000: None.

FREDERICKSBURG (INDEPENDENT CITY)

715 Princess Ann St   **Ph:** 540-372-1010
Fredericksburg, VA 22401   **Fax:** 540-372-1201
fredericksburgchamber.org

In northeastern VA on the Rappahannock River, 41 mi. southwest of Alexandria. Founded 1728; incorporated as a town in 1782; as a city in 1879. **Name Origin:** For Frederick Louis (1707-51), Prince of Wales, eldest son of King George II (1683-1760) of Great Britain.

---

*Source: Personal per capita income data are from the Bureau of Economic Analysis; per capita income data are from the Bureau of the Census. See Introduction for explanation of differences.

Fredericksburg (Independent City) (cont'd)

Area (sq mi): 10.52 (land 10.52; water 0). **Pop per sq mi:** 1970.7.

Pop 2005: 20,732. **State rank:** 76. **Pop change:** 2000-20005 +7.5%; 1990-2000 +1.3%. **Pop 2000:** 19,279 (White 71.4%; Black or African American 20.4%; Hispanic or Latino 4.9%; Asian 1.5%; Other 4.9%). **Foreign born:** 5.2%. **Median age:** 30.3.

Income 2000: per capita $21,527; median household $34,585; **Pop below poverty level:** 15.5%. ***Personal per capita income 2000-2003:** $28,359-$30,493 (includes Spotsylvania County & Fredericksburg).

Unemployment 2004: 4.9%. **Change from 2000:** +0.9%. **Median travel time to work:** 24.6 minutes. **Working outside county of residence:** 57.9%.

Cities with pop over 10,000: Fredericksburg ⛪ (20,458).

GALAX (INDEPENDENT CITY)

111 E Grayson St   **Ph:** 276-236-5773
Galax, VA 24333   **Fax:** 276-236-2889
www.ingalax.net

In southern VA, southwest of Roanoke. Incorporated as a town in 1906; as a city in 1954. **Name Origin:** For the mountain evergreen plant, which grows abundantly in the area. Originally called Bonaparte.

Area (sq mi): 8.23 (land 8.23; water 0). **Pop per sq mi:** 811.2.

Pop 2005: 6,676. **State rank:** 126. **Pop change:** 2000-20005 -2.4%; 1990-2000 +2.5%. **Pop 2000:** 6,837 (White 81.2%; Black or African American 6.3%; Hispanic or Latino 11.1%; Asian 0.7%; Other 7%). **Foreign born:** 8.6%. **Median age:** 39.8.

Income 2000: per capita $17,447; median household $28,236; **Pop below poverty level:** 18.6%. ***Personal per capita income 2000-2003:** $20,000-$21,476 (includes Carroll County & Galax).

Unemployment 2004: 5.5%. **Change from 2000:** -2.8%. **Median travel time to work:** 15.7 minutes. **Working outside county of residence:** 40.3%.

Cities with pop over 10,000: None.

GILES COUNTY

501 Wenonah Ave   **Ph:** 540-921-1722
Pearisburg, VA 24134   **Fax:** 540-921-3825
www.gilescounty.org

On the southwestern border of VA, west of Roanoke; organized Jan 16, 1806 from Montgomery and Tazewell counties, VA, and Monroe County (now WV). **Name Origin:** For William Branch Giles (1762-1830), U.S. senator from VA (1804-15) and governor (1827-30).

Area (sq mi): 360.4 (land 357.33; water 3.07). **Pop per sq mi:** 47.8.

Pop 2005: 17,098. **State rank:** 87. **Pop change:** 2000-20005 +2.6%; 1990-2000 +1.8%. **Pop 2000:** 16,657 (White 96.9%; Black or African American 1.6%; Hispanic or Latino 0.6%; Asian 0.2%; Other 0.8%). **Foreign born:** 0.8%. **Median age:** 40.2.

Income 2000: per capita $18,396; median household $34,927; **Pop below poverty level:** 9.5%. ***Personal per capita income 2000-2003:** $20,813-$21,926.

Unemployment 2004: 4.9%. **Change from 2000:** -2%. **Median travel time to work:** 28.2 minutes. **Working outside county of residence:** 46.3%.

Cities with pop over 10,000: None.

GLOUCESTER COUNTY

PO Box 329   **Ph:** 804-693-4042
Gloucester, VA 23061   **Fax:** 804-693-6004
www.co.gloucester.va.us

On the central eastern border of VA, on east bank of the York River; organized 1651 from York County. **Name Origin:** For Henry, Duke of Gloucester (1639-60), brother of Charles II (1630-85) and James II (1633-1701) of England.

Area (sq mi): 288 (land 216.61; water 71.39). **Pop per sq mi:** 174.4.

Pop 2005: 37,787. **State rank:** 44. **Pop change:** 2000-20005 +8.6%; 1990-2000 +15.4%. **Pop 2000:** 34,780 (White 85.7%; Black or African American 10.3%; Hispanic or Latino 1.6%; Asian 0.7%; Other 2.3%). **Foreign born:** 1.9%. **Median age:** 38.

Income 2000: per capita $19,990; median household $45,421; **Pop below poverty level:** 7.7%. ***Personal per capita income 2000-2003:** $34,463-$36,480.

Unemployment 2004: 3%. **Change from 2000:** +0.6%. **Median travel time to work:** 33.9 minutes. **Working outside county of residence:** 59.3%.

Cities with pop over 10,000: None.

GOOCHLAND COUNTY

1800 Sandy Hook Rd   **Ph:** 804-556-5800
Goochland, VA 23063   **Fax:** 804-556-4617
www.co.goochland.va.us

In central VA, northwest of Richmond; organized Feb 1, 1727 from Henrico County. **Name Origin:** For Sir William Gooch (1681-1751), governor of the colony of VA (1727-49).

Area (sq mi): 289.99 (land 284.43; water 5.56). **Pop per sq mi:** 68.1.

Pop 2005: 19,360. **State rank:** 79. **Pop change:** 2000-20005 +14.8%; 1990-2000 +19.1%. **Pop 2000:** 16,863 (White 72.3%; Black or African American 25.6%; Hispanic or Latino 0.9%; Asian 0.5%; Other 1.2%). **Foreign born:** 2%. **Median age:** 40.5.

Income 2000: per capita $29,105; median household $56,307; **Pop below poverty level:** 6.9%. ***Personal per capita income 2000-2003:** $40,589-$42,442.

Unemployment 2004: 3.3%. **Change from 2000:** +1.1%. **Median travel time to work:** 32.1 minutes. **Working outside county of residence:** 72%.

Cities with pop over 10,000: None.

GRAYSON COUNTY

129 Davis St PO Box 130   **Ph:** 276-773-2231
Independence, VA 24348   **Fax:** 276-773-3338
www.ls.net/~grayson/index.html

On the southwestern border of VA, east of Bristol, TN; organized Nov 7, 1792 from Wythe County. **Name Origin:** For Col. William Grayson (1736/40-90), an officer in the Revolutionary War, member of the Continental Congress (1785-87), and U.S. senator from VA (1789-90).

⛪ *County Seat*

Grayson County (cont'd)

Area (sq mi): 445.9 (land 442.64; water 3.26). **Pop per sq mi:** 37.

Pop 2005: 16,366. **State rank:** 89. **Pop change:** 2000-20005 -8.7%; 1990-2000 +10.1%. **Pop 2000:** 17,917 (White 90.9%; Black or African American 6.8%; Hispanic or Latino 1.5%; Asian 0.1%; Other 1.4%). **Foreign born:** 1.2%. **Median age:** 40.5.

Income 2000: per capita $16,768; median household $28,676; **Pop below poverty level:** 13.6%. *****Personal per capita income 2000-2003:** $18,768-$20,136.

Unemployment 2004: 4.9%. **Change from 2000:** -5.7%. **Median travel time to work:** 29 minutes. **Working outside county of residence:** 68.1%.

Cities with pop over 10,000: None.

GREENE COUNTY

22 Court St   **Ph:** 434-985-5208
Stanardsville, VA 22973   **Fax:** 434-985-6723
www.gcva.us

In north-central VA, north of Charlottesville; organized Jan 24, 1838 from Orange County. **Name Origin:** For Gen. Nathanael Greene (1742-86), hero of the Revolutionary War, quartermaster general (1778-80), and commander of the Army of the South (1780).

Area (sq mi): 156.96 (land 156.58; water 0.39). **Pop per sq mi:** 111.2.

Pop 2005: 17,418. **State rank:** 84. **Pop change:** 2000-20005 +14.3%; 1990-2000 +48%. **Pop 2000:** 15,244 (White 90.3%; Black or African American 6.4%; Hispanic or Latino 1.3%; Asian 0.4%; Other 2%). **Foreign born:** 1.6%. **Median age:** 35.5.

Income 2000: per capita $19,478; median household $45,931; **Pop below poverty level:** 6.6%. *****Personal per capita income 2000-2003:** $22,149-$24,495.

Unemployment 2004: 2.8%. **Change from 2000:** +0.8%. **Median travel time to work:** 28.6 minutes. **Working outside county of residence:** 72.7%.

Cities with pop over 10,000: None.

GREENSVILLE COUNTY

337 S Main St   **Ph:** 434-348-4215
Emporia, VA 23847   **Fax:** 434-348-4020
www.greensvillecountyva.gov

On the southeastern border of VA, south of Richmond; organized Oct 16, 1780 from Brunswick County. **Name Origin:** For either Gen. Nathanael Greene (1742-86) or Sir Richard Grenville (1542-91), leader of the Roanoke settlement.

Area (sq mi): 296.81 (land 295.44; water 1.37). **Pop per sq mi:** 37.5.

Pop 2005: 11,088. **State rank:** 112. **Pop change:** 2000-20005 -4.1%; 1990-2000 +30.6%. **Pop 2000:** 11,560 (White 38.6%; Black or African American 59.7%; Hispanic or Latino 0.9%; Asian 0.4%; Other 0.9%). **Foreign born:** 0.3%. **Median age:** 38.1.

Income 2000: per capita $14,632; median household $32,002; **Pop below poverty level:** 14.7%. *****Personal per capita income 2000-2003:** $17,388-$18,312 (includes Greensville County & Emporia).

Unemployment 2004: 6.9%. **Change from 2000:** +3.3%. **Median travel time to work:** 22.4 minutes. **Working outside county of residence:** 59.6%.

Cities with pop over 10,000: None.

HALIFAX COUNTY

134 S Main St   **Ph:** 434-476-3300
Halifax, VA 24558   **Fax:** 434-476-3384
www.halifax.com/county

On the central southern border of VA, southeast of Lynchburg; organized Feb 27, 1752 from Lunenburg County. Added the former independent city of South Boston effective June 30, 1995. **Name Origin:** For George Montagu Dunk (1716-71), 2nd Earl of Halifax, English statesman and a strong supporter of trade with the American colonies.

Area (sq mi): 829.56 (land 819.3; water 10.27). **Pop per sq mi:** 44.3.

Pop 2005: 36,284. **State rank:** 47. **Pop change:** 2000-20005 -2.9%; 1990-2000 +28.7%. **Pop 2000:** 37,355 (White 59.7%; Black or African American 38%; Hispanic or Latino 1.2%; Asian 0.2%; Other 1.4%). **Foreign born:** 1%. **Median age:** 40.7.

Income 2000: per capita $16,353; median household $29,929; **Pop below poverty level:** 15.7%. *****Personal per capita income 2000-2003:** $19,592-$20,644.

Unemployment 2004: 7.7%. **Change from 2000:** -1.6%. **Median travel time to work:** 25.1 minutes. **Working outside county of residence:** 22%.

Cities with pop over 10,000: None.

HAMPTON (INDEPENDENT CITY)

22 Lincoln St   **Ph:** 757-727-6000
Hampton, VA 23669
www.hampton.va.us

In southeastern VA, 7 mi. northeast of Newport News. Founded 1680; incorporated as a city in 1952. **Name Origin:** For Hampton Creek, earlier called the Southampton River, itself named for Henry Wriothesley (1573-1624), 3rd Earl of Southampton.

Area (sq mi): 136.23 (land 51.78; water 84.45). **Pop per sq mi:** 2811.5.

Pop 2005: 145,579. **State rank:** 12. **Pop change:** 2000-20005 -0.6%; 1990-2000 +9.5%. **Pop 2000:** 146,437 (White 48.5%; Black or African American 44.7%; Hispanic or Latino 2.8%; Asian 1.8%; Other 3.9%). **Foreign born:** 3.9%. **Median age:** 34.

Income 2000: per capita $19,774; median household $39,532; **Pop below poverty level:** 11.3%. *****Personal per capita income 2000-2003:** $23,945-$27,236.

Unemployment 2004: 4.9%. **Change from 2000:** +1.1%. **Median travel time to work:** 21.8 minutes. **Working outside county of residence:** 48.1%.

Cities with pop over 10,000: None.

HANOVER COUNTY

7516 County Complex Rd PO Box 470   **Ph:** 804-365-6000
Hanover, VA 23069   **Fax:** 804-365-6234
www.co.hanover.va.us

In east-central VA, north of Richmond; organized 1720 from New

---

Source: Personal per capita income data are from the Bureau of Economic Analysis; per capita income data are from the Bureau of the Census. See Introduction for explanation of differences.

Hanover County (cont'd)

Kent (prior to stateshood). **Name Origin:** For Hanover, the British royal house, which began with George I (1660-1727), the Duke of Hanover. The name was changed to Windsor during World War I to sound less German.

Area (sq mi): 474.08 (land 472.68; water 1.4). **Pop per sq mi:** 206.1.

Pop 2005: 97,426. **State rank:** 17. **Pop change:** 2000-20005 +12.9%; 1990-2000 +36.4%. **Pop 2000:** 86,320 (White 87.8%; Black or African American 9.3%; Hispanic or Latino 1%; Asian 0.8%; Other 1.5%). **Foreign born:** 1.8%. **Median age:** 37.4.

Income 2000: per capita $25,120; median household $59,223; **Pop below poverty level:** 3.6%. ***Personal per capita income 2000-2003:** $31,451-$33,980.

Unemployment 2004: 2.9%. **Change from 2000:** +0.5%. **Median travel time to work:** 25.4 minutes. **Working outside county of residence:** 64.7%.

Cities with pop over 10,000: None.

HARRISONBURG (INDEPENDENT CITY)

345 S Main St   **Ph:** 540-432-7701
Harrisonburg, VA 22801   **Fax:** 540-432-7778
www.ci.harrisonburg.va.us

In northern VA, 23 mi. northeast of Staunton. Founded in 1780; incorporated as a town in 1849; as a city in 1916. Serves as county seat for Rockingham County. **Name Origin:** For Thomas Harrison, who gave fifty acres for the town site.

Area (sq mi): 17.59 (land 17.56; water 0.03). **Pop per sq mi:** 2302.8.

Pop 2005: 40,438. **State rank:** 40. **Pop change:** 2000-20005 -0.1%; 1990-2000 +31.8%. **Pop 2000:** 40,468 (White 80.1%; Black or African American 5.9%; Hispanic or Latino 8.8%; Asian 3.1%; Other 6.1%). **Foreign born:** 9.2%. **Median age:** 22.6.

Income 2000: per capita $14,898; median household $29,949; **Pop below poverty level:** 30.1%. ***Personal per capita income 2000-2003:** $22,054-$24,240 (includes Rockingham County & Harrisonburg).

Unemployment 2004: 3.3%. **Change from 2000:** +1.3%. **Median travel time to work:** 14.8 minutes. **Working outside county of residence:** 29.9%.

Cities with pop over 10,000: Harrisonburg 🏛 (41,066).

HENRICO COUNTY

PO Box 27032   **Ph:** 804-501-4202
Richmond, VA 23273   **Fax:** 804-501-5214
www.co.henrico.va.us

In east-central VA, north of Petersburg; original county; organized 1634. **Name Origin:** For the lost town of Henricus (or Henrico), destroyed by Indians in the Massacre of 1622; itself named for Prince Henry Frederick (1594-1612), son of James I (1566-1625) of England. Originally called *Henricopolis* (the Greek suffix *-polis* 'city of Henry').

Area (sq mi): 244.6 (land 238.06; water 6.54). **Pop per sq mi:** 1178.6.

Pop 2005: 280,581. **State rank:** 5. **Pop change:** 2000-20005 +7%; 1990-2000 +20.4%. **Pop 2000:** 262,300 (White 67.9%; Black or African American 24.7%; Hispanic or Latino 2.3%; Asian 3.6%; Other 2.8%). **Foreign born:** 6.7%. **Median age:** 36.

Income 2000: per capita $26,410; median household $49,185; **Pop below poverty level:** 6.2%. ***Personal per capita income 2000-2003:** $35,143-$37,059.

Unemployment 2004: 3.4%. **Change from 2000:** +0.1%. **Median travel time to work:** 21.6 minutes. **Working outside county of residence:** 44.9%.

Cities with pop over 10,000: None.

HENRY COUNTY

PO Box 7   **Ph:** 276-634-4601
Collinsville, VA 24078   **Fax:** 276-634-4781
www.martinsville.com

On central southern border of VA, south of Roanoke; organized Oct 7, 1776 from Pittsylvania County. **Name Origin:** For Patrick Henry (1736-99), patriot, governor of VA (1776-79; 1784-86), and statesman, famous for proclaiming, 'Give me liberty or give me death.'

Area (sq mi): 384.39 (land 382.35; water 2.04). **Pop per sq mi:** 147.8.

Pop 2005: 56,501. **State rank:** 32. **Pop change:** 2000-20005 -2.5%; 1990-2000 +1.7%. **Pop 2000:** 57,930 (White 72.7%; Black or African American 22.7%; Hispanic or Latino 3.5%; Asian 0.4%; Other 2.5%). **Foreign born:** 2.7%. **Median age:** 39.3.

Income 2000: per capita $17,110; median household $31,816; **Pop below poverty level:** 11.7%. ***Personal per capita income 2000-2003:** $21,574-$23,309 (includes Henry County & Martinsville).

Unemployment 2004: 9.3%. **Change from 2000:** +0.7%. **Median travel time to work:** 22.5 minutes. **Working outside county of residence:** 35.2%.

Cities with pop over 10,000: None.

HIGHLAND COUNTY

Main St PO Box 190   **Ph:** 540-468-2447
Monterey, VA 24465   **Fax:** 540-468-3447
www.highlandcova.org

On the central western border of VA, west of Staunton; organized Mar 19, 1847 from Bath County, VA, and Pendleton County (now WV). **Name Origin:** For its location in the Allegheny Mountains.

Area (sq mi): 415.86 (land 415.86; water 0). **Pop per sq mi:** 6.

Pop 2005: 2,475. **State rank:** 134. **Pop change:** 2000-20005 -2.4%; 1990-2000 -3.8%. **Pop 2000:** 2,536 (White 98.9%; Black or African American 0.1%; Hispanic or Latino 0.5%; Asian 0.1%; Other 0.6%). **Foreign born:** 0.4%. **Median age:** 46.

Income 2000: per capita $15,976; median household $29,732; **Pop below poverty level:** 12.6%. ***Personal per capita income 2000-2003:** $23,765-$24,895.

Unemployment 2004: 3.1%. **Change from 2000:** +0.8%. **Median travel time to work:** 32 minutes. **Working outside county of residence:** 27%.

Cities with pop over 10,000: None.

🏛 *County Seat*

HOPEWELL (INDEPENDENT CITY)

300 N Main St **Ph:** 804-541-2243
Hopewell, VA 23860 **Fax:** 804-541-2248
www.ci.hopewell.va.us

In southeastern VA at the confluence of the James and Appomattox rivers, 10 mi. northeast of Petersburg. Incorporated as Hopewell in 1916. **Name Origin:** Established as Charles City Point by Sir Thomas Dale (?-1619) in 1613. Town called City Point until 1913 when Du Pont de Nemours and Co. established a settlement for their workers on Hopewell Farm, itself named by the former owner for the ship on which he arrived in VA.

Area (sq mi): 10.82 (land 10.24; water 0.58). **Pop per sq mi:** 2215.8.

Pop 2005: 22,690. **State rank:** 72. **Pop change:** 2000-20005 +1.5%; 1990-2000 -3.2%. **Pop 2000:** 22,354 (White 61.1%; Black or African American 33.5%; Hispanic or Latino 2.9%; Asian 0.8%; Other 3.5%). **Foreign born:** 1.9%. **Median age:** 35.

Income 2000: per capita $16,338; median household $33,196; **Pop below poverty level:** 14.9%. ***Personal per capita income 2000-2003:** $22,565-$23,502 (includes Prince George County & Hopewell).

Unemployment 2004: 5.5%. **Change from 2000:** +0.1%. **Median travel time to work:** 22.4 minutes. **Working outside county of residence:** 70.2%.

Cities with pop over 10,000: Hopewell ⛪ (22,369).

ISLE OF WIGHT COUNTY

PO Box 80 **Ph:** 757-365-6204
Isle of Wight, VA 23397 **Fax:** 757-357-9171
www.co.isle-of-wight.va.us

In southeastern VA, on the west bank of the James River. Organized 1634 as Warrascoyak County from Upper Norfolk (which was organized 1636 from New Norfolk County and renamed Nansemond County in 1642-43); name changed in 1637. **Name Origin:** For the island off the southern coast of England. Originally named for the local Indians.

Area (sq mi): 362.76 (land 315.87; water 46.89). **Pop per sq mi:** 105.8.

Pop 2005: 33,417. **State rank:** 50. **Pop change:** 2000-20005 +12.4%; 1990-2000 +18.7%. **Pop 2000:** 29,728 (White 70.6%; Black or African American 27.1%; Hispanic or Latino 0.9%; Asian 0.3%; Other 1.5%). **Foreign born:** 1.1%. **Median age:** 38.9.

Income 2000: per capita $20,235; median household $45,387; **Pop below poverty level:** 8.3%. ***Personal per capita income 2000-2003:** $27,122-$29,084.

Unemployment 2004: 3.3%. **Change from 2000:** +0.5%. **Median travel time to work:** 29.9 minutes. **Working outside county of residence:** 63.4%.

Cities with pop over 10,000: None.

JAMES CITY COUNTY

PO Box 8784 **Ph:** 757-253-6728
Williamsburg, VA 23187 **Fax:** 757-253-6833
www.james-city.va.us

In southeastern VA, on the east bank of James River; original county, organized 1634. **Name Origin:** For James I (1566-1625),

king of England; also king of Scotland as James VI; son of Mary, Queen of Scots.

Area (sq mi): 179.71 (land 142.92; water 36.79). **Pop per sq mi:** 402.5.

Pop 2005: 57,525. **State rank:** 31. **Pop change:** 2000-20005 +19.6%; 1990-2000 +38%. **Pop 2000:** 48,102 (White 81%; Black or African American 14.4%; Hispanic or Latino 1.7%; Asian 1.5%; Other 2.1%). **Foreign born:** 4.1%. **Median age:** 40.8.

Income 2000: per capita $29,256; median household $55,594; **Pop below poverty level:** 6.4%. ***Personal per capita income 2000-2003:** $34,850-$38,466 (includes James City County & Williamsburg).

Unemployment 2004: 3.2%. **Change from 2000:** +1.1%. **Median travel time to work:** 24.6 minutes. **Working outside county of residence:** 57.4%.

Cities with pop over 10,000: Williamsburg ⛪ (11,465).

KING GEORGE COUNTY

9483 Kings Hwy Suite 3 **Ph:** 540-775-3322
King George, VA 22485 **Fax:** 540-775-5466
www.king-george.va.us

On the northeastern coast of VA, on west bank of the Potomac River; organized Nov 2, 1720 from Richmond and Westmoreland counties. **Name Origin:** For King George I of England (1660-1727).

Area (sq mi): 187.79 (land 180; water 7.79). **Pop per sq mi:** 114.7.

Pop 2005: 20,637. **State rank:** 77. **Pop change:** 2000-20005 +22.8%; 1990-2000 +24.2%. **Pop 2000:** 16,803 (White 76.5%; Black or African American 18.7%; Hispanic or Latino 1.8%; Asian 1%; Other 2.7%). **Foreign born:** 1.3%. **Median age:** 35.1.

Income 2000: per capita $21,562; median household $49,882; **Pop below poverty level:** 5.6%. ***Personal per capita income 2000-2003:** $27,877-$30,425.

Unemployment 2004: 2.9%. **Change from 2000:** +1.1%. **Median travel time to work:** 31 minutes. **Working outside county of residence:** 46%.

Cities with pop over 10,000: None.

KING & QUEEN COUNTY

PO Box 177 **Ph:** 804-785-5975
King & Queen Court House, VA 23085 **Fax:** 804-785-5999
www.kingandqueenco.net

In east-central VA, northeast of Richmond; organized Apr 16, 1691 from New Kent County. **Name Origin:** For King William (1650-1702) and Queen Mary (1662-94) of England.

Area (sq mi): 326.33 (land 316.26; water 10.06). **Pop per sq mi:** 21.5.

Pop 2005: 6,796. **State rank:** 124. **Pop change:** 2000-20005 +2.5%; 1990-2000 +5.4%. **Pop 2000:** 6,630 (White 60.9%; Black or African American 35.7%; Hispanic or Latino 0.9%; Asian 0.3%; Other 2.9%, including 1.4% American Indian/Alaska Native). **Foreign born:** 0.9%. **Median age:** 40.9.

Income 2000: per capita $17,236; median household $35,941; **Pop below poverty level:** 10.9%. ***Personal per capita income 2000-2003:** $23,359-$25,418.

---

*Source: Personal per capita income data are from the Bureau of Economic Analysis; per capita income data are from the Bureau of the Census. See Introduction for explanation of differences.

King & Queen County (cont'd)

Unemployment 2004: 3.7%. **Change from 2000:** -0.2%. **Median travel time to work:** 37.1 minutes. **Working outside county of residence:** 75.6%.

Cities with pop over 10,000: None.

KING WILLIAM COUNTY
PO Box 215   **Ph:** 804-769-4927
King William, VA 23086   **Fax:** 804-769-4964
www.co.king-william.va.us

In east-central VA, northeast of Richmond; organized Dec 5, 1702 from King and Queen County. **Name Origin:** For William III of England (1650-1702).

Area (sq mi): 285.65 (land 275.43; water 10.22). **Pop per sq mi:** 53.5.

Pop 2005: 14,732. **State rank:** 96. **Pop change:** 2000-20005 +12.1%; 1990-2000 +20.5%. **Pop 2000:** 13,146 (White 73.4%; Black or African American 22.8%; Hispanic or Latino 0.9%; Asian 0.4%; Other 2.9%, including 1.5% American Indian/Alaska Native). **Foreign born:** 1.2%. **Median age:** 37.

Income 2000: per capita $21,928; median household $49,876; **Pop below poverty level:** 5.5%. ***Personal per capita income 2000-2003:** $27,285-$29,147.

Unemployment 2004: 3.2%. **Change from 2000:** -0.5%. **Median travel time to work:** 34.9 minutes. **Working outside county of residence:** 70.1%.

Cities with pop over 10,000: None.

LANCASTER COUNTY
PO Box 99   **Ph:** 804-462-5611
Lancaster, VA 22503
www.lancova.com

On the central eastern coast of VA, on east bank of the Rappahannock River; organized 1652 from York and Northumberland counties. **Name Origin:** For the city in England, former home of many early settlers who escaped from Oliver Cromwell's (1599-1658) reign.

Area (sq mi): 231.35 (land 133.14; water 98.2). **Pop per sq mi:** 87.1.

Pop 2005: 11,593. **State rank:** 111. **Pop change:** 2000-20005 +0.2%; 1990-2000 +6.2%. **Pop 2000:** 11,567 (White 69.6%; Black or African American 28.9%; Hispanic or Latino 0.6%; Asian 0.3%; Other 0.8%). **Foreign born:** 1.7%. **Median age:** 49.8.

Income 2000: per capita $24,663; median household $33,239; **Pop below poverty level:** 12.5%. ***Personal per capita income 2000-2003:** $30,372-$32,736.

Unemployment 2004: 5.2%. **Change from 2000:** -2.6%. **Median travel time to work:** 23.6 minutes. **Working outside county of residence:** 26.2%.

Cities with pop over 10,000: None.

LEE COUNTY
PO Box 367   **Ph:** 276-346-7714
Jonesville, VA 24263   **Fax:** 276-346-7712
www.leecountyvachamber.org

On the southwestern border of VA, west of Kingsport, TN; organized

Oct 25, 1792 from Russell County. **Name Origin:** For Henry 'Lighthorse Harry' Lee (1756-1818), VA soldier, statesman, governor (1792-95), and U.S. representative (1799-1801); father of Robert E. Lee (1807-70).

Area (sq mi): 437.32 (land 437.13; water 0.18). **Pop per sq mi:** 54.2.

Pop 2005: 23,686. **State rank:** 69. **Pop change:** 2000-20005 +0.4%; 1990-2000 -3.7%. **Pop 2000:** 23,589 (White 98.1%; Black or African American 0.4%; Hispanic or Latino 0.5%; Asian 0.2%; Other 0.9%). **Foreign born:** 0.5%. **Median age:** 39.7.

Income 2000: per capita $13,625; median household $22,972; **Pop below poverty level:** 23.9%. ***Personal per capita income 2000-2003:** $17,376-$20,261.

Unemployment 2004: 5.2%. **Change from 2000:** -0.3%. **Median travel time to work:** 29.5 minutes. **Working outside county of residence:** 38%.

Cities with pop over 10,000: None.

LEXINGTON (INDEPENDENT CITY)
300 E Washington St   **Ph:** 540-463-7133
Lexington, VA 24450   **Fax:** 540-463-5310
www.ci.lexington.va.us

In south-central VA, northeast of Roanoke. Established in 1778; incorporated as a town in 1874; as a city in 1965. Serves as county seat for Rockbridge County. **Name Origin:** Probably for the village in MA where the first battle of the American Revolution was fought.

Area (sq mi): 2.49 (land 2.49; water 0). **Pop per sq mi:** 2721.3.

Pop 2005: 6,776. **State rank:** 125. **Pop change:** 2000-20005 -1.3%; 1990-2000 -1.3%. **Pop 2000:** 6,867 (White 85%; Black or African American 10.4%; Hispanic or Latino 1.6%; Asian 1.9%; Other 1.7%). **Foreign born:** 4%. **Median age:** 23.3.

Income 2000: per capita $16,497; median household $28,982; **Pop below poverty level:** 21.6%. ***Personal per capita income 2000-2003:** $21,778-$23,612 (includes Rockbridge County, Buena Vista & Lexington).

Unemployment 2004: 4.4%. **Change from 2000:** +2.8%. **Median travel time to work:** 10.5 minutes. **Working outside county of residence:** 57.9%.

Cities with pop over 10,000: None.

LOUDOUN COUNTY
1 Harrison St SE PO Box 7000   **Ph:** 703-777-0200
Leesburg, VA 20177   **Fax:** 703-777-0325
www.co.loudoun.va.us

On northeastern border of VA, northwest of Washington, D.C.; organized Mar 25, 1757 from Fairfax County. **Name Origin:** For John Campbell (1705-82), 4th Earl of Loudoun, commander in chief of British forces during the French and Indian Wars.

Area (sq mi): 521.1 (land 519.85; water 1.25). **Pop per sq mi:** 491.5.

Pop 2005: 255,518. **State rank:** 6. **Pop change:** 2000-20005 +50.7%; 1990-2000 +96.9%. **Pop 2000:** 169,599 (White 79.6%; Black or African American 6.9%; Hispanic or Latino 5.9%; Asian 5.3%; Other 5%). **Foreign born:** 11.3%. **Median age:** 33.6.

Income 2000: per capita $33,530; median household $80,648; **Pop below poverty level:** 2.8%. ***Personal per capita income 2000-2003:** $41,124-$38,269.

Loudoun County (cont'd)

Unemployment 2004: 2.3%. **Change from 2000:** -0.6%. **Median travel time to work:** 30.8 minutes. **Working outside county of residence:** 58.5%.

Cities with pop over 10,000: Leesburg 🏛 (34,828).

LOUISA COUNTY

1 Woolfolk Ave   **Ph:** 540-967-0401
Louisa, VA 23093   **Fax:** 540-967-3411
www.louisacounty.com

In east-central VA, east of Charlottesville; organized May 6, 1742 from Hanover County. **Name Origin:** For Louisa, queen of Denmark (1724-51), daughter of George II (1683-1760) of England.

Area (sq mi): 510.79 (land 497.14; water 13.65). **Pop per sq mi:** 60.4.

Pop 2005: 30,020. **State rank:** 57. **Pop change:** 2000-20005 +17.1%; 1990-2000 +26.1%. **Pop 2000:** 25,627 (White 76.2%; Black or African American 21.6%; Hispanic or Latino 0.7%; Asian 0.2%; Other 1.6%). **Foreign born:** 1.3%. **Median age:** 38.8.

Income 2000: per capita $19,479; median household $39,402; **Pop below poverty level:** 10.2%. ***Personal per capita income 2000-2003:** $25,657-$27,491.

Unemployment 2004: 3.6%. **Change from 2000:** -0.9%. **Median travel time to work:** 36 minutes. **Working outside county of residence:** 63.6%.

Cities with pop over 10,000: None.

LUNENBURG COUNTY

11435 Courthouse Rd   **Ph:** 434-696-2230
Lunenburg, VA 23952   **Fax:** 434-696-3931
www.lunenburgva.org

In south-central VA, southwest of Richmond; organized 1746 from Brunswick County. **Name Origin:** For King George II (1683-1760) of England who retained the German title, Duke of Brunswick.

Area (sq mi): 432.38 (land 431.7; water 0.68). **Pop per sq mi:** 30.6.

Pop 2005: 13,194. **State rank:** 103. **Pop change:** 2000-20005 +0.4%; 1990-2000 +15.1%. **Pop 2000:** 13,146 (White 58.5%; Black or African American 38.6%; Hispanic or Latino 1.8%; Asian 0.2%; Other 2%). **Foreign born:** 1.2%. **Median age:** 40.5.

Income 2000: per capita $14,951; median household $27,899; **Pop below poverty level:** 20%. ***Personal per capita income 2000-2003:** $17,579-$19,286.

Unemployment 2004: 4.8%. **Change from 2000:** -1.3%. **Median travel time to work:** 30 minutes. **Working outside county of residence:** 52.6%.

Cities with pop over 10,000: None.

LYNCHBURG (INDEPENDENT CITY)

900 Church St   **Ph:** 434-847-1443
Lynchburg, VA 24504   **Fax:** 434-847-1536
www.ci.lynchburg.va.us

In south-central VA, northeast of Roanoke. Established 1786; incorporated as a town in 1805; as a city in 1852. **Name Origin:** For John Lynch, owner of the original town site.

Area (sq mi): 49.76 (land 49.39; water 0.37). **Pop per sq mi:** 1356.

Pop 2005: 66,973. **State rank:** 26. **Pop change:** 2000-20005 +2.6%; 1990-2000 -1.2%. **Pop 2000:** 65,269 (White 66%; Black or African American 29.7%; Hispanic or Latino 1.3%; Asian 1.3%; Other 2.4%). **Foreign born:** 3.2%. **Median age:** 35.1.

Income 2000: per capita $18,263; median household $32,234; **Pop below poverty level:** 15.9%. ***Personal per capita income 2000-2003:** $23,783-$25,297 (includes Campbell County & Lynchburg).

Unemployment 2004: 5%. **Change from 2000:** +0.5%. **Median travel time to work:** 16.8 minutes. **Working outside county of residence:** 20.6%.

Cities with pop over 10,000: Lynchburg 🏛 (64,932).

MADISON COUNTY

1 Main St   **Ph:** 540-948-6888
Madison, VA 22727   **Fax:** 540-948-3759
www.madison-va.com

In north-central VA, northeast of Charlottesville; organized May 1, 1793 from Culpeper County. **Name Origin:** For James Madison (1751-1836), fourth U.S. president.

Area (sq mi): 321.78 (land 321.42; water 0.36). **Pop per sq mi:** 41.7.

Pop 2005: 13,398. **State rank:** 102. **Pop change:** 2000-20005 +7%; 1990-2000 +4.8%. **Pop 2000:** 12,520 (White 86.3%; Black or African American 11.4%; Hispanic or Latino 0.8%; Asian 0.5%; Other 1.3%). **Foreign born:** 2.2%. **Median age:** 40.

Income 2000: per capita $18,636; median household $39,856; **Pop below poverty level:** 9.6%. ***Personal per capita income 2000-2003:** $23,189-$25,054.

Unemployment 2004: 3%. **Change from 2000:** +1.2%. **Median travel time to work:** 30.3 minutes. **Working outside county of residence:** 58.4%.

Cities with pop over 10,000: None.

MANASSAS (INDEPENDENT CITY)

PO Box 560   **Ph:** 703-257-8200
Manassas, VA 20108   **Fax:** 703-335-0042
www.manassascity.org

In northeastern VA, 25 mi. west of Alexandria. Established 1852; incorporated as a town in 1874; as a city in 1975. Serves as county seat for Prince William County. **Name Origin:** For its location at the Manassas junction of the Manassas Gap Railroad and the Orange and Alexandria Railroad.

Area (sq mi): 9.96 (land 9.93; water 0.02). **Pop per sq mi:** 3783.4.

Pop 2005: 37,569. **State rank:** 45. **Pop change:** 2000-20005 +6.9%; 1990-2000 +25.7%. **Pop 2000:** 35,135 (White 66.3%; Black or African American 12.9%; Hispanic or Latino 15.1%; Asian 3.4%; Other 11.7%). **Foreign born:** 14.2%. **Median age:** 31.3.

Income 2000: per capita $24,453; median household $60,409; **Pop below poverty level:** 6.3%. ***Personal per capita income 2000-2003:** $31,038-$32,849 (includes Prince William County, Manassas & Manassas Park).

Unemployment 2004: 3.1%. **Change from 2000:** -0.2%. **Median travel time to work:** 32.4 minutes. **Working outside county of residence:** 75.3%.

---

*Source: Personal per capita income data are from the Bureau of Economic Analysis; per capita income data are from the Bureau of the Census. See Introduction for explanation of differences.

Manassas (Independent City) (cont'd)

Cities with pop over 10,000: Manassas 🏛 (37,615).

MANASSAS PARK (INDEPENDENT CITY)

1 Park Center Ct   **Ph:** 703-335-8800
Manassas Park, VA 20111   **Fax:** 703-335-0053
www.cityofmanassaspark.us

In northeastern VA, west of Alexandria. Established in 1955; incorporated as a town in 1957; as a city in 1975. Annexed part of Prince William County effective December 31, 1990. **Name Origin:** For the nearby city of Manassas.

Area (sq mi): 2.49 (land 2.49; water 0). **Pop per sq mi:** 4667.5.

Pop 2005: 11,622. **State rank:** 110. **Pop change:** 2000-20005 +12.9%; 1990-2000 +52.8%. **Pop 2000:** 10,290 (White 67.2%; Black or African American 11.2%; Hispanic or Latino 15%; Asian 4.1%; Other 11.9%). **Foreign born:** 15%. **Median age:** 30.3.

Income 2000: per capita $21,048; median household $60,794; **Pop below poverty level:** 5.2%. ***Personal per capita income 2000-2003·** $31,038-$32,849 (includes Prince William County, Manassas & Manassas Park).

Unemployment 2004: 2.7%. **Change from 2000:** +1.2%. **Median travel time to work:** 35.6 minutes. **Working outside county of residence:** 90.8%.

Cities with pop over 10,000: None.

MARTINSVILLE (INDEPENDENT CITY)

PO Box 1112   **Ph:** 276-656-5180
Martinsville, VA 24114   **Fax:** 276-403-5280
www.ci.martinsville.va.us

In southern VA, 32 mi. west of Danville. Founded 1791; incorporated as a town in 1873; as a city in 1928. Serves as county seat for Henry County. **Name Origin:** For Gen. Joseph Martin (1740-1808), pioneer settler and army officer who represented the county in the General Assembly when the town was established.

Area (sq mi): 11.01 (land 10.96; water 0.05). **Pop per sq mi:** 1361.8.

Pop 2005: 14,925. **State rank:** 95. **Pop change:** 2000-20005 -3.2%; 1990-2000 -4.6%. **Pop 2000:** 15,416 (White 54.1%; Black or African American 42.5%; Hispanic or Latino 2.3%; Asian 0.5%; Other 1.6%). **Foreign born:** 2.7%. **Median age:** 40.8.

Income 2000: per capita $17,251; median household $27,441; **Pop below poverty level:** 19.2%. ***Personal per capita income 2000-2003:** $21,574-$23,309 (includes Henry County & Martinsville).

Unemployment 2004: 12.1%. **Change from 2000:** +1%. **Median travel time to work:** 18.1 minutes. **Working outside county of residence:** 56.1%.

Cities with pop over 10,000: Martinsville 🏛 (15,039).

MATHEWS COUNTY

PO Box 463   **Ph:** 804-725-2550
Mathews, VA 23109   **Fax:** 804-725-7456
www.co.mathews.va.us

On the southeastern border of VA, on the western shore of Chesapeake Bay; organized 1791 from Gloucester County. **Name Origin:** For Thomas Mathews, American Revolutionary general and patriot.

Area (sq mi): 251.96 (land 85.68; water 166.28). **Pop per sq mi:** 107.3.

Pop 2005: 9,194. **State rank:** 117. **Pop change:** 2000-20005 -0.1%; 1990-2000 +10.3%. **Pop 2000:** 9,207 (White 86.8%; Black or African American 11.3%; Hispanic or Latino 0.8%; Asian 0.2%; Other 1.2%). **Foreign born:** 2.2%. **Median age:** 46.2.

Income 2000: per capita $23,610; median household $43,222; **Pop below poverty level:** 0%. ***Personal per capita income 2000 2003·** $30,511-$35,117.

Unemployment 2004: 3.1%. **Change from 2000:** +0.4%. **Median travel time to work:** 45.8 minutes. **Working outside county of residence:** 60.8%.

Cities with pop over 10,000: None.

MECKLENBURG COUNTY

393 Washington St   **Ph:** 434-738-6191
Boydton, VA 23917   **Fax:** 434-738-6861
www.mecklenburgva.com

On the central southern border of VA, southwest of Richmond; organized Mar 1, 1765 from Lunenburg County. **Name Origin:** For Charlotte Sophia, Princess of Mecklenburg-Strelitz (1744-1818), wife of George III (1738-1820) of England.

Area (sq mi): 679.29 (land 623.93; water 55.36). **Pop per sq mi:** 52.1.

Pop 2005: 32,529. **State rank:** 53. **Pop change:** 2000-20005 +0.5%; 1990-2000 +10.7%. **Pop 2000:** 32,380 (White 58.7%; Black or African American 39.1%; Hispanic or Latino 1.2%; Asian 0.3%; Other 1.4%). **Foreign born:** 1.6%. **Median age:** 40.9.

Income 2000: per capita $17,171; median household $31,380; **Pop below poverty level:** 15.5%. ***Personal per capita income 2000-2003:** $20,468-$22,052.

Unemployment 2004: 6.7%. **Change from 2000:** -0.5%. **Median travel time to work:** 25.5 minutes. **Working outside county of residence:** 23.3%.

Cities with pop over 10,000: None.

MIDDLESEX COUNTY

PO Box 158   **Ph:** 804-758-5317
Saluda, VA 23149   **Fax:** 804-758-8637
www.co.middlesex.va.us

On the southeastern border of VA, along the west bank of the Rappahannock River; organized Sep 21, 1674 from Lancaster County. **Name Origin:** For an ancient county in England, most of which became part of Greater London in 1965. The suffix -*sex* is Old Norman from 'camp' or 'military headquarters.'

Area (sq mi): 210.75 (land 130.3; water 80.46). **Pop per sq mi:** 80.5.

Pop 2005: 10,493. **State rank:** 114. **Pop change:** 2000-20005 +5.6%; 1990-2000 +14.8%. **Pop 2000:** 9,932 (White 78.3%; Black or African American 20.1%; Hispanic or Latino 0.6%; Asian 0.1%; Other 1.3%). **Foreign born:** 2.1%. **Median age:** 46.8.

Income 2000: per capita $22,708; median household $36,875; **Pop below poverty level:** 13%. ***Personal per capita income 2000-2003:** $26,422-$28,444.

🏛 *County Seat*

Middlesex County (cont'd)

Unemployment 2004: 3.1%. **Change from 2000:** +1.4%. **Median travel time to work:** 35.1 minutes. **Working outside county of residence:** 50.5%.

Cities with pop over 10,000: None.

MONTGOMERY COUNTY

755 Roanoke St   **Ph:** 540-382-6954
Christiansburg, VA 24073   **Fax:** 540-382-6943
www.montva.com

In western VA, west of Roanoke; organized Oct 7, 1776 from Fincastle (organized 1772 from Botetourt County and abolished 1777), Botetourt, and Pulaski counties. **Name Origin:** For Gen. Richard Montgomery (1736-75), American Revolutionary War officer who captured Montreal, Canada.

Area (sq mi): 389.43 (land 388.22; water 1.21). **Pop per sq mi:** 217.2.

Pop 2005: 84,303. **State rank:** 21. **Pop change:** 2000-20005 +0.8%; 1990-2000 +13.1%. **Pop 2000:** 83,629 (White 89.1%; Black or African American 3.7%; Hispanic or Latino 1.6%; Asian 4%; Other 2.3%). **Foreign born:** 5.8%. **Median age:** 25.9.

Income 2000: per capita $17,077; median household $32,330; **Pop below poverty level:** 23.2%. ***Personal per capita income 2000-2003:** $18,979-$21,136 (includes Montgomery County & Radford).

Unemployment 2004: 3.2%. **Change from 2000:** +0.1%. **Median travel time to work:** 19.2 minutes. **Working outside county of residence:** 22.8%.

Cities with pop over 10,000: Blacksburg (39,212); Christiansburg 🏛 (17,495).

NELSON COUNTY

84 Courthouse Sq   **Ph:** 434-263-7000
Lovingston, VA 22949   **Fax:** 434-263-7004
www.nelsoncounty.com

In west-central VA, southwest of Charlottesville; organized 1808 from Amherst County. **Name Origin:** For Thomas Nelson (1738-89), member of the Continental Congress, signer of the Declaration of Independence, and governor of VA (1781).

Area (sq mi): 474.31 (land 472.35; water 1.95). **Pop per sq mi:** 32.

Pop 2005: 15,101. **State rank:** 94. **Pop change:** 2000-20005 +4.5%; 1990-2000 +13%. **Pop 2000:** 14,445 (White 81.4%; Black or African American 14.9%; Hispanic or Latino 2.1%; Asian 0.2%; Other 2.2%). **Foreign born:** 1.9%. **Median age:** 42.8.

Income 2000: per capita $22,230; median household $36,769; **Pop below poverty level:** 12.1%. ***Personal per capita income 2000-2003:** $24,936-$26,325.

Unemployment 2004: 3.4%. **Change from 2000:** -0.1%. **Median travel time to work:** 33.1 minutes. **Working outside county of residence:** 59%.

Cities with pop over 10,000: None.

NEW KENT COUNTY

PO Box 98   **Ph:** 804-966-9520
New Kent, VA 23124   **Fax:** 804-966-9528
www.newkent.com

In east-central VA, east of Richmond; organized Nov 20, 1654 from York County. **Name Origin:** For Kent, England.

Area (sq mi): 223.48 (land 209.55; water 13.93). **Pop per sq mi:** 76.9.

Pop 2005: 16,107. **State rank:** 91. **Pop change:** 2000-20005 +19.6%; 1990-2000 +28.9%. **Pop 2000:** 13,462 (White 79.7%; Black or African American 16.2%; Hispanic or Latino 1.3%; Asian 0.5%; Other 3%, including 1.3% American Indian/Alaska Native). **Foreign born:** 0.9%. **Median age:** 38.4.

Income 2000: per capita $22,893; median household $53,595; **Pop below poverty level:** 4.9%. ***Personal per capita income 2000-2003:** $27,341-$29,280.

Unemployment 2004: 3.3%. **Change from 2000:** -0.1%. **Median travel time to work:** 34 minutes. **Working outside county of residence:** 80.7%.

Cities with pop over 10,000: None.

NEWPORT NEWS (INDEPENDENT CITY)

2400 Washington Ave   **Ph:** 757-926-8411
Newport News, VA 23607   **Fax:** 757-926-3503
www.newport-news.va.us

In southeastern VA at the mouth of the James River and the entrance to Hampton Roads, 11 mi. northwest of Norfolk. Established in 1880; incorporated as a city in 1896. **Name Origin:** Possibly for Sir Christopher Newport and Sir William Newce, the latter name changed by folk etymology. In 1619 called Newportes Newce.

Area (sq mi): 119.05 (land 68.29; water 50.76). **Pop per sq mi:** 2634.3.

Pop 2005: 179,899. **State rank:** 11. **Pop change:** 2000-20005 -0.1%; 1990-2000 +5.9%. **Pop 2000:** 180,150 (White 52%; Black or African American 39.1%; Hispanic or Latino 4.2%; Asian 2.3%; Other 5.1%). **Foreign born:** 4.8%. **Median age:** 32.

Income 2000: per capita $17,843; median household $36,597; **Pop below poverty level:** 13.8%. ***Personal per capita income 2000-2003:** $21,913-$25,233.

Unemployment 2004: 4.7%. **Change from 2000:** +0.6%. **Median travel time to work:** 23 minutes. **Working outside county of residence:** 43.9%.

Cities with pop over 10,000: Newport News 🏛 (181,913); Hampton 🏛 (145,951).

NORFOLK (INDEPENDENT CITY)

810 Union St Rm 1101   **Ph:** 757-664-4242
Norfolk, VA 23510   **Fax:** 757-664-4239
www.norfolk.gov

In southeastern VA on the Elizabeth River just south of Hampton Roads. Established 1682; incorporated as a town in 1736; as a city in 1845. Major port; distribution center for nearby coal-mining regions. Site of Norfolk Naval Base, largest naval installation in the U.S.; headquarters of the Atlantic Command of the North

*Source: Personal per capita income data are from the Bureau of Economic Analysis; per capita income data are from the Bureau of the Census. See Introduction for explanation of differences.

746

Norfolk (Independent City) (cont'd)

Atlantic Treaty Organization (NATO). Site of Old Dominion University. **Name Origin:** For the county in England, former home of Adam Thoroughgood, an early settler.

Area (sq mi): 96.3 (land 53.73; water 42.58). **Pop per sq mi:** 4317.

Pop 2005: 231,954. **State rank:** 7. **Pop change:** 2000-20005 -1%; 1990-2000 -10.3%. **Pop 2000:** 234,403 (White 47%; Black or African American 44.1%; Hispanic or Latino 3.8%; Asian 2.8%; Other 4.8%). **Foreign born:** 5%. **Median age:** 29.6.

Income 2000: per capita $17,372; median household $31,815; **Pop below poverty level:** 19.4%. ***Personal per capita income 2000-2003:** $23,546-$25,895.

Unemployment 2004: 5.4%. **Change from 2000:** -0.3%. **Median travel time to work:** 21.7 minutes. **Working outside county of residence:** 33.5%.

Cities with pop over 10,000: Norfolk 🏛 (237,835).

NORTHAMPTON COUNTY

PO Box 36   **Ph:** 757-678-0465
Eastville, VA 23347   **Fax:** 757-678-5410
www.co.northampton.va.us

On the southern border of Delmarva peninsula, bounded on the west by Chesapeake Bay and on the east by the Atlantic Ocean. Original county; organized 1634 as Accawmack County; name changed 1642-43. **Name Origin:** Possibly for Spencer Compton (1601-32), 2nd Earl of Northampton.

Area (sq mi): 795.34 (land 207.37; water 587.97). **Pop per sq mi:** 65.3.

Pop 2005: 13,548. **State rank:** 101. **Pop change:** 2000-20005 +3.5%; 1990-2000 +0.2%. **Pop 2000:** 13,093 (White 52.5%; Black or African American 43%; Hispanic or Latino 3.5%; Asian 0.2%; Other 3.5%). **Foreign born:** 3.4%. **Median age:** 42.4.

Income 2000: per capita $16,591; median household $28,276; **Pop below poverty level:** 20.5%. ***Personal per capita income 2000-2003:** $20,841-$24,057.

Unemployment 2004: 4.3%. **Change from 2000:** +0.3%. **Median travel time to work:** 21.7 minutes. **Working outside county of residence:** 22.8%.

Cities with pop over 10,000: None.

NORTHUMBERLAND COUNTY

PO Box 217   **Ph:** 804-580-3700
Heathsville, VA 22473   **Fax:** 804-580-2261
www.co.northumberland.va.us

On central eastern coast of VA, on Chesapeake Bay; organized Oct 12, 1648 from Chicacoun Indian District. **Name Origin:** For the county in England, former home of many early settlers.

Area (sq mi): 285.67 (land 192.3; water 93.36). **Pop per sq mi:** 66.9.

Pop 2005: 12,874. **State rank:** 104. **Pop change:** 2000-20005 +5%; 1990-2000 +16.5%. **Pop 2000:** 12,259 (White 71.8%; Black or African American 26.6%; Hispanic or Latino 0.9%; Asian 0.2%; Other 1%). **Foreign born:** 1.6%. **Median age:** 50.1.

Income 2000: per capita $22,917; median household $38,129; **Pop below poverty level:** 12.3%. ***Personal per capita income 2000-2003:** $24,596-$27,511.

Unemployment 2004: 4.5%. **Change from 2000:** -2.3%. **Median travel time to work:** 28.4 minutes. **Working outside county of residence:** 53.2%.

Cities with pop over 10,000: None.

NORTON (INDEPENDENT CITY)

PO Box 618   **Ph:** 276-679-1160
Norton, VA 24273   **Fax:** 276-679-3510
www.nortonva.org

In southwestern VA. Incorporated as a town in 1894; as a city in 1954. **Name Origin:** For Eckstein Norton, Louisville and National Railroad president, 1886-91. Originally called Prince's Flats, probably for William Prince, a settler in the area about 1787.

Area (sq mi): 7.53 (land 7.53; water 0). **Pop per sq mi:** 488.3.

Pop 2005: 3,677. **State rank:** 133. **Pop change:** 2000-20005 -5.8%; 1990-2000 -8.1%. **Pop 2000:** 3,904 (White 90.9%; Black or African American 6.1%; Hispanic or Latino 0.9%; Asian 1%; Other 1.3%). **Foreign born:** 1.1%. **Median age:** 39.

Income 2000: per capita $16,024; median household $22,788; **Pop below poverty level:** 22.8%. ***Personal per capita income 2000-2003:** $18,469-$20,474 (includes Wise County & Norton).

Unemployment 2004: 5.3%. **Change from 2000:** +0.2%. **Median travel time to work:** 18.8 minutes. **Working outside county of residence:** 40.9%.

Cities with pop over 10,000: None.

NOTTOWAY COUNTY

325 W Court House Rd   **Ph:** 434-645-9043
Nottoway, VA 23955   **Fax:** 434-645-2201

In south-central VA, southwest of Richmond; organized 1789 from Amelia County. **Name Origin:** For the local Indian tribe related to the Iroquois. The name, given to them by their neighbours, means 'rattlesnake' in the sense of 'untrustworthy enemy.' Their own name *Cheroenhaka* is believed to mean 'fork of a stream,' perhaps to signify a favorite campsite.

Area (sq mi): 316.1 (land 314.65; water 1.45). **Pop per sq mi:** 49.5.

Pop 2005: 15,560. **State rank:** 93. **Pop change:** 2000-20005 -1%; 1990-2000 +4.9%. **Pop 2000:** 15,725 (White 56.7%; Black or African American 40.6%; Hispanic or Latino 1.6%; Asian 0.4%; Other 1.8%). **Foreign born:** 1.4%. **Median age:** 38.6.

Income 2000: per capita $15,552; median household $30,866; **Pop below poverty level:** 20.1%. ***Personal per capita income 2000-2003:** $20,452-$22,293.

Unemployment 2004: 4.4%. **Change from 2000:** +0.7%. **Median travel time to work:** 29.1 minutes. **Working outside county of residence:** 38.3%.

Cities with pop over 10,000: None.

🏛 *County Seat*

ORANGE COUNTY

112 W Main St Suite 202 PO Box 111   **Ph:** 540-672-3313
Orange, VA 22960   **Fax:** 276-672-1679
www.orangecova.com

In north-central VA, northeast of Charlottesville; organized Feb 1, 1734 from Spotsylvania County. **Name Origin:** For the European ruling family of Orange-Nassau, one of whose princes married Princess Anne, daughter of King George II (1683-1760).

Area (sq mi): 343.41 (land 341.7; water 1.7). **Pop per sq mi:** 88.5.

Pop 2005: 30,246. **State rank:** 56. **Pop change:** 2000-20005 +16.9%; 1990-2000 +20.8%. **Pop 2000:** 25,881 (White 83.6%; Black or African American 13.8%; Hispanic or Latino 1.3%; Asian 0.3%; Other 1.5%). **Foreign born:** 1.9%. **Median age:** 40.4.

Income 2000: per capita $21,107; median household $42,889; **Pop below poverty level:** 9.2%. ***Personal per capita income 2000-2003:** $24,961-$26,432.

Unemployment 2004: 3%. **Change from 2000:** +0%. **Median travel time to work:** 33.1 minutes. **Working outside county of residence:** 55.3%.

Cities with pop over 10,000: None.

PAGE COUNTY

117 S Court St   **Ph:** 540-743-4142
Luray, VA 22835   **Fax:** 540-743-4533
www.co.page.va.us

In north-central VA, north of Charlottesville; organized Mar 30, 1831 from Rockingham and Shenandoah counties. **Name Origin:** For John Page (1743-1808), U.S. representative from VA (1789-97) and governor (1802-05).

Area (sq mi): 314.09 (land 311.13; water 2.97). **Pop per sq mi:** 76.6.

Pop 2005: 23,831. **State rank:** 68. **Pop change:** 2000-20005 +2.8%; 1990-2000 +6.9%. **Pop 2000:** 23,177 (White 95.7%; Black or African American 2.2%; Hispanic or Latino 1.1%; Asian 0.2%; Other 1.3%). **Foreign born:** 1.5%. **Median age:** 39.

Income 2000: per capita $16,321; median household $33,359; **Pop below poverty level:** 12.5%. ***Personal per capita income 2000-2003:** $20,667-$21,490.

Unemployment 2004: 5.1%. **Change from 2000:** +1.8%. **Median travel time to work:** 32.5 minutes. **Working outside county of residence:** 37.8%.

Cities with pop over 10,000: None.

PATRICK COUNTY

PO Box 148   **Ph:** 276-694-7213
Stuart, VA 24171   **Fax:** 276-694-6943
www.co.patrick.va.us

On the southwestern border of VA, southwest of Roanoke; organized Nov 26, 1790 from Henry County. **Name Origin:** For Patrick Henry (1736-99), patriot, governor of VA (1776-79; 1784-86), and statesman, famous for proclaiming, 'Give me liberty or give me death.'

Area (sq mi): 485.87 (land 483.14; water 2.72). **Pop per sq mi:** 39.8.

Pop 2005: 19,209. **State rank:** 80. **Pop change:** 2000-20005 -1%; 1990-2000 +11.1%. **Pop 2000:** 19,407 (White 91%; Black or African

American 6.2%; Hispanic or Latino 1.9%; Asian 0.2%; Other 1.8%). **Foreign born:** 1.5%. **Median age:** 40.5.

Income 2000: per capita $15,574; median household $28,705; **Pop below poverty level:** 13.4%. ***Personal per capita income 2000-2003:** $18,019-$20,385.

Unemployment 2004: 7.6%. **Change from 2000:** -0.9%. **Median travel time to work:** 27.9 minutes. **Working outside county of residence:** 44.8%.

Cities with pop over 10,000: None.

PETERSBURG (INDEPENDENT CITY)

City Hall 135 N Union St   **Ph:** 804-733-2301
Petersburg, VA 23803   **Fax:** 804-732-9212
www.petersburg-va.org

In southeastern VA at the head of navigation of the Appomattox River, 23 mi. south of Richmond. **Name Origin:** Named by William Bryd II (1674-1744) for Peter Jones, his companion on expeditions into the VA backcountry. Founded in 1645 as Fort Henry, a trading post; name changed in 1748 when incorporated as a town; incorporated as a city in 1850.

Area (sq mi): 23.19 (land 22.88; water 0.3). **Pop per sq mi:** 1425.

Pop 2005: 32,604. **State rank:** 52. **Pop change:** 2000-20005 -3.4%; 1990-2000 -12.1%. **Pop 2000:** 33,740 (White 18.2%; Black or African American 79%; Hispanic or Latino 1.4%; Asian 0.7%; Other 1.8%). **Foreign born:** 2.3%. **Median age:** 36.9.

Income 2000: per capita $15,989; median household $28,851; **Pop below poverty level:** 19.6%. ***Personal per capita income 2000-2003:** $24,506-$26,729 (includes Dinwiddie County, Colonial Heights & Petersburg).

Unemployment 2004: 7.6%. **Change from 2000:** +1.2%. **Median travel time to work:** 23.3 minutes. **Working outside county of residence:** 60.6%.

Cities with pop over 10,000: None.

PITTSYLVANIA COUNTY

11 Bank St 2nd Fl   **Ph:** 434-432-7879
Chatham, VA 24531   **Fax:** 434-432-7915
www.pittgov.org

On the central southern border of VA, south of Lynchburg; organized Nov 6, 1766 from Halifax County. **Name Origin:** For William Pitt (the Elder; 1708-78), 1st Earl of Chatham, prime minister of England and supporter of the American colonies; with the addition of *-sylvania* 'Pitt's woods.'

Area (sq mi): 978.18 (land 970.76; water 7.42). **Pop per sq mi:** 63.7.

Pop 2005: 61,854. **State rank:** 29. **Pop change:** 2000-20005 +0.2%; 1990-2000 +10.9%. **Pop 2000:** 61,745 (White 74.4%; Black or African American 23.7%; Hispanic or Latino 1.2%; Asian 0.2%; Other 1.1%). **Foreign born:** 1%. **Median age:** 39.6.

Income 2000: per capita $16,991; median household $35,153; **Pop below poverty level:** 11.8%. ***Personal per capita income 2000-2003:** $21,486-$23,310 (includes Pittsylvania County & Danville).

Unemployment 2004: 6.2%. **Change from 2000:** -2.2%. **Median travel time to work:** 25.7 minutes. **Working outside county of residence:** 66%.

Cities with pop over 10,000: None.

---

*Source: Personal per capita income data are from the Bureau of Economic Analysis; per capita income data are from the Bureau of the Census. See Introduction for explanation of differences.

POQUOSON (INDEPENDENT CITY)

500 City Hall Ave   **Ph:** 757-868-3000
Poquoson, VA 23662   **Fax:** 757-868-3101
www.ci.poquoson.va.us

In southeastern VA, 9 mi. north of Newport News. Established as a post office between 1885 and 1888; incorporated as a town in 1952; as a city in 1976. **Name Origin:** From an Algonquian term probably meaning 'swamp' or 'overflowed land.'

Area (sq mi): 78.43 (land 15.52; water 62.91). **Pop per sq mi:** 761.

Pop 2005: 11,811. **State rank:** 108. **Pop change:** 2000-20005 +2.1%; 1990-2000 +5.1%. **Pop 2000:** 11,566 (White 95.5%; Black or African American 0.7%; Hispanic or Latino 1.1%; Asian 1.6%; Other 1.5%). **Foreign born:** 2.9%. **Median age:** 39.5.

Income 2000: per capita $25,336; median household $60,920; **Pop below poverty level:** 4.5%. ***Personal per capita income 2000-2003:** $29,709-$33,139 (includes York County & Poquoson).

Unemployment 2004: 2.9%. **Change from 2000:** +0.6%. **Median travel time to work:** 24 minutes. **Working outside county of residence:** 78%.

Cities with pop over 10,000: Poquoson ⚏ (11,700).

PORTSMOUTH (INDEPENDENT CITY)

PO Box 820   **Ph:** 757-393-8746
Portsmouth, VA 23705   **Fax:** 757-393-5378
www.portsmouth.va.us

In southeastern VA on the Elizabeth River opposite of Norfolk. Established 1752; incorporated as a town in 1836; as a city in 1858. **Name Origin:** Named by town founder, William Crawford, for the city in England.

Area (sq mi): 46.62 (land 33.16; water 13.46). **Pop per sq mi:** 3020.8.

Pop 2005: 100,169. **State rank:** 16. **Pop change:** 2000-20005 -0.4%; 1990-2000 -3.2%. **Pop 2000:** 100,565 (White 45.1%; Black or African American 50.6%; Hispanic or Latino 1.7%; Asian 0.8%; Other 2.8%). **Foreign born:** 1.6%. **Median age:** 34.5.

Income 2000: per capita $16,507; median household $33,742; **Pop below poverty level:** 16.2%. ***Personal per capita income 2000-2003:** $21,403-$25,171.

Unemployment 2004: 5.6%. **Change from 2000:** +0.2%. **Median travel time to work:** 23.8 minutes. **Working outside county of residence:** 54.7%.

Cities with pop over 10,000: Portsmouth ⚏ (99,291).

POWHATAN COUNTY

PO Box 37   **Ph:** 804-598-5660
Powhatan, VA 23139   **Fax:** 804-598-5608
www.powhatanva.com

In east-central VA, west of Richmond; organized May 5, 1777 from Cumberland and Chesterfield counties. **Name Origin:** For chief Powhatan (c.1550-1618), the leader of a confederacy of 32 tribes, whose Indian name was Wahunsonacock; father of Pocahontas (c.1595-1617). Name is believed to mean 'falls in a current of water' or 'at the falls.'

Area (sq mi): 262.4 (land 261.28; water 1.12). **Pop per sq mi:** 101.8.

Pop 2005: 26,598. **State rank:** 61. **Pop change:** 2000-20005 +18.9%; 1990-2000 +46%. **Pop 2000:** 22,377 (White 81%; Black or African American 16.9%; Hispanic or Latino 0.8%; Asian 0.2%; Other 1.3%). **Foreign born:** 1.5%. **Median age:** 36.8.

Income 2000: per capita $24,104; median household $53,992; **Pop below poverty level:** 5.7%. ***Personal per capita income 2000-2003:** $27,169-$27,273.

Unemployment 2004: 2.9%. **Change from 2000:** +0.8%. **Median travel time to work:** 34.8 minutes. **Working outside county of residence:** 76.8%.

Cities with pop over 10,000: None.

PRINCE EDWARD COUNTY

111 South St   **Ph:** 434-392-5145
Farmville, VA 23901
www.co.prince-edward.va.us

In south-central VA, southeast of Lynchburg; organized 1754 from Amelia County. **Name Origin:** For Prince Edward Augustus (1767-1820), son of George III (1738-1820) of England and father of Queen Victoria (1819-1901).

Area (sq mi): 353.85 (land 352.76; water 1.09). **Pop per sq mi:** 58.

Pop 2005: 20,455. **State rank:** 78. **Pop change:** 2000-20005 +3.7%; 1990-2000 +13.9%. **Pop 2000:** 19,720 (White 61.8%; Black or African American 35.8%; Hispanic or Latino 0.9%; Asian 0.5%; Other 1.5%). **Foreign born:** 1.4%. **Median age:** 31.5.

Income 2000: per capita $14,510; median household $31,301; **Pop below poverty level:** 18.9%. ***Personal per capita income 2000-2003:** $16,275-$17,004.

Unemployment 2004: 4.8%. **Change from 2000:** +0.9%. **Median travel time to work:** 25.1 minutes. **Working outside county of residence:** 28.8%.

Cities with pop over 10,000: None.

PRINCE GEORGE COUNTY

6602 Courts Dr PO Box 68   **Ph:** 804-733-2600
Prince George, VA 23875   **Fax:** 804-732-3604
www.princegeorgeva.org

In southeastern VA, southeast of Richmond; organized 1703 from Charles City County. **Name Origin:** For George of Denmark (1653-1708), husband of Queen Anne (1665-1714) of England.

Area (sq mi): 281.85 (land 265.62; water 16.23). **Pop per sq mi:** 138.3.

Pop 2005: 36,725. **State rank:** 46. **Pop change:** 2000-20005 +11.1%; 1990-2000 +20.6%. **Pop 2000:** 33,047 (White 59.1%; Black or African American 32.5%; Hispanic or Latino 4.9%; Asian 1.7%; Other 4.8%). **Foreign born:** 4.5%. **Median age:** 32.1.

Income 2000: per capita $20,196; median household $49,877; **Pop below poverty level:** 8%. ***Personal per capita income 2000-2003:** $22,565-$23,502 (includes Prince George County & Hopewell).

Unemployment 2004: 4.2%. **Change from 2000:** +0.8%. **Median travel time to work:** 22 minutes. **Working outside county of residence:** 55%.

Cities with pop over 10,000: Petersburg ⚏ (32,757).

⚏ *County Seat*

PRINCE WILLIAM COUNTY

1 County Complex Ct   **Ph:** 703-792-6600
Prince William, VA 22192   **Fax:** 703-792-7484
www.pwcgov.org

On the northeastern border of VA, southwest of Alexandria; organized 1731 from King George and Stafford counties. Part annexed to Manassas Park (independent) city effective December 31, 1990. **Name Origin:** For Prince William Augustus (1721-65), Duke of Cumberland, son of George II (1683-1760) of England.

Area (sq mi): 348.36 (land 337.78; water 10.58). **Pop per sq mi:** 1032.

Pop 2005: 348,588. **State rank:** 3. **Pop change:** 2000-20005 +24.1%; 1990-2000 +30.2%. **Pop 2000:** 280,813 (White 64.7%; Black or African American 18.8%; Hispanic or Latino 9.7%; Asian 3.8%; Other 8.4%). **Foreign born:** 11.5%. **Median age:** 31.9.

Income 2000: per capita $25,641; median household $65,960; **Pop below poverty level:** 4.4%. ***Personal per capita income 2000-2003:** $31,038-$32,849 (includes Prince William County, Manassas & Manassas Park).

Unemployment 2004: 2.8%. **Change from 2000:** +0.4%. **Median travel time to work:** 36.9 minutes. **Working outside county of residence:** 66.5%.

Cities with pop over 10,000: Manassas Park 🏛 (11,519).

PULASKI COUNTY

143 3rd St NW Suite 1   **Ph:** 540-980-7705
Pulaski, VA 24301   **Fax:** 540-980-7717
www.pulaskicounty.org

In southwestern VA, southwest of Roanoke; organized Mar 30, 1839 from Montgomery and Wythe counties. **Name Origin:** For Count Casimir Pulaski (1747-79), Polish soldier who fought for America during the Revolutionary War.

Area (sq mi): 329.59 (land 320.57; water 9.03). **Pop per sq mi:** 109.4.

Pop 2005: 35,081. **State rank:** 49. **Pop change:** 2000-20005 -0.1%; 1990-2000 +1.8%. **Pop 2000:** 35,127 (White 92.1%; Black or African American 5.6%; Hispanic or Latino 1%; Asian 0.3%; Other 1.5%). **Foreign born:** 0.6%. **Median age:** 40.3.

Income 2000: per capita $18,973; median household $33,873; **Pop below poverty level:** 13.1%. ***Personal per capita income 2000-2003:** $22,920-$25,241.

Unemployment 2004: 5.9%. **Change from 2000:** -4.2%. **Median travel time to work:** 21.3 minutes. **Working outside county of residence:** 34.6%.

Cities with pop over 10,000: None.

RADFORD (INDEPENDENT CITY)

619 2nd St   **Ph:** 540-731-3603
Radford, VA 24141   **Fax:** 540-731-3699
www.radford.va.us

In western VA, 14 mi. northeast of Pulaski. **Name Origin:** Previously called Lovely Mount, English Ferry, Ingle's Ferry, and Central Depot. Established as the town of Central City in 1885; incorporated in 1887. Name changed in 1890 to honor the original landowner, Dr. John Blair Radford; incorporated as a city in 1892.

Area (sq mi): 10.19 (land 9.82; water 0.37). **Pop per sq mi:** 1484.2.

Pop 2005: 14,575. **State rank:** 98. **Pop change:** 2000-20005 -8.1%; 1990-2000 -0.5%. **Pop 2000:** 15,859 (White 87.6%; Black or African American 8.1%; Hispanic or Latino 1.2%; Asian 1.4%; Other 2.2%). **Foreign born:** 2.5%. **Median age:** 22.8.

Income 2000: per capita $14,289; median household $24,654; **Pop below poverty level:** 31.4%. ***Personal per capita income 2000-2003:** $18,979-$21,136 (includes Montgomery County & Radford).

Unemployment 2004: 4.6%. **Change from 2000:** +0%. **Median travel time to work:** 16.1 minutes. **Working outside county of residence:** 47.6%.

Cities with pop over 10,000: Radford 🏛 (14,770).

RAPPAHANNOCK COUNTY

290 Gay St PO Box 519   **Ph:** 540-675-5330
Washington, VA 22747   **Fax:** 540-675-3698
www.rappahannockcountyva.gov

In north-central VA, west of Arlington; organized Feb 8, 1833 from Culpeper County (not to be confused with Old Rappahannock County, with county seat at Lancaster, organized 1656 from Lancaster County and abolished 1692). **Name Origin:** For the Rappahannock River.

Area (sq mi): 266.83 (land 266.57; water 0.26). **Pop per sq mi:** 27.3.

Pop 2005: 7,271. **State rank:** 120. **Pop change:** 2000-20005 +4.1%; 1990-2000 +5.5%. **Pop 2000:** 6,983 (White 91.8%; Black or African American 5.4%; Hispanic or Latino 1.3%; Asian 0.2%; Other 1.7%). **Foreign born:** 3.2%. **Median age:** 42.6.

Income 2000: per capita $23,863; median household $45,943; **Pop below poverty level:** 7.6%. ***Personal per capita income 2000-2003:** $27,459-$30,423.

Unemployment 2004: 2.5%. **Change from 2000:** +0.9%. **Median travel time to work:** 38.7 minutes. **Working outside county of residence:** 56.7%.

Cities with pop over 10,000: None.

RICHMOND COUNTY

101 Court Cir   **Ph:** 804-333-3781
Warsaw, VA 22572   **Fax:** 804-333-5396
www.co.richmond.va.us

In east-central VA, on the north bank of the Rappahannock River; organized Apr 16, 1692 from Old Rappahannock County, which was organized 1656 from Lancaster County and abolished in 1692. **Name Origin:** For Richmond, Surrey, England.

Area (sq mi): 216.38 (land 191.46; water 24.92). **Pop per sq mi:** 47.6.

Pop 2005: 9,114. **State rank:** 118. **Pop change:** 2000-20005 +3.5%; 1990-2000 +21.1%. **Pop 2000:** 8,809 (White 63.8%; Black or African American 33.2%; Hispanic or Latino 2.1%; Asian 0.3%; Other 1.8%). **Foreign born:** 1.9%. **Median age:** 40.3.

Income 2000: per capita $16,675; median household $33,026; **Pop below poverty level:** 15.4%. ***Personal per capita income 2000-2003:** $18,074-$19,264.

Unemployment 2004: 5.6%. **Change from 2000:** +2.1%. **Median travel time to work:** 28.6 minutes. **Working outside county of residence:** 54.2%.

*Source: Personal per capita income data are from the Bureau of Economic Analysis; per capita income data are from the Bureau of the Census.
See Introduction for explanation of differences.

Richmond County (cont'd)

Cities with pop over 10,000: None.

RICHMOND (INDEPENDENT CITY)
900 E Broad St Rm 201   **Ph:** 804-780-7970
Richmond, VA 23219   **Fax:** 804-646-7987
www.ci.richmond.va.us

In southeastern VA, northwest of Norfolk. State capital; founded 1742. Major commercial (tobacco products, chemicals, printed material); cultural, educational (Univ. of Richmond and others); and historical center. Capital of the Confederate States of America 1861-65. Established in 1742; incorporated as a town in 1782; as a city in 1842. Serves as county seat for Henrico County. **Name Origin:** Probably for Richmond, Surrey, England.

Area (sq mi): 62.55 (land 60.07; water 2.48). **Pop per sq mi:** 3225.9.

Pop 2005: 193,777. **State rank:** 10. **Pop change:** 2000-20005 - 2%; 1990-2000 -2.6%. **Pop 2000:** 197,790 (White 37.7%; Black or African American 57.2%; Hispanic or Latino 2.6%; Asian 1.2%; Other 3.3%). **Foreign born:** 3.9%. **Median age:** 33.9.

Income 2000: per capita $20,337; median household $31,121; **Pop below poverty level:** 21.4%. ***Personal per capita income 2000-2003:** $29,853-$33,705.

Unemployment 2004: 5.6%. **Change from 2000:** +0.6%. **Median travel time to work:** 22.1 minutes. **Working outside county of residence:** 42%.

Cities with pop over 10,000: Richmond ⛪ (192,494).

ROANOKE COUNTY
5204 Bernard Dr   **Ph:** 540-772-2006
Roanoke, VA 24018   **Fax:** 540-772-2193
www.co.roanoke.va.us

In west-central VA, west of Lynchburg; organized Mar 30, 1838 from Botetourt and Montgomery counties. **Name Origin:** From an Indian word spelled Roanoak by the first English settlers. Indians applied it to an island, meaning 'place where white shells are found' or perhaps 'shells which are used for money.' Or possibly named for the lost colony of Roanoke.

Area (sq mi): 251.04 (land 250.87; water 0.18). **Pop per sq mi:** 351.5.

Pop 2005: 88,172. **State rank:** 20. **Pop change:** 2000-20005 +2.8%; 1990-2000 +8.1%. **Pop 2000:** 85,778 (White 93%; Black or African American 3.4%; Hispanic or Latino 1%; Asian 1.6%; Other 1.4%). **Foreign born:** 3.1%. **Median age:** 40.9.

Income 2000: per capita $24,637; median household $47,689; **Pop below poverty level:** 4.5%. ***Personal per capita income 2000-2003:** $30,422-$32,951 (includes Roanoke County & Salem).

Unemployment 2004: 3.1%. **Change from 2000:** +1.2%. **Median travel time to work:** 20.7 minutes. **Working outside county of residence:** 66.8%.

Cities with pop over 10,000: None.

ROANOKE (INDEPENDENT CITY)
215 Church Ave SW   **Ph:** 540-853-2000
Roanoke, VA 24011   **Fax:** 540-853-1138
www.roanokeva.gov

In south-central VA, southwest of Lynchburg. Established in 1852 as Big Lick, for the large salt marsh where deer fed; incorporated in 1874. Name changed to Roanoke in 1882, became a city 1884. Convention and railroad center. **Name Origin:** From an Indian name applied to an island, possibly meaning '(place to find) shells that are used for money' or 'place where white shells are found.'

Area (sq mi): 42.91 (land 42.88; water 0.03). **Pop per sq mi:** 2160.2.

Pop 2005: 92,631. **State rank:** 18. **Pop change:** 2000-20005 -2.4%; 1990-2000 -1.5%. **Pop 2000:** 94,911 (White 68.8%; Black or African American 26.7%; Hispanic or Latino 1.5%; Asian 1.2%; Other 2.7%). **Foreign born:** 3.1%. **Median age:** 37.6.

Income 2000: per capita $18,468; median household $30,719; **Pop below poverty level:** 15.9%. ***Personal per capita income 2000-2003:** $24,698-$28,814.

Unemployment 2004: 4.6%. **Change from 2000:** +1%. **Median travel time to work:** 19.3 minutes. **Working outside county of residence:** 38%.

Cities with pop over 10,000: Roanoke ⛪ (92,352).

ROCKBRIDGE COUNTY
150 S Main St   **Ph:** 540-463-4361
Lexington, VA 24450   **Fax:** 540-463-5981
www.co.rockbridge.va.us

In west-central VA, northwest of Lynchburg; organized Mar 1, 1778 from Augusta and Botetourt counties. **Name Origin:** For the Natural Bridge or Rock Bridge, the most famous feature in the area.

Area (sq mi): 600.98 (land 599.63; water 1.35). **Pop per sq mi:** 35.4.

Pop 2005: 21,242. **State rank:** 75. **Pop change:** 2000-20005 +2.1%; 1990-2000 +13.4%. **Pop 2000:** 20,808 (White 95%; Black or African American 3%; Hispanic or Latino 0.6%; Asian 0.4%; Other 1.2%). **Foreign born:** 2%. **Median age:** 40.4.

Income 2000: per capita $18,356; median household $36,035; **Pop below poverty level:** 9.6%. ***Personal per capita income 2000-2003:** $21,778-$23,612 (includes Rockbridge County, Buena Vista & Lexington).

Unemployment 2004: 3%. **Change from 2000:** +0.3%. **Median travel time to work:** 25.1 minutes. **Working outside county of residence:** 45.7%.

Cities with pop over 10,000: None.

ROCKINGHAM COUNTY
Court Sq   **Ph:** 540-564-3000
Harrisonburg, VA 22801   **Fax:** 540-564-3127
www.co.rockingham.va.us

On the northwestern border of VA, northwest of Charlottesville; organized Mar 1, 1778 from Augusta County. **Name Origin:** For Charles Watson Wentworth (1730-82), 2nd Marquess of Rockingham, prime minister of England who was largely responsible for the repeal of the Stamp Act.

Area (sq mi): 853.29 (land 851.15; water 2.14). **Pop per sq mi:** 83.7.

Rockingham County (cont'd)

Pop 2005: 71,251. **State rank:** 23. **Pop change:** 2000-20005 +5.2%; 1990-2000 +17.8%. **Pop 2000:** 67,725 (White 94.4%; Black or African American 1.4%; Hispanic or Latino 3.3%; Asian 0.3%; Other 1.7%). **Foreign born:** 3.3%. **Median age:** 37.5.

Income 2000: per capita $18,795; median household $40,748; **Pop below poverty level:** 8.2%. ***Personal per capita income 2000-2003:** $22,054-$24,240 (includes Rockingham County & Harrisonburg).

Unemployment 2004: 2.7%. **Change from 2000:** +0.8%. **Median travel time to work:** 22.8 minutes. **Working outside county of residence:** 52.2%.

Cities with pop over 10,000: None.

RUSSELL COUNTY

121 E Main St PO Box 1208   **Ph:** 276-889-8000
Lebanon, VA 24266   **Fax:** 276-889-8011
www.russellcountyva.org

In southwestern VA, north of Bristol, TN; organized May 1, 1786 from Washington County. **Name Origin:** For William Russell (1758-1825), VA officer in the Revolutionary War and statesman.

Area (sq mi): 476.77 (land 474.66; water 2.11). **Pop per sq mi:** 61.

Pop 2005: 28,949. **State rank:** 59. **Pop change:** 2000-20005 -4.5%; 1990-2000 +5.7%. **Pop 2000:** 30,308 (White 95.6%; Black or African American 3.1%; Hispanic or Latino 0.8%; Asian 0%; Other 0.8%). **Foreign born:** 0.4%. **Median age:** 38.7.

Income 2000: per capita $14,863; median household $26,834; **Pop below poverty level:** 16.3%. ***Personal per capita income 2000-2003:** $18,514-$20,533.

Unemployment 2004: 5.8%. **Change from 2000:** -1.5%. **Median travel time to work:** 31.2 minutes. **Working outside county of residence:** 40.5%.

Cities with pop over 10,000: None.

SALEM (INDEPENDENT CITY)

114 N Broad St   **Ph:** 540-375-3016
Salem, VA 24153   **Fax:** 540-375-4048
www.ci.salem.va.us

In west-central VA, 8 mi. west of Roanoke. Laid out 1802; established in 1806. Incorporated as a town in 1836; as a city in 1968. Serves as county seat for Roanoke County. **Name Origin:** For Salem, NJ, former home of an early settler.

Area (sq mi): 14.59 (land 14.59; water 0). **Pop per sq mi:** 1689.8.

Pop 2005: 24,654. **State rank:** 67. **Pop change:** 2000-20005 -0.4%; 1990-2000 +4.2%. **Pop 2000:** 24,747 (White 91.3%; Black or African American 5.9%; Hispanic or Latino 0.8%; Asian 1%; Other 1.2%). **Foreign born:** 2.1%. **Median age:** 39.2.

Income 2000: per capita $20,091; median household $38,997; **Pop below poverty level:** 6.7%. ***Personal per capita income 2000-2003:** $30,422-$32,951 (includes Roanoke County & Salem).

Unemployment 2004: 3.4%. **Change from 2000:** +1%. **Median travel time to work:** 17 minutes. **Working outside county of residence:** 53.6%.

Cities with pop over 10,000: Salem 🏛 (24,347).

SCOTT COUNTY

112 Water St Suite 1   **Ph:** 276-386-6521
Gate City, VA 24251   **Fax:** 276-386-9198
www.scottcountyva.com

In southwest VA, north of Kingsport, TN; organized 1814 from Lee, Russell, and Washington counties. **Name Origin:** For Gen. Winfield Scott (1786-1866), VA officer during the War of 1812 and the Mexican War; general in chief of the U.S. Army (1841-61) and commander of the Union armies at the beginning of the Civil War.

Area (sq mi): 538.63 (land 536.58; water 2.05). **Pop per sq mi:** 42.8.

Pop 2005: 22,962. **State rank:** 71. **Pop change:** 2000-20005 -1.9%; 1990-2000 +0.9%. **Pop 2000:** 23,403 (White 98.2%; Black or African American 0.6%; Hispanic or Latino 0.4%; Asian 0.1%; Other 0.7%). **Foreign born:** 0.3%. **Median age:** 41.4.

Income 2000: per capita $15,073; median household $27,339; **Pop below poverty level:** 16.8%. ***Personal per capita income 2000-2003:** $17,857-$20,279.

Unemployment 2004: 5.5%. **Change from 2000:** +0.6%. **Median travel time to work:** 30.6 minutes. **Working outside county of residence:** 60.5%.

Cities with pop over 10,000: None.

SHENANDOAH COUNTY

600 N Main St Suite 102   **Ph:** 540-459-6165
Woodstock, VA 22664   **Fax:** 540-459-6168
www.co.shenandoah.va.us

On the northeastern border of VA, northeast of Harrisonburg; organized as Dunmore County May 15, 1772 from Frederick County; name changed 1778. **Name Origin:** For the Shenandoah River.

Area (sq mi): 512.53 (land 512.2; water 0.32). **Pop per sq mi:** 76.5.

Pop 2005: 39,184. **State rank:** 43. **Pop change:** 2000-20005 +11.7%; 1990-2000 +10.9%. **Pop 2000:** 35,075 (White 94.2%; Black or African American 1.2%; Hispanic or Latino 3.4%; Asian 0.3%; Other 2.9%). **Foreign born:** 3.1%. **Median age:** 40.9.

Income 2000: per capita $19,755; median household $39,173; **Pop below poverty level:** 8.2%. ***Personal per capita income 2000-2003:** $23,805-$25,219.

Unemployment 2004: 3%. **Change from 2000:** +0.9%. **Median travel time to work:** 27.1 minutes. **Working outside county of residence:** 34.8%.

Cities with pop over 10,000: None.

SMYTH COUNTY

109 W Main St Rm 144   **Ph:** 276-782-4044
Marion, VA 24354   **Fax:** 276-782-4045
www.smythcounty.org

In southwestern VA, northeast of Bristol, TN; organized Feb 23, 1832 from Washington and Wythe counties. **Name Origin:** For Gen. Alexander Smyth (1765-1830), U.S. representative from VA (1817-25; 1827-30).

Area (sq mi): 452.31 (land 452.09; water 0.22). **Pop per sq mi:** 72.2.

*Source: Personal per capita income data are from the Bureau of Economic Analysis; per capita income data are from the Bureau of the Census. See Introduction for explanation of differences.

Smyth County (cont'd)

Pop 2005: 32,640. **State rank:** 51. **Pop change:** 2000-20005 -1.3%; 1990-2000 +2.2%. **Pop 2000:** 33,081 (White 96.4%; Black or African American 1.9%; Hispanic or Latino 0.9%; Asian 0.2%; Other 1.1%). **Foreign born:** 0.5%. **Median age:** 40.

Income 2000: per capita $16,105; median household $30,083; **Pop below poverty level:** 13.3% *Personal per capita income 2000-2003:** $19,722-$21,794.

Unemployment 2004: 5.3%. **Change from 2000:** -3.5%. **Median travel time to work:** 22.5 minutes. **Working outside county of residence:** 20.3%.

Cities with pop over 10,000: None.

SOUTHAMPTON COUNTY

PO Box 190   **Ph:** 757-653-2200
Courtland, VA 23837   **Fax:** 757-653-2547
www.southamptoncounty.org

In southeastern VA, west of Norfolk; organized Apr 30, 1749 from Isle of Wight and Nansemond counties. Site of Nat Turner's (1800-31) Rebellion (1831). Part annexed to Franklin (independent) city effective December 31, 1995. **Name Origin:** For Henry Wriothesley (1573-1624), 3rd Earl of Southampton, English statesman and patron of William Shakespeare (1564-1616).

Area (sq mi): 602.35 (land 599.56; water 2.8). **Pop per sq mi:** 29.3.

Pop 2005: 17,585. **State rank:** 82. **Pop change:** 2000-20005 +0.6%; 1990-2000 -0.4%. **Pop 2000:** 17,482 (White 55.8%; Black or African American 42.9%; Hispanic or Latino 0.7%; Asian 0.2%; Other 1%). **Foreign born:** 0.3%. **Median age:** 38.6.

Income 2000: per capita $16,930; median household $33,995; **Pop below poverty level:** 14.6%. *Personal per capita income 2000-2003:** $23,046-$24,646 (includes Southampton County & Franklin).

Unemployment 2004: 4.2%. **Change from 2000:** +1.6%. **Median travel time to work:** 26.6 minutes. **Working outside county of residence:** 62.2%.

Cities with pop over 10,000: None.

SPOTSYLVANIA COUNTY

1905 Courthouse Rd   **Ph:** 540-582-7010
Spotsylvania, VA 22553   **Fax:** 540-582-9308
www.spotsylvania.va.us

In east-central VA, north of Richmond; organized 1721 from Essex, King William, and King and Queen counties. **Name Origin:** For Alexander Spotswood (1676-1740), lieutenant governor of the colony of VA (1710-22). Name is a combination of *Spots*wood and *sylvania* 'woodlands,' a play on the surname.

Area (sq mi): 412.27 (land 400.86; water 11.41). **Pop per sq mi:** 290.7.

Pop 2005: 116,549. **State rank:** 15. **Pop change:** 2000-20005 +28.9%; 1990-2000 +57.5%. **Pop 2000:** 90,395 (White 81.4%; Black or African American 12.5%; Hispanic or Latino 2.8%; Asian 1.4%; Other 3.2%). **Foreign born:** 3.2%. **Median age:** 34.3.

Income 2000: per capita $22,536; median household $57,525; **Pop below poverty level:** 4.7%. *Personal per capita income 2000-2003:** $28,359-$30,493 (includes Spotsylvania County & Fredericksburg).

Unemployment 2004: 2.5%. **Change from 2000:** +0.8%. **Median travel time to work:** 37.1 minutes. **Working outside county of residence:** 63.8%.

Cities with pop over 10,000: None.

STAFFORD COUNTY

1300 Court House Rd   **Ph:** 540-658-8605
Stafford, VA 22554   **Fax:** 540-658-7643
www.co.stafford.va.us

On the northeastern coast of VA, on west bank of upper Potomac River; organized 1664 from Westmoreland County. Part of the facility is also in Prince William County. **Name Origin:** For the county of Staffordshire, England.

Area (sq mi): 279.95 (land 270.35; water 9.59). **Pop per sq mi:** 436.

Pop 2005: 117,874. **State rank:** 14. **Pop change:** 2000-20005 +27.5%; 1990-2000 +51%. **Pop 2000:** 92,446 (White 80.1%; Black or African American 12.1%; Hispanic or Latino 3.6%; Asian 1.6%; Other 4.3%). **Foreign born:** 4%. **Median age:** 33.1.

Income 2000: per capita $24,762; median household $66,809; **Pop below poverty level:** 3.5%. *Personal per capita income 2000-2003:** $28,747-$30,178.

Unemployment 2004: 2.5%. **Change from 2000:** +0.8%. **Median travel time to work:** 37.7 minutes. **Working outside county of residence:** 70.9%.

Cities with pop over 10,000: None.

STAUNTON (INDEPENDENT CITY)

116 W Beverly St   **Ph:** 540-332-3800
Staunton, VA 24401   **Fax:** 540-332-3807
www.staunton.va.us

In north-central VA, 35 mi. northwest of Charlottesville. Laid out in 1748; established as a town in 1761. Incorporated as a town in 1801; as a city in 1871. Serves as county seat for Augusta County. **Name Origin:** For Rebecca Staunton, wife of colonial governor William Gooch.

Area (sq mi): 19.71 (land 19.71; water 0). **Pop per sq mi:** 1184.

Pop 2005: 23,337. **State rank:** 70. **Pop change:** 2000-20005 -2.2%; 1990-2000 -2.5%. **Pop 2000:** 23,853 (White 82.7%; Black or African American 14%; Hispanic or Latino 1.1%; Asian 0.5%; Other 2.3%). **Foreign born:** 2%. **Median age:** 39.8.

Income 2000: per capita $19,161; median household $32,941; **Pop below poverty level:** 11.7%. *Personal per capita income 2000-2003:** $24,053-$25,847 (includes Augusta County, Staunton & Waynesboro).

Unemployment 2004: 3.4%. **Change from 2000:** +0.9%. **Median travel time to work:** 19.9 minutes. **Working outside county of residence:** 54.1%.

Cities with pop over 10,000: Staunton ⛫ (23,840).

⛫ *County Seat*

SUFFOLK (INDEPENDENT CITY)
441 Market St
Suffolk, VA 23434
www.suffolk.va.us

Ph: 757-923-2085
Fax: 757-923-2091

In southeastern VA on the Nansemond River, 18 mi. southwest of Portsmouth. Established in 1742; incorporated as a town in 1808; as a city in 1910. **Name Origin:** For the county in England.

Area (sq mi): 429.07 (land 400.02; water 29.05). **Pop per sq mi:** 197.5.

Pop 2005: 78,994. **State rank:** 22. **Pop change:** 2000-20005 +24.1%; 1990-2000 +22.1%. **Pop 2000:** 63,677 (White 53.3%; Black or African American 43.5%; Hispanic or Latino 1.3%; Asian 0.8%; Other 1.9%). **Foreign born:** 1.9%. **Median age:** 36.

Income 2000: per capita $18,836; median household $41,115; **Pop below poverty level:** 13.2%. ***Personal per capita income 2000-2003:** $25,319-$26,975.

Unemployment 2004: 4%. **Change from 2000:** +0.5%. **Median travel time to work:** 27.3 minutes. **Working outside county of residence:** 60.1%.

Cities with pop over 10,000: Suffolk 🏛 (76,586).

SURRY COUNTY
PO Box 65
Surry, VA 23883
www.surrycounty.govoffice2.com

Ph: 757-294-5271
Fax: 757-294-5204

On southeastern coast of VA, on south bank of the James River; organized 1652 from James City County. **Name Origin:** For Surrey, England; spelling is a clerical error.

Area (sq mi): 310.31 (land 279.09; water 31.22). **Pop per sq mi:** 25.1.

Pop 2005: 7,013. **State rank:** 122. **Pop change:** 2000-20005 +2.7%; 1990-2000 +11.1%. **Pop 2000:** 6,829 (White 46.4%; Black or African American 51.6%; Hispanic or Latino 0.7%; Asian 0.1%; Other 1.3%). **Foreign born:** 0.5%. **Median age:** 39.4.

Income 2000: per capita $16,682; median household $37,558; **Pop below poverty level:** 10.8%. ***Personal per capita income 2000-2003:** $21,243-$22,629.

Unemployment 2004: 4%. **Change from 2000:** -1.4%. **Median travel time to work:** 39 minutes. **Working outside county of residence:** 70.3%.

Cities with pop over 10,000: None.

SUSSEX COUNTY
20233 Thornton Sq
Sussex, VA 23884
sussexcounty.govoffice.com

Ph: 434-246-5511
Fax: 434-246-6013

In southeastern VA, south of Richmond; organized 1754 from Surry County. **Name Origin:** For the county in England.

Area (sq mi): 492.83 (land 490.73; water 2.1). **Pop per sq mi:** 24.6.

Pop 2005: 12,071. **State rank:** 107. **Pop change:** 2000-20005 -3.5%; 1990-2000 +22%. **Pop 2000:** 12,504 (White 36.3%; Black or African American 62.1%; Hispanic or Latino 0.8%; Asian 0.1%; Other 1.3%). **Foreign born:** 1%. **Median age:** 37.6.

Income 2000: per capita $14,670; median household $31,007; **Pop below poverty level:** 16.1%. ***Personal per capita income 2000-2003:** $19,025-$20,838.

Unemployment 2004: 6.6%. **Change from 2000:** +2.6%. **Median travel time to work:** 27.9 minutes. **Working outside county of residence:** 55.7%.

Cities with pop over 10,000: None.

TAZEWELL COUNTY
PO Box 968
Tazewell, VA 24651
www.tazewellcounty.org

Ph: 276-988-1222
Fax: 276-988-7501

On the southwestern border of VA, northeast of Bristol, TN; organized 1800 from Russell and Wythe counties. **Name Origin:** For Henry Tazewell (1753-99), VA legislator, chief justice (1785-93), and U.S. senator (1794-99).

Area (sq mi): 519.89 (land 519.74; water 0.15). **Pop per sq mi:** 86.2.

Pop 2005: 44,795. **State rank:** 37. **Pop change:** 2000-20005 +0.4%; 1990-2000 -3%. **Pop 2000:** 44,598 (White 95.8%; Black or African American 2.3%; Hispanic or Latino 0.5%; Asian 0.6%; Other 1%). **Foreign born:** 1%. **Median age:** 40.7.

Income 2000: per capita $15,282; median household $27,304; **Pop below poverty level:** 15.3%. ***Personal per capita income 2000-2003:** $20,326-$22,353.

Unemployment 2004: 4.6%. **Change from 2000:** +0.2%. **Median travel time to work:** 26.6 minutes. **Working outside county of residence:** 31.9%.

Cities with pop over 10,000: None.

VIRGINIA BEACH (INDEPENDENT CITY)
2401 Courthouse Dr Municipal Ctr Bldg 1
Virginia Beach, VA 23456
www.vbgov.com

Ph: 757-427-4242
Fax: 757-427-5626

In southeastern VA on the Atlantic Ocean, 18 mi. east of Norfolk. Incorporated as a town in 1906; as a city in 1952. **Name Origin:** This noted oceanside resort is named for the state.

Area (sq mi): 497.33 (land 248.29; water 249.03). **Pop per sq mi:** 1765.7.

Pop 2005: 438,415. **State rank:** 2. **Pop change:** 2000-20005 +3.1%; 1990-2000 +8.2%. **Pop 2000:** 425,257 (White 69.5%; Black or African American 19%; Hispanic or Latino 4.2%; Asian 4.9%; Other 4.7%). **Foreign born:** 6.6%. **Median age:** 32.7.

Income 2000: per capita $22,365; median household $48,705; **Pop below poverty level:** 6.5%. ***Personal per capita income 2000-2003:** $30,118-$32,848.

Unemployment 2004: 3.6%. **Change from 2000:** +0.6%. **Median travel time to work:** 23.9 minutes. **Working outside county of residence:** 42.5%.

Cities with pop over 10,000: Virginia Beach 🏛 (440,098).

WARREN COUNTY
220 N Commerce Ave Suite 100
Front Royal, VA 22630
www.warrencountyva.net

Ph: 540-636-4600
Fax: 540-636-6066

In north-central VA, west of Arlington; organized Mar 9, 1836 from

*Source: Personal per capita income data are from the Bureau of Economic Analysis; per capita income data are from the Bureau of the Census.
See Introduction for explanation of differences.

754

Warren County (cont'd)

Frederick and Shenandoah counties. **Name Origin:** For Gen. Joseph Warren (1741-75), Revolutionary War patriot and member of the Committee of Safety who dispatched Paul Revere (1735-1818) on his famous ride.

Area (sq mi): 216.32 (land 213.7; water 2.63). **Pop per sq mi:** 166.4.

Pop 2005: 35,556. **State rank:** 18. **Pop change:** 2000-20005 +12.6%; 1990-2000 +20.8%. **Pop 2000:** 31,584 (White 91.7%; Black or African American 4.8%; Hispanic or Latino 1.6%; Asian 0.4%; Other 2.1%). **Foreign born:** 2.1%. **Median age:** 37.1.

Income 2000: per capita $19,841; median household $42,422; **Pop below poverty level:** 8.5%. ***Personal per capita income 2000-2003:** $25,925-$27,064.

Unemployment 2004: 3.2%. **Change from 2000:** +0.4%. **Median travel time to work:** 39.1 minutes. **Working outside county of residence:** 55.5%.

Cities with pop over 10,000: Front Royal 🏛 (14,210).

WASHINGTON COUNTY

205 Academy Dr   **Ph:** 276-676-6202
Abingdon, VA 24210   **Fax:** 276-676-6201
www.washcova.com

On the southwestern border of VA, north of Bristol, TN; organized Oct 7, 1776 from Fincastle (organized 1772 from Botetourt County and abolished 1777) and Montgomery counties. **Name Origin:** For George Washington (1732-99), American patriot and first U.S. president.

Area (sq mi): 565.98 (land 562.86; water 3.12). **Pop per sq mi:** 92.5.

Pop 2005: 52,085. **State rank:** 34. **Pop change:** 2000-20005 +1.9%; 1990-2000 +11.4%. **Pop 2000:** 51,103 (White 97%; Black or African American 1.3%; Hispanic or Latino 0.6%; Asian 0.3%; Other 0.8%). **Foreign born:** 0.9%. **Median age:** 40.3.

Income 2000: per capita $18,350; median household $32,742; **Pop below poverty level:** 10.9%. ***Personal per capita income 2000-2003:** $23,044-$25,307 (includes Washington County & Bristol).

Unemployment 2004: 4.7%. **Change from 2000:** -1.2%. **Median travel time to work:** 24.2 minutes. **Working outside county of residence:** 41.1%.

Cities with pop over 10,000: None.

WAYNESBORO (INDEPENDENT CITY)

503 W Main St   **Ph:** 540-942-6600
Waynesboro, VA 22980   **Fax:** 540-942-6671
www.waynesboro.va.us

In north-central VA, in the Shenandoah Valley at the foot of the Blue Ridge Mountains, 12 mi. southeast of Staunton. Laid out in 1797; established as a town in 1801. Incorporated as a town in 1834; as a city in 1948. Annexed part of Augusta County effective July 1, 1994. **Name Origin:** For Gen. Anthony Wayne (1745-96), PA soldier and statesman, nicknamed 'Mad Anthony' for his daring during the American Revolution.

Area (sq mi): 15.38 (land 15.36; water 0.02). **Pop per sq mi:** 1384.7.

Pop 2005: 21,269. **State rank:** 74. **Pop change:** 2000-20005 +9%; 1990-2000 +5.2%. **Pop 2000:** 19,520 (White 84.5%; Black or African American 10%; Hispanic or Latino 3.3%; Asian 0.6%; Other 3%). **Foreign born:** 2.4%. **Median age:** 38.9.

Income 2000: per capita $17,932; median household $32,686; **Pop below poverty level:** 12.8%. ***Personal per capita income 2000-2003:** $24,053-$25,847 (includes Augusta County, Staunton & Waynesboro).

Unemployment 2004: 3.6%. **Change from 2000:** -0.5%. **Median travel time to work:** 19.3 minutes. **Working outside county of residence:** 54.9%.

Cities with pop over 10,000: Waynesboro 🏛 (20,755).

WESTMORELAND COUNTY

PO Box 1000   **Ph:** 804-493-0130
Montross, VA 22520   **Fax:** 804-493-0134
www.westmoreland-county.org

On the central eastern coast of VA, along the west bank of the Potomac River; organized Jul 5, 1653 from Northumberland County. **Name Origin:** For the county in England.

Area (sq mi): 252.64 (land 229.18; water 23.46). **Pop per sq mi:** 75.2.

Pop 2005: 17,227. **State rank:** 86. **Pop change:** 2000-20005 +3%; 1990-2000 +8%. **Pop 2000:** 16,718 (White 64.1%; Black or African American 30.9%; Hispanic or Latino 3.5%; Asian 0.4%; Other 3.3%). **Foreign born:** 3.1%. **Median age:** 42.8.

Income 2000: per capita $19,473; median household $35,797; **Pop below poverty level:** 14.7%. ***Personal per capita income 2000-2003:** $23,136-$24,832.

Unemployment 2004: 4.4%. **Change from 2000:** -0.7%. **Median travel time to work:** 37.1 minutes. **Working outside county of residence:** 59.1%.

Cities with pop over 10,000: None.

WILLIAMSBURG (INDEPENDENT CITY)

401 Lafayette St   **Ph:** 757-220-6100
Williamsburg, VA 23185   **Fax:** 757-220-6107
www.ci.williamsburg.va.us

In southeastern VA on the peninsula between the James and York rivers, 27 mi. northwest of Newport News. Capital of VA, 1699-1780. Site of College of William and Mary. Serves as county seat for James City County. **Name Origin:** Established in 1633 as Middle Plantation. Renamed in 1699 for William III (1650-1702), king of England; incorporated as a city in 1884.

Area (sq mi): 8.67 (land 8.54; water 0.13). **Pop per sq mi:** 1376.

Pop 2005: 11,751. **State rank:** 109. **Pop change:** 2000-20005 -2.1%; 1990-2000 +4.1%. **Pop 2000:** 11,998 (White 77.9%; Black or African American 13.3%; Hispanic or Latino 2.5%; Asian 4.6%; Other 2.7%). **Foreign born:** 5.2%. **Median age:** 22.6.

Income 2000: per capita $18,483; median household $37,093; **Pop below poverty level:** 18.3%. ***Personal per capita income 2000-2003:** $34,850-$38,466 (includes James City County & Williamsburg).

🏛 *County Seat*

Williamsburg (independent City) (cont'd)

Unemployment 2004: 7.7%. **Change from 2000:** +1.7%. **Median travel time to work:** 18 minutes. **Working outside county of residence:** 47.8%.

Cities with pop over 10,000: None.

WINCHESTER (INDEPENDENT CITY)

5 N Kent St   **Ph:** 540-667-5770
Winchester, VA 22601   **Fax:** 540-545-8711
www.ci.winchester.va.us

In northern VA, in the Shenandoah Valley, 70 mi. northwest of Alexandria. Settled 1738; established in 1752. Incorporated as a town in 1779; as a city in 1874. Serves as county seat for Frederick County. **Name Origin:** Named by James Wood, one of the town founders, for Winchester, England, his birthplace. Previously called Opequon, Frederick's Town, and Fredericktown.

Area (sq mi): 9.33 (land 9.33; water 0). **Pop per sq mi:** 2692.3.

Pop 2005: 25,119. **State rank:** 64. **Pop change:** 2000-20005 +6.5%; 1990-2000 +7.5%. **Pop 2000:** 23,585 (White 79.4%; Black or African American 10.5%; Hispanic or Latino 6.5%; Asian 1.6%; Other 5.8%). **Foreign born:** 6.8%. **Median age:** 35.2.

Income 2000: per capita $20,500; median household $34,335; **Pop below poverty level:** 13.2%. *Personal per capita income 2000-2003: $27,238-$28,791 (includes Frederick County & Winchester).

Unemployment 2004: 3.2%. **Change from 2000:** +0.2%. **Median travel time to work:** 20.1 minutes. **Working outside county of residence:** 49.1%.

Cities with pop over 10,000: Winchester ⛫ (24,779).

WISE COUNTY

PO Box 570   **Ph:** 276-328-2321
Wise, VA 24293   **Fax:** 276-328-9780
www.wisecounty.org

On the southwestern border of VA, north of Kingsport, TN; organized Feb 16, 1856 from Lee, Russell, and Scott counties. **Name Origin:** For Gen. Henry A. Wise (1806-76), U.S. representative from VA (1833-44), governor (1856-60), and Confederate Army officer.

Area (sq mi): 405.22 (land 404.04; water 1.18). **Pop per sq mi:** 103.9.

Pop 2005: 41,997. **State rank:** 39. **Pop change:** 2000-20005 +4.7%; 1990-2000 +1.4%. **Pop 2000:** 40,123 (White 96.4%; Black or African American 1.8%; Hispanic or Latino 0.7%; Asian 0.3%; Other 1.1%). **Foreign born:** 0.5%. **Median age:** 37.8.

Income 2000: per capita $14,271; median household $26,149; **Pop below poverty level:** 20%. *Personal per capita income 2000-2003: $18,469-$20,474 (includes Wise County & Norton).

Unemployment 2004: 5%. **Change from 2000:** -0.6%. **Median travel time to work:** 23.6 minutes. **Working outside county of residence:** 37.6%.

Cities with pop over 10,000: None.

WYTHE COUNTY

340 S 6th St   **Ph:** 276-223-6020
Wytheville, VA 24382   **Fax:** 276-223-6030
www.wytheco.org

In southwestern VA, southwest of Roanoke; organized May 1, 1790 from Montgomery County. **Name Origin:** For George Wythe (1726-1806), VA patriot, first law professor in the U.S., member of the House of Burgesses (1758-68), and signer of the Declaration of Independence.

Area (sq mi): 464.62 (land 463.24; water 1.37). **Pop per sq mi:** 61.4.

Pop 2005: 28,421. **State rank:** 60. **Pop change:** 2000-20005 +3%; 1990-2000 +8.4%. **Pop 2000:** 27,599 (White 95.4%; Black or African American 2.9%; Hispanic or Latino 0.6%; Asian 0.4%; Other 1%). **Foreign born:** 0.5%. **Median age:** 39.4.

Income 2000: per capita $17,639; median household $32,235; **Pop below poverty level:** 11%. *Personal per capita income 2000-2003: $20,229-$21,677.

Unemployment 2004: 4.6%. **Change from 2000:** -5.1%. **Median travel time to work:** 24.2 minutes. **Working outside county of residence:** 30.3%.

Cities with pop over 10,000: None.

YORK COUNTY

300 Ballard St PO Box 316   **Ph:** 757-890-3450
Yorktown, VA 23690   **Fax:** 757-890-3459
www.co.york.va.us

On the southeastern coast of VA, on the west bank of the York River; original county; organized as Charles River Shire 1634; name changed 1642. **Name Origin:** Renamed York for Charles (1600-49), Duke of York, later King Charles I; this to avoid confusion of the original name, Charles River, with Charles City (County).

Area (sq mi): 215.52 (land 105.65; water 109.87). **Pop per sq mi:** 584.6.

Pop 2005: 61,758. **State rank:** 30. **Pop change:** 2000-20005 +9.7%; 1990-2000 +32.7%. **Pop 2000:** 56,297 (White 78.5%; Black or African American 13.4%; Hispanic or Latino 2.7%; Asian 3.2%; Other 3.3%). **Foreign born:** 5.2%. **Median age:** 36.5.

Income 2000: per capita $24,560; median household $57,956; **Pop below poverty level:** 3.5%. *Personal per capita income 2000-2003: $29,709-$33,139 (includes York County & Poquoson).

Unemployment 2004: 2.9%. **Change from 2000:** +0.7%. **Median travel time to work:** 23.7 minutes. **Working outside county of residence:** 76.6%.

Cities with pop over 10,000: None.

Source: Personal per capita income data are from the Bureau of Economic Analysis; per capita income data are from the Bureau of the Census. See Introduction for explanation of differences.

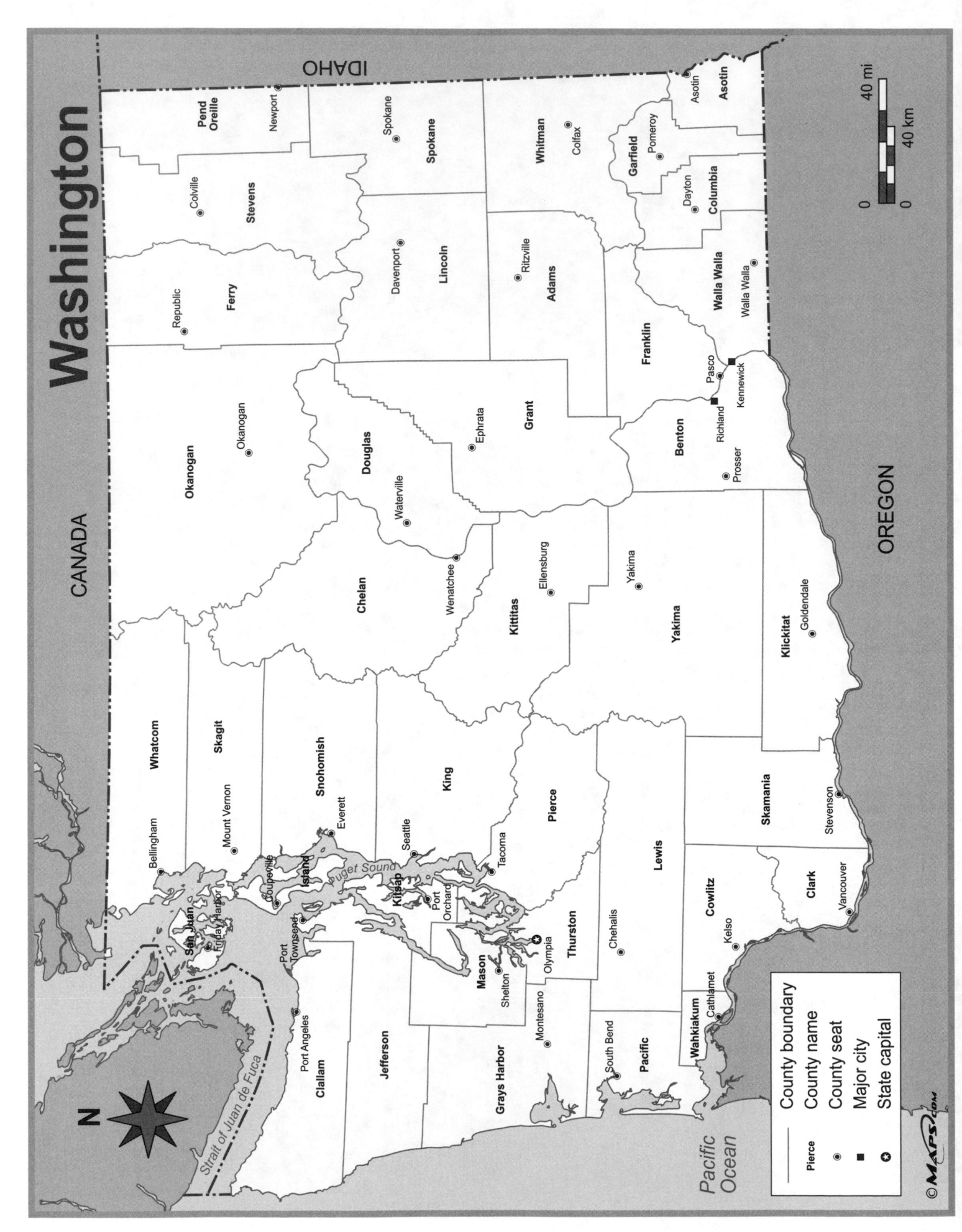

Washington

CANADA

IDAHO

OREGON

Pacific
Ocean

Strait of Juan de Fuca

Puget Sound

Pend Oreille — Newport
Stevens — Colville
Ferry — Republic
Okanogan — Okanogan
Spokane — Spokane
Whitman — Colfax
Garfield — Pomeroy
Asotin — Asotin
Lincoln — Davenport
Adams — Ritzville
Columbia — Dayton
Walla Walla — Walla Walla
Franklin — Pasco
Benton — Richland, Kennewick, Prosser
Douglas — Waterville
Grant — Ephrata
Chelan — Wenatchee
Kittitas — Ellensburg
Yakima — Yakima
Klickitat — Goldendale
Whatcom — Bellingham
Skagit — Mount Vernon
Snohomish — Everett
King — Seattle
Pierce — Tacoma
Island — Coupeville
San Juan — Friday Harbor
Kitsap — Port Orchard
Skamania — Stevenson
Clark — Vancouver
Lewis — Chehalis
Cowlitz — Kelso
Jefferson — Port Townsend
Clallam — Port Angeles
Mason — Shelton
Thurston — Olympia
Grays Harbor — Montesano
Pacific — South Bend
Wahkiakum — Cathlamet

N

Legend:
— County boundary
Pierce — County name
⊙ County seat
■ Major city
✪ State capital

40 mi
40 km
0

© MAPS.com

Washington

WASHINGTON STATE INFORMATION
access.wa.gov   **Ph:** 360-753-5000

Area (sq mi): 71,299.64 (land 66,544.06; water 4755.58). **Pop per sq mi:** 94.5.

Pop 2005: 6,287,759. **Pop change:** 2000-20005 +6.7%; 1990-2000 +21.1%. **Pop 2000:** 5,894,121 (White 78.9%; Black or African American 3.2%; Hispanic or Latino 7.5%; Asian 5.5%; Other 9.5%, including 1.6% American Indian/Alaska Native). **Foreign born:** 10.4%. **Median age:** 35.3.

Income 2000: per capita $22,973, median household $45,776, **Pop below poverty level:** 10.6%. ***Personal per capita income 2000-2003:** $31,779-$33,254.

Unemployment 2004: 6.3%. **Change from 2000:** +1.3%. **Median travel time to work:** 25.5 minutes. **Working outside county of residence:** 18.2%.

ADAMS COUNTY
210 W Broadway   **Ph:** 509-659-3257
Ritzville, WA 99169   **Fax:** 509-659-0118
www.co.adams.wa.us

In southeast WA, southwest of Spokane; organized Nov 28, 1883 (prior to statehood) from Whitman County. **Name Origin:** For John Adams (1735-1826), second U.S. president.

Area (sq mi): 1929.69 (land 1924.96; water 4.73). **Pop per sq mi:** 8.7.

Pop 2005: 16,803. **State rank:** 31. **Pop change:** 2000-20005 +2.3%; 1990-2000 +20.8%. **Pop 2000:** 16,428 (White 50.9%; Black or African American 0.3%; Hispanic or Latino 47.1%; Asian 0.6%; Other 34.1%). **Foreign born:** 22.9%. **Median age:** 29.6.

Income 2000: per capita $13,534; median household $33,888; **Pop below poverty level:** 18.2%. ***Personal per capita income 2000-2003:** $20,467-$22,099.

Unemployment 2004: 7.9%. **Change from 2000:** -2.9%. **Median travel time to work:** 17.7 minutes. **Working outside county of residence:** 19.8%.

Cities with pop over 10,000: None.

ASOTIN COUNTY
135 2nd St   **Ph:** 509-243-2081
Asotin, WA 99402   **Fax:** 509-243-4978
www.co.asotin.wa.us

On the southeastern border of WA; organized Oct 27, 1883 (prior to statehood) from Garfield County. **Name Origin:** For Asotin Creek,

which runs through the county; Nez Perce word meaning 'eel creek.'

Area (sq mi): 640.69 (land 635.34; water 5.34). **Pop per sq mi:** 33.3.

Pop 2005: 21,178. **State rank:** 29. **Pop change:** 2000-20005 +3.1%; 1990-2000 +16.7%. **Pop 2000:** 20,551 (White 94.5%; Black or African American 0.2%; Hispanic or Latino 2%; Asian 0.5%; Other 3.7%, including 1.3% American Indian/Alaska Native). **Foreign born:** 1.8%. **Median age:** 38.8.

Income 2000: per capita $17,748; median household $33,524; **Pop below poverty level:** 15.4%. ***Personal per capita income 2000-2003:** $23,716-$26,905.

Unemployment 2004: 6.6%. **Change from 2000:** +1.8%. **Median travel time to work:** 16.8 minutes. **Working outside county of residence:** 56.4%.

Cities with pop over 10,000: None.

BENTON COUNTY
7122 W Okanogan Pl MS C   **Ph:** 509-735-8388
Kennewick, WA 99336
www.co.benton.wa.us

On the south-central border of WA; organized Mar 8, 1905 from Yakima and Klickitat counties. **Name Origin:** For Thomas Hart Benton (1782-1858), U.S. journalist and statesman; nicknamed 'Old Bullion' for championing the use of gold and silver currency rather than paper money.

Area (sq mi): 1760.12 (land 1703.09; water 57.03). **Pop per sq mi:** 92.7.

Pop 2005: 157,950. **State rank:** 10. **Pop change:** 2000-20005 +10.9%; 1990-2000 +26.6%. **Pop 2000:** 142,475 (White 81.7%; Black or African American 0.9%; Hispanic or Latino 12.5%; Asian 2.2%; Other 10.6%). **Foreign born:** 8.5%. **Median age:** 34.4.

Income 2000: per capita $21,301; median household $47,044; **Pop below poverty level:** 10.3%. ***Personal per capita income 2000-2003:** $26,559-$29,689.

Unemployment 2004: 5.9%. **Change from 2000:** -0.6%. **Median travel time to work:** 21.5 minutes. **Working outside county of residence:** 20.1%.

Cities with pop over 10,000: Kennewick 🏛 (60,118); Richland (43,427).

CHELAN COUNTY
350 Orondo Ave   **Ph:** 509-667-6380
Wenatchee, WA 98801   **Fax:** 509-667-6611
www.co.chelan.wa.us

In north-central WA, east of Seattle; organized Mar 13, 1899 from

Chelan County (cont'd)

Kittitas and Okanogan counties. **Name Origin:** For Chelan Lake; from a Salish Indian tribal name, *tsill-anne*, said to mean 'deep water.'

Area (sq mi): 2993.62 (land 2921.37; water 72.25). **Pop per sq mi:** 23.9.

Pop 2005: 69,791. **State rank:** 17. **Pop change:** 2000-20005 +4.8%; 1990-2000 +27.5%. **Pop 2000:** 66,616 (White 77.4%; Black or African American 0.3%; Hispanic or Latino 19.3%; Asian 0.7%; Other 15.4%, including 1% American Indian/Alaska Native). **Foreign born:** 12.9%. **Median age:** 36.3.

Income 2000: per capita $19,273; median household $37,316; **Pop below poverty level:** 12.4%. ***Personal per capita income 2000-2003:** $25,101-$27,492.

Unemployment 2004: 6.9%. **Change from 2000:** -2.6%. **Median travel time to work:** 17.7 minutes. **Working outside county of residence:** 12.3%.

Cities with pop over 10,000: Wenatchee 🏛 (29,022).

CLALLAM COUNTY

223 E 4th St Suite 2   **Ph:** 360-452-7831
Port Angeles, WA 98362   **Fax:** 360-417-2493
www.clallam.net

On the northwest coast of WA, bordered on the north by the Strait of Juan de Fuca; organized as Clalm County Apr 26,1854 (prior to statehood) from Jefferson County; spelling changed soon after. **Name Origin:** For the Indian tribe; name means 'strong people.'

Area (sq mi): 2670.34 (land 1739.45; water 930.89). **Pop per sq mi:** 40.1.

Pop 2005: 69,689. **State rank:** 18. **Pop change:** 2000-20005 +8%; 1990-2000 +14.3%. **Pop 2000:** 64,525 (White 87.4%; Black or African American 0.8%; Hispanic or Latino 3.4%; Asian 1.1%; Other 8.9%, including 5.1% American Indian/Alaska Native). **Foreign born:** 4.5%. **Median age:** 43.8.

Income 2000: per capita $19,517; median household $36,449; **Pop below poverty level:** 12.5%. ***Personal per capita income 2000-2003:** $24,617-$27,737.

Unemployment 2004: 6.9%. **Change from 2000:** -0.9%. **Median travel time to work:** 21.4 minutes. **Working outside county of residence:** 6.4%.

Cities with pop over 10,000: Port Angeles 🏛 (18,635).

CLARK COUNTY

1200 Franklin St   **Ph:** 360-397-2000
Vancouver, WA 98660   **Fax:** 360-397-6099
www.co.clark.wa.us

On the southwestern border of WA, north of Portland, OR; original county. Organized as Vancouver County Dec 21, 1845 (prior to statehood); name changed Sep 3, 1849. **Name Origin:** For William Clark (1770-1838), explorer and co-leader of the Lewis and Clark expedition (1804-06).

Area (sq mi): 656.22 (land 628.22; water 27.99). **Pop per sq mi:** 642.7.

Pop 2005: 403,766. **State rank:** 5. **Pop change:** 2000-20005 +17%; 1990-2000 +45%. **Pop 2000:** 345,238 (White 86.6%; Black or African American 1.7%; Hispanic or Latino 4.7%; Asian 3.2%; Other 6.3%). **Foreign born:** 8.5%. **Median age:** 34.2.

Income 2000: per capita $21,448; median household $48,376; **Pop below poverty level:** 9.1%. ***Personal per capita income 2000-2003:** $28,890-$29,357.

Unemployment 2004: 7.5%. **Change from 2000:** +0.4%. **Median travel time to work:** 24.7 minutes. **Working outside county of residence:** 35.1%.

Cities with pop over 10,000: Vancouver 🏛 (155,053); Camas (16,089); Battle Ground (13,001); Washougal (10,134).

COLUMBIA COUNTY

341 E Main St   **Ph:** 509-382-4542
Dayton, WA 99328   **Fax:** 509-382-2490
www.columbiaco.com

On the southeastern border of WA; organized Nov 11, 1875 (prior to statehood) from Walla Walla County. **Name Origin:** For the Columbia River.

Area (sq mi): 873.53 (land 868.81; water 4.71). **Pop per sq mi:** 4.8.

Pop 2005: 4,129. **State rank:** 37. **Pop change:** 2000-20005 +1.6%; 1990-2000 +1%. **Pop 2000:** 4,064 (White 90.7%; Black or African American 0.2%; Hispanic or Latino 6.3%; Asian 0.4%; Other 5.6%, including 1% American Indian/Alaska Native). **Foreign born:** 3.2%. **Median age:** 42.4.

Income 2000: per capita $17,374; median household $33,500; **Pop below poverty level:** 12.6%. ***Personal per capita income 2000-2003:** $27,591-$26,320.

Unemployment 2004: 8%. **Change from 2000:** -3.4%. **Median travel time to work:** 18.7 minutes. **Working outside county of residence:** 25.6%.

Cities with pop over 10,000: None.

COWLITZ COUNTY

312 SW 1st Ave   **Ph:** 360-577-3016
Kelso, WA 98626   **Fax:** 360-577-2323
www.co.cowlitz.wa.us

In southwestern WA, north of Portland, OR; organized Apr 21, 1854 (prior to statehood) from Lewis County. **Name Origin:** For the Cowlitz River, which flows through the county; from an Indian tribal name; meaning uncertain but possibly 'river of shifting sand.'

Area (sq mi): 1166.33 (land 1138.64; water 27.69). **Pop per sq mi:** 85.5.

Pop 2005: 97,325. **State rank:** 12. **Pop change:** 2000-20005 +4.7%; 1990-2000 +13.2%. **Pop 2000:** 92,948 (White 89.9%; Black or African American 0.5%; Hispanic or Latino 4.6%; Asian 1.3%; Other 6.3%, including 1.5% American Indian/Alaska Native). **Foreign born:** 3.7%. **Median age:** 36.9.

Income 2000: per capita $18,583; median household $39,797; **Pop below poverty level:** 14%. ***Personal per capita income 2000-2003:** $23,665-$25,039.

Unemployment 2004: 8.5%. **Change from 2000:** -2.5%. **Median travel time to work:** 21.3 minutes. **Working outside county of residence:** 14.4%.

---

*Source: Personal per capita income data are from the Bureau of Economic Analysis; per capita income data are from the Bureau of the Census.
See Introduction for explanation of differences.

Cowlitz County (cont'd)

Cities with pop over 10,000: Longview (35,943); Kelso ⛪ (11,820).

DOUGLAS COUNTY

203 Ranier St
Waterville, WA 99050
www.douglascountywa.net

Ph: 509-745-8537
Fax: 509-745-9045

In east-central WA, west of Spokane; organized Nov 28, 1883 (prior to statehood) from Lincoln County, just four days after Lincoln Co. was formed. **Name Origin:** For Stephen Arnold Douglas (1813-61), U.S. orator and statesman.

Area (sq mi): 1848.69 (land 1820.53; water 28.17). **Pop per sq mi:** 19.2.

Pop 2005: 34,977. **State rank:** 26. **Pop change:** 2000-20005 +7.3%; 1990-2000 +24.4%. **Pop 2000:** 32,603 (White 77.2%; Black or African American 0.3%; Hispanic or Latino 19.7%; Asian 0.5%; Other 14.5%, including 1.1% American Indian/Alaska Native). **Foreign born:** 13.5%. **Median age:** 35.7.

Income 2000: per capita $17,148; median household $38,464; **Pop below poverty level:** 14.4%. ***Personal per capita income 2000-2003:** $21,509-$22,834.

Unemployment 2004: 6.3%. **Change from 2000:** -1.3%. **Median travel time to work:** 19.1 minutes. **Working outside county of residence:** 57.4%.

Cities with pop over 10,000: None.

FERRY COUNTY

290 E Tessie Ave
Republic, WA 99166
www.ferry-county.com

Ph: 509-775-5229
Fax: 509-775-5230

On northeastern border of WA, northwest of Spokane; organized as Eureka County Jan 12, 1899 from Stevens County; name changed Feb 16, 1899. Northern half is part of Colville National Forest; southern half comprises the Colville Indian Reservation. **Name Origin:** For Elisha Peyre Ferry (1825-95), first governor of WA (1889-93).

Area (sq mi): 2257.46 (land 2203.98; water 53.48). **Pop per sq mi:** 3.4.

Pop 2005: 7,542. **State rank:** 36. **Pop change:** 2000-20005 +3.9%; 1990-2000 +15.3%. **Pop 2000:** 7,260 (White 74.9%; Black or African American 0.2%; Hispanic or Latino 2.8%; Asian 0.3%; Other 24.1%, including 18.3% American Indian/Alaska Native). **Foreign born:** 2.5%. **Median age:** 40.

Income 2000: per capita $15,019; median household $30,388; **Pop below poverty level:** 19%. ***Personal per capita income 2000-2003:** $17,265-$18,955.

Unemployment 2004: 10.7%. **Change from 2000:** -3.8%. **Median travel time to work:** 24 minutes. **Working outside county of residence:** 21.4%.

Cities with pop over 10,000: None.

FRANKLIN COUNTY

1016 N 4th Ave
Pasco, WA 99301
www.co.franklin.wa.us

Ph: 509-545-3535
Fax: 509-545-3573

In southeastern WA; organized Nov 28, 1883 (prior to statehood) from Whitman County. **Name Origin:** For Benjamin Franklin (1706-90), U.S. patriot, diplomat, and statesman.

Area (sq mi): 1265.35 (land 1242.4; water 22.95). **Pop per sq mi:** 50.7.

Pop 2005: 63,011. **State rank:** 19. **Pop change:** 2000-20005 +27.7%; 1990-2000 +31.7%. **Pop 2000:** 49,347 (White 47.6%; Black or African American 2.5%; Hispanic or Latino 46.7%; Asian 1.6%; Other 33.9%). **Foreign born:** 25.2%. **Median age:** 28.

Income 2000: per capita $15,459; median household $38,991; **Pop below poverty level:** 19.2%. ***Personal per capita income 2000-2003:** $19,258-$20,757.

Unemployment 2004: 7.5%. **Change from 2000:** -1.9%. **Median travel time to work:** 20.9 minutes. **Working outside county of residence:** 41%.

Cities with pop over 10,000: Pasco ⛪ (42,290).

GARFIELD COUNTY

789 Main St
Pomeroy, WA 99347
www.palouse.org/garfield.htm

Ph: 509-843-3731
Fax: 509-843-1224

In southeastern WA; organized Nov 29, 1881 (prior to statehood) from Columbia County. **Name Origin:** For James Abram Garfiesld (1831-81), twentieth U.S. president.

Area (sq mi): 718.19 (land 710.55; water 7.64). **Pop per sq mi:** 3.3.

Pop 2005: 2,344. **State rank:** 39. **Pop change:** 2000-20005 -2.2%; 1990-2000 +6.6%. **Pop 2000:** 2,397 (White 96.1%; Black or African American 0%; Hispanic or Latino 2%; Asian 0.7%; Other 2.9%). **Foreign born:** 1%. **Median age:** 43.

Income 2000: per capita $16,992; median household $33,398; **Pop below poverty level:** 14.2%. ***Personal per capita income 2000-2003:** $24,225-$23,832.

Unemployment 2004: 5.2%. **Change from 2000:** +1.5%. **Median travel time to work:** 18.3 minutes. **Working outside county of residence:** 20.5%.

Cities with pop over 10,000: None.

GRANT COUNTY

35 C St NW
Ephrata, WA 98823
www.co.grant.wa.us

Ph: 509-754-2011
Fax: 509-754-6098

In east-central WA; organized Feb 24, 1909 from Douglas County. **Name Origin:** For Ulysses Simpson Grant (1822-85), Civil War general and eighteenth U.S. president.

Area (sq mi): 2791.29 (land 2681.06; water 110.23). **Pop per sq mi:** 30.3.

Pop 2005: 81,229. **State rank:** 13. **Pop change:** 2000-20005 +8.7%; 1990-2000 +36.4%. **Pop 2000:** 74,698 (White 65.4%; Black or African American 1%; Hispanic or Latino 30.1%; Asian 0.9%; Other 21.7%, including 1.2% American Indian/Alaska Native). **Foreign born:** 17.1%. **Median age:** 31.1.

Grant County (cont'd)

Income 2000: per capita $15,037; median household $35,276; **Pop below poverty level:** 17.4%. ***Personal per capita income 2000-2003:** $20,173-$21,756.

Unemployment 2004: 8.1%. **Change from 2000:** -2.2%. **Median travel time to work:** 17.7 minutes. **Working outside county of residence:** 7%.

Cities with pop over 10,000: Moses Lake (16,453).

GRAYS HARBOR COUNTY
102 W Broadway St Rm 203   **Ph:** 360-249-3842
Montesano, WA 98563   **Fax:** 360-249-6381
www.co.grays-harbor.wa.us

On the west-central coast of WA, E of Olympia; organized as Chehalis County Apr 14, 1854 (prior to statehood); name changed Mar 15, 1915. **Name Origin:** For Robert Gray (1755-1806), an American who discovered Grays Harbor and named it *Bulfinch* for an owner of his ship. Formerly called *Puerto Grek* by Spanish explorer Martinez y Zayas and *Whidbey* or *Whitbey Harbor* by British explorer David Douglas.

Area (sq mi): 2224.44 (land 1916.89; water 307.55). **Pop per sq mi:** 37.

Pop 2005: 70,900. **State rank:** 16. **Pop change:** 2000-20005 +5.5%; 1990-2000 +4.7%. **Pop 2000:** 67,194 (White 86.5%; Black or African American 0.3%; Hispanic or Latino 4.8%; Asian 1.2%; Other 10.2%, including 4.7% American Indian/Alaska Native). **Foreign born:** 4.2%. **Median age:** 38.8.

Income 2000: per capita $16,799; median household $34,160; **Pop below poverty level:** 16.1%. ***Personal per capita income 2000-2003:** $21,953-$23,467.

Unemployment 2004: 8.3%. **Change from 2000:** -2.3%. **Median travel time to work:** 22.4 minutes. **Working outside county of residence:** 12.6%.

Cities with pop over 10,000: Aberdeen (16,364).

ISLAND COUNTY
PO Box 5000   **Ph:** 360-679-7354
Coupeville, WA 98239   **Fax:** 360-679-7381
www.islandcounty.net

In northwestern WA, bounded on the north by Deception Pass, on the east by Skagit Bay, on the south by Admiralty Inlet, and on the west by the Strait of Juan de Fuca. Organized Jan 6, 1853 (prior to statehood) from either King County or Thurston County. **Name Origin:** So named because the county is wholly composed of islands.

Area (sq mi): 517.39 (land 208.43; water 308.95). **Pop per sq mi:** 380.2.

Pop 2005: 79,252. **State rank:** 14. **Pop change:** 2000-20005 +10.8%; 1990-2000 +18.9%. **Pop 2000:** 71,558 (White 85.1%; Black or African American 2.4%; Hispanic or Latino 4%; Asian 4.2%; Other 6.2%, including 1% American Indian/Alaska Native). **Foreign born:** 6.4%. **Median age:** 37.

Income 2000: per capita $21,472; median household $45,513; **Pop below poverty level:** 7%. ***Personal per capita income 2000-2003:** $26,567-$28,278.

Unemployment 2004: 6.6%. **Change from 2000:** +1.9%. **Median travel time to work:** 28.8 minutes. **Working outside county of residence:** 32.1%.

Cities with pop over 10,000: Oak Harbor (21,660).

JEFFERSON COUNTY
PO Box 1220   **Ph:** 360-385-9100
Port Townsend, WA 98368   **Fax:** 360-385-9382
www.co.jefferson.wa.us

On the northwestern coast of WA, E of Seattle; original county; organized Dec 23, 1852 (prior to statehood). **Name Origin:** For Thomas Jefferson (1743-1826), U.S. patriot and statesman; third U.S. president.

Area (sq mi): 2183.52 (land 1814.23; water 369.29). **Pop per sq mi:** 15.8.

Pop 2005: 28,666. **State rank:** 27. **Pop change:** 2000-20005 +10.5%; 1990-2000 +28.8%. **Pop 2000:** 25,953 (White 91%; Black or African American 0.4%; Hispanic or Latino 2.1%; Asian 1.2%; Other 6.2%, including 2.3% American Indian/Alaska Native). **Foreign born:** 4%. **Median age:** 47.1.

Income 2000: per capita $22,211; median household $37,869; **Pop below poverty level:** 11.3%. ***Personal per capita income 2000-2003:** $28,418-$31,097.

Unemployment 2004: 5.9%. **Change from 2000:** +0.1%. **Median travel time to work:** 26 minutes. **Working outside county of residence:** 19.9%.

Cities with pop over 10,000: None.

KING COUNTY
701 5th Ave Suite 3210   **Ph:** 206-296-4040
Seattle, WA 98104   **Fax:** 206-296-0194
www.metrokc.gov

In west-central WA, bounded on west by Puget Sound; organized Dec 22, 1852 (prior to statehood) from Thurston County. **Name Origin:** For William Rufus King (1786-1853), U.S. senator from AL (1819-44; 1848-52) and vice president for six weeks before his death. In 1986 it was decided the name would honor Martin Luther King, Jr. (1929-68), slain civil rights leader.

Area (sq mi): 2306.53 (land 2126.04; water 180.48). **Pop per sq mi:** 843.6.

Pop 2005: 1,793,583. **State rank:** 1. **Pop change:** 2000-20005 +3.3%; 1990-2000 +15.2%. **Pop 2000:** 1,737,034 (White 73.4%; Black or African American 5.4%; Hispanic or Latino 5.5%; Asian 10.8%; Other 8.1%). **Foreign born:** 15.4%. **Median age:** 35.7.

Income 2000: per capita $29,521; median household $53,157; **Pop below poverty level:** 8.4%. ***Personal per capita income 2000-2003:** $44,438-$45,334.

Unemployment 2004: 5.1%. **Change from 2000:** +0%. **Median travel time to work:** 26.5 minutes. **Working outside county of residence:** 6.8%.

Cities with pop over 10,000: 22 (see page 39 for cities).

---

*Source: Personal per capita income data are from the Bureau of Economic Analysis; per capita income data are from the Bureau of the Census. See Introduction for explanation of differences.

KITSAP COUNTY

614 Division St MS 4
Port Orchard, WA 98366
www.kitsapgov.com

Ph: 360-337-7146
Fax: 360-337-4632

A peninsula in western WA, bounded on east by Puget Sound, west of Seattle. Organized as Slaughter County Jan 16, 1857 (prior to statehood) from Jefferson and King counties; name changed Jul 13, 1857. **Name Origin:** For an Indian chief, whose name means 'brave,' said to have saved area settlers by warning them of a planned massacre. Originally named for Lt. W.A. Slaughter (?-1855).

Area (sq mi): 565.98 (land 395.97; water 170.01). **Pop per sq mi:** 607.8.

Pop 2005: 240,661. **State rank:** 6. **Pop change:** 2000-20005 +3.7%; 1990-2000 +22.3%. **Pop 2000:** 231,969 (White 82.2%; Black or African American 2.9%; Hispanic or Latino 4.1%; Asian 4.4%; Other 8.4%, including 1.6% American Indian/Alaska Native). **Foreign born:** 5.7%. **Median age:** 35.8.

Income 2000: per capita $22,317; median household $46,840; **Pop below poverty level:** 8.8%. *****Personal per capita income 2000-2003:** $29,493-$32,140

Unemployment 2004: 5.9%. **Change from 2000:** -0.1%. **Median travel time to work:** 32.5 minutes. **Working outside county of residence:** 23%.

Cities with pop over 10,000: Bremerton (35,967); Bainbridge Island (21,910).

KITTITAS COUNTY

205 W 5th Ave Rm 108
Ellensburg, WA 98926
www.co.kittitas.wa.us

Ph: 509-962-7508
Fax: 509-962-7679

In central WA, southeast of Tacoma; organized Nov 2, 1883 (prior to statehood) from Yakima County. **Name Origin:** Probably from a subtribal name of the Yakima Indians. Meaning uncertain, with 'shoal people' most appropriate, but 'land of bread' has also been suggested, as has 'gray gravel bank,' said to refer to a gravel bank on a river shoal.

Area (sq mi): 2333.11 (land 2297.19; water 35.93). **Pop per sq mi:** 16.

Pop 2005: 36,841. **State rank:** 25. **Pop change:** 2000-20005 +10.4%; 1990-2000 +24.8%. **Pop 2000:** 33,362 (White 89.4%; Black or African American 0.7%; Hispanic or Latino 5%; Asian 2.2%; Other 5.3%). **Foreign born:** 5.3%. **Median age:** 31.4.

Income 2000: per capita $18,928; median household $32,546; **Pop below poverty level:** 19.6%. *****Personal per capita income 2000-2003:** $23,028-$24,048.

Unemployment 2004: 6.5%. **Change from 2000:** +0%. **Median travel time to work:** 22 minutes. **Working outside county of residence:** 16.1%.

Cities with pop over 10,000: Ellensburg 🏛 (16,385).

KLICKITAT COUNTY

205 S Columbus Ave Rm 204 MS CH3
Goldendale, WA 98620
www.klickitatcounty.org

Ph: 509-773-5744
Fax: 509-773-4559

On central southern border of WA; original county; organized Dec

20, 1859 (prior to statehood). **Name Origin:** For an Indian nation that lived in the area; name possibly means 'beyond' or 'those who live beyond the mountain,' or even 'thief.'

Area (sq mi): 1904.18 (land 1872.37; water 31.8). **Pop per sq mi:** 10.6.

Pop 2005: 19,839. **State rank:** 30. **Pop change:** 2000-20005 +3.5%; 1990-2000 +15.3%. **Pop 2000:** 19,161 (White 85.2%; Black or African American 0.3%; Hispanic or Latino 7.8%; Asian 0.7%; Other 11.4%, including 3.5% American Indian/Alaska Native). **Foreign born:** 6%. **Median age:** 39.5.

Income 2000: per capita $16,502; median household $34,267; **Pop below poverty level:** 17%. *****Personal per capita income 2000-2003:** $22,520 $24,046.

Unemployment 2004: 9.2%. **Change from 2000:** -5.9%. **Median travel time to work:** 21.9 minutes. **Working outside county of residence:** 26.5%.

Cities with pop over 10,000: None.

LEWIS COUNTY

360 NW North St
Chehalis, WA 98532
fortress.wa.gov/lewisco/home

Ph: 360-748-9121
Fax: 360-748-1639

In southwestern WA, south of Tacoma; original county; organized Dec 21, 1845 (prior to statehood). **Name Origin:** For Meriwether Lewis (1774-1809), co-leader of the Lewis and Clark expedition (1804-06).

Area (sq mi): 2436.26 (land 2407.64; water 28.63). **Pop per sq mi:** 30.1.

Pop 2005: 72,449. **State rank:** 15. **Pop change:** 2000-20005 +5.6%; 1990-2000 +15.6%. **Pop 2000:** 68,600 (White 90.6%; Black or African American 0.4%; Hispanic or Latino 5.4%; Asian 0.7%; Other 6%, including 1.2% American Indian/Alaska Native). **Foreign born:** 4.1%. **Median age:** 38.4.

Income 2000: per capita $17,082; median household $35,511; **Pop below poverty level:** 14%. *****Personal per capita income 2000-2003:** $22,246-$23,694.

Unemployment 2004: 8.3%. **Change from 2000:** -1.1%. **Median travel time to work:** 25.7 minutes. **Working outside county of residence:** 20.1%.

Cities with pop over 10,000: Centralia (15,250).

LINCOLN COUNTY

450 Logan St
Davenport, WA 99122
www.co.lincoln.wa.us

Ph: 509-725-1401
Fax: 509-725-1150

In eastern WA, W of Spokane; organized Nov 24, 1883 (prior to statehood) from Spokane County. **Name Origin:** For Abraham Lincoln (1809-65), sixteenth U.S. president.

Area (sq mi): 2339.71 (land 2311.21; water 28.51). **Pop per sq mi:** 4.5.

Pop 2005: 10,381. **State rank:** 35. **Pop change:** 2000-20005 +1.9%; 1990-2000 +14.9%. **Pop 2000:** 10,184 (White 94.6%; Black or African American 0.2%; Hispanic or Latino 1.9%; Asian 0.2%; Other 3.9%, including 1.6% American Indian/Alaska Native). **Foreign born:** 1.2%. **Median age:** 42.8.

🏛 *County Seat*

Lincoln County (cont'd)

Income 2000: per capita $17,888; median household $35,255; **Pop below poverty level:** 12.6%. ***Personal per capita income 2000-2003:** $22,376-$23,817.

Unemployment 2004: 6.4%. **Change from 2000:** +1.1%. **Median travel time to work:** 22.1 minutes. **Working outside county of residence:** 27.7%.

Cities with pop over 10,000: None.

MASON COUNTY
PO Box 340   **Ph:** 360-427-9670
Shelton, WA 98584
www.co.mason.wa.us

In western WA, bordered on east by Puget Sound, west of Tacoma; organized as Sawamish County Mar 13, 1854 from Thurston County; name changed Jan 8, 1864. **Name Origin:** For Charles H. Mason (?-1859), secretary and sometimes acting governor of WA Territory.

Area (sq mi): 1051.03 (land 961.06; water 89.97). **Pop per sq mi:** 56.6.

Pop 2005: 54,359. **State rank:** 21. **Pop change:** 2000-20005 +10%; 1990-2000 +28.9%. **Pop 2000:** 49,405 (White 86.3%; Black or African American 1.2%; Hispanic or Latino 4.8%; Asian 1.1%; Other 9.2%, including 3.7% American Indian/Alaska Native). **Foreign born:** 4.4%. **Median age:** 40.3.

Income 2000: per capita $18,056; median household $39,586; **Pop below poverty level:** 12.2%. ***Personal per capita income 2000-2003:** $22,794-$24,689.

Unemployment 2004: 7.4%. **Change from 2000:** -0.5%. **Median travel time to work:** 30.8 minutes. **Working outside county of residence:** 43.3%.

Cities with pop over 10,000: None.

OKANOGAN COUNTY
149 N 3rd St   **Ph:** 509-422-7275
Okanogan, WA 98840   **Fax:** 509-422-7277
www.okanogancounty.org

On the central northern border of WA; organized Feb 2, 1888 (prior to statehood) from Stevens County. **Name Origin:** For the Okanogan River, which traverses the county. From a Salish Indian name possibly meaning 'meeting place [of water]' for the confluence of the Okanogan and Columbia rivers, or 'rendezvous' because they met here for their potlaches.

Area (sq mi): 5315.16 (land 5268.07; water 47.09). **Pop per sq mi:** 7.6.

Pop 2005: 39,782. **State rank:** 24. **Pop change:** 2000-20005 +0.6%; 1990-2000 +18.6%. **Pop 2000:** 39,564 (White 71.7%; Black or African American 0.3%; Hispanic or Latino 14.4%; Asian 0.4%; Other 24%, including 11.5% American Indian/Alaska Native). **Foreign born:** 10.2%. **Median age:** 38.2.

Income 2000: per capita $14,900; median household $29,726; **Pop below poverty level:** 21.3%. ***Personal per capita income 2000-2003:** $20,609-$23,095.

Unemployment 2004: 7.8%. **Change from 2000:** -3%. **Median travel time to work:** 19.6 minutes. **Working outside county of residence:** 9%.

Cities with pop over 10,000: None.

PACIFIC COUNTY
PO Box 67   **Ph:** 360-875-9300
South Bend, WA 98586   **Fax:** 360-875-9321
www.co.pacific.wa.us

On the southwestern coast of WA; original county; organized Feb 4, 1851 (prior to statehood). **Name Origin:** For the Pacific Ocean, which forms the county's western border.

Area (sq mi): 1223.5 (land 932.97; water 290.52). **Pop per sq mi:** 23.1.

Pop 2005: 21,579. **State rank:** 28. **Pop change:** 2000-20005 +2.8%; 1990-2000 +11.1%. **Pop 2000:** 20,984 (White 88%; Black or African American 0.2%; Hispanic or Latino 5%; Asian 2.1%; Other 7.1%, including 2.4% American Indian/Alaska Native). **Foreign born:** 6%. **Median age:** 45.8.

Income 2000: per capita $17,322; median household $31,209; **Pop below poverty level:** 14.4%. ***Personal per capita income 2000-2003:** $21,175-$23,395.

Unemployment 2004: 7.6%. **Change from 2000:** -1.4%. **Median travel time to work:** 20.7 minutes. **Working outside county of residence:** 17.4%.

Cities with pop over 10,000: None.

PEND OREILLE COUNTY
229 S Garden Ave   **Ph:** 509-447-2435
Newport, WA 99156   **Fax:** 509-447-2734
www.co.pend-oreille.wa.us

On northeastern border of WA; organized Mar 1, 1911 from Stevens County. **Name Origin:** For the Pend Oreille River, which runs through the county, or for the name given to the Kalispel Indians by French-Canadian traders; from the French meaning 'pendant ears' because the Indians wore ear ornaments that probably lengthened their lobes.

Area (sq mi): 1425.32 (land 1400.27; water 25.05). **Pop per sq mi:** 9.1.

Pop 2005: 12,673. **State rank:** 33. **Pop change:** 2000-20005 +8%; 1990-2000 +31.6%. **Pop 2000:** 11,732 (White 92.2%; Black or African American 0.1%; Hispanic or Latino 2.1%; Asian 0.6%; Other 5.7%, including 2.9% American Indian/Alaska Native). **Foreign born:** 2%. **Median age:** 41.9.

Income 2000: per capita $15,731; median household $31,677; **Pop below poverty level:** 18.1%. ***Personal per capita income 2000-2003:** $20,736-$22,009.

Unemployment 2004: 8.7%. **Change from 2000:** -1.4%. **Median travel time to work:** 31.5 minutes. **Working outside county of residence:** 38%.

Cities with pop over 10,000: None.

*Source: Personal per capita income data are from the Bureau of Economic Analysis; per capita income data are from the Bureau of the Census. See Introduction for explanation of differences.

PIERCE COUNTY

930 Tacoma Ave S Rm 110   **Ph:** 253-798-3495
Tacoma, WA 98402   **Fax:** 253-798-3428
www.co.pierce.wa.us

In west-central WA at the southeastern end of Puget Sound; original county; organized Dec 22, 1852 (prior to statehood). **Name Origin:** For Franklin Pierce (1804-69), fourteenth U.S. president.

Area (sq mi): 1806.6 (land 1678.01; water 127.58). **Pop per sq mi:** 449.

Pop 2005: 753,787. **State rank:** 2. **Pop change:** 2000-20005 +7.6%; 1990-2000 +19.6%. **Pop 2000:** 700,820 (White 76%; Black or African American 7%; Hispanic or Latino 5.5%; Asian 5.1%; Other 9.5%, including 1.4% American Indian/Alaska Native). **Foreign born:** 8.1%. **Median age:** 34.1.

Income 2000: per capita $20,948; median household $45,204; **Pop below poverty level:** 10.5%. ***Personal per capita income 2000-2003:** $27,580-$29,989.

Unemployment 2004: 7.1%. **Change from 2000:** +0.7%. **Median travel time to work:** 28.4 minutes. **Working outside county of residence:** 29.6%.

Cities with pop over 10,000: Tacoma ⏛ (196,094); Lakewood (58,070); Puyallup (35,496); University Place (30,399); Bonney Lake (14,142).

SAN JUAN COUNTY

350 Court St Rm 7   **Ph:** 360-378-2163
Friday Harbor, WA 98250   **Fax:** 360-378-3967
www.co.san-juan.wa.us

Islands in northwestern WA, bounded on west and northwest by Haro Strait, on north and northeast by Georgia Strait, and on south by Juan de Fuca Strait. Organized Oct 31, 1873 (prior to statehood) from Whatcom County. **Name Origin:** For Saint John the Baptist, cousin and baptizer of Jesus. Some sources suggest the county may have been named for San Juan Island, for Juan Francisco de Eliza, governor of the Spanish settlement at Nootka Sound in the late 18th century, or for Juan de Fuca, supposedly a Greek navigator in Spanish service.

Area (sq mi): 621.07 (land 174.92; water 446.15). **Pop per sq mi:** 87.3.

Pop 2005: 15,274. **State rank:** 32. **Pop change:** 2000-20005 +8.5%; 1990-2000 +40.3%. **Pop 2000:** 14,077 (White 93.7%; Black or African American 0.3%; Hispanic or Latino 2.4%; Asian 0.9%; Other 3.8%). **Foreign born:** 5.9%. **Median age:** 47.4.

Income 2000: per capita $30,603; median household $43,491; **Pop below poverty level:** 9.2%. ***Personal per capita income 2000-2003:** $37,620-$39,260.

Unemployment 2004: 4.5%. **Change from 2000:** +0.5%. **Median travel time to work:** 15.8 minutes. **Working outside county of residence:** 6.3%.

Cities with pop over 10,000: None.

SKAGIT COUNTY

205 W Kincaid St Rm 103   **Ph:** 360-336-9440
Mount Vernon, WA 98273
www.skagitcounty.net

In northwestern WA, bordered on west by upper Puget Sound, north of Seattle. Organized Nov 28, 1883 (prior to statehood) from Whatcom County. **Name Origin:** For the Indian tribe; meaning of name is unknown.

Area (sq mi): 1920.47 (land 1735.14; water 185.33). **Pop per sq mi:** 65.2.

Pop 2005: 113,171. **State rank:** 11. **Pop change:** 2000-20005 +9.9%; 1990-2000 +29.4%. **Pop 2000:** 102,979 (White 83%; Black or African American 0.4%; Hispanic or Latino 11.2%; Asian 1.5%; Other 11.7%, including 1.9% American Indian/Alaska Native). **Foreign born:** 8.8%. **Median age:** 37.2.

Income 2000: per capita $21,256; median household $42,381; **Pop below poverty level:** 11.1%. ***Personal per capita income 2000-2003:** $27,283-$30,144.

Unemployment 2004: 6.8%. **Change from 2000:** -0.6%. **Median travel time to work:** 25.1 minutes. **Working outside county of residence:** 21.7%.

Cities with pop over 10,000: Mount Vernon ⏛ (28,821); Anacortes (15,764).

SKAMANIA COUNTY

240 Vancouver Ave   **Ph:** 509-427-9430
Stevenson, WA 98648   **Fax:** 509-427-7386
www.skamaniacounty.org

On the southern border of WA, northeast of Portland, OR; organized Mar 9, 1854 (prior to statehood) from Clark County. **Name Origin:** From the Indian name for parts of the Columbia River, which forms the county's southern border. The usual interpretation is 'swift water.'

Area (sq mi): 1683.86 (land 1656.44; water 27.42). **Pop per sq mi:** 6.4.

Pop 2005: 10,664. **State rank:** 34. **Pop change:** 2000-20005 +8%; 1990-2000 +19.1%. **Pop 2000:** 9,872 (White 90.4%; Black or African American 0.3%; Hispanic or Latino 4%; Asian 0.5%; Other 7%, including 2.2% American Indian/Alaska Native). **Foreign born:** 3.5%. **Median age:** 38.7.

Income 2000: per capita $18,002; median household $39,317; **Pop below poverty level:** 13.1%. ***Personal per capita income 2000-2003:** $22,445-$22,758.

Unemployment 2004: 8.6%. **Change from 2000:** -2.5%. **Median travel time to work:** 29.2 minutes. **Working outside county of residence:** 52.3%.

Cities with pop over 10,000: None.

SNOHOMISH COUNTY

3000 Rockefeller Ave MS 605   **Ph:** 425-388-3466
Everett, WA 98201   **Fax:** 425-388-3806
www1.co.snohomish.wa.us

In northwestern WA, bordered on west by Puget Sound, northeast of Seattle. Organized Jan 14, 1861 (prior to statehood) from Island County. **Name Origin:** For the Snohomish Indians; name is believed to mean 'tidewater people' or 'union.'

Area (sq mi): 2196.41 (land 2089.06; water 107.35). **Pop per sq mi:** 314.

Pop 2005: 655,944. **State rank:** 3. **Pop change:** 2000-20005 +8.2%; 1990-2000 +30.1%. **Pop 2000:** 606,024 (White 83.4%; Black or

⏛ *County Seat*

Snohomish County (cont'd)

African American 1.7%; Hispanic or Latino 4.7%; Asian 5.8%; Other 7%, including 1.4% American Indian/Alaska Native). **Foreign born:** 9.7%. **Median age:** 34.7.

Income 2000: per capita $23,417; median household $53,060; **Pop below poverty level:** 6.9%. ***Personal per capita income 2000-2003:** $30,393-$31,964.

Unemployment 2004: 5.6%. **Change from 2000:** +0.2%. **Median travel time to work:** 29.6 minutes. **Working outside county of residence:** 37.2%.

Cities with pop over 10,000: 9 (see page 39 for cities).

SPOKANE COUNTY

1116 W Broadway Ave   **Ph:** 509-477-2265
Spokane, WA 99260   **Fax:** 509-477-2274
www.spokanecounty.org

On central eastern border of WA; organized Jan 29, 1864 (prior to statehood) from Stevens County (an earlier Spokane County was merged with Stevens County in 1863). It is the only WA county with township governments in each township. **Name Origin:** For the Spokane Indians, or for the city or river also named for the tribe. The meaning of the name is uncertain; possibly 'sun people' or 'children of the sun', or the name may be from Chief Illum Spokane, whose village was at the base of what became known as Spokane Falls.

Area (sq mi): 1780.72 (land 1763.64; water 17.09). **Pop per sq mi:** 249.9.

Pop 2005: 440,706. **State rank:** 4. **Pop change:** 2000-20005 +5.4%; 1990-2000 +15.7%. **Pop 2000:** 417,939 (White 89.8%; Black or African American 1.6%; Hispanic or Latino 2.8%; Asian 1.9%; Other 5.2%, including 1.4% American Indian/Alaska Native). **Foreign born:** 4.5%. **Median age:** 35.4.

Income 2000: per capita $19,233; median household $37,308; **Pop below poverty level:** 12.3%. ***Personal per capita income 2000-2003:** $26,010-$27,218.

Unemployment 2004: 6.5%. **Change from 2000:** -0.1%. **Median travel time to work:** 21.2 minutes. **Working outside county of residence:** 3.4%.

Cities with pop over 10,000: Spokane 🏛 (196,721); Spokane Valley (81,189); Cheney (10,076).

STEVENS COUNTY

215 S Oak St   **Ph:** 509-684-3751
Colville, WA 99114   **Fax:** 509-684-8310
www.co.stevens.wa.us

On the northeastern border of WA, northwest of Spokane; original county. Organized 1854 (prior to statehood). **Name Origin:** For Gen. Isaac Ingalls Stevens (1818-62), an officer in the Mexican-American War and the Civil War; first governor of WA Territory (1853-57).

Area (sq mi): 2540.64 (land 2478.3; water 62.34). **Pop per sq mi:** 17.

Pop 2005: 42,013. **State rank:** 22. **Pop change:** 2000-20005 +4.9%; 1990-2000 +29.5%. **Pop 2000:** 40,066 (White 89.1%; Black or African American 0.3%; Hispanic or Latino 1.8%; Asian 0.5%;

Other 9.3%, including 5.7% American Indian/Alaska Native). **Foreign born:** 2.4%. **Median age:** 39.2.

Income 2000: per capita $15,895; median household $34,673; **Pop below poverty level:** 15.9%. ***Personal per capita income 2000-2003:** $19,598-$21,089.

Unemployment 2004: 8.3%. **Change from 2000:** -2.6%. **Median travel time to work:** 27 minutes. **Working outside county of residence:** 29.2%.

Cities with pop over 10,000: None.

THURSTON COUNTY

2000 Lakeridge Dr SW Bldg 2   **Ph:** 360-786-5430
Olympia, WA 98502   **Fax:** 360-753-4033
www.co.thurston.wa.us

In west-central WA at the southern end of Puget Sound, southwest of Tacoma; organized Jan 12, 1852 (prior to statehood) from Lewis County. **Name Origin:** For Samuel Royal Thurston (1816-54), first delegate to Congress from the Oregon territory (1849-51).

Area (sq mi): 773.64 (land 727.02; water 46.62). **Pop per sq mi:** 314.8.

Pop 2005: 228,867. **State rank:** 8. **Pop change:** 2000-20005 +10.4%; 1990-2000 +28.6%. **Pop 2000:** 207,355 (White 83.4%; Black or African American 2.4%; Hispanic or Latino 4.5%; Asian 4.4%; Other 7.6%, including 1.5% American Indian/Alaska Native). **Foreign born:** 6.1%. **Median age:** 36.5.

Income 2000: per capita $22,415; median household $46,975; **Pop below poverty level:** 8.8%. ***Personal per capita income 2000-2003:** $29,250-$31,343.

Unemployment 2004: 5.7%. **Change from 2000:** +0%. **Median travel time to work:** 24.4 minutes. **Working outside county of residence:** 26.6%.

Cities with pop over 10,000: Olympia 🏛 (43,982); Lacey (32,981); Tumwater (13,182).

WAHKIAKUM COUNTY

PO Box 116   **Ph:** 360-795-3558
Cathlamet, WA 98612   **Fax:** 360-795-8813
www.co.wahkiakum.wa.us

On the southwestern border of WA at the mouth of the Columbia River; organized Apr 25, 1854 (prior to statehood) from Lewis County. **Name Origin:** For a Chinook tribe and chief, Wakiacum, a name believed to mean 'tall trees' or 'big timber.' The spelling was probably changed to reflect the Indian pronunciation.

Area (sq mi): 286.69 (land 264.24; water 22.45). **Pop per sq mi:** 14.6.

Pop 2005: 3,849. **State rank:** 38. **Pop change:** 2000-20005 +0.7%; 1990-2000 +14.9%. **Pop 2000:** 3,824 (White 92.7%; Black or African American 0.3%; Hispanic or Latino 2.6%; Asian 0.5%; Other 5.8%, including 1.6% American Indian/Alaska Native). **Foreign born:** 1.3%. **Median age:** 44.4.

Income 2000: per capita $19,063; median household $39,444; **Pop below poverty level:** 8.1%. ***Personal per capita income 2000-2003:** $22,493-$24,570.

*Source: Personal per capita income data are from the Bureau of Economic Analysis; per capita income data are from the Bureau of the Census. See Introduction for explanation of differences.

Wahkiakum County (cont'd)

Unemployment 2004: 7.5%. **Change from 2000:** +0.2%. **Median travel time to work:** 28.1 minutes. **Working outside county of residence:** 45.6%.

Cities with pop over 10,000: None.

WALLA WALLA COUNTY
315 W Main St
Walla Walla, WA 99362
www.co.walla-walla.wa.us
Ph: 509-527-3200
Fax: 509-527-3235

On the southeastern border of WA; original county; organized Apr 25, 1854 (prior to statehood). **Name Origin:** Apparently for a small tribe, closely related to the Nez Perce, which took its name from the Walla Walla River, 'place of many waters,' referring to the many tributaries, springs, and streams in the area. Lewis and Clark recorded the name as *Wollah Wollah*.

Area (sq mi): 1299.25 (land 1270.51; water 28.74). **Pop per sq mi:** 45.3.

Pop 2005: 57,558. **State rank:** 20. **Pop change:** 2000-20005 +4.3%; 1990-2000 +13.9%. **Pop 2000:** 55,180 (White 78.8%, Black or African American 1.7%; Hispanic or Latino 15.7%; Asian 1.1%; Other 11.8%). **Foreign born:** 9.4%. **Median age:** 34.9.

Income 2000: per capita $16,509; median household $35,900; **Pop below poverty level:** 15.1%. *****Personal per capita income 2000-2003:** $22,643-$24,417.

Unemployment 2004: 6.1%. **Change from 2000:** -0.4%. **Median travel time to work:** 15.2 minutes. **Working outside county of residence:** 13.7%.

Cities with pop over 10,000: Walla Walla 🏛 (30,272).

WHATCOM COUNTY
311 Grand Ave Rm 301
Bellingham, WA 98225
www.co.whatcom.wa.us
Ph: 360-676-6777
Fax: 360-676-6693

On the northwestern border of WA, bordered on west by Georgia Strait; organized Mar 9, 1854 (prior to statehood) from Island County. **Name Origin:** From the Lummi Indian word *what-coom* or *whuks-qua-koos-ta-qua*, said to mean 'noisy, rumbling water,' referring to Whatcom Falls on Bellingham Bay.

Area (sq mi): 2503.55 (land 2119.53; water 384.02). **Pop per sq mi:** 86.6.

Pop 2005: 183,471. **State rank:** 9. **Pop change:** 2000-20005 +10%; 1990-2000 +30.5%. **Pop 2000:** 166,814 (White 86.2%; Black or African American 0.7%; Hispanic or Latino 5.2%; Asian 2.8%; Other 8.1%, including 2.8% American Indian/Alaska Native). **Foreign born:** 9.8%. **Median age:** 34.

Income 2000: per capita $20,025; median household $40,005; **Pop below poverty level:** 14.2%. *****Personal per capita income 2000-2003:** $24,241-$26,617.

Unemployment 2004: 5.7%. **Change from 2000:** -1.1%. **Median travel time to work:** 20.8 minutes. **Working outside county of residence:** 9.1%.

Cities with pop over 10,000: Bellingham 🏛 (72,992); Lynden (10,456).

WHITMAN COUNTY
400 N Main St
Colfax, WA 99111
www.co.whitman.wa.us
Ph: 509-397-4622
Fax: 509-397-6355

On the southeastern border of WA, S of Spokane; organized Nov 29, 1871 (prior to statehood) from Stevens County. **Name Origin:** For Dr. Marcus Whitman (1802-47), massacred leader of a missionary colony.

Area (sq mi): 2177.6 (land 2159.37; water 18.23). **Pop per sq mi:** 18.6.

Pop 2005: 40,170. **State rank:** 23. **Pop change:** 2000-20005 -1.4%; 1990-2000 +5.1%. **Pop 2000:** 40,740 (White 86.7%; Black or African American 1.5%; Hispanic or Latino 3%; Asian 5.5%; Other 4.8%). **Foreign born:** 7.7%. **Median age:** 24.7.

Income 2000: per capita $15,298; median household $28,584; **Pop below poverty level:** 25.6%. *****Personal per capita income 2000-2003:** $19,821-$20,465.

Unemployment 2004: 4.4%. **Change from 2000:** +1.9%. **Median travel time to work:** 15.6 minutes. **Working outside county of residence:** 11.5%.

Cities with pop over 10,000: Pullman (25,022).

YAKIMA COUNTY
128 N 2nd St Rm 323
Yakima, WA 98901
www.co.yakima.wa.us
Ph: 509-574-1430
Fax: 509-574-1473

In south-central WA; organized Jan 1, 1865 (prior to statehood) from Indian Territory. **Name Origin:** For a tribe of Shahaptian Indians; name is believed to mean either 'runaway,' for a chief's errant daughter, or possibly 'black bear.'

Area (sq mi): 4311.61 (land 4296.23; water 15.38). **Pop per sq mi:** 53.9.

Pop 2005: 231,586. **State rank:** 7. **Pop change:** 2000-20005 +4%; 1990-2000 +17.9%. **Pop 2000:** 222,581 (White 56.5%; Black or African American 1%; Hispanic or Latino 35.9%; Asian 1%; Other 32.5%, including 4.5% American Indian/Alaska Native). **Foreign born:** 16.9%. **Median age:** 31.2.

Income 2000: per capita $15,606; median household $34,828; **Pop below poverty level:** 19.7%. *****Personal per capita income 2000-2003:** $22,070-$23,916.

Unemployment 2004: 8.6%. **Change from 2000:** -2.7%. **Median travel time to work:** 19.4 minutes. **Working outside county of residence:** 4.6%.

Cities with pop over 10,000: Yakima 🏛 (80,891); Sunnyside (14,216).

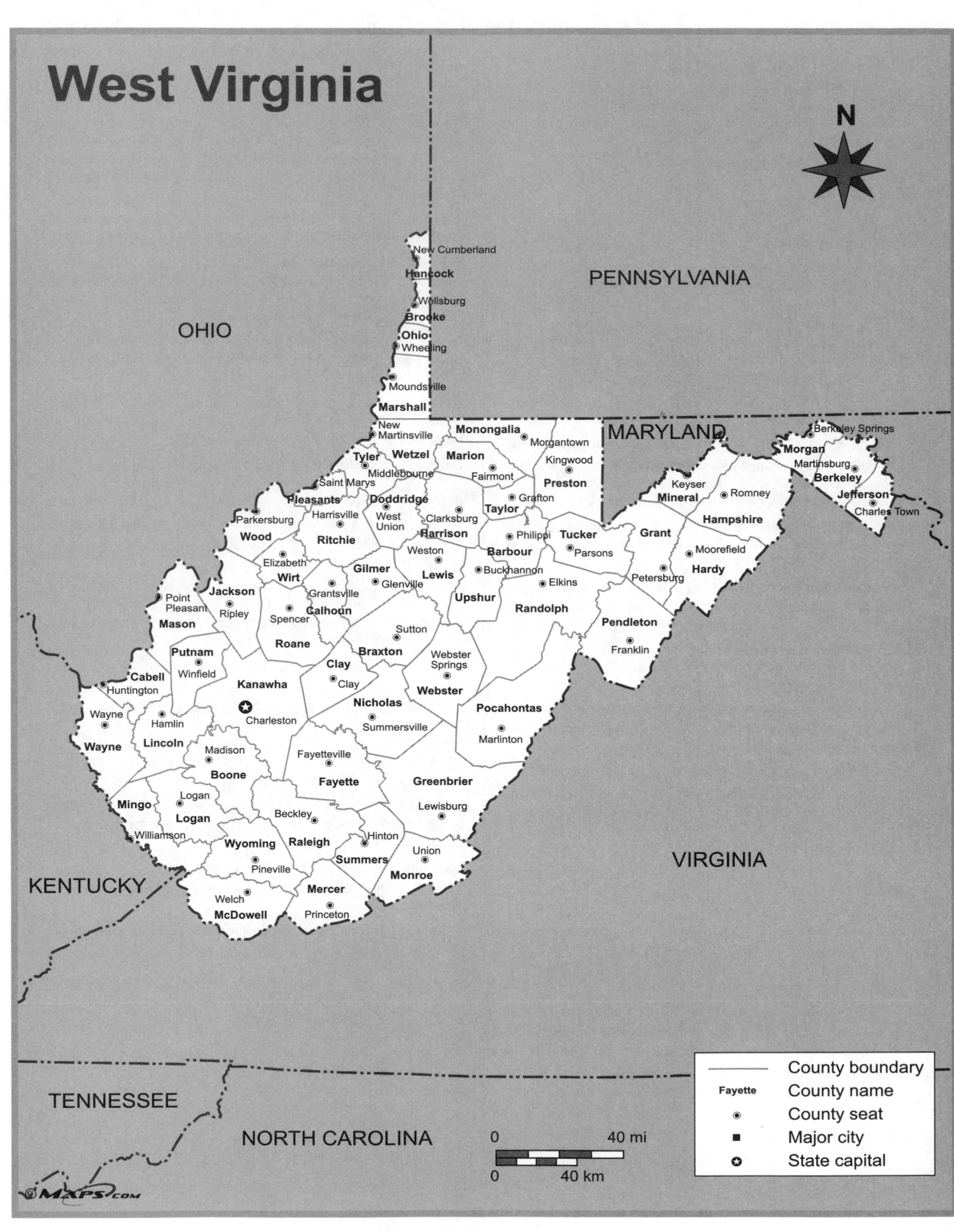

West Virginia

N

PENNSYLVANIA

OHIO

New Cumberland

Hancock

Wellsburg

Brooke

Ohio
Wheeling

Moundsville

Marshall

MARYLAND

Berkeley Springs

Morgan
Martinsburg

Berkeley

Jefferson
Charles Town

New
Martinsville

Monongalia

Morgantown

Kingwood

Preston

Keyser

Mineral

Romney

Hampshire

Tyler
Wetzel
Marion

Middlebourne
Fairmont

Saint Marys

Pleasants
Doddridge
Taylor

Grafton

Parkersburg
Harrisville
West
Union
Clarksburg

Grant

Moorefield

Wood
Ritchie
Harrison

Philippi
Tucker
Parsons

Hardy

Petersburg

Elizabeth

Gilmer
Weston

Barbour
Buckhannon

Wirt

Glenville

Lewis
Elkins

Jackson

Grantsville

Randolph

Point
Pleasant
Ripley

Calhoun

Upshur

Pendleton

Mason
Spencer

Roane
Sutton

Franklin

Putnam
Braxton

Webster
Springs

Cabell
Winfield

Clay

Huntington
Kanawha
Clay

Webster

Pocahontas

Wayne
Charleston

Nicholas

Marlinton

Hamlin
Summersville

Lincoln
Madison

Fayetteville

Wayne

Boone
Fayette

Greenbrier

Logan

Lewisburg

Mingo
Beckley

Logan

Hinton

Williamson

Wyoming
Raleigh

Union

Pineville
Summers
Monroe

Welch
Mercer

McDowell
Princeton

KENTUCKY

VIRGINIA

TENNESSEE

NORTH CAROLINA

0   40 mi

0   40 km

— County boundary
Fayette   County name
⊙   County seat
■   Major city
✪   State capital

©MAPS.com

West Virginia

WEST VIRGINIA STATE INFORMATION
www.wv.gov   **Ph:** 304-558-3456

Area (sq mi): 24,229.76 (land 24,077.73; water 152.03). **Pop per sq mi:** 75.5.

Pop 2005: 1,816,856. **Pop change:** 2000-20005 +0.5%; 1990-2000 +0.8%. **Pop 2000:** 1,808,344 (White 94.6%; Black or African American 3.2%; Hispanic or Latino 0.7%; Asian 0.5%; Other 1.3%). **Foreign born:** 1.1%. **Median age:** 38.9.

Income 2000: per capita $16,477; median household $29,696; **Pop below poverty level:** 17.9%. ***Personal per capita income 2000-2003:** $21,900-$24,542.

Unemployment 2004: 5.3%. **Change from 2000:** -0.2%. **Median travel time to work:** 26.2 minutes. **Working outside county of residence:** 31.4%.

BARBOUR COUNTY
8 N Main St   **Ph:** 304-457-2232
Philippi, WV 26416   **Fax:** 304-457-2790

In northern WV, southeast of Clarksburg; organized Mar 3, 1843 from Harrison, Lewis, and Randolph counties. **Name Origin:** For Philip Pendleton Barbour (1783-1841), U.S. representative from VA (1814-25; 1827-30) and associate justice of the U.S. Supreme Court (1836-41).

Area (sq mi): 342.75 (land 340.79; water 1.96). **Pop per sq mi:** 46.

Pop 2005: 15,689. **State rank:** 37. **Pop change:** 2000-20005 +0.8%; 1990-2000 -0.9%. **Pop 2000:** 15,557 (White 97%; Black or African American 0.5%; Hispanic or Latino 0.5%; Asian 0.3%; Other 1.8%). **Foreign born:** 0.5%. **Median age:** 38.7.

Income 2000: per capita $12,440; median household $24,729; **Pop below poverty level:** 22.6%. ***Personal per capita income 2000-2003:** $16,878-$19,551.

Unemployment 2004: 6.4%. **Change from 2000:** -1.4%. **Median travel time to work:** 28 minutes. **Working outside county of residence:** 44.9%.

Cities with pop over 10,000: None.

BERKELEY COUNTY
100 W King St Rm 1   **Ph:** 304-264-1925
Martinsburg, WV 25401   **Fax:** 304-267-1794
www.berkeleycountycomm.org

In eastern panhandle of WV, southwest of Hagerstown, MD; organized Feb 10, 1772 (prior to statehood) from Frederick County (in VA). **Name Origin:** For Norborne Berkeley (1718-70), Lord

Botetourt, member of the British Parliament and colonial governor of VA (1768-70) who favored the colonists.

Area (sq mi): 321.58 (land 321.14; water 0.44). **Pop per sq mi:** 290.8.

Pop 2005: 93,394. **State rank:** 3. **Pop change:** 2000-20005 +23%; 1990-2000 +28.1%. **Pop 2000:** 75,905 (White 91.9%; Black or African American 4.7%; Hispanic or Latino 1.5%; Asian 0.5%; Other 2.1%). **Foreign born:** 1.7%. **Median age:** 35.8.

Income 2000: per capita $17,982; median household $38,763; **Pop below poverty level:** 11.5%. ***Personal per capita income 2000-2003:** $23,250-$25,276.

Unemployment 2004: 4.2%. **Change from 2000:** +0.5%. **Median travel time to work:** 28.8 minutes. **Working outside county of residence:** 43.8%.

Cities with pop over 10,000: Martinsburg 🏛 (15,635).

BOONE COUNTY
200 State St   **Ph:** 304-369-3925
Madison, WV 25130   **Fax:** 304-369-7329
www.boonecountywv.org

In southwestern WV, south of Charleston; organized Mar 11, 1847 from Kanawha, Cabell, and Logan counties. **Name Origin:** For Daniel Boone (1734?-1820), U.S. frontiersman and KY pioneer, onetime resident of the nearby Kanawha Valley.

Area (sq mi): 503.18 (land 502.98; water 0.2). **Pop per sq mi:** 51.1.

Pop 2005: 25,703. **State rank:** 26. **Pop change:** 2000-20005 +0.7%; 1990-2000 -1.3%. **Pop 2000:** 25,535 (White 98.2%; Black or African American 0.7%; Hispanic or Latino 0.5%; Asian 0.1%; Other 0.7%). **Foreign born:** 0.4%. **Median age:** 38.8.

Income 2000: per capita $14,453; median household $25,669; **Pop below poverty level:** 22%. ***Personal per capita income 2000-2003:** $19,329-$20,175.

Unemployment 2004: 5%. **Change from 2000:** -0.5%. **Median travel time to work:** 33.8 minutes. **Working outside county of residence:** 45.4%.

Cities with pop over 10,000: None.

BRAXTON COUNTY
300 Main St PO Box 486   **Ph:** 304-765-2833
Sutton, WV 26601   **Fax:** 304-765-2093
www.braxtonwv.org/CourtHouse.htm

In central WV, northeast of Charleston; organized Jan 15, 1836 from Kanawha, Lewis, Nicholas, and Randolph counties. **Name Origin:** For Carter Braxton (1736-97), VA House of Burgesses

Braxton County (cont'd)

(1767-71; 1775), a signer of the Declaration of Independence, and a member of the council of state (1786-91; 1794-97).

Area (sq mi): 516.17 (land 513.48; water 2.69). **Pop per sq mi:** 28.9.

Pop 2005: 14,851. **State rank:** 39. **Pop change:** 2000-20005 +1%; 1990-2000 +13.1%. **Pop 2000:** 14,702 (White 97.6%; Black or African American 0.7%; Hispanic or Latino 0.4%; Asian 0.1%; Other 1.1%). **Foreign born:** 0.2%. **Median age:** 39.6.

Income 2000: per capita $13,349; median household $24,412; **Pop below poverty level:** 22%. ***Personal per capita income 2000-2003:** $15,587-$17,562.

Unemployment 2004: 6%. **Change from 2000:** -2%. **Median travel time to work:** 36.7 minutes. **Working outside county of residence:** 29.5%.

Cities with pop over 10,000: None.

BROOKE COUNTY

632 Main St   **Ph:** 304-737-3661
Wellsburg, WV 26070   **Fax:** 304-737-4023

In northern panhandle of WV, east of Steubenville, OH; organized Nov 30, 1796 from Ohio County. **Name Origin:** For Robert Brooke (1751-99), governor of VA (1794-96) and attorney general (1798).

Area (sq mi): 92.26 (land 88.85; water 3.41). **Pop per sq mi:** 275.9.

Pop 2005: 24,515. **State rank:** 27. **Pop change:** 2000-20005 -3.7%; 1990-2000 -5.7%. **Pop 2000:** 25,447 (White 97.6%; Black or African American 0.8%; Hispanic or Latino 0.4%; Asian 0.3%; Other 0.9%). **Foreign born:** 1.1%. **Median age:** 41.2.

Income 2000: per capita $17,131; median household $32,981; **Pop below poverty level:** 11.7%. ***Personal per capita income 2000-2003:** $22,384-$24,418.

Unemployment 2004: 7.3%. **Change from 2000:** +2.8%. **Median travel time to work:** 23.9 minutes. **Working outside county of residence:** 47.9%.

Cities with pop over 10,000: None.

CABELL COUNTY

750 5th Ave Rm 108   **Ph:** 304-526-8625
Huntington, WV 25701   **Fax:** 304-526-8632
www.cabellcounty.org

On western border of WV along the Ohio River, west of Charleston; organized Jan 2, 1809 from Kanawha County. **Name Origin:** For William H. Cabell (1772-1853), governor of VA (1805-08) and judge of various courts (1808; 1811; 1830).

Area (sq mi): 288.02 (land 281.59; water 6.43). **Pop per sq mi:** 333.9.

Pop 2005: 94,031. **State rank:** 2. **Pop change:** 2000-20005 -2.8%; 1990-2000 +0%. **Pop 2000:** 96,784 (White 92.9%; Black or African American 4.3%; Hispanic or Latino 0.7%; Asian 0.8%; Other 1.5%). **Foreign born:** 1.3%. **Median age:** 37.5.

Income 2000: per capita $17,638; median household $28,479; **Pop below poverty level:** 19.2%. ***Personal per capita income 2000-2003:** $23,638-$26,289.

Unemployment 2004: 4.8%. **Change from 2000:** +0.1%. **Median travel time to work:** 21.7 minutes. **Working outside county of residence:** 19.3%.

Cities with pop over 10,000: Huntington 🏛 (49,891).

CALHOUN COUNTY

PO Box 230   **Ph:** 304-354-6725
Grantsville, WV 26147   **Fax:** 304-354-6725

In central WV, southeast of Parkersburg; organized Mar 5, 1856 from Gilmer County. **Name Origin:** For John Caldwell Calhoun (1782-1850), U.S. statesman and champion of Southern causes.

Area (sq mi): 280.64 (land 280.62; water 0.02). **Pop per sq mi:** 26.3.

Pop 2005: 7,387. **State rank:** 51. **Pop change:** 2000-20005 -2.6%; 1990-2000 -3.8%. **Pop 2000:** 7,582 (White 98.6%; Black or African American 0.1%; Hispanic or Latino 0.6%; Asian 0.1%; Other 0.8%). **Foreign born:** 0.6%. **Median age:** 41.3.

Income 2000: per capita $11,491; median household $21,578; **Pop below poverty level:** 25.1%. ***Personal per capita income 2000-2003:** $15,660-$17,045.

Unemployment 2004: 9.4%. **Change from 2000:** -6%. **Median travel time to work:** 38 minutes. **Working outside county of residence:** 45.6%.

Cities with pop over 10,000: None.

CLAY COUNTY

PO Box 190   **Ph:** 304-587-4259
Clay, WV 25043   **Fax:** 304-587-7329

In central WV, east of Charleston; organized Mar 29, 1858 from Braxton and Nicholas counties. **Name Origin:** For Henry Clay (1777-1852), U.S. senator from KY, known as the 'Great Pacificator' for his advocacy of compromise to avert national crises.

Area (sq mi): 343.82 (land 342.4; water 1.42). **Pop per sq mi:** 30.2.

Pop 2005: 10,356. **State rank:** 45. **Pop change:** 2000-20005 +0.3%; 1990-2000 +3.5%. **Pop 2000:** 10,330 (White 97.9%; Black or African American 0.1%; Hispanic or Latino 0.4%; Asian 0%; Other 1.7%). **Foreign born:** 0.1%. **Median age:** 36.8.

Income 2000: per capita $12,021; median household $22,120; **Pop below poverty level:** 27.5%. ***Personal per capita income 2000-2003:** $13,713-$15,383.

Unemployment 2004: 7.5%. **Change from 2000:** +0.4%. **Median travel time to work:** 45 minutes. **Working outside county of residence:** 52.8%.

Cities with pop over 10,000: None.

DODDRIDGE COUNTY

118 E Court St Rm 102   **Ph:** 304-873-2631
West Union, WV 26456   **Fax:** 304-873-1840

In northern WV, west of Clarksburg; organized Feb 4, 1845 from Harrison, Tyler, Ritchie, and Lewis counties. **Name Origin:** For Philip Doddridge (1773-1832), VA house of delegates (1815-16; 1822-23; 1828-29) and U.S. representative (1829-32).

Area (sq mi): 320.48 (land 320.43; water 0.05). **Pop per sq mi:** 23.3.

Pop 2005: 7,476. **State rank:** 50. **Pop change:** 2000-20005 +1%; 1990-2000 +5.8%. **Pop 2000:** 7,403 (White 98%; Black or African

*Source: Personal per capita income data are from the Bureau of Economic Analysis; per capita income data are from the Bureau of the Census.
See Introduction for explanation of differences.

770

Doddridge County (cont'd)

American 0.3%; Hispanic or Latino 0.6%; Asian 0.1%; Other 1.2%). **Foreign born:** 0.6%. **Median age:** 38.7.

Income 2000: per capita $13,507; median household $26,744; **Pop below poverty level:** 19.8%. ***Personal per capita income 2000-2003:** $16,724-$17,731.

Unemployment 2004: 5%. **Change from 2000:** +0.6%. **Median travel time to work:** 38 minutes. **Working outside county of residence:** 68.9%.

Cities with pop over 10,000: None.

FAYETTE COUNTY

100 Court St   **Ph:** 304-574-4348
Fayetteville, WV 25840   **Fax:** 304-574-4314
www.fayettecounty.com

In south-central WV, north of Beckley; organized Feb 28, 1831 from Kanawha, Greenbrier, Nicholas, and Logan counties. **Name Origin:** For the Marquis de Lafayette (1757-1834), French statesman and soldier who fought with the Americans during the Revolutionary War.

Area (sq mi): 668.36 (land 663.93; water 4.43). **Pop per sq mi:** 70.5.

Pop 2005: 46,823. **State rank:** 12. **Pop change:** 2000-20005 -1.6%; 1990-2000 -0.8%. **Pop 2000:** 47,579 (White 92.2%; Black or African American 5.6%; Hispanic or Latino 0.7%; Asian 0.3%; Other 1.3%). **Foreign born:** 0.8%. **Median age:** 39.6.

Income 2000: per capita $13,809; median household $24,788; **Pop below poverty level:** 21.7%. ***Personal per capita income 2000-2003:** $18,237-$20,337.

Unemployment 2004: 6.2%. **Change from 2000:** -0.5%. **Median travel time to work:** 28 minutes. **Working outside county of residence:** 42.7%.

Cities with pop over 10,000: None.

GILMER COUNTY

10 Howard St   **Ph:** 304-462-7641
Glenville, WV 26351   **Fax:** 304-462-8855

In central WV, southwest of Clarksburg; organized Feb 3, 1845 from Lewis and Kanawha counties. **Name Origin:** For Thomas Walker Gilmer (1802-44), VA legislator, governor (1840-41), U.S. representative (1841-44), and U.S. secretary of the Navy (1844).

Area (sq mi): 340.07 (land 340.05; water 0.02). **Pop per sq mi:** 20.4.

Pop 2005: 6,950. **State rank:** 53. **Pop change:** 2000-20005 -2.9%; 1990-2000 -6.6%. **Pop 2000:** 7,160 (White 96.9%; Black or African American 0.9%; Hispanic or Latino 0.7%; Asian 0.6%; Other 1.2%). **Foreign born:** 1%. **Median age:** 36.8.

Income 2000: per capita $12,498; median household $22,857; **Pop below poverty level:** 25.9%. ***Personal per capita income 2000-2003:** $17,531-$19,988.

Unemployment 2004: 4.5%. **Change from 2000:** -0.6%. **Median travel time to work:** 30.2 minutes. **Working outside county of residence:** 28.6%.

Cities with pop over 10,000: None.

GRANT COUNTY

5 Highland Ave   **Ph:** 304-257-4422
Petersburg, WV 26847   **Fax:** 304-257-9645
www.grantcounty-wv.com

In eastern panhandle of WV, southwest of Cumberland, MD; organized Feb 14, 1866 from Hardy County. **Name Origin:** For Ulysses Simpson Grant (1822-85), Civil War general and eighteenth U.S. president.

Area (sq mi): 480.19 (land 477.21; water 2.99). **Pop per sq mi:** 24.5.

Pop 2005: 11,673. **State rank:** 43. **Pop change:** 2000-20005 +3.3%; 1990-2000 +8.4%. **Pop 2000:** 11,299 (White 97.9%; Black or African American 0.7%; Hispanic or Latino 0.5%; Asian 0.1%; Other 0.9%). **Foreign born:** 0.5%. **Median age:** 39.3.

Income 2000: per capita $15,696; median household $28,916; **Pop below poverty level:** 16.3%. ***Personal per capita income 2000-2003:** $20,912-$23,505.

Unemployment 2004: 6.7%. **Change from 2000:** +1.6%. **Median travel time to work:** 26.9 minutes. **Working outside county of residence:** 35.4%.

Cities with pop over 10,000: None.

GREENBRIER COUNTY

PO Box 506   **Ph:** 304-647-6602
Lewisburg, WV 24901   **Fax:** 304-647-6694
www.greenbrierwv.com

On southeastern border of WV, northeast of Beckley; organized Oct 20, 1778 from Montgomery and Botetourt counties (in VA). **Name Origin:** For the principal river of the county, whose name refers to the thorny vine *Smilax rotundifolia* found abundantly on its banks.

Area (sq mi): 1024.43 (land 1021.26; water 3.17). **Pop per sq mi:** 34.3.

Pop 2005: 35,027. **State rank:** 16. **Pop change:** 2000-20005 +1.7%; 1990-2000 -0.7%. **Pop 2000:** 34,453 (White 94.7%; Black or African American 3%; Hispanic or Latino 0.7%; Asian 0.2%; Other 1.5%). **Foreign born:** 0.6%. **Median age:** 41.6.

Income 2000: per capita $16,247; median household $26,927; **Pop below poverty level:** 18.2%. ***Personal per capita income 2000-2003:** $20,952-$23,680.

Unemployment 2004: 5.7%. **Change from 2000:** -0.5%. **Median travel time to work:** 24.3 minutes. **Working outside county of residence:** 16.9%.

Cities with pop over 10,000: None.

HAMPSHIRE COUNTY

PO Box 806   **Ph:** 304-822-5112
Romney, WV 26757   **Fax:** 304-822-4039
www.co.hampshire.wv.us

In eastern panhandle of WV, southeast of Cumberland, MD. Oldest county of what is now WV; organized Feb 27, 1754 from Frederick and Augusta counties (in VA). **Name Origin:** For the county in England.

Area (sq mi): 644.62 (land 641.72; water 2.9). **Pop per sq mi:** 34.3.

Pop 2005: 22,025. **State rank:** 32. **Pop change:** 2000-20005 +9%; 1990-2000 +22.5%. **Pop 2000:** 20,203 (White 97.7%; Black or

Hampshire County (cont'd)

African American 0.8%; Hispanic or Latino 0.6%; Asian 0.2%; Other 0.9%). **Foreign born:** 0.6%. **Median age:** 38.5.

Income 2000: per capita $14,851; median household $31,666; **Pop below poverty level:** 16.3%. ***Personal per capita income 2000-2003:** $18,758-$19,929.

Unemployment 2004: 4.5%. **Change from 2000:** +0%. **Median travel time to work:** 39.7 minutes. **Working outside county of residence:** 56.6%.

Cities with pop over 10,000: None.

HANCOCK COUNTY

PO Box 367   **Ph:** 304-564-3311
New Cumberland, WV 26047   **Fax:** 304-564-5941

In northern panhandle of WV, northeast of Steubenville, OH; organized Jan 15, 1848 from Brooke County. **Name Origin:** For John Hancock (1737-93), noted signer of the Declaration of Independence, governor of MA (1780-85; 1787-93), and statesman.

Area (sq mi): 88.35 (land 82.82; water 5.53). **Pop per sq mi:** 378.5.

Pop 2005: 31,350. **State rank:** 18. **Pop change:** 2000-20005 -4%; 1990-2000 -7.3%. **Pop 2000:** 32,667 (White 95.8%; Black or African American 2.3%; Hispanic or Latino 0.7%; Asian 0.3%; Other 0.9%). **Foreign born:** 1.8%. **Median age:** 41.7.

Income 2000: per capita $17,724; median household $33,759; **Pop below poverty level:** 11.1%. ***Personal per capita income 2000-2003:** $22,603-$25,062.

Unemployment 2004: 7.6%. **Change from 2000:** +3.9%. **Median travel time to work:** 21.6 minutes. **Working outside county of residence:** 53.8%.

Cities with pop over 10,000: Weirton (19,691).

HARDY COUNTY

204 Washington St Rm 111   **Ph:** 304-530-0250
Moorefield, WV 26836   **Fax:** 304-530-0251
hardycountywv.com

In eastern panhandle of WV, south of Cumberland, MD; organized Oct 17, 1786 from Hampshire County. **Name Origin:** For Samuel Hardy (1758-85), member of VA house of delegates (1780) and a member of the Continental Congress (1783-85).

Area (sq mi): 584.48 (land 583.39; water 1.09). **Pop per sq mi:** 22.8.

Pop 2005: 13,287. **State rank:** 42. **Pop change:** 2000-20005 +4.9%; 1990-2000 +15.4%. **Pop 2000:** 12,669 (White 96.5%; Black or African American 1.9%; Hispanic or Latino 0.7%; Asian 0.1%; Other 1.1%). **Foreign born:** 0.5%. **Median age:** 38.9.

Income 2000: per capita $15,859; median household $31,846; **Pop below poverty level:** 13.1%. ***Personal per capita income 2000-2003:** $19,159-$21,236.

Unemployment 2004: 3.9%. **Change from 2000:** +1.2%. **Median travel time to work:** 26 minutes. **Working outside county of residence:** 31%.

Cities with pop over 10,000: None.

HARRISON COUNTY

301 W Main St County Courthouse   **Ph:** 304-624-8611
Clarksburg, WV 26301   **Fax:** 304-624-8575
www.harrisoncountywv.com

In northern WV, southwest of Fairmont; organized May 3, 1784 from Monongalia, Randolph, and Ohio counties. **Name Origin:** For Benjamin Harrison (1726-91), a signer of the Declaration of Independence, governor of VA (1782-84), and father of President William Harrison (1773-1841).

Area (sq mi): 416.6 (land 416.04; water 0.56). **Pop per sq mi:** 164.3.

Pop 2005: 68,369. **State rank:** 7. **Pop change:** 2000-20005 -0.4%; 1990-2000 -1%. **Pop 2000:** 68,652 (White 95.8%; Black or African American 1.6%; Hispanic or Latino 1%; Asian 0.6%; Other 1.2%). **Foreign born:** 1.4%. **Median age:** 39.2.

Income 2000: per capita $16,810; median household $30,562; **Pop below poverty level:** 17.2%. ***Personal per capita income 2000-2003:** $24,034-$27,320.

Unemployment 2004: 5.3%. **Change from 2000:** +0.3%. **Median travel time to work:** 22.2 minutes. **Working outside county of residence:** 16.4%.

Cities with pop over 10,000: Clarksburg 🏛 (16,522).

JACKSON COUNTY

PO Box 800   **Ph:** 304-372-2011
Ripley, WV 25271   **Fax:** 304-372-1107

On western border of WV along the Ohio River, south of Parkersburg; organized May 1, 1831 from Kanawha, Mason, and Wood counties. **Name Origin:** For Andrew Jackson (1767-1845), seventh U.S. president.

Area (sq mi): 471.59 (land 465.79; water 5.8). **Pop per sq mi:** 61.

Pop 2005: 28,403. **State rank:** 21. **Pop change:** 2000-20005 +1.4%; 1990-2000 +7.9%. **Pop 2000:** 28,000 (White 98.6%; Black or African American 0.1%; Hispanic or Latino 0.3%; Asian 0.2%; Other 0.9%). **Foreign born:** 0.5%. **Median age:** 38.8.

Income 2000: per capita $16,205; median household $32,434; **Pop below poverty level:** 15.2%. ***Personal per capita income 2000-2003:** $19,988-$21,284.

Unemployment 2004: 6.3%. **Change from 2000:** +0.3%. **Median travel time to work:** 27.1 minutes. **Working outside county of residence:** 31.4%.

Cities with pop over 10,000: None.

JEFFERSON COUNTY

PO Box 208   **Ph:** 304-728-3215
Charles Town, WV 25414   **Fax:** 304-728-1957
www.jeffersoncountywv.org

In eastern panhandle of WV, south of Hagerstown, MD; organized Jan 8, 1801 from Berkeley County. **Name Origin:** For Thomas Jefferson (1743-1826), U.S. patriot and statesman; third U.S. president.

Area (sq mi): 211.57 (land 209.53; water 2.03). **Pop per sq mi:** 234.8.

Pop 2005: 49,206. **State rank:** 11. **Pop change:** 2000-20005 +16.6%; 1990-2000 +17.4%. **Pop 2000:** 42,190 (White 90%; Black

*Source: Personal per capita income data are from the Bureau of Economic Analysis; per capita income data are from the Bureau of the Census. See Introduction for explanation of differences.

772

Jefferson County (cont'd)

or African American 6.1%; Hispanic or Latino 1.7%; Asian 0.6%; Other 2.3%). **Foreign born:** 2.1%. **Median age:** 36.8.

Income 2000: per capita $20,441; median household $44,374; **Pop below poverty level:** 10.3%. ***Personal per capita income 2000-2003:** $26,621-$29,072.

Unemployment 2004: 3.2%. **Change from 2000:** +0.7%. **Median travel time to work:** 36.8 minutes. **Working outside county of residence:** 55.1%.

Cities with pop over 10,000: None.

KANAWHA COUNTY

409 Virginia St E   **Ph:** 304-357-0130
Charleston, WV 25301   **Fax:** 304-357-0585
www.kanawha.us

In west-central WV, east of Huntington; organized Nov 14, 1788 from Greenbrier County (WV) and Montgomery County (in VA). **Name Origin:** For the Kanawha River, which traverses it; named for an Indian tribe, possibly the Conoy of Algonquian linguistic stock. The name has been said to mean 'hurricane.'

Area (sq mi): 910.99 (land 903.1; water 7.89). **Pop per sq mi:** 214.3.

Pop 2005: 193,559. **State rank:** 1. **Pop change:** 2000-20005 -3.3%; 1990-2000 -3.6%. **Pop 2000:** 200,073 (White 90.1%; Black or African American 7%; Hispanic or Latino 0.6%; Asian 0.8%; Other 1.7%). **Foreign born:** 1.4%. **Median age:** 40.2.

Income 2000: per capita $20,354; median household $33,766; **Pop below poverty level:** 14.4%. ***Personal per capita income 2000-2003:** $28,775-$32,789.

Unemployment 2004: 4.8%. **Change from 2000:** +0.8%. **Median travel time to work:** 21.9 minutes. **Working outside county of residence:** 8.7%.

Cities with pop over 10,000: Charleston 🏛 (51,685); South Charleston (12,869); Saint Albans (11,173).

LEWIS COUNTY

110 Center Ave PO Box 87   **Ph:** 304-269-8215
Weston, WV 26452   **Fax:** 304-269-8202
www.stonewallcountry.com

In north-central WV, south of Clarksburg; organized Dec 18, 1816 from Harrison and Randolph counties. **Name Origin:** For Charles Lewis (?-1774), a soldier killed during the Revolutionary War.

Area (sq mi): 389.75 (land 382.14; water 7.61). **Pop per sq mi:** 45.

Pop 2005: 17,199. **State rank:** 33. **Pop change:** 2000-20005 +1.7%; 1990-2000 -1.8%. **Pop 2000:** 16,919 (White 98.1%; Black or African American 0.1%; Hispanic or Latino 0.5%; Asian 0.3%; Other 1%). **Foreign born:** 0.5%. **Median age:** 40.1.

Income 2000: per capita $13,933; median household $27,066; **Pop below poverty level:** 19.9%. ***Personal per capita income 2000-2003:** $18,675-$21,486.

Unemployment 2004: 5.3%. **Change from 2000:** -0.6%. **Median travel time to work:** 25.7 minutes. **Working outside county of residence:** 32.8%.

Cities with pop over 10,000: None.

LINCOLN COUNTY

PO Box 497   **Ph:** 304-824-7990
Hamlin, WV 25523   **Fax:** 304-824-2444
www.co.lincoln.wv.us

In southwestern WV, southwest of Charleston; organized Feb 23, 1867 from Boone, Cabell, and Kanawha counties. **Name Origin:** For Abraham Lincoln (1809-65), sixteenth U.S. president.

Area (sq mi): 438.59 (land 437.43; water 1.16). **Pop per sq mi:** 51.1.

Pop 2005: 22,374. **State rank:** 31. **Pop change:** 2000-20005 +1.2%; 1990-2000 +3.4%. **Pop 2000:** 22,108 (White 98.5%; Black or African American 0.1%; Hispanic or Latino 0.5%; Asian 0.1%; Other 0.9%). **Foreign born:** 0%. **Median age:** 37.4.

Income 2000: per capita $13,073; median household $22,662; **Pop below poverty level:** 27.9%. ***Personal per capita income 2000-2003:** $15,520-$17,251.

Unemployment 2004: 6.3%. **Change from 2000:** -2.2%. **Median travel time to work:** 39.2 minutes. **Working outside county of residence:** 67.1%.

Cities with pop over 10,000: None.

LOGAN COUNTY

300 Stratton St Rm 101   **Ph:** 304-792-8600
Logan, WV 25601   **Fax:** 304-792-8621
www.logancountychamberofcommerce.com

In southwestern WV, west of Beckley; organized Jan 12, 1824 from Cabell and Kanawha counties (WV), and Giles and Tazewell counties (in VA). **Name Origin:** For John Logan (1725-80), a Mingo Indian chief originally named *Tah-gah-jute*, who was educated by James Logan of PA.

Area (sq mi): 455.61 (land 454.21; water 1.4). **Pop per sq mi:** 79.8.

Pop 2005: 36,237. **State rank:** 15. **Pop change:** 2000-20005 -3.9%; 1990-2000 -12.4%. **Pop 2000:** 37,710 (White 95.9%; Black or African American 2.6%; Hispanic or Latino 0.5%; Asian 0.3%; Other 0.8%). **Foreign born:** 0.5%. **Median age:** 39.3.

Income 2000: per capita $14,102; median household $24,603; **Pop below poverty level:** 24.1%. ***Personal per capita income 2000-2003:** $19,059-$22,851.

Unemployment 2004: 5.8%. **Change from 2000:** +0.3%. **Median travel time to work:** 30.2 minutes. **Working outside county of residence:** 25.9%.

Cities with pop over 10,000: None.

MARION COUNTY

PO Box 1267   **Ph:** 304-367-5440
Fairmont, WV 26555   **Fax:** 304-367-5448
www.marioncountywv.com

In northern WV, southwest of Morgantown; organized Jan 14, 1842 from Harrison and Monongalia counties. **Name Origin:** For Gen. Francis Marion (c.1732-95), SC soldier and legislator, known as 'The Swamp Fox' for his tactics during the Revolutionary War.

Area (sq mi): 311.49 (land 309.69; water 1.8). **Pop per sq mi:** 182.5.

Pop 2005: 56,509. **State rank:** 9. **Pop change:** 2000-20005 -0.2%; 1990-2000 -1.1%. **Pop 2000:** 56,598 (White 94.5%; Black or African American 3.2%; Hispanic or Latino 0.7%; Asian 0.4%; Other 1.2%). **Foreign born:** 1%. **Median age:** 39.9.

🏛 *County Seat*

Marion County (cont'd)

Income 2000: per capita $16,246; median household $28,626; **Pop below poverty level:** 16.3%. ***Personal per capita income 2000-2003:** $22,441-$25,172.

Unemployment 2004: 4.9%. **Change from 2000:** -0.5%. **Median travel time to work:** 23.9 minutes. **Working outside county of residence:** 32%.

Cities with pop over 10,000: Fairmont 🏛 (18,992).

MARSHALL COUNTY

PO Box 459   **Ph:** 304-845-1220
Moundsville, WV 26041   **Fax:** 304-845-5891
www.marshallcountytourism.com

In northern panhandle of WV, southeast of Wheeling; organized Mar 12, 1835 from Ohio County. **Name Origin:** For John Marshall (1755-1835), American jurist and fourth Chief Justice of the U.S. Supreme Court (1801-35).

Area (sq mi): 312.18 (land 306.99; water 5.19). **Pop per sq mi:** 111.9.

Pop 2005: 34,337. **State rank:** 17. **Pop change:** 2000-20005 -3.3%; 1990-2000 -4.9%. **Pop 2000:** 35,519 (White 97.9%; Black or African American 0.4%; Hispanic or Latino 0.6%; Asian 0.3%; Other 0.9%). **Foreign born:** 0.7%. **Median age:** 40.4.

Income 2000: per capita $16,472; median household $30,989; **Pop below poverty level:** 16.6%. ***Personal per capita income 2000-2003:** $20,938-$23,006.

Unemployment 2004: 6%. **Change from 2000:** -0.2%. **Median travel time to work:** 26.4 minutes. **Working outside county of residence:** 53.9%.

Cities with pop over 10,000: None.

MASON COUNTY

200 6th St   **Ph:** 304-675-1110
Point Pleasant, WV 25550   **Fax:** 304-675-4982

On western border of WV along the Ohio River, northeast of Huntington; organized Jan 2, 1804 from Kanawha County. **Name Origin:** For George Mason (1725-92), VA statesman and author of the VA Declaration of Rights, a model for the American Bill of Rights.

Area (sq mi): 444.8 (land 431.85; water 12.95). **Pop per sq mi:** 59.7.

Pop 2005: 25,761. **State rank:** 25. **Pop change:** 2000-20005 -0.8%; 1990-2000 +3.1%. **Pop 2000:** 25,957 (White 98%; Black or African American 0.5%; Hispanic or Latino 0.5%; Asian 0.3%; Other 0.9%). **Foreign born:** 0.5%. **Median age:** 39.7.

Income 2000: per capita $14,804; median household $27,134; **Pop below poverty level:** 19.9%. ***Personal per capita income 2000-2003:** $18,753-$20,187.

Unemployment 2004: 8%. **Change from 2000:** -2.8%. **Median travel time to work:** 28.5 minutes. **Working outside county of residence:** 47.1%.

Cities with pop over 10,000: None.

MCDOWELL COUNTY

90 Wyoming St Suite 109   **Ph:** 304-436-8544
Welch, WV 24801   **Fax:** 304-436-8576

On southern border of WV, southwest of Beckley; organized Feb 20, 1858 from Tazewell County (in VA). **Name Origin:** For James McDowell (1796-1851), member of the VA house of delegates (1830-35; 1838), governor (1842-46), and U.S. representative (1846-51).

Area (sq mi): 534.9 (land 534.72; water 0.18). **Pop per sq mi:** 45.4.

Pop 2005: 24,273. **State rank:** 29. **Pop change:** 2000-20005 -11.2%; 1990-2000 -22.4%. **Pop 2000:** 27,329 (White 86.7%; Black or African American 11.9%; Hispanic or Latino 0.5%; Asian 0.1%; Other 1%). **Foreign born:** 0.5%. **Median age:** 40.5.

Income 2000: per capita $10,174; median household $16,931; **Pop below poverty level:** 37.7%. ***Personal per capita income 2000-2003:** $14,484-$16,962.

Unemployment 2004: 10.3%. **Change from 2000:** +3.4%. **Median travel time to work:** 32.6 minutes. **Working outside county of residence:** 27.2%.

Cities with pop over 10,000: None.

MERCER COUNTY

1501 Main St   **Ph:** 304-487-8311
Princeton, WV 24740   **Fax:** 304-487-9842
www.mccvb.com

On southern border of WV, southeast of Beckley; organized Mar 17, 1837 from Giles and Tazewell counties (in VA). **Name Origin:** For Gen. Hugh Mercer (1721-77), Revolutionary War officer and physician.

Area (sq mi): 420.69 (land 420.43; water 0.26). **Pop per sq mi:** 146.5.

Pop 2005: 61,589. **State rank:** 8. **Pop change:** 2000-20005 -2.2%; 1990-2000 -3.1%. **Pop 2000:** 62,980 (White 92.2%; Black or African American 5.8%; Hispanic or Latino 0.5%; Asian 0.5%; Other 1.1%). **Foreign born:** 0.8%. **Median age:** 40.2.

Income 2000: per capita $15,564; median household $26,628; **Pop below poverty level:** 19.7%. ***Personal per capita income 2000-2003:** $21,604-$24,251.

Unemployment 2004: 5.6%. **Change from 2000:** +1.1%. **Median travel time to work:** 24.9 minutes. **Working outside county of residence:** 21.4%.

Cities with pop over 10,000: Bluefield (11,222).

MINERAL COUNTY

150 Armstrong St   **Ph:** 304-788-3924
Keyser, WV 26726   **Fax:** 304-788-4109
www.mineralcountywv.com

In eastern panhandle of WV, southwest of Cumberland, MD; organized Feb 1, 1866 from Hampshire County. **Name Origin:** For its mineral resources, particularly coal.

Area (sq mi): 329.13 (land 327.73; water 1.4). **Pop per sq mi:** 82.5.

Pop 2005: 27,028. **State rank:** 23. **Pop change:** 2000-20005 -0.2%; 1990-2000 +1.4%. **Pop 2000:** 27,078 (White 95.7%; Black or African American 2.5%; Hispanic or Latino 0.6%; Asian 0.2%; Other 1.1%). **Foreign born:** 0.6%. **Median age:** 39.1.

Mineral County (cont'd)

Income 2000: per capita $15,384; median household $31,149; **Pop below poverty level:** 14.7%. *Personal per capita income 2000-2003: $20,079-$22,294.

Unemployment 2004: 6.1%. **Change from 2000:** -0.1%. **Median travel time to work:** 29.2 minutes. **Working outside county of residence:** 56.4%.

Cities with pop over 10,000: None.

MINGO COUNTY

PO Box 1197   **Ph:** 304-235-0381
Williamson, WV 25661   **Fax:** 304-235-0365

On southwestern border of WV, southeast of Huntington; organized Jan 30, 1895 from Logan County. **Name Origin:** For the Indian tribe of Iroquoian linguistic stock. The name derives from Algonquian *Mingwe*, probably 'stealthy, treacherous.'

Area (sq mi): 423.64 (land 422.61; water 1.03). **Pop per sq mi:** 64.4.

Pop 2005: 27,210. **State rank:** 22. **Pop change:** 2000-20005 -3.7%; 1990-2000 -16.3%. **Pop 2000:** 28,253 (White 96%; Black or African American 2.3%; Hispanic or Latino 0.5%; Asian 0.2%; Other 1%). **Foreign born:** 0.3%. **Median age:** 37.2.

Income 2000: per capita $12,445; median household $21,347; **Pop below poverty level:** 29.7%. *Personal per capita income 2000-2003: $19,381-$20,344.

Unemployment 2004: 7%. **Change from 2000:** +0.1%. **Median travel time to work:** 29.6 minutes. **Working outside county of residence:** 37.1%.

Cities with pop over 10,000: None.

MONONGALIA COUNTY

243 High St Rm 123   **Ph:** 304-291-7230
Morgantown, WV 26505   **Fax:** 304-291-7233
www.co.monongalia.wv.us

On northern border with PA, north of Fairmont; organized Oct 7, 1776 from District of West Augusta. **Name Origin:** Variant spelling for the Monongahela River, which traverses the county.

Area (sq mi): 365.89 (land 361.16; water 4.73). **Pop per sq mi:** 233.7.

Pop 2005: 84,386. **State rank:** 5. **Pop change:** 2000-20005 +3.1%; 1990-2000 +8.4%. **Pop 2000:** 81,866 (White 91.6%; Black or African American 3.4%; Hispanic or Latino 1%; Asian 2.5%; Other 1.9%). **Foreign born:** 3.8%. **Median age:** 30.4.

Income 2000: per capita $17,106; median household $28,625; **Pop below poverty level:** 22.8%. *Personal per capita income 2000-2003: $23,339-$27,685.

Unemployment 2004: 3.4%. **Change from 2000:** +1.2%. **Median travel time to work:** 20.6 minutes. **Working outside county of residence:** 13%.

Cities with pop over 10,000: Morgantown 🏛 (28,160).

MONROE COUNTY

PO Box 350   **Ph:** 304-772-3096
Union, WV 24983   **Fax:** 304-772-4191
www.travelmonroe.com

On southeastern border of WV, southeast of Beckley; organized Jan 14, 1779 from Greenbrier County (WV) and Botetourt County (in VA). **Name Origin:** For James Monroe (1758-1831), fifth U.S. president.

Area (sq mi): 473.66 (land 473.37; water 0.3). **Pop per sq mi:** 28.5.

Pop 2005: 13,507. **State rank:** 41. **Pop change:** 2000-20005 -7.4%; 1990-2000 +17.5%. **Pop 2000:** 14,583 (White 92.2%; Black or African American 6%; Hispanic or Latino 0.5%; Asian 0.2%; Other 1.1%). **Foreign born:** 0.5%. **Median age:** 39.7.

Income 2000: per capita $17,435; median household $27,575; **Pop below poverty level:** 16.2%. *Personal per capita income 2000-2003: $18,093-$19,483.

Unemployment 2004: 4.4%. **Change from 2000:** +0.4%. **Median travel time to work:** 35 minutes. **Working outside county of residence:** 60.1%.

Cities with pop over 10,000: None.

MORGAN COUNTY

77 Fairfax St Suite 1A   **Ph:** 304-258-8547
Berkeley Springs, WV 25411   **Fax:** 304-258-8545
www.morgancountyeda.com/gov

In eastern panhandle of WV, west of Hagerstown, MD; organized Feb 9, 1820 from Berkeley and Hampshire counties. **Name Origin:** For Gen. Daniel Morgan (1736-1802), an officer in the Revolutionary War and U.S. representative from VA (1797-99).

Area (sq mi): 229.67 (land 228.98; water 0.68). **Pop per sq mi:** 70.

Pop 2005: 16,022. **State rank:** 36. **Pop change:** 2000-20005 +7.2%; 1990-2000 +23.2%. **Pop 2000:** 14,943 (White 97.7%; Black or African American 0.6%; Hispanic or Latino 0.8%; Asian 0.1%; Other 1%). **Foreign born:** 1.4%. **Median age:** 40.7.

Income 2000: per capita $18,109; median household $35,016; **Pop below poverty level:** 10.4%. *Personal per capita income 2000-2003: $23,572-$26,684.

Unemployment 2004: 4.1%. **Change from 2000:** +0.6%. **Median travel time to work:** 36.3 minutes. **Working outside county of residence:** 60.5%.

Cities with pop over 10,000: None.

NICHOLAS COUNTY

700 Main St Suite 2   **Ph:** 304-872-7848
Summersville, WV 26651   **Fax:** 304-872-9600

In central WV, east of Charleston; organized Jan 30, 1818 from Greenbrier, Kanawha, and Randolph counties. **Name Origin:** For Wilson Cary Nicholas (1761-1820), U.S. senator from VA (1799-1804), U.S. representative (1807-09), and governor (1814-16).

Area (sq mi): 654.4 (land 648.63; water 5.77). **Pop per sq mi:** 40.8.

Pop 2005: 26,464. **State rank:** 24. **Pop change:** 2000-20005 -0.4%; 1990-2000 -0.8%. **Pop 2000:** 26,562 (White 98.5%; Black or African American 0.1%; Hispanic or Latino 0.5%; Asian 0.2%; Other 0.8%). **Foreign born:** 0.6%. **Median age:** 39.4.

Nicholas County (cont'd)

Income 2000: per capita $15,207; median household $26,974; **Pop below poverty level:** 19.2%. ***Personal per capita income 2000-2003:** $19,604-$20,989.

Unemployment 2004: 5.4%. **Change from 2000:** -0.6%. **Median travel time to work:** 28.9 minutes. **Working outside county of residence:** 24.7%.

Cities with pop over 10,000: None.

OHIO COUNTY
1500 Chapline St Rm 205   **Ph:** 304-234-3656
Wheeling, WV 26003   **Fax:** 304-234-3829

In northern panhandle of WV, southeast of Steubenville, OH; organized Oct 7, 1776 from Augusta County. **Name Origin:** For the Ohio River, which forms its western border.

Area (sq mi): 108.86 (land 106.18; water 2.68). **Pop per sq mi:** 424.9.

Pop 2005: 45,112. **State rank:** 13. **Pop change:** 2000-20005 -4.9%; 1990-2000 -6.8%. **Pop 2000:** 47,427 (White 94.1%; Black or African American 3.6%; Hispanic or Latino 0.5%; Asian 0.8%; Other 1.1%). **Foreign born:** 1.3%. **Median age:** 40.6.

Income 2000: per capita $17,734; median household $30,836; **Pop below poverty level:** 15.8%. ***Personal per capita income 2000-2003:** $27,132-$30,349.

Unemployment 2004: 5.1%. **Change from 2000:** +1.6%. **Median travel time to work:** 19.5 minutes. **Working outside county of residence:** 26.2%.

Cities with pop over 10,000: Wheeling ⚒ (29,891).

PENDLETON COUNTY
PO Box 1167   **Ph:** 304-358-2505
Franklin, WV 26807   **Fax:** 304-358-2473
www.pendletoncounty.net/pccom/

In eastern panhandle of WV; organized Dec 4, 1788 from Hardy County (WV) and Augusta and Rockingham counties (in VA). **Name Origin:** For Edmund Pendleton (1721-1803), VA House of Burgesses (1752-54), VA House of Delegates (1776-77), and presiding judge of VA court of appeals (1779).

Area (sq mi): 698.15 (land 697.87; water 0.28). **Pop per sq mi:** 11.2.

Pop 2005: 7,844. **State rank:** 49. **Pop change:** 2000-20005 -4.3%; 1990-2000 +1.8%. **Pop 2000:** 8,196 (White 95.8%; Black or African American 2.1%; Hispanic or Latino 0.9%; Asian 0.2%; Other 1.4%). **Foreign born:** 0.7%. **Median age:** 41.1.

Income 2000: per capita $15,805; median household $30,429; **Pop below poverty level:** 11.4%. ***Personal per capita income 2000-2003:** $20,328-$22,307.

Unemployment 2004: 3.8%. **Change from 2000:** +0.7%. **Median travel time to work:** 35.4 minutes. **Working outside county of residence:** 39.5%.

Cities with pop over 10,000: None.

PLEASANTS COUNTY
301 Court Ln Rm 101   **Ph:** 304-684-7542
Saint Marys, WV 26170   **Fax:** 304-684-7569

On northwestern border of WV, northeast of Parkersburg; organized Mar 29, 1851 from Ritchie, Tyler, and Wood counties. **Name Origin:** For James Pleasants, Jr. (1769-1836), U.S. representative from VA (1811-19), U.S. senator (1819-22), and governor (1822-25).

Area (sq mi): 134.59 (land 130.73; water 3.86). **Pop per sq mi:** 56.4.

Pop 2005: 7,376. **State rank:** 52. **Pop change:** 2000-20005 -1.8%; 1990-2000 -0.4%. **Pop 2000:** 7,514 (White 98%; Black or African American 0.5%; Hispanic or Latino 0.4%; Asian 0.2%; Other 1.1%). **Foreign born:** 0.5%. **Median age:** 38.9.

Income 2000: per capita $16,920; median household $32,736; **Pop below poverty level:** 13.7%. ***Personal per capita income 2000-2003:** $21,249-$25,255.

Unemployment 2004: 6.1%. **Change from 2000:** -0.7%. **Median travel time to work:** 24.4 minutes. **Working outside county of residence:** 51.2%.

Cities with pop over 10,000: None.

POCAHONTAS COUNTY
900C 10th Ave   **Ph:** 304-799-4549
Marlinton, WV 24954   **Fax:** 304-799-6947
www.pocahontascountywv.com

On central eastern border of WV; organized Dec 21, 1821 from Pendleton, Randolph, and Greenbrier counties (WV) and Bath County (in VA). **Name Origin:** For Indian princess Pocahontas (1595?-1617), daughter of Chief Powhatan (1550?-1618), whom she convinced to spare the life of VA colonist John Smith (c.1580-1631).

Area (sq mi): 941.85 (land 940.29; water 1.56). **Pop per sq mi:** 9.4.

Pop 2005: 8,851. **State rank:** 48. **Pop change:** 2000-20005 -3.1%; 1990-2000 +1.4%. **Pop 2000:** 9,131 (White 98%; Black or African American 0.8%; Hispanic or Latino 0.4%; Asian 0.1%; Other 0.8%). **Foreign born:** 0.6%. **Median age:** 41.9.

Income 2000: per capita $14,384; median household $26,401; **Pop below poverty level:** 17.1%. ***Personal per capita income 2000-2003:** $20,144-$22,808.

Unemployment 2004: 6.1%. **Change from 2000:** -1.2%. **Median travel time to work:** 31.3 minutes. **Working outside county of residence:** 16.3%.

Cities with pop over 10,000: None.

PRESTON COUNTY
101 W Main St Rm 201   **Ph:** 304-329-0070
Kingwood, WV 26537   **Fax:** 304-329-0198

On northern border of WV, east of Morgantown; organized Jan 19, 1818 from Monongalia and Ranolph counties. **Name Origin:** For James Patton Preston (1774-1843), VA legislator, officer in the War of 1812, and governor of VA (1816-19).

Area (sq mi): 651.39 (land 648.32; water 3.06). **Pop per sq mi:** 46.5.

Pop 2005: 30,115. **State rank:** 19. **Pop change:** 2000-20005 +2.7%; 1990-2000 +1%. **Pop 2000:** 29,334 (White 98.3%; Black or African American 0.3%; Hispanic or Latino 0.6%; Asian 0.1%; Other 0.6%). **Foreign born:** 0.6%. **Median age:** 39.1.

---

*Source: Personal per capita income data are from the Bureau of Economic Analysis; per capita income data are from the Bureau of the Census. See Introduction for explanation of differences.

Preston County (cont'd)

Income 2000: per capita $13,596; median household $27,927; **Pop below poverty level:** 18.3%. ***Personal per capita income 2000-2003:** $18,373-$20,984.

Unemployment 2004: 5.2%. **Change from 2000:** +0.6%. **Median travel time to work:** 30.2 minutes. **Working outside county of residence:** 45.4%.

Cities with pop over 10,000: None.

PUTNAM COUNTY
3389 Winfield Rd   **Ph:** 304-586-0202
Winfield, WV 25213   **Fax:** 304-586-0280
www.putnamcounty.org

In western WV, northwest of Charleston; organized Mar 11, 1848 from Kanawha, Mason, and Cabell counties. **Name Origin:** For Gen. Israel Putnam (1718-90), Revolutionary War officer and American commander at the Battle of Bunker Hill.

Area (sq mi): 350.4 (land 346.23; water 4.17). **Pop per sq mi:** 157.2.

Pop 2005: 54,443. **State rank:** 10. **Pop change:** 2000-20005 +5.5%; 1990-2000 +20.4%. **Pop 2000:** 51,589 (White 97.6%; Black or African American 0.6%; Hispanic or Latino 0.5%; Asian 0.6%; Other 0.9%). **Foreign born:** 1%. **Median age:** 37.7.

Income 2000: per capita $20,471; median household $41,892; **Pop below poverty level:** 9.3%. ***Personal per capita income 2000-2003:** $25,106-$27,759.

Unemployment 2004: 4.6%. **Change from 2000:** +0.9%. **Median travel time to work:** 27.1 minutes. **Working outside county of residence:** 58.9%.

Cities with pop over 10,000: None.

RALEIGH COUNTY
215 Main St   **Ph:** 304-255-9126
Beckley, WV 25801   **Fax:** 304-255-9355

In south-central WV, southeast of Charleston; organized Jan 23, 1850 from Fayette County. **Name Origin:** For Sir Walter Raleigh (1522?-1618), British naval commander and first lord proprietor of the colony of VA (1584-1603).

Area (sq mi): 609.34 (land 606.93; water 2.41). **Pop per sq mi:** 130.4.

Pop 2005: 79,167. **State rank:** 6. **Pop change:** 2000-20005 -0.1%; 1990-2000 +3.1%. **Pop 2000:** 79,220 (White 88.9%; Black or African American 8.5%; Hispanic or Latino 0.9%; Asian 0.7%; Other 1.1%). **Foreign born:** 1.2%. **Median age:** 39.5.

Income 2000: per capita $16,233; median household $28,181; **Pop below poverty level:** 18.5%. ***Personal per capita income 2000-2003:** $21,672-$24,368.

Unemployment 2004: 5.3%. **Change from 2000:** +1.1%. **Median travel time to work:** 26.3 minutes. **Working outside county of residence:** 18.3%.

Cities with pop over 10,000: Beckley 🏛 (16,994).

RANDOLPH COUNTY
PO Box 368   **Ph:** 304-636-0543
Elkins, WV 26241   **Fax:** 304-636-0544

In east-central WV; organized May 5, 1787 from Harrison County. **Name Origin:** For Edmund Jennings Randolph (1753-1813), governor of VA (1786-88), first U.S. attorney general (1789), and U.S. secretary of state (1794-95).

Area (sq mi): 1039.92 (land 1039.72; water 0.2). **Pop per sq mi:** 27.5.

Pop 2005: 28,571. **State rank:** 20. **Pop change:** 2000-20005 +1.1%; 1990-2000 +1.7%. **Pop 2000:** 28,262 (White 97.2%; Black or African American 1.1%; Hispanic or Latino 0.7%; Asian 0.4%; Other 0.9%). **Foreign born:** 0.7%. **Median age:** 38.8.

Income 2000: per capita $14,918; median household $27,299; **Pop below poverty level:** 18%. ***Personal per capita income 2000-2003:** $20,396-$23,589.

Unemployment 2004: 5.5%. **Change from 2000:** -0.4%. **Median travel time to work:** 22.5 minutes. **Working outside county of residence:** 16.2%.

Cities with pop over 10,000: None.

RITCHIE COUNTY
115 E Main St Rm 201   **Ph:** 304-643-2164
Harrisville, WV 26362   **Fax:** 304-643-2906

In north-central WV, east of Parkersburg; organized Feb 18, 1843 from Harrison, Lewis, and Wood counties. **Name Origin:** For Thomas Ritchie (1778-1854), newspaper owner and editor of the Richmond *Enquirer* (1804-45) and manager of the Washington, DC *Union* (1845-51).

Area (sq mi): 453.58 (land 453.51; water 0.07). **Pop per sq mi:** 23.2.

Pop 2005: 10,540. **State rank:** 44. **Pop change:** 2000-20005 +1.9%; 1990-2000 +1.1%. **Pop 2000:** 10,343 (White 98.3%; Black or African American 0.1%; Hispanic or Latino 0.5%; Asian 0.1%; Other 1.1%). **Foreign born:** 0.3%. **Median age:** 39.9.

Income 2000: per capita $15,175; median household $27,332; **Pop below poverty level:** 19.1%. ***Personal per capita income 2000-2003:** $18,805-$20,210.

Unemployment 2004: 6.6%. **Change from 2000:** -1.5%. **Median travel time to work:** 32.9 minutes. **Working outside county of residence:** 40.9%.

Cities with pop over 10,000: None.

ROANE COUNTY
200 Main St   **Ph:** 304-927-2860
Spencer, WV 25276   **Fax:** 304-927-2489

In west-central WV, northeast of Charleston; organized Mar 11, 1856 from Kanawha, Jackson, and Gilmer counties. **Name Origin:** For Spencer Roane (1762-1822), justice of the VA supreme court of appeals and son-in-law of Patrick Henry (1736-99).

Area (sq mi): 483.75 (land 483.57; water 0.18). **Pop per sq mi:** 31.9.

Pop 2005: 15,407. **State rank:** 38. **Pop change:** 2000-20005 -0.3%; 1990-2000 +2.2%. **Pop 2000:** 15,446 (White 98%; Black or African American 0.2%; Hispanic or Latino 0.7%; Asian 0.2%; Other 1%). **Foreign born:** 0.6%. **Median age:** 39.5.

🏛 *County Seat*

Roane County (cont'd)

Income 2000: per capita $13,195; median household $24,511; **Pop below poverty level:** 22.6%. ***Personal per capita income 2000-2003:** $17,285-$18,117.

Unemployment 2004: 7.9%. **Change from 2000:** -5.5%. **Median travel time to work:** 34.8 minutes. **Working outside county of residence:** 40.4%.

Cities with pop over 10,000: None.

SUMMERS COUNTY

PO Box 97　　　　　　　　**Ph:** 304-466-7104
Hinton, WV 25951　　　　**Fax:** 304-466-7146
www.summerscvb.com

In southern WV, east of Beckley; organized Feb 27, 1871 from Greenbrier, Monroe, and Mercer counties. **Name Origin:** For George William Summers (1804-68), U.S. representative from VA (1831-45) and judge of VA's eighteenth judicial circuit (1852-58).

Area (sq mi): 367.72 (land 361.17; water 6.54). **Pop per sq mi:** 38.

Pop 2005: 13,740. **State rank:** 40. **Pop change:** 2000-20005 +5.7%; 1990-2000 -8.5%. **Pop 2000:** 12,999 (White 96.1%; Black or African American 2.2%; Hispanic or Latino 0.5%; Asian 0.1%; Other 1.2%). **Foreign born:** 0.4%. **Median age:** 43.4.

Income 2000: per capita $12,419; median household $21,147; **Pop below poverty level:** 24.4%. ***Personal per capita income 2000-2003:** $14,800-$17,325.

Unemployment 2004: 6.1%. **Change from 2000:** -0.3%. **Median travel time to work:** 33.3 minutes. **Working outside county of residence:** 44.1%.

Cities with pop over 10,000: None.

TAYLOR COUNTY

214 W Main St　　　　　　**Ph:** 304-265-1401
Grafton, WV 26354　　　　**Fax:** 304-265-3016

In northern WV, south of Fairmont; organized Jan 19, 1844 from Harrison, Barbour, and Marion counties. **Name Origin:** For Col. John Taylor (1754-1824), officer in the Revolutionary War and U.S. senator from VA (1792-94; 1803; 1822-24).

Area (sq mi): 175.69 (land 172.78; water 2.91). **Pop per sq mi:** 94.3.

Pop 2005: 16,291. **State rank:** 35. **Pop change:** 2000-20005 +1.3%; 1990-2000 +6.2%. **Pop 2000:** 16,089 (White 97.7%; Black or African American 0.8%; Hispanic or Latino 0.6%; Asian 0.2%; Other 0.9%). **Foreign born:** 0.6%. **Median age:** 39.1.

Income 2000: per capita $13,681; median household $27,124; **Pop below poverty level:** 20.3%. ***Personal per capita income 2000-2003:** $17,140-$19,503.

Unemployment 2004: 4.9%. **Change from 2000:** -0.6%. **Median travel time to work:** 25.2 minutes. **Working outside county of residence:** 56.7%.

Cities with pop over 10,000: None.

TUCKER COUNTY

215 1st St Suite 3　　　　**Ph:** 304-478-2414
Parsons, WV 26287　　　　**Fax:** 304-478-2217
www.canaanvalley.org

In eastern WV, southeast of Clarksburg; organized Mar 7, 1856 from Randolph County. **Name Origin:** For Capt. Henry Saint George Tucker (1780-1848), cavalry officer in the War of 1812, U.S. representative from VA (1815-19), and president of the VA court of appeals (1831-41).

Area (sq mi): 421.11 (land 418.87; water 2.24). **Pop per sq mi:** 16.6.

Pop 2005: 6,943. **State rank:** 54. **Pop change:** 2000-20005 -5.2%; 1990-2000 -5.3%. **Pop 2000:** 7,321 (White 98.7%; Black or African American 0.1%; Hispanic or Latino 0.2%; Asian 0%; Other 1.1%). **Foreign born:** 0.2%. **Median age:** 42.

Income 2000: per capita $16,349; median household $26,250; **Pop below poverty level:** 18.1%. ***Personal per capita income 2000-2003:** $18,738-$21,831.

Unemployment 2004: 6.5%. **Change from 2000:** +0.9%. **Median travel time to work:** 30.1 minutes. **Working outside county of residence:** 26%.

Cities with pop over 10,000: None.

TYLER COUNTY

PO Box 66　　　　　　　　**Ph:** 304-758-2102
Middlebourne, WV 26149　　**Fax:** 304-758-2126

On northwestern border of WV along the Ohio River, west of Fairmont; organized Dec 6, 1814 from Ohio County. **Name Origin:** For John Tyler (1747-1813), judge in the VA general court (1789-1808), governor (1808-11), and father of U.S. President John Tyler (1790-1862).

Area (sq mi): 260.69 (land 257.56; water 3.14). **Pop per sq mi:** 36.3.

Pop 2005: 9,340. **State rank:** 47. **Pop change:** 2000-20005 -2.6%; 1990-2000 -2.1%. **Pop 2000:** 9,592 (White 99%; Black or African American 0%; Hispanic or Latino 0.4%; Asian 0.1%; Other 0.5%). **Foreign born:** 0.3%. **Median age:** 40.8.

Income 2000: per capita $15,216; median household $29,290; **Pop below poverty level:** 16.6%. ***Personal per capita income 2000-2003:** $17,114-$19,795.

Unemployment 2004: 7.3%. **Change from 2000:** +2%. **Median travel time to work:** 30.5 minutes. **Working outside county of residence:** 47.9%.

Cities with pop over 10,000: None.

UPSHUR COUNTY

40 W Main St Rm 101　　　**Ph:** 304-472-1068
Buckhannon, WV 26201　　**Fax:** 304-472-1029
www.buchamber.com

In central WV, south of Clarksburg; organized Mar 26, 1851 from Randolph, Barbour, and Lewis counties. **Name Origin:** For Abel Parker Upshur (1791-1844), judge in VA courts (1826-41), U.S. secretary of the Navy (1841-43), and U.S. secretary of state (1843-44).

Area (sq mi): 354.86 (land 354.76; water 0.1). **Pop per sq mi:** 66.8.

*Source: Personal per capita income data are from the Bureau of Economic Analysis; per capita income data are from the Bureau of the Census. See Introduction for explanation of differences.

Upshur County (cont'd)

Pop 2005: 23,712. **State rank:** 30. **Pop change:** 2000-20005 +1.3%; 1990-2000 +2.3%. **Pop 2000:** 23,404 (White 97.7%; Black or African American 0.6%; Hispanic or Latino 0.6%; Asian 0.3%; Other 0.9%). **Foreign born:** 0.4%. **Median age:** 37.4.

Income 2000: per capita $13,559; median household $26,973; **Pop below poverty level:** 20%. ***Personal per capita income 2000-2003:** $17,899-$19,412.

Unemployment 2004: 5.4%. **Change from 2000:** +0.1%. **Median travel time to work:** 25.4 minutes. **Working outside county of residence:** 24.9%.

Cities with pop over 10,000: None.

WAYNE COUNTY

PO Box 248   **Ph:** 304-272-6369
Wayne, WV 25570   **Fax:** 304-272-5318

On southwestern border of WV, south of Huntington; organized Jan 18, 1842 from Cabell County. **Name Origin:** For Gen. Anthony Wayne (1745-96), PA soldier and statesman, nicknamed 'Mad Anthony' for his daring during the Revolutionary War.

Area (sq mi): 512.19 (land 505.79; water 6.4). **Pop per sq mi:** 83.2.

Pop 2005: 42,091. **State rank:** 14. **Pop change:** 2000-20005 -1.9%; 1990-2000 +3%. **Pop 2000:** 42,903 (White 98.4%; Black or African American 0.1%; Hispanic or Latino 0.5%; Asian 0.2%; Other 0.9%). **Foreign born:** 0.6%. **Median age:** 38.4.

Income 2000: per capita $14,906; median household $27,352; **Pop below poverty level:** 19.6%. ***Personal per capita income 2000-2003:** $17,279-$20,068.

Unemployment 2004: 5.3%. **Change from 2000:** -0.3%. **Median travel time to work:** 28.3 minutes. **Working outside county of residence:** 63%.

Cities with pop over 10,000: None.

WEBSTER COUNTY

2 Court Sq Rm G1   **Ph:** 304-847-2508
Webster Springs, WV 26288   **Fax:** 304-847-5780
www.websterwv.com

In central WV; organized Jan 10, 1860 from Braxton, Nicholas, and Randolph counties. **Name Origin:** For Daniel Webster (1782-1852), U.S. statesman and orator from MA.

Area (sq mi): 556.15 (land 555.97; water 0.18). **Pop per sq mi:** 17.6.

Pop 2005: 9,804. **State rank:** 46. **Pop change:** 2000-20005 +0.9%; 1990-2000 -9.4%. **Pop 2000:** 9,719 (White 98.8%; Black or African American 0%; Hispanic or Latino 0.4%; Asian 0.1%; Other 0.8%). **Foreign born:** 0.4%. **Median age:** 40.4.

Income 2000: per capita $12,284; median household $21,055; **Pop below poverty level:** 31.8%. ***Personal per capita income 2000-2003:** $14,128-$16,458.

Unemployment 2004: 5.6%. **Change from 2000:** -1.7%. **Median travel time to work:** 31.5 minutes. **Working outside county of residence:** 27.8%.

Cities with pop over 10,000: None.

WETZEL COUNTY

PO Box 156   **Ph:** 304-455-8224
New Martinsville, WV 26155   **Fax:** 304-455-5256

In north WV below its northern panhandle, south of Wheeling; organized Jan 10, 1846 from Tyler County. **Name Origin:** For Lewis Wetzel (1764-1808), an Indian fighter and scout.

Area (sq mi): 361.37 (land 359.22; water 2.14). **Pop per sq mi:** 47.7.

Pop 2005: 17,117. **State rank:** 34. **Pop change:** 2000-20005 -3.3%; 1990-2000 -8.1%. **Pop 2000:** 17,693 (White 98.6%; Black or African American 0.1%; Hispanic or Latino 0.4%; Asian 0.3%; Other 0.6%). **Foreign born:** 0.4%. **Median age:** 40.4.

Income 2000: per capita $16,818; median household $30,935; **Pop below poverty level:** 19.8%. ***Personal per capita income 2000-2003:** $20,830-$23,393.

Unemployment 2004: 8.7%. **Change from 2000:** +0.2%. **Median travel time to work:** 29.4 minutes. **Working outside county of residence:** 35.8%.

Cities with pop over 10,000: None.

WIRT COUNTY

PO Box 53   **Ph:** 304-275-4271
Elizabeth, WV 26143   **Fax:** 304-275-3418

In west-central WV, southeast of Parkersburg; organized Jan 19, 1848 from Wood and Jackson counties. **Name Origin:** For William Wirt (1774-1838), who in 1807 prosecuted the case against Aaron Burr (1756-1836), and was an army officer in the War of 1812 and U.S. attorney general (1817-29).

Area (sq mi): 234.83 (land 232.99; water 1.85). **Pop per sq mi:** 25.3.

Pop 2005: 5,896. **State rank:** 55. **Pop change:** 2000-20005 +0.4%; 1990-2000 +13.1%. **Pop 2000:** 5,873 (White 98.3%; Black or African American 0.3%; Hispanic or Latino 0.3%; Asian 0.1%; Other 1%). **Foreign born:** 0.3%. **Median age:** 37.9.

Income 2000: per capita $14,000; median household $30,748; **Pop below poverty level:** 19.6%. ***Personal per capita income 2000-2003:** $16,084-$17,447.

Unemployment 2004: 7.1%. **Change from 2000:** -2.9%. **Median travel time to work:** 32.2 minutes. **Working outside county of residence:** 67.4%.

Cities with pop over 10,000: None.

WOOD COUNTY

PO Box 1474   **Ph:** 304-424-1850
Parkersburg, WV 26102   **Fax:** 304-424-1864
www.woodcountywv.com

On northwestern border of WV along the Ohio River, west of Clarksburg; organized Dec 21, 1798 from Harrison and Kanawha counties. **Name Origin:** For Gen. James Wood (1747-1813), Indian fighter, officer in the Revolutionary War, and governor of VA (1796-99).

Area (sq mi): 376.94 (land 367.29; water 9.65). **Pop per sq mi:** 237.

Pop 2005: 87,047. **State rank:** 4. **Pop change:** 2000-20005 -1.1%; 1990-2000 +1.2%. **Pop 2000:** 87,986 (White 96.9%; Black or African American 1%; Hispanic or Latino 0.6%; Asian 0.5%; Other 1.1%). **Foreign born:** 1.1%. **Median age:** 39.3.

Wood County (cont'd)

Income 2000: per capita $18,073; median household $33,285; **Pop below poverty level:** 13.9%. ***Personal per capita income 2000-2003:** $23,823-$25,942.

Unemployment 2004: 5.4%. **Change from 2000:** +0.7%. **Median travel time to work:** 19.8 minutes. **Working outside county of residence:** 15.8%.

Cities with pop over 10,000: Parkersburg ⚊ (32,159); Vienna (10,767).

WYOMING COUNTY

PO Box 309
Pineville, WV 24874

Ph: 304-732-8000
Fax: 304-732-9659

In southern WV, southwest of Beckley; organized Jan 26, 1850 from Logan County. **Name Origin:** For the Wyoming Valley of PA; the name was popularized by the 1809 Thomas Campbell (1777-1844) poem 'Gertrude of Wyoming' about the Indian attack on the Wyoming Valley in 1778.

Area (sq mi): 501.82 (land 500.88; water 0.94). **Pop per sq mi:** 48.9.

Pop 2005: 24,479. **State rank:** 28. **Pop change:** 2000-20005 -4.8%; 1990-2000 -11.3%. **Pop 2000:** 25,708 (White 98.1%; Black or African American 0.6%; Hispanic or Latino 0.5%; Asian 0.1%; Other 0.7%). **Foreign born:** 0.2%. **Median age:** 40.1.

Income 2000: per capita $14,220; median household $23,932; **Pop below poverty level:** 25.1%. ***Personal per capita income 2000-2003:** $16,572-$19,114.

Unemployment 2004: 6.5%. **Change from 2000:** +0.7%. **Median travel time to work:** 35.3 minutes. **Working outside county of residence:** 36.9%.

Cities with pop over 10,000: None.

Source: Personal per capita income data are from the Bureau of Economic Analysis; per capita income data are from the Bureau of the Census. See Introduction for explanation of differences.

Wisconsin

Lake Superior

Apostle Islands

MICHIGAN

N

Superior
Washburn
Ashland
Hurley

Douglas
Bayfield
Iron

Hayward
Ashland
Vilas
Eagle River
Florence
Florence

Burnett
Grantsburg
Washburn
Sawyer
Phillips
Oneida
Rhinelander
Forest
Crandon

Shell Lake

Price

Balsam Lake
Ladysmith
Lincoln
Langlade
Marinette

Polk
Barron
Rusk
Taylor
Merrill
Antigo

Barron
Medford
Menominee
Oconto
Marinette

Hudson
Chippewa
Chippewa Falls
Wausau
Keshena
Door
Sturgeon Bay

St. Croix
Dunn
Eau Claire
Marathon
Shawano
Oconto
Green Bay

Ellsworth
Menomonie
Eau Claire
Clark
Shawano
Kewaunee

Pierce
Durand
Neillsville
Stevens Point
Green Bay
Kewaunee

Pepin
Whitehall
Wood
Waupaca
Outagamie
Brown

Buffalo
Alma
Black River Falls
Wisconsin Rapids
Portage
Waupaca
Appleton
Manitowoc

Trempealeau
Jackson
Wautoma
Winnebago
Calumet
Manitowoc

La Crosse
Sparta
Friendship
Waushara
Oshkosh
Chilton

MINNESOTA
La Crosse
Monroe
Juneau
Marquette
Green Lake
Fond du Lac
Sheboygan

Mauston
Adams
Montello
Green Lake
Sheboygan

Viroqua
Baraboo
Portage
Fond Du Lac

Vernon
Richland
Sauk
Columbia
Dodge
West Bend
Ozaukee
Port Washington

IOWA
Crawford
Richland Center
Juneau
Washington
Milwaukee

Prairie du Chien
Iowa
Madison
Jefferson
Waukesha

Grant
Dodgeville
Dane
Jefferson
Waukesha
Milwaukee

Lancaster
Lafayette
Green
Rock
Walworth
Racine
Racine

Darlington
Monroe
Janesville
Elkhorn
Kenosha

Beloit
Kenosha

ILLINOIS

MICHIGAN

Lake Michigan

Green Bay

Legend

— County boundary
Taylor County name
⊙ County seat
■ Major city
✪ State capital

0 — 50 mi
0 — 50 km

© MAPS.com

Wisconsin

WISCONSIN STATE INFORMATION

www.wisconsin.gov   **Ph:** 608-266-2211

Area (sq mi): 65,497.82 (land 54310.1; water 11,187.72). **Pop per sq mi:** 101.9.

Pop 2005: 5,536,201. **Pop change:** 2000-20005 +3.2%; 1990-2000 +9.6%. **Pop 2000:** 5,363,675 (White 87.3%; Black or African American 5.7%; Hispanic or Latino 3.6%; Asian 1.7%; Other 3.7%). **Foreign born:** 3.6%. **Median age:** 36.

Income 2000: per capita $21,271; median household $43,791; **Pop below poverty level:** 8.7%. ***Personal per capita income 2000-2003:** $28,570-$30,685.

Unemployment 2004: 5%. **Change from 2000:** +1.6%. **Median travel time to work:** 20.8 minutes. **Working outside county of residence:** 26.1%.

ADAMS COUNTY

PO Box 278   **Ph:** 608-339-4200
Friendship, WI 53934   **Fax:** 608-339-4514
www.adamscountywi.com

In south-central WI, west of Oshkosh; organized Mar 11, 1848 (prior to statehood) from Portage County. **Name Origin:** For John Adams (1735-1826), second U.S. president.

Area (sq mi): 688.51 (land 647.74; water 40.78). **Pop per sq mi:** 32.2.

Pop 2005: 20,828. **State rank:** 51. **Pop change:** 2000-20005 +11.7%; 1990-2000 +18.9%. **Pop 2000:** 18,643 (White 96.7%; Black or African American 0.3%; Hispanic or Latino 1.4%; Asian 0.3%; Other 1.7%). **Foreign born:** 2.3%. **Median age:** 44.5.

Income 2000: per capita $17,777; median household $33,408; **Pop below poverty level:** 10.4%. ***Personal per capita income 2000-2003:** $20,395-$22,804.

Unemployment 2004: 6.6%. **Change from 2000:** +1.9%. **Median travel time to work:** 26.9 minutes. **Working outside county of residence:** 54.4%.

Cities with pop over 10,000: None.

ASHLAND COUNTY

201 W Main St Rm 202   **Ph:** 715-682-7000
Ashland, WI 54806   **Fax:** 715-682-7032
www.co.ashland.wi.us

On central northern border of WI, bordered on north by Lake Superior; organized Mar 27, 1860 from unorganized territory. **Name Origin:** For the abundant ash trees, probably *Fraxinus americana*, or for the KY home of Henry Clay (1777-1852), U.S. senator

known as the 'Great Pacificator' for his advocacy of compromise to avert national crises.

Area (sq mi): 2293.73 (land 1043.82; water 1249.91). **Pop per sq mi:** 15.9.

Pop 2005: 16,627. **State rank:** 59. **Pop change:** 2000-20005 -1.4%; 1990-2000 +3.4%. **Pop 2000:** 16,866 (White 86.7%; Black or African American 0.2%; Hispanic or Latino 1.1%; Asian 0.3%; Other 12.3%, including 10.3% American Indian/Alaska Native). **Foreign born:** 1%. **Median age:** 36.9.

Income 2000: per capita $16,069; median household $31,628; **Pop below poverty level:** 11.9%. ***Personal per capita income 2000-2003:** $21,271-$23,204.

Unemployment 2004: 5.9%. **Change from 2000:** -1.7%. **Median travel time to work:** 15.8 minutes. **Working outside county of residence:** 14.5%.

Cities with pop over 10,000: None.

BARRON COUNTY

330 E LaSalle Ave Rm 210   **Ph:** 715-537-6200
Barron, WI 54812   **Fax:** 715-537-6277
www.co.barron.wi.us

In west-central WI, east of Saint Paul, MN; organized as Dallas County Mar 19, 1859; name changed Mar 4, 1869. **Name Origin:** For Henry D. Barron, state senator and judge of the WI circuit court. Originally for George Dallas (1792-1864), U.S. vice president (1845-49).

Area (sq mi): 890.02 (land 862.84; water 27.18). **Pop per sq mi:** 53.1.

Pop 2005: 45,834. **State rank:** 29. **Pop change:** 2000-20005 +1.9%; 1990-2000 +10.3%. **Pop 2000:** 44,963 (White 97.1%; Black or African American 0.1%; Hispanic or Latino 1%; Asian 0.3%; Other 1.8%). **Foreign born:** 1.2%. **Median age:** 38.8.

Income 2000: per capita $18,091; median household $37,275; **Pop below poverty level:** 8.8%. ***Personal per capita income 2000-2003:** $23,029-$24,922.

Unemployment 2004: 5.5%. **Change from 2000:** +0%. **Median travel time to work:** 19.2 minutes. **Working outside county of residence:** 14.1%.

Cities with pop over 10,000: None.

BAYFIELD COUNTY

PO Box 878   **Ph:** 715-373-6100
Washburn, WI 54891   **Fax:** 715-373-6153
www.bayfieldcounty.org

On northwestern border of WI, east of Duluth, MN; organized as

Bayfield County (cont'd)

LaPointe County Feb 19, 1845 (prior to statehood) from Ashland County; name changed Apr 12, 1866. **Name Origin:** For Henry W. Bayfield, an admiral in the British navy.

Area (sq mi): 2041.53 (land 1476.25; water 565.28). **Pop per sq mi:** 10.3.

Pop 2005: 15,145. **State rank:** 66. **Pop change:** 2000-20005 +0.9%; 1990-2000 +7.2%. **Pop 2000:** 15,013 (White 88.2%; Black or African American 0.1%; Hispanic or Latino 0.6%; Asian 0.3%; Other 11.2%, including 9.4% American Indian/Alaska Native). **Foreign born:** 1.2%. **Median age:** 42.1.

Income 2000: per capita $16,407; median household $33,390; **Pop below poverty level:** 12.5%. ***Personal per capita income 2000-2003:** $21,441-$22,660.

Unemployment 2004: 6.2%. **Change from 2000:** -0.1%. **Median travel time to work:** 20.9 minutes. **Working outside county of residence:** 43.2%.

Cities with pop over 10,000: None.

BROWN COUNTY

305 E Walnut   **Ph:** 920-448-4016
Green Bay, WI 54301   **Fax:** 920-448-4498
www.co.brown.wi.us

In central-eastern WI, at southern end of Green Bay; organized Oct 26, 1818 (prior to statehood) from a territorial county; annexed part of Shawano and Oconto counties in 1919. **Name Origin:** For Gen. Jacob Jennings Brown (1775-1828), an officer in the War of 1812 and commander of the U.S. Army (1821-28).

Area (sq mi): 615.42 (land 528.68; water 86.75). **Pop per sq mi:** 452.

Pop 2005: 238,987. **State rank:** 4. **Pop change:** 2000-20005 +5.4%; 1990-2000 +16.5%. **Pop 2000:** 226,778 (White 89.6%; Black or African American 1.2%; Hispanic or Latino 3.8%; Asian 2.2%; Other 5.5%, including 2.3% American Indian/Alaska Native). **Foreign born:** 3.9%. **Median age:** 34.2.

Income 2000: per capita $21,784; median household $46,447; **Pop below poverty level:** 6.9%. ***Personal per capita income 2000-2003:** $29,812-$32,076.

Unemployment 2004: 4.5%. **Change from 2000:** +0.7%. **Median travel time to work:** 17.5 minutes. **Working outside county of residence:** 8.4%.

Cities with pop over 10,000: 6 (see page 39 for cities).

BUFFALO COUNTY

407 S 2nd St   **Ph:** 608-685-6209
Alma, WI 54610   **Fax:** 608-685-6213
www.buffalocounty.com

On central western border of WI, southeast of Saint Paul, MN; organized Jul 6, 1853. **Name Origin:** For the herds of buffalo that once roamed here.

Area (sq mi): 709.58 (land 684.47; water 25.11). **Pop per sq mi:** 20.4.

Pop 2005: 13,968. **State rank:** 67. **Pop change:** 2000-20005 +1.2%; 1990-2000 +1.6%. **Pop 2000:** 13,804 (White 98.2%; Black or African American 0.1%; Hispanic or Latino 0.6%; Asian 0.3%; Other 0.9%). **Foreign born:** 0.6%. **Median age:** 39.2.

Income 2000: per capita $18,123; median household $37,200; **Pop below poverty level:** 7.5%. ***Personal per capita income 2000-2003:** $27,225-$29,083.

Unemployment 2004: 4.5%. **Change from 2000:** +0.3%. **Median travel time to work:** 24.4 minutes. **Working outside county of residence:** 51.6%.

Cities with pop over 10,000: None.

BURNETT COUNTY

7410 County Rd K Box 115   **Ph:** 715-349-2147
Siren, WI 54872   **Fax:** 715-349-7659
www.burnettcounty.com/gov

On northwestern border of WI; organized Mar 31, 1856 from Polk County. **Name Origin:** For Thomas P. Burnett (?-1846), lawyer and WI territorial legislator.

Area (sq mi): 880.38 (land 821.52; water 58.86). **Pop per sq mi:** 20.1.

Pop 2005: 16,528. **State rank:** 61. **Pop change:** 2000-20005 +5.4%; 1990-2000 +19.8%. **Pop 2000:** 15,674 (White 92.9%; Black or African American 0.4%; Hispanic or Latino 0.8%; Asian 0.2%; Other 6.2%, including 4.5% American Indian/Alaska Native). **Foreign born:** 1.2%. **Median age:** 44.1.

Income 2000: per capita $17,712; median household $34,218; **Pop below poverty level:** 8.8%. ***Personal per capita income 2000-2003:** $21,211-$22,796.

Unemployment 2004: 5.4%. **Change from 2000:** -0.1%. **Median travel time to work:** 26.8 minutes. **Working outside county of residence:** 33%.

Cities with pop over 10,000: None.

CALUMET COUNTY

206 Court St   **Ph:** 920-849-2361
Chilton, WI 53014   **Fax:** 920-849-1469
www.co.calumet.wi.us

In east-central WI, east of Lake Winnebago; organized Dec 7, 1836 (prior to statehood) from a territorial county. **Name Origin:** French *chalumet* 'tube' or 'little reed'; extended to the Indians' 'peace pipe.'

Area (sq mi): 397.03 (land 319.84; water 77.19). **Pop per sq mi:** 138.

Pop 2005: 44,137. **State rank:** 32. **Pop change:** 2000-20005 +8.6%; 1990-2000 +18.5%. **Pop 2000:** 40,631 (White 96.1%; Black or African American 0.3%; Hispanic or Latino 1.1%; Asian 1.5%; Other 1.4%). **Foreign born:** 2.1%. **Median age:** 35.2.

Income 2000: per capita $21,919; median household $52,569; **Pop below poverty level:** 3.5%. ***Personal per capita income 2000-2003:** $28,660-$31,880.

Unemployment 2004: 4%. **Change from 2000:** +0.1%. **Median travel time to work:** 19.3 minutes. **Working outside county of residence:** 59.2%.

Cities with pop over 10,000: None.

---

*Source: Personal per capita income data are from the Bureau of Economic Analysis; per capita income data are from the Bureau of the Census. See Introduction for explanation of differences.

CHIPPEWA COUNTY

711 N Bridge St   **Ph:** 715-726-7980
Chippewa Falls, WI 54729   **Fax:** 715-726-7987
www.co.chippewa.wi.us

In west-central WI, east of Saint Paul, MN; organized Feb 3, 1845 (prior to statehood) from Crawford County. (A former county of the same name existed at the time of the 1830 census, covering much of what is now Douglas, Bayfield, Ashland, Iron, and Vilas counties). **Name Origin:** For the Chippewa River, which flows through it and near whose headwaters lived the Chippewa (properly Ojibway) Indians. Name means 'puckered', and refers to the seam in their moccasins.

Area (sq mi): 1041.32 (land 1010.43; water 30.89). **Pop per sq mi:** 59.3.

Pop 2005: 59,950. **State rank:** 24. **Pop change:** 2000-20005 +8.6%; 1990-2000 +5.4%. **Pop 2000:** 55,195 (White 97.5%; Black or African American 0.2%; Hispanic or Latino 0.5%; Asian 0.9%; Other 1.1%). **Foreign born:** 0.9%. **Median age:** 37.6.

Income 2000: per capita $18,243; median household $39,596; **Pop below poverty level:** 8.2%. ***Personal per capita income 2000-2003:** $25,018-$25,999.

Unemployment 2004: 5.6%. **Change from 2000:** -0.2%. **Median travel time to work:** 21.4 minutes. **Working outside county of residence:** 34.1%.

Cities with pop over 10,000: Chippewa Falls 🏛 (12,721).

CLARK COUNTY

517 Court St   **Ph:** 715-743-5148
Neillsville, WI 54456   **Fax:** 715-743-5154
www.co.clark.wi.us

In west-central WI; organized 1853 from Marathon County. **Name Origin:** For Gen. George Rogers Clark (1752-1818), officer in the Revolutionary War and frontiersman in the Northwest Territory.

Area (sq mi): 1219.08 (land 1215.64; water 3.44). **Pop per sq mi:** 28.

Pop 2005: 34,098. **State rank:** 41. **Pop change:** 2000-20005 +1.6%; 1990-2000 +6%. **Pop 2000:** 33,557 (White 97.5%; Black or African American 0.1%; Hispanic or Latino 1.2%; Asian 0.3%; Other 1.6%). **Foreign born:** 1.2%. **Median age:** 35.9.

Income 2000: per capita $15,100; median household $34,577; **Pop below poverty level:** 12.7%. ***Personal per capita income 2000-2003:** $20,468-$22,227.

Unemployment 2004: 5.6%. **Change from 2000:** -2%. **Median travel time to work:** 20.8 minutes. **Working outside county of residence:** 33.4%.

Cities with pop over 10,000: None.

COLUMBIA COUNTY

PO Box 177   **Ph:** 608-742-9654
Portage, WI 53901   **Fax:** 608-742-9602
www.co.columbia.wi.us

In south-central WI, northwest of Milwaukee; organized Feb 3, 1846 (prior to statehood) from Portage, Brown, and Crawford counties. **Name Origin:** Feminine form of Columbus, a poetic and honorific reference to Christopher Columbus (1451-1506) and America.

Area (sq mi): 795.7 (land 773.79; water 21.91). **Pop per sq mi:** 71.5.

Pop 2005: 55,364. **State rank:** 26. **Pop change:** 2000-20005 +5.5%; 1990-2000 +16.4%. **Pop 2000:** 52,468 (White 96.2%; Black or African American 0.9%; Hispanic or Latino 1.6%; Asian 0.3%; Other 1.6%). **Foreign born:** 1.3%. **Median age:** 38.

Income 2000: per capita $21,014; median household $45,064; **Pop below poverty level:** 5.2%. ***Personal per capita income 2000-2003:** $28,933-$30,846.

Unemployment 2004: 4.6%. **Change from 2000:** -0.4%. **Median travel time to work:** 24.7 minutes. **Working outside county of residence:** 47.5%.

Cities with pop over 10,000: Portage 🏛 (10,010).

CRAWFORD COUNTY

220 N Beaumont Rd   **Ph:** 608-326-0200
Prairie du Chien, WI 53821   **Fax:** 608-326-0213
www.wisconline.com/counties/crawford/

On southwestern border of WI; organized Oct 26, 1818 (prior to statehood) from a territorial county. **Name Origin:** For Fort Crawford, or possibly for Willliam Harris Crawford (1772-1834), U.S. senator from GA (1807-13), U.S. secretary of war (1815-16), and U.S. secretary of the treasury (1816-25).

Area (sq mi): 599.22 (land 572.69; water 26.53). **Pop per sq mi:** 29.9.

Pop 2005: 17,134. **State rank:** 57. **Pop change:** 2000-20005 -0.6%; 1990-2000 +8.2%. **Pop 2000:** 17,243 (White 96.8%; Black or African American 1.4%; Hispanic or Latino 0.7%; Asian 0.3%; Other 1.1%). **Foreign born:** 0.7%. **Median age:** 38.9.

Income 2000: per capita $16,833; median household $34,135; **Pop below poverty level:** 10.2%. ***Personal per capita income 2000-2003:** $20,723-$22,628.

Unemployment 2004: 5.3%. **Change from 2000:** +0.2%. **Median travel time to work:** 21.8 minutes. **Working outside county of residence:** 27.5%.

Cities with pop over 10,000: None.

DANE COUNTY

210 ML King Jr Blvd Rm 112   **Ph:** 608-266-4121
Madison, WI 53703
www.co.dane.wi.us

In south-central WI, west of Milwaukee; organized Dec 7, 1836 (prior to statehood) from Iowa County. **Name Origin:** For Nathan Dane (1725-1835), U.S. representative from MA (1782-85) who proposed the Ordinance of 1787 establishing the Northwest Territory.

Area (sq mi): 1238.32 (land 1201.89; water 36.42). **Pop per sq mi:** 381.2.

Pop 2005: 458,106. **State rank:** 2. **Pop change:** 2000-20005 +7.4%; 1990-2000 +16.2%. **Pop 2000:** 426,526 (White 87.4%; Black or African American 4%; Hispanic or Latino 3.4%; Asian 3.5%; Other 3.5%). **Foreign born:** 6.3%. **Median age:** 33.2.

Income 2000: per capita $24,985; median household $49,223; **Pop below poverty level:** 9.4%. ***Personal per capita income 2000-2003:** $33,539-$36,455.

Unemployment 2004: 3.1%. **Change from 2000:** +1.1%. **Median**

🏛 *County Seat*

Dane County (cont'd)

travel time to work: 19.9 minutes. **Working outside county of residence:** 5.4%.

Cities with pop over 10,000: Madison 🏛 (220,332); Sun Prairie (24,464); Fitchburg (21,821); Middleton (15,956); Stoughton (12,692).

DODGE COUNTY
127 E Oak St   **Ph:** 920-386-3602
Juneau, WI 53039   **Fax:** 920-386-3928
www.co.dodge.wi.us

In southeastern WI, west of Milwaukee; organized Dec 7, 1836 (prior to statehood) from territorial county. **Name Origin:** For Gen. Henry Dodge (1782-1867), an officer in the War of 1812 and Black Hawk War, first governor of WI Territory (1836-41;1845-48), and U.S. senator from WI (1848-57).

Area (sq mi): 906.99 (land 882.28; water 24.71). **Pop per sq mi:** 99.9.

Pop 2005: 88,103. **State rank:** 17. **Pop change:** 2000-20005 +2.6%; 1990-2000 +12.2%. **Pop 2000:** 85,897 (White 93.8%; Black or African American 2.5%; Hispanic or Latino 2.5%; Asian 0.3%; Other 1.9%). **Foreign born:** 1.6%. **Median age:** 37.

Income 2000: per capita $19,574; median household $45,190; **Pop below poverty level:** 5.3%. ***Personal per capita income 2000-2003:** $25,514-$26,048.

Unemployment 2004: 5.3%. **Change from 2000:** +0%. **Median travel time to work:** 20.8 minutes. **Working outside county of residence:** 40.2%.

Cities with pop over 10,000: Beaver Dam (15,015); Waupun (10,552).

DOOR COUNTY
PO Box 670   **Ph:** 920-746-2200
Sturgeon Bay, WI 54235   **Fax:** 920-746-2330
www.co.door.wi.gov

On the peninsula in northeast WI, bordered on west by Green Bay and on east by Lake Michigan; organized Feb 11,1851 from Brown County. **Name Origin:** Origin uncertain. A legendary incident involving Indians is said to be the reason the strait between Washington Island and the peninsula is named in French *La Porte des Morts*, 'Door of the Dead.' Or possibly 'the door' refers to the entrance to Green Bay. The county later took the name from the strait.

Area (sq mi): 2369.83 (land 482.72; water 1887.11). **Pop per sq mi:** 58.7.

Pop 2005: 28,349. **State rank:** 44. **Pop change:** 2000-20005 +1.4%; 1990-2000 +8.8%. **Pop 2000:** 27,961 (White 97.4%; Black or African American 0.2%; Hispanic or Latino 1%; Asian 0.3%; Other 1.7%). **Foreign born:** 1.5%. **Median age:** 42.9.

Income 2000: per capita $21,356; median household $38,813; **Pop below poverty level:** 6.4%. ***Personal per capita income 2000-2003:** $29,123-$30,657.

Unemployment 2004: 6%. **Change from 2000:** +0.8%. **Median travel time to work:** 17.8 minutes. **Working outside county of residence:** 11.4%.

Cities with pop over 10,000: None.

DOUGLAS COUNTY
1313 Belknap St   **Ph:** 715-395-1341
Superior, WI 54880   **Fax:** 715-395-1421
www.douglascountywi.org

On northwestern border of WI, at southwestern end of Lake Superior; organized Feb 9, 1854 from unorganized territory. **Name Origin:** For Stephen Arnold Douglas (1813-61), U.S. orator and statesman.

Area (sq mi): 1479.91 (land 1309.13; water 170.78). **Pop per sq mi:** 33.8.

Pop 2005: 44,208. **State rank:** 31. **Pop change:** 2000-20005 +2.1%; 1990-2000 +3.7%. **Pop 2000:** 43,287 (White 94.9%; Black or African American 0.6%; Hispanic or Latino 0.7%; Asian 0.6%; Other 3.4%, including 1.8% American Indian/Alaska Native). **Foreign born:** 1.6%. **Median age:** 37.7.

Income 2000: per capita $17,638; median household $35,226; **Pop below poverty level:** 11%. ***Personal per capita income 2000-2003:** $22,612-$23,568.

Unemployment 2004: 5.7%. **Change from 2000:** +0.6%. **Median travel time to work:** 20.9 minutes. **Working outside county of residence:** 35.2%.

Cities with pop over 10,000: Superior 🏛 (26,947).

DUNN COUNTY
800 Wilson Ave   **Ph:** 715-232-1677
Menomonie, WI 54751   **Fax:** 715-232-2534
dunncountywi.govoffice2.com

In west-central WI, east of Saint Paul, MN; organized Feb 3, 1854 from Chippewa County **Name Origin:** For Charles Dunn, a legislator and first chief justice of WI Territory.

Area (sq mi): 863.91 (land 852.03; water 11.89). **Pop per sq mi:** 49.

Pop 2005: 41,708. **State rank:** 35. **Pop change:** 2000-20005 +4.6%; 1990-2000 +11%. **Pop 2000:** 39,858 (White 95.6%; Black or African American 0.3%; Hispanic or Latino 0.8%; Asian 2.1%; Other 1.5%). **Foreign born:** 2.1%. **Median age:** 30.6.

Income 2000: per capita $17,520; median household $38,753; **Pop below poverty level:** 12.9%. ***Personal per capita income 2000-2003:** $21,964-$22,885.

Unemployment 2004: 4.5%. **Change from 2000:** +0.4%. **Median travel time to work:** 21.8 minutes. **Working outside county of residence:** 34.7%.

Cities with pop over 10,000: Menomonie 🏛 (15,195).

EAU CLAIRE COUNTY
721 Oxford Ave   **Ph:** 715-839-4803
Eau Claire, WI 54703   **Fax:** 715-839-4854
www.co.eau-claire.wi.us

In west-central WI, east of Saint Paul, MN; organized Oct 6, 1856 from Clark County. **Name Origin:** For Eau Clair River, which runs through it; French transliteration of an Indian word meaning 'clear water.'

Area (sq mi): 645.28 (land 637.64; water 7.64). **Pop per sq mi:** 147.6.

*Source: Personal per capita income data are from the Bureau of Economic Analysis; per capita income data are from the Bureau of the Census. See Introduction for explanation of differences.

786

Eau Claire County (cont'd)

Pop 2005: 94,089. **State rank:** 16. **Pop change:** 2000-20005 +1%; 1990-2000 +9.3%. **Pop 2000:** 93,142 (White 94.4%; Black or African American 0.5%; Hispanic or Latino 0.9%; Asian 2.5%; Other 1.9%). **Foreign born:** 2.2%. **Median age:** 32.4.

Income 2000: per capita $19,250; median household $39,219; **Pop below poverty level:** 10.9%. ***Personal per capita income 2000-2003:** $25,934-$27,469.

Unemployment 2004: 4.2%. **Change from 2000:** +0.1%. **Median travel time to work:** 17.3 minutes. **Working outside county of residence:** 17.8%.

Cities with pop over 10,000: Eau Claire 🏛 (62,576).

FLORENCE COUNTY

PO Box 410   **Ph:** 715-528-3201
Florence, WI 54121   **Fax:** 715-528-4762
www.florencewisconsin.com

On northeastern border of WI; organized Mar 18, 1882 from Marinette and Oconto counties. **Name Origin:** For Florence Terry Hulst, wife of an early developer and mine owner, Dr. N. P. Hulst.

Area (sq mi): 497.46 (land 488.03; water 9.43). **Pop per sq mi:** 10.2.

Pop 2005: 4,974. **State rank:** 71. **Pop change:** 2000-20005 -2.2%; 1990-2000 +10.8%. **Pop 2000:** 5,088 (White 97.9%; Black or African American 0.2%; Hispanic or Latino 0.5%; Asian 0.3%; Other 1.3%). **Foreign born:** 0.6%. **Median age:** 41.9.

Income 2000: per capita $18,328; median household $34,750; **Pop below poverty level:** 9.1%. ***Personal per capita income 2000-2003:** $21,750-$24,146.

Unemployment 2004: 6%. **Change from 2000:** -0.7%. **Median travel time to work:** 20.3 minutes. **Working outside county of residence:** 62.1%.

Cities with pop over 10,000: None.

FOND DU LAC COUNTY

PO Box 1557   **Ph:** 920-929-3000
Fond du Lac, WI 54936   **Fax:** 920-929-3293
www.co.fond-du-lac.wi.us

In east-central WI; organized Dec 7, 1836 (prior to statehood) from a territorial county. **Name Origin:** For its location at the southern end of Lake Winnebago; French 'end of the lake,' transliterated from *Wanikamiu*, name of an Indian village, with the similar meaning 'farthest point of the lake.'

Area (sq mi): 765.8 (land 722.91; water 42.89). **Pop per sq mi:** 137.4.

Pop 2005: 99,337. **State rank:** 15. **Pop change:** 2000-20005 +2.1%; 1990-2000 +8%. **Pop 2000:** 97,296 (White 95.1%; Black or African American 0.9%; Hispanic or Latino 2%; Asian 0.9%; Other 2%). **Foreign born:** 2%. **Median age:** 36.9.

Income 2000: per capita $20,022; median household $45,578; **Pop below poverty level:** 5.8%. ***Personal per capita income 2000-2003:** $27,716-$29,951.

Unemployment 2004: 4.6%. **Change from 2000:** +0.3%. **Median travel time to work:** 18.7 minutes. **Working outside county of residence:** 27.9%.

Cities with pop over 10,000: Fond du Lac 🏛 (42,408).

FOREST COUNTY

200 E Madison St   **Ph:** 715-478-2422
Crandon, WI 54520   **Fax:** 715-478-5175
www.forestcountywi.com

On northeastern border of WI; organized Apr 11, 1885 from Langlade and Oconto counties. **Name Origin:** Descriptively named for the forests in the area.

Area (sq mi): 1046.4 (land 1014.05; water 32.34). **Pop per sq mi:** 9.8.

Pop 2005: 9,961. **State rank:** 68. **Pop change:** 2000-20005 -0.6%; 1990-2000 +14.2%. **Pop 2000:** 10,024 (White 85.5%; Black or African American 1.2%; Hispanic or Latino 1.1%; Asian 0.2%; Other 12.7%, including 11.3% American Indian/Alaska Native). **Foreign born:** 1.1%. **Median age:** 39.9.

Income 2000: per capita $16,451; median household $32,023; **Pop below poverty level:** 13.1%. ***Personal per capita income 2000-2003:** $18,808-$21,975.

Unemployment 2004: 6.1%. **Change from 2000:** -0.4%. **Median travel time to work:** 23 minutes. **Working outside county of residence:** 24.9%.

Cities with pop over 10,000: None.

GRANT COUNTY

111 S Jefferson St   **Ph:** 608-723-2675
Lancaster, WI 53813   **Fax:** 608-723-4048
grantcounty.org/govt/index.html

On southwestern border of WI; organized Dec 8, 1836 (prior to statehood) from Iowa County. **Name Origin:** For the Grant River, which runs through it; itself named for a trapper and Indian trader who lived on the banks.

Area (sq mi): 1183.31 (land 1147.85; water 35.46). **Pop per sq mi:** 43.3.

Pop 2005: 49,671. **State rank:** 28. **Pop change:** 2000-20005 +0.1%; 1990-2000 +0.7%. **Pop 2000:** 49,597 (White 97.9%; Black or African American 0.5%; Hispanic or Latino 0.6%; Asian 0.5%; Other 0.7%). **Foreign born:** 1%. **Median age:** 35.9.

Income 2000: per capita $16,764; median household $36,268; **Pop below poverty level:** 11.2%. ***Personal per capita income 2000-2003:** $22,290-$24,116.

Unemployment 2004: 4.5%. **Change from 2000:** -0.8%. **Median travel time to work:** 20.4 minutes. **Working outside county of residence:** 29.9%.

Cities with pop over 10,000: None.

GREEN COUNTY

1016 16th Ave   **Ph:** 608-328-9430
Monroe, WI 53566   **Fax:** 608-328-2835
greencounty.org

On central southern border of WI, south of Madison; organized Dec 8, 1836 (prior to statehood) from Iowa County. **Name Origin:** For Gen. Nathanael Greene (1742-86), Revolutionary War officer and quartermaster general (1778-80). The missing *e* not explained.

Area (sq mi): 584.56 (land 583.99; water 0.58). **Pop per sq mi:** 60.2.

Green County (cont'd)

Pop 2005: 35,165. **State rank:** 40. **Pop change:** 2000-20005 +4.5%; 1990-2000 +10.9%. **Pop 2000:** 33,647 (White 97.7%; Black or African American 0.3%; Hispanic or Latino 1%; Asian 0.3%; Other 1.4%). **Foreign born:** 1.3%. **Median age:** 37.9.

Income 2000: per capita $20,795; median household $43,228; **Pop below poverty level:** 5.1%. ***Personal per capita income 2000-2003:** $26,910-$28,542.

Unemployment 2004: 4.5%. **Change from 2000:** -0.3%. **Median travel time to work:** 22.3 minutes. **Working outside county of residence:** 33.6%.

Cities with pop over 10,000: Monroe 🏛 (10,583).

GREEN LAKE COUNTY
PO Box 3188   **Ph:** 920-294-4005
Green Lake, WI 54941   **Fax:** 920-294-4009
www.co.green-lake.wi.us

In east-central WI, west of Lake Winnebago; organized Mar 5, 1858 from Marquette District. **Name Origin:** For the large lake in the middle of the county, named for the color of the water.

Area (sq mi): 380.44 (land 354.28; water 26.15). **Pop per sq mi:** 54.1.

Pop 2005: 19,168. **State rank:** 55. **Pop change:** 2000-20005 +0.3%; 1990-2000 +2.4%. **Pop 2000:** 19,105 (White 96.7%; Black or African American 0.2%; Hispanic or Latino 2.1%; Asian 0.3%; Other 1.7%). **Foreign born:** 1.8%. **Median age:** 40.9.

Income 2000: per capita $19,024; median household $39,462; **Pop below poverty level:** 7%. ***Personal per capita income 2000-2003:** $25,758-$26,962.

Unemployment 2004: 5.6%. **Change from 2000:** +0%. **Median travel time to work:** 22.4 minutes. **Working outside county of residence:** 43.7%.

Cities with pop over 10,000: None.

IOWA COUNTY
222 N Iowa St Suite 102   **Ph:** 608-935-5445
Dodgeville, WI 53533   **Fax:** 608-935-3024
www.iowacounty.org

In southwestern WI, west of Madison; organized Oct 9, 1829 (prior to statehood) from a territorial county. **Name Origin:** For either the Iowa River, or the Iowa Indians. Name is a French version of the Dakota name for the tribe, variously *Ayuhwa, Ouaouia, Aiouez,* and *Ioways* 'the sleepy ones.'

Area (sq mi): 768.08 (land 762.67; water 5.41). **Pop per sq mi:** 30.9.

Pop 2005: 23,569. **State rank:** 48. **Pop change:** 2000-20005 +3.5%; 1990-2000 +13.1%. **Pop 2000:** 22,780 (White 98.5%; Black or African American 0.2%; Hispanic or Latino 0.3%; Asian 0.3%; Other 0.8%). **Foreign born:** 0.6%. **Median age:** 37.1.

Income 2000: per capita $19,497; median household $42,518; **Pop below poverty level:** 7.3%. ***Personal per capita income 2000-2003:** $25,446-$27,308.

Unemployment 2004: 3.9%. **Change from 2000:** +0.2%. **Median travel time to work:** 24.7 minutes. **Working outside county of residence:** 36.5%.

Cities with pop over 10,000: None.

IRON COUNTY
300 Taconite St   **Ph:** 715-561-3375
Hurley, WI 54534   **Fax:** 715-561-2928
www.ironcountywi.com

On central northern border of WI; organized Mar 1, 1893 from Ashland and Oneida counties. **Name Origin:** For the huge deposits of iron ore found in the Mesabi Range.

Area (sq mi): 919.24 (land 757.23; water 162.01). **Pop per sq mi:** 8.8.

Pop 2005: 6,649. **State rank:** 70. **Pop change:** 2000-20005 -3.1%; 1990-2000 +11.5%. **Pop 2000:** 6,861 (White 97.9%; Black or African American 0.1%; Hispanic or Latino 0.7%; Asian 0.1%; Other 1.5%). **Foreign born:** 1.8%. **Median age:** 45.

Income 2000: per capita $17,371; median household $29,580; **Pop below poverty level:** 11.1%. ***Personal per capita income 2000-2003:** $20,772-$22,912.

Unemployment 2004: 8.8%. **Change from 2000:** +1.9%. **Median travel time to work:** 19.8 minutes. **Working outside county of residence:** 45.5%.

Cities with pop over 10,000: None.

JACKSON COUNTY
307 Main St   **Ph:** 715-284-0208
Black River Falls, WI 54615   **Fax:** 715-284-0270
www.co.jackson.wi.us

In west-central WI, northwest of Madison; organized Feb 11, 1853 from Crawford County. **Name Origin:** For Andrew Jackson (1767-1845), seventh U.S. president.

Area (sq mi): 1000.11 (land 987.32; water 12.79). **Pop per sq mi:** 20.

Pop 2005: 19,758. **State rank:** 54. **Pop change:** 2000-20005 +3.4%; 1990-2000 +15.1%. **Pop 2000:** 19,100 (White 89%; Black or African American 2.3%; Hispanic or Latino 1.9%; Asian 0.2%; Other 8%, including 6.2% American Indian/Alaska Native). **Foreign born:** 1.9%. **Median age:** 37.6.

Income 2000: per capita $17,604; median household $37,015; **Pop below poverty level:** 9.6%. ***Personal per capita income 2000-2003:** $22,877-$26,084.

Unemployment 2004: 5.4%. **Change from 2000:** +0.2%. **Median travel time to work:** 21.2 minutes. **Working outside county of residence:** 25.3%.

Cities with pop over 10,000: None.

JEFFERSON COUNTY
320 S Main St Rm 109   **Ph:** 920-674-7140
Jefferson, WI 53549   **Fax:** 920-674-7368
www.co.jefferson.wi.us

In southeastern WI, east of Milwaukee; organized Dec 7, 1836 from Dodge and Waukesha counties. **Name Origin:** For Thomas Jefferson (1743-1826), U.S. patriot and statesman; third U.S. president. Others claim it was named for Jefferson County, NY, former home of some prominent early settlers.

Area (sq mi): 582.75 (land 557.01; water 25.73). **Pop per sq mi:** 142.4.

---

*Source: Personal per capita income data are from the Bureau of Economic Analysis; per capita income data are from the Bureau of the Census. See Introduction for explanation of differences.

Jefferson County (cont'd)

Pop 2005: 79,328. **State rank:** 20. **Pop change:** 2000-20005 +7.2%; 1990-2000 +9.2%. **Pop 2000:** 74,021 (White 94.3%; Black or African American 0.3%; Hispanic or Latino 4.1%; Asian 0.4%; Other 2.8%). **Foreign born:** 2.8%. **Median age:** 36.6.

Income 2000: per capita $21,236; median household $46,901; **Pop below poverty level:** 5.7%. ***Personal per capita income 2000-2003:** $27,927-$29,330.

Unemployment 2004: 4.9%. **Change from 2000:** +1%. **Median travel time to work:** 21 minutes. **Working outside county of residence:** 39.5%.

Cities with pop over 10,000: Watertown (22,824); Fort Atkinson (11,870).

JUNEAU COUNTY
220 E State St
Mauston, WI 53948
www.juneaucounty.com

Ph: 608-847-9300
Fax: 608-847-9402

In south-central WI, northwest of Madison; organized Oct 13, 1856 from Adams County. **Name Origin:** For Solomon Juneau (1793-1856), early French trader, the first postmaster and first mayor of Milwaukee, called 'the father of the city.'

Area (sq mi): 804.13 (land 767.61; water 36.53). **Pop per sq mi:** 34.8.

Pop 2005: 26,725. **State rank:** 46. **Pop change:** 2000-20005 +9.9%; 1990-2000 +12.3%. **Pop 2000:** 24,316 (White 95.9%; Black or African American 0.3%; Hispanic or Latino 1.4%; Asian 0.4%; Other 2.6%, including 1.3% American Indian/Alaska Native). **Foreign born:** 1.5%. **Median age:** 39.4.

Income 2000: per capita $17,892; median household $35,335; **Pop below poverty level:** 10.1%. ***Personal per capita income 2000-2003:** $21,336-$22,382.

Unemployment 2004: 6.3%. **Change from 2000:** -2.8%. **Median travel time to work:** 22.1 minutes. **Working outside county of residence:** 33.2%.

Cities with pop over 10,000: None.

KENOSHA COUNTY
1010 56th St
Kenosha, WI 53140
www.co.kenosha.wi.us

Ph: 262-653-2552
Fax: 262-653-2564

On southeastern border of WI; organized Jan 30, 1850 from Racine County. **Name Origin:** For the name of Potawatomi (Algonquian) Indian villages, meaning 'pike' or 'pickerel,' for the abundance of this fish in the local creeks.

Area (sq mi): 754.31 (land 272.83; water 481.48). **Pop per sq mi:** 588.4.

Pop 2005: 160,544. **State rank:** 7. **Pop change:** 2000-20005 +7.3%; 1990-2000 +16.7%. **Pop 2000:** 149,577 (White 85.1%; Black or African American 5.1%; Hispanic or Latino 7.2%; Asian 0.9%; Other 5.6%). **Foreign born:** 4.8%. **Median age:** 34.8.

Income 2000: per capita $21,207; median household $46,970; **Pop below poverty level:** 7.5%. ***Personal per capita income 2000-2003:** $27,726-$29,117.

Unemployment 2004: 5.8%. **Change from 2000:** +0.9%. **Median travel time to work:** 25.3 minutes. **Working outside county of residence:** 43.8%.

Cities with pop over 10,000: Kenosha 🏛 (93,798); Pleasant Prairie (18,483).

KEWAUNEE COUNTY
613 Dodge St
Kewaunee, WI 54216
www.kewauneeco.org

Ph: 920-388-7144
Fax: 920-388-3199

On the peninsula in eastern WI, bordered on west by Green Bay and on east by Lake Michigan; organized Apr 16, 1852 from Manitowoc County. **Name Origin:** A Potawatomi word whose meaning is unclear; possibly 'to cross a point,' referring to the river between Green Bay and Lake Michigan or 'prairie hen' or 'wild duck.'

Area (sq mi): 1084.52 (land 342.64; water 741.89). **Pop per sq mi:** 60.8.

Pop 2005: 20,840. **State rank:** 50. **Pop change:** 2000-20005 +3.2%; 1990-2000 +6.9%. **Pop 2000:** 20,187 (White 98.2%; Black or African American 0.2%; Hispanic or Latino 0.8%; Asian 0.1%; Other 1.2%). **Foreign born:** 0.9%. **Median age:** 37.5.

Income 2000: per capita $18,456; median household $43,824; **Pop below poverty level:** 5.8%. ***Personal per capita income 2000-2003:** $25,044-$25,536.

Unemployment 2004: 4.4%. **Change from 2000:** +0.2%. **Median travel time to work:** 22.5 minutes. **Working outside county of residence:** 44.6%.

Cities with pop over 10,000: None.

LA CROSSE COUNTY
400 N 4th St Rm 1210
La Crosse, WI 54601
www.co.la-crosse.wi.us

Ph: 608-785-9581
Fax: 608-785-9741

On southwestern border of WI, northwest of Madison; organized Mar 1, 1851 from unorganized territory. **Name Origin:** For the village of the same name, from the French name for an Indian game *baggataway*, from a resemblance they saw to their tennis game, played with a racquet that resembled a bishop's crozier or cross.

Area (sq mi): 479.92 (land 452.74; water 27.18). **Pop per sq mi:** 240.7.

Pop 2005: 108,958. **State rank:** 13. **Pop change:** 2000-20005 +1.7%; 1990-2000 +9.4%. **Pop 2000:** 107,120 (White 93.7%; Black or African American 0.9%; Hispanic or Latino 0.9%; Asian 3.2%; Other 1.7%). **Foreign born:** 2.5%. **Median age:** 33.5.

Income 2000: per capita $19,800; median household $39,472; **Pop below poverty level:** 10.7%. ***Personal per capita income 2000-2003:** $26,015-$28,284.

Unemployment 2004: 4%. **Change from 2000:** +0.3%. **Median travel time to work:** 17.3 minutes. **Working outside county of residence:** 8.5%.

Cities with pop over 10,000: La Crosse 🏛 (50,695); Onalaska (15,622).

LAFAYETTE COUNTY

626 Main St PO Box 40   **Ph:** 608-776-4850
Darlington, WI 53530   **Fax:** 608-776-8893
www.co.lafayette.wi.gov

On southwestern border of WI, southwest of Madison; organized Jan 31, 1846 (prior to statehood) from Iowa County. **Name Origin:** For the Marquis de Lafayette (1757-1834), French statesman and soldier who fought with the Americans during the Revolutionary War.

Area (sq mi): 634.56 (land 633.57; water 1). **Pop per sq mi:** 25.7.

Pop 2005: 16,310. **State rank:** 62. **Pop change:** 2000-20005 +1.1%; 1990-2000 +0.4%. **Pop 2000:** 16,137 (White 98.7%; Black or African American 0.1%; Hispanic or Latino 0.6%; Asian 0.2%; Other 0.6%). **Foreign born:** 0.8%. **Median age:** 38.1.

Income 2000: per capita $16,811; median household $37,220; **Pop below poverty level:** 9.1%. *Personal per capita income 2000-2003: $20,739-$21,983.

Unemployment 2004: 4.4%. **Change from 2000:** -0.8%. **Median travel time to work:** 23.9 minutes. **Working outside county of residence:** 46.3%.

Cities with pop over 10,000: None.

LANGLADE COUNTY

800 Clermont St   **Ph:** 715-627-6200
Antigo, WI 54409   **Fax:** 715-627-6303
www.co.langlade.wi.us

In northeastern WI, northeast of Wausau; organized Feb 27, 1879 as New County from Oconto County; name changed Feb 19, 1880. **Name Origin:** For Charles Michael de Langlade (1729-1800), an Indian leader who fought with the French against the British in the French and Indian War and with the British against the Americans during the Revolutionary War; he established the first permanent settlement at Green Bay (1764). Some claim for his father, Augustin de Langlade (1695-1771), a French settler who married an Indian woman.

Area (sq mi): 887.88 (land 872.67; water 15.2). **Pop per sq mi:** 23.8.

Pop 2005: 20,735. **State rank:** 52. **Pop change:** 2000-20005 +0%; 1990-2000 +6.3%. **Pop 2000:** 20,740 (White 97.4%; Black or African American 0.1%; Hispanic or Latino 0.8%; Asian 0.3%; Other 1.6%). **Foreign born:** 1%. **Median age:** 40.5.

Income 2000: per capita $16,960; median household $33,168; **Pop below poverty level:** 10.1%. *Personal per capita income 2000-2003: $21,949-$23,739.

Unemployment 2004: 6.4%. **Change from 2000:** -1.4%. **Median travel time to work:** 20.3 minutes. **Working outside county of residence:** 18.9%.

Cities with pop over 10,000: None.

LINCOLN COUNTY

1110 E Main St   **Ph:** 715-536-0312
Merrill, WI 54452   **Fax:** 715-536-6528
www.co.lincoln.wi.us

In northeastern WI, north of Wausau; organized Mar 4, 1874 from Marathon County. **Name Origin:** For Abraham Lincoln (1809-65), sixteenth U.S. president.

Area (sq mi): 907.05 (land 883.3; water 23.75). **Pop per sq mi:** 34.3.

Pop 2005: 30,319. **State rank:** 42. **Pop change:** 2000-20005 +2.3%; 1990-2000 +9.8%. **Pop 2000:** 29,641 (White 97.4%; Black or African American 0.4%; Hispanic or Latino 0.8%; Asian 0.4%; Other 1.4%). **Foreign born:** 1.6%. **Median age:** 38.9.

Income 2000: per capita $17,940; median household $39,120; **Pop below poverty level:** 6.9%. *Personal per capita income 2000-2003: $22,982-$24,725.

Unemployment 2004: 5.5%. **Change from 2000:** -0.3%. **Median travel time to work:** 19.2 minutes. **Working outside county of residence:** 27.8%.

Cities with pop over 10,000: Merrill 🏛 (10,153).

MANITOWOC COUNTY

PO Box 2000   **Ph:** 920-683-4030
Manitowoc, WI 54221   **Fax:** 920-683-2733
www.co.manitowoc.wi.us

On central eastern coast of WI, south of Green Bay; organized Dec 7, 1836 (prior to statehood) from a territorial county. **Name Origin:** From an Indian name probably meaning 'land of the spirit,' possibly with a connotation of evil.

Area (sq mi): 1493.87 (land 591.53; water 902.34). **Pop per sq mi:** 138.5.

Pop 2005: 81,949. **State rank:** 19. **Pop change:** 2000-20005 -1.1%; 1990-2000 +3.1%. **Pop 2000:** 82,887 (White 95%; Black or African American 0.3%; Hispanic or Latino 1.6%; Asian 2%; Other 1.8%). **Foreign born:** 2.3%. **Median age:** 38.3.

Income 2000: per capita $20,285; median household $43,286; **Pop below poverty level:** 6.1%. *Personal per capita income 2000-2003: $26,152-$27,807.

Unemployment 2004: 6%. **Change from 2000:** +0.3%. **Median travel time to work:** 18.2 minutes. **Working outside county of residence:** 20.2%.

Cities with pop over 10,000: Manitowoc 🏛 (33,906); Two Rivers (12,163).

MARATHON COUNTY

500 Forest St   **Ph:** 715-261-1500
Wausau, WI 54403   **Fax:** 715-261-1515
www.co.marathon.wi.us

In central WI, east of Eau Claire; organized Feb 9, 1850 from Portage County. **Name Origin:** For the site of the famous battle in Greece (490 B.C.).

Area (sq mi): 1576.14 (land 1544.96; water 31.18). **Pop per sq mi:** 83.5.

Pop 2005: 128,941. **State rank:** 10. **Pop change:** 2000-20005 +2.5%; 1990-2000 +9%. **Pop 2000:** 125,834 (White 93.4%; Black or African American 0.3%; Hispanic or Latino 0.8%; Asian 4.5%; Other 1.3%). **Foreign born:** 3.5%. **Median age:** 36.3.

Income 2000: per capita $20,703; median household $45,165; **Pop below poverty level:** 6.6%. *Personal per capita income 2000-2003: $27,244-$29,992.

Unemployment 2004: 4.3%. **Change from 2000:** +0.2%. **Median travel time to work:** 18.4 minutes. **Working outside county of residence:** 13.2%.

Source: Personal per capita income data are from the Bureau of Economic Analysis; per capita income data are from the Bureau of the Census. See Introduction for explanation of differences.

Marathon County (cont'd)

Cities with pop over 10,000: Wausau ⚊ (37,173); Weston (12,736).

MARINETTE COUNTY

1926 Hall Ave
Marinette, WI 54143
www.marinettecounty.com
Ph: 715-732-7406
Fax: 715-732-7532

On northeastern border of WI, north of Green Bay; organized Feb 27, 1879 from Oconto County. **Name Origin:** For Marguerite Chevallier (1784-1865), a successful female fur trader, also known as *Marinette*, a combined form of Marie Antoinette (1755-93), then Queen of France.

Area (sq mi): 1550.07 (land 1401.76; water 148.32). **Pop per sq mi:** 31.

Pop 2005: 43,406. **State rank:** 33. **Pop change:** 2000-20005 +0.1%; 1990-2000 +7%. **Pop 2000:** 43,384 (White 97.6%; Black or African American 0.2%; Hispanic or Latino 0.7%; Asian 0.3%; Other 1.4%). **Foreign born:** 1.2%. **Median age:** 40.5.

Income 2000: per capita $17,492; median household $35,256; **Pop below poverty level:** 8.3%. ***Personal per capita income 2000-2003:** $22,706-$25,448.

Unemployment 2004: 6.2%. **Change from 2000:** -0.5%. **Median travel time to work:** 20.1 minutes. **Working outside county of residence:** 24.7%.

Cities with pop over 10,000: Marinette ⚊ (11,374).

MARQUETTE COUNTY

PO Box 186
Montello, WI 53949
www.co.marquette.wi.us
Ph: 608-297-9136
Fax: 608-297-7609

In south- central WI, west of Lake Winnebago; established Dec 7, 1836 (prior to statehood) from Marquette District. **Name Origin:** For Jacques Marquette (1637-75), French missonary known as Pere Marquette; explorer with Louis Jolliet (1645-1700) of the Wisconsin and Mississippi Rivers.

Area (sq mi): 464.42 (land 455.49; water 8.94). **Pop per sq mi:** 33.5.

Pop 2005: 15,237. **State rank:** 63. **Pop change:** 2000-20005 -3.8%; 1990-2000 +28.5%. **Pop 2000:** 15,832 (White 92%; Black or African American 3.4%; Hispanic or Latino 2.7%; Asian 0.3%; Other 2.6%, including 1% American Indian/Alaska Native). **Foreign born:** 1.5%. **Median age:** 40.9.

Income 2000: per capita $16,924; median household $35,746; **Pop below poverty level:** 7.7%. ***Personal per capita income 2000-2003:** $20,567-$22,590.

Unemployment 2004: 6.5%. **Change from 2000:** -0.8%. **Median travel time to work:** 25.9 minutes. **Working outside county of residence:** 49.7%.

Cities with pop over 10,000: None.

MENOMINEE COUNTY

PO Box 279
Keshena, WI 54135
www.wisconline.com/counties/menominee/
Ph: 715-799-3311
Fax: 715-799-1322

In east-central WI, northwest of Lake Winnebago; organized May 1, 1961 from Shawano and Oconto counties. **Name Origin:** For the Menominee Indians, a tribe of Algonquian linguistic stock, who lived in the lake region where wild rice grows. The name probably means 'wild rice people.'

Area (sq mi): 364.99 (land 357.96; water 7.03). **Pop per sq mi:** 12.8.

Pop 2005: 4,580. **State rank:** 72. **Pop change:** 2000-20005 +0.4%; 1990-2000 +17.3%. **Pop 2000:** 4,562 (White 11.5%; Black or African American 0.1%; Hispanic or Latino 2.7%; Asian 0%; Other 88.3%, including 87.3% American Indian/Alaska Native). **Foreign born:** 2.7%. **Median age:** 27.7.

Income 2000: per capita $10,625; median household $29,440; **Pop below poverty level:** 28.8%. ***Personal per capita income 2000-2003:** $15,966-$18,449.

Unemployment 2004: 10.7%. **Change from 2000:** -0.9%. **Median travel time to work:** 18.4 minutes. **Working outside county of residence:** 20.1%.

Cities with pop over 10,000: None.

MILWAUKEE COUNTY

901 N 9th St
Milwaukee, WI 53233
www.co.milwaukee.wi.us
Ph: 414-278-4067
Fax: 414-278-4075

On southeastern coast of WI; organized Aug 25, 1835 (prior to statehood). **Name Origin:** An Algonquian word of uncertain meaning; possibly 'rich beautiful land' or 'gathering place by the river.' The area had long been a council ground for different tribes.

Area (sq mi): 1189.7 (land 241.56; water 948.14). **Pop per sq mi:** 3815.4.

Pop 2005: 921,654. **State rank:** 1. **Pop change:** 2000-20005 -2%; 1990-2000 -2%. **Pop 2000:** 940,164 (White 62.1%; Black or African American 24.6%; Hispanic or Latino 8.8%; Asian 2.6%; Other 7.1%). **Foreign born:** 6.8%. **Median age:** 33.7.

Income 2000: per capita $19,939; median household $38,100; **Pop below poverty level:** 15.3%. ***Personal per capita income 2000-2003:** $28,226-$31,419.

Unemployment 2004: 6.3%. **Change from 2000:** +0.7%. **Median travel time to work:** 21.9 minutes. **Working outside county of residence:** 19.3%.

Cities with pop over 10,000: 13 (see page 39 for cities).

MONROE COUNTY

202 S 'K' St
Sparta, WI 54656
www.co.monroe.wi.us
Ph: 608-269-8705
Fax: 608-269-8747

In southwestern WI, east of La Crosse; organized Mar 21, 1854 from unorganized territory. **Name Origin:** For James Monroe (1758-1831), fifth U.S. president.

Area (sq mi): 908.29 (land 900.77; water 7.52). **Pop per sq mi:** 47.3.

Pop 2005: 42,644. **State rank:** 34. **Pop change:** 2000-20005 +4.3%; 1990-2000 +11.6%. **Pop 2000:** 40,899 (White 95.7%; Black or African American 0.5%; Hispanic or Latino 1.8%; Asian 0.5%; Other 2.4%). **Foreign born:** 1.8%. **Median age:** 36.8.

Income 2000: per capita $17,056; median household $37,170; **Pop below poverty level:** 12%. ***Personal per capita income 2000-2003:** $21,666-$23,467.

⚊ *County Seat*

Monroe County (cont'd)

Unemployment 2004: 4.2%. **Change from 2000:** -1.2%. **Median travel time to work:** 19 minutes. **Working outside county of residence:** 19.4%.

Cities with pop over 10,000: None.

OCONTO COUNTY

301 Washington St   **Ph:** 920-834-6800
Oconto, WI 54153   **Fax:** 920-834-6867
www.co.oconto.wi.us

On northeastern coast of WI, bordered on east by Green Bay; organized Feb 6, 1851 from unorganized territory. **Name Origin:** For the Oconto River, which flows through it; from a Menominee word of unclear meaning, possibly 'place of the pike fish' or 'red river.'

Area (sq mi): 1149.04 (land 997.97; water 151.07). **Pop per sq mi:** 37.7.

Pop 2005: 37,666. **State rank:** 38. **Pop change:** 2000-20005 +5.7%; 1990-2000 +17.9%. **Pop 2000:** 35,634 (White 97.4%; Black or African American 0.1%; Hispanic or Latino 0.7%; Asian 0.2%; Other 1.9%). **Foreign born:** 0.7%. **Median age:** 38.8.

Income 2000: per capita $19,016; median household $41,201; **Pop below poverty level:** 7.1%. ***Personal per capita income 2000-2003:** $23,900-$24,842.

Unemployment 2004: 6.1%. **Change from 2000:** -0.7%. **Median travel time to work:** 25.8 minutes. **Working outside county of residence:** 49.6%.

Cities with pop over 10,000: None.

ONEIDA COUNTY

PO Box 400   **Ph:** 715-369-6144
Rhinelander, WI 54501   **Fax:** 715-369-6230
www.co.oneida.wi.gov

In north-central WI; organized Apr 11, 1885 from Lincoln County. **Name Origin:** For the Oneida Indians, one of the Five Nations of the Iroquois. The name is thought to mean 'stone people,' perhaps in praise of their bravery.

Area (sq mi): 1235.88 (land 1124.5; water 111.38). **Pop per sq mi:** 32.9.

Pop 2005: 36,994. **State rank:** 39. **Pop change:** 2000-20005 +0.6%; 1990-2000 +16.1%. **Pop 2000:** 36,776 (White 97.3%; Black or African American 0.3%; Hispanic or Latino 0.7%; Asian 0.3%; Other 1.7%). **Foreign born:** 1%. **Median age:** 42.4.

Income 2000: per capita $19,746; median household $37,619; **Pop below poverty level:** 7.4%. ***Personal per capita income 2000-2003:** $26,393-$28,646.

Unemployment 2004: 5.8%. **Change from 2000:** +0.4%. **Median travel time to work:** 17.8 minutes. **Working outside county of residence:** 16.6%.

Cities with pop over 10,000: None.

OUTAGAMIE COUNTY

410 S Walnut St   **Ph:** 920-832-5077
Appleton, WI 54911   **Fax:** 920-832-2200
www.co.outagamie.wi.us

In east-central WI, west of Green Bay; organized Feb 17, 1851 from Brown County. **Name Origin:** Ojibway *O-dug-am-eeg* 'dwellers on the other side,' in reference to the Fox Indians.

Area (sq mi): 644.4 (land 640.34; water 4.06). **Pop per sq mi:** 267.1.

Pop 2005: 171,006. **State rank:** 6. **Pop change:** 2000-20005 +6.2%; 1990-2000 +14.6%. **Pop 2000:** 160,971 (White 93%; Black or African American 0.5%; Hispanic or Latino 2%; Asian 2.2%; Other 3.3%, including 1.5% American Indian/Alaska Native). **Foreign born:** 3.1%. **Median age:** 34.4.

Income 2000: per capita $21,943; median household $49,613; **Pop below poverty level:** 4.7%. ***Personal per capita income 2000-2003:** $29,078-$30,952.

Unemployment 2004: 4.7%. **Change from 2000:** +1%. **Median travel time to work:** 18.1 minutes. **Working outside county of residence:** 29.7%.

Cities with pop over 10,000: Appleton ⛪ (70,293); Kaukauna (14,463); Little Chute (10,791).

OZAUKEE COUNTY

PO Box 994   **Ph:** 262-284-8110
Port Washington, WI 53074   **Fax:** 262-284-8100
www.co.ozaukee.wi.us

On southestern coast of WI, north of Milwaukee, organized Mar 7, 1853 from Milwaukee County. **Name Origin:** Said to be the true name of the main Sauk Indian tribe; meaning is either 'people at the mouth of the river' (the Ojibway name for the tribe), or 'yellow earth,' from their tradition that the first Sauk male sprang from yellow earth.

Area (sq mi): 1116.2 (land 231.95; water 884.26). **Pop per sq mi:** 371.1.

Pop 2005: 86,072. **State rank:** 18. **Pop change:** 2000-20005 +4.6%; 1990-2000 +13%. **Pop 2000:** 82,317 (White 95.8%; Black or African American 0.9%; Hispanic or Latino 1.3%; Asian 1.1%; Other 1.2%). **Foreign born:** 3.3%. **Median age:** 38.9.

Income 2000: per capita $31,947; median household $62,745; **Pop below poverty level:** 2.6%. ***Personal per capita income 2000-2003:** $46,092-$47,527.

Unemployment 2004: 3.6%. **Change from 2000:** +0.6%. **Median travel time to work:** 22.1 minutes. **Working outside county of residence:** 48.4%.

Cities with pop over 10,000: Mequon (23,793); Grafton (11,588); Cedarburg (11,303); Port Washington ⛪ (10,890).

PEPIN COUNTY

740 7th Ave W   **Ph:** 715-672-8857
Durand, WI 54736   **Fax:** 715-672-8677
www.co.pepin.wi.us

On central western border of WI, southeast of Saint Paul, MN; organized Feb 25, 1858 from Chippewa County. **Name Origin:** For Pepin Lake, a widening of the Mississippi River. Named before 1700 by French explorers either for a member of the Duluth

**Source: Personal per capita income data are from the Bureau of Economic Analysis; per capita income data are from the Bureau of the Census.
See Introduction for explanation of differences.*

792

Pepin County (cont'd)

expedition, or for the French king, Pepin le Bref (715-768), the father of Charlemagne (742-814).

Area (sq mi): 248.68 (land 232.28; water 16.4). **Pop per sq mi:** 31.8.

Pop 2005: 7,380. **State rank:** 69. **Pop change:** 2000-20005 +2.3%; 1990-2000 +1.5%. **Pop 2000:** 7,213 (White 98.7%; Black or African American 0.1%; Hispanic or Latino 0.3%; Asian 0.2%; Other 0.8%). **Foreign born:** 0.6%. **Median age:** 38.7.

Income 2000: per capita $18,288; median household $37,609; **Pop below poverty level:** 9.1%. ***Personal per capita income 2000-2003:** $23,109-$24,407.

Unemployment 2004: 5%. **Change from 2000:** -0.9%. **Median travel time to work:** 25.7 minutes. **Working outside county of residence:** 46.2%.

Cities with pop over 10,000: None.

PIERCE COUNTY

414 W Main St PO Box 119
Ellsworth, WI 54011
www.co.pierce.wi.us

Ph: 715-273-6796
Fax: 715-273-6061

On central western border of WI, east of Saint Paul, MN, organized Mar 14, 1853 from Saint Croix County. **Name Origin:** For Franklin Pierce (1804-69), fourteenth U.S. president.

Area (sq mi): 591.59 (land 576.49; water 15.1). **Pop per sq mi:** 67.8.

Pop 2005: 39,102. **State rank:** 37. **Pop change:** 2000-20005 +6.2%; 1990-2000 +12.3%. **Pop 2000:** 36,804 (White 97.5%; Black or African American 0.2%; Hispanic or Latino 0.8%; Asian 0.4%; Other 1.3%). **Foreign born:** 1%. **Median age:** 32.1.

Income 2000: per capita $20,172; median household $49,551; **Pop below poverty level:** 7.7%. ***Personal per capita income 2000-2003:** $25,770-$27,963.

Unemployment 2004: 4.2%. **Change from 2000:** +0.2%. **Median travel time to work:** 25.1 minutes. **Working outside county of residence:** 59.4%.

Cities with pop over 10,000: River Falls (13,019).

POLK COUNTY

100 Polk County Plaza Suite 110
Balsam Lake, WI 54810
www.co.polk.wi.us

Ph: 715-485-9271
Fax: 715-485-9104

On central western border of WI, northeast of Saint Paul, MN; organized Mar 14, 1853 from Saint Croix County. **Name Origin:** For James Knox Polk (1795-1849), eleventh U.S. president.

Area (sq mi): 956.28 (land 917.27; water 39.01). **Pop per sq mi:** 48.3.

Pop 2005: 44,329. **State rank:** 30. **Pop change:** 2000-20005 +7.3%; 1990-2000 +18.8%. **Pop 2000:** 41,319 (White 97.1%; Black or African American 0.2%; Hispanic or Latino 0.8%; Asian 0.3%; Other 2%, including 1.1% American Indian/Alaska Native). **Foreign born:** 1%. **Median age:** 38.7.

Income 2000: per capita $19,129; median household $41,183; **Pop below poverty level:** 7.1%. ***Personal per capita income 2000-2003:** $23,404-$24,201.

Unemployment 2004: 5.4%. **Change from 2000:** -0.6%. **Median travel time to work:** 28.7 minutes. **Working outside county of residence:** 38.3%.

Cities with pop over 10,000: None.

PORTAGE COUNTY

1516 Church St
Stevens Point, WI 54481
www.co.portage.wi.us

Ph: 715-346-1351
Fax: 715-346-1486

In east-central WI, northwest of Lake Winnebago; organized Dec 7, 1836 (prior to statehood) from territorial county in the area now occupied by much of Columbia County, expanded northward in 1841 (into territory from Crawford County); Columbia County detached in 1846. **Name Origin:** For the portage of canoes or other craft between the Fox and Wisconsin rivers.

Area (sq mi): 822.76 (land 806.31; water 16.45). **Pop per sq mi:** 83.8.

Pop 2005: 67,585. **State rank:** 23. **Pop change:** 2000-20005 +0.6%; 1990-2000 +9.4%. **Pop 2000:** 67,182 (White 94.9%; Black or African American 0.3%; Hispanic or Latino 1.4%; Asian 2.2%; Other 1.7%). **Foreign born:** 2.2%. **Median age:** 33.

Income 2000: per capita $19,854; median household $43,487; **Pop below poverty level:** 9.5%. ***Personal per capita income 2000-2003:** $24,837-$27,464.

Unemployment 2004: 4.8%. **Change from 2000:** +0.3%. **Median travel time to work:** 18.3 minutes. **Working outside county of residence:** 19%.

Cities with pop over 10,000: Stevens Point ⚏ (24,283); Plover (11,155).

PRICE COUNTY

126 Cherry St
Phillips, WI 54555
www.co.price.wi.us

Ph: 715-339-3325
Fax: 715-339-3089

In north-central WI, northwest of Wausau; organized Feb 26, 1879 from Chippewa and Lincoln counties. **Name Origin:** For William Thompson Price (1824-86), WI jurist, legislator, and U.S. representative (1883-86).

Area (sq mi): 1278.43 (land 1252.56; water 25.87). **Pop per sq mi:** 12.2.

Pop 2005: 15,220. **State rank:** 64. **Pop change:** 2000-20005 -3.8%; 1990-2000 +1.4%. **Pop 2000:** 15,822 (White 97.7%; Black or African American 0.1%; Hispanic or Latino 0.7%; Asian 0.3%; Other 1.3%). **Foreign born:** 0.6%. **Median age:** 41.7.

Income 2000: per capita $17,837; median household $35,249; **Pop below poverty level:** 8.9%. ***Personal per capita income 2000-2003:** $21,863-$24,361.

Unemployment 2004: 4.6%. **Change from 2000:** -2.4%. **Median travel time to work:** 18.9 minutes. **Working outside county of residence:** 17%.

Cities with pop over 10,000: None.

RACINE COUNTY

730 Wisconsin Ave   **Ph:** 262-636-3121
Racine, WI 53403   **Fax:** 262-636-3491
www.racineco.com

On southeastern coast of WI, south of Milwaukee; organized Dec 7, 1836 (prior to statehood) from territorial county. **Name Origin:** French 'root,' referring to the county's principal town, located on the Root River, which had so many roots growing out of its banks that navigation was difficult.

Area (sq mi): 791.9 (land 333.1; water 458.81). **Pop per sq mi:** 587.5.

Pop 2005: 195,708. **State rank:** 5. **Pop change:** 2000-20005 +3.6%; 1990-2000 +7.9%. **Pop 2000:** 188,831 (White 79.6%; Black or African American 10.5%; Hispanic or Latino 7.9%; Asian 0.7%; Other 5.8%). **Foreign born:** 4.1%. **Median age:** 36.1.

Income 2000: per capita $21,772; median household $48,059; **Pop below poverty level:** 8.4%. ***Personal per capita income 2000-2003:** $28,776-$31,271.

Unemployment 2004: 6%. **Change from 2000:** -0.7%. **Median travel time to work:** 22 minutes. **Working outside county of residence:** 31.8%.

Cities with pop over 10,000: Mount Pleasant (25,389); Racine 🏛 (80,108); Burlington (11,043).

RICHLAND COUNTY

181 W Seminary St PO Box 310   **Ph:** 608-647-2197
Richland Center, WI 53581   **Fax:** 608-647-6134
www.co.richland.wi.us

In southwestern WI, northwest of Madison; organized Feb 18, 1842 (prior to statehood) from Crawford, Sauk, and Iowa counties. **Name Origin:** For the fertile soil, and possibly because an early settler came from Richland Co., IA.

Area (sq mi): 589.38 (land 586.2; water 3.18). **Pop per sq mi:** 31.4.

Pop 2005: 18,403. **State rank:** 56. **Pop change:** 2000-20005 +2.7%; 1990-2000 +2.3%. **Pop 2000:** 17,924 (White 97.9%; Black or African American 0.2%; Hispanic or Latino 0.9%; Asian 0.2%; Other 1.3%). **Foreign born:** 1%. **Median age:** 39.2.

Income 2000: per capita $17,042; median household $33,998; **Pop below poverty level:** 10.1%. ***Personal per capita income 2000-2003:** $20,917-$23,829.

Unemployment 2004: 4.5%. **Change from 2000:** -0.3%. **Median travel time to work:** 24.1 minutes. **Working outside county of residence:** 32.7%.

Cities with pop over 10,000: None.

ROCK COUNTY

51 S Main St   **Ph:** 608-757-5660
Janesville, WI 53545   **Fax:** 608-757-5662
www.co.rock.wi.us

On central southern border of WI, southeast of Madison; organized Dec 7, 1836 (prior to statehood) from a territorial county. **Name Origin:** For the Rock River, which flows through it.

Area (sq mi): 726.2 (land 720.47; water 5.73). **Pop per sq mi:** 218.7.

Pop 2005: 157,538. **State rank:** 9. **Pop change:** 2000-20005 +3.4%; 1990-2000 +9.2%. **Pop 2000:** 152,307 (White 89.2%; Black or

African American 4.6%; Hispanic or Latino 3.9%; Asian 0.8%; Other 3.6%). **Foreign born:** 3.3%. **Median age:** 35.9.

Income 2000: per capita $20,895; median household $45,517; **Pop below poverty level:** 7.3%. ***Personal per capita income 2000-2003:** $26,174-$28,256.

Unemployment 2004: 5.6%. **Change from 2000:** -0.8%. **Median travel time to work:** 20.3 minutes. **Working outside county of residence:** 22.4%.

Cities with pop over 10,000: Janesville 🏛 (61,604); Beloit (35,803).

RUSK COUNTY

311 Miner Ave E   **Ph:** 715-532-2100
Ladysmith, WI 54848   **Fax:** 715-532-2237
www.ruskcounty.org

In northwestern WI, northeast of Saint Paul, MN; organized May 15, 1901 as Gates County from Chippewa County; name changed Jun 19, 1905. **Name Origin:** For Col. Jeremiah McLain Rusk (1830-93), an officer in the Civil War, statesman, governor of WI (1882-89), and U.S. secretary of agriculture (1889-93).

Area (sq mi): 930.89 (land 913.13; water 17.77). **Pop per sq mi:** 16.6.

Pop 2005: 15,198. **State rank:** 65. **Pop change:** 2000-20005 -1%; 1990-2000 +1.8%. **Pop 2000:** 15,347 (White 97.4%; Black or African American 0.5%; Hispanic or Latino 0.8%; Asian 0.3%; Other 1.6%). **Foreign born:** 1.7%. **Median age:** 40.

Income 2000: per capita $15,563; median household $31,344; **Pop below poverty level:** 11.8%. ***Personal per capita income 2000-2003:** $19,333-$20,461.

Unemployment 2004: 6.4%. **Change from 2000:** -0.9%. **Median travel time to work:** 21.6 minutes. **Working outside county of residence:** 17.9%.

Cities with pop over 10,000: None.

SAINT CROIX COUNTY

1101 Carmichael Rd   **Ph:** 715-386-4600
Hudson, WI 54016   **Fax:** 715-381-4400
www.co.saint-croix.wi.us

On central western border of WI, east of Saint Paul, MN; organized Jan 9, 1840 (prior to statehood) from a territorial county. **Name Origin:** For the river, which flows through it; French 'holy cross,' probably for an early French explorer of that name who drowned in it.

Area (sq mi): 735.81 (land 721.82; water 13.98). **Pop per sq mi:** 106.9.

Pop 2005: 77,144. **State rank:** 21. **Pop change:** 2000-20005 +22.2%; 1990-2000 +25.7%. **Pop 2000:** 63,155 (White 97.4%; Black or African American 0.3%; Hispanic or Latino 0.8%; Asian 0.6%; Other 1.3%). **Foreign born:** 1.1%. **Median age:** 35.

Income 2000: per capita $23,937; median household $54,930; **Pop below poverty level:** 4%. ***Personal per capita income 2000-2003:** $30,670-$31,091.

Unemployment 2004: 4.8%. **Change from 2000:** +0.3%. **Median travel time to work:** 26.1 minutes. **Working outside county of residence:** 51.3%.

Cities with pop over 10,000: Hudson 🏛 (10,754).

Source: Personal per capita income data are from the Bureau of Economic Analysis; per capita income data are from the Bureau of the Census.
See Introduction for explanation of differences.

SAUK COUNTY

505 Broadway
Baraboo, WI 53913
www.co.sauk.wi.us

Ph: 608-355-3286
Fax: 608-355-3522

In south-central WI, northwest of Madison; organized Jan 11, 1840 (prior to statehood) from a territorial county. **Name Origin:** Shortened form of Saukie, a local Indian tribe; French form is *Sac*. Meaning of the name is unclear: possibly 'something sprouting up' or 'yellow earth' from which their tradition says their first male sprang.

Area (sq mi): 848.43 (land 837.63; water 10.8). **Pop per sq mi:** 68.9.

Pop 2005: 57,746. **State rank:** 25. **Pop change:** 2000-20005 +4.6%; 1990-2000 +17.6%. **Pop 2000:** 55,225 (White 96.4%; Black or African American 0.3%; Hispanic or Latino 1.7%; Asian 0.3%; Other 2.1%). **Foreign born:** 1.9%. **Median age:** 37.3.

Income 2000: per capita $19,695; median household $41,941; **Pop below poverty level:** 7.2%. *****Personal per capita income 2000-2003:** $26,348-$28,780.

Unemployment 2004: 4.4%. **Change from 2000:** +0.8%. **Median travel time to work:** 20.3 minutes. **Working outside county of residence:** 20.8%.

Cities with pop over 10,000: Baraboo ⛫ (10,771).

SAWYER COUNTY

PO Box 836
Hayward, WI 54843
www.sawyercountygov.org

Ph: 715-634-4866
Fax: 715-634-3666

In northwestern WI, north of Eau Claire; organized Mar 10, 1883 from Ashland and Chippewa counties. **Name Origin:** For Philetus Sawyer (1816-1900), U.S. representative from WI (1865-75) and U.S. senator (1881-93).

Area (sq mi): 1350.32 (land 1256.42; water 93.9). **Pop per sq mi:** 13.5.

Pop 2005: 16,975. **State rank:** 58. **Pop change:** 2000-20005 +4.8%; 1990-2000 +14.2%. **Pop 2000:** 16,196 (White 81.4%; Black or African American 0.3%; Hispanic or Latino 0.9%; Asian 0.3%; Other 17.6%, including 16.1% American Indian/Alaska Native). **Foreign born:** 1.6%. **Median age:** 42.1.

Income 2000: per capita $17,634; median household $32,287; **Pop below poverty level:** 12.7%. *****Personal per capita income 2000-2003:** $22,200-$23,921.

Unemployment 2004: 5.9%. **Change from 2000:** +0.2%. **Median travel time to work:** 18.4 minutes. **Working outside county of residence:** 16.2%.

Cities with pop over 10,000: None.

SHAWANO COUNTY

311 N Main St
Shawano, WI 54166
www.co.shawano.wi.us

Ph: 715-526-9150
Fax: 715-524-5157

In east-central WI, northwest of Green Bay; organized Feb 16, 1853 from Oconto County. **Name Origin:** For Shawano Lake, a Menominee word probably meaning 'to the south.'

Area (sq mi): 909.33 (land 892.51; water 16.82). **Pop per sq mi:** 46.3.

Pop 2005: 41,335. **State rank:** 36. **Pop change:** 2000-20005 +1.7%; 1990-2000 +9.4%. **Pop 2000:** 40,664 (White 91.2%; Black or African American 0.2%; Hispanic or Latino 1%; Asian 0.3%; Other 7.8%, including 6.3% American Indian/Alaska Native). **Foreign born:** 1%. **Median age:** 38.5.

Income 2000: per capita $17,991; median household $38,069; **Pop below poverty level:** 7.9%. *****Personal per capita income 2000-2003:** $22,165-$23,941.

Unemployment 2004: 5%. **Change from 2000:** -0.4%. **Median travel time to work:** 22.8 minutes. **Working outside county of residence:** 40.8%.

Cities with pop over 10,000: None.

SHEBOYGAN COUNTY

508 New York Ave
Sheboygan, WI 53081
www.co.sheboygan.wi.us

Ph: 920-459-3003
Fax: 920-459-0304

On central eastern coast of WI, southeast of Lake Winnebago; organized Dec 7, 1836 (prior to statehood) from a territorial county. **Name Origin:** For the Sheboygan River, from an Algonquian word whose meaning is unclear: possibly either 'reed like,' 'something that pierces,' or 'thundering under the ground.'

Area (sq mi): 1270.97 (land 513.63; water 757.34). **Pop per sq mi:** 223.1.

Pop 2005: 114,610. **State rank:** 12. **Pop change:** 2000-20005 +1.7%; 1990-2000 +8.4%. **Pop 2000:** 112,646 (White 91.1%; Black or African American 1.1%; Hispanic or Latino 3.4%; Asian 3.3%; Other 3%). **Foreign born:** 4.3%. **Median age:** 36.8.

Income 2000: per capita $21,509; median household $46,237; **Pop below poverty level:** 5.2%. *****Personal per capita income 2000-2003:** $28,814 $31,251.

Unemployment 2004: 4.4%. **Change from 2000:** +0.6%. **Median travel time to work:** 16.9 minutes. **Working outside county of residence:** 12.1%.

Cities with pop over 10,000: Sheboygan ⛫ (49,020).

TAYLOR COUNTY

224 S 2nd St
Medford, WI 54451
www.co.taylor.wi.us

Ph: 715-748-1460
Fax: 715-748-1415

In north-central WI, northwest of Wausau; organized Mar 4, 1875 from Clark and Lincoln counties. **Name Origin:** For William Robert Taylor (1820-1909), governor of WI (1874-76), known as the 'farmer governor.'

Area (sq mi): 984.49 (land 974.86; water 9.63). **Pop per sq mi:** 20.3.

Pop 2005: 19,766. **State rank:** 53. **Pop change:** 2000-20005 +0.4%; 1990-2000 +4.1%. **Pop 2000:** 19,680 (White 98.3%; Black or African American 0.1%; Hispanic or Latino 0.6%; Asian 0.2%; Other 1%). **Foreign born:** 0.9%. **Median age:** 37.4.

Income 2000: per capita $17,570; median household $38,502; **Pop below poverty level:** 9.8%. *****Personal per capita income 2000-2003:** $21,013-$23,020.

Unemployment 2004: 5.2%. **Change from 2000:** -0.6%. **Median travel time to work:** 18.5 minutes. **Working outside county of residence:** 17.5%.

⛫ *County Seat*

Taylor County (cont'd)

Cities with pop over 10,000: None.

TREMPEALEAU COUNTY

36245 Main St   **Ph:** 715-538-2311
Whitehall, WI 54773   **Fax:** 715-538-4210
www.tremplocounty.com

On central western border of WI, southeast of Saint Paul, MN; organized Jan 27, 1854 from Chippewa County. **Name Origin:** For the town at the foot of a high elevation surrounded by water; French transliteration *la montagne qui termpe a l'eau* of an Indian word probably meaning 'mountain drenched with water.' The Trempealeau River forms the lower western border of the county.

Area (sq mi): 741.98 (land 734.08; water 7.9). **Pop per sq mi:** 37.9.

Pop 2005: 27,812. **State rank:** 45. **Pop change:** 2000-20005 +3%; 1990-2000 +6.9%. **Pop 2000:** 27,010 (White 98.3%; Black or African American 0.1%; Hispanic or Latino 0.9%; Asian 0.1%; Other 1%). **Foreign born:** 0.8%. **Median age:** 38.3.

Income 2000: per capita $17,681; median household $37,889; **Pop below poverty level:** 8.3%. ***Personal per capita income 2000-2003:** $23,274-$25,242.

Unemployment 2004: 4.7%. **Change from 2000:** -1.1%. **Median travel time to work:** 21.9 minutes. **Working outside county of residence:** 29.2%.

Cities with pop over 10,000: None.

VERNON COUNTY

Courthouse Annex Rm 108   **Ph:** 608-637-5380
Viroqua, WI 54665   **Fax:** 608-637-5556
www.wisconline.com/counties/vernon/

On southwestern border of WI, southwest of Madison; organized as Bad Axe County Mar 1, 1851 from Richland and Crawford counties; name changed Mar 22, 1862. **Name Origin:** For either Mount Vernon, first U.S. President George Washington's (1732-99) home overlooking the Potomac River in VA, or for George Vernon Weeks, a friend of the county judge. Originally for the Bad Ax River, which traverses it.

Area (sq mi): 816.41 (land 794.87; water 21.54). **Pop per sq mi:** 36.6.

Pop 2005: 29,055. **State rank:** 43. **Pop change:** 2000-20005 +3.6%; 1990-2000 +9.5%. **Pop 2000:** 28,056 (White 98.4%; Black or African American 0.1%; Hispanic or Latino 0.7%; Asian 0.2%; Other 0.9%). **Foreign born:** 0.8%. **Median age:** 39.1.

Income 2000: per capita $15,859; median household $33,178; **Pop below poverty level:** 14.2%. ***Personal per capita income 2000-2003:** $19,234-$20,950.

Unemployment 2004: 4.6%. **Change from 2000:** -0.4%. **Median travel time to work:** 23.7 minutes. **Working outside county of residence:** 36.8%.

Cities with pop over 10,000: None.

VILAS COUNTY

330 Court St   **Ph:** 715-479-3600
Eagle River, WI 54521   **Fax:** 715-479-3605
www.co.vilas.wi.us

On central northern border of WI; organized Apr 12, 1893 from Oneida County. **Name Origin:** For Col. William Freeman Vilas (1840-1908), officer in the Civil War, U.S. postmaster general (1885-88), U.S. secretary of the interior (1888-89), and U.S. senator from WI (1891-97).

Area (sq mi): 1017.85 (land 873.72; water 144.13). **Pop per sq mi:** 25.6.

Pop 2005: 22,330. **State rank:** 49. **Pop change:** 2000-20005 +6.2%; 1990-2000 +18.8%. **Pop 2000:** 21,033 (White 89.2%; Black or African American 0.2%; Hispanic or Latino 0.9%; Asian 0.2%; Other 10%, including 9.1% American Indian/Alaska Native). **Foreign born:** 2.4%. **Median age:** 45.8.

Income 2000: per capita $18,361; median household $33,759; **Pop below poverty level:** 8%. ***Personal per capita income 2000-2003:** $24,497-$25,664.

Unemployment 2004: 6%. **Change from 2000:** +0.8%. **Median travel time to work:** 17.9 minutes. **Working outside county of residence:** 28.7%.

Cities with pop over 10,000: None.

WALWORTH COUNTY

PO Box 1001   **Ph:** 262-741-4241
Elkhorn, WI 53121   **Fax:** 262-741-4287
www.co.walworth.wi.us

On southeastern border of WI, southwest of Milwaukee; organized Dec 7, 1836 (prior to statehood) from a territorial county. **Name Origin:** For Col. Reuben Hyde Walworth (1788-1867), officer in the War of 1812, jurist, and U.S. representative from NY (1821-23); unconfirmed nominee to the U.S. Supreme Court (1844).

Area (sq mi): 576.5 (land 555.31; water 21.19). **Pop per sq mi:** 179.8.

Pop 2005: 99,844. **State rank:** 14. **Pop change:** 2000-20005 +6.5%; 1990-2000 +25%. **Pop 2000:** 93,759 (White 91.1%; Black or African American 0.8%; Hispanic or Latino 6.5%; Asian 0.7%; Other 3.9%). **Foreign born:** 5.4%. **Median age:** 35.1.

Income 2000: per capita $21,229; median household $46,274; **Pop below poverty level:** 8.4%. ***Personal per capita income 2000-2003:** $27,293-$27,626.

Unemployment 2004: 4.3%. **Change from 2000:** +0.6%. **Median travel time to work:** 24 minutes. **Working outside county of residence:** 36.6%.

Cities with pop over 10,000: Whitewater (14,215).

WASHBURN COUNTY

PO Box 639   **Ph:** 715-468-4600
Shell Lake, WI 54871   **Fax:** 715-468-4725
www.co.washburn.wi.us

In northwestern WI; organized Mar 27, 1883 from Burnett County. **Name Origin:** For Cadwallader Colden Washburn (1818-82), U.S. representative (1855-61; 1867-71) and governor of WI (1872-74).

Area (sq mi): 853.06 (land 809.68; water 43.37). **Pop per sq mi:** 20.5.

*Source: Personal per capita income data are from the Bureau of Economic Analysis; per capita income data are from the Bureau of the Census. See Introduction for explanation of differences.

Washburn County (cont'd)

Pop 2005: 16,601. **State rank:** 60. **Pop change:** 2000-20005 +3.5%; 1990-2000 +16.4%. **Pop 2000:** 16,036 (White 96.7%; Black or African American 0.2%; Hispanic or Latino 0.9%; Asian 0.2%; Other 2.3%, including 1% American Indian/Alaska Native). **Foreign born:** 1%. **Median age:** 42.1.

Income 2000: per capita $17,341, median household $33,716; **Pop below poverty level:** 9.9%. ***Personal per capita income 2000-2003:** $21,324-$22,794.

Unemployment 2004: 6.1%. **Change from 2000:** -0.2%. **Median travel time to work:** 22.4 minutes. **Working outside county of residence:** 30.7%.

Cities with pop over 10,000: None.

WASHINGTON COUNTY

432 E Washington St PO Box 1986   **Ph:** 262-335-4305
West Bend, WI 53095   **Fax:** 262-306-2208
www.co.washington.wi.us

In southeastern WI, northwest of Milwaukee; organized Dec 7, 1836 (prior to statehood) from a territorial county. **Name Origin:** For George Washington (1732-99), American patriot and first U.S. president.

Area (sq mi): 435.89 (land 430.82; water 5.07). **Pop per sq mi:** 292.8.

Pop 2005: 126,158. **State rank:** 11. **Pop change:** 2000-20005 +7.4%; 1990-2000 +23.3%. **Pop 2000:** 117,493 (White 96.9%; Black or African American 0.4%; Hispanic or Latino 1.3%; Asian 0.6%; Other 1.4%). **Foreign born:** 1.9%. **Median age:** 36.6.

Income 2000: per capita $24,319; median household $57,033; **Pop below poverty level:** 3.6%. ***Personal per capita income 2000-2003:** $33,604-$35,196.

Unemployment 2004: 4.5%. **Change from 2000:** +0.7%. **Median travel time to work:** 23.2 minutes. **Working outside county of residence:** 49.6%.

Cities with pop over 10,000: West Bend 🏛 (29,302); Germantown (19,104); Hartford (12,625).

WAUKESHA COUNTY

1320 Pewaukee Rd Rm 120   **Ph:** 262-548-7010
Waukesha, WI 53188   **Fax:** 262-548-7722
www.waukeshacounty.gov

In southeastern WI, west of Milwaukee; organized Jan 31, 1846 (prior to statehood) from Milwaukee County. **Name Origin:** For the Fox River and the Fox Indian tribe, from Potawatomi *wakusheg* 'foxes.'

Area (sq mi): 580.48 (land 555.58; water 24.91). **Pop per sq mi:** 682.1.

Pop 2005: 378,971. **State rank:** 3. **Pop change:** 2000-20005 +5%; 1990-2000 +18.4%. **Pop 2000:** 360,767 (White 94.2%; Black or African American 0.7%; Hispanic or Latino 2.6%; Asian 1.5%; Other 2%). **Foreign born:** 3.6%. **Median age:** 38.1.

Income 2000: per capita $29,164; median household $62,839; **Pop below poverty level:** 2.7%. ***Personal per capita income 2000-2003:** $41,033-$41,551.

Unemployment 2004: 4.2%. **Change from 2000:** +0.9%. **Median travel time to work:** 22.2 minutes. **Working outside county of residence:** 38%.

Cities with pop over 10,000: 7 (see page 39 for cities).

WAUPACA COUNTY

811 Harding St   **Ph:** 715-258-6200
Waupaca, WI 54981   **Fax:** 715-258-6212
www.co.waupaca.wi.us

In east-central WI, west of Green Bay; organized Feb 17, 1851 from Winnebago and Brown counties. **Name Origin:** From an Indian name of various interpretations; the most probable is 'place of clear water.'

Area (sq mi): 765.33 (land 751.09; water 14.24). **Pop per sq mi:** 70.

Pop 2005: 52,563. **State rank:** 27. **Pop change:** 2000-20005 +1.6%; 1990-2000 +12.2%. **Pop 2000:** 51,731 (White 97.2%; Black or African American 0.2%; Hispanic or Latino 1.4%; Asian 0.3%; Other 1.6%). **Foreign born:** 1%. **Median age:** 38.5.

Income 2000: per capita $18,664; median household $40,910; **Pop below poverty level:** 6.8%. ***Personal per capita income 2000-2003:** $24,798-$26,863.

Unemployment 2004: 5.2%. **Change from 2000:** +0.2%. **Median travel time to work:** 21 minutes. **Working outside county of residence:** 32.8%.

Cities with pop over 10,000: None.

WAUSHARA COUNTY

209 S Saint Marie St   **Ph:** 920-787-0441
Wautoma, WI 54982   **Fax:** 920-787-0481
www.1waushara.com

In east-central WI, west of Lake Winnebago; organized Feb 15, 1851 from Marquette County. **Name Origin:** From an Indian word possibly meaning 'good land river' or for a Winnebago word meaning 'foxes.' Corruption of the name of a Winnebago chief, an ancient Winnebago village, and the Indian name for Fox Lake.

Area (sq mi): 637.39 (land 626.03; water 11.36). **Pop per sq mi:** 39.6.

Pop 2005: 24,789. **State rank:** 47. **Pop change:** 2000-20005 +7.1%; 1990-2000 +19.4%. **Pop 2000:** 23,154 (White 94.8%; Black or African American 0.3%; Hispanic or Latino 3.7%; Asian 0.3%; Other 2.6%). **Foreign born:** 2%. **Median age:** 42.1.

Income 2000: per capita $18,144; median household $37,000; **Pop below poverty level:** 9.1%. ***Personal per capita income 2000-2003:** $20,913-$21,762.

Unemployment 2004: 5.7%. **Change from 2000:** -0.1%. **Median travel time to work:** 27.1 minutes. **Working outside county of residence:** 47.5%.

Cities with pop over 10,000: None.

WINNEBAGO COUNTY

PO Box 2808   **Ph:** 920-236-4800
Oshkosh, WI 54903   **Fax:** 920-303-3025
www.co.winnebago.wi.us

In east-central WI, west of Lake Winnebago; organized Jan 6, 1840 (prior to statehood) from Brown County. **Name Origin:** For the

Winnebago County (cont'd)

Winnebago Indians, a tribe of Siouan linguistic stock; their name believed to mean 'fish eaters.'

Area (sq mi): 578.7 (land 438.58; water 140.12). **Pop per sq mi:** 363.6.

Pop 2005: 159,482. **State rank:** 8. **Pop change:** 2000-20005 +1.7%; 1990-2000 +11.7%. **Pop 2000:** 156,763 (White 93.9%; Black or African American 1.1%; Hispanic or Latino 2%; Asian 1.8%; Other 2.1%). **Foreign born:** 2.8%. **Median age:** 35.4.

Income 2000: per capita $21,706; median household $44,445; **Pop below poverty level:** 6.7%. ***Personal per capita income 2000-2003:** $28,217-$30,359.

Unemployment 2004: 4.5%. **Change from 2000:** +1%. **Median travel time to work:** 17.8 minutes. **Working outside county of residence:** 25.5%.

Cities with pop over 10,000: Oshkosh 🏛 (63,515); Neenah (24,557); Menasha (16,363).

WOOD COUNTY

PO Box 8095   **Ph:** 715-421-8460
Wisconsin Rapids, WI 54495   **Fax:** 715-421-8808
www.co.wood.wi.us

In central WI, southwest of Wausau; organized Mar 29, 1856 from Portage County. **Name Origin:** For Joseph Wood, legislator, county judge, and mayor of Grand Rapids.

Area (sq mi): 809.46 (land 792.78; water 16.68). **Pop per sq mi:** 94.9.

Pop 2005: 75,234. **State rank:** 22. **Pop change:** 2000-20005 -0.4%; 1990-2000 +2.6%. **Pop 2000:** 75,555 (White 95.9%; Black or African American 0.3%; Hispanic or Latino 0.9%; Asian 1.6%; Other 1.7%). **Foreign born:** 2.1%. **Median age:** 38.

Income 2000: per capita $20,203; median household $41,595; **Pop below poverty level:** 6.5%. ***Personal per capita income 2000-2003:** $27,622-$30,401.

Unemployment 2004: 5.7%. **Change from 2000:** +0.4%. **Median travel time to work:** 17.4 minutes. **Working outside county of residence:** 14.9%.

Cities with pop over 10,000: Marshfield (18,644); Wisconsin Rapids 🏛 (17,845).

*Source: Personal per capita income data are from the Bureau of Economic Analysis; per capita income data are from the Bureau of the Census. See Introduction for explanation of differences.

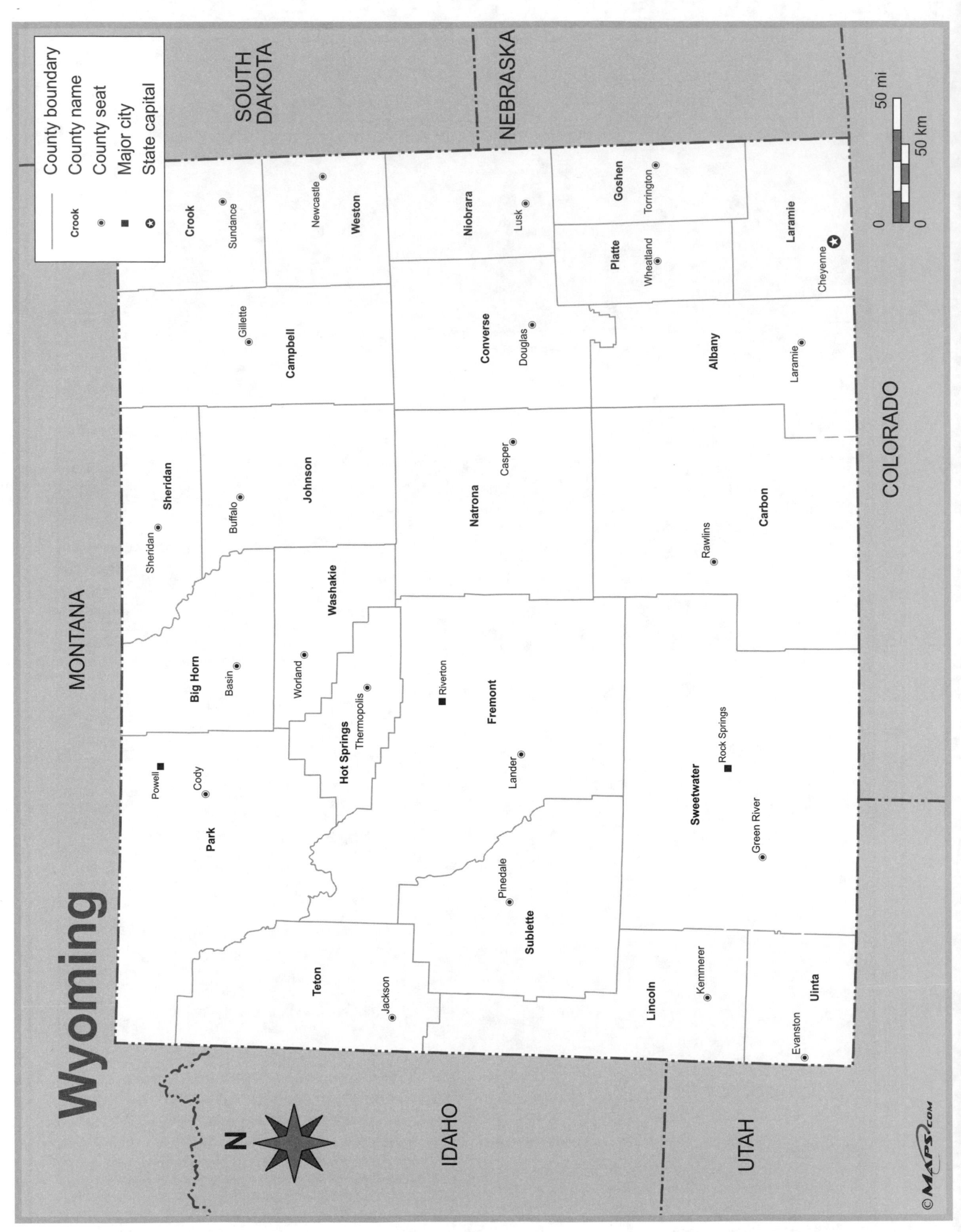

Wyoming

WYOMING STATE INFORMATION

wyoming.gov   **Ph:** 307-777-7220

Area (sq mi): 97,813.56 (land 97100.4; water 713.16). **Pop per sq mi:** 5.2.

Pop 2005: 509,294. **Pop change:** 2000-20005 +3.1%; 1990-2000 +8.9%. **Pop 2000:** 493,782 (White 88.9%; Black or African American 0.8%; Hispanic or Latino 6.4%; Asian 0.6%; Other 6.7%, including 2.3% American Indian/Alaska Native). **Foreign born:** 2.3%. **Median age:** 36.2.

Income 2000: per capita $19,134; median household $37,892; **Pop below poverty level:** 11.4%. ***Personal per capita income 2000-2003:** $28,460-$32,433.

Unemployment 2004: 3.9%. **Change from 2000:** +0.1%. **Median travel time to work:** 17.8 minutes. **Working outside county of residence:** 7.9%.

ALBANY COUNTY

525 Grand Ave County Courthouse Rm 202   **Ph:** 307-721-2541

Laramie, WY 82070   **Fax:** 307-721-2544

www.co.albany.wy.us

On the southeastern border of WY, west of Cheyenne; organized Dec 16, 1868 (prior to statehood) from Laramie County. **Name Origin:** For Albany, NY, former home of Charles D. Bradley, a member of the legislature.

Area (sq mi): 4308.79 (land 4272.75; water 36.04). **Pop per sq mi:** 7.2.

Pop 2005: 30,890. **State rank:** 6. **Pop change:** 2000-20005 -3.5%; 1990-2000 +4%. **Pop 2000:** 32,014 (White 87.5%; Black or African American 1.1%; Hispanic or Latino 7.5%; Asian 1.7%; Other 5.9%, including 1% American Indian/Alaska Native). **Foreign born:** 3.8%. **Median age:** 26.7.

Income 2000: per capita $16,706; median household $28,790; **Pop below poverty level:** 21%. ***Personal per capita income 2000-2003:** $23,335-$28,077.

Unemployment 2004: 3.1%. **Change from 2000:** +1.1%. **Median travel time to work:** 13.6 minutes. **Working outside county of residence:** 6.4%.

Cities with pop over 10,000: Laramie ⛫ (26,441).

BIG HORN COUNTY

420 W 'C' St   **Ph:** 307-568-2357

Basin, WY 82410   **Fax:** 307-568-9375

www.bighorncountywy.gov

On the central northern border of WY; organized 1896 from Fremont and Johnson counties. **Name Origin:** For the Big Horn River, which traverses the county, and the Big Horn Mountains, which form its eastern border; both are named for the bighorn sheep in the area.

Area (sq mi): 3158.96 (land 3136.99; water 21.97). **Pop per sq mi:** 3.6.

Pop 2005: 11,333. **State rank:** 15. **Pop change:** 2000-20005 -1.1%; 1990-2000 +8.9%. **Pop 2000:** 11,461 (White 91.9%; Black or African American 0.1%; Hispanic or Latino 6.2%; Asian 0.2%; Other 5.8%). **Foreign born:** 2.2%. **Median age:** 38.7.

Income 2000: per capita $15,086; median household $32,682; **Pop below poverty level:** 14.1%. ***Personal per capita income 2000-2003:** $20,640-$24,082.

Unemployment 2004: 4.7%. **Change from 2000:** -0.3%. **Median travel time to work:** 15.7 minutes. **Working outside county of residence:** 13.3%.

Cities with pop over 10,000: None.

CAMPBELL COUNTY

PO Box 3010   **Ph:** 307-682-7285

Gillette, WY 82717   **Fax:** 307-687-6455

ccg.co.campbell.wy.us

On northeastern border of WY; organized Feb 13, 1911 from Crook and Weston counties. **Name Origin:** Probably for Gen. John Allen Campbell (1835-80), Civil War officer and first territorial governor of WY (1869-75); or possibly for Robert Campbell, member of an expedition into the Missouri River area in 1822.

Area (sq mi): 4801.56 (land 4796.76; water 4.8). **Pop per sq mi:** 7.8.

Pop 2005: 37,405. **State rank:** 4. **Pop change:** 2000-20005 +11%; 1990-2000 +14.7%. **Pop 2000:** 33,698 (White 94.1%; Black or African American 0.2%; Hispanic or Latino 3.5%; Asian 0.3%; Other 3.4%). **Foreign born:** 1.7%. **Median age:** 32.2.

Income 2000: per capita $20,063; median household $49,536; **Pop below poverty level:** 7.6%. ***Personal per capita income 2000-2003:** $27,351-$30,777.

Unemployment 2004: 3.1%. **Change from 2000:** +0.2%. **Median travel time to work:** 20.1 minutes. **Working outside county of residence:** 3.1%.

Cities with pop over 10,000: Gillette ⛫ (22,260).

⛫ *County Seat*

CARBON COUNTY

PO Box 6   **Ph:** 307-328-2668
Rawlins, WY 82301   **Fax:** 307-328-2669
www.wyomingcarboncounty.com

On the central southern border of WY; organized Dec 16, 1868 (prior to statehood) from Laramie County. **Name Origin:** For vast coal deposits within its boundaries.

Area (sq mi): 7964.03 (land 7896.14; water 67.89). **Pop per sq mi:** 1.9.

Pop 2005: 15,331. **State rank:** 12. **Pop change:** 2000-20005 -2%; 1990-2000 -6.1%. **Pop 2000:** 15,639 (White 82.4%; Black or African American 0.7%; Hispanic or Latino 13.8%; Asian 0.7%; Other 8.7%, including 1.3% American Indian/Alaska Native). **Foreign born:** 2.9%. **Median age:** 38.9.

Income 2000: per capita $18,375; median household $36,060; **Pop below poverty level:** 12.9%. *****Personal per capita income 2000-2003:** $23,663-$27,479.

Unemployment 2004: 4.6%. **Change from 2000:** +0.2%. **Median travel time to work:** 13.7 minutes. **Working outside county of residence:** 5.7%.

Cities with pop over 10,000: None.

CONVERSE COUNTY

107 N 5th St Suite 114   **Ph:** 307-358-2244
Douglas, WY 82633   **Fax:** 307-358-5998
www.conversecounty.org

In east-central WY, east of Casper; organized Mar 9, 1888 (prior to statehood) from Albany County. **Name Origin:** For Amasa Converse (1842-85), WY Territory official and Cheyenne businessman who established the Converse Cattle Company.

Area (sq mi): 4265.1 (land 4254.72; water 10.38). **Pop per sq mi:** 3.

Pop 2005: 12,766. **State rank:** 13. **Pop change:** 2000-20005 +5.9%; 1990-2000 +8.3%. **Pop 2000:** 12,052 (White 91.9%; Black or African American 0.1%; Hispanic or Latino 5.5%; Asian 0.3%; Other 4.9%). **Foreign born:** 1.9%. **Median age:** 37.5.

Income 2000: per capita $18,744; median household $39,603; **Pop below poverty level:** 11.6%. *****Personal per capita income 2000-2003:** $25,251-$29,566.

Unemployment 2004: 4%. **Change from 2000:** -0.2%. **Median travel time to work:** 25.9 minutes. **Working outside county of residence:** 23.6%.

Cities with pop over 10,000: None.

CROOK COUNTY

309 Cleveland St   **Ph:** 307-283-1323
Sundance, WY 82729   **Fax:** 307-283-3038
www.newedc.net/crook/index.htm

On the northeastern border of WY, northeast of Gillette; created Dec 8, 1875 (prior to statehood). **Name Origin:** For Gen. George H. Crook (1829-90), officer in the Oregon Territory and Indian fighter; called 'Gray Fox' by the Shoshones.

Area (sq mi): 2870.52 (land 2858.59; water 11.93). **Pop per sq mi:** 2.2.

Pop 2005: 6,182. **State rank:** 21. **Pop change:** 2000-20005 +5%; 1990-2000 +11.2%. **Pop 2000:** 5,887 (White 97.3%; Black or African American 0.1%; Hispanic or Latino 0.9%; Asian 0.1%; Other 2%, including 1% American Indian/Alaska Native). **Foreign born:** 0.9%. **Median age:** 40.2.

Income 2000: per capita $17,379; median household $35,601; **Pop below poverty level:** 9.1%. *****Personal per capita income 2000-2003:** $24,845-$30,721.

Unemployment 2004: 3.8%. **Change from 2000:** +0%. **Median travel time to work:** 22.4 minutes. **Working outside county of residence:** 27.7%.

Cities with pop over 10,000: None.

FREMONT COUNTY

450 N 2nd St Rm 220   **Ph:** 307-332-2405
Lander, WY 82520   **Fax:** 307-332-1132
www.fremontcounty.org

In west-central WY, west of Casper; organized Mar 5, 1884 (prior to statehood) from Sweetwater County. **Name Origin:** For John Charles Fremont (1813-90), soldier and explorer who led five expeditions to the West, U.S. senator from CA (1850-51), and governor of the AZ Territory (1878-81).

Area (sq mi): 9265.8 (land 9182.27; water 83.53). **Pop per sq mi:** 4.

Pop 2005: 36,491. **State rank:** 5. **Pop change:** 2000-20005 +1.9%; 1990-2000 +6.4%. **Pop 2000:** 35,804 (White 74.6%; Black or African American 0.1%; Hispanic or Latino 4.4%; Asian 0.3%; Other 23.1%, including 19.7% American Indian/Alaska Native). **Foreign born:** 0.8%. **Median age:** 37.7.

Income 2000: per capita $16,519; median household $32,503; **Pop below poverty level:** 17.6%. *****Personal per capita income 2000-2003:** $23,123-$25,754.

Unemployment 2004: 5.2%. **Change from 2000:** -1.2%. **Median travel time to work:** 17.1 minutes. **Working outside county of residence:** 4.8%.

Cities with pop over 10,000: None.

GOSHEN COUNTY

2125 E 'A' St PO Box 160   **Ph:** 307-532-4051
Torrington, WY 82240   **Fax:** 307-532-7375
goshencounty.org

On the southeastern border of WY, northeast of Cheyenne; created Feb 9, 1911 from Platte and Laramie counties. **Name Origin:** For Goshen Hole Valley, which was probably named for the Biblical Egyptian home of the Israelites before the Exodus; generally interpreted as 'land of abundance or plenty.'

Area (sq mi): 2232.16 (land 2225.32; water 6.84). **Pop per sq mi:** 5.5.

Pop 2005: 12,243. **State rank:** 14. **Pop change:** 2000-20005 -2.4%; 1990-2000 +1.3%. **Pop 2000:** 12,538 (White 89.1%; Black or African American 0.2%; Hispanic or Latino 8.8%; Asian 0.2%; Other 5.8%). **Foreign born:** 1.9%. **Median age:** 40.

Income 2000: per capita $15,965; median household $32,228; **Pop below poverty level:** 13.9%. *****Personal per capita income 2000-2003:** $22,561-$25,786.

Source: Personal per capita income data are from the Bureau of Economic Analysis; per capita income data are from the Bureau of the Census. See Introduction for explanation of differences.

Goshen County (cont'd)

Unemployment 2004: 4.3%. **Change from 2000:** +0.7%. **Median travel time to work:** 18.7 minutes. **Working outside county of residence:** 20.2%.

Cities with pop over 10,000: None.

HOT SPRINGS COUNTY

415 Arapahoe St
Thermopolis, WY 82443
www.hscounty.com

Ph: 307-864 3515
Fax: 307-864-3333

In west-central WY; created Feb 9, 1911 from Fremont, Johnson, and Big Horn counties. **Name Origin:** For the hot springs located in the county seat.

Area (sq mi): 2006.21 (land 2003.89; water 2.32). **Pop per sq mi:** 2.3.

Pop 2005: 4,537. **State rank:** 22. **Pop change:** 2000-20005 -7.1%; 1990-2000 +1.5%. **Pop 2000:** 4,882 (White 94.5%; Black or African American 0.3%; Hispanic or Latino 2.4%; Asian 0.2%; Other 3.4%, including 1.5% American Indian/Alaska Native). **Foreign born:** 1.3%. **Median age:** 44.2.

Income 2000: per capita $16,858; median household $29,888; **Pop below poverty level:** 10.6%. ***Personal per capita income 2000-2003:** $23,496-$28,312.

Unemployment 2004: 3.9%. **Change from 2000:** -0.4%. **Median travel time to work:** 14.6 minutes. **Working outside county of residence:** 11.8%.

Cities with pop over 10,000: None.

JOHNSON COUNTY

76 N Main St
Buffalo, WY 82834
www.johnsoncountywyoming.org

Ph: 307-684-7272
Fax: 307-684-2708

In north-central WY, north of Casper; created as Pease County Dec 8, 1875 (prior to statehood) from Pease County; name changed Dec 13, 1879. **Name Origin:** For E.P. Johnson, a Cheyenne lawyer. Originally named for Dr. E. L. Pease.

Area (sq mi): 4174.71 (land 4166.28; water 8.42). **Pop per sq mi:** 1.9.

Pop 2005: 7,721. **State rank:** 18. **Pop change:** 2000-20005 +9.1%; 1990-2000 +15.1%. **Pop 2000:** 7,075 (White 95.7%; Black or African American 0.1%; Hispanic or Latino 2.1%; Asian 0.1%; Other 2.8%). **Foreign born:** 0.8%. **Median age:** 43.

Income 2000: per capita $19,030; median household $34,012; **Pop below poverty level:** 10.1%. ***Personal per capita income 2000-2003:** $24,647-$29,671.

Unemployment 2004: 3.4%. **Change from 2000:** +0.3%. **Median travel time to work:** 19.6 minutes. **Working outside county of residence:** 12.9%.

Cities with pop over 10,000: None.

LARAMIE COUNTY

309 W 20th St
Cheyenne, WY 82001
webgate.co.laramie.wy.us

Ph: 307-633-4264
Fax: 307-633-4240

On the southeastern border of WY; first county in WY; created Jan 9, 1867 (prior to statehood). **Name Origin:** For Jacques LaRamie (?-c.1818), a respected French-Canadian trapper killed by Indians near the river, which was later named for him. Also spelled *LaRamie* or *LaRamee*.

Area (sq mi): 2687.63 (land 2686.05; water 1.58). **Pop per sq mi:** 31.7.

Pop 2005: 85,163. **State rank:** 1. **Pop change:** 2000-20005 +4.4%; 1990-2000 +11.6%. **Pop 2000:** 81,607 (White 83.2%; Black or African American 2.6%; Hispanic or Latino 10.9%; Asian 1%; Other 7.5%). **Foreign born:** 2.9%. **Median age:** 35.3.

Income 2000: per capita $19,634; median household $39,607; **Pop below poverty level:** 9.1%. ***Personal per capita income 2000-2003:** $28,052-$32,529.

Unemployment 2004: 4.5%. **Change from 2000:** +1%. **Median travel time to work:** 16.3 minutes. **Working outside county of residence:** 5.8%.

Cities with pop over 10,000: Cheyenne 🏛 (55,362).

LINCOLN COUNTY

PO Box 670
Kemmerer, WY 83101
www.lcwy.org

Ph: 307-877-9056
Fax: 307-877-3101

On the southwestern border of WY; created Feb 20, 1911 from Uinta County. **Name Origin:** For Abraham Lincoln (1809-65), sixteenth U.S. president.

Area (sq mi): 4089.01 (land 4069.09; water 19.92). **Pop per sq mi:** 3.9.

Pop 2005: 15,999. **State rank:** 11. **Pop change:** 2000-20005 +9.8%; 1990-2000 +15.4%. **Pop 2000:** 14,573 (White 96.1%; Black or African American 0.1%; Hispanic or Latino 2.2%; Asian 0.2%; Other 2.6%). **Foreign born:** 1.4%. **Median age:** 36.8.

Income 2000: per capita $17,533; median household $40,794; **Pop below poverty level:** 9%. ***Personal per capita income 2000-2003:** $23,057-$27,156.

Unemployment 2004: 3.9%. **Change from 2000:** -1.5%. **Median travel time to work:** 25.1 minutes. **Working outside county of residence:** 21%.

Cities with pop over 10,000: None.

NATRONA COUNTY

200 N Center St
Casper, WY 82601
www.natronacounty-wy.gov

Ph: 307-235-9210
Fax: 307-235-9367

In east-central WY; created Mar 9, 1888 (prior to statehood) from Carbon County. **Name Origin:** For the mineral natron, or trona, a sodium carbonate, found in the area.

Area (sq mi): 5375.72 (land 5339.88; water 35.83). **Pop per sq mi:** 13.1.

Pop 2005: 69,799. **State rank:** 2. **Pop change:** 2000-20005 +4.9%; 1990-2000 +8.7%. **Pop 2000:** 66,533 (White 91.7%; Black or African American 0.8%; Hispanic or Latino 4.9%; Asian 0.4%; Other 4.6%, including 1% American Indian/Alaska Native). **Foreign born:** 1.8%. **Median age:** 36.4.

Natrona County (cont'd)

Income 2000: per capita $18,913; median household $36,619; **Pop below poverty level:** 11.8%. ***Personal per capita income 2000-2003:** $33,905-$35,599.

Unemployment 2004: 3.7%. **Change from 2000:** -0.4%. **Median travel time to work:** 16.7 minutes. **Working outside county of residence:** 4.9%.

Cities with pop over 10,000: Casper ⏛ (51,240).

NIOBRARA COUNTY

424 S Elm St PO Box 420   **Ph:** 307-334-2211
Lusk, WY 82225   **Fax:** 307-334-3013
www.newedc.net/niobrara/index.htm

On the central eastern border of WY, east of Casper, created Feb 14, 1911 from Converse County. **Name Origin:** For the Niobrara River, which flows through the county, or for the Niobrara Indian tribe; from an Omaha-Poca Indian word *ni obthantha ko* 'spreading water river.'

Area (sq mi): 2627.9 (land 2625.81; water 2.09). **Pop per sq mi:** 0.9.

Pop 2005: 2,286. **State rank:** 23. **Pop change:** 2000-20005 -5%; 1990-2000 -3.7%. **Pop 2000:** 2,407 (White 97.1%; Black or African American 0.1%; Hispanic or Latino 1.5%; Asian 0.1%; Other 1.7%). **Foreign born:** 0.7%. **Median age:** 42.8.

Income 2000: per capita $15,757; median household $29,701; **Pop below poverty level:** 13.4%. ***Personal per capita income 2000-2003:** $24,588-$30,241.

Unemployment 2004: 3.8%. **Change from 2000:** +0.5%. **Median travel time to work:** 14.8 minutes. **Working outside county of residence:** 7%.

Cities with pop over 10,000: None.

PARK COUNTY

1002 Sheridan Ave   **Ph:** 307-754-8600
Cody, WY 82414   **Fax:** 307-527-8626
www.parkcounty.us

On the northwestern border of WY; organized Feb 15, 1909 from Sweetwater, Fremont, and Big Horn counties. **Name Origin:** For Yellowstone National Park, which forms the northwestern part of the county.

Area (sq mi): 6968.51 (land 6942.39; water 26.11). **Pop per sq mi:** 3.8.

Pop 2005: 26,664. **State rank:** 8. **Pop change:** 2000-20005 +3.4%; 1990-2000 +11.3%. **Pop 2000:** 25,786 (White 94.5%; Black or African American 0.1%; Hispanic or Latino 3.7%; Asian 0.4%; Other 3.1%). **Foreign born:** 1.8%. **Median age:** 39.8.

Income 2000: per capita $18,020; median household $35,829; **Pop below poverty level:** 12.7%. ***Personal per capita income 2000-2003:** $27,088-$30,133.

Unemployment 2004: 4.1%. **Change from 2000:** -0.3%. **Median travel time to work:** 17.6 minutes. **Working outside county of residence:** 6.6%.

Cities with pop over 10,000: None.

PLATTE COUNTY

PO Box 728   **Ph:** 307-322-3555
Wheatland, WY 82201   **Fax:** 307-322-2245

In southeastern WY, north of Cheyenne; created Feb 9, 1911 from Laramie County. **Name Origin:** For the North Platte River, which flows through the county; French 'flat' or 'still.'

Area (sq mi): 2110.9 (land 2084.93; water 25.97). **Pop per sq mi:** 4.1.

Pop 2005: 8,619. **State rank:** 16. **Pop change:** 2000-20005 -2.1%; 1990-2000 +8.1%. **Pop 2000:** 8,807 (White 92.9%; Black or African American 0.2%; Hispanic or Latino 5.3%; Asian 0.2%; Other 3.5%). **Foreign born:** 1.5%. **Median age:** 41.2.

Income 2000: per capita $17,530; median household $33,866; **Pop below poverty level:** 11.7%. ***Personal per capita income 2000-2003:** $25,383-$27,609.

Unemployment 2004: 5.1%. **Change from 2000:** +1.2%. **Median travel time to work:** 14.5 minutes. **Working outside county of residence:** 9.9%.

Cities with pop over 10,000: None.

SHERIDAN COUNTY

224 S Main St Suite B-2   **Ph:** 307-674-2500
Sheridan, WY 82801
www.sheridancounty.com

On the central northern border of WY; created Mar 9, 1888 from Johnson County. **Name Origin:** For the county's major town and county seat, itself named for Gen. Philip Henry Sheridan (1831-88), Union officer during the Civil War and commander in chief of the U.S. army (1883-88).

Area (sq mi): 2527.07 (land 2523.32; water 3.75). **Pop per sq mi:** 10.9.

Pop 2005: 27,389. **State rank:** 7. **Pop change:** 2000-20005 +3.1%; 1990-2000 +12.7%. **Pop 2000:** 26,560 (White 94.6%; Black or African American 0.2%; Hispanic or Latino 2.4%; Asian 0.4%; Other 3.5%, including 1.3% American Indian/Alaska Native). **Foreign born:** 1.6%. **Median age:** 40.6.

Income 2000: per capita $19,407; median household $34,538; **Pop below poverty level:** 10.7%. ***Personal per capita income 2000-2003:** $29,829-$33,461.

Unemployment 2004: 3.9%. **Change from 2000:** -0.1%. **Median travel time to work:** 17.8 minutes. **Working outside county of residence:** 8.3%.

Cities with pop over 10,000: Sheridan ⏛ (16,118).

SUBLETTE COUNTY

PO Box 250   **Ph:** 307-367-4372
Pinedale, WY 82941   **Fax:** 307-367-6396
www.visitsublettecounty.com

In west-central WY; organized Feb 15, 1921 from Fremont County. **Name Origin:** For William Lewis Sublette (1799-1845), fur trader and explorer of the Rocky Mountain region.

Area (sq mi): 4935.66 (land 4882.57; water 53.08). **Pop per sq mi:** 1.4.

*Source: Personal per capita income data are from the Bureau of Economic Analysis; per capita income data are from the Bureau of the Census. See Introduction for explanation of differences.

Sublette County (cont'd)

Pop 2005: 6,926. **State rank:** 19. **Pop change:** 2000-20005 +17%; 1990-2000 +22.2%. **Pop 2000:** 5,920 (White 96.4%; Black or African American 0.2%; Hispanic or Latino 1.9%; Asian 0.2%; Other 2.1%). **Foreign born:** 1.6%. **Median age:** 39.8.

Income 2000: per capita $20,056; median household $39,044; **Pop below poverty level:** 9.7%. ***Personal per capita income 2000 2003:** $27,678-$33,936.

Unemployment 2004: 2.3%. **Change from 2000:** +0.2%. **Median travel time to work:** 20.2 minutes. **Working outside county of residence:** 12.6%.

Cities with pop over 10,000: None.

SWEETWATER COUNTY
PO Box 730   **Ph:** 307-872-6400
Green River, WY 82935   **Fax:** 307-872-6337
www.co.sweet.wy.us

On the southern border of WY; largest county in WY. Created as Carter County Dec 27, 1867 (prior to statehood) from Laramie County; name changed Dec 13, 1869. **Name Origin:** For the Sweetwater River, which flows through Fremont County, at that time still a part of Sweetwater County. Originally named for Judge W.A. Carter.

Area (sq mi): 10,491.17 (land 10425.3; water 65.87). **Pop per sq mi:** 3.6.

Pop 2005: 37,975. **State rank:** 3. **Pop change:** 2000-20005 +1%; 1990-2000 -3.1%. **Pop 2000:** 37,613 (White 86.9%; Black or African American 0.7%; Hispanic or Latino 9.4%; Asian 0.6%; Other 7%, including 1% American Indian/Alaska Native). **Foreign born:** 2.7%. **Median age:** 34.2.

Income 2000: per capita $19,575; median household $46,537; **Pop below poverty level:** 7.8%. ***Personal per capita income 2000-2003:** $29,501-$32,941.

Unemployment 2004: 3.5%. **Change from 2000:** -1.1%. **Median travel time to work:** 21.1 minutes. **Working outside county of residence:** 4.5%.

Cities with pop over 10,000: Rock Springs (18,746); Green River 🏛 (11,807).

TETON COUNTY
PO Box 1727   **Ph:** 307-733-4430
Jackson, WY 83001   **Fax:** 307-739-8681
www.tetonwyo.org

On the northwestern border of WY; created Feb 15, 1921 from Lincoln County. **Name Origin:** For the Teton Mountains.

Area (sq mi): 4221.8 (land 4007.76; water 214.04). **Pop per sq mi:** 4.7.

Pop 2005: 19,032. **State rank:** 10. **Pop change:** 2000-20005 +4.3%; 1990-2000 +63.4%. **Pop 2000:** 18,251 (White 91.3%; Black or African American 0.1%; Hispanic or Latino 6.5%; Asian 0.5%; Other 5.6%). **Foreign born:** 5.9%. **Median age:** 35.

Income 2000: per capita $38,260; median household $54,614; **Pop below poverty level:** 6%. ***Personal per capita income 2000-2003:** $62,831-$73,897.

Unemployment 2004: 3.3%. **Change from 2000:** +1.1%. **Median travel time to work:** 17.1 minutes. **Working outside county of residence:** 3.5%.

Cities with pop over 10,000: None.

UINTA COUNTY
PO Box 810   **Ph:** 307-783-0306
Evanston, WY 82931   **Fax:** 307-783-0376
www.uintacounty.com

On the southwestern border of WY; original county, organized Dec 1, 1869 (prior to statehood); smallest county in WY. **Name Origin:** For the Uintah Mountains or the Uinta Indian tribe.

Area (sq mi): 2087.56 (land 2081.66; water 5.9). **Pop per sq mi:** 9.6.

Pop 2005: 19,939. **State rank:** 9. **Pop change:** 2000-20005 +1%; 1990-2000 +5.5%. **Pop 2000:** 19,742 (White 92.2%; Black or African American 0.1%; Hispanic or Latino 5.3%; Asian 0.3%; Other 5.4%). **Foreign born:** 2.5%. **Median age:** 31.4.

Income 2000: per capita $16,994; median household $44,544; **Pop below poverty level:** 9.9%. ***Personal per capita income 2000-2003:** $23,084-$28,760.

Unemployment 2004: 4.1%. **Change from 2000:** -0.9%. **Median travel time to work:** 20.9 minutes. **Working outside county of residence:** 16.6%.

Cities with pop over 10,000: Evanston 🏛 (11,407).

WASHAKIE COUNTY
PO Box 260   **Ph:** 307-347-3131
Worland, WY 82401   **Fax:** 307-347-9366
www.washakiecounty.net

In north-central WY; created Feb 9, 1911 from Big Horn and Johnson counties. **Name Origin:** For Washakie (1804-1900), the Shoshone Indian chief and ally of the whites; meaning of name is uncertain but possibly 'rattler,' for the one he made and used to lead his men to battle.

Area (sq mi): 2242.75 (land 2240.06; water 2.69). **Pop per sq mi:** 3.5.

Pop 2005: 7,933. **State rank:** 17. **Pop change:** 2000-20005 -4.3%; 1990-2000 -1.2%. **Pop 2000:** 8,289 (White 86.2%; Black or African American 0.1%; Hispanic or Latino 11.5%; Asian 0.7%; Other 9%). **Foreign born:** 2.4%. **Median age:** 39.4.

Income 2000: per capita $17,780; median household $34,943; **Pop below poverty level:** 14.1%. ***Personal per capita income 2000-2003:** $25,678-$30,709.

Unemployment 2004: 4.1%. **Change from 2000:** -0.4%. **Median travel time to work:** 12.5 minutes. **Working outside county of residence:** 6.3%.

Cities with pop over 10,000: None.

WESTON COUNTY
1 W Main St   **Ph:** 307-746-4744
Newcastle, WY 82701   **Fax:** 307-746-9505

On the northeastern border of WY; organized Mar 12, 1890 from Crook County. **Name Origin:** For John B. Weston, geologist and surveyor who located large anthracite deposits that eventually brought the railroad to WY.

🏛 *County Seat*

805

Weston County (cont'd)

Area (sq mi): 2400.07 (land 2397.86; water 2.21). **Pop per sq mi:** 2.8.

Pop 2005: 6,671. **State rank:** 20. **Pop change:** 2000-20005 +0.4%; 1990-2000 +1.9%. **Pop 2000:** 6,644 (White 94.8%; Black or African American 0.1%; Hispanic or Latino 2.1%; Asian 0.2%; Other 3.7%, including 1.3% American Indian/Alaska Native). **Foreign born:** 0.8%. **Median age:** 40.7.

Income 2000: per capita $17,366; median household $32,348; **Pop below poverty level:** 9.9%. ***Personal per capita income 2000-2003:** $27,021-$31,370.

Unemployment 2004: 4%. **Change from 2000:** -0.3%. **Median travel time to work:** 21.7 minutes. **Working outside county of residence:** 17.5%.

Cities with pop over 10,000: None.

**Source: Personal per capita income data are from the Bureau of Economic Analysis; per capita income data are from the Bureau of the Census.
See Introduction for explanation of differences.*

Statistical Tables (County Rankings)

Counties Ranked by Population (2005)

Los Angeles County, CA	9,935,475
Cook County, IL	5,303,683
Harris County, TX	3,693,050
Maricopa County, AZ	3,635,528
Orange County, CA	2,988,072
San Diego County, CA	2,933,462
Kings County, NY	2,486,235
Miami-Dade County, FL	2,376,014
Dallas County, TX	2,305,454
Queens County, NY	2,241,600
Wayne County, MI	1,998,217
San Bernardino County, CA	1,963,535
Riverside County, CA	1,946,419
King County, WA	1,793,583
Broward County, FL	1,777,638
Clark County, NV	1,710,551
Santa Clara County, CA	1,699,052
Tarrant County, TX	1,620,479
New York County, NY	1,593,200
Bexar County, TX	1,518,370
Suffolk County, NY	1,474,927
Philadelphia County, PA	1,463,281
Middlesex County, MA	1,459,011
Alameda County, CA	1,448,905
Sacramento County, CA	1,363,482

Counties Ranked by Population Growth (2000-2005)

Maricopa County, AZ	563,379
Los Angeles County, CA	416,137
Riverside County, CA	401,032
Clark County, NV	334,786
Harris County, TX	292,472
San Bernardino County, CA	254,101
Tarrant County, TX	174,260
Collin County, TX	167,782
Broward County, FL	154,620
Orange County, CA	141,783
Will County, IL	140,547
Sacramento County, CA	139,983
Gwinnett County, GA	137,825
Palm Beach County, FL	137,364
Hillsborough County, FL	133,204
Orange County, FL	126,679
Bexar County, TX	125,439
Miami-Dade County, FL	122,652
Denton County, TX	121,666
Wake County, NC	120,969
San Diego County, CA	119,629
Fort Bend County, TX	109,198
Hidalgo County, TX	108,812
Lee County, FL	103,870
Mecklenburg County, NC	100,918

Counties Ranked by Percentage of Population Growth (2000-2005)

Flagler County, FL	+53.3%
Loudoun County, VA	+50.7%
Rockwall County, TX	+46.1%
Kendall County, IL	+45.8%
Forsyth County, GA	+42.7%
Douglas County, CO	+41.9%
Henry County, GA	+40.6%
Newton County, GA	+39.9%
Lincoln County, SD	+38.3%
Lyon County, NV	+37.7%
Paulding County, GA	+37.6%
Delaware County, OH	+36.6%
Osceola County, FL	+34.3%
Collin County, TX	+34.1%
Scott County, MN	+33.9%
Williamson County, TX	+33.4%
Spencer County, KY	+33.0%
Hamilton County, IN	+31.7%
Union County, NC	+31.7%
Lake County, FL	+31.6%
Washington County, UT	+31.6%
Saint Johns County, FL	+31.2%
Fort Bend County, TX	+30.8%
Camden County, NC	+30.2%
Barrow County, GA	+29.9%

Counties Ranked by Population Loss (2000-2005)

Cook County, IL	-73,058
Wayne County, MI	-62,945
Cuyahoga County, OH	-58,661
Philadelphia County, PA	-54,269
Allegheny County, PA	-45,825
Hamilton County, OH	-38,651
San Francisco City & County, CA	-37,307
Suffolk County, MA	-35,379
Orleans Parish, LA	-29,811
Erie County, NY	-19,562
Milwaukee County, WI	-18,510
Ramsey County, MN	-16,115
Saint Louis County, MO	-11,649
Montgomery County, OH	-11,627
Boulder County, CO	-10,848
San Mateo County, CA	-7,551
Lucas County, OH	-6,825
Kanawha County, WV	-6,514
Luzerne County, PA	-6,389
Middlesex County, MA	-6,385
Santa Cruz County, CA	-5,936
Trumbull County, OH	-5,820
Wichita County, TX	-5,770
Hudson County, NJ	-5,454
Jefferson County, AL	-4,818

Counties Ranked by Percentage of Population Loss (2000-2005)

Kalawao County, HI	-24.5%
Treasure County, MT	-20.0%
Stonewall County, TX	-19.0%
Esmeralda County, NV	-18.9%
Blaine County, NE	-17.0%
Sheridan County, ND	-16.4%
Issaquena County, MS	-16.1%
Arthur County, NE	-14.9%
Thomas County, NE	-14.5%
Sheridan County, MT	-14.2%
Lake & Peninsula Borough, AK	-13.9%
King County, TX	-13.8%
Eureka County, NV	-13.5%
Hidalgo County, NM	-13.4%
Jones County, SD	-13.4%
Ness County, KS	-12.9%
Garden County, NE	-12.9%
Haakon County, SD	-12.9%
Potter County, SD	-12.7%
Cheyenne County, CO	-12.5%
Throckmorton County, TX	-12.5%
Kiowa County, CO	-12.3%
Oliver County, ND	-12.2%
Campbell County, SD	-12.2%
Taliaferro County, GA	-12.1%
Greeley County, KS	-12.1%
Lane County, KS	-12.1%

Counties Having the Most Cities with Populations of 10,000+
(see page 31 for a full county-by-county list of cities with populations over 10,000)

Los Angeles County, CA	.79	Miami-Dade County, FL	.19
Cook County, IL	.79	Saint Louis County, MO	.19
Cuyahoga County, OH	.34	Dallas County, TX	.19
Orange County, CA	.33	Contra Costa County, CA	.18
Bergen County, NJ	.30	Tarrant County, TX	.18
Broward County, FL	.24	San Diego County, CA	.17
DuPage County, IL	.24	Hennepin County, MN	.17
Wayne County, MI	.24	Maricopa County, AZ	.15
Riverside County, CA	.22	Palm Beach County, FL	.15
San Bernardino County, CA	.22	San Mateo County, CA	.14
King County, WA	.22	Santa Clara County, CA	.14
Lake County, IL	.21	Westchester County, NY	.14
Oakland County, MI	.20		

Counties Ranked by Population Growth (1990-2000)

Maricopa County, AZ	950,048
Los Angeles County, CA	656,174
Clark County, NV	634,306
Harris County, TX	582,379
Orange County, CA	435,733
Riverside County, CA	374,974
Broward County, FL	367,530
Dallas County, TX	366,089
Miami-Dade County, FL	316,268
San Diego County, CA	315,817
San Bernardino County, CA	291,054
Queens County, NY	277,781
Tarrant County, TX	276,116
Cook County, IL	271,674
Palm Beach County, FL	267,666
Travis County, TX	235,873
Gwinnett County, GA	235,538
King County, WA	229,715
Collin County, TX	227,639
Orange County, FL	218,853
Bexar County, TX	207,537
Wake County, NC	204,466
Hidalgo County, TX	185,918
Santa Clara County, CA	185,008
Mecklenburg County, NC	184,021

Counties Ranked by Percentage of Population Growth (1990-2000)

Douglas County, CO	+191.0%
Forsyth County, GA	+123.2%
Elbert County, CO	+106.0%
Henry County, GA	+103.2%
Park County, CO	+102.4%
Loudoun County, VA	+96.9%
Paulding County, GA	+96.3%
Summit County, UT	+91.6%
Boise County, ID	+90.1%
Eagle County, CO	+90.0%
Collin County, TX	+86.2%
Washington County, UT	+86.1%
Clark County, NV	+85.5%
Archuleta County, CO	+85.2%
Summit County, CO	+82.8%
Nye County, NV	+82.7%
Custer County, CO	+81.9%
San Miguel County, CO	+80.5%
Williamson County, TX	+79.1%
Gilmer County, GA	+75.5%
Teton County, ID	+74.4%
Flagler County, FL	+73.6%
Spencer County, KY	+73.0%
Lyon County, NV	+72.5%
Dawson County, GA	+69.7%

Counties Ranked by Highest Population Density (2005)

New York County, NY	69,390.2
Kings County, NY	35,210.8
Bronx County, NY	32,300.5
Queens County, NY	20,520.0
San Francisco City & County, CA	15,836.9
Hudson County, NJ	12,926.1
Suffolk County, MA	11,183.0
Philadelphia County, PA	10,831.9
Richmond County, NY	7,944.1
Arlington County, VA	7,575.0
Essex County, NJ	6,264.8
Cook County, IL	5,608.3
Union County, NJ	5,145.3
Nassau County, NY	4,650.1
Bergen County, NJ	3,854.3
Milwaukee County, WI	3,815.4
Orange County, CA	3,785.2
Denver City & County, CO	3,638.2
Pinellas County, FL	3,315.3
Wayne County, MI	3,253.6
Ramsey County, MN	3,177.0
Delaware County, PA	3,016.4
Cuyahoga County, OH	2,912.4
DuPage County, IL	2,785.0
Passaic County, NJ	2,693.4

Counties Ranked by Lowest Population Density (2005)

Denali Borough, AK	0.1
Lake & Peninsula Borough, AK	0.1
Loving County, TX	0.1
North Slope Borough, AK	0.1
Yakutat City & Borough, AK	0.1
Esmeralda County, NV	0.2
Northwest Arctic Borough, AK	0.2
Eureka County, NV	0.3
Garfield County, MT	0.3
Harding County, NM	0.3
Kenedy County, TX	0.3
King County, TX	0.3
Petroleum County, MT	0.3
Aleutians East Borough, AK	0.4
Carter County, MT	0.4
Lincoln County, NV	0.4
Terrell County, TX	0.4
Arthur County, NE	0.5
Catron County, NM	0.5
Clark County, ID	0.5
Harding County, SD	0.5
Powder River County, MT	0.5
McPherson County, NE	0.6
Prairie County, MT	0.6
Slope County, ND	0.6

Counties Ranked by Per Capita Income (1999)
Data compiled by *Bureau of the Census*

Marin County, CA	$44,962
New York County, NY	$42,922
Pitkin County, CO	$40,811
Fairfield County, CT	$38,350
Teton County, WY	$38,260
Somerset County, NJ	$37,970
Arlington County, VA	$37,706
Morris County, NJ	$36,964
Fairfax County, VA	$36,888
Westchester County, NY	$36,726
Hunterdon County, NJ	$36,370
San Mateo County, CA	$36,045
Montgomery County, MD	$35,684
San Miguel County, CO	$35,329
Douglas County, CO	$34,848
Los Alamos County, NM	$34,646
San Francisco County, CA	$34,556
Summit County, UT	$33,767
Bergen County, NJ	$33,638
Loudoun County, VA	$33,530
Collin County, TX	$33,345
Hamilton County, IN	$33,109
Santa Clara County, CA	$32,795
Oakland County, MI	$32,534
Williamson County, TN	$32,496

Counties Ranked by Personal Per Capita Income (2003)
Data compiled by *Bureau of Economic Analysis*

New York County, NY	$84,044
Teton County, WY	$73,897
Loving County, TX	$72,063
Pitkin County, CO	$68,504
Marin County, CA	$65,642
Fairfield County, CT	$60,803
Arlington County, VA	$56,888
Morris County, NJ	$55,796
San Francisco City & County, CA	$55,720
Westchester County, NY	$55,557
Somerset County, NJ	$55,443
Hunterdon County, NJ	$55,196
Fairfax County, VA*	$53,984
Montgomery County, MD	$52,854
San Mateo County, CA	$52,841
Bergen County, NJ	$51,758
Nassau County, NY	$50,242
Montgomery County, PA	$49,429
Nantucket County, MA	$49,361
Oakland County, MI	$49,048
Fulton County, GA	$48,647
Los Alamos County, NM	$48,541
Norfolk County, MA	$48,238
Ozaukee County, WI	$47,527
Chester County, PA	$47,480

*Includes Fairfax County, Fairfax City & Falls Church

Counties Ranked by Highest Percentage Below Poverty (2000)
Data compiled by *Bureau of the Census*

Buffalo County, SD	56.9%
Shannon County, SD	52.3%
Starr County, TX	50.9%
Ziebach County, SD	49.9%
Todd County, SD	48.3%
Owsley County, KY	45.4%
Zavala County, TX	41.8%
Holmes County, MS	41.1%
Corson County, SD	41.0%
East Carroll Parish, LA	40.5%
Brooks County, TX	40.2%
Kalawao County, HI	40.1%
Wilcox County, AL	39.9%
Clay County, KY	39.7%
Bennett County, SD	39.2%
Sioux County, ND	39.2%
Sumter County, AL	38.7%
Sharkey County, MS	38.3%
Humphreys County, MS	38.2%
Apache County, AZ	37.8%
McDowell County, WV	37.7%
Wilkinson County, MS	37.7%
Martin County, KY	37.0%
Madison Parish, LA	36.7%
Magoffin County, KY	36.6%

Counties Ranked by Lowest Percentage Below Poverty (2000)
Data compiled by *Bureau of the Census*

Loving County, TX	0.0%
Douglas County, CO	2.1%
Fayette County, GA	2.6%
Hunterdon County, NJ	2.6%
Ozaukee County, WI	2.6%
Waukesha County, WI	2.7%
Loudoun County, VA	2.8%
Hamilton County, IN	2.9%
Los Alamos County, NM	2.9%
Washington County, MN	2.9%
Hancock County, IN	3.0%
Kendall County, IL	3.0%
Johnson County, KS	3.4%
Livingston County, MI	3.4%
Monroe County, IL	3.4%
Scott County, MN	3.4%
Calumet County, WI	3.5%
Carver County, MN	3.5%
Stafford County, VA	3.5%
York County, VA	3.5%
Dakota County, MN	3.6%
DuPage County, IL	3.6%
Hanover County, VA	3.6%
Hendricks County, IN	3.6%
Washington County, WI	3.6%

Counties Ranked by Growth of Personal Per Capita Income (2000-2003)

Data compiled by *Bureau of Economic Analysis*

Castro County, TX	$13,102
Wheeler County, NE	$12,179
Teton County, WY	$11,066
Borden County, TX	$8,859
Arthur County, NE	$8,522
Keya Paha County, NE	$8,509
Clear Creek County, CO	$7,776
Towner County, ND	$7,748
Wells County, ND	$7,477
Glasscock County, TX	$7,400
Arlington County, VA	$7,333
Blaine County, NE	$7,074
Renville County, ND	$6,997
Sheridan County, ND	$6,980
Sioux County, NE	$6,964
Banner County, NE	$6,956
Sheridan County, KS	$6,956
Lynn County, TX	$6,876
Los Alamos County, NM	$6,854
Nelson County, ND	$6,743
Assumption Parish, LA	$6,740
North Slope Borough, AK	$6,653
Jewell County, KS	$6,436
Talbot County, MD	$6,360
Cheyenne County, CO	$6,352

Counties Ranked by Percentage Growth of Personal Per Capita Income (2000-2003)

Data compiled by *Bureau of Economic Analysis*

Arthur County, NE	95.3%
Blaine County, NE	73.5%
Loup County, NE	71.9%
Sioux County, NE	56.5%
Keya Paha County, NE	55.2%
Wheeler County, NE	51.4%
Borden County, TX	49.8%
Hooker County, NE	48.0%
Castro County, TX	44.7%
McPherson County, NE	43.6%
Grant County, NE	41.7%
Glasscock County, TX	40.8%
Banner County, NE	40.1%
Thomas County, NE	39.7%
Issaquena County, MS	39.1%
Sheridan County, ND	37.3%
Lynn County, TX	37.1%
Assumption Parish, LA	35.2%
Sherman County, NE	34.5%
Wells County, ND	33.1%
Martin County, TX	32.7%
Madison Parish, LA	32.6%
Rock County, NE	32.5%
Edwards County, TX	32.4%
Lee County, AR	32.4%

Counties Ranked by Percentage Rise in Unemployment (2000-2004)

Data compiled by *Bureau of Labor Statistics*

Woods County, OK	5.4%
Allendale County, SC	5.2%
Aleutians East Borough, AK	4.5%
Concho County, TX	4.5%
Okfuskee County, OK	4.1%
Seminole County, OK	4.1%
Collingsworth County, TX	4.0%
Crowley County, CO	4.0%
Hancock County, WV	3.9%
Pickaway County, OH	3.9%
Coke County, TX	3.6%
Coal County, OK	3.5%
Leslie County, KY	3.5%
Madison County, TX	3.5%
Monroe County, OH	3.5%
Briscoe County, TX	3.4%
Foard County, TX	3.4%
Hughes County, OK	3.4%
McDowell County, WV	3.4%
Mitchell County, TX	3.4%
Greensville County, VA	3.3%
Jasper County, IA	3.3%
Jones County, TX	3.3%
Kiowa County, CO	3.3%
Madison County, OH	3.3%
Tama County, IA	3.3%

Counties Ranked by Percentage Drop in Unemployment (2000-2004)

Data compiled by *Bureau of Labor Statistics*

Dickenson County, VA	-10.7%
San Juan County, CO	-10.3%
Presidio County, TX	-9.0%
Yuma County, AZ	-9.0%
Maverick County, TX	-8.1%
Issaquena County, MS	-8.0%
Luna County, NM	-8.0%
Big Horn County, MT	-7.8%
Monroe County, KY	-7.8%
Dewey County, SD	-7.7%
Ziebach County, SD	-7.4%
Holmes County, MS	-7.3%
Carter County, KY	-6.5%
Chickasaw County, MS	-6.4%
Telfair County, GA	-6.3%
Washington County, AL	-6.2%
Carroll County, VA	-6.1%
Calhoun County, WV	-6.0%
Lincoln County, GA	-6.0%
Klickitat County, WA	-5.9%
Yancey County, NC	-5.9%
Grayson County, VA	-5.7%
Taliaferro County, GA	-5.7%
Roane County, WV	-5.5%
Winston County, MS	-5.5%

Counties Ranked by Highest Median Age

Kalawao County, HI 58.6
Charlotte County, FL 54.3
Llano County, TX 53.0
Citrus County, FL 52.6
McIntosh County, ND 51.0
Sarasota County, FL 50.5
Flagler County, FL 50.4
Northumberland County, VA 50.1
Highlands County, FL 50.0
Lancaster County, VA 49.8
Hickory County, MO 49.7
Hernando County, FL 49.5
Sumter County, FL 49.2
Alcona County, MI 49.0
Divide County, ND 49.0
Prairie County, MT 48.9
Sierra County, NM 48.9
Curry County, OR 48.8
Harding County, NM 48.7
Towns County, GA 48.6
Baxter County, AR 48.1
Sheridan County, ND 48.1
Wheeler County, OR 48.1
Catron County, NM 47.8
McPherson County, SD 47.6

Counties Ranked by Lowest Median Age

Shannon County, SD 20.6
Madison County, ID 20.7
Todd County, SD 21.7
Cusseta-Chattahoochee County, GA 23.2
Utah County, UT 23.3
Buffalo County, SD 23.4
Brazos County, TX 23.6
Ziebach County, SD 23.8
Cache County, UT 23.9
Northwest Arctic Borough, AK 23.9
Riley County, KS 23.9
Sioux County, ND 23.9
Iron County, UT 24.2
Whitman County, WA 24.7
Oktibbeha County, MS 24.8
Clay County, SD 24.9
Liberty County, GA 25.0
Onslow County, NC 25.0
Isabella County, MI 25.1
Sanpete County, UT 25.3
Athens-Clarke County, GA 25.4
San Juan County, UT 25.5
Claiborne County, MS 25.6
Athens County, OH 25.7
Montgomery County, VA 25.9

Most Common U.S. County Names

Washington 31
Franklin 25
Jefferson 25
Jackson 24
Lincoln 24
Madison 20
Clay 18
Montgomery 18
Union 18
Marion 17
Monroe 17
Wayne 16
Grant 15
Greene 14
Warren 14
Carroll 13
Adams 12
Clark 12
Douglas 12
Johnson 12
Lake 12
Lee 12
Marshall 12
Polk 12

Counties Ranked by Percentage of Residents Born Outside U.S.

Miami-Dade County, FL 50.9%
Queens County, NY 46.1%
Hudson County, NJ 38.5%
Kings County, NY 37.8%
Maverick County, TX 37.8%
Santa Cruz County, AZ 37.7%
Starr County, TX 36.9%
San Francisco City & County, CA 36.8%
Los Angeles County, CA 36.2%
Presidio County, TX 35.8%
Santa Clara County, CA 34.1%
Hudspeth County, TX 33.2%
San Mateo County, CA 32.3%
Imperial County, CA 32.2%
Orange County, CA 29.9%
Hidalgo County, TX 29.5%
New York County, NY 29.4%
Bronx County, NY 29.0%
Monterey County, CA 29.0%
Webb County, TX 29.0%
Clark County, ID 28.2%
Arlington County, VA 27.8%
Colusa County, CA 27.6%
El Paso County, TX 27.4%
Seward County, KS 27.4%

Counties Ranked by Total Area (square miles)

North Slope Borough, AK 94,762.64
Northwest Arctic Borough, AK 40,762.00
Lake & Peninsula Borough, AK 30,906.96
Matanuska-Susitna Borough, AK 25,259.79
Kenai Peninsula Borough, AK 24,754.60
San Bernardino County, CA 20,105.32
Coconino County, AZ 18,661.21
Nye County, NV 18,158.73
Elko County, NV 17,202.94
Aleutians East Borough, AK 15,011.60
Mohave County, AZ 13,469.71
Denali Borough, AK 12,774.53
Kodiak Island Borough, AK 12,023.67

Apache County, AZ 11,218.42
Lincoln County, NV 10,636.77
Sweetwater County, WY 10,491.17
Inyo County, CA 10,226.98
Harney County, OR 10,226.49
Navajo County, AZ 9,959.49
Malheur County, OR 9,929.99
Humboldt County, NV 9,657.87
Yakutat City & Borough, AK 9,459.28
Fremont County, WY 9,265.80
Maricopa County, AZ 9,224.27
Pima County, AZ 9,188.83

Counties Index